Open Secrets

The Encyclopedia of Congressional Money & Politics

Open Secrets

The Encyclopedia of Congressional Money & Politics

Larry Makinson
Joshua Goldstein
Center for Responsive Politics

Congressional Quarterly Inc.
1414 22nd Street N.W.
Washington, D.C. 20037

Library of Congress Cataloging-in-Publication Data

Makinson, Larry.
    Open secrets: the encyclopedia of congressional money & politics/Larry Makinson, Joshua Goldstein. — [3rd ed.]
      p.   cm.
    Includes index.
    ISBN 1-56802-026-0
    1. Campaign funds—United States.   2. Political action committees—United States.
3. United States.   Congress—Elections, 1992.
I. Goldstein, Joshua, 1966- .   II. Title.
JK1991.M26   1994
324.7'8'0973—dc20   94-18138
                                                                 CIP

Editorial, Research & Production Staff

Author/Editors:	Larry Makinson & Joshua Goldstein
Assistant Editor:	Sheila Krumholz
Research Assistants:	Amy Taylor
	Kristen Hubbard
Intern Assistants:	Michael Baranek
	Marni Ezra
	Trista Gaiotti
	Sherri Stevens

Acknowledgments

More than 18 months of painstaking research and production went into the publication of the third edition of this reference work and dozens of people and organizations were extremely helpful in the process. The publication of *Open Secrets* was a project of the Center for Responsive Politics and the information contained in this book would never have emerged in this form or any other without the untiring efforts of the Center's director, Ellen Miller, to win the enthusiasm and support of the foundations whose grants made it possible. The staff of the Federal Election Commission provided invaluable assistance, as usual. Kent Cooper, the FEC's Assistant Staff Director for Public Disclosure has offered advice, assistance and encouragement at every step of this project from its earliest days to its completion. Michael Dickerson, chief of the Public Records Office, has graciously and expertly assisted several generations of Center staffers in finding the buried treasures within the FEC's filing cabinets and microfilm readers. Bob Biersack, the FEC's Supervisory Statistician and chief computer guru, provided critical assistance at many points in the project — and deserves special thanks for making major improvements to the FEC's on-line database. Particular thanks also goes to Jacqueline R. Duobinis of the Center's National Library on Money & Politics for her invaluable assistance at many stages of this project, and for her blessed predilection for never throwing away a scrap of paper that has anything to do with money and politics. Finally, the authors extend their appreciation to the small but amazingly hard-working staff of the Center for Responsive Politics, who endured many trying moments during the months and years of research that have gone into successive editions of this book.

The funding that made this book possible came from major grants from the Joyce Foundation, the Florence & John Schumann Foundation, the Carnegie Corporation of America and the Rockefeller Family Associates.

The Center for Responsive Politics

The Center for Responsive Politics is a non-profit, non-partisan research group in Washington, D.C. Founded in 1983 by former Senators Frank Church (D-Idaho) and Hugh Scott (R-Pa), it specializes in the study of Congress, and particularly the role that money plays in its elections and actions. The Center's National Library on Money & Politics provides custom research for news organizations and others, using a computerized database that combines contributor classifications with current and historical federal campaign records. The Center's funding comes from a variety of foundations. It serves as a non-partisan resource for the public, the academic community and the news media. Interested readers can contact the Center at 202-857-0044 or by writing to Center for Responsive Politics, 1320 19th St. NW, Suite 700, Washington, DC 20036.

Contents

Introduction

This third edition of *Open Secrets* represents a major step forward in unraveling the patterns by which corporations, interest groups and wealthy individuals seek to influence both public policy and the outcome of federal elections.

The first edition of this book, following the 1988 elections, examined only contributions made through political action committees, or PACs. This was not because we were under any illusion that PACs were the whole story, but rather because they were the most obvious — and easily identified — givers in federal campaigns. We knew then (and know even better now) that contributions from individuals are a crucial element of election financing. But we didn't have the resources to do the full job in that first edition, so PACs were the first step.

The second edition of the book, which covered the 1990 elections, did examine individual contributors, adding an important new dimension to our knowledge of where members of Congress get the money that keeps them in office. It was particularly important in analyzing Senate races, since senators typically get only one-quarter of their campaign dollars from PACs. The research also revealed a number of facts that were suspected but never before documented. Among the more noteworthy was uncovering the "bundling" of large sums of individual contributions from Wall Street securities firms and Washington law and lobbying firms to members of Congress. Even more important, an examination of the individual contributions revealed that total donations from lawyers and lobbyists were triple the amount previously reported. But there were limitations too in that second edition. Because of limited staffing and time, we were unable to examine contributions made to losing candidates for Congress, so a large block of campaign money was never analyzed, and the totals given by the largest contributors were undercounted.

In this third edition of *Open Secrets*, with the addition of Josh Goldstein as co-author and primary researcher, we expanded our scope to examine *all* individual contributions — to winners and losers alike. Because of that, and because 1992 was a presidential election year, the volume of data (and money) examined in this edition was three times greater than in the previous edition. The authors, and other staffers and interns at the Center for Responsive Politics, reviewed over 850,000 individual contributions, finding the connections between families of contributors and identifying the financial interests of tens of thousands of companies. That work will now continue year-round, as we prepare for the 1994 elections and the next edition of *Open Secrets*.

That fourth edition, which will cover the 1994 elections, will represent another quantum leap forward. For the first time we will be able to give information on contributions from individuals to every senator over their entire six-year terms of office. This will make it possible to show contributions to Senate committees for a full six years, thus providing a much more accurate picture of each committee's chief supporters than has been available in the past.

Other horizons remain to be explored as well. One of our top priorities is offering *Open Secrets* not only in printed form, but in an interactive electronic format on CD-ROM. Some day reasonably soon, thousands of curious citizens will be able to sit down at their home computers — or a computer in their local library — and ask their own questions (like how much money did the oil and gas industry give to representatives from Texas, for example, or which members on the Agriculture Committee got the most from dairy interests). On that day we will have achieved the long-range goal that the *Open Secrets* project started with — namely, to take the secrets heretofore known only to Washington insiders and truly make them public information, available to everybody everywhere.

The information in this edition, the previous editions, and all future editions of *Open Secrets*, is presented in as clear and straightforward a manner as is possible. The authors feel no need to editorialize. There are no shortage of opinions in the nation's capital — or elsewhere in the country, for that matter. Our aim is to present the facts as clearly and understandably as possible, and let readers draw their own conclusions about the role of money in our American political system.

Larry Makinson/Joshua Goldstein
Center for Responsive Politics
April 1994

Scope, Limitations & Methodology

The job of gathering the material that made it possible to produce this book was both arduous and complicated. So that readers can understand the procedures that were used and the limitations that apply — and so other researchers can replicate the work on a state or local level — the following section explains how the data was collected and analyzed.

The starting point for this book was the official record of campaign contributions made to congressional and presidential candidates in the 1992 elections. That data was provided both by candidates and by political action committees, and was collected and computerized by the Federal Election Commission in Washington, D.C. Using those computer tapes, the authors, assistant editor and several additional staffers undertook the laborious task of identifying the contributors — both PACs and individuals — by industry and interest group.

What's Included in this Study

The primary focus of this book is on the 535 members of the U.S. Congress. Each member has a two-page contribution profile that details the industries and individual companies, labor unions and other organizations that contributed to his or her campaign. (Those profiles begin on page 176 for the Senate and 378 for the House of Representatives. They are arranged alphabetically within each house.)

Profiles of each of the 37 standing committees of the House and Senate are also presented, showing which industries and interest groups contributed most heavily to members of that committee. Those listings begin on page 96.

An industry-by-industry breakdown of contributor groups (beginning on page 42) examines in detail which segments of the business, labor and ideological communities give the biggest share of dollars to members of Congress. The top contributors within each sector are listed, as are the top recipients in the House and Senate.

At the end of the book, a directory of political action committees is included. This brief statistical overview shows the general patterns by which each PAC that gave $20,000 or more distributed its money. The PAC profiles begin on page 1249.

What's Missing

For one thing, **names**. The purpose of this report was to identify the industries, interests and specific organizations that are funding congressional campaigns. Knowing that a contributor works for Dow Chemical or Chase Manhattan is useful information. Knowing that the contributor's name is Harold Smith and that his wife's name is Millie is not. The contributor listings throughout this book therefore list individuals' employers and affiliations, but not their names. Though federal laws require disclosure of contributors giving $200 or more, the authors of this book were sensitive to the issue of privacy — particularly in the case of individuals contributing to ideological PACs. For readers who do wish to look up individual names, the original records at the Federal Election Commission do provide that information. Names can even be searched electronically through the FEC's on-line database.

Small individual contributors — those giving $200 or less — are also not listed, except in the aggregate. In the pie charts that accompany each member's contribution profile, the total received from small contributions is included. But since the candidates themselves list only the totals and do not itemize where the dollars came from, neither does this book. It is entirely possible, of course, that many of those small contributions came from the same sources that made big contributions.

Unknown contributors. Federal law requires that candidates identify all contributors who gave $200 or more to their campaign. Individual contributors are supposed to be identified by name, address, occupation and employer. In many cases, however, they are not. In researching the federal records, the authors found many thousands of cases of unidentified (or under-identified) contributors. In almost every case, names and addresses were provided, but quite often information on employer and occupation was left blank, incomplete, or so generic as to be useless in identifying the contributor's financial interest.

In all, of the approximately $298 million in individual contributions of $200 or more that went to federal candidates in the 1992 elections, the authors were able to classify 71 percent. Among elected members of Congress whose profiles appear in this book, the rate was over 75 percent. The breakdown of the unidentified dollars is as follows:

- **No employer listed or found:** ....**$33.5 million**

By far the worst offenders in identifying their contributors' economic affiliations were the presidential candidates — Bill Clinton, George Bush and Ross Perot, in particular. Most candidates for Congress identified the occupations and employers of all but a small portion of their contributors. Those members of the House and Senate who left the most blanks in their disclosure reports are identified on page 35.

- **Employer listed but category unknown:** ....**$34.4 million**

With over 70,000 individual companies to identify, the task of finding them all and filling in their classifications was simply impossible, given our limitations of staff and time. As the Center refines and updates its database, we hope to reduce this figure in future editions of *Open Secrets.*

- **Homemakers, students and other non-income earners:** .... **$13.6 million**

Where contributors' occupations were listed as "homemaker," "housewife," or some equivalent, the Center tried to match them with an income-earning spouse. In many, many cases this was possible. It is a common practice for wealthy contributors to double their effective limit by giving both personally and with their spouse. In some cases this even extends to children, who are often identified by occupation as "student." Whenever the source of the family's income could not be determined, the contribution was put into this category — with one exception. Persons with no income who contributed both to candidates and to political action committees — whether corporate or ideological — were assigned the classification of the PAC they contributed to.

- **Generic occupation/impossible to assign category:** ....**$3.0 million**

When a candidate identifies a contributor as "businessman" or "entrepreneur," classifying them in the right category becomes a hopeless task. Fortunately, many of these generic contributors gave to more than one candidate, sometimes enabling us to discover their employer or occupation.

Contributions from individuals who gave before 1989. Members of the U.S. Senate run for reelection every six years. Classifying their PAC contributions from previous election cycles was a difficult, but possible task. Identifying their *individual* contributors in those previous cycles, however, was beyond the capability of our limited time and staff. Consequently, contribution profiles of senators in this book include only PACs for the years prior to 1989.

How this Book Was Prepared

The first step in this project — and one that began in 1989 with the original edition of *Open Secrets* — was creating a classification system for the industries and interest groups that make political contributions. Since a majority of PACs and individual contributors come from the business world, the starting point was the system of Standard Industrial Codes (SIC codes) developed by the U.S. government's Office of Management and Budget. The SIC codes are used widely by reference organizations, such as Standard & Poors, that publish business directories. The codes were then streamlined to eliminate fine lines of distinction between industries and to make them more relevant to the political realities of congressional committee jurisdictions.

No similar codes cover non-business groups, so the Center developed its own, both for labor unions and for ideological and single-issue PACs. During the course of the project the classification system underwent a continual evolution, as the real world patterns of political giving gradually became apparent. A complete list of the categories — with the totals each contributed — is included in Appendix A, beginning on page 1314.

Classifying the Contributions

The contemporary American business world does not lend itself to simple classification. Modern corporations are often extremely diversified in their lines of business — and in their political interests — and in recent years many have been buying and selling subsidiaries almost routinely. To allow for this, the Center developed a multi-level system for classifying corporate PACs and other diversified contributors. A primary code was assigned, based on the company's primary business or profit center. Secondary codes were then added to account for subsidiary interests contributing more than 10 percent of the company's revenues or profits.

These multiple codes were then matched against the committee assignments of the candidates who received contributions. If the committee's jurisdiction did not relate to the PAC's main category, but did relate to a secondary code, that secondary code was used to classify the contribution. For example, a contribution from the Boeing PAC to a member of the Armed Services Committee was classified as a defense contribution. A similar contribution to a non-incumbent, or to someone sitting on a non-defense committee, would be classified under Boeing's primary category as an aircraft manufacturer. This system

was used to determine unique codes for each contribution made to congressional candidates during the 1991-92 election cycle.

Classifying contributions from individuals presented a new level of complexity. While it is generally safe to assume that a PAC is giving to further its economic interests, it is quite another matter to try to divine the motivations behind an individual's contribution to a politician. The Center's approach was not even to try. Rather, *the classifications in this book are based on the economic interests of the contributor's employer or line of business*. The only exception to this rule is in the case of individuals who have contributed to ideological or single-interest PACs. In that case, the contributor was generally assigned the same category as the PAC *if* they contributed to a candidate who received money from the PAC as well.

The following example illustrates the methodology: If a real estate developer contributes both to a pro-Israel PAC and to a candidate who received direct contributions from one or more pro-Israel PACs, the contribution would be classified under "pro-Israel." If the donor gave to someone who got no money from pro-Israel PACs, it would be classified under "real estate."

"Homemakers" and Other Non-Income Earners

If one to were take at face value the occupations and employers listed on federal campaign finance reports, one would quickly come to the conclusion that the biggest political interest group in the nation is made up of "homemakers" and "housewives." In fact, the use of contributions by spouses and other family members is common practice among wealthy contributors. Whenever a connection could be found between students, homemakers, or other non-income earners and a member of the household who did earn an income, the breadwinner's classification was used for all family members. Thus, a bank president, his wife and children would all be classified under "commercial banking" unless the wife listed a different occupation or employer, in which case she would be classified separately.

The only exception to this rule was in the case of ideological contributors. Non-income earning family members are not classified as ideological givers unless they themselves have contributed to an ideological PAC.

Compilation and Publication

Once all the data was collected and categorized, the final step was to arrange it in some order that would make it comprehensible — both for our own analysis and for readers of this book. Viewing the mountains of data that this book covers from only one angle would be limiting at best, so the information is presented here from a number of perspectives. Profiles cover not only the finances of individual members of Congress, but of PACs, congressional committees and specific industries as well. Wherever possible, the data is presented graphically, so readers can view not just the detail in the numbers, but also the patterns. In all, the book contains more than 3,000 charts and graphs.

Technical Notes

This entire project, from the first drafts of foundation proposals to the compiling of the databases, the charting and final desktop publishing, was done using Apple Macintosh™ computers. A large ensemble of software was used to gather and report the data. The workhorses included: FoxBase+/Mac™ and Panorama II™ for database work, DeltaGraph Professional™ for the charts and graphs, Microsoft Word™ for word processing, and Aldus PageMaker™ for final page layout.

The research to identify the thousands of PACs and individual contributors was done in libraries (primarily the Library of Congress), over the telephone, and in the Center's own growing library of reference materials. Standard & Poor's *Register of Corporations, Directors and Executives* was an invaluable reference work in identifying companies and matching the names of corporate officials and directors. *Washington Representatives*, published by Columbia Books, is the definitive guide to Washington lobbyists and was a constantly-appreciated reference tool. Also immensely useful was the *Yellow Book* series of business and congressional directories published by Monitor Publishing of Washington, DC.

Even with the vast resources of the Library of Congress and the dozens of business directories the Center consulted, the classification of the thousands of small businesses whose owners and officials gave money would not have been possible without the newly emerging medium of electronic reference works. Three CD-ROMs in particular proved to be worth more than their weight in gold: *Dun's Business Locator*, published by Dun & Bradstreet Information Services, was indispensable. On a single disk it classifies more than 10 million American businesses. Standard & Poors *Corporations CD-ROM* provides extremely valuable details on the business activities of the same public and privately-held corporations listed in their hardcover volume. Finally, the *Martindale-Hubbell Law Directory on CD-ROM* made it possible to identify an unprecedented number of law firms and individual attorneys — a particularly valuable resource considering that 86 percent of lawyers' contributions in the 1992 elections came from individuals, not PACs. Without those CD-ROMs, tens of thousands of small businesses and professionals identified on these pages would have been impossible to classify.

1.

The Big Picture

Open Secrets

The Price of Admission

. . . to the House of Representatives

Even when adjusted for inflation, the cost of a seat in the U.S. House of Representatives took a big leap forward in 1992. Just two years earlier, the cost of the average winning House campaign was $407,000. In 1992, the average House seat cost $543,000. Another telling statistic: in 1990, 11 House candidates waged campaigns costing $1 million or more. In 1992, the number of million-dollar campaigns soared to 46.

Several factors combined to boost the cost of a campaign, but the overriding factor was an increase in serious competition in districts all across the nation. Incumbents spent more to counteract widespread public anger with Congress, and to raise their profile among new constituents, as district lines were reapportioned. Reapportionment, combined with a surge in congressional retirements, opened many more seats than usual, creating open-seat races that traditionally cost more to win than incumbents spend to defend themselves. In 1992, however, that tradition fell, as incumbents spent more on average than open seat winners.

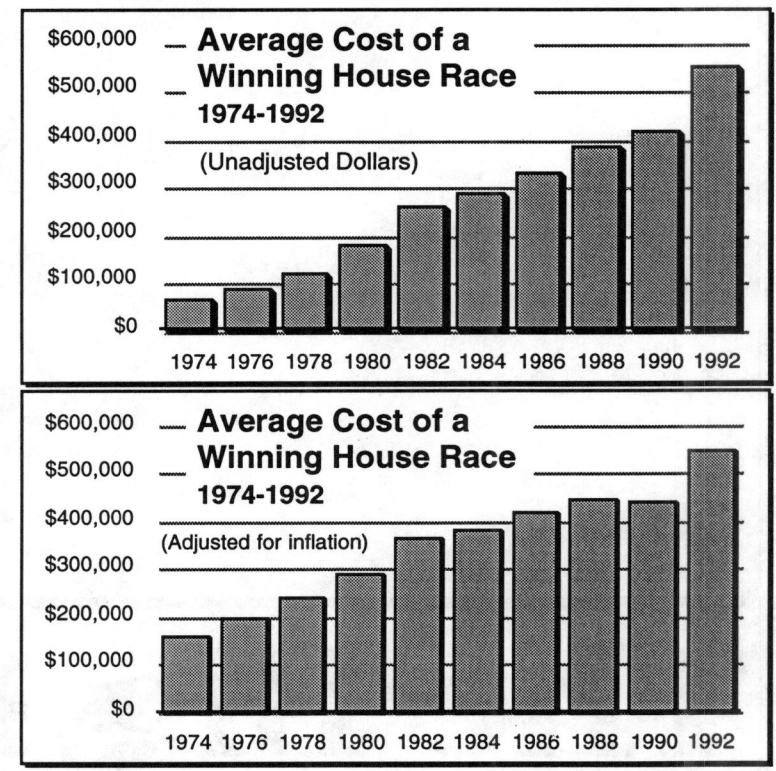

Source: Federal Election Commission and Center for Responsive Politics

. . . to the Senate

While average spending figures offer good yardsticks for measuring the rising cost of seats in the U.S. House of Representatives — where all 435 seats are up for election every two years — they are more problematic in the Senate. For one thing, only one-third of the 100 Senate seats are up for election in a given year, and a sample of 33 or 34 races is less reliable when measuring averages. For another thing, the costs of Senate races in a particular year can vary dramatically depending on which states are holding elections that year. In years when the largest states — such as New York and California — have races, average costs tend to be higher.

Over the past three elections, the cost of a winning Senate campaign has remained steady at around $4 million, but variations in spending have been wide. The chart below gives a sense of those variations in recent years, by highlighting the most and least expensive successful Senate campaigns in each of the last four elections.

Year	Most Expensive	State	Least Expensive	State
1986	$11,571,587	Calif	$883,977	Utah
1988	$14,656,367	Calif	$790,710	Hawaii
1990	$17,761,579	NC	$533,632	Kansas
1992	$14,958,095	NY	$1,095,154	NH

The most expensive Senate campaign ever waged was Jesse Helms' $17.8 million reelection race in 1990. The costliest race in 1992 was that of New York Republican Alfonse D'Amato, which totalled just under $15 million.

The Spending Gap Between Incumbents and Challengers

For years there has been a large — and widening — gap in the financial resources available to U.S. House incumbents versus those of candidates running to unseat them. In the 1992 elections, the spending gap between challengers and incumbents widened farther than ever. The average incumbent spent $578,475 in 1992. The average challenger (counting unopposed races as $0) spent $148,127. That left a gap of more than $430,000 between the ins and outs.

The chart at right gives a graphic perspective to the differences. Spending for both groups increased in 1992, but even though challengers spent more than ever, the rise in incumbent spending far outstripped the increase for challengers.

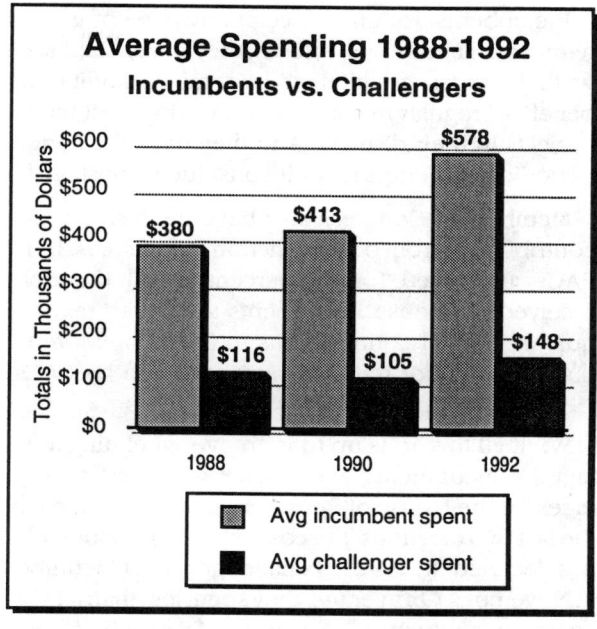

Fewer Incumbents Skating to Easy Victories

For the first time in years, there actually *was* competition in races for the U.S. House of Representatives. The great majority of incumbents won, as they usually do, but there were far fewer runaways than in previous years. The comparative pie charts below show the story. In 1988 most incumbents breezed to victory with little difficulty. In 1990, the number of close and marginal races nearly doubled. In 1992, barely half the winners captured more than 60 percent of the vote. The large number of open seat contests was the biggest reason, but incumbents also found their vote totals squeezed by better-funded challengers than in years past, and a rising restlessness among voters who were more willing than ever to give new candidates the benefit of the doubt.

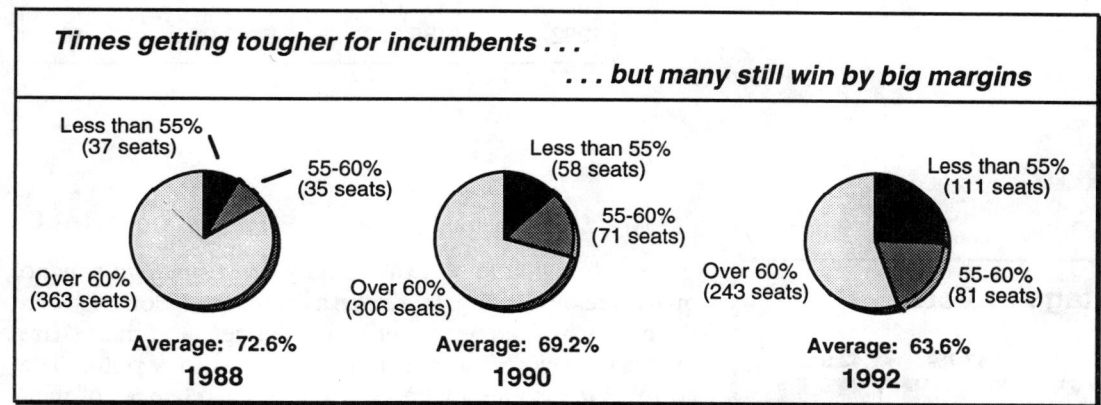

The Dollars and Cents of Incumbency

Incumbents, for any office at any level of government, have always enjoyed a natural advantage at election time. Their names are already well known, they have established a record of service for all to see, and if they have served their constituents well, the voters are likely to be reminded of it time and again come election time. Congressional incumbents also have the benefit of regular news coverage during their term in office — coverage which often gives them credit for federal grants and projects in their districts. And they have the congressional franking privilege, enabling them to send correspondence and periodic newsletters to their constituents postage free.

Members of Congress also have the inside lock on contributions from political action committees. In 1992 PACs accounted for 43 percent of all the dollars received by House incumbents and more than one-quarter of total contributions to Senators. More than three-quarters of the dollars contributed by PACs in 1992 went to incumbents.

What all this adds up to is an overwhelming advantage by incumbents over challengers, particularly in races for the House of Representatives. Yet for each of the last two elections, the cost of beating an incumbent has declined. In 1992, 19 challengers beat incumbents in November. On average, they spent less than $435,000 against incumbents who averaged $840,000 defending their seats. Of the 19, only one spent more than the incumbent they defeated, indicating once again that beating incumbents doesn't require outspending them, but rather raising enough money to be visible. (Five other incumbents in November lost to fellow incumbents; another 19 incumbents lost their seats in the primaries).

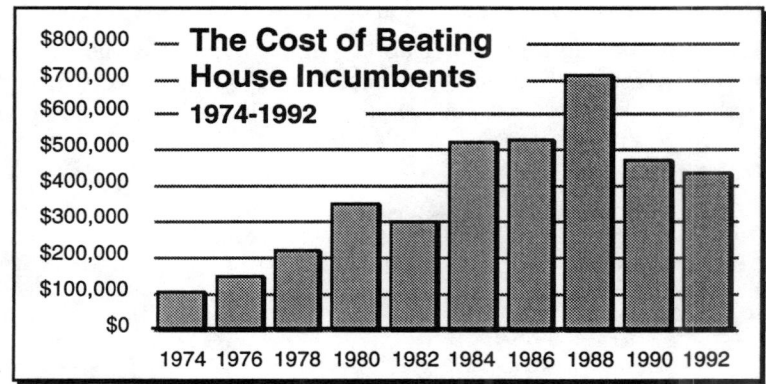

NOTE: Does not include races between two incumbents

Year	Average Challenger	Average Incumbent	No.
1974	$100,435	$101,102	40
1976	$144,720	$154,774	12
1978	$217,083	$200,607	19
1980	$343,093	$286,559	31
1982	$296,273	$453,459	23
1984	$518,781	$463,070	17
1986	$523,308	$562,139	6
1988	$703,740	$876,678	7
1990	$462,546	$631,025	16
1992	$435,829	$840,922	19

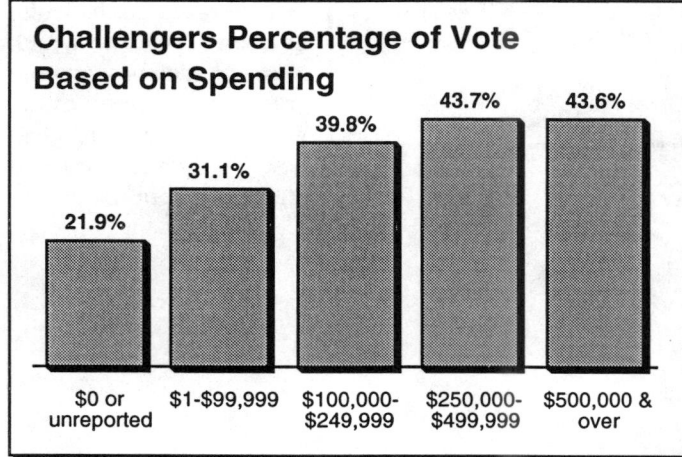

Even though adding extra money to a campaign was no guarantee of winning, there was a clear correlation between the amount of money spent by challengers and their share of the total votes on election day — up to a point. The correlation also held when comparing the chances of winning, as seen in the chart below.

Amount Spent by Challenger	Odds of Winning
$0 or unreported	0
$1-$99,999	0
$100,000-$249,999	13:1
$250,000-$499,999	4:1
$500,000 & over	2:1

Reelection Rates through the Years

Reelection rates for incumbents in both the House and Senate dipped below the 90 percent mark in 1992, to 88.3 percent in the House and 82.8 percent in the Senate.

What the figures don't show— particularly in the House of Representatives — is that a number of congressional incumbents who might have faced difficult races in 1992 decided not to seek reelection, and retired instead. But what the charts do show is that even in one of the most turbulent elections in recent decades, the great majority of incumbents were still able to hold onto their seats — regardless of the voters' low opinion of Congress in general.

The charts also show a contrast in reelection patterns between the House and Senate. Senate races tend to be more competitive than House races, as both parties usually attract (and support) credible candidates. They are also more subject to major swings in the political temperament, as in 1980 when the Reagan landslide swept nine Senate Democrats out of office, shifting control of that body to the Republicans.

Reelection rates in the House have proved much more stable over the years. The last time the reelection rate for House members dropped below 80 percent was in 1948.

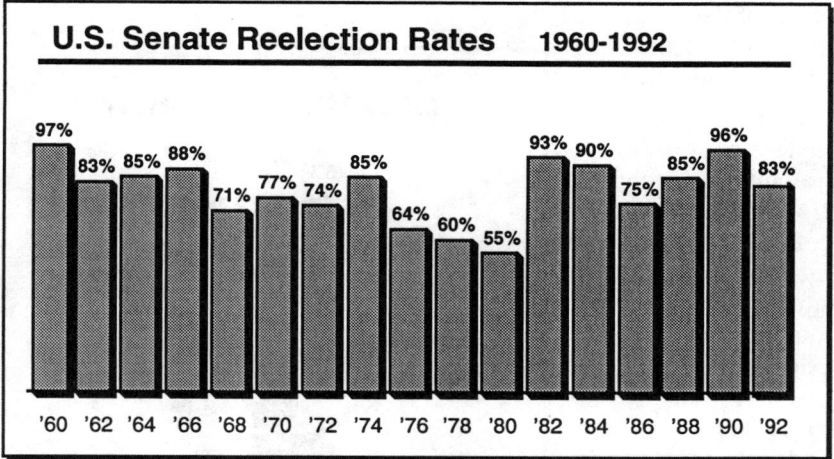

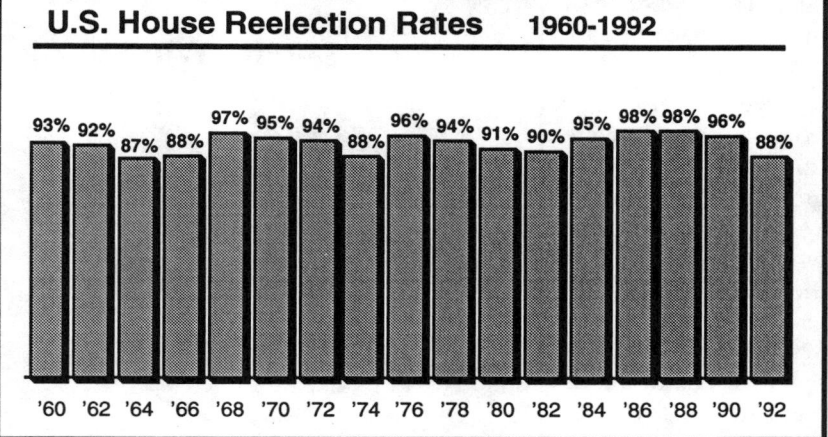

The High Cost of Losing

As Ross Perot could readily testify after his experience in the 1992 elections, an abundance of money doesn't always bring victory on election day. Like Perot, half of the 10 biggest-spending challengers in races for the U.S. House were defeated at the polls in November. But that ratio was a big improvement over previous elections. In 1990, seven of the 10

The 10 Top-Spending Challengers in House Races

Challenger	Party	District	Spent	Vote Pct	Outcome
Michael Huffington	Rep	Calif 22	$5,435,177	52.5%	Won
Dick Chrysler	Rep	Mich 8	$1,761,841	46.3%	Lost
Linda Bean	Rep	Maine 1	$1,441,720	35.0%	Lost
Gwen Margolis	Dem	Fla 22	$936,960	37.1%	Lost
Mark Neumann	Rep	Wis 1	$920,174	40.7%	Lost
James M. Talent	Rep	Mo 2	$916,868	50.4%	Won
H.L. "Bill" Richardson	Rep	Calif 3	$841,530	40.3%	Lost
Martin T. Meehan	Dem	Mass 5	$811,459	52.2%	Won
James C. Greenwood	Rep	Pa 8	$726,702	51.9%	Won
Martin R. Hoke	Rep	Ohio 10	$681,166	56.8%	Won

top-spending challengers lost; in 1988 nine of the 10 lost. More than $5 million from his personal bank account did help California Republican Michael Huffington win a seat in Congress, but runners-up Dick Chrysler and Linda Bean both suffered expensive losses despite their personal fortunes.

Where the Money Came From

The dollars that drove winning campaigns in 1992 came from different mixes of sources depending on the office and the status of the candidate. These pie charts highlight the differences.

Political action committees were most important to incumbent House members, who collected 43 percent of their revenues from that source. PACs were less important — but still a sizeable slice of the overall funding pie — to Senate incumbents and to new House winners. They were least important to Senate newcomers.

Large contributions from individuals were important to all groups — particularly Senate incumbents, who drew 39 percent of their dollars from individual donors giving $200 or more. Small individual contributions were most important to freshman senators — a possible reflection of the

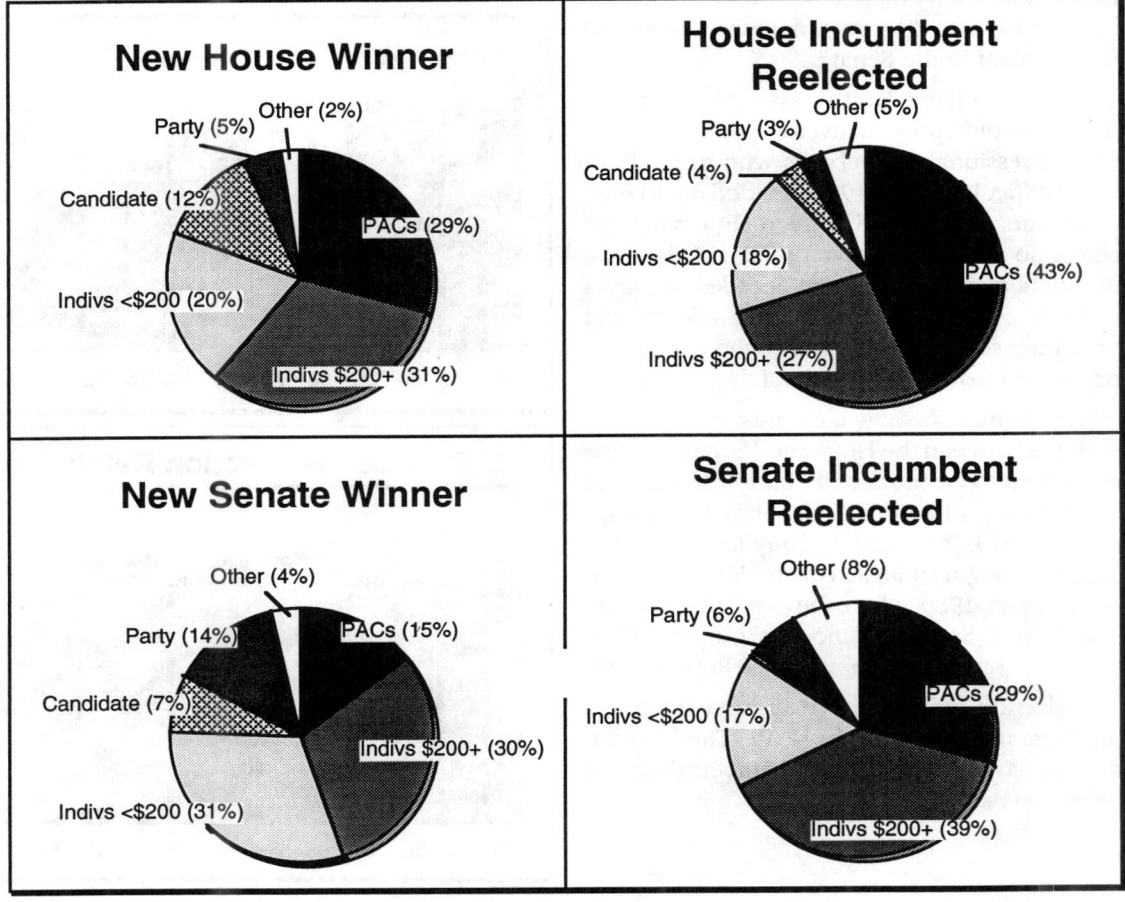

grass roots financial support that helped elect four women candidates to the U.S. Senate. Only one senator drew a majorty of campaign dollars from small donations in 1992: Democrat Carol Moseley-Braun of Illinois. California's Barbara Boxer drew the largest dollar amount in that category — just over $5 million from contributions under $200.

Another fact of political financing that is clear from these charts is the relatively minor role that candidates' personal funds play in most campaigns — particularly among incumbents.

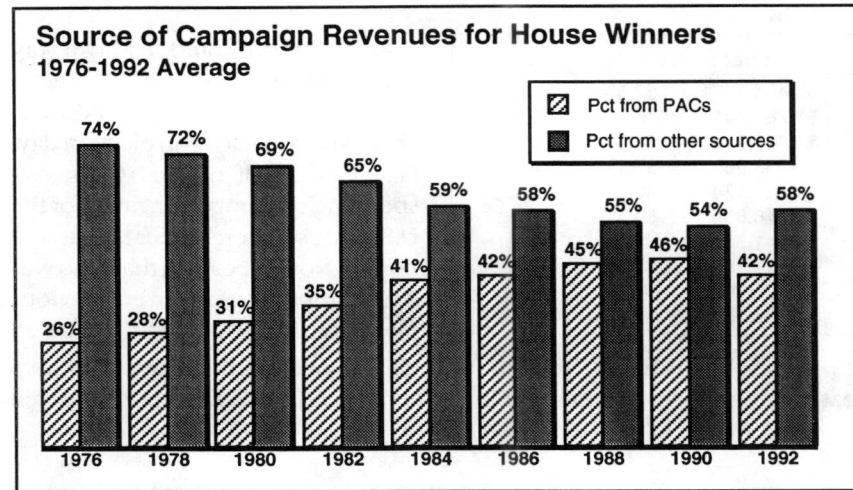

Sources: Federal Election Commission and Center for Responsive Politics

A Small Decline in PAC Dependency

The long-term trend toward greater PAC dependency among U.S. House winners reversed itself in 1992, albeit modestly. Though it may have been the beginnings of a new anti-PAC trend among incumbents feeling the heat from voters, the dip was more likely due to the unusually large number of non-incumbents who won office in 1992. As the charts on the following page indicate clearly, PACs give far more heavily to incumbents than to newcomers.

Source of PAC Funds — House Freshmen vs. Incumbents

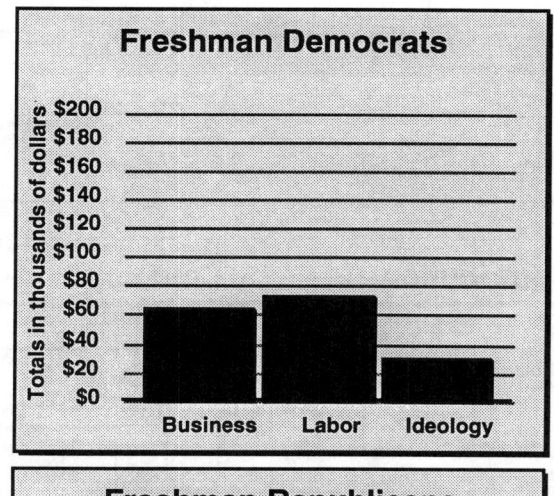

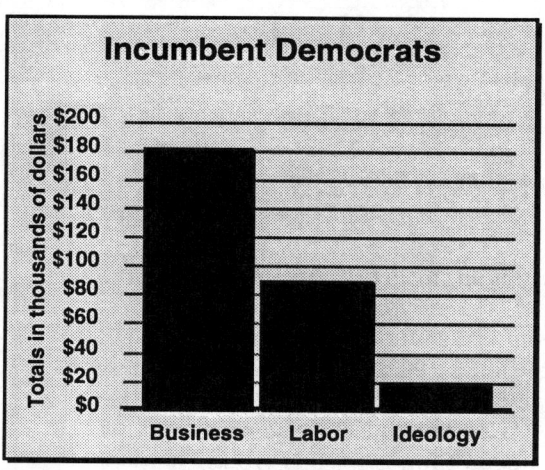

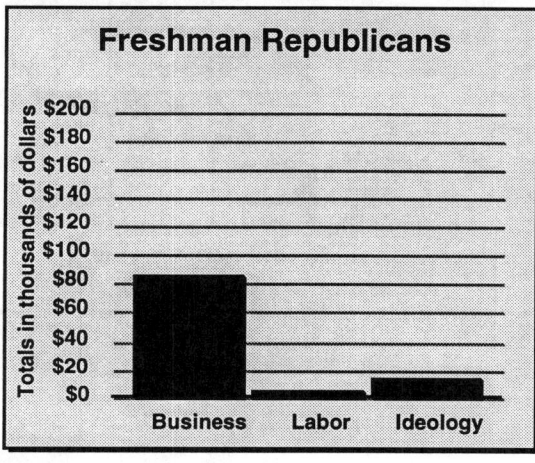

When PAC receipts are clustered into three distinct groups — business, labor and ideological — significant contrasts in the source of PAC funds can be seen between Democrats and Republicans, and between freshman members of Congress versus incumbents. The biggest source of funds for newly-elected Democrats comes from Labor PACs, which gave an average of more than $71,000 per Democratic winner in the 1992 elections. That is slightly more than the freshman Democrats got from all business PACs combined. Ideological and single-issue PACs are also an important source of funds for newly-elected Democrats.

Once the House Democrats have served one or more terms in Congress, the complexion of their PAC contributions shifts significantly. Labor dollars are still an important source of campaign revenues, but they are swamped by the combined dollars collected from business PACs. Ideological PACs, meanwhile, play only a minor part in the reelection war chests collected by Democratic House incumbents.

Republicans — whether freshmen or incumbents — collect the great preponderance of their PAC dollars from business interests. Labor PACs are almost non-existent for newly-elected Republicans, and ideological PACs provide less than half the dollars for freshman Republicans than they do for Democrats. As Republicans take office and seek reelection, their proportion of business dollars continues to vastly outweigh their combined contributions from labor and ideological groups. Labor and ideological PACs also come closer into balance.

Among both Democrats and Republicans, one trend is consistent. Incumbents — whatever the mix of business, labor and ideological PACs that give to their campaigns — routinely draw far more total PAC dollars than candidates who have not yet won election to Congress.

Where Newcomers Found the Money . . .

Freshman Democrats

PAC contributions from organized labor were the single biggest source of campaign funds for most freshman Democrats who broke into the House of Representatives in 1992. On average, the new Democratic members received just over $71,000 from labor PACs. Ideological PACs were another important source of funds for this group. Many of the most promising challengers and open seat candidates drew contributions from "leadership PACs" operated by Democratic members of Congress. Financial interests and lawyers were the other leading sources of funds for freshman Democrats. Most of those dollars came through individual contributions.

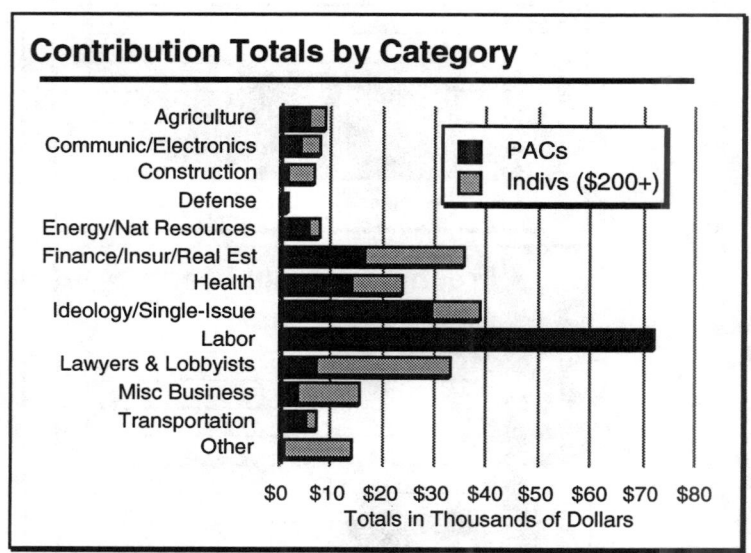

Freshman Republicans

Newly-elected Republicans had a markedly different contribution profile from their Democratic colleagues. Financial interests and miscellaneous business contributors were the two leading sources of campaign cash for the GOP freshman. Both those groups gave about half their money through PACs and half through large contributions from individuals. Health industry contributors — primarily doctors and other health professionals — were another important source of funds, providing about $25,000 to the average new Republican member of Congress. The remainder of the Republicans' dollars came from a wide cross-section of business groups.

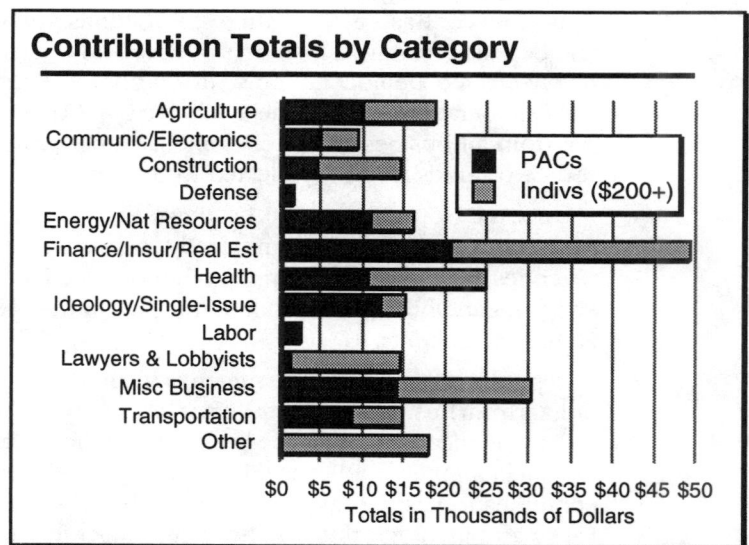

Where Incumbents Found the Money . . .

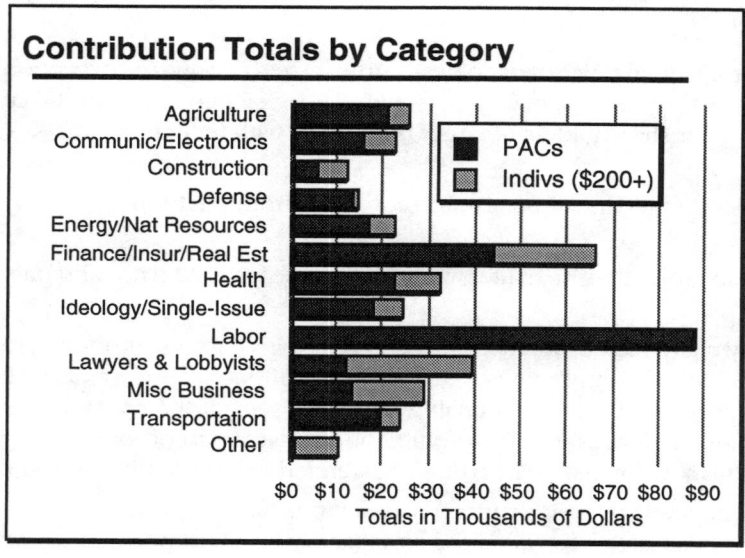

Contribution Totals by Category

Agriculture
Communic/Electronics
Construction
Defense
Energy/Nat Resources
Finance/Insur/Real Est
Health
Ideology/Single-Issue
Labor
Lawyers & Lobbyists
Misc Business
Transportation
Other

■ PACs
▨ Indivs ($200+)

$0 $10 $20 $30 $40 $50 $60 $70 $80 $90
Totals in Thousands of Dollars

Once they've been elected to Congress — and received their committee assignments — Democrats begin to receive contributions from many business groups that rarely give to non-incumbents. Organized labor continues to be an important source of campaign funds, but not nearly as important as it is to freshman Democrats. The finance/insurance/real estate sector is by far the most important source among business groups for incumbent Democrats. The "second tier" of business contributors is led by lawyers & lobbyists, but there is wide variation among members in the mix of different industries. The industry patterns to individual members tend to parallel their committee assignments as well as the economic profile of their home district.

Incumbent Republicans

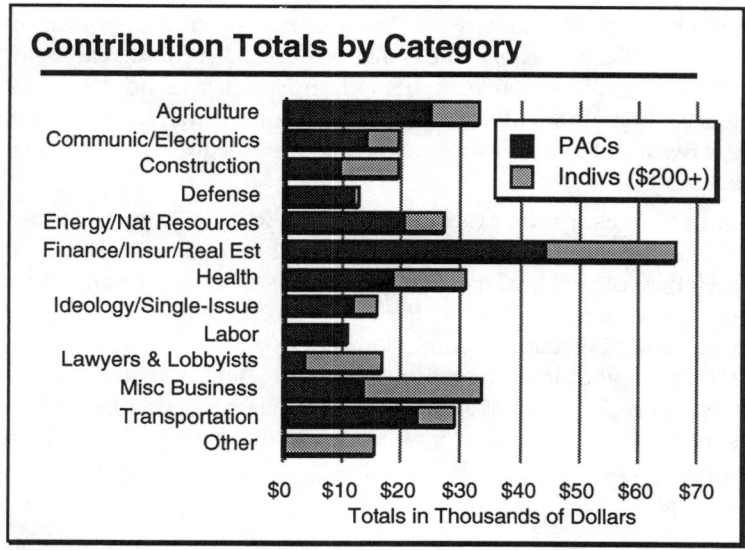

Contribution Totals by Category

Agriculture
Communic/Electronics
Construction
Defense
Energy/Nat Resources
Finance/Insur/Real Est
Health
Ideology/Single-Issue
Labor
Lawyers & Lobbyists
Misc Business
Transportation
Other

■ PACs
▨ Indivs ($200+)

$0 $10 $20 $30 $40 $50 $60 $70
Totals in Thousands of Dollars

By a wide margin, the finance/insurance/real estate sector is the leading source of campaign funds to incumbent House Republicans. Other important sectors include agriculture, energy, health, transportation, and miscellaneous business — though Republican incumbents drew significant funds from all other business sectors as well. Like their Democratic colleagues, most Republican incumbents get only a small proportion of their funds from ideological groups. Their share of labor PAC dollars, while still small in comparison to Democrats, is significantly higher than that received by Republican freshmen.

Rules of the Game

The rules that govern the financing of elections can be complicated enough to keep a small army of Washington lawyers perpetually employed. But federal election laws are not so complicated that the average voter can't figure out the basics. Outlined below is an overview of the rules. Significant changes in these laws were under consideration by the 103rd Congress, but any new rules are not likely to take effect before the 1996 elections.

Who Can Contribute and Who Cannot

Any American citizen can contribute funds to candidates for federal office or to political parties. There is only one exception to this broad rule: individuals and owners of sole proprietorships that have contracts with the federal government. (That prohibition does not extend to employees, partners, officers or shareholders of larger businesses with federal contracts — many of whom are active contributors).

Foreign nationals who do not have permanent residence in the United States are prohibited from contributing to *any* political candidates in the U.S. — at the federal, state, or local level.

Cash contributions exceeding an aggregate of $100 are also prohibited, no matter where they come from. And no candidate can accept an anonymous donation of more than $50.

Corporations, labor unions, national banks and federally chartered corporations are also prohibited from contributing to federal campaigns or parties — though they may make unlimited contributions to the parties' "soft money" accounts (see page 16). They may also organize political action committees (or "PACs") that enable the employees of the company, or members of the union, to pool their resources and deliver their funds as a bloc. The prohibition against direct corporate giving has been a part of federal law since the passage of the Tillman Act in 1907. The ban was extended to labor unions in 1943.

In recent years, the issue of political action committees operated by foreign-owned corporations has become contentious — particularly since a growing number of American companies have been acquired by Japanese and European investors. The Federal Election Commission has ruled that such companies *may* operate political action committees as long as American citizens are the only contributors to the PAC.

The Birth of PACs

When Congress acted in 1943 to ban direct contributions from labor unions to federal candidates, organized labor was quick to react. That same year, the first modern "political action committee" was formed by the Congress of Industrial Organization (which later merged with the American Federation of Labor to form the AFL-CIO). The dollars the PAC distributed came not from the union treasury, but from voluntary contributions by its members. While such an arrangement was not explicitly sanctioned by federal law, neither was it prohibited. Over the next 30 years the idea gradually caught on as other labor unions, then corporations and business groups, formed PACs of their own. But many groups held back. PACs were still a loophole in federal election laws — tolerated, but not officially sanctioned.

In 1974, amid the post-Watergate climate of political reform, Congress gave PACs the green light. In its 1974 amendments to the Federal Election Campaign Act, Congress specifically sanctioned the formation of "political committees" to enable employees of corporations, members of labor unions, or members of professional groups, trade associations or any other political group to pool their dollars and give to the candidates of their choice. At the same time, it gave PACs higher contribution limits than individual contributors, and set up the Federal Election Commission (FEC) to oversee elections and to collect and monitor campaign finance reports filed by PACs and candidates. It was an opening of the floodgates. By the end of 1974, 608 political action committees were officially recognized by the FEC. By 1992 that number had grown to more than 4,700. The dollars they pumped into federal elections mushroomed from $12.5 million in 1976 to nearly $189 million in 1992. The great majority of those dollars — then and now — went to finance the campaigns of incumbent members of Congress.

Contribution Limits

Candidates for Congress can spend as much money as they can raise, whether from their own pockets or from those of contributors. No spending limits apply. Contributors to federal campaigns, on the other hand, do face limits in what they can give to a federal candidate or a national political party. The limits were set as part of the 1974 Federal Election Campaign Act, and they are summarized in the chart below:

Federal Campaign Spending Limits

	To any candidate or candidate committee	To any national party committee	To any PAC or other political committee	Total
Time period	per election*	per calendar year	per calendar year	per calendar year
Individual can give...	$1,000	$20,000	$5,000	$25,000
Multicandidate Committee† can give...	$5,000	$15,000	$5,000	No limit
Other Political Committee can give...	$1,000	$20,000	$5,000	No limit

SOURCE: Federal Election Commission

* Primary and general elections count as two separate elections; so this contribution can be effectively doubled during a normal election year in states with primaries.

† Multicandidate committees are those with more than 50 contributors, that have been registered for at least six months, and (with the exception of state party committees) have made contributions to five or more federal candidates.

Enforcement of the Campaign Laws

Enforcement of the federal campaign laws lies in the hands of the six-member Federal Election Commission in Washington, D.C. Appointed by the president to serve staggered six-year terms, commission members are traditionally split 3-3 between Republicans and Democrats.

The 3-3 split is also common in many of the commission's votes on rulings that would likely benefit one party over the other. Many analysts and commentators have contended that the institutional paralysis which sometimes results was exactly what the drafters of the Federal Election Campaign Act had in mind — namely, to keep the commission from being too vigilant or activist in its enforcement.

Over the years, the commission has come under considerable attack by critics on both sides of the political fence for its lack of direction in enforcing and interpreting the campaign finance law. While the commissioners have fairly regularly cited candidates and fined their campaigns for relatively minor offenses (and occasionally for serious ones), they have been unable to reach consensus on many larger issues affecting the conduct of federal elections.

One area for which the FEC has received well-deserved praise, however, is in its role as a provider of campaign finance information to the public. The FEC has collected millions of pages of detailed records since 1975 on the financing of federal elections, and citizens curious about the identity of their representatives' financial backers can find a wealth of information in the FEC's files.

Public Disclosure

By law, every candidate for federal office must file periodic reports with the Federal Election Commission in Washington, D.C., detailing both the income and expenditures of their campaign. Copies of these reports, which are timed to coincide with various high points in the two-year election cycle, must also be filed in the candidate's home state with the state election commission or equivalent agency.

Individual contributors who give an aggregate of $200 or more must be identified by name, address, occupation and employer. All PAC and party contributions, no matter how large or small, must also be itemized.

In addition, PACs themselves must file reports four times a year with the FEC in Washington, detailing both the contributions received by the PAC and the names of candidates and other groups that received the PAC's donations. While PACs are required to file at least quarterly, they may choose to file monthly if they wish — and many of the larger PACs do.

When it compiles the official records of PAC contributions, and records them on its computers, the FEC uses the reports filed by the PACs — *not* those filed by the candidates. Because of this, occasional discrepancies are inevitable between the contributions reported by the candidates and those recorded in the FEC's official records. In itemizing those contributions, this book relies on the official FEC data.

Filing Deadlines

Members of Congress and candidates for Congress must file their FEC reports according to the schedules shown in the following charts. Each report must list the candidate's contributions and expenditures during the reporting period. As the charts show, the schedules vary during election years and off years. In the course of a typical election year, a candidate for Congress may file as many as seven reports. In other years, only two reports are required.

Election Year Reporting Deadlines

Reports	Deadline	Period covered
Pre-election reports	12 days before primary election	Up to 20 days before the election
	12 days before general election	Up to 20 days before the election
Post-general report	30 days after general election	Up to 20 days after the election
Quarterly reports	Apr 15	Jan 1 - Mar 31
	Jul 15	Apr 1 - Jun 30
	Oct 15	Jul 1 - Sep 30
	Jan 31	Oct 1 - Dec 31 of previous year

NOTE: If two of the above deadlines closely coincide, a single report may be sufficient.

Non-election Year Reporting Deadlines

Reports	Deadline	Period covered
Semi-annual reports	Jul 31	Jan 1 - Jun 30
	Jan 31	Jul 1 - Dec 31 of previous year

Where to Find a Candidate's Reports

Any member of the public can view current and past campaign spending reports filed by their own representatives in Congress, or those of any other candidate for federal office. The central repository for these reports is the Public Records office of the Federal Election Commission at 999 E Street NW, Washington, D.C. 20463. The FEC's toll-free phone number is 1-800-424-9530. In the Washington area, the number is 202-219-4140.

The FEC also maintains a number of remote computer terminals around the country, generally in the offices of the secretary of state or the state election commission. As of April 1994, some 28 states were equipped with FEC terminals. Computer printouts of candidate or PAC reports can be ordered either from the FEC in Washington or from these state offices with terminals. A nominal charge is made for the materials, generally calculated on the cost of reproducing each page. One caveat: itemized contribution reports for major campaigns, such as those for the U.S. Senate, can be quite lengthy, even when reduced to computer printouts. Browsing through them (and in some cases even picking them up and carrying them out the door) can be quite an effort.

Federal campaign records are also available on-line to anyone with a computer, a modem, and an interest in obtaining the information. The on-line fee is $20 an hour and new subscribers must first request the service in writing and include a deposit before receiving their password. Among the reports available on-line are full contribution reports for any candidate or group of candidates (such as the congressional delegation from a particular state) and any PAC or groups of PACs. Recent FEC news releases are also available on line.

Copies of the candidates' FEC filings are also available in the candidate's home state. The reports are filed with the secretary of state's office or the state election commission, or whichever other agency in the state monitors elections.

In addition to campaign reports, the FEC also publishes pre-election and post-election reports listing summary statistics on campaign spending and fundraising by federal candidates, as well as a number of informative brochures outlining federal campaign laws and how they apply to candidates, PACs and contributors.

National Library on Money & Politics

The Federal Election Commission is no longer the only source for campaign finance data. The non-profit, non-partisan National Library on Money & Politics (a project of the Center for Responsive Politics) maintains a computer database that takes the raw FEC data and classifies each contribution by the same system of industry and interest group categories used throughout this book.

The Library was established primarily to work with news organizations, academic researchers and others who want to follow the trends and specifics of who's funding federal elections. It can prepare custom reports analyzing the contributions of any member of Congress or other federal candidate. Reports can also be compiled on the spending patterns of a particular company, industry, or interest group.

The Library's computerized databases include FEC data going back several election cycles. It also has access to congressional voting records, so reports can be compiled comparing a member of Congress' voting pattern with his or her contributions.

Standard reports are priced from $10 to $25, depending on their complexity. Custom reports can be done on an hourly fee schedule.

For more information or to place an order for a report, the Library can be reached at 202-857-0318.

Deciphering the Candidates' FEC Reports

Sifting through a candidate's FEC reports is not always an enlightening experience. Many candidates, instead of entering the full name of a PAC, often enter the PAC's informal acronym. Even if you knew, for example, that the Association of Trial Lawyers of America was the nation's largest PAC representing lawyers, you might not be able to decode the PAC's shorthand name — ATLA — when it appears on a candidate's report.

Making matters worse, there are no conventions to PAC acronyms and no FEC guidelines to ensure that each PAC uses a unique name. In fact, there are many duplications of shortened PAC names. "APAC," for example, is the informal acronym of at least three PACs: The Alltel Corporation PAC, the American Society of Association Executives PAC, and the Armco Employees PAC. Many other duplicates can also be found among the more than 4,700 currently-registered political action committees.

Aside from the acronyms, most PAC names are fairly self-explanatory — at least in naming the organization that sponsors them. There is nothing mysterious, for example, about the Boeing Company PAC or the Mid-America Dairymen PAC. Identification becomes more difficult when the PAC sponsor is less well known and the company's name offers no hint of its line of business. Without consulting a corporate directory on the shelves of the nearest library, for example, one might not know that Malone & Hyde is a major food wholesaler, that the Kaman Corporation is a defense contractor, or that the Summa Corporation runs a Las Vegas hotel and casino.

Many other PACs, particularly ideological or single-issue PACs, have names that can be maddeningly obscure. Few casual observers would guess, for example, that the "Fund for Southern Progress" is actually the leadership PAC of South Carolina Governor Carroll Campbell, or that the "Committee for a Level Playing Field" represents banks that want Congress to allow them to begin offering stock brokerage services.

To assist those wanting to decipher the mysteries of PAC names that appear on candidates' FEC filings, the final section of this book (beginning on page 1251) identifies the primary interests of each PAC that gave $20,000 or more in the 1992 election cycle. But new PACs do spring up each election year, so the job of classifying the more obscure ones is a never-ending task.

Individual contributors present a different set of problems. Though candidates are required by law to list the name, address, occupation and employer of each contributor who gives $200 or more, this information is often incomplete. In the process of analyzing individual contributions undertaken for this book, these shortcomings stood out in stark relief. Some typical problems:

- **Missing information.** Federal election law requires that candidates for federal office make their "best effort" to obtain full information on employers and occupations of their contributors, and to report this information on their campaign filings for all contributors giving $200 or more. In 1993 the FEC finally served notice that it will begin to enforce the rule, which has long been ignored by some candidates since penalties have rarely been imposed for non-compliance. Most candidates are conscientious and do list the information for the great majority of their contributors. A few do not. A list of the leading offenders in the 1992 election can be found on page 35.

- **Incomplete information.** Sometimes the information listed by candidates is so generic that it is impossible to trace the economic interest of the contributor. "Businessman" or "Executive" is one example. "Self-employed" is another. Another commonly used euphemism is to identify contributors only by the term "consultant." The Center's analysis has found that many of these "consultants" — particular those from the Washington, DC area — turn out to be lobbyists.

- **Unemployed spouses and children.** If one were to take at face value the reports filed by candidates, one might come to the conclusion that the single most powerful constituency in America today is that of "homemakers" and "housewives." According to the reports filed by federal candidates for Congress in the 1992 elections, "housewives, homemakers, home managers, *executive* home managers" and various other variations on the theme contributed some $22.4 million — higher than any other listed occupation. In reality, the money that supplied these donations came overwhelmingly not from the "homemaker" but from her (or his) spouse. The same can be said of contributors identified as "students." In the research that went into this book, the Center took great pains to try to identify the spouses (or parents) of unemployed contributors. In many cases this was possible by comparing addresses, dates of contributions, etc. Where the connection with the income-earner was found, the contribution was classified as having the same economic interest as that of the person earning the family income.

Independent Expenditures

Direct contributions to candidates are not the only outlet for political action committees wishing to influence elections. "Independent expenditures" — funds spent independently by PACs to either support or oppose a candidate — offer another potentially powerful option. Unlike regular PAC gifts to campaigns, which cannot exceed $10,000 for the typical election cycle, independent expenditures can total any amount at all. They may directly attack or support a candidate by name, but the expenditures (or the advertising they support) cannot be made in conjunction or coordination with the campaign or staff of any candidate. In all, some 222 PACs and individuals spent more than $11.1 million on independent expenditures during the 1992 elections. About $4.4 million of that was directed at the presidential race, the rest was spent trying to influence congressional campaigns.

A total of 72 groups spent $10,000 or more on independent campaigns. Of those, 17 ran campaigns exceeding $100,000. The chart below lists the chief contributors of independent expenditures in 1992 and the top beneficiaries and targets of their funds.

Top PACs Making Independent Expenditures in 1992

PAC Name	Total	Top Beneficiaries/Targets	Amount	For/Agn	Office
Presidential Victory Committee	$2,057,757	George Bush	$2,057,757	For	Pres
National Right to Life PAC	$1,614,440	George Bush	$795,290	For	Pres
		Mike DeWine (R-Ohio)	$27,644	For	Senate
		Don Davis (R-NC)	$27,419	For	House
American Medical Assn	$1,024,210	Vic Fazio (D-Calif)	$255,085	For	House
		Bob Packwood (R-Ore)	$227,808	For	Senate
		Scott McInnis (R-Colo)	$184,910	For	House
		Michael A. Andrews (D-Texas)	$118,985	For	House
		Gary Franks (R-Conn)	$81,254	For	House
		Scott L. Klug (R-Wis)	$80,968	For	House
		Tony Meeker (R-Ore)	$75,200	For	House
National Assn of Realtors	$999,016	Les AuCoin (D-Ore)	$329,289	For	Senate
		Rod Chandler (R-Wash)	$169,950	For	Senate
		E. Clay Shaw Jr. (R-Fla)	$125,209	For	House
		Beryl Anthony Jr (D-Ark)	$100,000	For	House
		Ben Nighthorse Campbell (D-Colo)	$98,953	For	Senate
		Newt Gingrich (R-Ga)	$60,000	For	House
		Tom McMillen (D-Md)	$49,300	For	House
		Ronald K. Machtley (R-RI)	$45,100	For	House
National Rifle Assn	$957,666	Gene Green (D-Texas)	$139,468	For	House
		Mike Synar (D-Okla)	$137,574	Against	House
		Beryl Anthony Jr (D-Ark)	$86,412	Against	House
		W.A. Drew Edmondson (D-Okla)	$76,930	For	House
		Paul Coverdell (R-Ga)	$61,844	For	Senate
		Tom Coleman (R-Ga)	$61,209	Against	House
		Dan Glickman (D-Kan)	$52,080	Against	House
		Harris Wofford (D-Pa)	$40,292	Against	Senate
		Bill McCuen (D-Ark)	$30,137	For	House
		Pat Danner (D-Mo)	$25,890	For	House
National Abortion Rights Action League	$718,756	Russell Feingold (D-Wis)	$148,426	For	Senate
		Steven D. Pierce (R-Mass)	$144,091	Against	House
		Ben Nighthorse Campbell (D-Colo)	$137,487	For	
		Pat Williams (D-Mont)	$77,885	For	House
		Judith M. Ryan (R-Calif)	$59,827	For	House
		Robert Abrams (D-NY)	$47,930	For	Senate
		Alfonse M. D'Amato (R-NY)	$44,583	Against	Senate
		Dick Thornburgh (R-Pa)	$30,869	Against	Senate
Freedom Leadership PAC	$191,584	Bill Clinton	$190,597	Against	Pres

"Soft Money" — The Sky's the Limit

In the eyes of many observers — and many political practitioners who make use of it — the principal loophole in the federal campaign spending law is something that has come to be called "soft money." In the broadest sense, soft money encompasses any contributions not regulated by federal election laws. The exemption was made to encourage "party-building" activities which benefit the political parties in general, but not specific candidates. In reality, though, the loophole has emerged as the parties' primary means of raising tens of millions of dollars from wealthy contributors during the fall presidential campaigns, when direct contributions to candidates are prohibited. They are also used to support congressional candidates in key battleground states during off-year elections.

Technically, soft money contributions are supposed to be used only for state and local political activities — such as voter registration, get-out-the-vote drives and bumper stickers — and for such generic party-building activities as TV ads supporting the Democratic and Republican platforms, but not naming specific candidates. Typically, however, the funds pay for much more — including office overhead, the purchase of expensive computer equipment, and other behind-the-scenes expenses — thus freeing up other contributions to the party to be used directly to support candidates.

During the 1992 presidential campaign, the Democratic and Republican parties raised an estimated $34 million and $48 million respectively in soft money contributions on the national level alone. The exact figures will never be known (except to the parties), however, because much of the soft money was contributed directly to state and local political committees. Under new rules which took effect Jan. 1, 1991, soft money contributions to the national parties must now be reported to the Federal Election Commission. Even so, soft money can still be given with virtually no strings attached. This offers four main benefits to soft money contributors and recipients:

- **Soft money is not subject to any contribution limits.** Contributions to candidates or federal party committees are subject to specific limits (outlined in the chart on page 11). Soft money contributions can be made for any amount at all. The list on the facing page shows just how high the biggest contributions were in the 1991-92 election cycle.

- **Soft money contributions can be made by anyone — including groups prohibited from making contributions to federal candidates or parties.** In federal campaigns, corporations and labor unions are explicitly prohibited from making direct contributions to federal candidates, federal parties, or federal PACs. Their soft money contributions are subject only to the restrictions passed by the legislatures in the individual states where the contributions are made. Many states currently allow corporate and labor union contributions.

- **Soft money offers an extra means of political giving for individuals who've already given the maximum to candidates and federal parties.** Under the federal election laws, individual contributors are limited to an annual maximum of $25,000 in contributions to all candidates, PACs and national parties. Once they've "maxed out" they can give no more — except in soft money. Using this device, wealthy contributors, often with the encouragement of the national parties, have been able to give substantially more than the nominal limit.

- **Soft money offers a way for corporations, unions and wealthy contributors to directly support presidential candidates in the fall elections.** Since 1974, when Congress authorized the $1 checkoff on federal income tax returns (Since raised to $3), presidential elections have been publicly financed. While presidential candidates can (and do) raise millions during the primary election battles for the nomination, once the parties have officially nominated their candidate at their party conventions, no more private contributions are allowed. Because of the soft money loophole, however, the period during the fall campaign has turned into the most intensive period of political fundraising in American politics. In 1988 the Republicans even organized an exclusive club — called "Team 100" — made up of soft money contributors who gave $100,000 or more. Several Team 100 members were later appointed ambassadors to foreign nations after the Bush administration took office. In 1992, Team 100 was back, giving more than ever. Not to be outdone, the Democrats created a new circle of elite givers called the "Managing Trustees." Admission to this blue-chip group requires giving or raising at least $200,000 in soft money.

Top Soft Money Contributors in 1991-92

Contributor	Amount	To Repubs	To Dems	Industry
Archer-Daniels-Midland*	$1,374,500	$1,107,000	$267,500	Agricultural Svcs & Prod/Transport
RJR Nabisco*	$875,305	$529,305	$346,000	Tobacco/Food Products
Atlantic Richfield Co*	$857,958	$579,641	$278,317	Oil & Gas/Chemicals/Coal
Philip Morris*	$816,580	$589,080	$227,500	Tobacco/Beer
Joseph E Seagram & Sons*	$731,637	$524,727	$206,910	Beer, Wine & Liquor
American Financial Corp	$715,000	$715,000	$0	Insurance
US Tobacco	$652,768	$525,004	$127,764	Tobacco
International Marketing Bureau	$633,770	$633,770	$0	Business Services
Merrill Lynch*	$594,900	$485,100	$109,800	Securities & Investment
New Jersey Gala '92	$566,286	$0	$566,286	Democratic/Liberal
National Education Assn	$423,752	$7,750	$416,002	Public Sector Unions
United Steelworkers*	$404,876	$0	$404,876	Bldg Trades/Industrial Unions
Time Warner*	$398,573	$100,240	$298,333	TV & Movies/Publishing
Chevron Corp	$361,760	$256,372	$105,388	Oil & Gas
Occidental Petroleum	$336,030	$224,080	$111,950	Oil & Gas/Chemicals
Sony Corp of America	$332,650	$100,000	$232,650	TV & Movies/Electronics
American Intertrade Group*	$322,800	$322,800	$0	Business Services
Tobacco Institute	$317,202	$164,927	$152,275	Tobacco
Alida Rockefeller Messinger	$300,650	$0	$300,650	Philanthropist
Goldman, Sachs & Co*	$293,520	$248,520	$45,000	Securities & Investment
Limited Inc	$288,600	$247,100	$41,500	Retail Sales
Revlon Group Inc	$286,700	$140,000	$146,700	Cosmetics
Anheuser-Busch*	$279,280	$108,080	$171,200	Beer, Wine & Liquor
Lawrence Kadish	$276,200	$276,200	$0	Real Estate
Communications Workers of America	$275,680	$0	$275,680	Bldg Trades/Industrial Unions
Swanee Hunt	$262,200	$0	$262,200	Philanthropist
Bechtel Group*	$259,797	$124,347	$135,450	General Contractors
MCA Inc*	$257,730	$20,000	$237,730	TV & Movie Prod/Distribution
American Fedn of State/County/Munic Employees*	$256,574	$0	$256,574	Public Sector Unions
United States Surgical Corp	$255,200	$232,400	$22,800	Pharmaceuticals/Health Prod
Bell Atlantic*	$252,325	$159,700	$92,625	Telephone Utilities
International Assn of Firefighters	$250,869	$10,450	$240,419	Public Sector Unions
Brown-Foreman Corp*	$250,449	$250,449	$0	Beer, Wine & Liquor
Henley Group Inc*	$250,000	$200,000	$50,000	Pharmaceuticals/Health Prod
Forstmann, Little & Co*	$245,000	$245,000	$0	Securities & Investment
Kohlberg, Kravis & Roberts*	$240,000	$200,000	$40,000	Securities & Investment
Morgan Stanley & Co*	$238,827	$130,977	$107,850	Securities & Investment
United Auto Workers	$236,965	$0	$236,965	Bldg Trades/Industrial Unions
Lazard Freres & Co*	$236,500	$20,000	$216,500	Securities & Investment
Sheet Metal Workers Union*	$234,500	$0	$234,500	Bldg Trades/Industrial Unions
Thomas J. Watson	$234,000	$84,000	$150,000	Computer Equipment & Svcs
Peter B. Lewis	$231,300	$0	$231,300	Insurance
Connell Co	$225,100	$0	$225,100	Crop Prod & Basic Processing
Pacific Telesis Group	$223,927	$142,627	$81,300	Telephone Utilities
Mesa Limited Partnership	$221,100	$219,600	$1,500	Oil & Gas
Coca-Cola Co*	$218,830	$160,127	$58,703	Food & Beverage
Waste Management Inc*	$213,057	$155,327	$57,730	Waste Management
Merle C. Chambers	$210,200	$0	$210,200	Oil & Gas
Agenda for the 90's	$210,000	$0	$210,000	Democratic/Liberal
Peter & Eileen Norton	$210,000	$0	$210,000	Computer Software

* Total came from more than one affiliate or subsidiary.

The above list includes contributions made to the Democratic and Republican National Committees, as well as the National Republican Senatorial Committee, the Democratic Senatorial Campaign Committee, the National Republican Congressional Committee, the Democratic Congressional Campaign Committee, the President's Dinner Committee and the Democratic Congressional Dinner Committee.

The Role of PACs

Political action committees were born in the 1940s out of a perceived political necessity. When labor unions were prohibited from spending union treasury funds to contribute to federal candidates, they invented the idea of pooling donations from their members and presenting *that* money to the candidates instead. The idea appealed not only to labor unions, but to business and ideological groups as well, though the lack of a formal federal sanction for PACs kept many groups from setting up their own committees. When Congress passed the 1974 amendments to the Federal Election Campaign Act, officially sanctioning the concept of "political committees," the great PAC rush began. In recent years, the number of political action committees has stabilized, and even begun to decline. Total PAC dollars, however, continue to rise — particularly to House and Senate incumbents.

More than 4,700 political action committees were officially registered at the close of the 1992 election year. Of those, just over 3,100 actually contributed funds to federal candidates. Many of those PACs were small-scale operations, sponsored by small busi-

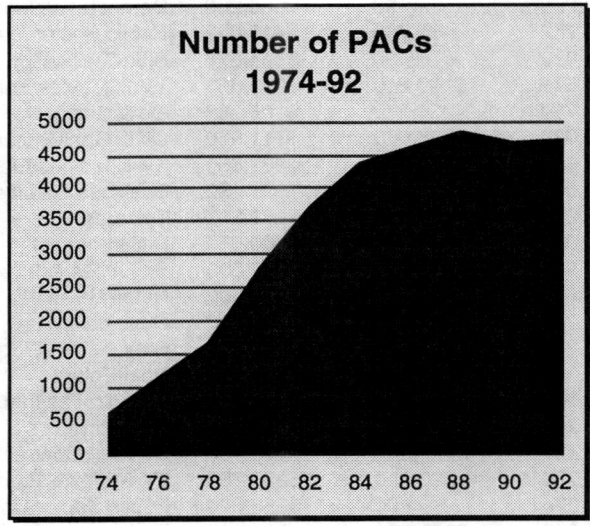

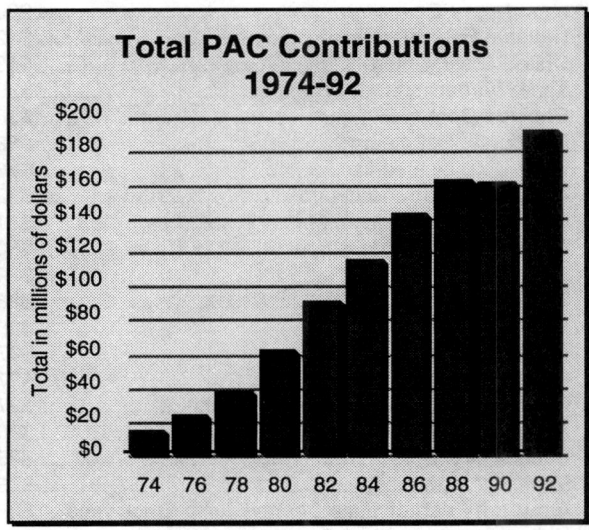

nesses, political clubs, or labor union locals, and contributed only to candidates in their own state or region. Only one out of four of the registered PACs gave $20,000 or more to federal candidates, but those that did accounted for over 94 percent of all PAC giving. The chart below shows the relative distribution of small, medium and large PACs, and their respective spending power in the 1992 elections.

Biggest PACs Deliver the Biggest Punch

This many PACs...	Gave this much money...	for this total impact...
1637	$0	
1496	Less than $10,000	
407	$10,000-$19,999	
499	$20,000-$49,999	
294	$50,000-$99,999	
398	$100,000 or more	

As is evident from this chart, the real power of PACs lies not in their numbers, but in the dollars they can deliver. In 1992, as in every year since PACs emerged as an important force in federal elections, a comparatively small number of large PACs delivered the biggest share of the money. Less than one-tenth of the total PAC community provided nearly three-fourths of all the dollars in the 1991-92 election cycle. On the other side of the spectrum, over 1,600 PACs — more than a third of all registered political action committees — made no contributions at all to congressional candidates.

With Outstretched Hands . . .

The financial clout of PACs is not something that has been forced upon members of Congress over their objections. Modern campaign techniques, centered around 30-second TV spots and highly targeted direct mail appeals, have prompted many incumbents to hire campaign consultants, pollsters, media advisors, fund-raisers and a retinue of specialists who are the behind-the-scenes operatives of today's high-tech campaigns. The pressures of raising the money it takes to pay for them all have forced nearly every incumbent to spend an increasing amount of time appealing to PACs and other large contributors for funds. Because of their higher contribution limits ($5,000 per election, versus $1,000 per election for individuals), PACs offer the most convenient means of raising large sums of campaign cash quickly.

In contrast to the pro-forma reelection races that many incumbents have enjoyed in recent years, the 1992 elections were worrisome for nearly every member of Congress. Those shown in the tables below relied the most heavily on PACs to provide the funds that helped them weather the political storm. (Dan Coats, the Senate leader, ran in both 1990 and 1992).

Top Recipients of PAC Contributions

House Members (1991-92)

Name	PAC Rcpts	Total Rcpts
Richard A. Gephardt (D-Mo)	$1,240,597	$3,238,479
Vic Fazio (D-Calif)	$1,147,938	$1,993,452
Dan Rostenkowski (D-Ill)	$961,937	$1,587,234
David E. Bonior (D-Mich)	$934,589	$1,295,553
John D. Dingell (D-Mich)	$767,931	$1,112,141
Newt Gingrich (R-Ga)	$756,347	$2,507,668
Steny H. Hoyer (D-Md)	$705,642	$1,304,867
Martin Frost (D-Texas)	$666,804	$1,241,725
Al Swift (D-Wash)	$649,844	$914,905
Charles Wilson (D-Texas)	$638,825	$1,188,912

Senate Members (1987-92)

Name	PAC Rcpts	Total Rcpts
Daniel R. Coats (R-Ind)	$2,349,342	$7,727,256
Lloyd Bentsen (D-Texas)	$2,349,054	$9,614,793
Arlen Specter (R-Pa)	$2,011,791	$10,463,911
Frank R. Lautenberg (D-NJ)	$1,884,342	$9,033,987
Phil Gramm (R-Texas)	$1,848,480	$18,457,261
Tom Harkin (D-Iowa)	$1,834,857	$5,867,588
Tom Daschle (D-SD)	$1,832,046	$4,122,119
Dave Durenberger (R-Minn)	$1,723,548	$6,388,791
Christopher S. Bond (R-Mo)	$1,717,017	$5,087,184
Richard C. Shelby (D-Ala)	$1,690,444	$3,778,582

. . . And 26 Members Who "Just Said No" to PACs

In an era when more and more voters are equating PAC contributions with "special interests," a growing number of House and Senate candidates are making an issue of running without the support of PACs. Twelve House incumbents turned down PAC contributions in the 1992 elections. So did nine newly-elected members. In the Senate, four incumbents have either refused PAC funds in the past or vowed not to accept any in the future. Here's the list of those who took the No-PAC Pledge.

1992 House Incumbents Who Took No PAC Funds

Name	Party	District	'92 Vote Pct
Bill Archer	Rep	Texas 7	100.0%
Anthony C. Beilenson	Dem	Calif 24	55.5%
Jim Cooper	Dem	Tenn 5	64.1%
Philip M. Crane	Rep	Ill 8	55.7%
Bill Goodling	Rep	Pa 19	45.3%
Bill Gradison	Rep	Ohio 2	70.1%
Andrew Jacobs Jr.	Dem	Ind 10	64.0%
Jim Leach	Rep	Iowa 1	68.1%
Edward J. Markey	Dem	Mass 7	62.1%
Romano L. Mazzoli	Dem	Ky 3	52.7%
William H. Natcher	Dem	Ky 2	61.4%
Glenn Poshard	Dem	Ill 19	69.1%
Ralph Regula	Rep	Ohio 16	63.7%
Mike Synar	Dem	Okla 2	55.5%

1992 House Freshmen Who Took No PAC Funds

Name	Party	District	'92 Vote Pct
Scotty Baesler	Dem	Ky 6	60.7%
Terry Everett	Rep	Ala 2	49.5%
Peter Hoekstra	Rep	Mich 2	63.0%
Martin R. Hoke	Rep	Ohio 10	56.8%
Steve Horn	Rep	Calif 38	48.6%
Michael Huffington	Rep	Calif 22	52.5%
Martin T. Meehan	Dem	Mass 5	52.2%
Nick Smith	Rep	Mich 7	87.6%
Peter Torkildsen	Rep	Mass 6	54.8%

Senate Incumbents Elected Without PAC Funds

Name	Party	State
David Boren	Dem	Okla
Herb Kohl	Dem	Wis
John Kerry	Dem	Mass

As the anti-PAC sentiment grows around the country, other members are likely to join the list. One prominent incumbent who announced early he would take no PAC funds in his 1994 reelection bid was Massachusetts Democrat Ted Kennedy. At least one of the candidates, however, had second thoughts. Freshman Republican Congressman Terry Everett of Alabama took no PAC funds until he was elected, but accepted them in 1993 after he took office.

The Patterns in PAC Contributions

Pragmatism — not partisanship and not political philosophy — appears to be the guiding principle behind many PAC contributions to congressional candidates, at least in the world of business PACs. Of the nearly 1,600 PACs that gave $10,000 or more in the 1992 elections, 92 percent gave to members of both parties. About one-third of those top-spending PACs — nearly all of them within the business community — split their dollars fairly evenly between Democrats and Republicans, giving no more than 60 percent of their money to either side. Ideological and labor PACs were far more likely to concentrate their funds with candidates of a single political party, as seen in the chart below.

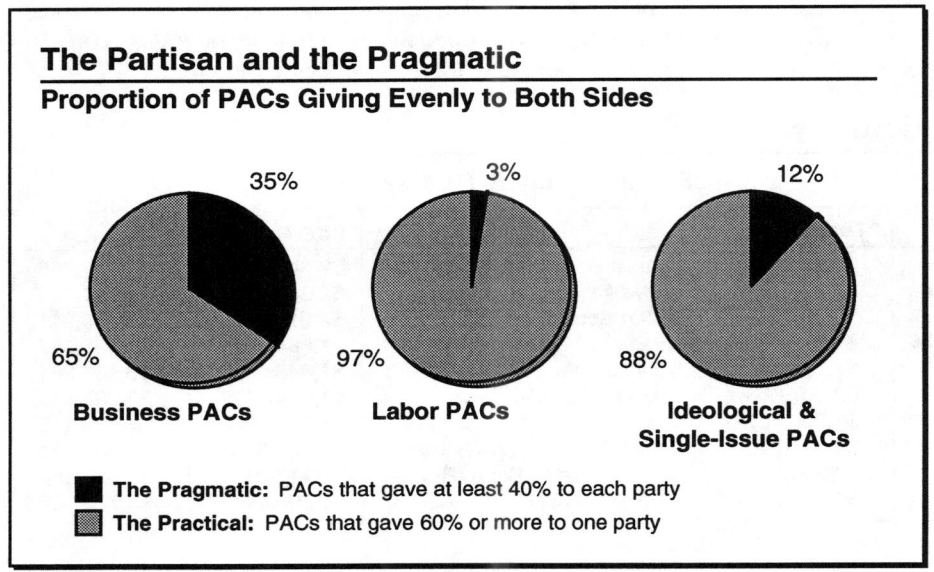

The Partisan and the Pragmatic

Proportion of PACs Giving Evenly to Both Sides

35%   3%   12%

65%   97%   88%

Business PACs   **Labor PACs**   **Ideological & Single-Issue PACs**

■ **The Pragmatic:** PACs that gave at least 40% to each party
▨ **The Practical:** PACs that gave 60% or more to one party

The Big Three Sectors: Business, Labor & Ideological/Single-Issue

While it is certainly possible to learn something about PAC behavior by looking at the overall patterns of PACs, it can be far more revealing to examine the many different segments of the PAC community one by one. It quickly becomes apparent that different groups of PACs behave differently. Labor and ideological PACs, for instance, distribute their money in a quite a different pattern from business PACs — as the charts on this page show.

Business PACs gave almost exactly the same amount to Democrats as Republicans. Ideological PACs favored Democrats two-to-one. And labor PACs, long the stalwarts of the Democratic Party, favored the party's candidates by a ratio of 16-to-one when handing out their contributions.

The overwhelming proportion of labor contributions to Democratic candidates tips the scale in favor of that party in overall PAC contributions, even though business PACs as a group gave nearly three times as much as labor PACs, and nearly twice as much as labor and ideological PACs combined. (See the chart on the facing page.)

Within these three main categories of PACs many other patterns can be found. The rest of the book explores their differences and similarities in detail.

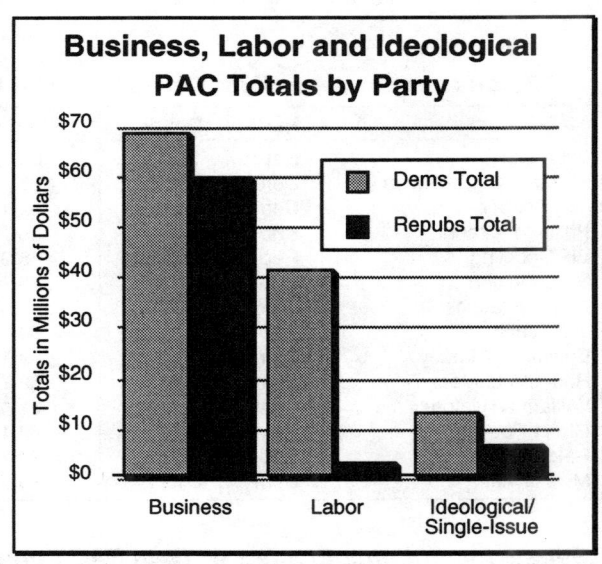

Business, Labor and Ideological PAC Totals by Party

Totals in Millions of Dollars

$70 / $60 / $50 / $40 / $30 / $20 / $10 / $0

▨ Dems Total
■ Repubs Total

Business   Labor   Ideological/ Single-Issue

The World of PACs from Three Different Angles

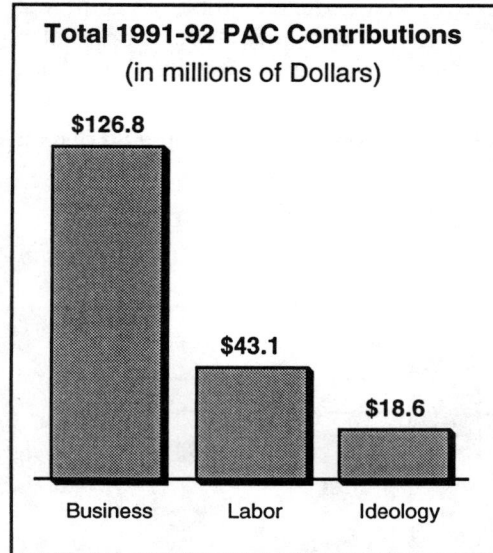

Total 1991-92 PAC Contributions
(in millions of Dollars)

$126.8 — Business
$43.1 — Labor
$18.6 — Ideology

The dollar power of business PACs can be clearly seen in the chart at left. With nearly $127 million in contributions to federal candidates in the 1992 election cycle, PACs representing every industry from car dealers to morticians sought to help their political friends and win their favor. Compared to labor and ideological/single-issue PACs, their dollar power was overwhelming.

A different story emerges when you turn the chart on its ear and break apart the business PACs into their individual sectors. No business sector comes close to offering either party the dollars that labor PACs produce for Democrats. While business PACs were giving relatively equal amounts to members of both parties, labor put 94 percent of its PAC dollars into Democratic campaigns. Even ideological and single-issue PACs rank high compared with the many diverse components of business PACs.

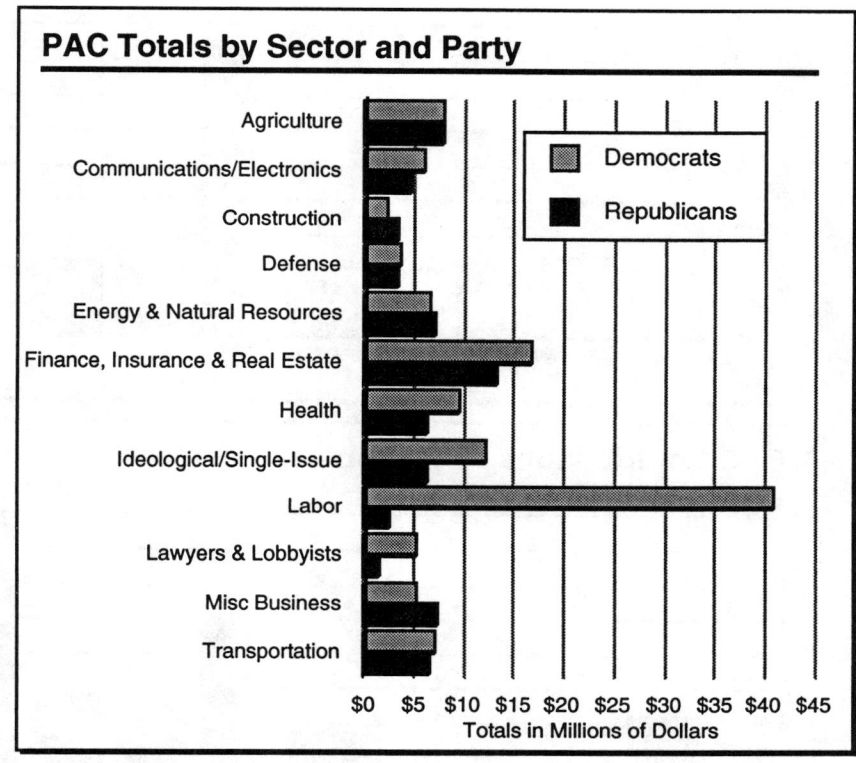

PAC Totals by Sector and Party

- Agriculture
- Communications/Electronics
- Construction
- Defense
- Energy & Natural Resources
- Finance, Insurance & Real Estate
- Health
- Ideological/Single-Issue
- Labor
- Lawyers & Lobbyists
- Misc Business
- Transportation

Democrats
Republicans

$0 $5 $10 $15 $20 $25 $30 $35 $40 $45
Totals in Millions of Dollars

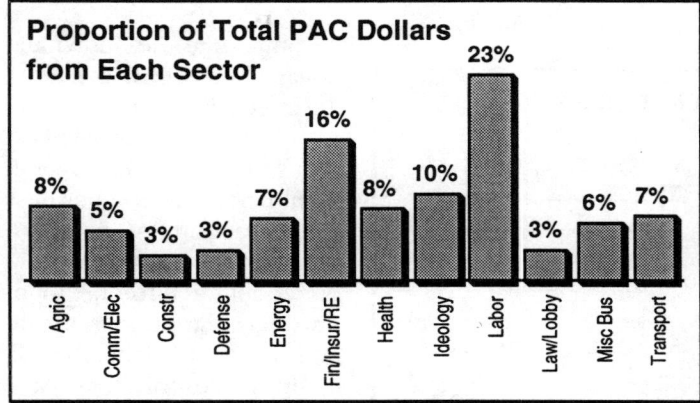

Proportion of Total PAC Dollars from Each Sector

8% — Agric
5% — Comm/Elec
3% — Constr
3% — Defense
7% — Energy
16% — Fin/Insur/RE
8% — Health
10% — Ideology
23% — Labor
3% — Law/Lobby
6% — Misc Bus
7% — Transport

After labor, the financial sector was the biggest PAC contributor to congressional campaigns, supplying 16 percent of all PAC dollars given in the 1992 elections. Banks, investment firms, insurance companies and real estate agents and developers combined to make it the biggest segment by far within the community of business PACs. What the charts on these pages don't show (but what can be seen in the pages that follow) is that PACs are only one source of campaign cash for members of Congress. When large individual contributions are added in, the picture changes again. Financial interests move to the top, lawyers rise to financial prominence from almost nowhere, and the dollars from organized labor are buried under an avalanche of dollars from business interests.

PACs and Individual Contributions Compared

The charts below illustrate the similarities and contrasts in spending patterns between individual contributors and PACs. Two sectors in particular are strikingly different — organized labor and lawyers and lobbyists. Nearly all the Labor dollars are delivered through political action committees. Looking only at PAC contributions therefore strongly overstates the political punch of labor unions. The charts at the bottom of the page underline this even more.

Lawyers and lobbyists, on the other hand, are dramatically undercounted when looking only at PACs. Some 86 percent of the legal community's contributions come from individuals, not PACs.

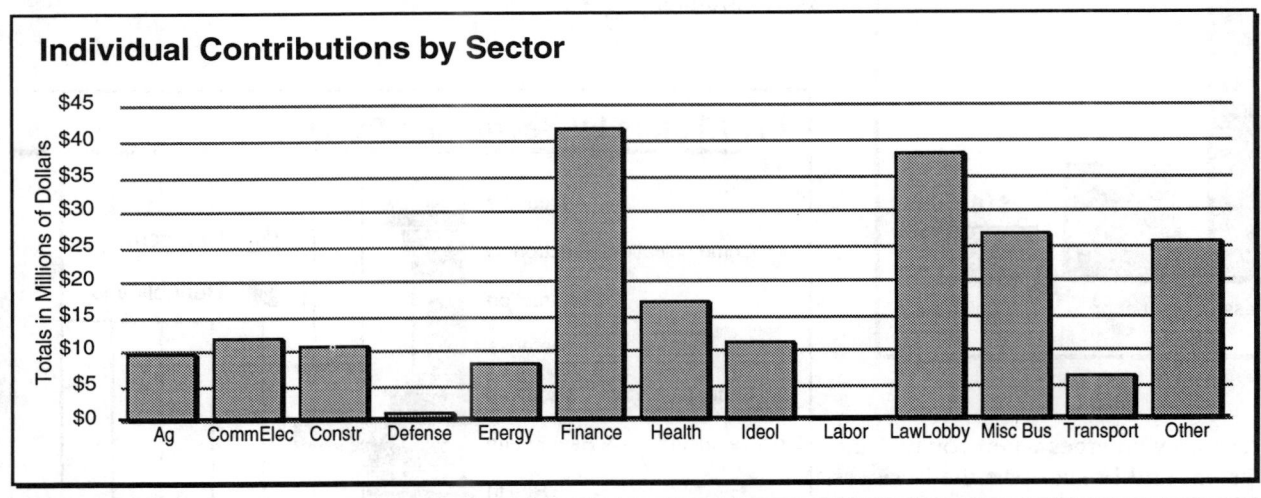

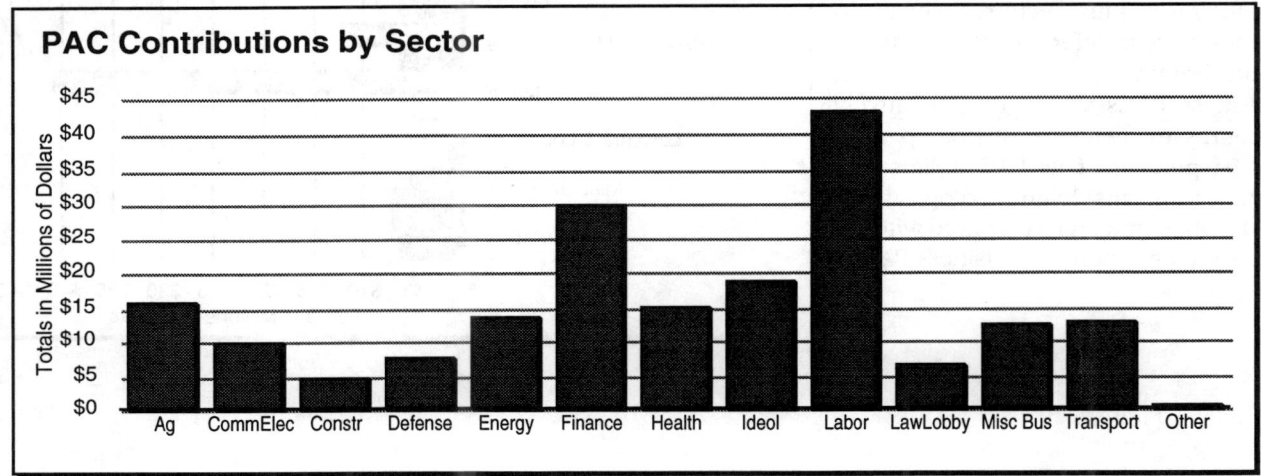

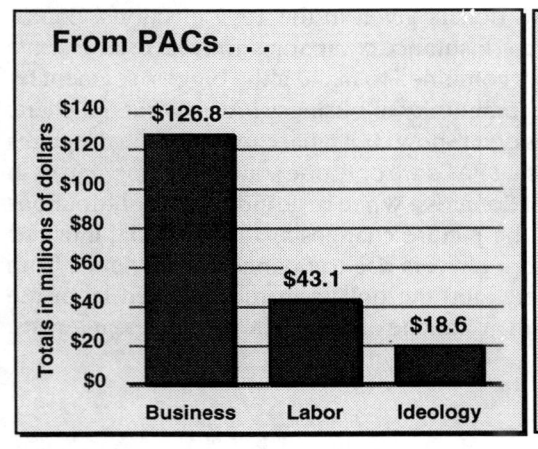

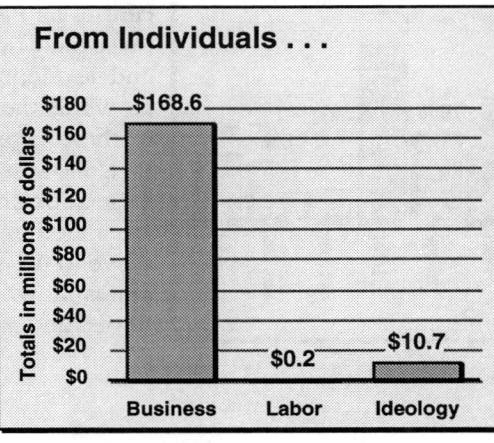

Comparing the individual dollars versus PAC dollars in the three large sectors of business, labor and ideological groups, shows the overall dominance of the business sector. Among PAC contributions, business outspends labor about three-to-one. In individual contributions, the ratio soars out of sight. Overall, business contributors gave $295 million in 1991-92. Organized labor gave $43 million. Ideological groups' combined total was $29 million.

Where the Individual Dollars* Came From: Top Metro Areas

Totals in Millions of Dollars

New York	$23.8
Los Angeles	$21.9
Washington	$17.4
Chicago	$8.8
Boston	$8.3
Philadelphia	$8.1
San Francisco	$7.5
Houston	$5.4
Atlanta	$4.8
Nassau County, NY	$4.6
Dallas	$4.2
Anaheim	$4.1
Miami	$3.7
St. Louis	$3.5
Bridgeport/Fairfield, Conn	$3.5
Newark, NJ	$3.3
San Diego	$3.2
Pittsburgh	$3.1
Cleveland	$3.0
Detroit	$3.0

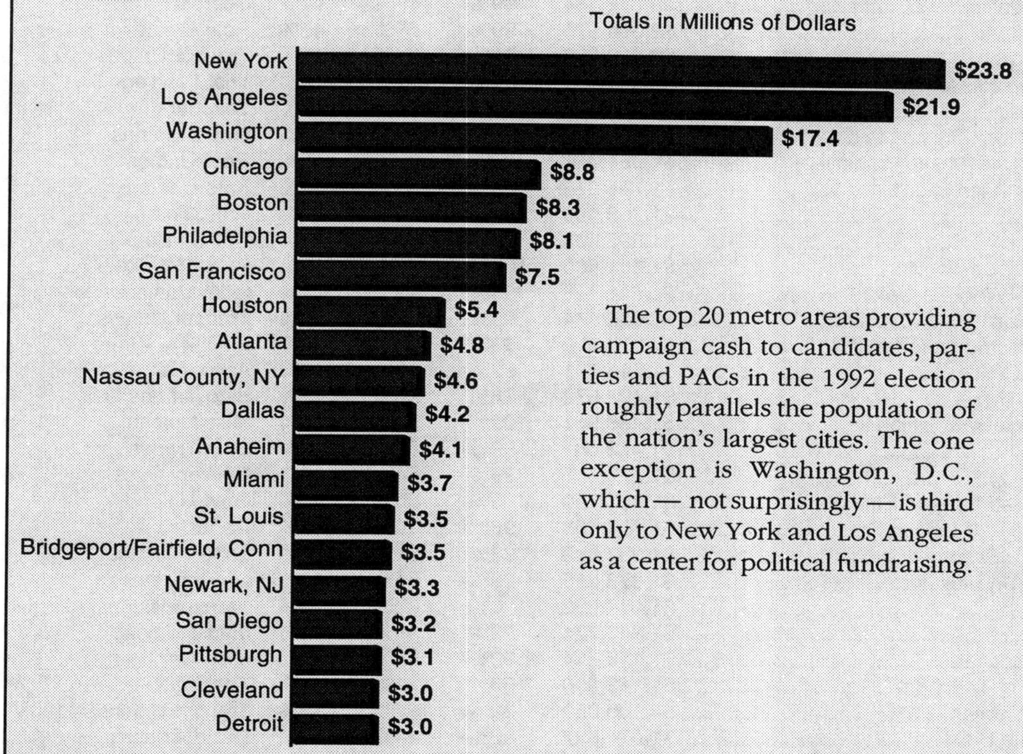

The top 20 metro areas providing campaign cash to candidates, parties and PACs in the 1992 election roughly parallels the population of the nation's largest cities. The one exception is Washington, D.C., which — not surprisingly — is third only to New York and Los Angeles as a center for political fundraising.

* Contributions of $200 and above

Where the PAC Dollars Came From: Top Metro Areas

Totals in Millions of Dollars

Washington	$91.4
New York	$12.9
Chicago	$9.6
San Francisco	$4.9
Los Angeles	$4.5
Detroit	$3.8
Bridgeport/Fairfield, Conn	$2.9
Houston	$2.9
Cleveland	$2.8
Pittsburgh	$2.5
St. Louis	$2.3
Dallas	$2.2
Atlanta	$1.8
Philadelphia	$1.8
Newark, NJ	$1.6
Birmingham, Ala	$1.6
Kansas City	$1.5
Boston	$1.5
Minneapolis	$1.4
Greensboro, NC	$1.2

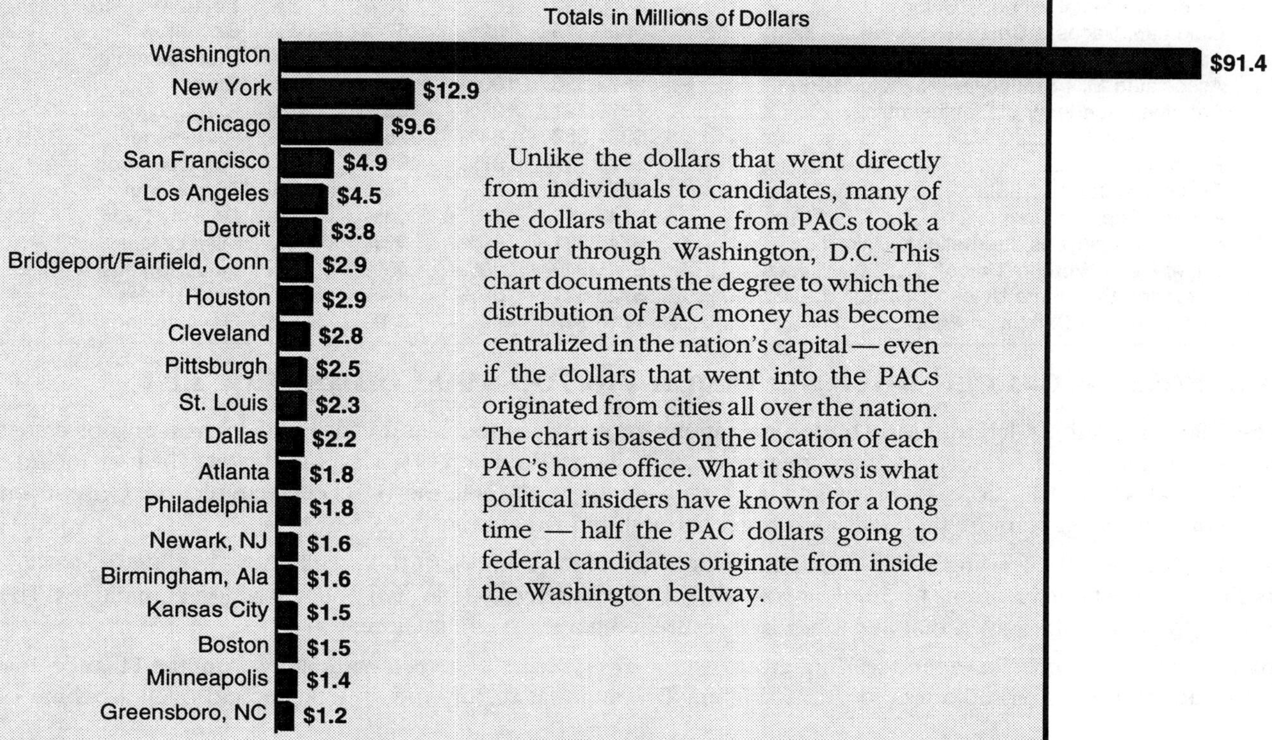

Unlike the dollars that went directly from individuals to candidates, many of the dollars that came from PACs took a detour through Washington, D.C. This chart documents the degree to which the distribution of PAC money has become centralized in the nation's capital — even if the dollars that went into the PACs originated from cities all over the nation. The chart is based on the location of each PAC's home office. What it shows is what political insiders have known for a long time — half the PAC dollars going to federal candidates originate from inside the Washington beltway.

23

Serious Money: The Top 100 Contributors

Rank	Contributor	Total	PAC Pct	Dem Pct	Rep Pct	Principal Category
1	American Medical Assn*	$3,245,544	99%+	49%	51%	Doctors
2	National Assn of Realtors	$2,954,973	99%+	55%	45%	Real Estate
3	Teamsters Union*	$2,532,956	99%+	94%	5%	Transpt Unions
4	Assn of Trial Lawyers of America	$2,361,135	100%	92%	8%	Trial Lawyers
5	National Education Assn*	$2,360,017	99%+	95%	3%	Teachers
6	United Auto Workers*	$2,251,489	99%+	98%	1%	Manuf Unions
7	American Fedn of St/Cnty/Munic Employees*	$1,954,063	99%+	97%	2%	Govt Unions
8	National Auto Dealers Assn	$1,784,375	100%	39%	61%	Auto Dealers
9	National Rifle Assn	$1,736,446	99%+	36%	63%	Pro-Guns
10	American Bankers Assn*	$1,692,508	99%+	50%	49%	Comml Banks
11	National Assn of Letter Carriers*	$1,661,880	100%	90%	10%	Postal Workers
12	Machinists/Aerospace Workers Union*	$1,641,746	99%+	97%	1%	Indust Unions
13	Marine Engineers Union*	$1,605,574	99%+	73%	27%	Transpt Unions
14	Intl Brotherhood of Electrical Workers*	$1,575,999	99%+	96%	3%	Electrical Wrkrs
15	American Institute of CPA's	$1,544,701	99%+	56%	44%	Accountants
16	Carpenters & Joiners Union*	$1,493,572	98%	94%	5%	Bldg Trades
17	Food & Commercial Workers Union	$1,488,961	100%	97%	2%	Misc Unions
18	Laborers Union*	$1,472,681	99%+	94%	5%	Bldg Trades
19	United Parcel Service	$1,472,357	99%	54%	46%	Delivery Svcs
20	National Assn of Retired Federal Employees	$1,437,250	100%	80%	19%	Govt Unions
21	American Dental Assn*	$1,434,408	99%+	60%	40%	Dentists
22	AT&T*	$1,397,883	93%	61%	39%	Long Distance
23	National Assn of Life Underwriters	$1,373,955	99%+	54%	46%	Life Insurance
24	Air Line Pilots Assn	$1,279,093	100%	87%	13%	Transpt Unions
25	United Steelworkers	$1,267,774	99%	99%	1%	Indust Unions
26	AFL-CIO*	$1,118,214	99%+	97%	2%	Misc Unions
27	American Federation of Teachers	$1,112,350	100%	99%	2%	Teachers
28	United Transportation Union	$1,100,050	99%+	97%	3%	Transpt Unions
29	National Assn of Home Builders*	$1,074,827	99%+	44%	56%	Resid Constr
30	Communications Workers of America*	$1,012,468	99%+	98%	1%	Indust Unions
31	RJR Nabisco*	$1,004,848	95%	55%	45%	Tobacco/Food
32	Emily's List	$999,755	37%	98%	0%	Women's Issues
33	Plumbers/Pipefitters Union*	$992,638	99%+	95%	4%	Bldg Trades
34	National Beer Wholesalers Assn	$977,081	100%	38%	62%	Beer Distrib
35	Seafarers International Union*	$970,476	99%+	92%	8%	Transpt Unions
36	BellSouth Corp*	$963,353	92%	59%	41%	Phone Utilities
37	National Cmte to Preserve Social Security	$941,650	99%+	88%	12%	Sr Citizens
38	American Postal Workers Union*	$900,390	100%	96%	3%	Postal Workers
39	Goldman, Sachs & Co	$898,545	22%	67%	33%	Securities
40	American Express*	$881,820	38%	69%	30%	Stocks/Credit
41	Associated Milk Producers	$877,550	100%	79%	21%	Dairy
42	American Academy of Ophthalmology	$870,227	99%+	63%	37%	Eye Doctors
43	General Electric*	$851,852	84%	58%	42%	Aerospace
44	Philip Morris*	$775,147	87%	59%	41%	Tobacco/Food
45	General Motors*	$771,474	88%	53%	46%	Auto Manuf
46	Federal Express Corp	$747,445	99%+	68%	32%	Delivery Svcs
47	Service Employees International Union	$745,931	99%+	98%	1%	Misc Unions
48	Sheet Metal Workers Union*	$745,749	99%+	95%	3%	Indust Unions
49	Operating Engineers Union*	$723,524	98%	89%	11%	Bldg Trades
50	Human Rights Campaign Fund	$718,590	99%+	92%	6%	Gay/Lesbian

Labor PACs, Financial Interests Dominate Top 100 Contributor List

These 100 corporations, labor unions, trade associations, professional societies and assorted interest groups were the top contributors in the 1992 elections. Together, they gave a combined $95 million to federal candidates. The total includes some $89 million in PAC contributions — nearly half the total given by all PACs in the 1991-92 election cycle. Only seven of the top 100 contributors gave more than half their funds through individual donations.

Labor unions were the leading sector, accounting for 29 positions in the Top 100. In all, those leading unions gave over $36 million in direct contributions to candidates — almost all of it delivered through political action committees. The figure is particularly remarkable given that all labor PACs combined gave just $43 million.

Financial interests were the second leading group on the Top 100 list. Nineteen companies from the Finance, Insurance & Real Estate sector dispensed a total of $13.4 million. Topping that sector, and ranking second overall behind only the

Rank	Contributor	Total	PAC Pct	Dem Pct	Rep Pct	Principal Category
51	Union Pacific Corp*	$713,390	96%	33%	67%	Railroads
52	National PAC	$684,000	100%	65%	35%	Pro-Israel
53	Waste Management Inc*	$683,558	78%	62%	38%	Waste Mgmt
54	Associated General Contractors*	$677,899	99%	24%	76%	Genl Contract
55	American Chiropractic Assn*	$658,596	99%+	73%	27%	Chiropractors
56	National Cmte for an Effective Congress	$651,250	99%+	100%	0%	Dem/Liberal
57	National Cable Television Assn	$644,249	99%	54%	46%	Cable TV
58	Prudential Insurance*	$640,040	63%	59%	41%	Insurance
59	US Tobacco*	$636,120	69%	34%	66%	Tobacco
60	GTE Corp*	$631,869	97%	52%	48%	Phone Utilities
61	Merrill Lynch*	$627,864	30%	51%	48%	Securities
62	ACRE (Action Cmte for Rural Electric)*	$627,155	100%	74%	26%	Rural Electric
63	American Hospital Assn*	$617,102	95%	69%	31%	Hospitals
64	Sierra Club	$612,130	99%+	96%	3%	Environment
65	Independent Insurance Agents of America	$589,798	100%	60%	40%	Insurance
66	Time Warner*	$583,089	24%	76%	24%	Movies/Publish
67	American Council of Life Insurance	$581,880	99%+	59%	40%	Life Insurance
68	Credit Union National Assn*	$581,830	99%+	67%	33%	Credit Unions
69	National Restaurant Assn*	$571,197	99%+	23%	77%	Restaurants
70	International Assn of Firefighters*	$565,353	100%	94%	6%	Firefighters
71	Ameritech Corp*	$562,342	92%	55%	45%	Phone Utilities
72	Ironworkers Union*	$551,480	99%+	92%	7%	Bldg Trades
73	American Family Corp	$550,000	91%	61%	39%	Health Insur
74	Chicago Mercantile Exchange	$549,500	90%	74%	26%	Commodities
75	Auto Dealers & Drivers for Free Trade	$538,550	100%	38%	62%	Import Auto Dlrs
76	Akin, Gump et al	$538,228	57%	79%	21%	Law/Lobby
77	Martin Marietta Corp	$536,335	95%	51%	49%	Air Defense
78	Food Marketing Institute	$531,778	100%	35%	65%	Food Stores
79	National Rural Letter Carriers Assn	$526,528	100%	86%	14%	Postal Workers
80	Dow Chemical*	$525,569	82%	22%	78%	Chemicals
81	National Assn of Broadcasters	$522,400	95%	55%	45%	Entertainment
82	National Abortion Rights Action League*	$517,705	100%	94%	8%	Pro-Choice
83	Women's Campaign Fund	$513,067	100%	76%	22%	Womens Issues
84	Rubber Cork Linoleum & Plastic Workers	$505,730	100%	100%	0%	Indust Unions
85	Atlantic Richfield	$493,092	66%	25%	74%	Oil & Gas
86	Aircraft Owners & Pilots Assn	$482,695	100%	56%	44%	Air Transport
87	Americans for Free International Trade	$475,150	100%	20%	80%	Import Auto Dlrs
88	JP Morgan & Co	$473,175	89%	56%	44%	Comml Banks
89	Morgan Stanley & Co	$470,781	47%	54%	46%	Securities
90	General Dynamics	$464,055	94%	61%	39%	Air Defense
91	United Mine Workers	$459,600	100%	98%	2%	Mining Unions
92	CSX Corp*	$453,750	93%	53%	47%	RR/Sea Trans
93	Metropolitan Life Insurance*	$453,564	81%	57%	43%	Insur/Real Est
94	Blue Cross & Blue Shield Assn*	$453,134	75%	59%	41%	Health Insur
95	Pepsico*	$452,363	66%	26%	63%	Soft Drinks/Rest
96	Textron Inc	$446,570	89%	64%	36%	Air Defense
97	League of Conservation Voters*	$443,062	97%	93%	7%	Environment
98	KidsPAC	$440,600	100%	95%	4%	Child Rights
99	Arthur Andersen & Co	$440,377	48%	56%	44%	Accountants
100	C&S/Sovran Corp*	$436,867	99%+	61%	38%	Comml Banks

* Contributions came from more than one affiliate or subsidiary.

NOTE: Contributors with PAC percents of "99%+" gave more than 99.5% but less than 100% of their contributions through PACs.

American Medical Association, was the National Association of Realtors, whose PAC contributed nearly $3 million to some 540 federal candidates.

Ideological and single-interest groups, led by the National Rifle Association, held 11 of the Top 100 slots. The Transportation and Communications/Electronics sectors ranked next, with eight contributors each.

A total of 31 contributors gave $1 million or more in the 1992 elections. Just outside that select circle was Emily's List, the leading women's rights group, whose PAC and individual supporters gave $999,755 that could be traced by the Center. The group claims to have bundled up to $6 million in contributions in the last election — the great bulk of it directed by the PAC toward a roster of favored candidates, but paid directly by individuals. That figure is impossible to verify, since much of it came in contributions under $200 that need not be itemized by candidates.

Individual Givers: A Counterpoint to the PACs

While much of the attention by the public and the news media is concentrated on contributions from political action committees, an entirely different community of contributors has quietly been filling the campaign coffers of candidates. Individual contributors giving $200 or more accounted for more than $289 million in contributions to congressional and presidential candidates in the 1992 elections. The Center's research, which eventually resulted in the identification and classification of approximately 71 percent of that $289 million, shows that many of the same industries and interest groups that have come to dominate the PAC world also give heavily through individual contributions.

The biggest contributors of all were lawyers and lobbyists, who delivered $37.7 million in individual contributions to federal candidates — six times as much as they gave through PACs. The Finance, Insurance & Real Estate sector ranked second, accounting for nearly $30 million in individual donations. In contrast to its high profile in the world of PACs, organized labor was scarcely in evidence among individual donors; nearly all of labor's dollars were delivered through PACs. Defense contractors were also very small players compared with other industries. A chart comparing each sector's PAC and individual contributions can be found on page 22.

Who Gives Individually

One notable pattern that emerges from a study of individual versus PAC giving is that, by and large, PACs are an instrument of large organizations, while individual givers tend to be connected with smaller companies. A clear example of this can be seen in the oil industry, where a discernible split can be found in the spending patterns of large oil companies versus small ones. Nearly all the dollars delivered by major oil companies — such as Exxon, Atlantic Richfield, or Mobil — are funneled through PACs. Few oil executives from these companies make substantial contributions directly to candidates. Among smaller companies — known in the trade as "independents" — PACs are rare and most of the dollars are given as individual contributions.

That trend is consistent among a cross-section of American industries. Firms that are big enough to form PACs tend to use them as their primary means of delivering campaign dollars. Firms that are smaller tend to rely on individual donations. The one exception to the rule is in the case of small businesses connected with nationwide organizations — such as doctors, Realtors, or trial lawyers. Those groups often give both ways — directly through individual contributions, and again through the PAC of their national affiliate.

Wall Street and Washington Lawyers Lead Individual Givers

Another pattern that emerges from examining individual contributions is that certain industries, whether large or small, tend to prefer individual contributions to PACs. Most noteworthy among these are the securities industry based on Wall Street and the influential community of lobbyists and lawyers concentrated in Washington, DC.

Some of the biggest contributors (seen in the chart on the facing page) give both through PACs and individually. Some of them also tend to deliver large bundles of contributions to selected candidates. The "bundling" of individual contributions from a group of executives within a particular company has become a popular means of supporting favored candidates. PACs alone are limited to a maximum $10,000 contribution during a normal election cycle. But a group of, say, a dozen vice presidents or partners in a law firm, can easily give much more than that, particularly if their spouses (and sometimes children) add contributions of their own. A list of the biggest "bundled" contributions to candidates in the 1992 elections can be found on pages 28 and 29.

The chart on the opposite page shows the biggest individual contributors in 1991-92. Goldman, Sachs & Co., the Wall Street investment firm, was the biggest of all, giving more than $700,000 in individual donations. The biggest recipient of that money was Bill Clinton — in fact, Goldman, Sachs was the number one contributor to his campaign. (The firm also gave substantial sums to George Bush.) Emily's List, the women's rights PAC that used bundling as its primary tool for directing tens of thousands of dollars to favored women candidates, was second. The total shown here is very conservative. It includes only "earmarked" individual funds coordinated by the PAC and funds from major Emily's List donors who also gave large individual donations directly to candidates the PAC supported.

American Express ranked third. The bulk of their funds were delivered through the company's chief securities subsidiary, Shearson Lehman Brothers. In all, 12 securities firms ranked among the top 30 individual contributors.

But the biggest cluster of contributors on the top 50 list were law firms. Thirteen of them show up on the list, and though their home offices are based in cities around the nation, 11 of the 13 (all but Milberg, Weiss and Wachtell, Lipton) also maintain offices in the nation's capital. The line between legal work and lobbying is often a thin one in Washington, and nearly all

Top 50 Individual Contributors

Rank	Contributor	Individual Total	Grand Total	Category
1	Goldman, Sachs & Co	$704,237	$898,545	Securities
2	Emily's List	$634,437	$999,755	Womens Issues
3	American Express*	$546,545	$881,820	Stocks/Credit
4	Time Warner*	$445,089	$583,089	Movies/Publish
5	Merrill Lynch*	$436,600	$627,864	Securities
6	Cassidy & Associates	$372,666	$372,666	Lobbyists
7	Walt Disney Co*	$304,384	$401,834	Movies/Resorts
8	Skadden, Arps et al	$254,849	$350,566	Law/Lobby
9	Forest City Enterprises Inc	$252,833	$252,833	Real Est Devel
10	Morgan Stanley & Co	$250,585	$470,781	Securities
11	Prudential Insurance*	$239,205	$640,040	Insurance
12	US House of Representatives	$239,171	$239,171	Govt
13	Bear Stearns & Co	$233,885	$233,885	Securities
14	Akin, Gump et al	$233,572	$538,228	Law/Lobby
15	PaineWebber*	$233,372	$318,847	Securities
16	Arthur Andersen & Co	$230,504	$440,377	Accountants
17	Salomon Brothers	$230,035	$285,885	Securities
18	Smith Barney	$219,846	$234,702	Securities
19	First Boston Corp	$219,121	$315,621	Securities
20	Gallo Winery	$217,984	$217,984	Wine
21	Lazard Freres & Co	$214,450	$214,450	Securities
22	University of California*	$206,915	$206,915	Universities
23	US Tobacco*	$197,870	$636,120	Tobacco
24	Ernst & Young	$183,357	$419,653	Accountants
25	Latham & Watkins	$180,389	$180,389	Law/Lobby
26	Williams & Jensen	$178,795	$269,264	Law/Lobby
27	Bear, Stearns & Co	$178,145	$267,095	Securities
28	Okeelanta Corp	$170,800	$170,800	Sugar
29	Atlantic Richfield	$169,558	$493,092	Oil & Gas
30	Equitable Life*	$169,182	$308,857	Insur/Securities
31	Jones, Day et al	$168,529	$344,611	Law/Lobby
32	Hospice Care Inc	$163,150	$163,150	Nursing Homes
33	Patton, Boggs & Blow	$160,937	$160,937	Law/Lobby
34	O'Melveny & Myers	$160,509	$160,509	Law/Lobby
35	Deloitte & Touche	$158,026	$282,530	Accountants
36	Waste Management Inc*	$153,069	$683,558	Waste Mgmt
37	MacAndrews & Forbes Group	$147,750	$147,750	Personal Prod Mfg
38	Milberg, Weiss et al	$146,700	$146,700	Law/Lobby
39	Gibson, Dunn & Crutcher	$145,595	$145,595	Law/Lobby
40	Wachtell, Lipton et al	$144,300	$144,300	Law/Lobby
41	KPMG Peat Marwick	$141,930	$141,930	Accountants
42	Sony Corp*	$141,635	$141,635	Movies
43	General Electric*	$140,136	$823,486	Aerospace
44	Mintz, Levin et al	$136,171	$136,171	Law/Lobby
45	US Senate	$135,875	$135,875	Government
46	MCA Inc*	$134,543	$317,193	Movies/TV
47	Amway Corp	$133,271	$149,121	Direct Sales
48	Wunder, Diefenderfer et al	$132,416	$132,416	Law/Lobby
49	Republic National Bank of New York	$125,550	$125,550	Comml Banks
50	Willkie, Farr & Gallagher	$124,550	$124,550	Law/Lobby

* Contributions came from more than one affiliate or subsidiary.

the firms maintain a high-profile presence on Capitol Hill. So does Cassidy & Associates, the Washington lobbying firm that ranked sixth on the top 50 list. One of Cassidy's partners early in the election cycle was Bob Farmer, chief fundraiser for Michael Dukakis in the 1988 presidential election and later for Bill Clinton in the 1992 campaign.

Four firms that operate major Hollywood movie studios also appeared on the top 50 list — Time Warner, Disney, Sony and MCA. They too share the stockbrokers' and lawyers' penchant for relying more heavily on individual donations than on corporate PACs.

Bundles of Money: Biggest Contributions in the 1992 Elections

In the Senate . . .

Despite the fact that political action committees are limited to a maximum of $10,000 in one election cycle and individuals are limited to $2,000, a total of 21 Senators received contributions of $20,000 or more from a single company or interest group in the 1992 elections. Most of the dollars were given through individual contributions from company executives and their families, supplemented in many cases by PAC funds. But the biggest bundling operation at all in 1992 was not a corporation, but an ideological PAC — Emily's List, the women's rights group that raised money for female Democrats and helped elect four of them to the U.S. Senate.

The Center was able to identify just under $1 million in contributions from Emily's List. The money came from three sources — the PAC itself, which handed out $365,318 directly; "earmarked" contributions forwarded by the PAC but counted as individual donations; and direct contributions to women candidates made by donors to the PAC. Nearly all those individual contributions were coordinated (at least informally) by Emily's List, but they do not count against the PAC's $10,000 limit. The total the Center found was almost certainly only the tip of the iceberg. Individual contributions under $200 are not itemized under federal rules, and many of the donations the group coordinated were undoubtedly in that range. The PAC itself claimed to have raised $6 million for women candidates in the 1992 elections. Nearly all of it went to Democrats.

Barbara Boxer was by far the biggest recipient of Emily's List money. The $130,000 the Center tracked to her campaign was the biggest bundle of the year by any group. Carol Moseley-Braun ranked second, with $83,000. The year's two other female Senate winners — Dianne Feinstein of California and Patty Murray of Washington state — also got help from Emily's List, but their totals were much lower. The only other ideological group on the top bundler list was the Council for a Livable World, a pro-peace group that also used earmarks and bundled individual gifts to give Barbara Boxer nearly $34,000.

The bulk of the biggest bundle list at left did come primarily from business executives and their families. Securities firms, which traditionally have been the most active bundlers, accounted for nine of the top contributions shown here. Three law firms also made the list.

These were not the only top bundles of the 1992 election. The list includes only those to candidates who were actually elected.

Biggest Contributions to Senators

Contributor	Total	Type	Recipient
Emily's List	$130,405	PAC/Ind	Barbara Boxer (D-Calif)
Emily's List	$83,190	PAC/Ind	Carol Moseley-Braun (D-Ill)
Bear, Stearns & Co	$62,051	Indiv	Alfonse M. D'Amato (R-NY)
Eli Lilly & Co	$44,650	PAC/Ind	Daniel R. Coats (R-Ind)
Time Warner*	$38,000	PAC/Ind	Bob Packwood (R-Ore)
Council for a Livable World	$33,894	PAC/Ind	Barbara Boxer (D-Calif)
Goldman, Sachs & Co	$32,600	Indiv	Alfonse M. D'Amato (R-NY)
Disney Channel*	$32,250	Indiv	Patrick J. Leahy (D-Vt)
Anheuser-Busch	$31,250	PAC/Ind	Christopher S. Bond (R-Mo)
Salomon Brothers	$31,000	PAC/Ind	Bob Dole (R-Kan)
McDonnell Douglas	$30,735	PAC/Ind	Christopher S. Bond (R-Mo)
Greenwich Capital Markets	$29,250	Indiv	Christopher J. Dodd (D-Conn)
Flowers Industries	$28,750	PAC/Ind	Paul Coverdell (R-Ga)
Morgan Stanley & Co	$28,450	PAC/Ind	Alfonse M. D'Amato (R-NY)
Time Warner*	$27,500	PAC/Ind	Christopher J. Dodd (D-Conn)
Seafarers International Union*	$26,000	PAC	Dianne Feinstein (D-Calif)
Republic National Bank of New York	$26,000	Indiv	Daniel K. Inouye (D-Hawaii)
US Tobacco Co	$25,200	PAC/Ind	Christopher J. Dodd (D-Conn)
Merrill Lynch	$24,605	PAC/Ind	Alfonse M. D'Amato (R-NY)
University of California System*	$24,445	Indiv	Barbara Boxer (D-Calif)
Arkla Inc	$24,300	PAC/Ind	Dale Bumpers (D-Ark)
Waste Management Inc	$24,187	PAC/Ind	Bob Dole (R-Kan)
Mitchell, Williams et al	$23,750	Indiv	Dale Bumpers (D-Ark)
Smith Barney	$23,600	PAC/Ind	Alfonse M. D'Amato (R-NY)
BellSouth Corp	$23,550	Indiv	Ernest F. Hollings (D-SC)
Merrill Lynch	$23,500	PAC/Ind	Christopher J. Dodd (D-Conn)
Barrack, Rodos & Bacine	$23,500	PAC/Ind	Harris Wofford (D-Pa)
Coopers & Lybrand	$22,990	PAC/Ind	Alfonse M. D'Amato (R-NY)
National Assn of Broadcasters	$22,886	PAC/Ind	Ernest F. Hollings (D-SC)
Jones, Day et al	$22,850	PAC/Ind	Paul Coverdell (R-Ga)
Warner-Lambert	$22,750	PAC/Ind	Frank R. Lautenberg (D-NJ)
Albertson's Inc	$22,700	Indiv	Dirk Kempthorne (R-Idaho)
Monsanto Co	$22,700	PAC/Ind	Christopher S. Bond (R-Mo)
Tyson Foods	$22,500	PAC/Ind	Dale Bumpers (D-Ark)
BankAmerica Corp	$22,300	PAC/Ind	Dianne Feinstein (D-Calif)
Goldman, Sachs & Co	$22,000	PAC/Ind	Christopher J. Dodd (D-Conn)
Conseco Inc	$22,000	Indiv	Daniel R. Coats (R-Ind)

* Contributions came from more than one affiliate or subsidiary.

In the House . . .

The biggest bundle of cash delivered to any House member in the 1992 election went to freshman Republican Michael Castle of Delaware. Castle's top benefactor was MBNA Corp., a Delaware-based bank holding company. Castle was hardly an unknown political figure in his home state. He was its governor before his election to Congress.

Dow Chemical executives and their families bestowed over $55,000 on Republican Dave Camp, whose district includes the corporation's home office in Midland, Mich. Camp got an additional $9,500 from Dow Corning. Those two companies combined in the 1992 election to give Camp just over $100,000 in contributions.

Emily's List, the group which boosted the campaigns of Democratic women in both the House and Senate, bundled big donations to congressional newcomers Anna Eshoo of California, Elizabeth Furse of Oregon, and Karen Shepherd of Utah. As with their contributions to Senate candidates, these totals are undoubtedly low as they do not include individual contribution under $200.

Emily's List was the only ideological group represented in the list below. All the others were business groups, with the notable exception of the top contributors to freshman Democrat Robert Menendez of New Jersey. Menendez, who served as mayor of Union City, N.J. before winning election to Congress, got more than $28,000 in large contributions from employees of its municipal government. He got an additional $30,150 from the Union City School Board.

In all, some 29 House members drew contributions of $20,000 or more from a single source in the 1992 elections. The biggest recipient of all was House Majority Leader Dick Gephardt, who collected large donations from five different contributors — $43,350 from Anheuser-Busch; $22,185 from the Wall Street investment firm of Salomon Brothers; $21,500 from the law firm of Sills, Cummis et al; $21,000 from the Gallo Winery and $20,000 from the St. Louis Law firm of Thompson & Mitchell.

Biggest Contributions to House Members

Contributor	Total	Type	Recipient
MBNA Corp	$61,300	PAC/Ind	Michael N. Castle (R-Del)
Dow Chemical	$55,319	PAC/Ind	Dave Camp (R-Mich)
Emily's List	$43,839	PAC/Ind	Anna G. Eshoo (D-Calif)
Anheuser-Busch	$43,350	PAC/Ind	Richard A. Gephardt (D-Mo)
Stephens Inc	$40,500	Indiv	Ray Thornton (D-Ark)
Anesthesia Professional Assn Inc	$38,000	Indiv	E. Clay Shaw Jr. (R-Fla)
Hospice Care Inc	$36,000	Indiv	Carrie Meek (D-Fla)
Schnitzer Steel Industries	$32,328	Indiv	Dick Swett (D-NH)
Jones, Day et al	$31,400	PAC/Ind	Jane Harman (D-Calif)
Union City Board of Education	$30,150	Indiv	Robert Menendez (D-NJ)
Corning Inc	$30,050	Indiv	Amo Houghton (R-NY)
Kirkpatrick & Lockhart	$29,975	PAC/Ind	Rick Santorum (R-Pa)
Emily's List	$29,105	PAC/Ind	Elizabeth Furse (D-Ore)
Cabletron Systems Inc	$28,940	Indiv	Bill Zeliff (R-NH)
Union City (NJ) Municipal Govt	$28,350	Indiv	Robert Menendez (D-NJ)
Veco International Inc	$27,790	Indiv	Don Young (R-Alaska)
Forest City Enterprises Inc	$25,350	Indiv	Eric D. Fingerhut (D-Ohio)
Chrysler Corp	$25,200	PAC/Ind	John D. Dingell (D-Mich)
Emily's List	$25,005	PAC/Ind	Karen Shepherd (D-Utah)
Latham & Watkins	$23,500	Indiv	C. Christopher Cox (R-Calif)
Ford Motor Co	$23,000	PAC/Ind	John D. Dingell (D-Mich)
Forest City Enterprises Inc	$23,000	Indiv	Louis Stokes (D-Ohio)
Beneficial Management Corp	$22,850	PAC/Ind	Dick Zimmer (R-NJ)
United Steelworkers	$22,500	PAC	Gene Green (D-Texas)
Archer-Daniels-Midland Corp	$22,300	PAC/Ind	Robert H. Michel (R-Ill)
Salomon Brothers	$22,185	Indiv	Richard A. Gephardt (D-Mo)
Guardsmark Inc	$21,750	Indiv	Don Sundquist (R-Tenn)
Sills, Cummis et al	$21,500	Indiv	Richard A. Gephardt (D-Mo)
Gallo Winery	$21,000	Indiv	Richard A. Gephardt (D-Mo)
Golden Rule Insurance Co	$20,565	PAC/Ind	Newt Gingrich (R-Ga)
Chicago Mercantile Exchange	$20,250	PAC/Ind	Dan Rostenkowski (D-Ill)

* Contributions came from more than one affiliate or subsidiary.

Leading Categories of Individual Contributions

Contributions from lawyers towered over all other industries and interest groups among individual contributions made to congressional candidates in the 1992 elections. In all, attorneys gave over $32 million of their personal funds — twice as much as the second leading category, retirees. Securities dealers and investment firms were next, followed by doctors, real estate agents, insurance agents and executives, lobbyists and real estate developers.

Pro-Israel contributors ranked ninth on the list, with nearly $3.4 million in contributions. This total was compiled by counting individuals who had contributed $200 or more both to a pro-Israel PAC and to a candidate who was supported by pro-Israel PACs. Because of that conservative criteria for counting ideological contributors, the actual total of pro-Israel givers can be safely assumed to be considerably higher.

Retirees, whose total contributions put them in second place behind only lawyers, includes all individuals who described themselves as "retired," except those who were classified as ideological contributors because of contributions to ideological or single-issue PACs.

Category	Total from Individuals	Grand Total
Attorneys & law firms	$32,182,674	$38,233,716
Retired	$15,930,210	$15,930,210
Security brokers & investment companies	$8,607,241	$10,383,262
Physicians	$8,174,796	$11,939,475
Real estate agents & managers	$4,556,362	$7,626,300
Insurance companies, brokers & agents, diversified	$4,191,395	$9,109,055
Lobbyists & public relations	$4,084,934	$4,353,571
Real estate developers & subdividers	$3,484,524	$3,797,455
Pro-Israel	$3,378,436	$7,401,113
Commercial banks & bank holding companies	$2,999,119	$10,349,223
Civil servant/public employee	$2,995,085	$2,995,085
Construction, unclassified	$2,634,132	$2,634,132
Investment banking	$2,496,011	$3,149,515
Business services	$2,447,213	$2,520,185
Accountants	$2,395,128	$4,877,052
Schools & colleges	$2,355,025	$2,355,025
Motion picture/TV production & distribution	$2,261,460	$2,596,760
Investors	$2,163,731	$2,163,731
Women's issues	$2,159,244	$3,725,735
Public works, industrial & commercial construction	$2,111,875	$3,623,909
Real estate	$1,936,926	$1,937,926
Building operators and managers	$1,876,581	$1,903,331
Finance, insurance & real estate, diversified or unclassified	$1,757,658	$1,757,658
Management consultants & services	$1,694,609	$1,697,109
Conservative/Republican	$1,685,903	$2,479,934
Restaurants & drinking establishments	$1,639,522	$2,994,793
Crop production & basic processing	$1,637,380	$1,748,430
Independent oil & gas producers	$1,525,308	$2,048,958
Registered foreign agents	$1,467,682	$1,467,682
Book, newspaper & periodical publishing	$1,463,934	$1,674,934
Auto dealers, new & used	$1,426,894	$3,211,769
Oil & gas	$1,280,446	$1,645,123
Liberal/Democrat	$1,268,347	$2,658,027
Advertising & public relations services	$1,233,583	$1,256,983
Misc physician specialists	$1,214,166	$2,182,598
Hospitals	$1,205,446	$2,369,306
Industrial/commercial equipment & materials	$1,170,428	$1,651,109
Liquor wholesalers	$1,091,909	$2,273,554
Health, unclassified & diversified	$1,088,045	$1,088,045
Cable & satellite TV production & distribution	$1,013,955	$2,226,214

The $8.6 million from securities executives, plus the $2.5 million from individuals involved in investment banking, illustrates the tendency of those in the securities and investment industry to favor individual contributions over PACs. Many of the larger Wall Street firms bundled contributions from partners, brokers and their families to deliver sizable contributions to particularly favored candidates. Those donations were often supplemented by PAC contributions from the parent firm.

Real estate brokers, developers and investors were also very much in evidence with individual contributions. Developers in particular were far more likely to give individually than through political action committees. Bankers and insurance executives were also high on the list of individual contributors, but those industries did tend to give large sums through PACs as well.

Industry Support of Democrats & Republicans

The widespread assumption that labor unions support Democrats while business groups support Republicans is only partially true — and in many cases is downright wrong. Organized labor is indeed heavily Democratic in its politics and its campaign contributions, though Republicans on committees important to labor often receive substantial financial support from unions. But the world of business is much more diverse in its political orientation than most casual observers realize. Overall, business groups split their dollars nearly evenly between Democrats and Republicans in Congress. It is common even for individual companies to support both parties — sometimes even in the same race.

Even among industries and individual businesses that are Republican in their politics, there is a tendency — presumably born of hard-headed pragmatism — to ensure a favorable reception on Capitol Hill by giving to members on both sides of the aisle. That inclination is strengthened by the fact that Democrats hold solid majorities in both the House and Senate. In that environment, virtually no bill becomes law without wide support among Democratic members — a fact that business groups must take into account, whatever their political orientation.

A glance at the charts at right illustrates several noteworthy patterns in the sectors' contributions during 1992. Most obvious is the contrast in Labor dollars between Republicans and Democrats. Also clear, both from the charts and the bottom line below is that Democrats received considerably more money overall than Republicans in the 1992 elections.

Other interesting findings can be seen by looking more closely. The finance, insurance and real estate sector, for example, is the heaviest business contributor to both parties. Moreover, the bankers, Realtors, insurance agents and others that make up that sector gave more to Democrats than to Republicans. Lawyers and lobbyists were even more strongly Democratic in their contributions, as were ideological and single-issue contributors.

A more detailed examination of the spending patterns in each of these sectors can be found in the Industry Profiles section beginning on page 41. A closer look at the individual categories most important to members of each party can be found on the following two pages.

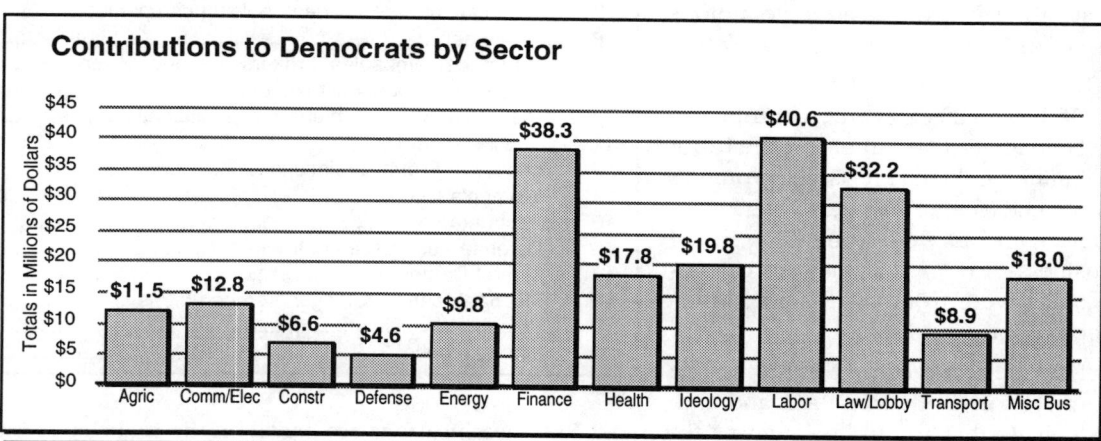

Contributions to Democrats by Sector

(Totals in Millions of Dollars)

Agric	Comm/Elec	Constr	Defense	Energy	Finance	Health	Ideology	Labor	Law/Lobby	Transport	Misc Bus
$11.5	$12.8	$6.6	$4.6	$9.8	$38.3	$17.8	$19.8	$40.6	$32.2	$8.9	$18.0

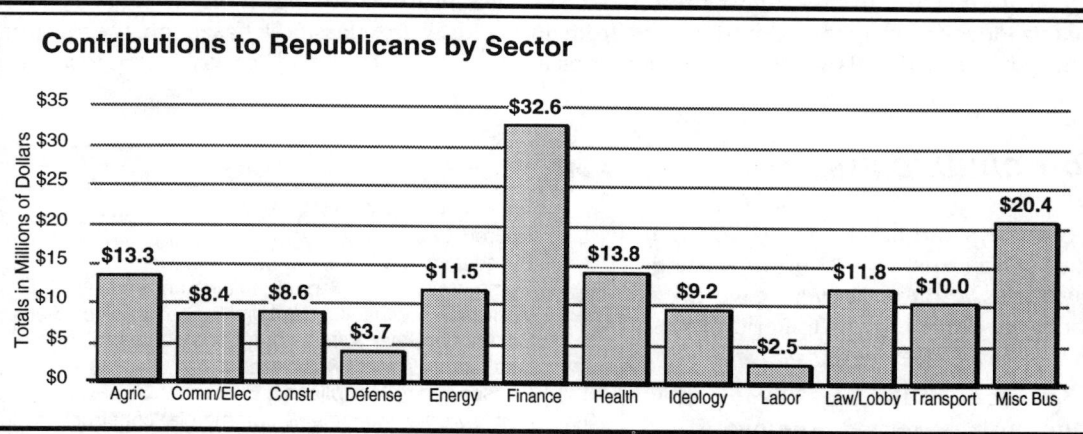

Contributions to Republicans by Sector

(Totals in Millions of Dollars)

Agric	Comm/Elec	Constr	Defense	Energy	Finance	Health	Ideology	Labor	Law/Lobby	Transport	Misc Bus
$13.3	$8.4	$8.6	$3.7	$11.5	$32.6	$13.8	$9.2	$2.5	$11.8	$10.0	$20.4

Sector	To Democrats	To Republicans
Agriculture	$11,533,853	$13,315,969
Communic/Electronics	$12,758,180	$8,391,147
Construction	$6,584,436	$8,617,049
Defense	$4,609,451	$3,714,903
Energy/Natural Resources	$9,794,836	$11,518,607
Finance/Insur/Real Estate	$38,321,025	$32,574,212
Health	$17,774,140	$13,780,085
Ideological/Single-Issue	$19,790,462	$9,161,539
Labor	$40,610,113	$2,471,102
Lawyers & Lobbyists	$32,160,897	$11,827,725
Transportation	$8,940,802	$10,020,890
Misc Business	$17,962,336	$20,354,469
GRAND TOTAL	**$160,439,956**	**$134,115,056**

Top-Dollar Categories to Each Party

Listed below are the industry and interest group categories that gave the most money to congressional Democrats and Republicans in the 1992 elections. A complete listing of categories used throughout this book, and the totals they provided in contributions, can be found in Appendix A, which begins on page 1314.

To Democrats . . .

Lawyers and labor unions provided the biggest financial assistance to Democratic candidates in the 1992 elections. Attorneys and law firms were by far the leading single category giving to Democrats, though taken as a whole, unions contributed more heavily than any other sector.

Of the top 20 categories contributing to Democrats, five came from the Labor community, three (Pro-Israel, women's issues and Liberal/Democrat) were ideological, and 11 were from the world of business. Among the business categories, six were from the finance, insurance & real estate sector.

The category totals in this list include contributions both from PACs and individuals. In this list, and throughout the book, PAC classifications are based on the industry or interests of the sponsoring organization or company. Contributions from individuals are classified based on the occupation or employer of the contributor. Individuals are classified as ideological givers only if they made contributions to an ideological/single-issue PAC.

Rank	Category	To Democrats	Dem Pct
1	Attorneys & law firms	$27,990,120	73.2%
2	Retired	$7,150,286	44.9%
3	Manufacturing unions	$6,767,277	98.0%
4	Building trades unions	$6,466,973	93.7%
5	Security brokers & investment companies	$6,083,313	58.6%
6	Physicians	$5,978,992	50.1%
7	Commercial banks & bank holding companies	$5,422,745	52.4%
8	Pro-Israel	$5,289,881	71.5%
9	Insurance companies, brokers & agents, diversified	$4,280,150	47.0%
10	Real estate agents & managers	$4,040,672	53.0%
11	US Postal Service unions & associations	$3,419,083	89.5%
12	Teachers unions	$3,340,592	96.1%
13	Lobbyists & public relations	$3,164,061	72.7%
14	Women's issues	$3,138,406	84.2%
15	Accountants	$2,680,609	55.0%
16	Defense aerospace contractors	$2,635,229	55.5%
17	Liberal/Democrat	$2,612,692	98.3%
18	Mechant marine & longshoremen unions	$2,572,292	82.3%
19	Telephone utilities	$2,504,997	55.4%
20	Life insurance	$2,441,220	57.0%

To Republicans . . .

Attorneys and law firms also topped the Republicans' Top 20 list of leading categories, though lawyers gave only about one-third as much to Republicans as they did to Democrats.

Seventeen of the top 20 categories were business related. The two ideological categories were Pro-Israel and Conservative/Republican. Retirees ranked second on the list both for Republicans and Democrats.

The finance, insurance & real estate sector accounted for seven of the Republicans' top 20 categories — more than any other sector.

Rank	Category	To Republicans	Repub Pct
1	Attorneys & law firms	$10,175,425	26.6%
2	Retired	$8,556,245	53.7%
3	Physicians	$5,869,848	49.2%
4	Commercial banks & bank holding companies	$4,915,548	47.5%
5	Insurance companies, brokers & agents, diversified	$4,817,610	52.9%
6	Security brokers & investment companies	$4,268,926	41.1%
7	Real estate agents & managers	$3,537,494	46.4%
8	Conservative/Republican	$2,406,051	97.0%
9	Public works, industrial & commercial construction	$2,227,578	61.5%
10	Accountants	$2,183,101	44.8%
11	Pro-Israel	$2,110,670	28.5%
12	Defense aerospace contractors	$2,110,299	44.4%
13	Auto dealers, new & used	$2,047,417	63.8%
14	Telephone utilities	$2,009,499	44.5%
15	Major (multinational) oil & gas producers	$1,998,225	74.0%
16	Restaurants & drinking establishments	$1,929,286	64.4%
17	Life insurance	$1,839,779	43.0%
18	Pharmaceutical manufacturing	$1,662,422	52.8%
19	Real estate developers & subdividers	$1,619,235	42.6%
20	Chemicals	$1,495,770	68.5%

The Most Heavily Partisan Categories

These were the categories that gave most heavily to one party or the other during the 1991-92 election cycle. The categories have been pared to include only those that accounted for $50,000 or more in contributions to one party.

To Democrats . . .

Labor unions dominate the list of most-partisan categories giving to Democrats. As a group, organized labor delivered 94 percent of its campaign dollars to Democratic candidates, making it by far the most important sector for Democrats. In fact, the strong partisanship of labor unions accounts for much of the overall edge in fundraising that congressional Democrats enjoyed over their Republican opponents.

In all, 15 of the 20 most partisan categories on the Democrats' list were from the Labor sector. The remaining five were from ideological & single-issue groups.

Rank	Category	To Democrats	Dem Pct
1	Other unions	$164,063	100.0%
2	Democratic leadership PAC	$1,341,037	99.9%
3	Human rights	$74,057	99.4%
4	Labor unions	$858,015	98.7%
5	Liberal/Democrat	$2,612,692	98.3%
6	Communications & hi-tech unions	$1,401,740	98.3%
7	Other commercial unions	$730,799	98.1%
8	Manufacturing unions	$6,767,277	98.0%
9	Mining unions	$448,100	97.5%
10	State & local govt employee unions	$1,902,863	97.3%
11	Retail trade unions	$1,476,986	97.2%
12	Other transportation unions	$1,238,150	97.1%
13	Railroad unions	$1,571,421	96.8%
14	Energy-related unions (non-mining)	$132,840	96.4%
15	Teachers unions	$3,340,592	96.1%
16	IBEW (Intl Brotherhood of Electrical Workers)	$1,512,817	96.0%
17	Children's rights	$433,800	95.6%
18	Food service & related unions	$539,950	94.7%
19	Teamsters union	$2,392,539	94.5%
20	Environmental policy	$1,536,840	94.1%

To Republicans . . .

Ideological and single-issue contributors accounted for four of the five most heavily partisan categories giving to Republicans, and six of the top 20. But a number of business categories were also heavily Republican in their giving.

Note that the partisan percentages of the Republicans' top supporters drop off quickly after the ideological categories at the top. Even the most conservative business groups tend to give at least a token share of their campaign dollars to candidates of both parties. The Republicans have no ideological stronghold comparable to the Democrats' rock-solid union money.

Rank	Category	To Republicans	Repub Pct
1	Republican leadership PAC	$845,393	99.2%
2	Labor, anti-union	$367,406	98.2%
3	Conservative/Republican	$2,406,051	97.0%
4	Fiscal & tax policy	$107,154	96.2%
5	Builders associations	$178,828	92.8%
6	Pro-business organizations	$130,501	91.1%
7	Abortion policy, Pro-Life	$432,460	88.9%
8	Direct sales	$176,112	83.9%
9	Paper packaging materials	$407,700	81.2%
10	Farm machinery & equipment	$256,947	80.2%
11	Animal feed & health products	$102,112	79.6%
12	Small business organizations	$293,146	79.4%
13	Air freight	$39,950	78.3%
14	Construction equipment	$247,150	77.6%
15	Hardware & tools	$62,265	77.2%
16	Truck & trailer manufacturers	$66,900	77.1%
17	Plastics & rubber processing & products	$400,543	75.9%
18	Forestry & forest products	$947,396	75.6%
19	Defense policy, pro-military	$144,385	75.2%
20	Truck/automotive parts & accessories	$628,661	74.8%

In-State vs. Out-of-State Contributions

Highest Percent of Out-of-State Contributions: US House*

Rank	Name	Out-of-state Pct	Out-of-state Total
1	David R. Obey (D-Wis)	93.8%	$76,470
2	Earl Pomeroy (D-ND)	89.0%	$55,077
3	Lee H. Hamilton (D-Ind)	87.6%	$132,800
4	Nick J. Rahall II (D-WVa)	85.5%	$71,500
5	Dick Swett (D-NH)	85.3%	$317,718
6	Sidney R. Yates (D-Ill)	83.6%	$131,350
7	Pete Stark (D-Calif)	83.4%	$91,550
8	Bruce F. Vento (D-Minn)	80.5%	$16,750
9	Les Aspin (D-Wis)	79.5%	$405,850
10	Bernard Sanders (I-Vt)	78.9%	$49,825
11	Charlie Rose (D-NC)	76.9%	$46,700
12	Patricia Schroeder (D-Colo)	76.5%	$110,503
13	Richard A. Gephardt (D-Mo)	75.9%	$1,230,248
14	William D. Ford (D-Mich)	74.3%	$55,700
15	William L. Clay (D-Mo)	72.4%	$18,818
16	Joseph M. McDade (R-Pa)	68.9%	$63,150
17	John T. Myers (R-Ind)	64.6%	$18,350
18	Jack Brooks (D-Texas)	63.3%	$58,276
19	Mike Espy (D-Miss)	62.5%	$26,500
20	Timothy J. Penny (D-Minn)	61.1%	$7,000

* Among members with $10,000 or more in individual contributions.

Most House members drew the bulk of their large individual contributions (76 percent on average) from within their own state. Many collected less than 10 percent of their cash from out-of-state contributors. Of the 435 members of the House of Representatives, only 47 drew the majority of their large individual contributions from outside their home states. The 20 members in the chart at left had the highest proportion of out-of-state contributions from large individual contributors.

All the totals on this page include only large individual contributions ($200 and above). Smaller contributions are not itemized, so it is not possible to check where they came from. PAC contributions are not counted, since many PACs with local affiliates maintain their headquarters in Washington, D.C. or other major cities.

Highest Percent of Out-of-State Contributions: US Senate

Rank	Name	Out-of-state Pct	Out-of-state Total
1	Byron L. Dorgan (D-ND)	100.0%	$146,200
2	Kent Conrad (D-ND)	93.8%	$673,334
3	Patrick J. Leahy (D-Vt)	90.0%	$812,156
4	Orrin G. Hatch (R-Utah)	89.0%	$1,982,816
5	Joseph R. Biden Jr. (D-Del)	87.7%	$1,375,960
6	Larry Pressler (R-SD)	86.7%	$1,447,824
7	Tom Daschle (D-SD)	84.3%	$1,836,522
8	Bob Dole (R-Kan)	79.2%	$1,468,458
9	Bob Packwood (R-Ore)	78.0%	$3,513,276
10	Claiborne Pell (D-RI)	77.7%	$1,445,166

Senators were much more likely than House members to draw substantial support from out-of-state contributors — particularly those senators from small states. The more prominent senators have developed national constituencies that help out with campaign cash at election time. Even those less well known can often corral dollars from party loyalists in major financial and political centers such as New York, Los Angeles, Washington and Chicago.

Two senators with high out-of-state percentages who were not included on this list were Tom Harkin and Bob Kerrey. Most of the money they raised in the 1991-92 was not for their Senate reelections, but for their presidential campaigns, where in-state/out-of-state ratios do not apply.

The 10 senators on the list at right got the highest proportion of large individual contributions from within the borders of their own states. The list includes four members — Lauch Faircloth, Dianne Feinstein, Barbara Boxer and Paul Coverdell — who won election to the Senate for the first time in 1992.

Highest Percent of In-State Contributions: US Senate

Rank	Name	In-state Pct	In-state Total
1	Lauch Faircloth (R-NC)	85.0%	$1,711,318
2	Connie Mack (R-Fla)	84.6%	$5,090,194
3	Phil Gramm (R-Texas)	83.8%	$15,081,604
4	Dianne Feinstein (D-Calif)	83.4%	$6,621,980
5	Barbara Boxer (D-Calif)	82.9%	$5,907,594
6	Nancy Kassebaum (R-Kan)	82.5%	$254,398
7	Slade Gorton (R-Wash)	81.4%	$1,706,514
8	Alfonse M. D'Amato (R-NY)	81.3%	$10,514,058
9	Daniel R. Coats (R-Ind)	81.0%	$4,870,192
10	Paul Coverdell (R-Ga)	79.8%	$3,103,796

Unidentified Contributors

While nearly every political action committee was identified and categorized by the Center, many thousands of *individual* contributors remain unclassified. Of the $289 million in large individual contributions that went to candidates for Congress and the presidency in the 1991-92 election cycle, the Center was able to identify and classify 71 percent. Of the remaining $85 million which was not identified . . .

- $34.4 million was given by contributors who did list their employers. The Center, however, was unable to identify the types of business these companies were engaged in — mainly due to limitations of staff and time.

- $13.6 million came from homemakers, students and other non-income earners whose income-earning spouses or parents were not found.

- $3.0 million came from individuals whose listed occupations were so generic they could not be classified. Examples are "businessman," "entrepreneur" and "self-employed."

- $33.5 million came from people whose occupation and employer was not listed at all. In many cases, the Center was able to discover the missing information by searching for other contributions by the same individuals. But a large portion of these contributors remain unclassified.

Federal law requires candidates to disclose the name, address, occupation and employer of each contributor giving $200 or more to their campaign. Most members of Congress complied with that requirement, providing information on all but a tiny fraction of their contributors. Some members, however, were less forthcoming. The following lists show the members of Congress with the biggest information gaps in their 1991-92 disclosure reports.

Senators Who Disclosed the Least in 1991-92

Rank	Name	Pct with No Employer Listed	Total No Employer Listed	Total Identified by Center	Final Total with No Employer Known	Final Pct with No Employer Known
1	Carol Moseley-Braun (D-Ill)	65.5%	$1,206,553	$601,758	$604,795	32.8%
2	Robert F. Bennett (R-Utah)	61.9%	$122,741	$61,000	$61,741	31.1%
3	Bob Kerrey (D-Neb)*	58.4%	$1,710,105	$750,968	$959,137	32.8%
4	Tom Harkin (D-Iowa)*	57.3%	$920,334	$416,794	$503,540	31.3%
5	Bob Packwood (R-Ore)	47.4%	$944,304	$649,291	$295,013	14.8%
6	Charles E. Grassley (R-Iowa)	38.8%	$211,856	$123,850	$88,006	16.1%
7	Daniel K. Inouye (D-Hawaii)	35.3%	$562,620	$259,102	$303,518	19.1%
8	Dennis DeConcini (D-Ariz)	29.2%	$50,950	$26,000	$24,950	14.3%
9	Ben Nighthorse Campbell (D-Colo)	29.0%	$163,401	$95,551	$67,850	12.0%
10	Alfonse M. D'Amato (R-NY)	24.6%	$896,040	$290,010	$606,030	16.7%

* Includes contributions to his 1992 presidential campaign.

House Members Who Disclosed the Least in 1991-92

Rank	Name	Pct with No Employer Listed	Total No Employer Listed	Total Identified by Center	Final Total with No Employer Known	Final Pct with No Employer Known
1	Eddie Bernice Johnson (D-Texas)	94.1%	$79,210	$37,630	$41,580	49.4%
2	Bobby L. Rush (D-Ill)	72.7%	$69,000	$28,950	$40,050	42.2%
3	Walter R. Tucker (D-Calif)	72.3%	$95,192	$23,525	$71,667	54.5%
4	Earl F. Hilliard (D-Ala)	60.0%	$69,800	$49,175	$20,625	17.7%
5	Melvin Watt (D-NC)	57.9%	$78,540	$35,750	$42,790	31.6%
6	Albert R. Wynn (D-Md)	56.5%	$69,386	$25,700	$43,686	35.6%
7	Fred Grandy (R-Iowa)	53.2%	$29,750	$15,250	$14,500	25.9%
8	Ron Klink (D-Pa)	52.3%	$18,940	$7,340	$11,600	32.0%
9	Philip M. Crane (R-Ill)	52.2%	$73,032	$30,306	$42,726	30.5%
10	Alcee L. Hastings (D-Fla)	49.4%	$71,650	$30,250	$41,400	28.5%
11	John T. Doolittle (R-Calif)	46.2%	$92,980	$48,225	$44,755	22.3%
12	Calvin Dooley (D-Calif)	45.9%	$66,879	$38,204	$28,675	19.7%
13	Edolphus Towns (D-NY)	45.6%	$76,935	$30,250	$46,685	27.7%
14	Nydia M. Velazquez (D-NY)	44.7%	$49,050	$14,900	$34,150	31.1%
15	Ed Pastor (D-Ariz)	44.2%	$150,172	$82,825	$67,347	19.8%
16	Major R. Owens (D-NY)	43.9%	$8,575	$0	$8,575	43.9%
17	Jay C. Kim (R-Calif)	39.8%	$127,960	$21,850	$106,110	33.0%
18	Eva Clayton (D-NC)	39.8%	$25,502	$16,300	$9,202	14.4%
19	Jim Clyburn (D-SC)	37.7%	$35,384	$18,850	$16,534	17.6%
20	Richard E. Neal (D-Mass)	36.5%	$28,000	$9,550	$18,450	24.0%

Targeting the Committees

One of the first patterns that becomes apparent when reviewing the political contributions to incumbents in Congress is that the member's profile of contributors tends to parallel his or her committee assignments. Members of the Banking Committees of the House or Senate, for example, typically receive substantial contributions from commercial banks, savings & loans, as well as related (and sometimes competing) industries, like securities firms and insurance companies. Members sitting on industry-specific committees (like the House Merchant Marine and Fisheries Committee) often receive funds both from business interests involved in the industry and from Labor PACs whose members provide the industry's work force. The consistency of these patterns can be seen on the member profile pages (beginning on page 171) and in the committee profiles that begin on page 94.

It can also be seen in the following charts that show the average contributions given by selected industry groups to members of various committees in the House of Representatives. The charts focus on House committees because industry contribution patterns are clearer there than in the Senate. House members generally have only one or two major committee assignments, while most senators must split their attention among three or four different committees. In addition, because senators face the voters only once every six years, the volume of dollars flowing to specific Senate committees tends to have more to do with the number of committee members seeking reelection than with the overall agenda of either the committee or the contributors.

Agriculture

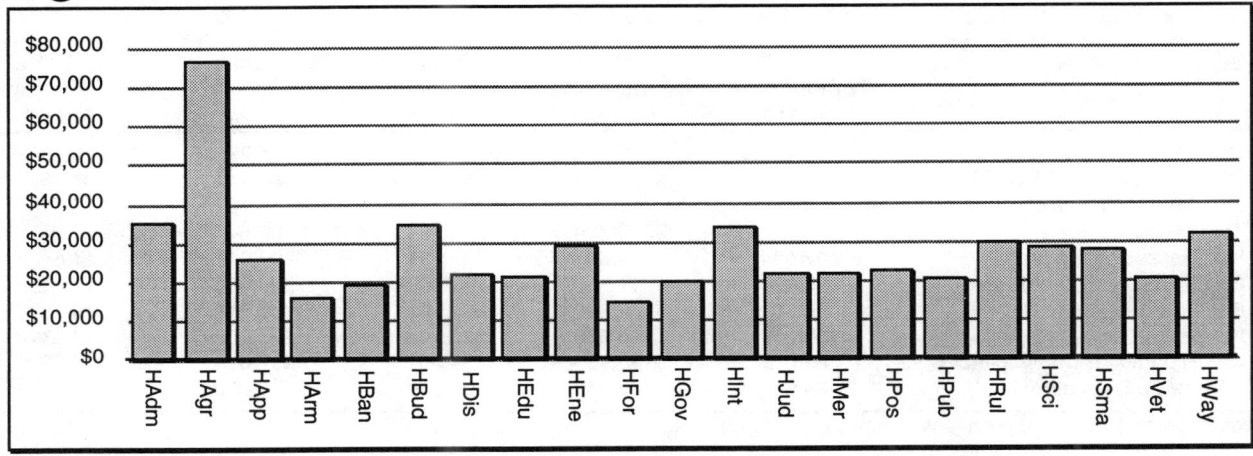

House Committee Key

HAdm	House Administration
HAgr	House Agriculture
HApp	House Appropriations
HArm	House Armed Services
HBan	House Banking, Finance & Urban Affairs
HBud	House Budget
HDis	House District of Columbia
HEdu	House Education & Labor
HEne	House Energy & Commerce
HFor	House Foreign Affairs
HGov	House Government Operations
HInt	House Interior & Insular Affairs
HJud	House Judiciary
HMer	House Merchant Marine & Fisheries
HPos	House Post Office & Civil Service
HPub	House Public Works & Transportation
HRul	House Rules
HSci	House Science, Space & Technology
HSma	House Small Business
HVet	House Veterans' Affairs
HWay	House Ways and Means

The chart above illustrates the correlation between industry spending and members' committee assignments. Agricultural industry contributors concentrated the biggest portion of their campaign dollars on the committee that most affects their business. Members of the House Agriculture Committee received an average of $76,000 from farmers, ranchers, pesticide manufacturers, and other agricultural interests during the 1991-92 election cycle.

Communications/Electronics

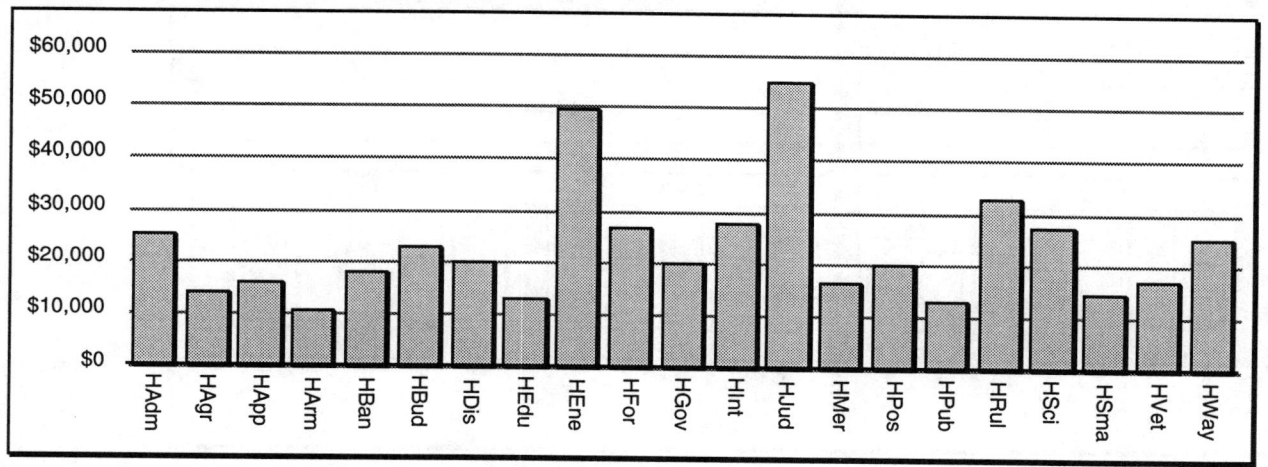

The Judiciary and Energy & Commerce committees attracted the biggest share of contributions from the communications and electronics sector. The Telecommunications and Finance subcommittee of Energy & Commerce is particularly important to telephone utilities and to TV and radio broadcasters. Both groups were major contributors to that committee. Hollywood film studios and TV broadcasters also gave heavily to the Judiciary Committee, which rules on such matters as copyright laws affecting the motion picture industry.

Defense

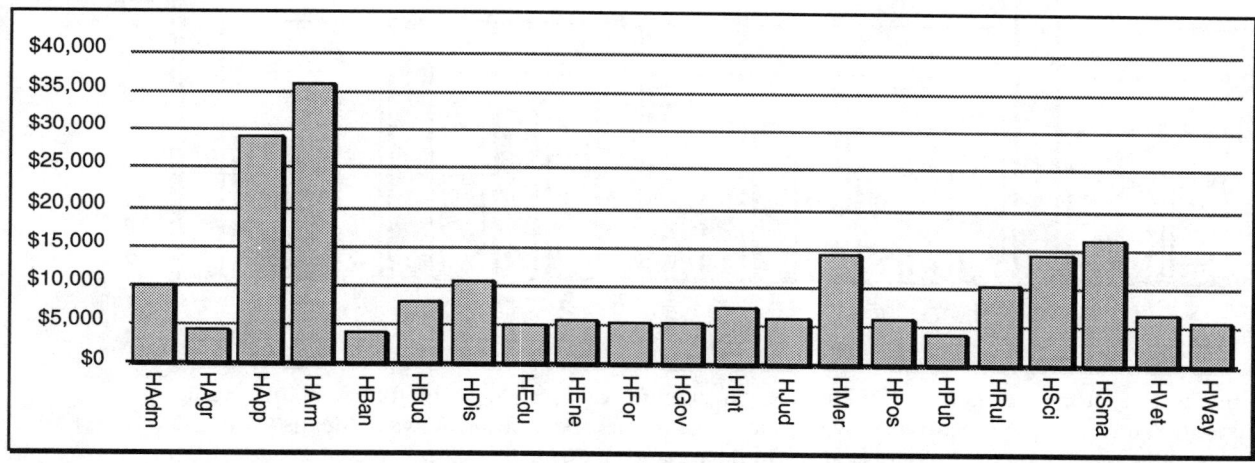

Defense contractors took careful aim at the Appropriations and Armed Services Committees when dispensing their dollars in the 1992 election. Armed Services makes crucial decisions on weapons systems and overall military budget priorities. Appropriations allocates the money to pay for it all. Both are crucial to the defense industry, particularly as defense spending winds down after the close of the Cold War and the dissolution of the former Soviet Union.

Energy & Natural Resources

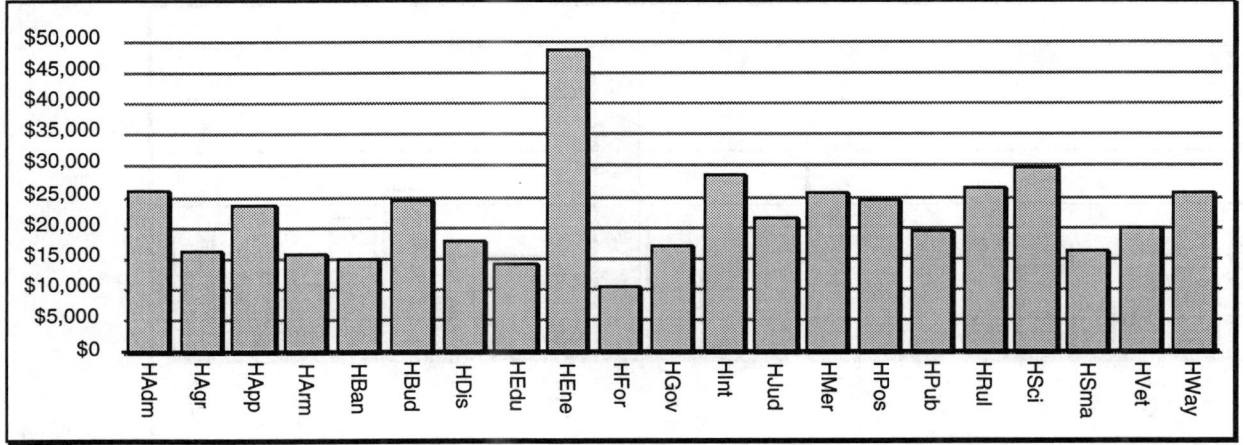

The Energy and Commerce Committee, with direct responsibility for the nation's energy policy, was the biggest beneficiary of campaign funds from the oil and gas industry. The committee's energy money was also boosted by large contributions from electric utilities.

Finance, Insurance & Real Estate

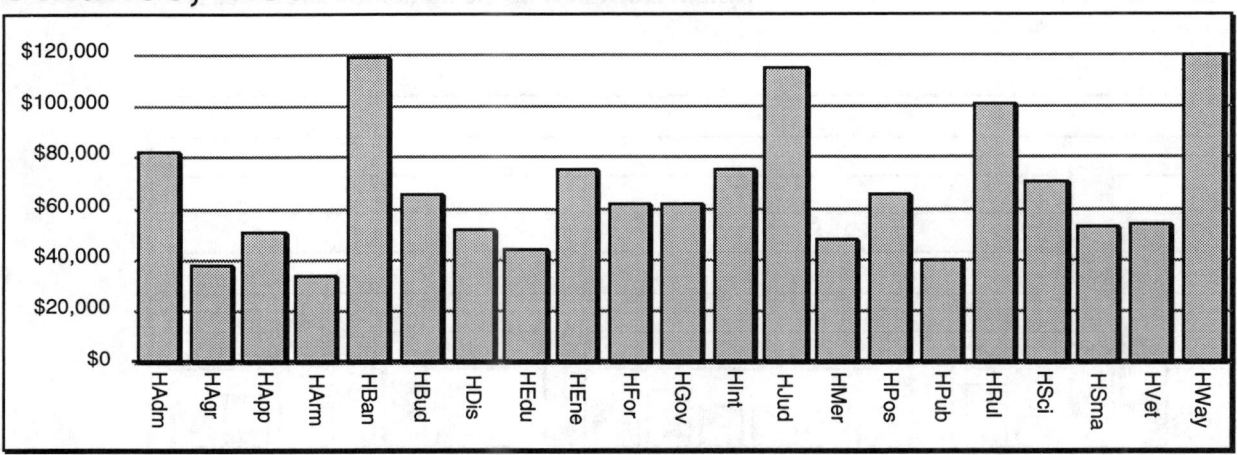

Within the financial sector, commercial banks gave an average of $36,000 to members of the Banking Committee. Insurance interests gave nearly $48,000 on average to members of the Ways & Means Committee. Securities & investment interests gave heavily both to Judiciary and to Ways & Means.

Health

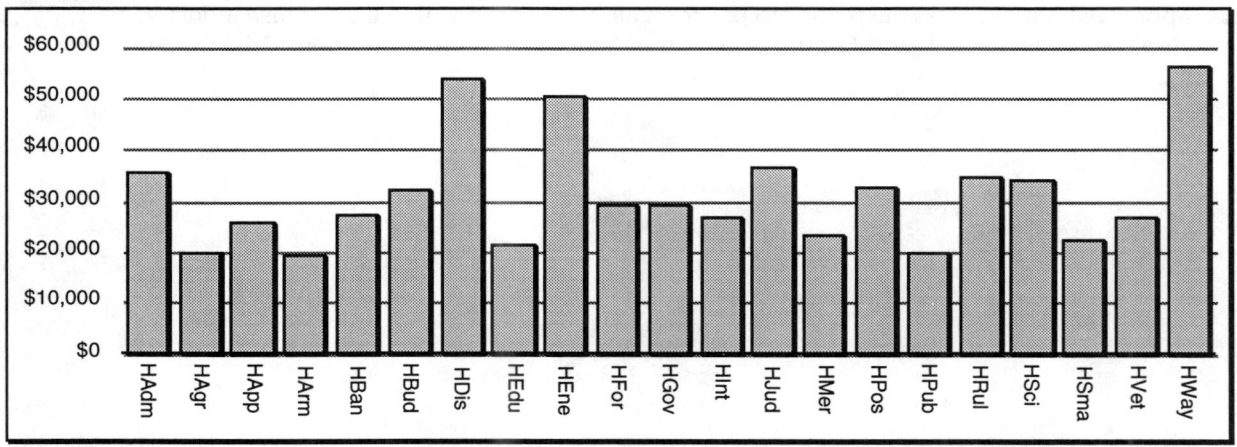

Both Energy & Commerce and Ways & Means have subcommittees dealing with Health matters. Both panels got generous funding from doctors, hospitals, pharmaceutical companies and other health care interests.

Labor

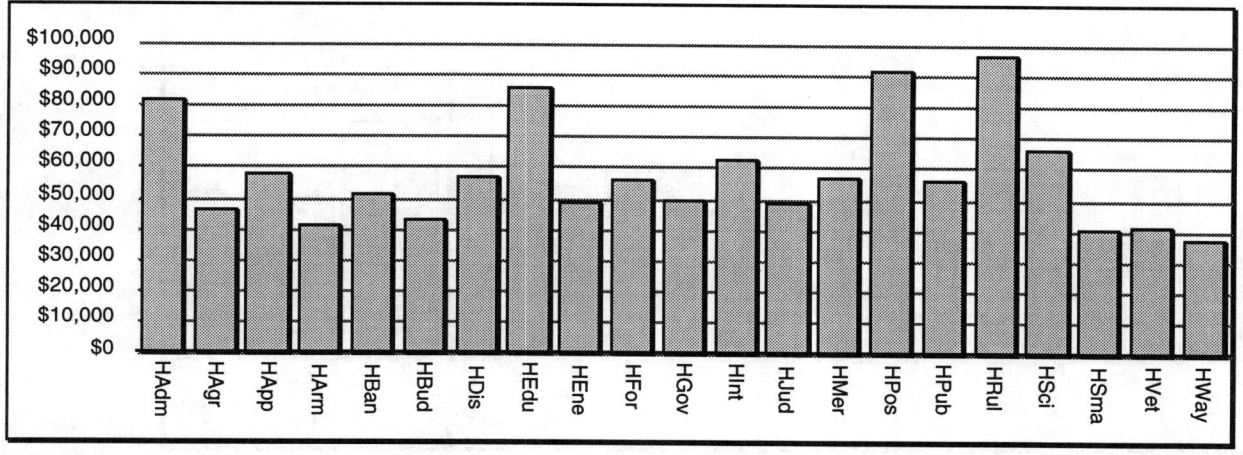

With 94 percent of its campaign dollars going to Democrats, organized Labor for the most part gave its dollars to Democratic members without regard to their committee assignments. But the Energy & Labor Committee and Post Office & Civil Service Committee — both particularly important to public sector unions — got extra, as did members of the Rules Committee.

Lawyer & Lobbyists

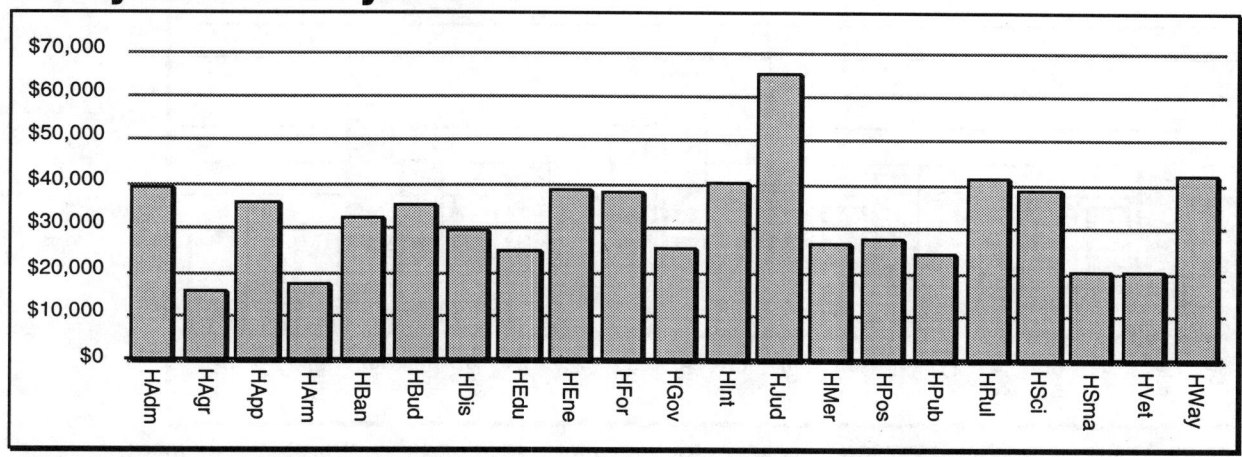

The House Judiciary Committee stood above all others in contributions from lawyers and lobbyists. Trial lawyers are most interested in combatting any movement toward tort reform. Lobbyists, perhaps the most pragmatic group of any contributors, give to all committees, largely to ensure access on behalf of their clients.

Transportation

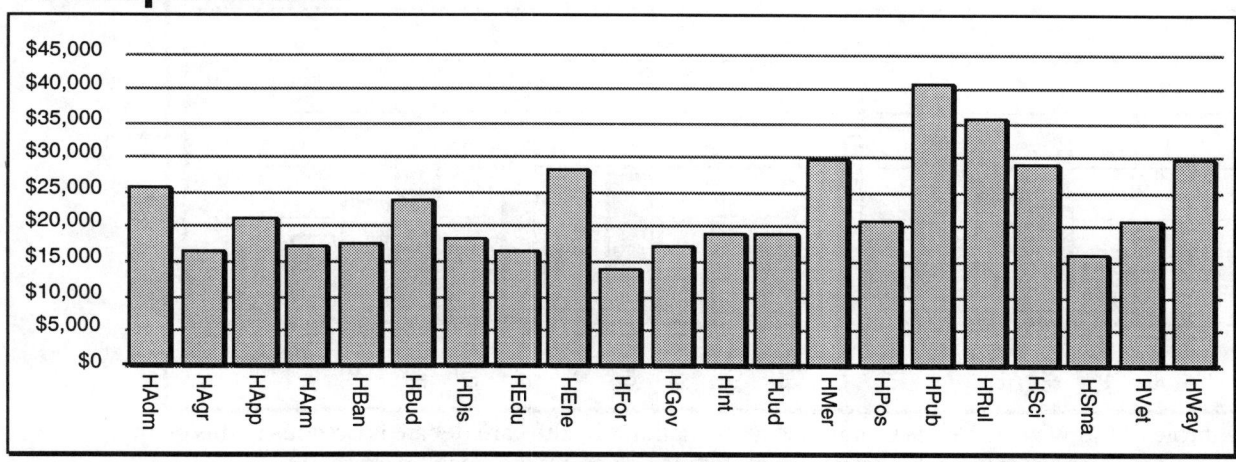

Not surprisingly, the Public Works and Transportation Committee was the biggest recipient of transport industry dollars. The Merchant Marine & Fisheries Committee got the most from shipping interests.

Construction

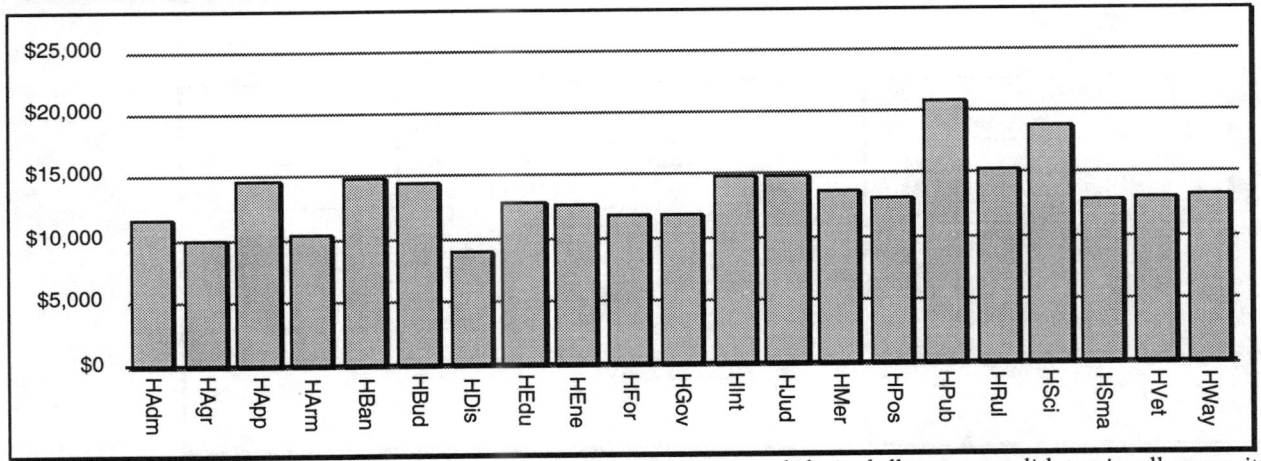

Builders groups and others within the construction sector spread their dollars to candidates in all committees. Public Works and Transportation Committee members, whose jurisdiction includes major federal building projects, got the most.

Ideological/Single-Issue

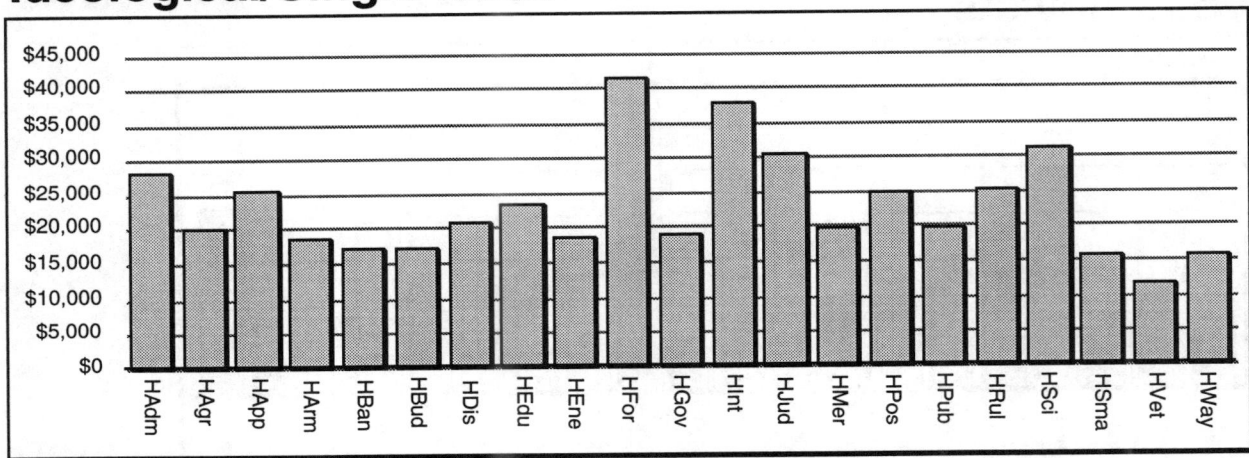

The House Foreign Affairs Committee drew the most in contributions from ideological contributors. The leader there was pro-Israel groups, which gave more than $18,000 per member. Environmental groups favored the Interior Committee; the Sierra Club was the committee's biggest single contributor.

Health & Insurance

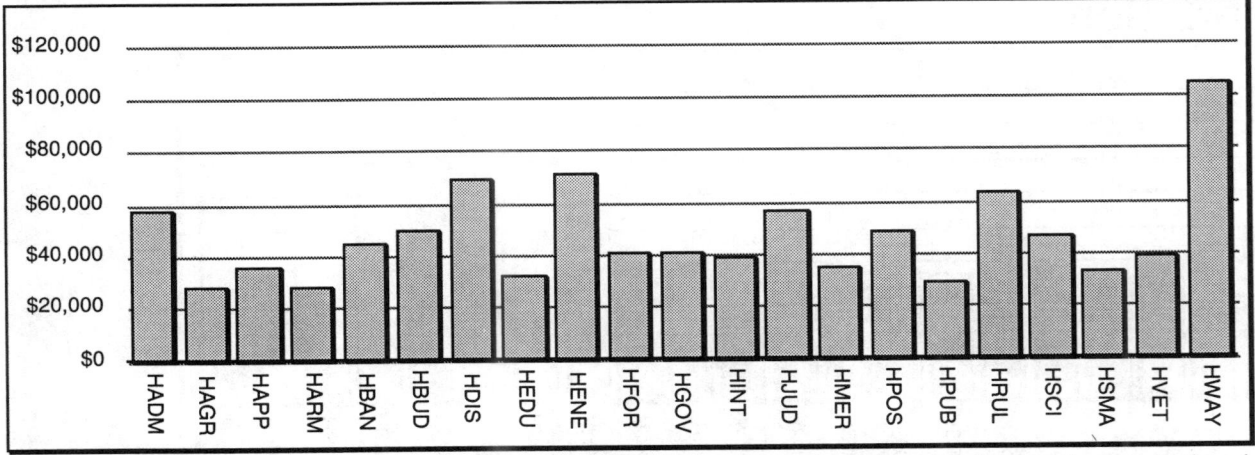

The preeminent role of the Ways & Means Committee in the nation's health care debate is obvious in this chart, which combines dollars given by insurance companies with those given by the health care sector.

2.

Industry Profiles

Industry Profiles in Brief

With today's expensive election campaigns, and the almost infinite spectrum of legislation considered on Capitol Hill, members of Congress draw their campaign funds from dozens of different industries and interests. The industry profiles on the following pages provide the details on which industries are the biggest givers and which members are the biggest recipients of their funds. The profiles have two sections: one shows graphically where the money comes from and where it goes. The other gives more detail about the smaller categories within each industry. Following is a thumbnail sketch of each of the 12 main industry and interest group sectors:

Agriculture .... $24.9 million

An important player in Washington that has maintained its longtime influence despite the decline of the family farm, agricultural contributors gave nearly $25 million in contributions to congressional and presidential candidates in 1991-92. Crop production and processing was the sector's leading source of campaign funds, but it accounted for only one-quarter of the sector's total dollars. The rest came from a wide range of affiliated industries, from food processors and supermarkets to pesticide and fertilizer manufacturers, tobacco companies, dairy farmers, poultry and livestock producers, and the forest products industry.

Communications/Electronics .... $21.2 million

The big money here comes from two main sources: the telecommunications industry (primarily local and long distance telephone companies) and the entertainment industry, made up mainly of the TV and motion picture industries. The phone company money comes predominantly from AT&T and the regional Bell systems. Nearly nine-tenths of that money was delivered through political action committees. The broadcasting and movie money — which tilted heavily toward Democratic candidates — came mostly through individual donors rather than PACs.

Construction .... $15.2 million

General contractors engaged in commercial, industrial, utility and highway construction were the biggest single source of campaign funds within the construction sector. Overall they outspent home builders by nearly three-to-one. Other notable sources of contributions were more specialized subcontractors, engineering and architectural firms, and building materials suppliers. A close partner of the construction industry, often weathering the same economic ups and downs, is the real estate industry, which is included separately in the Finance, Insurance & Real Estate sector, described below.

Defense .... $8.3 million

While every one of the 12 main industry and interest group sectors increased their giving in 1992, the Defense sector grew the least. That reflects the industry's continuing post-Cold War economic slump. Within the sector, defense aerospace contractors gave about twice as much as defense electronics firms. Overall, nearly 90 percent of the Defense industry's contributions came from PACs.

Energy & Natural Resources .... $21.3 million

Oil and gas producers supplied the biggest share of campaign dollars from this sector, as they have consistently over the years. In 1991-92 they gave $9.2 million to congressional and presidential candidates. Natural gas pipeline companies added another $2.4 million. The other big givers here were the nation's electric utilities, which doled out nearly $4.6 million — nearly 90 percent of it through PACs.

Finance, Insurance & Real Estate .... $71.1 million

This is the giant of all the contributor sectors, providing more than $71 million to federal candidates in the 1992 elections. Within the sector, four heavyweight industries provided most of the money — real estate interests gave $16.5 million, the securities & investment industry gave $15.9 million, insurance companies and agents gave $14.9 million, and commercial

banks passed out $11.2 million to candidates for Congress and the presidency. Two-thirds of the banking and insurance contributions came from political action committees, while three-quarters of the real estate and securities money came from individuals.

Health ....$31.7 million

With a complete overhaul of the nation's health care system looming at the top of the agenda of both Congress and the White House, the nation's health providers dramatically boosted their political contributions in the 1992 elections. Physicians and other health professionals led the way, providing more than $21 million in campaign cash to federal candidates. Pharmaceutical companies and health products manufacturers added another $4.4 million, and hospital and nursing homes gave $3.6 million. The insurance industry, included in the financial category above, added nearly $15 million of its own, bringing the combined health & insurance outlay to more than $46 million in the 1992 elections.

Lawyers & Lobbyists ....$44.1 million

When looking at PAC contributions alone, lawyers and lobbyists appear to be a second-tier player among business sectors, but a closer examination of their contributions finds that that is due more to the way they give than to how much they give. Fully 86 percent of the contributions from lawyers and lobbyists came through individual donations, and when added to the PAC dollars, their overall total during 1991-92 rose to more than $44 million — second only to the Finance, Insurance & Real Estate sector. Democrats were the main beneficiaries, capturing nearly three-quarters of the total contributions.

Miscellaneous Business ....$38.5 million

This catchall category includes everything from steelmakers to beer distributors, restaurants to casinos, chemical companies to advertising agencies. Major contributor groups within the sector include the food & beverage industries ($4 million), the alcohol industry ($4 million), chemical manufacturers ($3 million), and a wide collection of business services and manufacturing companies.

Transportation ....$19.0 million

The automotive and air transport industries were the biggest givers within the transportation sector during 1991-92, though within those groups much of the money came not from airlines and automakers, but from auto dealers and from the nation's two giant delivery services, UPS and Federal Express. The air transport sector was also boosted by the presence of the widely-diversified General Electric. Though known by consumers mostly for its light bulbs and home appliances, GE's biggest revenue source is from its aerospace division, which makes jet engines for both commercial airliners and the military.

Labor ....$43.3 million

Though the number of union members continues to dwindle nationwide, and the political impact of organized labor has been in a long decline — witness their inability to derail the NAFTA agreement — labor unions remain a financial stalwart of the Democratic Party. Union PACs, which account for 99 percent of the labor contributions, delivered $40.6 million to Democratic candidates in the 1992 election. Republicans got $2.5 million.

Ideological/Single-Issue ....$29.3 million

While the most highly-publicized ideological groups tend to be the National Rifle Association and abortion groups, the biggest source of campaign funds among ideological and single-issue groups continues to be the large nationwide network of pro-Israel PACs. The biggest growth in 1992, however, came from Women's Groups — led by Emily's List. Though the Center was able to track more than $3.7 million from women's issue PACs and individual contributors, that number is undoubtedly much lower than the actual figure, since only contributions of $200 and above are itemized under federal law and many of the women's group donations were for smaller amounts.

Business Contributors

Where the money came from . . .

By far the largest source of campaign contributions — for both congressional and presidential candidates — are the corporations, trade associations and professional groups that are loosely classified under the label of "business" contributors. The PACs and individual contributors in this group come from every sector of American industry — sectors which are explored in greater detail on the pages that follow. Together, giving both through PACs and individuals, business groups delivered nearly $300 million to federal candidates in the 1992 elections.

The Finance, Insurance & Real Estate sector was far and away the largest, providing more than $71 million in contributions. Lawyers and lobbyists — one of the smallest business sectors if one looks at PAC contributions alone — ranked second overall in their giving. Eight-six percent of their campaign dollars came not from PACs but from individuals.

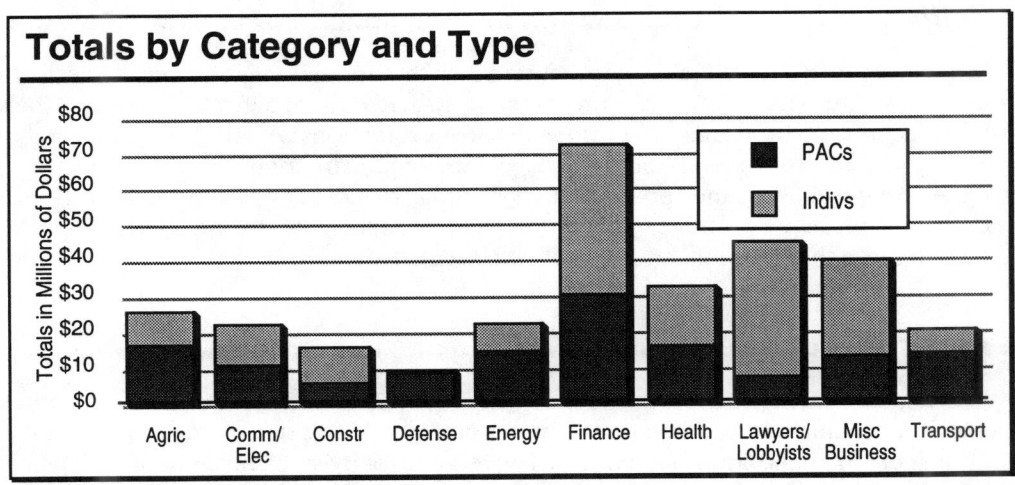

Totals by Category and Type

Category	Total	From PACs	PAC Pct	From Indivs	Indiv Pct
Agriculture	$24,892,124	$15,556,854	62%	$9,335,270	38%
Communic/Electronics	$21,232,464	$9,712,904	46%	$11,519,560	54%
Construction	$15,246,489	$4,730,644	31%	$10,515,845	69%
Defense	$8,328,760	$7,398,411	89%	$930,349	11%
Energy/Natural Resources	$21,341,235	$13,532,584	63%	$7,808,651	37%
Finance/Insur/Real Estate	$71,091,876	$29,617,353	42%	$41,474,523	58%
Health	$31,710,239	$14,932,301	47%	$16,777,938	53%
Lawyers & Lobbyists	$44,058,744	$6,319,679	14%	$37,739,065	86%
Misc Business	$38,478,007	$12,234,888	32%	$26,243,119	68%
Transportation	$18,989,690	$12,767,017	67%	$6,222,673	33%
Total	**$295,369,628**	**$126,802,635**	**43%**	**$168,566,993**	**57%**

Top 20 Business Contributors

Rank	Total	Contributor	Category	PAC Pct	Dem Pct	Repub Pct	To Dems / To Repubs
1	$3,245,544	American Medical Assn*	Doctors	100%	49%	51%	
2	$2,954,973	National Assn of Realtors	Real Estate	100%	55%	45%	
3	$2,361,135	Assn of Trial Lawyers of America	Trial Lawyers	100%	92%	8%	
4	$1,784,375	National Auto Dealers Assn	Auto Dealers	100%	39%	61%	
5	$1,692,508	American Bankers Assn*	Comml Banks	99%	50%	49%	
6	$1,544,701	American Institute of CPA's	Accountants	100%	56%	44%	
7	$1,472,357	United Parcel Service	Delivery Svcs	99%	54%	46%	
8	$1,434,408	American Dental Assn*	Dentists	100%	60%	40%	
9	$1,397,883	AT&T*	Long Distance	93%	61%	39%	
10	$1,373,955	National Assn of Life Underwriters	Life Insurance	100%	54%	46%	
11	$1,074,827	National Assn of Home Builders*	Resid Constr	100%	44%	56%	
12	$1,004,848	RJR Nabisco*	Tobacco/Food	95%	55%	45%	
13	$977,081	National Beer Wholesalers Assn	Beer Distrib	100%	38%	62%	
14	$963,353	BellSouth Corp*	Phone Utilities	92%	59%	41%	
15	$898,545	Goldman, Sachs & Co	Securities	22%	67%	33%	
16	$881,820	American Express*	Stocks/Credit	38%	69%	30%	
17	$877,550	Associated Milk Producers	Dairy	100%	79%	21%	
18	$870,227	American Academy of Ophthalmology	Eye Doctors	100%	63%	37%	
19	$823,486	General Electric*	Aerospace	86%	60%	43%	
20	$775,147	Philip Morris*	Tobacco/Food	87%	59%	41%	

* Contributions came from more than one affiliate or subsidiary.

Where the money went . . .

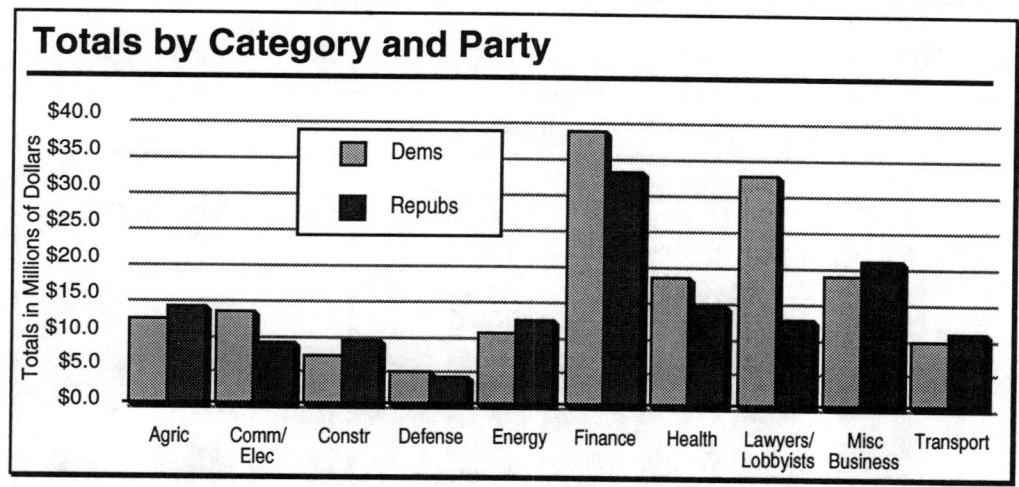

Totals by Category and Party

Category	Total	To Dems	Dem Pct	To Repubs	Repub Pct
Agriculture	$24,892,124	$11,533,853	46%	$13,315,969	53%
Communic/Electronics	$21,232,464	$12,758,180	60%	$8,391,147	40%
Construction	$15,246,489	$6,584,436	43%	$8,617,049	57%
Defense	$8,328,760	$4,609,451	55%	$3,714,903	45%
Energy/Natural Resources	$21,341,235	$9,794,836	46%	$11,518,607	54%
Finance/Insur/Real Estate	$71,091,876	$38,321,025	54%	$32,574,212	46%
Health	$31,710,239	$17,774,140	56%	$13,780,085	43%
Lawyers & Lobbyists	$44,058,744	$32,160,897	73%	$11,827,725	27%
Misc Business	$38,478,007	$17,962,336	47%	$20,354,469	53%
Transportation	$18,989,690	$8,940,802	47%	$10,020,890	53%
Total	**$295,369,628**	**$160,439,956**	**54%**	**$134,115,056**	**45%**

Overall, Democrats attracted a slight majority of the dollars from within the business community — a fact that many might find surprising, since most business groups tend to be more Republican in their political outlook. Whatever their personal preferences, however, the one quality that marks nearly all business groups is their pragmatism. Bluntly speaking, the Democrats control both houses of Congress with sizable majorities. Since the 1992 election, they also control the White House. Business leaders know well that if legislation is to succeed, the majority party is going to have to go along with it.

Most sectors within the business community split their dollars fairly evenly between Republicans and Democrats. The most notable exception was the legal community, which gave nearly three-quarters of its dollars to Democrats. The communications & electronics sector also favored Democrats by a fairly wide margin — primarily because of the heavily Democratic-leaning entertainment industry based in Hollywood and New York. The most heavily Republican sector was the construction industry, which gave 57 percent of its dollars to GOP candidates.

The Top 20 contributor chart on the opposite page illustrates an important point about contributions in American politics: the biggest overall contributors tend to be political action committees that represent large nationwide organizations or Fortune 500 companies. But behind those headline-grabbing leaders are tens of thousands of smaller organizations — law firms, doctors' offices, insurance agents, and every other kind of business from beer wholesalers to casinos. Individually they are small enough not to attract attention. Together, however, their donations amount to tens of millions of dollars. To fully reveal the patterns by which industries and interest groups make their opinions heard in Washington, one must aggregate *all* the contributors — large and small — into specific categories. That is the approach taken throughout this book and it will reveal many surprising (and not so surprising) patterns on these pages, and in the committee and member profiles that follow.

The totals on these pages, and in all others in the Industry Profile section of this book, reflect contributions both to congressional and presidential candidates. They do not include small contributions, however, as federal law does not require any itemization of individual donations under $200. What these pages do show are the patterns in giving from major contributors — political action committees, and those individuals giving $200 or more. Those two groups together provide the great majority of dollars that fuel the ever more expensive machinery of modern American elections.

Agriculture

Where the money came from . . .

The agriculture sector encompasses thousands of independent farmers, ranchers and dairy producers from Maine to California, but that's just the half of it. Also included in this widely diversified category are commodities brokers, lumber companies, grocery wholesalers, pesticide manufacturers and giant food industry conglomerates making everything from cigarettes to frozen pizzas. In all, the industry contributed nearly $25 million to federal campaigns in the 1992 elections. About 62 percent came from political action committees and just over half went to Republican candidates.

Within the farming community, the heaviest crop of dollars came from sugar growers and dairy producers, though detailed classifications were not always possible since many contributors described themselves simply as "farmers." More than 80 percent of the tobacco and dairy money was delivered through PACs, while cattle ranchers and poultry producers were the groups most likely to give through individual contributions.

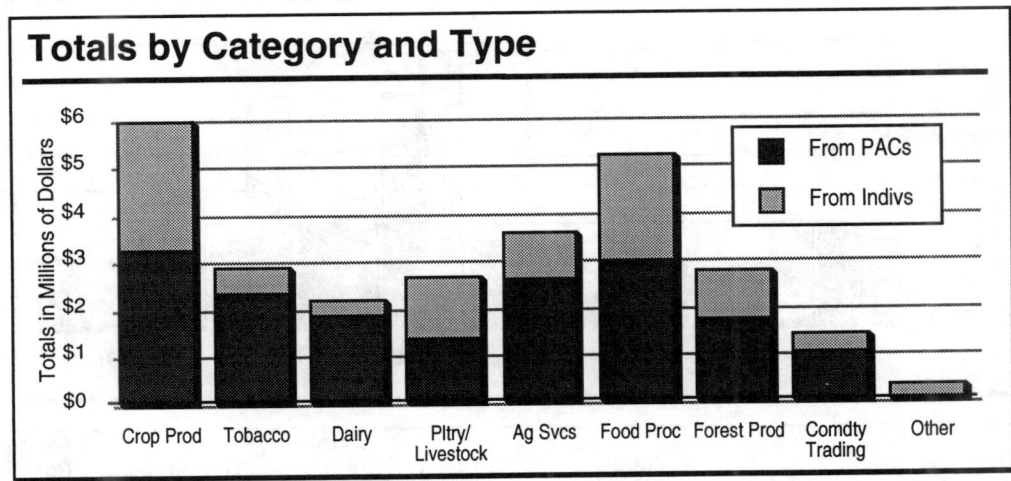

Totals by Category and Type

Category	Total	From PACs	PAC Pct	From Indivs	Indiv Pct
Crop Production/Processing	$5,868,649	$3,197,726	54%	$2,670,923	46%
Tobacco	$2,818,861	$2,280,012	81%	$538,849	19%
Dairy	$2,107,911	$1,753,112	83%	$354,799	17%
Poultry & Livestock	$2,551,679	$1,266,751	50%	$1,284,928	50%
Agricultural Services/Products	$3,470,020	$2,522,628	73%	$947,392	27%
Food Processing & Sales	$5,108,064	$2,886,974	57%	$2,221,090	43%
Forest Products	$2,709,343	$1,649,651	61%	$1,059,692	39%
Commodity Trading*	$1,325,102	$959,300	72%	$365,802	28%
Other & Unclassified	$257,597	$0	0%	$257,597	100%
TOTAL	**$24,892,124**	**$15,556,854**	**62%**	**$9,335,270**	**38%**

* Listed for information only. Total is included under Finance/Insurance/Real Estate.

Top 20 Agriculture Contributors

Rank	Total	Contributor	Category	PAC Pct	Dem Pct	Repub Pct	To Dems / To Repubs
1	$1,004,848	RJR Nabisco*	Tobacco/Food	95%	55%	45%	
2	$877,550	Associated Milk Producers	Dairy	100%	79%	21%	
3	$775,147	Philip Morris*	Tobacco/Food	87%	59%	41%	
4	$636,120	US Tobacco*	Tobacco	69%	34%	66%	
5	$531,778	Food Marketing Institute	Food Stores	100%	35%	65%	
6	$427,470	National Cattlemen's Assn*	Livestock	99%	44%	55%	
7	$345,650	Archer-Daniels-Midland Corp	Grain Traders	82%	51%	49%	
8	$345,071	Mid-America Dairymen	Dairy	100%	74%	26%	
9	$313,588	ConAgra Inc	Food Products	96%	30%	69%	
10	$311,707	American Sugarbeet Growers Assn	Sugar	100%	68%	32%	
11	$301,000	American Veterinary Medical Assn	Veterinarians	100%	59%	41%	
12	$297,015	American Crystal Sugar Corp	Sugar	100%	71%	29%	
13	$266,010	Tyson Foods	Poultry	65%	86%	14%	
14	$252,850	Winn-Dixie Stores	Food Stores	90%	37%	63%	
15	$248,650	Westvaco Corp	Paper/Pulp	99%	21%	79%	
16	$237,980	Anheuser-Busch	Beer	53%	54%	46%	
17	$221,860	International Paper Co	Paper/Pulp	99%	10%	90%	
18	$199,000	Freeport-McMoRan Inc	Ag Chemicals	67%	58%	42%	
19	$197,925	American Sugar Cane League	Sugar	100%	76%	24%	
20	$189,200	Tobacco Institute	Tobacco	97%	51%	49%	

* Contributions came from more than one affiliate or subsidiary.

Where the money went . . .

Totals by Category and Party

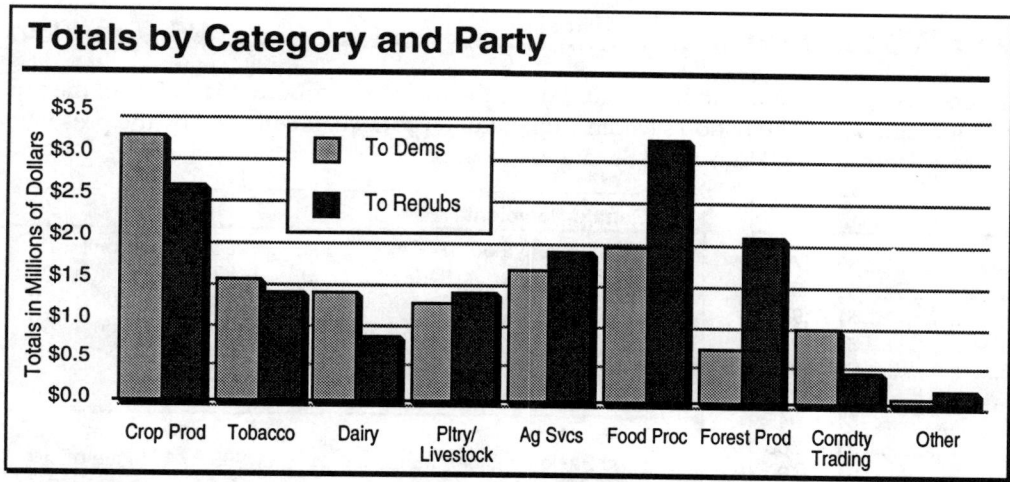

Category	Total	To Dems	Dem Pct	To Repubs	Repub Pct
Crop Production/Processing	$5,868,649	$3,229,687	55%	$2,629,576	45%
Tobacco	$2,818,861	$1,494,566	53%	$1,322,876	47%
Dairy	$2,107,911	$1,324,596	63%	$783,315	37%
Poultry & Livestock	$2,551,679	$1,201,531	47%	$1,346,698	53%
Agricultural Services/Products	$3,470,020	$1,619,109	47%	$1,844,911	53%
Food Processing & Sales	$5,108,064	$1,900,655	37%	$3,187,590	62%
Forest Products	$2,709,343	$678,905	25%	$2,028,438	75%
Commodity Trading*	$1,325,102	$936,452	71%	$387,150	29%
Other & Unclassified	$257,597	$84,804	33%	$172,565	67%
TOTAL	**$24,892,124**	**$11,533,853**	**46%**	**$13,315,969**	**53%**

* Listed for information only. Total is included under Finance/Insurance/Real Estate.

Overall, the agriculture sector gave a slight majority of its campaign dollars to Republicans, though there were wide variations within the sector. Most partisan was the forest products industry, which gave three-quarters of its money to Republicans. Dairy farmers, however, preferred Democrats nearly two-to-one.

California Republican John Seymour tapped successfully into the huge agribusiness industry of his home state, collecting more than half a million dollars in the 1992 election. The voters, however, preferred Dianne Feinstein. Only two of the remaining top recipients in the Senate held seats on the Agriculture Committee, though all came from states where farming is an important part of the economy.

In the House, farm-state incumbents drew the heaviest support from the agriculture sector. Five of the top 10 also sat on the House Agriculture Committee. Texas Democrat Kika de la Garza, who ranked seventh, is the committee's chairman. Ron Marlenee, the top-ranking recipient, lost his seat in a showdown with fellow incumbent Pat Williams, after Montana lost one of its two seats in Congress due to reapportionment. Marlenee, a conservative Republican, got most of the business support, but Williams, a liberal Democrat, was the winner in a close, bitterly-fought race.

Top 10 Senate Recipients

Rank	Name	Amount	Status	W/L
1	John F. Seymour (R-Calif)	$553,503	Incumb	L
2	Wyche Fowler Jr. (D-Ga)	$381,699	Incumb	L
3	Christopher S. Bond (R-Mo)	$293,303	Incumb	W
4	Bob Kasten (R-Wis)	$285,235	Incumb	L
5	Dale Bumpers (D-Ark)	$262,420	Incumb	W
6	Rod Chandler (R-Wash)	$251,707	Open	L
7	Paul Coverdell (R-Ga)	$230,707	Chall	W
8	Bob Dole (R-Kan)	$225,881	Incumb	W
9	Dirk Kempthorne (R-Idaho)	$222,886	Open	W
10	Don Nickles (R-Okla)	$217,228	Incumb	W

Top 10 House Recipients

Rank	Name	Amount	Status	W/L
1	Ron Marlenee (R-Mont)	$187,305	Incumb	L
2	Jerry Huckaby (D-La)	$186,374	Incumb	L
3	Charles Hatcher (D-Ga)	$176,621	Incumb	L
4	Vic Fazio (D-Calif)	$160,739	Incumb	W
5	Wally Herger (R-Calif)	$155,748	Incumb	W
6	Calvin Dooley (D-Calif)	$145,723	Incumb	W
7	E. "Kika" de la Garza (D-Texas)	$145,099	Incumb	W
8	Charles W. Stenholm (D-Texas)	$144,303	Incumb	W
9	Bill Emerson (R-Mo)	$143,925	Incumb	W
10	Tom Coleman (R-Mo)	$136,225	Incumb	L

Closeup on Agriculture

Crop Production & Basic Processing ....$5.9 million

Though this category includes farmers raising every crop under the sun, six of the top 10 contributors (and five of the top six) were sugar growers. California's preeminence as the nation's leading agricultural producer is reflected by the presence of five Californians on the list of top recipients among House and Senate candidates.

Top Contributors

1	American Sugarbeet Growers Assn	$311,707
2	American Crystal Sugar Corp	$297,015
3	American Sugar Cane League	$197,925
4	National Cotton Council	$184,989
5	Okeelanta Corp	$170,800
6	Florida Sugar Cane League	$167,075
7	Ocean Spray Cranberries	$145,945
8	Sunkist Growers	$134,360
9	Southern Minn Beet Sugar Co-op	$120,400
10	Sun-Diamond Growers*	$106,685

* Contributions came from more than one affiliate or subsidiary.

Top Senate Recipients

1	John F. Seymour (R-Calif)	$226,537	Incumb	L
2	Wyche Fowler Jr. (D-Ga)	$137,651	Incumb	L
3	Dale Bumpers (D-Ark)	$78,720	Incumb	W
4	Kent Conrad (D-ND)	$72,890	Incumb	W
5	Tom Campbell (R-Calif)	$60,078	Open	L

Top House Recipients

1	Jerry Huckaby (D-La)	$131,424	Incumb	L
2	Vic Fazio (D-Calif)	$95,774	Incumb	W
3	Charles Hatcher (D-Ga)	$91,121	Incumb	L
4	Calvin Dooley (D-Calif)	$82,122	Incumb	W
5	Wally Herger (R-Calif)	$76,165	Incumb	W

Tobacco ....$2.8 million

The nation's most controversial agricultural related industry, still supported by federal subsidies, delivered $2.8 million to federal candidates in the 1992 election. A number of tobacco state lawmakers appear on the list of biggest recipients, as expected. The only non-incumbent on the list was Oklahoma Democrat Drew Edmondson, who opposed Mike Synar, a longtime tobacco industry foe. Edmondson lost in the primary, and Synar was reelected despite the tobacco industry's efforts to unseat him.

Top Contributors

1	RJR Nabisco*	$1,004,848
2	Philip Morris*	$775,147
3	US Tobacco*	$636,120
4	Tobacco Institute	$189,200
5	Pinkerton Tobacco	$66,475

* Contributions came from more than one affiliate or subsidiary.

Top Senate Recipients

1	Wendell H. Ford (D-Ky)	$68,148	Incumb	W
2	Bob Kasten (R-Wis)	$62,502	Incumb	L
3	Wyche Fowler Jr. (D-Ga)	$43,000	Incumb	L
4	Christopher J. Dodd (D-Conn)	$35,700	Incumb	W
5	Terry Sanford (D-NC)	$34,250	Incumb	L

Top House Recipients

1	Drew Edmondson (D-Okla)	$53,830	Chall	L
2	Thomas J. Bliley Jr. (R-Va)	$38,991	Incumb	W
3	Sam M. Gibbons (D-Fla)	$25,250	Incumb	W
4	Charles Hatcher (D-Ga)	$24,950	Incumb	L
5	Richard A. Gephardt (D-Mo)	$22,848	Incumb	W

Dairy ....$2.1 million

Price supports to the dairy industry have long been a staple of federal agricultural policy. In return, the industry has been generous to Capitol Hill lawmakers seeking reelection. Overall, Democrats got 63 percent of their campaign dollars in 1991-92.

Top Contributors

1	Associated Milk Producers	$877,550
2	Mid-America Dairymen	$345,071
3	Dairymen Inc*	$173,874
4	Milk Industry Foundation	$132,600
5	Milk Marketing Inc	$84,700

* Contributions came from more than one affiliate or subsidiary.

Top Senate Recipients

1	Bob Kasten (R-Wis)	$36,035	Incumb	L
2	Ben Nighthorse Campbell (D-Colo)	$26,600	Open	W
3	Arlen Specter (R-Pa)	$26,250	Incumb	W
4	John F. Seymour (R-Calif)	$25,600	Incumb	L
5	Charles E. Grassley (R-Iowa)	$22,950	Incumb	W

Top House Recipients

1	Jill L. Long (D-Ind)	$23,500	Incumb	W
2	Wayne Allard (R-Colo)	$21,100	Incumb	W
3	Harold L. Volkmer (D-Mo)	$20,500	Incumb	W
4	Jim Jontz (D-Ind)	$18,250	Incumb	L
5	Charles W. Stenholm (D-Texas)	$18,000	Incumb	W

Agricultural Services & Products ....$3.5 million

The support industries that provide everything from fertilizers and pesticides to crop insurance form a major segment of the agriculture sector's contributions to Congress. The top contributor in this category, Archer-Daniels-Midland, a giant agribusiness firm that is the nation's largest supplier of ethanol, was also the biggest contributor of "soft money" in the 1992 elections. ADM gave over $1.3 million in soft money — most of it to the Republican National Committee in support of President Bush's reelection.

Top Contributors

1	Archer-Daniels-Midland Corp	$345,650
2	American Veterinary Medical Assn	$301,000
3	Freeport-McMoRan Inc	$199,000
4	Farm Credit Council	$170,023
5	American Assn of Crop Insurers	$152,726
6	Deere & Co*	$140,710
7	Cargill Inc	$134,850
8	Alabama Farm Bureau Federation	$131,231
9	National Council of Farmer Co-ops	$128,000
10	Land O'Lakes Inc	$80,525

* Contributions came from more than one affiliate or subsidiary.

Top Senate Recipients

1	John F. Seymour (R-Calif)	$92,299	Incumb	L
2	Bob Dole (R-Kan)	$65,500	Incumb	W
3	Christopher S. Bond (R-Mo)	$64,134	Incumb	W
4	Charles E. Grassley (R-Iowa)	$60,429	Incumb	W
5	Wyche Fowler Jr. (D-Ga)	$57,848	Incumb	L

Top House Recipients

1	Tom Coleman (R-Mo)	$40,850	Incumb	L
2	E. "Kika" de la Garza (D-Texas)	$37,670	Incumb	W
3	Charles W. Stenholm (D-Texas)	$29,000	Incumb	W
4	Pat Roberts (R-Kan)	$27,500	Incumb	W
5	Robert H. Michel (R-Ill)	$26,982	Incumb	W

Food Processing & Sales ....$5.1 million

This category encompasses the companies that provide most of the groceries we find on supermarket shelves, as well as the supermarkets themselves and grocery wholesalers. The industry favored Republican candidates by a wide margin.

Top Contributors

1	Food Marketing Institute	$531,778
2	ConAgra Inc	$313,588
3	Winn-Dixie Stores	$252,850
4	General Mills*	$205,683
5	Flowers Industries	$187,200
6	Fleming Companies Inc	$181,650
7	American Meat Institute	$107,129
8	Connell Rice & Sugar Co	$92,638
9	Nestle Enterprises Inc	$83,867
10	National Wholesale Grocers Assn	$83,839

* Contributions came from more than one affiliate or subsidiary.

Top Senate Recipients

1	John F. Seymour (R-Calif)	$89,560	Incumb	L
2	Christopher S. Bond (R-Mo)	$86,875	Incumb	W
3	Dirk Kempthorne (R-Idaho)	$79,982	Open	W
4	Arlen Specter (R-Pa)	$70,700	Incumb	W
5	Paul Coverdell (R-Ga)	$70,150	Chall	W

Top House Recipients

1	Michael D. Crapo (R-Idaho)	$38,750	Open	W
2	Tom Coleman (R-Mo)	$30,250	Incumb	L
3	Pete von Reichbauer (R-Wash)	$28,870	Open	L
4	H. Martin Lancaster (D-NC)	$28,550	Incumb	W
5	Charles W. Stenholm (D-Texas)	$28,528	Incumb	W

Forest Products ....$2.7 million

Candidates from the Pacific Northwest were the biggest recipients of dollars from the forest products industry. This was the most Republican-leaning industry within the agriculture sector. Only one dollar in every four went to Democrats.

Top Contributors

1	Westvaco Corp	$248,400
2	International Paper Co	$221,860
3	Weyerhaeuser Co*	$180,423
4	Georgia-Pacific Corp	$137,442
5	Champion International Corp	$127,612
6	Simpson Investment Co	$112,575
7	Scott Paper Co	$84,148
8	Union Camp Corp	$82,810
9	Boise Cascade	$82,507
10	Potlatch Corp	$78,828

* Contributions came from more than one affiliate or subsidiary.

Top Senate Recipients

1	Rod Chandler (R-Wash)	$132,193	Open	L
2	Bob Packwood (R-Ore)	$107,400	Incumb	W
3	Dirk Kempthorne (R-Idaho)	$83,554	Open	W
4	Paul Coverdell (R-Ga)	$71,995	Chall	W
5	Bob Kasten (R-Wis)	$64,200	Incumb	L

Top House Recipients

1	Tony Meeker (R-Ore)	$63,975	Open	L
2	Bob Smith (R-Ore)	$43,762	Incumb	W
3	Pat Fiske (R-Wash)	$40,300	Chall	L
4	Steve Buyer (R-Ind)	$39,698	Chall	W
5	Jennifer Dunn (R-Wash)	$28,868	Open	W

Communications & Electronics

Where the money came from . . .

Increasingly, the thread that ties the American nation together is an electronic one. We plug into television for the day's news, weather, football games and soap operas. We flash faxes by the millions across the continent each business day. Our telephones are never far from reach, whether we're in the backyard, the interstate, or 30,000 feet in the air. And our computers — desktop, laptop, or palm-of-the-hand varieties — are becoming more ubiquitous and more necessary every day. We are a nation plugged in, and our unceasing appetite for instant news, communications and entertainment have spawned industries that have become an increasingly important sector of the American economy.

Since much of the telecommunications industry comes under federal regulation, decisions made in Washington can mean billions to the industry. Both sides know it, and the flow of dollars to federal campaigns reflects that fact. In the 1992 elections this sector contributed more than $21 million to congressional and presidential campaigns.

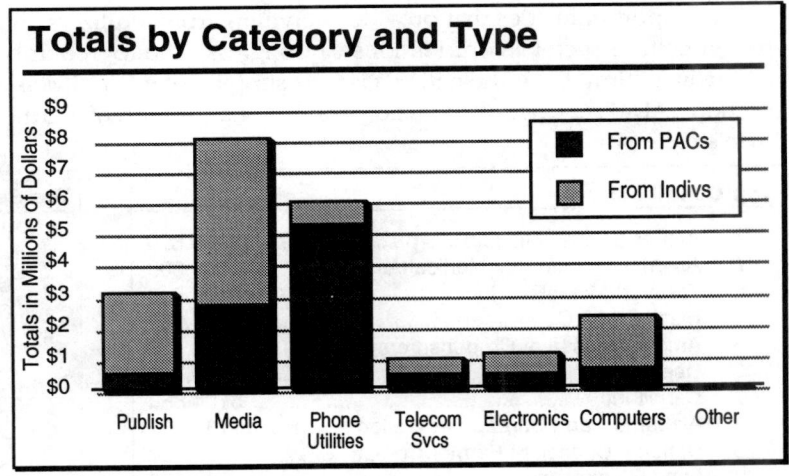

Totals by Category and Type

Category	Total	From PACs	PAC Pct	From Indivs	Indiv Pct
Publishing	$3,059,581	$465,102	15%	$2,594,479	85%
Media/Entertainment	$8,018,782	$2,598,430	32%	$5,420,352	68%
Telephone Utilities	$5,904,399	$5,167,442	88%	$736,957	12%
Telecom Equipment & Svcs	$909,340	$449,199	49%	$460,141	51%
Electronics Mfg & Services	$1,088,233	$455,250	42%	$632,983	58%
Computer Equipment & Svcs	$2,212,954	$576,981	26%	$1,635,973	74%
Other & Unclassified	$39,175	$500	1%	$38,675	99%
TOTAL	**$21,232,464**	**$9,712,904**	**46%**	**$11,519,560**	**54%**

The two most generous segments of the communications/electronics sector were the Media & Entertainment industries — which includes TV and motion picture production as well as the Cable TV and recorded music industries — and the nation's network of local and long distance telephone utilities. Most of the media dollars came through individual contributions, while the phone companies gave most of their money through political action committees.

Top 20 Communications & Electronics Contributors

Rank	Total	Contributor	Category	PAC Pct	Dem Pct	Repub Pct	To Dems / To Repubs
1	$1,397,883	AT&T*	Long Distance	93%	61%	39%	
2	$963,353	BellSouth Corp*	Phone Utilities	92%	59%	41%	
3	$644,249	National Cable Television Assn	Cable TV	99%	54%	46%	
4	$631,869	GTE Corp*	Phone Utilities	97%	52%	48%	
5	$583,089	Time Warner*	Movies/Publish	24%	76%	24%	
6	$562,342	Ameritech Corp*	Phone Utilities	92%	55%	45%	
7	$522,400	National Assn of Broadcasters	Entertainment	95%	55%	45%	
8	$432,910	United Telecommunications*	Phone Utilities	98%	33%	67%	
9	$401,834	Walt Disney Co*	Movies/Resorts	24%	77%	23%	
10	$331,512	Pacific Telesis Group	Phone Utilities	94%	63%	37%	
11	$325,113	US West*	Phone Utilities	82%	54%	46%	
12	$317,193	MCA Inc*	Movies/TV	58%	84%	16%	
13	$311,690	Southwestern Bell	Phone Utilities	80%	59%	41%	
14	$270,011	Bell Atlantic*	Phone Utilities	87%	56%	43%	
15	$258,377	Westinghouse Electric*	Electronics	83%	56%	43%	
16	$242,750	Corning Glass Works	Telecom Equip	100%	39%	61%	
17	$237,745	NYNEX Corp*	Phone Utilities	86%	50%	50%	
18	$220,680	Harris Corp	Electronics	94%	3%	96%	
19	$194,661	Hallmark Cards	Publishing	74%	22%	78%	
20	$179,210	ASCAP	Music Prod	97%	87%	13%	

* Contributions came from more than one affiliate or subsidiary.

Where the money went . . .

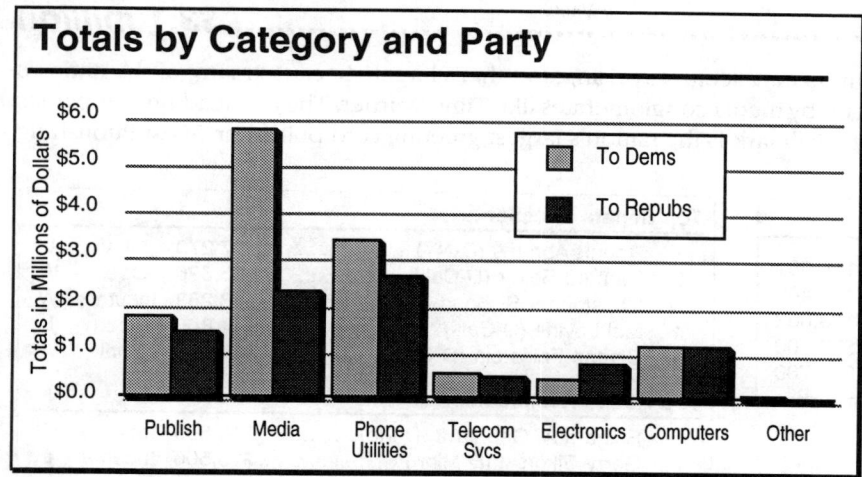

Totals by Category and Party

The Hollywood film community — both the studios and the stars — have always shown a strong preference for Democrats, a fact clearly reflected in the chart on the left. Telephone utilities were more even handed, though they too gave a majority of their dollars to Democratic candidates. Overall, the sector's 60-40 split in favor of Democrats was the second biggest of any business sector. Only lawyers and lobbyists were more supportive of the Democratic party.

Category	Total	To Dems	Dem Pct	To Repubs	Repub Pct
Publishing	$3,059,581	$1,678,693	55%	$1,354,284	44%
Media/Entertainment	$8,018,782	$5,746,780	72%	$2,252,427	28%
Telephone Utilities	$5,904,399	$3,333,625	56%	$2,565,484	43%
Telecom Equipment & Svcs	$909,340	$473,469	52%	$434,669	48%
Electronics Mfg & Services	$1,088,233	$401,368	37%	$683,515	63%
Computer Equipment & Svcs	$2,212,954	$1,099,595	50%	$1,086,243	49%
Other & Unclassified	$39,175	$24,650	63%	$14,525	37%
TOTAL	**$21,232,464**	**$12,758,180**	**60%**	**$8,391,147**	**40%**

Californians were the prime recipients of communications/electronics money in the 1992 elections in U.S. Senate races — a reflection of the fact that both Hollywood and Silicon Valley lie within the Golden State. The fact that both of California's Senate seats were up for election in 1992 was also a major factor. Oregon's Bob Packwood, ranking Republican on the Senate Commerce Committee's Communications subcommittee, was the top beneficiary of telephone and telecommunications industry money.

In the House, Majority Leader Dick Gephardt led all other members in donations from the sector. Five of the top 10 House recipients held seats on the influential Energy & Commerce Committee, which regulates telecommunications policy. John Dingell is the committee's chairman. Mike Synar, Don Ritter and Tom McMillen all sat on the panel's Telecommunications and Finance Subcommittee in 1992.

Top 10 Senate Recipients

Rank	Name	Amount	Status	W/L
1	Mel Levine (D-Calif)	$499,165	Open	L
2	Barbara Boxer (D-Calif)	$489,034	Open	W
3	Dianne Feinstein (D-Calif)	$382,515	Chall	W
4	Bob Packwood (R-Ore)	$331,850	Incumb	W
5	Arlen Specter (R-Pa)	$248,875	Incumb	W
6	Tom Campbell (R-Calif)	$234,488	Open	L
7	Robert Abrams (D-NY)	$231,370	Chall	L
8	John F. Seymour (R-Calif)	$223,658	Incumb	L
9	Ernest F. Hollings (D-SC)	$210,612	Incumb	W
10	Christopher J. Dodd (D-Conn)	$206,268	Incumb	W

Top 10 House Recipients

Rank	Name	Amount	Status	W/L
1	Richard A. Gephardt (D-Mo)	$191,855	Incumb	W
2	Mike Synar (D-Okla)	$130,354	Incumb	W
3	John D. Dingell (D-Mich)	$126,350	Incumb	W
4	Don Ritter (R-Pa)	$111,074	Incumb	L
5	Howard L. Berman (D-Calif)	$102,350	Incumb	W
6	Al Swift (D-Wash)	$99,000	Incumb	W
7	Vic Fazio (D-Calif)	$91,200	Incumb	W
8	David E. Bonior (D-Mich)	$88,150	Incumb	W
9	Tom McMillen (D-Md)	$86,200	Incumb	L
10	Jack Brooks (D-Texas)	$83,900	Incumb	W

Closeup on Communications & Electronics

Printing & Publishing ....$3.1 million

The list of leading publishing industry contributors may seem surprising, but that's largely because many of the nation's best known publishing houses have been bought up by media conglomerates like Time Warner. The two leading companies in the list below have long been politically active. Hallmark is the nation's largest greeting card publisher. West Publishing is the leading supplier of legal texts.

Top Contributors	
1	Hallmark Cards $194,661
2	West Publishing $140,400
3	Printing Industries of America $118,002
4	RR Donnelley & Sons $77,700
5	Forbes Inc $41,700

Top Senate Recipients			
1	Robert Abrams (D-NY) $97,270	Chall	L
2	Barbara Boxer (D-Calif) $55,526	Open	W
3	Christopher S. Bond (R-Mo) $48,288	Incumb	W
4	Mel Levine (D-Calif) $44,800	Open	L
5	Dianne Feinstein (D-Calif) $44,015	Chall	W

Top House Recipients			
1	Richard A. Gephardt (D-Mo) $18,850	Incumb	W
2	Gerry Sikorski (D-Minn) $15,500	Incumb	L
3	Tom Coleman (R-Mo) $14,300	Incumb	L
4	Patricia Schroeder (D-Colo) $14,281	Incumb	W
5	Mike Synar (D-Okla) $12,950	Incumb	W

TV & Movies Production/Distribution ....$5.8 million

Two distinct categories of contributors make up this group — the Hollywood-based TV and motion picture industry that produces much of the nation's mass-market entertainment, and the nationwide network of TV and radio broadcasters, represented primarily by the National Association of Broadcasters. While the broadcasters delivered most of their dollars through the NAB's political action committee, a major share of the movie money came from individuals. Time Warner and Disney both ranked among the 10 largest sources of individual contributions in the 1992 elections.

Top Contributors	
1	Time Warner* $583,089
2	National Assn of Broadcasters $522,400
3	Walt Disney Co* $399,834
4	MCA Inc* $317,193
5	Paramount Communications* $174,005
6	Sony Corp* $141,635
7	Creative Artists Agency Inc $66,702
8	CBS Inc $64,483
9	Interscope Group $62,800
10	Fox Inc $62,650

* Contributions came from more than one affiliate or subsidiary.

Plenty of Hollywood stars donated money to presidential and congressional candidates, but their dollars were small compared to those of the studio chiefs, producers, agents and other behind-the-scenes figures in the film community. One thing they all shared was a strong inclination to direct their dollars to Democrats.

Broadcasters too gave most of their dollars to Democratic candidates, but their distribution of funds was much more evenly balanced. Overall, commercial radio and TV operators gave 57 percent of their money to Democrats, while the TV and motion picture industries gave Democrats well over 80 percent of their dollars.

The biggest recipients of the entertainment industry's generosity were Californians. Democratic Congressman Mel Levine of Los Angeles made a run for the U.S. Senate, but never made it past the primary. Even so, he captured more media money than successful candidates Barbara Boxer and Dianne Feinstein.

In the House, two LA-area incumbents — Howard Berman and Anthony Beilenson — collected respectable sums from the TV and movie industry. So did House Majority Leader Dick Gephardt, who was one of Hollywood's favorites when he ran for president in 1988.

Top Senate Recipients			
1	Mel Levine (D-Calif) $370,925	Open	L
2	Barbara Boxer (D-Calif) $361,944	Open	W
3	Dianne Feinstein (D-Calif) $251,956	Chall	W
4	Christopher J. Dodd (D-Conn) $126,000	Incumb	W
5	Gray Davis (D-Calif) $112,500	Chall	L

Top House Recipients			
1	Howard L. Berman (D-Calif) $66,750	Incumb	W
2	Richard A. Gephardt (D-Mo) $64,755	Incumb	W
3	Anthony C. Beilenson (D-Calif) $48,150	Incumb	W
4	John D. Dingell (D-Mich) $39,550	Incumb	W
5	Mike Synar (D-Okla) $39,374	Incumb	W

Cable TV ....$2.2 million

One segment of the TV and entertainment industry politically sensitive enough to merit special attention is the cable TV industry. Its spending patterns were similar to that of over-the-air broadcasters — 55 percent of their money went to Democrats — but their issues were unique. Unlike broadcasters, most cable companies operate regulated monopolies. Besides facing occasional conflicts with broadcast stations and the major networks, they also come under fire from time to time from disgruntled customers who complain about bad service, high subscription rates and no alternatives. Under pressure, Congress finally acted in 1993 to beef up regulation and lower rates, but many cable operators used the opportunity to raise their rates, or to pare down the list of channels in their "basic" cable package.

Top Contributors	
1 National Cable Television Assn	$644,249
2 Tele-Communications Inc*	$162,400
3 Comcast Corp	$154,740
4 Viacom International*	$150,825
5 Turner Broadcasting System	$89,270
6 Adelphia Communications	$56,400
7 Cablevision Systems Corp	$53,000
8 Jones International	$42,950
9 Cox Cable Communications	$35,000
10 Home Shopping Network Inc	$32,830

* Contributions came from more than one affiliate or subsidiary.

Top Senate Recipients			
1 Bob Packwood (R-Ore)	$120,650	Incumb	W
2 Arlen Specter (R-Pa)	$57,600	Incumb	W
3 Wyche Fowler Jr. (D-Ga)	$54,649	Incumb	L
4 Alfonse M. D'Amato (R-NY)	$53,025	Incumb	W
5 Richard C. Shelby (D-Ala)	$52,000	Incumb	W

Top House Recipients			
1 Peter H. Kostmayer (D-Pa)	$31,999	Incumb	L
2 Mike Synar (D-Okla)	$31,380	Incumb	W
3 Bill Richardson (D-NM)	$29,000	Incumb	W
4 Tom McMillen (D-Md)	$27,650	Incumb	L
5 Richard A. Gephardt (D-Mo)	$25,600	Incumb	W

Telephone Utilities ....$5.9 million

As the phrase "information superhighway" has emerged as the buzzword of the 90s, telephone utilities have begun moving quickly to take advantage of new opportunities to wire the nation's homes and offices with the next generation of telecommunications and entertainment services. The plans on their drawing boards have often put them at odds with the cable TV industry, though a few of the regional "Baby Bells" have begun acquiring cable companies themselves, so that no matter what the "superhighway's" eventual mix of cable and telephone services, they'll be covered.

The dollars they have steadily pumped into federal campaigns have helped guarantee that Congress listens when the phone utilities talk. They spent nearly $6 million in the 1992 elections, splitting it fairly evenly between Democrats (56 percent) and Republicans (44 percent).

Top Contributors	
1 AT&T*	$1,397,883
2 BellSouth Corp*	$963,153
3 GTE Corp*	$631,869
4 Ameritech Corp*	$562,342
5 United Telecommunications*	$432,910
6 Pacific Telesis Group	$331,512
7 US West*	$325,113
8 Southwestern Bell	$311,690
9 Bell Atlantic*	$270,011
10 NYNEX Corp*	$237,295

Top Senate Recipients			
1 Bob Packwood (R-Ore)	$83,750	Incumb	W
2 Ernest F. Hollings (D-SC)	$76,551	Incumb	W
3 Wendell H. Ford (D-Ky)	$54,000	Incumb	W
4 Charles E. Grassley (R-Iowa)	$47,066	Incumb	W
5 Rod Chandler (R-Wash)	$46,850	Open	L

Top House Recipients			
1 David E. Bonior (D-Mich)	$49,250	Incumb	W
2 Richard A. Gephardt (D-Mo)	$46,250	Incumb	W
3 Jim Slattery (D-Kan)	$46,050	Incumb	W
4 Al Swift (D-Wash)	$43,850	Incumb	W
5 Don Ritter (R-Pa)	$43,300	Incumb	L

* Contributions came from more than one affiliate or subsidiary.

On Capitol Hill, the primary centers for debate on telecommunications policy are the House Energy and Commerce Committee and the Senate Commerce, Science and Transportation Committee. Oregon Republican Bob Packwood, the ranking Republican on the Commerce Committee's Communications Subcommittee, led all other recipients of phone company money in 1992. The number two recipient, Ernest Hollings of South Carolina, chairs the full committee.

Construction

Where the money came from . . .

Home builders, public works contractors, project management firms, architects, engineers and a host of assorted contractors supplying everything from plumbing to air conditioning to cement make up this sector of American business — the nation's construction industry.

Many construction firms — particularly the largest ones — are dependent for major portions of their work on decisions made in Washington. Government contracts to build new highways, bridges, dams and other public works projects can bring substantial amounts of business to a host of construction-related contractors and suppliers as well.

Home builders have a different perspective on federal policies. Instead of keeping an eye on the public works committees of Congress, they're more affected by the Banking committees, which set policies that can deeply affect the housing market.

The pattern of construction industry contributions reflects the nature of the industry. Unlike some industries that are dominated by large corporations, many contractors and subcontractors are relatively small shops that operate independently. Because of this, more than two-thirds of the sector's campaign dollars came from individual donors rather than political action committees. Even the two PACs that dominated the top contributors list — the National Association of Home Builders and Associated General Contractors — are nationwide trade associations that represent thousands of independent builders and suppliers.

Differentiating between home builders and public works contractors is not always easy, when analyzing campaign finance reports. Many contributors simply put "builder" as their occupation, giving no clue whether they concentrate on commercial, residential or industrial construction. Many other construction firms are diversified and do it all. In dealing with such contributors this book classifies them under the "general contractors" category.

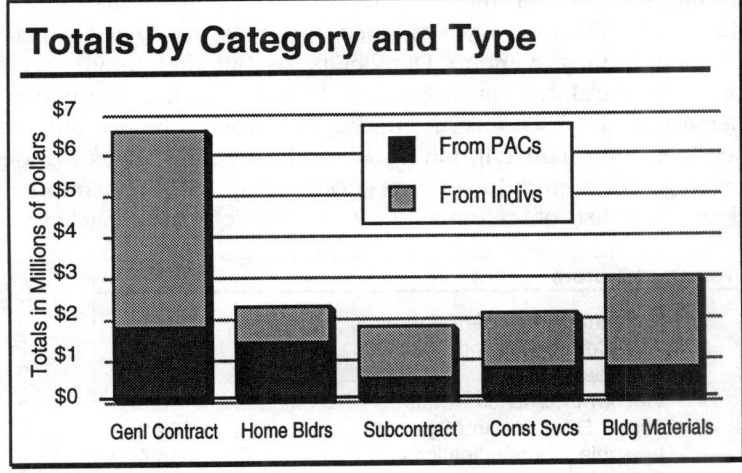

Totals by Category and Type

Category	Total	From PACs	PAC Pct	From Indivs	Indiv Pct
General Contractors	$6,500,194	$1,696,184	26%	$4,804,010	74%
Home Builders	$2,216,175	$1,318,292	59%	$897,883	41%
Special Trade Contractors	$1,686,428	$401,601	24%	$1,284,827	76%
Construction Services	$1,974,020	$656,253	33%	$1,317,767	67%
Building Materials	$2,869,672	$658,314	23%	$2,211,358	77%
TOTAL	**$15,246,489**	**$4,730,644**	**31%**	**$10,515,845**	**69%**

Top 20 Construction Contributors

Rank	Total	Contributor	Category	PAC Pct	Dem Pct	Repub Pct	To Dems / To Repubs
1	$1,074,827	National Assn of Home Builders*	Resid Constr	100%	44%	56%	
2	$677,899	Associated General Contractors*	Genl Contract	99%	24%	76%	
3	$353,558	Fluor Corp*	Heavy Constr	95%	44%	56%	
4	$203,580	National Utility Contractors Assn	Utility Constr	100%	38%	62%	
5	$191,877	Bechtel Corp	Heavy Constr	74%	53%	47%	
6	$184,150	Associated Builders & Contractors	Builders Assn	100%	8%	92%	
7	$163,500	National Electrical Contractors Assn	Subcontractors	100%	15%	85%	
8	$161,901	Sheet Metal/Air Conditioning Contractors	Subcontractors	100%	5%	94%	
9	$128,703	CH2M Hill	Engineers	95%	47%	53%	
10	$116,375	Morrison-Knudsen	General Contractors	93%	63%	37%	
11	$97,930	Caterpillar Tractor	Constr Equip	94%	12%	88%	
12	$95,500	American Consulting Engineers Council	Engineers	100%	47%	53%	
13	$87,770	Walter Industries*	Building Materials	87%	82%	18%	
14	$84,307	Brown & Root	Heavy Constr	96%	27%	73%	
15	$82,340	Manufactured Housing Institute	Mobile Homes	99%	49%	50%	
16	$82,050	National Soc of Professional Engineers	Engineers	100%	39%	61%	
17	$76,607	Jacobs Engineering Group	Engineers	83%	65%	35%	
18	$69,034	Owens-Corning Fiberglas	Bldg Materials	92%	34%	66%	
19	$63,300	Edward C Levy Co	Bldg Materials	0%	35%	65%	
20	$58,100	Vulcan Materials Co	Bldg Materials	76%	53%	47%	

* Contributions came from more than one affiliate or subsidiary.

Where the money went . . .

Totals by Category and Party

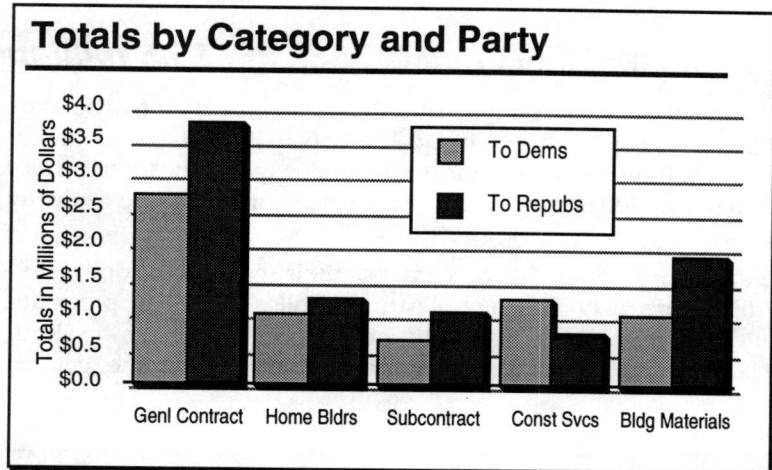

By and large, builders prefer Republicans. Some 57 percent of the sector's contributions went to Republican candidates — the most heavily Republican tilt of any sector. Only the construction services industry — engineers, architects and the like — gave a majority of its dollars to Democrats.

Category	Total	To Dems	Dem Pct	To Repubs	Repub Pct
General Contractors	$6,500,194	$2,717,136	42%	$3,767,141	58%
Home Builders	$2,216,175	$991,851	45%	$1,222,374	55%
Special Trade Contractors	$1,686,428	$645,098	38%	$1,031,913	61%
Construction Services	$1,974,020	$1,223,955	62%	$746,390	38%
Building Materials	$2,869,672	$1,006,396	35%	$1,849,231	64%
TOTAL	**$15,246,489**	**$6,584,436**	**43%**	**$8,617,049**	**57%**

New York Republican Alfonse D'Amato was the leading congressional recipient of construction industry money in the 1992 elections. The top 10 list of Senate candidates was dominated by Republicans. Among House members, the party split was even. The leading House recipient, Bud Shuster of Pennsylvania, is ranking Republican on the Public Works and Transportation Committee's Surface Transportation Subcommittee — the panel that oversees highway construction. Democrat Norman Mineta, who ranked third, chairs that subcommittee. Fifth-ranking Robert Roe, who retired after the 1992 elections, chaired the full committee.

Top 10 Senate Recipients

Rank	Name	Amount	Status	W/L
1	Alfonse M. D'Amato (R-NY)	$224,990	Incumb	W
2	John F. Seymour (R-Calif)	$212,584	Incumb	L
3	Arlen Specter (R-Pa)	$196,820	Incumb	W
4	Dick Thornburgh (R-Pa)	$190,550	Chall	L
5	Daniel R. Coats (R-Ind)	$189,735	Incumb	W
6	Christopher S. Bond (R-Mo)	$149,418	Incumb	W
7	Bob Kasten (R-Wis)	$137,820	Incumb	L
8	Dianne Feinstein (D-Calif)	$129,220	Chall	W
9	Bob Graham (D-Fla)	$122,335	Incumb	W
10	Tom Campbell (R-Calif)	$115,762	Open	L

Top 10 House Recipients

Rank	Name	Amount	Status	W/L
1	Bud Shuster (R-Pa)	$105,500	Incumb	W
2	Richard A. Gephardt (D-Mo)	$81,297	Incumb	W
3	Norman Y. Mineta (D-Calif)	$66,500	Incumb	W
4	Ron Marlenee (R-Mont)	$63,672	Incumb	L
5	Robert A. Roe (D-NJ)	$63,650	Incumb	Ret
6	Bill Paxon (R-NY)	$63,185	Incumb	W
7	Bob Carr (D-Mich)	$52,300	Incumb	W
8	Joe Moakley (D-Mass)	$50,600	Incumb	W
9	Spencer Bachus (R-Ala)	$48,425	Chall	W
10	Newt Gingrich (R-Ga)	$47,400	Incumb	W

Closeup on Construction

General Contractors ....$6.5 million

The leading contributor in this category, the Associated General Contractors, is the nation's largest organization of builders concentrating mainly on commercial, industrial and public works construction. Though the Top 10 list includes a number of large nationwide construction firms — like Fluor, Bechtel and Brown & Root — most of the industry is made up of smaller local contractors. Their dollars tend to come primarily through individual contributions, since their companies are generally too small to operate political action committees of their own.

Overall, general contractors and related builders' groups gave 58 percent of their campaign dollars to Republicans. This contrasts with many other industries that may be Republican in philosophy but pragmatically Democratic in their campaign contributions. The Democrats currently hold solid majorities in both houses of Congress and thereby control all committee and subcommittee chairmanships as well as the general flow of legislation.

Top Contributors	
1	Associated General Contractors* $677,899
2	Fluor Corp* $353,558
3	National Utility Contractors Assn $203,580
4	Halliburton Co* $196,319
5	Bechtel Corp $191,877
6	Associated Builders & Contractors $184,150
7	Morrison-Knudsen $116,375
8	Brown & Root $79,807
9	Suffolk Construction Co $45,300
10	HB Zachry Co $36,299

* Contributions came from more than one affiliate or subsidiary.

Top Senate Recipients			
1	John F. Seymour (R-Calif) $97,038	Incumb	L
2	Alfonse M. D'Amato (R-NY) $96,590	Incumb	W
3	Dick Thornburgh (R-Pa) $82,950	Chall	L
4	Arlen Specter (R-Pa) $74,100	Incumb	W
5	Dianne Feinstein (D-Calif) $65,220	Chall	W

Top House Recipients			
1	Bud Shuster (R-Pa) $57,750	Incumb	W
2	Ron Marlenee (R-Mont) $49,322	Incumb	L
3	Richard A. Gephardt (D-Mo) $34,985	Incumb	W
4	Bill Paxon (R-NY) $31,950	Incumb	W
5	Joe Moakley (D-Mass) $31,600	Incumb	W

Home Builders ....$2.2 million

This segment of the construction industry closely follows the ups and downs of interest rates and federal housing policies, as opposed to the level of funding for major public works projects. In that sense, home builders' legislative interests are similar to those of the real estate industry — particularly real estate developers. In many cases, the line between real estate and construction is a thin one; many companies engage in both. This book distinguishes between the two, however, as does the federal government's Standard Industrial Classification Index. The real estate industry deals primarily in the financial end of the business and is classified under finance in this book. Builders deal more in hammers, nails and road graders, and are classified in construction.

The National Association of Home Builders is the industry's main trade association, and by far its leading contributor. Both the PAC and individual contributors split their dollars fairly evenly between the parties. Republicans collected 55 percent in all.

Top Senate Recipients			
1	Daniel R. Coats (R-Ind) $70,300	Incumb	W
2	John F. Seymour (R-Calif) $36,646	Incumb	L
3	Les AuCoin (D-Ore) $26,100	Chall	L
4	Gray Davis (D-Calif) $24,750	Chall	L
5	Paul Coverdell (R-Ga) $24,550	Chall	W

Top House Recipients			
1	William J. Hughes (D-NJ) $35,850	Incumb	W
2	Robert H. Michel (R-Ill) $21,500	Incumb	W
3	Thomas J. Bliley Jr. (R-Va) $20,450	Incumb	W
4	Leonard R. Sendelsky (D-NJ) $18,800	Chall	L
5	Dennis Hastert (R-Ill) $17,400	Incumb	W

Top Contributors	
1	National Assn of Home Builders* $1,074,827
2	Manufactured Housing Institute $82,340
3	Perry-Houston Interests $53,000
4	Toll Brothers Inc $49,550
5	Rural Builders of America PAC $40,750

* Contributions came from more than one affiliate or subsidiary.

Construction Services ....$2.0 million

Architects, engineers and construction management specialists are an important (and politically active) segment of the construction industry. Big engineering firms are often competing for federal contracts. They are also clearly affected by upturns and downturns in construction cycles. The leading contributor in this category, the engineering firm of CH2M Hill is involved not only in construction engineering, but in environmental services as well. The company is a major federal contractor for hazardous waste cleanup projects.

One practical problem in classifying donors from this category is the lack of specificity in contributors' declared occupations. Contributors who put down "engineer" as their occupation could be involved in any number of industries. For that reason, only "structural engineers," "civil engineers," or others clearly identified with the construction industry were classified in this category. The overall total for this category, therefore, is almost certainly understated.

Top Contributors

1	CH2M Hill	$128,703
2	American Consulting Engineers Council	$95,500
3	National Soc of Professional Engineers	$82,050
4	Jacobs Engineering Group	$76,607
5	Parsons Brinckerhoff Inc	$52,750
6	Kaiser Engineers Inc	$49,896
7	Stone & Webster	$48,406
8	Sverdrup Corp	$37,950
9	American Institute of Architects	$36,125
10	Parsons Corp*	$31,750

* Contributions came from more than one affiliate or subsidiary.

Top Senate Recipients

1	Daniel K. Inouye (D-Hawaii)	$24,400	Incumb	W
2	Christopher S. Bond (R-Mo)	$24,300	Incumb	W
3	John F. Seymour (R-Calif)	$23,950	Incumb	L
4	Wyche Fowler Jr. (D-Ga)	$22,900	Incumb	L
5	John B. Breaux (D-La)	$22,258	Incumb	W

Top House Recipients

1	Norman Y. Mineta (D-Calif)	$29,850	Incumb	W
2	Robert A. Roe (D-NJ)	$21,300	Incumb	†
3	Richard A. Gephardt (D-Mo)	$21,262	Incumb	W
4	Robert E. Andrews (D-NJ)	$20,225	Incumb	W
5	Bob Carr (D-Mich)	$19,250	Incumb	W

† Did not seek reelection in 1992

Building Materials & Equipment ....$2.9 million

These are the companies that supply everything from gravel to earth movers to high-speed elevators in skyscrapers. Those involved in road building projects are particularly affected by federal decisions, especially those on the public works committees.

Top Contributors

1	Caterpillar Tractor	$97,930
2	Walter Industries*	$87,770
3	Owens-Corning Fiberglas	$69,034
4	Edward C Levy Co	$63,300
5	Vulcan Materials Co*	$58,100
6	American Supply Assn	$55,525
7	National Crushed Stone Assn	$50,875
8	Dravo Corp	$48,800
9	Cubic Corp	$47,797
10	National Concrete Masonry Assn	$45,509

* Contributions came from more than one affiliate or subsidiary.

Top Senate Recipients

1	Daniel R. Coats (R-Ind)	$57,150	Incumb	W
2	Dick Thornburgh (R-Pa)	$55,750	Chall	L
3	Paul Coverdell (R-Ga)	$49,341	Chall	W
4	Arlen Specter (R-Pa)	$47,200	Incumb	W
5	Christopher S. Bond (R-Mo)	$46,751	Incumb	W

Top House Recipients

1	Bud Shuster (R-Pa)	$31,500	Incumb	W
2	Don Ritter (R-Pa)	$17,910	Incumb	L
3	Harris W. Fawell (R-Ill)	$16,674	Incumb	W
4	Steve Buyer (R-Ind)	$15,240	Chall	W
5	Sam M. Gibbons (D-Fla)	$14,300	Incumb	W

Defense

Where the money came from . . .

Defense contractors have always been influential players in congressional politics, though the dollars they dispensed in the 1992 elections were fairly modest by contemporary standards. In all, the defense sector gave $8.3 million to federal candidates. Nearly nine-tenths of it was delivered through political action committees sponsored by corporations.

That figure can be considered to be quite conservative, however. Few U.S. corporations rely on defense work for the majority of their income, but many firms do some defense work or have defense-related subsidiaries. Under the system used to compile this book, contributions from PACs or employees of those firms were counted as defense related only if they were given to a member sitting on the Armed Services or Appropriations committees — panels that deal specifically with defense policy and defense spending. Most contributions from Boeing, for example, are classified under air transport, since Boeing makes most of its money from the sale of commercial, not military, aircraft. Many other major defense contractors — from General Motors to General Electric to AT&T — fall in the same category

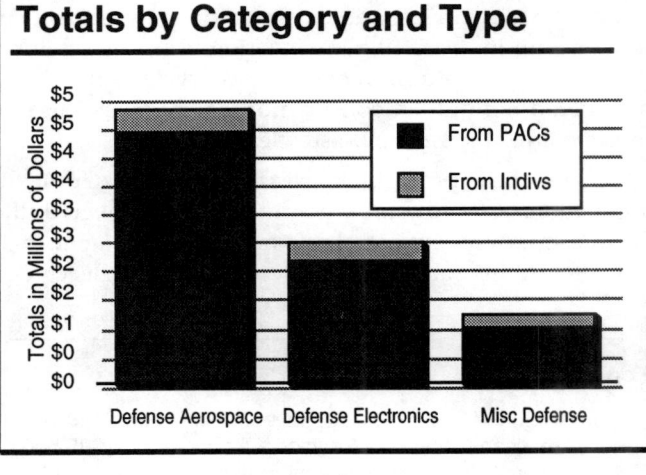

Totals by Category and Type

Category	Total	From PACs	PAC Pct	From Indivs	Indiv Pct
Defense Aerospace	$4,748,928	$4,359,923	92%	$389,005	8%
Defense Electronics	$2,433,503	$2,088,860	86%	$344,643	14%
Misc Defense	$1,146,329	$949,628	83%	$196,701	17%
TOTAL	**$8,328,760**	**$7,398,411**	**89%**	**$930,349**	**11%**

If one were to include *all* contributions from those big corporations as defense related (effectively double-counting the dollars since they serve more than one purpose) the sector's total would be much higher.

Top 20 Defense Contributors

Rank	Total	Contributor	Category	PAC Pct	Dem Pct	Repub Pct	To Dems / To Repubs
1	$536,335	Martin Marietta Corp	Air Defense	95%	51%	49%	
2	$464,055	General Dynamics	Air Defense	94%	61%	39%	
3	$446,570	Textron Inc	Air Defense	89%	64%	36%	
4	$377,515	Northrop Corp	Air Defense	95%	46%	53%	
5	$376,383	Rockwell International	Air Defense	90%	46%	54%	
6	$371,643	McDonnell Douglas*	Air Defense	81%	53%	47%	
7	$366,537	Lockheed Corp	Air Defense	92%	54%	46%	
8	$312,300	General Atomics	Misc Defense	98%	65%	35%	
9	$311,531	Chrysler Corp*	Air Defense	82%	71%	29%	
10	$307,100	Raytheon*	Air Defense	93%	64%	36%	
11	$300,040	United Technologies	Air Defense	95%	56%	44%	
12	$297,145	General Motors*†	Def Electronics	92%	55%	45%	
13	$256,526	Grumman Corp	Air Defense	98%	66%	34%	
14	$226,965	Loral Corp	Def Electronics	65%	77%	23%	
15	$221,084	Allied-Signal	Air Defense	89%	51%	49%	
16	$198,700	Tenneco Inc	Naval Ships	86%	55%	45%	
17	$197,425	AT&T†	Def Electronics	100%	70%	30%	
18	$194,575	General Electric†	Air Defense	98%	64%	36%	
19	$186,374	E-Systems Inc*	Def Electronics	89%	53%	46%	
20	$166,325	TRW Inc	Def Electronics	92%	51%	49%	

* Contributions came from more than one affiliate or subsidiary.　　　　† Includes defense operations only.

Where the money went . . .

Totals by Category and Party

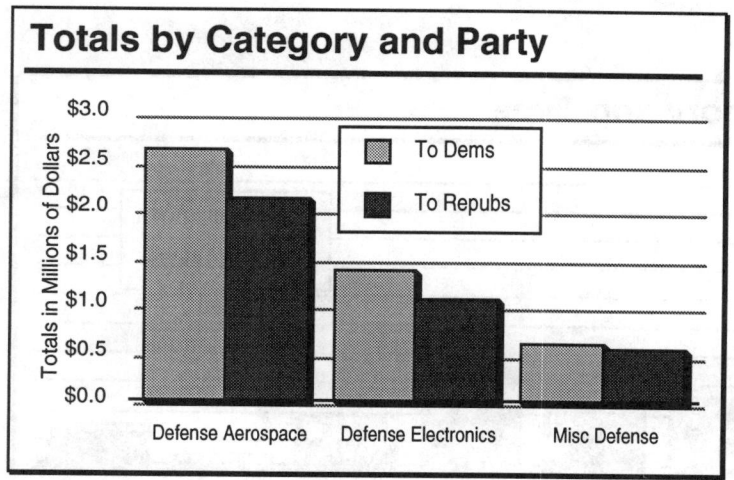

Category	Total	To Dems	Dem Pct	To Repubs	Repub Pct
Defense Aerospace	$4,748,928	$2,635,229	55%	$2,110,299	44%
Defense Electronics	$2,433,503	$1,371,777	56%	$1,061,220	44%
Misc Defense	$1,146,329	$602,445	53%	$543,384	47%
TOTAL	**$8,328,760**	**$4,609,451**	**55%**	**$3,714,903**	**45%**

Considering the traditionally conservative slant to the defense industry and the military services, it is somewhat surprising that the industry delivered 55 percent of its campaign dollars to Democrats in the 1992 elections. This is a classic example of political pragmatism at work. Democrats control both houses of Congress (and the Pentagon and White House too, after Bill Clinton's election). They therefore hold the power of the purse over the defense industry. Whatever their personal political preferences, defense contractors have learned to accommodate both sides of the aisle when pulling out their checkbooks.

Though the federal government's annual defense budget is voted on by the entire House and Senate, defense industry lobbyists spend most of their time concentrating on the Armed Services and Appropriations committees in each house. Armed Services sets the military policy, but the Appropriations panels — particularly the Defense Appropriations subcommittees — actually allocate the hundreds of billions of dollars the federal government spends annually on defense. Consequently, members of those committees receive by far the biggest proportion of defense industry contributions. Of the top 20 House and Senate recipients of defense dollars in 1992, eight served in the Armed Services committees and 12 sat on Appropriations.

John Murtha, the top defense contributor in Congress, is chairman of the House Defense Appropriations Subcommittee. Les Aspin, the number two recipient, was head of the House Armed Services Committee until he resigned his seat in early 1993 to become Secretary of Defense in the Clinton administration.

Top 10 Senate Recipients

Rank	Name	Amount	Status	W/L
1	Daniel R. Coats (R-Ind)	$175,350	Incumb	W
2	Arlen Specter (R-Pa)	$147,849	Incumb	W
3	John Glenn (D-Ohio)	$145,595	Incumb	W
4	Don Nickles (R-Okla)	$139,700	Incumb	W
5	Richard C. Shelby (D-Ala)	$139,675	Incumb	W
6	John McCain (R-Ariz)	$130,900	Incumb	W
7	Barbara A. Mikulski (D-Md)	$129,287	Incumb	W
8	Bob Kasten (R-Wis)	$126,450	Incumb	L
9	Alfonse M. D'Amato (R-NY)	$104,030	Incumb	W
10	Daniel K. Inouye (D-Hawaii)	$101,500	Incumb	W

Top 10 House Recipients

Rank	Name	Amount	Status	W/L
1	John P. Murtha (D-Pa)	$230,200	Incumb	W
2	Les Aspin (D-Wis)	$220,875	Incumb	W
3	Charles Wilson (D-Texas)	$210,650	Incumb	W
4	Dave McCurdy (D-Okla)	$129,450	Incumb	W
5	Herbert H. Bateman (R-Va)	$103,750	Incumb	W
6	Norm Dicks (D-Wash)	$98,963	Incumb	W
7	Richard Ray (D-Ga)	$92,050	Incumb	L
8	Vic Fazio (D-Calif)	$92,025	Incumb	W
9	Joseph M. McDade (R-Pa)	$91,350	Incumb	W
10	C. W. Bill Young (R-Fla)	$91,250	Incumb	W

Energy & Natural Resources

Where the money came from . . .

In a nation that grew to world prominence by exploiting its abundant natural resources, then building new industries on the strength of its home-grown oil, gas, minerals and electricity, it is not surprising that energy producers pack a powerful political punch on Capitol Hill.

The oil & gas industry was by far the biggest contributor within the sector, sending more than $9.2 million to congressional and presidential candidates in the 1992 elections. About half that money came from political action committees — mainly from large multinational oil companies. Another $2.4 million came from operators of natural gas pipelines that connect the southwestern oil and gas fields with consumers around the country.

The electric utilities lent power to their political arguments with over $4.5 million in contributions, most of it from PACs. Mining interests gave $1.8 million; half of that came from coal mine operators. Overall, the energy & natural resources sector gave $21.3 million to federal candidates in the 1992 elections.

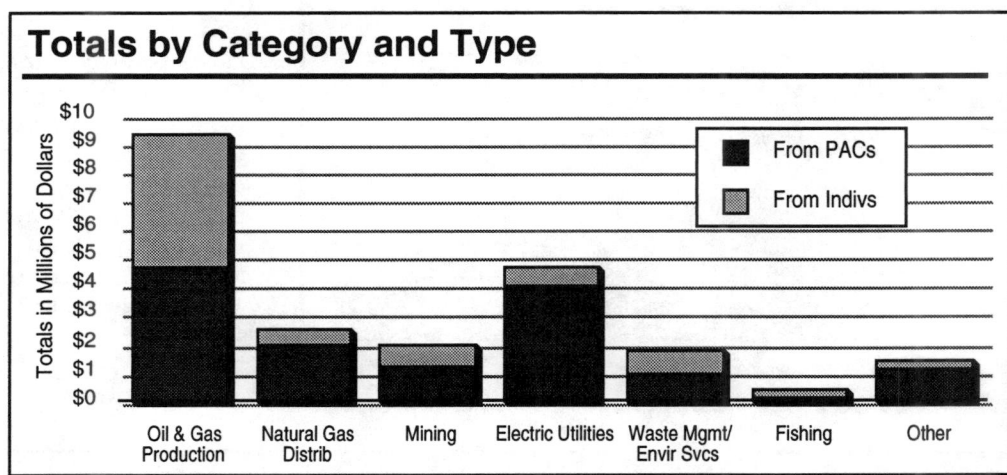

Totals by Category and Type

Category	Total	From PACs	PAC Pct	From Indivs	Indiv Pct
Oil & Gas Prod/Marketing	$9,234,077	$4,579,941	50%	$4,654,136	50%
Natural Gas Distribution	$2,393,866	$1,827,800	76%	$566,066	24%
Mining	$1,844,760	$1,118,704	61%	$726,056	39%
Electric Utilities	$4,555,470	$3,975,798	87%	$579,672	13%
Waste Mgmt/Environ Svcs	$1,717,181	$903,363	53%	$813,818	47%
Commercial Fishing	$314,209	$108,909	35%	$205,300	65%
Other & Unclassified	$1,281,672	$1,018,069	79%	$263,603	21%
TOTAL	**$21,341,235**	**$13,532,584**	**63%**	**$7,808,651**	**37%**

Top 20 Energy & Natural Resource Contributors

Rank	Total	Contributor	Category	PAC Pct	Dem Pct	Repub Pct	To Dems / To Repubs
1	$683,558	Waste Management Inc*	Waste Mgmt	78%	62%	38%	
2	$627,155	ACRE (Action Cmte for Rural Electric)*	Rural Electric	100%	74%	26%	
3	$493,092	Atlantic Richfield	Oil & Gas	66%	25%	74%	
4	$420,581	Chevron Corp	Oil & Gas	92%	28%	72%	
5	$397,825	Coastal Corp*	Natural Gas	84%	72%	28%	
6	$364,541	Southern Co*	Electric Utilities	87%	58%	42%	
7	$358,060	Exxon Corp	Oil & Gas	92%	19%	81%	
8	$348,250	Cooper Industries	Power Plant Constr	99%	2%	97%	
9	$306,450	Occidental Petroleum*†	Oil & Gas	83%	52%	48%	
10	$298,650	Southern California Edison	Electric Utilities	89%	76%	24%	
11	$293,200	Amoco Corp	Oil & Gas	90%	24%	75%	
12	$267,123	Petroleum Marketers Assn*	Oil & Gas	100%	37%	63%	
13	$245,398	Mobil Oil	Oil & Gas	80%	11%	88%	
14	$245,277	USX Corp*	Oil & Gas	76%	53%	47%	
15	$244,648	National Coal Assn	Coal Mining	98%	25%	75%	
16	$237,752	Columbia Gas System*	Natural Gas	100%	51%	54%	
17	$237,000	Texas Utilities Co*	Electric Utilities	97%	61%	39%	
18	$217,748	Ashland Oil*	Oil & Gas	86%	39%	61%	
19	$204,291	Phillips Petroleum	Oil & Gas	84%	27%	73%	
20	$195,330	Texaco	Oil & Gas	90%	30%	70%	

* Contributions came from more than one affiliate or subsidiary.　　　　　† Does not include Occidental's non-oil operations.

Where the money went . . .

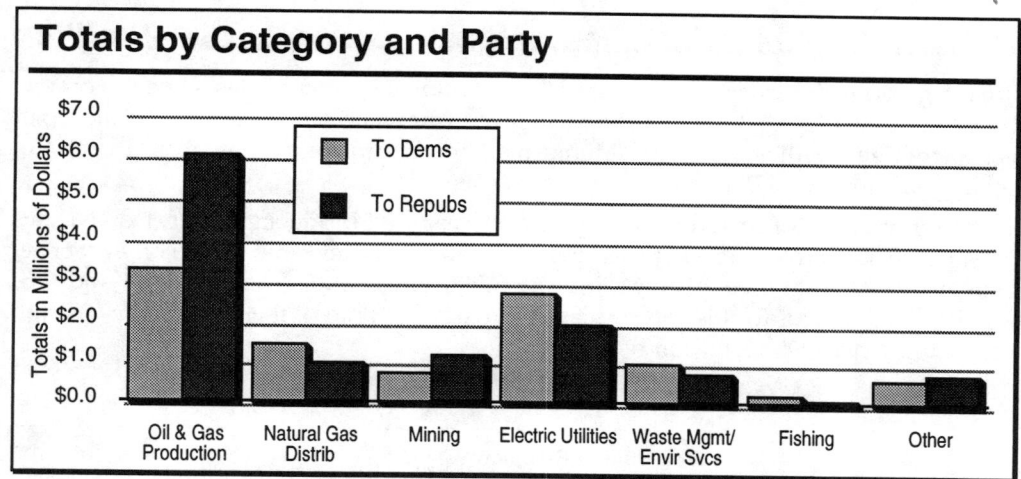

Totals by Category and Party

To Dems · *To Repubs*

The oil & gas industry distinctly prefers Republican candidates, as seen clearly in the chart on the left. It favored them by a nearly two-to-one margin over Democrats — a ratio that has been consistent over the years. Natural gas distributors, electric utilities and waste management firms slightly favored Democrats. Miners mostly backed the GOP. In all, 54 percent of the energy sector's campaign dollars wound up in the hands of Republicans.

Category	Total	To Dems	Dem Pct	To Repubs	Repub Pct
Oil & Gas Prod/Marketing	$9,234,077	$3,209,243	35%	$6,006,774	65%
Natural Gas Distribution	$2,393,866	$1,408,863	59%	$981,771	41%
Mining	$1,844,760	$709,468	38%	$1,135,092	62%
Electric Utilities	$4,555,470	$2,655,368	58%	$1,897,952	42%
Waste Mgmt/Environ Svcs	$1,717,181	$994,557	58%	$719,424	42%
Commercial Fishing	$314,209	$227,892	73%	$85,817	27%
Other & Unclassified	$1,281,672	$589,445	46%	$691,777	54%
TOTAL	**$21,341,235**	**$9,794,836**	**46%**	**$11,518,607**	**54%**

Republican Don Nickles of Oklahoma received more than twice as much from the energy sector as anyone else in Congress in 1992. Four other colleagues of his on the Senate Energy and Natural Resources Committee also appear on the Senate's top 10 recipient list—John Seymour, Wendell Ford, Richard Shelby and Frank Murkowski.

Oil-state congressmen dominated the Top 10 list in the House, led by Don Young of Alaska, who is ranking minority member of the House Interior Committee. Mike Synar of Oklahoma ranked second overall. Behind him were four Texans and Montana Republican Ron Marlenee, whose 1992 race against fellow incumbent Pat Williams was a flashpoint between energy versus environmental interests. The only representatives on the list from non-energy-rich states were House Majority Leader Dick Gephardt and Indiana Democrat Phil Sharp, who chairs the Energy and Power Subcommittee of the powerful House Energy and Commerce Committee.

Top 10 Senate Recipients

Rank	Name	Amount	Status	W/L
1	Don Nickles (R-Okla)	$572,766	Incumb	W
2	John B. Breaux (D-La)	$281,125	Incumb	W
3	John F. Seymour (R-Calif)	$271,125	Incumb	L
4	Wendell H. Ford (D-Ky)	$259,950	Incumb	W
5	Arlen Specter (R-Pa)	$242,316	Incumb	W
6	Richard C. Shelby (D-Ala)	$240,889	Incumb	W
7	Christopher S. Bond (R-Mo)	$218,789	Incumb	W
8	Bob Dole (R-Kan)	$217,437	Incumb	W
9	Frank H. Murkowski (R-Alaska)	$213,827	Incumb	W
10	Daniel R. Coats (R-Ind)	$210,795	Incumb	W

Top 10 House Recipients

Rank	Name	Amount	Status	W/L
1	Don Young (R-Alaska)	$181,497	Incumb	W
2	Mike Synar (D-Okla)	$146,474	Incumb	W
3	Richard A. Gephardt (D-Mo)	$144,800	Incumb	W
4	Joe L. Barton (R-Texas)	$137,282	Incumb	W
5	Jack Fields (R-Texas)	$126,605	Incumb	W
6	Philip R. Sharp (D-Ind)	$116,791	Incumb	W
7	Michael A. Andrews (D-Texas)	$116,050	Incumb	W
8	Harold Rogers (R-Ky)	$112,475	Incumb	W
9	Martin Frost (D-Texas)	$109,850	Incumb	W
10	Ron Marlenee (R-Mont)	$104,669	Incumb	L

Closeup on Energy & Natural Resources

Oil & Gas Production & Marketing ....$9.2 million

The oil industry looks at itself as having two main divisions: the "major" multinational oil companies—like Exxon and Mobil—and the smaller operators called "independents." Both groups tend to give to the same candidates, for the most part preferring Republicans to Democrats, but they deliver their dollars by different methods. The major oil companies give almost all their donations through corporate PACs, while the independents give mainly as individuals.

All of the top recipients of oil money in both the House and Senate come from major oil-producing states. Don Nickles of Oklahoma led them all, with over $405,000 in contributions. Republican Phil Gramm of Texas ranked third on the Senate list even though he didn't run in 1992. Gramm has his eye on the 1996 presidential nomination, and has continued his fund-raising even though it's an off-year for his Senate seat. A longtime favorite of the oil industry, Gramm raised over $600,000 from the industry during his 1990 reelection race.

Top Contributors

1	Atlantic Richfield	$472,142
2	Chevron Corp	$420,581
3	Exxon Corp	$358,060
4	Occidental Petroleum*†	$306,450
5	Amoco Corp	$293,200
6	Petroleum Marketers Assn*	$267,123
7	Mobil Oil	$245,398
8	USX Corp*	$243,277
9	Ashland Oil*	$215,798
10	Phillips Petroleum	$204,291

* Contributions came from more than one affiliate or subsidiary.
† Does not include Occidental's non-oil operations

Top Senate Recipients

1	Don Nickles (R-Okla)	$405,371	Incumb	W
2	John Seymour (R-Calif)	$152,250	Incumb	L
3	Phil Gramm (R-Texas)	$146,275	Incumb	†
4	Frank H. Murkowski (R-Alaska)	$143,827	Incumb	W
5	John B. Breaux (D-La)	$129,750	Incumb	W

Top House Recipients

1	Mike Synar (D-Okla)	$112,348	Incumb	W
2	Don Young (R-Alaska)	$108,095	Incumb	W
3	Jack Fields (R-Texas)	$76,705	Incumb	W
4	Pete Geren (D-Texas)	$73,105	Incumb	W
5	Sam Johnson (R-Texas)	$72,925	Incumb	W

† Did not run for election in 1992

Natural Gas Distribution ....$2.4 million

Quite apart from drilling for oil, refining it and marketing it in gas stations, there is another distinct industry involved in interstate transportation of natural gas. Gas pipelines criss-cross the nation, connecting the energy-rich oil patch states with the energy-hungry Northeast, Midwest and Southeast. Because of the interstate nature of the business, pipeline carriers are heavily regulated by the federal government. In contrast to the strongly Republican tilt of oil producers, the natural gas industry gives the majority of its dollars to Democrats.

Top Contributors

1	Coastal Corp*	$397,825
2	Columbia Gas System*	$241,852
3	Enron Corp	$187,850
4	Enserch Corp	$151,785
5	Arkla Inc*	$121,505
6	Panhandle Eastern Corp*	$116,350
7	Pacific Enterprises	$104,230
8	Interstate Natural Gas Assn	$96,443
9	Michigan Consolidated Gas	$86,900
10	Williams Companies	$69,236

* Contributions came from more than one affiliate or subsidiary.

Top Senate Recipients

1	Don Nickles (R-Okla)	$68,350	Incumb	W
2	Bob Dole (R-Kan)	$63,750	Incumb	W
3	John B. Breaux (D-La)	$46,175	Incumb	W
4	Dale Bumpers (D-Ark)	$46,150	Incumb	W
5	Wendell H. Ford (D-Ky)	$45,250	Incumb	W

Top House Recipients

1	Michael A. Andrews (D-Texas)	$32,400	Incumb	W
2	Charles Wilson (D-Texas)	$30,900	Incumb	W
3	Philip R. Sharp (D-Ind)	$26,716	Incumb	W
4	Jack Fields (R-Texas)	$24,800	Incumb	W
5	Greg Laughlin (D-Texas)	$24,550	Incumb	W

Mining..$1.8 million

Two distinct branches of the mining industry provide the bulk of its campaign dollars. Coal miners gave $918,000 in the last election, while companies dealing with metal mining and processing gave $685,000. Diversified interests, non-metal miners and mining services and equipment manufacturers gave the rest.

Kentuckians Wendell Ford in the Senate and Harold Rogers in the House led all other recipients of mining dollars. Both got the bulk of that money from coal mine operators in their home state and in nearby West Virginia.

Not included in these totals—but important in areas dealing with federal regulation of mine safety and other issues—are contributions from the United Mine Workers Union, classified under Labor. The UMW's political action committee gave $459,600 during the 1991-92 election cycle. Ninety-eight percent of it went to Democrats, in sharp contrast with their employers, the mining industry, which gave 62 percent of its dollars to Republicans.

Top Contributors	
1 National Coal Assn	$244,648
2 Phelps Dodge Corp	$96,049
3 Cyprus Minerals Co	$86,323
4 Reynolds Metals	$86,248
5 Drummond Co	$78,350
6 Peabody Coal	$78,213
7 Pittston Co	$60,350
8 Alcoa	$45,450
9 United Co	$40,450
10 Cleveland-Cliffs Iron Co	$38,400

* Contributions came from more than one affiliate or subsidiary.

Top Senate Recipients			
1 Wendell H. Ford (D-Ky)	$61,000	Incumb	W
2 Harry Reid (D-Nev)	$49,900	Incumb	W
3 John McCain (R-Ariz)	$34,617	Incumb	W
4 Arlen Specter (R-Pa)	$34,000	Incumb	W
5 Dick Thornburgh (R-Pa)	$33,650	Chall	L

Top House Recipients			
1 Harold Rogers (R-Ky)	$60,625	Incumb	W
2 John E. Jones (R-Pa)	$31,500	Open	L
3 Barbara F. Vucanovich (R-Nev)	$25,100	Incumb	W
4 Ron Marlenee (R-Mont)	$23,520	Incumb	L
5 Earl F. Hilliard (D-Ala)	$21,500	Open	W

Electric Utilities ....$4.6 million

Cleaning up their smokestacks in compliance with Clean Air legislation is a major preoccupation of many electric utilities, particularly those whose clouds of pollution have been responsible for much of the acid rain in the Northeast. The federal government's many rules governing the operation of utilities are another important issue, as is the perennial issue of nuclear power and the disposal of nuclear waste.

Big metropolitan area utilities are not the only ones with a strong voice on Capitol Hill. The largest single political contributor in the industry is the Action Committee for Rural Electrification (or ACRE), a PAC that represents the interests of the nation's rural electric cooperatives. The top contributor list also includes a number of holding companies that control smaller state-based utilities. Southern Co., for example, is the parent of Alabama Power, Georgia Power, Gulf Power and Mississippi Power.

Three of the top Senate recipients — Kent Conrad, Wendell Ford and Richard Shelby — sit on the Senate Energy and Natural Resources Committee. All five of the top House recipients hold seats on the House Energy and Commerce Committee, which regulates the electric utility industry.

Top Contributors	
1 ACRE (Action Cmte for Rural Electric)*	$627,155
2 Southern Co*	$364,541
3 Southern California Edison	$298,650
4 Texas Utilities Co*	$237,000
5 Entergy Corp*	$149,125
6 Pacific Gas & Electric	$147,175
7 American Electric Power*	$130,909
8 Detroit Edison	$103,870
9 Philadelphia Electric	$102,250
10 FPL Group Inc*	$97,950

* Contributions came from more than one affiliate or subsidiary.

Top Senate Recipients			
1 Kent Conrad (D-ND)	$67,500	Incumb	W
2 Wendell H. Ford (D-Ky)	$64,750	Incumb	W
3 Arlen Specter (R-Pa)	$63,566	Incumb	W
4 Richard C. Shelby (D-Ala)	$53,491	Incumb	W
5 Bob Graham (D-Fla)	$50,750	Incumb	W

Top House Recipients			
1 Tom McMillen (D-Md)	$53,550	Incumb	L
2 Philip R. Sharp (D-Ind)	$50,675	Incumb	W
3 Joe L. Barton (R-Texas)	$37,400	Incumb	W
4 Ralph M. Hall (D-Texas)	$37,050	Incumb	W
5 Don Ritter (R-Pa)	$33,536	Incumb	L

Finance, Insurance & Real Estate

Where the money came from . . .

If doctors, lawyers, oil companies and defense contractors are tidy pots of gold to congressional and presidential candidates, the financial sector is the mother lode. The combined giving by banks, insurance companies, real estate interests and other finance-related businesses amounted to more than $71 million in the 1991-92 election cycle — vastly more than any other industry or interest group.

Within the sector, the methods of delivering campaign dollars varied widely. Commercial banks gave two-thirds of their money through political action committees, as did the insurance industry. Securities brokers and real estate agents gave three dollars out of every four through individual contributions. Accountants split the difference equally between PACs and individuals. Wall Street brokerage houses in particular tended to use individual contributions from their executives (and their families) to bundle large sums to favored candidates — much more than they could have given through a single PAC. Federal regulation is a preoccupation for nearly every segment of the financial community. Insurance companies in particular were scrambling to protect their interests as national health insurance began to advance on the nation's political agenda in the '92 elections.

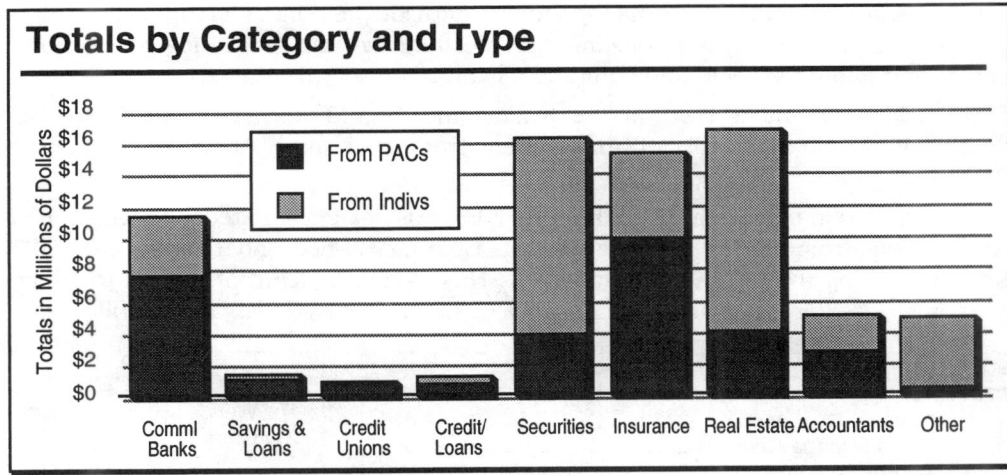

Totals by Category and Type

Category	Total	From PACs	PAC Pct	From Indivs	Indiv Pct
Commercial Banks	$11,196,321	$7,411,954	66%	$3,784,367	34%
Savings & Loans	$1,318,827	$927,898	70%	$390,929	30%
Credit Unions	$697,305	$664,910	95%	$32,395	5%
Finance/Credit Companies	$1,042,551	$572,678	55%	$469,873	45%
Securities & Investment	$15,936,222	$3,692,967	23%	$12,243,255	77%
Insurance	$14,944,778	$9,724,432	65%	$5,220,346	35%
Real Estate	$16,472,555	$3,907,233	24%	$12,565,322	76%
Accountants	$4,877,052	$2,481,924	51%	$2,395,128	49%
Other & Unclassified	$4,606,265	$233,357	5%	$4,372,908	95%
TOTAL	**$71,091,876**	**$29,617,353**	**42%**	**$41,474,523**	**58%**

Top 20 Finance, Insurance & Real Estate Contributors

Rank	Total	Contributor	Category	PAC Pct	Dem Pct	Repub Pct	To Dems / To Repubs
1	$2,954,973	National Assn of Realtors	Real Estate	100%	55%	45%	
2	$1,692,508	American Bankers Assn*	Comml Banks	99%	50%	49%	
3	$1,544,701	American Institute of CPA's	Accountants	100%	56%	44%	
4	$1,373,955	National Assn of Life Underwriters	Life Insurance	100%	54%	46%	
5	$898,545	Goldman, Sachs & Co	Securities	22%	67%	33%	
6	$881,820	American Express*	Stocks/Credit	38%	69%	30%	
7	$640,040	Prudential Insurance*	Insurance	63%	59%	41%	
8	$627,864	Merrill Lynch*	Securities	30%	51%	48%	
9	$589,798	Independent Insurance Agents of America	Insurance	100%	60%	40%	
10	$581,880	American Council of Life Insurance	Life Insurance	99%	59%	40%	
11	$581,830	Credit Union National Assn*	Credit Unions	100%	67%	33%	
12	$550,000	American Family Corp	Health Insur	91%	61%	39%	
13	$549,500	Chicago Mercantile Exchange	Commodities	90%	74%	26%	
14	$473,175	JP Morgan & Co	Comml Banks	89%	56%	44%	
15	$470,781	Morgan Stanley & Co	Securities	47%	54%	46%	
16	$453,564	Metropolitan Life Insurance*	Insur/Real Est	81%	57%	43%	
17	$453,134	Blue Cross & Blue Shield Assn*	Health Insur	75%	59%	41%	
18	$440,377	Arthur Andersen & Co	Accountants	48%	56%	44%	
19	$436,867	C&S/Sovran Corp*	Comml Banks	99%	61%	38%	
20	$419,653	Ernst & Young	Accountants	56%	55%	45%	

* Contributions came from more than one affiliate or subsidiary.

Where the money went . . .

Totals by Category and Party

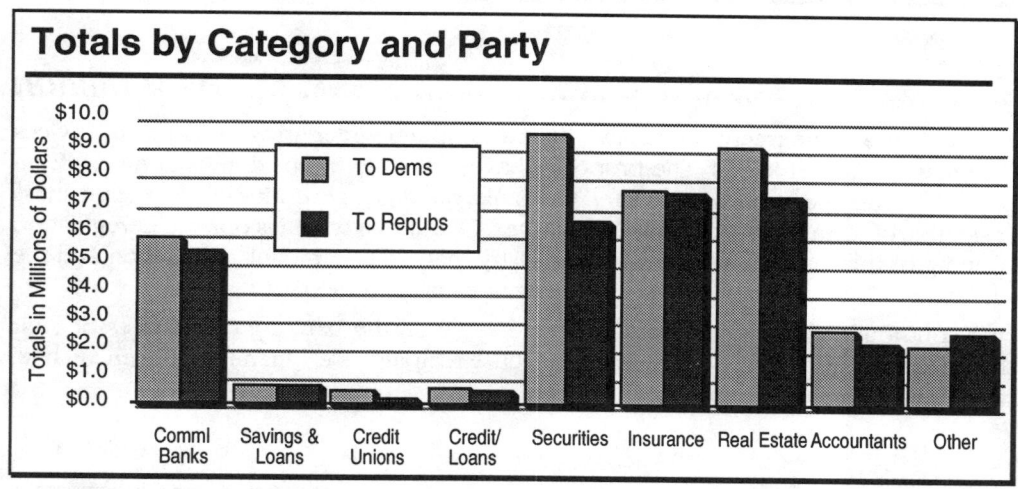

Category	Total	To Dems	Dem Pct	To Repubs	Repub Pct
Commercial Banks	$11,196,321	$5,827,443	52%	$5,353,698	48%
Savings & Loans	$1,318,827	$697,567	53%	$621,260	47%
Credit Unions	$697,305	$455,030	65%	$242,275	35%
Finance/Credit Companies	$1,042,551	$534,043	51%	$508,508	49%
Securities & Investment	$15,936,222	$9,507,816	60%	$6,389,133	40%
Insurance	$14,944,778	$7,506,107	50%	$7,425,126	50%
Real Estate	$16,472,555	$9,045,991	55%	$7,347,431	45%
Accountants	$4,877,052	$2,680,609	55%	$2,183,101	45%
Other & Unclassified	$4,606,265	$2,066,419	45%	$2,503,680	54%
TOTAL	**$71,091,876**	**$38,321,025**	**54%**	**$32,574,212**	**46%**

Keenly attuned to the value of careful investments, the financial community took pains to spread its dollars widely on both sides of the political aisle. Democrats got a narrow 54 percent majority of the overall dollars. That proportion was fairly consistent throughout the sector. The widest variance came among credit unions, which backed Democrats nearly two-to-one, and in the "other & unclassified" group, which gave a majority of its dollars to Republicans. That group consisted primarily of contributors who identified themselves only as "investors."

New York is the center of the nation's financial community and the 1992 race for the U.S. Senate in that state saw the biggest concentration of finance industry dollars. Robert Abrams, the Democratic loser against Alfonse D'Amato, was the top overall recipient. D'Amato ranked second. Elizabeth Holtzman, who lost to Abrams in the Democratic primary, collected $774,000 — most of it from the securities industry.

Three New Yorkers also showed up on the House's Top 10 list, but the leader there was Missouri's Dick Gephardt, the House Majority Leader who collected more than $575,000 in finance sector contributions for his reelection campaign. Gephardt's money was fairly evenly split between insurance, securities and real estate.

Top 10 Senate Recipients

Rank	Name	Amount	Status	W/L
1	Robert Abrams (D-NY)	$1,222,788	Chall	L
2	Alfonse M. D'Amato (R-NY)	$1,102,983	Incumb	W
3	Christopher J. Dodd (D-Conn)	$949,575	Incumb	W
4	John F. Seymour (R-Calif)	$869,275	Incumb	L
5	Tom Campbell (R-Calif)	$828,631	Open	L
6	Arlen Specter (R-Pa)	$817,527	Incumb	W
7	Dianne Feinstein (D-Calif)	$780,413	Chall	W
8	Elizabeth Holtzman (D-NY)	$774,360	Chall	L
9	Christopher S. Bond (R-Mo)	$650,059	Incumb	W
10	Mel Levine (D-Calif)	$628,700	Open	L

Top 10 House Recipients

Rank	Name	Amount	Status	W/L
1	Richard A. Gephardt (D-Mo)	$575,673	Incumb	W
2	Charles E. Schumer (D-NY)	$407,246	Incumb	W
3	Dan Rostenkowski (D-Ill)	$403,798	Incumb	W
4	Newt Gingrich (R-Ga)	$274,247	Incumb	W
5	Vic Fazio (D-Calif)	$272,781	Incumb	W
6	Marty Russo (D-Ill)	$252,349	Incumb	L
7	Thomas J. Downey (D-NY)	$244,800	Incumb	L
8	Stephen L. Neal (D-NC)	$220,050	Incumb	W
9	Tom McMillen (D-Md)	$210,835	Incumb	L
10	John J. LaFalce (D-NY)	$206,997	Incumb	W

Closeup on Finance, Insurance & Real Estate

Commercial Banks ....$11.2 million

Banking deregulation — allowing banks to operate freely across state lines and offer a wider array of financial services — remains high on the agenda of the nation's largest banks. The proposals have met wide opposition in Congress from competing interests, particularly insurance companies who want to keep the banks out of the securities brokerage business — something that's become a major sideline of insurance companies themselves. Non-industry critics oppose deregulation for different reasons. It was the loosening of rules in the savings & loan industry that led to rampant speculation and the eventual near-collapse of the industry, which is now being bailed out at enormous taxpayer expense.

Four of the five leaders in banking contributions in the House and Senate serve on the banking committees of their respective houses. Dan Coats was the only exception in the Senate. The top House recipient, freshman Republican Michael Castle, served as governor of Delaware before joining Congress.

Top Contributors

1	American Bankers Assn*	$1,692,508
2	JP Morgan & Co	$473,175
3	C&S/Sovran Corp*	$436,867
4	Citicorp*	$409,902
5	Independent Bankers Assn	$401,060
6	BankAmerica Corp*	$377,723
7	Barnett Banks Inc	$335,764
8	Chase Manhattan*	$303,328
9	Chemical Bank	$164,050
10	First Chicago Corp	$136,703

* Contributions came from more than one affiliate or subsidiary.

Top Senate Recipients

1	Christopher S. Bond (R-Mo)	$158,918	Incumb	W
2	Richard C. Shelby (D-Ala)	$125,828	Incumb	W
3	Terry Sanford (D-NC)	$125,400	Incumb	L
4	Daniel R. Coats (R-Ind)	$97,035	Incumb	W
5	Christopher J. Dodd (D-Conn)	$96,300	Incumb	W

Top House Recipients

1	Michael N. Castle (R-Del)	$123,800	Open	W
2	Stephen L. Neal (D-NC)	$112,900	Incumb	W
3	John J. LaFalce (D-NY)	$103,450	Incumb	W
4	Peter Hoagland (D-Neb)	$92,300	Incumb	W
5	Richard H. Baker (R-La)	$91,900	Incumb	W

Securities & Investment ....$15.9 million

While a number of top Wall Street investment firms do sponsor PACs, the preferred method for handing out contributions in the securities industry is through individual donations — often bundled in large amounts to their favorite candidates. Of the 30 biggest contributors of individual donations in the 1992 elections, 11 were securities firms. Goldman, Sachs was the biggest of all. It was also the single biggest supporter of Bill Clinton's campaign. Elizabeth Holtzman, who as New York City Comptroller was responsible for arranging the city's bond sales, led all other recipients from the industry. She lost in the Democratic primary to Robert Abrams, the number two recipient. Abrams, in turn, lost to incumbent Alfonse D'Amato, number three on the top recipient list.

Top Contributors

1	Goldman, Sachs & Co	$898,545
2	American Express/Shearson Lehman Bros*	$881,820
3	Merrill Lynch*	$627,864
4	Chicago Mercantile Exchange	$549,500
5	Morgan Stanley & Co	$470,781
6	Chicago Board of Trade	$346,750
7	PaineWebber*	$318,847
8	First Boston Corp	$315,621
9	Salomon Brothers	$285,885
10	Bear, Stearns & Co	$267,095

* Contributions came from more than one affiliate or subsidiary.

Top Senate Recipients

1	Elizabeth Holtzman (D-NY)	$636,880	Chall	L
2	Robert Abrams (D-NY)	$610,010	Chall	L
3	Alfonse M. D'Amato (R-NY)	$457,151	Incumb	W
4	Christopher J. Dodd (D-Conn)	$341,484	Incumb	W
5	Tom Campbell (R-Calif)	$264,700	Open	L

Top House Recipients

1	Charles E. Schumer (D-NY)	$221,996	Incumb	W
2	Richard A. Gephardt (D-Mo)	$141,207	Incumb	W
3	Dan Rostenkowski (D-Ill)	$124,600	Incumb	W
4	Nita M. Lowey (D-NY)	$99,740	Incumb	W
5	Bill Green (R-NY)	$96,000	Incumb	L

Insurance ....$14.9 million

Another giant of the financial world, the nation's insurance industry was one of the biggest contributors to congressional campaigns in the 1992 elections. Two-thirds of its money came from political action committees and much of it was targeted at members of committees concerned with tax policy, and with the redrafting of the nation's health insurance system.

Christopher Dodd, the industry's top recipient in 1992, represents the state that is home to some of the nation's largest insurance firms. Two other Connecticut lawmakers — Barbara Kennelly and Nancy Johnson — made the top 5 list in the House. Both sit on the powerful Ways & Means Committee, whose chairman, Dan Rostenkowski, ranked second on the list. The only non-incumbent on the leading recipients list was Earl Pomeroy, who served as North Dakota's insurance commissioner before his election to Congress.

Top Contributors

1	National Assn of Life Underwriters	$1,373,855
2	Prudential Insurance*	$639,540
3	Independent Insurance Agents of America	$589,798
4	American Council of Life Insurance	$581,880
5	American Family Corp	$550,000
6	Metropolitan Life Insurance*	$453,564
7	Blue Cross & Blue Shield Assn*	$412,359
8	Equitable Life*	$308,857
9	Massachusetts Mutual Life Insurance	$307,641
10	Northwestern Mutual Life	$288,829

* Contributions came from more than one affiliate or subsidiary.

Top Senate Recipients

1	Christopher J. Dodd (D-Conn)	$225,896	Incumb	W
2	Arlen Specter (R-Pa)	$199,494	Incumb	W
3	Christopher S. Bond (R-Mo)	$176,786	Incumb	W
4	Daniel R. Coats (R-Ind)	$174,248	Incumb	W
5	Bob Packwood (R-Ore)	$164,260	Incumb	W

Top House Recipients

1	Richard A. Gephardt (D-Mo)	$157,889	Incumb	W
2	Dan Rostenkowski (D-Ill)	$144,198	Incumb	W
3	Barbara B. Kennelly (D-Conn)	$111,305	Incumb	W
4	Earl Pomeroy (D-ND)	$98,628	Open	W
5	Nancy L. Johnson (R-Conn)	$95,305	Incumb	W

Real Estate ....$16.5 million

Investing in land and developing it with new and valuable buildings has been a thriving business fueling the American economy since the vast Eastern forests first began to be peeled back to make way for the villages, towns and farms of colonial settlers. The frantic building boom and real estate heyday of the 1980s gave way to a sobering crash in the early 90s in many markets around the nation. Some — particularly in California — have still not recovered, though the industry as a whole is rebounding with the gradually improving economy.

Campaign dollars from the real estate industry poured in heavily in 1991-92. The Realtors PAC gave more money to federal candidates than any other political action committee (though the American Medical Association gave more when state-based affiliates were added in). Despite their giant PAC, however, three-quarters of the real estate industry's money came from individuals.

Top Contributors

1	National Assn of Realtors	$2,954,973
2	Forest City Enterprises Inc	$252,833
3	Mortgage Bankers Assn of America	$221,200
4	JMB Realty Corp	$132,331
5	American Land Title Assn	$103,389
6	AKT Development Co	$94,982
7	Federal National Mortgage Assn	$93,775
8	Henry Crown & Co	$85,500
9	Carr-Gottstein Inc	$84,976
10	Sudler Companies	$82,750

* Contributions came from more than one affiliate or subsidiary.

Top Senate Recipients

1	John F. Seymour (R-Calif)	$414,017	Incumb	L
2	Robert Abrams (D-NY)	$270,718	Chall	L
3	Mel Levine (D-Calif)	$248,160	Open	L
4	Gray Davis (D-Calif)	$245,200	Chall	L
5	Dianne Feinstein (D-Calif)	$226,258	Chall	W

Top House Recipients

1	Richard A. Gephardt (D-Mo)	$125,677	Incumb	W
2	Charles E. Schumer (D-NY)	$83,000	Incumb	W
3	Bob Filner (D-Calif)	$62,950	Open	W
4	Newt Gingrich (R-Ga)	$56,459	Incumb	W
5	Bill Baker (R-Calif)	$55,567	Open	W

Health

Where the money came from . . .

For years — in fact, for decades — campaign dollars from medical PACs and from thousands of individual doctors, dentists, chiropractors, pharmacists, nursing home operators and all other manner of health care providers have been flowing generously toward Washington. But as the long march toward some form of national health insurance (or an industry acceptable alternative) enters the final stages of political battle, the pace of giving has surged to extraordinary new levels. In the 1991-92 election season, the health care sector gave $31.7 million to federal candidates — nearly double the amount identified by the Center just two years earlier.

Two thirds of that money came from physicians and other health care professionals. The rest came from hospitals, pharmaceutical companies and a variety of other health industry givers. The American Medical Association's political action committee, and its network of state-based affiliates, was the single biggest giver. In fact, the AMA ranked as the overall number one contributor to federal campaigns in the 1992 elections. But as a glance at the chart below makes clear, the AMA is hardly alone. Many other medical professionals — from ophthalmologists to root canal specialists — have national associations with PACs of their own. So do dozens of other health industry corporations.

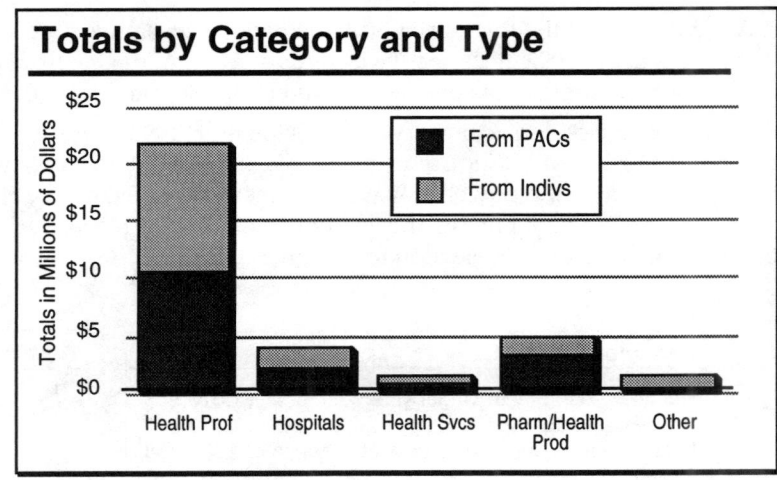

Totals by Category and Type

Category	Total	From PACs	PAC Pct	From Indivs	Indiv Pct
Health Professionals	$21,421,791	$9,959,465	46%	$11,462,326	54%
Hospitals/Nursing Homes	$3,638,760	$1,658,859	46%	$1,979,901	54%
Health Services	$1,122,272	$341,563	30%	$780,709	70%
Pharmaceuticals/Health Prod	$4,439,371	$2,972,414	67%	$1,466,957	33%
Other & Unclassified	$1,088,045	$0	0%	$1,088,045	100%
TOTAL	**$31,710,239**	**$14,932,301**	**47%**	**$16,777,938**	**53%**

Top 20 Health Contributors

Rank	Total	Contributor	Category	PAC Pct	Dem Pct	Repub Pct	To Dems / To Repubs
1	$3,245,544	American Medical Assn*	Doctors	100%	49%	51%	
2	$1,434,408	American Dental Assn*	Dentists	100%	60%	40%	
3	$870,227	American Academy of Ophthalmology	Eye Doctors	100%	63%	37%	
4	$658,596	American Chiropractic Assn*	Chiropractors	100%	73%	27%	
5	$617,102	American Hospital Assn*	Hospitals	95%	69%	31%	
6	$401,000	American Podiatry Assn	Doctors	100%	70%	30%	
7	$398,366	American Optometric Assn	Eye Doctors	100%	69%	31%	
8	$383,269	American Health Care Assn	Nursing Homes	99%	66%	33%	
9	$332,925	American College of Emerg'cy Physicians	Doctors	99%	73%	26%	
10	$311,019	American Nurses Assn	Nurses	100%	91%	9%	
11	$276,743	Assn for the Advancement of Psychology	Psychology	99%	90%	10%	
12	$258,330	Eli Lilly & Co	Pharmaceut	76%	21%	79%	
13	$217,780	Pfizer Inc	Pharmaceut	86%	47%	53%	
14	$207,331	Schering-Plough Corp	Pharmaceut	90%	51%	49%	
15	$199,166	American Physical Therapy Assn	Phys Therapists	100%	73%	27%	
16	$196,772	Glaxo Inc	Pharmaceut	89%	57%	43%	
17	$182,900	Federation of American Health Systems	Hospitals	98%	59%	41%	
18	$180,926	Merck & Co	Pharmaceut	80%	57%	43%	
19	$176,475	Bristol-Myers Squibb	Pharmaceut	72%	38%	62%	
20	$165,430	American Psychiatric Assn	Psychiatrists	100%	87%	12%	

* Contributions came from more than one affiliate or subsidiary.

Where the money went . . .

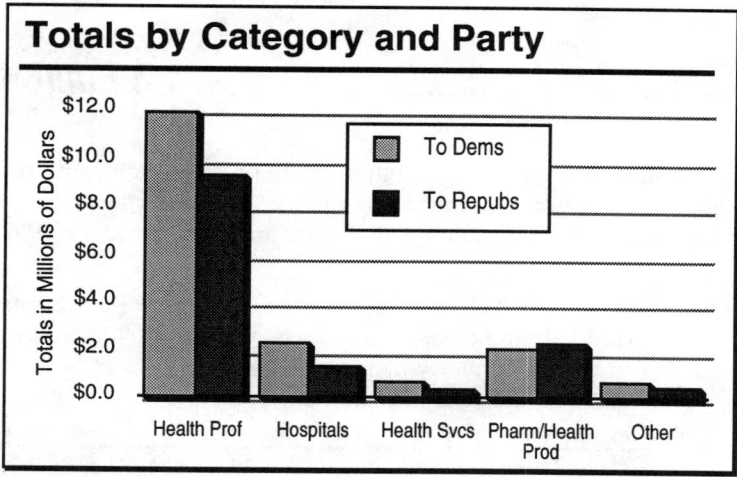

Totals by Category and Party

Overall, 54 percent of the medical community's campaign dollars went to Democrats. As with many other sectors, however, there were wide variations within the industry. Psychiatrists, psychologists and nurses were the most heavily Democratic, giving more than 80 percent of their dollars to candidates of that party. Pharmacists and chiropractors gave 70 percent to Democrats. The pharmaceutical industry leaned in the opposite direction, though not as far. Overall, they gave 53 percent of their campaign dollars to Republicans.

Category	Total	To Dems	Dem Pct	To Repubs	Repub Pct
Health Professionals	$21,421,791	$11,932,900	56%	$9,354,345	44%
Hospitals/Nursing Homes	$3,638,760	$2,350,484	65%	$1,279,291	35%
Health Services	$1,122,272	$726,279	65%	$393,428	35%
Pharmaceuticals/Health Prod	$4,439,371	$2,104,593	47%	$2,332,128	53%
Other & Unclassified	$1,088,045	$659,884	61%	$420,893	39%
TOTAL	**$31,710,239**	**$17,774,140**	**56%**	**$13,780,085**	**43%**

Republican Arlen Specter of Pennsylvania led all recipients of health care contributions in the 1992 elections, with $364,000. Bob Packwood, the number three recipient, is ranking Republican on the Senate Finance Committee — one of the key panels overseeing health care reform legislation.

Among House members, the top contributor list was led by Majority Leader Dick Gephardt. He was followed by Democrats Henry Waxman and Pete Stark, chairmen of the two key subcommittees (in the Energy & Commerce and Ways & Means Committees) that will write the new health care legislation.

Top 10 Senate Recipients

Rank	Name	Amount	Status	W/L
1	Arlen Specter (R-Pa)	$364,403	Incumb	W
2	Dianne Feinstein (D-Calif)	$329,029	Chall	W
3	Bob Packwood (R-Ore)	$299,400	Incumb	W
4	Barbara Boxer (D-Calif)	$284,897	Open	W
5	Daniel R. Coats (R-Ind)	$272,394	Incumb	W
6	John McCain (R-Ariz)	$251,989	Incumb	W
7	Tom Daschle (D-SD)	$244,999	Incumb	W
8	Christopher S. Bond (R-Mo)	$230,783	Incumb	W
9	Bob Graham (D-Fla)	$212,571	Incumb	W
10	Tom Campbell (R-Calif)	$208,759	Open	L

Top 10 House Recipients

Rank	Name	Amount	Status	W/L
1	Richard A. Gephardt (D-Mo)	$282,230	Incumb	W
2	Henry A. Waxman (D-Calif)	$203,199	Incumb	W
3	Pete Stark (D-Calif)	$193,401	Incumb	W
4	Vic Fazio (D-Calif)	$124,730	Incumb	W
5	E. Clay Shaw Jr. (R-Fla)	$115,445	Incumb	W
6	Newt Gingrich (R-Ga)	$114,360	Incumb	W
7	Robert G. Torricelli (D-NJ)	$113,600	Incumb	W
8	Gerry Sikorski (D-Minn)	$112,510	Incumb	L
9	Steny H. Hoyer (D-Md)	$109,174	Incumb	W
10	Michael Bilirakis (R-Fla)	$108,830	Incumb	W

Closeup on Health

Health Professionals ....$21.4 million

Doctors, dentists, psychiatrists, pathologists, chiropractors, pharmacists and a host of other health professionals form this segment of the medical industry that is far and away the biggest contributor to political campaigns. And while the political action committees representing these professionals are among the largest in the nation, half the dollars they gave in the 1992 elections came from individuals.

Eclipsing all other groups in this category were physicians and physician specialists. Among those specialties, optometrists and ophthalmologists were the most generous, giving $1.7 million to federal candidates. Psychiatrists and psychologists gave $920,000. Dentists opened their wallets wide and handed out $2.3 million of their own.

Top Contributors

1	American Medical Assn*	$3,225,110
2	American Dental Assn*	$1,434,408
3	American Academy of Ophthalmology	$870,227
4	American Chiropractic Assn*	$658,596
5	American Podiatry Assn	$401,000
6	American Optometric Assn	$398,366
7	American College of Emergency Physicians	$332,925
8	American Nurses Assn	$311,019
9	Assn for the Advancement of Psychology	$276,743
10	American Physical Therapy Assn	$199,166

* Contributions came from more than one affiliate or subsidiary.

Top Senate Recipients

1	Dianne Feinstein (D-Calif)	$222,087	Chall	W
2	Arlen Specter (R-Pa)	$217,685	Incumb	W
3	Barbara Boxer (D-Calif)	$212,294	Open	W
4	Bob Graham (D-Fla)	$154,081	Incumb	W
5	John McCain (R-Ariz)	$149,006	Incumb	W

Top House Recipients

1	Henry A. Waxman (D-Calif)	$126,049	Incumb	W
2	Pete Stark (D-Calif)	$113,401	Incumb	W
3	Richard A. Gephardt (D-Mo)	$98,630	Incumb	W
4	E. Clay Shaw Jr. (R-Fla)	$95,895	Incumb	W
5	Don Weidner (R-Fla)	$95,600	Open	L

Hospitals & Nursing Homes..$3.6 million

Physicians are not the only ones with a stake in the current and future state of health care. Hospitals and nursing homes are also major players in the industry, with billions of dollars at stake in the details of federal health care policy. During the 1991-92 election cycle, hospital PACs and individual administrators and executives gave nearly $2.4 million to federal candidates. Nursing home operators gave an additional $1.2 million. Both groups gave just under two-thirds of their dollars to Democrats.

Top Contributors

1	American Hospital Assn*	$616,602
2	Federation of American Health Systems	$182,900
3	Hospice Care Inc	$163,150
4	Manor Healthcare Corp	$96,200
5	Natl Assn of Private Psychiatric Hospitals	$92,950

* Contributions came from more than one affiliate or subsidiary.

Top Senate Recipients

1	Bob Packwood (R-Ore)	$68,675	Incumb	W
2	Dianne Feinstein (D-Calif)	$42,750	Chall	W
3	Tom Daschle (D-SD)	$42,700	Incumb	W
4	Bob Kerrey (D-Neb)	$39,100	Incumb	†
5	John F. Seymour (R-Calif)	$36,450	Incumb	L

Top House Recipients

1	Richard A. Gephardt (D-Mo)	$66,500	Incumb	W
2	Carrie Meek (D-Fla)	$44,500	Open	W
3	Pete Stark (D-Calif)	$32,000	Incumb	W
4	Henry A. Waxman (D-Calif)	$31,250	Incumb	W
5	Joseph D. Early (D-Mass)	$25,400	Incumb	L

Health Services ....$1.1 million

The Health Services classification covers a wide variety of health industry companies that provide services of one sort or another to the public at large. The biggest cluster of dollars within the group comes from health maintenance organizations, or HMO's, that offer their clients full medical services from on-staff doctors. (Many of the largest insurance companies also sponsor HMO's; those are not included here. Also in this category are companies providing home care services, and medical laboratories.

Top Contributors

1	Family Health Program Inc	$120,363
2	US Healthcare Inc	$79,868
3	Pacificare Health Systems	$69,100
4	American Ambulance Assn	$55,425
5	National Assn for Home Care	$32,982

Top Senate Recipients

1	Arlen Specter (R-Pa)	$30,118	Incumb	W
2	John F. Seymour (R-Calif)	$29,338	Incumb	L
3	Tom Campbell (R-Calif)	$23,050	Open	L
4	Gray Davis (D-Calif)	$21,800	Chall	L
5	Dianne Feinstein (D-Calif)	$21,042	Chall	W

Top House Recipients

1	Richard A. Gephardt (D-Mo)	$57,950	Incumb	W
2	Pete Stark (D-Calif)	$24,250	Incumb	W
3	Newt Gingrich (R-Ga)	$15,700	Incumb	W
4	Henry A. Waxman (D-Calif)	$15,500	Incumb	W
5	Vic Fazio (D-Calif)	$14,750	Incumb	W

Pharmaceuticals & Health Products ....$4.4 million

Pharmaceutical manufacturers are the one segment of the health care community that gave more money to Republicans in the 1992 elections than to Democrats. In that sense, their pattern of giving more closely reflects that of the manufacturing sector than the health care industry. Drug companies and health products manufacturers contributed $4.4 million to federal candidates. Two-thirds of the dollars came from PACs.

Top Contributors

1	Eli Lilly & Co	$258,330
2	Pfizer Inc	$217,780
3	Merck & Co	$211,943
4	Schering-Plough Corp	$207,331
5	Glaxo Inc	$196,772
6	Bristol-Myers Squibb	$176,475
7	Abbott Laboratories	$165,393
8	Upjohn Co	$151,900
9	Ciba-Geigy Corp	$144,400
10	Warner-Lambert	$142,555

Top Senate Recipients

1	Daniel R. Coats (R-Ind)	$112,850	Incumb	W
2	Frank R. Lautenberg (D-NJ)	$103,500	Incumb	†
3	Bob Packwood (R-Ore)	$96,825	Incumb	W
4	Christopher J. Dodd (D-Conn)	$80,298	Incumb	W
5	John McCain (R-Ariz)	$67,233	Incumb	W

Top House Recipients

1	Dick Zimmer (R-NJ)	$49,250	Incumb	W
2	Dan Rostenkowski (D-Ill)	$45,500	Incumb	W
3	Richard A. Gephardt (D-Mo)	$41,500	Incumb	W
4	Thomas J. Bliley Jr. (R-Va)	$35,000	Incumb	W
5	Charles B. Rangel (D-NY)	$34,200	Incumb	W

Leading Health & Insurance Recipients in Congress

The lists on these two pages show at a glance which members of the House and Senate received the biggest contributions from a combination of health and insurance industry supporters. Though these groups are classified separately in this book (insurance is included under the Finance, Insurance & Real Estate sector), both will be fundamentally affected by the outcome of the current health care debate in Congress and both are lobbying as mightily as they can to preserve their financial interests.

The Senate totals include money received over each member's full six-year term (or less if they were elected after 1988). House totals cover only those contributions received in the 1992 elections.

Top Senate Recipients

Rank	Name	Total	Health	Insurance
1	Phil Gramm (R-Texas)	$869,561	$623,564	$245,997
2	Daniel R. Coats (R-Ind)	$832,593	$516,886	$315,707
3	Arlen Specter (R-Pa)	$796,682	$531,479	$265,203
4	John D. Rockefeller IV (D-WVa)	$639,977	$482,327	$157,650
5	Bill Bradley (D-NJ)	$576,970	$312,586	$264,384
6	Tom Daschle (D-SD)	$507,373	$321,849	$185,524
7	Christopher J. Dodd (D-Conn)	$494,155	$210,797	$283,358
8	Christopher S. Bond (R-Mo)	$481,419	$261,083	$220,336
9	Tom Harkin (D-Iowa)	$475,905	$352,752	$123,153
10	Dave Durenberger (R-Minn)	$467,159	$308,217	$158,942
11	Bob Packwood (R-Ore)	$465,964	$302,600	$163,364
12	Bob Dole (R-Kan)	$444,689	$186,100	$258,589
13	Alfonse M. D'Amato (R-NY)	$430,456	$233,600	$196,856
14	Lloyd Bentsen (D-xTex)	$423,855	$191,705	$232,150
15	Dianne Feinstein (D-Calif)	$401,539	$329,029	$72,510
16	Frank R. Lautenberg (D-NJ)	$373,150	$222,400	$150,750
17	Richard C. Shelby (D-Ala)	$371,150	$226,100	$145,050
18	Max Baucus (D-Mont)	$367,209	$188,435	$178,774
19	Don Nickles (R-Okla)	$365,042	$183,550	$181,492
20	Charles E. Grassley (R-Iowa)	$364,792	$192,569	$172,223
21	Bob Graham (D-Fla)	$357,201	$226,071	$131,130
22	Orrin G. Hatch (R-Utah)	$355,290	$226,798	$128,492
23	John McCain (R-Ariz)	$350,514	$257,139	$93,375
24	Mitch McConnell (R-Ky)	$336,206	$215,050	$121,156
25	Barbara Boxer (D-Calif)	$331,647	$286,897	$44,750
26	John B. Breaux (D-La)	$299,354	$167,042	$132,312
27	Hank Brown (R-Colo)	$297,893	$115,004	$182,889
28	Paul Simon (D-Ill)	$293,849	$236,474	$57,375
29	Harry Reid (D-Nev)	$278,622	$234,622	$44,000
30	Connie Mack (R-Fla)	$277,045	$178,950	$98,095
31	Ernest F. Hollings (D-SC)	$274,575	$142,555	$132,020
32	John H. Chafee (R-RI)	$260,733	$146,400	$114,333
33	Carl Levin (D-Mich)	$260,136	$167,502	$92,634
34	Paul Coverdell (R-Ga)	$257,091	$145,729	$111,362
35	John Glenn (D-Ohio)	$252,301	$173,351	$78,950
36	Al Gore (D-Tenn)	$231,326	$127,750	$103,576
37	Howell Heflin (D-Ala)	$230,646	$111,615	$119,031
38	Harris Wofford (D-Pa)	$227,925	$156,425	$71,500
39	John C. Danforth (R-Mo)	$223,275	$89,650	$133,625
40	Larry Pressler (R-SD)	$220,398	$89,900	$130,498
41	John Kerry (D-Mass)	$219,625	$142,725	$76,900
42	Daniel Patrick Moynihan (D-NY)	$213,147	$119,180	$93,967
43	Jesse Helms (R-NC)	$208,185	$135,245	$72,940
44	Wendell H. Ford (D-Ky)	$205,859	$81,300	$124,559
45	Barbara A. Mikulski (D-Md)	$205,723	$178,723	$27,000
46	Dennis DeConcini (D-Ariz)	$203,056	$97,656	$105,400
47	Donald W. Riegle Jr. (D-Mich)	$197,450	$79,500	$117,950
48	George J. Mitchell (D-Maine)	$196,883	$106,759	$90,124
49	Jim Sasser (D-Tenn)	$196,765	$89,715	$107,050
50	Richard G. Lugar (R-Ind)	$194,365	$119,400	$74,965

It should be emphasized that the health care debate is a complex one. Different segments within both the health and insurance communities have interests that often conflict with others in their industry. Neither group speaks with a single voice, nor do the interests of the health community necessarily coincide with those of insurance carriers. These lists do indicate, however, which members of Congress have gotten the biggest financial support from each industry. These are the members that the industries are counting on the most, and for that reason the combined list is offered here.

Top House Recipients

Rank	Name	Total	Health	Insurance
1	Richard A. Gephardt (D-Mo)	$440,119	$282,230	$157,889
2	Dan Rostenkowski (D-Ill)	$238,598	$94,400	$144,198
3	Henry A. Waxman (D-Calif)	$224,449	$203,199	$21,250
4	Pete Stark (D-Calif)	$221,901	$193,401	$28,500
5	Vic Fazio (D-Calif)	$215,029	$124,730	$90,299
6	Newt Gingrich (R-Ga)	$198,873	$114,360	$84,513
7	E. Clay Shaw Jr. (R-Fla)	$185,545	$115,445	$70,100
8	Nancy L. Johnson (R-Conn)	$171,505	$76,200	$95,305
9	Barbara B. Kennelly (D-Conn)	$151,705	$40,400	$111,305
10	David E. Bonior (D-Mich)	$148,925	$82,650	$66,275
11	Michael A. Andrews (D-Texas)	$147,325	$81,160	$66,165
12	Steny H. Hoyer (D-Md)	$146,924	$109,174	$37,750
13	Sander Levin (D-Mich)	$143,596	$100,597	$42,999
14	Jim Bunning (R-Ky)	$142,632	$67,559	$75,073
15	Charles B. Rangel (D-NY)	$138,570	$84,275	$54,295
16	John D. Dingell (D-Mich)	$136,300	$76,050	$60,250
17	Benjamin L. Cardin (D-Md)	$136,000	$93,800	$42,200
18	Robert G. Torricelli (D-NJ)	$135,050	$113,600	$21,450
19	Michael Bilirakis (R-Fla)	$130,080	$108,830	$21,250
20	Earl Pomeroy (D-ND)	$127,328	$28,700	$98,628
21	J. Roy Rowland (D-Ga)	$123,200	$105,950	$17,250
22	Thomas J. Bliley Jr. (R-Va)	$116,738	$87,050	$29,688
23	Sam M. Gibbons (D-Fla)	$113,999	$53,050	$60,949
24	Bill Richardson (D-NM)	$108,610	$90,260	$18,350
25	Jim Bacchus (D-Fla)	$108,430	$98,530	$9,900
26	Martin Frost (D-Texas)	$107,150	$76,600	$30,550
27	Butler Derrick (D-SC)	$106,550	$49,900	$56,650
28	Don Sundquist (R-Tenn)	$106,011	$53,850	$52,161
29	Ileana Ros-Lehtinen (R-Fla)	$103,813	$88,085	$15,728
30	Jim Slattery (D-Kan)	$101,849	$55,150	$46,699
31	Dick Zimmer (R-NJ)	$101,822	$76,375	$25,447
32	Jim McCrery (R-La)	$100,100	$74,100	$26,000
33	Robert T. Matsui (D-Calif)	$99,273	$68,423	$30,850
34	Fred Grandy (R-Iowa)	$98,346	$40,847	$57,499
35	Bill Paxon (R-NY)	$97,500	$46,900	$50,600
36	J. J. Pickle (D-Texas)	$97,106	$49,397	$47,709
37	Bill Zeliff (R-NH)	$96,152	$53,010	$43,142
38	Bill McCollum (R-Fla)	$94,850	$60,400	$34,450
39	Rosa DeLauro (D-Conn)	$91,168	$61,468	$29,700
40	Peter Deutsch (D-Fla)	$90,750	$38,600	$52,150
41	Jack Kingston (R-Ga)	$89,672	$53,352	$36,320
42	Jim Ramstad (R-Minn)	$88,120	$50,445	$37,675
43	Robert H. Michel (R-Ill)	$86,473	$46,025	$40,448
44	Gary L. Ackerman (D-NY)	$84,650	$63,600	$21,050
45	Sam Johnson (R-Texas)	$83,584	$64,459	$19,125
46	Bill Thomas (R-Calif)	$82,899	$39,050	$43,849
47	Dan Burton (R-Ind)	$82,709	$36,805	$45,904
48	John Bryant (D-Texas)	$81,039	$64,189	$16,850
49	Jerry Lewis (R-Calif)	$80,789	$41,289	$39,500
50	Hamilton Fish Jr. (R-NY)	$80,600	$17,900	$62,700

Lawyers & Lobbyists

Where the money came from . . .

Lawyers, lobbyists and lawmakers have had a long and close relationship ever since modern democracy made its emergence on the world political scene. Indeed, many individuals have passed through all three professions in succession: lawyers winning election and becoming lawmakers, then retiring from office and becoming high-paid lobbyists. Congress has always had more lawyers than members of any other profession, and the number of former lawmakers who make the transition from Capitol Hill to K Street — the heart of Washington's lobbying district — is large and continually growing.

But little of that can be seen from tracking PAC contributions alone. Indeed, compared with other industry sectors, the legal community seems quite small. Legal industry PACs, led by the Association of Trial Lawyers of America, gave just $6.3 million in the 1992 elections. But in this case, following the PACs leads to a misleading conclusion. In fact, lawyers and lobbyists were responsible for $44 million in all — more than any other business sector except finance. But 86 percent of those dollars were delivered through individual contributions, not PACs. To journalists and other observers keeping a close watch on PAC donations, the full extent of the lawyers' giving was practically invisible.

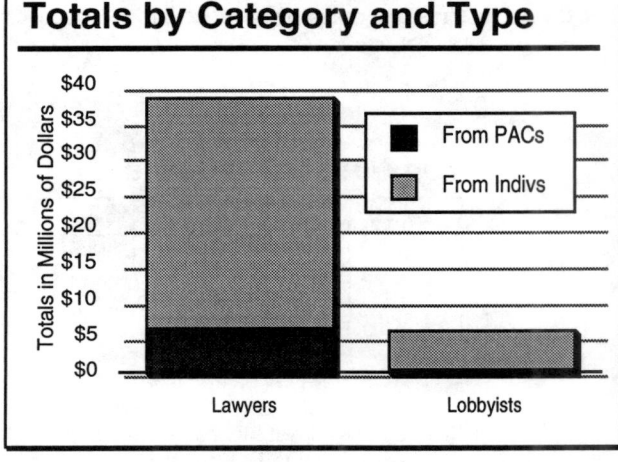

Totals by Category and Type

Category	Total	From PACs	PAC Pct	From Indivs	Indiv Pct
Lawyers/Law Firms	$38,237,491	$6,051,042	16%	$32,186,449	84%
Lobbyists/Foreign Agents	$5,821,253	$268,637	5%	$5,552,616	95%
TOTAL	**$44,058,744**	**$6,319,679**	**14%**	**$37,739,065**	**86%**

Even with the research that went into this book, many questions about the role of lawyers and lobbyists are unanswered. Many lawyers failed to put the name of their law firm, simply filling in "attorney" as their employer. And federal lobbying laws are so porous that the number of registered lobbyists is widely understood to be only a fraction of the number of Washington-area lawyers who routinely perform lobbying services for clients.

In this book, contributions from attorneys are classified under the lobbyist category only if the contributor was an officially registered lobbyist. The total lobbying dollars can therefore safely be considered to be extremely conservative. A new classification in this year's Open Secrets is that of "foreign agent." These are a particular class of Washington lobbyist who represents a foreign government or corporation in dealings with the federal government. Most, but not all registered foreign agents are also lobbyists, just as most, but not all lobbyists are also attorneys.

Top 20 Lawyer & Lobbyist Contributors

Rank	Total	Contributor	Category	PAC Pct	Dem Pct	Repub Pct	To Dems	To Repubs
1	$2,361,135	Assn of Trial Lawyers of America	Trial Lawyers	100%	92%	8%		
2	$538,228	Akin, Gump et al	Law/Lobby	57%	79%	21%		
3	$372,666	Cassidy & Associates	Lobbyists	0%	77%	23%		
4	$350,566	Skadden, Arps et al	Law/Lobby	27%	77%	23%		
5	$344,611	Jones, Day et al	Law/Lobby	51%	57%	43%		
6	$269,264	Williams & Jensen	Law/Lobby	34%	70%	30%		
7	$250,342	Verner, Liipfert et al	Law/Lobby	70%	87%	13%		
8	$203,374	Vinson & Elkins	Law/Lobby	59%	53%	47%		
9	$183,192	Preston, Gates et al	Law/Lobby	63%	68%	32%		
10	$180,389	Latham & Watkins	Law/Lobby	0%	57%	43%		
11	$179,224	Arnold & Porter*	Law/Lobby	60%	81%	19%		
12	$168,596	Manatt, Phelps et al	Law/Lobby	42%	83%	17%		
13	$160,937	Patton, Boggs & Blow	Law/Lobby	0%	80%	20%		
14	$160,509	O'Melveny & Myers	Law/Lobby	0%	56%	44%		
15	$159,619	Powell, Goldstein et al	Law/Lobby	77%	89%	11%		
16	$152,294	Kirkpatrick & Lockhart	Law/Lobby	45%	34%	66%		
17	$148,900	Hogan & Hartson	Law/Lobby	35%	83%	17%		
18	$147,741	Baker & Botts	Law/Lobby	50%	40%	60%		
19	$146,700	Milberg, Weiss et al	Law/Lobby	0%	99%	1%		
20	$145,595	Gibson, Dunn & Crutcher	Law/Lobby	0%	63%	37%		

* Contributions came from more than one affiliate or subsidiary.

Where the money went . . .

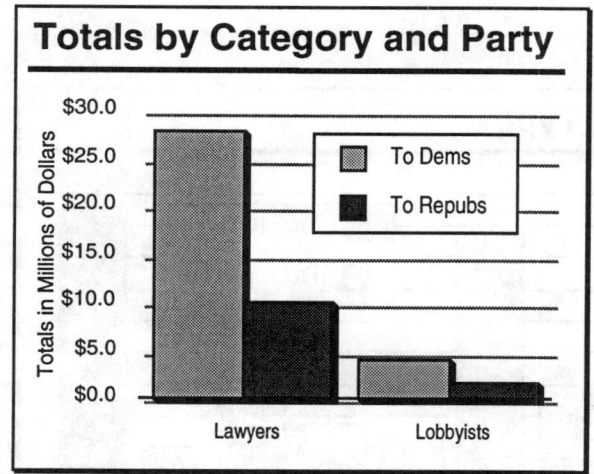

Totals by Category and Party

Totals in Millions of Dollars

□ To Dems
■ To Repubs

Lawyers   Lobbyists

By nearly a three-to-one margin, individual lawyers and their PACs favored Democrats over Republicans in their contributions. That was the strongest tilt by any business sector to either party.

Category	Total	To Dems	Dem Pct	To Repubs	Repub Pct
Lawyers/Law Firms	$38,237,491	$27,992,570	73%	$10,176,750	27%
Lobbyists/Foreign Agents	$5,821,253	$4,168,327	72%	$1,650,975	28%
TOTAL	**$44,058,744**	**$32,160,897**	**73%**	**$11,827,725**	**27%**

The biggest recipients from the legal community were nearly all Democrats. The only exception was Republican Senator Arlen Specter of Pennsylvania. Specter sits on the Senate Judiciary Committee, a panel of key importance to lawyers.

New York Democrat Robert Abrams was the top overall recipient in Congress. He collected nearly a million dollars from lawyers and lobbyists in his abortive attempt to oust Republican incumbent Alfonse D'Amato. Dick Gephardt led all House members, with nearly $370,000 in contributions.

Because of their heavy reliance on individual contributions, and the fact that many law firms bundled large numbers of contributions to particularly favored candidates, law firms were prominent on the list of the year's biggest individual contributors. In all, 13 law firms ranked among the top 50 individual contributors in the 1992 elections, as did Cassidy & Associates, a Washington lobbying group.

Top 10 Senate Recipients

Rank	Name	Amount	Status	W/L
1	Robert Abrams (D-NY)	$996,806	Chall	L
2	Harris Wofford (D-Pa)	$724,065	Incumb	W
3	Dianne Feinstein (D-Calif)	$707,149	Chall	W
4	Barbara Boxer (D-Calif)	$680,582	Open	W
5	Mel Levine (D-Calif)	$638,625	Open	L
6	Arlen Specter (R-Pa)	$544,605	Incumb	W
7	Wyche Fowler Jr. (D-Ga)	$425,231	Incumb	L
8	Ernest F. Hollings (D-SC)	$412,467	Incumb	W
9	Bob Graham (D-Fla)	$398,539	Incumb	W
10	Richard C. Shelby (D-Ala)	$390,213	Incumb	W

Top 10 House Recipients

Rank	Name	Amount	Status	W/L
1	Richard A. Gephardt (D-Mo)	$369,892	Incumb	W
2	Vic Fazio (D-Calif)	$165,504	Incumb	W
3	Jane Harman (D-Calif)	$148,925	Open	W
4	Mike Synar (D-Okla)	$143,121	Incumb	W
5	Gerry Sikorski (D-Minn)	$140,726	Incumb	L
6	Steny H. Hoyer (D-Md)	$140,217	Incumb	W
7	Lynn Schenk (D-Calif)	$139,642	Open	W
8	Martin Frost (D-Texas)	$137,162	Incumb	W
9	Marty Russo (D-Ill)	$136,265	Incumb	L
10	Robert G. Torricelli (D-NJ)	$131,800	Incumb	W

Miscellaneous Business

Where the money came from . . .

This catchall category encompasses a wide diversity of businesses from many different industries — from steel manufacturers to travel agents to funeral directors. Most of the industries here have an interest in many different legislative matters, but — aside from tax laws — few of those issues are concentrated under the jurisdiction of a particular committee.

Miscellaneous manufacturers and distributors comprised the biggest single group within the sector, both in PAC and individual contributions. The companies in this group manufacture everything from machine tools to cosmetics. Other large groups were the food & beverage industry (which includes restaurants, soft drink makers and bottlers — but not food manufacturers, who are classified under agriculture); the beer & liquor industry, retail sales, and "business services," which covers such fields as advertising, business consulting and employment agencies. Overall, two-thirds of the dollars in this sector came from individual contributors rather than PACs.

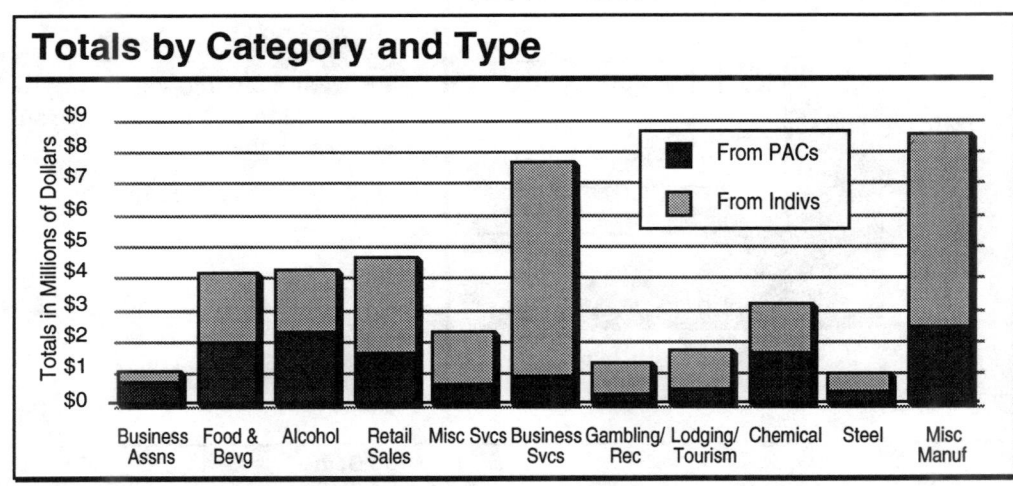

Totals by Category and Type

Category	Total	From PACs	PAC Pct	From Indivs	Indiv Pct
Business Associations	$934,666	$656,618	70%	$278,048	30%
Food & Beverage	$4,064,037	$1,854,399	46%	$2,209,638	54%
Beer, Wine & Liquor	$4,079,617	$2,139,202	52%	$1,940,415	48%
Retail Sales	$4,530,113	$1,500,376	33%	$3,029,737	67%
Misc Services	$2,174,644	$529,793	24%	$1,644,851	76%
Business Services	$7,502,660	$780,951	10%	$6,721,709	90%
Gambling/Live Entertainment	$1,212,097	$251,445	21%	$960,652	79%
Lodging/Tourism	$1,595,139	$401,600	25%	$1,193,539	75%
Chemicals	$3,088,619	$1,517,729	49%	$1,570,890	51%
Steel Production	$870,603	$276,646	32%	$593,957	68%
Misc Manufacturing/Distrib	$8,425,812	$2,326,129	28%	$6,099,683	72%
TOTAL	**$38,478,007**	**$12,234,888**	**32%**	**$26,243,119**	**68%**

Top 20 Miscellaneous Business Contributors

Rank	Total	Contributor	Category	PAC Pct	Dem Pct	Repub Pct	To Dems / To Repubs
1	$977,081	National Beer Wholesalers Assn	Beer Distrib	100%	38%	62%	
2	$571,197	National Restaurant Assn*	Restaurants	100%	23%	77%	
3	$525,569	Dow Chemical*	Chemicals	82%	22%	78%	
4	$452,363	Pepsico*	Soft Drinks/Rest	66%	26%	63%	
5	$368,000	Stone Container Corp	Paper Packging	96%	11%	89%	
6	$296,434	McDonald's Corp	Restaurants	79%	29%	71%	
7	$295,287	National Fedn of Independent Business	Business Assns	99%	13%	86%	
8	$284,649	Intl Council of Shopping Centers	Retail Sales	99%	41%	59%	
9	$277,260	FMC Corp	Chemicals	94%	36%	64%	
10	$267,090	Coca-Cola Co*	Soft Drinks	81%	59%	41%	
11	$258,600	Joseph E Seagram & Sons	Liquor/Wine	80%	83%	17%	
12	$232,134	Outdoor Advertising Assn of America	Billboards	91%	64%	36%	
13	$217,984	Gallo Winery	Wine	0%	68%	32%	
14	$198,890	JC Penney Co	Retail Sales	98%	57%	43%	
15	$190,800	Hoechst Celanese Corp	Synth Fibers	98%	47%	53%	
16	$187,050	Brown-Forman Distillers	Liquor	83%	21%	79%	
17	$178,228	Wine & Spirits Wholesalers of America	Liquor Whlsale	100%	66%	33%	
18	$176,700	Monsanto Co*	Chemicals	81%	27%	73%	
19	$163,075	Burlington Industries	Textiles	91%	77%	23%	
20	$152,895	WR Grace & Co	Chemicals	88%	37%	63%	

* Contributions came from more than one affiliate or subsidiary.

Where the money went . . .

Totals by Category and Party

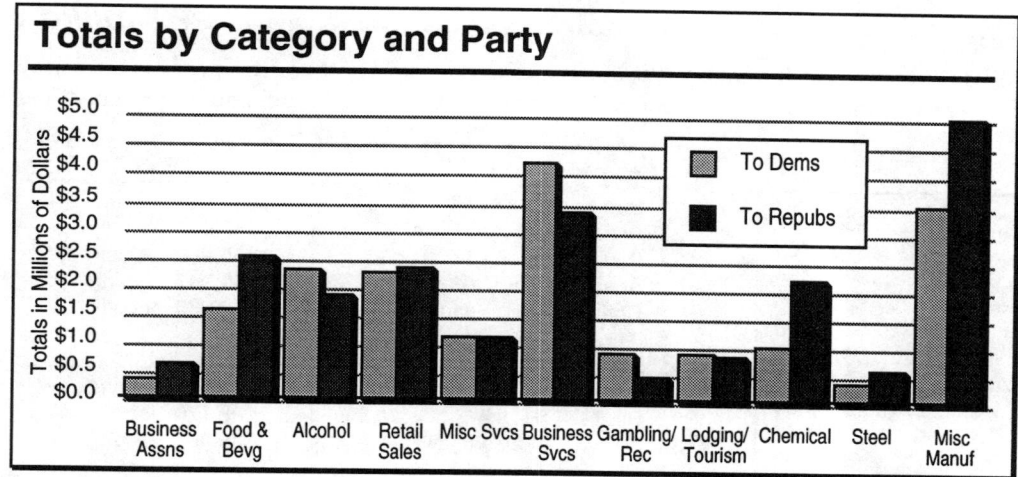

Category	Total	To Dems	Dem Pct	To Repubs	Repub Pct
Business Associations	$934,666	$310,721	33%	$612,979	66%
Food & Beverage	$4,064,037	$1,551,573	38%	$2,498,459	61%
Beer, Wine & Liquor	$4,079,617	$2,280,813	56%	$1,796,554	44%
Retail Sales	$4,530,113	$2,212,503	49%	$2,299,822	51%
Misc Services	$2,174,644	$1,083,112	50%	$1,084,086	50%
Business Services	$7,502,660	$4,161,485	55%	$3,285,390	44%
Gambling/Live Entertainment	$1,212,097	$807,481	67%	$400,268	33%
Lodging/Tourism	$1,595,139	$804,005	50%	$783,367	49%
Chemicals	$3,088,619	$970,808	31%	$2,110,998	68%
Steel Production	$870,603	$328,442	38%	$540,913	62%
Misc Manufacturing/Distrib	$8,425,812	$3,451,393	41%	$4,941,633	59%
TOTAL	**$38,478,007**	**$17,962,336**	**47%**	**$20,354,469**	**53%**

Democrats fared best among casinos and gambling interests. They also got a majority of the dollars from the liquor industry and from the diverse "business services" category. Republicans collected most of the dollars from everyone else — particularly the chemical, steel and food & beverage industries, and from the wide variety of manufacturing companies.

Leading recipients in this category most typically are candidates who raised large sums from all groups of contributors. House Majority Leader Richard Gephardt, who led all House recipients, was typical in that regard. His campaign raised over $3 million in contributions and his name was at or near the top of the Top 10 recipients list in eight of the 12 sector classifications. Overall, Republicans held seven of the top 10 Senate spots under the Miscellaneous Business sector, and accounted for six of the top 10 in the House of Representatives.

Top 10 Senate Recipients

Rank	Name	Amount	Status	W/L
1	Robert Abrams (D-NY)	$607,115	Chall	L
2	Arlen Specter (R-Pa)	$557,725	Incumb	W
3	Bob Kasten (R-Wis)	$532,099	Incumb	L
4	Alfonse M. D'Amato (R-NY)	$435,505	Incumb	W
5	Christopher S. Bond (R-Mo)	$422,928	Incumb	W
6	Dianne Feinstein (D-Calif)	$405,469	Chall	W
7	Dick Thornburgh (R-Pa)	$396,316	Chall	L
8	John F. Seymour (R-Calif)	$392,389	Incumb	L
9	Paul Coverdell (R-Ga)	$369,908	Chall	W
10	Mel Levine (D-Calif)	$368,898	Open	L

Top 10 House Recipients

Rank	Name	Amount	Status	W/L
1	Richard A. Gephardt (D-Mo)	$378,121	Incumb	W
2	Newt Gingrich (R-Ga)	$244,434	Incumb	W
3	Dan Rostenkowski (D-Ill)	$215,507	Incumb	W
4	Don Ritter (R-Pa)	$151,669	Incumb	L
5	Bud Shuster (R-Pa)	$135,050	Incumb	W
6	Jim Ramstad (R-Minn)	$119,643	Incumb	W
7	Bill Zeliff (R-NH)	$119,254	Incumb	W
8	Vic Fazio (D-Calif)	$116,631	Incumb	W
9	Barbara F. Vucanovich (R-Nev)	$108,745	Incumb	W
10	Robert G. Torricelli (D-NJ)	$104,100	Incumb	W

Closeup on Miscellaneous Business

Food & Beverage ....$4.1 million

This group includes restaurants and drinking establishments, soft drink manufacturers and bottlers, fish processors, candy manufacturers, and companies that make food additives. More general food processors and manufacturers are classified under the Agriculture sector.

Top Contributors

1	National Restaurant Assn*	$569,197
2	Pepsico*	$452,363
3	McDonald's Corp	$296,434
4	Coca-Cola Co*	$267,090
5	S&A Restaurant Corp	$143,500
6	Pepsi-Cola General Bottlers	$79,695
7	Chili's Inc	$70,000
8	National Soft Drink Assn	$64,264
9	ARA Services Inc	$57,947
10	Delaware North Companies	$54,300

* Contributions came from more than one affiliate or subsidiary.

Top Senate Recipients

1	Bob Kasten (R-Wis)	$64,856	Incumb	L
2	Dick Thornburgh (R-Pa)	$58,500	Chall	L
3	Paul Coverdell (R-Ga)	$55,280	Chall	W
4	Arlen Specter (R-Pa)	$50,947	Incumb	W
5	Christopher S. Bond (R-Mo)	$49,235	Incumb	W

Top House Recipients

1	Newt Gingrich (R-Ga)	$72,049	Incumb	W
2	Bill Zeliff (R-NH)	$28,170	Incumb	W
3	John J. LaFalce (D-NY)	$28,094	Incumb	W
4	Dan Rostenkowski (D-Ill)	$28,000	Incumb	W
5	Drew Edmondson (D-Okla)	$22,800	Chall	L

Beer, Wine & Liquor ....$4.1 million

Beer & liquor wholesalers were the biggest contributors in this group, accounting for $2.3 million. Wine & spirit manufacturers gave over $1.3 million. Beer manufacturers, led by Anheuser-Busch, gave a total of $348,000.

Top Contributors

1	National Beer Wholesalers Assn	$977,081
2	Joseph E Seagram & Sons	$258,600
3	Anheuser-Busch	$237,980
4	Gallo Winery	$217,984
5	Brown-Forman Distillers	$187,050
6	Wine & Spirits Wholesalers of America	$178,228
7	Wine Institute	$108,276
8	Smirnoff/Inglenook Distributors	$84,000
9	Distilled Spirits Council	$68,401
10	Southern Wine & Spirits	$64,250

Top Senate Recipients

1	John F. Seymour (R-Calif)	$88,477	Incumb	L
2	Robert Abrams (D-NY)	$66,700	Chall	L
3	Tom Daschle (D-SD)	$61,639	Incumb	W
4	Wendell H. Ford (D-Ky)	$58,050	Incumb	W
5	Christopher S. Bond (R-Mo)	$55,950	Incumb	W

Top House Recipients

1	Richard A. Gephardt (D-Mo)	$151,100	Incumb	W
2	Dan Rostenkowski (D-Ill)	$57,000	Incumb	W
3	Vic Fazio (D-Calif)	$53,750	Incumb	W
4	Frank Riggs (R-Calif)	$35,878	Incumb	L
5	Martin Frost (D-Texas)	$26,750	Incumb	W

Retail Sales ....$4.5 million

Department and variety stores led the spending in this category, which includes retail stores of all types as well as catalog and direct mail houses, vending machine operators and door-to-door sales companies.

Top Contributors

1	Intl Council of Shopping Centers	$284,649
2	Sears*	$220,926
3	JC Penney Co	$198,890
4	May Department Stores	$151,800
5	Amway Corp	$149,121
6	National Assn of Convenience Stores	$106,195
7	National Assn of Chain Drug Stores	$91,050
8	Wal-Mart Stores	$84,725
9	Dayton Hudson Corp	$69,250
10	Spiegel Inc	$68,650

* Contributions came from more than one affiliate or subsidiary.

Top Senate Recipients

1	Robert Abrams (D-NY)	$119,415	Chall	L
2	Arlen Specter (R-Pa)	$76,407	Incumb	W
3	Dianne Feinstein (D-Calif)	$68,300	Chall	W
4	Christopher S. Bond (R-Mo)	$59,017	Incumb	W
5	Bob Packwood (R-Ore)	$55,307	Incumb	W

Top House Recipients

1	Dan Rostenkowski (D-Ill)	$49,507	Incumb	W
2	Bob McEwen (R-Ohio)	$36,650	Incumb	L
3	Richard A. Gephardt (D-Mo)	$30,400	Incumb	W
4	Newt Gingrich (R-Ga)	$21,600	Incumb	W
5	Bill Baker (R-Calif)	$17,750	Open	W

Chemical & Related Manufacturing ....$3.1 million

Because of strict federal regulations on pollution control, clean air standards and hazardous waste cleanup, the chemical industry has long been one of the most politically active segments of the manufacturing sector. It is also one of the most conservative, delivering two-thirds of its campaign dollars to Republicans.

Top Contributors

1	Dow Chemical*	$525,569
2	FMC Corp	$277,260
3	Monsanto Co*	$175,000
4	WR Grace & Co	$152,895
5	Procter & Gamble	$110,100
6	Air Products & Chemicals Inc	$106,750
7	Dial Corp	$97,200
8	El du Pont de Nemours & Co*	$83,604
9	Philipp Brothers Chemical	$81,660
10	Nalco Chemical Co	$79,550

* Contributions came from more than one affiliate or subsidiary.

Top Senate Recipients

1	Dick Thornburgh (R-Pa)	$69,350	Chall	L
2	Christopher S. Bond (R-Mo)	$68,165	Incumb	W
3	Bob Kasten (R-Wis)	$56,886	Incumb	L
4	Arlen Specter (R-Pa)	$54,800	Incumb	W
5	Richard Williamson (R-Ill)	$43,400	Chall	L

Top House Recipients

1	Dave Camp (R-Mich)	$64,819	Incumb	W
2	Don Ritter (R-Pa)	$39,229	Incumb	L
3	James C. Greenwood (R-Pa)	$22,500	Chall	W
4	Jack Fields (R-Texas)	$21,050	Incumb	W
5	W.J. "Billy" Tauzin (D-La)	$20,350	Incumb	W

Misc. Manufacturing & Distributing ....$8.4 million

Once the backbone of American industry, this diverse group of manufacturers and distributors supply everything from office copiers to running shoes, blue jeans to jewelry, light bulbs to tin cans. Its dollars went mainly to Republicans, and its legislative interests range from occupational safety standards to product liability laws to the North American Free Trade Agreement.

Top Contributors

1	Stone Container Corp	$368,000
2	Hoechst Celanese Corp	$190,800
3	MacAndrews & Forbes Group	$147,750
4	Friedkin Industries	$106,500
5	American Furniture Manufacturers Assn	$86,750
6	Schnitzer Steel Industries	$81,602
7	Minnesota Mining & Manufacturing (3M)	$76,750
8	Nike Inc	$74,099
9	Maytag Co	$59,200
10	National Tooling & Machining Assn	$58,260

Top Senate Recipients

1	Robert Abrams (D-NY)	$164,750	Chall	L
2	Bob Kasten (R-Wis)	$164,031	Incumb	L
3	Arlen Specter (R-Pa)	$137,000	Incumb	W
4	Alfonse M. D'Amato (R-NY)	$114,984	Incumb	W
5	Daniel R. Coats (R-Ind)	$108,733	Incumb	W

Top House Recipients

1	Newt Gingrich (R-Ga)	$56,900	Incumb	W
2	Dick Swett (D-NH)	$49,828	Incumb	W
3	Jim Ramstad (R-Minn)	$47,825	Incumb	W
4	Richard A. Gephardt (D-Mo)	$46,750	Incumb	W
5	James M. Talent (R-Mo)	$41,987	Chall	W

Transportation

Where the money came from . . .

In a nation that spans more than 2,000 miles from coast to coast, and another 1,000 from border to border, the transportation of goods, services and people from one location to another has always been a major industry. From the days when the railroads opened up the American West, transportation companies have relied on allies in Congress to keep their business rolling along. Likewise, competing segments within the industry — railroads versus truckers, for example — have often sought to improve their market position at their competitors' expense.

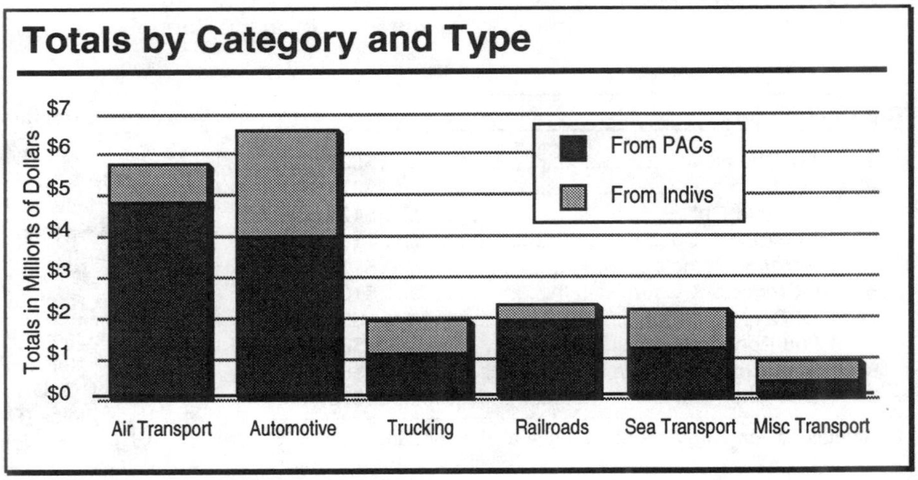
Totals by Category and Type
$7
$6
$5
$4
$3
$2
$1
$0
Totals in Millions of Dollars
From PACs
From Indivs
Air Transport
Automotive
Trucking
Railroads
Sea Transport
Misc Transport

In the 1992 elections the automotive and air transport industries were the biggest contributors to federal candidates, though most of the dollars did not come from airlines and automakers. Rather, it was the two biggest overnight delivery carriers — Federal Express and UPS — that were the leaders in air transport, along with General Electric, whose aerospace division provides its biggest source of revenues. And it was auto dealers — not the manufacturers — who led the way in spending in the automotive sector.

Category	Total	From PACs	PAC Pct	From Indivs	Indiv Pct
Air Transport/Aerospace	$5,655,211	$4,713,363	83%	$941,848	17%
Automotive	$6,494,504	$3,861,991	59%	$2,632,513	41%
Trucking	$1,821,556	$1,019,949	56%	$801,607	44%
Railroads	$2,179,996	$1,780,081	82%	$399,915	18%
Sea Transport	$2,062,351	$1,112,724	54%	$949,627	46%
Misc Transport	$776,072	$278,909	36%	$497,163	64%
TOTAL	**$18,989,690**	**$12,767,017**	**67%**	**$6,222,673**	**33%**

Contributions through political action committees were the most common form of delivering dollars from transportation interests. Two dollars out of every three came from PACs.

Top 20 Transportation Contributors

Rank	Total	Contributor	Category	PAC Pct	Dem Pct	Repub Pct
1	$1,784,375	National Auto Dealers Assn	Auto Dealers	100%	39%	61%
2	$1,472,357	United Parcel Service	Delivery Svcs	99%	54%	46%
3	$851,852	General Electric*	Aerospace	84%	58%	42%
4	$771,474	General Motors*	Auto Manuf	88%	53%	46%
5	$747,445	Federal Express Corp	Delivery Svcs	99%	68%	32%
6	$713,390	Union Pacific Corp*	Railroads	96%	33%	67%
7	$538,550	Auto Dealers & Drivers for Free Trade	Import Auto Dlrs	100%	38%	62%
8	$482,695	Aircraft Owners & Pilots Assn	Air Transport	100%	56%	44%
9	$475,150	Americans for Free International Trade	Import Auto Dlrs	100%	20%	80%
10	$453,750	CSX Corp*	RR/Sea Trans	93%	53%	47%
11	$385,003	Boeing Co	Aircraft Manuf	87%	54%	46%
12	$380,508	Ford Motor Co	Auto Manuf	85%	54%	46%
13	$359,019	American Trucking Assns	Trucking	99%	62%	38%
14	$316,481	Burlington Northern*	Railroads	93%	71%	29%
15	$298,469	American Airlines	Airlines	86%	70%	30%
16	$239,697	Norfolk Southern Corp*	Railroads	96%	63%	37%
17	$229,876	United Airlines	Airlines	86%	56%	44%
18	$223,850	Eaton Corp	Auto Parts	98%	7%	93%
19	$185,539	Northwest Airlines	Airlines	84%	66%	33%
20	$173,659	Yellow Freight System	Trucking	98%	68%	32%

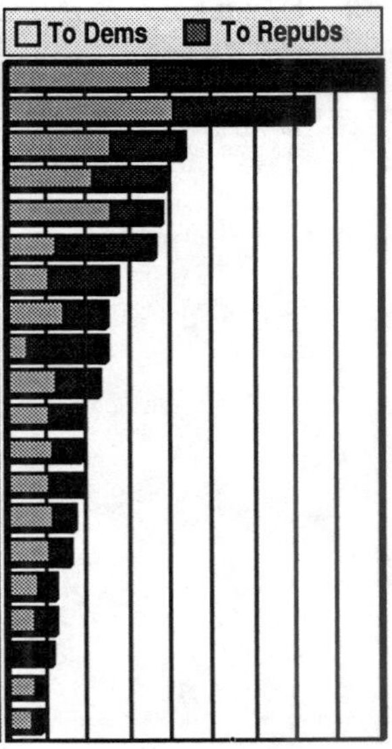
To Dems
To Repubs

* Contributions came from more than one affiliate or subsidiary.

Where the money went . . .

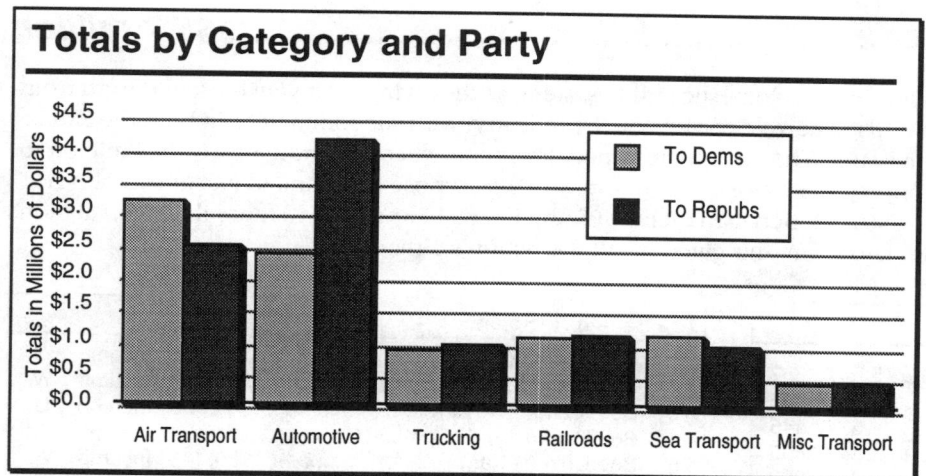

Totals by Category and Party

Totals in Millions of Dollars — categories: Air Transport, Automotive, Trucking, Railroads, Sea Transport, Misc Transport

☐ To Dems
■ To Repubs

Overall, the transportation sector split its campaign dollars fairly evenly, with Republicans collecting slightly more than half the money. The air transport and sea transport industries tipped slightly in favor of Democrats, while the automotive industry — particularly auto dealers — were the heaviest backers of the GOP.

Category	Total	To Dems	Dem Pct	To Repubs	Repub Pct
Air Transport/Aerospace	$5,655,211	$3,176,333	56%	$2,471,648	44%
Automotive	$6,494,504	$2,345,000	36%	$4,137,394	64%
Trucking	$1,821,556	$872,935	48%	$948,021	52%
Railroads	$2,179,996	$1,051,616	48%	$1,126,374	52%
Sea Transport	$2,062,351	$1,122,733	54%	$939,218	46%
Misc Transport	$776,072	$372,185	48%	$398,235	51%
TOTAL	**$18,989,690**	**$8,940,802**	**47%**	**$10,020,890**	**53%**

Several committees in Congress deal specifically with transportation issues, and their members were among the top recipients from the industry. In the upper chamber, the Senate Commerce and Transportation Committee is the focal point. Five of the top six Senate recipients (all but John Seymour) were members of that committee. So was 10th ranking John McCain.

In the House, the Public Works and Transportation Committee is the industry's chief overseer. The leading House recipient, Norman Mineta, chairs the committee's Surface Transportation Subcommittee. Three others among the top 10 — Pete Geren, Bud Shuster and Robert Roe — also served on the panel in 1992. Roe was chairman of the full committee.

Top 10 Senate Recipients

Rank	Name	Amount	Status	W/L
1	Bob Packwood (R-Ore)	$260,937	Incumb	W
2	John F. Seymour (R-Calif)	$238,746	Incumb	L
3	Bob Kasten (R-Wis)	$236,575	Incumb	L
4	John B. Breaux (D-La)	$205,718	Incumb	W
5	Ernest F. Hollings (D-SC)	$192,875	Incumb	W
6	Wendell H. Ford (D-Ky)	$187,920	Incumb	W
7	Christopher S. Bond (R-Mo)	$168,122	Incumb	W
8	Rod Chandler (R-Wash)	$161,627	Open	L
9	Bob Dole (R-Kan)	$155,937	Incumb	W
10	John McCain (R-Ariz)	$152,191	Incumb	W

Top 10 House Recipients

Rank	Name	Amount	Status	W/L
1	Norman Y. Mineta (D-Calif)	$174,359	Incumb	W
2	Richard A. Gephardt (D-Mo)	$146,996	Incumb	W
3	Bob Carr (D-Mich)	$129,330	Incumb	W
4	John D. Dingell (D-Mich)	$120,050	Incumb	W
5	Pete Geren (D-Texas)	$107,709	Incumb	W
6	Dan Rostenkowski (D-Ill)	$100,750	Incumb	W
7	Newt Gingrich (R-Ga)	$93,365	Incumb	W
8	David E. Bonior (D-Mich)	$88,925	Incumb	W
9	Bud Shuster (R-Pa)	$88,425	Incumb	W
10	Robert A. Roe (D-NJ)	$87,650	Incumb	Ret

Closeup on Transportation

Air Transport ....$5.7 million

Besides being among the most frequent fliers on the domestic airline system, as they wing their way back and forth from their far-flung districts, members of Congress also keep a close eye on the industry, with subcommittees in both the House and Senate dealing specifically with aviation issues. The industry returned the attention, contributing nearly $5.7 million to federal campaigns in the 1992 elections. Topping the list of contributors was UPS, whose PAC ranked just ahead of AT&T as the largest corporate PAC in the nation in 1991-92. Between them, UPS and Federal Express gave more than $2.2 million to federal candidates. That was almost double the amount given by all the nation's airlines.

Top Contributors	
1 United Parcel Service	$1,472,357
2 General Electric*	$785,636
3 Federal Express Corp	$747,445
4 Aircraft Owners & Pilots Assn	$482,695
5 Boeing Co	$385,003
6 American Airlines	$298,469
7 United Airlines	$216,526
8 Northwest Airlines	$185,539
9 Delta Airlines	$151,970
10 Texas Air	$110,550

* Contributions came from more than one affiliate or subsidiary.

Top Senate Recipients			
1 Wendell H. Ford (D-Ky)	$106,745	Incumb	W
2 John McCain (R-Ariz)	$64,615	Incumb	W
3 Bob Kasten (R-Wis)	$61,880	Incumb	L
4 Bob Packwood (R-Ore)	$61,437	Incumb	W
5 Bob Dole (R-Kan)	$59,775	Incumb	W

Top House Recipients			
1 Bob Carr (D-Mich)	$72,940	Incumb	W
2 Pete Geren (D-Texas)	$63,800	Incumb	W
3 Norman Y. Mineta (D-Calif)	$59,944	Incumb	W
4 James M. Inhofe (R-Okla)	$46,725	Incumb	W
5 Newt Gingrich (R-Ga)	$46,615	Incumb	W

Automotive ....$6.5 million

The Big Three automakers took a backseat to auto dealers when it came to handing out federal campaign contributions in the '92 elections. The National Auto Dealers Association more than doubled the dollars of General Motors, giving nearly $1.8 million. Meanwhile, two PACs representing dealers of Japanese imports — Auto Dealers & Drivers for Free Trade, and Americans for Free International Trade — combined for another million dollars in contributions. Though the PACs represent U.S. dealers, they lobby in favor of generous import quotas for Japanese automakers.

In recent years the increasing incursion of Japanese autos on American highways have made bilateral trade issues paramount in the minds of GM, Ford, Chrysler and their numerous suppliers and support industries. Emission controls, safety standards and requirements for fuel economy are other perennial issues that keep the path well-worn between Detroit and Washington.

Top Contributors	
1 National Auto Dealers Assn	$1,784,375
2 General Motors*	$771,474
3 Auto Dealers & Drivers for Free Trade	$538,550
4 Americans for Free International Trade	$475,150
5 Ford Motor Co	$344,904
6 Eaton Corp	$223,850
7 Prince Corp	$58,000
8 Enterprise Rent-a-Car	$55,000
9 Ryder System Inc	$51,961
10 Paccar Inc	$48,450

* Contributions came from more than one affiliate or subsidiary.

Top Senate Recipients			
1 John F. Seymour (R-Calif)	$104,500	Incumb	L
2 Bob Kasten (R-Wis)	$86,679	Incumb	L
3 Daniel R. Coats (R-Ind)	$72,433	Incumb	W
4 Bob Packwood (R-Ore)	$64,400	Incumb	W
5 Lauch Faircloth (R-NC)	$53,600	Chall	W

Top House Recipients			
1 John D. Dingell (D-Mich)	$75,150	Incumb	W
2 Richard A. Gephardt (D-Mo)	$50,500	Incumb	W
3 Don Sundquist (R-Tenn)	$33,400	Incumb	W
4 E. Clay Shaw Jr. (R-Fla)	$29,650	Incumb	W
5 Newt Gingrich (R-Ga)	$29,200	Incumb	W

Trucking ....$1.8 million

Top Contributors

1	American Trucking Assns	$359,019
2	Yellow Freight System	$172,409
3	Roadway Services Inc*	$100,425
4	Consolidated Freightways	$93,400
5	National Assn of Truck Stop Operators	$57,903

* Contributions came from more than one affiliate or subsidiary.

Top Senate Recipients

1	Ernest F. Hollings (D-SC)	$43,629	Incumb	W
2	Bob Kasten (R-Wis)	$30,666	Incumb	L
3	Bob Packwood (R-Ore)	$29,800	Incumb	W
4	Rod Chandler (R-Wash)	$29,150	Open	L
5	Christopher S. Bond (R-Mo)	$26,934	Incumb	W

Top House Recipients

1	Norman Y. Mineta (D-Calif)	$45,665	Incumb	W
2	Richard A. Gephardt (D-Mo)	$26,246	Incumb	W
3	Nick J. Rahall II (D-WVa)	$24,300	Incumb	W
4	Robert A. Roe (D-NJ)	$21,350	Incumb	†
5	Bud Shuster (R-Pa)	$18,750	Incumb	W

† Did not seek reelection in 1992

Trucking companies have an abiding interest in a variety of federal issues, particularly related to the interstate highway system. When the truckers lobbied Congress in 1991 to allow giant triple-trailer rigs on the nation's interstates, they ran into an onslaught of negative publicity from their rivals in the railroad industry. It was an example of the inter-industry competition that is often played out in the halls of Congress. Both sides lobbied heavily, but in the end the truckers' proposal was derailed.

Railroads ....$2.2 million

Top Contributors

1	Union Pacific Corp*	$713,390
2	Burlington Northern*	$316,481
3	Norfolk Southern Corp*	$239,697
4	CSX Corp†	$195,275
5	Southern Pacific Transportation Co	$119,700

* Contributions came from more than one affiliate or subsidiary.
† Does not include CSX's non-railroad subsidiaries.

Top Senate Recipients

1	Bob Packwood (R-Ore)	$43,850	Incumb	W
2	Christopher S. Bond (R-Mo)	$31,250	Incumb	W
3	Ernest F. Hollings (D-SC)	$31,051	Incumb	W
4	Arlen Specter (R-Pa)	$28,677	Incumb	W
5	Charles E. Grassley (R-Iowa)	$28,250	Incumb	W

Top House Recipients

1	Al Swift (D-Wash)	$41,250	Incumb	W
2	Don Ritter (R-Pa)	$32,375	Incumb	L
3	Norman Y. Mineta (D-Calif)	$29,000	Incumb	W
4	Bud Shuster (R-Pa)	$25,954	Incumb	W
5	Dan Rostenkowski (D-Ill)	$25,750	Incumb	W

Sea Transport ....$2.1 million

The American Merchant Marine fleet has seen more prosperous days, but shipping companies still managed to give $2.1 million to federal candidates in the 1992 elections. Sea transport unions gave an additional $3.1 million, often to the same members of Congress. Both labor and management are struggling to keep the merchant marine afloat in the face of fierce foreign competition.

Top Contributors

1	Sea-Land Corp	$175,375
2	American President Lines	$120,282
3	National Marine Manufacturers Assn	$73,000
4	Cruise PAC	$66,500
5	American Waterways Operators	$66,294

Top Senate Recipients

1	John B. Breaux (D-La)	$90,868	Incumb	W
2	Daniel K. Inouye (D-Hawaii)	$51,250	Incumb	W
3	John F. Seymour (R-Calif)	$41,016	Incumb	L
4	Dianne Feinstein (D-Calif)	$39,600	Chall	W
5	Bob Packwood (R-Ore)	$38,200	Incumb	W

Top House Recipients

1	Helen Delich Bentley (R-Md)	$53,230	Incumb	W
2	Gerry E. Studds (D-Mass)	$50,900	Incumb	W
3	W.J. "Billy" Tauzin (D-La)	$34,700	Incumb	W
4	Don Young (R-Alaska)	$33,750	Incumb	W
5	Jack Fields (R-Texas)	$33,000	Incumb	W

Labor

Where the money came from . . .

The 17 million Americans who are members of organized labor unions represent a cross-section of the workforce that is as diverse as one can imagine. Union members drive trucks, deliver mail, build skyscrapers, teach children, print newspapers, and manufacture everything from bombers to safety pins. Even individual unions can be amazingly diverse. Teamsters, for example, can be found not only behind the wheels of tractor-trailers, but in canneries, dairies, building sites and even in police departments.

Despite their diversity, however, the political action committees operated by labor unions have always been rock-solid supporters of the Democratic party. Of the $43.3 million they pumped

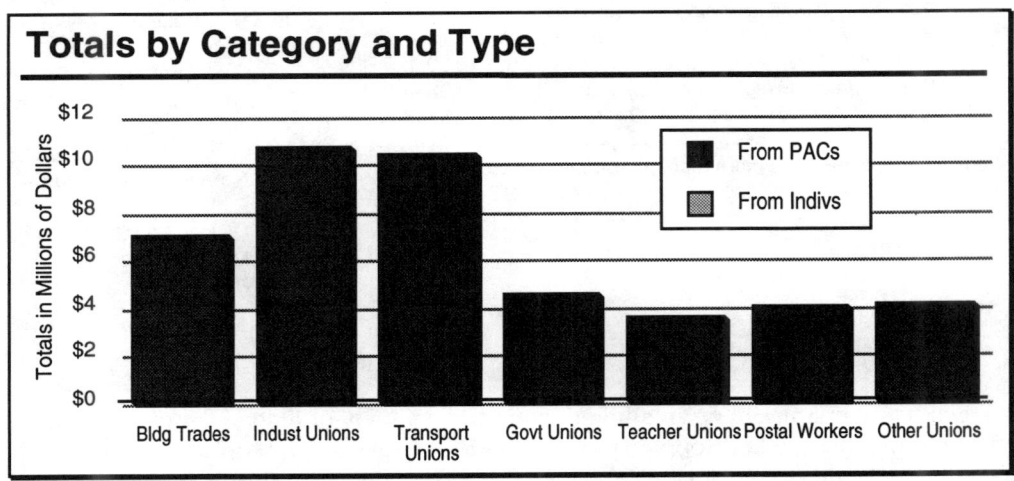

Totals by Category and Type

Category	Total	From PACs	PAC Pct	From Indivs	Indiv Pct
Building Trade Unions	$6,904,679	$6,828,879	99%	$75,800	1%
Industrial Unions	$10,505,946	$10,460,319	100%	$45,627	0%
Transportation Unions	$10,220,734	$10,195,513	100%	$25,221	0%
Government Worker Unions	$4,449,066	$4,440,668	100%	$8,398	0%
Teacher Unions	$3,477,117	$3,461,747	100%	$15,370	0%
Postal Service Unions	$3,822,198	$3,815,298	100%	$6,900	0%
Other Unions	$3,919,857	$3,867,229	99%	$52,628	1%
TOTAL	**$43,299,597**	**$43,069,653**	**99%**	**$229,944**	**1%**

into federal campaigns in the 1992 elections, 94 percent went to Democrats. No other sector of the PAC community is as partisan in its distribution of funds. Nor does any sector give as heavily through PACs.

As the 1994 elections approach, however, the unions may be rethinking their strategies. Deeply stung by their defeat in the passage of the North American Free Trade Agreement in 1993, many labor leaders vowed to withhold their traditional support of Democrats who voted for NAFTA. They may also be stung by changes in the campaign finance laws that reduce

Top 20 Labor Contributors

Rank	Total	Contributor	Category	PAC Pct	Dem Pct	Repub Pct	To Dems / To Repubs
1	$2,532,956	Teamsters Union*	Transpt Unions	100%	94%	5%	
2	$2,360,017	National Education Assn*	Teachers	100%	95%	3%	
3	$2,251,489	United Auto Workers*	Manuf Unions	100%	98%	1%	
4	$1,954,063	American Fedn of St/Cnty/Munic Emps*	Govt Unions	100%	97%	2%	
5	$1,661,880	National Assn of Letter Carriers*	Postal Workers	100%	90%	10%	
6	$1,641,746	Machinists/Aerospace Workers Union*	Indust Unions	100%	97%	1%	
7	$1,605,574	Marine Engineers Union*	Transpt Unions	100%	73%	27%	
8	$1,575,999	Intl Brotherhood of Electrical Workers*	Electrical Wrkrs	99%	96%	3%	
9	$1,493,572	Carpenters & Joiners Union*	Bldg Trades	98%	94%	5%	
10	$1,488,961	Food & Commercial Workers Union	Misc Unions	100%	97%	2%	
11	$1,472,681	Laborers Union*	Bldg Trades	100%	94%	5%	
12	$1,437,250	National Assn Retired Federal Employees	Govt Unions	100%	80%	19%	
13	$1,279,093	Air Line Pilots Assn	Transpt Unions	100%	87%	13%	
14	$1,267,774	United Steelworkers	Indust Unions	99%	99%	1%	
15	$1,118,214	AFL-CIO*	Misc Unions	99%	97%	2%	
16	$1,112,350	American Federation of Teachers	Teachers	100%	99%	2%	
17	$1,100,050	United Transportation Union	Transpt Unions	100%	97%	3%	
18	$1,012,468	Communications Workers of America*	Indust Unions	100%	98%	1%	
19	$992,638	Plumbers/Pipefitters Union*	Bldg Trades	100%	95%	4%	
20	$970,476	Seafarers International Union*	Transpt Unions	100%	92%	8%	

* Contributions came from more than one affiliate or subsidiary.

Where the money went . . .

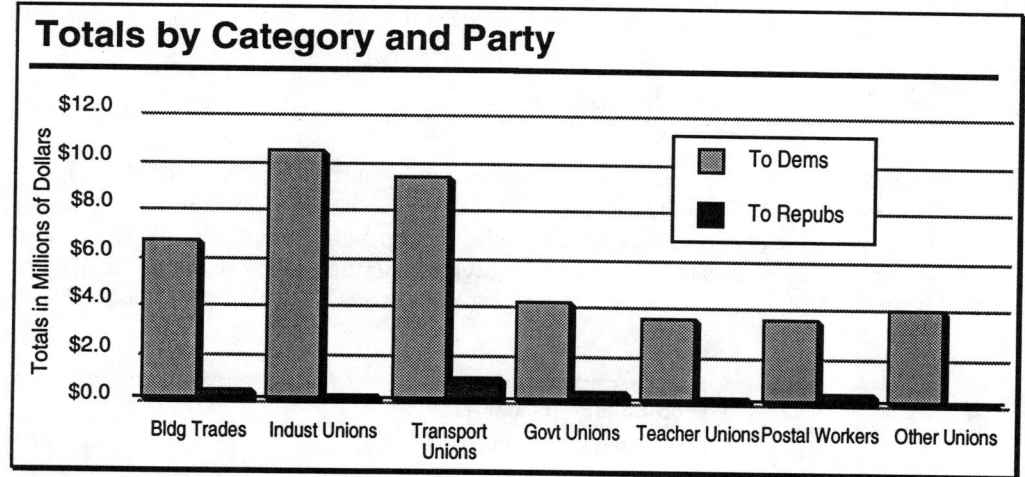

Totals by Category and Party

Category	Total	To Dems	Dem Pct	To Repubs	Repub Pct
Building Trade Unions	$6,904,679	$6,466,973	94%	$385,856	6%
Industrial Unions	$10,505,946	$10,262,774	98%	$172,172	2%
Transportation Unions	$10,220,734	$9,253,260	91%	$945,024	9%
Government Worker Unions	$4,449,066	$4,048,998	91%	$391,568	9%
Teacher Unions	$3,477,117	$3,340,592	96%	$107,325	3%
Postal Service Unions	$3,822,198	$3,419,083	89%	$394,115	10%
Other Unions	$3,919,857	$3,818,433	97%	$75,042	2%
TOTAL	**$43,299,597**	**$40,610,113**	**94%**	**$2,471,102**	**6%**

the power of PACs — the source of nearly 100 percent of their contributions.

In the study undertaken for this book, only $230,000 was identified as individual contributions by labor union members. Partly this reflects the fact that it is virtually impossible to tell who is or is not a union member by looking at their occupation (unless they work for the union itself). But it is also likely, given the economic makeup of the individuals who do make large contributions, that few union members have the resources or the inclination to write $500 or $1,000 checks to politicians.

Indeed, pooling small individual donations into large contributions from political action committees was an invention of labor unions back in the 1940s. Only later did it catch on in the business world.

Within the labor community there was a general consistency in spending patterns, though transport unions were the most likely to cross the aisle and give to Republicans. This was particularly true of the merchant marine unions.

In picking their candidates, labor PACs tend to concentrate their dollars on races where strong pro-union incumbents are facing a serious challenge. Unions are also far more likely than business PACs to underwrite the efforts of promising challengers. Still, 64 percent of the labor PACs' dollars went to incumbents in 1992. The remainder was split evenly between challengers and candidates in open seat races.

Though they tend to give as a bloc, labor unions can be separated into several distinct classes. Public sector unions — representing local, state and federal government workers, postal employees and teachers — are a growing segment of the labor community. Transportation unions are another major sector. Building trades and manufacturing unions are the mainstream of the popular image of union members, though their numbers are dwindling in the face of growing anti-union sentiment among businesses and (before the '92 elections) 12 successive years of Republican administrations.

Top 10 Senate Recipients

Rank	Name	Amount	Status	W/L
1	Harris Wofford (D-Pa)	$463,979	Incumb	W
2	Wyche Fowler Jr. (D-Ga)	$401,649	Incumb	L
3	John Glenn (D-Ohio)	$368,823	Incumb	W
4	Barbara Boxer (D-Calif)	$326,944	Open	W
5	Les AuCoin (D-Ore)	$309,526	Chall	L
6	Dianne Feinstein (D-Calif)	$298,602	Chall	W
7	Joseph H. Hogsett (D-Ind)	$297,940	Chall	L
8	Christopher J. Dodd (D-Conn)	$296,509	Incumb	W
9	Wayne Owens (D-Utah)	$293,699	Open	L
10	Carol Moseley-Braun (D-Ill)	$282,198	Chall	W

Top 10 House Recipients

Rank	Name	Amount	Status	W/L
1	John W. Olver (D-Mass)	$343,599	Incumb	W
2	David E. Bonior (D-Mich)	$286,688	Incumb	W
3	Pat Williams (D-Mont)	$282,709	Incumb	W
4	William D. Ford (D-Mich)	$282,200	Incumb	W
5	Mary Rose Oakar (D-Ohio)	$255,235	Incumb	L
6	Frank Pallone Jr. (D-NJ)	$255,030	Incumb	W
7	Gerry Sikorski (D-Minn)	$247,800	Incumb	L
8	Dale E. Kildee (D-Mich)	$244,135	Incumb	W
9	Dave Nagle (D-Iowa)	$243,563	Incumb	L
10	Vic Fazio (D-Calif)	$242,326	Incumb	W

Closeup on Labor

Building Trades Unions ....$6.9 million

Carpenters, laborers, plumbers, bricklayers — the union names are like job descriptions of the workforce that built much of the American skyline, and transformed the countryside from meadows and forests to cities and superhighways. Like the construction industry that employs them, their jobs are dependent on a healthy and growing economy. They are also dependent on labor laws that cover issues ranging from worksite safety to union organizing rules. Many of the top recipients of the building trades' PAC money come from the Northeastern and Midwest "rust belt" states where union membership is highest.

Top Contributors

1	Carpenters & Joiners Union*	$1,493,572
2	Laborers Union*	$1,472,681
3	Plumbers/Pipefitters Union*	$992,638
4	Sheet Metal Workers Union*	$745,749
5	Operating Engineers Union*	$723,524
6	Ironworkers Union*	$551,480
7	Boilermakers Union*	$425,054
8	Painters & Allied Trades Union*	$283,252
9	Bricklayers Union	$239,200
10	Heat/Frost/Asbestos Workers Union	$40,800

* Contributions came from more than one affiliate or subsidiary.

Top Senate Recipients

1	Harris Wofford (D-Pa)	$86,350	Incumb	W
2	John Glenn (D-Ohio)	$63,625	Incumb	W
3	Joseph H. Hogsett (D-Ind)	$58,250	Chall	L
4	Wayne Owens (D-Utah)	$57,250	Open	L
5	Dianne Feinstein (D-Calif)	$54,502	Chall	W

Top House Recipients

1	John W. Olver (D-Mass)	$86,000	Incumb	W
2	Pat Williams (D-Mont)	$60,750	Incumb	W
3	Frank Pallone Jr. (D-NJ)	$58,350	Incumb	W
4	Robert E. Andrews (D-NJ)	$56,123	Incumb	W
5	Dale E. Kildee (D-Mich)	$51,240	Incumb	W

Industrial Unions ....$10.5 million

Of all the sectors within organized labor, none had more at stake in the NAFTA debate than the manufacturing and industrial workers whose jobs may exported to Mexico as their employers try to compete with foreign exports by cutting labor costs. Many jobs in this sector have already headed south — from rustbelt states to the non-union sunbelt, leaving thousands of union workers in states like Michigan and Pennsylvania with little alternative but to pack up and follow along, and take whatever work they can find.

Like all other unions, their contributions have always been heavily Democratic, but the NAFTA loss may prompt a second look at the way they invest their campaign cash in 1994.

Top Contributors

1	United Auto Workers*	$2,251,489
2	Machinists/Aerospace Workers Union*	$1,641,746
3	Intl Brotherhood of Electrical Workers*	$1,575,999
4	United Steelworkers	$1,267,774
5	Communications Workers of America*	$1,012,468
6	Rubber Cork Linoleum & Plastic Workers	$505,730
7	United Mine Workers	$459,600
8	Electronic Machine Furniture Workers	$307,102
9	Amalgamated Clothing & Textile Workers*	$297,242
10	Ladies Garment Workers Union	$296,301

* Contributions came from more than one affiliate or subsidiary.

Top Senate Recipients

1	Harris Wofford (D-Pa)	$154,600	Incumb	W
2	Wyche Fowler Jr. (D-Ga)	$102,500	Incumb	L
3	Joseph H. Hogsett (D-Ind)	$100,850	Chall	L
4	Les AuCoin (D-Ore)	$98,500	Chall	L
5	Robert Abrams (D-NY)	$92,342	Chall	L

Top House Recipients

1	Gene Green (D-Texas)	$78,000	Open	W
2	John W. Olver (D-Mass)	$74,250	Incumb	W
3	Pat Williams (D-Mont)	$73,190	Incumb	W
4	Mary Rose Oakar (D-Ohio)	$72,700	Incumb	L
5	David E. Bonior (D-Mich)	$67,978	Incumb	W

Transportation Unions...$10.2 million

The Teamsters is the largest and best known of the transportation unions, but it's got plenty of company from unions that represent longshoremen, transit workers, railroad employees, airline pilots and a host of other transport workers who move people and goods across the nation's land, sea and air lanes. This is the one sector of the labor community most likely to give to Republicans, particularly if they sit on committees important to the transportation industry. That support is relative, however. Even the merchant marine unions, which gave the most to Republicans, still gave 82 percent of their dollars to Democrats.

Top Contributors

1	Teamsters Union*	$2,532,956
2	Marine Engineers Union*	$1,605,574
3	Air Line Pilots Assn	$1,279,093
4	United Transportation Union	$1,100,050
5	Seafarers International Union*	$970,476
6	Amalgamated Transit Union	$428,690
7	Transport Workers Union*	$422,730
8	Trans Comm International Union	$421,230
9	Brotherhood of Locomotive Engineers*	$262,969
10	Assn of Flight Attendants	$221,100

* Contributions came from more than one affiliate or subsidiary.

Top Senate Recipients

1	Barbara Boxer (D-Calif)	$105,250	Open	W
2	Dianne Feinstein (D-Calif)	$103,550	Chall	W
3	Les AuCoin (D-Ore)	$93,901	Chall	L
4	Wyche Fowler Jr. (D-Ga)	$91,300	Incumb	L
5	Patty Murray (D-Wash)	$82,500	Open	W

Top House Recipients

1	Gerry Sikorski (D-Minn)	$75,500	Incumb	L
2	David E. Bonior (D-Mich)	$73,400	Incumb	W
3	Frank Pallone Jr. (D-NJ)	$67,630	Incumb	W
4	Dave Nagle (D-Iowa)	$63,184	Incumb	L
5	Bob Carr (D-Mich)	$60,750	Incumb	W

Public Sector Unions ....$11.7 million

The one segment of the labor community that is actually growing, public sector workers hold down jobs in government offices, classrooms, post offices, fire houses and precinct stations that stretch from coast to coast and extend to all levels of government — state, federal and local. The one thing they have in common is that their paychecks ultimately are paid by taxpayers' money. Postal workers gave the most from within this group in 1991-92, a total of $3.8 million. Not far behind were teachers' unions that gave a combined $3.5 million.

Top Contributors

1	National Education Assn*	$2,360,017
2	American Fedn of St/Cnty/Munic Employ's*	$1,954,063
3	National Assn of Letter Carriers*	$1,661,880
4	National Assn Retired Federal Employees	$1,437,250
5	American Federation of Teachers	$1,092,600
6	American Postal Workers Union*	$900,390
7	International Assn of Firefighters*	$565,353
8	National Rural Letter Carriers Assn	$526,528
9	National Assn of Postmasters	$340,695
10	National League of Postmasters	$216,400

* Contributions came from more than one affiliate or subsidiary.

Top Senate Recipients

1	Wyche Fowler Jr. (D-Ga)	$94,750	Incumb	L
2	Terry Sanford (D-NC)	$74,793	Incumb	L
3	Wayne Owens (D-Utah)	$71,250	Open	L
4	Les AuCoin (D-Ore)	$65,425	Chall	L
5	Robert Abrams (D-NY)	$63,450	Chall	L

Top House Recipients

1	Gerry Sikorski (D-Minn)	$78,900	Incumb	L
2	Mary Rose Oakar (D-Ohio)	$78,850	Incumb	L
3	Dave Nagle (D-Iowa)	$63,780	Incumb	L
4	Peter H. Kostmayer (D-Pa)	$53,277	Incumb	L
5	John W. Olver (D-Mass)	$52,500	Incumb	W

Ideological/Single-Issue

Where the money came from . . .

A world apart from the pragmatic and largely bipartisan business PACs and the Democratically-aligned labor PACs are the third family of political givers — those organized not around a business or union, but an idea, cause or political party. Ideological and single-issue PACs have become significant players on the political landscape, as the women's rights PACs proved in the last election. In all, ideological PACs and their supporters delivered $29.3 million in the 1992 elections. Within this diverse community are political activists who represent every shade of political viewpoint, and many of them spend much of their money and time working to counteract the efforts of their adversaries. For issues which stir deep divisions among the American public—such as abortion, gun control, or defense spending — PACs have coalesced around both sides.

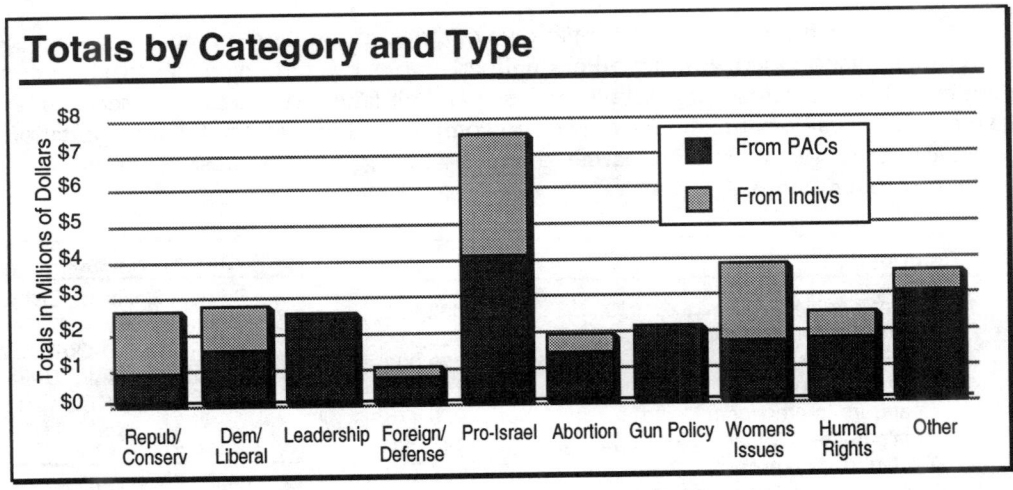

Totals by Category and Type

Category	Total	From PACs	PAC Pct	From Indivs	Indiv Pct
Republican/Conservative	$2,479,934	$794,031	32%	$1,685,903	68%
Democratic/Liberal	$2,658,027	$1,389,680	52%	$1,268,347	48%
Leadership PACs	$2,440,935	$2,428,435	99%	$12,500	1%
Foreign & Defense Policy	$918,162	$611,010	67%	$307,152	33%
Pro-Israel	$7,401,113	$4,022,677	54%	$3,378,436	46%
Abortion Policy	$1,804,175	$1,276,900	71%	$527,275	29%
Gun Policy	$2,024,067	$1,987,192	98%	$36,875	2%
Women's Issues	$3,725,735	$1,566,491	42%	$2,159,244	58%
Human Rights	$2,335,435	$1,623,606	70%	$711,829	30%
Other Issues	$3,544,331	$2,943,340	83%	$600,991	17%
TOTAL	**$29,331,914**	**$18,643,362**	**64%**	**$10,688,552**	**36%**

In addition to the PACs, the study that led to this book examined giving by individuals aligned with PACs who made individual contributions of their own directly to candidates. To be classified as an "ideological" giver, a contributor had to

Top 20 Ideological/Single-Issue Contributors

Rank	Total	Contributor	Category	PAC Pct	Dem Pct	Repub Pct
1	$1,736,446	National Rifle Assn	Pro-Guns	100%	36%	63%
2	$999,755	Emily's List	Womens Issues	37%	98%	0%
3	$941,650	Natl Cmte to Preserve Social Security	Sr Citizens	100%	88%	13%
4	$718,590	Human Rights Campaign Fund	Gay/Lesbian	99%	92%	6%
5	$684,000	National PAC	Pro-Israel	100%	65%	35%
6	$651,250	National Cmte for an Effective Congress	Dem/Liberal	100%	100%	0%
7	$612,130	Sierra Club	Environment	99%	96%	3%
8	$517,705	National Abortion Rights Action League*	Pro-Choice	100%	94%	8%
9	$513,067	Women's Campaign Fund	Womens Issues	100%	76%	22%
10	$443,062	League of Conservation Voters*	Environment	97%	93%	7%
11	$440,600	KidsPAC	Child Rights	100%	95%	4%
12	$400,736	Campaign America (Bob Dole)	Repub Leaders	97%	0%	100%
13	$329,451	National Organization for Women	Womens Issues	98%	89%	8%
14	$290,934	Right to Life*	Pro-Life	100%	13%	87%
15	$286,200	Voters for Choice	Pro-Choice	93%	89%	10%
16	$279,750	Hollywood Women's Political Cmte	Dem/Liberal	100%	99%	0%
17	$266,965	Hudson Valley PAC	Pro-Israel	100%	65%	35%
18	$244,056	House Leadership Fund (Tom Foley)	Dem Leaders	100%	100%	0%
19	$230,829	Council for a Livable World	Pro-Peace	56%	99%	0%
20	$221,950	National Council of Senior Citizens	Sr Citizens	100%	100%	0%

* Contributions came from more than one affiliate or subsidiary.

Where the money went . . .

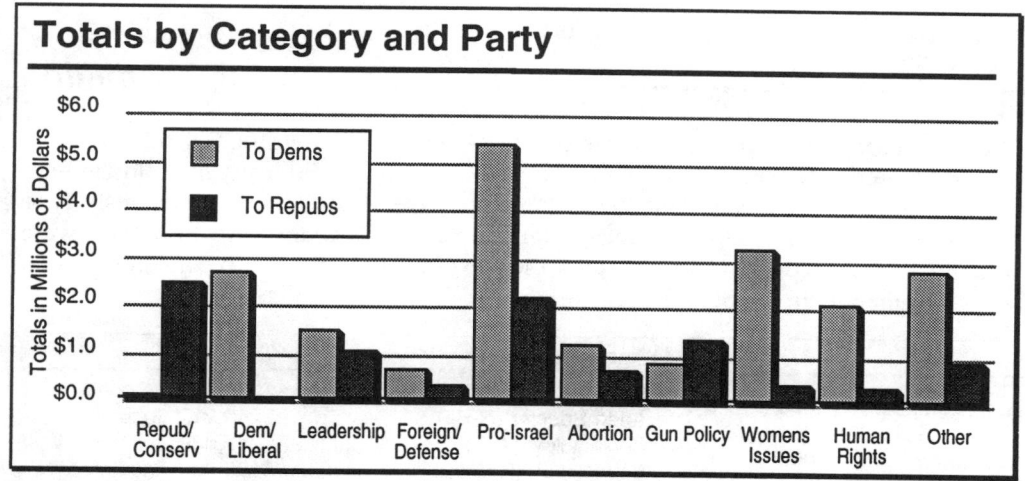

Totals by Category and Party

Category	Total	To Dems	Dem Pct	To Repubs	Repub Pct
Republican/Conservative	$2,479,934	$61,683	2%	$2,406,051	97%
Democratic/Liberal	$2,658,027	$2,612,692	98%	$25,700	1%
Leadership PACs	$2,440,935	$1,429,723	59%	$1,010,712	41%
Foreign & Defense Policy	$918,162	$607,997	66%	$279,696	30%
Pro-Israel	$7,401,113	$5,289,881	71%	$2,110,670	29%
Abortion Policy	$1,804,175	$1,162,980	64%	$630,595	35%
Gun Policy	$2,024,067	$786,554	39%	$1,232,563	61%
Women's Issues	$3,725,735	$3,138,406	84%	$339,488	9%
Human Rights	$2,335,435	$2,000,217	86%	$312,818	13%
Other Issues	$3,544,331	$2,700,329	76%	$813,246	23%
TOTAL	**$29,331,914**	**$19,790,462**	**67%**	**$9,161,539**	**31%**

give $200 or more both to an ideological or single-issue PAC and to a candidate who received funds from that PAC. Using that conservative criteria, the Center was able to identify another $10.7 million of ideological contributions.

The single biggest interest group within this community — in terms of dollars delivered to candidates — were those interested in strong U.S. ties with Israel. Pro-Israel PACs and individuals gave a combined $7.4 million to federal candidates in the 1992 elections, twice as much as any other ideological group. Women's rights PACs were second, dramatically increasing their giving from 1990 and in the process helping elect four new women to the U.S. Senate.

Other major contribution groups included broad-based conservative and liberal PACs, "leadership PACs" run by members of Congress and other political figures, PACs supporting environmental issues, groups

opposing organized labor, defending the rights of gays and lesbians, supporting or attacking the right to legal abortions, and groups involved in every issue from gun control to animal rights. There were also a variety of ethnic and minority PACs whose interests revolve around a specific segment of the American population, as well as the interests of the citizens in their homelands. Hispanic-Americans support no fewer than five individual PACs. Others promote the interests of Armenian-, Albanian-, Greek-, Korean-, Turkish-, Italian- and African-Americans; and there are PACs representing both American Indians and Indo-Americans from India.

Though they may represent every issue under the sun (and a few, like the SpacePAC, *beyond* the sun) one thing most single-issue and ideological PACs do have in common is a tendency to back candidates from one political party or the other. They also have a higher-than-normal tendency to give money to challengers — something the more pragmatic business PACs do only a tiny proportion of the time.

Top 10 Senate Recipients

Rank	Name	Amount	Status	W/L
1	Barbara Boxer (D-Calif)	$843,555	Open	W
2	Dianne Feinstein (D-Calif)	$542,956	Chall	W
3	Carol Moseley-Braun (D-Ill)	$451,135	Chall	W
4	Robert Abrams (D-NY)	$409,964	Chall	L
5	Lynn Yeakei (D-Pa)	$394,285	Chall	L
6	Harris Wofford (D-Pa)	$390,625	Incumb	W
7	Mel Levine (D-Calif)	$358,125	Open	L
8	Arlen Specter (R-Pa)	$337,153	Incumb	W
9	Bob Packwood (R-Ore)	$305,102	Incumb	W
10	Wyche Fowler Jr. (D-Ga)	$295,850	Incumb	L

Top 10 House Recipients

Rank	Name	Amount	Status	W/L
1	Anna G. Eshoo (D-Calif)	$169,441	Open	W
2	Elizabeth Furse (D-Ore)	$150,439	Open	W
3	Rosa DeLauro (D-Conn)	$149,893	Incumb	W
4	John W. Olver (D-Mass)	$136,683	Incumb	W
5	Gerry E. Studds (D-Mass)	$133,918	Incumb	W
6	Joan Kelly Horn (D-Mo)	$131,028	Incumb	L
7	Sam Gejdenson (D-Conn)	$129,360	Incumb	W
8	Peter H. Kostmayer (D-Pa)	$128,947	Incumb	L
9	Vic Fazio (D-Calif)	$128,450	Incumb	W
10	Anita Perez Ferguson (D-Calif)	$123,676	Chall	L

Closeup on Ideology/Single-Issue

Pro-Israel...$7.4 million

The biggest single source of contributions among ideological groups came from PACs supporting strong U.S. relations with Israel. In all, some 55 pro-Israel PACs contributed to federal campaigns in the 1992 elections, as did many more individuals who gave to the PACs and also gave to favored candidates in tight races. The money went mainly, but not exclusively to Democrats. Indeed, three of the biggest recipients in 1992 — Arlen Specter, Bob Packwood and Bob Kasten — were Republicans. Instead of spreading token payments to dozens of candidates, the pro-Israel groups tend to concentrate their contributions in a handful of key races — generally in the Senate.

Top Contributors

1	National PAC	$684,000
2	Hudson Valley PAC	$266,965
3	Women's Alliance for Israel	$209,000
4	Joint Action Cmte for Political Affairs	$205,000
5	Washington PAC	$202,020
6	Citizens Organized PAC	$192,750
7	Desert Caucus	$178,550
8	Americans for Good Government Inc	$166,750
9	Florida Congressional Committee	$158,250
10	Women's Pro-Israel National PAC	$155,550

Top Senate Recipients

1	Mel Levine (D-Calif)	$285,525	Open	L
2	Arlen Specter (R-Pa)	$249,210	Incumb	W
3	Bob Packwood (R-Ore)	$241,636	Incumb	W
4	Bob Kasten (R-Wis)	$198,599	Incumb	L
5	Daniel K. Inouye (D-Hawaii)	$190,155	Incumb	W

Top House Recipients

1	Sam Gejdenson (D-Conn)	$88,060	Incumb	W
2	Mel Reynolds (D-Ill)	$80,671	Chall	W
3	Les Aspin (D-Wis)	$79,850	Incumb	W
4	Eric D. Fingerhut (D-Ohio)	$72,950	Open	W
5	Dick Swett (D-NH)	$60,157	Incumb	W

Womens Issues ....$3.7 million

The much-trumpeted "Year of the Woman" in 1992 was helped along significantly by a virtual explosion in funds directed to and by women's rights PACs that aimed their considerable financial resources at electing a record new crop of women to the U.S. Congress. Leading the charge, and organizing the most money, was Emily's List, a Washington-based PAC that aims to elect Democratic women not just through direct PAC contributions, but by "bundling" hundreds and even thousands of individual donations from around the country and delivering them to the women with the most likely chances of winning. Though Emily's List claimed to have raised $6 million in contributions, the Center was able to confirm only $1 million in contributions using the conservative criteria outlined on the previous two pages. One reason that so much of the money was "invisible" was likely that most of it came in small contributions. Federal election law requires itemization only of contributions of $200 and above. Candidates receiving gifts below that amount need not identify the source; they only need to give the total.

Whatever their financial impact however, Emily's List and the rest of the women's issue PACs emerged as a major political force in 1992. Their impact is not likely to fade any time soon.

Top Contributors

1	Emily's List	$999,755
2	Women's Campaign Fund	$513,067
3	National Organization for Women	$329,451
4	National Womens Political Caucus	$207,520
5	Wish List	$86,509

Top Senate Recipients

1	Barbara Boxer (D-Calif)	$378,286	Open	W
2	Dianne Feinstein (D-Calif)	$223,878	Chall	W
3	Carol Moseley-Braun (D-Ill)	$185,717	Chall	W
4	Lynn Yeakel (D-Pa)	$142,211	Chall	L
5	Patty Murray (D-Wash)	$100,783	Open	W

Top House Recipients

1	Anna G. Eshoo (D-Calif)	$93,751	Open	W
2	Elizabeth Furse (D-Ore)	$60,305	Open	W
3	Elaine Baxter (D-Iowa)	$53,956	Chall	L
4	Karen Shepherd (D-Utah)	$48,255	Open	W
5	Lynn H. Taborsak (I-Conn)	$45,316	Chall	L

1992 Leadership PAC Roster

Since members of Congress often raise funds for their Leadership PACs at the same time they're collecting money for their reelection campaigns, it may be instructive to know which members have PACs and how much they give out. The list below shows all leadership PACs operated by members of Congress and other prominent party officials that made contributions to candidates in the 1992 elections.

Members of Congress

PAC Name	Sponsor	1992 Contributions
15th District Committee	Rep Edward Madigan (R-Ill)	$225
24th Congressional District of California PAC	Rep Henry Waxman (D-Calif)	$79,000
America's Leaders' Fund	Rep Dan Rostenkowski (D-Ill)	$120,703
AmeriPAC: The Fund for a Greater America	Rep Steny Hoyer (D-Md)	$31,500
Arizona Leadership for America	Sen Dennis DeConcini (D-Ariz)	$5,523
Bluegrass Committee	Sen Mitch McConnell (R-Ky)	$5,750
Campaign America	Sen Bob Dole (R-Kans)	$400,736
Campaign for America	Sen Frank Lautenberg (D-NJ)	$26,000
Catch the Spirit PAC	Sen Bob Kasten (R-Wisc)	$10,000
Citizens for Competitive America	Sen Ernest Hollings (D-SC)	$6,000
Committee for a Demoratic Consensus	Sen Alan Cranston (D-Calif)	$89,446
Committee for a Progressive Congress	Rep David Obey (D-Wis)	$500
Committee for America's Future	Sen Robert Byrd (D-WVa)	$47,000
Committee for Democratic Action	Sen Howard Metzenbaum (D-Ohio)	$17,250
Committee for Democratic Opportunity	Rep William Gray III (D-Pa)	$3,500
Congressional Black Caucus	Rep William Clay (D-Mo)	$6,500
Conservative Democratic PAC	Rep Charles Stenholm (D-Tex)	$16,250
Conservative Opportunities Society	Rep Newt Gingrich (R-Ga)	$1,000
Conservative Victory Fund	Sen Steve Symms (R-Idaho)	$19,298
Democratic Congressional Fund	Rep Joe Moakley (D-Mass)	$870
Democrats for the Future	Rep Beryl Anthony (D-Ark)	$11,000
Effective Government Committee	Rep Richard Gephardt (D-Mo)	$204,425
Fund for a Democratic Majority	Sen Edward Kennedy (D-Mass)	$185,530
Fund for a Republican Majority	Sen Ted Stevens (R-Alaska)	$3,000
Fund for Effective Leadership	Rep Neal Smith (D-Iowa)	$3,000
Fund for the Future Committee	Sen John Danforth (R-Mo)	$6,999
Future Leaders PAC	Rep Jerry Lewis (R-Calif)	$22,205
GOPAC	Rep Newt Gingrich (R-Ga)	$10,614
House Leadership Fund	Rep Thomas Foley (D-Wash)	$244,056
Lone Star Fund	Rep Martin Frost (D-Texas)	$38,500
Modern PAC	Rep Bill Green (R-NY)	$7,100
National Congressional Club	Sen Jesse Helms (R-NC)	$34,476
New Frontier Leadership PAC	Rep Norman Lent (R-NY)	$21,550
New Majority Leadership PAC	Rep Vin Weber (R-Minn)	$38,054
New Republican Majority Fund	Sen Trent Lott (R-Miss)	$4,500
Pelican PAC	Sen Bennett Johnston (D-La)	$93,284
People Helping People	Rep Maxine Waters (D-Calif)	$13,000
Policy Innovation PAC	Rep Dick Armey (R-Texas)	$1,000
Republican Leader's Fund	Rep Bob Michel (R-Ill)	$169,000
Senate Majority Fund	Sen Daniel Inouye (D-Hawaii)	$8,000
Senate Victory Fund	Sen Thad Cochran (R-Miss)	$107,000
Victory USA	Rep Vic Fazio (D-Calif)	$91,100

Other Notable Officials

PAC Name	Sponsor	1992 Contributions
America 2000 Fund	Former Gov Jim Thompson (R-Ill)	$19,950
America First PAC	Pat Buchanan	$2,750
Americans Concerned for Tomorrow	Geraldine Ferraro	$1,510
Americans for the Republic	Pat Robertson	$1,000
Citizens for the Republic	Ronald Reagan	$6,000
Committee for an Affordable New Jersey	Gov Christine Todd Whitman (R-NJ)	$61,500
DC Montana Committee	Former Sen Lee Metcalf (D-Mont)	$1,000
Democratic Candidate Fund	Former Rep Tip O'Neill (D-Mass)	$14,950
Fund for Southern Progress	Gov Carroll Campbell (R-SC)	$42,500
Majority Congress Committee	Former Rep Jim Wright (D-Texas)	$100
Participation 2000	Gov Richard Celeste (D-Ohio)	$8,824
San Franciscans Getting Things Done	Art Agnos (former SF Mayor)	$2,500

A Potpourri of Issue PACs

Like metal filings drawn to a magnet, political action committees have coalesced around virtually every issue of interest — or dispute — among Americans. The amounts spent by one group versus another, and the proportions within each camp that go to Democrats versus Republicans, offer a fascinating glimpse at the political strategies of these specialized interest groups. The following mini-profiles present the highlights, combining dollars that came both from PACs and from individuals supporting the PACs' policies through direct contributions to candidates.

Abortion

A total of 27 Pro-Life PACs and 13 Pro-Choice PACs contributed to federal candidates in the 1992 elections. Most of the Pro-Life PACs were organized under the national Right to Life organization, and that group's national PAC gave the biggest share of the group's money.

As can be seen from the chart at right, the Pro-Choice forces were decidedly Democratic in their contributions. Pro-Life groups mainly supported Republicans.

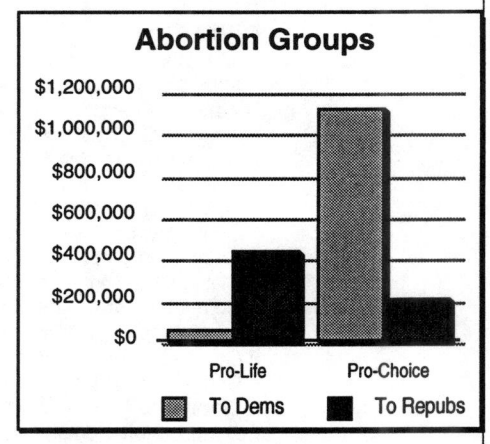

Abortion Groups

Pro-Life	
Right to Life*	$290,934
Pro-Choice	
National Abortion Rights Action League*	$517,705
Voters for Choice	$286,200

* Contributions came from more than one affiliate or subsidiary.

Gun Control vs. Gun Ownership

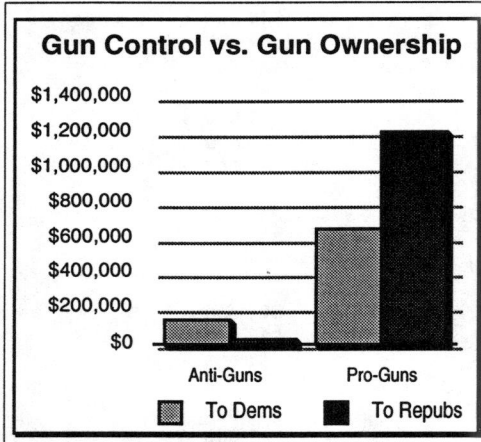

Gun Control vs. Gun Ownership

The National Rifle Association had the strongest presence by far among PACs dealing with the issue of gun control vs. gun owners' rights. Long an influential lobby on Capitol Hill, the NRA Political Victory Fund was the biggest ideological PAC in the nation in 1992, delivering over $1.7 million to 346 candidates — more than double what they gave two years earlier. Playing David to the NRA's Goliath was Handgun Control Inc., the anti-gun PAC organized by Sarah and Jim Brady. Despite the huge NRA financial advantage, the Brady Bill finally became law in 1993, requiring a seven-day waiting period for purchasers of firearms.

Pro-Guns	
National Rifle Assn	$1,736,446
Anti-Guns	
Handgun Control Inc	$156,112

The Left and the Right

A total of 101 ideological PACs on both the left and right of the political spectrum contributed to federal candidates in the 1992 election. Along with Leadership PACs operated by members of Congress, these tend to be the most partisan of all PACs, giving virtually all their funds to candidates of one party or the other.

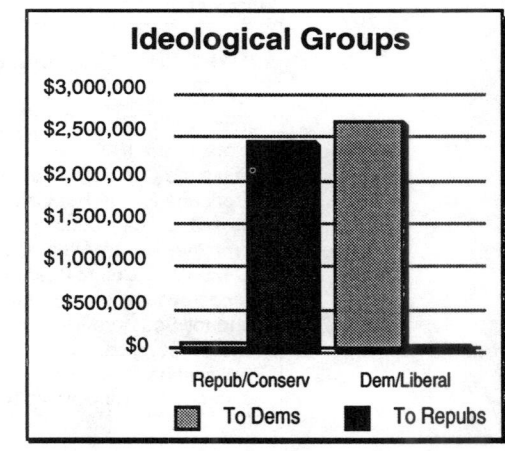

Ideological Groups

Republican/Conservative PACs	
Eagle Forum	$148,361
Conservative Victory Committee	$96,022
Democratic/Liberal PACs	
National Cmte for an Effective Congress	$650,750
Hollywood Women's Political Cmte	$278,500
Independent Action	$116,318
Fifth Horseman PAC	$109,000

Human Rights

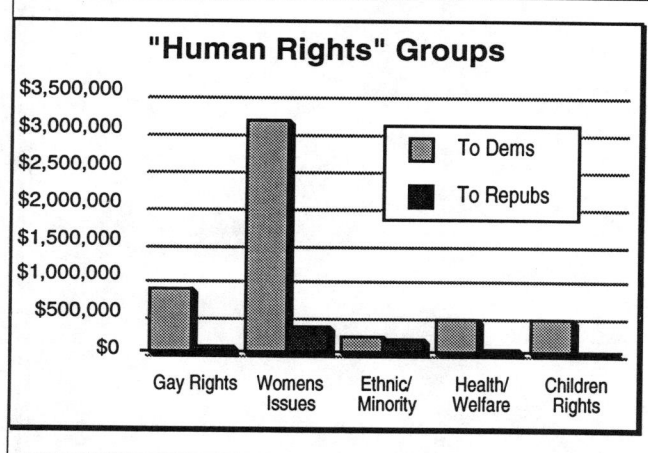

"Human Rights" Groups

Groups seeking to improve the lot of the women, children, gays and ethnic minorities were all active with political contributions in the 1992 elections — none more so than the women's groups whose spending helped elect a record crop of women to Congress. Democrats were by far the biggest beneficiaries of the human rights groups' spending.

Gay/Lesbian Rights
Human Rights Campaign Fund $713,040
Womens Issues (see list on page 90) $3,725,735
Ethnic/Minority $365,619
Children's Rights
KidsPAC $440,600
Health/Welfare
National Community Action Foundation $120,350

War and Peace

The end of the Cold War and the dissolution of the Soviet Union greatly diminished the threat of global nuclear war, shifting the focus of debate between the pro-military and pro-peace PACs. The level of defense spending in the post Cold War era remains a concern of both groups, though their perspectives — and the distribution of their dollars — are at opposite poles.

Pro-Military
Veterans of Foreign Wars $102,675
Council for National Defense $55,995
Pro-Peace
Council for a Livable World* $230,829

* Contributions came from more than one affiliate or subsidiary.

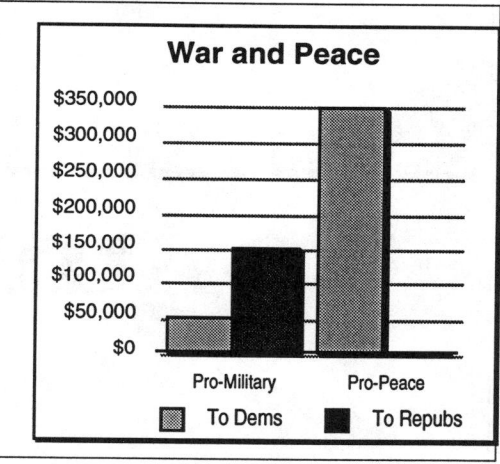

Other Single-Issue Groups

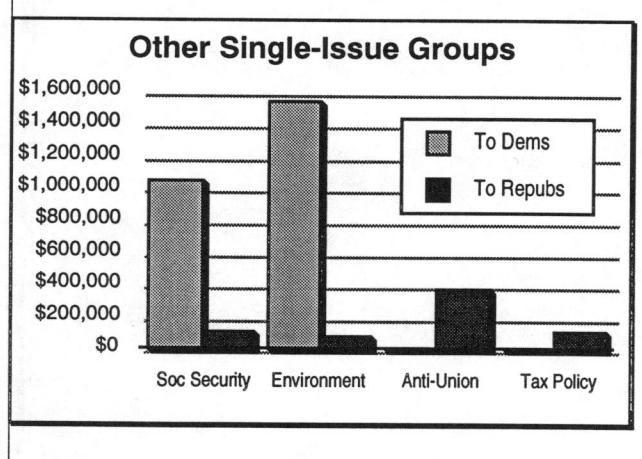

Of the remaining single-issue groups the largest are those advocating protection of the social security and medicare programs for senior citizens, along with environmental PACs and organizations seeking to reduce the influence of labor unions in the American workplace. Among the anti-union PACs, the Public Service Research Council specifically opposes unionism among public employees.

Elderly/Social Security
National Cmte to Preserve Social Security $941,650
National Council of Senior Citizens $221,750
Environmental Issues
Sierra Club...$608,680
League of Conservation Voters...................................$413,139
Anti-Union
Right to Work PAC $205,151
Public Service Research Council $140,553
Tax Policy $111,404

3.

Committee Profiles

Open Secrets

Introduction to the Committee Profiles

Most of the work that Congress does in shaping legislation takes place not on the floor of the House and Senate, but in meetings of committees and subcommittees. It is at this level that the language of bills is crafted, revised and debated, that congressional hearings are held and investigations directed. For all these reasons, much of the attention of industry and interest group lobbyists — and contributors — is focused on deliberations within the specific committees that oversee their particular industry or interest. The section which follows examines the patterns in political contributions made in 1991-92 to members of each of the 37 standing committees of the House and Senate.

What the profiles contain

• Names of the chairman and ranking minority member of each committee and the ratio of seats between Democrats and Republicans.

• A full description of the committee's jurisdiction.

• A listing of each subcommittee, with its chairman and ranking minority member.

• A roster listing each committee member, and showing the totals they received in 1991-92 from PACs and from individual contributors giving $200 or more. The members are arranged in descending order of the amount they received. The rosters include all members who served on the committee during the 102nd Congress — whether or not they ran for reelection in 1992.

• Top 20 contributors to members of that committee, including both PACs and individual contributors of $200 and more.

• Total contributions to all members of that committee from 13 broad categories of industries and interests.

• A spotlight on the 15 largest industry and interest group sectors that contributed to committee members during 1991-92. This is a more detailed breakdown of the general categories. For example, the general chart groups all finance, insurance and real estate contributors into one broad category. The spotlight chart breaks them down further, into commercial banks, insurance companies, real estate, etc.

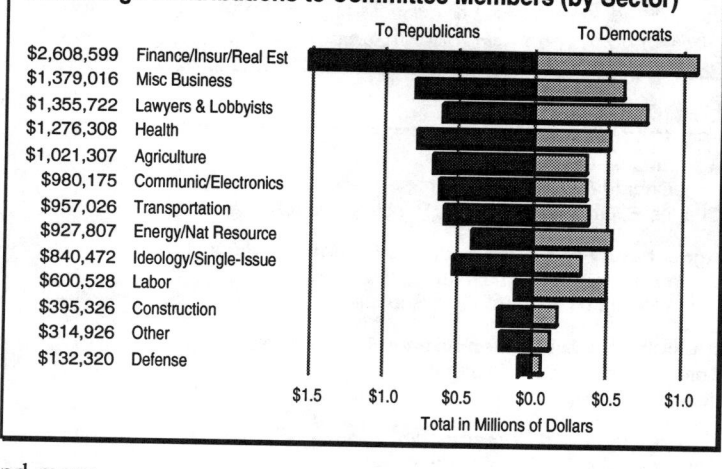

Total Large Contributions to Committee Members (by Sector)

To Republicans — To Democrats

$2,608,599	Finance/Insur/Real Est
$1,379,016	Misc Business
$1,355,722	Lawyers & Lobbyists
$1,276,308	Health
$1,021,307	Agriculture
$980,175	Communic/Electronics
$957,026	Transportation
$927,807	Energy/Nat Resource
$840,472	Ideology/Single-Issue
$600,528	Labor
$395,326	Construction
$314,926	Other
$132,320	Defense

$1.5 $1.0 $0.5 $0.0 $0.5 $1.0
Total in Millions of Dollars

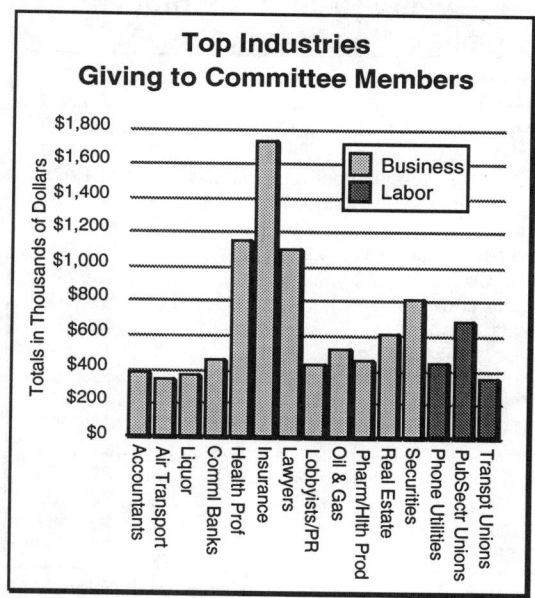

Top Industries Giving to Committee Members

Totals in Thousands of Dollars

Business / Labor

Accountants, Air Transport, Liquor, Comml Banks, Health Prof, Insurance, Lawyers, Lobbyists/PR, Oil & Gas, Pharm/Hlth Prod, Real Estate, Securities, Phone Utilities, PubSectr Unions, Transpt Unions

"Generic" Committees and "Specific" Committees

The format and information shown on the committee pages varies with the jurisdictional scope of the committee. Some "generic" committees (for example, the tax-writing committees or those dealing with foreign relations, veterans' affairs, or government operations) affect a broad range of industries and interest groups more or less equally. Other committees — such as Agriculture, Armed Services, or Banking — have jurisdictions which focus on specific industries.

In generic committees, the contribution totals shown for committee members refer to the total dollars received by that member from *all* PACs and *all* individual contributors giving $200 or more. In the specific committees, the figure refers to the total received *only from those contributors whose interests coincide with the committee's jurisdiction.*

"Specific" committees also include one additional chart, highlighting those interests most directly affected by the committee's actions.

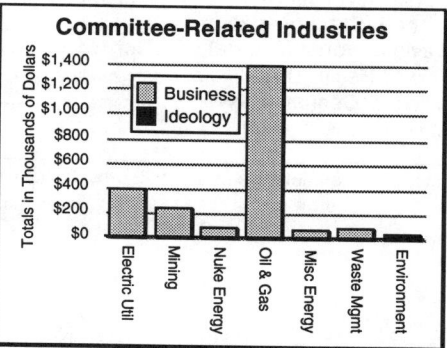

Committee-Related Industries

Totals in Thousands of Dollars

Business / Ideology

Electric Util, Mining, Nuke Energy, Oil & Gas, Misc Energy, Waste Mgmt, Environment

Senate Agriculture, Nutrition and Forestry Committee

Patrick J. Leahy (D-Vt), Chairman
Richard G. Lugar (R-Ind), Ranking Republican

Party Ratio: 10 Democrats
8 Republicans

Jurisdiction: (1) Agricultural economics and research; (2) Agricultural extension services and experiment stations; (3) Agricultural production, marketing and stabilization of prices; (4) Agriculture and agricultural commodities; (5) Animal industry and diseases; (6) Crop insurance and soil conservation; (7) Farm credit and farm security; (8) Food from fresh waters; (9) Food stamp programs; (10) Forestry and forest reserves and wilderness areas other than those created from the public domain; (11) Home economics; (12) Home nutrition; (13) Inspection of livestock, meat and agricultural products; (14) Pests and pesticides; (15) Plant industry, soils and agricultural engineering; (16) Rural development, rural electrification and watershed; (17) School nutrition programs. In addition, the committee is mandated to study and review matters relating to food, nutrition and hunger — both in the U.S. and in foreign countries — and rural areas, and to report on these matters periodically.

Subcommittees

Agricultural Credit
Kent Conrad (D-ND), Chairman
Charles E. Grassley (R-Iowa), Ranking Republican

Agricultural Production and Stabilization of Prices
David Pryor (D-Ark), Chairman
Jesse Helms (R-NC), Ranking Republican

Agricultural Research and General Legislation
Tom Daschle (D-SD), Chairman
John Seymour (R-Calif), Ranking Republican

Conservation and Forestry
Wyche Fowler Jr. (D-Ga), Chairman
Larry E. Craig (R-Idaho), Ranking Republican

Domestic and Foreign Marketing and Product Promotion
David L. Boren (D-Okla), Chairman
Thad Cochran (R-Miss), Ranking Republican

Nutrition and Investigations
Tom Harkin (D-Iowa), Chairman
Mitch McConnell (R-Ky), Ranking Republican

Rural Development and Rural Electrification
Howell Heflin (D-Ala), Chairman
Thad Cochran (R-Miss), Ranking Republican

Total Agriculture-Related Contributions to Committee Members

	Total from Cmte-Related Contribs	Pct of Member's Lg Contribs
John F. Seymour (R-Calif)	$567,003	11%
Wyche Fowler Jr. (D-Ga)	$432,449	12%
Bob Dole (R-Kan)	$262,381	13%
Charles E. Grassley (R-Iowa)	$221,752	14%
Tom Daschle (D-SD)	$204,694	9%
Kent Conrad (D-ND)	$183,780	15%
Bob Kerrey (D-Neb)†	$139,379	4%
Tom Harkin (D-Iowa)†	$87,099	4%
Richard G. Lugar (R-Ind)	$78,750	13%
Patrick J. Leahy (D-Vt)	$74,160	11%
Thad Cochran (R-Miss)	$30,750	58%
Jesse Helms (R-NC)	$29,088	13%
Larry E. Craig (R-Idaho)	$13,750	53%
David L. Boren (D-Okla)	$5,500	16%
Howell Heflin (D-Ala)	$3,250	18%
Mitch McConnell (R-Ky)	$3,125	4%
Max Baucus (D-Mont)	$1,000	14%

† Includes contributions to his 1992 presidential campaign

	Top 20 Agriculture-Related Contributors to Committee Members in 1991-92	
1	Archer-Daniels-Midland Corp	$55,000
2	Chicago Board of Trade	$54,500
3	Chicago Mercantile Exchange	$53,750
4	Philip Morris*	$53,000
5	American Assn of Crop Insurers	$51,976
6	ACRE (Action Cmte for Rural Electrification)*	$48,000
7	ConAgra Inc	$43,500
8	Associated Milk Producers	$37,000
9	US Tobacco Co	$36,500
10	Sun-Diamond Growers*	$34,000
11	Tyson Foods	$32,500
12	American Crystal Sugar Corp	$32,000
13	Food Marketing Institute	$29,500
14	National Pork Producers Council	$27,603
15	National Cattlemen's Assn*	$26,500
16	RJR Nabisco	$24,000
17	American Sugarbeet Growers Assn	$23,766
18	Okeelanta Corp	$23,500
19	National Cotton Council	$23,451
20	Mid-America Dairymen	$23,000

* Contributions came from more than one affiliate or subsidiary.

Members in **bold italics** ran for reelection in 1992

Summary

Dairy, sugar, tobacco and a variety of other agricultural subsidies and programs come under the jurisdiction of the Senate Agriculture Committee, making this panel crucially important to the nation's agriculture and food processing industries.

Like other Senate committees, however, the contribution patterns to committee members do not always draw a direct line between the industries and committee members. Since most Senators have four committee assignments, no one committee tends to dominate their contribution profiles. Likewise, the amount of money going to committee members varies greatly from year to year, depending on how many members are up for reelection and whether they come from big (high-budget) states, or small ones. Nevertheless, as seen in the chart at right, the agriculture industry was one of the leading sources of funds for committee members in 1991-92.

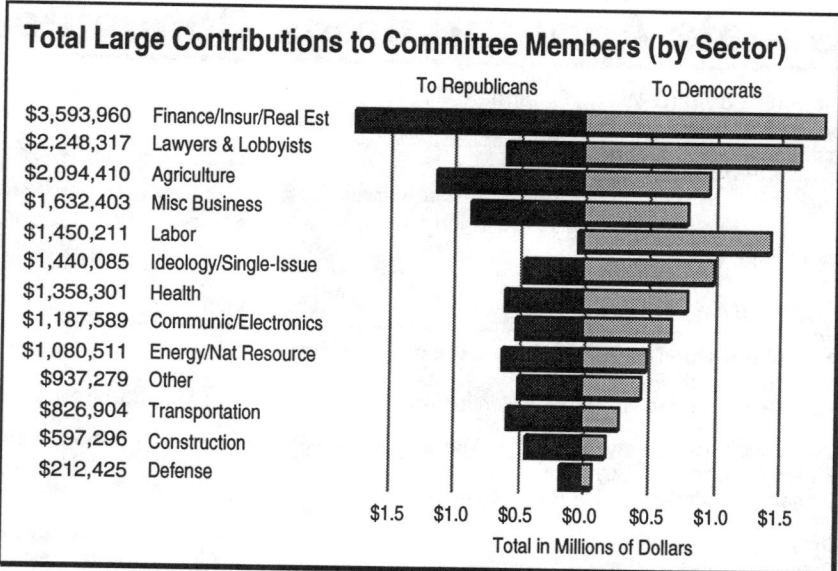

Total Large Contributions to Committee Members (by Sector)

$3,593,960	Finance/Insur/Real Est
$2,248,317	Lawyers & Lobbyists
$2,094,410	Agriculture
$1,632,403	Misc Business
$1,450,211	Labor
$1,440,085	Ideology/Single-Issue
$1,358,301	Health
$1,187,589	Communic/Electronics
$1,080,511	Energy/Nat Resource
$937,279	Other
$826,904	Transportation
$597,296	Construction
$212,425	Defense

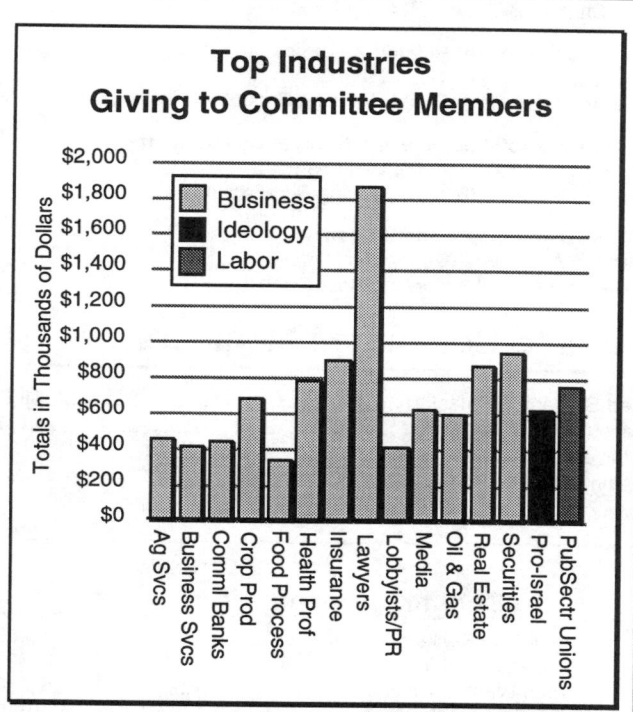

Top Industries Giving to Committee Members

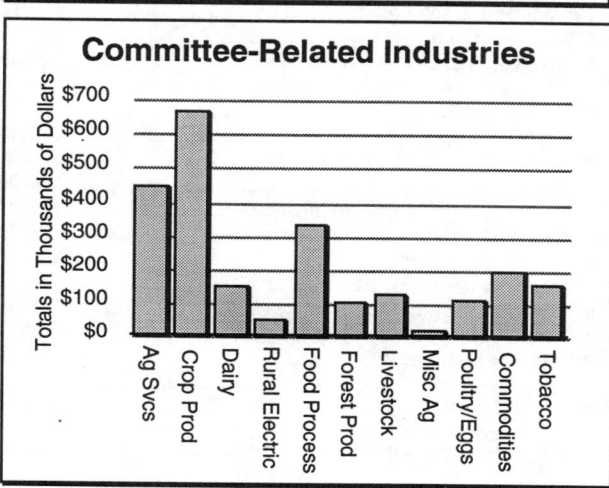

Committee-Related Industries

Leading Industries Giving to Committee Members

Business

Agricultural Services/Products	$444,213
Business Services	$393,448
Commercial Banks	$428,138
Crop Production & Basic Processing	$661,671
Food Processing & Sales	$330,141
Health Professionals	$767,074
Insurance	$881,578
Lawyers/Law Firms	$1,848,698
Lobbyists/PR	$399,619
Media/Entertainment	$612,899
Oil & Gas	$578,346
Real Estate	$856,523
Securities & Investment	$928,370

Ideological/Single-Issue

Pro-Israel	$609,358

Labor

Public Sector Unions	$731,053

Leading Committee-Related Industries Giving to Committee Members

Business

Agricultural Services/Products	$444,213
Crop Production & Basic Processing	$661,671
Dairy	$145,290
Rural Electric Utilities	$50,000
Food Processing & Sales	$330,141
Forestry & Forest Products	$103,675
Livestock	$125,780
Poultry & Eggs	$112,400
Commodity Trading	$193,000
Tobacco	$151,500
Misc Agriculture	$19,740

Senate Appropriations Committee

Robert C. Byrd (D-WVa), Chairman
Mark O. Hatfield (R-Ore), Ranking Republican

Party Ratio: 16 Democrats
13 Republicans

Jurisdiction: (1) Appropriation of the revenue for the support of the Government; (2) Rescission of appropriations contained in appropriation acts; (3) The amount of new spending authority . . . which is to be effective for a fiscal year. Other committees of Congress may *authorize* the government to spend money on various projects and programs, but only the Appropriations committees of the House and Senate *appropriate* the funds.

Subcommittees

Agriculture, Rural Development and Related Agencies
Dale Bumpers (D-Ark), Chairman
Thad Cochran (R-Miss), Ranking Republican

Commerce, Justice and State, the Judiciary and Related Agencies
Ernest F. Hollings (D-SC), Chairman
Warren B. Rudman (R-NH), Ranking Republican

Defense
Daniel K. Inouye (D-Hawaii), Chairman
Ted Stevens (R-Alaska), Ranking Republican

District of Columbia
Brock Adams (D-Wash), Chairman
Christopher S. Bond (R-Mo), Ranking Republican

Energy and Water Development
J. Bennett Johnston (D-La), Chairman
Mark O. Hatfield (R-Ore), Ranking Republican

Foreign Operations
Patrick J. Leahy (D-Vt), Chairman
Bob Kasten (R-Wis), Ranking Republican

Interior and Related Agencies
Robert C. Byrd (D-WVa), Chairman
Don Nickles (R-Okla), Ranking Republican

Labor, Health and Human Services, Education and Related Agencies
Tom Harkin (D-Iowa), Chairman
Arlen Specter (R-Pa), Ranking Republican

Legislative Branch
Harry Reid (D-Nev), Chairman
Slade Gorton (R-Wash), Ranking Republican

Military Construction
Jim Sasser (D-Tenn), Chairman
Phil Gramm (R-Texas), Ranking Republican

Transportation and Related Agencies
Frank Lautenberg (D-NJ), Chairman
Alfonse M. D'Amato (R-NY), Ranking Republican

Treasury, Postal Service and General Government
Dennis DeConcini (D-Ariz), Chairman
Pete V. Domenici (R-NM), Ranking Republican

VA, HUD and Independent Agencies
Barbara A. Mikulski (D-Md), Chairwoman
Jake Garn (R-Utah), Ranking Republican

Total PAC and Large Individual Contributions to Committee Members

Arlen Specter (R-Pa) $5,296,607
Alfonse M. D'Amato (R-NY)....................$4,607,894
Bob Kasten (R-Wis) $4,009,220
Wyche Fowler Jr. (D-Ga) $3,516,212
Bob Kerrey (D-Neb)† $3,409,573
Christopher S. Bond (R-Mo)...................$3,232,383
Don Nickles (R-Okla) $2,591,195
Daniel K. Inouye (D-Hawaii) $2,398,729
Ernest F. Hollings (D-SC) $2,318,965
Tom Harkin (D-Iowa)† $2,149,567
Phil Gramm (R-Texas) $1,964,503
Harry Reid (D-Nev) $1,845,018
Dale Bumpers (D-Ark)............................$1,648,431
Barbara A. Mikulski (D-Md) $1,578,220
Kent Conrad (D-ND) $1,238,407
Frank R. Lautenberg (D-NJ) $1,129,924
Brock Adams (D-Wash) $701,536
Patrick J. Leahy (D-Vt) $662,722
Dennis DeConcini (D-Ariz) $362,639
Slade Gorton (R-Wash) $280,422
Jim Sasser (D-Tenn) $152,231
Robert C. Byrd (D-WVa) $139,000
Mark O. Hatfield (R-Ore) $96,200
Thad Cochran (R-Miss) $52,600
J. Bennett Johnston (D-La) $43,950
Pete V. Domenici (R-NM) $17,700

Members in **bold italics** ran for reelection in 1992

† Includes contributions to his 1992 presidential campaign

Ted Stevens (R-Alaska) $8,050
Jake Garn (R-Utah) $1,000
Warren B. Rudman (R-NH) $0
Quentin N. Burdick (D-ND) ....-$900

Top 20 Contributors to Committee Members in 1991-92	
1 American Bankers Assn*	$108,450
2 General Electric*	$105,825
3 Time Warner*	$99,250
4 American Dental Assn	$98,100
5 American Federation of Teachers	$97,000
6 Assn of Trial Lawyers of America	$97,000
7 United Parcel Service	$94,550
8 Merrill Lynch*	$93,214
9 National Assn of Realtors	$90,450
10 National Assn of Letter Carriers*	$90,040
11 National PAC	$90,000
12 National Assn of Life Underwriters	$87,000
13 National Cable Television Assn	$86,750
14 American Express*	$86,100
15 National Beer Wholesalers Assn	$85,700
16 National Assn of Broadcasters	$85,186
17 United Transportation Union	$83,800
18 Goldman, Sachs & Co	$83,501
19 US Tobacco*	$82,270
20 Philip Morris*	$80,980

* Contributions came from more than one affiliate or subsidiary.

Summary

The Appropriations Committee is the largest committee in the U.S. Senate; its 29 members have the job of doling out the dollars it takes to keep the government running. This makes its decisions especially important to those businesses that rely heavily on government contracts.

As seen dramatically in the chart below, contributions from lawyers and law firms towered over those of all other industries giving to members of the committee. That pattern was not specifically related to the Appropriations Committee — in fact the same pattern can be found in nearly every Senate committee. The reason has less to do with the effect of committee decisions on the legal profession than it does with the fact that lawyers and lobbyists represent a diverse collection of clients whose interests *are* affected by congressional decisions.

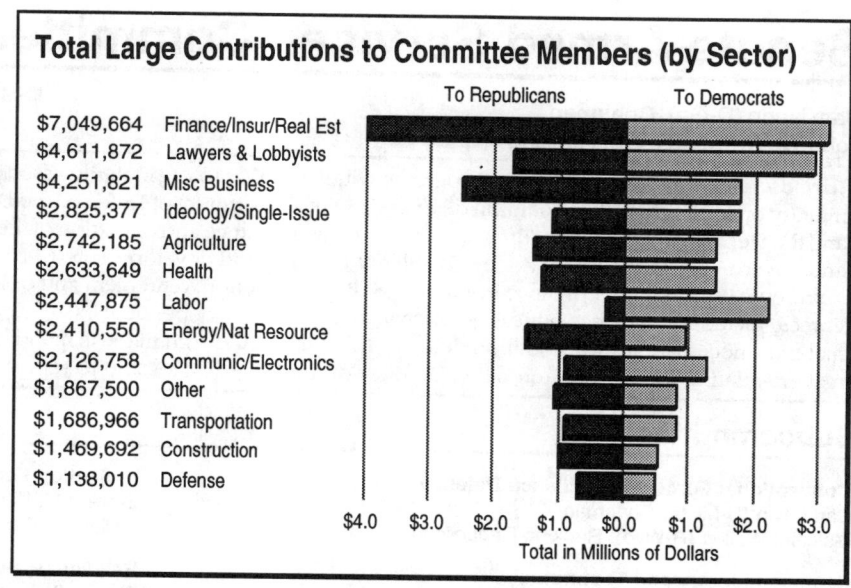

Total Large Contributions to Committee Members (by Sector)

$7,049,664	Finance/Insur/Real Est
$4,611,872	Lawyers & Lobbyists
$4,251,821	Misc Business
$2,825,377	Ideology/Single-Issue
$2,742,185	Agriculture
$2,633,649	Health
$2,447,875	Labor
$2,410,550	Energy/Nat Resource
$2,126,758	Communic/Electronics
$1,867,500	Other
$1,686,966	Transportation
$1,469,692	Construction
$1,138,010	Defense

Total in Millions of Dollars

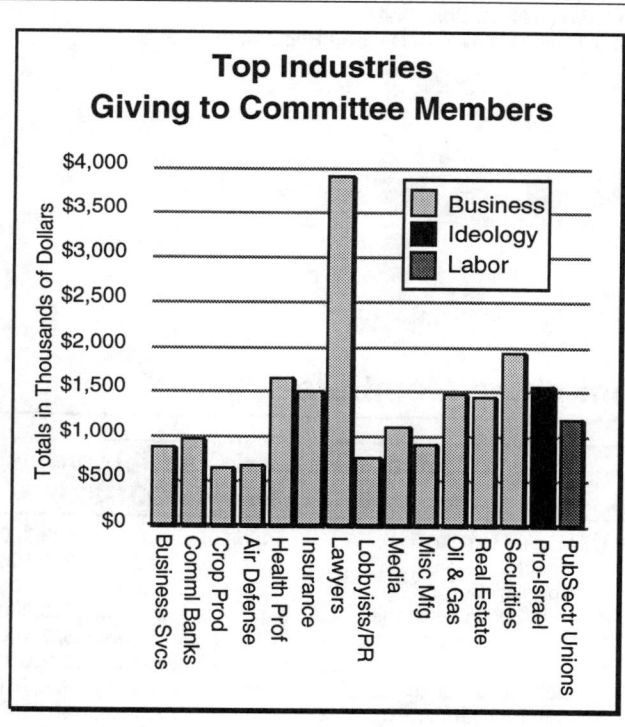

Top Industries Giving to Committee Members

(Business, Ideology, Labor)

Totals in Thousands of Dollars

Business Svcs, Comml Banks, Crop Prod, Air Defense, Health Prof, Insurance, Lawyers, Lobbyists/PR, Media, Misc Mfg, Oil & Gas, Real Estate, Securities, Pro-Israel, PubSectr Unions

Leading Industries Giving to Committee Members

Business

Business Services	$840,036
Commercial Banks	$939,786
Crop Production & Basic Processing	$628,261
Defense Aerospace	$655,178
Health Professionals	$1,620,535
Insurance	$1,489,334
Lawyers/Law Firms	$3,878,193
Lobbyists/PR	$733,679
Media/Entertainment	$1,077,620
Misc Manufacturing & Distributing	$871,653
Oil & Gas	$1,444,090
Real Estate	$1,410,402
Securities & Investment	$1,906,250

Ideological/Single-Issue

Pro-Israel	$1,545,837

Labor

Public Sector Unions	$1,156,886

Senate Armed Services Committee

Sam Nunn (D-Ga), Chairman
John W. Warner (R-Va), Ranking Republican

Party Ratio: 11 Democrats
9 Republicans

Jurisdiction: (1) Aeronautical and space activities peculiar to or primarily associated with the development of weapons systems or military operations; (2) The common defense; (3) The Department of Defense, the Department of the Army, the Department of the Navy and the Department of the Air Force, generally; (4) Maintenance and operation of the Panama Canal, including administration, sanitation and government of the Canal Zone; (5) Military research and development; (6) National security aspects of nuclear energy; (7) Naval petroleum reserves, except those in Alaska; (8) Pay, promotion, retirement and other benefits and privileges of members of the Armed Forces, including overseas education of civilian and military dependents; (9) Selective Service System; and (10) Strategic and critical materials necessary for the common defense. In addition, the committee is mandated to study and review, on a comprehensive basis, matters relating to the common defense policy of the United States and to report on them from time to time.

Subcommittees

Conventional Forces and Alliance Defense
Carl Levin (D-Mich), Chairman
Malcolm Wallop (R-Wyo), Ranking Republican

Defense Industry and Technology
Jeff Bingaman (D-NM), Chairman
Daniel R. Coats (R-Ind), Ranking Republican

Manpower and Personnel
John Glenn (D-Ohio), Chairman
John McCain (R-Ariz), Ranking Republican

Projection Forces and Regional Defense
Edward M. Kennedy (D-Mass), Chairman
William S. Cohen (R-Maine), Ranking Republican

Readiness, Sustainability and Support
Alan J. Dixon (D-Ill), Chairman
Trent Lott (R-Miss), Ranking Republican

Strategic Forces and Nuclear Deterrence
Jim Exon (D-Neb), Chairman
Strom Thurmond (R-SC), Ranking Republican

Total Defense-Related Contributions to Committee Members

	Total from Cmte-Related Contribs	Pct of Member's Lg Contribs
Daniel R. Coats (R-Ind)	$175,998	6%
John Glenn (D-Ohio)	$151,572	6%
Richard C. Shelby (D-Ala)	$142,175	6%
John McCain (R-Ariz)	$138,821	6%
Alan J. Dixon (D-Ill)	$93,312	7%
Tim Wirth (D-Colo)	$48,214	5%
Trent Lott (R-Miss)	$20,750	6%
Robert C. Byrd (D-WVa)	$11,500	8%
Connie Mack (R-Fla)	$8,000	1%
Malcolm Wallop (R-Wyo)	$6,000	11%
John W. Warner (R-Va)	$2,850	58%
William S. Cohen (R-Maine)	$2,000	4%
Robert C. Smith (R-NH)	$1,250	26%
Strom Thurmond (R-SC)	$1,000	31%
Sam Nunn (D-Ga)	$695	0%
Jim Exon (D-Neb)	$426	4%

	Top 20 Defense-Related Contributors to Committee Members in 1991-92	
1	Martin Marietta Corp	$43,750
2	General Motors*	$35,500
3	Northrop Corp	$29,300
4	Rockwell International	$29,050
5	United Technologies	$27,400
6	Loral Corp	$27,000
7	General Dynamics	$26,101
8	Allied-Signal	$25,750
9	McDonnell Douglas*	$25,500
10	Boeing Co	$23,500
11	Grumman Corp	$22,800
12	Lockheed Corp	$22,750
13	General Electric	$20,500
14	GTE Corp	$20,000
15	Litton Industries	$19,000
16	BDM International	$18,300
17	Textron Inc	$18,000
18	FMC Corp	$17,500
19	AT&T	$14,500
20	Gencorp Inc	$14,100

* Contributions came from more than one affiliate or subsidiary.

Members in **bold italics** ran for reelection in 1992

Summary

Defense aerospace and electronics contractors were the biggest defense-related contributors to members of the Senate Armed Services Committee, but the chart at right reveals that overall the defense industry was not one of the top sources of campaign cash for committee members. This is due partly to the fact that senators routinely sit on three or four major committees, and as many as a dozen subcommittees. That tends to broaden the spectrum of interests that contribute to their campaigns.

The defense industry also gives much less to Congress as a whole than any other business sector. The $8.3 million that defense contractors gave in 1991-92 compares with $44 million from lawyers and lobbyists, for example, $24 million from agriculture interests, and more than $71 million from the finance/insurance/real estate sector.

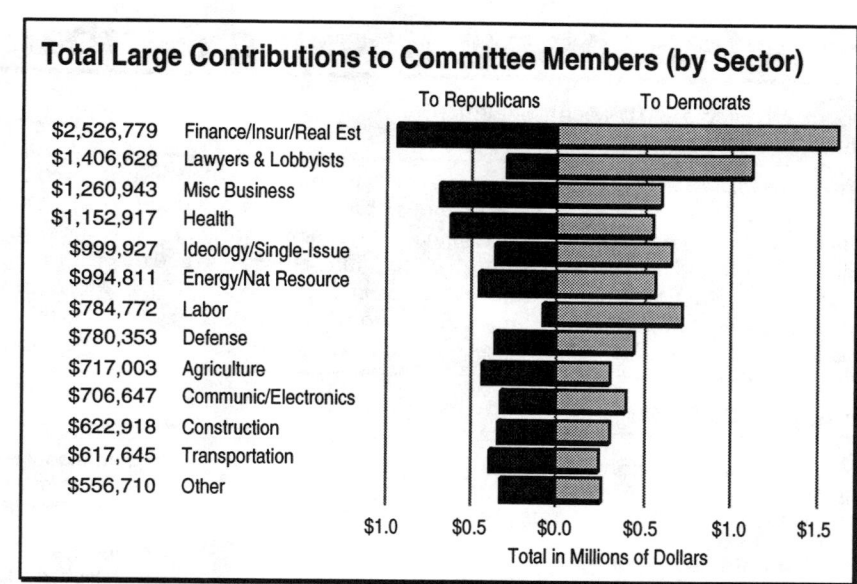

Total Large Contributions to Committee Members (by Sector)

		To Republicans	To Democrats
$2,526,779	Finance/Insur/Real Est		
$1,406,628	Lawyers & Lobbyists		
$1,260,943	Misc Business		
$1,152,917	Health		
$999,927	Ideology/Single-Issue		
$994,811	Energy/Nat Resource		
$784,772	Labor		
$780,353	Defense		
$717,003	Agriculture		
$706,647	Communic/Electronics		
$622,918	Construction		
$617,645	Transportation		
$556,710	Other		

Total in Millions of Dollars

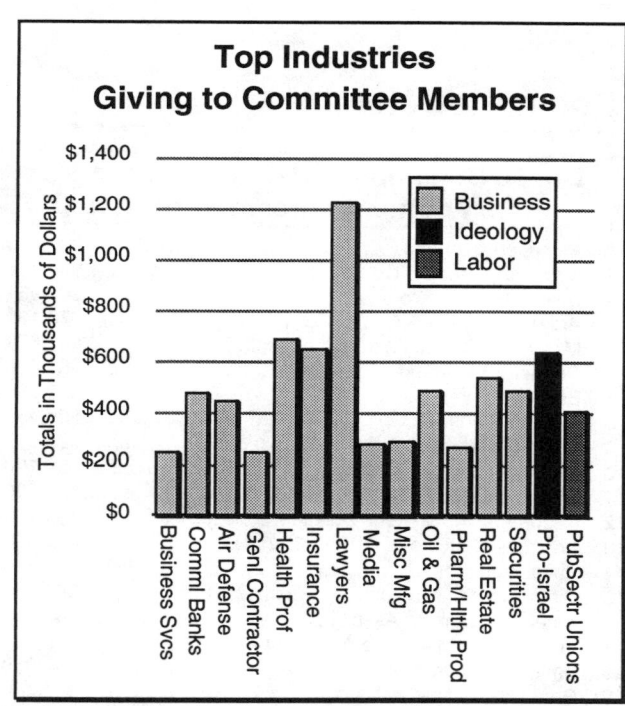

Top Industries Giving to Committee Members

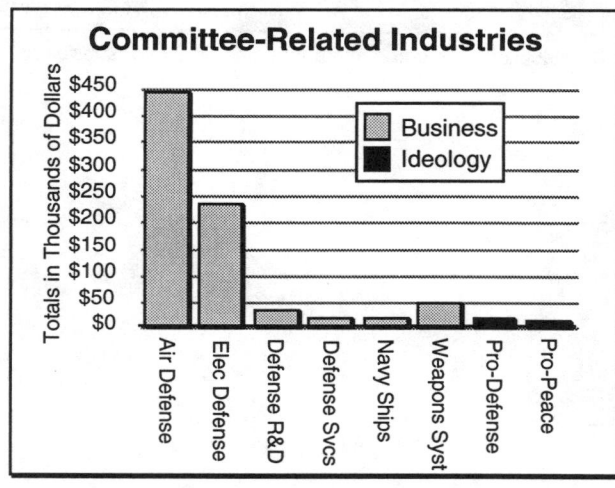

Committee-Related Industries

Leading Industries
Giving to Committee Members

Business

Business Services	$234,221
Commercial Banks	$465,963
Defense Aerospace	$438,147
General Contractors	$237,911
Health Professionals	$678,861
Insurance	$639,372
Lawyers/Law Firms	$1,216,367
Media/Entertainment	$271,212
Misc Manufacturing & Distributing	$275,017
Oil & Gas	$480,425
Pharmaceuticals/Health Products	$254,662
Real Estate	$525,084
Securities & Investment	$477,011

Ideological/Single-Issue

Pro-Israel	$625,228

Labor

Public Sector Unions	$393,801

Leading Industries
Giving to Committee Members

Business

Defense Aerospace	$438,147
Defense Electronics	$230,520
Defense R&D	$32,500
Defense Services	$15,294
Defense Shipbuilders	$16,500
Weapons Systems	$47,392

Ideological/Single-Issue

Pro-Defense	$15,569
Pro-Peace	$8,641

Senate Banking, Housing & Urban Affairs Committee

Donald W. Riegle Jr. (D-Mich), Chairman
Jake Garn (R-Utah), Ranking Republican

Party Ratio: 12 Democrats
9 Republicans

Jurisdiction: (1) Banks, banking and financial institutions; (2) Financial aid to commerce and industry; (3) Deposit insurance; (4) Public and private housing (including veterans' housing); (5) Federal monetary policy (including Federal Reserve System); (6) Money and credit, including currency and coinage; (7) Issuance and redemption of notes; (8) Control of prices of commodities, rents and services; (9) Urban development and urban mass transit; (10) Economic stabilization and defense production; (11) Export controls; (12) Export and foreign trade promotion; (13) Nursing home construction; (14) Renegotiation of Government contracts. In addition, the committee is mandated to study and review matters relating to international economic policy as it affects U.S. monetary affairs, credit, and financial institutions, economic growth, urban affairs and credit and to report on these matters periodically.

Subcommittees

Consumer and Regulatory Affairs
Alan J. Dixon (D-Ill), Chairman
Christopher S. Bond (R-Mo), Ranking Republican

Housing and Urban Affairs
Alan Cranston (D-Calif), Chairman
Alfonse M. D'Amato (R-NY), Ranking Republican

International Finance and Monetary Policy
Paul S. Sarbanes (D-Md), Chairman
Connie Mack (R-Fla), Ranking Republican

Securities
Christopher J. Dodd (D-Conn), Chairman
Phil Gramm (R-Texas), Ranking Republican

Total Committee-Related Contributions to Committee Members

	Total from Cmte-Related Contribs	Pct of Member's Lg Contribs
Alfonse M. D'Amato (R-NY)	$1,143,033	25%
Christopher J. Dodd (D-Conn)	$967,075	31%
Arlen Specter (R-Pa)	$844,347	16%
Christopher S. Bond (R-Mo)	$683,648	21%
Richard C. Shelby (D-Ala)	$453,828	18%
Bob Graham (D-Fla)	$432,157	17%
Alan J. Dixon (D-Ill)	$385,379	28%
Terry Sanford (D-NC)	$378,974	21%
Phil Gramm (R-Texas)	$344,374	18%
Tim Wirth (D-Colo)	$260,446	24%
John Kerry (D-Mass)	$130,524	27%
Connie Mack (R-Fla)	$125,703	17%
Jim Sasser (D-Tenn)	$47,806	31%
Richard H. Bryan (D-Nev)	$33,900	12%
Donald W. Riegle Jr. (D-Mich)	$27,000	15%
William V. Roth Jr. (R-Del)	$9,500	34%
Pete V. Domenici (R-NM)	$7,300	41%
Paul S. Sarbanes (D-Md)	$750	4%
Nancy Landon Kassebaum (R-Kan)	-$750	7%
Alan Cranston (D-Calif)	-$48,000	18%

Top 20 Commitee-Related Contributors to Committee Members in 1991-92

1	American Express*	$88,725
2	Goldman, Sachs & Co	$84,766
3	Bear, Stearns & Co	$80,951
4	Arthur Andersen & Co	$70,199
5	Merrill Lynch	$69,679
6	Coopers & Lybrand	$63,840
7	Ernst & Young	$60,396
8	Morgan Stanley & Co	$58,450
9	Equitable Life*	$56,575
10	National Assn of Realtors	$56,100
11	National Assn of Life Underwriters	$56,000
12	National Assn of Home Builders	$55,250
13	American Institute of CPA's	$51,000
14	Price Waterhouse	$46,775
15	Cigna Corp	$44,950
16	American Bankers Assn	$44,000
17	Independent Insurance Agents of America	$42,999
18	American Council of Life Insurance	$42,069
19	Credit Union National Assn*	$41,500
20	Smith Barney	$41,256

* Contributions came from more than one affiliate or subsidiary.

Members in **bold italics** ran for reelection in 1992

Summary

The banking industry, a heavily regulated sector of American business, has become much more diversified in recent years, offering an ever-widening array of financial services. This diversification has come about as Congress (and the banking committees in particular) have gradually lifted many restrictions governing the industry. But banks are anxious for considerably more freedom — the ability to branch into stock brokerage services, for example — and the Senate Banking Committee is one of the central battlegrounds for the ongoing debate.

The issue of bank deregulation, of course, concerns not only banks but also their competitors — particularly major insurance companies who have become increasingly active in the securities field themselves. And, like many other committees in the Senate, contributions from lawyers and lobbyists (representing either their own interests or those of their clients) were substantial.

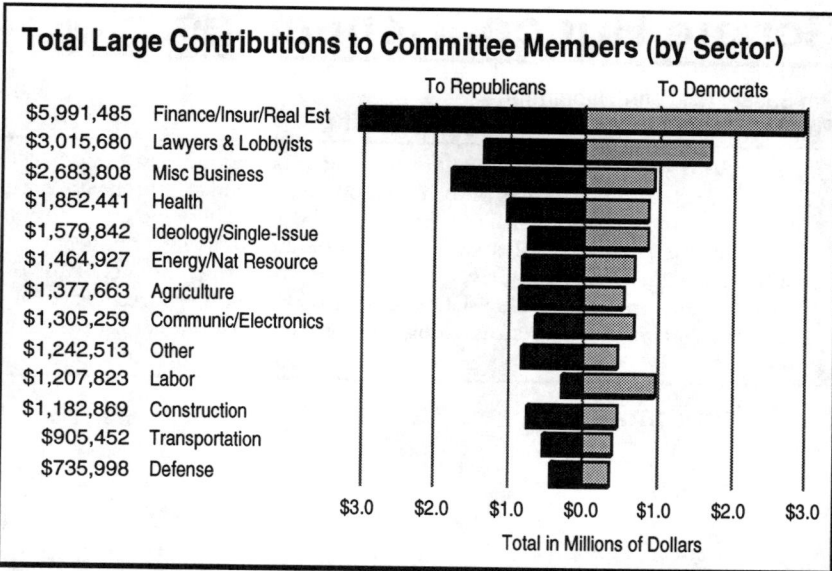

Total Large Contributions to Committee Members (by Sector)

$5,991,485	Finance/Insur/Real Est
$3,015,680	Lawyers & Lobbyists
$2,683,808	Misc Business
$1,852,441	Health
$1,579,842	Ideology/Single-Issue
$1,464,927	Energy/Nat Resource
$1,377,663	Agriculture
$1,305,259	Communic/Electronics
$1,242,513	Other
$1,207,823	Labor
$1,182,869	Construction
$905,452	Transportation
$735,998	Defense

Total in Millions of Dollars

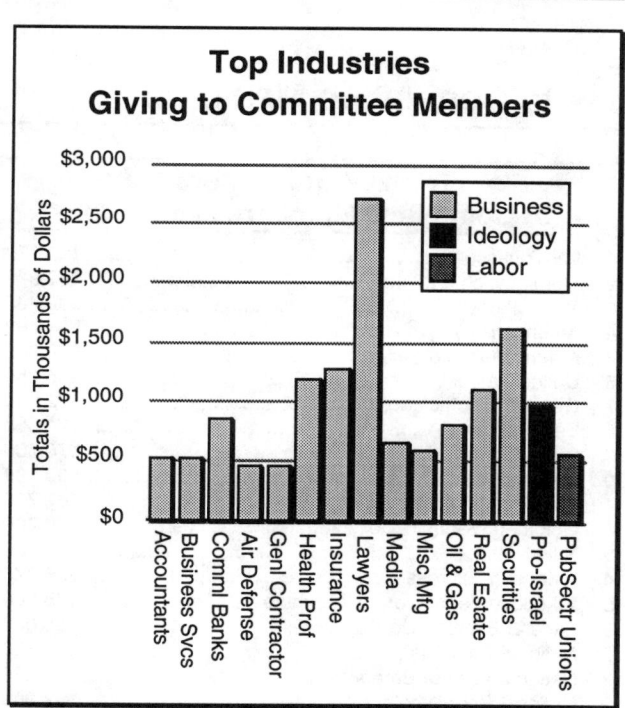

Top Industries Giving to Committee Members

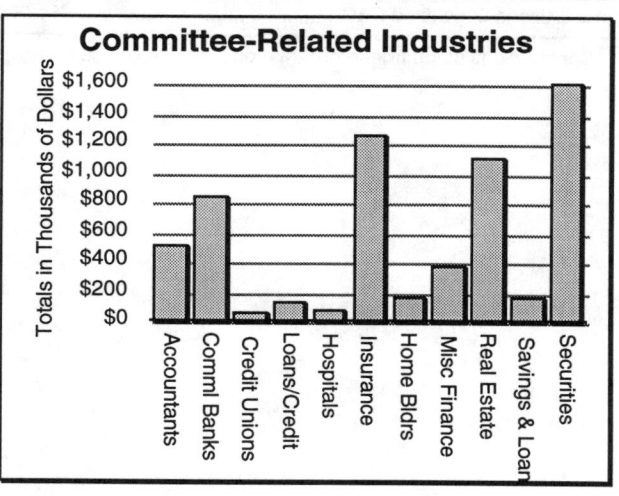

Committee-Related Industries

Leading Industries Giving to Committee Members

Business

Accountants	$505,919
Business Services	$505,605
Commercial Banks	$833,476
Defense Aerospace	$452,499
General Contractors	$451,194
Health Professionals	$1,166,535
Insurance	$1,255,163
Lawyers/Law Firms	$2,700,544
Media/Entertainment	$628,115
Misc Manufacturing & Distributing	$567,322
Oil & Gas	$779,616
Real Estate	$1,095,443
Securities & Investment	$1,590,906

Ideological/Single-Issue

Pro-Israel	$961,088

Labor

Public Sector Unions	$555,353

Leading Committee-Related Industries Giving to Committee Members

Business

Accountants	$505,919
Commercial Banks	$833,476
Credit Unions	$50,000
Finance/Credit Companies	$131,371
Hospitals/Nursing Homes	$79,070
Insurance	$1,255,163
Home Builders	$156,439
Misc Finance	$375,180
Real Estate	$1,095,443
Savings & Loans	$154,027
Securities & Investment	$1,590,906

Senate Budget Committee

Jim Sasser (D-Tenn), Chairman
Pete V. Domenici (R-NM), Ranking Republican

Party Ratio: 12 Democrats
9 Republicans

Jurisdiction: (1) To report the matters needing to be reported by it under Titles III and IV of the Congressional Budget Act of 1974; (2) To make continuing studies of the effect on budget outlays of relevant existing and proposed legislation and to report the results of such studies to the Senate on a recurring basis; (3) To request and evaluate continuing studies of tax expenditures, to devise methods of coordinating tax expenditures, policies and programs with direct budget outlays, and to report the results of such studies to the Senate on a recurring basis; (4) To review, on a continuing basis, the conduct by the Congressional Budget Office of its functions and duties; (5) To consider impoundment legislation required to be jointly referred to it, the Appropriations Committee, and other Senate Committees . . . and (6) To consider matters affecting the Congressional Budget process required to be referred to it and the Governmental Affairs Committee.

No Subcommittees

Total PAC and Large Individual Contributions to Committee Members

Bob Kasten (R-Wis)	$4,009,220
Wyche Fowler Jr. (D-Ga)	$3,516,212
Christopher S. Bond (R-Mo)	$3,232,383
Christopher J. Dodd (D-Conn)	$3,167,767
Don Nickles (R-Okla)	$2,591,195
Ernest F. Hollings (D-SC)	$2,318,965
Phil Gramm (R-Texas)	$1,964,503
Terry Sanford (D-NC)	$1,803,161
Charles E. Grassley (R-Iowa)	$1,593,319
Kent Conrad (D-ND)	$1,238,407
Frank R. Lautenberg (D-NJ)	$1,129,924
Tim Wirth (D-Colo)	$1,067,928
Trent Lott (R-Miss)	$372,060
Steve Symms (R-Idaho)	$188,078
Donald W. Riegle Jr. (D-Mich)	$180,405
Jim Sasser (D-Tenn)	$152,231
Paul Simon (D-Ill)	$59,392
J. Bennett Johnston (D-La)	$43,950
Pete V. Domenici (R-NM)	$17,700
Jim Exon (D-Neb)	$10,176
Hank Brown (R-Colo)	-$1,813

Top 20 Contributors to Committee Members in 1991-92

1	US Tobacco*	$102,770
2	Merrill Lynch*	$99,919
3	Time Warner*	$92,450
4	American Bankers Assn*	$84,700
5	American Dental Assn	$76,000
6	United Parcel Service	$75,050
7	General Electric*	$72,950
8	BellSouth Corp*	$71,669
9	Philip Morris*	$70,530
10	National Assn of Life Underwriters	$69,500
11	American Institute of CPA's	$67,750
12	Goldman, Sachs & Co	$66,700
13	RJR Nabisco*	$66,500
14	American Express*	$66,375
15	American Federation of Teachers	$65,000
16	Federal Express Corp	$65,000
17	National Rifle Assn	$64,850
18	National Assn of Broadcasters	$63,336
19	National Beer Wholesalers Assn	$62,200
20	Citizens Organized PAC	$61,000

* Contributions came from more than one affiliate or subsidiary.

Members in **bold italics** ran for reelection in 1992

Summary

Perhaps no other document in the Western World is so important to so many people, yet understood by so few, as the federal government's annual budget. Weighty, befuddling, sometimes self-contradictory, and inevitably the subject of political wrangling and intense negotiation between Congress and the administration, the budget is the blueprint for federal spending and programs for the coming fiscal year. This is the committee charged with shaping that budget into something both sides can live with.

In recent years the budget deficit has been an ever-growing preoccupation of this committee. Finding ways to reduce it — at least on paper — has been a sometimes all-consuming task. Since federal spending — and the deficit in particular — affects the overall American economy, many industries have a more than casual interest in the committee's work. Not surprisingly, the financial sector was the biggest overall contributor to committee members.

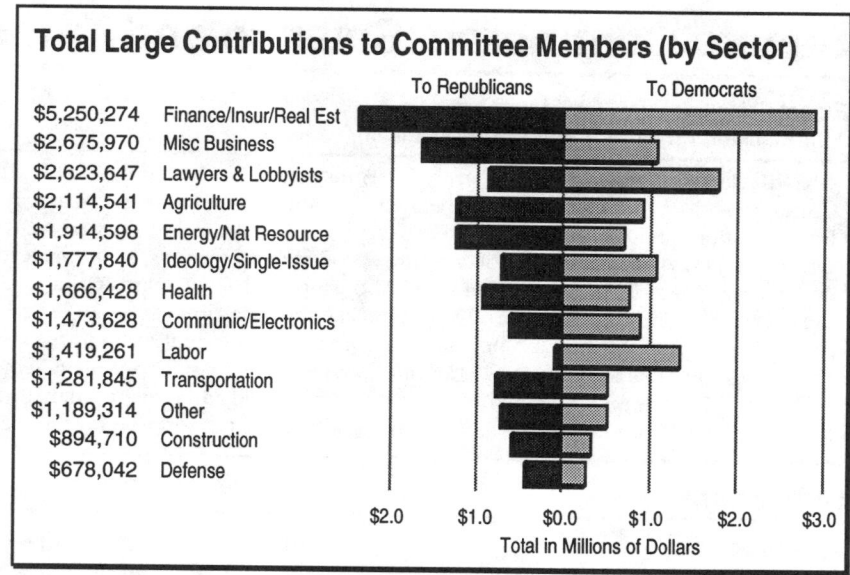

Total Large Contributions to Committee Members (by Sector)

$5,250,274	Finance/Insur/Real Est
$2,675,970	Misc Business
$2,623,647	Lawyers & Lobbyists
$2,114,541	Agriculture
$1,914,598	Energy/Nat Resource
$1,777,840	Ideology/Single-Issue
$1,666,428	Health
$1,473,628	Communic/Electronics
$1,419,261	Labor
$1,281,845	Transportation
$1,189,314	Other
$894,710	Construction
$678,042	Defense

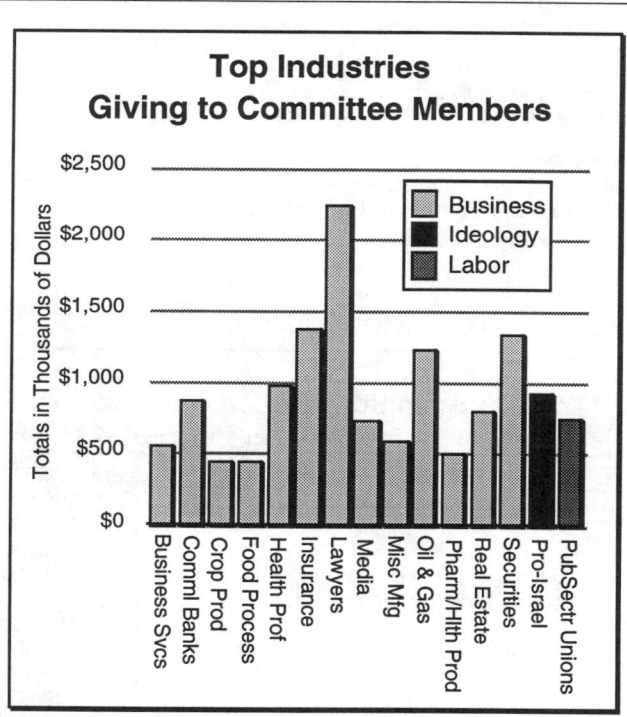

Top Industries Giving to Committee Members

Totals in Thousands of Dollars

Business
Ideology
Labor

Business Svcs, Comml Banks, Crop Prod, Food Process, Health Prof, Insurance, Lawyers, Media, Misc Mfg, Oil & Gas, Pharm/Hlth Prod, Real Estate, Securities, Pro-Israel, PubSector Unions

Leading Industries Giving to Committee Members

Business

Business Services	$520,920
Commercial Banks	$857,697
Crop Production & Basic Processing	$423,700
Food Processing & Sales	$418,920
Health Professionals	$951,550
Insurance	$1,353,599
Lawyers/Law Firms	$2,232,021
Media/Entertainment	$702,259
Misc Manufacturing & Distributing	$572,722
Oil & Gas	$1,205,804
Pharmaceuticals/Health Products	$472,161
Real Estate	$777,678
Securities & Investment	$1,309,114

Ideological/Single-Issue

Pro-Israel	$908,735

Labor

Public Sector Unions	$733,819

Senate Commerce, Science and Transportation Committee

Ernest F. Hollings (D-SC), Chairman
John C. Danforth (R-Mo), Ranking Republican

Party Ratio: 11 Democrats
9 Republicans

Jurisdiction: (1) Interstate commerce; (2) Transportation; (3) Regulation of interstate common carriers, including railroads, buses, trucks, vessels, pipelines and civil aviation; (4) Merchant marine and navigation; (5) Marine and ocean navigation, safety, and transportation, including navigational aspects of deepwater ports; (6) Coast Guard; (7) Inland waterways, except construction; (8) Communications; (9) Regulation of consumer products and services, including testing related to toxic substances, other than pesticides, and except for credit, financial services and housing; (10) The Panama Canal and interoceanic canals generally, except as referred to the Committee on Armed Services; (11) Standards and measurement; (12) Highway safety; (13) Science, engineering, and technology research and development and policy; (14) Nonmilitary aeronautical and space sciences; (15) Transportation and commerce aspects of Outer Continental Shelf lands; (16) Marine fisheries; (17) Coastal Zone Management; (18) Oceans, weather and atmospheric activities; (19) Sports. In addition, the committee is mandated to study and review all matters relating to science and technology, oceans policy, transportation, communications and consumer affairs, and to report on these matters periodically.

Subcommittees

Aviation
Wendell H. Ford (D-Ky), Chairman
John McCain (R-Ariz), Ranking Republican

Communications
Daniel K. Inouye (D-Hawaii), Chairman
Bob Packwood (R-Ore), Ranking Republican

Consumer
Richard H. Bryan (D-Nev), Chairman
Slade Gorton (R-Wash), Ranking Republican

Foreign Commerce and Tourism
John D. Rockefeller IV (D-WVa), Chairman
Conrad Burns (R-Mont), Ranking Republican

Merchant Marine
John B. Breaux (D-La), Chairman
Trent Lott (R-Miss), Ranking Republican

Science, Technology and Space
Al Gore (D-Tenn), Chairman
Larry Pressler (R-SD), Ranking Republican

Surface Transportation
Jim Exon (D-Neb), Chairman
Bob Kasten (R-Wis), Ranking Republican

National Ocean Policy Study
Ernest F. Hollings (D-SC), Chairman
Ted Stevens (R-Alaska), Ranking Republican

Total Committee-Related Contributions to Committee Members

	Total from Cmte-Related Contribs	Pct of Member's Lg Contribs
Bob Packwood (R-Ore)	$922,144	28%
Ernest F. Hollings (D-SC)	$917,053	40%
John B. Breaux (D-La)	$776,464	35%
Wendell H. Ford (D-Ky)	$648,886	33%
Bob Kasten (R-Wis)	$634,030	16%
Daniel K. Inouye (D-Hawaii)	$487,600	20%
John McCain (R-Ariz)	$439,106	20%
Lloyd Bentsen (D-Tex)	$265,409	34%
John Kerry (D-Mass)	$145,573	30%
Trent Lott (R-Miss)	$127,700	34%
Conrad Burns (R-Mont)	$102,868	40%
Slade Gorton (R-Wash)	$88,448	32%
Richard H. Bryan (D-Nev)	$51,890	18%
Larry Pressler (R-SD)	$31,000	29%
John D. Rockefeller IV (D-WVa)	$20,000	10%
John C. Danforth (R-Mo)	$17,500	55%
Charles S. Robb (D-Va)	$7,100	54%
Jim Exon (D-Neb)	$5,750	57%
Ted Stevens (R-Alaska)	$5,250	65%
Al Gore (D-Tenn)	$500	5%

Top 20 Committee-Related Contributors to Committee Members in 1991-92

1	National Assn of Broadcasters	$82,386
2	Marine Engineers Union*	$65,500
3	CSX Corp*	$55,500
4	United Parcel Service	$55,050
5	National Assn of Life Underwriters	$54,500
6	National Auto Dealers Assn	$54,000
7	General Electric*	$51,900
8	Federal Express Corp	$51,000
9	Time Warner*	$50,500
10	GTE Corp*	$49,800
11	American Trucking Assns	$49,243
12	Union Pacific Corp	$48,951
13	Aircraft Owners & Pilots Assn	$46,000
14	American Family Corp	$45,500
15	National Cable Television Assn	$44,250
16	Auto Dealers & Drivers for Free Trade	$44,000
17	Air Line Pilots Assn	$42,500
18	American Council of Life Insurance	$40,783
19	BellSouth Corp*	$39,850
20	Americans for Free International Trade	$39,000

* Contributions came from more than one affiliate or subsidiary.

Members in ***bold italics*** ran for reelection in 1992

Summary

Under the wide umbrella of the Senate Commerce Committee's jurisdiction falls a variety of industries and interests ranging from cable TV operators to telephone utilities, railroads to barge lines to interstate truckers. Disputes between competing segments within those industries ensure a perennially heavy schedule on the committee's agenda. This is also the committee that wrestles with the issue of product liability laws, pitting lawyers on the one side against manufacturers on the other — with a host of other groups falling somewhere in between.

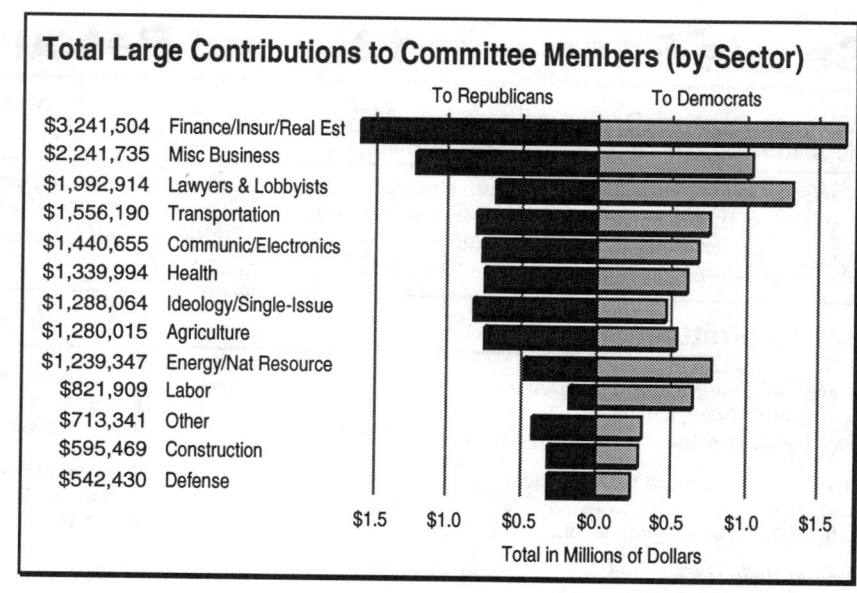

Total Large Contributions to Committee Members (by Sector)

	To Republicans	To Democrats
$3,241,504	Finance/Insur/Real Est	
$2,241,735	Misc Business	
$1,992,914	Lawyers & Lobbyists	
$1,556,190	Transportation	
$1,440,655	Communic/Electronics	
$1,339,994	Health	
$1,288,064	Ideology/Single-Issue	
$1,280,015	Agriculture	
$1,239,347	Energy/Nat Resource	
$821,909	Labor	
$713,341	Other	
$595,469	Construction	
$542,430	Defense	

Total in Millions of Dollars

Top Industries Giving to Committee Members

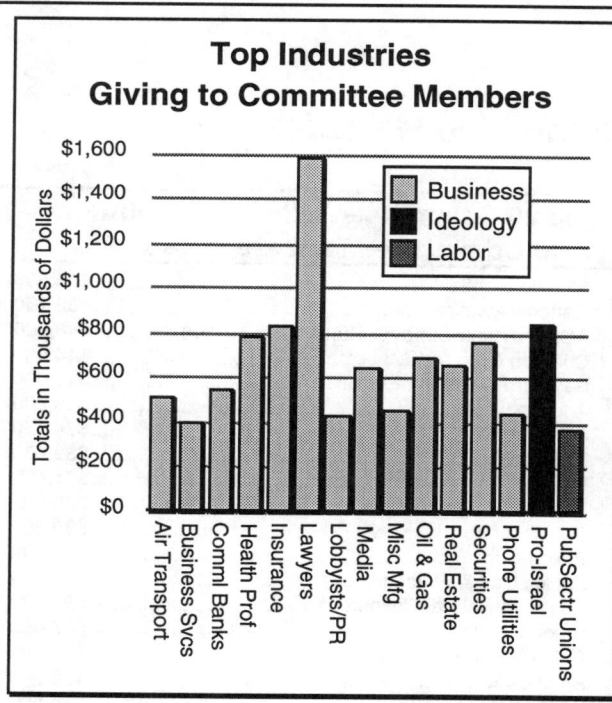

Committee-Related Industries

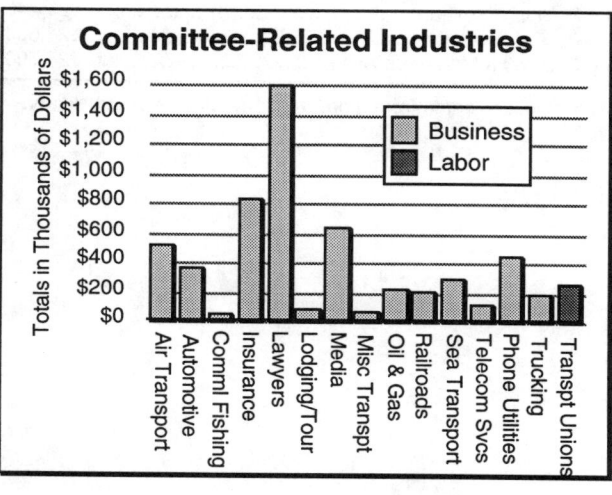

Leading Industries Giving to Committee Members

Business

Air Transport	$500,362
Business Services	$388,197
Commercial Banks	$531,428
Health Professionals	$771,020
Insurance	$822,470
Lawyers/Law Firms	$1,575,445
Lobbyists/PR	$417,469
Media/Entertainment	$634,986
Misc Manufacturing & Distributing	$444,621
Oil & Gas	$683,819
Real Estate	$643,205
Securities & Investment	$749,909
Telephone Utilities	$431,616

Ideological/Single-Issue

Pro-Israel	$829,757

Labor

Public Sector Unions	$364,373

Leading Committee-Related Industries Giving to Committee Members

Business

Air Transport	$500,362
Automotive	$347,774
Commercial Fishing	$38,783
Insurance	$822,470
Lawyers/Law Firms	$1,575,445
Lodging/Tourism	$75,850
Media/Entertainment	$634,986
Misc Transport	$48,800
Oil & Gas	$210,153
Railroads	$187,227
Sea Transport	$274,518
Telecom Services & Equipment	$109,103
Telephone Utilities	$431,616
Trucking	$178,309

Labor

Transportation Unions	$253,250

Senate Energy and Natural Resources Committee

J. Bennett Johnston (D-La), Chairman
Malcolm Wallop (R-Wyo), Ranking Republican

Party Ratio: 11 Democrats
9 Republicans

> **Jurisdiction:** Oversight and legislative responsibilities, including (1) Strategic petroleum reserves; (2) Intergovernmental Relations; (3) Outer continental shelf leasing; (4) Investigation and oversight; (5) International energy affairs; (6) Global climate change; (7) Natural gas pricing and regulation; (8) Utility policy; (9) Nuclear waste and insurance programs; (10) Territorial affairs, including commonwealths; (11) Free Associated States; and (12) Antarctica.

Subcommittees

Energy Regulation and Conservation
Tim Wirth (D-Colo), Chairman
Don Nickles (R-Okla), Ranking Republican

Energy Research and Development
Wendell H. Ford (D-Ky), Chairman
Pete V. Domenici (R-NM), Ranking Republican

Mineral Resources Development and Production
Jeff Bingaman (D-NM), Chairman
Larry E. Craig (R-Idaho), Ranking Republican

Public Lands, National Parks and Forests
Dale Bumpers (D-Ark), Chairman
Frank H. Murkowski (R-Alaska), Ranking Republican

Water and Power
Bill Bradley (D-NJ), Chairman
Conrad Burns (R-Mont), Ranking Republican

Total Committee-Related Contributions to Committee Members

	Total from Cmte-Related Contribs	Pct of Member's Lg Contribs
Don Nickles (R-Okla)	$572,766	22%
John F. Seymour (R-Calif)	$271,625	5%
Wendell H. Ford (D-Ky)	$259,950	13%
Richard C. Shelby (D-Ala)	$241,889	10%
Frank H. Murkowski (R-Alaska)	$204,227	15%
Kent Conrad (D-ND)	$185,172	15%
Wyche Fowler Jr. (D-Ga)	$170,534	5%
Dale Bumpers (D-Ark)	$170,366	10%
Tim Wirth (D-Colo)	$92,203	9%
Conrad Burns (R-Mont)	$32,850	13%
Malcolm Wallop (R-Wyo)	$19,965	38%
Daniel K. Akaka (D-Hawaii)	$13,650	3%
Jeff Bingaman (D-NM)	$8,818	5%
Mark O. Hatfield (R-Ore)	$8,500	9%
J. Bennett Johnston (D-La)	$7,500	17%
Paul Wellstone (D-Minn)	$6,100	4%
Larry E. Craig (R-Idaho)	$1,500	6%
Pete V. Domenici (R-NM)	$500	3%
Bill Bradley (D-NJ)	-$150	0%

Top 20 Committee-Related Contributors to Committee Members in 1991-92

1	Atlantic Richfield	$55,633
2	General Atomics	$52,750
3	ACRE (Action Cmte for Rural Electrification)*	$48,500
4	Chevron Corp	$44,000
5	Southern California Edison	$42,000
6	Arkla Inc	$38,200
7	Southern Co*	$34,250
8	Mobil Oil	$32,000
9	National Coal Assn	$31,499
10	Waste Management Inc	$30,650
11	Coastal Corp	$30,000
12	Exxon Corp	$28,700
13	Pacific Gas & Electric	$28,500
14	Southern Natural Resources	$27,300
15	Union Pacific Corp	$27,000
16	Columbia Gas System*	$25,600
17	Amoco Corp	$25,500
18	Halliburton Co*	$25,500
19	Phillips Petroleum	$25,446
20	Pacific Enterprises	$24,500
20	Petroleum Marketers Assn	$24,500

* Contributions came from more than one affiliate or subsidiary.

Members in **bold italics** ran for reelection in 1992

Summary

Oil & gas policies, the interstate transportation of natural gas, the ever-deepening problem of nuclear waste disposal and a host of other energy-related issues are the primary concern of the Senate Energy and Natural Resources Committee. Its domain, and the scope of its jurisdiction, range from oilfields on the North Slope of Alaska to the ice fields of Antarctica and the oil and mineral-rich deposits beneath the seabeds of the outer continental shelf.

As the world's largest consumer of energy, and one of its largest producers, America's economic health has long been tied to the fortunes of the oil & gas industry — though the interests of the nation and the industry do not always coincide. Balancing those interests, and setting the nation's energy policy, is the charge of this committee.

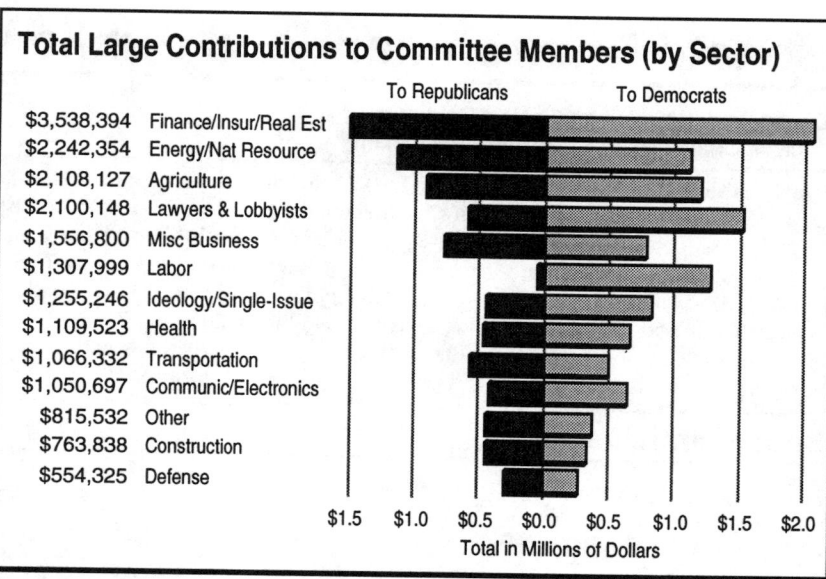

Total Large Contributions to Committee Members (by Sector)

$3,538,394	Finance/Insur/Real Est
$2,242,354	Energy/Nat Resource
$2,108,127	Agriculture
$2,100,148	Lawyers & Lobbyists
$1,556,800	Misc Business
$1,307,999	Labor
$1,255,246	Ideology/Single-Issue
$1,109,523	Health
$1,066,332	Transportation
$1,050,697	Communic/Electronics
$815,532	Other
$763,838	Construction
$554,325	Defense

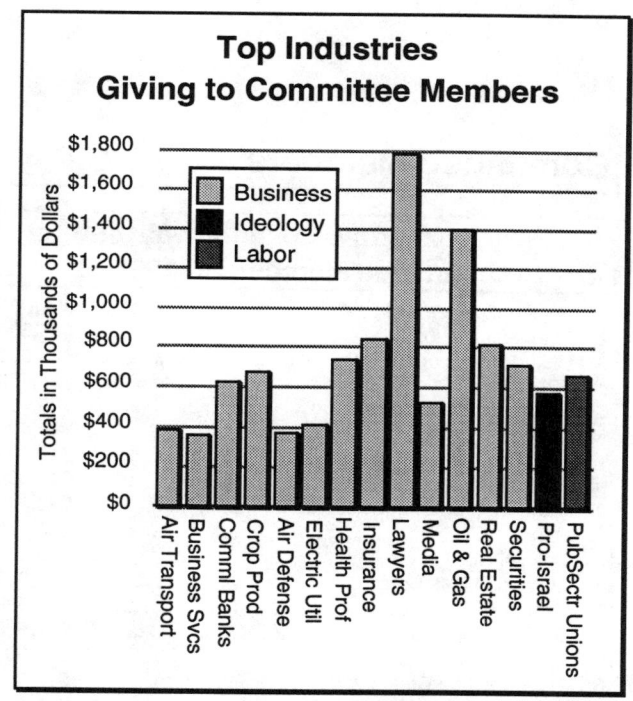

Top Industries Giving to Committee Members

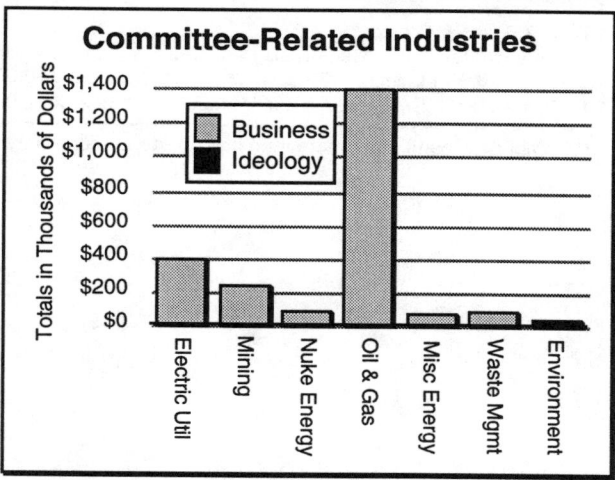

Committee-Related Industries

Leading Industries Giving to Committee Members

Business

Air Transport	$361,979
Business Services	$347,726
Commercial Banks	$614,187
Crop Production & Basic Processing	$665,323
Defense Aerospace	$354,775
Electric Utilities	$390,318
Health Professionals	$728,162
Insurance	$827,114
Lawyers/Law Firms	$1,766,978
Media/Entertainment	$511,881
Oil & Gas	$1,380,334
Real Estate	$806,213
Securities & Investment	$705,082

Ideological/Single-Issue

Pro-Israel	$566,321

Labor

Public Sector Unions	$649,561

Leading Committee-Related Industries Giving to Committee Members

Business

Electric Utilities	$390,318
Mining	$227,794
Nuclear Energy	$72,750
Oil & Gas	$1,380,334
Misc Energy	$72,225
Waste Management	$81,400

Ideological/Single-Issue

Environmental Issues	$37,211

Senate Environment and Public Works Committee

Daniel Patrick Moynihan (D-NY), Chairman
John H. Chafee (R-RI), Ranking Republican

Party Ratio: 10 Democrats
7 Republicans

Jurisdiction: (1) Environmental policy; (2) Environmental research and development; (3) Ocean dumping; (4) Fisheries and wildlife; (5) Environmental aspects of Outer Continental Shelf lands; (6) Solid waste disposal and recycling; (7) Environmental effects of toxic substances, other than pesticides; (8) Water resources; (9) Flood control and improvements of rivers and harbors, including environmental aspects of deepwater ports; (10) Public works, bridges and dams; (11) Water pollution; (12) Air pollution; (13) Noise pollution; (14) Nonmilitary environmental regulation and control of nuclear energy; (15) Regional economic development; (16) Construction and maintenance of highways; (17) Public buildings and improved grounds of the United States generally, including Federal buildings in the District of Columbia. In addition, the committee is mandated to study and review matters relating to environmental protection, resource utilization and conservation, and to report on these matters periodically.

Subcommittees

Environmental Protection
Max Baucus (D-Mont), Chairman
John H. Chafee (R-RI), Ranking Republican

Nuclear Regulation
Bob Graham (D-Fla), Chairman
Alan K. Simpson (R-Wyo), Ranking Republican

Superfund, Ocean and Water Protection
Frank Lautenberg (D-NJ), Chairman
Dave Durenberger (R-Minn), Ranking Republican

Toxic Substances, Environmental Oversight, Research and Development
Harry Reid (D-Nev), Chairman
John W. Warner (R-Va), Ranking Republican

Water Resources, Transportation and Infrastructure
Daniel Patrick Moynihan (D-NY), Chairman
Steve Symms (R-Idaho), Ranking Republican

Total Committee-Related Contributions to Committee Members

	Total from Cmte-Related Contribs	Pct of Member's Lg Contribs
Bob Graham (D-Fla)	$286,175	11%
Harry Reid (D-Nev)	$270,594	15%
Harris Wofford (D-Pa)†	$214,048	6%
Frank R. Lautenberg (D-NJ)	$107,374	10%
Daniel Patrick Moynihan (D-NY)	$92,987	16%
Joseph I. Lieberman (D-Conn)	$83,660	9%
Steve Symms (R-Idaho)	$34,250	18%
John H. Chafee (R-RI)	$15,050	12%
Dave Durenberger (R-Minn)	$13,050	5%
Alan K. Simpson (R-Wyo)	$3,000	21%
Robert C. Smith (R-NH)	$1,500	32%
Max Baucus (D-Mont)	$1,000	14%
James M. Jeffords (R-Vt)	$1,000	14%
John W. Warner (R-Va)	$1,000	20%

† Wofford's election was in 1991

Top 20 Committee Related Contributors to Committee Members in 1991-92

1	Marine Engineers Union*	$31,000
2	Teamsters Union	$27,500
3	United Transportation Union	$26,500
4	FPL Group Inc*	$26,250
5	Chambers Development Co	$25,000
6	Seafarers International Union	$18,000
7	Auto Dealers & Drivers for Free Trade	$15,000
8	Waste Management Inc	$14,500
9	Browning-Ferris Industries	$13,640
10	General Electric	$13,400
11	Coastal Corp	$13,000
12	Amerada Hess Corp	$12,000
13	Cyprus Minerals Co	$11,500
14	General Public Utilities	$11,500
15	Yellow Freight System	$11,500
16	ACRE (Action Cmte for Rural Electrification)	$11,000
17	ITEL Corp	$11,000
18	WR Grace & Co	$11,000
19	American Trucking Assns	$10,081
20	Occidental Petroleum	$10,000
20	Sierra Pacific Resources	$10,000

* Contributions came from more than one affiliate or subsidiary.

Members in **bold italics** ran for reelection in 1992

Summary

"Infrastructure" is not a glamorous word or a particularly inspiring political cause, but it is crucial to the health of the nation. The building and maintenance of the nation's highways, waterways and other public facilities is a central concern of this committee — and of many of the industries that supply campaign dollars to committee members.

But there is another side to development, one that often *does* inspire political action — the effect that our modern industrial infrastructure has on the environment of the planet. That too is a major preoccupation of this committee.

The heavy Democratic tilt in contributors to the committee (as seen in the chart at right) is due to the fact that the only three committee members who faced election campaigns in 1991-92 were all Democrats.

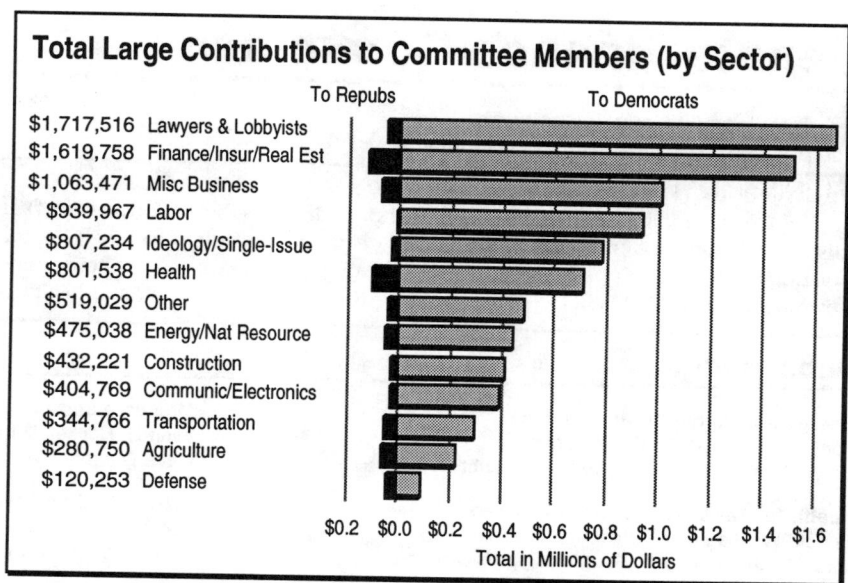

Total Large Contributions to Committee Members (by Sector)

	To Repubs	To Democrats
$1,717,516	Lawyers & Lobbyists	
$1,619,758	Finance/Insur/Real Est	
$1,063,471	Misc Business	
$939,967	Labor	
$807,234	Ideology/Single-Issue	
$801,538	Health	
$519,029	Other	
$475,038	Energy/Nat Resource	
$432,221	Construction	
$404,769	Communic/Electronics	
$344,766	Transportation	
$280,750	Agriculture	
$120,253	Defense	

Total in Millions of Dollars

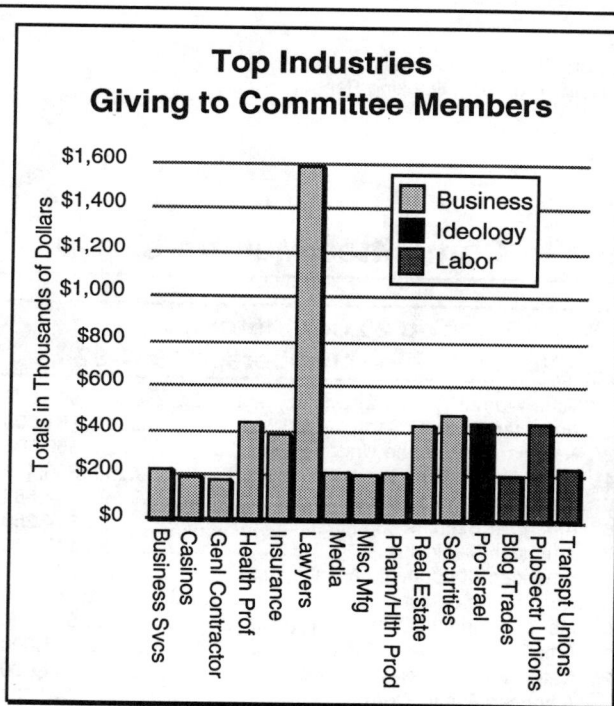

Top Industries Giving to Committee Members

Totals in Thousands of Dollars

Legend: Business, Ideology, Labor

Business Svcs, Casinos, Genl Contractor, Health Prof, Insurance, Lawyers, Media, Misc Mfg, Pharm/Hlth Prod, Real Estate, Securities, Pro-Israel, Bldg Trades, PubSectr Unions, Transpt Unions

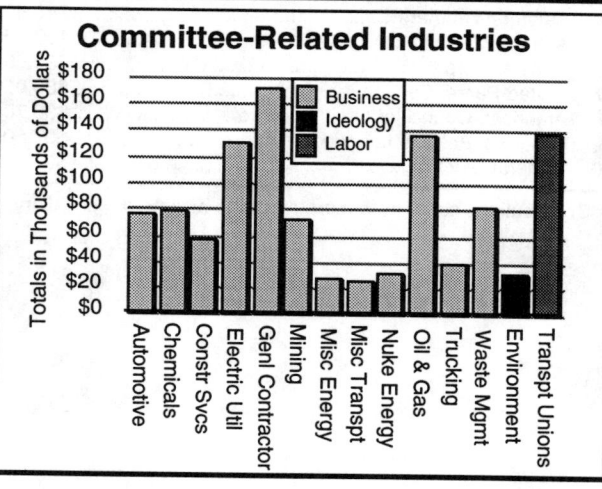

Committee-Related Industries

Totals in Thousands of Dollars

Legend: Business, Ideology, Labor

Automotive, Chemicals, Constr Svcs, Electric Util, Genl Contractor, Mining, Misc Energy, Misc Transport, Nuke Energy, Oil & Gas, Trucking, Waste Mgmt, Environment, Transpt Unions

Leading Industries Giving to Committee Members

Business

Business Services	$218,531
Casinos/Gambling	$175,909
General Contractors	$171,498
Health Professionals	$433,148
Insurance	$367,919
Lawyers/Law Firms	$1,574,065
Media/Entertainment	$199,000
Misc Manufacturing & Distributing	$185,710
Pharmaceuticals/Health Products	$201,750
Real Estate	$422,250
Securities & Investment	$460,158

Ideological/Single-Issue

Pro-Israel	$433,176

Labor

Building Trade Unions	$191,629
Public Sector Unions	$424,399
Transportation Unions	$227,350

Leading Committee-Related Industries Giving to Committee Members

Business

Automotive	$73,750
Chemical & Related Manufacturing	$76,950
Construction Services	$54,773
Electric Utilities	$129,100
General Contractors	$171,498
Mining	$70,650
Misc Energy	$24,912
Misc Transport	$22,750
Nuclear Energy	$28,650
Oil & Gas	$136,386
Trucking	$37,981
Waste Management	$79,840

Ideological/Single-Issue

Environmental Issues	$29,248

Labor

Transportation Unions	$137,100

Senate Finance Committee

Lloyd Bentsen (D-Texas), Chairman
Bob Packwood (R-Ore), Ranking Republican

Party Ratio: 11 Democrats
9 Republicans

Jurisdiction: (1) Except as provided in the Congressional Budget Act of 1974, revenue measures generally; (2) Except as provided in the Congressional Budget Act of 1974, the bonded debt of the United States; (3) The deposit of public moneys; (4) Customs, collection districts and ports of entry and delivery; (5) Reciprocal trade agreements; (6) Transportation of dutiable goods; (7) Revenue measures relating to the insular possessions; (8) Tariffs and import quotas, and matters related thereto; (9) National social security; (10) General revenue sharing; (11) Health programs under the Social Security Act and health programs financed by a specific tax or trust fund.

Subcommittees

Energy and Agricultural Taxation
Tom Daschle (D-SD), Chairman
Steve Symms (R-Idaho), Ranking Republican

Health for Families and the Uninsured
Donald W. Riegle Jr. (D-Mich), Chairman
John H. Chafee (R-RI), Ranking Republican

Deficits, Debt Management and International Debt
Bill Bradley (D-NJ), Chairman
Orrin G. Hatch (R-Utah), Ranking Republican

International Trade
Max Baucus (D-Mont), Chairman
John C. Danforth (R-Mo), Ranking Republican

Medicare and Long-Term Care
John D. Rockefeller IV (D-WVa), Chairman
Dave Durenberger (R-Minn), Ranking Republican

Private Retirement Plans and Oversight of the Internal Revenue Service
David Pryor (D-Ark), Chairman
Charles E. Grassley (R-Iowa), Ranking Republican

Social Security and Family Policy
Daniel Patrick Moynihan (D-NY), Chairman
Bob Dole (R-Kan), Ranking Republican

Taxation
David L. Boren (D-Okla), Chairman
William V. Roth Jr. (R-Del), Ranking Republican

Total PAC and Large Individual Contributions to Committee Members

Bob Packwood (R-Ore) $3,300,513
John B. Breaux (D-La) $2,225,056
Tom Daschle (D-SD) $2,157,690
Bob Dole (R-Kan) $1,949,015
Charles E. Grassley (R-Iowa) $1,593,319
Lloyd Bentsen (D-Tex) $774,065
Daniel Patrick Moynihan (D-NY) $584,201
Orrin G. Hatch (R-Utah) $364,798
Dave Durenberger (R-Minn) $275,339
John D. Rockefeller IV (D-WVa) $191,950
Steve Symms (R-Idaho) $188,078
Donald W. Riegle Jr. (D-Mich) $180,405
John H. Chafee (R-RI) $128,550
David L. Boren (D-Okla) $34,306
John C. Danforth (R-Mo) $31,975
William V. Roth Jr. (R-Del) $28,210
Max Baucus (D-Mont) $7,000
George J. Mitchell (D-Maine) $4,000
Bill Bradley (D-NJ) $1,215

	Top 20 Contributors to Committee Members in 1991-92	
1	Time Warner*	$61,500
2	American Bankers Assn	$51,300
3	National Assn of Life Underwriters	$50,500
4	Union Pacific Corp	$50,449
5	Waste Management Inc	$44,687
6	American Express*	$44,250
7	American Medical Assn*	$43,790
8	American Chiropractic Assn*	$42,747
9	National Rifle Assn	$42,600
10	Metropolitan Life/Century 21*	$42,490
11	American Institute of CPA's	$41,000
12	National Cable Television Assn	$41,000
13	American Family Corp	$40,500
14	Salomon Brothers	$40,500
15	American Health Care Assn	$39,750
16	Coastal Corp	$39,000
17	United Parcel Service	$39,000
18	American Council of Life Insurance	$38,782
19	Laborers' Political League	$37,500
20	General Electric	$37,175

* Contributions came from more than one affiliate or subsidiary.

Members in **bold italics** ran for reelection in 1992

Summary

As the Senate committee charged with debating and defining the nation's tax laws, the Senate Finance Committee is one of the most important panels in Congress to virtually every industry in America. It is also one of the most heavily lobbied committees, particularly when major revisions to the tax code are under consideration.

These days, however, the committee's most notable assignment has to do not with taxes, but with health care. As one of the Senate's lead committees charged with remaking the nation's health insurance system, the committee is at the center of the biggest political firestorm to engulf Capitol Hill in years. Even in 1992, before the election of Bill Clinton brought health care reform firmly onto Congress's front burner, the money from health professionals and insurance firms was on the rise. It will undoubtedly continue to flow generously to committee members as the debate intensifies.

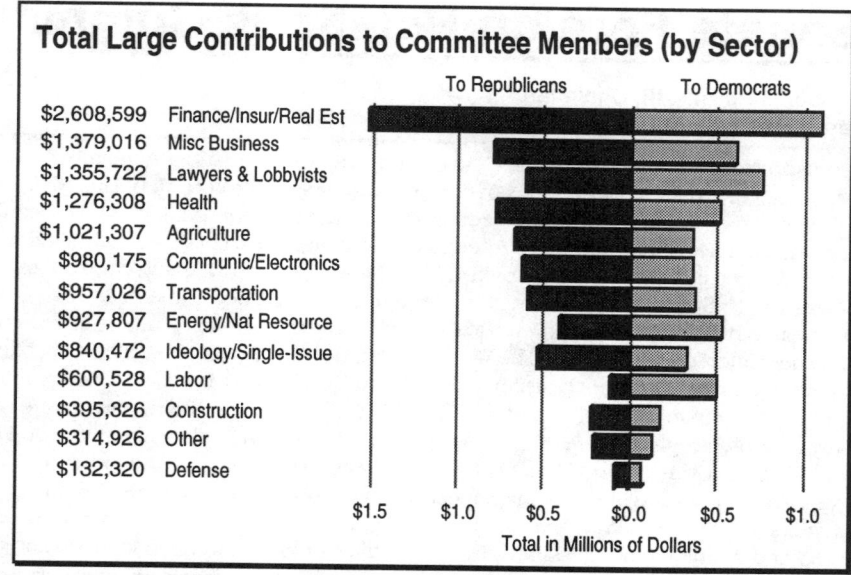

Total Large Contributions to Committee Members (by Sector)

$2,608,599	Finance/Insur/Real Est
$1,379,016	Misc Business
$1,355,722	Lawyers & Lobbyists
$1,276,308	Health
$1,021,307	Agriculture
$980,175	Communic/Electronics
$957,026	Transportation
$927,807	Energy/Nat Resource
$840,472	Ideology/Single-Issue
$600,528	Labor
$395,326	Construction
$314,926	Other
$132,320	Defense

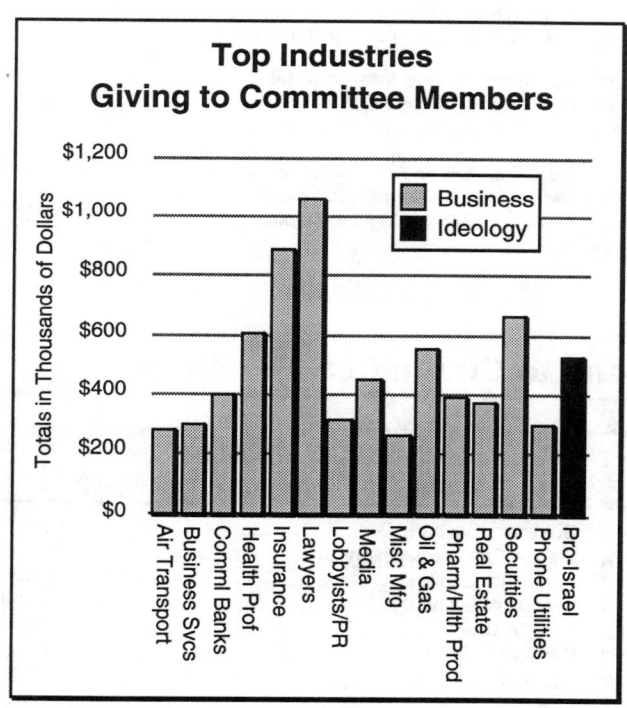

Top Industries Giving to Committee Members

Leading Industries Giving to Committee Members

Business

Air Transport	$268,577
Business Services	$286,203
Commercial Banks	$387,203
Health Professionals	$600,629
Insurance	$877,060
Lawyers/Law Firms	$1,050,623
Lobbyists/PR	$305,099
Media/Entertainment	$438,725
Misc Manufacturing & Distributing	$251,316
Oil & Gas	$542,517
Pharmaceuticals/Health Products	$380,104
Real Estate	$363,291
Securities & Investment	$657,633
Telephone Utilities	$290,275

Ideological/Single-Issue

Pro-Israel	$521,597

Senate Foreign Relations Committee

Claiborne Pell (D-RI), Chairman
Jesse Helms (R-NC), Ranking Republican

Party Ratio: 11 Democrats
8 Republicans

Jurisdiction: (1) Relations of the United States with foreign nations generally; (2) Treaties and executive agreements, except reciprocal trade agreements; (3) Boundaries of the United States; (4) Protection of United States citizens abroad and expatriation; (5) Intervention abroad and declarations of war; (6) Foreign economic, military, technical and humanitarian assistance;(7) United Nations and its affiliated organizations; (8) International conferences and congresses; (9) Diplomatic service; (10) International law as it relates to foreign policy; (11) Oceans and international environmental and scientific affairs as they relate to foreign policy; (12) International activities of the American National Red Cross and the International Committee of the Red Cross; (13) International aspects of nuclear energy, including nuclear transfer policy; (14) Foreign loans; (15) Measures to foster commercial intercourse with foreign nations and to safeguard American business interests abroad; (16) The World Bank group, the regional development banks and other international organizations established primarily for development assistance purposes; (17) The International Monetary Fund and other international organizations established primarily for international monetary purposes (except that, at the request of the Committee on Banking, Housing and Urban Affairs, any proposed legislation relating to such subjects reported by the Committee on Foreign Relations shall be referred to the Committee on Banking, Housing and Urban Affairs); (18) Acquisition of land and buildings for embassies and legations in foreign countries; (19) National security and international aspects of trusteeships of the United States. In addition, the committee is mandated to study and review matters relating to the national security policy, foreign policy, and international economic policy as it relates to foreign policy of the U.S., and matters relating to food, hunger and nutrition in foreign countries, and to report on these matters periodically.

Subcommittees

African Affairs
Paul Simon (D-Ill), Chairman
Nancy Landon Kassebaum (R-Kan), Ranking Republican

East Asian and Pacific Affairs
Alan Cranston (D-Calif), Chairman
Frank H. Murkowski (R-Alaska), Ranking Republican

European Affairs
Joseph R. Biden Jr. (D-Del), Chairman
Larry Pressler (R-SD), Ranking Republican

International Economic Policy, Trade, Oceans and Environment
Paul S. Sarbanes (D-Md), Chairman
Mitch McConnell (R-Ky), Ranking Republican

Near Eastern and South Asian Affairs
Terry Sanford (D-NC), Chairman
James M. Jeffords (R-Vt), Ranking Republican

Terrorism, Narcotics and International Operations
John Kerry (D-Mass), Chairman
Hank Brown (R-Colo), Ranking Republican

Western Hemisphere and Peace Corps Affairs
Christopher J. Dodd (D-Conn), Chairman
Richard G. Lugar (R-Ind), Ranking Republican

Total PAC and Large Individual Contributions to Committee Members

Harris Wofford (D-Pa) †	$3,309,396
Christopher J. Dodd (D-Conn)	$3,167,767
Terry Sanford (D-NC)	$1,803,161
Frank H. Murkowski (R-Alaska)	$1,362,732
Richard G. Lugar (R-Ind)	$607,269
Daniel Patrick Moynihan (D-NY)	$584,201
John Kerry (D-Mass)	$483,997
Jesse Helms (R-NC)	$224,478
Larry Pressler (R-SD)	$105,350
Mitch McConnell (R-Ky)	$75,650
Paul Simon (D-Ill)	$59,392
Paul S. Sarbanes (D-Md)	$17,148
Charles S. Robb (D-Va)	$13,100
James M. Jeffords (R-Vt)	$6,950
Joseph R. Biden Jr. (D-Del)	$4,000
Hank Brown (R-Colo)	-$1,813
Claiborne Pell (D-RI)	-$4,100
Nancy Landon Kassebaum (R-Kan)	-$10,250
Alan Cranston (D-Calif)	-$272,198

† Wofford's election was in 1991

Members in **bold italics** ran for reelection in 1992

Top 20 Contributors to Committee Members in 1991-92

1	Goldman, Sachs & Co	$43,100
2	Marine Engineers Union*	$41,500
3	American Express*	$40,625
4	Laborers Union*	$39,300
5	Time Warner*	$37,500
6	General Electric*	$36,950
7	US Tobacco	$34,700
8	AT&T	$32,693
9	American Fedn of St/Cnty/Munic Employees	$32,500
10	Federal Express Corp	$32,500
11	Mintz, Levin et al	$31,471
12	Greenwich Capital Markets	$30,250
13	American Federation of Teachers	$30,000
14	MacAndrews & Forbes Group	$29,250
15	American Bankers Assn*	$29,000
16	United Auto Workers	$28,000
17	Barrack, Rodos & Bacine	$27,500
18	Chicago Mercantile Exchange	$27,000
19	National Education Assn	$27,000
20	Merrill Lynch	$26,930

* Contributions came from more than one affiliate or subsidiary.

Summary

The Senate Foreign Relations Committee may be the one committee in Congress that is more important to the world at large than to the community of PACs and other high-level contributors here at home. Since foreign nationals and their governments are prohibited from making direct contributions to U.S. candidates, they must find other means to make their voices heard when the committee debates such issues as the level and focus of American foreign aid.

One group of major contributors that is squarely focused on the committee's deliberations, however, is the community of Pro-Israel PACs and their individual supporters. In all, they delivered over $400,000 to committee members in 1991-92. The two biggest recipients during the last election were Harris Wofford, who collected $172,000 from Pro-Israel groups, and Christopher Dodd, who got $150,000.

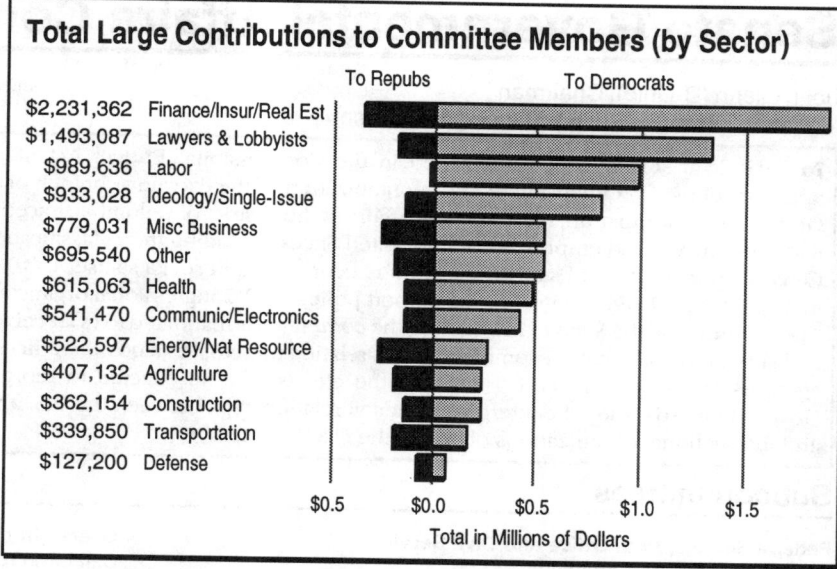

Total Large Contributions to Committee Members (by Sector)

$2,231,362	Finance/Insur/Real Est
$1,493,087	Lawyers & Lobbyists
$989,636	Labor
$933,028	Ideology/Single-Issue
$779,031	Misc Business
$695,540	Other
$615,063	Health
$541,470	Communic/Electronics
$522,597	Energy/Nat Resource
$407,132	Agriculture
$362,154	Construction
$339,850	Transportation
$127,200	Defense

Total in Millions of Dollars

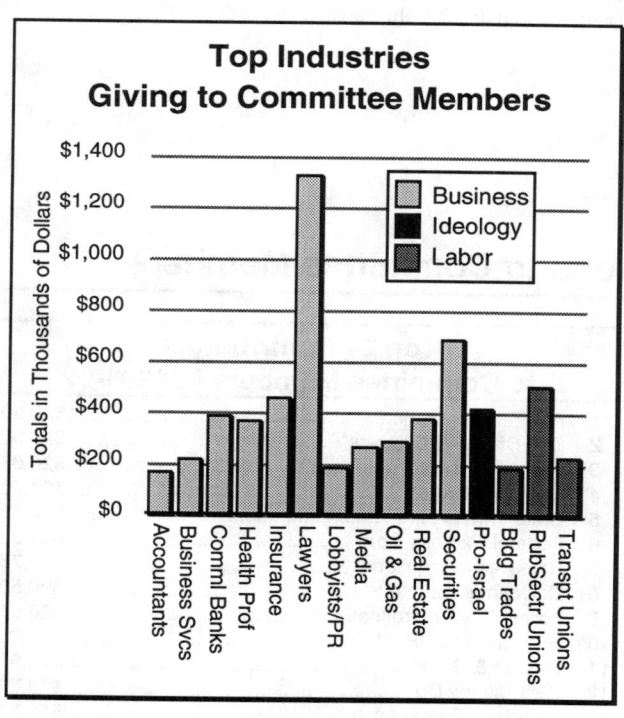

Top Industries Giving to Committee Members

Legend: Business, Ideology, Labor

Totals in Thousands of Dollars

Accountants, Business Svcs, Comml Banks, Health Prof, Insurance, Lawyers, Lobbyists/PR, Media, Oil & Gas, Real Estate, Securities, Pro-Israel, Bldg Trades, PubSectr Unions, Transpt Unions

Leading Industries Giving to Committee Members

Business

Accountants	$157,089
Business Services	$209,959
Commercial Banks	$375,670
Health Professionals	$360,289
Insurance	$441,760
Lawyers/Law Firms	$1,319,910
Lobbyists/PR	$173,177
Media/Entertainment	$252,696
Oil & Gas	$274,263
Real Estate	$364,362
Securities & Investment	$677,695

Ideological/Single-Issue

Pro-Israel	$404,800

Labor

Building Trade Unions	$174,550
Public Sector Unions	$500,958
Transportation Unions	$212,456

115

Senate Governmental Affairs Committee

John Glenn (D-Ohio), Chairman
William V. Roth Jr. (R-Del), Ranking Republican

Party Ratio: 8 Democrats
6 Republicans

Jurisdiction: (1) Except as provided in the Congressional Budget Act of 1974, budget and accounting measures, other than appropriations; (2) Organization and reorganization of the executive branch of the Government; (3) Intergovernmental relations; (4) Government information; (5) Municipal affairs of the District of Columbia, except appropriations therefor; (6) Federal Civil Service; (7) Status of officers and employees of the United States, including their classification, compensation and benefits; (8) Postal Service; (9) Census and collection of statistics, including economic and social statistics; (10) Archives of the United States; (11) Organization and management of United States nuclear export policy; (12) Congressional organization, except for any part of the matter that amends the rules or orders of the Senate. In addition, the committee is mandated to (a) receive and examine reports of the U.S. Comptroller General and submit to the Senate recommendations relating thereto; (b) study the efficiency, economy and effectiveness of the Government's agencies and departments; (c) evaluate the effects of laws enacted to reorganize the legislative and executive branches of the Government; (d) study the intergovernmental relationships between the U.S. and the states and municipalities, and between the U.S. and international organizations of which the U.S. is a member.

Subcommittees

Federal Service, Post Office and Civil Service
David Pryor (D-Ark), Chairman
Ted Stevens (R-Alaska), Ranking Republican

General Service, Federalism and the District of Columbia
Jim Sasser (D-Tenn), Chairman
John Seymour (R-Calif), Ranking Republican

Government Information and Regulation
Herb Kohl (D-Wis), Chairman
Warren B. Rudman (R-NH), Ranking Republican

Oversight of Government Management
Carl Levin (D-Mich), Chairman
William S. Cohen (R-Maine), Ranking Republican

Permanent Subcommittee on Investigations
Sam Nunn (D-Ga), Chairman
William V. Roth Jr. (R-Del), Ranking Republican

Total PAC and Large Individual Contributions to Committee Members

John F. Seymour (R-Calif) $5,126,165
John Glenn (D-Ohio) $2,486,349
Joseph I. Lieberman (D-Conn) $906,337
Daniel K. Akaka (D-Hawaii) $415,958
Jim Sasser (D-Tenn) $152,231
William S. Cohen (R-Maine) $46,200
William V. Roth Jr. (R-Del) $28,210
Ted Stevens (R-Alaska) $8,050
Carl Levin (D-Mich) $2,400
Herb Kohl (D-Wis) $0
Warren B. Rudman (R-NH) $0
Sam Nunn (D-Ga) .... -$35,089

Top 20 Contributors to Committee Members in 1991-92	
1 AT&T	$30,900
2 Sun-Diamond Growers*	$27,000
3 Atlantic Richfield	$26,650
4 General Motors*	$24,000
5 Gallo Winery	$22,482
6 Federal Express Corp	$21,000
7 Rockwell International	$20,750
8 Occidental Petroleum	$20,500
9 Forest City Enterprises Inc	$20,000
10 Hudson Valley PAC	$20,000
11 Procter & Gamble	$19,800
12 Walt Disney Co*	$18,750
13 American Dental Assn	$18,500
14 National Assn of Home Builders	$18,500
15 Plumbers/Pipefitters Union*	$18,500
16 Lockheed Corp	$17,900
17 Teamsters Union	$17,500
18 General Electric	$17,450
19 Waste Management Inc	$17,150
20 United Parcel Service	$16,700

* Contributions came from more than one affiliate or subsidiary.

Members in **bold italics** ran for reelection in 1992

Summary

Other committees of Congress have more direct relevance to particular industries or interest groups than Senate Governmental Affairs, which focuses more on the government itself. The federal civil service and postal system do fall within its purview, as does reorganization of executive branch agencies. Affairs relating to the District of Columbia are also debated here.

With the exception of money that came from PACs representing postal workers, the breakdown of contributions by industry and sector among Government Affairs members is more likely affected by the members' other committee assignments than by work specifically done on this committee.

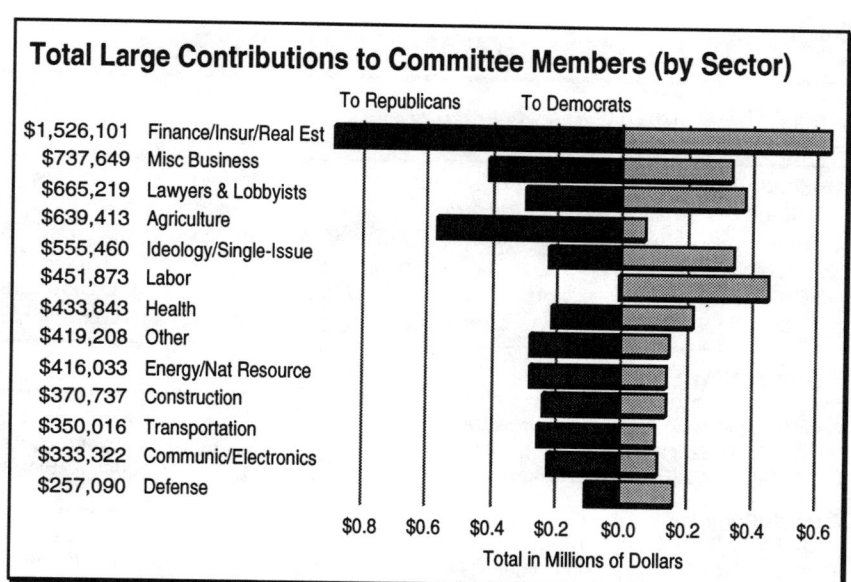

Total Large Contributions to Committee Members (by Sector)

	To Republicans / To Democrats
$1,526,101	Finance/Insur/Real Est
$737,649	Misc Business
$665,219	Lawyers & Lobbyists
$639,413	Agriculture
$555,460	Ideology/Single-Issue
$451,873	Labor
$433,843	Health
$419,208	Other
$416,033	Energy/Nat Resource
$370,737	Construction
$350,016	Transportation
$333,322	Communic/Electronics
$257,090	Defense

Total in Millions of Dollars

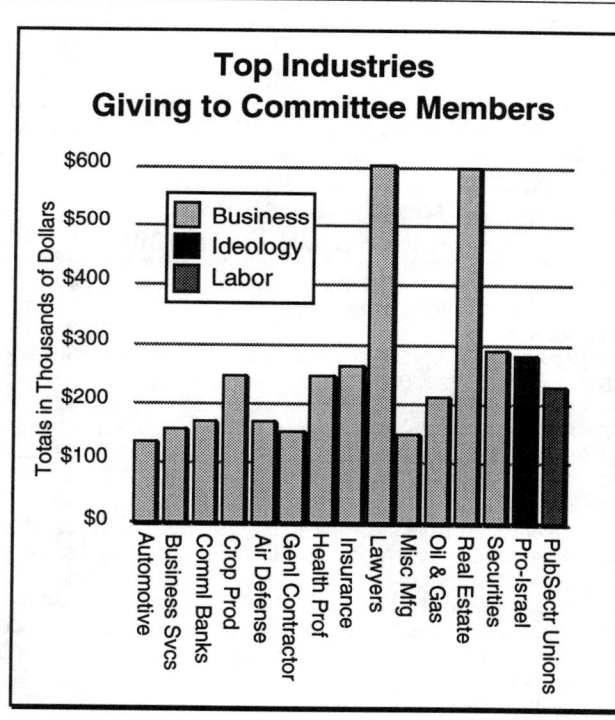

Top Industries Giving to Committee Members

Totals in Thousands of Dollars

- Business
- Ideology
- Labor

(Automotive, Business Svcs, Comml Banks, Crop Prod, Air Defense, Genl Contractor, Health Prof, Insurance, Lawyers, Misc Mfg, Oil & Gas, Real Estate, Securities, Pro-Israel, PubSectr Unions)

Leading Industries Giving to Committee Members

Business

Automotive	$131,100
Business Services	$153,950
Commercial Banks	$166,367
Crop Production & Basic Processing	$243,087
Defense Aerospace	$166,146
General Contractors	$146,891
Health Professionals	$243,906
Insurance	$259,099
Lawyers/Law Firms	$598,449
Misc Manufacturing & Distributing	$144,700
Oil & Gas	$208,150
Real Estate	$595,467
Securities & Investment	$284,831

Ideological/Single-Issue

Pro-Israel	$275,112

Labor

Public Sector Unions	$223,950

Senate Judiciary Committee

Joseph R. Biden Jr. (D-Del), Chairman
Strom Thurmond (R-SC), Ranking Republican

Party Ratio: 8 Democrats
6 Republicans

> **Jurisdiction:** All areas not delegated to the subcommittees, including but not limited to: (1) Nominations; (2) Holidays, commemorations, Federal charters and celebrations; (3) Department of Justice oversight, authorization and budget; (4) Revision and codification of the statutes of the United States; (5) Criminal justice, including (a) criminal laws, (b) criminal judicial proceedings, (c) Rules of Criminal Procedure, (d) national penitentiaries, (e) Bureau of Prisons, (f) U.S. Parole Commission, (g) oversight of the Criminal Division of the U.S. Department of Justice, (h) juvenile justice, (i) Youthful Offenders Act, (j) oversight of the Office of Justice Programs. (Excluded from (5) above is criminal legislation delegated to the Subcommittee on the Constitution.)

Subcommittees

Antitrust, Monopolies and Business Rights
Howard M. Metzenbaum (D-Ohio), Chairman
Strom Thurmond (R-SC), Ranking Republican

Constitution
Paul Simon (D-Ill), Chairman
Arlen Specter (R-Pa), Ranking Republican

Courts and Administrative Practice
Howell Heflin (D-Ala), Chairman
Charles E. Grassley (R-Iowa), Ranking Republican

Immigration and Refugee Affairs
Edward M. Kennedy (D-Mass), Chairman
Alan K. Simpson (R-Wyo), Ranking Republican

Patents, Copyrights and Trademarks
Dennis DeConcini (D-Ariz), Chairman
Orrin G. Hatch (R-Utah), Ranking Republican

Technology and the Law
Patrick J. Leahy (D-Vt), Chairman
Hank Brown (R-Colo), Ranking Republican

Total PAC and Large Individual Contributions to Committee Members

Arlen Specter (R-Pa) $5,296,607
Charles E. Grassley (R-Iowa) $1,593,319
Edward M. Kennedy (D-Mass) $797,580
Patrick J. Leahy (D-Vt) $662,722
Orrin G. Hatch (R-Utah) $364,798
Dennis DeConcini (D-Ariz) $362,639
Paul Simon (D-Ill) $59,392
Howell Heflin (D-Ala) $18,200
Alan K. Simpson (R-Wyo) $14,000
Joseph R. Biden Jr. (D-Del) $4,000
Strom Thurmond (R-SC) $3,230
Herb Kohl (D-Wis) $0
Hank Brown (R-Colo) ....-$1,813

#	Top 20 Contributors to Committee Members in 1991-92	
1	Walt Disney Co*	$38,750
2	National Assn of Independent Insurers	$30,500
3	MCA Inc*	$27,200
4	American Chiropractic Assn	$24,998
5	Morgan, Lewis & Bockius	$23,000
6	General Electric	$22,675
7	National Beer Wholesalers Assn	$22,000
8	Reed, Smith et al	$21,800
9	ConAgra Inc	$21,500
10	Sears*	$21,200
11	American Institute of CPA's	$21,100
12	American Bankers Assn*	$21,000
13	Union Pacific Corp	$20,750
14	National Assn of Realtors	$20,509
15	Citizens Concerned for the Natl Interest	$20,000
16	Citizens Organized PAC	$20,000
17	General Motors*	$20,000
18	National Cable Television Assn	$20,000
19	National Rifle Assn	$19,800
20	Dechert, Price & Rhoads	$19,125

* Contributions came from more than one affiliate or subsidiary.

Members in **bold italics** ran for reelection in 1992

Summary

Though it is most known to the public for its sometimes dramatic hearings on the confirmation of presidential appointments to the Supreme Court, cabinet positions and other top government posts, the Senate Judiciary Committee is also important to a wide range of businesses and industries — none more so than lawyers. From the criminal justice system to antitrust legislation to copyright and patent law, to new areas of the law arising from the birth of new high-tech industries, the committee plays a major role in defining the system of laws that governs the nation.

All that was overshadowed during 1991-92, however, by the committee's nationally televised hearings on the confirmation of Clarence Thomas to the Supreme Court — and most particularly by several members' heavy-handed treatment of witness Anita Hill. The committee's treatment of Hill ignited a firestorm of outrage among women across the nation, and was a catalyst in the decision of a record number of women to seek office themselves. The controversy also helped bring about a massive increase in fund-raising for women's issue PACs — money that helped elect four new women to the U.S. Senate in 1992.

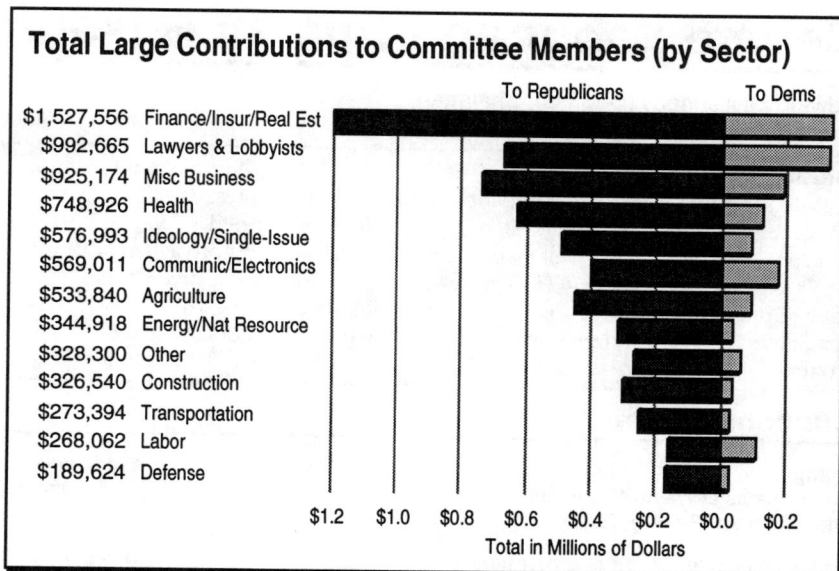

Total Large Contributions to Committee Members (by Sector)

$1,527,556	Finance/Insur/Real Est
$992,665	Lawyers & Lobbyists
$925,174	Misc Business
$748,926	Health
$576,993	Ideology/Single-Issue
$569,011	Communic/Electronics
$533,840	Agriculture
$344,918	Energy/Nat Resource
$328,300	Other
$326,540	Construction
$273,394	Transportation
$268,062	Labor
$189,624	Defense

Total in Millions of Dollars

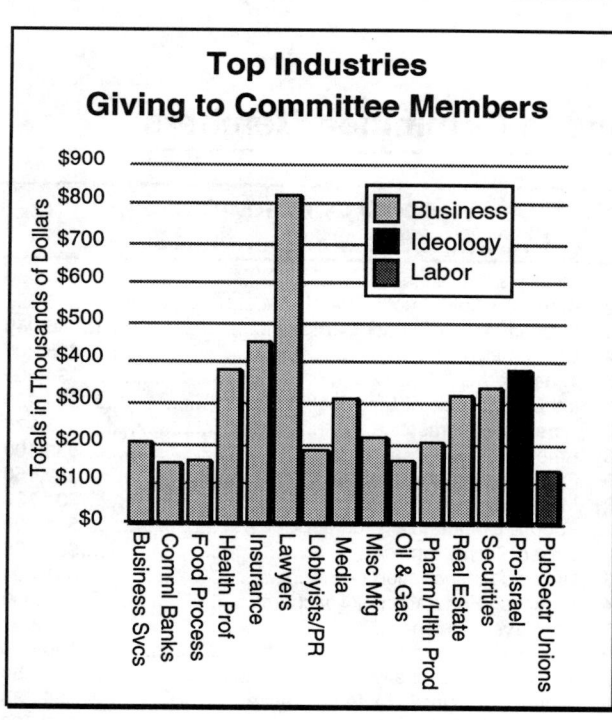

Top Industries Giving to Committee Members

Totals in Thousands of Dollars

- Business
- Ideology
- Labor

Business Svcs, Comml Banks, Food Process, Health Prof, Insurance, Lawyers, Lobbyists/PR, Media, Misc Mfg, Oil & Gas, Pharm/Hlth Prod, Real Estate, Securities, Pro-Israel, PubSectr Unions

Leading Industries Giving to Committee Members

Business

Business Services	$195,105
Commercial Banks	$142,424
Food Processing & Sales	$151,828
Health Professionals	$377,673
Insurance	$448,567
Lawyers/Law Firms	$813,458
Lobbyists/PR	$179,207
Media/Entertainment	$306,805
Misc Manufacturing & Distributing	$211,627
Oil & Gas	$149,102
Pharmaceuticals/Health Products	$194,860
Real Estate	$311,248
Securities & Investment	$331,869

Ideological/Single-Issue

Pro-Israel	$378,107

Labor

Public Sector Unions	$128,126

Senate Labor and Human Resources Committee

Edward M. Kennedy (D-Mass), Chairman
Orrin G. Hatch (R-Utah), Ranking Republican

Party Ratio: 10 Democrats
7 Republicans

Jurisdiction: (1) Education, labor, health and public welfare; (2) Labor standards and labor statistics; (3) Wages and hours of labor; (4) Child labor; (5) Mediation and arbitration of labor disputes; (6) Convict labor and the entry of goods made by convicts into interstate commerce; (7) Regulation of foreign laborers; (8) Handicapped individuals; (9) Equal employment opportunity; (10) Occupational safety and health, including the welfare of miners; (11) Private pension plans; (12) Aging; (13) Railway labor and retirement; (14) Public health; (15) Arts and humanities; (16) Gallaudet College, Howard University and Saint Elizabeths Hospital; (17) Biomedical research and development; (18) Student loans; (19) Agricultural colleges; (20) Domestic activities of the American Red Cross. The committee is also mandated to study and review matters relating to health, education and training, and public welfare, and to report thereon from time to time.

Subcommittees

Aging
Brock Adams(D-Wash), Chairman
Thad Cochran (R-Miss), Ranking Republican

Children, Family, Drugs and Alcoholism
Christopher J. Dodd (D-Conn), Chairman
Daniel R. Coats (R-Ind), Ranking Republican

Education, Arts and Humanities
Claiborne Pell (D-RI), Chairman
Nancy Landon Kassebaum (R-Kan), Ranking Republican

Employment and Productivity
Paul Simon (D-Ill), Chairman
Strom Thurmond (R-SC), Ranking Republican

Disability Policy
Tom Harkin (D-Iowa), Chairman
Dave Durenberger (R-Minn), Ranking Republican

Labor
Howard M. Metzenbaum (D-Ohio), Chairman
James M. Jeffords (R-Vt), Ranking Republican

Total PAC and Large Individual Contributions to Committee Members

Christopher J. Dodd (D-Conn) $3,167,767
Daniel R. Coats (R-Ind) $2,825,825
Tom Harkin (D-Iowa)† $2,149,567
Barbara A. Mikulski (D-Md) $1,578,220
Edward M. Kennedy (D-Mass) $797,580
Brock Adams (D-Wash) $701,536
Orrin G. Hatch (R-Utah) $364,798
Dave Durenberger (R-Minn) $275,339
Jeff Bingaman (D-NM) $192,522
Paul Wellstone (D-Minn) $142,017
Paul Simon (D-Ill) $59,392
Thad Cochran (R-Miss) $52,600
James M. Jeffords (R-Vt) $6,950
Strom Thurmond (R-SC) $3,230
Claiborne Pell (D-RI) ....-$4,100
Nancy Landon Kassebaum (R-Kan) ....-$10,250

† Includes contributions to his 1992 presidential campaign

Top 20 Contributors to Committee Members in 1991-92

1	Eli Lilly & Co	$49,650
2	American Chiropractic Assn*	$45,698
3	National Assn of Letter Carriers*	$36,040
4	US Tobacco Co	$35,200
5	Time Warner*	$34,500
6	Intl Brotherhood of Electrical Workers	$34,450
7	American Express*	$33,375
8	American Dental Assn	$33,100
9	Seafarers International Union*	$32,150
10	Merrill Lynch	$31,730
11	Food & Commercial Workers Union	$31,500
12	United Technologies*	$31,100
13	United Transportation Union	$31,000
14	American Federation of Teachers	$30,000
15	Bricklayers Union	$30,000
16	Marine Engineers Union*	$30,000
17	Aetna Life & Casualty	$29,350
18	American Council of Life Insurance	$29,284
19	Greenwich Capital Markets	$29,250
20	United Auto Workers	$28,807

* Contributions came from more than one affiliate or subsidiary.

Members in **bold italics** ran for reelection in 1992

Summary

The Senate Labor Committee is the birthplace for many of the standards and rules that govern the American workplace. As such, it is of natural interest to the nation's labor unions, which gave more than a million dollars in contributions to its members in 1991-92. But decisions about labor conditions affect not only workers, but also their employers, who must live by the rules. Consequently, many of the issues discussed and debated by the committee are closely followed by a wide cross-section of business interests. And those businesses delivered substantial campaign contributions to committee members.

The Labor committee's cash profile reveals another important fact about the relationship between business and labor contributors: if PACs alone are counted, organized labor ranks as the single largest industry group giving to committee members (followed closely by ideological PACs). But if *all* contributors are included — PACs *and* individuals giving $200 or more — labor falls to fourth place. This illustrates the fact that business contributors give heavily both through PACs and individuals, while labor gives almost all its contributions through PACs. Because of that, looking at PAC contributions alone substantially overstates the cash clout of organized labor in American politics and understates the clout of business interests.

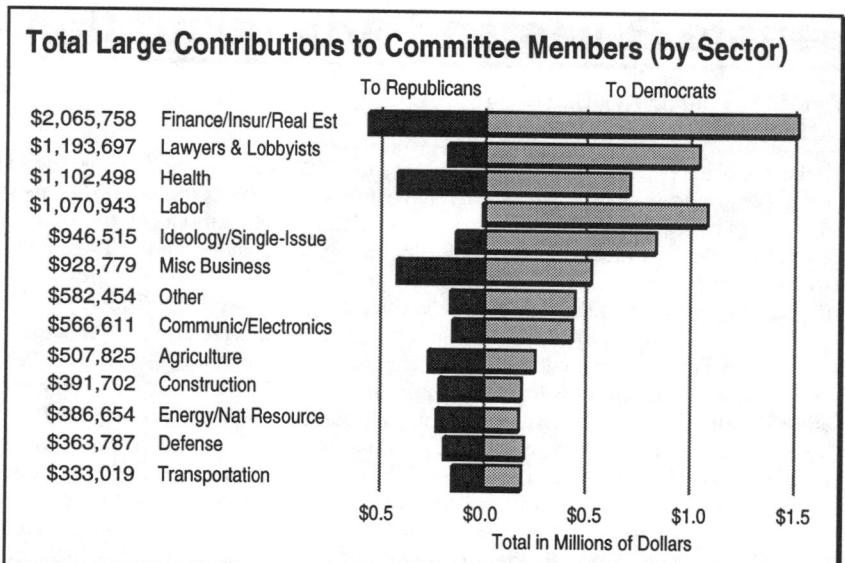

Total Large Contributions to Committee Members (by Sector)

$2,065,758	Finance/Insur/Real Est
$1,193,697	Lawyers & Lobbyists
$1,102,498	Health
$1,070,943	Labor
$946,515	Ideology/Single-Issue
$928,779	Misc Business
$582,454	Other
$566,611	Communic/Electronics
$507,825	Agriculture
$391,702	Construction
$386,654	Energy/Nat Resource
$363,787	Defense
$333,019	Transportation

Total in Millions of Dollars

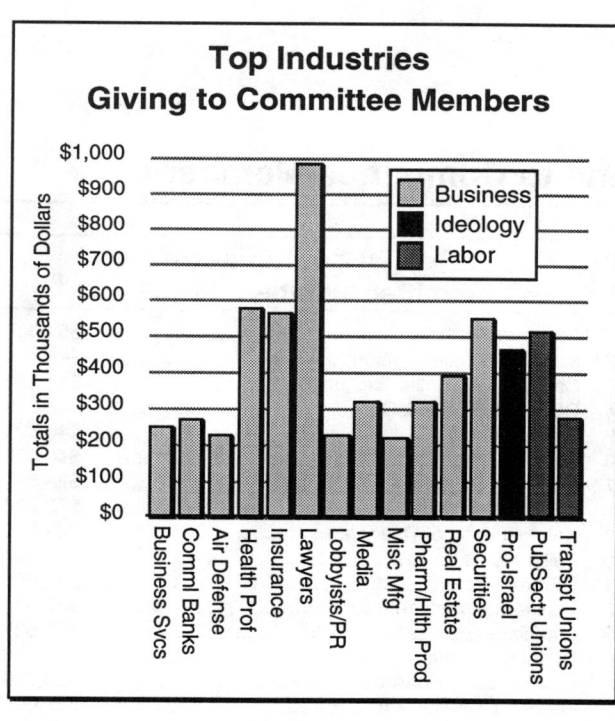

Top Industries Giving to Committee Members

Leading Industries Giving to Committee Members

Business

Business Services	$236,999
Commercial Banks	$258,625
Defense Aerospace	$216,917
Health Professionals	$566,633
Insurance	$556,008
Lawyers/Law Firms	$973,678
Lobbyists/PR	$220,019
Media/Entertainment	$308,203
Misc Manufacturing & Distributing	$212,985
Pharmaceuticals/Health Products	$309,427
Real Estate	$381,554
Securities & Investment	$539,303

Ideological/Single-Issue

Pro-Israel	$452,950

Labor

Public Sector Unions	$507,217
Transportation Unions	$271,256

Senate Rules and Administration Committee

Wendell H. Ford (D-Ky), Chairman
Ted Stevens (R-Alaska), Ranking Republican

Party Ratio: 9 Democrats
7 Republicans

Jurisdiction: (1) Administration of the Senate Office Buildings and the Senate wing of the Capitol, including the assignment of office space; (2) Congressional organization relative to rules and procedures, and Senate rules and regulations, including floor and gallery rules; (3) Corrupt practices; (4) Credentials and qualifications of Members of the Senate, contested elections, and acceptance of incompatible offices; (5) Federal elections generally, including the election of the President, Vice President, and Members of the Congress; (6) Government Printing Office and the printing and correction of the *Congressional Record*, as well as those matters provided for under rule XI; (7) Meetings of the Congress and attendance of Members; (8) Payment of money out of the contingent fund of the Senate or creating a charge upon the same (except that any resolution relating to substantive matter within the jurisdiction of any other standing committee of the Senate shall be first referred to such committee); (9) Presidential succession; (10) Purchase of books and manuscripts and erection of monuments to the memory of individuals; (11) Senate Library and statuary, art and pictures in the Capitol and Senate Office Buildings; (12) Services to the Senate, including the Senate restaurant; (13) United States Capitol and congressional office buildings, the Library of Congress, the Smithsonian Institution (and the incorporation of similar institutions), and the Botanic Garden. The committee is also mandated to (A) make a continuing study of the organization and operation of the Congress of the United States and recommend improvements in such organization and operation with a view toward strengthening the Congress, simplifying its operations, improving its relationships with other branches of the U.S. Government, and enabling it to better meet its responsibilities under the Constitution of the United States; and (B) identify any court proceeding or action which, in its opinion, is of vital interest to the Congress as a constitutionally established institution of the Federal Government and call such proceeding or action to the attention of the Senate.

No Subcommittees

Total PAC and Large Individual Contributions to Committee Members

Christopher J. Dodd (D-Conn)	$3,167,767
Daniel K. Inouye (D-Hawaii)	$2,398,729
Bob Dole (R-Kan)	$1,949,015
Wendell H. Ford (D-Ky)	$1,981,781
Brock Adams (D-Wash)	$701,536
Daniel Patrick Moynihan (D-NY)	$584,201
Dennis DeConcini (D-Ariz)	$362,639
Jesse Helms (R-NC)	$224,478
Robert C. Byrd (D-WVa)	$139,000
Mark O. Hatfield (R-Ore)	$96,200
Mitch McConnell (R-Ky)	$75,650
Al Gore (D-Tenn)	$10,112
Ted Stevens (R-Alaska)	$8,050
John W. Warner (R-Va)	$4,925
Jake Garn (R-Utah)	$1,000
Claiborne Pell (D-RI)	-$4,100

Top 20 Contributors to Committee Members in 1991-92

1	Salomon Brothers	$51,000
2	Marine Engineers Union*	$46,000
3	Chicago Mercantile Exchange	$44,250
4	Goldman, Sachs & Co	$42,000
5	Time Warner*	$40,500
6	Cassidy & Associates	$40,060
7	American Bankers Assn	$39,500
8	US Tobacco Co	$39,200
9	National Assn of Realtors	$39,100
10	Philip Morris*	$38,848
11	Laborers Union*	$37,800
12	Waste Management Inc	$37,687
13	American Express*	$37,625
14	General Electric	$36,350
15	United Parcel Service	$36,250
16	Federal Express Corp	$36,000
17	Teamsters Union	$35,000
18	Akin, Gump et al	$34,349
19	AFL-CIO*	$33,950
20	American Institute of CPA's	$32,250

* Contributions came from more than one affiliate or subsidiary.

Members in **bold italics** ran for reelection in 1992

Summary

In any legislative body, the key to success often lies in a mastery of the body's rules and procedures. Those rules — from the assignment of office space to the conducting of business on the Senate floor and even the rules governing federal elections — are debated within this committee.

As part of its role in setting election procedures, the committee is also at center stage in revising the laws governing campaign financing. The rules governing PACs, the spending limits and reporting requirements of contributors to federal campaigns, the oversight of the process by the Federal Election Commission — all these elements of American elections fall within the jurisdiction of the Senate Rules Committee.

Total Large Contributions to Committee Members (by Sector)

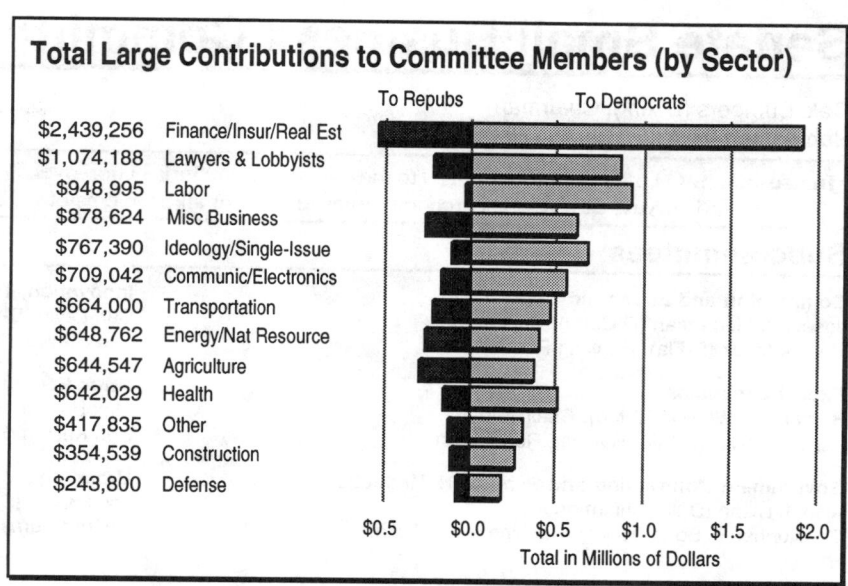

$2,439,256	Finance/Insur/Real Est
$1,074,188	Lawyers & Lobbyists
$948,995	Labor
$878,624	Misc Business
$767,390	Ideology/Single-Issue
$709,042	Communic/Electronics
$664,000	Transportation
$648,762	Energy/Nat Resource
$644,547	Agriculture
$642,029	Health
$417,835	Other
$354,539	Construction
$243,800	Defense

Total in Millions of Dollars

Top Industries Giving to Committee Members

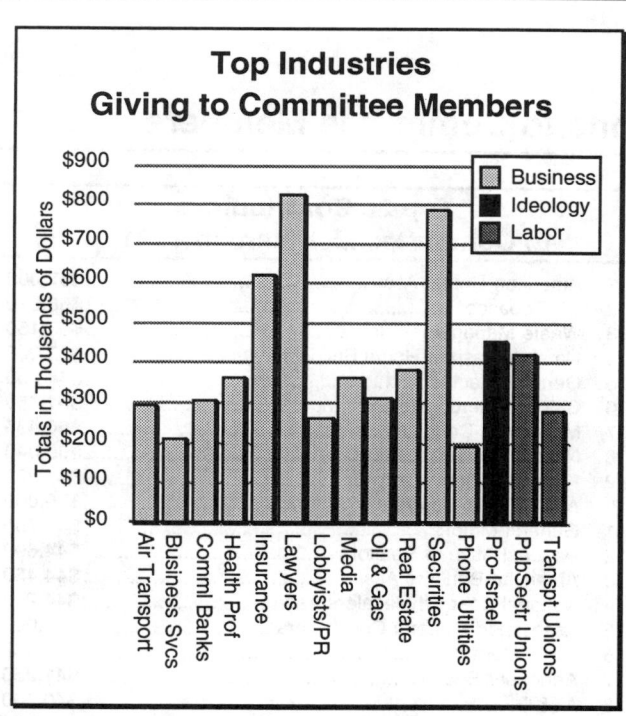

Leading Industries Giving to Committee Members

Business

Air Transport	$284,270
Business Services	$202,988
Commercial Banks	$302,365
Health Professionals	$360,254
Insurance	$615,401
Lawyers/Law Firms	$818,078
Lobbyists/PR	$256,110
Media/Entertainment	$359,460
Oil & Gas	$308,536
Real Estate	$377,629
Securities & Investment	$778,749
Telephone Utilities	$181,272

Ideological/Single-Issue

Pro-Israel	$448,455

Labor

Public Sector Unions	$417,979
Transportation Unions	$272,600

Senate Small Business Committee

Dale Bumpers (D-Ark), Chairman
Bob Kasten (R-Wis), Ranking Republican

Party Ratio: 11 Democrats
8 Republicans

> **Jurisdiction:** (1) All legislation referred to the committee; (2) Jurisdiction over all matters related to the Small Business Administration; (3) Study and survey, through research and investigation, of all problems of American small business enterprises.

Subcommittees

Competition and Economic Opportunity
Joseph I. Lieberman (D-Conn), Chairman
Connie Mack (R-Fla), Ranking Republican

Export Expansion
Barbara A. Mikulski (D-Md), Chairwoman
Larry Pressler (R-SD), Ranking Republican

Government Contracting and Paperwork Reduction
Alan J. Dixon (D-Ill), Chairman
Christopher S. Bond (R-Mo), Ranking Republican

Innovation, Technology and Productivity
Carl Levin (D-Mich), Chairman
Ted Stevens (R-Alaska), Ranking Republican

Rural Economy and Family Farming
Max Baucus (D-Mont), Chairman
Bob Kasten (R-Wis), Ranking Republican

Urban and Minority-Owned Business Development
John Kerry (D-Mass), Chairman
Conrad Burns (R-Mont), Ranking Republican

Total PAC and Large Individual Contributions to Committee Members

John F. Seymour (R-Calif) $5,126,165
Bob Kasten (R-Wis) $4,009,220
Harris Wofford (D-Pa)[1] $3,309,396
Christopher S. Bond (R-Mo) $3,232,383
Tom Harkin (D-Iowa)[2] $2,149,567
Dale Bumpers (D-Ark) *$1,648,431*
Barbara A. Mikulski (D-Md) $1,578,220
Alan J. Dixon (D-Ill) $1,383,511
Joseph I. Lieberman (D-Conn) $906,337
Connie Mack (R-Fla) $726,909
John Kerry (D-Mass) $483,997
Conrad Burns (R-Mont) $256,346
Paul Wellstone (D-Minn) $142,017
Larry Pressler (R-SD) $105,350
Malcolm Wallop (R-Wyo) $53,215
Ted Stevens (R-Alaska) $8,050
Max Baucus (D-Mont) $7,000
Carl Levin (D-Mich) $2,400
Sam Nunn (D-Ga) .... -$35,089

[1] Wofford's election was in 1991
[2] Includes contributions to his 1992 presidential campaign

Top 20 Contributors to Committee Members in 1991-92	
1 American Dental Assn	$57,000
2 US Tobacco*	$55,570
3 Waste Management Inc	$55,150
4 National Assn of Home Builders	$55,000
5 General Electric*	$54,200
6 Chicago Mercantile Exchange	$51,650
7 McDonnell Douglas*	$50,435
8 National Assn of Letter Carriers*	$50,040
9 Federal Express Corp	$47,300
10 Assn of Trial Lawyers of America	$46,000
11 General Motors*	$44,750
12 National Assn of Realtors	$44,699
13 American Bankers Assn*	$44,450
14 National Beer Wholesalers Assn	$44,200
15 Associated General Contractors	$42,000
16 Philip Morris*	$41,532
17 Anheuser-Busch	$41,250
18 AT&T	$40,200
19 National Assn of Life Underwriters	$40,000
20 National PAC	$40,000

* Contributions came from more than one affiliate or subsidiary.

Members in **bold italics** ran for reelection in 1992

Summary

Its statement of jurisdiction is the shortest of all Senate committees, but the expanse of that jurisdiction reaches into every city and town across America. Overseeing the concerns of small business — from the corner grocery to the family farm — is the committee's charge, and considering the fact that both the corner grocery and the family farm are endangered species in America today, the concerns of small business are large indeed.

As with most committees in the Senate, the single biggest source of campaign funds to committee members came from the Finance/ Insurance/Real Estate sector, while lawyers and law firms, as seen in the chart below, were the top-ranking industry.

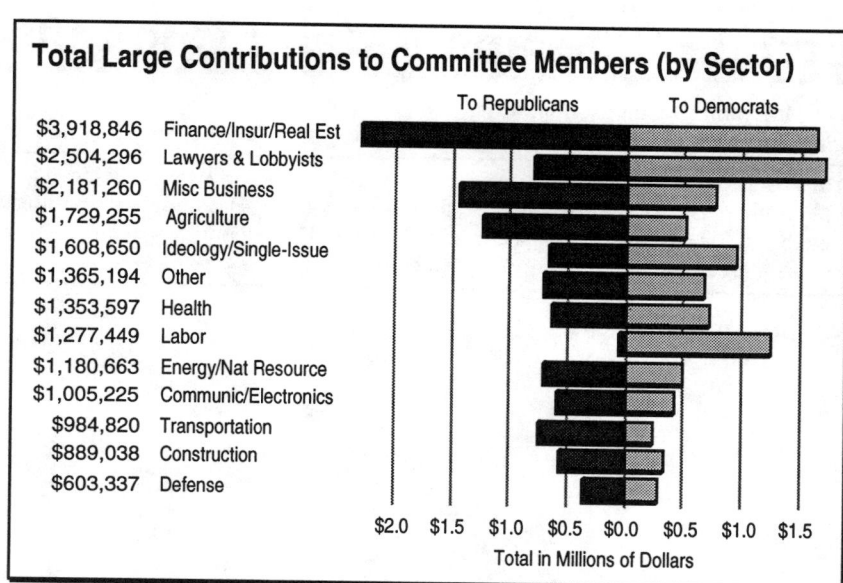

Total Large Contributions to Committee Members (by Sector)

$3,918,846	Finance/Insur/Real Est
$2,504,296	Lawyers & Lobbyists
$2,181,260	Misc Business
$1,729,255	Agriculture
$1,608,650	Ideology/Single-Issue
$1,365,194	Other
$1,353,597	Health
$1,277,449	Labor
$1,180,663	Energy/Nat Resource
$1,005,225	Communic/Electronics
$984,820	Transportation
$889,038	Construction
$603,337	Defense

Total in Millions of Dollars

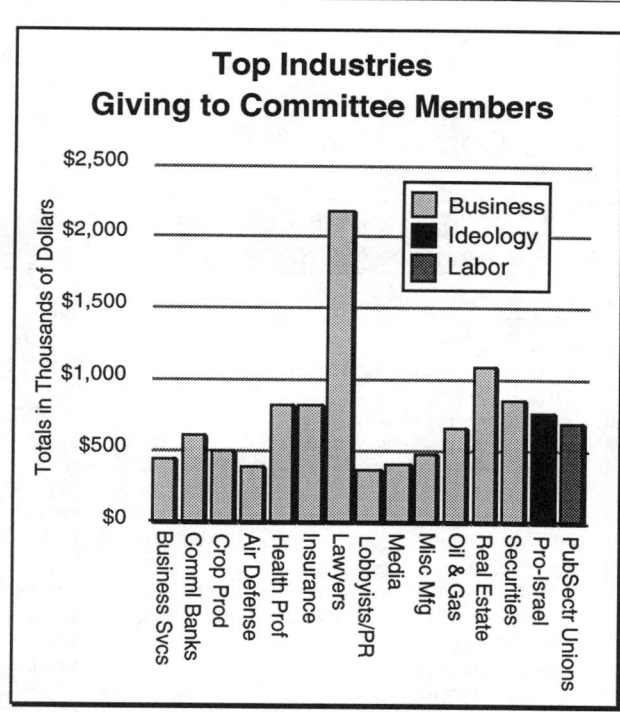

Top Industries Giving to Committee Members

Totals in Thousands of Dollars

Business
Ideology
Labor

Business Svcs, Comml Banks, Crop Prod, Air Defense, Health Prof, Insurance, Lawyers, Lobbyists/PR, Media, Misc Mfg, Oil & Gas, Real Estate, Securities, Pro-Israel, PubSectr Unions

Leading Industries Giving to Committee Members

Business

Business Services	$421,158
Commercial Banks	$581,747
Crop Production & Basic Processing	$472,052
Defense Aerospace	$371,657
Health Professionals	$798,840
Insurance	$795,009
Lawyers/Law Firms	$2,159,383
Lobbyists/PR	$344,913
Media/Entertainment	$388,310
Misc Manufacturing & Distributing	$456,494
Oil & Gas	$630,754
Real Estate	$1,057,133
Securities & Investment	$834,177

Ideological/Single-Issue

Pro-Israel	$747,366

Labor

Public Sector Unions	$665,052

Senate Veterans' Affairs Committee

Alan Cranston (D-Calif), Chairman
Arlen Specter (R-Pa), Ranking Republican

Party Ratio: 7 Democrats
5 Republicans

Jurisdiction: Veterans' measures generally; (2) Pensions of all wars of the U.S., general and special; (3) Life insurance issued by the Government on account of service in the Armed Forces; (4) Compensation of veterans; (5) Vocational rehabilitation and education of veterans; (6) Veterans' hospitals, medical care and treatment of veterans; (7) Soldiers' and sailors' civil relief; (8) Readjustment of servicemen to civil life; (9) National cemeteries.

No Subcommittees

Total PAC and Large Individual Contributions to Committee Members

Arlen Specter (R-Pa) $5,296,607
Bob Graham (D-Fla) $2,508,277
Tom Daschle (D-SD) $2,157,690
Frank H. Murkowski (R-Alaska) $1,362,732
Daniel K. Akaka (D-Hawaii) $415,958
Dennis DeConcini (D-Ariz) $362,639
John D. Rockefeller IV (D-WVa) $191,950
Alan K. Simpson (R-Wyo) $14,000
James M. Jeffords (R-Vt) $6,950
George J. Mitchell (D-Maine) $4,000
Strom Thurmond (R-SC) $3,230
Alan Cranston (D-Calif) .... -$272,198

	Top 20 Contributors to Committee Members in 1991-92	
1	National Cable Television Assn	$35,000
2	American Dental Assn	$34,500
3	Marine Engineers Union*	$34,000
4	National Assn of Life Underwriters	$33,000
5	General Electric	$30,100
6	National Assn of Realtors	$29,350
7	American Medical Assn*	$28,224
8	American Bankers Assn*	$27,900
9	Laborers Union*	$27,500
10	National Assn of Home Builders	$27,500
11	FPL Group Inc*	$26,750
12	Aircraft Owners & Pilots Assn	$25,500
13	Independent Insurance Agents of America	$25,499
14	American Institute of CPA's	$25,250
15	Desert Caucus	$25,000
16	United Transportation Union	$25,000
17	Barnett Banks Inc	$24,676
18	American Federation of Teachers	$24,500
19	Assn of Trial Lawyers of America	$24,500
20	National Venture Capital Assn	$24,500

* Contributions came from more than one affiliate or subsidiary.

Members in **bold italics** ran for reelection in 1992

Summary

Insurance companies and health professionals were among the major contributors to the Senate Veterans Affairs Committee in 1991-92, ranking only behind lawyers and law firms among business groups. While government life insurance to veterans does fall within its jurisdiction, as does the VA hospital system, most of the committee's work does not directly affect any particular segments of American business in a major way. Perhaps because of this, the Veterans Affairs Committee has never been a central focus of political fundraising on Capitol Hill.

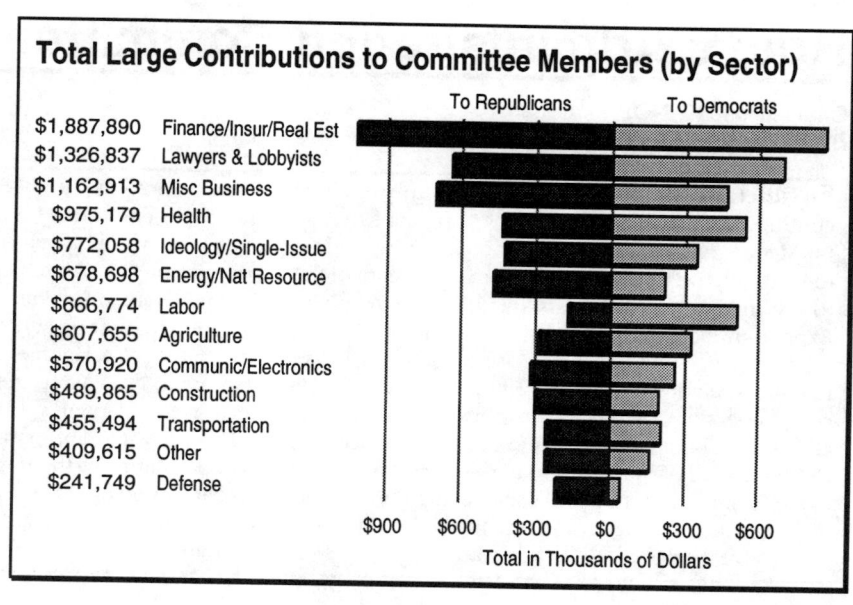

Total Large Contributions to Committee Members (by Sector)

Amount	Sector
$1,887,890	Finance/Insur/Real Est
$1,326,837	Lawyers & Lobbyists
$1,162,913	Misc Business
$975,179	Health
$772,058	Ideology/Single-Issue
$678,698	Energy/Nat Resource
$666,774	Labor
$607,655	Agriculture
$570,920	Communic/Electronics
$489,865	Construction
$455,494	Transportation
$409,615	Other
$241,749	Defense

To Republicans   To Democrats

$900 $600 $300 $0 $300 $600
Total in Thousands of Dollars

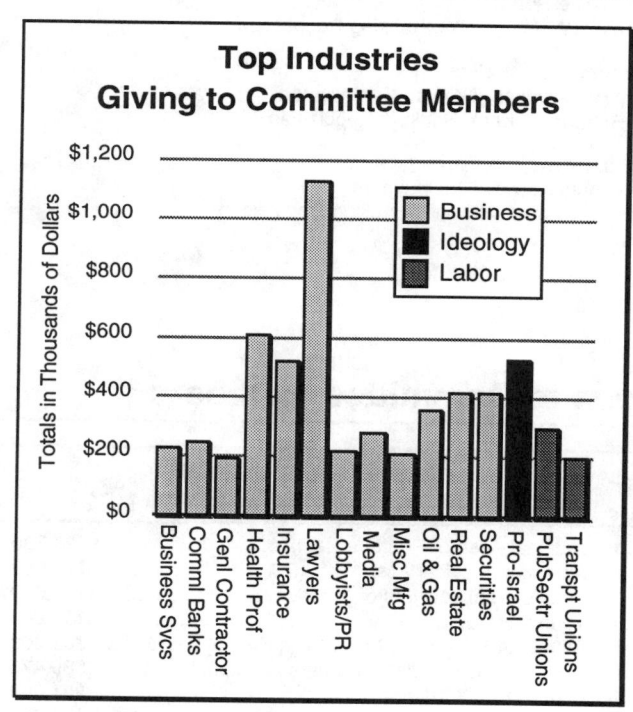

Top Industries Giving to Committee Members

Totals in Thousands of Dollars

Legend: Business, Ideology, Labor

Industries: Business Svcs, Comml Banks, Genl Contractor, Health Prof, Insurance, Lawyers, Lobbyists/PR, Media, Misc Mfg, Oil & Gas, Real Estate, Securities, Pro-Israel, PubSectr Unions, Transpt Unions

Leading Industries
Giving to Committee Members

Business

Business Services	$221,572
Commercial Banks	$236,427
General Contractors	$187,451
Health Professionals	$592,640
Insurance	$510,449
Lawyers/Law Firms	$1,115,646
Lobbyists/PR	$211,191
Media/Entertainment	$268,331
Misc Manufacturing & Distributing	$204,500
Oil & Gas	$345,727
Real Estate	$405,991
Securities & Investment	$408,255

Ideological/Single-Issue

Pro-Israel	$522,171

Labor

Public Sector Unions	$292,020
Transportation Unions	$193,500

House Administration Committee

Charlie Rose (D-NC), Chairman
Bill Thomas (R-Calif), Ranking Republican

Party Ratio: 15 Democrats
9 Republicans

Jurisdiction: (1) Appropriations from the contingent fund; (2) Auditing and settling of all accounts which may be charged to the contingent fund; (3) Employment of persons by the House, including clerks for Members and committees, and reporters of debates; (4) Matters relating to the Library of Congress and the House Library; statuary and pictures; acceptance or purchase of works of art for the Capitol; the Botanic Gardens; management of the Library of Congress, purchase of books and manuscripts; erection of monuments to the memory of individuals; (5) Matters relating to the Smithsonian Institution and the incorporation of similar institutions; (6) Expenditure of contingent fund of the House; (7) Matters relating to printing and correction of the Congressional Record; (8) Measures relating to accounts of the House generally; (9) Measures relating to assignment of office space for Members and committees; (10) measures relating to the disposition of useless executive papers; (11) Measures relating to the election of the President, Vice President or Members of Congress; corrupt practices; contested elections; credentials and qualifications; and Federal elections generally; (12) Measures relating to services to the House, including the House Restaurant, parking facilities and administration of the House office Buildings and of the House wing of the Capitol; (13) Measures relating to the travel of Members of the House; (14) Measures relating to the raising, reporting and use of campaign contributions for candidates for office of Representative in the House of Representatives and of Resident Commissioner to the United States from Puerto Rico; (15) Measures relating to the compensation, retirement and other benefits of the Members, officers and employees of the Congress.

Subcommittees

Accounts
Joseph M. Gaydos (D-Pa), Chairman
Paul E. Gillmor (R-Ohio), Ranking Republican

Elections
Al Swift (D-Wash), Chairman
Bob Livingston (R-La), Ranking Republican

Libraries and Memorials
William L. Clay (D-Mo), Chairman
Bill Barrett (R-Neb), Ranking Republican

Office Systems
Sam Gejdenson (D-Conn), Chairman
James T. Walsh (R-NY), Ranking Republican

Personnel and Police
Mary Rose Oakar (D-Ohio), Chairwoman
Pat Roberts (R-Kan), Ranking Republican

Procurement and Printing
Frank Annunzio (D-Ill), Chairman
Mickey Edwards (R-Okla), Ranking Republican

Total PAC and Large Individual Contributions to Committee Members

Newt Gingrich (R-Ga) $1,419,505
Steny H. Hoyer (D-Md) $1,091,486
Martin Frost (D-Texas) $1,079,404
Marty Russo (D-Ill) $990,657
Mary Rose Oakar (D-Ohio) $860,393
Al Swift (D-Wash)..$781,229
Sam Gejdenson (D-Conn) $571,167
Dale E. Kildee (D-Mich) $558,660
Thomas J. Manton (D-NY) $516,378
Bill Thomas (R-Calif) $469,226
Mickey Edwards (R-Okla) $388,827
Charlie Rose (D-NC) $323,975
Bill Barrett (R-Neb) $301,454
Leon E. Panetta (D-Calif) $300,800
William L. Clay (D-Mo) $282,938
William H. Gray III (D-Pa)† $267,995
Gerald D. Kleczka (D-Wis) $261,040
Robert L. Livingston (R-La) $231,250
Pat Roberts (R-Kan) $223,912
Paul E. Gillmor (R-Ohio) $205,782
James T. Walsh (R-NY) $136,553
Joe Kolter (D-Pa) $117,475
Bill Dickinson (R-Ala) $54,780
Joseph M. Gaydos (D-Pa) $45,800
Frank Annunzio (D-Ill) $42,720

Top 20 Contributors to Committee Members in 1991-92	
1 National Assn of Realtors	$127,780
2 American Medical Assn*	$122,950
3 Assn of Trial Lawyers of America	$110,500
4 Teamsters Union*	$107,000
5 American Fedn of St/Cnty/Munic Employees	$89,600
6 National Assn of Letter Carriers	$89,475
7 United Auto Workers	$81,000
8 National Education Assn	$78,500
9 Carpenters & Joiners Union*	$78,000
10 National Assn Retired Federal Employees	$76,500
11 American Bankers Assn*	$74,170
12 Air Line Pilots Assn	$70,500
13 Laborers Union*	$69,450
14 United Parcel Service	$65,925
15 Marine Engineers Union*	$63,500
16 American Postal Workers Union	$63,000
17 American Institute of CPA's	$62,100
18 Machinists/Aerospace Workers Union	$62,000
19 AT&T	$61,000
20 National Assn of Life Underwriters	$60,000

* Contributions came from more than one affiliate or subsidiary.

† Resigned in September 1991

Summary

Since the Committee on House Administration is more concerned with matters internal to the House than to the world of industry and commerce beyond it, the pattern of contributions to its members closely parallels that of the rest of Congress. In fact, 16 of the Top 20 contributors to committee members also rank among the top 20 contributors to Congress as a whole.

In one respect, the committee does figure prominently in the world of money and politics on Capital Hill. Its subcommittee on Elections is the panel that oversees the drafting of changes in the nation's campaign finance laws.

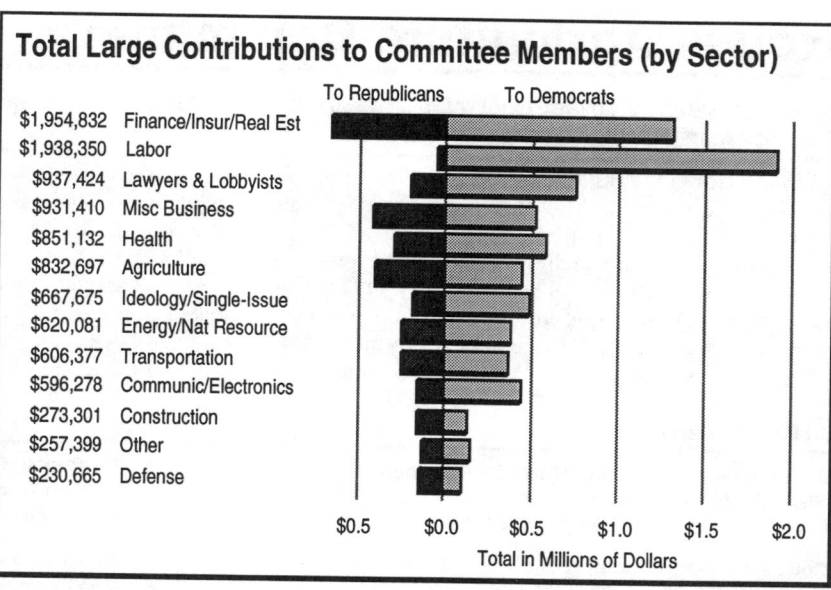

Total Large Contributions to Committee Members (by Sector)

Amount	Sector
$1,954,832	Finance/Insur/Real Est
$1,938,350	Labor
$937,424	Lawyers & Lobbyists
$931,410	Misc Business
$851,132	Health
$832,697	Agriculture
$667,675	Ideology/Single-Issue
$620,081	Energy/Nat Resource
$606,377	Transportation
$596,278	Communic/Electronics
$273,301	Construction
$257,399	Other
$230,665	Defense

To Republicans   To Democrats

Total in Millions of Dollars

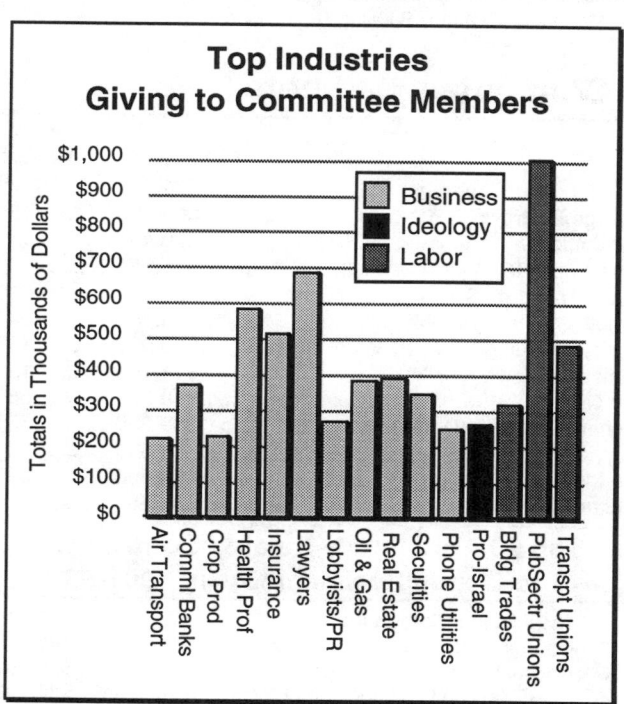

Top Industries Giving to Committee Members

Totals in Thousands of Dollars

Business
Ideology
Labor

Leading Industries Giving to Committee Members

Business

Air Transport	$211,549
Commercial Banks	$358,416
Crop Production & Basic Processing	$219,275
Health Professionals	$573,407
Insurance	$504,013
Lawyers/Law Firms	$677,887
Lobbyists/PR	$259,537
Oil & Gas	$376,093
Real Estate	$386,228
Securities & Investment	$338,133
Telephone Utilities	$238,870

Ideological/Single-Issue

Pro-Israel	$256,537

Labor

Building Trade Unions	$309,500
Public Sector Unions	$1,000,666
Transportation Unions	$474,330

House Agriculture Committee

Kika de la Garza (D-Texas), Chairman
Tom Coleman (R-Mo), Ranking Republican

Party Ratio: 27 Democrats
18 Republicans

Jurisdiction: (1) Adulteration of seeds, insect pests, and protection of birds and animals in forest reserves; (2) Agriculture generally; (3) Agricultural and industrial chemistry; (4) Agricultural colleges and experimental stations; (5) Agricultural economics and research; (6) Agricultural education extension services; (7) Agricultural production and marketing and stabilization of prices of agricultural products and commodities (not including distribution outside the United States); (8) Animal industry and diseases of animals; (9) Crop insurance and soil conservation; (10) Dairy industry; (11) Entomology and plant quarantine; (12) Extension of farm credit and farm security; (13) Forestry in general, and forest reserves other than those created from the public domain; (14) Human nutrition and home economics; (15) Inspection of livestock and meat products; (16) Plant industry, soils, and agricultural engineering; (17) Rural electrification; (18) Commodities exchanges; (19) Rural development.

Subcommittees

Conservation, Credit and Rural Development
Glenn English (D-Okla), Chairman
Bob Smith (R-Ore), Ranking Republican

Cotton, Rice and Sugar
Jerry Huckaby (D-La), Chairman
Bill Emerson (R-Mo), Ranking Republican

Department Operations, Research and Foreign Agriculture
Charlie Rose (D-NC), Chairman
Pat Roberts (R-Kan), Ranking Republican

Livestock, Dairy and Poultry
Charles W. Stenholm (D-Texas), Chairman
Steve Gunderson (R-Wis), Ranking Republican

Tobacco and Peanuts
Charlie Hatcher (D-Ga), Chairman
Larry J. Hopkins (R-Ky), Ranking Republican

Wheat, Soybeans and Feed Grains
Dan Glickman (D-Kan), Chairman
Ron Marlenee (R-Mont), Ranking Republican

Total Agriculture-Related Contributions to Committee Members

	Total from Cmte-Related Contribs	Pct of Member's Lg Contribs
Ron Marlenee (R-Mont)	$191,805	24%
Jerry Huckaby (D-La)	$189,374	48%
Charles Hatcher (D-Ga)	$180,121	52%
Wally Herger (R-Calif)	$159,098	39%
E. "Kika" de la Garza (D-Texas)	$157,599	72%
Tom Coleman (R-Mo)	$148,475	36%
Calvin Dooley (D-Calif)	$148,223	39%
Charles W. Stenholm (D-Texas)	$148,003	44%
Bill Emerson (R-Mo)	$146,925	36%
Ben Nighthorse Campbell (D-Colo)†	$121,574	9%
Bob Smith (R-Ore)	$118,487	47%
Bill Sarpalius (D-Texas)	$114,781	25%
Jim Nussle (R-Iowa)	$97,682	18%
Pat Roberts (R-Kan)	$97,525	44%
Richard Stallings (D-Idaho)†	$96,430	12%
Steve Gunderson (R-Wis)	$93,316	30%
Glenn English (D-Okla)	$92,550	32%
Wayne Allard (R-Colo)	$90,038	23%
Charlie Rose (D-NC)	$89,275	28%
Gary Condit (D-Calif)	$89,272	38%
Tom Lewis (R-Fla)	$87,793	41%
Dan Glickman (D-Kan)	$71,100	10%
Mike Espy (D-Miss)	$68,350	24%
Collin C. Peterson (D-Minn)	$68,267	20%
John A. Boehner (R-Ohio)	$67,538	20%
Dave Camp (R-Mich)	$67,255	19%
Harold L. Volkmer (D-Mo)	$67,008	25%
Thomas W. Ewing (R-Ill)	$65,189	17%
Bill Barrett (R-Neb)	$64,890	22%
Jill L. Long (D-Ind)	$61,500	21%
Larry Combest (R-Texas)	$57,380	33%
Dave Nagle (D-Iowa)	$56,555	10%
Leon E. Panetta (D-Calif)	$55,900	19%
Tim Johnson (D-SD)	$54,775	20%

	Total from Cmte-Related Contribs	Pct of Member's Lg Contribs
George E. Brown Jr. (D-Calif)	$52,550	8%
Jim Jontz (D-Ind)	$50,450	12%
Mike Kopetski (D-Ore)	$41,337	12%
Robin Tallon (D-SC)	$38,950	41%
Timothy J. Penny (D-Minn)	$35,450	34%
Harley O. Staggers Jr. (D-WVa)	$20,000	11%
James T. Walsh (R-NY)	$16,100	12%
Jim Olin (D-Va)	$10,075	38%
Richard Stallings (D-Idaho)	$9,850	15%
Larry J. Hopkins (R-Ky)	$5,500	100%
Sid Morrison (R-Wash)	$4,000	39%
Walter B. Jones (D-NC)	$3,650	22%

Top 20 Agriculture-Related Contributors to Committee Members in 1991-92

1	Associated Milk Producers	$165,300
2	ConAgra Inc	$98,450
3	National Cattlemen's Assn*	$92,550
4	ACRE (Action Cmte for Rural Electrification)*	$82,750
5	American Crystal Sugar Corp	$80,400
6	Chicago Mercantile Exchange	$78,950
7	RJR Nabisco	$72,250
8	Mid-America Dairymen	$72,150
9	Food Marketing Institute	$68,970
10	American Veterinary Medical Assn	$68,500
11	American Sugarbeet Growers Assn	$68,150
12	American Assn of Crop Insurers	$63,900
13	National Cotton Council	$63,105
14	Philip Morris*	$62,345
15	National Broiler Council	$48,200
16	Chicago Board of Trade	$46,850
17	Farm Credit Council	$46,755
18	American Meat Institute	$41,581
19	National Council of Farmer Co-ops	$39,400
20	National Pork Producers Council	$38,551

† Ran for US Senate in 1992

* Contributions came from more than one affiliate or subsidiary.

Summary

Farmers and agribusiness corporations involved in the production of crops were the leading source of campaign funds for members of the House Agriculture committee, but committee members also drew contributions from many other agriculture-related industries. Dairy farmers, agricultural chemical manufacturers, and a wide variety of agricultural service companies were also major sources of cash, as were livestock and poultry producers, commodities brokers, tobacco companies and timber and paper producers. Within the crop production sector, sugar growers led all other groups by a wide margin — a reflection of the importance of sugar in the American diet and also the role of federal subsidies in sweetening the growers' profits.

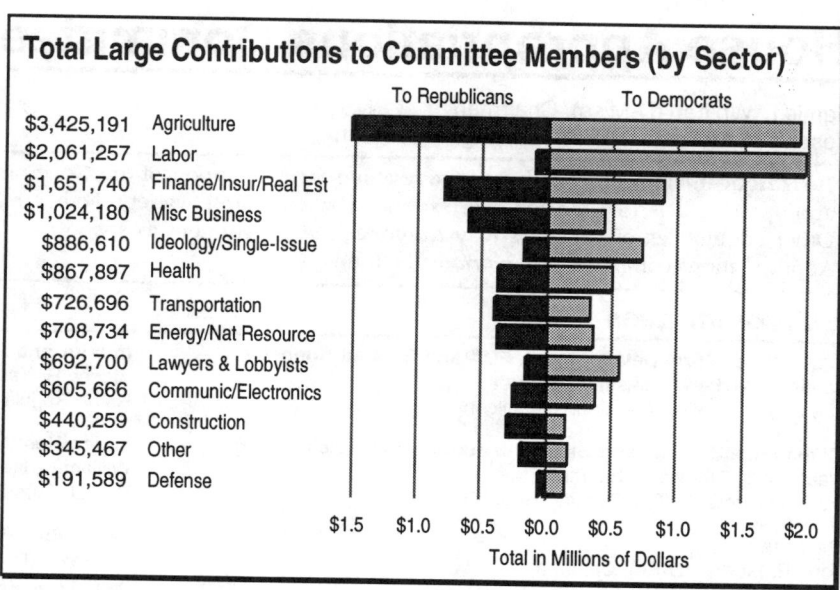

Total Large Contributions to Committee Members (by Sector)

$3,425,191	Agriculture
$2,061,257	Labor
$1,651,740	Finance/Insur/Real Est
$1,024,180	Misc Business
$886,610	Ideology/Single-Issue
$867,897	Health
$726,696	Transportation
$708,734	Energy/Nat Resource
$692,700	Lawyers & Lobbyists
$605,666	Communic/Electronics
$440,259	Construction
$345,467	Other
$191,589	Defense

Total in Millions of Dollars

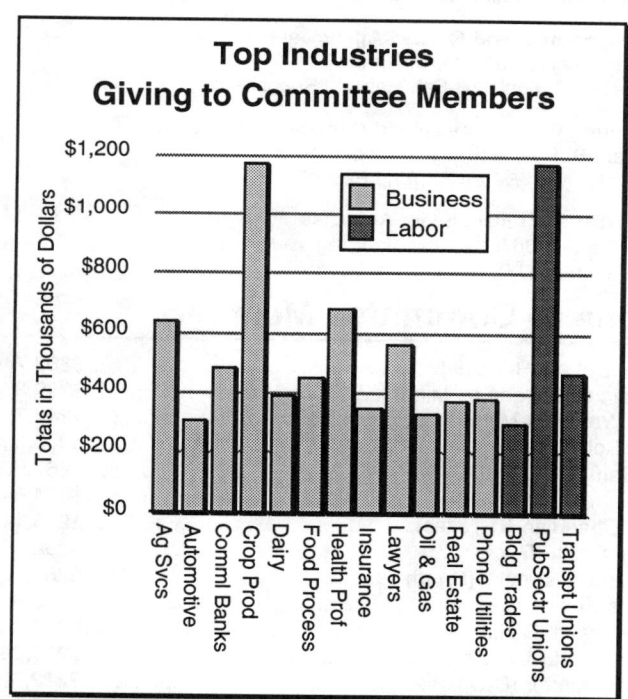

Top Industries Giving to Committee Members

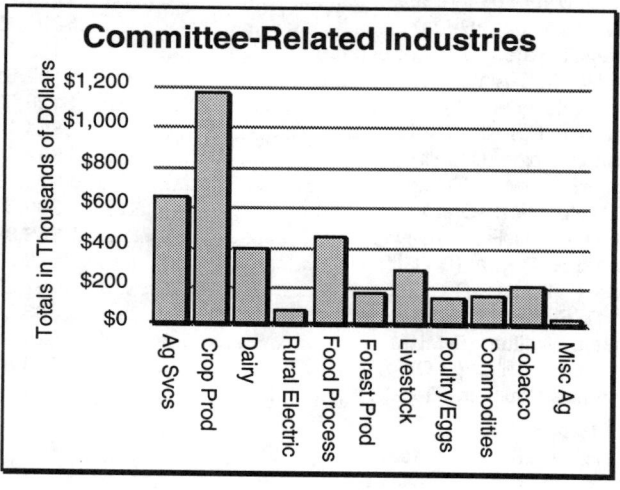

Committee-Related Industries

Leading Industries Giving to Committee Members

Business

Agricultural Services/Products	$635,119
Automotive	$299,553
Commercial Banks	$473,528
Crop Production & Basic Processing	$1,159,173
Dairy	$386,841
Food Processing & Sales	$445,664
Health Professionals	$673,127
Insurance	$336,975
Lawyers/Law Firms	$550,513
Oil & Gas	$318,900
Real Estate	$367,019
Telephone Utilities	$377,720

Labor

Building Trade Unions	$287,345
Public Sector Unions	$1,159,005
Transportation Unions	$458,234

Leading Committee-Related Industries Giving to Committee Members

Business

Agricultural Services/Products	$635,119
Crop Production & Basic Processing	$1,159,173
Dairy	$386,841
Rural Electric Utilities	$74,050
Food Processing & Sales	$445,664
Forestry & Forest Products	$163,214
Livestock	$278,092
Poultry & Eggs	$135,050
Commodity Trading	$150,150
Tobacco	$196,346
Misc Agriculture	$25,692

131

House Appropriations Committee

Jamie L. Whitten (D-Miss), Chairman
Joseph M. McDade (R-Pa), Ranking Republican

Party Ratio: 37 Democrats
22 Republicans

Jurisdiction: (1) Appropriation of the revenue for the support of the Government; (2) Rescissions of appropriations contained in appropriation acts; (3) Transfers of unexpended balances, and a variety of other duties involving the appropriation of government funds. Other committees of Congress may *authorize* the government to spend money on various projects and programs, but only the Appropriations committee *appropriates* the funds.

Subcommittees

Agriculture, Rural Development, FDA and Related Agencies
Jamie L. Whitten (D-Miss), Chairman
Joe Skeen (R-NM), Ranking Republican

Commerce, Justice, and State, the Judiciary and Related Agencies
Neal Smith (D-Iowa), Chairman
Harold Rogers (R-Ky), Ranking Republican

Defense
John P. Murtha (D-Pa), Chairman
Joseph M. McDade (R-Pa), Ranking Republican

District of Columbia
Julian C. Dixon (D-Calif), Chairman
Dean A. Gallo (R-NJ), Ranking Republican

Energy and Water Development
Tom Bevill (D-Ala), Chairman
John T. Myers (R-Ind), Ranking Republican

Foreign Operations, Export Financing and Related Programs
David R. Obey (D-Wis), Chairman
Mickey Edwards (R-Okla), Ranking Republican

Interior and Related Agencies
Sidney R. Yates (D-Ill), Chairman
Ralph Regula (R-Ohio), Ranking Republican

Labor, Health and Human Services, Education and Related Agencies
William H. Natcher (D-Ky), Chairman
Carl D. Pursell (R-Mich), Ranking Republican

Legislative Branch
Vic Fazio (D-Calif), Chairman
Jerry Lewis (R-Calif), Ranking Republican

Military Construction
W. G. "Bill" Hefner (D-NC), Chairman
Bill Lowery (R-Calif), Ranking Republican

Transportation and Related Agencies
William Lehman (D-Fla), Chairman
Lawrence Coughlin (R-Pa), Ranking Republican

Treasury, Postal Service and General Government
Edward R. Roybal (D-Calif), Chairman
Frank R. Wolf (R-Va), Ranking Republican

VA, HUD and Independent Agencies
Bob Traxler (D-Mich), Chairman
Bill Green (R-NY), Ranking Republican

Total PAC and Large Individual Contributions to Committee Members

Vic Fazio (D-Calif)	$1,715,706
Les AuCoin (D-Ore)[1]	$1,672,141
Steny H. Hoyer (D-Md)	$1,091,486
Charles Wilson (D-Texas)	$1,089,956
Bob Carr (D-Mich)	$951,370
John P. Murtha (D-Pa)	$876,783
Robert J. Mrazek (D-NY)	$788,458
Bill Green (R-NY)	$635,158
Joseph D. Early (D-Mass)	$595,518
Ronald D. Coleman (D-Texas)	$590,272
Chester G. Atkins (D-Mass)	$526,348
Harold Rogers (R-Ky)	$505,082
Richard J. Durbin (D-Ill)	$493,702
Barbara F. Vucanovich (R-Nev)	$471,113
Norm Dicks (D-Wash)	$469,728
W. G. "Bill" Hefner (D-NC)	$457,667
David E. Skaggs (D-Colo)	$454,221
Jerry Lewis (R-Calif)	$435,220
Dean A. Gallo (R-NJ)	$427,809
Bill Lowery (R-Calif)	$423,953
Alan B. Mollohan (D-WVa)	$393,925
Mickey Edwards (R-Okla)	$388,827
Nancy Pelosi (D-Calif)	$387,813
Bill Alexander (D-Ark)	$371,886
David R. Obey (D-Wis)	$346,125
John Porter (R-Ill)	$341,385
Jim Ross Lightfoot (R-Iowa)	$340,475
Joseph M. McDade (R-Pa)	$334,623
David Price (D-NC)	$323,455
Frank R. Wolf (R-Va)	$312,158
Tom DeLay (R-Texas)	$307,744
Martin Olav Sabo (D-Minn)	$290,309
Vin Weber (R-Minn)	$282,753
Jim Kolbe (R-Ariz)	$273,343
William H. Gray III (D-Pa)[2]	$267,995
William Lehman (D-Fla)	$264,643
Jim Chapman (D-Texas)	$263,149
Neal Smith (D-Iowa)	$262,542
Peter J. Visclosky (D-Ind)	$262,476
Louis Stokes (D-Ohio)	$260,657
Joe Skeen (R-NM)	$240,363
Robert L. Livingston (R-La)	$231,250
Marcy Kaptur (D-Ohio)	$222,325
John T. Myers (R-Ind)	$215,708
C. W. Bill Young (R-Fla)	$207,150
Sidney R. Yates (D-Ill)	$189,164
Tom Bevill (D-Ala)	$187,810
Bob Traxler (D-Mich)	$126,528
Lawrence J. Smith (D-Fla)	$84,743
Julian C. Dixon (D-Calif)	$82,489
Bernard J. Dwyer (D-NJ)	$77,875
Ralph Regula (R-Ohio)	$69,513
Matthew F. McHugh (D-NY)	$68,890
Edward R. Roybal (D-Calif)	$68,625
Lindsay Thomas (D-Ga)	$67,278
Carl D. Pursell (R-Mich)	$63,000
Jamie L. Whitten (D-Miss)	$29,300
Clarence E. Miller (R-Ohio)	$18,800
Lawrence Coughlin (R-Pa)	-$1,045

[1] Ran for Senate in 1992
[2] Resigned in September 1991

Summary

Businesses and industries that rely heavily on government contracts keep a sharp eye on the activities of the congressional appropriations committees — particularly defense contractors, whose fortunes may rise or fall depending on decisions reached by these panels. John Murtha, the Pennsylvania Democrat who chairs the Defense Appropriations subcommittee, collected over $230,000 from defense contractors in 1991-92, once again leading all other House recipients in defense dollars. Democrat Charles Wilson of Texas wasn't far behind, with over $210,000 from the defense sector. In all, eight of the 13 members of Murtha's subcommittee drew $50,000 or more from defense industry contributors.

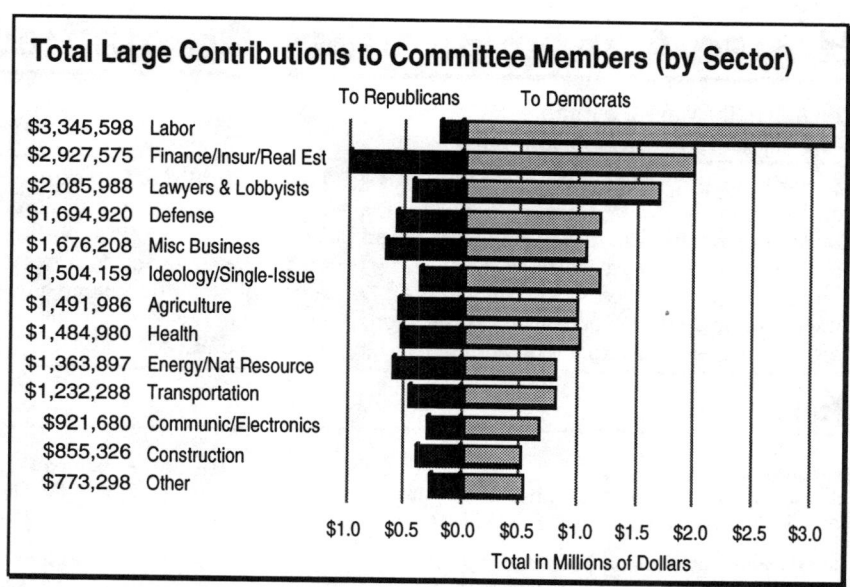

Total Large Contributions to Committee Members (by Sector)

$3,345,598	Labor
$2,927,575	Finance/Insur/Real Est
$2,085,988	Lawyers & Lobbyists
$1,694,920	Defense
$1,676,208	Misc Business
$1,504,159	Ideology/Single-Issue
$1,491,986	Agriculture
$1,484,980	Health
$1,363,897	Energy/Nat Resource
$1,232,288	Transportation
$921,680	Communic/Electronics
$855,326	Construction
$773,298	Other

Total in Millions of Dollars

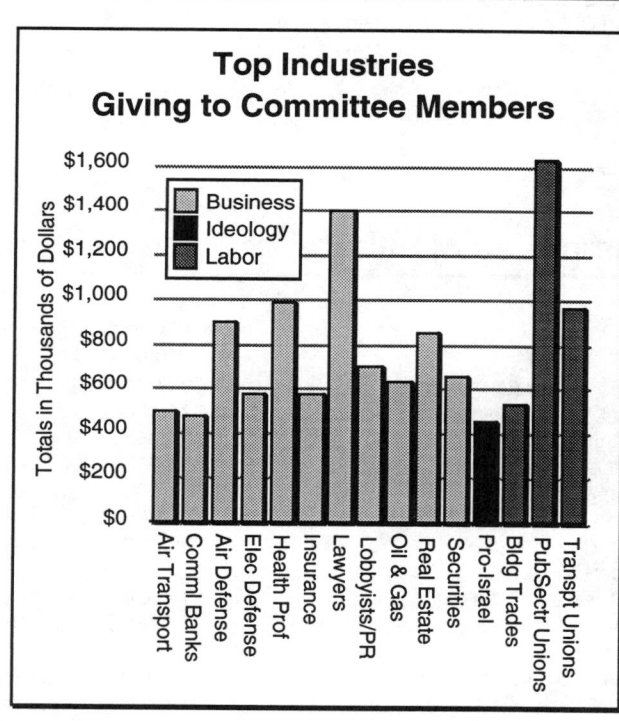

Top Industries Giving to Committee Members

Top 20 Contributors to Committee Members in 1991-92

1	National Assn of Realtors	$276,510
2	American Medical Assn*	$246,599
3	Teamsters Union*	$217,670
4	United Auto Workers	$169,650
5	Air Line Pilots Assn	$165,000
6	National Education Assn*	$162,250
7	American Dental Assn	$148,289
8	Marine Engineers Union*	$147,250
9	National Rifle Assn	$143,550
10	Assn of Trial Lawyers of America	$139,350
11	American Fedn of St/Cnty/Munic Employees	$138,950
12	AT&T*	$137,995
13	United Parcel Service	$136,174
14	Laborers Union*	$128,750
15	National Assn Retired Federal Employees	$128,500
16	Carpenters & Joiners Union	$121,950
17	National Assn of Letter Carriers*	$121,800
18	United Transportation Union	$116,100
19	National Auto Dealers Assn	$108,000
20	General Motors*	$107,250

* Contributions came from more than one affiliate or subsidiary.

Leading Industries
Giving to Committee Members

Business

Air Transport	$487,543
Commercial Banks	$459,294
Defense Aerospace	$888,875
Defense Electronics	$568,250
Health Professionals	$983,543
Insurance	$567,517
Lawyers/Law Firms	$1,390,579
Lobbyists/PR	$695,409
Oil & Gas	$628,613
Real Estate	$839,331
Securities & Investment	$649,279

Ideological/Single-Issue

Pro-Israel	$439,055

Labor

Building Trade Unions	$527,046
Public Sector Unions	$1,617,281
Transportation Unions	$960,681

House Armed Services Committee

Les Aspin (D-Wis), Chairman
Bill Dickinson (R-Ala), Ranking Republican

Party Ratio: 32 Democrats
21 Republicans

> **Jurisdiction:** (1) Common defense generally; (2) The Department of Defense generally, including the Departments of the Army, Navy, and Air Force; (3) Ammunition depots, forts, arsenals, Army, Navy, and Air Force reservations and establishments; (4) Conservation, development, and use of naval petroleum and oil shale reserves; (5) Pay, promotion, retirement, and other benefits and privileges of members of the armed forces; (6) Scientific research and development in support of the armed services; (7) Selective service; (8) Size and composition of the Army, Navy and Air Force; (9) Soldiers' and sailors' homes; (10) Strategic and critical materials necessary for the common defense; (11) Military applications of nuclear energy. The committee also has oversight duties with respect to international arms control and disarmament, and military dependents' education.

Subcommittees

Investigations
Nicholas Mavroules (D-Mass), Chairman
Larry J. Hopkins (R-Ky), Ranking Republican

Military Installations and Facilities
Patricia Schroeder (D-Colo), Chairwoman
David O'B. Martin (R-NY), Ranking Republican

Military Personnel and Compensation
Beverly B. Byron (D-Md), Chairwoman
Herbert H. Bateman (R-Va), Ranking Republican

Procurement and Military Nuclear Systems
Les Aspin (D-Wis), Chairman
Bill Dickinson (R-Ala), Ranking Republican

Readiness
Earl Hutto (D-Fla), Chairman
John R. Kasich (R-Ohio), Ranking Republican

Research and Development
Ronald V. Dellums (D-Calif), Chairman
Robert W. Davis (R-Mich), Ranking Republican

Seapower and Strategic and Critical Materials
Charles E. Bennett (D-Fla), Chairman
Floyd D. Spence (R-SC), Ranking Republican

Total Defense-Related Contributions to Committee Members

	Total from Cmte-Related Contribs	Pct of Member's Lg Contribs
Les Aspin (D-Wis)	$222,125	21%
Dave McCurdy (D-Okla)	$129,450	27%
Herbert H. Bateman (R-Va)	$103,750	19%
Richard Ray (D-Ga)	$92,800	17%
Duncan Hunter (R-Calif)	$81,167	19%
Nicholas Mavroules (D-Mass)	$77,200	15%
Randy "Duke" Cunningham (R-Calif)	$72,055	14%
Chet Edwards (D-Texas)	$58,950	13%
Gary Franks (R-Conn)	$54,959	11%
Marilyn Lloyd (D-Tenn)	$51,750	15%
Ike Skelton (D-Mo)	$49,700	20%
Beverly B. Byron (D-Md)	$49,500	32%
H. Martin Lancaster (D-NC)	$47,000	10%
Barbara Boxer (D-Calif)†	$45,720	1%
George "Buddy" Darden (D-Ga)	$44,700	14%
Albert G. Bustamante (D-Texas)	$43,200	11%
H. James Saxton (R-NJ)	$41,955	10%
Norman Sisisky (D-Va)	$39,550	20%
Jim McCrery (R-La)	$39,300	7%
Robert W. Davis (R-Mich)	$38,250	27%
Ronald K. Machtley (R-RI)	$38,025	11%
James V. Hansen (R-Utah)	$36,750	20%
Bill Dickinson (R-Ala)	$36,700	67%
Curt Weldon (R-Pa)	$36,323	13%
Earl Hutto (D-Fla)	$34,850	18%
Bob Stump (R-Ariz)	$34,065	18%
Floyd D. Spence (R-SC)	$32,850	27%
Jon Kyl (R-Ariz)	$31,920	7%
George J. Hochbrueckner (D-NY)	$30,300	8%

	Total from Cmte-Related Contribs	Pct of Member's Lg Contribs
Gene Taylor (D-Miss)	$29,270	12%
Frank McCloskey (D-Ind)	$26,400	8%
Dennis M. Hertel (D-Mich)	$26,045	15%
James Bilbray (D-Nev)	$23,950	6%
John M. Spratt Jr. (D-SC)	$23,900	10%
Owen B. Pickett (D-Va)	$22,650	10%
Glen Browder (D-Ala)	$22,500	14%
Robert K. Dornan (R-Calif)	$20,350	6%
Joel Hefley (R-Colo)	$18,000	16%
G. V. "Sonny" Montgomery (D-Miss)	$17,750	13%
Thomas H. Andrews (D-Maine)	$17,161	3%
John R. Kasich (R-Ohio)	$16,850	7%
John Tanner (D-Tenn)	$16,450	8%
Michael R. McNulty (D-NY)	$13,650	11%
Arthur Ravenel Jr. (R-SC)	$13,000	7%
Thomas M. Foglietta (D-Pa)	$12,000	4%
Solomon P. Ortiz (D-Texas)	$10,950	5%
Andy Ireland (R-Fla)	$7,100	9%
Ben Blaz (R-Guam)	$4,950	7%
Patricia Schroeder (D-Colo)	$4,500	2%
Lane Evans (D-Ill)	$3,500	2%
Neil Abercrombie (D-Hawaii)	$1,750	1%
Ronald V. Dellums (D-Calif)	$1,000	1%
David O'B. Martin (R-NY)	$0	0%
Charles E. Bennett (D-Fla)	-$1,000	0%

† Ran for US Senate in 1992

Summary

The demise of the Soviet Union and a general warming in international relations may be welcome news to most Americans, but it also signals hard times for the nation's defense industry. The House and Senate Armed Services and Appropriations committees are the key congressional panels wrestling with the problem of downsizing the military without crippling the American defense industry.

The patterns of contributions within the committee reflects the industry's concern. Defense contractors delivered nearly $2 million in contributions to House Armed Services members in the 1992 elections, and the Top 20 list of contributors bears a close resemblance to the Pentagon's list of top contractors.

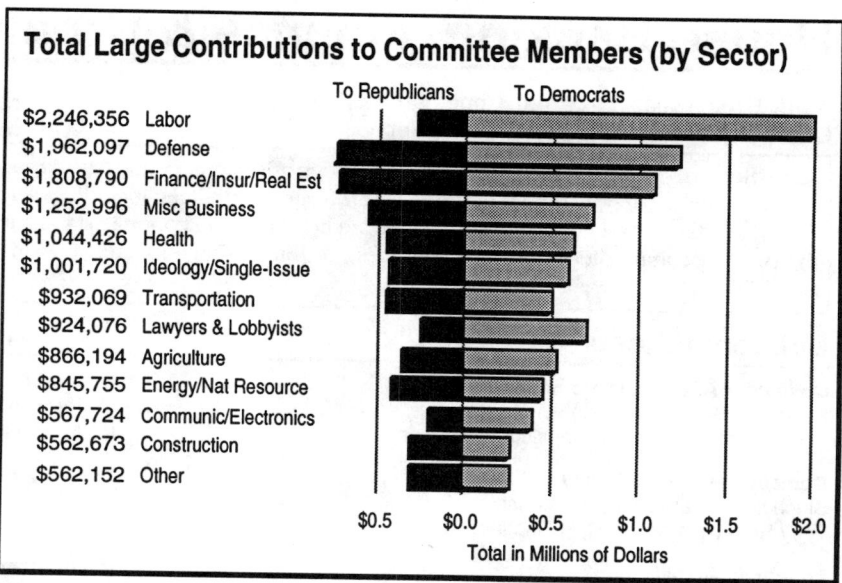

Total Large Contributions to Committee Members (by Sector)

$2,246,356	Labor
$1,962,097	Defense
$1,808,790	Finance/Insur/Real Est
$1,252,996	Misc Business
$1,044,426	Health
$1,001,720	Ideology/Single-Issue
$932,069	Transportation
$924,076	Lawyers & Lobbyists
$866,194	Agriculture
$845,755	Energy/Nat Resource
$567,724	Communic/Electronics
$562,673	Construction
$562,152	Other

Total in Millions of Dollars

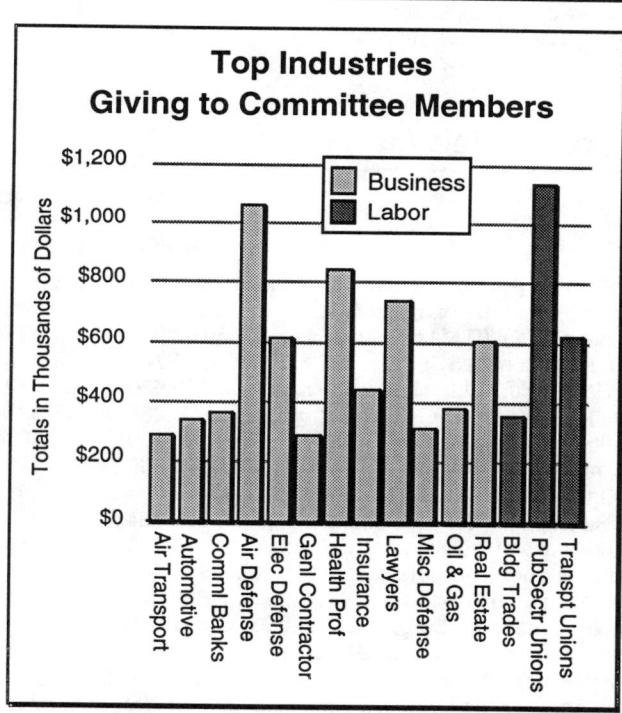

Top Industries Giving to Committee Members

Totals in Thousands of Dollars

Business / Labor

Air Transport, Automotive, Comml Banks, Air Defense, Elec Defense, Genl Contractor, Health Prof, Insurance, Lawyers, Misc Defense, Oil & Gas, Real Estate, Bldg Trades, PubSectr Unions, Transpt Unions

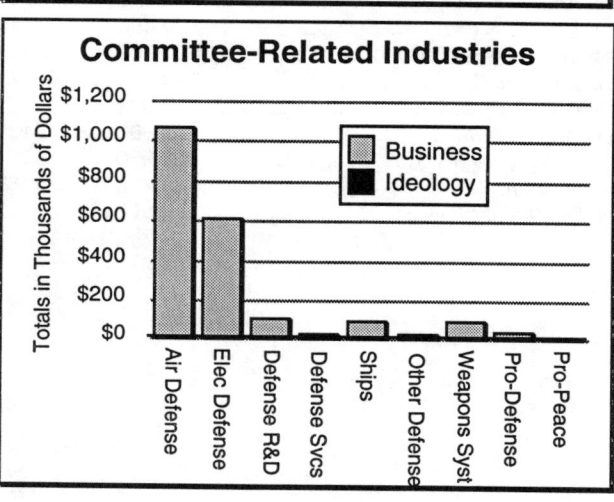

Committee-Related Industries

Totals in Thousands of Dollars

Business / Ideology

Air Defense, Elec Defense, Defense R&D, Defense Svcs, Ships, Other Defense, Weapons Syst, Pro-Defense, Pro-Peace

Top 20 Defense-Related Contributors to Committee Members in 1991-92

1	General Dynamics	$105,600
2	Textron Inc	$104,250
3	Martin Marietta Corp	$97,700
4	AT&T	$79,200
5	McDonnell Douglas*	$78,275
6	Lockheed Corp	$76,720
7	Grumman Corp	$72,775
8	Raytheon	$72,525
9	General Electric	$69,500
10	Rockwell International	$67,250
11	General Motors*	$62,450
12	General Atomics	$59,900
13	Northrop Corp	$54,400
14	LTV Aerospace & Defense Co	$52,000
15	Tenneco Inc	$48,000
16	United Technologies	$45,600
17	Boeing Co	$45,000
18	E-Systems*	$44,400
19	Colt Industries	$41,400
20	GTE Corp	$39,900

* Contributions came from more than one affiliate or subsidiary.

Leading Industries Giving to Committee Members

Business

Defense Aerospace	$1,054,470
Defense Electronics	$603,482
Defense R&D	$97,200
Defense Services	$20,600
Naval Ships	$86,645
Weapons Systems	$84,500
Other Defense	$15,200

Ideological/Single-Issue

Pro-Defense	$35,462
Pro-Peace	$4,261

House Banking, Finance & Urban Affairs Committee

Henry B. Gonzalez (D-Texas), Chairman
Chalmers P. Wylie (R-Ohio), Ranking Republican

Party Ratio: 31 Democrats
20 Republicans

Jurisdiction: (1) Banks and banking, including deposit insurance and Federal monetary policy; (2) money and credit, including currency and the issuance of notes and redemption thereof; gold and silver, including the coinage thereof; valuation and revaluation of the dollar; (3) Urban development; (4) Public and private housing; (5) Economic stabilization, defense production, renegotiation, and control of the price of commodities, rents and services; (6) International finance; (7) Financial aid to commerce and industry; (8) International financial and monetary organizations.

Subcommittees

Consumer Affairs and Coinage
Esteban E. Torres (D-Calif), Chairman
Al McCandless (R-Calif), Ranking Republican

Domestic Monetary Policy
Stephen L. Neal (D-NC), Chairman
Toby Roth (R-Wis), Ranking Republican

Economic Stabilization
Thomas R. Carper (D-Del), Chairman
Tom Ridge (R-Pa), Ranking Republican

Financial Institutions Supervision, Regulation and Insurance
Frank Annunzio (D-Ill), Chairman
Chalmers P. Wylie (R-Ohio), Ranking Republican

General Oversight and Investigations
Carroll Hubbard Jr. (D-Ky), Chairman
Bill McCullum (R-Fla), Ranking Republican

Housing and Community Development
Henry B. Gonzalez (D-Texas), Chairman
Marge Roukema (R-NJ), Ranking Republican

International Development, Finance, Trade and Monetary Policy
Mary Rose Oakar (D-Ohio), Chairwoman
Jim Leach (R-Iowa), Ranking Republican

Policy Research and Insurance
Ben Erdreich (D-Ala), Chairman
Doug Bereuter (R-Neb), Ranking Republican

Total Committee-Related Contributions to Committee Members

	Total from Cmte-Related Contribs	Pct of Member's Lg Contribs		Total from Cmte-Related Contribs	Pct of Member's Lg Contribs
Tom Campbell (R-Calif)†	$842,114	23%	Cliff Stearns (R-Fla)	$97,888	37%
Charles E. Schumer (D-NY)	$407,746	60%	Bruce F. Vento (D-Minn)	$97,375	43%
Stephen L. Neal (D-NC)	$223,550	52%	Richard E. Neal (D-Mass)	$92,318	33%
Richard H. Baker (R-La)	$209,775	36%	Liz J. Patterson (D-SC)	$90,720	34%
John J. LaFalce (D-NY)	$208,997	43%	John W. Cox Jr. (D-Ill)	$80,570	21%
Bill Paxon (R-NY)	$197,392	31%	Floyd H. Flake (D-NY)	$76,264	39%
Mary Rose Oakar (D-Ohio)	$192,061	22%	Gerald D. Kleczka (D-Wis)	$73,000	28%
Peter Hoagland (D-Neb)	$191,329	32%	Dick Armey (R-Texas)	$71,500	24%
Ben Erdreich (D-Ala)	$170,600	30%	Bill Orton (D-Utah)	$67,294	26%
Larry LaRocco (D-Idaho)	$155,197	33%	Mel Hancock (R-Mo)	$66,324	23%
Toby Roth (R-Wis)	$149,475	37%	Charles Luken (D-Ohio)	$66,025	36%
James P. Moran Jr. (D-Va)	$148,558	21%	Paul E. Gillmor (R-Ohio)	$65,342	32%
Sam Johnson (R-Texas)	$143,975	24%	Craig Thomas (R-Wyo)	$63,675	20%
Tom Ridge (R-Pa)	$143,410	34%	Carroll Hubbard Jr. (D-Ky)	$61,950	50%
Jim Bacchus (D-Fla)	$143,300	19%	John J. "Jimmy" Duncan Jr. (R-Tenn)	$57,615	28%
Bill McCollum (R-Fla)	$141,600	28%	Kweisi Mfume (D-Md)	$52,390	28%
Joseph P. Kennedy II (D-Mass)	$137,536	23%	Frank Annunzio (D-Ill)	$32,220	75%
Marge Roukema (R-NJ)	$133,485	38%	Ted Weiss (D-NY)	$30,450	11%
Jim Nussle (R-Iowa)	$132,525	24%	Esteban E. Torres (D-Calif)	$27,600	21%
Frank Riggs (R-Calif)	$132,139	27%	Maxine Waters (D-Calif)	$20,475	12%
Jim Slattery (D-Kan)	$122,894	20%	Thomas R. Carper (D-Del)	$9,063	85%
Gary L. Ackerman (D-NY)	$121,975	21%	Jim Leach (R-Iowa)	$7,800	13%
Al McCandless (R-Calif)	$119,799	44%	Bernard Sanders (I-Vt)	$2,950	1%
Paul E. Kanjorski (D-Pa)	$111,400	42%	Henry B. Gonzalez (D-Texas)	$1,700	6%
Barney Frank (D-Mass)	$109,293	36%	Doug Barnard Jr. (D-Ga)	$900	22%
Doug Bereuter (R-Neb)	$105,931	47%			
Chalmers P. Wylie (R-Ohio)	$102,520	77%			

† Ran for U.S. Senate in 1992

Summary

Commercial banks were the leading (but hardly the only) major contributor to members of the House Banking Committee in 1991-92, since no committee in the House is as important to the heavily-regulated banking industry. The issue of bank deregulation has been high on the committee's agenda in recent years, as Congress tries to shore up the sagging fortunes of many of the nation's leading financial institutions. This is the same committee that in the early 1980s loosened the rules governing savings & loans — thereby setting the stage for what became the most expensive political scandal (and subsequent bailout) in American history.

Aside from banking and financial interests, the committee also deals with housing issues — a fact that helped attract nearly $1.3 million dollars in contributions from the real estate and home building industries.

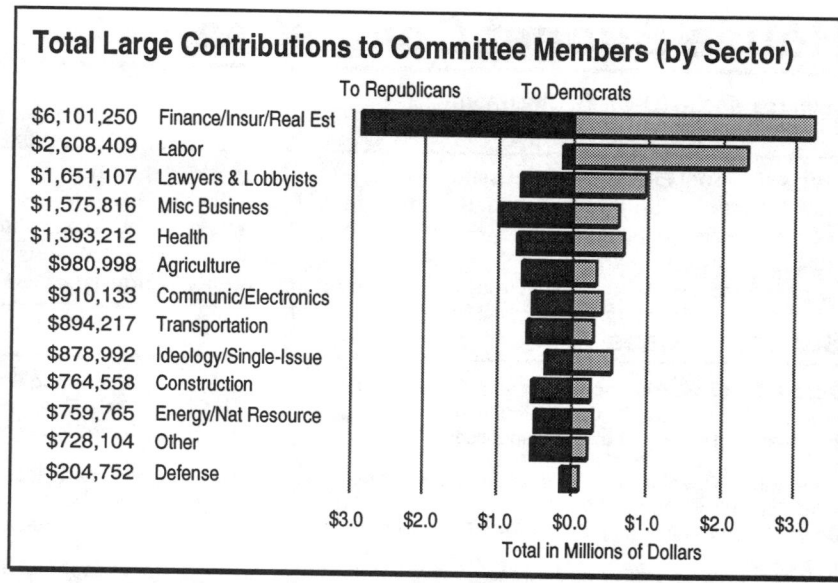

Total Large Contributions to Committee Members (by Sector)

	To Republicans / To Democrats
$6,101,250	Finance/Insur/Real Est
$2,608,409	Labor
$1,651,107	Lawyers & Lobbyists
$1,575,816	Misc Business
$1,393,212	Health
$980,998	Agriculture
$910,133	Communic/Electronics
$894,217	Transportation
$878,992	Ideology/Single-Issue
$764,558	Construction
$759,765	Energy/Nat Resource
$728,104	Other
$204,752	Defense

Total in Millions of Dollars
$3.0 $2.0 $1.0 $0.0 $1.0 $2.0 $3.0

Top Industries Giving to Committee Members

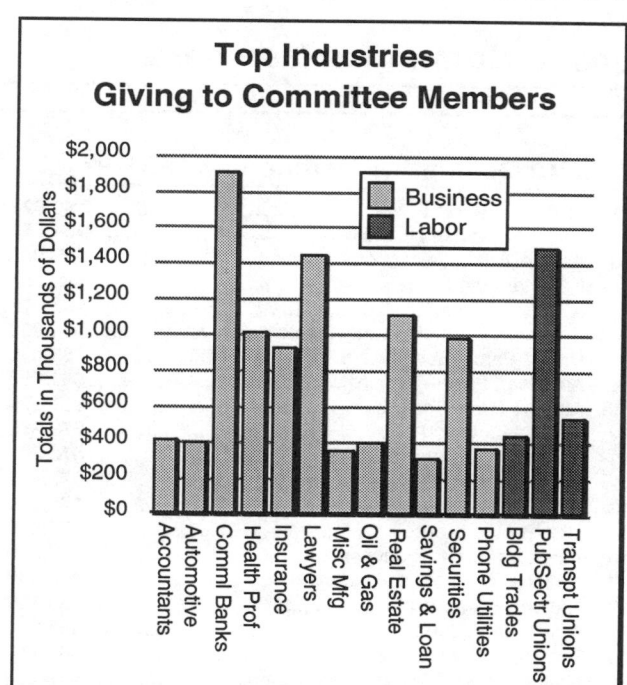

Totals in Thousands of Dollars. Legend: Business, Labor.

Categories: Accountants, Automotive, Comml Banks, Health Prof, Insurance, Lawyers, Misc Mfg, Oil & Gas, Real Estate, Savings & Loan, Securities, Phone Utilities, Bldg Trades, PubSectr Unions, Transpt Unions

Committee-Related Industries

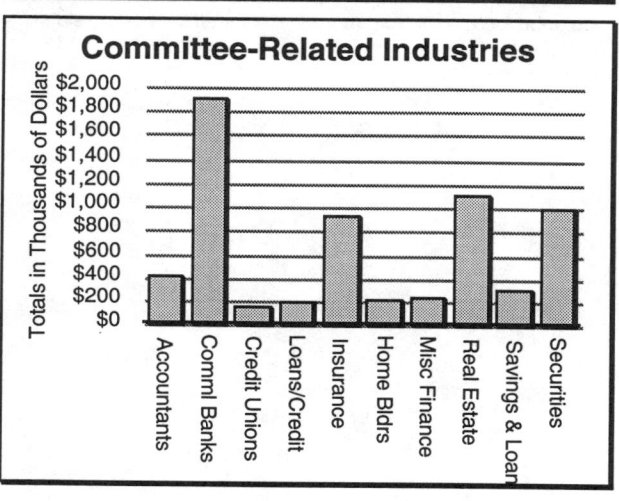

Totals in Thousands of Dollars.

Categories: Accountants, Comml Banks, Credit Unions, Loans/Credit, Insurance, Home Bldrs, Misc Finance, Real Estate, Savings & Loan, Securities

Top 20 Committee-Related Contributors to Committee Members in 1991-92

1	National Assn of Realtors	$316,733
2	American Bankers Assn*	$305,965
3	American Institute of CPA's	$224,350
4	JP Morgan & Co	$153,500
5	National Assn of Life Underwriters	$120,000
6	National Assn of Home Builders	$110,196
7	Credit Union National Assn*	$108,450
8	Chase Manhattan	$100,650
9	Citicorp	$99,900
10	US League of Savings Assns*	$94,169
11	Citizens & Southern National Bank	$92,850
12	Barnett Banks Inc	$75,950
13	BankAmerica Corp*	$66,750
14	Independent Bankers Assn	$64,807
15	American Council of Life Insurance	$60,769
16	American Express*	$59,900
17	Goldman, Sachs & Co	$55,358
18	Household International Inc	$54,650
19	Bankers Trust	$54,400
20	Associated Credit Bureaus	$51,950

* Contributions came from more than one affiliate or subsidiary.

Leading Committee-Related Industries Giving to Committee Members

Business

Accountants	$390,834
Commercial Banks	$1,893,409
Credit Unions	$144,446
Finance/Credit Companies	$188,900
Insurance	$912,372
Home Builders	$210,734
Misc Finance	$217,307
Real Estate	$1,092,077
Savings & Loans	$290,739
Securities & Investment	$971,166

House Budget Committee

Leon E. Panetta (D-Calif), Chairman
Bill Gradison (R-Ohio), Ranking Republican

Party Ratio: 23 Democrats
14 Republicans

Jurisdiction: (1) To report the matters required to be reported by it under titles III and IV of the Congressional Budget Act of 1974; (2) To make continuing studies of the effect on budget outlays of relevant existing and proposed legislation and to report the results of such studies to the House on a recurring basis; (3) To request and evaluate continuing studies of tax expenditures, to devise methods of coordinating tax expenditures, policies, and programs with direct budget outlays, and to report the results of such studies to the House on a recurring basis; and (4) To review, on a continuing basis, the conduct by the Congressional Budget Office of its functions and duties.

Subcommittees

Budget Process, Reconciliation and Enforcement
Anthony C. Beilenson (D-Calif), Chairman
Bill Thomas (R-Calif), Ranking Republican

Community Development and Natural Resources
Mike Espy (D-Miss), Chairman
Helen Delich Bentley (R-Md), Ranking Republican

Defense, Foreign Policy and Space
Richard J. Durbin (D-Ill), Chairman
Jim McCrery (R-La), Ranking Republican

Economic Policy, Projections and Revenues
Dale E. Kildee (D-Mich), Chairman
Amo Houghton (R-NY), Ranking Republican

Human Resources
James L. Oberstar (D-Minn), Chairman
John R. Kasich (R-Ohio), Ranking Republican

Urgent Fiscal Issues
Frank J. Guarini (D-NY), Chairman
Harold Rogers(R-Ky), Ranking Republican

Total PAC and Large Individual Contributions to Committee Members

Richard A. Gephardt (D-Mo) $2,870,796
Helen Delich Bentley (R-Md) $657,606
Bill Paxon (R-NY) $640,187
Jim McCrery (R-La) $565,170
Dale E. Kildee (D-Mich) $558,660
John Bryant (D-Texas) $525,038
Robert T. Matsui (D-Calif) $521,339
Harold Rogers (R-Ky) $505,082
Howard L. Berman (D-Calif) $498,862
Anthony C. Beilenson (D-Calif) $497,109
Rick Santorum (R-Pa) $494,739
Richard J. Durbin (D-Ill) $493,702
Bill Thomas (R-Calif) $469,226
Jerry Huckaby (D-La) $392,884
Lewis F. Payne Jr. (D-Va) $364,257
Louise M. Slaughter (D-NY) $357,247
Mike Parker (D-Miss) $339,891
William E. Dannemeyer (R-Calif)† $339,067
Charles W. Stenholm (D-Texas) $335,166
Barney Frank (D-Mass) $304,428
Alex McMillan (R-NC) $301,050
Leon E. Panetta (D-Calif) $300,800
Martin Olav Sabo (D-Minn) $290,309
Amo Houghton (R-NY) $288,678
Mike Espy (D-Miss) $280,598
Jim Kolbe (R-Ariz) $273,343
John R. Kasich (R-Ohio) $255,254
James L. Oberstar (D-Minn) $247,230
John M. Spratt Jr. (D-SC) $238,600
Bob Wise (D-WVa) $219,450
Christopher Shays (R-Conn) $214,388
Frank J. Guarini (D-NJ) $81,498
Bernard J. Dwyer (D-NJ) $77,875
Jim Cooper (D-Tenn) $65,275
John Miller (R-Wash) $65,000
Bill Gradison (R-Ohio) $40,509
Don J. Pease (D-Ohio) .... -$9,849

Top 20 Contributors to Committee Members in 1991-92

1	American Medical Assn*	$180,624
2	National Assn of Realtors	$154,559
3	Assn of Trial Lawyers of America	$93,000
4	National Auto Dealers Assn	$89,700
5	AT&T	$85,075
6	American Fedn of St/Cnty/Munic Employees	$84,000
7	United Parcel Service	$82,490
8	American Bankers Assn*	$81,250
9	Air Line Pilots Assn	$81,000
10	Teamsters Union	$79,300
11	American Institute of CPA's	$78,000
12	National Assn of Letter Carriers*	$77,925
13	National Education Assn	$75,000
14	United Auto Workers	$72,850
15	Associated Milk Producers	$70,500
16	National Assn of Life Underwriters	$70,500
17	National Rifle Assn	$68,100
18	American Federation of Teachers	$65,000
19	BellSouth Corp*	$60,150
20	National Assn Retired Federal Employees	$57,500

* Contributions came from more than one affiliate or subsidiary.

† Ran for U.S. Senate in 1992

Summary

Along with its counterpart in the Senate, the House Budget Committee is the panel in Congress chiefly responsible for putting together the federal government's annual budget. That assignment, though important to the nation as a whole, is not focused directly on any one industry or interest group — so the patterns in campaign contributions are typical of Congress as a whole. The financial sector was the biggest funder of committee members' 1992 campaigns. Organized labor was second, delivering its dollars overwhelmingly to Democrats.

Total Large Contributions to Committee Members (by Sector)

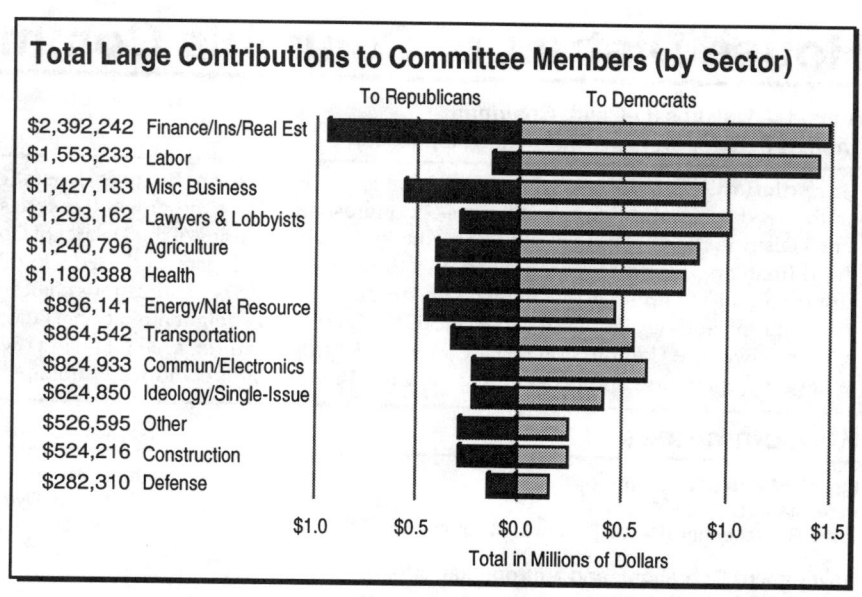

$2,392,242	Finance/Ins/Real Est
$1,553,233	Labor
$1,427,133	Misc Business
$1,293,162	Lawyers & Lobbyists
$1,240,796	Agriculture
$1,180,388	Health
$896,141	Energy/Nat Resource
$864,542	Transportation
$824,933	Commun/Electronics
$624,850	Ideology/Single-Issue
$526,595	Other
$524,216	Construction
$282,310	Defense

Total in Millions of Dollars

Top Industries Giving to Committee Members

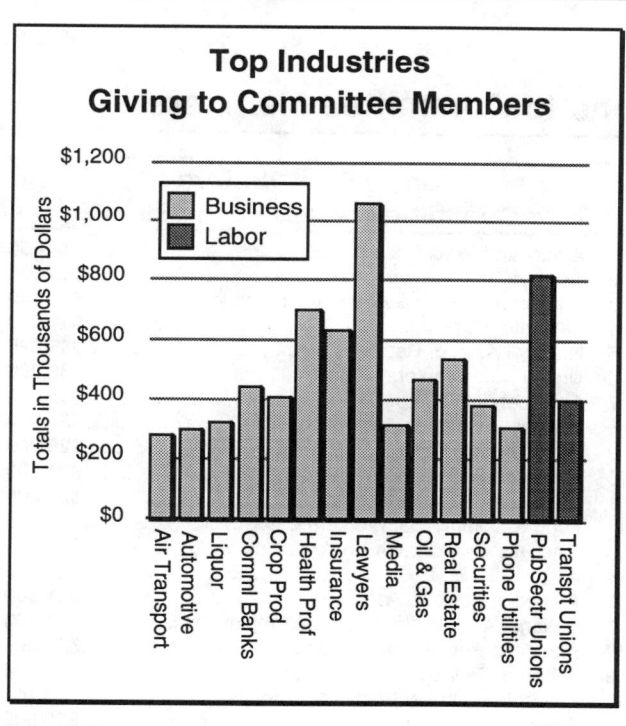

Leading Industries Giving to Committee Members

Business

Air Transport	$272,201
Automotive	$291,547
Beer, Wine & Liquor	$310,540
Commercial Banks	$430,649
Crop Production & Basic Processing	$401,774
Health Professionals	$690,414
Insurance	$621,265
Lawyers/Law Firms	$1,051,616
Media/Entertainment	$301,855
Oil & Gas	$456,957
Real Estate	$529,925
Securities & Investment	$377,447
Telephone Utilities	$297,410

Labor

Public Sector Unions	$811,129
Transportation Unions	$393,970

House District of Columbia Committee

Ronald V. Dellums (D-Calif), Chairman
Thomas J. Bliley Jr. (R-Va), Ranking Republican

Party Ratio: 7 Democrats
4 Republicans

Jurisdiction: (1) Local government, delegated authority, form, finances, operations and programs, of local government bodies, as authorized by . . . the U.S. Constitution—"Congress shall have the power to exercise exclusive legislation in all cases whatsoever over such District . . ."; (2) Political status, jurisdiction and boundaries of the District of Columbia; (3) The annual federal payment — pension fund financing for police, firefighters and teachers; (4) Delegate to the House of Representatives; courts: organization, operations; appointment and removal mechanisms and term of judges; (5) Organizations chartered by Congress: determination of tax-exempt status; (6) Planning and design of the national capital: (a) building height limitation, National Capital Planning Commission, protection of Old Georgetown, the Commission of Fine Arts; (7) Metropolitan regional affairs: (a) Washington Metropolitan Area Transit Authority, (b) emergency planning and procedures, Potomac River shoreline and water quality improvement; (8) The International Community.

Subcommittees

Fiscal Affairs and Health
Pete Stark (D-Calif), Chairman
Dana Rohrabacher (R-Calif), Ranking Republican

Government Operations and Metropolitan Affairs
Alan Wheat (D-Mo), Chairman
Larry Combest (R-Texas), Ranking Republican

Judiciary and Education
Mervyn M. Dymally (D-Calif), Chairman
Bill Lowery (R-Calif), Ranking Republican

Total PAC and Large Individual Contributions to Committee Members

Sander Levin (D-Mich) $791,756
Thomas J. Bliley Jr. (R-Va) $557,531
Pete Stark (D-Calif) $455,572
Bill Lowery (R-Calif) $423,953
Alan Wheat (D-Mo) $414,621
Dana Rohrabacher (R-Calif) $282,873
William H. Gray III (D-Pa)† $267,995
Jim McDermott (D-Wash) $213,735
Ronald V. Dellums (D-Calif) $196,021
Larry Combest (R-Texas) $175,084
Mervyn M. Dymally (D-Calif) $144,911
Eleanor Holmes Norton (D-DC) $136,975

† Resigned in September 1991

Top 20 Contributors to Committee Members in 1991-92

1	American Medical Assn*	$64,450
2	Assn of Trial Lawyers of America	$45,000
3	American Fedn of St/Cnty/Munic Employees	$41,000
4	Teamsters Union	$41,000
5	National Assn of Realtors	$38,825
6	United Auto Workers	$35,900
7	American Institute of CPA's	$32,000
8	National Education Assn	$29,350
9	Air Line Pilots Assn	$28,000
10	American Federation of Teachers	$24,500
11	American Chiropractic Assn	$23,000
12	Food & Commercial Workers Union	$23,000
13	Machinists/Aerospace Workers Union	$22,800
14	AT&T	$21,975
15	American Bankers Assn	$21,500
16	National Assn Retired Federal Employees	$21,500
17	American Postal Workers Union	$20,500
18	Laborers' Political League	$20,400
19	Intl Brotherhood of Electrical Workers	$20,100
20	American Podiatry Assn	$20,000

* Contributions came from more than one affiliate or subsidiary.

Summary

Unlike every other city in America, the nation's capital is governed only partly by its own elected officials, and partly by the U.S. Congress, which has overseen the city's affairs since the District of Columbia was created in 1790. The degree of congressional control has lessened over the years and the city now enjoys most benefits of home rule. But the Congress still controls a major part of the city's purse strings, and decisions made in this committee affect the lives of every resident of Washington.

Since D.C. is not a state, its residents do not elect their own representative, but rather a "delegate," like those who represent Puerto Rico, the Virgin Islands, Guam and American Samoa. Delegates do not have full voting rights on the House floor, but they are entitled to debate and vote on issues within the committees on which they serve.

This second-class status has long rankled D.C. residents. In 1990, in addition to electing their delegate to Congress, the district's voters also elected two "shadow Senators" — one of them the Rev. Jesse Jackson — to lobby for statehood. Unlike the D.C. delegate, the shadow Senators enjoy no official status in Congress, formal or otherwise.

Total Large Contributions to Committee Members (by Sector)

To Republicans — To Democrats

Amount	Sector
$614,475	Labor
$587,778	Health
$563,759	Finance/Insur/Real Est
$318,036	Lawyers & Lobbyists
$290,109	Misc Business
$235,332	Agriculture
$225,672	Ideology/Single-Issue
$212,916	Communic/Electronics
$198,374	Transportation
$191,932	Energy/Nat Resource
$120,826	Other
$114,815	Defense
$95,580	Construction

Total in Thousands of Dollars

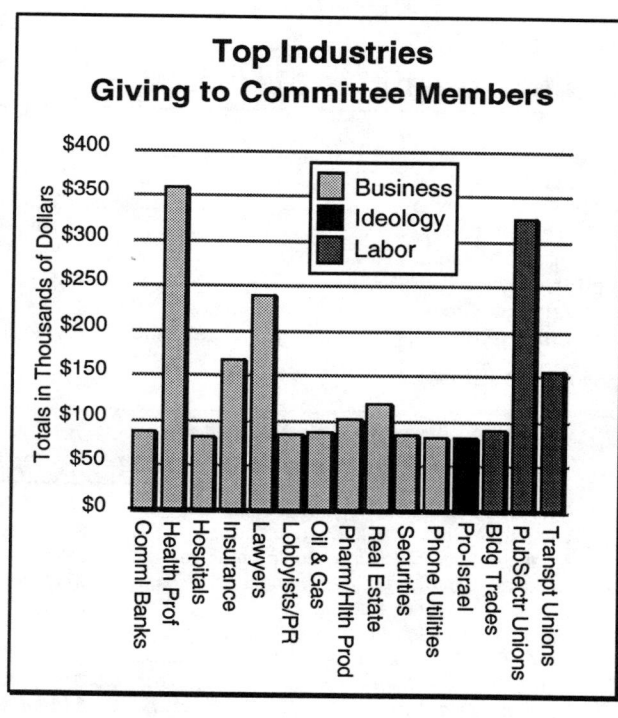

Top Industries Giving to Committee Members

Totals in Thousands of Dollars

Legend: Business, Ideology, Labor

Categories: Comml Banks, Health Prof, Hospitals, Insurance, Lawyers, Lobbyists/PR, Oil & Gas, Pharm/Hlth Prod, Real Estate, Securities, Phone Utilities, Pro-Israel, Bldg Trades, PubSect Unions, Transpt Unions

Leading Industries Giving to Committee Members

Business

Commercial Banks	$83,590
Health Professionals	$356,163
Hospitals/Nursing Homes	$79,600
Insurance	$164,087
Lawyers/Law Firms	$237,201
Lobbyists/PR	$80,835
Oil & Gas	$83,875
Pharmaceuticals/Health Products	$99,150
Real Estate	$116,829
Securities & Investment	$83,125
Telephone Utilities	$77,985

Ideological/Single-Issue

Pro-Israel	$77,750

Labor

Building Trade Unions	$86,540
Public Sector Unions	$321,700
Transportation Unions	$154,050

House Education and Labor Committee

William D. Ford (D-Mich), Chairman
Bill Goodling (R-Pa), Ranking Republican

Party Ratio: 24 Democrats
15 Republicans

> **Jurisdiction:** (1) Measures relating to education or labor generally; (2) Child labor; (3) Columbia Institution for the Deaf, Dumb and Blind; Howard University; Freedman's Hospital; (4) Convict labor and the entry of goods made by convicts into interstate commerce; (5) Labor standards; (6) Labor statistics; (7) Mediation and arbitration of labor disputes; (8) Regulation or prevention of importation of foreign laborers under contract; (9) Food programs for children in schools; (10) United States Employees' Compensation Commission; (11) Vocational rehabilitation; (12) Wages and hours of labor; (13) Welfare of miners; (14) Work incentives programs. The committee also has a special oversight function with respect to domestic educational programs and institutions, and programs of student assistance, which are within the Jurisdiction of other committees.

Subcommittees

Elementary, Secondary and Vocational Education
Dale E. Kildee (D-Mich), Chairman
Bill Goodling (R-Pa), Ranking Republican

Employment Opportunities
Carl C. Perkins (D-Ky), Chairman
Steve Gunderson (R-Wis), Ranking Republican

Health and Safety
Joseph M. Gaydos (D-Pa), Chairman
Paul B. Henry (R-Mich), Ranking Republican

Human Resources
Matthew G. Martinez (D-Calif), Chairman
Harris W. Fawell (R-Ill), Ranking Republican

Labor-Management Relations
Pat Williams (D-Mont), Chairman
Marge Roukema (R-NJ), Ranking Republican

Labor Standards
Austin J. Murphy (D-Pa), Chairman
Thomas E. Petri (R-Wis), Ranking Republican

Postsecondary Education
William D. Ford (D-Mich), Chairman
Tom Coleman (R-Mo), Ranking Republican

Total PAC and Large Individual Contributions to Committee Members

John W. Olver (D-Mass)	$859,467
Nita M. Lowey (D-NY)	$831,320
Pat Williams (D-Mont)	$730,984
Ed Pastor (D-Ariz)	$695,569
William D. Ford (D-Mich)	$585,175
John F. Reed (D-RI)	$580,186
Dale E. Kildee (D-Mich)	$558,660
Scott L. Klug (R-Wis)	$528,430
Randy "Duke" Cunningham (R-Calif)	$498,935
Jolene Unsoeld (D-Wash)	$476,934
Robert E. Andrews (D-NJ)	$473,741
Harris W. Fawell (R-Ill)	$428,241
Tom Coleman (R-Mo)	$417,087
Susan Molinari (R-NY)	$415,370
Tim Roemer (D-Ind)	$411,948
George Miller (D-Calif)	$393,005
Mickey Edwards (R-Okla)	$388,827
William J. Jefferson (D-La)	$350,974
Marge Roukema (R-NJ)	$349,324
John A. Boehner (R-Ohio)	$343,332
Steve Gunderson (R-Wis)	$310,242
Bill Barrett (R-Neb)	$301,454
Dick Armey (R-Texas)	$294,990
William L. Clay (D-Mo)	$282,938
Donald M. Payne (D-NJ)	$262,191
Cass Ballenger (R-NC)	$253,875
Tom Petri (R-Wis)	$237,318
Charles A. Hayes (D-Ill)	$223,251
Austin J. Murphy (D-Pa)	$191,323
Paul B. Henry (R-Mich)	$187,298
Craig Washington (D-Texas)	$171,250
Tom Sawyer (D-Ohio)	$169,407
Patsy T. Mink (D-Hawaii)	$168,358

Carl C. Perkins (D-Ky)	$160,275
Matthew G. Martinez (D-Calif)	$110,291
Major R. Owens (D-NY)	$109,744
Jose E. Serrano (D-NY)	$108,900
Bill Goodling (R-Pa)	$95,579
Joseph M. Gaydos (D-Pa)	$45,800
Ron de Lugo (D-Virgin Is)	$44,050
Steve Bartlett (R-Texas)†	$4,592

† Resigned in March 1991

Top 20 Contributors to Committee Members in 1991-92

1	American Medical Assn*	$207,800
2	Teamsters Union*	$195,600
3	American Fedn of St/Cnty/Munic Employees	$174,197
4	National Assn of Realtors	$173,960
5	United Auto Workers	$163,900
6	National Education Assn	$147,750
7	Assn of Trial Lawyers of America	$145,500
8	Carpenters & Joiners Union*	$142,700
9	Laborers Union*	$140,800
10	Machinists/Aerospace Workers Union	$133,875
11	Intl Brotherhood of Electrical Workers*	$129,800
12	American Federation of Teachers	$126,475
13	National Assn Retired Federal Employees	$119,750
14	Food & Commercial Workers Union	$118,791
15	Marine Engineers Union*	$115,774
16	National Assn of Letter Carriers*	$111,950
17	Air Line Pilots Assn	$109,000
18	American Postal Workers Union	$106,300
19	United Parcel Service	$96,055
20	Plumbers/Pipefitters Union*	$94,850

* Contributions came from more than one affiliate or subsidiary.

Summary

Not surprisingly, labor unions dominate the political contributions to members of the Education and Labor Committee, giving twice as much as any other sector. But decisions made by this panel affect virtually every American business, whether or not they employ union workers. Minimum wage laws, safety rules, and dozens of other labor-related standards and regulations fall within the purview of this committee.

Organized unions do have an enormous stake in the issues debated here and they accounted for 16 of the top 20 contributors to the committee and $3.4 million in contributions overall to committee members. Still, despite the tens of millions of dollars that labor groups donate to Congress every election cycle, their political clout has been in serious decline in recent years. The unions' embarrassing defeat on the North American Free Trade Agreement in November 1993 was a particularly painful one for labor leaders, as many of their Democratic allies sided against them and voted yes on NAFTA. Many unions vowed retribution against those Democrats in the 1994 elections.

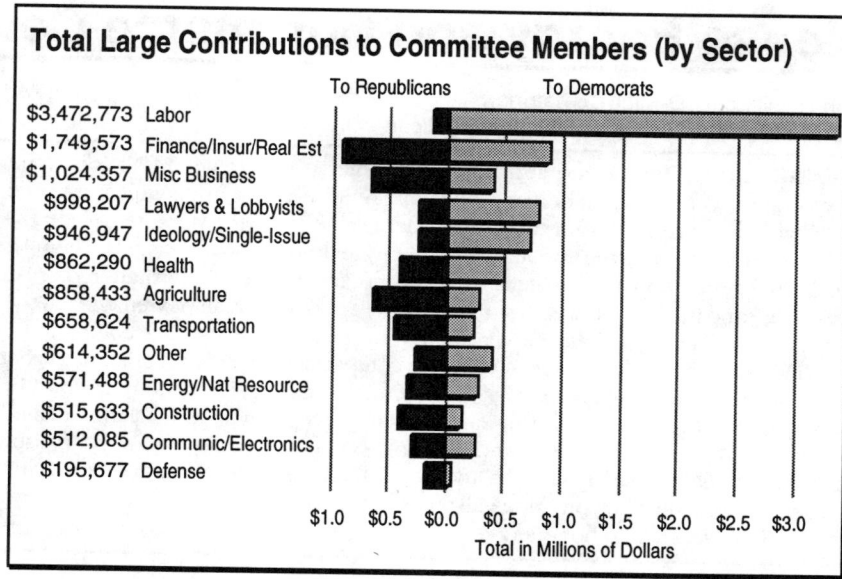

Total Large Contributions to Committee Members (by Sector)

$3,472,773	Labor
$1,749,573	Finance/Insur/Real Est
$1,024,357	Misc Business
$998,207	Lawyers & Lobbyists
$946,947	Ideology/Single-Issue
$862,290	Health
$858,433	Agriculture
$658,624	Transportation
$614,352	Other
$571,488	Energy/Nat Resource
$515,633	Construction
$512,085	Communic/Electronics
$195,677	Defense

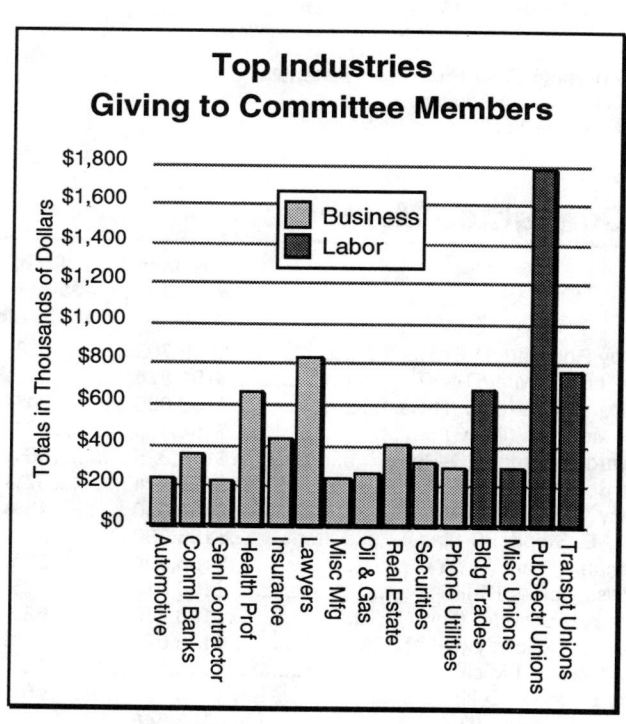

Top Industries Giving to Committee Members

Leading Industries Giving to Committee Members

Business

Automotive	$222,089
Commercial Banks	$344,860
General Contractors	$214,473
Health Professionals	$652,356
Insurance	$418,607
Lawyers/Law Firms	$822,477
Misc Manufacturing & Distributing	$224,785
Oil & Gas	$250,576
Real Estate	$399,967
Securities & Investment	$298,068
Telephone Utilities	$280,953

Labor

Building Trade Unions	$663,118
Misc Unions	$284,096
Public Sector Unions	$1,768,015
Transportation Unions	$757,544

143

House Energy and Commerce Committee

John D. Dingell (D-Mich), Chairman
Norman F. Lent (R-NY), Ranking Republican

Party Ratio: 27 Democrats
16 Republicans

Jurisdiction: (1) Interstate and foreign commerce generally; (2) National energy policy generally; (3) Measures relating to the exploration, production, storage, supply, marketing, pricing, and regulation of energy resources, including all fossil fuels, solar energy, and other unconventional or renewable energy resources; (4) Measures relating to the conservation of energy resources; (5) Measures relating to the commercial application of energy technology; (6) Measures relating to energy information generally; (7) Measures relating to (A) the generation and marketing of power (except by federally chartered or Federal regional power marketing authorities), (B) the reliability and interstate transmission of, and rate making for, all power, and (C) the siting of generation facilities; except the installation of interconnections between Government waterpower projects. (The committee's jurisdiction extends both to nuclear and nonnuclear facilities and energy). (8) Interstate energy compacts; (9) Measures relating to general management of the Department of Energy, and the management and all functions of the Federal Energy Regulatory Commission; (10) Inland waterways; (11) Railroads, including railroad labor, railroad retirement and unemployment, except revenue measures related thereto; (12) Regulation of interstate and foreign communication; (13) Securities and exchanges; (14) Consumer affairs and consumer protection; (15) Travel and tourism; (16) Public health and quarantine; (17) Health and health facilities, except health care supported by payroll deductions; (18) Biomedical research and development. The committee also has special oversight functions with respect to all laws, programs, and Government activities affecting nuclear and other energy.

Subcommittees

Commerce, Consumer Protection and Competitiveness
Cardiss Collins(D-Ill), Chairwoman
Alex McMillan (R-NC), Ranking Republican

Energy and Power
Philip R. Sharp (D-Ind), Chairman
Carlos J. Moorhead (R-Calif), Ranking Republican

Health and the Environment
Henry A. Waxman (D-Calif), Chairman
William E. Dannemeyer (R-Calif), Ranking Republican

Oversight and Investigations
John D. Dingell (D-Mich), Chairman
Thomas J. Bliley Jr. (R-Va), Ranking Republican

Telecommunications and Finance
Edward J. Markey (D-Mass), Chairman
Matthew J. Rinaldo (R-NJ), Ranking Republican

Transportation and Hazardous Materials
Al Swift (D-Wash), Chairman
Don Ritter (R-Pa), Ranking Republican

Total Committee-Related Contributions to Committee Members

	Total from Cmte-Related Contribs	Pct of Member's Lg Contribs		Total from Cmte-Related Contribs	Pct of Member's Lg Contribs
John D. Dingell (D-Mich)	$592,072	59%	J. Roy Rowland (D-Ga)	$206,702	62%
Mike Synar (D-Okla)	$477,411	55%	Edolphus Towns (D-NY)	$191,874	45%
Tom McMillen (D-Md)	$462,755	43%	Carlos J. Moorhead (R-Calif)	$190,000	64%
Joe L. Barton (R-Texas)	$390,781	52%	Alex McMillan (R-NC)	$186,150	62%
Don Ritter (R-Pa)	$387,889	51%	Edward J. Markey (D-Mass)	$185,325	56%
Jack Fields (R-Texas)	$387,707	57%	Dan Schaefer (R-Colo)	$177,424	57%
Al Swift (D-Wash)	$386,873	50%	Sonny Callahan (R-Ala)	$168,650	48%
Henry A. Waxman (D-Calif)	$375,949	64%	Gerry E. Studds (D-Mass)	$166,730	22%
Gerry Sikorski (D-Minn)	$346,842	45%	Norman F. Lent (R-NY)	$163,394	69%
Jim Slattery (D-Kan)	$334,348	55%	Cardiss Collins (D-Ill)	$156,312	62%
Thomas J. Bliley Jr. (R-Va)	$320,443	57%	James H. Scheuer (D-NY)	$136,435	62%
Bill Richardson (D-NM)	$310,231	57%	Clyde C. Holloway (R-La)	$126,075	47%
Peter H. Kostmayer (D-Pa)	$309,646	33%	Fred Upton (R-Mich)	$125,370	38%
W.J. "Billy" Tauzin (D-La)	$298,791	54%	Terry L. Bruce (D-Ill)	$123,497	56%
Rick Boucher (D-Va)	$282,400	57%	Dennis E. Eckart (D-Ohio)	$98,548	53%
Philip R. Sharp (D-Ind)	$278,241	54%	Ron Wyden (D-Ore)	$78,575	56%
John Bryant (D-Texas)	$274,391	52%	Matthew J. Rinaldo (R-NJ)	$72,592	58%
Thomas J. Manton (D-NY)	$264,282	51%	Claude Harris (D-Ala)	$68,209	59%
Michael Bilirakis (R-Fla)	$262,073	52%	William E. Dannemeyer (R-Calif)†	$38,230	11%
Ralph M. Hall (D-Texas)	$261,913	61%	Jim Cooper (D-Tenn)	$27,556	42%
Richard H. Lehman (D-Calif)	$255,340	36%			
Michael G. Oxley (R-Ohio)	$229,750	61%			
Dennis Hastert (R-Ill)	$212,996	50%			

† Ran for Senate in 1992

Summary

One glance at the volume of campaign dollars flowing into the reelection campaigns of Energy and Commerce Committee members is enough to see why a seat on this committee is considered a plum assignment on Capitol Hill. Its jurisdiction gives it important influence over some of the most politically active industries in America: oil & gas, health care, telecommunications, finance and a host of smaller industries and interests.

After the election of Bill Clinton in 1992 and the elevation of health care reform to the top of the political agenda, the committee became even more important to American business. Along with the Ways & Means Committee, it is the lead panel charged with drafting the details of the nation's new health care policy.

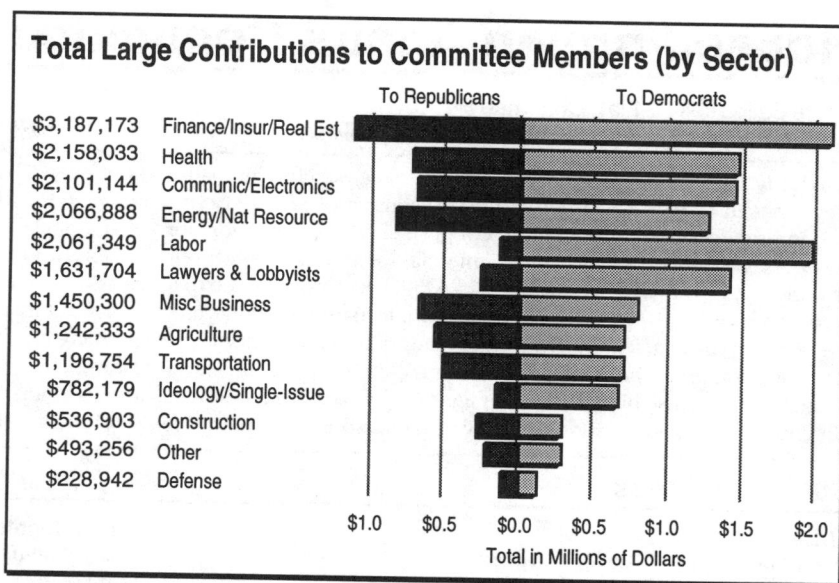

Total Large Contributions to Committee Members (by Sector)

	To Republicans	To Democrats
$3,187,173	Finance/Insur/Real Est	
$2,158,033	Health	
$2,101,144	Communic/Electronics	
$2,066,888	Energy/Nat Resource	
$2,061,349	Labor	
$1,631,704	Lawyers & Lobbyists	
$1,450,300	Misc Business	
$1,242,333	Agriculture	
$1,196,754	Transportation	
$782,179	Ideology/Single-Issue	
$536,903	Construction	
$493,256	Other	
$228,942	Defense	

Total in Millions of Dollars

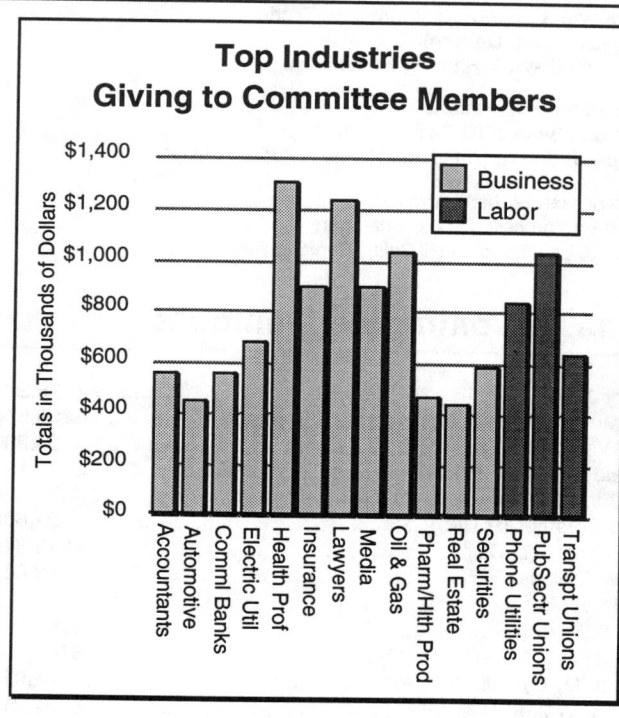

Top Industries Giving to Committee Members

Top 20 Committe-Related Contributors to Committee Members in 1991-92

1	American Medical Assn*	$255,196
2	National Cable Television Assn	$186,049
3	American Dental Assn	$148,750
4	Assn of Trial Lawyers of America	$143,500
5	AT&T	$132,975
6	National Assn of Broadcasters	$127,150
7	National Auto Dealers Assn	$119,250
8	American Bankers Assn*	$118,850
9	United Transportation Union	$116,200
10	American Family Corp	$104,250
11	Ameritech Corp*	$99,950
12	BellSouth Corp*	$94,350
13	American Hospital Assn	$90,836
14	American Academy of Ophthalmology	$86,500
15	National Assn of Life Underwriters	$78,000
16	Burlington Northern*	$76,099
17	Union Pacific Corp	$68,499
18	GTE Corp	$66,220
19	Pacific Telesis Group	$65,550
20	Viacom International	$63,550

* Contributions came from more than one affiliate or subsidiary.

Leading Committee-Related Industries Giving to Committee Members

Business

Automotive	$435,365
Chemical & Related Manufacturing	$238,434
Commercial Banks	$550,395
Electric Utilities	$662,184
Health Professionals	$1,300,449
Hospitals/Nursing Homes	$277,402
Insurance	$888,736
Lawyers/Law Firms	$1,221,667
Media/Entertainment	$885,435
Oil & Gas	$1,028,721
Pharmaceuticals/Health Products	$453,079
Railroads	$271,323
Securities & Investment	$578,953
Telephone Utilities	$826,335

Labor

Transportation Unions	$181,450

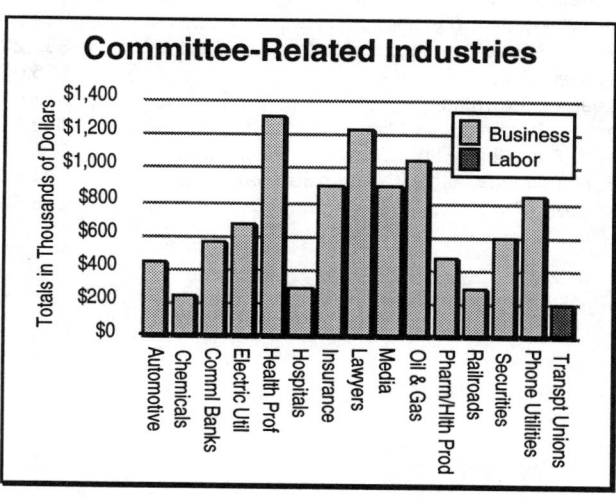

Committee-Related Industries

145

House Foreign Affairs Committee

Dante B. Fascell (D-Fla), Chairman
William S. Broomfield (R-Mich), Ranking Republican

Party Ratio: 26 Democrats
17 Republicans

Jurisdiction: (1) Relations of the United States with foreign nations generally; (2) Acquisition of land and buildings for embassies and legations in foreign countries; (3) Establishment of boundary lines between the United States and foreign nations; (4) Foreign loans; (5) International conferences and congresses; (6) Intervention abroad and declarations of war; (7) Measures relating to the diplomatic service; (8) Measures to foster commercial intercourse with foreign nations and to safeguard American business interests abroad; (9) Neutrality; (10) Protection of American citizens abroad and expatriation; (11) The American National Red Cross; (12) United Nations Organizations; (13) Measures relating to international economic policy; (14) Export controls, including non-proliferation of nuclear technology and nuclear hardware; (15) International commodity agreements (other than those involving sugar), including all agreements for cooperation in the export of nuclear technology and nuclear hardware; (16) Trading with the enemy; (17) International education. The committee also has special oversight functions with respect to customs administration, intelligence activities relating to foreign policy, international financial and monetary organizations, and international fishing agreements.

Subcommittees

Africa
Mervyn M. Dymally (D-Calif), Chairman
Dan Burton (R-Ind), Ranking Republican

Arms Control, International Security and Science
Dante B. Fascell (D-Fla), Chairman
William S. Broomfield (R-Mich), Ranking Republican

Asian and Pacific Affairs
Stephen J. Solarz (D-NY), Chairman
Jim Leach (R-Iowa), Ranking Republican

Europe and the Middle East
Lee H. Hamilton (D-Ind), Chairman
Benjamin A. Gilman (R-NY), Ranking Republican

Human Rights and International Organizations
Gus Yatron (D-Pa), Chairman
Doug Bereuter (R-Neb), Ranking Republican

International Economic Policy and Trade
Sam Gejdenson (D-Conn), Chairman
Toby Roth (R-Wis), Ranking Republican

International Operations
Howard L. Berman (D-Calif), Chairman
Olympia J. Snowe (R-Maine), Ranking Republican

Western Hemisphere Affairs
Robert G. Torricelli (D-NJ), Chairman
Robert J. Lagomarsino (R-Calif), Ranking Republican

Total PAC and Large Individual Contributions to Committee Members

Mel Levine (D-Calif)†	$4,106,254
Wayne Owens (D-Utah)†	$1,507,026
Robert G. Torricelli (D-NJ)	$940,467
Peter H. Kostmayer (D-Pa)	$936,117
Gerry E. Studds (D-Mass)	$758,331
Sam Gejdenson (D-Conn)	$571,167
Gary L. Ackerman (D-NY)	$570,150
Stephen J. Solarz (D-NY)	$500,753
Howard L. Berman (D-Calif)	$498,862
Ileana Ros-Lehtinen (R-Fla)	$483,059
Elton Gallegly (R-Calif)	$458,469
Dan Burton (R-Ind)	$447,425
Olympia J. Snowe (R-Maine)	$444,140
Benjamin A. Gilman (R-NY)	$400,750
Toby Roth (R-Wis)	$399,470
Eliot L. Engel (D-NY)	$366,480
Lee H. Hamilton (D-Ind)	$352,150
Frank McCloskey (D-Ind)	$339,669
Thomas M. Foglietta (D-Pa)	$334,781
Harry A. Johnston (D-Fla)	$303,042
Robert J. Lagomarsino (R-Calif)	$299,079
Antonio J. Colorado-Laguna (D-Puerto Rico)	$297,325
Amo Houghton (R-NY)	$288,678
Henry J. Hyde (R-Ill)	$278,227
Jan Meyers (R-Kan)	$265,614
Ted Weiss (D-NY)	$264,980
Donald M. Payne (D-NJ)	$262,191
Bill Orton (D-Utah)	$255,564
Doug Bereuter (R-Neb)	$223,833
Tom Lantos (D-Calif)	$219,848
Porter J. Goss (R-Fla)	$212,049
Austin J. Murphy (D-Pa)	$191,323
Tom Sawyer (D-Ohio)	$169,407
Christopher H. Smith (R-NJ)	$149,555
Mervyn M. Dymally (D-Calif)	$144,911
Howard Wolpe (D-Mich)	$134,215
Bill Goodling (R-Pa)	$95,579
Edward F. Feighan (D-Ohio)	$83,348
Ben Blaz (R-Guam)	$69,200
John Miller (R-Wash)	$65,000
Jim Leach (R-Iowa)	$59,058
William S. Broomfield (R-Mich)	$33,950
Dante B. Fascell (D-Fla)	$32,565
Eni F. H. Faleomavaega (D-Amer Samoa)	$24,703
Gus Yatron (D-Pa)	$18,500

† Ran for U.S. Senate in 1992

Summary

Though its agenda spans foreign policy issues around the world, the House Foreign Affairs Committee is not a center of great interest for a majority of the PAC community or among other major political contributors. There is one important exception, however — ideological and single-issue groups whose main focus is foreign policy. Within that group, none is more formidable on Capitol Hill than supporters of strong U.S. ties to Israel. Pro-Israel PACs and their members are heavy contributors to Congress as a whole (giving more than $7.4 million in the 1992 elections), and to this committee in particular. Foreign Affairs members received a combined $827,000 from pro-Israel contributors in the last election cycle — an average of more than $19,000 per member. Overall, however, most of the pro-Israel dollars went not to House members, but to Senators.

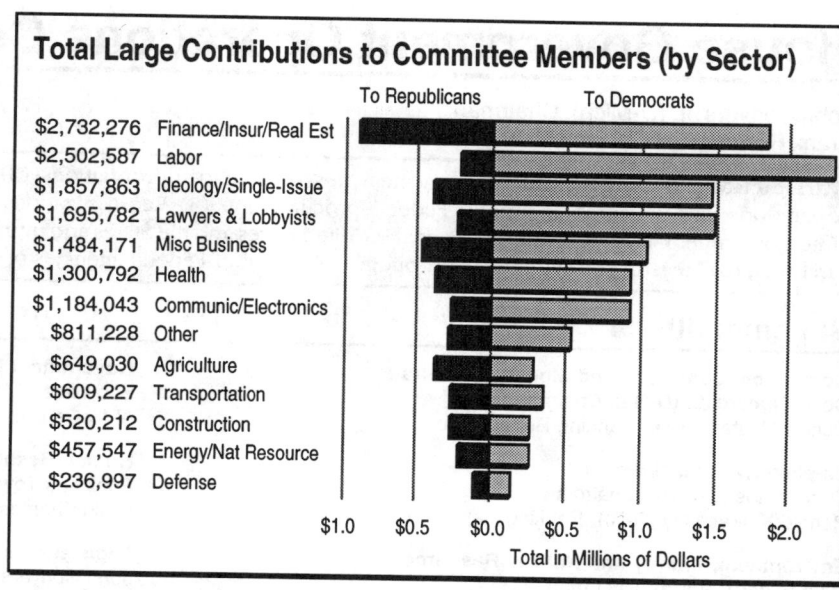

Total Large Contributions to Committee Members (by Sector)

$2,732,276	Finance/Insur/Real Est
$2,502,587	Labor
$1,857,863	Ideology/Single-Issue
$1,695,782	Lawyers & Lobbyists
$1,484,171	Misc Business
$1,300,792	Health
$1,184,043	Communic/Electronics
$811,228	Other
$649,030	Agriculture
$609,227	Transportation
$520,212	Construction
$457,547	Energy/Nat Resource
$236,997	Defense

Total in Millions of Dollars

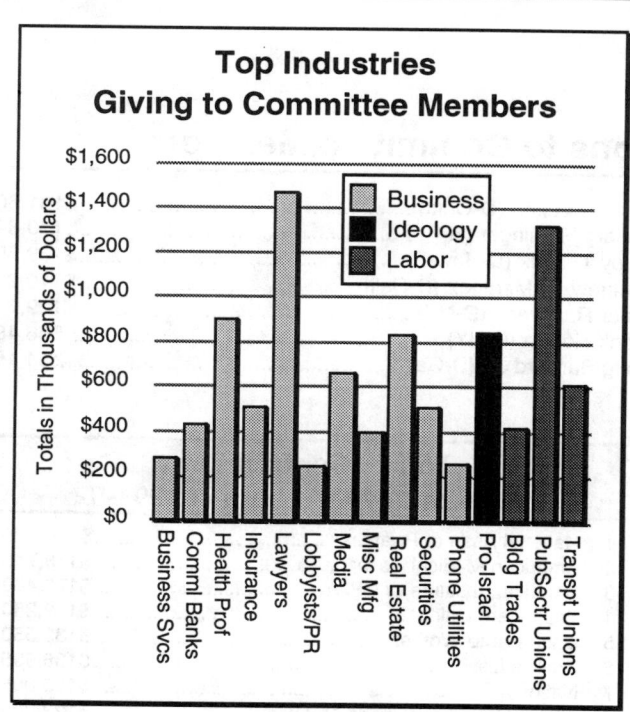

Top Industries Giving to Committee Members

Totals in Thousands of Dollars

Business
Ideology
Labor

Business Svcs, Comml Banks, Health Prof, Insurance, Lawyers, Lobbyists/PR, Media, Misc Mfg, Real Estate, Securities, Phone Utilities, Pro-Israel, Bldg Trades, PubSectr Unions, Transpt Unions

Top 20 Contributors to Committee Members in 1991-92

1	National Assn of Realtors	$193,144
2	American Medical Assn*	$172,200
3	Teamsters Union*	$162,175
4	United Auto Workers	$145,755
5	American Fedn of St/Cnty/Munic Employees	$136,777
6	Assn of Trial Lawyers of America	$132,500
7	Marine Engineers Union*	$125,500
8	National PAC	$117,000
9	National Education Assn	$115,525
10	National Assn Retired Federal Employees	$112,000
11	National Assn of Letter Carriers	$107,225
12	AT&T*	$90,780
13	Laborers Union*	$89,750
14	Air Line Pilots Assn	$87,000
15	Carpenters & Joiners Union*	$85,300
16	Intl Brotherhood of Electrical Workers*	$80,492
17	Machinists/Aerospace Workers Union	$78,425
18	Food & Commercial Workers Union	$76,199
19	American Federation of Teachers	$75,750
20	American Postal Workers Union	$71,750

* Contributions came from more than one affiliate or subsidiary.

Leading Industries Giving to Committee Members

Business

Business Services	$274,146
Commercial Banks	$421,996
Health Professionals	$892,199
Insurance	$495,788
Lawyers/Law Firms	$1,461,148
Lobbyists/PR	$234,634
Media/Entertainment	$642,494
Misc Manufacturing & Distributing	$378,944
Real Estate	$820,108
Securities & Investment	$493,368
Telephone Utilities	$250,197

Ideological/Single-Issue

Pro-Israel	$827,012

Labor

Building Trade Unions	$408,150
Public Sector Unions	$1,311,935
Transportation Unions	$605,850

House Government Operations Committee

John Conyers Jr. (D-Mich), Chairman
Frank Horton (R-NY), Ranking Republican

Party Ratio: 24 Democrats
15 Republicans

Jurisdiction: (1) Budget and accounting measures, other than appropriations; (2) The overall economy and efficiency of Government operations and activities, including Federal procurement; (3) Reorganizations in the executive branch of the Government; (4) Intergovernmental relationships between the United States and the States and municipalities, and general revenue sharing; (5) National archives; (6) Measures providing for off-budget treatment of Federal agencies or programs.

Subcommittees

Commerce, Consumer and Monetary Affairs
Doug Barnard Jr. (D-Ga), Chairman
Dennis Hastert (R-Ill), Ranking Republican

Employment and Housing
Tom Lantos (D-Calif), Chairman
Ronald K. Machtley (R-RI), Ranking Republican

Environment, Energy and Natural Resources
Mike Synar (D-Okla), Chairman
William F. Clinger Jr. (R-Pa), Ranking Republican

Government Activities and Transportation
Barbara Boxer (D-Calif), Chairwoman
C. Christopher Cox (R-Calif), Ranking Republican

Government Information, Justice and Agriculture
Bob Wise (D-WVa), Chairman
Al McCandless (R-Calif), Ranking Republican

Human Resources and Intergovernmental Relations
Edolphus Towns (D-NY), Chairman
Craig Thomas (R-Wyo), Ranking Republican

Legislation and National Security
John Conyers Jr. (D-Mich), Chairman
Frank Horton (R-NY), Ranking Republican

Total PAC and Large Individual Contributions to Committee Members

Barbara Boxer (D-Calif)†	$4,591,641
Mike Synar (D-Okla)	$862,475
Rosa DeLauro (D-Conn)	$811,235
Dick Zimmer (R-NJ)	$752,478
Bill Zeliff (R-NH)	$621,554
Henry A. Waxman (D-Calif)	$584,505
Ben Erdreich (D-Ala)	$573,700
Scott L. Klug (R-Wis)	$528,430
Jon Kyl (R-Ariz)	$486,876
Ileana Ros-Lehtinen (R-Fla)	$483,059
C. Christopher Cox (R-Calif)	$480,795
Dennis Hastert (R-Ill)	$429,221
Stephen L. Neal (D-NC)	$428,370
Edolphus Towns (D-NY)	$424,274
Albert G. Bustamante (D-Texas)	$399,962
John W. Cox Jr. (D-Ill)	$389,715
Ronald K. Machtley (R-RI)	$355,191
Collin C. Peterson (D-Minn)	$342,787
Craig Thomas (R-Wyo)	$312,050
Steven H. Schiff (R-NM)	$297,300
Glenn English (D-Okla)	$289,271
Ray Thornton (D-Ark)	$280,048
John Conyers Jr. (D-Mich)	$273,450
Al McCandless (R-Calif)	$271,107
Ted Weiss (D-NY)	$264,980
Donald M. Payne (D-NJ)	$262,191
Gerald D. Kleczka (D-Wis)	$261,040
David L. Hobson (R-Ohio)	$251,230
Cardiss Collins (D-Ill)	$250,761
Gary Condit (D-Calif)	$233,244
Tom Lantos (D-Calif)	$219,848
Bob Wise (D-WVa)	$219,450
Christopher Shays (R-Conn)	$214,388
Bernard Sanders (I-Vt)	$209,885
Charles Luken (D-Ohio)	$181,600
William F. Clinger (R-Pa)	$170,817
Patsy T. Mink (D-Hawaii)	$168,358
Matthew G. Martinez (D-Calif)	$110,291
Major R. Owens (D-NY)	$109,744
Frank Horton (R-NY)	$66,481
Doug Barnard Jr. (D-Ga)	$4,150

Top 20 Contributors to Committee Members in 1991-92

1	National Assn of Realtors	$220,625
2	American Medical Assn*	$178,745
3	American Institute of CPA's	$173,400
4	Teamsters Union*	$149,250
5	United Auto Workers	$139,550
6	Emily's List	$136,995
7	National Education Assn	$135,005
8	Assn of Trial Lawyers of America	$123,350
9	National Assn Retired Federal Employees	$120,000
10	American Fedn of St/Cnty/Munic Employees	$118,397
11	American Bankers Assn*	$108,150
12	United Parcel Service	$102,580
13	Machinists/Aerospace Workers Union	$97,000
14	AT&T*	$93,885
15	National Auto Dealers Assn	$91,700
16	Marine Engineers Union*	$86,500
16	Air Line Pilots Assn	$86,500
18	Food & Commercial Workers Union	$86,098
19	Associated Milk Producers	$80,900
20	Laborers Union*	$79,000
20	National Assn of Letter Carriers	$79,000

* Contributions came from more than one affiliate or subsidiary.

† Ran for US Senate in 1992

Summary

Despite a name which might make it seem preoccupied with affairs inside the federal bureaucracy, the Government Operations Committee has a wide-ranging jurisdiction that touches upon large segments of American business. Among other things, this committee has an important say in the reorganization of executive branch agencies — something that can have important repercussions on heavily-regulated industries.

Banking and other financial interests were an important element in the members' contribution profile. The panel's Commerce, Consumer and Monetary Affairs subcommittee is of particular interest to that industry.

Lawyers, doctors and labor unions representing public employees were also important sources of contributions.

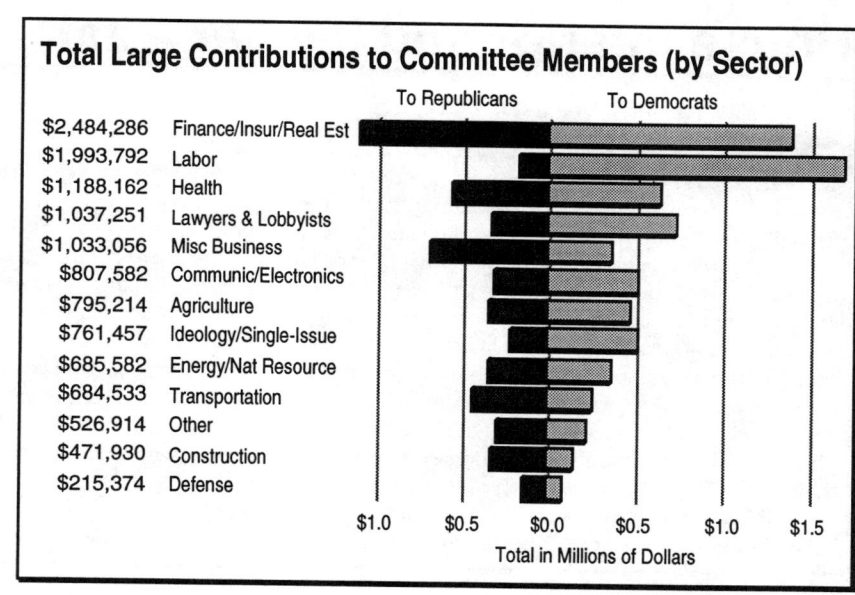

Total Large Contributions to Committee Members (by Sector)

$2,484,286	Finance/Insur/Real Est
$1,993,792	Labor
$1,188,162	Health
$1,037,251	Lawyers & Lobbyists
$1,033,056	Misc Business
$807,582	Communic/Electronics
$795,214	Agriculture
$761,457	Ideology/Single-Issue
$685,582	Energy/Nat Resource
$684,533	Transportation
$526,914	Other
$471,930	Construction
$215,374	Defense

Total in Millions of Dollars

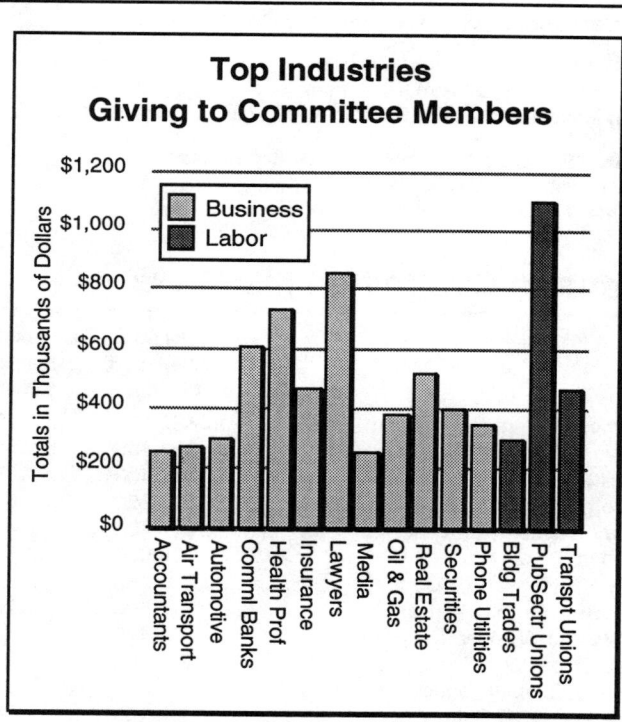

Top Industries Giving to Committee Members

Totals in Thousands of Dollars

Legend: Business, Labor

(Industries: Accountants, Air Transport, Automotive, Comml Banks, Health Prof, Insurance, Lawyers, Media, Oil & Gas, Real Estate, Securities, Phone Utilities, Bldg Trades, PubSectr Unions, Transpt Unions)

Leading Industries Giving to Committee Members

Business

Accountants	$249,080
Air Transport	$260,930
Automotive	$288,621
Commercial Banks	$596,030
Health Professionals	$724,579
Insurance	$459,905
Lawyers/Law Firms	$844,450
Media/Entertainment	$243,024
Oil & Gas	$376,510
Real Estate	$509,681
Securities & Investment	$388,500
Telephone Utilities	$337,088

Labor

Building Trade Unions	$287,120
Public Sector Unions	$1,091,179
Transportation Unions	$462,375

149

House Interior and Insular Affairs Committee

George Miller (D-Calif), Chairman
Don Young (R-Alaska), Ranking Republican

Party Ratio: 26 Democrats
16 Republicans

Jurisdiction: (1) Forest reserves and national parks created from the public domain; (2) Forfeiture of land grants and alien ownership, including alien ownership of mineral lands; (3) Geological survey; (4) Interstate compacts relating to apportionment of waters for irrigation purposes; (5) Irrigation and reclamation, including water supply for reclamation projects, and easements of public lands for irrigation projects, and acquisition of private lands when necessary to complete irrigation project; (6) Measures relating to the care and management of Indians, including the care and allotment of Indian lands and general and special measures relating to claims which are paid out of Indian funds; (7) Measures relating generally to the insular possessions of the United States, except those affecting the revenue and appropriations; (8) Military parks and battlefields; national cemeteries administered by the Secretary of the Interior, and parks within the District of Columbia; (9) Mineral land laws and claims and entries thereunder; (10) Mineral resources of the public lands; (11) Mining interest generally; (12) Mining schools and experimental stations; (13) Petroleum conservation on the public lands and conservation of the radium supply in the United States; (14) Preservation of historic ruins and objects of interest on the public domain; (15) Public lands generally, including entry, easements, and grazing thereon; (16) Relations of the United States with the Indians and the Indian tribes; (17) Regulation of the domestic nuclear energy industry, including regulation of research and development reactors and nuclear regulatory research. The committee also has special oversight functions with respect to all programs affecting Indians and nonmilitary nuclear energy and research and development including the disposal of nuclear waste.

Subcommittees

Energy and the Environment
Peter H. Kostmayer (D-Pa), Chairman
John J. Rhodes III (R-Ariz), Ranking Republican

General Oversight and Investigations
Richard H. Lehman (D-Calif), Chairman
Ben Blaz (R-Guam), Ranking Republican

Insular and International Affairs
Ron de Lugo (D-Virgin Islands), Chairman
Robert J. Lagomarsino (R-Calif), Ranking Republican

Mining and Natural Resources
Nick J. Rahall II (D-WVa), Chairman
Barbara Vucanocich (R-Nev), Ranking Republican

National Parks and Public Lands
Bruce F. Vento (D-Minn), Chairman
Ron Marlenee (R-Mont), Ranking Republican

Water, Power and Offshore Energy Resources
George Miller (D-Calif), Chairman
James V. Hansen (R-Utah), Ranking Republican

Total PAC and Large Individual Contributions to Committee Members

	Total from Cmte-Related Contribs	Pct of Member's Lg Contribs		Total from Cmte-Related Contribs	Pct of Member's Lg Contribs
Don Young (R-Alaska)	$174,251	26%	James V. Hansen (R-Utah)	$27,125	14%
Ron Marlenee (R-Mont)	$130,069	16%	Beverly B. Byron (D-Md)	$24,450	16%
Philip R. Sharp (D-Ind)	$114,641	22%	Dick Schulze (R-Pa)	$22,400	13%
Ben Nighthorse Campbell (D-Colo)†	$112,166	9%	George "Buddy" Darden (D-Ga)	$20,350	6%
Charles H. Taylor (R-NC)	$70,475	15%	Larry LaRocco (D-Idaho)	$19,186	4%
Wayne Owens (D-Utah)†	$68,959	5%	Robert J. Lagomarsino (R-Calif)	$18,050	6%
Craig Thomas (R-Wyo)	$66,050	21%	Sam Gejdenson (D-Conn)	$15,125	3%
John J. Rhodes III (R-Arizona)	$59,700	14%	Austin J. Murphy (D-Pa)	$13,500	7%
Bob Smith (R-Ore)	$58,012	23%	Edward J. Markey (D-Mass)	$11,475	3%
Barbara F. Vucanovich (R-Nev)	$55,200	12%	Peter Hoagland (D-Neb)	$11,000	2%
Pat Williams (D-Mont)	$52,526	7%	John J. "Jimmy" Duncan Jr. (R-Tenn)	$10,800	5%
John T. Doolittle (R-Calif)	$52,200	12%	Joel Hefley (R-Colo)	$10,150	9%
George Miller (D-Calif)	$48,341	12%	Calvin Dooley (D-Calif)	$9,780	3%
Richard H. Lehman (D-Calif)	$47,750	7%	John Lewis (D-Ga)	$8,250	3%
Bill Richardson (D-NM)	$47,062	9%	Harry A. Johnston (D-Fla)	$7,150	2%
Mel Levine (D-Calif)†	$45,084	1%	Peter A. DeFazio (D-Ore)	$6,750	4%
Wayne Allard (R-Colo)	$38,288	10%	Neil Abercrombie (D-Hawaii)	$4,300	2%
Peter H. Kostmayer (D-Pa)	$37,443	4%	Bruce F. Vento (D-Minn)	$4,296	2%
Elton Gallegly (R-Calif)	$35,222	8%	Antonio J. Colorado-Laguna (D-Puerto Rico)	$3,500	1%
Richard H. Baker (R-La)	$34,000	6%	Tim Johnson (D-SD)	$3,500	1%
Jim Jontz (D-Ind)	$29,318	7%	Eni F. H. Faleomavaega (D-Amer Samoa)	$2,000	8%
Nick J. Rahall II (D-WVa)	$27,325	8%	Ron de Lugo (D-Virgin Is)	$1,500	3%
			Charles E. Schumer (D-NY)	$1,400	0%

† Ran for US Senate in 1992

Summary

Debates over the use and disposal of public lands are a central focus of the House Interior Committee — a focus that makes it vitally important to states in the western U.S., where much of the land is still federally owned. The committee is also vital to mining, oil & gas and other industries that extract natural resources from public lands through federal leases. In recent years the committee has been a battleground for issues that pit the interests of industry versus those of environmentalists. The committee is also important to American territories and possessions, from Puerto Rico to American Samoa.

With the opening of the 103rd Congress in 1993, the committee officially changed its name to the House Natural Resources Committee. Its jurisdiction remains the same.

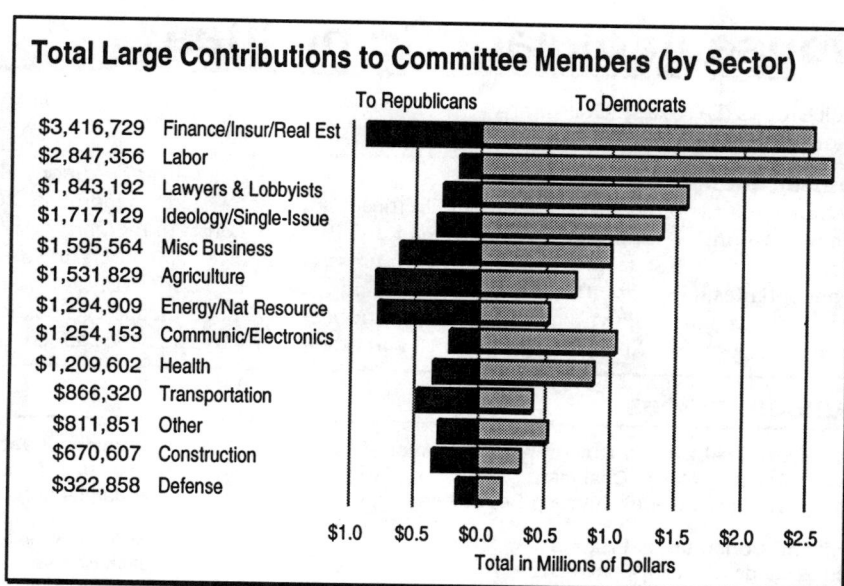

Total Large Contributions to Committee Members (by Sector)

	To Republicans	To Democrats
$3,416,729	Finance/Insur/Real Est	
$2,847,356	Labor	
$1,843,192	Lawyers & Lobbyists	
$1,717,129	Ideology/Single-Issue	
$1,595,564	Misc Business	
$1,531,829	Agriculture	
$1,294,909	Energy/Nat Resource	
$1,254,153	Communic/Electronics	
$1,209,602	Health	
$866,320	Transportation	
$811,851	Other	
$670,607	Construction	
$322,858	Defense	

Total in Millions of Dollars

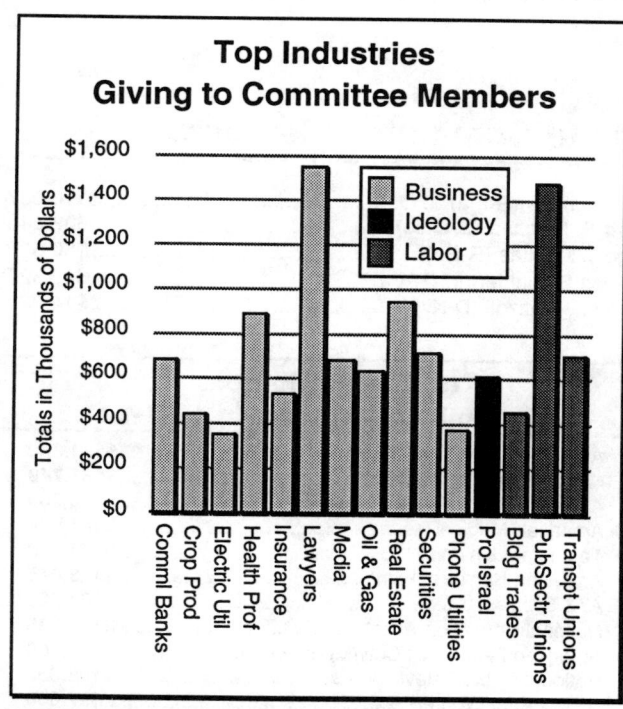

Top Industries Giving to Committee Members

Totals in Thousands of Dollars

- Business
- Ideology
- Labor

Comml Banks, Crop Prod, Electric Util, Health Prof, Insurance, Lawyers, Media, Oil & Gas, Real Estate, Securities, Phone Utilities, Pro-Israel, Bldg Trades, PubSectr Unions, Transpt Unions

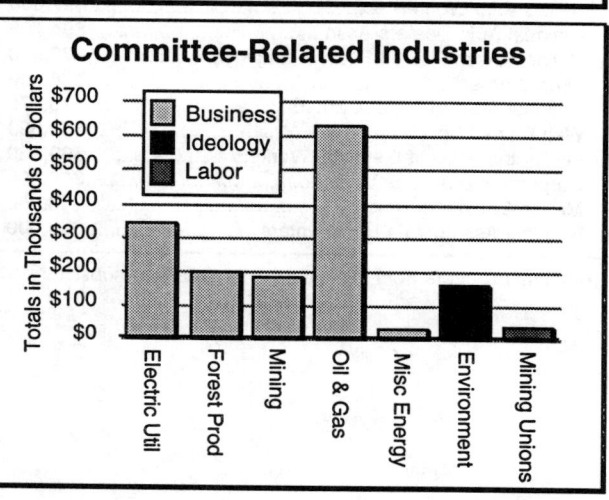

Committee-Related Industries

Totals in Thousands of Dollars

- Business
- Ideology
- Labor

Electric Util, Forest Prod, Mining, Oil & Gas, Misc Energy, Environment, Mining Unions

Top 20 Committe-Related Contributors to Committee Members in 1991-92

1	Sierra Club	$61,752
2	Atlantic Richfield	$53,283
3	ACRE (Action Cmte for Rural Electrification)*	$51,651
4	Chevron Corp	$45,400
5	United Mine Workers	$42,100
6	Southern California Edison	$39,230
7	League of Conservation Voters	$34,207
8	Exxon Corp	$31,300
9	Veco International Inc	$27,790
10	Pacific Gas & Electric	$27,600
11	Amoco Corp	$25,050
12	National Coal Assn	$24,400
13	Southern Co*	$20,775
14	Coastal Corp	$20,000
15	Phelps Dodge Corp	$17,100
16	Louisiana-Pacific Corp	$16,600
17	Cyprus Minerals Co	$16,500
18	Occidental Petroleum*	$15,350
18	Shell Oil	$15,350
20	Columbia Gas System*	$15,100

* Contributions came from more than one affiliate or subsidiary.

Leading Committee-Related Industries Giving to Committee Members

Business

Electric Utilities	$337,268
Forestry & Forest Products	$189,343
Mining	$177,569
Oil & Gas	$626,932
Misc Energy	$28,500

Ideological/Single-Issue

Environmental Issues	$153,741

Labor

Mining Unions	$34,600

House Judiciary Committee

Jack Brooks (D-Texas), Chairman
Hamilton Fish Jr. (R-NY), Ranking Republican

Party Ratio: 21 Democrats
13 Republicans

> **Jurisdiction:** (1) Judicial proceedings, civil and criminal generally; (2) Apportionment of Representatives; (3) Bankruptcy, mutiny, espionage and counterfeiting; (4) Civil liberties; (5) Constitutional amendments; (6) Federal courts and judges; (7) Immigration and naturalization; (8) Interstate compacts generally; (9) Local courts in the Territories and possessions; (10) Measures relating to claims against the United States; (11) Meetings of Congress, attendance of Members and their acceptance of incompatible offices; (12) National penitentiaries; (13) Patent Office; (14) Patents, copyrights, and trademarks; (15) Presidential succession; (16) Protection of trade and commerce against unlawful restraints and monopolies; (17) Revision and codification of the Statutes of the United States; (18) State and territorial boundary lines; (19) Communist and other subversive activities affecting the internal security of the United States.

Subcommittees

Administrative Law and Governmental Relations
Barney Frank (D-Mass), Chairman
George W. Gekas (R-Pa), Ranking Republican

Civil and Constitutional Rights
Don Edwards (D-Calif), Chairman
Henry J. Hyde (R-Ill), Ranking Republican

Intellectual Property and Judicial Administration
William J. Hughes (D-NJ), Chairman
Carlos J. Moorhead (R-Calif), Ranking Republican

Criminal Justice
Charles E. Schumer (D-NY), Chairman
F. James Sensenbrenner Jr. (R-Wis), Ranking Republican

Economic and Commercial Law
Jack Brooks (D-Texas), Chairman
Hamilton Fish Jr. (R-NY), Ranking Republican

International Law, Immigration and Refugees
Romano L. Mazzoli (D-Ky), Chairman
Bill McCollum (R-Fla), Ranking Republican

Total PAC and Large Individual Contributions to Committee Members

Mel Levine (D-Calif)[1]	$4,106,254
Tom Campbell (R-Calif)[1]	$3,593,778
Mike Synar (D-Okla)	$862,475
Dan Glickman (D-Kan)	$730,001
Jim Ramstad (R-Minn)	$712,432
Charles E. Schumer (D-NY)	$677,473
Peter Hoagland (D-Neb)	$605,817
John F. Reed (D-RI)	$580,186
Jack Brooks (D-Texas)	$540,283
John Bryant (D-Texas)	$525,038
Bill McCollum (R-Fla)	$514,575
Howard L. Berman (D-Calif)	$498,862
Rick Boucher (D-Va)	$493,959
Hamilton Fish Jr. (R-NY)	$401,550
William J. Hughes (D-NJ)	$362,262
George F. Allen (R-Va)	$357,906
Mike Kopetski (D-Ore)	$351,542
Lamar Smith (R-Texas)	$329,635
J. Howard Coble (R-NC)	$307,546
Barney Frank (D-Mass)	$304,428
Steven H. Schiff (R-NM)	$297,300
Carlos J. Moorhead (R-Calif)	$294,740
George E. Sangmeister (D-Ill)	$278,286
Henry J. Hyde (R-Ill)	$278,227
Patricia Schroeder (D-Colo)	$278,131
John Conyers Jr. (D-Mich)	$273,450
Don Edwards (D-Calif)	$221,785
Harley O. Staggers Jr. (D-WVa)	$188,168
Craig Washington (D-Texas)	$171,250
F. James Sensenbrenner Jr. (R-Wis)	$131,020

Craig T. James (R-Fla)	$116,087
Edward F. Feighan (D-Ohio)	$83,348
George W. Gekas (R-Pa)	$80,810
D. French Slaughter Jr. (R-Va)[2]	$43,525
Romano L. Mazzoli (D-Ky)	$14,923

Top 20 Contributors to Committee Members in 1991-92

1	American Institute of CPA's	$181,800
2	National Assn of Realtors	$167,749
3	Assn of Trial Lawyers of America	$159,500
4	American Medical Assn*	$141,084
5	Teamsters Union	$124,000
6	American Bankers Assn*	$113,075
7	AT&T	$108,520
8	National Education Assn*	$106,685
9	American Fedn of St/Cnty/Munic Employees	$103,600
10	National Cable Television Assn	$102,650
11	United Auto Workers	$97,600
12	National Auto Dealers Assn	$94,700
13	National Assn Retired Federal Employees	$79,500
14	Time Warner*	$78,200
15	National Assn of Letter Carriers*	$73,775
16	Walt Disney Co*	$72,599
17	Intl Brotherhood of Electrical Workers	$69,450
18	Carpenters & Joiners Union	$68,300
19	Marine Engineers Union*	$63,850
20	National Assn of Life Underwriters	$63,000

* Contributions came from more than one affiliate or subsidiary.

[1] Ran for U.S. Senate in 1992
[2] Resigned in November 1991

Summary

The shape of the American judicial and criminal justice system is the central focus of the House Judiciary Committee. It is a role that makes it important not only to lawyers, but to every sector of the American business community as well. As is true in most committees of Congress, the financial industry provided the biggest level of support to committee members — nearly $3.9 million in 1991-92. But attorneys and lobbyists were particularly active in this committee, delivering a combined $2.2 million, mostly through individual contributions as opposed to PACs. The average committee member received nearly $65,000 from lawyers and lobbyists in the 1992 elections — the highest average from the legal community to any House committee.

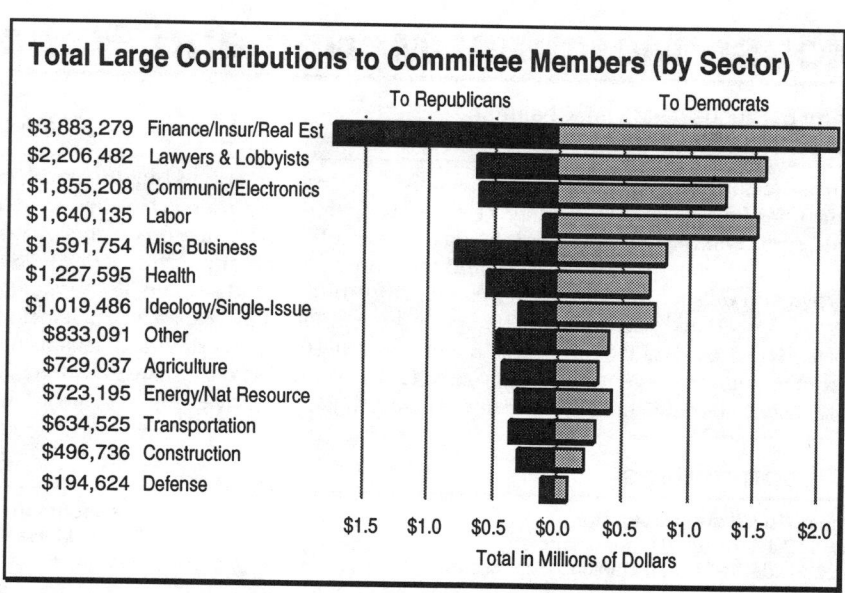

Total Large Contributions to Committee Members (by Sector)

$3,883,279	Finance/Insur/Real Est	
$2,206,482	Lawyers & Lobbyists	
$1,855,208	Communic/Electronics	
$1,640,135	Labor	
$1,591,754	Misc Business	
$1,227,595	Health	
$1,019,486	Ideology/Single-Issue	
$833,091	Other	
$729,037	Agriculture	
$723,195	Energy/Nat Resource	
$634,525	Transportation	
$496,736	Construction	
$194,624	Defense	

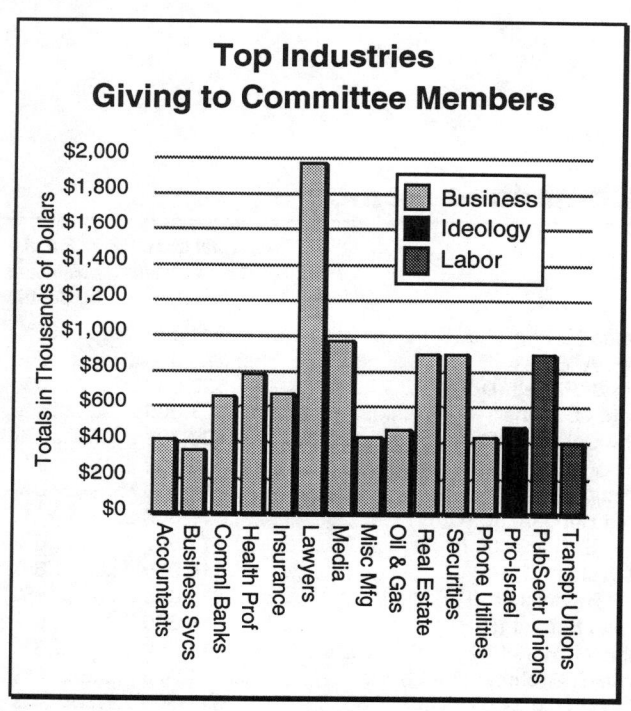

Top Industries Giving to Committee Members

Leading Industries Giving to Committee Members

Business

Accountants	$396,210
Business Services	$341,340
Commercial Banks	$635,557
Health Professionals	$761,747
Insurance	$653,673
Lawyers/Law Firms	$1,948,788
Media/Entertainment	$951,484
Misc Manufacturing & Distributing	$406,994
Oil & Gas	$458,554
Real Estate	$880,096
Securities & Investment	$881,061
Telephone Utilities	$415,155

Ideological/Single-Issue

Pro-Israel	$464,539

Labor

Public Sector Unions	$885,274
Transportation Unions	$382,789

House Merchant Marine and Fisheries Committee

Gerry E. Studds (D-Mass), Chairman
Robert W. Davis (R-Mich), Ranking Republican

Party Ratio: 28 Democrats
17 Republicans

Jurisdiction: (1) Merchant marine generally; (2) Oceanography and marine affairs, including coastal zone management; (3) Coast Guard, including lifesaving service, lighthouses, lightships and ocean derelicts; (4) Fisheries and wildlife, including research, restoration, refuges and conservation; (5) Measures relating to the regulation of common carriers by water (except matters subject to the jurisdiction of the Interstate Commerce Commission) and to the inspection of merchant marine vessels, lights and signals, lifesaving equipment and fire protection on such vessels; (6) Merchant marine officers and seamen; (7) Navigation and the laws relating thereto, including pilotage; (8) Panama Canal and the maintenance and operation of the Panama Canal, including the administration, sanitation and government of the Canal Zone; and interoceanic canals generally; (9) Registering and licensing of vessels and small boats; (10) Rules and international arrangements to prevent collisions at sea; (11) United States Coast Guard and Merchant Marine Academies, and State maritime academies; (12) International fishing agreements. The committee also oversees offshore oil and gas matters on the U.S. Outer Continental Shelf.

Subcommittees

Coast Guard and Navigation
W. J. "Billy" Tauzin (D-La), Chairman
Jack Fields (R-Texas), Ranking Republican

Fisheries and Wildlife Conservation and Environment
Gerry E. Studds (D-Mass), Chairman
Don Young (R-Alaska), Ranking Republican

Merchant Marine
Carroll Hubbard Jr. (D-Ky), Acting Chairman
Norman F. Lent (R-NY), Ranking Republican

Oceanography and Great Lakes
Dennis M. Hertel (D-Mich), Chairman
Herbert H. Bateman (R-Va), Ranking Republican

Oversight and Investigations
William O. Lipinski (D-Ill), Chairman
H. James Saxton (R-NJ), Ranking Republican

Total Committee-Related Contributions to Committee Members

	Total from Cmte-Related Contribs	Pct of Member's Lg Contribs
Don Young (R-Alaska)	$171,797	25%
Gerry E. Studds (D-Mass)	$125,454	17%
Jack Fields (R-Texas)	$107,105	16%
Helen Delich Bentley (R-Md)	$88,630	13%
Jolene Unsoeld (D-Wash)	$78,952	17%
W.J. "Billy" Tauzin (D-La)	$70,700	13%
Frank Pallone Jr. (D-NJ)	$66,635	9%
Randy "Duke" Cunningham (R-Calif)	$61,848	12%
Greg Laughlin (D-Texas)	$44,338	8%
James M. Inhofe (R-Okla)	$43,305	12%
Herbert H. Bateman (R-Va)	$38,700	7%
H. James Saxton (R-NJ)	$33,748	8%
Nita M. Lowey (D-NY)	$33,050	4%
William J. Jefferson (D-La)	$32,400	9%
Gene Taylor (D-Miss)	$31,050	12%
William J. Hughes (D-NJ)	$30,300	8%
George J. Hochbrueckner (D-NY)	$29,850	8%
John T. Doolittle (R-Calif)	$29,050	7%
Thomas J. Manton (D-NY)	$28,533	6%
Robert W. Davis (R-Mich)	$27,600	19%
H. Martin Lancaster (D-NC)	$26,700	6%
John F. Reed (D-RI)	$26,500	5%
Wally Herger (R-Calif)	$24,150	6%
Thomas M. Foglietta (D-Pa)	$24,050	7%
Robert A. Borski (D-Pa)	$23,550	5%
Owen B. Pickett (D-Va)	$23,232	10%
William O. Lipinski (D-Ill)	$21,000	4%
Sonny Callahan (R-Ala)	$20,700	6%
Solomon P. Ortiz (D-Texas)	$19,300	9%
Earl Hutto (D-Fla)	$18,750	10%
Carroll Hubbard Jr. (D-Ky)	$17,600	14%
Lucien E. Blackwell (D-Pa)	$17,500	6%
Curt Weldon (R-Pa)	$16,250	6%
Arthur Ravenel Jr. (R-SC)	$14,425	8%
Norman F. Lent (R-NY)	$14,300	6%
Dennis M. Hertel (D-Mich)	$14,250	8%
Wayne T. Gilchrest (R-Md)	$11,973	6%
J. Howard Coble (R-NC)	$11,300	4%
Bob Clement (D-Tenn)	$8,750	2%
Robin Tallon (D-SC)	$8,050	9%
Stephen J. Solarz (D-NY)	$5,350	1%
Glenn M. Anderson (D-Calif)	$5,000	17%
Walter B. Jones (D-NC)	$3,750	23%
Charles E. Bennett (D-Fla)	$3,000	18%
Eni F. H. Faleomavaega (D-Amer Samoa)	$2,600	11%
Porter J. Goss (R-Fla)	$1,000	0%

Summary

The House Merchant Marine and Fisheries Committee presents an interesting example of one of the often-overlooked realities of PAC giving in Congress — that the interests of labor unions and businesses are not always in conflict. Foreign competition and a dwindling American presence on the open seas have put labor and business together in trying to preserve what is left of the increasingly imperiled U.S. merchant marine. While the two sides do have their differences, they often work to achieve consensus on issues of basic interest to the survival of the industry.

Oil & gas producers and exploration companies also pay close attention to this committee's deliberations, as this is the panel that wrangles over the economic and environmental repercussions of offshore oil drilling.

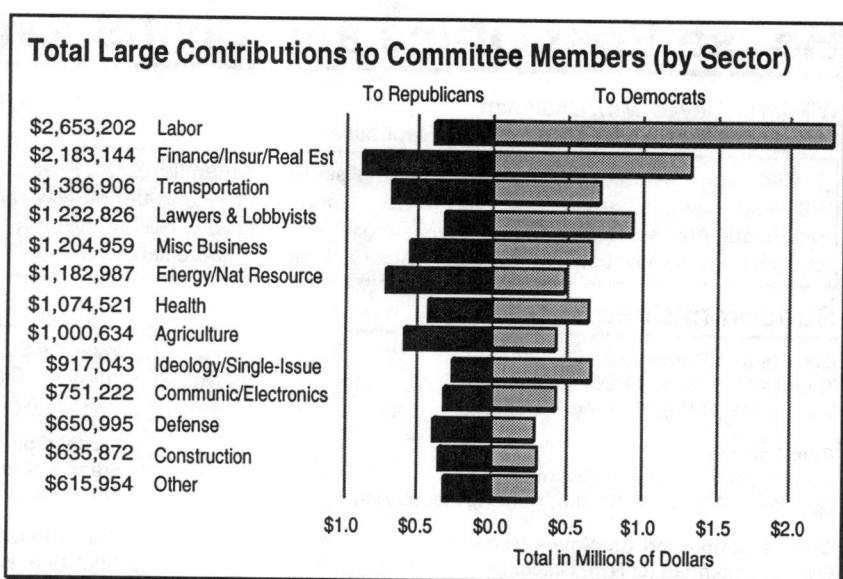

Total Large Contributions to Committee Members (by Sector)

$2,653,202	Labor
$2,183,144	Finance/Insur/Real Est
$1,386,906	Transportation
$1,232,826	Lawyers & Lobbyists
$1,204,959	Misc Business
$1,182,987	Energy/Nat Resource
$1,074,521	Health
$1,000,634	Agriculture
$917,043	Ideology/Single-Issue
$751,222	Communic/Electronics
$650,995	Defense
$635,872	Construction
$615,954	Other

Total in Millions of Dollars

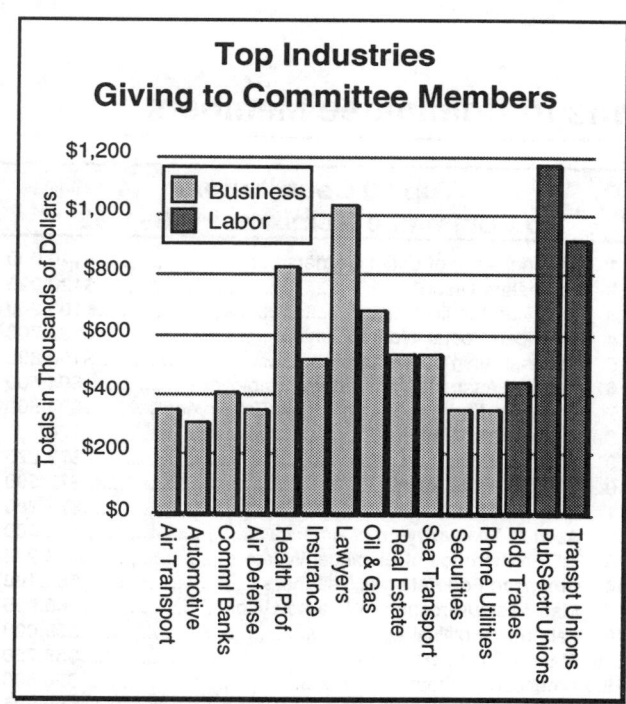

Top Industries Giving to Committee Members

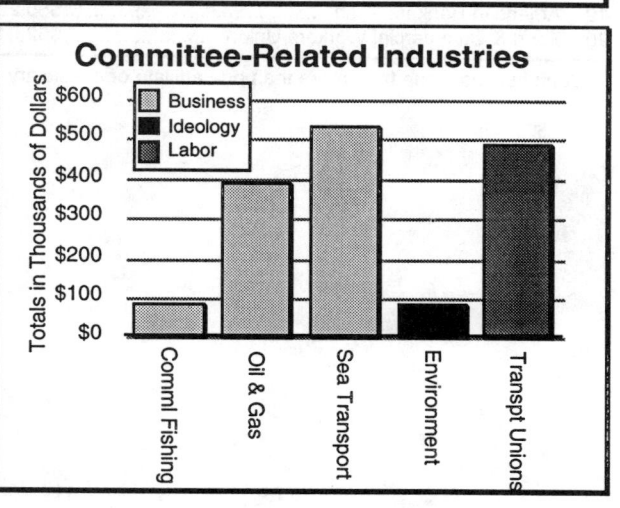

Committee-Related Industries

Top 20 Committee-Related Contributors to Committee Members in 1991-92

1	Marine Engineers Union*	$232,974
2	Seafarers International Union*	$161,700
3	CSX Corp*	$89,375
4	Sierra Club	$45,144
5	Atlantic Richfield	$41,950
6	International Longshoremens Assn	$39,050
7	Exxon Corp	$33,450
8	Chevron Corp	$33,200
9	American Pilots Assn	$28,700
10	Masters, Mates & Pilots Union	$27,900
11	Veco International Inc	$27,790
12	American President Lines	$27,200
13	American Waterways Operators	$20,500
14	BP America	$20,050
15	Matson Navigation	$19,600
16	Crowley Maritime	$19,050
17	Shell Oil	$17,950
18	Occidental Petroleum*	$17,600
19	Cruise PAC	$17,500
20	Amoco Corp	$17,250

* Contributions came from more than one affiliate or subsidiary.

Leading Committee-Related Industries Giving to Committee Members

Business

Commercial Fishing	$81,084
Oil & Gas	$383,493
Sea Transport	$530,799

Ideological/Single-Issue

Environmental Issues	$80,075

Labor

Sea Transport Unions	$480,624

House Post Office and Civil Service Committee

William L. Clay (D-Mo), Chairman
Benjamin A. Gilman (R-NY), Ranking Republican

Party Ratio: 14 Democrats
8 Republicans

Jurisdiction: (1) Census and the collection of statistics generally; (2) All Federal Civil Service, including intergovernmental personnel; (3) Postal-savings banks; (4) Postal Service generally, including the railway mail service, and measures relating to ocean mail and pneumatic-tube service; but excluding post roads; (5) Status of officers and employees of the United States, including their compensation, classification and retirement; (6) Hatch Act; (7) Holidays and celebrations; (8) Population and demography.

Subcommittees

Census and Population
Thomas C. Sawyer (D-Ohio), Chairman
Tom Ridge (R-Pa), Ranking Republican

Civil Service
Gerry Sikorski (D-Minn), Chairman
Constance A. Morella (R-Md), Ranking Republican

Compensation and Employee Benefits
Gary L. Ackerman (D-NY), Chairman
John T. Myers (R-Ind), Ranking Republican

Human Resources
Paul E. Kanjorski (D-Pa), Chairman
Dan Burton (R-Ind), Ranking Republican

Investigations
William L. Clay (D-Mo), Chairman
Rod Chandler (R-Wash), Ranking Republican

Postal Operations and Services
Frank McCloskey (D-Ind), Chairman
Frank Horton (R-NY), Ranking Republican

Postal Personnel and Modernization
Charles A. Hayes (D-Ill), Chairman
Don Young (R-Alaska), Ranking Republican

Total PAC and Large Individual Contributions to Committee Members

Rod Chandler (R-Wash)† $2,094,096
Mary Rose Oakar (D-Ohio) $860,393
Gerry Sikorski (D-Minn) $775,497
James P. Moran Jr. (D-Va) $715,363
Don Young (R-Alaska) $679,879
Gary L. Ackerman (D-NY) $570,150
Dan Burton (R-Ind) $447,425
Tom Ridge (R-Pa) $416,370
Benjamin A. Gilman (R-NY) $400,750
Frank McCloskey (D-Ind) $339,669
William L. Clay (D-Mo) $282,938
Constance A. Morella (R-Md) $282,091
Patricia Schroeder (D-Colo) $278,131
Paul E. Kanjorski (D-Pa) $265,662
Charles A. Hayes (D-Ill) $223,251
Barbara-Rose Collins (D-Mich) $217,646
John T. Myers (R-Ind) $215,708
Tom Sawyer (D-Ohio) $169,407
Mervyn M. Dymally (D-Calif) $144,911
Eleanor Holmes Norton (D-DC) $136,975
Michael R. McNulty (D-NY) $126,126
Frank Horton (R-NY) $66,481
Gus Yatron (D-Pa) $18,500

---

† Ran for U.S. Senate in 1992

Top 20 Contributors to Committee Members in 1991-92

1	National Assn of Letter Carriers	$140,000
2	Teamsters Union*	$120,025
3	American Medical Assn*	$103,900
4	American Postal Workers Union*	$102,700
5	National Assn of Realtors	$100,890
6	National Assn Retired Federal Employees	$94,500
7	American Fedn of St/Cnty/Munic Employees	$92,500
8	United Auto Workers	$78,705
9	National Education Assn	$77,975
10	Air Line Pilots Assn	$77,500
11	United Parcel Service	$71,280
12	Assn of Trial Lawyers of America	$69,500
13	Intl Brotherhood of Electrical Workers*	$63,992
14	American Federation of Teachers	$61,100
15	Machinists/Aerospace Workers Union*	$60,925
16	Laborers' Political League	$59,000
17	Marine Engineers Union*	$56,750
18	American Institute of CPA's	$56,600
19	American Bankers Assn*	$55,225
20	Food & Commercial Workers Union	$52,843

* Contributions came from more than one affiliate or subsidiary.

Summary

Steelworkers, teamsters and assembly line operators may be popularly thought of as the mainstream of organized labor, but government employees and postal workers are an increasingly powerful segment of the labor community — and one which has weighed in heavily with PAC contributions to members of Congress. The Post Office and Civil Service Committee is of particular interest to government and postal PACs, since it debates crucial issues ranging from salaries to government workers' participation in political activities.

Public sector unions (which includes postal workers, government unions and teacher unions) gave an average of nearly $56,000 to committee members — far more than to any other House committee. Non-government unions were also generous to committee members. In all, committee members received an average of more than $95,000 from labor unions.

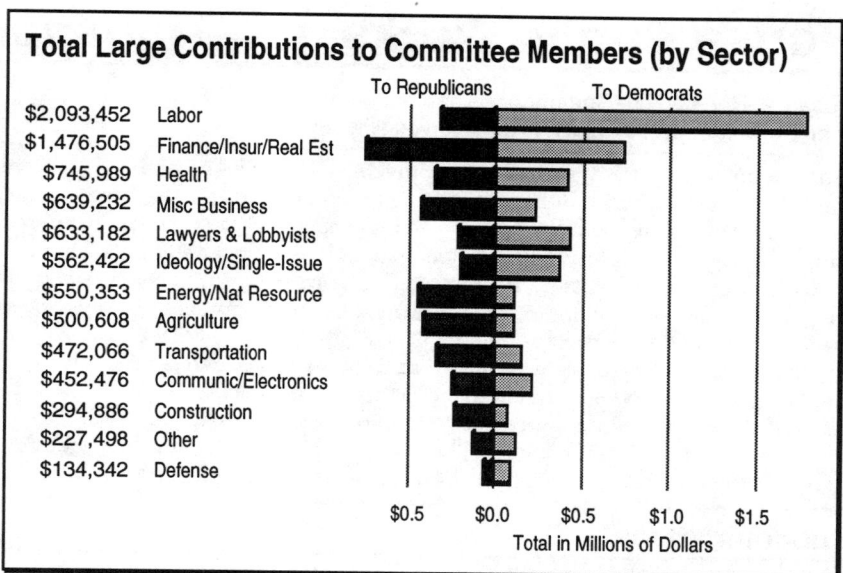

Total Large Contributions to Committee Members (by Sector)

$2,093,452	Labor
$1,476,505	Finance/Insur/Real Est
$745,989	Health
$639,232	Misc Business
$633,182	Lawyers & Lobbyists
$562,422	Ideology/Single-Issue
$550,353	Energy/Nat Resource
$500,608	Agriculture
$472,066	Transportation
$452,476	Communic/Electronics
$294,886	Construction
$227,498	Other
$134,342	Defense

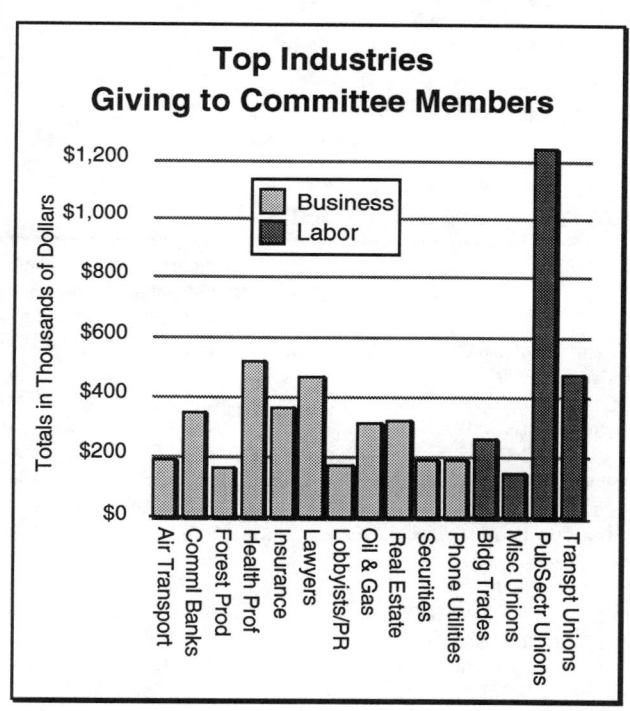

Top Industries Giving to Committee Members

Leading Industries Giving to Committee Members

Business

Air Transport	$183,702
Commercial Banks	$337,929
Forestry & Forest Products	$162,424
Health Professionals	$511,800
Insurance	$359,428
Lawyers/Law Firms	$462,893
Lobbyists/PR	$170,289
Oil & Gas	$305,630
Real Estate	$313,400
Securities & Investment	$188,170
Telephone Utilities	$186,035

Labor

Building Trade Unions	$258,185
Misc Unions	$138,535
Public Sector Unions	$1,230,032
Transportation Unions	$466,700

House Public Works and Transportation Committee

Robert A. Roe (D-NJ), Chairman
John Paul Hammerschmidt (R-Ark), Ranking Republican

Party Ratio: 34 Democrats
21 Republicans

Jurisdiction: (1) Flood control and improvement of rivers and harbors; (2) Measures relating to the Capitol Building and the Senate and the House Office Buildings; (3) Measures relating to the construction or maintenance of roads and post roads, other than appropriations therefor; but no bill providing general legislation in relation to roads may contain any provision for any specific road, nor may any bill in relation to a specific road embrace a provision in relation to any other specific road; (4) Measures relating to the construction or reconstruction, maintenance and care of the buildings and grounds of the Botanic Garden, the Library of Congress, and the Smithsonian Institution; (5) Measures relating to the purchase of sites and construction of post offices, customhouses, Federal courthouses, and Government buildings within the District of Columbia; (6) Oil and other pollution of navigable waters; (7) Public buildings and occupied or improved grounds of the United States generally; (8) Public works for the benefit of navigation, including bridges and dams (other than international bridges and dams); (9) Water power; (10) Transportation, including civil aviation except railroads, railroad labor and pensions; (11) Roads and the safety thereof; (12) Water transportation subject to the jurisdiction of the Interstate Commerce Commission; (13) Related transportation regulatory agencies, except (A) the Interstate Commerce Commission as it relates to railroads, (B) Federal Railroad Administration, and (C) Amtrak.

Subcommittees

Aviation
James L. Oberstar (D-Minn), Chairman
William F. Clinger Jr. (R-Pa), Ranking Republican

Economic Development
Joe Kolter (D-Pa), Chairman
Helen Delich Bentley (R-Md), Ranking Republican

Investigations and Oversight
Robert A. Borski (D-Pa), Chairman
Ron Packard (R-Calif), Ranking Republican

Public Buildings and Grounds
Gus Savage (D-Ill), Chairman
James M. Inhofe (R-Okla), Ranking Republican

Surface Transportation
Norman Y. Mineta (D-Calif), Chairman
Bud Shuster (R-Pa), Ranking Republican

Water Resources
Henry J. Nowak (D-NY), Chairman
Thomas E. Petri (R-Wis), Ranking Republican

Total Committee-Related Contributions to Committee Members

	Total from Cmte-Related Contribs	Pct of Member's Lg Contribs		Total from Cmte-Related Contribs	Pct of Member's Lg Contribs
Norman Y. Mineta (D-Calif)	$297,809	36%	Tim Valentine (D-NC)	$64,550	19%
Bud Shuster (R-Pa)	$196,925	38%	Tom Petri (R-Wis)	$63,390	27%
Robert A. Roe (D-NJ)	$180,300	43%	Bud Cramer (D-Ala)	$60,200	19%
Frank Pallone Jr. (D-NJ)	$163,871	22%	Mel Hancock (R-Mo)	$59,400	21%
Pete Geren (D-Texas)	$155,138	21%	John Lewis (D-Ga)	$59,250	19%
Helen Delich Bentley (R-Md)	$150,290	23%	Sherwood Boehlert (R-NY)	$57,270	21%
Greg Laughlin (D-Texas)	$137,529	25%	Bill Brewster (D-Okla)	$56,000	15%
William O. Lipinski (D-Ill)	$120,650	26%	Bill Emerson (R-Mo)	$55,260	14%
Nick J. Rahall II (D-WVa)	$107,840	33%	Peter A. DeFazio (D-Ore)	$54,550	29%
Robert A. Borski (D-Pa)	$103,545	24%	Dick Nichols (R-Kan)	$53,324	22%
Bob Clement (D-Tenn)	$101,566	22%	Thomas W. Ewing (R-Ill)	$50,760	13%
James L. Oberstar (D-Minn)	$97,680	40%	John J. "Jimmy" Duncan Jr. (R-Tenn)	$49,400	24%
James M. Inhofe (R-Okla)	$97,575	28%	Barbara-Rose Collins (D-Mich)	$48,450	22%
Rosa DeLauro (D-Conn)	$97,361	12%	Ben Jones (D-Ga)	$45,250	21%
Ron Packard (R-Calif)	$96,023	44%	George E. Sangmeister (D-Ill)	$45,190	16%
Joan Kelly Horn (D-Mo)	$93,950	17%	David L. Hobson (R-Ohio)	$44,400	18%
Bill Zeliff (R-NH)	$93,500	15%	Lucien E. Blackwell (D-Pa)	$44,370	16%
Jimmy Hayes (D-La)	$93,130	26%	Joe Kolter (D-Pa)	$38,950	33%
Dick Swett (D-NH)	$91,910	12%	Cass Ballenger (R-NC)	$37,350	15%
C. Christopher Cox (R-Calif)	$83,790	17%	Paul E. Gillmor (R-Ohio)	$34,100	17%
Jerry F. Costello (D-Ill)	$83,700	21%	Gus Savage (D-Ill)	$32,550	32%
Pete Peterson (D-Fla)	$81,957	24%	Douglas Applegate (D-Ohio)	$24,368	29%
Lewis F. Payne Jr. (D-Va)	$80,700	22%	James A. Traficant Jr. (D-Ohio)	$23,500	19%
Susan Molinari (R-NY)	$72,150	17%	Eleanor Holmes Norton (D-DC)	$19,300	14%
Frank Riggs (R-Calif)	$69,924	14%	Glenn M. Anderson (D-Calif)	$16,050	55%
Charles H. Taylor (R-NC)	$68,172	15%	Ron de Lugo (D-Virgin Is)	$15,750	36%
Mike Parker (D-Miss)	$66,755	20%	Glenn Poshard (D-Ill)	$3,650	8%
William F. Clinger (R-Pa)	$65,325	38%	John Paul Hammerschmidt (R-Ark)	$1,524	100%
			Henry J. Nowak (D-NY)	$0	0%

Summary

The biggest contributors on this committee are related to the transportation industry — and those interests are represented not only by the airlines, trucking companies, railroads and freight services, but by the labor unions representing the people who drive the trucks, pilot the planes and ride the rails across America. Together, transportation companies and transport unions gave nearly $3.3 million to the committee's members during the 1991-92 election cycle.

The committee also earmarks billions of dollars in federally-funded public works projects that are built each year in every congressional district in the nation — projects that employ thousands of construction workers and supply important revenues to the nation's builders and other construction-related businesses. Here too the contributions came both from the business and labor sectors, though most businesses gave more to Republicans and the labor PACs heavily favored Democrats.

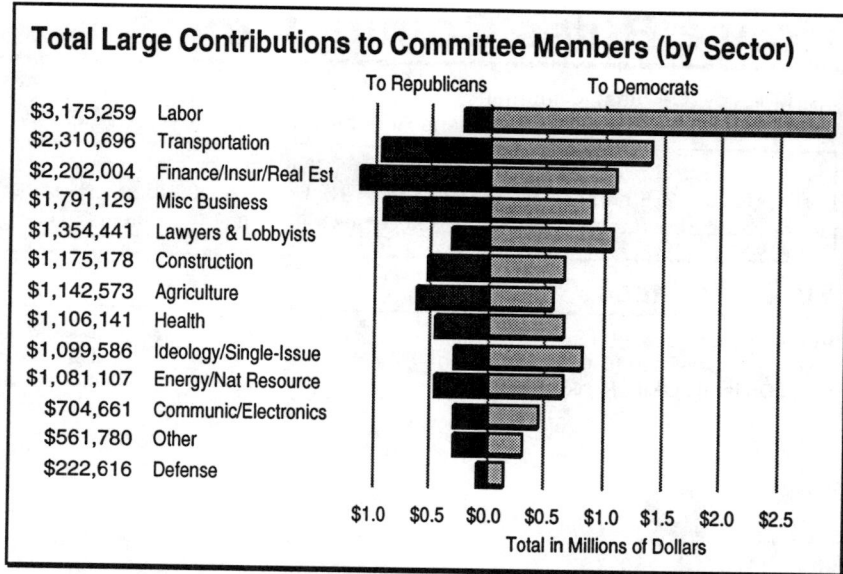

Total Large Contributions to Committee Members (by Sector)

To Republicans   To Democrats

$3,175,259	Labor
$2,310,696	Transportation
$2,202,004	Finance/Insur/Real Est
$1,791,129	Misc Business
$1,354,441	Lawyers & Lobbyists
$1,175,178	Construction
$1,142,573	Agriculture
$1,106,141	Health
$1,099,586	Ideology/Single-Issue
$1,081,107	Energy/Nat Resource
$704,661	Communic/Electronics
$561,780	Other
$222,616	Defense

$1.0 $0.5 $0.0 $0.5 $1.0 $1.5 $2.0 $2.5
Total in Millions of Dollars

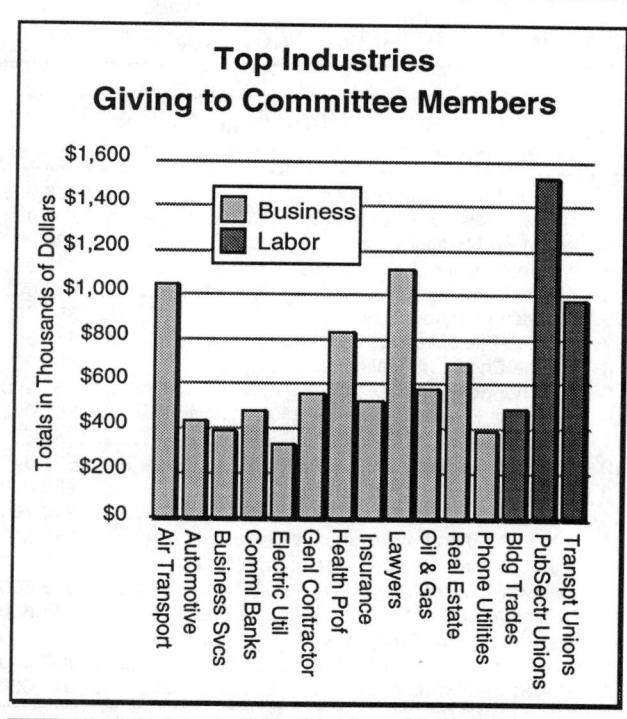

Top Industries Giving to Committee Members

Legend: Business, Labor

Totals in Thousands of Dollars

Industries: Air Transport, Automotive, Business Svcs, Comml Banks, Electric Util, Genl Contractor, Health Prof, Insurance, Lawyers, Oil & Gas, Real Estate, Phone Utilities, Bldg Trades, PubSectr Unions, Transpt Unions

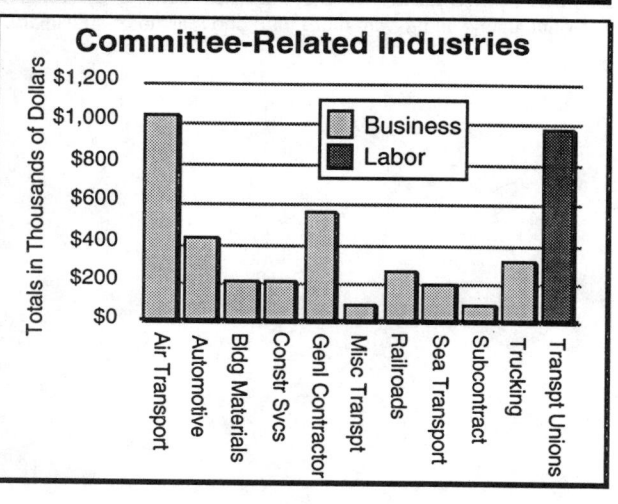

Committee-Related Industries

Legend: Business, Labor

Totals in Thousands of Dollars

Industries: Air Transport, Automotive, Bldg Materials, Const Svcs, Genl Contractor, Misc Transpt, Railroads, Sea Transport, Subcontract, Trucking, Transpt Unions

Top 20 Committee-Related Contributors to Committee Members in 1991-92

1	United Parcel Service	$241,000
2	Federal Express Corp	$211,145
3	Air Line Pilots Assn	$208,000
4	Teamsters Union*	$186,898
5	National Auto Dealers Assn	$181,900
6	Marine Engineers Union*	$134,850
7	Aircraft Owners & Pilots Assn	$128,000
8	Associated General Contractors*	$84,399
9	American Airlines	$77,150
10	United Transportation Union	$76,348
11	Seafarers International Union	$70,500
12	National Utility Contractors Assn	$62,330
13	CSX Corp*	$61,250
14	American Trucking Assns	$59,875
15	Norfolk Southern*	$59,500
16	Amalgamated Transit Union	$54,750
17	Auto Dealers & Drivers for Free Trade	$53,500
18	Union Pacific Corp	$51,359
19	Transport Workers Union	$51,280
20	United Airlines	$48,600

* Contributions came from more than one affiliate or subsidiary.

Leading Committee-Related Industries Giving to Committee Members

Business

Air Transport	$1,037,213
Automotive	$422,482
Building Materials & Equipment	$195,229
Construction Services	$202,970
General Contractors	$543,595
Misc Transport	$87,525
Railroads	$247,036
Sea Transport	$188,468
Special Trade Contractors	$82,456
Trucking	$307,271

Labor

Transportation Unions	$965,126

House Rules Committee

Joe Moakley (D-Mass), Chairman
Gerald B. H. Solomon (R-NY), Ranking Republican

Party Ratio: 9 Democrats
4 Republicans

Jurisdiction: (1) The rules and joint rules (other than rules or joint rules relating to the Code of Official Conduct), and order of business of the House; (2) Emergency waivers (under the Congressional Budget Act of 1974) of the required reporting date for bills and resolutions authorizing new budget authority; (3) Recesses and final adjournments of Congress.

Subcommittees

Rules of the House
Anthony C. Beilenson (D-Calif), Chairman
David Dreier (R-Calif), Ranking Republican

The Legislative Process
Butler Derrick (D-SC), Chairman
James H. Quillen (R-Tenn), Ranking Republican

Total PAC and Large Individual Contributions to Committee Members

David E. Bonior (D-Mich) $1,113,713
Martin Frost (D-Texas) $1,079,404
Joe Moakley (D-Mass) $649,823
Butler Derrick (D-SC) $581,380
Anthony C. Beilenson (D-Calif) $497,109
Bob McEwen (R-Ohio) $462,448
Alan Wheat (D-Mo) $414,621
Bart Gordon (D-Tenn) $403,510
Louise M. Slaughter (D-NY) $357,247
David Dreier (R-Calif) $346,008
James H. Quillen (R-Tenn) $334,744
Gerald B. H. Solomon (R-NY) $315,143
Tony P. Hall (D-Ohio) $256,344

Top 20 Contributors to Committee Members in 1991-92

1	Assn of Trial Lawyers of America	$105,000
2	National Assn of Realtors	$91,879
3	American Medical Assn*	$86,200
4	National Assn of Letter Carriers	$76,390
5	American Institute of CPA's	$65,000
6	American Bankers Assn*	$59,450
7	Air Line Pilots Assn	$57,500
8	Marine Engineers Union*	$54,200
9	National Education Assn	$53,900
10	American Fedn of St/Cnty/Munic Employees	$53,000
11	National Assn of Life Underwriters	$52,500
12	United Transportation Union	$51,640
13	Federal Express Corp	$50,000
14	United Auto Workers	$49,760
15	Intl Brotherhood of Electrical Workers	$47,500
16	National Assn Retired Federal Employees	$47,500
17	BellSouth Corp*	$45,500
18	Teamsters Union*	$45,500
19	Associated Milk Producers	$44,000
20	Seafarers International Union	$42,500
20	United Steelworkers	$42,500

* Contributions came from more than one affiliate or subsidiary.

Summary

On the floor of the U.S. Senate, any Senator can offer an amendment to a bill under discussion, whether or not the amendment is germane to the bill itself. In the House, with its 435 members, such a policy could lead to a nightmare of legislative gridlock. To prevent that, the House is far more structured in its legislative procedures. Before any bill is brought to the House floor, specific rules are determined over whether amendments can be offered, and if so what type. Those rules — and a variety of other important legislative guidelines — are determined by the House Rules Committee.

While the shape of those rules can be important to a bill's passage, they do not specifically affect any particular industry or interest group more than any other. Correspondingly, PAC contributions to the committee came from a diversity of sources and were reflective of the overall patterns of PAC giving to members of Congress in general.

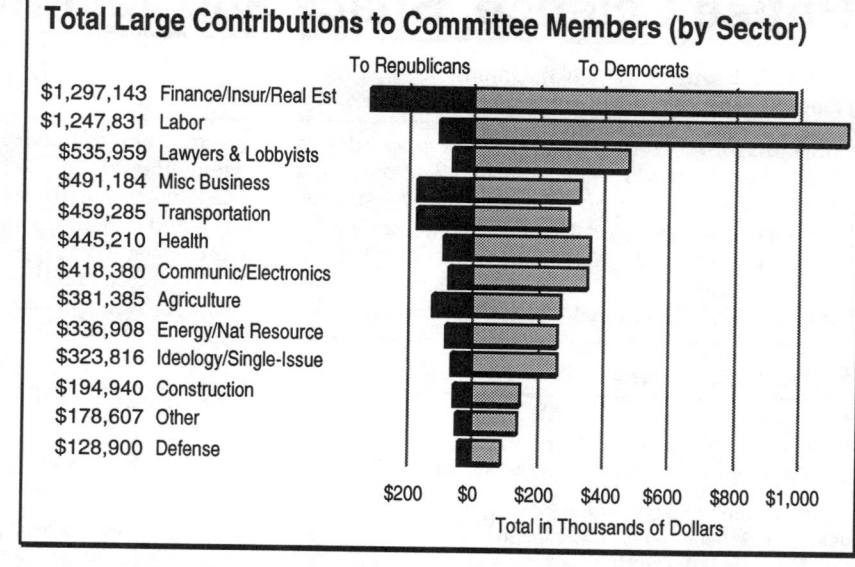

Total Large Contributions to Committee Members (by Sector)

$1,297,143	Finance/Insur/Real Est
$1,247,831	Labor
$535,959	Lawyers & Lobbyists
$491,184	Misc Business
$459,285	Transportation
$445,210	Health
$418,380	Communic/Electronics
$381,385	Agriculture
$336,908	Energy/Nat Resource
$323,816	Ideology/Single-Issue
$194,940	Construction
$178,607	Other
$128,900	Defense

Total in Thousands of Dollars

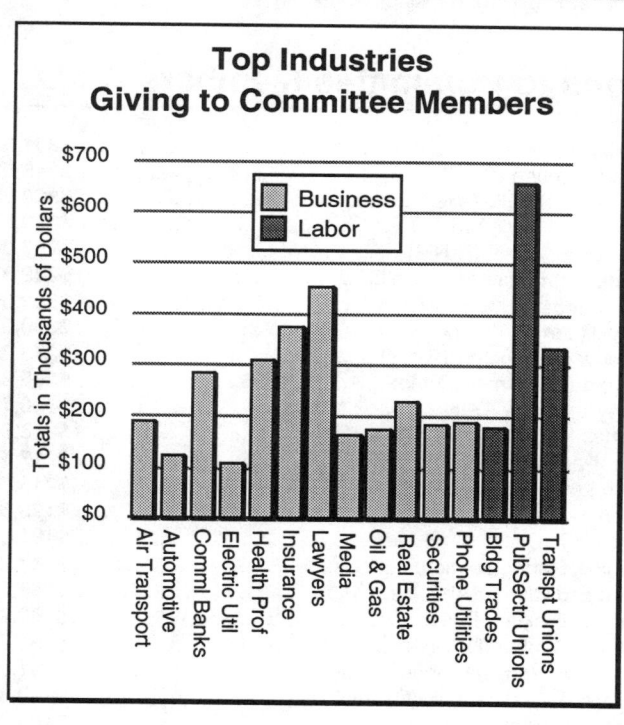

Top Industries Giving to Committee Members

Legend: Business, Labor

Leading Industries Giving to Committee Members

Business

Air Transport	$182,605
Automotive	$115,950
Commercial Banks	$276,589
Electric Utilities	$101,490
Health Professionals	$301,960
Insurance	$367,263
Lawyers/Law Firms	$448,730
Media/Entertainment	$156,130
Oil & Gas	$169,570
Real Estate	$224,079
Securities & Investment	$177,500
Telephone Utilities	$183,900

Labor

Building Trade Unions	$172,600
Public Sector Unions	$653,838
Transportation Unions	$329,710

House Science, Space and Technology Committee

George E. Brown Jr. (D-Calif), Chairman
Robert S. Walker (R-Pa), Ranking Republican

Party Ratio: 33 Democrats
20 Republicans

Jurisdiction: (1) Astronautical research and development, including resources, personnel, equipment and facilities; (2) Bureau of Standards, standardization of weights and measures and the metric system; (3) National Aeronautics and Space Administration; (4) National Aeronautics and Space Council; (5) National Science Foundation; (6) Outer space, including exploration and control thereof; (7) Science scholarships; (8) Scientific research, development, and demonstration, and projects therefor, and all federally owned or operated nonmilitary energy laboratories; (9) Civil aviation research and development; (10) Environmental research and development; (11) All energy research, development, and demonstration, and projects therefor, and all federally owned or operated nonmilitary energy laboratories; (12) National Weather Service. The committee also has oversight with respect to all nonmilitary research and development.

Subcommittees

Energy
Marilyn Lloyd (D-Tenn), Chairwoman
Sid Morrison (R-Wash), Ranking Republican

Environment
James H. Scheuer (D-NY), Chairman
Don Ritter (R-Pa), Ranking Republican

Investigations and Oversight
Howard Wolpe (D-Mich), Chairman
Sherwood Boehlert (R-NY),Ranking Republican

Science
Rick Boucher (D-Va), Chairman
Ron Packard (R-Calif), Ranking Republican

Space
Ralph M. Hall (D-Texas), Chairman
F. James Sensenbrenner Jr. (R-Wis), Ranking Republican

Technology and Competitiveness
Tim Valentine (D-NC), Chairman
Tom Lewis (R-Fla), Ranking Republican

Total PAC and Large Individual Contributions to Committee Members

Tom Campbell (R-Calif)[1]	$3,593,778
Tom McMillen (D-Md)	$1,065,639
Robert G. Torricelli (D-NJ)	$940,467
John W. Olver (D-Mass)	$859,467
Norman Y. Mineta (D-Calif)	$818,018
Richard Stallings (D-Idaho)[1]	$810,812
Dick Swett (D-NH)	$766,645
Don Ritter (R-Pa)	$764,400
Jim Bacchus (D-Fla)	$759,216
Dick Zimmer (R-NJ)	$752,478
Joe L. Barton (R-Texas)	$746,490
Dan Glickman (D-Kan)	$730,001
Pete Geren (D-Texas)	$725,500
George E. Brown Jr. (D-Calif)	$671,601
Sam Johnson (R-Texas)	$608,534
Joan Kelly Horn (D-Mo)	$567,392
Dave Nagle (D-Iowa)	$547,441
Rick Boucher (D-Va)	$493,959
Dave McCurdy (D-Okla)	$484,850
Ralph M. Hall (D-Texas)	$431,623
John J. Rhodes III (R-Ariz)	$429,710
Harris W. Fawell (R-Ill)	$428,241
Tim Roemer (D-Ind)	$411,948
Jerry F. Costello (D-Ill)	$404,080
Eliot L. Engel (D-NY)	$366,480
George F. Allen (R-Va)	$357,906
Jimmy Hayes (D-La)	$356,638
Marilyn Lloyd (D-Tenn)	$353,972
Mike Kopetski (D-Ore)	$351,542
Tim Valentine (D-NC)	$345,522
Lamar Smith (R-Texas)	$329,635
Bud Cramer (D-Ala)	$323,585
Steven H. Schiff (R-NM)	$297,300
Dana Rohrabacher (R-Calif)	$282,873
Constance A. Morella (R-Md)	$282,091
Ray Thornton (D-Ark)	$280,048
Sherwood Boehlert (R-NY)	$278,396
Harold L. Volkmer (D-Mo)	$265,808
Terry L. Bruce (D-Ill)	$220,147
James H. Scheuer (D-NY)	$218,318
Ron Packard (R-Calif)	$217,119
Tom Lewis (R-Fla)	$215,067
John Tanner (D-Tenn)	$195,689
Wayne T. Gilchrest (R-Md)	$191,810
Paul B. Henry (R-Mich)	$187,298
Glen Browder (D-Ala)	$166,713
Carl C. Perkins (D-Ky)	$160,275
Howard Wolpe (D-Mich)	$134,215
F. James Sensenbrenner Jr. (R-Wis)	$131,020
James A. Traficant Jr. (D-Ohio)	$120,870
Robert S. Walker (R-Pa)	$103,416
Richard Stallings (D-Idaho)	$63,868
D. French Slaughter Jr. (R-Va)[2]	$43,525
Sid Morrison (R-Wash)	$10,340
Henry J. Nowak (D-NY)	$573

[1] Ran for U.S. Senate in 1992
[2] Resigned in November 1991

Summary

As the mainstream of the American economy has shifted away from the old heavy industrial base and into new high-tech and information industries, the attention of Congress has come to focus more and more on the legal and political ramifications of emerging technologies and the post-industrial economy. Much of the legislative debate on these new industries — and the unique new problems and legal challenges they present — has fallen under the jurisdiction of the Science, Space and Technology Committee. Formed in 1959, a year after the Russians launched Sputnik, the committee has also been deeply involved with the U.S. space program and NASA.

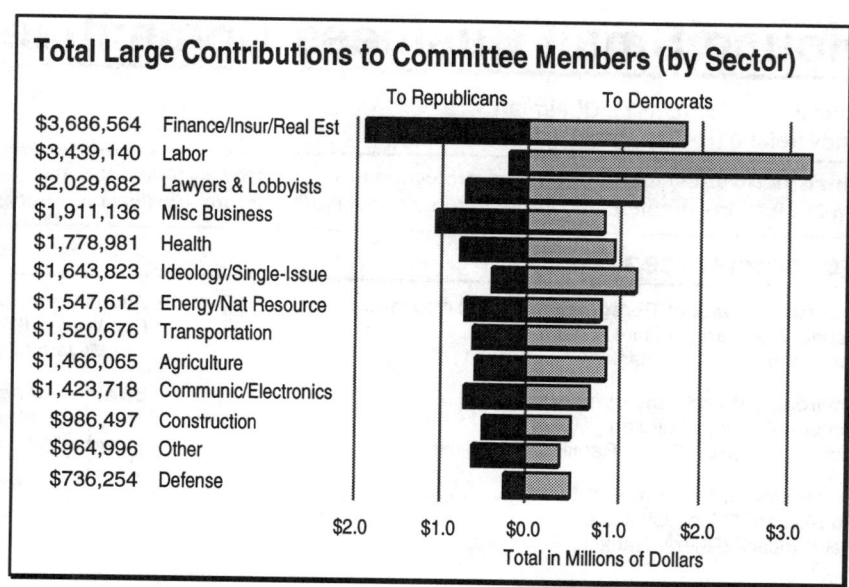

Total Large Contributions to Committee Members (by Sector)

		To Republicans	To Democrats
$3,686,564	Finance/Insur/Real Est		
$3,439,140	Labor		
$2,029,682	Lawyers & Lobbyists		
$1,911,136	Misc Business		
$1,778,981	Health		
$1,643,823	Ideology/Single-Issue		
$1,547,612	Energy/Nat Resource		
$1,520,676	Transportation		
$1,466,065	Agriculture		
$1,423,718	Communic/Electronics		
$986,497	Construction		
$964,996	Other		
$736,254	Defense		

$2.0 $1.0 $0.0 $1.0 $2.0 $3.0

Total in Millions of Dollars

Top Industries Giving to Committee Members

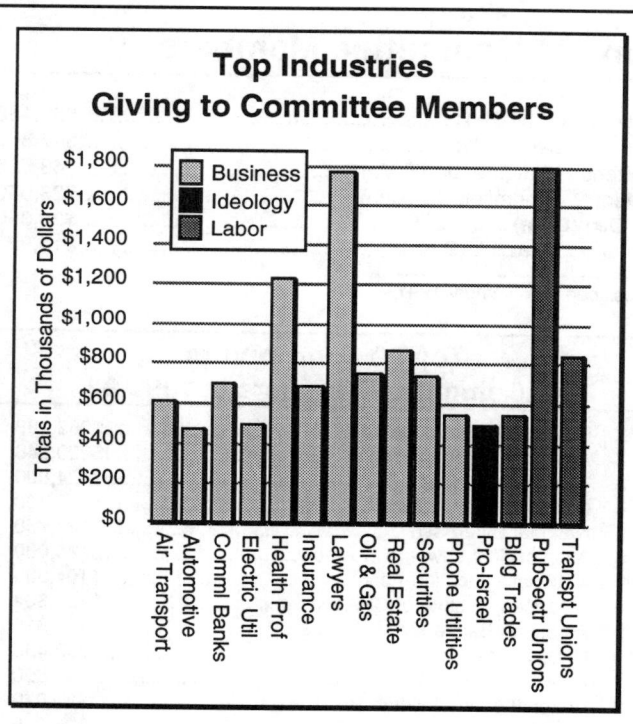

Totals in Thousands of Dollars

$1,800 — $1,600 — $1,400 — $1,200 — $1,000 — $800 — $600 — $400 — $200 — $0

Legend: Business, Ideology, Labor

Air Transport, Automotive, Comml Banks, Electric Util, Health Prof, Insurance, Lawyers, Oil & Gas, Real Estate, Securities, Phone Utilities, Pro-Israel, Bldg Trades, PubSectr Unions, Transpt Unions

Top 20 Contributors to Committee Members in 1991-92

1	American Medical Assn*	$304,029
2	National Assn of Realtors	$250,675
3	Assn of Trial Lawyers of America	$223,650
4	Teamsters Union*	$206,250
5	National Education Assn*	$200,650
6	National Auto Dealers Assn	$183,300
7	United Auto Workers	$179,700
8	National Assn Retired Federal Employees	$162,000
9	Machinists/Aerospace Workers Union*	$155,900
10	Marine Engineers Union*	$147,500
11	Intl Brotherhood of Electrical Workers*	$145,482
12	American Fedn of St/Cnty/Munic Employees	$143,899
13	American Bankers Assn*	$143,690
14	National Assn of Letter Carriers*	$138,015
15	Food & Commercial Workers Union	$134,985
16	Air Line Pilots Assn	$133,500
17	AT&T*	$127,800
18	United Parcel Service	$121,990
19	Carpenters & Joiners Union*	$116,815
20	Laborers Union*	$113,000

* Contributions came from more than one affiliate or subsidiary.

Leading Industries Giving to Committee Members

Business

Air Transport	$602,283
Automotive	$455,353
Commercial Banks	$683,715
Electric Utilities	$486,997
Health Professionals	$1,217,447
Insurance	$677,888
Lawyers/Law Firms	$1,759,927
Oil & Gas	$747,143
Real Estate	$854,953
Securities & Investment	$729,083
Telephone Utilities	$532,785

Ideological/Single-Issue

Pro-Israel	$478,667

Labor

Building Trade Unions	$533,010
Public Sector Unions	$1,782,651
Transportation Unions	$828,934

House Small Business Committee

John J. LaFalce (D-NY), Chairman
Andy Ireland (R-Fla), Ranking Republican

Party Ratio: 27 Democrats
17 Republicans

> **Jurisdiction:** (1) Assistance to and protection of small business, including financial aid; (2) Participation of small-business enterprises in Federal procurement and Government contracts. The committee also has oversight with respect to the problems of small business.

Subcommittees

Antitrust, Impact of Deregulation and Privatization
Dennis E. Eckart (D-Ohio), Chairman
Joel Hefley (R-Colo), Ranking Republican

Environment and Employment
Jim Olin (D-Va), Chairman
Richard H. Baker (R-La), Ranking Republican

Procurement, Tourism and Rural Development
Ike Skelton (D-Mo), Chairman
Mel Hancock (R-Mo), Ranking Republican

Regulation, Business Opportunities and Energy
Ron Wyden (D-Ore), Chairman
Jan Meyers (R-Kan), Ranking Republican

SBA, the General Economy and Minority Enterprise Development
John J. LaFalce (D-NY), Chairman
Andy Ireland (R-Fla), Ranking Republican

Total PAC and Large Individual Contributions to Committee Members

Jim Ramstad (R-Minn)	$712,432
Ed Pastor (D-Ariz)	$695,569
Thomas H. Andrews (D-Maine)	$623,990
Bill Zeliff (R-NH)	$621,554
Sam Johnson (R-Texas)	$608,534
Richard H. Baker (R-La)	$589,721
Richard Ray (D-Ga)	$531,178
Gary Franks (R-Conn)	$518,787
Nicholas Mavroules (D-Mass)	$498,298
John J. LaFalce (D-NY)	$483,431
H. Martin Lancaster (D-NC)	$478,515
Robert E. Andrews (D-NJ)	$473,741
Bill Sarpalius (D-Texas)	$456,536
James Bilbray (D-Nev)	$413,557
Wayne Allard (R-Colo)	$392,891
George F. Allen (R-Va)	$357,906
Ronald K. Machtley (R-RI)	$355,191
Dave Camp (R-Mich)	$354,181
Charles Hatcher (D-Ga)	$349,500
John A. Boehner (R-Ohio)	$343,332
Joseph M. McDade (R-Pa)	$334,623
Mel Hancock (R-Mo)	$282,537
Richard E. Neal (D-Mass)	$279,091
John Conyers Jr. (D-Mich)	$273,450
Jan Meyers (R-Kan)	$265,614
Neal Smith (D-Iowa)	$262,542
Bill Orton (D-Utah)	$255,564
Ike Skelton (D-Mo)	$242,876
Norman Sisisky (D-Va)	$200,384
Floyd H. Flake (D-NY)	$194,650
Kweisi Mfume (D-Md)	$188,034
Dennis E. Eckart (D-Ohio)	$186,930
Larry Combest (R-Texas)	$175,084
Ron Wyden (D-Ore)	$141,075
Esteban E. Torres (D-Calif)	$133,106
Joel Hefley (R-Colo)	$113,075
Jose E. Serrano (D-NY)	$108,900
Gus Savage (D-Ill)	$100,500

Andy Ireland (R-Fla)	$82,488
Glenn Poshard (D-Ill)	$47,862
D. French Slaughter Jr. (R-Va)†	$43,525
William S. Broomfield (R-Mich)	$33,950
Jim Olin (D-Va)	$26,350
Romano L. Mazzoli (D-Ky)	$14,923

† Resigned in November 1991

Top 20 Contributors to Committee Members in 1991-92

1	National Assn of Realtors	$262,138
2	American Medical Assn*	$220,348
3	Teamsters Union*	$134,000
4	National Auto Dealers Assn	$130,700
5	National Rifle Assn	$124,750
6	Assn of Trial Lawyers of America	$124,000
7	National Education Assn*	$104,300
8	American Institute of CPA's	$101,804
9	American Bankers Assn*	$94,615
10	United Auto Workers	$93,450
11	National Assn Retired Federal Employees	$89,500
12	National Assn of Home Builders	$87,649
13	Laborers Union*	$85,275
14	AT&T	$85,225
15	Dow Chemical*	$82,519
16	Marine Engineers Union*	$78,250
17	National Beer Wholesalers Assn	$78,100
18	American Fedn of St/Cnty/Munic Employees	$71,300
19	United Parcel Service	$71,270
20	Food & Commercial Workers Union	$70,448

* Contributions came from more than one affiliate or subsidiary.

Summary

Small businesses have always been an important constituency of Congress. Every congressional district in the land has its local chamber of commerce, with its bankers, lawyers, doctors, insurance agents and real estate brokers — many of whom take a keen interest in those items of federal government policy that affect their businesses.

Judging by the patterns in contributions to committee members, those doctors, lawyers, bankers and brokers paid the closest attention of all. Financial industry contributors led all others overall, just as they did in contributions to Congress as a whole. And as on most committees, organized labor PACs were a major source of funds for Democrats.

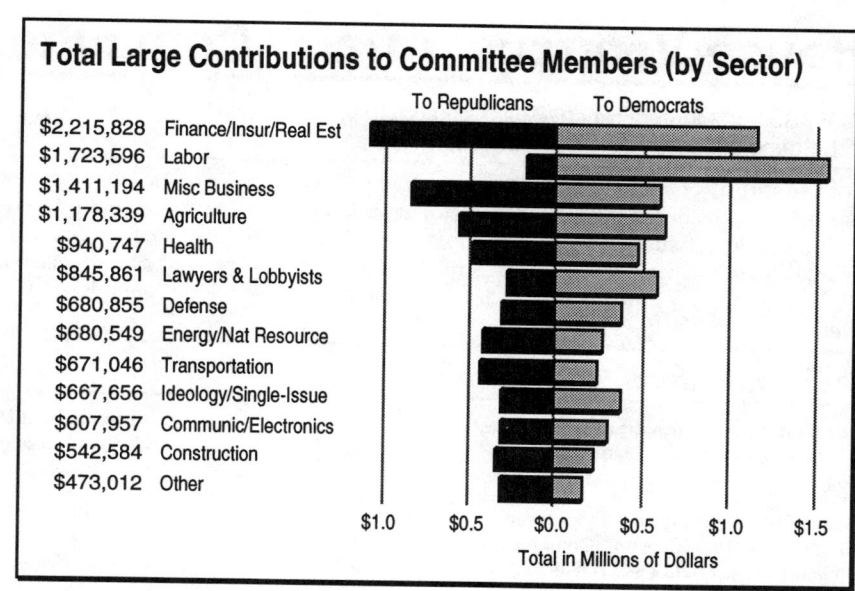

Total Large Contributions to Committee Members (by Sector)

Amount	Sector
$2,215,828	Finance/Insur/Real Est
$1,723,596	Labor
$1,411,194	Misc Business
$1,178,339	Agriculture
$940,747	Health
$845,861	Lawyers & Lobbyists
$680,855	Defense
$680,549	Energy/Nat Resource
$671,046	Transportation
$667,656	Ideology/Single-Issue
$607,957	Communic/Electronics
$542,584	Construction
$473,012	Other

Total in Millions of Dollars

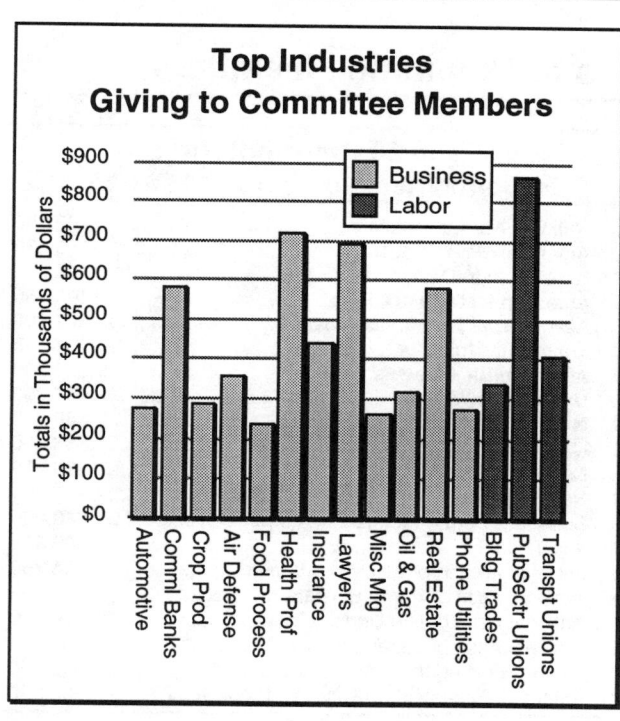

Top Industries Giving to Committee Members

Leading Industries Giving to Committee Members

Business

Automotive	$268,098
Commercial Banks	$579,373
Crop Production & Basic Processing	$278,416
Defense Aerospace	$352,305
Food Processing & Sales	$230,312
Health Professionals	$708,427
Insurance	$433,744
Lawyers/Law Firms	$686,867
Misc Manufacturing & Distributing	$252,299
Oil & Gas	$312,679
Real Estate	$576,209
Telephone Utilities	$267,252

Labor

Building Trade Unions	$331,599
Public Sector Unions	$860,843
Transportation Unions	$403,056

House Veterans' Affairs Committee

G. V. "Sonny" Montgomery (D-Miss), Chairman
Bob Stump (R-Ariz), Ranking Republican

Party Ratio: 21 Democrats
13 Republicans

Jurisdiction: (1) Veterans' measures generally; (2) Cemeteries of the United States in which veterans of any war or conflict are or may be buried, whether in the United States or abroad, except cemeteries administered by the Secretary of the Interior; (3) Compensation, vocational rehabilitation and education of veterans; (4) Life insurance issued by the Government on account of service in the Armed Forces; (5) Pensions of all the wars of the United States, general and special; (6) Compensation for service-related disability; (7) Readjustment of servicemen to civil life; (8) Soldiers' and sailors' civil relief; (9) Veterans' hospitals, medical care, and treatment of veterans.

Subcommittees

Compensation, Pension and Insurance
Douglas Applegate (D-Ohio), Chairman
Bob Stump (R-Ariz), Ranking Republican

Education, Training and Employment
Timothy J. Penny (D-Minn), Chairman
Christopher H. Smith (R-NJ), Ranking Republican

Hospitals and Health Care
G. V. "Sonny" Montgomery (D-Miss), Chairman
John Paul Hammerschmidt (R-Ark), Ranking Republican

Housing and Memorial Affairs
Harley O. Staggers Jr. (D-WVa), Chairman
Dan Burton (R-Ind), Ranking Republican

Oversight and Investigations
Lane Evans (D-Ill), Chairman
Michael Bilirakis (R-Fla), Ranking Republican

Total PAC and Large Individual Contributions to Committee Members

Pete Geren (D-Texas)	$725,500
Bill Paxon (R-NY)	$640,187
Jim Slattery (D-Kan)	$611,113
Joseph P. Kennedy II (D-Mass)	$598,296
Michael Bilirakis (R-Fla)	$506,808
Rick Santorum (R-Pa)	$494,739
Bob Clement (D-Tenn)	$466,453
Dan Burton (R-Ind)	$447,425
Chet Edwards (D-Texas)	$439,199
Tom Ridge (R-Pa)	$416,370
Bill Brewster (D-Okla)	$368,096
Pete Peterson (D-Fla)	$335,730
J. Roy Rowland (D-Ga)	$332,098
Jill L. Long (D-Ind)	$291,363
George E. Sangmeister (D-Ill)	$278,286
Liz J. Patterson (D-SC)	$266,558
Cliff Stearns (R-Fla)	$261,910
Dick Nichols (R-Kan)	$247,150
Owen B. Pickett (D-Va)	$225,835
Lane Evans (D-Ill)	$222,293
Don Edwards (D-Calif)	$221,785
Ben Jones (D-Ga)	$218,345
Bob Stump (R-Ariz)	$192,525
Harley O. Staggers Jr. (D-WVa)	$188,168
Maxine Waters (D-Calif)	$171,652
Christopher H. Smith (R-NJ)	$149,555
G. V. "Sonny" Montgomery (D-Miss)	$140,243
Chalmers P. Wylie (R-Ohio)	$132,770
Floyd D. Spence (R-SC)	$120,600
Craig T. James (R-Fla)	$116,087
Claude Harris (D-Ala)	$114,701
Timothy J. Penny (D-Minn)	$104,943
Douglas Applegate (D-Ohio)	$84,591
John Paul Hammerschmidt (R-Ark)	$1,524

Top 20 Contributors to Committee Members in 1991-92

1	National Assn of Realtors	$187,250
2	American Medical Assn*	$165,660
3	National Auto Dealers Assn	$126,850
4	American Institute of CPA's	$100,950
5	Assn of Trial Lawyers of America	$92,000
6	Teamsters Union*	$91,098
7	American Bankers Assn*	$89,200
8	United Auto Workers	$87,750
9	National Rifle Assn	$86,850
10	United Parcel Service	$86,700
11	National Education Assn*	$79,600
12	National Assn Retired Federal Employees	$77,000
13	BellSouth Corp*	$73,200
14	AT&T	$69,950
15	Intl Brotherhood of Electrical Workers	$64,750
16	National Assn of Home Builders	$64,699
17	National Assn of Life Underwriters	$64,500
18	National Assn of Letter Carriers*	$62,950
19	Marine Engineers Union*	$58,250
20	American Fedn of St/Cnty/Munic Employees	$58,000

* Contributions came from more than one affiliate or subsidiary.

Summary

The profile — and problems — of America's veterans have changed considerably over the past generation. The postwar boom of the late 1940s and early 50s, when veterans of World War II and Korea came home to raise new families, build new suburbs and go on to college with the G.I. Bill has been replaced by the postwar trauma of Vietnam era vets, many of whom have still not been able to shake off the war's lingering effects.

The Gulf War added a new class of combat veterans, many of whom came not from the regular ranks of active services but from reserve units all around the nation. They have since been joined by yet another group of veterans — those whose military careers are ending prematurely due to the post-Cold War downsizing of the active military. The Veterans Affairs committee pays close attention to the needs of all these ex-servicemen and women, but the scope of its political contributions reflect no special patterns apart from those of Congress as a whole.

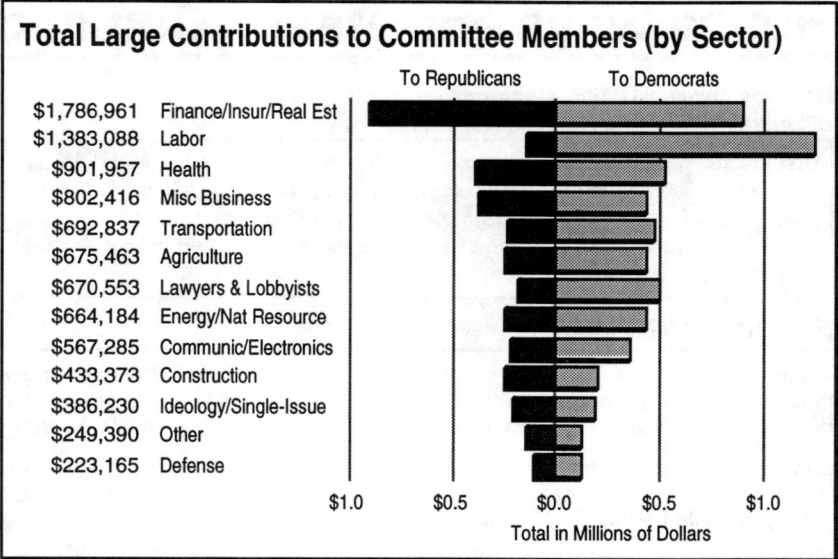

Total Large Contributions to Committee Members (by Sector)

$1,786,961	Finance/Insur/Real Est	
$1,383,088	Labor	
$901,957	Health	
$802,416	Misc Business	
$692,837	Transportation	
$675,463	Agriculture	
$670,553	Lawyers & Lobbyists	
$664,184	Energy/Nat Resource	
$567,285	Communic/Electronics	
$433,373	Construction	
$386,230	Ideology/Single-Issue	
$249,390	Other	
$223,165	Defense	

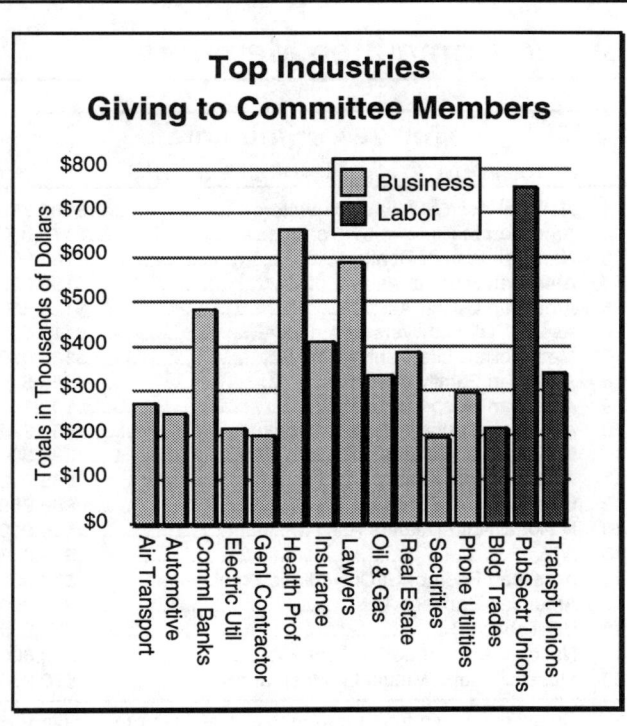

Top Industries Giving to Committee Members

Leading Industries Giving to Committee Members

Business

Air Transport	$268,739
Automotive	$243,824
Commercial Banks	$478,062
Electric Utilities	$210,830
General Contractors	$194,920
Health Professionals	$654,216
Insurance	$401,298
Lawyers/Law Firms	$582,055
Oil & Gas	$330,677
Real Estate	$379,317
Securities & Investment	$186,025
Telephone Utilities	$291,860

Labor

Building Trade Unions	$207,585
Public Sector Unions	$750,781
Transportation Unions	$333,572

House Ways and Means Committee

Dan Rostenkowski (D-Ill), Chairman
Bill Archer (R-Texas), Ranking Republican

Party Ratio: 23 Democrats
13 Republicans

Jurisdiction: (1) Customs, collection districts, and ports of entry and delivery; (2) Reciprocal trade agreements; (3) Revenue measures generally; (4) Revenue measures relating to the insular possessions; (5) The bonded debt of the United States; (6) The deposit of public moneys; (7) Transportation of dutiable goods; (8) Tax-exempt foundations and charitable trusts; (9) National social security, except (a) health care and facilities programs that are supported form general revenues as opposed to payroll deductions, and (b) work incentive programs.

Subcommittees

Health
Pete Stark (D-Calif), Chairman
Bill Gradison (R-Ohio), Ranking Republican

Human Resources
Harold E. Ford (D-Tenn), Chairman
E. Clay Shaw Jr. (R-Fla), Ranking Republican

Oversight
J. J. Pickle (D-Texas), Chairman
Dick Schulze (R-Pa), Ranking Republican

Select Revenue Measures
Charles B. Rangel (D-NY), Chairman
Guy Vander Jagt (R-Mich), Ranking Republican

Social Security
Andrew Jacobs Jr. (D-Ind), Chairman
Jim Bunning (R-Ky), Ranking Republican

Trade
Sam M. Gibbons (D-Fla), Chairman
Philip M. Crane (R-Ill), Ranking Republican

Total PAC and Large Individual Contributions to Committee Members

Rod Chandler (R-Wash)†	$2,094,096
Jim Moody (D-Wis)†	$1,448,240
Dan Rostenkowski (D-Ill)	$1,302,759
Marty Russo (D-Ill)	$990,657
Byron Dorgan (D-ND)†	$870,676
Thomas J. Downey (D-NY)	$864,993
Michael A. Andrews (D-Texas)	$802,333
Sander Levin (D-Mich)	$791,756
E. Clay Shaw Jr. (R-Fla)	$773,302
Beryl Anthony Jr. (D-Ark)	$769,360
Jim Bunning (R-Ky)	$713,831
Sam M. Gibbons (D-Fla)	$617,249
Don Sundquist (R-Tenn)	$590,627
Guy Vander Jagt (R-Mich)	$537,329
Robert T. Matsui (D-Calif)	$521,339
Charles B. Rangel (D-NY)	$491,425
Bill Thomas (R-Calif)	$469,226
Nancy L. Johnson (R-Conn)	$467,506
Benjamin L. Cardin (D-Md)	$466,793
Pete Stark (D-Calif)	$455,572
Barbara B. Kennelly (D-Conn)	$436,004
J. J. Pickle (D-Texas)	$373,514
Fred Grandy (R-Iowa)	$351,733
Raymond J. McGrath (R-NY)	$257,974
William J. Coyne (D-Pa)	$229,882
Jim McDermott (D-Wash)	$213,735
Harold E. Ford (D-Tenn)	$189,768
Dick Schulze (R-Pa)	$170,375
Philip M. Crane (R-Ill)	$137,894
Frank J. Guarini (D-NJ)	$81,498
Brian Donnelly (D-Mass)	$62,450
Bill Archer (R-Texas)	$44,679
Bill Gradison (R-Ohio)	$40,509
Ed Jenkins (D-Ga)	$9,440
Andrew Jacobs Jr. (D-Ind)	$3,050
Don J. Pease (D-Ohio)	-$9,849

† U.S. Senate candidate in 1992

Top 20 Contributors to Committee Members in 1991-92

1	National Assn of Life Underwriters	$185,755
2	American Institute of CPA's	$172,347
3	National Assn of Realtors	$161,600
4	American Medical Assn*	$150,529
5	American Dental Assn	$126,850
6	Assn of Trial Lawyers of America	$113,500
7	Metropolitan Life/Century 21*	$103,030
8	American Family Corp	$95,500
9	American Hospital Assn*	$93,100
10	American Council of Life Insurance	$92,994
11	National Education Assn	$91,300
12	Air Line Pilots Assn	$88,093
13	United Parcel Service	$86,255
14	National Auto Dealers Assn	$86,000
15	AT&T	$79,050
15	American Fedn of St/Cnty/Munic Employees	$79,050
17	American Bankers Assn*	$77,000
18	US Tobacco*	$76,250
19	National Assn of Letter Carriers	$70,800
20	Massachusetts Mutual Life Insurance	$70,200

* Contributions came from more than one affiliate or subsidiary.

Summary

No committee in the House of Representatives — and possibly in all of Congress — is more important to as wide a breath of industries, interests and political contributors as Ways and Means. Along with its counterpart, the Senate Finance Committee, this is where the first drafts of the nation's tax laws are written and where the final chapters (along with footnotes, abridgments and special exceptions) are hammered into shape. Ways and Means operates in an arcane world of lawyers and tax accountants, where every comma, semicolon and parenthetical addendum can mean millions or billions of dollars to individual companies and industries.

A quick glance at the Top Industries chart below spotlights another crucial jurisdiction of the committee. Along with the Energy & Commerce Committee, it is the lead panel in redrafting federal health care policy — and thus is of extreme interest to insurance companies and doctors' groups. The insurance industry, which has been a consistent supporter of Ways and Means members over the years, gave its members an average of more than $47,000 in the 1992 elections.

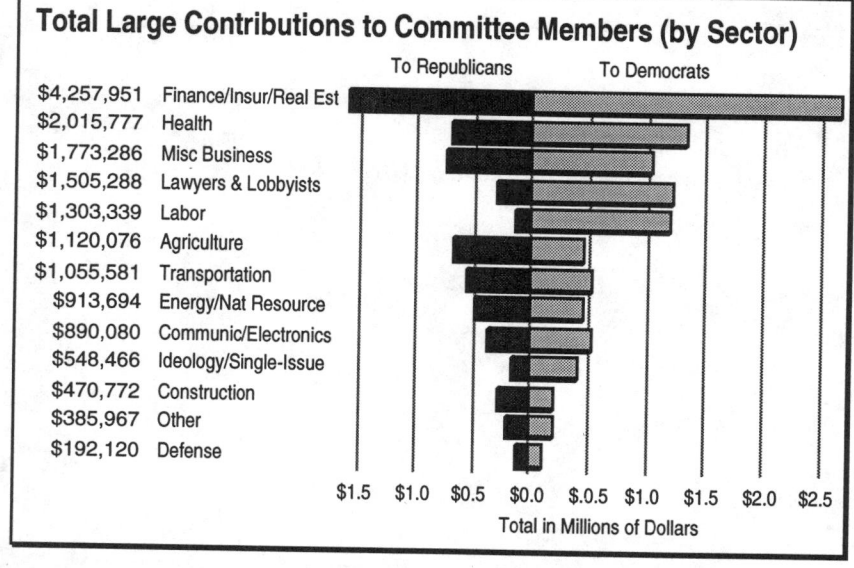

Total Large Contributions to Committee Members (by Sector)

		To Republicans	To Democrats
$4,257,951	Finance/Insur/Real Est		
$2,015,777	Health		
$1,773,286	Misc Business		
$1,505,288	Lawyers & Lobbyists		
$1,303,339	Labor		
$1,120,076	Agriculture		
$1,055,581	Transportation		
$913,694	Energy/Nat Resource		
$890,080	Communic/Electronics		
$548,466	Ideology/Single-Issue		
$470,772	Construction		
$385,967	Other		
$192,120	Defense		

Total in Millions of Dollars

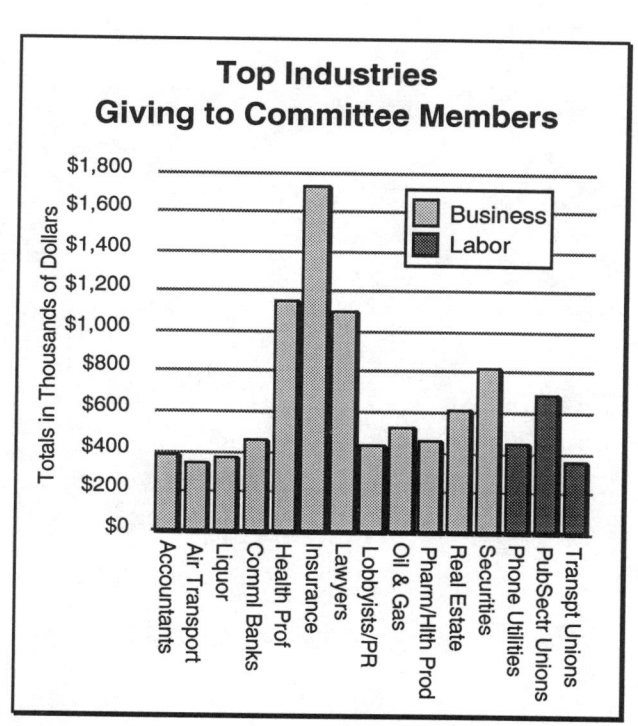

Top Industries Giving to Committee Members

Totals in Thousands of Dollars

Business / Labor

Accountants, Air Transport, Liquor, Comml Banks, Health Prof, Insurance, Lawyers, Lobbyists/PR, Oil & Gas, Pharm/Hlth Prod, Real Estate, Securities, Phone Utilities, PubSect Unions, Transpt Unions

**Leading Industries
Giving to Committee Members**

Business

Accountants	$362,317
Air Transport	$335,191
Beer, Wine & Liquor	$361,664
Commercial Banks	$440,980
Health Professionals	$1,138,791
Insurance	$1,713,765
Lawyers/Law Firms	$1,090,096
Lobbyists/PR	$415,192
Oil & Gas	$511,136
Pharmaceuticals/Health Products	$447,454
Real Estate	$594,532
Securities & Investment	$803,065
Telephone Utilities	$438,110

Labor

Public Sector Unions	$671,346
Transportation Unions	$338,403

4.

Member Profiles

Open Secrets

What's included in the Member Profiles

Vital Statistics

Member's name, party affiliation, state and congressional district

Henry A. Waxman, D-Calif (29)

Year first elected to this seat in Congress

First elected: 1974

1991-92 Total Receipts:	$682,214
1992 Year-end Cash:	$432,414

Total receipts in the 1992 campaign, as reported by the candidate to the Federal Election Commission. In the case of Senators, the contributions cover the six year period from 1987 through 1992.

Cash on hand at the end of the 1992. This too comes from the candidate's FEC filings. It is the bank balance the member reported in his or her campaign committee as of December 31, 1992. Note that the figure does not include outstanding debts.

Energy and Commerce
Commerce, Consumer Protection and Competitiveness; Health and the Environment (Chairman)

Government Operations
Commerce, Consumer and Monetary Affairs; Human Resources and Intergovernmental Relations

Select Committee on Aging

1992 committee and subcommittee assignments. These are the committee assignments held by the member at the time of the 1992 election. When the 103rd Congress convened in January 1993 many members assumed new committee assignments, so these listings may no longer be current. They were current, however, when PACs and other contributors were deciding whether to place their contributions during the 1992 elections season. Current 1993-94 committee assignments are listed for members who were elected to Congress for the first time in 1992.

Sources of Campaign Revenues

The first pie chart on the page gives the broad breakdown of where the member's campaign funds came from. The figures to the right provide the dollar amounts and percentage of total revenues for each source. The sources are:

PACs. Contributions from political action committees. A detailed breakdown of which PACs gave from which industries is itemized in the Leading Contributors section below.

Source of Funds in 1992 Election		
Source	**Total**	**Pct**
■ PACs	$402,915	58%
▨ Indivs $200+	$119,691	28%
☐ Indivs under $200	$36,537	5%
▨ Other	$62,019	9%
Party	$0	0%
Candidate	$11,248	2%

Indivs $200+. These are contributions of $200 or more made by individuals. Under federal law, each of these contributions must be itemized and the contributor identified by name, address, employer and occupation. Like the PACs, these contributions have been classified by industry and interest group, and listed in the Leading Contributors section.

Indivs under $200. Contributions from individuals who gave $200 or less. The FEC does not require that these contributions be itemized, but only reported in the aggregate. This figure was derived by subtracting the itemized contributions from the total individual contributions reported by the member.

Other. This covers funds from all other sources, including (but not limited to) party contributions and funds from the candidate's own pocket. This figures was calculated by subtracting the member's total contributions from the amount they received from PACs and individuals.

Party. This figure is included in the "Other" total. It covers both direct contributions made to the candidate's campaign committee and coordinated expenditures made by the party on his or her behalf.

Candidate. Money the member contributed or loaned to his or her own campaign. Note that many successful candidates later reimburse themselves for these expenses.

NOTE: Percentages listed to the right of the dollar amounts will add up to more than 100%, since party and candidate totals are already included in "Other."

Source of PAC Dollars by Sector

This chart shows at a glance what proportion of a member's campaign funds came from Business, Labor and Ideological PACs. The totals only apply to PACs, and do not include contributions received from individuals.

Source of PAC Dollars by Sector		
Source	**Total**	**Pct**
■ Business	$308,500	78%
▨ Labor	$63,750	16%
☐ Ideology/Single Issue	$21,564	5%

In-State vs. Out-of-State Contributions

This chart shows where a member's large individual contributions come from geographically. It covers only those donations received from individuals giving $200 or more. Smaller individual contributions are not itemized, so it is not possible to tell where they came from. And PAC contributions are *not* included in the total since many PACs have central headquarters in Washington or other cities, even though they may have offices or members within the congressman's home district. An example would be the Realtors PAC, headquartered in Chicago but having members in every congressional district from Florida to Alaska. In the 1992 elections, House members tended to get a large majority of their dollars from within their home states. On average, senators received about 45 percent of their funds from out-of-state.

In-State vs. Out-of-State Contributions*		
Source	**Total**	**Pct**
☐ In-State	$125,341	66%
■ Out-of-state	$63,850	34%
No state listed	$1,500	
* by large individual contributors ($200 & above)		

PAC Totals by Category

In order to allow for easy comparison of the sources of campaign funds among different candidate, each contribution was grouped into one of 13 broad categories. This chart shows how much the member got from each, as well as showing the proportion of funds from PACs and individuals within each group. The categories are:

Agriculture. Includes farmers and all other segments of the agriculture industry, including food processors and supermarkets. Also covers timber companies and paper manufacturers.

Communications/Electronics. This includes telecommunications, broadcasting, TV & movie production, printing and publishing, and the computer and electronics industries.

Construction and related services and equipment.

Defense. Defense contractors (like Boeing or General Motors) that earn most of their revenues from non-defense activities are *not* classified as defense unless the member sits on a defense-related committee.

Energy & Natural Resources. Besides the oil & gas industry, this includes electric utilities, mining companies, waste management and related industries.

Finance, Insurance & Real Estate. Includes banks, stock brokerage and investment firms, insurance and real estate companies, accountants, commodities brokers and all other financial services.

Health. Includes health professionals, hospitals, nursing homes, pharmaceutical companies and others providing health services or products.

Ideology/Single-Issue. Also includes "leadership" PACs.

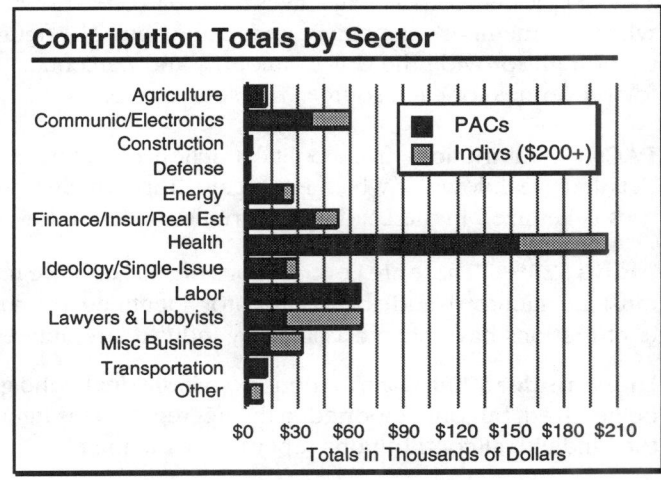

Labor. Includes all varieties of labor union PACs and individual gifts from union officials.

Lawyers & Lobbyists. Includes law firms and lawyers' professional associations, as well as firms specializing in lobbying and in politically-related public relations counseling.

Miscellaneous Business. This includes a variety of manufacturing, sales and service-related companies not classified elsewhere.

Transportation. Also includes non-defense aerospace manufacturers.

Other. Includes companies that do not fit easily into the other categories as well as non-profits and others whose business or ideological interests could not be determined.

Spending in the Last Three Elections

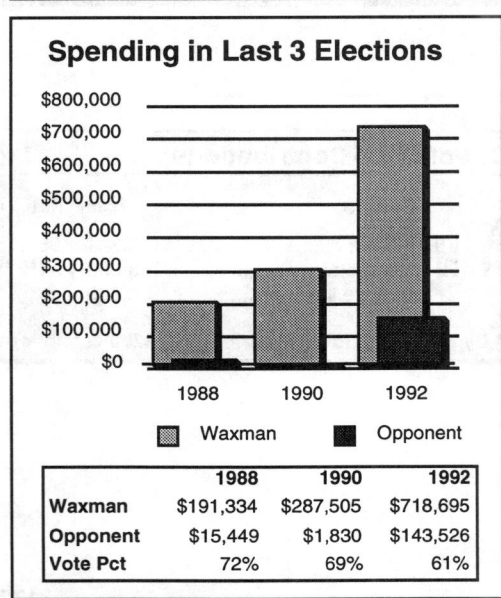

This chart shows at a glance the level of competition — both in votes and spending — that the member faced in his or her last three elections. It compares spending by the member and their chief opponents, and lists the percentage of the vote that the member received in each election.

One trend that these charts tend to show is that spending by incumbents in congressional elections is directly related to the spending of their opponents. Since 1992 was a particularly contentious election year, and since every incumbent faced new blocks of constituents due to reapportionment, spending shot up considerably in most districts around the nation. So did spending by challengers.

Unusually large expenditures by an incumbent against a challenger with little or no money may indicate a costly challenge in the primary election — or it may be a sign that the member is building up his or her name recognition as a prelude to seeking higher office.

As a point of comparison, the average winning U.S. House campaign in 1992 cost $543,000. Successful Senate races averaged about $4 million, though spending ranged widely depending on the size of the state.

Leading Contributors Profile

This is a detailed itemization of the specific contributors, industries and interest groups that contributed to the member's 1992 campaign. Business contributors are named first, followed by Labor unions, Ideological/Single-Issue groups and finally "Other & Unknown." Within those broad areas, the listings are hierarchical. The total for each of the 13 major contributor sectors (Agriculture, Defense, Health, etc.) is given first. This number corresponds to the total in the category bar chart at the bottom of the page. Beneath the sector totals are more detailed categories, and beneath those are the listings of actual contributors and the amounts they gave. To the right of the amount is an abbreviated code that indicates whether the money came from PACs, individuals, or a combination of the two. If the total came from more than one subsidiary or affiliate of the listed contributor, it will be followed by an asterisk. Names of individual contributors are *not* listed unless the contributor put down his or her name as their employer — for example, Henry Jones MD.

To make the source of each member's funds as clear as possible, PACs are listed in most cases not by their formal names, but by the name of their sponsoring or affiliated organization. This sponsorship may be formal or informal. Many PACs are officially connected with their parent organizations, while others may be legally "non-connected" even though its members all work for the same company or belong to the same union. The listing of corporate or union sponsors is *not* intended to imply that the organization contributed out of its corporate or union treasury. Such contributions are prohibited under federal law. Rather, PAC contributions come from *employees* of a company or *members* of a union — not from the organization itself.

Agriculture	$10,700	
Agricultural Services/Products **$6,000**		
American Veterinary Medical Assn $5,000		PAC
Food Processing & Sales **$3,500**		
None over $2,000		

Communications/Electronics	$58,250	
Media/Entertainment **$44,750**		
MCA Inc $7,000		PAC/Ind
National Assn of Broadcasters $5,000		PAC
National Cable Television Assn $5,000		PAC
Recording Industry Assn of America $3,000		PAC/Ind
Paramount Communications* $2,500		PAC
Capitol-EMI Music $2,000		Indiv
Falcon Cable TV $2,000		Indiv
Viacom International $2,000		PAC
Walt Disney Co* $2,000		Indiv
Warner Brothers $2,000		Indiv
Telephone Utilities **$11,500**		
AT&T $4,000		PAC
Pacific Telesis Group $4,000		PAC
Telecom Services & Equipment **$2,000**		
None over $2,000		

Construction	$3,000	
None over $2,000		

Energy & Natural Resources	$26,000	
Oil & Gas **$13,500**		
Pacific Enterprises $6,000		PAC
Electric Utilities **$10,500**		
Southern California Edison $7,000		PAC/Ind

In the case of individual contributions, the name listed is that of the contributor's employer (or the company they own). Whenever a contributor listed "housewife," "homemaker," "student," or some other non-income-producing occupation, every attempt was made to match the contributor with their income-earning spouse or parents. Where the income-earner in the family was found, the contributions from all non-income-earning members of the family are included in the breadwinner's total.

Most contributions listed in the "Ideological/Single-Issue" sector came from political action committees, but those PAC dollars may be supplemented by contributions from individuals as well. Individual contributions were classified as "ideological" only if the donor gave both to an ideological PAC and to a candidate supported by that same PAC.

Careful readers may notice that a particular company or PAC may sometimes appear under different categories in different members' profiles. This is because many companies have multiple interests. To accommodate that fact, the book uses a system which recognizes both primary and secondary classifications for diversified companies. In cases where a member's committee assignments coincide with a secondary classification, the secondary code is the one used. For example: the Boeing Co. gets most of its revenues from the manufacture and sale of commercial aircraft. It is also a major defense contractor. If one of Boeing's contributions goes to a member of a defense-related committee, it is counted under Defense. If the member sits only on non-defense committees, it's counted under Transportation.

While every attempt was made to itemize as many contributions as possible, space limitations require that many contributions go unlisted. Where possible, every contribution of $1,000 or more was included. Where a member had too many contributions to fit on his or her two-page profile, the threshold amount for listed contributions was raised. In some cases only contributions of $5,000 or even $10,000 and above are listed. The exact threshold amount can be found by looking carefully at categories where the category total is listed, but no contributions are itemized. In the example above, the member's threshold was $2,000 — as seen in the listings that say "None over $2,000."

Daniel K. Akaka (D-Hawaii)

First elected: 1990

1989-92 Total Rcpts:	$2,237,549
1992 Year-end Cash:	$69,280
Current term expires:	1994

1991-92 Committees & Subcommittees

Energy and Natural Resources
Energy Regulation and Conservation (Vice Chairman); Energy Research and Development; Public Lands, National Parks and Forests

Governmental Affairs
Federal Services, Post Office and Civil Service; General Services, Federalism and the District of Columbia; Oversight of Government Management

Veterans' Affairs

Select Committee on Indian Affairs

Leading Contributors

Business

Agriculture	$67,000

Crop Production & Basic Processing $27,850
   None over $7,500
Tobacco $8,750
   None over $7,500
Dairy $11,900
   None over $7,500

Communications/Electronics	$53,300

Media/Entertainment $26,100
   National Cable Television Assn .... $10,000   PAC
Telephone Utilities $18,700
   None over $7,500

Construction	$126,185

General Contractors $12,200
   None over $7,500
Home Builders $12,000
   None over $7,500
Construction Services $95,185
   RM Towill Corp .... $8,450   Indiv

Source of Funds: 1987-1992

Source	Total	Pct
PACs	$1,005,009	43%
Indivs $200+	$873,303	37%
Indivs under $200	$285,311	12%
Other	$192,692	8%
Candidate	$0	0%
Party	$118,766	5%

Source of PAC Dollars by Sector

Source	Total	Pct
Business	$388,007	39%
Labor	$409,750	42%
Ideological/Single-Issue ..	$184,952	19%

In-State vs. Out-of-State Contributions*

Source	Total	Pct
In-State	$643,013	74%
Out-of-state	$230,430	26%
No state listed	$3,500	

* by large individual contributors ($200 & above)

Defense	$24,900

Defense Aerospace $10,400
   None over $7,500
Defense Electronics $10,000
   AT&T .... $10,000   PAC

Energy & Natural Resources	$43,050

Oil & Gas $19,700
   None over $7,500
Electric Utilities $16,850
   ACRE (Action Cmte for Rural Electrification) ..... $10,500   PAC

Finance, Insurance & Real Estate	$173,510

Commercial Banks $35,960
   American Bankers Assn .... $10,000   PAC
Securities & Investment $20,500
   Chicago Mercantile Exchange .... $10,500   PAC/Ind
Insurance $31,400
   National Assn of Life Underwriters ...... $9,000   PAC
Real Estate $50,500
   National Assn of Realtors .... $8,600   PAC
Accountants $13,400
   None over $7,500
Misc Finance $10,250
   None over $7,500

Health	$62,520

Health Professionals $51,720
   None over $7,500
Hospitals/Nursing Homes $8,150
   None over $7,500

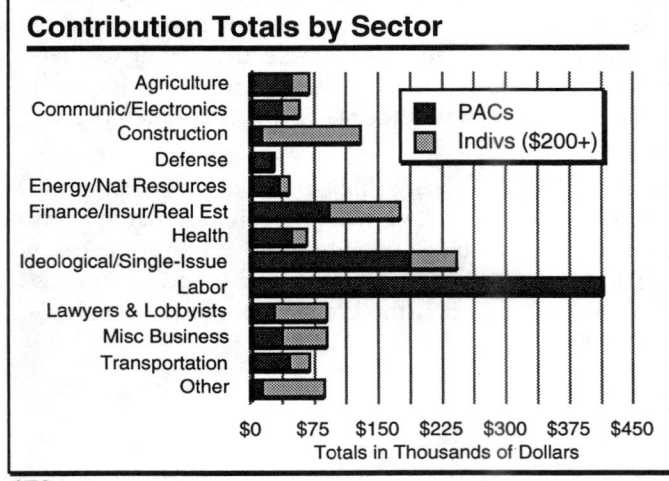

Contribution Totals by Sector

Agriculture
Communic/Electronics
Construction
Defense
Energy/Nat Resources
Finance/Insur/Real Est
Health
Ideological/Single-Issue
Labor
Lawyers & Lobbyists
Misc Business
Transportation
Other

■ PACs
▨ Indivs ($200+)

$0 $75 $150 $225 $300 $375 $450
Totals in Thousands of Dollars

Lawyers & Lobbyists — $86,767

Lawyers & Lobbyists $86,767
    Assn of Trial Lawyers of America ....$10,000 PAC

Misc Business — $85,120

Retail Sales $16,450
    None over $7,500

Business Services $11,450
    None over $7,500

Casinos/Gambling $13,170
    None over $7,500

Lodging/Tourism $13,050
    None over $7,500

Misc Manufacturing & Distributing $9,500
    None over $7,500

Transportation — $64,700

Air Transport $20,450
    None over $7,500

Automotive $12,300
    None over $7,500

Sea Transport $25,150
    Alexander & Baldwin Inc ....$9,250 PAC/Ind
    Matson Navigation ....$7,500 PAC/Ind

Labor

Labor — $412,050

Building Trade Unions $74,000
    Laborers' Western Political League ....$15,000 PAC
    Operating Engineers Union* ....$12,000 PAC
    Sheet Metal Workers Union ....$12,000 PAC
    Carpenters & Joiners Union ....$11,000 PAC
    Plumbers/Pipefitters Union* ....$11,000 PAC

Industrial Unions — $93,000
    Intl Brotherhood of Electrical Workers ....$12,000 PAC
    Amalgamated Clothing & Textile Workers ....$10,000 PAC
    American Federation of Teachers.....................$10,000 PAC
    Communications Workers of America ....$10,000 PAC
    Machinists/Aerospace Workers Union ....$10,000 PAC
    United Auto Workers ....$10,000 PAC
    United Steelworkers ....$10,000 PAC

Transportation Unions — $107,500
    Seafarers International Union* ....$16,000 PAC
    Teamsters Union ....$12,500 PAC
    Marine Engineers Union* ....$11,000 PAC
    Longshoremen's & Warehousemen's Union ....$10,500 PAC
    Air Line Pilots Assn ....$10,000 PAC
    United Transportation Union ....$10,000 PAC

Public Sector Unions — $97,150
    American Fedn of St/Cnty/Munic Employees ....$15,000 PAC
    National Education Assn ....$12,000 PAC
    American Postal Workers Union ....$11,000 PAC
    National Assn of Letter Carriers ....$10,000 PAC
    National Rural Letter Carriers Assn ....$10,000 PAC
    National Treasury Employees Union ....$10,000 PAC
    Natl Assn of Retired Federal Employees ....$10,000 PAC

Misc Unions — $40,400
    Food & Commercial Workers Union ....$10,000 PAC
    AFL-CIO ....$9,000 PAC
    Service Employees International Union ....$7,500 PAC

Ideological/Single-Issue

Ideological/Single-Issue — $240,702

Democratic/Liberal $46,550
    None over $7,500

Leadership PACs $35,500
    Fund for a Democratic Majority (Ted Kennedy) .$10,000 PAC
    Senate Majority Fund (Daniel Inouye) ....$10,000 PAC

Pro-Israel $107,900
    Citizens Organized PAC ....$10,000 PAC
    Joint Action Cmte for Political Affairs ....$10,000 PAC
    National PAC ....$10,000 PAC

Human Rights $21,799
    KidsPAC ....$10,000 PAC
    Human Rights Campaign Fund..........................$9,999 PAC

Misc Issues..$17,476
    National Cmte to Preserve Social Security ....$10,000 PAC

Other & Unknown

Other — $84,170

Other $13,650
    National Assn of Social Workers ....$10,000 PAC

Civil Servants/Public Officials............................$19,401
    State of Hawaii ....$8,222 Indiv

Education $17,779
    None over $7,500

Retired $32,340
    None over $7,500

Unknown — $342,038
    Homemakers/Non-income earners $15,100
    No Employer Listed or Found $182,908
    Employer Listed/Category Unknown................$137,450
        None over $7,500

---

* Contributions came from more than one affiliate or
subsidiary.

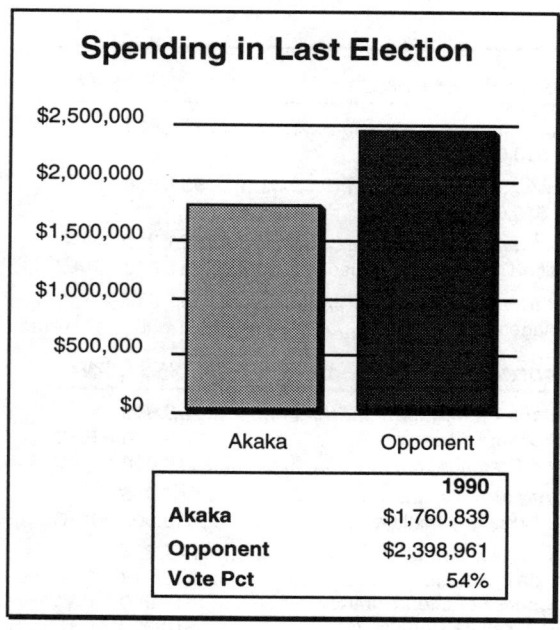

Spending in Last Election

	1990
Akaka	$1,760,839
Opponent	$2,398,961
Vote Pct	54%

Max Baucus (D-Mont)

First elected: 1978

1987-92 Total Rcpts:	$3,104,032
1992 Year-end Cash:	$311,797
Current term expires:	1996

1991-92 Committees & Subcommittees

Agriculture, Nutrition and Forestry
Agricultural Production and Stabilization of Prices; Conservation and Forestry; Domestic and Foreign Marketing and Product Promotion

Environment and Public Works
Environmental Protection (Chairman); Superfund, Ocean and Water Protection; Toxic Substances, Environmental Oversight, Research and Development

Finance
International Trade (Chairman); Medicare and Long Term Care; Taxation

Small Business
Innovation, Technology and Productivity; Rural Economy and Family Farming (Chairman)

Joint Committee on Taxation

Leading Contributors

Business

Agriculture		$158,927
Crop Production & Basic Processing		**$29,800**
None over $10,000		
Tobacco		**$11,750**
None over $10,000		
Poultry & Eggs		**$13,000**
Tyson Foods	$11,000	PAC/Ind
Livestock		**$23,850**
None over $10,000		
Agricultural Services/Products		**$37,570**
None over $10,000		
Food Processing & Sales		**$11,200**
None over $10,000		
Forestry & Forest Products		**$26,257**
None over $10,000		

Communications/Electronics		$132,052
Media/Entertainment		**$69,152**
MCA Inc	$14,000	PAC/Ind
National Cable Television Assn	$10,000	PAC

Source of Funds: 1987-1992

Source	Total	Pct
■ PACs	$1,659,483	51%
▨ Indivs $200+	$880,198	27%
☐ Indivs under $200	$375,931	12%
▨ Other	$311,152	10%
Candidate	$0	0%
Party	$122,732	4%

Source of PAC Dollars by Sector

Source	Total	Pct
■ Business	$1,213,868	74%
▨ Labor	$267,580	16%
☐ Ideological/Single-Issue	$164,790	10%

In-State vs. Out-of-State Contributions*

Source	Total	Pct
☐ In-State	$203,085	23%
■ Out-of-state	$676,613	77%
No state listed	$500	

* by large individual contributors ($200 & above)

Telephone Utilities		**$35,600**
None over $10,000		
Computer Equipment & Services		**$11,000**
None over $10,000		

Construction		$45,950
General Contractors		**$16,000**
None over $10,000		
Home Builders		**$11,750**
None over $10,000		
Building Materials & Equipment		**$10,000**
None over $10,000		

Defense		$3,500

Energy & Natural Resources		$162,871
Oil & Gas		**$58,915**
None over $10,000		
Mining		**$31,950**
None over $10,000		
Electric Utilities		**$26,200**
ACRE (Action Cmte for Rural Electrification)	$10,000	PAC
Waste Management		**$31,556**
Waste Management Inc	$14,957	PAC/Ind

Finance, Insurance & Real Estate		$531,540
Commercial Banks		**$80,600**
American Bankers Assn	$10,000	PAC
JP Morgan & Co	$10,000	PAC
Securities & Investment		**$143,366**
Investment Company Institute	$10,000	PAC
Insurance		**$178,774**
New York Life	$12,274	PAC/Ind
American Council of Life Insurance	$10,000	PAC
National Assn of Life Underwriters	$10,000	PAC

Contribution Totals by Sector

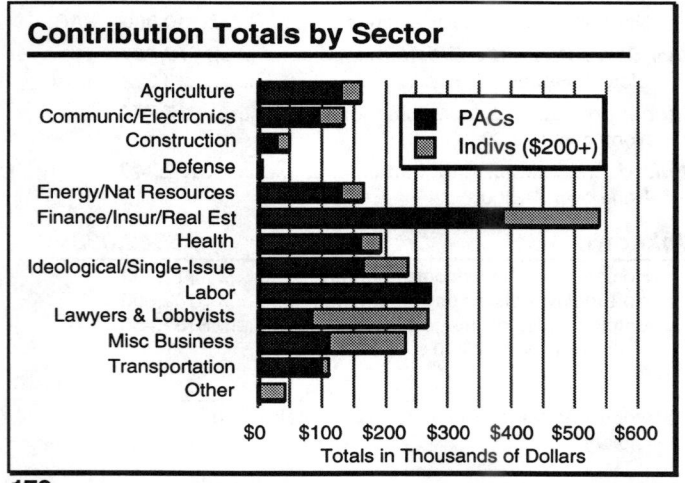

Legend: ■ PACs ▨ Indivs ($200+)

Categories: Agriculture, Communic/Electronics, Construction, Defense, Energy/Nat Resources, Finance/Insur/Real Est, Health, Ideological/Single-Issue, Labor, Lawyers & Lobbyists, Misc Business, Transportation, Other

Axis: $0 $100 $200 $300 $400 $500 $600
Totals in Thousands of Dollars

Real Estate	....	$54,200	
None over $10,000			
Accountants	....	$34,950	
American Institute of CPA's	....	$10,000	PAC
Misc Finance	....	$20,450	
Employee Stock Ownership Assn	....	$10,000	PAC

Health — $188,435

Health Professionals	....	$101,890	
American Academy of Ophthalmology	....	$12,000	PAC
Hospitals/Nursing Homes	....	$45,045	
Federation of American Health Systems	....	$10,000	PAC
Pharmaceuticals/Health Products	....	$38,000	
None over $10,000			

Lawyers & Lobbyists — $263,745

Lawyers & Lobbyists	....	$263,745	
Assn of Trial Lawyers of America	....	$18,000	PAC
Willkie, Farr & Gallagher	....	$16,750	Indiv
Marks, Murase & White	....	$14,000	Indiv

Misc Business — $227,332

Food & Beverage	....	$13,920	
None over $10,000			
Beer, Wine & Liquor	....	$51,822	
National Beer Wholesalers Assn	....	$10,000	PAC
Retail Sales	....	$40,700	
None over $10,000			
Business Services	....	$15,200	
None over $10,000			
Casinos/Gambling	....	$11,000	
None over $10,000			
Chemical & Related Manufacturing	....	$14,500	
None over $10,000			
Misc Manufacturing & Distributing	....	$48,150	
Columbia Falls Aluminum Co	....	$11,000	Indiv
Liz Claiborne Inc	....	$10,450	Indiv

Transportation — $109,900

Air Transport	....	$33,500	
None over $10,000			

Automotive	....	$12,000	
None over $10,000			
Trucking	....	$14,750	
None over $10,000			
Railroads	....	$43,650	
Union Pacific Corp	....	$10,000	PAC

Labor

Labor — $267,580

Building Trade Unions	....	$48,500	
Operating Engineers Union	....	$15,000	PAC
Carpenters & Joiners Union	....	$10,000	PAC
Industrial Unions	....	$66,000	
American Federation of Teachers	....	$10,000	PAC
Communications Workers of America	....	$10,000	PAC
Intl Brotherhood of Electrical Workers	....	$10,000	PAC
Machinists/Aerospace Workers Union	....	$10,000	PAC
National Education Assn	....	$10,000	PAC
Transportation Unions	....	$73,950	
United Transportation Union	....	$11,000	PAC
Air Line Pilots Assn	....	$10,000	PAC
Teamsters Union	....	$10,000	PAC
Public Sector Unions	....	$54,800	
American Fedn of St/Cnty/Munic Employees	....	$10,000	PAC
National Assn of Letter Carriers	....	$10,000	PAC
Misc Unions	....	$24,330	
None over $10,000			

Ideological/Single-Issue

Ideological/Single-Issue — $232,095

Democratic/Liberal	....	$38,305	
None over $10,000			
Leadership PACs	....	$20,500	
None over $10,000			
Pro-Israel	....	$115,100	
Citizens Organized PAC	....	$10,000	PAC
National PAC	....	$10,000	PAC
Washington PAC	....	$10,000	PAC
Pro-Choice	....	$14,750	
National Abortion Rights Action League	....	$10,000	PAC
Misc Issues	....	$16,911	
None over $10,000			

Other & Unknown

Other — $38,550

Retired	....	$23,650	
None over $10,000			

Unknown — $115,709

Homemakers/Non-income earners	....	$20,300
No Employer Listed or Found	....	$22,900
Employer Listed/Category Unknown	....	$71,759
None over $10,000		

Independent expenditures supporting Baucus
American Academy of Ophthalmology $81,000

Independent expenditures opposing Baucus
Council for National Defense $18,487

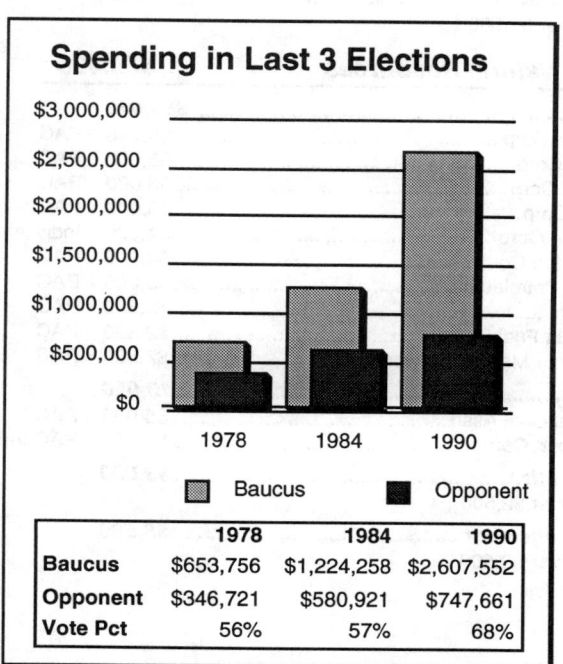

Spending in Last 3 Elections

	1978	1984	1990
Baucus	$653,756	$1,224,258	$2,607,552
Opponent	$346,721	$580,921	$747,661
Vote Pct	56%	57%	68%

Legend: Baucus / Opponent

Robert F. Bennett (R-Utah)

First elected: 1992

1991-92 Total Rcpts:	$3,457,116
1992 Year-end Cash:	$173,424
Current term expires:	1998

1993-94 Committees & Subcommittees

Banking, Housing and Urban Affairs
Economic Stabilization and Rural Development; International Finance and Monetary Policy

Energy and Natural Resources
Mineral Resources Development and Production; Public Lands, National Parks and Forests; Water and Power (Ranking Republican)

Small Business
Export Expansion and Agricultural Development; Innovation, Manufacturing and Technology

Joint Economic Committee

Leading Contributors

Business

Agriculture		$33,500	
Crop Production & Basic Processing		**$3,500**	
None over $2,500			
Livestock		**$5,300**	
National Cattlemen's Assn*		$4,500	PAC
Agricultural Services/Products		**$3,000**	
None over $2,500			
Food Processing & Sales		**$15,750**	
Pepsico Inc		$5,000	PAC
Forestry & Forest Products		**$4,000**	
None over $2,500			

Communications/Electronics		$32,864	
Media/Entertainment		**$10,114**	
National Assn of Broadcasters		$6,114	PAC
Telephone Utilities		**$12,000**	
United Telecommunications		$5,000	PAC
AT&T		$4,000	PAC
Electronics Mfg & Services		**$5,000**	
Harris Corp		$5,000	PAC
Computer Equipment & Services		**$4,500**	
WordPerfect Corp		$3,000	Indiv

Source of Funds: 1987-1992

Source	Total	Pct
■ PACs	$379,110	11%
▨ Indivs $200+	$198,306	6%
☐ Indivs under $200	$58,194	2%
⊠ Other	$2,964,627	82%
Candidate	$2,797,004	78%
Party	$143,121	4%

Source of PAC Dollars by Sector

Source	Total	Pct
■ Business	$370,477	93%
▨ Labor	$0	0%
☐ Ideological/Single-Issue	$28,000	7%

In-State vs. Out-of-State Contributions*

Source	Total	Pct
☐ In-State	$137,606	71%
■ Out-of-state	$56,750	29%
No state listed	$0	

*** by large individual contributors ($200 & above)**

Construction		$14,200	
General Contractors		**$7,200**	
Associated General Contractors		$2,500	PAC
Special Trade Contractors		**$3,000**	
Sheet Metal/Air Conditioning Contractors		$3,000	PAC

Defense		$21,500	
Defense Aerospace		**$17,500**	
Martin Marietta Corp		$5,000	PAC
Thiokol		$4,000	PAC
Allied-Signal		$2,500	PAC
Defense Electronics		**$3,000**	
None over $2,500			

Energy & Natural Resources		$80,498	
Oil & Gas		**$60,048**	
Chevron Corp		$5,748	PAC
Amoco Corp		$5,000	PAC
Coastal Corp		$5,000	PAC
Exxon Corp		$5,000	PAC
Coalinga Corp		$4,000	Indiv
Halliburton Co		$4,000	PAC
Phillips Petroleum		$3,000	PAC
Mobil Oil		$2,500	PAC
Mountain Fuel Supply		$2,500	PAC
Petroleum Marketers Assn		$2,500	PAC
Mining		**$13,950**	
National Coal Assn		$5,000	PAC
Kennecott Corp		$4,150	PAC/Ind
Electric Utilities		**$3,000**	
None over $2,500			
Waste Management		**$3,500**	
None over $2,500			

Contribution Totals by Sector

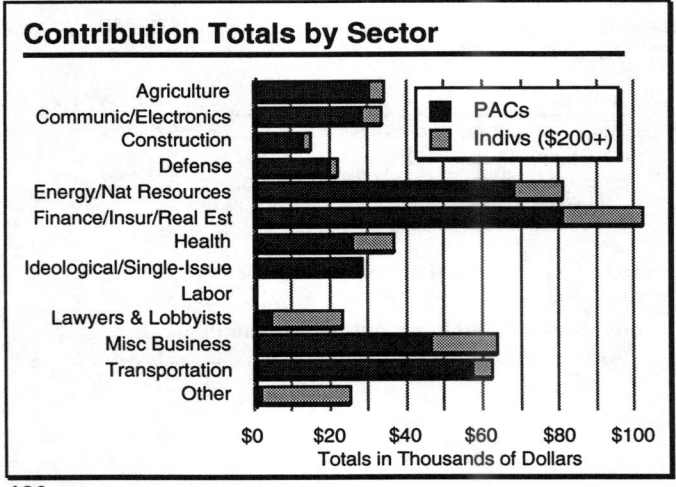

Agriculture, Communic/Electronics, Construction, Defense, Energy/Nat Resources, Finance/Insur/Real Est, Health, Ideological/Single-Issue, Labor, Lawyers & Lobbyists, Misc Business, Transportation, Other

■ PACs
▨ Indivs ($200+)

$0 $20 $40 $60 $80 $100
Totals in Thousands of Dollars

Finance, Insurance & Real Estate — $101,711

Commercial Banks $24,150
- American Bankers Assn .... $10,000 — PAC
- First Security Bank .... $3,000 — Indiv

Credit Unions $2,500
- Credit Union National Assn .... $2,500 — PAC

Finance/Credit Companies $3,300
- None over $2,500

Securities & Investment $14,561
- Dean Witter .... $6,150 — PAC/Ind

Insurance $40,750
- Torchmark Corp .... $6,000 — PAC
- American Family Corp .... $5,000 — PAC
- National Assn of Life Underwriters .... $5,000 — PAC
- National Assn of Independent Insurers .... $3,000 — PAC

Real Estate $7,500
- National Assn of Realtors .... $5,000 — PAC

Accountants $5,250
- American Institute of CPA's .... $5,000 — PAC

Misc Finance $2,700
- None over $2,500

Health — $36,150

Health Professionals $18,150
- American Medical Assn .... $5,000 — PAC
- American Podiatry Assn .... $2,500 — PAC

Hospitals/Nursing Homes $3,500
- None over $2,500

Pharmaceuticals/Health Products $10,500
- Schering-Plough Corp .... $2,500 — PAC

Lawyers & Lobbyists — $22,700

Lawyers & Lobbyists $22,700
- Timmons & Co .... $2,950 — Indiv

Misc Business — $63,265

Business Associations $3,040
- None over $2,500

Food & Beverage $14,000
- McDonald's Corp .... $5,000 — PAC
- Slaymaker Restaurants .... $2,500 — Indiv

Retail Sales — $6,375
- None over $2,500

Business Services — $6,650
- None over $2,500

Lodging/Tourism — $6,000
- Marriott Corp .... $4,000 — PAC

Chemical & Related Manufacturing — $12,450
- Huntsman Chemical Corp .... $4,000 — Indiv

Misc Manufacturing & Distributing — $12,500
- Brush Wellman .... $5,000 — PAC
- Stone Container Corp .... $3,000 — PAC

Transportation — $61,750

Air Transport $13,000
- United Parcel Service .... $5,000 — PAC
- General Electric .... $4,000 — PAC

Automotive $26,750
- Americans for Free International Trade .... $10,000 — PAC
- National Auto Dealers Assn .... $10,000 — PAC

Trucking $6,000
- None over $2,500

Railroads $13,000
- Union Pacific Corp .... $10,000 — PAC

Sea Transport $3,000
- None over $2,500

Ideological/Single-Issue

Ideological/Single-Issue — $28,000

Republican/Conservative $2,600
- Eagle Forum .... $2,500 — PAC

Leadership PACs $12,000
- Campaign America (Bob Dole) .... $10,000 — PAC

Gun Rights/Gun Control $9,900
- National Rifle Assn .... $9,900 — PAC

Misc Issues $3,000
- None over $2,500

Other & Unknown

Other — $24,550

Non-Profit Institutions $7,100
- Franklin Institute .... $7,100 — Indiv

Education $4,750
- None over $2,500

Retired $11,700
- None over $2,500

Unknown — $77,595
- No Employer Listed or Found $61,741
- Generic Occupation/Category Unknown $2,500
- Employer Listed/Category Unknown $11,854
  - None over $2,500

Independent expenditures supporting Bennett
- National Right to Life PAC $2,607

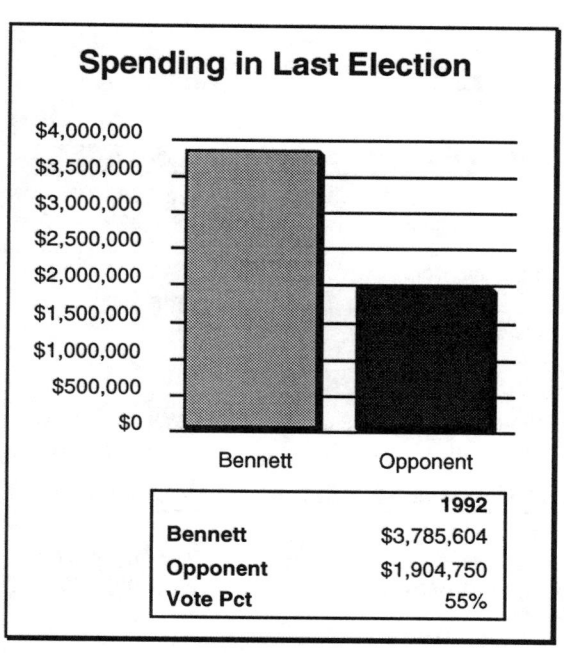

Spending in Last Election

	1992
Bennett	$3,785,604
Opponent	$1,904,750
Vote Pct	55%

---

* Contributions came from more than one affiliate or subsidiary.

Lloyd Bentsen (D-Texas)

First elected: 1970

1987-92 Total Rcpts: $9,614,793
1992 Year-end Cash: $691,634

1991-92 Committees & Subcommittees

Commerce, Science and Transportation
Aviation; Communications; Merchant Marine; National Ociean Policy Study; Science Technology and Space

Finance (Chairman)
International Trade; Medicare and Long Term Care; Taxation

Joint Economic Committee

Joint Committee on Taxation (Chairman)

Leading Contributors

NOTE: The bulk of Bentsen's large individual contributions do not appear in the listings below. His last election was in 1988, and this book lists individual contributions only from 1989-1992.

Business

Agriculture $153,550

Crop Production & Basic Processing $32,750
   None over $10,000

Tobacco $13,000
   None over $10,000

Dairy $17,500
   None over $10,000

Livestock $18,400
   National Cattlemen's Assn* .... $10,000 PAC

Agricultural Services/Products $25,500
   None over $10,000

Food Processing & Sales $22,900
   None over $10,000

Forestry & Forest Products $19,500
   None over $10,000

Communications/Electronics $139,735

Media/Entertainment $48,215
   MCA Inc .... $10,000 PAC

Telephone Utilities $41,220
   AT&T .... $10,000 PAC
   GTE Corp* .... $10,000 PAC

Computer Equipment & Services $26,500
   None over $10,000

Source of Funds: 1987-1992

Source	Total	Pct
■ PACs	$2,349,054	23%
▨ Indivs $200+	$5,120,143	51%
□ Indivs under $200	$1,482,241	15%
⊠ Other	$1,111,270	11%
Candidate	$0	0%
Party	$447,915	4%

Source of PAC Dollars by Sector

Source	Total	Pct
■ Business	$2,097,916	88%
▨ Labor	$184,999	8%
□ Ideological/Single-Issue	$94,331	4%

In-State vs. Out-of-State Contributions*

Source	Total	Pct
□ In-State	$3,310,166	65%
▨ Out-of-state	$1,804,477	35%
No state listed	$4,500	

* by large individual contributors ($200 & above)

Construction $96,925

General Contractors $36,000
   Associated General Contractors .... $10,000 PAC

Home Builders $17,500
   National Assn of Home Builders .... $10,000 PAC

Construction Services $15,425
   None over $10,000

Building Materials & Equipment $27,500
   None over $10,000

Defense $91,817

Defense Aerospace $57,750
   None over $10,000

Defense Electronics $13,317
   None over $10,000

Misc Defense $20,750
   Litton Industries .... $10,000 PAC

Energy & Natural Resources $347,837

Oil & Gas $252,587
   Internorth Inc .... $15,000 PAC
   Enserch Corp .... $10,500 PAC/Ind
   Panhandle Eastern Corp .... $10,000 PAC/Ind

Mining $15,500
   None over $10,000

Electric Utilities $53,250
   None over $10,000

Waste Management $18,000
   Waste Management Inc .... $10,000 PAC

Finance, Insurance & Real Estate $745,122

Commercial Banks $118,825
   Allied Bankshares .... $10,000 PAC
   American Bankers Assn .... $10,000 PAC

Contribution Totals by Sector

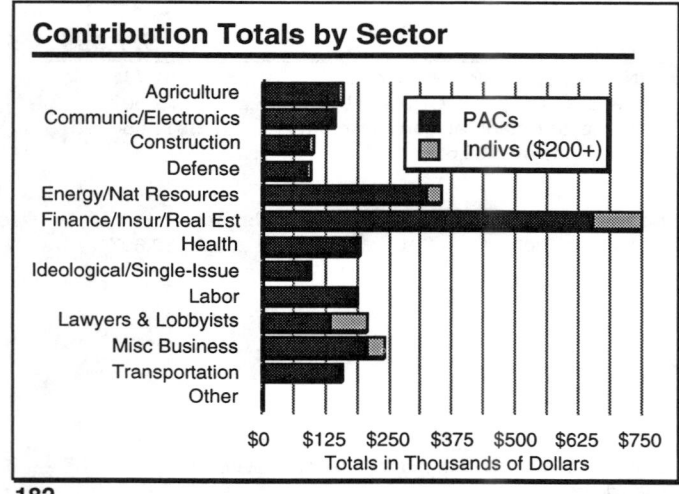

Agriculture
Communic/Electronics
Construction
Defense
Energy/Nat Resources
Finance/Insur/Real Est
Health
Ideological/Single-Issue
Labor
Lawyers & Lobbyists
Misc Business
Transportation
Other

■ PACs
▨ Indivs ($200+)

$0 $125 $250 $375 $500 $625 $750
Totals in Thousands of Dollars

Savings & Loans **$47,372**
US League of Savings Assns .... $10,000   PAC

Credit Unions **$10,000**
Credit Union National Assn .... $10,000   PAC

Finance/Credit Companies **$35,500**
Beneficial Management Corp .... $10,000   PAC/Ind
Gulf + Western Industries .... $10,000   PAC

Securities & Investment **$158,850**
Goldman, Sachs & Co .... $16,500   PAC/Ind
First Boston Corp .... $12,000   PAC/Ind
Chicago Board of Trade .... $10,000   PAC
Chicago Mercantile Exchange .... $10,000   PAC
Investment Company Institute .... $10,000   PAC
National Venture Capital Assn .... $10,000   PAC
Salomon Brothers .... $10,000   PAC

Insurance **$232,150**
American Family Corp .... $10,000   PAC
Cigna Corp .... $10,000   PAC
National Assn of Life Underwriters .... $10,000   PAC
United Services Automobile Assn Group .... $10,000   PAC

Real Estate **$93,300**
National Realty Cmte .... $10,000   PAC
Trammell Crow Co .... $10,000   PAC/Ind

Accountants **$23,375**
American Institute of CPA's .... $10,000   PAC

Misc Finance **$25,750**
None over $10,000

Health $191,705

Health Professionals **$84,955**
American Dental Assn .... $10,000   PAC

Hospitals/Nursing Homes **$56,500**
American Health Care Assn .... $10,000   PAC
American Hospital Assn .... $10,000   PAC
Federation of American Health Systems .... $10,000   PAC

Pharmaceuticals/Health Products **$48,250**
None over $10,000

Lawyers & Lobbyists $204,632

Lawyers & Lobbyists **$204,632**
Bracewell & Patterson .... $11,000   PAC/Ind
Assn of Trial Lawyers of America .... $10,000   PAC
Johnson & Gibbs .... $10,000   PAC
Jones, Day et al .... $10,000   PAC

Spending in Last 3 Elections

	1976	1982	1988
Bensten	$1,237,910	$4,971,342	$9,467,641
Opponent	$665,058	$4,138,736	$1,353,345
Vote Pct	57%	59%	59%

Misc Business   **$235,575**

Food & Beverage **$27,050**
National Restaurant Assn .... $10,000   PAC

Beer, Wine & Liquor **$49,800**
Gallo Winery .... $12,000   Indiv
National Beer Wholesalers Assn .... $10,000   PAC

Retail Sales **$39,000**
None over $10,000

Misc Services **$12,000**
American Assn of Equipment Lessors .... $10,000   PAC

Business Services **$13,200**
None over $10,000

Chemical & Related Manufacturing **$23,200**
None over $10,000

Misc Manufacturing & Distributing **$29,500**
None over $10,000

Transportation $156,030

Air Transport **$51,990**
None over $10,000

Automotive **$41,700**
National Auto Dealers Assn .... $10,000   PAC

Trucking **$25,500**
American Trucking Assns .... $10,000   PAC

Railroads **$24,500**
Union Pacific Corp .... $10,000   PAC

Labor

Labor   **$184,999**

Building Trade Unions **$18,020**
None over $10,000

Industrial Unions **$36,400**
None over $10,000

Transportation Unions **$50,500**
Marine Engineers Union* .... $10,000   PAC
Teamsters Union* .... $10,000   PAC

Public Sector Unions **$42,750**
American Fedn of St/Cnty/Munic Employees .... $11,000   PAC

Misc Unions **$37,329**
Food & Commercial Workers Union .... $11,329   PAC

Ideological/Single-Issue

Ideological/Single-Issue   **$94,331**

Leadership PACs **$21,525**
Cmte for a Demo Consensus (Alan Cranston) .. $11,000   PAC

Pro-Israel **$35,200**
None over $10,000

Human Rights **$10,000**
KidsPAC .... $10,000   PAC

Other & Unknown

Unknown   **$70,424**

Employer Listed/Category Unknown $58,824
None over $10,000

Independent expenditures supporting Bentsen
National Cmte to Preserve Social Security $51,085

---

* Contributions came from more than one affiliate or subsidiary.

Joseph R. Biden Jr. (D-Del)

First elected: 1972

1987-92 Total Rcpts:	$2,160,291
1992 Year-end Cash:	$46,943
Current term expires:	1996

1991-92 Committees & Subcommittees

Foreign Relations
East Asian and Pacific Affairs; European Affairs (Chairman); International Economic Policy, Trade, Oceans and Environment

Judiciary (Chairman)
Juvenile Justice

Leading Contributors

Business

Agriculture	$9,000
None over $5,000	

Communications/Electronics	$131,704

Printing & Publishing $10,250
None over $5,000

Media/Entertainment $79,754
Gulf + Western Industries	$10,000	PAC
National Cable Television Assn	$10,000	PAC
Warner Brothers	$9,000	PAC/Ind
Paramount Pictures	$6,550	Indiv
MCA Inc	$6,000	PAC/Ind

Telephone Utilities $41,150
AT&T	$11,500	PAC
Bell Atlantic	$8,500	PAC/Ind
BellSouth Corp*	$5,000	PAC

Construction	$35,375

General Contractors $8,250
None over $5,000

Home Builders $8,925
| National Assn of Home Builders | $7,500 | PAC |

Special Trade Contractors $9,100
| Forest Electric Corp | $7,000 | Indiv |

Building Materials & Equipment $9,000
None over $5,000

Contribution Totals by Sector

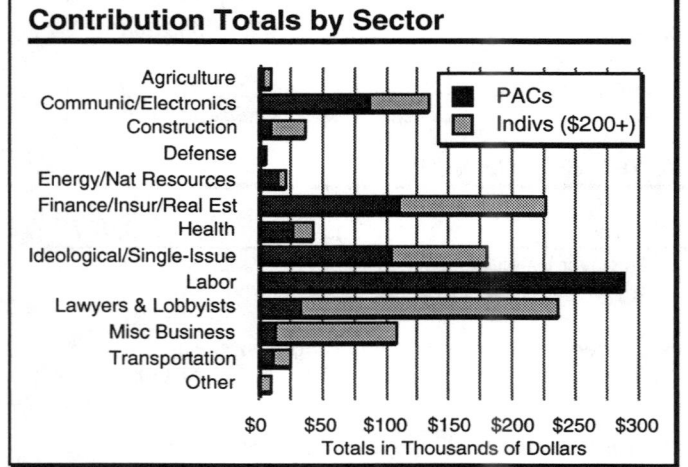

Totals in Thousands of Dollars

(legend: ■ PACs, ▨ Indivs ($200+))

Categories: Agriculture, Communic/Electronics, Construction, Defense, Energy/Nat Resources, Finance/Insur/Real Est, Health, Ideological/Single-Issue, Labor, Lawyers & Lobbyists, Misc Business, Transportation, Other — scale $0 $50 $100 $150 $200 $250 $300

Source of Funds: 1987-1992

Source	Total	Pct
■ PACs	$681,241	31%
▨ Indivs $200+	$784,792	36%
□ Indivs under $200	$438,211	20%
▨ Other	$306,079	14%
Candidate	$0	0%
Party	$50,032	2%

Source of PAC Dollars by Sector

Source	Total	Pct
■ Business	$302,854	44%
▨ Labor	$285,649	41%
□ Ideological/Single-Issue	$102,363	15%

In-State vs. Out-of-State Contributions*

Source	Total	Pct
□ In-State	$96,812	12%
■ Out-of-state	$687,980	88%
No state listed	$0	

* by large individual contributors ($200 & above)

Energy & Natural Resources	$20,600

Oil & Gas $11,350
None over $5,000

Finance, Insurance & Real Estate	$224,125

Commercial Banks $35,100
| American Bankers Assn | $10,000 | PAC |
| JP Morgan & Co | $7,500 | PAC |

Finance/Credit Companies $5,000
None over $5,000

Securities & Investment $35,275
| Chicago Mercantile Exchange | $7,000 | PAC/Ind |

Insurance $34,125
None over $5,000

Real Estate $69,175
National Assn of Realtors	$9,125	PAC
Richard I Rubin & Co	$6,000	Indiv
Century 21 Real Estate	$5,000	PAC
Mack Co	$5,000	Indiv

Accountants $35,700
| American Institute of CPA's | $10,000 | PAC |
| Schooler, Weinstein et al | $9,000 | Indiv |

Misc Finance $8,750
None over $5,000

Health	$41,900

Health Professionals $27,900
| American Academy of Ophthalmology | $5,000 | PAC |
| American Dental Assn | $5,000 | PAC |

Pharmaceuticals/Health Products $10,000
None over $5,000

Lawyers & Lobbyists — $233,650

Lawyers & Lobbyists $233,650
- Milberg, Weiss et al .... $12,250   Indiv
- Assn of Trial Lawyers of America .... $10,000   PAC
- Brobyn & Forceno .... $10,000   Indiv
- Skadden, Arps et al .... $8,250   Indiv
- Shaw, Licitra, Eisenberg et al .... $7,000   Indiv
- Kreindler & Kreindler .... $5,000   Indiv
- Wagner, Cunningham et al .... $5,000   Indiv

Misc Business — $106,550

Beer, Wine & Liquor $6,500
- None over $5,000

Retail Sales $19,000
- None over $5,000

Business Services $18,200
- Guardian Service Industries .... $8,000   Indiv

Chemical & Related Manufacturing $25,000
- EI du Pont de Nemours & Co .... $13,500   Indiv
- Jesup Group .... $8,000   Indiv

Misc Manufacturing & Distributing $19,000
- None over $5,000

Transportation — $24,575

Automotive $10,125
- None over $5,000

Trucking $8,000
- None over $5,000

Labor

Labor — $285,649

Building Trade Unions $49,150
- Laborers' Political League .... $10,500   PAC
- Carpenters & Joiners Union .... $10,000   PAC
- Sheet Metal Workers Union .... $10,000   PAC
- Plumbers/Pipefitters Union* .... $5,500   PAC
- Operating Engineers Union .... $5,000   PAC

Industrial Unions $85,500
- Intl Brotherhood of Electrical Workers* ... $10,500   PAC
- American Federation of Teachers .... $10,000   PAC
- Communications Workers of America ... $10,000   PAC
- Machinists/Aerospace Workers Union ... $10,000   PAC
- United Auto Workers .... $10,000   PAC
- United Steelworkers .... $10,000   PAC
- National Education Assn .... $7,000   PAC
- Boilermakers Union .... $6,000   PAC

Transportation Unions $86,000
- Air Line Pilots Assn .... $10,000   PAC
- Marine Engineers Union* .... $10,000   PAC
- Seafarers International Union .... $10,000   PAC
- Teamsters Union .... $10,000   PAC
- Transport Workers Union .... $8,000   PAC
- United Transportation Union .... $7,000   PAC
- Amalgamated Transit Union .... $5,000   PAC
- Assn of Flight Attendants .... $5,000   PAC
- Maintenance of Way Employees .... $5,000   PAC
- Trans Comm International Union .... $5,000   PAC

Public Sector Unions $41,750
- National Assn of Letter Carriers .... $10,000   PAC
- American Postal Workers Union .... $7,500   PAC
- American Fedn of St/Cnty/Munic Employees ... $6,000   PAC
- Natl Assn of Retired Federal Employees ... $5,000   PAC

Misc Unions $23,249
- Food & Commercial Workers Union ..... $10,000   PAC
- AFL-CIO .... $5,000   PAC

Ideological/Single-Issue

Ideological/Single-Issue — $177,513

Democratic/Liberal $41,750
- Agenda for the 90's .... $10,000   PAC
- Religion and Tolerance PAC .... $10,000   PAC
- National Cmte for an Effective Congress ... $6,000   PAC
- Democrats for the 80's .... $5,000   PAC

Leadership PACs $7,000
- Fund for a Democratic Majority (Ted Kennedy) ... $5,000   PAC

Foreign & Defense Policy $5,563
- Free Cuba PAC .... $5,000   PAC

Pro-Israel $99,900
- Citizens Organized PAC .... $10,000   PAC
- Delaware Valley PAC .... $6,000   PAC
- National PAC .... $5,000   PAC
- San Franciscans for Good Government ... $5,000   PAC
- Washington PAC .... $5,000   PAC

Human Rights $14,500
- Armenian-American PAC .... $5,000   PAC
- KidsPAC .... $5,000   PAC

Misc Issues $8,050
- National Cmte to Preserve Social Security ... $5,000   PAC

Other & Unknown

Other — $8,062
- None over $5,000

Unknown — $179,205
- Homemakers/Non-income earners $40,075
- No Employer Listed or Found $76,200
- Generic Occupation/Category Unknown ... $7,250
- Employer Listed/Category Unknown $55,680
  - None over $5,000

Independent expenditures opposing Biden
- American Citizens for Political Action ... $19,200

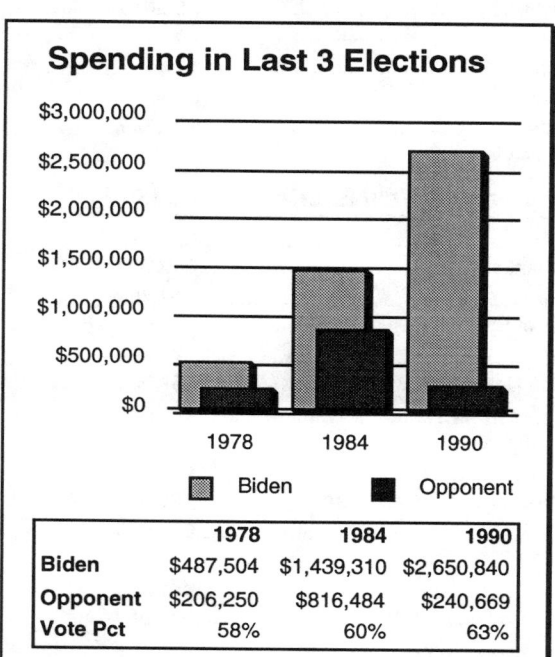

Spending in Last 3 Elections

Legend: ▨ Biden   ■ Opponent

	1978	1984	1990
Biden	$487,504	$1,439,310	$2,650,840
Opponent	$206,250	$816,484	$240,669
Vote Pct	58%	60%	63%

---

* Contributions came from more than one affiliate or subsidiary.

Jeff Bingaman (D-NM)

First elected: 1982

1987-92 Total Rcpts:	$3,697,569
1992 Year-end Cash:	$466,031
Current term expires:	1994

1991-92 Committees & Subcommittees

Armed Services
Defense Industry and Technology (Chairman); Readiness, Sustainability and Support; Strategic Forces and Nuclear Deterrence

Energy and Natural Resources
Energy Research and Development; Mineral Resources Development and Production (Chairman); Public Lands, National Parks and Forests

Labor and Human Resources
Children, Families, Drugs and Alcoholism; Education, Arts and Humanities; Employment and Productivity

Select Committee on Ethics

Joint Economic Committee

Leading Contributors

NOTE: The bulk of Bingaman's large individual contributions do not appear in the listings below. His last election was in 1988, and this book lists individual contributions only from 1989-1992.

Business

Agriculture	$59,653

Crop Production & Basic Processing	$21,745
None over $6,000	
Dairy	$13,633
Associated Milk Producers	$7,000 PAC
Livestock	$7,496
None over $6,000	
Food Processing & Sales	$8,364
None over $6,000	

Communications/Electronics	$23,479

Media/Entertainment	$7,316
None over $6,000	
Computer Equipment & Services	$7,665
None over $6,000	

Construction	$25,087

General Contractors	$10,481
None over $6,000	
Home Builders	$11,416
National Assn of Home Builders	$9,500 PAC

Source of Funds: 1987-1992

Source	Total	Pct
■ PACs	$1,087,814	29%
▦ Indivs $200+	$989,324	26%
□ Indivs under $200	$1,259,155	34%
▨ Other	$408,228	11%
Candidate	$0	0%
Party	$46,952	1%

Source of PAC Dollars by Sector

Source	Total	Pct
■ Business	$572,987	53%
▦ Labor	$273,400	25%
□ Ideological/Single-Issue	$240,444	22%

In-State vs. Out-of-State Contributions*

Source	Total	Pct
□ In-State	$616,804	63%
■ Out-of-state	$369,520	37%
No state listed	$3,000	

*** by large individual contributors ($200 & above)**

Defense	$127,116

Defense Aerospace	$64,415
Textron Inc	$10,000 PAC
McDonnell Douglas*	$6,000 PAC
Defense Electronics	$46,551
AT&T	$6,000 PAC
Misc Defense	$16,150
None over $6,000	

Energy & Natural Resources	$129,590

Oil & Gas	$88,313
Chevron Corp	$7,000 PAC
Atlantic Richfield	$6,319 PAC/Ind
El Paso Co	$6,000 PAC
Mining	$10,697
None over $6,000	
Electric Utilities	$24,382
None over $6,000	

Finance, Insurance & Real Estate	$139,710

Commercial Banks	$27,168
American Bankers Assn	$10,000 PAC
Savings & Loans	$8,498
US League of Savings Assns	$6,000 PAC
Credit Unions	$7,500
Credit Union National Assn	$7,500 PAC
Securities & Investment	$18,663
None over $6,000	
Insurance	$36,245
National Assn of Life Underwriters	$6,000 PAC
Real Estate	$17,645
None over $6,000	
Accountants	$15,830
American Institute of CPA's	$10,000 PAC

Contribution Totals by Sector

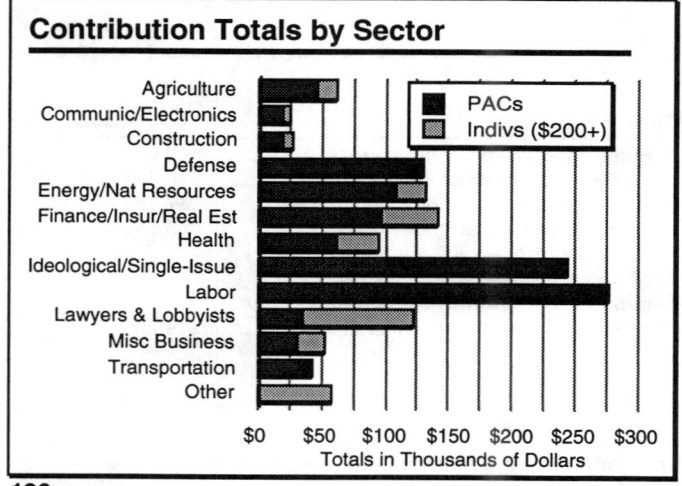

Categories: Agriculture, Communic/Electronics, Construction, Defense, Energy/Nat Resources, Finance/Insur/Real Est, Health, Ideological/Single-Issue, Labor, Lawyers & Lobbyists, Misc Business, Transportation, Other

Legend: ■ PACs ▦ Indivs ($200+)

Totals in Thousands of Dollars ($0, $50, $100, $150, $200, $250, $300)

Misc Finance $8,161
    None over $6,000

Health $93,195

Health Professionals $60,118
    None over $6,000

Hospitals/Nursing Homes $21,666
    American Hospital Assn .... $9,000   PAC

Lawyers & Lobbyists $120,789

Lawyers & Lobbyists $120,789
    Assn of Trial Lawyers of America .... $10,000   PAC
    Sutin, Thayer & Browne .... $6,828   Indiv

Misc Business $51,717

Food & Beverage $7,166
    None over $6,000

Retail Sales $14,578
    None over $6,000

Business Services $11,106
    None over $6,000

Transportation $40,965

Air Transport $11,833
    Federal Express Corp .... $7,000   PAC

Automotive $16,299
    National Auto Dealers Assn .... $10,000   PAC

Railroads $7,000
    None over $6,000

Labor

Labor $273,400

Building Trade Unions $57,000
    Carpenters & Joiners Union .... $10,000   PAC
    Laborers' Political League .... $10,000   PAC
    Operating Engineers Union .... $10,000   PAC
    Sheet Metal Workers Union .... $10,000   PAC
    Plumbers/Pipefitters Union .... $7,000   PAC

Industrial Unions $66,450
    American Federation of Teachers .... $10,000   PAC
    Intl Brotherhood of Electrical Workers .... $10,000   PAC

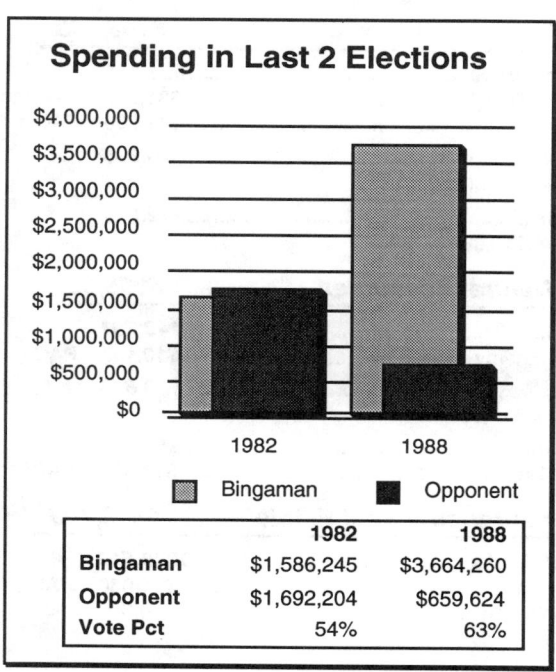

Spending in Last 2 Elections

	1982	1988
Bingaman	$1,586,245	$3,664,260
Opponent	$1,692,204	$659,624
Vote Pct	54%	63%

    Machinists/Aerospace Workers Union .... $10,000   PAC
    National Education Assn .... $10,000   PAC
    United Steelworkers .... $10,000   PAC

Transportation Unions $72,250
    United Auto Workers .... $10,000   PAC
    United Transportation Union .... $10,000   PAC
    Teamsters Union .... $8,750   PAC
    Marine Engineers Union* .... $8,500   PAC
    Air Line Pilots Assn .... $7,500   PAC

Public Sector Unions $56,200
    American Fedn of St/Cnty/Munic Employees .... $10,000   PAC
    National Assn of Letter Carriers .... $10,000   PAC
    Natl Assn of Retired Federal Employees .... $10,000   PAC
    American Postal Workers Union .... $9,000   PAC

Misc Unions $21,500
    AFL-CIO .... $8,500   PAC
    Food & Commercial Workers Union .... $8,000   PAC

Ideological/Single-Issue

Ideological/Single-Issue $241,107

Democratic/Liberal $22,156
    Democrats for the 80's .... $10,000   PAC
    National Cmte for an Effective Congress .... $9,993   PAC

Leadership PACs $33,994
    Cmte for a Demo Consensus (Alan Cranston) .. $10,000   PAC
    Senate Majority Fund (Daniel Inouye) .... $10,000   PAC
    Pelican PAC (Bennett Johnston) .... $9,994   PAC

Pro-Israel $137,100
    Citizens Organized PAC .... $10,000   PAC
    Delaware Valley PAC .... $10,000   PAC
    Desert Caucus .... $10,000   PAC
    Hudson Valley PAC .... $10,000   PAC
    National PAC .... $10,000   PAC
    Pacific PAC .... $10,000   PAC
    Washington PAC .... $9,000   PAC

Pro-Choice $11,000
    National Abortion Rights Action League .... $6,000   PAC

Human Rights $10,000
    KidsPAC .... $10,000   PAC

Misc Issues $15,907
    National Cmte to Preserve Social Security .... $8,000   PAC
    Sierra Club .... $6,907   PAC

Other & Unknown

Other $57,133

Civil Servants/Public Officials $16,902
    None over $6,000

Education $11,160
    None over $6,000

Retired $22,826
    None over $6,000

Other $6,245
    None over $6,000

Unknown $111,864

    Homemakers/Non-income earners $14,237
    No Employer Listed or Found $10,303
    Employer Listed/Category Unknown $83,910
      Sandia National Labs .... $6,829   Indiv

Independent expenditures opposing Bingaman
    National Conservative PAC $79,099
    Council for National Defense $6,044

* Contributions came from more than one affiliate or subsidiary.

Christopher S. Bond (R-Mo)

First elected: 1986

1987-92 Total Rcpts: $5,087,184
1992 Year-end Cash: $106,621
Current term expires: 1998

1991-92 Committees & Subcommittees

Appropriations
Agriculture, Rural Development and Related Agencies; District of Columbia (Ranking Republican); Legislative Branch; VA, HUD and Independent Agencies

Banking, Housing and Urban Affairs
Consumer and Regulatory Affairs (Ranking Republican); Housing and Urban Affairs; Securities

Budget

Small Business
Government Contracting and Paperwork Reduction (Ranking Republican); Rural Economy and Family Farming

Leading Contributors

Business

Agriculture $360,178

Crop Production & Basic Processing $45,150
  None over $10,000
Tobacco $31,000
  US Tobacco Co .... $10,000   PAC
Dairy $27,369
  Mid-America Dairymen .... $13,000   PAC
Livestock $20,125
  None over $10,000
Agricultural Services/Products $78,009
  None over $10,000
Food Processing & Sales $102,125
  ConAgra Inc .... $10,000   PAC
  Food Marketing Institute .... $10,000   PAC
Forestry & Forest Products $46,400
  None over $10,000

Communications/Electronics $159,901

Printing & Publishing $52,288
  Hallmark Cards .... $20,241   PAC/Ind
Media/Entertainment $21,650
  None over $10,000
Telephone Utilities $63,263
  United Telecommunications .... $12,500   PAC/Ind
  Southwestern Bell .... $11,950   PAC/Ind
  AT&T .... $10,000   PAC

Source of Funds: 1987-1992

Source	Total	Pct
PACs	$1,717,017	31%
Indivs $200+	$2,205,472	40%
Indivs under $200	$840,262	15%
Other	$757,947	14%
Candidate	$9,386	0%
Party	$433,514	8%

Source of PAC Dollars by Sector

Source	Total	Pct
Business	$1,659,348	92%
Labor	$30,000	2%
Ideological/Single-Issue	$114,751	6%

In-State vs. Out-of-State Contributions*

Source	Total	Pct
In-State	$1,702,683	77%
Out-of-state	$497,514	23%
No state listed	$825	

* by large individual contributors ($200 & above)

Electronics Mfg & Services $15,000
  None over $10,000

Construction $183,368

General Contractors $66,048
  Associated General Contractors .... $10,000   PAC
  Heavy Constructors Assn .... $10,000   PAC
Home Builders $23,319
  National Assn of Home Builders .... $10,000   PAC
Construction Services $25,550
  Sverdrup Corp .... $15,950   PAC/Ind
Building Materials & Equipment $58,501
  None over $10,000

Defense $106,393

Defense Aerospace $84,155
  McDonnell Douglas .... $31,735   PAC/Ind
  Allied-Signal .... $11,500   PAC/Ind
Defense Electronics $10,238
  None over $10,000
Misc Defense $12,000
  None over $10,000

Energy & Natural Resources $235,039

Oil & Gas $142,701
  Mustang Energy Corp .... $10,167   PAC
Mining $23,619
  None over $10,000
Electric Utilities $50,600
  Utilicorp United Inc .... $13,500   PAC/Ind

Finance, Insurance & Real Estate $848,109

Commercial Banks $226,543
  Bankers Trust .... $11,000   PAC
  Boatman's Bank .... $10,350   Indiv

Contribution Totals by Sector

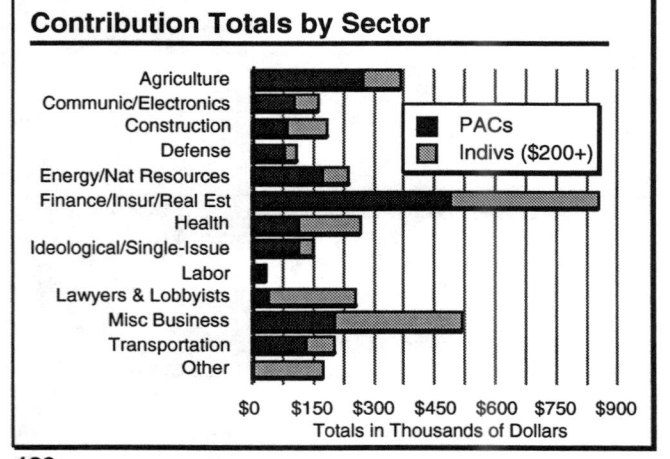

Agriculture
Communic/Electronics
Construction
Defense
Energy/Nat Resources
Finance/Insur/Real Est
Health
Ideological/Single-Issue
Labor
Lawyers & Lobbyists
Misc Business
Transportation
Other

■ PACs
▨ Indivs ($200+)

$0 $150 $300 $450 $600 $750 $900
Totals in Thousands of Dollars

| Mercantile Bancorp | $10,150 | PAC |
| Chase Manhattan | $10,000 | PAC |

Savings & Loans **$13,169**
  None over $10,000

Credit Unions **$14,500**
  Credit Union National Assn ....$12,000 PAC

Finance/Credit Companies **$36,367**
  None over $10,000

Securities & Investment **$142,795**
  Edward D Jones & Co ....$15,200 Indiv

Insurance **$220,336**
  National Assn of Independent Insurers ....$10,500 PAC
  Blue Cross & Blue Shield Assn* ....$10,300 PAC/Ind
  Travelers Corp ....$10,250 PAC/Ind
  National Assn of Life Underwriters..................$10,000 PAC

Real Estate **$95,550**
  None over $10,000

Accountants **$59,875**
  None over $10,000

Misc Finance **$38,974**
  None over $10,000

Health $261,083

Health Professionals **$138,593**
  American Dental Assn.....................................$10,000 PAC
  American Medical Assn* ....$10,000 PAC

Hospitals/Nursing Homes **$34,866**
  None over $10,000

Pharmaceuticals/Health Products **$66,544**
  Eli Lilly & Co ....$10,000 PAC

Misc Health **$17,930**
  None over $10,000

Lawyers & Lobbyists $248,961

Lawyers & Lobbyists.. **$248,961**
  None over $10,000

Misc Business $510,303

Food & Beverage **$56,735**
  Russell Stover Candies Inc ....$10,000 Indiv

Beer, Wine & Liquor **$63,700**
  Anheuser-Busch...$32,000 PAC/Ind

Spending in Last 2 Elections

	1986	**1992**
Bond	$5,396,255	$4,797,665
Opponent	$4,377,661	$1,112,187
Vote Pct	53%	52%

Retail Sales... **$73,792**
  May Department Stores ....$12,500 PAC/Ind
  Bass Pro Shops ....$10,192 Indiv

Misc Services **$17,974**
  None over $10,000

Business Services **$52,219**
  None over $10,000

Lodging/Tourism **$17,737**
  None over $10,000

Chemical & Related Manufacturing **$83,790**
  Monsanto Co ....$24,950 PAC/Ind
  Mallinckrodt Inc ....$10,000 PAC

Misc Manufacturing & Distributing **$114,063**
  Emerson Electric ....$24,300 PAC/Ind
  Hunter Engineering ....$10,000 PAC

Transportation $197,672

Air Transport.. **$62,370**
  Sabreliner Corp ....$16,000 PAC/Ind

Automotive **$61,649**
  None over $10,000

Trucking... **$29,034**
  Yellow Freight System ....$11,309 PAC/Ind

Railroads **$36,250**
  Kansas City Southern ....$15,500 PAC/Ind
  Union Pacific Corp ....$10,000 PAC

Labor

Labor $30,300

Public Sector Unions **$21,250**
  None over $10,000

Ideological/Single-Issue

Ideological/Single-Issue $145,691

Republican/Conservative **$11,955**
  None over $10,000

Leadership PACs.. **$22,386**
  Campaign America (Bob Dole) ....$10,000 PAC

Pro-Israel **$80,450**
  Desert Caucus ....$10,000 PAC
  St Louisians for Better Government..................$10,000 PAC

Gun Rights/Gun Control **$14,850**
  National Rifle Assn...$14,850 PAC

Other & Unknown

Other $171,656

Civil Servants/Public Officials...........................**$27,625**
  State of Missouri ....$10,675 Indiv

Education **$17,063**
  None over $10,000

Retired **$118,918**
  None over $10,000

Unknown $539,217

  Homemakers/Non-income earners $144,600
  No Employer Listed or Found $153,532
  Generic Occupation/Category Unknown $14,475
  Employer Listed/Category Unknown................$226,610
    None over $10,000

---

* Contributions came from more than one affiliate or
subsidiary.

David L. Boren (D-Okla)

First elected: 1978

1987-92 Total Rcpts:	$1,726,669
1992 Year-end Cash:	$7,103
Current term expires:	1996

1991-92 Committees & Subcommittees

Agriculture, Nutrition and Forestry
Agricultural Credit; Agricultural Production and Stabilization of Prices; Domestic and Foreign Marketing and Product Promotion (Chairman)

Finance
Energy and Agricultural Taxation; International Trade; Taxation (Chairman)

Select Committee on Intelligence (Chairman)

Leading Contributors

Business

Agriculture — $67,000

Crop Production & Basic Processing $15,450
  None over $2,500

Poultry & Eggs $6,000
  None over $2,500

Livestock $22,000
  None over $2,500

Agricultural Services/Products $6,600
  Farmland Industries .... $5,150   Indiv

Food Processing & Sales $7,450
  None over $2,500

Forestry & Forest Products $3,000
  None over $2,500

Misc Agriculture $6,500
  None over $2,500

Communications/Electronics — $35,580

Printing & Publishing $9,100
  None over $2,500

Media/Entertainment $16,850
  None over $2,500

Telephone Utilities $5,080
  None over $2,500

Source of Funds: 1987-1992

Source	Total	Pct
PACs	$0	0%
Indivs $200+	$1,406,799	81%
Indivs under $200	$196,265	11%
Other	$134,105	8%
Candidate	$1,500	0%
Party	$17,500	1%

Source of PAC Dollars by Sector

No PAC contributions reported

Source	Total	Pct
Business	$0	0%
Labor	$0	0%
Ideological/Single-Issue	$0	0%

In-State vs. Out-of-State Contributions*

Source	Total	Pct
In-State	$782,711	56%
Out-of-state	$620,588	44%
No state listed	$3,500	

*** by large individual contributors ($200 & above)**

Construction — $24,150

General Contractors $13,450
  None over $2,500

Construction Services $4,400
  None over $2,500

Building Materials & Equipment $5,600
  None over $2,500

Defense — $3,750

Energy & Natural Resources — $201,360

Oil & Gas $186,760
Phillips Petroleum	$6,700	Indiv
Sooner Pipe & Supply	$6,200	Indiv
Arkla Inc	$5,500	Indiv
Bass Brothers Enterprises	$5,000	Indiv
Williams Companies	$5,000	Indiv
Mobil Oil	$3,750	Indiv
Kerr-McGee	$3,700	Indiv
Austin Production Co	$3,500	Indiv
Holden Energy Corp	$3,500	Indiv
Amoco Corp	$3,200	Indiv
Daube Co	$3,000	Indiv
Freeport-McMoRan Inc	$3,000	Indiv
Enron Corp	$2,500	Indiv

Mining $4,600
  None over $2,500

Misc Energy $3,350
  None over $2,500

Environmental Svcs/Equipment $2,500
  None over $2,500

Contribution Totals by Sector

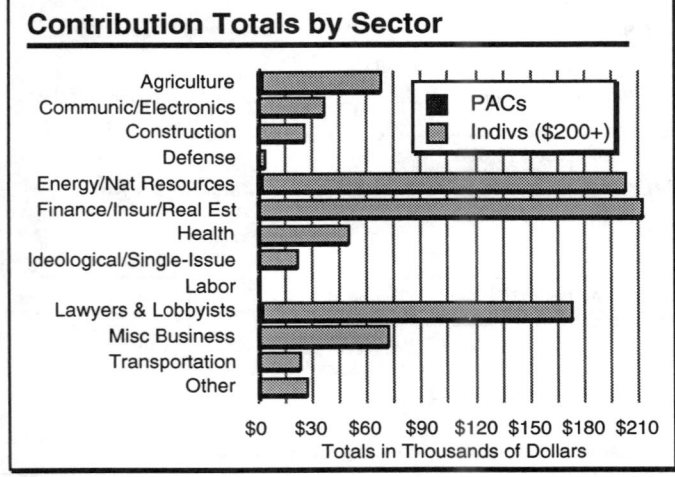

Agriculture
Communic/Electronics
Construction
Defense
Energy/Nat Resources
Finance/Insur/Real Est
Health
Ideological/Single-Issue
Labor
Lawyers & Lobbyists
Misc Business
Transportation
Other

■ PACs
▨ Indivs ($200+)

$0 $30 $60 $90 $120 $150 $180 $210
Totals in Thousands of Dollars

Finance, Insurance & Real Estate — $211,580

Commercial Banks $48,580
    First National Bank/OK .... $4,000   Indiv
    Citizens National Bank .... $2,500   Indiv

Securities & Investment $49,350
    Mayfield Fund .... $3,250   Indiv
    Merrill Lynch .... $3,000   Indiv
    Salomon Brothers .... $3,000   Indiv
    Stifel, Nicolaus & Co .... $2,950   Indiv

Insurance $39,350
    CL Frates & Co .... $3,000   Indiv

Real Estate $45,800
    Trammell Crow Co .... $4,500   Indiv
    Rose Associates .... $2,500   Indiv

Accountants $4,600
    None over $2,500

Misc Finance $21,400
    Related Capital Corp .... $3,000   Indiv

Health — $49,220

Health Professionals $34,020
    None over $2,500

Hospitals/Nursing Homes $8,950
    None over $2,500

Pharmaceuticals/Health Products $5,000
    None over $2,500

Lawyers & Lobbyists — $172,450

Lawyers & Lobbyists $172,450
    McClure, Trotter & Mentz .... $6,000   Indiv
    Akin, Gump et al .... $5,000   Indiv
    Marks, Murase & White .... $5,000   Indiv
    Williams & Jensen .... $4,500   Indiv
    Charls E Walker Associates .... $3,000   Indiv
    Hughes & Luce .... $3,000   Indiv
    Riddle & Brown .... $3,000   Indiv
    Vinson & Elkins .... $3,000   Indiv
    O'Sullivan, Graev & Karabell .... $2,500   Indiv

Misc Business — $70,251

Business Associations $3,000
    None over $2,500

Food & Beverage $5,975
    None over $2,500

Beer, Wine & Liquor $4,250
    None over $2,500

Retail Sales $11,100
    None over $2,500

Misc Services $5,500
    None over $2,500

Business Services $16,550
    None over $2,500

Misc Manufacturing & Distributing $19,576
    Acker Industries .... $3,500   Indiv
    Estee Lauder Inc .... $3,000   Indiv

Transportation — $22,500

Automotive $13,550
    None over $2,500

Trucking $4,700
    None over $2,500

Ideological/Single-Issue

Ideological/Single-Issue — $21,050

Republican/Conservative $2,500
    None over $2,500

Democratic/Liberal $4,450
    None over $2,500

Pro-Israel $13,000
    None over $2,500

Other & Unknown

Other — $26,325

Civil Servants/Public Officials $3,525
    None over $2,500

Education $6,800
    None over $2,500

Retired $13,700
    None over $2,500

Unknown — $169,029

    Homemakers/Non-income earners $45,473
    No Employer Listed or Found $15,325
    Generic Occupation/Category Unknown $5,000
    Employer Listed/Category Unknown $103,231
        Furst, Rudman .... $4,000   Indiv
        M&M Battery Co .... $3,500   Indiv

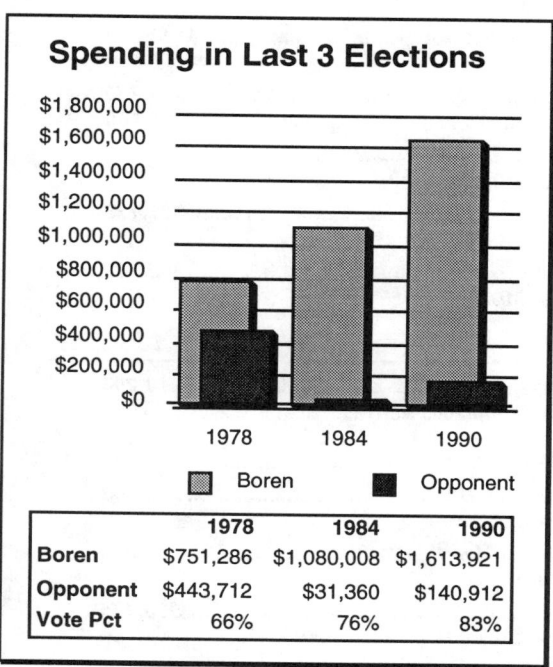

Spending in Last 3 Elections

	1978	1984	1990
Boren	$751,286	$1,080,008	$1,613,921
Opponent	$443,712	$31,360	$140,912
Vote Pct	66%	76%	83%

Legend: ▨ Boren   ■ Opponent

Barbara Boxer (D-Calif)

First elected: 1992
1991-92 Total Rcpts: $10,348,571
1992 Year-end Cash: $18,459
Current term expires: 1998

1991-92 House Committee Assignments

Armed Services
Investigations; Military Personnel and Compensation; Research and Development

Government Operations
Government Activities and Transportation (Chairwoman)

Select Committee on Children, Youth and Families

Leading Contributors

Business

Agriculture	$42,200

Dairy $10,600
None over $10,000

Food Processing & Sales $11,050
None over $10,000

Communications/Electronics	$476,771

Printing & Publishing $58,026
None over $10,000

Media/Entertainment $378,395
Paramount Pictures .... $21,555 Indiv
MCA Inc* .... $16,926 PAC/Ind
Disney Channel* .... $14,726 PAC/Ind
Time Warner* .... $14,425 Indiv
Creative Artists Agency .... $11,902 Indiv

Telephone Utilities $13,275
None over $10,000

Computer Equipment & Services $22,775
None over $10,000

Construction	$62,601

General Contractors $10,000
None over $10,000

Home Builders $12,763
None over $10,000

Construction Services $21,788
None over $10,000

Contribution Totals by Sector

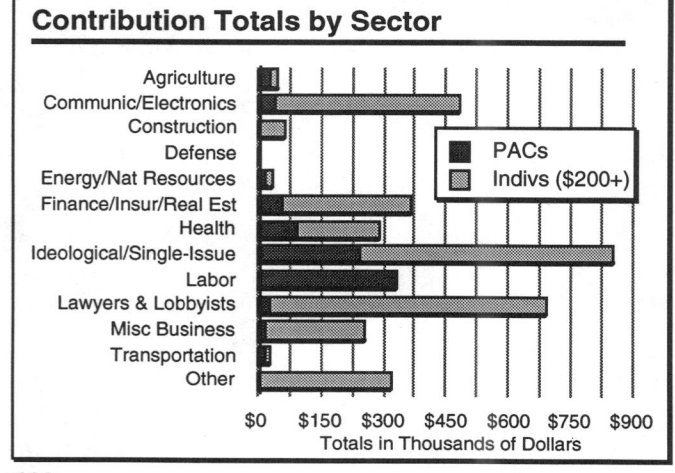

Agriculture
Communic/Electronics
Construction
Defense
Energy/Nat Resources
Finance/Insur/Real Est
Health
Ideological/Single-Issue
Labor
Lawyers & Lobbyists
Misc Business
Transportation
Other

■ PACs
▨ Indivs ($200+)

$0 $150 $300 $450 $600 $750 $900
Totals in Thousands of Dollars

Source of Funds: 1987-1992

Source	Total	Pct
■ PACs	$900,355	7%
▨ Indivs $200+	$3,739,711	31%
☐ Indivs under $200	$5,019,837	41%
☒ Other	$2,449,750	20%
Candidate	$3,000	0%
Party	$1,761,082	15%

Source of PAC Dollars by Sector

Source	Total	Pct
■ Business	$277,633	33%
▨ Labor	$324,205	38%
☐ Ideological/Single-Issue	$241,392	29%

In-State vs. Out-of-State Contributions*

Source	Total	Pct
☐ In-State	$2,953,797	83%
■ Out-of-state	$610,866	17%
No state listed	$0	

* by large individual contributors ($200 & above)

Building Materials & Equipment $10,550
None over $10,000

Energy & Natural Resources	$32,840

Electric Utilities $18,215
Southern California Edison .... $14,965 PAC/Ind

Finance, Insurance & Real Estate	$362,864

Commercial Banks $19,550
None over $10,000

Finance/Credit Companies $11,163
None over $10,000

Securities & Investment $113,528
None over $10,000

Insurance $44,750
Massachusetts Mutual Life Insurance .... $10,000 PAC

Real Estate $96,166
None over $10,000

Accountants $27,175
None over $10,000

Misc Finance $42,682
None over $10,000

Health	$286,897

Health Professionals $214,294
American Chiropractic Assn .... $10,000 PAC
American Nurses Assn .... $10,000 PAC
Cooperative of American Physicians .... $10,000 PAC

Hospitals/Nursing Homes $26,203
None over $10,000

Pharmaceuticals/Health Products $21,050
None over $10,000

Misc Health $16,175
None over $10,000

Lawyers & Lobbyists — $687,082

Lawyers & Lobbyists **$687,082**
Latham & Watkins	$15,270	Indiv
O'Melveny & Myers	$14,250	PAC/Ind
Manatt, Phelps & Phillips	$11,250	Indiv
Heller, Ehrman et al	$10,415	Indiv
Assn of Trial Lawyers of America	$10,000	PAC

Misc Business — $250,348

Beer, Wine & Liquor **$20,857**
None over $10,000

Retail Sales **$39,945**
None over $10,000

Misc Services **$17,580**
None over $10,000

Business Services **$110,200**
None over $10,000

Misc Manufacturing & Distributing **$22,529**
None over $10,000

Transportation — $27,834

Labor

Labor — $327,244

Building Trade Unions **$42,500**
Carpenters & Joiners Union	$10,500	PAC

Industrial Unions **$69,000**
Communications Workers of America	$10,000	PAC
Intl Brotherhood of Electrical Workers	$10,000	PAC
Machinists/Aerospace Workers Union	$10,000	PAC
United Auto Workers	$10,000	PAC

Transportation Unions **$105,250**
Seafarers International Union*	$15,000	PAC
Air Line Pilots Assn	$10,000	PAC
Intl Longshoremen's/Warehousemen's Union	$10,000	PAC
United Transportation Union	$10,000	PAC

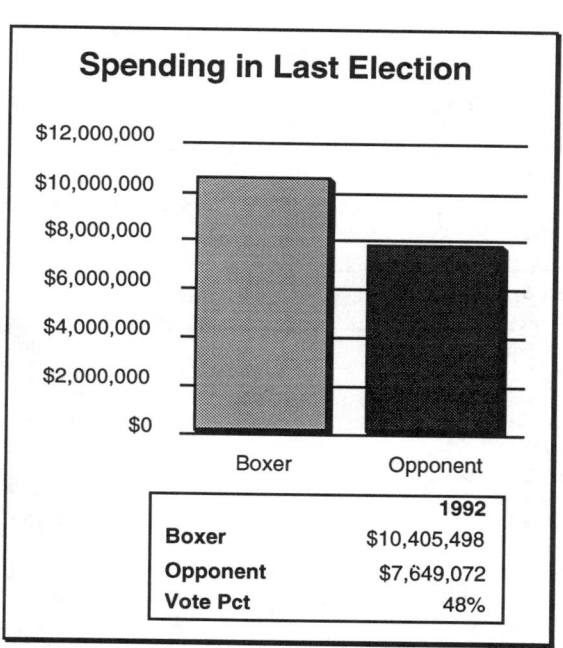

Spending in Last Election

	1992
Boxer	$10,405,498
Opponent	$7,649,072
Vote Pct	48%

Public Sector Unions **$72,405**
American Federation of Teachers*	$10,500	PAC
American Fedn of St/Cnty/Munic Employees	$10,000	PAC
National Assn of Letter Carriers	$10,000	PAC
National Assn Retired Federal Employees	$10,000	PAC
National Education Assn	$10,000	PAC

Misc Unions **$38,089**
AFL-CIO	$10,000	PAC
Food & Commercial Workers Union	$10,000	PAC
Service Employees International Union	$10,000	PAC

Ideological/Single-Issue

Ideological/Single-Issue — **$847,555**

Democratic/Liberal **$111,416**
None over $10,000

Leadership PACs **$28,000**
Fund for a Democratic Majority (Ted Kennedy)	$10,000	PAC

Foreign & Defense Policy **$43,170**
Council for a Livable World	$33,894	PAC/Ind

Pro-Israel **$71,190**
Joint Action Cmte for Political Affairs	$10,000	PAC

Pro-Choice **$50,665**
Voters for Choice	$12,000	PAC/Ind
National Abortion Rights Action League	$10,000	PAC

Womens Issues **$379,286**
Emily's List	$130,405	PAC/Ind
National Organization for Women	$10,711	PAC/Ind
National Womens Political Caucus	$10,400	PAC/Ind
Women's Campaign Fund	$10,000	PAC
Women's Political Committee	$10,000	PAC

Human Rights **$72,329**
Women for:	$10,402	PAC/Ind
Human Rights Campaign Fund	$10,000	PAC

Misc Issues **$83,449**
None over $10,000

Other & Unknown

Other — $312,992

Non-Profit Institutions **$10,025**
None over $10,000

Civil Servants/Public Officials **$43,499**
None over $10,000

Education **$80,202**
University of California System*	$24,445	Indiv

Retired **$147,026**
None over $10,000

Other **$32,240**
None over $10,000

Unknown — $880,013
Homemakers/Non-income earners	$83,695
No Employer Listed or Found	$513,740
Generic Occupation/Category Unknown	$31,153
Employer Listed/Category Unknown	$244,925

None over $10,000

Independent expenditures supporting Boxer
California Democratic Voter Checklist	$10,700

Independent expenditures opposing Boxer
Eagle Forum	$20,391

* Contributions came from more than one affiliate or subsidiary.

Bill Bradley (D-NJ)

First elected: 1978

1987-92 Total Rcpts: $11,674,727
1992 Year-end Cash: $53,941
Current term expires: 1996

1991-92 Committees & Subcommittees

Energy and Natural Resources
Energy Regulation and Conservation; Public Lands, National Parks and Forests; Water and Power (Chairman)

Finance
Health for Families and the Uninsured; Deficits, Debt Management and International Debt (Chairman); International Trade

Select Committee on Intelligence

Special Aging

Leading Contributors

Business

Agriculture	$75,775

Food Processing & Sales $37,825
None over $12,500

Communications/Electronics	$528,477

Printing & Publishing $95,887
None over $12,500

Media/Entertainment $341,142
Time Warner* .... $48,525 PAC/Ind
Walt Disney Co/Disney Channel* .... $41,415 PAC/Ind
Creative Artists Agency .... $16,760 Indiv

Telephone Utilities $43,442
AT&T* .... $14,050 PAC/Ind

Telecom Services & Equipment $15,750
None over $12,500

Computer Equipment & Services $24,000
None over $12,500

Construction	$199,701

General Contractors $99,550
None over $12,500

Home Builders $28,301
None over $12,500

Special Trade Contractors $19,800
None over $12,500

Construction Services $25,300
None over $12,500

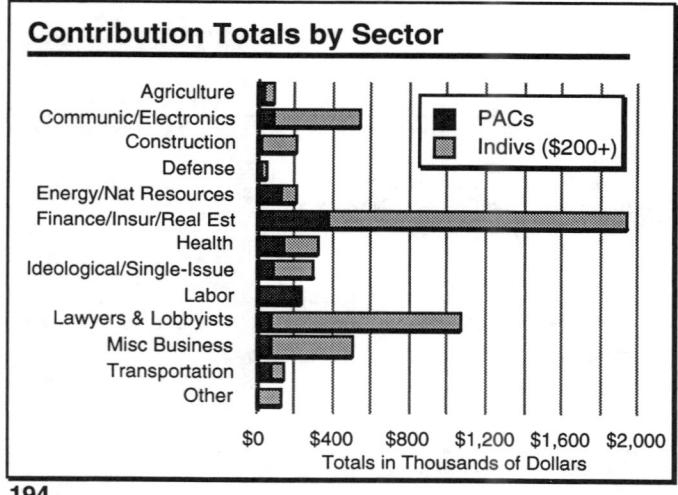

Contribution Totals by Sector

- Agriculture
- Communic/Electronics
- Construction
- Defense
- Energy/Nat Resources
- Finance/Insur/Real Est
- Health
- Ideological/Single-Issue
- Labor
- Lawyers & Lobbyists
- Misc Business
- Transportation
- Other

PACs
Indivs ($200+)

$0 $400 $800 $1,200 $1,600 $2,000
Totals in Thousands of Dollars

194

Source of Funds: 1987-1992

Source	Total	Pct
■ PACs	$1,284,694	11%
▨ Indivs $200+	$7,896,209	66%
☐ Indivs under $200	$1,549,737	13%
⊠ Other	$1,264,639	11%
Candidate	$410	0%
Party	$320,552	3%

Source of PAC Dollars by Sector

Source	Total	Pct
■ Business	$978,023	77%
▨ Labor	$220,600	17%
☐ Ideological/Single-Issue	$77,560	6%

In-State vs. Out-of-State Contributions*

Source	Total	Pct
☐ In-State	$2,353,520	30%
■ Out-of-state	$5,512,524	70%
No state listed	$30,450	

* by large individual contributors ($200 & above)

Building Materials & Equipment $26,750
None over $12,500

Defense	$38,200

Defense Aerospace $25,500
Allied-Signal .... $14,000 PAC/Ind

Energy & Natural Resources	$197,404

Oil & Gas $85,842
Occidental Petroleum* .... $16,350 PAC/Ind

Mining $17,000
None over $12,500

Electric Utilities $50,762
None over $12,500

Waste Management $29,350
None over $12,500

Finance, Insurance & Real Estate	$1,929,799

Commercial Banks $170,690
None over $12,500

Savings & Loans $18,392
None over $12,500

Finance/Credit Companies $16,550
None over $12,500

Securities & Investment $959,048
American Express* .... $82,800 PAC/Ind
Goldman, Sachs & Co .... $50,100 Indiv
Salomon Brothers .... $47,550 Indiv
Bear, Stearns & Co .... $40,225 Indiv
Smith Barney .... $38,350 PAC/Ind
Prudential Securities .... $38,142 PAC/Ind
Morgan Stanley & Co .... $31,425 PAC/Ind
First Boston Corp .... $30,450 PAC/Ind
Merrill Lynch .... $26,550 PAC/Ind
Equitable/Donaldson, Lufkin & Jenrette* .... $21,200 PAC/Ind
Allen & Co .... $15,900 Indiv
Princeton Venture Research .... $13,050 Indiv

Insurance $264,384
    Chubb Corp ....$15,000   PAC/Ind
Real Estate $311,008
    None over $12,500
Accountants $103,635
    Ernst & Young ....$15,400   PAC/Ind
    Price Waterhouse ....$14,125   PAC/Ind
Misc Finance $83,092
    None over $12,500

Health $312,586

Health Professionals $126,584
    None over $12,500
Hospitals/Nursing Homes $39,542
    None over $12,500
Health Services $15,750
    None over $12,500
Pharmaceuticals/Health Products $118,260
    Warner-Lambert ....$25,500   PAC/Ind
    Merck & Co ....$13,650   PAC/Ind

Lawyers & Lobbyists $1,059,963

Lawyers & Lobbyists $1,059,963
    Skadden, Arps et al ....$35,200   PAC/Ind
    Willkie, Farr & Gallagher ....$34,250   Indiv
    Bryan, Cave et al ....$26,753   Indiv
    Sills, Cummis et al ....$22,460   Indiv
    Spear, Leeds & Kellogg ....$22,400   PAC/Ind
    Dewey, Ballantine et al ....$17,060   Indiv
    Wilson, Sonsini et al ....$15,200   Indiv
    Webster & Sheffield ....$15,000   Indiv
    Cleary, Gottlieb et al ....$14,500   Indiv
    Weil, Gotshal & Manges ....$13,100   Indiv
    Milberg, Weiss et al ....$13,000   Indiv
    Wachtell, Lipton et al ....$12,500   Indiv
    Waters, McPherson et al ....$12,500   Indiv

Misc Business $495,808

Food & Beverage $28,900
    None over $12,500
Beer, Wine & Liquor $24,787
    None over $12,500
Retail Sales $76,006
    None over $12,500

Spending in Last 3 Elections

	1978	1984	1990
Bradley	$1,688,499	$4,566,758	$12,475,527
Opponent	$1,418,931	$956,398	$801,660
Vote Pct	55%	64%	50%

Business Services $117,584
    None over $12,500
Recreation/Live Entertainment $16,400
    None over $12,500
Misc Business $16,875
    None over $12,500
Chemical & Related Manufacturing $19,100
    None over $12,500
Misc Manufacturing & Distributing $140,164
    None over $12,500

Transportation $133,085

Air Transport $30,442
    None over $12,500
Automotive $52,950
    None over $12,500
Trucking $16,200
    None over $12,500
Sea Transport $13,701
    None over $12,500

Labor

Labor $227,500

Building Trade Unions $67,400
    Operating Engineers Union* ....$13,100   PAC/Ind
Industrial Unions $41,750
    None over $12,500
Transportation Unions $48,750
    None over $12,500
Public Sector Unions $43,800
    None over $12,500
Misc Unions $25,800
    None over $12,500

Ideological/Single-Issue

Ideological/Single-Issue $281,524

Democratic/Liberal $76,330
    None over $12,500
Pro-Israel $143,234
    None over $12,500
Womens Issues $21,400
    None over $12,500

Other & Unknown

Other $122,890

Civil Servants/Public Officials $27,364
    None over $12,500
Education $39,226
    None over $12,500
Retired $41,400
    None over $12,500

Unknown $1,311,316

    Homemakers/Non-income earners $481,526
    No Employer Listed or Found $41,118
    Generic Occupation/Category Unknown $16,884
    Employer Listed/Category Unknown $771,788
        None over $12,500

---

* Contributions came from more than one affiliate or
subsidiary.

John B. Breaux (D-La)

First elected: 1986

1987-92 Total Rcpts:	$3,481,494
1992 Year-end Cash:	$1,522,344
Current term expires:	1998

1991-92 Committees & Subcommittees

Commerce, Science and Transportation
Communications; Merchant Marine (Chairman); National Ocean Policy Study; Surface Transportation

Finance
Energy and Agricultural Taxation; International Trade; Social Security and Family Policy

Special Aging

Leading Contributors

Business

Agriculture	$205,838

Crop Production & Basic Processing $69,080
American Sugar Cane League .... $8,500 PAC

Tobacco $21,800
None over $7,500

Poultry & Eggs $12,000
Tyson Foods .... $9,000 Indiv

Livestock $8,500
None over $7,500

Agricultural Services/Products $32,350
CF Industries .... $8,500 PAC

Food Processing & Sales $32,150
Malone & Hyde Inc .... $10,000 PAC

Forestry & Forest Products $24,058
None over $7,500

Communications/Electronics	$186,650

Media/Entertainment $97,200
National Cable Television Assn .... $12,000 PAC
Sony Corp/Columbia Pictures* .... $7,500 Indiv

Telephone Utilities $57,550
None over $7,500

Telecom Services & Equipment $17,500
ITEL Corp .... $7,500 PAC

Contribution Totals by Sector

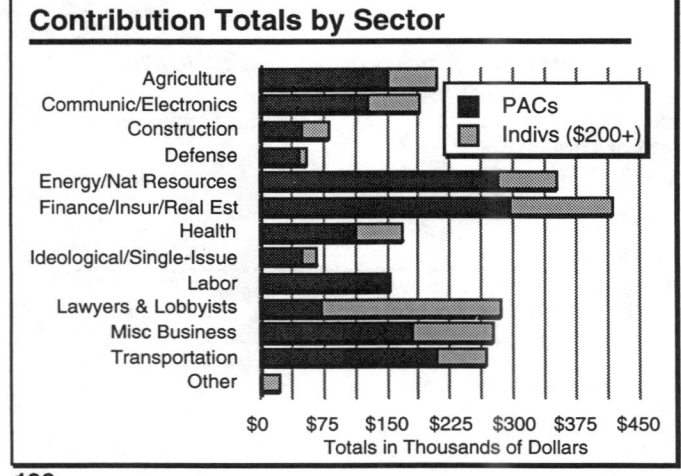

Totals in Thousands of Dollars

Source of Funds: 1987-1992

Source	Total	Pct
PACs	$1,678,505	48%
Indivs $200+	$1,144,883	33%
Indivs under $200	$413,468	12%
Other	$275,168	8%
Candidate	$0	0%
Party	$30,530	1%

Source of PAC Dollars by Sector

Source	Total	Pct
Business	$1,503,943	88%
Labor	$150,973	9%
Ideological/Single-Issue	$48,350	3%

In-State vs. Out-of-State Contributions*

Source	Total	Pct
In-State	$480,603	42%
Out-of-state	$656,830	58%
No state listed	$0	

by large individual contributors ($200 & above)

Construction	$80,058

General Contractors $30,600
Fluor Corp .... $11,000 PAC

Construction Services $27,908
None over $7,500

Building Materials & Equipment $12,650
None over $7,500

Defense	$54,452

Defense Aerospace $34,820
Textron Inc .... $9,370 PAC/Ind

Defense Electronics $11,632
None over $7,500

Misc Defense $8,000
None over $7,500

Energy & Natural Resources	$348,349

Oil & Gas $211,675
Arkla Inc .... $16,070 PAC/Ind
Chevron Corp .... $11,000 PAC
Amoco Corp .... $10,000 PAC
Occidental Petroleum* .... $9,000 PAC
Exxon Corp .... $8,700 PAC/Ind

Mining $19,250
None over $7,500

Nuclear Energy $9,400
None over $7,500

Misc Energy $13,300
Babcock & Wilcox* .... $7,500 PAC

Electric Utilities $55,900
None over $7,500

Waste Management $15,724
None over $7,500

Commercial Fishing $21,700
National Fisheries Institute .... $13,250 PAC

Finance, Insurance & Real Estate — $413,611

Commercial Banks $81,081
    American Bankers Assn .... $10,400   PAC/Ind

Securities & Investment $112,899
    National Venture Capital Assn .... $9,999   PAC
    Bear, Stearns & Co .... $9,500   PAC/Ind
    Chicago Board of Trade .... $9,000   PAC
    PaineWebber .... $8,000   PAC/Ind
    Princeton Venture Research .... $8,000   Indiv
    American Express* .... $7,500   PAC/Ind

Insurance $132,312
    American Family Corp .... $11,000   PAC
    National Assn of Life Underwriters .... $10,000   PAC

Real Estate $49,350
    National Assn of Realtors .... $8,000   PAC

Accountants $16,199
    None over $7,500

Misc Finance $13,370
    None over $7,500

Health — $167,042

Health Professionals $94,242
    Assn for the Advancement of Psychology .... $10,387   PAC/Ind

Hospitals/Nursing Homes $27,150
    None over $7,500

Pharmaceuticals/Health Products $39,700
    None over $7,500

Lawyers & Lobbyists — $282,631

Lawyers & Lobbyists $282,631
    Assn of Trial Lawyers of America .... $10,000   PAC
    Milberg, Weiss et al .... $9,250   Indiv
    Bergreen & Bergreen .... $8,000   Indiv

Misc Business — $272,546

Food & Beverage $37,450
    ARA Services Inc .... $10,000   PAC
    National Restaurant Assn .... $10,000   PAC

Beer, Wine & Liquor $40,036
    National Beer Wholesalers Assn .... $10,000   PAC

Retail Sales $30,257
    International Council of Shopping Centers .... $10,000   PAC

Business Services $58,050
    Outdoor Advertising Assn of America .... $12,000   PAC/Ind

Casinos/Gambling $21,753
    Circus Circus Enterprises .... $10,753   PAC/Ind

Lodging/Tourism $8,000
    None over $7,500

Chemical & Related Manufacturing $39,100
    None over $7,500

Misc Manufacturing & Distributing $23,650
    None over $7,500

Transportation — $263,778

Air Transport $61,650
    Textron Inc .... $10,000   PAC

Automotive $40,400
    Americans for Free International Trade .... $10,000   PAC
    Auto Dealers & Drivers for Free Trade .... $10,000   PAC

Trucking $22,330
    None over $7,500

Railroads $16,500
    None over $7,500

Sea Transport $116,098
    American President Lines .... $12,298   PAC/Ind
    CSX Corp* .... $11,000   PAC/Ind
    Lykes Brothers Steamship Co .... $10,100   PAC/Ind
    Crescent River Port Pilots .... $8,500   PAC

Labor

Labor — $150,973

Building Trade Unions $38,000
    Laborers' Political League .... $11,000   PAC

Industrial Unions $17,000
    None over $7,500

Transportation Unions $58,750
    Seafarers International Union* .... $15,500   PAC
    Air Line Pilots Assn .... $10,000   PAC
    United Transportation Union .... $10,000   PAC

Public Sector Unions $30,723
    None over $7,500

Ideological/Single-Issue

Ideological/Single-Issue — $64,050

Democratic/Liberal $8,850
    None over $7,500

Pro-Israel $26,350
    None over $7,500

Gun Rights/Gun Control $10,900
    National Rifle Assn .... $9,900   PAC

Other & Unknown

Other — $20,100
    None over $7,500

Unknown — $179,774
    Homemakers/Non-income earners $27,100
    No Employer Listed or Found $29,325
    Generic Occupation/Category Unknown $17,900
    Employer Listed/Category Unknown $105,349
      None over $7,500

---

* Contributions came from more than one affiliate or subsidiary.

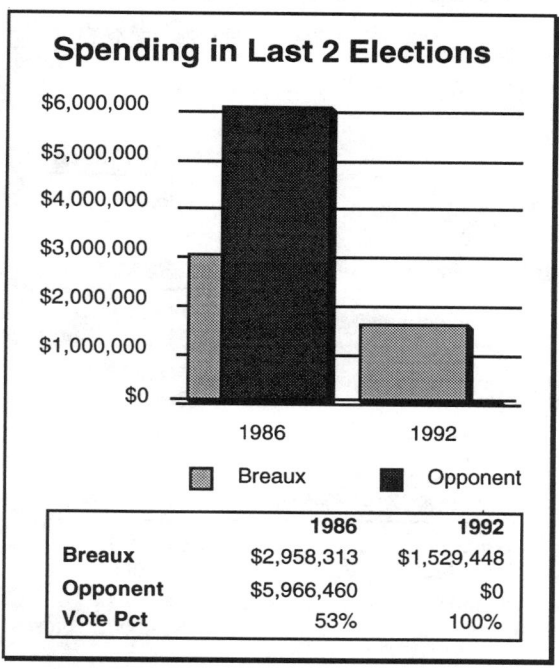

Spending in Last 2 Elections

	1986	1992
Breaux	$2,958,313	$1,529,448
Opponent	$5,966,460	$0
Vote Pct	53%	100%

Legend: Breaux, Opponent

Hank Brown (R-Colo)

First elected: 1990

1989-92 Total Rcpts:	$4,288,022
1992 Year-end Cash:	$426,326
Current term expires:	1996

1991-92 Committees & Subcommittees

Budget

Foreign Relations
East Asian and Pacific Affairs; European Affairs; Terrorism, Narcotics and International Operations (Ranking Republican)

Judiciary
Juvenile Justice (Ranking Republican); Technology and the Law (Ranking Republican)

Select Committee on POW/MIA Affairs

Leading Contributors

Business

Agriculture	$205,268

Crop Production & Basic Processing $26,050
  None over $10,000

Tobacco $27,000
  US Tobacco Co .... $10,000 PAC

Livestock $20,300
  None over $10,000

Agricultural Services/Products $20,376
  None over $10,000

Food Processing & Sales $49,942
  None over $10,000

Forestry & Forest Products $45,500
  Westvaco Corp .... $13,000 PAC
  Union Camp Corp .... $10,000 PAC

Communications/Electronics	$173,275

Printing & Publishing $12,000
  None over $10,000

Media/Entertainment $54,670
  Tele-Communications Inc .... $10,000 PAC

Telephone Utilities $54,505
  US West Inc .... $20,255 PAC/Ind
  AT&T .... $10,000 PAC

Source of Funds: 1987-1992

Source	Total	Pct
■ PACs	$1,386,475	30%
▨ Indivs $200+	$1,398,852	31%
□ Indivs under $200	$605,088	13%
▨ Other	$1,165,399	26%
Candidate	$0	0%
Party	$267,792	6%

Source of PAC Dollars by Sector

Source	Total	Pct
■ Business	$1,242,103	90%
▨ Labor.........................	$22,000	2%
□ Ideological/Single-Issue ..	$109,450	8%

In-State vs. Out-of-State Contributions*

Source	Total	Pct
□ In-State	$957,887	70%
■ Out-of-state.....................	$407,483	30%
No state listed	$33,482	

* by large individual contributors ($200 & above)

Electronics Mfg & Services $23,750
  Storagetek Corp .... $10,750 Indiv
  Harris Corp .... $10,000 PAC

Computer Equipment & Services $18,850
  None over $10,000

Construction	$140,150

General Contractors $54,150
  None over $10,000

Home Builders $16,250
  None over $10,000

Special Trade Contractors $33,000
  Sheet Metal/Air Conditioning Contractors .... $10,000 PAC

Construction Services $15,500
  None over $10,000

Building Materials & Equipment $21,250
  None over $10,000

Defense	$52,275

Defense Aerospace $36,025
  None over $10,000

Energy & Natural Resources	$245,018

Oil & Gas $153,991
  Amoco Corp .... $10,000 PAC

Mining $48,377
  Cyprus Minerals Co .... $25,177 PAC/Ind

Electric Utilities $23,350
  None over $10,000

Finance, Insurance & Real Estate	$566,581

Commercial Banks $43,245
  American Bankers Assn .... $10,000 PAC

Securities & Investment $117,101
  Salomon Brothers .... $19,000 PAC/Ind

Contribution Totals by Sector

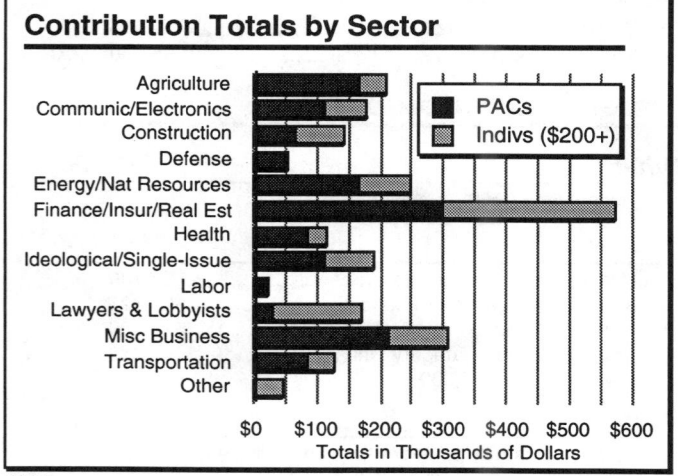

Agriculture
Communic/Electronics
Construction
Defense
Energy/Nat Resources
Finance/Insur/Real Est
Health
Ideological/Single-Issue
Labor
Lawyers & Lobbyists
Misc Business
Transportation
Other

■ PACs
▨ Indivs ($200+)

$0 $100 $200 $300 $400 $500 $600
Totals in Thousands of Dollars

Insurance	$182,889	
National Assn of Independent Insurers	$10,000	PAC
National Assn of Life Underwriters	$10,000	PAC
Real Estate	**$102,625**	
National Assn of Realtors	$10,500	PAC
American Resort & Residential Devel Assn	$10,000	PAC
Accountants	**$66,817**	
American Institute of CPA's	$10,000	PAC
Misc Finance	**$40,404**	
None over $10,000		

Health $115,004

Health Professionals	$70,204	
American Academy of Ophthalmology	$10,000	PAC
American Dental Assn	$10,000	PAC
Hospitals/Nursing Homes	**$18,650**	
None over $10,000		
Pharmaceuticals/Health Products	**$24,900**	
None over $10,000		

Lawyers & Lobbyists $167,010

Lawyers & Lobbyists	$167,010	
Kirkland & Ellis	$14,000	PAC/Ind
Brownstein, Hyatt et al	$13,050	Indiv

Misc Business $300,566

Business Associations	$18,607	
National Fedn of Independent Business	$13,000	PAC
Food & Beverage	**$40,250**	
National Restaurant Assn	$10,000	PAC
S&A Restaurant Corp	$10,000	PAC
Beer, Wine & Liquor	**$39,508**	
Coors Industries	$10,000	PAC
Retail Sales	**$35,427**	
International Council of Shopping Centers	$10,000	PAC
Business Services	**$27,116**	
None over $10,000		

Spending in Last Election

	1990
Brown	$3,723,911
Opponent	$1,943,422
Vote Pct	56%

Lodging/Tourism	$15,620	
None over $10,000		
Chemical & Related Manufacturing	**$56,999**	
None over $10,000		
Misc Manufacturing & Distributing	**$45,500**	
None over $10,000		

Transportation $126,240

Air Transport	$31,390	
Texas Air	$10,000	PAC
Automotive	**$32,250**	
National Auto Dealers Assn	$10,000	PAC
Trucking	**$31,300**	
None over $10,000		
Railroads	**$28,000**	
Union Pacific Corp	$10,000	PAC

Labor

Labor $22,000

Public Sector Unions	$13,500	
None over $10,000		

Ideological/Single-Issue

Ideological/Single-Issue $185,984

Republican/Conservative	$42,184	
National Republican Senatorial Cmte	$12,250	Indiv
Leadership PACs	**$19,000**	
None over $10,000		
Pro-Israel	**$100,800**	
Desert Caucus	$10,000	PAC
Human Rights	**$10,000**	
National Albanian American PAC	$10,000	PAC
Misc Issues	**$11,500**	
None over $10,000		

Other & Unknown

Other $44,049

Civil Servants/Public Officials	$14,400	
None over $10,000		
Retired	**$21,980**	
None over $10,000		

Unknown $451,735

Homemakers/Non-income earners	$39,193
No Employer Listed or Found	$278,997
Employer Listed/Category Unknown	$123,795
None over $10,000	

Independent expenditures supporting Brown
National Assn of Realtors $186,589

Richard H. Bryan (D-Nev)

First elected: 1988

1987-92 Total Rcpts:	$3,482,447
1992 Year-end Cash:	$201,859
Current term expires:	1994

1991-92 Committees & Subcommittees

Banking, Housing and Urban Affairs
Consumer and Regulatory Affairs; Housing and Urban Affairs

Commerce, Science and Transportation
Consumer (Chairman); Foreign Commerce and Tourism; Science, Technology and Space

Select Committee on Ethics

Joint Economic Committee

Leading Contributors

NOTE: The bulk of Bryan's large individual contributions do not appear in the listings below. His last election was in 1988, and this book lists individual contributions only from 1989-1992.

Business

Agriculture — $25,050

Dairy $6,000
    None over $5,000

Agricultural Services/Products $11,000
    American Veterinary Medical Assn ..... $5,000   PAC

Communications/Electronics — $33,025

Media/Entertainment $8,250
    None over $5,000

Telephone Utilities $19,275
    None over $5,000

Construction — $46,015

General Contractors $15,250
    None over $5,000

Home Builders $18,965
    National Assn of Home Builders ..... $10,000   PAC

Energy & Natural Resources — $31,100

Oil & Gas $15,000
    None over $5,000

Mining $11,400
    None over $5,000

Source of Funds: 1987-1992

Source	Total	Pct
■ PACs	$944,977	26%
▨ Indivs $200+	$1,958,225	55%
☐ Indivs under $200	$377,672	11%
☒ Other	$309,322	9%
Candidate	$100,135	3%
Party	$107,749	3%

Source of PAC Dollars by Sector

Source	Total	Pct
■ Business	$438,882	48%
▨ Labor	$311,800	34%
☐ Ideological/Single-Issue	$172,761	19%

In-State vs. Out-of-State Contributions*

Source	Total	Pct
☐ In-State	$1,406,008	72%
■ Out-of-state	$538,967	28%
No state listed	$13,250	

*** by large individual contributors ($200 & above)**

Finance, Insurance & Real Estate — $169,851

Commercial Banks $18,150
    American Bankers Assn ..... $5,000   PAC

Savings & Loans $7,752
    None over $5,000

Credit Unions $12,000
    Credit Union National Assn ..... $12,000   PAC

Securities & Investment $20,250
    Chicago Mercantile Exchange ..... $5,000   PAC
    Salomon Brothers ..... $5,000   PAC

Insurance $61,699
    Independent Insurance Agents of America ..... $14,999   PAC
    National Assn of Life Underwriters ..... $10,000   PAC
    National Assn of Prof Insurance Agents ..... $7,000   PAC

Real Estate $37,700
    Del Webb Corp ..... $8,250   PAC
    National Assn of Realtors ..... $6,000   PAC

Misc Finance $6,550
    None over $5,000

Health — $80,767

Health Professionals $74,667
    American Academy of Ophthalmology ..... $10,000   PAC
    American Nurses Assn ..... $7,000   PAC
    American Dental Assn ..... $5,000   PAC
    American Optometric Assn ..... $5,000   PAC

Lawyers & Lobbyists — $65,890

Lawyers & Lobbyists $65,890
    Assn of Trial Lawyers of America ..... $10,000   PAC

Misc Business — $161,766

Beer, Wine & Liquor $43,500
    Deluca Liquor & Wine Ltd ..... $14,000   Indiv
    Southern Wine & Spirits ..... $14,000   PAC/Ind
    Joseph E Seagram & Sons ..... $6,000   PAC

Contribution Totals by Sector

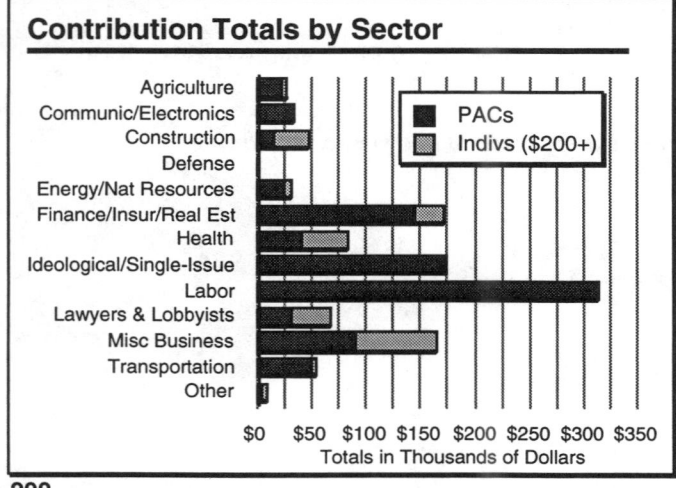

Legend: PACs (black), Indivs ($200+) (gray)

Categories: Agriculture, Communic/Electronics, Construction, Defense, Energy/Nat Resources, Finance/Insur/Real Est, Health, Ideological/Single-Issue, Labor, Lawyers & Lobbyists, Misc Business, Transportation, Other

Scale: $0 $50 $100 $150 $200 $250 $300 $350
Totals in Thousands of Dollars

Retail Sales **$6,750**
    None over $5,000

Casinos/Gambling **$84,016**
California Hotel & Casino PAC	$10,000	PAC
Bally Manufacturing Corp	$9,500	PAC
Gold Strike Inn & Casino	$8,000	Indiv
Harrah's	$8,000	PAC/Ind
Nevada Landing Hotel & Casino	$8,000	Indiv
Circus Circus Enterprises	$5,766	PAC
Showboat Inc	$5,000	PAC
Summa Corp	$5,000	PAC
Union Plaza	$5,000	PAC

Transportation $52,250

Air Transport **$16,500**
Federal Express Corp	$7,000	PAC

Automotive **$9,250**
National Auto Dealers Assn	$5,000	PAC

Trucking **$10,500**
Yellow Freight System	$7,500	PAC

Railroads **$13,000**
    None over $5,000

Labor

Labor $311,800

Building Trade Unions **$61,000**
Carpenters & Joiners Union	$10,000	PAC
Ironworkers Union	$10,000	PAC
Laborers' Western Political League	$10,000	PAC
Operating Engineers Union	$10,000	PAC
Plumbers/Pipefitters Union	$10,000	PAC
Bricklayers Union	$5,000	PAC
Sheet Metal Workers Union	$5,000	PAC

Industrial Unions **$77,300**
American Federation of Teachers	$10,000	PAC
Communications Workers of America	$10,000	PAC
Intl Brotherhood of Electrical Workers	$10,000	PAC
Machinists/Aerospace Workers Union	$10,000	PAC
National Education Assn	$10,000	PAC
United Steelworkers	$7,500	PAC
Amalgamated Clothing & Textile Workers	$5,000	PAC
Ladies Garment Workers Union	$5,000	PAC

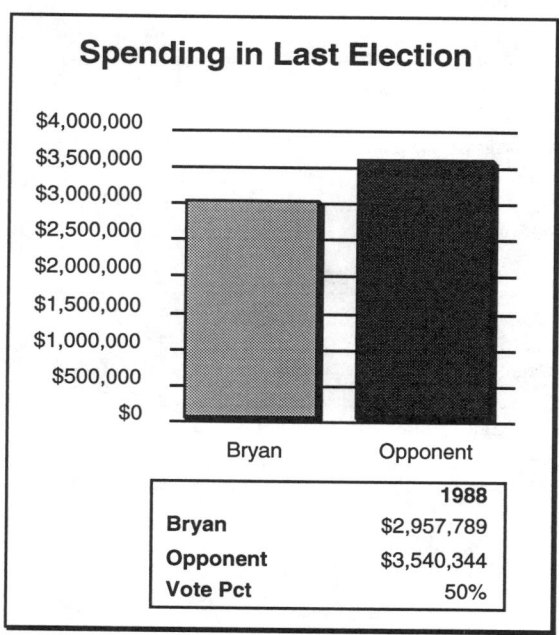

Spending in Last Election

	1988
Bryan	$2,957,789
Opponent	$3,540,344
Vote Pct	50%

Transportation Unions **$88,250**
Marine Engineers Union	$15,000	PAC
Air Line Pilots Assn	$10,000	PAC
Seafarers International Union	$10,000	PAC
Teamsters Union	$10,000	PAC
United Auto Workers	$10,000	PAC
United Transportation Union	$10,000	PAC
Amalgamated Transit Union	$7,500	PAC
Trans Comm International Union	$6,500	PAC

Public Sector Unions **$50,750**
National Assn of Letter Carriers	$11,000	PAC
American Fedn of St/Cnty/Munic Employees	$10,000	PAC
Natl Assn of Retired Federal Employees	$10,000	PAC
National Treasury Employees Union	$8,000	PAC
American Postal Workers Union	$5,000	PAC

Misc Unions **$34,500**
AFL-CIO	$10,000	PAC
Food & Commercial Workers Union	$10,000	PAC
Hotel/Restaurant Employees Union	$6,500	PAC
Service Employees International Union	$5,500	PAC

Ideological/Single-Issue

Ideological/Single-Issue $172,761

Democratic/Liberal **$21,306**
Democrats for the 80's	$10,000	PAC
Religion and Tolerance PAC	$5,000	PAC

Leadership PACs **$24,000**
Cmte for a Demo Consensus (Alan Cranston)	$10,000	PAC
Senate Majority Fund (Daniel Inouye)	$10,000	PAC

Pro-Israel **$85,660**
Hudson Valley PAC	$15,410	PAC
Joint Action Cmte for Political Affairs	$10,000	PAC
Washington PAC	$10,000	PAC
Citizens Organized PAC	$5,000	PAC
Desert Caucus	$5,000	PAC
MOPAC	$5,000	PAC
National PAC	$5,000	PAC
Pacific PAC	$5,000	PAC
San Franciscans for Good Government	$5,000	PAC

Human Rights **$18,000**
KidsPAC	$10,000	PAC
Pakistani Physicians PAC	$5,500	PAC

Misc Issues **$18,095**
National Cmte to Preserve Social Security	$10,000	PAC
National Council of Senior Citizens	$5,000	PAC

Other & Unknown

Other $8,500

Retired **$6,000**
    None over $5,000

Unknown $74,900

Homemakers/Non-income earners	$31,950
Generic Occupation/Category Unknown	$8,200
Employer Listed/Category Unknown	$33,250

    None over $5,000

Independent expenditures supporting Bryan
    National Cmte to Preserve Social Security $28,410

Independent expenditures opposing Bryan
    Auto Dealers & Drivers for Free Trade $23,450

Dale Bumpers (D-Ark)

First elected: 1974

1987-92 Total Rcpts:	$2,063,717
1992 Year-end Cash:	$172,582
Current term expires:	1998

1991-92 Committees & Subcommittees

Appropriations
Agriculture, Rural Development and Related Agencies (Chairman); Commerce, Justice, State, the Judiciary and Related Agencies; Defense; Interior and Related Agencies; Labor, Health and Human Services, Education and Related Agencies

Energy and Natural Resources
Energy Research and Development; Mineral Resources Development and Production; Public Lands, National Parks and Forests (Chairman)

Small Business (Chairman)

Leading Contributors

Business

Agriculture	$270,870

Crop Production & Basic Processing	$79,970	
Riceland Foods	$7,500	PAC/Ind

Tobacco	$6,500
None over $6,000	

Dairy	$21,500	
Associated Milk Producers	$10,000	PAC
Mid-America Dairymen	$10,000	PAC

Poultry & Eggs	$69,750	
Tyson Foods	$22,500	PAC/Ind
Hudson Foods Inc	$9,000	Indiv
National Broiler Council	$6,000	PAC

Livestock	$8,200
None over $6,000	

Agricultural Services/Products	$29,550	
Farm Credit Council	$8,000	PAC

Food Processing & Sales	$23,650	
ConAgra Inc	$10,000	PAC/Ind

Forestry & Forest Products	$31,750	
Georgia-Pacific Corp	$10,000	PAC
International Paper Co	$8,000	PAC

Communications/Electronics	$65,900

Printing & Publishing	$9,900
None over $6,000	

Contribution Totals by Sector

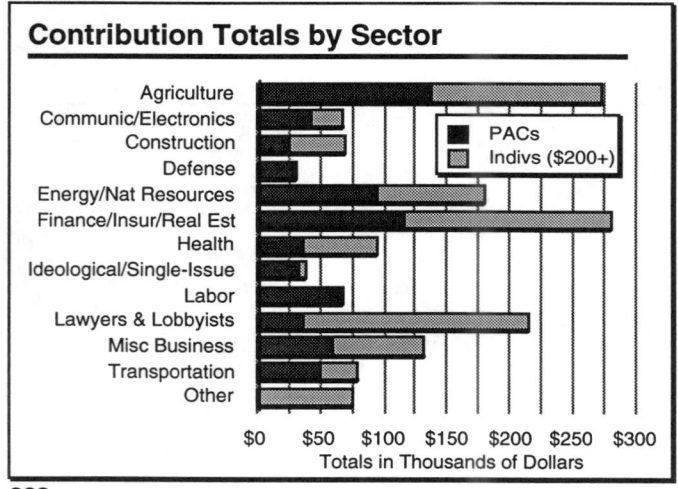

Agriculture
Communic/Electronics
Construction
Defense
Energy/Nat Resources
Finance/Insur/Real Est
Health
Ideological/Single-Issue
Labor
Lawyers & Lobbyists
Misc Business
Transportation
Other

■ PACs
▨ Indivs ($200+)

$0 $50 $100 $150 $200 $250 $300
Totals in Thousands of Dollars

Source of Funds: 1987-1992

Source	Total	Pct
■ PACs	$723,585	34%
▨ Indivs $200+	$1,022,142	48%
□ Indivs under $200	$198,241	9%
▧ Other	$165,023	8%
Candidate	$0	0%
Party	$45,274	2%

Source of PAC Dollars by Sector

Source	Total	Pct
■ Business	$613,423	86%
▨ Labor	$65,600	9%
□ Ideological/Single-Issue	$31,091	4%

In-State vs. Out-of-State Contributions*

Source	Total	Pct
□ In-State	$800,344	78%
■ Out-of-state	$221,798	22%
No state listed	$0	

* by large individual contributors ($200 & above)

Media/Entertainment	$27,000	
MCA Inc	$14,000	PAC/Ind

Telephone Utilities	$26,500	
AT&T	$6,000	PAC

Construction	$67,350

General Contractors	$28,900
None over $6,000	

Home Builders	$6,500
None over $6,000	

Construction Services	$10,150
None over $6,000	

Building Materials & Equipment	$18,800
None over $6,000	

Defense	$29,100

Defense Aerospace	$13,600
None over $6,000	

Defense Electronics	$9,500
None over $6,000	

Misc Defense	$6,000
None over $6,000	

Energy & Natural Resources	$178,366

Oil & Gas	$101,300	
Arkla Inc	$24,300	PAC/Ind
Murphy Oil	$9,500	PAC/Ind

Mining	$7,250
None over $6,000	

Nuclear Energy	$7,500	
General Atomics	$6,000	PAC

Electric Utilities	$52,016	
Entergy Corp*	$12,250	PAC/Ind
ACRE (Action Cmte for Rural Electrification)	$10,000	PAC

Waste Management $6,500
None over $6,000

Finance, Insurance & Real Estate $277,950

Commercial Banks $76,050
American Bankers Assn .... $10,000   PAC
Worthen Banking Corp .... $8,500   PAC/Ind
Independent Bankers Assn .... $7,000   PAC

Credit Unions $7,300
Credit Union National Assn .... $7,000   PAC

Securities & Investment $39,800
Chicago Mercantile Exchange .... $10,000   PAC
Stephens Inc .... $7,500   Indiv

Insurance $55,550
National Assn of Life Underwriters .... $10,000   PAC

Real Estate $57,400
National Assn of Realtors .... $10,000   PAC
Cooper Communities Inc .... $7,000   Indiv

Accountants $13,150
None over $6,000

Misc Finance $24,450
None over $6,000

Health $93,525

Health Professionals $66,775
St Michael Hospital .... $6,000   Indiv

Hospitals/Nursing Homes $8,500
None over $6,000

Pharmaceuticals/Health Products $13,500
None over $6,000

Lawyers & Lobbyists $213,550

Lawyers & Lobbyists $213,550
Mitchell, Williams et al .... $25,250   Indiv
Assn of Trial Lawyers of America .... $10,000   PAC
Friday, Eldredge & Clark .... $9,000   Indiv
Mayer, Brown & Platt .... $6,350   Indiv

Misc Business $129,775

Business Associations $11,500
None over $6,000

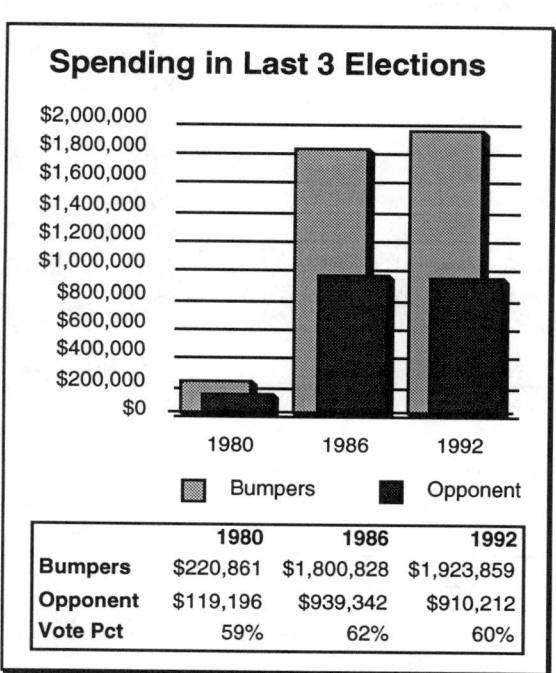

Spending in Last 3 Elections

	1980	1986	1992
Bumpers	$220,861	$1,800,828	$1,923,859
Opponent	$119,196	$939,342	$910,212
Vote Pct	59%	62%	60%

Bumpers   Opponent

Food & Beverage $19,325
None over $6,000

Beer, Wine & Liquor $20,250
National Beer Wholesalers Assn .... $6,000   PAC

Retail Sales $14,550
None over $6,000

Misc Services $6,000
None over $6,000

Business Services $17,300
None over $6,000

Lodging/Tourism $10,000
Gaston's Resort .... $6,000   Indiv

Chemical & Related Manufacturing $7,800
None over $6,000

Misc Manufacturing & Distributing $15,450
None over $6,000

Transportation $77,000

Air Transport $23,050
United Parcel Service .... $7,500   PAC
General Electric .... $6,000   PAC

Automotive $26,700
National Auto Dealers Assn .... $10,000   PAC

Trucking $7,250
None over $6,000

Railroads $13,500
None over $6,000

Labor

Labor $66,350

Transportation Unions $18,550
United Transportation Union .... $7,000   PAC
Marine Engineers Union .... $6,000   PAC

Public Sector Unions $38,300
National Assn of Letter Carriers .... $10,000   PAC
National Education Assn .... $7,500   PAC
National Rural Letter Carriers Assn .... $6,000   PAC

Ideological/Single-Issue

Ideological/Single-Issue $37,591

Leadership PACs $10,000
None over $6,000

Pro-Israel $13,000
None over $6,000

Other & Unknown

Other $73,355

Civil Servants/Public Officials $13,500
None over $6,000

Education $20,255
University of Arkansas .... $10,080   Indiv

Retired $37,100
None over $6,000

Unknown $147,799

Homemakers/Non-income earners $45,300
Employer Listed/Category Unknown $100,200
None over $6,000

---

* Contributions came from more than one affiliate or
subsidiary.

Conrad Burns (R-Mont)

First elected: 1988

1987-92 Total Rcpts:	$1,641,252
1992 Year-end Cash:	$205,240
Current term expires:	1994

1991-92 Committees & Subcommittees

Commerce, Science and Transportation
Communications; Foreign Commerce and Tourism (Ranking Republican); Surface Transportation

Energy and Natural Resources
Energy Research and Development; Public Lands, National Parks and Forests; Water and Power (Ranking Republican)

Small Business
Rural Economy and Family Farming; Urban and Minority-Owned Business Development (Ranking Republican)

Special Aging

Leading Contributors

NOTE: The bulk of Burns' large individual contributions do not appear in the listings below. His last election was in 1988, and this book lists individual contributions only from 1989-1992.

Business

Agriculture	$94,800

Crop Production & Basic Processing $31,350
American Crystal Sugar Corp $4,000	PAC
JG Boswell Co $2,500	PAC
Minn-Dak Farmers Co-op $2,500	PAC

Tobacco $14,000
RJR Nabisco $5,000	PAC
US Tobacco Co $5,000	PAC
Philip Morris $2,500	PAC

Livestock $11,900
None over $2,500

Agricultural Services/Products $7,400
None over $2,500

Food Processing & Sales $16,150
| Flowers Industries .... $5,000 | PAC |
| ConAgra Inc .... $3,000 | PAC |

Forestry & Forest Products $10,000
| International Paper Co .... $5,000 | PAC |

Communications/Electronics	$89,500

Printing & Publishing $5,996
| Printing Industries of America .... $4,996 | PAC |

Source of Funds: 1987-1992

Source	Total	Pct
PACs	$663,143	38%
Indivs $200+	$433,581	25%
Indivs under $200	$291,624	17%
Other	$371,716	21%
Candidate	$0	0%
Party	$118,812	7%

Source of PAC Dollars by Sector

Source	Total	Pct
Business	$456,848	79%
Labor.............................	$0	0%
Ideological/Single-Issue ..	$118,455	21%

In-State vs. Out-of-State Contributions*

Source	Total	Pct
In-State	$126,954	30%
Out-of-state	$296,127	70%
No state listed	$10,500	

*** by large individual contributors ($200 & above)**

Media/Entertainment $14,500
| Tele-Communications Inc .... $5,000 | PAC |

Telephone Utilities $41,500
AT&T $8,500	PAC
United Telecommunications $5,000	PAC
GTE Corp $4,000	PAC
BellSouth Services $3,500	PAC
Contel $3,000	PAC
Mountain Bell $3,000	PAC
US West Inc $2,500	PAC

Telecom Services & Equipment $8,304
None over $2,500

Electronics Mfg & Services $13,000
| Cooper Industries .... $10,000 | PAC |

Computer Equipment & Services $6,200
| Tamsco .... $4,000 | Indiv |

Construction	$28,950

General Contractors $13,050
| Associated General Contractors .... $10,000 | PAC |

Special Trade Contractors $7,250
| Sheet Metal/Air Conditioning Contractors .... $5,000 | PAC |

Building Materials & Equipment $8,150
| Manville Corp .... $3,000 | PAC |

Defense	$11,500

Defense Aerospace $6,500
None over $2,500

Defense Electronics $3,000
| Harris Corp .... $3,000 | PAC |

Energy & Natural Resources	$71,050

Oil & Gas $39,850
| Dallas Energy PAC .... $5,000 | PAC |
| Petroleum Marketers Assn .... $5,000 | PAC |

Contribution Totals by Sector

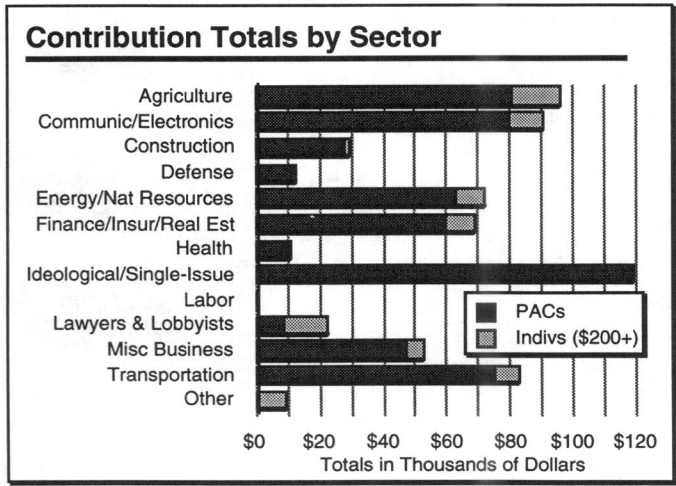

Agriculture
Communic/Electronics
Construction
Defense
Energy/Nat Resources
Finance/Insur/Real Est
Health
Ideological/Single-Issue
Labor
Lawyers & Lobbyists
Misc Business
Transportation
Other

PACs
Indivs ($200+)

$0 $20 $40 $60 $80 $100 $120
Totals in Thousands of Dollars

| Mining | $15,100 |
| Cyprus Minerals Co | $3,000 | PAC |

| Electric Utilities | $11,700 |
| None over $2,500 | | |

| Waste Management | $3,000 |
| Waste Management Inc | $3,000 | PAC |

Finance, Insurance & Real Estate $68,410

Commercial Banks	$18,449
American Bankers Assn	$10,000	PAC
Independent Bankers Assn	$3,000	PAC

| Securities & Investment | $7,700 |
| None over $2,500 | | |

Insurance	$35,661
National Assn of Independent Insurers	$5,000	PAC
Torchmark Corp	$5,000	PAC
Independent Insurance Agents of America	$4,061	PAC
National Assn of Life Underwriters	$3,000	PAC
Aetna Life & Casualty	$2,500	PAC

| Real Estate | $4,600 |
| None over $2,500 | | |

Health $10,250

| Pharmaceuticals/Health Products | $8,750 |
| None over $2,500 | | |

Lawyers & Lobbyists $22,011

| Lawyers & Lobbyists | $22,011 |
| Preston, Gates et al | $3,000 | PAC/Ind |

Misc Business $52,137

| Business Associations | $4,436 |
| National Fedn of Independent Business | $4,436 | PAC |

| Food & Beverage | $5,000 |
| National Restaurant Assn | $3,000 | PAC |

| Beer, Wine & Liquor | $3,000 |
| None over $2,500 | | |

| Retail Sales | $3,000 |
| None over $2,500 | | |

| Business Services | $7,300 |
| Dun & Bradstreet | $2,500 | PAC |

| Lodging/Tourism | $6,550 |
| None over $2,500 | | |

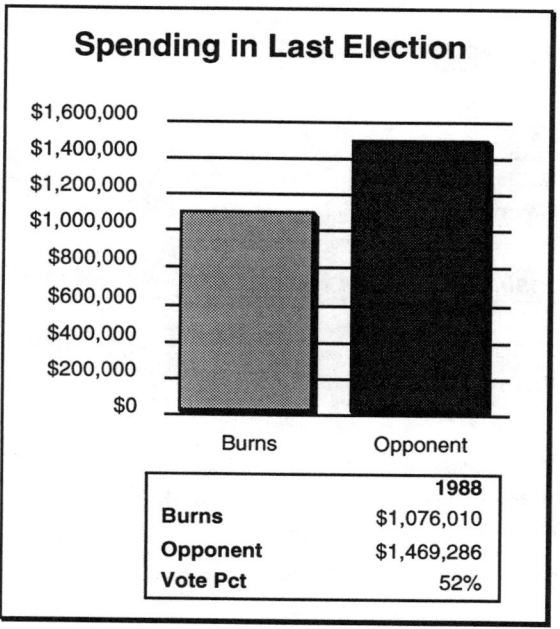

Spending in Last Election

	1988
Burns	$1,076,010
Opponent	$1,469,286
Vote Pct	52%

| Misc Business | $2,500 |
| None over $2,500 | | |

| Chemical & Related Manufacturing | $5,600 |
| NL Industries | $3,500 | PAC |

Misc Manufacturing & Distributing	$13,250
Corning Glass Works	$3,000	PAC
Borg-Warner	$2,500	PAC
General Electric	$2,500	PAC

Transportation $82,314

Air Transport	$21,000
Federal Express Corp	10,000	PAC
Texas Air	$5,000	PAC

Automotive	$28,900
Auto Dealers & Drivers for Free Trade	$12,000	PAC
National Auto Dealers Assn	$6,000	PAC
Eaton Corp	$4,000	PAC
General Motors	$4,000	PAC

| Trucking | $12,964 |
| American Trucking Assns | $5,214 | PAC |

Railroads	$18,050
Burlington Northern	$10,550	PAC/Ind
Union Pacific Corp	$3,500	PAC

Ideological/Single-Issue

Ideological/Single-Issue $118,455

| Republican/Conservative | $3,950 |
| Conservatives Acting Together | $2,500 | PAC |

Leadership PACs	$56,000
Campaign America (Bob Dole)	$10,000	PAC
Catch the Spirit PAC (Bob Kasten)	$10,000	PAC
Citizens for the Republic (Ronald Reagan)	$5,000	PAC
Fund for America's Future (George Bush)	$5,000	PAC
Leadership - USA (James McClure)	$5,000	PAC
Republican Majority Fund (Richard Lugar)	$5,000	PAC
Heartland PAC of Missouri (Kit Bond)	$4,500	PAC
Plaid PAC (Rudy Boschwitz)	$4,000	PAC
Fund for a Republican Majority (Ted Stevens)	$3,000	PAC

Foreign & Defense Policy	$9,000
Council for National Defense	$5,000	PAC
National Security PAC	$4,000	PAC

Pro-Israel	$36,005
Hudson Valley PAC	$9,205	PAC
National PAC	$5,000	PAC
Women's Pro-Israel National PAC	$5,000	PAC

Misc Issues	$12,500
Public Service Research Council	$5,000	PAC
Ruff PAC	$3,500	PAC
Right to Work PAC	$3,000	PAC

Other & Unknown

Other $8,500

| Retired | $7,200 |
| None over $2,500 | | |

Unknown $51,104

Homemakers/Non-income earners	$4,200
No Employer Listed or Found	$19,755
Employer Listed/Category Unknown	$25,549
None over $2,500		

Independent expenditures supporting Burns
Associated Builders & Contractors $5,000

Robert C. Byrd (D-WVa)

First elected: 1958

1987-92 Total Rcpts:	$1,721,118
1992 Year-end Cash:	$703,378
Current term expires:	1994

1991-92 Committees & Subcommittees

Appropriations (Chairman)
Defense; Energy and Water Development; Interior and Related Agencies (Chairman); Labor, Health and Human Services, Education and Related Agencies; Transportation and Related Agencies

Armed Services
Conventional Forces and Alliance Defense; Defense Industry and Technology; Manpower and Personnel

Rules and Administration

Leading Contributors

NOTE: The bulk of Byrd's large individual contributions do not appear in the listings below. His last election was in 1988, and this book lists individual contributions only from 1989-1992.

Business

Agriculture — $78,800

Crop Production & Basic Processing $12,000
    None over $6,000
Tobacco $13,000
    Philip Morris .... $8,000 PAC
Dairy $9,500
    None over $6,000
Agricultural Services/Products $12,000
    None over $6,000
Food Processing & Sales $11,500
    None over $6,000
Forestry & Forest Products $18,300
    Westvaco Corp .... $6,000 PAC

Communications/Electronics — $41,928

Media/Entertainment $9,000
    None over $6,000
Telephone Utilities $26,928
    None over $6,000

Source of Funds: 1987-1992

Source	Total	Pct
PACs	$1,040,264	60%
Indivs $200+	$305,522	18%
Indivs under $200	$65,260	4%
Other	$310,172	18%
Candidate	$0	0%
Party	$100	0%

Source of PAC Dollars by Sector

Source	Total	Pct
Business	$744,964	72%
Labor	$234,050	23%
Ideological/Single-Issue	$59,250	6%

In-State vs. Out-of-State Contributions*

Source	Total	Pct
In-State	$70,622	23%
Out-of-state	$233,650	77%
No state listed	$1,250	

*** by large individual contributors ($200 & above)**

Construction — $41,000

General Contractors $29,000
    Associated General Contractors .... $20,000 PAC
Home Builders $12,000
    National Assn of Home Builders .... $10,000 PAC

Defense — $105,666

Defense Aerospace $70,500
    Lockheed Corp .... $10,000 PAC
    Northrop Corp .... $10,000 PAC
Defense Electronics $26,166
    AT&T .... $7,666 PAC
Misc Defense $9,000
    None over $6,000

Energy & Natural Resources — $127,150

Oil & Gas $55,350
    Occidental Petroleum .... $8,000 PAC
Mining $22,500
    Peabody Coal .... $7,000 PAC
Electric Utilities $38,300
    American Electric Power .... $13,000 PAC

Finance, Insurance & Real Estate — $156,971

Commercial Banks $25,000
    American Bankers Assn .... $11,000 PAC
Savings & Loans $11,000
    US League of Savings Assns .... $10,000 PAC
Credit Unions $10,000
    Credit Union National Assn .... $10,000 PAC
Securities & Investment $43,600
    Chicago Board of Trade .... $12,000 PAC
    Chicago Mercantile Exchange .... $12,000 PAC
    Morgan Stanley & Co .... $8,000 PAC

Contribution Totals by Sector

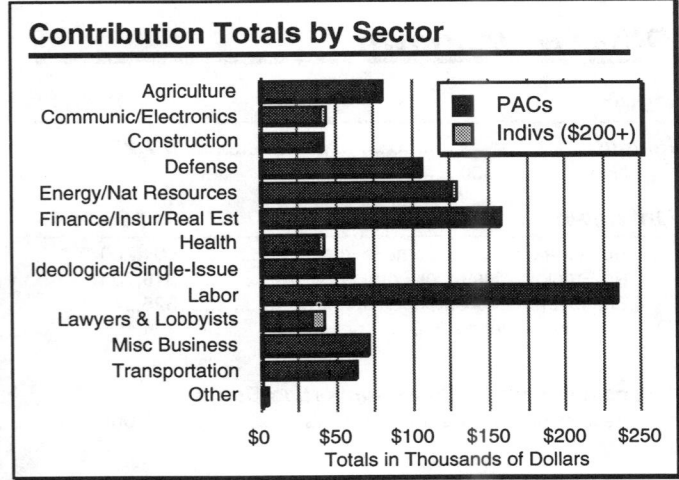

Agriculture, Communic/Electronics, Construction, Defense, Energy/Nat Resources, Finance/Insur/Real Est, Health, Ideological/Single-Issue, Labor, Lawyers & Lobbyists, Misc Business, Transportation, Other

Legend: PACs, Indivs ($200+)

$0 $50 $100 $150 $200 $250
Totals in Thousands of Dollars

| Insurance | $39,021 | |
| None over $6,000 | | |

Real Estate **$15,350**
    National Assn of Realtors .... $11,000   PAC

Accountants **$8,000**
    American Institute of CPA's .... $7,000   PAC

Health $40,750

Health Professionals **$31,750**
    None over $6,000

Lawyers & Lobbyists $40,000

Lawyers & Lobbyists **$40,000**
    Assn of Trial Lawyers of America .... $10,000   PAC
    Camp, Barsh & Tate .... $7,000   PAC/Ind

Misc Business $69,850

Beer, Wine & Liquor **$17,000**
    National Beer Wholesalers Assn .... $11,000   PAC

Retail Sales **$8,100**
    None over $6,000

Business Services **$9,000**
    Outdoor Advertising Assn of America .... $6,000   PAC

Chemical & Related Manufacturing **$8,000**
    None over $6,000

Misc Manufacturing & Distributing **$8,000**
    None over $6,000

Textiles **$12,250**
    None over $6,000

Transportation $61,349

Air Transport **$17,000**
    Federal Express Corp .... $10,000   PAC

Automotive **$6,500**
    None over $6,000

Trucking **$12,499**
    American Trucking Assns .... $6,999   PAC

Railroads **$20,100**
    CSX Corp* .... $7,000   PAC

Labor

Labor $234,050

Building Trade Unions **$50,000**
    Laborers' Political League .... $12,000   PAC
    Carpenters & Joiners Union .... $10,000   PAC
    Operating Engineers Union .... $10,000   PAC
    Sheet Metal Workers Union .... $10,000   PAC

Industrial Unions **$48,700**
    National Education Assn .... $9,000   PAC
    Ladies Garment Workers Union .... $8,000   PAC
    United Mine Workers .... $7,500   PAC
    Amalgamated Clothing & Textile Workers .... $7,000   PAC
    Intl Brotherhood of Electrical Workers .... $7,000   PAC
    Machinists/Aerospace Workers Union .... $6,000   PAC

Transportation Unions **$68,700**
    Teamsters Union .... $12,500   PAC
    Seafarers International Union .... $12,000   PAC
    Marine Engineers Union* .... $11,000   PAC
    United Transportation Union .... $10,000   PAC
    Amalgamated Transit Union .... $8,500   PAC
    United Auto Workers .... $6,000   PAC

Public Sector Unions **$47,050**
    National Assn of Letter Carriers .... $10,000   PAC
    American Postal Workers Union .... $7,000   PAC
    American Fedn of St/Cnty/Munic Employees ...... $6,000   PAC
    National Rural Letter Carriers Assn .... $6,000   PAC
    Natl Assn of Retired Federal Employees .... $6,000   PAC

Misc Unions **$19,600**
    AFL-CIO .... $9,000   PAC
    Food & Commercial Workers Union .... $6,000   PAC

Ideological/Single-Issue

Ideological/Single-Issue $59,250

Democratic/Liberal **$6,000**
    Democrats for the 80's .... $6,000   PAC

Leadership PACs **$12,500**
    Senate Majority Fund (Daniel Inouye) ...... $10,000   PAC

Foreign & Defense Policy **$7,000**
    None over $6,000

Pro-Israel **$10,000**
    None over $6,000

Human Rights **$7,000**
    None over $6,000

Misc Issues **$10,800**
    National Cmte to Preserve Social Security .... $9,000   PAC

Independent expenditures supporting Byrd
    National Cmte to Preserve Social Security $8,146

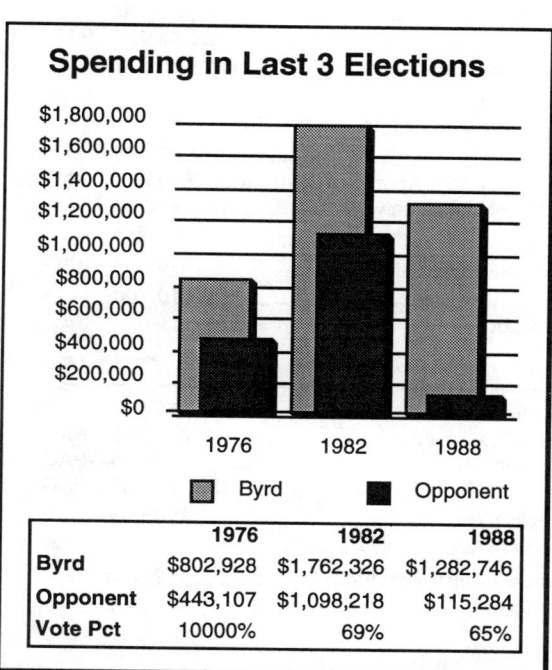

Spending in Last 3 Elections

	1976	1982	1988
Byrd	$802,928	$1,762,326	$1,282,746
Opponent	$443,107	$1,098,218	$115,284
Vote Pct	10000%	69%	65%

Byrd   Opponent

---

* Contributions came from more than one affiliate or subsidiary.

Ben Nighthorse Campbell (D-Colo)

First elected: 1992

1991-92 Total Rcpts:	$1,594,544
1992 Year-end Cash:	$46,741
Current term expires:	1998

1991-92 House Committee Assignments

Agriculture
Department Operations, Research and Foreign Agriculture; Livestock, Dairy and Poultry

Interior and Insular Affairs
Mining and Natural Resources; National Parks and Public Lands; Water, Power and Offshore Energy Resources

Leading Contributors

Business

Agriculture	$100,974

Crop Production & Basic Processing	$29,025	
Sun World International	$5,750	Indiv
Tobacco	**$9,499**	
None over $5,000		
Dairy	**$26,600**	
Dairymens Mountain Assn	$10,000	PAC
Associated Milk Producers	$5,000	PAC
Livestock	**$7,950**	
None over $5,000		
Agricultural Services/Products	**$19,400**	
ConAgra Inc	$5,000	PAC

Communications/Electronics	$52,555

Printing & Publishing	$6,450	
None over $5,000		
Media/Entertainment	**$29,000**	
Walt Disney Co	$6,500	Indiv
Jones International	$5,000	PAC
Telephone Utilities	**$12,950**	
US West Inc	$5,550	PAC/Ind
AT&T	$5,300	PAC

Construction	$8,300
None over $5,000	

Contribution Totals by Sector

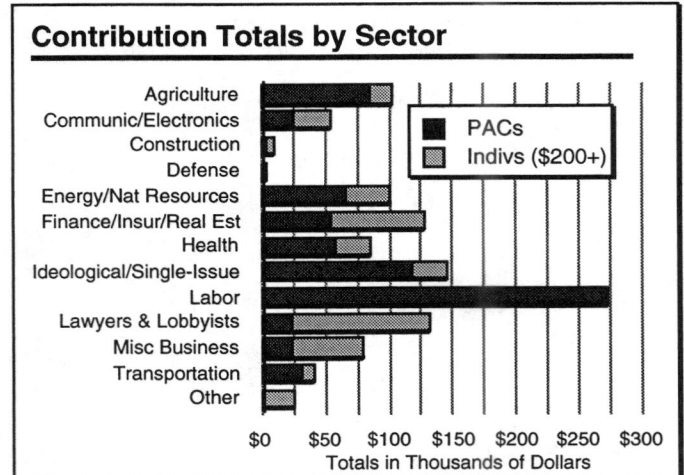

Agriculture
Communic/Electronics
Construction
Defense
Energy/Nat Resources
Finance/Insur/Real Est
Health
Ideological/Single-Issue
Labor
Lawyers & Lobbyists
Misc Business
Transportation
Other

■ PACs
▨ Indivs ($200+)

$0 $50 $100 $150 $200 $250 $300
Totals in Thousands of Dollars

Source of Funds: 1987-1992

Source	Total	Pct
■ PACs	$739,286	40%
▨ Indivs $200+	$563,849	30%
☐ Indivs under $200	$266,793	14%
▨ Other..............................	$286,915	15%
Candidate	$539	0%
Party	$262,299	14%

Source of PAC Dollars by Sector

Source	Total	Pct
■ Business	$361,366	48%
▨ Labor	$270,150	36%
☐ Ideological/Single-Issue ..	$116,038	16%

In-State vs. Out-of-State Contributions*

Source	Total	Pct
☐ In-State	$275,786	49%
■ Out-of-state	$288,063	51%
No state listed	$0	

*** by large individual contributors ($200 & above)**

Energy & Natural Resources	$98,718

Oil & Gas	$58,918	
Amoco Corp	$9,000	PAC
Chevron Corp	$7,800	PAC
Mining	**$15,300**	
None over $5,000		
Electric Utilities	**$15,200**	
ACRE (Action Cmte for Rural Electrification)	$10,000	PAC

Finance, Insurance & Real Estate	$126,170

Commercial Banks	$10,900	
American Bankers Assn	$5,000	PAC
Securities & Investment	**$47,700**	
Apollo Advisors...	$7,000	Indiv
Chicago Mercantile Exchange	$5,000	PAC
Insurance	**$22,070**	
Independent Insurance Agents of America	$10,000	PAC
National Assn of Life Underwriters	$5,000	PAC
Real Estate	**$31,650**	
National Assn of Realtors	$10,000	PAC
Misc Finance	**$10,300**	
None over $5,000		

Health	$83,115

Health Professionals	$56,500	
American Medical Assn*	$10,500	PAC
American Dental Assn	$10,000	PAC
American Academy of Ophthalmology	$8,000	PAC
Hospitals/Nursing Homes	**$15,065**	
New Boston General Hospital	$6,565	Indiv
Pharmaceuticals/Health Products	**$8,800**	
None over $5,000		

Lawyers & Lobbyists — $129,763

Lawyers & Lobbyists — $129,763
Assn of Trial Lawyers of America	$10,000	PAC
Haddon, Morgan & Foreman	$6,000	Indiv
Kogovsek & Associates	$5,350	Indiv

Misc Business — $76,900

Retail Sales — $12,750
None over $5,000

Misc Services — $7,250
None over $5,000

Business Services — $16,400
Chotin Group Corp	$7,000	Indiv

Lodging/Tourism — $11,000
None over $5,000

Misc Manufacturing & Distributing — $13,100
None over $5,000

Textiles — $6,300
Burlington Industries	$5,000	PAC

Transportation — $39,750

Air Transport — $12,750
Aircraft Owners & Pilots Assn	$10,000	PAC

Automotive — $7,300
Americans for Free International Trade	$5,000	PAC

Railroads — $13,700
Union Pacific Corp	$7,850	PAC/Ind

Labor

Labor — $270,150

Building Trade Unions — $44,800
Carpenters & Joiners Union	$10,000	PAC
Laborers' Political League	$10,000	PAC
Plumbers/Pipefitters Union	$10,000	PAC
Sheet Metal Workers Union	$7,500	PAC

Industrial Unions — $72,650
Communications Workers of America	$10,000	PAC
Intl Brotherhood of Electrical Workers	$10,000	PAC
Machinists/Aerospace Workers Union	$10,000	PAC
United Steelworkers	$10,000	PAC
United Auto Workers	$9,500	PAC
United Mine Workers	$7,500	PAC

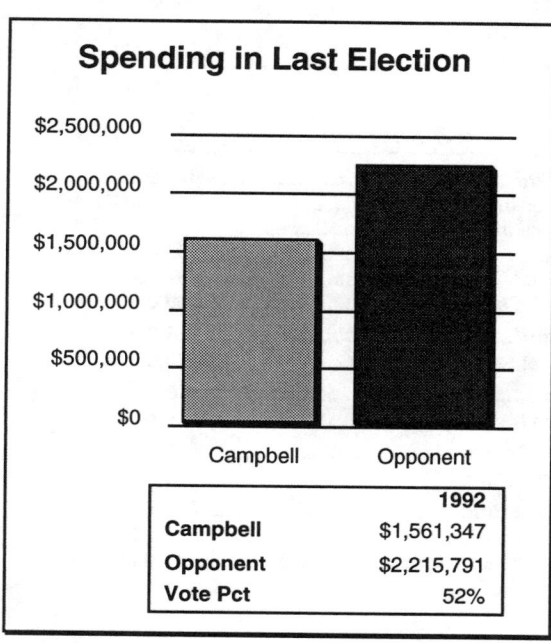

Spending in Last Election

	1992
Campbell	$1,561,347
Opponent	$2,215,791
Vote Pct	52%

Transportation Unions — $68,350
Marine Engineers Union*	$11,000	PAC
Air Line Pilots Assn	$10,000	PAC
Teamsters Union	$10,000	PAC
United Transportation Union	$10,000	PAC
Amalgamated Transit Union	$7,000	PAC
Trans Comm International Union	$5,100	PAC
Assn of Flight Attendants	$5,000	PAC

Public Sector Unions — $55,100
National Education Assn	$10,000	PAC
National Rural Letter Carriers Assn	$10,000	PAC
American Postal Workers Union	$6,600	PAC
National Assn of Letter Carriers	$6,000	PAC
National Assn Retired Federal Employees	$6,000	PAC
American Federation of Teachers	$5,600	PAC

Misc Unions — $29,250
AFL-CIO	$9,450	PAC
Food & Commercial Workers Union	$7,500	PAC
Service Employees International Union	$7,500	PAC

Ideological/Single-Issue

Ideological/Single-Issue — $144,088

Democratic/Liberal — $20,300
Fifth Horseman PAC	$10,000	PAC

Leadership PACs — $12,985
Fund for a Democratic Majority (Ted Kennedy)	$5,000	PAC

Pro-Israel — $36,950
Joint Action Cmte for Political Affairs	$6,500	PAC
Desert Caucus	$5,000	PAC
St Louisians for Better Government	$5,000	PAC

Abortion Policy — $13,036
None over $5,000

Gun Rights/Gun Control — $7,250
None over $5,000

Human Rights — $17,969
KidsPAC	$10,000	PAC
Human Rights Campaign Fund	$5,069	PAC

Misc Issues — $34,348
National Council of Senior Citizens	$10,000	PAC
National Cmte to Preserve Social Security	$9,100	PAC
Greenvote	$5,000	PAC
League of Conservation Voters	$5,000	PAC

Other & Unknown

Other — $23,070

Retired — $14,070
None over $5,000

Unknown — $156,350
Homemakers/Non-income earners	$12,200
No Employer Listed or Found	$67,850
Generic Occupation/Category Unknown	$5,000
Employer Listed/Category Unknown	$71,300
None over $5,000	

Independent expenditures supporting Campbell
National Abortion Rights Action League	$137,487
National Assn of Realtors	$98,953

---

* Contributions came from more than one affiliate or subsidiary.

John H. Chafee (R-RI)

First elected: 1976

1987-92 Total Rcpts:	$2,783,322
1992 Year-end Cash:	$188,821
Current term expires:	1994

1991-92 Committees & Subcommittees

Environment and Public Works (Ranking Republican)
Environmental Protection (Ranking Republican); Water Resources, Transportation and Infrastructure

Finance
Health for Families and the Uninsured (Ranking Republican); International Trade; Medicare and Long Term Care

Select Committee on Intelligence

Leading Contributors

NOTE: The bulk of Chafee's large individual contributions do not appear in the listings below. His last election was in 1988, and this book lists individual contributions only from 1989-1992.

Business

Agriculture		$52,750
Food Processing & Sales	**$24,250**	
ConAgra Inc	$6,000	PAC
Forestry & Forest Products	**$17,000**	
None over $6,000		

Communications/Electronics		$79,135
Printing & Publishing	**$10,200**	
Hallmark Cards	$8,000	PAC
Media/Entertainment	**$15,100**	
None over $6,000		
Telephone Utilities	**$29,185**	
AT&T	$10,400	PAC
NYNEX Corp*	$7,000	PAC
Electronics Mfg & Services	**$16,900**	
None over $6,000		

Construction		$71,500
General Contractors	**$34,050**	
National Utility Contractors Assn	$7,500	PAC
Construction Services	**$11,650**	
None over $6,000		
Building Materials & Equipment	**$17,400**	
None over $6,000		

Contribution Totals by Sector

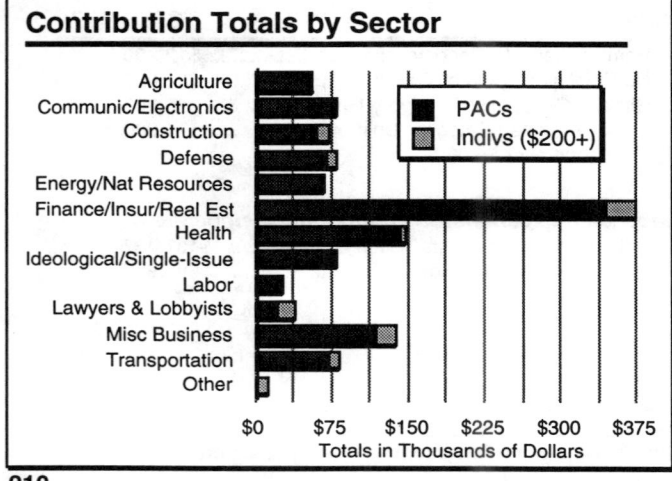

Agriculture
Communic/Electronics
Construction
Defense
Energy/Nat Resources
Finance/Insur/Real Est
Health
Ideological/Single-Issue
Labor
Lawyers & Lobbyists
Misc Business
Transportation
Other

■ PACs
▨ Indivs ($200+)

$0 $75 $150 $225 $300 $375
Totals in Thousands of Dollars

Source of Funds: 1987-1992

Source	Total	Pct
■ PACs	$1,117,520	39%
▨ Indivs $200+	$707,579	24%
☐ Indivs under $200	$763,721	26%
▨ Other	$302,985	10%
Candidate	$0	0%
Party	$108,483	4%

Source of PAC Dollars by Sector

Source	Total	Pct
■ Business	$1,011,354	91%
▨ Labor	$24,650	2%
☐ Ideological/Single-Issue	$76,840	7%

In-State vs. Out-of-State Contributions*

Source	Total	Pct
☐ In-State	$324,252	46%
■ Out-of-state	$378,677	54%
No state listed	$4,650	

*** by large individual contributors ($200 & above)**

Defense		$77,961
Defense Aerospace	**$55,111**	
Textron Inc	$20,250	PAC/Ind
General Dynamics	$6,500	PAC
United Technologies	$6,500	PAC
Defense Electronics	**$19,100**	
Harris Corp	$10,000	PAC

Energy & Natural Resources		$66,279
Oil & Gas	**$15,635**	
None over $6,000		
Mining	**$10,500**	
None over $6,000		
Electric Utilities	**$12,960**	
None over $6,000		
Waste Management	**$15,500**	
Waste Management Inc	$9,000	PAC

Finance, Insurance & Real Estate		$373,025
Commercial Banks	**$104,208**	
American Bankers Assn*	$10,500	PAC
Barnett Banks Inc	$10,000	PAC
Citicorp	$9,000	PAC
Bank of Boston*	$7,500	PAC
JP Morgan & Co	$6,000	PAC
Savings & Loans	**$16,350**	
US League of Savings Assns	$8,000	PAC
Credit Unions	**$6,425**	
Credit Union National Assn	$6,400	PAC
Finance/Credit Companies	**$11,000**	
None over $6,000		
Securities & Investment	**$63,534**	
American Express*	$7,250	PAC
Chicago Mercantile Exchange	$6,000	PAC

Insurance $114,333
   Aetna Life & Casualty .... $10,000   PAC
   Torchmark Corp .... $8,666   PAC
   Independent Insurance Agents of America .... $6,650   PAC

Real Estate *$30,125*
   Mortgage Bankers Assn of America .... $11,000   PAC

Accountants *$20,700*
   American Institute of CPA's .... $10,000   PAC

Misc Finance *$6,350*
   None over $6,000

Health $146,400

Health Professionals *$78,050*
   American Dental Assn .... $10,000   PAC
   American Medical Assn .... $10,000   PAC
   American Academy of Ophthalmology .... $9,000   PAC

Hospitals/Nursing Homes *$25,100*
   American Hospital Assn .... $11,000   PAC

Pharmaceuticals/Health Products *$41,850*
   None over $6,000

Lawyers & Lobbyists $37,675

Lawyers & Lobbyists *$37,675*
   None over $6,000

Misc Business $136,129

Business Associations *$7,121*
   None over $6,000

Food & Beverage *$16,800*
   National Restaurant Assn .... $7,000   PAC

Beer, Wine & Liquor *$14,700*
   None over $6,000

Retail Sales *$11,407*
   None over $6,000

Business Services *$17,850*
   Dun & Bradstreet .... $7,500   PAC

Chemical & Related Manufacturing *$18,500*
   None over $6,000

Misc Manufacturing & Distributing *$39,050*
   Stanley Works .... $8,400   PAC

Transportation $79,950

Air Transport *$22,500*
   Federal Express Corp .... $8,000   PAC
   United Parcel Service .... $7,500   PAC

Automotive *$17,900*
   None over $6,000

Trucking *$6,650*
   None over $6,000

Railroads *$14,000*
   Union Pacific Corp .... $11,000   PAC

Sea Transport *$11,000*
   None over $6,000

Misc Transport *$7,900*
   None over $6,000

Labor

Labor   *$24,650*

Building Trade Unions *$8,000*
   Laborers' Political League .... $8,000   PAC

Public Sector Unions *$14,050*
   None over $6,000

Ideological/Single-Issue

Ideological/Single-Issue   *$76,840*

Leadership PACs *$29,500*
   Republican Majority Fund (Richard Lugar) .... $10,000   PAC
   Campaign America (Bob Dole) .... $7,000   PAC
   Fund for America's Future (George Bush) .... $6,000   PAC

Pro-Choice *$7,000*
   None over $6,000

Human Rights *$12,000*
   Human Rights Campaign Fund .... $10,000   PAC

Misc Issues *$22,400*
   Sierra Club .... $9,000   PAC
   League of Conservation Voters .... $7,289   PAC

Other & Unknown

Other   *$11,550*

Retired *$6,200*
   None over $6,000

Unknown $68,050

   No Employer Listed or Found $22,800
   Employer Listed/Category Unknown $40,150
      None over $6,000

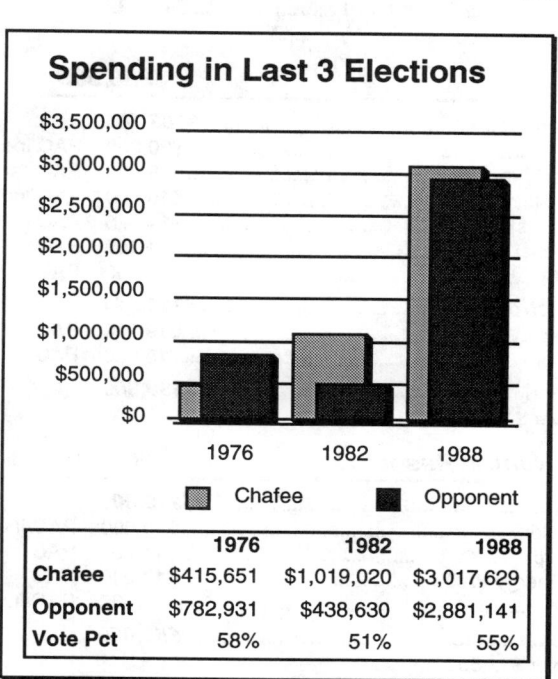

Spending in Last 3 Elections

	1976	1982	1988
Chafee	$415,651	$1,019,020	$3,017,629
Opponent	$782,931	$438,630	$2,881,141
Vote Pct	58%	51%	55%

* Contributions came from more than one affiliate or subsidiary.

211

Daniel R. Coats (R-Ind)

First elected: 1990 (app'ted 1988)

1989-92 Total Rcpts:	$7,727,256
1992 Year-end Cash:	$183,495
Current term expires:	1998

1991-92 Committees & Subcommittees

Armed Services
Conventional Forces and Alliance Defense; Defense Industry and Technology (Ranking Republican); Readiness, Sustainability and Support

Labor and Human Resources
Aging; Children, Families, Drugs and Alcoholism (Ranking Republican); Education, Arts and Humanities; Employment and Productivity

Leading Contributors

Business

Agriculture	$343,700	
Crop Production & Basic Processing	**$18,700**	
None over $12,500		
Tobacco	**$52,000**	
US Tobacco Co	$18,000	PAC
RJR Nabisco	$13,000	PAC
Dairy	**$14,125**	
None over $12,500		
Agricultural Services/Products	**$68,800**	
Navistar International	$15,250	PAC
Food Processing & Sales	**$118,025**	
Food Marketing Institute	$12,500	PAC
Forestry & Forest Products	**$52,750**	
International Paper Co	$15,000	PAC

Communications/Electronics	$234,770	
Printing & Publishing	**$50,650**	
None over $12,500		
Media/Entertainment	**$60,900**	
National Assn of Broadcasters	$17,500	PAC/Ind
National Cable Television Assn	$15,000	PAC
Telephone Utilities	**$72,170**	
Ameritech Corp*	$16,620	PAC
United Telecommunications	$13,000	PAC
Telecom Services & Equipment	**$12,750**	
None over $12,500		
Computer Equipment & Services	**$34,050**	
Ontario Corp	$24,800	PAC/Ind

Contribution Totals by Sector

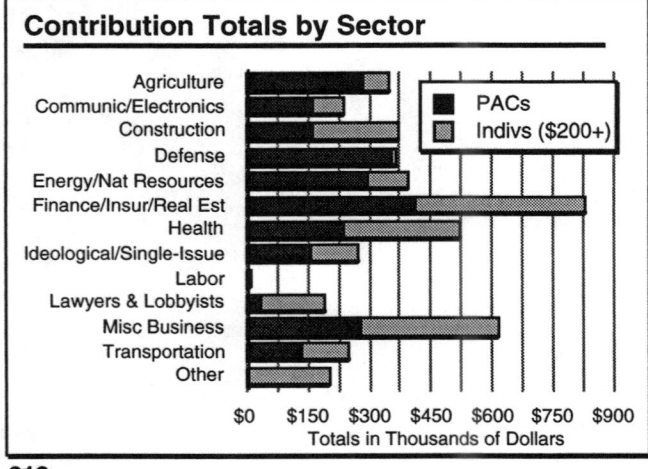

Totals in Thousands of Dollars

Source of Funds: 1987-1992

Source	Total	Pct
PACs	$2,349,342	27%
Indivs $200+	$3,006,881	35%
Indivs under $200	$1,614,125	19%
Other	$1,660,452	19%
Candidate	$0	0%
Party	$903,544	10%

Source of PAC Dollars by Sector

Source	Total	Pct
Business	$2,303,439	94%
Labor	$6,500	0%
Ideological/Single-Issue	$153,033	6%

In-State vs. Out-of-State Contributions*

Source	Total	Pct
In-State	$2,435,096	81%
Out-of-state	$570,285	19%
No state listed	$-1,000	

* by large individual contributors ($200 & above)

Construction	$366,802	
General Contractors	**$106,960**	
Associated General Contractors	$20,000	PAC
Associated Builders & Contractors	$15,000	PAC
Home Builders	**$88,150**	
National Assn of Home Builders	$20,000	PAC
Special Trade Contractors	**$57,400**	
Sheet Metal/Air Conditioning Contractors	$16,000	PAC
Construction Services	**$15,000**	
None over $12,500		
Building Materials & Equipment	**$99,292**	
None over $12,500		

Defense	$358,589	
Defense Aerospace	**$203,745**	
United Technologies	$20,000	PAC/Ind
Northrop Corp	$18,000	PAC
General Motors	$15,500	PAC/Ind
Martin Marietta Corp	$14,375	PAC
Allied-Signal	$14,250	PAC
Boeing Co	$14,000	PAC
Defense Electronics	**$116,544**	
GTE Corp	$19,000	PAC
Harris Corp	$15,000	PAC
Misc Defense	**$38,300**	
None over $12,500		

Energy & Natural Resources	$389,795	
Oil & Gas	**$210,000**	
Amoco Corp	$20,500	PAC/Ind
USX Corp*	$14,700	PAC
Dallas Energy PAC	$14,000	PAC
Mobil Oil	$13,000	PAC/Ind
Mining	**$52,050**	
None over $12,500		
Misc Energy	**$22,400**	
Cooper Industries	$12,500	PAC

Electric Utilities **$87,045**
  Public Service Co of Indiana .... $20,950   PAC/Ind

Finance, Insurance & Real Estate $821,441

Commercial Banks **$171,460**
  American Bankers Assn .... $20,000   PAC
  Bank One .... $17,750   Indiv
  Mercantile National Bank .... $13,500   Indiv
  Merchants National Corp .... $13,000   PAC/Ind

Savings & Loans **$15,450**
  None over $12,500

Securities & Investment **$128,240**
  Salomon Brothers .... $30,225   PAC/Ind
  Chicago Mercantile Exchange .... $16,500   PAC
  City Securities Corp .... $12,750   Indiv

Insurance **$315,707**
  Conseco Inc .... $22,000   Indiv
  American Council of Life Insurance .... $19,284   PAC
  National Assn of Independent Insurers .... $18,374   PAC
  Blue Cross & Blue Shield Assn* .... $18,000   PAC/Ind
  National Assn of Life Underwriters .... $17,500   PAC
  Travelers Corp .... $17,269   PAC
  Lincoln National Corp .... $13,900   PAC/Ind

Real Estate **$92,850**
  National Assn of Realtors .... $18,000   PAC

Accountants **$44,825**
  None over $12,500

Misc Finance **$38,525**
  None over $12,500

Health $516,886

Health Professionals **$239,412**
  American Medical Assn* .... $20,000   PAC
  American Dental Assn .... $16,000   PAC

Hospitals/Nursing Homes **$47,050**
  American Hospital Assn .... $13,050   PAC

Pharmaceuticals/Health Products **$219,820**
  Eli Lilly & Co .... $96,350   PAC/Ind

Lawyers & Lobbyists $187,771

Lawyers & Lobbyists **$187,771**
  Barnes & Thornburg .... $23,800   Indiv

Misc Business $611,257

Food & Beverage **$82,895**
  Pizza Hut Inc* .... $17,200   Indiv
  National Restaurant Assn .... $17,000   PAC

Beer, Wine & Liquor **$16,200**
  None over $12,500

Retail Sales **$51,454**
  None over $12,500

Business Services **$77,669**
  Whiteco Industries .... $13,500   Indiv

Lodging/Tourism **$21,350**
  None over $12,500

Chemical & Related Manufacturing **$76,833**
  None over $12,500

Steel Production **$31,950**
  None over $12,500

Misc Manufacturing & Distributing **$200,233**
  Accurate Castings Inc .... $13,450   Indiv

Transportation $246,258

Air Transport **$31,600**
  None over $12,500

Automotive **$122,933**
  National Auto Dealers Assn .... $18,500   PAC
  Auto Dealers & Drivers for Free Trade .... $15,000   PAC

Trucking **$28,225**
  North American Van Lines .... $12,950   PAC/Ind

Railroads **$35,800**
  Union Pacific Corp .... $19,000   PAC

Misc Transport **$18,450**
  None over $12,500

Ideological/Single-Issue

Ideological/Single-Issue $267,930

Republican/Conservative **$83,097**
  National Republican Senatorial Cmte .... $28,200   Indiv

Leadership PACs **$33,500**
  Campaign America (Bob Dole) .... $16,000   PAC

Pro-Israel **$102,900**
  National PAC .... $15,000   PAC
  Hudson Valley PAC .... $13,500   PAC

Gun Rights/Gun Control **$19,800**
  National Rifle Assn .... $19,800   PAC

Other & Unknown

Other $199,788

Civil Servants/Public Officials **$15,714**
  None over $12,500

Education **$15,950**
  None over $12,500

Retired **$156,174**
  None over $12,500

Unknown $966,766

  Homemakers/Non-income earners $165,499
  No Employer Listed or Found $498,151
  Generic Occupation/Category Unknown $15,483
  Employer Listed/Category Unknown $287,133
    None over $12,500

---

* Contributions came from more than one affiliate or
subsidiary.

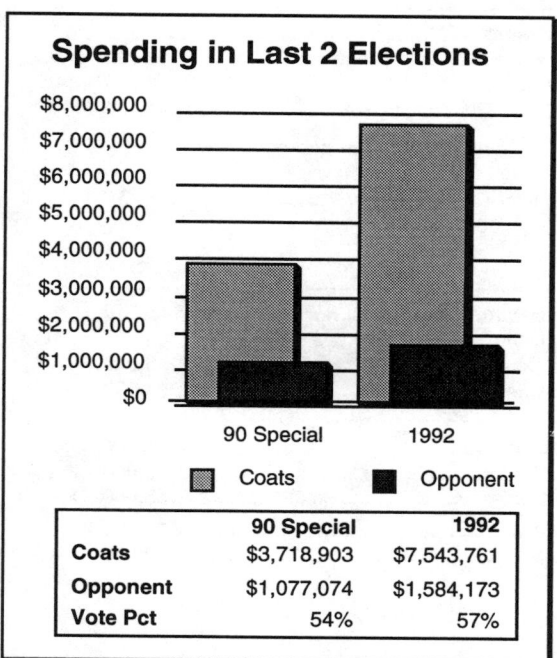

Spending in Last 2 Elections

	90 Special	1992
Coats	$3,718,903	$7,543,761
Opponent	$1,077,074	$1,584,173
Vote Pct	54%	57%

Thad Cochran (R-Miss)

First elected: 1978

1987-92 Total Rcpts:	$1,491,775
1992 Year-end Cash:	$764,610
Current term expires:	1996

1991-92 Committees & Subcommittees

Agriculture, Nutrition and Forestry
Agricultural Production and Stabilization of Prices; Domestic and Foreign Marketing and Product Promotion (Ranking Republican); Rural Development and Rural Electrification (Ranking Republican)

Appropriations
Agriculture, Rural Development and Related Agencies (Ranking Republican); Defense; Energy and Water Development; Interior and Related Agencies; Labor, Health and Human Services, Education and Related Agencies

Labor and Human Resources
Aging (Ranking Republican); Education, Arts and Humanities; Labor

Select Committee on Indian Affairs

Leading Contributors

Business

Agriculture $308,775

Crop Production & Basic Processing $136,125
National Cotton Council	$8,000	PAC
Riceland Foods	$6,500	PAC/Ind
American Sugar Cane League	$6,000	PAC
American Crystal Sugar Corp	$5,000	PAC
JG Boswell Co	$5,000	PAC
Sun-Diamond Growers*	$4,000	PAC

Tobacco $22,450
Philip Morris	$10,000	PAC
US Tobacco Co	$5,000	PAC

Dairy $12,625
Dairymen Inc-Mississippi	$6,000	PAC

Poultry & Eggs $13,500
National Broiler Council	$4,500	PAC

Livestock $13,200
Tennessee Walking Horse Breeders	$5,000	PAC

Agricultural Services/Products $42,500
Alabama Farm Bureau Federation	$4,000	PAC
American Assn of Crop Insurers	$4,000	PAC

Food Processing & Sales $44,875
Food Marketing Institute	$11,000	PAC
ConAgra Inc	$5,000	PAC
Malone & Hyde Inc	$5,000	PAC

Contribution Totals by Sector

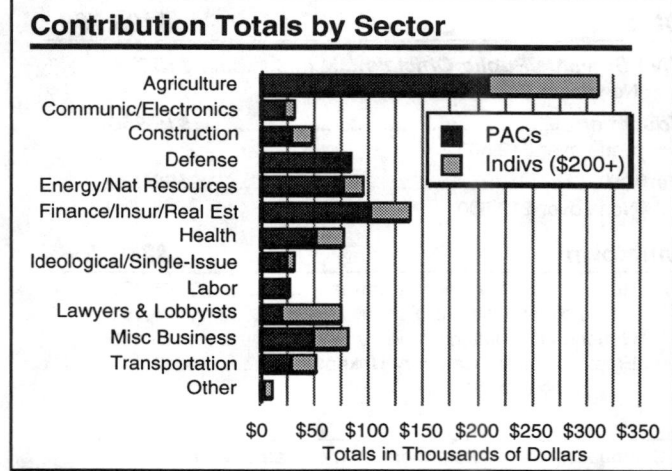

Agriculture
Communic/Electronics
Construction
Defense
Energy/Nat Resources
Finance/Insur/Real Est
Health
Ideological/Single-Issue
Labor
Lawyers & Lobbyists
Misc Business
Transportation
Other

■ PACs
▨ Indivs ($200+)

$0 $50 $100 $150 $200 $250 $300 $350
Totals in Thousands of Dollars

Source of Funds: 1987-1992

Source	Total	Pct
■ PACs	$673,406	45%
▨ Indivs $200+	$394,630	26%
□ Indivs under $200	$145,152	10%
▨ Other	$294,763	20%
Candidate	$0	0%
Party	$16,176	1%

Source of PAC Dollars by Sector

Source	Total	Pct
■ Business	$654,606	93%
▨ Labor	$25,050	4%
□ Ideological/Single-Issue	$22,850	3%

In-State vs. Out-of-State Contributions*

Source	Total	Pct
□ In-State	$300,680	76%
▨ Out-of-state	$93,950	24%
No state listed	$0	

* by large individual contributors ($200 & above)

Forestry & Forest Products $19,000
International Paper Co	$8,000	PAC
Westvaco Corp	$4,000	PAC

Misc Agriculture $4,500
None over $4,000

Communications/Electronics $29,030

Media/Entertainment $6,000
None over $4,000

Telephone Utilities $17,130
BellSouth Corp*	$10,750	PAC/Ind

Construction $46,375

General Contractors $29,375
Associated General Contractors	$5,000	PAC
Fluor Corp	$4,125	PAC
National Utility Contractors Assn	$4,000	PAC

Home Builders $6,250
None over $4,000

Building Materials & Equipment $6,750
None over $4,000

Defense $81,050

Defense Aerospace $45,050
Lockheed Corp	$5,000	PAC
Northrop Corp	$5,000	PAC
Colt Industries	$4,000	PAC
McDonnell Douglas*	$4,000	PAC

Defense Electronics $24,500
Hughes Aircraft	$6,000	PAC
Litton Industries	$5,000	PAC

Misc Defense $11,500
FMC Corp	$4,000	PAC

Energy & Natural Resources · $92,350

Oil & Gas **$59,350**
   Chevron Corp .... $5,500   PAC
   Mobil Oil .... $5,000   PAC

Misc Energy **$7,500**
   McDermott Inc .... $4,000   PAC

Electric Utilities **$20,000**
   ACRE (Action Cmte for Rural Electrification)* ..... $6,000   PAC
   Southern Co* .... $4,000   PAC

Finance, Insurance & Real Estate · $136,458

Commercial Banks **$28,816**
   American Bankers Assn .... $10,000   PAC

Securities & Investment **$22,885**
   Equitable Financial Services .... $5,000   PAC
   Salomon Brothers .... $4,500   PAC

Insurance **$53,232**
   National Assn of Life Underwriters............ $5,500   PAC
   American Council of Life Insurance .... $4,000   PAC
   Equitable Financial Services .... $4,000   PAC
   Travelers Corp .... $4,000   PAC

Real Estate **$14,500**
   None over $4,000

Accountants **$8,125**
   American Institute of CPA's .... $4,625   PAC

Misc Finance **$4,900**
   None over $4,000

Health · $75,600

Health Professionals **$55,850**
   American Medical Assn............................... $9,650   PAC
   American Academy of Ophthalmology .... $5,000   PAC
   American Dental Assn .... $5,000   PAC
   American Assn Oral & Maxillofacial Surgeons .... $5,000   PAC

Hospitals/Nursing Homes **$9,000**
   None over $4,000

Pharmaceuticals/Health Products **$9,000**
   None over $4,000

Lawyers & Lobbyists · $71,950

Lawyers & Lobbyists **$71,950**
   Assn of Trial Lawyers of America .... $5,000   PAC

Misc Business · $79,364

Food & Beverage **$14,985**
   None over $4,000

Retail Sales **$19,000**
   JE Nellson Co .... $5,000   Indiv

Business Services **$9,125**
   None over $4,000

Misc Business **$4,125**
   None over $4,000

Steel Production **$8,000**
   Schnitzer Steel Industries .... $7,000   Indiv

Misc Manufacturing & Distributing **$9,750**
   None over $4,000

Textiles **$4,000**
   None over $4,000

Transportation · $49,500

Air Transport **$14,000**
   Federal Express Corp .... $9,000   PAC

Automotive **$13,250**
   Auto Dealers & Drivers for Free Trade .... $4,000   PAC

Railroads **$5,000**
   None over $4,000

Sea Transport **$13,500**
   None over $4,000

Labor

Labor · $25,050

Transportation Unions **$20,000**
   Marine Engineers Union* .... $11,500   PAC
   Seafarers International Union .... $7,500   PAC

Public Sector Unions **$5,050**
   None over $4,000

Ideological/Single-Issue

Ideological/Single-Issue · $29,100

Leadership PACs **$7,000**
   Campaign America (Bob Dole) .... $5,000   PAC

Pro-Israel **$13,500**
   National PAC .... $5,000   PAC

Gun Rights/Gun Control **$4,950**
   National Rifle Assn .... $4,950   PAC

Other & Unknown

Other · $9,500

Education **$5,000**
   None over $4,000

Unknown · $62,584

   Homemakers/Non-income earners $13,975
   No Employer Listed or Found $15,100
   Employer Listed/Category Unknown $32,659
     None over $4,000

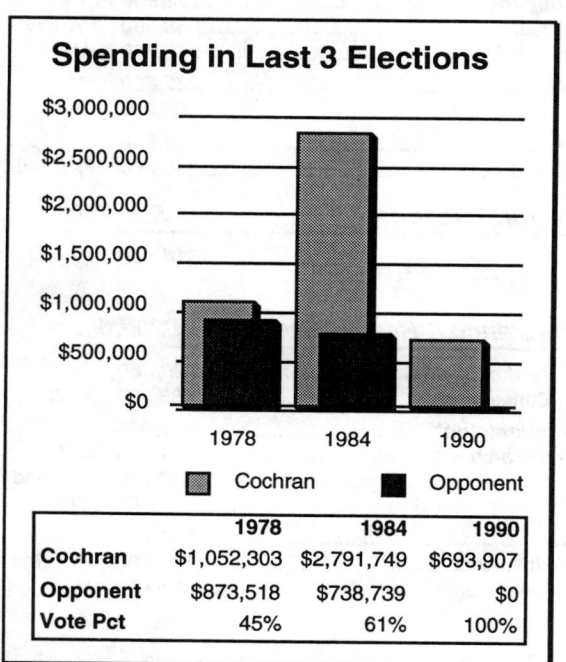

Spending in Last 3 Elections

	1978	1984	1990
Cochran	$1,052,303	$2,791,749	$693,907
Opponent	$873,518	$738,739	$0
Vote Pct	45%	61%	100%

Legend: ▨ Cochran   ■ Opponent

---

* Contributions came from more than one affiliate or subsidiary.

William S. Cohen (R-Maine)

First elected: 1978

1987-92 Total Rcpts:	$1,557,640
1992 Year-end Cash:	$26,547
Current term expires:	1996

1991-92 Committees & Subcommittees

Armed Services
Conventional Forces and Alliance Defense; Projection Forces and Regional Defense (Ranking Republican); Strategic Forces and Nuclear Deterrence

Governmental Affairs
Government Information and Regulation; Oversight of Government Management (Ranking Republican); Permanent Subcommittee on Investigations

Special Aging (Ranking Republican)

Leading Contributors

Business

Agriculture	$72,394

Crop Production & Basic Processing **$7,092**
    None over $5,000

Dairy **$10,700**
    Associated Milk Producers .... $7,000 PAC

Agricultural Services/Products **$6,000**
    None over $5,000

Food Processing & Sales **$13,500**
    None over $5,000

Forestry & Forest Products **$30,602**
    International Paper Co .... $10,000 PAC

Communications/Electronics	$59,292

Printing & Publishing **$6,700**
    None over $5,000

Media/Entertainment **$35,892**
    Time Warner* .... $18,000 Indiv
    National Cable Television Assn .... $9,000 PAC

Telephone Utilities **$6,000**
    None over $5,000

Computer Equipment & Services **$6,500**
    None over $5,000

Source of Funds: 1987-1992

Source	Total	Pct
■ PACs	$558,253	33%
▦ Indivs $200+	$569,336	34%
☐ Indivs under $200	$247,041	15%
⊠ Other	$305,480	18%
Candidate	$0	0%
Party	$122,470	7%

Source of PAC Dollars by Sector

Source	Total	Pct
■ Business	$418,602	75%
▦ Labor	$35,750	6%
☐ Ideological/Single-Issue ..	$104,901	19%

In-State vs. Out-of-State Contributions*

Source	Total	Pct
☐ In-State	$133,561	24%
■ Out-of-state	$433,775	76%
No state listed	$2,000	

* by large individual contributors ($200 & above)

Construction	$59,525

General Contractors **$25,775**
    Associated General Contractors .... $10,000 PAC

Home Builders **$11,350**
    National Assn of Home Builders .... $7,500 PAC

Construction Services **$6,750**
    None over $5,000

Building Materials & Equipment **$11,400**
    None over $5,000

Defense	$98,450

Defense Aerospace **$52,900**
    Colt Industries .... $6,500 PAC/Ind
    Lockheed Corp .... $5,000 PAC

Defense Electronics **$25,800**
    AT&T .... $5,000 PAC

Misc Defense **$19,750**
    Bath Iron Works .... $10,500 PAC/Ind

Energy & Natural Resources	$24,750

Oil & Gas **$14,000**
    None over $5,000

Finance, Insurance & Real Estate	$233,000

Commercial Banks **$20,050**
    American Bankers Assn .... $6,000 PAC

Securities & Investment **$71,900**
    Chicago Research & Trading Group .... $21,000 Indiv
    Morgan Stanley & Co .... $17,200 PAC/Ind
    National Venture Capital Assn .... $5,000 PAC

Insurance **$51,250**
    Unum Life Insurance Co .... $10,000 PAC/Ind
    National Assn of Life Underwriters ...... $5,000 PAC

Contribution Totals by Sector

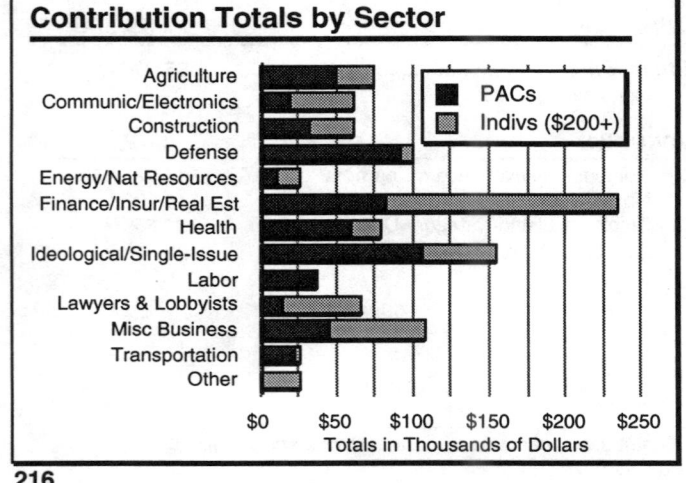

Agriculture
Communic/Electronics
Construction
Defense
Energy/Nat Resources
Finance/Insur/Real Est
Health
Ideological/Single-Issue
Labor
Lawyers & Lobbyists
Misc Business
Transportation
Other

■ PACs
▦ Indivs ($200+)

$0 $50 $100 $150 $200 $250
Totals in Thousands of Dollars

Real Estate	......	$61,350	
National Assn of Realtors	......	$9,550	PAC
Charles E Smith Companies	......	$5,000	Indiv
Henry Crown & Co	......	$5,000	Indiv
Accountants	......	**$9,000**	
American Institute of CPA's	......	$5,000	PAC
Misc Finance	......	**$13,450**	
None over $5,000			

Health $76,950

Health Professionals	......	$53,200	
American Medical Assn	......	$10,000	PAC
American Academy of Ophthalmology	......	$7,000	PAC
American Dental Assn	......	$5,000	PAC
Hospitals/Nursing Homes	......	**$11,500**	
American Hospital Assn	......	$5,000	PAC
Pharmaceuticals/Health Products	......	**$11,250**	
None over $5,000			

Lawyers & Lobbyists $64,200

| Lawyers & Lobbyists | ...... | $64,200 | |
| Assn of Trial Lawyers of America | ...... | $10,000 | PAC |

Misc Business $106,818

Food & Beverage	......	$5,528	
None over $5,000			
Beer, Wine & Liquor	......	**$5,500**	
None over $5,000			
Retail Sales	......	**$8,440**	
None over $5,000			
Business Services	......	**$12,650**	
None over $5,000			
Lodging/Tourism	......	**$7,050**	
None over $5,000			
Chemical & Related Manufacturing	......	**$13,000**	
Avery Inc	......	$5,000	PAC
Contran Corp	......	$5,000	PAC/Ind
Misc Manufacturing & Distributing	......	**$25,900**	
Revlon Inc	......	$8,000	Indiv
Textiles	......	**$15,450**	
None over $5,000			

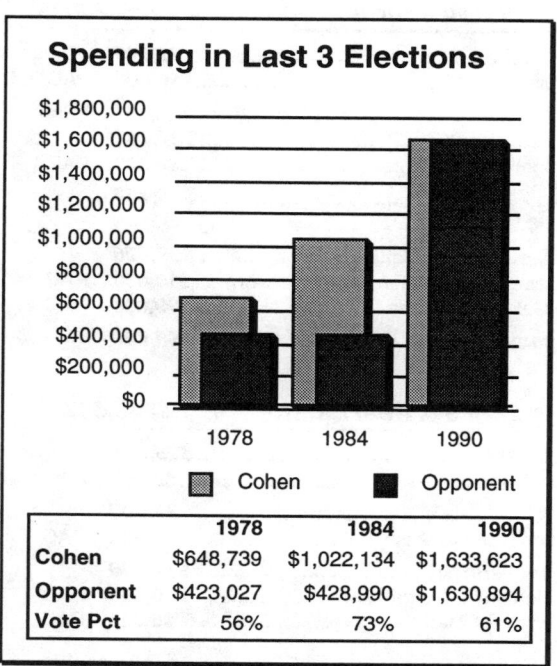

Spending in Last 3 Elections

	1978	1984	1990
Cohen	$648,739	$1,022,134	$1,633,623
Opponent	$423,027	$428,990	$1,630,894
Vote Pct	56%	73%	61%

Transportation $24,700

Air Transport	......	$13,250	
Federal Express Corp	......	$7,000	PAC
Automotive	......	**$7,450**	
None over $5,000			

Labor

Labor $35,750

Transportation Unions	......	$17,000	
Marine Engineers Union*	......	$10,000	PAC
Public Sector Unions	......	**$14,750**	
Natl Assn of Retired Federal Employees	......	$6,000	PAC

Ideological/Single-Issue

Ideological/Single-Issue $152,351

Leadership PACs	......	$5,640	
None over $5,000			
Foreign & Defense Policy	......	**$6,000**	
Free Cuba PAC	......	$5,000	PAC
Pro-Israel	......	**$114,750**	
Citizens Organized PAC	......	$10,000	PAC
National PAC	......	$10,000	PAC
Washington PAC	......	$8,000	PAC
Citizens Concerned for the National Interest	......	$5,000	PAC
Hudson Valley PAC	......	$5,000	PAC
Mid Manhattan PAC	......	$5,000	PAC
San Franciscans for Good Government	......	$5,000	PAC
Women's Alliance for Israel	......	$5,000	PAC
Women's Pro-Israel National PAC	......	$5,000	PAC
Human Rights	......	**$7,500**	
Human Rights Campaign Fund	......	$5,000	PAC
Misc Issues	......	**$7,461**	
None over $5,000			

Other & Unknown

Other $24,768

| Retired | ...... | $17,668 | |
| None over $5,000 | | | |

Unknown $97,291

Homemakers/Non-income earners	......	$16,400
No Employer Listed or Found	......	$8,191
Generic Occupation/Category Unknown	......	$6,850
Employer Listed/Category Unknown	......	$65,850
None over $5,000		

---

* Contributions came from more than one affiliate or
subsidiary.

Kent Conrad (D-ND)

First elected: 1986

1987-92 Total Rcpts:	$2,524,425
1992 Year-end Cash:	$132,101
Current term expires:	1994

1991-92 Committees & Subcommittees

Agriculture, Nutrition and Forestry
Agricultural Credit (Chairman); Agricultural Production and Stabilization of Prices; Domestic and Foreign Marketing and Product Promotion

Appropriations
Agriculture, Rural Development and Related Agencies; Energy and Water Development; Interior and Related Agencies; Labor, Health and Human Services, Education and Related Agencies

Budget

Energy and Natural Resources
Mineral Resources Development and Production; Public Lands, National Parks and Forests; Water and Power (Vice Chairman)

Select Committee on Indian Affairs

Leading Contributors

Business

Agriculture	$284,650

Crop Production & Basic Processing	**$125,555**	
American Crystal Sugar Corp	$18,000	PAC
American Sugarbeet Growers Assn	$11,000	PAC
Sun-Diamond Growers*	$10,200	PAC
Tobacco	**$21,355**	
Philip Morris	$8,355	PAC
Dairy	**$25,750**	
Mid-America Dairymen	$10,000	PAC
Associated Milk Producers	$9,000	PAC
Poultry & Eggs	**$14,500**	
None over $7,500		
Livestock	**$16,950**	
National Cattlemen's Assn*	$8,000	PAC
Agricultural Services/Products	**$57,450**	
American Assn of Crop Insurers	$10,000	PAC
Food Processing & Sales	**$22,500**	
ConAgra Inc	$7,500	PAC

Communications/Electronics	$46,500

Media/Entertainment	**$19,500**	
None over $7,500		

Source of Funds: 1987-1992

Source	Total	Pct
■ PACs	$1,502,985	57%
▨ Indivs $200+	$361,541	14%
☐ Indivs under $200	$214,034	8%
⊠ Other	$550,141	21%
Candidate	$0	0%
Party	$104,276	4%

Source of PAC Dollars by Sector

Source	Total	Pct
■ Business	$1,067,417	69%
▨ Labor	$330,738	21%
☐ Ideological/Single-Issue	$145,441	9%

In-State vs. Out-of-State Contributions*

Source	Total	Pct
☐ In-State	$22,124	6%
■ Out-of-state	$336,667	94%
No state listed	$2,000	

*** by large individual contributors ($200 & above)**

Telephone Utilities	**$16,500**	
None over $7,500		

Construction	$19,250

General Contractors	**$8,500**	
None over $7,500		
Home Builders	**$7,500**	
National Assn of Home Builders	$7,500	PAC

Defense	$9,500

Defense Aerospace	**$8,500**	
None over $7,500		

Energy & Natural Resources	$279,266

Oil & Gas	**$121,649**	
Ashland Oil	$10,000	PAC/Ind
Coastal Corp	$8,000	PAC
Mining	**$27,742**	
National Coal Assn	$9,929	PAC
Nuclear Energy	**$15,750**	
None over $7,500		
Electric Utilities	**$99,425**	
ACRE (Action Cmte for Rural Electrification)	$10,000	PAC
Southern California Edison	$9,000	PAC
Waste Management	**$8,000**	
None over $7,500		

Finance, Insurance & Real Estate	$245,517

Commercial Banks	**$25,829**	
Independent Bankers Assn	$9,000	PAC
Credit Unions	**$7,500**	
Credit Union National Assn	$7,500	PAC
Securities & Investment	**$71,500**	
Chicago Mercantile Exchange	$10,000	PAC
Chicago Board of Trade	$8,000	PAC

Contribution Totals by Sector

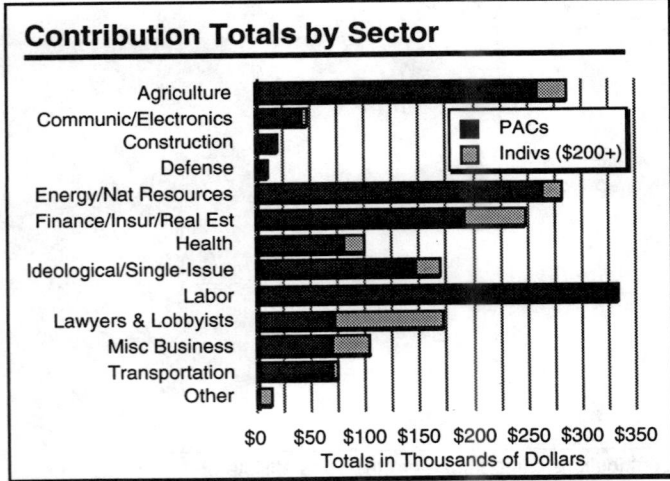

Legend: PACs, Indivs ($200+)

Categories: Agriculture, Communic/Electronics, Construction, Defense, Energy/Nat Resources, Finance/Insur/Real Est, Health, Ideological/Single-Issue, Labor, Lawyers & Lobbyists, Misc Business, Transportation, Other

$0 $50 $100 $150 $200 $250 $300 $350
Totals in Thousands of Dollars

Insurance **$92,838**
    Independent Insurance Agents of America .... $14,388 PAC
    National Assn of Life Underwriters .... $10,000 PAC
    American Council of Life Insurance .... $8,500 PAC

Real Estate **$26,150**
    National Assn of Realtors .... $7,500 PAC

Accountants **$18,500**
    None over $7,500

Health $98,115

Health Professionals **$54,409**
    American Chiropractic Assn .... $9,500 PAC

Hospitals/Nursing Homes **$23,456**
    American Hospital Assn .... $11,956 PAC

Health Services **$10,500**
    US Healthcare Inc .... $10,000 Indiv

Pharmaceuticals/Health Products **$9,750**
    None over $7,500

Lawyers & Lobbyists $169,862

Lawyers & Lobbyists **$169,862**
    Assn of Trial Lawyers of America .... $10,000 PAC

Misc Business $101,450

Food & Beverage **$10,800**
    None over $7,500

Beer, Wine & Liquor **$28,000**
    National Beer Wholesalers Assn .... $12,500 PAC

Retail Sales **$13,750**
    None over $7,500

Business Services **$23,800**
    None over $7,500

Misc Manufacturing & Distributing **$10,250**
    None over $7,500

Transportation $73,750

Air Transport **$32,000**
    United Parcel Service .... $9,500 PAC
    Federal Express Corp .... $8,000 PAC

Automotive **$18,500**
    Auto Dealers & Drivers for Free Trade .... $10,000 PAC

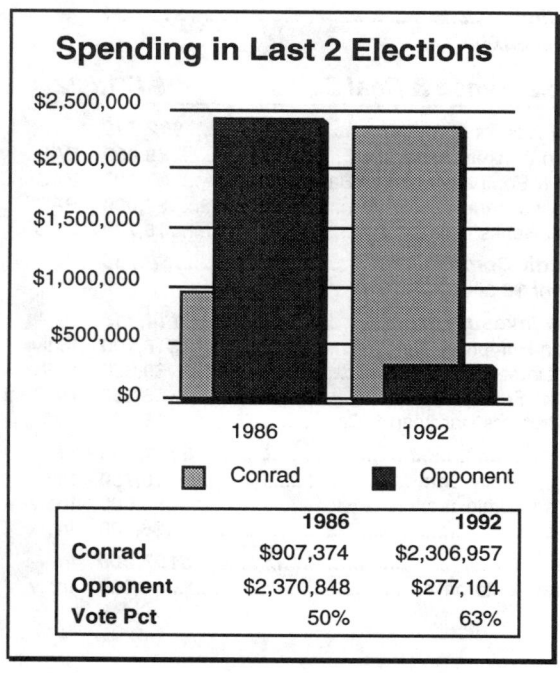

Spending in Last 2 Elections

	1986	1992
Conrad	$907,374	$2,306,957
Opponent	$2,370,848	$277,104
Vote Pct	50%	63%

Railroads **$15,000**
    None over $7,500

Labor

Labor $331,238

Building Trade Unions **$51,378**
    Carpenters & Joiners Union .... $10,378 PAC
    Laborers' Political League .... $10,000 PAC
    Operating Engineers Union .... $10,000 PAC
    Sheet Metal Workers Union .... $10,000 PAC

Industrial Unions **$68,700**
    Intl Brotherhood of Electrical Workers .... $10,000 PAC
    Machinists/Aerospace Workers Union .... $10,000 PAC
    United Auto Workers .... $10,000 PAC
    United Mine Workers .... $10,000 PAC
    United Steelworkers .... $10,000 PAC

Transportation Unions **$76,500**
    Marine Engineers Union .... $10,000 PAC
    Seafarers International Union .... $10,000 PAC
    Teamsters Union .... $10,000 PAC
    United Transportation Union .... $10,000 PAC

Public Sector Unions **$107,360**
    American Federation of Teachers...................... $20,000 PAC
    National Rural Letter Carriers Assn .... $11,000 PAC
    National Treasury Employees Union .... $10,560 PAC
    American Fedn of St/Cnty/Munic Employees .... $10,000 PAC
    American Postal Workers Union .... $10,000 PAC
    National Assn of Letter Carriers .... $10,000 PAC
    National Assn Retired Federal Employees .... $8,000 PAC
    National Assn of Postmasters .... $7,550 PAC

Misc Unions **$27,300**
    Service Employees International Union .... $10,000 PAC

Ideological/Single-Issue

Ideological/Single-Issue $167,741

Democratic/Liberal **$19,991**
    Fifth Horseman PAC .... $10,000 PAC

Leadership PACs **$11,500**
    None over $7,500

Pro-Israel **$90,300**
    Washington PAC .... $9,000 PAC

Human Rights **$22,000**
    KidsPAC .... $10,000 PAC
    National Community Action Foundation .... $10,000 PAC

Misc Issues **$11,000**
    National Cmte to Preserve Social Security .... $9,500 PAC

Other & Unknown

Other $12,350

    None over $7,500

Unknown $52,453

    Homemakers/Non-income earners $9,200
    Employer Listed/Category Unknown $39,003
        None over $7,500

---

* Contributions came from more than one affiliate or
subsidiary.

Paul Coverdell (R-Ga)

First elected: 1992

1991-92 Total Rcpts:	$3,297,110
1992 Year-end Cash:	$136,055
Current term expires:	1998

1993-94 Committees & Subcommittees

Agriculture, Nutrition and Forestry
Agricultural Credit; Domestic and Foreign Marketing and Product Promotion; Rural Development and Rural Electrification (Ranking Republican)

Foreign Relations
Near Eastern and South Asian Affairs; Terrorism, Narcotics and International Operations; Western Hemisphere and Peace Corps Affairs (Ranking Republican)

Small Business
Export Expansion and Agricultural Development (Ranking Republican); Rural Economy and Family Farming

Leading Contributors

Business

Agriculture $231,307

Crop Production & Basic Processing **$34,450**	
WC Bradley Co $12,800	Indiv
Poultry & Eggs **$12,000**	
None over $6,000	
Agricultural Services/Products **$34,212**	
Lasseter Tractor Co $6,500	Indiv
Food Processing & Sales **$70,150**	
Flowers Industries $28,750	PAC/Ind
American Bakers Assn $8,500	PAC
Forestry & Forest Products **$72,595**	
Westvaco Corp $6,000	PAC

Communications/Electronics $58,833

Printing & Publishing **$18,558**	
None over $6,000	
Electronics Mfg & Services **$14,500**	
Harris Corp $7,000	PAC
Computer Equipment & Services **$17,575**	
American Software Inc $7,000	Indiv

Construction $116,041

General Contractors **$25,850**	
None over $6,000	
Home Builders **$21,550**	
John Wieland Homes $6,700	Indiv

Source of Funds: 1987-1992

Source	Total	Pct
PACs	$651,966	15%
Indivs $200+	$1,953,532	45%
Indivs under $200	$602,721	14%
Other	$1,111,377	26%
Candidate	$7,518	0%
Party	$1,022,486	24%

Source of PAC Dollars by Sector

Source	Total	Pct
Business	$498,940	86%
Labor..............................	$0	0%
Ideological/Single-Issue	$81,040	14%

In-State vs. Out-of-State Contributions*

Source	Total	Pct
In-State	$1,551,898	80%
Out-of-state	$391,554	20%
No state listed	$0	

* by large individual contributors ($200 & above)

Special Trade Contractors **$14,900**	
None over $6,000	
Building Materials & Equipment **$48,741**	
Apex Supply Co $6,887	Indiv
Space Master Internation $6,000	Indiv

Defense $4,000

Energy & Natural Resources $111,200

Oil & Gas **$79,950**	
Onyx Petroleum Co $6,000	Indiv
Misc Energy **$9,000**	
Cooper Industries $9,000	PAC
Electric Utilities **$11,000**	
None over $6,000	

Finance, Insurance & Real Estate $471,822

Commercial Banks **$62,319**	
American Bankers Assn* $8,000	PAC
Citizens & Southern National Bank $7,500	PAC/Ind
CB&T Bancshares $7,000	PAC
SunTrust Banks* $6,700	PAC
Finance/Credit Companies **$8,750**	
None over $6,000	
Securities & Investment **$114,115**	
Robinson-Humphrey Co $15,100	Indiv
Oppenheimer & Co $9,300	Indiv
Prudential Securities $6,250	PAC/Ind
Brown Brothers Harriman & Co $6,000	Indiv
Insurance **$111,362**	
American Family Corp $8,750	Indiv
Integrated Administration Services $8,000	Indiv
Powell & Co $6,000	Indiv
Real Estate **$107,600**	
Woodcrest Enterprises $8,000	Indiv

Contribution Totals by Sector

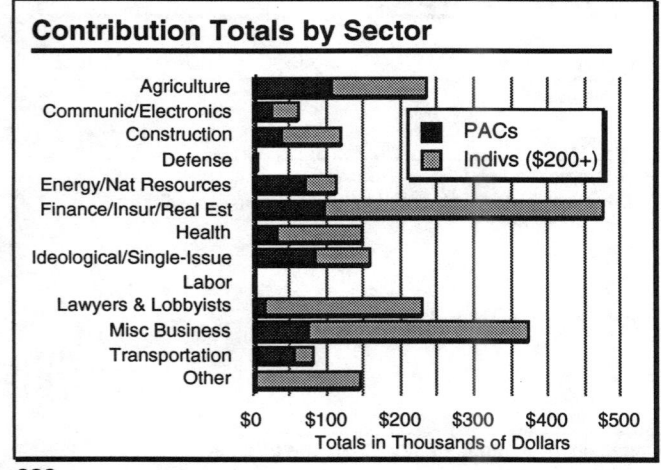

PACs
Indivs ($200+)

Agriculture
Communic/Electronics
Construction
Defense
Energy/Nat Resources
Finance/Insur/Real Est
Health
Ideological/Single-Issue
Labor
Lawyers & Lobbyists
Misc Business
Transportation
Other

$0 $100 $200 $300 $400 $500
Totals in Thousands of Dollars

Accountants	$24,326	
Ernst & Young	$6,400	Indiv
Misc Finance	**$39,050**	
None over $6,000		

Health $145,729

Health Professionals	$103,358	
American Medical Assn	$11,900	PAC
Hospitals/Nursing Homes	**$8,040**	
None over $6,000		
Health Services	**$8,500**	
None over $6,000		
Pharmaceuticals/Health Products	**$19,231**	
None over $6,000		
Misc Health	**$6,600**	
None over $6,000		

Lawyers & Lobbyists $226,287

Lawyers & Lobbyists	$226,287	
Jones, Day et al	$23,350	PAC/Ind
King & Spalding	$21,150	Indiv
Parker, Hudson et al	$18,126	Indiv
Sutherland, Asbill & Brennan	$13,600	Indiv
Arnall, Golden & Gregory	$9,200	Indiv
Alston & Bird	$7,831	Indiv
Powell, Goldstein et al	$6,400	PAC/Ind

Misc Business $369,908

Business Associations	$9,112	
None over $6,000		
Food & Beverage	**$55,280**	
Waffle House Inc	$18,850	Indiv
Coca-Cola Co	$8,950	PAC/Ind
Beer, Wine & Liquor	**$10,000**	
None over $6,000		
Retail Sales	**$24,850**	
T&S Hardwoods Inc	$6,900	Indiv
Misc Services	**$16,067**	
Rollins Inc	$9,000	Indiv
Business Services	**$100,255**	
BEI Holdings Inc	$12,300	Indiv
Norrell Corp	$8,730	Indiv
Coverdell & Co	$8,250	Indiv
RJM Group Inc	$7,000	Indiv

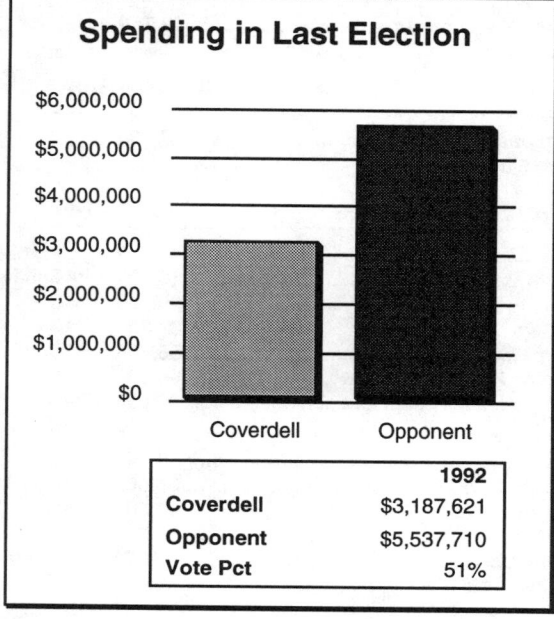

Spending in Last Election

	1992
Coverdell	$3,187,621
Opponent	$5,537,710
Vote Pct	51%

Lodging/Tourism	$12,150	
None over $6,000		
Chemical & Related Manufacturing	**$21,600**	
None over $6,000		
Misc Manufacturing & Distributing	**$86,650**	
Carson Products Co	$10,900	Indiv
Central Metals Co	$6,700	Indiv
Mode Inc	$6,500	Indiv
Textiles	**$28,244**	
S Lichtenberg & Co	$11,000	Indiv
Beaulien of America	$6,700	Indiv

Transportation $77,221

Air Transport	$8,950	
United Parcel Service	$6,000	PAC
Automotive	**$43,199**	
None over $6,000		
Trucking	**$6,000**	
None over $6,000		
Railroads	**$16,572**	
Union Pacific Corp	$10,072	PAC

Ideological/Single-Issue

Ideological/Single-Issue $155,765

Republican/Conservative	$79,485	
Loose Group	$15,000	PAC
Coverdell for Senate Committee	$11,995	Indiv
Leadership PACs	**$34,000**	
Campaign America (Bob Dole)	$21,000	PAC
Fund for Southern Progress (Carroll Campbell)	$6,000	PAC
Pro-Life	**$8,930**	
None over $6,000		
Gun Rights/Gun Control	**$9,900**	
National Rifle Assn	$9,900	PAC
Human Rights	**$6,000**	
None over $6,000		
Misc Issues	**$15,050**	
None over $6,000		

Other & Unknown

Other $141,195

Civil Servants/Public Officials	$24,100	
US Peace Corps	$7,050	Indiv
Education	**$20,304**	
American European Corp	$11,104	Indiv
Retired	**$94,241**	
None over $6,000		

Unknown $426,204

Unknown	$6,000	
Homemakers/Non-income earners	$49,728	
No Employer Listed or Found	$233,964	
Generic Occupation/Category Unknown	$7,100	
Employer Listed/Category Unknown	$133,412	
None over $6,000		

Independent expenditures supporting Coverdell

National Rifle Assn	$61,844
National Right to Life PAC	$15,327
Minnesota Citizens Concerned for Life	$8,585

* Contributions came from more than one affiliate or subsidiary.

Larry E. Craig (R-Idaho)

First elected: 1990

1989-92 Total Rcpts:	$1,784,600
1992 Year-end Cash:	$58,562
Current term expires:	1996

1991-92 Committees & Subcommittees

Agriculture, Nutrition and Forestry
Agricultural Credit; Conservation and Forestry (Ranking Republican); Rural Development and Rural Electrification

Energy and Natural Resources
Energy Research and Development; Mineral Resources Development and Production (Ranking Republican); Public Lands, National Parks and Forests

Special Aging

Leading Contributors

Business

Agriculture — $231,833

Crop Production & Basic Processing	**$36,180**	
American Sugarbeet Growers Assn	$5,800	PAC
JG Boswell Co	$5,000	PAC
Tobacco	**$11,550**	
None over $5,000		
Dairy	**$8,200**	
None over $5,000		
Livestock	**$18,750**	
National Cattlemen's Assn*	$6,800	PAC
Agricultural Services/Products	**$18,524**	
None over $5,000		
Food Processing & Sales	**$53,309**	
ConAgra Inc	$6,500	PAC
Albertson's Inc	$6,000	Indiv
JR Simplot Co	$5,309	PAC/Ind
Flowers Industries	$5,000	PAC
Pepsico Inc	$5,000	PAC
Forestry & Forest Products	**$80,320**	
Boise Cascade	$20,000	PAC/Ind
Potlatch Corp	$8,750	PAC/Ind
Bennett Lumber Products	$5,500	Indiv
International Paper Co	$5,000	PAC

Communications/Electronics — $40,000

Media/Entertainment	**$6,500**	
None over $5,000		
Telephone Utilities	**$17,500**	
US West Inc	$7,000	PAC

Contribution Totals by Sector

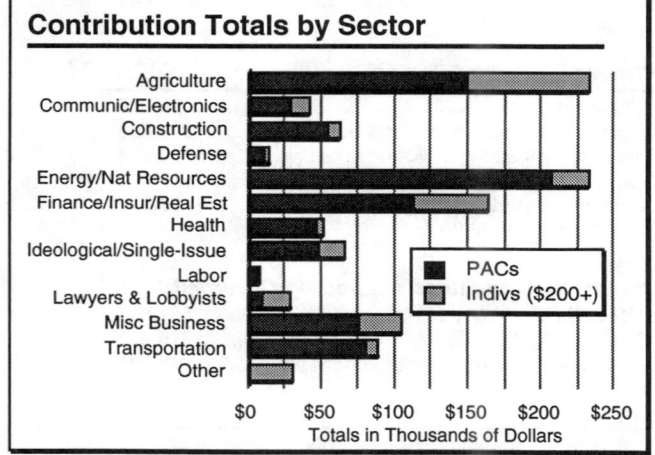

Totals in Thousands of Dollars

Source of Funds: 1987-1992

Source	Total	Pct
■ PACs	$818,479	43%
■ Indivs $200+	$365,911	19%
☐ Indivs under $200	$384,757	20%
⊠ Other	$336,077	18%
Candidate	$0	0%
Party	$120,624	6%

Source of PAC Dollars by Sector

Source	Total	Pct
■ Business	$763,490	93%
■ Labor	$6,300	1%
☐ Ideological/Single-Issue	$47,223	6%

In-State vs. Out-of-State Contributions*

Source	Total	Pct
☐ In-State	$198,753	54%
■ Out-of-state	$166,658	46%
No state listed	$500	

* by large individual contributors ($200 & above)

Telecom Services & Equipment	**$5,000**	
None over $5,000		
Electronics Mfg & Services	**$5,000**	
None over $5,000		

Construction — $61,700

General Contractors	**$24,700**	
Morrison-Knudsen	$7,000	PAC/Ind
Associated General Contractors	$5,300	PAC
Home Builders	**$9,500**	
National Assn of Home Builders	$8,500	PAC
Special Trade Contractors	**$9,000**	
National Electrical Contractors Assn	$7,000	PAC
Construction Services	**$8,750**	
None over $5,000		
Building Materials & Equipment	**$9,750**	
None over $5,000		

Defense — $13,300

Defense Aerospace	**$10,800**	
None over $5,000		

Energy & Natural Resources — $232,314

Oil & Gas	**$122,308**	
Amoco Corp	$10,500	PAC/Ind
Atlantic Richfield	$9,500	PAC
Chevron Corp	$7,858	PAC
Exxon Corp	$5,500	PAC/Ind
Dallas Energy PAC	$5,000	PAC
Mobil Oil	$5,000	PAC
Union Oil	$5,000	PAC
Mining	**$58,456**	
FMC Corp	$8,000	PAC
Cyprus Minerals Co	$7,500	PAC
Peabody Coal	$6,500	PAC
Arch Mineral Corp	$5,656	PAC/Ind
National Coal Assn	$5,000	PAC

Nuclear Energy $7,250
  None over $5,000

Misc Energy $8,150
  Cooper Industries .... $5,000   PAC

Electric Utilities $36,150
  Idaho Power Co .... $6,500   PAC/Ind
  ACRE (Action Cmte for Rural Electrification) .... $5,000   PAC

Finance, Insurance & Real Estate $162,579

Commercial Banks $20,225
  American Bankers Assn .... $10,000   PAC

Credit Unions $8,000
  Credit Union National Assn .... $8,000   PAC

Securities & Investment $20,250
  Salomon Brothers .... $8,000   PAC/Ind

Insurance $52,800
  National Assn of Life Underwriters .... $10,000   PAC

Real Estate $37,700
  National Assn of Realtors .... $10,000   PAC

Accountants $12,750
  American Institute of CPA's .... $10,000   PAC

Misc Finance $10,354
  None over $5,000

Health $50,650

Health Professionals $34,950
  American Medical Assn .... $10,000   PAC
  American Academy of Ophthalmology .... $5,000   PAC
  American Assn Oral & Maxillofacial Surgeons .... $5,000   PAC

Hospitals/Nursing Homes $6,200
  American Hospital Assn .... $5,200   PAC

Pharmaceuticals/Health Products $9,500
  None over $5,000

Lawyers & Lobbyists $27,108

Lawyers & Lobbyists $27,108
  None over $5,000

Misc Business $102,772

Business Associations $11,827
  National Fedn of Independent Business .... $8,040   PAC

Food & Beverage $12,250
  National Restaurant Assn .... $5,000   PAC

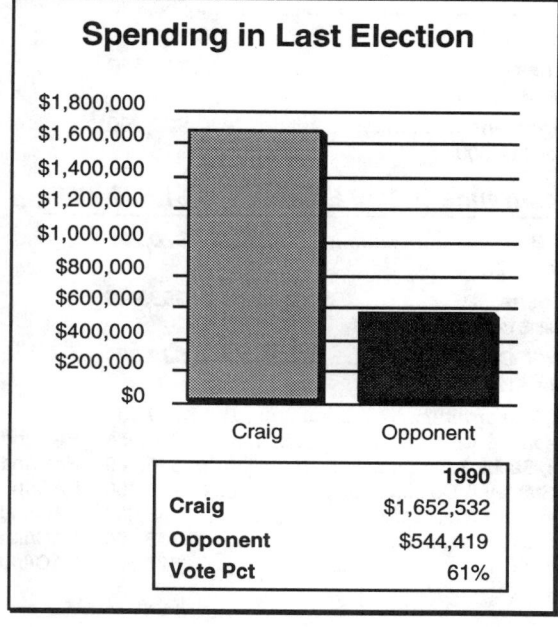

Spending in Last Election

	1990
Craig	$1,652,532
Opponent	$544,419
Vote Pct	61%

Beer, Wine & Liquor $10,150
  None over $5,000

Retail Sales $13,000
  International Council of Shopping Centers .... $5,000   PAC

Business Services $7,994
  None over $5,000

Lodging/Tourism $5,050
  None over $5,000

Misc Business $5,050
  None over $5,000

Chemical & Related Manufacturing $17,250
  Contran Corp .... $5,000   Indiv

Misc Manufacturing & Distributing $17,000
  None over $5,000

Transportation $86,665

Air Transport $23,100
  Aircraft Owners & Pilots Assn .... $5,000   PAC

Automotive $27,150
  National Auto Dealers Assn .... $6,300   PAC
  Auto Dealers & Drivers for Free Trade .... $6,000   PAC

Trucking $6,595
  None over $5,000

Railroads $23,370
  Union Pacific Corp .... $10,500   PAC

Labor

Labor $6,300

Public Sector Unions $6,000
  National Assn of Letter Carriers .... $5,000   PAC

Ideological/Single-Issue

Ideological/Single-Issue $65,123

Republican/Conservative $12,450
  None over $5,000

Leadership PACs $20,284
  Senate Victory Fund (Thad Cochran) .... $5,000   PAC

Pro-Israel $13,900
  None over $5,000

Gun Rights/Gun Control $10,689
  National Rifle Assn .... $9,689   PAC

Misc Issues $7,800
  None over $5,000

Other & Unknown

Other $29,225

Retired $23,625
  None over $5,000

Unknown $74,855

  No Employer Listed or Found $33,400
  Generic Occupation/Category Unknown $8,800
  Employer Listed/Category Unknown $28,650
    None over $5,000

Independent expenditures supporting Craig
  National Assn of Realtors $109,363
  National Right to Life PAC $7,736

* Contributions came from more than one affiliate or
subsidiary.

Alfonse M. D'Amato (R-NY)

First elected: 1980

1987-92 Total Rcpts:	$11,246,373
1992 Year-end Cash:	$144,716
Current term expires:	1998

1991-92 Committees & Subcommittees

Appropriations
Defense; Foreign Operations; Transportation and Related Agencies (Ranking Republican); Treasury, Postal Service and General Government; VA, HUD and Independent Agencies

Banking, Housing and Urban Affairs
Housing and Urban Affairs (Ranking Republican); Securities

Select Committee on Intelligence

Leading Contributors

Business

Agriculture	**$174,685**

Crop Production & Basic Processing	$36,090
None over $12,500	
Tobacco	$28,950
None over $12,500	
Food Processing & Sales	$72,300
None over $12,500	

Communications/Electronics	**$209,298**

Printing & Publishing	$34,000	
None over $12,500		
Media/Entertainment	$108,125	
Cablevision Systems Corp	$18,000	PAC/Ind
Telephone Utilities	$19,673	
None over $12,500		
Telecom Services & Equipment	$15,550	
None over $12,500		
Computer Equipment & Services	$19,850	
None over $12,500		

Construction	**$326,415**

General Contractors	$121,715
None over $12,500	
Home Builders	$47,300
None over $12,500	
Special Trade Contractors	$97,200
None over $12,500	

Contribution Totals by Sector

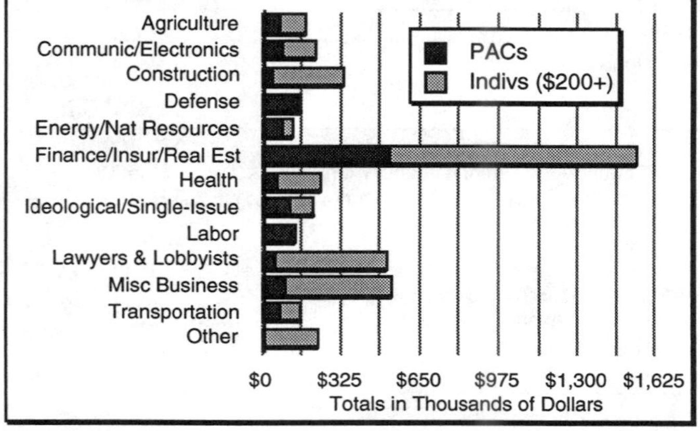

Agriculture
Communic/Electronics
Construction
Defense
Energy/Nat Resources
Finance/Insur/Real Est
Health
Ideological/Single-Issue
Labor
Lawyers & Lobbyists
Misc Business
Transportation
Other

PACs
Indivs ($200+)

$0 $325 $650 $975 $1,300 $1,625
Totals in Thousands of Dollars

Source of Funds: 1987-1992

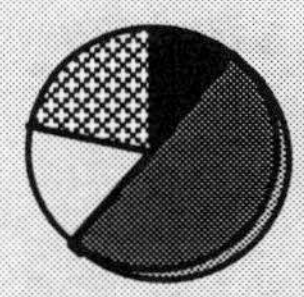

Source	Total	Pct
PACs	$1,349,131	11%
Indivs $200+	$6,511,908	51%
Indivs under $200	$2,124,916	17%
Other	$2,846,850	22%
Candidate	$0	0%
Party	$1,586,432	12%

Source of PAC Dollars by Sector

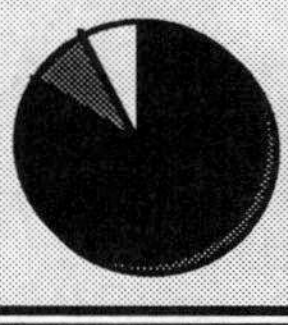

Source	Total	Pct
Business	$1,174,372	84%
Labor	$124,400	9%
Ideological/Single-Issue	$107,552	8%

In-State vs. Out-of-State Contributions*

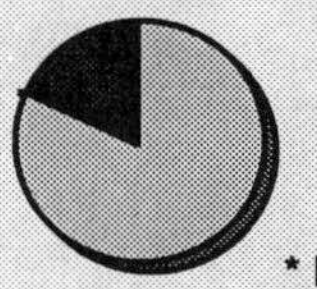

Source	Total	Pct
In-State	$5,257,029	81%
Out-of-state	$1,207,639	19%
No state listed	$7,500	

by large individual contributors ($200 & above)

Construction Services	$22,450
None over $12,500	
Building Materials & Equipment	$37,750
None over $12,500	

Defense	**$145,730**

Defense Aerospace	$72,600	
None over $12,500		
Defense Electronics	$58,830	
Harris Corp	$22,880	PAC/Ind
Misc Defense	$14,300	
None over $12,500		

Energy & Natural Resources	**$120,590**

Oil & Gas	$68,190
None over $12,500	
Electric Utilities	$16,550
None over $12,500	
Waste Management	$25,350
None over $12,500	

Finance, Insurance & Real Estate	**$1,539,784**

Commercial Banks	$70,225	
None over $12,500		
Savings & Loans	$93,980	
None over $12,500		
Finance/Credit Companies	$32,884	
None over $12,500		
Securities & Investment	$610,651	
Bear, Stearns & Co	$68,051	PAC/Ind
Goldman, Sachs & Co	$50,700	PAC/Ind
Morgan Stanley & Co	$45,450	PAC/Ind
Smith Barney	$35,600	PAC/Ind
American Express*	$35,100	PAC/Ind
Merrill Lynch	$28,605	PAC/Ind

PaineWebber	$17,250	PAC/Ind
Brown Brothers Harriman & Co	$14,500	Indiv
First Boston Corp	$13,500	PAC/Ind

Insurance **$196,856**
Reliance Group Holdings ....$13,000 PAC/Ind

Real Estate **$328,973**
None over $12,500

Accountants **$132,115**
Coopers & Lybrand	$22,990	PAC/Ind
Arthur Andersen & Co	$15,750	PAC/Ind
KPMG Peat Marwick	$14,800	Indiv
Ernst & Young	$12,500	PAC/Ind

Misc Finance **$63,100**
None over $12,500

Health $233,600

Health Professionals **$140,450**
American Medical Assn* ....$13,400 PAC

Hospitals/Nursing Homes **$47,725**
None over $12,500

Pharmaceuticals/Health Products **$25,050**
None over $12,500

Lawyers & Lobbyists $505,035

Lawyers & Lobbyists **$505,035**
None over $12,500

Misc Business $528,131

Food & Beverage **$54,860**
None over $12,500

Beer, Wine & Liquor **$46,100**
None over $12,500

Retail Sales **$67,050**
None over $12,500

Misc Services **$14,100**
None over $12,500

Business Services **$101,970**
None over $12,500

Lodging/Tourism **$28,500**
None over $12,500

Chemical & Related Manufacturing **$25,216**
None over $12,500

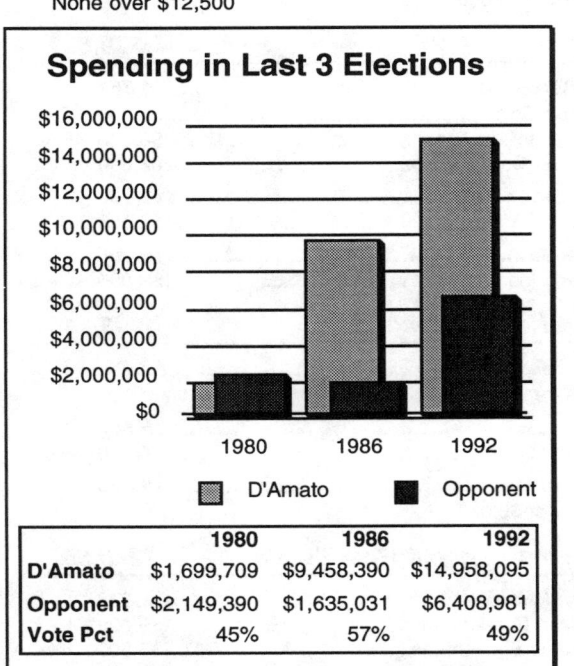

Spending in Last 3 Elections

	1980	1986	1992
D'Amato	$1,699,709	$9,458,390	$14,958,095
Opponent	$2,149,390	$1,635,031	$6,408,981
Vote Pct	45%	57%	49%

Legend: ▨ D'Amato   ■ Opponent

Misc Manufacturing & Distributing **$136,690**
None over $12,500

Textiles **$18,200**
None over $12,500

Transportation $152,355

Air Transport **$38,830**
None over $12,500

Automotive **$24,975**
None over $12,500

Railroads **$22,800**
None over $12,500

Sea Transport **$21,600**
None over $12,500

Misc Transport **$32,150**
None over $12,500

Labor

Labor $129,200

Building Trade Unions **$43,700**
Operating Engineers Union* ....$13,200 PAC/Ind

Transportation Unions **$75,100**
Teamsters Union* ....$13,500 PAC/Ind

Ideological/Single-Issue

Ideological/Single-Issue $204,187

Republican/Conservative **$17,060**
None over $12,500

Leadership PACs **$23,000**
Campaign America (Bob Dole) ....$14,000 PAC/Ind

Pro-Israel **$110,702**
None over $12,500

Human Rights **$22,875**
None over $12,500

Other & Unknown

Other $223,521

Other **$22,200**
None over $12,500

Civil Servants/Public Officials **$51,930**
None over $12,500

Education **$38,960**
None over $12,500

Retired **$103,806**
None over $12,500

Unknown $1,810,977

Homemakers/Non-income earners	$277,212
No Employer Listed or Found	$712,530
Generic Occupation/Category Unknown	$12,860
Employer Listed/Category Unknown	$806,875
National Right to Life PAC	$16,102

None over $12,500

Independent expenditures opposing D'Amato
National Abortion Rights Action League $44,583

* Contributions came from more than one affiliate or subsidiary.

John C. Danforth (R-Mo)

First elected: 1976

1987-92 Total Rcpts:	$4,268,154
1992 Year-end Cash:	$645,961
Current term expires:	1994

1991-92 Committees & Subcommittees

Commerce, Science and Transportation (Ranking Republican)
National Ocean Policy Study

Finance
International Trade (Ranking Republican); Medicare and Long Term Care; Taxation

Select Committee on Intelligence

Leading Contributors

NOTE: The bulk of Danforth's large individual contributions do not appear in the listings below. His last election was in 1988, and this book lists individual contributions only from 1989-1992.

Business

Agriculture — $77,120

Dairy **$12,500**
    Mid-America Dairymen .... $10,000   PAC
Agricultural Services/Products **$22,800**
    None over $6,000
Food Processing & Sales **$18,720**
    None over $6,000
Forestry & Forest Products **$10,000**
    None over $6,000

Communications/Electronics — $124,925

Printing & Publishing **$11,500**
    Hallmark Cards .... $9,000   PAC
Media/Entertainment **$31,150**
    None over $6,000
Telephone Utilities **$47,571**
    AT&T .... $8,000   PAC
    United Telecommunications .... $6,000   PAC
Telecom Services & Equipment **$9,204**
    None over $6,000
Electronics Mfg & Services **$13,500**
    None over $6,000
Computer Equipment & Services **$12,000**
    None over $6,000

Source of Funds: 1987-1992

Source	Total	Pct
PACs	$1,200,406	26%
Indivs $200+	$1,562,989	34%
Indivs under $200	$1,098,547	24%
Other	$700,316	15%
Candidate	$0	0%
Party	$294,104	6%

Source of PAC Dollars by Sector

Source	Total	Pct
Business	$1,130,319	93%
Labor	$10,000	1%
Ideological/Single-Issue	$78,287	6%

In-State vs. Out-of-State Contributions*

Source	Total	Pct
In-State	$1,024,552	66%
Out-of-state	$536,987	34%
No state listed	$1,450	

*** by large individual contributors ($200 & above)**

Construction — $59,250

General Contractors **$22,250**
    Associated General Contractors .... $10,000   PAC
    Heavy Constructors Assn .... $6,000   PAC
Home Builders **$10,500**
    National Assn of Home Builders .... $10,000   PAC
Special Trade Contractors **$10,500**
    Sheet Metal/Air Conditioning Contractors ...... $6,000   PAC
Construction Services **$8,500**
    None over $6,000
Building Materials & Equipment **$7,500**
    None over $6,000

Defense — $79,861

Defense Aerospace **$44,361**
    Northrop Corp .... $8,000   PAC
    Rockwell International .... $8,000   PAC
    Lockheed Corp .... $6,000   PAC
Defense Electronics **$19,500**
    Emerson Electric .... $10,000   PAC
Misc Defense **$16,000**
    Tenneco Inc .... $7,000   PAC

Energy & Natural Resources — $93,140

Oil & Gas **$52,455**
    None over $6,000
Mining **$18,500**
    Peabody Coal .... $6,000   PAC
Electric Utilities **$13,685**
    None over $6,000

Finance, Insurance & Real Estate — $270,657

Commercial Banks **$32,048**
    American Bankers Assn .... $9,000   PAC
    Boatmens Bankshares .... $8,500   PAC

Contribution Totals by Sector

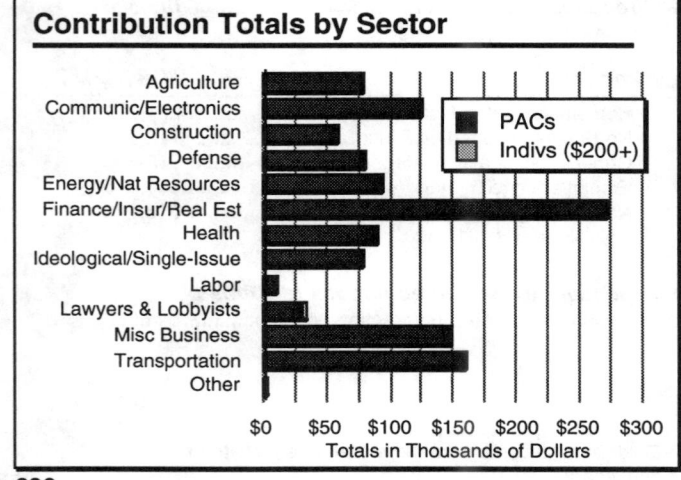

Categories (top to bottom): Agriculture, Communic/Electronics, Construction, Defense, Energy/Nat Resources, Finance/Insur/Real Est, Health, Ideological/Single-Issue, Labor, Lawyers & Lobbyists, Misc Business, Transportation, Other

Legend: ■ PACs   ▨ Indivs ($200+)

Totals in Thousands of Dollars ($0, $50, $100, $150, $200, $250, $300)

Savings & Loans	$17,000	
US League of Savings Assns	$9,000	PAC
Securities & Investment	**$50,084**	
Goldman, Sachs & Co	$10,000	PAC
Insurance	**$133,625**	
National Assn of Life Underwriters	$10,000	PAC
Business Mens Assurance Co	$9,000	PAC
National Assn of Prof Insurance Agents	$8,000	PAC
Independent Insurance Agents of America	$7,999	PAC
General American Life Insurance	$6,500	PAC
Real Estate	**$10,900**	
None over $6,000		
Accountants	**$19,500**	
American Institute of CPA's	$7,000	PAC

Health $89,650

Health Professionals	**$33,200**	
American Medical Assn	$8,500	PAC
American Academy of Ophthalmology	$7,000	PAC
Hospitals/Nursing Homes	**$16,050**	
American Health Care Assn	$6,500	PAC
Pharmaceuticals/Health Products	**$40,400**	
None over $6,000		

Lawyers & Lobbyists $32,836

| **Lawyers & Lobbyists** | **$32,836** | |
| None over $6,000 | | |

Misc Business $147,649

Food & Beverage	**$8,300**	
None over $6,000		
Beer, Wine & Liquor	**$25,649**	
National Beer Wholesalers Assn	$7,149	PAC
Retail Sales	**$14,307**	
May Department Stores	$7,250	PAC
Business Services	**$9,500**	
None over $6,000		
Chemical & Related Manufacturing	**$35,590**	
Monsanto Co	$10,765	PAC/Ind

Steel Production	$6,500	
None over $6,000		
Misc Manufacturing & Distributing	**$29,900**	
None over $6,000		

Transportation $159,576

Air Transport	**$47,500**	
McDonnell Douglas	$10,000	PAC
Federal Express Corp	$8,000	PAC
Boeing Co	$6,500	PAC
United Parcel Service	$6,000	PAC
Automotive	**$38,150**	
Chrysler Corp	$8,000	PAC
Trucking	**$27,614**	
Yellow Freight System	$7,000	PAC
Railroads	**$36,100**	
Kansas City Southern	$10,000	PAC
Union Pacific Corp	$8,000	PAC

Labor

| Labor | $10,500 |
| None over $6,000 | |

Ideological/Single-Issue

Ideological/Single-Issue	**$78,287**	
Leadership PACs	**$22,000**	
None over $6,000		
Pro-Israel	**$37,500**	
St Louisians for Better Government	$10,000	PAC
Human Rights	**$9,000**	
None over $6,000		

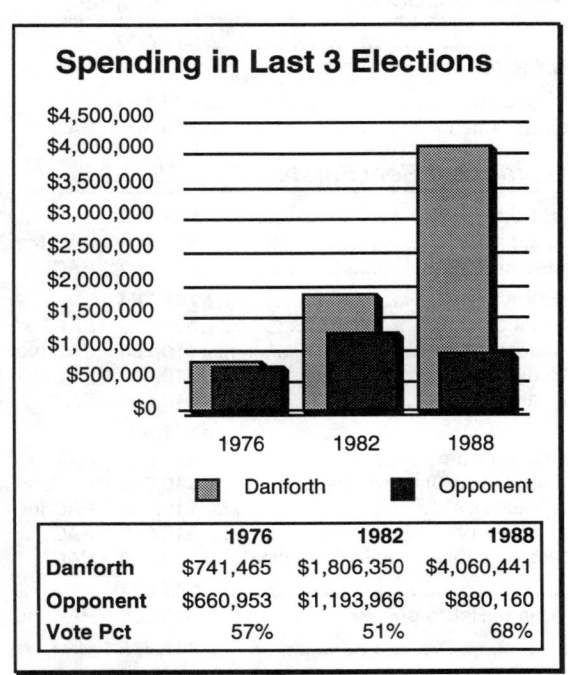

Spending in Last 3 Elections

	1976	1982	1988
Danforth	$741,465	$1,806,350	$4,060,441
Opponent	$660,953	$1,193,966	$880,160
Vote Pct	57%	51%	68%

Legend: ▨ Danforth ■ Opponent

Tom Daschle (D-SD)

1991-92 Committees & Subcommittees

Agriculture, Nutrition and Forestry
Agricultural Credit; Agricultural Research and General Legislation (Chairman); Rural Development and Rural Electrification

Finance
Energy and Agricultural Taxation (Chairman); International Trade; Medicare and Long Term Care

Veterans' Affairs

Select Committee on Indian Affairs

Select Committee on POW/MIA Affairs

Leading Contributors

Business

Agriculture	$244,408

Crop Production & Basic Processing $65,583
None over $10,000

Tobacco $17,750
None over $10,000

Dairy $24,000
Associated Milk Producers .... $10,000   PAC

Poultry & Eggs $13,000
None over $10,000

Livestock $24,550
None over $10,000

Agricultural Services/Products $67,125
Archer-Daniels-Midland Corp .... $13,500   PAC/Ind
American Assn of Crop Insurers .... $10,000   PAC

Food Processing & Sales $31,400
None over $10,000

Communications/Electronics	$152,585

Printing & Publishing $18,250
None over $10,000

Media/Entertainment $62,500
Time Warner* .... $11,000   PAC/Ind

Contribution Totals by Sector

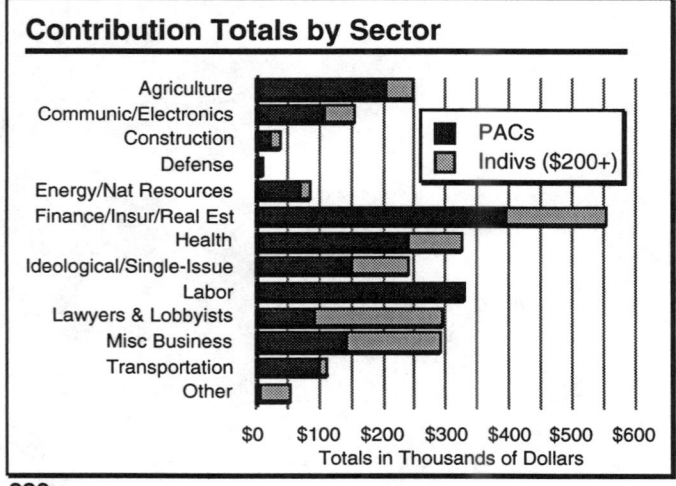

Totals in Thousands of Dollars

First elected: 1986

1987-92 Total Rcpts:	$4,122,119
1992 Year-end Cash:	$192,096
Current term expires:	1998

Source of Funds: 1987-1992

Source	Total	Pct
PACs	$1,832,046	44%
Indivs $200+	$1,090,003	26%
Indivs under $200	$952,098	23%
Other	$323,352	8%
Candidate	$0	0%
Party	$75,380	2%

Source of PAC Dollars by Sector

Source	Total	Pct
Business	$1,357,107	74%
Labor	$323,850	18%
Ideological/Single-Issue	$149,760	8%

In-State vs. Out-of-State Contributions*

Source	Total	Pct
In-State	$170,492	16%
Out-of-state	$918,261	84%
No state listed	$500	

* by large individual contributors ($200 & above)

Telephone Utilities $57,585
None over $10,000

Computer Equipment & Services $10,000
None over $10,000

Construction	$35,700

Home Builders $12,000
None over $10,000

Defense	$11,000

Energy & Natural Resources	$80,920

Oil & Gas $39,000
None over $10,000

Electric Utilities $28,170
ACRE (Action Cmte for Rural Electrification) ..... $10,500   PAC

Finance, Insurance & Real Estate	$548,236

Commercial Banks $93,162
Citicorp .... $12,499   PAC/Ind
American Bankers Assn .... $12,000   PAC

Securities & Investment $147,784
Salomon Brothers .... $27,250   PAC/Ind
Chicago Mercantile Exchange .... $10,750   PAC/Ind
Chicago Board of Options Exchange .... $10,000   PAC
Chicago Board of Trade .... $10,000   PAC

Insurance $185,524
American Family Corp .... $11,000   PAC
National Assn of Life Underwriters .... $10,500   PAC/Ind
Prudential Insurance .... $10,500   PAC/Ind
American Council of Life Insurance .... $10,000   PAC
Independent Insurance Agents of America .... $10,000   PAC

Real Estate $75,291
National Assn of Realtors .... $10,500   PAC/Ind

Accountants $21,475
None over $10,000

Misc Finance $12,750
   None over $10,000

Health $321,849

Health Professionals $179,549
   American Chiropractic Assn* .... $12,249   PAC
   American Academy of Ophthalmology .... $11,000   PAC
   American Podiatry Assn .... $11,000   PAC
   American Dental Assn .... $10,000   PAC
   American Medical Assn .... $10,000   PAC
   American Soc Cataract/Refractive Surgery .... $10,000   PAC
   Assn for the Advancement of Psychology .... $10,000   PAC

Hospitals/Nursing Homes $63,700
   Hospice Care Inc .... $18,500   Indiv
   American Health Care Assn .... $10,000   PAC
   American Hospital Assn .... $10,000   PAC

Health Services $13,500
   None over $10,000

Pharmaceuticals/Health Products $58,650
   Invacare Corp .... $15,000   PAC/Ind

Lawyers & Lobbyists $291,165

Lawyers & Lobbyists $291,165
   Mansour, Gavin et al .... $12,500   Indiv
   Cassidy & Associates .... $11,674   Indiv
   Assn of Trial Lawyers of America .... $10,000   PAC

Misc Business $287,897

Food & Beverage $21,750
   None over $10,000

Beer, Wine & Liquor $88,139
   Gallo Winery .... $18,000   Indiv
   Wine Institute .... $13,000   PAC/Ind
   Florida Distillers Co .... $10,000   Indiv

Retail Sales $47,776
   None over $10,000

Business Services $46,500
   None over $10,000

Casinos/Gambling $21,232
   None over $10,000

Misc Manufacturing & Distributing $22,550
   None over $10,000

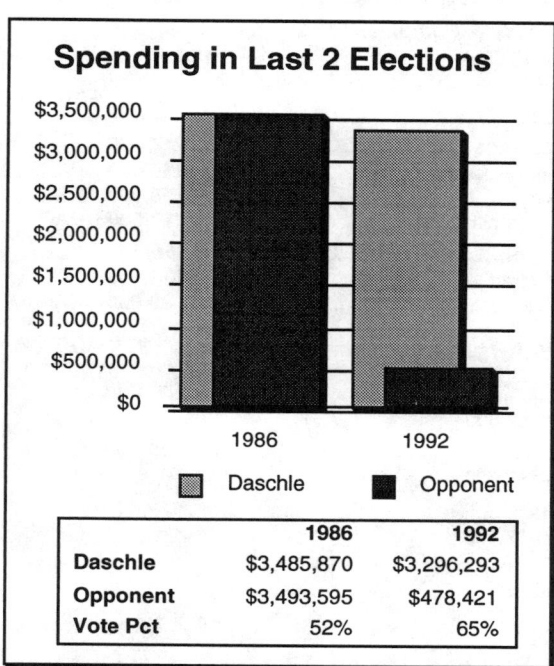

Spending in Last 2 Elections

	1986	1992
Daschle	$3,485,870	$3,296,293
Opponent	$3,493,595	$478,421
Vote Pct	52%	65%

Transportation $111,124

Air Transport $60,500
   Aircraft Owners & Pilots Assn .... $11,000   PAC
   Federal Experss Corp .... $10,000   PAC

Automotive $17,250
   None over $10,000

Railroads $16,499
   None over $10,000

Labor

Labor $325,100

Building Trade Unions $46,500
   Carpenters & Joiners Union .... $10,000   PAC
   Laborers' Political League .... $10,000   PAC

Industrial Unions $72,075
   Intl Brotherhood of Electrical Workers* .... $10,250   PAC/Ind
   Communications Workers of America .... $10,000   PAC
   Machinists/Aerospace Workers Union .... $10,000   PAC
   United Auto Workers .... $10,000   PAC
   United Steelworkers .... $10,000   PAC

Transportation Unions $78,000
   Marine Engineers Union* .... $12,500   PAC
   Air Line Pilots Assn .... $10,000   PAC
   Seafarers International Union .... $10,000   PAC
   Teamsters Union .... $10,000   PAC
   United Transportation Union .... $10,000   PAC

Public Sector Unions $85,475
   National Assn of Letter Carriers .... $11,000   PAC
   American Federation of Teachers .... $10,000   PAC
   American Fedn of St/Cnty/Munic Employees .... $10,000   PAC

Misc Unions $43,050
   Food & Commercial Workers Union .... $15,000   PAC

Ideological/Single-Issue

Ideological/Single-Issue $236,886

Democratic/Liberal $22,015
   None over $10,000

Pro-Israel $161,961
   Citizens Organized PAC .... $10,000   PAC
   Desert Caucus .... $10,000   PAC
   Washington PAC .... $10,000   PAC
   Women's Alliance for Israel .... $10,000   PAC

Human Rights $16,400
   KidsPAC .... $10,000   PAC

Misc Issues $12,250
   National Cmte to Preserve Social Security .... $10,000   PAC

Other & Unknown

Other $53,400

Civil Servants/Public Officials $12,000
   None over $10,000

Retired $20,600
   None over $10,000

Unknown $163,848

   Homemakers/Non-income earners $30,300
   No Employer Listed or Found $33,350
   Generic Occupation/Category Unknown $16,600
   Employer Listed/Category Unknown $83,098
      None over $10,000

* Contributions came from more than one affiliate or
subsidiary.

Dennis DeConcini (D-Ariz)

First elected: 1976

1987-92 Total Rcpts:	$3,487,272
1992 Year-end Cash:	$269,245
Current term expires:	1994

1991-92 Committees & Subcommittees

Appropriations
Defense; Energy and Water Development; Foreign Operations; Interior and Related Agencies; Treasury, Postal Service and General Government (Chairman)

Judiciary
Antitrust, Monopolies and Business Rights; Constitution; Patents, Copyrights and Trademarks (Chairman)

Rules and Administration

Veterans' Affairs

Select Committee on Indian Affairs

Select Committee on Intelligence

Joint Committee on the Library

Joint Committee on Printing

Leading Contributors

NOTE: The bulk of DeConcini's large individual contributions do not appear in the listings below. His last election was in 1988, and this book lists individual contributions only from 1989-1992.

Business

Agriculture $101,199

Crop Production & Basic Processing	**$40,750**	
Sunkist Growers	$8,000	PAC
Tobacco	**$9,999**	
Philip Morris	$7,999	PAC
Livestock	**$8,650**	
None over $7,500		
Agricultural Services/Products	**$10,250**	
None over $7,500		
Food Processing & Sales	**$17,000**	
None over $7,500		
Forestry & Forest Products	**$11,550**	
None over $7,500		

Source of Funds: 1987-1992

Source	Total	Pct
PACs	$1,289,492	36%
Indivs $200+	$1,338,439	38%
Indivs under $200	$559,985	16%
Other	$351,256	10%
Candidate	$0	0%
Party	$51,900	1%

Source of PAC Dollars by Sector

Source	Total	Pct
Business	$999,342	78%
Labor	$179,700	14%
Ideological/Single-Issue	$109,564	8%

In-State vs. Out-of-State Contributions*

Source	Total	Pct
In-State	$620,982	47%
Out-of-state	$712,107	53%
No state listed	$2,000	

* by large individual contributors ($200 & above)

Communications/Electronics $117,472

Media/Entertainment	**$84,972**	
MCA Inc	$11,000	PAC
Turner Broadcasting System	$10,000	PAC
Telephone Utilities	**$15,500**	
None over $7,500		

Construction $39,983

General Contractors	**$10,500**	
None over $7,500		
Home Builders	**$16,983**	
National Assn of Home Builders	$10,000	PAC
Building Materials & Equipment	**$7,500**	
None over $7,500		

Defense $136,569

Defense Aerospace	**$77,800**	
Allied-Signal	$9,000	PAC
Textron Inc	$8,000	PAC
General Dynamics	$7,500	PAC
Defense Electronics	**$56,769**	
Hughes Aircraft	$11,300	PAC
AT&T	$9,000	PAC

Energy & Natural Resources $79,600

Oil & Gas	**$30,050**	
None over $7,500		
Mining	**$23,400**	
None over $7,500		
Electric Utilities	**$19,650**	
None over $7,500		

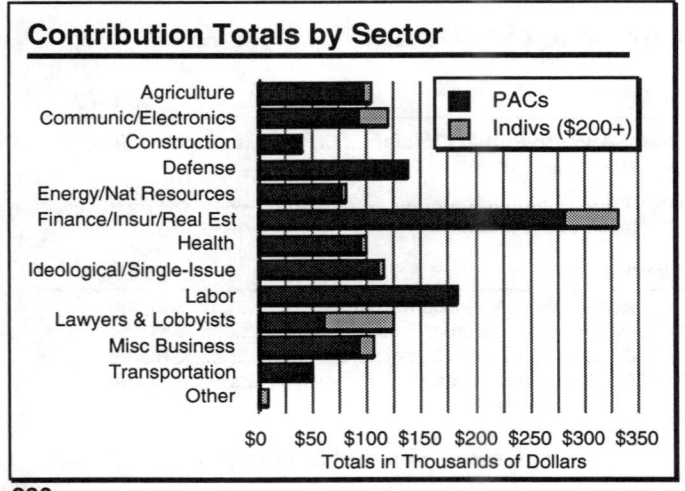

Contribution Totals by Sector

Agriculture
Communic/Electronics
Construction
Defense
Energy/Nat Resources
Finance/Insur/Real Est
Health
Ideological/Single-Issue
Labor
Lawyers & Lobbyists
Misc Business
Transportation
Other

■ PACs
▨ Indivs ($200+)

$0 $50 $100 $150 $200 $250 $300 $350
Totals in Thousands of Dollars

Finance, Insurance & Real Estate $328,150

Commercial Banks **$44,950**
    JP Morgan & Co ....$10,000 PAC
    American Bankers Assn ....$9,000 PAC

Savings & Loans **$16,650**
    US League of Savings Assns ....$9,000 PAC

Credit Unions **$8,750**
    Credit Union National Assn ....$8,500 PAC

Finance/Credit Companies **$9,000**
    None over $7,500

Securities & Investment **$56,000**
    Chicago Mercantile Exchange ....$14,000 PAC
    Dean Witter ....$11,000 PAC

Insurance **$105,400**
    National Assn of Independent Insurers ....$14,000 PAC
    National Assn of Life Underwriters.....................$12,000 PAC

Real Estate **$47,750**
    Estes Co ....$8,500 PAC

Accountants **$27,550**
    American Institute of CPA's ....$15,000 PAC

Misc Finance **$12,100**
    None over $7,500

Health $97,656

Health Professionals **$34,500**
    American Medical Assn........................$7,500 PAC

Pharmaceuticals/Health Products **$57,156**
    Warner-Lambert ....$13,000 PAC/Ind

Lawyers & Lobbyists $121,212

Lawyers & Lobbyists **$121,212**
    Assn of Trial Lawyers of America ......$11,000 PAC
    Akin, Gump et al ....$9,000 PAC/Ind

Misc Business $104,613

Beer, Wine & Liquor **$37,663**
    National Beer Wholesalers Assn ....$12,000 PAC

Retail Sales **$13,250**
    None over $7,500

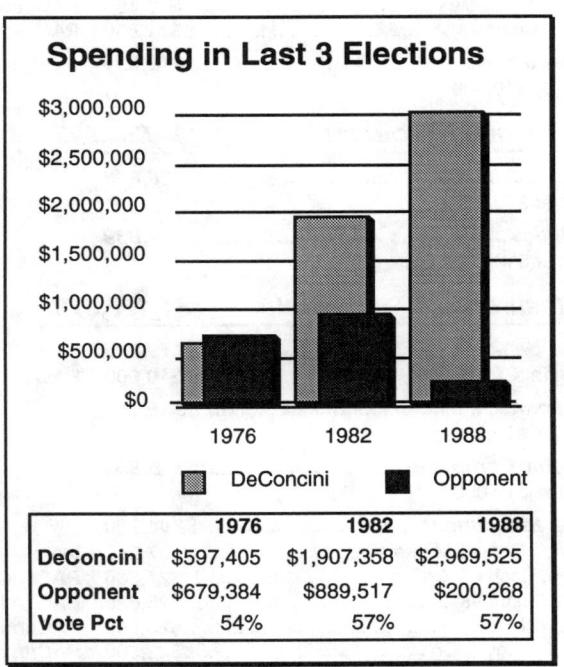

Spending in Last 3 Elections

DeConcini / Opponent

	1976	1982	1988
DeConcini	$597,405	$1,907,358	$2,969,525
Opponent	$679,384	$889,517	$200,268
Vote Pct	54%	57%	57%

Business Services **$12,000**
    None over $7,500

Lodging/Tourism **$7,850**
    None over $7,500

Chemical & Related Manufacturing **$9,800**
    None over $7,500

Misc Manufacturing & Distributing **$8,900**
    None over $7,500

Transportation $47,850

Air Transport **$26,550**
    Federal Express Corp ....$7,500 PAC
    United Parcel Service ....$7,500 PAC

Automotive **$10,300**
    None over $7,500

Labor

Labor $179,700

Building Trade Unions **$24,850**
    Laborers' Western Political League ....$10,000 PAC

Industrial Unions **$26,200**
    Intl Brotherhood of Electrical Workers ....$9,000 PAC

Transportation Unions **$45,000**
    Air Line Pilots Assn ....$10,000 PAC
    Marine Engineers Union* ....$10,000 PAC
    Teamsters Union ....$8,000 PAC

Public Sector Unions **$70,070**
    National Assn of Letter Carriers ....$10,000 PAC
    Natl Assn of Retired Federal Employees ....$10,000 PAC
    American Postal Workers Union ....$8,000 PAC

Misc Unions **$13,580**
    None over $7,500

Ideological/Single-Issue

Ideological/Single-Issue $113,564

Leadership PACs **$35,329**
    Senate Majority Fund (Daniel Inouye) ....$10,000 PAC

Foreign & Defense Policy **$7,750**
    None over $7,500

Pro-Israel **$47,750**
    Washington PAC ....$10,000 PAC

Human Rights **$9,000**
    None over $7,500

Other & Unknown

Other $7,500
    None over $7,500

Unknown $80,479

    No Employer Listed or Found $36,774
    Employer Listed/Category Unknown $40,755
        None over $7,500

Independent expenditures supporting DeConcini
    National Cmte to Preserve Social Security $20,780

---

* Contributions came from more than one affiliate or subsidiary.

Christopher J. Dodd (D-Conn)

First elected: 1980

1987-92 Total Rcpts:	$4,342,880
1992 Year-end Cash:	$62,777
Current term expires:	1998

1991-92 Committees & Subcommittees

Banking, Housing and Urban Affairs
Housing and Urban Affairs; Securities (Chairman)

Budget

Foreign Relations
East Asian and Pacific Affairs; International Economic Policy, Trade, Oceans and Environment; Western Hemisphere and Peace Corps Affairs (Chairman)

Labor and Human Resources
Aging; Children, Families, Drugs and Alcoholism (Chairman); Education, Arts and Humanities; Labor

Rules and Administration

Leading Contributors

Business

Agriculture		$95,800

Crop Production & Basic Processing $12,250
None over $10,000

Tobacco $37,700
US Tobacco Co .... $26,200 PAC/Ind

Food Processing & Sales $15,550
None over $10,000

Forestry & Forest Products $13,000
None over $10,000

Communications/Electronics		$219,018

Printing & Publishing $21,350
None over $10,000

Media/Entertainment $147,900
Time Warner* .... $28,500 PAC/Ind
Sony Corp/Columbia Pictures* .... $11,750 Indiv

Telephone Utilities $29,268
None over $10,000

Telecom Services & Equipment $15,250
None over $10,000

Construction		$95,200

General Contractors $36,950
None over $10,000

Contribution Totals by Sector

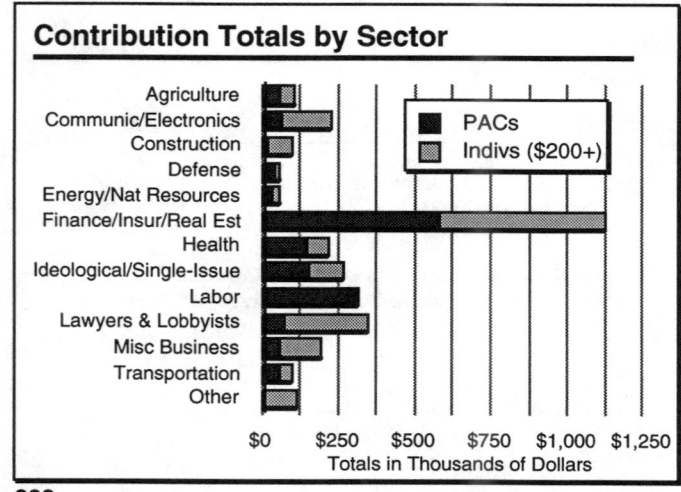

Totals in Thousands of Dollars

Source of Funds: 1987-1992

Source	Total	Pct
PACs	$1,530,634	33%
Indivs $200+	$2,049,367	45%
Indivs under $200	$539,909	12%
Other	$462,439	10%
Candidate	$0	0%
Party	$239,469	5%

Source of PAC Dollars by Sector

Source	Total	Pct
Business	$1,067,880	70%
Labor	$306,609	20%
Ideological/Single-Issue	$146,525	10%

In-State vs. Out-of-State Contributions*

Source	Total	Pct
In-State	$927,833	46%
Out-of-state	$1,106,234	54%
No state listed	$1,750	

* by large individual contributors ($200 & above)

Home Builders $14,950
None over $10,000

Special Trade Contractors $10,400
None over $10,000

Construction Services $12,450
None over $10,000

Building Materials & Equipment $20,450
Ply-Gem Industries .... $11,000 Indiv

Defense		$53,934

Defense Aerospace $41,100
United Technologies .... $15,150 PAC/Ind
General Dynamics .... $11,650 PAC/Ind

Defense Electronics $12,834
None over $10,000

Energy & Natural Resources		$54,922

Oil & Gas $28,683
None over $10,000

Electric Utilities $11,839
None over $10,000

Finance, Insurance & Real Estate		$1,120,378

Commercial Banks $119,575
JP Morgan & Co .... $10,000 PAC

Savings & Loans $39,142
None over $10,000

Finance/Credit Companies $15,850
None over $10,000

Securities & Investment $394,750
Greenwich Capital Markets .... $37,250 Indiv
Goldman, Sachs & Co .... $27,266 PAC/Ind
American Express* .... $25,625 PAC/Ind
Merrill Lynch .... $23,500 PAC/Ind
Morgan Stanley & Co .... $22,500 PAC/Ind
Salomon Brothers .... $18,000 Indiv

First Boston Corp .... $13,500 PAC/Ind
Chicago Mercantile Exchange .... $10,000 PAC
Donaldson, Lufkin & Jenrette .... $10,000 Indiv
Princeton Venture Research .... $10,000 Indiv

Insurance $283,358
ITT Corp* .... $26,325 PAC/Ind
Cigna Corp .... $23,200 PAC/Ind
Aetna Life & Casualty .... $20,100 PAC/Ind
Travelers Corp .... $14,000 PAC/Ind
Casualty & Surety Agents Assn .... $11,000 PAC
National Assn of Prof Insurance Agents .... $10,000 PAC
Textron Inc .... $10,000 PAC

Real Estate $153,503
Transcon Builders Inc .... $10,000 Indiv

Accountants $77,450
Coopers & Lybrand .... $11,900 PAC/Ind
Arthur Andersen & Co .... $11,000 PAC/Ind
Ernst & Young .... $11,000 PAC
Deloitte & Touche .... $10,000 PAC

Misc Finance $26,750
None over $10,000

Health $210,797

Health Professionals $98,324
US Surgical Corp .... $18,480 Indiv

Hospitals/Nursing Homes $12,400
None over $10,000

Pharmaceuticals/Health Products $91,798
None over $10,000

Lawyers & Lobbyists $339,250

Lawyers & Lobbyists $339,250
Verner, Liipfert et al .... $12,174 PAC/Ind

Misc Business $185,679

Beer, Wine & Liquor $28,850
None over $10,000

Business Services $50,104
None over $10,000

Chemical & Related Manufacturing $14,650
None over $10,000

Misc Manufacturing & Distributing $32,025
None over $10,000

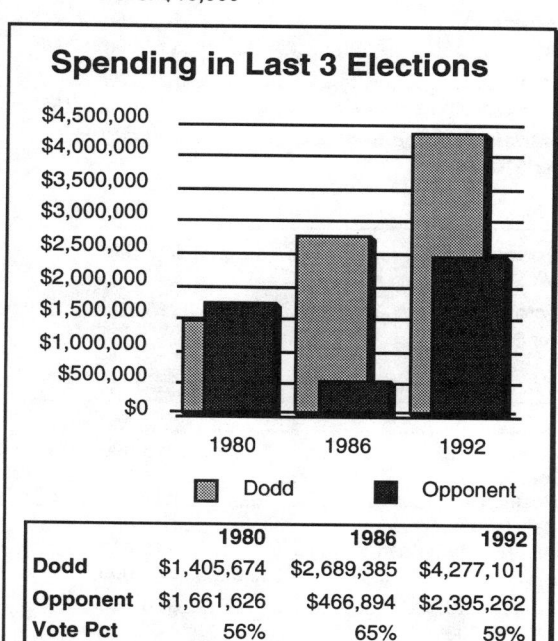

Spending in Last 3 Elections

	1980	1986	1992
Dodd	$1,405,674	$2,689,385	$4,277,101
Opponent	$1,661,626	$466,894	$2,395,262
Vote Pct	56%	65%	59%

Transportation $91,550

Air Transport $35,350
Federal Express Corp .... $10,000 PAC

Automotive $25,350
Auto Dealers & Drivers for Free Trade .... $10,000 PAC

Trucking $11,650
None over $10,000

Labor

Labor $307,009

Building Trade Unions $55,500
Bricklayers Union .... $10,000 PAC
Carpenters & Joiners Union* .... $10,000 PAC

Industrial Unions $72,450
Intl Brotherhood of Electrical Workers .... $10,200 PAC/Ind
Machinists/Aerospace Workers Union .... $10,000 PAC
United Auto Workers .... $10,000 PAC

Transportation Unions $74,000
Air Line Pilots Assn .... $10,000 PAC
Marine Engineers Union .... $10,000 PAC
Teamsters Union .... $10,000 PAC
United Transportation Union .... $10,000 PAC

Public Sector Unions $71,209
American Fedn of St/Cnty/Munic Employees .... $10,000 PAC
National Assn of Letter Carriers .... $10,000 PAC
National Assn Retired Federal Employees .... $10,000 PAC
National Education Assn .... $10,000 PAC

Misc Unions $33,850
Food & Commercial Workers Union .... $10,000 PAC
Service Employees International Union .... $10,000 PAC

Ideological/Single-Issue

Ideological/Single-Issue $256,810

Democratic/Liberal $25,985
None over $10,000

Leadership PACs $20,000
Fund for a Democratic Majority (Ted Kennedy) . $10,000 PAC

Pro-Israel $150,750
Citizens Organized PAC .... $10,000 PAC
Desert Caucus .... $10,000 PAC

Human Rights $39,500
KidsPAC .... $10,000 PAC
National Community Action Foundation .... $10,000 PAC

Other & Unknown

Other $110,990

Civil Servants/Public Officials $14,575
None over $10,000

Education $30,190
None over $10,000

Retired $55,125
None over $10,000

Unknown $408,607

Homemakers/Non-income earners $45,920
No Employer Listed or Found $156,253
Generic Occupation/Category Unknown $12,330
Employer Listed/Category Unknown $193,604
None over $10,000

* Contributions came from more than one affiliate or subsidiary.

Bob Dole (R-Kan)

First elected: 1968

1987-92 Total Rcpts:	$3,143,115
1992 Year-end Cash:	$1,756,483
Current term expires:	1998

1991-92 Committees & Subcommittees

Agriculture, Nutrition and Forestry
Agricultural Production and Stabilization of Prices; Agricultural Research and General Legislation; Nutrition and Investigations

Finance
Energy and Agricultural Taxation; Medicare and Long Term Care; Social Security and Family Policy (Ranking Republican)

Rules and Administration

Joint Committee on Taxation

Leading Contributors

Business

Agriculture — $430,350

Crop Production & Basic Processing	**$95,782**	
Sun-Diamond Growers*	$11,000	PAC
Tobacco	**$54,250**	
US Tobacco Co	$19,000	PAC/Ind
Philip Morris	$16,250	PAC/Ind
Dairy	**$40,000**	
Mid-America Dairymen	$11,000	PAC
Milk Industry Foundation	$11,000	PAC
Poultry & Eggs	**$16,500**	
None over $10,000		
Livestock	**$24,500**	
None over $10,000		
Agricultural Services/Products	**$88,250**	
Archer-Daniels-Midland Corp	$12,000	PAC/Ind
Food Processing & Sales	**$93,568**	
ConAgra Inc	$15,000	PAC
Forestry & Forest Products	**$17,500**	
None over $10,000		

Communications/Electronics — $229,600

Printing & Publishing	**$29,200**	
Hallmark Cards	$17,750	PAC/Ind
Media/Entertainment	**$62,500**	
Time Warner*	$11,000	PAC
National Cable Television Assn	$10,000	PAC

Contribution Totals by Sector

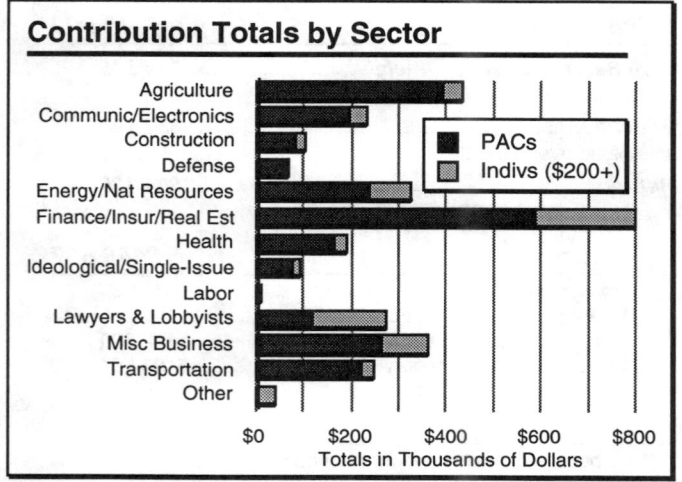

Totals in Thousands of Dollars

Source of Funds: 1987-1992

Source	Total	Pct
PACs	$1,597,189	50%
Indivs $200+	$927,728	29%
Indivs under $200	$125,489	4%
Other	$526,944	17%
Candidate	$42	0%
Party	$34,235	1%

Source of PAC Dollars by Sector

Source	Total	Pct
Business	$2,288,564	96%
Labor	$9,500	0%
Ideological/Single-Issue	$74,968	3%

In-State vs. Out-of-State Contributions*

Source	Total	Pct
In-State	$192,499	21%
Out-of-state	$734,229	79%
No state listed	$1,000	

* by large individual contributors ($200 & above)

Telephone Utilities	**$101,650**	
AT&T	$15,000	PAC
Pacific Telesis Group	$12,000	PAC
Southwestern Bell	$11,500	PAC
Bell Atlantic*	$11,000	PAC
Ameritech Corp	$10,000	PAC
United Telecommunications	$10,000	PAC
Electronics Mfg & Services	**$15,500**	
None over $10,000		
Computer Equipment & Services	**$13,250**	
None over $10,000		

Construction — $100,250

General Contractors	**$43,250**	
Fluor Corp	$17,000	PAC
Home Builders	**$21,500**	
National Assn of Home Builders	$15,000	PAC
Building Materials & Equipment	**$20,000**	
None over $10,000		

Defense — $66,104

Defense Aerospace	**$47,500**	
None over $10,000		
Defense Electronics	**$16,104**	
None over $10,000		

Energy & Natural Resources — $319,187

Oil & Gas	**$204,000**	
Coastal Corp	$18,000	PAC/Ind
Enron Corp	$14,500	PAC/Ind
Koch Industries	$14,000	PAC/Ind
Occidental Petroleum*	$11,000	PAC
Petroleum Marketers Assn	$10,000	PAC
Shell Oil	$10,000	PAC
Mining	**$18,000**	
None over $10,000		

Misc Energy $14,000
    None over $10,000

Electric Utilities $41,500
    ACRE (Action Cmte for Rural Electrification) ..... $10,000   PAC

Waste Management $42,187
    Waste Management Inc .... $29,187   PAC/Ind

Finance, Insurance & Real Estate $795,271

Commercial Banks $130,340
    Barnett Banks Inc .... $12,500   PAC
    American Bankers Assn .... $10,000   PAC

Savings & Loans $42,700
    None over $10,000

Securities & Investment $205,050
    Salomon Brothers .... $32,000   PAC/Ind
    Chicago Mercantile Exchange .... $10,750   PAC/Ind
    Chicago Board of Trade .... $10,000   PAC
    PaineWebber .... $10,000   PAC

Insurance $258,589
    Torchmark Corp .... $15,667   PAC/Ind
    Metropolitan Life Insurance .... $12,070   PAC
    Massachusetts Mutual Life Insurance .... $10,000   PAC
    National Assn of Life Underwriters .... $10,000   PAC

Real Estate $71,842
    National Assn of Realtors .... $14,999   PAC

Accountants $26,000
    None over $10,000

Misc Finance $37,750
    Stephens Overseas Services .... $10,600   PAC

Health $186,100

Health Professionals $62,750
    American Medical Assn* .... $10,000   PAC

Hospitals/Nursing Homes $48,850
    None over $10,000

Pharmaceuticals/Health Products $69,500
    Glaxo Inc .... $10,000   PAC

Lawyers & Lobbyists $267,617

Lawyers & Lobbyists $267,617
    Marks, Murase & White .... $14,000   Indiv
    Vinson & Elkins .... $13,000   PAC/Ind

Spending in Last 3 Elections

	1980	1986	1992
Dole	$1,224,494	$1,772,049	$2,169,603
Opponent	$339,987	$0	$249,359
Vote Pct	64%	70%	63%

Misc Business $358,728

Food & Beverage $38,500
    None over $10,000

Beer, Wine & Liquor $58,750
    Gallo Winery .... $20,000   Indiv
    National Beer Wholesalers Assn .... $12,000   PAC

Retail Sales $60,021
    Limited Inc .... $10,077   PAC
    International Council of Shopping Centers .... $10,000   PAC

Business Services $39,767
    None over $10,000

Lodging/Tourism $15,750
    Marriott Corp .... $10,000   PAC

Chemical & Related Manufacturing $26,190
    None over $10,000

Misc Manufacturing & Distributing $54,400
    None over $10,000

Textiles $26,500
    None over $10,000

Transportation $245,786

Air Transport $100,624
    Aircraft Owners & Pilots Assn .... $15,000   PAC
    Federal Express Corp .... $15,000   PAC
    Boeing Co .... $11,000   PAC/Ind
    Beech Aircraft .... $10,000   PAC
    United Parcel Service .... $10,000   PAC

Automotive $58,000
    Auto Dealers & Drivers for Free Trade .... $15,000   PAC
    Americans for Free International Trade .... $10,000   PAC
    National Auto Dealers Assn .... $10,000   PAC

Trucking $35,162
    Yellow Freight System .... $11,500   PAC

Railroads $36,000
    Union Pacific Corp .... $10,000   PAC

Sea Transport $11,000
    None over $10,000

Ideological/Single-Issue

Ideological/Single-Issue $91,168

Republican/Conservative $17,700
    None over $10,000

Leadership PACs $19,466
    None over $10,000

Human Rights $27,552
    National Albanian American PAC .... $10,000   PAC

Other & Unknown

Other $38,990

Retired $20,540
    None over $10,000

Unknown $117,518

    Homemakers/Non-income earners $32,450
    Generic Occupation/Category Unknown $10,200
    Employer Listed/Category Unknown $72,849
       None over $10,000

Independent expenditures supporting Dole
    American Citizens for Political Action $58,644

* Contributions came from more than one affiliate or
subsidiary.

Pete V. Domenici (R-NM)

First elected: 1972

1987-92 Total Rcpts: $2,231,577
1992 Year-end Cash: $111,153
Current term expires: 1996

1991-92 Committees & Subcommittees

Appropriations
Defense; Energy and Water Development; Interior and Related Agencies; Transportation and Related Agencies; Treasury, Postal Service and General Government (Ranking Republican)

Banking, Housing and Urban Affairs
Housing and Urban Affairs; International Finance and Monetary Policy

Budget (Ranking Republican)

Energy and Natural Resources
Energy Regulation and Conservation; Energy Research and Development (Ranking Republican); Public Lands, National Parks and Forests

Select Committee on Indian Affairs

Leading Contributors

Business

Agriculture	$91,150	
Crop Production & Basic Processing $19,700		
None over $6,000		
Tobacco $23,000		
Philip Morris $11,000	PAC/Ind	
Livestock $19,750		
National Cattlemen's Assn* $6,500	PAC	
Agricultural Services/Products $8,000		
None over $6,000		
Food Processing & Sales $9,375		
None over $6,000		

Communications/Electronics	$42,083	
Media/Entertainment $21,608		
National Assn of Broadcasters $7,000	PAC	
Telephone Utilities $11,500		
None over $6,000		

Source of Funds: 1987-1992

Source	Total	Pct
■ PACs	$901,574	38%
▨ Indivs $200+	$693,458	29%
☐ Indivs under $200	$420,274	18%
▥ Other	$340,531	14%
Candidate	$0	0%
Party	$124,260	5%

Source of PAC Dollars by Sector

Source	Total	Pct
■ Business	$814,774	92%
▨ Labor	$33,750	4%
☐ Ideological/Single-Issue	$41,750	5%

In-State vs. Out-of-State Contributions*

Source	Total	Pct
☐ In-State	$328,778	48%
■ Out-of-state	$363,430	52%
No state listed	$1,250	

* by large individual contributors ($200 & above)

Construction	$50,450	
General Contractors $22,500		
None over $6,000		
Home Builders $8,500		
None over $6,000		
Construction Services $7,000		
None over $6,000		
Building Materials & Equipment $6,950		
None over $6,000		

Defense	$100,842	
Defense Aerospace $53,900		
Northrop Corp $7,000	PAC	
Lockheed Corp $6,000	PAC	
Defense Electronics $32,712		
GTE Corp* $6,000	PAC	
Misc Defense $14,230		
BDM International $7,380	PAC/Ind	

Energy & Natural Resources	$368,064	
Oil & Gas $232,435		
Union Pacific Corp $8,000	PAC	
Columbia Gas System* $7,250	PAC	
Chevron Corp $6,500	PAC	
Amoco Corp $6,000	PAC	
Mobil Oil $6,000	PAC/Ind	
Mining $41,000		
Fluor Corp $6,000	PAC	
Nuclear Energy $13,000		
None over $6,000		
Misc Energy $13,279		
None over $6,000		

Contribution Totals by Sector

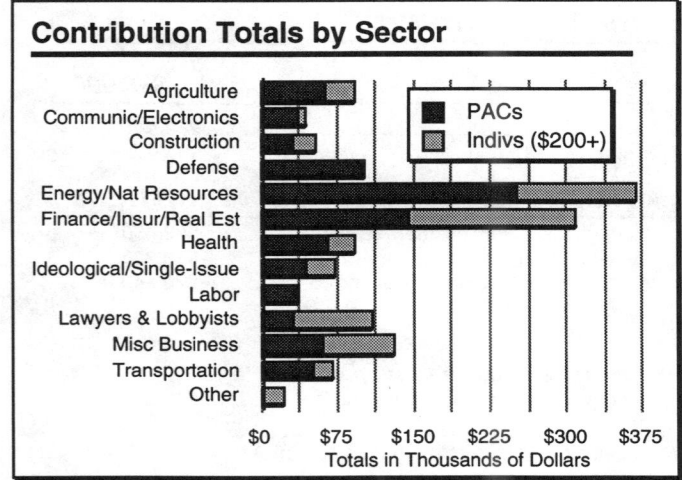

Agriculture
Communic/Electronics
Construction
Defense
Energy/Nat Resources
Finance/Insur/Real Est
Health
Ideological/Single-Issue
Labor
Lawyers & Lobbyists
Misc Business
Transportation
Other

■ PACs
▨ Indivs ($200+)

$0 $75 $150 $225 $300 $375
Totals in Thousands of Dollars

Electric Utilities *$54,350*
    Pacific Gas & Electric ....$7,000   PAC

Waste Management *$9,000*
    None over $6,000

Finance, Insurance & Real Estate   **$307,315**

Commercial Banks *$50,755*
    United New Mexico Financial Corp ....$11,900   PAC/Ind
    American Bankers Assn ....$10,000   PAC

Savings & Loans *$7,400*
    None over $6,000

Securities & Investment *$102,235*
    Salomon Brothers ....$46,800   PAC/Ind

Insurance *$61,682*
    Independent Insurance Agents of America ....$10,000   PAC
    National Assn of Life Underwriters ....$6,000   PAC

Real Estate *$59,118*
    National Assn of Realtors ....$7,000   PAC
    Drizin Real Estate Developers ....$6,000   Indiv

Accountants *$8,175*
    None over $6,000

Misc Finance *$17,200*
    None over $6,000

Health   **$90,050**

Health Professionals *$43,750*
    None over $6,000

Hospitals/Nursing Homes *$11,700*
    None over $6,000

Health Services *$6,000*
    Family Health Program Inc ....$6,000   PAC

Pharmaceuticals/Health Products *$27,100*
    None over $6,000

Lawyers & Lobbyists   **$106,523**

Lawyers & Lobbyists *$106,523*
    Dow, Lohnes & Albertson ....$9,000   Indiv

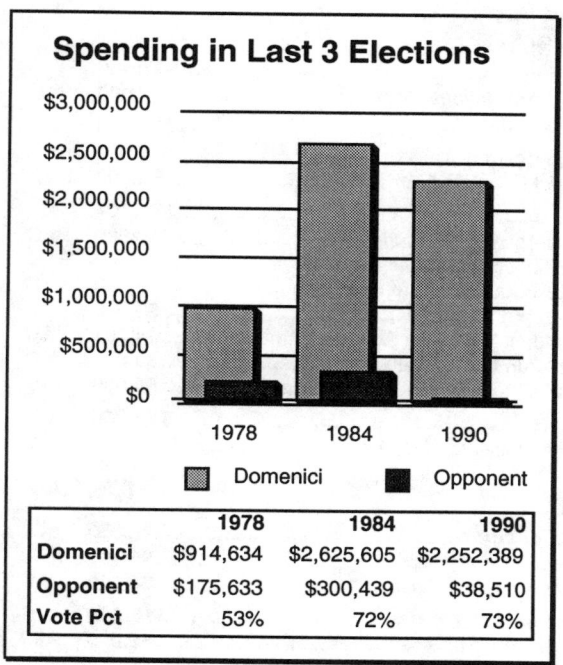

Spending in Last 3 Elections

	1978	1984	1990
Domenici	$914,634	$2,625,605	$2,252,389
Opponent	$175,633	$300,439	$38,510
Vote Pct	53%	72%	73%

■ Domenici   ■ Opponent

Misc Business   **$128,570**

Food & Beverage *$22,335*
    None over $6,000

Beer, Wine & Liquor *$19,600*
    National Beer Wholesalers Assn ....$10,000   PAC

Retail Sales *$26,150*
    None over $6,000

Business Services *$14,365*
    None over $6,000

Lodging/Tourism *$6,695*
    None over $6,000

Chemical & Related Manufacturing *$9,000*
    None over $6,000

Misc Manufacturing & Distributing *$12,800*
    None over $6,000

Transportation   **$68,700**

Air Transport *$24,000*
    Federal Express Corp ....$6,000   PAC
    Texas Air ....$6,000   PAC
    United Parcel Service ....$6,000   PAC

Automotive *$29,850*
    National Auto Dealers Assn ....$6,500   PAC

Trucking *$7,500*
    None over $6,000

Labor

Labor   **$33,750**

Public Sector Unions *$32,750*
    National Assn of Letter Carriers ....$7,000   PAC
    Natl Assn of Retired Federal Employees ....$7,000   PAC
    National Rural Letter Carriers Assn ....$6,000   PAC

Ideological/Single-Issue

Ideological/Single-Issue   **$71,300**

Republican/Conservative *$15,300*
    National Republican Senatorial Cmte ....$7,500   Indiv

Leadership PACs *$6,000*
    None over $6,000

Pro-Israel *$32,550*
    Desert Caucus ....$10,000   PAC

Human Rights *$8,000*
    None over $6,000

Other & Unknown

Other   **$19,555**

Retired *$9,930*
    None over $6,000

Unknown   **$121,380**

    Homemakers/Non-income earners $9,550
    No Employer Listed or Found $28,205
    Employer Listed/Category Unknown $79,375
        None over $6,000

* Contributions came from more than one affiliate or subsidiary.

Byron L. Dorgan (D-ND)

1991-92 House Committee Assignments

Ways and Means
Select Revenue Measures; Trade

Select Committee on Hunger

First elected: 1992

1991-92 Total Rcpts:	$1,061,651
1992 Year-end Cash:	$107,654
Current term expires:	1998

Leading Contributors

Business

Agriculture — $98,545

Crop Production & Basic Processing	**$26,295**	
American Crystal Sugar Corp	$5,000	PAC
Tobacco	**$12,000**	
US Tobacco Co	$5,000	PAC
Dairy	**$12,500**	
Associated Milk Producers	$10,000	PAC
Livestock	**$5,000**	
None over $4,000		
Agricultural Services/Products	**$27,150**	
Archer-Daniels-Midland Corp	$7,000	PAC/Ind
Food Processing & Sales	**$12,100**	
Winn-Dixie Stores	$5,000	PAC
Connell Rice & Sugar Co	$4,000	Indiv

Communications/Electronics — $27,962

Printing & Publishing	**$6,500**	
West Publishing	$5,000	PAC
Media/Entertainment	**$7,000**	
None over $4,000		
Telephone Utilities	**$10,962**	
AT&T	$6,000	PAC

Source of Funds: 1987-1992

Source	Total	Pct
PACs	$776,943	68%
Indivs $200+	$74,100	7%
Indivs under $200	$139,382	12%
Other	$144,273	13%
Candidate	$0	0%
Party	$73,047	6%

Source of PAC Dollars by Sector

Source	Total	Pct
Business	$500,814	65%
Labor	$219,300	28%
Ideological/Single-Issue	$51,162	7%

In-State vs. Out-of-State Contributions*

Source	Total	Pct
In-State	$0	0%
Out-of-state	$73,100	100%
No state listed	$1,000	

* by large individual contributors ($200 & above)

Energy & Natural Resources — $48,800

Oil & Gas	**$17,500**	
Ashland Oil	$5,000	PAC
Coastal Corp	$5,000	PAC
Mining	**$9,500**	
None over $4,000		
Electric Utilities	**$17,000**	
ACRE (Action Cmte for Rural Electrification)	$10,000	PAC

Finance, Insurance & Real Estate — $161,201

Commercial Banks	**$9,000**	
None over $4,000		
Credit Unions	**$11,500**	
Credit Union National Assn	$10,000	PAC
Securities & Investment	**$27,500**	
Chicago Board of Trade	$10,000	PAC
Chicago Mercantile Exchange	$5,000	PAC
Insurance	**$95,101**	
National Assn of Life Underwriters	$10,000	PAC
Massachusetts Mutual Life Insurance	$7,500	PAC
American Council of Life Insurance	$5,000	PAC
American Family Corp	$5,000	PAC
Independent Insurance Agents of America	$4,101	PAC
Metropolitan Life Insurance	$4,000	PAC
Pacific Mutual Life	$4,000	PAC
Accountants	**$11,900**	
American Institute of CPA's	$10,000	PAC

Health — $56,900

Health Professionals	**$38,850**	
American Dental Assn	$5,500	PAC
American Podiatry Assn	$4,000	PAC
Hospitals/Nursing Homes	**$11,250**	
American Hospital Assn	$5,000	PAC

Contribution Totals by Sector

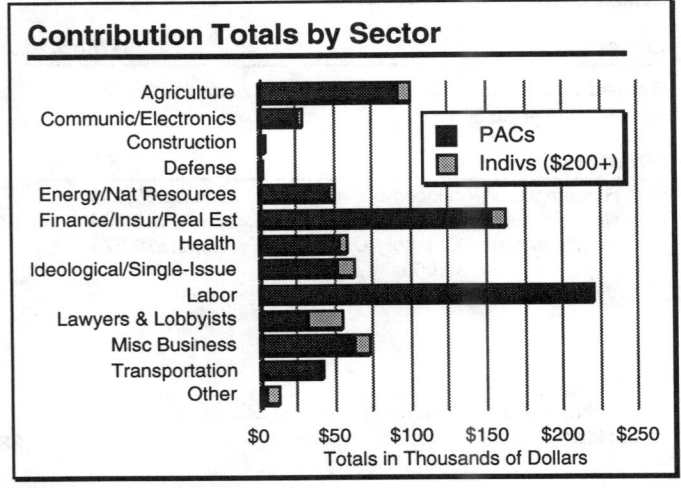

Legend: PACs, Indivs ($200+)

Categories: Agriculture, Communic/Electronics, Construction, Defense, Energy/Nat Resources, Finance/Insur/Real Est, Health, Ideological/Single-Issue, Labor, Lawyers & Lobbyists, Misc Business, Transportation, Other

Totals in Thousands of Dollars ($0, $50, $100, $150, $200, $250)

Lawyers & Lobbyists $54,249

Lawyers & Lobbyists $54,249
Assn of Trial Lawyers of America	$10,000	PAC
Opperman, Heins & Paquin	$4,999	PAC

Misc Business $71,957

Food & Beverage $19,250
National Restaurant Assn	$10,000	PAC
S&A Restaurant Corp	$4,500	PAC

Beer, Wine & Liquor $22,750
Joseph E Seagram & Sons	$4,500	PAC

Retail Sales $8,007
None over $4,000

Business Services $10,750
None over $4,000

Misc Manufacturing & Distributing $5,500
None over $4,000

Transportation $40,900

Air Transport $23,500
United Parcel Service	$7,500	PAC
Aircraft Owners & Pilots Assn	$5,000	PAC

Automotive $10,000
National Auto Dealers Assn	$5,500	PAC

Labor

Labor $219,300

Building Trade Unions $30,000
Laborers' Political League	$8,000	PAC
Carpenters & Joiners Union	$7,000	PAC
Plumbers/Pipefitters Union	$6,000	PAC

Industrial Unions $46,750
United Auto Workers	$9,500	PAC
Machinists/Aerospace Workers Union	$9,000	PAC
Communications Workers of America	$5,000	PAC
Intl Brotherhood of Electrical Workers	$5,000	PAC
United Steelworkers	$5,000	PAC
United Mine Workers	$4,000	PAC

Transportation Unions $52,250
United Transportation Union	$11,000	PAC
Air Line Pilots Assn	$10,000	PAC
Teamsters Union	$10,000	PAC
Marine Engineers Union	$7,500	PAC
Seafarers International Union	$5,000	PAC

Public Sector Unions $68,000
American Federation of Teachers	$10,000	PAC
National Assn of Letter Carriers	$10,000	PAC
National Education Assn	$10,000	PAC
National Rural Letter Carriers Assn	$10,000	PAC
American Postal Workers Union	$7,500	PAC
American Fedn of St/Cnty/Munic Employees	$6,000	PAC
National Assn Retired Federal Employees	$6,000	PAC

Misc Unions $22,300
AFL-CIO	$7,500	PAC
Food & Commercial Workers Union	$7,500	PAC
Service Employees International Union	$5,000	PAC

Ideological/Single-Issue

Ideological/Single-Issue $62,062

Democratic/Liberal $7,150
None over $4,000

Leadership PACs $5,000
None over $4,000

Foreign & Defense Policy $5,762
None over $4,000

Pro-Israel $22,700
National PAC	$5,000	PAC

Gun Rights/Gun Control $4,450
National Rifle Assn	$4,450	PAC

Human Rights $7,500
National Community Action Foundation	$4,000	PAC

Misc Issues $9,000
National Cmte to Preserve Social Security	$6,000	PAC

Other & Unknown

Other $11,100

Other $4,500
None over $4,000

Unknown $12,700
No Employer Listed or Found	$5,200	
None over $4,000		

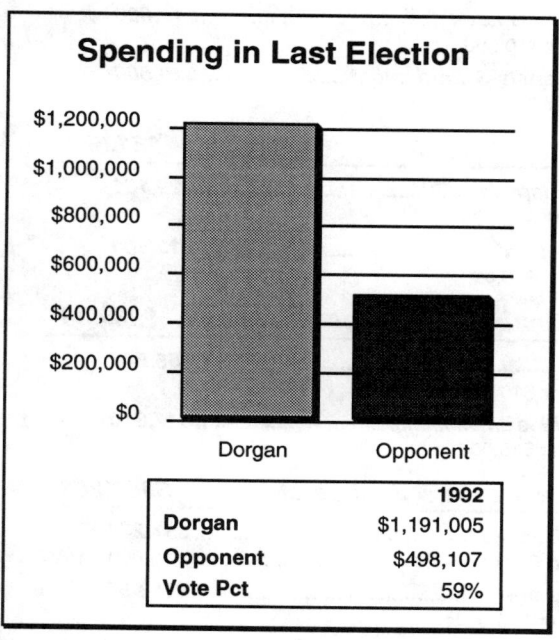

Spending in Last Election

	1992
Dorgan	$1,191,005
Opponent	$498,107
Vote Pct	59%

Dave Durenberger (R-Minn)

First elected: 1978

1987-92 Total Rcpts:	$6,388,791
1992 Year-end Cash:	$27,191
Current term expires:	1994

1991-92 Committees & Subcommittees

Environment and Public Works
Environmental Protection; Superfund, Ocean and Water Protection (Ranking Republican); Water Resources, Transportation and Infrastructure

Finance
Health for Families and the Uninsured; Medicare and Long Term Care (Ranking Republican); Social Security and Family Policy

Labor and Human Resources
Aging; Children, Families, Drugs and Alcoholism; Disability Policy (Ranking Republican); Employment and Productivity

Special Aging

Leading Contributors

NOTE: The bulk of Durenberger's large individual contributions do not appear in the listings below. His last election was in 1988, and this book lists individual contributions only from 1989-1992.

Business

Agriculture		$207,146
Crop Production & Basic Processing		$29,851
None over $10,000		
Tobacco		$15,266
None over $10,000		
Dairy		$28,400
None over $10,000		
Agricultural Services/Products		$37,950
Cargill Inc	$10,000	PAC
Food Processing & Sales		$50,550
None over $10,000		
Forestry & Forest Products		$31,029
None over $10,000		

Communications/Electronics		$93,147
Printing & Publishing		$13,112
None over $10,000		
Media/Entertainment		$12,250
None over $10,000		
Telephone Utilities		$32,785
None over $10,000		

Source of Funds: 1987-1992

Source	Total	Pct
■ PACs	$1,723,548	26%
▨ Indivs $200+	$1,191,717	18%
☐ Indivs under $200	$3,195,330	48%
▧ Other	$552,093	8%
Candidate	$0	0%
Party	$273,897	4%

Source of PAC Dollars by Sector

Source	Total	Pct
■ Business	$1,427,868	82%
▨ Labor	$69,872	4%
☐ Ideological/Single-Issue	$234,643	14%

In-State vs. Out-of-State Contributions*

Source	Total	Pct
☐ In-State	$749,796	63%
■ Out-of-state	$438,421	37%
No state listed	$1,500	

* by large individual contributors ($200 & above)

Electronics Mfg & Services		$17,000
Honeywell Inc	$10,000	PAC
Computer Equipment & Services		$15,500
None over $10,000		

Construction		$91,075
General Contractors		$26,000
None over $10,000		
Home Builders		$12,775
None over $10,000		
Special Trade Contractors		$21,000
National Electrical Contractors Assn	$12,000	PAC
Construction Services		$10,800
None over $10,000		
Building Materials & Equipment		$20,500
None over $10,000		

Defense		$51,661
Defense Aerospace		$29,161
None over $10,000		
Defense Electronics		$13,500
None over $10,000		

Energy & Natural Resources		$93,408
Oil & Gas		$56,848
None over $10,000		
Electric Utilities		$17,310
None over $10,000		

Finance, Insurance & Real Estate		$382,203
Commercial Banks		$51,241
American Bankers Assn	$10,000	PAC
Savings & Loans		$11,950
None over $10,000		

Contribution Totals by Sector

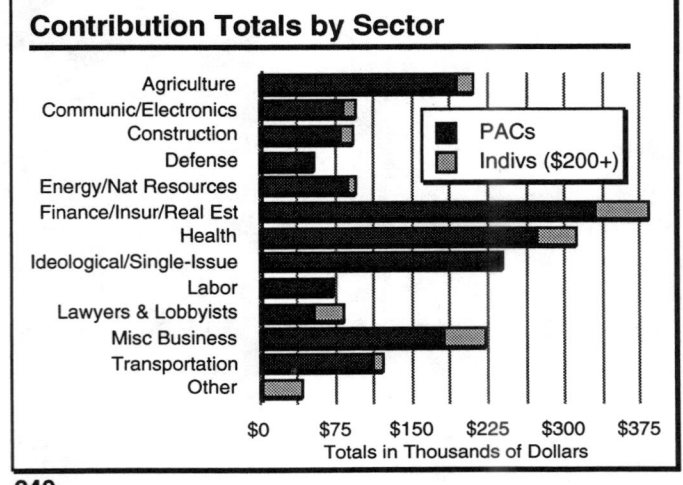

Agriculture
Communic/Electronics
Construction
Defense
Energy/Nat Resources
Finance/Insur/Real Est
Health
Ideological/Single-Issue
Labor
Lawyers & Lobbyists
Misc Business
Transportation
Other

■ PACs
☐ Indivs ($200+)

$0 $75 $150 $225 $300 $375
Totals in Thousands of Dollars

Securities & Investment	$81,680	
Chicago Mercantile Exchange	$11,000	PAC
Insurance	$158,942	
Massachusetts Mutual Life Insurance	$11,442	PAC
Real Estate	$31,190	
None over $10,000		
Accountants	$23,700	
None over $10,000		
Misc Finance	$16,000	
None over $10,000		

Health $308,217

Health Professionals	$122,896	
American Podiatry Assn	$14,000	PAC
Hospitals/Nursing Homes	$69,871	
American Hospital Assn	$17,550	PAC
Health Services	$10,500	
None over $10,000		
Pharmaceuticals/Health Products	$97,750	
Eli Lilly & Co	$10,000	PAC

Lawyers & Lobbyists $80,554

| Lawyers & Lobbyists | $80,554 | |
| Assn of Trial Lawyers of America | $10,000 | PAC |

Misc Business $220,239

Food & Beverage	$31,050	
None over $10,000		
Beer, Wine & Liquor	$17,446	
None over $10,000		
Retail Sales	$20,882	
None over $10,000		
Business Services	$33,250	
None over $10,000		
Chemical & Related Manufacturing	$25,900	
None over $10,000		
Steel Production	$12,400	
None over $10,000		
Misc Manufacturing & Distributing	$50,150	
None over $10,000		

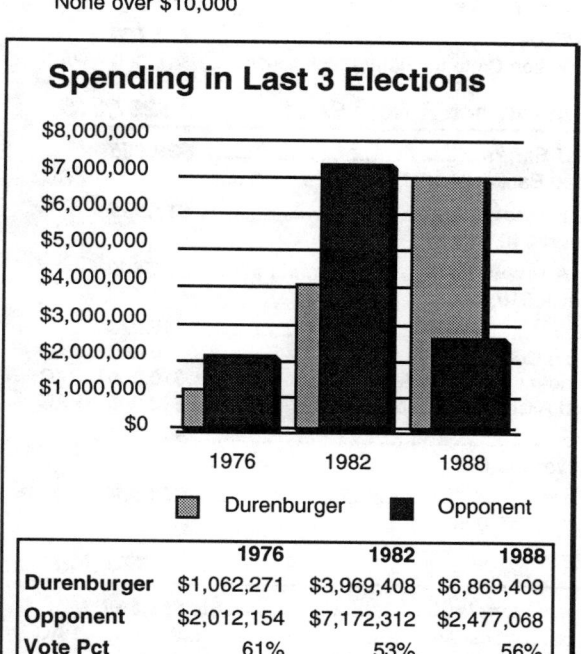

Spending in Last 3 Elections

	1976	1982	1988
Durenburger	$1,062,271	$3,969,408	$6,869,409
Opponent	$2,012,154	$7,172,312	$2,477,068
Vote Pct	61%	53%	56%

Transportation $117,986

Air Transport	$34,311	
None over $10,000		
Automotive	$38,500	
Auto Dealers & Drivers for Free Trade	$11,000	PAC
Trucking	$11,975	
None over $10,000		
Railroads	$28,200	
Union Pacific Corp	$10,000	PAC

Labor

Labor $69,872

Building Trade Unions	$13,000	
None over $10,000		
Transportation Unions	$35,000	
Teamsters Union*	$20,000	PAC
Air Line Pilots Assn	$10,000	PAC
Public Sector Unions	$14,500	
None over $10,000		

Ideological/Single-Issue

Ideological/Single-Issue $235,893

Leadership PACs	$30,505	
Republican Majority Fund (Richard Lugar)	$10,000	PAC
Pro-Israel	$168,000	
Citizens Organized PAC	$10,000	PAC
Delaware Valley PAC	$10,000	PAC
Desert Caucus	$10,000	PAC
Florida Congressional Cmte	$10,000	PAC
Joint Action Cmte for Political Affairs	$10,000	PAC
Maryland Assn for Concerned Citizens	$10,000	PAC
National PAC	$10,000	PAC
Pro-Life	$10,000	
Right to Life*	$10,000	PAC

Other & Unknown

Other $39,350

| Retired | $34,350 | |
| None over $10,000 | | |

Unknown $132,005

Homemakers/Non-income earners	$16,250	
No Employer Listed or Found	$34,855	
Employer Listed/Category Unknown	$75,400	
None over $10,000		

Independent expenditures supporting Durenberger
American Medical Assn $134,527

---

* Contributions came from more than one affiliate or subsidiary.

Jim Exon (D-Neb)

First elected: 1978

1987-92 Total Rcpts:	$2,705,658
1992 Year-end Cash:	$250,308
Current term expires:	1996

1991-92 Committees & Subcommittees

Armed Services
Manpower and Personnel; Projection Forces and Regional Defense; Strategic Forces and Nuclear Deterrence (Chairman)

Budget

Commerce, Science and Transportation
Aviation; Communications; Surface Transportation (Chairman)

Leading Contributors

Business

Agriculture	**$150,496**

Crop Production & Basic Processing	**$37,347**
None over $10,000	

Tobacco	**$12,499**
None over $10,000	

Dairy	**$24,000**	
Associated Milk Producers	$10,000	PAC
Mid-America Dairymen	$10,000	PAC

Agricultural Services/Products	**$30,550**	
Archer-Daniels-Midland Corp	$10,000	PAC

Food Processing & Sales	**$24,400**	
ConAgra Inc	$11,250	PAC/Ind

Communications/Electronics	**$153,977**

Media/Entertainment	**$65,767**	
National Assn of Broadcasters	$10,000	PAC
National Cable Television Assn	$10,000	PAC

Telephone Utilities	**$60,610**	
US West Inc	$13,293	PAC/Ind

Construction	**$32,950**

Construction Services	**$12,100**
None over $10,000	

Source of Funds: 1987-1992

Source	Total	Pct
■ PACs	$1,503,706	53%
▨ Indivs $200+	$538,756	19%
☐ Indivs under $200	$483,483	17%
⊠ Other	$302,809	11%
Candidate	$0	0%
Party	$123,096	4%

Source of PAC Dollars by Sector

Source	Total	Pct
■ Business	$1,073,158	71%
▨ Labor	$292,100	19%
☐ Ideological/Single-Issue	$140,400	9%

In-State vs. Out-of-State Contributions*

Source	Total	Pct
☐ In-State	$252,979	47%
■ Out-of-state	$285,777	53%
No state listed	$0	

* by large individual contributors ($200 & above)

Defense — **$160,763**

Defense Aerospace	**$96,837**	
Northrop Corp	$10,000	PAC

Defense Electronics	**$43,526**
None over $10,000	

Misc Defense	**$20,400**
None over $10,000	

Energy & Natural Resources — **$66,718**

Oil & Gas	**$35,468**
None over $10,000	

Electric Utilities	**$14,100**	
ACRE (Action Cmte for Rural Electrification)	$10,000	PAC

Finance, Insurance & Real Estate — **$297,615**

Commercial Banks	**$38,696**	
American Bankers Assn*	$10,000	PAC

Savings & Loans	**$11,500**
None over $10,000	

Securities & Investment	**$43,400**
None over $10,000	

Insurance	**$145,973**	
American Council of Life Insurance	$10,000	PAC
Independent Insurance Agents of America	$10,000	PAC
National Assn of Life Underwriters	$10,000	PAC

Real Estate	**$35,958**
None over $10,000	

Misc Finance	**$13,088**
None over $10,000	

Health — **$74,850**

Health Professionals	**$51,850**	
American Medical Assn	$10,000	PAC

Hospitals/Nursing Homes	**$11,500**
None over $10,000	

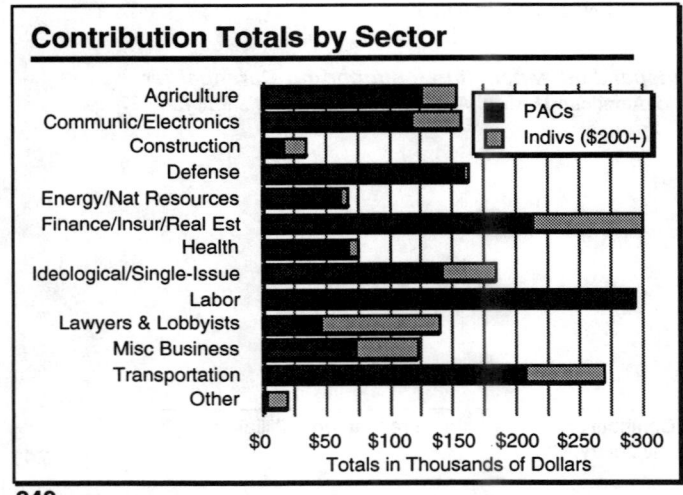

Contribution Totals by Sector

Agriculture, Communic/Electronics, Construction, Defense, Energy/Nat Resources, Finance/Insur/Real Est, Health, Ideological/Single-Issue, Labor, Lawyers & Lobbyists, Misc Business, Transportation, Other

■ PACs
▨ Indivs ($200+)

$0 $50 $100 $150 $200 $250 $300
Totals in Thousands of Dollars

Lawyers & Lobbyists $138,104

Lawyers & Lobbyists $138,104
   Kutak, Rock & Campbell .... $10,750 PAC/Ind

Misc Business $120,933

Food & Beverage $10,800
   None over $10,000

Beer, Wine & Liquor $20,000
   National Beer Wholesalers Assn .... $10,000 PAC

Retail Sales $10,800
   None over $10,000

Business Services $17,500
   None over $10,000

Casinos/Gambling $13,283
   None over $10,000

Misc Manufacturing & Distributing $23,050
   None over $10,000

Transportation $266,837

Air Transport $69,800
   United Parcel Service .... $11,000 PAC
   Aircraft Owners & Pilots Assn .... $10,000 PAC

Automotive $22,000
   National Auto Dealers Assn .... $10,000 PAC

Trucking $49,602
   None over $10,000

Railroads $101,315
   Union Pacific Corp .... $30,300 Indiv
   Burlington Northern .... $16,049 PAC/Ind
   Union Pacific Corp .... $10,000 PAC

Sea Transport $15,100
   None over $10,000

Labor

Labor $292,100

Building Trade Unions $28,300
   Carpenters & Joiners Union .... $10,000 PAC
   Laborers' Political League .... $10,000 PAC

Industrial Unions $75,500
   American Federation of Teachers .... $10,000 PAC
   Machinists/Aerospace Workers Union .... $10,000 PAC
   National Education Assn .... $10,000 PAC

Transportation Unions $109,300
   Air Line Pilots Assn .... $10,000 PAC
   Marine Engineers Union .... $10,000 PAC
   Seafarers International Union .... $10,000 PAC
   Teamsters Union .... $10,000 PAC
   Transport Workers Union .... $10,000 PAC
   United Transportation Union .... $10,000 PAC

Public Sector Unions $56,000
   American Postal Workers Union .... $10,000 PAC
   National Assn of Letter Carriers .... $10,000 PAC
   National Rural Letter Carriers Assn .... $10,000 PAC

Misc Unions $23,000
   AFL-CIO .... $10,000 PAC

Ideological/Single-Issue

Ideological/Single-Issue $180,947

Democratic/Liberal $23,652
   None over $10,000

Leadership PACs $41,000
   Cmte for America's Future (Robert Byrd) .... $10,000 PAC
   Fund for a Democratic Majority (Ted Kennedy) . $10,000 PAC
   Senate Majority Fund (Daniel Inouye) .... $10,000 PAC

Pro-Israel $88,405
   Citizens Organized PAC .... $10,000 PAC
   National PAC .... $10,000 PAC

Other & Unknown

Other $18,600
   None over $10,000

Unknown $94,074
   Homemakers/Non-income earners $19,386
   No Employer Listed or Found $23,432
   Employer Listed/Category Unknown $46,756
   None over $10,000

Spending in Last 3 Elections

	1978	1984	1990
Exon	$234,862	$843,393	$2,417,748
Opponent	$218,148	$583,632	$145,681
Vote Pct	68%	52%	59%

* Contributions came from more than one affiliate or subsidiary.

Lauch Faircloth (R-NC)

First elected: 1992

1991-92 Total Rcpts:	$2,960,437
1992 Year-end Cash:	$9,762
Current term expires:	1998

1993-94 Committees & Subcommittees

Armed Services
Defense Technology, Acquisition and Industrial Base; Force Requirements and Personnel; Military Readiness and Defense Infrastructure

Banking, Housing and Urban Affairs
Economic Stabilization and Rural Development (Ranking Republican); Housing and Urban Affairs; Securities

Environment and Public Works
Clean Air and Nuclear Regulation; Clean Water, Fisheries and Wildlife; Toxic Substances, Research and Development

Leading Contributors

Business

Agriculture — $195,350

Crop Production & Basic Processing $41,850
Cargill Inc .... $5,000   PAC

Tobacco $26,550
RJR Nabisco* .... $10,250   PAC/Ind
AC Monk & Co .... $5,000   Indiv
Philip Morris .... $5,000   PAC
Standard Commerical Tobacco .... $4,300   Indiv

Poultry & Eggs $19,650
Cuddy Farms .... $4,000   Indiv

Livestock $13,250
None over $4,000

Agricultural Services/Products $15,800
Deere & Co* .... $4,000   PAC

Food Processing & Sales $32,375
Lundy Packing Co .... $6,200   Indiv
Lance Inc .... $4,000   Indiv

Forestry & Forest Products $39,875
Weyerhaeuser Co .... $7,000   PAC
Federal Paperboard Co .... $6,500   PAC/Ind
International Paper Co .... $5,000   PAC

Source of Funds: 1987-1992

Source	Total	Pct
■ PACs	$375,255	11%
▨ Indivs $200+	$1,006,424	28%
□ Indivs under $200	$789,512	22%
▦ Other	$1,369,540	39%
Candidate	$760,530	21%
Party	$580,294	16%

Source of PAC Dollars by Sector

Source	Total	Pct
■ Business	$332,841	86%
■ Labor	$0	0%
□ Ideological/Single-Issue	$53,812	14%

In-State vs. Out-of-State Contributions*

Source	Total	Pct
□ In-State	$855,659	85%
■ Out-of-state	$150,765	15%
No state listed	$0	

* by large individual contributors ($200 & above)

Communications/Electronics — $45,325

Printing & Publishing $13,800
Hi-Torque Publications .... $4,000   Indiv

Media/Entertainment $12,500
National Cable Television Assn .... $10,000   PAC

Telephone Utilities $11,750
Southern Bell .... $4,000   PAC

Electronics Mfg & Services $5,000
Harris Corp .... $4,000   PAC

Construction — $88,650

General Contractors $34,900
Associated General Contractors .... $5,000   PAC

Home Builders $6,800
None over $4,000

Special Trade Contractors $14,250
Sheet Metal/Air Conditioning Contractors .... $4,500   PAC

Building Materials & Equipment $32,450
None over $4,000

Defense — $15,390

Defense Aerospace $11,400
Martin Marietta Corp .... $5,400   PAC/Ind

Energy & Natural Resources — $61,540

Oil & Gas $47,840
Coastal Corp .... $8,000   Indiv
Exxon Corp .... $7,500   PAC
Ashland Oil .... $5,000   PAC

Misc Energy $5,000
Cooper Industries .... $5,000   PAC

Electric Utilities $6,300
None over $4,000

Contribution Totals by Sector

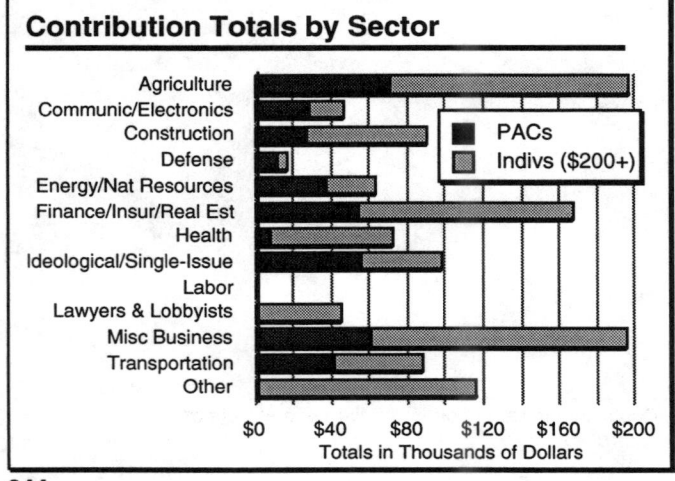

Agriculture	
Communic/Electronics	
Construction	
Defense	■ PACs
Energy/Nat Resources	▨ Indivs ($200+)
Finance/Insur/Real Est	
Health	
Ideological/Single-Issue	
Labor	
Lawyers & Lobbyists	
Misc Business	
Transportation	
Other	

$0 $40 $80 $120 $160 $200
Totals in Thousands of Dollars

Finance, Insurance & Real Estate — $165,904

Commercial Banks $17,300
None over $4,000

Securities & Investment $20,090
None over $4,000

Insurance $63,300
Jefferson-Pilot Corp .... $17,950   PAC/Ind
National Assn of Life Underwriters .... $10,000   PAC
Torchmark Corp .... $8,000   PAC/Ind

Real Estate $41,314
None over $4,000

Accountants $8,800
None over $4,000

Misc Finance $14,100
None over $4,000

Health — $70,756

Health Professionals $63,006
None over $4,000

Hospitals/Nursing Homes $5,000
None over $4,000

Lawyers & Lobbyists — $44,131

Lawyers & Lobbyists $44,131
None over $4,000

Misc Business — $193,941

Business Associations $8,541

Food & Beverage $30,800
McDonald's Corp .... $5,000   PAC
National Restaurant Assn .... $5,000   PAC
S&A Restaurant Corp .... $5,000   PAC

Retail Sales $25,725
None over $4,000

Misc Services $4,700
None over $4,000

Business Services $7,400
None over $4,000

Chemical & Related Manufacturing — $14,750
Dow Chemical .... $4,000   PAC

Steel Production $4,000
None over $4,000

Misc Manufacturing & Distributing $53,600
Packaging Co .... $4,600   Indiv
Broyhill Investments Inc .... $4,000   Indiv

Textiles $37,675
Glen Raven Mills .... $4,000   Indiv
Stonecutter Mills Corp .... $4,000   Indiv

Transportation — $86,549

Air Transport $11,999
None over $4,000

Automotive $53,600
Americans for Free International Trade ...... $10,000   PAC
Eaton Corp .... $5,000   PAC
National Auto Dealers Assn .... $5,000   PAC

Trucking $6,550
None over $4,000

Railroads $7,400
Union Pacific Corp .... $6,400   PAC

Misc Transport $4,000
None over $4,000

Ideological/Single-Issue

Ideological/Single-Issue — $97,162

Republican/Conservative $52,900
Conservative Victory Cmte .... $5,000   PAC
V-PAC .... $5,000   PAC

Leadership PACs $16,350
Campaign America (Bob Dole) .... $9,100   PAC
National Congressional Club (Jesse Helms) ...... $5,000   PAC

Gun Rights/Gun Control $9,900
National Rifle Assn .... $9,900   PAC

Misc Issues $17,050
Right to Work PAC .... $10,000   PAC

Other & Unknown

Other — $114,758

Civil Servants/Public Officials $8,450
None over $4,000

Education $4,200
None over $4,000

Retired $99,013
None over $4,000

Unknown — $215,621

Homemakers/Non-income earners $53,939
No Employer Listed or Found $77,045
Generic Occupation/Category Unknown $8,797
Employer Listed/Category Unknown $74,840
Wimbley-Gregory & Co .... $4,750   Indiv

Independent expenditures supporting Faircloth
National Right to Life PAC $14,598
National Rifle Assn $8,073

---

* Contributions came from more than one affiliate or subsidiary.

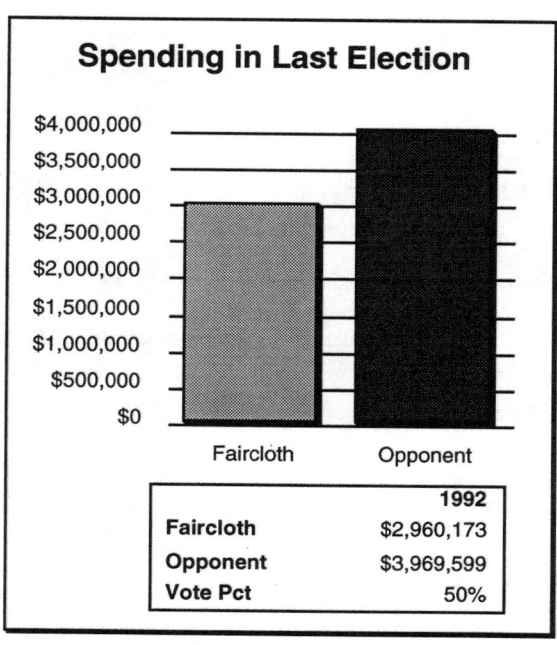

Spending in Last Election

	1992
Faircloth	$2,960,173
Opponent	$3,969,599
Vote Pct	50%

Russell Feingold (D-Wis)

First elected: 1992

1991-92 Total Rcpts:	$1,996,312
1992 Year-end Cash:	$26,855
Current term expires:	1998

1993-94 Committees & Subcommittees

Agriculture, Nutrition and Forestry
Agricultural Production and Stabilization of Prices; Domestic and Foreign Marketing and Product Promotion; Nutrition and Investigations

Foreign Relations
African Affairs; European Affairs; International Economic Policy, Trade, Oceans and Environment

Special Aging

Leading Contributors

Business

Agriculture		$20,450

Crop Production & Basic Processing	...............$12,500	
American Sugarbeet Growers Assn	...................$3,500	PAC
Agricultural Services/Products	...........................$3,800	
None over $3,000		

Communications/Electronics		$40,108

Printing & Publishing	....$8,750	
None over $3,000		
Media/Entertainment	....$20,150	
National Cable Television Assn	........................$10,000	PAC
Telephone Utilities	....$10,458	
AT&T	....$7,000	PAC

Construction		$11,430

General Contractors	....$7,130	
None over $3,000		

Finance, Insurance & Real Estate		$86,408

Commercial Banks	....$14,347	
Valley Bank of Nevada	....$3,000	Indiv
Savings & Loans	....$4,450	
None over $3,000		
Credit Unions	....$5,000	
Credit Union National Assn	..................................$5,000	PAC

Contribution Totals by Sector

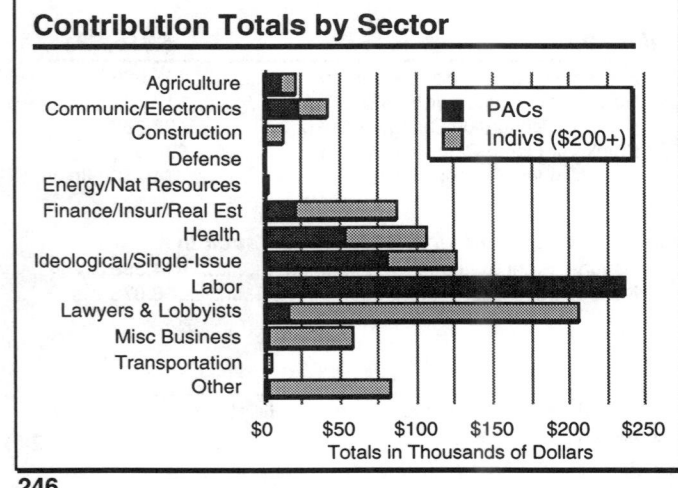

Agriculture
Communic/Electronics
Construction
Defense
Energy/Nat Resources
Finance/Insur/Real Est
Health
Ideological/Single-Issue
Labor
Lawyers & Lobbyists
Misc Business
Transportation
Other

■ PACs
▨ Indivs ($200+)

$0 $50 $100 $150 $200 $250
Totals in Thousands of Dollars

Source of Funds: 1987-1992

Source	Total	Pct
■ PACs	$457,563	19%
▨ Indivs $200+	$655,387	28%
☐ Indivs under $200	$821,228	35%
☒ Other	$442,931	19%
Candidate	$175	0%
Party	$380,797	16%

Source of PAC Dollars by Sector

Source	Total	Pct
■ Business	$122,075	28%
▨ Labor	$234,200	54%
☐ Ideological/Single-Issue	$78,986	18%

In-State vs. Out-of-State Contributions*

Source	Total	Pct
☐ In-State	$465,716	69%
■ Out-of-state	$210,591	31%
No state listed	$0	

* by large individual contributors ($200 & above)

Securities & Investment	....$13,750	
None over $3,000		
Insurance	....$9,886	
National Assn of Life Underwriters	.......................$3,000	PAC
Real Estate	....$32,975	
Chen Investment Properties	................................$4,050	Indiv
Yacht Club Condominiums	...................................$4,000	Indiv
Accountants	....$3,000	
None over $3,000		

Health		$104,595

Health Professionals	....$86,345	
American Chiropractic Assn	...............................$10,000	PAC
American Physical Therapy Assn	.........................$7,000	PAC
American Optometric Assn	...................................$5,500	PAC
American Psychiatric Assn	....................................$5,000	PAC
American Academy of Ophthalmology	.................$4,000	PAC
American Podiatry Assn	....$3,500	PAC
Physician's Plus Group	....$3,500	Indiv
American Occupational Therapy Assn	................$3,200	PAC
Hospitals/Nursing Homes	....................................$7,700	
None over $3,000		
Pharmaceuticals/Health Products	.....................$3,650	
None over $3,000		
Misc Health	....$5,150	
None over $3,000		

Lawyers & Lobbyists		$204,367

Lawyers & Lobbyists	....$204,367	
Foley & Lardner	....$14,175	Indiv
Habush, Habush & Davis	....................................$11,225	Indiv
Assn of Trial Lawyers of America	.....................$10,000	PAC
Warshafsky, Rotter et al	....$6,500	Indiv
Godfrey & Kahn	....$4,950	Indiv
Previant, Goldbert, Uelman & Assoc	..................$4,450	Indiv

Misc Business — $56,916

Beer, Wine & Liquor $3,400
  None over $3,000

Retail Sales $6,400
  None over $3,000

Misc Services $5,350
  None over $3,000

Business Services $15,990
  Manpower Inc .... $3,250   Indiv

Lodging/Tourism $4,350
  None over $3,000

Misc Business $6,750
  Conney Safety Products Co .... $4,000   Indiv

Misc Manufacturing & Distributing $7,927
  None over $3,000

Transportation — $4,500

Labor

Labor — $234,650

Building Trade Unions $28,600
Carpenters & Joiners Union	$10,000	PAC
Laborers Union*	$7,000	PAC
Plumbers/Pipefitters Union	$5,000	PAC

Industrial Unions $75,500
Communications Workers of America	$10,000	PAC
United Steelworkers	$10,000	PAC
Rubber Cork Linoleum & Plastic Workers	$9,000	PAC
Intl Brotherhood of Electrical Workers	$7,500	PAC
United Auto Workers	$7,000	PAC
Amalgamated Clothing & Textile Workers	$5,000	PAC
Electronic Machine Furniture Workers	$5,000	PAC
Machinists/Aerospace Workers Union	$5,000	PAC
United Electrical Radio Machine Workers	$4,500	PAC
United Paperworkers	$3,500	PAC

Transportation Unions — $55,550
Air Line Pilots Assn	$10,000	PAC
Teamsters Union	$10,000	PAC
United Transportation Union	$9,000	PAC
Amalgamated Transit Union	$8,000	PAC
Trans Comm International Union	$6,000	PAC
Assn of Flight Attendants	$5,000	PAC
Brotherhood of Locomotive Engineers	$3,000	PAC

Public Sector Unions $42,800
American Fedn of St/Cnty/Munic Employees	$10,250	PAC/Ind
American Federation of Teachers	$10,000	PAC
National Education Assn	$10,000	PAC
International Assn of Firefighters	$5,000	PAC
National Assn Retired Federal Employees	$5,000	PAC

Misc Unions $32,200
AFL-CIO	$10,200	PAC/Ind
Food & Commercial Workers Union	$10,000	PAC
Service Employees International Union	$7,500	PAC

Ideological/Single-Issue

Ideological/Single-Issue — $124,409

Democratic/Liberal $27,407
Fifth Horseman PAC	$10,000	PAC
Hollywood Women's Political Cmte	$5,000	PAC

Foreign & Defense Policy $12,412
Council for a Livable World	$8,962	PAC/Ind

Pro-Israel $10,400
Multi-Issue PAC	$4,000	PAC

Pro-Choice $9,650
Voters for Choice	$3,500	PAC/Ind

Gun Rights/Gun Control $4,000
Handgun Control Inc	$4,000	PAC

Human Rights $23,048
KidsPAC	$10,000	PAC
Human Rights Campaign Fund	$8,000	PAC

Misc Issues $32,242
League of Conservation Voters	$6,500	PAC/Ind
National Cmte to Preserve Social Security	$6,500	PAC
Greenvote	$5,000	PAC/Ind
National Council of Senior Citizens	$5,000	PAC

Other & Unknown

Other — $80,179

Civil Servants/Public Officials $20,750
State of Wisconsin	$7,650	Indiv

Education $27,675
  None over $3,000

Retired $26,704
  None over $3,000

Other $3,800
  None over $3,000

Unknown — $149,906
Homemakers/Non-income earners	$17,800	
No Employer Listed or Found	$29,966	
Employer Listed/Category Unknown	$101,365	
William B Mark & Assoc	$3,000	Indiv

Independent expenditures supporting Feingold
  National Abortion Rights Action League $148,426

Independent expenditures opposing Feingold
  Wisconsin Right to Life $3,711

* Contributions came from more than one affiliate or subsidiary.

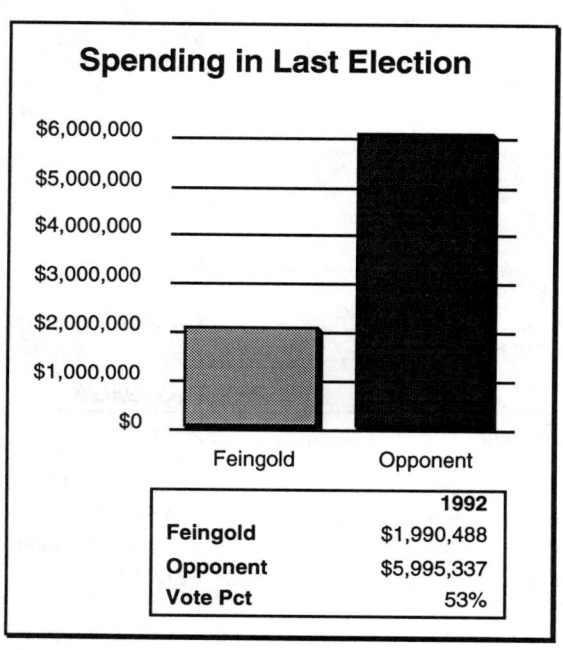

Spending in Last Election

	1992
Feingold	$1,990,488
Opponent	$5,995,337
Vote Pct	53%

Dianne Feinstein (D-Calif)

First elected: 1992

1991-92 Total Rcpts:	$8,114,032
1992 Year-end Cash:	$60,645
Current term expires:	1994

1993-94 Committees & Subcommittees

Appropriations
Agriculture, Rural Development and Related Agencies; District of Columbia; Foreign Operations; VA, HUD and Independent Agencies

Judiciary
Patents, Copyrights and Trademarks; Technology and the Law

Rules and Administration

Leading Contributors

Business

Agriculture		$133,748

Crop Production & Basic Processing	$40,493	
None over $10,000		

Agricultural Services/Products	$16,300	
None over $10,000		

Food Processing & Sales	$60,214	
Yucaipa Companies	$13,000	Indiv

Communications/Electronics		$374,515

Printing & Publishing	$44,015	
None over $10,000		

Media/Entertainment	$277,250	
MCA Inc*	$19,017	PAC/Ind
Disney Channel*	$16,854	PAC/Ind
Time Warner*	$13,400	PAC/Ind

Telephone Utilities	$22,250	
Pacific Telesis Group	$14,000	PAC/Ind

Telecom Services & Equipment	$12,250	
None over $10,000		

Construction		$137,220

General Contractors	$65,220	
Tutor-Saliba Corp	$15,000	Indiv

Home Builders	$23,500	
None over $10,000		

Special Trade Contractors	$19,200	
None over $10,000		

Construction Services	$19,250	
None over $10,000		

Source of Funds: 1987-1992

Source	Total	Pct
PACs	$933,999	10%
Indivs $200+	$3,978,994	41%
Indivs under $200	$2,761,796	29%
Other	$1,948,606	20%
Candidate	$77,695	1%
Party	$1,509,363	16%

Source of PAC Dollars by Sector

Source	Total	Pct
Business	$448,254	49%
Labor	$296,052	33%
Ideological/Single-Issue	$162,583	18%

In-State vs. Out-of-State Contributions*

Source	Total	Pct
In-State	$3,310,990	83%
Out-of-state	$657,571	17%
No state listed	$0	

* by large individual contributors ($200 & above)

Defense		$16,550
None over $10,000		

Energy & Natural Resources		$72,050

Oil & Gas	$24,550	
None over $10,000		

Electric Utilities	$26,500	
Southern California Edison	$15,750	PAC/Ind

Finance, Insurance & Real Estate		$780,413

Commercial Banks	$77,100	
BankAmerica Corp	$22,300	PAC/Ind
Wells Fargo	$11,800	PAC/Ind

Securities & Investment	$235,553	
Shearson Lehman Brothers	$15,250	PAC/Ind
Princeton Venture Research	$12,000	Indiv
Bear, Stearns & Co	$11,750	PAC/Ind
Merrill Lynch	$11,400	PAC/Ind

Insurance	$72,510	
None over $10,000		

Real Estate	$226,258	
None over $10,000		

Accountants	$63,799	
None over $10,000		

Misc Finance	$87,225	
None over $10,000		

Health		$329,029

Health Professionals	$222,087	
American Chiropractic Assn	$10,000	PAC
American Medical Assn	$10,000	PAC

Hospitals/Nursing Homes	$42,750	
National Medical Enterprises Inc	$10,550	PAC/Ind

Health Services	$21,042	
None over $10,000		

Contribution Totals by Sector

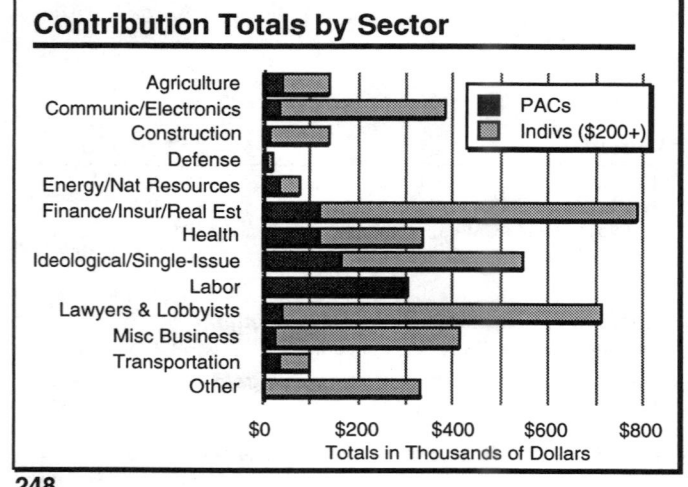

Legend: ■ PACs   ▨ Indivs ($200+)

Categories: Agriculture, Communic/Electronics, Construction, Defense, Energy/Nat Resources, Finance/Insur/Real Est, Health, Ideological/Single-Issue, Labor, Lawyers & Lobbyists, Misc Business, Transportation, Other

Totals in Thousands of Dollars: $0, $200, $400, $600, $800

Pharmaceuticals/Health Products **$31,300**
Syntex (USA) Inc ....$10,000 PAC

Lawyers & Lobbyists $707,149

Lawyers & Lobbyists **$707,149**
Milberg, Weiss et al ....$21,700 Indiv
Gibson, Dunn & Crutcher ....$20,325 Indiv
Howard, Rice et al ....$16,000 Indiv
O'Melveny & Myers ....$13,650 PAC/Ind
Morrison & Foerster ....$13,000 Indiv
Cotchett, Illston et al ....$12,000 Indiv
Manatt, Phelps & Phillips ....$11,850 PAC/Ind
Pillsbury, Madison & Sutro ....$11,500 PAC/Ind
Heller, Ehrman et al ....$11,250 Indiv
Latham & Watkins ....$10,300 Indiv
Assn of Trial Lawyers of America ....$10,000 PAC

Misc Business $405,469

Food & Beverage **$20,920**
None over $10,000

Beer, Wine & Liquor **$37,800**
Joseph E Seagram & Sons ....$11,500 PAC/Ind

Retail Sales **$68,300**
None over $10,000

Business Services **$141,579**
None over $10,000

Lodging/Tourism **$24,050**
None over $10,000

Misc Manufacturing & Distributing **$63,150**
None over $10,000

Transportation $93,117

Air Transport **$23,750**
Northwest Airlines ....$10,500 Indiv

Sea Transport **$39,600**
None over $10,000

Labor

Labor $298,602

Building Trade Unions **$54,502**
Operating Engineers Union* ....$11,500 PAC
Carpenters & Joiners Union ....$10,000 PAC

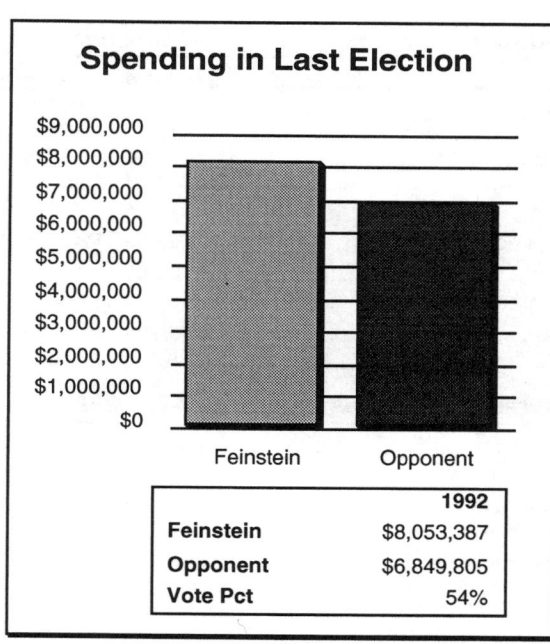

Spending in Last Election

	1992
Feinstein	$8,053,387
Opponent	$6,849,805
Vote Pct	54%

Industrial Unions **$51,750**
Intl Brotherhood of Electrical Workers ....$10,000 PAC
United Auto Workers ....$10,000 PAC

Transportation Unions **$103,550**
Seafarers International Union* ....$26,000 PAC
Marine Engineers Union* ....$14,500 PAC
Teamsters Union* ....$10,300 PAC/Ind
Air Line Pilots Assn ....$10,000 PAC
Assn of Flight Attendants ....$10,000 PAC
United Transportation Union ....$10,000 PAC

Public Sector Unions **$51,300**
National Assn of Letter Carriers ....$10,000 PAC
National Education Assn ....$10,000 PAC

Misc Unions **$37,500**
AFL-CIO ....$10,000 PAC
Food & Commercial Workers Union ....$10,000 PAC
Service Employees International Union ....$10,000 PAC

Ideological/Single-Issue

Ideological/Single-Issue $542,956

Democratic/Liberal **$61,750**
Hollywood Women's Political Cmte ....$10,000 PAC

Leadership PACs **$17,000**
Fund for a Democratic Majority (Ted Kennedy) .$10,000 PAC

Pro-Israel **$135,975**
None over $10,000

Pro-Choice **$21,850**
None over $10,000

Womens Issues **$223,878**
Emily's List ....$12,736 PAC/Ind
Women's Campaign Fund ....$10,000 PAC
Women's Political Committee ....$10,000 PAC

Human Rights **$51,653**
Human Rights Campaign Fund ....$10,500 PAC/Ind

Misc Issues **$25,050**
None over $10,000

Other & Unknown

Other $326,778

Civil Servants/Public Officials **$59,530**
None over $10,000

Education **$59,624**
University of California System* ....$20,800 Indiv

Retired **$187,424**
None over $10,000

Other **$15,000**
None over $10,000

Unknown $676,787

Homemakers/Non-income earners $166,909
No Employer Listed or Found $53,659
Generic Occupation/Category Unknown $20,600
Employer Listed/Category Unknown $430,619
None over $10,000

Independent expenditures supporting Feinstein
Your Pro-Choice Voter Guide $12,345
California Democratic Voter Checklist $10,700

Independent expenditures opposing Feinstein
English Language PAC $49,718

*Contributions came from more than one affiliate or subsidiary.

Wendell H. Ford (D-Ky)

First elected: 1974

1987-92 Total Rcpts:	$2,386,966
1992 Year-end Cash:	$438,224
Current term expires:	1998

1991-92 Committees & Subcommittees

Commerce, Science and Transportation
Aviation (Chairman); Communications; Consumer; National Ocean Policy Study

Energy and Natural Resources
Energy Research and Development (Chairman); Mineral Resources Development and Production; Water and Power

Rules and Administration (Chairman)

Joint Committee on Printing (Vice Chairman)

Leading Contributors

Business

Agriculture — $182,879

Crop Production & Basic Processing **$35,105**
  None over $7,500

Tobacco **$68,724**
  Philip Morris .... $14,598 — PAC/Ind
  Brown & Williamson Tobacco .... $10,800 — PAC/Ind
  US Tobacco Co .... $10,000 — PAC

Dairy **$14,700**
  Dairymen Inc-Kentucky .... $8,000 — PAC

Livestock **$12,000**
  None over $7,500

Agricultural Services/Products **$21,500**
  Archer-Daniels-Midland Corp .... $8,000 — PAC

Food Processing & Sales **$14,850**
  None over $7,500

Forestry & Forest Products **$15,000**
  None over $7,500

Communications/Electronics — $96,800

Media/Entertainment **$29,000**
  National Assn of Broadcasters .... $10,000 — PAC

Telephone Utilities **$55,000**
  BellSouth Corp* .... $10,000 — PAC
  Bell Atlantic .... $9,000 — PAC

Source of Funds: 1987-1992

Source	Total	Pct
PACs	$1,334,613	55%
Indivs $200+	$689,913	29%
Indivs under $200	$122,550	5%
Other	$272,193	11%
Candidate	$0	0%
Party	$32,303	1%

Source of PAC Dollars by Sector

Source	Total	Pct
Business	$1,051,843	80%
Labor	$239,750	18%
Ideological/Single-Issue	$30,251	2%

In-State vs. Out-of-State Contributions*

Source	Total	Pct
In-State	$399,644	58%
Out-of-state	$288,769	42%
No state listed	$0	

* by large individual contributors ($200 & above)

Construction — $56,650

General Contractors **$16,250**
  None over $7,500

Home Builders **$9,500**
  National Assn of Home Builders .... $9,000 — PAC

Construction Services **$12,700**
  None over $7,500

Building Materials & Equipment **$12,000**
  None over $7,500

Defense — $14,500

Defense Aerospace **$12,500**
  None over $7,500

Energy & Natural Resources — $266,450

Oil & Gas **$108,700**
  Transco Energy Co* .... $13,000 — PAC/Ind
  Ashland Oil .... $11,950 — PAC/Ind
  Panhandle Eastern Corp .... $8,000 — PAC/Ind
  Columbia Gas System* .... $7,500 — PAC

Mining **$61,000**
  National Coal Assn .... $8,500 — PAC/Ind

Nuclear Energy **$12,500**
  General Atomics .... $9,000 — PAC

Electric Utilities **$69,250**
  Kentucky Utilities Co .... $8,000 — PAC

Finance, Insurance & Real Estate — $291,290

Commercial Banks **$47,900**
  American Bankers Assn .... $10,500 — PAC

Savings & Loans **$8,500**
  None over $7,500

Securities & Investment **$44,715**
  Chicago Mercantile Exchange .... $11,000 — PAC/Ind

Contribution Totals by Sector

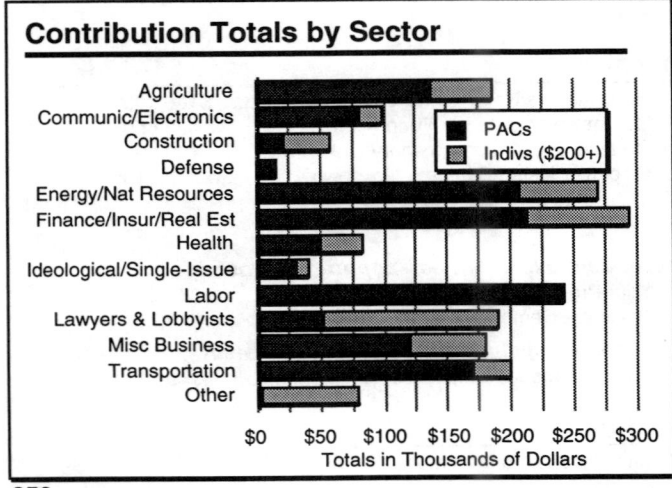

Legend: ■ PACs ▨ Indivs ($200+)

Categories: Agriculture, Communic/Electronics, Construction, Defense, Energy/Nat Resources, Finance/Insur/Real Est, Health, Ideological/Single-Issue, Labor, Lawyers & Lobbyists, Misc Business, Transportation, Other

$0 $50 $100 $150 $200 $250 $300
Totals in Thousands of Dollars

Insurance	$124,559	
American Council of Life Insurance	$13,499	PAC
Capital Holding Corp	$10,000	PAC
Independent Insurance Agents of America	$9,810	PAC
National Assn of Life Underwriters	$7,500	PAC
Real Estate	**$32,291**	
National Assn of Realtors	$10,000	PAC
Accountants	**$23,475**	
American Institute of CPA's	$10,250	PAC

Health $81,300

Health Professionals	$52,550	
American Dental Assn	$10,000	PAC
Hospitals/Nursing Homes	**$23,250**	
Humana Inc	$12,000	PAC/Ind

Lawyers & Lobbyists $188,057

Lawyers & Lobbyists	$188,057	
Akin, Gump et al	$12,099	PAC/Ind
Cassidy & Associates	$8,000	Indiv

Misc Business $177,559

Food & Beverage	$17,895	
None over $7,500		
Beer, Wine & Liquor	**$58,050**	
Brown-Forman Distillers	$11,500	PAC/Ind
Joseph E Seagram & Sons	$8,000	PAC
Retail Sales	**$12,157**	
None over $7,500		
Business Services	**$39,207**	
None over $7,500		
Lodging/Tourism	**$9,250**	
None over $7,500		
Misc Manufacturing & Distributing	**$16,500**	
None over $7,500		

Spending in Last 3 Elections

	Ford	Opponent

	1980	1986	1992
Ford	$491,522	$1,321,029	$2,207,813
Opponent	$7,262	$58,572	$335,304
Vote Pct	65%	74%	63%

Transportation	$196,920	
Air Transport	**$111,745**	
Delta Airlines	$11,500	PAC/Ind
American Assn of Airport Executives	$11,483	PAC/Ind
Aircraft Owners & Pilots Assn	$10,000	PAC
Federal Express Corp	$10,000	PAC
United Parcel Service	$9,750	PAC/Ind
American Airlines	$8,500	PAC/Ind
Automotive	**$29,550**	
National Auto Dealers Assn	$9,000	PAC
Trucking	**$15,250**	
None over $7,500		
Railroads	**$27,875**	
Union Pacific Corp	$10,000	PAC
Sea Transport	**$11,000**	
None over $7,500		

Labor

Labor	$240,250	
Building Trade Unions	**$28,700**	
Laborers' Political League	$9,000	PAC
Industrial Unions	**$61,950**	
United Auto Workers	$10,000	PAC
United Steelworkers	$10,000	PAC
United Mine Workers	$8,500	PAC
Transportation Unions	**$66,650**	
Marine Engineers Union*	$13,500	PAC
Air Line Pilots Assn	$10,000	PAC
Teamsters Union	$10,000	PAC
Public Sector Unions	**$62,450**	
National Rural Letter Carriers Assn	$11,000	PAC
American Fedn of St/Cnty/Munic Employees	$10,000	PAC
National Assn of Letter Carriers	$9,000	PAC
American Federation of Teachers	$8,500	PAC
Misc Unions	**$20,500**	
None over $7,500		

Ideological/Single-Issue

Ideological/Single-Issue	$38,801	
Pro-Israel	**$13,300**	
None over $7,500		
Misc Issues	**$8,000**	
None over $7,500		

Other & Unknown

Other	$76,847	
Civil Servants/Public Officials	**$26,582**	
Commonwealth of Kentucky	$7,782	Indiv
Education	**$13,525**	
None over $7,500		
Retired	**$33,740**	
None over $7,500		

Unknown	$106,704	
Homemakers/Non-income earners	$18,350	
Employer Listed/Category Unknown	$85,163	
None over $7,500		

---

* Contributions came from more than one affiliate or subsidiary.

John Glenn (D-Ohio)

First elected: 1974

1987-92 Total Rcpts:	$4,245,138
1992 Year-end Cash:	$109,668
Current term expires:	1998

1991-92 Committees & Subcommittees

Armed Services
Conventional Forces and Alliance Defense; Manpower and Personnel (Chairman); Strategic Forces and Nuclear Deterrence

Governmental Affairs (Chairman)
Permanent Subcommittee on Investigations (Vice Chairman)

Select Committee on Intelligence

Special Aging

Leading Contributors

Business

Agriculture	$38,155
None over $10,000	

Communications/Electronics	$79,240

Printing & Publishing	$18,450	
American Greetings Corp	$12,000	Indiv
Media/Entertainment	$16,826	
None over $10,000		
Telephone Utilities	$21,164	
None over $10,000		
Computer Equipment & Services	$15,300	
None over $10,000		

Construction	$69,783

General Contractors	$35,283	
Fluor Corp	$10,608	PAC
Construction Services	$16,250	
None over $10,000		
Building Materials & Equipment	$12,500	
None over $10,000		

Defense	$168,845

Defense Aerospace	$86,801	
Rockwell International	$10,000	PAC
Defense Electronics	$55,700	
Loral Corp	$17,000	PAC/Ind

Contribution Totals by Sector

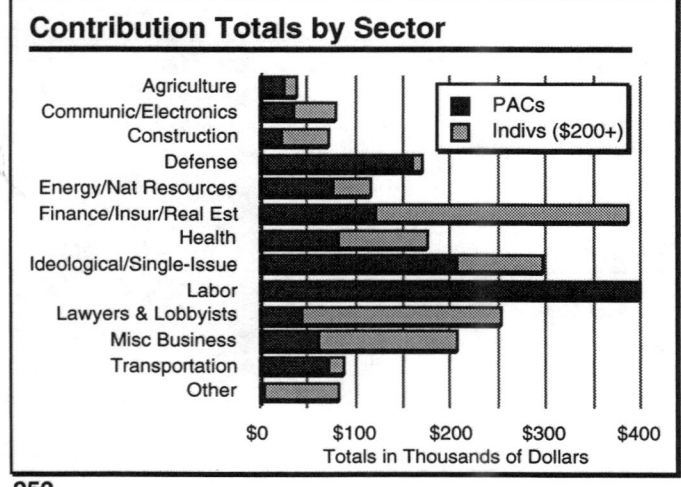

Totals in Thousands of Dollars

Source of Funds: 1987-1992

Source	Total	Pct
■ PACs	$1,254,197	26%
▨ Indivs $200+	$1,523,088	31%
□ Indivs under $200	$548,472	11%
▨ Other	$1,592,562	32%
Candidate	$706,818	14%
Party	$673,181	14%

Source of PAC Dollars by Sector

Source	Total	Pct
■ Business	$687,399	53%
▨ Labor	$394,898	31%
□ Ideological/Single-Issue	$203,045	16%

In-State vs. Out-of-State Contributions*

Source	Total	Pct
□ In-State	$808,310	55%
■ Out-of-state	$666,578	45%
No state listed	$3,250	

* by large individual contributors ($200 & above)

Misc Defense	$26,344	
None over $10,000		

Energy & Natural Resources	$113,958

Oil & Gas	$31,650	
Occidental Petroleum	$10,000	PAC
Electric Utilities	$34,525	
ACRE (Action Cmte for Rural Electrification)*	$10,000	PAC
Waste Management	$28,533	
Waste Management Inc	$14,000	PAC/Ind
Mid-American Waste Systems	$10,833	PAC/Ind

Finance, Insurance & Real Estate	$383,700

Commercial Banks	$48,250	
Banc One Corp	$12,500	PAC/Ind
Securities & Investment	$79,150	
Chicago Mercantile Exchange	$10,000	PAC
Insurance	$78,950	
None over $10,000		
Real Estate	$120,500	
None over $10,000		
Accountants	$27,650	
American Institute of CPA's	$10,000	PAC
Misc Finance	$18,450	
None over $10,000		

Health	$173,351

Health Professionals	$121,951	
American Chiropractic Assn*	$12,300	PAC
Hospitals/Nursing Homes	$22,400	
None over $10,000		
Health Services	$11,750	
None over $10,000		
Pharmaceuticals/Health Products	$10,750	
None over $10,000		

Lawyers & Lobbyists — $251,131

Lawyers & Lobbyists **$251,131**
- Jones, Day et al .... $12,250 PAC/Ind

Misc Business — $203,450

Food & Beverage **$11,500**
- None over $10,000

Retail Sales **$45,950**
- None over $10,000

Business Services **$40,450**
- None over $10,000

Chemical & Related Manufacturing **$25,550**
- Procter & Gamble .... $18,300 PAC/Ind

Steel Production **$10,000**
- None over $10,000

Misc Manufacturing & Distributing **$47,900**
- None over $10,000

Transportation — $85,350

Air Transport **$45,250**
- Aircraft Owners & Pilots Assn .... $15,000 PAC
- Federal Express Corp .... $10,000 PAC

Automotive **$15,350**
- None over $10,000

Misc Transport **$10,500**
- None over $10,000

Labor

Labor — **$396,473**

Building Trade Unions **$73,625**
- Laborers' Political League .... $12,000 PAC
- Carpenters & Joiners Union .... $10,000 PAC
- Ironworkers Union .... $10,000 PAC
- Plumbers/Pipefitters Union* .... $10,000 PAC
- Sheet Metal Workers Union .... $10,000 PAC

Industrial Unions **$88,450**
- Intl Brotherhood of Electrical Workers .... $12,500 PAC
- Communications Workers of America .... $10,000 PAC
- Electronic Machine Furniture Workers .... $10,000 PAC
- Machinists/Aerospace Workers Union .... $10,000 PAC
- Rubber Cork Linoleum & Plastic Workers .... $10,000 PAC
- United Auto Workers .... $10,000 PAC

Transportation Unions **$76,000**
- Air Line Pilots Assn .... $10,000 PAC
- Seafarers International Union .... $10,000 PAC
- Teamsters Union .... $10,000 PAC
- United Transportation Union .... $10,000 PAC

Public Sector Unions **$121,200**
- National Rural Letter Carriers Assn .... $14,000 PAC
- American Postal Workers Union .... $11,000 PAC
- National Treasury Employees Union .... $11,000 PAC
- National Assn of Postmasters .... $10,400 PAC
- American Federation of Teachers .... $10,000 PAC
- American Fedn of St/Cnty/Munic Employees ... $10,000 PAC
- National Assn of Letter Carriers .... $10,000 PAC
- National Assn Retired Federal Employees .... $10,000 PAC
- National Education Assn .... $10,000 PAC

Misc Unions **$37,198**
- Service Employees International Union .... $10,000 PAC

Ideological/Single-Issue

Ideological/Single-Issue — **$293,989**

Democratic/Liberal **$22,212**
- None over $10,000

Leadership PACs **$24,000**
- Fund for a Democratic Majority (Ted Kennedy) . $10,000 PAC
- Natl Council on Public Policy (John Glenn) ...... $10,000 PAC

Pro-Israel **$182,400**
- Citizens Organized PAC .... $10,000 PAC
- Desert Caucus .... $10,000 PAC
- Hudson Valley PAC .... $10,000 PAC
- National PAC .... $10,000 PAC

Pro-Choice **$15,200**
- National Abortion Rights Action League .... $10,000 PAC

Human Rights **$11,500**
- None over $10,000

Misc Issues **$23,250**
- None over $10,000

Other & Unknown

Other — **$81,200**

Civil Servants/Public Officials **$22,750**
- None over $10,000

Education **$19,700**
- None over $10,000

Retired **$36,050**
- None over $10,000

Unknown — **$455,305**
- Homemakers/Non-income earners $25,260
- No Employer Listed or Found $330,520
- Employer Listed/Category Unknown $95,275
  - None over $10,000

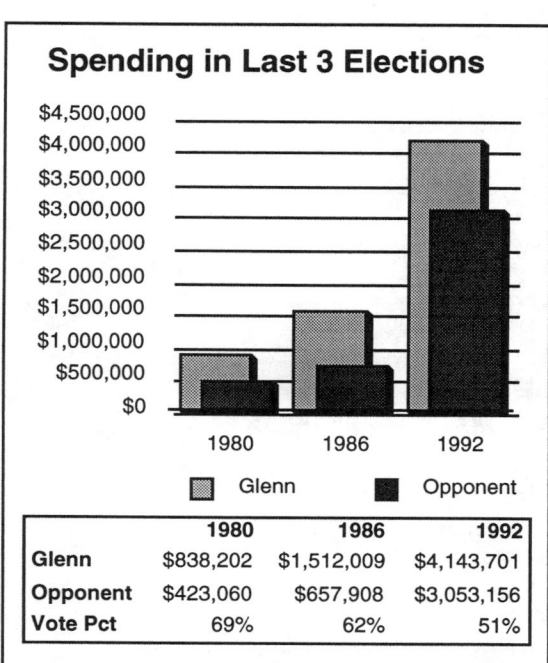

Spending in Last 3 Elections

	1980	1986	1992
Glenn	$838,202	$1,512,009	$4,143,701
Opponent	$423,060	$657,908	$3,053,156
Vote Pct	69%	62%	51%

Glenn ☐   Opponent ■

* Contributions came from more than one affiliate or subsidiary.

253

Al Gore (D-Tenn)

First elected: 1984

1987-92 Total Rcpts: $2,488,698
1992 Year-end Cash: $291,115

1991-92 Committees & Subcommittees

Armed Services
Defense Industry and Technology; Projection Forces and Regional Defense; Strategic Forces and Nuclear Deterrence

Commerce, Science and Transportation
Communications; Consumer; National Ocean Policy Study; Science, Technology and Space (Chairman); Surface Transportation

Rules and Administration

Joint Committee on Printing

Joint Economic Committee

Leading Contributors

Business

Agriculture	$92,340

Crop Production & Basic Processing $19,550
None over $10,000

Tobacco $11,190
None over $10,000

Dairy $19,000
Associated Milk Producers .... $10,000 PAC

Agricultural Services/Products $13,750
None over $10,000

Food Processing & Sales $20,500
None over $10,000

Communications/Electronics	$212,499

Printing & Publishing $20,250
West Publishing .... $12,000 PAC/Ind

Media/Entertainment $82,550
Walt Disney Co/Disney Channel* .... $22,000 PAC/Ind
MCA Inc* .... $10,800 PAC/Ind
Time Warner* .... $10,000 PAC/Ind

Telephone Utilities $79,449
BellSouth Corp* .... $14,500 PAC
US Telephone Assn .... $12,000 PAC
Bell Atlantic .... $10,000 PAC

Telecom Services & Equipment $17,742
None over $10,000

Source of Funds: 1987-1992

Source	Total	Pct
PACs	$1,044,316	41%
Indivs $200+	$1,053,735	42%
Indivs under $200	$190,255	8%
Other	$242,992	10%
Candidate	$0	0%
Party	$42,600	2%

Source of PAC Dollars by Sector

Source	Total	Pct
Business	$1,019,479	66%
Labor	$396,387	26%
Ideological/Single-Issue	$121,250	8%

In-State vs. Out-of-State Contributions*

Source	Total	Pct
In-State	$251,034	24%
Out-of-state	$795,401	76%
No state listed	$7,300	

* by large individual contributors ($200 & above)

Construction	$72,052

General Contractors $20,050
None over $10,000

Home Builders $12,250
None over $10,000

Construction Services $22,252
None over $10,000

Building Materials & Equipment $11,000
None over $10,000

Defense	$121,078

Defense Aerospace $67,450
None over $10,000

Defense Electronics $41,915
None over $10,000

Misc Defense $11,713
None over $10,000

Energy & Natural Resources	$91,038

Oil & Gas $41,149
Occidental Petroleum* .... $12,049 PAC/Ind

Electric Utilities $20,000
ACRE (Action Cmte for Rural Electrification) ..... $10,000 PAC

Waste Management $18,316
None over $10,000

Finance, Insurance & Real Estate	$385,472

Commercial Banks $70,950
American Bankers Assn .... $10,000 PAC

Securities & Investment $72,000
Chicago Mercantile Exchange .... $10,000 PAC

Insurance $103,576
None over $10,000

Real Estate $88,046
None over $10,000

Contribution Totals by Sector

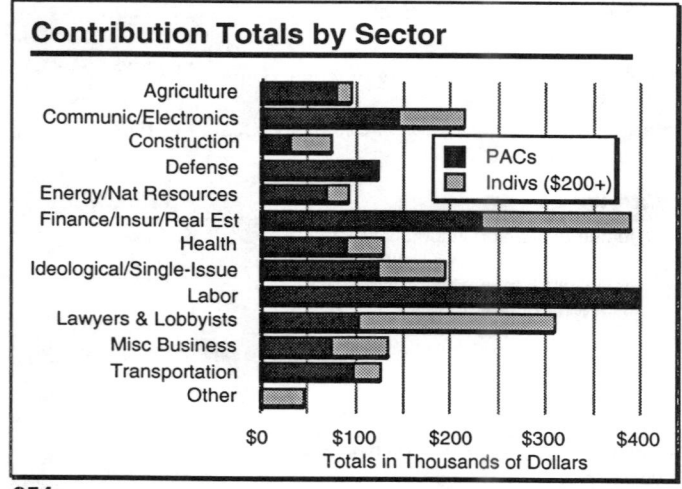

Agriculture
Communic/Electronics
Construction
Defense
Energy/Nat Resources
Finance/Insur/Real Est
Health
Ideological/Single-Issue
Labor
Lawyers & Lobbyists
Misc Business
Transportation
Other

PACs
Indivs ($200+)

$0 $100 $200 $300 $400
Totals in Thousands of Dollars

Accountants $20,250
   None over $10,000

Misc Finance $15,850
   None over $10,000

Health $127,750

Health Professionals $75,050
   None over $10,000

Hospitals/Nursing Homes $19,650
   None over $10,000

Pharmaceuticals/Health Products $26,550
   None over $10,000

Lawyers & Lobbyists $307,042

Lawyers & Lobbyists $307,042
   Opperman, Heins & Paquin .... $10,691 PAC/Ind
   Assn of Trial Lawyers of America .... $10,000 PAC
   Marks, Murase & White .... $10,000 Indiv

Misc Business $131,148

Food & Beverage $20,498
   None over $10,000

Beer, Wine & Liquor $10,400
   None over $10,000

Retail Sales $17,250
   None over $10,000

Business Services $22,300
   None over $10,000

Lodging/Tourism $18,500
   None over $10,000

Misc Manufacturing & Distributing $24,200
   None over $10,000

Transportation $123,179

Air Transport $44,500
   None over $10,000

Automotive $19,900
   None over $10,000

Trucking $18,521
   None over $10,000

Railroads $23,058
   None over $10,000

Sea Transport $15,200
   None over $10,000

Labor

Labor $396,887

Building Trade Unions $84,543
   Sheet Metal Workers Union .... $15,000 PAC
   Plumbers/Pipefitters Union* .... $13,000 PAC
   Laborers Union* .... $12,300 PAC
   Bricklayers Union .... $12,000 PAC
   Operating Engineers Union .... $12,000 PAC

Industrial Unions $95,574
   Intl Brotherhood of Electrical Workers .... $15,000 PAC
   Communications Workers of America .... $14,274 PAC
   Ladies Garment Workers Union .... $10,750 PAC
   American Federation of Teachers .... $10,000 PAC
   Machinists/Aerospace Workers Union .... $10,000 PAC
   United Steelworkers .... $10,000 PAC

Transportation Unions $94,500
   Seafarers International Union .... $13,000 PAC
   Air Line Pilots Assn .... $12,500 PAC
   Amalgamated Transit Union .... $11,000 PAC
   Teamsters Union .... $11,000 PAC
   Trans Comm International Union .... $10,000 PAC

Public Sector Unions $92,100
   American Postal Workers Union .... $15,000 PAC
   National Assn of Letter Carriers .... $15,000 PAC
   National Education Assn .... $11,000 PAC
   American Fedn of St/Cnty/Munic Employees .... $10,000 PAC
   Natl Assn of Retired Federal Employees .... $10,000 PAC

Misc Unions $30,170
   None over $10,000

Ideological/Single-Issue

Ideological/Single-Issue $190,605

Democratic/Liberal $37,750
   National Cmte for an Effective Congress .... $10,000 PAC

Leadership PACs $19,250
   None over $10,000

Pro-Israel $115,905
   Citizens Organized PAC .... $10,000 PAC
   Desert Caucus .... $10,000 PAC
   National PAC .... $10,000 PAC

Other & Unknown

Other $44,025

Education $12,250
   None over $10,000

Retired $17,175
   None over $10,000

Unknown $255,624

   Homemakers/Non-income earners $34,300
   No Employer Listed or Found $119,950
   Employer Listed/Category Unknown $94,924
      None over $10,000

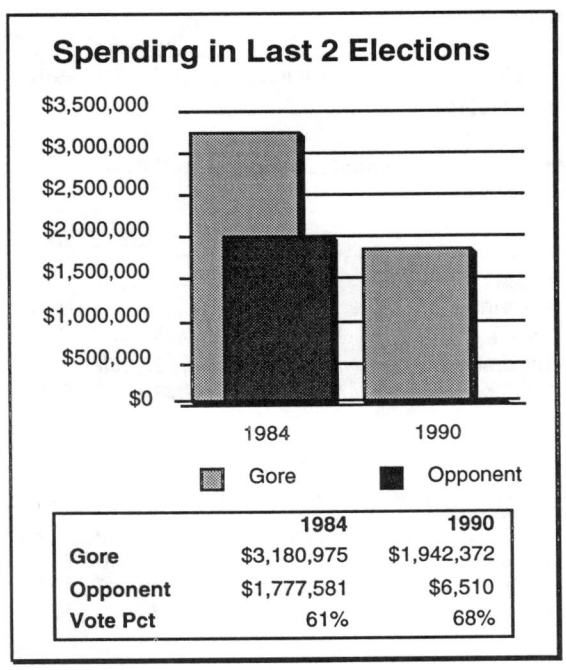

Spending in Last 2 Elections

	1984	1990
Gore	$3,180,975	$1,942,372
Opponent	$1,777,581	$6,510
Vote Pct	61%	68%

---

* Contributions came from more than one affiliate or subsidiary.

Slade Gorton (R-Wash)

First elected: 1980 *(out of office 87-88)*

1987-92 Total Rcpts:	$3,364,943
1992 Year-end Cash:	$128,708
Current term expires:	1994

1991-92 Committees & Subcommittees

Appropriations
District of Columbia; Interior and Related Agencies; Labor, Health and Human Services, Education and Related Agencies; Legislative Branch (Ranking Republican)

Commerce, Science and Transportation
Aviation; Communications; Consumer (Ranking Republican); National Ocean Policy Study

Select Committee on Ethics

Select Committee on Indian Affairs

Select Committee on Intelligence

Leading Contributors

NOTE: The bulk of Gorton's large individual contributions do not appear in the listings below. His last election was in 1988, and this book lists individual contributions only from 1989-1992.

Business

Agriculture	$173,237

Crop Production & Basic Processing **$6,700**
    None over $6,000

Dairy **$9,000**
    None over $6,000

Agricultural Services/Products **$12,400**
    None over $6,000

Food Processing & Sales **$54,749**
    Food Marketing Institute .... $6,000   PAC
    Services Group of America .... $6,000   PAC

Forestry & Forest Products **$82,688**
    Simpson Investment Co .... $20,000   PAC/Ind
    Weyerhaeuser Co .... $12,100   PAC/Ind
    Boise Cascade .... $6,000   PAC

Communications/Electronics	$120,600

Printing & Publishing **$10,000**
    None over $6,000

Media/Entertainment **$23,250**
    Assn of Independent Television Stations .... $9,000   PAC

Contribution Totals by Sector

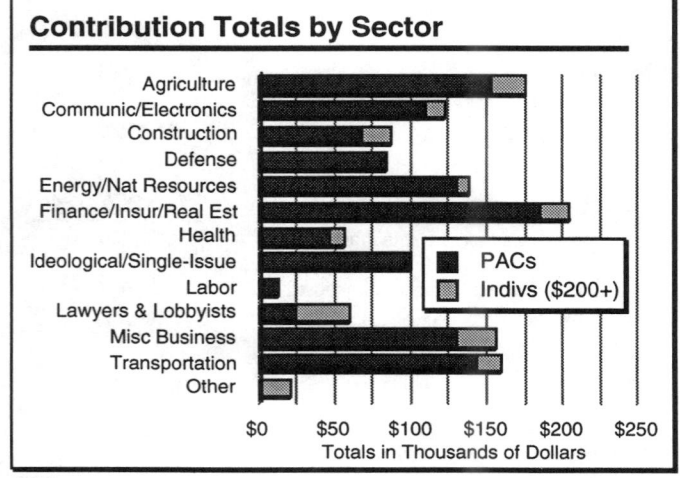

Totals in Thousands of Dollars

Source of Funds: 1987-1992

Source	Total	Pct
■ PACs	$1,190,089	32%
▨ Indivs $200+	$1,054,957	28%
□ Indivs under $200	$932,856	25%
⊠ Other	$541,647	15%
Candidate	$90,000	2%
Party	$354,606	10%

Source of PAC Dollars by Sector

Source	Total	Pct
■ Business	$1,061,855	91%
▨ Labor	$12,500	1%
□ Ideological/Single-Issue	$98,119	8%

In-State vs. Out-of-State Contributions*

Source	Total	Pct
□ In-State	$853,257	81%
■ Out-of-state	$194,800	19%
No state listed	$6,900	

*** by large individual contributors ($200 & above)**

Telephone Utilities **$54,100**
    AT&T .... $11,500   PAC
    Contel .... $6,000   PAC

Telecom Services & Equipment **$12,500**
    None over $6,000

Electronics Mfg & Services **$15,750**
    Cooper Industries .... $10,000   PAC

Construction	$85,450

General Contractors **$36,200**
    Associated General Contractors .... $10,000   PAC
    National Utility Contractors Assn .... $8,000   PAC

Home Builders **$7,250**
    None over $6,000

Special Trade Contractors **$21,800**
    Sheet Metal/Air Conditioning Contractors .... $12,000   PAC

Construction Services **$9,100**
    None over $6,000

Building Materials & Equipment **$11,100**
    None over $6,000

Defense	$81,750

Defense Aerospace **$42,500**
    Rockwell International .... $8,000   PAC
    Northrop Corp .... $7,000   PAC

Defense Electronics **$25,250**
    Harris Corp .... $10,000   PAC

Misc Defense **$14,000**
    None over $6,000

Energy & Natural Resources	$137,450

Oil & Gas **$81,450**
    Chevron Corp .... $10,000   PAC
    Dallas Energy PAC .... $10,000   PAC
    Amoco Corp .... $8,000   PAC

Mining	$9,400	
None over $6,000		
Electric Utilities	**$20,350**	
Puget Sound Power & Light $7,750		PAC/Ind
Commercial Fishing	**$20,750**	
National Fisheries Institute $15,000		PAC

Finance, Insurance & Real Estate $203,534

Commercial Banks	**$66,805**	
American Bankers Assn* $11,250		PAC
SeaFirst Bank $11,250		PAC
US Bancorp $8,000		PAC/Ind
Savings & Loans	**$18,550**	
US League of Savings Assns* $10,500		PAC
Securities & Investment	**$19,000**	
Chicago Mercantile Exchange $7,500		PAC
Insurance	**$65,179**	
National Assn of Independent Insurers $6,000		PAC
Real Estate	**$18,750**	
National Assn of Realtors $8,000		PAC
Accountants	**$8,750**	
None over $6,000		
Misc Finance	**$6,000**	
None over $6,000		

Health $55,750

Health Professionals	**$34,250**	
American Academy of Ophthalmology $10,000		PAC
American Medical Assn $10,000		PAC
Pharmaceuticals/Health Products	**$15,500**	
None over $6,000		

Lawyers & Lobbyists $58,721

Lawyers & Lobbyists	**$58,721**	
Davis, Wright et al $6,375		Indiv

Misc Business $155,489

Business Associations	**$13,432**	
National Fedn of Independent Business $9,569		PAC
Food & Beverage	**$42,499**	
National Restaurant Assn $6,000		PAC

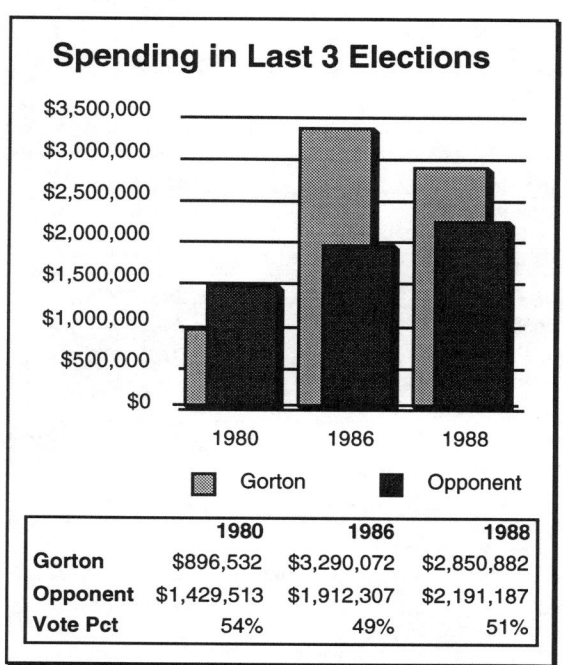

Spending in Last 3 Elections

	1980	1986	1988
Gorton	$896,532	$3,290,072	$2,850,882
Opponent	$1,429,513	$1,912,307	$2,191,187
Vote Pct	54%	49%	51%

Retail Sales	**$11,757**	
None over $6,000		
Business Services	**$15,750**	
Dun & Bradstreet $6,500		PAC
Chemical & Related Manufacturing	**$26,500**	
Dow Chemical* $6,000		PAC
Misc Manufacturing & Distributing	**$28,750**	
None over $6,000		

Transportation $157,999

Air Transport	**$51,800**	
Boeing Co $16,750		PAC/Ind
Texas Air $10,000		PAC
Federal Express Corp $7,000		PAC
Automotive	**$31,400**	
Auto Dealers & Drivers for Free Trade $12,000		PAC
Eaton Corp $6,000		PAC
National Auto Dealers Assn $6,000		PAC
Trucking	**$22,750**	
Paccar Inc $10,750		PAC/Ind
Railroads	**$21,799**	
Union Pacific Corp $9,000		PAC
Sea Transport	**$27,300**	
Sea-Land Corp $6,000		PAC

Labor

Labor $12,500

Transportation Unions	**$8,500**	
Marine Engineers Union* $7,500		PAC

Ideological/Single-Issue

Ideological/Single-Issue $98,369

Leadership PACs	**$53,502**	
Republican Majority Fund (Richard Lugar) $10,000		PAC
Campaign America (Bob Dole) $8,002		PAC
Catch the Spirit PAC (Bob Kasten) $8,000		PAC
Foreign & Defense Policy	**$11,117**	
National Security PAC $6,000		PAC
Pro-Israel	**$21,750**	
None over $6,000		

Other & Unknown

Other $20,000

Retired	**$18,050**	
None over $6,000		

Unknown $63,023

Homemakers/Non-income earners $17,250	
No Employer Listed or Found $8,562	
Employer Listed/Category Unknown $35,461	
None over $6,000	

Independent expenditures supporting Gorton
National Council of Senior Citizens $10,486

---

* Contributions came from more than one affiliate or subsidiary.

Bob Graham (D-Fla)

First elected: 1986

1987-92 Total Rcpts: $3,696,833
1992 Year-end Cash: $354,763
Current term expires: 1998

1991-92 Committees & Subcommittees

Banking, Housing and Urban Affairs
Housing and Urban Affairs; International Finance and Monetary Policy

Environment and Public Works
Environmental Protection; Nuclear Regulation (Chairman); Water Resources, Transportation and Infrastructure

Veterans' Affairs

Special Aging

Leading Contributors

Business

Agriculture		$147,850

Crop Production & Basic Processing	$65,000	
Okeelanta Corp	$10,000	Indiv

Livestock	$10,550	
None over $7,500		

Agricultural Services/Products	$25,950	
None over $7,500		

Food Processing & Sales	$29,450	
Food Marketing Institute	$10,000	PAC

Communications/Electronics		$157,215

Media/Entertainment	$104,900	
Walt Disney Co	$32,000	PAC/Ind
MCA Inc	$19,700	PAC/Ind
National Cable Television Assn	$10,000	PAC
Time Warner*	$8,000	Indiv

Telephone Utilities	$25,115	
BellSouth Corp*	$8,140	PAC/Ind

Computer Equipment & Services	$8,250	
None over $7,500		

Construction		$132,335

General Contractors	$47,801	
National Utility Contractors Assn	$9,000	PAC

Home Builders	$22,350	
None over $7,500		

Special Trade Contractors	$10,650	
None over $7,500		

Contribution Totals by Sector

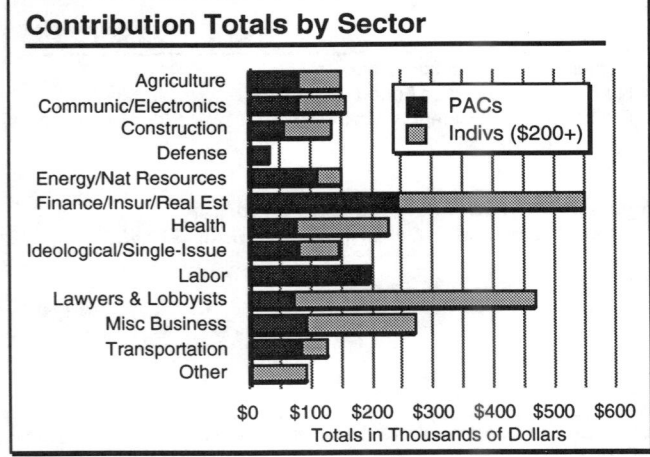

Agriculture
Communic/Electronics
Construction
Defense
Energy/Nat Resources
Finance/Insur/Real Est
Health
Ideological/Single-Issue
Labor
Lawyers & Lobbyists
Misc Business
Transportation
Other

■ PACs
▨ Indivs ($200+)

$0 $100 $200 $300 $400 $500 $600
Totals in Thousands of Dollars

Source of Funds: 1987-1992

Source	Total	Pct
■ PACs	$1,172,508	31%
▨ Indivs $200+	$1,864,046	50%
□ Indivs under $200	$327,783	9%
▧ Other	$370,271	10%
Candidate	$0	0%
Party	$37,775	1%

Source of PAC Dollars by Sector

Source	Total	Pct
■ Business	$907,325	77%
▨ Labor	$192,154	16%
□ Ideological/Single-Issue	$76,600	7%

In-State vs. Out-of-State Contributions*

Source	Total	Pct
□ In-State	$1,248,077	67%
■ Out-of-state	$603,344	33%
No state listed	$5,250	

*** by large individual contributors ($200 & above)**

Construction Services	$19,134	
None over $7,500		

Building Materials & Equipment	$32,400	
Jim Walter Corp	$11,000	PAC/Ind

Defense		$32,750

Defense Aerospace	$20,250	
None over $7,500		

Energy & Natural Resources		$149,740

Oil & Gas	$42,650	
Occidental Petroleum	$10,000	PAC/Ind

Mining	$8,250	
None over $7,500		

Nuclear Energy	$13,250	
None over $7,500		

Electric Utilities	$55,250	
Florida Power & Light	$24,250	PAC/Ind

Waste Management	$24,340	
Waste Management Inc	$8,500	PAC

Finance, Insurance & Real Estate		$546,047

Commercial Banks	$61,276	
Barnett Banks Inc	$9,676	Indiv

Finance/Credit Companies	$10,500	
None over $7,500		

Securities & Investment	$114,816	
Goldman, Sachs & Co	$10,716	PAC/Ind
Chicago Mercantile Exchange	$9,000	PAC

Insurance	$131,130	
American Family Corp	$10,000	PAC/Ind
National Assn of Life Underwriters	$10,000	PAC
Independent Insurance Agents of America	$9,999	PAC

Real Estate	$140,950	
National Assn of Realtors	$8,000	PAC

Accountants $41,425
   None over $7,500

Misc Finance $38,150
   None over $7,500

Health $226,071

Health Professionals $163,581
   None over $7,500

Hospitals/Nursing Homes $25,340
   Hospice Care Inc .... $10,750   Indiv

Pharmaceuticals/Health Products $22,300
   None over $7,500

Lawyers & Lobbyists $463,670

Lawyers & Lobbyists $463,670
   Holland & Knight .... $19,900   PAC/Ind
   Assn of Trial Lawyers of America .... $10,000   PAC
   Stuzin & Camner .... $9,226   PAC/Ind
   Steel, Hector & Davis .... $7,850   Indiv

Misc Business $265,442

Food & Beverage $17,500
   None over $7,500

Beer, Wine & Liquor $24,450
   None over $7,500

Retail Sales $48,542
   None over $7,500

Business Services $47,350
   None over $7,500

Casinos/Gambling $23,950
   Circus Circus Enterprises .... $9,000   PAC/Ind

Lodging/Tourism $13,050
   None over $7,500

Chemical & Related Manufacturing $23,950
   WR Grace & Co .... $9,000   PAC

Misc Manufacturing & Distributing $38,350
   None over $7,500

Transportation $124,784

Air Transport $41,884
   Federal Express Corp .... $11,000   PAC
   United Parcel Service .... $8,000   PAC

Spending in Last 2 Elections

	1986	1992
Graham	$6,173,663	$3,130,543
Opponent	$7,129,409	$242,251
Vote Pct	55%	65%

Automotive $24,850
   None over $7,500

Trucking.. $14,800
   None over $7,500

Railroads $19,000
   CSX Corp* .... $8,750   PAC/Ind

Sea Transport $16,250
   None over $7,500

Labor

Labor $193,354

Building Trade Unions $28,825
   Laborers Union* .... $10,500   PAC

Industrial Unions $18,250
   Communications Workers of America .... $10,000   PAC

Transportation Unions $79,000
   Air Line Pilots Assn .... $10,000   PAC
   Marine Engineers Union* .... $10,000   PAC
   Teamsters Union .... $10,000   PAC
   United Transportation Union .... $10,000   PAC
   Transport Workers Union .... $9,000   PAC
   Amalgamated Transit Union .... $8,500   PAC

Public Sector Unions $56,780
   American Federation of Teachers .... $10,000   PAC

Misc Unions... $10,499
   None over $7,500

Ideological/Single-Issue

Ideological/Single-Issue $145,300

Democratic/Liberal $18,050
   None over $7,500

Foreign & Defense Policy $9,500
   None over $7,500

Pro-Israel $89,500
   Florida Congressional Cmte .... $10,000   PAC
   Washington PAC .... $7,500   PAC

Human Rights $8,500
   None over $7,500

Misc Issues... $12,500
   National Cmte to Preserve Social Security .... $10,000   PAC

Other & Unknown

Other $90,040

Civil Servants/Public Officials............................ $17,600
   None over $7,500

Education $14,550
   None over $7,500

Retired $53,890
   None over $7,500

Unknown $373,279

   Homemakers/Non-income earners $68,727
   No Employer Listed or Found $118,564
   Generic Occupation/Category Unknown $11,175
   Employer Listed/Category Unknown................ $174,713
      None over $7,500

---

* Contributions came from more than one affiliate or subsidiary.

259

Phil Gramm (R-Texas)

First elected: 1984

1987-92 Total Rcpts:	$18,457,261
1992 Year-end Cash:	$5,921,738
Current term expires:	1996

1991-92 Committees & Subcommittees

Appropriations
Commerce, Justice, State, the Judiciary and Related Agencies; Labor, Health and Human Services, Education and Related Agencies; Military Construction (Ranking Republican); VA, HUD and Independent Agencies

Banking, Housing and Urban Affairs
Housing and Urban Affairs; Securities (Ranking Republican)

Budget

Source of Funds: 1987-1992

Source	Total	Pct
PACs	$1,848,480	9%
Indivs $200+	$9,004,499	46%
Indivs under $200	$5,478,760	28%
Other	$3,246,833	17%
Candidate	$0	0%
Party	$1,121,311	6%

Source of PAC Dollars by Sector

Source	Total	Pct
Business	$1,744,190	95%
Labor	$25,700	1%
Ideological/Single-Issue	$65,350	4%

In-State vs. Out-of-State Contributions*

Source	Total	Pct
In-State	$7,540,802	84%
Out-of-state	$1,453,663	16%
No state listed	$8,584	

* by large individual contributors ($200 & above)

Leading Contributors

Business

Agriculture — $635,384

Crop Production & Basic Processing $88,485
None over $12,500

Tobacco $25,000
None over $12,500

Livestock $224,959
Texas & Southwestern Cattle Raisers .... $12,500 — PAC

Agricultural Services/Products $52,050
None over $12,500

Food Processing & Sales $170,715
McLane Co .... $13,850 — PAC/Ind

Forestry & Forest Products $41,275
None over $12,500

Misc Agriculture $13,450
None over $12,500

Communications/Electronics — $212,342

Printing & Publishing $39,375
None over $12,500

Media/Entertainment $48,450
None over $12,500

Telephone Utilities $33,675
None over $12,500

Electronics Mfg & Services $25,926
None over $12,500

Computer Equipment & Services $54,641
Sterling Software .... $20,000 — Indiv

Contribution Totals by Sector

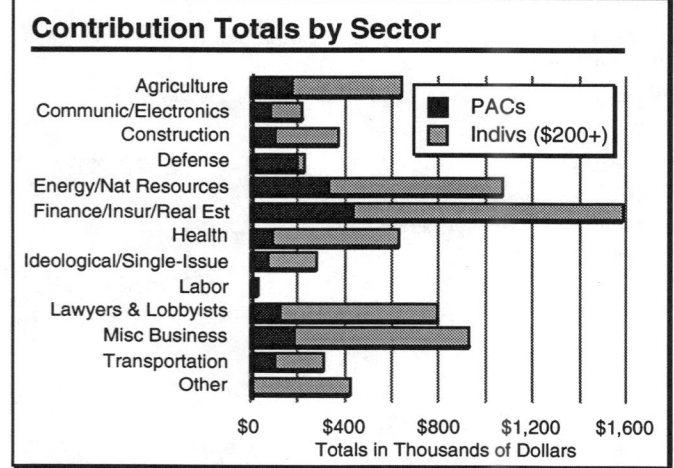

Agriculture
Communic/Electronics
Construction
Defense
Energy/Nat Resources
Finance/Insur/Real Est
Health
Ideological/Single-Issue
Labor
Lawyers & Lobbyists
Misc Business
Transportation
Other

- PACs
- Indivs ($200+)

$0 $400 $800 $1,200 $1,600
Totals in Thousands of Dollars

Construction — $363,736

General Contractors $143,775
None over $12,500

Home Builders $50,650
None over $12,500

Special Trade Contractors $40,250
None over $12,500

Construction Services $51,425
None over $12,500

Building Materials & Equipment $77,636
None over $12,500

Defense — $216,947

Defense Aerospace $109,282
Northrop Corp .... $12,500 — PAC/Ind

Defense Electronics $78,015
None over $12,500

Misc Defense $29,650
None over $12,500

Energy & Natural Resources — $1,061,464

Oil & Gas $881,649
Quintana Petroleum .... $24,000 — Indiv
Mesa Limited Partnership .... $23,250 — Indiv
Exxon Corp .... $13,650 — PAC/Ind
Atlantic Richfield .... $12,525 — PAC/Ind
Occidental Petroleum* .... $12,500 — PAC/Ind

Mining $35,000
None over $12,500

Misc Energy $49,115
None over $12,500

Electric Utilities $69,650
None over $12,500

Waste Management $22,800
None over $12,500

Finance, Insurance & Real Estate $1,572,150

Commercial Banks $331,646
  First City Bancorp of Texas* .... $52,403   PAC/Ind
  NCNB Corp* .... $18,000   PAC/Ind
Savings & Loans $47,250
  None over $12,500
Credit Unions $15,178
  None over $12,500
Finance/Credit Companies $23,914
  None over $12,500
Securities & Investment $226,310
  American Express* .... $14,750   PAC/Ind
Insurance $245,997
  None over $12,500
Real Estate $293,280
  None over $12,500
Accountants $89,632
  None over $12,500
Misc Finance $298,943
  None over $12,500

Health $623,564

Health Professionals $512,599
  None over $12,500
Hospitals/Nursing Homes $26,105
  None over $12,500
Pharmaceuticals/Health Products $67,810
  Behrens Inc .... $12,500   Indiv

Lawyers & Lobbyists $784,900

Lawyers & Lobbyists $784,900
  Baker & Botts .... $30,175   PAC/Ind
  Fulbright & Jaworski .... $18,600   PAC/Ind
  Akin, Gump et al .... $18,100   PAC/Ind
  Vinson & Elkins .... $15,500   PAC/Ind
  Johnson & Gibbs .... $13,800   PAC/Ind
  Bracewell & Patterson .... $12,550   PAC/Ind

Misc Business $914,394

Business Associations $26,989
  None over $12,500
Food & Beverage $88,985
  None over $12,500

Spending in Last 2 Elections

	1984	1990
Gramm	$9,452,357	$12,474,887
Opponent	$5,889,458	$1,677,087
Vote Pct	59%	60%

Beer, Wine & Liquor $40,775
  None over $12,500
Retail Sales $109,262
  None over $12,500
Misc Services $61,225
  None over $12,500
Business Services $165,433
  None over $12,500
Lodging/Tourism $26,750
  None over $12,500
Chemical & Related Manufacturing $117,225
  Contran Corp .... $18,000   PAC/Ind
Steel Production $18,900
  None over $12,500
Misc Manufacturing & Distributing $219,225
  Rock-Tenn Co .... $14,000   Indiv

Transportation $306,718

Air Transport $75,568
  Texas Air .... $18,000   PAC/Ind
Automotive $120,800
  None over $12,500
Trucking $29,200
  None over $12,500
Railroads $28,350
  None over $12,500
Sea Transport $44,900
  None over $12,500

Labor

Labor $26,050

Transportation Unions $21,300
  Teamsters Union* .... $21,000   PAC

Ideological/Single-Issue

Ideological/Single-Issue $266,887

Republican/Conservative $135,412
  National Republican Senatorial Cmte .... $46,600   Indiv
Pro-Israel $75,775
  None over $12,500
Misc Issues $13,050
  None over $12,500

Other & Unknown

Other $411,752

Civil Servants/Public Officials $55,900
  None over $12,500
Education $63,100
  None over $12,500
Retired $281,712
  None over $12,500

Unknown $2,193,498

  Homemakers/Non-income earners $422,319
  No Employer Listed or Found $958,980
  Generic Occupation/Category Unknown $63,575
  Employer Listed/Category Unknown $746,555
    None over $12,500

---

* Contributions came from more than one affiliate or subsidiary.

Charles E. Grassley (R-Iowa)

First elected: 1980

1987-92 Total Rcpts:	$2,833,489
1992 Year-end Cash:	$821,030
Current term expires:	1998

1991-92 Committees & Subcommittees

Agriculture, Nutrition and Forestry
Agricultural Credit (Ranking Republican); Agricultural Production and Stabilization of Prices; Domestic and Foreign Marketing and Product Promotion

Budget

Finance
International Trade; Medicare and Long Term Care; Private Retirement Plans and Oversight of the Internal Revenue Service (Ranking Republican)

Judiciary
Courts and Administrative Practice (Ranking Republican); Patents, Copyrights and Trademarks

Select Committee on POW/MIA Affairs

Special Aging

Leading Contributors

Business

Agriculture	$208,952

Crop Production & Basic Processing $26,020
None over $6,000

Tobacco $15,000
None over $6,000

Dairy $24,450
Associated Milk Producers .... $8,000 PAC

Poultry & Eggs $14,000
None over $6,000

Livestock $11,053
National Pork Producers Council .... $7,053 PAC

Agricultural Services/Products $64,429
Archer-Daniels-Midland Corp .... $10,000 PAC
Deere & Co .... $8,450 PAC
American Assn of Crop Insurers .... $7,979 PAC

Food Processing & Sales $47,000
ConAgra Inc .... $10,000 PAC
Iowa Packing Co .... $8,000 Indiv

Forestry & Forest Products $7,000
None over $6,000

Contribution Totals by Sector

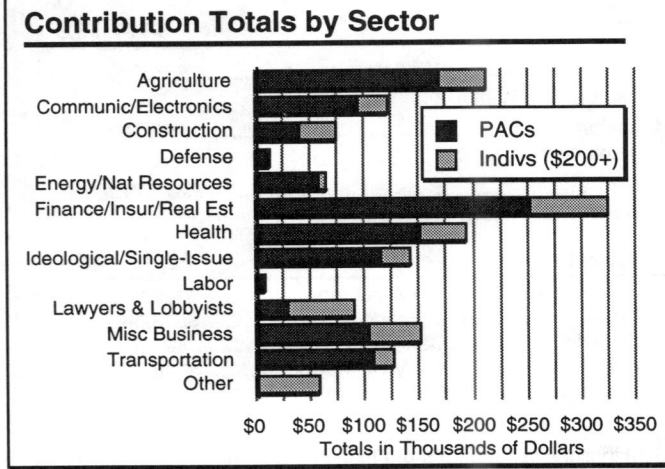

Totals in Thousands of Dollars

Source of Funds: 1987-1992

Source	Total	Pct
■ PACs	$1,033,084	33%
▨ Indivs $200+	$582,536	19%
☐ Indivs under $200	$797,758	26%
▨ Other	$681,836	22%
Candidate	$0	0%
Party	$261,725	8%

Source of PAC Dollars by Sector

Source	Total	Pct
■ Business	$999,077	89%
▨ Labor	$8,000	1%
☐ Ideological/Single-Issue ..	$113,950	10%

In-State vs. Out-of-State Contributions*

Source	Total	Pct
☐ In-State	$345,029	60%
■ Out-of-state	$233,607	40%
No state listed	$0	

* by large individual contributors ($200 & above)

Communications/Electronics	$120,371

Printing & Publishing $24,500
None over $6,000

Media/Entertainment $36,900
National Cable Television Assn .... $10,000 PAC
National Assn of Broadcasters .... $7,650 PAC
Heritage Communications .... $6,500 PAC/Ind

Telephone Utilities $47,066
GTE Corp .... $7,150 PAC
AT&T .... $7,000 PAC
Ameritech Corp .... $6,666 PAC
BellSouth Corp* .... $6,000 PAC

Computer Equipment & Services $6,905
None over $6,000

Construction	$72,100

General Contractors $26,250
Associated General Contractors* .... $11,000 PAC

Home Builders $8,500
None over $6,000

Special Trade Contractors $6,200
None over $6,000

Building Materials & Equipment $26,650
None over $6,000

Defense	$11,000

Defense Aerospace $7,250
None over $6,000

Energy & Natural Resources	$63,000

Oil & Gas $23,250
None over $6,000

Mining $11,500
None over $6,000

Electric Utilities **$16,000**
    ACRE (Action Cmte for Rural Electrification)* ..... $6,500   PAC

Waste Management **$7,500**
    Waste Management Inc .... $6,500   PAC/Ind

Finance, Insurance & Real Estate $323,347

Commercial Banks **$43,510**
    American Bankers Assn .... $10,000   PAC
    Independent Bankers Assn .... $8,000   PAC

Securities & Investment **$43,580**
    Chicago Mercantile Exchange .... $9,500   PAC
    Chicago Board of Trade .... $7,000   PAC

Insurance **$172,223**
    National Assn of Independent Insurers .... $10,500   PAC
    American Family Corp .... $10,000   PAC
    National Assn of Life Underwriters .... $10,000   PAC
    Principal Mutual Life Insurance .... $9,399   PAC
    American Council of Life Insurance .... $8,284   PAC
    Mutual of Omaha .... $7,000   PAC/Ind
    Independent Insurance Agents of America .... $6,200   PAC

Real Estate **$21,450**
    National Assn of Realtors .... $10,000   PAC

Accountants **$15,950**
    American Institute of CPA's .... $10,000   PAC

Misc Finance **$13,750**
    None over $6,000

Health $192,569

Health Professionals **$101,540**
    American Chiropractic Assn .... $10,000   PAC
    American Medical Assn .... $9,473   PAC

Hospitals/Nursing Homes **$29,200**
    American Health Care Assn .... $10,000   PAC
    American Hospital Assn .... $8,000   PAC

Pharmaceuticals/Health Products **$60,079**
    Pfizer Inc .... $6,000   PAC

Lawyers & Lobbyists $87,670

Lawyers & Lobbyists **$87,670**
    Weil, Gotshal & Manges .... $8,200   Indiv
    McClure, Trotter & Mentz .... $7,000   Indiv

Spending in Last 3 Elections

	1980	1986	1992
Grassley	$2,183,028	$2,844,222	$2,448,806
Opponent	$1,750,680	$255,673	$410,894
Vote Pct	54%	66%	70%

Misc Business   **$148,901**

Food & Beverage **$13,160**
    None over $6,000

Beer, Wine & Liquor **$16,000**
    National Beer Wholesalers Assn .... $9,000   PAC

Retail Sales **$24,257**
    None over $6,000

Business Services **$26,200**
    Outdoor Advertising Assn of America .... $8,500   PAC

Chemical & Related Manufacturing **$15,750**
    None over $6,000

Misc Manufacturing & Distributing **$33,234**
    Maytag Co .... $6,250   PAC/Ind

Transportation $124,589

Air Transport **$24,250**
    General Electric .... $7,000   PAC
    United Parcel Service .... $6,500   PAC

Automotive **$44,750**
    National Auto Dealers Assn .... $10,000   PAC
    Auto Dealers & Drivers for Free Trade .... $9,000   PAC

Trucking **$20,789**
    American Trucking Assns .... $7,039   PAC

Railroads **$31,750**
    Union Pacific Corp .... $11,000   PAC/Ind

Labor

Labor $8,000

Public Sector Unions **$8,000**
    None over $6,000

Ideological/Single-Issue

Ideological/Single-Issue $139,750

Republican/Conservative **$6,250**
    None over $6,000

Leadership PACs **$15,000**
    Campaign America (Bob Dole) .... $10,000   PAC

Foreign & Defense Policy **$8,000**
    None over $6,000

Pro-Israel **$82,600**
    Citizens Concerned for the National Interest ..... $10,000   PAC
    Citizens Organized PAC .... $10,000   PAC

Gun Rights/Gun Control **$9,900**
    National Rifle Assn .... $9,900   PAC

Misc Issues **$11,000**
    National Cmte to Preserve Social Security .... $7,000   PAC

Other & Unknown

Other $57,676

Education **$12,050**
    University of Iowa .... $7,050   Indiv

Retired **$36,976**
    None over $6,000

Unknown $144,888

    Homemakers/Non-income earners $11,750
    No Employer Listed or Found $92,256
    Employer Listed/Category Unknown $40,121
      None over $6,000

* Contributions came from more than one affiliate or subsidiary.

Judd Gregg (R-NH)

1993-94 Committees & Subcommittees

Budget

Foreign Relations
European Affairs; Near Eastern and South Asian Affairs

Labor and Human Resources
Aging (Ranking Republican); Children, Family, Drugs and Alcoholism; Education, Arts and Humanities; Employment and Productivity

First elected: 1992

1991-92 Total Rcpts:	$991,938
1992 Year-end Cash:	$115,162
Current term expires:	1998

Leading Contributors

Business

Agriculture	$39,300	
Tobacco	**$3,000**	
None over $2,500		
Agricultural Services/Products	**$8,500**	
None over $2,500		
Food Processing & Sales	**$15,500**	
Winn-Dixie Stores	$5,000	PAC
Pepsico Inc	$2,500	PAC
Forestry & Forest Products	**$12,000**	
None over $2,500		

Communications/Electronics	$45,000	
Printing & Publishing	**$4,500**	
Hallmark Cards	$2,500	PAC
Telephone Utilities	**$11,750**	
United Telecommunications	$7,000	PAC
Electronics Mfg & Services	**$4,750**	
Bell Controls	$2,500	Indiv
Computer Equipment & Services	**$21,500**	
Cabletron Systems Inc	$17,000	Indiv

Construction	$26,650	
General Contractors	**$18,150**	
Associated General Contractors	$5,000	PAC
Speedway Inc	$5,000	Indiv
Special Trade Contractors	**$2,500**	
None over $2,500		

Contribution Totals by Sector

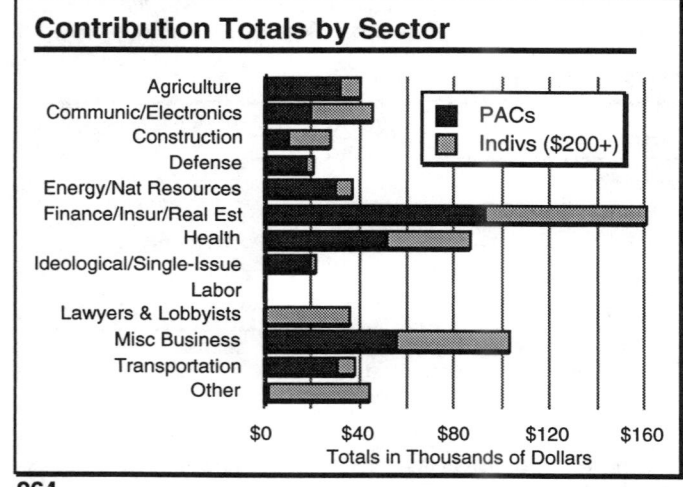

Agriculture
Communic/Electronics
Construction
Defense
Energy/Nat Resources
Finance/Insur/Real Est
Health
Ideological/Single-Issue
Labor
Lawyers & Lobbyists
Misc Business
Transportation
Other

■ PACs
▨ Indivs ($200+)

$0 $40 $80 $120 $160
Totals in Thousands of Dollars

Source of Funds: 1987-1992

Source	Total	Pct
■ PACs	$367,605	33%
▨ Indivs $200+	$417,204	37%
□ Indivs under $200	$158,922	14%
▨ Other	$176,186	16%
Candidate	$0	0%
Party	$127,979	11%

Source of PAC Dollars by Sector

Source	Total	Pct
■ Business	$332,554	95%
▨ Labor	$0	0%
□ Ideological/Single-Issue	$19,050	5%

In-State vs. Out-of-State Contributions*

Source	Total	Pct
□ In-State	$268,424	65%
■ Out-of-state	$146,080	35%
No state listed	$0	

*** by large individual contributors ($200 & above)**

Defense	$19,800	
Defense Aerospace	**$7,500**	
Martin Marietta Corp	$3,500	PAC
Defense Electronics	**$11,300**	
Raytheon	$7,000	PAC
Lockheed Sanders Inc	$3,300	Indiv

Energy & Natural Resources	$35,965	
Oil & Gas	**$29,405**	
Exxon Corp	$7,500	PAC
Sun Co	$3,000	PAC
Mobil Oil	$2,500	PAC
Waste Management	**$3,710**	
Wheelabrator Technologies	$3,710	PAC/Ind

Finance, Insurance & Real Estate	$159,605	
Commercial Banks	**$27,150**	
American Bankers Assn	$10,000	PAC
JP Morgan & Co	$5,000	PAC
Savings & Loans	**$2,750**	
None over $2,500		
Finance/Credit Companies	**$6,000**	
American Financial Services Assn	$3,000	PAC
Beneficial Management Corp	$3,000	PAC/Ind
Securities & Investment	**$26,800**	
Bear, Stearns & Co	$5,000	Indiv
Dean Witter	$3,000	PAC/Ind
Morgan Stanley & Co	$3,000	Indiv
First Boston Corp	$2,750	Indiv
American Express*	$2,500	PAC/Ind

Insurance **$68,909**
   Independent Insurance Agents of America ....$10,000 PAC
   National Assn of Life Underwriters....................$10,000 PAC
   National Assn of Independent Insurers ....$6,000 PAC
   Liberty Mutual Insurance ....$5,000 PAC
   Prudential Insurance ....$3,500 PAC
   Travelers Corp ....$3,000 PAC
   Mutual of Omaha...$2,500 PAC

Real Estate **$22,246**
   New England Development ....$6,000 Indiv

Accountants **$2,750**
   Arthur Andersen & Co ....$2,750 Indiv

Misc Finance **$3,000**
   None over $2,500

Health   **$85,651**

Health Professionals **$33,301**
   American Academy of Ophthalmology ....$5,000 PAC
   American Medical Assn.......................................$5,000 PAC
   American Assn Oral & Maxillofacial Surgeons ....$3,000 PAC
   American Society of Anesthesiologists ....$2,500 PAC

Hospitals/Nursing Homes **$9,750**
   McKerley Management Services ....$4,000 Indiv

Pharmaceuticals/Health Products **$42,600**
   Henley Group Inc ....$21,350 PAC/Ind
   Eli Lilly & Co ....$4,000 PAC
   Abbott Laboratories ....$3,000 PAC
   Pfizer Inc ....$3,000 PAC

Lawyers & Lobbyists   **$34,900**

Lawyers & Lobbyists **$34,900**
   Rath, Young et al ....$4,000 Indiv
   Wiggin & Nourie ....$2,500 Indiv

Misc Business   **$102,570**

Business Associations **$7,540**
   National Fedn of Independent Business ....$4,500 PAC

Food & Beverage **$11,250**
   National Restaurant Assn ....$3,500 PAC

Beer, Wine & Liquor **$8,200**
   National Beer Wholesalers Assn ....$5,000 PAC

Retail Sales **$12,750**
   None over $2,500

Business Services **$11,530**
   None over $2,500

Casinos/Gambling **$4,000**
   Hinsdale Greyhound Racing Assn ....$4,000 Indiv

Lodging/Tourism **$4,500**
   None over $2,500

Misc Business **$3,000**
   None over $2,500

Chemical & Related Manufacturing **$10,300**
   None over $2,500

Misc Manufacturing & Distributing **$26,800**
   Tyco Laboratories ....$4,000 Indiv
   National Screw Machines Products Assn ....$3,000 PAC
   Simplex Wire & Cable ....$3,000 Indiv
   Grinnell Corp ....$2,700 Indiv

Transportation   **$37,330**

Air Transport **$12,250**
   United Parcel Service ....$6,000 PAC

Automotive **$16,830**
   Americans for Free International Trade ....$5,000 PAC
   National Auto Dealers Assn ....$5,000 PAC

Railroads **$6,000**
   Union Pacific Corp ....$6,000 PAC

Ideological/Single-Issue

Ideological/Single-Issue   **$21,050**

Leadership PACs **$9,000**
   Campaign America (Bob Dole) ....$5,000 PAC
   Senate Victory Fund (Thad Cochran) ....$3,000 PAC

Gun Rights/Gun Control **$5,950**
   National Rifle Assn ....$5,950 PAC

Other & Unknown

Other   **$43,350**

Civil Servants/Public Officials **$5,950**
   State of New Hampshire ....$2,500 Indiv

Retired **$32,650**
   None over $2,500

Unknown   **$118,637**

   Homemakers/Non-income earners $26,900
   No Employer Listed or Found $40,334
   Employer Listed/Category Unknown $50,903
      Capital Distributors......................................$3,000 Indiv

Independent expenditures supporting Gregg
   National Right to Life PAC $2,638

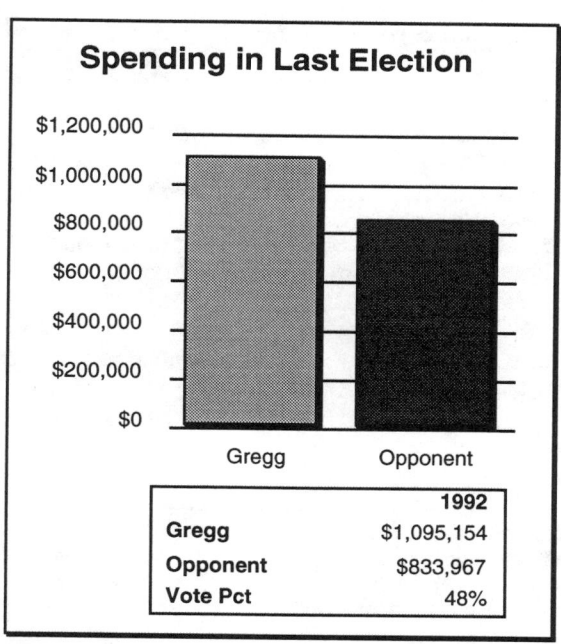

Spending in Last Election

	1992
Gregg	$1,095,154
Opponent	$833,967
Vote Pct	48%

---

* Contributions came from more than one affiliate or subsidiary.

Tom Harkin (D-Iowa)

First elected: 1984

1987-92 Total Rcpts:	$5,867,588
1992 Year-end Cash:	$78,831
Current term expires:	1996

1991-92 Committees & Subcommittees

Agriculture, Nutrition and Forestry
Agricultural Production and Stabilization of Prices; Domestic and Foreign Marketing and Product Promotion; Nutrition and Investigations (Chairman)

Appropriations
Agriculture, Rural Development and Related Agencies; Defense; Foreign Operations; Labor, Health and Human Services, Education and Related Agencies (Chairman); Transportation and Related Agencies

Labor and Human Resources
Children, Families, Drugs and Alcoholism; Employment and Productivity; Disability Policy (Chairman); Labor

Small Business
Competitiveness and Economic Opportunity; Export Expansion

Leading Contributors

NOTE: Harkin's profile includes contributions received in his 1992 presidential campaign.

Business

Agriculture $257,424

Crop Production & Basic Processing	**$77,089**	
American Crystal Sugar Corp	$13,000	PAC
Dairy	**$35,500**	
Associated Milk Producers	$15,000	PAC
Poultry & Eggs	**$31,000**	
Tyson Foods	$13,000	PAC/Ind
Agricultural Services/Products	**$72,735**	
Archer-Daniels-Midland Corp	$15,000	PAC
American Assn of Crop Insurers	$13,500	PAC
Food Processing & Sales	**$26,500**	
None over $12,500		

Communications/Electronics $111,464

Printing & Publishing	**$17,724**	
None over $12,500		
Media/Entertainment	**$73,600**	
None over $12,500		

Construction $42,000

General Contractors	**$16,200**	
None over $12,500		

Source of Funds: 1987-1992

Source	Total	Pct
PACs	$1,834,857	30%
Indivs $200+	$1,830,539	29%
Indivs under $200	$2,023,539	33%
Other	$530,476	9%
Candidate	$0	0%
Party	$351,823	6%

Source of PAC Dollars by Sector

Source	Total	Pct
Business	$1,058,169	48%
Labor	$681,100	31%
Ideological/Single-Issue	$459,163	21%

In-State vs. Out-of-State Contributions*

Source	Total	Pct
In-State	$418,815	13%
Out-of-state	$2,863,577	87%
No state listed	$9,450	

* by large individual contributors ($200 & above)

Defense $71,690

Defense Aerospace	**$33,250**	
None over $12,500		
Defense Electronics	**$34,740**	
None over $12,500		

Energy & Natural Resources $69,500

Oil & Gas	**$51,000**	
Occidental Petroleum*	$20,000	PAC/Ind
Michigan Consolidated Gas	$15,500	PAC
Electric Utilities	**$12,500**	
None over $12,500		

Finance, Insurance & Real Estate $491,416

Commercial Banks	**$56,011**	
None over $12,500		
Savings & Loans	**$17,000**	
None over $12,500		
Securities & Investment	**$107,650**	
Chicago Mercantile Exchange	$15,000	PAC
Refco Inc	$15,000	Indiv
Chicago Board of Trade	$12,500	PAC
Insurance	**$123,153**	
American Council of Life Insurance	$14,000	PAC
Real Estate	**$158,025**	
None over $12,500		
Misc Finance	**$16,250**	
None over $12,500		

Health $352,752

Health Professionals	**$244,127**	
American Chiropractic Assn	$18,000	PAC
American Physical Therapy Assn	$16,750	PAC
Assn for the Advancement of Psychology	$15,137	PAC
Hospitals/Nursing Homes	**$45,200**	
American Hospital Assn	$12,500	PAC

Contribution Totals by Sector

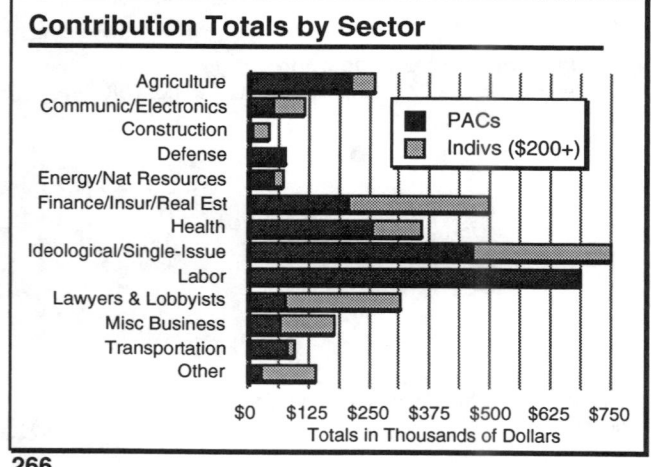

Agriculture, Communic/Electronics, Construction, Defense, Energy/Nat Resources, Finance/Insur/Real Est, Health, Ideological/Single-Issue, Labor, Lawyers & Lobbyists, Misc Business, Transportation, Other

PACs / Indivs ($200+)

$0 $125 $250 $375 $500 $625 $750
Totals in Thousands of Dollars

Health Services	$13,200
None over $12,500	
Pharmaceuticals/Health Products	$43,250
None over $12,500	

Lawyers & Lobbyists — $311,294

Lawyers & Lobbyists	$311,294	
Akin, Gump et al	$14,150	PAC/Ind

Misc Business — $176,694

Food & Beverage	$21,044
None over $12,500	
Beer, Wine & Liquor	$17,500
None over $12,500	
Retail Sales	$20,400
None over $12,500	
Business Services	$44,100
None over $12,500	
Misc Manufacturing & Distributing	$29,450
None over $12,500	

Transportation — $93,930

Air Transport	$41,600
None over $12,500	
Automotive	$13,530
None over $12,500	
Sea Transport	$15,750
None over $12,500	

Labor

Labor — $681,948

Building Trade Unions	$120,175	
Bricklayers Union	$16,000	PAC
Operating Engineers Union*	$16,000	PAC
Plumbers/Pipefitters Union*	$16,000	PAC
Sheet Metal Workers Union	$16,000	PAC
Laborers' Political League	$15,500	PAC
Industrial Unions	$182,150	
United Mine Workers	$17,500	PAC
Amalgamated Clothing & Textile Workers	$16,000	PAC
United Steelworkers	$15,500	PAC

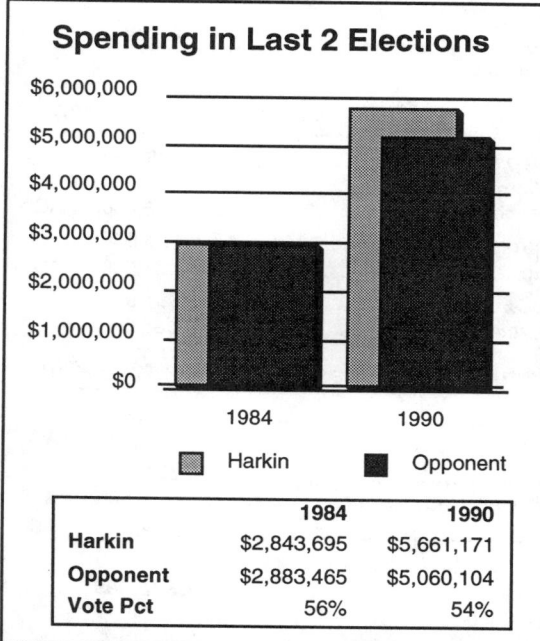

Spending in Last 2 Elections

	1984	1990
Harkin	$2,843,695	$5,661,171
Opponent	$2,883,465	$5,060,104
Vote Pct	56%	54%

	$15,000	PAC
Boilermakers Union	$15,000	PAC
Communications Workers of America	$15,000	PAC
Machinists/Aerospace Workers Union	$15,000	PAC
Rubber Cork Linoleum & Plastic Workers	$15,000	PAC
United Auto Workers	$14,000	PAC
Transportation Unions	$164,560	
Seafarers International Union*	$22,650	PAC
Teamsters Union	$16,000	PAC
United Transportation Union	$15,700	PAC
Air Line Pilots Assn	$15,000	PAC
Amalgamated Transit Union	$15,000	PAC
Public Sector Unions	$147,563	
American Postal Workers Union	$19,000	PAC
American Fedn of St/Cnty/Munic Employees	$15,448	PAC/Ind
National Assn of Letter Carriers*	$15,040	PAC
American Federation of Teachers	$15,000	PAC
National Education Assn	$15,000	PAC
Misc Unions	$67,500	
Food & Commercial Workers Union	$19,000	PAC
AFL-CIO	$13,000	PAC

Ideological/Single-Issue

Ideological/Single-Issue — $743,863

Democratic/Liberal	$159,758	
Independent Action	$14,750	PAC
Leadership PACs	$53,000	
None over $12,500		
Foreign & Defense Policy	$45,142	
None over $12,500		
Pro-Israel	$353,450	
National PAC	$15,000	PAC
Pro-Choice	$21,900	
None over $12,500		
Human Rights	$40,090	
National Community Action Foundation	$13,500	PAC
Misc Issues	$54,023	
National Cmte to Preserve Social Security	$15,000	PAC

Other & Unknown

Other — $136,880

Other	$22,650
None over $12,500	
Education	$59,001
None over $12,500	
Retired	$43,629
None over $12,500	

Unknown — $403,094

Homemakers/Non-income earners	$47,651
No Employer Listed or Found	$256,969
Employer Listed/Category Unknown	$90,874
None over $12,500	

Independent expenditures supporting Harkin

National Abortion Rights Action League*	$112,444
National Cmte to Preserve Social Security	$34,808

Independent expenditures opposing Harkin

Council for National Defense	$18,487
Mid-America Conservative PAC	$18,068
National Rifle Assn	$13,579

* Contributions came from more than one affiliate or subsidiary.

Orrin G. Hatch (R-Utah)

First elected: 1976

1987-92 Total Rcpts:	$4,574,487
1992 Year-end Cash:	$438,741
Current term expires:	1994

1991-92 Committees & Subcommittees

Finance
Health for Families and the Uninsured; Deficits, Debt Management and International Debt (Ranking Republican); International Trade

Judiciary
Antitrust, Monopolies and Business Rights; Constitution; Patents, Copyrights and Trademarks (Ranking Republican)

Labor and Human Resources (Ranking Republican)
Children, Families, Drugs and Alcoholism; Disability Policy; Education, Arts and Humanities; Labor

Leading Contributors

NOTE: The bulk of Hatch's large individual contributions do not appear in the listings below. His last election was in 1988, and this book lists individual contributions only from 1989-1992.

Business

Agriculture — $142,757

Crop Production & Basic Processing $17,296
    None over $6,000

Agricultural Services/Products $21,150
    None over $6,000

Food Processing & Sales $66,611
    Food Marketing Institute .... $8,500   PAC
    Herbalife of America .... $8,000   Indiv
    ConAgra Inc .... $6,000   PAC

Forestry & Forest Products $25,000
    None over $6,000

Communications/Electronics — $107,156

Media/Entertainment $55,570
    MCA Inc* .... $15,400   PAC/Ind
    Assn of Independent Television Stations .... $6,000   PAC

Telephone Utilities $28,686
    AT&T .... $9,400   PAC

Electronics Mfg & Services $6,500
    None over $6,000

Computer Equipment & Services $8,400
    None over $6,000

Source of Funds: 1987-1992

Source	Total	Pct
PACs	$1,375,748	30%
Indivs $200+	$1,118,658	24%
Indivs under $200	$1,600,647	35%
Other	$494,584	11%
Candidate	$0	0%
Party	$15,150	0%

Source of PAC Dollars by Sector

Source	Total	Pct
Business	$1,272,046	94%
Labor	$13,000	1%
Ideological/Single-Issue	$69,820	5%

In-State vs. Out-of-State Contributions*

Source	Total	Pct
In-State	$122,250	11%
Out-of-state	$991,408	89%
No state listed	$1,500	

* by large individual contributors ($200 & above)

Construction — $113,000

General Contractors $61,500
    Fluor Corp .... $17,000   PAC
    Associated General Contractors .... $10,750   PAC
    Associated Builders & Contractors .... $10,000   PAC
    National Utility Contractors Assn .... $7,500   PAC

Home Builders $7,500
    None over $6,000

Special Trade Contractors $25,500
    Wall & Ceiling/Gypsum Drywall Contr .... $7,000   PAC
    National Electrical Contractors Assn .... $6,000   PAC
    Sheet Metal/Air Conditioning Contractors .... $6,000   PAC

Construction Services $6,500
    None over $6,000

Building Materials & Equipment $12,000
    None over $6,000

Defense — $69,100

Defense Aerospace $36,150
    Northrop Corp .... $8,500   PAC
    United Technologies .... $6,000   PAC

Defense Electronics $21,050
    Harris Corp .... $7,500   PAC

Misc Defense $11,900
    Litton Industries .... $6,000   PAC

Energy & Natural Resources — $116,285

Oil & Gas $73,850
    BP America .... $10,000   PAC

Mining $20,850
    Cyprus Minerals Co .... $8,500   PAC

Misc Energy $6,000
    None over $6,000

Electric Utilities $10,085
    None over $6,000

Contribution Totals by Sector

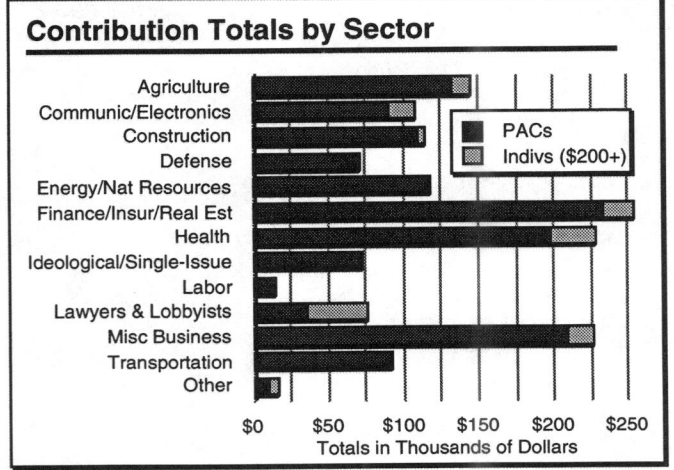

Agriculture, Communic/Electronics, Construction, Defense, Energy/Nat Resources, Finance/Insur/Real Est, Health, Ideological/Single-Issue, Labor, Lawyers & Lobbyists, Misc Business, Transportation, Other

■ PACs
▨ Indivs ($200+)

$0 $50 $100 $150 $200 $250
Totals in Thousands of Dollars

Finance, Insurance & Real Estate — $252,238

Commercial Banks $27,312
    American Bankers Assn .... $11,000   PAC

Securities & Investment $21,400
    None over $6,000

Insurance $128,492
    National Assn of Independent Insurers .... $19,750   PAC
    Travelers Corp .... $9,000   PAC
    Sears/Allstate* .... $8,000   PAC
    American Council of Life Insurance .... $7,000   PAC
    National Assn of Prof Insurance Agents .... $6,000   PAC

Real Estate $29,434
    National Assn of Realtors .... $9,600   PAC

Accountants $22,500
    American Institute of CPA's .... $10,000   PAC

Health — $226,798

Health Professionals $86,098
    American Podiatry Assn .... $11,000   PAC
    American Academy of Ophthalmology .... $10,000   PAC
    American Medical Assn .... $10,000   PAC
    American Dental Assn .... $8,800   PAC
    American Chiropractic Assn .... $6,998   PAC

Hospitals/Nursing Homes $31,300
    American Hospital Assn .... $6,000   PAC

Health Services $8,700
    None over $6,000

Pharmaceuticals/Health Products $100,200
    Allergan Inc .... $7,400   Indiv
    Ciba-Geigy Corp .... $7,000   PAC

Lawyers & Lobbyists — $74,050

Lawyers & Lobbyists $74,050
    Delany & Associates .... $10,000   Indiv

Misc Business — $225,176

Food & Beverage $53,919
    National Restaurant Assn .... $12,000   PAC
    General Mills Restaurants .... $7,500   PAC
    S&A Restaurant Corp .... $6,500   PAC

Beer, Wine & Liquor $18,500
    National Beer Wholesalers Assn .... $15,000   PAC

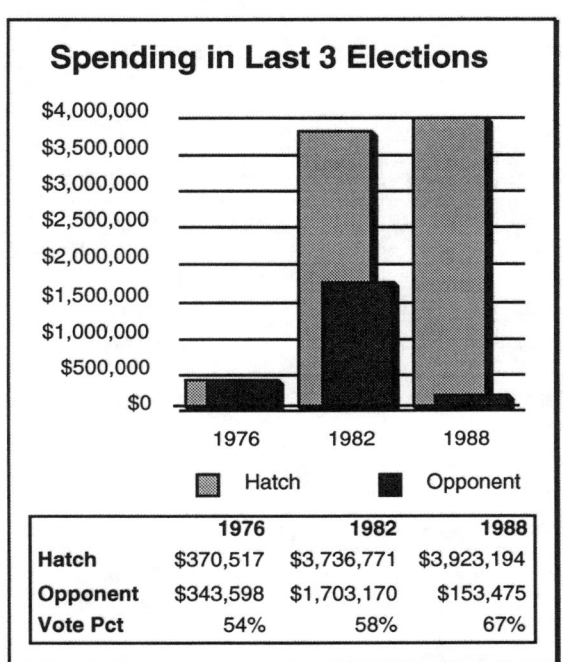

Spending in Last 3 Elections

	1976	1982	1988
Hatch	$370,517	$3,736,771	$3,923,194
Opponent	$343,598	$1,703,170	$153,475
Vote Pct	54%	58%	67%

Retail Sales $23,764
    None over $6,000

Business Services $23,600
    None over $6,000

Lodging/Tourism $15,000
    Marriott Corp .... $7,500   PAC

Chemical & Related Manufacturing $21,400
    None over $6,000

Steel Production $8,500
    None over $6,000

Misc Manufacturing & Distributing $36,090
    Brush Wellman .... $8,000   PAC

Textiles $10,500
    None over $6,000

Transportation — $90,556

Air Transport $29,357
    Federal Express Corp .... $10,400   PAC
    Texas Air .... $7,000   PAC

Automotive $26,500
    General Motors.................................... $7,350   PAC
    Auto Dealers & Drivers for Free Trade .... $7,000   PAC

Trucking $8,899
    None over $6,000

Railroads $21,500
    Union Pacific Corp .... $15,000   PAC

Labor

Labor — $13,000

Transportation Unions $12,000
    United Transportation Union .... $6,000   PAC

Ideological/Single-Issue

Ideological/Single-Issue — $71,570

Republican/Conservative $12,396
    None over $6,000

Leadership PACs $18,916
    Catch the Spirit PAC (Bob Kasten) .... $10,000   PAC

Foreign & Defense Policy $16,664
    National Security PAC .... $6,009   PAC

Gun Rights/Gun Control $7,950
    National Rifle Assn .... $7,950   PAC

Other & Unknown

Other — $15,800

Education $8,800
    None over $6,000

Retired $6,000
    None over $6,000

Unknown — $43,320

    Homemakers/Non-income earners $10,500
    No Employer Listed or Found $6,820
    Employer Listed/Category Unknown $24,000
    None over $6,000

Independent expenditures supporting Hatch
    American Citizens for Political Action $153,166
    National Security PAC $58,345

---

* Contributions came from more than one affiliate or subsidiary.

269

Mark O. Hatfield (R-Ore)

First elected: 1966

1987-92 Total Rcpts:	$2,550,434
1992 Year-end Cash:	$4,716
Current term expires:	1996

1991-92 Committees & Subcommittees

Appropriations (Ranking Republican)
Commerce, Justice, State, the Judiciary and Related Agencies;
Energy and Water Development (Ranking Republican); Foreign
Operations; Labor, Health and Human Services, Education and
Related Agencies; Transportation and Related Agencies

Energy and Natural Resources
Energy Regulation and Conservation; Public Lands, National Parks
and Forests; Water and Power

Rules and Administration

Joint Committee on the Library

Joint Committee on Printing

Leading Contributors

Business

Agriculture — $241,999

Crop Production & Basic Processing $13,900
None over $7,500

Agricultural Services/Products $11,200
None over $7,500

Food Processing & Sales $21,499
None over $7,500

Forestry & Forest Products $183,100
Willamette Industries	$12,400	PAC/Ind
South Coast Lumber	$10,500	Indiv
Georgia-Pacific Corp	$9,000	PAC
International Paper Co	$9,000	PAC
Weyerhaeuser Co	$9,000	PAC

Communications/Electronics — $109,430

Printing & Publishing $7,600
None over $7,500

Media/Entertainment $39,200
National Cable Television Assn	$10,000	PAC

Telephone Utilities $44,565
AT&T	$9,000	PAC
US West Inc	$8,965	PAC/Ind

Computer Equipment & Services $11,065
None over $7,500

Contribution Totals by Sector

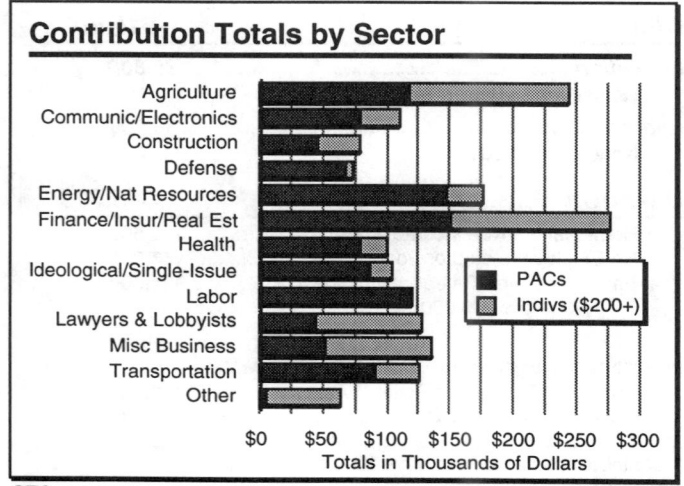

Agriculture
Communic/Electronics
Construction
Defense
Energy/Nat Resources
Finance/Insur/Real Est
Health
Ideological/Single-Issue
Labor
Lawyers & Lobbyists
Misc Business
Transportation
Other

■ PACs
□ Indivs ($200+)

$0 $50 $100 $150 $200 $250 $300
Totals in Thousands of Dollars

Source of Funds: 1987-1992

Source	Total	Pct
■ PACs	$1,061,844	38%
▨ Indivs $200+	$929,419	33%
□ Indivs under $200	$306,902	11%
▧ Other	$496,560	18%
Candidate	$0	0%
Party	$244,291	9%

Source of PAC Dollars by Sector

Source	Total	Pct
■ Business	$860,208	81%
▨ Labor	$117,927	11%
□ Ideological/Single-Issue	$86,287	8%

In-State vs. Out-of-State Contributions*

Source	Total	Pct
□ In-State	$545,111	59%
■ Out-of-state	$382,585	41%
No state listed	$1,723	

*** by large individual contributors ($200 & above)**

Construction — $78,628

General Contractors $27,700
Associated General Contractors	$10,000	PAC

Home Builders $10,500
None over $7,500

Construction Services $18,428
None over $7,500

Building Materials & Equipment $18,000
None over $7,500

Defense — $72,750

Defense Aerospace $42,500
None over $7,500

Defense Electronics $19,750
None over $7,500

Misc Defense $10,500
None over $7,500

Energy & Natural Resources — $173,307

Oil & Gas $84,957
Union Pacific Corp	$8,000	PAC

Mining $28,350
None over $7,500

Misc Energy $8,000
None over $7,500

Electric Utilities $35,750
None over $7,500

Waste Management $15,250
Waste Management Inc	$8,000	PAC

Finance, Insurance & Real Estate — $275,181

Commercial Banks $50,300
US Bancorp	$11,000	PAC/Ind
American Bankers Assn	$10,000	PAC

Savings & Loans **$11,350**
    None over $7,500

Securities & Investment **$65,650**
    Salomon Brothers ....$21,000   PAC/Ind

Insurance **$66,281**
    None over $7,500

Real Estate **$47,800**
    National Assn of Realtors ....$9,550   PAC

Misc Finance **$20,800**
    WIG Securities ....$8,000   Indiv

Health $99,650

Health Professionals **$68,400**
    American Medical Assn ....$10,000   PAC

Hospitals/Nursing Homes **$7,500**
    None over $7,500

Pharmaceuticals/Health Products **$22,500**
    None over $7,500

Lawyers & Lobbyists $125,856

Lawyers & Lobbyists **$125,856**
    Schwabe, Williamson & Wyatt ....$10,450   Indiv
    Neill & Co ....$10,000   Indiv
    Cassidy & Associates ....$7,500   Indiv

Misc Business $134,616

Food & Beverage **$11,050**
    None over $7,500

Retail Sales **$25,450**
    Fred Meyer Inc ....$7,800   PAC/Ind

Business Services **$13,000**
    None over $7,500

Lodging/Tourism **$13,000**
    None over $7,500

Misc Manufacturing & Distributing **$45,868**
    Nike Inc ....$17,500   PAC/Ind

Transportation $124,250

Air Transport **$42,500**
    Federal Express Corp ....$9,000   PAC
    United Parcel Service ....$8,500   PAC

Automotive **$24,200**
    Auto Dealers & Drivers for Free Trade .....$7,500   PAC

Trucking **$11,050**
    None over $7,500

Railroads **$16,000**
    None over $7,500

Sea Transport **$26,500**
    None over $7,500

Labor

Labor $117,927

Building Trade Unions **$21,850**
    Carpenters & Joiners Union ....$7,500   PAC

Industrial Unions **$13,000**
    National Education Assn ....$7,500   PAC

Transportation Unions **$48,300**
    Marine Engineers Union ....$14,000   PAC
    Air Line Pilots Assn ....$10,000   PAC
    Teamsters Union ....$10,000   PAC

Public Sector Unions **$32,277**
    None over $7,500

Ideological/Single-Issue

Ideological/Single-Issue $102,427

Republican/Conservative **$8,540**
    None over $7,500

Leadership PACs **$34,500**
    Campaign America (Bob Dole) ....$10,000   PAC

Human Rights **$35,200**
    National Community Action Foundation ....$17,000   PAC

Misc Issues **$8,700**
    None over $7,500

Other & Unknown

Other $61,603

Education **$17,350**
    Oregon Health Sciences University ....$7,500   Indiv

Retired **$30,681**
    None over $7,500

Unknown $190,267

    Homemakers/Non-income earners $28,400
    No Employer Listed or Found $69,148
    Employer Listed/Category Unknown $87,495
        None over $7,500

Independent expenditures supporting Hatfield
    National Cmte to Preserve Social Security $25,435
    National Right to Life PAC $21,803

Spending in Last 3 Elections

	1978	1984	1990
Hatfield	$223,874	$605,557	$2,749,232
Opponent	$38,976	$255,244	$1,479,099
Vote Pct	62%	67%	54%

Howell Heflin (D-Ala)

First elected: 1978

1987-92 Total Rcpts:	$4,103,630
1992 Year-end Cash:	$962,661
Current term expires:	1996

1991-92 Committees & Subcommittees

Agriculture, Nutrition and Forestry
Agricultural Production and Stabilization of Prices; Conservation and Forestry; Rural Development and Rural Electrification (Chairman)

Judiciary
Antitrust, Monopolies and Business Rights; Courts and Administrative Practice (Chairman); Patents, Copyrights and Trademarks

Leading Contributors

Business

Agriculture		$421,222
Crop Production & Basic Processing	**$162,361**	
National Cotton Council	$10,250	PAC/Ind
Southeastern Peanut Assn	$10,000	PAC
Tobacco	**$15,200**	
None over $10,000		
Dairy	**$17,772**	
None over $10,000		
Poultry & Eggs	**$22,500**	
Tyson Foods	$10,000	PAC/Ind
Livestock	**$24,284**	
None over $10,000		
Agricultural Services/Products	**$84,175**	
American Assn of Crop Insurers	$10,000	PAC
Food Processing & Sales	**$28,716**	
None over $10,000		
Forestry & Forest Products	**$56,050**	
International Paper Co	$10,000	PAC
Misc Agriculture	**$10,164**	
None over $10,000		

Communications/Electronics		$168,394
Printing & Publishing	**$30,832**	
West Publishing	$24,000	PAC/Ind
Media/Entertainment	**$56,029**	
Time Warner*	$14,000	PAC/Ind

Contribution Totals by Sector

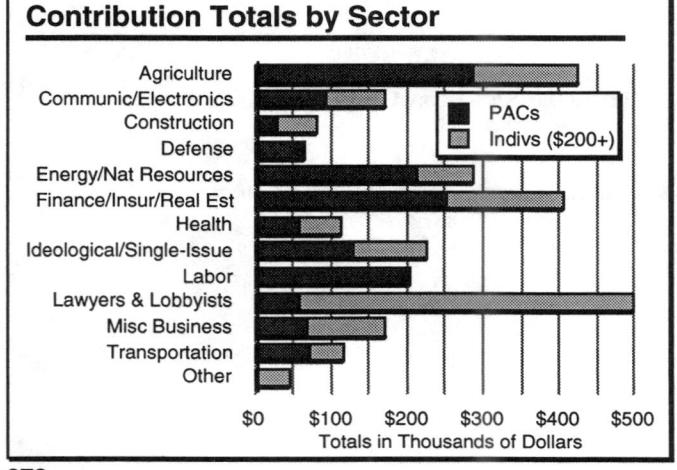

- Agriculture
- Communic/Electronics
- Construction
- Defense
- Energy/Nat Resources
- Finance/Insur/Real Est
- Health
- Ideological/Single-Issue
- Labor
- Lawyers & Lobbyists
- Misc Business
- Transportation
- Other

■ PACs
▨ Indivs ($200+)

$0 $100 $200 $300 $400 $500
Totals in Thousands of Dollars

Source of Funds: 1987-1992

Source	Total	Pct
■ PACs	$1,490,083	35%
▨ Indivs $200+	$1,703,513	40%
□ Indivs under $200	$354,438	8%
▨ Other	$712,906	17%
Candidate	$0	0%
Party	$157,310	4%

Source of PAC Dollars by Sector

Source	Total	Pct
■ Business	$1,166,926	78%
▨ Labor	$199,950	13%
□ Ideological/Single-Issue	$126,100	8%

In-State vs. Out-of-State Contributions*

Source	Total	Pct
□ In-State	$904,963	53%
■ Out-of-state	$798,050	47%
No state listed	$500	

*** by large individual contributors ($200 & above)**

Telephone Utilities		$49,700
BellSouth Corp*	$14,600	PAC/Ind
AT&T	$10,000	PAC
Computer Equipment & Services	**$24,536**	
Colsa Inc	$11,336	Indiv

Construction		$76,748
General Contractors	**$22,098**	
None over $10,000		
Home Builders	**$13,000**	
None over $10,000		
Construction Services	**$12,250**	
None over $10,000		
Building Materials & Equipment	**$27,200**	
None over $10,000		

Defense		$63,737
Defense Aerospace	**$44,037**	
None over $10,000		
Defense Electronics	**$12,300**	
None over $10,000		

Energy & Natural Resources		$283,359
Oil & Gas	**$149,615**	
Amoco Corp	$10,500	PAC/Ind
Mining	**$58,500**	
Drummond Co	$16,200	PAC/Ind
FMC Corp	$10,000	PAC
Electric Utilities	**$57,000**	
Southern Co*	$13,500	PAC/Ind
ACRE (Action Cmte for Rural Electrification)	$10,000	PAC

Finance, Insurance & Real Estate — $402,851

Commercial Banks $78,175
    Amsouth Bancorp .... $10,250 PAC/Ind
    American Bankers Assn .... $10,000 PAC

Finance/Credit Companies $11,279
    None over $10,000

Securities & Investment $71,583
    Chicago Board of Trade .... $12,000 PAC/Ind
    Chicago Mercantile Exchange .... $10,500 PAC/Ind

Insurance $119,031
    National Assn of Independent Insurers .... $10,350 PAC
    American Council of Life Insurance .... $10,000 PAC
    American Family Corp .... $10,000 PAC
    National Assn of Life Underwriters .... $10,000 PAC

Real Estate $78,133
    None over $10,000

Accountants $21,550
    American Institute of CPA's .... $10,000 PAC

Misc Finance $10,350
    None over $10,000

Health — $111,615

Health Professionals $61,115
    American Medical Assn .... $10,000 PAC

Hospitals/Nursing Homes $11,300
    None over $10,000

Pharmaceuticals/Health Products $30,150
    Henley Group Inc .... $10,000 PAC

Lawyers & Lobbyists — $496,064

Lawyers & Lobbyists $496,064
    Assn of Trial Lawyers of America ...... $10,000 PAC
    Hollis, Pittman et al .... $10,000 Indiv

Misc Business — $166,911

Food & Beverage $17,999
    None over $10,000

Beer, Wine & Liquor $13,200
    None over $10,000

Retail Sales $22,564
    None over $10,000

Misc Services $11,750
    None over $10,000

Business Services $27,300
    None over $10,000

Misc Manufacturing & Distributing $37,532
    None over $10,000

Textiles $14,250
    None over $10,000

Transportation — $112,450

Air Transport $37,650
    None over $10,000

Automotive $31,000
    None over $10,000

Trucking $18,700
    None over $10,000

Sea Transport $12,900
    None over $10,000

Labor

Labor — $200,150

Building Trade Unions $36,700
    Laborers' Political League .... $10,000 PAC

Industrial Unions $60,500
    Machinists/Aerospace Workers Union .... $10,000 PAC
    National Education Assn .... $10,000 PAC

Transportation Unions $55,000
    Air Line Pilots Assn .... $10,000 PAC
    Seafarers International Union .... $10,000 PAC
    Teamsters Union .... $10,000 PAC

Public Sector Unions $38,450
    None over $10,000

Ideological/Single-Issue

Ideological/Single-Issue — $221,236

Democratic/Liberal $25,000
    None over $10,000

Pro-Israel $169,986
    Americans for Good Government ...... $10,000 PAC
    Citizens Organized PAC .... $10,000 PAC

Other & Unknown

Other — $43,132

Education $25,732
    None over $10,000

Unknown — $230,323

    Homemakers/Non-income earners $36,893
    No Employer Listed or Found $52,030
    Employer Listed/Category Unknown $138,200
        None over $10,000

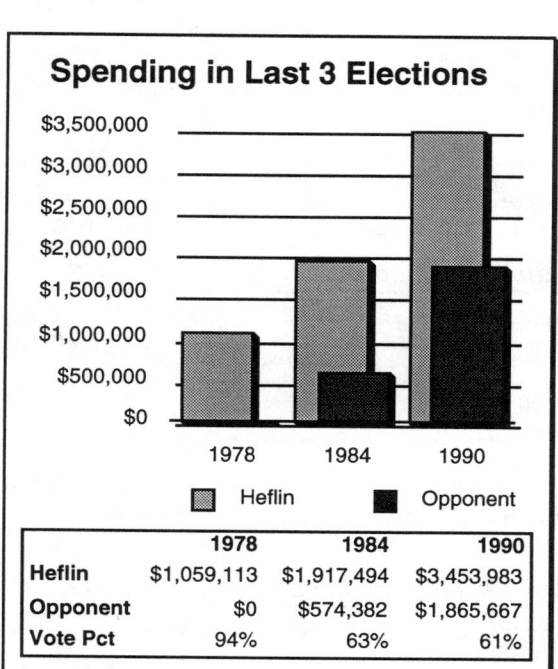

Spending in Last 3 Elections

	1978	1984	1990
Heflin	$1,059,113	$1,917,494	$3,453,983
Opponent	$0	$574,382	$1,865,667
Vote Pct	94%	63%	61%

Heflin   ■ Opponent

---

* Contributions came from more than one affiliate or
subsidiary.

Jesse Helms (R-NC)

First elected: 1972

1987-92 Total Rcpts:	$20,382,361
1992 Year-end Cash:	$1,387
Current term expires:	1996

1991-92 Committees & Subcommittees

Agriculture, Nutrition and Forestry
Agricultural Production and Stabilization of Prices (Ranking Republican); Conservation and Forestry; Domestic and Foreign Marketing and Product Promotion; Nutrition and Investigations

Foreign Relations (Ranking Republican)
African Affairs; Western Hemisphere and Peace Corps Affairs

Rules and Administration

Select Committees on POW/MIA Affairs

Leading Contributors

Business

Agriculture	$317,661

Crop Production & Basic Processing **$60,557**
National Cotton Council ....$7,000 PAC

Tobacco **$58,530**
US Tobacco Co ....$12,250 PAC
RJR Nabisco ....$10,000 PAC
Philip Morris ....$9,500 PAC
Tobacco Institute ....$7,000 PAC

Dairy **$17,219**
Dairymen Inc* ....$9,500 PAC

Poultry & Eggs **$24,750**
Showell Farms ....$6,000 Indiv

Livestock **$22,425**
None over $6,000

Agricultural Services/Products **$52,364**
Archer-Daniels-Midland Corp ....$7,000 PAC

Food Processing & Sales **$42,140**
None over $6,000

Forestry & Forest Products **$35,075**
Union Camp Corp ....$6,000 PAC

Communications/Electronics	$78,664

Printing & Publishing **$14,100**
None over $6,000

Media/Entertainment **$19,470**
National Cable Television Assn ....$10,000 PAC

Source of Funds: 1987-1992

Source	Total	Pct
■ PACs	$884,724	4%
▨ Indivs $200+	$2,968,074	14%
☐ Indivs under $200	$16,055,851	77%
⊠ Other	$995,888	5%
Candidate	$0	0%
Party	$522,176	2%

Source of PAC Dollars by Sector

Source	Total	Pct
■ Business	$728,840	83%
▨ Labor	$1,000	0%
☐ Ideological/Single-Issue ..	$147,467	17%

In-State vs. Out-of-State Contributions*

Source	Total	Pct
☐ In-State	$1,497,675	51%
■ Out-of-state	$1,465,478	49%
No state listed	$4,921	

* by large individual contributors ($200 & above)

Telephone Utilities **$25,032**
Southern Bell ....$9,000 PAC
AT&T ....$6,250 PAC/Ind

Electronics Mfg & Services **$10,500**
None over $6,000

Construction	$109,425

General Contractors **$48,780**
Associated General Contractors* ....$10,500 PAC

Home Builders **$15,500**
National Assn of Home Builders ....$8,000 PAC

Special Trade Contractors **$14,565**
Wall & Ceiling/Gypsum Drywall Contr ....$6,500 PAC

Building Materials & Equipment **$26,950**
None over $6,000

Defense	$31,250

Defense Aerospace **$25,200**
Northrop Corp ....$6,000 PAC

Energy & Natural Resources	$110,073

Oil & Gas **$58,203**
Amoco Corp ....$7,000 PAC

Misc Energy **$9,500**
None over $6,000

Electric Utilities **$31,120**
Duke Power Co ....$11,300 PAC/Ind
Carolina Power & Light ....$10,320 PAC/Ind

Waste Management **$6,000**
None over $6,000

Finance, Insurance & Real Estate	$270,917

Commercial Banks **$57,450**
American Bankers Assn ....$10,000 PAC
NCNB Corp ....$7,250 PAC/Ind

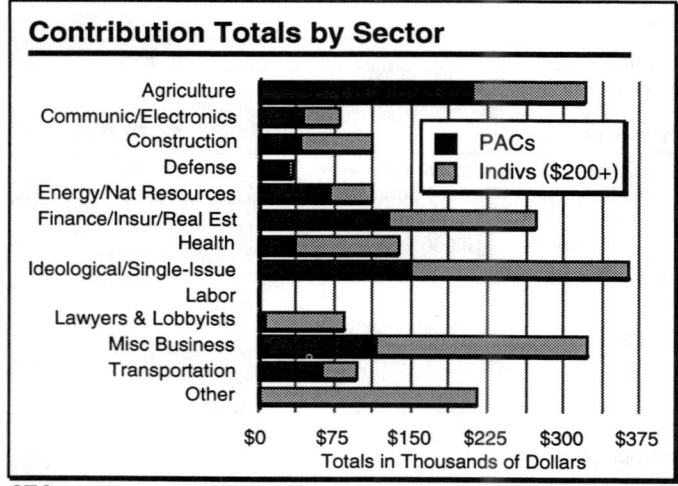

Contribution Totals by Sector

Agriculture
Communic/Electronics
Construction
Defense
Energy/Nat Resources
Finance/Insur/Real Est
Health
Ideological/Single-Issue
Labor
Lawyers & Lobbyists
Misc Business
Transportation
Other

■ PACs
▨ Indivs ($200+)

$0 $75 $150 $225 $300 $375
Totals in Thousands of Dollars

Securities & Investment $36,084
   Sanford C Bernstein & Co .... $9,384   Indiv

Insurance **$72,940**
   Jefferson-Pilot Corp .... $13,750   PAC/Ind
   American Family Corp .... $10,000   PAC
   National Assn of Life Underwriters .... $7,500   PAC

Real Estate **$71,048**
   National Assn of Realtors .... $10,000   PAC
   First Union Corp .... $6,000   PAC

Misc Finance **$22,095**
   None over $6,000

Health $135,245

Health Professionals $115,269
   American Medical Assn .... $10,000   PAC

Pharmaceuticals/Health Products **$14,300**
   Glaxo Inc .... $10,000   PAC

Lawyers & Lobbyists $82,675

Lawyers & Lobbyists $82,675
   None over $6,000

Misc Business $320,692

Business Associations **$17,679**
   National Fedn of Independent Business .... $7,000   PAC

Food & Beverage **$32,205**
   Hardee's Food Systems .... $7,500   PAC/Ind

Beer, Wine & Liquor **$6,000**
   None over $6,000

Retail Sales **$39,203**
   None over $6,000

Misc Services **$15,101**
   None over $6,000

Business Services **$22,540**
   None over $6,000

Chemical & Related Manufacturing **$19,750**
   Contran Corp .... $8,000   Indiv

Misc Manufacturing & Distributing **$80,540**
   American Furniture Manufacturers Assn .... $10,000   PAC

Textiles **$69,004**
   Burlington Industries .... $11,500   PAC/Ind
   American Textile Manufacturers Institute .... $8,000   PAC
   Milliken & Co .... $7,000   Indiv

Transportation   *$93,989*

Air Transport **$31,276**
   American Airlines .... $6,100   PAC
   Texas Air .... $6,000   PAC

Automotive **$37,265**
   Auto Dealers & Drivers for Free Trade .... $10,000   PAC
   National Auto Dealers Assn .... $10,000   PAC

Trucking **$9,848**
   None over $6,000

Misc Transport **$7,250**
   None over $6,000

Ideological/Single-Issue

Ideological/Single-Issue $363,298

Republican/Conservative $198,999
   Conservative Victory Cmte .... $10,000   PAC
   National Republican Senatorial Cmte .... $6,000   Indiv

Leadership PACs **$33,150**
   Campaign America (Bob Dole) .... $10,000   PAC
   National Congressional Club (Jesse Helms) .... $6,210   PAC

Foreign & Defense Policy **$19,955**
   None over $6,000

Pro-Israel **$24,750**
   Hudson Valley PAC .... $6,000   PAC

Pro-Life **$20,625**
   None over $6,000

Gun Rights/Gun Control **$16,150**
   National Rifle Assn .... $9,950   PAC

Human Rights **$10,000**
   National Albanian American PAC .... $8,500   PAC

Misc Issues **$37,669**
   Public Service Research Council .... $10,000   PAC
   Right to Work PAC .... $10,000   PAC

Other & Unknown

Other $212,402

Civil Servants/Public Officials $16,136
   None over $6,000

Education **$19,593**
   Bowman Gray School of Medicine .... $6,550   Indiv

Retired **$172,273**
   None over $6,000

Unknown $1,547,973

   Homemakers/Non-income earners $73,001
   No Employer Listed or Found $1,316,709
   Generic Occupation/Category Unknown $27,497
   Employer Listed/Category Unknown $130,766
     None over $6,000

Independent expenditures supporting Helms
   National Right to Life PAC $140,117
   Council for National Defense $94,766
   Conservative Campaign Fund $47,914
   National Rifle Assn $7,621

Independent expenditures opposing Helms
   National Abortion Rights Action League $315,907
   Human Rights Campaign Fund $65,974
   North Carolina Senate Vote 90 .... $46,594
   Robert D. Rodman $12,719
   National Abortion Rights Action Lge/NC $7,497

---

* Contributions came from more than one affiliate or
subsidiary.

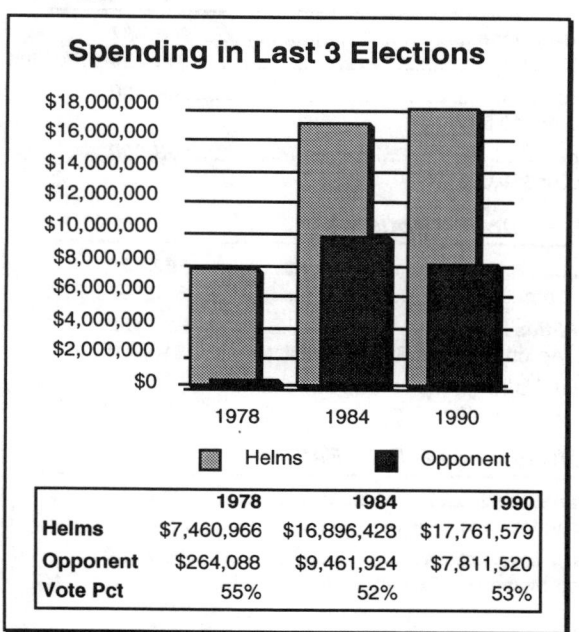

Spending in Last 3 Elections

	1978	1984	1990
Helms	$7,460,966	$16,896,428	$17,761,579
Opponent	$264,088	$9,461,924	$7,811,520
Vote Pct	55%	52%	53%

Legend: ▨ Helms   ■ Opponent

Ernest F. Hollings (D-SC)

First elected: 1966

1987-92 Total Rcpts:	$4,016,311
1992 Year-end Cash:	$25,336
Current term expires:	1998

1991-92 Committees & Subcommittees

Appropriations
Commerce, Justice, State, the Judiciary and Related Agencies (Chairman); Defense; Energy and Water Development; Interior and Related Agencies; Labor, Health and Human Services, Education and Related Agencies

Budget

Commerce, Science and Transportation (Chairman)
Communications; Foreign Commerce and Tourism; Surface Transportation; National Ocean Policy Study (Chairman)

Select Committee on Intelligence

Leading Contributors

Business

Agriculture	$178,550

Crop Production & Basic Processing **$35,500**
　None over $10,000

Tobacco **$41,463**
　Philip Morris ....$12,463　PAC/Ind

Poultry & Eggs **$13,000**
　None over $10,000

Agricultural Services/Products **$19,250**
　None over $10,000

Food Processing & Sales **$40,087**
　None over $10,000

Forestry & Forest Products **$15,750**
　None over $10,000

Communications/Electronics	$437,168

Printing & Publishing **$13,750**
　None over $10,000

Media/Entertainment **$236,731**
　Time Warner* ....$31,500　PAC/Ind
　MCA Inc* ....$26,800　PAC/Ind
　National Assn of Broadcasters ....$24,886　PAC/Ind
　National Cable Television Assn ....$10,000　PAC

Telephone Utilities **$140,837**
　BellSouth Corp* ....$44,700　PAC/Ind
　Pacific Telesis Group ....$15,249　PAC/Ind
　Bell Atlantic ....$12,000　PAC/Ind
　Ameritech Corp* ....$10,000　PAC

Contribution Totals by Sector

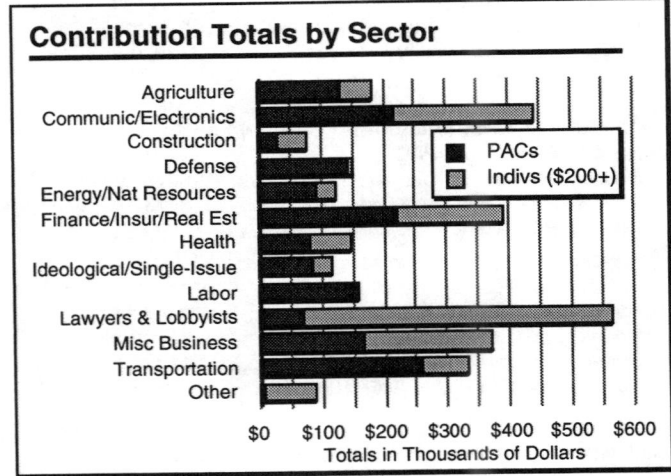

PACs
Indivs ($200+)

Agriculture
Communic/Electronics
Construction
Defense
Energy/Nat Resources
Finance/Insur/Real Est
Health
Ideological/Single-Issue
Labor
Lawyers & Lobbyists
Misc Business
Transportation
Other

$0　$100　$200　$300　$400　$500　$600
Totals in Thousands of Dollars

Source of Funds: 1987-1992

Source	Total	Pct
■ PACs	$1,611,270	39%
▨ Indivs $200+	$1,843,549	44%
□ Indivs under $200	$307,930	7%
▨ Other	$411,067	10%
Candidate	$0	0%
Party	$157,505	4%

Source of PAC Dollars by Sector

Source	Total	Pct
■ Business	$1,384,881	85%
▨ Labor	$153,850	9%
□ Ideological/Single-Issue	$83,400	5%

In-State vs. Out-of-State Contributions*

Source	Total	Pct
□ In-State	$603,584	33%
▨ Out-of-state	$1,224,465	67%
No state listed	$0	

*** by large individual contributors ($200 & above)**

Telecom Services & Equipment **$19,250**
　None over $10,000

Electronics Mfg & Services **$14,100**
　None over $10,000

Computer Equipment & Services **$12,500**
　None over $10,000

Construction	$73,133

General Contractors **$39,150**
　Fluor Corp ....$10,000　PAC

Building Materials & Equipment **$14,500**
　None over $10,000

Defense	$147,834

Defense Aerospace **$64,734**
　Allied-Signal ....$11,284　PAC/Ind

Defense Electronics **$49,500**
　None over $10,000

Misc Defense **$33,600**
　None over $10,000

Energy & Natural Resources	$121,831

Oil & Gas **$67,436**
　Scana Corp ....$10,000　PAC

Electric Utilities **$31,462**
　ACRE (Action Cmte for Rural Electrification) .....$10,000　PAC

Commercial Fishing **$10,333**
　None over $10,000

Finance, Insurance & Real Estate	$386,691

Commercial Banks **$75,550**
　American Bankers Assn ....$10,000　PAC

Securities & Investment **$69,150**
　Chicago Mercantile Exchange ....$10,000　PAC

Insurance **$132,020**
    Colonial Life & Accident Insurance ....$15,500   PAC/Ind
    National Assn of Life Underwriters.....................$10,000   PAC

Real Estate **$65,991**
    National Assn of Realtors ....$10,000   PAC

Accountants **$22,980**
    None over $10,000

Health

Health   **$142,555**

Health Professionals **$107,200**
    American Dental Assn ....$10,000   PAC

Hospitals/Nursing Homes **$12,000**
    None over $10,000

Health Services **$10,750**
    None over $10,000

Lawyers & Lobbyists

Lawyers & Lobbyists   **$559,192**

Lawyers & Lobbyists **$559,192**
    McNair Law Firm ....$13,700   Indiv
    Emond & Vines ....$13,000   Indiv
    King & Spalding ....$12,225   PAC/Ind
    Verner, Liipfert et al ....$10,000   PAC/Ind

Misc Business

Misc Business   **$368,430**

Food & Beverage **$35,450**
    None over $10,000

Beer, Wine & Liquor **$31,973**
    None over $10,000

Retail Sales...**$29,457**
    None over $10,000

Business Services **$58,500**
    None over $10,000

Lodging/Tourism **$22,500**
    None over $10,000

Chemical & Related Manufacturing **$17,028**
    None over $10,000

Misc Manufacturing & Distributing **$36,742**
    None over $10,000

Textiles **$107,530**
    Burlington Industries ....$14,250   PAC/Ind
    American Textile Manufacturers Institute...........$10,000   PAC

Spending in Last 3 Elections

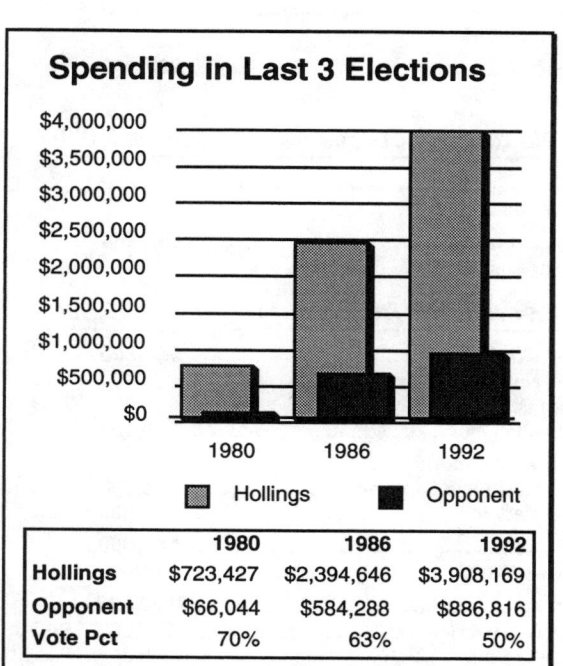

	1980	1986	1992
Hollings	$723,427	$2,394,646	$3,908,169
Opponent	$66,044	$584,288	$886,816
Vote Pct	70%	63%	50%

Transportation   **$330,894**

Air Transport **$88,895**
    Federal Express Corp ....$10,000   PAC
    United Parcel Service...$10,000   PAC

Automotive **$35,000**
    National Auto Dealers Assn ....$10,000   PAC

Trucking...**$67,879**
    American Trucking Assns ....$13,329   PAC/Ind
    Yellow Freight System ....$11,000   PAC/Ind

Railroads **$53,551**
    None over $10,000

Sea Transport **$63,319**
    None over $10,000

Misc Transport..**$22,250**
    None over $10,000

Labor

Labor   **$153,850**

Building Trade Unions **$11,000**
    None over $10,000

Industrial Unions **$23,300**
    Amalgamated Clothing & Textile Workers ....$10,000   PAC
    Ladies Garment Workers Union ....$10,000   PAC

Transportation Unions **$57,000**
    Marine Engineers Union* ....$10,000   PAC
    Seafarers International Union ....$10,000   PAC
    United Transportation Union ....$10,000   PAC

Public Sector Unions **$54,250**
    National Assn of Letter Carriers ....$13,500   PAC
    American Federation of Teachers.......................$12,000   PAC

Ideological/Single-Issue

Ideological/Single-Issue   **$114,400**

Leadership PACs **$17,500**
    None over $10,000

Foreign & Defense Policy **$12,250**
    None over $10,000

Pro-Israel **$33,000**
    None over $10,000

Human Rights **$14,750**
    None over $10,000

Misc Issues..**$12,500**
    None over $10,000

Other & Unknown

Other   **$87,913**

Civil Servants/Public Officials............................**$14,300**
    None over $10,000

Education **$35,063**
    Medical University of South Carolina ....$23,263   Indiv

Retired **$33,300**
    None over $10,000

Unknown   **$337,489**

    Homemakers/Non-income earners $57,549
    No Employer Listed or Found $13,875
    Employer Listed/Category Unknown................$265,015
      None over $10,000

* Contributions came from more than one affiliate or subsidiary.

277

Daniel K. Inouye (D-Hawaii)

First elected: 1962

1987-92 Total Rcpts:	$2,936,821
1992 Year-end Cash:	$11,907
Current term expires:	1998

1991-92 Committees & Subcommittees

Appropriations
Commerce, Justice, State, the Judiciary and Related Agencies; Defense (Chairman); Foreign Operations; Labor, Health and Human Services, Education and Related Agencies; Military Construction

Commerce, Science and Transportation
Aviation; Communications (Chairman); Merchant Marine; National Ocean Policy Study; Surface Transportation

Rules and Administration

Select Committee on Indian Affairs (Chairman)

Leading Contributors

Business

Agriculture	$58,000

Crop Production & Basic Processing $21,650
  None over $6,000
Tobacco $9,000
  None over $6,000
Agricultural Services/Products $8,550
  None over $6,000
Food Processing & Sales $7,800
  None over $6,000

Communications/Electronics	$147,700

Printing & Publishing $10,550
  None over $6,000
Media/Entertainment $76,350
  National Assn of Broadcasters .... $10,500 PAC/Ind
  National Cable Television Assn .... $10,250 PAC/Ind
Telephone Utilities $31,800
  GTE Corp* .... $10,300 PAC/Ind
  AT&T .... $10,000 PAC/Ind
Telecom Services & Equipment $17,250
  McCaw Cellular Communications .... $10,000 PAC/Ind
Computer Equipment & Services $9,500
  None over $6,000

Construction	$64,200

General Contractors $16,900
  Grace Pacific Corp .... $9,000 Indiv

Contribution Totals by Sector

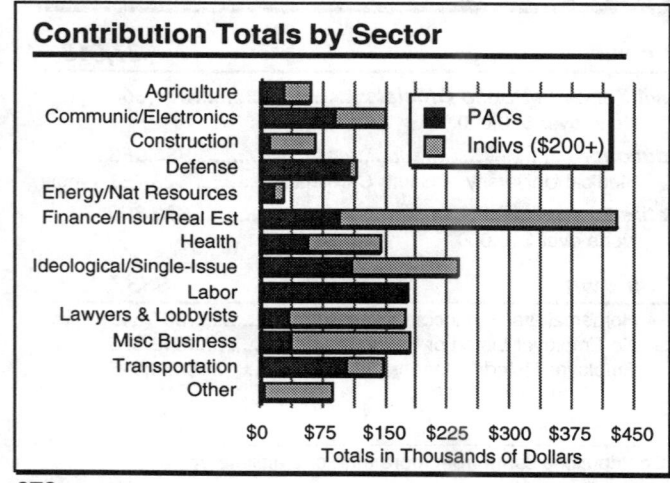

Agriculture
Communic/Electronics
Construction
Defense
Energy/Nat Resources
Finance/Insur/Real Est
Health
Ideological/Single-Issue
Labor
Lawyers & Lobbyists
Misc Business
Transportation
Other

■ PACs
▨ Indivs ($200+)

$0 $75 $150 $225 $300 $375 $450
Totals in Thousands of Dollars

Source of Funds: 1987-1992

Source	Total	Pct
■ PACs	$856,665	29%
▨ Indivs $200+	$1,607,550	54%
☐ Indivs under $200	$267,700	9%
▧ Other	$252,062	8%
Candidate	$0	0%
Party	$47,156	2%

Source of PAC Dollars by Sector

Source	Total	Pct
■ Business	$565,543	67%
▨ Labor	$173,136	20%
☐ Ideological/Single-Issue	$109,350	13%

In-State vs. Out-of-State Contributions*

Source	Total	Pct
☐ In-State	$399,049	25%
■ Out-of-state	$1,193,151	75%
No state listed	$0	

*** by large individual contributors ($200 & above)**

Home Builders $9,050
  None over $6,000
Construction Services $24,400
  None over $6,000
Building Materials & Equipment $8,250
  None over $6,000

Defense	$113,500

Defense Aerospace $64,250
  General Dynamics .... $11,500 PAC/Ind
  Northrop Corp .... $6,500 PAC
  Martin Marietta Corp .... $6,000 PAC
Defense Electronics $26,250
  None over $6,000
Misc Defense $23,000
  None over $6,000

Energy & Natural Resources	$27,050

Oil & Gas $12,250
  None over $6,000
Misc Energy $6,250
  None over $6,000

Finance, Insurance & Real Estate	$425,598

Commercial Banks $68,700
  Republic National Bank of New York .... $26,000 Indiv
  American Bankers Assn .... $10,000 PAC
  First Hawaiian Inc .... $10,000 PAC
Securities & Investment $138,550
  Chicago Mercantile Exchange .... $10,500 PAC/Ind
  Odyssey Partners .... $9,000 Indiv
Insurance $42,050
  None over $6,000
Real Estate $102,398
  National Assn of Realtors .... $6,600 PAC
  JMB Realty Corp .... $6,250 PAC/Ind

Accountants **$32,200**
None over $6,000

Misc Finance **$35,500**
None over $6,000

Health $141,905

Health Professionals **$104,555**
American Chiropractic Assn ....$10,000   PAC
American Podiatry Assn ....$10,000   PAC
Assn for the Advancement of Psychology ....$9,993   PAC

Hospitals/Nursing Homes **$22,100**
None over $6,000

Health Services **$9,000**
None over $6,000

Lawyers & Lobbyists $171,330

Lawyers & Lobbyists **$171,330**
Cassidy & Associates.....................................$17,500   Indiv
Assn of Trial Lawyers of America ....$10,000   PAC

Misc Business $178,800

Business Associations **$9,000**
None over $6,000

Retail Sales.. **$16,750**
None over $6,000

Misc Services **$7,500**
None over $6,000

Business Services **$38,150**
None over $6,000

Casinos/Gambling **$6,000**
Circus Circus Enterprises ....$6,000   PAC/Ind

Lodging/Tourism **$7,150**
None over $6,000

Misc Business **$19,050**
Aviv Judaica Imports ....$8,000   Indiv

Chemical & Related Manufacturing **$11,150**
None over $6,000

Misc Manufacturing & Distributing **$47,000**
Evvco Enterprises ....$6,000   Indiv

Textiles... **$6,750**
None over $6,000

Transportation **$145,420**

Air Transport **$53,850**
Aloha Airlines ....$10,000   Indiv
General Electric ....$8,950   PAC
United Parcel Service ....$6,000   PAC

Automotive **$21,820**
Auto Dealers & Drivers for Free Trade ....$9,000   PAC

Sea Transport **$55,250**
Alexander & Baldwin Inc ....$11,000   PAC/Ind

Labor

Labor **$173,136**

Building Trade Unions **$36,400**
Carpenters & Joiners Union ....$10,000   PAC
Laborers Union* ....$10,000   PAC
Operating Engineers Union* ....$8,000   PAC

Industrial Unions **$20,500**
Intl Brotherhood of Electrical Workers ....$6,000   PAC
United Auto Workers ....$6,000   PAC

Transportation Unions **$64,500**
Marine Engineers Union* ....$11,000   PAC
Seafarers International Union* ....$10,700   PAC
Air Line Pilots Assn ....$10,000   PAC
Intl Longshoremen's/Warehousemen's Union .....$6,800   PAC

Public Sector Unions **$37,100**
American Fedn of St/Cnty/Munic Employees ....$10,000   PAC
National Assn of Letter Carriers ....$10,000   PAC

Misc Unions.. **$14,636**
AFL-CIO ....$6,500   PAC

Ideological/Single-Issue

Ideological/Single-Issue **$235,488**

Democratic/Liberal **$10,833**
None over $6,000

Leadership PACs...................................... **$15,000**
None over $6,000

Pro-Israel **$190,155**
Citizens Organized PAC ....$10,000   PAC
National PAC ....$10,000   PAC
Women's Alliance for Israel ....$10,000   PAC
Hudson Valley PAC ....$7,500   PAC

Human Rights **$16,250**
None over $6,000

Other & Unknown

Other **$84,824**

Civil Servants/Public Officials.................. **$8,784**
None over $6,000

Education **$13,450**
None over $6,000

Retired **$52,090**
None over $6,000

Other **$10,250**
None over $6,000

Unknown **$482,878**

Homemakers/Non-income earners $41,950
No Employer Listed or Found $305,518
Generic Occupation/Category Unknown $11,300
Employer Listed/Category Unknown $124,110
None over $6,000

---

* Contributions came from more than one affiliate or
subsidiary.

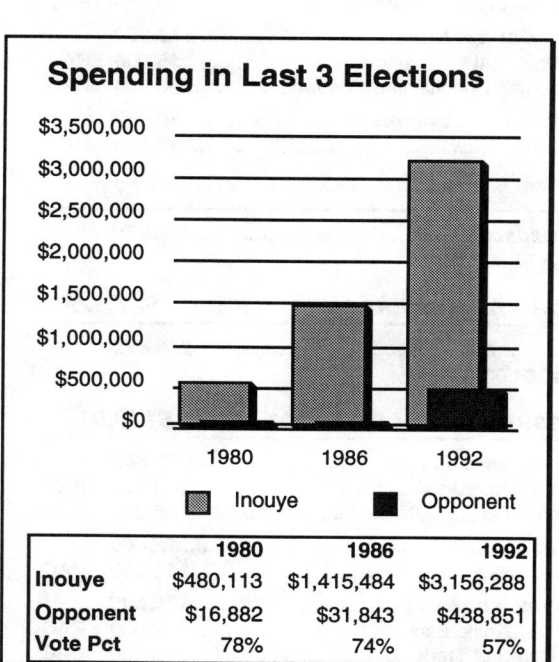

Spending in Last 3 Elections

	1980	1986	1992
Inouye	$480,113	$1,415,484	$3,156,288
Opponent	$16,882	$31,843	$438,851
Vote Pct	78%	74%	57%

James M. Jeffords (R-Vt)

First elected: 1988
1987-92 Total Rcpts: $1,138,169
1992 Year-end Cash: $342,620
Current term expires: 1994

1991-92 Committees & Subcommittees

Environment and Public Works
Environmental Protection; Toxic Substances, Environmental Oversight, Research and Development; Water Resources, Transportation and Infrastructure

Foreign Relations
Near Eastern and South Asian Affairs (Ranking Republican); Terrorism, Narcotics and International Operations; Western Hemisphere and Peace Corps Affairs

Labor and Human Resources
Children, Families, Drugs and Alcoholism; Disability Policy; Education, Arts and Humanities; Labor (Ranking Republican)

Veterans' Affairs

Special Aging

Leading Contributors

NOTE: The bulk of Jefford's large individual contributions do not appear in the listings below. His last election was in 1988, and this book lists individual contributions only from 1989-1992.

Business

Agriculture $102,150

Crop Production & Basic Processing $13,800
None over $4,000

Tobacco $4,500
None over $4,000

Dairy $45,300
Agri-Mark Inc .... $10,500 PAC
Mid-America Dairymen .... $10,000 PAC
Associated Milk Producers .... $9,100 PAC
Dairymen Inc .... $6,000 PAC
Land O'Lakes Inc .... $4,500 PAC

Agricultural Services/Products $19,321
None over $4,000

Food Processing & Sales $13,629
None over $4,000

Forestry & Forest Products $4,000
None over $4,000

Source of Funds: 1987-1992

Source	Total	Pct
PACs	$699,422	56%
Indivs $200+	$116,372	9%
Indivs under $200	$107,573	9%
Other	$322,535	26%
Candidate	$0	0%
Party	$107,733	9%

Source of PAC Dollars by Sector

Source	Total	Pct
Business	$524,816	77%
Labor	$96,092	14%
Ideological/Single-Issue	$58,024	9%

In-State vs. Out-of-State Contributions*

Source	Total	Pct
In-State	$28,672	25%
Out-of-state	$86,700	75%
No state listed	$1,000	

* by large individual contributors ($200 & above)

Communications/Electronics $32,909

Telephone Utilities $19,909
AT&T .... $4,500 PAC

Electronics Mfg & Services $5,500
Cooper Industries .... $5,000 PAC

Construction $59,116

General Contractors $23,200
Associated General Contractors .... $10,000 PAC
National Utility Contractors Assn .... $7,000 PAC

Home Builders $11,779
National Assn of Home Builders .... $8,279 PAC

Special Trade Contractors $12,000
National Electrical Contractors Assn .... $5,000 PAC
Sheet Metal/Air Conditioning Contractors ... $5,000 PAC

Building Materials & Equipment $9,637
Manville Corp .... $5,000 PAC

Defense $13,279

Defense Aerospace $11,279
None over $4,000

Energy & Natural Resources $27,529

Oil & Gas $16,879
None over $4,000

Finance, Insurance & Real Estate $110,917

Commercial Banks $23,300
American Bankers Assn .... $10,000 PAC
JP Morgan & Co .... $5,000 PAC

Credit Unions $6,000
Credit Union National Assn .... $6,000 PAC

Securities & Investment $25,500
Chicago Mercantile Exchange .... $10,000 PAC
Chicago Board of Trade .... $8,000 PAC

Contribution Totals by Sector

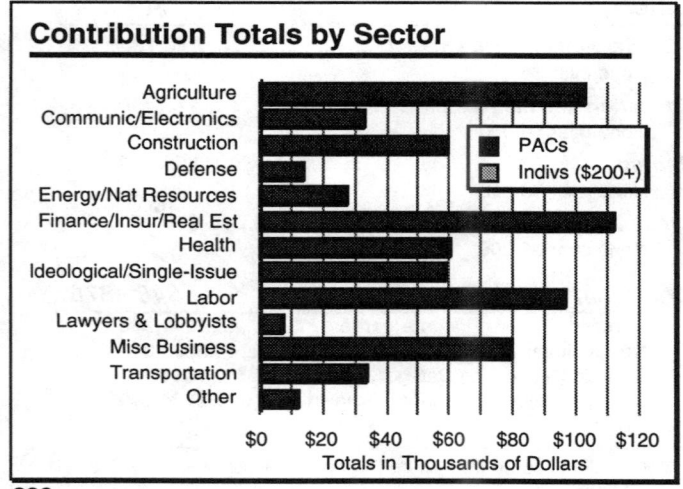

Agriculture
Communic/Electronics
Construction
Defense
Energy/Nat Resources
Finance/Insur/Real Est
Health
Ideological/Single-Issue
Labor
Lawyers & Lobbyists
Misc Business
Transportation
Other

PACs
Indivs ($200+)

$0 $20 $40 $60 $80 $100 $120
Totals in Thousands of Dollars

Insurance **$36,158**
    National Assn of Life Underwriters .... $5,000 PAC
Real Estate **$11,500**
    National Assn of Realtors .... $10,000 PAC
Accountants **$4,959**
    American Institute of CPA's .... $4,959 PAC

Health $59,687

Health Professionals **$35,733**
    American Academy of Ophthalmology .... $10,000 PAC
Hospitals/Nursing Homes **$7,500**
    None over $4,000
Pharmaceuticals/Health Products **$16,454**
    None over $4,000

Lawyers & Lobbyists $6,979

Lawyers & Lobbyists **$6,979**
    None over $4,000

Misc Business $78,900

Food & Beverage **$15,500**
    McDonald's Corp .... $5,000 PAC
Beer, Wine & Liquor **$6,500**
    None over $4,000
Retail Sales **$10,600**
    None over $4,000
Business Services **$5,000**
    None over $4,000
Chemical & Related Manufacturing **$12,850**
    None over $4,000
Misc Manufacturing & Distributing **$14,850**
    None over $4,000

Transportation   **$33,550**

Air Transport **$6,050**
    None over $4,000
Automotive **$15,000**
    Auto Dealers & Drivers for Free Trade .... $8,000 PAC
Trucking **$8,500**
    None over $4,000
Railroads **$4,000**
    None over $4,000

Labor

Labor $96,092

Industrial Unions **$18,371**
    National Education Assn .... $10,000 PAC
    American Federation of Teachers .... $5,000 PAC
Transportation Unions **$34,350**
    Air Line Pilots Assn .... $10,000 PAC
    Teamsters Union .... $10,000 PAC
    United Transportation Union .... $6,600 PAC
Public Sector Unions **$37,500**
    American Fedn of St/Cnty/Munic Employees .... $10,000 PAC
    National Assn of Letter Carriers .... $10,000 PAC
    Natl Assn of Retired Federal Employees .... $6,000 PAC
    American Postal Workers Union .... $5,000 PAC
Misc Unions **$5,371**
    None over $4,000

Ideological/Single-Issue

Ideological/Single-Issue $58,024

Leadership PACs **$20,622**
    Campaign America (Bob Dole) .... $5,000 PAC
    Republican Majority Fund (Richard Lugar) .... $5,000 PAC
    Catch the Spirit PAC (Bob Kasten) .... $4,500 PAC
Foreign & Defense Policy **$5,569**
    Council for a Livable World .... $5,569 PAC
Pro-Israel **$17,750**
    Desert Caucus .... $5,000 PAC
Human Rights **$8,850**
    Human Rights Campaign Fund .... $5,000 PAC

Other & Unknown

Other $12,200

Education **$11,200**
    Assn of Independent Colleges & Schools .... $6,000 PAC
    Natl Assn of Trade/Technical Schools .... $5,000 PAC

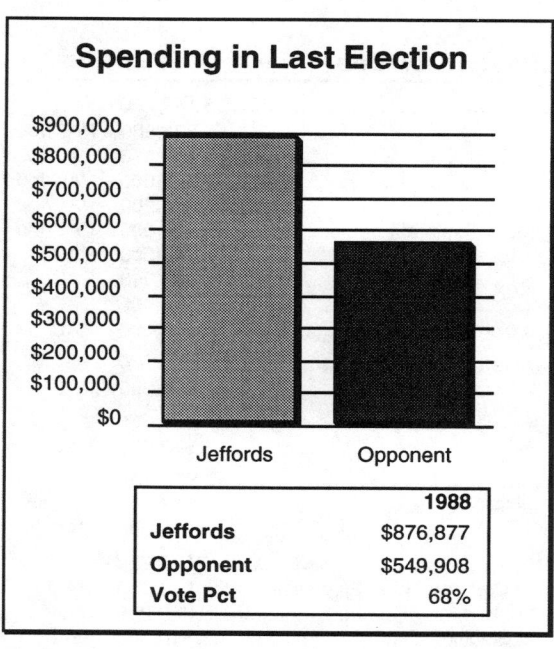

Spending in Last Election

	1988
Jeffords	$876,877
Opponent	$549,908
Vote Pct	68%

J. Bennett Johnston (D-La)

First elected: 1972

1987-92 Total Rcpts:	$4,671,888
1992 Year-end Cash:	$874,800
Current term expires:	1996

1991-92 Committees & Subcommittees

Appropriations
Defense; Energy and Water Development (Chairman); Foreign Operations; Interior and Related Agencies; VA, HUD and Independent Agencies

Budget

Energy and Natural Resources (Chairman)

Special Aging

Leading Contributors

Business

Agriculture	**$170,658**

Crop Production & Basic Processing $61,118
    None over $10,000

Tobacco $16,890
    None over $10,000

Dairy $10,500
    None over $10,000

Agricultural Services/Products $28,800
    None over $10,000

Food Processing & Sales $19,650
    None over $10,000

Forestry & Forest Products $26,000
    None over $10,000

Communications/Electronics	**$101,800**

Printing & Publishing $12,000
    None over $10,000

Media/Entertainment $61,200
    MCA Inc* .... $24,200   PAC/Ind

Computer Equipment & Services $16,000
    None over $10,000

Construction	**$90,500**

General Contractors $30,900
    None over $10,000

Home Builders $16,500
    National Assn of Home Builders .... $10,000   PAC

Contribution Totals by Sector

Horizontal bar chart with legend: PACs (black), Indivs ($200+) (gray)

Categories: Agriculture, Communic/Electronics, Construction, Defense, Energy/Nat Resources, Finance/Insur/Real Est, Health, Ideological/Single-Issue, Labor, Lawyers & Lobbyists, Misc Business, Transportation, Other

X-axis: $0 $100 $200 $300 $400 $500 $600 $700
Totals in Thousands of Dollars

Source of Funds: 1987-1992

Source	Total	Pct
■ PACs	$1,468,090	30%
▨ Indivs $200+	$1,370,135	28%
☐ Indivs under $200	$924,013	19%
⊠ Other	$1,057,650	22%
Candidate	$0	0%
Party	$148,000	3%

Source of PAC Dollars by Sector

Source	Total	Pct
■ Business	$1,220,448	82%
▨ Labor	$138,100	9%
☐ Ideological/Single-Issue ..	$136,360	9%

In-State vs. Out-of-State Contributions*

Source	Total	Pct
☐ In-State	$598,712	44%
■ Out-of-state	$768,123	56%
No state listed	$3,300	

*** by large individual contributors ($200 & above)**

Construction Services $32,800
    None over $10,000

Defense	**$188,914**

Defense Aerospace $106,950
    Textron Inc .... $11,200   PAC
    Northrop Corp .... $11,000   PAC/Ind
    Allied-Signal .... $10,000   PAC
    General Dynamics .... $10,000   PAC

Defense Electronics $51,964
    AT&T .... $10,000   PAC
    Westinghouse Electric .... $10,000   PAC

Misc Defense $30,000
    None over $10,000

Energy & Natural Resources	**$663,550**

Oil & Gas $344,750
    Arkla Inc .... $26,850   PAC/Ind
    Mobil Oil .... $19,000   PAC/Ind
    Atlantic Richfield .... $15,000   PAC/Ind
    Exxon Corp .... $11,200   PAC/Ind
    Louisiana Land & Exploration .... $11,000   PAC/Ind
    Chevron Corp .... $10,000   PAC
    Coastal Corp .... $10,000   PAC
    Enserch Corp .... $10,000   PAC
    Union Pacific Corp .... $10,000   PAC

Mining $45,100
    Fluor Corp .... $10,000   PAC

Nuclear Energy $20,000
    General Electric .... $10,000   PAC

Misc Energy $57,250
    Stone & Webster .... $21,000   PAC/Ind
    Bechtel Corp .... $10,000   PAC

Electric Utilities $176,950
    ACRE (Action Cmte for Rural Electrification)* ... $11,000   PAC
    Caithness Geothermal .... $10,000   Indiv
    Pacific Gas & Electric .... $10,000   PAC
    Southern California Edison .... $10,000   PAC

| Waste Management | $14,000 |
| None over $10,000 | |

Finance, Insurance & Real Estate — $306,785

Commercial Banks	$44,760	
American Bankers Assn	$10,000	PAC
Securities & Investment	$72,150	
Salomon Brothers	$16,000	PAC/Ind
Chicago Mercantile Exchange	$10,000	PAC
Insurance	$70,966	
National Assn of Life Underwriters	$10,000	PAC
Real Estate	$70,360	
None over $10,000		
Accountants	$17,950	
American Institute of CPA's	$10,000	PAC
Misc Finance	$26,799	
None over $10,000		

Health — $104,500

Health Professionals	$59,600
None over $10,000	
Hospitals/Nursing Homes	$13,950
None over $10,000	
Health Services	$18,050
None over $10,000	

Lawyers & Lobbyists — $305,150

| Lawyers & Lobbyists | $305,150 | |
| Assn of Trial Lawyers of America | $10,000 | PAC |

Misc Business — $143,369

Beer, Wine & Liquor	$32,550	
National Beer Wholesalers Assn	$10,500	PAC
Retail Sales	$17,350	
None over $10,000		
Business Services	$17,800	
None over $10,000		
Chemical & Related Manufacturing	$10,350	
None over $10,000		

Steel Production	$11,250
None over $10,000	
Misc Manufacturing & Distributing	$28,500
None over $10,000	

Transportation — $122,650

Air Transport	$34,000	
Federal Express Corp	$10,000	PAC
Automotive	$23,150	
None over $10,000		
Railroads	$12,500	
None over $10,000		
Sea Transport	$44,500	
None over $10,000		

Labor

Labor — $138,100

Building Trade Unions	$31,000	
Plumbers/Pipefitters Union	$10,000	PAC
Industrial Unions	$34,250	
None over $10,000		
Transportation Unions	$33,500	
Seafarers International Union	$10,000	PAC
Teamsters Union*	$10,000	PAC
Public Sector Unions	$26,050	
None over $10,000		
Misc Unions	$13,300	
None over $10,000		

Ideological/Single-Issue

Ideological/Single-Issue — $210,737

Democratic/Liberal	$19,575	
None over $10,000		
Leadership PACs	$30,090	
Pelican PAC (Bennett Johnston)	$18,090	PAC
Pro-Israel	$129,802	
Women's Alliance for Israel	$10,000	PAC

Other & Unknown

Other — $50,585

Civil Servants/Public Officials	$11,450
None over $10,000	
Education	$12,585
None over $10,000	
Retired	$19,800
None over $10,000	

Unknown — $255,245

Homemakers/Non-income earners	$44,850
No Employer Listed or Found	$59,550
Generic Occupation/Category Unknown	$26,650
Employer Listed/Category Unknown	$124,195
None over $10,000	

Independent expenditures supporting Johnston

National Assn of Realtors	$158,811
Auto Dealers & Drivers for Free Trade	$93,750
National Cmte to Preserve Social Security	$23,519

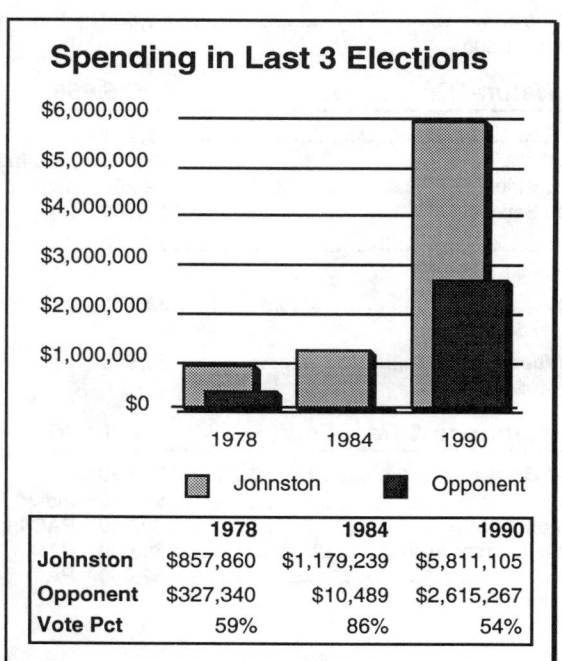

Spending in Last 3 Elections

	1978	1984	1990
Johnston	$857,860	$1,179,239	$5,811,105
Opponent	$327,340	$10,489	$2,615,267
Vote Pct	59%	86%	54%

---

* Contributions came from more than one affiliate or subsidiary.

Nancy Landon Kassebaum (R-Kan)

First elected: 1978

1987-92 Total Rcpts:	$529,612
1992 Year-end Cash:	$172,579
Current term expires:	1996

1991-92 Committees & Subcommittees

Banking, Housing and Urban Affairs
Housing and Urban Affairs; International Finance and Monetary Policy

Foreign Relations
African Affairs (Ranking Republican); International Economic Policy, Trade, Oceans and Environment; Western Hemisphere and Peace Corps Affairs

Labor and Human Resources
Children, Families, Drugs and Alcoholism; Education, Arts and Humanities (Ranking Republican); Employment and Productivity

Select Committee on Indian Affairs

Select Committee on POW/MIA Affairs

Leading Contributors

Business

Agriculture $28,150

Crop Production & Basic Processing **$4,450**		
Cargill Inc $2,000	PAC/Ind
Tobacco **$3,000**		
RJR Nabisco $2,000	PAC
Agricultural Services/Products **$10,250**		
Cereal Food Processors $3,000	Indiv
American Veterinary Medical Assn $2,000	PAC
Food Processing & Sales **$5,750**		
Pepsico Inc $3,000	PAC
Forestry & Forest Products **$2,000**		
None over $1,500		

Communications/Electronics $21,700

Printing & Publishing **$10,500**		
Sosland Companies Inc $7,000	Indiv
Hallmark Cards $2,500	PAC/Ind
Media/Entertainment **$3,200**		
National Cable Television Assn $2,000	PAC
Telephone Utilities **$6,000**		
AT&T $2,000	PAC
United Telecommunications $2,000	PAC/Ind

Source of Funds: 1987-1992

Source	Total	Pct
■ PACs	$177,088	29%
▨ Indivs $200+	$156,249	26%
☐ Indivs under $200	$87,383	14%
⊠ Other	$183,594	30%
Candidate	$0	0%
Party	$74,702	12%

Source of PAC Dollars by Sector

Source	Total	Pct
■ Business	$157,288	93%
▨ Labor	$2,750	2%
☐ Ideological/Single-Issue	$9,300	5%

In-State vs. Out-of-State Contributions*

Source	Total	Pct
☐ In-State	$127,199	82%
■ Out-of-state	$27,050	18%
No state listed	$2,000	

***by large individual contributors ($200 & above)**

Construction $16,200

General Contractors **$6,700**		
Associated General Contractors $2,000	PAC
Fluor Corp $2,000	PAC
Home Builders **$3,500**		
National Assn of Home Builders $2,000	PAC
Construction Services **$1,500**		
None over $1,500		
Building Materials & Equipment **$3,500**		
None over $1,500		

Defense $3,250

Defense Electronics **$2,000**		
None over $1,500		

Energy & Natural Resources $26,658

Oil & Gas **$18,208**		
Mobil Oil $3,000	PAC/Ind
Koch Industries $2,250	Indiv
KPL Gas Service $2,000	PAC
Mining **$2,500**		
None over $1,500		
Misc Energy **$2,000**		
None over $1,500		
Electric Utilities **$2,950**		
None over $1,500		

Finance, Insurance & Real Estate $81,180

Commercial Banks **$33,850**		
Mission Hills Bank $5,000	Indiv
BankAmerica Corp $2,750	PAC/Ind
American Bankers Assn $2,000	PAC
Citicorp $2,000	PAC
JP Morgan & Co $2,000	PAC

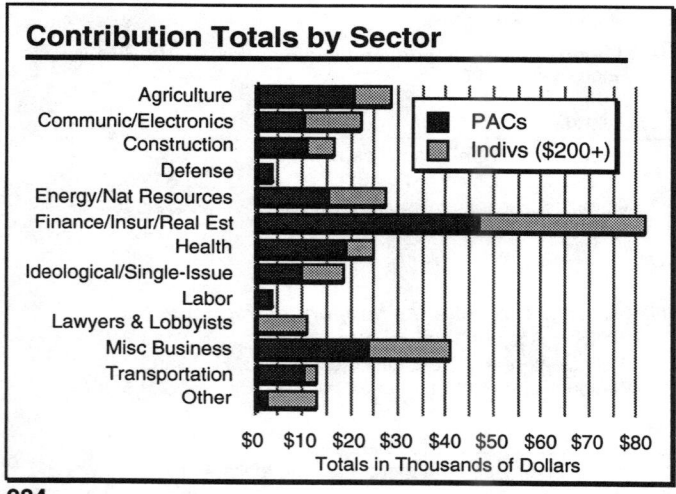

Contribution Totals by Sector

Agriculture
Communic/Electronics
Construction
Defense
Energy/Nat Resources
Finance/Insur/Real Est
Health
Ideological/Single-Issue
Labor
Lawyers & Lobbyists
Misc Business
Transportation
Other

■ PACs
▨ Indivs ($200+)

$0 $10 $20 $30 $40 $50 $60 $70 $80
Totals in Thousands of Dollars

| Savings & Loans | .... | $2,600 | |
| US League of Savings Assns | .... | $2,000 | PAC |

Finance/Credit Companies $1,500
None over $1,500

Securities & Investment $11,250
Salomon Brothers .... $2,000 PAC/Ind
American Express* .... $1,750 PAC

Insurance $11,930
None over $1,500

Real Estate $10,250
National Assn of Realtors .... $2,000 PAC
National Parking Assn .... $2,000 PAC

Accountants $5,000
American Institute of CPA's .... $2,000 PAC

Misc Finance $3,800
None over $1,500

Health $24,400

Health Professionals $11,700
American Dental Assn .... $2,000 PAC
American Medical Assn .... $2,000 PAC

Hospitals/Nursing Homes $3,000
None over $1,500

Pharmaceuticals/Health Products $9,500
Marion Laboratories .... $2,000 PAC/Ind

Lawyers & Lobbyists $10,650

Lawyers & Lobbyists $10,650
None over $1,500

Misc Business $40,150

Food & Beverage $9,300
National Pizza Co .... $2,000 Indiv
National Restaurant Assn .... $2,000 PAC
S&A Restaurant Corp .... $2,000 PAC

Beer, Wine & Liquor $4,000
National Beer Wholesalers Assn .... $2,000 PAC

Retail Sales $7,450
International Council of Shopping Centers .... $2,000 PAC

Misc Services $2,200
None over $1,500

Business Services $3,000
None over $1,500

Lodging/Tourism $3,000
None over $1,500

Chemical & Related Manufacturing $3,000
Dow Chemical* .... $2,000 PAC

Misc Manufacturing & Distributing $6,950
Coleman Co .... $2,000 Indiv

Transportation $12,300

Air Transport $4,300
None over $1,500

Automotive $3,000
National Auto Dealers Assn .... $2,000 PAC

Railroads $4,000
Union Pacific Corp .... $2,000 PAC

Labor

Labor $3,050

Public Sector Unions $2,250
None over $1,500

Ideological/Single-Issue

Ideological/Single-Issue $18,050

Republican/Conservative $7,500
National Republican Senatorial Cmte .... $6,000 Indiv

Leadership PACs $4,000
Campaign America (Bob Dole) .... $2,000 PAC
Republican Majority Fund (Richard Lugar) .... $2,000 PAC

Pro-Israel $3,000
National PAC .... $2,000 PAC

Other & Unknown

Other $12,650

Education $3,200
Assn of Independent Colleges & Schools............ $2,000 PAC

Retired $8,450
None over $1,500

Unknown $40,449

Homemakers/Non-income earners $11,250
No Employer Listed or Found $5,750
Generic Occupation/Category Unknown $2,250
Employer Listed/Category Unknown $20,199
Chisholm Enterprises .... $1,500 Indiv

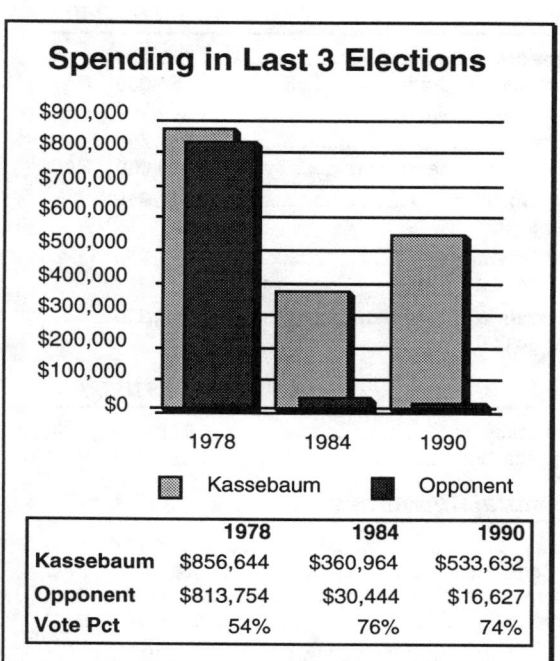

Spending in Last 3 Elections

	1978	1984	1990
Kassebaum	$856,644	$360,964	$533,632
Opponent	$813,754	$30,444	$16,627
Vote Pct	54%	76%	74%

Legend: Kassebaum / Opponent

---

* Contributions came from more than one affiliate or subsidiary.

Dirk Kempthorne (R-Idaho)

First elected: 1992

1991-92 Total Rcpts:	$1,351,127
1992 Year-end Cash:	$45,789
Current term expires:	1998

1993-94 Committees & Subcommittees

Armed Services
Coalition Defense and Reinforcing Forces; Defense Technology, Acquisition and Industrial Base; Nuclear Deterrence, Arms Control and Defense Intelligence

Environment and Public Works
Clean Air and Nuclear Regulation; Clean Water, Fisheries and Wildlife; Water Resources, Transportation, Public Buildings and Economic Development

Small Business
Innovation, Manufacturing and Technology; Rural Economy and Family Farming

Leading Contributors

Business

Agriculture	$222,886	
Crop Production & Basic Processing	**$19,200**	
Cargill Inc	$5,000	PAC
American Sugarbeet Growers Assn	$4,000	PAC
Tobacco	**$10,000**	
US Tobacco Co	$5,000	PAC
Livestock	**$17,750**	
None over $4,000		
Agricultural Services/Products	**$8,400**	
None over $4,000		
Food Processing & Sales	**$79,982**	
Albertson's Inc	$22,700	Indiv
JR Simplot Co	$6,500	PAC/Ind
ConAgra Inc	$5,000	PAC
Fleming Companies Inc	$5,000	PAC
Food Marketing Institute	$5,000	PAC
Pepsico Inc	$5,000	PAC
American Bakers Assn	$4,000	PAC
Forestry & Forest Products	**$83,554**	
Boise Cascade	$18,757	PAC/Ind
Potlatch Corp	$12,828	PAC/Ind
International Paper Co	$7,500	PAC
Willamette Industries	$5,000	PAC

Source of Funds: 1987-1992

Source	Total	Pct
PACs	$595,416	40%
Indivs $200+	$365,291	25%
Indivs under $200	$336,021	23%
Other	$186,433	13%
Candidate	$0	0%
Party	$132,034	9%

Source of PAC Dollars by Sector

Source	Total	Pct
Business	$559,865	94%
Labor	$0	0%
Ideological/Single-Issue	$36,450	6%

In-State vs. Out-of-State Contributions*

Source	Total	Pct
In-State	$268,413	74%
Out-of-state	$95,878	26%
No state listed	$0	

* by large individual contributors ($200 & above)

Communications/Electronics	$54,000	
Printing & Publishing	**$9,500**	
Printing Industries of America	$4,000	PAC/Ind
Media/Entertainment	**$12,250**	
National Cable Television Assn	$5,000	PAC
Telephone Utilities	**$15,500**	
United Telecommunications	$8,000	PAC
Electronics Mfg & Services	**$12,250**	
Hewlett-Packard	$5,250	PAC/Ind
Harris Corp	$5,000	PAC

Construction	$60,360	
General Contractors	**$22,420**	
Associated General Contractors	$5,000	PAC
Fluor Corp	$5,000	PAC
Home Builders	**$10,750**	
National Assn of Home Builders	$10,000	PAC
Special Trade Contractors	**$7,940**	
None over $4,000		
Construction Services	**$6,200**	
None over $4,000		
Building Materials & Equipment	**$13,050**	
None over $4,000		

Defense	$16,647	
Defense Aerospace	**$11,750**	
Martin Marietta Corp	$5,000	PAC

Energy & Natural Resources	$113,307	
Oil & Gas	**$75,507**	
Chevron Corp	$10,000	PAC
Amoco Corp	$6,000	PAC
Exxon Corp	$6,000	PAC
Atlantic Richfield	$5,000	PAC
Mobil Oil	$5,000	PAC
Mapco Inc	$4,000	PAC

Contribution Totals by Sector

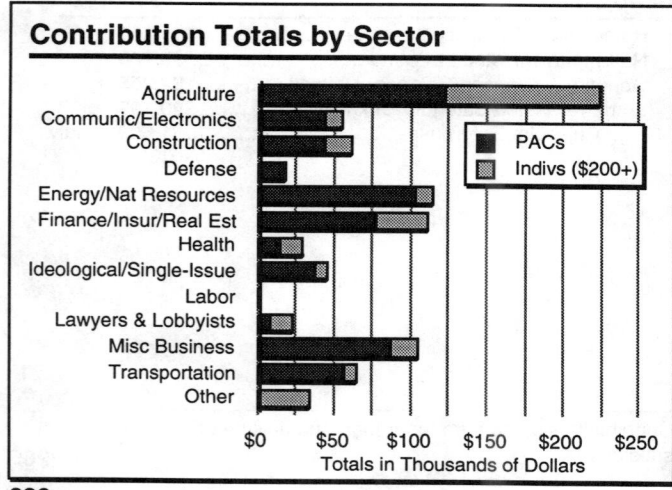

Agriculture
Communic/Electronics
Construction
Defense
Energy/Nat Resources
Finance/Insur/Real Est
Health
Ideological/Single-Issue
Labor
Lawyers & Lobbyists
Misc Business
Transportation
Other

PACs
Indivs ($200+)

$0 $50 $100 $150 $200 $250
Totals in Thousands of Dollars

Mining		$21,050
Cyprus Minerals Co	$5,000	PAC
National Coal Assn	$5,000	PAC

Misc Energy		$5,500
Cooper Industries	$5,000	PAC

Electric Utilities		$8,750
None over $4,000		

Finance, Insurance & Real Estate — $110,300

Commercial Banks		$24,700
American Bankers Assn*	$9,000	PAC
Barnett Banks Inc	$4,500	PAC
West One Bancorp	$4,000	PAC/Ind

Securities & Investment		$5,500
None over $4,000		

Insurance		$46,504
National Assn of Independent Insurers	$5,450	PAC
National Assn of Life Underwriters	$5,000	PAC
Independent Insurance Agents of America	$4,602	PAC

Real Estate		$15,170
None over $4,000		

Accountants		$7,676
American Institute of CPA's	$7,000	PAC

Misc Finance		$9,750
None over $4,000		

Health — $27,742

Health Professionals		$13,412
None over $4,000		

Pharmaceuticals/Health Products		$11,000
Eli Lilly & Co	$5,000	PAC

Lawyers & Lobbyists — $20,770

Lawyers & Lobbyists		$20,770
None over $4,000		

Misc Business — $103,391

Food & Beverage		$20,500
National Restaurant Assn	$6,000	PAC

Beer, Wine & Liquor		$6,000
National Beer Wholesalers Assn	$5,000	PAC

Retail Sales		$15,000
None over $4,000		

Business Services		$8,630
None over $4,000		

Lodging/Tourism		$4,000
None over $4,000		

Misc Business		$5,000
National Assn of Wholesale-Distributors	$4,000	PAC

Chemical & Related Manufacturing		$24,000
FMC Corp	$10,000	PAC
Monsanto Co	$5,000	PAC
Dow Chemical	$4,000	PAC

Misc Manufacturing & Distributing		$10,560
None over $4,000		

Transportation — $62,560

Air Transport		$14,500
United Parcel Service	$6,000	PAC
General Electric	$5,000	PAC

Automotive		$33,060
Americans for Free International Trade	$10,000	PAC
National Auto Dealers Assn	$10,000	PAC
Eaton Corp	$4,000	PAC

Railroads		$10,500
Union Pacific Corp	$10,500	PAC/Ind

Ideological/Single-Issue

Ideological/Single-Issue		$43,950

Republican/Conservative		$7,100
None over $4,000		

Leadership PACs		$18,250
Campaign America (Bob Dole)	$10,000	PAC
Senate Victory Fund (Thad Cochran)	$4,000	PAC

Gun Rights/Gun Control		$4,950
National Rifle Assn	$4,950	PAC

Misc Issues		$11,000
Right to Work PAC	$5,000	PAC
Public Service Research Council	$4,000	PAC

Other & Unknown

Other		$32,895

Civil Servants/Public Officials		$6,060
None over $4,000		

Retired		$23,365
None over $4,000		

Unknown		$92,798
Homemakers/Non-income earners	$10,232	
No Employer Listed or Found	$27,415	
Employer Listed/Category Unknown	$52,851	
JB Scott Enterprises	$4,000	Indiv

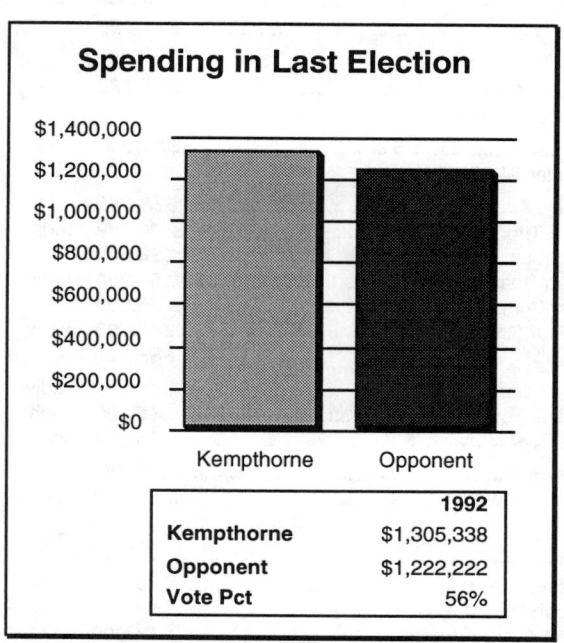

Spending in Last Election

	1992
Kempthorne	$1,305,338
Opponent	$1,222,222
Vote Pct	56%

* Contributions came from more than one affiliate or subsidiary.

287

Edward M. Kennedy (D-Mass)

First elected: 1962

1987-92 Total Rcpts:	$4,270,784
1992 Year-end Cash:	$748,063
Current term expires:	1994

1991-92 Committees & Subcommittees

Armed Services
Manpower and Personnel; Projection Forces and Regional Defense (Chairman); Strategic Forces and Nuclear Deterrence

Judiciary
Constitution; Immigration and Refugee Affairs (Chairman); Patents, Copyrights and Trademarks

Labor and Human Resources (Chairman)
Children, Families, Drugs and Alcoholism; Education, Arts and Humanities; Labor

Joint Economic Committee

Leading Contributors

NOTE: The bulk of Kennedy's large individual contributions do not appear in the listings below. His last election was in 1988, and this book lists individual contributions only from 1989-1992.

Business

Agriculture		$11,600

Food Processing & Sales $4,000
    None over $4,000

Communications/Electronics		$47,931

Printing & Publishing $5,000
    None over $4,000
Media/Entertainment $26,831
    MCA Inc ....$4,861   PAC
Telephone Utilities $6,500
    None over $4,000
Computer Equipment & Services $6,800
    None over $4,000

Construction		$23,350

General Contractors $8,250
    None over $4,000
Home Builders $5,000
    None over $4,000
Special Trade Contractors $4,000
    None over $4,000
Construction Services $4,500
    None over $4,000

Contribution Totals by Sector

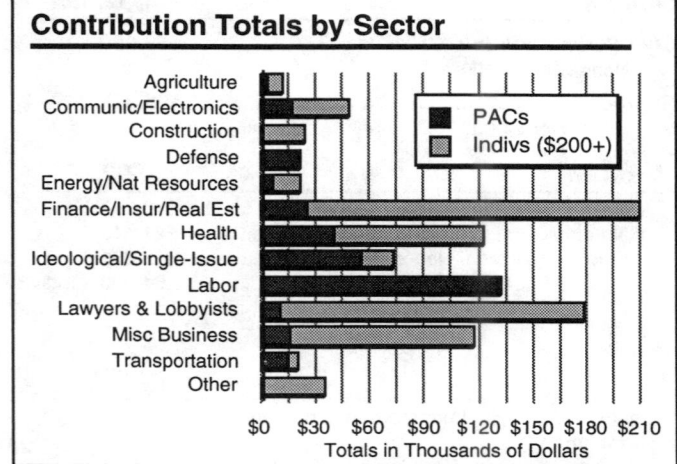

PACs
Indivs ($200+)

Agriculture
Communic/Electronics
Construction
Defense
Energy/Nat Resources
Finance/Insur/Real Est
Health
Ideological/Single-Issue
Labor
Lawyers & Lobbyists
Misc Business
Transportation
Other

$0 $30 $60 $90 $120 $150 $180 $210
Totals in Thousands of Dollars

288

Source of Funds: 1987-1992

Source	Total	Pct
PACs	$326,691	8%
Indivs $200+	$2,721,461	63%
Indivs under $200	$977,990	23%
Other	$263,442	6%
Candidate	$0	0%
Party	$18,800	0%

Source of PAC Dollars by Sector

Source	Total	Pct
Business	$150,006	45%
Labor	$130,500	39%
Ideological/Single-Issue	$54,230	16%

In-State vs. Out-of-State Contributions*

Source	Total	Pct
In-State	$815,888	30%
Out-of-state	$1,899,573	70%
No state listed	$6,000	

* by large individual contributors ($200 & above)

Defense		$20,700

Defense Aerospace $16,200
    None over $4,000
Defense Electronics $5,500
    None over $4,000

Energy & Natural Resources		$21,202

Oil & Gas $14,202
    Global Petroleum Corp ....$6,702   Indiv
    Occidental Petroleum ....$5,000   PAC

Finance, Insurance & Real Estate		$208,017

Commercial Banks $11,295
    None over $4,000
Securities & Investment $47,133
    None over $4,000
Insurance $21,800
    None over $4,000
Real Estate $73,889
    Maguire Thomas Partners ....$6,989   Indiv
    Finch Group ....$6,500   Indiv
    Tishman Realty & Construction ....$6,000   Indiv
    Beacon Companies ....$5,000   Indiv
    Cloverleaf Group Inc ....$5,000   Indiv
Accountants $25,650
    Arthur Andersen & Co ....$9,250   Indiv
    Deloitte & Touche ....$5,500   Indiv
    KPMG Peat Marwick ....$4,000   Indiv
Misc Finance $25,750
    First Winthrop Corp ....$4,500   Indiv

Health		$121,975

Health Professionals $40,000
    American Dental Assn ....$4,000   PAC
    National Assn of Pharmacists ....$4,000   PAC

Hospitals/Nursing Homes **$40,000**
    Hospice Care Inc .... $8,000   Indiv
    Continental Health Affiliates .... $6,000   Indiv
Health Services **$11,000**
    None over $4,000
Pharmaceuticals/Health Products **$20,250**
    None over $4,000
Misc Health **$10,725**
    Park Health Care Services .... $4,000   Indiv

Lawyers & Lobbyists $177,809

Lawyers & Lobbyists **$177,809**
    Morgan, Lewis & Bockius .... $10,000   Indiv
    Peabody & Brown .... $8,630   Indiv
    Mintz, Levin et al .... $8,050   Indiv
    Cooley, Manion et al .... $8,000   Indiv
    Fox, Weinberg & Bennett .... $6,000   Indiv
    Wunder, Diefenderfer et al .... $4,016   Indiv
    Esanu, Katsky et al .... $4,000   Indiv
    Manatt, Phelps & Phillips .... $4,000   PAC/Ind
    Weitz & Luxenberg .... $4,000   Indiv

Misc Business $116,142

Food & Beverage **$8,750**
    Coca-Cola Co .... $4,000   PAC/Ind
Beer, Wine & Liquor **$7,000**
    None over $4,000
Retail Sales **$11,800**
    None over $4,000
Business Services **$34,933**
    Advacare Diagnostics .... $4,000   Indiv
Chemical & Related Manufacturing **$4,160**
    None over $4,000
Misc Manufacturing & Distributing **$33,249**
    Anwelt Corp .... $4,000   Indiv
Textiles **$4,000**
    None over $4,000

Transportation $19,800

Air Transport **$8,000**
    Federal Express Corp .... $5,000   PAC
Automotive **$7,500**
    None over $4,000

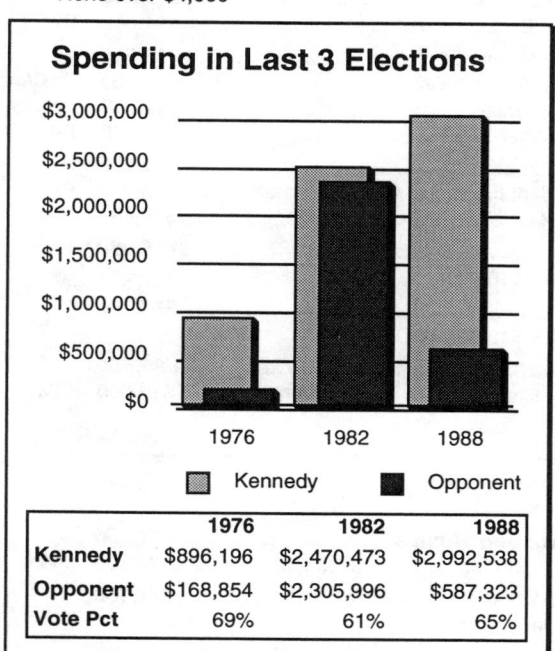

Spending in Last 3 Elections

	1976	1982	1988
Kennedy	$896,196	$2,470,473	$2,992,538
Opponent	$168,854	$2,305,996	$587,323
Vote Pct	69%	61%	65%

Legend: Kennedy / Opponent

Labor

Labor $131,000

Building Trade Unions **$32,000**
    Bricklayers Union .... $10,000   PAC
    Operating Engineers Union* .... $10,000   PAC
    Sheet Metal Workers Union .... $5,000   PAC
Industrial Unions **$40,500**
    Communications Workers of America .... $6,000   PAC
    Amalgamated Clothing & Textile Workers ... $5,000   PAC
    American Federation of Teachers .... $5,000   PAC
    Intl Brotherhood of Electrical Workers .... $5,000   PAC
    Ladies Garment Workers Union .... $5,000   PAC
    United Mine Workers .... $5,000   PAC
    United Steelworkers .... $5,000   PAC
Transportation Unions **$28,000**
    United Auto Workers .... $5,500   PAC
    Air Line Pilots Assn .... $5,000   PAC
    Amalgamated Transit Union .... $5,000   PAC
    United Transportation Union .... $5,000   PAC
Public Sector Unions **$15,500**
    American Fedn of St/Cnty/Munic Employees ...... $5,000   PAC
Misc Unions **$15,000**
    AFL-CIO .... $5,000   PAC
    Food & Commercial Workers Union .... $5,000   PAC
    Service Employees International Union .... $5,000   PAC

Ideological/Single-Issue

Ideological/Single-Issue $72,230

Democratic/Liberal **$14,244**
    Hollywood Women's Political Cmte .... $5,000   PAC
Leadership PACs **$7,750**
    Senate Majority Fund (Daniel Inouye) .... $5,000   PAC
Pro-Israel **$31,250**
    Pacific PAC .... $10,000   PAC
    National PAC .... $5,000   PAC
Human Rights **$10,379**
    KidsPAC .... $5,000   PAC

Other & Unknown

Other $33,925

Education **$8,000**
    None over $4,000
Retired **$20,925**
    None over $4,000

Unknown $120,640

    Homemakers/Non-income earners $31,590
    Employer Listed/Category Unknown $102,150
        Kalos Kagathon Inc .... $4,000   Indiv

Independent expenditures supporting Kennedy
    National Cmte to Preserve Social Security $21,832
Independent expenditures opposing Kennedy
    American Citizens for Political Action $167,950
    National Congressional Club $91,429
    East Coast Conservative PAC $21,858
    Mid-America Conservative PAC $14,641
    Life Amendment PAC $7,555
    Conservative Campaign Fund $4,560

---

* Contributions came from more than one affiliate or subsidiary.

Bob Kerrey (D-Neb)

First elected: 1988

1987-92 Total Rcpts:	$4,091,163
1992 Year-end Cash:	$91,304
Current term expires:	1994

1991-92 Committees & Subcommittees

Agriculture, Nutrition and Forestry
Agricultural Production and Stabilization of Prices; Agricultural Research and General Legislation; Nutrition and Investigations

Appropriations
Agriculture, Rural Development and Related Agencies; District of Columbia; Treasury, Postal Service and General Government; VA, HUD and Independent Agencies

Select Committee on Intelligence

Select Committee on POW/MIA Affairs

Leading Contributors

NOTE: Kerry's profile includes contributions received in his 1992 presidential campaign, but it does not include individual donations he collected in his 1988 senatorial campaign. This book lists individual contributions only from 1989-1992.

Business

Agriculture $169,174

Crop Production & Basic Processing $37,200
    None over $10,000

Tobacco $15,250
    None over $10,000

Dairy $23,500
    None over $10,000

Livestock $17,275
    None over $10,000

Agricultural Services/Products $39,599
    American Assn of Crop Insurers .... $11,999   PAC

Food Processing & Sales $32,500
    ConAgra Inc .... $12,000   PAC

Communications/Electronics $224,831

Printing & Publishing $21,969
    None over $10,000

Media/Entertainment $121,950
    None over $10,000

Telephone Utilities $58,162
    US West Inc* .... $18,610   PAC/Ind

Source of Funds: 1987-1992

Source	Total	Pct
PACs	$1,066,363	25%
Indivs $200+	$1,200,994	28%
Indivs under $200	$1,628,420	39%
Other	$324,160	8%
Candidate	$102,500	2%
Party	$128,774	3%

Source of PAC Dollars by Sector

Source	Total	Pct
Business	$673,967	48%
Labor	$468,605	34%
Ideological/Single-Issue	$254,825	18%

In-State vs. Out-of-State Contributions*

Source	Total	Pct
In-State	$857,584	21%
Out-of-state	$3,179,271	79%
No state listed	$5,500	

* by large individual contributors ($200 & above)

Construction $58,425

Construction Services $16,975
    Leo A Daly Co .... $12,000   Indiv

Defense $11,500

    None over $10,000

Energy & Natural Resources $65,655

Oil & Gas $37,900
    None over $10,000

Finance, Insurance & Real Estate $539,396

Commercial Banks $49,836
    American Bankers Assn* .... $11,000   PAC

Securities & Investment $215,825
    Goldman, Sachs & Co .... $13,000   PAC/Ind
    Whale Securities .... $12,000   Indiv
    PaineWebber .... $11,750   PAC/Ind

Insurance $90,625
    Independent Insurance Agents of America .... $15,000   PAC
    Mutual of Omaha* .... $13,850   PAC

Real Estate $116,060
    None over $10,000

Accountants $17,000
    None over $10,000

Misc Finance $35,550
    America First Resource Management .... $10,000   PAC

Health $174,900

Health Professionals $93,200
    None over $10,000

Hospitals/Nursing Homes $51,350
    Hospice Care Inc .... $27,100   Indiv

Pharmaceuticals/Health Products $21,900
    None over $10,000

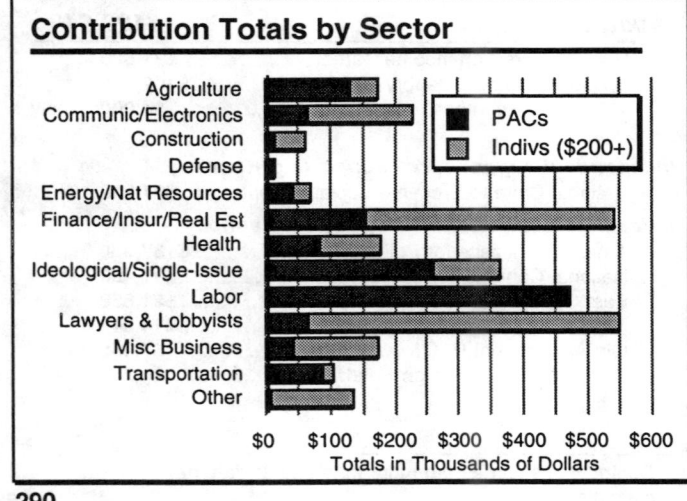

Contribution Totals by Sector

Agriculture, Communic/Electronics, Construction, Defense, Energy/Nat Resources, Finance/Insur/Real Est, Health, Ideological/Single-Issue, Labor, Lawyers & Lobbyists, Misc Business, Transportation, Other

Legend: PACs / Indivs ($200+)

$0 $100 $200 $300 $400 $500 $600
Totals in Thousands of Dollars

Lawyers & Lobbyists $546,039

Lawyers & Lobbyists $505,266
- Greenberg, Traurig et al .... $18,583   PAC/Ind
- Assn of Trial Lawyers of America .... $15,000   PAC
- Kutak, Rock & Campbell .... $12,700   PAC/Ind

Transportation $103,000

Air Transport $48,250
- Federal Express Corp .... $18,000   PAC

Automotive $16,950
- None over $10,000

Railroads $21,250
- Union Pacific Corp .... $11,000   PAC

Misc Business $168,224

Food & Beverage $26,500
- None over $10,000

Retail Sales $31,000
- None over $10,000

Business Services $48,000
- None over $10,000

Misc Manufacturing & Distributing $19,500
- None over $10,000

Labor

Labor $469,105

Building Trade Unions $87,250
- Carpenters & Joiners Union .... $15,000   PAC
- Sheet Metal Workers Union .... $15,000   PAC
- Laborers' Political League .... $14,000   PAC
- Plumbers/Pipefitters Union .... $13,000   PAC
- Operating Engineers Union* .... $11,000   PAC

Industrial Unions $115,700
- Communications Workers of America .... $15,000   PAC
- Intl Brotherhood of Electrical Workers .... $15,000   PAC
- Machinists/Aerospace Workers Union .... $15,000   PAC
- United Auto Workers .... $15,000   PAC
- United Steelworkers .... $15,000   PAC
- Rubber Cork Linoleum & Plastic Workers .... $10,900   PAC
- Amalgamated Clothing & Textile Workers .... $10,000   PAC

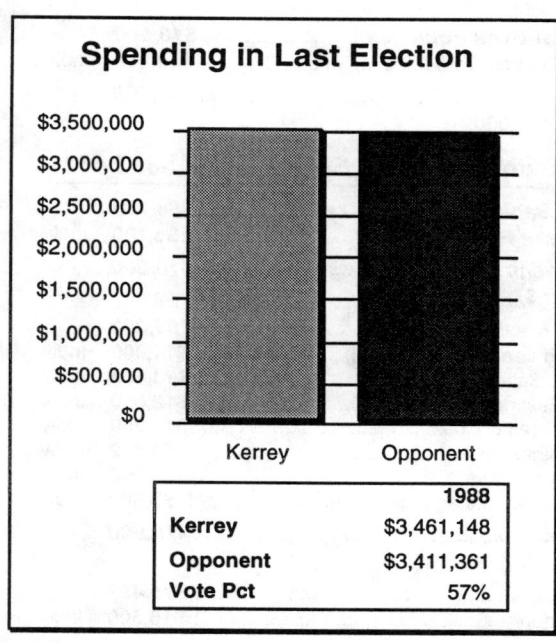

Spending in Last Election

	1988
Kerrey	$3,461,148
Opponent	$3,411,361
Vote Pct	57%

Transportation Unions $114,750
- United Transportation Union .... $20,000   PAC
- Teamsters Union .... $16,000   PAC
- Air Line Pilots Assn .... $15,000   PAC
- Marine Engineers Union .... $15,000   PAC
- Trans Comm International Union .... $13,500   PAC
- Seafarers International Union .... $13,000   PAC/Ind

Public Sector Unions $106,405
- American Federation of Teachers .... $15,000   PAC
- American Fedn of St/Cnty/Munic Employees .... $15,000   PAC
- National Education Assn .... $15,000   PAC
- National Assn of Letter Carriers .... $13,000   PAC
- National Treasury Employees Union .... $11,000   PAC
- American Postal Workers Union .... $10,000   PAC

Misc Unions $45,000
- Food & Commercial Workers Union .... $15,000   PAC
- AFL-CIO .... $10,000   PAC

Ideological/Single-Issue

Ideological/Single-Issue $358,798

Democratic/Liberal $85,878
- Democrats for the 80's .... $10,000   PAC
- Religion and Tolerance PAC .... $10,000   PAC

Leadership PACs $50,124
- Senate Majority Fund (Daniel Inouye) .... $15,000   PAC
- Cmte for a Democratic Consensus (Alan Cranston) $10,000   PAC

Foreign & Defense Policy $17,725
- None over $10,000

Pro-Israel $133,750
- Washington PAC .... $11,000   PAC
- National PAC .... $10,000   PAC

Womens Issues $15,667
- None over $10,000

Misc Issues $27,888
- National Cmte to Preserve Social Secur .... $10,000   PAC

Other & Unknown

Other $133,206

Civil Servants/Public Officials $37,431
- None over $10,000

Education $25,475
- None over $10,000

Retired $57,050
- None over $10,000

Unknown $1,204,683
- Homemakers/Non-income earners $63,400
- No Employer Listed or Found $943,887
- Generic Occupation/Category Unknown $26,271
- Employer Listed/Category Unknown $171,125
  - None over $10,000

Independent expenditures opposing Kerry
- East Coast Conservative PAC $30,035
- Mid-America Conservative PAC $13,306

---

* Contributions came from more than one affiliate or subsidiary.

John Kerry (D-Mass)

First elected: 1984

1987-92 Total Rcpts:	$7,573,317
1992 Year-end Cash:	$119,651
Current term expires:	1996

1991-92 Committees & Subcommittees

Banking, Housing and Urban Affairs
Consumer and Regulatory Affairs; Housing and Urban Affairs

Commerce, Science and Transportation
Aviation; Communications; Science, Technology and Space; National Ocean Policy Study (Vice Chairman)

Foreign Relations
East Asian and Pacific Affairs; Terrorism, Narcotics and International Operations (Chairman); Western Hemisphere and Peace Corps Affairs

Small Business
Innovation, Technology and Productivity; Rural Economy and Family Farming; Urban and Minority-Owned Business Development (Chairman)

Select Committee on POW/MIA Affairs (Chairman)

Leading Contributors

Business

Agriculture	$40,450

Food Processing & Sales	$29,700
None over $7,500	

Communications/Electronics	$336,171

Printing & Publishing	$37,750
None over $7,500	

Media/Entertainment	$239,125	
Time Warner*	$40,500	Indiv
Walt Disney Co/Disney Channel*	$11,500	Indiv
Continental Cablevision	$10,375	Indiv
MCA Inc	$10,000	Indiv

Telephone Utilities	$14,225
None over $7,500	

Computer Equipment & Services	$30,371
None over $7,500	

Construction	$144,750

General Contractors	$63,150
None over $7,500	

Home Builders	$15,950
None over $7,500	

Contribution Totals by Sector

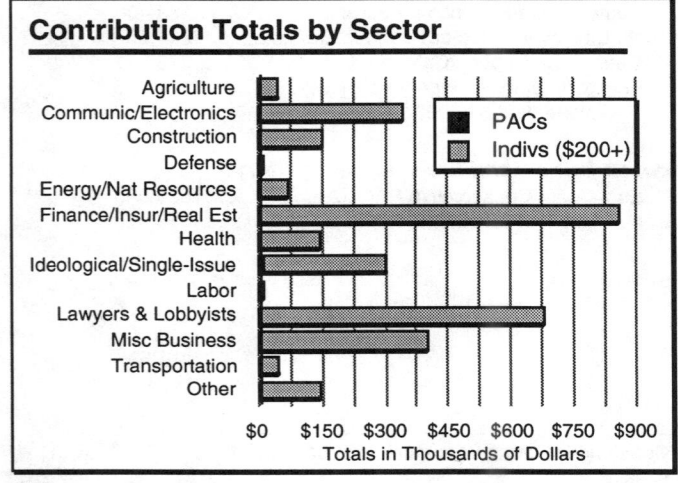

Categories (top to bottom): Agriculture, Communic/Electronics, Construction, Defense, Energy/Nat Resources, Finance/Insur/Real Est, Health, Ideological/Single-Issue, Labor, Lawyers & Lobbyists, Misc Business, Transportation, Other

Legend: ■ PACs ▨ Indivs ($200+)

$0 $150 $300 $450 $600 $750 $900
Totals in Thousands of Dollars

Source of Funds: 1987-1992

Source	Total	Pct
■ PACs	$0	0%
▨ Indivs $200+	$4,418,261	55%
☐ Indivs under $200	$2,864,109	36%
▨ Other	$769,195	10%
Candidate	$170,000	2%
Party	$485,273	6%

Source of PAC Dollars by Sector

No PAC contributions reported

Source	Total	Pct
■ Business	$0	0%
▨ Labor	$0	0%
☐ Ideological/Single-Issue	$0	0%

In-State vs. Out-of-State Contributions*

Source	Total	Pct
☐ In-State	$2,483,088	56%
■ Out-of-state	$1,934,673	44%
No state listed	$500	

* by large individual contributors ($200 & above)

Special Trade Contractors	$18,000
None over $7,500	

Construction Services	$28,900
None over $7,500	

Building Materials & Equipment	$18,750
None over $7,500	

Defense	$10,084

Defense Electronics	$8,184
None over $7,500	

Energy & Natural Resources	$68,050

Oil & Gas	$30,300	
Edward Callan Interests	$12,000	Indiv

Environmental Svcs/Equipment	$13,500	
Thermo Electron Corp	$13,000	Indiv

Waste Management	$8,000
None over $7,500	

Finance, Insurance & Real Estate	$853,441

Commercial Banks	$84,703	
Fleet/Norstar Financial Group*	$8,700	Indiv

Savings & Loans	$10,800
None over $7,500	

Securities & Investment	$209,092	
Thomas H Lee Co	$14,800	Indiv
Goldman, Sachs & Co	$13,500	Indiv
Aldrich, Eastman & Waltch	$12,500	Indiv
Lazard Freres & Co	$10,250	Indiv
Meuse, Rinker et al	$8,842	Indiv
American Express*	$7,900	Indiv
First Financial Management Corp	$7,500	Indiv

Insurance	$76,900
None over $7,500	

Real Estate	$335,497	
Finch Group	$15,500	Indiv

New England Development	$12,500	Indiv
Beacon Companies	$11,250	Indiv
Maric Inc	$10,750	Indiv
Boston Capital Partners	$8,750	Indiv

Accountants **$55,749**
None over $7,500

Misc Finance **$74,000**
None over $7,500

Health $142,725

Health Professionals **$57,575**
None over $7,500

Hospitals/Nursing Homes **$43,550**
None over $7,500

Pharmaceuticals/Health Products **$23,000**
Advanced Magnetics .... $8,600 Indiv

Misc Health **$11,900**
None over $7,500

Lawyers & Lobbyists $670,205

Lawyers & Lobbyists **$670,205**

Mintz, Levin et al	$58,946	Indiv
Hale & Dorr	$20,500	Indiv
Foley, Hoag & Eliot	$20,250	Indiv
Goulston & Storrs	$10,300	Indiv
Milberg, Weiss et al	$10,000	Indiv
Donahue & Donahue	$8,000	Indiv
Kaye, Scholer et al	$7,500	Indiv

Misc Business $396,535

Food & Beverage **$39,600**
None over $7,500

Beer, Wine & Liquor **$41,206**
United Liquors .... $13,500 Indiv
Williams Distributing Corp .... $7,906 Indiv

Retail Sales **$33,325**
None over $7,500

Misc Services **$10,750**
None over $7,500

Business Services **$108,558**
Hill, Holiday et al .... $8,000 Indiv

Lodging/Tourism **$37,400**
None over $7,500

Spending in Last 2 Elections

	1984	1990
Kerry	$2,070,000	$8,063,933
Opponent	$4,180,961	$5,177,801
Vote Pct	55%	57%

Chemical & Related Manufacturing **$10,950**
None over $7,500

Misc Manufacturing & Distributing **$91,846**
MacAndrews & Forbes Group .... $17,000 Indiv
Revlon Inc .... $13,000 Indiv
Luz International Ltd .... $8,000 Indiv

Textiles **$8,950**
None over $7,500

Transportation $42,483

Air Transport **$8,983**
None over $7,500

Automotive **$18,250**
None over $7,500

Sea Transport **$8,200**
None over $7,500

Labor

Labor $7,750

None over $7,500

Ideological/Single-Issue

Ideological/Single-Issue $298,766

Democratic/Liberal **$81,257**
None over $7,500

Foreign & Defense Policy **$24,250**
None over $7,500

Pro-Israel **$121,045**
None over $7,500

Pro-Choice **$12,450**
None over $7,500

Womens Issues **$10,400**
None over $7,500

Human Rights **$22,950**
None over $7,500

Misc Issues **$25,414**
None over $7,500

Other & Unknown

Other $143,557

Civil Servants/Public Officials **$18,522**
None over $7,500

Education **$58,400**
None over $7,500

Retired **$48,635**
None over $7,500

Other **$12,300**
None over $7,500

Unknown $959,841

Homemakers/Non-income earners	$134,695
No Employer Listed or Found	$346,351
Generic Occupation/Category Unknown	$13,500
Employer Listed/Category Unknown	$465,295

None over $7,500

Independent expenditures opposing Kerry
East Coast Conservative PAC $30,035
Mid-America Conservative PAC $13,306
Council for National Defense $8,547

---

* Contributions came from more than one affiliate or
subsidiary.

Herb Kohl (D-Wis)

First elected: 1988

1987-92 Total Rcpts:	$8,371,609
1992 Year-end Cash:	$1,530
Current term expires:	1994

1991-92 Committees & Subcommittees

Governmental Affairs
Government Information and Regulation (Chairman); Oversight of Government Management; Permanent Subcommittee on Investigations

Judiciary
Courts and Administrative Practice; Technology and the Law; Juvenile Justice (Chairman)

Select Committee on POW/MIA Affairs

Special Aging

Leading Contributors

NOTES: Kohl reported taking no PAC funds during his 1988 Senate campaign. The PAC listed below did report making a contribution, however, and that contribution is recorded in the official FEC records.

The bulk of Kohl's large individual contributions from that 1988 campaign do not appear in the listings below. This book lists individual contributions only from 1989-1992.

Business

Agriculture $1,000

Crop Production & Basic Processing $1,000
    None over $1,000

Transportation $2,000

Automotive $2,000
    None over $1,000

Source of Funds: 1987-1992

Source	Total	Pct
PACs	$1,500	0%
Indivs $200+	$413,211	5%
Indivs under $200	$246,531	3%
Other	$7,710,367	92%
Candidate	$7,258,071	87%
Party	$0	0%

Source of PAC Dollars by Sector

No PAC contributions reported

Source	Total	Pct
Business	$0	0%
Labor	$1,500	100%
Ideological/Single-Issue	$0	0%

In-State vs. Out-of-State Contributions*

Source	Total	Pct
In-State	$201,136	49%
Out-of-state	$206,575	51%
No state listed	$5,500	

* by large individual contributors ($200 & above)

Contribution Totals by Sector

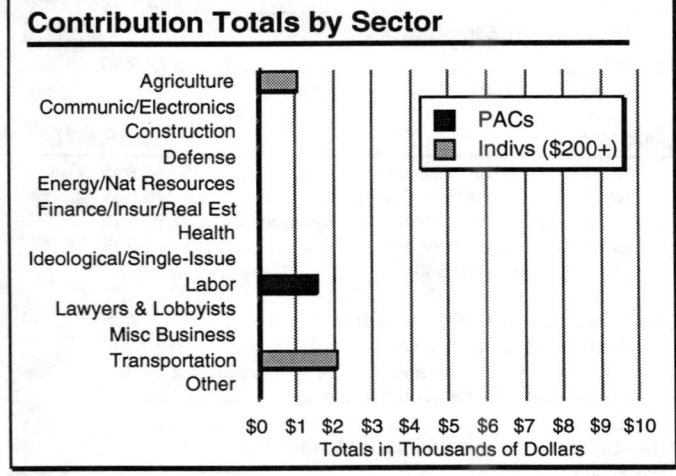

Agriculture
Communic/Electronics
Construction
Defense
Energy/Nat Resources
Finance/Insur/Real Est
Health
Ideological/Single-Issue
Labor
Lawyers & Lobbyists
Misc Business
Transportation
Other

■ PACs
▨ Indivs ($200+)

$0 $1 $2 $3 $4 $5 $6 $7 $8 $9 $10
Totals in Thousands of Dollars

Labor

Labor	$1,500

Misc Unions **$1,500**

    Bakery, Confectionery & Tobacco Workers .... $1,500   PAC

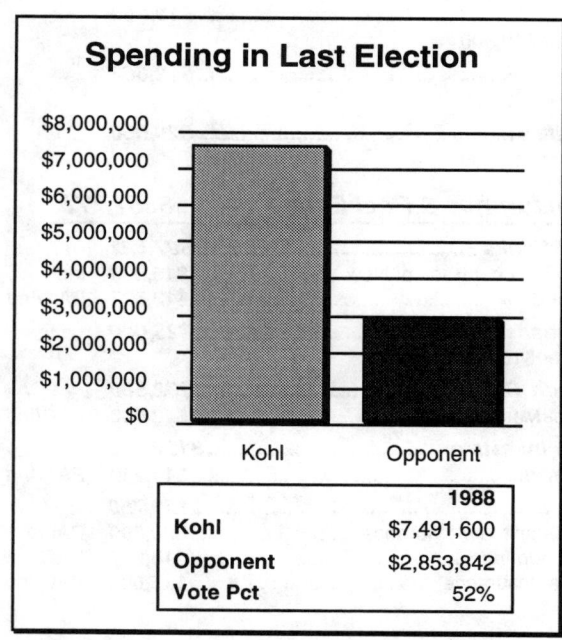

Spending in Last Election

	1988
Kohl	$7,491,600
Opponent	$2,853,842
Vote Pct	52%

Frank R. Lautenberg (D-NJ)

First elected: 1982

1987-92 Total Rcpts:	$9,033,987
1992 Year-end Cash:	$902,271
Current term expires:	1994

1991-92 Committees & Subcommittees

Appropriations
Commerce, Justice, State, the Judiciary and Related Agencies; Defense; Foreign Operations; Transportation and Related Agencies (Chairman); VA, HUD and Independent Agencies

Budget

Environment and Public Works
Environmental Protection; Superfund, Ocean and Water Protection (Chairman); Water Resources, Transportation and Infrastructure

Leading Contributors

NOTE: The bulk of Lautenberg's large individual contributions do not appear in the listings below. His last election was in 1988, and this book lists individual contributions only from 1989-1992.

Business

Agriculture $45,250

Food Processing & Sales $16,250
  None over $12,500

Communications/Electronics $141,073

Media/Entertainment $61,500
  None over $12,500

Telephone Utilities $36,700
  Bell Atlantic* .... $15,500   PAC/Ind
  AT&T .... $12,500   PAC/Ind

Telecom Services & Equipment $13,500
  None over $12,500

Computer Equipment & Services $21,623
  None over $12,500

Construction $138,412

General Contractors $56,400
  None over $12,500

Home Builders $20,000
  None over $12,500

Special Trade Contractors $13,000
  None over $12,500

Source of Funds: 1987-1992

Source	Total	Pct
PACs	$1,884,342	20%
Indivs $200+	$4,738,313	49%
Indivs under $200	$1,641,816	17%
Other	$1,329,256	14%
Candidate	$330,000	3%
Party	$559,740	6%

Source of PAC Dollars by Sector

Source	Total	Pct
Business	$1,066,623	57%
Labor	$377,302	20%
Ideological/Single-Issue	$421,405	23%

In-State vs. Out-of-State Contributions*

Source	Total	Pct
In-State	$2,259,598	48%
Out-of-state	$2,412,315	52%
No state listed	$64,000	

* by large individual contributors ($200 & above)

Construction Services $32,012
  None over $12,500

Building Materials & Equipment $17,000
  None over $12,500

Defense $65,700

Defense Aerospace $42,500
  Allied-Signal .... $23,000   PAC/Ind

Defense Electronics $19,700
  None over $12,500

Energy & Natural Resources $75,812

Oil & Gas $18,850
  None over $12,500

Misc Energy $12,662
  None over $12,500

Electric Utilities $29,000
  None over $12,500

Finance, Insurance & Real Estate $557,772

Commercial Banks $97,622
  Republic National Bank of New York .... $15,000   Indiv
  Chemical Bank .... $12,525   PAC/Ind

Savings & Loans $25,000
  None over $12,500

Finance/Credit Companies $32,500
  Beneficial Management Corp .... $23,000   PAC/Ind

Securities & Investment $102,000
  Merrill Lynch .... $14,250   PAC/Ind

Insurance $150,750
  Mutual Benefit Life Insurance .... $20,000   PAC
  Home Group Inc .... $15,000   PAC
  Prudential Insurance .... $15,000   PAC/Ind

Contribution Totals by Sector

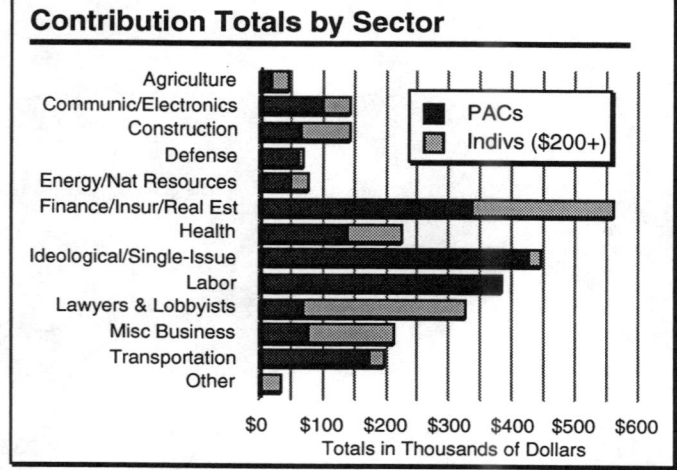

Agriculture
Communic/Electronics
Construction
Defense
Energy/Nat Resources
Finance/Insur/Real Est
Health
Ideological/Single-Issue
Labor
Lawyers & Lobbyists
Misc Business
Transportation
Other

■ PACs
▨ Indivs ($200+)

$0 $100 $200 $300 $400 $500 $600
Totals in Thousands of Dollars

Real Estate $109,400
  None over $12,500

Accountants $27,750
  None over $12,500

Health $222,400

Health Professionals $21,750
  None over $12,500

Pharmaceuticals/Health Products $186,400
  Warner-Lambert .... $36,250   PAC/Ind
  Merck & Co .... $22,500   PAC/Ind
  American Cyanimid .... $20,000   PAC
  Johnson & Johnson .... $20,000   PAC/Ind
  Schering-Plough Corp .... $13,000   PAC/Ind
  Hoffman-La Roche .... $12,500   PAC

Lawyers & Lobbyists $321,450

Lawyers & Lobbyists $321,450
  Waters, McPherson et al .... $20,500   Indiv
  Sills, Cummis et al .... $19,000   Indiv
  Wilentz, Goldman & Spitzer .... $18,250   Indiv
  Lowenstein, Sandler et al .... $15,750   Indiv
  Crummy, Del Deo et al .... $15,000   Indiv

Misc Business $211,450

Retail Sales $44,500
  Big M Inc .... $15,000   Indiv

Business Services $39,000
  None over $12,500

Chemical & Related Manufacturing $19,500
  None over $12,500

Misc Manufacturing & Distributing $59,250
  Winer Industries .... $13,000   Indiv

Textiles $13,500
  None over $12,500

Transportation $195,828

Air Transport $92,550
  Federal Express Corp .... $20,000   PAC
  United Parcel Service .... $14,000   PAC

Automotive $24,450
  None over $12,500

Trucking $25,928
  None over $12,500

Railroads $26,600
  None over $12,500

Misc Transport $14,800
  None over $12,500

Labor

Labor $377,302

Building Trade Unions $61,500
  Laborers' Political League .... $13,000   PAC

Industrial Unions $92,800
  None over $12,500

Transportation Unions $107,302
  None over $12,500

Public Sector Unions $73,500
  None over $12,500

Misc Unions $42,200
  None over $12,500

Ideological/Single-Issue

Ideological/Single-Issue $442,655

Democratic/Liberal $38,238
  None over $12,500

Leadership PACs $63,813
  None over $12,500

Foreign & Defense Policy $18,926
  None over $12,500

Pro-Israel $250,250
  None over $12,500

Pro-Choice $16,000
  None over $12,500

Human Rights $17,800
  None over $12,500

Misc Issues $31,628
  None over $12,500

Other & Unknown

Other $33,750

Retired $15,500
  None over $12,500

Unknown $304,185

  Homemakers/Non-income earners $99,400
  No Employer Listed or Found $18,750
  Employer Listed/Category Unknown $180,550
    None over $12,500

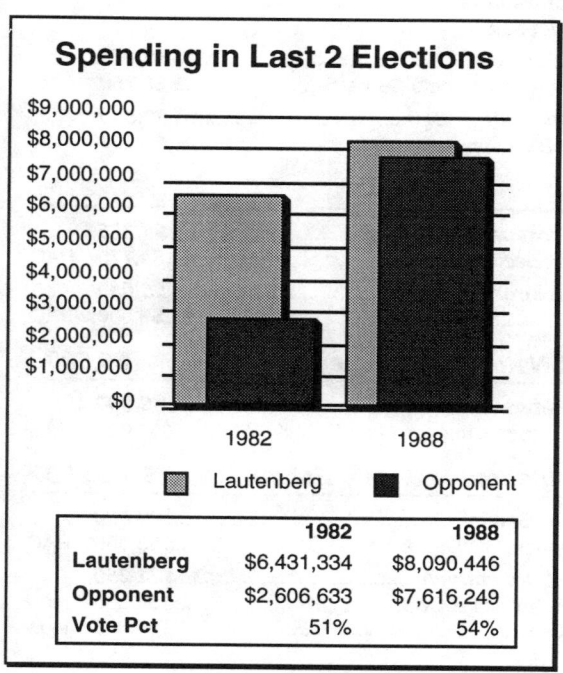

Spending in Last 2 Elections

	1982	1988
Lautenberg	$6,431,334	$8,090,446
Opponent	$2,606,633	$7,616,249
Vote Pct	51%	54%

---

* Contributions came from more than one affiliate or subsidiary.

Patrick J. Leahy (D-Vt)

1991-92 Committees & Subcommittees

Agriculture, Nutrition and Forestry (Chairman)

Appropriations
Defense; Foreign Operations (Chairman); Interior and Related Agencies; VA, HUD and Independent Agencies

Judiciary
Patents, Copyrights and Trademarks; Technology and the Law (Chairman)

Leading Contributors

Business

Agriculture		$86,785

Crop Production & Basic Processing	$36,320	
Riceland Foods	$4,700	PAC/Ind
Sunkist Growers	$3,000	PAC
Sun World International	$2,500	Indiv

Poultry & Eggs	$4,000	
None over $2,500		

Livestock	$2,500	
None over $2,500		

Agricultural Services/Products	$19,500	
American Veterinary Medical Assn	$2,500	PAC

Food Processing & Sales	$19,625	
ConAgra Inc	$5,000	PAC
Gel Spice Co	$4,000	Indiv
General Mills	$3,000	PAC

Communications/Electronics		$114,850

Printing & Publishing	$5,750	
None over $2,500		

Media/Entertainment	$86,100	
Disney Channel*	$32,250	Indiv
Time Warner*	$6,500	PAC/Ind
MCA Inc	$5,450	PAC/Ind
ASCAP	$3,000	PAC
Recording Industry Assn of America	$3,000	PAC

Contribution Totals by Sector

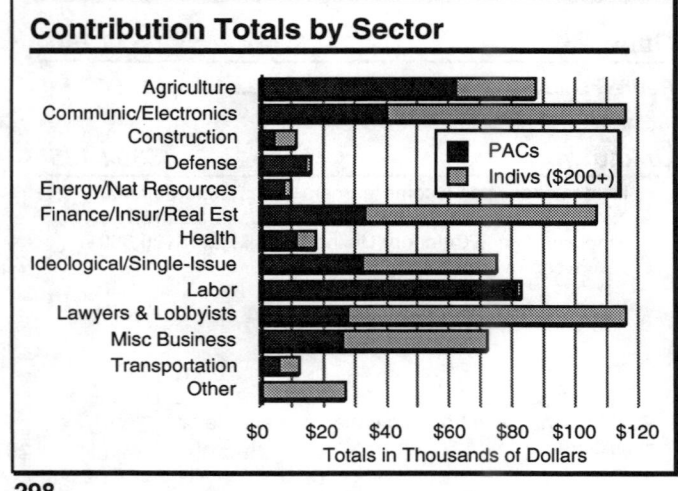

Totals in Thousands of Dollars

Telephone Utilities	$14,000	
Ameritech Corp	$3,500	PAC
AT&T	$3,000	PAC
BellSouth Corp*	$3,000	PAC
GTE Corp	$2,500	PAC

Telecom Services & Equipment	$2,500	
None over $2,500		

Computer Equipment & Services	$6,500	
None over $2,500		

Construction		$11,370

General Contractors	$3,500	
None over $2,500		

Home Builders	$3,870	
National Assn of Home Builders	$3,750	PAC

Building Materials & Equipment	$3,500	
Mintzer Brothers Inc	$3,250	Indiv

Defense		$15,325

Defense Aerospace	$9,275	
General Electric	$4,775	PAC

Defense Electronics	$5,050	
AT&T	$3,000	PAC

Energy & Natural Resources		$9,500

Electric Utilities	$6,000	
ACRE (Action Cmte for Rural Electrification)	$5,000	PAC

Finance, Insurance & Real Estate		$105,950

Commercial Banks	$5,000	
Independent Bankers Assn	$3,000	PAC

Securities & Investment	$22,250	
Joseph Stechler & Co	$4,000	Indiv
Kassko Inc	$4,000	Indiv

Insurance **$26,850**
    Independent Insurance Agents of America ....$6,000 PAC
    American Council of Life Insurance ....$5,000 PAC

Real Estate **$34,500**
    Landow & Co ....$5,000 Indiv
    Retrovest Associates Inc ....$3,000 Indiv

Accountants **$5,600**
    Coopers & Lybrand ....$3,000 PAC/Ind
    Ernst & Young ....$2,500 PAC

Misc Finance **$9,000**
    None over $2,500

Health   **$17,450**

Health Professionals **$12,950**
    None over $2,500

Lawyers & Lobbyists   **$115,420**

Lawyers & Lobbyists **$115,420**
    Assn of Trial Lawyers of America ....$10,000 PAC
    Marks, Murase & White ....$6,150 Indiv
    Holland & Knight ....$4,250 PAC/Ind
    Neill & Co ....$3,500 Indiv
    Akin, Gump et al ....$3,100 PAC/Ind
    Cassidy & Associates ....$3,000 Indiv
    Griffin, Johnson & Associates ....$3,000 Indiv
    Long Law Firm ....$3,000 Indiv
    Piper & Marbury ....$2,850 Indiv
    Podesta Associates ....$2,757 Indiv
    Swidler & Berlin ....$2,750 PAC/Ind
    Milberg, Weiss et al ....$2,500 Indiv
    Preston, Gates et al ....$2,500 PAC/Ind

Misc Business   **$71,206**

Beer, Wine & Liquor **$24,250**
    Wine Institute ....$10,000 PAC
    Gallo Winery ....$6,000 Indiv
    National Beer Wholesalers Assn ....$3,000 PAC
    Mondavi Winery ....$2,500 Indiv

Retail Sales **$15,256**
    E-II Holdings ....$5,000 Indiv

Business Services **$18,050**
    Dun & Bradstreet ....$3,750 PAC/Ind

Misc Manufacturing & Distributing **$7,200**
    None over $2,500

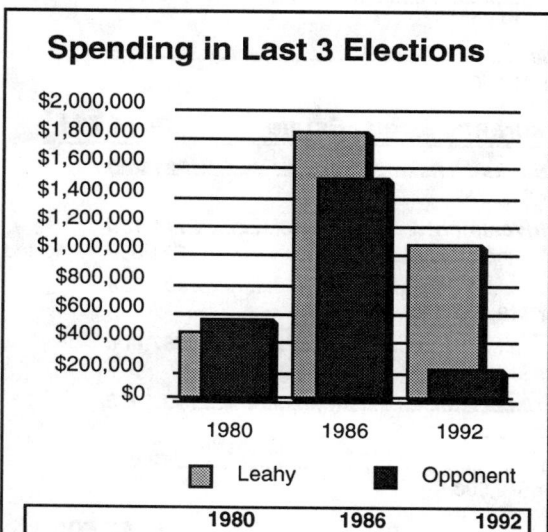

Spending in Last 3 Elections

	1980	1986	1992
Leahy	$434,644	$1,812,584	$1,039,793
Opponent	$532,904	$1,502,304	$195,737
Vote Pct	50%	63%	54%

Transportation   **$11,500**

Air Transport **$9,000**
    United Parcel Service ....$4,000 PAC
    Claneil Enterprises ....$3,000 Indiv

Labor

Labor   **$81,800**

Building Trade Unions **$14,500**
    Laborers' Political League ....$5,000 PAC
    Operating Engineers Union ....$3,000 PAC
    Carpenters & Joiners Union ....$2,500 PAC

Industrial Unions **$22,000**
    Communications Workers of America ....$5,000 PAC
    Intl Brotherhood of Electrical Workers ....$5,000 PAC
    Machinists/Aerospace Workers Union ....$5,000 PAC

Transportation Unions **$19,500**
    Teamsters Union ....$5,000 PAC
    Marine Engineers Union* ....$4,000 PAC
    Trans Comm International Union ....$3,000 PAC
    United Transportation Union ....$3,000 PAC
    Amalgamated Transit Union ....$2,500 PAC

Public Sector Unions **$21,000**
    American Federation of Teachers ....$5,000 PAC
    American Fedn of St/Cnty/Munic Employees ......$5,000 PAC
    National Assn of Letter Carriers ....$3,000 PAC
    National Assn of Postmasters ....$2,500 PAC

Misc Unions **$4,800**
    Hotel/Restaurant Employees Union ....$3,000 PAC

Ideological/Single-Issue

Ideological/Single-Issue   **$74,430**

Democratic/Liberal **$17,200**
    Hollywood Women's Political Cmte ....$5,000 PAC
    National Cmte for an Effective Congress ....$5,000 PAC

Pro-Israel **$29,297**
    None over $2,500

Human Rights **$13,250**
    KidsPAC ....$10,000 PAC

Misc Issues **$10,988**
    National Cmte to Preserve Social Security ....$6,000 PAC

Other & Unknown

Other   **$26,435**

Education **$5,535**
    None over $2,500

Retired **$16,600**
    None over $2,500

Other **$2,500**
    None over $2,500

Unknown   **$52,814**

    Homemakers/Non-income earners $9,350
    No Employer Listed or Found $15,264
    Employer Listed/Category Unknown $26,450
        None over $2,500

---

* Contributions came from more than one affiliate or
subsidiary.

Carl Levin (D-Mich)

First elected: 1978

1987-92 Total Rcpts:	$7,232,932
1992 Year-end Cash:	$92,319
Current term expires:	1996

1991-92 Committees & Subcommittees

Armed Services
Conventional Forces and Alliance Defense (Chairman); Readiness, Sustainability and Support; Strategic Forces and Nuclear Deterrence

Governmental Affairs
Government Information and Regulation; Oversight of Government Management (Chairman); Permanent Subcommittee on Investigations

Small Business
Innovation, Technology and Productivity (Chairman); Rural Economy and Family Farming

Leading Contributors

Business

Agriculture	$92,625

Crop Production & Basic Processing $22,750
None over $12,500

Dairy $18,500
None over $12,500

Agricultural Services/Products $15,750
None over $12,500

Food Processing & Sales $26,375
None over $12,500

Communications/Electronics	$144,940

Printing & Publishing $20,637
None over $12,500

Media/Entertainment $96,298
   MCA Inc* .... $20,300   PAC/Ind

Telephone Utilities $18,105
None over $12,500

Construction	$94,980

General Contractors $35,380
None over $12,500

Home Builders $17,600
None over $12,500

Contribution Totals by Sector

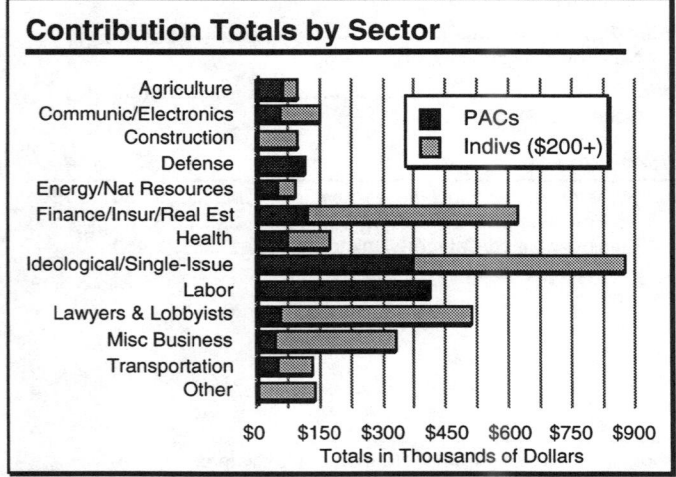

Totals in Thousands of Dollars

Source of Funds: 1987-1992

Source	Total	Pct
PACs	$1,373,622	18%
Indivs $200+	$3,036,345	39%
Indivs under $200	$2,274,983	30%
Other...........................	$1,003,467	13%
Candidate	$0	0%
Party	$455,485	6%

Source of PAC Dollars by Sector

Source	Total	Pct
Business	$605,994	44%
Labor	$403,690	29%
Ideological/Single-Issue ..	$367,542	27%

In-State vs. Out-of-State Contributions*

Source	Total	Pct
In-State	$1,222,394	40%
Out-of-state	$1,812,951	60%
No state listed	$1,000	

* by large individual contributors ($200 & above)

Special Trade Contractors $17,200
None over $12,500

Construction Services $13,550
None over $12,500

Defense	$113,274

Defense Aerospace $64,600
None over $12,500

Defense Electronics $41,424
None over $12,500

Energy & Natural Resources	$88,239

Oil & Gas $45,844
None over $12,500

Electric Utilities $27,975
None over $12,500

Finance, Insurance & Real Estate	$614,714

Commercial Banks $21,280
None over $12,500

Securities & Investment $114,150
   Salomon Brothers .... $21,500   PAC/Ind

Insurance $92,634
None over $12,500

Real Estate $287,000
None over $12,500

Accountants $37,925
None over $12,500

Misc Finance $52,400
None over $12,500

Health	$167,502

Health Professionals $116,407
None over $12,500

Hospitals/Nursing Homes $26,295
    None over $12,500

Pharmaceuticals/Health Products $15,450
    None over $12,500

Lawyers & Lobbyists $507,808

Lawyers & Lobbyists $507,808
    None over $12,500

Misc Business $328,455

Retail Sales $57,440
    None over $12,500

Misc Services $13,160
    None over $12,500

Business Services $67,742
    None over $12,500

Lodging/Tourism $14,744
    None over $12,500

Chemical & Related Manufacturing $24,000
    None over $12,500

Steel Production $14,400
    None over $12,500

Misc Manufacturing & Distributing $93,188
    None over $12,500

Transportation $130,943

Air Transport $29,823
    None over $12,500

Automotive $83,700

Chrysler Corp	$22,800	PAC/Ind
General Motors	$16,500	PAC/Ind
Ford Motor Co	$12,650	Indiv

Labor

Labor $405,280

Building Trade Unions $77,290
    None over $12,500

Industrial Unions $105,800
    None over $12,500

Transportation Unions $101,150
    None over $12,500

Public Sector Unions $74,940
    None over $12,500

Misc Unions $46,100
    None over $12,500

Ideological/Single-Issue

Ideological/Single-Issue $867,590

Democratic/Liberal $127,580
    None over $12,500

Leadership PACs $31,000
    None over $12,500

Foreign & Defense Policy $18,427
    None over $12,500

Pro-Israel $572,648
    None over $12,500

Pro-Choice $20,600
    None over $12,500

Womens Issues $15,300
    None over $12,500

Human Rights $56,160
    None over $12,500

Misc Issues $18,875
    None over $12,500

Other & Unknown

Other $136,883

Civil Servants/Public Officials $17,745
    None over $12,500

Education $30,400
    None over $12,500

Retired $70,424
    None over $12,500

Other $13,464
    None over $12,500

Unknown $603,488

Homemakers/Non-income earners	$159,194
No Employer Listed or Found	$80,270
Generic Occupation/Category Unknown	$118,925
Employer Listed/Category Unknown	$245,099

    None over $12,500

Independent expenditures opposing Levin
    Council for National Defense $18,487

Spending in Last 3 Elections

	1978	1984	1990
Levin	$971,775	$3,504,962	$7,082,164
Opponent	$1,681,550	$1,765,786	$2,417,705
Vote Pct	52%	52%	57%

* Contributions came from more than one affiliate or subsidiary.

Joseph I. Lieberman (D-Conn)

First elected: 1988

1987-92 Total Rcpts:	$4,052,725
1992 Year-end Cash:	$702,453
Current term expires:	1994

1991-92 Committees & Subcommittees

Environment and Public Works
Environmental Protection; Toxic Substances, Environmental Oversight, Research and Development; Water Resources, Transportation and Infrastructure

Governmental Affairs
General Services, Federalism and the District of Columbia; Government Information and Regulation; Oversight of Government Management; Permanent Subcommittee on Investigations

Small Business
Competitiveness and Economic Opportunity (Chairman); Export Expansion; Government Contracting and Paperwork Reduction

Leading Contributors

NOTE: The bulk of Lieberman's large individual contributions do not appear in the listings below. His last election was in 1988, and this book lists individual contributions only from 1989-1992.

Business

Agriculture	$25,650

Dairy	**$8,500**	
Mid-America Dairymen	$6,000	PAC

Communications/Electronics	$38,150

Printing & Publishing	**$6,000**
None over $5,000	
Media/Entertainment	**$6,750**
None over $5,000	
Telephone Utilities	**$7,250**
None over $5,000	
Computer Equipment & Services	**$9,250**
None over $5,000	

Construction	$53,510

General Contractors	**$16,360**	
None over $5,000		
Home Builders	**$9,000**	
National Assn of Home Builders	$5,000	PAC
Special Trade Contractors	**$9,750**	
None over $5,000		
Building Materials & Equipment	**$14,500**	
O&G Industries Inc	$5,000	Indiv

Contribution Totals by Sector

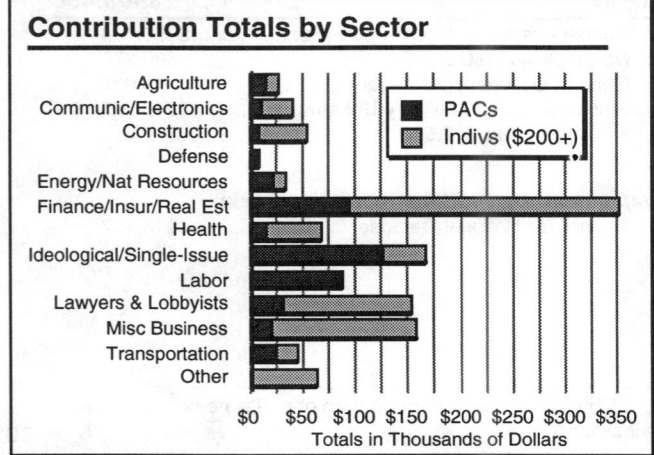

■ PACs
▨ Indivs ($200+)

Agriculture
Communic/Electronics
Construction
Defense
Energy/Nat Resources
Finance/Insur/Real Est
Health
Ideological/Single-Issue
Labor
Lawyers & Lobbyists
Misc Business
Transportation
Other

$0 $50 $100 $150 $200 $250 $300 $350
Totals in Thousands of Dollars

Source of Funds: 1987-1992

Source	Total	Pct
■ PACs	$482,375	11%
▨ Indivs $200+	$2,356,473	55%
☐ Indivs under $200	$1,032,460	24%
⊠ Other	$422,090	10%
Candidate	$50,000	1%
Party	$240,673	6%

Source of PAC Dollars by Sector

Source	Total	Pct
■ Business	$239,333	53%
▨ Labor	$86,200	19%
☐ Ideological/Single-Issue	$124,322	28%

In-State vs. Out-of-State Contributions*

Source	Total	Pct
☐ In-State	$1,045,894	45%
■ Out-of-state	$1,277,559	55%
No state listed	$33,020	

***by large individual contributors ($200 & above)**

Defense	$8,500

Defense Aerospace	**$6,500**
None over $5,000	

Energy & Natural Resources	$33,300

Oil & Gas	**$8,550**	
None over $5,000		
Electric Utilities	**$11,500**	
United Illuminating Co	$6,500	PAC
Waste Management	**$6,000**	
None over $5,000		

Finance, Insurance & Real Estate	$348,576

Commercial Banks	**$19,610**	
None over $5,000		
Savings & Loans	**$5,100**	
None over $5,000		
Securities & Investment	**$130,716**	
American Express*	$17,750	PAC/Ind
Goldman, Sachs & Co	$16,500	PAC/Ind
First Boston Corp	$7,000	PAC/Ind
Greenwich Capital Markets	$6,250	Indiv
Merrill Lynch	$5,750	PAC/Ind
Donaldson, Lufkin & Jenrette	$5,250	PAC/Ind
Bear, Stearns & Co	$5,066	PAC/Ind
Lazard Freres & Co	$5,000	Indiv
Insurance	**$70,400**	
Travelers Corp	$6,000	PAC/Ind
Insurance Assn of Connecticut	$5,000	PAC
National Assn of Life Underwriters	$5,000	PAC
Real Estate	**$94,200**	
None over $5,000		
Accountants	**$7,300**	
None over $5,000		
Misc Finance	**$20,500**	
None over $5,000		

Health — $65,470

Health Professionals $33,570
   American Dental Assn .... $5,000   PAC
Hospitals/Nursing Homes $14,900
   None over $5,000
Pharmaceuticals/Health Products $11,750
   None over $5,000
Misc Health $5,000
   None over $5,000

Lawyers & Lobbyists — $150,623

Lawyers & Lobbyists $150,623
   Verner, Liipfert et al .... $9,135   PAC/Ind
   Stroock & Stroock & Lavan .... $5,250   Indiv
   Robinson & Cole .... $5,000   PAC/Ind

Misc Business — $156,560

Beer, Wine & Liquor $8,500
   None over $5,000
Retail Sales $19,850
   None over $5,000
Misc Services $6,000
   None over $5,000
Business Services $31,000
   None over $5,000
Lodging/Tourism $9,000
   St George's Hotel .... $6,000   Indiv
Chemical & Related Manufacturing $24,000
   Philipp Brothers Chemical .... $8,000   Indiv
Misc Manufacturing & Distributing $44,960
   Triangle Industries .... $5,000   PAC
Textiles $5,750
   None over $5,000

Transportation — $44,200

Air Transport $9,750
   None over $5,000
Automotive $23,200
   Auto Dealers & Drivers for Free Trade .... $6,000   PAC
   Textron Inc .... $5,000   PAC
Sea Transport $8,500
   None over $5,000

Spending in Last Election

	1988
Lieberman	$2,570,779
Opponent	$2,731,294
Vote Pct	50%

Labor

Labor — $86,700

Industrial Unions $18,000
   American Federation of Teachers .... $5,000   PAC
   Communications Workers of America .... $5,000   PAC
   Intl Brotherhood of Electrical Workers .... $5,000   PAC
Transportation Unions $19,000
   Teamsters Union .... $7,500   PAC
   United Auto Workers .... $5,500   PAC/Ind
Public Sector Unions $35,200
   American Postal Workers Union .... $8,000   PAC
   National Treasury Employees Union .... $7,000   PAC
   American Fedn of St/Cnty/Munic Employees ...... $5,000   PAC
   National Assn of Letter Carriers .... $5,000   PAC
Misc Unions $12,000
   Food & Commercial Workers Union .... $5,000   PAC
   Service Employees International Union .... $5,000   PAC

Ideological/Single-Issue

Ideological/Single-Issue — $165,672

Democratic/Liberal $10,600
   Democrats for the 80's .... $10,000   PAC
Leadership PACs $40,567
   Pelican PAC (Bennett Johnston) .... $10,000   PAC
   Cmte for a Demo Consensus (Alan Cranston) .... $8,000   PAC
   Democratic Candidate Fund (Tip O'Neill) ...... $5,500   PAC
   Campaign for America (Frank Lautenberg) .... $5,000   PAC
   Senate Majority Fund (Daniel Inouye) .... $5,000   PAC
Foreign & Defense Policy $16,074
   Council for a Livable World .... $9,085   PAC
   Free Cuba PAC .... $6,989   PAC
Pro-Israel $81,818
   North Jersey PAC .... $8,000   PAC
   Hudson Valley PAC .... $7,500   PAC
   Women's Pro-Israel National PAC .... $5,916   PAC
   National PAC .... $5,000   PAC
Human Rights $5,500
   KidsPAC .... $5,000   PAC
Misc Issues $10,013
   League of Conservation Voters .... $5,199   PAC

Other & Unknown

Other — $61,000

Education $16,650
   None over $5,000
Retired $35,700
   None over $5,000
Other $5,900
   None over $5,000

Unknown — $205,060

   Homemakers/Non-income earners $47,400
   No Employer Listed or Found $35,250
   Generic Occupation/Category Unknown $7,100
   Employer Listed/Category Unknown $115,310
      Scharf Brothers .... $8,000   Indiv
      M&M Investments .... $6,000   Indiv

* Contributions came from more than one affiliate or subsidiary.

Trent Lott (R-Miss)

First elected: 1988

1987-92 Total Rcpts:	$4,162,080
1992 Year-end Cash:	$379,192
Current term expires:	1994

1991-92 Committees & Subcommittees

Armed Services
Projection Forces and Regional Defense; Readiness, Sustainability and Support (Ranking Republican); Strategic Forces and Nuclear Deterrence

Budget

Commerce, Science and Transportation
Merchant Marine (Ranking Republican); National Ocean Policy Study; Science, Technology and Space; Surface Transportation

Select Committee on Ethics

Leading Contributors

NOTE: The bulk of Lott's large individual contributions do not appear in the listings below. His last election was in 1988, and this book lists individual contributions only from 1989-1992.

Business

Agriculture $190,060

Crop Production & Basic Processing **$20,500**
  None over $6,000

Tobacco **$18,000**
  RJR Nabisco ....$7,000   PAC

Agricultural Services/Products **$26,900**
  None over $6,000

Food Processing & Sales **$62,200**
  Food Marketing Institute ....$11,000   PAC
  ConAgra Inc ....$6,000   PAC
  Winn-Dixie Stores ....$6,000   PAC

Forestry & Forest Products **$47,760**
  International Paper Co ....$10,010   PAC

Communications/Electronics $106,000

Media/Entertainment **$28,500**
  None over $6,000

Telephone Utilities **$43,500**
  BellSouth Corp* ....$10,000   PAC/Ind

Telecom Services & Equipment **$7,000**
  None over $6,000

Electronics Mfg & Services **$13,000**
  None over $6,000

Source of Funds: 1987-1992

Source	Total	Pct
■ PACs	$1,270,711	29%
▨ Indivs $200+	$1,404,822	32%
☐ Indivs under $200	$814,347	19%
▧ Other	$861,599	20%
Candidate	$0	0%
Party	$189,399	4%

Source of PAC Dollars by Sector

Source	Total	Pct
■ Business	$1,087,803	88%
▨ Labor	$23,050	2%
☐ Ideological/Single-Issue ..	$131,343	11%

In-State vs. Out-of-State Contributions*

Source	Total	Pct
☐ In-State	$866,807	62%
■ Out-of-state	$538,015	38%
No state listed	$0	

* by large individual contributors ($200 & above)

Computer Equipment & Services **$7,000**
  None over $6,000

Construction $81,476

General Contractors **$23,550**
  None over $6,000

Home Builders **$17,500**
  National Assn of Home Builders ....$10,000   PAC

Special Trade Contractors **$10,000**
  None over $6,000

Construction Services **$7,176**
  None over $6,000

Building Materials & Equipment **$23,250**
  None over $6,000

Defense $93,750

Defense Aerospace **$50,000**
  Northrop Corp ....$8,000   PAC
  Lockheed Corp ....$7,000   PAC
  Martin Marietta Corp ....$6,000   PAC
  United Technologies ....$6,000   PAC

Defense Electronics **$22,250**
  Harris Corp ....$10,000   PAC

Misc Defense **$21,500**
  Tenneco Inc...$6,000   PAC

Energy & Natural Resources $154,000

Oil & Gas **$83,250**
  Chevron Corp ....$10,000   PAC
  Amoco Corp ....$7,000   PAC

Mining **$11,000**
  None over $6,000

Electric Utilities **$40,250**
  Southern Co* ....$19,000   PAC

Waste Management **$7,000**
  None over $6,000

Contribution Totals by Sector

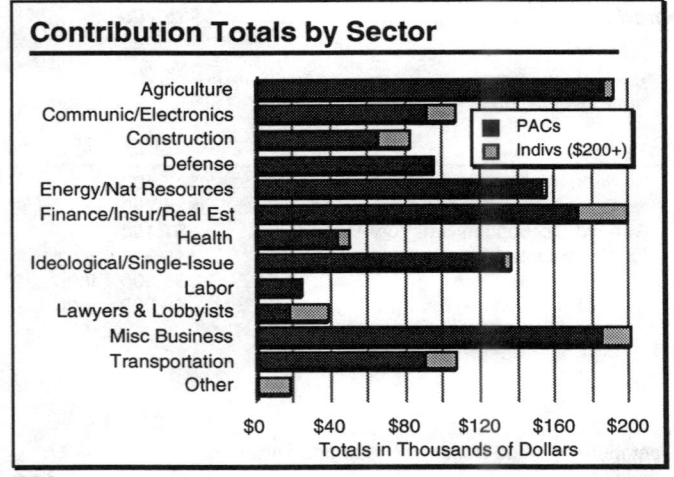

Agriculture
Communic/Electronics
Construction
Defense
Energy/Nat Resources
Finance/Insur/Real Est
Health
Ideological/Single-Issue
Labor
Lawyers & Lobbyists
Misc Business
Transportation
Other

■ PACs
▨ Indivs ($200+)

$0 $40 $80 $120 $160 $200
Totals in Thousands of Dollars

Commercial Fishing **$8,000**
  National Fisheries Institute ....$8,000 PAC

Finance, Insurance & Real Estate $198,200

Commercial Banks **$43,650**
  Bank of Mississippi ....$6,000 PAC

Savings & Loans **$10,600**
  None over $6,000

Securities & Investment **$20,000**
  Chicago Mercantile Exchange ....$6,000 PAC

Insurance **$67,500**
  National Assn of Life Underwriters...................$11,000 PAC
  Torchmark Corp ....$7,000 PAC
  Independent Insurance Agents of America.........$6,000 PAC

Real Estate **$31,000**
  National Assn of Realtors ....$9,000 PAC

Accountants **$9,500**
  None over $6,000

Misc Finance **$8,750**
  None over $6,000

Health $49,400

Health Professionals **$21,900**
  None over $6,000

Pharmaceuticals/Health Products **$23,750**
  None over $6,000

Lawyers & Lobbyists $37,650

Lawyers & Lobbyists **$37,650**
  None over $6,000

Misc Business $199,417

Business Associations **$8,909**
  None over $6,000

Food & Beverage **$30,350**
  McDonald's Corp ....$10,000 PAC

Beer, Wine & Liquor **$7,500**
  None over $6,000

Retail Sales **$18,757**
  None over $6,000

Business Services **$13,000**
  None over $6,000

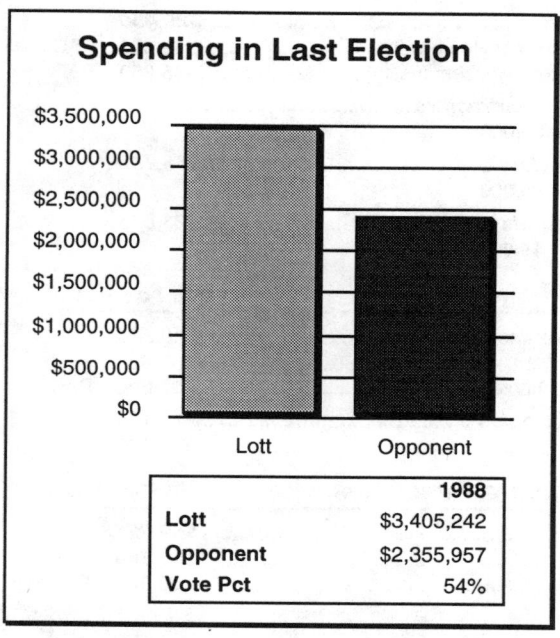

Spending in Last Election

	1988
Lott	$3,405,242
Opponent	$2,355,957
Vote Pct	54%

Lodging/Tourism **$9,200**
  None over $6,000

Chemical & Related Manufacturing **$29,100**
  Dow Chemical* ....$10,000 PAC
  FMC Corp ....$7,000 PAC

Misc Manufacturing & Distributing **$49,000**
  American Furniture Manufacturers Assn ....$8,500 PAC

Textiles **$14,200**
  None over $6,000

Transportation $105,750

Air Transport **$46,750**
  Federal Express Corp ....$14,000 PAC
  United Parcel Service ....$9,000 PAC

Automotive **$22,000**
  Auto Dealers & Drivers for Free Trade ....$7,000 PAC

Trucking **$6,750**
  None over $6,000

Railroads **$13,250**
  Union Pacific Corp ....$11,750 PAC

Sea Transport **$15,500**
  None over $6,000

Labor

Labor $23,050

Transportation Unions **$17,000**
  Marine Engineers Union* ....$12,000 PAC

Ideological/Single-Issue

Ideological/Single-Issue $135,343

Republican/Conservative **$22,653**
  None over $6,000

Leadership PACs **$52,627**
  Republican Majority Fund (Richard Lugar) ....$10,000 PAC
  Campaign America (Bob Dole) ....$7,000 PAC
  New Republican Victory Fund (Trent Lott) ....$6,000 PAC

Foreign & Defense Policy **$13,585**
  National Security PAC ....$8,000 PAC

Pro-Israel **$19,000**
  National PAC ....$10,000 PAC

Gun Rights/Gun Control **$6,000**
  None over $6,000

Misc Issues **$17,500**
  Public Service Research Council ....$10,000 PAC

Other & Unknown

Other $16,800

Retired **$13,550**
  None over $6,000

Unknown $31,460

  Homemakers/Non-income earners $9,160
  No Employer Listed or Found $10,550
  Employer Listed/Category Unknown $10,750
    None over $6,000

Independent expenditures supporting Lott
  National Assn of Realtors $348,498
  Auto Dealers & Drivers for Free Trade $319,126
  National Security PAC.....................................$50,202

---

* Contributions came from more than one affiliate or
subsidiary.

Richard G. Lugar (R-Ind)

First elected: 1976

1987-92 Total Rcpts:	$4,583,235
1992 Year-end Cash:	$1,346,212
Current term expires:	1994

1991-92 Committees & Subcommittees

Agriculture, Nutrition and Forestry (Ranking Republican)

Foreign Relations
East Asian and Pacific Affairs; International Economic Policy, Trade, Oceans and Environment; Western Hemisphere and Peace Corps Affairs (Ranking Republican)

Leading Contributors

NOTE: The bulk of Lugar's large individual contributions do not appear in the listings below. His last election was in 1988, and this book lists individual contributions only from 1989-1992.

Business

Agriculture	$302,355	
Crop Production & Basic Processing	**$51,750**	
Peanut Butter & Nut Processors Assn	$5,000	PAC
Dairy	**$10,400**	
None over $5,000		
Poultry & Eggs	**$10,250**	
None over $5,000		
Livestock	**$12,500**	
None over $5,000		
Agricultural Services/Products	**$90,820**	
Indiana Farm Bureau	$10,000	PAC
Archer-Daniels-Midland Corp	$7,500	PAC
Eli Lilly & Co	$7,000	PAC
FMC Corp	$6,000	PAC
Dow Chemical*	$5,000	PAC
Navistar International	$5,000	PAC
Pfizer Inc	$5,000	PAC
Food Processing & Sales	**$97,135**	
ConAgra Inc	$13,500	PAC
Food Marketing Institute	$11,170	PAC
Pepsico Inc	$5,000	PAC
Forestry & Forest Products	**$26,250**	
Westvaco Corp	$10,000	PAC

Communications/Electronics	$93,336	
Printing & Publishing	**$14,750**	
None over $5,000		

Source of Funds: 1987-1992

Source	Total	Pct
■ PACs	$969,840	20%
▨ Indivs $200+	$1,596,090	33%
□ Indivs under $200	$1,669,513	35%
▤ Other	$531,981	11%
Candidate	$0	0%
Party	$184,189	4%

Source of PAC Dollars by Sector

Source	Total	Pct
■ Business	$935,382	96%
▨ Labor	$3,000	0%
□ Ideological/Single-Issue	$36,811	4%

In-State vs. Out-of-State Contributions*

Source	Total	Pct
□ In-State	$1,203,548	75%
■ Out-of-state	$391,792	25%
No state listed	$750	

*** by large individual contributors ($200 & above)**

Media/Entertainment	**$19,400**	
None over $5,000		
Telephone Utilities	**$34,936**	
AT&T	$11,750	PAC
Ameritech Corp*	$7,936	PAC/Ind
Electronics Mfg & Services	**$5,250**	
None over $5,000		
Computer Equipment & Services	**$15,500**	
Ontario Corp	$10,500	PAC/Ind

Construction	$102,215	
General Contractors	**$34,550**	
Associated General Contractors	$10,000	PAC
Associated Builders & Contractors	$5,000	PAC
Home Builders	**$29,450**	
National Assn of Home Builders	$9,500	PAC
Manufactured Housing Institute	$5,250	PAC
Special Trade Contractors	**$8,500**	
None over $5,000		
Construction Services	**$6,100**	
None over $5,000		
Building Materials & Equipment	**$23,615**	
None over $5,000		

Defense	$57,420	
Defense Aerospace	**$40,820**	
Northrop Corp	$7,000	PAC
United Technologies	$5,500	PAC
Defense Electronics	**$12,100**	
Harris Corp	$5,000	PAC

Energy & Natural Resources	$106,980	
Oil & Gas	**$59,625**	
Amoco Corp	$5,750	PAC/Ind
Mobil Oil	$5,500	PAC/Ind

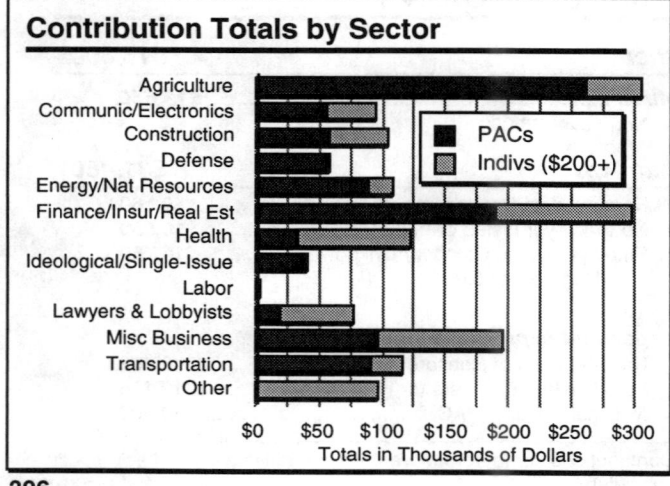

Contribution Totals by Sector

Agriculture
Communic/Electronics
Construction
Defense
Energy/Nat Resources
Finance/Insur/Real Est
Health
Ideological/Single-Issue
Labor
Lawyers & Lobbyists
Misc Business
Transportation
Other

■ PACs
▨ Indivs ($200+)

$0 $50 $100 $150 $200 $250 $300
Totals in Thousands of Dollars

Mining	$15,230	
Alcoa	$5,000	PAC

Electric Utilities	$16,375	
ACRE (Action Cmte for Rural Electrification)*	$6,375	PAC

Waste Management	$9,250	
Waste Management Inc	$6,250	PAC/Ind

Finance, Insurance & Real Estate — $295,676

Commercial Banks	$72,911	
American Bankers Assn	$8,500	PAC
Merchants National Corp	$6,530	PAC/Ind

Savings & Loans	$12,000	
US League of Savings Assns*	$9,750	PAC

Securities & Investment	$69,500	
Chicago Board of Trade	$6,250	PAC/Ind
Equitable/Donaldson, Lufkin & Jenrette*	$6,000	PAC
Chicago Mercantile Exchange	$5,000	PAC

Insurance	$74,965	
Lincoln National Corp	$7,750	PAC
National Assn of Life Underwriters	$7,750	PAC
National Assn of Independent Insurers	$6,050	PAC
National Assn of Prof Insurance Agents	$5,000	PAC

Real Estate	$41,450	
National Assn of Realtors	$10,000	PAC

Accountants	$6,100	
None over $5,000		

Misc Finance	$9,700	
None over $5,000		

Health — $119,400

Health Professionals	$86,400	
American Medical Assn	$6,000	PAC
American Academy of Ophthalmology	$5,000	PAC

Hospitals/Nursing Homes	$8,350	
None over $5,000		

Pharmaceuticals/Health Products	$23,150	
Eli Lilly & Co	$8,250	Indiv

Lawyers & Lobbyists — $76,140

Lawyers & Lobbyists	$76,140	
Ice, Miller et al	$5,450	Indiv
Barnes & Thornburg	$5,000	Indiv

Spending in Last 3 Elections

	1976	1982	1988
Lugar	$727,720	$2,973,791	$3,244,601
Opponent	$654,279	$870,023	$306,836
Vote Pct	59%	54%	68%

Misc Business	$193,009	
Business Associations	$6,978	
None over $5,000		
Food & Beverage	$27,125	
None over $5,000		
Beer, Wine & Liquor	$8,200	
None over $5,000		
Retail Sales	$20,000	
None over $5,000		
Misc Services	$6,306	
None over $5,000		
Business Services	$37,450	
None over $5,000		
Lodging/Tourism	$7,609	
None over $5,000		
Chemical & Related Manufacturing	$12,750	
None over $5,000		
Misc Manufacturing & Distributing	$58,141	
None over $5,000		

Transportation — $113,825

Air Transport	$37,450	
Federal Express Corp	$11,875	PAC
United Parcel Service	$7,475	PAC

Automotive	$44,875	
Auto Dealers & Drivers for Free Trade	$10,500	PAC
National Auto Dealers Assn	$8,000	PAC
General Motors	$6,125	PAC

Trucking	$9,500	
None over $5,000		

Railroads	$8,000	
None over $5,000		

Sea Transport	$7,750	
Totem Ocean Trailer Express	$5,250	PAC

Labor

Labor	$3,000
None over $5,000	

Ideological/Single-Issue

Ideological/Single-Issue	$40,061	
Leadership PACs	$17,311	
Campaign America (Bob Dole)	$8,000	PAC
Republican Majority Fund (Richard Lugar)	$5,000	PAC
Pro-Israel	$6,500	
National PAC	$5,000	PAC

Other & Unknown

Other	$94,195	
Education	$12,200	
None over $5,000		
Retired	$71,795	
None over $5,000		

Unknown	$226,875	
Homemakers/Non-income earners	$44,525	
No Employer Listed or Found	$28,750	
Employer Listed/Category Unknown	$149,850	
None over $5,000		

* Contributions came from more than one affiliate or subsidiary.

Connie Mack (R-Fla)

First elected: 1988

1987-92 Total Rcpts: $7,589,143
1992 Year-end Cash: $413,863
Current term expires: 1994

1991-92 Committees & Subcommittees

Armed Services
Defense Industry and Technology; Projection Forces and Regional Defense; Readiness, Sustainability and Support

Banking, Housing and Urban Affairs
Housing and Urban Affairs; International Finance and Monetary Policy (Ranking Republican); Securities

Small Business
Competitiveness and Economic Opportunity (Ranking Republican); Rural Economy and Family Farming; Urban and Minority-Owned Business Development

Joint Economic Committee

Leading Contributors

NOTE: The bulk of Mack's large individual contributions do not appear in the listings below. His last election was in 1988, and this book lists individual contributions only from 1989-1992.

Business

Agriculture $187,780

Crop Production & Basic Processing **$40,300**
    None over $7,500

Tobacco **$20,550**
    US Tobacco Co .... $8,000   PAC/Ind

Agricultural Services/Products **$21,900**
    None over $7,500

Food Processing & Sales **$55,550**
    Winn-Dixie Stores .... $8,800   PAC/Ind

Forestry & Forest Products **$31,700**
    None over $7,500

Communications/Electronics $120,415

Printing & Publishing **$15,475**
    None over $7,500

Media/Entertainment **$30,640**
    Walt Disney Co .... $10,000   PAC/Ind

Telephone Utilities **$51,650**
    Southern Bell .... $13,900   PAC

Electronics Mfg & Services **$12,150**
    Cooper Industries .... $10,000   PAC

Source of Funds: 1987-1992

Source	Total	Pct
PACs	$1,433,619	17%
Indivs $200+	$3,082,257	36%
Indivs under $200	$2,643,290	31%
Other	$1,323,924	16%
Candidate	$0	0%
Party	$893,947	11%

Source of PAC Dollars by Sector

Source	Total	Pct
Business	$1,188,278	85%
Labor	$25,750	2%
Ideological/Single-Issue ..	$176,641	13%

In-State vs. Out-of-State Contributions*

Source	Total	Pct
In-State	$2,545,097	85%
Out-of-state	$462,660	15%
No state listed	$68,000	

* by large individual contributors ($200 & above)

Construction $133,118

General Contractors **$44,185**
    Associated General Contractors .... $10,000   PAC

Home Builders **$21,800**
    National Assn of Home Builders .... $10,000   PAC

Special Trade Contractors **$21,250**
    National Electrical Contractors Assn .... $10,000   PAC

Construction Services **$10,700**
    None over $7,500

Building Materials & Equipment **$35,183**
    None over $7,500

Defense $77,150

Defense Aerospace **$41,400**
    United Technologies .... $8,500   PAC/Ind

Defense Electronics **$19,250**
    Harris Corp .... $10,750   PAC/Ind

Misc Defense **$16,500**
    None over $7,500

Energy & Natural Resources $173,140

Oil & Gas **$108,260**
    Dallas Energy PAC .... $10,000   PAC
    Amoco Corp .... $8,000   PAC
    Chevron Corp .... $7,700   PAC
    Mobil Oil .... $7,500   PAC

Electric Utilities **$51,380**
    Southern Co* .... $10,500   PAC
    Teco Energy Inc .... $9,220   PAC/Ind
    Florida Power & Light .... $7,500   PAC/Ind

Waste Management **$8,500**
    None over $7,500

Contribution Totals by Sector

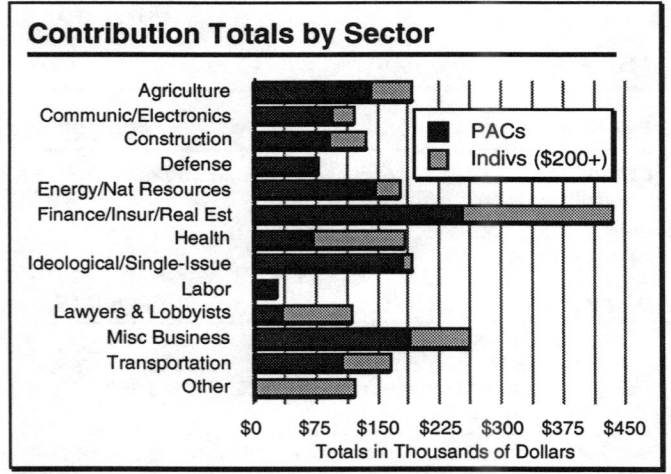

Legend: PACs / Indivs ($200+)

Agriculture
Communic/Electronics
Construction
Defense
Energy/Nat Resources
Finance/Insur/Real Est
Health
Ideological/Single-Issue
Labor
Lawyers & Lobbyists
Misc Business
Transportation
Other

$0 $75 $150 $225 $300 $375 $450
Totals in Thousands of Dollars

Finance, Insurance & Real Estate $431,903

Commercial Banks $104,990
    American Bankers Assn* .... $12,000   PAC
    Barnett Banks Inc .... $11,000   PAC
    JP Morgan & Co .... $9,500   PAC

Savings & Loans $21,570
    None over $7,500

Securities & Investment $40,850
    None over $7,500

Insurance $98,095
    JM Family Enterprises .... $9,400   Indiv

Real Estate $101,468
    National Assn of Realtors .... $11,200   PAC

Accountants $19,310
    None over $7,500

Misc Finance $36,620
    None over $7,500

Health $178,950

Health Professionals $130,860
    American Medical Assn* .... $12,200   PAC
    American Dental Assn .... $10,000   PAC

Hospitals/Nursing Homes $16,710
    None over $7,500

Pharmaceuticals/Health Products $19,900
    None over $7,500

Lawyers & Lobbyists $117,454

Lawyers & Lobbyists $117,454
    Holland & Knight .... $16,600   PAC/Ind

Misc Business $257,740

Business Associations $14,839
    National Fedn of Independent Business .... $9,699   PAC

Food & Beverage $44,710
    None over $7,500

Beer, Wine & Liquor $21,830
    None over $7,500

Retail Sales $28,547
    None over $7,500

Business Services $19,880
    None over $7,500

Spending in Last Election

	1988
Mack	$5,171,639
Opponent	$3,521,180
Vote Pct	50%

Chemical & Related Manufacturing $46,050
    Dow Chemical* .... $10,000   PAC
    FMC Corp .... $10,000   PAC

Misc Manufacturing & Distributing $50,793
    None over $7,500

Transportation $162,873

Air Transport $39,120
    Federal Express Corp .... $10,000   PAC
    Eastern Airlines .... $9,250   PAC

Automotive $63,433
    Auto Dealers & Drivers for Free Trade .... $12,000   PAC
    Eaton Corp .... $8,000   PAC

Trucking $20,920
    None over $7,500

Railroads $11,750
    None over $7,500

Sea Transport $25,650
    None over $7,500

Labor

Labor $25,750

Transportation Unions $20,000
    Marine Engineers Union* .... $18,000   PAC

Ideological/Single-Issue

Ideological/Single-Issue $190,341

Republican/Conservative $29,850
    None over $7,500

Leadership PACs $57,457
    Catch the Spirit PAC (Bob Kasten) .... $11,077   PAC
    Campaign America (Bob Dole) .... $10,880   PAC
    Citizens for the Republic (Ronald Reagan) .... $10,000   PAC

Foreign & Defense Policy $24,219
    Free Cuba PAC .... $10,000   PAC
    National Security PAC .... $7,969   PAC

Pro-Israel $39,522
    None over $7,500

Misc Issues $27,543
    Public Service Research Council .... $9,700   PAC

Other & Unknown

Other $119,320

Retired $109,240
    None over $7,500

Unknown $420,051

    Homemakers/Non-income earners $27,773
    No Employer Listed or Found $195,420
    Generic Occupation/Category Unknown $18,065
    Employer Listed/Category Unknown $178,043
      None over $7,500

Independent expenditures supporting Mack
    Auto Dealers & Drivers for Free Trade $326,050
    National Right to Life PAC $48,225
    National Security PAC $42,821
    Council for National Defense $7,542

Independent expenditures opposing Mack
    National Council of Senior Citizens $17,375

* Contributions came from more than one affiliate or
subsidiary.

John McCain (R-Ariz)

First elected: 1986

1987-92 Total Rcpts:	$3,623,397
1992 Year-end Cash:	$5,927
Current term expires:	1998

1991-92 Committees & Subcommittees

Armed Services
Conventional Forces and Alliance Defense; Manpower and Personnel (Ranking Republican); Projection Forces and Regional Defense

Commerce, Science and Transportation
Aviation (Ranking Republican); Communications; Consumer

Select Committee on Indian Affairs (Co-Chairman)

Select Committee on POW/MIA Affairs

Special Aging

Leading Contributors

Business

Agriculture		$151,752
Crop Production & Basic Processing **$37,377**		
Sunkist Growers $10,000	PAC	
Tobacco **$19,500**		
RJR Nabisco $9,000	PAC	
Livestock **$20,925**		
None over $7,500		
Agricultural Services/Products **$19,450**		
Salt River Valley Water Users $8,500	PAC	
Food Processing & Sales **$39,450**		
Food Marketing Institute $10,000	PAC	
Forestry & Forest Products **$9,100**		
None over $7,500		

Communications/Electronics		$130,749
Printing & Publishing **$10,450**		
None over $7,500		
Media/Entertainment **$32,800**		
National Assn of Broadcasters $10,000	PAC	
Telephone Utilities **$47,500**		
None over $7,500		
Telecom Services & Equipment **$27,799**		
Motorola Inc $12,499	PAC/Ind	
Computer Equipment & Services **$11,200**		
None over $7,500		

Source of Funds: 1987-1992

Source	Total	Pct
■ PACs $1,236,237		31%
▨ Indivs $200+ $1,086,543		27%
☐ Indivs under $200 .... $1,073,029		27%
⊠ Other $571,723		14%
Candidate $3,000		0%
Party $344,135		9%

Source of PAC Dollars by Sector

Source	Total	Pct
■ Business $1,145,938		87%
▨ Labor $52,950		4%
☐ Ideological/Single-Issue .. $118,173		9%

In-State vs. Out-of-State Contributions*

Source	Total	Pct
☐ In-State $673,015		62%
▨ Out-of-state $413,078		38%
No state listed $250		

* by large individual contributors ($200 & above)

Construction		$83,196
General Contractors **$34,879**		
None over $7,500		
Home Builders **$11,000**		
None over $7,500		
Special Trade Contractors **$8,200**		
None over $7,500		
Construction Services **$8,500**		
None over $7,500		
Building Materials & Equipment **$20,617**		
None over $7,500		

Defense		$143,190
Defense Aerospace **$65,790**		
Allied-Signal $10,500	PAC/Ind	
McDonnell Douglas* $10,000	PAC	
Defense Electronics **$52,700**		
None over $7,500		
Misc Defense **$24,700**		
None over $7,500		

Energy & Natural Resources		$161,122
Oil & Gas **$88,305**		
Atlantic Richfield $11,000	PAC/Ind	
Exxon Corp $7,500	PAC	
Mining **$38,417**		
Phelps Dodge Corp $14,250	PAC/Ind	
Cyprus Minerals Co $9,917	PAC/Ind	
Electric Utilities **$20,950**		
None over $7,500		

Finance, Insurance & Real Estate		$337,044
Commercial Banks **$73,605**		
American Bankers Assn $10,000	PAC	
BankAmerica Corp $10,000	PAC/Ind	
Valley National Bank of Arizona $7,850	PAC/Ind	

Contribution Totals by Sector

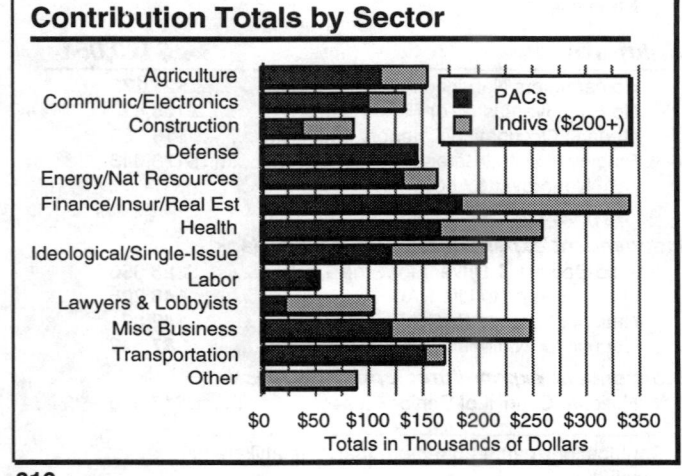

Agriculture
Communic/Electronics
Construction
Defense
Energy/Nat Resources
Finance/Insur/Real Est
Health
Ideological/Single-Issue
Labor
Lawyers & Lobbyists
Misc Business
Transportation
Other

■ PACs
☐ Indivs ($200+)

$0 $50 $100 $150 $200 $250 $300 $350
Totals in Thousands of Dollars

Securities & Investment	......	$41,800	
Chicago Mercantile Exchange	......	$10,000	PAC

Insurance	......	$93,375	
National Assn of Life Underwriters	......	$10,000	PAC

Real Estate	......	$79,215	
Del Webb Corp	......	$10,035	PAC/Ind

Accountants	......	$19,700	
American Institute of CPA's	......	$7,500	PAC

Misc Finance **$20,100**
None over $7,500

Health $257,139

Health Professionals	......	$152,756	
American Dental Assn	......	$10,000	PAC
American Podiatry Assn	......	$10,000	PAC
American Medical Assn	......	$9,700	PAC

Hospitals/Nursing Homes	......	$24,200	
Natl Assn of Private Psychiatric Hosp	......	$7,500	PAC

Health Services **$7,950**
None over $7,500

Pharmaceuticals/Health Products **$67,883**
None over $7,500

Lawyers & Lobbyists $102,970

Lawyers & Lobbyists **$102,970**
None over $7,500

Misc Business $245,691

Food & Beverage	......	$44,050	
S&A Restaurant Corp	......	$9,000	PAC

Beer, Wine & Liquor	......	$60,250	
Hensley & Co	......	$15,200	Indiv
National Beer Wholesalers Assn	......	$10,000	PAC

Retail Sales **$23,557**
None over $7,500

Misc Services **$8,801**
None over $7,500

Business Services **$25,750**
None over $7,500

Casinos/Gambling **$12,250**
None over $7,500

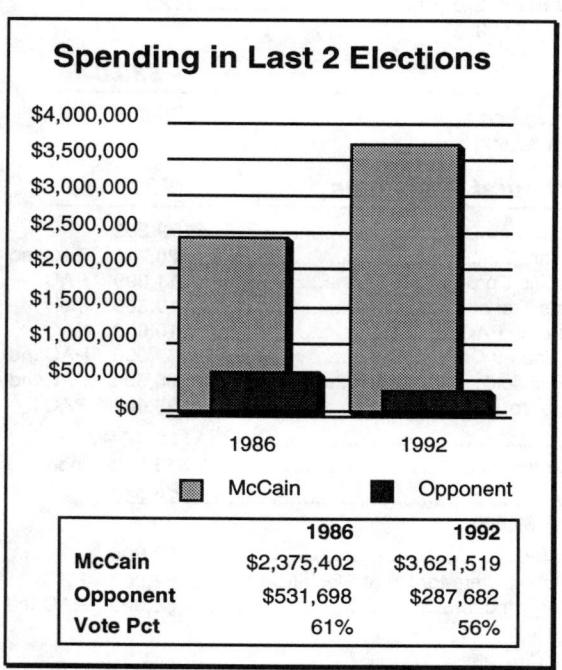

Spending in Last 2 Elections

	1986	1992
McCain	$2,375,402	$3,621,519
Opponent	$531,698	$287,682
Vote Pct	61%	56%

McCain / Opponent

Misc Business **$10,692**
None over $7,500

Chemical & Related Manufacturing **$20,916**
None over $7,500

Misc Manufacturing & Distributing **$27,150**
None over $7,500

Transportation $167,441

Air Transport	......	$74,365	
Aircraft Owners & Pilots Assn	......	$10,000	PAC
Federal Express Corp	......	$10,000	PAC
General Electric	......	$9,000	PAC
America West Airlines	......	$7,900	PAC/Ind

Automotive	......	$47,575	
Americans for Free International Trade	......	$10,000	PAC
Auto Dealers & Drivers for Free Trade	......	$10,000	PAC
National Auto Dealers Assn	......	$10,000	PAC

Trucking **$7,800**
None over $7,500

Railroads	......	$20,251	
Union Pacific Corp	......	$8,251	PAC

Sea Transport **$11,000**
None over $7,500

Labor

Labor $52,950

Transportation Unions	......	$17,500	
Marine Engineers Union*	......	$13,000	PAC

Public Sector Unions	......	$35,450	
National Assn of Letter Carriers	......	$10,000	PAC
National Assn Retired Federal Employees	......	$10,000	PAC

Ideological/Single-Issue

Ideological/Single-Issue $204,389

Republican/Conservative **$30,116**
None over $7,500

Leadership PACs	......	$17,000	
Campaign America (Bob Dole)	......	$10,000	PAC

Foreign & Defense Policy	......	$17,921	
Free Cuba PAC	......	$10,000	PAC

Pro-Israel **$110,802**
None over $7,500

Gun Rights/Gun Control	......	$10,100	
National Rifle Assn	......	$9,900	PAC

Misc Issues **$14,450**
None over $7,500

Other & Unknown

Other $86,949

Education **$8,600**
None over $7,500

Retired **$69,649**
None over $7,500

Unknown $275,557

Homemakers/Non-income earners	......	$28,500
No Employer Listed or Found	......	$141,163
Employer Listed/Category Unknown	......	$97,694

None over $7,500

---

* Contributions came from more than one affiliate or subsidiary.

Mitch McConnell (R-Ky)

First elected: 1984

1987-92 Total Rcpts:	$5,108,185
1992 Year-end Cash:	$233,458
Current term expires:	1996

1991-92 Committees & Subcommittees

Agriculture, Nutrition and Forestry
Agricultural Production and Stabilization of Prices; Domestic and Foreign Marketing and Product Promotion; Nutrition and Investigations (Ranking Republican)

Foreign Relations
East Asian and Pacific Affairs; International Economic Policy, Trade, Oceans and Environment (Ranking Republican); Terrorism, Narcotics and International Operations

Rules and Administration

Leading Contributors

Business

Agriculture	$375,235

Crop Production & Basic Processing $39,500
   None over $7,500

Tobacco $61,400
   Philip Morris ....$11,250   PAC/Ind
   RJR Nabisco ....$11,000   PAC/Ind
   US Tobacco Co ....$10,000   PAC

Dairy $30,100
   Dairymen Inc* ....$9,750   PAC/Ind

Poultry & Eggs $12,500
   None over $7,500

Livestock $69,335
   Tennessee Walking Horse Breeders .... $10,000   PAC

Agricultural Services/Products $57,225
   None over $7,500

Food Processing & Sales $71,375
   Pepsico Inc ....$9,919   PAC

Forestry & Forest Products $25,000
   None over $7,500

Misc Agriculture $8,800
   None over $7,500

Communications/Electronics	$76,250

Printing & Publishing $15,525
   None over $7,500

Telephone Utilities $35,725
   AT&T ....$9,750   PAC
   Cincinnati Bell ....$8,025   PAC

Source of Funds: 1987-1992

Source	Total	Pct
■ PACs	$1,171,112	22%
▨ Indivs $200+	$2,252,729	42%
☐ Indivs under $200	$941,148	17%
⊠ Other	$1,043,770	19%
Candidate	$0	0%
Party	$300,574	6%

Source of PAC Dollars by Sector

Source	Total	Pct
■ Business	$985,912	85%
▨ Labor	$3,000	0%
☐ Ideological/Single-Issue	$177,200	15%

In-State vs. Out-of-State Contributions*

Source	Total	Pct
☐ In-State	$1,583,600	70%
■ Out-of-state	$669,129	30%
No state listed	$0	

* by large individual contributors ($200 & above)

Electronics Mfg & Services $10,000
   Harris Corp ....$10,000   PAC

Computer Equipment & Services $10,000
   None over $7,500

Construction	$144,325

General Contractors $56,850
   None over $7,500

Home Builders $26,975
   National Assn of Home Builders .... $10,000   PAC

Special Trade Contractors $12,500
   None over $7,500

Building Materials & Equipment $42,250
   None over $7,500

Defense	$30,045

Defense Aerospace $25,045
   None over $7,500

Energy & Natural Resources	$390,966

Oil & Gas $199,292
   Ashland Oil ....$20,718   PAC/Ind
   Union Pacific Corp ....$11,999   PAC
   Texas Gas Transmission ....$10,300   Indiv
   Dallas Energy PAC ....$10,000   PAC
   Transco Energy Co* ....$9,500   PAC/Ind
   Atlantic Richfield ....$8,500   PAC/Ind
   Chevron Corp ....$8,000   PAC

Mining $118,374
   Addington Inc ....$16,000   Indiv

Misc Energy $8,250
   None over $7,500

Electric Utilities $52,800
   ACRE (Action Cmte for Rural Electrification) .... $9,000   PAC
   Teco Energy Inc ....$8,000   PAC/Ind

Contribution Totals by Sector

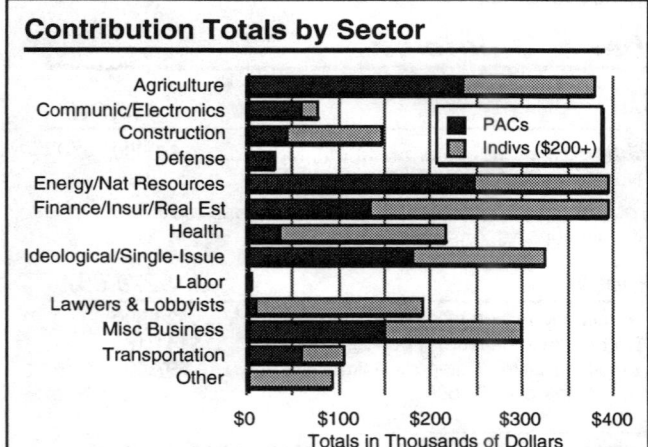

Agriculture, Communic/Electronics, Construction, Defense, Energy/Nat Resources, Finance/Insur/Real Est, Health, Ideological/Single-Issue, Labor, Lawyers & Lobbyists, Misc Business, Transportation, Other

■ PACs   ▨ Indivs ($200+)

$0 $100 $200 $300 $400
Totals in Thousands of Dollars

Finance, Insurance & Real Estate — $391,643

Commercial Banks $83,650
   American Bankers Assn .... $10,000 PAC

Securities & Investment $43,010
   None over $7,500

Insurance $121,156
   Capital Holding Corp .... $12,499 PAC/Ind
   American Financial Corp .... $11,700 Indiv
   Independent Insurance Agents of America .... $7,500 PAC
   National Assn of Life Underwriters .... $7,500 PAC

Real Estate $83,700
   None over $7,500

Accountants $35,475
   American Institute of CPA's .... $9,625 PAC

Misc Finance $16,550
   None over $7,500

Health — $215,050

Health Professionals $181,875
   None over $7,500

Hospitals/Nursing Homes $26,425
   None over $7,500

Lawyers & Lobbyists — $189,218

Lawyers & Lobbyists $189,218
   Wyatt, Tarrant & Combs .... $7,634 Indiv

Misc Business — $296,242

Business Associations $11,388
   None over $7,500

Food & Beverage $33,610
   None over $7,500

Beer, Wine & Liquor $47,172
   Brown-Forman Distillers .... $14,000 PAC/Ind
   National Beer Wholesalers Assn .... $9,000 PAC

Retail Sales $20,700
   None over $7,500

Business Services $37,095
   Dun & Bradstreet .... $7,625 PAC/Ind

Lodging/Tourism $13,551
   None over $7,500

Spending in Last 2 Elections

	1984	1990
McConnell	$1,776,128	$5,399,428
Opponent	$2,380,239	$3,016,967
Vote Pct	50%	52%

Chemical & Related Manufacturing $30,100
   None over $7,500

Steel Production $15,500
   None over $7,500

Misc Manufacturing & Distributing $57,400
   None over $7,500

Textiles $12,000
   None over $7,500

Transportation — $102,950

Air Transport $25,550
   United Parcel Service .... $8,650 PAC/Ind
   Federal Express Corp .... $8,000 PAC

Automotive $48,500
   None over $7,500

Railroads $8,450
   None over $7,500

Sea Transport $10,900
   None over $7,500

Labor

Labor — $3,000

Ideological/Single-Issue

Ideological/Single-Issue — $321,750

Republican/Conservative $51,100
   National Republican Senatorial Cmte .... $36,500 Indiv

Leadership PACs $13,500
   None over $7,500

Pro-Israel $230,400
   Citizens Organized PAC .... $10,000 PAC
   Delaware Valley PAC .... $10,000 PAC
   Desert Caucus .... $10,000 PAC
   Florida Congressional Cmte .... $10,000 PAC
   Maryland Assn for Concerned Citizens .... $10,000 PAC
   Women's Pro-Israel National PAC .... $10,000 PAC
   Washington PAC .... $9,000 PAC

Misc Issues $20,000
   Public Service Research Council .... $10,000 PAC
   Right to Work PAC .... $10,000 PAC

Other & Unknown

Other — $91,049

Civil Servants/Public Officials $26,839
   None over $7,500

Education $20,750
   None over $7,500

Retired $37,460
   None over $7,500

Unknown — $548,166
   Homemakers/Non-income earners $149,692
   No Employer Listed or Found $174,731
   Generic Occupation/Category Unknown $45,850
   Employer Listed/Category Unknown $177,893
     None over $7,500

Independent expenditures supporting McConnell
   American Citizens for Political Action $16,313
   National Rifle Assn $7,579

* Contributions came from more than one affiliate or
subsidiary.

Howard M. Metzenbaum (D-Ohio)

First elected: 1976

1987-92 Total Rcpts: $7,312,533
1992 Year-end Cash: $0
Current term expires: 1994

1991-92 Committees & Subcommittees

Environment and Public Works
Environmental Protection; Superfund, Ocean and Water Protection;
Water Resources, Transportation and Infrastructure

Judiciary
Antitrust, Monopolies and Business Rights (Chairman); Constitution;
Courts and Administrative Practice

Labor and Human Resources
Aging; Disability Policy; Education, Arts and Humanities; Labor
(Chairman)

Select Committee on Intelligence

Leading Contributors

NOTE: The bulk of Metzenbaum's large individual contributions do not
appear in the listings below. His last election was in 1988, and this book
lists individual contributions only from 1989-1992.

Business

Agriculture	$11,400

None over $6,000

Communications/Electronics	$41,085

Media/Entertainment $18,085
  None over $6,000
Telephone Utilities $21,500
  AT&T .... $9,000   PAC

Construction	$14,125

Building Materials & Equipment $10,025
  Philips Industries .... $10,000   PAC

Defense	$6,500

None over $6,000

Energy & Natural Resources	$17,105

Oil & Gas $10,105
  None over $6,000

Source of Funds: 1987-1992

Source	Total	Pct
PACs	$1,025,894	13%
Indivs $200+	$2,949,302	37%
Indivs under $200	$2,890,451	36%
Other	$1,174,595	15%
Candidate	$0	0%
Party	$727,709	9%

Source of PAC Dollars by Sector

Source	Total	Pct
Business	$267,765	26%
Labor	$346,730	34%
Ideological/Single-Issue	$404,929	40%

In-State vs. Out-of-State Contributions*

Source	Total	Pct
In-State	$991,863	34%
Out-of-state	$1,954,939	66%
No state listed	$2,500	

*** by large individual contributors ($200 & above)**

Finance, Insurance & Real Estate	$34,800

Securities & Investment $19,500
  None over $6,000

Health	$46,000

Health Professionals $41,000
  American Podiatry Assn .... $10,000   PAC

Lawyers & Lobbyists	$38,250

Lawyers & Lobbyists $38,250
  Kirkland & Ellis .... $9,000   PAC
  Fine, Kaplan & Black .... $6,000   PAC

Misc Business	$33,500

Retail Sales $6,500
  None over $6,000
Steel Production $7,500
  None over $6,000
Misc Manufacturing & Distributing $8,250
  None over $6,000

Transportation	$25,000

Air Transport $17,000
  Federal Express Corp .... $10,000   PAC

Contribution Totals by Sector

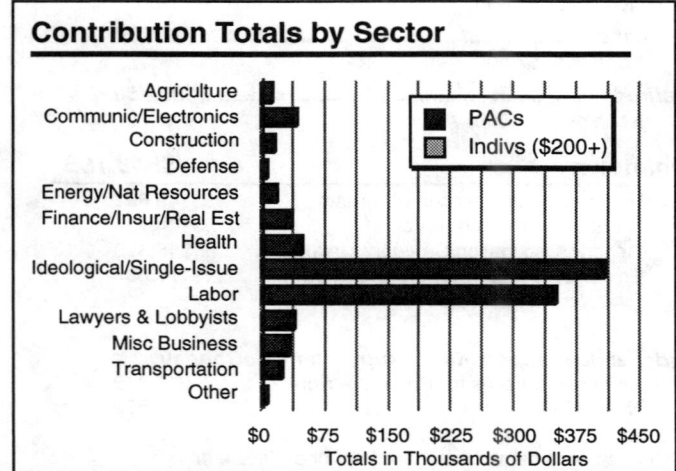

Agriculture
Communic/Electronics
Construction
Defense
Energy/Nat Resources
Finance/Insur/Real Est
Health
Ideological/Single-Issue
Labor
Lawyers & Lobbyists
Misc Business
Transportation
Other

■ PACs
▨ Indivs ($200+)

$0 $75 $150 $225 $300 $375 $450
Totals in Thousands of Dollars

Labor

Labor	$346,730

Building Trade Unions $56,480
Bricklayers Union	$10,000	PAC
Carpenters & Joiners Union	$10,000	PAC
Laborers' Political League	$9,000	PAC
Operating Engineers Union*	$7,980	PAC
Ironworkers Union	$7,000	PAC

Industrial Unions $126,450
Amalgamated Clothing & Textile Workers	$10,000	PAC
American Federation of Teachers	$10,000	PAC
Boilermakers Union	$10,000	PAC
Electronic Machine Furniture Workers	$10,000	PAC
Intl Brotherhood of Electrical Workers	$10,000	PAC
Ladies Garment Workers Union	$10,000	PAC
Machinists/Aerospace Workers Union	$10,000	PAC
National Education Assn	$10,000	PAC
United Steelworkers	$10,000	PAC
United Mine Workers	$9,900	PAC

Transportation Unions $90,800
Air Line Pilots Assn	$10,000	PAC
Amalgamated Transit Union	$10,000	PAC
Seafarers International Union	$10,000	PAC
United Transportation Union	$10,000	PAC
Transport Workers Union	$8,000	PAC
Maintenance of Way Employees	$7,500	PAC
Trans Comm International Union	$7,500	PAC
Assn of Flight Attendants	$6,000	PAC

Public Sector Unions $41,000
American Postal Workers Union	$10,000	PAC
Natl Assn of Retired Federal Employees	$10,000	PAC

Misc Unions $32,000
Service Employees International Union	$10,000	PAC

Ideological/Single-Issue

Ideological/Single-Issue	$404,929

Democratic/Liberal $44,796
Democrats for the 80's	$10,000	PAC
Religion and Tolerance PAC	$10,000	PAC
National Cmte for an Effective Congress	$9,996	PAC
Independent Action	$7,000	PAC

Leadership PACs $51,500
Campaign for America (Frank Lautenberg)	$10,000	PAC
Cmte for a Demo Consensus (Alan Cranston) ..	$10,000	PAC
Senate Majority Fund (Daniel Inouye)	$10,000	PAC

Foreign & Defense Policy $11,787
Council for a Livable World	$6,743	PAC

Pro-Israel $245,085
Citizens Organized PAC	$10,000	PAC
Delaware Valley PAC	$10,000	PAC
Desert Caucus	$10,000	PAC
Florida Congressional Cmte	$10,000	PAC
Garden State PAC	$10,000	PAC
Hudson Valley PAC	$10,000	PAC
Joint Action Cmte for Political Affairs	$10,000	PAC
Maryland Assn for Concerned Citizens	$10,000	PAC
MOPAC	$10,000	PAC
Multi-Issue PAC	$10,000	PAC
National PAC	$10,000	PAC
Ocean State PAC	$10,000	PAC
Pacific PAC	$10,000	PAC
San Franciscans for Good Government	$10,000	PAC
Washington PAC	$9,000	PAC
Arizona Politically Interested Citizens	$8,000	PAC
National Action Committee	$8,000	PAC
Sacramento Area Good Government Assn	$8,000	PAC
Heartland PAC	$7,500	PAC
Mid Manhattan PAC	$7,500	PAC

Pro-Choice $15,000
National Abortion Rights Action League	$10,000	PAC

Gun Rights/Gun Control $7,500
Handgun Control Inc	$7,500	PAC

Human Rights $6,050
None over $6,000

Misc Issues $23,211
National Cmte to Preserve Social Security	$10,000	PAC
Sierra Club	$9,936	PAC

Other & Unknown

Other	$6,200

None over $6,000

Independent expenditures supporting Metzenbaum
National Cmte to Preserve Social Security	$45,060

Independent expenditures opposing Metzenbaum
Americans United	$412,169
Life Amendment PAC	$18,455
Mid-America Conservative PAC	$17,489
Ruff PAC	$17,466
Conservative Victory Committee	$12,379
American Citizens for Political Action	$8,796
Council for National Defense	$6,044

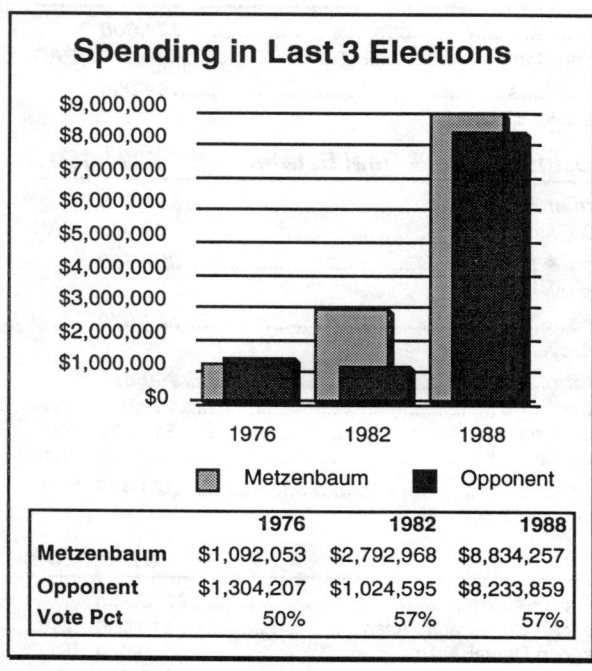

Spending in Last 3 Elections

	1976	1982	1988
Metzenbaum	$1,092,053	$2,792,968	$8,834,257
Opponent	$1,304,207	$1,024,595	$8,233,859
Vote Pct	50%	57%	57%

---

* Contributions came from more than one affiliate or subsidiary.

Barbara A. Mikulski (D-Md)

First elected: 1986

1987-92 Total Rcpts:	$3,789,523
1992 Year-end Cash:	$269,145
Current term expires:	1998

1991-92 Committees & Subcommittees

Appropriations
Foreign Operations; Legislative Branch; Transportation and Related Agencies; Treasury, Postal Service and General Government; VA, HUD and Independent Agencies (Chairwoman)

Labor and Human Resources
Children, Families, Drugs and Alcoholism; Education, Arts and Humanities; Employment and Productivity; Labor

Small Business
Export Expansion (Chairwoman); Urban and Minority-Owned Business Development

Leading Contributors

Business

Agriculture	$46,987

Crop Production & Basic Processing $12,287
None over $7,500

Agricultural Services/Products $8,950
None over $7,500

Food Processing & Sales $14,750
None over $7,500

Communications/Electronics	$93,170

Printing & Publishing $8,800
None over $7,500

Media/Entertainment $38,800
None over $7,500

Telephone Utilities $16,620
None over $7,500

Telecom Services & Equipment $10,000
Comsat .... $10,000 PAC

Computer Equipment & Services $15,800
None over $7,500

Construction	$44,850

General Contractors $16,000
None over $7,500

Home Builders $13,400
None over $7,500

Construction Services $11,200
None over $7,500

Contribution Totals by Sector

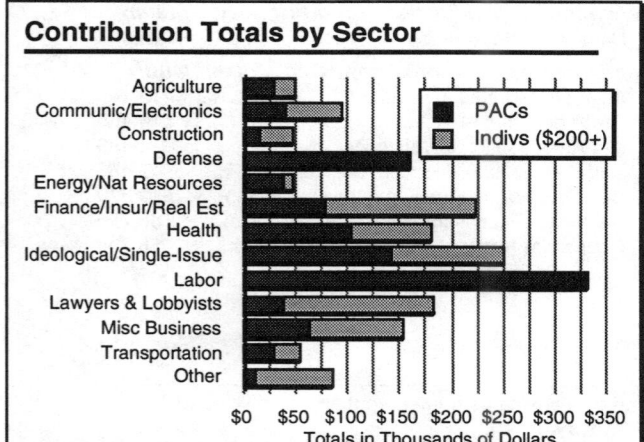

Agriculture
Communic/Electronics
Construction
Defense
Energy/Nat Resources
Finance/Insur/Real Est
Health
Ideological/Single-Issue
Labor
Lawyers & Lobbyists
Misc Business
Transportation
Other

■ PACs
▨ Indivs ($200+)

$0 $50 $100 $150 $200 $250 $300 $350
Totals in Thousands of Dollars

Source of Funds: 1987-1992

Source	Total	Pct
■ PACs	$1,067,306	28%
▨ Indivs $200+	$1,027,890	27%
☐ Indivs under $200	$1,404,180	37%
⊠ Other	$323,955	8%
Candidate	$0	0%
Party	$33,808	1%

Source of PAC Dollars by Sector

Source	Total	Pct
■ Business	$576,278	55%
▨ Labor	$328,844	31%
☐ Ideological/Single-Issue ..	$140,498	13%

In-State vs. Out-of-State Contributions*

Source	Total	Pct
☐ In-State	$541,162	53%
■ Out-of-state	$483,978	47%
No state listed	$0	

*** by large individual contributors ($200 & above)**

Defense	$159,137

Defense Aerospace $95,237
Allied-Signal .... $10,000 PAC
General Electric .... $10,000 PAC
UNC Inc .... $9,987 PAC
Boeing Co .... $9,000 PAC

Defense Electronics $49,200
Westinghouse Electric .... $8,500 PAC

Misc Defense $14,700
None over $7,500

Energy & Natural Resources	$46,850

Oil & Gas $23,600
Coastal Corp .... $8,000 PAC

Electric Utilities $9,000
None over $7,500

Finance, Insurance & Real Estate	$221,150

Commercial Banks $37,275
MNC Financial Inc .... $9,000 PAC

Securities & Investment $32,550
None over $7,500

Insurance $27,000
None over $7,500

Real Estate $90,550
Landow & Co .... $10,000 Indiv
National Assn of Realtors .... $10,000 PAC
Rouse Co .... $7,750 Indiv

Accountants $23,449
None over $7,500

Health	$178,723

Health Professionals $115,735
American Chiropractic Assn .... $10,000 PAC
American Dental Assn .... $10,000 PAC
American Medical Assn* .... $10,000 PAC

American Optometric Assn ....$10,000 PAC
Hospitals/Nursing Homes............................**$32,319**
American Hospital Assn ....$9,469 PAC
Misc Health **$16,969**
None over $7,500

Lawyers & Lobbyists $180,150

Lawyers & Lobbyists....................................**$180,150**
Assn of Trial Lawyers of America ....$10,000 PAC
Akin, Gump et al ....$8,000 PAC/Ind

Misc Business $150,914

Food & Beverage **$18,900**
None over $7,500

Beer, Wine & Liquor **$17,600**
National Beer Wholesalers Assn ....$8,500 PAC

Retail Sales..**$24,050**
None over $7,500

Business Services **$37,414**
Outdoor Advertising Assn of America ....$9,884 PAC/Ind

Lodging/Tourism **$9,800**
None over $7,500

Steel Production **$9,600**
None over $7,500

Misc Manufacturing & Distributing....................**$11,500**
None over $7,500

Transportation $53,450

Air Transport **$23,750**
Aircraft Owners & Pilots Assn ....$8,000 PAC

Sea Transport...**$10,450**
None over $7,500

Labor

Labor $329,344

Building Trade Unions **$60,000**
Bricklayers Union ....$10,000 PAC
Laborers' Political League ....$10,000 PAC
Sheet Metal Workers Union ....$10,000 PAC
Carpenters & Joiners Union ....$9,250 PAC

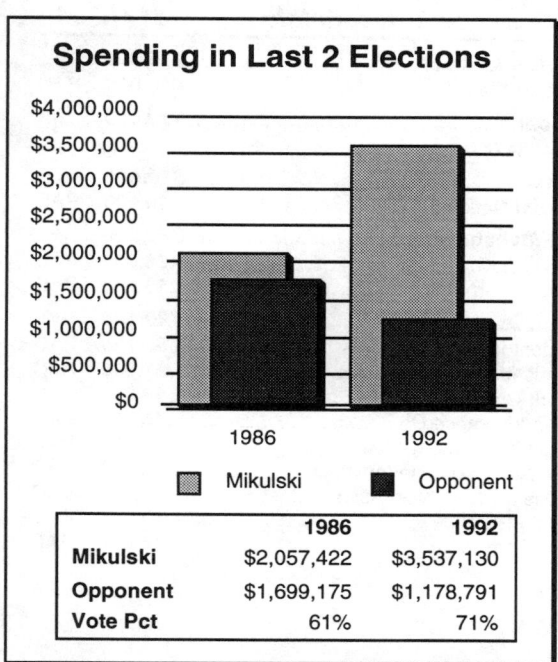

Spending in Last 2 Elections

	1986	1992
Mikulski	$2,057,422	$3,537,130
Opponent	$1,699,175	$1,178,791
Vote Pct	61%	71%

Mikulski   Opponent

Industrial Unions **$69,807**
Intl Brotherhood of Electrical Workers ....$10,000 PAC
Machinists/Aerospace Workers Union ....$10,000 PAC
United Auto Workers ....$9,057 PAC
Amalgamated Clothing & Textile Workers* ....$9,000 PAC

Transportation Unions **$80,500**
Marine Engineers Union* ....$10,500 PAC
Seafarers International Union ....$10,000 PAC
Teamsters Union ....$10,000 PAC
United Transportation Union ....$10,000 PAC
Masters, Mates & Pilots Union ....$8,000 PAC

Public Sector Unions **$93,087**
American Fedn of St/Cnty/Munic Employees ....$10,205 PAC
American Postal Workers Union ....$10,100 PAC
American Federation of Teachers.....................$10,000 PAC
National Assn of Letter Carriers ....$10,000 PAC
National Treasury Employees Union ....$10,000 PAC
National Education Assn ....$9,207 PAC

Misc Unions..**$25,950**
Service Employees International Union ....$10,000 PAC
Food & Commercial Workers Union ....$9,500 PAC

Ideological/Single-Issue

Ideological/Single-Issue $247,855

Democratic/Liberal **$21,850**
None over $7,500

Leadership PACs..**$17,150**
Fund for a Democratic Majority (Ted Kennedy) .$10,000 PAC

Pro-Israel **$118,950**
Desert Caucus ....$10,000 PAC
Women's Alliance for Israel ....$10,000 PAC

Pro-Choice...**$19,000**
National Abortion Rights Action League ....$8,500 PAC

Womens Issues..**$45,292**
Women's Campaign Fund ....$10,000 PAC

Human Rights **$9,600**
None over $7,500

Misc Issues...**$13,870**
None over $7,500

Other & Unknown

Other $85,083

Civil Servants/Public Officials...........................**$7,750**
None over $7,500

Education **$24,200**
None over $7,500

Retired **$29,933**
None over $7,500

Other **$20,700**
National Assn of Social Workers ....$9,000 PAC

Unknown $241,281

Homemakers/Non-income earners $29,700
No Employer Listed or Found $76,420
Generic Occupation/Category Unknown $8,700
Employer Listed/Category Unknown.................$126,461
None over $7,500

Independent expenditures opposing Mikulski
Citizens for Informed Voters $11,867
East Coast Conservative PAC $10,474
Mid-America Conservative PAC $9,486

---

* Contributions came from more than one affiliate or subsidiary.

George J. Mitchell (D-Maine)

First elected: 1982 *(App'ted 1980)*

1987-92 Total Rcpts:	$1,966,727
1992 Year-end Cash:	$477,648
Current term expires:	1994

1991-92 Committees & Subcommittees

Environment and Public Works
Environmental Protection; Superfund, Ocean and Water Protection; Water Resources, Transportation and Infrastructure

Finance
Health for Families and the Uninsured; International Trade; Medicare and Long Term Care

Veterans' Affairs

Leading Contributors

NOTE: The bulk of Mitchell's large individual contributions do not appear in the listings below. His last election was in 1988, and this book lists individual contributions only from 1989-1992.

Business

Agriculture — $39,900

Crop Production & Basic Processing $14,500
    None over $4,000
Tobacco $8,000
    Philip Morris .... $4,000   PAC
Food Processing & Sales $6,500
    None over $4,000

Communications/Electronics — $28,000

Media/Entertainment $14,000
    None over $4,000
Telephone Utilities $11,750
    AT&T .... $5,000   PAC

Construction — $20,000

General Contractors $10,500
    Associated General Contractors .... $5,000   PAC
Home Builders $8,500
    Walter Industries .... $4,000   PAC

Source of Funds: 1987-1992

Source	Total	Pct
■ PACs	$739,141	37%
▨ Indivs $200+	$593,164	30%
☐ Indivs under $200	$378,125	19%
▨ Other	$264,325	13%
Candidate	$0	0%
Party	$8,028	0%

Source of PAC Dollars by Sector

Source	Total	Pct
■ Business	$506,423	68%
▨ Labor	$144,300	19%
☐ Ideological/Single-Issue	$93,418	13%

In-State vs. Out-of-State Contributions*

Source	Total	Pct
☐ In-State	$176,569	30%
■ Out-of-state	$416,595	70%
No state listed	$0	

* by large individual contributors ($200 & above)

Defense — $20,500

Defense Aerospace $16,500
    Lockheed Corp .... $5,000   PAC
Misc Defense $5,000
    Bath Iron Works .... $5,000   PAC

Energy & Natural Resources — $27,000

Oil & Gas $10,500
    None over $4,000
Electric Utilities $6,000
    None over $4,000

Finance, Insurance & Real Estate — $171,764

Commercial Banks $15,000
    American Bankers Assn .... $10,000   PAC
Savings & Loans $10,000
    None over $4,000
Credit Unions $10,000
    Credit Union National Assn .... $10,000   PAC
Securities & Investment $22,500
    EF Hutton .... $6,000   PAC
    First Boston Corp .... $5,000   PAC
Insurance $90,124
    Independent Insurance Agents of America .... $7,724   PAC
    Massachusetts Mutual Life Insurance .... $7,000   PAC
    Torchmark Corp .... $6,000   PAC
    Unum Life Insurance Co .... $5,400   PAC
    Equitable Financial Services .... $5,000   PAC
    National Assn of Life Underwriters ... $5,000   PAC
    Blue Cross & Blue Shield Assn .... $4,000   PAC
    Prudential Insurance .... $4,000   PAC
    Travelers Corp .... $4,000   PAC

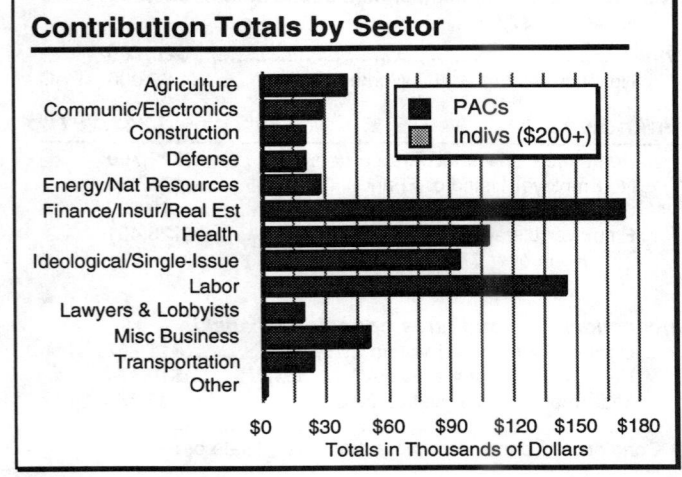

Contribution Totals by Sector

Agriculture, Communic/Electronics, Construction, Defense, Energy/Nat Resources, Finance/Insur/Real Est, Health, Ideological/Single-Issue, Labor, Lawyers & Lobbyists, Misc Business, Transportation, Other

- ■ PACs
- ▨ Indivs ($200+)

$0 $30 $60 $90 $120 $150 $180
Totals in Thousands of Dollars

Real Estate **$14,000**
   Mortgage Bankers Assn of America .... $10,000 PAC

Accountants **$7,000**
   American Institute of CPA's .... $5,000 PAC

Health   **$106,759**

Health Professionals **$52,509**
   American Dental Assn .... $6,000 PAC
   American Podiatry Assn .... $5,000 PAC
   Anesthesia Service Medical Group .... $5,000 PAC
   National Assn of Pharmacists .... $5,000 PAC
   American Academy of Ophthalmology .... $4,000 PAC
   American Chiropractic Assn .... $4,000 PAC
   Co-op of American Physicians .... $4,000 PAC

Hospitals/Nursing Homes **$31,000**
   American Health Care Assn .... $9,500 PAC
   American Hospital Assn .... $5,000 PAC
   Federation of American Health Systems .... $5,000 PAC
   Manor Healthcare Corp .... $4,000 PAC

Health Services **$7,000**
   National Assn for Home Care .... $5,000 PAC

Pharmaceuticals/Health Products **$16,250**
   Pfizer Inc .... $4,000 PAC

Lawyers & Lobbyists   **$19,500**

Lawyers & Lobbyists **$19,500**
   Assn of Trial Lawyers of America .... $5,500 PAC

Misc Business   **$50,500**

Beer, Wine & Liquor **$17,000**
   National Beer Wholesalers Assn .... $6,000 PAC

Retail Sales **$7,000**
   None over $4,000

Business Services **$4,000**
   Dun & Bradstreet .... $4,000 PAC

Chemical & Related Manufacturing **$5,000**
   None over $4,000

Misc Manufacturing & Distributing **$5,000**
   None over $4,000

Textiles **$5,000**
   None over $4,000

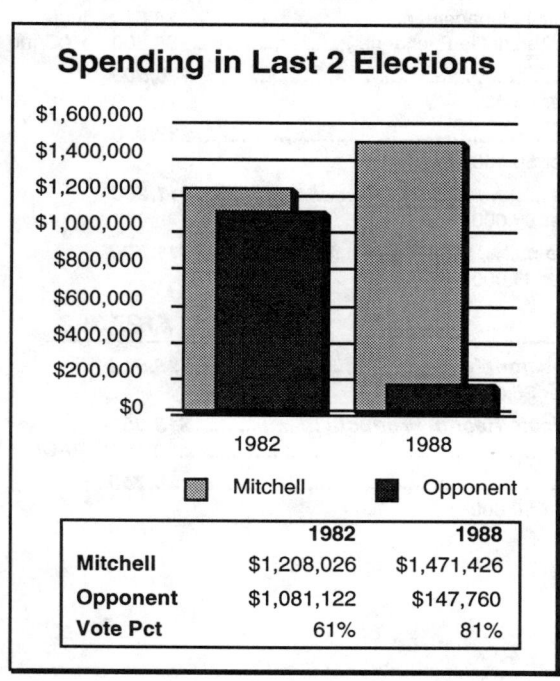

Spending in Last 2 Elections

	1982	1988
Mitchell	$1,208,026	$1,471,426
Opponent	$1,081,122	$147,760
Vote Pct	61%	81%

Transportation   **$23,500**

Air Transport **$13,500**
   Aircraft Owners & Pilots Assn .... $4,000 PAC
   Federal Express Corp .... $4,000 PAC

Automotive **$4,500**
   None over $4,000

Trucking **$4,500**
   None over $4,000

Labor

Labor   **$144,300**

Building Trade Unions **$20,500**
   Operating Engineers Union .... $5,000 PAC
   Sheet Metal Workers Union .... $5,000 PAC

Industrial Unions **$35,000**
   Machinists/Aerospace Workers Union .... $15,000 PAC
   Communications Workers of America .... $5,000 PAC
   Ladies Garment Workers Union .... $5,000 PAC

Transportation Unions **$41,000**
   Marine Engineers Union .... $10,000 PAC
   Air Line Pilots Assn .... $5,000 PAC
   Maintenance of Way Employees .... $5,000 PAC
   United Auto Workers .... $5,000 PAC
   United Transportation Union .... $4,000 PAC

Public Sector Unions **$36,300**
   American Postal Workers Union .... $6,000 PAC
   American Fedn of St/Cnty/Munic Employees ...... $5,000 PAC
   National Assn of Letter Carriers .... $5,000 PAC
   National Treasury Employees Union .... $5,000 PAC
   Natl Assn of Retired Federal Employees .... $5,000 PAC

Misc Unions **$11,500**
   AFL-CIO .... $7,000 PAC

Ideological/Single-Issue

Ideological/Single-Issue   **$93,418**

Democratic/Liberal **$10,034**
   Democrats for the 80's .... $5,000 PAC

Leadership PACs **$10,000**
   Cmte for a Demo Consensus (Alan Cranston) .... $5,000 PAC
   Fund for a Democratic Majority (Ted Kennedy) ... $5,000 PAC

Foreign & Defense Policy **$10,384**
   Council for a Livable World .... $5,384 PAC
   Free Cuba PAC .... $5,000 PAC

Pro-Israel **$58,500**
   Citizens Organized PAC .... $10,000 PAC
   Desert Caucus .... $10,000 PAC
   Pacific PAC .... $10,000 PAC
   National PAC .... $5,000 PAC
   San Franciscans for Good Government .... $5,000 PAC
   Hudson Valley PAC .... $4,000 PAC

Human Rights **$6,000**
   KidsPAC .... $5,000 PAC

Independent expenditures supporting Mitchell
   League of Conservation Voters $8,731

Carol Moseley-Braun (D-Ill)

First elected: 1992
1991-92 Total Rcpts: $6,774,890
1992 Year-end Cash: $30,144
Current term expires: 1998

1993-94 Committees & Subcommittees

Banking, Housing and Urban Affairs
Housing and Urban Affairs; Securities

Judiciary
Courts and Administrative Practice; Juvenile Justice

Small Business
Export Expansion and Agricultural Development; Urban and Minority-Owned Business Development

Leading Contributors

Business

Agriculture	$35,600

Tobacco $7,500
   None over $6,000
Agricultural Services/Products $10,500
   None over $6,000
Food Processing & Sales $10,000
   None over $6,000

Communications/Electronics	$69,256

Printing & Publishing $16,300
   None over $6,000
Media/Entertainment $22,350
   None over $6,000
Telephone Utilities $18,406
   Ameritech Corp* .... $6,900   PAC/Ind
   AT&T .... $6,350   PAC/Ind
Computer Equipment & Services $8,700
   None over $6,000

Construction	$23,675

General Contractors $10,175
   None over $6,000
Construction Services $8,100
   None over $6,000

Source of Funds: 1987-1992

Source	Total	Pct
PACs	$762,931	11%
Indivs $200+	$1,841,595	25%
Indivs under $200	$3,826,304	53%
Other	$807,395	11%
Candidate	$2,114	0%
Party	$463,335	6%

Source of PAC Dollars by Sector

Source	Total	Pct
Business	$246,861	34%
Labor	$280,048	38%
Ideological/Single-Issue	$203,869	28%

In-State vs. Out-of-State Contributions*

Source	Total	Pct
In-State	$1,072,158	62%
Out-of-state	$668,183	38%
No state listed	$0	

* by large individual contributors ($200 & above)

Energy & Natural Resources	$20,900

Oil & Gas $6,075
   None over $6,000
Waste Management $8,175
   Waste Management Inc .... $7,675   PAC/Ind

Finance, Insurance & Real Estate	$229,473

Commercial Banks $48,163
   None over $6,000
Securities & Investment $85,560
   Ariel Capital Management .... $8,810   Indiv
   Chicago Mercantile Exchange .... $6,500   PAC/Ind
Insurance $28,500
   None over $6,000
Real Estate $39,950
   None over $6,000
Accountants $11,200
   None over $6,000
Misc Finance $11,500
   None over $6,000

Health	$127,392

Health Professionals $98,912
   None over $6,000
Pharmaceuticals/Health Products $13,850
   Glaxo Inc .... $8,000   PAC/Ind
Misc Health $6,750
   None over $6,000

Contribution Totals by Sector

Agriculture
Communic/Electronics
Construction
Defense
Energy/Nat Resources
Finance/Insur/Real Est
Health
Ideological/Single-Issue
Labor
Lawyers & Lobbyists
Misc Business
Transportation
Other

■ PACs
▨ Indivs ($200+)

$0 $75 $150 $225 $300 $375 $450
Totals in Thousands of Dollars

Lawyers & Lobbyists — $356,893

Lawyers & Lobbyists — $356,893
Sidley & Austin	$11,600	Indiv
Kirkland & Ellis	$10,950	PAC/Ind
Assn of Trial Lawyers of America	$10,000	PAC
Corboy & Demetrio	$9,000	Indiv
Jenner & Block	$8,350	Indiv
Wildman, Harrold et al	$7,400	Indiv
Rose, Klein & Marias	$7,250	Indiv
Mayer, Brown & Platt	$7,100	Indiv

Misc Business — $108,410

Beer, Wine & Liquor — $8,965
None over $6,000

Retail Sales — $10,330
None over $6,000

Misc Services — $7,500
None over $6,000

Business Services — $39,700
None over $6,000

Misc Manufacturing & Distributing — $23,950
William Levine Inc	$6,200	Indiv

Transportation — $26,160

Air Transport — $15,720
None over $6,000

Labor

Labor — $282,198

Building Trade Unions — $35,850
Laborers' Political League	$10,000	PAC

Industrial Unions — $74,998
Machinists/Aerospace Workers Union	$10,000	PAC
United Auto Workers	$10,000	PAC
Communications Workers of America	$9,998	PAC
United Mine Workers	$7,500	PAC

Transportation Unions — $68,550
Air Line Pilots Assn	$10,000	PAC
Assn of Flight Attendants	$10,000	PAC
Teamsters Union	$10,000	PAC

Public Sector Unions — $63,000
American Fedn of St/Cnty/Munic Employees	$12,500	PAC
American Federation of Teachers	$10,000	PAC
National Assn of Letter Carriers	$10,000	PAC
National Education Assn	$10,000	PAC

Misc Unions — $39,800
AFL-CIO	$10,000	PAC
Food & Commercial Workers Union	$10,000	PAC
Service Employees International Union	$10,000	PAC

Ideological/Single-Issue

Ideological/Single-Issue — $451,135

Democratic/Liberal — $57,220
Fifth Horseman PAC	$10,000	PAC
Hollywood Women's Political Cmte	$6,000	PAC

Leadership PACs — $29,350
Fund for a Democratic Majority (Ted Kennedy)	$10,000	PAC

Foreign & Defense Policy — $22,872
Council for a Livable World	$10,448	PAC/Ind
Illinois SANE/Freeze	$6,840	PAC

Pro-Israel — $49,450
Multi-Issue PAC	$6,500	PAC

Pro-Choice — $37,010
Voters for Choice	$10,000	PAC
National Abortion Rights Action League	$8,000	PAC

Womens Issues — $185,717
Emily's List	$83,190	PAC/Ind
National Organization for Women	$9,882	PAC/Ind
Women's Campaign Fund	$8,000	PAC
National Womens Political Caucus	$7,500	PAC

Human Rights — $41,798
KidsPAC	$10,000	PAC
Human Rights Campaign Fund	$9,998	PAC

Misc Issues — $26,718
Sierra Club	$7,000	PAC

Other & Unknown

Other — $110,178

Non-Profit Institutions — $9,050
None over $6,000

Civil Servants/Public Officials — $19,250
None over $6,000

Education — $32,530
None over $6,000

Retired — $37,968
None over $6,000

Other — $11,380
None over $6,000

Unknown — $736,717
Homemakers/Non-income earners	$23,500
No Employer Listed or Found	$604,795
Generic Occupation/Category Unknown	$10,300
Employer Listed/Category Unknown	$96,658

None over $6,000

---

* Contributions came from more than one affiliate or subsidiary.

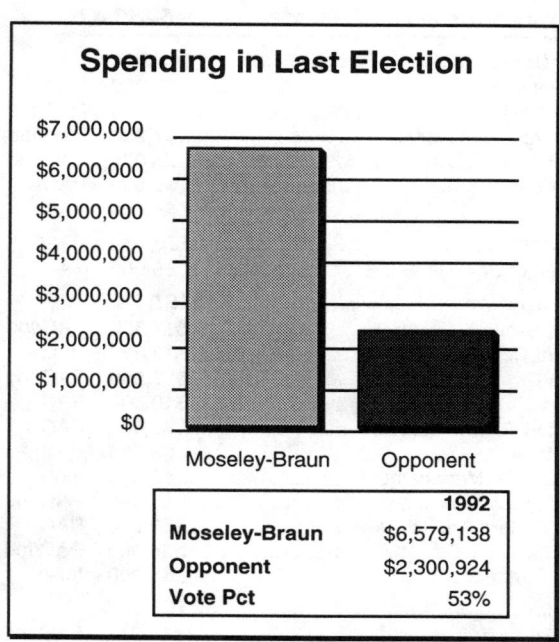

Spending in Last Election

	1992
Moseley-Braun	$6,579,138
Opponent	$2,300,924
Vote Pct	53%

Daniel Patrick Moynihan (D-NY)

First elected: 1976

1987-92 Total Rcpts:	$5,665,268
1992 Year-end Cash:	$854,325
Current term expires:	1994

1991-92 Committees & Subcommittees

Environment and Public Works (Chairman)
Environmental Protection; Nuclear Regulation; Water Resources, Transportation and Infrastructure (Chairman)

Finance
International Trade; Private Retirement Plans and Oversight of the Internal Revenue Service; Social Security and Family Policy (Chairman)

Foreign Relations
African Affairs; Near Eastern and South Asian Affairs; Terrorism, Narcotics and International Operations

Rules and Administration

Joint Committee on the Library

Joint Committee on Taxation

Leading Contributors

NOTE: The bulk of Moynihan's large individual contributions do not appear in the listings below. His last election was in 1988, and this book lists individual contributions only from 1989-1992.

Business

Agriculture — $16,650
None over $6,000

Communications/Electronics — $81,668

Printing & Publishing $23,000
None over $6,000
Media/Entertainment $26,200
None over $6,000
Telephone Utilities $24,968
AT&T .... $9,000 PAC

Construction — $84,337

General Contractors $47,260
Associated General Contractors .... $10,000 PAC
National Utility Contractors Assn .... $8,500 PAC
Slattery Associates .... $7,000 Indiv
Construction Services $19,577
None over $6,000

Contribution Totals by Sector

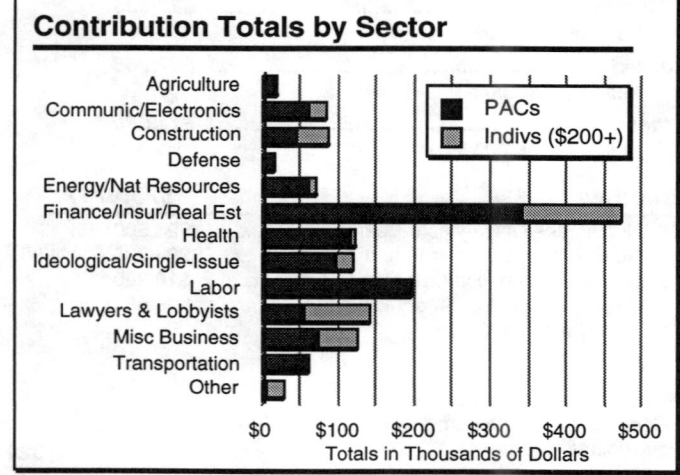

Totals in Thousands of Dollars

Source of Funds: 1987-1992

Source	Total	Pct
■ PACs	$1,074,411	19%
■ Indivs $200+	$1,597,561	28%
□ Indivs under $200	$2,618,548	46%
⊠ Other	$444,704	8%
Candidate	$0	0%
Party	$69,956	1%

Source of PAC Dollars by Sector

Source	Total	Pct
■ Business	$820,904	74%
■ Labor	$194,854	18%
□ Ideological/Single-Issue	$93,746	8%

In-State vs. Out-of-State Contributions*

Source	Total	Pct
□ In-State	$1,144,995	72%
■ Out-of-state	$444,541	28%
No state listed	$7,000	

* by large individual contributors ($200 & above)

Defense — $14,250

Defense Aerospace $12,000
None over $6,000

Energy & Natural Resources — $70,050

Oil & Gas $33,000
Amerada Hess Corp .... $8,000 Indiv
Electric Utilities $14,300
None over $6,000
Waste Management $10,000
None over $6,000

Finance, Insurance & Real Estate — $469,414

Commercial Banks $69,575
Norstar Bancorp .... $9,000 PAC
Chemical Bank .... $7,750 PAC/Ind
Manufacturers Hanover .... $7,250 PAC/Ind
Citicorp .... $6,025 PAC/Ind
American Bankers Assn .... $6,000 PAC
Bankers Trust .... $6,000 PAC
Savings & Loans $30,494
US League of Savings Assns* .... $9,000 PAC
Securities & Investment $191,178
Goldman, Sachs & Co .... $17,500 PAC/Ind
Investment Company Institute .... $13,822 PAC
American Express* .... $11,000 PAC/Ind
EF Hutton .... $10,000 PAC
First Boston Corp .... $9,000 PAC
PaineWebber .... $8,750 PAC
Alliance Capital Management .... $8,000 Indiv
Bear, Stearns & Co .... $7,000 PAC/Ind
National Venture Capital Assn .... $7,000 PAC
Morgan Stanley & Co .... $6,000 PAC/Ind
Odyssey Partners .... $6,000 Indiv
Insurance $93,967
Continental Insurance .... $12,312 PAC/Ind
Metropolitan Life Insurance .... $8,655 PAC

Real Estate	$50,200	
National Assn of Realtors	$7,000	PAC
Accountants	**$17,000**	
American Institute of CPA's	$10,000	PAC
Misc Finance	**$12,250**	
None over $6,000		

Health — $119,180

Health Professionals	$67,930	
American Medical Assn*	$9,000	PAC
American Academy of Ophthalmology	$8,000	PAC
Assn for the Advancement of Psychology	$7,680	PAC
American Physical Therapy Assn	$7,000	PAC
Hospitals/Nursing Homes	**$16,750**	
None over $6,000		
Pharmaceuticals/Health Products	**$33,500**	
Pfizer Inc	$6,000	PAC

Lawyers & Lobbyists — $140,056

Lawyers & Lobbyists	$140,056	
Willkie, Farr & Gallagher	$22,500	Indiv
Assn of Trial Lawyers of America	$10,000	PAC
Verner, Liipfert et al	$9,500	PAC/Ind
Dickstein, Shapiro & Morin	$7,000	PAC/Ind
Paul, Weiss et al	$6,750	Indiv
Skadden, Arps et al	$6,500	PAC/Ind

Misc Business — $122,942

Food & Beverage	$8,250	
None over $6,000		
Retail Sales	**$13,650**	
None over $6,000		
Business Services	**$19,500**	
None over $6,000		
Chemical & Related Manufacturing	**$12,000**	
None over $6,000		
Steel Production	**$9,100**	
None over $6,000		
Misc Manufacturing & Distributing	**$37,500**	
Triangle Industries	$10,000	PAC
Avon Products	$8,000	PAC
M Fabrikant & Sons	$6,000	Indiv

Spending in Last 3 Elections

| | Moynihan | Opponent |

	1976	1982	1988
Moynihan	$1,210,796	$2,708,660	$5,468,516
Opponent	$2,101,424	$117,875	$528,989
Vote Pct	54%	65%	67%

Transportation	$59,475	
Air Transport	$27,975	
Federal Express Corp	$8,000	PAC
United Parcel Service	$7,500	PAC
Trucking	**$8,000**	
None over $6,000		
Railroads	**$13,000**	
None over $6,000		

Labor

Labor	$194,854	
Building Trade Unions	$50,704	
Laborers Union*	$12,750	PAC
Operating Engineers Union*	$9,000	PAC
Carpenters & Joiners Union*	$8,500	PAC
Bricklayers Union	$6,000	PAC
Industrial Unions	**$32,300**	
Intl Brotherhood of Electrical Workers	$8,500	PAC
Transportation Unions	**$61,350**	
Teamsters Union	$13,000	PAC
Transport Workers Union*	$9,000	PAC
Air Line Pilots Assn	$7,500	PAC
United Transportation Union	$7,500	PAC
Marine Engineers Union*	$7,000	PAC
International Longshoremen's Assn	$6,150	PAC
Public Sector Unions	**$26,500**	
National Assn of Letter Carriers	$9,000	PAC
Misc Unions	**$24,000**	
AFL-CIO	$11,000	PAC

Ideological/Single-Issue

Ideological/Single-Issue	$116,796	
Democratic/Liberal	$26,527	
National Cmte for an Effective Congress	$9,990	PAC
Religion and Tolerance PAC	$6,000	PAC
Leadership PACs	**$20,000**	
Senate Majority Fund (Daniel Inouye)	$10,000	PAC
Pro-Israel	**$42,300**	
None over $6,000		
Human Rights	**$10,500**	
None over $6,000		
Misc Issues	**$8,500**	
National Cmte to Preserve Social Security	$6,000	PAC

Other & Unknown

Other	$27,700	
Retired	$15,950	
None over $6,000		

Unknown	$122,718	
Homemakers/Non-income earners	$14,550	
No Employer Listed or Found	$14,008	
Employer Listed/Category Unknown	$91,160	
None over $6,000		

Independent expenditures supporting Moynihan
National Cmte to Preserve Social Security $63,570

Independent expenditures opposing Moynihan
National Conservative PAC $8,722
Council for National Defense $6,044

* Contributions came from more than one affiliate or
subsidiary.

Frank H. Murkowski (R-Alaska)

First elected: 1980
1987-92 Total Rcpts:	$1,887,991
1992 Year-end Cash:	$31,081
Current term expires:	1998

1991-92 Committees & Subcommittees

Energy and Natural Resources
Energy Regulation and Conservation; Mineral Resources Development and Production; Public Lands, National Parks and Forests (Ranking Republican)

Foreign Relations
East Asian and Pacific Affairs (Ranking Republican); International Economic Policy, Trade, Oceans and Environment; Near Eastern and South Asian Affairs

Veterans' Affairs

Select Committee on Indian Affairs

Select Committee on Intelligence (Vice Chairman)

Leading Contributors

Business

Agriculture	$65,311
Tobacco	$13,500
None over $6,000	
Agricultural Services/Products	$6,101
None over $6,000	
Food Processing & Sales	$17,500
ConAgra Inc	$8,000 PAC
Forestry & Forest Products	$18,260
None over $6,000	

Communications/Electronics	$76,249
Printing & Publishing	$6,799
None over $6,000	
Media/Entertainment	$14,000
National Cable Television Assn	$10,000 PAC
Telephone Utilities	$30,750
BellSouth Corp*	$9,500 PAC
Telecom Services & Equipment	$7,000
None over $6,000	
Electronics Mfg & Services	$7,200
None over $6,000	
Computer Equipment & Services	$10,500
None over $6,000	

Contribution Totals by Sector

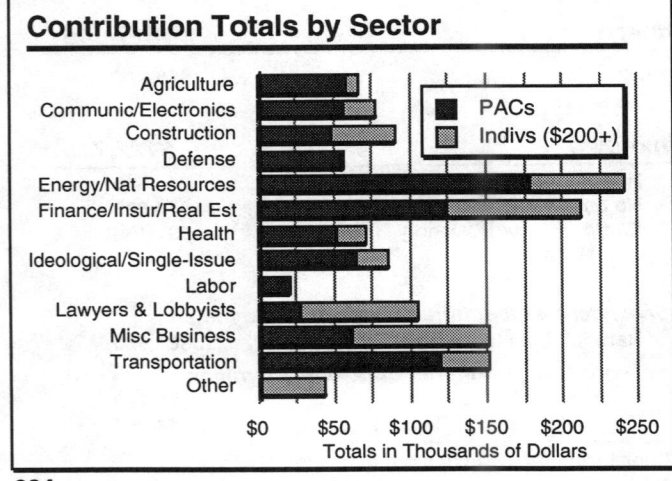

Totals in Thousands of Dollars

Source of Funds: 1987-1992

Source	Total	Pct
PACs	$771,841	38%
Indivs $200+	$675,386	33%
Indivs under $200	$223,498	11%
Other	$368,131	18%
Candidate	$1,425	0%
Party	$150,865	7%

Source of PAC Dollars by Sector

Source	Total	Pct
Business	$768,092	90%
Labor	$19,500	2%
Ideological/Single-Issue	$63,850	8%

In-State vs. Out-of-State Contributions*

Source	Total	Pct
In-State	$207,214	31%
Out-of-state	$453,172	69%
No state listed	$500	

* by large individual contributors ($200 & above)

Construction	$88,950
General Contractors	$53,550
Associated General Contractors	$10,000 PAC
Fluor Corp	$9,500 PAC
Associated Builders & Contractors	$6,000 PAC
Home Builders	$6,500
None over $6,000	
Construction Services	$16,000
None over $6,000	
Building Materials & Equipment	$8,000
None over $6,000	

Defense	$55,000
Defense Aerospace	$44,000
Martin Marietta Corp	$8,000 PAC
Northrop Corp	$8,000 PAC
Defense Electronics	$8,000
None over $6,000	

Energy & Natural Resources	$239,072
Oil & Gas	$166,327
Atlantic Richfield	$12,550 PAC/Ind
Chevron Corp	$10,000 PAC
Amoco Corp	$8,000 PAC
Halliburton Co	$8,000 PAC
Mapco Inc	$8,000 PAC
BP America	$7,750 PAC/Ind
Exxon Corp	$7,500 PAC
Mobil Oil	$7,500 PAC
Veco International Inc	$6,947 Indiv
Shell Oil	$6,000 PAC/Ind
Mining	$25,025
None over $6,000	
Misc Energy	$8,500
None over $6,000	

Electric Utilities	$14,950	
None over $6,000		
Waste Management	$6,250	
Waste Management Inc	$6,000	PAC
Commercial Fishing	$14,520	
None over $6,000		

Finance, Insurance & Real Estate $210,370

Commercial Banks	$70,750	
American Bankers Assn	$10,000	PAC
Barnett Banks Inc	$10,000	PAC
Credit Unions	$6,000	
Credit Union National Assn	$6,000	PAC
Securities & Investment	$30,680	
Chicago Mercantile Exchange	$6,000	PAC
National Venture Capital Assn	$6,000	PAC
Insurance	$42,250	
American International Group	$9,000	PAC
National Assn of Life Underwriters	$7,500	PAC
Real Estate	$34,306	
Cook Inlet Region Inc	$6,500	Indiv
National Assn of Realtors	$6,500	PAC
Accountants	$8,000	
None over $6,000		
Misc Finance	$17,000	
None over $6,000		

Health $70,025

Health Professionals	$51,025	
American Medical Assn	$10,825	PAC
American Dental Assn	$10,000	PAC
American Podiatry Assn	$6,000	PAC
Pharmaceuticals/Health Products	$14,500	
Eli Lilly & Co	$7,000	PAC

Lawyers & Lobbyists $103,486

| Lawyers & Lobbyists | $103,486 | |
| Hopkins & Sutter | $7,000 | PAC/Ind |

Misc Business $150,159

| Food & Beverage | $45,563 | |
| None over $6,000 | | |

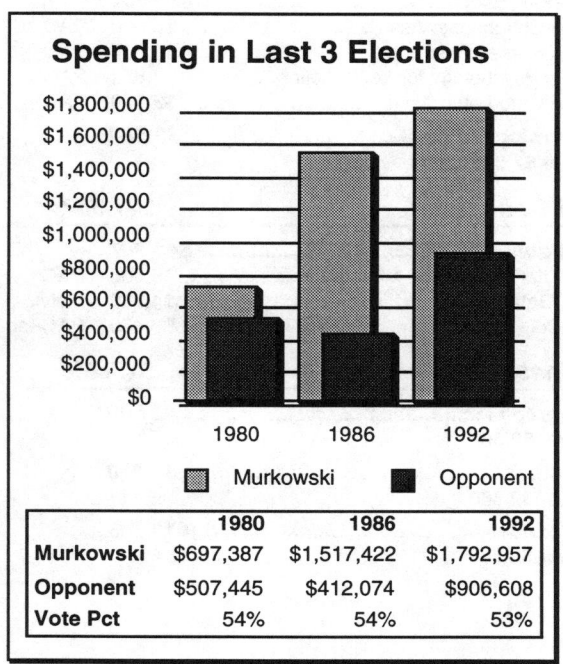

Spending in Last 3 Elections

	1980	1986	1992
Murkowski	$697,387	$1,517,422	$1,792,957
Opponent	$507,445	$412,074	$906,608
Vote Pct	54%	54%	53%

Beer, Wine & Liquor	$13,750	
National Beer Wholesalers Assn	$7,500	PAC
Retail Sales	$11,250	
None over $6,000		
Business Services	$37,000	
Naegele Outdoor Advertising	$6,500	Indiv
Lodging/Tourism	$18,400	
None over $6,000		

Transportation $149,159

Air Transport	$58,244	
Aircraft Owners & Pilots Assn	$10,000	PAC
Federal Express Corp	$9,500	PAC
General Electric	$8,000	PAC
Boeing Co	$7,000	PAC/Ind
Automotive	$23,400	
Americans for Free International Trade	$10,000	PAC
Trucking	$6,750	
None over $6,000		
Railroads	$20,250	
Union Pacific Corp	$9,500	PAC
Sea Transport	$38,780	
Sea-Land Corp	$9,000	PAC

Labor

Labor $19,700

| Transportation Unions | $13,500 | |
| Marine Engineers Union* | $11,000 | PAC |

Ideological/Single-Issue

Ideological/Single-Issue $84,602

Republican/Conservative	$14,752	
None over $6,000		
Leadership PACs	$15,950	
Campaign America (Bob Dole)	$10,000	PAC
Pro-Israel	$31,000	
Hudson Valley PAC	$6,500	PAC
Washington PAC	$6,000	PAC
Gun Rights/Gun Control	$10,900	
National Rifle Assn	$9,900	PAC
Misc Issues	$6,000	
None over $6,000		

Other & Unknown

Other $43,100

Civil Servants/Public Officials	$7,500	
None over $6,000		
Education	$11,500	
St John's University	$8,000	Indiv
Retired	$22,600	
None over $6,000		

Unknown $151,145

Homemakers/Non-income earners	$23,531	
No Employer Listed or Found	$39,877	
Generic Occupation/Category Unknown	$8,400	
Employer Listed/Category Unknown	$79,337	
Hongsong International Co	$6,000	Indiv

* Contributions came from more than one affiliate or subsidiary.

Patty Murray (D-Wash)

First elected: 1992

1991-92 Total Rcpts:	$1,496,204
1992 Year-end Cash:	$154,166
Current term expires:	1998

1993-94 Committees & Subcommittees

Appropriations
District of Columbia; Interior and Related Agencies; Labor, Health and Human Services, Education and Related Agencies; Legislative Branch

Banking, Housing and Urban Affairs
International Finance and Monetary Policy; Securities

Budget

Leading Contributors

Business

Agriculture		$11,250
Crop Production & Basic Processing		$4,000
None over $2,500		
Dairy		$2,500
None over $2,500		
Forestry & Forest Products		$2,750
None over $2,500		

Communications/Electronics		$21,483
Printing & Publishing		$8,700
None over $2,500		
Media/Entertainment		$2,750
None over $2,500		
Telecom Services & Equipment		$3,000
McCaw Cellular Communications	$3,000	PAC/Ind
Computer Equipment & Services		$5,283
None over $2,500		

Construction		$1,400

Energy & Natural Resources		$24,900
Oil & Gas		$3,800
Western Pioneer Inc	$2,500	Indiv
Commercial Fishing		$20,500
American Factory Trawler Assn	$5,250	PAC/Ind
Arctic Alaska Fisheries Corp	$5,000	PAC
Fishing Co of Alaska	$4,000	Indiv

Source of Funds: 1987-1992

Source	Total	Pct
■ PACs	$438,766	23%
▨ Indivs $200+	$327,387	17%
☐ Indivs under $200	$666,996	35%
▧ Other	$459,511	24%
Candidate	$8,376	0%
Party	$396,456	21%

Source of PAC Dollars by Sector

Source	Total	Pct
■ Business	$68,835	16%
▨ Labor	$257,400	59%
☐ Ideological/Single-Issue	$113,205	26%

In-State vs. Out-of-State Contributions*

Source	Total	Pct
☐ In-State	$193,511	59%
■ Out-of-state	$133,176	41%
No state listed	$0	

* by large individual contributors ($200 & above)

Finance, Insurance & Real Estate		$23,600
Commercial Banks		$7,750
BankAmerica Corp*	$4,000	PAC
Securities & Investment		$6,350
None over $2,500		
Insurance		$3,500
None over $2,500		
Misc Finance		$2,750
None over $2,500		

Health		$39,652
Health Professionals		$31,602
American Chiropractic Assn	$5,000	PAC
American Nurses Assn	$4,000	PAC
Women in Psychology for Legis Action	$3,852	PAC
American Optometric Assn	$2,500	PAC
Hospitals/Nursing Homes		$3,500
None over $2,500		

Lawyers & Lobbyists		$41,367
Lawyers & Lobbyists		$41,367
Assn of Trial Lawyers of America	$5,000	PAC
Preston, Gates et al	$4,750	Indiv
Perkins Coie	$3,450	PAC/Ind

Misc Business		$23,268
Food & Beverage		$2,500
None over $2,500		
Retail Sales		$3,250
None over $2,500		
Business Services		$13,785
None over $2,500		

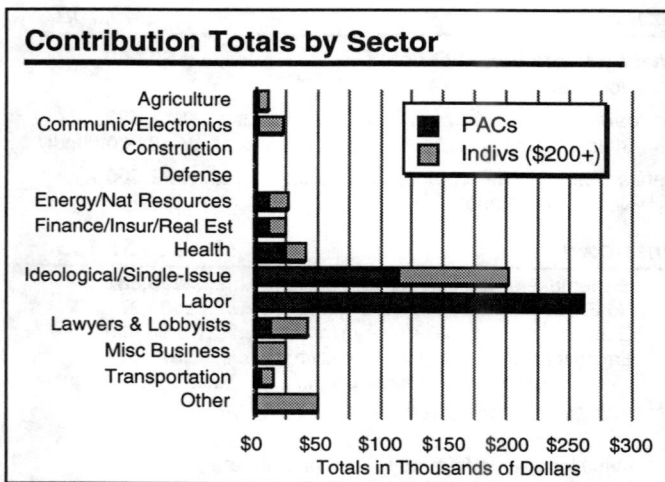

Contribution Totals by Sector

Agriculture
Communic/Electronics
Construction
Defense
Energy/Nat Resources
Finance/Insur/Real Est
Health
Ideological/Single-Issue
Labor
Lawyers & Lobbyists
Misc Business
Transportation
Other

■ PACs
▨ Indivs ($200+)

$0 $50 $100 $150 $200 $250 $300
Totals in Thousands of Dollars

Transportation $13,890

Air Transport $3,890
   None over $2,500

Sea Transport $9,000
   Stevedoring Services of America .... $6,500   Indiv

Labor

Labor $258,400

Building Trade Unions $37,700
   Carpenters & Joiners Union .... $10,000   PAC
   Laborers Union* .... $7,500   PAC
   Ironworkers Union .... $5,500   PAC
   Plumbers/Pipefitters Union .... $5,000   PAC
   Sheet Metal Workers Union .... $5,000   PAC
   Operating Engineers Union* .... $3,500   PAC

Industrial Unions $40,750
   United Auto Workers .... $10,000   PAC
   Intl Brotherhood of Electrical Workers .... $6,000   PAC
   Machinists/Aerospace Workers Union .... $5,000   PAC
   United Steelworkers .... $5,000   PAC
   Communications Workers of America .... $4,000   PAC
   Boilermakers Union .... $3,000   PAC
   Oil, Chemical & Atomic Workers Union .... $2,750   PAC

Transportation Unions $82,500
   Seafarers International Union* .... $11,500   PAC
   Air Line Pilots Assn .... $10,000   PAC
   Assn of Flight Attendants .... $10,000   PAC
   Intl Longshoremen's/Warehousemen's Union ... $10,000   PAC
   Teamsters Union .... $10,000   PAC
   United Transportation Union .... $10,000   PAC
   Brotherhood of Locomotive Engineers .... $6,000   PAC
   Amalgamated Transit Union .... $5,000   PAC
   Marine Engineers Union .... $5,000   PAC
   Trans Comm International Union .... $2,500   PAC

Public Sector Unions $58,250
   American Federation of Teachers .... $10,000   PAC
   American Fedn of St/Cnty/Munic Employees .... $10,000   PAC
   National Assn of Letter Carriers .... $10,000   PAC
   National Education Assn .... $10,000   PAC
   National Assn Retired Federal Employees .... $5,000   PAC
   National Rural Letter Carriers Assn .... $5,000   PAC
   International Assn of Firefighters .... $3,500   PAC
   American Postal Workers Union .... $2,500   PAC

Misc Unions $39,200
   AFL-CIO .... $10,000   PAC
   Food & Commercial Workers Union .... $10,000   PAC
   Service Employees International Union .... $10,000   PAC
   Office & Professional Employees Union .... $5,000   PAC
   Bakery, Confectionery & Tobacco Workers .... $3,000   PAC

Ideological/Single-Issue

Ideological/Single-Issue $199,789

Democratic/Liberal $17,016
   Hollywood Women's Political Cmte .... $5,000   PAC

Leadership PACs $8,000
   Fund for a Democratic Majority (Ted Kennedy) ... $5,000   PAC

Pro-Israel $8,000
   None over $2,500

Pro-Choice $13,250
   National Abortion Rights Action League .... $5,000   PAC

Womens Issues $100,783
   Emily's List .... $11,686   PAC/Ind
   National Womens Political Caucus .... $10,000   PAC
   Women's Campaign Fund .... $10,000   PAC
   National Organization for Women .... $7,097   PAC

Human Rights $18,800
   KidsPAC .... $10,000   PAC
   Human Rights Campaign Fund .... $5,000   PAC
   National Community Action Foundation .... $3,500   PAC

Misc Issues $32,000
   National Council of Senior Citizens .... $10,000   PAC
   Sierra Club .... $9,900   PAC
   League of Conservation Voters .... $4,200   PAC

Other & Unknown

Other $48,897

Civil Servants/Public Officials $11,310
   State of Washington .... $5,560   Indiv

Education $10,551
   None over $2,500

Retired $23,250
   None over $2,500

Other $2,936
   None over $2,500

Unknown $60,431

   Homemakers/Non-income earners $8,630
   No Employer Listed or Found $25,185
   Generic Occupation/Category Unknown $2,950
   Employer Listed/Category Unknown $23,666
     None over $2,500

Independent expenditures opposing Murray
   Daniel L. Matthews $8,000

---

* Contributions came from more than one affiliate or subsidiary.

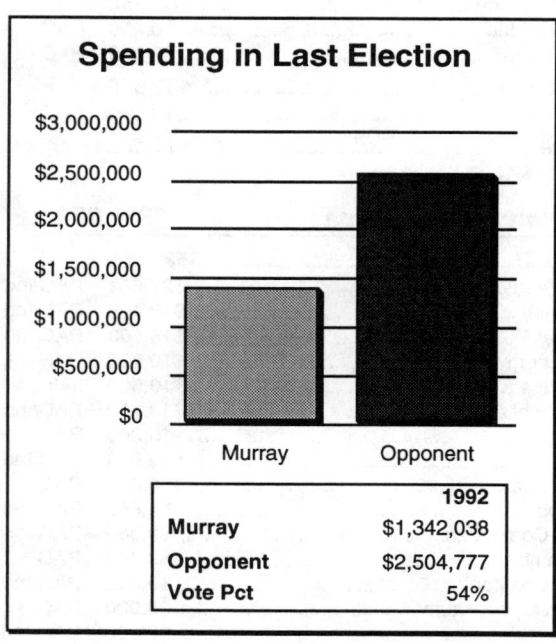

Spending in Last Election

	1992
Murray	$1,342,038
Opponent	$2,504,777
Vote Pct	54%

Don Nickles (R-Okla)

First elected: 1980

1987-92 Total Rcpts:	$3,686,883
1992 Year-end Cash:	$569,953
Current term expires:	1998

1991-92 Committees & Subcommittees

Appropriations
Agriculture, Rural Development and Related Agencies; Energy and Water Development; Foreign Operations; Interior and Related Agencies (Ranking Republican); VA, HUD and Independent Agencies

Budget

Energy and Natural Resources
Energy Regulation and Conservation (Ranking Republican); Energy Research and Development; Mineral Resources Development and Production

Select Committee on Indian Affairs

Leading Contributors

Business

Agriculture		$229,978
Crop Production & Basic Processing		**$25,700**
None over $7,500		
Tobacco		**$30,000**
US Tobacco Co	$11,000	PAC/Ind
Dairy		**$11,800**
None over $7,500		
Poultry & Eggs		**$8,000**
None over $7,500		
Livestock		**$40,850**
National Cattlemen's Assn*	$7,500	PAC
Agricultural Services/Products		**$19,550**
None over $7,500		
Food Processing & Sales		**$62,600**
Fleming Companies Inc	$9,500	PAC/Ind
Forestry & Forest Products		**$28,278**
None over $7,500		

Communications/Electronics		$99,370
Printing & Publishing		**$22,970**
None over $7,500		
Media/Entertainment		**$39,750**
National Assn of Broadcasters	$10,000	PAC
National Cable Television Assn	$10,000	PAC
Telephone Utilities		**$27,200**
Southwestern Bell	$10,300	PAC/Ind

Source of Funds: 1987-1992

Source	Total	Pct
■ PACs	$1,187,070	30%
▨ Indivs $200+	$1,558,971	39%
□ Indivs under $200	$497,556	12%
▥ Other	$736,268	18%
Candidate	$0	0%
Party	$292,982	7%

Source of PAC Dollars by Sector

Source	Total	Pct
■ Business	$1,219,480	93%
▨ Labor	$4,250	0%
□ Ideological/Single-Issue	$90,200	7%

In-State vs. Out-of-State Contributions*

Source	Total	Pct
□ In-State	$1,191,267	76%
■ Out-of-state	$367,704	24%
No state listed	$0	

by large individual contributors ($200 & above)

Construction		$106,127
General Contractors		**$41,327**
Associated Builders & Contractors	$10,000	PAC
Home Builders		**$12,000**
None over $7,500		
Special Trade Contractors		**$14,000**
National Electrical Contractors Assn	$10,000	PAC
Building Materials & Equipment		**$27,600**
None over $7,500		

Defense		$142,050
Defense Aerospace		**$84,950**
General Electric	$9,950	PAC
Northrop Corp	$8,000	PAC
Defense Electronics		**$43,600**
AT&T	$8,000	PAC
Misc Defense		**$13,500**
None over $7,500		

Energy & Natural Resources		$636,834
Oil & Gas		**$531,189**
Phillips Petroleum	$27,881	PAC/Ind
Kerr-McGee	$18,400	PAC/Ind
Occidental Petroleum*	$14,500	PAC/Ind
Holden Energy Corp	$10,500	Indiv
Sooner Pipe & Supply	$10,500	Indiv
Atlantic Richfield	$10,100	PAC/Ind
Exxon Corp	$10,000	PAC
Mobil Oil	$10,000	PAC/Ind
Union Pacific Corp	$10,000	PAC
Mapco Inc	$9,550	PAC/Ind
Chevron Corp	$9,000	PAC
Dow Chemical	$9,000	PAC
Williams Companies	$9,000	PAC/Ind
Columbia Gas System*	$8,000	PAC
Koch Industries	$8,000	PAC/Ind

Contribution Totals by Sector

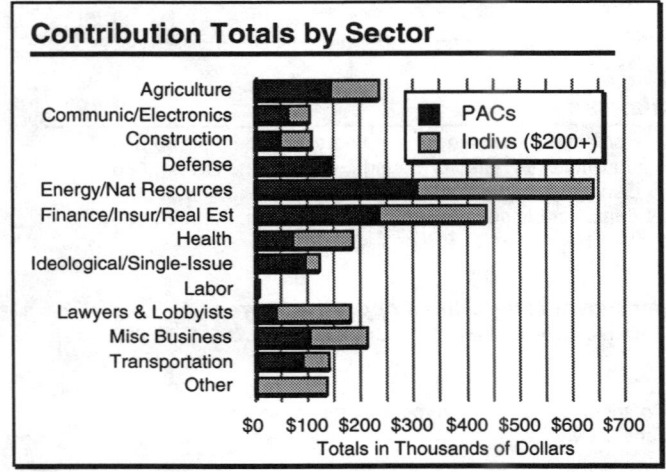

Agriculture
Communic/Electronics
Construction
Defense
Energy/Nat Resources
Finance/Insur/Real Est
Health
Ideological/Single-Issue
Labor
Lawyers & Lobbyists
Misc Business
Transportation
Other

■ PACs
▥ Indivs ($200+)

$0 $100 $200 $300 $400 $500 $600 $700
Totals in Thousands of Dollars

Mining	....	**$33,650**	
	Fluor Corp	$10,000	PAC

Misc Energy	....	**$16,000**
	None over $7,500	

Electric Utilities	....	**$36,495**
	None over $7,500	

Waste Management	....	**$15,000**
	None over $7,500	

Finance, Insurance & Real Estate — $432,049

Commercial Banks	....	**$80,418**	
	American Bankers Assn	$10,000	PAC
	First National Bank	$8,700	Indiv

Securities & Investment	....	**$47,755**
	None over $7,500	

Insurance	....	**$181,492**	
	Casualty & Surety Agents Assn	$12,000	PAC
	Torchmark Corp	$11,167	PAC/Ind
	Independent Insurance Agents of America	$10,000	PAC
	Massachusetts Mutual Life Insurance	$10,000	PAC
	National Assn of Life Underwriters	$9,500	PAC
	American Council of Life Insurance	$9,285	PAC
	Prudential Insurance	$9,000	PAC
	National Assn of Independent Insurers	$8,500	PAC

Real Estate	....	**$39,650**	
	National Assn of Realtors	$10,000	PAC

Accountants	....	**$19,800**	
	American Institute of CPA's	$9,500	PAC

Misc Finance	....	**$56,300**
	None over $7,500	

Health — $183,550

Health Professionals	....	**$133,100**	
	American Medical Assn*	$12,000	PAC
	American Dental Assn	$10,000	PAC

Hospitals/Nursing Homes	....	**$12,450**
	None over $7,500	

Pharmaceuticals/Health Products	....	**$32,550**
	None over $7,500	

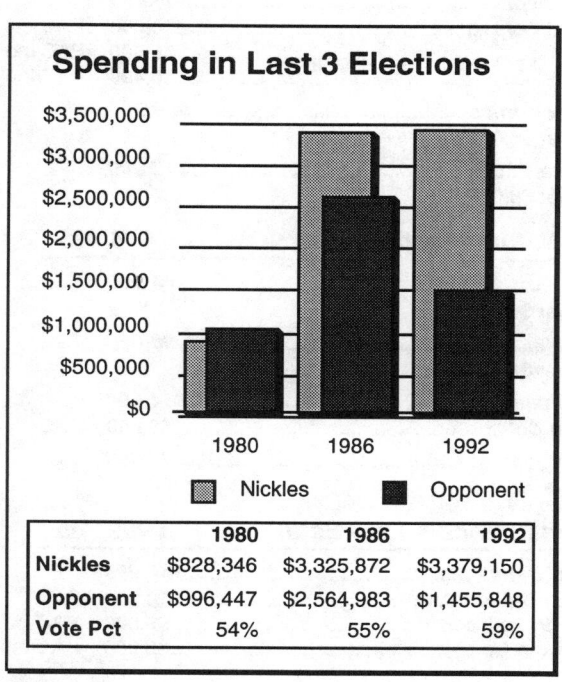

Spending in Last 3 Elections

	1980	1986	1992
Nickles	$828,346	$3,325,872	$3,379,150
Opponent	$996,447	$2,564,983	$1,455,848
Vote Pct	54%	55%	59%

Legend: Nickles, Opponent

Lawyers & Lobbyists — $178,770

Lawyers & Lobbyists	....	**$178,770**	
	Akin, Gump et al	$8,403	PAC/Ind
	Williams & Jensen	$8,000	PAC/Ind

Misc Business — $209,326

Food & Beverage	....	**$24,260**
	None over $7,500	

Beer, Wine & Liquor	....	**$17,034**	
	National Beer Wholesalers Assn	$10,000	PAC

Retail Sales	....	**$22,645**
	None over $7,500	

Business Services	....	**$51,250**
	None over $7,500	

Chemical & Related Manufacturing	....	**$19,000**
	None over $7,500	

Misc Manufacturing & Distributing	....	**$31,500**
	None over $7,500	

Transportation — $137,300

Air Transport	....	**$42,250**	
	Federal Express Corp	$10,000	PAC
	United Parcel Service	$9,000	PAC

Automotive	....	**$53,650**	
	Auto Dealers & Drivers for Free Trade	$11,000	PAC
	Americans for Free International Trade	$10,000	PAC
	National Auto Dealers Assn	$8,000	PAC

Trucking	....	**$21,500**
	None over $7,500	

Railroads	....	**$10,500**
	None over $7,500	

Ideological/Single-Issue

Ideological/Single-Issue		**$117,400**

Republican/Conservative	....	**$13,450**
	None over $7,500	

Leadership PACs	....	**$16,000**	
	Campaign America (Bob Dole)	$10,000	PAC

Pro-Israel	....	**$42,800**
	None over $7,500	

Gun Rights/Gun Control	....	**$9,900**	
	National Rifle Assn	$9,900	PAC

Human Rights	....	**$12,500**	
	National Albanian American PAC	$10,000	PAC

Misc Issues	....	**$15,000**
	None over $7,500	

Other & Unknown

Other		**$131,250**

Civil Servants/Public Officials	....	**$18,400**
	None over $7,500	

Retired	....	**$97,150**
	None over $7,500	

Unknown		**$261,234**

	Homemakers/Non-income earners	$68,950
	No Employer Listed or Found	$11,684
	Employer Listed/Category Unknown	$179,650
	None over $7,500	

---

* Contributions came from more than one affiliate or subsidiary.

Sam Nunn (D-Ga)

First elected: 1972

1987-92 Total Rcpts:	$2,245,900
1992 Year-end Cash:	$1,381,700
Current term expires:	1996

1991-92 Committees & Subcommittees

Armed Services (Chairman)

Governmental Affairs
Government Information and Regulation; Oversight of Government Management; Permanent Subcommittee on Investigations (Chairman)

Small Business
Government Contracting and Paperwork Reduction; Rural Economy and Family Farming; Urban and Minority-Owned Business Development

Leading Contributors

Business

Agriculture	$132,660

Crop Production & Basic Processing $22,050
　　None over $6,000

Tobacco $15,000
　　RJR Nabisco .... $6,000　PAC/Ind

Dairy $10,000
　　None over $6,000

Poultry & Eggs $14,200
　　None over $6,000

Agricultural Services/Products $24,910
　　None over $6,000

Food Processing & Sales $8,450
　　None over $6,000

Forestry & Forest Products $35,300
　　Georgia-Pacific Corp .... $6,750　PAC/Ind

Communications/Electronics	$84,770

Printing & Publishing $7,160
　　None over $6,000

Media/Entertainment $42,140
　　Time Warner* .... $21,340　Indiv

Telephone Utilities $21,960
　　BellSouth Corp* .... $7,710　PAC/Ind
　　Coastal Utilities Inc .... $7,000　Indiv

Telecom Services & Equipment $10,000
　　Metromedia Co .... $6,000　Indiv

Source of Funds: 1987-1992

Source	Total	Pct
■ PACs	$613,157	27%
▨ Indivs $200+	$1,042,798	46%
☐ Indivs under $200	$101,265	5%
⊠ Other	$488,680	22%
Candidate	$0	0%
Party	$0	0%

Source of PAC Dollars by Sector

Source	Total	Pct
■ Business	$564,664	91%
▨ Labor	$40,500	7%
☐ Ideological/Single-Issue	$12,217	2%

In-State vs. Out-of-State Contributions*

Source	Total	Pct
☐ In-State	$715,395	69%
■ Out-of-state	$327,403	31%
No state listed	$0	

* by large individual contributors ($200 & above)

Construction	$81,550

General Contractors $51,260
　　None over $6,000

Home Builders $6,660
　　None over $6,000

Special Trade Contractors $7,050
　　None over $6,000

Building Materials & Equipment $11,650
　　None over $6,000

Defense	$114,084

Defense Aerospace $69,499
　　Lockheed Corp .... $10,000　PAC
　　Textron Inc .... $6,500　PAC/Ind
　　General Electric .... $6,400　PAC/Ind

Defense Electronics $29,585
　　None over $6,000

Misc Defense $15,000
　　None over $6,000

Energy & Natural Resources	$74,825

Oil & Gas $44,100
　　None over $6,000

Mining $8,050
　　None over $6,000

Electric Utilities $14,690
　　Southern Co* .... $6,000　PAC

Waste Management $6,000
　　None over $6,000

Finance, Insurance & Real Estate	$409,745

Commercial Banks $67,995
　　American Bankers Assn .... $10,000　PAC
　　Barnett Banks Inc .... $8,000　PAC
　　C&S/Sovran Corp* .... $8,000　PAC/Ind

Contribution Totals by Sector

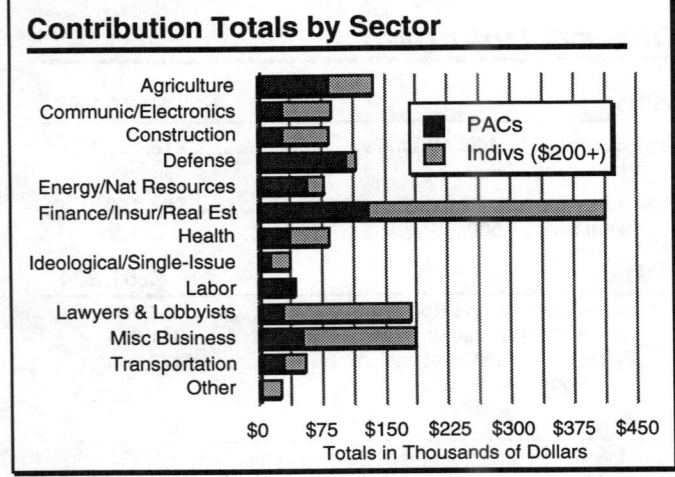

Agriculture
Communic/Electronics
Construction
Defense
Energy/Nat Resources
Finance/Insur/Real Est
Health
Ideological/Single-Issue
Labor
Lawyers & Lobbyists
Misc Business
Transportation
Other

■ PACs
▨ Indivs ($200+)

$0　$75　$150　$225　$300　$375　$450
Totals in Thousands of Dollars

Savings & Loans	....	$7,050

Savings & Loans $7,050
None over $6,000

Securities & Investment $122,220
  Goldman, Sachs & Co .... $46,660   PAC/Ind
  Invesco Capital Management .... $6,000   Indiv

Insurance $62,390
  American Family Corp .... $10,000   PAC

Real Estate $101,500
  National Assn of Realtors .... $10,000   PAC
  Ocmulgee Fields Inc .... $6,000   Indiv

Accountants $17,000
  American Institute of CPA's .... $10,000   PAC

Misc Finance $26,590
None over $6,000

Health — $82,450

Health Professionals $52,300
None over $6,000

Hospitals/Nursing Homes $9,200
None over $6,000

Health Services $7,500
  Home Health Care of Georgia .... $7,000   Indiv

Pharmaceuticals/Health Products $10,500
None over $6,000

Lawyers & Lobbyists — $178,654

Lawyers & Lobbyists $178,654
  King & Spalding .... $20,280   Indiv
  Sutherland, Asbill & Brennan .... $11,000   Indiv
  Sullivan & Cromwell .... $9,000   Indiv
  Kilpatrick & Cody .... $7,710   Indiv
  Jones, Osteen et al .... $7,000   Indiv
  Assn of Trial Lawyers of America .... $6,000   PAC

Spending in Last 3 Elections

	1978	1984	1990
Nunn	$548,814	$729,843	$1,245,042
Opponent	$0	$0	$0
Vote Pct	83%	80%	100%

Misc Business — $182,040

Food & Beverage $20,150
  Coca-Cola Co .... $7,000   PAC/Ind

Beer, Wine & Liquor $28,650
  National Beer Wholesalers Assn .... $7,500   PAC

Retail Sales $20,000
None over $6,000

Business Services $17,050
None over $6,000

Lodging/Tourism $15,180
None over $6,000

Misc Manufacturing & Distributing $55,110
  Rock-Tenn Co .... $21,000   Indiv

Textiles $6,000
None over $6,000

Transportation — $51,670

Air Transport $18,770
None over $6,000

Automotive $16,250
None over $6,000

Sea Transport $6,150
None over $6,000

Labor

Labor — $40,500

Transportation Unions $13,000
None over $6,000

Public Sector Unions $17,000
None over $6,000

Ideological/Single-Issue

Ideological/Single-Issue — $36,177

Pro-Israel $28,610
None over $6,000

Other & Unknown

Other — $24,275

Retired $14,150
None over $6,000

Unknown — $173,639

  Homemakers/Non-income earners $28,385
  No Employer Listed or Found $15,364
  Employer Listed/Category Unknown $129,890
    None over $6,000

Independent expenditures opposing Nunn
  American Citizens for Political Action $19,200

* Contributions came from more than one affiliate or subsidiary.

Bob Packwood (R-Ore)

First elected: 1968

1987-92 Total Rcpts:	$8,228,212
1992 Year-end Cash:	$887,627
Current term expires:	1998

1991-92 Committees & Subcommittees

Commerce, Science and Transportation
Communications (Ranking Republican); Foreign Commerce and Tourism; National Ocean Policy Study; Surface Transportation

Finance (Ranking Republican)
International Trade; Medicare and Long Term Care; Taxation

Joint Committee on Taxation

Leading Contributors

Business

Agriculture		$192,100
Crop Production & Basic Processing	$14,800	
None over $10,000		
Tobacco	$23,000	
None over $10,000		
Agricultural Services/Products	$13,250	
None over $10,000		
Food Processing & Sales	$17,000	
None over $10,000		
Forestry & Forest Products	$108,900	
International Paper Co	$10,000	PAC

Communications/Electronics		$331,776
Printing & Publishing	$40,475	
Hallmark Cards	$11,500	PAC/Ind
Media/Entertainment	$178,051	
Time Warner*	$38,000	PAC/Ind
National Assn of Broadcasters	$12,000	PAC/Ind
National Cable Television Assn	$10,126	PAC
Tele-Communications Inc	$10,000	PAC
Telephone Utilities	$84,500	
US West Inc	$14,250	PAC/Ind
GTE Corp	$10,000	PAC
Telecom Services & Equipment	$10,250	
None over $10,000		
Electronics Mfg & Services	$10,000	
None over $10,000		

Source of Funds: 1987-1992

Source	Total	Pct
■ PACs	$1,274,358	15%
▨ Indivs $200+	$2,268,996	27%
□ Indivs under $200	$3,972,302	47%
▨ Other	$987,717	12%
Candidate	$0	0%
Party	$275,161	3%

Source of PAC Dollars by Sector

Source	Total	Pct
■ Business	$1,057,057	81%
▨ Labor	$94,000	7%
□ Ideological/Single-Issue	$155,150	12%

In-State vs. Out-of-State Contributions*

Source	Total	Pct
□ In-State	$496,553	22%
■ Out-of-state	$1,756,638	78%
No state listed	$2,800	

* by large individual contributors ($200 & above)

Construction		$47,381
General Contractors	$10,930	
None over $10,000		
Building Materials & Equipment	$21,400	
None over $10,000		

Energy & Natural Resources		$100,503
Oil & Gas	$56,142	
None over $10,000		
Mining	$17,000	
None over $10,000		
Electric Utilities	$11,500	
None over $10,000		

Finance, Insurance & Real Estate		$572,248
Commercial Banks	$75,535	
American Bankers Assn	$12,500	PAC
Citicorp	$11,250	PAC/Ind
Securities & Investment	$162,140	
American Express*	$11,500	PAC/Ind
Investment Company Institute	$10,000	PAC
Insurance	$163,364	
Metropolitan Life Insurance	$14,104	PAC/Ind
American Council of Life Insurance	$11,000	PAC/Ind
American Family Corp	$10,000	PAC
National Assn of Life Underwriters	$10,000	PAC
Real Estate	$88,975	
None over $10,000		
Accountants	$35,500	
American Institute of CPA's	$10,000	PAC
Misc Finance	$41,850	
None over $10,000		

Contribution Totals by Sector

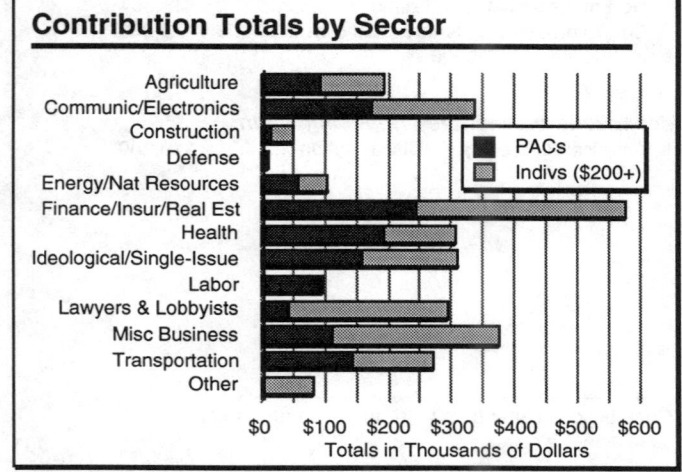

Agriculture
Communic/Electronics
Construction
Defense
Energy/Nat Resources
Finance/Insur/Real Est
Health
Ideological/Single-Issue
Labor
Lawyers & Lobbyists
Misc Business
Transportation
Other

■ PACs
▨ Indivs ($200+)

$0 $100 $200 $300 $400 $500 $600
Totals in Thousands of Dollars

Health — $302,600

Health Professionals $115,050
    American Medical Assn .... $11,000   PAC/Ind
    American Academy of Ophthalmology .... $10,000   PAC
    American Chiropractic Assn .... $10,000   PAC

Hospitals/Nursing Homes $69,675
    American Hospital Assn .... $14,000   PAC/Ind
    Federation of American Health Systems .... $11,000   PAC/Ind
    American Health Care Assn .... $10,000   PAC

Health Services $18,500
    Pacificare Health Systems .... $10,750   PAC/Ind

Pharmaceuticals/Health Products $96,825
    Eli Lilly & Co .... $10,500   PAC/Ind

Lawyers & Lobbyists — $288,575

Lawyers & Lobbyists $288,575
    McDermott, Will & Emery .... $16,000   Indiv
    Assn of Trial Lawyers of America .... $10,000   PAC

Misc Business — $370,930

Food & Beverage $48,133
    National Restaurant Assn .... $10,000   PAC

Beer, Wine & Liquor $24,990
    None over $10,000

Retail Sales $57,057
    May Department Stores .... $15,500   PAC/Ind

Business Services $65,400
    None over $10,000

Lodging/Tourism $11,000
    None over $10,000

Chemical & Related Manufacturing $25,750
    None over $10,000

Misc Manufacturing & Distributing $105,650
    Nike Inc .... $15,750   PAC/Ind

Transportation — $266,687

Air Transport $63,937
    United Parcel Service .... $10,000   PAC

Automotive $65,650
    Auto Dealers & Drivers for Free Trade .... $10,000   PAC

Trucking $29,800
    American Trucking Assns .... $10,000   PAC/Ind

Railroads $45,850
    Union Pacific Corp .... $10,000   PAC

Sea Transport $41,200
    None over $10,000

Misc Transport $20,250
    Falcon Shipping Group .... $10,000   Indiv

Labor

Labor — $95,000

Building Trade Unions $25,000
    None over $10,000

Transportation Unions $22,000
    Marine Engineers Union .... $11,000   PAC/Ind
    Air Line Pilots Assn .... $10,000   PAC

Public Sector Unions $25,000
    National Assn of Letter Carriers .... $10,000   PAC

Misc Unions $20,000
    Food & Commercial Workers Union .... $10,000   PAC
    Hotel/Restaurant Employees Union .... $10,000   PAC

Ideological/Single-Issue

Ideological/Single-Issue — $306,252

Leadership PACs $15,000
    Campaign America (Bob Dole) .... $10,000   PAC

Pro-Israel $242,536
    Citizens Concerned for the National Interest ..... $10,000   PAC
    Citizens Organized PAC .... $10,000   PAC
    Desert Caucus .... $10,000   PAC
    Florida Congressional Cmte .... $10,000   PAC
    National PAC .... $10,000   PAC
    Washington PAC .... $10,000   PAC
    Women's Alliance for Israel .... $10,000   PAC

Pro-Choice $16,726
    None over $10,000

Other & Unknown

Other — $79,820

Retired $55,445
    None over $10,000

Unknown — $602,081

    Homemakers/Non-income earners $20,100
    No Employer Listed or Found $452,898
    Employer Listed/Category Unknown $120,608
      None over $10,000

Independent expenditures supporting Packwood
    American Medical Assn $227,808
    Auto Dealers & Drivers for Free Trade $65,539

Independent expenditures opposing Packwood
    Life Amendment PAC $17,902

Spending in Last 3 Elections

	1980	1986	1992
Packwood	$1,534,607	$7,491,360	$7,547,173
Opponent	$195,035	$64,139	$2,629,397
Vote Pct	52%	63%	52%

(Bar chart: Packwood (gray), Opponent (black))

---

* Contributions came from more than one affiliate or subsidiary.

Claiborne Pell (D-RI)

First elected: 1960

1987-92 Total Rcpts:	$2,233,158
1992 Year-end Cash:	$101,208
Current term expires:	1996

1991-92 Committees & Subcommittees

Foreign Relations (Chairman)
International Economic Policy, Trade, Oceans and Environment; Terrorism, Narcotics and International Operations

Labor and Human Resources
Aging; Children, Families, Drugs and Alcoholism; Education, Arts and Humanities (Chairman)

Rules and Administration

Joint Committee on the Library (Chairman)

Leading Contributors

Business

Agriculture $20,600

Food Processing & Sales $6,750
  None over $6,000

Communications/Electronics $73,700

Printing & Publishing $9,150
  None over $6,000
Media/Entertainment $38,600
  Walt Disney Co/Disney Channel* .... $7,400 PAC/Ind
Telephone Utilities $11,500
  AT&T .... $6,000 PAC

Construction $32,850

General Contractors $8,500
  None over $6,000
Home Builders $15,200
  National Assn of Home Builders .... $10,000 PAC

Defense $28,850

Defense Aerospace $22,650
  Textron Inc .... $19,250 PAC/Ind

Energy & Natural Resources $39,000

Oil & Gas $26,350
  Occidental Petroleum .... $19,500 PAC/Ind

Contribution Totals by Sector

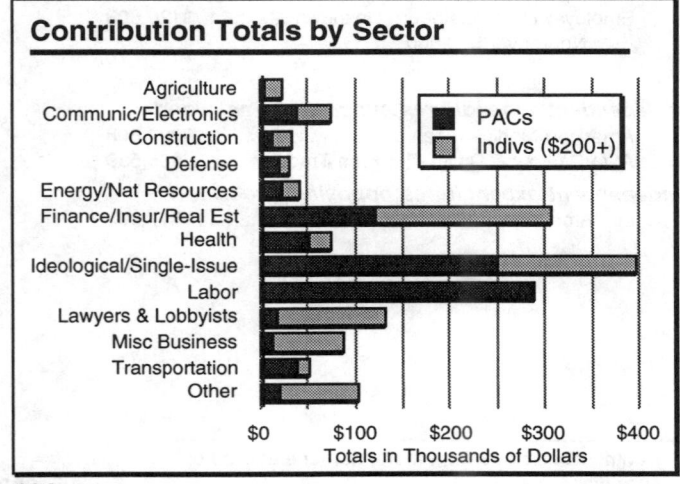

Agriculture
Communic/Electronics
Construction
Defense
Energy/Nat Resources
Finance/Insur/Real Est
Health
Ideological/Single-Issue
Labor
Lawyers & Lobbyists
Misc Business
Transportation
Other

PACs
Indivs ($200+)

$0 $100 $200 $300 $400
Totals in Thousands of Dollars

Source of Funds: 1987-1992

Source	Total	Pct
PACs	$881,512	39%
Indivs $200+	$941,250	41%
Indivs under $200	$182,188	8%
Other	$278,042	12%
Candidate	$0	0%
Party	$49,834	2%

Source of PAC Dollars by Sector

Source	Total	Pct
Business	$327,214	38%
Labor	$285,150	33%
Ideological/Single-Issue	$247,293	29%

In-State vs. Out-of-State Contributions*

Source	Total	Pct
In-State	$207,442	22%
Out-of-state	$722,583	78%
No state listed	$11,225	

* by large individual contributors ($200 & above)

Finance, Insurance & Real Estate $305,031

Commercial Banks $56,414
  Citicorp .... $10,999 PAC/Ind
  Fleet/Norstar Financial Group* .... $10,150 Indiv
  American Bankers Assn .... $10,000 PAC
  Norstar Bancorp .... $6,050 PAC
Credit Unions $6,200
  None over $6,000
Finance/Credit Companies $6,750
  None over $6,000
Securities & Investment $59,050
  National Venture Capital Assn .... $10,000 PAC
Insurance $56,500
  Independent Insurance Agents of America ... $10,000 PAC
  National Assn of Life Underwriters .... $10,000 PAC
Real Estate $79,600
  None over $6,000
Accountants $19,700
  None over $6,000
Misc Finance $16,817
  None over $6,000

Health $73,637

Health Professionals $64,887
  American Podiatry Assn .... $10,000 PAC
  American Chiropractic Assn .... $6,000 PAC

Lawyers & Lobbyists $128,960

Lawyers & Lobbyists $128,960
  Edwards & Angell .... $7,400 Indiv

Misc Business $85,685

Food & Beverage $9,735
  None over $6,000

Beer, Wine & Liquor **$8,425**
　None over $6,000

Business Services **$14,075**
　None over $6,000

Misc Manufacturing & Distributing **$32,100**
　General Electric .... $6,000　PAC

Transportation　　　　　　　　$48,650

Air Transport **$27,500**
　Federal Express Corp .... $10,000　PAC
　United Parcel Service .... $9,000　PAC

Automotive **$13,000**
　Auto Dealers & Drivers for Free Trade .... $10,500　PAC

Labor

Labor　　　　　　　　$285,350

Building Trade Unions **$53,000**
　Bricklayers Union .... $10,000　PAC
　Carpenters & Joiners Union .... $10,000　PAC
　Laborers' Political League .... $10,000　PAC
　Operating Engineers Union .... $7,000　PAC

Industrial Unions **$90,150**
　American Federation of Teachers .... $10,200　PAC/Ind
　Communications Workers of America .... $10,000　PAC
　Intl Brotherhood of Electrical Workers .... $10,000　PAC
　Machinists/Aerospace Workers Union .... $10,000　PAC
　National Education Assn .... $10,000　PAC
　United Steelworkers .... $10,000　PAC
　Amalgamated Clothing & Textile Workers .... $7,000　PAC
　Boilermakers Union .... $6,500　PAC

Transportation Unions **$61,550**
　Seafarers International Union .... $10,000　PAC
　Teamsters Union .... $10,000　PAC
　Amalgamated Transit Union .... $7,300　PAC
　Assn of Flight Attendants .... $7,000　PAC
　United Transportation Union .... $7,000　PAC
　Transport Workers Union .... $6,000　PAC

Public Sector Unions **$54,650**
　American Fedn of St/Cnty/Munic Employees .... $10,000　PAC
　American Postal Workers Union .... $10,000　PAC
　National Assn of Letter Carriers .... $10,000　PAC
　Natl Assn of Retired Federal Employees .... $10,000　PAC

Misc Unions **$26,000**
　Service Employees International Union .... $10,000　PAC
　AFL-CIO .... $8,000　PAC

Ideological/Single-Issue

Ideological/Single-Issue　　　$393,544

Democratic/Liberal **$49,890**
　None over $6,000

Leadership PACs **$25,238**
　Cmte for a Demo Consensus (Alan Cranston) .. $10,000　PAC
　Fund for a Democratic Majority (Ted Kennedy) . $10,000　PAC

Foreign & Defense Policy **$9,434**
　None over $6,000

Pro-Israel **$231,411**
　Citizens Organized PAC .... $10,000　PAC
　Delaware Valley PAC .... $10,000　PAC
　Desert Caucus .... $10,000　PAC
　National PAC .... $10,000　PAC
　Washington PAC .... $10,000　PAC
　Florida Congressional Cmte .... $7,500　PAC
　Hudson Valley PAC .... $7,500　PAC
　Multi-Issue PAC .... $6,000　PAC

Human Rights **$53,221**
　National Albanian American PAC .... $14,971　PAC
　Human Rights Campaign Fund .... $10,000　PAC
　KidsPAC .... $10,000　PAC

Misc Issues **$16,450**
　None over $6,000

Other & Unknown

Other　　　　　　　　$100,600

Non-Profit Institutions **$9,000**
　None over $6,000

Education **$48,200**
　Assn of Independent Colleges & Schools .... $10,000　PAC
　Natl Assn of Trade/Technical Schools .... $6,000　PAC

Retired **$26,400**
　None over $6,000

Other **$13,650**
　None over $6,000

Unknown　　　　　　　　$204,450

　Homemakers/Non-income earners $41,000
　No Employer Listed or Found $60,050
　Generic Occupation/Category Unknown $9,400
　Employer Listed/Category Unknown $94,000
　　None over $6,000

Independent expenditures supporting Pell
　National Cmte to Preserve Social Security $14,781

Independent expenditures opposing Pell
　American Citizens for Political Action $22,384
　Council for National Defense $9,940

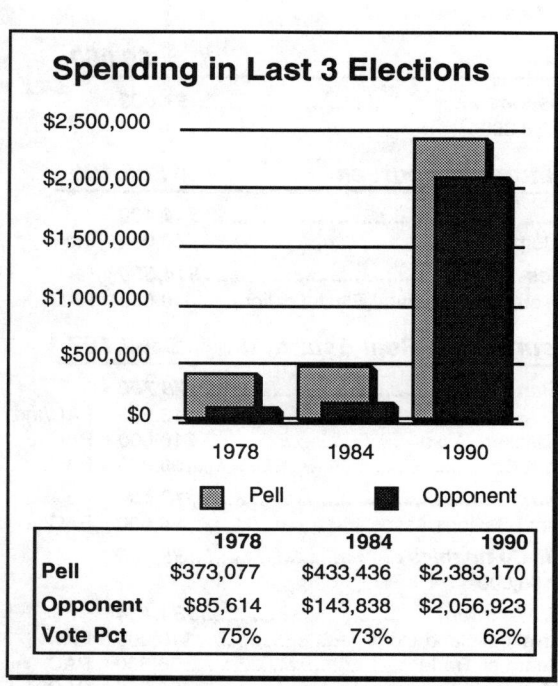

Spending in Last 3 Elections

	1978	1984	1990
Pell	$373,077	$433,436	$2,383,170
Opponent	$85,614	$143,838	$2,056,923
Vote Pct	75%	73%	62%

* Contributions came from more than one affiliate or
subsidiary.

Larry Pressler (R-SD)

First elected: 1978

1987-92 Total Rcpts:	$2,458,596
1992 Year-end Cash:	$393,410
Current term expires:	1996

1991-92 Committees & Subcommittees

Commerce, Science and Transportation
Communications; Science, Technology and Space (Ranking Republican); National Ocean Policy Study; Surface Transportation

Foreign Relations
European Affairs (Ranking Republican); Near Eastern and South Asian Affairs

Small Business
Export Expansion (Ranking Republican); Rural Economy and Family Farming

Special Aging

Leading Contributors

Business

Agriculture	$117,025

Crop Production & Basic Processing	$20,250	
None over $6,000		
Tobacco	**$18,000**	
None over $6,000		
Dairy	**$22,125**	
Mid-America Dairymen	$10,000	PAC
Associated Milk Producers	$7,500	PAC
Poultry & Eggs	**$8,500**	
None over $6,000		
Agricultural Services/Products	**$22,075**	
None over $6,000		
Food Processing & Sales	**$14,825**	
None over $6,000		
Forestry & Forest Products	**$6,250**	
None over $6,000		

Communications/Electronics	$132,419

Media/Entertainment	$58,319	
Walt Disney Co/Disney Channel*	$11,469	PAC/Ind
National Assn of Broadcasters	$8,000	PAC
Telephone Utilities	**$41,750**	
AT&T	$9,750	PAC
Telecom Services & Equipment	**$21,500**	
Comsat	$6,000	PAC

Contribution Totals by Sector

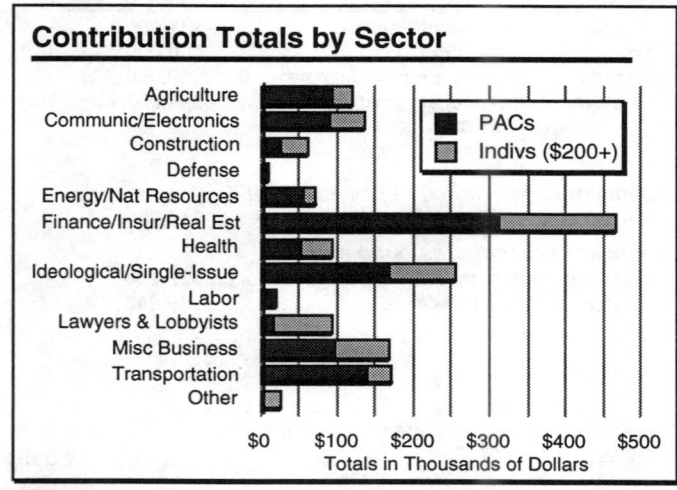

Agriculture
Communic/Electronics
Construction
Defense
Energy/Nat Resources
Finance/Insur/Real Est
Health
Ideological/Single-Issue
Labor
Lawyers & Lobbyists
Misc Business
Transportation
Other

■ PACs
▨ Indivs ($200+)

$0 $100 $200 $300 $400 $500
Totals in Thousands of Dollars

Source of Funds: 1987-1992

Source	Total	Pct
■ PACs	$1,043,647	40%
▨ Indivs $200+	$848,512	33%
☐ Indivs under $200	$230,528	9%
⊠ Other	$456,972	18%
Candidate	$0	0%
Party	$121,063	5%

Source of PAC Dollars by Sector

Source	Total	Pct
■ Business	$862,322	83%
▨ Labor	$17,500	2%
☐ Ideological/Single-Issue	$163,750	16%

In-State vs. Out-of-State Contributions*

Source	Total	Pct
☐ In-State	$111,300	13%
■ Out-of-state	$723,912	87%
No state listed	$9,300	

by large individual contributors ($200 & above)

Construction	$59,025

General Contractors	$23,425	
Associated General Contractors	$10,000	PAC
Home Builders	**$9,350**	
None over $6,000		
Special Trade Contractors	**$8,000**	
None over $6,000		
Construction Services	**$8,250**	
Leo A Daly Co	$6,000	Indiv
Building Materials & Equipment	**$10,000**	
None over $6,000		

Defense	$9,000

Defense Aerospace	$7,000
None over $6,000	

Energy & Natural Resources	$68,100

Oil & Gas	$44,400	
Coalinga Corp	$6,000	Indiv
Electric Utilities	**$14,500**	
ACRE (Action Cmte for Rural Electrification)	$10,000	PAC

Finance, Insurance & Real Estate	$462,107

Commercial Banks	$79,750	
Citicorp	$13,000	PAC/Ind
American Bankers Assn	$10,000	PAC
JP Morgan & Co	$6,000	PAC
Savings & Loans	**$13,500**	
US League of Savings Assns	$6,000	PAC
Finance/Credit Companies	**$8,000**	
None over $6,000		
Securities & Investment	**$84,434**	
Archer-Daniels-Midland Corp	$10,000	PAC
Chicago Board of Trade	$6,500	PAC
Chicago Mercantile Exchange	$6,000	PAC

Insurance	$130,498	
American Family Corp	$14,500	PAC
National Assn of Prof Insurance Agents	$12,500	PAC
National Assn of Independent Insurers	$10,999	PAC
National Assn of Life Underwriters	$10,000	PAC
American Council of Life Insurance	$9,999	PAC
Independent Insurance Agents of America	$6,000	PAC
Real Estate	**$80,900**	
National Assn of Realtors	$7,000	PAC
Drizin Real Estate Developers	$6,000	Indiv
Accountants	**$19,375**	
American Institute of CPA's	$9,625	PAC
Misc Finance	**$45,650**	
Stephens Overseas Services	$18,000	PAC
America First Resource Management	$10,000	PAC

Health · $89,900

Health Professionals	$67,050	
American Medical Assn	$10,000	PAC
Pharmaceuticals/Health Products	**$14,950**	
None over $6,000		

Lawyers & Lobbyists · $92,550

Lawyers & Lobbyists	$92,550	
Marks, Murase & White	$10,000	Indiv

Misc Business · $165,046

Business Associations	$6,074	
None over $6,000		
Food & Beverage	**$17,935**	
None over $6,000		
Beer, Wine & Liquor	**$13,000**	
National Beer Wholesalers Assn	$9,000	PAC
Retail Sales	**$24,249**	
None over $6,000		
Business Services	**$27,325**	
Dun & Bradstreet	$8,625	PAC/Ind

Spending in Last 3 Elections

	1978	1984	1990
Pressler	$449,541	$938,709	$2,136,850
Opponent	$152,006	$166,426	$1,323,770
Vote Pct	67%	74%	52%

Lodging/Tourism	$15,400	
None over $6,000		
Chemical & Related Manufacturing	**$14,500**	
None over $6,000		
Misc Manufacturing & Distributing	**$31,687**	
None over $6,000		

Transportation · $167,100

Air Transport	$38,850	
Federal Express Corp	$9,000	PAC
Automotive	**$23,500**	
Auto Dealers & Drivers for Free Trade	$7,000	PAC
Trucking	**$25,950**	
Consolidated Freightways	$6,000	PAC
Railroads	**$56,800**	
Union Pacific Corp	$11,000	PAC
Chicago & North Western Transport	$10,000	PAC
Burlington Northern	$9,000	PAC
Sea Transport	**$16,250**	
C Ventures Inc	$8,000	Indiv

Labor

Labor · $17,500

Transportation Unions	$11,000	
Air Line Pilots Assn	$10,000	PAC

Ideological/Single-Issue

Ideological/Single-Issue · $251,197

Republican/Conservative	$37,600	
National Republican Senatorial Cmte	$28,150	Indiv
Leadership PACs	**$26,000**	
Campaign America (Bob Dole)	$16,000	PAC/Ind
Senate Victory Fund (Thad Cochran)	$6,000	PAC
Foreign & Defense Policy	**$10,000**	
None over $6,000		
Pro-Israel	**$120,345**	
Citizens Organized PAC	$10,000	PAC
Desert Caucus	$10,000	PAC
Florida Congressional Cmte	$10,000	PAC
Washington PAC	$8,000	PAC
Hudson Valley PAC	$6,500	PAC
Gun Rights/Gun Control	**$13,400**	
National Rifle Assn	$13,400	PAC
Human Rights	**$39,602**	
National Albanian American PAC	$20,000	PAC

Other & Unknown

Other · $24,900

Retired	$14,850	
None over $6,000		

Unknown · $151,115

Homemakers/Non-income earners	$18,500	
No Employer Listed or Found	$64,465	
Generic Occupation/Category Unknown	$8,450	
Employer Listed/Category Unknown	$59,700	
None over $6,000		

---

* Contributions came from more than one affiliate or subsidiary.

David Pryor (D-Ark)

First elected: 1978

1987-92 Total Rcpts:	$1,513,481
1992 Year-end Cash:	$804,911
Current term expires:	1996

1991-92 Committees & Subcommittees

Agriculture, Nutrition and Forestry
Agricultural Production and Stabilization of Prices (Chairman); Domestic and Foreign Marketing and Product Promotion; Nutrition and Investigations; Rural Development and Rural Electrification

Finance
Medicare and Long Term Care; Private Retirement Plans and Oversight of the Internal Revenue Service (Chairman); Taxation

Governmental Affairs
Federal Services, Post Office and Civil Service (Chairman); Oversight of Government Management; Permanent Subcommittee on Investigations

Special Aging (Chairman)

Leading Contributors

Business

Agriculture		$227,183	
Crop Production & Basic Processing		**$87,383**	
Riceland Foods		$10,250	PAC/Ind
National Cotton Council		$8,434	PAC
Federal Compress & Warehouse Co		$5,000	Indiv
Tobacco		**$10,500**	
Philip Morris		$4,500	PAC
Dairy		**$12,000**	
Mid-America Dairymen		$5,000	PAC
Associated Milk Producers		$4,000	PAC
Poultry & Eggs		**$36,500**	
Tyson Foods		$11,500	PAC/Ind
Hudson Foods Inc		$5,000	Indiv
Livestock		**$6,850**	
None over $4,000			
Agricultural Services/Products		**$26,700**	
None over $4,000			
Food Processing & Sales		**$29,250**	
Malone & Hyde Inc		$5,000	PAC
Forestry & Forest Products		**$12,000**	
International Paper Co		$5,000	PAC
Misc Agriculture		**$6,000**	
None over $4,000			

Contribution Totals by Sector

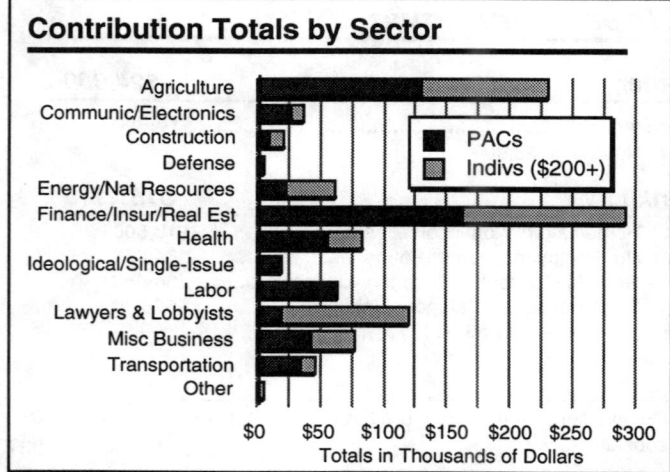

Totals in Thousands of Dollars

Source of Funds: 1987-1992

Source	Total	Pct
■ PACs	$581,201	38%
▨ Indivs $200+	$634,124	42%
□ Indivs under $200	$50,137	3%
⊠ Other	$248,019	16%
Candidate	$0	0%
Party	$0	0%

Source of PAC Dollars by Sector

Source	Total	Pct
■ Business	$495,952	87%
▨ Labor	$61,550	11%
□ Ideological/Single-Issue	$15,313	3%

In-State vs. Out-of-State Contributions*

Source	Total	Pct
□ In-State	$454,724	72%
■ Out-of-state	$179,400	28%
No state listed	$0	

* by large individual contributors ($200 & above)

Communications/Electronics		$36,250	
Printing & Publishing		**$7,000**	
None over $4,000			
Media/Entertainment		**$4,250**	
None over $4,000			
Telephone Utilities		**$20,000**	
AT&T		$4,500	PAC
Computer Equipment & Services		**$4,000**	
None over $4,000			

Construction		$20,950	
General Contractors		**$16,950**	
Associated General Contractors		$5,000	PAC

Defense		$5,200	
Defense Aerospace		**$4,000**	
None over $4,000			

Energy & Natural Resources		$61,250	
Oil & Gas		**$46,750**	
Arkla Inc		$21,250	Indiv
Murphy Oil Co		$4,500	Indiv
Mining		**$5,000**	
None over $4,000			
Electric Utilities		**$8,500**	
Entergy Corp*		$4,000	PAC/Ind

Finance, Insurance & Real Estate		$289,252	
Commercial Banks		**$51,150**	
Union National Bank/Little Rock		$6,000	Indiv
American Bankers Assn		$5,000	PAC
Savings & Loans		**$7,500**	
None over $4,000			
Credit Unions		**$4,500**	
None over $4,000			

Securities & Investment **$62,890**
    Stephens Inc .... $13,200 Indiv
    Chicago Board of Trade .... $6,000 PAC
    National Venture Capital Assn .... $6,000 PAC
    Salomon Brothers .... $6,000 PAC/Ind
    Equitable Financial Services .... $5,000 PAC
    Lazard Freres & Co .... $4,000 Indiv

Insurance **$83,762**
    Blue Cross & Blue Shield Assn* .... $6,000 PAC/Ind
    National Assn of Life Underwriters .... $5,000 PAC
    American Council of Life Insurance .... $4,362 PAC
    Independent Insurance Agents of America .... $4,000 PAC
    Rebsamen Insurance .... $4,000 Indiv
    Travelers Corp .... $4,000 PAC

Real Estate **$32,300**
    American Resort & Residential Devel Assn .... $5,500 PAC
    Century 21 Real Estate .... $5,000 PAC

Accountants **$31,350**
    American Institute of CPA's .... $10,000 PAC
    Frost & Co .... $7,000 Indiv
    Erwin & Co .... $5,000 Indiv

Misc Finance **$14,800**
    Stephens Overseas Services .... $5,000 PAC

Health $81,500

Health Professionals **$57,000**
    American Dental Assn .... $5,000 PAC
    American Soc Cataract/Refractive Surgery .... $5,000 PAC
    National Assn of Pharmacists .... $4,000 PAC

Hospitals/Nursing Homes **$13,000**
    None over $4,000

Pharmaceuticals/Health Products **$9,000**
    None over $4,000

Lawyers & Lobbyists $118,817

Lawyers & Lobbyists **$118,817**
    Mitchell Firm .... $12,000 Indiv
    Arnold, Grobmyer & Haley .... $5,000 Indiv
    Assn of Trial Lawyers of America .... $5,000 PAC
    Wilson & Assoc .... $4,000 Indiv

Misc Business   **$75,900**

Business Associations **$5,250**
    None over $4,000
Food & Beverage **$9,000**
    None over $4,000
Retail Sales **$17,750**
    Wal-Mart Stores .... $4,000 Indiv
Misc Services **$8,800**
    None over $4,000
Business Services **$6,700**
    None over $4,000
Lodging/Tourism **$4,500**
    None over $4,000
Chemical & Related Manufacturing **$4,000**
    None over $4,000
Misc Manufacturing & Distributing **$12,900**
    None over $4,000

Transportation $45,700

Air Transport **$10,500**
    Federal Express Corp .... $6,000 PAC
Automotive **$15,000**
    National Auto Dealers Assn .... $5,000 PAC
Trucking **$12,000**
    Arkansas Best Corp .... $5,500 PAC/Ind
Railroads **$5,000**
    None over $4,000

Labor

Labor   **$61,550**

Industrial Unions **$9,000**
    American Federation of Teachers .... $5,000 PAC
Transportation Unions **$8,200**
    None over $4,000
Public Sector Unions **$38,350**
    National Rural Letter Carriers Assn .... $6,000 PAC
    National Assn of Letter Carriers .... $5,000 PAC
    Natl Assn of Retired Federal Employees .... $5,000 PAC
    American Postal Workers Union .... $4,000 PAC

Ideological/Single-Issue

Ideological/Single-Issue   **$18,063**

Leadership PACs **$5,000**
    Fund for a Democratic Majority (Ted Kennedy) ... $5,000 PAC
Pro-Israel **$6,000**
    National PAC .... $5,000 PAC

Other & Unknown

Other   **$5,250**

Civil Servants/Public Officials **$4,500**
    None over $4,000

Unknown   **$96,299**

    Homemakers/Non-income earners $23,600
    No Employer Listed or Found $15,500
    Employer Listed/Category Unknown $55,199
        Wallace, Dover & Dix .... $4,000 Indiv

---

Spending in Last 3 Elections

	1978	1984	1990
Pryor	$774,824	$1,761,115	$673,941
Opponent	$19,208	$1,072,879	$0
Vote Pct	77%	57%	100%

---

* Contributions came from more than one affiliate or subsidiary.

Harry Reid (D-Nev)

1991-92 Committees & Subcommittees

Appropriations
Energy and Water Development; Interior and Related Agencies;
Labor, Health and Human Services, Education and Related Agencies;
Legislative Branch (Chairman); Military Construction

Environment and Public Works
Nuclear Regulation; Toxic Substances, Environmental Oversight,
Research and Development (Chairman); Water Resources, Transportation and Infrastructure

Select Committee on Indian Affairs

Select Committee on POW/MIA Affairs

Special Aging

Leading Contributors

Business

Agriculture		$57,583
Tobacco	$11,000	
None over $10,000		
Agricultural Services/Products	$16,800	
None over $10,000		

Communications/Electronics		$78,500
Media/Entertainment	$51,000	
National Cable Television Assn	$10,000	PAC
Telephone Utilities	$13,500	
None over $10,000		

Construction		$119,077
General Contractors	$58,327	
None over $10,000		
Home Builders	$22,000	
None over $10,000		
Special Trade Contractors	$10,000	
None over $10,000		
Building Materials & Equipment	$19,500	
None over $10,000		

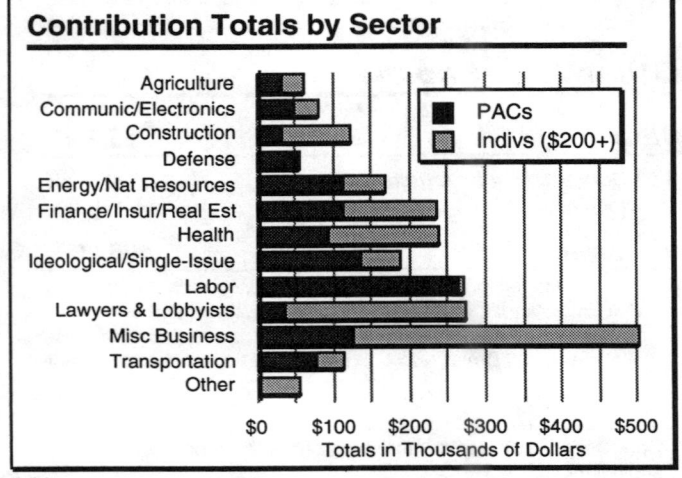
First elected: 1986

1987-92 Total Rcpts:	$3,371,146
1992 Year-end Cash:	$144,835
Current term expires:	1998

Source of Funds: 1987-1992

Source	Total	Pct
■ PACs	$1,098,689	31%
▨ Indivs $200+	$1,772,875	50%
☐ Indivs under $200	$156,090	4%
▨ Other	$511,953	14%
Candidate	$0	0%
Party	$168,461	5%

Source of PAC Dollars by Sector

Source	Total	Pct
■ Business	$695,975	64%
▨ Labor	$262,314	24%
☐ Ideological/Single-Issue ..	$133,771	12%

In-State vs. Out-of-State Contributions*

Source	Total	Pct
☐ In-State	$1,193,897	67%
■ Out-of-state	$575,478	33%
No state listed	$3,500	

* by large individual contributors ($200 & above)

Defense		$52,653
Defense Aerospace	$30,078	
None over $10,000		
Defense Electronics	$14,575	
None over $10,000		

Energy & Natural Resources		$165,686
Oil & Gas	$47,086	
Bass Brothers Enterprises	$10,000	PAC
Mining	$61,000	
None over $10,000		
Electric Utilities	$21,100	
Sierra Pacific Resources	$11,000	PAC
Waste Management	$29,500	
Silver State Disposal Service	$12,000	Indiv

Finance, Insurance & Real Estate		$232,562
Commercial Banks	$36,000	
American Bankers Assn	$10,000	PAC
Valley Bank of Nevada	$10,000	Indiv
Securities & Investment	$18,862	
None over $10,000		
Insurance	$44,000	
National Assn of Life Underwriters	$10,000	PAC
Real Estate	$94,200	
National Assn of Realtors	$12,000	PAC
Summa Corp	$12,000	PAC/Ind
Del Webb Corp	$10,500	PAC/Ind
Accountants	$12,250	
None over $10,000		
Misc Finance	$16,250	
None over $10,000		

Health $234,622

Health Professionals $185,272
    American Chiropractic Assn .... $10,000   PAC

Hospitals/Nursing Homes $25,350
    None over $10,000

Pharmaceuticals/Health Products $12,000
    None over $10,000

Lawyers & Lobbyists $271,153

Lawyers & Lobbyists $271,153
    Lionel, Sawyer & Collins .... $16,216   Indiv
    Assn of Trial Lawyers of America .... $10,000   PAC

Misc Business $498,896

Food & Beverage $16,386
    None over $10,000

Beer, Wine & Liquor $18,000
    None over $10,000

Retail Sales $25,750
    None over $10,000

Business Services $68,600
    Outdoor Advertising Assn of America .... $11,500   PAC/Ind

Casinos/Gambling $259,177
    Circus Circus Enterprises.................................. $23,500   PAC/Ind
    Palace Station Hotel & Casino .... $14,500   Indiv
    Lady Luck Casino & Hotel .... $14,000   Indiv
    Union Plaza .... $13,800   PAC
    Showboat Inc .... $13,000   PAC
    Harrah's .... $12,500   PAC/Ind
    Bally Manufacturing Corp* .... $11,468   PAC
    Caesar's World .... $10,800   PAC/Ind
    Golden Nugget Hotel .... $10,000   Indiv
    Mirage Hotel & Casino .... $10,000   Indiv

Lodging/Tourism $48,633
    None over $10,000

Chemical & Related Manufacturing $11,250
    None over $10,000

Misc Manufacturing & Distributing $26,600
    None over $10,000

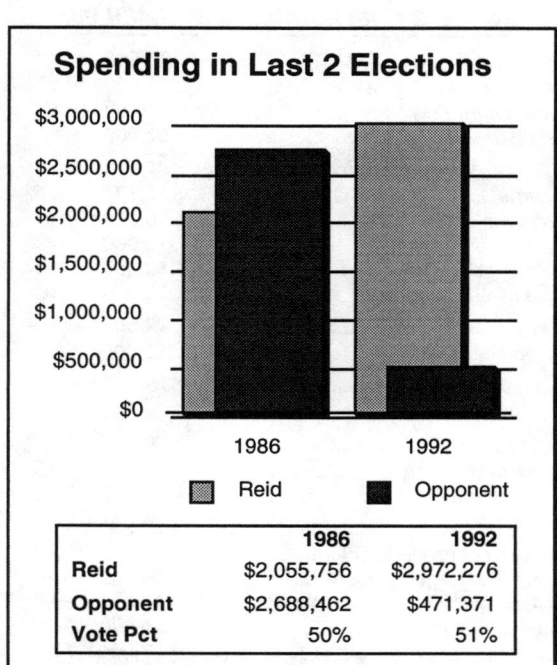

Spending in Last 2 Elections

	1986	1992
Reid	$2,055,756	$2,972,276
Opponent	$2,688,462	$471,371
Vote Pct	50%	51%

Transportation $109,944

Air Transport $25,726
    None over $10,000

Automotive $35,000
    None over $10,000

Trucking $21,018
    None over $10,000

Misc Transport $15,000
    None over $10,000

Labor

Labor $266,314

Building Trade Unions $54,454
    Carpenters & Joiners Union .... $10,000   PAC
    Laborers Union* .... $10,000   PAC

Industrial Unions $43,750
    Intl Brotherhood of Electrical Workers .... $10,000   PAC
    Machinists/Aerospace Workers Union .... $10,000   PAC

Transportation Unions $67,000
    Air Line Pilots Assn .... $10,000   PAC
    Marine Engineers Union .... $10,000   PAC
    Teamsters Union .... $10,000   PAC

Public Sector Unions $65,549
    American Federation of Teachers...................... $10,000   PAC
    National Assn of Letter Carriers .... $10,000   PAC

Misc Unions $35,561
    Food & Commercial Workers Union .... $10,000   PAC

Ideological/Single-Issue

Ideological/Single-Issue $185,138

Leadership PACs $24,100
    Cmte for a Demo Consensus (Alan Cranston) .. $10,000   PAC

Pro-Israel $104,574
    Desert Caucus .... $10,000   PAC

Gun Rights/Gun Control $11,450
    None over $10,000

Human Rights $11,500
    None over $10,000

Misc Issues $19,150
    National Cmte to Preserve Social Security .... $10,000   PAC

Other & Unknown

Other $51,850

Retired $32,300
    None over $10,000

Unknown $377,276

    Homemakers/Non-income earners $112,952
    No Employer Listed or Found $44,800
    Employer Listed/Category Unknown................ $215,774
      None over $10,000

Independent expenditures supporting Reid
    Auto Dealers & Drivers for Free Trade $60,000

---

* Contributions came from more than one affiliate or
  subsidiary.

Donald W. Riegle Jr. (D-Mich)

First elected: 1976

1987-92 Total Rcpts:	$3,776,831
1992 Year-end Cash:	$544,242
Current term expires:	1994

1991-92 Committees & Subcommittees

Banking, Housing and Urban Affairs (Chairman)

Budget

Finance
Health for Families and the Uninsured (Chairman); Deficits, Debt Management and International Debt; International Trade

Leading Contributors

NOTE: The bulk of Riegle's large individual contributions do not appear in the listings below. His last election was in 1988, and this book lists individual contributions only from 1989-1992.

Business

Agriculture $57,643

Crop Production & Basic Processing $13,443
  None over $6,000
Tobacco $8,500
  None over $6,000
Dairy $9,500
  Associated Milk Producers ....$6,000   PAC
Food Processing & Sales $10,500
  None over $6,000
Forestry & Forest Products $6,000
  None over $6,000

Communications/Electronics $56,170

Media/Entertainment $16,070
  None over $6,000
Telephone Utilities $30,850
  AT&T ....$9,000   PAC
  Michigan Bell Telephone ....$6,250   PAC

Construction $27,500

Home Builders $19,500
  National Assn of Home Builders ....$8,000   PAC
Building Materials & Equipment $6,000
  None over $6,000

Contribution Totals by Sector

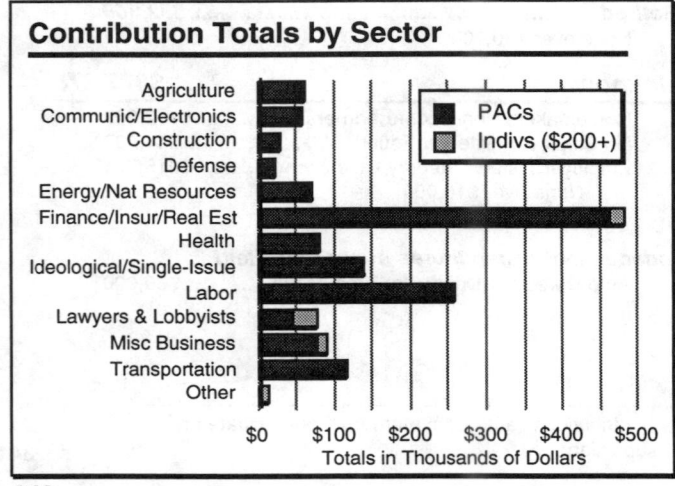

Totals in Thousands of Dollars

- Agriculture
- Communic/Electronics
- Construction
- Defense
- Energy/Nat Resources
- Finance/Insur/Real Est
- Health
- Ideological/Single-Issue
- Labor
- Lawyers & Lobbyists
- Misc Business
- Transportation
- Other

Legend: ■ PACs ▨ Indivs ($200+)

$0 $100 $200 $300 $400 $500

Source of Funds: 1987-1992

Source	Total	Pct
■ PACs	$1,389,410	37%
■ Indivs $200+	$1,282,520	34%
□ Indivs under $200	$511,794	14%
▨ Other	$600,157	16%
Candidate	$0	0%
Party	$7,050	0%

Source of PAC Dollars by Sector

Source	Total	Pct
■ Business	$989,811	72%
▨ Labor	$255,955	19%
□ Ideological/Single-Issue	$134,346	10%

In-State vs. Out-of-State Contributions*

Source	Total	Pct
□ In-State	$322,920	25%
■ Out-of-state	$958,600	75%
No state listed	$1,000	

* by large individual contributors ($200 & above)

Defense $20,000

Defense Aerospace $14,800
  Rockwell International ....$8,600   PAC

Energy & Natural Resources $67,460

Oil & Gas $22,775
  Coastal Corp ....$6,750   PAC
Electric Utilities $33,322
  Consumers Power Co ....$8,000   PAC
  Detroit Edison ....$6,500   PAC

Finance, Insurance & Real Estate $480,035

Commercial Banks $103,825
  JP Morgan & Co ....$10,000   PAC
  American Bankers Assn* ....$9,100   PAC
  Bankers Trust ....$7,000   PAC
  Citicorp ....$7,000   PAC
Savings & Loans $59,175
  Columbia S&L (Beverly Hills) ....$10,000   PAC
  Home Savings of America ....$10,000   PAC
  Mercury Savings & Loan ....$9,500   PAC
  US League of Savings Assns* ....$8,000   PAC
Credit Unions $9,500
  Credit Union National Assn* ....$8,500   PAC
Finance/Credit Companies $15,621
  None over $6,000
Securities & Investment $88,949
  Chicago Board of Trade ....$6,500   PAC
  National Venture Capital Assn ....$6,000   PAC
Insurance $117,950
  National Assn of Life Underwriters ....$10,000   PAC
  Casualty & Surety Agents Assn ....$9,000   PAC
  National Assn of Prof Insurance Agents ....$9,000   PAC
  TransAmerica Corp* ....$9,000   PAC
  Independent Insurance Agents of America ....$7,000   PAC
  Equitable Financial Services ....$6,000   PAC

Real Estate	$46,765	
Mortgage Bankers Assn of America	$10,000	PAC
National Assn of Realtors	$8,250	PAC
Century 21 Real Estate/Met Life*	$7,000	PAC
Accountants	**$23,000**	
American Institute of CPA's	$8,000	PAC
Misc Finance	**$15,250**	
None over $6,000		

Health $79,500

Health Professionals	$53,150	
American Podiatry Assn	$7,500	PAC
American Academy of Ophthalmology	$6,000	PAC
American Soc Cataract/Refractive Surgery	$6,000	PAC
Assn for the Advancement of Psychology	$6,000	PAC
Hospitals/Nursing Homes	**$14,500**	
None over $6,000		
Pharmaceuticals/Health Products	**$11,850**	
None over $6,000		

Lawyers & Lobbyists $75,292

Lawyers & Lobbyists	$75,292	
None over $6,000		

Misc Business $86,371

Beer, Wine & Liquor	$30,371	
National Beer Wholesalers Assn	$8,000	PAC
Joseph E Seagram & Sons	$6,000	PAC
Retail Sales	**$9,500**	
None over $6,000		
Business Services	**$8,000**	
None over $6,000		
Misc Manufacturing & Distributing	**$23,000**	
Triangle Industries	$10,000	PAC

Transportation $113,477

Air Transport	$44,270	
Federal Express Corp	$7,000	PAC
Automotive	**$42,706**	
Chrysler Corp	$15,956	PAC/Ind
General Motors	$7,250	PAC

Trucking	$14,601	
American Trucking Assns	$6,601	PAC
Railroads	**$9,900**	
None over $6,000		

Labor

Labor	$255,955	
Building Trade Unions	**$41,700**	
Laborers' Political League	$13,000	PAC
Carpenters & Joiners Union	$10,000	PAC
Ironworkers Union	$6,000	PAC
Industrial Unions	**$84,200**	
Communications Workers of America	$11,000	PAC
Machinists/Aerospace Workers Union	$10,000	PAC
United Steelworkers	$10,000	PAC
National Education Assn	$9,700	PAC
Intl Brotherhood of Electrical Workers	$7,500	PAC
Electronic Machine Furniture Workers	$6,000	PAC
Transportation Unions	**$58,000**	
Teamsters Union	$12,500	PAC
Air Line Pilots Assn	$10,500	PAC
United Transportation Union	$6,000	PAC
Public Sector Unions	**$42,700**	
American Fedn of St/Cnty/Munic Employees	$11,000	PAC
Natl Assn of Retired Federal Employees	$10,000	PAC
National Assn of Letter Carriers	$6,000	PAC
Misc Unions	**$29,355**	
AFL-CIO	$10,000	PAC
Food & Commercial Workers Union	$9,155	PAC

Ideological/Single-Issue

Ideological/Single-Issue	$135,346	
Democratic/Liberal	**$21,090**	
Democrats for the 80's	$10,000	PAC
National Cmte for an Effective Congress	$9,990	PAC
Leadership PACs	**$25,500**	
Senate Majority Fund (Daniel Inouye)	$10,000	PAC
Fund for a Democratic Majority (Ted Kennedy)	$7,500	PAC
Foreign & Defense Policy	**$10,656**	
None over $6,000		
Pro-Israel	**$52,750**	
Citizens Organized PAC	$10,000	PAC
Human Rights	**$11,250**	
KidsPAC	$6,000	PAC
Misc Issues	**$12,600**	
National Cmte to Preserve Social Security	$11,000	PAC

Other & Unknown

Other	$12,000
None over $6,000	

Unknown	$10,575
Employer Listed/Category Unknown	$10,575
None over $6,000	

Independent expenditures supporting Riegle
National Cmte to Preserve Social Security $37,790

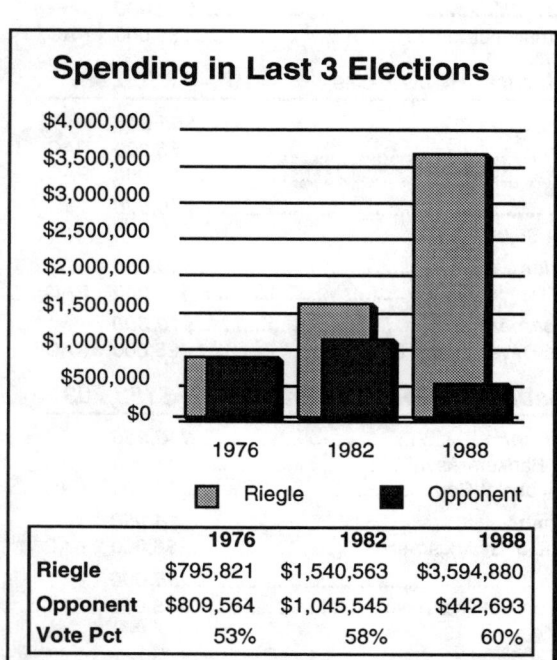

Spending in Last 3 Elections

	1976	1982	1988
Riegle	$795,821	$1,540,563	$3,594,880
Opponent	$809,564	$1,045,545	$442,693
Vote Pct	53%	58%	60%

■ Riegle   ■ Opponent

---

* Contributions came from more than one affiliate or subsidiary.

343

Charles S. Robb (D-Va)

First elected: 1988

1987-92 Total Rcpts:	$3,329,658
1992 Year-end Cash:	$-249
Current term expires:	1994

1991-92 Committees & Subcommittees

Commerce, Science and Transportation
Consumer; National Ocean Policy Study; Science, Technology and Space; Surface Transportation

Foreign Relations
East Asian and Pacific Affairs; Near Eastern and South Asian Affairs; Western Hemisphere and Peace Corps Affairs

Select Committee on POW/MIA Affairs

Leading Contributors

NOTE: The bulk of Robb's large individual contributions do not appear in the listings below. His last election was in 1988, and this book lists individual contributions only from 1989-1992.

Business

Agriculture $78,150

Crop Production & Basic Processing $11,050
    None over $5,000
Tobacco $17,000
    Philip Morris .... $5,000   PAC
Dairy $8,100
    Associated Milk Producers .... $5,000   PAC
Agricultural Services/Products $6,500
    None over $5,000
Food Processing & Sales $18,500
    Food Marketing Institute .... $5,000   PAC
Forestry & Forest Products $15,000
    Westvaco Corp .... $5,000   PAC

Communications/Electronics $64,050

Media/Entertainment $17,500
    MCA Inc .... $5,000   PAC
    National Cable Television Assn .... $5,000   PAC
Telephone Utilities $32,250
    AT&T .... $10,000   PAC
Computer Equipment & Services $8,250
    None over $5,000

Source of Funds: 1987-1992

Source	Total	Pct
PACs	$960,357	27%
Indivs $200+	$1,839,667	52%
Indivs under $200	$400,414	11%
Other	$307,595	9%
Candidate	$16,065	0%
Party	$178,375	5%

Source of PAC Dollars by Sector

Source	Total	Pct
Business	$737,357	78%
Labor	$134,750	14%
Ideological/Single-Issue	$76,000	8%

In-State vs. Out-of-State Contributions*

Source	Total	Pct
In-State	$1,231,245	67%
Out-of-state	$607,922	33%
No state listed	$0	

by large individual contributors ($200 & above)

Construction $35,850

General Contractors $11,500
    Associated General Contractors .... $10,000   PAC
Home Builders $13,500
    National Assn of Home Builders .... $10,000   PAC

Defense $63,500

Defense Aerospace $36,500
    Textron Inc .... $10,000   PAC
Defense Electronics $17,000
    TRW Inc .... $5,000   PAC
Misc Defense $10,000
    BDM International .... $5,000   PAC

Energy & Natural Resources $106,967

Oil & Gas $55,847
    Amoco Corp .... $5,000   PAC
    Mobil Oil .... $5,000   PAC
Mining $10,570
    None over $5,000
Electric Utilities $26,050
    Dominion Resources Inc .... $10,000   PAC
Waste Management $10,500
    Chambers Development Co .... $5,000   PAC

Finance, Insurance & Real Estate $183,703

Commercial Banks $40,250
    American Bankers Assn* .... $11,000   PAC
    Crestar Financial Corp .... $5,000   PAC
Savings & Loans $6,950
    US League of Savings Assns .... $6,000   PAC
Credit Unions $5,000
    Credit Union National Assn .... $5,000   PAC

Contribution Totals by Sector

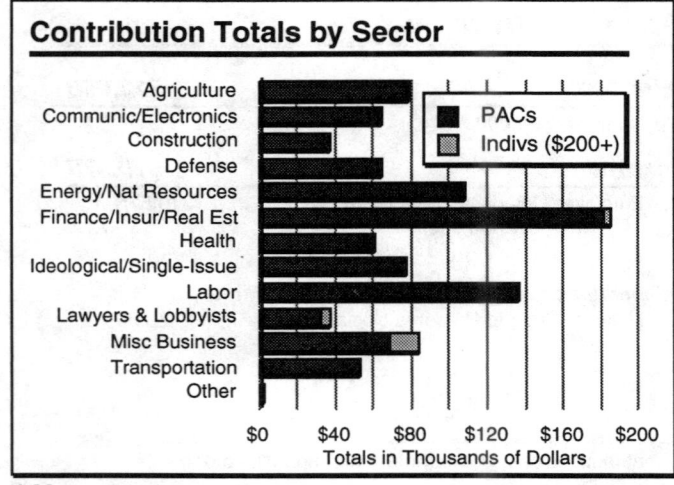

- Agriculture
- Communic/Electronics
- Construction
- Defense
- Energy/Nat Resources
- Finance/Insur/Real Est
- Health
- Ideological/Single-Issue
- Labor
- Lawyers & Lobbyists
- Misc Business
- Transportation
- Other

Legend: ■ PACs   ▨ Indivs ($200+)

$0 $40 $80 $120 $160 $200
Totals in Thousands of Dollars

Securities & Investment	$37,500	
Chicago Board of Trade	$5,000	PAC
Chicago Mercantile Exchange	$5,000	PAC
Merrill Lynch	$5,000	PAC
Shearson Lehman Brothers	$5,000	PAC

Insurance	$56,753	
Blue Cross & Blue Shield Assn*	$10,500	PAC
National Assn of Life Underwriters	$10,000	PAC
Independent Insurance Agents of America	$5,753	PAC
American Family Corp	$5,000	PAC

Real Estate	$25,250	
National Assn of Realtors	$11,000	PAC

Accountants	$9,000	
American Institute of CPA's	$5,000	PAC

Health — $60,132

Health Professionals	$39,584	
American Medical Assn	$9,000	PAC
American Academy of Ophthalmology	$7,500	PAC
American Dental Assn	$5,000	PAC
American Optometric Assn	$5,000	PAC

Hospitals/Nursing Homes	$5,048	
None over $5,000		

Pharmaceuticals/Health Products	$15,000	
None over $5,000		

Lawyers & Lobbyists — $35,950

Lawyers & Lobbyists	$35,950	
Assn of Trial Lawyers of America	$5,000	PAC

Misc Business — $82,705

Food & Beverage	$27,050	
Chesapeake Bay Seafood	$10,000	Indiv

Beer, Wine & Liquor	$8,500	
None over $5,000		

Retail Sales	$10,750	
None over $5,000		

Chemical & Related Manufacturing	$7,500	
None over $5,000		

Misc Manufacturing & Distributing	$16,555	
None over $5,000		

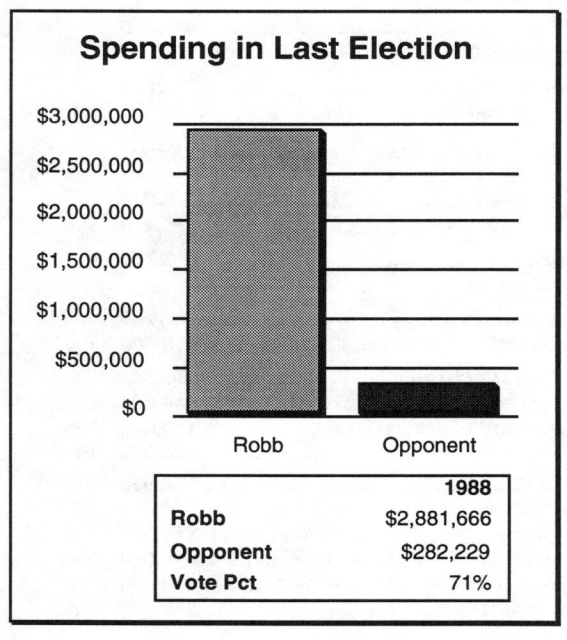

Spending in Last Election

	1988
Robb	$2,881,666
Opponent	$282,229
Vote Pct	71%

Transportation	$52,400	
Air Transport	**$19,500**	
Federal Express Corp	$9,000	PAC
Automotive	**$11,800**	
National Auto Dealers Assn	$5,000	PAC
Trucking	**$7,500**	
None over $5,000		
Railroads	**$9,600**	
Union Pacific Corp	$5,000	PAC

Labor

Labor	$134,750	
Building Trade Unions	**$22,750**	
Carpenters & Joiners Union	$8,500	PAC
Laborers' Political League	$7,000	PAC
Industrial Unions	**$21,700**	
National Education Assn	$11,000	PAC
Intl Brotherhood of Electrical Workers	$7,500	PAC
Transportation Unions	**$52,050**	
Marine Engineers Union*	$15,000	PAC
Seafarers International Union	$12,500	PAC
Teamsters Union*	$5,250	PAC
Air Line Pilots Assn	$5,000	PAC
United Transportation Union	$5,000	PAC
Public Sector Unions	**$24,250**	
Natl Assn of Retired Federal Employees	$7,000	PAC
American Fedn of St/Cnty/Munic Employees	$5,000	PAC
National Assn of Letter Carriers	$5,000	PAC
Misc Unions	**$14,000**	
Food & Commercial Workers Union	$5,000	PAC

Ideological/Single-Issue

Ideological/Single-Issue	$76,000	
Democratic/Liberal	**$6,000**	
Democrats for the 80's	$6,000	PAC
Leadership PACs	**$22,500**	
Cmte for a Demo Consensus (Alan Cranston)	$10,000	PAC
Pelican PAC (Bennett Johnston)	$5,000	PAC
Senate Majority Fund (Daniel Inouye)	$5,000	PAC
Foreign & Defense Policy	**$5,000**	
Free Cuba PAC	$5,000	PAC
Pro-Israel	**$33,000**	
National PAC	$10,000	PAC
Citizens Organized PAC	$5,000	PAC
Washington PAC	$5,000	PAC
Misc Issues	**$5,500**	
National Cmte to Preserve Social Security	$5,000	PAC

Other & Unknown

Unknown	$6,490	
None over $5,000		

---

* Contributions came from more than one affiliate or subsidiary.

John D. Rockefeller IV (D-WVa)

First elected: 1984

1987-92 Total Rcpts:	$3,858,133
1992 Year-end Cash:	$530,633
Current term expires:	1996

1991-92 Committees & Subcommittees

Commerce, Science and Transportation
Foreign Commerce and Tourism (Chairman); Science, Technology and Space; Surface Transportation

Finance
Health for Families and the Uninsured; International Trade; Medicare and Long Term Care (Chairman)

Veterans' Affairs

Leading Contributors

Business

Agriculture	$107,261

Crop Production & Basic Processing $24,050
None over $10,000

Tobacco $11,811
None over $10,000

Agricultural Services/Products $16,500
None over $10,000

Food Processing & Sales $25,500
Pepsico Inc .... $10,000 PAC/Ind

Forestry & Forest Products $10,500
None over $10,000

Communications/Electronics	$173,723

Printing & Publishing $16,450
None over $10,000

Media/Entertainment $91,307
Time Warner* .... $32,000 PAC/Ind
Walt Disney Co* .... $10,700 PAC/Ind
National Cable Television Assn .... $10,000 PAC

Telephone Utilities $31,716
None over $10,000

Telecom Services & Equipment $26,000
None over $10,000

Construction	$80,350

General Contractors $33,750
None over $10,000

Source of Funds: 1987-1992

Source	Total	Pct
■ PACs	$1,445,478	37%
▨ Indivs $200+	$1,840,495	47%
☐ Indivs under $200	$312,655	8%
⊠ Other	$350,617	9%
Candidate	$0	0%
Party	$91,112	2%

Source of PAC Dollars by Sector

Source	Total	Pct
■ Business	$1,140,740	76%
▨ Labor	$240,500	16%
☐ Ideological/Single-Issue	$112,013	8%

In-State vs. Out-of-State Contributions*

Source	Total	Pct
☐ In-State	$606,386	33%
■ Out-of-state	$1,232,109	67%
No state listed	$2,000	

* by large individual contributors ($200 & above)

Home Builders $17,400
National Assn of Home Builders .... $10,000 PAC

Building Materials & Equipment $14,650
None over $10,000

Defense	$11,100

Defense Aerospace $10,100
None over $10,000

Energy & Natural Resources	$230,924

Oil & Gas $119,600
USX Corp* .... $13,000 PAC/Ind

Mining $59,900
None over $10,000

Electric Utilities $27,250
None over $10,000

Waste Management $12,174
None over $10,000

Finance, Insurance & Real Estate	$640,608

Commercial Banks $78,558
American Bankers Assn .... $10,400 PAC

Savings & Loans $12,750
None over $10,000

Credit Unions $10,000
Credit Union National Assn .... $10,000 PAC

Securities & Investment $150,750
Goldman, Sachs & Co .... $14,000 PAC/Ind
Chicago Mercantile Exchange .... $10,000 PAC
National Venture Capital Assn .... $10,000 PAC

Insurance $157,650
Equitable Life* .... $11,000 PAC/Ind
Independent Insurance Agents of America .... $11,000 PAC
American Council of Life Insurance .... $10,000 PAC
National Assn of Prof Insurance Agents .... $10,000 PAC
Prudential Insurance .... $10,000 PAC

Contribution Totals by Sector

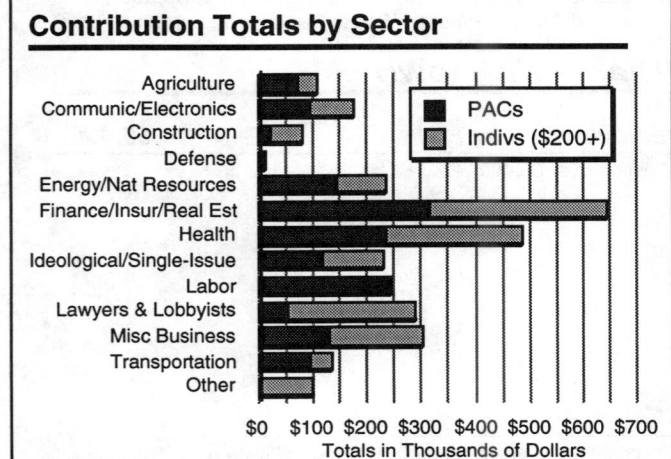

Agriculture
Communic/Electronics
Construction
Defense
Energy/Nat Resources
Finance/Insur/Real Est
Health
Ideological/Single-Issue
Labor
Lawyers & Lobbyists
Misc Business
Transportation
Other

■ PACs
▨ Indivs ($200+)

$0 $100 $200 $300 $400 $500 $600 $700
Totals in Thousands of Dollars

Real Estate	....	$169,675	
Cafaro Co	....	$10,250	Indiv
National Assn of Realtors	....	$10,000	PAC

Accountants	....	**$44,575**	
Arthur Andersen & Co	....	$14,475	PAC/Ind
American Institute of CPA's	....	$10,000	PAC

| **Misc Finance** | .... | **$13,400** | |
| None over $10,000 | | | |

Health — $482,327

Health Professionals	....	**$278,752**	
American Academy of Ophthalmology	....	$10,000	PAC
American Soc Cataract/Refractive Surgery	....	$10,000	PAC

Hospitals/Nursing Homes	....	**$106,375**	
Humana Inc	....	$13,250	PAC/Ind
American Health Care Assn	....	$10,000	PAC
American Hospital Assn	....	$10,000	PAC
Federation of American Health Systems	....	$10,000	PAC

| **Health Services** | .... | **$27,550** | |
| American Ambulance & Oxygen Service | .... | $16,000 | Indiv |

| **Pharmaceuticals/Health Products** | .... | **$57,250** | |
| National Intergroup Inc | .... | $11,000 | PAC/Ind |

Lawyers & Lobbyists — $286,720

| **Lawyers & Lobbyists** | .... | **$286,720** | |
| None over $10,000 | | | |

Misc Business — $300,639

| **Food & Beverage** | .... | **$12,450** | |
| None over $10,000 | | | |

| **Beer, Wine & Liquor** | .... | **$32,250** | |
| None over $10,000 | | | |

| **Retail Sales** | .... | **$38,350** | |
| None over $10,000 | | | |

| **Business Services** | .... | **$40,650** | |
| None over $10,000 | | | |

| **Lodging/Tourism** | .... | **$21,049** | |
| None over $10,000 | | | |

| **Steel Production** | .... | **$46,450** | |
| None over $10,000 | | | |

| **Misc Manufacturing & Distributing** | .... | **$48,100** | |
| None over $10,000 | | | |

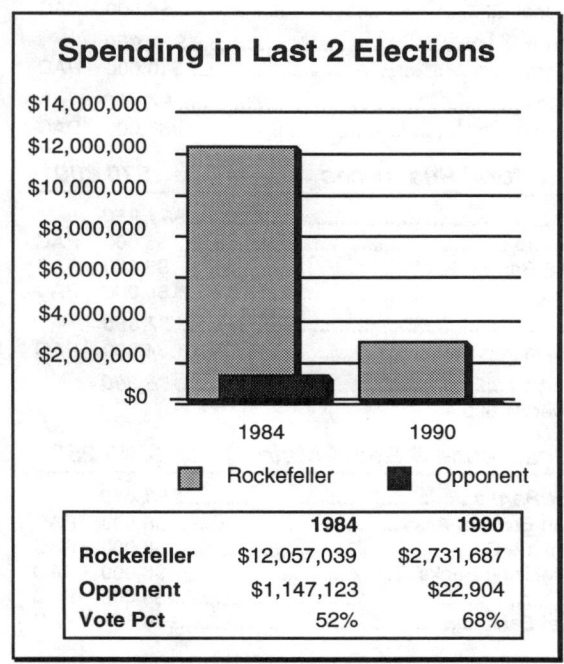

Spending in Last 2 Elections

	1984	1990
Rockefeller	$12,057,039	$2,731,687
Opponent	$1,147,123	$22,904
Vote Pct	52%	68%

| **Transportation** | | **$131,950** |

| **Air Transport** | .... | **$41,650** | |
| None over $10,000 | | | |

| **Automotive** | .... | **$52,600** | |
| None over $10,000 | | | |

| **Trucking** | .... | **$16,950** | |
| American Trucking Assns | .... | $10,000 | PAC |

| **Railroads** | .... | **$12,500** | |
| None over $10,000 | | | |

Labor

| **Labor** | | **$241,500** |

Building Trade Unions	....	**$52,500**	
Laborers Union*	....	$10,250	PAC/Ind
Carpenters & Joiners Union	....	$10,000	PAC
Operating Engineers Union	....	$10,000	PAC
Sheet Metal Workers Union	....	$10,000	PAC

Industrial Unions	....	**$69,500**	
American Federation of Teachers	....	$10,000	PAC
Intl Brotherhood of Electrical Workers	....	$10,000	PAC

Transportation Unions	....	**$63,000**	
Air Line Pilots Assn	....	$10,000	PAC
Marine Engineers Dist 2 Maritime Officers	....	$10,000	PAC
Seafarers International Union	....	$10,000	PAC
Teamsters Union	....	$10,000	PAC

| **Public Sector Unions** | .... | **$41,250** | |
| National Assn of Letter Carriers | .... | $10,000 | PAC |

| **Misc Unions** | .... | **$15,250** | |
| None over $10,000 | | | |

Ideological/Single-Issue

| **Ideological/Single-Issue** | | **$226,613** |

| **Democratic/Liberal** | .... | **$30,750** | |
| None over $10,000 | | | |

| **Leadership PACs** | .... | **$12,250** | |
| None over $10,000 | | | |

| **Pro-Israel** | .... | **$133,550** | |
| Desert Caucus | .... | $10,000 | PAC |

| **Human Rights** | .... | **$21,500** | |
| KidsPAC | .... | $10,000 | PAC |

| **Misc Issues** | .... | **$12,250** | |
| None over $10,000 | | | |

Other & Unknown

| **Other** | | **$96,732** |

| **Retired** | .... | **$47,380** | |
| None over $10,000 | | | |

| **Other** | .... | **$26,050** | |
| None over $10,000 | | | |

| **Unknown** | | **$306,101** |

Homemakers/Non-income earners	....	$72,854
No Employer Listed or Found	....	$70,750
Employer Listed/Category Unknown	....	$157,397
None over $10,000		

Independent expenditures supporting Rockefeller
American Citizens for Political Action $64,769

---

* Contributions came from more than one affiliate or subsidiary.

William V. Roth Jr. (R-Del)

First elected: 1970

1987-92 Total Rcpts:	$1,945,816
1992 Year-end Cash:	$69,658
Current term expires:	1994

1991-92 Committees & Subcommittees

Banking, Housing and Urban Affairs
Housing and Urban Affairs; Securities

Finance
Health for Families and the Uninsured; International Trade; Taxation (Ranking Republican)

Governmental Affairs (Ranking Republican)
Permanent Subcommittee on Investigations (Ranking Republican)

Joint Economic Committee

Leading Contributors

NOTE: The bulk of Roth's large individual contributions do not appear in the listings below. His last election was in 1988, and this book lists individual contributions only from 1989-1992.

Business

Agriculture $39,766

Crop Production & Basic Processing *$4,000*
   None over $4,000

Agricultural Services/Products *$4,500*
   None over $4,000

Food Processing & Sales *$6,000*
   None over $4,000

Forestry & Forest Products *$15,600*
   Westvaco Corp .... $6,000   PAC
   International Paper Co .... $5,000   PAC

Communications/Electronics $43,100

Media/Entertainment *$4,000*
   None over $4,000

Telephone Utilities *$26,400*
   AT&T .... $8,400   PAC
   Bell Atlantic .... $7,000   PAC

Electronics Mfg & Services *$4,750*
   None over $4,000

Contribution Totals by Sector

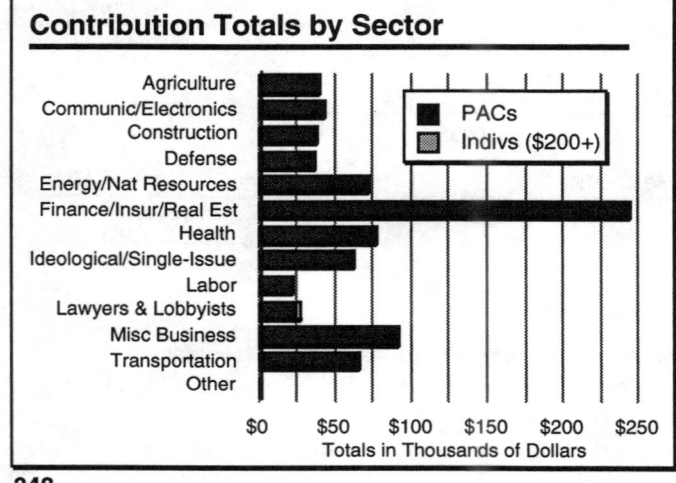

Totals in Thousands of Dollars

Source of Funds: 1987-1992

Source	Total	Pct
■ PACs	$809,256	39%
▨ Indivs $200+	$647,235	32%
□ Indivs under $200	$395,176	19%
⊠ Other	$198,180	10%
Candidate	$0	0%
Party	$104,031	5%

Source of PAC Dollars by Sector

Source	Total	Pct
■ Business	$724,611	90%
▨ Labor	$22,000	3%
□ Ideological/Single-Issue	$61,725	8%

In-State vs. Out-of-State Contributions*

Source	Total	Pct
□ In-State	$434,863	68%
■ Out-of-state	$208,372	32%
No state listed	$4,000	

***** by large individual contributors ($200 & above)**

Construction $37,750

General Contractors *$21,250*
   Associated General Contractors ...... $10,000   PAC
   Associated Builders & Contractors ... $5,000   PAC
   National Utility Contractors Assn ..... $4,500   PAC

Special Trade Contractors *$8,500*
   National Electrical Contractors Assn . $5,000   PAC

Building Materials & Equipment *$4,500*
   None over $4,000

Defense $35,350

Defense Aerospace *$14,000*
   Allied-Signal .... $4,500   PAC

Defense Electronics *$13,950*
   Harris Corp .... $10,000   PAC

Misc Defense *$7,400*
   Tenneco Inc .... $5,000   PAC

Energy & Natural Resources $70,800

Oil & Gas *$51,950*
   Amoco Corp .... $5,000   PAC
   Columbia Gas System* .... $5,000   PAC
   Texaco .... $5,000   PAC

Mining *$7,500*
   Cyprus Minerals Co .... $4,000   PAC

Electric Utilities *$6,350*
   None over $4,000

Finance, Insurance & Real Estate $243,250

Commercial Banks *$53,450*
   American Bankers Assn .... $8,500   PAC
   JP Morgan & Co .... $8,000   PAC
   Marine Midland Banks .... $6,000   PAC
   Citicorp .... $5,000   PAC
   Chemical Bank .... $4,500   PAC

| Savings & Loans | $10,000 | |
| US League of Savings Assns | $7,500 | PAC |

| Finance/Credit Companies | $9,250 | |
| Beneficial Management Corp | $4,000 | PAC |

Securities & Investment	$59,750	
National Venture Capital Assn	$9,000	PAC
Merrill Lynch	$6,000	PAC
Shearson Lehman Brothers	$5,500	PAC
EF Hutton	$5,000	PAC
Salomon Brothers	$5,000	PAC
Securities Industry Assn	$4,250	PAC

Insurance	$83,800	
National Assn of Independent Insurers	$9,000	PAC
American International Group	$6,000	PAC
American Council of Life Insurance	$5,000	PAC
Independent Insurance Agents of America	$5,000	PAC
National Assn of Life Underwriters	$5,000	PAC
Torchmark Corp	$5,000	PAC
Aetna Life & Casualty	$4,000	PAC
Cigna Corp	$4,000	PAC

| Real Estate | $5,500 | |
| None over $4,000 | | |

| Accountants | $17,000 | |
| American Institute of CPA's | $10,000 | PAC |

Health — $76,000

Health Professionals	$38,500	
American Academy of Ophthalmology	$10,000	PAC
American Medical Assn	$10,000	PAC
American Optometric Assn	$4,000	PAC

| Hospitals/Nursing Homes | $8,250 | |
| None over $4,000 | | |

Pharmaceuticals/Health Products	$29,250	
Birstol-Myers Squibb	$4,000	PAC
ICI Americas Inc	$4,000	PAC

Lawyers & Lobbyists — $25,625

| Lawyers & Lobbyists | $25,625 | |
| Assn of Trial Lawyers of America | $9,500 | PAC |

| Misc Business | $91,320 | |

Food & Beverage	$21,500	
National Restaurant Assn	$7,000	PAC
S&A Restaurant Corp	$6,000	PAC

| Beer, Wine & Liquor | $10,210 | |
| National Beer Wholesalers Assn | $4,000 | PAC |

| Retail Sales | $10,707 | |
| None over $4,000 | | |

| Business Services | $4,500 | |
| None over $4,000 | | |

| Misc Business | $4,000 | |
| None over $4,000 | | |

| Chemical & Related Manufacturing | $11,500 | |
| FMC Corp | $4,000 | PAC |

| Misc Manufacturing & Distributing | $21,500 | |
| None over $4,000 | | |

Transportation — $64,650

| Air Transport | $15,400 | |
| United Parcel Service | $6,000 | PAC |

Automotive	$31,750	
National Auto Dealers Assn	$10,000	PAC
Auto Dealers & Drivers for Free Trade	$8,000	PAC
Chrysler Corp	$4,000	PAC

| Trucking | $5,750 | |
| None over $4,000 | | |

| Railroads | $10,000 | |
| Union Pacific Corp | $6,000 | PAC |

Labor

| Labor | $22,000 | |

Public Sector Unions	$21,000	
Natl Assn of Retired Federal Employees	$6,000	PAC
National Assn of Letter Carriers	$5,000	PAC

Ideological/Single-Issue

| Ideological/Single-Issue | $61,725 | |

Leadership PACs	$20,000	
Republican Majority Fund (Richard Lugar)	$10,000	PAC
Catch the Spirit PAC (Bob Kasten)	$5,000	PAC
Campaign America (Bob Dole)	$4,000	PAC

| Foreign & Defense Policy | $8,605 | |
| Council for National Defense | $5,605 | PAC |

Pro-Israel	$13,500	
Washington PAC	$6,000	PAC
Delaware Valley PAC	$5,000	PAC

| Gun Rights/Gun Control | $4,950 | |
| National Rifle Assn | $4,950 | PAC |

| Misc Issues | $13,070 | |
| Public Service Research Council | $10,000 | PAC |

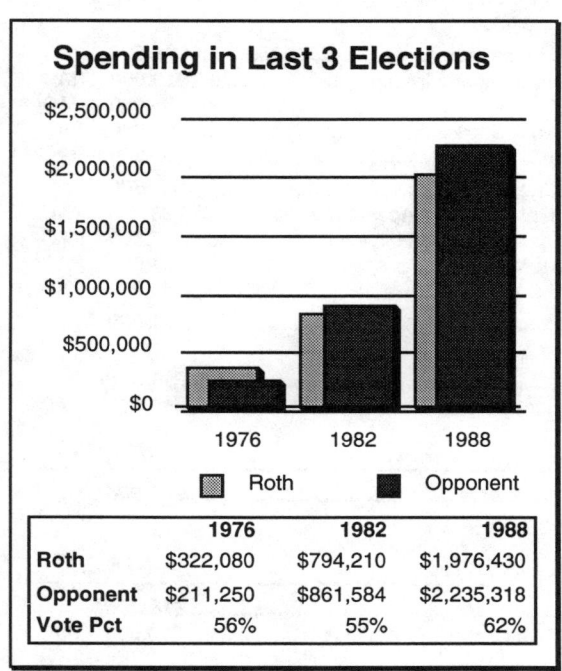

Spending in Last 3 Elections

Legend: Roth, Opponent

	1976	1982	1988
Roth	$322,080	$794,210	$1,976,430
Opponent	$211,250	$861,584	$2,235,318
Vote Pct	56%	55%	62%

* Contributions came from more than one affiliate or subsidiary.

Paul S. Sarbanes (D-Md)

First elected: 1976

1987-92 Total Rcpts:	$1,547,244
1992 Year-end Cash:	$12,862
Current term expires:	1994

1991-92 Committees & Subcommittees

Banking, Housing and Urban Affairs
Housing and Urban Affairs; International Finance and Monetary Policy (Chairman)

Foreign Relations
European Affairs; International Economic Policy, Trade, Oceans and Environment (Chairman); Near Eastern and South Asian Affairs

Joint Economic Committee (Chairman)

Leading Contributors

NOTE: The bulk of Sarbanes's large individual contributions do not appear in the listings below. His last election was in 1988, and this book lists individual contributions only from 1989-1992.

Business

Agriculture		$10,500
Dairy		**$7,000**
Associated Milk Producers	$3,000	PAC
Dairymen Inc	$3,000	PAC
Food Processing & Sales		**$2,500**
None over $2,500		

Communications/Electronics		$10,750
Media/Entertainment		**$3,000**
None over $2,500		
Telephone Utilities		**$4,750**
None over $2,500		

Construction		$23,000
Home Builders		**$11,750**
National Assn of Home Builders	$10,000	PAC
Building Materials & Equipment		**$9,250**
Westvaco Corp	$6,000	PAC

Defense		$4,050
Defense Aerospace		**$3,000**
None over $2,500		

Source of Funds: 1987-1992

Source	Total	Pct
■ PACs	$601,858	38%
▨ Indivs $200+	$521,702	33%
□ Indivs under $200	$332,263	21%
⊠ Other	$117,921	7%
Candidate	$0	0%
Party	$26,500	2%

Source of PAC Dollars by Sector

Source	Total	Pct
■ Business	$234,950	39%
▨ Labor	$285,775	48%
□ Ideological/Single-Issue	$80,133	13%

In-State vs. Out-of-State Contributions*

Source	Total	Pct
□ In-State	$185,395	36%
■ Out-of-state	$336,307	64%
No state listed	$0	

* by large individual contributors ($200 & above)

Energy & Natural Resources		$7,000
Electric Utilities		**$3,000**
ACRE (Action Cmte for Rural Electrification)	$3,000	PAC

Finance, Insurance & Real Estate		$108,700
Commercial Banks		**$13,200**
American Bankers Assn	$5,000	PAC
Independent Bankers Assn	$3,500	PAC
Savings & Loans		**$10,000**
US League of Savings Assns	$5,500	PAC
Finance/Credit Companies		**$6,000**
None over $2,500		
Securities & Investment		**$31,500**
Investment Company Institute	$10,000	PAC
First Boston Corp	$5,000	PAC
Alex Brown & Sons	$4,000	PAC
EF Hutton	$2,500	PAC
Insurance		**$28,800**
Independent Insurance Agents of America	$8,000	PAC
National Assn of Life Underwriters	$7,500	PAC
Casualty & Surety Agents Assn	$4,000	PAC
Travelers Corp	$3,000	PAC
Real Estate		**$8,500**
None over $2,500		
Accountants		**$8,450**
American Institute of CPA's	$5,000	PAC

Health		$14,000
Health Professionals		**$10,000**
None over $2,500		

Lawyers & Lobbyists		$18,200
Lawyers & Lobbyists		**$18,200**
Assn of Trial Lawyers of America	$10,000	PAC

Contribution Totals by Sector

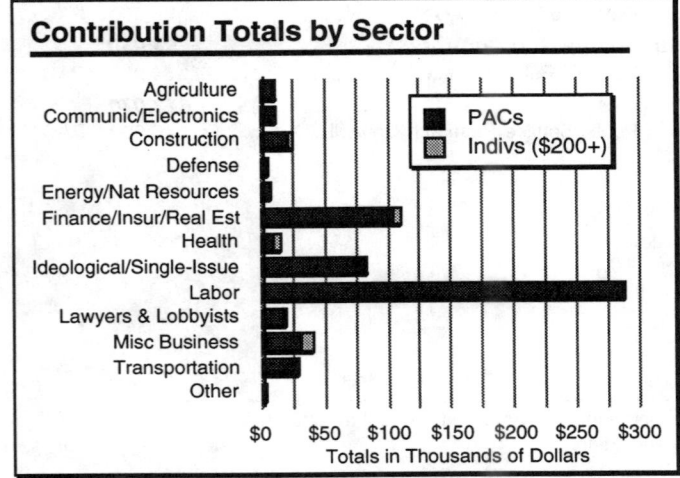

- Agriculture
- Communic/Electronics
- Construction
- Defense
- Energy/Nat Resources
- Finance/Insur/Real Est
- Health
- Ideological/Single-Issue
- Labor
- Lawyers & Lobbyists
- Misc Business
- Transportation
- Other

Legend: ■ PACs ▨ Indivs ($200+)

$0 $50 $100 $150 $200 $250 $300
Totals in Thousands of Dollars

Misc Business $38,398

Food & Beverage **$5,298**
    None over $2,500

Beer, Wine & Liquor **$13,000**
    National Beer Wholesalers Assn ....$9,000 PAC
    Joseph E Seagram & Sons ....$4,000 PAC

Steel Production **$5,250**
    Bethlehem Steel ....$3,000 PAC

Misc Manufacturing & Distributing **$10,000**
    Triangle Industries ....$5,000 PAC
    General Electric ....$3,000 PAC

Transportation $26,900

Air Transport **$11,000**
    Aircraft Owners & Pilots Assn ....$4,000 PAC
    United Parcel Service...$3,000 PAC

Automotive **$7,300**
    Chrysler Corp ....$4,000 PAC

Trucking **$4,600**
    American Trucking Assns ....$3,500 PAC

Railroads **$3,000**
    None over $2,500

Labor

Labor $285,775

Building Trade Unions **$45,200**
    Carpenters & Joiners Union ....$10,000 PAC
    Sheet Metal Workers Union ....$10,000 PAC
    Laborers' Political League ....$7,000 PAC
    Operating Engineers Union ....$7,000 PAC
    Plumbers/Pipefitters Union...................................$4,000 PAC
    Baltimore Bldg/Const Trades Council ....$3,500 PAC
    Bricklayers Union ....$3,000 PAC

Industrial Unions **$81,225**
    American Federation of Teachers.......................$10,000 PAC
    Intl Brotherhood of Electrical Workers ....$10,000 PAC
    National Education Assn ....$10,000 PAC
    United Steelworkers ....$10,000 PAC
    Communications Workers of America ....$7,500 PAC

    Boilermakers Union ....$7,000 PAC
    Ladies Garment Workers Union ....$7,000 PAC
    Machinists/Aerospace Workers Union ....$7,000 PAC
    Clothing & Textile Workers/Baltimore ....$4,500 PAC

Transportation Unions **$84,000**
    Marine Engineers Union* ....$11,000 PAC
    Masters, Mates & Pilots Union ....$10,000 PAC
    Seafarers International Union ....$10,000 PAC
    Teamsters Union ....$10,000 PAC
    United Auto Workers ....$10,000 PAC
    United Transportation Union ....$7,500 PAC
    Air Line Pilots Assn ....$5,000 PAC
    International Longshoremen's Assn ....$5,000 PAC
    Trans Comm International Union ....$4,500 PAC
    Amalgamated Transit Union ....$4,000 PAC

Public Sector Unions **$54,950**
    American Fedn of St/Cnty/Munic Employees ....$10,000 PAC
    National Assn of Letter Carriers ....$10,000 PAC
    Natl Assn of Retired Federal Employees ....$10,000 PAC
    American Postal Workers Union ....$8,000 PAC
    National Rural Letter Carriers Assn ....$5,000 PAC
    American Federation of Govt Employees ....$3,200 PAC

Misc Unions **$20,400**
    Food & Commercial Workers Union ....$7,100 PAC
    AFL-CIO ....$6,800 PAC
    Service Employees International Union ....$2,500 PAC

Ideological/Single-Issue

Ideological/Single-Issue $81,133

Democratic/Liberal **$11,533**
    Democrats for the 80's ....$5,000 PAC
    National Cmte for an Effective Congress ....$4,996 PAC

Leadership PACs **$17,000**
    Pelican PAC (Bennett Johnston) ....$5,000 PAC
    Senate Majority Fund (Daniel Inouye) ....$5,000 PAC
    Cmte for a Demo Consensus (Alan Cranston) ....$3,500 PAC

Foreign & Defense Policy **$2,600**
    Council for a Livable World ....$2,600 PAC

Pro-Israel **$37,000**
    Washington PAC ....$10,000 PAC
    Hudson Valley PAC...$6,000 PAC
    National PAC ....$5,000 PAC
    St Louisians for Better Government ....$5,000 PAC
    San Franciscans for Good Government ....$2,500 PAC

Human Rights **$11,900**
    Dynamis ....$5,000 PAC
    KidsPAC ....$3,500 PAC

Other & Unknown

Other $3,100

    None over $2,500

Unknown $12,600

    Homemakers/Non-income earners $7,300
    Employer Listed/Category Unknown $3,000
        None over $2,500

Independent expenditures supporting Sarbanes
    National Cmte to Preserve Social Security $15,526

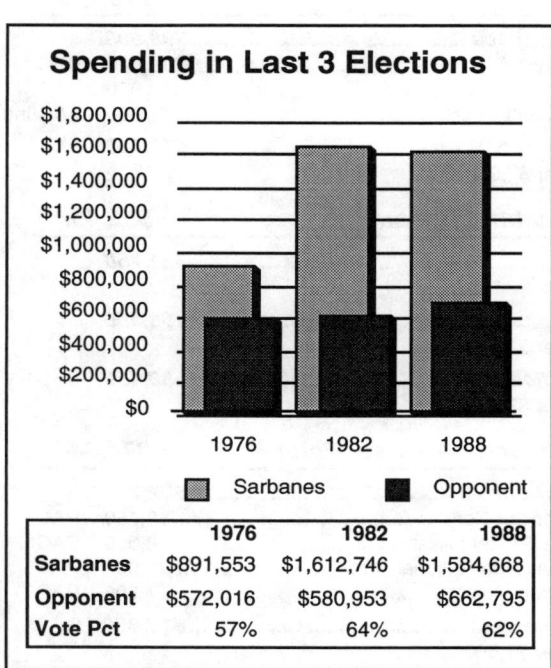

Spending in Last 3 Elections

	1976	1982	1988
Sarbanes	$891,553	$1,612,746	$1,584,668
Opponent	$572,016	$580,953	$662,795
Vote Pct	57%	64%	62%

---

* Contributions came from more than one affiliate or subsidiary.

Jim Sasser (D-Tenn)

First elected: 1976

1987-92 Total Rcpts:	$3,474,892
1992 Year-end Cash:	$281,527
Current term expires:	1994

1991-92 Committees & Subcommittees

Appropriations
Commerce, Justice, State, the Judiciary and Related Agencies; Defense; Energy and Water Development; Military Construction (Chairman); Transportation and Related Agencies

Banking, Housing and Urban Affairs
Housing and Urban Affairs; Securities

Budget (Chairman)

Governmental Affairs
Federal Services, Post Office and Civil Service; General Services, Federalism and the District of Columbia (Chairman); Permanent Subcommittee on Investigations

Leading Contributors

NOTE: The bulk of Jefford's large individual contributions do not appear in the listings below. His last election was in 1988, and this book lists individual contributions only from 1989-1992.

Business

Agriculture $107,150

Crop Production & Basic Processing $23,150
   None over $7,500

Tobacco $24,000
   None over $7,500

Dairy $16,500
   None over $7,500

Agricultural Services/Products $10,250
   None over $7,500

Food Processing & Sales $20,850
   None over $7,500

Communications/Electronics $43,000

Media/Entertainment $9,850
   None over $7,500

Telephone Utilities $23,750
   AT&T .... $12,000   PAC

Source of Funds: 1987-1992

Source	Total	Pct
◼ PACs	$1,492,529	43%
▨ Indivs $200+	$1,161,777	33%
◻ Indivs under $200	$624,128	18%
▨ Other	$214,958	6%
Candidate	$0	0%
Party	$18,500	1%

Source of PAC Dollars by Sector

Source	Total	Pct
◼ Business	$1,040,415	70%
▨ Labor	$300,750	20%
◻ Ideological/Single-Issue ..	$144,046	10%

In-State vs. Out-of-State Contributions*

Source	Total	Pct
◻ In-State	$781,369	67%
◼ Out-of-state	$379,892	33%
No state listed	$516	

* by large individual contributors ($200 & above)

Construction $69,450

General Contractors $17,050
   None over $7,500

Home Builders $13,750
   National Assn of Home Builders .... $9,500   PAC

Special Trade Contractors $19,000
   None over $7,500

Building Materials & Equipment $13,250
   None over $7,500

Defense $119,300

Defense Aerospace $93,900
   Textron Inc .... $10,500   PAC
   Boeing Co .... $9,000   PAC
   Martin Marietta Corp .... $7,500   PAC/Ind

Defense Electronics $18,400
   None over $7,500

Energy & Natural Resources $52,450

Oil & Gas $21,750
   None over $7,500

Mining $8,500
   None over $7,500

Electric Utilities $9,150
   None over $7,500

Finance, Insurance & Real Estate $374,346

Commercial Banks $92,740
   First American Corp .... $9,750   PAC
   American Bankers Assn .... $8,000   PAC
   First Tennessee National Corp .... $8,000   PAC
   C&S/Sovran Corp* .... $7,500   PAC

Savings & Loans $19,850
   None over $7,500

Contribution Totals by Sector

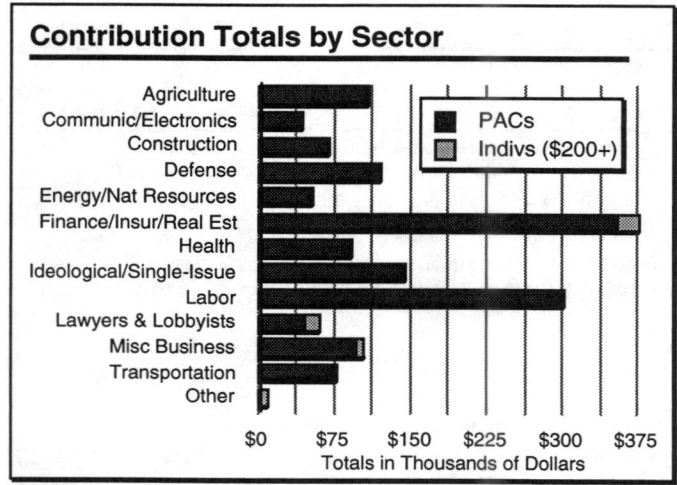

Agriculture
Communic/Electronics
Construction
Defense
Energy/Nat Resources
Finance/Insur/Real Est
Health
Ideological/Single-Issue
Labor
Lawyers & Lobbyists
Misc Business
Transportation
Other

◼ PACs
▨ Indivs ($200+)

$0 $75 $150 $225 $300 $375
Totals in Thousands of Dollars

Credit Unions	$8,250	
None over $7,500		

Securities & Investment **$87,306**
Smith Barney	$10,356	PAC/Ind
First Boston Corp	$9,500	PAC
Chicago Mercantile Exchange	$9,000	PAC
Investment Company Institute	$8,000	PAC

Insurance **$107,050**
Independent Insurance Agents of America	$12,000	PAC
National Assn of Prof Insurance Agents	$10,500	PAC
National Assn of Life Underwriters	$9,000	PAC

Real Estate **$30,900**
| National Assn of Realtors | $9,000 | PAC |

Accountants **$18,000**
| American Institute of CPA's | $9,500 | PAC |

Health $89,715

Health Professionals **$55,615**
American Dental Assn	$10,000	PAC
American Medical Assn	$10,000	PAC
National Assn of Pharmacists	$8,490	PAC

Hospitals/Nursing Homes **$27,000**
| None over $7,500 | | |

Lawyers & Lobbyists $57,575

Lawyers & Lobbyists **$57,575**
| Assn of Trial Lawyers of America | $9,000 | PAC |

Misc Business $102,300

Food & Beverage **$15,700**
| None over $7,500 | | |

Beer, Wine & Liquor **$32,750**
| National Beer Wholesalers Assn | $11,000 | PAC |

Lodging/Tourism **$8,500**
| None over $7,500 | | |

Misc Manufacturing & Distributing **$9,550**
| None over $7,500 | | |

Textiles **$9,000**
| None over $7,500 | | |

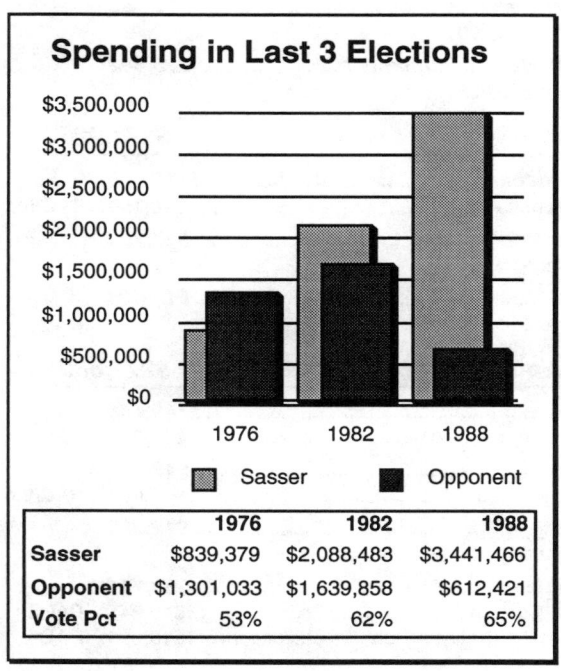

Spending in Last 3 Elections

	1976	1982	1988
Sasser	$839,379	$2,088,483	$3,441,466
Opponent	$1,301,033	$1,639,858	$612,421
Vote Pct	53%	62%	65%

Legend: ▨ Sasser ■ Opponent

Transportation	$74,479	

Air Transport **$26,250**
| Federal Express Corp | $10,000 | PAC |

Automotive **$17,000**
| National Auto Dealers Assn | $10,000 | PAC |

Trucking **$18,729**
| None over $7,500 | | |

Labor

Labor	$300,750	

Building Trade Unions **$51,000**
Plumbers/Pipefitters Union	$13,000	PAC
Operating Engineers Union	$10,000	PAC
Sheet Metal Workers Union	$10,000	PAC
Laborers' Political League	$9,000	PAC
Carpenters & Joiners Union	$8,000	PAC

Industrial Unions **$87,000**
Communications Workers of America	$10,000	PAC
Machinists/Aerospace Workers Union	$10,000	PAC
United Steelworkers	$10,000	PAC
National Education Assn	$9,500	PAC

Transportation Unions **$73,500**
Teamsters Union	$12,500	PAC
Air Line Pilots Assn	$10,000	PAC
United Auto Workers	$10,000	PAC
Marine Engineers Union*	$8,500	PAC
Amalgamated Transit Union	$7,500	PAC

Public Sector Unions **$72,000**
American Fedn of St/Cnty/Munic Employees	$10,000	PAC
American Postal Workers Union	$10,000	PAC
National Assn of Letter Carriers	$10,000	PAC
Natl Assn of Retired Federal Employees	$10,000	PAC
National Rural Letter Carriers Assn	$8,000	PAC

Misc Unions **$17,250**
| AFL-CIO | $9,500 | PAC |

Ideological/Single-Issue

Ideological/Single-Issue	$144,046	

Democratic/Liberal **$9,991**
| None over $7,500 | | |

Leadership PACs **$23,500**
| Senate Majority Fund (Daniel Inouye) | $10,000 | PAC |

Foreign & Defense Policy **$10,579**
| None over $7,500 | | |

Pro-Israel **$84,000**
Citizens Organized PAC	$10,000	PAC
Desert Caucus	$10,000	PAC
Hudson Valley PAC	$10,000	PAC

Human Rights **$9,000**
| None over $7,500 | | |

Other & Unknown

Other	$8,400	
None over $7,500		

Unknown	$14,050	
Employer Listed/Category Unknown	$8,800	
None over $7,500		

---

* Contributions came from more than one affiliate or
subsidiary.

Richard C. Shelby (D-Ala)

First elected: 1986

1987-92 Total Rcpts:	$3,778,582
1992 Year-end Cash:	$1,112,139
Current term expires:	1998

1991-92 Committees & Subcommittees

Armed Services
Conventional Forces and Alliance Defense; Projection Forces and Regional Defense; Readiness, Sustainability and Support

Banking, Housing and Urban Affairs
Housing and Urban Affairs; Securities

Energy and Natural Resources
Energy Regulation and Conservation; Energy Research and Development (Vice Chairman); Mineral Resources Development and Production

Special Aging

Leading Contributors

Business

Agriculture	$192,956

Crop Production & Basic Processing $43,456	
None over $10,000	
Tobacco $24,750	
None over $10,000	
Dairy $13,500	
None over $10,000	
Poultry & Eggs $11,000	
None over $10,000	
Agricultural Services/Products $20,250	
None over $10,000	
Food Processing & Sales $42,200	
None over $10,000	
Forestry & Forest Products $29,050	
None over $10,000	

Communications/Electronics	$164,600

Printing & Publishing $14,250		
None over $10,000		
Media/Entertainment $67,500		
Comcast Corp $10,000	PAC
National Cable Television Assn $10,000	PAC
Telephone Utilities $21,500		
None over $10,000		

Contribution Totals by Sector

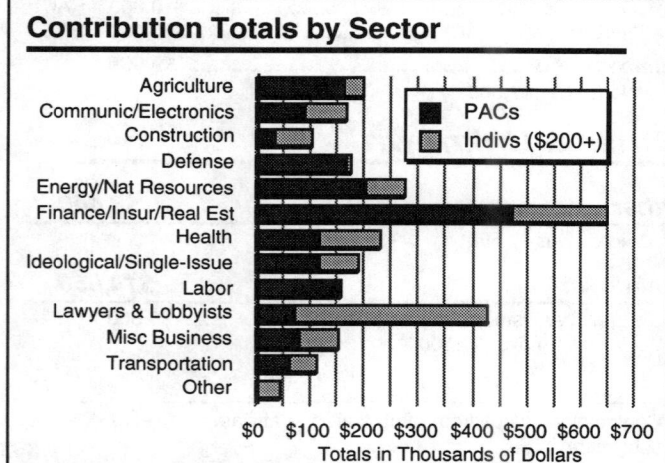

Totals in Thousands of Dollars

Source of Funds: 1987-1992

Source	Total	Pct
■ PACs	$1,690,444	43%
▨ Indivs $200+	$1,497,748	38%
▢ Indivs under $200	$226,992	6%
▨ Other	$484,335	12%
Candidate	$0	0%
Party	$120,937	3%

Source of PAC Dollars by Sector

Source	Total	Pct
■ Business	$1,426,446	84%
▨ Labor	$156,000	9%
▢ Ideological/Single-Issue ..	$115,400	7%

In-State vs. Out-of-State Contributions*

Source	Total	Pct
▢ In-State	$1,035,950	69%
■ Out-of-state	$461,298	31%
No state listed	$0	

* by large individual contributors ($200 & above)

Electronics Mfg & Services $29,250		
American Instrument Co $10,000	Indiv
Computer Equipment & Services $23,500		
Colsa Inc $13,000	Indiv
Intergraph Corp $10,000	PAC

Construction	$99,932

General Contractors $43,400	
None over $10,000	
Home Builders $14,550	
None over $10,000	
Construction Services $12,000	
None over $10,000	
Building Materials & Equipment $26,482	
None over $10,000	

Defense	$171,925

Defense Aerospace $112,075		
Martin Marietta Corp $10,750	PAC/Ind
Defense Electronics $47,250		
None over $10,000		
Misc Defense $12,600		
None over $10,000		

Energy & Natural Resources	$271,889

Oil & Gas $149,148		
Southern Natural Resources $10,000	PAC
Mining $40,000		
Drummond Co $18,000	PAC/Ind
Nuclear Energy $12,000		
None over $10,000		
Electric Utilities $58,741		
Southern Co* $19,241	PAC/Ind
ACRE (Action Cmte for Rural Electrification) $10,000	PAC

Finance, Insurance & Real Estate $646,025

Commercial Banks $208,324
- Bankers Trust ....$10,250 PAC/Ind
- American Bankers Assn ....$10,000 PAC
- Amsouth Bancorp ....$10,000 PAC
- Central Bancshares of the South ....$10,000 PAC
- JP Morgan & Co ....$10,000 PAC

Savings & Loans $19,250
- None over $10,000

Credit Unions $12,000
- Credit Union National Assn* ....$10,000 PAC

Finance/Credit Companies $21,500
- None over $10,000

Securities & Investment $99,801
- Chicago Board of Trade ....$10,000 PAC
- Chicago Mercantile Exchange ....$10,000 PAC

Insurance $145,050
- American Family Corp ....$11,250 Indiv
- Torchmark Corp ....$11,000 PAC/Ind
- American Family Corp ....$10,000 PAC
- National Assn of Life Underwriters ....$10,000 PAC

Real Estate $93,550
- National Assn of Realtors ....$10,000 PAC

Accountants $25,000
- None over $10,000

Health $226,100

Health Professionals $150,050
- American Chiropractic Assn ....$10,000 PAC
- American Dental Assn ....$10,000 PAC
- American Medical Assn ....$10,000 PAC

Hospitals/Nursing Homes $24,100
- None over $10,000

Pharmaceuticals/Health Products $36,450
- None over $10,000

Lawyers & Lobbyists $423,147

Lawyers & Lobbyists $423,147
- Cunningham, Bounds et al ....$15,000 Indiv
- Balch & Bingham ....$11,650 Indiv
- Assn of Trial Lawyers of America ....$10,000 PAC
- Hogan, Smith et al ....$10,000 Indiv

Spending in Last 2 Elections

	1986	1992
Shelby	$2,259,167	$2,520,141
Opponent	$4,865,276	$146,552
Vote Pct	50%	65%

Misc Business $151,500

Food & Beverage $19,750
- None over $10,000

Beer, Wine & Liquor $15,700
- None over $10,000

Retail Sales $31,500
- None over $10,000

Business Services $19,650
- None over $10,000

Chemical & Related Manufacturing $13,750
- None over $10,000

Misc Manufacturing & Distributing $22,750
- None over $10,000

Transportation $107,750

Air Transport $26,500
- None over $10,000

Automotive $40,500
- Auto Dealers & Drivers for Free Trade ....$10,000 PAC
- National Auto Dealers Assn ....$10,000 PAC

Trucking $12,250
- None over $10,000

Sea Transport $17,750
- None over $10,000

Labor

Labor $156,000

Building Trade Unions $28,000
- None over $10,000

Industrial Unions $37,500
- None over $10,000

Transportation Unions $46,000
- Air Line Pilots Assn ....$10,000 PAC
- Marine Engineers Union* ....$10,000 PAC
- Teamsters Union ....$10,000 PAC

Public Sector Unions $34,000
- None over $10,000

Ideological/Single-Issue

Ideological/Single-Issue $183,930

Pro-Israel $148,330
- Americans for Good Government ....$15,000 PAC
- Desert Caucus ....$10,000 PAC

Misc Issues $15,000
- None over $10,000

Other & Unknown

Other $44,375

Education $20,150
- None over $10,000

Retired $17,600
- None over $10,000

Unknown $162,065
- Homemakers/Non-income earners $46,500
- Employer Listed/Category Unknown................$112,565
  - None over $10,000

---

* Contributions came from more than one affiliate or subsidiary.

Paul Simon (D-III)

First elected: 1984

1987-92 Total Rcpts:	$9,018,774
1992 Year-end Cash:	$540,483
Current term expires:	1996

1991-92 Committees & Subcommittees

Budget

Foreign Relations
African Affairs (Chairman); European Affairs; Terrorism, Narcotics and International Operations

Judiciary
Antitrust, Monopolies and Business Rights; Constitution (Chairman); Immigration and Refugee Affairs

Labor and Human Resources
Education, Arts and Humanities; Employment and Productivity (Chairman); Disability Policy

Select Committee on Indian Affairs

Leading Contributors

Business

Agriculture	$133,001

Crop Production & Basic Processing	$31,450	
None over $12,500		
Dairy	$27,750	
Mid-America Dairymen	$13,000	PAC
Agricultural Services/Products	$28,300	
Archer-Daniels-Midland Corp	$15,000	PAC
Food Processing & Sales	$32,001	
None over $12,500		

Communications/Electronics	$195,143

Printing & Publishing	$29,900	
None over $12,500		
Media/Entertainment	$136,722	
Time Warner*	$20,000	PAC/Ind
National Cable Television Assn	$15,000	PAC
Telephone Utilities	$19,171	
None over $12,500		

Construction	$60,440

General Contractors	$19,050	
None over $12,500		
Home Builders	$13,000	
None over $12,500		

Contribution Totals by Sector

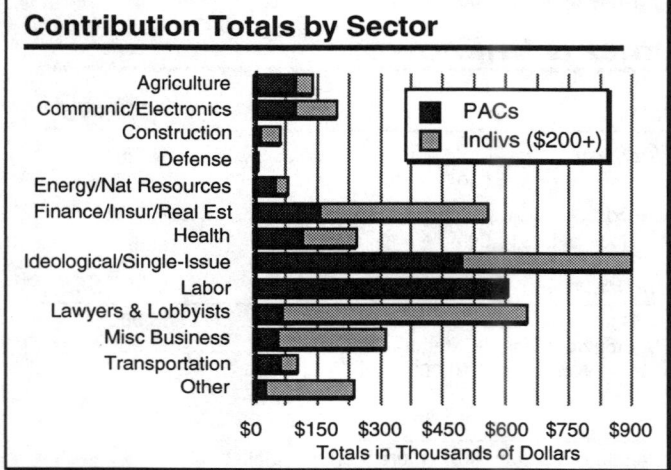

PACs
Indivs ($200+)

Agriculture
Communic/Electronics
Construction
Defense
Energy/Nat Resources
Finance/Insur/Real Est
Health
Ideological/Single-Issue
Labor
Lawyers & Lobbyists
Misc Business
Transportation
Other

$0 $150 $300 $450 $600 $750 $900
Totals in Thousands of Dollars

Source of Funds: 1987-1992

Source	Total	Pct
■ PACs	$1,487,275	15%
▨ Indivs $200+	$3,136,940	32%
□ Indivs under $200	$3,931,978	40%
⊠ Other	$1,370,427	14%
Candidate	$30,000	0%
Party	$907,846	9%

Source of PAC Dollars by Sector

Source	Total	Pct
■ Business	$706,828	40%
▨ Labor	$589,920	33%
□ Ideological/Single-Issue	$485,099	27%

In-State vs. Out-of-State Contributions*

Source	Total	Pct
□ In-State	$1,539,057	50%
■ Out-of-state	$1,548,272	50%
No state listed	$49,000	

* by large individual contributors ($200 & above)

Construction Services	$16,650	
None over $12,500		

Energy & Natural Resources	$79,735

Oil & Gas	$34,700	
Occidental Petroleum	$16,000	PAC/Ind
Electric Utilities	$18,600	
None over $12,500		
Waste Management	$20,500	
Waste Management Inc	$16,000	PAC/Ind

Finance, Insurance & Real Estate	$553,085

Commercial Banks	$69,470	
First Chicago Corp	$16,260	PAC/Ind
Securities & Investment	$141,876	
Chicago Board of Trade	$27,950	PAC/Ind
Chicago Mercantile Exchange	$15,550	PAC/Ind
Insurance	$57,375	
American International Group	$15,000	PAC/Ind
Real Estate	$210,434	
JMB Realty Corp	$28,600	PAC/Ind
Accountants	$23,665	
None over $12,500		
Misc Finance	$26,115	
None over $12,500		

Health	$236,474

Health Professionals	$159,724	
None over $12,500		
Hospitals/Nursing Homes	$46,375	
American Hospital Assn	$12,500	PAC/Ind
Misc Health	$14,375	
None over $12,500		

Lawyers & Lobbyists — $644,496

Lawyers & Lobbyists **$644,496**
- Mayer, Brown & Platt .... $18,200 — Indiv
- Kirkland & Ellis .... $16,750 — PAC/Ind
- Jenner & Block .... $15,575 — PAC/Ind

Misc Business — $309,312

Food & Beverage **$27,856**
- None over $12,500

Beer, Wine & Liquor **$15,718**
- None over $12,500

Retail Sales **$38,055**
- None over $12,500

Business Services **$51,400**
- None over $12,500

Chemical & Related Manufacturing **$15,500**
- None over $12,500

Steel Production **$14,675**
- None over $12,500

Misc Manufacturing & Distributing **$99,533**
- William Levine Inc .... $14,250 — Indiv

Transportation — $98,683

Air Transport **$32,883**
- None over $12,500

Automotive **$30,850**
- None over $12,500

Railroads **$27,200**
- None over $12,500

Labor

Labor — **$598,676**

Building Trade Unions **$102,962**
- Laborers Union* .... $16,750 — PAC/Ind
- Bricklayers Union .... $15,000 — PAC
- Ironworkers Union .... $15,000 — PAC
- Carpenters & Joiners Union .... $14,500 — PAC

Industrial Unions **$193,891**
- United Mine Workers .... $20,500 — PAC/Ind
- Intl Brotherhood of Electrical Workers* .... $15,860 — PAC/Ind

- Machinists/Aerospace Workers Union .... $15,400 — PAC/Ind
- American Federation of Teachers .... $15,000 — PAC
- Communications Workers of America .... $15,000 — PAC
- National Education Assn .... $15,000 — PAC
- United Steelworkers .... $15,000 — PAC
- Amalgamated Clothing & Textile Workers* .... $13,400 — PAC
- Ladies Garment Workers Union .... $12,656 — PAC
- Rubber Cork Linoleum & Plastic Workers .... $12,500 — PAC

Transportation Unions **$139,873**
- Marine Engineers Union* .... $15,000 — PAC
- Seafarers International Union .... $15,000 — PAC
- United Transportation Union .... $15,000 — PAC
- Teamsters Union* .... $14,900 — PAC

Public Sector Unions **$94,550**
- National Assn of Letter Carriers .... $17,700 — PAC/Ind
- American Postal Workers Union .... $16,000 — PAC

Misc Unions **$67,400**
- Food & Commercial Workers Union .... $15,000 — PAC
- Service Employees International Union .... $15,000 — PAC
- AFL-CIO .... $12,500 — PAC

Ideological/Single-Issue

Ideological/Single-Issue — **$891,959**

Democratic/Liberal **$174,434**
- Independent Action .... $24,000 — PAC
- Democrats for the 80's .... $17,000 — PAC
- Religion and Tolerance PAC .... $15,000 — PAC

Leadership PACs **$49,511**
- None over $12,500

Foreign & Defense Policy **$42,904**
- None over $12,500

Pro-Israel **$466,567**
- National PAC .... $15,000 — PAC

Pro-Choice **$19,550**
- None over $12,500

Womens Issues **$13,150**
- None over $12,500

Human Rights **$69,774**
- None over $12,500

Misc Issues **$46,719**
- National Cmte to Preserve Social Security .... $15,000 — PAC

Other & Unknown

Other — **$235,295**

Civil Servants/Public Officials **$21,235**
- None over $12,500

Education **$113,357**
- None over $12,500

Retired **$68,398**
- None over $12,500

Other **$21,100**
- None over $12,500

Unknown — **$841,751**
- Homemakers/Non-income earners $108,445
- No Employer Listed or Found $480,956
- Generic Occupation/Category Unknown $22,230
- Employer Listed/Category Unknown $232,217
  - None over $12,500

Independent expenditures opposing Simon
- Council for National Defense $18,487

---

* Contributions came from more than one affiliate or subsidiary.

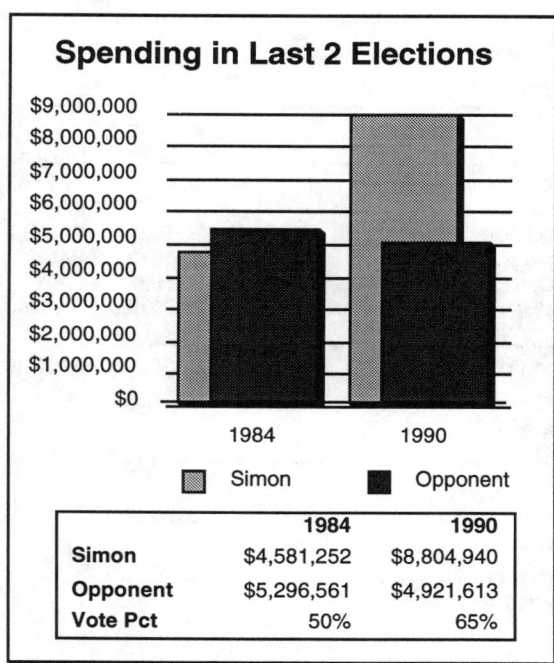

Spending in Last 2 Elections

	1984	1990
Simon	$4,581,252	$8,804,940
Opponent	$5,296,561	$4,921,613
Vote Pct	50%	65%

Legend: Simon, Opponent

Alan K. Simpson (R-Wyo)

First elected: 1978

1987-92 Total Rcpts:	$1,633,044
1992 Year-end Cash:	$256,869
Current term expires:	1996

1991-92 Committees & Subcommittees

Environment and Public Works
Environmental Protection; Nuclear Regulation (Ranking Republican); Superfund, Ocean and Water Protection

Judiciary
Immigration and Refugee Affairs (Ranking Republican); Patents, Copyrights and Trademarks

Veterans' Affairs

Special Aging

Leading Contributors

Business

Agriculture — $85,600

Crop Production & Basic Processing $14,250
  None over $5,000

Tobacco $11,000
  Philip Morris .... $8,000 PAC

Livestock $21,800
  None over $5,000

Agricultural Services/Products $14,850
  None over $5,000

Food Processing & Sales $12,200
  None over $5,000

Forestry & Forest Products $10,000
  None over $5,000

Communications/Electronics — $88,306

Printing & Publishing $5,213
  None over $5,000

Media/Entertainment $42,793
  Paramount Pictures .... $10,500 Indiv
  National Cable Television Assn .... $7,000 PAC
  Gulf + Western Industries .... $5,000 PAC

Telephone Utilities $30,300
  AT&T .... $5,000 PAC

Electronics Mfg & Services $5,000
  Harris Corp .... $5,000 PAC

Source of Funds: 1987-1992

Source	Total	Pct
PACs	$794,246	46%
Indivs $200+	$473,193	27%
Indivs under $200	$50,010	3%
Other	$421,216	24%
Candidate	$22,000	1%
Party	$105,621	6%

Source of PAC Dollars by Sector

Source	Total	Pct
Business	$785,871	97%
Labor	$6,000	1%
Ideological/Single-Issue	$16,600	2%

In-State vs. Out-of-State Contributions*

Source	Total	Pct
In-State	$127,493	27%
Out-of-state	$345,700	73%
No state listed	$0	

* by large individual contributors ($200 & above)

Construction — $53,750

General Contractors $32,500
  Fluor Corp .... $10,000 PAC
  Associated General Contractors .... $5,000 PAC

Home Builders $7,500
  National Assn of Home Builders .... $6,500 PAC

Construction Services $5,500
  None over $5,000

Building Materials & Equipment $5,250
  None over $5,000

Defense — $22,500

Defense Aerospace $20,000
  None over $5,000

Energy & Natural Resources — $193,781

Oil & Gas $110,450
  Mobil Oil .... $8,000 PAC/Ind
  Amoco Corp .... $6,500 PAC/Ind
  Coastal Corp .... $6,000 PAC
  Atlantic Richfield .... $5,000 PAC
  Chevron Corp .... $5,000 PAC
  Enserch Corp .... $5,000 PAC
  Occidental Petroleum* .... $5,000 PAC/Ind

Mining $32,750
  Drummond Co .... $6,000 PAC/Ind

Nuclear Energy $8,300
  None over $5,000

Misc Energy $5,781
  None over $5,000

Electric Utilities $26,500
  None over $5,000

Waste Management $9,750
  Waste Management Inc .... $5,000 PAC/Ind

Contribution Totals by Sector

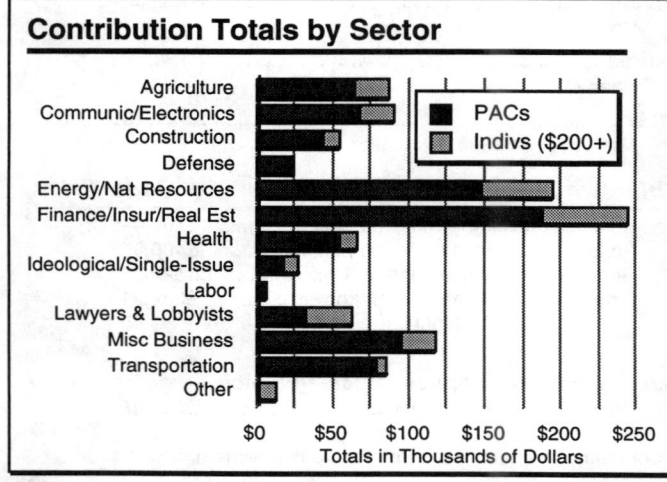

Legend: ■ PACs　■ Indivs ($200+)

Categories: Agriculture, Communic/Electronics, Construction, Defense, Energy/Nat Resources, Finance/Insur/Real Est, Health, Ideological/Single-Issue, Labor, Lawyers & Lobbyists, Misc Business, Transportation, Other

Totals in Thousands of Dollars
$0　$50　$100　$150　$200　$250

Finance, Insurance & Real Estate — $242,700

Commercial Banks **$29,250**
    American Bankers Assn ....$10,000   PAC

Securities & Investment **$35,050**
    Chicago Mercantile Exchange ....$5,000   PAC
    Salomon Brothers ....$5,000   PAC

Insurance **$113,050**
    Torchmark Corp ....$13,000   PAC/Ind
    National Assn of Independent Insurers ....$10,000   PAC
    National Assn of Life Underwriters...................$10,000   PAC
    Massachusetts Mutual Life Insurance ....$7,000   PAC
    Equitable Financial Services ....$5,800   PAC/Ind
    American Council of Life Insurance ....$5,000   PAC
    American Family Corp ....$5,000   PAC
    American International Group ....$5,000   PAC

Real Estate **$35,000**
    National Assn of Realtors ....$9,000   PAC

Accountants **$17,200**
    American Institute of CPA's ....$10,000   PAC

Misc Finance **$7,850**
    None over $5,000

Health — $64,450

Health Professionals **$33,200**
    American Academy of Ophthalmology ....$5,000   PAC
    American Dental Assn ....$5,000   PAC

Pharmaceuticals/Health Products **$24,250**
    None over $5,000

Lawyers & Lobbyists — $60,825

Lawyers & Lobbyists **$60,825**
    Assn of Trial Lawyers of America ....$10,000   PAC

Spending in Last 3 Elections

	1978	1984	1990
Simpson	$439,805	$702,643	$1,443,298
Opponent	$143,749	$0	$6,243
Vote Pct	62%	78%	64%

Simpson   Opponent

Misc Business — $116,621

Food & Beverage **$11,981**
    None over $5,000

Beer, Wine & Liquor **$20,500**
    National Beer Wholesalers Assn ....$10,000   PAC

Retail Sales **$14,000**
    None over $5,000

Business Services **$13,000**
    Dun & Bradstreet ....$6,000   PAC/Ind

Chemical & Related Manufacturing **$35,500**
    FMC Corp ....$10,000   PAC

Misc Manufacturing & Distributing **$7,500**
    None over $5,000

Transportation — $83,700

Air Transport **$31,500**
    Federal Express Corp ....$12,000   PAC
    Aircraft Owners & Pilots Assn ....$5,000   PAC
    Texas Air ....$5,000   PAC

Automotive **$29,950**
    Auto Dealers & Drivers for Free Trade ....$9,000   PAC
    National Auto Dealers Assn ....$5,000   PAC

Railroads **$18,250**
    Union Pacific Corp ....$7,750   PAC/Ind

Labor

Labor — **$6,000**
    None over $5,000

Ideological/Single-Issue

Ideological/Single-Issue — **$26,850**

Republican/Conservative **$6,100**
    None over $5,000

Leadership PACs **$6,500**
    Campaign America (Bob Dole) ....$6,000   PAC/Ind

Human Rights **$5,000**
    KidsPAC ....$5,000   PAC

Other & Unknown

Other — **$11,500**

Retired **$11,000**
    None over $5,000

Unknown — **$70,944**

    Homemakers/Non-income earners $19,950
    No Employer Listed or Found $27,350
    Generic Occupation/Category Unknown $6,187
    Employer Listed/Category Unknown $17,457
        None over $5,000

---

* Contributions came from more than one affiliate or subsidiary.

Robert C. Smith (R-NH)

First elected: 1990

1989-92 Total Rcpts:	$1,537,492
1992 Year-end Cash:	$46,190
Current term expires:	1996

1991-92 Committees & Subcommittees

Armed Services
Defense Industry and Technology; Manpower and Personnel; Strategic Forces and Nuclear Deterrence

Environment and Public Works
Superfund, Ocean and Water Protection; Water Resources, Transportation and Infrastructure

Select Committee on POW/MIA Affairs

Joint Economic Committee

Leading Contributors

Business

Agriculture	$69,550	
Tobacco	**$12,000**	
None over $5,000		
Food Processing & Sales	**$24,500**	
Flowers Industries	$5,000	PAC
Forestry & Forest Products	**$25,350**	
International Paper Co	$10,000	PAC
Manville Corp	$5,000	PAC

Communications/Electronics	$35,011	
Telephone Utilities	**$16,400**	
None over $5,000		
Computer Equipment & Services	**$8,661**	
None over $5,000		

Construction	$94,850	
General Contractors	**$46,600**	
Associated General Contractors	$10,000	PAC
National Utility Contractors Assn	$5,000	PAC
Home Builders	**$6,500**	
National Assn of Home Builders	$6,500	PAC
Special Trade Contractors	**$20,150**	
National Electrical Contractors Assn	$5,000	PAC
Sheet Metal/Air Conditioning Contractors	$5,000	PAC
Building Materials & Equipment	**$16,750**	
None over $5,000		

Contribution Totals by Sector

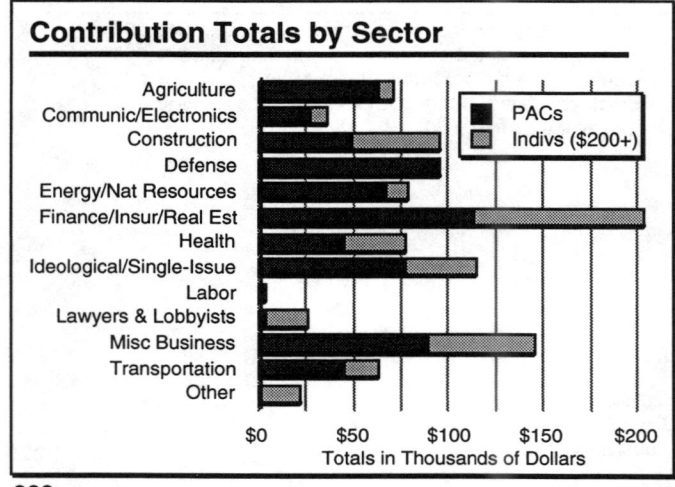

Totals in Thousands of Dollars

Source of Funds: 1987-1992

Source	Total	Pct
■ PACs	$665,831	39%
▨ Indivs $200+	$423,737	25%
□ Indivs under $200	$237,264	14%
▧ Other	$359,076	21%
Candidate	$0	0%
Party	$148,416	9%

Source of PAC Dollars by Sector

Source	Total	Pct
■ Business	$585,380	88%
▨ Labor	$3,050	0%
□ Ideological/Single-Issue	$76,401	11%

In-State vs. Out-of-State Contributions*

Source	Total	Pct
□ In-State	$277,687	66%
■ Out-of-state	$144,550	34%
No state listed	$1,500	

* by large individual contributors ($200 & above)

Defense	$94,500	
Defense Aerospace	**$55,000**	
United Technologies	$7,000	PAC
Lockheed Corp	$6,000	PAC
Henley Group Inc	$5,000	PAC
Northrop Corp	$5,000	PAC
Defense Electronics	**$28,000**	
AT&T	$8,000	PAC
Harris Corp	$5,000	PAC
Misc Defense	**$11,500**	
None over $5,000		

Energy & Natural Resources	$77,500	
Oil & Gas	**$42,800**	
Amoco Corp	$5,000	PAC
Mobil Oil	$5,000	PAC
Misc Energy	**$5,500**	
Cooper Industries	$5,000	PAC
Electric Utilities	**$20,400**	
None over $5,000		

Finance, Insurance & Real Estate	$201,535	
Commercial Banks	**$37,550**	
American Bankers Assn	$10,000	PAC
JP Morgan & Co	$5,000	PAC
Savings & Loans	**$5,250**	
None over $5,000		
Securities & Investment	**$23,135**	
Salomon Brothers	$11,500	PAC/Ind
Insurance	**$74,675**	
National Assn of Life Underwriters	$10,000	PAC
National Assn of Prof Insurance Agents	$6,500	PAC
National Assn of Independent Insurers	$6,357	PAC
Independent Insurance Agents of America	$6,268	PAC

Real Estate **$44,225**
    National Assn of Realtors .... $10,000 PAC
    Lakeshore Realty .... $5,000 Indiv

Accountants **$6,750**
    None over $5,000

Misc Finance **$7,950**
    None over $5,000

Health $76,050

Health Professionals **$40,250**
    American Academy of Ophthalmology .... $10,000 PAC
    American Medical Assn .... $10,000 PAC

Hospitals/Nursing Homes **$10,700**
    None over $5,000

Pharmaceuticals/Health Products **$22,650**
    Henley Group Inc .... $11,250 Indiv

Lawyers & Lobbyists $24,380

Lawyers & Lobbyists **$24,380**
    None over $5,000

Misc Business $144,147

Business Associations **$11,348**
    National Fedn of Independent Business .... $9,000 PAC

Food & Beverage **$25,860**
    National Restaurant Assn .... $10,000 PAC
    McDonald's Corp .... $6,000 PAC

Retail Sales **$10,250**
    International Council of Shopping Centers .... $5,000 PAC

Business Services **$19,738**
    None over $5,000

Lodging/Tourism **$6,300**
    None over $5,000

Misc Business **$6,500**
    None over $5,000

Chemical & Related Manufacturing **$26,000**
    Contran Corp .... $14,000 PAC/Ind

Misc Manufacturing & Distributing **$25,550**
    None over $5,000

Transportation $62,000

Air Transport **$17,600**
    Texas Air .... $6,500 PAC
    Aircraft Owners & Pilots Assn .... $5,600 PAC

Automotive **$32,200**
    National Auto Dealers Assn .... $10,000 PAC
    Auto Dealers & Drivers for Free Trade .... $8,500 PAC

Railroads **$6,000**
    Union Pacific Corp .... $6,000 PAC

Ideological/Single-Issue

Ideological/Single-Issue $112,901

Republican/Conservative **$31,500**
    National Republican Senatorial Cmte .... $20,000 Indiv

Leadership PACs **$26,000**
    Campaign America (Bob Dole) .... $10,000 PAC
    Senate Victory Fund (Thad Cochran) .... $6,500 PAC

Pro-Israel **$27,000**
    Hudson Valley PAC .... $6,000 PAC
    National PAC .... $5,000 PAC

Gun Rights/Gun Control **$10,000**
    National Rifle Assn .... $10,000 PAC

Misc Issues **$11,300**
    Public Service Research Council .... $5,500 PAC

Other & Unknown

Other $21,664

Civil Servants/Public Officials **$5,150**
    None over $5,000

Retired **$14,714**
    None over $5,000

Unknown $96,680

    Homemakers/Non-income earners $13,000
    No Employer Listed or Found $19,381
    Employer Listed/Category Unknown $61,199
        None over $5,000

Independent expenditures supporting Smith
    Auto Dealers & Drivers for Free Trade $357,600
    National Assn of Realtors $141,774
    National Right to Life PAC $13,756

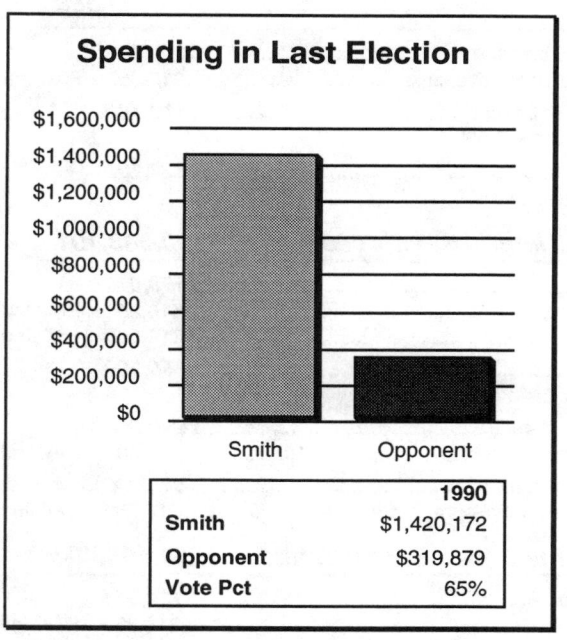

Spending in Last Election

	1990
Smith	$1,420,172
Opponent	$319,879
Vote Pct	65%

---

* Contributions came from more than one affiliate or subsidiary.

361

Arlen Specter (R-Pa)

First elected: 1980

1987-92 Total Rcpts:	$10,463,911
1992 Year-end Cash:	$51,128
Current term expires:	1998

1991-92 Committees & Subcommittees

Appropriations
Agriculture, Rural Development and Related Agencies; Defense; Energy and Water Development; Foreign Operations; Labor, Health and Human Services, Education and Related Agencies (Ranking Republican)

Banking, Housing and Urban Affairs
Consumer and Regulatory Affairs; Housing and Urban Affairs

Judiciary
Antitrust, Monopolies and Business Rights; Constitution (Ranking Republican)

Veterans' Affairs (Ranking Republican)

Special Aging

Leading Contributors

Business

Agriculture	$241,400

Crop Production & Basic Processing	$26,300
None over $12,500	
Dairy	$30,950
None over $12,500	
Agricultural Services/Products	$30,000
None over $12,500	
Food Processing & Sales	$82,700
None over $12,500	
Forestry & Forest Products	$50,950
None over $12,500	

Communications/Electronics	$301,125

Printing & Publishing	$53,800	
None over $12,500		
Media/Entertainment	$126,825	
Adelphia Communications	$15,000	Indiv
Telephone Utilities	$38,700	
Bell Atlantic*	$15,550	PAC/Ind
Electronics Mfg & Services	$35,700	
None over $12,500		
Computer Equipment & Services	$35,000	
None over $12,500		

Contribution Totals by Sector

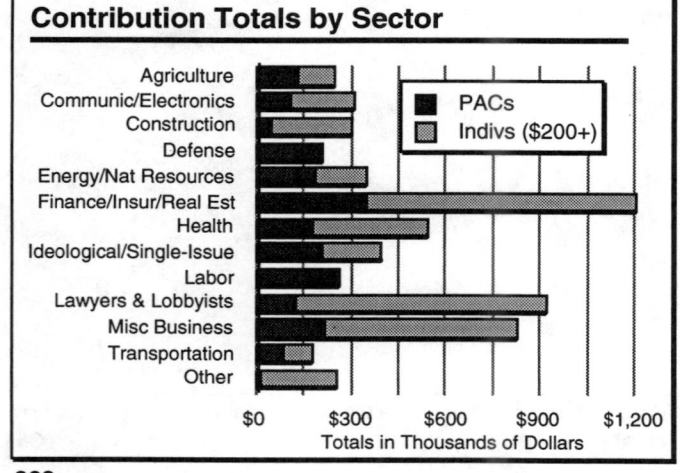

Totals in Thousands of Dollars

Source of Funds: 1987-1992

Source	Total	Pct
■ PACs	$2,011,791	17%
▨ Indivs $200+	$6,118,043	53%
□ Indivs under $200	$1,775,317	15%
⊠ Other	$1,608,569	14%
Candidate	$0	0%
Party	$1,049,809	9%

Source of PAC Dollars by Sector

Source	Total	Pct
■ Business	$1,565,915	77%
▨ Labor	$254,900	13%
□ Ideological/Single-Issue	$206,273	10%

In-State vs. Out-of-State Contributions*

Source	Total	Pct
□ In-State	$4,109,296	70%
■ Out-of-state	$1,755,897	30%
No state listed	$192,600	

*** by large individual contributors ($200 & above)**

Construction	$297,040

General Contractors	$128,050
None over $12,500	
Home Builders	$33,770
None over $12,500	
Special Trade Contractors	$43,700
None over $12,500	
Construction Services	$25,250
None over $12,500	
Building Materials & Equipment	$66,270
None over $12,500	

Defense	$204,899

Defense Aerospace	$104,699	
Rockwell International	$12,650	PAC/Ind
Defense Electronics	$73,100	
None over $12,500		
Misc Defense	$27,100	
None over $12,500		

Energy & Natural Resources	$343,191

Oil & Gas	$158,075	
USX Corp*	$16,250	PAC/Ind
Sun Co	$12,500	PAC/Ind
Mining	$50,500	
None over $12,500		
Electric Utilities	$90,866	
Philadelphia Electric	$18,000	PAC/Ind
Waste Management	$32,700	
Chambers Development Co	$17,750	PAC/Ind

Finance, Insurance & Real Estate	$1,195,484

Commercial Banks	$132,574	
Mellon Bank	$14,350	PAC/Ind
PNC Financial Corp*	$12,700	PAC/Ind

Finance/Credit Companies	$29,134	
Advanta Corp	$12,500	Indiv
Securities & Investment	**$261,825**	
Federated Investors Inc	$19,500	PAC/Ind
Goldman, Sachs & Co	$14,750	PAC/Ind
Soros Fund Management	$14,500	Indiv
Insurance	**$265,203**	
Reliance Group Holdings	$16,044	PAC/Ind
Cigna Corp	$15,250	PAC/Ind
Real Estate	**$319,448**	
National Assn of Realtors	$13,200	PAC
Accountants	**$95,250**	
None over $12,500		
Misc Finance	**$72,050**	
None over $12,500		

Health — $531,479

Health Professionals	$294,135
None over $12,500	
Hospitals/Nursing Homes	**$50,050**
None over $12,500	
Health Services	**$39,618**
US Healthcare Inc	$25,318 PAC/Ind
Pharmaceuticals/Health Products	**$108,326**
None over $12,500	
Misc Health	**$39,350**
None over $12,500	

Lawyers & Lobbyists — $911,005

Lawyers & Lobbyists	$911,005	
Dechert, Price & Rhoads	$40,125	Indiv
Reed, Smith et al	$32,100	PAC/Ind
Wolf, Block et al	$32,050	PAC/Ind
Blank, Rome et al	$28,883	Indiv
Schnader, Harrison et al	$22,300	PAC/Ind
Morgan, Lewis & Bockius	$18,000	Indiv
Kirkpatrick & Lockhart	$15,050	PAC/Ind
Assn of Trial Lawyers of America	$15,000	PAC
Duane, Morris & Heckscher	$13,250	Indiv

Misc Business — $816,125

| Food & Beverage | $67,447 | |
| ARA Services Inc | $14,697 | PAC/Ind |

Spending in Last 3 Elections

	1980	1986	1992
Specter	$1,488,588	$6,451,649	$9,744,696
Opponent	$633,861	$3,898,017	$5,028,669
Vote Pct	51%	56%	49%

Retail Sales	$122,007	
Rite Aid Corp	$17,300	PAC/Ind
Business Services	**$129,272**	
None over $12,500		
Chemical & Related Manufacturing	**$97,000**	
Air Products & Chemicals Inc	$22,000	PAC/Ind
Rohm & Haas Co	$15,000	PAC/Ind
Steel Production	**$63,208**	
None over $12,500		
Misc Manufacturing & Distributing	**$206,700**	
MacAndrews & Forbes Group	$14,000	Indiv
PPG Industries	$13,000	PAC/Ind
Textiles	**$31,900**	
None over $12,500		

Transportation — $174,929

Air Transport	$38,100
None over $12,500	
Automotive	**$51,050**
None over $12,500	
Trucking	**$19,052**
None over $12,500	
Railroads	**$46,177**
None over $12,500	

Labor

Labor — $254,900

Building Trade Unions	$83,700	
Operating Engineers Union*	$14,000	PAC
Industrial Unions	**$36,700**	
None over $12,500		
Transportation Unions	**$64,500**	
None over $12,500		
Public Sector Unions	**$65,500**	
None over $12,500		

Ideological/Single-Issue

Ideological/Single-Issue — $385,053

Republican/Conservative	$31,920
None over $12,500	
Leadership PACs	**$15,500**
None over $12,500	
Pro-Israel	**$275,960**
None over $12,500	

Other & Unknown

Other — $248,475

Education	$89,875	
University of Pennsylvania	$17,200	Indiv
Retired	**$119,550**	
None over $12,500		

Unknown — $2,037,818

Homemakers/Non-income earners	$245,032
No Employer Listed or Found	$1,050,380
Generic Occupation/Category Unknown	$19,250
Employer Listed/Category Unknown	$722,156
None over $12,500	

* Contributions came from more than one affiliate or subsidiary.

Ted Stevens (R-Alaska)

First elected: 1970 *(App'ted 1968)*

1987-92 Total Rcpts:	$1,709,700	
1992 Year-end Cash:	$45,715	
Current term expires:	1996	

1991-92 Committees & Subcommittees

Appropriations
Commerce, Justice, State, the Judiciary and Related Agencies; Defense (Ranking Republican); Interior and Related Agencies; Labor, Health and Human Services, Education and Related Agencies; Military Construction

Commerce, Science and Transportation
Aviation; Communications; Merchant Marine; National Ocean Policy Study (Ranking Republican); Science, Technology and Space

Governmental Affairs
Federal Services, Post Office and Civil Service (Ranking Republican); General Services, Federalism and the District of Columbia; Oversight of Government Management; Permanent Subcommittee on Investigations

Rules and Administration (Ranking Republican)

Small Business
Export Expansion; Innovation, Technology and Productivity (Ranking Republican)

Joint Committee on the Library

Joint Committee on Printing

Leading Contributors

Business

Agriculture — $36,250

Crop Production & Basic Processing	**$14,250**
None over $5,000	
Food Processing & Sales	**$10,875**
None over $5,000	

Communications/Electronics — $148,310

Media/Entertainment	**$90,610**	
National Cable Television Assn	$9,999	PAC
Tele-Communications Inc	$7,820	PAC
Viacom International	$6,000	PAC
Gulf + Western Industries	$5,000	PAC
Home Shopping Network Inc	$5,000	PAC
MCA Inc	$5,000	PAC/Ind
National Assn of Broadcasters	$5,000	PAC

Source of Funds: 1987-1992

Source	Total	Pct
PACs	$937,427	51%
Indivs $200+	$437,974	24%
Indivs under $200	$86,086	5%
Other	$366,235	20%
Candidate	$0	0%
Party	$118,022	6%

Source of PAC Dollars by Sector

Source	Total	Pct
Business	$780,145	84%
Labor	$112,300	12%
Ideological/Single-Issue	$38,848	4%

In-State vs. Out-of-State Contributions*

Source	Total	Pct
In-State	$146,402	34%
Out-of-state	$290,572	66%
No state listed	$1,000	

* by large individual contributors ($200 & above)

Telephone Utilities	**$40,500**	
Pacific Telesis Group	$6,000	PAC
BellSouth Corp	$5,000	PAC

Construction — $34,025

General Contractors	**$18,675**	
Associated General Contractors	$5,000	PAC

Defense — $199,275

Defense Aerospace	**$113,275**	
Lockheed Corp	$12,000	PAC
General Dynamics	$10,000	PAC
Textron Inc	$10,000	PAC
United Technologies	$10,000	PAC
McDonnell Douglas*	$9,000	PAC
Grumman Corp	$7,000	PAC
Colt Industries	$6,900	PAC/Ind
General Electric	$6,500	PAC
Allied-Signal	$6,000	PAC
Boeing Co	$5,500	PAC
Martin Marietta Corp	$5,375	PAC
LTV Aerospace & Defense Co	$5,000	PAC
Rockwell International	$5,000	PAC
Defense Electronics	**$59,000**	
AT&T	$7,500	PAC
Hughes Aircraft	$7,000	PAC
Harris Corp	$5,000	PAC
Raytheon	$5,000	PAC
Misc Defense	**$27,000**	
BDM International	$5,000	PAC
CSX Corp*	$5,000	PAC

Energy & Natural Resources — $139,071

Oil & Gas	**$100,100**	
BP America	$11,600	PAC/Ind
Atlantic Richfield	$7,450	PAC/Ind
Veco Inc	$7,000	Indiv
Shell Oil	$5,000	PAC
Texaco	$5,000	PAC

Contribution Totals by Sector

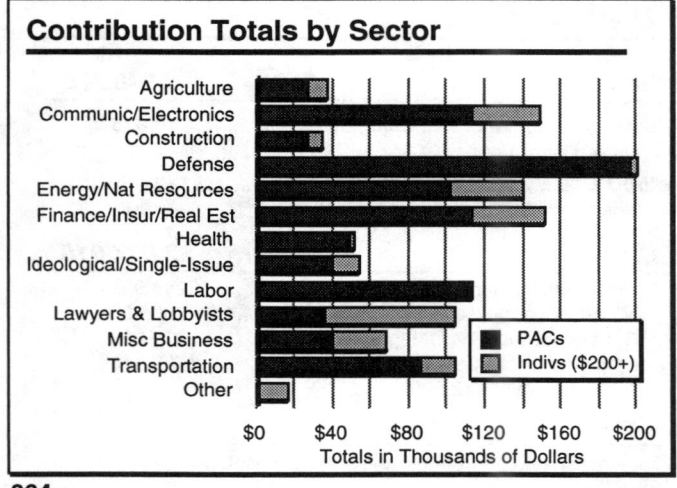

Agriculture
Communic/Electronics
Construction
Defense
Energy/Nat Resources
Finance/Insur/Real Est
Health
Ideological/Single-Issue
Labor
Lawyers & Lobbyists
Misc Business
Transportation
Other

- PACs
- Indivs ($200+)

$0 $40 $80 $120 $160 $200
Totals in Thousands of Dollars

Mining	$9,000
None over $5,000	
Electric Utilities	$11,500
None over $5,000	
Waste Management	$7,000
Waste Management Inc ...$6,500 PAC/Ind	
Commercial Fishing	$9,221
None over $5,000	

Finance, Insurance & Real Estate — $150,817

Commercial Banks ...$20,850
American Bankers Assn ...$10,000 PAC
Securities & Investment ...$27,635
None over $5,000
Insurance ...$58,232
Aetna Life & Casualty ...$9,000 PAC/Ind
American Council of Life Insurance ...$6,000 PAC
National Assn of Life Underwriters ...$5,000 PAC
Real Estate ...$30,775
National Assn of Realtors ...$10,000 PAC

Health — $50,500

Health Professionals ...$31,500
American Academy of Ophthalmology ...$6,000 PAC
American Chiropractic Assn ...$6,000 PAC
American Dental Assn ...$5,000 PAC
Hospitals/Nursing Homes ...$7,500
None over $5,000
Pharmaceuticals/Health Products ...$10,500
None over $5,000

Lawyers & Lobbyists — $103,750

Lawyers & Lobbyists ...$103,750
Assn of Trial Lawyers of America ...$5,000 PAC

Misc Business — $67,285

Food & Beverage ...$8,985
None over $5,000
Beer, Wine & Liquor ...$9,500
None over $5,000

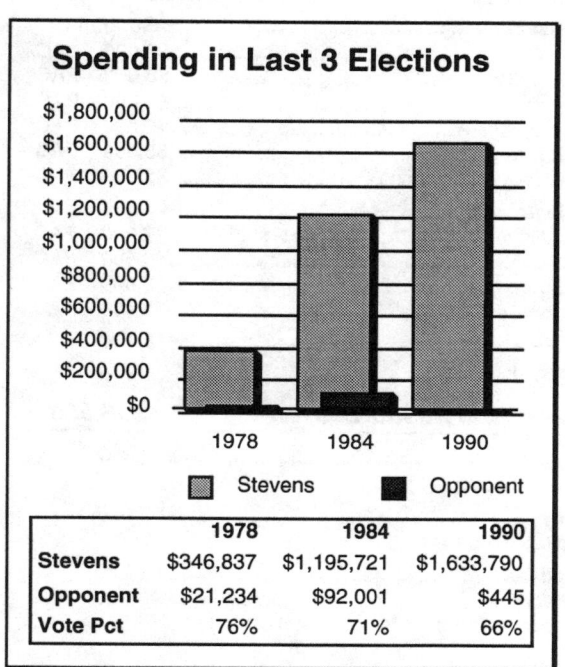

Spending in Last 3 Elections

	1978	1984	1990
Stevens	$346,837	$1,195,721	$1,633,790
Opponent	$21,234	$92,001	$445
Vote Pct	76%	71%	66%

Retail Sales	$10,950
None over $5,000	
Lodging/Tourism	$13,500
None over $5,000	

Transportation — $102,637

Air Transport ...$49,887
Federal Express Corp ...$15,712 PAC
Aircraft Owners & Pilots Assn ...$10,000 PAC
Texas Air ...$6,000 PAC
Automotive ...$15,750
Auto Dealers & Drivers for Free Trade ...$5,000 PAC
Trucking ...$10,500
None over $5,000
Sea Transport ...$19,250
None over $5,000

Labor

Labor — $112,550

Building Trade Unions ...$18,000
Plumbers/Pipefitters Union ...$6,000 PAC
Laborers' Political League ...$5,000 PAC
Operating Engineers Union ...$5,000 PAC
Transportation Unions ...$36,750
Air Line Pilots Assn ...$10,000 PAC
Teamsters Union* ...$8,750 PAC/Ind
Marine Engineers Union* ...$7,500 PAC
Seafarers International Union ...$5,000 PAC
Public Sector Unions ...$52,800
American Postal Workers Union ...$7,500 PAC
National Assn of Letter Carriers ...$7,500 PAC
American Federation of Govt Employees ...$6,000 PAC
National Rural Letter Carriers Assn ...$6,000 PAC

Ideological/Single-Issue

Ideological/Single-Issue — $53,598

Leadership PACs ...$6,600
Campaign America (Bob Dole) ...$5,000 PAC
Pro-Israel ...$22,250
National PAC ...$5,000 PAC
Human Rights ...$11,500
KidsPAC ...$5,000 PAC

Other & Unknown

Other — $15,900

Retired ...$8,150
None over $5,000

Unknown — $68,399

Homemakers/Non-income earners ...$9,730
No Employer Listed or Found ...$23,347
Generic Occupation/Category Unknown ...$9,950
Employer Listed/Category Unknown ...$25,372
None over $5,000

Independent expenditures supporting Stevens
National Rifle Assn ...$5,247

---

* Contributions came from more than one affiliate or subsidiary.

Strom Thurmond (R-SC)

First elected: 1954

1987-92 Total Rcpts: $2,240,505
1992 Year-end Cash: $160,843
Current term expires: 1996

1991-92 Committees & Subcommittees

Armed Services
Conventional Forces and Alliance Defense; Readiness, Sustainability and Support; Strategic Forces and Nuclear Deterrence (Ranking Republican)

Judiciary (Ranking Republican)
Antitrust, Monopolies and Business Rights (Ranking Republican); Courts and Administrative Practice

Labor and Human Resources
Children, Families, Drugs and Alcoholism; Education, Arts and Humanities; Employment and Productivity (Ranking Republican); Labor

Veterans' Affairs

Leading Contributors

Business

Agriculture — $96,050

Crop Production & Basic Processing	**$17,650**	
None over $5,000		
Tobacco	**$10,750**	
RJR Nabisco	$6,000	PAC
Poultry & Eggs	**$6,000**	
None over $5,000		
Agricultural Services/Products	**$9,500**	
None over $5,000		
Food Processing & Sales	**$26,000**	
Food Marketing Institute	$5,000	PAC
Pepsico Inc	$5,000	PAC
Forestry & Forest Products	**$19,900**	
Georgia-Pacific Corp	$5,000	PAC

Communications/Electronics — $41,900

Media/Entertainment	**$15,500**	
National Cable Television Assn	$5,000	PAC
Telephone Utilities	**$18,750**	
BellSouth Corp*	$5,000	PAC/Ind

Source of Funds: 1987-1992

Source	Total	Pct
PACs	$657,282	26%
Indivs $200+	$609,803	24%
Indivs under $200	$793,225	32%
Other	$438,060	18%
Candidate	$0	0%
Party	$257,865	10%

Source of PAC Dollars by Sector

Source	Total	Pct
Business	$623,302	96%
Labor	$2,250	0%
Ideological/Single-Issue	$26,250	4%

In-State vs. Out-of-State Contributions*

Source	Total	Pct
In-State	$328,830	54%
Out-of-state	$279,973	46%
No state listed	$1,000	

* by large individual contributors ($200 & above)

Construction — $68,350

General Contractors	**$35,400**	
Fluor Corp	$10,000	PAC
Associated General Contractors	$5,000	PAC
Home Builders	**$10,000**	
National Assn of Home Builders	$6,000	PAC
Construction Services	**$9,200**	
None over $5,000		
Building Materials & Equipment	**$10,750**	
None over $5,000		

Defense — $119,900

Defense Aerospace	**$59,300**	
Northrop Corp	$8,000	PAC
McDonnell Douglas*	$6,000	PAC
Textron Inc	$6,000	PAC
General Dynamics	$5,000	PAC
Lockheed Corp	$5,000	PAC
LTV Aerospace & Defense Co	$5,000	PAC
Defense Electronics	**$41,500**	
Hughes Aircraft	$7,000	PAC
AT&T	$6,500	PAC
Harris Corp	$5,000	PAC
Westinghouse Electric	$5,000	PAC
Misc Defense	**$19,100**	
None over $5,000		

Energy & Natural Resources — $58,600

Oil & Gas	**$27,800**	
None over $5,000		
Misc Energy	**$7,000**	
None over $5,000		
Electric Utilities	**$16,800**	
Scana Corp	$6,000	PAC
ACRE (Action Cmte for Rural Electrification)	$5,500	PAC

Contribution Totals by Sector

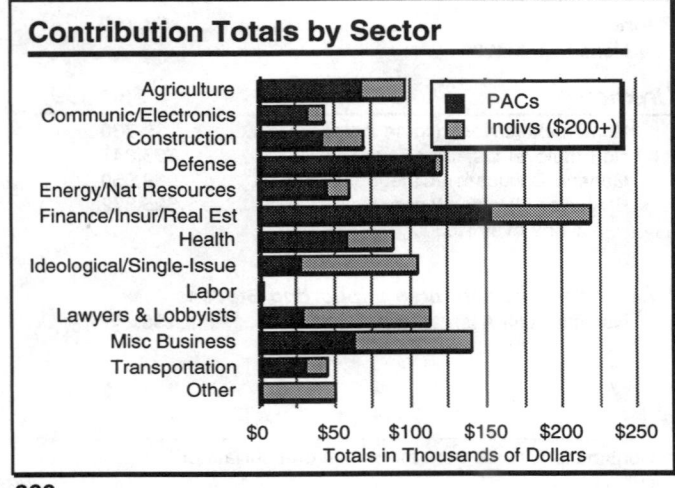

Bar chart legend: ■ PACs, ▨ Indivs ($200+)

Categories: Agriculture, Communic/Electronics, Construction, Defense, Energy/Nat Resources, Finance/Insur/Real Est, Health, Ideological/Single-Issue, Labor, Lawyers & Lobbyists, Misc Business, Transportation, Other

Scale: $0, $50, $100, $150, $200, $250
Totals in Thousands of Dollars

Finance, Insurance & Real Estate — $217,342

Commercial Banks *$53,150*
- C&S/Sovran Corp* .... $14,250 — PAC/Ind
- NCNB Corp* .... $12,500 — PAC/Ind
- American Bankers Assn .... $10,000 — PAC
- South Carolina National Bank .... $6,000 — PAC/Ind

Securities & Investment *$12,535*
- None over $5,000

Insurance *$80,357*
- Colonial Life & Accident Insurance .... $11,000 — PAC/Ind
- National Assn of Life Underwriters .... $7,500 — PAC
- National Assn of Independent Insurers .... $6,357 — PAC
- American Council of Life Insurance .... $5,000 — PAC
- American Family Corp .... $5,000 — PAC

Real Estate *$43,800*
- National Assn of Realtors .... $7,750 — PAC
- Drizin Real Estate Developers .... $6,000 — Indiv
- Century 21 Real Estate .... $5,000 — PAC

Accountants *$14,250*
- American Institute of CPA's .... $10,000 — PAC

Misc Finance *$9,500*
- None over $5,000

Health — $87,380

Health Professionals *$65,250*
- American Medical Assn .... $10,000 — PAC
- Pee Dee Pathologist .... $7,000 — Indiv
- American Chiropractic Assn .... $5,000 — PAC
- American Dental Assn .... $5,000 — PAC
- American Optometric Assn .... $5,000 — PAC
- American Podiatry Assn .... $5,000 — PAC
- American Assn Oral & Maxillofacial Surgeons .... $5,000 — PAC

Hospitals/Nursing Homes *$6,000*
- None over $5,000

Pharmaceuticals/Health Products *$16,130*
- None over $5,000

Lawyers & Lobbyists — $111,600

Lawyers & Lobbyists *$111,600*
- Assn of Trial Lawyers of America .... $10,000 — PAC
- Thompson, Mann & Hutson .... $10,000 — Indiv

Misc Business — $138,960

Food & Beverage *$17,860*
- None over $5,000

Retail Sales *$10,300*
- None over $5,000

Business Services *$10,750*
- None over $5,000

Chemical & Related Manufacturing *$12,700*
- None over $5,000

Steel Production *$12,500*
- Macalloy Corp .... $11,500 — Indiv

Misc Manufacturing & Distributing *$23,350*
- Hoechst Celanese Corp .... $5,000 — PAC

Textiles *$41,150*
- Milliken & Co .... $6,000 — Indiv

Transportation — $43,550

Air Transport *$18,250*
- Federal Express Corp .... $6,000 — PAC

Automotive *$7,700*
- None over $5,000

Trucking *$8,000*
- None over $5,000

Sea Transport *$5,500*
- None over $5,000

Ideological/Single-Issue

Ideological/Single-Issue — $103,414

Republican/Conservative *$71,534*
- National Republican Senatorial Cmte .... $6,000 — Indiv

Leadership PACs *$11,000*
- Campaign America (Bob Dole) .... $10,000 — PAC

Foreign & Defense Policy *$5,180*
- None over $5,000

Gun Rights/Gun Control *$9,900*
- National Rifle Assn .... $9,900 — PAC

Misc Issues *$5,550*
- None over $5,000

Other & Unknown

Other — $48,170

Education *$9,900*
- None over $5,000

Retired *$31,720*
- None over $5,000

Unknown — $113,439
- Homemakers/Non-income earners $27,050
- No Employer Listed or Found $20,814
- Employer Listed/Category Unknown $65,375
  - None over $5,000

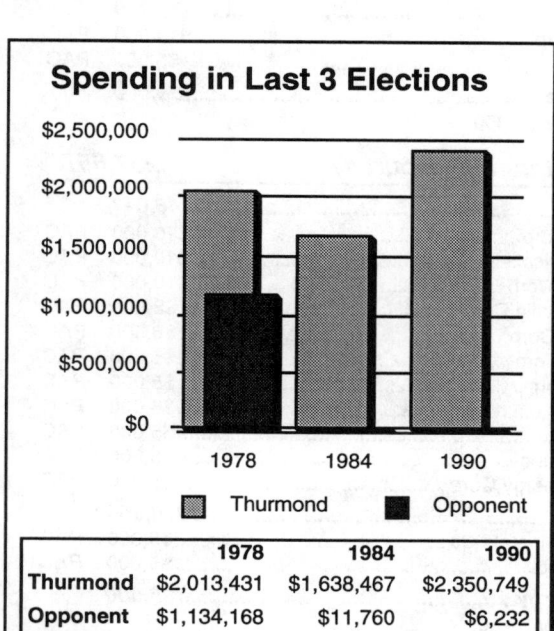

Spending in Last 3 Elections

	1978	1984	1990
Thurmond	$2,013,431	$1,638,467	$2,350,749
Opponent	$1,134,168	$11,760	$6,232
Vote Pct	56%	67%	64%

Legend: Thurmond / Opponent

* Contributions came from more than one affiliate or subsidiary.

367

Malcolm Wallop (R-Wyo)

First elected: 1976

1987-92 Total Rcpts:	$1,680,549
1992 Year-end Cash:	$143,400
Current term expires:	1994

1991-92 Committees & Subcommittees

Armed Services
Conventional Forces and Alliance Defense (Ranking Republican);
Manpower and Personnel; Strategic Forces and Nuclear Deterrence

Energy and Natural Resources (Ranking Republican)

Small Business
Export Expansion; Rural Economy and Family Farming

Leading Contributors

NOTE: The bulk of Jefford's large individual contributions do not appear in the listings below. His last election was in 1988, and this book lists individual contributions only from 1989-1992.

Business

Agriculture	$81,657

Crop Production & Basic Processing	$20,508	
None over $5,000		
Tobacco	**$17,916**	
Philip Morris	$6,250	PAC/Ind
RJR Nabisco	$6,000	PAC
Livestock	**$11,400**	
National Cattlemen's Assn*	$6,000	PAC
Agricultural Services/Products	**$8,500**	
None over $5,000		
Food Processing & Sales	**$12,333**	
None over $5,000		
Forestry & Forest Products	**$10,500**	
None over $5,000		

Communications/Electronics	$46,727

Media/Entertainment	**$11,500**
None over $5,000	
Telephone Utilities	**$22,261**
None over $5,000	
Electronics Mfg & Services	**$5,030**
None over $5,000	
Computer Equipment & Services	**$5,000**
None over $5,000	

Source of Funds: 1987-1992

Source	Total	Pct
PACs	$1,009,852	56%
Indivs $200+	$301,992	17%
Indivs under $200	$196,637	11%
Other	$281,483	16%
Candidate	$0	0%
Party	$109,415	6%

Source of PAC Dollars by Sector

Source	Total	Pct
Business	$916,807	91%
Labor	$6,000	1%
Ideological/Single-Issue	$82,510	8%

In-State vs. Out-of-State Contributions*

Source	Total	Pct
In-State	$83,937	28%
Out-of-state	$217,555	72%
No state listed	$500	

* by large individual contributors ($200 & above)

Construction	$33,000

General Contractors	**$17,750**	
Associated General Contractors	$10,000	PAC
Special Trade Contractors	**$8,000**	
None over $5,000		

Defense	$84,111

Defense Aerospace	**$53,111**	
Rockwell International	$14,000	PAC
Northrop Corp	$7,500	PAC
Textron Inc	$7,500	PAC
Defense Electronics	**$23,000**	
Harris Corp	$10,000	PAC
TRW Inc	$5,000	PAC
Misc Defense	**$8,000**	
None over $5,000		

Energy & Natural Resources	$237,557

Oil & Gas	**$146,017**	
Amoco Corp	$10,000	PAC
Atlantic Richfield	$10,000	PAC
Chevron Corp	$10,000	PAC
Union Pacific Corp	$8,000	PAC
Enserch Corp	$6,500	PAC
Coastal Corp	$5,500	PAC
Exxon Corp	$5,000	PAC
Mobil Oil	$5,000	PAC
Shell Oil	$5,000	PAC
Tenneco Inc	$5,000	PAC
Valero Energy Corp	$5,000	PAC
Mining	**$30,500**	
Cyprus Minerals Co	$5,000	PAC
Mapco Inc	$5,000	PAC
Nuclear Energy	**$5,500**	
None over $5,000		

Contribution Totals by Sector

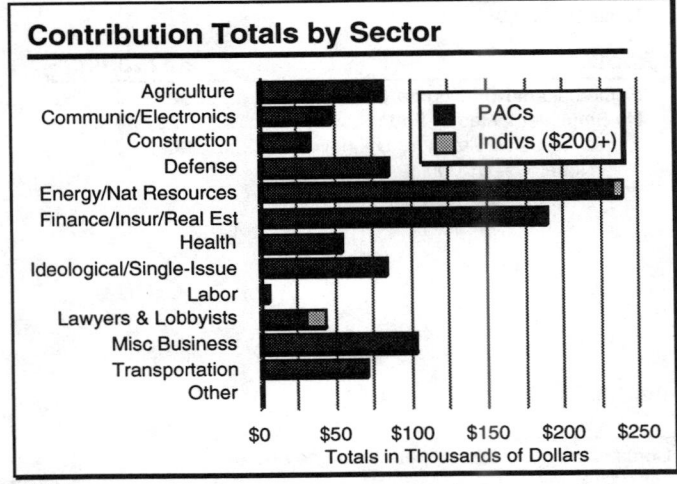

Agriculture, Communic/Electronics, Construction, Defense, Energy/Nat Resources, Finance/Insur/Real Est, Health, Ideological/Single-Issue, Labor, Lawyers & Lobbyists, Misc Business, Transportation, Other

Legend: PACs, Indivs ($200+)

$0 $50 $100 $150 $200 $250
Totals in Thousands of Dollars

Misc Energy **$8,750**		
None over $5,000		
Electric Utilities **$39,325**		
Pacific Gas & Electric $8,250	PAC	
Waste Management **$7,465**		
None over $5,000		

Finance, Insurance & Real Estate $188,743

Commercial Banks **$22,833**		
American Bankers Assn $11,000	PAC	
JP Morgan & Co $6,000	PAC	
Savings & Loans **$5,000**		
None over $5,000		
Securities & Investment **$49,417**		
National Venture Capital Assn $10,000	PAC	
Merrill Lynch $6,667	PAC	
EF Hutton $5,000	PAC	
Insurance **$78,943**		
Torchmark Corp $8,834	PAC	
National Assn of Independent Insurers $6,000	PAC	
Aetna Life & Casualty $5,000	PAC	
American Council of Life Insurance $5,000	PAC	
Real Estate **$9,300**		
None over $5,000		
Accountants **$18,500**		
American Institute of CPA's $10,000	PAC	
Deloitte & Touche $5,000	PAC	

Health $53,000

Health Professionals **$30,000**		
American Medical Assn $10,000	PAC	
American Academy of Ophthalmology $8,000	PAC	
American Dental Assn $6,000	PAC	
Pharmaceuticals/Health Products **$19,000**		
Abbott Laboratories $5,000	PAC	

Lawyers & Lobbyists $41,750

Lawyers & Lobbyists **$41,750**		
None over $5,000		

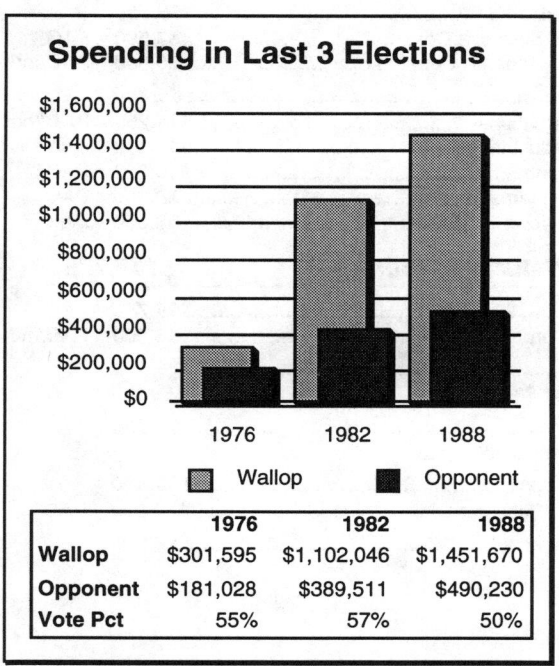

Spending in Last 3 Elections

	1976	1982	1988
Wallop	$301,595	$1,102,046	$1,451,670
Opponent	$181,028	$389,511	$490,230
Vote Pct	55%	57%	50%

Misc Business $102,402

Business Associations **$7,603**		
None over $5,000		
Food & Beverage **$12,300**		
National Restaurant Assn $5,000	PAC	
Beer, Wine & Liquor **$18,000**		
National Beer Wholesalers Assn $11,000	PAC	
Retail Sales **$8,666**		
None over $5,000		
Business Services **$8,750**		
None over $5,000		
Casinos/Gambling **$6,000**		
Nevada Resort Assn $6,000	PAC	
Chemical & Related Manufacturing **$19,250**		
FMC Corp $10,000	PAC	
Misc Manufacturing & Distributing **$9,833**		
None over $5,000		

Transportation $69,010

Air Transport **$21,083**		
United Parcel Service $7,500	PAC	
Automotive **$26,700**		
Auto Dealers & Drivers for Free Trade $10,000	PAC	
National Auto Dealers Assn $10,000	PAC	
Trucking **$11,727**		
American Trucking Assns $5,077	PAC	
Railroads **$7,000**		
None over $5,000		

Labor

Labor $6,000

Ideological/Single-Issue

Ideological/Single-Issue $82,510

Leadership PACs **$34,297**		
Campaign America (Bob Dole) $10,000	PAC	
Republican Majority Fund (Richard Lugar) $10,000	PAC	
Fund for a Republican Majority (Ted Stevens) $5,000	PAC	
Foreign & Defense Policy **$7,211**		
National Security PAC $5,009	PAC	
Pro-Israel **$10,733**		
Hudson Valley PAC $5,233	PAC	
Gun Rights/Gun Control **$9,764**		
National Rifle Assn $8,764	PAC	
Misc Issues **$13,155**		
Public Service Research Council $7,000	PAC	
Right to Work PAC $5,905	PAC	

Independent expenditures supporting Wallop
Auto Dealers & Drivers for Free Trade $88,862
National Security PAC.....................................$58,728

---

* Contributions came from more than one affiliate or subsidiary.

John W. Warner (R-Va)

First elected: 1978

1987-92 Total Rcpts:	$1,892,918
1992 Year-end Cash:	$160,162
Current term expires:	1996

1991-92 Committees & Subcommittees

Armed Services (Ranking Republican)

Environment and Public Works
Environmental Protection; Toxic Substances, Environmental Oversight, Research and Development (Ranking Republican); Water Resources, Transportation and Infrastructure

Rules and Administration

Select Committee on Intelligence

Leading Contributors

Business

Agriculture	$98,240

Crop Production & Basic Processing $17,850
None over $6,000

Tobacco $23,000
None over $6,000

Dairy $6,625
None over $6,000

Food Processing & Sales $21,375
None over $6,000

Forestry & Forest Products $19,000
None over $6,000

Communications/Electronics	$45,500

Printing & Publishing $6,250
None over $6,000

Media/Entertainment $8,500
None over $6,000

Telephone Utilities $12,500
None over $6,000

Computer Equipment & Services $13,000
None over $6,000

Construction	$111,325

General Contractors $51,825
   Miller & Smith Co .... $9,000   Indiv

Home Builders $25,000
None over $6,000

Source of Funds: 1987-1992

Source	Total	Pct
PACs	$765,385	38%
Indivs $200+	$801,460	40%
Indivs under $200	$28,093	1%
Other	$401,770	20%
Candidate	$0	0%
Party	$103,790	5%

Source of PAC Dollars by Sector

Source	Total	Pct
Business	$734,409	94%
Labor	$34,350	4%
Ideological/Single-Issue	$11,750	2%

In-State vs. Out-of-State Contributions*

Source	Total	Pct
In-State	$512,365	64%
Out-of-state	$289,110	36%
No state listed	$-15	

*** by large individual contributors ($200 & above)**

Special Trade Contractors $15,000
   William A Hazel Inc .... $11,000   Indiv

Construction Services $7,000
None over $6,000

Building Materials & Equipment $12,500
None over $6,000

Defense	$206,692

Defense Aerospace $74,982
   McDonnell Douglas* .... $6,000   PAC
   Northrop Corp .... $6,000   PAC

Defense Electronics $66,360
   Computer Sciences Corp .... $7,500   PAC
   Planning Research Corp .... $6,000   PAC/Ind

Misc Defense $65,350
   BDM International .... $14,250   PAC/Ind
   Unified Industries Inc .... $11,000   Indiv
   Tenneco Inc .... $10,000   PAC
   Mantech International .... $8,850   PAC
   Newport News Shipbuilding .... $6,000   Indiv

Energy & Natural Resources	$119,775

Oil & Gas $59,750
   Amoco Corp .... $6,500   PAC/Ind

Mining $21,025
None over $6,000

Misc Energy $7,000
None over $6,000

Electric Utilities $23,500
   Dominion Resources Inc .... $10,000   PAC

Waste Management $7,000
None over $6,000

Contribution Totals by Sector

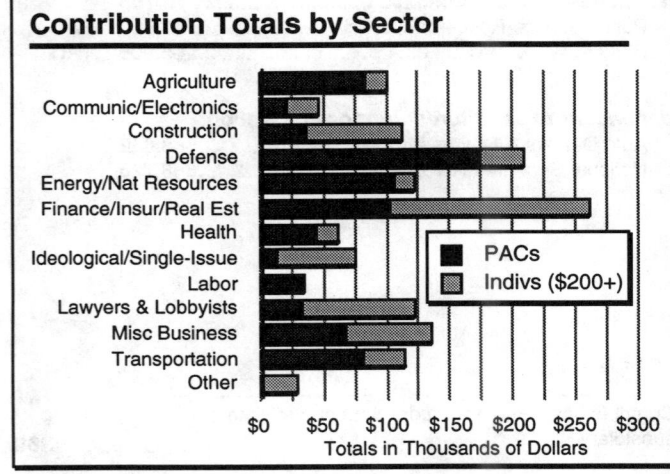

Agriculture
Communic/Electronics
Construction
Defense
Energy/Nat Resources
Finance/Insur/Real Est
Health
Ideological/Single-Issue
Labor
Lawyers & Lobbyists
Misc Business
Transportation
Other

PACs
Indivs ($200+)

$0 $50 $100 $150 $200 $250 $300
Totals in Thousands of Dollars

Finance, Insurance & Real Estate $257,967

Commercial Banks *$44,000*
   Barnett Banks Inc ....$11,000   PAC
   American Bankers Assn ....$10,000   PAC
   C&S/Sovran Corp* ....$7,400   PAC/Ind

Securities & Investment *$23,385*
   None over $6,000

Insurance *$26,232*
   None over $6,000

Real Estate *$124,725*
   Hazel-Peterson Companies ....$10,000   Indiv
   Mark Winkler Co ....$10,000   Indiv
   National Assn of Realtors.................................$10,000   PAC
   Cavalier Land Development Corp ....$6,000   Indiv
   Drizin Real Estate Developers ....$6,000   Indiv

Accountants *$16,125*
   American Institute of CPA's ....$9,625   PAC

Misc Finance *$18,000*
   None over $6,000

Health $61,195

Health Professionals *$32,445*
   None over $6,000

Pharmaceuticals/Health Products *$26,750*
   None over $6,000

Lawyers & Lobbyists $119,620

Lawyers & Lobbyists....................................*$119,620*
   McGuire, Woods et al ....$10,000   PAC

Misc Business $133,545

Beer, Wine & Liquor *$6,000*
   National Beer Wholesalers Assn ....$6,000   PAC

Retail Sales...*$30,000*
   None over $6,000

Business Services *$37,725*
   Dun & Bradstreet ....$6,725   PAC/Ind

Lodging/Tourism *$9,150*
   None over $6,000

Spending in Last 3 Elections

	1978	1984	1990
Warner	$2,897,237	$2,786,140	$1,311,131
Opponent	$832,773	$492,201	$0
Vote Pct	50%	70%	81%

Chemical & Related Manufacturing *$21,750*
   Ethyl Corp ....$7,000   PAC/Ind

Misc Manufacturing & Distributing *$12,500*
   None over $6,000

Transportation $112,650

Air Transport *$46,500*
   Worldcorp Inc ....$10,000   PAC
   Federal Express Corp ....$8,000   PAC

Automotive *$24,800*
   National Auto Dealers Assn ....$6,500   PAC

Trucking..*$8,000*
   None over $6,000

Railroads *$21,450*
   None over $6,000

Sea Transport...*$9,900*
   None over $6,000

Labor

Labor $34,350

Transportation Unions *$26,000*
   Marine Engineers Union* ....$10,000   PAC
   Seafarers International Union ....$7,000   PAC

Public Sector Unions *$7,350*
   None over $6,000

Ideological/Single-Issue

Ideological/Single-Issue $74,050

Republican/Conservative *$57,900*
   None over $6,000

Leadership PACs...*$6,415*
   None over $6,000

Other & Unknown

Other $28,385

Retired *$15,975*
   None over $6,000

Unknown $179,475

   Homemakers/Non-income earners $24,550
   No Employer Listed or Found $45,825
   Employer Listed/Category Unknown...............$103,900
      None over $6,000

---

* Contributions came from more than one affiliate or
subsidiary.

371

Paul Wellstone (D-Minn)

First elected: 1990

1989-92 Total Rcpts: $2,063,410
1992 Year-end Cash: $3,390
Current term expires: 1996

1991-92 Committees & Subcommittees

Energy and Natural Resources
Energy Regulation and Conservation; Energy Research and Development; Public Lands, National Parks and Forests

Labor and Human Resources
Children, Families, Drugs and Alcoholism; Education, Arts and Humanities; Labor

Small Business
Rural Economy and Family Farming; Urban and Minority-Owned Business Development

Select Committee on Indian Affairs

Leading Contributors

Business

Agriculture	$20,738

Crop Production & Basic Processing	$11,288	
American Crystal Sugar Corp	$8,000	PAC
Agricultural Services/Products	**$6,750**	
None over $2,500		

Communications/Electronics	$21,895

Printing & Publishing	$8,950	
None over $2,500		
Telephone Utilities	**$5,000**	
AT&T	$5,000	PAC
Computer Equipment & Services	**$6,695**	
None over $2,500		

Construction	$2,550
None over $2,500	

Energy & Natural Resources	$5,700

Electric Utilities	$5,500	
ACRE (Action Cmte for Rural Electrification)	$5,000	PAC

Finance, Insurance & Real Estate	$18,000

Securities & Investment	$13,950	
Mailman Brothers	$4,000	Indiv

Source of Funds: 1987-1992

Source	Total	Pct
PACs	$413,024	19%
Indivs $200+	$268,838	12%
Indivs under $200	$1,306,276	59%
Other	$227,772	10%
Candidate	$0	0%
Party	$152,500	7%

Source of PAC Dollars by Sector

Source	Total	Pct
Business	$61,605	15%
Labor	$273,686	66%
Ideological/Single-Issue	$79,132	19%

In-State vs. Out-of-State Contributions*

Source	Total	Pct
In-State	$172,346	68%
Out-of-state	$82,617	32%
No state listed	$13,875	

* by large individual contributors ($200 & above)

Health	$19,125

Health Professionals	$14,375
None over $2,500	
Hospitals/Nursing Homes	**$2,700**
None over $2,500	

Lawyers & Lobbyists	$41,606

Lawyers & Lobbyists	$41,606	
Assn of Trial Lawyers of America	$10,000	PAC
Kaplan-Strangis	$6,946	Indiv
Faegre & Benson	$2,750	PAC/Ind

Misc Business	$15,515

Business Services	$3,610	
None over $2,500		
Misc Manufacturing & Distributing	**$6,005**	
None over $2,500		

Transportation	$3,925
None over $2,500	

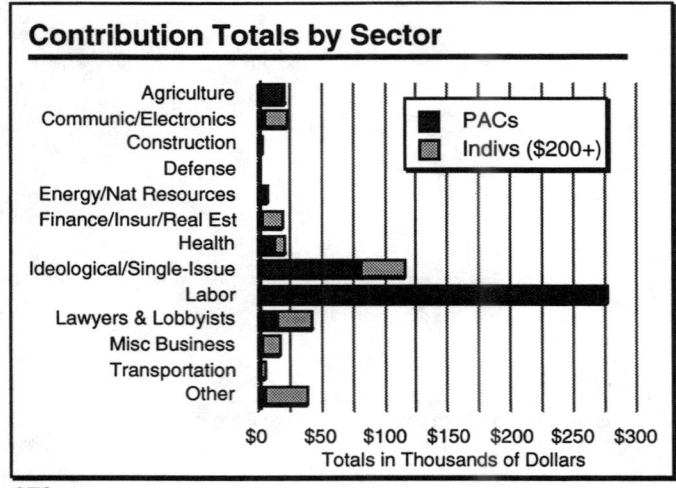

Contribution Totals by Sector

- Agriculture
- Communic/Electronics
- Construction
- Defense
- Energy/Nat Resources
- Finance/Insur/Real Est
- Health
- Ideological/Single-Issue
- Labor
- Lawyers & Lobbyists
- Misc Business
- Transportation
- Other

Legend: ■ PACs ▨ Indivs ($200+)

$0 $50 $100 $150 $200 $250 $300
Totals in Thousands of Dollars

Labor

Labor	$273,986	

Building Trade Unions **$32,400**
Carpenters & Joiners Union	$10,000	PAC
Laborers' Political League	$10,000	PAC
Plumbers/Pipefitters Union	$5,500	PAC
Operating Engineers Union	$3,500	PAC

Industrial Unions **$98,050**
American Federation of Teachers	$10,000	PAC
Communications Workers of America	$10,000	PAC
Intl Brotherhood of Electrical Workers	$10,000	PAC
Machinists/Aerospace Workers Union	$10,000	PAC
National Education Assn	$10,000	PAC
United Auto Workers	$10,000	PAC
United Steelworkers	$10,000	PAC
Amalgamated Clothing & Textile Workers	$6,000	PAC
Oil, Chemical & Atomic Workers Union	$4,300	PAC
United Paperworkers	$4,000	PAC
Electronic Machine Furniture Workers	$3,500	PAC
United Mine Workers	$3,500	PAC

Transportation Unions **$46,750**
Teamsters Union*	$10,000	PAC
Transport Workers Union	$9,000	PAC
Air Line Pilots Assn	$7,500	PAC
Amalgamated Transit Union	$5,000	PAC
United Transportation Union	$5,000	PAC
Trans Comm International Union	$3,500	PAC

Public Sector Unions **$62,036**
National Assn of Letter Carriers*	$15,800	PAC
American Fedn of St/Cnty/Munic Employees	$10,000	PAC
American Postal Workers Union	$10,000	PAC
Natl Assn of Retired Federal Employees	$7,636	PAC
National Treasury Employees Union	$4,000	PAC
National Assn Retired Federal Employees	$3,000	PAC
American Federation of Govt Employees	$2,500	PAC
National League of Postmasters	$2,500	PAC

Misc Unions **$34,750**
AFL-CIO	$10,000	PAC
Food & Commercial Workers Union	$10,000	PAC
Office & Professional Employees Union	$5,500	PAC
Service Employees International Union	$3,000	PAC

Ideological/Single-Issue

Ideological/Single-Issue	$115,095	

Democratic/Liberal **$35,742**
Independent Action	$5,500	PAC
National Cmte for an Effective Congress	$5,000	PAC
Democrats for the 80's	$2,500	PAC

Leadership PACs **$5,727**
| Fund for a Democratic Majority (Ted Kennedy) | $3,500 | PAC |

Foreign & Defense Policy **$6,500**
| None over $2,500 | | |

Pro-Choice **$6,784**
| National Abortion Rights Action League | $3,084 | PAC |

Gun Rights/Gun Control **$4,500**
| Handgun Control Inc | $4,500 | PAC |

Womens Issues **$9,775**
| None over $2,500 | | |

Human Rights **$15,530**
Human Rights Campaign Fund	$5,330	PAC
KidsPAC	$5,000	PAC
National Community Action Foundation	$5,000	PAC

Misc Issues **$29,287**
National Cmte to Preserve Social Security	$10,000	PAC
National Council of Senior Citizens	$5,000	PAC
Sierra Club	$4,000	PAC
Greenvote	$3,740	PAC

Other & Unknown

Other	$37,408	

Civil Servants/Public Officials **$7,958**
| State of Minnesota | $3,500 | Indiv |

Education **$13,410**
| University of Minnesota | $3,200 | Indiv |

Retired **$9,890**
| None over $2,500 | | |

Other **$4,900**
| National Assn of Social Workers | $4,200 | PAC |

Unknown	$111,918	

Homemakers/Non-income earners	$4,800	
No Employer Listed or Found	$86,281	
Generic Occupation/Category Unknown	$6,000	
Employer Listed/Category Unknown	$14,837	
None over $2,500		

Independent expenditures opposing Wellstone
| American Citizens for Political Action | $4,368 | |

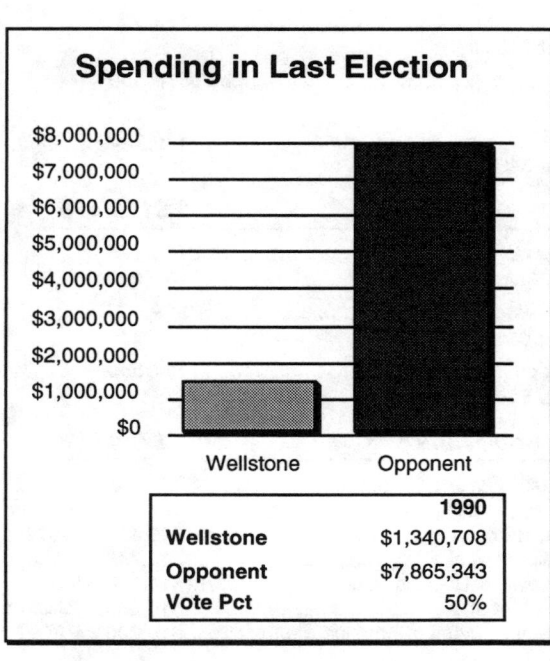

Spending in Last Election

	1990
Wellstone	$1,340,708
Opponent	$7,865,343
Vote Pct	50%

---

* Contributions came from more than one affiliate or subsidiary.

Harris Wofford (D-Pa)

First elected: 1991

1991-92 Total Rcpts:	$3,982,806
1992 Year-end Cash:	$454,565
Current term expires:	1994

1991-92 Committees & Subcommittees

Environment and Public Works
Superfund, Ocean and Water Protection; Toxic Substances, Environmental Oversight, Research and Development

Foreign Relations
International Economic Policy, Trade, Oceans and Environment; Near Eastern and South Asian Affairs; Western Hemisphere and Peace Corps Affairs

Small Business
Export Expansion; Rural Economy and Family Farming

Leading Contributors

Business

Agriculture		$37,250

Crop Production & Basic Processing $12,500
   None over $10,000

Communications/Electronics		$104,450

Printing & Publishing $29,650
   None over $10,000
Media/Entertainment $42,550
   None over $10,000
Telephone Utilities $12,500
   AT&T .... $10,000   PAC

Construction		$65,150

General Contractors $15,350
   None over $10,000
Building Materials & Equipment $29,300
   None over $10,000

Defense		$10,000

   None over $10,000

Energy & Natural Resources		$121,650

Oil & Gas $43,900
   None over $10,000
Nuclear Energy $14,000
   None over $10,000

Source of Funds: 1987-1992

Source	Total	Pct
■ PACs	$1,031,159	21%
▤ Indivs $200+	$2,275,987	46%
☐ Indivs under $200	$500,413	10%
⊠ Other.......................	$1,163,838	23%
Candidate	$2,000	0%
Party	$988,591	20%

Source of PAC Dollars by Sector

Source	Total	Pct
■ Business	$402,824	39%
▤ Labor	$453,500	44%
☐ Ideological/Single-Issue ..	$173,335	17%

In-State vs. Out-of-State Contributions*

Source	Total	Pct
☐ In-State	$1,120,056	49%
■ Out-of-state	$1,151,525	51%
No state listed	$0	

* by large individual contributors ($200 & above)

Electric Utilities $23,750
   None over $10,000
Waste Management $31,500
   Chambers Development Co .... $17,000   PAC/Ind

Finance, Insurance & Real Estate		$344,950

Commercial Banks $17,500
   None over $10,000
Securities & Investment $134,000
   Chicago Mercantile Exchange .... $12,000   PAC/Ind
Insurance $71,500
   None over $10,000
Real Estate $79,500
   None over $10,000
Accountants $10,500
   None over $10,000
Misc Finance $18,450
   None over $10,000

Health		$156,425

Health Professionals $103,175
   American Chiropractic Assn .... $10,000   PAC
Hospitals/Nursing Homes $29,300
   None over $10,000
Health Services $11,550
   None over $10,000

Lawyers & Lobbyists		$724,065

Lawyers & Lobbyists $724,065
   Barrack, Rodos & Bacine .... $23,500   PAC/Ind
   Schnader, Harrison et al .... $20,450   PAC/Ind
   Verner, Liipfert et al .... $12,749   PAC/Ind
   Morgan, Lewis & Bockius .... $11,250   Indiv
   Reed, Smith et al .... $10,600   PAC/Ind
   Assn of Trial Lawyers of America .... $10,000   PAC

Contribution Totals by Sector

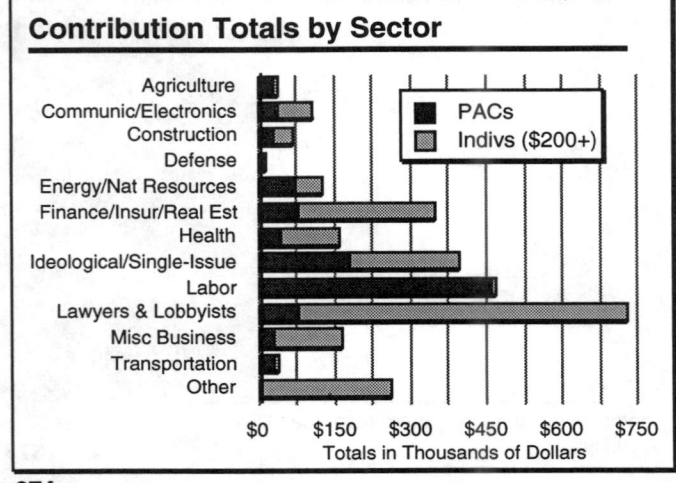

Totals in Thousands of Dollars

Misc Business — $162,845

Food & Beverage $16,000
  None over $10,000
Retail Sales $20,350
  None over $10,000
Business Services $45,945
  None over $10,000
Casinos/Gambling $11,000
  None over $10,000
Misc Manufacturing & Distributing $28,250
  None over $10,000

Transportation — $33,600

Air Transport $20,500
  None over $10,000

Labor

Labor — $463,979

Building Trade Unions $86,350
  Carpenters & Joiners Union .... $15,000 PAC
  Laborers' Political League .... $15,000 PAC
  Sheet Metal Workers Union .... $15,000 PAC
  Operating Engineers Union .... $10,000 PAC
  Plumbers/Pipefitters Union .... $10,000 PAC
Industrial Unions $154,600
  Communications Workers of America* .... $15,000 PAC
  United Auto Workers .... $15,000 PAC
  United Mine Workers .... $15,000 PAC
  United Steelworkers .... $15,000 PAC
  Electronic Machine Furniture Workers .... $12,500 PAC
  Amalgamated Clothing & Textile Workers .... $11,000 PAC
  Boilermakers Union .... $10,000 PAC
  Glass Molders Pottery Plastics Workers .... $10,000 PAC
  Machinists/Aerospace Workers Union .... $10,000 PAC
  Rubber Cork Linoleum & Plastic Workers .... $10,000 PAC

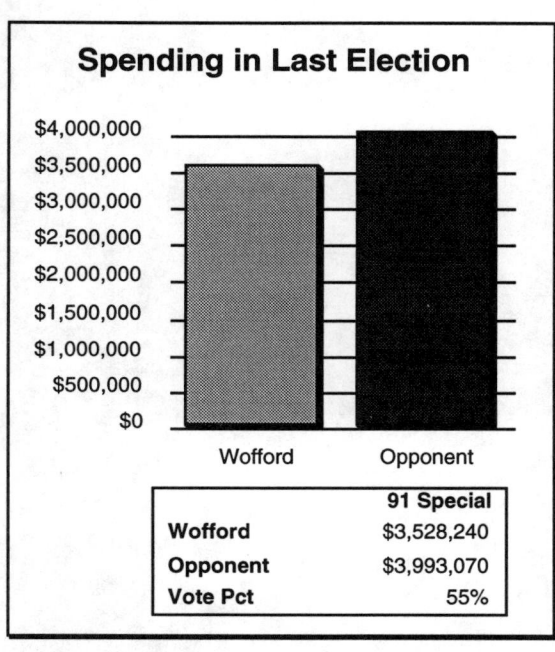

Spending in Last Election

	91 Special
Wofford	$3,528,240
Opponent	$3,993,070
Vote Pct	55%

Transportation Unions $79,250
  Amalgamated Transit Union .... $11,000 PAC
  Air Line Pilots Assn .... $10,000 PAC
  Marine Engineers Union* .... $10,000 PAC
  Seafarers International Union .... $10,000 PAC
  United Transportation Union .... $10,000 PAC
Public Sector Unions $94,750
  American Federation of Teachers..................... $15,000 PAC
  American Fedn of St/Cnty/Munic Employees .... $15,000 PAC
  American Postal Workers Union .... $15,000 PAC
Misc Unions $49,029
  Service Employees International Union .... $15,700 PAC/Ind
  Food & Commercial Workers Union .... $10,000 PAC

Ideological/Single-Issue

Ideological/Single-Issue — $390,625

Democratic/Liberal $84,430
  National Cmte for an Effective Congress .... $10,000 PAC
Leadership PACs $41,446
  Fund for a Democratic Majority (Ted Kennedy) . $10,000 PAC
Foreign & Defense Policy $11,451
  None over $10,000
Pro-Israel $172,450
  Citizens Organized PAC .... $10,000 PAC
Womens Issues $14,350
  None over $10,000
Human Rights $35,800
  Human Rights Campaign Fund .... $10,000 PAC
  KidsPAC .... $10,000 PAC
Misc Issues $26,198
  None over $10,000

Other & Unknown

Other — $259,039

Civil Servants/Public Officials $35,150
  Commonwealth of Pennsylvania .... $14,950 Indiv
Education $80,950
  University of Pennsylvania .... $13,200 Indiv
Retired $128,414
  None over $10,000
Other $10,275
  None over $10,000

Unknown — $435,368

  Homemakers/Non-income earners $116,750
  No Employer Listed or Found $172,036
  Generic Occupation/Category Unknown $14,300
  Employer Listed/Category Unknown $132,282
    None over $10,000

Independent expenditures supporting Wofford
  National Council of Senior Citizens $53,099
Independent expenditures opposing Wofford
  National Rifle Assn $40,292

---

* Contributions came from more than one affiliate or
  subsidiary.

Member Profiles
U.S. House of Representatives

pen Secrets

Neil Abercrombie, D-Hawaii (1)

First elected: 1990

1991-92 Total Receipts: $359,336
1992 Year-end Cash: $33,907

1991-92 Committees & Subcommittees

Armed Services
Military Installations and Facilities; Readiness

Interior and Insular Affairs
Geberal Oversight and California Desert Lands; National Parks and Public Lands; Water, Power and Offshore Energy

Select Committee on Aging

Leading Contributors

Business

Agriculture	$9,400	
Crop Production & Basic Processing	**$5,400**	
US Beet Sugar Assn	$1,500	PAC
Florida Sugar Cane League	$1,000	PAC
Dairy	**$2,500**	
Associated Milk Producers	$2,000	PAC
Misc Agriculture	**$1,000**	
Agriculture Concepts Inc	$1,000	Indiv

Communications/Electronics	$4,426	
Printing & Publishing	**$1,000**	
None over $1,000		
Media/Entertainment	**$1,500**	
Pacific Theaters Agency	$1,000	Indiv
Telephone Utilities	**$1,926**	
AT&T	$1,200	PAC/Ind

Construction	$13,800	
General Contractors	**$4,500**	
Morrison-Knudsen	$2,500	PAC
Obayashi Corp	$2,000	Indiv
Home Builders	**$2,500**	
National Assn of Home Builders	$2,500	PAC
Special Trade Contractors	**$1,000**	
T Kashiwagi Tractor Service	$1,000	Indiv
Construction Services	**$5,800**	
Engineers Surveyors Hawaii	$1,400	Indiv
Kilohana Corp	$1,000	PAC
Mitsunaga Associates	$1,000	Indiv

Source of Funds in 1992 Election

Source	Total	Pct
■ PACs	$176,568	48%
▦ Indivs $200+	$49,203	13%
☐ Indivs under $200	$69,991	19%
▨ Other	$73,782	20%
Candidate	$0	0%
Party	$10,658	3%

Source of PAC Dollars by Sector

Source	Total	Pct
■ Business	$66,226	34%
▦ Labor	$115,800	60%
☐ Ideology/Single Issue	$11,000	6%

In-State vs. Out-of-State Contributions*

Source	Total	Pct
☐ In-State	$36,403	74%
■ Out-of-state	$12,800	26%
No state listed	$0	

by large individual contributors ($200 & above)

Defense	$1,750	
Defense Aerospace	**$1,000**	
None over $1,000		

Energy & Natural Resources	$5,300	
Oil & Gas	**$1,800**	
Pacific Resources	$1,300	PAC
Electric Utilities	**$1,500**	
ACRE (Action Cmte for Rural Electrification)	$1,000	PAC
Waste Management	**$1,500**	
Waste Management Inc	$1,500	PAC

Finance, Insurance & Real Estate	$26,253	
Commercial Banks	**$4,700**	
First Hawaiian Inc	$2,000	PAC
Bancorp Hawaii	$1,500	PAC
Savings & Loans	**$1,100**	
None over $1,000		
Credit Unions	**$1,000**	
None over $1,000		
Securities & Investment	**$1,250**	
American Express	$1,000	PAC
Insurance	**$1,750**	
American Council of Life Insurance	$1,000	PAC
Real Estate	**$16,200**	
National Assn of Realtors	$15,000	PAC

Health	$2,850	
Health Professionals	**$2,850**	
American Nurses Assn	$1,000	PAC

Contribution Totals by Sector

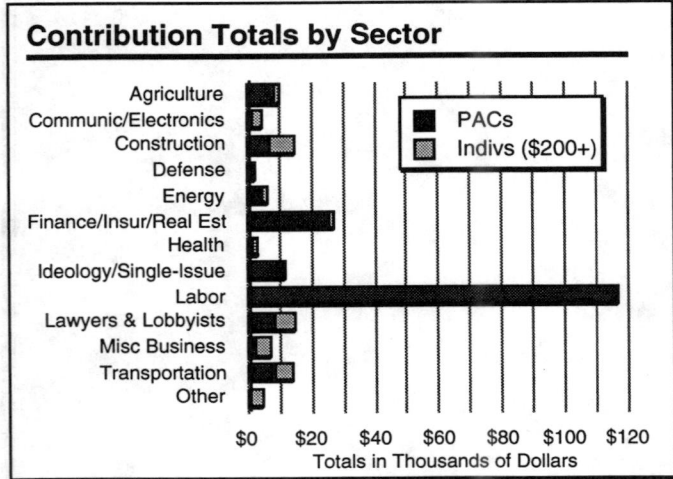

Agriculture
Communic/Electronics
Construction
Defense
Energy
Finance/Insur/Real Est
Health
Ideology/Single-Issue
Labor
Lawyers & Lobbyists
Misc Business
Transportation
Other

■ PACs
▦ Indivs ($200+)

$0 $20 $40 $60 $80 $100 $120
Totals in Thousands of Dollars

Lawyers & Lobbyists — $14,050

Lawyers & Lobbyists **$14,050**
Assn of Trial Lawyers of America	$8,000	PAC
Cassidy & Associates	$1,750	Indiv
Dwyer, Imanaka & Scharaff	$1,000	Indiv
Murray, Scheer & Montgomery	$1,000	Indiv

Misc Business — $6,600

Beer, Wine & Liquor **$1,000**
Gallo Winery	$1,000	Indiv

Business Services **$3,300**
Loomis & Pollock Inc	$2,000	Indiv

Transportation — $14,000

Air Transport **$3,800**
Aloha Airlines	$2,800	Indiv
United Airlines	$1,000	PAC

Automotive **$1,200**
None over $1,000

Railroads **$1,000**
AEG Westinghouse Transport Systems	$1,000	PAC

Sea Transport **$8,000**
Alexander & Baldwin Inc	$2,500	PAC/Ind
Matson Navigation	$2,500	PAC
American Hawaii Cruises	$1,000	Indiv
Charter Boat Fishing	$1,000	Indiv
Sea-Land Corp	$1,000	PAC

Labor

Labor — $115,800

Building Trade Unions **$20,150**
Carpenters & Joiners Union	$5,000	PAC
Laborers Union*	$5,000	PAC
Plumbers/Pipefitters Union*	$5,000	PAC
Operating Engineers Union*	$3,000	PAC
Ironworkers Union	$1,000	PAC

Industrial Unions **$29,250**
United Auto Workers	$8,500	PAC
Intl Brotherhood of Electrical Workers	$7,000	PAC
Machinists/Aerospace Workers Union	$6,000	PAC
Boilermakers Union	$3,500	PAC
Amalgamated Clothing & Textile Workers	$1,000	PAC
Communications Workers of America	$1,000	PAC
Ladies Garment Workers Union	$1,000	PAC
Rubber Cork Linoleum & Plastic Workers	$1,000	PAC

Transportation Unions **$30,100**
Seafarers International Union*	$8,550	PAC
Marine Engineers Union*	$6,000	PAC
Teamsters Union	$6,000	PAC
Air Line Pilots Assn	$3,500	PAC
Intl Longshoremen's/Warehousemen's Union	$3,000	PAC
United Transportation Union	$1,500	PAC

Public Sector Unions **$26,300**
American Fedn of St/Cnty/Munic Employees	$5,500	PAC
National Education Assn	$5,000	PAC
National Assn of Letter Carriers	$4,000	PAC
American Postal Workers Union	$3,500	PAC
National Assn Retired Federal Employees	$3,000	PAC
National Assn of Postmasters	$2,000	PAC
International Assn of Firefighters	$1,300	PAC
National League of Postmasters	$1,000	PAC

Misc Unions **$10,000**
Food & Commercial Workers Union	$4,000	PAC
Hotel/Restaurant Employees Union	$3,500	PAC
AFL-CIO	$1,500	PAC
Service Employees International Union	$1,000	PAC

Ideological/Single-Issue

Ideological/Single-Issue — $11,000

Democratic/Liberal **$2,500**
National Cmte for an Effective Congress	$2,500	PAC

Leadership PACs **$1,000**
Victory USA (Vic Fazio)	$1,000	PAC

Pro-Choice **$1,000**
Voters for Choice	$1,000	PAC

Human Rights **$3,000**
Human Rights Campaign Fund	$3,000	PAC

Misc Issues **$3,500**
National Cmte to Preserve Social Security	$3,000	PAC

Other & Unknown

Other — $4,450

Civil Servants/Public Officials **$1,250**
US Veterans Administration	$1,000	Indiv

Education **$2,200**
University of Hawaii	$1,700	Indiv

Unknown — $12,550
Homemakers/Non-income earners	$1,500	
Employer Listed/Category Unknown	$9,650	
Campbell Estates	$2,000	Indiv
GMP Associates Inc	$1,000	Indiv
Wilber Smith Associates	$1,000	Indiv

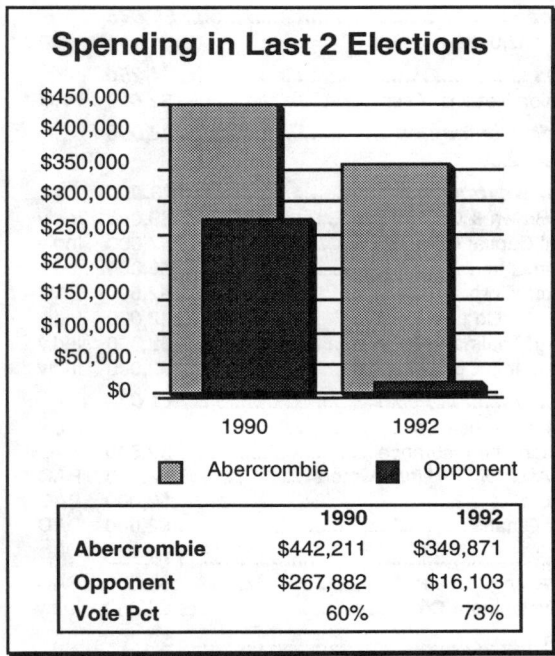

Spending in Last 2 Elections

	1990	1992
Abercrombie	$442,211	$349,871
Opponent	$267,882	$16,103
Vote Pct	60%	73%

---

* Contributions came from more than one affiliate or subsidiary.

Gary L. Ackerman, D-NY (5)

First elected: 1983

1991-92 Total Receipts: $688,551
1992 Year-end Cash: $28,412

1991-92 Committees & Subcommittees

Banking, Finance and Urban Affairs
General Oversight and Investigations

Foreign Affairs
Arms Control, International Security and Science; Asian and Pacific Affairs; Europe and the Middle East

Post Office and Civil Service
Compensation and Employee Benefits (Chairman)

Select Committee on Hunger

Leading Contributors

Business

Agriculture	$6,350	
Crop Production & Basic Processing	$4,225	
None over $2,000		

Communications/Electronics	$19,250	
Printing & Publishing	$4,900	
Excelsior Graphics	$2,000	Indiv
Media/Entertainment	$6,100	
Kenmare Productions	$4,000	Indiv
Telephone Utilities	$4,250	
AT&T	$2,000	PAC
Electronics Mfg & Services	$2,000	
None over $2,000		
Computer Equipment & Services	$2,000	
None over $2,000		

Construction	$15,125	
General Contractors	$5,375	
Amrit Construction Co	$3,000	Indiv
Home Builders	$7,250	
Shie Jie Enterprises	$3,750	Indiv
Berkson's Building Inc	$3,000	Indiv
Special Trade Contractors	$2,500	
None over $2,000		

Source of Funds in 1992 Election

Source	Total	Pct
■ PACs	$357,925	52%
▦ Indivs $200+	$215,681	31%
□ Indivs under $200	$48,203	7%
▨ Other	$67,279	10%
Candidate	$20,000	3%
Party	$987	0%

Source of PAC Dollars by Sector

Source	Total	Pct
■ Business	$152,625	42%
▦ Labor	$185,400	51%
□ Ideology/Single Issue	$22,500	6%

In-State vs. Out-of-State Contributions*

Source	Total	Pct
□ In-State	$149,225	74%
■ Out-of-state	$51,950	26%
No state listed	$8,450	

* by large individual contributors ($200 & above)

Energy & Natural Resources	$4,149	
Oil & Gas	$2,024	
None over $2,000		
Electric Utilities	$2,125	
None over $2,000		

Finance, Insurance & Real Estate	$114,725	
Commercial Banks	$19,250	
Citicorp	$6,750	PAC/Ind
JP Morgan & Co	$5,000	PAC
Bankers Trust	$2,000	PAC
Great Eastern Bank	$2,000	Indiv
Savings & Loans	$5,975	
None over $2,000		
Credit Unions	$4,250	
Credit Union National Assn	$2,500	PAC
Finance/Credit Companies	$2,000	
None over $2,000		
Securities & Investment	$38,000	
Hibbard, Brown & Co	$9,000	Indiv
Forest Hill Capital Corp	$7,000	Indiv
SF Investments	$6,000	Indiv
First Boston Corp	$2,500	PAC
LC Wegard & Co	$2,000	Indiv
Ladenberg, Thalmann & Co	$2,000	Indiv
Oppenheimer & Co	$2,000	Indiv
Insurance	$21,050	
Transtate Insurance Co	$4,000	Indiv
Metropolitan Life Insurance	$2,500	PAC
National Assn of Life Underwriters	$2,500	PAC
Loews Corp*	$2,000	PAC
Mutual of Omaha	$2,000	PAC
Real Estate	$18,750	
National Assn of Realtors	$8,000	PAC
Muss Development Co	$6,250	Indiv
Accountants	$2,700	
None over $2,000		

Contribution Totals by Sector

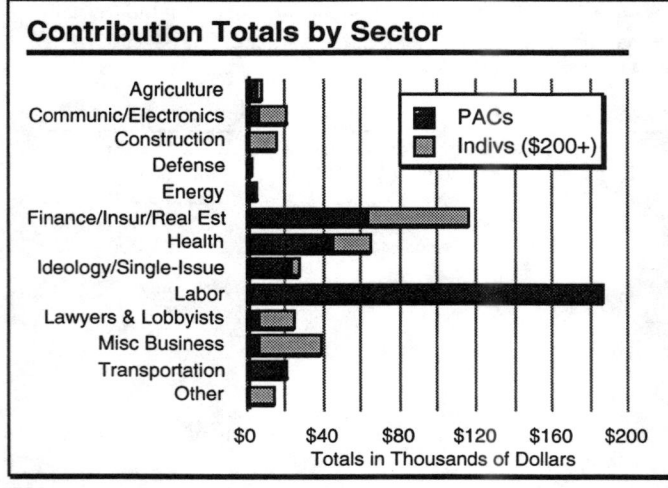

Agriculture
Communic/Electronics
Construction
Defense
Energy
Finance/Insur/Real Est
Health
Ideology/Single-Issue
Labor
Lawyers & Lobbyists
Misc Business
Transportation
Other

■ PACs
▦ Indivs ($200+)

$0 $40 $80 $120 $160 $200
Totals in Thousands of Dollars

Health $63,600

Health Professionals **$45,350**
    American Medical Assn* ....$10,000   PAC
    American Podiatry Assn ....$7,000   PAC
    Assn for the Advancement of Psychology ....$3,500   PAC
    American Chiropractic Assn ....$2,000   PAC

Hospitals/Nursing Homes **$3,250**
    None over $2,000

Health Services **$3,500**
    None over $2,000

Pharmaceuticals/Health Products **$11,500**
    Medco Containment Services ....$8,000   PAC
    Medicis Corp ....$2,000   Indiv

Lawyers & Lobbyists $24,200

Lawyers & Lobbyists **$24,200**
    Assn of Trial Lawyers of America ....$3,500   PAC
    Chen & Swift ....$2,000   Indiv
    Lowey, Dannenberg et al ....$2,000   Indiv

Misc Business $37,225

Food & Beverage **$3,575**
    Ben's Best Deli ....$2,500   Indiv

Retail Sales **$9,800**
    Toys-R-Us Inc ....$2,000   Indiv

Business Services **$12,000**
    Esmor Inc ....$4,000   Indiv
    Advo-System Inc ....$3,000   PAC

Misc Manufacturing & Distributing **$9,000**
    Rosco Inc ....$3,250   Indiv
    Emlin Cosmetics ....$2,000   Indiv

Transportation $19,450

Air Transport **$4,000**
    United Parcel Service ....$4,000   PAC

Automotive **$13,700**
    Auto Dealers & Drivers for Free Trade ....$10,000   PAC
    National Auto Dealers Assn ....$3,500   PAC

Labor

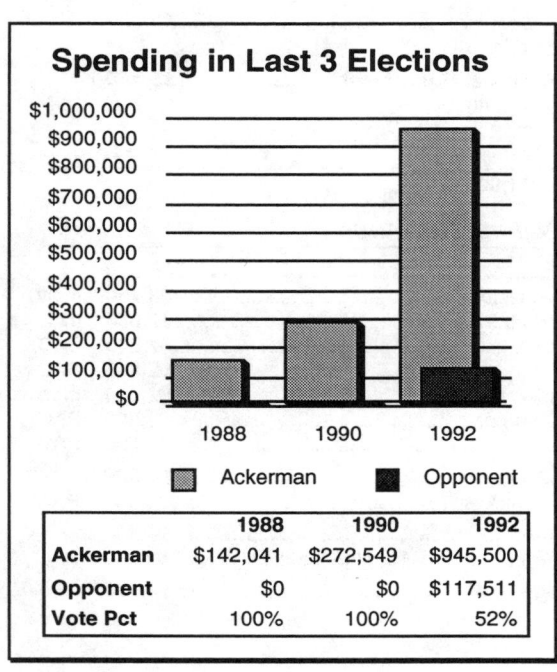

Spending in Last 3 Elections

	1988	1990	1992
Ackerman	$142,041	$272,549	$945,500
Opponent	$0	$0	$117,511
Vote Pct	100%	100%	52%

Legend: ▨ Ackerman   ■ Opponent

Labor $185,650

Building Trade Unions **$26,000**
    Ironworkers Union ....$9,500   PAC
    Carpenters & Joiners Union* ....$6,000   PAC
    Laborers' Political League ....$5,000   PAC

Industrial Unions **$28,750**
    Intl Brotherhood of Electrical Workers ....$10,000   PAC
    United Auto Workers ....$6,000   PAC
    Machinists/Aerospace Workers Union ....$4,500   PAC
    Ladies Garment Workers Union ....$2,000   PAC

Transportation Unions **$37,000**
    United Transportation Union ....$7,500   PAC
    Air Line Pilots Assn ....$5,000   PAC
    Teamsters Union ....$5,000   PAC
    Marine Engineers Union* ....$4,500   PAC
    International Longshoremen's Assn ....$4,000   PAC
    National Air Traffic Controllers Assn ....$2,500   PAC

Public Sector Unions **$87,250**
    National Assn Retired Federal Employees ....$12,000   PAC
    American Federation of Teachers......................$10,000   PAC
    American Fedn of St/Cnty/Munic Employees ....$10,000   PAC
    American Postal Workers Union ....$10,000   PAC
    National Assn of Letter Carriers ....$10,000   PAC
    National Education Assn ....$10,000   PAC
    National Assn of Postmasters ....$4,300   PAC
    American Federation of Govt Employees ....$4,000   PAC
    International Assn of Firefighters ....$3,000   PAC
    National Treasury Employees Union ....$3,000   PAC
    Federal Managers' Assn ....$2,500   PAC
    National Rural Letter Carriers Assn ....$2,500   PAC
    National League of Postmasters ....$2,000   PAC

Misc Unions **$6,650**
    Food & Commercial Workers Union ....$3,500   PAC

Ideological/Single-Issue

Ideological/Single-Issue $26,200

Democratic/Liberal **$2,500**
    National Cmte for an Effective Congress ....$2,500   PAC

Leadership PACs **$3,500**
    None over $2,000

Pro-Israel **$13,700**
    National PAC ....$5,000   PAC

Misc Issues **$3,750**
    National Cmte to Preserve Social Security ....$3,750   PAC

Other & Unknown

Other $13,125

Retired **$4,700**
    None over $2,000

Other **$5,250**
    None over $2,000

Unknown $39,601

    Homemakers/Non-income earners $3,000
    No Employer Listed or Found $11,200
    Generic Occupation/Category Unknown $2,800
    Employer Listed/Category Unknown $22,601
        Kingray ....$2,000   Indiv

---

* Contributions came from more than one affiliate or subsidiary.

Wayne Allard, R-Colo (4)

First elected: 1990

1991-92 Total Receipts: $474,315
1992 Year-end Cash: $6,808

1991-92 Committees & Subcommittees

Agriculture
Conservation, Credit and Rural Development; Department Operations, Research and Foreign Agriculture; Livestock, Dairy and Poultry

Interior and Insular Affairs
Energy and the Environment; Water, Power and Offshore Energy Resources

Small Business
Antitrust, Impact of Deregulation and Ecology; Procurement, Tourism and Rural Development; SBA, the General Economy and Minority Enterprise Development

Leading Contributors

Business

Agriculture	$86,688	
Crop Production & Basic Processing	**$9,700**	
None over $1,500		
Tobacco	**$4,350**	
US Tobacco Co	$2,000	PAC
Dairy	**$21,100**	
Dairymens Mountain Assn	$5,350	PAC
Associated Milk Producers	$4,000	PAC
Leprino Foods Co	$2,000	Indiv
Royal Crest Dairy	$1,900	Indiv
Milk Industry Foundation	$1,850	PAC
Milk Marketing Inc	$1,500	PAC
Poultry & Eggs	**$2,850**	
None over $1,500		
Livestock	**$8,888**	
Horton Cattle Co	$2,200	Indiv
National Cattlemen's Assn*	$1,850	PAC
National Pork Producers Council	$1,500	PAC
Agricultural Services/Products	**$25,850**	
American Veterinary Medical Assn	$10,000	PAC
Farm Credit Council	$2,000	PAC
Aerial Sprayers Inc	$1,750	Indiv
Food Processing & Sales	**$12,600**	
ConAgra Inc	$7,000	PAC/Ind

Source of Funds in 1992 Election

Source	Total	Pct
PACs	$223,765	47%
Indivs $200+	$137,925	29%
Indivs under $200	$42,099	9%
Other	$70,526	15%
Candidate	$0	0%
Party	$10,000	2%

Source of PAC Dollars by Sector

Source	Total	Pct
Business	$215,540	84%
Labor	$23,450	9%
Ideology/Single Issue	$16,200	6%

In-State vs. Out-of-State Contributions*

Source	Total	Pct
In-State	$128,751	95%
Out-of-state	$7,400	5%
No state listed	$1,550	

by large individual contributors ($200 & above)

Communications/Electronics — $18,850

Media/Entertainment	**$11,200**	
Tele-Communications Inc	$7,000	PAC
Telephone Utilities	**$5,300**	
AT&T	$2,850	PAC
Computer Equipment & Services	**$1,850**	
None over $1,500		

Construction — $16,300

General Contractors	**$8,850**	
Phelps-Tointon Inc	$3,000	Indiv
Associated General Contractors	$2,350	PAC
Construction Services	**$2,500**	
None over $1,500		
Building Materials & Equipment	**$3,450**	
None over $1,500		

Defense — $1,600

None over $1,500

Energy & Natural Resources — $40,488

Oil & Gas	**$28,638**	
Associated Natural Gas	$3,750	Indiv
Benson Mineral Group	$2,888	Indiv
Shell Oil	$2,500	PAC
Chevron Corp	$2,100	PAC
Tom Vessels Oil & Gas	$2,000	Indiv
Amoco Corp	$1,500	PAC
Exxon Corp	$1,500	PAC
Mining	**$4,000**	
National Coal Assn	$1,500	PAC
Electric Utilities	**$4,300**	
ACRE (Action Cmte for Rural Electrification)	$2,350	PAC
Waste Management	**$2,550**	
None over $1,500		

Contribution Totals by Sector

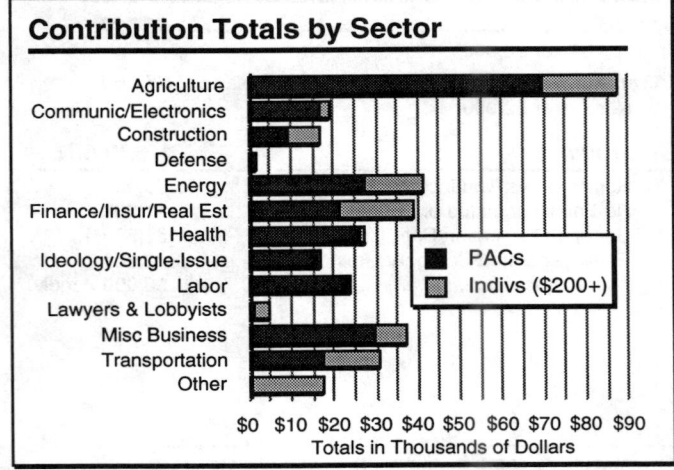

Agriculture
Communic/Electronics
Construction
Defense
Energy
Finance/Insur/Real Est
Health
Ideology/Single-Issue
Labor
Lawyers & Lobbyists
Misc Business
Transportation
Other

■ PACs
▨ Indivs ($200+)

$0 $10 $20 $30 $40 $50 $60 $70 $80 $90
Totals in Thousands of Dollars

Finance, Insurance & Real Estate $38,150

Commercial Banks **$8,250**
    First Interstate Bank ....$2,000   Indiv
    Independent Bankers Assn ....$1,850   PAC
    Colorado National Bank ....$1,500   Indiv

Insurance **$2,500**
    None over $1,500

Real Estate **$17,650**
    National Assn of Realtors........................$10,000   PAC
    Broe Companies ....$2,000   Indiv

Accountants **$4,800**
    Pedersen & Allard CPA ....$2,300   Indiv
    American Institute of CPA's ....$1,500   PAC

Misc Finance **$2,700**
    Carl M Williams & Assoc ....$2,000   Indiv

Health $27,094

Health Professionals **$20,944**
    American Medical Assn............................$9,794   PAC
    American Dental Assn ....$3,350   PAC
    American Academy of Ophthalmology ....$2,000   PAC
    American College of Emergency Physicians ......$2,000   PAC

Hospitals/Nursing Homes **$2,700**
    American Hospital Assn ....$2,000   PAC

Pharmaceuticals/Health Products **$3,450**
    None over $1,500

Lawyers & Lobbyists $4,500

Lawyers/Law Firms **$4,500**
    None over $1,500

Misc Business $36,646

Business Associations **$2,350**
    National Fedn of Independent Business ....$2,350   PAC

Food & Beverage **$2,500**
    National Restaurant Assn ....$2,000   PAC

Beer, Wine & Liquor **$9,850**
    National Beer Wholesalers Assn ....$6,850   PAC
    Coors Industries ....$2,000   PAC

Retail Sales **$3,500**
    None over $1,500

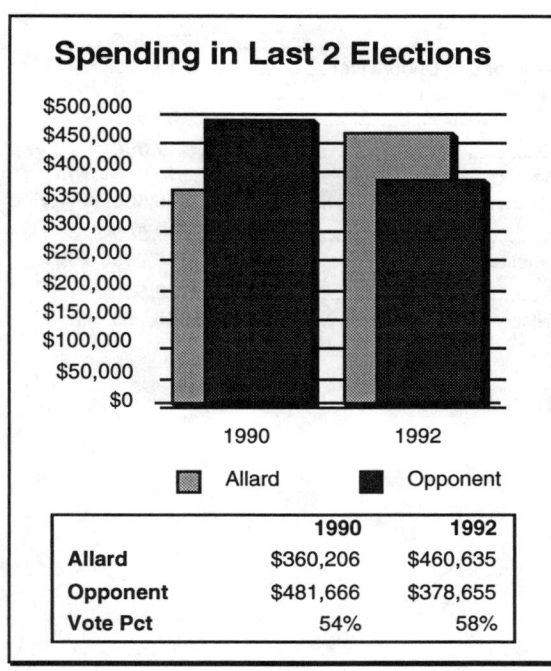

Spending in Last 2 Elections

	1990	1992
Allard	$360,206	$460,635
Opponent	$481,666	$378,655
Vote Pct	54%	58%

Legend: Allard, Opponent

Misc Services **$2,751**
    None over $1,500

Business Services **$2,300**
    None over $1,500

Chemical & Related Manufacturing **$6,945**
    Dow Chemical ....$2,000   PAC
    Hach Chemical Corp ....$2,000   Indiv

Misc Manufacturing & Distributing **$6,000**
    Stone Container Corp ....$3,500   PAC

Transportation $30,300

Air Transport **$4,000**
    United Parcel Service ....$3,000   PAC

Automotive **$9,850**
    National Auto Dealers Assn ....$3,350   PAC
    Americans for Free International Trade ....$2,000   PAC

Trucking **$12,000**
    Northwest Transport Service ....$9,000   Indiv

Railroads **$3,450**
    Union Pacific Corp ....$2,250   PAC

Labor

Labor $23,450

Building Trade Unions **$2,500**
    Laborers' Political League ....$2,000   PAC

Industrial Unions **$3,500**
    United Auto Workers ....$2,500   PAC

Transportation Unions **$4,350**
    Marine Engineers Dist 2 Maritime Offices ....$4,000   PAC

Public Sector Unions **$13,100**
    National Assn of Letter Carriers ....$5,000   PAC
    National Education Assn ....$5,000   PAC
    National Assn Retired Federal Employees ....$3,000   PAC

Ideological/Single-Issue

Ideological/Single-Issue $16,200

Gun Rights/Gun Control **$9,900**
    National Rifle Assn ....$9,900   PAC

Human Rights **$3,750**
    Human Rights Campaign Fund ....$2,500   PAC

Other & Unknown

Other $16,792

Retired **$15,092**
    None over $1,500

Unknown $35,833

    Homemakers/Non-income earners $3,550
    No Employer Listed or Found $14,400
    Generic Occupation/Category Unknown $4,250
    Employer Listed/Category Unknown $13,633
      None over $1,500

Independent expenditures supporting Allard
    National Right to Life PAC $1,834

---

* Contributions came from more than one affiliate or subsidiary.

Michael A. Andrews, D-Texas (25)

First elected: 1982

1991-92 Total Receipts: $974,838
1992 Year-end Cash: $388,519

1991-92 Committees & Subcommittees

Ways and Means
Human Resources; Select Revenue Measures

Leading Contributors

Business

Agriculture	$28,000

Crop Production & Basic Processing $6,250
   None over $5,000

Food Processing & Sales $8,650
   None over $5,000

Communications/Electronics	$39,850

Media/Entertainment $6,750
   None over $5,000

Telephone Utilities $16,850
   None over $5,000

Computer Equipment & Services $10,000
   None over $5,000

Construction	$20,350

General Contractors $8,350
   None over $5,000

Home Builders $5,750
   None over $5,000

Defense	$18,000

Defense Aerospace $7,500
   None over $5,000

Misc Defense $9,500
   Tenneco Inc .... $6,500   PAC

Source of Funds in 1992 Election

Source	Total	Pct
PACs	$526,931	54%
Indivs $200+	$256,659	26%
Indivs under $200	$62,394	6%
Other	$130,091	13%
Candidate	$0	0%
Party	$1,587	0%

Source of PAC Dollars by Sector

Source	Total	Pct
Business	$497,524	91%
Labor	$40,850	8%
Ideology/Single Issue	$5,650	1%

In-State vs. Out-of-State Contributions*

Source	Total	Pct
In-State	$210,949	82%
Out-of-state	$45,610	18%
No state listed	$0	

by large individual contributors ($200 & above)

Energy & Natural Resources	$116,050

Oil & Gas $99,300
   Coastal Corp .... $7,500   PAC/Ind
   Shell Oil .... $6,000   PAC/Ind
   Chevron Corp .... $5,000   PAC

Electric Utilities $7,500
   None over $5,000

Finance, Insurance & Real Estate	$203,065

Commercial Banks $28,500
   None over $5,000

Securities & Investment $41,200
   None over $5,000

Insurance $66,165
   National Assn of Life Underwriters .... $10,000   PAC
   American International Group Inc .... $6,000   PAC
   Prudential Insurance .... $5,500   PAC

Real Estate $39,000
   National Assn of Realtors .... $10,000   PAC
   Trammell Crow Co .... $6,500   PAC/Ind

Accountants $10,500
   American Institute of CPA's .... $5,000   PAC

Misc Finance $12,500
   Ranieri, Wilson & Co .... $6,750   Indiv

Contribution Totals by Sector

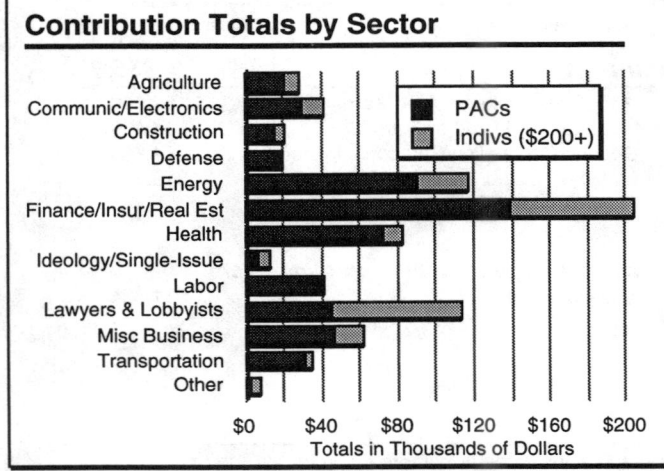

Legend: ■ PACs ▨ Indivs ($200+)

Agriculture, Communic/Electronics, Construction, Defense, Energy, Finance/Insur/Real Est, Health, Ideology/Single-Issue, Labor, Lawyers & Lobbyists, Misc Business, Transportation, Other

$0 $40 $80 $120 $160 $200
Totals in Thousands of Dollars

Health $81,160

Health Professionals **$49,410**
American Medical Assn ....$10,000 PAC
American Academy of Ophthalmology ....$5,000 PAC
American Dental Assn ....$5,000 PAC
American Society of Anesthesiologists ....$5,000 PAC

Hospitals/Nursing Homes **$11,750**
American Hospital Assn ....$7,500 PAC

Pharmaceuticals/Health Products **$17,000**
None over $5,000

Lawyers & Lobbyists $111,639

Lawyers & Lobbyists **$111,639**
Vinson & Elkins ....$10,360 PAC/Ind
McClure, Trotter & Mentz ....$6,700 Indiv
Assn of Trial Lawyers of America ....$6,500 PAC
Jamail & Kolius ....$5,200 Indiv
Baker & Botts ....$5,000 PAC/Ind

Misc Business $60,765

Beer, Wine & Liquor **$6,250**
None over $5,000

Retail Sales **$13,927**
International Council of Shopping Centers ....$8,000 PAC

Business Services **$6,860**
None over $5,000

Chemical & Related Manufacturing **$16,580**
Dow Chemical ....$5,750 PAC/Ind

Misc Manufacturing & Distributing **$6,000**
None over $5,000

Transportation $34,500

Air Transport **$8,000**
None over $5,000

Automotive **$13,250**
National Auto Dealers Assn ....$5,500 PAC

Railroads **$6,500**
None over $5,000

Labor

Labor $40,850

Industrial Unions **$11,000**
None over $5,000

Transportation Unions **$9,400**
Seafarers International Union ....$7,100 PAC

Public Sector Unions **$18,450**
National Education Assn ....$10,000 PAC

Ideological/Single-Issue

Ideological/Single-Issue $11,978
None over $5,000

Other & Unknown

Other $6,400
None over $5,000

Unknown $29,726
Employer Listed/Category Unknown $20,300
None over $5,000

Independent expenditures supporting Andrews
American Medical Assn $118,985
National Assn of Realtors $21,095

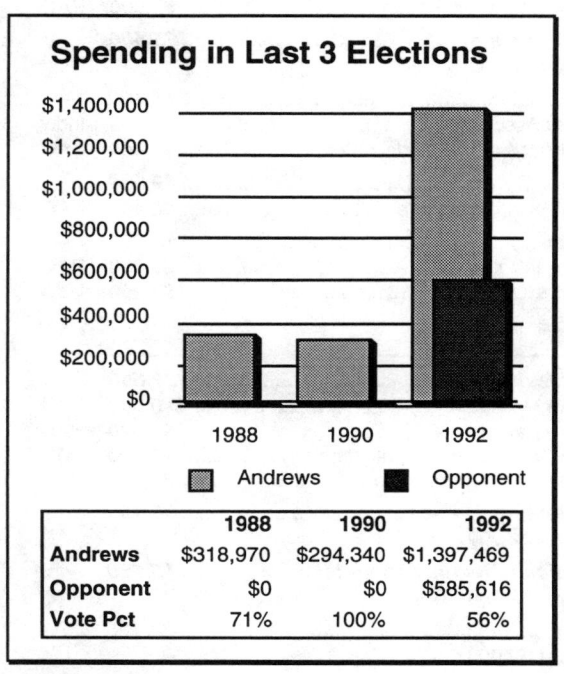

Spending in Last 3 Elections

	1988	1990	1992
Andrews	$318,970	$294,340	$1,397,469
Opponent	$0	$0	$585,616
Vote Pct	71%	100%	56%

Robert E. Andrews, D-NJ (1)

First elected: 1990

1991-92 Total Receipts: $738,301
1992 Year-end Cash: $1,284

1991-92 Committees & Subcommittees

Education and Labor
Employment Opportunities; Health and Safety; Postsecondary Education

Small Business
Antitrust, Impact of Deregulation and Ecology; Regulation, Business Opportunity and Energy

Select Committee on Narcotics Abuse and Control

Leading Contributors

Business

Agriculture	$13,550	
Crop Production & Basic Processing **$2,500**		
None over $2,000		
Tobacco **$2,900**		
US Tobacco Co	$2,000	PAC
Dairy **$2,000**		
Associated Milk Producers	$2,000	PAC
Food Processing & Sales **$5,000**		
Connell Rice & Sugar Co	$2,000	Indiv

Communications/Electronics	$14,650	
Media/Entertainment **$5,800**		
None over $2,000		
Telephone Utilities **$7,800**		
Bell Atlantic*	$4,500	PAC

Construction	$30,675	
General Contractors **$5,450**		
Clyde N Lattimer Construction	$2,000	Indiv
Home Builders **$4,500**		
National Assn of Home Builders	$4,500	PAC
Construction Services **$20,225**		
Remington & Vernick	$5,500	Indiv
O'Brien-Kreitzberg Associates	$3,300	Indiv
Garrison Architects	$3,000	Indiv

Source of Funds in 1992 Election

Source	Total	Pct
■ PACs	$345,800	46%
▨ Indivs $200+	$140,725	19%
☐ Indivs under $200	$188,207	25%
⊠ Other.............................	$75,353	10%
Candidate	$0	0%
Party	$13,534	2%

Source of PAC Dollars by Sector

Source	Total	Pct
■ Business	$147,893	44%
▨ Labor	$165,973	49%
☐ Ideology/Single Issue	$23,000	7%

In-State vs. Out-of-State Contributions*

Source	Total	Pct
☐ In-State	$108,900	80%
▨ Out-of-state	$26,525	20%
No state listed	$0	

* by large individual contributors ($200 & above)

Energy & Natural Resources	$15,049	
Oil & Gas **$3,400**		
Coastal Corp	$2,000	PAC
Electric Utilities **$9,849**		
Public Service Electric & Gas	$4,599	PAC

Finance, Insurance & Real Estate	$45,719	
Commercial Banks **$5,400**		
None over $2,000		
Credit Unions **$2,000**		
Credit Union National Assn	$2,000	PAC
Securities & Investment **$5,400**		
None over $2,000		
Insurance **$17,100**		
Gallagher Associates Inc	$7,000	Indiv
National Assn of Life Underwriters	$2,000	PAC
Real Estate **$9,500**		
National Assn of Realtors	$8,400	PAC
Accountants **$5,050**		
American Institute of CPA's	$3,050	PAC
Bowman & Co	$2,000	Indiv

Health	$45,350	
Health Professionals **$31,650**		
American Medical Assn*	$10,000	PAC
American Dental Assn	$5,500	PAC
American Academy of Ophthalmology	$3,000	PAC
American Chiropractic Assn	$2,000	PAC
Hospitals/Nursing Homes **$5,150**		
None over $2,000		
Pharmaceuticals/Health Products **$5,650**		
None over $2,000		
Misc Health **$2,100**		
None over $2,000		

Contribution Totals by Sector

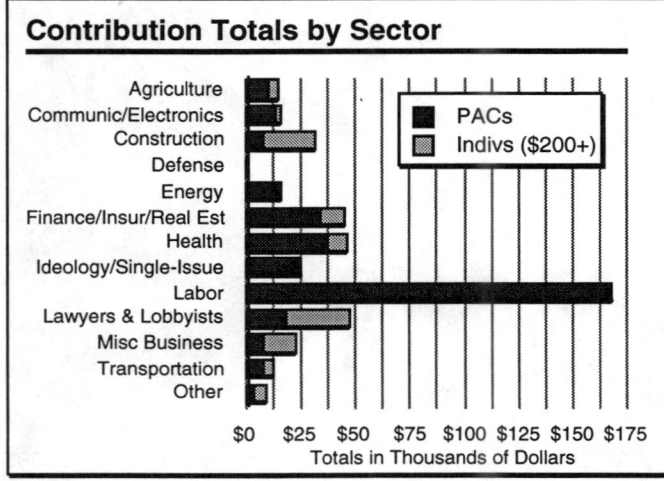

Agriculture
Communic/Electronics
Construction
Defense
Energy
Finance/Insur/Real Est
Health
Ideology/Single-Issue
Labor
Lawyers & Lobbyists
Misc Business
Transportation
Other

- ■ PACs
- ▨ Indivs ($200+)

$0 $25 $50 $75 $100 $125 $150 $175
Totals in Thousands of Dollars

Lawyers & Lobbyists — $46,650

Lawyers & Lobbyists **$46,650**
- Assn of Trial Lawyers of America ....$10,000 — PAC
- Cassidy & Associates ....$4,050 — Indiv
- Reid & Priest ....$3,050 — PAC/Ind
- Higgins, Slachetka & Long ....$3,000 — Indiv
- Wolf, Block et al ....$2,500 — PAC
- Greenberg, Traurig et al ....$2,000 — PAC/Ind
- Riccardelli & Rosa ....$2,000 — Indiv

Misc Business — $22,300

Food & Beverage **$3,750**
- None over $2,000

Beer, Wine & Liquor **$4,000**
- National Beer Wholesalers Assn ....$2,000 — PAC

Retail Sales **$3,300**
- None over $2,000

Business Services **$4,300**
- None over $2,000

Steel Production **$2,000**
- Professional Steel Tech Inc ....$2,000 — Indiv

Transportation — $11,900

Air Transport **$4,500**
- General Electric* ....$2,500 — Indiv

Automotive **$2,300**
- National Auto Dealers Assn ....$2,000 — PAC

Sea Transport **$3,000**
- Holt Cargo Systems ....$3,000 — Indiv

Labor

Labor — $166,223

Building Trade Unions **$56,123**
- Carpenters & Joiners Union ....$10,900 — PAC
- Plumbers/Pipefitters Union* ....$10,850 — PAC
- Laborers' Political League ....$8,400 — PAC
- Sheet Metal Workers Union ....$7,500 — PAC
- Operating Engineers Union* ....$6,125 — PAC
- Ironworkers Union ....$4,500 — PAC
- Bricklayers Union ....$2,400 — PAC

Industrial Unions — $28,750
- Electrical Radio & Machine Workers ....$6,250 — PAC
- United Auto Workers ....$5,900 — PAC
- Intl Brotherhood of Electrical Workers* ....$5,100 — PAC
- United Steelworkers ....$2,000 — PAC

Transportation Unions **$36,950**
- Teamsters Union ....$11,000 — PAC
- Marine Engineers Union* ....$8,000 — PAC
- Seafarers International Union ....$5,400 — PAC
- Amalgamated Transit Union ....$2,500 — PAC
- Transport Workers Union ....$2,500 — PAC
- United Transportation Union ....$2,000 — PAC

Public Sector Unions **$37,600**
- American Fedn of St/Cnty/Munic Employees ......$9,000 — PAC
- National Assn Retired Federal Employees ....$6,000 — PAC
- National Education Assn ....$5,900 — PAC
- American Federation of Teachers ....$5,000 — PAC
- International Assn of Firefighters ....$3,000 — PAC
- National Assn of Letter Carriers ....$3,000 — PAC
- American Postal Workers Union ....$2,900 — PAC
- National Rural Letter Carriers Assn ....$2,000 — PAC

Misc Unions **$6,800**
- Food & Commercial Workers Union ....$3,400 — PAC
- Service Employees International Union ....$2,000 — PAC

Ideological/Single-Issue

Ideological/Single-Issue — $24,000

Democratic/Liberal **$2,500**
- National Cmte for an Effective Congress ....$2,500 — PAC

Pro-Israel **$4,750**
- None over $2,000

Pro-Choice **$5,000**
- National Abortion Rights Action League ....$3,000 — PAC

Human Rights **$6,000**
- Human Rights Campaign Fund ....$2,000 — PAC
- Indian-American PAC/NJ State Chapter ....$2,000 — PAC
- KidsPAC ....$2,000 — PAC

Misc Issues **$5,000**
- National Cmte to Preserve Social Security ....$4,500 — PAC

Other & Unknown

Other — $8,650

Civil Servants/Public Officials **$4,000**
- County of Camden ....$2,300 — Indiv

Education **$2,300**
- None over $2,000

Unknown — $28,325
- Employer Listed/Category Unknown $29,025
  - ST Hudson Engineers Inc ....$2,500 — Indiv
  - Consulting Engineer Services ....$2,000 — Indiv
  - Richter & Scaramella ....$2,000 — Indiv

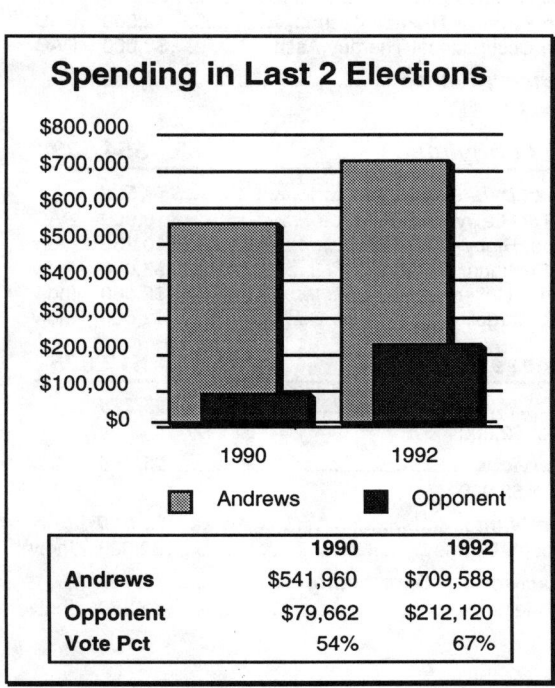

Spending in Last 2 Elections

	1990	1992
Andrews	$541,960	$709,588
Opponent	$79,662	$212,120
Vote Pct	54%	67%

Legend: Andrews, Opponent

* Contributions came from more than one affiliate or subsidiary.

Thomas H. Andrews, D-Maine (1)

First elected: 1990

1991-92 Total Receipts: $861,034
1992 Year-end Cash: $52,269

1991-92 Committees & Subcommittees

Armed Services
Research and Development; Seapower and Strategic and Critical Materials

Small Business
Exports, Tax Policy and Special Problems

Leading Contributors

Business

Agriculture		**$7,062**
Dairy	**$3,500**	
Associated Milk Producers	$3,000	PAC

Communications/Electronics		**$16,750**
Printing & Publishing	**$5,100**	
None over $2,000		
Telephone Utilities	**$7,000**	
BellSouth Corp*	$2,500	PAC
AT&T	$2,000	PAC

Construction		**$6,050**
None over $2,000		

Defense		**$12,500**
Defense Aerospace	**$6,000**	
None over $2,000		
Misc Defense	**$5,000**	
Bath Iron Works	$3,500	PAC/Ind

Energy & Natural Resources		**$3,900**
None over $2,000		

Finance, Insurance & Real Estate		**$58,377**
Commercial Banks	**$4,432**	
None over $2,000		
Securities & Investment	**$10,945**	
Boston Co	$2,000	Indiv
Insurance	**$8,500**	
Unum Life Insurance Co	$3,700	PAC/Ind

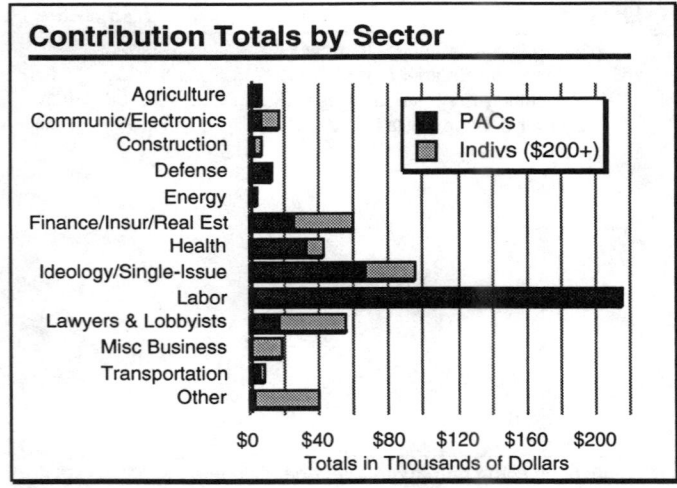

Contribution Totals by Sector

Legend: ■ PACs, ▨ Indivs ($200+)

Categories: Agriculture, Communic/Electronics, Construction, Defense, Energy, Finance/Insur/Real Est, Health, Ideology/Single-Issue, Labor, Lawyers & Lobbyists, Misc Business, Transportation, Other

Scale: $0 $40 $80 $120 $160 $200
Totals in Thousands of Dollars

Source of Funds in 1992 Election

Source	Total	Pct
■ PACs	$392,357	43%
▨ Indivs $200+	$240,109	26%
☐ Indivs under $200	$217,186	24%
▧ Other....................................	$61,584	7%
Candidate	$0	0%
Party	$50,502	6%

Source of PAC Dollars by Sector

Source	Total	Pct
■ Business	$105,720	28%
▨ Labor	$213,200	55%
☐ Ideology/Single Issue	$65,511	17%

In-State vs. Out-of-State Contributions*

Source	Total	Pct
☐ In-State	$134,990	56%
■ Out-of-state	$103,542	43%
No state listed	$577	

* by large individual contributors ($200 & above)

Real Estate	**$25,250**	
National Assn of Realtors	$11,000	PAC
Tishman Realty & Construction	$5,000	Indiv
Accountants	**$2,750**	
None over $2,000		

Health		**$42,210**
Health Professionals	**$37,260**	
American Chiropractic Assn	$5,000	PAC
American Academy of Ophthalmology	$3,500	PAC
American College of Emergency Physicians	$3,000	PAC
National Assn of Pharmacists	$2,600	PAC
American Nurses Assn	$2,500	PAC
American Physical Therapy Assn	$2,500	PAC
American Occupational Therapy Assn	$2,000	PAC
Hospitals/Nursing Homes	**$2,700**	
None over $2,000		

Lawyers & Lobbyists		**$54,500**
Lawyers & Lobbyists	**$54,500**	
Assn of Trial Lawyers of America	$16,000	PAC
McTeague, Higby et al	$10,250	Indiv
Jacobs, Persinger & Parker	$3,000	Indiv
Bornstein & Hoverdale	$2,500	Indiv
Tureen & Margolin	$2,000	Indiv

Misc Business		**$17,325**
Retail Sales	**$5,375**	
None over $2,000		
Business Services	**$5,150**	
None over $2,000		
Casinos/Gambling	**$2,000**	
Scarborough Downs	$2,000	Indiv
Misc Manufacturing & Distributing	**$2,950**	
Toms of Maine	$2,450	Indiv

Transportation	$7,900

Air Transport $2,800
   None over $2,000

Sea Transport..$2,750
   None over $2,000

Labor

Labor	$213,200

Building Trade Unions **$31,550**
Carpenters & Joiners Union $8,750	PAC
Painters & Allied Trades Union $5,500	PAC
Laborers' Political League $5,000	PAC
Sheet Metal Workers Union $3,500	PAC
Plumbers/Pipefitters Union $3,000	PAC
Bricklayers Union $2,500	PAC
Ironworkers Union $2,000	PAC

Industrial Unions **$58,800**
Machinists/Aerospace Workers Union $15,000	PAC
United Auto Workers $10,000	PAC
Intl Brotherhood of Electrical Workers $7,500	PAC
United Steelworkers $7,000	PAC
Boilermakers Union $6,000	PAC
United Paperworkers $3,500	PAC
Amalgamated Clothing & Textile Workers $3,000	PAC
Communications Workers of America $3,000	PAC
Rubber Cork Linoleum & Plastic Workers $2,000	PAC

Transportation Unions **$47,000**
Teamsters Union $10,000	PAC
Seafarers International Union $9,000	PAC
Air Line Pilots Assn $7,500	PAC
Marine Engineers Union* $6,500	PAC
United Transportation Union $6,000	PAC
International Longshoremen's Assn $2,000	PAC

Public Sector Unions **$52,350**
American Fedn of St/Cnty/Munic Employees $11,000	PAC
National Education Assn $10,000	PAC
National Assn Retired Federal Employees $8,000	PAC
National Assn of Letter Carriers $7,500	PAC
American Postal Workers Union $4,000	PAC
International Assn of Firefighters $3,500	PAC
American Federation of Teachers $3,000	PAC

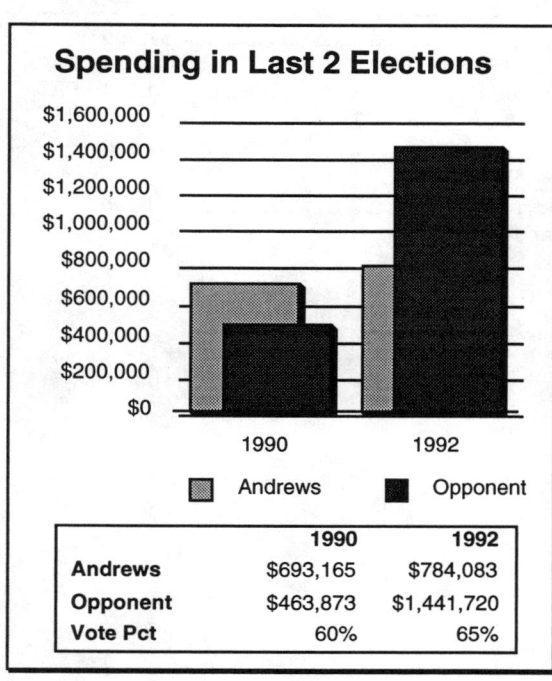

Spending in Last 2 Elections

Andrews (light bars) / Opponent (dark bars)

	1990	1992
Andrews	$693,165	$784,083
Opponent	$463,873	$1,441,720
Vote Pct	60%	65%

Misc Unions	$23,500
Food & Commercial Workers Union $7,500	PAC
AFL-CIO $7,000	PAC
Service Employees International Union $6,000	PAC

Ideological/Single-Issue

Ideological/Single-Issue	$94,361

Democratic/Liberal **$13,825**
| National Cmte for an Effective Congress ....$5,000 | PAC |
| Hollywood Women's Political Cmte ....$2,500 | PAC |

Leadership PACs **$4,000**
| House Leadership Fund (Tom Foley) ....$2,000 | PAC |

Foreign & Defense Policy **$5,161**
   None over $2,000

Pro-Israel **$4,250**
   None over $2,000

Pro-Choice..**$8,250**
| National Abortion Rights Action League ....$4,000 | PAC |
| Voters for Choice ....$2,000 | PAC |

Gun Rights/Gun Control **$4,065**
| Handgun Control Inc ....$4,065 | PAC |

Womens Issues...**$2,450**
   None over $2,000

Human Rights **$11,500**
| Human Rights Campaign Fund ....$8,500 | PAC |
| KidsPAC ....$3,000 | PAC |

Misc Issues...**$40,860**
Sierra Club $9,000	PAC
Greenvote..$6,000	PAC
National Cmte to Preserve Social Security $5,500	PAC
League of Conservation Voters $4,460	PAC/Ind
National Council of Senior Citizens....................$2,000	PAC

Other & Unknown

Other	$39,150

Non-Profit Institutions.................................**$4,200**
| Foundation for Hearing Aid Research ....$2,000 | Indiv |

Civil Servants/Public Officials............................**$2,150**
   None over $2,000

Education **$6,750**
| Gorham School Department ....$2,000 | Indiv |

Retired **$16,450**
   None over $2,000

Other **$9,600**
| National Assn of Social Workers.........................$2,000 | PAC |
| Unitarian Universalist Church ....$2,000 | Indiv |

Unknown	$50,705
Homemakers/Non-income earners $5,800	
No Employer Listed or Found $19,575	
Employer Listed/Category Unknown $23,680	
   None over $2,000

Independent expenditures supporting Andrews
   National Cmte to Preserve Social Security $3,236

---

* Contributions came from more than one affiliate or
subsidiary.

Douglas Applegate, D-Ohio (18)

First elected: 1976

1991-92 Total Receipts:	$117,262
1992 Year-end Cash:	$176,449

1991-92 Committees & Subcommittees

Public Works and Transportation
Economic Development; Surface Transportation; Water Resources

Veterans' Affairs
Compensation, Pension and Insurance (Chairman); Hospitals and Health Care

Leading Contributors

Business

Agriculture $7,700

Crop Production & Basic Processing	**$2,500**	
Florida Sugar Cane League	$1,000	PAC
Dairy	**$3,000**	
Associated Milk Producers	$3,000	PAC
Livestock	**$1,000**	
National Cattlemen's Assn	$1,000	PAC
Food Processing & Sales	**$1,000**	
Food Marketing Institute	$1,000	PAC

Communications/Electronics $4,000

Telephone Utilities	**$4,000**	
AT&T	$2,500	PAC
Ohio Bell Telephone	$1,000	PAC

Construction $2,000

General Contractors	**$1,500**	
National Utility Contractors Assn	$1,500	PAC

Energy & Natural Resources $8,000

Oil & Gas	**$3,050**	
Columbia Gas of Ohio	$1,200	PAC
Electric Utilities	**$4,650**	
American Electric Power*	$2,650	PAC
ACRE (Action Cmte for Rural Electrification)	$1,000	PAC

Source of Funds in 1992 Election

Source	Total	Pct
■ PACs	$88,170	68%
▨ Indivs $200+	$1,250	1%
□ Indivs under $200	$6,275	5%
▧ Other	$33,730	26%
Candidate	$0	0%
Party	$12,463	10%

Source of PAC Dollars by Sector

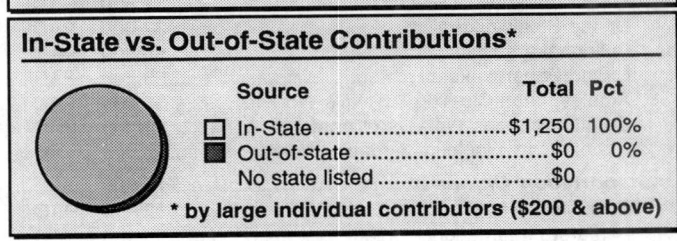

Source	Total	Pct
■ Business	$41,220	50%
▨ Labor	$39,098	47%
□ Ideology/Single Issue	$2,023	2%

In-State vs. Out-of-State Contributions*

Source	Total	Pct
□ In-State	$1,250	100%
■ Out-of-state	$0	0%
No state listed	$0	

* by large individual contributors ($200 & above)

Finance, Insurance & Real Estate $6,500

Real Estate	**$6,000**	
National Assn of Realtors	$6,000	PAC

Misc Business $1,750
None over $1,000

Health $2,000

Pharmaceuticals/Health Products	**$1,000**
None over $1,000	

Transportation $9,770

Air Transport	**$7,200**	
United Parcel Service	$4,200	PAC
United Airlines	$1,500	PAC
Aircraft Owners & Pilots Assn	$1,000	PAC
Trucking	**$1,520**	
None over $1,000		
Misc Transport	**$1,000**	
None over $1,000		

Contribution Totals by Sector

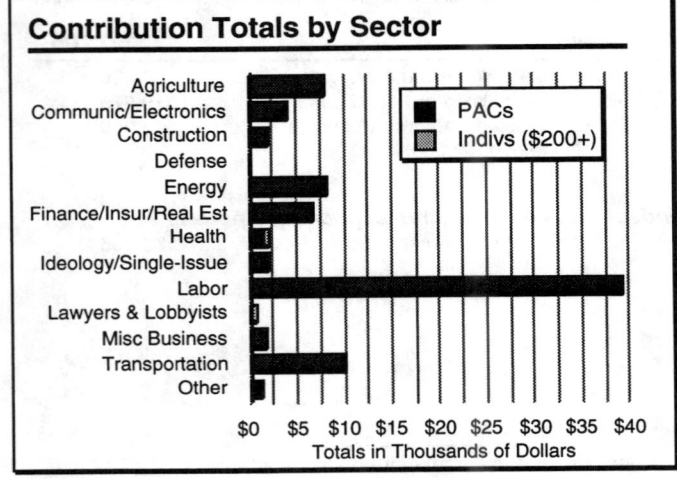

Agriculture
Communic/Electronics
Construction
Defense
Energy
Finance/Insur/Real Est
Health
Ideology/Single-Issue
Labor
Lawyers & Lobbyists
Misc Business
Transportation
Other

■ PACs
▨ Indivs ($200+)

$0 $5 $10 $15 $20 $25 $30 $35 $40
Totals in Thousands of Dollars

Labor

Labor	$39,098

Building Trade Unions **$4,000**
    Laborers' Political League ....$2,000 PAC
    AFL-CIO Bldg/Construction Trades Dept ....$1,000 PAC
    Operating Engineers Union ....$1,000 PAC

Industrial Unions **$13,000**
    United Auto Workers ....$5,000 PAC
    Boilermakers Union...$4,000 PAC
    Intl Brotherhood of Electrical Workers ....$1,000 PAC

Transportation Unions **$13,098**
    Air Line Pilots Assn ....$7,500 PAC
    Teamsters Union/Ohio ....$1,098 PAC
    Assn of Flight Attendants ....$1,000 PAC
    Marine Engineers Dist 2 Maritime Offices ....$1,000 PAC
    United Transportation Union ....$1,000 PAC

Public Sector Unions.. **$6,500**
    International Assn of Firefighters ....$3,000 PAC
    American Fedn of St/Cnty/Munic Employees ......$1,000 PAC
    American Postal Workers Union ....$1,000 PAC
    National Assn Retired Federal Employees ....$1,000 PAC

Misc Unions.. **$2,500**
    Food & Commercial Workers Union ....$1,500 PAC

Ideological/Single-Issue

Ideological/Single-Issue	$2,023

Misc Issues.. **$1,500**
    National Cmte to Preserve Social Security ....$1,000 PAC

Other & Unknown

Other	$1,000

Education **$1,000**
    Congressional Choice PAC NJ ....$1,000 PAC

Spending in Last 3 Elections

	1988	1990	1992
Applegate	$86,061	$94,754	$102,335
Opponent	$7,095	$0	$25,460
Vote Pct	77%	74%	68%

* Contributions came from more than one affiliate or subsidiary.

Bill Archer, R-Texas (7)

First elected: 1970

1991-92 Total Receipts:	$121,947
1992 Year-end Cash:	$671,097

1991-92 Committees & Subcommittees

Ways and Means (Ranking Republican)

Joint Committee on Taxation

Leading Contributors

Business

Agriculture — $2,500

Livestock $1,500
    None over $1,000

Food Processing & Sales $1,000
    Randall's Food Markets .... $1,000   Indiv

Energy & Natural Resources — $4,200

Oil & Gas $4,200
    Panhandle Eastern Corp .... $4,000   Indiv

Finance, Insurance & Real Esta — $19,429

Insurance $18,179
    Management Compensation Group .... $4,600   Indiv
    CLU Insurance .... $2,600   Indiv
    Security Life of Denver .... $1,600   Indiv
    Cominsky-Kaufman Inc .... $1,400   Indiv

Health — $4,250

Health Professionals $4,250
    None over $1,000

Source of Funds in 1992 Election

Source	Total	Pct
■ PACs	$0	0%
▦ Indivs $200+	$45,375	37%
☐ Indivs under $200	$3,567	3%
▨ Other	$73,005	60%
Candidate	$0	0%
Party	$225	0%

Source of PAC Dollars by Sector

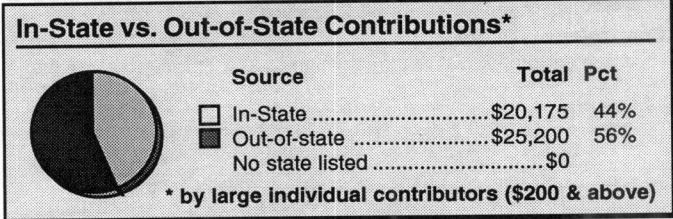

No PAC contributions reported

Source	Total	Pct
■ Business	$0	0%
▦ Labor	$0	0%
☐ Ideology/Single Issue	$0	0%

In-State vs. Out-of-State Contributions*

Source	Total	Pct
☐ In-State	$20,175	44%
■ Out-of-state	$25,200	56%
No state listed	$0	

* by large individual contributors ($200 & above)

Lawyers & Lobbyists — $2,950

Lawyers & Lobbyists $2,950
    Carl Arnold & Associates .... $1,000   Indiv
    McClure, Trotter & Mentz .... $1,000   Indiv

Misc Business — $5,500

Beer, Wine & Liquor $4,500
    Florida Distillers Co .... $2,000   Indiv
    Todhunter International Inc .... $2,000   Indiv

Contribution Totals by Sector

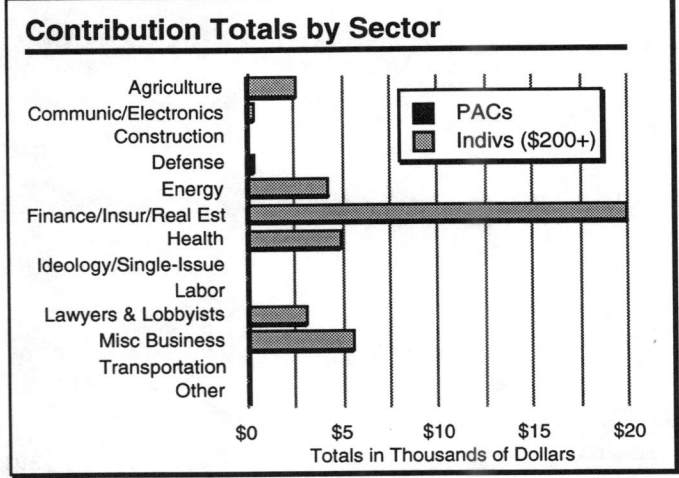

Legend: ■ PACs   ▦ Indivs ($200+)

Categories: Agriculture, Communic/Electronics, Construction, Defense, Energy, Finance/Insur/Real Est, Health, Ideology/Single-Issue, Labor, Lawyers & Lobbyists, Misc Business, Transportation, Other

Totals in Thousands of Dollars ($0, $5, $10, $15, $20)

Other & Unknown

Unknown $5,350

Employer Listed/Category Unknown $5,150
CM Alliance ....$1,000   Indiv

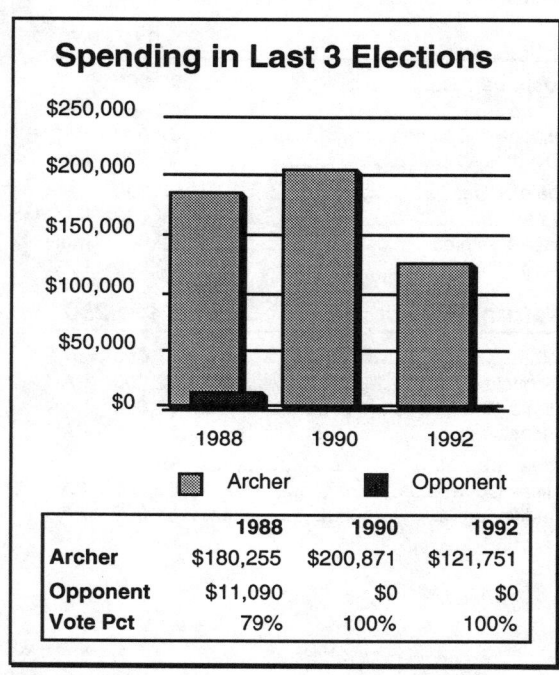

Spending in Last 3 Elections

	1988	1990	1992
Archer	$180,255	$200,871	$121,751
Opponent	$11,090	$0	$0
Vote Pct	79%	100%	100%

Dick Armey, R-Texas (26)

First elected: 1984

1991-92 Total Receipts: $483,928
1992 Year-end Cash: $351,112

1991-92 Committees & Subcommittees

Banking, Finance and Urban Affairs
Consumer Affairs and Coinage; Economic Stabilization; Housing and Community Development

Education and Labor
Labor-Management Relations; Labor Standards; Postsecondary Education

Joint Economic Committee

Leading Contributors

Business

Agriculture		$22,550
Crop Production & Basic Processing		**$1,500**
Peanut Butter & Nut Processors Assn	$1,500	PAC
Tobacco		**$3,000**
RJR Nabisco	$1,500	PAC
Dairy		**$2,000**
None over $1,500		
Poultry & Eggs		**$2,500**
Pilgrim's Pride Co	$2,000	Indiv
Livestock		**$2,700**
None over $1,500		
Agricultural Services/Products		**$3,500**
Garvey Enterprises Inc	$2,000	Indiv
Food Processing & Sales		**$6,350**
Food Marketing Institute	$3,000	PAC

Communications/Electronics		$18,150
Media/Entertainment		**$1,950**
None over $1,500		
Telephone Utilities		**$8,200**
GTE Corp	$2,700	PAC/Ind
Southwestern Bell	$2,000	PAC
AT&T	$1,500	PAC
BellSouth Corp	$1,500	PAC
Computer Equipment & Services		**$6,250**
Collmer Semiconductor	$2,000	Indiv
Sterling Software	$1,500	Indiv

Source of Funds in 1992 Election

Source	Total	Pct
■ PACs	$194,110	40%
▨ Indivs $200+	$101,668	21%
☐ Indivs under $200	$121,317	25%
▨ Other	$66,833	14%
Candidate	$0	0%
Party	$70	0%

Source of PAC Dollars by Sector

Source	Total	Pct
■ Business	$184,797	96%
▨ Labor	$0	0%
☐ Ideology/Single Issue	$7,525	4%

In-State vs. Out-of-State Contributions*

Source	Total	Pct
☐ In-State	$92,968	91%
▨ Out-of-state	$8,700	9%
No state listed	$0	

* by large individual contributors ($200 & above)

Construction		$21,950
General Contractors		**$7,750**
Dal Mac Construction	$2,000	Indiv
National Utility Contractors Assn	$1,500	PAC
Home Builders		**$6,000**
Fox & Jacobs	$2,000	Indiv
Perry-Houston Insterests	$2,000	Indiv
Construction Services		**$1,750**
None over $1,500		
Building Materials & Equipment		**$5,950**
CGF Industries Inc	$2,000	Indiv

Defense		$17,250
Defense Aerospace		**$9,000**
Northrop Corp	$2,500	PAC
LTV Aerospace & Defense Co	$2,000	PAC
General Dynamics	$1,500	PAC
Defense Electronics		**$8,250**
E-Systems Inc	$4,250	PAC/Ind
Electrospace Systems	$2,000	Indiv
Imo Industries Inc	$2,000	PAC

Energy & Natural Resources		$31,250
Oil & Gas		**$21,450**
Atlantic Richfield	$2,000	PAC
Bass Brothers Enterprises	$2,000	Indiv
Dresser Industries	$1,500	PAC
Electric Utilities		**$8,300**
Texas Utilities Co*	$3,000	PAC
Houston Industries	$1,500	PAC

Contribution Totals by Sector

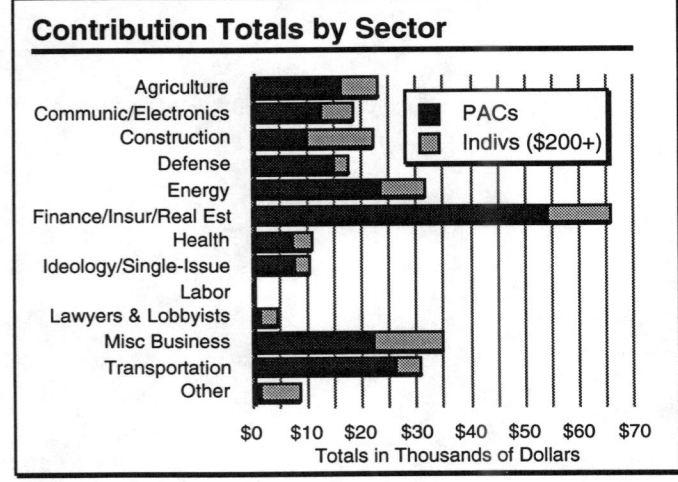

- Agriculture
- Communic/Electronics
- Construction
- Defense
- Energy
- Finance/Insur/Real Est
- Health
- Ideology/Single-Issue
- Labor
- Lawyers & Lobbyists
- Misc Business
- Transportation
- Other

■ PACs
▨ Indivs ($200+)

$0 $10 $20 $30 $40 $50 $60 $70
Totals in Thousands of Dollars

Finance, Insurance & Real Estate — $65,500

Commercial Banks **$24,000**
- Chase Manhattan .... $5,000 — PAC
- Citizens & Southern National Bank .... $3,000 — PAC
- JP Morgan & Co .... $2,500 — PAC
- American Bankers Assn .... $2,000 — PAC
- Barnett Banks Inc .... $2,000 — PAC
- Chemical Bank .... $2,000 — PAC
- Citicorp .... $2,000 — PAC
- NCNB Texas .... $1,500 — PAC

Savings & Loans **$2,000**
- US League of Savings Assns .... $1,500 — PAC

Credit Unions **$2,000**
- Credit Union National Assn .... $1,500 — PAC

Finance/Credit Companies **$3,500**
- Associated Credit Bureaus .... $2,000 — PAC

Securities & Investment **$3,750**
- None over $1,500

Insurance **$9,500**
- Health Insurance Assn of America .... $2,000 — PAC

Real Estate **$12,750**
- National Assn of Realtors .... $4,500 — PAC
- Ebby Halliday Realtors .... $1,500 — Indiv
- Southmark Corp .... $1,500 — PAC

Accountants **$2,000**
- American Institute of CPA's .... $2,000 — PAC

Misc Finance **$6,000**
- Phillips-Smith Specialty Retail .... $1,500 — Indiv

Health — $10,650

Health Professionals **$8,400**
- American Medical Assn .... $4,350 — PAC

Pharmaceuticals/Health Products **$2,250**
- None over $1,500

Lawyers & Lobbyists — $4,100

Lawyers & Lobbyists **$4,100**
- None over $1,500

Misc Business — $34,191

Food & Beverage **$4,700**
- Chili's Inc .... $2,000 — PAC

Beer, Wine & Liquor **$2,019**
- None over $1,500

Retail Sales **$6,272**
- None over $1,500

Business Services **$3,750**
- Figgie International .... $1,500 — PAC
- National Banner Co .... $1,500 — Indiv

Misc Business **$2,000**
- John G Mahler Co .... $2,000 — Indiv

Chemical & Related Manufacturing **$3,000**
- WR Grace & Co.. $1,500 — PAC

Misc Manufacturing & Distributing **$11,200**
- Stone Container Corp .... $2,500 — PAC
- Hoechst Celanese Corp .... $2,000 — PAC
- AE Petsche Co Inc .... $1,500 — Indiv

Transportation — $30,125

Air Transport **$9,500**
- American Airlines .... $3,000 — PAC
- United Parcel Service .... $3,000 — PAC

Automotive **$14,875**
- National Auto Dealers Assn .... $5,000 — PAC
- Americans for Free International Trade .... $2,500 — PAC
- Auto Dealers & Drivers for Free Trade .... $2,500 — PAC

Trucking **$2,750**
- Paccar Inc .... $1,500 — PAC

Railroads **$2,500**
- None over $1,500

Ideological/Single-Issue

Ideological/Single-Issue — $10,025

Republican/Conservative **$3,025**
- None over $1,500

Misc Issues **$5,500**
- Right to Work PAC .... $5,000 — PAC

Other & Unknown

Other — $8,410

Civil Servants/Public Officials **$1,500**
- Small Business Administration .... $1,500 — Indiv

Retired **$5,410**
- None over $1,500

Unknown — $20,839
- No Employer Listed or Found $6,250
- Employer Listed/Category Unknown $12,589
  - None over $1,500

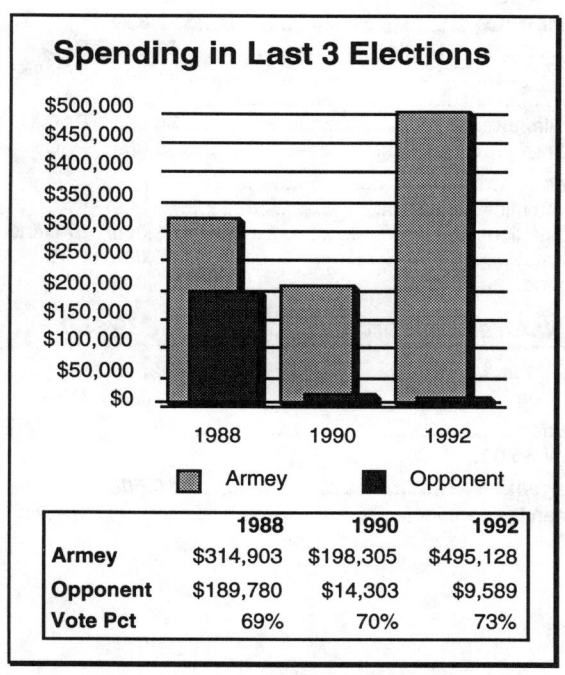

Spending in Last 3 Elections

	1988	1990	1992
Armey	$314,903	$198,305	$495,128
Opponent	$189,780	$14,303	$9,589
Vote Pct	69%	70%	73%

Legend: Armey / Opponent

---

* Contributions came from more than one affiliate or subsidiary.

395

Les Aspin, D-Wis (1)

First elected: 1970

1991-92 Total Receipts: $1,369,976
1992 Year-end Cash: $131,742

1991-92 Committees & Subcommittees

Armed Services (Chairman)
Procurement and Military Nuclear Systems (Chairman)

Leading Contributors

Business

Agriculture	$32,450

Tobacco $5,100
    None over $5,000

Dairy $5,600
    None over $5,000

Food Processing & Sales $15,650
    None over $5,000

Communications/Electronics	$30,100

Printing & Publishing $7,700
    None over $5,000

Electronics Mfg & Services $5,050
    None over $5,000

Computer Equipment & Services $8,600
    None over $5,000

Construction	$24,050

General Contractors $10,350
    None over $5,000

Construction Services $8,650
    None over $5,000

Source of Funds in 1992 Election

Source	Total	Pct
■ PACs	$535,125	39%
▨ Indivs $200+	$511,675	37%
□ Indivs under $200	$246,894	18%
▧ Other.................................	$85,981	6%
Candidate	$0	0%
Party	$14,099	1%

Source of PAC Dollars by Sector

Source	Total	Pct
■ Business	$412,175	73%
▨ Labor	$99,750	18%
□ Ideology/Single Issue	$52,450	9%

In-State vs. Out-of-State Contributions*

Source	Total	Pct
□ In-State	$104,825	21%
■ Out-of-state.....................	$405,850	79%
No state listed	$1,000	

* by large individual contributors ($200 & above)

Defense	$220,875

Defense Aerospace $116,975
General Dynamics.................................	$12,750	PAC/Ind
Martin Marietta Corp	$11,750	PAC/Ind
Textron Inc	$10,750	PAC/Ind
Colt Industries	$10,000	PAC
General Electric	$9,000	PAC
Lockheed Corp	$8,500	PAC/Ind
McDonnell Douglas*	$6,500	PAC
United Technologies	$6,000	PAC
Rockwell International	$5,600	PAC/Ind
Grumman Corp....................................	$5,000	PAC

Defense Electronics $62,850
Raytheon	$9,000	PAC
Loral Corp	$7,500	PAC/Ind
AT&T	$7,000	PAC
Hughes Aircraft...................................	$5,500	PAC
Kaman Corp	$5,000	PAC

Misc Defense $41,050
General Atomics	$9,000	PAC
BDM International	$6,000	PAC/Ind
FMC Corp	$5,000	PAC
Tenneco Inc..	$5,000	PAC

Energy & Natural Resources	$39,350

Oil & Gas.. $14,500
| Enserch Corp .... | $5,000 | PAC |

Electric Utilities... $8,100
    None over $5,000

Waste Management $10,500
| Waste Management Inc .... | $9,500 | PAC/Ind |

Contribution Totals by Sector

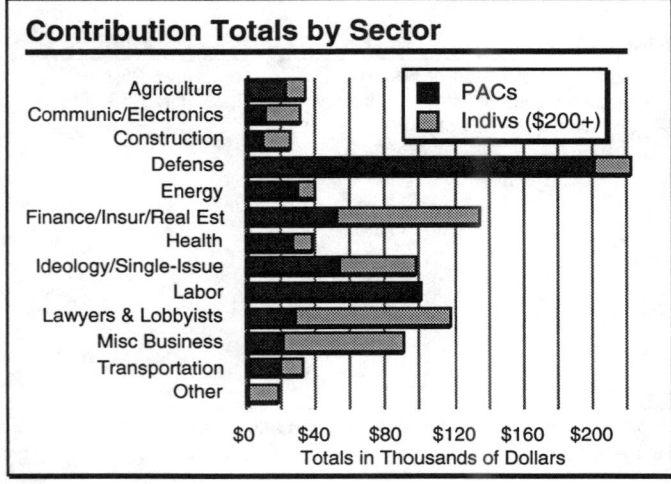

Legend: ■ PACs ▨ Indivs ($200+)

Agriculture, Communic/Electronics, Construction, Defense, Energy, Finance/Insur/Real Est, Health, Ideology/Single-Issue, Labor, Lawyers & Lobbyists, Misc Business, Transportation, Other

$0 $40 $80 $120 $160 $200
Totals in Thousands of Dollars

Finance, Insurance & Real Estate — $130,700

Commercial Banks $26,200
   American Bankers Assn .... $5,000   PAC

Securities & Investment $42,850
   Shearson Lehman Brothers .... $6,000   PAC/Ind
   Investment Company Institute .... $5,000   PAC

Insurance $16,050
   Northwestern Mutual Life .... $5,000   PAC

Real Estate $29,150
   National Assn of Realtors .... $7,000   PAC
   Henry Crown & Co .... $6,000   Indiv

Accountants $5,450
   None over $5,000

Misc Finance $6,750
   None over $5,000

Health — $37,300

Health Professionals $33,850
   American Chiropractic Assn .... $10,000   PAC
   American Dental Assn .... $10,000   PAC

Lawyers & Lobbyists — $116,200

Lawyers & Lobbyists $116,200
   Assn of Trial Lawyers of America .... $10,000   PAC
   Hyjek & Fix .... $10,000   Indiv

Misc Business — $89,200

Beer, Wine & Liquor $16,500
   National Beer Wholesalers Assn .... $6,000   PAC

Business Services $11,150
   None over $5,000

Chemical & Related Manufacturing $6,900
   None over $5,000

Steel Production $12,200
   None over $5,000

Misc Manufacturing & Distributing $24,550
   None over $5,000

Transportation — $31,700

Air Transport $13,900
   None over $5,000

Sea Transport $7,550
   None over $5,000

Labor

Labor — $99,750

Building Trade Unions $21,000
   Laborers' Political League .... $6,000   PAC
   Bricklayers Union .... $5,500   PAC

Industrial Unions $23,100
   United Auto Workers .... $10,000   PAC
   Machinists/Aerospace Workers Union .... $8,000   PAC

Transportation Unions $23,850
   Marine Engineers Union* .... $9,500   PAC
   Teamsters Union .... $7,500   PAC
   Seafarers International Union .... $5,500   PAC

Public Sector Unions $22,050
   National Education Assn .... $7,700   PAC

Misc Unions $9,750
   Office & Professional Employees Union .... $5,000   PAC

Ideological/Single-Issue

Ideological/Single-Issue — $98,250

Pro-Israel $79,850
   Citizens Organized PAC .... $5,000   PAC
   National PAC .... $5,000   PAC

Other & Unknown

Other — $17,200

Education $7,550
   None over $5,000

Retired $7,000
   None over $5,000

Unknown — $109,225

   No Employer Listed or Found $51,050
   Employer Listed/Category Unknown $52,625
    None over $5,000 ....

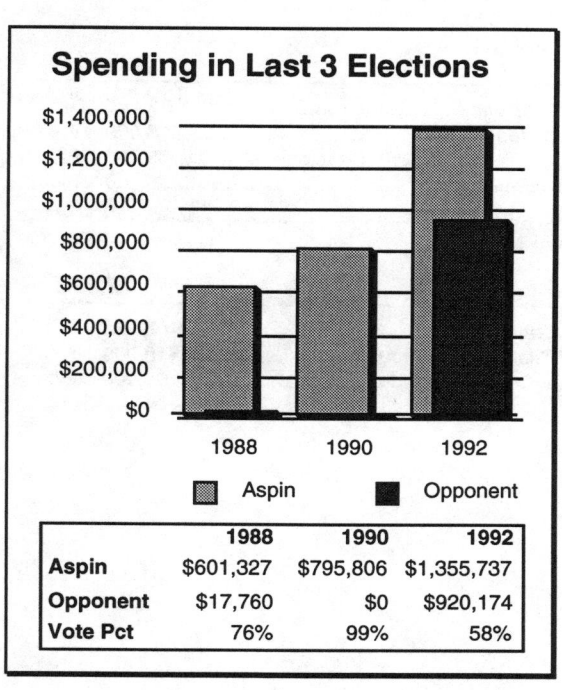

Spending in Last 3 Elections

	1988	1990	1992
Aspin	$601,327	$795,806	$1,355,737
Opponent	$17,760	$0	$920,174
Vote Pct	76%	99%	58%

Legend: Aspin, Opponent

* Contributions came from more than one affiliate or subsidiary.

397

Jim Bacchus, D-Fla (15)

First elected: 1990

1991-92 Total Receipts: $842,030
1992 Year-end Cash: $23,893

1991-92 Committees & Subcommittees

Banking, Finance and Urban Affairs
Financial Institutions Supervision, Regulation and Insurance;
International Development, Finance, Trade and Monetary Policy

Science, Space and Technology
Science; Space; Technology and Competitiveness

Select Committee on Children, Youth and Families

Leading Contributors

Business

Agriculture	$30,150

Crop Production & Basic Processing $24,650
  None over $5,000

Communications/Electronics	$24,650

Telephone Utilities $13,950
  AT&T .... $6,500 PAC

Construction	$22,750

General Contractors $7,200
  None over $5,000
Home Builders $7,050
  None over $5,000
Construction Services $5,750
  None over $5,000

Defense	$21,600

Defense Aerospace $21,300
  Lockheed Corp .... $5,500 PAC
  Martin Marietta Corp .... $5,000 PAC

Energy & Natural Resources	$13,600

Electric Utilities $6,300
  None over $5,000

Source of Funds in 1992 Election

Source	Total	Pct
PACs	$465,347	54%
Indivs $200+	$277,435	32%
Indivs under $200	$72,049	8%
Other	$47,821	6%
Candidate	$0	0%
Party	$25,712	3%

Source of PAC Dollars by Sector

Source	Total	Pct
Business	$259,576	54%
Labor	$177,548	37%
Ideology/Single Issue	$44,657	9%

In-State vs. Out-of-State Contributions*

Source	Total	Pct
In-State	$257,835	93%
Out-of-state	$19,400	7%
No state listed	$200	

* by large individual contributors ($200 & above)

Finance, Insurance & Real Estate	$136,250

Commercial Banks $62,650
  American Bankers Assn .... $12,500 PAC
  Central Bancshares of the South .... $10,000 PAC
  Barnett Banks Inc .... $7,250 PAC
Insurance $9,900
  None over $5,000
Real Estate $37,250
  National Assn of Realtors .... $10,000 PAC
Accountants $6,250
  None over $5,000

Health	$98,530

Health Professionals $86,480
  American Medical Assn* .... $15,000 PAC
  American Academy of Ophthalmology ... $5,330 PAC
  American Dental Assn .... $5,000 PAC
Hospitals/Nursing Homes $5,450
  None over $5,000

Lawyers & Lobbyists	$72,296

Lawyers & Lobbyists $72,296
  Assn of Trial Lawyers of America .... $10,000 PAC
  Akerman, Senterfitt & Eidson .... $6,100 Indiv

Contribution Totals by Sector

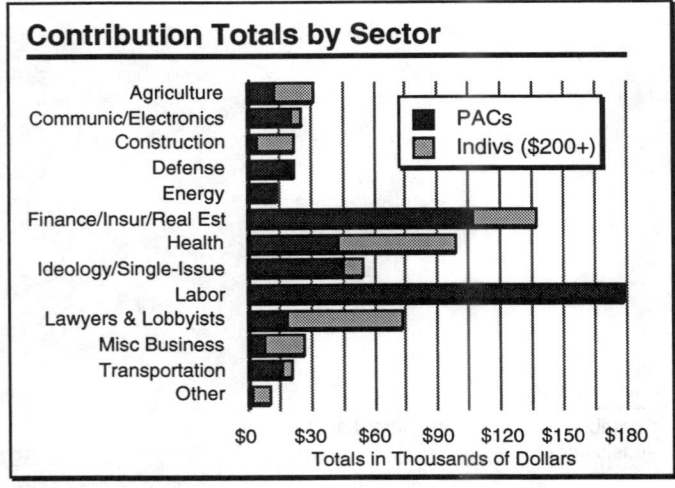

Agriculture, Communic/Electronics, Construction, Defense, Energy, Finance/Insur/Real Est, Health, Ideology/Single-Issue, Labor, Lawyers & Lobbyists, Misc Business, Transportation, Other

■ PACs   ▨ Indivs ($200+)

$0 $30 $60 $90 $120 $150 $180
Totals in Thousands of Dollars

Misc Business	**$26,200**
Lodging/Tourism *$6,250*
None over $5,000

Transportation	**$21,050**
Air Transport *$7,250*
None over $5,000
Automotive *$8,250*
National Auto Dealers Assn .... $6,000 PAC

Labor

Labor	**$177,748**

Building Trade Unions *$22,000*
   Carpenters & Joiners Union .... $5,500 PAC
   Painters & Allied Trades Union .... $5,000 PAC

Industrial Unions *$37,700*
   Machinists/Aerospace Workers Union .... $10,000 PAC
   United Steelworkers .... $7,500 PAC
   Intl Brotherhood of Electrical Workers* .... $7,200 PAC
   Communications Workers of America .... $7,000 PAC
   United Auto Workers .... $6,000 PAC

Transportation Unions *$43,000*
   Marine Engineers Union* .... $11,000 PAC
   Teamsters Union .... $10,000 PAC
   Air Line Pilots Assn .... $5,000 PAC

Public Sector Unions *$53,549*
   American Federation of Teachers .... $10,000 PAC
   National Assn of Letter Carriers .... $10,000 PAC
   National Education Assn .... $10,000 PAC
   American Fedn of St/Cnty/Munic Employees ...... $9,999 PAC

Misc Unions *$21,499*
   Food & Commercial Workers Union .... $9,999 PAC
   AFL-CIO .... $6,500 PAC

Ideological/Single-Issue

Ideological/Single-Issue	**$53,957**

Democratic/Liberal *$5,250*
   None over $5,000

Leadership PACs *$5,450*
   None over $5,000

Pro-Israel *$11,500*
   None over $5,000

Pro-Choice *$9,500*
   National Abortion Rights Action League .... $6,000 PAC

Misc Issues *$14,750*
   Sierra Club .... $7,500 PAC

Other & Unknown

Other	**$9,700**

Retired *$5,000*
   None over $5,000

Unknown	**$50,735**

   Homemakers/Non-income earners $15,800
   No Employer Listed or Found $5,100
   Generic Occupation/Category Unknown $7,150
   Employer Listed/Category Unknown $22,685
     None over $5,000

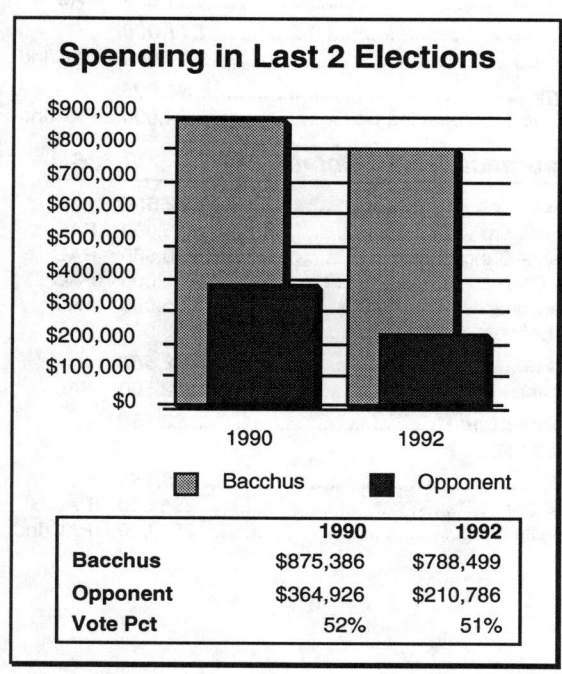

Spending in Last 2 Elections

	1990	1992
Bacchus	$875,386	$788,499
Opponent	$364,926	$210,786
Vote Pct	52%	51%

* Contributions came from more than one affiliate or subsidiary.

Spencer Bachus, R-Ala (6)

First elected: 1992

1991-92 Total Receipts: $499,206
1992 Year-end Cash: $15,660

1993-94 Committees & Subcommittees

Banking, Finance and Urban Affairs
Consumer Credit and Insurance; Financial Institutions Supervision, Regulation and Deposit Insurance; Housing and Community Development

Veterans' Affairs
Oversight and Investigations

Leading Contributors

Business

Agriculture	$16,750	
Agricultural Services/Products	**$12,000**	
Alabama Farm Bureau Federation	$10,000	PAC
Food Processing & Sales	**$2,500**	
Flowers Industries	$2,000	PAC

Communications/Electronics	$17,950	
Printing & Publishing	**$3,000**	
Jefferson News Co	$2,500	Indiv
Media/Entertainment	**$6,000**	
McDonald Group Cable TV	$4,000	Indiv
HBO Inc	$2,000	Indiv
Telephone Utilities	**$2,450**	
Southern Bell	$2,000	PAC
Electronics Mfg & Services	**$5,500**	
American Instrument Co	$4,000	Indiv

Construction	$48,425	
General Contractors	**$30,425**	
Cornerstone Properties	$9,025	Indiv
Associated Builders & Contractors	$5,000	PAC
Harbert Corp	$3,000	Indiv
Acton Homes	$2,000	Indiv
Ellard Contracting	$2,000	Indiv
Dunn Investment Co/Dunn Construction Co	$3,250	Indiv
Home Builders	**$4,500**	
Speir Construction	$2,000	Indiv
National Assn of Home Builders	$1,500	PAC

Source of Funds in 1992 Election

Source	Total	Pct
■ PACs	$150,307	28%
▨ Indivs $200+	$306,877	56%
☐ Indivs under $200	$23,317	4%
▧ Other	$63,692	12%
Candidate	$0	0%
Party	$62,508	11%

Source of PAC Dollars by Sector

Source	Total	Pct
■ Business	$120,701	92%
▨ Labor	$0	0%
☐ Ideology/Single Issue	$11,085	8%

In-State vs. Out-of-State Contributions*

Source	Total	Pct
☐ In-State	$297,177	98%
▨ Out-of-state	$5,750	2%
No state listed	$3,450	

* by large individual contributors ($200 & above)

Special Trade Contractors	$2,250	
None over $1,500		
Building Materials & Equipment	**$10,000**	
Vulcan Materials Co	$5,250	PAC/Ind
Altec Industries Inc	$2,000	Indiv
Pinson Valley Millworks	$1,500	Indiv

Energy & Natural Resources	$29,100	
Oil & Gas	**$13,600**	
Tidmore Oil	$3,000	Indiv
Chevron Corp	$2,000	PAC
Amoco Corp	$1,500	PAC
Mining	**$11,000**	
Drummond Co	$11,000	PAC/Ind
Nuclear Energy	**$4,000**	
Southern Nuclear Operating Co	$4,000	PAC/Ind

Finance, Insurance & Real Estate	$98,136	
Commercial Banks	**$42,500**	
Amsouth Bancorp	$15,000	PAC
First Alabama Bancshares	$10,500	PAC
Southtrust Corp	$8,000	PAC
Central Bancshares of the South	$5,000	PAC
American Bankers Assn	$2,500	PAC
Credit Unions	**$2,500**	
Alabama Credit Union Assn	$2,500	PAC
Securities & Investment	**$2,150**	
None over $1,500		
Insurance	**$15,150**	
Torchmark Corp	$5,000	PAC
Protective Life Corp	$2,000	PAC/Ind

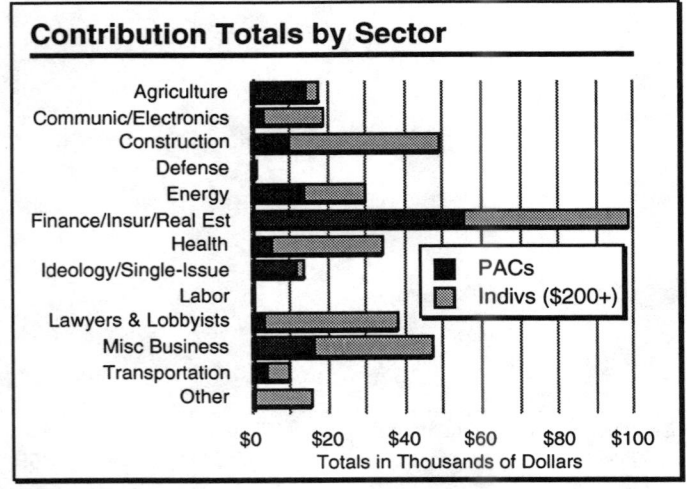

Contribution Totals by Sector

Agriculture
Communic/Electronics
Construction
Defense
Energy
Finance/Insur/Real Est
Health
Ideology/Single-Issue
Labor
Lawyers & Lobbyists
Misc Business
Transportation
Other

■ PACs
▨ Indivs ($200+)

$0 $20 $40 $60 $80 $100
Totals in Thousands of Dollars

Real Estate	$29,236	
Polar-Bek & Baker	$6,000	Indiv
Colonial Properties Inc	$4,000	Indiv
Thompson Realty Corp	$3,000	Indiv
Southeastern Property Management	$2,000	Indiv
Sunbelt Properties	$2,000	Indiv
LBH Properties	$1,836	Indiv
Hubbard Realty	$1,500	Indiv
Accountants	**$6,350**	
American Institute of CPA's	$2,000	PAC
Pearce, Bevill et al	$2,000	Indiv

Health $33,325

Health Professionals	$25,625	
Retina & Vitreous Assoc	$10,000	Indiv
Brookwood Orthopedics Assn	$5,500	Indiv
Healthsouth Rehabilitation Corp	$2,500	PAC
Alabama Orthopaedic & Spine Center	$2,000	Indiv
Ami Columbiana Family Health Center	$2,000	Indiv
Hospitals/Nursing Homes	**$2,500**	
None over $1,500		
Health Services	**$4,000**	
Healthsouth Rehabilitation Corp	$4,000	Indiv

Lawyers & Lobbyists $37,274

Lawyers & Lobbyists	$37,274	
Balch & Bingham	$7,875	Indiv
Stephens, Millirons et al	$6,000	Indiv
Clark & Scott	$4,000	Indiv
Lange, Simpson et al	$2,950	Indiv
Maynard, Cooper et al	$2,000	PAC
Burr & Forman	$1,800	Indiv
Amer, Cunningham, Brennan & Co	$1,500	Indiv

Misc Business $46,701

Business Associations	$3,500	
National Fedn of Independent Business	$2,000	PAC
Business Industry PAC	$1,500	PAC
Food & Beverage	**$5,700**	
None over $1,500		
Retail Sales	**$2,650**	
None over $1,500		

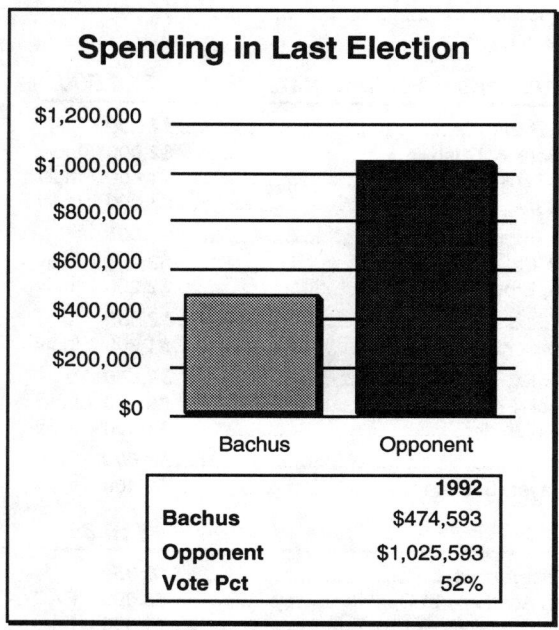

Spending in Last Election

	1992
Bachus	$474,593
Opponent	$1,025,593
Vote Pct	52%

Business Services	$4,250	
Masada Corp	$2,000	Indiv
Ebsco Industries Inc	$1,500	Indiv
Chemical & Related Manufacturing	**$8,250**	
Dow Chemical	$5,000	PAC
American Household Products	$3,000	Indiv
Steel Production	**$7,000**	
American Cast Iron & Pipe Co	$4,000	Indiv
Misc Manufacturing & Distributing	**$14,400**	
McWane Inc	$5,000	Indiv
Amerex Corp	$3,000	Indiv
Precision Grinding Co	$2,000	Indiv
Stone Container Corp	$1,500	PAC

Transportation $9,200

Air Transport	$1,500	
None over $1,500		
Automotive	**$4,700**	
Eaton Corp	$2,000	PAC
McCarty Ford	$2,000	Indiv
Misc Transport	**$1,750**	
Carter Brothers Mfg Co	$1,750	Indiv

Ideological/Single-Issue

Ideological/Single-Issue	$13,085	
Republican/Conservative	**$2,517**	
None over $1,500		
Pro-Israel	**$3,500**	
Americans for Good Government Inc	$2,500	PAC
Pro-Life	**$2,500**	
Republican National Coalition for Life	$2,500	PAC
Misc Issues	**$3,250**	
Right to Work PAC	$2,250	PAC

Other & Unknown

Other	$15,322	
Civil Servants/Public Officials	**$9,372**	
Jefferson County	$4,922	Indiv
City of Birmingham	$2,000	Indiv
Retired	**$5,950**	
None over $1,500		

Unknown	$72,145	
Homemakers/Non-income earners	$15,470	
No Employer Listed or Found	$4,900	
Employer Listed/Category Unknown	$51,275	
Atlas Technology Inc	$4,200	Indiv
Goodwyn Investment Co	$3,000	Indiv
Spain, Gillon et al	$3,000	Indiv
ND Co	$2,200	Indiv
JLG Industries	$2,000	Indiv
McCain Investments Co	$2,000	Indiv
Miller Sales Co	$2,000	Indiv
Grogan Associates	$1,500	Indiv
Holliman, Shockley & Kelly	$1,500	Indiv
Jamisar Inc	$1,500	Indiv

Independent expenditures supporting Bachus
National Right to Life PAC $4,065

Scotty Baesler, D-Ky (6)

First elected: 1992

1991-92 Total Receipts:	$301,557
1992 Year-end Cash:	$27,830

1993-94 Committees & Subcommittees

Agriculture
Environment, Credit and Rural Development; Foreign Agriculture and Hunger; Specialty Crops and Natural Resources

Education and Labor
Human Resources

Veterans' Affairs
Hospitals and Health Care

Leading Contributors

NOTE: Baesler reported taking no PAC funds in the 1992 campaign. The PACs listed below did report making contributions to the candidate, however, and those contributions are recorded in the official FEC records.

Business

Agriculture		$13,502
Crop Production & Basic Processing		**$6,752**
None over $1,000		
Tobacco		**$1,000**
None over $1,000		
Livestock		**$4,500**
None over $1,000		
Agricultural Services/Products		**$1,250**
East Kentucky Investment Co	$1,250	Indiv

Communications/Electronics		$2,000
Media/Entertainment		**$1,750**
Kentucky New Era	$1,000	Indiv

Construction		$20,200
General Contractors		**$10,950**
Central Rock Mineral Co	$2,250	Indiv
Barco Inc	$1,700	Indiv
Clermont Construction Co	$1,000	Indiv
Wiseman Homes	$1,000	Indiv
Woolpart Construction	$1,000	Indiv

Source of Funds in 1992 Election

Source	Total	Pct
■ PACs	$0	0%
▨ Indivs $200+	$184,851	58%
☐ Indivs under $200	$112,812	35%
⊠ Other	$23,678	7%
Candidate	$0	0%
Party	$19,784	6%

Source of PAC Dollars by Sector

No PAC contributions reported

Source	Total	Pct
■ Business	$4,500	100%
▨ Labor	$0	0%
☐ Ideology/Single Issue	$0	0%

In-State vs. Out-of-State Contributions*

Source	Total	Pct
☐ In-State	$180,901	99%
■ Out-of-state	$2,250	1%
No state listed	$0	

* by large individual contributors ($200 & above)

Home Builders		$6,000
Ball Homes Inc	$3,000	Indiv
Parrott, Ely & Hurt	$3,000	Indiv
Construction Services		**$2,500**
None over $1,000		

Energy & Natural Resources		$9,150
Oil & Gas		**$4,000**
Ashland Oil	$3,000	Indiv
Century Offshore Management	$1,000	Indiv
Electric Utilities		**$3,400**
Kentucky Utilities Co	$3,400	Indiv
Waste Management		**$1,000**
None over $1,000		

Finance, Insurance & Real Estate		$24,500
Commercial Banks		**$4,900**
Central Bank & Trust	$2,000	Indiv
Republic Bank & Trust Co	$1,400	Indiv
Central Bank	$1,000	Indiv
Securities & Investment		**$5,000**
Dupree & Co	$2,500	Indiv
Johnston, Brown et al	$2,250	Indiv
Insurance		**$2,550**
Kentucky Central Insurance	$1,300	Indiv
Real Estate		**$8,650**
Southcreek Properties	$3,000	Indiv
Farmer Enterprises	$1,900	Indiv
Accountants		**$2,650**
Miller, Mayer, Sullivan	$2,400	Indiv

Health		$19,350
Health Professionals		**$18,850**
American Academy of Ophthalmology	$3,000	PAC
American Dental Assn	$1,000	PAC

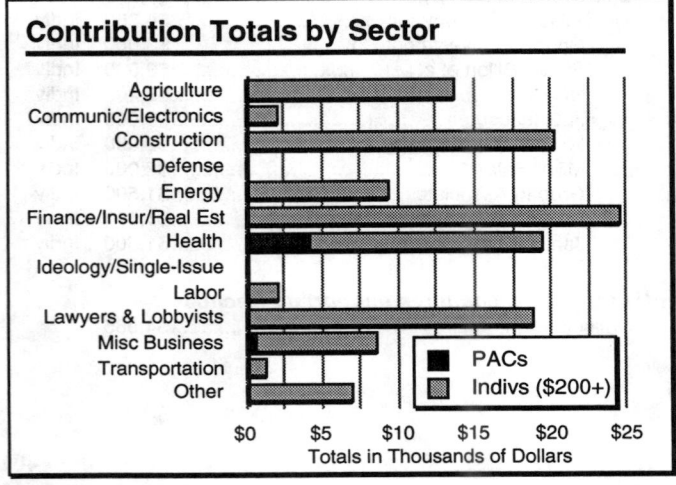

Contribution Totals by Sector

Agriculture
Communic/Electronics
Construction
Defense
Energy
Finance/Insur/Real Est
Health
Ideology/Single-Issue
Labor
Lawyers & Lobbyists
Misc Business
Transportation
Other

■ PACs
▨ Indivs ($200+)

$0 $5 $10 $15 $20 $25
Totals in Thousands of Dollars

Lawyers & Lobbyists $18,671

Lawyers & Lobbyists	**$18,671**	
Henry, Wats et al	$6,000	Indiv
Greenebaum, Doll & McDonald	$2,271	Indiv
Gallion, Baker, Bray	$1,000	Indiv
Harper, Ferguson, Davis	$1,000	Indiv

Misc Business $8,332

Retail Sales	**$1,882**	
Haworth, Meyer & Boleyn Inc	$1,000	Indiv
Misc Services	**$2,500**	
Kerr Brothers Funeral Home	$1,000	Indiv
Richardson Funeral Home	$1,000	Indiv
Misc Business	**$1,000**	
WT Young Storage Co	$1,000	Indiv
Misc Manufacturing & Distributing	**$2,000**	
Baker Iron & Metal Co	$2,000	Indiv

Transportation $1,250

Automotive	**$1,250**	
None over $1,000		

Labor

Labor $2,000

Transportation Unions	**$2,000**	
United Transportation Union	$2,000	Indiv

Other & Unknown

Other $6,846

Education	**$1,725**	
Fayette County Schools	$1,000	Indiv
Retired	**$4,300**	
None over $1,000		

Unknown $61,850

Homemakers/Non-income earners	$14,450	
No Employer Listed or Found	$2,200	
Generic Occupation/Category Unknown	$3,000	
Employer Listed/Category Unknown	$42,200	
JM Crawford & Associates	$4,000	Indiv
Quest Engineers Inc	$3,500	Indiv
GRW Engineers Inc	$3,000	Indiv
Mass-Hamilton Group	$3,000	Indiv
EA Partners	$2,000	Indiv
American Engineering Co	$1,500	Indiv
Philip Mullins Co	$1,500	Indiv
Commonwealth Technology	$1,300	Indiv
Am-Dor Reporting Service	$1,000	Indiv
Congelton, Morris, Thorup & Assoc	$1,000	Indiv
East Ky Power Cooperative	$1,000	Indiv
H-H-R Contractors	$1,000	Indiv
Midwest	$1,000	Indiv
Nesbitt Engineering	$1,000	Indiv
Phillips Tree Experts	$1,000	Indiv
Ross-Feldman	$1,000	Indiv

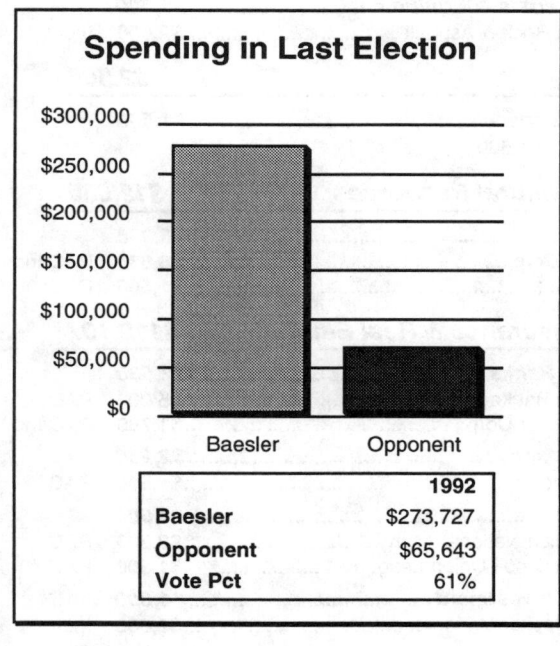

Spending in Last Election

	1992
Baesler	$273,727
Opponent	$65,643
Vote Pct	61%

Bill Baker, R-Calif (10)

1993-94 Committees & Subcommittees

Public Works and Transportation
Economic Development; Investigations and Oversight; Surface Transportation

Science, Space and Technology
Energy

Leading Contributors

Business

Agriculture — $29,150

Crop Production & Basic Processing $3,250
  None over $1,500

Tobacco $3,500
  RJR Nabisco .... $2,000   PAC
  US Tobacco Co .... $1,500   PAC

Dairy $6,000
  Dreyer's Grand Ice Cream Inc .... $4,500   Indiv

Livestock $3,300
  None over $1,500

Agricultural Services/Products $3,000
  None over $1,500

Food Processing & Sales $3,500
  None over $1,500

Forestry & Forest Products $6,350
  Clearprint Paper Co .... $2,000   Indiv
  Louisiana-Pacific Corp .... $2,000   Indiv

Communications/Electronics — $15,250

Media/Entertainment $2,500
  None over $1,500

Telephone Utilities $4,250
  United Telecommunications .... $1,500   PAC

Telecom Services & Equipment $2,000
  Engineered Safety Device .... $1,750   Indiv

Electronics Mfg & Services $3,250
  Electro-Test Inc .... $2,250   Indiv

Computer Equipment & Services $3,250
  Howard Enterprises .... $2,000   Indiv

Contribution Totals by Sector

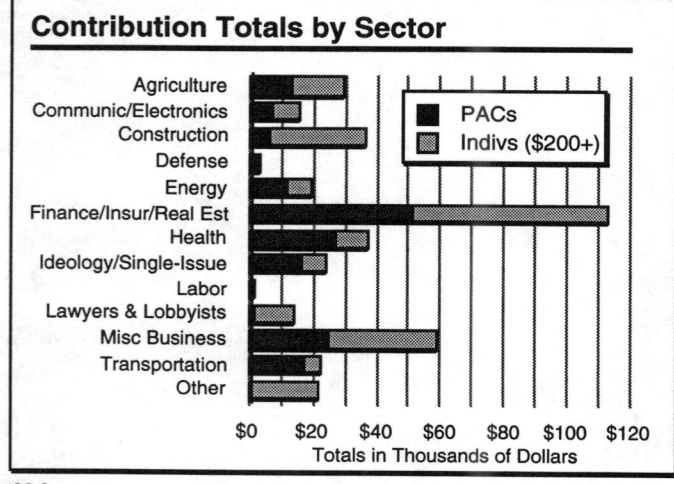

Totals in Thousands of Dollars

First elected: 1992

1991-92 Total Receipts: $708,485
1992 Year-end Cash: $1,704

Source of Funds in 1992 Election

Source	Total	Pct
PACs	$177,800	25%
Indivs $200+	$316,381	44%
Indivs under $200	$145,484	20%
Other	$78,320	11%
Candidate	$50,000	7%
Party	$10,630	1%

Source of PAC Dollars by Sector

Source	Total	Pct
Business	$157,405	90%
Labor	$1,000	1%
Ideology/Single Issue	$15,774	9%

In-State vs. Out-of-State Contributions*

Source	Total	Pct
In-State	$303,865	97%
Out-of-state	$8,550	3%
No state listed	$0	

* by large individual contributors ($200 & above)

Construction — $36,450

General Contractors $19,250
  Gregory Group Inc .... $3,000   Indiv
  Security Owners Corp .... $3,000   Indiv
  Associated General Contractors .... $2,500   PAC
  Cortese Investment Co .... $1,500   Indiv

Home Builders $2,750
  Braddock & Logan .... $1,500   Indiv

Special Trade Contractors $3,000
  Conco Cement Co .... $1,500   Indiv

Construction Services $5,950
  Santina & Thompson .... $2,000   Indiv

Building Materials & Equipment $5,500
  American Rock & Asphalt .... $2,000   Indiv

Defense — $2,500

Defense Aerospace $1,500
  None over $1,500

Energy & Natural Resources — $19,086

Oil & Gas $16,336
  Chevron Corp .... $8,836   PAC/Ind
  Shell Oil .... $1,500   PAC

Finance, Insurance & Real Estate — $112,107

Commercial Banks $12,030
  American Bankers Assn* .... $5,000   PAC
  BankAmerica Corp .... $1,780   PAC/Ind

Savings & Loans $2,250
  CalFed Inc .... $1,500   PAC

Credit Unions $4,000
  Credit Union National Assn .... $2,500   PAC
  California Credit Union League .... $1,500   PAC

Securities & Investment $4,000
  Andron Capitol Management .... $2,000   Indiv

Insurance — $21,150

National Assn of Life Underwriters	$5,000	PAC
Associated Claims Management	$2,000	Indiv
Capitol Guaranty Corp	$2,000	Indiv
Myron V Carlso Insurance	$2,000	Indiv
Nationwide Corp*	$2,000	PAC

Real Estate — $55,567

National Assn of Realtors	$10,000	PAC
Chapman & Wilson	$6,000	Indiv
Bedford Properties	$5,750	PAC/Ind
Reynolds & Brown Development Co	$3,000	Indiv
Ponderosa Homes Inc	$2,000	Indiv
Balco Properties Ltd	$1,500	Indiv
Bedayn Associates	$1,500	Indiv
Sunset Development Co	$1,500	Indiv

Accountants — $6,500

American Institute of CPA's	$2,500	PAC

Misc Finance — $6,160

Merchants Collection Assoc	$2,160	Indiv
Woodard Industries	$1,500	Indiv

Health — $36,175

Health Professionals — $28,375

American Medical Assn	$7,500	PAC
American Academy of Ophthalmology	$6,000	PAC
American Dental Assn	$4,000	PAC
Foundation Health Corp	$1,500	Indiv

Hospitals/Nursing Homes — $4,500
None over $1,500

Pharmaceuticals/Health Products — $2,500
None over $1,500

Lawyers & Lobbyists — $13,250

Lawyers & Lobbyists — $13,250
None over $1,500

Misc Business — $61,009

Food & Beverage — $7,515

Herman Goelitz Candy Co	$2,000	Indiv

Beer, Wine & Liquor — $7,500

Wente Bros Winery	$3,000	Indiv
National Beer Wholesalers Assn	$2,000	PAC

Retail Sales — $17,750

Simpson Co	$6,000	Indiv
Kleinfelder Group	$4,250	Indiv
Longs Drugs Stores Inc	$2,200	PAC
Ethan Allen Gallery	$1,500	Indiv

Business Services — $2,800
None over $1,500

Lodging/Tourism — $1,750
None over $1,500

Chemical & Related Manufacturing — $6,500

Dow Chemical	$3,000	PAC
Clorox Co	$1,500	PAC/Ind

Misc Manufacturing & Distributing — $14,650

Institutional Financial Service	$5,900	Indiv
Stone Container Corp	$2,000	PAC
Owens-Illinois	$1,500	PAC

Transportation — $21,625

Air Transport — $3,500

United Parcel Service	$3,250	PAC/Ind

Automotive — $12,500

National Auto Dealers Assn	$5,000	PAC

Trucking — $1,750
None over $1,500

Railroads — $2,500

Union Pacific Corp	$2,500	PAC

Ideological/Single-Issue

Ideological/Single-Issue — $23,524

Republican/Conservative — $16,024

Lincoln Club of Northern California	$6,000	PAC
Lincoln Club of Orange County	$2,500	PAC

Leadership PACs — $2,250
None over $1,500

Foreign & Defense Policy — $2,000
None over $1,500

Misc Issues — $2,250
None over $1,500

Other & Unknown

Other — $21,403

Retired — $18,153
None over $1,500

Other — $1,750
None over $1,500

Unknown — $94,565

Homemakers/Non-income earners	$7,224	
No Employer Listed or Found	$26,785	
Generic Occupation/Category Unknown	$1,600	
Employer Listed/Category Unknown	$58,956	
Schaffer Laboratories	$2,500	Indiv
Bissel & Karn Inc	$2,000	Indiv
Floratec	$1,500	Indiv
Pac West Development Co	$1,500	Indiv
Richland Development Corp	$1,500	Indiv

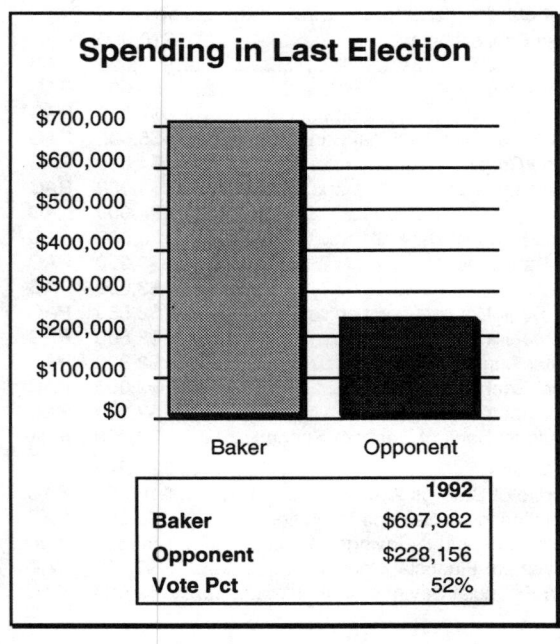

Spending in Last Election

	1992
Baker	$697,982
Opponent	$228,156
Vote Pct	52%

---

* Contributions came from more than one affiliate or subsidiary.

Richard H. Baker, R-La (6)

First elected: 1986

1991-92 Total Receipts: $711,147
1992 Year-end Cash: $7,999

1991-92 Committees & Subcommittees

Banking, Finance and Urban Affairs
Consumer Affairs and Coinage; Financial Institutions Supervision, Regulation and Insurance; Housing and Community Development

Interior and Insular Affairs
Energy and the Environment; General Oversight and California Desert Lands

Small Business
Environment and Employment (Ranking Republican)

Leading Contributors

Business

Agriculture — $21,750

Crop Production & Basic Processing ... **$3,300**
 None over $2,000

Livestock ... **$4,200**
 Jack Lawton Inc ... $3,500 Indiv

Agricultural Services/Products ... **$5,300**
 Freeport-McMoRan Inc ... $3,000 PAC

Food Processing & Sales ... **$2,500**
 None over $2,000

Forestry & Forest Products ... **$3,750**
 None over $2,000

Communications/Electronics — $13,450

Printing & Publishing ... **$2,200**
 None over $2,000

Telephone Utilities ... **$9,500**
 BellSouth Corp* ... $6,000 PAC
 AT&T ... $3,500 PAC

Construction — $23,850

General Contractors ... **$11,650**
 Merit Construction ... $2,000 Indiv

Home Builders ... **$6,300**
 Essen Development ... $3,000 Indiv
 National Assn of Home Builders ... $2,800 PAC

Construction Services ... **$2,750**
 None over $2,000

Contribution Totals by Sector

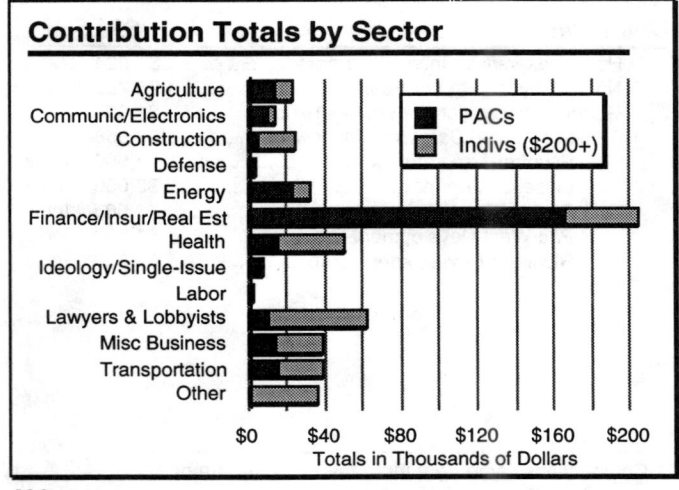

	PACs	Indivs ($200+)
Agriculture		
Communic/Electronics		
Construction		
Defense		
Energy		
Finance/Insur/Real Est		
Health		
Ideology/Single-Issue		
Labor		
Lawyers & Lobbyists		
Misc Business		
Transportation		
Other		

$0 $40 $80 $120 $160 $200
Totals in Thousands of Dollars

Source of Funds in 1992 Election

Source	Total	Pct
PACs	$267,350	38%
Indivs $200+	$314,696	44%
Indivs under $200	$113,844	16%
Other	$15,257	2%
Candidate	$0	0%
Party	$2,659	0%

Source of PAC Dollars by Sector

Source	Total	Pct
Business	$268,225	98%
Labor	$1,500	1%
Ideology/Single Issue	$5,300	2%

In-State vs. Out-of-State Contributions*

Source	Total	Pct
In-State	$297,946	95%
Out-of-state	$16,750	5%
No state listed	$0	

* by large individual contributors ($200 & above)

Defense — $3,600

Defense Aerospace ... **$2,800**
 None over $2,000

Energy & Natural Resources — $31,850

Oil & Gas ... **$15,300**
 Taylor Energy Co ... $2,800 Indiv

Mining ... **$6,750**
 Dravo Corp ... $5,000 PAC

Electric Utilities ... **$8,200**
 Entergy Corp* ... $3,800 PAC
 Central Louisiana Electric ... $2,500 PAC

Finance, Insurance & Real Estate — $203,475

Commercial Banks ... **$91,900**
 American Bankers Assn ... $10,000 PAC
 JP Morgan & Co ... $10,000 PAC
 Chase Manhattan ... $8,000 PAC
 BankAmerica Corp ... $7,000 PAC
 Citizens & Southern National Bank ... $5,000 PAC
 Banc One Corp ... $4,000 PAC
 Bankers Trust ... $4,000 PAC
 MBNA Corp ... $4,000 PAC
 Louisiana National Bank ... $3,500 PAC
 Barnett Banks Inc ... $3,000 PAC
 Citicorp ... $3,000 PAC
 Assn of Bank Holding Companies ... $2,550 PAC
 Continental Illinois Corp ... $2,500 PAC
 Consumer Bankers Assn ... $2,300 PAC
 Chemical Bank ... $2,000 PAC
 First Chicago Corp ... $2,000 PAC
 First National Bank of Denham Springs ... $2,000 Indiv

Savings & Loans ... **$25,325**
 US League of Savings Assns* ... $10,525 PAC
 National Council of Savings Institutions ... $2,800 PAC
 Pelican Homestead & Savings ... $2,500 Indiv
 Great Western Financial Corp ... $2,000 PAC
 Western Financial Savings Bank ... $2,000 PAC

Finance/Credit Companies *$14,850*
    Household International Inc ....$10,500 PAC/Ind

Securities & Investment *$8,150*
    Dean Witter ....$2,300 PAC

Insurance *$23,200*
    American Family Corp ....$3,000 PAC
    National Assn of Life Underwriters..............$3,000 PAC
    American International Group Inc ....$2,300 PAC

Real Estate *$27,800*
    National Assn of Realtors ....$7,300 PAC
    Mortgage Bankers Assn of America ....$6,000 PAC
    JC Canizaro Interests.........................$4,000 Indiv

Accountants *$6,400*
    American Institute of CPA's ....$4,000 PAC

Misc Finance *$5,250*
    Noland Investments ....$3,500 Indiv

Health   **$49,000**

Health Professionals *$33,150*
    Louisiana Medical Assn ....$10,000 PAC
    Our Lady of the Lake Hospital ....$2,000 Indiv

Hospitals/Nursing Homes *$10,850*
    General Health Inc ....$2,950 Indiv

Pharmaceuticals/Health Products *$4,000*
    None over $2,000

Lawyers & Lobbyists   **$61,400**

Lawyers & Lobbyists *$61,400*
    Jones, Walker et al ....$5,700 PAC/Ind
    Breazeale, Sachse & Wilson ....$4,700 Indiv
    Cashe, Lewis et al ....$4,400 Indiv
    Fayard & Fayard ....$3,500 Indiv
    Adams & Reese ....$2,700 PAC/Ind
    Arnold & Porter* ....$2,000 PAC
    Baldwin & Haspel ....$2,000 Indiv
    Lippman, Mafouz et al ....$2,000 Indiv
    McNulty, O'Connor et al ....$2,000 Indiv
    Porteous, Hainkel et al ....$2,000 Indiv

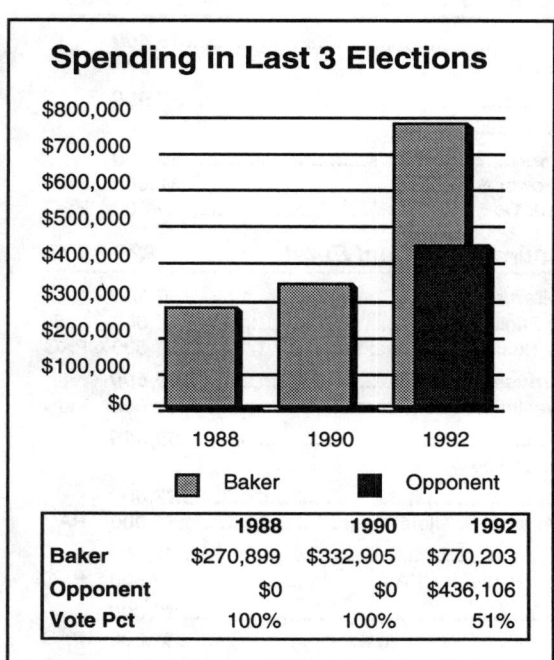

Spending in Last 3 Elections

	1988	1990	1992
Baker	$270,899	$332,905	$770,203
Opponent	$0	$0	$436,106
Vote Pct	100%	100%	51%

Misc Business   **$37,150**

Food & Beverage *$3,000*
    None over $2,000

Beer, Wine & Liquor *$5,500*
    National Beer Wholesalers Assn ....$4,000 PAC

Retail Sales *$5,900*
    None over $2,000

Business Services *$12,750*
    AME Inc ....$5,000 Indiv
    Lamar Outdoor Advertising Corp ....$2,250 Indiv

Chemical & Related Manufacturing *$4,900*
    None over $2,000

Transportation   **$37,600**

Air Transport *$3,800*
    United Parcel Service ....$3,000 PAC

Automotive *$14,900*
    National Auto Dealers Assn ....$4,000 PAC
    Duplessis Cadillac ....$2,350 Indiv
    Woodfin-Smith Pontiac ....$2,250 Indiv

Trucking *$10,600*
    CM Penn & Sons ....$6,600 Indiv

Railroads *$3,000*
    Union Pacific Corp ....$3,000 PAC

Sea Transport *$5,300*
    Gulf Intracoastal Marine ....$2,500 Indiv
    Bollinger Machine Shop & Shipyards ....$2,000 Indiv

Labor

Labor   **$2,000**
    None over $2,000

Ideological/Single-Issue

Ideological/Single-Issue   **$7,300**

Pro-Israel *$3,000*
    Louisiana for American Security ....$3,000 PAC

Misc Issues *$2,300*
    None over $2,000

Other & Unknown

Other   **$34,800**

Civil Servants/Public Officials *$2,950*
    None over $2,000

Education *$3,500*
    None over $2,000

Retired *$27,350*
    None over $2,000

Unknown   **$62,496**
    Homemakers/Non-income earners $12,000
    No Employer Listed or Found $13,275
    Employer Listed/Category Unknown $37,221
        None over $2,000

---

* Contributions came from more than one affiliate or
subsidiary.

Cass Ballenger, R-NC (10)

First elected: 1986

1991-92 Total Receipts:	$277,122
1992 Year-end Cash:	$19,700

1991-92 Committees & Subcommittees

Education and Labor
Health and Safety; Labor-Management Relations; Select Education (Ranking Republican)

Public Works and Transportation
Aviation; Economic Development; Water Resources

Leading Contributors

Business

Agriculture $34,225

Crop Production & Basic Processing *$3,625*
   None over $1,500

Tobacco *$12,250*
   RJR Nabisco* .... $8,750   Indiv
   Philip Morris .... $2,500   PAC

Poultry & Eggs *$4,500*
   National Broiler Council .... $1,500   PAC
   Perdue Farms .... $1,500   Indiv
   Tyson Foods .... $1,500   PAC

Agricultural Services/Products *$2,500*
   None over $1,500

Food Processing & Sales *$7,000*
   Merchants Distributors Inc .... $2,000   Indiv

Forestry & Forest Products *$3,750*
   Westvaco Corp .... $2,000   PAC

Communications/Electronics $14,250

Printing & Publishing *$2,250*
   Hickory Printing Co .... $1,500   Indiv

Telephone Utilities *$12,000*
   Southern Bell .... $9,000   PAC
   United Telecommunications .... $1,500   PAC

Source of Funds in 1992 Election

Source	Total	Pct
■ PACs	$167,925	61%
▨ Indivs $200+	$88,650	32%
☐ Indivs under $200	$10,437	4%
⊠ Other	$10,110	4%
Candidate	$0	0%
Party	$70	0%

Source of PAC Dollars by Sector

Source	Total	Pct
■ Business	$155,325	94%
▨ Labor	$500	0%
☐ Ideology/Single Issue	$9,400	6%

In-State vs. Out-of-State Contributions*

Source	Total	Pct
☐ In-State	$81,400	92%
■ Out-of-state	$7,250	8%
No state listed	$0	

* by large individual contributors ($200 & above)

Construction $13,350

General Contractors *$7,000*
   Associated General Contractors .... $2,500   PAC
   National Utility Contractors Assn .... $2,000   PAC
   Shook & Tarton Investment Co .... $1,500   Indiv

Building Materials & Equipment *$3,100*
   None over $1,500

Defense $4,500

Defense Aerospace *$4,500*
   None over $1,500

Energy & Natural Resources $13,950

Oil & Gas *$6,400*
   None over $1,500

Mining *$2,000*
   None over $1,500

Electric Utilities *$5,300*
   Carolina Power & Light .... $2,000   PAC
   Duke Power Co .... $1,500   PAC

Finance, Insurance & Real Estate $26,300

Commercial Banks *$6,300*
   Wachovia Bank & Trust .... $2,500   Indiv
   Citizens & Southern National Bank .... $1,500   PAC

Securities & Investment *$2,500*
   Salem Investment Counselors .... $2,000   Indiv

Insurance *$5,000*
   None over $1,500

Real Estate *$7,000*
   National Assn of Realtors .... $6,000   PAC

Accountants *$2,500*
   American Institute of CPA's .... $2,500   PAC

Misc Finance *$3,000*
   Employee Stock Ownership Assn .... $1,500   PAC

Contribution Totals by Sector

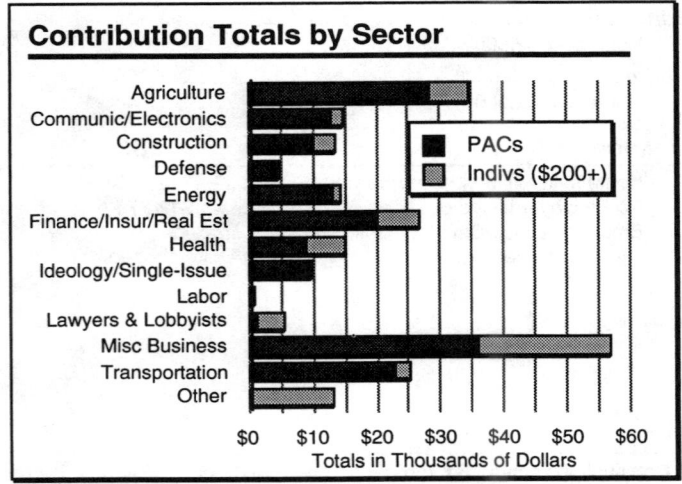

Legend: ■ PACs, ▨ Indivs ($200+)

Sectors (top to bottom): Agriculture, Communic/Electronics, Construction, Defense, Energy, Finance/Insur/Real Est, Health, Ideology/Single-Issue, Labor, Lawyers & Lobbyists, Misc Business, Transportation, Other

X-axis: $0, $10, $20, $30, $40, $50, $60 — Totals in Thousands of Dollars

Health $14,950

Health Professionals **$8,800**
     American Medical Assn.....................................$2,350   PAC
     American Dental Assn ....$2,000   PAC

Hospitals/Nursing Homes **$2,000**
     None over $1,500

Pharmaceuticals/Health Products **$4,150**
     Glaxo Inc ....$2,000   PAC

Lawyers & Lobbyists $5,000

Lawyers & Lobbyists **$5,000**
     None over $1,500

Misc Business $56,750

Business Associations **$1,500**
     None over $1,500

Food & Beverage **$2,500**
     National Restaurant Assn ....$2,000   PAC

Beer, Wine & Liquor **$4,500**
     National Beer Wholesalers Assn ....$3,500   PAC

Retail Sales **$2,700**
     None over $1,500

Business Services **$2,300**
     None over $1,500

Chemical & Related Manufacturing **$8,050**
     FMC Corp ....$2,500   PAC
     WR Grace & Co ....$1,500   PAC

Misc Manufacturing & Distributing **$18,750**
     American Furniture Manufacturers Assn ....$3,500   PAC
     Hoechst Celanese Corp ....$2,500   PAC
     Century Furniture Co ....$2,000   Indiv
     Broyhill Investments Inc ....$1,500   Indiv
     Classic Leather Inc...$1,500   Indiv
     Sock Manufacturing ....$1,500   Indiv

Textiles **$15,950**
     Burlington Industries ....$4,500   PAC
     American Textile Machinery Assn ....$1,500   PAC
     American Textile Manufacturers Institute ....$1,500   PAC

Transportation $25,000

Air Transport **$12,500**
     United Parcel Service ....$4,500   PAC
     Aircraft Owners & Pilots Assn ....$4,000   PAC

Automotive **$5,500**
     National Auto Dealers Assn ....$3,500   PAC
     Auto Dealers & Drivers for Free Trade ....$1,500   PAC

Trucking **$5,500**
     Carolina Freight Carriers ....$2,000   PAC/Ind

Railroads **$1,500**
     None over $1,500

Ideological/Single-Issue

Ideological/Single-Issue $9,400

Leadership PACs **$5,000**
     National Congressional Club (Jesse Helms) ....$5,000   PAC

Gun Rights/Gun Control **$2,000**
     National Rifle Assn ....$2,000   PAC

Other & Unknown

Other $12,950

Civil Servants/Public Officials **$4,000**
     State of North Carolina ....$3,000   Indiv

Education **$2,750**
     Bowman Gray School of Medicine ....$1,500   Indiv

Retired **$6,200**
     None over $1,500

Unknown $22,750

     Homemakers/Non-income earners $3,000
     No Employer Listed or Found $1,950
     Employer Listed/Category Unknown $17,550
         Edward Aycoth & Co ....$2,000   Indiv

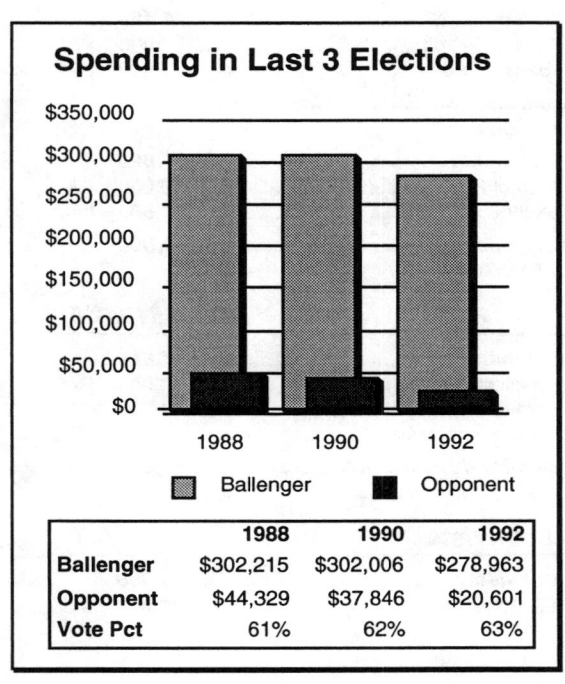

Spending in Last 3 Elections

	1988	1990	1992
Ballenger	$302,215	$302,006	$278,963
Opponent	$44,329	$37,846	$20,601
Vote Pct	61%	62%	63%

* Contributions came from more than one affiliate or
   subsidiary.

James A. Barcia, D-Mich (5)

1993-94 Committees & Subcommittees

First elected: 1992

1991-92 Total Receipts: $283,843
1992 Year-end Cash: $689

Public Works and Transportation
Economic Development; Investigations and Oversight; Water Resources and the Environment

Science, Space and Technology
Science; Space

Leading Contributors

Business

Agriculture	$8,950	
Crop Production & Basic Processing	$1,700	
None over $1,000		
Tobacco	$3,000	
RJR Nabisco	$2,000	PAC
Livestock	$1,000	
None over $1,000		
Agricultural Services/Products	$1,250	
None over $1,000		
Food Processing & Sales	$1,500	
Pepsico Inc	$1,000	PAC

Communications/Electronics	$6,750	
Media/Entertainment	$1,500	
Comcast Corp	$1,000	PAC
Telephone Utilities	$3,500	
AT&T	$2,500	PAC

Construction	$7,300	
General Contractors	$2,550	
National Utility Contractors Assn	$1,000	PAC
Special Trade Contractors	$2,750	
Northern Boiler	$1,500	Indiv
Construction Services	$1,050	
Wade-Trim Group Inc	$1,050	Indiv

Source of Funds in 1992 Election

Source	Total	Pct
PACs	$137,751	47%
Indivs $200+	$76,030	26%
Indivs under $200	$43,249	15%
Other	$37,016	13%
Candidate	$10,692	4%
Party	$10,203	3%

Source of PAC Dollars by Sector

Source	Total	Pct
Business	$85,150	62%
Labor	$37,200	27%
Ideology/Single Issue	$16,051	12%

In-State vs. Out-of-State Contributions*

Source	Total	Pct
In-State	$64,584	97%
Out-of-state	$2,000	3%
No state listed	$200	

* by large individual contributors ($200 & above)

Energy & Natural Resources	$13,800	
Oil & Gas	$9,500	
Ashland Oil	$2,000	PAC
Ken Mattis Inc	$1,000	Indiv
Michigan Consolidated Gas	$1,000	PAC
Phillips Petroleum	$1,000	PAC
Electric Utilities	$3,500	
Consumers Power Co	$2,000	PAC
Detroit Edison	$1,000	PAC

Finance, Insurance & Real Estate	$17,250	
Commercial Banks	$4,450	
National Bank of Detroit	$2,000	PAC
American Bankers Assn	$1,000	PAC
Insurance	$2,750	
None over $1,000		
Real Estate	$7,800	
National Assn of Realtors	$5,000	PAC
Re/Max Realty	$1,500	Indiv
Accountants	$1,000	
None over $1,000		

Health	$19,816	
Health Professionals	$17,816	
American Medical Assn	$10,000	PAC
American Academy of Ophthalmology	$4,000	PAC
American Optometric Assn	$1,000	PAC
Pharmaceuticals/Health Products	$1,500	
Eli Lilly & Co	$1,000	PAC

Lawyers & Lobbyists	$5,850	
Lawyers & Lobbyists	$5,850	
Ackerman & Ackerman	$2,000	Indiv

Contribution Totals by Sector

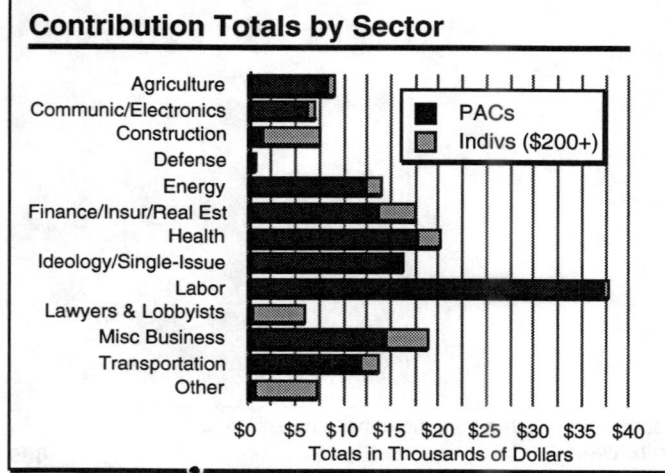

- Agriculture
- Communic/Electronics
- Construction
- Defense
- Energy
- Finance/Insur/Real Est
- Health
- Ideology/Single-Issue
- Labor
- Lawyers & Lobbyists
- Misc Business
- Transportation
- Other

■ PACs
▨ Indivs ($200+)

$0 $5 $10 $15 $20 $25 $30 $35 $40
Totals in Thousands of Dollars

Misc Business $18,674

Food & Beverage $1,150
   None over $1,000

Beer, Wine & Liquor $3,750
   National Beer Wholesalers Assn ....$2,000   PAC

Retail Sales $3,174
   None over $1,000

Business Services $1,000
   None over $1,000

Chemical & Related Manufacturing $5,000
   Dow Chemical ....$4,500   PAC

Misc Manufacturing & Distributing $3,350
   None over $1,000

Transportation $13,500

Air Transport $5,000
   United Parcel Service ....$5,000   PAC

Automotive $5,450
   Eaton Corp ....$2,000   PAC
   National Auto Dealers Assn ....$1,500   PAC

Trucking $1,250
   Lee Wood Trucking ....$1,250   Indiv

Railroads $1,500
   Union Pacific Corp ....$1,500   PAC

Labor

Labor $37,700

Building Trade Unions $12,300
   Sheet Metal Workers Union ....$3,750   PAC
   Carpenters & Joiners Union ....$3,500   PAC
   Plumbers/Pipefitters Union* ....$2,500   PAC
   Laborers' Political League ....$1,500   PAC

Industrial Unions $9,000
   United Auto Workers ....$5,000   PAC
   United Steelworkers ....$2,000   PAC
   AFL-CIO Allied Industrial Wrkrs ....$1,000   PAC
   Communications Workers of America ....$1,000   PAC

Transportation Unions $5,000
   Teamsters Union ....$5,000   PAC

Public Sector Unions $7,600
   National Education Assn ....$5,000   PAC
   American Fedn of St/Cnty/Munic Employees ......$1,600   PAC
   National Rural Letter Carriers Assn ....$1,000   PAC

Misc Unions $3,800
   Food & Commercial Workers Union ....$2,500   PAC

Ideological/Single-Issue

Ideological/Single-Issue $16,051

Leadership PACs $3,000
   Conservative Demo PAC (Charles Stenholm) .....$1,000   PAC
   Effective Government Cmte (Dick Gephardt) ......$1,000   PAC
   House Leadership Fund (Tom Foley) ....$1,000   PAC

Pro-Israel $1,000
   MOPAC ....$1,000   PAC

Pro-Life $4,601
   Right to Life* ....$4,601   PAC

Gun Rights/Gun Control $7,450
   National Rifle Assn ....$4,950   PAC
   Safari Club International ....$2,500   PAC

Other & Unknown

Other $6,909

Civil Servants/Public Officials $1,550
   None over $1,000

Education $1,121
   None over $1,000

Retired $3,738
   None over $1,000

Unknown $32,635

   Homemakers/Non-income earners $1,133
   No Employer Listed or Found $14,577
   Generic Occupation/Category Unknown $6,300
   Employer Listed/Category Unknown $10,625
      Lakeshore Diagnostic Ultrasound ....$1,600   Indiv
      Dore Enterprises ....$1,100   Indiv
      Damn Yankees World Wide ....$1,000   Indiv
      Enkon Environmental Services Inc ....$1,000   Indiv

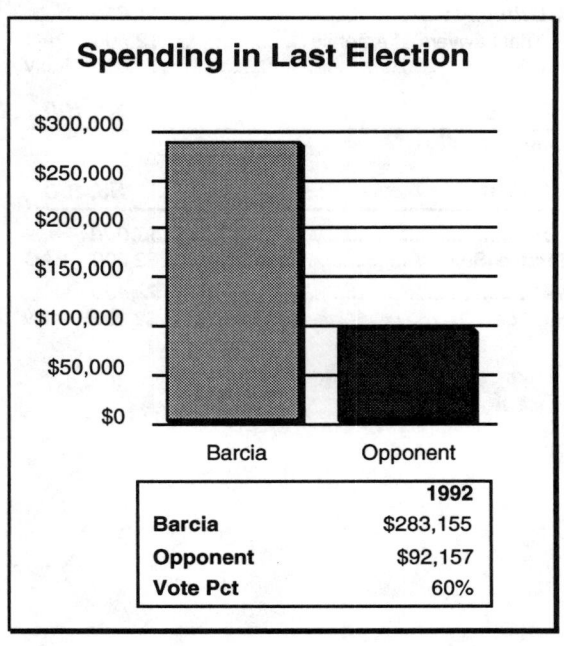

Spending in Last Election

	1992
Barcia	$283,155
Opponent	$92,157
Vote Pct	60%

---

* Contributions came from more than one affiliate or
  subsidiary.

Tom Barlow, D-Ky (1)

First elected: 1992

1991-92 Total Receipts: $220,396
1992 Year-end Cash: $6,864

1993-94 Committees & Subcommittees

Agriculture
Environment, Credit and Rural Development; Foreign Agriculture and Hunger; General Farm Commodities

Merchant Marine and Fisheries
Coast Guard and Navigation

Natural Resources
Energy and Mineral Resources

Leading Contributors

Business

Agriculture	$8,750	
Crop Production & Basic Processing	**$1,500**	
None over $1,000		
Tobacco	**$2,750**	
Philip Morris	$1,000	PAC
Dairy	**$2,500**	
Associated Milk Producers	$1,000	PAC
Dairymen Inc-Kentucky	$1,000	PAC
Poultry & Eggs	**$1,000**	
National Broiler Council	$1,000	PAC

Communications/Electronics	$1,800	
Telephone Utilities	**$1,800**	
AT&T	$1,000	PAC

Energy & Natural Resources	$3,250	
Oil & Gas	**$1,000**	
None over $1,000		
Waste Management	**$1,500**	
Waste Management Inc	$1,500	PAC

Finance, Insurance & Real Estate	$8,400	
Commercial Banks	**$1,400**	
None over $1,000		
Insurance	**$2,500**	
Kentucky Central Life Insurance Co	$1,000	PAC
LWD Inc	$1,000	Indiv

Source of Funds in 1992 Election

Source	Total	Pct
PACs	$105,850	48%
Indivs $200+	$22,460	10%
Indivs under $200	$31,003	14%
Other	$61,233	28%
Candidate	$48,437	22%
Party	$9,150	4%

Source of PAC Dollars by Sector

Source	Total	Pct
Business	$33,300	34%
Labor	$58,000	60%
Ideology/Single Issue	$5,500	6%

In-State vs. Out-of-State Contributions*

Source	Total	Pct
In-State	$18,460	83%
Out-of-state	$3,900	17%
No state listed	$0	

*** by large individual contributors ($200 & above)**

Real Estate	$3,000	
National Assn of Realtors	$3,000	PAC
Accountants	**$1,000**	
American Institute of CPA's	$1,000	PAC

Health	$5,500	
Health Professionals	**$5,500**	
American Dental Assn	$2,500	PAC
American Academy of Ophthalmology	$1,000	PAC
American Chiropractic Assn	$1,000	PAC
American Optometric Assn	$1,000	PAC

Lawyers & Lobbyists	$5,650	
Lawyers & Lobbyists	**$5,650**	
Assn of Trial Lawyers of America	$2,500	PAC
Ferreri & Fogle	$1,000	Indiv

Misc Business	$1,400	
None over $1,000		

Transportation	$6,450	
Air Transport	**$3,000**	
United Parcel Service	$2,500	PAC
Automotive	**$2,450**	
Paducah Ford	$2,000	Indiv

Contribution Totals by Sector

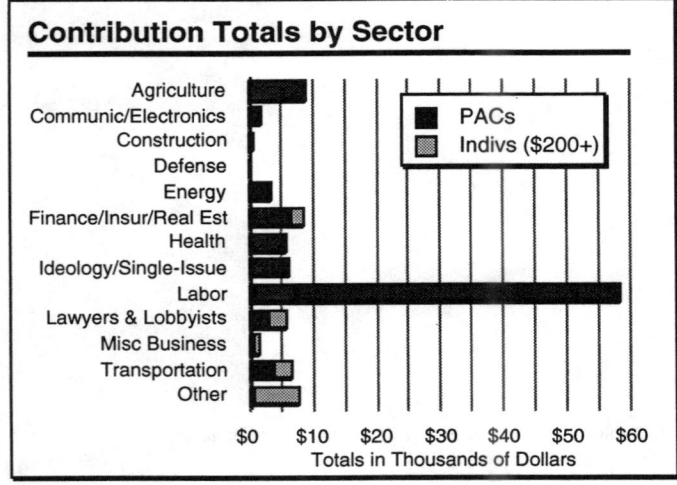

■ PACs
▨ Indivs ($200+)

Agriculture
Communic/Electronics
Construction
Defense
Energy
Finance/Insur/Real Est
Health
Ideology/Single-Issue
Labor
Lawyers & Lobbyists
Misc Business
Transportation
Other

$0 $10 $20 $30 $40 $50 $60
Totals in Thousands of Dollars

Labor

Labor	$58,400

Building Trade Unions **$4,900**
   Carpenters & Joiners Union ....$1,400 PAC/Ind
   Laborers' Political League ....$1,000 PAC
   Plumbers/Pipefitters Union ....$1,000 PAC
   Sheet Metal Workers Union ....$1,000 PAC

Industrial Unions **$26,000**
   Machinists/Aerospace Workers Union ....$10,000 PAC
   Rubber Cork Linoleum & Plastic Workers ....$5,000 PAC
   United Auto Workers ....$5,000 PAC
   United Mine Workers ....$2,500 PAC
   Boilermakers Union ....$1,000 PAC
   Communications Workers of America ....$1,000 PAC
   Intl Brotherhood of Electrical Workers ....$1,000 PAC

Transportation Unions **$9,000**
   Teamsters Union ....$3,500 PAC
   Seafarers International Union ....$2,500 PAC
   Air Line Pilots Assn ....$1,000 PAC
   United Transportation Union ....$1,000 PAC

Public Sector Unions **$13,500**
   National Assn of Letter Carriers ....$3,000 PAC
   National Education Assn ....$3,000 PAC
   American Fedn of St/Cnty/Munic Employees ......$2,500 PAC
   National Assn Retired Federal Employees ....$2,000 PAC
   International Assn of Firefighters ....$1,000 PAC
   National Rural Letter Carriers Assn ....$1,000 PAC

Misc Unions **$5,000**
   Food & Commercial Workers Union ....$2,500 PAC
   Bakery, Confectionery & Tobacco Workers ....$1,500 PAC
   Service Employees International Union ....$1,000 PAC

Ideological/Single-Issue

Ideological/Single-Issue	$5,750

Leadership PACs **$4,500**
   America's Leaders' Fund (Dan Rostenkowski) ....$1,000 PAC
   Effective Government Cmte (Dick Gephardt) ......$1,000 PAC
   House Leadership Fund (Tom Foley) ....$1,000 PAC
   Victory USA (Vic Fazio) ....$1,000 PAC

Misc Issues **$1,250**
   National Cmte to Preserve Social Security ....$1,000 PAC

Other & Unknown

Other	$7,310

Civil Servants/Public Officials **$1,910**
   US House of Representatives ....$1,000 Indiv

Retired **$4,900**
   None over $1,000

Unknown	$5,800

   Generic Occupation/Category Unknown $1,000
   Employer Listed/Category Unknown $4,300
      McHenry Brass Inc ....$1,000 Indiv

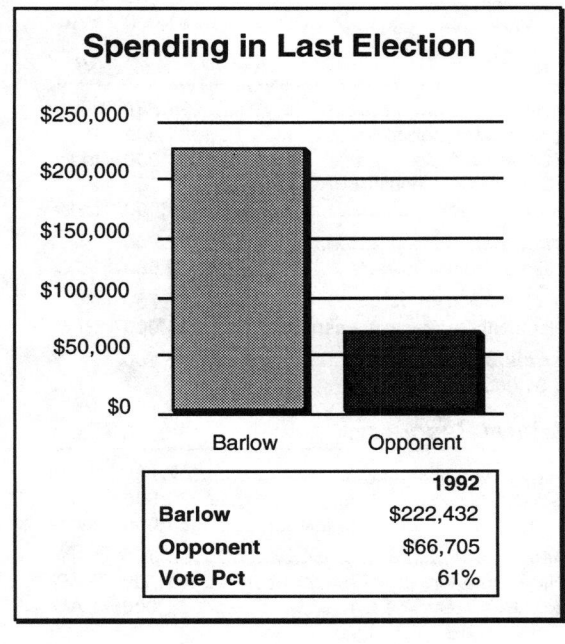

Spending in Last Election

	1992
Barlow	$222,432
Opponent	$66,705
Vote Pct	61%

Bill Barrett, R-Neb (3)

First elected: 1990

1991-92 Total Receipts: $454,589
1992 Year-end Cash: $17,315

1991-92 Committees & Subcommittees

Administration
Accounts; Libraries and Memorials (Ranking Republican)

Agriculture
Conservation, Credit and Rural Development; Department Operations, Research and Foreign Agriculture; Wheat, Soybeans and Feed Grains

Education and Labor
Human Resources; Labor-Management Relations; Postsecondary Education

Joint Committee on the Library

Select Committee on Children, Youth and Families

Leading Contributors

Business

Agriculture	$63,190	
Crop Production & Basic Processing	**$11,825**	
American Sugarbeet Growers Assn	$2,300	PAC
American Crystal Sugar Corp	$1,500	PAC
Southern Minn Beet Sugar Co-op	$1,125	PAC
Amalgamated Sugar Co	$1,000	PAC
Great Lakes Sugar Beet Growers	$1,000	PAC
Tobacco	**$1,800**	
RJR Nabisco	$1,300	PAC
Dairy	**$4,650**	
Associated Milk Producers	$3,000	PAC
Poultry & Eggs	**$3,700**	
United Egg Assn	$2,000	PAC
Livestock	**$6,965**	
National Cattlemen's Assn*	$2,900	PAC
Sand Livestock Systems	$1,450	Indiv
Agricultural Services/Products	**$14,850**	
Farm Credit Council	$1,550	PAC
T&L Irrigation	$1,500	Indiv
American Assn of Nurserymen	$1,250	PAC
Society of American Florists	$1,250	PAC
American Assn of Crop Insurers	$1,000	PAC

Source of Funds in 1992 Election

Source	Total	Pct
PACs	$197,525	43%
Indivs $200+	$107,839	24%
Indivs under $200	$139,391	31%
Other	$9,834	2%
Candidate	$0	0%
Party	$3,650	1%

Source of PAC Dollars by Sector

Source	Total	Pct
Business	$187,874	96%
Labor	$1,000	1%
Ideology/Single Issue	$7,250	4%

In-State vs. Out-of-State Contributions*

Source	Total	Pct
In-State	$97,930	94%
Out-of-state	$6,150	6%
No state listed	$0	

* by large individual contributors ($200 & above)

American Veterinary Medical Assn	$1,000	PAC
Dow Chemical	$1,000	PAC
Farmland Industries	$1,000	PAC
PMS Feed Supply	$1,000	Indiv
Food Processing & Sales	**$19,400**	
ConAgra Inc	$10,000	PAC
Fleming Companies Inc	$3,000	PAC
Food Marketing Institute	$2,800	PAC
American Meat Institute	$1,050	PAC

Communications/Electronics	$10,550	
Telephone Utilities	**$9,100**	
US West Inc	$2,750	PAC/Ind
AT&T	$2,250	PAC
GTE Corp	$1,000	PAC

Construction	$12,300	
General Contractors	**$6,550**	
Associated General Contractors	$1,300	PAC
Hawkins Construction Co	$1,000	Indiv
Nebraska Construction Industry PAC	$1,000	PAC
Peter Kiewit Sons Inc	$1,000	Indiv
Home Builders	**$2,900**	
National Assn of Home Builders	$2,900	PAC
Special Trade Contractors	**$1,750**	
National Electrical Contractors Assn	$1,000	PAC
Building Materials & Equipment	**$1,100**	
None over $1,000		

Energy & Natural Resources	$11,958	
Oil & Gas	**$7,758**	
KN Energy Inc	$1,500	PAC/Ind
Beard Oil Co	$1,000	Indiv
Electric Utilities	**$2,300**	
ACRE (Action Cmte for Rural Electrification)	$1,300	PAC
Northwestern Public Service Co	$1,000	PAC

Contribution Totals by Sector

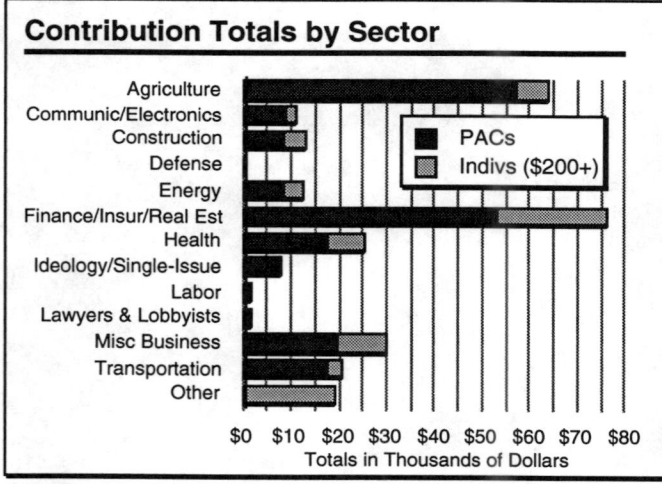

Agriculture
Communic/Electronics
Construction
Defense
Energy
Finance/Insur/Real Est
Health
Ideology/Single-Issue
Labor
Lawyers & Lobbyists
Misc Business
Transportation
Other

PACs
Indivs ($200+)

$0 $10 $20 $30 $40 $50 $60 $70 $80
Totals in Thousands of Dollars

Finance, Insurance & Real Estate — $77,548

Commercial Banks $27,741
American Bankers Assn*	$10,000	PAC
Independent Bankers Assn	$2,300	PAC
Bank of St Edward	$2,000	Indiv
Union Bank	$2,000	Indiv
First State Bank	$1,500	Indiv
Firstier Financial Inc	$1,500	PAC
Farmers State Bank	$1,450	Indiv
Cozad State Bank	$1,000	Indiv
Norwest Corp	$1,000	PAC

Securities & Investment $2,008
None over $1,000

Insurance $28,049
Mutual of Omaha	$4,899	PAC/Ind
National Assn of Prof Insurance Agents	$1,900	PAC
National Assn of Independent Insurers	$1,500	PAC
Ryder, Rosacker, McCue	$1,500	Indiv
American Council of Life Insurance	$1,400	PAC
Health Insurance Assn of America	$1,250	PAC
Blue Cross & Blue Shield Assn	$1,150	PAC
Principal Mutual Life Insurance	$1,150	PAC
Casualty & Surety Agents Assn	$1,000	PAC

Real Estate $12,700
National Assn of Realtors	$12,000	PAC

Accountants $4,450
American Institute of CPA's	$3,000	PAC

Misc Finance $2,100
America First Resource Management	$1,000	PAC

Health — $24,700

Health Professionals $19,400
American Medical Assn	$12,200	PAC
American Optometric Assn	$1,500	PAC
American Assn Oral & Maxillofacial Surgeons	$1,000	PAC
American Dental Assn	$1,000	PAC

Hospitals/Nursing Homes $3,750
Lantis Enterprises Inc	$2,400	Indiv

Pharmaceuticals/Health Products $1,250
Ciba-Geigy Corp	$1,150	PAC/Ind

Lawyers & Lobbyists — $2,200

Lawyers & Lobbyists $2,200
Gross & Welch	$1,200	Indiv

Spending in Last 2 Elections

	1990	1992
Barrett	$624,575	$412,993
Opponent	$457,655	$90,570
Vote Pct	51%	72%

Misc Business — $29,851

Food & Beverage $4,750
National Restaurant Assn	$3,350	PAC

Beer, Wine & Liquor $3,201
National Beer Wholesalers Assn	$2,000	PAC

Retail Sales $5,300
Cabela's Inc	$2,500	Indiv

Misc Services $2,200
Ideal Cleaners	$1,000	Indiv
National Pest Control Assn	$1,000	PAC

Business Services $2,200
None over $1,000

Chemical & Related Manufacturing $2,150
Dow Chemical	$1,000	PAC

Misc Manufacturing & Distributing $7,900
Valmont Industries	$6,000	PAC/Ind
Stone Container Corp	$1,400	PAC

Transportation — $20,008

Air Transport $5,500
United Parcel Service	$2,500	PAC
Aircraft Owners & Pilots Assn	$1,500	PAC
Federal Express Corp	$1,000	PAC

Automotive $9,108
National Auto Dealers Assn	$4,800	PAC
Americans for Free International Trade	$1,000	PAC
Auto Dealers & Drivers for Free Trade	$1,000	PAC
HP Smith Motors	$1,000	Indiv

Trucking $1,700
None over $1,000

Railroads $3,700
Union Pacific Corp	$2,500	PAC

Labor

Labor — $1,000

Public Sector Unions $1,000
National Assn Retired Federal Employees	$1,000	PAC

Ideological/Single-Issue

Ideological/Single-Issue — $7,250

Gun Rights/Gun Control $6,850
National Rifle Assn	$6,850	PAC

Other & Unknown

Other — $18,800

Education $1,000
Educational Management	$1,000	Indiv

Retired $17,800
None over $1,000

Unknown — $22,099
Homemakers/Non-income earners	$4,600	
Employer Listed/Category Unknown	$17,058	
Nedelco	$1,500	Indiv
H&H Distributing	$1,000	Indiv
PMS Feed Supply	$1,000	Indiv

---

* Contributions came from more than one affiliate or subsidiary.

Thomas Barrett, D-Wis (5)

First elected: 1992

1991-92 Total Receipts: $358,639
1992 Year-end Cash: $39,162

1993-94 Committees & Subcommittees

Banking, Finance and Urban Affairs
Consumer Credit and Insurance; Financial Institutions Supervision, Regulation and Deposit Insurance; Housing and Community Development

Government Operations
Human Resources and Intergovernmental Relations

Natural Resources
Oversight and Investigations

Leading Contributors

Business

Agriculture		$6,250

Tobacco	...$2,000	
Philip Morris	$2,000	PAC/Ind
Dairy	**...$3,000**	
Associated Milk Producers	$2,000	PAC
Mid-America Dairymen	$1,000	PAC

Communications/Electronics		$8,000

Telephone Utilities	...$6,750	
Wisconsin Bell Telephone	$2,300	PAC/Ind
AT&T	$2,200	PAC
GTE Corp	$1,000	PAC
United Telecommunications	$1,000	PAC

Construction		$4,300

Home Builders	...$1,300	
National Assn of Home Builders	$1,000	PAC
Construction Services	**...$1,250**	
Howard, Needles et al	$1,000	Indiv
Building Materials & Equipment	**...$1,200**	
Fleck Controls Inc	$1,000	Indiv

Energy & Natural Resources		$2,550

Electric Utilities	...$1,550	
None over $1,000		

Contribution Totals by Sector

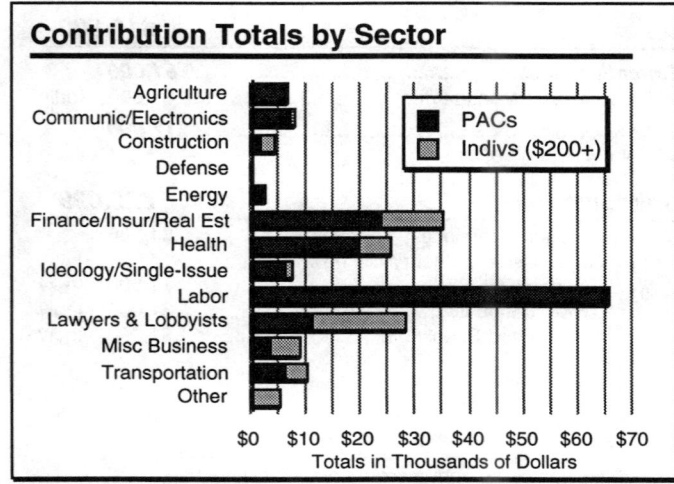

Totals in Thousands of Dollars

Source of Funds in 1992 Election

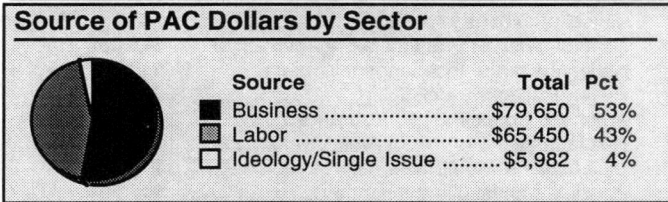

Source	Total	Pct
PACs	$154,526	42%
Indivs $200+	$65,926	18%
Indivs under $200	$123,753	34%
Other	$23,897	6%
Candidate	$2,166	1%
Party	$9,463	3%

Source of PAC Dollars by Sector

Source	Total	Pct
Business	$79,650	53%
Labor	$65,450	43%
Ideology/Single Issue	$5,982	4%

In-State vs. Out-of-State Contributions*

Source	Total	Pct
In-State	$59,208	91%
Out-of-state	$5,920	9%
No state listed	$0	

* by large individual contributors ($200 & above)

Finance, Insurance & Real Estate		$34,900

Commercial Banks	...$7,250	
Norwest Corp	$1,500	PAC
First Wisconsin Corp	$1,350	PAC
American Bankers Assn	$1,000	PAC
Credit Unions	**...$1,000**	
Credit Union National Assn	$1,000	PAC
Securities & Investment	**...$4,950**	
Dain Bosworth Inc	$1,000	Indiv
Lubar & Co	$1,000	Indiv
Smith Barney	$1,000	Indiv
Insurance	**...$11,100**	
Northwestern Mutual Life	$5,950	PAC/Ind
National Assn of Life Underwriters	$1,500	PAC
Blue Cross/Blue Shield of Wisconsin	$1,150	PAC
Real Estate	**...$8,100**	
National Assn of Realtors	$5,000	PAC
Dhaliwal Enterprises Inc	$1,000	Indiv
Accountants	**...$1,500**	
American Institute of CPA's	$1,500	PAC

Health		$25,144

Health Professionals	...$22,344	
American Medical Assn	$9,700	PAC
American Dental Assn	$3,000	PAC
American Academy of Ophthalmology	$2,000	PAC
American College of Emergency Physicians	$2,000	PAC
Hospitals/Nursing Homes	**...$2,000**	
None over $1,000		

Misc Business $8,599

Food & Beverage **$1,750**
Pepsi-Cola General Bottlers .... $1,000   PAC

Misc Services **$2,000**
American Assn of Equipment Lessors .... $2,000   PAC

Business Services **$1,760**
None over $1,000

Misc Manufacturing & Distributing **$2,550**
Fall River Group .... $2,000   Indiv

Lawyers & Lobbyists $27,972

Lawyers & Lobbyists **$27,972**
Assn of Trial Lawyers of America .... $10,000   PAC
Friebert, Finerty & St John .... $2,050   Indiv
Broydrick & Associates .... $2,002   Indiv
Quarles & Brady .... $1,450   Indiv
Schoendorf, Sorgi & Carlson .... $1,400   Indiv
Godfrey & Kahn .... $1,350   Indiv
Canellos & Storm .... $1,100   Indiv
CR Associates .... $1,020   Indiv
Habush, Habush & Davis .... $1,000   Indiv

Transportation $9,600

Air Transport **$5,400**
United Parcel Service .... $5,100   PAC/Ind

Automotive **$2,200**
National Auto Dealers Assn .... $2,000   PAC

Trucking **$1,100**
None over $1,000

Labor

Labor $65,450

Building Trade Unions **$10,500**
Laborers Union local #113 .... $3,500   PAC
Carpenters & Joiners Union .... $2,500   PAC
Sheet Metal Workers Union .... $2,500   PAC
Plumbers/Pipefitters Union .... $2,000   PAC

Industrial Unions **$14,350**
United Auto Workers .... $5,000   PAC
Communications Workers of America .... $3,000   PAC
Intl Brotherhood of Electrical Workers .... $2,000   PAC
Machinists/Aerospace Workers Union .... $2,000   PAC
United Steelworkers .... $2,000   PAC

Transportation Unions **$10,500**
Teamsters Union .... $5,000   PAC
Amalgamated Transit Union .... $1,500   PAC
Air Line Pilots Assn .... $1,000   PAC
Marine Engineers Union.................................. $1,000   PAC
United Transportation Union .... $1,000   PAC

Public Sector Unions **$25,250**
American Fedn of St/Cnty/Munic Employees .... $10,000   PAC
National Education Assn .... $10,000   PAC
National Assn of Letter Carriers .... $2,000   PAC
American Federation of Teachers...................... $1,500   PAC
National Assn Retired Federal Employees .... $1,000   PAC

Misc Unions **$4,850**
Food & Commercial Workers Union .... $2,500   PAC
Service Employees International Union .... $2,000   PAC

Ideological/Single-Issue

Ideological/Single-Issue $7,232

Democratic/Liberal **$1,682**
None over $1,000

Leadership PACs **$1,500**
Effective Government Cmte (Dick Gephardt) ...... $1,000   PAC

Pro-Choice **$1,000**
National Abortion Rights Action League .... $1,000   PAC

Misc Issues **$2,200**
Sierra Club .... $1,000   PAC

Other & Unknown

Other $5,087

Civil Servants/Public Officials **$2,287**
State of Wisconsin .... $1,637   Indiv

Retired **$1,900**
None over $1,000

Unknown $11,426

Homemakers/Non-income earners $3,500
Employer Listed/Category Unknown $7,676
None over $1,000

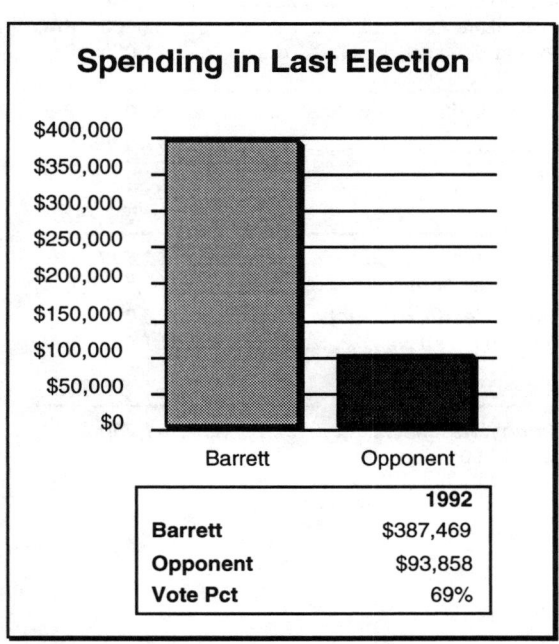

Spending in Last Election

	1992
Barrett	$387,469
Opponent	$93,858
Vote Pct	69%

Roscoe G. Bartlett, R-Md (6)

First elected: 1992

1991-92 Total Receipts: $271,371
1992 Year-end Cash: $3,933

1993-94 Committees & Subcommittees

Armed Services
Military Forces and Personnel; Research and Technology

Science, Space and Technology
Energy; Technology, Environment and Aviation

Leading Contributors

Business

Agriculture — $8,124

Crop Production & Basic Processing	**$1,300**	
Eaton Farms Inc	$1,000	Indiv
Food Processing & Sales	**$3,324**	
Flowers Industries	$2,000	PAC
Forestry & Forest Products	**$2,000**	
Westvaco Corp	$2,000	PAC

Communications/Electronics — $5,340

Printing & Publishing	**$1,000**	
Crown Enterprises	$1,000	Indiv
Telephone Utilities	**$2,300**	
Chesapeake & Potomac Telephone	$1,000	PAC
Electronics Mfg & Services	**$1,000**	
Harris Corp	$1,000	PAC

Construction — $13,200

General Contractors	**$5,100**	
Associated General Contractors	$1,500	PAC
Associated Builders & Contractors	$1,000	PAC
National Utility Contractors Assn	$1,000	PAC
Home Builders	**$2,900**	
National Assn of Home Builders	$2,000	PAC
Special Trade Contractors	**$3,200**	
Bouma Corp	$1,000	Indiv
Merillat Industries	$1,000	Indiv
Building Materials & Equipment	**$2,000**	
Independent Cement Corp	$1,000	Indiv
Lehigh Portland Cement Co	$1,000	PAC

Source of Funds in 1992 Election

Source	Total	Pct
■ PACs	$90,500	28%
▨ Indivs $200+	$47,089	15%
□ Indivs under $200	$53,652	17%
▧ Other	$126,790	40%
Candidate	$71,538	22%
Party	$51,573	16%

Source of PAC Dollars by Sector

Source	Total	Pct
■ Business	$71,654	86%
▨ Labor	$0	0%
□ Ideology/Single Issue	$11,724	14%

In-State vs. Out-of-State Contributions*

Source	Total	Pct
□ In-State	$24,889	54%
■ Out-of-state	$21,450	46%
No state listed	$750	

* by large individual contributors ($200 & above)

Energy & Natural Resources — $23,210

Oil & Gas	**$6,760**	
Columbia Gas System*	$2,310	PAC
Amoco Corp	$1,000	PAC
Phillips Petroleum	$1,000	PAC
Misc Energy	**$6,000**	
Cooper Industries	$6,000	PAC
Electric Utilities	**$10,450**	
Baltimore Gas & Electric	$5,500	PAC

Finance, Insurance & Real Estate — $9,805

Commercial Banks	**$3,050**	
American Bankers Assn	$2,000	PAC
First Maryland Bancorp	$1,050	PAC
Insurance	**$5,250**	
National Assn of Life Underwriters	$2,000	PAC
Real Estate	**$1,005**	
None over $1,000		

Health — $7,000

Health Professionals	**$4,500**	
Maryland Medical Assn	$2,500	PAC
Pharmaceuticals/Health Products	**$2,000**	
Schering-Plough Corp	$1,000	PAC

Lawyers & Lobbyists — $1,250

Lawyers & Lobbyists	**$1,250**	
None over $1,000		

Contribution Totals by Sector

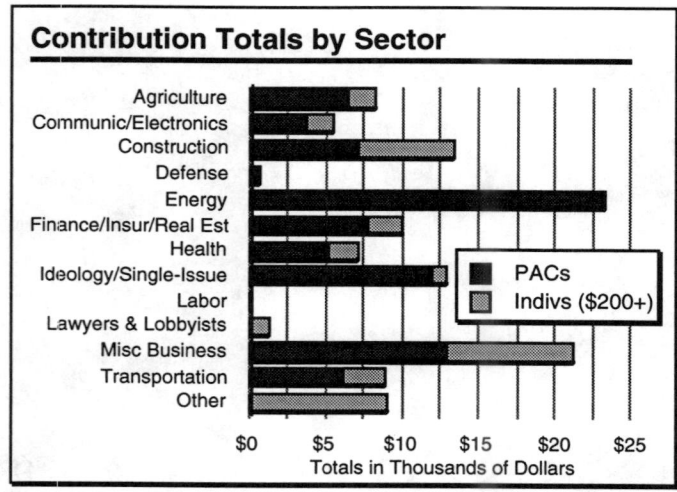

Totals in Thousands of Dollars

Legend: PACs, Indivs ($200+)

Sectors: Agriculture, Communic/Electronics, Construction, Defense, Energy, Finance/Insur/Real Est, Health, Ideology/Single-Issue, Labor, Lawyers & Lobbyists, Misc Business, Transportation, Other

Misc Business $21,034

Business Associations **$1,044**
   Business Industry PAC ....$1,044   PAC

Food & Beverage **$4,700**
   National Restaurant Assn ....$2,000   PAC
   Shamrock Restaurant ....$1,200   Indiv
   Hardee's Food Systems ....$1,000   PAC

Beer, Wine & Liquor **$1,000**
   Brown-Forman Distillers ....$1,000   PAC

Retail Sales **$7,690**
   Amway Corp ....$5,000   Indiv

Lodging/Tourism **$1,000**
   None over $1,000

Chemical & Related Manufacturing **$2,850**
   Dow Chemical ....$2,000   PAC

Misc Manufacturing & Distributing **$2,500**
   Stone Container Corp ....$1,500   PAC
   Smith & Butterfield Co ....$1,000   Indiv

Transportation $8,800

Automotive **$8,300**
   Americans for Free International Trade ....$2,000   PAC
   National Auto Dealers Assn ....$2,000   PAC
   Eaton Corp ....$1,500   PAC
   Great Lakes Mazda Distributors ....$1,000   Indiv
   Prince Corp ....$1,000   Indiv

Ideological/Single-Issue

Ideological/Single-Issue $12,724

Republican/Conservative **$4,774**
   Conservative Victory Committee ....$1,000   PAC
   Eagle Forum ....$1,000   PAC
   V-PAC ....$1,000   PAC

Leadership PACs **$3,000**
   Republican Leader's Fund (Bob Michel) ....$2,000   PAC

Pro-Life **$3,350**
   National Right to Life PAC ....$3,000   PAC

Misc Issues **$1,600**
   English First ....$1,000   PAC

Other & Unknown

Other $8,950

Civil Servants/Public Officials **$2,500**
   US Government ....$2,250   Indiv

Education **$1,000**
   National Business Institute ....$1,000   Indiv

Retired **$2,850**
   None over $1,000

Other **$2,600**
   US Navy ....$2,600   Indiv

Unknown $10,530

   No Employer Listed or Found $3,700
   Employer Listed/Category Unknown $6,080
      Dynamark Security ....$1,000   Indiv
      Hold Enterprises ....$1,000   Indiv

Independent expenditures supporting Bartlett
   National Right to Life PAC $6,931

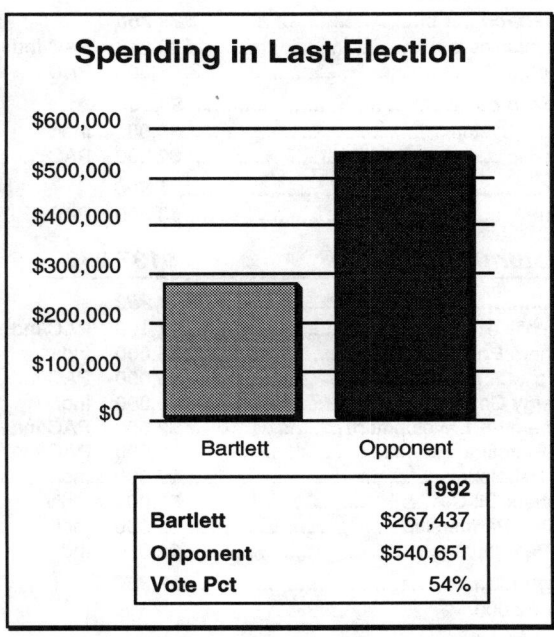

Spending in Last Election

	1992
Bartlett	$267,437
Opponent	$540,651
Vote Pct	54%

* Contributions came from more than one affiliate or subsidiary.

Joe L. Barton, R-Texas (6)

First elected: 1984
1991-92 Total Receipts: $1,018,595
1992 Year-end Cash: $7,022

1991-92 Committees & Subcommittees

Energy and Commerce
Commerce, Consumer Protection and Competitiveness; Energy and Power; Telecommunications and Finance

Science, Space and Technology
Energy

Leading Contributors

Business

Agriculture	$39,725

Crop Production & Basic Processing **$6,625**
  None over $2,000

Tobacco **$4,000**
  Philip Morris .... $2,000   PAC

Livestock **$6,050**
  National Cattlemen's Assn* .... $2,150   PAC

Agricultural Services/Products **$10,200**
  Texas Farm Bureau .... $2,500   PAC
  Gordon Boswell Flowers .... $2,250   Indiv
  Garvey Enterprises Inc .... $2,000   Indiv

Food Processing & Sales **$9,800**
  Standard Meat Co .... $2,000   Indiv

Communications/Electronics	$69,095

Media/Entertainment **$24,050**
  National Cable Television Assn .... $10,000   PAC
  Tele-Communications Inc .... $5,000   PAC

Telephone Utilities **$29,550**
  BellSouth Corp* .... $3,500   PAC
  GTE Corp .... $3,500   PAC
  United Telecommunications .... $3,500   PAC
  Ameritech Corp .... $3,250   PAC
  Southwestern Bell .... $2,750   PAC

Telecom Services & Equipment **$3,000**
  None over $2,000

Electronics Mfg & Services **$4,000**
  None over $2,000

Computer Equipment & Services **$5,745**
  None over $2,000

Contribution Totals by Sector

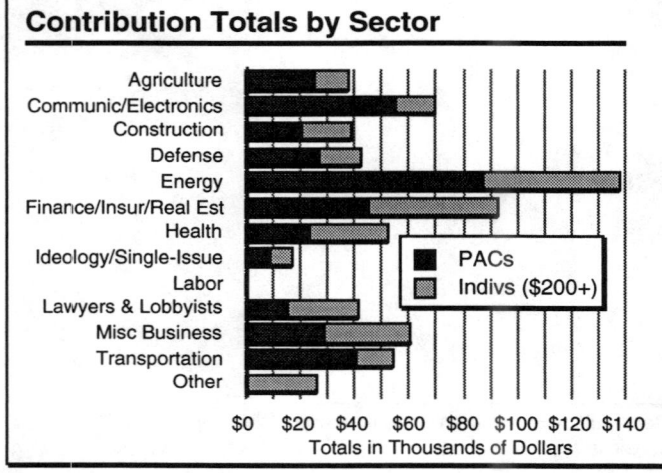

Totals in Thousands of Dollars

Source of Funds in 1992 Election

Source	Total	Pct
■ PACs	$374,046	37%
▨ Indivs $200+	$354,817	35%
☐ Indivs under $200	$160,273	16%
▧ Other	$129,459	13%
Candidate	$0	0%
Party	$-200	0%

Source of PAC Dollars by Sector

Source	Total	Pct
■ Business	$362,332	98%
▨ Labor	$500	0%
☐ Ideology/Single Issue	$8,141	2%

In-State vs. Out-of-State Contributions*

Source	Total	Pct
☐ In-State	$346,217	93%
■ Out-of-state	$28,050	7%
No state listed	$0	

* by large individual contributors ($200 & above)

Construction	$38,388

General Contractors **$10,950**
  Fluor Corp .... $3,000   PAC
  Associated General Contractors .... $2,650   PAC/Ind

Home Builders **$3,000**
  Perry-Houston Insterests .... $3,500   Indiv

Construction Services **$11,900**
  National Society of Professional Engineers .... $3,500   PAC

Building Materials & Equipment **$12,288**
  Southdown Corp .... $3,000   Indiv

Defense	$41,750

Defense Aerospace **$28,750**
  General Dynamics .... $19,250   PAC/Ind
  Textron Inc .... $6,000   PAC

Defense Electronics **$8,500**
  Electrospace Systems .... $6,000   Indiv
  E-Systems Inc .... $2,500   PAC

Misc Defense **$4,500**
  Insilco Corp .... $3,500   PAC

Energy & Natural Resources	$137,282

Oil & Gas **$90,282**
  Atlantic Richfield .... $7,100   PAC/Ind
  Bass Brothers Enterprises .... $5,000   Indiv
  Enron Corp .... $5,000   PAC/Ind
  Taylor Energy Co .... $2,800   Indiv
  Mitchell Energy & Development .... $2,500   PAC/Ind
  American Petrofina .... $2,000   PAC
  Anadarko Petroleum .... $2,000   Indiv
  Cross Timbers Oil Co .... $2,000   Indiv
  Mesa Limited Partnership .... $2,000   Indiv
  Quintana Petroleum .... $2,000   Indiv

Nuclear Energy **$2,350**
  None over $2,000

Misc Energy	$4,000	
Cooper Industries	$2,000	PAC
Electric Utilities	**$37,400**	
Texas Utilities Co	$6,750	PAC/Ind
Houston Industries	$4,000	PAC
Southern Co*	$2,200	PAC

Finance, Insurance & Real Estate $92,750

Commercial Banks	**$21,950**	
American Bankers Assn	$5,000	PAC
Independent Bankers Assn	$2,000	PAC
NCNB Texas	$2,000	PAC
Savings & Loans	**$4,500**	
Colonial Savings & Loan	$2,000	Indiv
Securities & Investment	**$12,750**	
Goldman, Sachs & Co	$4,000	PAC/Ind
Sutton Capital Associates	$2,000	Indiv
Insurance	**$16,250**	
American National Insurance Co	$3,500	PAC
Real Estate	**$17,850**	
National Assn of Realtors	$8,000	PAC
Accountants	**$10,150**	
American Institute of CPA's	$6,000	PAC
Misc Finance	**$9,300**	
None over $2,000		

Health $51,150

Health Professionals	**$37,600**	
American Medical Assn	$10,000	PAC
Medical Arts Clinic	$3,650	Indiv
American Academy of Ophthalmology	$2,500	PAC
American Dental Assn	$2,500	PAC
Hunt Consolidated Inc	$2,000	Indiv
Pharmaceuticals/Health Products	**$10,600**	
Alcon Laboratories	$3,000	Indiv
Behrens Inc	$2,000	Indiv

Lawyers & Lobbyists $41,000

Lawyers & Lobbyists	**$41,000**	
Jenkens & Gilchrist	$5,000	PAC
Winstead, Sechrest & Minick	$3,250	PAC/Ind
Lipnick & Gordon Co	$3,000	Indiv

Spending in Last 3 Elections

	1988	1990	1992
Barton	$654,260	$458,346	$1,422,644
Opponent	$17,414	$6,568	$13,751
Vote Pct	68%	67%	72%

Johnson & Gibbs	$2,750	PAC/Ind
Baker & Botts	$2,500	PAC
Hughes & Luce	$2,000	Indiv

Misc Business $59,637

Business Associations	**$4,279**	
Ennis Business Forms	$3,000	Indiv
Food & Beverage	**$5,450**	
None over $2,000		
Beer, Wine & Liquor	**$10,250**	
Brooks Distributing	$3,500	Indiv
Coors Distributing	$2,750	Indiv
Retail Sales	**$8,407**	
Tradewest Inc	$2,250	Indiv
Pier 1 Imports	$2,000	PAC
Misc Services	**$4,701**	
Club Corp International	$2,000	Indiv
Lodging/Tourism	**$2,000**	
Rosewood Hotel Group	$2,000	Indiv
Chemical & Related Manufacturing	**$9,950**	
Dow Chemical	$2,000	PAC
Misc Manufacturing & Distributing	**$12,100**	
Hoechst Celanese Corp	$3,000	PAC
Owens-Illinois	$2,000	PAC
Windway Capital Corp	$2,000	Indiv

Transportation $53,732

Air Transport	**$10,000**	
American Airlines	$4,500	PAC
United Parcel Service	$3,000	PAC
Automotive	**$19,450**	
National Auto Dealers Assn	$10,000	PAC
Martin Sprocket & Gear	$2,750	Indiv
Americans for Free International Trade	$2,000	PAC
Trucking	**$2,583**	
None over $2,000		
Railroads	**$20,699**	
Burlington Northern	$15,699	PAC/Ind
Union Pacific Corp	$2,000	PAC/Ind

Ideological/Single-Issue

Ideological/Single-Issue $16,952

Republican/Conservative	**$8,300**	
None over $2,000		
Gun Rights/Gun Control	**$5,450**	
National Rifle Assn	$5,450	PAC

Other & Unknown

Other $25,500

Retired	**$22,100**	
None over $2,000		

Unknown $79,029

Homemakers/Non-income earners	$24,132
No Employer Listed or Found	$12,600
Generic Occupation/Category Unknown	$10,950
Employer Listed/Category Unknown	$31,347
None over $2,000	

* Contributions came from more than one affiliate or subsidiary.

Herbert H. Bateman, R-Va (1)

First elected: 1982

1991-92 Total Receipts: $766,895
1992 Year-end Cash: $16,992

1991-92 Committees & Subcommittees

Armed Services
Military Personnel and Compensation (Ranking Republican);
Seapower and Strategic and Critical Materials

Merchant Marine and Fisheries
Coast Guard and Navigation; Merchant Marine; Oceanography, Great
Lakes and Outer Continental Shelf (Ranking Republican)

Leading Contributors

Business

Agriculture $34,075

Crop Production & Basic Processing	**$3,375**	
None over $2,500		
Tobacco	**$8,450**	
Philip Morris	$2,800	PAC
RJR Nabisco	$2,550	PAC
Agricultural Services/Products	**$3,300**	
None over $2,500		
Food Processing & Sales	**$5,450**	
None over $2,500		
Forestry & Forest Products	**$9,000**	
Westvaco Corp	$4,000	PAC
Chesapeake Corp of Virginia	$3,000	Indiv
Misc Agriculture	**$2,500**	
None over $2,500		

Communications/Electronics $12,350

Media/Entertainment	**$5,450**	
None over $2,500		
Telephone Utilities	**$4,100**	
None over $2,500		

Construction $33,750

General Contractors	**$18,700**	
CBC Enterprises Inc	$9,000	Indiv
Associated General Contractors	$2,500	PAC
Home Builders	**$4,000**	
National Assn of Home Builders	$4,000	PAC

Source of Funds in 1992 Election

Source	Total	Pct
PACs	$294,121	36%
Indivs $200+	$258,735	32%
Indivs under $200	$192,320	24%
Other	$66,476	8%
Candidate	$100	0%
Party	$54,757	7%

Source of PAC Dollars by Sector

Source	Total	Pct
Business	$255,571	91%
Labor	$16,350	6%
Ideology/Single Issue	$9,100	3%

In-State vs. Out-of-State Contributions*

Source	Total	Pct
In-State	$243,010	95%
Out-of-state	$13,550	5%
No state listed	$500	

* by large individual contributors ($200 & above)

Special Trade Contractors	**$3,750**	
None over $2,500		
Building Materials & Equipment	**$7,300**	
Lennox Industries	$2,500	PAC
Solite Corp	$2,500	Indiv

Defense $103,750

Defense Aerospace	**$37,500**	
McDonnell Douglas*	$4,350	PAC
Bionetics Corp	$3,500	Indiv
General Electric	$3,000	PAC
Northrop Corp	$3,000	PAC
Lockheed Corp	$2,600	PAC
Defense Electronics	**$29,900**	
Hughes Aircraft	$3,900	PAC
E-Systems Inc	$3,250	PAC
GTE Corp	$2,700	PAC
Raytheon	$2,500	PAC
Misc Defense	**$36,350**	
Newport News Shipbuilding	$15,550	Indiv
Tenneco Inc	$9,000	PAC
BDM International	$3,550	PAC/Ind

Energy & Natural Resources $42,300

Oil & Gas	**$21,150**	
Columbia Gas System*	$5,900	PAC
Cooper Industries	$3,000	PAC
Mining	**$5,750**	
Reynolds Metals	$4,000	PAC
Electric Utilities	**$7,750**	
ACRE (Action Cmte for Rural Electrification)	$3,000	PAC
Dominion Resources Inc	$2,500	PAC
Waste Management	**$2,500**	
None over $2,500		
Commercial Fishing	**$2,800**	
National Fisheries Institute	$2,800	PAC

Contribution Totals by Sector

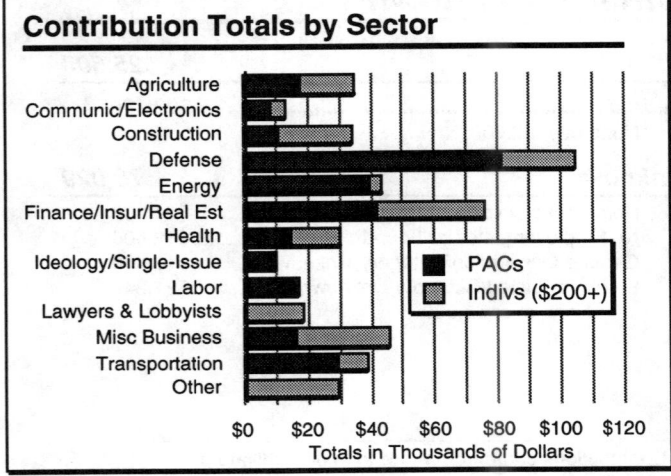

Agriculture
Communic/Electronics
Construction
Defense
Energy
Finance/Insur/Real Est
Health
Ideology/Single-Issue
Labor
Lawyers & Lobbyists
Misc Business
Transportation
Other

■ PACs
▨ Indivs ($200+)

$0 $20 $40 $60 $80 $100 $120
Totals in Thousands of Dollars

Finance, Insurance & Real Estate $75,700

Commercial Banks **$20,700**
    American Bankers Assn* ....$7,500 PAC
    Citizens & Southern National Bank ....$5,000 PAC

Securities & Investment **$6,700**
    None over $2,500

Insurance **$14,400**
    National Assn of Life Underwriters.....................$7,000 PAC

Real Estate **$27,800**
    National Assn of Realtors ....$5,300 PAC
    Kellam Energy Inc ....$3,900 Indiv
    J&R Enterprises ....$2,500 Indiv

Accountants **$3,600**
    None over $2,500

Health $29,800

Health Professionals **$25,550**
    American Dental Assn ....$6,000 PAC
    American Medical Assn..................................$4,450 PAC

Pharmaceuticals/Health Products **$4,000**
    None over $2,500

Lawyers & Lobbyists $18,250

Lawyers & Lobbyists **$18,250**
    Jones, Blechman et al ....$4,400 Indiv
    Patten, Wornom & Watkins ....$3,250 Indiv

Misc Business $44,811

Business Associations **$3,345**
    None over $2,500

Food & Beverage **$3,000**
    None over $2,500

Beer, Wine & Liquor **$6,000**
    National Beer Wholesalers Assn ....$2,500 PAC

Retail Sales **$12,000**
    Virginia Specialty Store ....$2,500 Indiv

Lodging/Tourism **$5,500**
    None over $2,500

Chemical & Related Manufacturing $4,000
    None over $2,500

Misc Manufacturing & Distributing **$7,915**
    Craft Machine Works ....$4,425 Indiv

Transportation $38,020

Air Transport **$4,500**
    None over $2,500

Automotive **$18,850**
    National Auto Dealers Assn ....$10,000 PAC

Sea Transport **$10,950**
    Norfolk Shipbuilding & Drydock Corp ....$2,750 PAC/Ind

Labor

Labor $16,350

Transportation Unions **$13,750**
    Marine Engineers Union* ....$8,250 PAC
    Seafarers International Union ....$3,500 PAC

Public Sector Unions **$2,600**
    None over $2,500

Ideological/Single-Issue

Ideological/Single-Issue $9,600

Gun Rights/Gun Control **$4,500**
    Handgun Control Inc ....$4,500 PAC

Misc Issues **$2,600**
    None over $2,500

Other & Unknown

Other $28,750

Education **$5,000**
    College of William & Mary ....$3,000 Indiv

Retired **$22,850**
    None over $2,500

Unknown $51,325

    Homemakers/Non-income earners $10,575
    Generic Occupation/Category Unknown $3,500
    Employer Listed/Category Unknown $35,850
        None over $2,500

Independent expenditures supporting Bateman
    Handgun Control Inc $18,252
    National Right to Life PAC $4,591

Independent expenditures opposing Bateman
    National Rifle Assn $6,598

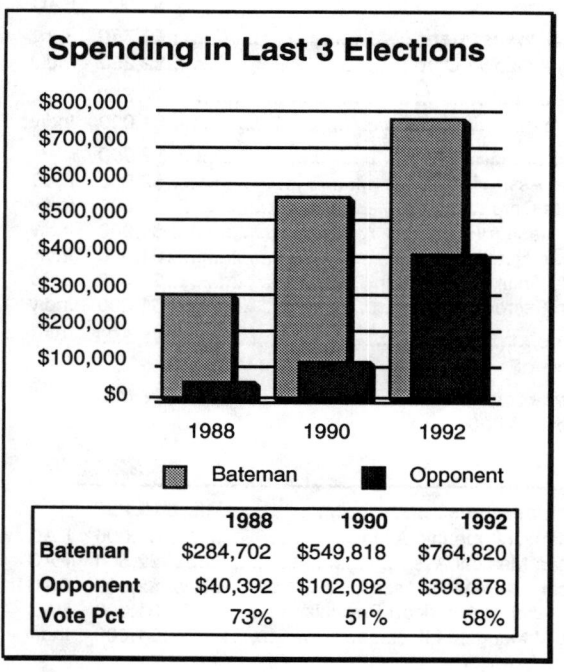

Spending in Last 3 Elections

	1988	1990	1992
Bateman	$284,702	$549,818	$764,820
Opponent	$40,392	$102,092	$393,878
Vote Pct	73%	51%	58%

Bateman   Opponent

* Contributions came from more than one affiliate or subsidiary.

Xavier Becerra, D-Calif (30)

First elected: 1992

1991-92 Total Receipts: $367,385
1992 Year-end Cash: $13,833

1993-94 Committees & Subcommittees

Education and Labor
Elementary, Secondary and Vocational Education; Labor-Management Relations; Postsecondary Education and Training

Judiciary
Intellectual Property and Judicial Administration; International Law, Immigration and Refugees

Science, Space and Technology
Technology, Environment and Aviation

Source of Funds in 1992 Election

Source	Total	Pct
■ PACs	$97,450	26%
▨ Indivs $200+	$96,900	26%
□ Indivs under $200	$91,096	24%
⊠ Other	$88,913	24%
Candidate	$59,000	16%
Party	$6,974	2%

Source of PAC Dollars by Sector

Source	Total	Pct
■ Business	$39,300	38%
▨ Labor	$53,050	51%
□ Ideology/Single Issue	$11,289	11%

In-State vs. Out-of-State Contributions*

Source	Total	Pct
□ In-State	$91,800	95%
■ Out-of-state	$4,850	5%
No state listed	$250	

*** by large individual contributors ($200 & above)**

Leading Contributors

Business

Agriculture $5,250

Crop Production & Basic Processing	**$2,000**	
None over $1,000		
Dairy	**$1,000**	
Associated Milk Producers	$1,000	PAC
Food Processing & Sales	**$1,250**	
Pepsico Inc	$1,000	PAC

Communications/Electronics $6,750

Printing & Publishing	**$1,000**	
Korea Times	$1,000	Indiv
Media/Entertainment	**$1,750**	
Warner Brothers	$1,000	Indiv
Telephone Utilities	**$2,500**	
AT&T	$1,000	PAC
Pacific Telesis Group	$1,000	PAC
Telecom Services & Equipment	**$1,000**	
New Bedford Panoramex Corp	$1,000	PAC

Construction $5,200

Home Builders	**$1,000**	
Neil Construction	$1,000	Indiv
Special Trade Contractors	**$2,000**	
All State Air Conditioning	$1,000	Indiv
Intercom Systems	$1,000	Indiv
Construction Services	**$1,200**	
None over $1,000		

Defense $1,750

Defense Aerospace	**$1,500**	
Northrop Corp	$1,000	PAC

Energy & Natural Resources $1,250

None over $1,000

Finance, Insurance & Real Estate $20,450

Commercial Banks	**$3,500**	
American Bankers Assn	$1,000	PAC
BankAmerica Corp	$1,000	PAC
Wells Fargo	$1,000	PAC
Securities & Investment	**$2,750**	
Saybrook Capital Corp	$2,250	Indiv
Insurance	**$1,750**	
ITT Corp	$1,000	Indiv
Real Estate	**$9,950**	
National Assn of Realtors	$2,500	PAC
Via Vista Corp	$2,000	Indiv
Steven Kasten Properties	$1,200	Indiv
American Housing Corp	$1,000	Indiv
Maguire Thomas Partners	$1,000	Indiv
Modern Escrow Co	$1,000	Indiv
Accountants	**$1,300**	
None over $1,000		
Misc Finance	**$1,000**	
None over $1,000		

Health $20,200

Health Professionals	**$15,250**	
American Chiropractic Assn	$5,000	PAC
American Medical Assn	$2,500	PAC
American Optometric Assn	$2,000	PAC
Cooperative of American Physicians	$1,000	PAC
Renato V Mungcal MD	$1,000	Indiv

Contribution Totals by Sector

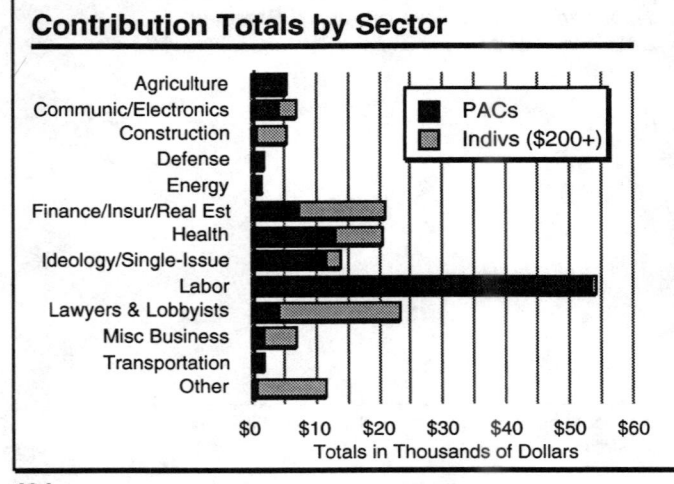

Legend: ■ PACs, ▨ Indivs ($200+)

Sectors (top to bottom): Agriculture, Communic/Electronics, Construction, Defense, Energy, Finance/Insur/Real Est, Health, Ideology/Single-Issue, Labor, Lawyers & Lobbyists, Misc Business, Transportation, Other

Axis: $0 $10 $20 $30 $40 $50 $60
Totals in Thousands of Dollars

Hospitals/Nursing Homes $1,000
    None over $1,000

Misc Health $2,750
    Community Health Foundation ....$1,250   Indiv

Lawyers & Lobbyists $22,800

Lawyers & Lobbyists $22,800
    Assn of Trial Lawyers of America ....$2,500   PAC
    Taylor, Roth et al ....$2,000   Indiv
    MARC Associates ....$1,750   Indiv
    Law Offices of Nicholas F Reyes ....$1,500   Indiv
    Ochoa & Sillas ....$1,150   Indiv
    Kampe & Hendrickson ....$1,000   Indiv
    Margolis, Hertzberg et al ....$1,000   Indiv
    O'Melveny & Myers ....$1,000   PAC
    Riordan & McKinzie ....$1,000   PAC/Ind
    Rosato & Samuels ....$1,000   Indiv
    Ross & Scott ....$1,000   Indiv

Misc Business $6,800

Food & Beverage $3,300
    Sanchez Family Corp ....$1,500   Indiv
    Pepsi-Cola Bottlers Assn ....$1,000   PAC

Business Services $2,500
    James Alan Co ....$1,000   Indiv
    People Works ....$1,000   Indiv

Transportation $1,850

Air Transport $1,200
    United Parcel Service ....$1,200   PAC

Labor

Labor $53,550

Building Trade Unions $5,500
    Laborers' Political League ....$3,000   PAC
    Painters & Allied Trades Union/Calif ....$2,500   PAC

Industrial Unions $15,500
    United Auto Workers ....$10,000   PAC
    Intl Brotherhood of Electrical Workers ....$2,500   PAC
    Machinists/Aerospace Workers Union ....$2,500   PAC

Transportation Unions $8,350
    Teamsters Union ....$5,000   PAC
    Air Line Pilots Assn ....$1,000   PAC
    Trans Comm International Union ....$1,000   PAC

Public Sector Unions $14,700
    National Education Assn ....$7,500   PAC
    American Fedn of St/Cnty/Munic Employees ......$4,500   PAC
    National Assn Retired Federal Employees ....$1,000   PAC

Misc Unions $9,500
    Service Employees International Union ....$5,000   PAC
    AFL-CIO ....$2,000   PAC
    Food & Commercial Workers Union ....$2,000   PAC

Ideological/Single-Issue

Ideological/Single-Issue $13,539

Leadership PACs $5,500
    America's Leaders' Fund (Dan Rostenkowski) ....$1,000   PAC
    Effective Government Cmte (Dick Gephardt) ......$1,000   PAC
    House Leadership Fund (Tom Foley) ....$1,000   PAC
    Johan Klehs Federal Cmte ....$1,000   PAC
    Victory USA (Vic Fazio) ....$1,000   PAC

Human Rights $4,750
    Hispanic PAC USA ....$2,000   PAC
    National Council of La Raza ....$1,000   Indiv

Misc Issues $1,564
    League of Conservation Voters ....$1,000   PAC

Other & Unknown

Other $11,200

Education $4,400
    University of Southern California ....$2,150   Indiv
    California State University ....$1,250   Indiv

Retired $5,550
    None over $1,000

Unknown $29,950

    No Employer Listed or Found $9,500
    Employer Listed/Category Unknown $19,950
        Abel & Associates ....$1,000   Indiv
        Borbon Inc ....$1,000   Indiv
        Classic-Couriers Inc ....$1,000   Indiv
        Perez & Associates ....$1,000   Indiv
        RS Plaza ....$1,000   Indiv

Spending in Last Election

	1992
Becerra	$353,551
Opponent	$57,063
Vote Pct	58%

Anthony C. Beilenson, D-Calif (24)

First elected: 1976

1991-92 Total Receipts: $739,415
1992 Year-end Cash: $12,478

1991-92 Committees & Subcommittees

Budget
Budget Process, Reconciliation and Enforcement (Chairman);
Defense, Foreign Policy and Space

Rules
Rules of the House (Chairman)

Leading Contributors

Business

Communications/Electronics	$57,050	
Printing & Publishing	**$5,500**	
None over $1,500		
Media/Entertainment	**$50,150**	
Warner Brothers	$3,750	Indiv
Walt Disney Co	$3,500	Indiv
Arthur Hiller Enterprises	$2,000	Indiv
Petunia Productions	$2,000	Indiv
Landsburg Co	$1,500	Indiv
Lorimar Production	$1,500	Indiv

Construction	$7,150	
General Contractors	**$3,950**	
Silverton Construction	$2,000	Indiv
Home Builders	**$1,500**	
None over $1,500		

Energy & Natural Resources	$1,750
None over $1,500	

Source of Funds in 1992 Election

Source	Total	Pct
■ PACs	$0	0%
▨ Indivs $200+	$496,859	63%
☐ Indivs under $200	$186,532	24%
▧ Other	$108,456	14%
Candidate	$50,000	6%
Party	$52,432	7%

Source of PAC Dollars by Sector

No PAC contributions reported

Source	Total	Pct
■ Business	$0	0%
▨ Labor	$0	0%
☐ Ideology/Single Issue	$0	0%

In-State vs. Out-of-State Contributions*

Source	Total	Pct
☐ In-State	$474,259	96%
■ Out-of-state	$20,250	4%
No state listed	$2,350	

* by large individual contributors ($200 & above)

Finance, Insurance & Real Estate	$81,300	
Savings & Loans	**$2,000**	
Royal Thrift & Loan Co	$2,000	Indiv
Finance/Credit Companies	**$2,000**	
Budget Finance Co	$2,000	Indiv
Insurance	**$15,800**	
Loews Corp	$4,000	Indiv
Price, Raffel & Associates	$4,000	Indiv
Greenspan Co	$3,000	Indiv
Real Estate	**$27,950**	
Kay Properties	$3,000	Indiv
Hapsmith Co	$1,500	Indiv
Paris Industrial Parks	$1,500	Indiv
RK Squire Co	$1,500	Indiv
Weiss Engineering & Development	$1,500	Indiv
Accountants	**$5,100**	
None over $1,500		
Misc Finance	**$26,700**	
Home Budget Loans	$10,250	Indiv
Timcor Financial Corp	$3,500	Indiv

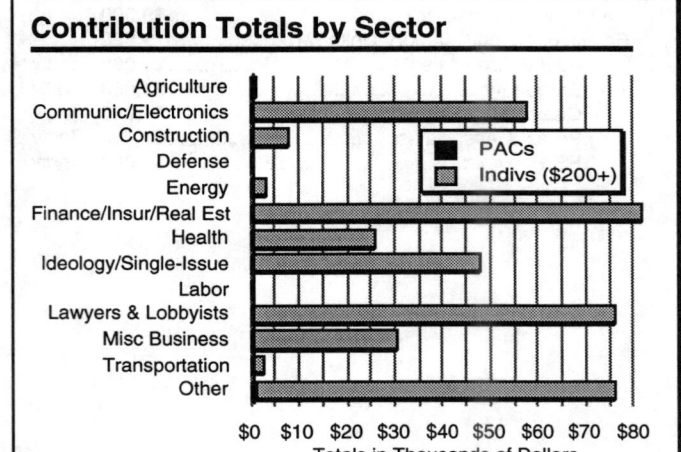

Contribution Totals by Sector

Legend: ■ PACs, ▨ Indivs ($200+)

Sectors: Agriculture, Communic/Electronics, Construction, Defense, Energy, Finance/Insur/Real Est, Health, Ideology/Single-Issue, Labor, Lawyers & Lobbyists, Misc Business, Transportation, Other

Totals in Thousands of Dollars ($0 $10 $20 $30 $40 $50 $60 $70 $80)

Health $25,250

Health Professionals $19,050
  None over $1,500
Hospitals/Nursing Homes $1,500
  None over $1,500
Pharmaceuticals/Health Products $3,000
  Diagnostic Products Corp ....$3,000   Indiv
Misc Health $1,500
  None over $1,500

Lawyers & Lobbyists $76,650

Lawyers & Lobbyists $76,650
  Rosenfeld, Meyer & Susman ....$3,750   Indiv
  Gibson, Dunn & Crutcher ....$2,750   Indiv
  Mitchell, Silverberg et al ....$2,400   Indiv
  Stutman, Treister & Glatt ....$2,200   Indiv
  Gang, Tyre et al ....$2,000   Indiv
  Irell & Manella ....$2,000   Indiv
  Freeman & Golden ....$1,800   Indiv
  Greenberg, Glusker et al ....$1,750   Indiv
  Latham & Watkins ....$1,750   Indiv

Misc Business $29,746

Retail Sales $4,000
  Chevaliar's Books ....$1,500   Indiv
Misc Services $2,000
  Ren-Mar Studios ....$2,000   Indiv
Business Services $8,000
  None over $1,500
Lodging/Tourism $3,750
  Ledler Corp ....$3,000   Indiv
Misc Business $4,996
  Bargain Wholesale ....$3,996   Indiv
Misc Manufacturing & Distributing $3,500
  Great River ....$1,500   Indiv
Textiles $1,500
  Bentley Mills ....$1,500   Indiv

Transportation $2,150

Automotive $2,150
  Executive Car Leasing ....$2,150   Indiv

Ideological/Single-Issue

Ideological/Single-Issue $47,550

Democratic/Liberal $7,200
  None over $1,500
Pro-Israel $20,650
  None over $1,500
Womens Issues $8,200
  None over $1,500
Human Rights $3,750
  None over $1,500
Misc Issues $7,750
  Santa Monica Mountains Conservancy ....$2,250   Indiv

Other & Unknown

Other $75,617

Civil Servants/Public Officials $8,200
  City of Los Angeles ....$3,250   Indiv
Education $6,250
  University of California System* ....$4,250   Indiv
Retired $59,167
  None over $1,500
Other $2,000
  None over $1,500

Unknown $91,896

  Homemakers/Non-income earners $21,800
  No Employer Listed or Found $26,394
  Generic Occupation/Category Unknown $5,350
  Employer Listed/Category Unknown $38,352
    Cain ....$2,000   Indiv
    Davis & Davis.....................................$2,000   Indiv
    Gendea, Raskoff et al ....$2,000   Indiv
    Institute for Fiduciary Education ....$2,000   Indiv
    Joshua Tree Manufacturing Co ....$2,000   Indiv
    Lainer Development Inc ....$2,000   Indiv
    Chi Gale Hayman Inc ....$1,500   Indiv

Independent expenditures supporting Beilenson
  United Teachers-Los Angeles $6,154
Independent expenditures opposing Beilenson
  Californians Against Corruption $3,658

Spending in Last 3 Elections

	1988	1990	1992
Beilenson	$140,486	$201,404	$772,463
Opponent	$100,956	$361,461	$469,714
Vote Pct	64%	62%	56%

Helen Delich Bentley, R-Md (2)

First elected: 1984

1991-92 Total Receipts: $959,100
1992 Year-end Cash: $130,463

1991-92 Committees & Subcommittees

Budget
Community Development and Natural Resources (Ranking Republican); Defense, Foreign Policy and Space; Human Resources

Merchant Marine and Fisheries

Public Works and Transportation
Economic Development (Ranking Republican); Public Buildings and Grounds; Water Resources

Select Committee on Aging

Leading Contributors

Business

Agriculture		$26,680
Crop Production & Basic Processing	$3,000	
None over $2,500		
Dairy	$4,500	
Associated Milk Producers	$3,000	PAC
Food Processing & Sales	$7,750	
None over $2,500		
Forestry & Forest Products	$5,500	
Westvaco Corp	$5,500	PAC

Communications/Electronics		$17,300
Printing & Publishing	$3,000	
None over $2,500		
Media/Entertainment	$4,000	
Mangione Family Enterprises	$3,000	Indiv
Telephone Utilities	$3,450	
None over $2,500		
Computer Equipment & Services	$5,250	
None over $2,500		

Construction		$36,990
General Contractors	$13,920	
National Utility Contractors Assn	$4,000	PAC
Associated General Contractors	$2,500	PAC
Home Builders	$3,900	
None over $2,500		

Source of Funds in 1992 Election

Source	Total	Pct
PACs	$240,620	25%
Indivs $200+	$425,896	44%
Indivs under $200	$275,391	29%
Other	$17,193	2%
Candidate	$0	0%
Party	$2,233	0%

Source of PAC Dollars by Sector

Source	Total	Pct
Business	$179,030	77%
Labor	$49,730	21%
Ideology/Single Issue	$3,250	1%

In-State vs. Out-of-State Contributions*

Source	Total	Pct
In-State	$299,056	70%
Out-of-state	$126,340	30%
No state listed	$0	

* by large individual contributors ($200 & above)

Special Trade Contractors	$9,350	
National Electrical Contractors Assn	$3,000	PAC
Construction Services	$4,850	
None over $2,500		
Building Materials & Equipment	$4,970	
None over $2,500		

Defense		$17,450
Defense Aerospace	$7,050	
None over $2,500		
Misc Defense	$9,400	
AAI Corp	$7,750	PAC/Ind

Energy & Natural Resources		$41,016
Oil & Gas	$22,166	
Occidental Petroleum	$5,000	PAC
Crown Central Petroleum	$4,840	PAC
Vane Brothers Co	$4,476	Indiv
Electric Utilities	$15,350	
Baltimore Gas & Electric	$10,000	PAC

Finance, Insurance & Real Estate		$75,855
Commercial Banks	$13,950	
MNC Financial Inc	$5,050	PAC
Savings & Loans	$4,170	
None over $2,500		
Securities & Investment	$8,170	
None over $2,500		
Insurance	$12,095	
Maggio-Onorato & Assoc	$3,895	Indiv
Real Estate	$24,570	
National Assn of Realtors	$6,500	PAC
Questar Properties Inc	$3,300	Indiv
AE Dott & Associates	$3,200	Indiv

Contribution Totals by Sector

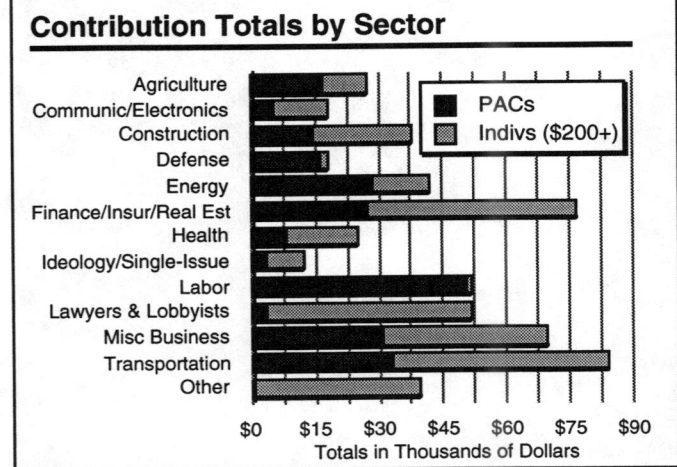

- PACs
- Indivs ($200+)

Agriculture
Communic/Electronics
Construction
Defense
Energy
Finance/Insur/Real Est
Health
Ideology/Single-Issue
Labor
Lawyers & Lobbyists
Misc Business
Transportation
Other

$0 $15 $30 $45 $60 $75 $90
Totals in Thousands of Dollars

Accountants $4,700
   None over $2,500

Misc Finance $8,200
   None over $2,500

Health $24,455

Health Professionals $18,605
   American Medical Assn .... $4,350   PAC

Pharmaceuticals/Health Products $3,000
   None over $2,500

Lawyers & Lobbyists $51,270

Lawyers & Lobbyists $51,270
   Venable, Baetjer & Howard .... $5,100   Indiv
   Hall, Levy & Marino .... $3,000   Indiv

Misc Business $69,170

Beer, Wine & Liquor $2,750
   None over $2,500

Retail Sales $2,650
   None over $2,500

Misc Services $4,350
   None over $2,500

Business Services $6,900
   None over $2,500

Casinos/Gambling $4,000
   Laurel Race Track .... $4,000   Indiv

Misc Business $7,300
   Belt's Distribution Services .... $3,000   Indiv

Steel Production $9,170
   Bethlehem Steel .... $5,970   PAC/Ind

Misc Manufacturing & Distributing $14,200
   United Industrial Corp .... $3,000   Indiv

Textiles $8,850
   Milliken & Co .... $4,000   Indiv
   Burlington Industries .... $3,200   PAC

Transportation $83,800

Air Transport $3,670
   None over $2,500

Automotive $9,050
   Auto Dealers & Drivers for Free Trade .... $3,000   PAC

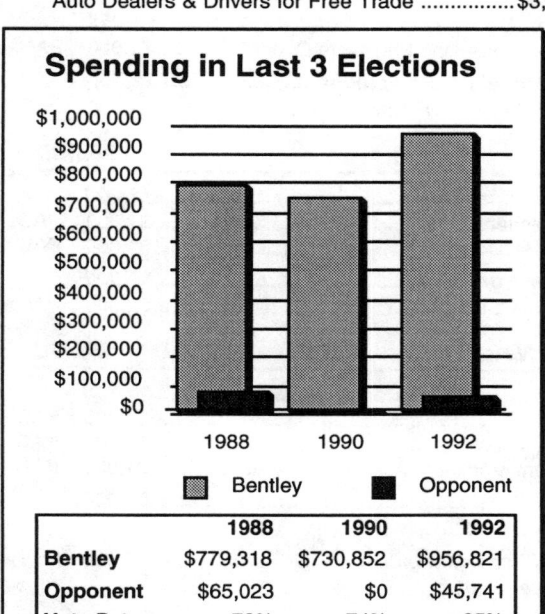

Spending in Last 3 Elections

	1988	1990	1992
Bentley	$779,318	$730,852	$956,821
Opponent	$65,023	$0	$45,741
Vote Pct	72%	74%	65%

Legend: Bentley / Opponent

Trucking $9,050
   Oceanic Ltd .... $4,000   Indiv

Sea Transport $55,230
   Great Lakes Dredge & Dock Co .... $6,800   PAC/Ind
   American Hawaii Cruises .... $4,000   Indiv
   Apex Marine Corp .... $4,000   Indiv
   Liberty Maritime Corp .... $4,000   Indiv
   CSX Corp* .... $3,400   PAC
   Crowley Maritime .... $3,400   PAC/Ind
   Ceres Terminals Inc .... $3,000   Indiv
   Keystone Shipping Co .... $2,650   Indiv
   Maersk Inc .... $2,650   PAC

Misc Transport $4,900
   None over $2,500

Labor

Labor $51,170

Building Trade Unions $9,950
   Baltimore Bldg & Constr Trades Council ...... $3,700   PAC
   Operating Engineers Union* .... $3,150   PAC

Industrial Unions $3,990
   Boilermakers Union .... $2,900   PAC

Transportation Unions $33,400
   Marine Engineers Union* .... $10,000   PAC
   Seafarers International Union .... $8,000   PAC
   Teamsters Union .... $4,800   PAC
   International Longshoremen's Assn ..... $3,550   PAC
   Air Line Pilots Assn .... $2,500   PAC

Public Sector Unions $3,830
   None over $2,500

Ideological/Single-Issue

Ideological/Single-Issue $11,800

Republican/Conservative $4,200
   None over $2,500

Pro-Israel $4,100
   None over $2,500

Other & Unknown

Other $39,155

Civil Servants/Public Officials $3,900
   None over $2,500

Education $4,850
   None over $2,500

Retired $26,705
   None over $2,500

Other $3,200
   None over $2,500

Unknown $111,495

   Homemakers/Non-income earners $13,610
   No Employer Listed or Found $42,905
   Generic Occupation/Category Unknown $2,920
   Employer Listed/Category Unknown $52,060
      Metropolitan Constract .... $2,750   Indiv

Independent expenditures opposing Bentley
   Maryland Coalition to Stop Ethnic Cleansing $27,210

---

* Contributions came from more than one affiliate or
  subsidiary.

Doug Bereuter, R-Neb (1)

First elected: 1978

1991-92 Total Receipts: $315,824
1992 Year-end Cash: $5,167

1991-92 Committees & Subcommittees

Banking, Finance and Urban Affairs
Financial Institutions Supervision, Regulation and Insurance; Housing and Community Development; International Development, Finance, Trade and Monetary Policy; Policy Research and Insurance (Ranking Republican)

Foreign Affairs
Human Rights and International Organizations (Ranking Republican); International Economic Policy and Trade

Select Committee on Hunger

Select Committee on Intelligence

Leading Contributors

Business

Agriculture	$35,150	
Crop Production & Basic Processing	**$9,100**	
Cargill Inc	$3,000	PAC
AG Processing Inc	$1,250	PAC
American Soybean Assn	$1,000	PAC
American Sugarbeet Growers Assn	$1,000	PAC
Continental Grain	$1,000	PAC
Florida Sugar Cane League	$1,000	PAC
Dairy	**$2,500**	
Milk Industry Foundation	$1,500	PAC
Poultry & Eggs	**$2,000**	
United Egg Assn	$2,000	PAC
Agricultural Services/Products	**$8,250**	
Farmland Industries	$1,250	PAC
American Assn of Crop Insurers	$1,000	PAC
Deere & Co	$1,000	PAC
Federal Agricultural Mortgage Corp	$1,000	PAC
Land O'Lakes Inc	$1,000	PAC
Food Processing & Sales	**$11,900**	
ConAgra Inc	$8,500	PAC
IBP Inc	$1,500	PAC

Source of Funds in 1992 Election

Source	Total	Pct
PACs	$194,482	62%
Indivs $200+	$29,577	9%
Indivs under $200	$82,866	26%
Other	$8,899	3%
Candidate	$0	0%
Party	$1,017	0%

Source of PAC Dollars by Sector

Source	Total	Pct
Business	$191,756	99%
Labor	$2,000	1%
Ideology/Single Issue	$500	0%

In-State vs. Out-of-State Contributions*

Source	Total	Pct
In-State	$23,877	81%
Out-of-state	$5,700	19%
No state listed	$0	

* by large individual contributors ($200 & above)

Communications/Electronics	$7,550	
Telephone Utilities	**$5,300**	
AT&T	$1,750	PAC
GTE Corp	$1,000	PAC

Construction	$9,650	
General Contractors	**$4,250**	
Brown & Root	$1,000	PAC
Hawkins Construction Co	$1,000	Indiv
Nebraska Construction Industry PAC	$1,000	PAC
Home Builders	**$1,800**	
None over $1,000		
Construction Services	**$1,250**	
American Consulting Engineers Council	$1,000	PAC
Building Materials & Equipment	**$2,350**	
National Concrete Masonry Assn	$1,600	PAC

Defense	$5,600	
Defense Aerospace	**$3,600**	
Martin Marietta Corp	$1,000	PAC
United Technologies	$1,000	PAC
Defense Electronics	**$2,000**	
E-Systems Inc	$2,000	PAC

Energy & Natural Resources	$6,700	
Oil & Gas	**$4,500**	
Enron Corp	$1,250	PAC
Dresser Industries	$1,000	PAC
Petroleum Marketers Assn	$1,000	PAC
Misc Energy	**$1,000**	
None over $1,000		
Electric Utilities	**$1,200**	
None over $1,000		

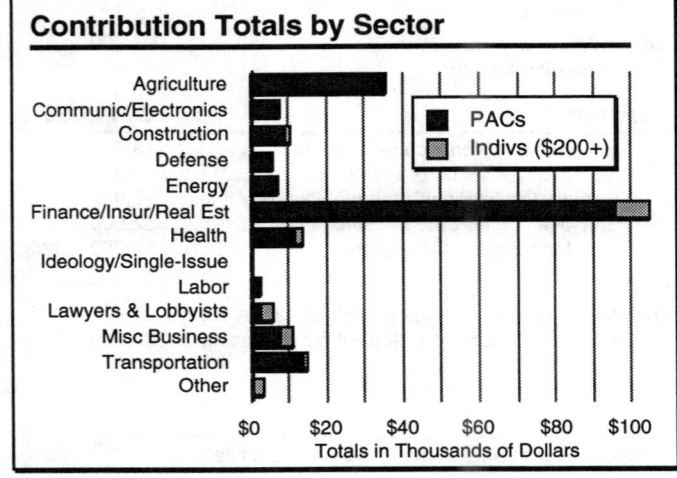

Contribution Totals by Sector

Legend: PACs, Indivs ($200+)

Categories: Agriculture, Communic/Electronics, Construction, Defense, Energy, Finance/Insur/Real Est, Health, Ideology/Single-Issue, Labor, Lawyers & Lobbyists, Misc Business, Transportation, Other

Totals in Thousands of Dollars ($0, $20, $40, $60, $80, $100)

Finance, Insurance & Real Estate — $104,131

Commercial Banks **$52,732**
American Bankers Assn	$10,000	PAC
Citicorp	$4,650	PAC
Chase Manhattan	$3,000	PAC
First Chicago Corp	$3,000	PAC
Norwest Corp	$3,000	PAC
Independent Bankers Assn	$2,582	PAC
JP Morgan & Co	$2,500	PAC
Barnett Banks Inc	$2,000	PAC
Firstier Financial Inc	$1,750	PAC
BankAmerica Corp	$1,500	PAC
Bankers Trust	$1,500	PAC
Chemical Bank	$1,500	PAC
Citizens & Southern National Bank	$1,500	PAC
Continental Illinois Corp	$1,500	PAC
Farmers & Merchants Bank	$1,450	Indiv
Consumer Bankers Assn	$1,000	PAC
National Bank of Commerce	$1,000	Indiv
Security Pacific Corp	$1,000	PAC
SunBanks	$1,000	PAC

Savings & Loans **$2,000**
US League of Savings Assns*	$1,500	PAC

Finance/Credit Companies **$1,500**
Associated Credit Bureaus	$1,500	PAC

Securities & Investment **$2,450**
None over $1,000

Insurance **$27,899**
Mutual of Omaha	$7,249	PAC/Ind
American Council of Life Insurance	$2,000	PAC
Allstate Insurance	$1,500	PAC
Northwestern Mutual Life	$1,500	PAC
United Services Automobile Assn Group	$1,500	PAC
Liberty Mutual Insurance	$1,000	PAC
Metropolitan Life Insurance	$1,000	PAC
Mortgage Insurance Companies of America	$1,000	PAC
National Assn of Independent Insurers	$1,000	PAC
Principal Mutual Life Insurance	$1,000	PAC
Travelers Corp	$1,000	PAC

Real Estate **$8,300**
National Assn of Realtors	$6,800	PAC

Accountants **$8,500**
American Institute of CPA's	$6,000	PAC
Ernst & Young	$1,000	PAC

Spending in Last 3 Elections

	1988	1990	1992
Bereuter	$221,530	$223,898	$365,386
Opponent	$96,278	$65,064	$84,533
Vote Pct	67%	65%	60%

Health — $13,100

Health Professionals **$8,400**
American Medical Assn*	$7,000	PAC

Hospitals/Nursing Homes **$1,200**
None over $1,000

Pharmaceuticals/Health Products **$3,500**
Ciba-Geigy Corp	$1,000	PAC
ICN Pharmaceuticals	$1,000	Indiv
SmithKline Beecham	$1,000	PAC

Lawyers & Lobbyists — $5,950

Lawyers & Lobbyists **$5,950**
Neill & Co	$1,500	Indiv
Preston, Gates et al	$1,000	PAC

Misc Business — $10,500

Food & Beverage **$1,000**
National Restaurant Assn	$1,000	PAC

Beer, Wine & Liquor **$1,750**
National Beer Wholesalers Assn	$1,250	PAC

Retail Sales **$1,500**
None over $1,000

Chemical & Related Manufacturing **$1,500**
Dial Corp	$1,000	PAC

Misc Manufacturing & Distributing **$2,900**
Valmont Industries	$1,000	PAC

Transportation — $14,102

Air Transport **$4,975**
General Electric	$1,750	PAC
Boeing Co	$1,000	PAC
United Parcel Service	$1,000	PAC

Automotive **$4,950**
National Auto Dealers Assn	$3,750	PAC

Trucking **$1,677**
None over $1,000

Railroads **$2,500**
Union Pacific Corp	$1,500	PAC
Burlington Northern	$1,000	PAC

Labor

Labor — **$2,000**

Public Sector Unions **$2,000**
National Assn Retired Federal Employees	$2,000	PAC

Ideological/Single-Issue

Ideological/Single-Issue — **$500**
None over $1,000

Other & Unknown

Other — **$2,850**

Retired **$2,400**
None over $1,000

Unknown — **$6,050**
Homemakers/Non-income earners	$1,150	
Employer Listed/Category Unknown	$4,900	
Atlantic Tele Network Inc	$1,000	Indiv

---

* Contributions came from more than one affiliate or subsidiary.

Howard L. Berman, D-Calif (26)

First elected: 1982

1991-92 Total Receipts:	$548,212
1992 Year-end Cash:	$26,077

1991-92 Committees & Subcommittees

Budget
Budget Process, Reconciliation and Enforcement; Defense, Foreign Policy and Space

Foreign Affairs
Arms Control, International Security and Science; International Operations (Chairman)

Judiciary
Economic and Commercial Law; International Law, Immigration and Refugees

Leading Contributors

Business

Agriculture	**$4,800**

Crop Production & Basic Processing $2,500
None over $2,000

Communications/Electronics	**$102,350**

Printing & Publishing $3,300
None over $2,000

Media/Entertainment $82,650

Time Warner*	$7,000	PAC
MCA Inc	$5,800	PAC/Ind
Disney Channel*	$5,300	Indiv
National Cable Television Assn	$4,800	PAC
Azoff Entertainment Co	$4,000	Indiv
Carolco Pictures Inc	$4,000	Indiv
Falcon Cable TV	$4,000	Indiv
Metropolitan Theatres Corp	$4,000	Indiv
Mirage Productions	$4,000	Indiv
Recording Industry Assn of America	$4,000	PAC/Ind
Paramount Communications	$3,000	PAC
New World Entertainment	$2,800	Indiv
BMI Music	$2,200	Indiv
ASCAP	$2,000	PAC
Andrew Adelson Co	$2,000	Indiv
Fox Inc	$2,000	PAC
Interscope Group	$2,000	Indiv
Sovereign Pictures	$2,000	Indiv
Weintraub Entertainment Group	$2,000	Indiv

Source of Funds in 1992 Election

Source	Total	Pct
■ PACs	$216,350	39%
▨ Indivs $200+	$284,648	51%
☐ Indivs under $200	$15,795	3%
▧ Other	$39,686	7%
Candidate	$0	0%
Party	$8,717	2%

Source of PAC Dollars by Sector

Source	Total	Pct
■ Business	$129,400	60%
▨ Labor	$77,750	36%
☐ Ideology/Single Issue	$7,064	3%

In-State vs. Out-of-State Contributions*

Source	Total	Pct
☐ In-State	$264,748	93%
■ Out-of-state	$19,900	7%
No state listed	$0	

*** by large individual contributors ($200 & above)**

Telephone Utilities $8,000

AT&T	$5,000	PAC
Pacific Telesis Group	$2,000	PAC

Telecom Services & Equipment $3,100
None over $2,000

Computer Equipment & Services $4,800

Tandon Corp	$4,000	Indiv

Construction	**$6,250**

General Contractors $2,450
None over $2,000

Construction Services $2,000

Parsons Brinckerhoff Inc	$2,000	Indiv

Defense | **$4,100**

Defense Aerospace $3,600

Lockheed Corp	$2,100	PAC

Energy & Natural Resources | **$5,500**

Oil & Gas $3,000
None over $2,000

Electric Utilities $2,000

Southern California Edison	$2,000	PAC

Finance, Insurance & Real Estate | **$69,600**

Commercial Banks $6,900

BankAmerica Corp	$2,100	PAC
American Bankers Assn	$2,000	PAC

Savings & Loans $7,500

Home Savings of America	$4,000	PAC
First Federal Savings Bank of California	$2,500	PAC

Finance/Credit Companies $2,000

East-West Capital Associates	$2,000	Indiv

Securities & Investment $4,500

Capital Insight	$2,000	Indiv

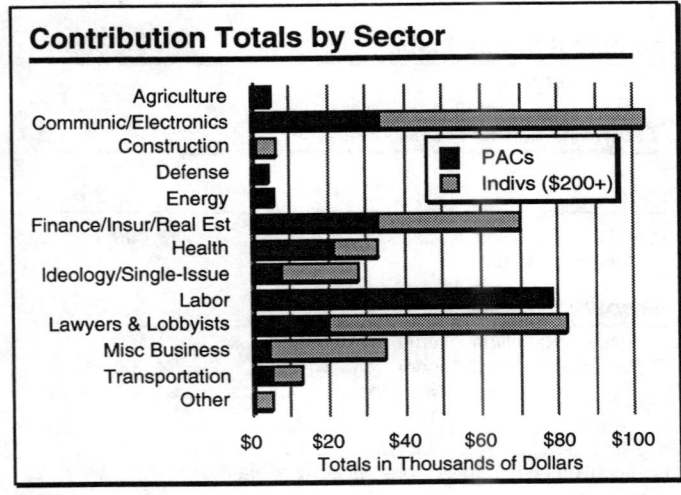

Contribution Totals by Sector

Agriculture
Communic/Electronics
Construction
Defense
Energy
Finance/Insur/Real Est
Health
Ideology/Single-Issue
Labor
Lawyers & Lobbyists
Misc Business
Transportation
Other

■ PACs
▨ Indivs ($200+)

$0 $20 $40 $60 $80 $100
Totals in Thousands of Dollars

Insurance	....	$11,950	
Allen Lawrence & Associates	....	$2,200	Indiv
TransAmerica Life Companies	....	$2,100	PAC

Real Estate	....	$25,900	
National Assn of Realtors	....	$6,000	PAC
Casden Co	....	$4,000	Indiv
Paris Industrial Parks	....	$4,000	Indiv
Amir Development Co	....	$2,000	Indiv
Irmas & Gold	....	$2,000	Indiv
Nobles Property Management Inc	....	$2,000	Indiv

Accountants	....	$6,750
None over $2,000		

Misc Finance	....	$4,100
None over $2,000		

Health $32,348

Health Professionals	....	$20,498	
American Medical Assn	....	$4,850	PAC
Cooperative of American Physicians	....	$4,500	PAC

Hospitals/Nursing Homes	....	$6,550	
American Hospital Assn	....	$2,500	PAC

Health Services	....	$2,400	
Family Health Program Inc	....	$2,000	PAC

Lawyers & Lobbyists $81,700

Lawyers & Lobbyists	....	$81,700	
Assn of Trial Lawyers of America	....	$10,000	PAC
Corinblit, Shapiro & Seltzer	....	$4,000	Indiv
Hochman, Salkin & Deroy	....	$4,000	Indiv
Gang, Tyre et al	....	$3,200	Indiv
Taylor, Roth et al	....	$3,000	Indiv
Fogel, Feldman et al	....	$2,000	Indiv
Howard Horn & Associates	....	$2,000	Indiv
Rose, Klein & Marias	....	$2,000	Indiv
Ziffren, Brittenham et al	....	$2,000	Indiv

Misc Business $34,350

Beer, Wine & Liquor	....	$10,900	
Gallo Winery	....	$4,000	Indiv
California Beer & Wine Wholesalers	....	$2,000	Indiv
Iron Horse Vineyards	....	$2,000	Indiv
Wine Institute	....	$2,000	PAC

Retail Sales	....	$4,000	
Desmonds Inc	....	$2,000	Indiv

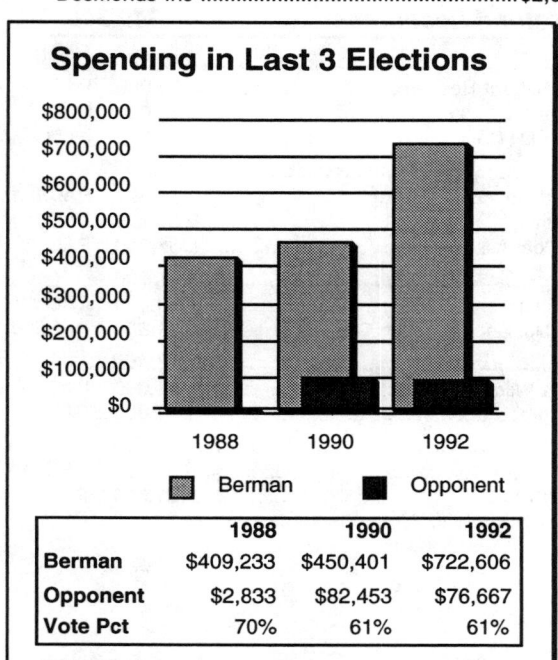

Spending in Last 3 Elections

	Betman	Opponent	

	1988	1990	1992
Berman	$409,233	$450,401	$722,606
Opponent	$2,833	$82,453	$76,667
Vote Pct	70%	61%	61%

Business Services	....	$13,300	
National Staff Network	....	$2,000	Indiv

Misc Manufacturing & Distributing	....	$4,950	
Occidental Coating Co	....	$4,000	Indiv

Transportation $12,400

Automotive	....	$10,000	
Executive Car Leasing	....	$4,000	Indiv
Americans for Free International Trade	....	$3,000	PAC
Galpin Motors	....	$3,000	Indiv

Labor

Labor $77,750

Building Trade Unions	....	$26,000	
Plumbers/Pipefitters Union	....	$10,000	PAC
Carpenters & Joiners Union	....	$7,000	PAC
Operating Engineers Union*	....	$4,500	PAC
Laborers' Political League	....	$3,000	PAC

Industrial Unions	....	$8,100	
United Auto Workers	....	$6,500	PAC

Transportation Unions	....	$13,250	
Air Line Pilots Assn	....	$6,000	PAC
Teamsters Union	....	$4,000	PAC

Public Sector Unions	....	$23,800	
American Fedn of St/Cnty/Munic Employees	....	$10,000	PAC
American Federation of Teachers	....	$5,000	PAC
National Assn Retired Federal Employees	....	$2,000	PAC
National Education Assn	....	$2,000	PAC

Misc Unions	....	$6,600	
Service Employees International Union	....	$2,500	PAC
Food & Commercial Workers Union	....	$2,300	PAC

Ideological/Single-Issue

Ideological/Single-Issue $27,314

Pro-Israel	....	$13,750
None over $2,000		

Pro-Choice	....	$2,000
None over $2,000		

Human Rights	....	$5,500	
KidsPAC	....	$2,000	PAC

Misc Issues	....	$4,064	
National Cmte to Preserve Social Security	....	$2,000	PAC
Santa Monica Mountains Conservancy	....	$2,000	Indiv

Other & Unknown

Other $4,850

Retired	....	$2,850
None over $2,000		

Unknown $35,550

Homemakers/Non-income earners	....	$8,900
No Employer Listed or Found	....	$14,050
Employer Listed/Category Unknown	....	$12,600
None over $2,000		

---

* Contributions came from more than one affiliate or subsidiary.

Tom Bevill, D-Ala (4)

1991-92 Committees & Subcommittees

Appropriations
Energy and Water Development (Chairman); Interior and Related Agencies; Military Construction

First elected: 1966

1991-92 Total Receipts: $318,198
1992 Year-end Cash: $365,281

Leading Contributors

Business

Agriculture	$12,150	
Crop Production & Basic Processing	**$3,250**	
Ocean Spray Cranberries Inc	$1,000	PAC
Poultry & Eggs	**$1,500**	
None over $1,000		
Agricultural Services/Products	**$4,100**	
Alabama Farm Bureau Federation	$2,100	PAC
Forestry & Forest Products	**$1,000**	
None over $1,000		

Communications/Electronics	$8,700	
Misc Communications/Electronics	**$1,000**	
None over $1,000		
Printing & Publishing	**$1,000**	
Thomas E Coker & Associates	$1,000	Indiv
Telephone Utilities	**$1,700**	
Southern Bell	$1,200	PAC
Electronics Mfg & Services	**$1,500**	
Pentastar Electronics Inc	$1,000	Indiv
Computer Equipment & Services	**$3,000**	
Intergraph Corp	$3,000	PAC

Construction	$17,850	
General Contractors	**$9,500**	
Ferguson-Williams Inc	$3,000	Indiv
Brown & Root	$1,000	PAC
Fluor Corp	$1,000	PAC
Pearce Construction Co	$1,000	Indiv
Whitaker Construction Co	$1,000	Indiv

Source of Funds in 1992 Election

Source	Total	Pct
■ PACs	$105,675	32%
▨ Indivs $200+	$83,310	25%
□ Indivs under $200	$49,044	15%
⊗ Other	$91,864	28%
Candidate	$0	0%
Party	$11,845	4%

Source of PAC Dollars by Sector

Source	Total	Pct
■ Business	$91,300	87%
▨ Labor	$11,200	11%
□ Ideology/Single Issue	$2,000	2%

In-State vs. Out-of-State Contributions*

Source	Total	Pct
□ In-State	$74,247	89%
■ Out-of-state	$9,063	11%
No state listed	$0	

* by large individual contributors ($200 & above)

Construction Services	**$5,100**	
Chambless & Associates	$1,000	Indiv
Building Materials & Equipment	**$2,750**	
Vulcan Materials Co	$2,000	PAC/Ind

Defense	$5,500	
Defense Aerospace	**$3,800**	
Lockheed Corp	$1,000	PAC
Martin Marietta Corp	$1,000	PAC
Rockwell International	$1,000	PAC
Defense Electronics	**$1,700**	
TRW Inc	$1,200	PAC

Energy & Natural Resources	$40,300	
Oil & Gas	**$10,600**	
Southern Natural Resources	$5,000	PAC
Alagasco Inc	$2,000	PAC
Williamson Oil Co	$1,000	Indiv
Mining	**$5,450**	
Drummond Co	$2,500	PAC/Ind
Dravo Corp	$1,250	PAC
National Coal Assn	$1,000	PAC
Nuclear Energy	**$11,500**	
General Atomics	$10,000	PAC
Southern Nuclear Operating Co	$1,500	PAC/Ind
Misc Energy	**$2,000**	
Babcock & Wilcox	$1,000	PAC
Bechtel Corp	$1,000	PAC
Electric Utilities	**$9,750**	
Alabama Power Co	$5,250	PAC/Ind
Southern Co*	$1,500	PAC
ACRE (Action Cmte for Rural Electrification)	$1,000	PAC

Contribution Totals by Sector

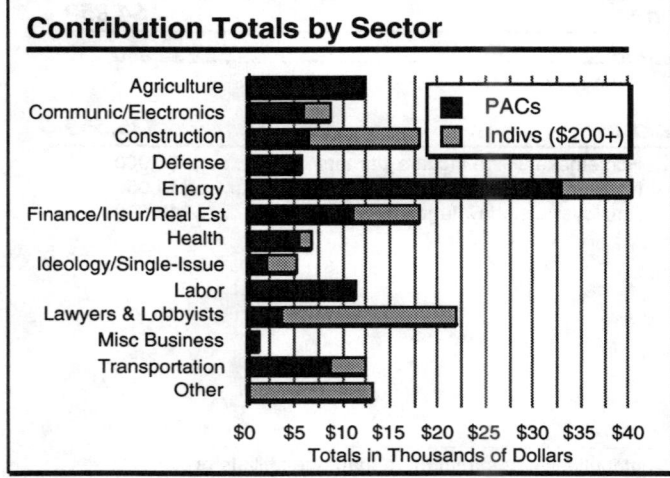

Agriculture
Communic/Electronics
Construction
Defense
Energy
Finance/Insur/Real Est
Health
Ideology/Single-Issue
Labor
Lawyers & Lobbyists
Misc Business
Transportation
Other

■ PACs
▨ Indivs ($200+)

$0 $5 $10 $15 $20 $25 $30 $35 $40
Totals in Thousands of Dollars

Finance, Insurance & Real Estate — $17,700

Commercial Banks $7,200
    Central Bancshares of the South .... $2,000 PAC
    First Bank of Fayette .... $1,500 Indiv
    Amsouth Bancorp .... $1,250 PAC

Insurance $6,000
    Torchmark Corp .... $5,000 PAC

Real Estate $4,250
    Hays Land Companies .... $1,000 Indiv
    Westminster Group .... $1,000 Indiv

Health — $6,600

Health Professionals $6,600
    American Medical Assn .... $2,850 PAC
    American Dental Assn .... $2,500 PAC

Lawyers & Lobbyists — $21,675

Lawyers & Lobbyists $21,675
    Wilson & King .... $2,500 Indiv
    McDaniel & McDaniel .... $2,000 Indiv
    Balch & Bingham .... $1,675 Indiv
    Assn of Trial Lawyers of America .... $1,000 PAC
    Fine, Geddie & Associates .... $1,000 Indiv
    Hogan & Hartson .... $1,000 PAC
    Sirote, Permutt et al .... $1,000 PAC
    Van Scoyoc Associates Inc .... $1,000 Indiv

Misc Business — $1,000

None over $1,000

Transportation — $12,250

Air Transport $1,500
    Boeing Co .... $1,500 PAC

Automotive $4,000
    National Auto Dealers Assn .... $4,000 PAC

Trucking $1,500
    Vernon Milling .... $1,000 Indiv

---

Railroads $1,000
    None over $1,000

Sea Transport $4,000
    American Waterways Operators .... $1,000 PAC

Labor

Labor — **$11,200**

Building Trade Unions $2,000
    Plumbers/Pipefitters Union .... $1,000 PAC

Industrial Unions $4,000
    United Auto Workers .... $2,000 PAC

Transportation Unions $1,000
    Marine Engineers Dist 2 Maritime Officers .... $1,000 PAC

Public Sector Unions $2,700
    National Assn Retired Federal Employees .... $1,000 PAC
    National Assn of Letter Carriers .... $1,000 PAC

Misc Unions $1,500
    Food & Commercial Workers Union .... $1,500 PAC

Ideological/Single-Issue

Ideological/Single-Issue — **$5,000**

Pro-Israel $4,000
    Americans for Good Government Inc .... $1,000 PAC

Gun Rights/Gun Control $1,000
    National Rifle Assn .... $1,000 PAC

Other & Unknown

Other — **$13,072**

Education $9,272
    University of Alabama .... $4,700 Indiv
    Bevill State College .... $2,025 Indiv
    Northwest Alabama Community College .... $1,000 Indiv

Retired $2,550
    None over $1,000

Other $1,000
    US Army .... $1,000 Indiv

Unknown — **$14,813**

    Homemakers/Non-income earners $2,313
    Employer Listed/Category Unknown $12,250
        CCSI Inc .... $1,000 Indiv
        Comptronics Inc .... $1,000 Indiv
        Nichols Research Corp .... $1,000 Indiv
        Summa Technology Inc .... $1,000 Indiv
        Terra First .... $1,000 Indiv

Spending in Last 3 Elections

	1988	1990	1992
Bevill	$130,642	$168,054	$519,416
Opponent	$0	$0	$20,117
Vote Pct	96%	100%	69%

---

* Contributions came from more than one affiliate or subsidiary.

435

James Bilbray, D-Nev (1)

First elected: 1986

1991-92 Total Receipts: $443,431
1992 Year-end Cash: $32,519

1991-92 Committees & Subcommittees

Armed Services
Military Installations and Facilities; Procurement and Military Nuclear Systems; Seapower and Strategic and Critical Materials

Small Business
Exports, Tax Policy and Special Problems; Procurement, Tourism and Rural Development

Select Committee on Aging

Leading Contributors

Business

Agriculture $8,125

Crop Production & Basic Processing $4,375
  None over $1,500

Tobacco $1,500
  None over $1,500

Dairy $1,500
  None over $1,500

Communications/Electronics $9,000

Media/Entertainment $3,500
  KLVX Channel 10 .... $1,500 Indiv

Telephone Utilities $2,250
  None over $1,500

Construction $6,850

General Contractors $1,500
  GKG Builders Inc .... $1,500 Indiv

Building Materials & Equipment $3,500
  Las Vegas Rock .... $3,000 Indiv

Defense $22,450

Defense Aerospace $16,850
  Grumman Corp .... $2,500 PAC
  Gencorp Inc .... $2,000 PAC
  LTV Aerospace & Defense Co .... $2,000 PAC
  Lockheed Corp .... $2,000 PAC
  Martin Marietta Corp .... $2,000 PAC
  Northrop Corp .... $1,500 PAC

Source of Funds in 1992 Election

Source	Total	Pct
■ PACs	$226,534	49%
▨ Indivs $200+	$186,055	40%
□ Indivs under $200	$12,611	3%
▧ Other	$40,013	9%
Candidate	$10,000	2%
Party	$22,432	5%

Source of PAC Dollars by Sector

Source	Total	Pct
■ Business	$114,452	50%
▨ Labor	$90,650	40%
□ Ideology/Single Issue	$22,400	10%

In-State vs. Out-of-State Contributions*

Source	Total	Pct
□ In-State	$159,905	86%
■ Out-of-state	$26,150	14%
No state listed	$0	

*** by large individual contributors ($200 & above)**

Defense Electronics $3,000
  Raytheon .... $2,000 PAC

Misc Defense $2,600
  None over $1,500

Energy & Natural Resources $19,800

Oil & Gas $5,000
  Southwest Gas Corp .... $2,000 PAC

Nuclear Energy $2,500
  General Atomics .... $2,500 PAC

Electric Utilities $4,000
  None over $1,500

Waste Management $7,000
  Silver State Disposal Service .... $6,000 Indiv

Finance, Insurance & Real Estate $50,200

Commercial Banks $7,250
  Valley Bank of Nevada .... $3,750 Indiv
  American Bankers Assn .... $1,500 PAC

Insurance $11,200
  National Assn of Life Underwriters .... $2,500 PAC
  Nevada Medical Liability Insurance .... $2,000 Indiv

Real Estate $28,200
  National Assn of Realtors .... $8,000 PAC
  Summa Corp .... $6,000 PAC
  Diversified Realty .... $4,250 Indiv
  Del Webb Corp .... $2,500 PAC
  Vista Group .... $2,000 Indiv

Accountants $1,500
  American Institute of CPA's .... $1,500 PAC

Misc Finance $1,500
  None over $1,500

Contribution Totals by Sector

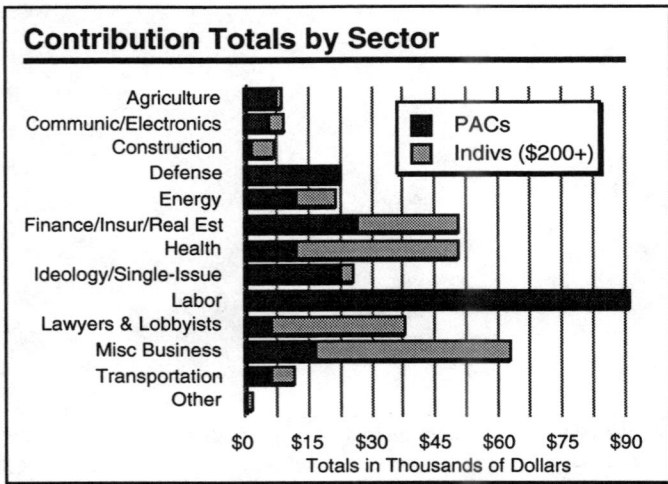

Agriculture
Communic/Electronics
Construction
Defense
Energy
Finance/Insur/Real Est
Health
Ideology/Single-Issue
Labor
Lawyers & Lobbyists
Misc Business
Transportation
Other

■ PACs
▨ Indivs ($200+)

$0 $15 $30 $45 $60 $75 $90
Totals in Thousands of Dollars

Health $50,200

Health Professionals **$44,700**
    American Medical Assn.............................$6,500   PAC
    American Academy of Ophthalmology ....$1,500   PAC
    Sierra Health Services ....$1,500   Indiv

Hospitals/Nursing Homes **$2,000**
    None over $1,500

Health Services **$3,000**
    Sierra Health Services ....$1,500   Indiv

Lawyers & Lobbyists $37,050

Lawyers & Lobbyists **$37,050**
    Assn of Trial Lawyers of America ....$5,000   PAC
    Lionel, Sawyer & Collins ....$4,000   Indiv
    Galatz, Earl et al ....$2,000   Indiv
    Goetz, Fitzpatrick & Flynn ....$2,000   Indiv
    Oshins, Brown & Singer ....$2,000   Indiv

Misc Business $61,887

Food & Beverage **$1,500**
    None over $1,500

Beer, Wine & Liquor **$1,500**
    None over $1,500

Retail Sales **$6,660**
    Schiff Enterprises ....$4,410   Indiv

Business Services **$6,850**
    Interface Group ....$3,000   Indiv

Casinos/Gambling **$38,227**
    Circus Circus Enterprises ....$6,000   PAC/Ind
    Whiskey Pete's Casino ....$5,000   Indiv
    California Hotel & Casino PAC ....$3,500   PAC
    Nevada Landing Hotel & Casino ....$3,000   Indiv
    Sahara Hotel & Casino ....$3,000   Indiv
    Harrah's ....$4,527   PAC
    Bally's Grand Inc ....$2,200   PAC
    Sands Hotel & Casino ....$2,000   Indiv
    Searchlight Nugget Casino ....$1,500   Indiv

Lodging/Tourism **$5,550**
    Transcontinental Properties ....$2,000   Indiv

Transportation $11,250

Automotive **$3,000**
    National Auto Dealers Assn ....$2,500   PAC

Misc Transport **$5,500**
    Ace Cab Co ....$2,000   Indiv

Labor

Labor $90,650

Building Trade Unions **$33,000**
    Carpenters & Joiners Union ....$7,500   PAC
    Ironworkers Union ....$7,500   PAC
    Operating Engineers Union* ....$5,500   PAC
    Laborers Union* ....$4,500   PAC
    Plumbers/Pipefitters Union ....$3,000   PAC
    Sheet Metal Workers Union ....$2,500   PAC
    AFL-CIO Bldg/Construction Trades Dept ....$1,500   PAC

Industrial Unions **$15,250**
    Intl Brotherhood of Electrical Workers ....$3,500   PAC
    United Auto Workers ....$3,000   PAC
    United Steelworkers ....$2,500   PAC
    Boilermakers Union ....$2,000   PAC
    Machinists/Aerospace Workers Union ....$2,000   PAC

Transportation Unions **$17,500**
    Air Line Pilots Assn ....$5,500   PAC
    Teamsters Union ....$5,000   PAC
    Marine Engineers Union* ....$4,000   PAC

Public Sector Unions **$19,500**
    National Education Assn ....$6,500   PAC
    American Postal Workers Union ....$3,500   PAC
    National Assn of Letter Carriers ....$3,000   PAC
    National Assn Retired Federal Employees ....$2,000   PAC
    American Fedn of St/Cnty/Munic Employees ....$1,500   PAC

Misc Unions **$5,400**
    AFL-CIO ....$2,000   PAC
    Food & Commercial Workers Union ....$1,700   PAC
    Hotel/Restaurant Employees Union ....$1,500   PAC

Ideological/Single-Issue

Ideological/Single-Issue $25,300

Democratic/Liberal **$2,500**
    National Cmte for an Effective Congress ....$2,500   PAC

Foreign & Defense Policy **$1,500**
    Veterans of Foreign Wars ....$1,500   PAC

Pro-Israel **$10,850**
    National PAC ....$5,000   PAC

Gun Rights/Gun Control **$5,950**
    National Rifle Assn ....$5,950   PAC

Misc Issues **$4,500**
    National Cmte to Preserve Social Security ....$4,000   PAC

Other & Unknown

Other $1,500
    None over $1,500

Unknown $19,295
    Homemakers/Non-income earners $4,750
    Employer Listed/Category Unknown $14,545
        Arcadia Corp ....$6,500   Indiv

---

* Contributions came from more than one affiliate or subsidiary.

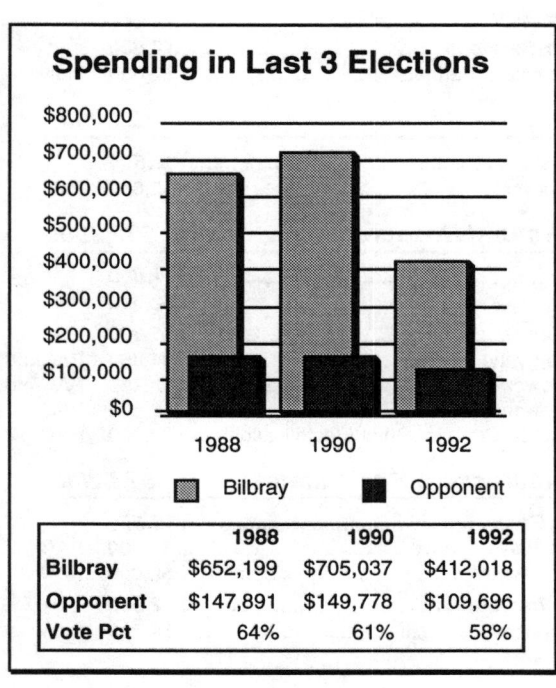

Spending in Last 3 Elections

Legend: ▩ Bilbray   ■ Opponent

	1988	1990	1992
Bilray	$652,199	$705,037	$412,018
Opponent	$147,891	$149,778	$109,696
Vote Pct	64%	61%	58%

Michael Bilirakis, R-Fla (9)

First elected: 1982

1991-92 Total Receipts: $779,124
1992 Year-end Cash: $1,923

1991-92 Committees & Subcommittees

Energy and Commerce
Commerce, Consumer Protection and Competitiveness; Health and the Environment; Telecommunications and Finance

Veterans' Affairs
Hospitals and Health Care; Oversight and Investigations (Ranking Republican)

Select Committee on Children, Youth and Families

Leading Contributors

Business

Agriculture — $44,500

Crop Production & Basic Processing	**$8,600**	
Cargill Inc	$3,000	PAC
Tobacco	**$12,700**	
RJR Nabisco	$5,000	PAC
US Tobacco Co	$2,500	PAC
Philip Morris	$2,000	PAC
Dairy	**$2,200**	
None over $2,000		
Agricultural Services/Products	**$7,500**	
Freeport-McMoRan Inc	$2,000	PAC
Food Processing & Sales	**$12,750**	
Food Marketing Institute	$2,500	PAC
Winn-Dixie Stores	$2,250	PAC/Ind

Communications/Electronics — $57,500

Misc Communications/Electronics	**$3,000**	
Pappas Telecasting Companies	$3,000	Indiv
Printing & Publishing	**$4,450**	
Pelam Investments	$4,000	Indiv
Media/Entertainment	**$25,300**	
National Assn of Broadcasters	$9,500	PAC
Adelphia Communications	$5,000	Indiv
Home Shopping Network Inc	$5,000	Indiv
National Cable Television Assn	$3,000	PAC
Telephone Utilities	**$17,250**	
Southern Bell	$7,000	PAC
GTE Corp	$2,000	PAC
United Telecommunications	$2,000	PAC

Contribution Totals by Sector

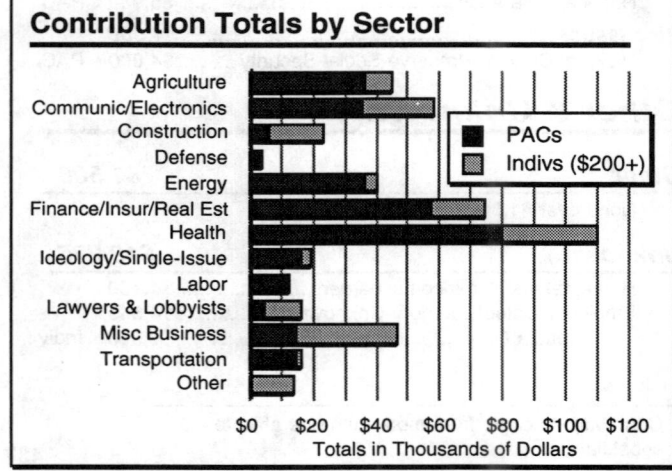

Totals in Thousands of Dollars

Source of Funds in 1992 Election

Source	Total	Pct
PACs	$312,710	38%
Indivs $200+	$194,458	23%
Indivs under $200	$255,906	31%
Other	$66,050	8%
Candidate	$0	0%
Party	$60,014	7%

Source of PAC Dollars by Sector

Source	Total	Pct
Business	$284,596	91%
Labor	$12,000	4%
Ideology/Single Issue	$15,350	5%

In-State vs. Out-of-State Contributions*

Source	Total	Pct
In-State	$148,612	77%
Out-of-state	$44,750	23%
No state listed	$1,000	

* by large individual contributors ($200 & above)

Telecom Services & Equipment	**$2,000**	
None over $2,000		
Electronics Mfg & Services	**$5,500**	
Harris Corp	$3,000	PAC
Audiovox Corp	$2,000	Indiv

Construction — $22,991

General Contractors	**$14,016**	
General Contractor	$4,000	Indiv
Associated General Contractors	$2,000	PAC
Home Builders	**$3,475**	
None over $2,000		
Construction Services	**$2,000**	
Spillis, Canela & Partners	$2,000	Indiv

Defense — $3,000

Misc Defense	**$2,500**	
Insilco Corp	$2,000	PAC

Energy & Natural Resources — $39,700

Oil & Gas	**$11,850**	
Ashland Oil	$2,500	PAC
Electric Utilities	**$25,300**	
Teco Energy Inc	$4,850	PAC/Ind
Florida Power & Light	$2,750	PAC/Ind
Florida Power Corp	$2,500	PAC
ACRE (Action Cmte for Rural Electrification)	$2,000	PAC

Finance, Insurance & Real Estate — $73,200

Commercial Banks	**$9,550**	
American Bankers Assn	$2,000	PAC
Barnett Banks Inc	$2,000	PAC
Securities & Investment	**$12,650**	
US Enterprises	$2,200	Indiv

Insurance	$21,250	
American Family Corp	$3,000	PAC
Blue Cross & Blue Shield Assn*	$3,000	PAC
Mutual of Omaha	$2,500	PAC

Real Estate	$16,250	
National Assn of Realtors	$10,000	PAC

Accountants	$13,250	
American Institute of CPA's	$10,000	PAC

Health — $108,830

Health Professionals	$77,994	
American Medical Assn	$10,200	PAC
American Dental Assn	$8,000	PAC
American Chiropractic Assn	$5,000	PAC
American College of Emergency Physicians	$5,000	PAC
American Podiatry Assn	$4,000	PAC
American Optometric Assn	$3,500	PAC
American Academy of Ophthalmology	$2,500	PAC
American Assn Oral & Maxillofacial Surgeons	$2,000	PAC

Hospitals/Nursing Homes	$12,036	
American Hospital Assn	$5,236	PAC
American Health Care Assn	$2,500	PAC

Pharmaceuticals/Health Products	$16,000	
Schering-Plough Corp	$2,000	PAC

Misc Health	$2,300	
None over $2,000		

Lawyers & Lobbyists — $15,593

Lawyers & Lobbyists	$15,593	
None over $2,000		

Misc Business — $45,982

Food & Beverage	$7,550	
None over $2,000		

Beer, Wine & Liquor	$4,682	
National Beer Wholesalers Assn	$3,000	PAC

Retail Sales	$6,000	
None over $2,000		

Spending in Last 3 Elections

	1988	1990	1992
Bilirakis	$193,901	$815,366	$774,818
Opponent	$0	$89,852	$265,192
Vote Pct	100%	58%	59%

Business Services	$9,800	
Tampa Machinery Auction	$4,000	Indiv

Lodging/Tourism	$4,000	
Palm Pavilion	$2,000	Indiv

Chemical & Related Manufacturing	$4,000	
None over $2,000		

Misc Manufacturing & Distributing	$7,500	
Danka Industries	$4,000	Indiv

Transportation — $15,600

Air Transport	$3,750	
United Parcel Service	$3,000	PAC

Automotive	$7,300	
National Auto Dealers Assn	$4,500	PAC

Railroads	$2,250	
None over $2,000		

Labor

Labor	$12,000	

Transportation Unions	$3,500	
Marine Engineers Dist 2 Maritime Offices	$3,500	PAC

Public Sector Unions	$8,500	
National Assn Retired Federal Employees	$7,000	PAC

Ideological/Single-Issue

Ideological/Single-Issue	$18,650	

Republican/Conservative	$4,000	
Eagle Forum	$2,000	PAC

Foreign & Defense Policy	$2,000	
Veterans of Foreign Wars	$2,000	PAC

Human Rights	$5,800	
Dynamis	$5,000	PAC

Misc Issues	$4,000	
National Cmte to Preserve Social Security	$3,000	PAC

Other & Unknown

Other	$13,510	

Civil Servants/Public Officials	$2,000	
State of Florida	$2,000	Indiv

Retired	$10,610	
None over $2,000		

Unknown	$35,752	
Homemakers/Non-income earners	$9,506	
Generic Occupation/Category Unknown	$3,070	
Employer Listed/Category Unknown	$21,176	
Persephone Co	$2,000	Indiv

Independent expenditures supporting Bilirakis		
National Right to Life PAC	$12,855	
National Cmte to Preserve Social Security	$8,203	

---

* Contributions came from more than one affiliate or subsidiary.

Sanford Bishop, D-Ga (2)

First elected: 1992

1991-92 Total Receipts: $354,989
1992 Year-end Cash: $3,737

1993-94 Committees & Subcommittees

Agriculture
Department Operations and Nutrition; General Farm Commodities; Specialty Crops and Natural Resources

Post Office and Civil Service
Postal Operations and Services

Veterans' Affairs
Hospitals and Health Care; Housing and Memorial Affairs

Leading Contributors

Business

Agriculture $14,160

Crop Production & Basic Processing	**$4,510**	
WC Bradley Co	$1,500	Indiv
Alabama Peanut Producers Assn	$1,000	PAC
Cargill Inc	$1,000	PAC
Tobacco	**$3,000**	
RJR Nabisco	$2,000	PAC
Poultry & Eggs	**$2,500**	
National Broiler Council	$1,500	PAC
Gold Kist	$1,000	PAC
Agricultural Services/Products	**$1,000**	
None over $1,000		
Food Processing & Sales	**$2,000**	
Pepsico Inc	$1,000	PAC

Communications/Electronics $3,000

Telephone Utilities	**$2,500**	
Southern Bell	$2,500	PAC

Construction $5,300

General Contractors	**$5,300**	
Hardaway Co	$3,000	PAC
Adams Construction Co	$1,000	Indiv

Source of Funds in 1992 Election

Source	Total	Pct
PACs	$144,510	40%
Indivs $200+	$96,177	27%
Indivs under $200	$62,752	17%
Other	$56,184	16%
Candidate	$25,000	7%
Party	$4,634	1%

Source of PAC Dollars by Sector

Source	Total	Pct
Business	$95,160	66%
Labor	$36,349	25%
Ideology/Single Issue	$12,250	9%

In-State vs. Out-of-State Contributions*

Source	Total	Pct
In-State	$84,077	88%
Out-of-state	$11,100	12%
No state listed	$1,000	

by large individual contributors ($200 & above)

Energy & Natural Resources $5,700

Oil & Gas	**$2,500**	
Atlanta Gas Light Co	$1,000	PAC
Electric Utilities	**$2,950**	
Southern Co*	$2,250	PAC

Finance, Insurance & Real Estate $59,590

Commercial Banks	**$28,000**	
CB&T Bancshares	$15,000	PAC
Synovus Financial Co	$5,250	Indiv
American Bankers Assn*	$2,250	PAC
Citizens & Southern National Bank	$2,000	PAC
Trust Co of Georgia	$1,750	PAC
Securities & Investment	**$1,250**	
Diaz-Verson Capital Investments	$1,250	Indiv
Insurance	**$21,640**	
American Family Corp	$17,000	Indiv
Blue Cross & Blue Shield Assn	$1,890	Indiv
National Assn of Life Underwriters	$1,500	PAC
Real Estate	**$7,150**	
National Assn of Realtors	$2,500	PAC
Smyre Realty Co	$1,200	Indiv
Ray M Wright Inc	$1,000	Indiv
Misc Finance	**$1,050**	
None over $1,000		

Contribution Totals by Sector

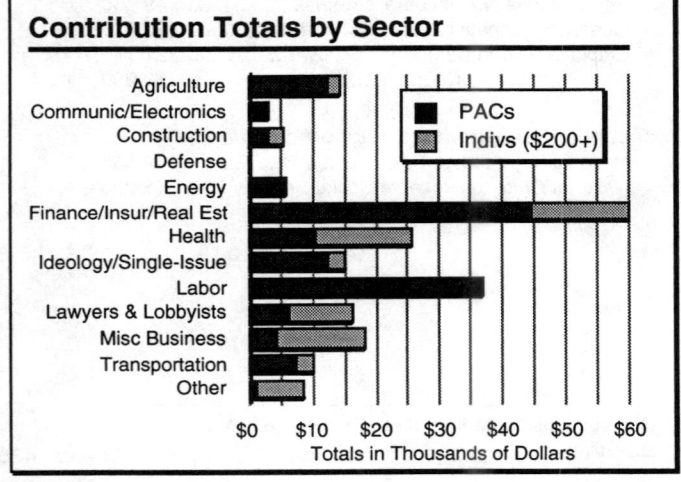

Agriculture
Communic/Electronics
Construction
Defense
Energy
Finance/Insur/Real Est
Health
Ideology/Single-Issue
Labor
Lawyers & Lobbyists
Misc Business
Transportation
Other

■ PACs
▨ Indivs ($200+)

$0 $10 $20 $30 $40 $50 $60
Totals in Thousands of Dollars

Health $25,250

Health Professionals **$20,150**
    American Dental Assn .... $4,000   PAC
    American Medical Assn... $2,500   PAC
    Emanuel Wilkes Ophthamologist .... $1,200   Indiv
    American Chiropractic Assn.................................. $1,000   PAC
    Kaufmann Diagnostic Clinic .... $1,000   Indiv

Hospitals/Nursing Homes **$2,100**
    American Hospital Assn .... $1,000   PAC

Misc Health **$3,000**
    Managed Healthcare Systems Inc .... $2,000   Indiv
    Medical Transcription .... $1,000   Indiv

Lawyers & Lobbyists $18,100

Lawyers & Lobbyists **$18,100**
    Assn of Trial Lawyers of America .... $5,000   PAC
    Butler, Wooten et al... $2,750   Indiv
    Pope, McGlamry et al... $2,100   Indiv
    King & Spalding .... $1,000   PAC
    Lamar, Archer & Cofrin .... $1,000   Indiv

Misc Business $17,700

Food & Beverage **$4,750**
    Coca-Cola Co .... $2,000   PAC
    Kentucky Fried Chicken .... $2,000   Indiv

Beer, Wine & Liquor **$5,500**
    Georgia Crown Distributing Co .... $4,000   Indiv
    National Beer Wholesalers Assn .... $1,000   PAC

Retail Sales **$1,500**
    Movin Man, The .... $1,000   Indiv

Misc Services **$2,600**
    Family Care Center .... $1,000   Indiv
    Progressive Funeral Home .... $1,000   Indiv

Lodging/Tourism **$2,250**
    Williams Investments .... $2,000   Indiv

Transportation $9,850

Air Transport **$4,600**
    United Parcel Service .... $4,000   PAC

Automotive **$5,000**
    Bill Heard Chevrolet .... $2,250   Indiv
    National Auto Dealers Assn .... $2,000   PAC

Spending in Last Election

	1992
Bishop	$351,252
Opponent	$181,421
Vote Pct	64%

Labor

Labor $36,349

Building Trade Unions **$2,500**
    Laborers' Political League .... $1,500   PAC
    Sheet Metal Workers Union .... $1,000   PAC

Industrial Unions **$7,050**
    Communications Workers of America .... $4,250   PAC
    United Auto Workers .... $2,500   PAC

Transportation Unions **$9,300**
    Teamsters Union .... $5,000   PAC
    Air Line Pilots Assn .... $1,000   PAC
    Marine Engineers Union...................................... $1,000   PAC
    United Transportation Union .... $1,000   PAC

Public Sector Unions **$11,500**
    National Education Assn .... $5,000   PAC
    American Fedn of St/Cnty/Munic Employees ...... $4,000   PAC
    National Assn Retired Federal Employees .... $1,000   PAC
    National Rural Letter Carriers Assn .... $1,000   PAC

Misc Unions.. **$5,999**
    AFL-CIO .... $2,500   PAC
    Food & Commercial Workers Union .... $2,499   PAC
    Service Employees International Union .... $1,000   PAC

Ideological/Single-Issue

Ideological/Single-Issue $14,750

Democratic/Liberal **$2,500**
    None over $1,000

Leadership PACs **$3,000**
    Effective Government Cmte (Dick Gephardt) ...... $1,000   PAC
    House Leadership Fund (Tom Foley) .... $1,000   PAC

Pro-Israel **$5,500**
    Florida Congressional Cmte .... $1,000   PAC
    National PAC .... $1,000   PAC

Pro-Choice.. **$1,750**
    National Abortion Rights Action League .... $1,500   PAC

Womens Issues **$1,000**
    National Organization for Women .... $1,000   PAC

Other & Unknown

Other $8,300

Civil Servants/Public Officials............................. **$1,300**
    None over $1,000

Education **$2,500**
    Columbus College School of Business .... $1,000   Indiv
    Mercer University .... $1,000   Indiv

Retired **$4,000**
    None over $1,000

Unknown $22,137

    Homemakers/Non-income earners $2,750
    No Employer Listed or Found $5,750
    Generic Occupation/Category Unknown $1,437
    Employer Listed/Category Unknown $12,200
        Southern Management Facilities .... $2,500   Indiv
        Dimensions International Inc .... $1,000   Indiv
        Keys Communications Group .... $1,000   Indiv
        Southeast Capitol Market Group .... $1,000   Indiv
        Southeastern Facility .... $1,000   Indiv
        Stonewall Jackson Investment Co .... $1,000   Indiv

---

* Contributions came from more than one affiliate or subsidiary.

Lucien E. Blackwell, D-Pa (2)

First elected: 1991

1991-92 Total Receipts: $313,413
1992 Year-end Cash: $16,359

1991-92 Committees & Subcommittees

Merchant Marine and Fisheries
Merchant Marine

Public Works and Transportation
Investigations and Oversight; Surface Transportation; Water Resources

Leading Contributors

Business

Agriculture		$3,050
Dairy	**$1,000**	
Associated Milk Producers	$1,000	PAC
Food Processing & Sales	**$1,250**	
Food Marketing Institute	$1,000	PAC

Communications/Electronics		$3,400
Media/Entertainment	**$2,000**	
QVC Network	$1,000	Indiv

Construction		$10,000
General Contractors	**$7,250**	
Kemrodco Development & Construction	$2,500	Indiv
Keating Construction Co	$2,000	Indiv
Construction Services	**$1,250**	
None over $1,000		

Defense		$4,750
Misc Defense	**$4,500**	
Unified Industries Inc	$4,500	Indiv

Energy & Natural Resources		$5,250
Electric Utilities	**$3,000**	
Philadelphia Electric	$2,500	PAC
Waste Management	**$1,000**	
Browning-Ferris Industries	$1,000	PAC

Source of Funds in 1992 Election

Source	Total	Pct
■ PACs	$157,610	49%
▨ Indivs $200+	$125,153	39%
☐ Indivs under $200	$26,545	8%
▨ Other	$11,635	4%
Candidate	$0	0%
Party	$7,680	2%

Source of PAC Dollars by Sector

Source	Total	Pct
■ Business	$36,970	26%
▨ Labor	$101,970	71%
☐ Ideology/Single Issue	$5,500	4%

In-State vs. Out-of-State Contributions*

Source	Total	Pct
☐ In-State	$101,931	83%
■ Out-of-state	$21,072	17%
No state listed	$1,800	

* by large individual contributors ($200 & above)

Finance, Insurance & Real Estate		$21,800
Commercial Banks	**$1,250**	
Provident National Bank	$1,250	PAC
Savings & Loans	**$1,050**	
None over $1,000		
Securities & Investment	**$1,000**	
None over $1,000		
Insurance	**$1,950**	
Blue Cross & Blue Shield Assn	$1,250	PAC/Ind
Real Estate	**$14,050**	
Pennrose Properties	$4,500	Indiv
Parkway Corp	$2,250	Indiv
Ate Kays Co	$1,500	Indiv
National Assn of Realtors	$1,500	PAC
Amerimar Realty Co	$1,250	Indiv
Accountants	**$2,500**	
American Institute of CPA's	$1,000	PAC

Health		$13,256
Health Professionals	**$7,331**	
Lomax Health Systems	$2,000	Indiv
Temple Group Inc	$1,250	Indiv
American Medical Assn	$1,000	PAC
Hospitals/Nursing Homes	**$2,425**	
Spruce Medical Center	$1,200	Indiv
Newman Medical Center	$1,000	Indiv
Pharmaceuticals/Health Products	**$1,000**	
SmithKline Beecham	$1,000	PAC
Misc Health	**$2,000**	
Managed Healthcare Systems Inc	$1,000	Indiv
Nelson Medical Group Inc	$1,000	Indiv

Contribution Totals by Sector

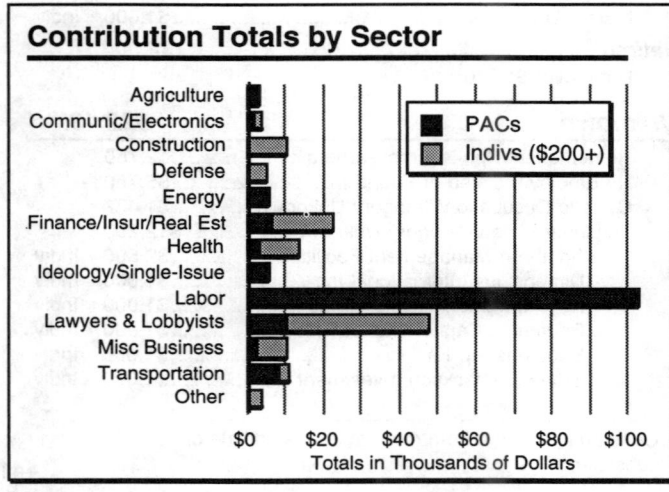

Legend: ■ PACs, ▨ Indivs ($200+)

Categories (top to bottom): Agriculture, Communic/Electronics, Construction, Defense, Energy, Finance/Insur/Real Est, Health, Ideology/Single-Issue, Labor, Lawyers & Lobbyists, Misc Business, Transportation, Other

X-axis: $0, $20, $40, $60, $80, $100
Totals in Thousands of Dollars

Lawyers & Lobbyists | $46,947

Lawyers & Lobbyists **$46,947**
SR Wojdak & Associates	$6,500	Indiv
Assn of Trial Lawyers of America	$5,000	PAC
Small, Margolin & Mirsky	$4,000	Indiv
Wolf, Block et al	$2,500	PAC/Ind
Dilworth, Paxson et al	$2,000	Indiv
Cassidy & Associates	$1,997	Indiv
Blank, Rome et al	$1,550	PAC/Ind
Delaware Valley Leadership Fund	$1,500	PAC
Reid & Priest	$1,500	PAC/Ind
Elliott & O'Brien	$1,000	Indiv
Paul, Reich & Myers	$1,000	Indiv
Singley & Associates	$1,000	Indiv

Misc Business | $9,950

Food & Beverage **$1,250**
None over $1,000

Business Services **$2,700**
PG Corbin & Co	$1,500	Indiv

Lodging/Tourism **$4,500**
Cobbs Creek International Travel	$4,000	Indiv

Chemical & Related Manufacturing **$1,250**
None over $1,000

Transportation | $10,370

Air Transport **$4,000**
United Parcel Service	$4,000	PAC

Trucking **$1,520**
None over $1,000

Sea Transport **$3,500**
Holt Cargo Systems	$1,000	Indiv
Society for Relief of Distressed Pilots	$1,000	PAC

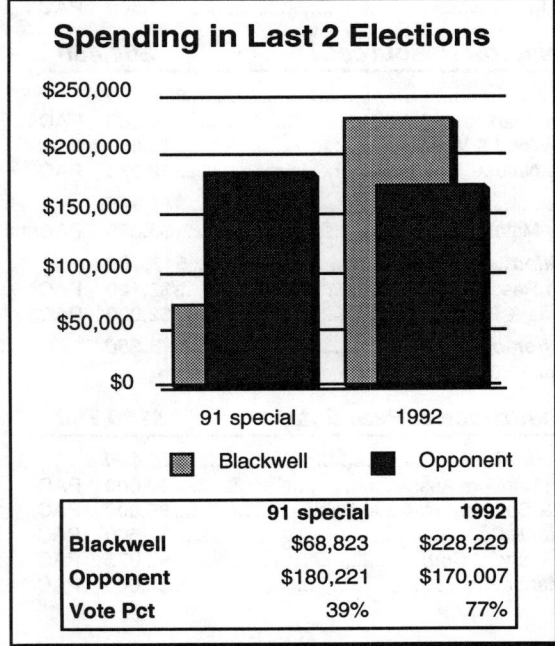

Spending in Last 2 Elections

	91 special	1992
Blackwell	$68,823	$228,229
Opponent	$180,221	$170,007
Vote Pct	39%	77%

Labor

Labor | $102,170

Building Trade Unions **$18,470**
Plumbers/Pipefitters Union*	$6,070	PAC
Roofers Union local #30	$3,000	PAC
Sheet Metal Workers Union	$3,000	PAC
Operating Engineers Union*	$1,250	PAC
Heat/Frost/Asbestos Workers #14	$1,000	PAC
Laborers' Political League	$1,000	PAC
Painters & Allied Trades Union	$1,000	PAC

Industrial Unions **$29,500**
Machinists/Aerospace Workers Union	$10,500	PAC
Communications Workers Union #13000	$5,500	PAC
United Auto Workers	$5,500	PAC
Intl Brotherhood of Electrical Workers*	$4,000	PAC
Amalgamated Clothing & Textile Workers	$1,500	PAC
Boilermakers Union	$1,000	PAC
Ladies Garment Workers Union	$1,000	PAC

Transportation Unions **$24,500**
International Longshoremen's Assn	$7,500	PAC
Seafarers International Union	$5,000	PAC
Air Line Pilots Assn	$3,500	PAC
Teamsters Union*	$3,000	PAC
Brotherhood of Locomotive Engineers	$1,000	PAC
Maintenance of Way Employees	$1,000	PAC
Marine Engineers Union*	$1,000	PAC
United Transportation Union	$1,000	PAC

Public Sector Unions **$23,000**
National Education Assn	$7,500	PAC
American Federation of Teachers	$5,000	PAC
American Fedn of St/Cnty/Munic Employees	$5,000	PAC
American Postal Workers Union	$4,000	PAC
National Assn of Letter Carriers	$1,000	PAC

Misc Unions **$6,700**
Food & Commercial Workers Union	$3,000	PAC
AFL-CIO	$2,500	PAC
Hotel/Restaurant Employees Union	$1,000	PAC

Ideological/Single-Issue

Ideological/Single-Issue | $5,500

Pro-Israel **$1,500**
Joint Action Cmte for Political Affairs	$1,000	PAC

Human Rights **$2,500**
Human Rights Campaign Fund	$2,500	PAC

Misc Issues **$1,500**
National Cmte to Preserve Social Security	$1,500	PAC

Other & Unknown

Other | $3,400

Civil Servants/Public Officials **$2,200**
City of Philadelphia	$2,200	Indiv

Unknown | $33,900

Unknown	$4,500	
Citizens Action PAC	$3,000	PAC
PAC 250	$1,000	PAC
No Employer Listed or Found	$16,050	
Generic Occupation/Category Unknown	$3,200	
Employer Listed/Category Unknown	$10,150	
Amoroso Brothers	$2,500	Indiv
Centra Associates	$1,000	Indiv
Hines, Goldberg et al	$1,000	Indiv

* Contributions came from more than one affiliate or
subsidiary.

Thomas J. Bliley Jr., R-Va (7)

First elected: 1980

1991-92 Total Receipts: $721,526
1992 Year-end Cash: $52,852

1991-92 Committees & Subcommittees

District of Columbia (Ranking Republican)
Fiscal Affairs and Health; Government Operations and Metropolitan Affairs; Judiciary and Education

Energy and Commerce
Health and the Environment; Oversight and Investigations (Ranking Republican); Telecommunications and Finance

Leading Contributors

Business

Agriculture	$89,044	
Crop Production & Basic Processing	**$7,025**	
None over $2,000		
Tobacco	**$38,991**	
Philip Morris	$12,491	PAC/Ind
US Tobacco Co	$11,000	PAC/Ind
RJR Nabisco	$7,000	PAC
Pinkerton Tobacco	$2,775	PAC
Agricultural Services/Products	**$5,500**	
None over $2,000		
Food Processing & Sales	**$22,279**	
National Food Processors Assn	$2,379	PAC
ConAgra Inc	$2,000	PAC
Food Marketing Institute	$2,000	PAC
Nabisco Brands Inc	$2,000	PAC
Pepsico Inc	$2,000	PAC
Forestry & Forest Products	**$14,249**	
Westvaco Corp	$6,250	PAC/Ind

Communications/Electronics	$51,575	
Printing & Publishing	**$2,800**	
None over $2,000		
Media/Entertainment	**$19,450**	
National Cable Television Assn	$10,000	PAC
Comcast Corp	$2,000	PAC
Viacom International	$2,000	PAC
Telephone Utilities	**$14,775**	
AT&T	$7,975	PAC
Bell Atlantic*	$2,050	PAC
Telecom Services & Equipment ...	**$11,300**	
Cable & Wireless North America ...	$2,500	Indiv

Contribution Totals by Sector

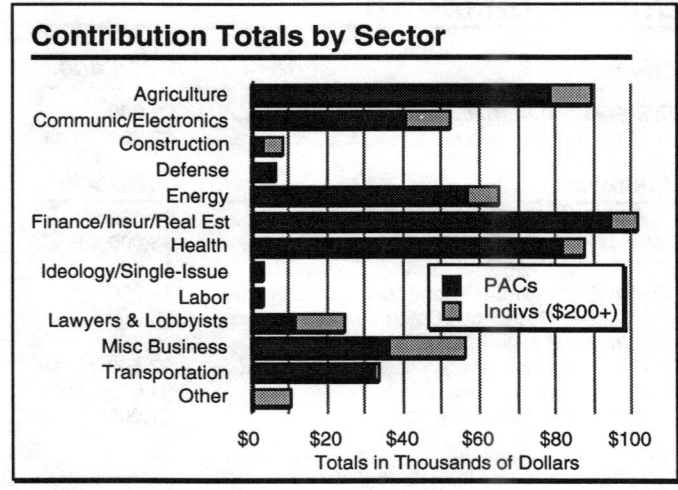

Totals in Thousands of Dollars

444

Source of Funds in 1992 Election

Source	Total	Pct
■ PACs	$441,292	61%
▨ Indivs $200+	$116,443	16%
□ Indivs under $200	$160,223	22%
⊠ Other	$3,568	0%
Candidate	$0	0%
Party	$83	0%

Source of PAC Dollars by Sector

Source	Total	Pct
■ Business	$436,388	99%
▨ Labor	$2,500	1%
□ Ideology/Single Issue	$2,200	0%

In-State vs. Out-of-State Contributions*

Source	Total	Pct
□ In-State	$86,495	74%
■ Out-of-state	$29,719	26%
No state listed	$229	

* by large individual contributors ($200 & above)

Computer Equipment & Services	$2,250	
None over $2,000		

Construction	$7,930	
General Contractors	**$2,340**	
None over $2,000		
Building Materials & Equipment ...	**$4,090**	
None over $2,000		

Defense	$6,000	
Defense Aerospace	**$2,000**	
None over $2,000		
Misc Defense	**$4,000**	
Tenneco Inc	$2,500	PAC

Energy & Natural Resources	$64,450	
Oil & Gas	**$31,125**	
Petroleum Marketers Assn	$5,000	PAC
Massey, Wood & West	$3,000	Indiv
Columbia Natural Resources	$2,275	PAC
Mining	**$11,375**	
Reynolds Metals	$3,875	PAC/Ind
Electric Utilities	**$17,450**	
Dominion Resources Inc	$3,100	PAC
Pacific Gas & Electric	$2,000	PAC
Waste Management	**:$3,250**	
None over $2,000		

Finance, Insurance & Real Estate	$100,792	
Commercial Banks	**$25,450**	
American Bankers Assn	$7,000	PAC
Citizens & Southern National Bank ...	$5,000	PAC
JP Morgan & Co	$2,500	PAC
Crestar Financial Corp	$2,375	PAC
Chase Manhattan	$2,000	PAC

Securities & Investment	$16,975	
Morgan Stanley & Co	$2,000	PAC

Insurance	$29,688	
American Council of Life Insurance	$2,438	PAC
Blue Cross & Blue Shield Assn*	$2,250	PAC
Travelers Corp	$2,000	PAC

Real Estate	$2,875	
None over $2,000		

Accountants	$24,154	
American Institute of CPA's	$10,000	PAC
Deloitte & Touche	$3,404	PAC
Coopers & Lybrand	$3,000	PAC
Ernst & Young	$3,000	PAC
Arthur Andersen & Co	$2,000	PAC
Price Waterhouse	$2,000	PAC

Health — $87,050

Health Professionals	$37,450	
American Chiropractic Assn	$5,000	PAC
American Podiatry Assn	$5,000	PAC
American Medical Assn	$4,600	PAC
American Dental Assn	$4,500	PAC
American College of Emergency Physicians	$2,000	PAC
American Optometric Assn	$2,000	PAC

Hospitals/Nursing Homes	$12,100	
American Hospital Assn	$3,000	PAC
American Health Care Assn	$2,500	PAC
Manor Healthcare Corp	$2,000	PAC

Health Services	$2,500	
None over $2,000		

Pharmaceuticals/Health Products	$35,000	
Upjohn Co	$2,750	PAC
American Home Products Corp	$2,000	PAC
Glaxo Inc	$2,000	PAC
Hoffman-La Roche	$2,000	PAC
Schering-Plough Corp	$2,000	PAC
Warner-Lambert	$2,000	PAC

Lawyers & Lobbyists — $23,723

Lawyers & Lobbyists	$23,723	
None over $2,000		

Spending in Last 3 Elections

	1988	1990	1992
Bliley	$366,816	$710,739	$698,964
Opponent	$0	$57,909	$0
Vote Pct	100%	65%	83%

Legend: Bliley / Opponent

Misc Business	$55,447	
Business Associations	**$2,000**	
Greater Washington Board of Trade	$2,000	PAC
Food & Beverage	**$4,600**	
None over $2,000		
Beer, Wine & Liquor	**$8,250**	
Smirnoff/Inglenook Distributors	$2,000	PAC
Retail Sales	**$5,207**	
None over $2,000		
Misc Services	**$2,500**	
National Funeral Directors Assn	$2,000	PAC
Business Services	**$4,240**	
None over $2,000		
Chemical & Related Manufacturing	**$13,850**	
Ethyl Corp	$8,850	PAC/Ind
Misc Manufacturing & Distributing	**$12,800**	
Dixie Container Corp	$3,000	Indiv
Hoechst Celanese Corp	$2,000	PAC
Stone Container Corp	$2,000	PAC

Transportation — $33,170

Air Transport	$5,790	
United Parcel Service	$3,290	PAC
Automotive	**$9,530**	
National Auto Dealers Assn	$5,000	PAC
Americans for Free International Trade	$2,000	PAC
Trucking	**$3,000**	
None over $2,000		
Railroads	**$12,100**	
CSX Corp*	$3,600	PAC/Ind
Union Pacific Corp	$2,500	PAC
Norfolk Southern Corp	$2,000	PAC
Sea Transport	**$2,000**	
None over $2,000		

Labor

Labor	$2,500	
Transportation Unions	**$2,000**	
Marine Engineers Dist 2 Maritime Offices	$2,000	PAC

Ideological/Single-Issue

Ideological/Single-Issue	$2,700	
None over $2,000		

Other & Unknown

Other	$10,000	
Retired	**$9,050**	
None over $2,000		

Unknown	$23,150	
No Employer Listed or Found	$3,000	
Employer Listed/Category Unknown	$18,050	
None over $2,000		

---

* Contributions came from more than one affiliate or subsidiary.

Peter Blute, R-Mass (3)

1993-94 Committees & Subcommittees

First elected: 1992

1991-92 Total Receipts:	$446,908
1992 Year-end Cash:	$4,753

Public Works and Transportation
Economic Development; Surface Transportation

Science, Space and Technology
Science; Technology, Environment and Aviation

Leading Contributors

Business

Agriculture		$2,200	
Crop Production & Basic Processing		**$1,000**	
Sawmill River Farm		$1,000	Indiv

Communications/Electronics		$6,625	
Printing & Publishing		**$1,700**	
Larkin Group		$1,000	Indiv
Media/Entertainment		**$1,800**	
Muirfield Village Golf Club		$1,800	Indiv
Electronics Mfg & Services		**$1,250**	
None over $1,000			
Computer Equipment & Services		**$1,875**	
EMC Corp		$1,375	Indiv

Construction		$6,700	
General Contractors		**$4,000**	
Associated General Contractors		$1,000	PAC
Morgan Construction		$1,000	Indiv
Plumb House Inc		$1,000	Indiv
Building Materials & Equipment		**$2,200**	
Logan Equipment		$1,700	Indiv

Defense		$1,275	
Defense Electronics		**$1,275**	
Raytheon Co		$1,275	Indiv

Source of Funds in 1992 Election

Source	Total	Pct
■ PACs	$43,910	9%
▨ Indivs $200+	$185,752	37%
☐ Indivs under $200	$202,732	40%
▨ Other	$68,233	14%
Candidate	$1,400	0%
Party	$59,723	12%

Source of PAC Dollars by Sector

Source	Total	Pct
■ Business	$33,300	80%
▨ Labor	$0	0%
☐ Ideology/Single Issue	$8,518	20%

In-State vs. Out-of-State Contributions*

Source	Total	Pct
☐ In-State	$160,252	87%
■ Out-of-state	$23,250	13%
No state listed	$2,250	

*** by large individual contributors ($200 & above)**

Energy & Natural Resources		$6,700	
Oil & Gas		**$3,250**	
Amoco Corp		$1,000	PAC
Exxon Corp		$1,000	PAC
Sun Co		$1,000	PAC
Commercial Fishing		**$1,500**	
National Fisheries Institute		$1,000	PAC

Finance, Insurance & Real Estate		$29,850	
Commercial Banks		**$2,500**	
None over $1,000			
Securities & Investment		**$7,250**	
Dean Witter		$1,500	PAC/Ind
Kidder, Peabody		$1,250	Indiv
Boston Co		$1,000	Indiv
Insurance		**$8,850**	
National Employee Benefit Services		$2,000	Indiv
Nathan Sallop Insurance		$1,450	Indiv
Aim Insurance Agency		$1,000	Indiv
Liberty Mutual Insurance		$1,000	PAC
Real Estate		**$3,700**	
Lynch, Murphy & Walsh		$1,500	Indiv
Charles River Properties		$1,000	Indiv
Accountants		**$4,800**	
American Institute of CPA's		$2,500	PAC
Misc Finance		**$2,500**	
Forward Financial Co		$1,500	Indiv

Contribution Totals by Sector

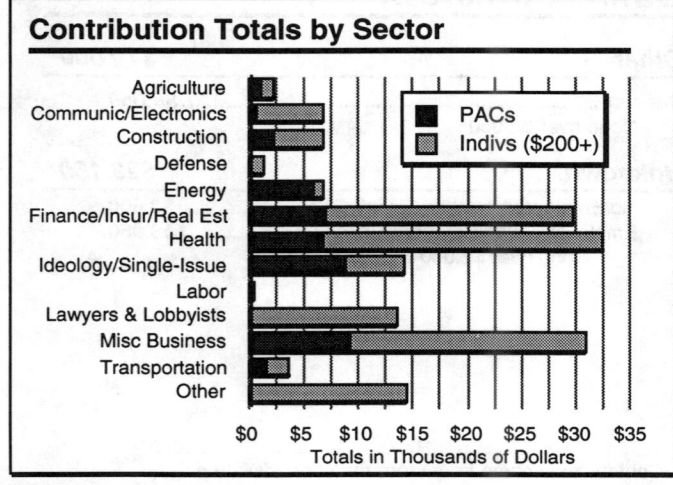

Legend: PACs (■); Indivs ($200+) (▨)

Sectors: Agriculture, Communic/Electronics, Construction, Defense, Energy, Finance/Insur/Real Est, Health, Ideology/Single-Issue, Labor, Lawyers & Lobbyists, Misc Business, Transportation, Other

Totals in Thousands of Dollars
$0 $5 $10 $15 $20 $25 $30 $35

Health $32,322

Health Professionals **$24,685**
    American Medical Assn .... $5,000 PAC
    Retina Consultants .... $1,700 Indiv
    College of American Pathologists .... $1,000 PAC

Hospitals/Nursing Homes **$2,937**
    Whittier Rehab Hospital .... $1,412 Indiv

Health Services **$1,000**
    None over $1,000

Misc Health **$3,200**
    Fallon Clinic .... $1,500 Indiv
    Trinet Health Care Consultants .... $1,000 Indiv

Lawyers & Lobbyists $13,700

Lawyers & Lobbyists **$13,700**
    Muldoon, Murphy & Faucette .... $2,000 Indiv
    Peters & Erskine .... $1,150 Indiv
    Choate, Hall & Stewart .... $1,000 Indiv
    Fletcher, Tilton & Whipple .... $1,000 Indiv

Misc Business $30,750

Business Associations **$2,200**
    National Fedn of Independent Business .... $1,500 PAC

Food & Beverage **$5,200**
    Chili's Inc .... $1,000 PAC
    Coca-Cola Bottling .... $1,000 Indiv
    National Restaurant Assn .... $1,000 PAC
    S&A Restaurant Corp .... $1,000 PAC

Beer, Wine & Liquor **$4,250**
    Consolidated Beverages .... $2,000 Indiv
    Colonial Wholesale Beverage .... $1,000 Indiv
    Quality Beverage Inc .... $1,000 Indiv

Retail Sales **$1,250**
    None over $1,000

Business Services **$4,400**
    Bain & Co .... $1,000 Indiv
    National Assn of Temporary Services .... $1,000 PAC

Lodging/Tourism **$1,000**
    None over $1,000

Chemical & Related Manufacturing **$1,250**
    Cabot Corp .... $1,250 Indiv

Steel Production **$4,750**
    Kervick Enterprises .... $4,750 Indiv

Misc Manufacturing & Distributing **$5,000**
    Vacuum Barrier Corp .... $2,000 Indiv

Textiles **$1,200**
    Stevens Linen Assoc .... $1,200 Indiv

Transportation $3,500

Automotive **$3,000**
    Muzi Ford City .... $2,000 Indiv
    Eaton Corp .... $1,000 PAC

Ideological/Single-Issue

Ideological/Single-Issue $14,098

Republican/Conservative **$5,348**
    None over $1,000

Leadership PACs **$3,000**
    Republican Leader's Fund (Bob Michel) .... $2,000 PAC
    Future Leaders PAC (Jerry Lewis) .... $1,000 PAC

Pro-Israel **$1,250**
    Congressional Action Cmte of Texas .... $1,000 PAC

Pro-Life **$1,250**
    Republican National Coalition for Life .... $1,000 PAC

Gun Rights/Gun Control **$2,000**
    National Rifle Assn .... $2,000 PAC

Misc Issues **$1,250**
    None over $1,000

Other & Unknown

Other $14,325

Civil Servants/Public Officials **$2,175**
    Commonwealth of Massachusetts .... $1,625 Indiv

Education **$1,700**
    Assumption College .... $1,000 Indiv

Retired **$10,450**
    None over $1,000

Unknown $65,275

    Homemakers/Non-income earners $6,650
    No Employer Listed or Found $38,775
    Generic Occupation/Category Unknown $2,000
    Employer Listed/Category Unknown $17,850
        Coghlin Electric .... $1,050 Indiv
        Arlington Heights Transportation .... $1,000 Indiv
        Dolphin Resource Group .... $1,000 Indiv
        Education Management Corp .... $1,000 Indiv
        Emerson Lane .... $1,000 Indiv
        Jen Nuffy Inc .... $1,000 Indiv
        TA Communications Partners .... $1,000 Indiv

Independent expenditures supporting Blute
    National Right to Life PAC $1,513

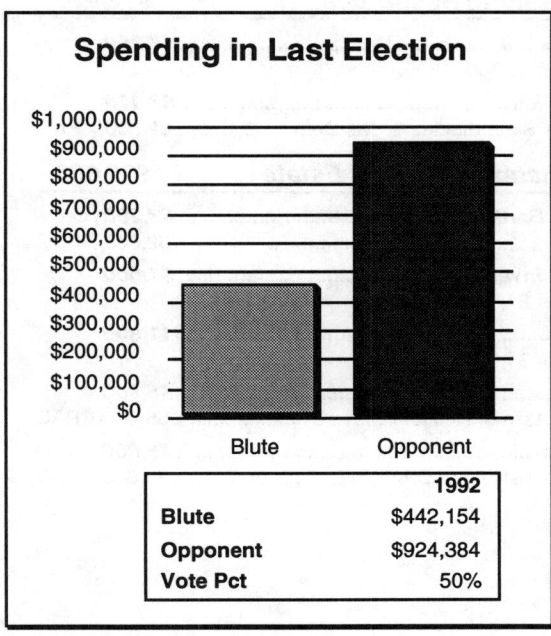

Spending in Last Election

	1992
Blute	$442,154
Opponent	$924,384
Vote Pct	50%

Sherwood Boehlert, R-NY (23)

First elected: 1982

1991-92 Total Receipts: $368,179
1992 Year-end Cash: $185,722

1991-92 Committees & Subcommittees

Public Works and Transportation
Aviation; Economic Development; Surface Transportation

Science, Space and Technology
Investigations and Oversight (Ranking Republican); Science

Select Committee on Aging

Leading Contributors

Business

Agriculture	$17,700

Crop Production & Basic Processing **$2,000**
    None over $1,500

Tobacco **$2,000**
    None over $1,500

Dairy **$7,750**
    Associated Milk Producers .... $4,000   PAC
    Agri-Mark Inc .... $2,000   PAC

Agricultural Services/Products **$3,000**
    None over $1,500

Food Processing & Sales **$2,700**
    Food Marketing Institute .... $1,500   PAC

Communications/Electronics	$15,650

Printing & Publishing **$5,000**
    Wolfe News .... $2,000   Indiv
    Cullman Ventures Inc .... $1,500   Indiv

Telephone Utilities **$4,000**
    New York Telephone .... $1,750   PAC/Ind
    AT&T .... $1,500   PAC

Telecom Services & Equipment **$1,500**
    None over $1,500

Electronics Mfg & Services **$3,500**
    Par Technology Inc .... $2,500   Indiv

Source of Funds in 1992 Election

Source	Total	Pct
PACs	$197,190	53%
Indivs $200+	$93,050	25%
Indivs under $200	$49,760	13%
Other	$31,679	9%
Candidate	$0	0%
Party	$5,043	1%

Source of PAC Dollars by Sector

Source	Total	Pct
Business	$123,247	66%
Labor	$54,830	30%
Ideology/Single Issue	$7,519	4%

In-State vs. Out-of-State Contributions*

Source	Total	Pct
In-State	$85,800	92%
Out-of-state	$7,000	8%
No state listed	$0	

* by large individual contributors ($200 & above)

Construction	$12,700

General Contractors **$5,500**
    Associated General Contractors .... $2,000   PAC

Construction Services **$2,200**
    None over $1,500

Building Materials & Equipment **$2,850**
    None over $1,500

Defense	$6,000

Defense Aerospace **$5,500**
    None over $1,500

Energy & Natural Resources	$12,920

Oil & Gas **$4,250**
    None over $1,500

Electric Utilities **$7,170**
    New York State Electric & Gas Corp .... $2,500   PAC

Finance, Insurance & Real Estate	$36,600

Commercial Banks **$7,200**
    Citicorp .... $2,000   PAC

Securities & Investment **$1,500**
    None over $1,500

Insurance **$11,900**
    None over $1,500

Real Estate **$6,800**
    National Assn of Realtors .... $6,000   PAC

Accountants **$5,800**
    American Institute of CPA's .... $5,000   PAC

Contribution Totals by Sector

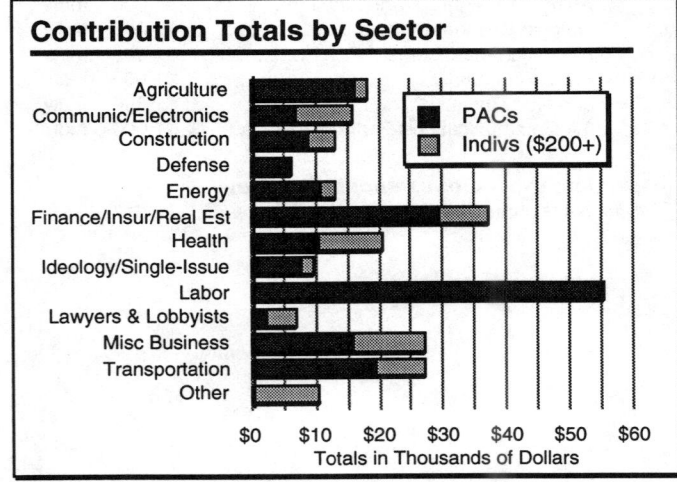

Agriculture
Communic/Electronics
Construction
Defense
Energy
Finance/Insur/Real Est
Health
Ideology/Single-Issue
Labor
Lawyers & Lobbyists
Misc Business
Transportation
Other

■ PACs
▨ Indivs ($200+)

$0 $10 $20 $30 $40 $50 $60
Totals in Thousands of Dollars

Health $20,300

Health Professionals **$18,300**
   American Medical Assn..........................$5,000   PAC
   American Dental Assn ....$2,000   PAC

Lawyers & Lobbyists $6,800

Lawyers & Lobbyists....................................**$6,800**
   Leboeuf, Lamb et al ....$2,500   PAC/Ind

Misc Business $28,307

Food & Beverage **$2,600**
   None over $1,500

Beer, Wine & Liquor **$5,000**
   Wine & Spirits Wholesalers of America ....$2,500   PAC

Retail Sales **$2,257**
   None over $1,500

Business Services **$1,550**
   None over $1,500

Lodging/Tourism **$1,850**
   None over $1,500

Chemical & Related Manufacturing **$3,000**
   None over $1,500

Misc Manufacturing & Distributing **$7,150**
   None over $1,500

Textiles...**$2,500**
   Raschel Fashion ....$2,000   Indiv

Transportation $26,570

Air Transport **$11,050**
   General Electric....................................$2,850   PAC/Ind
   Aircraft Owners & Pilots Assn ....$2,000   PAC
   United Parcel Service..........................$1,500   PAC

Automotive **$3,750**
   Utica Metal Products Inc ....$1,500   Indiv

Trucking...**$1,520**
   None over $1,500

Railroads **$6,750**
   None over $1,500

Misc Transport..**$2,750**
   Bus Industries of America ....$2,000   Indiv

Labor

Labor $54,830

Building Trade Unions **$12,500**
   Carpenters & Joiners Union ....$5,500   PAC
   Laborers' Political League ....$3,000   PAC
   Plumbers/Pipefitters Union..................$2,000   PAC

Industrial Unions **$4,750**
   None over $1,500

Transportation Unions **$19,250**
   Air Line Pilots Assn ....$10,000   PAC
   Teamsters Union ....$5,000   PAC
   Marine Engineers Dist 2 Maritime Offices ....$2,000   PAC

Public Sector Unions **$12,330**
   National Education Assn ....$3,000   PAC
   National Assn of Letter Carriers ....$2,500   PAC
   International Assn of Firefighters ....$2,000   PAC

Misc Unions..**$6,000**
   Food & Commercial Workers Union ....$5,500   PAC

Ideological/Single-Issue

Ideological/Single-Issue $9,519

Pro-Choice...**$6,519**
   Republicans for Choice ....$1,519   PAC
   National Abortion Rights Action League ....$1,500   PAC

Misc Issues...**$2,000**
   None over $1,500

Other & Unknown

Other $10,350

Education **$2,000**
   None over $1,500

Retired **$7,350**
   None over $1,500

Unknown $20,150

   Employer Listed/Category Unknown $18,900
    Norwich-Eaton.............................$3,200   Indiv
    Mann Block Associates ....$2,000   Indiv

Spending in Last 3 Elections

	1988	1990	1992
Boehlert	$145,883	$272,533	$372,109
Opponent	$0	$0	$63,220
Vote Pct	100%	84%	64%

Legend: Boehlert / Opponent

John A. Boehner, R-Ohio (8)

First elected: 1990

1991-92 Total Receipts: $555,139
1992 Year-end Cash: $31,376

1991-92 Committees & Subcommittees

Agriculture
Conservation, Credit and Rural Development; Cotton, Rice and Sugar; Department Operations, Research and Foreign Agriculture; Livestock, Dairy and Poultry

Education and Labor
Elementary, Secondary and Vocational Education; Health and Safety; Labor-Management Relations

Small Business
Exports, Tax Policy and Special Problems

Leading Contributors

Business

Agriculture	$64,488

Crop Production & Basic Processing **$13,868**
    American Sugarbeet Growers Assn .... $1,500   PAC

Tobacco **$8,503**
    RJR Nabisco .... $4,300   PAC
    Philip Morris .... $3,053   PAC

Dairy **$9,800**
    Milk Marketing Inc .... $6,350   PAC
    Milk Industry Foundation .... $1,550   PAC

Poultry & Eggs **$4,550**
    None over $1,500

Livestock **$3,400**
    National Cattlemen's Assn* .... $1,950   PAC

Agricultural Services/Products **$9,850**
    Ohio Farm Bureau Federation .... $2,000   PAC

Food Processing & Sales **$7,525**
    Food Marketing Institute .... $2,000   PAC

Forestry & Forest Products **$6,750**
    Westvaco Corp .... $2,000   PAC
    Mead Corp .... $1,500   PAC

Source of Funds in 1992 Election

Source	Total	Pct
■ PACs	$238,839	43%
▨ Indivs $200+	$107,699	19%
☐ Indivs under $200	$200,801	36%
▨ Other	$7,800	1%
Candidate	$0	0%
Party	$213	0%

Source of PAC Dollars by Sector

Source	Total	Pct
■ Business	$224,101	95%
▨ Labor	$1,450	1%
☐ Ideology/Single Issue	$10,082	4%

In-State vs. Out-of-State Contributions*

Source	Total	Pct
☐ In-State	$105,999	98%
■ Out-of-state	$1,700	2%
No state listed	$0	

***by large individual contributors ($200 & above)**

Communications/Electronics	$24,425

Media/Entertainment **$5,300**
    National Cable Television Assn .... $2,300   PAC
    Time Warner* .... $1,600   PAC

Telephone Utilities **$17,350**
    Ameritech Corp* .... $6,650   PAC
    AT&T .... $2,500   PAC
    BellSouth Corp* .... $2,350   PAC
    United Telecommunications .... $2,000   PAC

Construction	$31,541

General Contractors **$20,492**
    Joseph & Co .... $3,050   Indiv
    Associated General Contractors .... $2,050   PAC
    Ferguson Construction .... $1,600   Indiv
    National Utility Contractors Assn .... $1,500   PAC

Home Builders **$5,449**
    National Assn of Home Builders .... $4,999   PAC

Special Trade Contractors **$4,150**
    None over $1,500

Defense	$4,450

Defense Aerospace **$4,200**
    Lockheed Corp .... $1,650   PAC

Energy & Natural Resources	$17,434

Oil & Gas **$7,100**
    Ashland Oil .... $2,000   PAC
    Columbia Gas System* .... $1,550   PAC

Mining **$2,600**
    None over $1,500

Electric Utilities **$7,084**
    Dayton Power & Light .... $3,200   PAC

Contribution Totals by Sector

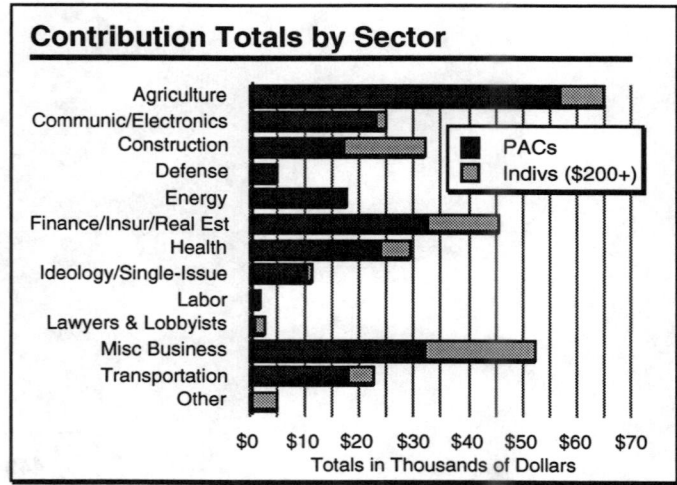

Agriculture
Communic/Electronics
Construction
Defense
Energy
Finance/Insur/Real Est
Health
Ideology/Single-Issue
Labor
Lawyers & Lobbyists
Misc Business
Transportation
Other

■ PACs
▨ Indivs ($200+)

$0 $10 $20 $30 $40 $50 $60 $70
Totals in Thousands of Dollars

Finance, Insurance & Real Estate — $45,208

Commercial Banks $8,592
   Second National Bank ....$2,700   Indiv
   American Bankers Assn* ....$2,500   PAC

Securities & Investment $7,025
   Gradison & Co ....$2,600   Indiv

Insurance $13,549
   Nationwide Corp ....$1,884   PAC

Real Estate $10,692
   National Assn of Realtors ....$8,000   PAC

Accountants $2,800
   American Institute of CPA's ....$2,000   PAC

Misc Finance $1,550
   None over $1,500

Health — $29,151

Health Professionals $24,342
   American Medical Assn ....$9,700   PAC
   American Academy of Ophthalmology ...$7,000   PAC
   American Dental Assn* ....$2,300   PAC
   American Chiropractic Assn* ....$1,500   PAC

Pharmaceuticals/Health Products $2,725
   None over $1,500

Lawyers & Lobbyists — $2,409

Lawyers & Lobbyists $2,409
   None over $1,500

Misc Business — $51,881

Food & Beverage $6,934
   National Restaurant Assn ....$2,900   PAC

Beer, Wine & Liquor $4,200
   National Beer Wholesalers Assn ....$3,000   PAC

Retail Sales $4,450
   None over $1,500

Misc Services $2,100
   None over $1,500

Business Services $3,882
   LM Berry & Co ....$1,882   PAC/Ind

Chemical & Related Manufacturing $3,450
   None over $1,500

Steel Production $4,100
   Armco Inc ....$2,800   PAC

Misc Manufacturing & Distributing ...$19,865
   Crown Equipment Corp ....$5,600   Indiv
   West Chester Marketing ....$2,680   Indiv
   Corning Glass Works ....$2,000   PAC
   Tipp Novelty Co ....$1,500   Indiv

Transportation — $22,376

Air Transport $5,075
   United Parcel Service ....$2,750   PAC

Automotive $13,267
   National Auto Dealers Assn ....$4,050   PAC
   Auto Dealers & Drivers for Free Trade ...$3,500   PAC
   Americans for Free International Trade ...$2,350   PAC
   Honda of America ....$1,500   Indiv

Misc Transport $2,034
   None over $1,500

Ideological/Single-Issue

Ideological/Single-Issue — $10,832

Republican/Conservative $6,375
   Southwest Ohio Concerned Citizens ...$4,875   PAC

Gun Rights/Gun Control $3,000
   National Rifle Assn ....$3,000   PAC

Other & Unknown

Other — $4,584

Retired $4,334
   None over $1,500

Unknown — $33,103

   No Employer Listed or Found $2,542
   Generic Occupation/Category Unknown ...$2,000
   Employer Listed/Category Unknown $27,361
      Busemeyer Co ....$4,700   Indiv
      Omni Knitting ....$1,542   Indiv

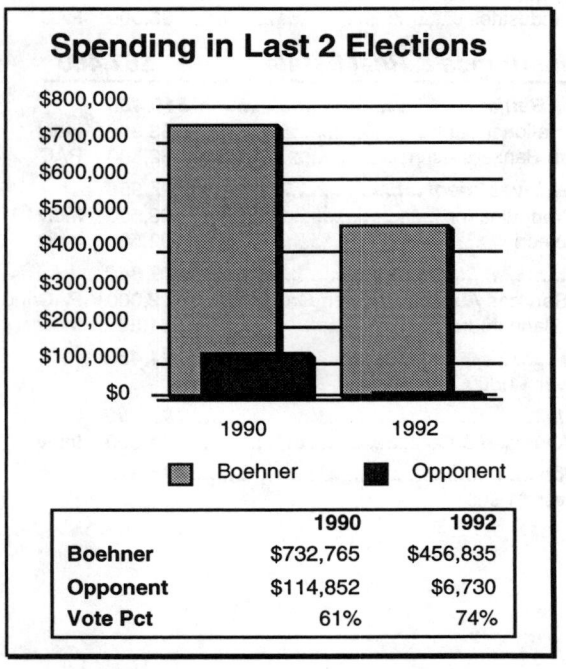

Spending in Last 2 Elections

	1990	1992
Boehner	$732,765	$456,835
Opponent	$114,852	$6,730
Vote Pct	61%	74%

* Contributions came from more than one affiliate or subsidiary.

451

Henry Bonilla, R-Texas (23)

First elected: 1992

1991-92 Total Receipts: $550,673
1992 Year-end Cash: -$5,359

1993-94 Committees & Subcommittees

Appropriations
District of Columbia; Labor, Health and Human Services, Education and Related Agencies

Leading Contributors

Business

Agriculture	$35,730	
Livestock **$24,330**		
Texas Cattle Feeders Assn $2,000	PAC	
Jones Cattle Co $1,500	Indiv	
Agricultural Services/Products **$5,950**		
Texas Farm Bureau $5,000	PAC	
Food Processing & Sales **$4,000**		
Flowers Industries $2,000	PAC	

Communications/Electronics	$17,100	
Printing & Publishing **$6,650**		
Harte-Hanks Communications $3,750	Indiv	
Media/Entertainment **$6,000**		
KENS-TV $2,750	Indiv	
National Assn of Broadcasters $2,000	PAC	
Telephone Utilities **$3,950**		
AT&T $1,500	PAC	

Construction	$17,200	
General Contractors **$9,450**		
HB Zachry Co $1,500	Indiv	
Home Builders **$2,500**		
None over $1,500		
Building Materials & Equipment **$4,250**		
Holt Companies $2,000	Indiv	

Defense	$1,750
None over $1,500	

Source of Funds in 1992 Election

Source	Total	Pct
■ PACs	$109,888	18%
▨ Indivs $200+	$301,176	51%
☐ Indivs under $200	$81,034	14%
⊠ Other	$103,075	17%
Candidate	$17,790	3%
Party	$68,000	11%

Source of PAC Dollars by Sector

Source	Total	Pct
■ Business	$96,881	92%
▨ Labor	$0	0%
☐ Ideology/Single Issue	$8,480	8%

In-State vs. Out-of-State Contributions*

Source	Total	Pct
☐ In-State	$287,926	98%
■ Out-of-state	$5,250	2%
No state listed	$1,000	

* by large individual contributors ($200 & above)

Energy & Natural Resources	$62,150	
Oil & Gas **$58,150**		
Valero Energy Corp $11,500	Indiv	
Diamond Shamrock Inc $6,250	PAC	
Ashland Oil $2,000	PAC	
Chevron Corp $2,000	PAC	
Killam Oil Co $2,000	Indiv	
Sun Co $2,000	PAC	
Granite Oil $1,500	Indiv	
PK Pipe & Tubing Inc $1,500	Indiv	
Tesoro Petroleum Corp $1,500	Indiv	
Misc Energy **$3,000**		
Cooper Industries $3,000	PAC	

Finance, Insurance & Real Estate	$67,460	
Commercial Banks **$10,400**		
Laredo National Bank $3,900	Indiv	
American Bankers Assn $2,500	PAC	
Securities & Investment **$7,950**		
Hixon Properties Inc $2,500	Indiv	
Merrill Lynch $2,500	Indiv	
Insurance **$29,840**		
United Services Automobile Assn Group $12,000	PAC/Ind	
Benefit Planners Inc $1,500	Indiv	
Real Estate **$4,450**		
None over $1,500		
Accountants **$3,300**		
Arthur Andersen & Co $1,900	Indiv	
Misc Finance **$11,520**		
None over $1,500		

Contribution Totals by Sector

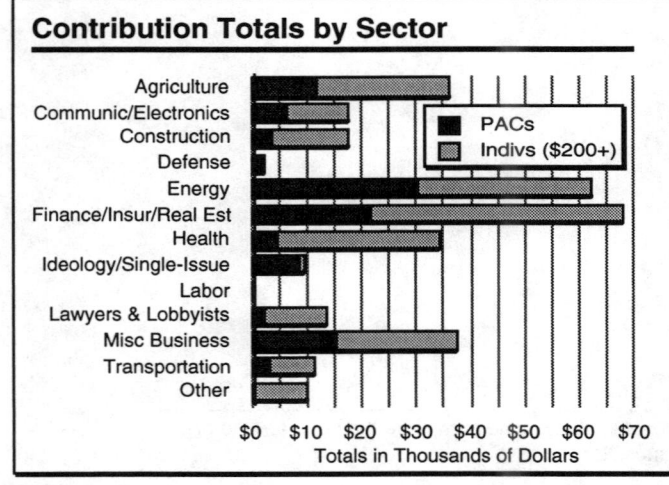

Agriculture
Communic/Electronics
Construction
Defense
Energy
Finance/Insur/Real Est
Health
Ideology/Single-Issue
Labor
Lawyers & Lobbyists
Misc Business
Transportation
Other

■ PACs
▨ Indivs ($200+)

$0 $10 $20 $30 $40 $50 $60 $70
Totals in Thousands of Dollars

Health $33,700

Health Professionals $27,700
    None over $1,500
Hospitals/Nursing Homes $2,200
    Humana Inc ....$2,200   PAC/Ind
Pharmaceuticals/Health Products $2,000
    None over $1,500

Lawyers & Lobbyists $13,428

Lawyers & Lobbyists $13,428
    None over $1,500

Misc Business $37,248

Business Associations $4,041
    National Fedn of Independent Business ....$3,000   PAC
Food & Beverage $4,250
    None over $1,500
Retail Sales $3,300
    None over $1,500
Misc Services $4,941
    Comet Cleaners ....$1,500   Indiv
    Harts for Hair ....$1,500   Indiv
Business Services $7,021
    None over $1,500
Lodging/Tourism $1,745
    None over $1,500
Misc Business $2,350
    None over $1,500
Chemical & Related Manufacturing $3,550
    Dow Chemical ....$3,000   PAC
Misc Manufacturing & Distributing $4,750
    Stone Container Corp ....$1,500   PAC

Transportation $11,150

Automotive $8,650
    Curtis C Gunn Inc ....$1,500   Indiv
Railroads $1,500
    None over $1,500

Ideological/Single-Issue

Ideological/Single-Issue $9,180

Republican/Conservative $2,680
    None over $1,500
Leadership PACs $5,000
    Republican Leader's Fund (Bob Michel) ....$3,000   PAC
Misc Issues $1,500
    None over $1,500

Other & Unknown

Other $9,800

Retired $7,750
    None over $1,500

Unknown $83,641

    Homemakers/Non-income earners $11,000
    No Employer Listed or Found $26,870
    Generic Occupation/Category Unknown $1,700
    Employer Listed/Category Unknown $44,071
        Newman Brothers Drilling ....$2,000   Indiv
        Don Johnson Co ....$1,608   Indiv
        La Gente Sales & Associates ....$1,500   Indiv

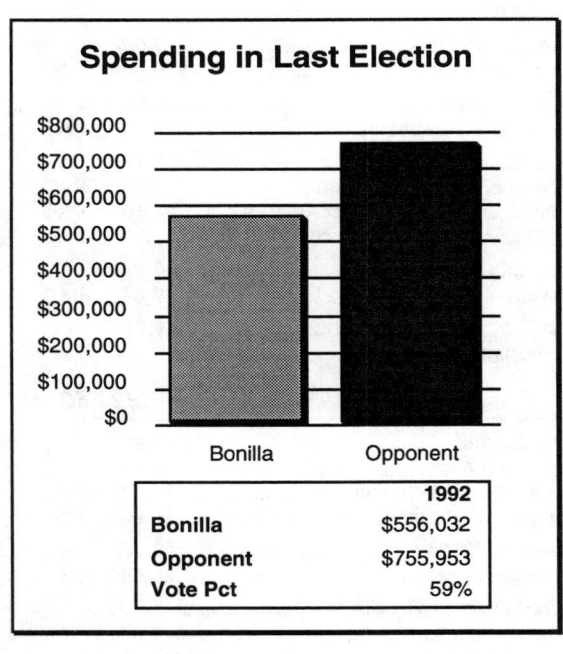

Spending in Last Election

	1992
Bonilla	$556,032
Opponent	$755,953
Vote Pct	59%

David E. Bonior, D-Mich (10)

First elected: 1976

1991-92 Total Receipts: $1,295,553
1992 Year-end Cash: $40,391

1991-92 Committees & Subcommittees

Rules
Rules of the House

Select Committee on Intelligence

Leading Contributors

Business

Agriculture $82,435

Crop Production & Basic Processing $32,675
  Sun-Diamond Growers* .... $10,000 PAC

Tobacco $18,000
  RJR Nabisco .... $9,500 PAC
  Philip Morris .... $6,500 PAC/Ind

Dairy $14,560
  Mid-America Dairymen .... $7,000 PAC
  Associated Milk Producers .... $6,500 PAC

Agricultural Services/Products $6,750
  None over $5,000

Food Processing & Sales $7,450
  None over $5,000

Communications/Electronics $88,150

Media/Entertainment $31,900
  National Cable Television Assn .... $10,000 PAC
  Comcast Corp .... $5,000 PAC

Telephone Utilities $49,250
  BellSouth Corp* .... $10,000 PAC
  Michigan Bell Telephone .... $7,200 PAC/Ind
  Pacific Telesis Group .... $7,000 PAC
  Ameritech Corp .... $6,500 PAC/Ind
  NYNEX Corp .... $5,000 PAC

Construction $18,830

Construction Services $8,730
  None over $5,000

Source of Funds in 1992 Election

Source	Total	Pct
PACs	$934,589	70%
Indivs $200+	$174,492	13%
Indivs under $200	$107,417	8%
Other	$109,625	8%
Candidate	$0	0%
Party	$59,470	4%

Source of PAC Dollars by Sector

Source	Total	Pct
Business	$576,864	61%
Labor	$283,798	30%
Ideology/Single Issue	$78,459	8%

In-State vs. Out-of-State Contributions*

Source	Total	Pct
In-State	$92,180	53%
Out-of-state	$82,312	47%
No state listed	$0	

* by large individual contributors ($200 & above)

Defense $17,600

Defense Aerospace $14,100
  Textron Inc .... $6,000 PAC

Energy & Natural Resources $42,100

Oil & Gas $19,900
  None over $5,000

Electric Utilities $17,200
  Consumers Power Co .... $8,500 PAC

Finance, Insurance & Real Estate $159,979

Commercial Banks $18,225
  None over $5,000

Credit Unions $10,000
  Credit Union National Assn* .... $10,000 PAC

Securities & Investment $28,600
  Chicago Mercantile Exchange .... $10,000 PAC

Insurance $66,275
  National Assn of Life Underwriters .... $10,000 PAC
  Independent Insurance Agents of America .... $8,500 PAC
  American Council of Life Insurance .... $5,000 PAC

Real Estate $20,279
  National Assn of Realtors .... $7,879 PAC

Accountants $11,250
  American Institute of CPA's .... $10,000 PAC

Health $82,650

Health Professionals $49,950
  American Dental Assn .... $9,000 PAC
  American Academy of Ophthalmology .... $5,000 PAC
  American College of Emergency Physicians .... $5,000 PAC

Hospitals/Nursing Homes $12,050
  American Hospital Assn .... $6,550 PAC

Pharmaceuticals/Health Products $15,250
  Upjohn Co .... $10,000 PAC/Ind

Contribution Totals by Sector

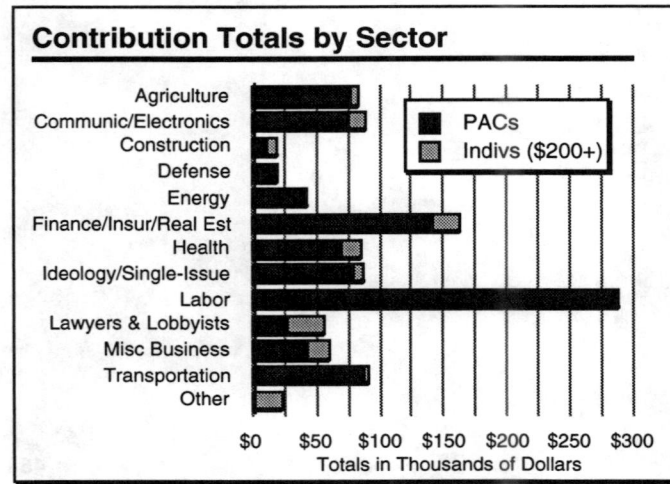

Agriculture, Communic/Electronics, Construction, Defense, Energy, Finance/Insur/Real Est, Health, Ideology/Single-Issue, Labor, Lawyers & Lobbyists, Misc Business, Transportation, Other

■ PACs
▨ Indivs ($200+)

$0 $50 $100 $150 $200 $250 $300
Totals in Thousands of Dollars

Lawyers & Lobbyists $55,540

Lawyers & Lobbyists $55,540
    Assn of Trial Lawyers of America ....$10,000 PAC

Misc Business $58,845

Food & Beverage $13,450
    None over $5,000

Beer, Wine & Liquor $17,895
    National Beer Wholesalers Assn ....$6,000 PAC

Retail Sales $10,700
    None over $5,000

Misc Manufacturing & Distributing $6,050
    None over $5,000

Transportation $88,925

Air Transport $30,475
    Federal Express Corp ....$10,000 PAC
    Northwest Airlines ....$8,950 PAC
    United Parcel Service.......................................$5,025 PAC

Automotive $19,150
    Ford Motor Co ....$8,900 PAC/Ind
    Chrysler Corp ....$8,000 PAC

Trucking $7,950
    None over $5,000

Railroads...$13,250
    None over $5,000

Sea Transport..$17,600
    National Marine Manufacturers Assn ....$10,000 PAC

Labor

Labor $286,688

Building Trade Unions $45,750
    Carpenters & Joiners Union ....$10,000 PAC
    Laborers' Political League ....$10,000 PAC
    Plumbers/Pipefitters Union* ....$8,550 PAC

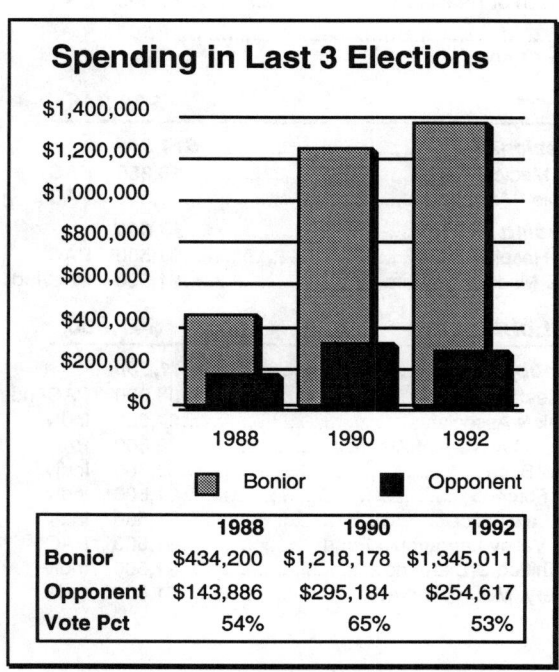

Spending in Last 3 Elections

	1988	1990	1992
Bonior	$434,200	$1,218,178	$1,345,011
Opponent	$143,886	$295,184	$254,617
Vote Pct	54%	65%	53%

Legend: ▨ Bonior   ■ Opponent

Industrial Unions $67,978
    Machinists/Aerospace Workers Union ....$10,000 PAC
    United Steelworkers ....$10,000 PAC
    United Mine Workers ....$9,000 PAC
    Communications Workers of America ....$8,998 PAC
    United Auto Workers ....$8,760 PAC
    Intl Brotherhood of Electrical Workers ....$7,500 PAC

Transportation Unions $73,400
    Air Line Pilots Assn ....$10,000 PAC
    Marine Engineers Union* ....$10,000 PAC
    Seafarers International Union ....$10,000 PAC
    Teamsters Union ....$10,000 PAC
    United Transportation Union ....$10,000 PAC
    Amalgamated Transit Union ....$5,000 PAC

Public Sector Unions $70,160
    American Fedn of St/Cnty/Munic Employees ....$10,000 PAC
    American Postal Workers Union ....$10,000 PAC
    National Education Assn ....$10,000 PAC
    National Assn of Letter Carriers ....$9,990 PAC
    American Federation of Teachers ....$9,850 PAC
    National Assn Retired Federal Employees ....$5,000 PAC

Misc Unions..$29,400
    Food & Commercial Workers Union ....$8,000 PAC
    AFL-CIO ....$7,000 PAC
    Office & Professional Employees Union ....$5,000 PAC
    Service Employees International Union ....$5,000 PAC

Ideological/Single-Issue

Ideological/Single-Issue $84,671

Democratic/Liberal $29,110
    12th District Democratic Cmte ....$10,000 PAC
    Clinton Township Democratic Club ....$10,000 PAC
    Philip A Hart Democratic Club ....$5,150 PAC

Leadership PACs $6,000
    None over $5,000

Foreign & Defense Policy $5,310
    None over $5,000

Human Rights $14,500
    KidsPAC ....$10,000 PAC

Misc Issues $25,749
    National Cmte to Preserve Social Security ....$10,000 PAC
    Sierra Club ....$7,499 PAC
    League of Conservation Voters ....$5,000 PAC

Other & Unknown

Other $22,225

Civil Servants/Public Officials............................$7,525
    None over $5,000

Education $7,125
    None over $5,000

Retired $6,075
    None over $5,000

Unknown $25,075
    Homemakers/Non-income earners $5,200
    Employer Listed/Category Unknown $17,775
        None over $5,000

---

* Contributions came from more than one affiliate or
subsidiary.

Robert A. Borski, D-Pa (3)

First elected: 1982

1991-92 Total Receipts: $512,477
1992 Year-end Cash: $3,481

1991-92 Committees & Subcommittees

Merchant Marine and Fisheries
Merchant Marine; Oversight and Investigations

Public Works and Transportation
Investigations and Oversight (Chairman); Public Buildings and Grounds; Water Resources

Select Committee on Aging

Leading Contributors

Business

Agriculture		$1,515
None over $1,500		

Communications/Electronics		$12,500
Media/Entertainment		$3,000
Comcast Corp	$2,000	PAC
Telephone Utilities		$9,000
AT&T	$8,000	PAC

Construction		$23,447
General Contractors		$10,950
Associated General Contractors	$2,000	PAC
Home Builders		$2,000
None over $1,500		
Construction Services		$6,000
None over $1,500		
Building Materials & Equipment		$3,497
Angelo Brothers Inc	$2,997	Indiv

Defense		$10,500
Defense Electronics		$9,000
SPD Technologies	$8,000	PAC

Energy & Natural Resources		$11,000
Oil & Gas		$4,000
None over $1,500		
Misc Energy		$2,000
None over $1,500		
Electric Utilities		$3,500
Philadelphia Electric	$2,500	PAC

Source of Funds in 1992 Election

Source	Total	Pct
PACs	$274,819	53%
Indivs $200+	$155,783	30%
Indivs under $200	$54,650	11%
Other	$28,862	6%
Candidate	$0	0%
Party	$1,787	0%

Source of PAC Dollars by Sector

Source	Total	Pct
Business	$115,348	42%
Labor	$149,395	55%
Ideology/Single Issue	$9,023	3%

In-State vs. Out-of-State Contributions*

Source	Total	Pct
In-State	$126,249	81%
Out-of-state	$28,868	19%
No state listed	$666	

* by large individual contributors ($200 & above)

Finance, Insurance & Real Estate — $36,850

Commercial Banks		$4,300
American Bankers Assn	$2,000	PAC
Securities & Investment		$5,500
Philadelphia Stock Exchange	$1,750	PAC/Ind
Insurance		$9,500
Penn Mutual Life Insurance	$3,500	PAC
Graham Co	$2,000	Indiv
Real Estate		$14,550
Linpro Co	$4,250	Indiv
National Assn of Realtors	$3,000	PAC
Accountants		$1,500
None over $1,500		

Health — $18,348

Health Professionals		$14,348
American Medical Assn	$6,350	PAC
Osteopathic PAC	$1,500	PAC
Hospitals/Nursing Homes		$3,000
American Hospital Assn	$1,500	PAC
Geriatric & Medical Centers Inc	$1,500	PAC/Ind

Lawyers & Lobbyists — $41,000

Lawyers & Lobbyists		$41,000
Reid & Priest	$6,000	PAC/Ind
SR Wojdak & Associates	$4,000	Indiv
Assn of Trial Lawyers of America	$2,500	PAC
Fineman & Bach	$2,000	Indiv
Brobyn & Forceno	$1,500	Indiv
Cameron Law Office	$1,500	Indiv
Delaware Valley Leadership Fund	$1,500	PAC
Lipsen, Whitten & Diamond	$1,500	Indiv
Montgomery, McCracken et al	$1,500	Indiv

Contribution Totals by Sector

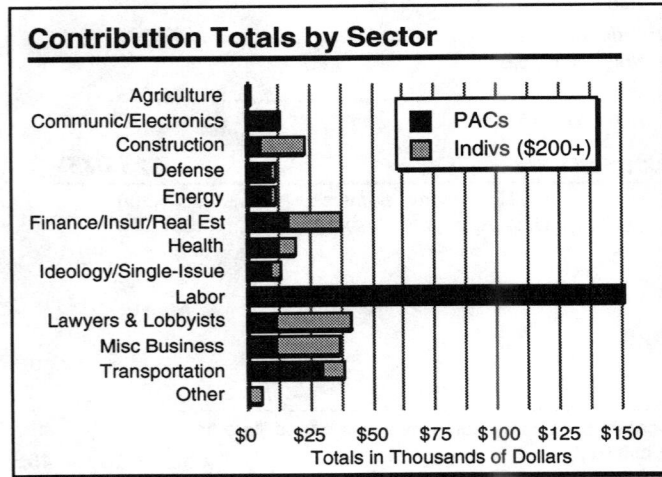

Agriculture, Communic/Electronics, Construction, Defense, Energy, Finance/Insur/Real Est, Health, Ideology/Single-Issue, Labor, Lawyers & Lobbyists, Misc Business, Transportation, Other

■ PACs ▨ Indivs ($200+)

$0 $25 $50 $75 $100 $125 $150
Totals in Thousands of Dollars

Misc Business $35,644

Beer, Wine & Liquor **$2,500**
    None over $1,500

Retail Sales **$3,750**
    United Vending Service .... $2,000   Indiv

Business Services **$9,725**
    Keystone Outdoor Advertising Inc .... $2,000   Indiv
    Outdoor Advertising Assn of America .... $2,000   PAC
    Lehrer, McGovern, Bovis Inc .... $1,500   Indiv

Chemical & Related Manufacturing **$7,323**
    Airwick Professional Products .... $2,500   Indiv
    Pennwalt Corp .... $2,000   PAC

Misc Manufacturing & Distributing **$11,000**
    Crown Cork & Seal Co .... $2,000   PAC
    Franklin Smelting & Refining Corp .... $2,000   Indiv
    Gold Metal Sporting Goods .... $2,000   Indiv
    United Refrigeration Inc .... $2,000   Indiv

Transportation $38,048

Air Transport **$3,500**
    United Parcel Service .... $2,000   PAC

Automotive **$5,250**
    Auto Dealers & Drivers for Free Trade .... $2,500   PAC
    Martin's Metal Specialties Inc .... $1,750   Indiv

Trucking **$4,500**
    Xpress Truck Lines Inc .... $1,500   Indiv

Railroads **$10,748**
    Consolidated Rail Corp .... $4,248   PAC
    Norfolk Southern Corp .... $1,500   PAC
    Safetran Systems Corp .... $1,500   Indiv

Sea Transport **$9,050**
    American Pilots Assn .... $2,500   PAC/Ind
    Sea-Land Corp .... $2,500   PAC
    Society for Relief of Distressed Pilots .... $2,000   PAC

Misc Transport **$5,000**
    American Bus Assn .... $3,000   PAC
    BDP International Inc .... $1,500   Indiv

---

Spending in Last 3 Elections

	1988	1990	1992
Borski	$250,480	$277,011	$664,231
Opponent	$23,101	$74,417	$215,321
Vote Pct	63%	60%	59%

Labor

Labor $149,695

Building Trade Unions **$31,895**
    Sheet Metal Workers Union .... $7,000   PAC
    Plumbers/Pipefitters Union* .... $5,645   PAC
    Carpenters & Joiners Union* .... $4,500   PAC
    Laborers' Political League .... $3,750   PAC
    Roofers Union local #30 .... $2,750   PAC
    Operating Engineers Union* .... $2,000   PAC
    Painters & Allied Trades Union .... $2,000   PAC

Industrial Unions **$32,000**
    United Auto Workers .... $10,000   PAC
    Intl Brotherhood of Electrical Workers* .... $5,500   PAC
    Machinists/Aerospace Workers Union .... $5,500   PAC
    Communications Workers Union #13000 .... $5,000   PAC
    Amalgamated Clothing & Textile Workers ...... $2,000   PAC

Transportation Unions **$44,050**
    Air Line Pilots Assn .... $10,000   PAC
    United Transportation Union .... $10,000   PAC
    Marine Engineers Dist 2 Maritime Offices ...... $6,000   PAC
    Transport Workers Union .... $5,000   PAC
    Seafarers International Union .... $3,000   PAC
    Amalgamated Transit Union .... $2,000   PAC
    International Longshoremen's Assn .... $2,000   PAC
    Masters, Mates & Pilots Union .... $1,500   PAC

Public Sector Unions **$34,500**
    National Assn Retired Federal Employees ...... $7,000   PAC
    American Fedn of St/Cnty/Munic Employees ... $6,500   PAC
    National Education Assn .... $6,000   PAC
    National Assn of Letter Carriers .... $5,000   PAC
    American Postal Workers Union .... $4,500   PAC
    International Assn of Firefighters .... $2,500   PAC

Misc Unions **$7,250**
    AFL-CIO .... $4,000   PAC
    Food & Commercial Workers Union .... $2,000   PAC

Ideological/Single-Issue

Ideological/Single-Issue $13,273

Democratic/Liberal **$3,500**
    National Cmte for an Effective Congress .... $2,500   PAC

Pro-Israel **$5,250**
    None over $1,500

Misc Issues **$4,000**
    National Cmte to Preserve Social Security ...... $4,000   PAC

Other & Unknown

Other $5,650

Retired **$3,900**
    None over $1,500

Unknown $33,479

    Homemakers/Non-income earners $7,500
    No Employer Listed or Found $6,500
    Generic Occupation/Category Unknown $1,500
    Employer Listed/Category Unknown $16,579
        None over $1,500

---

* Contributions came from more than one affiliate or
subsidiary.

Rick Boucher, D-Va (9)

First elected: 1982

1991-92 Total Receipts: $639,537
1992 Year-end Cash: $380,922

1991-92 Committees & Subcommittees

Energy and Commerce
Commerce, Consumer Protection and Competitiveness; Telecommunications and Finance; Transportation and Hazardous Materials

Judiciary
Intellectual Property and Judicial Administration

Science, Space and Technology
Science (Chairman); Technology and Competitiveness

Leading Contributors

Business

Agriculture	$34,500

Crop Production & Basic Processing	$2,500
None over $2,000	

Tobacco	$21,350	
RJR Nabisco	$10,000	PAC
Philip Morris	$4,950	PAC/Ind
US Tobacco Co	$3,000	PAC

Dairy	$2,500	
Dairymen Inc-Virginia	$2,000	PAC

Food Processing & Sales	$2,000
None over $2,000	

Communications/Electronics	$58,500

Media/Entertainment	$13,800	
National Assn of Broadcasters	$6,000	PAC
Fox Inc	$2,000	PAC
Primetime 24	$2,000	Indiv

Telephone Utilities	$34,900	
Ameritech Corp	$6,000	PAC
Bell Atlantic*	$4,000	PAC
US Telephone Assn	$3,500	PAC
United Telecommunications	$3,500	PAC
GTE Corp	$3,000	PAC
NYNEX Corp	$2,500	PAC
AT&T	$2,000	PAC
Alltel Corp	$2,000	PAC

Telecom Services & Equipment	$7,800	
Corning Glass Works	$2,500	PAC

Source of Funds in 1992 Election

Source	Total	Pct
■ PACs	$404,579	62%
▤ Indivs $200+	$89,500	14%
□ Indivs under $200	$65,899	10%
⊠ Other	$89,290	14%
Candidate	$0	0%
Party	$11,631	2%

Source of PAC Dollars by Sector

Source	Total	Pct
■ Business	$347,309	86%
▤ Labor	$50,750	13%
□ Ideology/Single Issue	$6,950	2%

In-State vs. Out-of-State Contributions*

Source	Total	Pct
□ In-State	$68,700	78%
■ Out-of-state	$19,950	22%
No state listed	$0	

*** by large individual contributors ($200 & above)**

Construction	$9,184	

Building Materials & Equipment	$7,184	
National Concrete Masonry Assn	$2,959	PAC

Defense	$9,000	

Defense Aerospace	$2,500
None over $2,000	

Defense Electronics	$4,500	
Raytheon	$3,000	PAC

Misc Defense	$2,000	
BDM International	$2,000	PAC

Energy & Natural Resources	$58,550	

Oil & Gas	$15,750	
Coastal Corp	$3,000	PAC

Mining	$10,000
None over $2,000	

Misc Energy	$2,250
None over $2,000	

Electric Utilities	$17,050	
Dominion Resources Inc	$3,000	PAC
ACRE (Action Cmte for Rural Electrification)	$2,500	PAC
Pacific Gas & Electric	$2,000	PAC

Waste Management	$13,500	
Chambers Development Co	$4,500	PAC
National Solid Wastes Management Assn	$4,000	PAC
Browning-Ferris Industries	$2,250	PAC

Finance, Insurance & Real Estate	$102,100	

Commercial Banks	$44,100	
American Bankers Assn	$10,000	PAC
JP Morgan & Co	$10,000	PAC
Citicorp	$3,500	PAC
Citizens & Southern National Bank	$3,500	PAC
Chemical Bank	$2,500	PAC

Contribution Totals by Sector

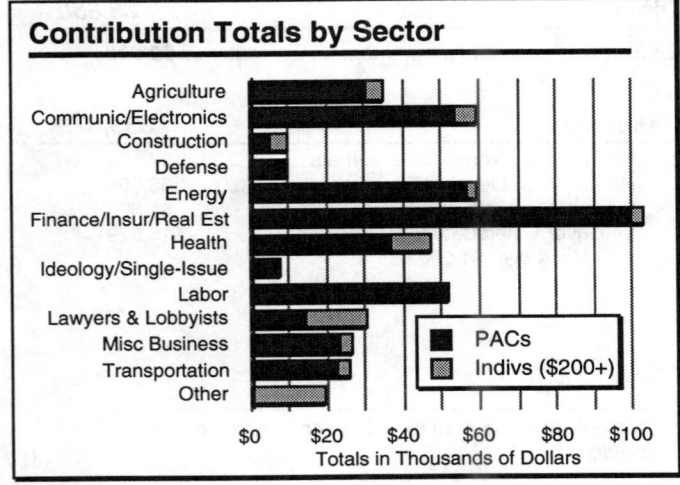

Agriculture
Communic/Electronics
Construction
Defense
Energy
Finance/Insur/Real Est
Health
Ideology/Single-Issue
Labor
Lawyers & Lobbyists
Misc Business
Transportation
Other

■ PACs
▤ Indivs ($200+)

$0 $20 $40 $60 $80 $100
Totals in Thousands of Dollars

Finance/Credit Companies	$2,000	
None over $2,000		

Securities & Investment	$12,000	
American Express*	$2,500	PAC
Dean Witter	$2,000	PAC
Securities Industry Assn	$2,000	PAC

Insurance	$19,350	
American Family Corp	$3,000	PAC

Real Estate	$2,500	
None over $2,000		

Accountants	$19,900	
American Institute of CPA's	$7,500	PAC
Price Waterhouse	$3,000	PAC
Arthur Andersen & Co	$2,000	PAC
Ernst & Young	$2,000	PAC
Deloitte & Touche	$2,000	PAC

Health $46,600

Health Professionals	$22,600	
American Dental Assn	$4,000	PAC
American Medical Assn	$3,000	PAC
National Assn of Pharmacists	$3,000	PAC

Hospitals/Nursing Homes	$2,250	
American Hospital Assn	$2,000	PAC

Pharmaceuticals/Health Products	$21,000	
Upjohn Co	$3,000	PAC
Warner-Lambert	$2,500	PAC/Ind
Genentech Inc	$2,000	PAC
Merck & Co	$2,000	PAC

Lawyers & Lobbyists $29,600

Lawyers & Lobbyists	$29,600	
Arnold & Porter*	$2,000	PAC
Kirkland & Ellis	$2,000	PAC

Spending in Last 3 Elections

	1988	1990	1992
Boucher	$606,420	$252,685	$660,452
Opponent	$154,515	$0	$104,589
Vote Pct	63%	97%	63%

Misc Business	$26,175	
Food & Beverage	$2,575	
None over $2,000		

Beer, Wine & Liquor	$2,000	
None over $2,000		

Retail Sales	$2,000	
None over $2,000		

Chemical & Related Manufacturing	$6,750	
Eastman Kodak/Chemicals Division	$2,000	PAC

Misc Manufacturing & Distributing	$8,500	
Hoechst Celanese Corp	$3,000	PAC
Institute of Scrap Recycling Industries	$2,750	PAC

Transportation $25,650

Air Transport	$7,000	
General Electric	$3,000	PAC
United Parcel Service	$2,500	PAC

Automotive	$8,300	
National Auto Dealers Assn	$5,000	PAC

Railroads	$6,500	
Burlington Northern	$2,500	PAC

Misc Transport	$2,850	
Pittston Co	$2,850	Indiv

Labor

Labor	$50,750	
Building Trade Unions	$5,500	
Carpenters & Joiners Union	$2,000	PAC
Laborers' Political League	$2,000	PAC

Industrial Unions	$12,500	
United Auto Workers	$5,500	PAC
Communications Workers of America	$2,500	PAC

Transportation Unions	$15,800	
Teamsters Union	$5,500	PAC
United Transportation Union	$4,000	PAC

Public Sector Unions	$15,450	
National Education Assn	$4,500	PAC
American Fedn of St/Cnty/Munic Employees	$4,000	PAC
National Assn of Letter Carriers	$2,000	PAC

Ideological/Single-Issue

Ideological/Single-Issue	$7,200	
Gun Rights/Gun Control	$6,950	
National Rifle Assn	$6,950	PAC

Other & Unknown

Other	$18,650	
Education	$3,950	
VPI & SU	$2,250	Indiv
Retired	$13,200	
None over $2,000		

Unknown	$17,500	
No Employer Listed or Found	$11,800	
Employer Listed/Category Unknown	$3,700	
None over $2,000		

* Contributions came from more than one affiliate or subsidiary.

459

Bill Brewster, D-Okla (3)

First elected: 1990

1991-92 Total Receipts: $423,953
1992 Year-end Cash: $39,867

1991-92 Committees & Subcommittees

Public Works and Transportation
Investigations and Oversight; Surface Transportation; Water Resources

Veterans' Affairs
Hospitals and Health Care; Housing and Memorial Affairs

Leading Contributors

Business

Agriculture		$37,150
Crop Production & Basic Processing **$2,500**		
Southwest Peanut Membership Org $1,500	PAC	
Tobacco **$7,250**		
RJR Nabisco $3,500	PAC	
Dairy **$4,500**		
Associated Milk Producers $4,000	PAC	
Poultry & Eggs **$6,250**		
Tyson Foods $2,500	PAC	
Livestock **$4,550**		
National Cattlemen's Assn* $3,000	PAC	
Agricultural Services/Products **$4,850**		
None over $1,500		
Food Processing & Sales **$6,250**		
Fleming Companies Inc $2,500	PAC	
Winn-Dixie Stores $2,000	PAC	

Communications/Electronics		$15,750
Printing & Publishing **$2,000**		
None over $1,500		
Telephone Utilities **$12,250**		
AT&T $3,000	PAC	
GTE Corp $3,000	PAC	
Southwestern Bell $3,000	PAC	

Source of Funds in 1992 Election

Source	Total	Pct
■ PACs	$266,973	62%
▨ Indivs $200+	$104,783	24%
☐ Indivs under $200	$43,394	10%
⊠ Other	$15,103	4%
Candidate	$0	0%
Party	$6,450	2%

Source of PAC Dollars by Sector

Source	Total	Pct
■ Business	$234,263	89%
▨ Labor	$15,350	6%
☐ Ideology/Single Issue	$13,700	5%

In-State vs. Out-of-State Contributions*

Source	Total	Pct
☐ In-State	$85,650	82%
■ Out-of-state	$19,133	18%
No state listed	$0	

* by large individual contributors ($200 & above)

Construction		$20,000
General Contractors **$12,750**		
Redfork Construction Co $2,000	Indiv	
Interstate Contracting Corp $1,500	Indiv	
Home Builders **$3,500**		
National Assn of Home Builders $3,000	PAC	
Construction Services **$2,500**		
National Society of Professional Engineers $1,500	PAC	

Defense		$3,750
Defense Aerospace **$2,000**		
None over $1,500		

Energy & Natural Resources		$71,800
Oil & Gas **$49,000**		
Holden Energy Corp $8,000	Indiv	
Sooner Pipe & Supply $2,750	Indiv	
Oneok Inc $2,250	PAC	
Columbia Gas System* $2,000	PAC	
Jordan Distributing Co $2,000	Indiv	
Mustang Fuel Corp $2,000	Indiv	
Arkla Inc $1,500	PAC	
Citgo Petroleum Corp $1,500	Indiv	
Koch Industries $1,500	PAC	
Mining **$2,250**		
None over $1,500		
Electric Utilities **$14,300**		
ACRE (Action Cmte for Rural Electrification)* $2,250	PAC	
Oklahoma Gas & Electric $2,250	PAC/Ind	
Southern Co* $2,000	PAC	
Texas Utilities Co* $2,000	PAC	
Central & South West Services* $1,500	PAC	
Waste Management **$5,500**		
Safe Tire Disposal Corp $5,000	Indiv	

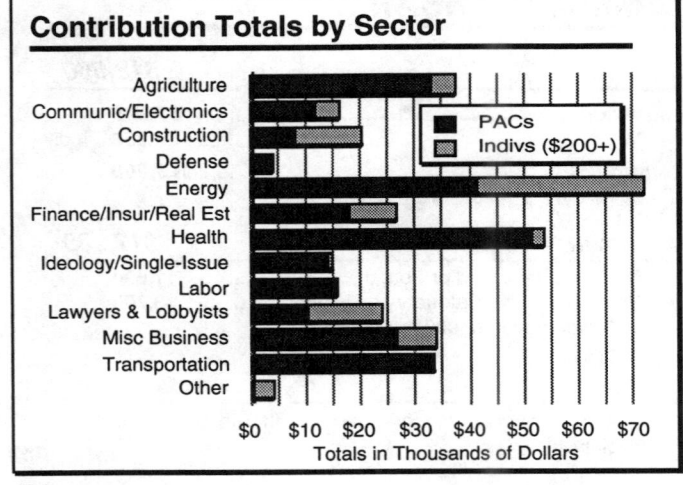

Contribution Totals by Sector

Agriculture
Communic/Electronics
Construction
Defense
Energy
Finance/Insur/Real Est
Health
Ideology/Single-Issue
Labor
Lawyers & Lobbyists
Misc Business
Transportation
Other

■ PACs
▨ Indivs ($200+)

$0 $10 $20 $30 $40 $50 $60 $70
Totals in Thousands of Dollars

Finance, Insurance & Real Estate $26,450

Commercial Banks $7,200
    The Bank ....$2,000 Indiv
Credit Unions $1,500
    Credit Union National Assn ....$1,500 PAC
Securities & Investment $3,250
    None over $1,500
Insurance $5,000
    None over $1,500
Real Estate $6,000
    National Assn of Realtors ....$5,500 PAC
Accountants $1,500
    None over $1,500
Misc Finance $1,500
    None over $1,500

Health $53,349

Health Professionals $34,599
    American Medical Assn* ....$10,000 PAC
    National Assn of Pharmacists ....$5,000 PAC
    American Pharmaceutical Assn ....$4,099 PAC
    American College of Emergency Physicians ....$3,000 PAC
    American Dental Assn ....$2,500 PAC
    American Academy of Ophthalmology ....$2,000 PAC
    American Physical Therapy Assn ....$1,500 PAC
Hospitals/Nursing Homes $5,250
    American Hospital Assn ....$2,500 PAC
Pharmaceuticals/Health Products $13,000
    National Wholesale Druggists Assn .....$2,000 PAC
    Glaxo Inc ....$1,500 PAC

Lawyers & Lobbyists $23,600

Lawyers & Lobbyists $23,600
    Assn of Trial Lawyers of America ....$5,500 PAC
    Williams & Jensen ....$5,000 Indiv
    Akin, Gump et al ....$1,500 PAC/Ind

Spending in Last 2 Elections

	1990	1992
Brewster	$446,766	$351,144
Opponent	$0	$6,023
Vote Pct	80%	75%

Misc Business $33,597

Food & Beverage $3,364
    National Restaurant Assn ....$1,500 PAC
Beer, Wine & Liquor $2,000
    National Beer Wholesalers Assn ....$1,500 PAC
Retail Sales..$16,000
    National Assn of Chain Drug Stores ....$10,000 PAC
Business Services $4,083
    None over $1,500
Chemical & Related Manufacturing $2,000
    None over $1,500
Misc Manufacturing & Distributing $3,250
    Corning Glass Works ....$2,000 PAC

Transportation $33,000

Air Transport.......................................$17,500
    United Parcel Service ....$7,500 PAC
    Federal Express Corp ....$4,000 PAC
    American Airlines ....$2,000 PAC
Automotive $2,500
    National Auto Dealers Assn ....$1,500 PAC
Trucking..$4,750
    American Trucking Assns ....$1,500 PAC
Railroads $7,750
    Union Pacific Corp ....$2,500 PAC
    Burlington Northern ....$2,000 PAC

Labor

Labor $15,350

Transportation Unions $6,500
    Air Line Pilots Assn ....$2,500 PAC
    Marine Engineers Dist 2 Maritime Offices ....$2,000 PAC
    United Transportation Union ....$1,500 PAC
Public Sector Unions $7,600
    National Assn of Letter Carriers ....$5,000 PAC
    National Education Assn ....$1,500 PAC

Ideological/Single-Issue

Ideological/Single-Issue $14,700

Gun Rights/Gun Control $9,450
    National Rifle Assn ....$8,450 PAC
Misc Issues...$3,250
    National Cmte to Preserve Social Security ....$2,000 PAC

Other & Unknown

Other $3,800

Retired $3,050
    None over $1,500

Unknown $15,800

    Homemakers/Non-income earners $3,500
    Employer Listed/Category Unknown $12,100
    Vacco Industries ....$2,000 Indiv

---

* Contributions came from more than one affiliate or
subsidiary.

461

Jack Brooks, D-Texas (9)

First elected: 1952

1991-92 Total Receipts: $606,926
1992 Year-end Cash: $465,327

1991-92 Committees & Subcommittees

Judiciary (Chairman)
Economic and Commercial Law (Chairman)

Select Committee on Narcotics Abuse and Control

Leading Contributors

Business

Agriculture	$20,950

Crop Production & Basic Processing $5,000
    None over $2,500

Tobacco $4,000
    None over $2,500

Food Processing & Sales $4,500
    None over $2,500

Forestry & Forest Products $3,000
    None over $2,500

Communications/Electronics	$83,900

Printing & Publishing $11,800
    West Publishing .... $8,000   PAC/Ind

Media/Entertainment $37,100
    National Cable Television Assn .... $10,000   PAC
    National Assn of Broadcasters .... $7,000   PAC
    Viacom International .... $5,000   PAC
    MCA Inc .... $4,000   PAC/Ind
    ASCAP .... $2,500   PAC

Telephone Utilities $25,500
    Ameritech Corp .... $5,000   PAC
    AT&T .... $4,000   PAC
    United Telecommunications .... $4,000   PAC
    GTE Corp .... $3,500   PAC
    Pacific Telesis Group .... $3,000   PAC

Computer Equipment & Services $6,750
    None over $2,500

Source of Funds in 1992 Election

Source	Total	Pct
PACs	$452,357	74%
Indivs $200+	$92,126	15%
Indivs under $200	$10,305	2%
Other	$52,575	9%
Candidate	$0	0%
Party	$1,806	0%

Source of PAC Dollars by Sector

Source	Total	Pct
Business	$340,057	76%
Labor	$90,700	20%
Ideology/Single Issue	$16,400	4%

In-State vs. Out-of-State Contributions*

Source	Total	Pct
In-State	$33,850	37%
Out-of-state	$58,276	63%
No state listed	$0	

* by large individual contributors ($200 & above)

Construction	$16,000

Home Builders $2,500
    National Assn of Home Builders .... $2,500   PAC

Construction Services $9,500
    American Consulting Engineers Council .. $2,500   PAC

Defense	$11,750

Defense Aerospace $9,500
    None over $2,500

Energy & Natural Resources	$33,500

Oil & Gas $25,200
    Coastal Corp .... $5,000   PAC
    USX Corp* .... $3,000   PAC

Electric Utilities $5,300
    Houston Industries .... $3,000   PAC

Finance, Insurance & Real Estate	$85,150

Commercial Banks $23,750
    Citizens & Southern National Bank ..... $6,500   PAC
    American Bankers Assn .... $4,000   PAC
    JP Morgan & Co .... $2,500   PAC

Finance/Credit Companies $5,000
    None over $2,500

Securities & Investment $13,500
    Morgan Stanley & Co .... $5,000   PAC

Insurance $14,000
    None over $2,500

Real Estate $12,500
    National Assn of Realtors .... $7,000   PAC

Accountants $13,400
    American Institute of CPA's .... $10,000   PAC

Contribution Totals by Sector

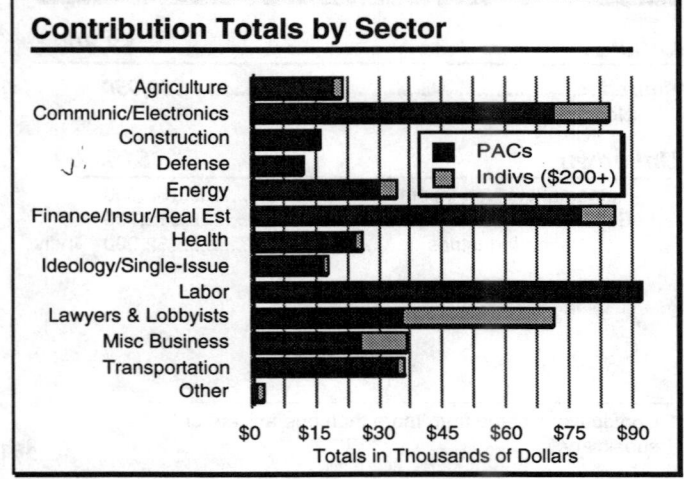

Agriculture
Communic/Electronics
Construction
Defense
Energy
Finance/Insur/Real Est
Health
Ideology/Single-Issue
Labor
Lawyers & Lobbyists
Misc Business
Transportation
Other

■ PACs
▨ Indivs ($200+)

$0 $15 $30 $45 $60 $75 $90
Totals in Thousands of Dollars

Health $25,700

Health Professionals **$14,500**
    National Assn of Pharmacists ....$5,000 PAC
    American Medical Assn.......................................$3,000 PAC
    American Pharmaceutical Assn ....$3,000 PAC

Pharmaceuticals/Health Products **$9,700**
    None over $2,500

Lawyers & Lobbyists $71,000

Lawyers & Lobbyists.. **$71,000**
    Assn of Trial Lawyers of America ....$10,000 PAC
    Cassidy & Associates...$9,250 Indiv
    Akin, Gump et al...$7,000 PAC/Ind
    Opperman & Paquin...$3,000 PAC
    Verner, Liipfert et al ....$3,000 PAC/Ind

Misc Business $36,007

Food & Beverage **$6,000**
    None over $2,500

Beer, Wine & Liquor **$4,500**
    National Beer Wholesalers Assn ....$2,500 PAC

Retail Sales... **$7,007**
    None over $2,500

Business Services **$8,500**
    Dun & Bradstreet...$4,000 PAC/Ind
    Alarm Industry Communications Cmte ....$3,000 PAC

Chemical & Related Manufacturing **$5,000**
    None over $2,500

Misc Manufacturing & Distributing **$2,500**
    None over $2,500

Transportation $35,476

Air Transport **$9,000**
    None over $2,500

Automotive **$13,000**
    National Auto Dealers Assn ....$10,000 PAC

Railroads.. **$10,226**
    Burlington Northern ....$2,500 PAC

Labor

Labor $91,700

Building Trade Unions **$20,500**
    Carpenters & Joiners Union ....$10,000 PAC
    Laborers' Political League ....$4,000 PAC

Industrial Unions **$15,000**
    None over $2,500

Transportation Unions **$27,700**
    Teamsters Union ....$7,500 PAC
    Seafarers International Union ....$6,000 PAC
    International Longshoremen's Assn....................$5,000 PAC
    Marine Engineers Union* ....$4,000 PAC

Public Sector Unions **$24,500**
    American Fedn of St/Cnty/Munic Employees ......$7,500 PAC
    National Education Assn ....$6,000 PAC
    American Postal Workers Union ....$4,500 PAC

Misc Unions... **$4,000**
    Hotel/Restaurant Employees Union ....$2,500 PAC

Ideological/Single-Issue

Ideological/Single-Issue $17,400

Gun Rights/Gun Control **$9,900**
    National Rifle Assn ....$9,900 PAC

Human Rights **$2,500**
    KidsPAC ....$2,500 PAC

Misc Issues.. **$4,000**
    National Cmte to Preserve Social Security ....$4,000 PAC

Other & Unknown

Other $2,250
    None over $2,500

Unknown $9,500
    Employer Listed/Category Unknown $8,500
        None over $2,500

Independent expenditures supporting Brooks
    National Rifle Assn $5,675

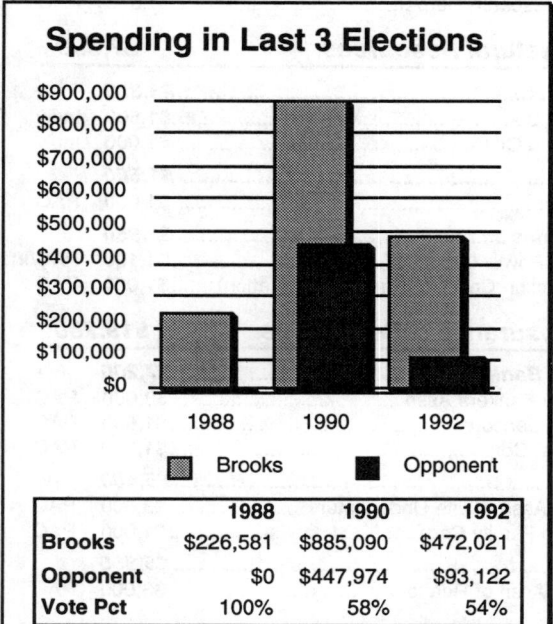

Spending in Last 3 Elections

	1988	1990	1992
Brooks	$226,581	$885,090	$472,021
Opponent	$0	$447,974	$93,122
Vote Pct	100%	58%	54%

Legend: Brooks / Opponent

---

* Contributions came from more than one affiliate or subsidiary.

463

Glen Browder, D-Ala (3)

First elected: 1989

1991-92 Total Receipts: $231,325
1992 Year-end Cash: $242,422

1991-92 Committees & Subcommittees

Armed Services
Military Installations and Facilities; Research and Development

Science, Space and Technology
Science; Space

Leading Contributors

Business

Agriculture	$16,050	
Crop Production & Basic Processing	**$3,150**	
Alabama Peanut Producers Assn	$1,000	PAC
Tobacco	**$3,700**	
RJR Nabisco	$2,000	PAC
Dairy	**$1,350**	
None over $1,000		
Poultry & Eggs	**$1,850**	
None over $1,000		
Agricultural Services/Products	**$4,500**	
Alabama Farm Bureau Federation	$4,000	PAC
Forestry & Forest Products	**$1,000**	
None over $1,000		

Communications/Electronics	$6,250	
Media/Entertainment	**$1,300**	
None over $1,000		
Telephone Utilities	**$2,000**	
Southern Bell	$2,000	PAC
Computer Equipment & Services	**$2,450**	
Colsa Inc	$2,000	Indiv

Construction	$3,550	
General Contractors	**$1,550**	
Hale Construction Co	$1,000	Indiv
Home Builders	**$1,000**	
None over $1,000		

Contribution Totals by Sector

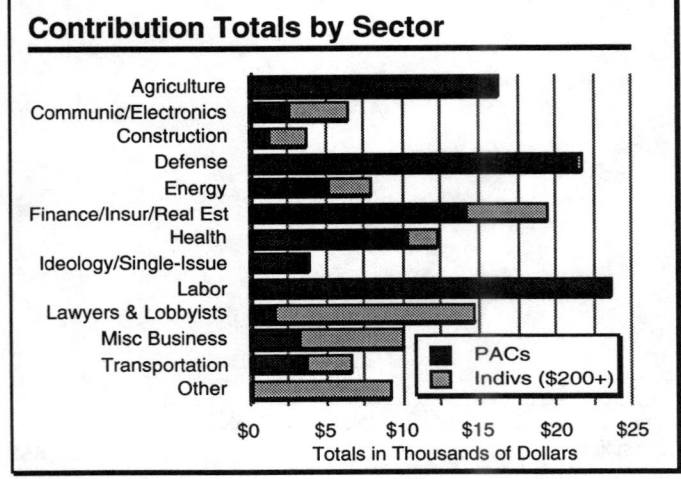

Agriculture
Communic/Electronics
Construction
Defense
Energy
Finance/Insur/Real Est
Health
Ideology/Single-Issue
Labor
Lawyers & Lobbyists
Misc Business
Transportation
Other

PACs
Indivs ($200+)

$0 $5 $10 $15 $20 $25
Totals in Thousands of Dollars

Source of Funds in 1992 Election

Source	Total	Pct
■ PACs	$105,550	45%
▨ Indivs $200+	$60,913	26%
□ Indivs under $200	$49,534	21%
▨ Other	$18,547	8%
Candidate	$0	0%
Party	$3,519	2%

Source of PAC Dollars by Sector

Source	Total	Pct
■ Business	$78,550	74%
▨ Labor	$23,550	22%
□ Ideology/Single Issue	$3,700	4%

In-State vs. Out-of-State Contributions*

Source	Total	Pct
□ In-State	$59,813	98%
■ Out-of-state	$1,100	2%
No state listed	$0	

*** by large individual contributors ($200 & above)**

Defense	$21,500	
Defense Aerospace	**$9,500**	
Boeing Co	$1,500	PAC
Rockwell International	$1,250	PAC/Ind
Thiokol	$1,000	PAC
Defense Electronics	**$6,000**	
AT&T	$3,000	PAC
Imo Industries Inc	$2,000	PAC
Misc Defense	**$6,000**	
General Atomics	$3,000	PAC
FMC Corp	$2,000	PAC
Atlantic Research Corp	$1,000	PAC

Energy & Natural Resources	$7,800	
Oil & Gas	**$3,350**	
Nolen Oil Co	$1,500	Indiv
McPherson Oil Co	$1,000	Indiv
Mining	**$1,500**	
Dravo Corp	$1,000	PAC
Electric Utilities	**$2,950**	
Alabama Power Co	$1,100	PAC/Ind
ACRE (Action Cmte for Rural Electrification)	$1,000	PAC

Finance, Insurance & Real Estate	$19,250	
Commercial Banks	**$7,200**	
American Bankers Assn	$3,000	PAC
Amsouth Bancorp	$1,600	PAC
Southtrust Corp	$1,000	PAC
Insurance	**$5,400**	
National Assn of Life Underwriters	$3,000	PAC
American Family Corp	$1,000	PAC
Real Estate	**$5,850**	
National Assn of Realtors	$3,000	PAC

Health $12,100

Health Professionals **$11,450**
American Medical Assn	$6,000	PAC
American Dental Assn	$2,350	PAC
American Academy of Ophthalmology	$1,000	PAC

Lawyers & Lobbyists $14,450

Lawyers & Lobbyists **$14,450**
Buttram & McWhorter	$2,000	Indiv
Morris, Haynes & Ingram	$1,250	Indiv
Assn of Trial Lawyers of America	$1,000	PAC
Gorham, Waldrep	$1,000	Indiv
Sirote, Permutt et al	$1,000	Indiv

Misc Business $9,850

Beer, Wine & Liquor **$1,000**
None over $1,000

Retail Sales **$1,000**
None over $1,000

Misc Services **$1,250**
Gray-Brown Funeral Home	$1,250	Indiv

Business Services **$2,950**
Miller Photographers	$2,450	Indiv

Misc Manufacturing & Distributing **$1,250**
None over $1,000

Textiles **$1,350**
None over $1,000

Transportation $6,450

Automotive **$3,000**
National Auto Dealers Assn	$3,000	PAC

Trucking **$2,550**
Floyd & Beasley Trucking Co	$2,000	Indiv

Labor

Labor $23,550

Building Trade Unions **$4,850**
Plumbers/Pipefitters Union	$2,000	PAC
Laborers' Political League	$1,500	PAC

Industrial Unions **$9,400**
United Auto Workers	$3,350	PAC
Intl Brotherhood of Electrical Workers	$2,000	PAC
Communications Workers of America	$1,000	PAC

Transportation Unions **$1,850**
Marine Engineers Dist 2 Maritime Offices	$1,000	PAC

Public Sector Unions **$5,250**
American Federation of Govt Employees	$1,350	PAC
National Assn Retired Federal Employees	$1,000	PAC
National Assn of Letter Carriers	$1,000	PAC

Misc Unions **$2,200**
Food & Commercial Workers Union	$1,850	PAC

Ideological/Single-Issue $3,700

Foreign & Defense Policy **$1,000**
Veterans of Foreign Wars	$1,000	PAC

Gun Rights/Gun Control **$1,000**
National Rifle Assn	$1,000	PAC

Misc Issues **$1,200**
National Cmte to Preserve Social Security	$1,700	PAC

Other & Unknown

Other $9,050

Education **$1,000**
None over $1,000

Retired **$7,250**
None over $1,000

Unknown $13,163

Homemakers/Non-income earners	$1,500	
Employer Listed/Category Unknown	$11,250	
Spliceco Inc	$4,000	Indiv
Blue Mountain Industries	$1,000	Indiv
CAS Inc	$1,000	Indiv
Dese Research & Engineering	$1,000	Indiv
Office of Hearings & Appeals	$1,000	Indiv

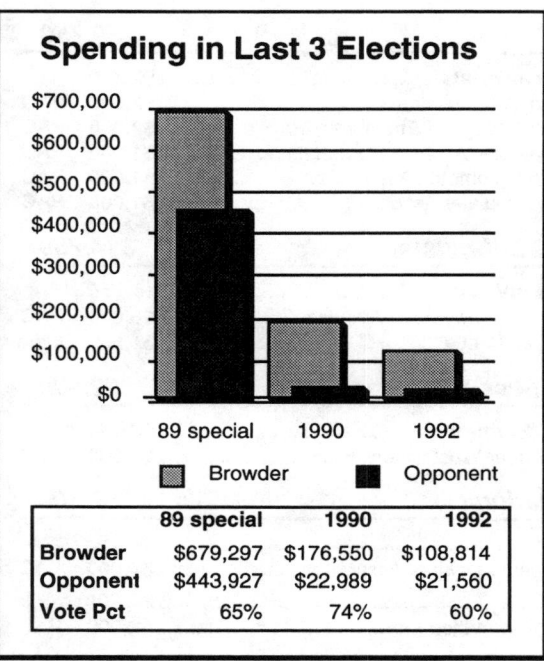

Spending in Last 3 Elections

	89 special	1990	1992
Browder	$679,297	$176,550	$108,814
Opponent	$443,927	$22,989	$21,560
Vote Pct	65%	74%	60%

Corrine Brown, D-Fla (3)

1993-94 Committees & Subcommittees

First elected: 1992
1991-92 Total Receipts: $293,084
1992 Year-end Cash: $1,398

Government Operations
Legislation and National Security

Public Works and Transportation
Aviation; Economic Development; Water Resources and the Environment

Veterans' Affairs
Hospitals and Health Care; Housing and Memorial Affairs

Leading Contributors

Business

Agriculture $5,100

Crop Production & Basic Processing	**$1,600**
United States Sugar Corp	$1,000 PAC
Tobacco	**$2,000**
RJR Nabisco	$1,500 PAC
Food Processing & Sales	**$1,500**
Winn-Dixie Stores	$1,500 PAC

Communications/Electronics $10,000

Telephone Utilities	**$9,750**
Southern Bell	$6,250 PAC
AT&T	$1,500 PAC
GTE Corp	$1,500 PAC

Construction $8,900

General Contractors	**$2,750**
Suffolk Construction Co	$1,000 Indiv
Building Materials & Equipment	**$5,650**
Florida Rock Industries	$4,150 PAC
Southdown Inc	$1,000 PAC

Energy & Natural Resources $5,050

Oil & Gas	**$1,250**
None over $1,000	
Electric Utilities	**$3,800**
ACRE (Action Cmte for Rural Electrification)	$1,500 PAC
Florida Power & Light	$1,000 PAC

Source of Funds in 1992 Election

Source	Total	Pct
■ PACs	$166,239	56%
▨ Indivs $200+	$35,673	12%
□ Indivs under $200	$81,981	28%
⊠ Other	$13,381	4%
Candidate	$6,000	2%
Party	$4,640	2%

Source of PAC Dollars by Sector

Source	Total	Pct
■ Business	$63,400	39%
▨ Labor	$56,565	35%
□ Ideology/Single Issue	$42,445	26%

In-State vs. Out-of-State Contributions*

Source	Total	Pct
□ In-State	$25,003	80%
■ Out-of-state	$6,120	20%
No state listed	$450	

* by large individual contributors ($200 & above)

Finance, Insurance & Real Estate $10,750

Commercial Banks	**$2,250**
Barnett Banks Inc	$2,000 PAC
Savings & Loans	**$1,000**
Florida League of Financial Institutions	$1,000 PAC
Insurance	**$3,800**
National Assn of Life Underwriters	$1,500 PAC
Fidelity Insurance Agency Inc	$1,000 PAC
Real Estate	**$3,500**
National Assn of Realtors	$2,500 PAC
First Union Corp	$1,000 PAC

Health $9,750

Health Professionals	**$9,750**
American Chiropractic Assn	$2,000 PAC
American College of Emergency Physicians	$2,000 PAC
Florida Medical Assn	$1,500 PAC
American Optometric Assn	$1,000 PAC
American Podiatry Assn	$1,000 PAC

Lawyers & Lobbyists $14,750

Lawyers & Lobbyists	**$14,750**
Assn of Trial Lawyers of America	$10,000 PAC
Brown, Terrell et al	$1,500 Indiv

Misc Business $2,800

Beer, Wine & Liquor	**$2,000**
National Beer Wholesalers Assn	$1,500 PAC

Transportation $7,100

Automotive	**$4,250**
National Auto Dealers Assn	$4,000 PAC
Railroads	**$2,000**
CSX Transportation Inc	$2,000 PAC

Contribution Totals by Sector

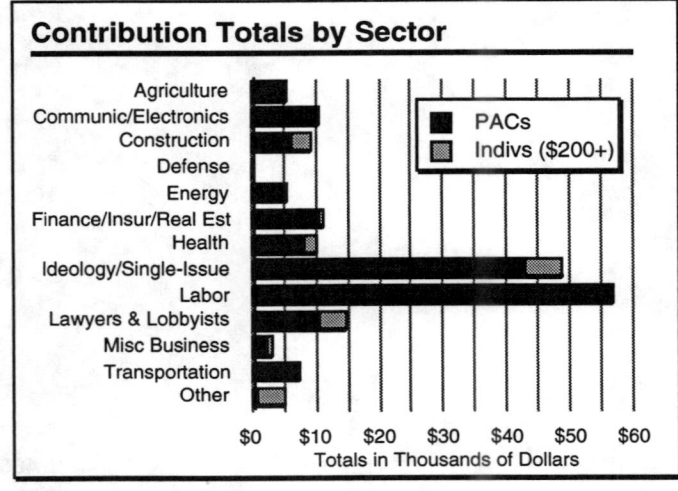

Agriculture
Communic/Electronics
Construction
Defense
Energy
Finance/Insur/Real Est
Health
Ideology/Single-Issue
Labor
Lawyers & Lobbyists
Misc Business
Transportation
Other

■ PACs
▨ Indivs ($200+)

$0 $10 $20 $30 $40 $50 $60
Totals in Thousands of Dollars

Labor

Labor $56,565

Building Trade Unions **$3,500**
   Laborers' Political League ....$2,000 PAC
   Sheet Metal Workers Union ....$1,000 PAC

Industrial Unions **$4,800**
   United Auto Workers ....$2,000 PAC
   United Steelworkers ....$2,000 PAC

Transportation Unions **$10,765**
   International Longshoremen's Assn ....$2,500 PAC
   Marine Engineers Union ....$2,000 PAC
   Teamsters Union ....$2,000 PAC
   United Transportation Union ....$1,500 PAC
   Seafarers International Union ....$1,000 PAC

Public Sector Unions **$33,000**
   American Fedn of St/Cnty/Munic Employees ....$12,500 PAC
   National Education Assn ....$12,500 PAC
   American Federation of Teachers ....$5,000 PAC
   National Assn Retired Federal Employees ....$3,000 PAC

Misc Unions **$4,500**
   Food & Commercial Workers Union ....$4,500 PAC

Ideological/Single-Issue

Ideological/Single-Issue $48,145

Democratic/Liberal **$1,100**
   Hollywood Women's Political Cmte ....$1,000 PAC

Leadership PACs **$6,950**
   People Helping People (Maxine Waters) ....$3,000 PAC
   Effective Government Cmte (Dick Gephardt) ......$1,450 PAC
   AmeriPAC (Steny Hoyer) ....$1,000 PAC
   Victory USA (Vic Fazio) ....$1,000 PAC

Foreign & Defense Policy **$3,500**
   Free Cuba PAC ....$2,500 PAC
   Veterans of Foreign Wars ....$1,000 PAC

Pro-Israel **$1,100**
   National PAC ....$1,000 PAC

Pro-Choice **$3,000**
   Voters for Choice ....$2,000 PAC
   National Abortion Rights Action League ....$1,000 PAC

Womens Issues **$26,745**
   Emily's List ....$13,395 PAC/Ind
   Women's Campaign Fund ....$6,000 PAC
   National Womens Political Caucus ....$3,000 PAC
   National Organization for Women ....$2,750 PAC

Human Rights **$4,500**
   Human Rights Campaign Fund ....$4,500 PAC

Misc Issues **$1,000**
   National Cmte to Preserve Social Security ....$1,000 PAC

Other & Unknown

Other $4,745

Education **$1,150**
   None over $1,000

Other **$3,295**
   None over $1,000

Unknown $14,428

   Homemakers/Non-income earners $1,700
   No Employer Listed or Found $5,100
   Generic Occupation/Category Unknown $5,658
   Employer Listed/Category Unknown $1,970
      None over $1,000

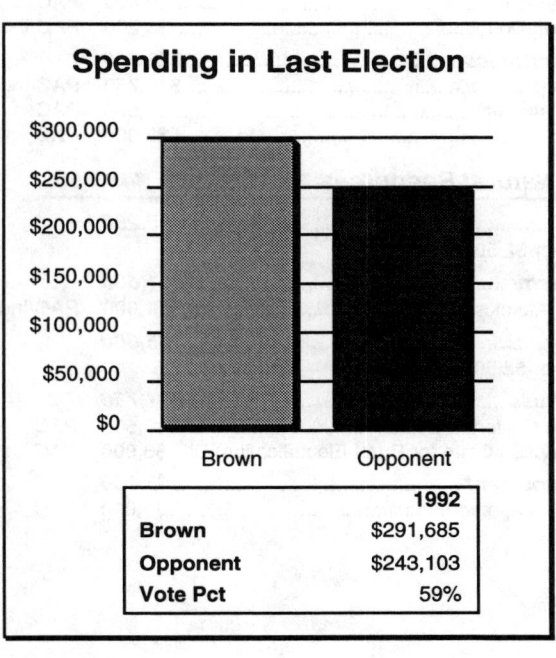

Spending in Last Election

	1992
Brown	$291,685
Opponent	$243,103
Vote Pct	59%

George E. Brown Jr., D-Calif (42)

First elected: 1962

1991-92 Total Receipts: $908,348
1992 Year-end Cash: $5,564

1991-92 Committees & Subcommittees

Agriculture
Department Operations, Research and Foreign Agriculture (Vice Chairman); Forests, Family Farms and Energy

Science, Space and Technology (Chairman)

Leading Contributors

Business

Agriculture	$48,550	
Crop Production & Basic Processing	**$21,300**	
Sunkist Growers	$7,000	PAC
Dairy	**$3,000**	
None over $2,500		
Agricultural Services/Products	**$17,950**	
American Veterinary Medical Assn	$10,000	PAC
Food Processing & Sales	**$3,800**	
None over $2,500		

Communications/Electronics	$48,576	
Media/Entertainment	**$5,550**	
None over $2,500		
Telephone Utilities	**$20,000**	
AT&T	$10,000	PAC
Pacific Telesis Group	$5,000	PAC
Telecom Services & Equipment	**$2,500**	
None over $2,500		
Electronics Mfg & Services	**$7,000**	
None over $2,500		
Computer Equipment & Services	**$12,176**	
None over $2,500		

Construction	$25,930	
General Contractors	**$5,780**	
None over $2,500		
Home Builders	**$9,500**	
Lewis Homes	$7,000	Indiv

Source of Funds in 1992 Election

Source	Total	Pct
■ PACs	$506,120	54%
▨ Indivs $200+	$188,854	20%
□ Indivs under $200	$191,698	20%
▣ Other	$53,108	6%
Candidate	$0	0%
Party	$36,732	4%

Source of PAC Dollars by Sector

Source	Total	Pct
■ Business	$251,463	52%
▨ Labor	$173,265	36%
□ Ideology/Single Issue	$57,769	12%

In-State vs. Out-of-State Contributions*

Source	Total	Pct
□ In-State	$111,829	59%
■ Out-of-state	$77,025	41%
No state listed	$0	

by large individual contributors ($200 & above)

Special Trade Contractors	$3,500	
Taber Co	$2,500	Indiv
Construction Services	**$5,650**	
National Society of Professional Engineers	$4,150	PAC

Defense	$65,562	
Defense Aerospace	**$43,062**	
General Dynamics	$7,500	PAC
Lockheed Corp	$7,462	PAC
Martin Marietta Corp	$6,000	PAC
Rockwell International	$5,500	PAC
Gencorp Inc	$3,700	PAC
Grumman Corp	$3,400	PAC
McDonnell Douglas	$3,200	PAC/Ind
Defense Electronics	**$22,500**	
Loral Corp	$12,750	PAC/Ind
Hughes Aircraft	$4,500	PAC
TRW Inc	$3,000	PAC

Energy & Natural Resources	$48,550	
Oil & Gas	**$5,250**	
None over $2,500		
Nuclear Energy	**$11,500**	
General Atomics	$11,000	PAC/Ind
Misc Energy	**$5,800**	
None over $2,500		
Electric Utilities	**$21,750**	
Southern California Edison	$10,500	PAC
ACRE (Action Cmte for Rural Electrification)	$3,000	PAC
Waste Management	**$3,250**	
Waste Management Inc	$3,000	PAC

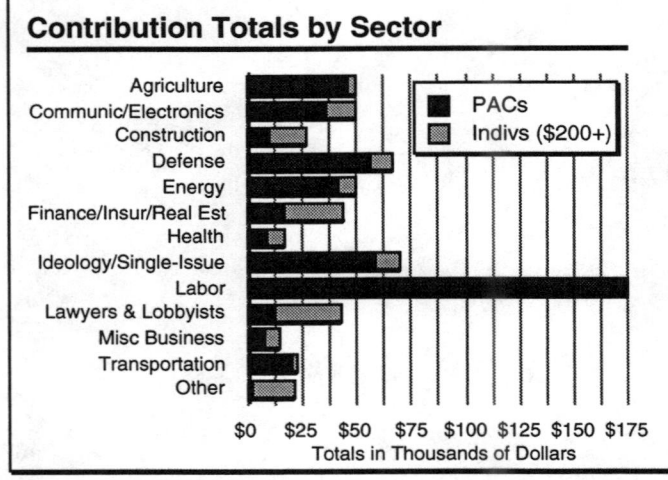

Contribution Totals by Sector

Categories: Agriculture, Communic/Electronics, Construction, Defense, Energy, Finance/Insur/Real Est, Health, Ideology/Single-Issue, Labor, Lawyers & Lobbyists, Misc Business, Transportation, Other

Legend: ■ PACs, ▨ Indivs ($200+)

Totals in Thousands of Dollars ($0, $25, $50, $75, $100, $125, $150, $175)

Finance, Insurance & Real Estate — $42,700

Commercial Banks **$2,650**
   None over $2,500

Securities & Investment **$2,500**
   None over $2,500

Insurance **$10,000**
   Life Partners Group Insurance .... $2,500   Indiv

Real Estate **$17,800**
   National Assn of Realtors .... $3,000   PAC
   Trammell Crow Co .... $3,000   PAC/Ind

Accountants **$2,500**
   None over $2,500

Misc Finance **$5,250**
   None over $2,500

Health — $16,100

Health Professionals **$13,750**
   None over $2,500

Lawyers & Lobbyists — $42,675

Lawyers & Lobbyists **$42,675**
   Assn of Trial Lawyers of America .... $5,000   PAC
   Templeton & Co .... $4,000   Indiv
   Marks, Murase & White .... $3,500   Indiv

Misc Business — $14,449

Misc Manufacturing & Distributing **$5,900**
   None over $2,500

Transportation — $22,000

Air Transport **$19,250**
   Boeing Co .... $7,000   PAC
   General Electric .... $5,000   PAC
   United Parcel Service .... $3,400   PAC

Labor

Labor   **$173,265**

Building Trade Unions **$23,065**
   Ironworkers Union .... $5,000   PAC
   Plumbers/Pipefitters Union .... $5,000   PAC
   Laborers Union* .... $4,000   PAC
   Operating Engineers Union* .... $4,000   PAC
   Sheet Metal Workers Union .... $2,500   PAC

Industrial Unions **$42,850**
   Machinists/Aerospace Workers Union .... $10,000   PAC
   United Auto Workers .... $10,000   PAC
   United Steelworkers .... $7,500   PAC
   Intl Brotherhood of Electrical Workers .... $5,000   PAC

Transportation Unions **$31,000**
   Air Line Pilots Assn .... $8,500   PAC
   Marine Engineers Union* .... $8,000   PAC
   Teamsters Union .... $7,500   PAC

Public Sector Unions **$50,250**
   American Fedn of St/Cnty/Munic Employees .... $10,000   PAC
   National Assn of Letter Carriers .... $10,000   PAC
   National Education Assn .... $10,000   PAC
   National Assn Retired Federal Employees .... $8,000   PAC
   American Federation of Teachers .... $5,000   PAC
   International Assn of Firefighters .... $3,000   PAC

Misc Unions **$26,100**
   Service Employees International Union .... $10,000   PAC
   AFL-CIO .... $8,000   PAC
   Food & Commercial Workers Union .... $6,400   PAC

Ideological/Single-Issue

Ideological/Single-Issue   **$69,369**

Democratic/Liberal **$11,950**
   Hollywood Women's Political Cmte .... $5,000   PAC
   National Cmte for an Effective Congress .... $2,500   PAC

Leadership PACs **$8,248**
   Cmte for a Demo Consensus (Alan Cranston) .... $3,500   PAC

Pro-Israel **$5,250**
   Joint Action Cmte for Political Affairs .... $2,500   PAC

Pro-Choice **$7,250**
   National Abortion Rights Action League .... $4,000   PAC

Human Rights **$9,250**
   Human Rights Campaign Fund .... $7,000   PAC

Misc Issues **$24,036**
   Sierra Club .... $9,997   PAC
   League of Conservation Voters .... $5,000   PAC
   National Cmte to Preserve Social Security .... $2,750   PAC

Other & Unknown

Other   **$20,975**

Non-Profit Institutions **$3,250**
   None over $2,500

Education **$7,200**
   University of California System* .... $2,500   Indiv

Retired **$9,025**
   None over $2,500

Unknown   **$32,900**

   Homemakers/Non-income earners $5,000
   No Employer Listed or Found $11,800
   Employer Listed/Category Unknown $15,850
     None over $2,500

* Contributions came from more than one affiliate or
subsidiary.

Spending in Last 3 Elections

	1988	1990	1992
Brown	$532,897	$822,686	$897,227
Opponent	$218,696	$538,156	$456,963
Vote Pct	54%	53%	51%

Legend: ▨ Brown   ■ Opponent

Sherrod Brown, D-Ohio (13)

First elected: 1992

1991-92 Total Receipts: $495,275
1992 Year-end Cash: $8,920

1993-94 Committees & Subcommittees

Energy and Commerce
Health and the Environment; Oversight and Investigations

Foreign Affairs
Asia and the Pacific; Europe and the Middle East

Post Office and Civil Service

Leading Contributors

Business

Agriculture			**$2,700**
Tobacco			...$1,500
None over $1,500			

Communications/Electronics			**$7,250**
Media/Entertainment			...$1,750
None over $1,500			
Telephone Utilities			...$5,000
AT&T	$2,000	PAC	
United Telecommunications	$2,000	PAC	

Construction			**$2,950**
General Contractors			...$1,750
None over $1,500			

Energy & Natural Resources			**$4,550**
Oil & Gas			...$2,900
None over $1,500			

Finance, Insurance & Real Estate			**$49,021**
Commercial Banks			...$8,250
American Bankers Assn*	$4,000	PAC	
National City Corp	$2,000	PAC	
Finance/Credit Companies			...$1,500
Gries Investment Co	$1,500	Indiv	
Securities & Investment			...$3,250
Shearson Lehman Brothers	$2,750	Indiv	

Source of Funds in 1992 Election

Source	Total	Pct
■ PACs	$263,816	51%
▦ Indivs $200+	$152,229	30%
□ Indivs under $200	$72,417	14%
⊠ Other	$23,995	5%
Candidate	$1,327	0%
Party	$22,516	4%

Source of PAC Dollars by Sector

Source	Total	Pct
■ Business	$68,195	27%
▦ Labor	$148,289	58%
□ Ideology/Single Issue	$40,551	16%

In-State vs. Out-of-State Contributions*

Source	Total	Pct
□ In-State	$129,179	85%
■ Out-of-state	$21,800	14%
No state listed	$1,250	

*** by large individual contributors ($200 & above)**

Real Estate			...$25,250
Forest City Enterprises Inc	$8,250	Indiv	
National Assn of Realtors	$5,000	PAC	
Transcon Builders Inc	$3,000	Indiv	
Spitzer Management Inc	$2,000	Indiv	
Thomas Fok & Associates	$2,000	Indiv	
Accountants			...$7,321
Arthur Andersen & Co	$3,000	PAC/Ind	
American Institute of CPA's	$2,000	PAC	

Health — **$28,200**

Health Professionals			...$24,200
American Chiropractic Assn*	$4,000	PAC	
American Dental Assn	$2,500	PAC	
American Medical Assn	$2,500	PAC	
American Academy of Ophthalmology	$2,000	PAC	
American Nurses Assn	$1,500	PAC	
Misc Health			...$3,000
Citizens Medical Corp	$2,000	Indiv	

Lawyers & Lobbyists — **$39,550**

Lawyers & Lobbyists			...$39,550
Assn of Trial Lawyers of America	$10,000	PAC	
Vorys, Sater et al	$2,250	PAC/Ind	
Kahn, Kleinman et al	$2,000	Indiv	
Jones, Day et al	$1,800	PAC/Ind	
Schwartz, Manes & Ruby	$1,500	Indiv	

Contribution Totals by Sector

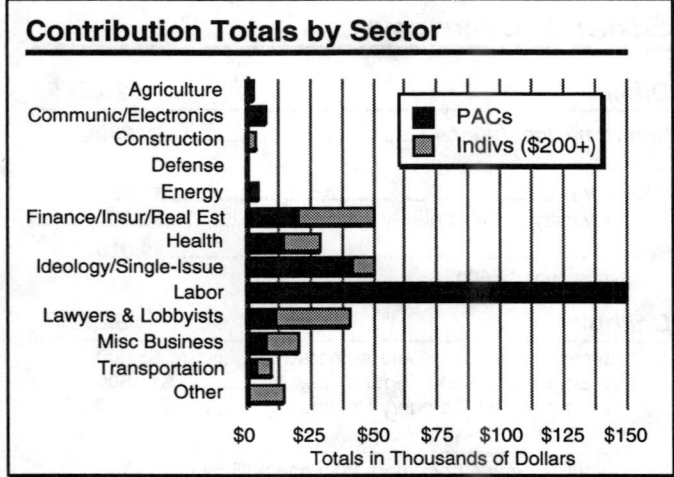

■ PACs
▦ Indivs ($200+)

Agriculture
Communic/Electronics
Construction
Defense
Energy
Finance/Insur/Real Est
Health
Ideology/Single-Issue
Labor
Lawyers & Lobbyists
Misc Business
Transportation
Other

$0 $25 $50 $75 $100 $125 $150
Totals in Thousands of Dollars

Misc Business — $19,295

Beer, Wine & Liquor *$2,000*
    Bay Distributors .... $2,000   Indiv
Retail Sales *$3,795*
    None over $1,500
Business Services *$3,550*
    Success Group Inc .... $2,000   Indiv
Misc Manufacturing & Distributing *$4,000*
    Kobacker Co .... $4,000   Indiv

Transportation — $8,950

Automotive *$5,750*
    Bush Leasing .... $2,000   Indiv
    Columbus Auto Auction..................... $2,000   Indiv
Railroads *$2,000*
    None over $1,500

Labor

Labor — $148,289

Building Trade Unions *$21,340*
    Carpenters & Joiners Union .... $10,000   PAC
    Sheet Metal Workers Union .... $5,000   PAC
    Laborers' Political League .... $2,000   PAC
    Plumbers/Pipefitters Union .... $2,000   PAC
Industrial Unions *$67,500*
    Communications Workers of America......... $10,000   PAC
    Intl Brotherhood of Electrical Workers ... $10,000   PAC
    Machinists/Aerospace Workers Union .... $10,000   PAC
    United Auto Workers .... $10,000   PAC
    United Steelworkers .... $10,000   PAC
    Electronic Machine Furniture Workers ..... $6,000   PAC
    Rubber Cork Linoleum & Plastic Workers ... $4,000   PAC
    United Mine Workers .... $3,000   PAC
Transportation Unions *$15,250*
    Teamsters Union* .... $5,000   PAC
    Air Line Pilots Assn .... $3,500   PAC
    International Longshoremen's Assn......... $1,500   PAC

Public Sector Unions *$30,200*
    National Education Assn .... $10,000   PAC
    National Assn of Letter Carriers .... $5,000   PAC
    National Assn Retired Federal Employees .. $4,000   PAC
    American Federation of Teachers .... $2,500   PAC
    American Fedn of St/Cnty/Munic Employees . $2,500   PAC
    National Rural Letter Carriers Assn ...... $2,500   PAC
    International Assn of Firefighters .... $2,000   PAC
Misc Unions *$13,999*
    Food & Commercial Workers Union .... $7,499   PAC
    AFL-CIO .... $2,500   PAC
    Service Employees International Union ..... $2,000   PAC

Ideological/Single-Issue

Ideological/Single-Issue — $49,301

Democratic/Liberal *$13,051*
    Fifth Horseman PAC .... $10,000   PAC
    National Cmte for an Effective Congress ... $2,500   PAC
Leadership PACs *$3,000*
    House Leadership Fund (Tom Foley) .... $2,000   PAC
Pro-Israel *$10,000*
    Heartland PAC .... $1,500   PAC
Pro-Choice *$4,000*
    Voters for Choice .... $2,000   PAC
Womens Issues *$1,500*
    None over $1,500
Human Rights *$5,500*
    Human Rights Campaign Fund .... $4,500   PAC
Misc Issues *$10,750*
    League of Conservation Voters .... $5,000   PAC
    Sierra Club .... $4,500   PAC

Other & Unknown

Other — $14,050

Civil Servants/Public Officials *$2,800*
    None over $1,500
Education *$3,000*
    Ohio Diesel Technical Institute Inc ...... $1,500   Indiv
Retired *$7,750*
    None over $1,500

Unknown — $34,658

    Homemakers/Non-income earners $5,505
    No Employer Listed or Found $9,053
    Employer Listed/Category Unknown $19,100
        National Feed Screw .... $3,500   Indiv
        State Government Consultants Inc ..... $1,800   Indiv

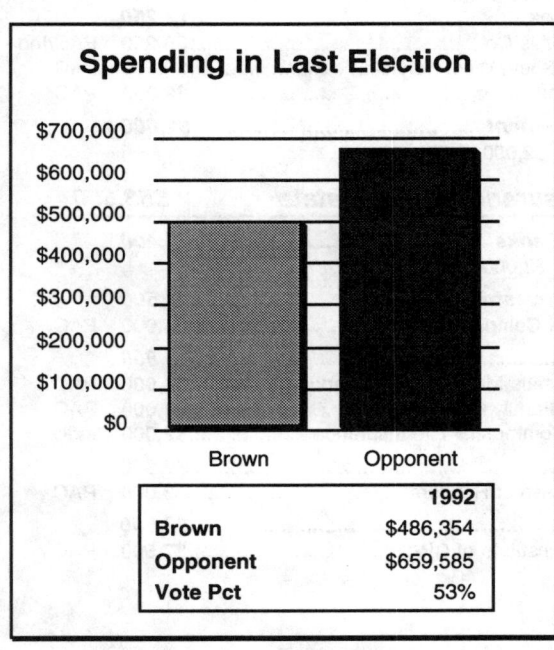

Spending in Last Election

	1992
Brown	$486,354
Opponent	$659,585
Vote Pct	53%

---

* Contributions came from more than one affiliate or subsidiary.

471

John Bryant, D-Texas (5)

First elected: 1982

1991-92 Total Receipts: $622,709
1992 Year-end Cash: $85,087

1991-92 Committees & Subcommittees

Budget
Defense, Foreign Policy and Space; Human Resources

Energy and Commerce
Health and the Environment; Oversight and Investigations; Telecommunications and Finance

Judiciary
Crime and Criminal Justice; Economic and Commercial Law; International Law, Immigration and Refugees

Leading Contributors

Business

Agriculture $28,575

Crop Production & Basic Processing $4,875
   None over $2,000

Tobacco $3,000
   None over $2,000

Dairy $8,000
   Associated Milk Producers .... $8,000   PAC

Livestock $2,000
   None over $2,000

Food Processing & Sales $7,500
   Pepsico Inc .... $2,000   Indiv
   Perrier Group of America .... $2,000   Indiv

Communications/Electronics $53,644

Printing & Publishing $3,500
   West Publishing .... $2,000   PAC

Media/Entertainment $21,300
   National Cable Television Assn .... $5,500   PAC
   Fox Inc .... $4,000   PAC
   National Assn of Broadcasters .... $4,000   PAC

Telephone Utilities $13,550
   AT&T .... $3,000   PAC
   GTE Corp .... $2,500   PAC
   MCI Telecommunications .... $2,250   PAC
   United Telecommunications .... $2,000   PAC

Source of Funds in 1992 Election

Source	Total	Pct
PACs	$353,133	56%
Indivs $200+	$162,416	26%
Indivs under $200	$86,237	14%
Other	$26,923	4%
Candidate	$0	0%
Party	$6,150	1%

Source of PAC Dollars by Sector

Source	Total	Pct
Business	$253,622	70%
Labor	$100,000	28%
Ideology/Single Issue	$9,000	2%

In-State vs. Out-of-State Contributions*

Source	Total	Pct
In-State	$137,816	85%
Out-of-state	$24,600	15%
No state listed	$0	

* by large individual contributors ($200 & above)

Telecom Services & Equipment $12,794
   DSC Communications Corp .... $9,544   PAC/Ind

Computer Equipment & Services $2,500
   Electronic Data Systems .... $2,500   PAC

Construction $5,250

General Contractors $3,500
   Williams Brothers Construction .... $2,000   Indiv

Energy & Natural Resources $31,300

Oil & Gas $16,050
   Northwest Oil Co .... $3,000   Indiv

Electric Utilities $12,250
   Texas Utilities Co .... $6,250   PAC/Ind
   Central & South West Services* .... $2,500   PAC
   Houston Industries .... $2,000   PAC

Waste Management $2,000
   None over $2,000

Finance, Insurance & Real Estate $53,550

Commercial Banks $4,400
   None over $2,000

Securities & Investment $11,500
   Investment Company Institute .... $4,000   PAC

Insurance $16,850
   Massachusetts Mutual Life Insurance .... $4,000   PAC
   American Family Corp .... $3,000   PAC
   Bankers Commercial Life Insurance .... $2,000   Indiv

Real Estate $9,800
   National Assn of Realtors .... $3,000   PAC

Accountants $9,500
   American Institute of CPA's .... $7,500   PAC

Contribution Totals by Sector

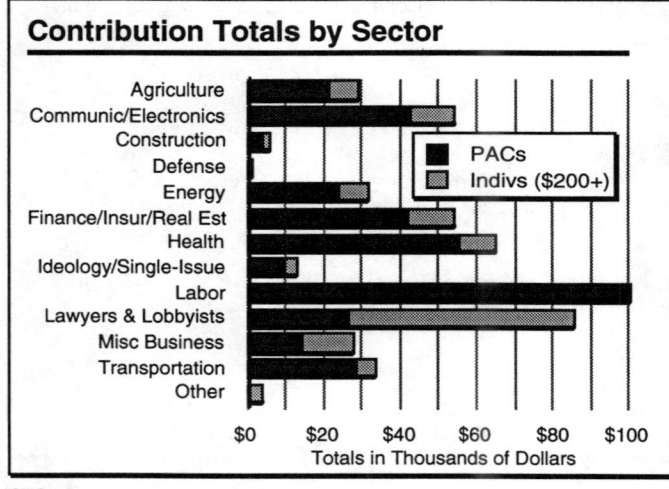

Legend: ■ PACs   ▨ Indivs ($200+)

Categories: Agriculture, Communic/Electronics, Construction, Defense, Energy, Finance/Insur/Real Est, Health, Ideology/Single-Issue, Labor, Lawyers & Lobbyists, Misc Business, Transportation, Other

$0 $20 $40 $60 $80 $100
Totals in Thousands of Dollars

Health — $64,189

Health Professionals **$41,189**
American Medical Assn*	$10,339	PAC
American Dental Assn	$6,500	PAC
American Academy of Ophthalmology	$4,500	PAC
American College of Emergency Physicians	$2,250	PAC
American Assn Oral & Maxillofacial Surgeons	$2,000	PAC

Hospitals/Nursing Homes **$10,750**
American Health Care Assn	$5,000	PAC
American Hospital Assn	$3,750	PAC

Health Services **$3,750**
None over $2,000

Pharmaceuticals/Health Products **$8,500**
Schering-Plough Corp	$2,000	PAC

Lawyers & Lobbyists — $84,973

Lawyers & Lobbyists **$84,973**
Assn of Trial Lawyers of America	$10,000	PAC
Baron & Budd	$6,000	Indiv
Misko, Howie et al	$2,500	Indiv
Akin, Gump et al	$2,250	PAC/Ind
Baldwin & Baldwin	$2,000	Indiv
Boyd & Associates	$2,000	Indiv
Hardy, Milutin et al	$2,000	Indiv
Johnson & Gibbs	$2,000	PAC
Winstead, Sechrest & Minick	$2,000	PAC

Misc Business — $27,007

Beer, Wine & Liquor **$8,250**
Miller of Dallas	$3,000	Indiv

Retail Sales **$3,007**
None over $2,000

Business Services **$5,500**
Alarm Industry Communications Cmte	$3,000	PAC

Misc Manufacturing & Distributing **$5,750**
Corning Glass Works	$2,000	PAC

Transportation — $33,035

Air Transport **$11,500**
American Airlines	$7,500	PAC
United Parcel Service	$2,000	PAC

Automotive **$15,535**
National Auto Dealers Assn	$10,000	PAC
WO Bankston Lincoln Mercury Saab	$2,257	Indiv
Sun Chevrolet Geo Oldsmobile	$2,000	Indiv

Railroads **$4,500**
Union Pacific Corp	$2,000	PAC

Labor

Labor — $100,000

Building Trade Unions **$6,500**
None over $2,000

Industrial Unions **$43,000**
United Steelworkers	$13,000	PAC
United Auto Workers	$10,000	PAC
Communications Workers of America	$7,000	PAC
Machinists/Aerospace Workers Union	$6,500	PAC
Intl Brotherhood of Electrical Workers	$5,000	PAC

Transportation Unions **$19,000**
Transport Workers Union	$8,000	PAC
Teamsters Union	$5,000	PAC
Air Line Pilots Assn	$2,000	PAC

Public Sector Unions **$23,000**
National Education Assn	$10,000	PAC
American Fedn of St/Cnty/Munic Employees	$5,000	PAC
National Assn of Letter Carriers	$3,000	PAC
American Postal Workers Union	$2,000	PAC

Misc Unions **$8,500**
Food & Commercial Workers Union	$6,000	PAC

Ideological/Single-Issue

Ideological/Single-Issue — $12,750

Democratic/Liberal **$2,750**
National Cmte for an Effective Congress	$2,500	PAC

Pro-Choice **$3,500**
None over $2,000

Misc Issues **$6,000**
National Cmte to Preserve Social Security	$2,500	PAC
League of Conservation Voters	$2,000	PAC

Other & Unknown

Other — $3,400

Retired **$2,150**
None over $2,000

Unknown — $26,365

Homemakers/Non-income earners	$7,000
Employer Listed/Category Unknown	$18,865
None over $2,000	

Spending in Last 3 Elections

	1988	1990	1992
Bryant	$646,218	$588,019	$795,462
Opponent	$179,201	$453,165	$43,942
Vote Pct	61%	60%	59%

---

* Contributions came from more than one affiliate or subsidiary.

473

Jim Bunning, R-Ky (4)

First elected: 1986

1991-92 Total Receipts: $946,781
1992 Year-end Cash: $59,618

1991-92 Committees & Subcommittees

Standards of Official Conduct

Ways and Means
Oversight; Social Security (Ranking Republicans)

Leading Contributors

Business

Agriculture — $63,650

Crop Production & Basic Processing	**$9,200**	
None over $2,500		
Tobacco	**$20,500**	
Philip Morris	$6,500	PAC/Ind
RJR Nabisco	$6,000	PAC
US Tobacco Co	$5,000	PAC
Livestock	**$4,500**	
Hermitage Farm	$3,000	Indiv
Agricultural Services/Products	**$5,750**	
None over $2,500		
Food Processing & Sales	**$16,200**	
Pepsico Inc	$3,000	PAC
Forestry & Forest Products	**$6,000**	
Westvaco Corp	$5,000	PAC

Communications/Electronics — $41,800

Telephone Utilities	**$33,550**	
Cincinnati Bell	$8,050	PAC
AT&T	$7,500	PAC
BellSouth Corp*	$4,500	PAC
Ameritech Corp	$3,000	PAC
Electronics Mfg & Services	**$2,500**	
None over $2,500		
Computer Equipment & Services	**$2,500**	
None over $2,500		

Source of Funds in 1992 Election

Source	Total	Pct
■ PACs	$435,491	45%
▨ Indivs $200+	$285,030	29%
□ Indivs under $200	$174,021	18%
⊠ Other	$77,791	8%
Candidate	$0	0%
Party	$36,552	4%

Source of PAC Dollars by Sector

Source	Total	Pct
■ Business	$422,647	98%
▨ Labor	$8,000	2%
□ Ideology/Single Issue	$1,914	0%

In-State vs. Out-of-State Contributions*

Source	Total	Pct
□ In-State	$228,820	82%
■ Out-of-state	$51,950	18%
No state listed	$0	

* by large individual contributors ($200 & above)

Construction — $23,750

General Contractors	**$13,250**	
Henry Fischer Builder	$3,000	Indiv
Associated General Contractors	$2,500	PAC
Home Builders	**$6,750**	
National Assn of Home Builders*	$4,250	PAC

Defense — $5,250

Defense Aerospace	**$3,500**	
None over $2,500		

Energy & Natural Resources — $56,040

Oil & Gas	**$31,840**	
Ashland Oil	$15,990	PAC/Ind
Mining	**$9,900**	
None over $2,500		
Electric Utilities	**$11,300**	
ACRE (Action Cmte for Rural Electrification)*	$2,500	PAC

Finance, Insurance & Real Estate — $178,023

Commercial Banks	**$39,600**	
American Bankers Assn*	$10,000	PAC
JP Morgan & Co	$5,500	PAC
Barnett Banks Inc	$3,500	PAC
Savings & Loans	**$5,000**	
US League of Savings Assns*	$5,000	PAC
Credit Unions	**$5,500**	
Credit Union National Assn*	$4,500	PAC
Securities & Investment	**$14,650**	
None over $2,500		

Contribution Totals by Sector

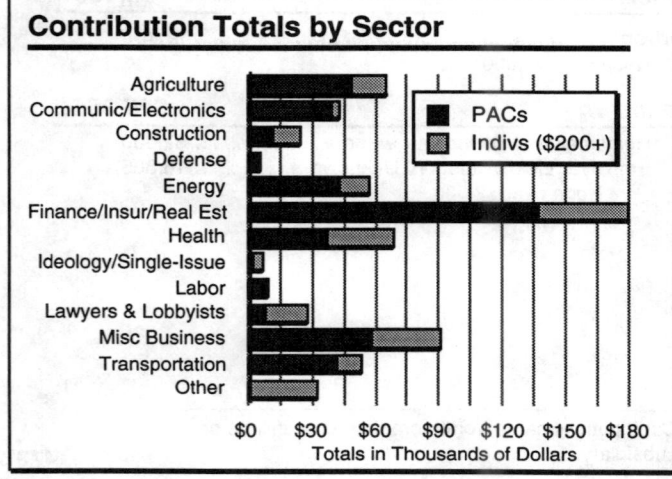

Agriculture
Communic/Electronics
Construction
Defense
Energy
Finance/Insur/Real Est
Health
Ideology/Single-Issue
Labor
Lawyers & Lobbyists
Misc Business
Transportation
Other

■ PACs
▨ Indivs ($200+)

$0 $30 $60 $90 $120 $150 $180
Totals in Thousands of Dollars

Insurance **$75,073**
    National Assn of Life Underwriters .... $7,500   PAC
    Independent Insurance Agents of America .... $6,323   PAC
    Mutual of Omaha .... $4,000   PAC
    Cigna Corp .... $3,500   PAC/Ind
    American Council of Life Insurance .... $3,000   PAC
    American Family Corp .... $3,000   PAC
    Beuttel-Youtsey Insurance .... $3,000   Indiv
    Capital Holding Corp .... $3,000   PAC
    Massachusetts Mutual Life Insurance .... $3,000   PAC
    National Assn of Independent Insurers .... $3,000   PAC
    Northwestern Mutual Life .... $3,000   PAC
    Putnam Agency Inc .... $2,500   Indiv

Real Estate **$20,400**
    National Assn of Realtors .... $6,500   PAC
    Stearns Co .... $4,000   Indiv

Accountants **$10,500**
    American Institute of CPA's .... $6,500   PAC

Misc Finance **$5,800**
    None over $2,500

Health
$67,559

Health Professionals **$52,809**
    American Medical Assn .... $10,000   PAC
    American Optometric Assn .... $4,000   PAC
    American Dental Assn .... $2,500   PAC
    Grefer & O'Brien .... $2,500   Indiv

Hospitals/Nursing Homes **$8,250**
    American Hospital Assn .... $3,500   PAC

Pharmaceuticals/Health Products **$6,500**
    None over $2,500

Lawyers & Lobbyists
$27,615

Lawyers & Lobbyists **$27,615**
    Assn of Trial Lawyers of America .... $2,500   PAC
    Greenebaum, Doll & McDonald .... $2,500   Indiv

Spending in Last 3 Elections

	1988	1990	1992
Bunning	$468,870	$563,409	$984,180
Opponent	$23,636	$76,580	$311,121
Vote Pct	74%	69%	62%

Misc Business **$89,740**

Food & Beverage **$14,250**
    National Restaurant Assn .... $3,500   PAC
    McDonald's Corp .... $3,000   PAC/Ind

Beer, Wine & Liquor **$25,500**
    Brown-Forman Distillers .... $11,500   PAC/Ind
    National Beer Wholesalers Assn .... $5,000   PAC
    Wine & Spirits Wholesalers of America .... $2,500   PAC

Retail Sales **$12,800**
    None over $2,500

Business Services **$5,200**
    None over $2,500

Chemical & Related Manufacturing **$4,000**
    None over $2,500

Steel Production **$5,000**
    Armco Inc .... $2,500   PAC

Misc Manufacturing & Distributing **$17,040**
    Deluxe Engraving Co .... $5,390   Indiv
    National Band & Tag .... $2,500   Indiv

Transportation
$52,650

Air Transport **$23,900**
    Federal Express Corp .... $6,000   PAC
    Comair .... $5,500   Indiv
    United Parcel Service .... $5,000   PAC
    Delta Airlines .... $3,000   PAC
    General Electric .... $2,900   PAC

Automotive **$17,250**
    Bob Sumerel Tire Co .... $4,500   Indiv
    National Auto Dealers Assn .... $4,000   PAC
    Auto Dealers & Drivers for Free Trade .... $2,500   PAC

Railroads **$6,000**
    Norfolk Southern Corp .... $2,500   PAC
    Union Pacific Corp .... $2,500   PAC

Sea Transport **$3,250**
    CSX Corp* .... $2,500   PAC/Ind

Labor

Labor **$8,000**

Transportation Unions **$4,500**
    Marine Engineers Union* .... $4,500   PAC

Public Sector Unions **$3,500**
    None over $2,500

Ideological/Single-Issue

Ideological/Single-Issue **$6,064**

Republican/Conservative **$3,950**
    None over $2,500

Other & Unknown

Other **$31,840**

Retired **$28,090**
    None over $2,500

Unknown **$61,850**

    Homemakers/Non-income earners $21,400
    Generic Occupation/Category Unknown $2,750
    Employer Listed/Category Unknown $37,000
        None over $2,500

---

* Contributions came from more than one affiliate or subsidiary.

Dan Burton, R-Ind (6)

First elected: 1982

1991-92 Total Receipts: $629,390
1992 Year-end Cash: $622,881

1991-92 Committees & Subcommittees

Foreign Affairs
Africa (Ranking Republican); Western Hemisphere Affairs

Post Office and Civil Service
Human Resources (Ranking Republican)

Veterans' Affairs
Hospitals and Health Care; Housing and Memorial Affairs (Ranking Republican)

Leading Contributors

Business

Agriculture	$29,700	
Tobacco	**$1,800**	
None over $1,500		
Dairy	**$9,500**	
Associated Milk Producers	$7,000	PAC
Livestock	**$1,500**	
None over $1,500		
Agricultural Services/Products	**$9,000**	
Indiana Farm Bureau	$5,000	PAC
Seabord Corp	$2,000	PAC
Food Processing & Sales	**$5,650**	
None over $1,500		

Communications/Electronics	$26,060	
Printing & Publishing	**$2,650**	
None over $1,500		
Media/Entertainment	**$6,300**	
Cardinal Communications Inc	$3,000	Indiv
Comcast Corp	$3,000	PAC
Telephone Utilities	**$12,110**	
Ameritech Corp*	$8,000	PAC
GTE Corp	$2,610	PAC
Computer Equipment & Services	**$5,000**	
IBM Corp	$2,000	Indiv

Construction	$18,934	
General Contractors	**$5,150**	
Associated General Contractors	$1,500	PAC

Contribution Totals by Sector

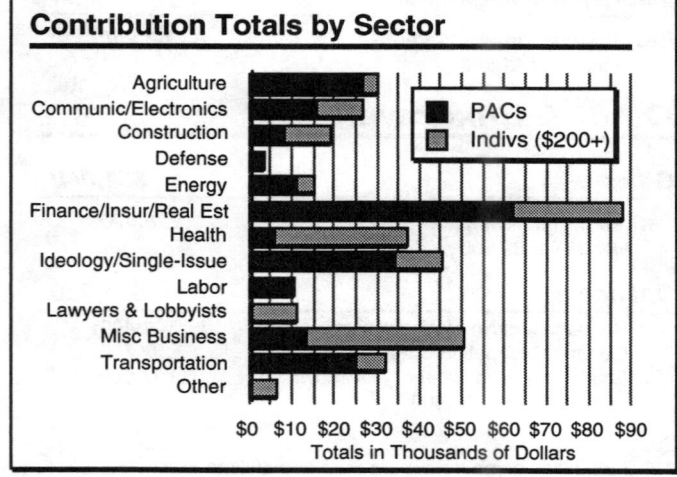

Totals in Thousands of Dollars

Source of Funds in 1992 Election

Source	Total	Pct
PACs	$208,385	33%
Indivs $200+	$236,952	38%
Indivs under $200	$115,557	18%
Other	$68,496	11%
Candidate	$0	0%
Party	$2,404	0%

Source of PAC Dollars by Sector

Source	Total	Pct
Business	$167,098	79%
Labor	$10,000	5%
Ideology/Single Issue	$33,850	16%

In-State vs. Out-of-State Contributions*

Source	Total	Pct
In-State	$101,225	43%
Out-of-state	$133,102	57%
No state listed	$2,150	

*** by large individual contributors ($200 & above)**

Home Builders	$3,550	
National Assn of Home Builders	$3,000	PAC
Special Trade Contractors	**$4,684**	
Sheet Metal/Air Conditioning Contractors	$2,084	PAC
Building Materials & Equipment	**$4,550**	
Asphalt Materials Inc	$3,300	Indiv

Defense	$3,000	
Defense Aerospace	**$3,000**	
Northrop Corp	$1,500	PAC

Energy & Natural Resources	$14,950	
Oil & Gas	**$8,200**	
Ashland Oil	$2,300	PAC
Dresser Industries	$1,500	PAC
Mesa Limited Partnership	$1,500	Indiv
Misc Energy	**$2,000**	
Babcock & Wilcox	$2,000	PAC
Electric Utilities	**$3,950**	
None over $1,500		

Finance, Insurance & Real Estate	$87,654	
Commercial Banks	**$7,000**	
Hasten Bancorp	$3,000	Indiv
Merchants National Corp	$2,000	PAC/Ind
Credit Unions	**$2,500**	
Credit Union National Assn	$2,500	PAC
Finance/Credit Companies	**$2,000**	
First Management Corp	$2,000	Indiv
Securities & Investment	**$6,750**	
Prudential Securities	$2,750	PAC
Insurance	**$45,904**	
National Assn of Life Underwriters	$7,000	PAC
Independent Insurance Agents of America	$6,550	PAC
American International Group Inc	$5,300	PAC
Golden Rule Insurance Co	$4,180	PAC/Ind

New England Mutual Life	$2,750	PAC
National Assn of Prof Insurance Agents	$2,589	PAC
Casualty & Surety Agents Assn	$2,250	PAC
American Council of Life Insurance	$2,000	PAC
Capitol Guaranty Corp	$2,000	Indiv
Chubb Corp	$1,500	PAC

Real Estate **$11,900**

National Assn of Realtors	$6,000	PAC
Mark III Development	$2,000	Indiv

Accountants **$7,400**

American Institute of CPA's	$6,000	PAC

Misc Finance **$3,800**
None over $1,500

Health — $36,805

Health Professionals **$32,050**

American Dental Assn	$2,000	PAC
American Medical Assn*	$1,500	PAC

Hospitals/Nursing Homes **$2,175**
None over $1,500

Pharmaceuticals/Health Products **$2,330**
None over $1,500

Lawyers & Lobbyists — $10,750

Lawyers & Lobbyists **$10,750**
None over $1,500

Misc Business — $49,815

Food & Beverage **$6,250**

Pizza Hut Inc	$2,000	Indiv

Beer, Wine & Liquor **$5,650**

Olinger Distributing Co	$5,650	Indiv

Retail Sales **$3,000**

Reliable Drug Stores Inc	$1,500	Indiv

Misc Services **$3,800**

Monarch Beverage Co	$2,000	Indiv

Business Services **$8,750**

Klipsch, Lanham & Associates	$5,000	Indiv
Russ Merritt Public Relations	$2,000	Indiv

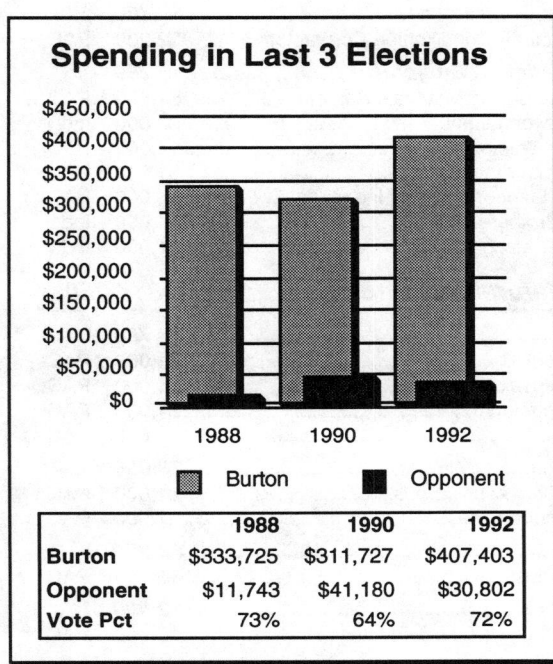

Spending in Last 3 Elections

	1988	1990	1992
Burton	$333,725	$311,727	$407,403
Opponent	$11,743	$41,180	$30,802
Vote Pct	73%	64%	72%

Misc Business	$1,500	
None over $1,500		

Misc Manufacturing & Distributing **$9,475**

Stone Container Corp	$2,300	PAC

Textiles **$8,750**

Milliken & Co	$4,000	Indiv
Burlington Industries	$3,000	PAC

Transportation — $31,700

Air Transport **$10,550**

United Parcel Service	$5,150	PAC
Federal Express Corp	$3,500	PAC
United Airlines	$1,500	PAC

Automotive **$17,000**

National Auto Dealers Assn	$7,000	PAC
Auto Dealers & Drivers for Free Trade	$2,000	PAC
Ford Motor Co	$2,000	PAC
General Motors	$1,650	PAC
Chrysler Corp	$1,500	PAC

Sea Transport **$3,000**

Amex International Inc	$3,000	Indiv

Labor

Labor — $10,000

Public Sector Unions **$9,500**

National Assn of Letter Carriers	$4,000	PAC
National Assn of Postmasters	$1,500	PAC
National League of Postmasters	$1,500	PAC

Ideological/Single-Issue

Ideological/Single-Issue — $44,800

Republican/Conservative **$1,750**
None over $1,500

Foreign & Defense Policy **$13,150**

Serbian Unity Congress	$5,400	PAC/Ind
Pakistan-American Friendship Society	$4,250	PAC
Free Cuba PAC	$1,500	PAC

Pro-Israel **$19,500**

National PAC	$5,000	PAC
Hudson Valley PAC	$3,000	PAC
Florida Congressional Cmte	$2,000	PAC
National Action Committee	$2,000	PAC

Gun Rights/Gun Control **$9,900**

National Rifle Assn	$9,900	PAC

Other & Unknown

Other — $6,210

Civil Servants/Public Officials **$2,810**

City of Frankfort	$1,860	Indiv

Education **$2,000**

Ball State University	$2,000	Indiv

Unknown — $77,047

Homemakers/Non-income earners	$6,160	
No Employer Listed or Found	$48,312	
Generic Occupation/Category Unknown	$2,250	
Employer Listed/Category Unknown	$20,325	
ENC Corp	$1,500	Indiv

---

* Contributions came from more than one affiliate or
subsidiary.

Steve Buyer, R-Ind (5)

First elected: 1992

1991-92 Total Receipts:	$392,885
1992 Year-end Cash:	$2,902

1993-94 Committees & Subcommittees

Armed Services
Military Forces and Personnel; Research and Technology

Veterans' Affairs
Hospitals and Health Care; Housing and Memorial Affairs

Leading Contributors

Business

Agriculture — $63,948

Crop Production & Basic Processing ... **$1,950**
    None over $1,000

Agricultural Services/Products ... **$11,500**
    Indiana Farm Bureau ... $10,000   PAC

Food Processing & Sales ... **$10,500**
    Marburger Foods ... $4,000   Indiv
    Flowers Industries ... $2,000   PAC
    Central Soya Co ... $1,000   PAC
    Interstate Bakeries Corp ... $1,000   Indiv

Forestry & Forest Products ... **$39,698**
    Willamette Industries ... $2,956   PAC
    Boise Cascade ... $2,500   PAC
    Westvaco Corp ... $2,000   PAC
    Weyerhaeuser Co ... $2,000   PAC
    National Forest Products Assn ... $1,692   PAC
    Medford Corp ... $1,500   PAC
    Potlatch Corp ... $1,500   PAC
    Simpson Investment Co ... $1,500   PAC
    Wetzel-Ovetti Lumber Co ... $1,500   Indiv
    International Paper Co ... $1,250   PAC
    DR Johnson Lumber Co ... $1,000   Indiv
    Pacific Lumber & Shipping Co ... $1,000   Indiv
    Riley Creek Lumber Co ... $1,000   Indiv
    SDS Lumber Co ... $1,000   Indiv
    Union Camp Corp ... $1,000   PAC
    Zir-Mac Forest Products Inc ... $1,000   Indiv

Communications/Electronics — $6,500

Printing & Publishing ... **$1,000**
    None over $1,000

Contribution Totals by Sector

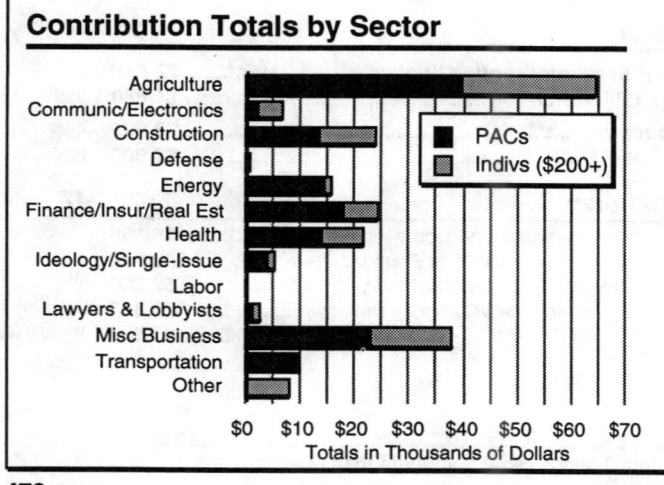

Agriculture
Communic/Electronics
Construction
Defense
Energy
Finance/Insur/Real Est
Health
Ideology/Single-Issue
Labor
Lawyers & Lobbyists
Misc Business
Transportation
Other

■ PACs
▨ Indivs ($200+)

$0 $10 $20 $30 $40 $50 $60 $70
Totals in Thousands of Dollars

Source of Funds in 1992 Election

Source	Total	Pct
■ PACs	$136,893	31%
▨ Indivs $200+	$108,038	24%
☐ Indivs under $200	$93,362	21%
▧ Other	$105,707	24%
Candidate	$30,626	7%
Party	$62,115	14%

Source of PAC Dollars by Sector

Source	Total	Pct
■ Business	$133,640	97%
▨ Labor	$0	0%
☐ Ideology/Single Issue	$3,797	3%

In-State vs. Out-of-State Contributions*

Source	Total	Pct
☐ In-State	$75,521	70%
■ Out-of-state	$32,517	30%
No state listed	$0	

* by large individual contributors ($200 & above)

Media/Entertainment ... **$2,000**
    Cardinal Communications Inc ... $2,000   Indiv

Telephone Utilities ... **$1,000**
    AT&T ... $1,000   PAC

Computer Equipment & Services ... **$2,000**
    Ontario Corp ... $2,000   Indiv

Construction — $24,170

General Contractors ... **$1,730**
    Associated General Contractors ... $1,000   PAC

Home Builders ... **$5,000**
    National Assn of Home Builders ... $5,000   PAC

Special Trade Contractors ... **$2,200**
    Sheet Metal/Air Conditioning Contractors ... $2,200   PAC

Building Materials & Equipment ... **$15,240**
    Lumber & Building Materials Dealers ... $2,600   PAC
    Cole Hardwood Lumber Inc ... $2,000   Indiv
    Caterpillar Tractor ... $1,000   PAC
    Crone Lumber Inc ... $1,000   Indiv
    Glen Oak Lumber & Milling Inc ... $1,000   Indiv
    Jackson Brothers Lumber ... $1,000   Indiv
    MacAllister Machine Co ... $1,000   Indiv

Energy & Natural Resources — $15,250

Oil & Gas ... **$6,750**
    Amoco Corp ... $1,000   PAC
    Exxon Corp ... $1,000   PAC
    Phillips Petroleum ... $1,000   PAC
    Sun Co ... $1,000   PAC

Mining ... **$3,000**
    National Coal Assn ... $1,000   PAC
    Phelps Dodge Corp ... $1,000   PAC

Misc Energy ... **$3,000**
    Cooper Industries ... $3,000   PAC

Electric Utilities ... **$2,500**
    Southern Indiana Gas & Electric ... $2,000   PAC

Finance, Insurance & Real Estate $24,050

Commercial Banks $7,000
    American Bankers Assn ....$3,000   PAC
    1st Source Corp ....$1,000   PAC
    Chase Manhattan ....$1,000   PAC
    First Source Bank......................................$1,000   Indiv
    Frances Slocum Bank ....$1,000   Indiv

Insurance $2,550
    None over $1,000

Real Estate $13,800
    National Assn of Realtors............................$10,000   PAC
    Grant Co Abstract ....$1,000   Indiv
    Mortgage Bankers Assn of America ....$1,000   PAC

Health $21,240

Health Professionals $8,118
    American Dental Assn ....$5,000   PAC

Hospitals/Nursing Homes $4,950
    American Health Care Assn..........................$2,000   PAC
    Tioga Pines Living Center Inc ....$1,700   Indiv
    Millers Merry Manor ....$1,000   Indiv

Pharmaceuticals/Health Products $7,500
    Eli Lilly & Co ....$6,000   PAC/Ind

Lawyers & Lobbyists $2,486

Lawyers & Lobbyists $2,486
    Jones, Day et al ....$1,000   PAC

Misc Business $37,592

Business Associations $3,041
    National Fedn of Independent Business ....$2,000   PAC
    Business Industry PAC ....$1,041   PAC

Food & Beverage $8,300
    National Restaurant Assn ....$2,500   PAC
    Coca-Cola Bottling ....$1,500   Indiv
    Brucker Enterprises Inc..............................$1,300   Indiv
    S&A Restaurant Corp ....$1,000   PAC

Beer, Wine & Liquor $4,000
    National Beer Wholesalers Assn ....$3,000   PAC

Retail Sales $1,250
    None over $1,000

Business Services $2,750
    Duke Inc ....$1,000   Indiv
    Whiteco Industries....................................$1,000   Indiv

Chemical & Related Manufacturing $1,500
    Landis Plastics Inc ....$1,000   Indiv

Misc Manufacturing & Distributing $15,250
    Stone Container Corp ....$5,000   PAC
    Accurate Castings Inc ....$3,000   Indiv
    Jordan Manufacturing ....$2,000   Indiv
    PPG Industries ....$1,000   PAC
    Shirt Shed Inc ....$1,000   Indiv
    Windway Capital Corp ....$1,000   Indiv

Transportation $9,800

Automotive $8,300
    National Auto Dealers Assn ....$5,000   PAC
    Eaton Corp ....$2,000   PAC
    Federal-Mogul Corp ....$1,000   PAC

Railroads $1,000
    Union Pacific Corp ....$1,000   PAC

Ideological/Single-Issue

Ideological/Single-Issue $5,043

Republican/Conservative.................................... $1,270
    Hoosiers Supporting Buyer for Congress ....$1,246   Indiv

Leadership PACs $1,000
    Republican Leader's Fund (Bob Michel) ....$1,000   PAC

Misc Issues $2,273
    Ruff PAC ....$1,273   PAC
    Public Service Research Council ....$1,000   PAC

Other & Unknown

Other $7,697

Civil Servants/Public Officials............................. $1,300
    State of New Jersey ....$1,000   Indiv

Retired $6,197
    None over $1,000

Unknown $26,949

    Homemakers/Non-income earners $7,979
    Employer Listed/Category Unknown $18,770
       Kellan Inc ....$1,900   Indiv
       Tippecanoe Beverages Inc ....$1,200   Indiv
       Gutchess International ....$1,000   Indiv
       Irving Brothers Gravel Inc ....$1,000   Indiv
       Monon Trailer ....$1,000   Indiv
       Redmen & Reese ....$1,000   Indiv
       Spiece Sales ....$1,000   Indiv
       Syndicate Sales Inc ....$1,000   Indiv
       US Coatings ....$1,000   Indiv
       Woodmizer ....$1,000   Indiv

Independent expenditures supporting Buyer
    National Right to Life PAC $3,036

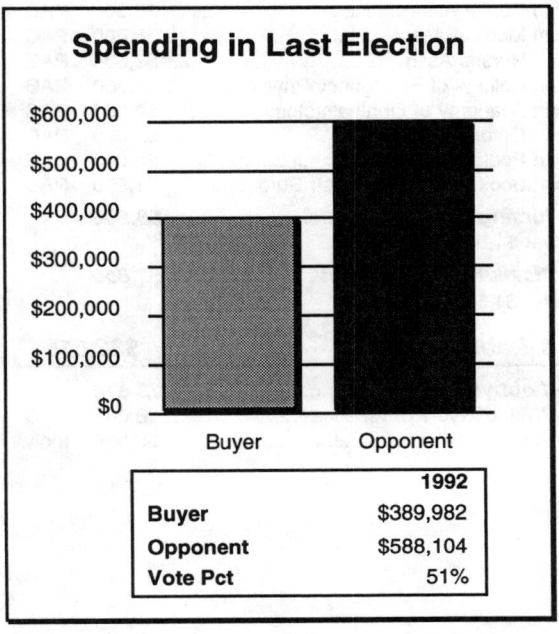

Spending in Last Election

	1992
Buyer	$389,982
Opponent	$588,104
Vote Pct	51%

---

* Contributions came from more than one affiliate or
subsidiary.

479

Leslie L. Byrne, D-Va (11)

First elected: 1992

1991-92 Total Receipts: $792,565
1992 Year-end Cash: $16,651

1993-94 Committees & Subcommittees

Post Office and Civil Service
Compensation and Employee Benefits

Public Works and Transportation
Investigations and Oversight; Surface Transportation; Water Resources and the Environment

Leading Contributors

Business

Agriculture $7,700

Tobacco	**$4,000**	
Philip Morris	$2,000	PAC
RJR Nabisco	$2,000	PAC
Dairy	**$2,000**	
None over $1,500		

Communications/Electronics $8,900

Telephone Utilities	**$2,100**	
None over $1,500		
Telecom Services & Equipment	**$2,000**	
Columbia Cellular Corp	$2,000	Indiv
Computer Equipment & Services	**$2,350**	
None over $1,500		

Construction $2,200

None over $1,500

Defense $3,550

None over $1,500

Energy & Natural Resources $6,964

Oil & Gas	**$3,576**	
None over $1,500		
Electric Utilities	**$1,750**	
None over $1,500		

Source of Funds in 1992 Election

Source	Total	Pct
PACs	$310,167	37%
Indivs $200+	$126,952	15%
Indivs under $200	$312,959	37%
Other	$95,729	11%
Candidate	$22,000	3%
Party	$66,392	8%

Source of PAC Dollars by Sector

Source	Total	Pct
Business	$92,669	30%
Labor	$149,249	48%
Ideology/Single Issue	$71,665	23%

In-State vs. Out-of-State Contributions*

Source	Total	Pct
In-State	$96,204	78%
Out-of-state	$27,398	22%
No state listed	$500	

* by large individual contributors ($200 & above)

Finance, Insurance & Real Estate $24,700

Commercial Banks	**$3,200**	
Virginia Bankers Assn	$1,500	PAC
Credit Unions	**$1,500**	
Credit Union National Assn	$1,500	PAC
Insurance	**$8,950**	
National Assn of Life Underwriters	$3,500	PAC
Real Estate	**$8,650**	
National Assn of Realtors	$5,000	PAC

Health $38,234

Health Professionals	**$30,634**	
American Dental Assn	$5,000	PAC
American Medical Assn	$5,000	PAC
American Nurses Assn	$2,634	PAC
American College of Emergency Physicians	$2,300	PAC
American Academy of Ophthalmology	$2,000	PAC
American Optometric Assn	$2,000	PAC
American Podiatry Assn	$2,000	PAC
American Soc Plastic & Reconstr Surgeons	$1,500	PAC
Hospitals/Nursing Homes	**$3,900**	
None over $1,500		
Pharmaceuticals/Health Products	**$1,850**	
None over $1,500		

Lawyers & Lobbyists $33,616

Lawyers & Lobbyists	**$33,616**	
Assn of Trial Lawyers of America	$10,000	PAC
Patton, Boggs & Blow	$2,016	Indiv

Contribution Totals by Sector

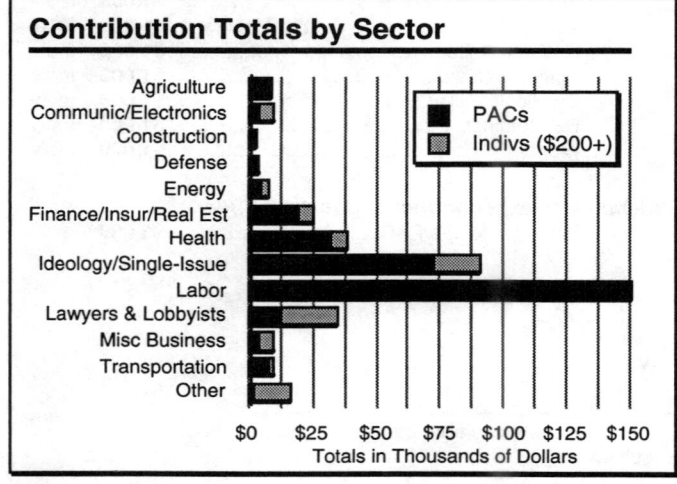

Totals in Thousands of Dollars

Misc Business $8,762

Business Associations **$2,500**
    Greater Washington Board of Trade ....$2,000 PAC
Beer, Wine & Liquor **$1,500**
    None over $1,500
Business Services **$4,062**
    None over $1,500

Transportation $8,950

Automotive **$6,700**
    National Auto Dealers Assn ....$5,000 PAC

Labor

Labor $149,749

Building Trade Unions **$14,850**
    Laborers' Political League ....$4,000 PAC
    Carpenters & Joiners Union ....$3,500 PAC
    Sheet Metal Workers Union ....$2,000 PAC
    Bricklayers Union ....$1,850 PAC
Industrial Unions **$52,800**
    Communications Workers of America...............$10,000 PAC
    Intl Brotherhood of Electrical Workers ....$10,000 PAC
    United Steelworkers ....$10,000 PAC
    Machinists/Aerospace Workers Union ....$6,500 PAC
    United Auto Workers ....$5,000 PAC
    United Mine Workers ....$4,000 PAC
    Boilermakers Union ....$2,000 PAC
    Graphic Communications Union ....$1,500 PAC
    Ladies Garment Workers Union...........................$1,500 PAC
Transportation Unions **$21,050**
    Teamsters Union ....$6,000 PAC
    Seafarers International Union ....$3,750 PAC
    United Transportation Union ....$3,000 PAC
    Air Line Pilots Assn ....$2,000 PAC
    Maintenance of Way Employees ....$1,500 PAC
    Trans Comm International Union ....$1,500 PAC

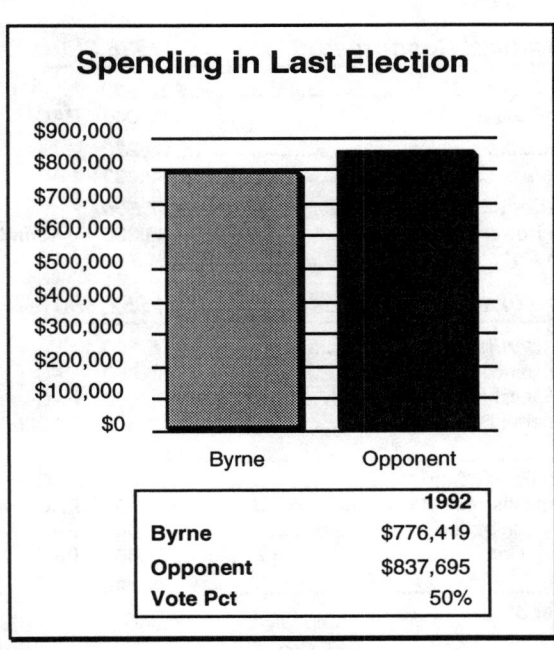

Spending in Last Election

	1992
Byrne	$776,419
Opponent	$837,695
Vote Pct	50%

Public Sector Unions $45,799

    National Assn of Letter Carriers ....$10,000 PAC
    National Education Assn ....$10,000 PAC
    International Assn of Firefighters ....$7,600 PAC
    American Fedn of St/Cnty/Munic Employees ......$4,999 PAC
    American Postal Workers Union ....$3,500 PAC
    American Federation of Govt Employees ....$2,000 PAC
    National Assn Retired Federal Employees ....$2,000 PAC
    National Rural Letter Carriers Assn ....$2,000 PAC
Misc Unions.. **$15,250**
    Food & Commercial Workers Union ....$7,500 PAC
    AFL-CIO ....$4,000 PAC
    Service Employees International Union ....$2,000 PAC
    Bakery, Confectionery & Tobacco Workers ....$1,500 PAC

Ideological/Single-Issue

Ideological/Single-Issue $90,115

Democratic/Liberal **$5,400**
    National Cmte for an Effective Congress ....$2,800 PAC
Leadership PACs.. **$3,000**
    None over $1,500
Foreign & Defense Policy **$3,788**
    Council for a Livable World ....$1,888 PAC
Pro-Israel **$3,500**
    None over $1,500
Pro-Choice... **$6,500**
    National Abortion Rights Action League ....$5,000 PAC
Gun Rights/Gun Control **$2,677**
    Handgun Control Inc ....$2,677 PAC
Womens Issues... **$36,530**
    Emily's List ....$10,430 PAC/Ind
    Women's Campaign Fund ....$9,000 PAC
    National Organization for Women ....$5,000 PAC
    National Womens Political Caucus ....$4,000 PAC
Human Rights **$7,518**
    Human Rights Campaign Fund.............................$7,518 PAC
Misc Issues... **$21,202**
    Sierra Club ....$5,000 PAC
    League of Conservation Voters ....$3,469 PAC
    New Jersey Environmental Federation ....$2,633 PAC
    National Council of Senior Citizens....................$2,000 PAC
    National Cmte to Preserve Social Security ....$1,750 PAC

Other & Unknown

Other $15,930

Civil Servants/Public Officials **$8,600**
    Fairfax County ....$1,550 Indiv
Education **$2,600**
    None over $1,500
Retired **$3,480**
    None over $1,500

Unknown $41,665

    Homemakers/Non-income earners $6,829
    No Employer Listed or Found $16,015
    Employer Listed/Category Unknown $18,821
    Sunshine Ventures.......................................$1,657 Indiv

Sonny Callahan, R-Ala (1)

Agricultural Services/Products

1991-92 Committees & Subcommittees

First elected: 1984
1991-92 Total Receipts: $376,087
1992 Year-end Cash: $228,837

Energy and Commerce
Energy and Power; Transportation and Hazardous Materials

Merchant Marine and Fisheries
Coast Guard and Navigation; Merchant Marine

Leading Contributors

Business

Agriculture	$51,974

Crop Production & Basic Processing $4,275
    None over $1,500

Tobacco $6,900
    RJR Nabisco .... $3,000   PAC
    Philip Morris .... $1,600   PAC

Dairy $4,500
    Dairy Fresh Corp .... $4,250   Indiv

Agricultural Services/Products $5,350
    Alabama Farm Bureau Federation .... $3,300   PAC

Food Processing & Sales $9,900
    Delchamps Inc .... $2,500   PAC/Ind
    Winn-Dixie Stores .... $1,500   PAC

Forestry & Forest Products $19,249
    International Paper Co .... $3,000   PAC
    Scott Paper Co .... $2,999   PAC
    Parsons & Whittemore Inc .... $2,500   Indiv
    Champion International Corp .... $1,800   PAC

Communications/Electronics	$20,500

Media/Entertainment $10,350
    National Cable Television Assn .... $5,000   PAC
    National Assn of Broadcasters .... $2,900   PAC

Telephone Utilities $7,250
    BellSouth Corp* .... $2,750   PAC
    AT&T .... $2,000   PAC

Computer Equipment & Services $1,800
    None over $1,500

Source of Funds in 1992 Election

Source	Total	Pct
■ PACs	$208,608	55%
▨ Indivs $200+	$117,700	31%
□ Indivs under $200	$24,235	6%
▨ Other	$25,544	7%
Candidate	$0	0%
Party	$19	0%

Source of PAC Dollars by Sector

Source	Total	Pct
■ Business	$212,754	90%
▨ Labor	$21,000	9%
□ Ideology/Single Issue	$3,400	1%

In-State vs. Out-of-State Contributions*

Source	Total	Pct
□ In-State	$106,050	91%
■ Out-of-state	$10,900	9%
No state listed	$0	

* by large individual contributors ($200 & above)

Construction	$20,850

General Contractors $8,800
    Associated General Contractors .... $2,800   PAC/Ind

Special Trade Contractors $3,500
    None over $1,500

Construction Services $2,250
    David Volkert & Associates .... $2,000   Indiv

Building Materials & Equipment $6,050
    Scotch Lumber Co .... $2,000   Indiv

Defense	$1,500

    None over $1,500

Energy & Natural Resources	$36,300

Oil & Gas $22,600
    Southern Natural Resources .... $2,000   PAC

Mining $3,250
    Dravo Corp .... $2,000   PAC

Electric Utilities $7,800
    Alabama Power Co .... $3,250   PAC/Ind
    Southern Co* .... $1,750   PAC

Finance, Insurance & Real Estate	$52,850

Commercial Banks $16,150
    Amsouth Bancorp .... $6,850   PAC
    Central Bancshares of the South .... $5,000   PAC
    First Alabama Bancshares .... $1,500   PAC/Ind

Insurance $22,800
    American Family Corp .... $9,000   PAC
    Massachusetts Mutual Life Insurance ... $2,000   PAC
    National Assn of Life Underwriters ...... $2,000   PAC
    Torchmark Corp .... $1,800   PAC

Real Estate $4,750
    None over $1,500

Contribution Totals by Sector

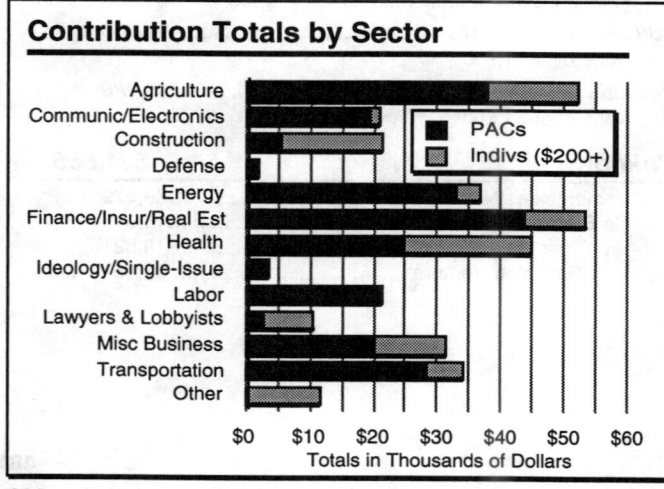

Totals in Thousands of Dollars

Accountants **$6,800**
    American Institute of CPA's .... $5,000   PAC
Misc Finance **$1,500**
    None over $1,500

Health $44,500

Health Professionals **$28,650**
    American Medical Assn .... $14,500   PAC
    American Dental Assn .... $3,000   PAC
Health Services **$8,000**
    Healthsouth Rehabilitation Corp .... $7,000   Indiv
Pharmaceuticals/Health Products **$4,600**
    Ciba-Geigy Corp .... $1,500   PAC/Ind
Misc Health **$2,150**
    Managed Healthcare Systems Inc .... $1,900   Indiv

Lawyers & Lobbyists $10,400

Lawyers & Lobbyists **$10,400**
    None over $1,500

Misc Business $30,900

Food & Beverage **$7,250**
    Morrison Inc .... $3,750   PAC/Ind
Beer, Wine & Liquor **$1,800**
    None over $1,500
Retail Sales **$2,300**
    None over $1,500
Misc Services **$2,250**
    None over $1,500
Chemical & Related Manufacturing **$7,100**
    Westvaco Corp .... $2,000   PAC
Misc Manufacturing & Distributing **$7,600**
    Ocal Inc .... $2,750   Indiv
    Stone Container Corp .... $2,300   PAC
Textiles **$1,550**
    None over $1,500

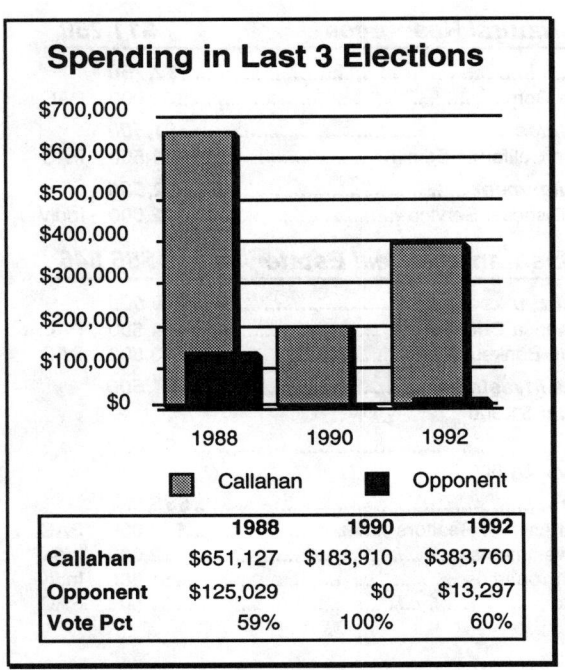

Spending in Last 3 Elections

	1988	1990	1992
Callahan	$651,127	$183,910	$383,760
Opponent	$125,029	$0	$13,297
Vote Pct	59%	100%	60%

Transportation $33,730

Air Transport **$4,730**
    United Parcel Service .... $3,100   PAC
Automotive **$10,600**
    National Auto Dealers Assn .... $4,800   PAC
    Americans for Free International Trade .... $2,000   PAC
    Auto Dealers & Drivers for Free Trade .... $1,500   PAC
Trucking **$2,800**
    None over $1,500
Railroads **$5,750**
    Norfolk Southern Corp .... $1,600   PAC
    Union Pacific Corp .... $1,500   PAC
Sea Transport **$9,350**
    CSX Corp* .... $1,600   PAC

Labor

Labor $21,000

Industrial Unions **$7,000**
    United Steelworkers .... $5,000   PAC
    Intl Brotherhood of Electrical Workers .... $2,000   PAC
Transportation Unions **$3,000**
    Marine Engineers Dist 2 Maritime Officers .... $3,000   PAC
Public Sector Unions **$11,000**
    American Fedn of St/Cnty/Munic Employees ...... $5,000   PAC
    National Assn of Letter Carriers .... $5,000   PAC

Ideological/Single-Issue

Ideological/Single-Issue $3,400

Gun Rights/Gun Control **$1,800**
    National Rifle Assn .... $1,800   PAC

Other & Unknown

Other $11,450

Civil Servants/Public Officials **$2,000**
    None over $1,500
Education **$1,750**
    None over $1,500
Retired **$7,700**
    None over $1,500

Unknown $14,750

    Homemakers/Non-income earners $3,000
    Employer Listed/Category Unknown $12,250
        None over $1,500

---

* Contributions came from more than one affiliate or
subsidiary.

Ken Calvert, R-Calif (43)

First elected: 1992

1991-92 Total Receipts: $423,001
1992 Year-end Cash: $934

1993-94 Committees & Subcommittees

Natural Resources
National Parks, Forests and Public Lands; Native American Affairs; Oversight and Investigations

Science, Space and Technology
Space; Technology, Environment and Aviation

Leading Contributors

Business

Agriculture		$24,100
Crop Production & Basic Processing		**$6,250**
None over $1,500		
Tobacco		**$2,000**
None over $1,500		
Dairy		**$5,750**
None over $1,500		
Agricultural Services/Products		**$4,750**
Nature's Recipe Pet Foods	$2,000	Indiv
Food Processing & Sales		**$3,000**
Tom's Farms	$1,500	Indiv

Communications/Electronics		$10,850
Printing & Publishing		**$5,600**
Lincoln Club of Riverside County	$4,600	PAC
Telephone Utilities		**$4,250**
AT&T	$1,500	PAC

Construction		$34,950
General Contractors		**$13,300**
Associated General Contractors	$2,500	PAC
Matich Brothers	$2,500	Indiv
All American Asphalt	$2,000	Indiv
EL Yeager Construction Co	$1,500	Indiv
Pennhill Co	$1,500	Indiv
Home Builders		**$4,150**
Fleetwood Enterprises	$2,650	PAC/Ind

Source of Funds in 1992 Election

Source	Total	Pct
■ PACs	$136,985	29%
▨ Indivs $200+	$221,223	47%
☐ Indivs under $200	$40,377	9%
⊠ Other	$70,641	15%
Candidate	$4,269	1%
Party	$54,512	12%

Source of PAC Dollars by Sector

Source	Total	Pct
■ Business	$111,463	84%
▨ Labor	$1,000	1%
☐ Ideology/Single Issue	$20,974	16%

In-State vs. Out-of-State Contributions*

Source	Total	Pct
☐ In-State	$210,223	95%
■ Out-of-state	$11,000	5%
No state listed	$0	

* by large individual contributors ($200 & above)

Special Trade Contractors		**$3,500**
GL Rawlings Corp	$2,000	Indiv
Building Materials & Equipment		**$13,000**
Johnson Machinery Co	$6,200	Indiv
Deleo Clay Tile Co Inc	$1,500	Indiv

Defense		$4,250
Defense Aerospace		**$2,250**
None over $1,500		
Defense Electronics		**$2,000**
None over $1,500		

Energy & Natural Resources		$11,750
Oil & Gas		**$7,750**
Chevron Corp	$2,000	PAC
Electric Utilities		**$1,500**
Southern California Edison	$1,500	PAC
Waste Management		**$2,500**
Newco Disposal Service	$2,000	Indiv

Finance, Insurance & Real Estate		$65,846
Commercial Banks		**$10,000**
BankAmerica Corp	$4,500	PAC/Ind
American Bankers Assn	$3,500	PAC
Securities & Investment		**$1,500**
None over $1,500		
Insurance		**$3,000**
None over $1,500		
Real Estate		**$36,921**
National Assn of Realtors	$10,000	PAC
DRR Investments	$2,000	Indiv
Foothill Properties	$1,500	Indiv
Irvine Co	$1,500	PAC

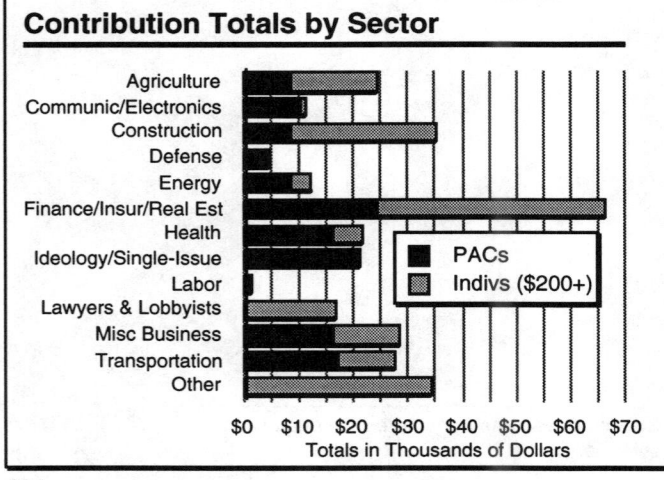

Contribution Totals by Sector

Agriculture
Communic/Electronics
Construction
Defense
Energy
Finance/Insur/Real Est
Health
Ideology/Single-Issue
Labor
Lawyers & Lobbyists
Misc Business
Transportation
Other

PACs
Indivs ($200+)

$0 $10 $20 $30 $40 $50 $60 $70
Totals in Thousands of Dollars

Accountants $3,750
    None over $1,500

Misc Finance $9,300
    None over $1,500

Health | $21,335

Health Professionals $19,335
    American Medical Assn* .... $4,188   PAC
    American Academy of Ophthalmology .... $4,000   PAC
    American Dental Assn .... $3,500   PAC

Hospitals/Nursing Homes $2,000
    None over $1,500

Lawyers & Lobbyists | $16,500

Lawyers & Lobbyists $16,500
    Clayson, Mann et al .... $2,000   Indiv

Misc Business | $27,930

Food & Beverage $4,850
    National Restaurant Assn .... $2,000   PAC
    McDonald's Corp .... $1,550   PAC/Ind

Beer, Wine & Liquor $7,500
    National Beer Wholesalers Assn .... $5,000   PAC

Retail Sales $6,055
    Ikon Inc .... $4,805   Indiv

Business Services $2,525
    Versacare Inc .... $2,000   Indiv

Chemical & Related Manufacturing $2,000
    None over $1,500

Misc Manufacturing & Distributing $3,250
    Stone Container Corp .... $1,500   PAC

Transportation | $27,250

Air Transport $4,000
    Hiser Helicopter Inc .... $2,000   Indiv
    United Parcel Service .... $2,000   PAC

Automotive $19,250
    National Auto Dealers Assn .... $10,000   PAC
    Phillips Pontiac Mazda & RV's .... $4,000   Indiv
    Americans for Free International Trade ..... $2,000   PAC
    Hemborg Ford .... $1,500   Indiv

Railroads $3,000
    Union Pacific Corp .... $2,500   PAC

Ideological/Single-Issue

Ideological/Single-Issue | $20,974

Republican/Conservative $2,524
    Lincoln Club of Orange County .... $2,500   PAC

Leadership PACs $3,000
    Fund for California's Future .... $2,000   PAC

Pro-Israel $6,000
    National PAC .... $5,000   PAC

Gun Rights/Gun Control $6,450
    National Rifle Assn .... $4,950   PAC
    Safari Club International .... $1,500   PAC

Misc Issues $3,000
    None over $1,500

Other & Unknown

Other | $33,700

Education $3,200
    None over $1,500

Retired $30,500
    None over $1,500

Unknown | $54,225

    Homemakers/Non-income earners $21,350
    Generic Occupation/Category Unknown $3,000
    Employer Listed/Category Unknown $29,875
        3-R Investments .... $4,000   Indiv
        Werner Corp .... $2,000   Indiv

Independent expenditures supporting Calvert
    California Medical Assn $2,500

Spending in Last Election

	1992
Calvert	$422,717
Opponent	$249,879
Vote Pct	47%

---

* Contributions came from more than one affiliate or
subsidiary.

Dave Camp, R-Mich (4)

First elected: 1990

1991-92 Total Receipts: $586,892
1992 Year-end Cash: $218

1991-92 Committees & Subcommittees

Agriculture
Cotton, Rice and Sugar; Wheat, Soybeans and Feed Grains

Small Business
Regulation, Business Opportunity and Energy; SBA, the General Economy and Minority Enterprise Development

Select Committee on Children, Youth and Families

Leading Contributors

Business

Agriculture	$63,855	
Crop Production & Basic Processing **$15,105**		
American Sugarbeet Growers Assn	$2,000	PAC
Great Lakes Sugar Beet Growers	$1,915	PAC
American Crystal Sugar Corp	$1,600	PAC
National Cotton Council	$1,500	PAC
Tobacco **$10,100**		
US Tobacco Co	$5,500	PAC
RJR Nabisco	$4,000	PAC
Dairy **$9,450**		
Associated Milk Producers	$4,000	PAC
Mid-America Dairymen	$2,000	PAC
Milk Marketing Inc	$1,600	PAC
Poultry & Eggs **$2,300**		
National Broiler Council	$1,500	PAC
Livestock **$3,200**		
National Cattlemen's Assn*	$2,100	PAC
Agricultural Services/Products **$9,100**		
Blossom's Flowers	$2,000	Indiv
Food Processing & Sales **$11,700**		
ConAgra Inc	$3,500	PAC
Food Marketing Institute	$1,800	PAC
Forestry & Forest Products **$2,900**		
None over $1,500		

Source of Funds in 1992 Election

Source	Total	Pct
■ PACs	$201,462	34%
▨ Indivs $200+	$164,076	28%
□ Indivs under $200	$119,339	20%
▧ Other	$102,015	17%
Candidate	$0	0%
Party	$6,427	1%

Source of PAC Dollars by Sector

Source	Total	Pct
■ Business	$178,155	94%
▨ Labor	$5,000	3%
□ Ideology/Single Issue	$6,950	4%

In-State vs. Out-of-State Contributions*

Source	Total	Pct
□ In-State	$148,226	90%
■ Out-of-state	$15,850	10%
No state listed	$0	

*** by large individual contributors ($200 & above)**

Communications/Electronics	$16,250	
Printing & Publishing **$2,600**		
Washington Post	$2,000	Indiv
Media/Entertainment **$1,600**		
None over $1,500		
Telephone Utilities **$11,550**		
Michigan Bell Telephone	$5,300	PAC
BellSouth Corp*	$3,350	PAC
GTE Corp	$2,400	PAC

Construction	$18,150	
General Contractors **$9,450**		
Associated Builders & Contractors	$2,500	PAC
Associated General Contractors	$2,500	PAC
Home Builders **$4,000**		
National Assn of Home Builders	$4,000	PAC
Special Trade Contractors **$3,250**		
Tri-County Drillers	$1,500	Indiv

Energy & Natural Resources	$21,550	
Oil & Gas **$8,700**		
Lease Management Inc	$1,500	Indiv
Misc Energy **$1,500**		
None over $1,500		
Electric Utilities **$10,250**		
Consumers Power Co	$5,500	PAC
Detroit Edison	$2,900	PAC
ACRE (Action Cmte for Rural Electrification)	$1,600	PAC

Contribution Totals by Sector

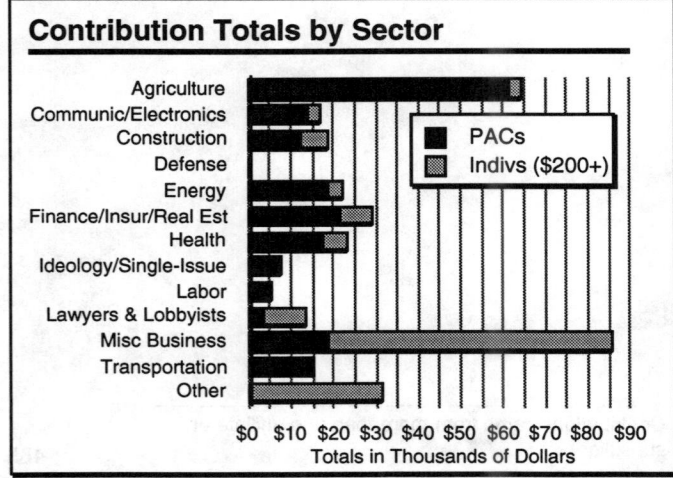

Agriculture
Communic/Electronics
Construction
Defense
Energy
Finance/Insur/Real Est
Health
Ideology/Single-Issue
Labor
Lawyers & Lobbyists
Misc Business
Transportation
Other

■ PACs
▨ Indivs ($200+)

$0 $10 $20 $30 $40 $50 $60 $70 $80 $90
Totals in Thousands of Dollars

Finance, Insurance & Real Estate — $28,700

Commercial Banks **$6,175**
    American Bankers Assn ....$2,000   PAC
Savings & Loans **$2,475**
    Wolverine Federal Savings & Loan.....................$1,975   Indiv
Securities & Investment **$2,100**
    None over $1,500
Insurance **$3,450**
    None over $1,500
Real Estate **$7,450**
    National Assn of Realtors ....$6,000   PAC
Accountants **$3,550**
    American Institute of CPA's ....$2,800   PAC
Misc Finance **$2,500**
    None over $1,500

Health — $22,861

Health Professionals **$18,400**
    American Medical Assn.................................$6,500   PAC
    American Dental Assn ....$2,950   PAC
    American Academy of Ophthalmology ....$2,000   PAC
    Rush Orthopedic Clinic ....$1,750   Indiv
    American Podiatry Assn ....$1,500   PAC
Pharmaceuticals/Health Products **$2,100**
    None over $1,500

Lawyers & Lobbyists — $12,795

Lawyers & Lobbyists **$12,795**
    Riecker, George et al ....$3,000   Indiv
    Assn of Trial Lawyers of America ....$2,500   PAC
    Porteous & White ....$2,250   Indiv
    Currie & Kendall ....$1,650   Indiv
    Tendler, Goldberg & Biggins ....$1,500   Indiv

Misc Business — $85,044

Food & Beverage **$3,350**
    National Restaurant Assn ....$1,800   PAC
Beer, Wine & Liquor **$1,650**
    None over $1,500
Retail Sales **$2,250**
    None over $1,500
Business Services **$3,300**
    Franklin Associates ....$2,000   Indiv
Chemical & Related Manufacturing **$64,819**
    Dow Chemical ....$55,319   PAC/Ind
    Dow Corning Corp ....$9,500   PAC/Ind
Misc Manufacturing & Distributing **$7,700**
    Corning Glass Works ....$2,000   PAC
    Stone Container Corp ....$2,000   PAC

Transportation — $14,800

Air Transport **$4,950**
    United Parcel Service ....$3,050   PAC
Automotive **$7,950**
    National Auto Dealers Assn ....$2,850   PAC
    General Motors..$1,900   PAC

Labor

Labor — $5,000

Transportation Unions **$2,000**
    Marine Engineers Union* ....$2,000   PAC
Public Sector Unions **$3,000**
    National Assn Retired Federal Employees ....$3,000   PAC

Ideological/Single-Issue

Ideological/Single-Issue — $6,950

Gun Rights/Gun Control **$4,950**
    National Rifle Assn ....$4,950   PAC

Other & Unknown

Other — $30,700

Education **$3,900**
    Midland Board of Education ....$2,000   Indiv
Retired **$25,850**
    None over $1,500

Unknown — $27,526

    Homemakers/Non-income earners $13,775
    Employer Listed/Category Unknown $12,400
      Doan Associates ....$3,000   Indiv

Spending in Last 2 Elections

	1990	1992
Camp	$657,229	$418,118
Opponent	$0	$15,650
Vote Pct	65%	63%

* Contributions came from more than one affiliate or subsidiary.

Charles T. Canady, R-Fla (12)

First elected: 1992

1991-92 Total Receipts: $158,527
1992 Year-end Cash: $1,792

1993-94 Committees & Subcommittees

Agriculture
Department Operations and Nutrition; Foreign Agriculture and Hunger

Judiciary
Civil and Constitutional Rights; Economic and Commercial Law;
International Law, Immigration and Refugees

Leading Contributors

Business

Agriculture	$19,600	
Crop Production & Basic Processing	**$7,200**	
Florida Citrus Mutual	$2,000	PAC
Ben Hill Griffin Inc	$1,250	Indiv
Cargill Inc	$1,000	PAC
Livestock	**$1,000**	
None over $1,000		
Agricultural Services/Products	**$2,050**	
None over $1,000		
Food Processing & Sales	**$7,400**	
Publix Super Markets	$3,050	Indiv
Fleming Companies Inc	$1,000	PAC
Food Marketing Institute	$1,000	PAC
JFI Corp	$1,000	Indiv
Winn-Dixie Stores	$1,000	PAC
Forestry & Forest Products	**$1,000**	
Westvaco Corp	$1,000	PAC

Communications/Electronics	$2,000	
Electronics Mfg & Services	**$2,000**	
Harris Corp	$2,000	PAC

Construction	$5,750	
General Contractors	**$2,700**	
Associated General Contractors	$1,000	PAC
Home Builders	**$2,000**	
National Assn of Home Builders	$1,000	PAC

Source of Funds in 1992 Election

	Source	Total	Pct
■	PACs	$53,311	25%
▨	Indivs $200+	$47,574	22%
□	Indivs under $200	$47,683	22%
▨	Other	$63,580	30%
	Candidate	$0	0%
	Party	$60,654	29%

Source of PAC Dollars by Sector

	Source	Total	Pct
■	Business	$41,350	82%
▨	Labor	$0	0%
□	Ideology/Single Issue	$8,974	18%

In-State vs. Out-of-State Contributions*

	Source	Total	Pct
□	In-State	$47,574	100%
■	Out-of-state	$0	0%
	No state listed	$0	

* by large individual contributors ($200 & above)

Energy & Natural Resources	$6,750	
Oil & Gas	**$3,000**	
Chevron Corp	$1,000	PAC
Exxon Corp	$1,000	PAC
Misc Energy	**$3,000**	
Cooper Industries	$3,000	PAC

Finance, Insurance & Real Estate	$11,700	
Insurance	**$4,150**	
None over $1,000		
Real Estate	**$5,600**	
National Assn of Realtors	$5,000	PAC
Misc Finance	**$1,000**	
None over $1,000		

Health	$4,550	
Health Professionals	**$4,050**	
American Chiropractic Assn	$2,000	PAC

Lawyers & Lobbyists	$4,900	
Lawyers & Lobbyists	**$4,900**	
Holland & Knight	$1,950	PAC/Ind
Lane Trohn	$1,500	Indiv
Connor & Assoc	$1,000	Indiv

Contribution Totals by Sector

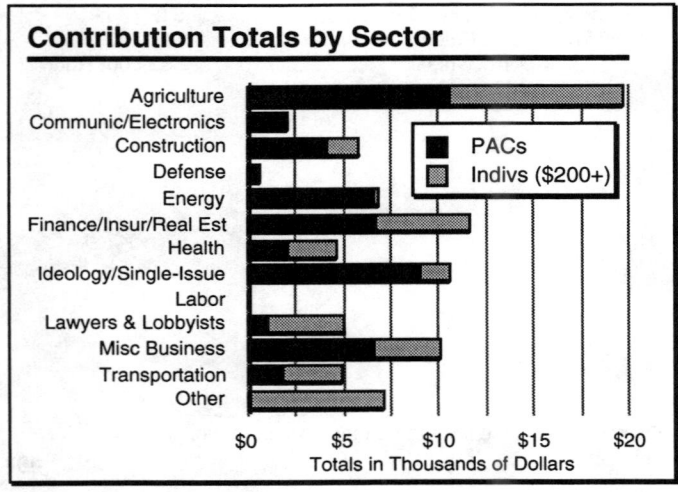

Agriculture
Communic/Electronics
Construction
Defense
Energy
Finance/Insur/Real Est
Health
Ideology/Single-Issue
Labor
Lawyers & Lobbyists
Misc Business
Transportation
Other

■ PACs
▨ Indivs ($200+)

$0　$5　$10　$15　$20
Totals in Thousands of Dollars

Misc Business $10,000

Business Associations $1,500
    National Fedn of Independent Business ....$1,500 PAC
Beer, Wine & Liquor $2,750
    Bernie Little Distributors ....$1,250 Indiv
    National Beer Wholesalers Assn ....$1,000 PAC
Business Services $1,000
    National Assn of Temporary Services ....$1,000 PAC
Lodging/Tourism $3,250
    Ocean Eleven Resorts ....$2,250 Indiv
    American Hotel & Motel Assn ....$1,000 PAC
Chemical & Related Manufacturing $1,500
    Dow Chemical ....$1,000 PAC

Transportation $4,800

Trucking $4,300
    Watkins Motor Lines Inc ....$1,800 Indiv
    Comcar Industries Inc ....$1,250 Indiv
    Watkins Associated Industries ....$1,250 PAC

Ideological/Single-Issue

Ideological/Single-Issue $11,474

Republican/Conservative $2,024
    None over $1,000
Leadership PACs $2,000
    Fund for Southern Progress (Carroll Campbell) ..$1,000 PAC
    Republican Leader's Fund (Bob Michel) ....$1,000 PAC
Gun Rights/Gun Control $4,950
    National Rifle Assn ....$4,950 PAC
Misc Issues $2,500
    Right to Work PAC ....$2,250 PAC

Other & Unknown

Other $7,037

Civil Servants/Public Officials $1,000
    Hillsborough Cty Board of Public Inst ....$1,000 Indiv
Retired $4,425
    None over $1,000
Other $1,412
    Scott Lake Baptist Church ....$1,412 Indiv

Unknown $9,837

    Homemakers/Non-income earners $1,300
    Employer Listed/Category Unknown $7,787
        Keelan ....$1,412 Indiv
        Lane, Trohn et al ....$1,000 Indiv

Independent expenditures supporting Canady
    National Right to Life PAC $3,853

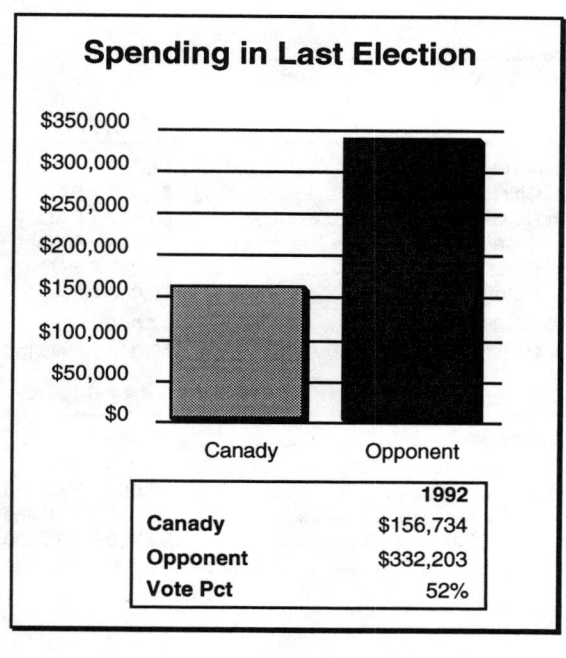

Spending in Last Election

	1992
Canady	$156,734
Opponent	$332,203
Vote Pct	52%

Maria Cantwell, D-Wash (1)

First elected: 1992

1991-92 Total Receipts: $657,454
1992 Year-end Cash: $3,209

1993-94 Committees & Subcommittees

Foreign Affairs
Economic Policy, Trade and Environment

Merchant Marine and Fisheries
Fisheries Management

Public Works and Transportation
Aviation; Surface Transportation

Leading Contributors

Business

Agriculture $7,300

Crop Production & Basic Processing $2,000
    None over $1,500

Forestry & Forest Products $3,300
    Pacific Lumber & Shipping Co .... $2,800   Indiv

Communications/Electronics $8,550

Media/Entertainment $2,250
    None over $1,500

Electronics Mfg & Services $1,650
    None over $1,500

Computer Equipment & Services $2,950
    Microsoft Corp .... $2,450   PAC/Ind

Energy & Natural Resources $20,400

Oil & Gas $3,000
    Western Pioneer Inc .... $2,500   Indiv

Commercial Fishing $16,750
    Royal Seafood Inc .... $5,000   Indiv
    Oceantrawl Inc .... $4,000   Indiv
    Fishing Co of Alaska .... $2,000   Indiv
    Morning Star Fisheries .... $2,000   Indiv
    Arctic Alaska Fisheries Corp .... $1,500   PAC

Source of Funds in 1992 Election

Source	Total	Pct
PACs	$287,003	42%
Indivs $200+	$140,967	21%
Indivs under $200	$183,849	27%
Other	$68,598	10%
Candidate	$0	0%
Party	$28,413	4%

Source of PAC Dollars by Sector

Source	Total	Pct
Business	$71,838	27%
Labor	$143,350	54%
Ideology/Single Issue	$51,832	19%

In-State vs. Out-of-State Contributions*

Source	Total	Pct
In-State	$113,917	88%
Out-of-state	$15,200	12%
No state listed	$500	

* by large individual contributors ($200 & above)

Finance, Insurance & Real Estate $26,900

Commercial Banks $6,250
    BankAmerica Corp* .... $2,000   PAC
    US Bancorp .... $2,000   PAC

Credit Unions $1,500
    Credit Union National Assn .... $1,500   PAC

Insurance $3,100
    None over $1,500

Real Estate $8,100
    Finkbeiner Development Inc .... $3,500   Indiv
    Dunson Equities Corp .... $2,000   Indiv

Accountants $3,250
    None over $1,500

Misc Finance $3,450
    None over $1,500

Health $29,827

Health Professionals $24,327
    American Chiropractic Assn .... $7,500   PAC
    American Dental Assn .... $5,577   PAC
    American College of Emergency Physicians .... $2,000   PAC
    American Nurses Assn .... $2,000   PAC
    American Optometric Assn .... $2,000   PAC

Pharmaceuticals/Health Products $4,000
    Immunex Corp .... $3,000   PAC/Ind

Lawyers & Lobbyists $34,952

Lawyers & Lobbyists $34,952
    Assn of Trial Lawyers of America .... $10,000   PAC
    Bogle & Gates .... $5,052   PAC/Ind
    Garvey, Schubert & Barer .... $3,250   PAC/Ind
    Preston, Gates et al .... $2,750   PAC/Ind
    Perkins Coie .... $2,700   PAC/Ind

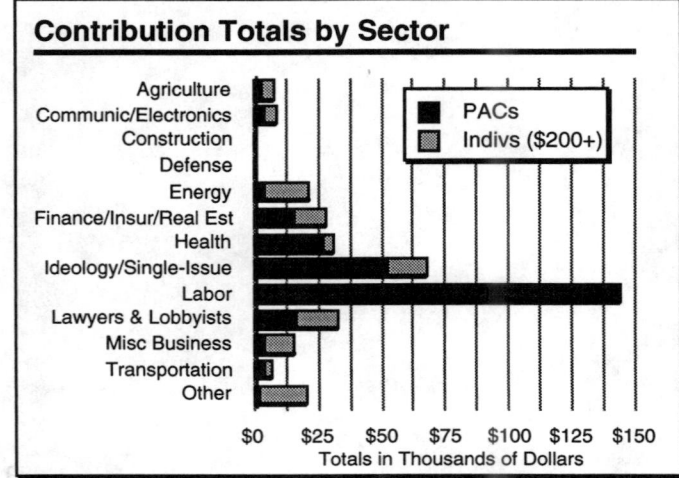

Contribution Totals by Sector

- PACs
- Indivs ($200+)

Agriculture
Communic/Electronics
Construction
Defense
Energy
Finance/Insur/Real Est
Health
Ideology/Single-Issue
Labor
Lawyers & Lobbyists
Misc Business
Transportation
Other

$0 $25 $50 $75 $100 $125 $150

Totals in Thousands of Dollars

Misc Business	$14,679

Food & Beverage	$7,275	
Golden Alaska Seafoods	$2,250	Indiv
Retail Sales	$2,250	
None over $1,500		
Business Services	$2,000	
None over $1,500		

Transportation	$5,705

Air Transport	$2,380
None over $1,500	
Sea Transport	$1,775
None over $1,500	

Labor

Labor	$143,350

Building Trade Unions	$17,500	
Carpenters & Joiners Union	$5,000	PAC
Laborers Union*	$4,000	PAC
Ironworkers Union	$2,500	PAC
Operating Engineers Union*	$2,000	PAC
Sheet Metal Workers Union	$2,000	PAC
Industrial Unions	$25,300	
Intl Brotherhood of Electrical Workers	$6,000	PAC
United Auto Workers	$5,500	PAC
Machinists/Aerospace Workers Union	$5,000	PAC
Communications Workers of America	$4,500	PAC
United Steelworkers	$2,500	PAC
Transportation Unions	$39,000	
Seafarers International Union*	$10,500	PAC
Teamsters Union*	$7,500	PAC
Marine Engineers Union*	$7,000	PAC
Intl Longshoremen's/Warehousemen's Union	$5,500	PAC
Amalgamated Transit Union	$2,000	PAC
United Transportation Union	$2,000	PAC

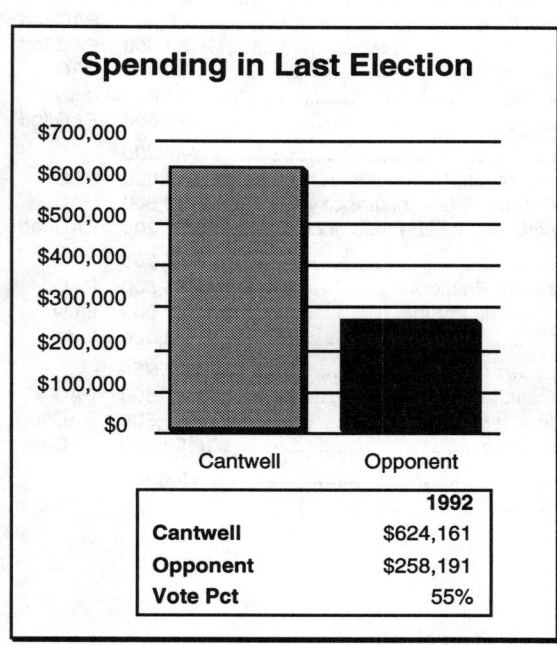

Spending in Last Election

	1992
Cantwell	$624,161
Opponent	$258,191
Vote Pct	55%

Public Sector Unions	$39,000	
American Fedn of St/Cnty/Munic Employees	$10,000	PAC
National Assn of Letter Carriers	$10,000	PAC
National Education Assn	$10,000	PAC
American Federation of Teachers	$3,000	PAC
International Assn of Firefighters	$2,000	PAC
National Assn Retired Federal Employees	$2,000	PAC
Misc Unions	$22,550	
Food & Commercial Workers Union	$10,000	PAC
AFL-CIO	$7,000	PAC
Service Employees International Union	$3,000	PAC
Bakery, Confectionery & Tobacco Workers	$2,000	PAC

Ideological/Single-Issue

Ideological/Single-Issue	$66,882	

Democratic/Liberal	$3,508	
National Cmte for an Effective Congress	$2,500	PAC
Leadership PACs	$3,000	
None over $1,500		
Foreign & Defense Policy	$1,778	
Council for a Livable World	$1,778	PAC/Ind
Pro-Israel	$2,950	
None over $1,500		
Pro-Choice	$2,000	
None over $1,500		
Womens Issues	$33,485	
Emily's List	$16,976	PAC/Ind
Women's Campaign Fund	$10,000	PAC
National Organization for Women	$3,259	PAC
National Womens Political Caucus	$3,000	PAC
Human Rights	$8,511	
Human Rights Campaign Fund	$7,511	PAC
Misc Issues	$11,150	
League of Conservation Voters	$4,000	PAC
Sierra Club	$2,500	PAC
National Council of Senior Citizens	$2,000	PAC

Other & Unknown

Other	$20,600	

Civil Servants/Public Officials	$5,300	
Center Township Assors Office	$1,500	Indiv
Education	$1,750	
University of Washington	$1,500	Indiv
Retired	$10,800	
None over $1,500		
Other	$2,750	
Estate of Arch MacDonald	$1,750	Indiv

Unknown	$28,467	
No Employer Listed or Found	$10,952	
Employer Listed/Category Unknown	$15,515	
Trinus Partners	$1,500	Indiv
Wolfe & Rodihan	$1,500	Indiv

---

* Contributions came from more than one affiliate or subsidiary.

Benjamin L. Cardin, D-Md (3)

First elected: 1986

1991-92 Total Receipts: $591,234
1992 Year-end Cash: $195,084

1991-92 Committees & Subcommittees

Standards of Official Conduct

Ways and Means
Health; Social Security

Leading Contributors

Business

Agriculture	$13,971	
Crop Production & Basic Processing	$4,171	
None over $1,500		
Tobacco	$2,450	
None over $1,500		
Food Processing & Sales	$3,750	
Food Marketing Institute	$1,550	PAC
Forestry & Forest Products	$2,000	
Westvaco Corp	$2,000	PAC

Communications/Electronics	$9,500	
Media/Entertainment	$1,950	
None over $1,500		
Telephone Utilities	$5,350	
Bell Atlantic*	$1,700	PAC

Construction	$8,100	
General Contractors	$4,050	
P Flanigan & Sons	$1,500	Indiv
Home Builders	$2,000	
None over $1,500		

Defense	$2,500	
None over $1,500		

Energy & Natural Resources	$9,775	
Oil & Gas	$2,850	
None over $1,500		
Electric Utilities	$4,450	
Baltimore Gas & Electric	$1,850	PAC

Contribution Totals by Sector

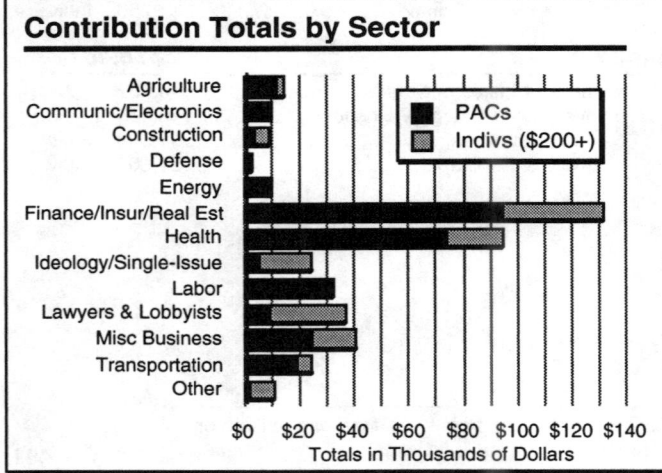

Totals in Thousands of Dollars

Source of Funds in 1992 Election

Source	Total	Pct
PACs	$292,553	48%
Indivs $200+	$175,758	29%
Indivs under $200	$45,183	7%
Other	$95,166	16%
Candidate	$0	0%
Party	$17,426	3%

Source of PAC Dollars by Sector

Source	Total	Pct
Business	$253,535	87%
Labor	$32,050	11%
Ideology/Single Issue	$5,150	2%

In-State vs. Out-of-State Contributions*

Source	Total	Pct
In-State	$152,808	87%
Out-of-state	$22,750	13%
No state listed	$0	

* by large individual contributors ($200 & above)

Finance, Insurance & Real Estate	$130,772	
Commercial Banks	$16,750	
American Bankers Assn	$5,000	PAC
Citicorp	$3,350	PAC
Citizens & Southern National Bank	$2,500	PAC
Savings & Loans	$2,700	
None over $1,500		
Finance/Credit Companies	$2,350	
None over $1,500		
Securities & Investment	$28,072	
Alex Brown Inc	$5,000	PAC
Assn of Private Pension Plans	$2,532	PAC
Goldman, Sachs & Co	$2,000	PAC/Ind
Legg Mason Inc	$2,000	PAC/Ind
National Venture Capital Assn	$2,000	PAC
CMS Companies	$1,600	Indiv
Merrill Lynch	$1,500	PAC/Ind
Insurance	$42,200	
National Assn of Life Underwriters	$10,000	PAC
American Council of Life Insurance	$2,500	PAC
Massachusetts Mutual Life Insurance	$2,200	PAC/Ind
Real Estate	$17,000	
National Assn of Realtors	$6,500	PAC
Regional Management Inc	$2,000	Indiv
Rouse Co	$2,000	Indiv
Accountants	$17,950	
American Institute of CPA's	$7,500	PAC
Arthur Andersen & Co	$2,500	PAC/Ind
Price Waterhouse	$2,500	PAC/Ind
Misc Finance	$2,500	
None over $1,500		

Health $93,800

Health Professionals $50,400
American Medical Assn	$9,700	PAC
American Dental Assn	$4,850	PAC
American Academy of Ophthalmology	$3,000	PAC
American Chiropractic Assn	$3,000	PAC
American Assn Oral & Maxillofacial Surgeons	$2,000	PAC
American Podiatry Assn	$2,000	PAC
American Optometric Assn	$1,850	PAC
Assn for the Advancement of Psychology	$1,700	PAC
American Physical Therapy Assn	$1,600	PAC
Cmte for Quality Orthopedic Health Care	$1,550	PAC

Hospitals/Nursing Homes $18,400
American Health Care Assn	$5,000	PAC
Meridian Health Care Inc	$3,000	Indiv
American Hospital Assn	$2,550	PAC
Manor Healthcare Corp	$2,500	PAC

Health Services $3,000
Homedco Inc	$1,500	PAC

Pharmaceuticals/Health Products $20,750
Kinetic Concepts Inc	$2,500	PAC
Schering-Plough Corp	$2,000	PAC
Medical Equipment Suppliers	$1,600	PAC
Invacare Corp	$1,500	PAC
Kirson Medical Equipment Co	$1,500	Indiv
Merck & Co	$1,500	PAC

Lawyers & Lobbyists $36,472

Lawyers & Lobbyists $36,472
Piper & Marbury	$5,200	Indiv
Gordon, Feinblatt et al	$2,900	Indiv
Gallagher, Evelius & Jones	$2,500	Indiv
Skadden, Arps et al	$1,500	PAC

Misc Business $40,200

Business Associations $3,000
Bethesda Engravers Ltd	$2,000	Indiv

Food & Beverage $3,700
National Restaurant Assn	$2,000	PAC

Beer, Wine & Liquor $8,700
Joseph E Seagram & Sons	$2,500	PAC
Smirnoff/Inglenook Distributors	$1,500	PAC

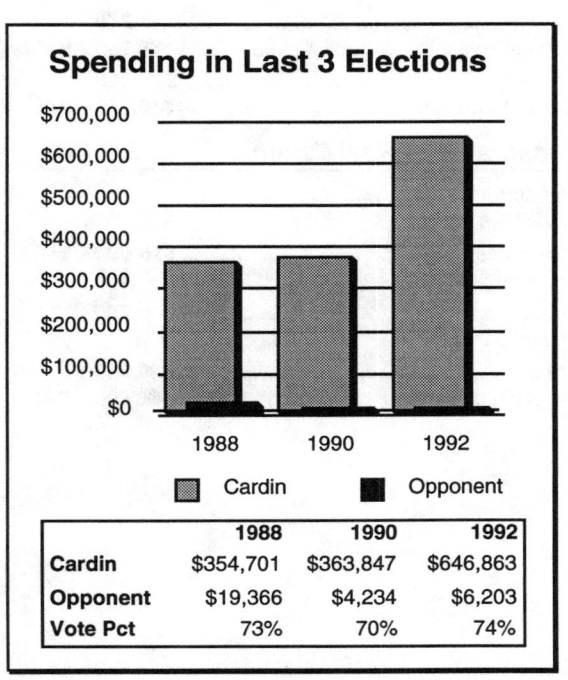

Spending in Last 3 Elections

	1988	1990	1992
Cardin	$354,701	$363,847	$646,863
Opponent	$19,366	$4,234	$6,203
Vote Pct	73%	70%	74%

Retail Sales $7,250
International Council of Shopping Centers	$2,000	PAC
Neighborcare Pharmacies	$1,500	Indiv

Business Services $4,700
None over $1,500

Chemical & Related Manufacturing $3,950
None over $1,500

Misc Manufacturing & Distributing $3,850
None over $1,500

Transportation $23,675

Air Transport $8,325
United Parcel Service	$3,700	PAC
Aircraft Owners & Pilots Assn	$2,000	PAC

Automotive $7,550
National Auto Dealers Assn	$2,000	PAC
Westminster Motor Co	$2,000	Indiv

Railroads $3,550
Union Pacific Corp	$2,000	PAC

Sea Transport $3,000
American Trading & Production	$1,750	Indiv

Labor

Labor $32,050

Building Trade Unions $4,150
Laborers' Political League	$2,000	PAC

Industrial Unions $4,400
None over $1,500

Transportation Unions $6,450
Air Line Pilots Assn	$1,500	PAC

Public Sector Unions $14,050
National Education Assn	$2,850	PAC
American Fedn of St/Cnty/Munic Employees	$2,050	PAC
National Assn Retired Federal Employees	$2,000	PAC
National Assn of Letter Carriers	$2,000	PAC

Misc Unions $3,000
Food & Commercial Workers Union	$1,500	PAC

Ideological/Single-Issue

Ideological/Single-Issue $23,450

Pro-Israel $17,650
None over $1,500

Misc Issues $2,400
National Cmte to Preserve Social Security	$2,400	PAC

Other & Unknown

Other $10,550

Education $3,450
None over $1,500

Retired $3,950
None over $1,500

Unknown $31,978
Homemakers/Non-income earners	$2,500
No Employer Listed or Found	$14,008
Employer Listed/Category Unknown	$15,270

None over $1,500

---

* Contributions came from more than one affiliate or subsidiary.

Bob Carr, D-Mich (8)

First elected: 1974

1991-92 Total Receipts: $1,107,973
1992 Year-end Cash: $9,399

1991-92 Committees & Subcommittees

Appropriations
Commerce, Justice, State and Judiciary and Related Agencies;
Transportation and Related Agencies

Select Committee on Hunger

Leading Contributors

Business

Agriculture	$36,800

Tobacco	$14,250	
RJR Nabisco	$9,000	PAC
Dairy	$6,500	
None over $5,000		
Agricultural Services/Products	$5,550	
None over $5,000		
Food Processing & Sales	$5,500	
None over $5,000		

Communications/Electronics	$39,550

Media/Entertainment	$17,450
None over $5,000	
Telephone Utilities	$12,500
None over $5,000	

Construction	$52,300

General Contractors	$24,250
None over $5,000	
Construction Services	$19,250
None over $5,000	
Building Materials & Equipment	$8,100
None over $5,000	

Source of Funds in 1992 Election

Source	Total	Pct
■ PACs	$564,303	50%
▨ Indivs $200+	$387,441	35%
☐ Indivs under $200	$93,686	8%
⊠ Other	$72,869	7%
Candidate	$0	0%
Party	$23,270	2%

Source of PAC Dollars by Sector

Source	Total	Pct
■ Business	$378,372	68%
▨ Labor	$132,063	24%
☐ Ideology/Single Issue	$48,994	9%

In-State vs. Out-of-State Contributions*

Source	Total	Pct
☐ In-State	$180,035	46%
■ Out-of-state	$207,406	54%
No state listed	$0	

* by large individual contributors ($200 & above)

Defense	$53,093

Defense Aerospace	$28,643	
Ford Motor Co	$6,500	PAC
Defense Electronics	$17,450	
AT&T	$5,500	PAC
Misc Defense	$7,000	
None over $5,000		

Energy & Natural Resources	$45,900

Oil & Gas	$12,450	
None over $5,000		
Nuclear Energy	$8,750	
KMS Fusion Inc	$8,750	PAC/Ind
Electric Utilities	$20,250	
Consumers Power Co	$10,000	PAC

Finance, Insurance & Real Estate	$77,870

Commercial Banks	$5,750	
None over $5,000		
Securities & Investment	$16,600	
None over $5,000		
Insurance	$14,700	
None over $5,000		
Real Estate	$29,250	
National Assn of Realtors	$8,500	PAC

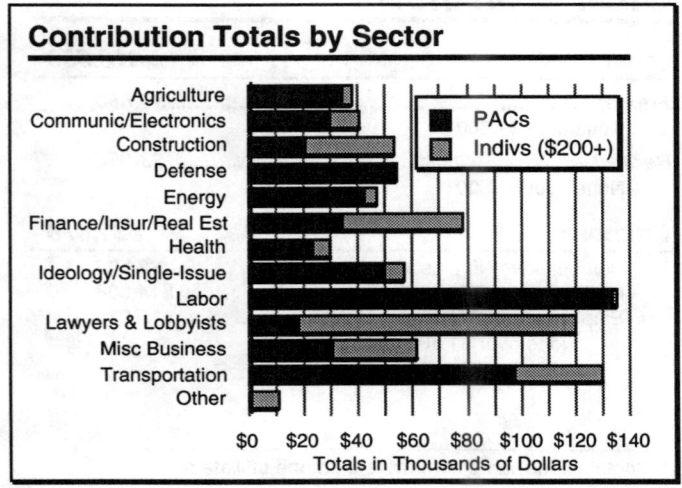

Contribution Totals by Sector

- Agriculture
- Communic/Electronics
- Construction
- Defense
- Energy
- Finance/Insur/Real Est
- Health
- Ideology/Single-Issue
- Labor
- Lawyers & Lobbyists
- Misc Business
- Transportation
- Other

Legend: ■ PACs, ▨ Indivs ($200+)

$0 $20 $40 $60 $80 $100 $120 $140
Totals in Thousands of Dollars

Health $29,250

Health Professionals **$22,100**
    American Medical Assn................................$6,850 PAC
    American Dental Assn ....$5,000 PAC

Lawyers & Lobbyists $119,403

Lawyers & Lobbyists...................................... **$119,403**
    Hubbell, Sawyer et al ....$5,000 Indiv

Misc Business $60,728

Beer, Wine & Liquor **$14,803**
    National Beer Wholesalers Assn ....$6,500 PAC
Retail Sales **$7,750**
    None over $5,000
Business Services **$12,900**
    None over $5,000
Casinos/Gambling **$7,000**
    None over $5,000
Misc Manufacturing & Distributing **$10,025**
    None over $5,000

Transportation $129,330

Air Transport **$72,940**
    Aircraft Owners & Pilots Assn ....$11,000 PAC
    Federal Express Corp ....$10,000 PAC
    Northwest Airlines ....$9,500 PAC
    Delta Airlines ....$8,000 PAC
    United Parcel Service ....$7,550 PAC
    American Airlines ....$5,500 PAC
Automotive **$18,300**
    General Motors ....$10,900 Indiv
Trucking **$14,990**
    American Trucking Assns ....$8,240 PAC
Railroads **$12,500**
    None over $5,000
Misc Transport **$8,150**
    None over $5,000

Labor

Labor $134,463

Building Trade Unions **$22,750**
    Carpenters & Joiners Union ....$6,500 PAC
Industrial Unions **$25,000**
    United Auto Workers ....$10,000 PAC
    Communications Workers of America ....$7,250 PAC
Transportation Unions **$60,750**
    Teamsters Union* ....$11,000 PAC
    Air Line Pilots Assn ....$10,000 PAC
    Marine Engineers Union* ....$10,000 PAC
    United Transportation Union ....$10,000 PAC
    Amalgamated Transit Union ....$6,000 PAC
Public Sector Unions **$17,900**
    National Education Assn ....$10,000 PAC
Misc Unions **$8,063**
    None over $5,000

Ideological/Single-Issue

Ideological/Single-Issue $56,374

Democratic/Liberal **$8,994**
    Ingham County Democratic Party ....$7,794 PAC
Pro-Israel **$25,830**
    National PAC ....$5,000 PAC
Gun Rights/Gun Control **$9,900**
    National Rifle Assn ....$9,900 PAC
Misc Issues **$5,900**
    None over $5,000

Other & Unknown

Other $10,200
    None over $5,000

Unknown $106,109
    Homemakers/Non-income earners $8,350
    No Employer Listed or Found $10,085
    Employer Listed/Category Unknown $82,524
        None over $5,000

Independent expenditures opposing Carr
    Public Citizen $40,161

Spending in Last 3 Elections

	1988	1990	1992
Carr	$504,217	$223,595	$1,355,199
Opponent	$81,586	$0	$1,761,841
Vote Pct	59%	100%	48%

* Contributions came from more than one affiliate or subsidiary.

Michael N. Castle, R-Del (1)

First elected: 1992

1991-92 Total Receipts: $708,671
1992 Year-end Cash: $17,929

1993-94 Committees & Subcommittees

Banking, Finance and Urban Affairs
Consumer Credit and Insurance; Housing and Community Development; International Development, Finance, Trade and Monetary Policy

Merchant Marine and Fisheries
Coast Guard and Navigation; Environment and Natural Resources

Leading Contributors

Business

Agriculture	$15,050	
Crop Production & Basic Processing	**$3,050**	
None over $1,500		
Poultry & Eggs	**$2,000**	
None over $1,500		
Food Processing & Sales	**$4,500**	
Pepsico Inc	$3,000	PAC
Forestry & Forest Products	**$3,500**	
Westvaco Corp	$2,000	PAC

Communications/Electronics	$13,250	
Printing & Publishing	**$4,000**	
Forbes Inc	$1,700	Indiv
Telephone Utilities	**$6,250**	
Diamond State Telephone Co	$2,150	PAC/Ind
Electronics Mfg & Services	**$1,500**	
None over $1,500		

Construction	$15,500	
General Contractors	**$9,000**	
James Julian Inc	$2,000	Indiv
Special Trade Contractors	**$2,500**	
Private Gardens	$2,000	Indiv
Construction Services	**$2,000**	
None over $1,500		

Defense	$1,500	
Misc Defense	**$1,500**	
None over $1,500		

Contribution Totals by Sector

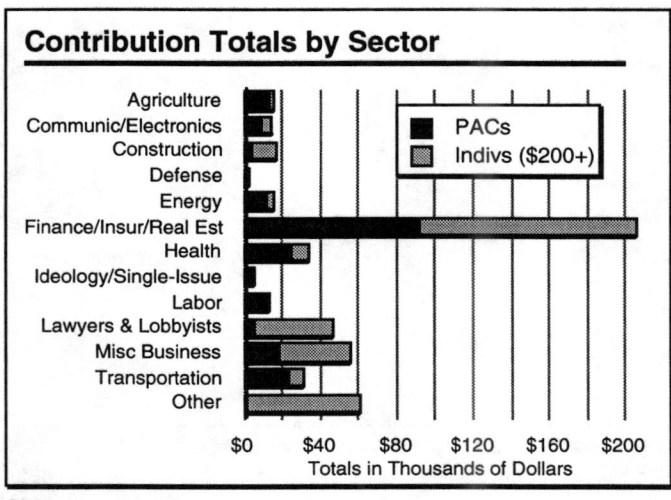

Agriculture
Communic/Electronics
Construction
Defense
Energy
Finance/Insur/Real Est
Health
Ideology/Single-Issue
Labor
Lawyers & Lobbyists
Misc Business
Transportation
Other

■ PACs
▨ Indivs ($200+)

$0 $40 $80 $120 $160 $200
Totals in Thousands of Dollars

Source of Funds in 1992 Election

Source	Total	Pct
■ PACs	$206,868	27%
▨ Indivs $200+	$371,370	48%
□ Indivs under $200	$101,399	13%
▧ Other	$96,503	12%
Candidate	$0	0%
Party	$82,469	11%

Source of PAC Dollars by Sector

Source	Total	Pct
■ Business	$192,427	93%
▨ Labor	$11,500	6%
□ Ideology/Single Issue	$2,500	1%

In-State vs. Out-of-State Contributions*

Source	Total	Pct
□ In-State	$239,720	65%
■ Out-of-state	$131,650	35%
No state listed	$0	

* by large individual contributors ($200 & above)

Energy & Natural Resources	$14,800	
Oil & Gas	**$10,050**	
Columbia Gas System	$2,750	PAC
Mining	**$2,000**	
None over $1,500		
Electric Utilities	**$1,750**	
None over $1,500		

Finance, Insurance & Real Estate	$205,400	
Commercial Banks	**$123,800**	
MBNA Corp	$61,300	PAC/Ind
Citicorp	$7,950	PAC
First USA Bank	$7,000	Indiv
Wilmington Trust Co	$6,100	PAC/Ind
Chase Manhattan	$6,000	PAC
JP Morgan & Co	$6,000	PAC/Ind
American Bankers Assn	$5,000	PAC
Bank of New York	$4,500	PAC
Delaware Trust Co	$2,500	Indiv
Meridian Bancorp	$1,800	PAC
Bankers Trust	$1,750	PAC/Ind
Chemical Bank	$1,500	PAC
Corestates Financial Corp	$1,500	PAC
First Chicago Corp	$1,500	PAC
Savings & Loans	**$1,500**	
US League of Savings Assns	$1,500	PAC
Finance/Credit Companies	**$24,750**	
Beneficial Management Corp	$17,000	PAC/Ind
Advanta Corp	$3,000	Indiv
American Financial Services Assn	$2,500	PAC
Household International Inc	$2,000	PAC
Securities & Investment	**$21,600**	
Dillon, Read & Co	$3,000	PAC/Ind
Goldman, Sachs & Co	$2,250	PAC/Ind
Dean Witter	$2,000	PAC/Ind
Merrill Lynch	$2,000	PAC/Ind
Shearson Lehman Brothers	$2,000	PAC/Ind
Donaldson, Lufkin & Jenrette	$1,500	PAC/Ind

Insurance	$12,100	
Torchmark Corp	$1,500	PAC

Real Estate	$14,400	
National Assn of Realtors	$5,000	PAC
Barness Organization	$2,000	Indiv
Toll Brothers Inc	$1,500	Indiv

Misc Finance	$5,250	
None over $1,500		

Health — $32,287

Health Professionals	$21,820	
American Medical Assn	$10,000	PAC
American Dental Assn	$3,120	PAC

Pharmaceuticals/Health Products	$9,467	
Merck & Co	$2,117	PAC

Lawyers & Lobbyists — $47,275

Lawyers & Lobbyists	$47,275	
Potter, Anderson & Corroon	$5,200	Indiv
Morris, Nichols et al	$4,300	Indiv
Richards, Layton & Finger	$3,000	Indiv
Dilworth, Paxson et al	$2,000	Indiv
Duane, Morris & Heckscher	$2,000	Indiv
Saul, Ewing et al	$2,000	Indiv
Skadden, Arps et al	$1,775	Indiv
Prickett, Jones et al	$1,750	Indiv
Black, Manafort et al	$1,500	Indiv
Montgomery, McCracken et al	$1,500	Indiv

Misc Business — $54,790

Business Associations	$1,540	
None over $1,500		

Food & Beverage	$1,500	
None over $1,500		

Beer, Wine & Liquor	$3,000	
National Beer Wholesalers Assn	$1,500	PAC

Retail Sales	$6,000	
Bootiful Shoes	$3,000	Indiv

Misc Services	$3,000	
Professional Leasing	$2,000	Indiv

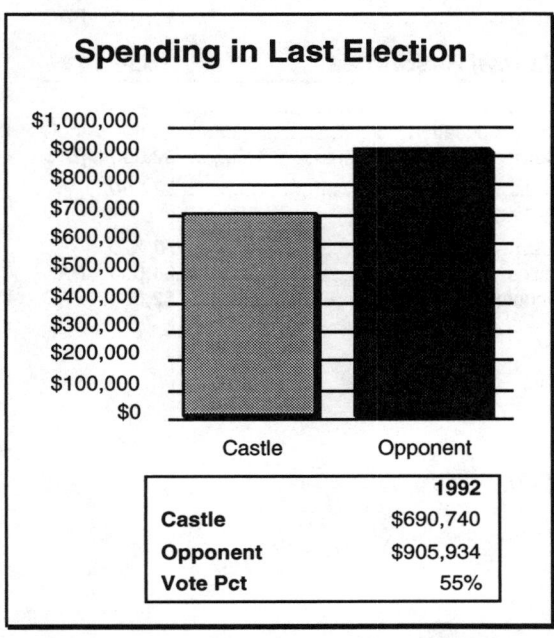

Spending in Last Election

	1992
Castle	$690,740
Opponent	$905,934
Vote Pct	55%

Business Services	$12,200	
Border Co	$2,000	Indiv
Tierney Group	$2,000	Indiv
Kekst & Co	$1,500	Indiv
Rockefeller Family & Assoc	$1,500	Indiv

Chemical & Related Manufacturing	$19,200	
EI du Pont de Nemours & Co	$8,250	Indiv
Hercules Inc	$3,500	Indiv
Standard Chlorine of Del	$2,000	Indiv
FMC Corp	$1,500	PAC

Misc Manufacturing & Distributing	$5,500	
WL Gore & Associates	$2,000	Indiv

Transportation — $30,400

Air Transport	$4,300	
United Parcel Service	$3,000	PAC

Automotive	$19,600	
National Auto Dealers Assn	$10,000	PAC
Winner Group	$2,000	Indiv

Trucking	$2,000	
Rollind Truck Leasing Corp	$2,000	Indiv

Railroads	$2,000	
Union Pacific Corp	$1,500	PAC

Sea Transport	$2,000	
None over $1,500		

Labor

Labor	$11,500

Public Sector Unions	$11,500	
National Education Assn	$10,000	PAC

Ideological/Single-Issue

Ideological/Single-Issue	$4,450

Republican/Conservative	$1,950	
None over $1,500		

Leadership PACs	$1,500	
None over $1,500		

Other & Unknown

Other	$60,170

Civil Servants/Public Officials	$3,280	
State of Delaware	$2,450	Indiv

Education	$1,800	
None over $1,500		

Retired	$52,890	
None over $1,500		

Unknown	$71,925

Homemakers/Non-income earners	$29,850	
Generic Occupation/Category Unknown	$3,500	
Employer Listed/Category Unknown	$37,875	
James T Cavanaugh & Associates	$4,000	Indiv
Carroll Engineering	$2,000	Indiv
Gerret Van S Copeland	$2,000	Indiv
Wierd Rose Co	$1,750	Indiv
Axess Corp	$1,500	Indiv
Frederick R Harris Inc	$1,500	Indiv

Jim Chapman, D-Texas (1)

First elected: 1986

1991-92 Total Receipts: $311,558
1992 Year-end Cash: $286,303

1991-92 Committees & Subcommittees

Appropriations
Energy and Water Development; Veterans Affairs, Housing and Urban Development, and Independent Agencies

Leading Contributors

Business

Agriculture	$35,431	
Crop Production & Basic Processing	**$6,200**	
Southwest Peanut Membership Org	$1,500	PAC
Tobacco	**$7,731**	
RJR Nabisco	$4,500	PAC
Philip Morris	$1,831	PAC
Dairy	**$10,000**	
Associated Milk Producers	$7,000	PAC
Mid-America Dairymen	$2,000	PAC
Poultry & Eggs	**$4,000**	
Pilgrim's Pride Co	$2,000	Indiv
Agricultural Services/Products	**$2,900**	
None over $1,500		
Food Processing & Sales	**$2,000**	
Flowers Industries	$2,000	PAC
Forestry & Forest Products	**$1,500**	
None over $1,500		

Communications/Electronics	$8,250	
Media/Entertainment	**$1,500**	
None over $1,500		
Telephone Utilities	**$4,500**	
Southwestern Bell	$2,000	PAC

Construction	$8,000	
General Contractors	**$4,500**	
Associated General Contractors	$2,000	PAC
Construction Services	**$1,500**	
None over $1,500		

Contribution Totals by Sector

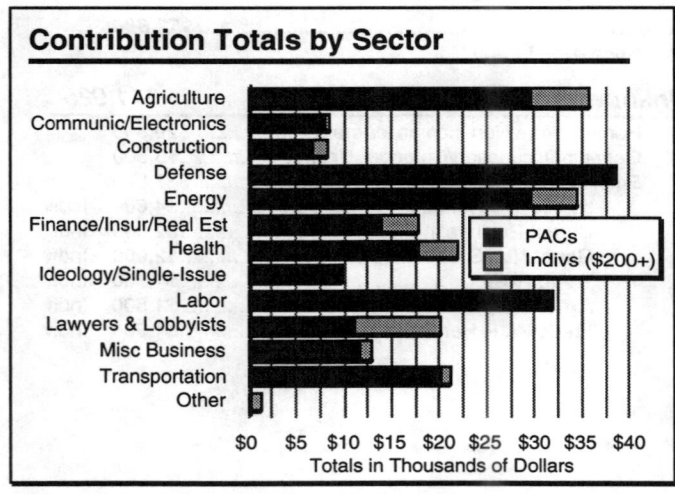

PACs
Indivs ($200+)

Agriculture
Communic/Electronics
Construction
Defense
Energy
Finance/Insur/Real Est
Health
Ideology/Single-Issue
Labor
Lawyers & Lobbyists
Misc Business
Transportation
Other

$0 $5 $10 $15 $20 $25 $30 $35 $40
Totals in Thousands of Dollars

Source of Funds in 1992 Election

Source	Total	Pct
■ PACs	$230,053	72%
▨ Indivs $200+	$36,795	12%
☐ Indivs under $200	$29,015	9%
▨ Other	$22,095	7%
Candidate	$0	0%
Party	$7,653	2%

Source of PAC Dollars by Sector

Source	Total	Pct
■ Business	$185,154	82%
▨ Labor	$31,700	14%
☐ Ideology/Single Issue	$9,500	4%

In-State vs. Out-of-State Contributions*

Source	Total	Pct
☐ In-State	$30,545	83%
▨ Out-of-state	$6,250	17%
No state listed	$0	

* by large individual contributors ($200 & above)

Defense	$38,500	
Defense Aerospace	**$18,000**	
McDonnell Douglas*	$2,500	PAC
Rockwell International	$2,500	PAC
General Dynamics	$2,000	PAC
Lockheed Corp	$2,000	PAC
General Electric	$1,500	PAC
Textron Inc	$1,500	PAC
Defense Electronics	**$16,500**	
E-Systems Inc	$4,000	PAC
GTE Corp	$4,000	PAC
AT&T	$2,000	PAC
Misc Defense	**$4,000**	
FMC Corp	$1,500	PAC
General Atomics	$1,500	PAC

Energy & Natural Resources	$34,143	
Oil & Gas	**$19,423**	
Wisenbaker Production Co	$3,000	Indiv
Coastal Corp	$2,000	PAC
Misc Energy	**$2,000**	
None over $1,500		
Electric Utilities	**$10,720**	
Texas Utilities Co*	$4,000	PAC
Houston Industries	$2,000	PAC

Finance, Insurance & Real Estate $17,575

Commercial Banks $6,350
    American Bankers Assn ....$2,000   PAC
Insurance $2,225
    None over $1,500
Real Estate $7,500
    National Assn of Realtors ....$6,000   PAC

Health $21,600

Health Professionals $15,500
    American Medical Assn ....$10,000   PAC
Hospitals/Nursing Homes $3,100
    American Hospital Assn ....$1,750   PAC
Pharmaceuticals/Health Products $2,000
    None over $1,500

Lawyers & Lobbyists $20,000

Lawyers & Lobbyists $20,000
    Assn of Trial Lawyers of America ....$5,000   PAC
    Akin, Gump et al ....$2,000   PAC
    Vinson & Elkins ....$1,500   PAC/Ind

Misc Business $12,650

Food & Beverage $2,500
    None over $1,500
Beer, Wine & Liquor $3,500
    National Beer Wholesalers Assn ....$1,500   PAC
Retail Sales $2,000
    International Council of Shopping Centers ....$1,500   PAC

Transportation $21,000

Air Transport $12,000
    Aircraft Owners & Pilots Assn ....$4,500   PAC
    United Parcel Service ....$2,500   PAC
    American Airlines ....$2,000   PAC
Automotive $5,000
    National Auto Dealers Assn ....$3,500   PAC
    Auto Dealers & Drivers for Free Trade ....$1,500   PAC
Railroads $2,500
    None over $1,500

Labor

Labor $31,700

Industrial Unions $8,000
    United Auto Workers ....$3,000   PAC
    Intl Brotherhood of Electrical Workers ....$2,500   PAC
    United Steelworkers ....$2,000   PAC
Transportation Unions $9,000
    United Transportation Union ....$3,000   PAC
    Teamsters Union ....$2,500   PAC
    Marine Engineers Dist 2 Maritime Officers ....$1,500   PAC
Public Sector Unions $13,700
    National Education Assn ....$10,000   PAC

Ideological/Single-Issue

Ideological/Single-Issue $9,500

Gun Rights/Gun Control $3,000
    National Rifle Assn ....$3,000   PAC
Misc Issues $6,500
    National Cmte to Preserve Social Security ....$6,000   PAC

Other & Unknown

Unknown $3,800

    Homemakers/Non-income earners $1,750
    Employer Listed/Category Unknown $1,800
      None over $1,500

Spending in Last 3 Elections

	1988	1990	1992
Chapman	$505,611	$463,377	$151,472
Opponent	$94,477	$408,677	$0
Vote Pct	62%	61%	100%

---

* Contributions came from more than one affiliate or subsidiary.

William L. Clay, D-Mo (1)

First elected: 1968

1991-92 Total Receipts: $328,937
1992 Year-end Cash: $124,500

1991-92 Committees & Subcommittees

Administration
Libraries and Memorials (Chairman)

Education and Labor
Labor-Management Relations; Labor Standards

Post Office and Civil Service (Chairman)
Investigations (Chairman)

Leading Contributors

Business

Agriculture $8,200

Tobacco	**$1,500**	
Philip Morris	$1,000	PAC
Dairy	**$3,500**	
Mid-America Dairymen	$2,000	PAC
Associated Milk Producers	$1,500	PAC
Poultry & Eggs	**$2,000**	
Perdue Farms	$2,000	Indiv

Communications/Electronics $9,510

Printing & Publishing	**$3,750**	
Magazine Publishers Assn	$1,500	PAC
Media/Entertainment	**$1,200**	
Time Warner	$1,000	PAC
Telephone Utilities	**$3,810**	
Southwestern Bell	$3,410	PAC/Ind

Construction $1,000

General Contractors	**$1,000**	
Fred Weber Inc	$1,000	Indiv

Energy & Natural Resources $1,500

Electric Utilities	**$1,000**	
ACRE (Action Cmte for Rural Electrification)	$1,000	PAC

Source of Funds in 1992 Election

Source	Total	Pct
■ PACs	$254,680	74%
▨ Indivs $200+	$26,228	8%
□ Indivs under $200	$14,203	4%
⊠ Other	$48,194	14%
Candidate	$0	0%
Party	$14,668	4%

Source of PAC Dollars by Sector

Source	Total	Pct
■ Business	$87,360	34%
▨ Labor	$156,600	61%
□ Ideology/Single Issue	$12,500	5%

In-State vs. Out-of-State Contributions*

Source	Total	Pct
□ In-State	$7,160	28%
■ Out-of-state	$18,818	72%
No state listed	$0	

*** by large individual contributors ($200 & above)**

Finance, Insurance & Real Estate $22,450

Commercial Banks	**$6,750**	
American Bankers Assn	$3,000	PAC
Boatmens Bankshares	$2,250	PAC
Mercantile Bancorp	$1,000	PAC
Securities & Investment	**$2,000**	
Prudential Securities	$1,000	PAC/Ind
Insurance	**$9,700**	
CNA Financial Corp	$5,000	PAC
Blue Cross & Blue Shield Assn*	$2,700	PAC
Principal Mutual Life Insurance	$1,000	PAC
Accountants	**$2,000**	
American Institute of CPA's	$2,000	PAC
Misc Finance	**$2,000**	
Healthcare Compare Corp	$2,000	PAC

Health $20,300

Health Professionals	**$11,300**	
American Medical Assn*	$3,000	PAC
Assn for the Advancement of Psychology	$3,000	PAC
American Assn Oral & Maxillofacial Surgeons	$2,000	PAC
American Assn Marriage/Family Therapy	$1,000	PAC
American Optometric Assn	$1,000	PAC
Health Services	**$3,000**	
Group Health Assn of America	$2,000	PAC
Family Health Program Inc	$1,000	PAC
Pharmaceuticals/Health Products	**$5,500**	
Medco Containment Services	$5,000	PAC

Contribution Totals by Sector

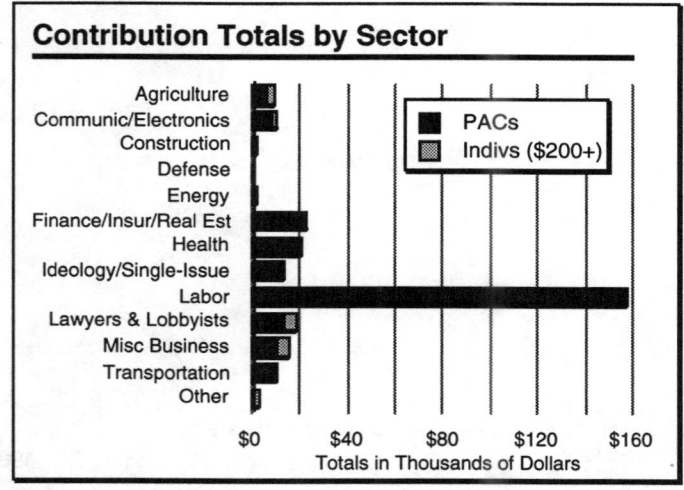

Totals in Thousands of Dollars

Lawyers & Lobbyists $18,300

Lawyers & Lobbyists **$18,300**
Assn of Trial Lawyers of America	$10,000	PAC
Swidler & Berlin	$2,000	PAC
Cameron Law Office	$1,000	Indiv
Shaw, Bransford & O'Rourke	$1,000	Indiv

Misc Business $15,478

Beer, Wine & Liquor **$1,400**
Anheuser-Busch	$1,400	Indiv

Retail Sales **$7,828**
Third Class Mail Assn	$2,000	PAC
Parcel Shippers Assn	$1,500	PAC
Direct Marketing Assn	$1,328	PAC/Ind
Publishers Clearing House	$1,000	Indiv

Misc Services **$1,000**
Mail Boxes Etc	$1,000	PAC

Business Services **$4,250**
Advo-System Inc	$2,500	PAC
Watson & Hughey	$1,000	Indiv

Transportation $9,450

Air Transport **$6,950**
United Parcel Service	$5,450	PAC
United Airlines	$1,000	PAC

Automotive **$2,000**
Warshawsky & Co/JC Whitney & Co	$2,000	PAC

Labor

Labor $156,600

Building Trade Unions **$20,200**
Laborers' Political League	$6,000	PAC
Carpenters & Joiners Union	$5,000	PAC
Plumbers/Pipefitters Union	$4,000	PAC
Painters & Allied Trades Union	$2,000	PAC
AFL-CIO Bldg/Construction Trades Dept	$1,000	PAC
Ironworkers Union	$1,000	PAC
Operating Engineers Union	$1,000	PAC

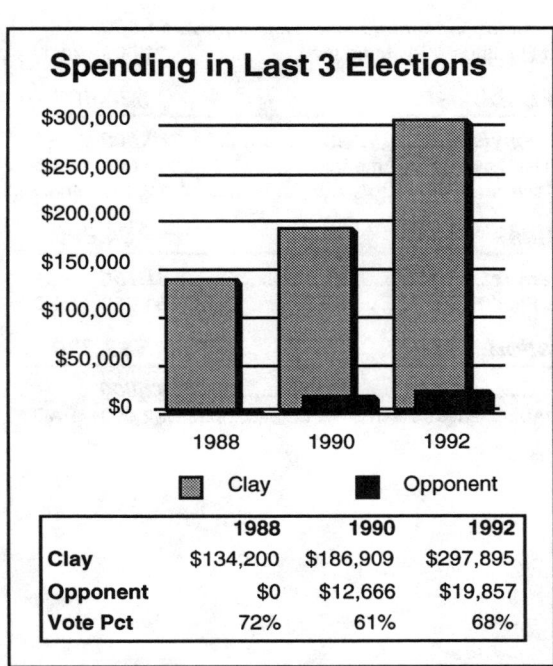

Spending in Last 3 Elections

	1988	1990	1992
Clay	$134,200	$186,909	$297,895
Opponent	$0	$12,666	$19,857
Vote Pct	72%	61%	68%

Industrial Unions $20,600
Machinists/Aerospace Workers Union	$5,000	PAC
Boilermakers Union	$3,000	PAC
Intl Brotherhood of Electrical Workers*	$3,000	PAC
United Auto Workers	$3,000	PAC
Communications Workers of America	$2,600	PAC
United Mine Workers	$1,500	PAC
Ladies Garment Workers Union	$1,200	PAC

Transportation Unions **$39,750**
Air Line Pilots Assn	$10,000	PAC
Teamsters Union	$6,000	PAC
Amalgamated Transit Union	$5,000	PAC
Marine Engineers Union*	$5,000	PAC
Seafarers International Union	$3,500	PAC
National Air Traffic Controllers Assn	$2,500	PAC
Transport Workers Union	$2,500	PAC
United Transportation Union	$2,500	PAC
International Longshoremen's Assn	$1,500	PAC

Public Sector Unions **$70,150**
American Fedn of St/Cnty/Munic Employees	$10,000	PAC
American Postal Workers Union	$10,000	PAC
National Assn of Letter Carriers	$10,000	PAC
National Assn Retired Federal Employees	$7,000	PAC
American Federation of Teachers	$5,000	PAC
National Assn of Postmasters	$4,250	PAC
National League of Postmasters	$4,000	PAC
Natl Star Route Mail Contractors Assn	$3,500	PAC
Federal Managers' Assn	$3,000	PAC
National Treasury Employees Union	$3,000	PAC
National Rural Letter Carriers Assn	$2,500	PAC
International Assn of Firefighters	$2,000	PAC
National Education Assn	$2,000	PAC
Natl Alliance of Postal/Fedl Employees	$1,100	PAC
American Federation of Govt Employees	$1,000	PAC
National Assn of Postal Supervisors	$1,000	PAC

Misc Unions **$5,900**
Food & Commercial Workers Union	$2,000	PAC
Hotel/Restaurant Employees Union	$1,500	PAC
AFL-CIO	$1,000	PAC
Bakery, Confectionery & Tobacco Workers	$1,000	PAC

Ideological/Single-Issue

Ideological/Single-Issue $12,700

Pro-Israel **$5,000**
National PAC	$5,000	PAC

Misc Issues **$7,700**
National Cmte to Preserve Social Security	$7,500	PAC

Other & Unknown

Other $2,600

Education **$1,200**
None over $1,000

Unknown $4,850
No Employer Listed or Found	$1,150
Employer Listed/Category Unknown	$3,200

None over $1,000

---

* Contributions came from more than one affiliate or subsidiary.

Eva Clayton, D-NC (1)

First elected: 1992

1991-92 Total Receipts: $521,382
1992 Year-end Cash: $258

1993-94 Committees & Subcommittees

Agriculture
Department Operations and Nutrition; Environment, Credit and Rural Development; Specialty Crops and Natural Resources

Small Business
Procurement, Taxation and Tourism; Rural Enterprises, Exports and the Environment

Leading Contributors

Business

Agriculture $15,000

Crop Production & Basic Processing	**$1,750**
None over $1,500	
Tobacco	**$5,000**
RJR Nabisco	$3,000 PAC
Philip Morris	$1,500 PAC
Dairy	**$3,000**
Associated Milk Producers	$2,000 PAC
Food Processing & Sales	**$1,500**
None over $1,500	

Communications/Electronics $7,450

Telephone Utilities	**$6,500**
Southern Bell	$3,500 PAC
United Telecommunications	$2,500 PAC

Energy & Natural Resources $3,200

Electric Utilities	**$3,200**
Carolina Power & Light	$1,700 PAC/Ind

Finance, Insurance & Real Estate $25,600

Commercial Banks	**$5,600**
Citizens & Southern National Bank	$2,000 PAC
Securities & Investment	**$1,500**
None over $1,500	
Insurance	**$3,500**
None over $1,500	
Real Estate	**$13,000**
National Assn of Realtors	$10,000 PAC
Shelton Companies	$2,000 Indiv

Contribution Totals by Sector

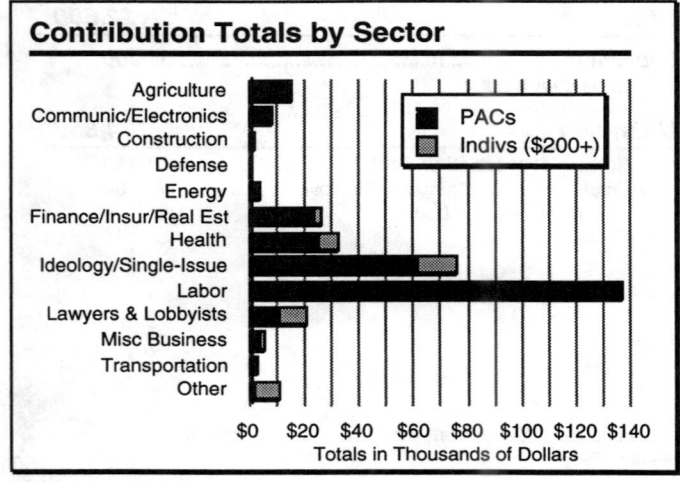

Totals in Thousands of Dollars

Source of Funds in 1992 Election

Source	Total	Pct
PACs	$281,415	54%
Indivs $200+	$64,046	12%
Indivs under $200	$137,712	26%
Other	$42,272	8%
Candidate	$17,665	3%
Party	$8,713	2%

Source of PAC Dollars by Sector

Source	Total	Pct
Business	$89,600	31%
Labor	$136,300	48%
Ideology/Single Issue	$60,449	21%

In-State vs. Out-of-State Contributions*

Source	Total	Pct
In-State	$36,851	59%
Out-of-state	$25,350	41%
No state listed	$1,420	

* by large individual contributors ($200 & above)

Health $32,000

Health Professionals	**$25,550**
American Dental Assn	$5,000 PAC
American Medical Assn	$5,000 PAC
American Academy of Ophthalmology	$3,000 PAC
American College of Emergency Physicians	$2,000 PAC
American Nurses Assn	$1,500 PAC
Hospitals/Nursing Homes	**$3,450**
American Hospital Assn	$1,500 PAC
Pharmaceuticals/Health Products	**$1,500**
None over $1,500	
Misc Health	**$1,500**
Managed Healthcare Systems Inc	$1,500 Indiv

Lawyers & Lobbyists $20,500

Lawyers & Lobbyists	**$20,500**
Assn of Trial Lawyers of America	$10,000 PAC
Kelly & Associates Inc	$2,000 Indiv

Misc Business $4,800

Food & Beverage	**$1,750**
Hardee's Food Systems	$1,750 PAC

Transportation $2,250

Automotive	**$2,000**
National Auto Dealers Assn	$2,000 PAC

Labor

Labor $136,300

Building Trade Unions **$8,500**
    Carpenters & Joiners Union .... $4,000 PAC
    Laborers' Political League .... $2,000 PAC

Industrial Unions **$47,800**
    United Auto Workers .... $11,000 PAC
    Machinists/Aerospace Workers Union .... $10,000 PAC
    Intl Brotherhood of Electrical Workers .... $5,000 PAC
    Communications Workers of America .... $5,000 PAC
    United Steelworkers .... $5,000 PAC
    Rubber Cork Linoleum & Plastic Workers .... $3,000 PAC
    Amalgamated Clothing & Textile Workers .... $2,000 PAC
    Electronic Machine Furniture Workers .... $2,000 PAC

Transportation Unions **$20,000**
    Teamsters Union .... $10,000 PAC
    Marine Engineers Union .... $2,500 PAC
    International Longshoremen's Assn .... $1,500 PAC
    United Transportation Union .... $1,500 PAC

Public Sector Unions **$36,500**
    National Education Assn .... $15,000 PAC
    American Fedn of St/Cnty/Munic Employees ...... $7,500 PAC
    American Postal Workers Union .... $3,500 PAC
    National Assn of Letter Carriers .... $3,500 PAC
    American Federation of Teachers .... $2,500 PAC
    American Federation of Govt Employees .... $1,500 PAC

Misc Unions **$23,500**
    AFL-CIO .... $10,000 PAC
    Food & Commercial Workers Union .... $8,500 PAC
    Bakery, Confectionery & Tobacco Workers .... $4,000 PAC

Ideological/Single-Issue

Ideological/Single-Issue $74,549

Democratic/Liberal **$13,250**
    Independent Action .... $5,000 PAC
    National Cmte for an Effective Congress .... $5,000 PAC
    Hollywood Women's Political Cmte .... $2,000 PAC

Leadership PACs **$4,385**
    None over $1,500

Foreign & Defense Policy **$1,600**
    None over $1,500

Pro-Israel **$3,000**
    None over $1,500

Pro-Choice **$1,518**
    None over $1,500

Womens Issues **$39,096**
    Emily's List .... $14,196 PAC/Ind
    Women's Campaign Fund .... $8,000 PAC
    National Organization for Women .... $5,500 PAC
    National Womens Political Caucus .... $2,500 PAC

Human Rights **$4,500**
    Human Rights Campaign Fund .... $4,500 PAC

Misc Issues **$6,200**
    Sierra Club .... $3,000 PAC

Other & Unknown

Other $10,200

Civil Servants/Public Officials **$2,200**
    None over $1,500

Education **$1,550**
    None over $1,500

Retired **$2,850**
    None over $1,500

Other **$2,850**
    National Assn of Social Workers .... $1,500 PAC

Unknown $17,621

    No Employer Listed or Found $9,202
    Employer Listed/Category Unknown $6,519
      None over $1,500

Spending in Last Election

	1992
Clayton	$520,919
Opponent	$6,131
Vote Pct	67%

Bob Clement, D-Tenn (5)

First elected: 1988

1991-92 Total Receipts:	$562,141
1992 Year-end Cash:	$127,237

1991-92 Committees & Subcommittees

Public Works and Transportation
Aviation; Surface Transportation; Water Resources

Veterans' Affairs
Education, Training and Employment; Housing and Memorial Affairs

Leading Contributors

Business

Agriculture	$33,475

Crop Production & Basic Processing $8,225
None over $2,000

Tobacco $12,500
RJR Nabisco .... $4,000 PAC
US Tobacco Co .... $3,500 PAC
Philip Morris .... $3,000 PAC

Dairy $3,500
None over $2,000

Livestock $3,500
Tennessee Walking Horse Breeders .... $2,500 PAC

Food Processing & Sales $2,000
None over $2,000

Communications/Electronics	$26,950

Media/Entertainment $5,750
None over $2,000

Telephone Utilities $16,450
BellSouth Corp* .... $9,600 PAC
AT&T .... $4,000 PAC

Construction	$20,840

General Contractors $10,100
None over $2,000

Home Builders $5,990
Haury & Smith .... $2,990 Indiv
National Assn of Home Builders .... $2,500 PAC

Building Materials & Equipment $2,250
None over $2,000

Source of Funds in 1992 Election

Source	Total	Pct
■ PACs	$288,762	51%
▨ Indivs $200+	$178,441	31%
□ Indivs under $200	$69,630	12%
▩ Other	$32,654	6%
Candidate	$0	0%
Party	$8,146	1%

Source of PAC Dollars by Sector

Source	Total	Pct
■ Business	$206,412	72%
▨ Labor	$72,600	25%
□ Ideology/Single Issue	$9,000	3%

In-State vs. Out-of-State Contributions*

Source	Total	Pct
□ In-State	$164,191	92%
■ Out-of-state	$14,250	8%
No state listed	$0	

* by large individual contributors ($200 & above)

Defense	$3,500

Defense Aerospace $3,000
Textron Inc .... $2,500 PAC

Energy & Natural Resources	$25,050

Oil & Gas $9,750
Cone Management Inc .... $2,000 Indiv

Nuclear Energy $2,100
None over $2,000

Electric Utilities $8,700
None over $2,000

Waste Management $2,500
None over $2,000

Finance, Insurance & Real Estate	$55,500

Commercial Banks $16,225
Third National Corp .... $3,600 PAC
Citizens & Southern National Bank .... $2,500 PAC
Bank of Putnam County .... $2,000 Indiv
First American Bank .... $2,000 PAC

Securities & Investment $5,000
JC Bradford & Co .... $2,250 Indiv

Insurance $8,225
None over $2,000

Real Estate $13,750
National Assn of Realtors .... $8,000 PAC

Accountants $5,000
Kraft Brothers .... $2,750 Indiv
American Institute of CPA's .... $2,000 PAC

Misc Finance $5,500
None over $2,000

Contribution Totals by Sector

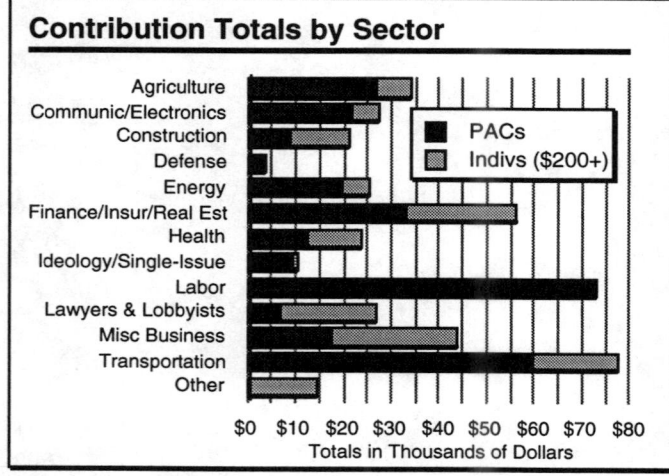

Legend: ■ PACs, ▨ Indivs ($200+)

Categories (top to bottom): Agriculture, Communic/Electronics, Construction, Defense, Energy, Finance/Insur/Real Est, Health, Ideology/Single-Issue, Labor, Lawyers & Lobbyists, Misc Business, Transportation, Other

X-axis: $0 $10 $20 $30 $40 $50 $60 $70 $80
Totals in Thousands of Dollars

Health $23,200

Health Professionals $15,700
    American Medical Assn .... $5,000 PAC
    Surgical Care Affiliates .... $2,000 Indiv

Hospitals/Nursing Homes $6,000
    Baptist Hospital .... $2,500 Indiv

Lawyers & Lobbyists $26,575

Lawyers & Lobbyists $26,575
    Assn of Trial Lawyers of America .... $5,000 PAC
    Boult, Cummings et al .... $2,000 Indiv

Misc Business $43,598

Food & Beverage $3,442
    None over $2,000

Beer, Wine & Liquor $7,816
    None over $2,000

Retail Sales $5,000
    None over $2,000

Misc Services $2,100
    None over $2,000

Business Services $11,150
    Fulton-Armstrong .... $2,000 Indiv
    Guardsmark Inc .... $2,000 Indiv

Lodging/Tourism $10,090
    Opryland USA .... $4,200 PAC

Misc Manufacturing & Distributing $2,500
    70 Wrecker Service .... $2,000 Indiv

Transportation $77,266

Air Transport $35,420
    Federal Express Corp .... $10,520 PAC/Ind
    United Parcel Service .... $10,000 PAC
    American Airlines .... $4,500 PAC
    Aircraft Owners & Pilots Assn .... $4,000 PAC

Automotive $15,250
    National Auto Dealers Assn .... $7,500 PAC
    Ford Motor Co .... $2,000 PAC
    Two Rivers Ford .... $2,000 Indiv

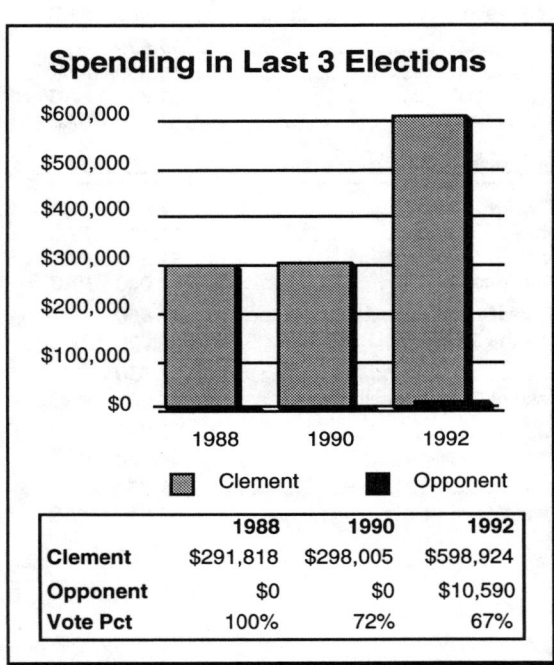

Spending in Last 3 Elections

	1988	1990	1992
Clement	$291,818	$298,005	$598,924
Opponent	$0	$0	$10,590
Vote Pct	100%	72%	67%

Trucking $13,346
    Paccar Inc .... $2,000 PAC

Railroads $2,500
    None over $2,000

Sea Transport $5,750
    Ingram Industries .... $2,000 Indiv

Misc Transport $5,000
    None over $2,000

Labor

Labor $72,600

Building Trade Unions $15,500
    Carpenters & Joiners Union .... $5,000 PAC
    Plumbers/Pipefitters Union .... $5,000 PAC
    Laborers' Political League .... $3,000 PAC
    Ironworkers Union .... $2,000 PAC

Industrial Unions $22,000
    United Auto Workers .... $6,500 PAC
    United Steelworkers .... $5,000 PAC
    Intl Brotherhood of Electrical Workers .... $4,000 PAC
    Communications Workers of America .... $3,000 PAC
    Machinists/Aerospace Workers Union .... $2,000 PAC

Transportation Unions $11,200
    Teamsters Union .... $2,000 PAC
    Transport Workers Union .... $2,000 PAC

Public Sector Unions $20,200
    National Assn Retired Federal Employees .... $7,000 PAC
    National Education Assn .... $4,500 PAC
    American Fedn of St/Cnty/Munic Employees ...... $2,500 PAC

Misc Unions $3,700
    Food & Commercial Workers Union .... $2,000 PAC

Ideological/Single-Issue

Ideological/Single-Issue $10,000

Leadership PACs $2,000
    House Leadership Fund (Tom Foley) .... $2,000 PAC

Misc Issues $5,000
    National Cmte to Preserve Social Security .... $5,000 PAC

Other & Unknown

Other $14,300

Civil Servants/Public Officials $4,750
    State of Tennessee .... $2,000 Indiv

Retired $8,550
    None over $2,000

Unknown $33,599

    No Employer Listed or Found $2,700
    Generic Occupation/Category Unknown $2,500
    Employer Listed/Category Unknown $26,670
        None over $2,000

---

* Contributions came from more than one affiliate or subsidiary.

William F. Clinger, R-Pa (5)

First elected: 1978

1991-92 Total Receipts:	$286,477
1992 Year-end Cash:	$96,640

1991-92 Committees & Subcommittees

Government Operations
Environment, Energy and Natural Resources (Ranking Republican)

Public Works and Transportation
Aviation (Ranking Republican); Surface Transportation; Water Resources

Select Committee on Narcotics Abuse and Control

Leading Contributors

Business

Agriculture — $9,275

Crop Production & Basic Processing	**$4,475**	
Ocean Spray Cranberries Inc	$1,500	PAC
Tobacco	**$1,750**	
Philip Morris	$1,050	PAC
Food Processing & Sales	**$1,050**	
None over $1,000		

Communications/Electronics — $10,050

Printing & Publishing	**$1,000**	
None over $1,000		
Telephone Utilities	**$7,850**	
AT&T	$3,500	PAC
GTE Corp	$1,750	PAC
Bell Telephone of Pennsylvania	$1,100	PAC
United Telecommunications	$1,000	PAC

Construction — $12,000

General Contractors	**$4,550**	
National Utility Contractors Assn	$3,500	PAC
Home Builders	**$2,150**	
National Assn of Home Builders	$2,150	PAC
Construction Services	**$3,400**	
American Consulting Engineers Council	$1,000	PAC
National Society of Professional Engineers	$1,000	PAC
Building Materials & Equipment	**$1,900**	
None over $1,000		

Source of Funds in 1992 Election

Source	Total	Pct
PACs	$142,894	50%
Indivs $200+	$28,750	10%
Indivs under $200	$101,846	36%
Other	$12,987	5%
Candidate	$0	0%
Party	$1,398	0%

Source of PAC Dollars by Sector

Source	Total	Pct
Business	$130,077	92%
Labor	$11,290	8%
Ideology/Single Issue	$700	0%

In-State vs. Out-of-State Contributions*

Source	Total	Pct
In-State	$22,850	79%
Out-of-state	$5,900	21%
No state listed	$0	

*** by large individual contributors ($200 & above)**

Defense — $1,450

Defense Aerospace	**$1,200**	
None over $1,000		

Energy & Natural Resources — $19,174

Oil & Gas	**$9,345**	
National Fuel Gas Corp	$1,600	PAC
Consolidated Natural Gas	$1,050	PAC
BP America	$1,000	PAC
Mining	**$3,350**	
National Coal Assn	$1,000	PAC
Electric Utilities	**$5,629**	
United Electric Coop	$1,900	Indiv
General Public Utilities	$1,650	PAC
Duquesne Light Co	$1,200	PAC

Finance, Insurance & Real Estate — $20,864

Commercial Banks	**$4,514**	
PennBancorp	$1,410	PAC
Marine Bank	$1,200	PAC
American Bankers Assn	$1,000	PAC
Securities & Investment	**$1,850**	
Goldman, Sachs & Co	$1,000	PAC
Insurance	**$2,350**	
National Assn of Life Underwriters	$2,000	PAC
Real Estate	**$6,200**	
National Assn of Realtors	$6,000	PAC
Accountants	**$5,350**	
American Institute of CPA's	$5,350	PAC

Contribution Totals by Sector

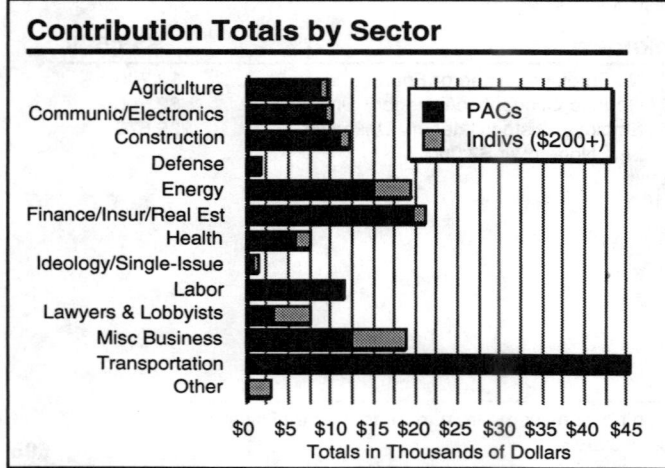

Agriculture
Communic/Electronics
Construction
Defense
Energy
Finance/Insur/Real Est
Health
Ideology/Single-Issue
Labor
Lawyers & Lobbyists
Misc Business
Transportation
Other

■ PACs
▨ Indivs ($200+)

$0 $5 $10 $15 $20 $25 $30 $35 $40 $45
Totals in Thousands of Dollars

Health $7,400

Health Professionals $5,550
  American Medical Assn .... $3,350   PAC

Pharmaceuticals/Health Products $1,500
  None over $1,000

Lawyers & Lobbyists $7,300

Lawyers & Lobbyists $7,300
  None over $1,000

Misc Business $18,589

Beer, Wine & Liquor $1,550
  None over $1,000

Business Services $4,089
  Accu Weather Inc .... $1,000   Indiv

Lodging/Tourism $1,000
  None over $1,000

Chemical & Related Manufacturing $4,000
  FMC Corp .... $1,000   PAC

Steel Production $2,350
  National Forge .... $2,000   Indiv

Misc Manufacturing & Distributing $3,800
  Owens-Illinois .... $1,700   PAC
  Corning Glass Works .... $1,000   PAC

Transportation $45,325

Air Transport $33,525
  Aircraft Owners & Pilots Assn .... $11,000   PAC
  United Parcel Service .... $6,850   PAC
  Texas Air .... $1,850   PAC
  Northwest Airlines .... $1,700   PAC
  Boeing Co .... $1,400   PAC
  American Airlines .... $1,200   PAC
  General Electric .... $1,050   PAC
  Delta Airlines .... $1,000   PAC
  Federal Express Corp .... $1,000   PAC
  United Airlines .... $1,000   PAC

Automotive $2,650
  National Auto Dealers Assn .... $2,050   PAC

Trucking $4,650
  American Trucking Assns .... $1,050   PAC
  North American Van Lines .... $1,000   PAC

Railroads $2,750
  Union Pacific Corp .... $1,000   PAC

Sea Transport $1,050
  None over $1,000

Labor

Labor $11,290

Transportation Unions $10,150
  Air Line Pilots Assn .... $5,000   PAC
  Marine Engineers Dist 2 Maritime Officers .... $2,000   PAC

Public Sector Unions $1,140
  None over $1,000

Ideological/Single-Issue

Ideological/Single-Issue $1,400

Gun Rights/Gun Control $1,400
  None over $1,000

Other & Unknown

Other $2,650

Retired $2,200
  None over $1,000

Unknown $4,050

  Homemakers/Non-income earners $2,650

Spending in Last 3 Elections

	1988	1990	1992
Clinger	$336,774	$338,431	$274,415
Opponent	$106,463	$6,765	$0
Vote Pct	62%	59%	100%

Jim Clyburn, D-SC (6)

1993-94 Committees & Subcommittees

Public Works and Transportation
Economic Development; Public Buildings and Grounds; Surface Transportation

Veterans' Affairs
Education, Training and Employment; Oversight and Investigations

First elected: 1992

1991-92 Total Receipts: $407,978
1992 Year-end Cash: $795

Leading Contributors

Business

Agriculture — $10,300

Tobacco	**$5,500**	
Philip Morris	$2,000	PAC
RJR Nabisco	$2,000	PAC
Ragsdale Tobacco	$1,000	Indiv
Food Processing & Sales	**$1,500**	
Pepsico Inc	$1,000	PAC
Forestry & Forest Products	**$1,500**	
None over $1,000		

Communications/Electronics — $8,750

Media/Entertainment	**$2,550**	
Black Entertainment Network	$1,000	Indiv
WYMB Radio	$1,000	Indiv
Telephone Utilities	**$4,700**	
Southern Bell	$3,000	PAC

Construction — $4,250

General Contractors	**$1,250**	
Fluor Corp	$1,000	PAC
Home Builders	**$2,250**	
National Assn of Home Builders	$2,000	PAC

Energy & Natural Resources — $14,250

Oil & Gas	**$3,000**	
Phillips Petroleum	$1,500	PAC

Electric Utilities	**$9,750**	
ACRE (Action Cmte for Rural Electrification)	$3,000	PAC
Carolina Power & Light	$3,000	PAC
Scana Corp	$2,500	PAC
Waste Management	**$1,500**	
Waste Management Inc	$1,000	PAC

Finance, Insurance & Real Estate — $29,650

Commercial Banks	**$18,150**	
C&S/Sovran Corp*	$8,000	PAC
Nations Bank	$2,500	Indiv
National Bank of South Carolina	$2,000	Indiv
South Carolina National Bank	$1,700	PAC
NCNB Corp	$1,500	Indiv
American Bankers Assn	$1,000	PAC
Securities & Investment	**$1,000**	
None over $1,000		
Insurance	**$7,950**	
Colonial Life & Accident Insurance	$3,450	PAC/Ind
Liberty Corp	$2,500	Indiv

Health — $18,000

Health Professionals	**$14,500**	
American Medical Assn	$5,000	PAC
American College of Emergency Physicians	$2,000	PAC
American Chiropractic Assn	$1,000	PAC
American Dental Assn	$1,000	PAC
American Optometric Assn	$1,000	PAC
Floyd Medical Associates	$1,000	Indiv
Hospitals/Nursing Homes	**$1,500**	
None over $1,000		
Misc Health	**$1,000**	
Managed Healthcare Systems Inc	$1,000	Indiv

Source of Funds in 1992 Election

Source	Total	Pct
PACs	$101,710	24%
Indivs $200+	$93,868	22%
Indivs under $200	$68,314	16%
Other	$166,096	39%
Candidate	$128,732	30%
Party	$22,010	5%

Source of PAC Dollars by Sector

Source	Total	Pct
Business	$83,630	65%
Labor	$28,500	22%
Ideology/Single Issue	$16,700	13%

In-State vs. Out-of-State Contributions*

Source	Total	Pct
In-State	$73,878	81%
Out-of-state	$17,890	19%
No state listed	$1,500	

* by large individual contributors ($200 & above)

Contribution Totals by Sector

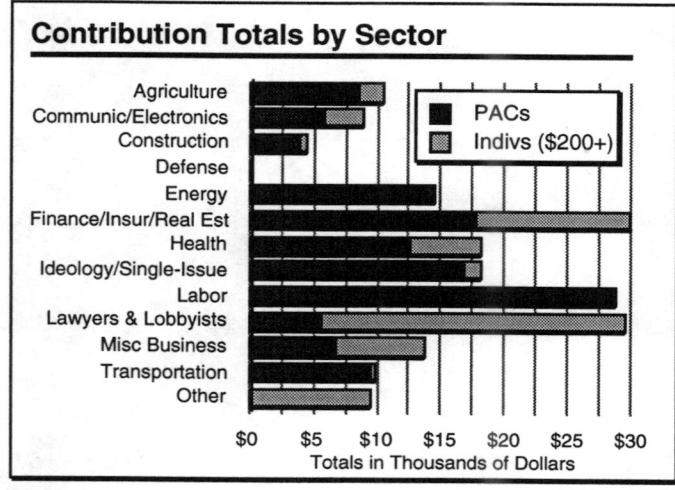

Agriculture
Communic/Electronics
Construction
Defense
Energy
Finance/Insur/Real Est
Health
Ideology/Single-Issue
Labor
Lawyers & Lobbyists
Misc Business
Transportation
Other

- PACs
- Indivs ($200+)

$0 $5 $10 $15 $20 $25 $30
Totals in Thousands of Dollars

Lawyers & Lobbyists $29,287

Lawyers & Lobbyists **$29,287**
- Assn of Trial Lawyers of America ....$5,000 PAC
- Winburn & Associates ....$2,000 Indiv
- Nelson, Mullins et al ....$1,650 Indiv
- McNair Law Firm ....$1,500 Indiv
- Bethea, Jordan & Griffin ....$1,000 Indiv
- Lewis, Babcock & Hawkins ....$1,000 Indiv

Misc Business $13,630

Business Associations **$1,030**
- Business Industry PAC ....$1,030 PAC

Misc Services **$1,500**
- American Assn of Equipment Lessors ....$1,500 PAC

Business Services **$2,500**
- Am-Pro Protective Agency ....$1,000 Indiv

Steel Production **$2,000**
- MacAlloy Corp ....$2,000 Indiv

Misc Manufacturing & Distributing **$2,250**
- Stone Container Corp ....$1,500 PAC

Textiles **$3,400**
- Greenwood Mills ....$1,000 Indiv
- Springs Mills ....$1,000 PAC

Transportation $9,800

Air Transport **$4,800**
- Federal Express Corp ....$3,500 PAC
- United Parcel Service ....$1,000 PAC

Automotive **$3,750**
- National Auto Dealers Assn ....$3,000 PAC

Railroads **$1,250**
- None over $1,000

Labor

Labor $28,500

Industrial Unions **$1,000**
- Communications Workers of America ....$1,000 PAC

Transportation Unions **$5,500**
- International Longshoremen's Assn ....$2,500 PAC
- Air Line Pilots Assn ....$1,500 PAC
- United Transportation Union ....$1,000 PAC

Public Sector Unions **$22,000**
- National Education Assn ....$10,000 PAC
- National Assn of Letter Carriers ....$4,000 PAC
- American Fedn of St/Cnty/Munic Employees ......$3,000 PAC
- National Assn Retired Federal Employees ....$2,500 PAC
- National Rural Letter Carriers Assn ....$1,000 PAC

Ideological/Single-Issue

Ideological/Single-Issue $17,950

Leadership PACs **$5,000**
- America's Leaders' Fund (Dan Rostenkowski) ....$1,000 PAC
- Citizens for Competitive Amer (Ernest Hollings) ..$1,000 PAC
- Effective Government Cmte (Dick Gephardt) ......$1,000 PAC
- House Leadership Fund (Tom Foley) ....$1,000 PAC
- Victory USA (Vic Fazio) ....$1,000 PAC

Pro-Israel **$3,850**
- South Carolinians for Representative Govt ....$2,100 PAC
- National PAC ....$1,000 PAC

Gun Rights/Gun Control **$4,950**
- National Rifle Assn ....$4,950 PAC

Human Rights **$2,900**
- Human Rights Campaign Fund ....$2,500 PAC

Misc Issues **$1,000**
- None over $1,000

Other & Unknown

Other $9,300

Civil Servants/Public Officials **$4,000**
- Town of Lamar ....$1,000 Indiv

Education **$1,450**
- None over $1,000

Retired **$3,650**
- None over $1,000

Unknown $28,431
- Homemakers/Non-income earners $2,250
- No Employer Listed or Found $16,534
- Generic Occupation/Category Unknown $1,200
- Employer Listed/Category Unknown $8,447
  - Delon, Hampton & Associates ....$1,000 Indiv
  - Fontaine Co ....$1,000 Indiv
  - Kneece & Kneece ....$1,000 Indiv

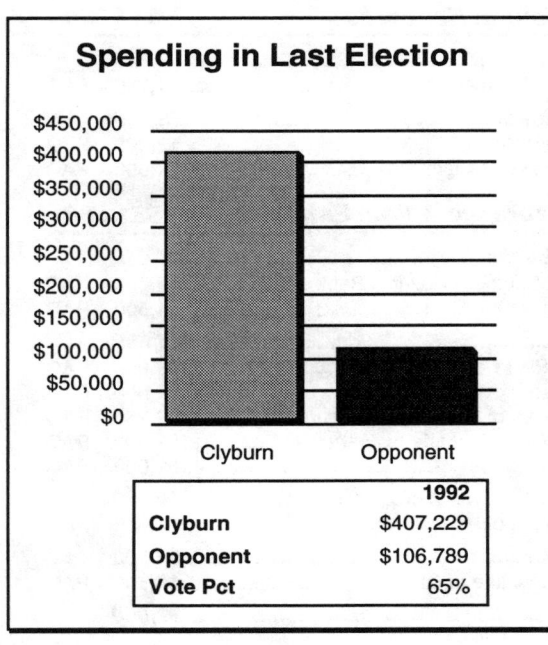

Spending in Last Election

	1992
Clyburn	$407,229
Opponent	$106,789
Vote Pct	65%

---

* Contributions came from more than one affiliate or subsidiary.

509

J. Howard Coble, R-NC (6)

First elected: 1984

1991-92 Total Receipts: $504,213
1992 Year-end Cash: $84,967

1991-92 Committees & Subcommittees

Judiciary
Civil and Constitutional Rights; Intellectual Property and Judicial Administration

Merchant Marine and Fisheries
Coast Guard and Navigation; Fisheries and Wildlife Conservation and the Environment

Select Committee on Narcotics Abuse and Control

Leading Contributors

Business

Agriculture	$31,540

Crop Production & Basic Processing **$3,500**
    None over $1,500

Tobacco **$16,640**
    RJR Nabisco .... $6,000   PAC
    US Tobacco Co .... $4,000   PAC/Ind
    Philip Morris .... $3,790   PAC

Food Processing & Sales **$4,900**
    None over $1,500

Forestry & Forest Products **$3,550**
    None over $1,500

Communications/Electronics	$35,997

Printing & Publishing **$2,167**
    West Publishing .... $1,500   PAC

Media/Entertainment **$14,950**
    National Cable Television Assn .... $6,000   PAC
    National Assn of Broadcasters .... $4,250   PAC
    ASCAP .... $2,000   PAC

Telephone Utilities **$17,380**
    AT&T .... $7,130   PAC/Ind
    Southern Bell .... $5,000   PAC
    United Telecommunications .... $1,900   PAC

Source of Funds in 1992 Election

Source	Total	Pct
■ PACs	$207,135	41%
▨ Indivs $200+	$101,591	20%
☐ Indivs under $200	$178,565	35%
⊠ Other	$16,922	3%
Candidate	$0	0%
Party	$9,779	2%

Source of PAC Dollars by Sector

Source	Total	Pct
■ Business	$193,190	93%
▨ Labor	$4,335	2%
☐ Ideology/Single Issue	$10,200	5%

In-State vs. Out-of-State Contributions*

Source	Total	Pct
☐ In-State	$92,221	92%
■ Out-of-state	$7,600	8%
No state listed	$0	

* by large individual contributors ($200 & above)

Construction	$11,300

General Contractors **$5,250**
    Ansco & Associates .... $2,000   Indiv

Home Builders **$2,950**
    None over $1,500

Building Materials & Equipment **$2,500**
    None over $1,500

Defense	$3,600

Defense Aerospace **$3,600**
    None over $1,500

Energy & Natural Resources	$14,850

Oil & Gas **$8,700**
    Petroleum Marketers Assn .... $1,750   PAC

Electric Utilities **$5,400**
    Duke Power Co .... $2,900   PAC
    Carolina Power & Light .... $1,500   PAC

Finance, Insurance & Real Estate	$51,600

Commercial Banks **$7,050**
    Citizens & Southern National Bank ...... $1,700   PAC
    Barnett Banks Inc .... $1,500   PAC

Insurance **$25,650**
    Jefferson-Pilot Corp .... $6,000   PAC
    National Assn of Life Underwriters .... $5,000   PAC
    National Assn of Independent Insurers ... $2,250   PAC
    American Council of Life Insurance ...... $2,000   PAC
    Travelers Corp .... $2,000   PAC

Real Estate **$10,350**
    National Assn of Realtors .... $6,500   PAC

Accountants **$5,500**
    American Institute of CPA's .... $5,500   PAC

Misc Finance **$2,000**
    None over $1,500

Contribution Totals by Sector

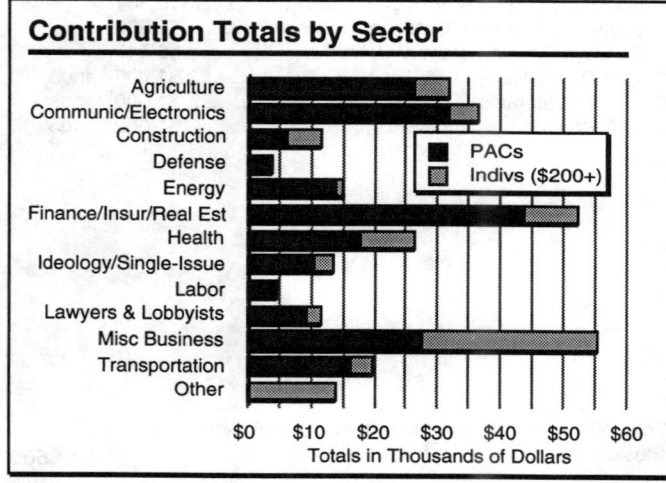

Agriculture
Communic/Electronics
Construction
Defense
Energy
Finance/Insur/Real Est
Health
Ideology/Single-Issue
Labor
Lawyers & Lobbyists
Misc Business
Transportation
Other

■ PACs
▨ Indivs ($200+)

$0 $10 $20 $30 $40 $50 $60
Totals in Thousands of Dollars

Health $26,100

Health Professionals $12,350
    American Medical Assn.............................$5,000   PAC
    Greensboro Radiology ....$2,100   Indiv
    Wesley Long Hospital ....$1,750   Indiv

Hospitals/Nursing Homes $3,600
    May Memorial Hospital...........................$2,000   Indiv

Pharmaceuticals/Health Products $10,150
    Ciba-Geigy Corp ....$1,900   PAC/Ind
    Glaxo Inc ....$1,850   PAC
    Hoffman-La Roche ....$1,850   PAC

Lawyers & Lobbyists $11,450

Lawyers & Lobbyists $11,450
    Assn of Trial Lawyers of America ....$5,500   PAC

Misc Business $54,894

Food & Beverage $2,800
    Triton Management ....$2,000   Indiv

Beer, Wine & Liquor $3,250
    National Beer Wholesalers Assn ....$2,500   PAC

Retail Sales $4,000
    None over $1,500

Business Services $2,050
    None over $1,500

Chemical & Related Manufacturing $4,650
    Kay Chemical Co ....$1,500   Indiv
    Procter & Gamble ....$1,500   PAC/Ind

Misc Manufacturing & Distributing $16,169
    American Furniture Manufacturers Assn ....$2,200   PAC
    Blue Bell Inc ....$2,000   PAC
    Levin Brothers ....$2,000   Indiv

Textiles $19,675
    Burlington Industries ....$5,000   PAC
    Glen Raven Mills ....$5,000   Indiv
    Cone Mills Corp ....$3,400   PAC/Ind
    Guilford Mills Inc ....$1,525   Indiv

Transportation $19,450

Air Transport $2,500
    United Parcel Service ....$1,650   PAC

Automotive $9,950
    National Auto Dealers Assn ....$3,850   PAC
    Americans for Free International Trade ....$2,000   PAC
    Auto Dealers & Drivers for Free Trade ....$2,000   PAC

Sea Transport $3,750
    None over $1,500

Misc Transport $1,500
    None over $1,500

Labor

Labor $4,335

Transportation Unions $3,000
    Marine Engineers Dist 2 Maritime Officers ....$3,000   PAC

Ideological/Single-Issue

Ideological/Single-Issue $13,200

Leadership PACs $5,300
    National Congressional Club (Jesse Helms) ....$5,300   PAC

Pro-Life $1,700
    Right to Life* ....$1,700   PAC

Gun Rights/Gun Control $2,850
    National Rifle Assn ....$2,850   PAC

Misc Issues $2,350
    None over $1,500

Other & Unknown

Other $13,700

Retired $11,350
    None over $1,500

Unknown $15,530

    Generic Occupation/Category Unknown $1,750
    Employer Listed/Category Unknown $11,780
        None over $1,500

Spending in Last 3 Elections

	1988	1990	1992
Coble	$738,088	$572,846	$435,093
Opponent	$583,013	$33,135	$26,411
Vote Pct	63%	67%	71%

---

* Contributions came from more than one affiliate or subsidiary.

Ronald D. Coleman, D-Texas (16)

First elected: 1982

1991-92 Total Receipts: $762,219
1992 Year-end Cash: $6,719

1991-92 Committees & Subcommittees

Appropriations
Transportation and Related Agencies; Treasury, Postal Service and General Government

Leading Contributors

Business

Agriculture	$32,625

Crop Production & Basic Processing **$10,475**
  American Crystal Sugar Corp .... $2,600 PAC
Tobacco **$6,200**
  Philip Morris .... $4,200 PAC/Ind
Dairy **$8,050**
  Associated Milk Producers .... $7,000 PAC
Agricultural Services/Products **$2,750**
  None over $2,500
Food Processing & Sales **$2,950**
  None over $2,500

Communications/Electronics	$9,400

Telephone Utilities **$4,900**
  Southwestern Bell .... $2,700 PAC/Ind
Computer Equipment & Services **$2,500**
  None over $2,500

Construction	$21,580

General Contractors **$5,700**
  Urban General Contractors .... $2,500 Indiv
Home Builders **$6,750**
  National Assn of Home Builders .... $3,750 PAC
Construction Services **$4,100**
  None over $2,500
Building Materials & Equipment **$3,750**
  Jobe Concrete .... $3,000 Indiv

Source of Funds in 1992 Election

Source	Total	Pct
■ PACs	$486,544	61%
▨ Indivs $200+	$132,991	17%
□ Indivs under $200	$70,882	9%
▩ Other	$102,220	13%
Candidate	$52,500	7%
Party	$36,018	5%

Source of PAC Dollars by Sector

Source	Total	Pct
■ Business	$213,949	47%
▨ Labor	$181,500	40%
□ Ideology/Single Issue	$61,832	14%

In-State vs. Out-of-State Contributions*

Source	Total	Pct
□ In-State	$117,191	88%
■ Out-of-state	$15,800	12%
No state listed	$0	

*** by large individual contributors ($200 & above)**

Defense	$28,750

Defense Aerospace **$20,050**
  Textron Inc .... $5,200 PAC
  Martin Marietta Corp .... $2,600 PAC
  General Dynamics .... $2,500 PAC
Defense Electronics **$7,100**
  None over $2,500

Energy & Natural Resources	$29,905

Oil & Gas **$20,605**
  Coastal Corp .... $3,000 PAC
Electric Utilities **$6,950**
  Texas Utilities Co* .... $3,000 PAC

Finance, Insurance & Real Estate	$43,071

Commercial Banks **$5,071**
  Texas Commerce Bank .... $2,721 PAC/Ind
Insurance **$12,300**
  National Assn of Life Underwriters .... $5,000 PAC
Real Estate **$14,950**
  National Assn of Realtors .... $9,000 PAC
Accountants **$5,000**
  American Institute of CPA's .... $3,500 PAC
Misc Finance **$3,500**
  None over $2,500

Health	$19,250

Health Professionals **$17,150**
  American Dental Assn .... $5,000 PAC
  American Medical Assn .... $5,000 PAC
  American Nurses Assn .... $2,500 PAC

Contribution Totals by Sector

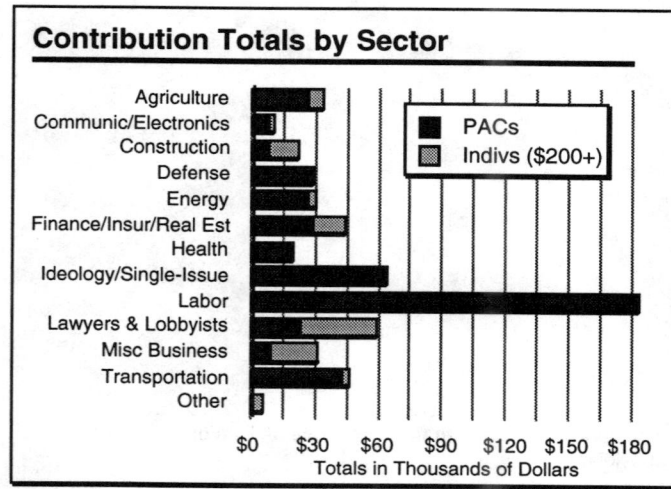

Agriculture, Communic/Electronics, Construction, Defense, Energy, Finance/Insur/Real Est, Health, Ideology/Single-Issue, Labor, Lawyers & Lobbyists, Misc Business, Transportation, Other

■ PACs
▨ Indivs ($200+)

$0 $30 $60 $90 $120 $150 $180
Totals in Thousands of Dollars

Lawyers & Lobbyists — $58,327

Lawyers & Lobbyists **$58,327**
Assn of Trial Lawyers of America	$10,500	PAC
Ginnings, Birkengack et al	$3,000	Indiv
Kemp, Smith et al	$2,950	Indiv
Grambling & Mounce	$2,650	Indiv

Misc Business — $30,757

Food & Beverage **$2,500**
None over $2,500

Beer, Wine & Liquor **$7,900**
None over $2,500

Retail Sales **$2,757**
None over $2,500

Business Services **$5,500**
None over $2,500

Misc Manufacturing & Distributing **$7,200**
American Garment Finishers Corp	$6,250	Indiv

Transportation — $45,150

Air Transport **$27,400**
American Airlines	$7,350	PAC
Federal Express Corp	$6,000	PAC
United Parcel Service	$5,050	PAC

Automotive **$8,950**
National Auto Dealers Assn	$7,000	PAC

Trucking **$3,450**
None over $2,500

Railroads **$3,850**
None over $2,500

Labor

Labor — **$182,250**

Building Trade Unions **$18,100**
Laborers' Political League	$6,500	PAC
Plumbers/Pipefitters Union	$4,000	PAC

Industrial Unions **$36,700**
United Auto Workers	$10,000	PAC
United Steelworkers	$10,000	PAC
Communications Workers of America	$5,500	PAC
Intl Brotherhood of Electrical Workers	$4,000	PAC

Transportation Unions **$53,250**
Air Line Pilots Assn	$10,000	PAC
Teamsters Union*	$10,000	PAC
United Transportation Union	$10,000	PAC
Seafarers International Union	$6,000	PAC
Marine Engineers Union*	$5,500	PAC
Amalgamated Transit Union	$3,500	PAC
Transport Workers Union	$2,500	PAC

Public Sector Unions **$55,600**
National Assn of Letter Carriers	$10,000	PAC
National Education Assn	$10,000	PAC
American Fedn of St/Cnty/Munic Employees	$8,000	PAC
National Assn Retired Federal Employees	$7,000	PAC
American Postal Workers Union	$6,500	PAC
International Assn of Firefighters	$3,000	PAC
National Assn of Postmasters	$2,900	PAC
American Federation of Teachers	$2,500	PAC

Misc Unions **$18,600**
AFL-CIO	$6,000	PAC
Food & Commercial Workers Union	$6,000	PAC
Service Employees International Union	$3,000	PAC

Ideological/Single-Issue

Ideological/Single-Issue — **$63,032**

Leadership PACs **$15,632**
House Leadership Fund (Tom Foley)	$8,132	PAC
Effective Government Cmte (Dick Gephardt)	$3,000	PAC
America's Leaders' Fund (Dan Rostenkowski)	$2,500	PAC

Pro-Israel **$16,400**
National PAC	$6,000	PAC
Joint Action Cmte for Political Affairs	$3,000	PAC

Gun Rights/Gun Control **$9,900**
National Rifle Assn	$9,900	PAC

Human Rights **$7,000**
Human Rights Campaign Fund	$4,500	PAC

Misc Issues **$12,600**
National Cmte to Preserve Social Security	$6,700	PAC
League of Conservation Voters	$5,000	PAC

Other & Unknown

Other — **$5,500**

Retired **$2,950**
None over $2,500

Unknown — **$20,675**
No Employer Listed or Found	$4,285
Employer Listed/Category Unknown	$14,190
None over $2,500	

Independent expenditures supporting Coleman
National Cmte to Preserve Social Security $5,010

Spending in Last 3 Elections

	1988	1990	1992
Coleman	$312,444	$286,407	$765,038
Opponent	$3,528	$0	$211,319
Vote Pct	100%	96%	52%

* Contributions came from more than one affiliate or subsidiary.

513

Barbara-Rose Collins, D-Mich (15)

First elected: 1990

1991-92 Total Receipts: $222,662
1992 Year-end Cash: $55,717

1991-92 Committees & Subcommittees

Post Office and Civil Service
Postal Personnel and Modernization

Public Works and Transportation
Aviation; Economic Development; Investigations and Oversight;
Water Resources

Select Committee on Children, Youth and Families

Leading Contributors

Business

Agriculture — $7,100

Tobacco	**$3,800**	
RJR Nabisco	$2,800	PAC
Dairy	**$1,250**	
Associated Milk Producers	$1,000	PAC
Food Processing & Sales	**$1,050**	
None over $1,000		

Communications/Electronics — $13,550

Media/Entertainment	**$5,500**	
National Cable Television Assn	$4,250	PAC
Barden Cablevision	$1,000	Indiv
Telephone Utilities	**$7,100**	
Michigan Bell Telephone	$6,100	PAC

Construction — $2,750

Building Materials & Equipment	**$1,000**	
None over $1,000		

Energy & Natural Resources — $8,850

Oil & Gas	**$3,750**	
Michigan Consolidated Gas	$1,900	PAC
Coastal Corp	$1,000	PAC
Electric Utilities	**$3,850**	
Detroit Edison	$3,050	PAC/Ind
Waste Management	**$1,250**	
Waste Management Inc	$1,000	PAC

Source of Funds in 1992 Election

Source	Total	Pct
■ PACs	$92,536	37%
■ Indivs $200+	$60,225	24%
□ Indivs under $200	$14,359	6%
▨ Other	$80,897	33%
Candidate	$0	0%
Party	$25,905	10%

Source of PAC Dollars by Sector

Source	Total	Pct
■ Business	$54,871	35%
■ Labor	$87,100	55%
□ Ideology/Single Issue	$15,200	10%

In-State vs. Out-of-State Contributions*

Source	Total	Pct
□ In-State	$53,525	90%
■ Out-of-state	$6,200	10%
No state listed	$500	

* by large individual contributors ($200 & above)

Finance, Insurance & Real Estate — $6,650

Commercial Banks	**$2,600**	
Comerica Inc	$1,350	PAC
Real Estate	**$2,500**	
None over $1,000		

Health — $4,650

Health Professionals	**$2,150**	
None over $1,000		
Hospitals/Nursing Homes	**$1,000**	
Michigan Health Center	$1,000	Indiv
Pharmaceuticals/Health Products	**$1,500**	
Upjohn Co	$1,500	PAC

Lawyers & Lobbyists — $5,550

Lawyers & Lobbyists	**$5,550**	
None over $1,000		

Misc Business — $8,446

Beer, Wine & Liquor	**$1,000**	
None over $1,000		
Business Services	**$5,496**	
Outdoor Advertising Assn of America	$2,596	PAC
Gannett Outdoor	$1,300	PAC

Transportation — $16,900

Air Transport	**$5,100**	
United Parcel Service	$2,800	PAC
Aircraft Owners & Pilots Assn	$1,000	PAC
Northwest Airlines	$1,000	PAC
Automotive	**$5,000**	
Ford Motor Co	$1,800	PAC
General Motors	$1,550	PAC

Contribution Totals by Sector

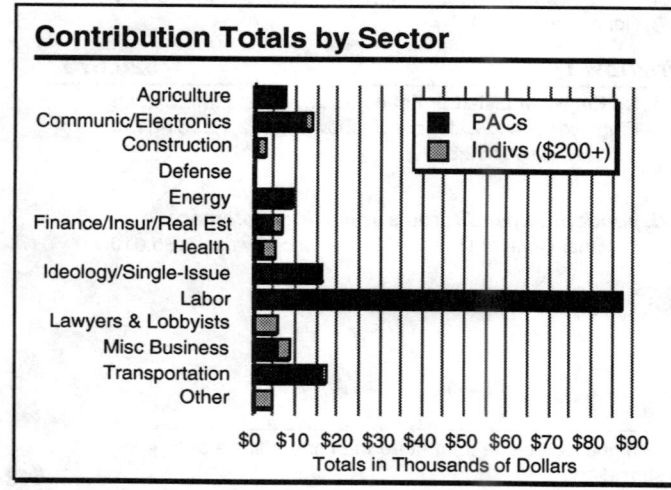

Agriculture, Communic/Electronics, Construction, Defense, Energy, Finance/Insur/Real Est, Health, Ideology/Single-Issue, Labor, Lawyers & Lobbyists, Misc Business, Transportation, Other

■ PACs   ▨ Indivs ($200+)

$0 $10 $20 $30 $40 $50 $60 $70 $80 $90
Totals in Thousands of Dollars

Trucking **$2,750**
    Central Transport Inc ....$1,000   Indiv
    Yellow Freight System ....$1,000   PAC

Railroads **$4,050**
    CSX Transportation Inc ....$1,300   PAC

Labor

Labor	**$87,100**

Building Trade Unions **$11,550**
    Carpenters & Joiners Union ....$5,500   PAC
    Laborers' Political League ....$3,000   PAC
    Plumbers/Pipefitters Union ....$2,200   PAC

Industrial Unions **$19,600**
    United Auto Workers ....$10,000   PAC
    Intl Brotherhood of Electrical Workers ....$3,000   PAC
    United Steelworkers ....$2,000   PAC
    Machinists/Aerospace Workers Union ....$1,800   PAC

Transportation Unions **$25,600**
    Teamsters Union ....$12,500   PAC
    Air Line Pilots Assn ....$4,500   PAC
    Brotherhood of Locomotive Engineers ....$1,500   PAC
    Marine Engineers Dist 2 Maritime Officers ...$1,500   PAC
    Trans Comm International Union ....$1,300   PAC
    Assn of Flight Attendants ....$1,000   PAC
    United Transportation Union ....$1,000   PAC

Public Sector Unions **$25,350**
    National Assn of Letter Carriers ....$6,000   PAC
    American Postal Workers Union ....$5,500   PAC
    National Education Assn ....$5,000   PAC
    American Fedn of St/Cnty/Munic Employees ...$3,500   PAC
    National Assn of Postmasters ....$1,800   PAC
    American Federation of Govt Employees .....$1,050   PAC

Misc Unions **$5,000**
    AFL-CIO ....$2,500   PAC
    Food & Commercial Workers Union ....$2,000   PAC

Ideological/Single-Issue

Ideological/Single-Issue	**$16,100**

Leadership PACs **$7,500**
    House Leadership Fund (Tom Foley) ....$5,000   PAC
    Effective Government Cmte (Dick Gephardt) ...$1,000   PAC
    Victory USA (Vic Fazio) ....$1,000   PAC

Foreign & Defense Policy **$1,000**
    Pakistan-American Friendship Society ....$1,000   PAC

Pro-Israel **$1,400**
    None over $1,000

Womens Issues **$2,500**
    National Womens Political Caucus ....$1,000   PAC
    Women's Campaign Fund ....$1,000   PAC

Human Rights **$1,000**
    Human Rights Campaign Fund ....$1,000   PAC

Misc Issues **$1,600**
    National Cmte to Preserve Social Security ...$1,600   PAC

Other & Unknown

Other	**$4,350**

Civil Servants/Public Officials **$1,025**
    None over $1,000

Retired **$2,375**
    None over $1,000

Unknown	**$35,650**

    No Employer Listed or Found $17,000
    Employer Listed/Category Unknown $17,700
        Consulting Engineering Associates ....$3,000   Indiv
        Forest Haven Ltc ....$1,500   Indiv
        Heritage Optical ....$1,400   Indiv
        CAS ....$1,250   Indiv
        Barbara Martin ....$1,000   Indiv
        Foster-Davis ....$1,000   Indiv
        Madison & Madison ....$1,000   Indiv
        Motor City ....$1,000   Indiv
        Prea-Rob ....$1,000   Indiv
        Sleepy Hollow ....$1,000   Indiv

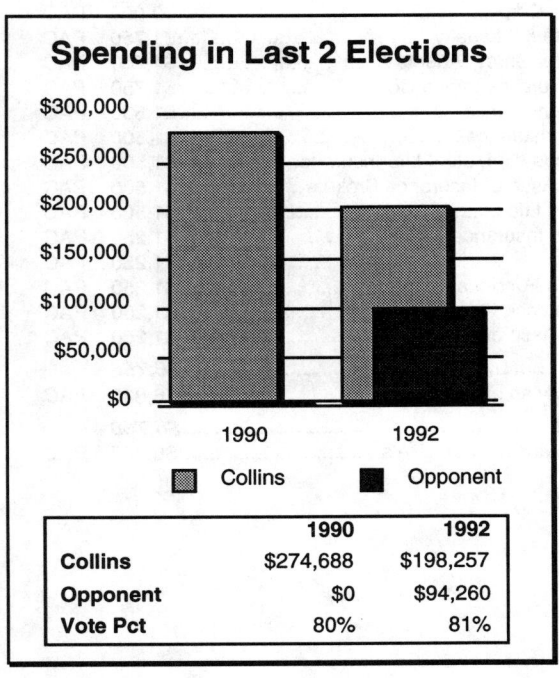

Spending in Last 2 Elections

	1990	1992
Collins	$274,688	$198,257
Opponent	$0	$94,260
Vote Pct	80%	81%

Cardiss Collins, D-III (7)

First elected: 1973

1991-92 Total Receipts: $344,933
1992 Year-end Cash: $49,167

1991-92 Committees & Subcommittees

Energy and Commerce
Commerce, Consumer Protection and Competitiveness (Chair-woman); Transportation and Hazardous Materials

Government Operations
Commerce, Consumer and Monetary Affairs; Legislation and National Security

Select Committee on Narcotics Abuse and Control

Leading Contributors

Business

Agriculture	$2,800

Crop Production & Basic Processing $1,300
 None over $1,000

Communications/Electronics	$23,850

Media/Entertainment *$8,000*
 Viacom International .... $2,000 PAC
 ASCAP .... $1,250 PAC
 Recording Industry Assn of America .... $1,250 PAC
 Walt Disney Co .... $1,250 Indiv

Telephone Utilities *$13,850*
 AT&T .... $4,000 PAC
 Ameritech Corp* .... $3,500 PAC
 BellSouth Corp* .... $2,500 PAC
 United Telecommunications .... $2,000 PAC

Construction	$1,000
 None over $1,000

Energy & Natural Resources	$3,500

Electric Utilities *$3,000*
 Detroit Edison .... $1,750 PAC

Finance, Insurance & Real Estate	$93,250

Commercial Banks *$5,500*
 Independent Bankers Assn .... $2,250 PAC
 Barnett Banks Inc .... $1,000 PAC
 Continental Illinois Corp .... $1,000 PAC

Source of Funds in 1992 Election

Source	Total	Pct
■ PACs	$285,067	82%
▨ Indivs $200+	$24,550	7%
☐ Indivs under $200	$1,912	1%
⊠ Other	$37,213	11%
Candidate	$423	0%
Party	$4,109	1%

Source of PAC Dollars by Sector

Source	Total	Pct
■ Business	$166,362	74%
▨ Labor	$57,349	25%
☐ Ideology/Single Issue	$2,500	1%

In-State vs. Out-of-State Contributions*

Source	Total	Pct
☐ In-State	$16,100	66%
■ Out-of-state	$8,450	34%
No state listed	$0	

* by large individual contributors ($200 & above)

Securities & Investment *$13,500*
 Chicago Mercantile Exchange .... $10,000 PAC
 Chicago Board of Trade .... $3,000 PAC

Insurance *$60,000*
 National Assn of Life Underwriters .... $7,000 PAC
 American Council of Life Insurance .... $4,000 PAC
 Independent Insurance Agents of America .... $4,000 PAC
 American Family Corp .... $3,000 PAC
 CNA Financial Corp .... $2,500 PAC
 Prudential Insurance .... $2,500 PAC
 Mutual of Omaha .... $2,000 PAC
 National Assn of Prof Insurance Agents .... $2,000 PAC
 Travelers Corp .... $2,000 PAC
 Aetna Life & Casualty .... $1,750 PAC
 Casualty & Surety Agents Assn .... $1,750 PAC
 Golden Rule Insurance Co .... $1,750 PAC
 Hartford Insurance .... $1,500 PAC
 Kemper Insurance .... $1,500 PAC
 Massachusetts Mutual Life Insurance .... $1,500 PAC
 National Assn of Insurance Brokers .... $1,500 PAC
 New York Life .... $1,500 PAC
 American Insurance Assn .... $1,250 PAC
 Cigna Corp .... $1,250 PAC
 Fireman's Fund Insurance .... $1,250 PAC
 John Hancock Financial Service .... $1,250 PAC
 National Assn of Life Companies .... $1,250 PAC

Real Estate *$6,750*
 National Assn of Realtors .... $6,000 PAC

Accountants *$6,750*
 American Institute of CPA's .... $6,250 PAC

Contribution Totals by Sector

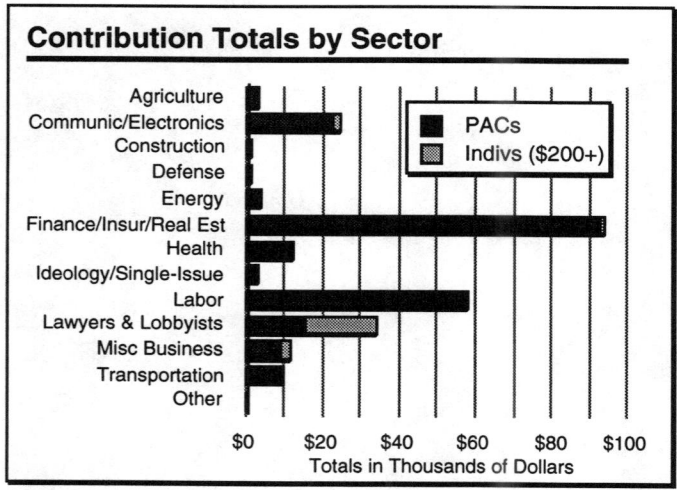

Agriculture
Communic/Electronics
Construction
Defense
Energy
Finance/Insur/Real Est
Health
Ideology/Single-Issue
Labor
Lawyers & Lobbyists
Misc Business
Transportation
Other

■ PACs
▨ Indivs ($200+)

$0 $20 $40 $60 $80 $100
Totals in Thousands of Dollars

Health $11,500

Health Professionals **$8,750**
American Dental Assn ....$2,750 PAC
American Academy of Ophthalmology ....$2,000 PAC
American Assn Oral & Maxillofacial Surgeons ....$1,000 PAC
National Assn of Pharmacists ....$1,000 PAC

Hospitals/Nursing Homes **$1,000**
American Health Care Assn..................................$1,000 PAC

Pharmaceuticals/Health Products **$1,750**
Proprietary Association ....$1,250 PAC

Lawyers & Lobbyists $33,912

Lawyers & Lobbyists **$33,912**
Assn of Trial Lawyers of America ....$10,000 PAC
Power, Rogers & Lavin ....$2,000 Indiv
Leonard M Ring & Associates............................$1,500 Indiv
Cameron Law Office ....$1,250 Indiv
Dickstein, Shapiro & Morin.................................$1,250 PAC
Robert A Clifford & Associates...........................$1,250 Indiv
Verner, Liipfert et al...$1,062 PAC
Anesi, Ozmon & Rodin..$1,000 Indiv
Demos & Burke Ltd ....$1,000 Indiv
Hilfman & Fogel ....$1,000 Indiv
Motherway & Glenn ....$1,000 Indiv
Pavalon & Gifford ....$1,000 Indiv
Thomas P Valenti & Associates ....$1,000 Indiv

Misc Business $10,850

Food & Beverage **$1,500**
McDonald's Corp ....$1,000 PAC

Beer, Wine & Liquor **$1,000**
None over $1,000

Retail Sales... **$3,750**
Sonicraft Inc ....$2,000 Indiv
JC Penney Co ....$1,250 PAC

Business Services **$1,250**
Borg-Warner ....$1,250 PAC

Misc Manufacturing & Distributing **$2,250**
Institute of Scrap Recycling Industries ....$1,250 PAC

Transportation $9,000

Air Transport **$4,250**
United Parcel Service ....$2,000 PAC
American Airlines ....$1,250 PAC

Automotive **$1,750**
Warshawsky & Co/JC Whitney & Co ....$1,000 PAC

Railroads **$3,000**
None over $1,000

Labor

Labor $57,349

Building Trade Unions **$4,250**
Laborers' Political League ....$2,000 PAC

Industrial Unions **$11,000**
United Auto Workers ....$3,750 PAC
Intl Brotherhood of Electrical Workers ....$2,500 PAC
Machinists/Aerospace Workers Union ....$1,500 PAC
Ladies Garment Workers Union ....$1,250 PAC

Transportation Unions **$16,650**
Air Line Pilots Assn ....$3,500 PAC
United Transportation Union ....$2,750 PAC
Teamsters Union ....$2,500 PAC
Marine Engineers Dist 2 Maritime Officers ....$2,000 PAC
Transport Workers Union ....$1,500 PAC
Trans Comm International Union ....$1,000 PAC

Public Sector Unions **$21,500**
National Education Assn ....$10,000 PAC
American Fedn of St/Cnty/Munic Employees ......$5,000 PAC
American Postal Workers Union ....$2,000 PAC
National Assn Retired Federal Employees ....$2,000 PAC
American Federation of Teachers ....$1,500 PAC

Misc Unions **$3,949**
Food & Commercial Workers Union ....$1,749 PAC
AFL-CIO ....$1,500 PAC
Hotel/Restaurant Employees Union ....$1,000 PAC

Ideological/Single-Issue

Ideological/Single-Issue $2,500

Human Rights **$1,250**
Human Rights Campaign Fund.............................$1,000 PAC

Misc Issues... **$1,250**
National Cmte to Preserve Social Security ....$1,250 PAC

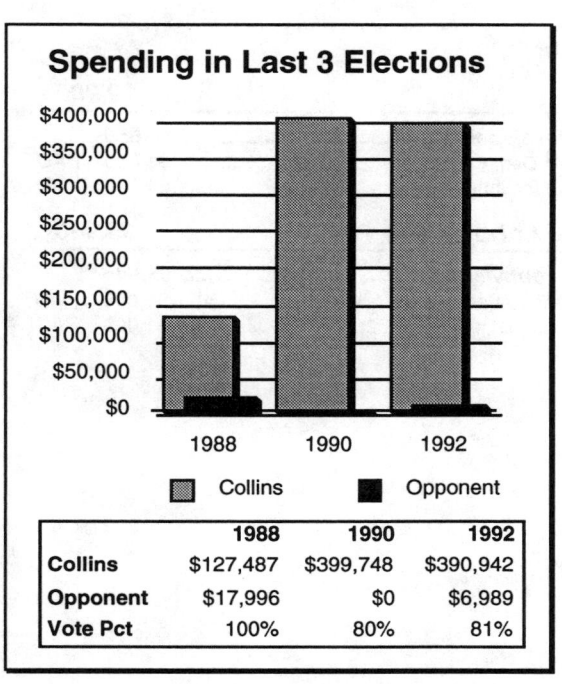

Spending in Last 3 Elections

	1988	1990	1992
Collins	$127,487	$399,748	$390,942
Opponent	$17,996	$0	$6,989
Vote Pct	100%	80%	81%

Legend: Collins, Opponent

---

* Contributions came from more than one affiliate or subsidiary.

Mac Collins, R-Ga (3)

First elected: 1992

1991-92 Total Receipts: $241,783
1992 Year-end Cash: $9,676

1993-94 Committees & Subcommittees

Public Works and Transportation
Aviation; Economic Development; Surface Transportation

Small Business
Rural Enterprises, Exports and the Environment; SBA Legislation and the General Economy

Leading Contributors

Business

Agriculture		$8,950
Forestry & Forest Products	**$8,200**	
Georgia-Pacific Corp	$5,000	PAC
Gilman Paper Co	$1,000	PAC
Union Camp Corp	$1,000	PAC

Communications/Electronics		$4,500
Printing & Publishing	**$1,500**	
Martino-White Printing	$1,500	Indiv
Telephone Utilities	**$3,000**	
Southern Bell	$1,500	PAC
AT&T	$1,000	PAC

Construction		$3,300
Home Builders	**$2,750**	
John Wieland Homes	$2,000	Indiv

Energy & Natural Resources		$10,200
Oil & Gas	**$3,950**	
Atlanta Gas Light Co	$1,000	PAC
Misc Energy	**$3,000**	
Cooper Industries	$3,000	PAC
Electric Utilities	**$3,000**	
Georgia Power Co	$3,000	PAC

Source of Funds in 1992 Election

Source	Total	Pct
■ PACs	$50,272	17%
■ Indivs $200+	$87,888	30%
□ Indivs under $200	$45,621	16%
⊠ Other	$107,002	37%
Candidate	$36,675	13%
Party	$55,000	19%

Source of PAC Dollars by Sector

Source	Total	Pct
■ Business	$37,800	69%
■ Labor	$3,000	6%
□ Ideology/Single Issue ...	$13,724	25%

In-State vs. Out-of-State Contributions*

Source	Total	Pct
□ In-State	$82,788	94%
■ Out-of-state	$5,100	6%
No state listed	$0	

* by large individual contributors ($200 & above)

Finance, Insurance & Real Estate		$20,330
Commercial Banks	**$5,450**	
Trust Co of Georgia	$1,600	PAC
Barnett Banks Inc	$1,000	PAC
Securities & Investment	**$2,000**	
Capital Formation Counselors	$1,000	Indiv
Insurance	**$8,125**	
American Family Corp	$6,250	Indiv
Real Estate	**$3,155**	
Woodcrest Enterprises	$1,000	Indiv
Misc Finance	**$1,000**	
None over $1,000 ·		

Health		$9,900
Health Professionals	**$8,650**	
American Dental Assn	$1,000	PAC
Hillis Eye Institute	$1,000	Indiv

Lawyers & Lobbyists		$5,946
Lawyers & Lobbyists	**$5,946**	
Bird & Associates	$1,000	Indiv
King & Spalding	$1,000	PAC

Contribution Totals by Sector

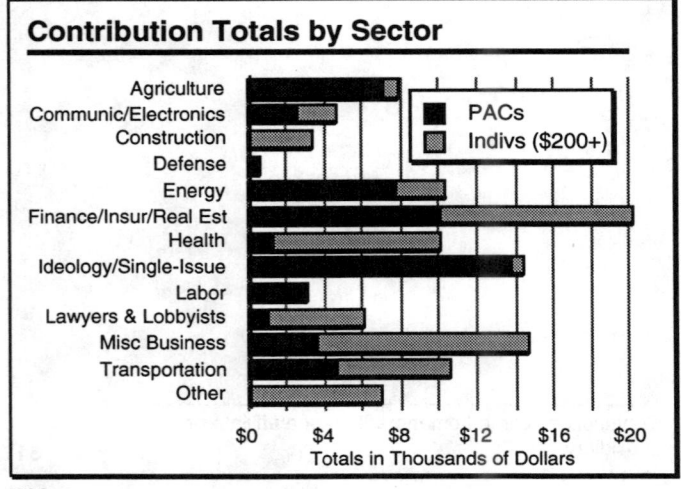

Agriculture
Communic/Electronics
Construction
Defense
Energy
Finance/Insur/Real Est
Health
Ideology/Single-Issue
Labor
Lawyers & Lobbyists
Misc Business
Transportation
Other

■ PACs
▨ Indivs ($200+)

$0 $4 $8 $12 $16 $20
Totals in Thousands of Dollars

Misc Business $14,500

Food & Beverage **$3,000**
    Chick-Fil-A ....$2,000   Indiv
    Waffle House Inc ....$1,000   Indiv

Beer, Wine & Liquor **$3,000**
    National Beer Wholesalers Assn ....$2,500   PAC

Business Services **$2,000**
    National Assn of Temporary Services ....$1,000   PAC
    Norrell Corp ....$1,000   Indiv

Misc Manufacturing & Distributing **$6,000**
    Jebco Manufacturing ....$5,000   Indiv
    Mode Inc ....$1,000   Indiv

Transportation $10,430

Air Transport **$5,530**
    United Parcel Service ....$4,250   PAC/Ind
    Delta Airlines ....$1,280   PAC/Ind

Automotive **$1,200**
    None over $1,000

Trucking **$3,500**
    Bennett Trucking Co ....$1,000   Indiv
    Transus Inc ....$1,000   Indiv

Labor

Labor $3,000

Public Sector Unions **$3,000**
    National Assn Retired Federal Employees ....$3,000   PAC

Ideological/Single-Issue

Ideological/Single-Issue $14,324

Republican/Conservative **$4,624**
    Loose Group ....$4,000   PAC

Leadership PACs **$3,500**
    Republican Leader's Fund (Bob Michel) ....$2,000   PAC
    Campaign America (Bob Dole) ....$1,500   PAC

Gun Rights/Gun Control **$4,950**
    National Rifle Assn ....$4,950   PAC

Other & Unknown

Other $6,893

Civil Servants/Public Officials **$1,088**
    None over $1,000

Retired **$5,805**
    None over $1,000

Unknown $30,139

    Homemakers/Non-income earners $6,244
    No Employer Listed or Found $8,500
    Employer Listed/Category Unknown $14,895
       Country Fed Meat Co ....$1,000   Indiv
       FC&A Associates ....$1,000   Indiv
       HBR Capital ....$1,000   Indiv
       McClain Int Inc ....$1,000   Indiv
       South Eastern Electronic Control ....$1,000   Indiv
       Sun Security Systems Telephone Sys ....$1,000   Indiv

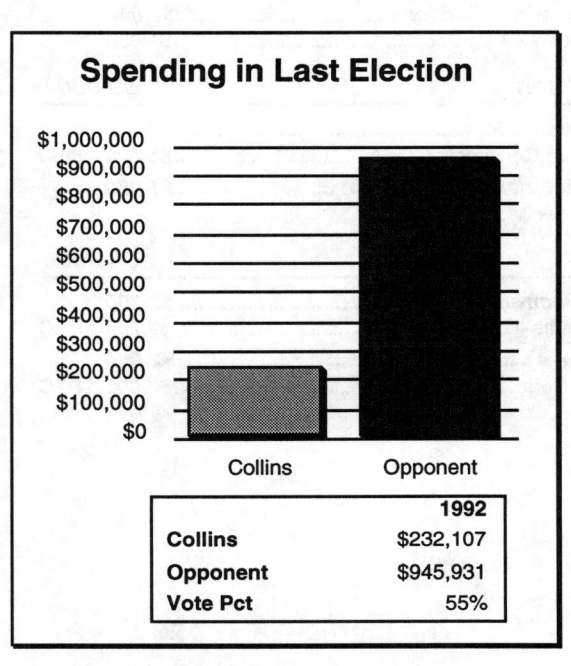

Spending in Last Election

	1992
Collins	$232,107
Opponent	$945,931
Vote Pct	55%

Larry Combest, R-Texas (19)

First elected: 1984

1991-92 Total Receipts: $241,559
1992 Year-end Cash: $173,124

1991-92 Committees & Subcommittees

Agriculture
Conservation, Credit and Rural Development; Cotton, Rice and Sugar; Peanuts and Tobacco

District of Columbia
Fiscal Affairs and Health; Government Operations and Metropolitan Affairs (Ranking Republican)

Small Business
Exports, Tax Policy and Special Problems (Ranking Republican)

Select Committee on Intelligence

Leading Contributors

Business

Agriculture — $54,530

Crop Production & Basic Processing $15,180
National Cotton Council	$2,805	PAC
Southern Minn Beet Sugar Co-op	$1,125	PAC
American Cotton Shippers Assn	$1,050	PAC
Ocho Gin	$1,000	Indiv

Tobacco $4,300
RJR Nabisco	$1,850	PAC
US Tobacco Co	$1,000	PAC

Dairy $3,400
Associated Milk Producers	$1,500	PAC
Milk Industry Foundation	$1,200	PAC

Poultry & Eggs $3,750
Pilgrim's Pride Co	$2,000	Indiv

Livestock $8,400
National Cattlemen's Assn*	$3,700	PAC
Texas & Southwestern Cattle Raisers	$2,000	PAC
AZTX Cattle Co	$1,500	Indiv

Agricultural Services/Products $8,800
Texas Farm Bureau	$2,500	PAC
Farmland Industries	$1,000	PAC

Food Processing & Sales $10,450
Fleming Companies Inc	$2,000	PAC
United Supermarkets Inc	$1,750	Indiv
Winn-Dixie Stores	$1,500	PAC
Food Marketing Institute	$1,400	PAC
Nabisco Brands Inc	$1,000	PAC
Pepsico Inc	$1,000	PAC

Communications/Electronics — $6,700

Telephone Utilities $4,700
GTE Corp	$2,000	PAC
Southwestern Bell	$1,500	PAC

Electronics Mfg & Services $1,050
Westinghouse Electric	$1,050	PAC

Construction — $5,000

General Contractors $3,500
Holloman Construction Co	$1,000	Indiv

Building Materials & Equipment $1,000
None over $1,000

Defense — $5,050

Defense Electronics $2,700
E-Systems Inc	$2,700	PAC

Misc Defense $2,000
Insilco Corp	$2,000	PAC

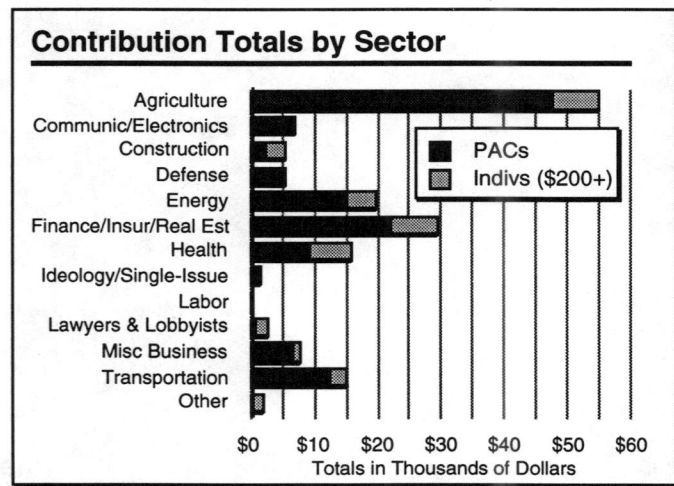

Contribution Totals by Sector

Agriculture
Communic/Electronics
Construction
Defense
Energy
Finance/Insur/Real Est
Health
Ideology/Single-Issue
Labor
Lawyers & Lobbyists
Misc Business
Transportation
Other

■ PACs
▨ Indivs ($200+)

$0 $10 $20 $30 $40 $50 $60
Totals in Thousands of Dollars

Energy & Natural Resources — $19,400

Oil & Gas **$10,900**
    Enserch Corp .... $1,500   PAC
    Atlantic Richfield .... $1,050   PAC

Electric Utilities **$7,300**
    Texas Utilities Co* .... $4,000   PAC
    Southwestern Public Service Co .... $2,450   PAC

Finance, Insurance & Real Estate — $29,000

Commercial Banks **$10,950**
    American Bankers Assn .... $5,000   PAC
    Amarillo National Bank .... $1,000   Indiv
    Ford Bank Group .... $1,000   Indiv

Securities & Investment **$4,950**
    Merrill Lynch .... $1,150   PAC/Ind
    Chicago Board of Trade .... $1,000   PAC
    Chicago Mercantile Exchange .... $1,000   PAC

Insurance **$3,100**
    Independent Insurance Agents of America .... $1,050   PAC
    American National Insurance Co .... $1,000   PAC

Real Estate **$8,250**
    National Assn of Realtors .... $7,250   PAC

Accountants **$1,250**
    American Institute of CPA's .... $1,000   PAC

Health — $15,651

Health Professionals **$13,601**
    American Medical Assn .... $7,350   PAC

Hospitals/Nursing Homes **$1,000**
    None over $1,000

Pharmaceuticals/Health Products **$1,050**
    None over $1,000

Lawyers & Lobbyists — $2,490

Lawyers & Lobbyists **$2,490**
    None over $1,000

Misc Business — $7,500

Beer, Wine & Liquor **$1,250**
    National Beer Wholesalers Assn .... $1,000   PAC

Chemical & Related Manufacturing **$1,350**
    Dow Chemical .... $1,000   PAC

Misc Manufacturing & Distributing **$1,000**
    Hoechst Celanese Corp .... $1,000   PAC

Textiles **$1,050**
    None over $1,000

Transportation — $14,650

Air Transport **$2,350**
    Federal Express Corp .... $1,000   PAC
    Goldstar Services .... $1,000   Indiv

Automotive **$9,950**
    National Auto Dealers Assn .... $6,700   PAC
    Auto Dealers & Drivers for Free Trade ..... $1,500   PAC

Railroads **$1,850**
    None over $1,000

Ideological/Single-Issue

Ideological/Single-Issue — $1,300
    None over $1,000

Other & Unknown

Other — $1,750

Retired **$1,000**
    None over $1,000

Unknown — $11,963
    Homemakers/Non-income earners $1,990
    Employer Listed/Category Unknown $9,123
      None over $1,000

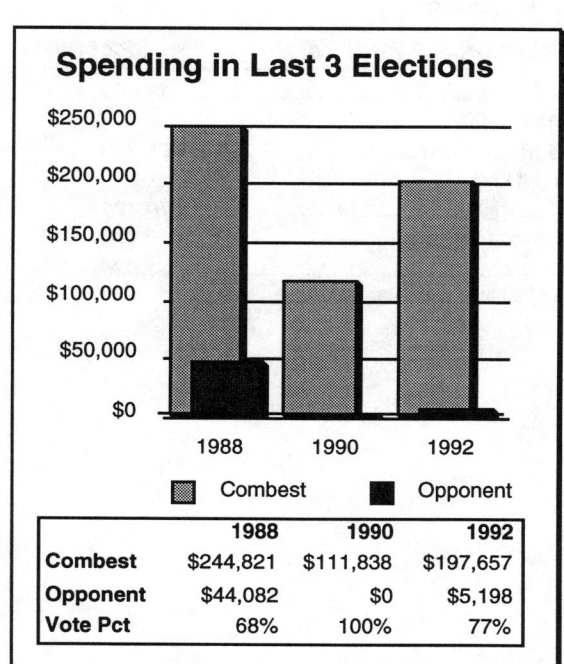

Spending in Last 3 Elections

	1988	1990	1992
Combest	$244,821	$111,838	$197,657
Opponent	$44,082	$0	$5,198
Vote Pct	68%	100%	77%

Legend: ▨ Combest   ■ Opponent

* Contributions came from more than one affiliate or subsidiary.

Gary Condit, D-Calif (18)

First elected: 1989

1991-92 Total Receipts:	$371,990
1992 Year-end Cash:	$66,029

1991-92 Committees & Subcommittees

Agriculture
Cotton, Rice and Sugar; Livestock, Dairy and Poultry

Government Operations
Government Activities and Transportation; Government Information, Justice and Agriculture

Leading Contributors

Business

Agriculture	$87,272

Crop Production & Basic Processing	$44,975	
Calcot Ltd	$3,575	PAC
National Cotton Council	$2,500	PAC
Sun-Diamond Growers*	$2,500	PAC
Sunkist Growers	$2,500	PAC
California Pistachio Assn	$1,500	PAC
Farmers' Rice Cooperative	$1,500	PAC
Tobacco	**$3,000**	
None over $1,500		
Dairy	**$13,302**	
Associated Milk Producers	$5,500	PAC
Western United Dairymens Assn	$3,052	PAC
Poultry & Eggs	**$3,500**	
None over $1,500		
Livestock	**$7,000**	
National Cattlemen's Assn*	$2,000	PAC
National Pork Producers Council	$1,500	PAC
Agricultural Services/Products	**$10,780**	
Farm Credit Council	$1,680	PAC
Food Processing & Sales	**$4,715**	
None over $1,500		

Communications/Electronics	$7,585

Printing & Publishing	$2,500	
None over $1,500		
Media/Entertainment	**$1,965**	
None over $1,500		
Telephone Utilities	**$2,620**	
Pacific Telesis Group	$1,620	PAC

Source of Funds in 1992 Election

Source	Total	Pct
PACs	$155,045	41%
Indivs $200+	$76,338	20%
Indivs under $200	$120,683	32%
Other	$25,338	7%
Candidate	$0	0%
Party	$5,564	1%

Source of PAC Dollars by Sector

Source	Total	Pct
Business	$110,037	70%
Labor	$42,869	27%
Ideology/Single Issue	$4,000	3%

In-State vs. Out-of-State Contributions*

Source	Total	Pct
In-State	$70,338	92%
Out-of-state	$6,000	8%
No state listed	$0	

*** by large individual contributors ($200 & above)**

Construction	$5,410

General Contractors	$3,960
None over $1,500	

Defense	$1,750

Defense Aerospace	$1,500	
Northrop Corp	$1,500	PAC

Energy & Natural Resources	$6,000

Electric Utilities	$5,000	
Pacific Gas & Electric	$3,000	PAC

Finance, Insurance & Real Estate	$22,605

Commercial Banks	$3,260	
None over $1,500		
Securities & Investment	**$1,750**	
None over $1,500		
Real Estate	**$10,125**	
National Assn of Realtors	$6,000	PAC
Accountants	**$4,920**	
American Institute of CPA's	$3,500	PAC

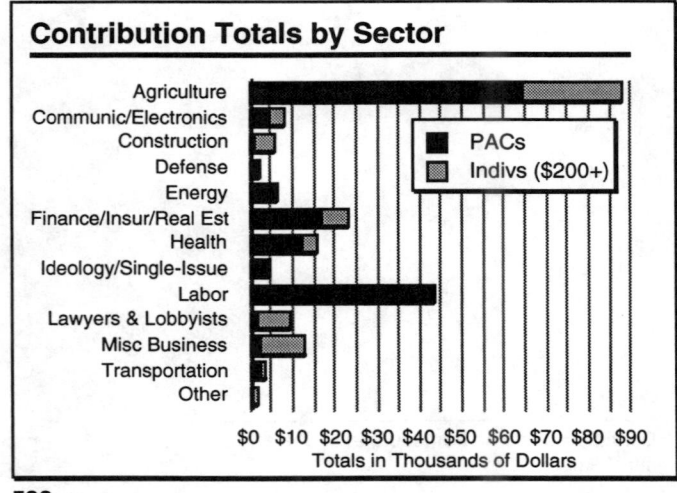

Contribution Totals by Sector

Agriculture
Communic/Electronics
Construction
Defense
Energy
Finance/Insur/Real Est
Health
Ideology/Single-Issue
Labor
Lawyers & Lobbyists
Misc Business
Transportation
Other

■ PACs
▨ Indivs ($200+)

$0 $10 $20 $30 $40 $50 $60 $70 $80 $90
Totals in Thousands of Dollars

Health	$15,001

Health Professionals	**$10,351**	
American Medical Assn*	$3,850	PAC
American Dental Assn	$1,500	PAC
Hospitals/Nursing Homes	**$3,150**	
None over $1,500		

Lawyers & Lobbyists	$9,600

Lawyers & Lobbyists	**$9,600**	
Will & Muys	$1,500	Indiv

Misc Business	$12,302

Beer, Wine & Liquor	**$9,302**	
Gallo Winery	$6,602	Indiv

Transportation	$2,850

None over $1,500	

Labor

Labor	$42,869

Building Trade Unions	**$9,380**	
Laborers Union*	$3,000	PAC
Ironworkers Union	$2,000	PAC
Plumbers/Pipefitters Union	$2,000	PAC
Industrial Unions	**$11,500**	
United Auto Workers	$4,000	PAC
Machinists/Aerospace Workers Union	$2,500	PAC
Intl Brotherhood of Electrical Workers	$2,000	PAC
Boilermakers Union	$1,500	PAC
Transportation Unions	**$10,800**	
Teamsters Union	$4,500	PAC
Air Line Pilots Assn	$2,500	PAC
Public Sector Unions	**$8,090**	
American Federation of Teachers	$2,000	PAC
National Assn Retired Federal Employees	$1,500	PAC
National Rural Letter Carriers Assn	$1,500	PAC
Misc Unions	**$3,099**	
Food & Commercial Workers Union	$1,999	PAC

Ideological/Single-Issue

Ideological/Single-Issue	$4,000

Gun Rights/Gun Control	**$1,500**	
National Rifle Assn	$1,500	PAC
Misc Issues	**$2,500**	
National Cmte to Preserve Social Security	$2,000	PAC

Other & Unknown

Other	$1,593

None over $1,500	

Unknown	$14,407

No Employer Listed or Found	$4,600
Employer Listed/Category Unknown	$7,957
None over $1,500	

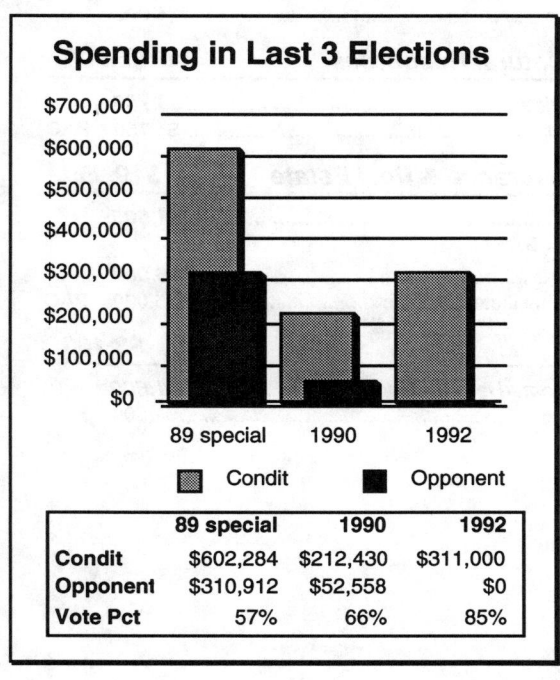

Spending in Last 3 Elections

	89 special	1990	1992
Condit	$602,284	$212,430	$311,000
Opponent	$310,912	$52,558	$0
Vote Pct	57%	66%	85%

* Contributions came from more than one affiliate or subsidiary.

John Conyers Jr., D-Mich (14)

First elected: 1964

1991-92 Total Receipts:	$380,072
1992 Year-end Cash:	$35,601

1991-92 Committees & Subcommittees

Government Operations (Chairman)
Legislation and National Security (Chairman)

Judiciary
Civil and Constitutional Rights; Economic and Commercial Law;
Intellectual Property and Judicial Administration

Small Business
SBA, the General Economy and Minority Enterprise Development

Leading Contributors

Business

Agriculture		$4,350
Dairy	**$2,500**	
Associated Milk Producers	$2,500	PAC

Communications/Electronics		$49,200
Printing & Publishing	**$7,800**	
West Publishing	$6,000	PAC/Ind
HDM Graphics	$1,800	Indiv
Media/Entertainment	**$7,200**	
ASCAP	$2,000	PAC
National Cable Television Assn	$2,000	PAC
Telephone Utilities	**$14,450**	
AT&T	$8,000	PAC
United Telecommunications	$3,000	PAC
Michigan Bell Telephone	$1,950	PAC
Computer Equipment & Services	**$18,750**	
Network Solutions Inc	$4,500	PAC
Computer Sciences Corp	$3,000	PAC
Metters Industries Inc	$2,250	Indiv
Computer & Communications Industry Assn	$1,500	PAC
Electronic Data Systems	$1,500	PAC
Technology Applications Inc	$1,500	Indiv

Source of Funds in 1992 Election

Source	Total	Pct
■ PACs	$207,008	52%
▨ Indivs $200+	$61,043	15%
☐ Indivs under $200	$49,674	13%
⊠ Other	$78,823	20%
Candidate	$0	0%
Party	$17,276	4%

Source of PAC Dollars by Sector

Source	Total	Pct
■ Business	$115,997	55%
▨ Labor	$92,560	44%
☐ Ideology/Single Issue	$3,700	2%

In-State vs. Out-of-State Contributions*

Source	Total	Pct
☐ In-State	$25,275	42%
■ Out-of-state	$34,768	58%
No state listed	$1,000	

***by large individual contributors ($200 & above)**

Construction		$8,900
General Contractors	**$1,700**	
None over $1,500		
Special Trade Contractors	**$4,250**	
Supreme Heating & Cooling	$2,000	Indiv
American Subcontractors Assn	$1,500	PAC
Construction Services	**$1,750**	
None over $1,500		

Defense		$6,750
Defense Aerospace	**$5,500**	
OAO Corp	$4,000	Indiv

Energy & Natural Resources		$5,500
Electric Utilities	**$3,750**	
Detroit Edison	$1,750	PAC

Finance, Insurance & Real Estate		$19,950
Real Estate	**$1,500**	
None over $1,500		
Accountants	**$16,000**	
American Institute of CPA's	$15,000	PAC

Health		$3,100
Pharmaceuticals/Health Products	**$1,500**	
Upjohn Co	$1,500	PAC

Contribution Totals by Sector

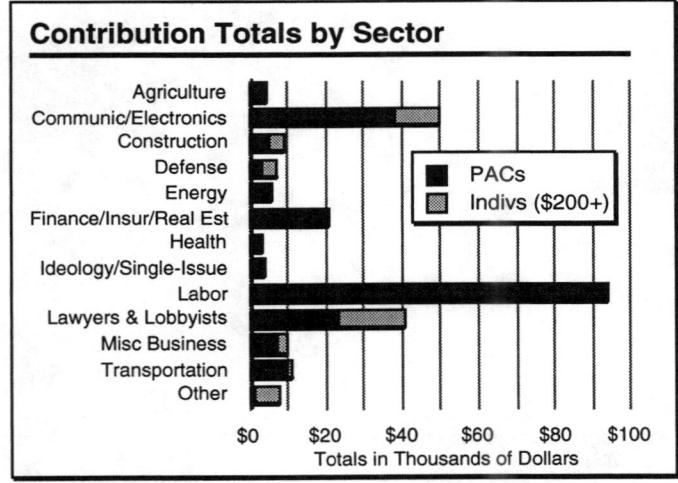

Legend: ■ PACs ▨ Indivs ($200+)

Categories: Agriculture, Communic/Electronics, Construction, Defense, Energy, Finance/Insur/Real Est, Health, Ideology/Single-Issue, Labor, Lawyers & Lobbyists, Misc Business, Transportation, Other

$0 $20 $40 $60 $80 $100
Totals in Thousands of Dollars

Lawyers & Lobbyists $40,180

Lawyers & Lobbyists $40,180
- Assn of Trial Lawyers of America ....$10,500 PAC
- Opperman & Paquin ....$5,262 PAC
- Cassidy & Associates ....$2,718 Indiv
- Crowell & Moring ....$2,000 PAC
- Milberg, Weiss et al ....$2,000 Indiv
- Shaw, Pittman et al ....$2,000 PAC
- Ackerman & Ackerman ....$1,925 Indiv

Misc Business $8,975

Business Associations $2,000
- None over $1,500

Food & Beverage $1,675
- None over $1,500

Business Services $2,750
- None over $1,500

Transportation $10,785

Air Transport $5,160
- United Parcel Service ....$3,060 PAC

Automotive $4,625
- Ford Motor Co ....$2,000 PAC
- Chrysler Corp ....$1,625 PAC

Labor

Labor $93,560

Building Trade Unions $12,210
- Laborers' Political League ....$4,000 PAC
- Carpenters & Joiners Union ....$3,000 PAC
- Plumbers/Pipefitters Union ....$2,260 PAC

Industrial Unions $16,550
- United Auto Workers ....$10,000 PAC
- Machinists/Aerospace Workers Union ....$2,000 PAC
- United Steelworkers ....$2,000 PAC

Transportation Unions $20,625
- Teamsters Union ....$10,000 PAC
- Marine Engineers Union* ....$3,500 PAC
- Air Line Pilots Assn ....$1,500 PAC
- United Transportation Union ....$1,500 PAC

Public Sector Unions $33,775
- American Postal Workers Union ....$5,950 PAC
- National Education Assn ....$5,000 PAC
- National Assn Retired Federal Employees ....$4,500 PAC
- American Fedn of St/Cnty/Munic Employees ......$3,900 PAC
- National Assn of Letter Carriers ....$3,500 PAC
- American Federation of Govt Employees ....$1,700 PAC
- National Assn of Postal Supervisors ....$1,500 PAC
- National League of Postmasters ....$1,500 PAC
- National Rural Letter Carriers Assn ....$1,500 PAC

Misc Unions $10,400
- Food & Commercial Workers Union ....$5,000 PAC
- AFL-CIO ....$3,500 PAC
- Service Employees International Union ....$1,500 PAC

Ideological/Single-Issue

Ideological/Single-Issue $3,700

Misc Issues $2,100
- National Cmte to Preserve Social Security ....$2,000 PAC

Other & Unknown

Other $7,300

Education $3,650
- Highland Park School Board ....$2,000 Indiv

Retired $2,650
- None over $1,500

Unknown $11,200

- No Employer Listed or Found $3,900
- Employer Listed/Category Unknown $6,400
  - None over $1,500

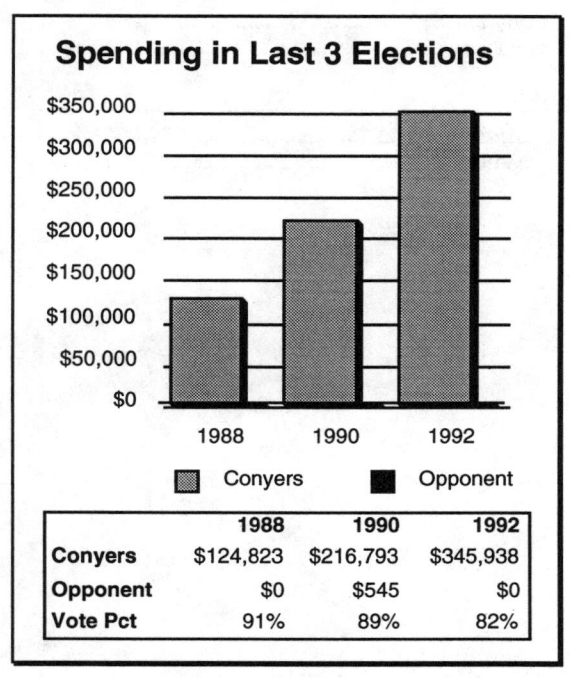

Spending in Last 3 Elections

	1988	1990	1992
Conyers	$124,823	$216,793	$345,938
Opponent	$0	$545	$0
Vote Pct	91%	89%	82%

* Contributions came from more than one affiliate or subsidiary.

Jim Cooper, D-Tenn (4)

First elected: 1982

1991-92 Total Receipts:	$164,092
1992 Year-end Cash:	$174,426

1991-92 Committees & Subcommittees

Budget
Defense, Foreign Policy and Space; Human Resources; Urgent Fiscal Issues

Energy and Commerce
Commerce, Consumer Protection and Competitiveness; Energy and Power; Telecommunications and Finance

Leading Contributors

NOTE: Cooper reported taking no PAC contributions in his 1992 campaign. The PACs listed below did report making contributions to him , however, and those contributions are recorded in the official FEC records.

Business

Agriculture $2,050

Food Processing & Sales $1,250
  Mike Rose Foods Inc ....$1,250   Indiv

Construction $4,050

General Contractors $1,800
  Maymead Inc ....$1,000   Indiv
Construction Services $1,000
  None over $1,000
Building Materials & Equipment $1,000
  Regal Corp ....$1,000   Indiv

Energy & Natural Resources $3,150

Oil & Gas $3,150
  Pilot Oil Corp ....$1,000   Indiv

Finance, Insurance & Real Estate $7,455

Commercial Banks $1,050
  Dominion Bankshares Corp ....$1,050   Indiv
Securities & Investment $3,500
  Levy, Harkins & Co ....$2,000   Indiv
  Gen Cap America Inc ....$1,000   Indiv
Real Estate $1,405
  None over $1,000
Accountants $1,000
  Davidson & Kruse ....$1,000   Indiv

Source of Funds in 1992 Election

Source	Total	Pct
■ PACs	$0	0%
▨ Indivs $200+	$60,775	36%
☐ Indivs under $200	$68,145	40%
▧ Other..............................	$40,018	24%
Candidate	$0	0%
Party	$7,746	5%

Source of PAC Dollars by Sector

No PAC contributions reported

Source	Total	Pct
■ Business	$2,500	50%
▨ Labor.................................	$0	0%
☐ Ideology/Single Issue	$2,500	50%

In-State vs. Out-of-State Contributions*

Source	Total	Pct
☐ In-State	$54,225	90%
■ Out-of-state	$6,050	10%
No state listed	$0	

* by large individual contributors ($200 & above)

Health $12,606

Health Professionals $4,750
  American Medical Assn ....$1,000   PAC
  Healthcorp ....$1,000   Indiv
Hospitals/Nursing Homes $6,356
  Healthtrust Inc ....$3,678   Indiv
  Hospital Corp of America ....$1,678   Indiv
Health Services $1,000
  None over $1,000

Lawyers & Lobbyists $7,250

Lawyers & Lobbyists..............................$7,250
  Chambliss, Bahner et al ....$1,000   Indiv

Misc Business $2,750

Beer, Wine & Liquor $1,000
  Brown-Forman Distillers ....$1,000   PAC

Contribution Totals by Sector

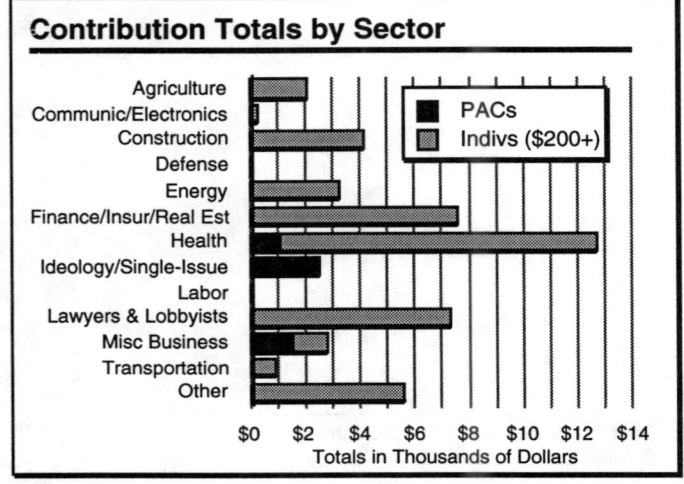

Totals in Thousands of Dollars

- PACs
- Indivs ($200+)

Agriculture
Communic/Electronics
Construction
Defense
Energy
Finance/Insur/Real Est
Health
Ideology/Single-Issue
Labor
Lawyers & Lobbyists
Misc Business
Transportation
Other

$0 $2 $4 $6 $8 $10 $12 $14

Ideological/Single-Issue

Ideological/Single-Issue	$2,500	

Democratic/Liberal $2,500
    National Cmte for an Effective Congress ....$2,500   PAC

Other & Unknown

Other	$5,500	

Civil Servants/Public Officials $1,000
    None over $1,000

Retired $4,500
    None over $1,000

Unknown	$16,889	

    No Employer Listed or Found $1,900
    Employer Listed/Category Unknown $14,689
        Bobo, Hunt & Bobo ....$1,000   Indiv
        Herman Grant Co ....$1,000   Indiv
        Mid-State Management Co ....$1,000   Indiv
        Modern Technical Services ....$1,000   Indiv
        Ritchie, Fels & Dillard ....$1,000   Indiv

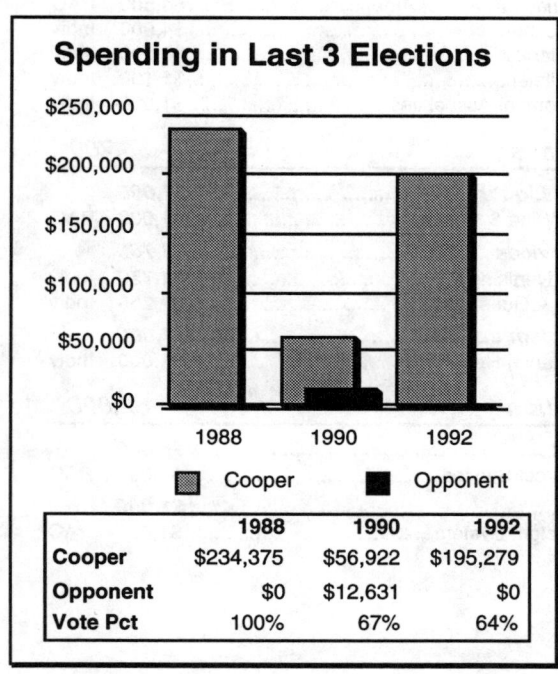

Spending in Last 3 Elections

	1988	1990	1992
Cooper	$234,375	$56,922	$195,279
Opponent	$0	$12,631	$0
Vote Pct	100%	67%	64%

Sam Coppersmith, D-Ariz (1)

First elected: 1992

1991-92 Total Receipts: $248,108
1992 Year-end Cash: $3,474

1993-94 Committees & Subcommittees

Public Works and Transportation
Aviation; Economic Development

Science, Space and Technology
Energy; Investigations and Oversight; Technology, Environment and Aviation

Leading Contributors

Business

Agriculture		$3,250
Agricultural Services/Products		$2,500
Salt River Valley Water Users	$2,500	PAC

Communications/Electronics		$5,119
Telephone Utilities		$1,500
AT&T	$1,000	PAC
Telecom Services & Equipment		$2,000
Bell Laboratories	$2,000	Indiv

Construction		$2,000
Construction Services		$1,000
Andrew Fredman Assoc	$1,000	Indiv
Building Materials & Equipment		$1,000
Empire Southwest Co	$1,000	Indiv

Finance, Insurance & Real Estate		$9,890
Securities & Investment		$1,450
None over $1,000		
Real Estate		$6,350
Del Webb Corp	$1,000	PAC
PNC Realty Holding Corp	$1,000	Indiv
Philadelphia Investment Corp	$1,000	Indiv
Misc Finance		$1,250
Consolidated Investments	$1,250	Indiv

Source of Funds in 1992 Election

Source	Total	Pct
■ PACs	$66,183	24%
▨ Indivs $200+	$98,934	36%
□ Indivs under $200	$44,319	16%
⊠ Other	$66,763	24%
Candidate	$31,019	11%
Party	$33,241	12%

Source of PAC Dollars by Sector

Source	Total	Pct
■ Business	$15,600	22%
▨ Labor	$34,999	50%
□ Ideology/Single Issue	$20,097	28%

In-State vs. Out-of-State Contributions*

Source	Total	Pct
□ In-State	$61,669	62%
■ Out-of-state	$37,265	38%
No state listed	$0	

* by large individual contributors ($200 & above)

Health		$5,350
Health Professionals		$3,400
None over $1,000		
Hospitals/Nursing Homes		$1,500
None over $1,000		

Lawyers & Lobbyists		$46,675
Lawyers & Lobbyists		$46,675
Lewis & Roca	$14,250	Indiv
Brown & Bain	$5,210	Indiv
Cohen, Milstein et al	$4,865	Indiv
Assn of Trial Lawyers of America	$4,500	PAC
Susman, Schermer et al	$4,000	Indiv
Blank & Blank	$1,500	Indiv
Snell & Wilmer	$1,100	Indiv
Parry & Romani Associates	$1,000	Indiv

Misc Business		$6,700
Beer, Wine & Liquor		$1,000
Southern Wine & Spirits	$1,000	PAC
Business Services		$3,750
Barash Advertising	$1,750	Indiv
Jamieson & Gutierrez	$1,250	Indiv
Lodging/Tourism		$1,000
Canyon Ranch Health Spa	$1,000	Indiv

Transportation		$2,000
Air Transport		$1,000
United Parcel Service	$1,000	PAC
Trucking		$1,000
Yellow Freight System	$1,000	PAC

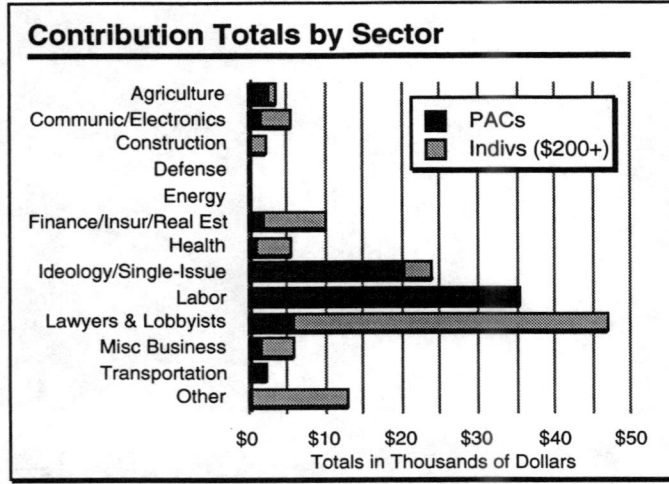

Contribution Totals by Sector

Legend: ■ PACs ▨ Indivs ($200+)

Categories: Agriculture, Communic/Electronics, Construction, Defense, Energy, Finance/Insur/Real Est, Health, Ideology/Single-Issue, Labor, Lawyers & Lobbyists, Misc Business, Transportation, Other

Totals in Thousands of Dollars ($0, $10, $20, $30, $40, $50)

Labor

Labor		$34,999
Building Trade Unions	**$3,500**	
Laborers' Western Political League	$1,000	PAC
Plumbers/Pipefitters Union	$1,000	PAC
Sheet Metal Workers Union	$1,000	PAC
Industrial Unions	**$6,499**	
Machinists/Aerospace Workers Union	$2,500	PAC
Intl Brotherhood of Electrical Workers	$2,000	PAC
United Steelworkers	$1,000	PAC
Transportation Unions	**$6,500**	
United Transportation Union	$3,000	PAC
Teamsters Union	$2,500	PAC
Public Sector Unions	**$13,500**	
National Education Assn	$5,000	PAC
Phoenix Firefighters #493	$3,500	PAC
American Fedn of St/Cnty/Munic Employees	$3,000	PAC
International Assn of Firefighters	$1,500	PAC
Misc Unions	**$5,000**	
Food & Commercial Workers Union	$2,500	PAC
AFL-CIO	$1,000	PAC
Bakery, Confectionery & Tobacco Workers	$1,000	PAC

Ideological/Single-Issue

Ideological/Single-Issue		$23,497
Democratic/Liberal	**$2,750**	
Independent Action	$2,000	PAC
Leadership PACs	**$1,000**	
Effective Government Cmte (Dick Gephardt)	$1,000	PAC
Pro-Israel	**$3,050**	
None over $1,000		
Pro-Choice	**$4,014**	
National Abortion Rights Action League	$3,014	PAC
Voters for Choice	$1,000	PAC
Womens Issues	**$1,000**	
None over $1,000		
Human Rights	**$3,000**	
Human Rights Campaign Fund	$2,500	PAC
Misc Issues	**$8,183**	
Sierra Club	$4,783	PAC
League of Conservation Voters	$3,000	PAC

Other & Unknown

Other		$12,500
Non-Profit Institutions	**$1,500**	
Phoenix Art Museum	$1,500	Indiv
Education	**$4,750**	
Rockefeller University	$2,000	Indiv
Retired	**$5,050**	
None over $1,000		
Other	**$1,000**	
Planned Parenthood	$1,000	Indiv

Unknown		$17,400
Homemakers/Non-income earners	$1,950	
No Employer Listed or Found	$2,850	
Employer Listed/Category Unknown	$12,350	
Paul Gibson & Associates	$2,000	Indiv
Chiefetz, Pierce et al	$1,000	Indiv
DM Griffith & Co	$1,000	Indiv

Spending in Last Election

	1992
Coppersmith	$244,633
Opponent	$452,348
Vote Pct	51%

Jerry F. Costello, D-Ill (12)

First elected: 1988
1991-92 Total Receipts: $503,778
1992 Year-end Cash: $171,227

1991-92 Committees & Subcommittees

Public Works and Transportation
Aviation; Surface Transportation; Water Resources

Science, Space and Technology
Energy; Science

Select Committee on Aging

Leading Contributors

Business

Agriculture		$5,907
Crop Production & Basic Processing		$1,700
None over $1,500		
Livestock		$2,275
None over $1,500		

Communications/Electronics		$7,900
Media/Entertainment		$3,000
None over $1,500		
Telephone Utilities		$4,650
AT&T	$1,750	PAC
GTE Corp	$1,500	PAC

Construction		$41,750
General Contractors		$20,875
Calhoun Construction	$2,000	Indiv
Keeley Brothers Construction	$2,000	Indiv
Korte-Plocher Construction Co	$2,000	Indiv
PCF Construction Inc	$2,000	Indiv
Bauer Brothers Construction	$1,750	Indiv
Special Trade Contractors		$6,750
Illinois Excavators	$2,000	Indiv
Construction Services		$12,375
Sverdrup Corp	$4,000	PAC
Tams Consultants Inc	$2,000	Indiv
Campbell Design Group	$1,500	Indiv
Thouvenot, Wade et al	$1,500	Indiv

Source of Funds in 1992 Election

Source	Total	Pct
■ PACs	$142,675	27%
▨ Indivs $200+	$258,850	50%
☐ Indivs under $200	$68,373	13%
▨ Other	$49,988	10%
Candidate	$0	0%
Party	$16,558	3%

Source of PAC Dollars by Sector

Source	Total	Pct
■ Business	$69,607	48%
▨ Labor	$70,900	49%
☐ Ideology/Single Issue	$4,723	3%

In-State vs. Out-of-State Contributions*

Source	Total	Pct
☐ In-State	$233,800	90%
■ Out-of-state	$25,050	10%
No state listed	$0	

* by large individual contributors ($200 & above)

Defense		$2,750
Defense Electronics		$2,000
AEL Industries Inc	$2,000	PAC

Energy & Natural Resources		$6,600
Electric Utilities		$2,500
Illinois Power Co	$1,500	PAC
Waste Management		$2,650
Metro East Sanitary Dist	$2,000	Indiv

Finance, Insurance & Real Estate		$37,675
Commercial Banks		$12,750
American Bankers Assn	$2,000	PAC
Magna Group Inc	$2,000	PAC/Ind
Mark Twain Illinois Bank	$2,000	Indiv
Boatmens Bankshares	$1,500	PAC
Securities & Investment		$3,500
Bridge Trading Co	$2,000	Indiv
Insurance		$7,000
Allsup & Associates Inc	$4,500	Indiv
Real Estate		$10,550
National Assn of Realtors	$7,000	PAC
Accountants		$2,875
None over $1,500		

Health		$23,600
Health Professionals		$17,200
American Medical Assn	$3,000	PAC
Hospitals/Nursing Homes		$4,000
Eldercare Inc	$2,000	Indiv

Contribution Totals by Sector

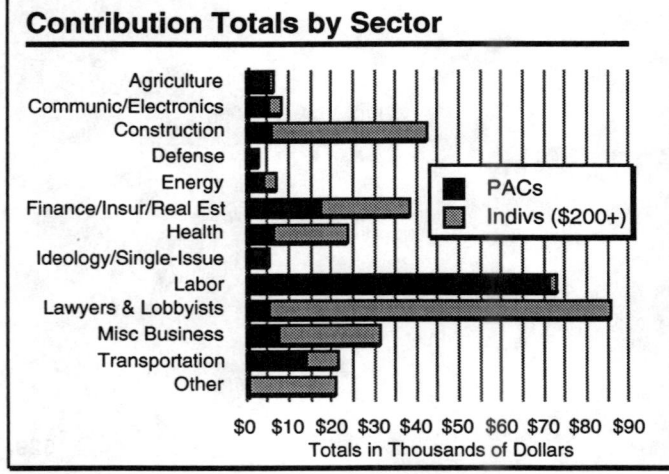

Agriculture
Communic/Electronics
Construction
Defense
Energy
Finance/Insur/Real Est
Health
Ideology/Single-Issue
Labor
Lawyers & Lobbyists
Misc Business
Transportation
Other

■ PACs
▨ Indivs ($200+)

$0 $10 $20 $30 $40 $50 $60 $70 $80 $90
Totals in Thousands of Dollars

Lawyers & Lobbyists	$85,000

Lawyers & Lobbyists $85,000
- Cook, Shevlin et al ....$8,000 — Indiv
- Assn of Trial Lawyers of America ....$5,000 — PAC
- Callis, Papa et al ....$3,000 — Indiv
- Bono, Goldenberg et al ....$2,250 — Indiv
- Chatham & Babka ....$2,000 — Indiv
- Heiligenstein & Badgley ....$2,000 — Indiv
- Kassly, Bone et al ....$2,000 — Indiv
- Pratt, Jones et al ....$2,000 — Indiv
- Rice Law Offices ....$2,000 — Indiv
- Ripplinger, Dixon & Johnson ....$2,000 — Indiv
- Thompson & Mitchell ....$2,000 — Indiv

Misc Business	$30,600

Business Associations $1,500
- Corridor 67 Inc ....$1,500 — PAC

Food & Beverage $1,500
- None over $1,500

Beer, Wine & Liquor $6,250
- Robert 'Chick' Fritz Inc ....$2,000 — Indiv

Retail Sales $3,500
- Liese Lumber Co ....$2,000 — Indiv

Misc Services $2,875
- None over $1,500

Business Services $8,775
- Auto Spa Car Wash ....$2,000 — Indiv

Misc Business $2,250
- National Assn of Water Companies ......$2,000 — PAC

Transportation	$21,150

Air Transport $6,800
- United Airlines ....$1,500 — PAC

Automotive $6,000
- Auffenberg Ford Lincoln ....$2,000 — Indiv
- National Auto Dealers Assn ....$2,000 — PAC

Trucking $4,850
- Beelman Trucking Co ....$2,000 — Indiv

Railroads $3,100
- None over $1,500

Spending in Last 3 Elections

	1988	1990	1992
Costello	$394,412	$394,896	$606,383
Opponent	$157,171	$26,230	$21,024
Vote Pct	53%	66%	71%

Labor

Labor	$72,650

Building Trade Unions $12,550
- Laborers Union* ....$3,750 — Indiv
- Ironworkers Union ....$3,500 — PAC
- Plumbers/Pipefitters Union....................$2,000 — PAC
- Operating Engineers Union* ....$1,500 — Indiv

Industrial Unions $27,100
- Machinists/Aerospace Workers Union* ....$10,000 — PAC
- United Mine Workers ....$6,600 — PAC
- Boilermakers Union ....$2,500 — PAC
- United Steelworkers ....$2,000 — PAC
- Intl Brotherhood of Electrical Workers ....$1,750 — PAC

Transportation Unions $17,900
- Teamsters Union ....$7,500 — PAC
- Air Line Pilots Assn ....$5,500 — PAC
- Amalgamated Transit Union ....$2,000 — PAC

Public Sector Unions $12,950
- National Education Assn ....$5,800 — PAC
- National Assn Retired Federal Employees ....$3,000 — PAC

Misc Unions..$2,150
- Food & Commercial Workers Union ......$1,900 — PAC

Ideological/Single-Issue

Ideological/Single-Issue	$4,723

Democratic/Liberal $2,500
- National Cmte for an Effective Congress ....$2,500 — PAC

Other & Unknown

Other	$20,375

Civil Servants/Public Officials $8,375
- St Clair County ....$2,625 — Indiv

Retired $10,750
- None over $1,500

Unknown	$43,400

- Homemakers/Non-income earners $9,250
- No Employer Listed or Found $5,600
- Generic Occupation/Category Unknown $1,500
- Employer Listed/Category Unknown $27,050
  - Hurst-Rosche Engineers ....$2,900 — Indiv
  - EJ Stone Co ....$2,000 — Indiv
  - Feder Builder & Rentals ....$2,000 — Indiv
  - Vollmer-Oates Inc ....$2,000 — Indiv
  - SCC ....$1,750 — Indiv

* Contributions came from more than one affiliate or subsidiary.

C. Christopher Cox, R-Calif (47)

First elected: 1988

1991-92 Total Receipts: $515,754
1992 Year-end Cash: $118,668

1991-92 Committees & Subcommittees

Government Operations
Government Activities and Transportation (Ranking Republican)

Public Works and Transportation
Aviation; Public Buildings and Grounds; Surface Transportation

Leading Contributors

Business

Agriculture $9,900

Agricultural Services/Products $3,200
    Archer-Daniels-Midland Corp .... $2,000 PAC
Food Processing & Sales $2,450
    None over $1,500
Misc Agriculture $2,000
    None over $1,500

Communications/Electronics $13,350

Media/Entertainment $4,000
    Walt Disney Co .... $1,500 PAC
Telephone Utilities $3,400
    None over $1,500
Telecom Services & Equipment $1,500
    Secomerica Inc .... $1,500 Indiv
Computer Equipment & Services $3,750
    AST Research .... $2,000 Indiv

Construction $45,500

General Contractors $25,700
    Fluor Corp .... $10,000 PAC
    National Utility Contractors Assn .... $2,000 PAC
    Steve P Rados Inc .... $1,900 Indiv
    Associated General Contractors .... $1,500 PAC
Home Builders $3,350
    None over $1,500
Special Trade Contractors $3,900
    Penhall Co .... $1,900 Indiv

Source of Funds in 1992 Election

Source	Total	Pct
■ PACs	$155,500	30%
▨ Indivs $200+	$321,030	62%
☐ Indivs under $200	$31,969	6%
▨ Other	$7,255	1%
Candidate	$0	0%
Party	$742	0%

Source of PAC Dollars by Sector

Source	Total	Pct
■ Business	$152,590	94%
▨ Labor	$1,750	1%
☐ Ideology/Single Issue	$8,500	5%

In-State vs. Out-of-State Contributions*

Source	Total	Pct
☐ In-State	$296,980	93%
■ Out-of-state	$20,950	7%
No state listed	$0	

* by large individual contributors ($200 & above)

Construction Services $7,500
    Boyle Engineering Corp .... $2,000 Indiv
    CH2M Hill .... $1,800 PAC/Ind
    Robert Bein, William Frost & Assoc .... $1,500 Indiv
Building Materials & Equipment $5,050
    None over $1,500

Defense $5,800

Defense Aerospace $4,400
    Rockwell International .... $2,550 Indiv

Energy & Natural Resources $12,700

Oil & Gas $9,300
    Koch Industries .... $3,000 PAC/Ind
    Evergreen Holdings .... $1,500 Indiv
Electric Utilities $1,800
    None over $1,500

Finance, Insurance & Real Estate $97,050

Commercial Banks $12,950
    American Bankers Assn .... $3,500 PAC
    Independent Bankers Assn .... $2,850 PAC
    Citicorp .... $1,600 PAC
Savings & Loans $4,850
    Plaza Savings & Loan .... $1,500 Indiv
Credit Unions $4,000
    Orange County Teachers Fed Credit Union .... $3,500 Indiv
Securities & Investment $12,500
    Hermes Investment Corp .... $2,000 Indiv
    Merrill Lynch .... $1,500 Indiv
Insurance $11,950
    Pacific Mutual Life .... $3,250 PAC
    National Assn of Life Underwriters .... $2,000 PAC

Contribution Totals by Sector

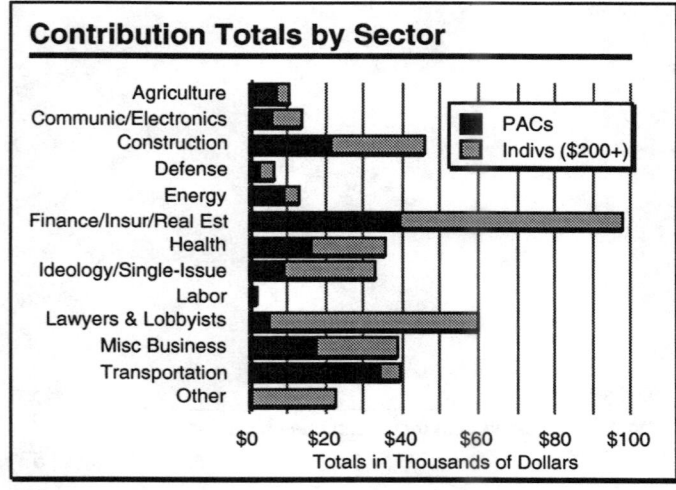

Agriculture
Communic/Electronics
Construction
Defense
Energy
Finance/Insur/Real Est
Health
Ideology/Single-Issue
Labor
Lawyers & Lobbyists
Misc Business
Transportation
Other

■ PACs
▨ Indivs ($200+)

$0 $20 $40 $60 $80 $100
Totals in Thousands of Dollars

Real Estate	....	$35,000	
National Assn of Realtors	.....................................$6,500		PAC
Angeles Corp	.....................................$4,000		Indiv
Meeker Development Co	.....................................$4,000		Indiv
Irvine Co	.....................................$2,500		PAC/Ind
First American Title Insurance Co	.....................................$2,000		Indiv
DL Bendetti Co	.....................................$1,500		Indiv
Fieldstone Co	.....................................$1,500		Indiv

Accountants	....	$7,300	
American Institute of CPA's	.....................................$5,350		PAC

Misc Finance	....	$7,100	
Dimensional Fund Advisors Inc	.....................................$4,500		Indiv

Health — $34,750

Health Professionals	....	$18,750	
American Medical Assn	.....................................$2,300		PAC
American Chiropractic Assn	.....................................$2,000		PAC

Health Services	....	$6,000	
Family Health Program Inc	.....................................$2,750		PAC
Homedco Inc	.....................................$1,750		PAC/Ind
Pacificare Health Systems	.....................................$1,500		PAC/Ind

Pharmaceuticals/Health Products	....	$4,750	
Baxter Healthcare Corp	.....................................$1,600		PAC

Misc Health	....	$4,000	
Chapin Medical Center	.....................................$4,000		Indiv

Lawyers & Lobbyists — $60,300

Lawyers & Lobbyists	....	$60,300	
Latham & Watkins	.....................................$23,500		Indiv
Riordan & McKinzie	.....................................$7,000		PAC/Ind
Gibson, Dunn & Crutcher	.....................................$2,500		Indiv
O'Melveny & Myers	.....................................$2,500		Indiv
Gilchrist & Rutter	.....................................$2,250		Indiv
McConnell/Ferguson Group	.....................................$1,900		Indiv
Allen, Matkins et al	.....................................$1,750		Indiv

Misc Business — $38,430

Food & Beverage	....	$5,000	
National Restaurant Assn	.....................................$2,000		PAC

Beer, Wine & Liquor	....	$4,350	
Straub Distributing Co	.....................................$2,350		Indiv
National Beer Wholesalers Assn	.....................................$1,500		PAC

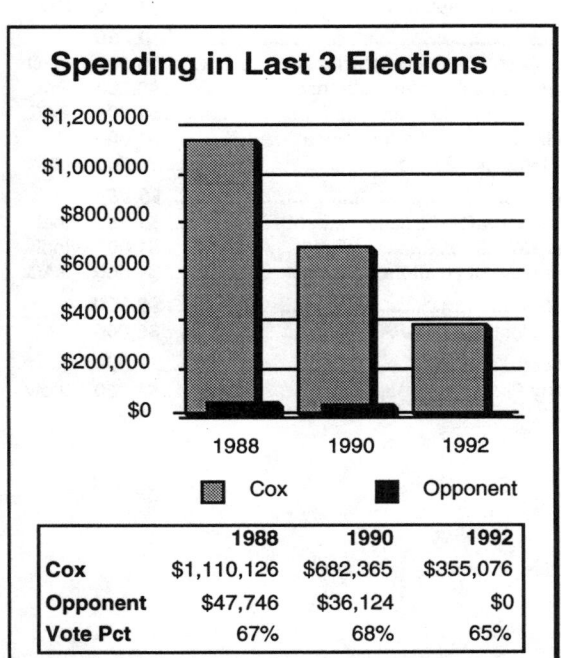

Spending in Last 3 Elections

	1988	1990	1992
Cox	$1,110,126	$682,365	$355,076
Opponent	$47,746	$36,124	$0
Vote Pct	67%	68%	65%

■ Cox ■ Opponent

Retail Sales	....	$5,350	
International Council of Shopping Centers	..........$2,000		PAC
Horton & Converse Pharmacies	.........................$1,500		Indiv

Misc Services	....	$2,000	
Amplicon Financial	....$2,000		Indiv

Business Services	....	$11,830	
Enniskerry Financial Ltd	......................................$2,500		Indiv

Lodging/Tourism	....	$1,650	
None over $1,500			

Chemical & Related Manufacturing	....	$1,850	
None over $1,500			

Steel Production	....	$1,850	
None over $1,500			

Misc Manufacturing & Distributing	....	$4,250	
Stone Container Corp	....$1,500		PAC

Transportation — $38,490

Air Transport	....	$24,690	
United Parcel Service	....$7,300		PAC
Federal Express Corp	....$5,000		PAC
Northrop Corp	....$1,600		PAC

Automotive	....	$11,100	
Auto Dealers & Drivers for Free Trade	...............$2,000		PAC
Rockwell International	....$2,000		PAC
Barwick Imports Inc	....$1,500		Indiv

Railroads	....	$2,700	
None over $1,500			

Labor

Labor	$1,750
None over $1,500	

Ideological/Single-Issue

Ideological/Single-Issue	$32,350

Republican/Conservative	....	$24,450	
None over $1,500			

Gun Rights/Gun Control	....	$2,500	
National Rifle Assn	....$2,000		PAC

Human Rights	....	$2,000	
None over $1,500			

Misc Issues	....	$2,600	
None over $1,500			

Other & Unknown

Other	$21,850

Civil Servants/Public Officials	....	$4,300	
None over $1,500			

Education	....	$2,900	
None over $1,500			

Retired	....	$14,650	
None over $1,500			

Unknown	$68,575
Homemakers/Non-income earners	...................$10,600
No Employer Listed or Found	............................$4,300
Generic Occupation/Category Unknown	............$5,400
Employer Listed/Category Unknown	................$48,250

Century Council	....$2,000	Indiv
Fusco, Williams et al	...................................$1,500	Indiv

William J. Coyne, D-Pa (14)

First elected: 1980

1991-92 Total Receipts:	$264,042
1992 Year-end Cash:	$167,604

1991-92 Committees & Subcommittees

Ways and Means
Health; Select Revenue Measures

Leading Contributors

Business

Agriculture — $2,000

Food Processing & Sales **$1,000**
   Nabisco Brands Inc .... $1,000   PAC

Communications/Electronics — $5,800

Telephone Utilities **$3,500**
   AT&T .... $2,500   PAC
Computer Equipment & Services **$1,000**
   Amdahl Corp .... $1,000   Indiv

Energy & Natural Resources — $12,750

Oil & Gas **$2,750**
   USX Corp .... $1,500   PAC/Ind
Mining **$2,000**
   Alcoa .... $1,000   PAC
   Drummond Co .... $1,000   PAC
Electric Utilities **$3,500**
   Southern Co* .... $1,500   PAC
Waste Management **$4,500**
   Chambers Development Co .... $4,000   PAC/Ind

Source of Funds in 1992 Election

Source	Total	Pct
■ PACs	$171,007	63%
▨ Indivs $200+	$69,125	25%
☐ Indivs under $200	$9,410	3%
⊠ Other	$23,852	9%
Candidate	$0	0%
Party	$9,352	3%

Source of PAC Dollars by Sector

Source	Total	Pct
■ Business	$89,957	56%
▨ Labor	$70,800	44%
☐ Ideology/Single Issue	$0	0%

In-State vs. Out-of-State Contributions*

Source	Total	Pct
☐ In-State	$50,750	73%
■ Out-of-state	$18,375	27%
No state listed	$0	

* by large individual contributors ($200 & above)

Finance, Insurance & Real Estate — $62,750

Commercial Banks **$3,600**
   American Bankers Assn .... $1,500   PAC
   Pittsburgh National Bank .... $1,000   PAC
Savings & Loans **$1,550**
   US League of Savings Assns* .... $1,050   PAC
Credit Unions **$5,000**
   Credit Union National Assn .... $5,000   PAC
Securities & Investment **$16,450**
   Federated Investors Inc .... $11,750   Indiv
   Federated Securities .... $1,500   Indiv
   Public Securities Assn .... $1,000   PAC
Insurance **$20,750**
   National Assn of Life Underwriters .... $6,000   PAC
   American Council of Life Insurance .... $3,000   PAC
   American Family Corp .... $1,000   PAC
   Connecticut Mutual Life Insurance .... $1,000   PAC
   Shevlin Financial Group .... $1,000   Indiv
Real Estate **$6,900**
   Howard Hanna Real Estate .... $1,250   Indiv
   Buncher Co .... $1,000   Indiv
   National Assn of Realtors .... $1,000   PAC
Accountants **$6,500**
   American Institute of CPA's .... $6,000   PAC
Misc Finance **$2,000**
   Allegheny Financial Group .... $1,000   Indiv

Contribution Totals by Sector

Legend: ■ PACs   ▨ Indivs ($200+)

Categories (top to bottom): Agriculture, Communic/Electronics, Construction, Defense, Energy, Finance/Insur/Real Est, Health, Ideology/Single-Issue, Labor, Lawyers & Lobbyists, Misc Business, Transportation, Other

X-axis: $0 $10 $20 $30 $40 $50 $60 $70
Totals in Thousands of Dollars

Health $30,782

Health Professionals $24,732
Assn for the Advancement of Psychology	$8,957	PAC
American Medical Assn*	$5,500	PAC
American Assn Oral & Maxillofacial Surgeons	$1,500	PAC
American Dental Assn	$1,500	PAC
American Soc Cataract/Refractive Surgery	$1,000	PAC

Pharmaceuticals/Health Products $5,250
Merck & Co	$1,500	PAC
Kinetic Concepts Inc	$1,000	PAC
Schering-Plough Corp	$1,000	PAC
SmithKline Beecham	$1,000	PAC

Lawyers & Lobbyists $19,050

Lawyers & Lobbyists $19,050
Assn of Trial Lawyers of America	$5,000	PAC
McClure, Trotter & Mentz	$4,000	Indiv
Houston, Houston & Donnelly	$1,000	Indiv
Kirkpatrick & Lockhart	$1,000	PAC
SR Wojdak & Associates	$1,000	Indiv

Misc Business $8,700

Beer, Wine & Liquor $3,000
Anheuser-Busch	$1,000	PAC
Wine & Spirits Wholesalers of America	$1,000	PAC

Business Services $3,500
None over $1,000

Transportation $3,250

Air Transport $1,000
None over $1,000

Railroads $1,000
None over $1,000

Labor

Labor $70,800

Building Trade Unions $11,250
Carpenters & Joiners Union	$5,000	PAC
Laborers' Political League	$3,000	PAC
Operating Engineers Union	$2,750	PAC
Plumbers/Pipefitters Union	$1,000	PAC

Industrial Unions $19,000
United Auto Workers	$5,000	PAC
United Steelworkers	$5,000	PAC
Communications Workers Union #13000	$3,000	PAC
Machinists/Aerospace Workers Union	$2,000	PAC
Rubber Cork Linoleum & Plastic Workers	$2,000	PAC
Intl Brotherhood of Electrical Workers	$1,000	PAC

Transportation Unions $14,500
Air Line Pilots Assn	$5,000	PAC
Marine Engineers Dist 2 Maritime Officers	$2,500	PAC
United Transportation Union	$2,500	PAC
Amalgamated Transit Union	$2,000	PAC
Seafarers International Union	$1,500	PAC
Transport Workers Union	$1,000	PAC

Public Sector Unions $23,050
National Education Assn	$8,000	PAC
American Federation of Teachers	$5,000	PAC
National Assn Retired Federal Employees	$3,000	PAC
American Fedn of St/Cnty/Munic Employees	$2,500	PAC
National Assn of Letter Carriers	$2,000	PAC
National Rural Letter Carriers Assn	$1,000	PAC

Misc Unions $3,000
Food & Commercial Workers Union	$2,500	PAC

Other & Unknown

Other $1,750

Retired $1,000
None over $1,000

Unknown $11,750
Homemakers/Non-income earners	$2,000	
Employer Listed/Category Unknown	$9,500	
Kabala & Geeseman	$1,000	Indiv

Spending in Last 3 Elections

	1988	1990	1992
Coyne	$80,730	$130,904	$323,937
Opponent	$0	$0	$98,526
Vote Pct	79%	72%	72%

* Contributions came from more than one affiliate or subsidiary.

535

Bud Cramer, D-Ala (5)

First elected: 1990

1991-92 Total Receipts: $400,693
1992 Year-end Cash: $32,112

1991-92 Committees & Subcommittees

Public Works and Transportation
Economic Development; Surface Transportation; Water Resources

Science, Space and Technology
Energy; Space

Select Committee on Children, Youth and Families

Leading Contributors

Business

Agriculture $22,300

Crop Production & Basic Processing **$5,250**		
Alabama Peanut Producers Assn $2,000	PAC
Tobacco **$3,350**		
RJR Nabisco $2,500	PAC
Dairy **$3,200**		
Associated Milk Producers $2,500	PAC
Poultry & Eggs **$1,850**		
None over $1,500		
Agricultural Services/Products **$6,050**		
Alabama Farm Bureau Federation $3,350	PAC
Alabama Farmers Co-op $1,500	Indiv

Communications/Electronics $25,650

Telephone Utilities **$7,000**		
South Central Bell Telephone $4,000	PAC
AT&T $3,000	PAC
Electronics Mfg & Services **$3,150**		
Teledyne Brown Engineering $1,800	Indiv
Computer Equipment & Services **$13,000**		
Intergraph Corp $10,000	PAC
Colsa Inc $2,000	Indiv

Source of Funds in 1992 Election

Source	Total	Pct
■ PACs	$222,075	53%
▨ Indivs $200+	$102,598	25%
□ Indivs under $200	$65,611	16%
▨ Other..............................	$25,049	6%
Candidate	$0	0%
Party	$14,790	4%

Source of PAC Dollars by Sector

Source	Total	Pct
■ Business	$154,137	70%
▨ Labor	$52,850	24%
□ Ideology/Single Issue	$14,100	6%

In-State vs. Out-of-State Contributions*

Source	Total	Pct
□ In-State	$99,898	97%
■ Out-of-state	$2,600	3%
No state listed	$0	

* by large individual contributors ($200 & above)

Construction $15,200

General Contractors **$6,650**		
None over $1,500		
Home Builders **$4,500**		
National Assn of Home Builders $2,500	PAC
Breland Homes $2,000	Indiv
Building Materials & Equipment **$2,550**		
None over $1,500		

Defense $9,600

Defense Aerospace **$7,650**		
Lockheed Corp $4,700	PAC/Ind
Rockwell International $2,950	PAC/Ind

Energy & Natural Resources $23,525

Oil & Gas **$12,050**		
Alagasco Inc $2,500	PAC
Spencer Companies $1,500	Indiv
Mining **$1,500**		
None over $1,500		
Electric Utilities **$7,675**		
Southern Co* $3,475	PAC
ACRE (Action Cmte for Rural Electrification) $1,850	PAC
Waste Management **$2,000**		
None over $1,500		

Contribution Totals by Sector

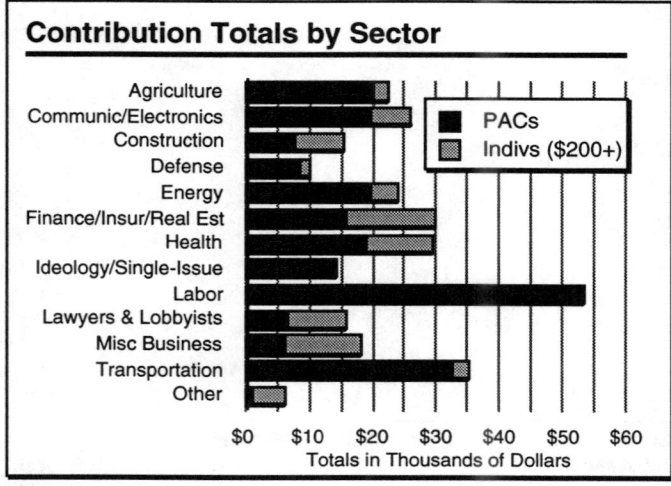

Agriculture, Communic/Electronics, Construction, Defense, Energy, Finance/Insur/Real Est, Health, Ideology/Single-Issue, Labor, Lawyers & Lobbyists, Misc Business, Transportation, Other

■ PACs   ▨ Indivs ($200+)

$0 $10 $20 $30 $40 $50 $60
Totals in Thousands of Dollars

Finance, Insurance & Real Estate $29,550

Commercial Banks **$9,500**
    Amsouth Bancorp ....$2,500 PAC
    Southtrust Corp ....$2,250 PAC
    Central Bancshares of the South ....$1,500 PAC

Insurance **$3,600**
    National Assn of Life Underwriters.....................$2,000 PAC

Real Estate **$11,450**
    Hays Land Companies ....$4,500 Indiv
    National Assn of Realtors ....$3,000 PAC

Accountants **$2,000**
    None over $1,500

Misc Finance **$1,750**
    None over $1,500

Health $29,212

Health Professionals **$27,462**
    American Medical Assn......................................$9,700 PAC
    American Academy of Ophthalmology ....$4,312 PAC

Hospitals/Nursing Homes **$1,550**
    None over $1,500

Lawyers & Lobbyists $15,598

Lawyers & Lobbyists...................................**$15,598**
    Assn of Trial Lawyers of America ....$6,000 PAC

Misc Business $18,000

Food & Beverage **$3,500**
    None over $1,500

Beer, Wine & Liquor **$1,850**
    None over $1,500

Retail Sales...**$3,200**
    Jimmy Smith Jewelers ....$1,600 Indiv

Business Services **$2,050**
    None over $1,500

Misc Manufacturing & Distributing **$4,000**
    Denbo Iron & Metal Co......................................$1,500 Indiv

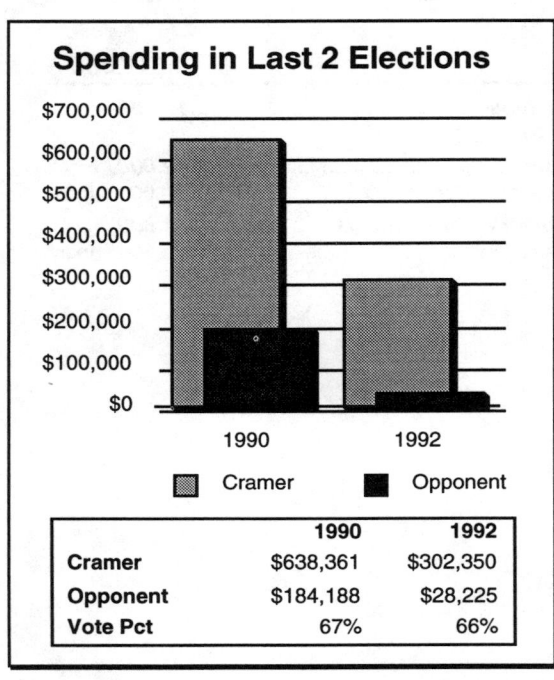

Spending in Last 2 Elections

	1990	1992
Cramer	$638,361	$302,350
Opponent	$184,188	$28,225
Vote Pct	67%	66%

Transportation $34,750

Air Transport **$21,200**
    United Parcel Service ....$4,700 PAC
    Boeing Co ....$3,850 PAC/Ind
    Grumman Corp ....$1,600 PAC

Automotive **$8,300**
    National Auto Dealers Assn ....$4,350 PAC
    Gencorp Inc ....$2,350 PAC

Trucking...**$3,050**
    None over $1,500

Railroads **$2,200**
    None over $1,500

Labor

Labor $52,850

Building Trade Unions **$4,600**
    Plumbers/Pipefitters Union................................$2,000 PAC
    Laborers' Political League ....$1,500 PAC

Industrial Unions **$21,900**
    United Auto Workers ....$7,350 PAC
    Intl Brotherhood of Electrical Workers ....$6,000 PAC
    Rubber Cork Linoleum & Plastic Workers ....$3,500 PAC
    Machinists/Aerospace Workers Union ....$2,200 PAC
    Communications Workers of America ....$1,500 PAC

Transportation Unions **$13,500**
    Air Line Pilots Assn ....$6,000 PAC
    Teamsters Union ....$2,500 PAC
    Marine Engineers Union* ....$2,000 PAC

Public Sector Unions **$10,600**
    American Fedn of St/Cnty/Munic Employees ......$5,000 PAC

Misc Unions..**$2,250**
    Food & Commercial Workers Union ....$1,500 PAC

Ideological/Single-Issue

Ideological/Single-Issue $14,100

Pro-Israel **$3,000**
    Americans for Good Government Inc ....$3,000 PAC

Pro-Choice..**$1,850**
    Voters for Choice ....$1,850 PAC

Gun Rights/Gun Control **$6,000**
    National Rifle Assn ....$6,000 PAC

Misc Issues...**$2,750**
    National Cmte to Preserve Social Security ....$2,750 PAC

Other & Unknown

Other $5,800

Civil Servants/Public Officials **$2,250**
    None over $1,500

Retired **$1,600**
    None over $1,500

Unknown $27,450

    Homemakers/Non-income earners $3,700
    Employer Listed/Category Unknown $23,750
        Anco Management Services Inc ....$2,750 Indiv
        Mid-South Testing Inc ....$1,750 Indiv

---

* Contributions came from more than one affiliate or subsidiary.

Philip M. Crane, R-Ill (8)

First elected: 1969

1991-92 Total Receipts:	$477,110
1992 Year-end Cash:	$64,211

1991-92 Committees & Subcommittees

Ways and Means
Social Security; Trade (Ranking Republican)

Leading Contributors

Business

Agriculture — $4,700

Crop Production & Basic Processing $2,300
    US Cane Sugar Refiners Assn .... $1,300   Indiv
Dairy $1,400
    None over $1,000

Communications/Electronics — $3,900

Printing & Publishing $2,850
    RR Donnelley & Sons .... $1,300   Indiv

Construction — $3,500

General Contractors $1,700
    Irby Construction Co .... $1,000   Indiv
Building Materials & Equipment $1,800
    Deltrol Controls .... $1,000   Indiv

Source of Funds in 1992 Election

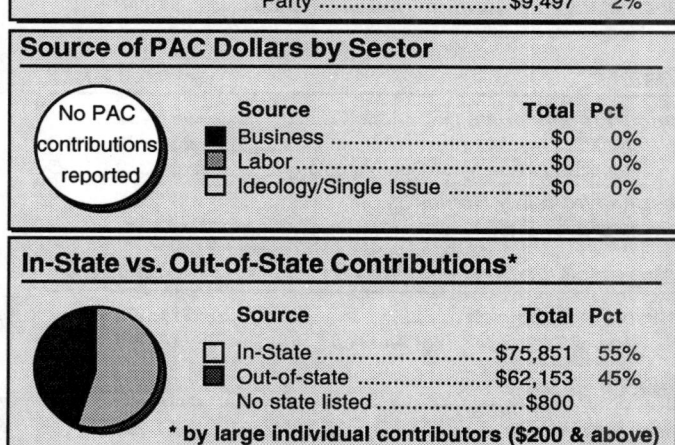

Source	Total	Pct
■ PACs	$0	0%
▨ Indivs $200+	$139,954	29%
☐ Indivs under $200	$311,384	65%
▨ Other	$30,269	6%
Candidate	$0	0%
Party	$9,497	2%

Source of PAC Dollars by Sector

No PAC contributions reported

Source	Total	Pct
■ Business	$0	0%
▨ Labor	$0	0%
☐ Ideology/Single Issue	$0	0%

In-State vs. Out-of-State Contributions*

Source	Total	Pct
☐ In-State	$75,851	55%
■ Out-of-state	$62,153	45%
No state listed	$800	

* by large individual contributors ($200 & above)

Finance, Insurance & Real Esta — $13,497

Savings & Loans $1,250
    Hoyne Savings & Loan Assn .... $1,250   Indiv
Securities & Investment $2,250
    Template Funds Management .... $1,000   Indiv
Insurance $1,997
    Travelers Corp .... $1,750   Indiv
Real Estate $2,500
    Kennedy Group Ltd .... $2,000   Indiv
Misc Finance $5,000
    None over $1,000

Health — $15,550

Health Professionals $8,450
    None over $1,000
Health Services $2,000
    Cancer Treatment Centers .... $2,000   Indiv
Pharmaceuticals/Health Products $4,600
    Baxter International Inc .... $4,800   Indiv

Contribution Totals by Sector

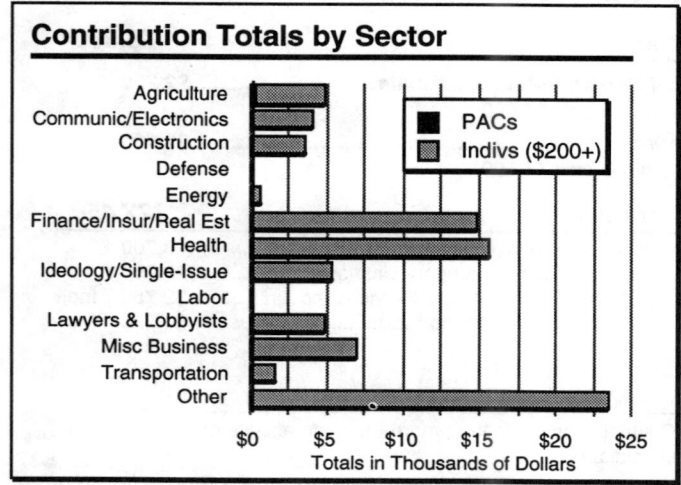

Legend: ■ PACs   ▨ Indivs ($200+)

Categories: Agriculture, Communic/Electronics, Construction, Defense, Energy, Finance/Insur/Real Est, Health, Ideology/Single-Issue, Labor, Lawyers & Lobbyists, Misc Business, Transportation, Other

Totals in Thousands of Dollars ($0, $5, $10, $15, $20, $25)

Lawyers & Lobbyists $4,650

Lawyers & Lobbyists **$4,650**
   Sidley & Austin .... $1,000 Indiv
   Stephen Munisteri & Associates .... $1,000 Indiv

Misc Business $6,725

Misc Manufacturing & Distributing **$6,075**
   Highland Supply Corp .... $2,250 Indiv
   Lane Industries .... $1,500 Indiv
   Cabay & Co .... $1,000 Indiv

Transportation $1,500

Air Transport **$1,500**
   Sundstrand Corp .... $1,000 Indiv

Ideological/Single-Issue

Ideological/Single-Issue $5,246

Republican/Conservative **$4,750**
   None over $1,000

Other & Unknown

Other $23,400

Retired **$22,150**
   None over $1,000
Other **$1,050**
   Serbian Orthodox Church .... $1,050 Indiv

Unknown $54,726

   Homemakers/Non-income earners $6,450
   No Employer Listed or Found $41,976
   Generic Occupation/Category Unknown $2,100
   Employer Listed/Category Unknown $4,200
      Crimson Corp .... $1,000 Indiv

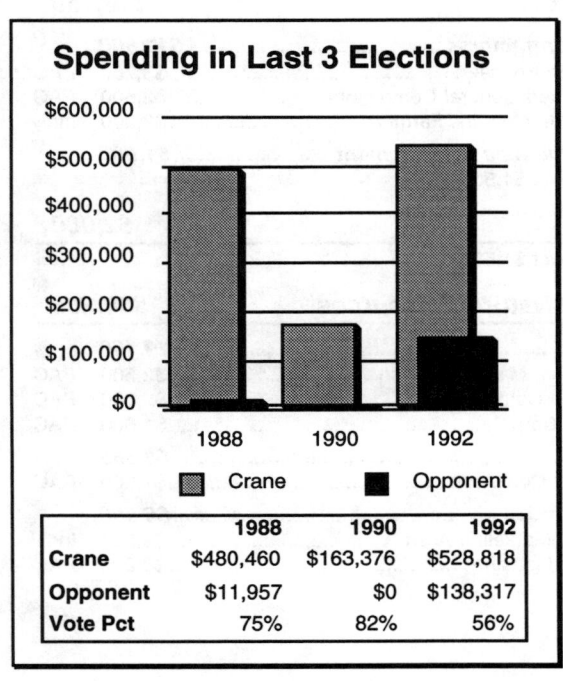

Spending in Last 3 Elections

	1988	1990	1992
Crane	$480,460	$163,376	$528,818
Opponent	$11,957	$0	$138,317
Vote Pct	75%	82%	56%

* Contributions came from more than one affiliate or subsidiary.

Michael D. Crapo, R-Idaho (2)

1993-94 Committees & Subcommittees

Energy and Commerce
Energy and Power; Transportation and Hazardous Materials

Leading Contributors

Business

Agriculture $91,400

Crop Production & Basic Processing **$12,550**
Amalgamated Sugar Co ....$2,000 PAC
Walker Farms ....$2,000 Indiv

Tobacco **$3,500**
RJR Nabisco .... $2,000 PAC

Dairy **$2,000**
None over $1,500

Livestock **$5,900**
National Cattlemen's Assn ....$1,500 PAC

Agricultural Services/Products **$2,250**
None over $1,500

Food Processing & Sales **$38,750**
Albertson's Inc .... $8,900 Indiv
King B Jerky .... $8,000 Indiv
JR Simplot Co .... $6,200 PAC/Ind
Ampco Foods Inc .... $2,500 PAC
Flowers Industries .... $2,000 PAC
Food Marketing Institute ....$1,500 PAC
Waremart Inc .... $1,500 Indiv
Winn-Dixie Stores .... $1,500 PAC

Forestry & Forest Products **$21,700**
Boise Cascade .... $9,000 PAC/Ind
Potlatch Corp .... $5,250 PAC/Ind
Bennett Lumber Products ....$2,000 Indiv

Misc Agriculture **$4,750**
None over $1,500

Source of Funds in 1992 Election

Source	Total	Pct
PACs	$226,899	40%
Indivs $200+	$149,771	26%
Indivs under $200	$121,237	21%
Other	$67,232	12%
Candidate	$20,193	4%
Party	$36,000	6%

Source of PAC Dollars by Sector

Source	Total	Pct
Business	$208,053	92%
Labor	$0	0%
Ideology/Single Issue	$19,268	8%

In-State vs. Out-of-State Contributions*

Source	Total	Pct
In-State	$134,711	91%
Out-of-state	$14,035	9%
No state listed	$1,000	

by large individual contributors ($200 & above)

Communications/Electronics $16,623

Printing & Publishing **$2,873**
Pioneer Newspapers Inc ....$2,373 Indiv

Telephone Utilities **$8,250**
US West Inc .... $4,250 PAC/Ind

Telecom Services & Equipment **$2,000**
Boston Technology .... $2,000 Indiv

Electronics Mfg & Services **$1,750**
None over $1,500

Construction $16,150

General Contractors **$11,500**
Morrison-Knudsen .... $3,750 PAC/Ind
Associated General Contractors .... $2,500 PAC
HK Contractors Inc/Farmer .... $2,000 Indiv

Building Materials & Equipment **$1,900**
None over $1,500

Defense $2,000
None over $1,500

Energy & Natural Resources $39,258

Oil & Gas **$19,100**
Petroleum Marketers Assn ....$2,500 PAC
Chevron Corp .... $2,000 PAC
Amoco Corp .... $1,500 PAC

Mining **$4,658**
National Coal Assn .... $1,500 PAC

Misc Energy **$6,500**
Ethanol Marketing Assn .... $3,500 Indiv
Cooper Industries .... $3,000 PAC

Contribution Totals by Sector

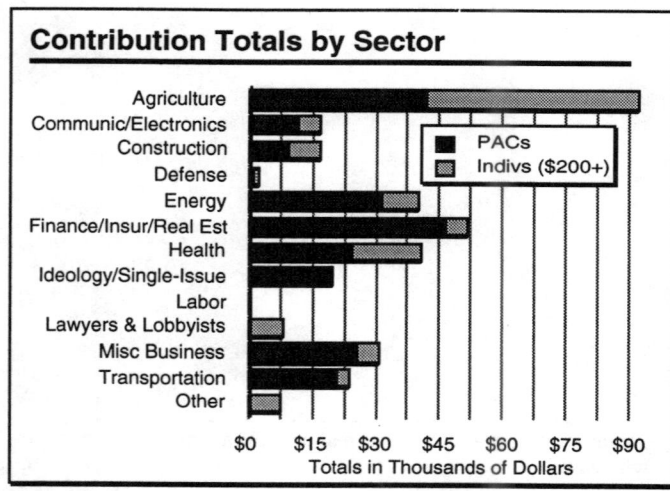

Agriculture
Communic/Electronics
Construction
Defense
Energy
Finance/Insur/Real Est
Health
Ideology/Single-Issue
Labor
Lawyers & Lobbyists
Misc Business
Transportation
Other

- PACs
- Indivs ($200+)

$0 $15 $30 $45 $60 $75 $90
Totals in Thousands of Dollars

Electric Utilities **$7,500**
    Idaho Power Co .... $4,650   PAC
    ACRE (Action Cmte for Rural Electrification) .... $1,750   PAC
Waste Management **$1,500**
    None over $1,500

Finance, Insurance & Real Estate $51,250

Commercial Banks **$13,750**
    American Bankers Assn* .... $10,500   PAC
    West One Bancorp .... $2,000   PAC
Insurance **$13,500**
    National Assn of Life Underwriters .... $6,500   PAC
Real Estate **$11,150**
    National Assn of Realtors .... $10,000   PAC
Accountants **$10,000**
    American Institute of CPA's .... $9,000   PAC

Health $40,096

Health Professionals **$33,296**
    American Medical Assn .... $9,546   PAC
    American Dental Assn .... $5,000   PAC
    American Academy of Ophthalmology .... $3,000   PAC
Hospitals/Nursing Homes **$2,800**
    None over $1,500
Pharmaceuticals/Health Products **$4,000**
    Melaleuca .... $2,000   Indiv

Lawyers & Lobbyists $8,560

Lawyers & Lobbyists **$8,560**
    Davis, Wright et al .... $1,850   Indiv
    Givens, Pursley et al .... $1,625   Indiv

Misc Business   **$30,107**

Business Associations **$3,206**
    National Fedn of Independent Business .... $2,000   PAC
Food & Beverage **$3,000**
    National Restaurant Assn .... $2,000   PAC
Beer, Wine & Liquor **$2,500**
    National Beer Wholesalers Assn .... $2,000   PAC
Retail Sales **$6,350**
    Lucero & Associates Inc .... $4,000   Indiv
Chemical & Related Manufacturing **$5,750**
    FMC Corp .... $2,500   PAC
    Dow Chemical .... $1,750   PAC
Misc Manufacturing & Distributing **$6,750**
    Stone Container Corp .... $5,000   PAC

Transportation $23,276

Air Transport **$2,250**
    United Parcel Service .... $1,500   PAC
Automotive **$12,526**
    National Auto Dealers Assn .... $10,000   PAC
Trucking **$2,500**
    Andrus Distributing .... $2,000   Indiv
Railroads **$5,500**
    Union Pacific Corp .... $5,500   PAC/Ind

Ideological/Single-Issue

Ideological/Single-Issue   **$19,568**

Leadership PACs **$7,000**
    Campaign America (Bob Dole) .... $3,000   PAC
    Republican Leader's Fund (Bob Michel) .... $2,000   PAC
    Idaho Cmte for a Conservative Majority .... $1,500   PAC
Gun Rights/Gun Control **$4,950**
    National Rifle Assn .... $4,950   PAC
Misc Issues **$4,250**
    Right to Work PAC .... $3,250   PAC

Other & Unknown

Other   **$7,442**

Retired **$6,300**
    None over $1,500

Unknown   **$31,837**

    No Employer Listed or Found $9,425
    Employer Listed/Category Unknown $21,412
        Sure Tracks .... $4,000   Indiv
        Farm Land Develpment Co .... $3,000   Indiv

Independent expenditures supporting Crapo
    National Right to Life PAC $3,226

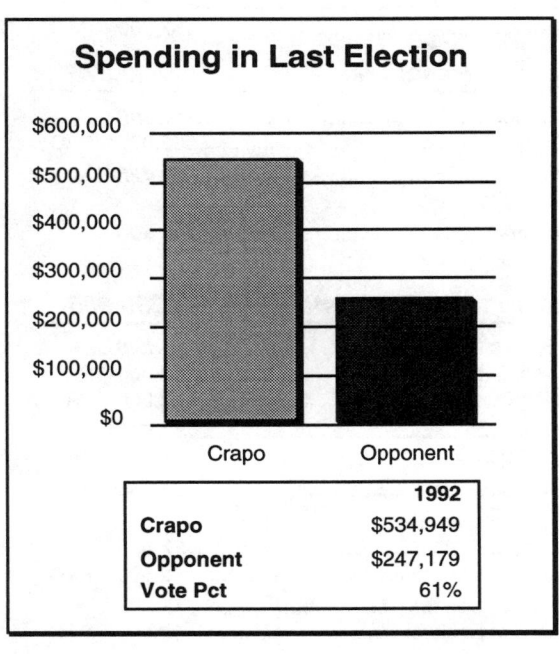

Spending in Last Election

	1992
Crapo	$534,949
Opponent	$247,179
Vote Pct	61%

* Contributions came from more than one affiliate or
  subsidiary.

Randy "Duke" Cunningham, R-Calif (51)

First elected: 1990

1991-92 Total Receipts: $907,606
1992 Year-end Cash: $19,196

1991-92 Committees & Subcommittees

Armed Services
Military Personnel and Compensation; Readiness; Research and Development

Education and Labor
Elementary, Secondary and Vocational Education; Select Education

Merchant Marine and Fisheries
Merchant Marine; Oversight and Investigations

Leading Contributors

Business

Agriculture	$16,700

Crop Production & Basic Processing $7,300
    None over $2,000

Tobacco $2,575
    None over $2,000

Livestock $2,900
    None over $2,000

Communications/Electronics	$18,225

Media/Entertainment $3,200
    None over $2,000

Telephone Utilities $2,650
    None over $2,000

Electronics Mfg & Services $5,000
    Titan Corp .... $3,200 Indiv

Computer Equipment & Services $5,375
    Questech Inc .... $3,225 Indiv

Construction	$20,850

General Contractors $11,050
    CE Wylie Construction Co .... $3,000 Indiv
    Associated General Contractors .... $2,500 PAC

Home Builders $2,250
    National Assn of Home Builders .... $2,000 PAC

Special Trade Contractors $3,250
    None over $2,000

Building Materials & Equipment $2,700
    None over $2,000

Source of Funds in 1992 Election

Source	Total	Pct
PACs	$260,441	29%
Indivs $200+	$242,472	27%
Indivs under $200	$370,484	41%
Other	$34,209	4%
Candidate	$0	0%
Party	$566	0%

Source of PAC Dollars by Sector

Source	Total	Pct
Business	$214,359	83%
Labor	$21,399	8%
Ideology/Single Issue	$22,575	9%

In-State vs. Out-of-State Contributions*

Source	Total	Pct
In-State	$186,522	78%
Out-of-state	$51,855	22%
No state listed	$500	

* by large individual contributors ($200 & above)

Defense	$68,455

Defense Aerospace $35,533
    General Dynamics .... $7,650 PAC/Ind
    Grumman Corp .... $4,550 PAC
    Sundstrand Corp .... $2,683 PAC
    Martin Marietta Corp .... $2,250 PAC
    Lockheed Corp .... $2,220 PAC
    Interlake Inc .... $2,050 PAC
    Northrop Corp .... $2,000 PAC

Defense Electronics $22,422
    Cubic Corp .... $7,947 PAC/Ind
    Hughes Aircraft .... $2,225 PAC

Misc Defense $10,500
    General Atomics .... $7,500 PAC

Energy & Natural Resources	$23,575

Oil & Gas $14,900
    Contran Corp .... $2,000 PAC

Electric Utilities $3,425
    None over $2,000

Waste Management $2,500
    None over $2,000

Finance, Insurance & Real Estate	$39,385

Commercial Banks $5,200
    American Bankers Assn .... $3,000 PAC
    BankAmerica Corp .... $2,200 PAC/Ind

Savings & Loans $2,525
    None over $2,000

Securities & Investment $2,600
    None over $2,000

Insurance $7,075
    National Assn of Life Underwriters .... $2,500 PAC

Real Estate $18,675
    National Assn of Realtors .... $9,225 PAC

Contribution Totals by Sector

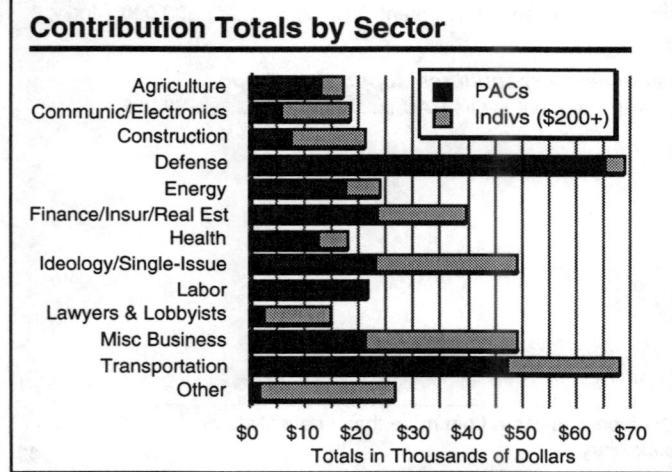

Agriculture
Communic/Electronics
Construction
Defense
Energy
Finance/Insur/Real Est
Health
Ideology/Single-Issue
Labor
Lawyers & Lobbyists
Misc Business
Transportation
Other

■ PACs
▨ Indivs ($200+)

$0 $10 $20 $30 $40 $50 $60 $70
Totals in Thousands of Dollars

Health $17,670

Health Professionals $14,195
    American Medical Assn .... $3,850 PAC
    American Dental Assn .... $2,725 PAC

Health Services $2,000
    None over $2,000

Lawyers & Lobbyists $14,775

Lawyers & Lobbyists $14,775
    None over $1,500

Misc Business $48,764

Business Associations $3,900
    Golden Eagle Club of San Diego County .... $2,900 PAC

Food & Beverage $6,214
    National Restaurant Assn .... $3,000 PAC

Beer, Wine & Liquor $4,500
    National Beer Wholesalers Assn .... $4,000 PAC

Retail Sales $6,100
    None over $2,000

Business Services $5,150
    Bob Baker Enterprises .... $2,500 Indiv

Lodging/Tourism $3,400
    None over $2,000

Steel Production $2,500
    Fontana Steel .... $2,000 Indiv

Misc Manufacturing & Distributing $9,850
    Mountain High Knitting .... $2,000 Indiv

Textiles $5,000
    Milliken & Co .... $5,000 Indiv

Transportation $67,719

Air Transport $15,345
    Aircraft Owners & Pilots Assn .... $5,500 PAC
    United Parcel Service .... $3,725 PAC
    North American Airlines .... $2,920 Indiv

Automotive $16,150
    National Auto Dealers Assn .... $9,000 PAC
    Auto Dealers & Drivers for Free Trade .... $2,000 PAC

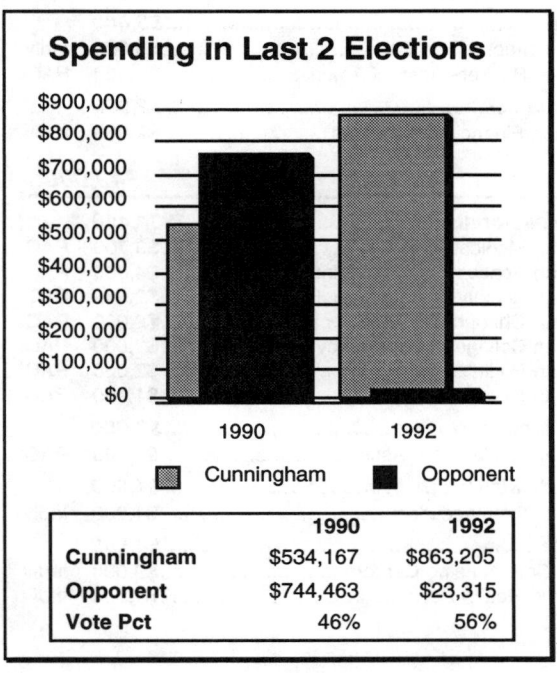

Spending in Last 2 Elections

	1990	1992
Cunningham	$534,167	$863,205
Opponent	$744,463	$23,315
Vote Pct	46%	56%

Legend: Cunningham, Opponent

Sea Transport $30,424
    National Steel & Shipbuilding .... $8,784 PAC
    Southwest Marine .... $6,300 PAC
    Continental Maritime .... $3,890 Indiv
    Atlantic Marine/Atlantic Dry Dock .... $2,450 PAC
    Maersk Inc .... $2,050 PAC

Misc Transport $5,000
    Alessio's Limousine .... $4,000 Indiv

Labor

Labor $21,399

Transportation Unions $18,024
    Seafarers International Union .... $9,000 PAC
    Marine Engineers Union* .... $8,524 PAC

Public Sector Unions $3,150
    National Assn Retired Federal Employees .... $2,750 PAC

Ideological/Single-Issue

Ideological/Single-Issue $48,743

Republican/Conservative $22,643
    None over $2,000

Foreign & Defense Policy $3,600
    Veterans of Foreign Wars .... $2,800 PAC

Pro-Israel $7,650
    None over $2,000

Gun Rights/Gun Control $11,900
    National Rifle Assn .... $9,900 PAC
    Safari Club International .... $2,000 PAC

Misc Issues $2,950
    None over $2,000

Other & Unknown

Other $27,020

Education $2,625
    None over $2,000

Retired $21,250
    None over $2,000

Unknown $65,655

    Homemakers/Non-income earners $7,045
    No Employer Listed or Found $11,725
    Employer Listed/Category Unknown $45,385
        Science & Applied Technologies .... $10,100 Indiv
        California West .... $2,000 Indiv

---

* Contributions came from more than one affiliate or
subsidiary.

Pat Danner, D-Mo (6)

1993-94 Committees & Subcommittees

Public Works and Transportation
Aviation; Economic Development; Surface Transportation

Small Business
Rural Enterprises, Exports and the Environment

First elected: 1992

1991-92 Total Receipts: $417,277
1992 Year-end Cash: $3,291

Leading Contributors

Business

Agriculture	$14,660

Crop Production & Basic Processing $3,410
    None over $1,000
Dairy $10,000
    Mid-America Dairymen .... $10,000   PAC

Communications/Electronics	$6,379

Printing & Publishing $4,379
    Tinnen Publishing .... $1,629   Indiv
    St Joseph News Press & Gazette .... $1,000   Indiv
Telephone Utilities $2,000
    AT&T .... $1,000   PAC
    Southwestern Bell .... $1,000   PAC

Construction	$3,679

General Contractors $2,300
    Heavy Constructors Assn .... $1,500   PAC
Building Materials & Equipment $1,379
    E&M Precast .... $1,129   Indiv

Energy & Natural Resources	$5,500

Oil & Gas $4,000
    Ashland Oil .... $2,000   PAC
    Phillips Petroleum .... $1,500   PAC
Electric Utilities $1,500
    ACRE (Action Cmte for Rural Electrification)* ..... $1,500   PAC

Source of Funds in 1992 Election

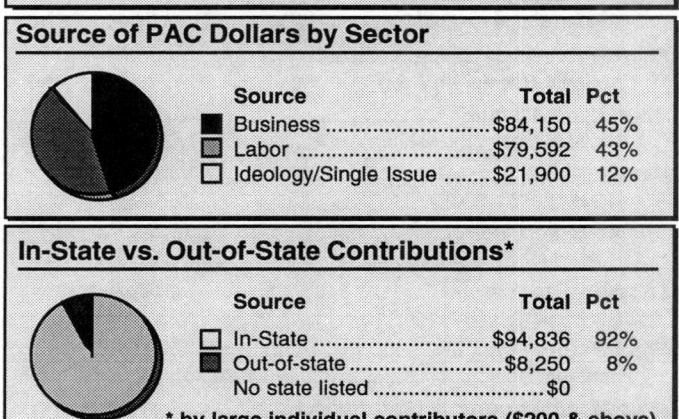

Source	Total	Pct
■ PACs	$183,992	41%
▨ Indivs $200+	$103,086	23%
□ Indivs under $200	$46,823	10%
▨ Other	$112,998	25%
Candidate	$64,800	14%
Party	$35,122	8%

Source of PAC Dollars by Sector

Source	Total	Pct
■ Business	$84,150	45%
▨ Labor	$79,592	43%
□ Ideology/Single Issue	$21,900	12%

In-State vs. Out-of-State Contributions*

Source	Total	Pct
□ In-State	$94,836	92%
■ Out-of-state	$8,250	8%
No state listed	$0	

* by large individual contributors ($200 & above)

Finance, Insurance & Real Estate	$24,250

Commercial Banks $4,550
    American Bankers Assn* .... $3,000   PAC
Credit Unions $1,550
    Credit Union National Assn .... $1,000   PAC
Finance/Credit Companies $1,750
    Household International Inc .... $1,500   PAC
Insurance $4,150
    General American Life Insurance .... $1,500   PAC
    New York Life Insurance .... $1,000   Indiv
Real Estate $8,800
    Hall's Abstract & Title Co .... $3,250   Indiv
    Mortgage Bankers Assn of America .... $1,000   PAC
Misc Finance $2,000
    Dickinson Financial Resources .... $2,000   Indiv

Health	$43,000

Health Professionals $34,450
    American Medical Assn .... $9,700   PAC
    American Academy of Ophthalmology ...... $4,000   PAC
    American Society of Anesthesiologists ..... $2,500   PAC
    American Chiropractic Assn .... $2,000   PAC
    American College of Emergency Physicians .... $2,000   PAC
    American Podiatry Assn .... $2,000   PAC
    American Psychiatric Assn .... $1,000   PAC
Hospitals/Nursing Homes $3,050
    American Health Care Assn .... $1,000   PAC
Pharmaceuticals/Health Products $1,000
    Phoenix Pharmaceutical .... $1,000   Indiv
Misc Health $4,500
    Tiffany Care Nursing Centers .... $3,000   Indiv
    Heartland Health Services .... $1,500   Indiv

Contribution Totals by Sector

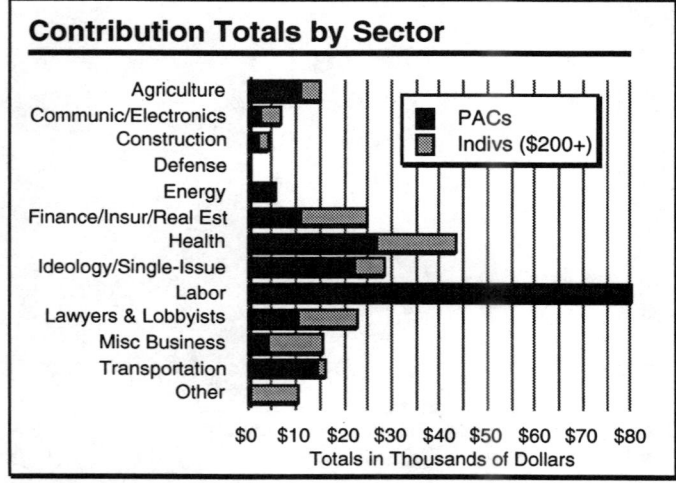

Agriculture, Communic/Electronics, Construction, Defense, Energy, Finance/Insur/Real Est, Health, Ideology/Single-Issue, Labor, Lawyers & Lobbyists, Misc Business, Transportation, Other

■ PACs
▨ Indivs ($200+)

$0 $10 $20 $30 $40 $50 $60 $70 $80
Totals in Thousands of Dollars

Lawyers & Lobbyists $22,250

Lawyers & Lobbyists $22,250
Assn of Trial Lawyers of America	$10,000	PAC
Armstrong, Teasdale et al	$1,000	Indiv
Robb & Robb	$1,000	Indiv

Misc Business $15,150

Food & Beverage $1,250
None over $1,000

Beer, Wine & Liquor $4,000
Bay Distributors	$2,000	Indiv
National Beer Wholesalers Assn	$1,500	PAC

Retail Sales $2,000
Eckard's Home Improvement	$1,000	Indiv

Misc Services $4,150
None over $1,000

Lodging/Tourism $1,000
Shamrock Motel	$1,000	Indiv

Misc Business $2,000
Artesian Ice & Cold Storage	$1,500	Indiv

Transportation $15,550

Automotive $10,300
National Auto Dealers Assn	$10,000	PAC

Trucking $4,500
American Trucking Assns	$1,500	PAC
Consolidated Freightways	$1,000	PAC
Slay Transportation Co	$1,000	Indiv

Labor

Labor $79,842

Building Trade Unions $14,350
Carpenters & Joiners Union	$10,000	PAC
Plumbers/Pipefitters Union*	$2,500	PAC
Laborers' Political League	$1,500	PAC

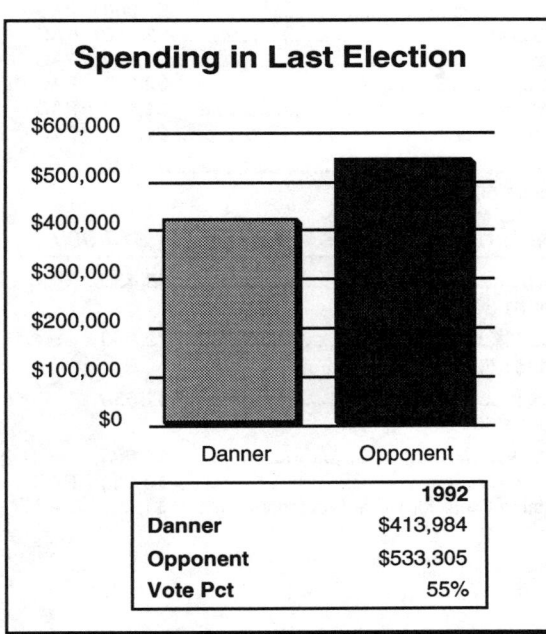

Spending in Last Election

	1992
Danner	$413,984
Opponent	$533,305
Vote Pct	55%

Industrial Unions $25,142
Machinists/Aerospace Workers Union*	$5,000	PAC
United Auto Workers	$5,000	PAC
United Mine Workers	$5,000	PAC
Intl Brotherhood of Electrical Workers	$4,000	PAC
Communications Workers of America	$2,142	PAC
United Steelworkers	$2,000	PAC
United Paperworkers	$1,000	PAC

Transportation Unions $20,550
Brotherhood of Locomotive Engineers	$7,800	PAC
Teamsters Union	$5,000	PAC
United Transportation Union	$3,000	PAC
Marine Engineers Union	$2,000	PAC
Seafarers International Union	$1,000	PAC

Public Sector Unions $13,800
National Education Assn	$5,000	PAC
American Fedn of St/Cnty/Munic Employees	$2,500	PAC
National Assn of Letter Carriers	$2,500	PAC
National Assn Retired Federal Employees	$2,000	PAC
International Assn of Firefighters	$1,500	PAC

Misc Unions $6,000
AFL-CIO	$4,500	PAC
Service Employees International Union	$1,000	PAC

Ideological/Single-Issue

Ideological/Single-Issue $28,600

Leadership PACs $4,000
Effective Government Cmte (Dick Gephardt)	$2,000	PAC
America's Leaders' Fund (Dan Rostenkowski)	$1,000	PAC
House Leadership Fund (Tom Foley)	$1,000	PAC

Pro-Israel $2,500
Chai PAC	$1,000	PAC
St Louisians for Better Government	$1,000	PAC

Gun Rights/Gun Control $9,900
National Rifle Assn	$9,900	PAC

Womens Issues $11,700
Women's Campaign Fund	$5,000	PAC

Other & Unknown

Other $10,000

Education $2,750
Proprietary School	$1,000	Indiv

Retired $6,250
None over $1,000

Other $1,000
None over $1,000

Unknown $19,868

No Employer Listed or Found	$1,450	
Generic Occupation/Category Unknown	$8,888	
Employer Listed/Category Unknown	$9,530	
John Lutjen & Assoc	$1,500	Indiv
Albert Joseph Investment Co	$1,000	Indiv
Jas B Nutter Co	$1,000	Indiv
Telephone Contact Inc	$1,000	Indiv

Independent expenditures supporting Danner
National Rifle Assn	$25,890	

---

* Contributions came from more than one affiliate or subsidiary.

George "Buddy" Darden, D-Ga (7)

First elected: 1983	
1991-92 Total Receipts:	$410,958
1992 Year-end Cash:	$650

1991-92 Committees & Subcommittees

Armed Services
Investigations; Research and Development

Interior and Insular Affairs
Energy and the Environment; Insular and International Affairs; National Parks and Public Lands

Standards of Official Conduct

Leading Contributors

Business

Agriculture	$26,550

Crop Production & Basic Processing	**$5,550**	
None over $1,500		
Tobacco	**$3,500**	
RJR Nabisco	$1,500	PAC
Dairy	**$2,500**	
Dairymen Inc-Georgia	$2,000	PAC
Poultry & Eggs	**$4,750**	
None over $1,500		
Agricultural Services/Products	**$1,500**	
None over $1,500		
Food Processing & Sales	**$5,500**	
Food Marketing Institute	$1,500	PAC
Forestry & Forest Products	**$2,750**	
None over $1,500		

Communications/Electronics	$10,300

Telephone Utilities	**$8,500**	
Southern Bell	$7,500	PAC
Computer Equipment & Services	**$1,500**	
None over $1,500		

Construction	$8,500

General Contractors	**$3,250**	
None over $1,500		
Home Builders	**$2,500**	
National Assn of Home Builders	$2,500	PAC

Source of Funds in 1992 Election

Source	Total	Pct
PACs	$225,940	55%
Indivs $200+	$92,185	22%
Indivs under $200	$70,355	17%
Other	$23,438	6%
Candidate	$0	0%
Party	$1,610	0%

Source of PAC Dollars by Sector

Source	Total	Pct
Business	$185,775	83%
Labor	$33,390	15%
Ideology/Single Issue	$5,250	2%

In-State vs. Out-of-State Contributions*

Source	Total	Pct
In-State	$79,735	87%
Out-of-state	$12,000	13%
No state listed	$0	

* by large individual contributors ($200 & above)

Defense — $44,200

Defense Aerospace	**$24,950**	
Lockheed Corp	$5,000	PAC
Rockwell International	$3,450	PAC/Ind
Textron Inc	$2,500	PAC
Boeing Co	$2,000	PAC
General Electric	$1,500	PAC
Grumman Corp	$1,500	PAC
Martin Marietta Corp	$1,500	PAC
McDonnell Douglas*	$1,500	PAC
United Technologies	$1,500	PAC
Defense Electronics	**$17,750**	
Diagnostic Retrieval Systems	$3,000	Indiv
AT&T	$2,000	PAC
Hughes Aircraft	$2,000	PAC
Loral Corp	$2,000	PAC
Raytheon	$2,000	PAC
E-Systems Inc	$1,500	PAC
Texas Instruments	$1,500	PAC
Misc Defense	**$1,500**	
None over $1,500		

Energy & Natural Resources — $19,900

Oil & Gas	**$8,450**	
None over $1,500		
Mining	**$2,850**	
None over $1,500		
Nuclear Energy	**$1,550**	
None over $1,500		
Electric Utilities	**$6,300**	
Southern Co*	$3,000	PAC
ACRE (Action Cmte for Rural Electrification)	$1,500	PAC

Contribution Totals by Sector

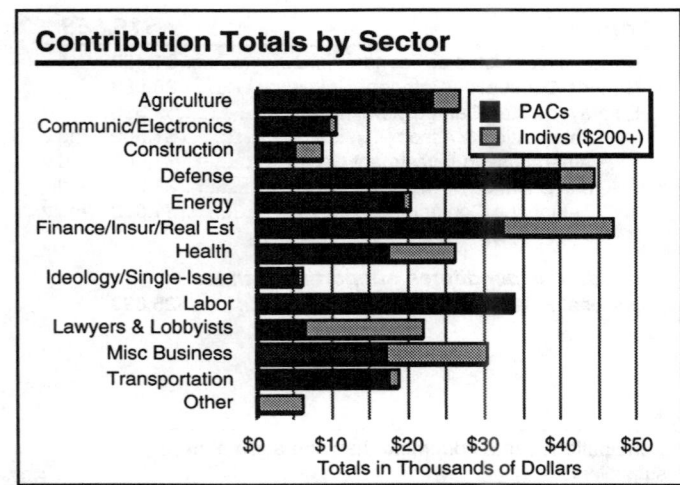

Agriculture
Communic/Electronics
Construction
Defense
Energy
Finance/Insur/Real Est
Health
Ideology/Single-Issue
Labor
Lawyers & Lobbyists
Misc Business
Transportation
Other

■ PACs
▨ Indivs ($200+)

$0 $10 $20 $30 $40 $50
Totals in Thousands of Dollars

Finance, Insurance & Real Estate $46,575

Commercial Banks **$17,625**
    Citizens & Southern National Bank ....$4,000   PAC
    Barnett Banks Inc ....$3,500   PAC
    American Bankers Assn* ....$2,500   PAC
    Bank South Corp ....$2,000   PAC
    Trust Co of Georgia ....$1,875   PAC
    Independent Bankers Assn ....$1,500   PAC

Finance/Credit Companies **$1,500**
    Nationwide Credit ....$1,500   Indiv

Securities & Investment **$1,500**
    None over $1,500

Insurance **$12,600**
    American Family Corp ....$4,500   PAC
    Georgia US Corp ....$1,500   PAC

Real Estate **$11,600**
    National Assn of Realtors ....$6,000   PAC
    Post Properties Inc ....$3,000   Indiv

Health $25,725

Health Professionals **$20,475**
    American Medical Assn ....$10,000   PAC
    American Chiropractic Assn ....$2,000   PAC

Hospitals/Nursing Homes **$2,000**
    None over $1,500

Health Services **$2,750**
    Central Health Services ....$1,500   Indiv

Lawyers & Lobbyists $21,900

Lawyers & Lobbyists **$21,900**
    King & Spalding ....$3,000   PAC
    Kilpatrick & Cody ....$2,050   Indiv
    Hicks, Maloof & Campbell ....$1,500   Indiv
    Troutman, Sanders et al ....$1,500   Indiv

Misc Business $30,100

Food & Beverage **$7,500**
    Coca-Cola Co ....$4,000   PAC/Ind
    National Restaurant Assn ....$1,500   PAC

Beer, Wine & Liquor **$6,250**
    National Beer Wholesalers Assn ....$3,500   PAC

Retail Sales **$1,750**
    None over $1,500

Misc Manufacturing & Distributing **$8,400**
    Rock-Tenn Co ....$5,000   Indiv

Textiles **$1,750**
    None over $1,500

Transportation $18,300

Air Transport **$5,500**
    United Parcel Service ....$4,000   PAC

Automotive **$5,500**
    National Auto Dealers Assn ....$5,000   PAC

Trucking **$4,500**
    Watkins Associated Industries ....$3,000   PAC

Railroads **$2,000**
    Norfolk Southern Corp ....$1,500   PAC

Labor

Labor $33,390

Industrial Unions **$19,000**
    United Auto Workers ....$6,000   PAC
    Communications Workers of America ....$5,000   PAC
    Machinists/Aerospace Workers Union ....$5,000   PAC
    Electronic Machine Furniture Workers ....$2,000   PAC

Transportation Unions **$6,500**
    Marine Engineers Dist 2 Maritime Officers ....$3,000   PAC
    Air Line Pilots Assn ....$2,500   PAC

Public Sector Unions **$6,000**
    National Assn Retired Federal Employees ....$3,000   PAC

Misc Unions **$1,890**
    Hotel/Restaurant Employees Union ....$1,890   PAC

Ideological/Single-Issue

Ideological/Single-Issue $5,750

Gun Rights/Gun Control **$2,000**
    National Rifle Assn ....$2,000   PAC

Misc Issues **$2,750**
    National Cmte to Preserve Social Security ....$2,750   PAC

Other & Unknown

Other $6,000

Education **$1,500**
    None over $1,500

Retired **$4,500**
    None over $1,500

Unknown $19,410

    Homemakers/Non-income earners $4,200
    Employer Listed/Category Unknown $14,010
        Cousins & Lipson ....$1,500   Indiv
        Newcomb & Boyd ....$1,500   Indiv

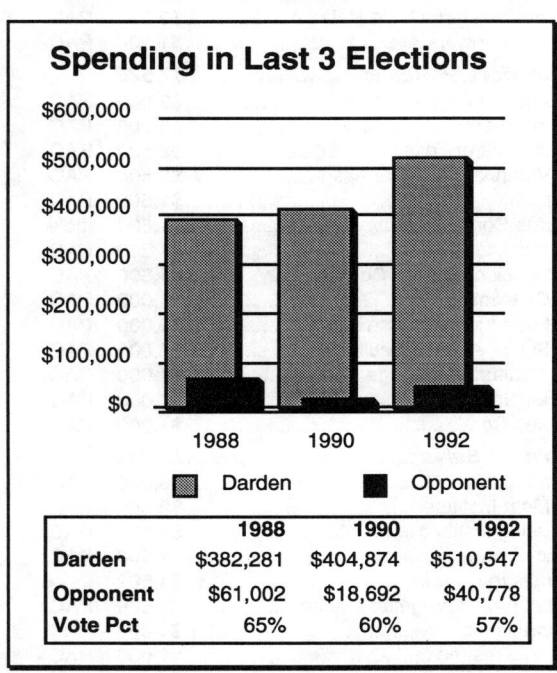

Spending in Last 3 Elections

	1988	1990	1992
Darden	$382,281	$404,874	$510,547
Opponent	$61,002	$18,692	$40,778
Vote Pct	65%	60%	57%

---

* Contributions came from more than one affiliate or subsidiary.

E. "Kika" de la Garza, D-Texas (15)

First elected: 1964

1991-92 Total Receipts:	$248,430
1992 Year-end Cash:	$118,307

1991-92 Committees & Subcommittees

Agriculture (Chairman)

Leading Contributors

Business

Agriculture	$145,099	

Crop Production & Basic Processing	$58,579	
National Cotton Council	$4,500	PAC
American Crystal Sugar Corp	$4,000	PAC
American Sugarbeet Growers Assn	$3,500	PAC
Florida Sugar Cane League	$3,500	PAC
Riceland Foods	$3,000	PAC/Ind
Desert Grape Growers League/California	$2,000	PAC
Sunkist Growers	$2,000	PAC
Texas Sugar Beet Growers Assn	$2,000	PAC
Texas Rice Producers Legislative Group	$1,989	PAC
Farmers' Rice Cooperative	$1,750	PAC
American Cotton Shippers Assn	$1,500	PAC
Minn-Dak Farmers Co-op	$1,500	PAC
Rio Grande Valley Sugar Growers	$1,500	PAC/Ind
Southern Minn Beet Sugar Co-op	$1,500	PAC
American Sugar Cane League	$1,000	PAC
Calcot Ltd	$1,000	PAC
Cargill Inc	$1,000	PAC
Imperial Holly Corp	$1,000	Indiv
Richard Peters Farms	$1,000	Indiv
Savannah Foods & Industries	$1,000	PAC
Sugar Cane Growers Co-op of Florida	$1,000	PAC
US Beet Sugar Assn	$1,000	PAC
US Cane Sugar Refiners Assn	$1,000	Indiv
United States Sugar Corp	$1,000	PAC
Western Growers Assn	$1,000	PAC
Western Peanut Growers Assn	$1,000	PAC

Tobacco	$3,500	
Philip Morris	$2,000	PAC
US Tobacco Co	$1,000	PAC

Contribution Totals by Sector

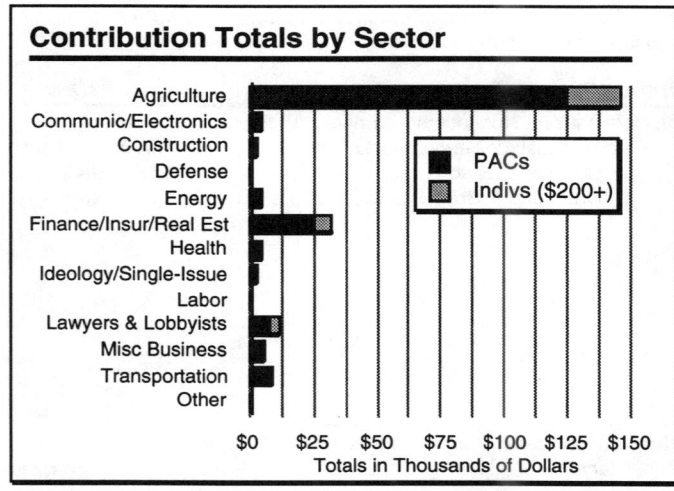

Agriculture
Communic/Electronics
Construction
Defense
Energy
Finance/Insur/Real Est
Health
Ideology/Single-Issue
Labor
Lawyers & Lobbyists
Misc Business
Transportation
Other

■ PACs
▨ Indivs ($200+)

$0 $25 $50 $75 $100 $125 $150
Totals in Thousands of Dollars

Source of Funds in 1992 Election

Source	Total	Pct
■ PACs	$184,825	73%
▨ Indivs $200+	$35,037	14%
☐ Indivs under $200	$26,545	10%
⊠ Other	$8,409	3%
Candidate	$742	0%
Party	$6,386	3%

Source of PAC Dollars by Sector

Source	Total	Pct
■ Business	$183,917	99%
▨ Labor	$0	0%
☐ Ideology/Single Issue	$2,000	1%

In-State vs. Out-of-State Contributions*

Source	Total	Pct
☐ In-State	$22,147	65%
■ Out-of-state	$11,890	35%
No state listed	$0	

* by large individual contributors ($200 & above)

Dairy	$4,000	
Associated Milk Producers	$1,000	PAC
Dairymen Inc	$1,000	PAC
Mid-America Dairymen	$1,000	PAC
Milk Industry Foundation	$1,000	PAC

Poultry & Eggs	$9,000	
National Turkey Federation	$3,000	PAC
National Broiler Council	$2,000	PAC
Pilgrim's Pride Co	$2,000	Indiv
United Egg Assn	$2,000	PAC

Livestock	$13,250	
National Cattlemen's Assn*	$6,000	PAC
Texas & Southwestern Cattle Raisers	$2,500	PAC
National Wool Growers Assn	$1,500	PAC

Agricultural Services/Products	$37,670	
American Assn of Crop Insurers	$9,000	PAC
Texas Farm Bureau	$5,000	PAC
Farm Credit Bank of Texas	$2,520	PAC
American Veterinary Medical Assn	$2,500	PAC
Dow Chemical	$1,500	PAC
Louis-Dreyfus Corp	$1,500	Indiv
Monsanto Co	$1,500	PAC
National Council of Farmer Co-ops	$1,500	PAC
American Cyanimid	$1,000	PAC
American Feed Industry Assn	$1,000	PAC
American Soc of Agric Consultants	$1,000	PAC
Federal Agricultural Mortgage Corp	$1,000	PAC
Land O'Lakes Inc	$1,000	PAC
Rohm & Haas Co	$1,000	PAC

Food Processing & Sales	$18,600	
ConAgra Inc	$6,000	PAC
American Meat Institute	$2,500	PAC
Food Marketing Institute	$2,500	PAC
Pepsico Inc	$2,000	PAC
Beef Products Inc	$1,500	Indiv
United Fresh Fruit & Vegetable Assn	$1,500	PAC
Nabisco Brands Inc	$1,000	PAC
Nestle Enterprises Inc	$1,000	PAC

Communications/Electronics $4,500

Telephone Utilities **$4,000**
    GTE Corp ....$1,500   PAC
    Southwestern Bell ....$1,500   PAC

Construction $2,750

General Contractors **$1,500**
    Associated General Contractors ....$1,500   PAC

Energy & Natural Resources $4,000

Oil & Gas **$2,000**
    Coastal Corp ....$1,000   PAC
Electric Utilities **$2,000**
    ACRE (Action Cmte for Rural Electrification) ....$1,000   PAC
    Central Power & Light ....$1,000   PAC

Finance, Insurance & Real Estate $31,055

Commercial Banks **$16,555**
    American Bankers Assn ....$5,000   PAC
    Texas Bancshares ....$4,947   Indiv
    Independent Bankers Assn ....$1,058   PAC
    Bankers Trust ....$1,000   PAC
    Chemical Bank ....$1,000   PAC
    JP Morgan & Co ....$1,000   PAC
Securities & Investment **$14,000**
    Chicago Mercantile Exchange ....$10,000   PAC
    New York Mercantile Exchange ....$1,500   PAC
    Chicago Board of Trade ....$1,000   PAC

Health $4,500

Health Professionals **$2,000**
    American Medical Assn......................$2,000   PAC
Pharmaceuticals/Health Products **$2,500**
    None over $1,000

Lawyers & Lobbyists $11,000

Lawyers & Lobbyists **$11,000**
    Assn of Trial Lawyers of America ....$5,000   PAC
    Hogan & Hartson ....$1,500   PAC/Ind
    Hopkins & Sutter ....$1,500   PAC
    Meyers & Associates ....$1,500   Indiv

Misc Business $5,000

Business Associations **$1,000**
    National Cooperative Business Assn ...$1,000   PAC
Beer, Wine & Liquor **$1,000**
    Smirnoff/Inglenook Distributors ....$1,000   PAC
Misc Services **$1,000**
    National Pest Control Assn ....$1,000   PAC
Chemical & Related Manufacturing **$1,500**
    Chemical Specialties Manufacturers Assn ....$1,000   PAC

Transportation $8,500

Air Transport **$1,500**
    Texas Air ....$1,000   PAC
Automotive **$6,500**
    National Auto Dealers Assn ....$6,500   PAC

Ideological/Single-Issue

Ideological/Single-Issue $2,000

Leadership PACs **$1,000**
    House Leadership Fund (Tom Foley) ....$1,000   PAC
Gun Rights/Gun Control **$1,000**
    National Rifle Assn ....$1,000   PAC

Other & Unknown

Unknown $1,550

    Employer Listed/Category Unknown $2,550
        Rice, Miller ....$1,000   Indiv

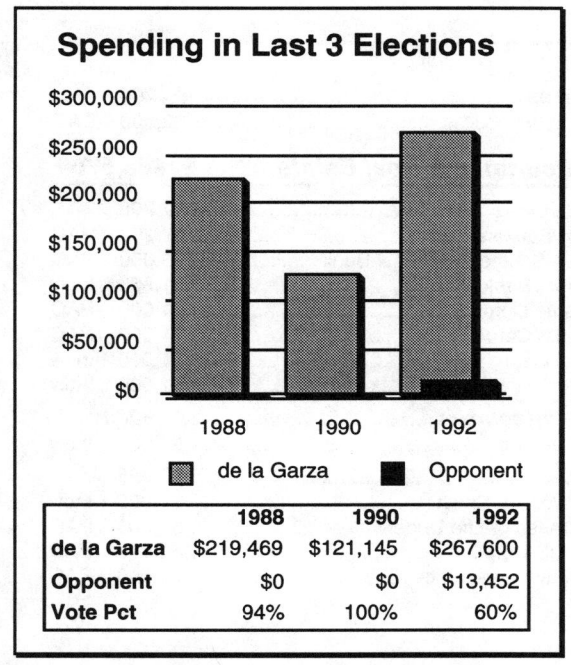

Spending in Last 3 Elections

	1988	1990	1992
de la Garza	$219,469	$121,145	$267,600
Opponent	$0	$0	$13,452
Vote Pct	94%	100%	60%

---

* Contributions came from more than one affiliate or subsidiary.

549

Nathan Deal, D-Ga (9)

1993-94 Committees & Subcommittees

Natural Resources
Energy and Mineral Resources; Oversight and Investigations

Public Works and Transportation
Economic Development; Water Resources and the Environment

Science, Space and Technology
Technology, Environment and Aviation

Leading Contributors

Business

Agriculture	$27,250	
Crop Production & Basic Processing	**$2,800**	
Cargill Inc	$1,000	PAC
Continental Grain	$1,000	PAC
Tobacco	**$1,000**	
None over $1,000		
Dairy	**$1,500**	
Dairymen Inc-Georgia	$1,000	PAC
Poultry & Eggs	**$10,050**	
Fieldale Farms Corp	$4,250	Indiv
Gold Kist	$2,500	PAC
National Broiler Council	$1,500	PAC
Livestock	**$2,000**	
National Cattlemen's Assn*	$1,500	PAC
Agricultural Services/Products	**$1,750**	
Hall County Farm Bureau	$1,250	Indiv
Food Processing & Sales	**$4,900**	
Fleming Companies Inc	$1,000	PAC
Winn-Dixie Stores	$1,000	PAC
Forestry & Forest Products	**$3,250**	
Georgia-Pacific Corp	$2,500	Indiv

Communications/Electronics	$6,750	
Printing & Publishing	**$3,000**	
Peeples Printing	$2,000	Indiv
Telephone Utilities	**$2,800**	
Southern Bell	$1,500	PAC
AT&T	$1,000	PAC

First elected: 1992

1991-92 Total Receipts:	$543,942
1992 Year-end Cash:	$1,461

Source of Funds in 1992 Election

Source	Total	Pct
■ PACs	$135,750	25%
▨ Indivs $200+	$134,084	25%
☐ Indivs under $200	$94,983	17%
⊠ Other	$179,125	33%
Candidate	$75,250	14%
Party	$5,150	1%

Source of PAC Dollars by Sector

Source	Total	Pct
■ Business	$119,500	84%
▥ Labor	$16,000	11%
☐ Ideology/Single Issue	$7,450	5%

In-State vs. Out-of-State Contributions*

Source	Total	Pct
☐ In-State	$131,434	98%
■ Out-of-state	$2,650	2%
No state listed	$0	

* by large individual contributors ($200 & above)

Construction	$3,100	
General Contractors	**$2,550**	
Associated General Contractors	$1,000	PAC

Energy & Natural Resources	$13,550	
Oil & Gas	**$8,100**	
Petroleum Marketers Assn	$1,350	PAC
Amoco Corp	$1,000	PAC
Atlanta Gas Light Co	$1,000	PAC
Mansfield Oil Co	$1,000	Indiv
North Georgia Petroleum	$1,000	Indiv
Phillips Petroleum	$1,000	PAC
Mining	**$1,500**	
None over $1,000		
Electric Utilities	**$3,200**	
Georgia Power Co	$2,500	PAC

Finance, Insurance & Real Estate	$48,575	
Commercial Banks	**$19,200**	
American Bankers Assn*	$7,200	PAC
Citizens & Southern National Bank	$3,000	PAC
Home Trust Bank	$1,600	Indiv
First Atlanta Corp	$1,500	PAC
Bank South Corp	$1,000	PAC
Northeast Georgia Bank	$1,000	Indiv
Rabun County Bank	$1,000	Indiv
Securities & Investment	**$1,500**	
Boring & Boring	$1,500	Indiv
Insurance	**$13,625**	
Turner, Wood & Smith	$4,000	Indiv
National Assn of Life Underwriters	$1,500	PAC
Georgia US Corp	$1,000	PAC
Liberty Mutual Insurance	$1,000	PAC

Contribution Totals by Sector

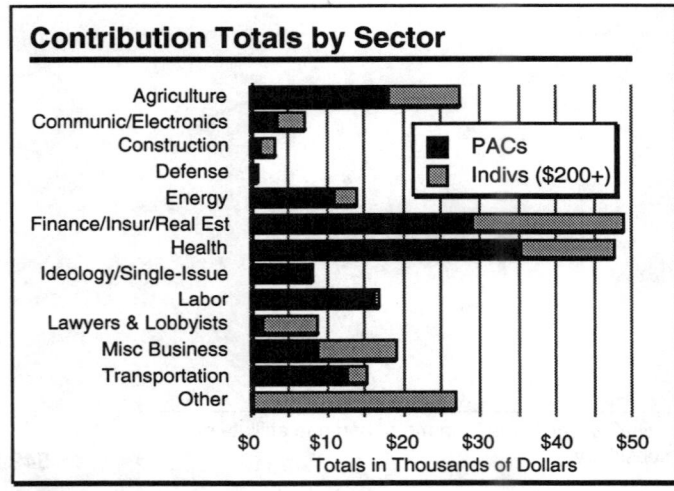

Agriculture
Communic/Electronics
Construction
Defense
Energy
Finance/Insur/Real Est
Health
Ideology/Single-Issue
Labor
Lawyers & Lobbyists
Misc Business
Transportation
Other

■ PACs
▨ Indivs ($200+)

$0 $10 $20 $30 $40 $50
Totals in Thousands of Dollars

Real Estate **$9,750**
    National Assn of Realtors .... $7,500 PAC
    Connolly Realty Service .... $1,000 Indiv

Misc Finance **$3,500**
    Gainesville Milling Co .... $3,500 Indiv

Health $47,250

Health Professionals **$34,750**
    American Medical Assn .... $14,700 PAC
    American Academy of Ophthalmology .... $6,000 PAC
    American Dental Assn .... $5,000 PAC
    American College of Emergency Physicians .... $2,000 PAC
    American Podiatry Assn .... $1,000 PAC

Hospitals/Nursing Homes **$5,750**
    Health Service Centers .... $2,000 Indiv
    American Hospital Assn .... $1,500 PAC

Health Services **$3,000**
    Gibson's Dental Design.............................. $2,000 Indiv
    Central Health Services .... $1,000 Indiv

Pharmaceuticals/Health Products **$2,000**
    Eli Lilly & Co .... $1,000 PAC
    Johnson & Johnson.................................. $1,000 PAC

Misc Health **$1,750**
    Tugaloo Home Health .... $1,250 Indiv

Lawyers & Lobbyists $8,368

Lawyers & Lobbyists **$8,368**
    King & Spalding .... $1,500 PAC/Ind

Misc Business $18,800

Food & Beverage **$3,250**
    Coca-Cola Co* .... $2,250 PAC
    Hardee's Food Systems .... $1,000 Indiv

Beer, Wine & Liquor **$2,250**
    National Beer Wholesalers Assn .... $1,000 PAC

Retail Sales **$4,550**
    Wayne Brothers Furniture .... $2,000 Indiv

Misc Manufacturing & Distributing **$6,000**
    Wilheit Packaging .... $3,500 Indiv
    Queen Carpets Corp .... $1,000 Indiv
    Stone Container Corp .... $1,000 PAC

Textiles **$1,750**
    Shaw Industries .... $1,500 Indiv

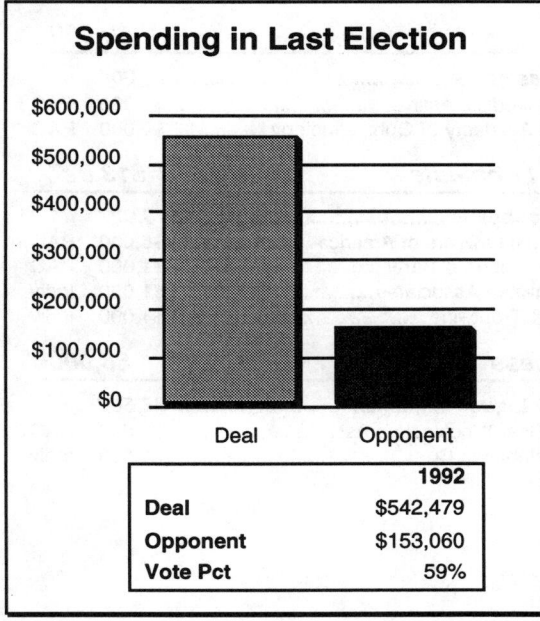

Spending in Last Election

	1992
Deal	$542,479
Opponent	$153,060
Vote Pct	59%

Transportation   **$15,050**

Air Transport **$5,300**
    United Parcel Service .... $4,500 PAC

Automotive **$6,500**
    National Auto Dealers Assn .... $4,000 PAC
    Slack Auto Parts Co .... $2,000 Indiv

Trucking **$1,750**
    Watkins Associated Industries .... $1,000 PAC

Railroads **$1,000**
    Union Pacific Corp .... $1,000 PAC

Labor

Labor   **$16,500**

Building Trade Unions **$1,000**
    Laborers' Political League .... $1,000 PAC

Industrial Unions **$1,500**
    Intl Brotherhood of Electrical Workers .... $1,000 PAC

Transportation Unions **$1,000**
    Air Line Pilots Assn .... $1,000 PAC

Public Sector Unions **$13,000**
    National Education Assn .... $10,500 PAC
    National Assn of Letter Carriers .... $1,500 PAC
    National Rural Letter Carriers Assn .... $1,000 PAC

Ideological/Single-Issue

Ideological/Single-Issue   **$7,750**

Democratic/Liberal **$3,250**
    National Cmte for an Effective Congress .... $2,950 PAC

Leadership PACs **$2,500**
    Effective Government Cmte (Dick Gephardt) ...... $1,000 PAC
    House Leadership Fund (Tom Foley) .... $1,000 PAC

Foreign & Defense Policy **$1,000**
    Veterans of Foreign Wars .... $1,000 PAC

Other & Unknown

Other   **$26,350**

Education **$3,250**
    Hall County Board of Education .... $3,000 Indiv

Retired **$22,400**
    None over $1,000

Unknown   **$36,991**

    Homemakers/Non-income earners $6,210
    Generic Occupation/Category Unknown $2,300
    Employer Listed/Category Unknown $27,681
        Walters Management .... $3,000 Indiv
        Citizens Management .... $2,303 Indiv
        Stowe Graphic Arts .... $2,000 Indiv
        Dixie Aluminum .... $1,400 Indiv
        Atlantastaff Inc .... $1,000 Indiv
        Cottrell Inc .... $1,000 Indiv
        Piedmont Laboratories .... $1,000 Indiv
        Premium Corp Services .... $1,000 Indiv

---

* Contributions came from more than one affiliate or subsidiary.

Peter A. DeFazio, D-Ore (4)

First elected: 1986

1991-92 Total Receipts: $248,887
1992 Year-end Cash: $43,563

1991-92 Committees & Subcommittees

Interior and Insular Affairs
Mining and Natural Resources; National Parks and Public Lands;
Water, Power and Offshore Energy Resources

Public Works and Transportation
Aviation; Water Resources

Select Committee on Aging

Leading Contributors

Business

Agriculture $10,750

Crop Production & Basic Processing *$2,750*		
American Sugarbeet Growers Assn.................... $1,000	PAC
Dairy *$5,000*		
Associated Milk Producers $2,500	PAC
Mid-America Dairymen $2,500	PAC
Forestry & Forest Products *$2,500*		
Willamette Industries $1,000	PAC

Communications/Electronics $3,000

Telephone Utilities *$3,000*		
US West Inc $1,500	PAC
AT&T $1,000	PAC

Construction $1,500

None over $1,000

Energy & Natural Resources $3,350

Mining *$1,000*		
Northwest Aluminum Co $1,000	Indiv
Electric Utilities *$1,750*		
None over $1,000		

Source of Funds in 1992 Election

Source	Total	Pct
PACs	$173,500	68%
Indivs $200+	$11,777	5%
Indivs under $200	$49,565	20%
Other	$18,936	7%
Candidate	$0	0%
Party	$5,441	2%

Source of PAC Dollars by Sector

Source	Total	Pct
Business	$75,150	42%
Labor	$94,500	53%
Ideology/Single Issue	$7,900	4%

In-State vs. Out-of-State Contributions*

Source	Total	Pct
In-State	$7,250	62%
Out-of-state	$4,527	38%
No state listed	$0	

* by large individual contributors ($200 & above)

Finance, Insurance & Real Estate $15,500

Commercial Banks *$4,750*		
American Bankers Assn $2,000	PAC
US Bancorp $2,000	PAC
Credit Unions *$2,000*		
Credit Union National Assn $2,000	PAC
Securities & Investment *$1,000*		
National Venture Capital Assn $1,000	PAC
Insurance *$1,000*		
National Assn of Life Underwriters $1,000	PAC
Real Estate *$6,500*		
National Assn of Realtors $6,000	PAC

Health $9,000

Health Professionals *$9,000*		
American Medical Assn $8,000	PAC
American Academy of Ophthalmology $1,000	PAC

Lawyers & Lobbyists $13,027

Lawyers & Lobbyists *$13,027*		
Assn of Trial Lawyers of America $5,000	PAC
Garvey, Schubert & Barer $1,000	PAC
Smith, Dawson Associates $1,000	Indiv
Williams & Troutwine $1,000	Indiv

Misc Business $5,000

Beer, Wine & Liquor *$2,500*		
National Beer Wholesalers Assn $1,500	PAC
Coast Distributing Co $1,000	Indiv

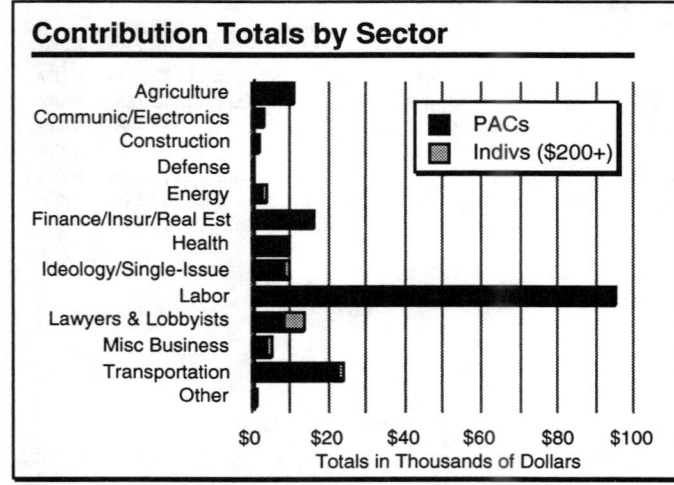

Contribution Totals by Sector

Agriculture
Communic/Electronics
Construction
Defense
Energy
Finance/Insur/Real Est
Health
Ideology/Single-Issue
Labor
Lawyers & Lobbyists
Misc Business
Transportation
Other

PACs
Indivs ($200+)

$0 $20 $40 $60 $80 $100
Totals in Thousands of Dollars

Transportation $23,050

Air Transport **$14,750**
    Aircraft Owners & Pilots Assn ....$10,000   PAC
    Federal Express Corp ....$2,500   PAC
    American Airlines ....$1,000   PAC

Automotive **$3,000**
    National Auto Dealers Assn ....$3,000   PAC

Trucking **$1,000**
    None over $1,000

Railroads **$3,500**
    Burlington Northern ....$1,000   PAC
    James-Furman & Co ....$1,000   Indiv

Labor

Labor $94,500

Building Trade Unions **$15,500**
    Carpenters & Joiners Union ....$8,000   PAC
    Laborers' Political League ....$2,500   PAC
    Plumbers/Pipefitters Union ....$2,000   PAC
    Operating Engineers Union ....$1,000   PAC
    Sheet Metal Workers Union ....$1,000   PAC

Industrial Unions **$25,000**
    Machinists/Aerospace Workers Union .....$10,000   PAC
    United Auto Workers ....$6,000   PAC
    Intl Brotherhood of Electrical Workers .....$4,500   PAC
    Boilermakers Union ....$2,000   PAC
    United Mine Workers ....$1,000   PAC
    United Steelworkers ....$1,000   PAC

Transportation Unions **$30,500**
    Air Line Pilots Assn ....$10,000   PAC
    Teamsters Union ....$5,000   PAC
    Marine Engineers Union* ....$4,000   PAC
    Amalgamated Transit Union ....$1,500   PAC
    Assn of Flight Attendants ....$1,500   PAC
    Transport Workers Union ....$1,500   PAC
    Brotherhood of Locomotive Engineers.....$1,000   PAC
    Intl Longshoremen's/Warehousemen's Union .....$1,000   PAC
    Maintenance of Way Employees ....$1,000   PAC
    National Air Traffic Controllers Assn ....$1,000   PAC
    Seafarers International Union ....$1,000   PAC
    Trans Comm International Union ....$1,000   PAC
    United Transportation Union ....$1,000   PAC

Public Sector Unions **$18,500**
    American Fedn of St/Cnty/Munic Employees ......$5,000   PAC
    National Assn of Letter Carriers ....$5,000   PAC
    National Education Assn* ....$3,500   PAC
    National Assn Retired Federal Employees ....$2,000   PAC
    American Postal Workers Union ....$1,000   PAC

Misc Unions **$5,000**
    AFL-CIO ....$2,000   PAC
    Food & Commercial Workers Union ....$2,000   PAC
    Service Employees International Union .....$1,000   PAC

Ideological/Single-Issue

Ideological/Single-Issue $9,150

Democratic/Liberal **$3,750**
    National Cmte for an Effective Congress ....$2,500   PAC

Human Rights **$1,000**
    Human Rights Campaign Fund ....$1,000   PAC

Misc Issues **$4,400**
    National Cmte to Preserve Social Security ....$4,000   PAC

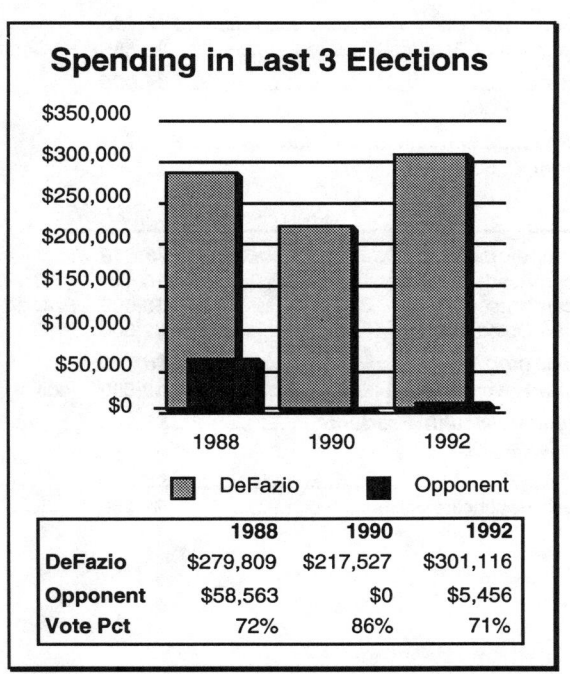

Spending in Last 3 Elections

	1988	1990	1992
DeFazio	$279,809	$217,527	$301,116
Opponent	$58,563	$0	$5,456
Vote Pct	72%	86%	71%

* Contributions came from more than one affiliate or subsidiary.

Rosa DeLauro, D-Conn (3)

First elected: 1990

1991-92 Total Receipts: $1,026,034
1992 Year-end Cash: $19,545

1991-92 Committees & Subcommittees

Government Operations
Employment and Housing; Human Resources and Intergovernmental Relations

Public Works and Transportation
Economic Development; Surface Transportation; Water Resources

Select Committee on Aging

Leading Contributors

Business

Agriculture	$9,725	
Dairy	**$6,250**	
Associated Milk Producers	$3,000	PAC
Mid-America Dairymen	$3,000	PAC

Communications/Electronics	$22,900	
Media/Entertainment	**$11,450**	
Cable Holdings Inc	$3,000	Indiv
Telephone Utilities	**$6,850**	
None over $2,500		

Construction	$24,111	
General Contractors	**$9,450**	
Fusco Corp	$3,000	Indiv
Special Trade Contractors	**$4,311**	
None over $2,500		
Construction Services	**$3,550**	
None over $2,500		
Building Materials & Equipment	**$6,800**	
None over $2,500		

Defense	$10,850	
Defense Aerospace	**$9,850**	
United Technologies	$7,000	PAC

Energy & Natural Resources	$7,400	
Oil & Gas	**$2,750**	
None over $2,500		
Electric Utilities	**$2,950**	
None over $2,500		

Source of Funds in 1992 Election

Source	Total	Pct
■ PACs	$493,531	47%
■ Indivs $200+	$319,674	30%
□ Indivs under $200	$194,936	19%
⊠ Other	$45,141	4%
Candidate	$0	0%
Party	$34,607	3%

Source of PAC Dollars by Sector

Source	Total	Pct
■ Business	$169,268	34%
■ Labor	$216,750	44%
□ Ideology/Single Issue	$105,543	21%

In-State vs. Out-of-State Contributions*

Source	Total	Pct
□ In-State	$187,631	59%
■ Out-of-state	$131,543	41%
No state listed	$0	

* by large individual contributors ($200 & above)

Finance, Insurance & Real Estate	$78,235	
Credit Unions	**$2,750**	
Credit Union National Assn	$2,750	PAC
Securities & Investment	**$10,200**	
Goldman, Sachs & Co	$4,000	PAC/Ind
Insurance	**$29,700**	
Independent Insurance Agents of America	$4,350	PAC
Aetna Life & Casualty	$4,250	PAC/Ind
Cigna Corp	$3,600	PAC/Ind
National Assn of Life Underwriters	$3,500	PAC
Hartford Insurance	$2,500	PAC
Real Estate	**$17,135**	
National Assn of Realtors	$8,585	PAC/Ind
Accountants	**$4,000**	
None over $2,500		
Misc Finance	**$11,400**	
None over $2,500		

Health	$61,468	
Health Professionals	**$35,618**	
American Academy of Ophthalmology	$10,418	PAC
American Nurses Assn	$3,500	PAC
American Optometric Assn	$2,500	PAC
Hospitals/Nursing Homes	**$6,750**	
Yale-New Haven Hospital	$2,500	Indiv
Pharmaceuticals/Health Products	**$8,700**	
None over $2,500		
Misc Health	**$8,850**	
Managed Healthcare Systems Inc	$3,250	Indiv

Contribution Totals by Sector

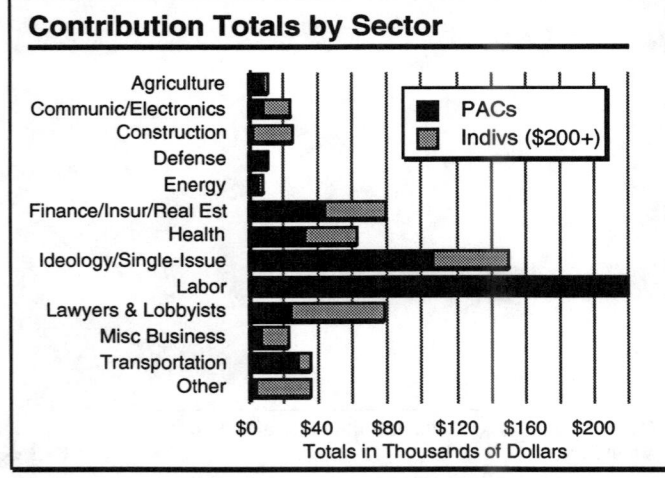

Agriculture, Communic/Electronics, Construction, Defense, Energy, Finance/Insur/Real Est, Health, Ideology/Single-Issue, Labor, Lawyers & Lobbyists, Misc Business, Transportation, Other

■ PACs
▨ Indivs ($200+)

$0 $40 $80 $120 $160 $200
Totals in Thousands of Dollars

Lawyers & Lobbyists $76,263

Lawyers & Lobbyists **$76,263**
Assn of Trial Lawyers of America .... $12,000 PAC
Fox, Weinberg & Bennett .... $5,000 Indiv
Akin, Gump et al .... $2,950 PAC/Ind

Misc Business $21,750

Beer, Wine & Liquor **$3,250**
None over $2,500
Business Services **$10,650**
None over $2,500

Transportation $34,100

Air Transport **$18,400**
United Parcel Service .... $9,550 PAC
Automotive **$5,800**
None over $2,500
Trucking **$5,450**
None over $2,500

Labor

Labor $217,500

Building Trade Unions **$30,850**
Carpenters & Joiners Union* .... $10,000 PAC
Laborers' Political League .... $8,000 PAC
Ironworkers Union .... $3,500 PAC
Plumbers/Pipefitters Union .... $3,000 PAC
Bricklayers Union .... $2,850 PAC
Industrial Unions **$58,800**
Intl Brotherhood of Electrical Workers .... $10,000 PAC
Machinists/Aerospace Workers Union .... $10,000 PAC
United Auto Workers .... $10,000 PAC
United Steelworkers .... $10,000 PAC
Connecticut Union of Telephone Workers .... $6,500 PAC
Electronic Machine Furniture Workers .... $2,500 PAC
Transportation Unions **$39,150**
Teamsters Union .... $10,000 PAC
Seafarers International Union .... $6,000 PAC
Air Line Pilots Assn .... $5,000 PAC
Marine Engineers Union* .... $5,000 PAC
Amalgamated Transit Union .... $2,500 PAC
Transport Workers Union .... $2,500 Indiv

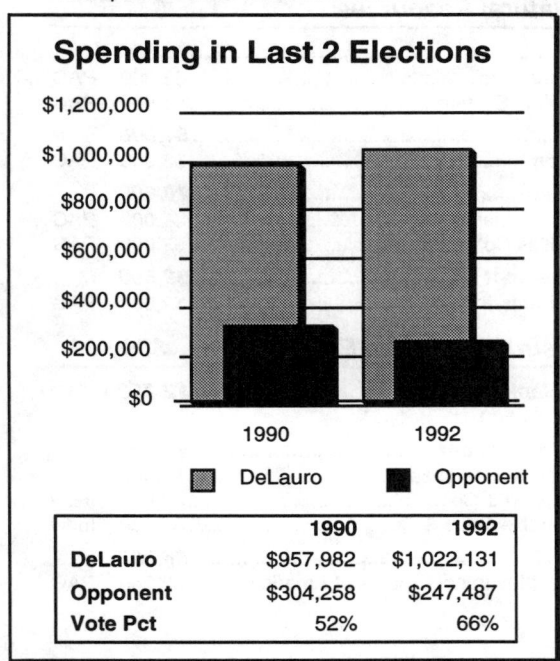

Spending in Last 2 Elections

	1990	1992
DeLauro	$957,982	$1,022,131
Opponent	$304,258	$247,487
Vote Pct	52%	66%

Public Sector Unions $63,950
American Federation of Teachers .... $10,000 PAC
American Fedn of St/Cnty/Munic Employees .... $10,000 PAC
National Education Assn .... $10,000 PAC
American Postal Workers Union .... $8,500 PAC
National Assn of Letter Carriers .... $7,000 PAC
National Assn Retired Federal Employees .... $5,000 PAC
International Assn of Firefighters .... $4,500 PAC
Misc Unions **$24,750**
Food & Commercial Workers Union .... $10,000 PAC
AFL-CIO .... $7,000 PAC
Service Employees International Union .... $4,000 PAC

Ideological/Single-Issue

Ideological/Single-Issue $149,893

Democratic/Liberal **$17,650**
Hollywood Women's Political Cmte .... $10,000 PAC
National Cmte for an Effective Congress .... $2,500 PAC
Leadership PACs **$6,524**
House Leadership Fund (Tom Foley) .... $4,024 PAC
Pro-Israel **$18,750**
None over $2,500
Pro-Choice **$13,100**
National Abortion Rights Action League .... $5,000 PAC
Voters for Choice .... $3,850 PAC/Ind
Womens Issues **$41,122**
Women's Campaign Fund .... $10,000 PAC
Emily's List .... $6,590 PAC/Ind
National Organization for Women .... $6,232 PAC
National Womens Political Caucus .... $5,000 PAC
Human Rights **$23,550**
KidsPAC .... $10,000 PAC
Human Rights Campaign Fund .... $6,000 PAC
Misc Issues **$25,500**
Sierra Club .... $8,750 PAC
Greenvote .... $5,250 PAC
National Cmte to Preserve Social Security .... $4,250 PAC

Other & Unknown

Other $34,457

Civil Servants/Public Officials **$5,807**
None over $2,500
Education **$11,750**
Yale University .... $2,975 Indiv
Retired **$10,100**
None over $2,500
Other **$4,800**
National Assn of Social Workers .... $3,000 PAC

Unknown $62,583

Homemakers/Non-income earners $4,400
No Employer Listed or Found $13,400
Generic Occupation/Category Unknown $2,625
Employer Listed/Category Unknown $42,158
None over $2,500

---

* Contributions came from more than one affiliate or
subsidiary.

Tom DeLay, R-Texas (22)

First elected: 1984

1991-92 Total Receipts: $341,516
1992 Year-end Cash: $46,466

1991-92 Committees & Subcommittees

Appropriations
District of Columbia; Military Construction; Transportation and Related Agencies

Leading Contributors

Business

Agriculture	**$21,800**	
Tobacco	**$10,300**	
RJR Nabisco	$4,000	PAC
Philip Morris	$2,000	PAC
Livestock	**$3,500**	
National Cattlemen's Assn*	$2,500	PAC
Food Processing & Sales	**$6,000**	
Randall's Food Markets	$2,000	Indiv
National Wholesale Grocers Assn	$1,500	PAC

Communications/Electronics	**$17,000**	
Media/Entertainment	**$1,500**	
National Assn of Broadcasters	$1,500	PAC
Telephone Utilities	**$11,500**	
Sugar Land Telephone Co	$3,000	Indiv
AT&T	$2,000	PAC
SLT Communications	$2,000	PAC/Ind
Southwestern Bell	$2,000	PAC
Computer Equipment & Services	**$3,000**	
None over $1,500		

Construction	**$24,250**	
General Contractors	**$15,500**	
Fluor Corp	$5,000	PAC
Associated General Contractors	$2,500	PAC
Brown & Root	$2,500	PAC
Home Builders	**$2,000**	
Perry-Houston Interests	$2,000	Indiv

Contribution Totals by Sector

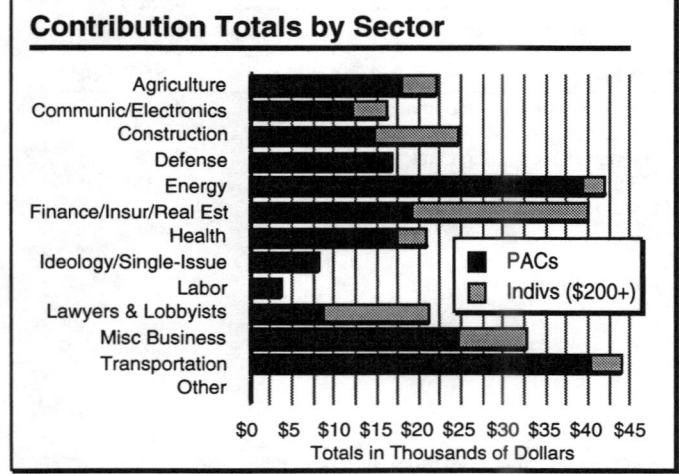

Agriculture
Communic/Electronics
Construction
Defense
Energy
Finance/Insur/Real Est
Health
Ideology/Single-Issue
Labor
Lawyers & Lobbyists
Misc Business
Transportation
Other

■ PACs
▨ Indivs ($200+)

$0 $5 $10 $15 $20 $25 $30 $35 $40 $45
Totals in Thousands of Dollars

Source of Funds in 1992 Election

Source	Total	Pct
■ PACs	$223,678	66%
▨ Indivs $200+	$87,365	26%
□ Indivs under $200	$22,483	7%
▣ Other	$7,990	2%
Candidate	$0	0%
Party	$70	0%

Source of PAC Dollars by Sector

Source	Total	Pct
■ Business	$208,879	95%
▨ Labor	$3,500	2%
□ Ideology/Single Issue	$8,000	4%

In-State vs. Out-of-State Contributions*

Source	Total	Pct
□ In-State	$78,365	91%
■ Out-of-state	$8,000	9%
No state listed	$1,000	

* by large individual contributors ($200 & above)

Special Trade Contractors	$2,500	
Houston Fence Co	$2,000	Indiv
Construction Services	**$3,750**	
None over $1,500		

Defense	**$16,500**	
Defense Aerospace	**$6,000**	
McDonnell Douglas*	$1,500	PAC
Defense Electronics	**$10,000**	
GTE Corp	$4,000	PAC
E-Systems Inc	$3,000	PAC
Imo Industries Inc	$2,000	PAC

Energy & Natural Resources	**$41,650**	
Oil & Gas	**$23,300**	
Baker Hughes Inc	$3,000	PAC/Ind
Columbia Gas System	$1,500	PAC
Misc Energy	**$4,000**	
Bechtel Corp	$3,000	PAC
Electric Utilities	**$10,600**	
Houston Industries	$4,000	PAC
Texas Utilities Co*	$2,000	PAC
Waste Management	**$2,500**	
Browning-Ferris Industries	$2,000	PAC

Finance, Insurance & Real Estate	**$39,598**	
Commercial Banks	**$2,750**	
None over $1,500		
Securities & Investment	**$9,400**	
Clive Runnells Enterprises	$2,000	Indiv
Gilder, Gagnon & Co	$2,000	Indiv
Underwood, Neuhaus & Co	$2,000	Indiv
Insurance	**$6,883**	
Independent Insurance Agents of America	$2,200	PAC

Real Estate $14,815
    National Assn of Realtors ....$6,000 PAC
    Michael Stevens Interest ....$3,000 Indiv
    Hale/Associates ....$2,000 Indiv
    Henry S Miller Co ....$2,000 Indiv

Accountants $2,500
    American Institute of CPA's ....$2,500 PAC

Misc Finance $3,250
    None over $1,500

Health $20,600

Health Professionals $16,900
    American Medical Assn ....$9,350 PAC
    American Dental Assn ....$4,000 PAC

Pharmaceuticals/Health Products $2,700
    Rhone-Poulenc Inc ....$2,500 PAC

Lawyers & Lobbyists $21,000

Lawyers & Lobbyists $21,000
    Akin, Gump et al ....$2,000 PAC
    Kee & Patterson ....$2,000 Indiv
    Pierce, Goodwin, Alexander ....$2,000 Indiv
    Baker & Botts ....$1,500 PAC

Misc Business $32,400

Food & Beverage $1,750
    None over $1,500

Beer, Wine & Liquor $2,250
    National Beer Wholesalers Assn ....$1,500 PAC

Retail Sales $6,000
    IW Marks Jewelers Inc ....$2,000 Indiv

Misc Services $3,000
    National Pest Control Assn ....$2,000 PAC

Business Services $3,900
    Secretary Tempower ....$1,500 Indiv

Chemical & Related Manufacturing ...$11,750
    Dow Chemical ....$7,000 PAC

Misc Manufacturing & Distributing $1,500
    None over $1,500

Transportation $43,846

Air Transport $17,827
    Aircraft Owners & Pilots Assn ....$7,000 PAC
    United Parcel Service ....$3,654 PAC
    Northwest Airlines ....$2,000 PAC
    American Airlines ....$1,500 PAC
    Texas Air ....$1,500 PAC

Automotive $10,000
    National Auto Dealers Assn ....$4,000 PAC
    Sterling McCall Toyota ....$2,500 Indiv
    Auto Dealers & Drivers for Free Trade .....$1,500 PAC

Trucking $3,519
    None over $1,500

Railroads $5,750
    Union Pacific Corp ....$1,500 PAC/Ind

Sea Transport $2,250
    None over $1,500

Misc Transport $4,500
    International Taxicab Assn ....$2,000 PAC

Labor

Labor $3,500

Transportation Unions $3,500
    Marine Engineers Dist 2 Retirees ....$2,000 PAC
    Air Line Pilots Assn ....$1,500 PAC

Ideological/Single-Issue

Ideological/Single-Issue $8,000

Pro-Life $2,500
    Republican National Coalition for Life ....$2,500 PAC

Gun Rights/Gun Control $2,000
    National Rifle Assn ....$1,500 PAC

Misc Issues $3,000
    Right to Work PAC ....$2,500 PAC

Other & Unknown

Unknown $17,600

    No Employer Listed or Found $3,700
    Employer Listed/Category Unknown $12,900
        Lichliter-Jameson & Assoc ....$2,000 Indiv

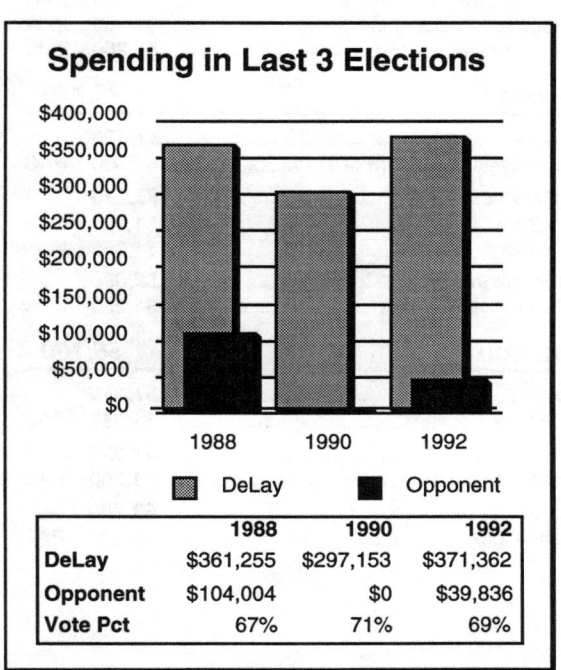

Spending in Last 3 Elections

	1988	1990	1992
DeLay	$361,255	$297,153	$371,362
Opponent	$104,004	$0	$39,836
Vote Pct	67%	71%	69%

* Contributions came from more than one affiliate or subsidiary.

Ronald V. Dellums, D-Calif (9)

First elected: 1970

1991-92 Total Receipts: $854,478
1992 Year-end Cash: $15,335

1991-92 Committees & Subcommittees

Armed Services
Research and Development (Chairman)

District of Columbia (Chairman)
Fiscal Affairs and Health; Judiciary and Education

Select Committee on Intelligence

Leading Contributors

Business

Agriculture	$2,800	
Tobacco	**$1,500**	
Philip Morris	$1,500	PAC

Communications/Electronics	$13,106	
Printing & Publishing	**$3,700**	
None over $1,000		
Media/Entertainment	**$5,406**	
Mutable Music Productions	$2,000	Indiv
Tabu Productions Inc	$1,056	Indiv
Telephone Utilities	**$3,000**	
AT&T	$2,000	PAC
Pacific Telesis Group	$1,000	PAC

Construction	$2,950	
Construction Services	**$2,250**	
Kaiser Engineers Inc	$1,500	PAC

Energy & Natural Resources	$1,050	
None over $1,000		

Finance, Insurance & Real Estate	$7,874	
Real Estate	**$5,074**	
Chapman & Wilson	$1,000	Indiv
National Assn of Realtors	$1,000	PAC
Misc Finance	**$1,500**	
None over $1,000		

Source of Funds in 1992 Election

Source	Total	Pct
■ PACs	$78,437	9%
▨ Indivs $200+	$107,021	12%
□ Indivs under $200	$529,218	62%
▧ Other	$145,216	17%
Candidate	$0	0%
Party	$5,564	1%

Source of PAC Dollars by Sector

Source	Total	Pct
■ Business	$30,850	34%
▨ Labor	$58,400	65%
□ Ideology/Single Issue	$1,000	1%

In-State vs. Out-of-State Contributions*

Source	Total	Pct
□ In-State	$64,420	60%
■ Out-of-state	$42,151	40%
No state listed	$0	

* by large individual contributors ($200 & above)

Health	$10,510	
Health Professionals	**$7,810**	
American Medical Assn	$2,500	PAC
Border Area Mental Health	$1,000	Indiv
Hospitals/Nursing Homes	**$2,000**	
Children's Hospital of Oakland	$1,000	Indiv
Merritt-Peralta Medical Center	$1,000	Indiv

Lawyers & Lobbyists	$17,506	
Lawyers & Lobbyists	**$17,506**	
Assn of Trial Lawyers of America	$10,000	PAC
Cambridge International Inc	$1,250	Indiv
Copeland, Hatfield & Lowery	$1,250	Indiv

Misc Business	$8,770	
Business Associations	**$1,500**	
Greater Washington Board of Trade	$1,500	PAC
Business Services	**$5,270**	
Caltech Serv	$1,250	Indiv
AMPB Security	$1,060	Indiv
Misc Manufacturing & Distributing	**$2,000**	
Leon Tempelsman & Son	$1,250	Indiv

Transportation	$6,100	
Air Transport	**$1,350**	
United Parcel Service	$1,350	PAC
Automotive	**$1,300**	
New United Motor Manufacturing Inc	$1,300	PAC
Sea Transport	**$3,200**	
Sea-Land Corp	$1,500	PAC

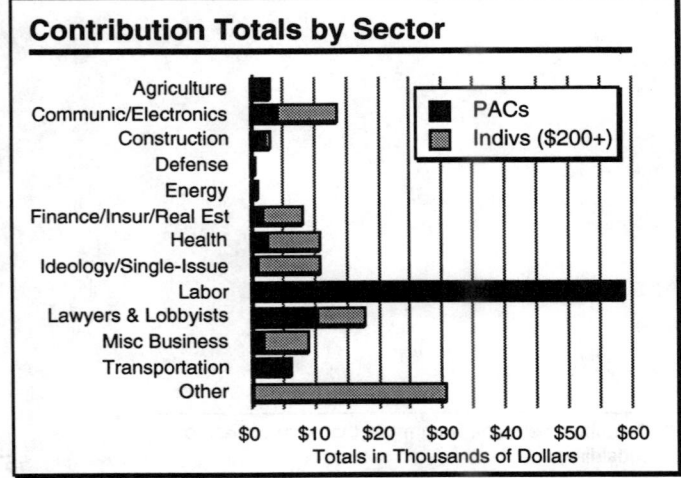

Contribution Totals by Sector

■ PACs
▨ Indivs ($200+)

Agriculture
Communic/Electronics
Construction
Defense
Energy
Finance/Insur/Real Est
Health
Ideology/Single-Issue
Labor
Lawyers & Lobbyists
Misc Business
Transportation
Other

$0 $10 $20 $30 $40 $50 $60
Totals in Thousands of Dollars

Labor

Labor — $58,400

Building Trade Unions **$8,300**
  Laborers' Political League .... $4,000   PAC
  Plumbers/Pipefitters Union .... $2,000   PAC
  AFL-CIO Bldg/Construction Trades Dept .... $1,500   PAC

Industrial Unions **$9,100**
  United Auto Workers .... $4,750   PAC
  Machinists/Aerospace Workers Union .... $1,050   PAC

Transportation Unions **$26,150**
  Teamsters Union .... $10,000   PAC
  Intl Longshoremen's/Warehousemen's Union ..... $9,000   PAC
  Seafarers International Union* .... $2,150   PAC
  Marine Engineers Union* .... $2,000   PAC

Public Sector Unions **$10,350**
  American Fedn of St/Cnty/Munic Employees ...... $5,000   PAC
  National Assn Retired Federal Employees .... $2,500   PAC
  National Education Assn .... $2,250   PAC
  American Postal Workers Union .... $1,500   PAC

Misc Unions **$4,500**
  Food & Commercial Workers Union .... $1,750   PAC
  Hotel/Restaurant Employees Union .... $1,000   PAC
  Service Employees International Union .... $1,000   PAC

Ideological/Single-Issue

Ideological/Single-Issue — $10,700

Democratic/Liberal **$5,000**
  None over $1,000

Womens Issues **$3,950**
  None over $1,000

Human Rights **$1,000**
  Human Rights Campaign Fund .... $1,000   PAC

Other & Unknown

Other — $30,356

Non-Profit Institutions **$4,750**
  Foundation for Hearing Aid Research .... $4,000   Indiv

Civil Servants/Public Officials **$2,000**
  District of Columbia City Council .... $1,000   Indiv
  Pennsylvania Department of Transportation .... $1,000   Indiv

Retired **$21,456**
  None over $1,000

Other **$1,500**
  Lef Foundation .... $1,000   Indiv

Unknown — $25,399

  Homemakers/Non-income earners $2,250
  No Employer Listed or Found $9,895
  Generic Occupation/Category Unknown $1,842
  Employer Listed/Category Unknown $11,412
    Mal Warwick Associates .... $1,056   Indiv
    AA Rosen Inc .... $1,000   Indiv
    Cinegon Group .... $1,000   Indiv

Independent expenditures opposing Dellums
  Conservative Campaign Fund $6,238

Spending in Last 3 Elections

	1988	1990	1992
Dellums	$1,174,676	$840,029	$921,771
Opponent	$7,071	$0	$559,970
Vote Pct	67%	61%	72%

* Contributions came from more than one affiliate or subsidiary.

Butler Derrick, D-SC (3)

First elected: 1974

1991-92 Total Receipts: $681,632
1992 Year-end Cash: $114,145

1991-92 Committees & Subcommittees

Rules
Legislative Process (Chairman)

Select Committee on Aging

Leading Contributors

Business

Agriculture	$54,813

Crop Production & Basic Processing $8,750
    None over $2,500

Tobacco $15,263
    RJR Nabisco .... $7,963   PAC
    Philip Morris .... $4,000   PAC

Dairy $8,750
    Associated Milk Producers .... $5,000   PAC

Poultry & Eggs $4,000
    None over $2,500

Agricultural Services/Products $3,750
    None over $2,500

Food Processing & Sales $10,750
    Winn-Dixie Stores .... $3,500   PAC
    Greenwood Packing Plant .... $3,000   Indiv

Communications/Electronics	$31,950

Media/Entertainment $13,000
    National Cable Television Assn .... $5,000   PAC
    Turner Broadcasting System .... $3,000   PAC

Telephone Utilities $14,200
    Southern Bell .... $7,500   PAC

Electronics Mfg & Services $2,500
    None over $2,500

Construction	$20,750

General Contractors $13,750
    Fluor Corp .... $10,000   PAC

Source of Funds in 1992 Election

Source	Total	Pct
■ PACs	$469,870	68%
▨ Indivs $200+	$115,312	17%
☐ Indivs under $200	$59,446	9%
⊠ Other	$41,744	6%
Candidate	$0	0%
Party	$4,890	1%

Source of PAC Dollars by Sector

Source	Total	Pct
■ Business	$411,318	88%
▨ Labor	$42,250	9%
☐ Ideology/Single Issue	$13,250	3%

In-State vs. Out-of-State Contributions*

Source	Total	Pct
☐ In-State	$81,262	71%
■ Out-of-state	$32,550	29%
No state listed	$500	

* by large individual contributors ($200 & above)

Construction Services $3,000
    Stone & Webster .... $3,000   PAC

Building Materials & Equipment $3,000
    None over $2,500

Defense	$4,850

Defense Aerospace $3,850
    None over $2,500

Energy & Natural Resources	$43,448

Oil & Gas $11,250
    None over $2,500

Mining $3,000
    None over $2,500

Nuclear Energy $3,948
    General Atomics .... $3,150   PAC

Misc Energy $4,000
    Bechtel Corp .... $3,500   PAC

Electric Utilities $17,250
    ACRE (Action Cmte for Rural Electrification) .... $3,750   PAC
    Carolina Power & Light .... $2,500   PAC
    Duke Power Co .... $2,500   PAC

Waste Management $3,500
    Waste Management Inc .... $3,500   PAC

Finance, Insurance & Real Estate	$168,850

Commercial Banks $48,750
    American Bankers Assn .... $10,000   PAC
    Citizens & Southern National Bank .... $5,550   PAC
    Citicorp .... $5,000   PAC
    Barnett Banks Inc .... $4,000   PAC
    Bankers Trust .... $3,500   PAC
    JP Morgan & Co .... $3,500   PAC
    NCNB Corp .... $3,250   PAC/Ind
    Independent Bankers Assn .... $2,500   PAC

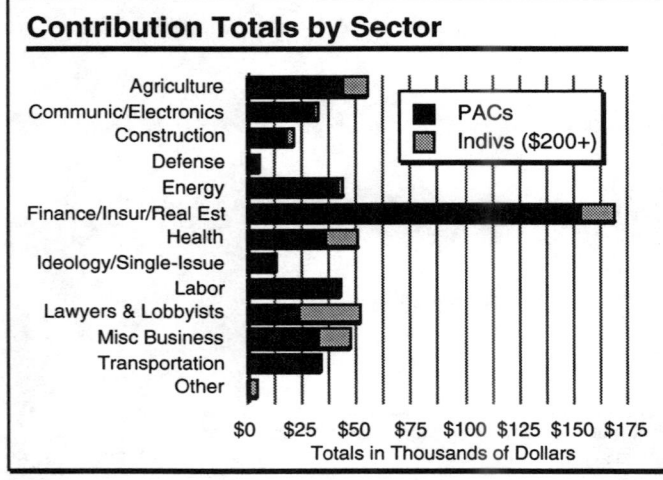

Contribution Totals by Sector

Agriculture
Communic/Electronics
Construction
Defense
Energy
Finance/Insur/Real Est
Health
Ideology/Single-Issue
Labor
Lawyers & Lobbyists
Misc Business
Transportation
Other

■ PACs
▨ Indivs ($200+)

$0 $25 $50 $75 $100 $125 $150 $175
Totals in Thousands of Dollars

Credit Unions		$8,000	
Credit Union National Assn		$7,500	PAC

Finance/Credit Companies		$6,500	
Household International Inc		$3,500	PAC

Securities & Investment		$15,500	
Chicago Mercantile Exchange		$4,500	PAC

Insurance		$56,650	
National Assn of Life Underwriters		$10,000	PAC
Independent Insurance Agents of America		$7,500	PAC
Colonial Life & Accident Insurance		$6,500	PAC/Ind
American Council of Life Insurance		$4,000	PAC
American Family Corp		$4,000	PAC

Real Estate		$16,450	
National Assn of Realtors		$8,000	PAC

Accountants		$12,500	
American Institute of CPA's		$10,000	PAC

Misc Finance		$2,500	
None over $2,500			

Health $49,900

Health Professionals		$29,000	
American Medical Assn		$10,000	PAC
American Dental Assn		$3,000	PAC

Hospitals/Nursing Homes		$9,000	
American Hospital Assn		$5,500	PAC

Pharmaceuticals/Health Products		$11,650	
Warner-Lambert		$5,000	PAC/Ind

Lawyers & Lobbyists $51,133

Lawyers & Lobbyists		$51,133	
Assn of Trial Lawyers of America		$10,000	PAC
Akin, Gump et al		$6,232	PAC/Ind
McNair Law Firm		$2,750	Indiv

Misc Business $46,386

Food & Beverage		$5,686	
None over $2,500			

Beer, Wine & Liquor		$6,750	
National Beer Wholesalers Assn		$4,500	PAC

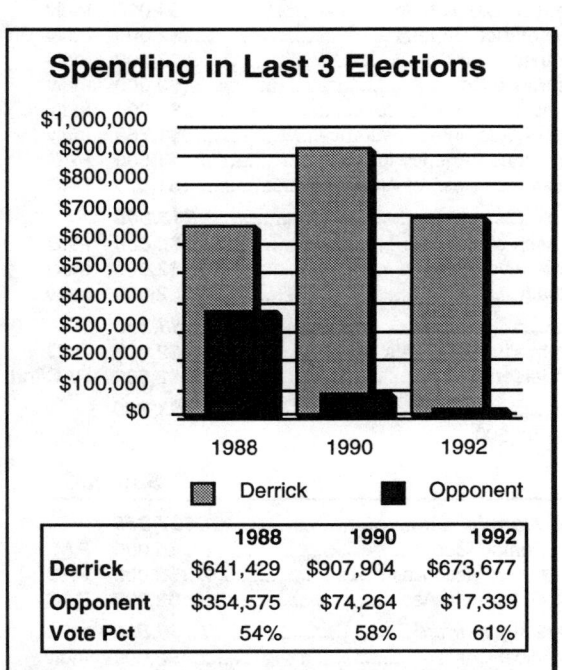

Spending in Last 3 Elections

	1988	1990	1992
Derrick	$641,429	$907,904	$673,677
Opponent	$354,575	$74,264	$17,339
Vote Pct	54%	58%	61%

Retail Sales		$2,500	
None over $2,500			

Chemical & Related Manufacturing		$7,750	
None over $2,500			

Textiles		$20,150	
Burlington Industries		$5,000	PAC
Delta Woodside Industries		$5,000	Indiv
American Textile Manufacturers Institute		$3,000	PAC
Springs Mills		$2,500	PAC

Transportation $33,250

Air Transport		$9,500	
United Parcel Service		$5,500	PAC

Automotive		$9,500	
National Auto Dealers Assn		$5,000	PAC

Trucking		$3,750	
None over $2,500			

Railroads		$8,500	
CSX Transportation Inc		$2,500	PAC

Labor

Labor $42,250

Transportation Unions		$20,000	
Marine Engineers Union*		$8,000	PAC
Seafarers International Union		$5,000	PAC
Air Line Pilots Assn		$3,500	PAC
United Transportation Union		$3,500	PAC

Public Sector Unions		$17,750	
National Assn of Letter Carriers		$6,500	PAC
National Assn Retired Federal Employees		$3,000	PAC
American Fedn of St/Cnty/Munic Employees		$2,500	PAC

Misc Unions		$2,500	
None over $2,500			

Ideological/Single-Issue

Ideological/Single-Issue $13,250

Democratic/Liberal		$2,500	
National Cmte for an Effective Congress		$2,500	PAC

Pro-Israel		$5,000	
National PAC		$5,000	PAC

Misc Issues		$5,250	
National Cmte to Preserve Social Security		$4,500	PAC

Other & Unknown

Other $3,300

None over $2,500

Unknown $17,250

Employer Listed/Category Unknown		$14,750
None over $2,500		

---

* Contributions came from more than one affiliate or subsidiary.

Peter Deutsch, D-Fla (20)

First elected: 1992

1991-92 Total Receipts: $835,010
1992 Year-end Cash: $17,277

1993-94 Committees & Subcommittees

Banking, Finance and Urban Affairs
Consumer Credit and Insurance; Financial Institutions Supervision, Regulation and Deposit Insurance; Housing and Community Development

Foreign Affairs
Europe and the Middle East; Western Hemisphere Affairs

Merchant Marine and Fisheries

Leading Contributors

Business

Agriculture	$13,600	
Crop Production & Basic Processing	$8,750	
Okeelanta Corp	$4,000	Indiv
United States Sugar Corp	$2,000	PAC
Tobacco	$2,500	
None over $1,500		

Communications/Electronics	$8,550	
Media/Entertainment	$2,000	
None over $1,500		
Telephone Utilities	$3,950	
None over $1,500		

Construction	$7,400	
General Contractors	$4,400	
Adler Group Inc	$2,000	Indiv
Church & Tower of Florida	$2,000	Indiv
Special Trade Contractors	$2,000	
None over $1,500		

Energy & Natural Resources	$6,000	
Electric Utilities	$3,500	
ACRE (Action Cmte for Rural Electric)	$2,000	PAC
Waste Management	$1,500	
None over $1,500		

Contribution Totals by Sector

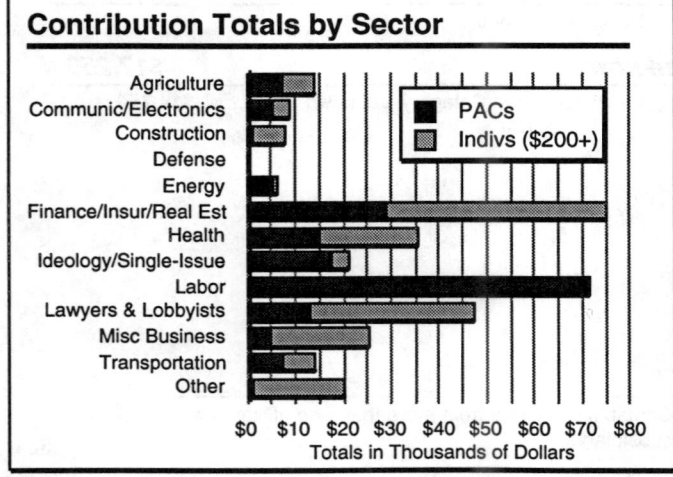

Agriculture
Communic/Electronics
Construction
Defense
Energy
Finance/Insur/Real Est
Health
Ideology/Single-Issue
Labor
Lawyers & Lobbyists
Misc Business
Transportation
Other

■ PACs
▨ Indivs ($200+)

$0 $10 $20 $30 $40 $50 $60 $70 $80
Totals in Thousands of Dollars

Source of Funds in 1992 Election

Source	Total	Pct
■ PACs	$168,826	20%
▨ Indivs $200+	$235,660	28%
☐ Indivs under $200	$69,150	8%
▦ Other	$3351,834	42%
Candidate	$343,240	41%
Party	$8,594	1%

Source of PAC Dollars by Sector

Source	Total	Pct
■ Business	$84,350	49%
▨ Labor	$71,150	41%
☐ Ideology/Single Issue	$16,920	10%

In-State vs. Out-of-State Contributions*

Source	Total	Pct
☐ In-State	$163,660	70%
■ Out-of-state	$71,750	30%
No state listed	$250	

* by large individual contributors ($200 & above)

Finance, Insurance & Real Estate	$74,600	
Commercial Banks	$5,300	
American Bankers Assn	$1,500	PAC
Savings & Loans	$2,000	
None over $1,500		
Securities & Investment	$2,900	
None over $1,500		
Insurance	$38,650	
Hallman & Lorber Associates	$5,500	Indiv
Phoenix American	$4,000	Indiv
Transportation Casualty Insurance	$4,000	Indiv
Assn of Insurance Brokers	$2,000	Indiv
Biscayne Insurance Co	$2,000	Indiv
Orion Insurance Co	$2,000	Indiv
Union General Insurance Co	$2,000	Indiv
Underwriters Guarantee Insurance	$1,750	Indiv
Fidelity Insurance Agency Inc	$1,500	PAC
Health Insurance Assn of America	$1,500	PAC
Real Estate	$13,800	
National Assn of Realtors	$5,000	PAC
Real Estate Investment	$2,000	Indiv
Swezy Realty	$2,000	Indiv
Accountants	$8,250	
American Institute of CPA's	$2,000	PAC
Arthur Andersen & Co	$2,000	PAC/Ind
Misc Finance	$3,700	
None over $1,500		

Health	$35,200	
Health Professionals	$27,350	
American Dental Assn	$5,000	PAC
American Chiropractic Assn	$2,000	PAC
American Optometric Assn	$2,000	PAC
Hospitals/Nursing Homes	$6,850	
Florida Medical Center	$2,000	Indiv
Humana Inc	$1,500	PAC

Lawyers & Lobbyists $47,200

Lawyers & Lobbyists **$44,700**
  Assn of Trial Lawyers of America .... $10,000   PAC
  Becker & Poliakoff ....$3,600   Indiv
  Greenberg, Traurig et al ....$3,500   PAC/Ind
  Kluger, Peretz et al ....$2,000   Indiv
  Michael Deutsch Esq ....$2,000   Indiv
  Panza, Maurer et al ....$1,500   Indiv

Transportation $13,600

Automotive **$7,500**
  National Auto Dealers Assn ....$4,000   PAC
  Alamo Rent-a-Car ....$3,000   Indiv
Sea Transport **$2,400**
  None over $1,500
Misc Transport **$3,200**
  Metro Limo Co ....$3,000   Indiv

Misc Business $24,600

Business Associations **$1,500**
  None over $1,500
Beer, Wine & Liquor **$9,500**
  Southern Wine & Spirits ....$7,500   PAC/Ind
Misc Services **$2,000**
  None over $1,500
Business Services **$4,400**
  Hudson Management Corp ....$1,500   Indiv
Misc Manufacturing & Distributing **$4,200**
  Kulmer ....$1,500   Indiv

Labor

Labor $71,150

Building Trade Unions **$6,000**
  Laborers' Political League ....$2,000   PAC
Industrial Unions **$11,550**
  Machinists/Aerospace Workers Union ....$5,000   PAC
  United Auto Workers ....$4,000   PAC
Transportation Unions **$22,350**
  Marine Engineers Union* ....$10,000   PAC
  Teamsters Union ....$5,000   PAC
  United Transportation Union ....$3,000   PAC
  International Longshoremens Assn ....$1,500   PAC

Public Sector Unions $29,750
  American Fedn of St/Cnty/Munic Employees ....$10,000   PAC
  National Education Assn ....$10,000   PAC
  National Assn of Letter Carriers ....$3,500   PAC
  American Federation of Teachers ....$2,500   PAC
  International Assn of Firefighters* ....$2,000   PAC
Misc Unions **$1,500**
  None over $1,500

Ideological/Single-Issue

Ideological/Single-Issue $20,620

Democratic/Liberal **$2,755**
  National Cmte for an Effective Congress ....$2,500   PAC
Leadership PACs **$3,000**
  None over $1,500
Pro-Israel **$7,000**
  None over $1,500
Womens Issues **$1,665**
  National Organization for Women ....$1,665   PAC
Human Rights **$2,750**
  Human Rights Campaign Fund ....$2,500   PAC
Misc Issues **$2,950**
  None over $1,500

Other & Unknown

Other $19,500

Education **$4,800**
  None over $1,500
Retired **$13,250**
  None over $1,500

Unknown $66,560
  Homemakers/Non-income earners $14,780
  No Employer Listed or Found $18,150
  Generic Occupation/Category Unknown $1,500
  Employer Listed/Category Unknown $32,130
    Hip ....$2,000   Indiv
    Roche Enterprises ....$2,000   Indiv
    Tingue, Brown & Co ....$2,000   Indiv
    Wagner, Francis et al ....$2,000   Indiv
    Amerijet ....$1,500   Indiv
    Wear-2-be-Seen ....$1,500   Indiv

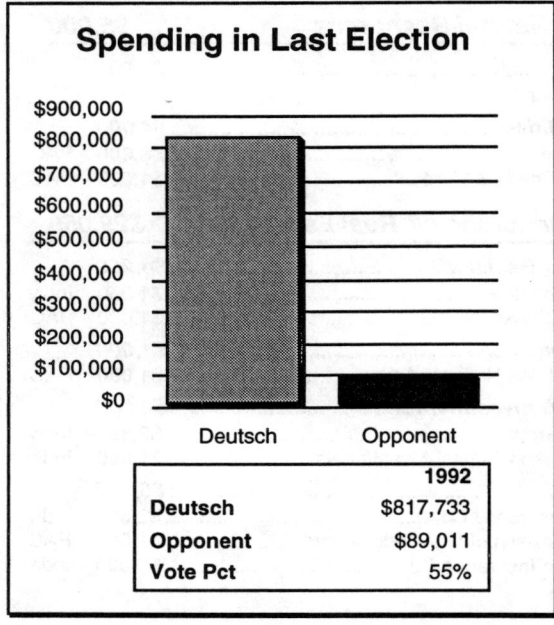

Spending in Last Election

	1992
Deutsch	$817,733
Opponent	$89,011
Vote Pct	55%

---

* Contributions came from more than one affiliate or subsidiary.

Lincoln Diaz-Balart, R-Fla (21)

First elected: 1992

1991-92 Total Receipts: $279,773
1992 Year-end Cash: $292

1993-94 Committees & Subcommittees

Foreign Affairs
Africa; International Operations

Merchant Marine and Fisheries
Coast Guard and Navigation; Merchant Marine

Leading Contributors

Business

Agriculture	$20,750	
Crop Production & Basic Processing	**$10,000**	
Okeelanta Corp	$6,000	Indiv
Flo-Sun Land Corp	$2,000	Indiv
United States Sugar Corp	$2,000	PAC
Tobacco	**$1,000**	
None over $1,000		
Agricultural Services/Products	**$6,500**	
Integrated World Enterprises	$3,000	Indiv
Integrated World Services	$1,000	Indiv
Inter American Transport Equip Co	$1,000	Indiv
Kelly Tractor	$1,000	Indiv
Food Processing & Sales	**$2,750**	
Winn-Dixie Stores	$1,500	PAC
Pepsico Inc	$1,000	PAC

Communications/Electronics	$15,000	
Printing & Publishing	**$5,000**	
Avanti Press Inc	$5,000	Indiv
Media/Entertainment	**$1,000**	
Adelphia Communications	$1,000	Indiv
Telephone Utilities	**$8,500**	
Southern Bell	$5,000	PAC
GTE Corp	$1,000	PAC
Peoples Telephone Co	$1,000	Indiv
United Telecommunications	$1,000	PAC

Source of Funds in 1992 Election

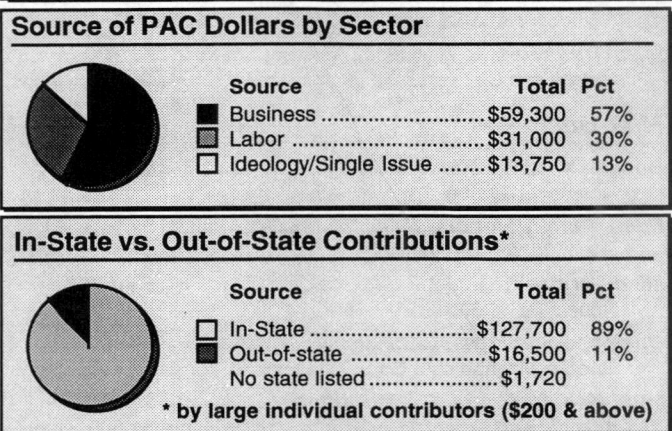

Source	Total	Pct
■ PACs	$83,800	30%
▨ Indivs $200+	$145,920	52%
□ Indivs under $200	$43,958	16%
▦ Other	$6,095	2%
Candidate	$0	0%
Party	$4	0%

Source of PAC Dollars by Sector

Source	Total	Pct
■ Business	$59,300	57%
▨ Labor	$31,000	30%
□ Ideology/Single Issue	$13,750	13%

In-State vs. Out-of-State Contributions*

Source	Total	Pct
□ In-State	$127,700	89%
■ Out-of-state	$16,500	11%
No state listed	$1,720	

*** by large individual contributors ($200 & above)**

Construction	$11,000	
General Contractors	**$3,000**	
Church & Tower of Florida	$2,500	Indiv
Home Builders	**$3,250**	
Cametco Construction	$1,250	Indiv
Adrian Investment Corp	$1,000	Indiv
National Assn of Home Builders	$1,000	PAC
Special Trade Contractors	**$1,250**	
None over $1,000		
Construction Services	**$1,000**	
None over $1,000		
Building Materials & Equipment	**$2,500**	
Rinker Materials Corp	$2,500	Indiv

Energy & Natural Resources	$5,000	
Oil & Gas	**$1,000**	
None over $1,000		
Electric Utilities	**$4,000**	
Southern Co*	$3,000	PAC
Florida Power & Light	$1,000	PAC

Finance, Insurance & Real Estate	$29,050	
Commercial Banks	**$4,250**	
Hamilton Bank	$1,950	Indiv
Barnett Banks Inc	$1,000	PAC
Credit Unions	**$1,000**	
Credit Union National Assn	$1,000	PAC
Securities & Investment	**$4,500**	
Besilu Group	$2,500	Indiv
Diaz-Verson Capital Investments	$1,000	Indiv
Insurance	**$6,300**	
Orion Insurance Co	$2,000	Indiv
National Assn of Life Underwriters	$1,500	PAC
Granada Insurance Co	$1,000	Indiv

Contribution Totals by Sector

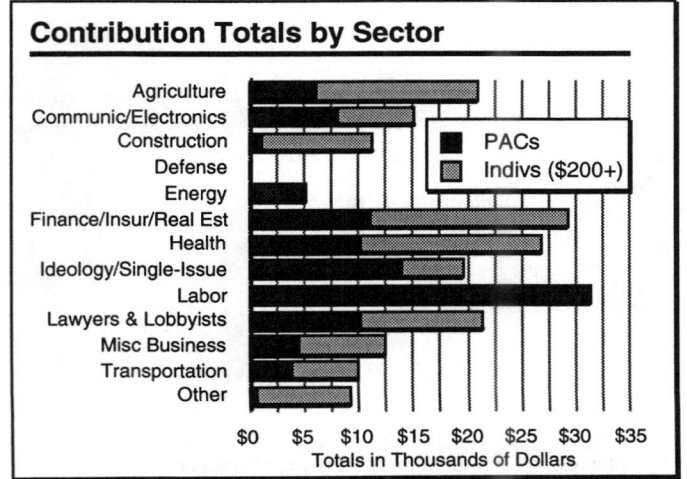

Agriculture, Communic/Electronics, Construction, Defense, Energy, Finance/Insur/Real Est, Health, Ideology/Single-Issue, Labor, Lawyers & Lobbyists, Misc Business, Transportation, Other

■ PACs ▨ Indivs ($200+)

$0 $5 $10 $15 $20 $25 $30 $35
Totals in Thousands of Dollars

Real Estate **$12,500**
    National Assn of Realtors ....$5,000 PAC
    Courtelis Co..$4,000 Indiv
    ROK Enterprises ....$1,000 Indiv

Health   **$26,650**

Health Professionals **$16,450**
    American Dental Assn ....$5,000 PAC
    American Optometric Assn ....$1,000 PAC
Hospitals/Nursing Homes **$5,500**
    American Hospital Assn ....$1,000 PAC
    Hospital Corp of America ....$1,000 PAC
    National Medical Enterprises Inc ....$1,000 PAC
    Palmetto General Hospital ....$1,000 Indiv
    Westchester General Hospital ....$1,000 Indiv
Pharmaceuticals/Health Products **$2,000**
    Pharmed Group ....$2,000 Indiv
Misc Health **$2,500**
    Physician Corp of America ....$1,000 Indiv
    South Florida Health Alliance ....$1,000 Indiv

Lawyers & Lobbyists   **$21,200**

Lawyers & Lobbyists **$21,200**
    Assn of Trial Lawyers of America ....$10,000 PAC
    Leesfield & Blackburn ....$2,000 Indiv
    Eric R Sisser Inc ....$1,000 Indiv
    Fowler, White et al ....$1,000 Indiv
    Martinez, Quintana et al ....$1,000 Indiv
    Sylvester Lukis & Associates ....$1,000 Indiv

Misc Business   **$12,150**

Food & Beverage **$2,000**
    Coca-Cola Co* ....$1,000 PAC
Beer, Wine & Liquor **$7,000**
    Eagle Brands Inc ....$5,000 Indiv
    National Beer Wholesalers Assn ....$1,000 PAC
    Southern Wine & Spirits ....$1,000 PAC
Casinos/Gambling **$1,000**
    Flagler Dog Track ....$1,000 Indiv

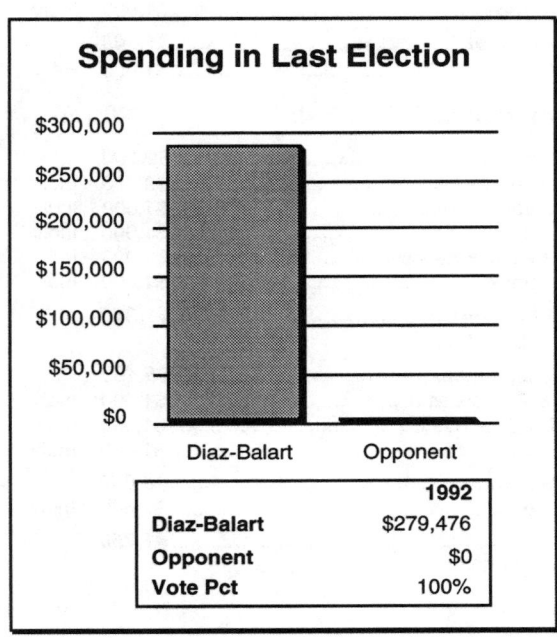

Spending in Last Election

	1992
Diaz-Balart	$279,476
Opponent	$0
Vote Pct	100%

Transportation **$9,750**

Automotive **$6,500**
    National Auto Dealers Assn ....$3,000 PAC
    Algus Enterprises ....$1,000 Indiv
    Metro Ford Inc ....$1,000 Indiv
    Williamson Cadillac ....$1,000 Indiv
Sea Transport.. **$3,000**
    Harrington & Co..$2,000 Indiv

Labor

Labor   **$31,000**

Building Trade Unions **$9,500**
    Carpenters & Joiners Union ....$7,500 PAC
    Plumbers/Pipefitters Union* ....$2,000 PAC
Industrial Unions **$3,500**
    Machinists/Aerospace Workers Union ....$2,500 PAC
    Ladies Garment Workers Union........................$1,000 PAC
Transportation Unions **$9,500**
    Teamsters Union ....$5,000 PAC
    Trans Comm International Union ....$3,000 PAC
Public Sector Unions **$6,500**
    National Assn of Letter Carriers ....$5,000 PAC
    American Federation of Teachers......................$1,000 PAC
Misc Unions... **$2,000**
    Food & Commercial Workers Union ....$2,000 PAC

Ideological/Single-Issue

Ideological/Single-Issue   **$20,500**

Leadership PACs **$1,500**
    Republican Leader's Fund (Bob Michel) ....$1,000 PAC
Foreign & Defense Policy **$14,750**
    Free Cuba PAC ....$10,000 PAC
Pro-Israel **$3,000**
    National Action Committee................................$1,000 PAC
    National PAC ....$1,000 PAC

Other & Unknown

Other   **$9,000**

Civil Servants/Public Officials **$1,000**
    State of Massachusetts ....$1,000 Indiv
Education **$5,500**
    Jearmi Enterprises ....$3,500 Indiv
Retired **$2,000**
    None over $1,000

Unknown   **$38,920**

    Homemakers/Non-income earners $5,750
    No Employer Listed or Found $12,670
    Generic Occupation/Category Unknown $8,100
        PAC ....$1,000 Indiv
    Employer Listed/Category Unknown $13,400
        Beltran Alexander & Assoc ....$2,000 Indiv
        Stinson, Lion & Bustamante ....$2,000 Indiv
        Tajar Corp ....$2,000 Indiv
        Harrington Corp/Fla ....$1,000 Indiv
        Urrechaga, Janus et al ....$1,000 Indiv

---

* Contributions came from more than one affiliate or subsidiary.

Jay Dickey, R-Ark (4)

1993-94 Committees & Subcommittees

First elected: 1992

1991-92 Total Receipts:	$405,965
1992 Year-end Cash:	$14,621

Agriculture
Environment, Credit and Rural Development; General Farm Commodities; Specialty Crops and Natural Resources

Natural Resources
National Parks, Forests and Public Lands; Oversight and Investigations

Small Business
Minority Enterprise, Finance and Urban Development, Regulation, Business Opportunities and Technology

Leading Contributors

NOTE: Dickey reported taking no PAC funds during his 1992 campaign. The PACs listed below did report making contributions, however, and those contributions are recorded in the official FEC records

Business

Agriculture $20,267

Crop Production & Basic Processing	$5,900	
Longfield Farms	$2,000	Indiv
Riceland Foods	$1,000	Indiv
Livestock	**$2,000**	
Arkansas Land & Cattle Co	$1,000	Indiv
Agricultural Services/Products	**$1,000**	
None over $1,000		
Food Processing & Sales	**$1,500**	
Meyer's Bakeries Inc	$1,250	Indiv
Forestry & Forest Products	**$9,867**	
Anthony Timberlands Inc	$2,000	Indiv
Ross Foundation	$1,747	Indiv
Stevens Forestry Service	$1,500	Indiv

Communications/Electronics $2,750

Telephone Utilities	$1,000	
AT&T	$1,000	PAC
Computer Equipment & Services	**$1,000**	
None over $1,000		

Source of Funds in 1992 Election

Source	Total	Pct
■ PACs	$0	0%
▨ Indivs $200+	$138,600	34%
□ Indivs under $200	$95,563	24%
▨ Other	$171,552	42%
Candidate	$124,000	31%
Party	$13,100	3%

Source of PAC Dollars by Sector

No PAC contributions reported

Source	Total	Pct
■ Business	$5,500	100%
▨ Labor	$0	0%
□ Ideology/Single Issue	$6	0%

In-State vs. Out-of-State Contributions*

Source	Total	Pct
□ In-State	$122,800	89%
■ Out-of-state	$15,550	11%
No state listed	$250	

* by large individual contributors ($200 & above)

Construction $5,140

General Contractors	$2,440	
None over $1,000		
Building Materials & Equipment	**$2,700**	
River Equipment Co	$1,000	Indiv
Trinity Lumber Co	$1,000	Indiv

Energy & Natural Resources $9,000

Oil & Gas	$7,500	
Murphy Oil	$3,000	Indiv
BBF Oil Co	$1,000	Indiv
Chesley Pruet Drilling Co	$1,000	Indiv
Mid South Sales Inc	$1,000	Indiv
Waste Management	**$1,000**	
Waste Management Inc	$1,000	PAC

Finance, Insurance & Real Estate $20,150

Commercial Banks	$9,000	
Walton Enterprises Inc	$2,000	Indiv
Arkansas Bank & Trust	$1,000	Indiv
Bank of Star City	$1,000	Indiv
Central Arkansas Bancshares	$1,000	Indiv
Twin City Bank	$1,000	Indiv
Securities & Investment	**$1,250**	
None over $1,000		
Real Estate	**$5,400**	
Lindsey & Associates	$1,000	Indiv
Pulaski Lenders Title Co	$1,000	Indiv
Stearns Co	$1,000	Indiv
Accountants	**$2,000**	
Erwin & Co	$1,000	Indiv
Misc Finance	**$1,750**	
None over $1,000		

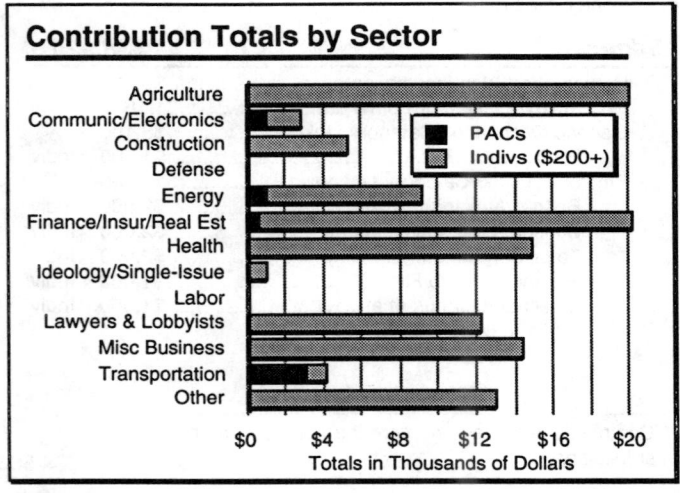

Contribution Totals by Sector

Agriculture
Communic/Electronics
Construction
Defense
Energy
Finance/Insur/Real Est
Health
Ideology/Single-Issue
Labor
Lawyers & Lobbyists
Misc Business
Transportation
Other

PACs
Indivs ($200+)

$0 $4 $8 $12 $16 $20
Totals in Thousands of Dollars

Health $14,824

Health Professionals $14,524
  None over $1,000

Lawyers & Lobbyists $12,100

Lawyers & Lobbyists $12,100
  Friday, Eldredge & Clark .... $5,200 Indiv
  Skokos, Coleman & Rainwa .... $2,000 Indiv
  Hilburn, Calhoun et al .... $1,000 Indiv
  Jack, Lyon & Jones .... $1,000 Indiv

Transportation $4,050

Air Transport $1,000
  United Parcel Service .... $1,000 PAC
Automotive $3,050
  National Auto Dealers Assn .... $2,000 PAC

Misc Business $14,250

Food & Beverage $3,000
  K-Mac Enterprises .... $1,500 Indiv
  Haynie Companies .... $1,000 Indiv
Beer, Wine & Liquor $1,500
  None over $1,000
Retail Sales $3,750
  Wal-Mart Stores .... $2,000 Indiv
  Gingles Department Store .... $1,250 Indiv
Misc Services $1,250
  Partee Flooring Mill .... $1,000 Indiv
Business Services $2,000
  None over $1,000
Chemical & Related Manufacturing $2,000
  Moline Paint Co .... $2,000 Indiv

Ideological/Single-Issue

Ideological/Single-Issue $1,006

Republican/Conservative $1,006
  Arkansas Republican Party .... $1,000 Indiv

Other & Unknown

Other $12,830

Education $2,250
  North Little Rock School District .... $1,000 Indiv
  Oklahoma State University .... $1,000 Indiv
Retired $10,580
  None over $1,000

Unknown $27,749

  Homemakers/Non-income earners $9,396
  No Employer Listed or Found $1,200
  Employer Listed/Category Unknown $17,143
    MacFarland Co .... $1,748 Indiv
    Arky House .... $1,000 Indiv
    Brenda Newman Interiors & Access .... $1,000 Indiv
    Harris & Harris of Kentucky .... $1,000 Indiv
    Jay Dickey Campaign Cmte .... $1,000 Indiv
    Suffolk Bloodstock .... $1,000 Indiv

Independent expenditures supporting Dickey
  National Right to Life PAC $2,874

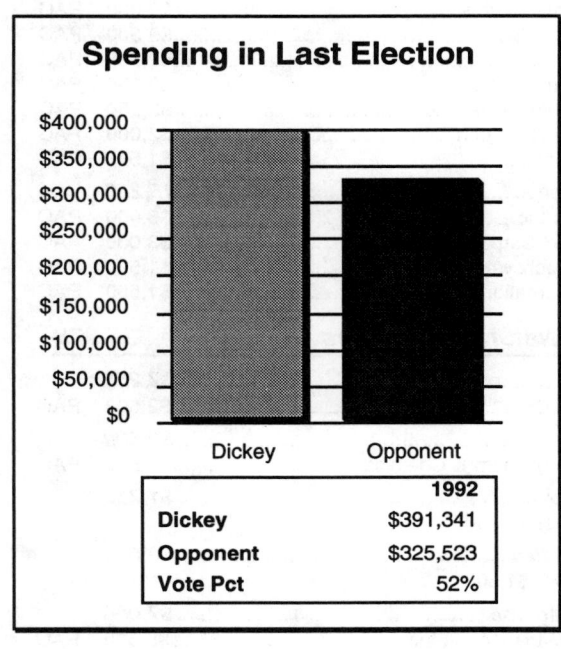

Spending in Last Election

	1992
Dickey	$391,341
Opponent	$325,523
Vote Pct	52%

Norm Dicks, D-Wash (6)

First elected: 1976
1991-92 Total Receipts: $546,865
1992 Year-end Cash: $55,882

1991-92 Committees & Subcommittees

Appropriations
Defense; Interior and Related Agencies; Military Construction

Select Committee on Intelligence

Leading Contributors

Business

Agriculture	$31,950	
Crop Production & Basic Processing	**$3,500**	
Ocean Spray Cranberries Inc	$1,500	PAC
Forestry & Forest Products	**$24,450**	
Weyerhaeuser Co*	$5,000	Indiv
Simpson Investment Co	$4,650	PAC/Ind
Manke Lumber Co	$1,500	Indiv
National Forest Products Assn	$1,500	PAC

Communications/Electronics	$15,120	
Media/Entertainment	**$3,750**	
National Assn of Broadcasters	$3,000	PAC
Telephone Utilities	**$4,250**	
US West Inc	$3,500	PAC
Telecom Services & Equipment	**$2,870**	
McCaw Cellular Communications	$2,870	PAC/Ind
Computer Equipment & Services	**$2,750**	
Electronic Data Systems	$1,500	PAC

Construction	$15,800	
General Contractors	**$9,500**	
Associated General Contractors	$2,250	PAC/Ind
Tucci & Sons	$2,250	Indiv
National Utility Contractors Assn	$1,500	PAC
Construction Services	**$4,500**	
None over $1,500		

Defense	$98,963	
Defense Aerospace	**$52,963**	
Northrop Corp	$8,000	PAC

Contribution Totals by Sector

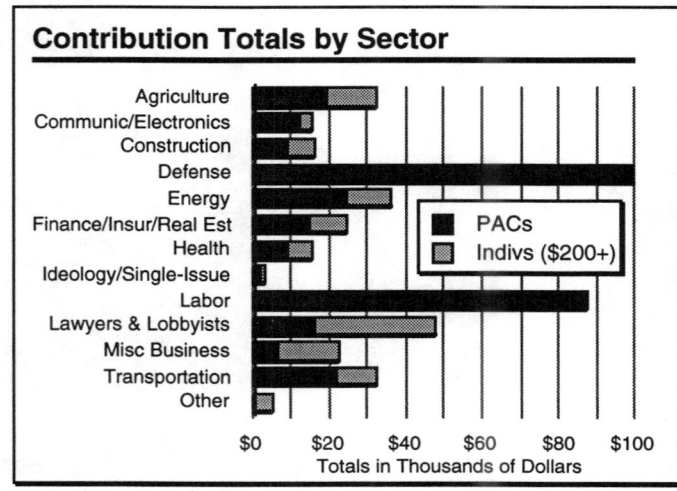

Agriculture
Communic/Electronics
Construction
Defense
Energy
Finance/Insur/Real Est
Health
Ideology/Single-Issue
Labor
Lawyers & Lobbyists
Misc Business
Transportation
Other

■ PACs
▨ Indivs ($200+)

$0 $20 $40 $60 $80 $100
Totals in Thousands of Dollars

Source of Funds in 1992 Election

Source	Total	Pct
■ PACs	$310,318	56%
▨ Indivs $200+	$153,648	28%
□ Indivs under $200	$59,245	11%
▨ Other	$30,898	6%
Candidate	$0	0%
Party	$7,894	1%

Source of PAC Dollars by Sector

Source	Total	Pct
■ Business	$227,634	72%
▨ Labor	$86,646	27%
□ Ideology/Single Issue	$1,300	0%

In-State vs. Out-of-State Contributions*

Source	Total	Pct
□ In-State	$115,623	75%
■ Out-of-state	$37,825	25%
No state listed	$200	

*** by large individual contributors ($200 & above)**

Boeing Co	$7,000	PAC
Textron Inc	$6,000	PAC
General Electric	$5,000	PAC
Lockheed Corp	$5,000	PAC
McDonnell Douglas*	$5,000	PAC
General Dynamics	$4,500	PAC
LTV Aerospace & Defense Co	$2,500	PAC
Martin Marietta Corp	$2,500	PAC
United Technologies	$2,000	PAC
Rockwell International	$1,500	PAC
Defense Electronics	**$30,750**	
Raytheon	$5,000	PAC
TRW Inc	$3,500	PAC
Hughes Aircraft	$3,000	PAC
Texas Instruments	$3,000	PAC
E-Systems Inc	$2,500	PAC
AT&T	$2,250	PAC
GTE Corp	$2,250	PAC
Westinghouse Electric	$2,250	PAC
Planning Research Corp	$2,000	PAC
Loral Corp	$1,500	PAC
Misc Defense	**$15,250**	
Tenneco Inc	$5,000	PAC
Sea-Land Corp	$3,000	PAC
Alliant Techsystems Inc	$1,500	PAC
BDM International	$1,500	PAC

Energy & Natural Resources	$35,975	
Oil & Gas	**$7,250**	
Enserch Corp	$2,000	PAC
Mining	**$2,500**	
Kaiser Aluminum & Chemical	$1,500	PAC
Misc Energy	**$1,750**	
None over $1,500		
Electric Utilities	**$3,600**	
None over $1,500		
Waste Management	**$7,000**	
Waste Management Inc	$5,500	PAC

Commercial Fishing $12,175
    American Factory Trawler Assn ....$2,625   PAC/Ind
    Royal Seafood Inc ....$1,500   Indiv

Finance, Insurance & Real Estate $23,823

Commercial Banks $6,325
    US Bancorp ....$3,000   PAC
    SeaFirst Bank ....$1,500   PAC

Savings & Loans $1,750
    None over $1,500

Securities & Investment $2,350
    None over $1,500

Insurance $5,250
    Delta Dental Plans Assn ....$2,000   PAC

Real Estate $7,148
    National Assn of Realtors ....$4,000   PAC

Health $15,500

Health Professionals $11,750
    American Medical Assn.......................................$5,000   PAC
    American Dental Assn ....$2,500   PAC

Pharmaceuticals/Health Products $2,000
    None over $1,500

Lawyers & Lobbyists $47,075

Lawyers & Lobbyists $47,075
    Preston, Gates et al ....$4,250   PAC/Ind
    Bogle & Gates ....$2,750   PAC/Ind
    Assn of Trial Lawyers of America ....$2,500   PAC
    Cassidy & Associates...$2,500   Indiv
    Paul Magliocchetti Associates ....$2,500   Indiv
    Denny Miller Associates ....$2,325   Indiv
    Garvey, Schubert & Barer ....$2,250   PAC/Ind
    Patton, Boggs & Blow ....$1,500   Indiv
    Winston & Strawn ....$1,500   Indiv

Misc Business $21,251

Food & Beverage $4,250
    None over $1,500

Beer, Wine & Liquor $2,051
    None over $1,500

Business Services $6,250
    None over $1,500

Spending in Last 3 Elections

	1988	1990	1992
Dicks	$288,168	$565,257	$617,460
Opponent	$37,620	$7,598	$6,861
Vote Pct	68%	61%	64%

Chemical & Related Manufacturing $3,500
    Puget Corp ....$2,000   Indiv

Misc Manufacturing & Distributing $3,250
    None over $1,500

Transportation $32,600

Air Transport...$11,500
    Boeing Co ....$4,500   Indiv
    United Airlines ....$1,500   PAC

Automotive $3,750
    Americans for Free International Trade ....$2,000   PAC

Trucking..$3,500
    Paccar Inc ....$2,000   PAC

Railroads $3,500
    Burlington Northern ....$3,500   PAC

Sea Transport...$9,850
    Stevedoring Services of America ....$2,500   Indiv
    Totem Ocean Trailer Express ....$2,250   PAC
    Cruise PAC...$1,500   PAC

Labor

Labor $86,646

Building Trade Unions $13,450
    Carpenters & Joiners Union ....$8,000   PAC
    Laborers' Political League ....$2,500   PAC

Industrial Unions $28,746
    Machinists/Aerospace Workers Union ....$13,746   PAC
    United Steelworkers ....$5,000   PAC
    Intl Brotherhood of Electrical Workers ....$3,500   PAC
    United Auto Workers ....$3,000   PAC
    Oil, Chemical & Atomic Workers Union ....$1,500   PAC

Transportation Unions $25,000
    Marine Engineers Union* ....$9,500   PAC
    Teamsters Union ....$6,000   PAC
    Seafarers International Union* ....$3,000   PAC
    Air Line Pilots Assn ....$2,500   PAC
    United Transportation Union ....$1,500   PAC

Public Sector Unions $16,950
    National Assn Retired Federal Employees ....$6,000   PAC
    American Fedn of St/Cnty/Munic Employees ......$3,450   PAC
    American Postal Workers Union ....$1,500   PAC

Misc Unions...$2,500
    Food & Commercial Workers Union ....$1,500   PAC

Ideological/Single-Issue

Ideological/Single-Issue $3,050
    None over $1,500

Other & Unknown

Other $4,750

Retired $4,000
    None over $1,500

Unknown $37,225
    Homemakers/Non-income earners $2,500
    No Employer Listed or Found $7,450
    Generic Occupation/Category Unknown $6,450
    Employer Listed/Category Unknown $20,325
        None over $1,500

---

* Contributions came from more than one affiliate or
subsidiary.

John D. Dingell, D-Mich (16)

First elected: 1955

1991-92 Total Receipts: $1,112,141
1992 Year-end Cash: $523,361

1991-92 Committees & Subcommittees

Energy and Commerce (Chairman)
Oversight and Investigations (Chairman)

Leading Contributors

Business

Agriculture — $45,550

Tobacco *$11,500*
   None over $5,000

Agricultural Services/Products *$8,500*
   American Veterinary Medical Assn .... $5,000 PAC

Food Processing & Sales *$12,500*
   None over $5,000

Communications/Electronics — $126,350

Printing & Publishing *$7,750*
   None over $5,000

Media/Entertainment *$59,050*
   National Assn of Broadcasters .... $10,000 PAC
   Paramount Communications .... $8,000 PAC
   Comcast Corp .... $5,000 PAC
   MCA Inc .... $5,000 PAC
   National Cable Television Assn .... $5,000 PAC
   Time Warner .... $5,000 PAC
   Viacom International .... $5,000 PAC

Telephone Utilities *$40,050*
   Ameritech Corp* .... $8,350 PAC

Telecom Services & Equipment *$14,000*
   None over $5,000

Construction — $19,450

General Contractors *$6,500*
   None over $5,000

Construction Services *$5,450*
   None over $5,000

Source of Funds in 1992 Election

Source	Total	Pct
PACs	$767,931	68%
Indivs $200+	$234,574	21%
Indivs under $200	$47,453	4%
Other	$79,589	7%
Candidate	$0	0%
Party	$17,556	2%

Source of PAC Dollars by Sector

Source	Total	Pct
Business	$629,707	83%
Labor	$116,725	15%
Ideology/Single Issue	$15,300	2%

In-State vs. Out-of-State Contributions*

Source	Total	Pct
In-State	$123,124	53%
Out-of-state	$108,250	47%
No state listed	$0	

* by large individual contributors ($200 & above)

Defense — $7,500

Defense Aerospace *$6,500*
   None over $5,000

Energy & Natural Resources — $94,750

Oil & Gas *$43,450*
   USX Corp* .... $5,000 PAC

Mining *$5,500*
   None over $5,000

Electric Utilities *$31,600*
   None over $5,000

Waste Management *$8,200*
   None over $5,000

Finance, Insurance & Real Estate — $166,700

Commercial Banks *$11,700*
   None over $5,000

Securities & Investment *$56,350*
   Federated Investors Inc .... $10,000 PAC/Ind
   Goldman, Sachs & Co .... $8,000 PAC/Ind
   Morgan Stanley & Co .... $5,000 PAC

Insurance *$60,250*
   Massachusetts Mutual Life Insurance .... $6,000 PAC
   American Council of Life Insurance .... $5,000 PAC

Real Estate *$12,700*
   None over $5,000

Accountants *$18,250*
   American Institute of CPA's .... $10,000 PAC

Contribution Totals by Sector

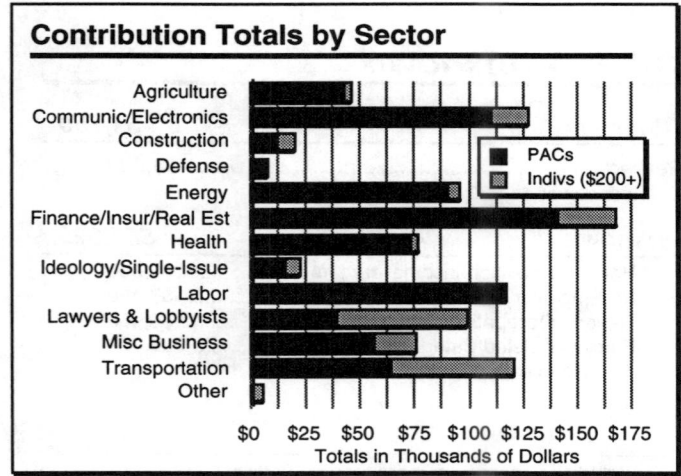

Legend: ■ PACs ▨ Indivs ($200+)

Agriculture
Communic/Electronics
Construction
Defense
Energy
Finance/Insur/Real Est
Health
Ideology/Single-Issue
Labor
Lawyers & Lobbyists
Misc Business
Transportation
Other

$0 $25 $50 $75 $100 $125 $150 $175
Totals in Thousands of Dollars

Health $76,050

Health Professionals **$35,650**
   American Chiropractic Assn .... $5,000 PAC
Hospitals/Nursing Homes **$7,250**
   None over $5,000
Pharmaceuticals/Health Products **$29,250**
   None over $5,000

Lawyers & Lobbyists $98,322

Lawyers & Lobbyists **$98,322**
   None over $5,000

Misc Business $74,429

Food & Beverage **$7,700**
   None over $5,000
Beer, Wine & Liquor **$17,450**
   Smirnoff/Inglenook Distributors .... $5,000 PAC
Retail Sales **$6,707**
   None over $5,000
Business Services **$5,350**
   None over $5,000
Chemical & Related Manufacturing **$7,700**
   None over $5,000
Misc Manufacturing & Distributing **$14,422**
   None over $5,000

Transportation $120,050

Air Transport **$18,700**
   United Parcel Service .... $8,200 PAC
   Aircraft Owners & Pilots Assn .... $5,000 PAC
Automotive **$75,150**
   Chrysler Corp .... $25,200 PAC/Ind
   Ford Motor Co .... $23,000 PAC/Ind
   General Motors .... $16,750 PAC/Ind
Railroads **$19,450**
   Union Pacific Corp .... $5,000 PAC

Labor

Labor $116,725

Building Trade Unions **$18,250**
   Carpenters & Joiners Union .... $5,000 PAC
   Sheet Metal Workers Union .... $5,000 PAC
Industrial Unions **$25,625**
   United Auto Workers .... $10,000 PAC
   Intl Brotherhood of Electrical Workers* .... $5,025 PAC
Transportation Unions **$38,700**
   Teamsters Union .... $10,000 PAC
   United Transportation Union .... $10,000 PAC
   Seafarers International Union .... $5,000 PAC
Public Sector Unions **$24,850**
   American Fedn of St/Cnty/Munic Employees ...... $7,750 PAC
   National Education Assn .... $5,000 PAC
Misc Unions **$9,300**
   Food & Commercial Workers Union .... $5,000 PAC

Ideological/Single-Issue

Ideological/Single-Issue $21,550

Pro-Israel **$5,000**
   None over $5,000
Human Rights **$5,000**
   KidsPAC .... $5,000 PAC

Other & Unknown

Unknown $23,850

   No Employer Listed or Found $7,925
   Employer Listed/Category Unknown $15,525
     None over $5,000

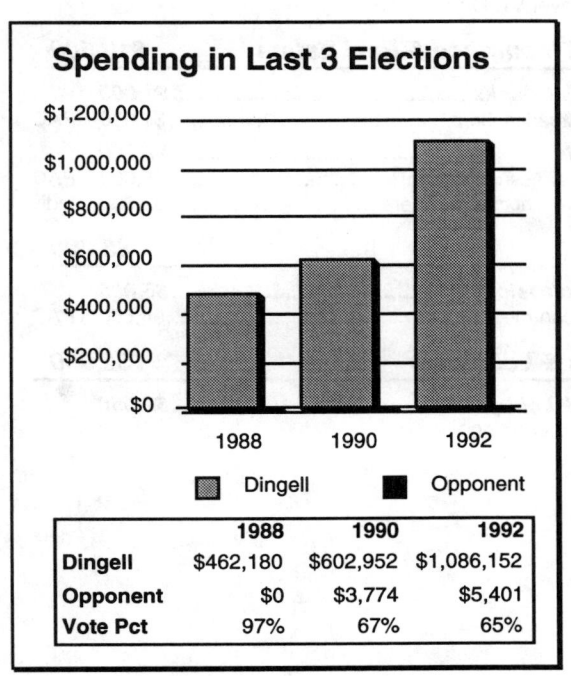

Spending in Last 3 Elections

	1988	1990	1992
Dingell	$462,180	$602,952	$1,086,152
Opponent	$0	$3,774	$5,401
Vote Pct	97%	67%	65%

* Contributions came from more than one affiliate or
subsidiary.

571

Julian C. Dixon, D-Calif (32)

First elected: 1978

1991-92 Total Receipts: $83,583
1992 Year-end Cash: $80,101

1991-92 Committees & Subcommittees

Appropriations
Defense; District of Columbia (Chairman)

Leading Contributors

Business

Agriculture	$2,500

Tobacco **$1,500**
    Tobacco Institute .... $1,000   PAC

Food Processing & Sales **$1,000**
    Connell Rice & Sugar Co .... $1,000   Indiv

Communications/Electronics	$6,650

Printing & Publishing **$1,000**
    Printco Graphic Arts .... $1,000   Indiv

Media/Entertainment **$3,650**
    MCA Inc .... $2,000   PAC/Ind
    Warner Brothers .... $1,000   Indiv

Telephone Utilities **$1,000**
    Pacific Telesis Group .... $1,000   PAC

Electronics Mfg & Services **$1,000**
    AVW Electronic Systems Inc .... $1,000   Indiv

Construction	$5,250

Home Builders **$1,000**
    National Assn of Home Builders .... $1,000   PAC

Construction Services **$3,000**
    Parsons Corp .... $1,000   PAC

Source of Funds in 1992 Election

Source	Total	Pct
■ PACs	$54,750	58%
▨ Indivs $200+	$27,150	29%
☐ Indivs under $200	$1,683	2%
▧ Other	$10,631	11%
Candidate	$0	0%
Party	$10,631	11%

Source of PAC Dollars by Sector

Source	Total	Pct
■ Business	$31,250	56%
▨ Labor	$18,000	33%
☐ Ideology/Single Issue	$6,089	11%

In-State vs. Out-of-State Contributions*

Source	Total	Pct
☐ In-State	$24,150	89%
■ Out-of-state	$3,000	11%
No state listed	$0	

* by large individual contributors ($200 & above)

Defense	$7,000

Defense Aerospace **$3,000**
    Textron Inc .... $2,000   PAC

Defense Electronics **$3,000**
    Hughes Aircraft .... $1,000   PAC
    ITT Corp .... $1,000   PAC

Misc Defense **$1,000**
    General Atomics .... $1,000   PAC

Energy & Natural Resources	$1,500

    None over $1,000

Finance, Insurance & Real Estate	$10,500

Commercial Banks **$1,000**
    BankAmerica Corp .... $1,000   PAC

Real Estate **$7,750**
    National Assn of Realtors .... $5,000   PAC
    Maguire Thomas Partners .... $2,000   Indiv

Health	$5,000

Health Professionals **$5,000**
    American Medical Assn .... $4,500   PAC

Lawyers & Lobbyists	$2,950

Lawyers & Lobbyists **$2,950**
    None over $1,000

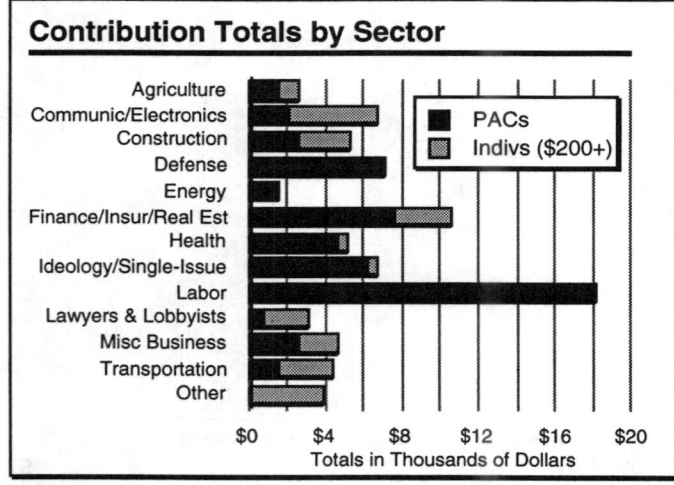

Contribution Totals by Sector

Legend: ■ PACs, ▨ Indivs ($200+)

Categories: Agriculture, Communic/Electronics, Construction, Defense, Energy, Finance/Insur/Real Est, Health, Ideology/Single-Issue, Labor, Lawyers & Lobbyists, Misc Business, Transportation, Other

Totals in Thousands of Dollars: $0, $4, $8, $12, $16, $20

Misc Business $4,500

Business Associations $1,000
    Greater Washington Board of Trade ....$1,000   PAC
Business Services $2,000
    CZ Wilson & Associates......................................$1,000   Indiv
Chemical & Related Manufacturing $1,000
    Dial Corp ....$1,000   PAC

Transportation $4,300

Air Transport $1,000
    United Parcel Service..$1,000   PAC
Automotive $1,800
    Mike Miller Toyota ....$1,000   Indiv
Sea Transport..$1,500
    Long Beach Naval Shipyard ....$1,000   Indiv

Labor

Labor $18,000

Building Trade Unions $2,500
    Laborers' Political League ....$2,000   PAC
Industrial Unions $3,000
    United Auto Workers ....$3,000   PAC
Transportation Unions $5,000
    Teamsters Union ....$5,000   PAC
Public Sector Unions...$5,500
    American Federation of Teachers ....$3,000   PAC
    American Postal Workers Union ....$1,000   PAC
    National Assn Retired Federal Employees ....$1,000   PAC
Misc Unions..$2,000
    Food & Commercial Workers Union ....$1,000   PAC
    Service Employees International Union ....$1,000   PAC

Ideological/Single-Issue

Ideological/Single-Issue $6,589

Pro-Israel $5,500
    National PAC ....$5,000   PAC

Other & Unknown

Other $3,800

Retired $2,500
    None over $1,000

Unknown $3,950

    Employer Listed/Category Unknown $3,950
        STD Research Corp ....$1,000   Indiv

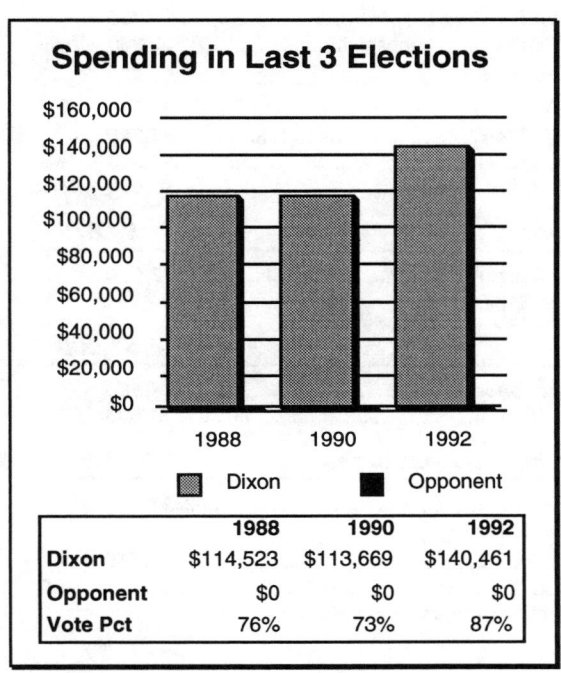

Spending in Last 3 Elections

	1988	1990	1992
Dixon	$114,523	$113,669	$140,461
Opponent	$0	$0	$0
Vote Pct	76%	73%	87%

Calvin Dooley, D-Calif (20)

First elected: 1990

1991-92 Total Receipts: $496,485
1992 Year-end Cash: $1,544

1991-92 Committees & Subcommittees

Agriculture
Cotton, Rice and Sugar; Department Operations, Research and Foreign Agriculture; Livestock, Dairy and Poultry

Interior and Insular Affairs
National Parks and Public Lands; Water, Power and Offshore Energy

Leading Contributors

Business

Agriculture $145,723

Crop Production & Basic Processing $82,122
Calcot Ltd	$7,870	PAC
California Almond Growers Exchange	$5,000	PAC
Sun-Diamond Growers*	$4,000	PAC
Sunkist Growers	$3,750	PAC
National Cotton Council	$3,400	PAC
Nichols Farms	$3,250	Indiv
California Pistachio Assn	$2,500	PAC
JG Boswell Co	$2,500	PAC
Jack Stone Farming	$2,500	Indiv
Conejo Farms	$2,000	Indiv
Harris Farms Inc	$2,000	Indiv
Dooley Farms	$1,900	Indiv
American Cotton Shippers Assn	$1,850	PAC
American Sugarbeet Growers Assn	$1,850	PAC
Double D Farms	$1,500	Indiv

Tobacco $2,550
None over $1,500

Dairy $12,939
Dairymans Co-op Creamery Assn	$4,125	PAC
Western United Dairymens Assn	$1,990	PAC
Mid-America Dairymen	$1,500	PAC

Poultry & Eggs $4,450
National Turkey Federation	$1,750	PAC
National Broiler Council	$1,700	PAC

Livestock $13,048
National Cattlemen's Assn*	$3,850	PAC
Price Giffen Associates	$2,450	Indiv
Errotabere Ranches	$1,748	Indiv
National Pork Producers Council	$1,600	PAC

Agricultural Services/Products $17,550
Friant Water PAC	$5,000	PAC
California Westside Farmers Inc	$2,500	PAC
American Veterinary Medical Assn	$2,000	PAC
California Farm Bureau Federation	$1,500	PAC

Food Processing & Sales $9,064
American Meat Institute	$2,414	PAC
Food Marketing Institute	$1,700	PAC

Misc Agriculture $3,500
Cap Ranches	$1,500	Indiv

Communications/Electronics $13,180

Misc Communications/Electronics $2,330
Pappas Telecasting Companies	$2,330	Indiv

Media/Entertainment $4,550
KMPH-TV	$1,500	Indiv

Telephone Utilities $5,250
Pacific Telesis Group	$2,300	PAC
BellSouth Corp*	$1,950	PAC

Construction $3,875

General Contractors $2,500
None over $1,500

Defense $1,500

Defense Aerospace $1,500
Northrop Corp	$1,500	PAC

Energy & Natural Resources $10,255

Oil & Gas $1,605
None over $1,500

Electric Utilities $7,550
Pacific Gas & Electric	$3,150	PAC
ACRE (Action Cmte for Rural Electrification)	$1,500	PAC

Source of Funds in 1992 Election

Source	Total	Pct
PACs	$242,583	49%
Indivs $200+	$145,584	29%
Indivs under $200	$97,655	20%
Other	$11,245	2%
Candidate	$0	0%
Party	$1,432	0%

Source of PAC Dollars by Sector

Source	Total	Pct
Business	$166,624	71%
Labor	$60,085	25%
Ideology/Single Issue	$9,313	4%

In-State vs. Out-of-State Contributions*

Source	Total	Pct
In-State	$139,184	96%
Out-of-state	$5,900	4%
No state listed	$500	

* by large individual contributors ($200 & above)

Contribution Totals by Sector

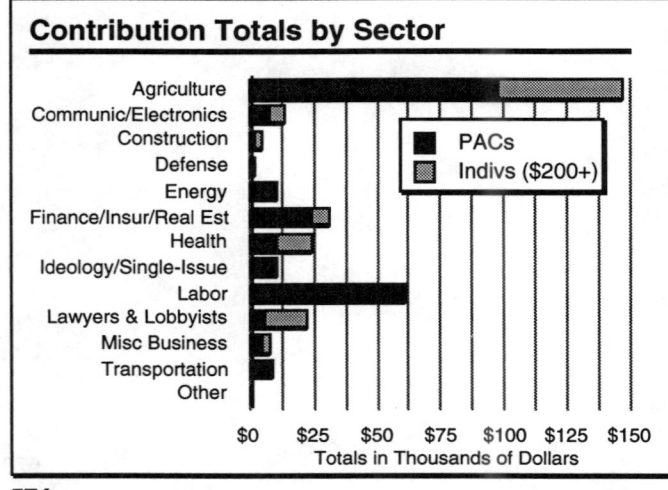

- Agriculture
- Communic/Electronics
- Construction
- Defense
- Energy
- Finance/Insur/Real Est
- Health
- Ideology/Single-Issue
- Labor
- Lawyers & Lobbyists
- Misc Business
- Transportation
- Other

■ PACs
▨ Indivs ($200+)

$0 $25 $50 $75 $100 $125 $150
Totals in Thousands of Dollars

Finance, Insurance & Real Estate $30,532

Commercial Banks **$10,450**
    American Bankers Assn .... $3,500   PAC
    BankAmerica Corp .... $2,000   PAC
    Independent Bankers Assn .... $1,700   PAC
    Wells Fargo .... $1,500   PAC

Securities & Investment **$2,332**
    None over $1,500

Insurance **$2,750**
    None over $1,500

Real Estate **$11,500**
    National Assn of Realtors .... $9,500   PAC

Accountants **$2,000**
    None over $1,500

Health $23,950

Health Professionals **$17,950**
    American Medical Assn .... $3,850   PAC
    American Academy of Ophthalmology .... $1,500   PAC

Hospitals/Nursing Homes **$3,750**
    California Assn of Hosp/Health Systems .... $1,750   PAC

Pharmaceuticals/Health Products **$2,000**
    None over $1,500

Lawyers & Lobbyists $22,023

Lawyers & Lobbyists **$22,023**
    Kahn, Soares & Conway .... $3,750   Indiv
    Sullivan & Worcester .... $2,000   PAC
    Bolen, Fransen & Boostrom .... $1,750   Indiv

Misc Business $7,300

Beer, Wine & Liquor **$2,100**
    None over $1,500

Transportation $8,200

Air Transport **$4,350**
    United Parcel Service .... $3,850   PAC

Automotive **$3,500**
    Auto Dealers & Drivers for Free Trade .... $1,500   PAC

Labor

Labor $60,085

Building Trade Unions **$15,600**
    Carpenters & Joiners Union .... $5,000   PAC
    Laborers' Political League .... $4,000   PAC
    Plumbers/Pipefitters Union .... $3,000   PAC
    Ironworkers Union .... $2,000   PAC

Industrial Unions **$13,550**
    United Auto Workers .... $5,350   PAC
    Intl Brotherhood of Electrical Workers .... $5,000   PAC
    Boilermakers Union .... $2,000   PAC

Transportation Unions **$12,150**
    Teamsters Union .... $7,500   PAC
    Air Line Pilots Assn .... $3,500   PAC

Public Sector Unions **$15,210**
    National Assn Retired Federal Employees .... $6,000   PAC
    National Assn of Letter Carriers .... $3,500   PAC
    National Education Assn .... $1,750   PAC

Misc Unions **$3,575**
    Food & Commercial Workers Union .... $1,650   PAC

Ideological/Single-Issue

Ideological/Single-Issue $9,813

Leadership PACs **$5,188**
    House Leadership Fund (Tom Foley) .... $3,188   PAC

Misc Issues **$2,525**
    National Cmte to Preserve Social Security .... $2,400   PAC

Other & Unknown

Unknown $44,670

    No Employer Listed or Found $28,675
    Employer Listed/Category Unknown $15,140
        Dooley Hill Associates .... $1,500   Indiv

Spending in Last 2 Elections

	1990	1992
Dooley	$538,354	$469,352
Opponent	$622,184	$133,757
Vote Pct	55%	65%

* Contributions came from more than one affiliate or
  subsidiary.

John T. Doolittle, R-Calif (4)

First elected: 1990

1991-92 Total Receipts: $610,104
1992 Year-end Cash: $217

1991-92 Committees & Subcommittees

Interior and Insular Affairs
Energy and the Environment; National Parks and Public Lands; Water, Power and Offshore Energy Resources

Merchant Marine and Fisheries
Fisheries and Wildlife Conservation and the Environment; Merchant Marine

Leading Contributors

Business

Agriculture	$55,650	
Crop Production & Basic Processing	**$15,575**	
California Almond Growers Exchange	$3,500	PAC
Sunkist Growers	$1,500	PAC
Dairy	**$2,150**	
None over $1,500		
Livestock	**$5,400**	
National Cattlemen's Assn*	$3,150	PAC
Agricultural Services/Products	**$3,625**	
None over $1,500		
Food Processing & Sales	**$8,200**	
Denio's Farmers Market	$2,000	Indiv
Pepsico Inc	$2,000	PAC
General Mills	$1,500	PAC/Ind
Forestry & Forest Products	**$16,700**	
Louisiana-Pacific Corp	$4,000	PAC
Simpson Investment Co	$3,850	PAC
Snider Lumber	$2,500	Indiv
Georgia-Pacific Corp	$2,100	PAC
Misc Agriculture	**$2,800**	
None over $1,500		

Communications/Electronics	$16,000	
Telephone Utilities	**$10,800**	
AT&T	$2,600	PAC
Pacific Telesis Group	$2,500	PAC
GTE Corp	$2,450	PAC
Roseville Telephone Co	$1,750	Indiv
Computer Equipment & Services	**$2,900**	
Electronic Data Systems	$1,600	PAC

Source of Funds in 1992 Election

Source	Total	Pct
■ PACs	$249,095	38%
▨ Indivs $200+	$201,079	31%
☐ Indivs under $200	$144,772	22%
☒ Other	$61,364	9%
Candidate	$0	0%
Party	$56,491	9%

Source of PAC Dollars by Sector

Source	Total	Pct
■ Business	$190,500	85%
▨ Labor	$7,200	3%
☐ Ideology/Single Issue	$25,875	12%

In-State vs. Out-of-State Contributions*

Source	Total	Pct
☐ In-State	$193,099	96%
■ Out-of-state	$7,305	4%
No state listed	$450	

* by large individual contributors ($200 & above)

Construction	$28,799	
General Contractors	**$16,349**	
Associated General Contractors	$2,500	PAC
CMSH Electrical	$2,100	Indiv
Teichert Inc	$1,749	Indiv
Ford Construction	$1,500	Indiv
Home Builders	**$6,450**	
John Mourier Construction	$4,000	Indiv
National Assn of Home Builders	$1,500	PAC
Building Materials & Equipment	**$5,000**	
Fibreboard Corp	$2,000	PAC
Meek's Building Supplies	$2,000	Indiv

Defense	$3,600	
Defense Aerospace	**$2,600**	
Northrop Corp	$1,850	PAC

Energy & Natural Resources	$36,000	
Oil & Gas	**$23,000**	
Chevron Corp	$4,750	PAC
Wickland Oil	$3,150	PAC
Atlantic Richfield	$2,000	PAC
Exxon Corp	$2,000	PAC
Halliburton Co	$2,000	PAC
Phillips Petroleum	$1,500	PAC
Mining	**$6,100**	
Lodestar Mining	$3,850	Indiv
Electric Utilities	**$6,400**	
Houston Industries	$2,000	PAC
Southern California Edison	$2,000	PAC
Pacific Gas & Electric	$1,850	PAC

Contribution Totals by Sector

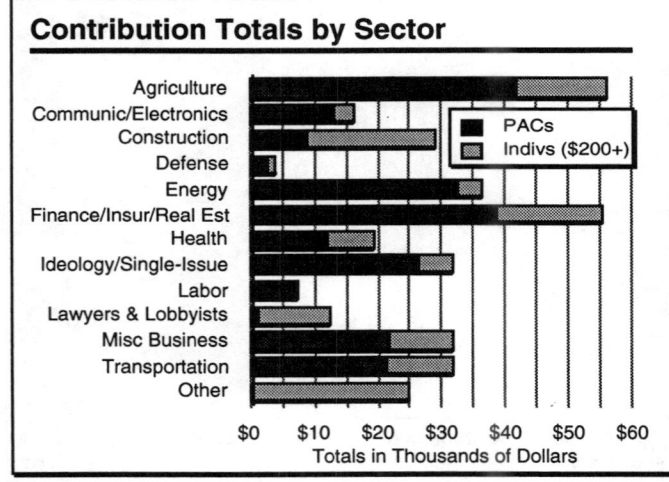

Agriculture
Communic/Electronics
Construction
Defense
Energy
Finance/Insur/Real Est
Health
Ideology/Single-Issue
Labor
Lawyers & Lobbyists
Misc Business
Transportation
Other

■ PACs
▨ Indivs ($200+)

$0 $10 $20 $30 $40 $50 $60
Totals in Thousands of Dollars

Finance, Insurance & Real Estate $54,900

Commercial Banks $21,825
     American Bankers Assn* .... $7,500   PAC
     Bank of Stockton .... $5,500   PAC
     BankAmerica Corp .... $3,200   PAC/Ind
     Barnett Banks Inc .... $2,000   PAC

Savings & Loans $4,750
     El Dorado Savings .... $2,750   Indiv
     Heart Federal Savings & Loan .... $1,500   Indiv

Insurance $7,000
     National Assn of Life Underwriters .... $3,000   PAC

Real Estate $16,550
     National Assn of Realtors .... $8,250   PAC
     Bishop Hawk Real Estate .... $2,800   Indiv

Accountants $1,650
     None over $1,500

Health $19,050

Health Professionals $18,700
     American Medical Assn .... $6,450   PAC
     American Academy of Ophthalmology .... $3,000   PAC

Lawyers & Lobbyists $12,150

Lawyers & Lobbyists $12,150
     None over $1,500

Misc Business $31,400

Business Associations $2,000
     National Fedn of Independent Business .... $2,000   PAC

Food & Beverage $4,950
     National Restaurant Assn .... $2,000   PAC

Beer, Wine & Liquor $2,250
     Capital Coors Co .... $2,000   Indiv

Retail Sales $5,750
     JC Penney Co .... $1,500   PAC

Business Services $4,350
     Harman Management Corp .... $4,000   Indiv

Spending in Last 2 Elections

	1990	1992
Doolittle	$517,668	$622,071
Opponent	$220,379	$375,190
Vote Pct	52%	50%

Lodging/Tourism $1,500
     Marriott Corp .... $1,500   PAC

Chemical & Related Manufacturing $3,000
     Dow Chemical .... $2,000   PAC

Misc Manufacturing & Distributing $6,500
     Stone Container Corp .... $5,000   PAC

Transportation $31,550

Air Transport $4,550
     United Parcel Service .... $3,350   PAC

Automotive $17,150
     National Auto Dealers Assn .... $5,850   PAC
     Senator Ford Inc .... $2,150   Indiv
     Americans for Free International Trade .... $2,000   PAC
     Auto Dealers & Drivers for Free Trade .... $2,000   PAC
     Snider AMC Jeep .... $1,750   Indiv

Trucking $2,600
     California Trucking Assn .... $1,900   Indiv

Railroads $2,750
     Union Pacific Corp .... $2,500   PAC

Sea Transport $3,500
     CSX Corp* .... $2,350   PAC

Labor

Labor $7,200

Transportation Unions $6,700
     Marine Engineers Union* .... $6,000   PAC

Ideological/Single-Issue

Ideological/Single-Issue $31,225

Republican/Conservative $7,550
     Eagle Forum .... $2,350   PAC

Pro-Life $7,575
     Republican National Coalition for Life .... $4,000   PAC
     California Pro Life Council .... $2,450   PAC

Gun Rights/Gun Control $10,750
     National Rifle Assn .... $9,500   PAC

Misc Issues $2,850
     None over $1,500

Other & Unknown

Other $24,525

Civil Servants/Public Officials $2,000
     None over $1,500

Retired $22,025
     None over $1,500

Unknown $72,380

     No Employer Listed or Found $44,755
     Generic Occupation/Category Unknown $1,500
     Employer Listed/Category Unknown $25,925
         Bring Marini .... $4,000   Indiv
         Hanzlick Enterprises .... $3,650   Indiv
         Westar Comm Inc .... $1,525   Indiv

Independent expenditures supporting Doolittle
     National Right to Life PAC $1,992

---

* Contributions came from more than one affiliate or
   subsidiary.

577

Robert K. Dornan, R-Calif (46)

First elected: 1976

1991-92 Total Receipts: $1,443,564
1992 Year-end Cash: $47,253

1991-92 Committees & Subcommittees

Armed Services
Research and Development; Seapower and Strategic and Critical Materials

Select Committee on Intelligence

Select Committee on Narcotics Abuse and Control

Leading Contributors

Business

Agriculture $13,900

Crop Production & Basic Processing	**$5,550**	
Eaton Farms Inc	$1,500	Indiv
Livestock	**$3,750**	
None over $1,000		
Agricultural Services/Products	**$1,500**	
Garvey Enterprises Inc	$1,000	Indiv
Misc Agriculture	**$3,000**	
Doheny Ranches	$3,000	Indiv

Communications/Electronics $5,500

Printing & Publishing	**$2,550**	
TV Fanfare Publications	$1,000	Indiv
Media/Entertainment	**$1,750**	
Walt Disney Co	$1,750	PAC/Ind
Telephone Utilities	**$1,000**	
Pacific Telesis Group	$1,000	PAC

Construction $10,000

General Contractors	**$3,000**	
Associated General Contractors	$2,500	PAC
Home Builders	**$1,000**	
Fleetwood Enterprises	$1,000	Indiv
Special Trade Contractors	**$1,750**	
National Roofing Contractors Assn	$1,000	PAC
Building Materials & Equipment	**$4,250**	
Orco Block Co	$1,700	Indiv
Deltrol Controls	$1,500	Indiv

Source of Funds in 1992 Election

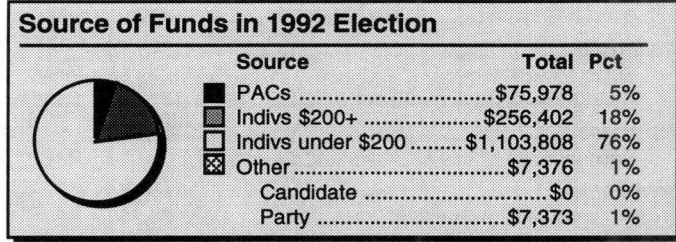

Source	Total	Pct
■ PACs	$75,978	5%
▨ Indivs $200+	$256,402	18%
☐ Indivs under $200	$1,103,808	76%
▣ Other	$7,376	1%
Candidate	$0	0%
Party	$7,373	1%

Source of PAC Dollars by Sector

Source	Total	Pct
■ Business	$57,500	66%
▨ Labor	$2,500	3%
☐ Ideology/Single Issue	$27,001	31%

In-State vs. Out-of-State Contributions*

Source	Total	Pct
☐ In-State	$97,415	42%
■ Out-of-state	$136,339	58%
No state listed	$0	

* by large individual contributors ($200 & above)

Defense $20,350

Defense Aerospace	**$13,500**	
Northrop Corp	$4,000	PAC
Lockheed Corp	$1,500	PAC
Martin Marietta Corp	$1,500	PAC
McDonnell Douglas*	$1,500	PAC
Rockwell International	$1,500	PAC
Boeing Co	$1,000	PAC
Grumman Corp	$1,000	PAC
Defense Electronics	**$6,500**	
Raytheon	$2,500	PAC
Cubic Corp	$1,000	PAC
Hughes Aircraft	$1,000	PAC

Energy & Natural Resources $7,607

Oil & Gas	**$6,807**	
None over $1,000		

Finance, Insurance & Real Estate $11,700

Commercial Banks	**$3,000**	
American Bankers Assn	$2,500	PAC
Insurance	**$1,000**	
None over $1,000		
Real Estate	**$6,450**	
National Assn of Realtors	$5,000	PAC
Misc Finance	**$1,000**	
None over $1,000		

Contribution Totals by Sector

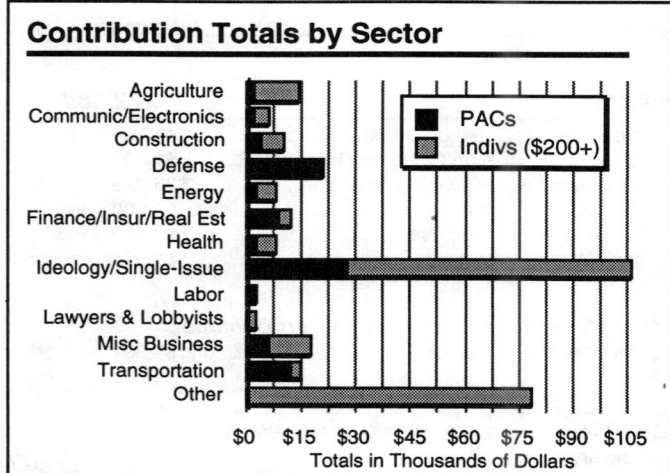

Agriculture
Communic/Electronics
Construction
Defense
Energy
Finance/Insur/Real Est
Health
Ideology/Single-Issue
Labor
Lawyers & Lobbyists
Misc Business
Transportation
Other

■ PACs
▨ Indivs ($200+)

$0 $15 $30 $45 $60 $75 $90 $105
Totals in Thousands of Dollars

Health $7,900

Health Professionals $7,900
   American Medical Assn .... $2,500   PAC

Lawyers & Lobbyists $2,500

Lawyers & Lobbyists $2,500
   Amer, Cunningham, Brennan & Co .... $1,000   Indiv

Misc Business $16,900

Food & Beverage $2,400
   National Restaurant Assn .... $1,000   PAC

Beer, Wine & Liquor $1,300
   National Beer Wholesalers Assn .... $1,000   PAC

Retail Sales $4,750
   Merl-Norman Cosmetics .... $3,800   Indiv

Business Services $1,300
   None over $1,000

Chemical & Related Manufacturing $1,250
   Sachem Inc .... $1,000   Indiv

Misc Manufacturing & Distributing $4,600
   Stone Container Corp .... $1,500   PAC
   Parker-Hannifin Corp .... $1,000   Indiv

Transportation $14,750

Air Transport $3,000
   United Parcel Service .... $2,000   PAC

Automotive $11,250
   National Auto Dealers Assn .... $5,500   PAC
   Auto Dealers & Drivers for Free Trade .... $2,500   PAC
   Avalon Glass & Mirror Co .... $2,000   Indiv
   Americans for Free International Trade .... $1,000   PAC

Labor

Labor $2,500

Transportation Unions $2,000
   Marine Engineers Dist 2 Retirees .... $2,000   PAC

Ideological/Single-Issue

Ideological/Single-Issue $105,385

Republican/Conservative $81,304
   Eagle Forum .... $2,500   PAC
   Conservative Victory Committee .... $2,000   PAC
   American Citizens for Political Action .... $1,000   PAC

Leadership PACs $1,500
   New Majority Leadership PAC (Vin Weber) ...... $1,000   PAC

Pro-Life $9,750
   National Right to Life PAC .... $5,000   PAC
   Pro-Life PAC of Orange County .... $2,500   PAC
   Republican National Coalition for Life .... $1,000   PAC

Gun Rights/Gun Control $6,950
   National Rifle Assn .... $6,950   PAC

Misc Issues $4,850
   Right to Work PAC .... $1,000   PAC

Other & Unknown

Other $77,618

Civil Servants/Public Officials $1,645
   US Department of Justice .... $1,445   Indiv

Retired $72,813
   None over $1,000

Other $2,660
   None over $1,000

Unknown $24,145

   Homemakers/Non-income earners $9,275
   No Employer Listed or Found $6,970
   Employer Listed/Category Unknown $7,900
     Heusser Enterprises .... $1,000   Indiv
     Kenneth & Leslie .... $1,000   Indiv
     Onter Corp .... $1,000   Indiv

Independent expenditures supporting Dornan
   California Pro Life Council $12,795
   National Right to Life PAC $4,597
   National Freedom PAC $1,430

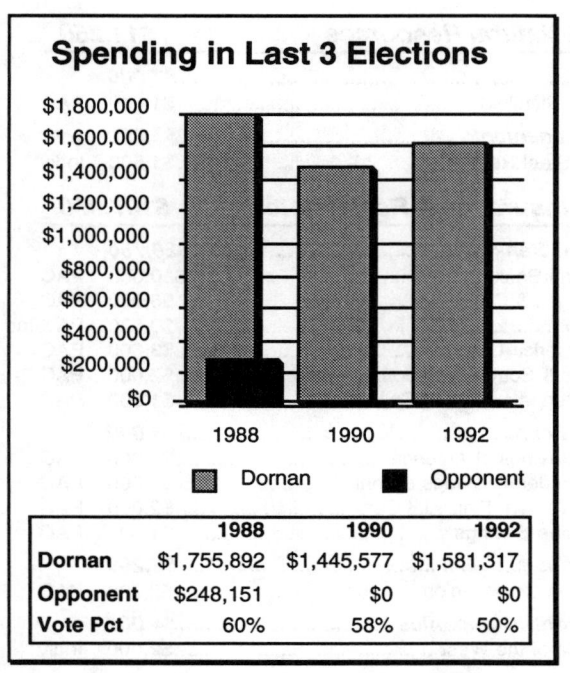

Spending in Last 3 Elections

	1988	1990	1992
Dornan	$1,755,892	$1,445,577	$1,581,317
Opponent	$248,151	$0	$0
Vote Pct	60%	58%	50%

Dornan   Opponent

* Contributions came from more than one affiliate or
  subsidiary.

David Dreier, R-Calif (28)

First elected: 1980

1991-92 Total Receipts: $646,323
1992 Year-end Cash: $2,026,109

1991-92 Committees & Subcommittees

Rules
Rules of the House (Ranking Republican)

Leading Contributors

Business

Agriculture	$25,250

Crop Production & Basic Processing **$7,250**
    Cypress Farms Inc .... $2,000   Indiv
    Sun World International .... $2,000   Indiv
    Sunkist Growers .... $2,000   PAC

Dairy **$1,500**
    None over $1,500

Livestock **$2,000**
    None over $1,500

Agricultural Services/Products **$4,000**
    Monrovia Nursery Co .... $2,750   Indiv

Food Processing & Sales **$5,750**
    Mexican American Grocers Assn .... $4,000   Indiv

Forestry & Forest Products **$1,750**
    None over $1,500

Misc Agriculture **$2,000**
    Doheny Ranches .... $2,000   Indiv

Communications/Electronics	$14,700

Printing & Publishing **$3,000**
    Pace Lithographers .... $2,000   Indiv

Media/Entertainment **$6,950**
    National Cable Television Assn .... $1,500   PAC

Telephone Utilities **$2,250**
    None over $1,500

Telecom Services & Equipment **$2,500**
    New Bedford Panoramex Corp .... $2,500   PAC

Source of Funds in 1992 Election

Source	Total	Pct
■ PACs	$131,350	20%
▨ Indivs $200+	$219,170	34%
☐ Indivs under $200	$41,585	6%
▩ Other	$254,218	39%
Candidate	$0	0%
Party	$0	0%

Source of PAC Dollars by Sector

Source	Total	Pct
■ Business	$125,800	99%
▨ Labor............................	$500	0%
☐ Ideology/Single Issue	$750	1%

In-State vs. Out-of-State Contributions*

Source	Total	Pct
☐ In-State	$202,420	93%
■ Out-of-state	$16,000	7%
No state listed	$0	

* by large individual contributors ($200 & above)

Construction	$16,250

General Contractors **$6,250**
    Associated General Contractors .... $1,500   PAC

Home Builders **$7,500**
    Matreyek Homes .... $4,000   Indiv
    Lewis Homes .... $2,000   Indiv

Construction Services **$1,750**
    Jacobs Engineering Group .... $1,500   Indiv

Defense	$1,500
    None over $1,500

Energy & Natural Resources	$11,250

Oil & Gas **$7,000**
    Atlantic Richfield .... $1,500   PAC

Waste Management **$3,000**
    Kaiser Steel Resources .... $1,500   Indiv

Finance, Insurance & Real Estate	$107,950

Commercial Banks **$29,750**
    American Bankers Assn .... $10,000   PAC
    JP Morgan & Co .... $5,000   PAC
    Citicorp .... $3,500   PAC/Ind
    BankAmerica Corp .... $3,000   PAC
    Citizens & Southern National Bank .... $2,000   PAC
    First Interstate Bank of California .... $1,500   PAC

Savings & Loans **$13,000**
    Home Savings of America .... $4,000   PAC
    Coast Federal Savings & Loan .... $2,000   PAC
    Great Western Financial Corp .... $2,000   PAC
    Guarantee Savings .... $1,500   PAC

Credit Unions **$2,200**
    California Credit Union League .... $2,200   PAC

Finance/Credit Companies **$4,000**
    Trust Co of the West .... $2,000   Indiv

Contribution Totals by Sector

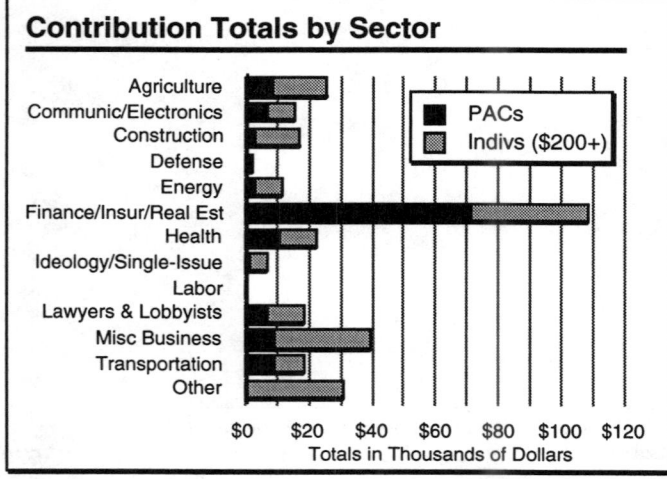

Agriculture
Communic/Electronics
Construction
Defense
Energy
Finance/Insur/Real Est
Health
Ideology/Single-Issue
Labor
Lawyers & Lobbyists
Misc Business
Transportation
Other

■ PACs
▨ Indivs ($200+)

$0 $20 $40 $60 $80 $100 $120
Totals in Thousands of Dollars

Securities & Investment $11,250
    Dean Witter ....$2,000 PAC
    Morgan Stanley & Co ....$2,000 PAC
    Provident Investment ....$2,000 Indiv

Insurance $13,750
    TransAmerica Corp* ....$2,500 PAC
    Holden Group ....$2,000 Indiv

Real Estate $21,000
    National Assn of Realtors ....$4,000 PAC
    Sierra Land Group ....$4,000 Indiv
    California Assn of Mortgage Brokers ...$2,000 PAC

Accountants $10,250
    American Institute of CPA's ....$5,000 PAC
    Parke Guptill & Co ....$3,750 Indiv

Misc Finance $2,750
    None over $1,500

Health $21,500

Health Professionals $17,000
    American Medical Assn ....$5,000 PAC
    Cooperative of American Physicians ...$4,000 PAC

Pharmaceuticals/Health Products $2,250
    None over $1,500

Lawyers & Lobbyists $18,050

Lawyers & Lobbyists $18,050
    Assn of Trial Lawyers of America ......$5,000 PAC
    Thomson & Nelson ....$2,250 Indiv

Misc Business $38,661

Food & Beverage $3,750
    In-N-Out Burger ....$2,000 Indiv

Beer, Wine & Liquor $3,500
    Foothill Beverage Co ....$3,000 Indiv

Retail Sales $3,750
    None over $1,500

Misc Services $2,911
    None over $1,500

Business Services $7,500
    American Building Maintenance Co .....$2,000 Indiv

Misc Manufacturing & Distributing $14,800
    Aerosol Services Co ....$3,000 Indiv
    Stone Container Corp ....$3,000 PAC
    Cheyo Inc ....$2,000 Indiv
    Highland Supply Corp ....$1,500 Indiv
    Rainbird Sprinklers ....$1,500 Indiv

Transportation $18,750

Air Transport $4,000
    United Parcel Service ....$3,000 PAC

Automotive $9,250
    Auto Dealers & Drivers for Free Trade .$2,000 PAC

Sea Transport $1,750
    None over $1,500

Misc Transport $3,250
    Durham Transportation ....$2,000 Indiv

Ideological/Single-Issue

Ideological/Single-Issue $6,250

Republican/Conservative $4,500
    None over $1,500

Other & Unknown

Other $30,450

Retired $27,450
    None over $1,500

Unknown $34,947

    Homemakers/Non-income earners $4,850
    Employer Listed/Category Unknown $28,559
        Rose Hills Co ....$1,809 Indiv
        McIntyre, Reenders Corp ....$2,000 Indiv

Spending in Last 3 Elections

	1988	1990	1992
Dreier	$186,183	$172,451	$290,128
Opponent	$0	$29,177	$23,493
Vote Pct	69%	64%	58%

---

* Contributions came from more than one affiliate or subsidiary.

John J. "Jimmy" Duncan Jr., R-Tenn (2)

First elected: 1988

1991-92 Total Receipts:	$258,496
1992 Year-end Cash:	$225,372

1991-92 Committees & Subcommittees

Banking, Finance and Urban Affairs
Domestic Monetary Policy; Financial Institutions Supervision, Regulation and Insurance; International Development, Finance, Trade and Monetary Policy

Interior and Insular Affairs
General Oversight and California Desert Lands; National Parks and Public Lands

Public Works and Transportation
Aviation; Public Buildings and Grounds; Surface Transportation

Select Committee on Aging

Leading Contributors

Business

Agriculture	$14,625	
Crop Production & Basic Processing $2,375		
None over $1,000		
Tobacco $2,750		
RJR Nabisco $1,350	PAC	
Dairy $3,800		
Associated Milk Producers $2,000	PAC	
Dairymen Inc-Tennessee $1,800	PAC	
Agricultural Services/Products $1,000		
None over $1,000		
Food Processing & Sales $3,300		
Winn-Dixie Stores $2,000	PAC	

Communications/Electronics	$5,900	
Telephone Utilities $4,400		
AT&T $2,700	PAC	

Source of Funds in 1992 Election

Source	Total	Pct
■ PACs	$162,509	62%
▨ Indivs $200+	$43,816	17%
□ Indivs under $200	$43,685	17%
⊠ Other	$11,317	4%
Candidate	$0	0%
Party	$3,157	1%

Source of PAC Dollars by Sector

Source	Total	Pct
■ Business	$147,690	90%
▨ Labor	$10,700	7%
□ Ideology/Single Issue	$5,900	4%

In-State vs. Out-of-State Contributions*

Source	Total	Pct
□ In-State	$38,616	88%
■ Out-of-state	$5,200	12%
No state listed	$0	

* by large individual contributors ($200 & above)

Construction	$14,299	
General Contractors $4,000		
National Utility Contractors Assn $1,500	PAC	
Nova Inc $1,000	Indiv	
Home Builders $3,799		
National Assn of Home Builders $2,499	PAC	
JS Doss & Associates $1,000	Indiv	
Building Materials & Equipment $5,500		
Regal Corp $2,000	Indiv	
Schubert Lumber Co $1,000	Indiv	

Defense	$1,650	
Defense Aerospace $1,650		
None over $1,000		

Energy & Natural Resources	$14,450	
Oil & Gas $2,700		
Petroleum Marketers Assn $1,000	PAC	
Mining $6,250		
Alcoa $1,600	PAC	
Appolo Fuels Inc $1,000	Indiv	
Nuclear Energy $2,650		
Gilbert Associates $1,500	PAC	
General Atomics $1,000	PAC	
Misc Energy $1,000		
None over $1,000		
Electric Utilities $1,050		
None over $1,000		

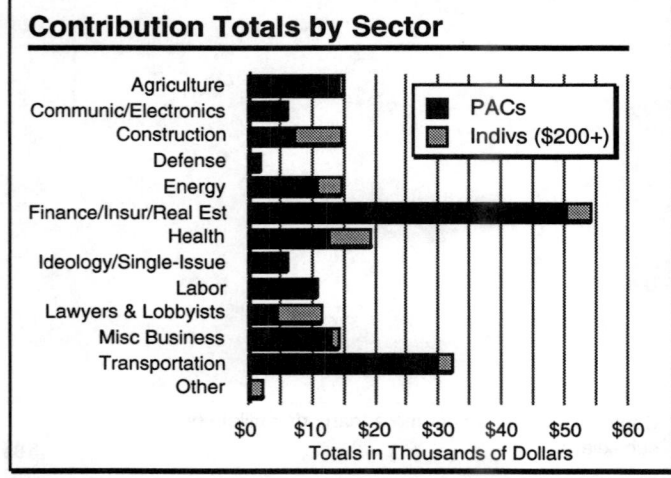

Contribution Totals by Sector

- Agriculture
- Communic/Electronics
- Construction
- Defense
- Energy
- Finance/Insur/Real Est
- Health
- Ideology/Single-Issue
- Labor
- Lawyers & Lobbyists
- Misc Business
- Transportation
- Other

■ PACs
▨ Indivs ($200+)

$0 $10 $20 $30 $40 $50 $60

Totals in Thousands of Dollars

Finance, Insurance & Real Estate $53,816

Commercial Banks **$9,950**
American Bankers Assn .... $2,500   PAC
Third National Corp .... $2,000   PAC
Bank of East Tennessee .... $1,300   Indiv
Barnett Banks Inc .... $1,000   PAC
Citizens & Southern National Bank .... $1,000   PAC
First Tennessee National Corp .... $1,000   PAC

Savings & Loans **$3,800**
US League of Savings Assns* .... $3,000   PAC

Credit Unions **$2,600**
Credit Union National Assn .... $2,000   PAC

Securities & Investment **$2,100**
Tudor Investment Corp .... $1,000   Indiv

Insurance **$18,526**
National Assn of Life Underwriters .... $7,500   PAC
Independent Insurance Agents of America .... $2,200   PAC
American Family Corp .... $2,000   PAC
National Assn of Prof Insurance Agents .... $1,526   PAC
American Council of Life Insurance .... $1,000   PAC
Casualty & Surety Agents Assn .... $1,000   PAC

Real Estate **$9,690**
National Assn of Realtors .... $7,440   PAC

Accountants **$5,000**
American Institute of CPA's .... $5,000   PAC

Misc Finance **$1,350**
None over $1,000

Health $18,950

Health Professionals **$14,700**
American Medical Assn .... $4,800   PAC
American Dental Assn .... $1,300   PAC
American Academy of Ophthalmology .... $1,000   PAC
American Podiatry Assn .... $1,000   PAC

Pharmaceuticals/Health Products **$2,300**
Schering-Plough Corp .... $2,000   PAC

Misc Health **$1,000**
Home Health Care .... $1,000   Indiv

Lawyers & Lobbyists $11,466

Lawyers & Lobbyists **$11,466**
Assn of Trial Lawyers of America .... $3,350   PAC
Webster, Chamberlain & Bean .... $1,200   Indiv

Misc Business $14,200

Beer, Wine & Liquor **$1,900**
None over $1,000

Retail Sales **$2,100**
Pardons Jewelers .... $1,000   Indiv

Chemical & Related Manufacturing **$2,700**
Eastman Kodak/Chemicals Division .... $1,200   PAC
Rohm & Haas Co .... $1,000   PAC

Misc Manufacturing & Distributing **$5,700**
Stone Container Corp .... $2,300   PAC
Maytag Co .... $1,000   PAC
Xerox Corp .... $1,000   PAC

Transportation $31,650

Air Transport **$16,100**
Federal Express Corp .... $9,000   PAC
United Parcel Service .... $4,600   PAC
Aircraft Owners & Pilots Assn .... $1,000   PAC

Automotive **$10,400**
National Auto Dealers Assn .... $7,500   PAC
Auto Dealers & Drivers for Free Trade .... $1,000   PAC
Matlock Tire Service .... $1,000   Indiv

Trucking **$2,000**
None over $1,000

Railroads **$2,300**
Norfolk Southern Corp .... $1,100   PAC

Labor

Labor $10,700

Transportation Unions **$7,500**
Marine Engineers Union* .... $5,000   PAC
Air Line Pilots Assn .... $2,500   PAC

Public Sector Unions **$3,200**
National Assn Retired Federal Employees .... $2,000   PAC

Ideological/Single-Issue

Ideological/Single-Issue $5,900

Gun Rights/Gun Control **$4,000**
National Rifle Assn .... $4,000   PAC

Misc Issues **$1,100**
National Cmte to Preserve Social Security .... $1,100   PAC

Other & Unknown

Other $2,000

Retired **$1,300**
None over $1,000

Unknown $8,500

Employer Listed/Category Unknown $8,000
   Coastal Supply Co .... $1,000   Indiv
   Phillips & Jordan .... $1,000   Indiv
   Pilot Castastrophe Serv .... $1,000   Indiv

---

* Contributions came from more than one affiliate or subsidiary.

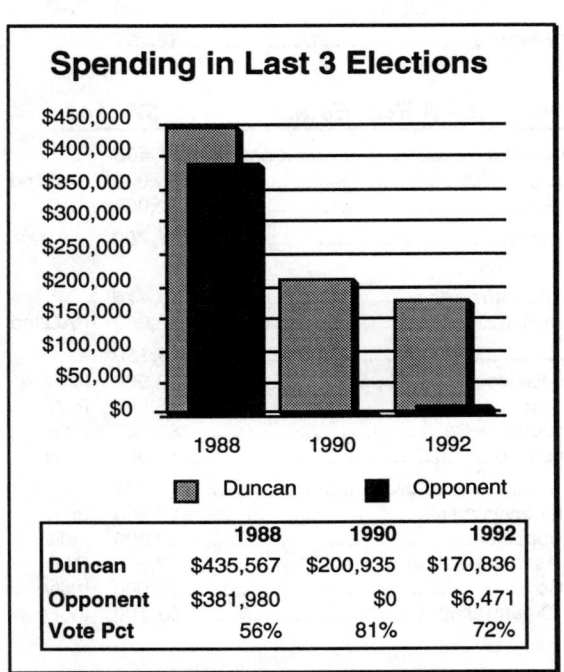

Spending in Last 3 Elections

	1988	1990	1992
Duncan	$435,567	$200,935	$170,836
Opponent	$381,980	$0	$6,471
Vote Pct	56%	81%	72%

Legend: ▨ Duncan   ■ Opponent

Jennifer Dunn, R-Wash (8)

First elected: 1992

1991-92 Total Receipts:	$684,207
1992 Year-end Cash:	$4,533

1993-94 Committees & Subcommittees

Administration
Accounts; Elections; Personnel and Police (Ranking Republican)

Public Works and Transportation
Aviation; Economic Development; Surface Transportation

Science, Space and Technology
Space

Joint Committee on the Organization of Congress

Leading Contributors

Business

Agriculture		$39,768

Agricultural Services/Products	**$2,650**	
None over $1,500		

Food Processing & Sales	**$6,750**	
Services Group of America	$3,000	PAC

Forestry & Forest Products	**$28,868**	
Weyerhaeuser Co*	$11,318	Indiv
Simpson Investment Co	$6,300	PAC/Ind
Port Blakely Tree Farms	$3,000	Indiv

Communications/Electronics		$16,075

Printing & Publishing	**$1,700**	
None over $1,500		

Media/Entertainment	**$2,100**	
None over $1,500		

Telephone Utilities	**$8,025**	
United Telecommunications	$3,000	PAC
US West Inc	$2,775	PAC

Telecom Services & Equipment	**$2,000**	
None over $1,500		

Computer Equipment & Services	**$1,500**	
None over $1,500		

Construction		$9,285

General Contractors	**$5,450**	
None over $1,500		

Special Trade Contractors	**$1,835**	
None over $1,500		

Contribution Totals by Sector

Agriculture
Communic/Electronics
Construction
Defense
Energy
Finance/Insur/Real Est
Health
Ideology/Single-Issue
Labor
Lawyers & Lobbyists
Misc Business
Transportation
Other

PACs
Indivs ($200+)

$0 $10 $20 $30 $40 $50 $60 $70
Totals in Thousands of Dollars

Source of Funds in 1992 Election

Source	Total	Pct
PACs	$168,373	24%
Indivs $200+	$220,927	31%
Indivs under $200	$271,617	38%
Other	$51,772	7%
Candidate	$0	0%
Party	$48,482	7%

Source of PAC Dollars by Sector

Source	Total	Pct
Business	$141,574	83%
Labor	$500	0%
Ideology/Single Issue	$28,361	17%

In-State vs. Out-of-State Contributions*

Source	Total	Pct
In-State	$188,927	87%
Out-of-state	$28,150	13%
No state listed	$250	

by large individual contributors ($200 & above)

Defense		$2,000

Defense Electronics	**$1,500**	
None over $1,500		

Energy & Natural Resources		$20,947

Oil & Gas	**$9,750**	
None over $1,500		

Mining	**$2,750**	
National Coal Assn	$1,500	PAC

Electric Utilities	**$5,350**	
Puget Sound Power & Light	$4,000	PAC

Commercial Fishing	**$2,097**	
None over $1,500		

Finance, Insurance & Real Estate		$71,141

Commercial Banks	**$11,600**	
US Bancorp	$4,000	PAC/Ind
SeaFirst Bank	$2,000	PAC

Savings & Loans	**$1,700**	
None over $1,500		

Securities & Investment	**$5,416**	
Merrill Lynch	$2,600	PAC/Ind

Insurance	**$16,150**	
CEM Associates	$3,500	Indiv
Safeco Corp	$3,500	PAC
Pemco Insurance Co	$2,300	Indiv
Meisenbach Co	$2,000	Indiv

Real Estate	**$25,125**	
Sarkowsky Investments	$3,500	Indiv
Safeco Properties	$3,000	Indiv
National Assn of Realtors	$2,500	PAC
Stearns Co	$2,000	Indiv
Barness Organization	$1,500	Indiv

Accountants	$5,000	
American Institute of CPA's	$2,500	PAC
Misc Finance	$6,150	
None over $1,500		

Health — $19,650

Health Professionals	$13,650	
American Medical Assn	$5,000	PAC
American Academy of Ophthalmology	$2,000	PAC
American College of Emergency Physicians	$2,000	PAC
American Dental Assn	$2,000	PAC
Pharmaceuticals/Health Products	$5,000	
Immunex Corp	$3,000	PAC/Ind

Lawyers & Lobbyists — $11,125

Lawyers & Lobbyists	$11,125	
Preston, Gates et al	$2,000	PAC/Ind

Misc Business — $46,269

Business Associations	$1,545	
None over $1,500		
Food & Beverage	$13,800	
Peter Pan Seafoods	$4,000	PAC/Ind
National Restaurant Assn	$3,500	PAC
Restaurants Unlimited	$2,000	Indiv
Pacific Seafood Processors	$1,650	PAC/Ind
Beer, Wine & Liquor	$8,102	
National Beer Wholesalers Assn	$5,000	PAC
Stimson Lane Ltd	$3,000	PAC
Retail Sales	$5,361	
None over $1,500		
Misc Services	$2,250	
American Assn of Equipment Lessors	$2,000	PAC
Business Services	$7,361	
Leisure Care Inc	$3,350	Indiv
Misc Manufacturing & Distributing	$5,700	
Ace Novelty	$2,000	Indiv
Esterline Corp	$2,000	Indiv

Transportation — $22,696

Air Transport	$6,950	
Boeing Co	$2,750	PAC/Ind
United Parcel Service	$2,000	PAC
Automotive	$3,200	
None over $1,500		
Trucking	$5,000	
Paccar Inc	$2,000	PAC/Ind
Railroads	$3,900	
Burlington Northern	$2,900	PAC
Sea Transport	$2,646	
Totem Ocean Trailer Express	$1,500	PAC

Ideological/Single-Issue

Ideological/Single-Issue — $36,061

Republican/Conservative	$9,304	
Leader PAC	$5,000	PAC
Leadership PACs	$1,972	
None over $1,500		
Pro-Israel	$1,750	
None over $1,500		
Womens Issues	$21,335	
Wish List	$11,285	PAC/Ind
Women's Campaign Fund	$10,000	PAC

Other & Unknown

Other — $34,225

Education	$2,000	
None over $1,500		
Retired	$31,075	
None over $1,500		

Unknown — $61,520

Homemakers/Non-income earners	$20,680	
Generic Occupation/Category Unknown	$2,000	
Employer Listed/Category Unknown	$38,390	
Careys Corp	$2,000	Indiv
Cosmer	$2,000	Indiv
E&H Co	$2,000	Indiv
Interstate Distributing Co	$2,000	Indiv
STI Industries	$1,500	Indiv

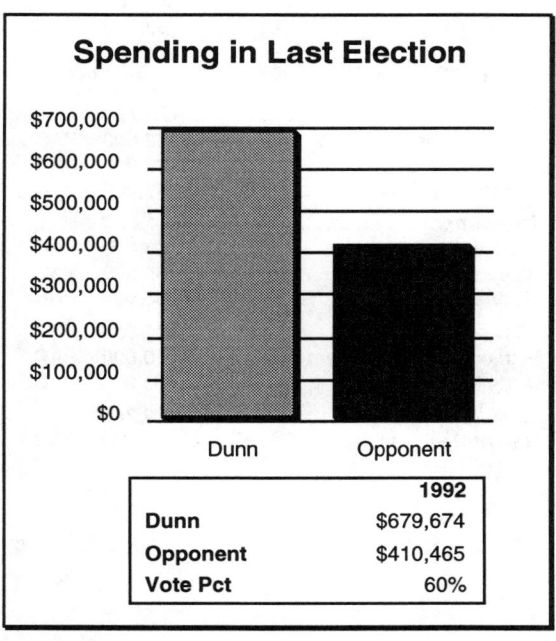

Spending in Last Election

	1992
Dunn	$679,674
Opponent	$410,465
Vote Pct	60%

---

* Contributions came from more than one affiliate or subsidiary.

Richard J. Durbin, D-III (20)

First elected: 1982

1991-92 Total Receipts: $666,110
1992 Year-end Cash: $51,822

1991-92 Committees & Subcommittees

Appropriations
Agriculture, Rural Development, Food and Drug Administration and Related Agencies; Transportation and Related Agencies

Budget
Defense, Foreign Policy and Space (Chairman); Economic Policy, Projections and Revenues; Human Resources

Select Committee on Children, Youth and Families

Leading Contributors

Business

Agriculture		$60,027
Crop Production & Basic Processing		**$12,900**
Sunkist Growers	$4,000	PAC
Dairy		**$4,500**
Mid-America Dairymen	$2,500	PAC
Poultry & Eggs		**$2,000**
None over $2,000		
Livestock		**$5,977**
National Pork Producers Council	$2,177	PAC
National Cattlemen's Assn*	$2,000	PAC
Agricultural Services/Products		**$16,700**
Archer-Daniels-Midland Corp	$9,500	PAC
Food Processing & Sales		**$17,950**
AE Staley Manufacturing Co	$7,000	PAC
Food Marketing Institute	$3,000	PAC
Connell Rice & Sugar Co	$2,000	Indiv

Communications/Electronics		$13,880
Media/Entertainment		**$5,250**
Brown & Associates	$3,500	Indiv
Telephone Utilities		**$6,930**
Illinois Bell Telephone	$2,750	PAC
AT&T	$2,250	PAC

Source of Funds in 1992 Election

Source	Total	Pct
■ PACs	$419,362	61%
▨ Indivs $200+	$79,255	12%
☐ Indivs under $200	$123,860	18%
⊠ Other	$60,578	9%
Candidate	$0	0%
Party	$19,995	3%

Source of PAC Dollars by Sector

Source	Total	Pct
■ Business	$242,797	59%
▨ Labor	$147,300	36%
☐ Ideology/Single Issue	$24,350	6%

In-State vs. Out-of-State Contributions*

Source	Total	Pct
☐ In-State	$42,605	54%
■ Out-of-state	$36,650	46%
No state listed	$0	

* by large individual contributors ($200 & above)

Construction		$7,550
Home Builders		**$2,500**
None over $2,000		
Construction Services		**$3,400**
Sverdrup Corp	$2,000	PAC

Energy & Natural Resources		$9,450
Oil & Gas		**$2,400**
None over $2,000		
Misc Energy		**$2,000**
None over $2,000		
Electric Utilities		**$2,750**
ACRE (Action Cmte for Rural Electrification)	$2,500	PAC

Finance, Insurance & Real Estate		$70,050
Commercial Banks		**$10,750**
American Bankers Assn	$2,000	PAC
Continental Illinois Corp	$2,000	PAC
Independent Bankers Assn	$2,000	PAC
Securities & Investment		**$21,000**
Chicago Board of Trade	$8,000	PAC
Chicago Mercantile Exchange	$5,000	PAC
American Express*	$3,000	PAC
Insurance		**$24,850**
National Assn of Life Underwriters	$10,000	PAC
Massachusetts Mutual Life Insurance	$3,000	PAC
Real Estate		**$10,250**
National Assn of Realtors	$8,000	PAC

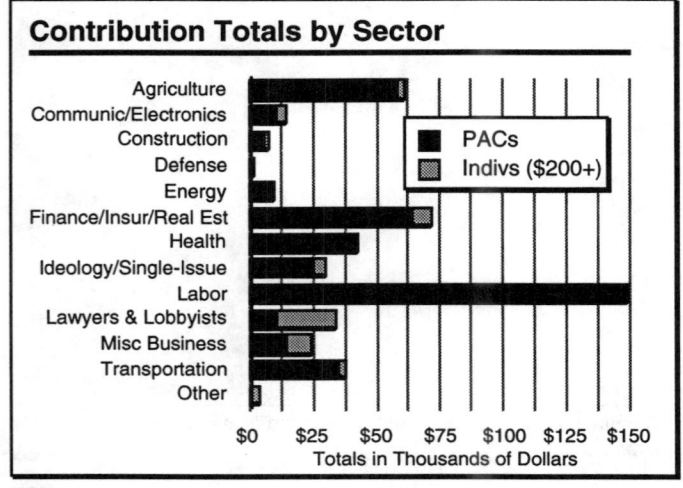

Contribution Totals by Sector

Agriculture
Communic/Electronics
Construction
Defense
Energy
Finance/Insur/Real Est
Health
Ideology/Single-Issue
Labor
Lawyers & Lobbyists
Misc Business
Transportation
Other

■ PACs
▨ Indivs ($200+)

$0 $25 $50 $75 $100 $125 $150
Totals in Thousands of Dollars

Health — $41,750

Health Professionals **$26,900**
    American Dental Assn .... $5,500 PAC
    American Medical Assn.................................. $5,000 PAC
    American Optometric Assn .... $2,000 PAC
    American Physical Therapy Assn .... $2,000 PAC

Hospitals/Nursing Homes **$7,100**
    American Hospital Assn .... $3,900 PAC

Pharmaceuticals/Health Products **$7,750**
    None over $2,000

Lawyers & Lobbyists — $34,150

Lawyers & Lobbyists **$34,150**
    Assn of Trial Lawyers of America .... $5,000 PAC
    Winston & Strawn .... $3,000 Indiv
    Cassidy & Associates .... $2,250 Indiv

Misc Business — $23,400

Beer, Wine & Liquor **$12,500**
    Gallo Winery .... $5,000 Indiv
    Wine Institute .... $2,500 PAC

Business Services **$2,750**
    Jasculca & Terman Associates .... $2,000 Indiv

Misc Manufacturing & Distributing **$2,200**
    None over $2,000

Transportation — $36,890

Air Transport **$19,340**
    Aircraft Owners & Pilots Assn .... $7,000 PAC
    American Airlines .... $4,000 PAC
    United Parcel Service .... $3,640 PAC
    United Airlines .... $2,000 PAC

Automotive **$2,500**
    None over $2,000

Trucking **$2,000**
    None over $2,000

Railroads **$11,750**
    Chicago & North Western Transport .... $2,000 PAC

Labor

Labor — $147,300

Building Trade Unions **$22,600**
    Carpenters & Joiners Union .... $6,000 PAC
    Laborers' Political League .... $4,500 PAC
    Sheet Metal Workers Union .... $3,500 PAC
    Plumbers/Pipefitters Union* .... $3,300 PAC
    Ironworkers Union .... $2,000 PAC

Industrial Unions **$33,250**
    Machinists/Aerospace Workers Union* .... $9,000 PAC
    United Mine Workers .... $7,000 PAC
    United Auto Workers .... $6,000 PAC
    Intl Brotherhood of Electrical Workers .... $3,500 PAC
    Boilermakers Union .... $2,500 PAC
    United Steelworkers .... $2,000 PAC

Transportation Unions **$39,000**
    Air Line Pilots Assn .... $10,000 PAC
    Teamsters Union .... $10,000 PAC
    United Transportation Union .... $7,500 PAC
    Amalgamated Transit Union .... $3,500 PAC
    Transport Workers Union .... $2,000 PAC

Public Sector Unions **$44,250**
    American Fedn of St/Cnty/Munic Employees .... $10,000 PAC
    National Education Assn .... $7,000 PAC
    National Assn Retired Federal Employees .... $6,000 PAC
    American Federation of Teachers .... $5,500 PAC
    National Rural Letter Carriers Assn .... $3,500 PAC
    National Assn of Letter Carriers .... $3,000 PAC
    American Postal Workers Union .... $2,500 PAC
    National Assn of Postmasters .... $2,250 PAC
    International Assn of Firefighters .... $2,000 PAC

Misc Unions **$8,200**
    Food & Commercial Workers Union .... $2,500 PAC
    Service Employees International Union .... $2,000 PAC

Ideological/Single-Issue

Ideological/Single-Issue — $30,100

Democratic/Liberal **$2,500**
    National Cmte for an Effective Congress .... $2,500 PAC

Leadership PACs **$4,700**
    America's Leaders' Fund (Dan Rostenkowski) .... $3,000 PAC

Pro-Israel **$7,500**
    None over $2,000

Human Rights **$9,000**
    KidsPAC .... $7,500 PAC

Misc Issues **$5,650**
    National Cmte to Preserve Social Security .... $4,500 PAC

Other & Unknown

Other — $3,205

    None over $2,000

Unknown — $14,450

    Homemakers/Non-income earners $2,700
    Employer Listed/Category Unknown $10,550
      None over $2,000

Spending in Last 3 Elections

	1988	1990	1992
Durbin	$251,634	$209,360	$921,659
Opponent	$57,708	$44,861	$278,357
Vote Pct	69%	66%	57%

---

* Contributions came from more than one affiliate or subsidiary.

587

Chet Edwards, D-Texas (11)

First elected: 1990

1991-92 Total Receipts: $462,342
1992 Year-end Cash: $43,902

1991-92 Committees & Subcommittees

Armed Services
Military Installations and Facilities; Research and Development

Veterans' Affairs
Compensation, Pension and Insurance; Hospitals and Health Care

Leading Contributors

Business

Agriculture — $39,110

Crop Production & Basic Processing	**$4,100**	
None over $2,000		
Tobacco	**$8,910**	
US Tobacco Co	$3,500	PAC
RJR Nabisco	$3,000	PAC
Dairy	**$4,700**	
Associated Milk Producers	$4,000	PAC
Poultry & Eggs	**$2,600**	
None over $2,000		
Livestock	**$2,000**	
National Cattlemen's Assn*	$2,000	PAC
Agricultural Services/Products	**$6,450**	
Texas Farm Bureau	$3,500	PAC
Wolfe the Florist	$2,000	Indiv
Food Processing & Sales	**$10,350**	
McLane Co	$8,000	PAC

Communications/Electronics — $9,750

Printing & Publishing	**$3,000**	
Temple Telegram	$2,000	Indiv
Telephone Utilities	**$3,750**	
Southwestern Bell	$2,000	PAC

Construction — $12,250

General Contractors	**$5,000**	
Karl May Construction	$2,000	Indiv
Home Builders	**$6,750**	
National Assn of Home Builders	$5,500	PAC

Contribution Totals by Sector

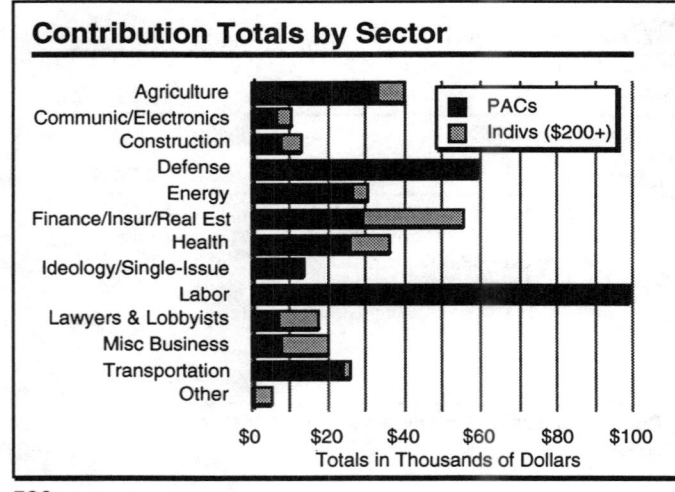

Totals in Thousands of Dollars

- PACs
- Indivs ($200+)

Agriculture, Communic/Electronics, Construction, Defense, Energy, Finance/Insur/Real Est, Health, Ideology/Single-Issue, Labor, Lawyers & Lobbyists, Misc Business, Transportation, Other

$0 $20 $40 $60 $80 $100

Source of Funds in 1992 Election

Source	Total	Pct
PACs	$317,975	68%
Indivs $200+	$106,939	23%
Indivs under $200	$32,923	7%
Other	$9,830	2%
Candidate	$0	0%
Party	$6,275	1%

Source of PAC Dollars by Sector

Source	Total	Pct
Business	$220,660	66%
Labor	$98,450	30%
Ideology/Single Issue	$13,150	4%

In-State vs. Out-of-State Contributions*

Source	Total	Pct
In-State	$101,339	95%
Out-of-state	$5,600	5%
No state listed	$0	

* by large individual contributors ($200 & above)

Defense — $58,450

Defense Aerospace	**$35,650**	
Textron Inc	$13,000	PAC
General Dynamics	$5,000	PAC
Martin Marietta Corp	$2,350	PAC
Lockheed Corp	$2,000	PAC
Defense Electronics	**$17,900**	
Chrysler Technologies Corp	$3,700	PAC
GTE Corp	$3,500	PAC
E-Systems Inc	$2,300	PAC
Imo Industries Inc	$2,000	PAC
Texas Instruments	$2,000	PAC
Misc Defense	**$4,900**	
None over $2,000		

Energy & Natural Resources — $29,940

Oil & Gas	**$11,940**	
Coastal Corp	$2,000	PAC
Montgomery Exploration Co	$2,000	Indiv
Electric Utilities	**$16,200**	
Texas Utilities Co*	$12,500	PAC

Finance, Insurance & Real Estate — $54,750

Commercial Banks	**$11,200**	
American Bankers Assn	$2,000	PAC
Citizens State Bank	$2,000	Indiv
Savings & Loans	**$3,000**	
Guardian Savings & Loan	$3,000	Indiv
Credit Unions	**$3,500**	
Credit Union National Assn	$3,500	PAC
Insurance	**$14,950**	
National Assn of Life Underwriters	$3,000	PAC
Primerica Life Insurance Co	$2,500	Indiv
Prudential Insurance	$2,500	PAC
Independent Insurance Agents of America	$2,000	PAC

Real Estate	....	$16,500	
National Assn of Realtors	....	$6,000	PAC
Rainbow International	....	$3,000	Indiv
First Worthing Co	....	$2,000	Indiv
RCS Investments	....	$2,000	Indiv
Accountants		**$3,600**	
Jaynes, Reitmeier et al	....	$3,000	Indiv

Health $35,525

Health Professionals	....	$26,375	
American Medical Assn	....	$10,000	PAC
American College of Emergency Physicians	....	$3,000	PAC
American Dental Assn	....	$2,500	PAC
Hospitals/Nursing Homes		**$7,150**	
Marwitz Brothers Inc	....	$2,000	Indiv
Pharmaceuticals/Health Products		**$2,000**	
None over $2,000			

Lawyers & Lobbyists $16,850

Lawyers & Lobbyists	....	$16,850	
Akin, Gump et al	....	$2,600	PAC/Ind
Busby & Associates	....	$2,000	Indiv

Misc Business $19,799

Food & Beverage	....	$2,500	
National Restaurant Assn*	....	$2,500	PAC
Beer, Wine & Liquor		**$3,750**	
National Beer Wholesalers Assn	....	$2,500	PAC
Retail Sales		**$6,700**	
J-Hawk Corp	....	$4,250	Indiv
Misc Manufacturing & Distributing		**$4,000**	
American Desk Manufacturing Co	....	$2,000	Indiv

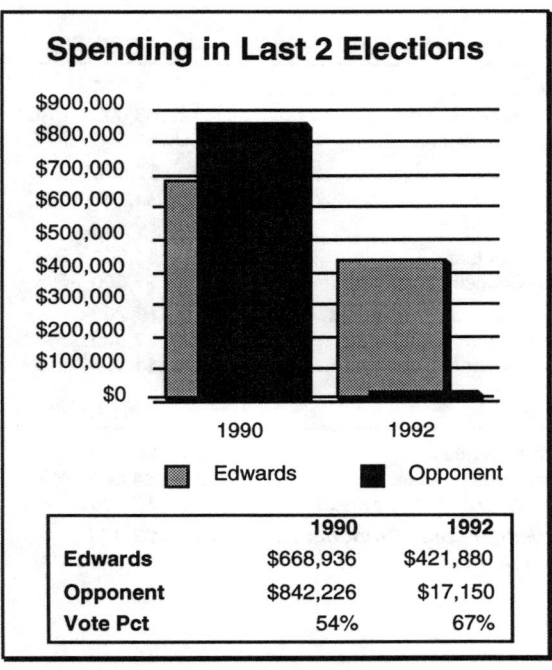

Spending in Last 2 Elections

	1990	1992
Edwards	$668,936	$421,880
Opponent	$842,226	$17,150
Vote Pct	54%	67%

Transportation $25,400

Air Transport	....	$10,850	
United Parcel Service	....	$4,850	PAC
Aircraft Owners & Pilots Assn	....	$3,500	PAC
American Airlines	....	$2,000	PAC
Automotive		**$11,500**	
National Auto Dealers Assn	....	$10,000	PAC
Railroads		**$2,200**	
None over $2,000			

Labor

Labor $98,450

Building Trade Unions	....	$10,350	
Plumbers/Pipefitters Union	....	$5,000	PAC
Laborers' Political League	....	$3,000	PAC
Industrial Unions		**$28,200**	
United Auto Workers	....	$10,000	PAC
Intl Brotherhood of Electrical Workers	....	$8,000	PAC
Communications Workers of America	....	$4,000	PAC
United Steelworkers	....	$4,000	PAC
Transportation Unions		**$26,200**	
Teamsters Union	....	$10,000	PAC
Seafarers International Union	....	$3,500	PAC
Transport Workers Union	....	$3,500	PAC
Air Line Pilots Assn	....	$2,500	PAC
United Transportation Union	....	$2,500	PAC
Public Sector Unions		**$24,950**	
National Education Assn	....	$10,000	PAC
American Fedn of St/Cnty/Munic Employees	....	$5,000	PAC
National Assn of Letter Carriers	....	$2,500	PAC
National Assn Retired Federal Employees	....	$2,000	PAC
Misc Unions		**$8,750**	
Food & Commercial Workers Union	....	$4,000	PAC
Office & Professional Employees Union	....	$3,500	PAC

Ideological/Single-Issue

Ideological/Single-Issue $13,150

Democratic/Liberal	....	$2,500	
National Cmte for an Effective Congress	....	$2,500	PAC
Pro-Israel		**$3,000**	
San Franciscans for Good Government	....	$2,000	PAC
Gun Rights/Gun Control		**$4,950**	
National Rifle Assn	....	$4,950	PAC
Misc Issues		**$2,200**	
National Cmte to Preserve Social Security	....	$2,200	PAC

Other & Unknown

Other $4,450

Retired	....	$2,750	
None over $2,000			

Unknown $21,325

Homemakers/Non-income earners	....	$2,000	
No Employer Listed or Found	....	$2,000	
Generic Occupation/Category Unknown	....	$3,500	
Employer Listed/Category Unknown	....	$13,825	
None over $2,000			

---

* Contributions came from more than one affiliate or subsidiary.

Don Edwards, D-Calif (16)

First elected: 1962

1991-92 Total Receipts: $249,478
1992 Year-end Cash: $13,687

1991-92 Committees & Subcommittees

Judiciary (Vice Chairman)
Administrative Law and Governmental Relations; Civil and Constitutional Rights (Chairman); Economic and Commercial Law

Veterans' Affairs (Vice Chairman)
Oversight and Investigations (Vice Chairman)

Leading Contributors

Business

Agriculture		$3,500
Crop Production & Basic Processing	**$2,000**	
Sunkist Growers	$1,500	PAC
Food Processing & Sales	**$1,500**	
Food Marketing Institute	$1,500	PAC

Communications/Electronics		$30,000
Printing & Publishing	**$1,500**	
West Publishing	$1,000	PAC
Media/Entertainment	**$7,450**	
National Cable Television Assn	$2,450	PAC
ASCAP	$1,000	PAC
National Music Publishers Assn	$1,000	Indiv
Sante D'Orazio Studio	$1,000	Indiv
Walt Disney Co	$1,000	PAC/Ind
Telephone Utilities	**$14,300**	
AT&T	$7,500	PAC
Pacific Telesis Group	$3,800	PAC
BellSouth Corp*	$1,500	PAC
Electronics Mfg & Services	**$2,000**	
Rolm Corp	$1,500	Indiv
Computer Equipment & Services	**$4,250**	
Amdahl Corp	$2,500	Indiv

Construction		$4,500
General Contractors	**$1,250**	
Yamaoka Builders Inc	$1,250	Indiv
Home Builders	**$2,250**	
National Assn of Home Builders	$1,000	PAC

Source of Funds in 1992 Election

Source	Total	Pct
PACs	$182,700	72%
Indivs $200+	$39,910	16%
Indivs under $200	$21,721	9%
Other	$10,561	4%
Candidate	$0	0%
Party	$5,564	2%

Source of PAC Dollars by Sector

Source	Total	Pct
Business	$89,575	49%
Labor	$83,125	46%
Ideology/Single Issue	$9,175	5%

In-State vs. Out-of-State Contributions*

Source	Total	Pct
In-State	$23,700	60%
Out-of-state	$15,710	40%
No state listed	$500	

*** by large individual contributors ($200 & above)**

Defense		$1,100
Defense Aerospace	**$1,100**	
None over $1,000		

Energy & Natural Resources		$5,500
Oil & Gas	**$1,500**	
Petroleum Marketers Assn	$1,000	PAC
Nuclear Energy	**$1,500**	
General Atomics	$1,500	PAC
Electric Utilities	**$2,000**	
Pacific Gas & Electric	$1,500	PAC

Finance, Insurance & Real Estate		$20,550
Commercial Banks	**$5,000**	
American Bankers Assn	$3,000	PAC
BankAmerica Corp	$1,500	PAC
Savings & Loans	**$1,000**	
US League of Savings Assns*	$1,000	PAC
Insurance	**$3,600**	
Pacific Mutual Life	$1,500	PAC
American Council of Life Insurance	$1,000	PAC
Real Estate	**$10,250**	
National Assn of Realtors	$7,500	PAC
Brown & Kaufman Properties	$1,000	Indiv

Health		$11,625
Health Professionals	**$8,300**	
American Medical Assn	$4,500	PAC
National Assn of Pharmacists	$2,000	PAC
Pharmaceuticals/Health Products	**$3,075**	
Syntex (USA) Inc	$2,825	PAC

Contribution Totals by Sector

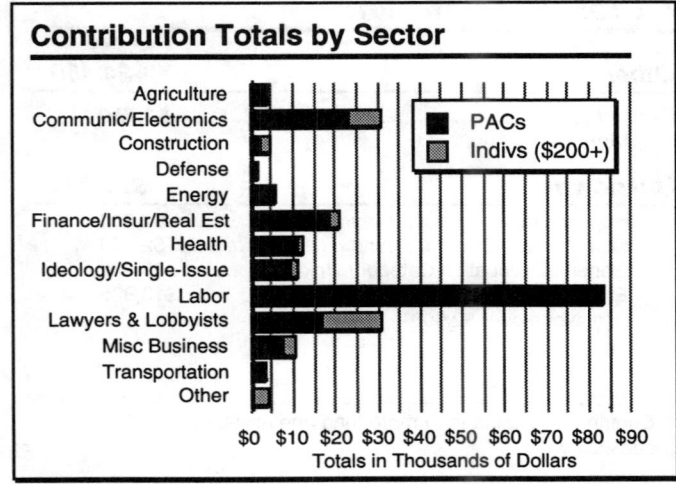

Agriculture, Communic/Electronics, Construction, Defense, Energy, Finance/Insur/Real Est, Health, Ideology/Single-Issue, Labor, Lawyers & Lobbyists, Misc Business, Transportation, Other

■ PACs
▨ Indivs ($200+)

$0 $10 $20 $30 $40 $50 $60 $70 $80 $90
Totals in Thousands of Dollars

Lawyers & Lobbyists $30,450

Lawyers & Lobbyists **$30,450**
Assn of Trial Lawyers of America ....$10,000   PAC
David Vienna & Associates ....$3,000   Indiv
Arnold & Porter ....$2,000   PAC
Akin, Gump et al ....$1,500   PAC
Wylie, McBride et al ....$1,200   Indiv
Davis, Polk & Wardwell ....$1,000   Indiv
Hopkins & Carley ....$1,000   Indiv
Manatt, Phelps et al ....$1,000   PAC
Pattison Fulton Government Relations ....$1,000   Indiv
Patton, Boggs & Blow ....$1,000   Indiv

Misc Business $9,850

Beer, Wine & Liquor **$1,500**
National Beer Wholesalers Assn ....$1,000   PAC

Business Services **$4,000**
Dun & Bradstreet ....$1,500   PAC
Regis McKenna Inc ....$1,500   Indiv

Steel Production **$1,000**
LTV Steel..$1,000   PAC

Transportation $3,210

Air Transport **$1,450**
United Parcel Service ....$1,450   PAC

Automotive **$1,760**
None over $1,000

Labor

Labor $83,125

Building Trade Unions **$15,200**
Carpenters & Joiners Union ....$5,000   PAC
Laborers' Political League ....$4,000   PAC
Plumbers/Pipefitters Union ....$2,000   PAC
AFL-CIO Bldg/Construction Trades Dept ....$1,150   PAC
Ironworkers Union ....$1,000   PAC

Industrial Unions **$13,750**
Intl Brotherhood of Electrical Workers ....$4,750   PAC
United Auto Workers ....$4,000   PAC
Machinists/Aerospace Workers Union ....$2,750   PAC
Ladies Garment Workers Union...........................$1,000   PAC

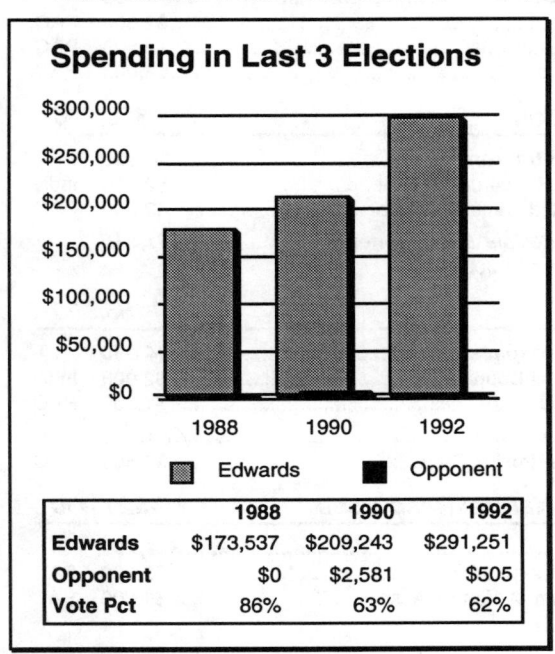

Spending in Last 3 Elections

	1988	1990	1992
Edwards	$173,537	$209,243	$291,251
Opponent	$0	$2,581	$505
Vote Pct	86%	63%	62%

Transportation Unions **$16,300**
Teamsters Union ....$10,000   PAC
Marine Engineers Dist 2 Maritime Officers ....$2,000   PAC
Amalgamated Transit Union ....$1,500   PAC
Intl Longshoremen's/Warehousemen's Union .....$1,000   PAC

Public Sector Unions **$30,375**
National Assn of Letter Carriers* ....$7,525   PAC
National Assn Retired Federal Employees ....$6,500   PAC
National Education Assn ....$6,200   PAC
American Fedn of St/Cnty/Munic Employees ......$5,000   PAC
American Postal Workers Union ....$2,600   PAC
National Assn of Postmasters ....$1,000   PAC

Misc Unions **$7,500**
Food & Commercial Workers Union ....$3,250   PAC
Service Employees International Union ....$2,000   PAC
AFL-CIO ....$1,750   PAC

Ideological/Single-Issue

Ideological/Single-Issue $10,625

Pro-Choice **$3,425**
National Abortion Rights Action League ....$2,000   PAC

Womens Issues **$1,200**
None over $1,000

Human Rights **$4,100**
Human Rights Campaign Fund.............................$3,000   PAC
Bay Area Municipal Elections Cmte ....$1,100   PAC

Misc Issues **$1,400**
National Cmte to Preserve Social Security ....$1,500   PAC

Other & Unknown

Other $3,900

Retired **$3,500**
None over $1,000

Unknown $3,850

Homemakers/Non-income earners $2,000
Employer Listed/Category Unknown $1,350
None over $1,000

---

* Contributions came from more than one affiliate or
subsidiary.

Bill Emerson, R-Mo (8)

First elected: 1980

1991-92 Total Receipts: $518,998
1992 Year-end Cash: $36,538

1991-92 Committees & Subcommittees

Agriculture
Cotton, Rice and Sugar (Ranking Republican); Domestic Marketing, Consumer Relations and Nutrition; Forests, Family Farms and Energy

Public Works and Transportation
Economic Development; Surface Transportation; Water Resources

Select Committee on Hunger (Ranking Republican)

Leading Contributors

Business

Agriculture	$143,925

Crop Production & Basic Processing	**$55,440**	
National Cotton Council	$5,350	PAC
Riceland Foods	$4,000	PAC/Ind
American Sugarbeet Growers Assn	$3,500	PAC
American Cotton Shippers Assn	$3,000	PAC
American Sugar Cane League	$3,000	PAC
American Crystal Sugar Corp	$2,500	PAC
Southern Minn Beet Sugar Co-op	$2,000	PAC
Amalgamated Sugar Co	$1,500	PAC/Ind
Florida Sugar Cane League	$1,500	PAC
US Beet Sugar Assn	$1,500	PAC
Tobacco	**$5,500**	
RJR Nabisco	$3,000	PAC
Tobacco Institute	$1,500	PAC
Dairy	**$12,000**	
Mid-America Dairymen	$5,000	PAC
Associated Milk Producers	$4,000	PAC
Dairymen Inc	$1,500	PAC
Poultry & Eggs	**$4,500**	
National Turkey Federation	$2,000	PAC
United Egg Assn	$1,500	PAC
Livestock	**$5,000**	
National Cattlemen's Assn*	$2,500	PAC
National Pork Producers Council	$1,500	PAC
Agricultural Services/Products	**$22,735**	
Missouri Farm Bureau/SE Dist	$5,000	PAC
Archer-Daniels-Midland Corp	$2,000	PAC
Farm Credit Council	$2,000	PAC
American Assn of Crop Insurers	$1,500	PAC

Contribution Totals by Sector

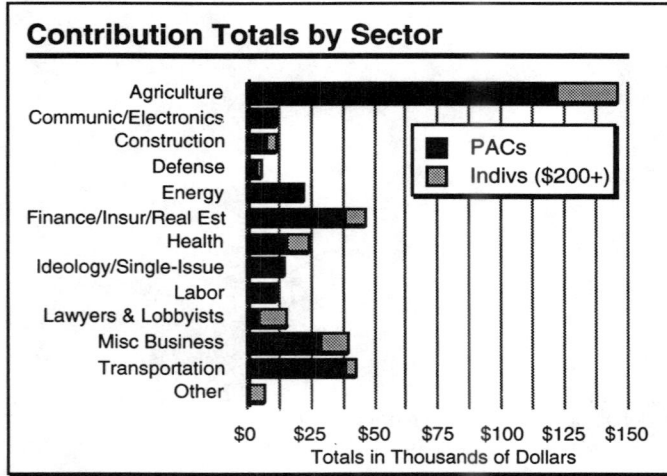

Agriculture
Communic/Electronics
Construction
Defense
Energy
Finance/Insur/Real Est
Health
Ideology/Single-Issue
Labor
Lawyers & Lobbyists
Misc Business
Transportation
Other

- PACs
- Indivs ($200+)

$0 $25 $50 $75 $100 $125 $150
Totals in Thousands of Dollars

Source of Funds in 1992 Election

Source	Total	Pct
■ PACs	$299,188	58%
▨ Indivs $200+	$96,315	19%
☐ Indivs under $200	$117,638	23%
▨ Other	$5,957	1%
Candidate	$0	0%
Party	$2,990	1%

Source of PAC Dollars by Sector

Source	Total	Pct
■ Business	$284,626	92%
▨ Labor	$11,250	4%
☐ Ideology/Single Issue	$14,005	5%

In-State vs. Out-of-State Contributions*

Source	Total	Pct
☐ In-State	$75,375	79%
▨ Out-of-state	$20,190	21%
No state listed	$250	

*** by large individual contributors ($200 & above)**

Food Processing & Sales	**$21,500**	
Fleming Companies Inc	$5,000	PAC
ConAgra Inc	$3,500	PAC
Food Marketing Institute	$2,500	PAC
Winn-Dixie Stores	$1,500	PAC
Forestry & Forest Products	**$17,250**	
Westvaco Corp	$6,000	PAC
Boise Cascade	$3,000	PAC
East Perry Lumber Co	$1,500	Indiv

Communications/Electronics	$11,050

Telephone Utilities	**$8,000**	
AT&T	$2,500	PAC
Southwestern Bell	$2,500	PAC
GTE Corp	$2,000	PAC

Construction	$10,996

General Contractors	**$8,500**	
Harrison Construction	$2,250	Indiv
Associated General Contractors	$2,000	PAC
Building Materials & Equipment	**$1,515**	
None over $1,500		

Defense	$5,550

Defense Aerospace	**$4,050**	
McDonnell Douglas	$2,000	Indiv
Lockheed Corp	$1,500	PAC
Defense Electronics	**$1,500**	
Esco Electronics Corp	$1,500	PAC

Energy & Natural Resources	$21,450

Oil & Gas	**$11,700**	
Coastal Corp	$2,000	PAC
Petroleum Marketers Assn	$1,500	PAC

Mining **$4,500**
   National Coal Assn .... $1,500 PAC

Electric Utilities **$5,000**
   Union Electric .... $2,000 PAC
   ACRE (Action Cmte for Rural Electrification) .... $1,500 PAC

Finance, Insurance & Real Estate $45,500

Commercial Banks **$12,500**
   American Bankers Assn .... $7,500 PAC
   Mercantile Bancorp .... $2,500 PAC
   Independent Bankers Assn .... $1,500 PAC

Securities & Investment **$2,500**
   None over $1,500

Insurance **$15,000**
   American Family Corp .... $8,500 Indiv
   National Assn of Life Underwriters................. $2,500 PAC

Real Estate **$14,250**
   National Assn of Realtors............................... $10,000 PAC
   Health Facilities Management Corp .... $3,500 Indiv

Health $23,350

Health Professionals **$18,600**
   American Medical Assn* .... $10,000 PAC
   American Dental Assn .... $2,000 PAC

Pharmaceuticals/Health Products **$3,500**
   Schering-Plough Corp .... $1,500 PAC

Lawyers & Lobbyists $14,125

Lawyers & Lobbyists **$14,125**
   Holland & Knight .... $3,000 PAC
   Jefferson Group .... $1,500 Indiv
   Olsson, Frank & Weeda .... $1,500 Indiv

Misc Business $38,500

Food & Beverage **$7,450**
   National Restaurant Assn .... $3,000 PAC

Beer, Wine & Liquor **$4,450**
   Bluff City Beer .... $2,450 Indiv
   National Beer Wholesalers Assn .... $2,000 PAC

Retail Sales **$1,500**
   None over $1,500

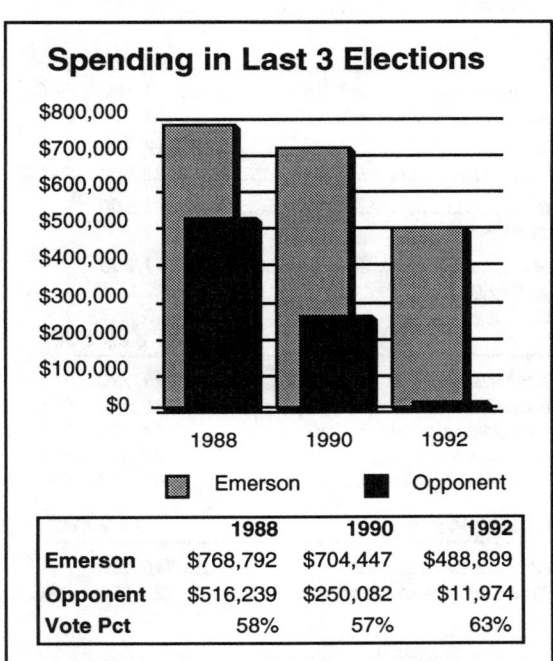

Spending in Last 3 Elections

	1988	1990	1992
Emerson	$768,792	$704,447	$488,899
Opponent	$516,239	$250,082	$11,974
Vote Pct	58%	57%	63%

◼ Emerson   ■ Opponent

Business Services **$1,900**
   None over $1,500

Lodging/Tourism **$2,850**
   Leuckel's Landing .... $2,000 Indiv

Chemical & Related Manufacturing **$4,500**
   FMC Corp .... $1,500 PAC
   Dial Corp .... $1,500 PAC

Misc Manufacturing & Distributing **$9,000**
   Hoechst Celanese Corp .... $2,500 PAC
   Corning Glass Works .... $2,000 PAC
   Stone Container Corp .... $2,000 PAC

Textiles **$4,500**
   American Textile Manufacturers Institute .... $2,500 PAC
   Burlington Industries .... $2,000 PAC

Transportation $41,495

Air Transport **$15,500**
   Federal Express Corp .... $4,000 PAC
   United Parcel Service .... $4,000 PAC
   Sabreliner Corp .... $3,500 PAC/Ind
   McDonnell Douglas .... $1,500 PAC

Automotive **$13,245**
   National Auto Dealers Assn .... $8,000 PAC
   Auto Dealers & Drivers for Free Trade .... $2,000 PAC

Trucking **$4,000**
   American Trucking Assns .... $1,500 PAC

Railroads **$5,500**
   Burlington Northern .... $1,500 PAC/Ind
   Kansas City Southern .... $1,500 PAC
   Union Pacific Corp .... $1,500 PAC

Sea Transport **$3,000**
   American Commercial Barge Line Co .... $1,500 PAC

Labor

Labor $11,250

Transportation Unions **$3,500**
   Marine Engineers Dist 2 Maritime Officers .... $2,500 PAC

Public Sector Unions **$7,750**
   National Assn Retired Federal Employees .... $4,000 PAC
   National Assn of Letter Carriers* .... $3,750 PAC

Ideological/Single-Issue

Ideological/Single-Issue $14,005

Gun Rights/Gun Control **$6,950**
   National Rifle Assn .... $6,950 PAC

Misc Issues **$5,555**
   National Cmte to Preserve Social Security .... $5,500 PAC

Other & Unknown

Other $6,550

Retired **$5,050**
   None over $1,500

Unknown $16,950

   Homemakers/Non-income earners $2,250
   No Employer Listed or Found $1,500
   Generic Occupation/Category Unknown $1,500
   Employer Listed/Category Unknown $11,700
      None over $1,500

---

* Contributions came from more than one affiliate or
subsidiary.

Eliot L. Engel, D-NY (17)

First elected: 1988

1991-92 Total Receipts: $440,835
1992 Year-end Cash: $8,107

1991-92 Committees & Subcommittees

Foreign Affairs
Europe and the Middle East; International Economic Policy and Trade; Western Hemisphere Affairs

Science, Space and Technology
Space; Technology and Competitiveness

Select Committee on Hunger

Leading Contributors

Business

Agriculture — $19,000

Crop Production & Basic Processing	**$9,750**	
American Sugarbeet Growers Assn	$2,000	PAC
US Cane Sugar Refiners Assn	$2,000	Indiv
American Crystal Sugar Corp	$1,500	PAC
Tobacco	**$4,500**	
RJR Nabisco	$3,500	PAC
Dairy	**$2,500**	
Associated Milk Producers	$2,000	PAC

Communications/Electronics — $8,650

Media/Entertainment	**$3,150**	
ASCAP	$1,500	PAC
Telephone Utilities	**$5,250**	
AT&T	$2,500	PAC
New York Telephone	$1,500	PAC

Defense — $4,500

Defense Aerospace	**$4,000**	
General Dynamics	$1,500	PAC

Energy & Natural Resources — $2,000

Electric Utilities	**$1,500**	
None over $1,500		

Source of Funds in 1992 Election

Source	Total	Pct
PACs	$285,450	65%
Indivs $200+	$80,030	18%
Indivs under $200	$66,617	15%
Other	$9,119	2%
Candidate	$0	0%
Party	$831	0%

Source of PAC Dollars by Sector

Source	Total	Pct
Business	$106,700	37%
Labor	$132,650	46%
Ideology/Single Issue	$47,200	16%

In-State vs. Out-of-State Contributions*

Source	Total	Pct
In-State	$46,330	59%
Out-of-state	$32,440	41%
No state listed	$960	

* by large individual contributors ($200 & above)

Finance, Insurance & Real Estate — $63,245

Commercial Banks	**$22,950**	
Citicorp	$6,600	PAC
Chase Manhattan	$2,500	PAC/Ind
Chemical Bank	$2,500	PAC
JP Morgan & Co	$2,500	PAC
American Bankers Assn	$2,000	PAC
Bankers Trust	$2,000	PAC
Savings & Loans	**$3,000**	
National Council of Savings Institutions*	$1,600	PAC
Credit Unions	**$3,000**	
Credit Union National Assn	$3,000	PAC
Securities & Investment	**$5,760**	
None over $1,500		
Insurance	**$7,750**	
Mutual Life Insurance of New York	$1,500	PAC
National Assn of Life Underwriters	$1,500	PAC
Real Estate	**$17,325**	
National Assn of Realtors	$8,000	PAC
Accountants	**$1,500**	
None over $1,500		
Misc Finance	**$1,960**	
None over $1,500		

Health — $29,630

Health Professionals	**$29,130**	
American Medical Assn*	$10,000	PAC
American Academy of Ophthalmology	$4,000	PAC
American Dental Assn	$2,000	PAC
American Nurses Assn	$1,500	PAC

Lawyers & Lobbyists — $19,800

Lawyers & Lobbyists	**$19,800**	
Assn of Trial Lawyers of America	$9,500	PAC

Contribution Totals by Sector

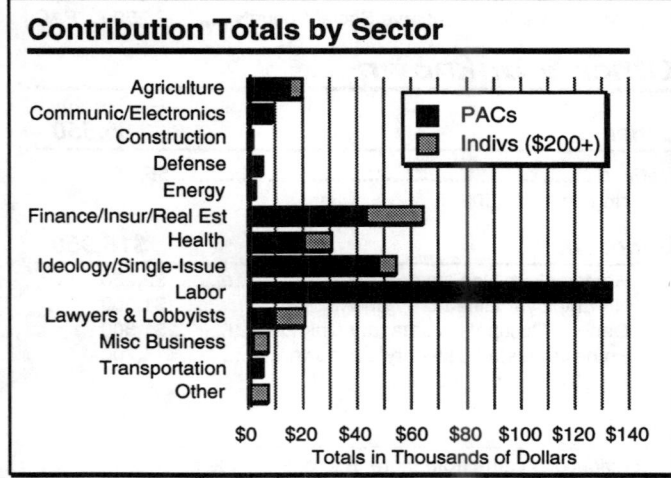

Legend: PACs (black); Indivs ($200+) (grey)

Categories: Agriculture, Communic/Electronics, Construction, Defense, Energy, Finance/Insur/Real Est, Health, Ideology/Single-Issue, Labor, Lawyers & Lobbyists, Misc Business, Transportation, Other

Scale: $0 $20 $40 $60 $80 $100 $120 $140
Totals in Thousands of Dollars

Misc Business   **$6,950**

Business Services $1,750
    None over $1,500

Transportation   **$4,550**

Air Transport $2,000
    None over $1,500

Automotive $1,800
    National Auto Dealers Assn ....$1,800   PAC

Labor

Labor   **$132,650**

Building Trade Unions **$21,750**
    Laborers' Political League ....$5,500   PAC
    Carpenters & Joiners Union ....$5,000   PAC
    Ironworkers Union ....$4,500   PAC
    Sheet Metal Workers Union ....$2,500   PAC
    AFL-CIO Bldg/Construction Trades Dept ....$2,000   PAC
    Plumbers/Pipefitters Union ....$1,500   PAC

Industrial Unions **$27,100**
    United Auto Workers ....$7,000   PAC
    Machinists/Aerospace Workers Union ....$6,000   PAC
    Intl Brotherhood of Electrical Workers ....$5,100   PAC
    Boilermakers Union ....$2,500   PAC
    United Steelworkers ....$2,000   PAC

Transportation Unions **$33,000**
    Teamsters Union ....$10,000   PAC
    Marine Engineers Union* ....$6,500   PAC
    Air Line Pilots Assn ....$5,000   PAC
    United Transportation Union ....$4,500   PAC
    Transport Workers Union ....$3,000   PAC

Public Sector Unions **$41,650**
    American Fedn of St/Cnty/Munic Employees ....$10,000   PAC
    American Federation of Teachers ....$9,500   PAC
    National Education Assn ....$8,000   PAC
    American Postal Workers Union ....$5,000   PAC
    National Assn Retired Federal Employees ....$4,000   PAC
    National Assn of Letter Carriers ....$2,500   PAC

Misc Unions...**$9,150**
    Food & Commercial Workers Union ....$5,650   PAC
    AFL-CIO ....$1,500   PAC

Ideological/Single-Issue

Ideological/Single-Issue   **$53,470**

Leadership PACs **$4,000**
    House Leadership Fund (Tom Foley) ....$2,000   PAC

Foreign & Defense Policy **$2,000**
    Free Cuba PAC ....$1,500   PAC

Pro-Israel **$25,870**
    National PAC ....$5,000   PAC
    Joint Action Cmte for Political Affairs ....$4,000   PAC
    Hudson Valley PAC ....$3,000   PAC
    Florida Congressional Cmte ....$2,000   PAC
    Maryland Assn for Concerned Citizens...............$1,500   PAC

Pro-Choice..**$5,050**
    National Abortion Rights Action League ....$2,500   PAC
    Voters for Choice ....$2,000   PAC

Human Rights **$12,800**
    Human Rights Campaign Fund...........................$6,000   PAC
    National Albanian American PAC ....$6,000   PAC

Misc Issues...**$3,500**
    National Cmte to Preserve Social Security ....$3,000   PAC

Other & Unknown

Other   **$6,300**

Education **$2,750**
    None over $1,500

Retired **$2,300**
    None over $1,500

Unknown   **$14,635**

    Homemakers/Non-income earners $1,985
    No Employer Listed or Found $4,450
    Employer Listed/Category Unknown....................$6,950
        None over $1,500

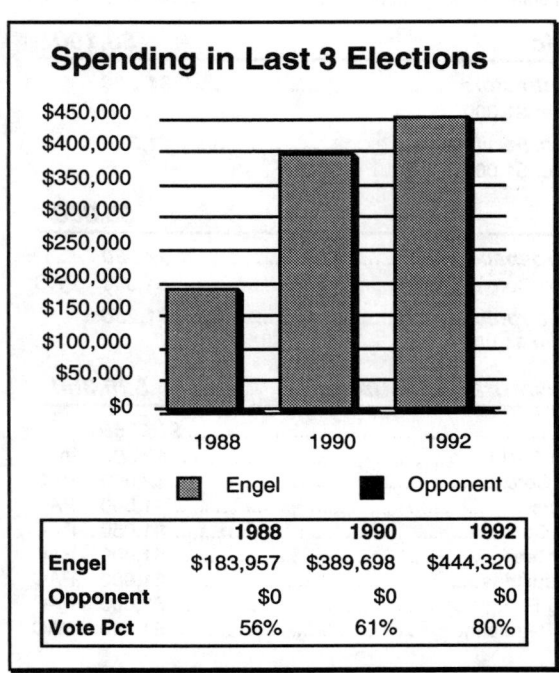

Spending in Last 3 Elections

	1988	1990	1992
Engel	$183,957	$389,698	$444,320
Opponent	$0	$0	$0
Vote Pct	56%	61%	80%

---

* Contributions came from more than one affiliate or subsidiary.

Glenn English, D-Okla (6)

First elected: 1974

1991-92 Total Receipts: $379,380
1992 Year-end Cash: $150,105

1991-92 Committees & Subcommittees

Agriculture
Conservation, Credit and Rural Development (Chairman); Peanuts and Tobacco; Wheat, Soybeans and Feed Grains

Government Operations
Government Activities and Transportation; Legislation and National Security

Leading Contributors
Business

Agriculture $63,050

Crop Production & Basic Processing $15,450
Southwest Peanut Membership Org	$1,850	PAC
American Crystal Sugar Corp	$1,500	PAC
National Cotton Council	$1,500	PAC
National Assn of Wheat Growers	$1,400	PAC
American Sugarbeet Growers Assn	$1,100	PAC
Florida Sugar Cane League	$1,000	PAC
Southern Minn Beet Sugar Co-op	$1,000	PAC

Tobacco $2,900
RJR Nabisco	$1,500	PAC

Dairy $9,500
Associated Milk Producers	$7,500	PAC
Dairymen Inc	$1,000	PAC
Mid-America Dairymen	$1,000	PAC

Poultry & Eggs $2,250
National Broiler Council	$1,250	PAC

Livestock $5,850
National Cattlemen's Assn*	$4,150	PAC
National Pork Producers Council	$1,000	PAC

Agricultural Services/Products $17,850
American Assn of Crop Insurers	$6,000	PAC
Farm Credit Council	$1,500	PAC
American Veterinary Medical Assn	$1,000	PAC
Farm Credit Bank of Texas	$1,000	PAC
Farmland Industries	$1,000	PAC
Seabord Corp	$1,000	PAC

Food Processing & Sales $9,250
ConAgra Inc	$3,500	PAC
Fleming Companies Inc	$2,000	PAC
American Meat Institute	$1,000	PAC
Connell Rice & Sugar Co	$1,000	Indiv
Food Marketing Institute	$1,000	PAC

Contribution Totals by Sector

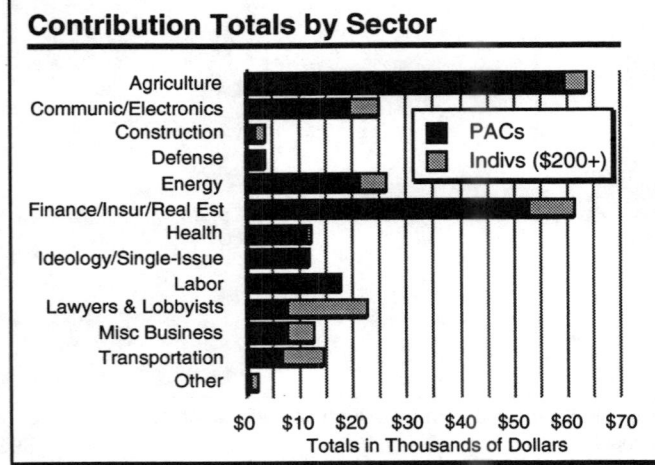

Totals in Thousands of Dollars

Source of Funds in 1992 Election

Source	Total	Pct
■ PACs	$203,400	49%
▨ Indivs $200+	$73,236	18%
☐ Indivs under $200	$75,779	18%
⊠ Other	$60,362	15%
Candidate	$0	0%
Party	$40,047	10%

Source of PAC Dollars by Sector

Source	Total	Pct
■ Business	$187,300	87%
▨ Labor	$17,449	8%
☐ Ideology/Single Issue	$11,286	5%

In-State vs. Out-of-State Contributions*

Source	Total	Pct
☐ In-State	$49,218	68%
■ Out-of-state	$23,518	32%
No state listed	$0	

*** by large individual contributors ($200 & above)**

Communications/Electronics $24,400

Telephone Utilities $22,150
AT&T	$4,000	PAC
GTE Corp	$3,500	PAC
US Telephone Assn	$2,500	PAC
National Telephone Co-op Assn	$1,850	PAC
Southwestern Bell	$1,800	PAC
US West Inc	$1,500	PAC
Dobson Telephone Co	$1,250	Indiv
National Rural Telecom Assn	$1,250	Indiv
Alltel Corp	$1,000	PAC
United Telecommunications	$1,000	PAC

Construction $3,100

General Contractors $1,300
None over $1,000

Construction Services $1,300
None over $1,000

Defense $3,300

Defense Aerospace $2,050
Lockheed Corp	$1,300	PAC

Defense Electronics $1,250
None over $1,000

Energy & Natural Resources $26,300

Oil & Gas $16,250
Mustang Fuel Corp	$2,500	Indiv
Coastal Corp	$2,000	PAC
Oneok Inc	$1,500	PAC
El Paso Co	$1,050	PAC
Kerr-McGee	$1,000	PAC
Koch Industries	$1,000	PAC
Mustang Energy Corp	$1,000	PAC
Phillips Petroleum	$1,000	PAC

Electric Utilities **$10,050**
    ACRE (Action Cmte for Rural Electrification)* .....$4,200 PAC
    Oklahoma Gas & Electric .... $2,300 PAC
    Public Service Co of Oklahoma .... $1,000 PAC
    Southwestern Public Service Co .... $1,000 PAC
    Western Farmers Electric Coop .... $1,000 PAC/Ind

Finance, Insurance & Real Estate $60,700

Commercial Banks **$13,900**
    American Bankers Assn* .... $5,100 PAC
    First National Bank .... $1,750 Indiv
    Independent Bankers Assn .... $1,400 PAC
    Norwest Corp .... $1,250 PAC
    Banc First .... $1,000 Indiv

Securities & Investment **$29,900**
    Chicago Mercantile Exchange .... $10,000 PAC
    Chicago Board of Trade .... $8,500 PAC
    Commodity Exchange Inc .... $4,300 PAC
    New York Mercantile Exchange .... $3,250 PAC
    National Venture Capital Assn .... $1,100 PAC
    Craig Capital Corp .... $1,000 Indiv
    New York Cotton Exchange .... $1,000 PAC

Insurance **$3,300**
    None over $1,000

Real Estate **$8,900**
    National Assn of Realtors .... $8,000 PAC

Accountants **$3,000**
    American Institute of CPA's .... $3,000 PAC

Misc Finance **$1,000**
    None over $1,000

Health $11,800

Health Professionals **$9,800**
    American Medical Assn* .... $6,300 PAC
    American Chiropractic Assn .... $2,000 PAC
    American Physical Therapy Assn .... $1,000 PAC

Pharmaceuticals/Health Products **$1,750**
    Ciba-Geigy Corp .... $1,000 PAC

Lawyers & Lobbyists $22,218

Lawyers & Lobbyists **$22,218**
    Assn of Trial Lawyers of America .... $2,500 PAC
    Akin, Gump et al .... $1,750 PAC/Ind
    Burson-Marsteller .... $1,500 PAC
    Hogan & Hartson .... $1,000 PAC/Ind
    Kerr, Irvine & Rhodes .... $1,000 Indiv
    Williams & Jensen .... $1,000 Indiv

Misc Business $12,350

Food & Beverage **$2,500**
    Applewoods Inc .... $2,000 Indiv

Beer, Wine & Liquor **$1,000**
    National Beer Wholesalers Assn .... $1,000 PAC

Retail Sales **$1,050**
    None over $1,000

Business Services **$3,000**
    A-Bear's Janitorial Service .... $1,000 Indiv
    Ram Group Ltd .... $1,000 Indiv

Misc Business **$1,300**
    National Rural Water Assn .... $1,300 PAC

Chemical & Related Manufacturing **$2,500**
    WR Grace & Co .... $2,000 PAC

Transportation $14,250

Air Transport **$4,200**
    American Airlines .... $1,600 PAC
    United Parcel Service .... $1,050 PAC

Automotive **$9,050**
    Fred Jones Industries .... $6,500 Indiv
    National Auto Dealers Assn .... $2,550 PAC

Labor

Labor $17,449

Public Sector Unions **$16,700**
    National Assn Retired Federal Employees .... $6,000 PAC
    American Fedn of St/Cnty/Munic Employees ...... $5,000 PAC
    National Rural Letter Carriers Assn .... $2,500 PAC
    National Assn of Letter Carriers .... $2,000 PAC
    International Assn of Firefighters .... $1,500 PAC

Ideological/Single-Issue

Ideological/Single-Issue $11,286

Gun Rights/Gun Control **$5,250**
    National Rifle Assn .... $5,250 PAC

Misc Issues **$6,013**
    Sierra Club .... $4,814 PAC
    National Cmte to Preserve Social Security .... $1,000 PAC

Other & Unknown

Other $2,000
    None over $1,000

Unknown $17,068
    No Employer Listed or Found $4,132
    Employer Listed/Category Unknown $12,686
      TCOM LP .... $3,000 Indiv
      Bogan Aerotech .... $1,000 Indiv
      Century Telephone Co .... $1,000 Indiv
      Cooper West Agency .... $1,000 Indiv
      Russell, Gravlin et al .... $1,000 Indiv

* Contributions came from more than one affiliate or
subsidiary.

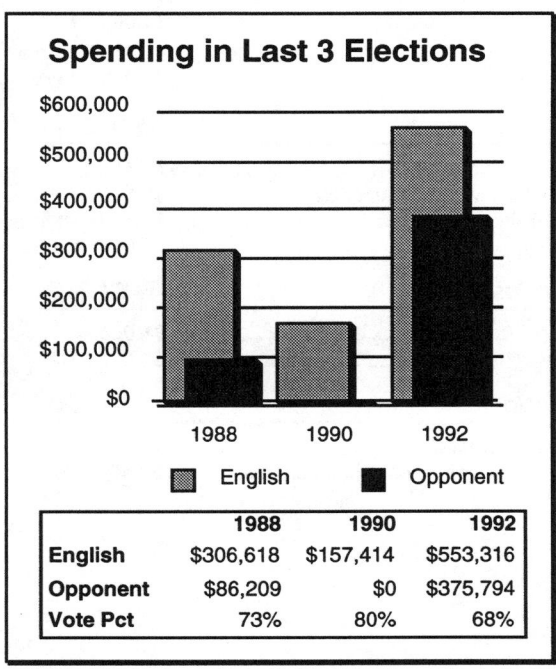

Spending in Last 3 Elections

	1988	1990	1992
English	$306,618	$157,414	$553,316
Opponent	$86,209	$0	$375,794
Vote Pct	73%	80%	68%

Legend: ▨ English   ■ Opponent

Karan English, D-Ariz (6)

1993-94 Committees & Subcommittees

First elected: 1992
1991-92 Total Receipts: $392,253
1992 Year-end Cash: $3,238

Education and Labor
Elementary, Secondary and Vocational Education; Postsecondary Education and Training

Natural Resources
National Parks Forests and Public Lands; Native American Affairs; Oversight and Investigations

Leading Contributors

Business

Agriculture — $5,000

Dairy	$1,500	
Associated Milk Producers	$1,000	PAC
Agricultural Services/Products	$2,500	
Salt River Valley Water Users	$2,500	PAC

Communications/Electronics — $3,800

Media/Entertainment	$1,250	
KTVK-TV	$1,000	Indiv
Telephone Utilities	$1,500	
Southwestern Bell	$1,000	PAC

Construction — $1,000

Building Materials & Equipment	$1,000	
Empire Southwest Co	$1,000	Indiv

Energy & Natural Resources — $2,600

Oil & Gas	$2,250	
Southwest Gas Corp	$1,000	PAC

Finance, Insurance & Real Estate — $9,250

Commercial Banks	$1,800	
American Bankers Assn	$1,500	PAC
Credit Unions	$1,000	
Credit Union National Assn	$1,000	PAC

Insurance	$1,000	
Insurance Information Institute	$1,000	Indiv
Real Estate	$3,950	
Del Webb Corp	$1,500	PAC/Ind

Health — $18,800

Health Professionals	$15,800	
American Medical Assn	$10,000	PAC
American Nurses Assn	$1,500	PAC
American Optometric Assn	$1,000	PAC
Hospitals/Nursing Homes	$1,000	
American Hospital Assn	$1,000	PAC
Health Services	$1,000	
Family Health Program Inc	$1,000	PAC
Misc Health	$1,000	
Fallon Clinic	$1,000	Indiv

Lawyers & Lobbyists — $10,557

Lawyers & Lobbyists	$10,557	
Assn of Trial Lawyers of America	$2,500	PAC
Brown & Bain	$1,650	Indiv
Patton, Boggs & Blow	$1,000	Indiv

Misc Business — $3,265

Beer, Wine & Liquor	$1,000	
Southern Wine & Spirits	$1,000	PAC

Transportation — $4,250

Automotive	$3,000	
National Auto Dealers Assn	$2,500	PAC

Source of Funds in 1992 Election

Source	Total	Pct
PACs	$135,087	34%
Indivs $200+	$60,402	15%
Indivs under $200	$161,480	41%
Other	$40,284	10%
Candidate	$33,742	8%
Party	$5,150	1%

Source of PAC Dollars by Sector

Source	Total	Pct
Business	$36,150	29%
Labor	$39,850	32%
Ideology/Single Issue	$50,275	40%

In-State vs. Out-of-State Contributions*

Source	Total	Pct
In-State	$34,390	64%
Out-of-state	$19,212	36%
No state listed	$0	

* by large individual contributors ($200 & above)

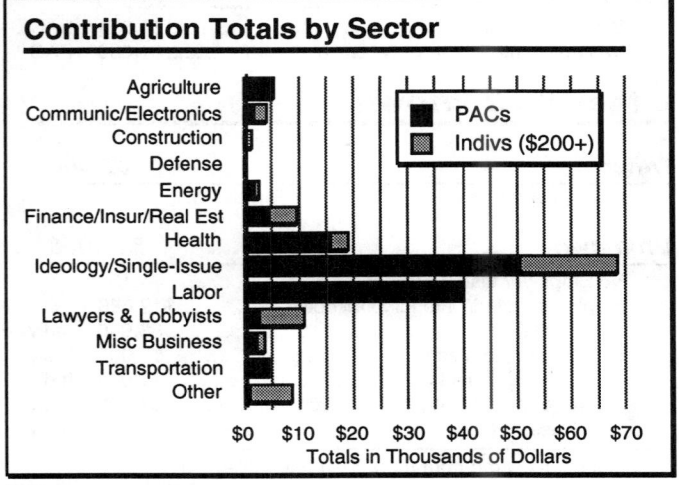

Contribution Totals by Sector

Agriculture
Communic/Electronics
Construction
Defense
Energy
Finance/Insur/Real Est
Health
Ideology/Single-Issue
Labor
Lawyers & Lobbyists
Misc Business
Transportation
Other

■ PACs
▨ Indivs ($200+)

$0 $10 $20 $30 $40 $50 $60 $70
Totals in Thousands of Dollars

Labor

Labor $39,850

Building Trade Unions $3,000
    Laborers' Political League ....$1,000   PAC
    Plumbers/Pipefitters Union ....$1,000   PAC
    Sheet Metal Workers Union ....$1,000   PAC

Industrial Unions $9,500
    Intl Brotherhood of Electrical Workers ......$3,500   PAC
    Machinists/Aerospace Workers Union ....$2,500   PAC
    United Steelworkers ....$2,500   PAC

Transportation Unions $4,500
    Assn of Flight Attendants ....$1,000   PAC
    Brotherhood of Locomotive Engineers ....$1,000   PAC
    Teamsters Union ....$1,000   PAC
    United Transportation Union ....$1,000   PAC

Public Sector Unions $14,700
    National Education Assn ....$10,000   PAC
    National Assn of Letter Carriers ....$2,500   PAC
    National Rural Letter Carriers Assn ....$1,000   PAC

Misc Unions $8,150
    Food & Commercial Workers Union ....$5,000   PAC
    AFL-CIO ....$1,000   PAC
    Bakery, Confectionery & Tobacco Workers ....$1,000   PAC
    Service Employees International Union ....$1,000   PAC

Ideological/Single-Issue

Ideological/Single-Issue $67,875

Democratic/Liberal $9,150
    National Cmte for an Effective Congress ....$5,000   PAC
    Hollywood Women's Political Cmte ....$1,000   PAC

Leadership PACs $1,500
    Effective Government Cmte (Dick Gephardt) ......$1,000   PAC

Foreign & Defense Policy $1,000
    Council for a Livable World ....$1,000   PAC

Pro-Israel $1,500
    None over $1,000

Pro-Choice $2,250
    National Abortion Rights Action League ....$2,000   PAC

Womens Issues $36,046
    Emily's List ....$16,046   PAC/Ind
    Women's Campaign Fund ....$10,000   PAC
    National Womens Political Caucus ....$5,000   PAC
    National Organization for Women ....$1,250   PAC

Human Rights $5,500
    Human Rights Campaign Fund ....$4,500   PAC
    Navajo Nation Washington Office ....$1,000   Indiv

Misc Issues $10,929
    League of Conservation Voters ....$5,879   PAC
    Sierra Club ....$2,000   PAC

Other & Unknown

Other $8,140

Education $1,140
    None over $1,000

Retired $5,750
    None over $1,000

Unknown $12,290

    Homemakers/Non-income earners $1,800
    No Employer Listed or Found $4,940
    Employer Listed/Category Unknown $5,550
        O'Connor & Associates ....$1,000   Indiv

Spending in Last Election

	1992
English	$389,015
Opponent	$654,960
Vote Pct	53%

Anna G. Eshoo, D-Calif (14)

First elected: 1992

1991-92 Total Receipts: $917,346
1992 Year-end Cash: $7,774

1993-94 Committees & Subcommittees

Merchant Marine and Fisheries
Environment and Natural Resources; Oceanography, Gulf of Mexico and the Outer Continental Shelf

Science, Space and Technology
Science; Space; Technology, Environment and Aviation

Leading Contributors

Business

Agriculture	$5,000
Dairy	$1,500

None over $1,500

Communications/Electronics	$11,850
Printing & Publishing	$1,650

None over $1,500

Media/Entertainment	$2,750

None over $1,500

Telephone Utilities	$2,000

None over $1,500

Electronics Mfg & Services	$2,450
Rolm Corp $2,000	Indiv

Computer Equipment & Services	$3,000

None over $1,500

Construction	$10,500
General Contractors	$4,500

None over $1,500

Construction Services	$5,500
O'Brien-Kreitzberg Associates $5,000	Indiv

Defense	$2,000
Defense Aerospace	$1,500

None over $1,500

Energy & Natural Resources	$3,500
Electric Utilities	$1,750

None over $1,500

Contribution Totals by Sector

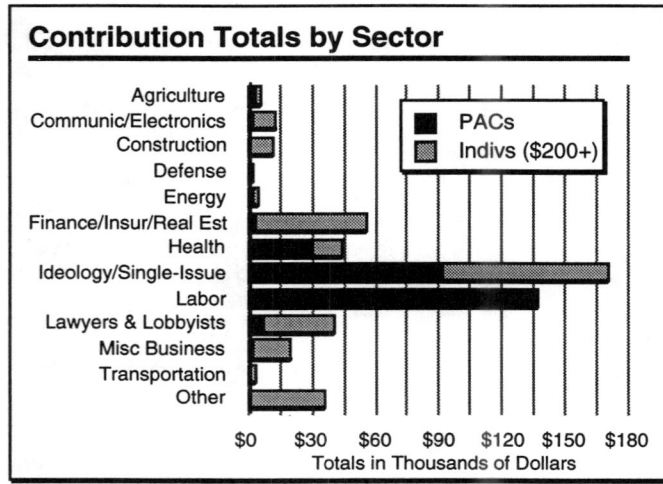

Totals in Thousands of Dollars

Finance, Insurance & Real Estate — $55,600

Commercial Banks	$2,250	
BankAmerica Corp	$2,000	PAC

Savings & Loans	$3,000	
World Savings & Loan	$3,000	Indiv

Finance/Credit Companies	$2,000	
Financial Leasing Services Inc	$2,000	Indiv

Securities & Investment	$9,500	
Bay Partners	$4,000	Indiv

Real Estate	$34,650	
Marcus & Millichap	$8,250	Indiv
Shamrock Group	$5,000	Indiv
Glenborough Corp	$3,000	Indiv
AKT Development Co	$2,250	Indiv
Hockey-Meier Co	$2,250	Indiv
EMD Properties	$1,500	Indiv

Misc Finance	$3,250	

None over $1,500

Health — $43,300

Health Professionals	$23,850	
American Medical Assn	$7,500	PAC
American Nurses Assn	$3,000	PAC
American College of Emergency Physicians	$2,000	PAC

Hospitals/Nursing Homes	$6,250	
American Hospital Assn	$1,500	PAC
California Assn of Hosp/Health Systems	$1,500	PAC

Health Services	$2,500	

None over $1,500

Pharmaceuticals/Health Products	$10,500	
Syntex (USA) Inc	$6,000	PAC
Alza Corp	$2,500	Indiv

Lawyers & Lobbyists — $39,850

Lawyers & Lobbyists $39,850
Assn of Trial Lawyers of America	$5,000	PAC
Cotchett, Illston et al	$3,000	Indiv
Ware & Freidenrich	$2,500	Indiv
Adams & Broadwell	$2,000	Indiv
Dewey, Ballantine et al	$2,000	Indiv
Haley, Purchio et al	$2,000	Indiv
Dickson & Ross	$1,500	Indiv
Kamber Group	$1,500	PAC/Ind
Kay & Stevens	$1,500	Indiv

Misc Business — $19,300

Beer, Wine & Liquor $1,500
Joseph E Seagram & Sons	$1,500	PAC/Ind

Misc Services $2,700
International Lease Finance Corp	$2,000	Indiv

Business Services $6,950
Regis McKenna Inc	$3,000	Indiv

Recreation/Live Entertainment $4,000
Robert Trent Jones International	$4,000	Indiv

Transportation — $2,500
None over $1,500

Labor

Labor — $135,549

Building Trade Unions $20,500
Carpenters & Joiners Union	$5,000	PAC
Plumbers/Pipefitters Union	$5,000	PAC
Laborers Union*	$4,000	PAC
Sheet Metal Workers Union	$2,500	PAC
Operating Engineers Union*	$2,000	PAC

Industrial Unions $30,000
United Auto Workers	$10,000	PAC
Machinists/Aerospace Workers Union	$7,500	PAC
United Steelworkers	$5,000	PAC
Communications Workers of America	$2,000	PAC
Intl Brotherhood of Electrical Workers	$2,000	PAC

Transportation Unions $21,050
Intl Longshoremen's/Warehousemen's Union	$6,000	PAC
Teamsters Union	$5,000	PAC
Marine Engineers Union	$2,500	PAC
Air Line Pilots Assn	$2,000	PAC

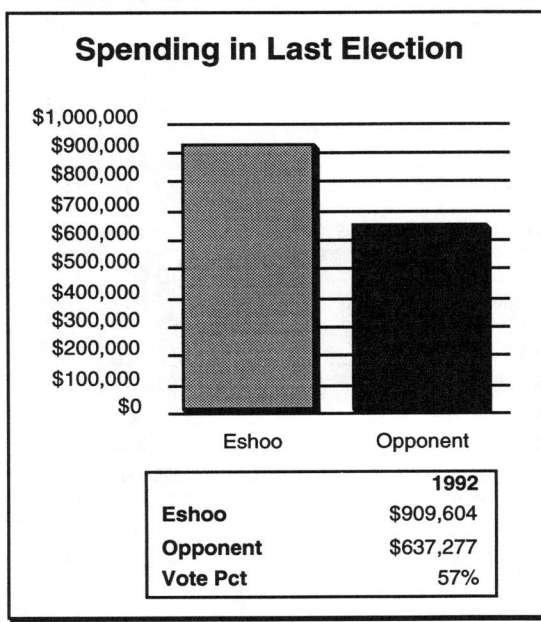

Spending in Last Election

	1992
Eshoo	$909,604
Opponent	$637,277
Vote Pct	57%

Public Sector Unions $43,000
American Fedn of St/Cnty/Munic Employees	$10,000	PAC
National Education Assn	$10,000	PAC
National Assn of Letter Carriers*	$8,000	PAC
American Federation of Teachers	$5,000	PAC
National Assn Retired Federal Employees	$5,000	PAC
International Assn of Firefighters	$1,500	PAC

Misc Unions $20,999
Service Employees International Union	$10,000	PAC
Food & Commercial Workers Union	$4,999	PAC
AFL-CIO	$3,500	PAC
Bakery, Confectionery & Tobacco Workers	$1,500	PAC

Ideological/Single-Issue

Ideological/Single-Issue — $169,441

Democratic/Liberal $18,955
Hollywood Women's Political Cmte	$10,000	PAC
National Cmte for an Effective Congress	$2,500	PAC

Leadership PACs $13,820
Fund for a Democratic Majority (Ted Kennedy)	$5,000	PAC
America's Leaders' Fund (Dan Rostenkowski)	$2,000	PAC

Foreign & Defense Policy $6,090
Council for a Livable World	$5,240	PAC/Ind

Pro-Israel $2,300
None over $1,500

Pro-Choice $7,700
Voters for Choice	$2,000	Indiv

Womens Issues $93,751
Emily's List	$43,839	PAC/Ind
Women's Campaign Fund	$10,000	PAC
Women's Political Committee	$7,000	PAC
National Organization for Women	$6,812	PAC
National Womens Political Caucus	$4,000	PAC

Human Rights $11,250
Human Rights Campaign Fund	$4,500	PAC
Women for:	$1,500	PAC

Misc Issues $15,575
League of Conservation Voters	$7,000	PAC
Sierra Club	$5,000	PAC
National Cmte to Preserve Social Security	$2,000	PAC

Other & Unknown

Other — $35,530

Civil Servants/Public Officials $11,950
California State Assembly	$2,750	Indiv
California Health Care Systems	$2,000	Indiv
San Mateo County	$2,000	Indiv

Education $12,850
University of California System*	$5,800	Indiv
Stanford University	$3,550	Indiv
St Anthony High School	$2,000	Indiv

Retired $7,900
None over $1,500

Unknown — $59,897
Homemakers/Non-income earners	$11,000	
No Employer Listed or Found	$13,750	
Generic Occupation/Category Unknown	$4,550	
Employer Listed/Category Unknown	$30,597	
Mareovich Inc	$3,000	Indiv
Ryzak & Associates	$2,000	Indiv

* Contributions came from more than one affiliate or subsidiary.

Mike Espy, D-Miss (2)

First elected: 1986

1991-92 Total Receipts: $299,560
1992 Year-end Cash: $113,887

1991-92 Committees & Subcommittees

Agriculture
Conservation, Credit and Rural Development; Cotton, Rice and Sugar (Vice Chairman); Domestic Marketing, Consumer Relations and Nutrition

Budget
Budget Process, Reconciliation and Enforcement; Community Development and Natural Resources (Chairman)

Select Committee on Hunger

Leading Contributors

Business

Agriculture	$65,500	
Crop Production & Basic Processing	**$20,675**	
American Crystal Sugar Corp	$3,100	PAC
National Cotton Council	$2,350	PAC
Riceland Foods	$2,000	PAC/Ind
Tobacco	**$8,150**	
RJR Nabisco	$3,050	PAC
Philip Morris	$2,000	PAC
Dairy	**$9,950**	
Associated Milk Producers	$6,000	PAC
Dairymen Inc-Mississippi	$2,950	PAC
Poultry & Eggs	**$3,150**	
National Broiler Council	$2,100	PAC
Livestock	**$2,050**	
National Cattlemen's Assn	$1,550	PAC
Agricultural Services/Products	**$9,075**	
Alabama Farm Bureau Federation	$2,100	PAC
National Council of Farmer Co-ops	$1,550	PAC
Food Processing & Sales	**$11,950**	
Food Marketing Institute	$3,550	PAC
Connell Rice & Sugar Co	$2,000	Indiv
ConAgra Inc	$1,900	PAC

Source of Funds in 1992 Election

Source	Total	Pct
■ PACs	$235,960	79%
▨ Indivs $200+	$42,383	14%
□ Indivs under $200	$21,167	7%
⊞ Other	$587	0%
Candidate	$0	0%
Party	$587	0%

Source of PAC Dollars by Sector

Source	Total	Pct
■ Business	$152,415	64%
▨ Labor	$67,900	28%
□ Ideology/Single Issue	$17,900	8%

In-State vs. Out-of-State Contributions*

Source	Total	Pct
□ In-State	$15,883	37%
■ Out-of-state	$26,500	63%
No state listed	$0	

* by large individual contributors ($200 & above)

Communications/Electronics — $18,350

Media/Entertainment	**$4,250**	
None over $1,500		
Telephone Utilities	**$13,850**	
BellSouth Corp*	$8,000	PAC
AT&T	$2,500	PAC
US Telephone Assn	$1,500	PAC

Construction — $6,250

Home Builders	**$5,000**	
Essen Development	$2,000	Indiv

Energy & Natural Resources — $14,000

Oil & Gas	**$2,500**	
None over $1,500		
Electric Utilities	**$8,650**	
Entergy Corp*	$2,500	PAC
Southern Co*	$2,050	PAC
ACRE (Action Cmte for Rural Electrification)*	$1,850	PAC
Waste Management	**$2,350**	
Waste Management Inc	$2,350	PAC

Finance, Insurance & Real Estate — $27,473

Commercial Banks	**$10,650**	
American Bankers Assn	$7,500	PAC
Independent Bankers Assn	$2,400	PAC
Savings & Loans	**$2,440**	
US League of Savings Assns	$1,940	PAC
Securities & Investment	**$5,000**	
Goldman, Sachs & Co	$2,500	PAC/Ind
Insurance	**$6,933**	
Prudential Insurance	$1,850	PAC
Real Estate	**$2,200**	
National Assn of Realtors	$1,700	PAC

Contribution Totals by Sector

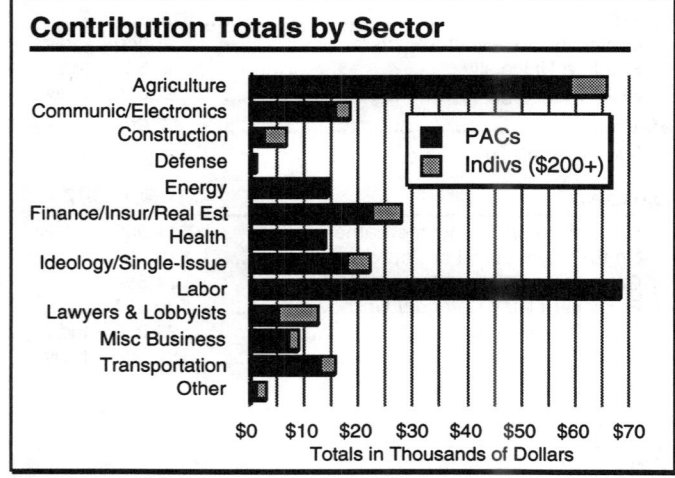

Agriculture
Communic/Electronics
Construction
Defense
Energy
Finance/Insur/Real Est
Health
Ideology/Single-Issue
Labor
Lawyers & Lobbyists
Misc Business
Transportation
Other

■ PACs
▨ Indivs ($200+)

$0 $10 $20 $30 $40 $50 $60 $70
Totals in Thousands of Dollars

Health | $13,700

Health Professionals **$6,600**	
American Medical Assn $2,350	PAC
Hospitals/Nursing Homes **$2,000**	
American Hospital Assn $1,500	PAC
Pharmaceuticals/Health Products **$5,100**	
None over $1,500	

Lawyers & Lobbyists | $12,140

Lawyers & Lobbyists **$12,140**	
Assn of Trial Lawyers of America $3,000	PAC

Misc Business | $8,550

Food & Beverage **$3,500**	
National Restaurant Assn $2,000	PAC
Chemical & Related Manufacturing **$1,500**	
None over $1,500	
Misc Manufacturing & Distributing **$2,000**	
None over $1,500	

Transportation | $15,450

Air Transport **$9,700**	
United Parcel Service $5,200	PAC
Federal Express Corp $4,000	PAC
Sea Transport **$4,250**	
Dixie Carriers Inc $1,500	PAC

Labor

Labor | $67,900

Building Trade Unions **$10,500**	
Plumbers/Pipefitters Union $5,500	PAC
Laborers' Political League $4,500	PAC
Industrial Unions **$20,850**	
United Auto Workers $6,350	PAC
Intl Brotherhood of Electrical Workers $6,000	PAC
United Steelworkers $5,000	PAC
Transportation Unions **$7,150**	
Teamsters Union $5,000	PAC
Public Sector Unions **$25,900**	
American Federation of Teachers $5,000	PAC
National Education Assn $5,000	PAC
American Postal Workers Union $4,200	PAC
National Assn of Letter Carriers $4,000	PAC
American Fedn of St/Cnty/Munic Employees $3,500	PAC
Misc Unions **$3,500**	
Food & Commercial Workers Union $2,000	PAC

Ideological/Single-Issue

Ideological/Single-Issue | $21,750

Pro-Israel **$5,650**	
City PAC $3,000	PAC
Pro-Choice **$1,800**	
None over $1,500	
Gun Rights/Gun Control **$9,900**	
National Rifle Assn $9,900	PAC
Misc Issues **$2,200**	
National Cmte to Preserve Social Security $2,200	PAC

Other & Unknown

Other | $2,950

None over $1,500	

Unknown | $5,550

Employer Listed/Category Unknown $5,550	
None over $1,500	

Spending in Last 3 Elections

	1988	1990	1992
Espy	$886,540	$365,825	$262,127
Opponent	$225,873	$0	$0
Vote Pct	65%	84%	76%

* Contributions came from more than one affiliate or subsidiary.

Lane Evans, D-Ill (17)

First elected: 1982

1991-92 Total Receipts:	$370,096
1992 Year-end Cash:	$25,957

1991-92 Committees & Subcommittees

Armed Services
Investigations; Procurement and Military Nuclear Systems; Readiness

Veterans' Affairs
Compensation, Pension and Insurance (Vice Chairman); Oversight and Investigations (Chairman)

Select Committee on Children, Youth and Families

Leading Contributors

Business

Agriculture		$8,225

Crop Production & Basic Processing	$2,375	
None over $1,000		
Dairy	$4,500	
Associated Milk Producers	$4,000	PAC

Communications/Electronics		$4,400

Printing & Publishing	$2,200	
Newsweb Corp	$2,000	Indiv
Telephone Utilities	$2,200	
AT&T	$1,500	PAC

Defense		$2,500

Defense Aerospace	$2,500	
Martin Marietta Corp	$1,000	PAC
McDonnell Douglas	$1,000	PAC

Energy & Natural Resources		$1,000

Electric Utilities	$1,000	
ACRE (Action Cmte for Rural Electrification)	$1,000	PAC

Finance, Insurance & Real Estate		$14,300

Commercial Banks	$1,000	
Shore Bank Corp	$1,000	Indiv
Securities & Investment	$6,000	
Chicago Board of Trade	$3,000	PAC
Sullivan & Proops	$2,000	Indiv
Chicago Mercantile Exchange	$1,000	PAC

Source of Funds in 1992 Election

Source	Total	Pct
■ PACs	$187,760	49%
▨ Indivs $200+	$34,733	9%
□ Indivs under $200	$136,968	36%
▨ Other	$22,879	6%
Candidate	$0	0%
Party	$12,394	3%

Source of PAC Dollars by Sector

Source	Total	Pct
■ Business	$43,475	23%
▨ Labor	$126,785	68%
□ Ideology/Single Issue	$17,500	9%

In-State vs. Out-of-State Contributions*

Source	Total	Pct
□ In-State	$34,533	100%
■ Out-of-state	$0	0%
No state listed	$0	

* by large individual contributors ($200 & above)

Insurance		$1,300
None over $1,000		
Real Estate		$5,500
National Assn of Realtors	$5,500	PAC

Health		$8,700

Health Professionals	$8,700	
American Chiropractic Assn	$5,000	PAC
International Chiropractors Assn	$2,500	PAC

Lawyers & Lobbyists		$20,533

Lawyers & Lobbyists	$20,533	
Assn of Trial Lawyers of America	$5,500	PAC
Hofeld & Schaffner	$3,500	Indiv
Burke, Wilson & McIlvaine	$2,000	Indiv
Power, Rogers & Lavin	$2,000	Indiv
Winstein, Kavensky et al	$1,500	Indiv
Cherry & Flynn	$1,000	Indiv
Demos & Burke Ltd	$1,000	Indiv

Misc Business		$4,700

Business Services	$1,250	
None over $1,000		
Misc Manufacturing & Distributing	$3,200	
Best Foam Fabricators	$3,000	PAC

Transportation		$3,200

Air Transport	$1,500	
United Airlines	$1,500	PAC
Railroads	$1,500	
Midland Manufacturing Corp	$1,000	Indiv

Contribution Totals by Sector

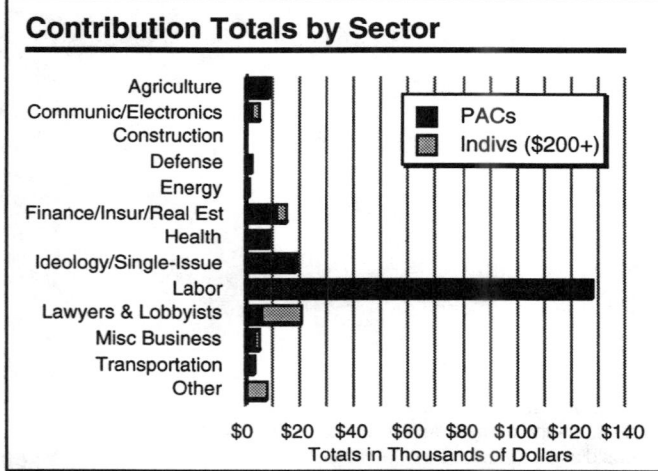

Legend: ■ PACs ▨ Indivs ($200+)

Categories (top to bottom): Agriculture, Communic/Electronics, Construction, Defense, Energy, Finance/Insur/Real Est, Health, Ideology/Single-Issue, Labor, Lawyers & Lobbyists, Misc Business, Transportation, Other

X-axis: $0 $20 $40 $60 $80 $100 $120 $140
Totals in Thousands of Dollars

Labor

Labor $126,785

Building Trade Unions $28,010
- Carpenters & Joiners Union .... $6,500   PAC
- Operating Engineers Union* .... $5,200   PAC
- Laborers' Political League .... $4,500   PAC
- Ironworkers Union .... $4,000   PAC
- Plumbers/Pipefitters Union* .... $3,210   PAC
- Sheet Metal Workers Union .... $2,500   PAC
- AFL-CIO Bldg/Construction Trades Dept .... $1,000   PAC

Industrial Unions $36,750
- Machinists/Aerospace Workers Union .... $10,000   PAC
- United Auto Workers .... $10,000   PAC
- Rubber Cork Linoleum & Plastic Workers .... $4,050   PAC
- Intl Brotherhood of Electrical Workers .... $4,000   PAC
- United Steelworkers .... $2,200   PAC
- Boilermakers Union .... $1,500   PAC
- Clothing & Textile Workers/Chicago .... $1,500   PAC
- United Mine Workers .... $1,500   PAC
- Graphic Communications Union .... $1,000   PAC
- Ladies Garment Workers Union .... $1,000   PAC

Transportation Unions $18,025
- Teamsters Union .... $10,000   PAC
- Marine Engineers Dist 2 Maritime Officers .... $2,500   PAC
- Seafarers International Union .... $2,000   PAC
- Air Line Pilots Assn .... $1,500   PAC

Public Sector Unions $36,400
- American Fedn of St/Cnty/Munic Employees .... $10,000   PAC
- National Education Assn .... $7,500   PAC
- National Assn Retired Federal Employees .... $6,000   PAC
- National Assn of Letter Carriers .... $5,000   PAC
- American Postal Workers Union .... $2,500   PAC
- International Assn of Firefighters .... $1,200   PAC
- National Assn of Postmasters .... $1,100   PAC

Misc Unions $7,600
- Food & Commercial Workers Union .... $2,600   PAC
- AFL-CIO .... $2,000   PAC
- Service Employees International Union .... $2,000   PAC
- Bakery, Confectionery & Tobacco Workers .... $1,000   PAC

Ideological/Single-Issue

Ideological/Single-Issue $18,000

Democratic/Liberal $2,500
- National Cmte for an Effective Congress .... $2,500   PAC

Foreign & Defense Policy $1,000
- Veterans of Foreign Wars .... $1,000   PAC

Pro-Israel $7,000
- National PAC .... $5,000   PAC
- Washington PAC .... $1,000   PAC

Human Rights $4,500
- Human Rights Campaign Fund .... $3,000   PAC
- KidsPAC .... $1,000   PAC

Misc Issues $3,000
- National Cmte to Preserve Social Security .... $3,000   PAC

Other & Unknown

Other $7,200

Education $1,000
- Northwestern University .... $1,000   Indiv

Retired $5,500
- None over $1,000

Unknown $2,750
- Homemakers/Non-income earners $2,000

Spending in Last 3 Elections

	1988	1990	1992
Evans	$471,233	$390,401	$374,415
Opponent	$124,993	$115,495	$115,569
Vote Pct	65%	67%	60%

---

* Contributions came from more than one affiliate or subsidiary.

Terry Everett, R-Ala (2)

1993-94 Committees & Subcommittees

First elected: 1992

1991-92 Total Receipts: $1,054,982
1992 Year-end Cash: $27,228

Agriculture
Foreign Agriculture and Hunger; Specialty Crops and Natural Resources

Armed Services
Military Installations and Facilities; Oversight and Investigations

Veterans' Affairs
Compensation, Pension and Insurance; Hospitals and Health Care; Oversight and Investigations

Leading Contributors

Business

Agriculture	**$3,150**	
Crop Production & Basic Processing	$2,600	
Weil Brothers Cotton	$1,500	Indiv

Communications/Electronics	**$5,250**	
Printing & Publishing	$3,250	
Boone Newspaper Inc	$1,000	Indiv
Crown Enterprises	$1,000	Indiv
Smith Newspapers	$1,000	Indiv
Electronics Mfg & Services	$2,000	
Techsonic Industries	$2,000	Indiv

Construction	**$12,650**	
General Contractors	$9,650	
Blount Inc	$6,000	Indiv
Dunning Construction	$1,000	Indiv
Home Builders	$1,300	
None over $1,000		
Special Trade Contractors	$1,000	
Merillat Industries	$1,000	Indiv

Source of Funds in 1992 Election

Source	Total	Pct
■ PACs	$0	0%
▦ Indivs $200+	$95,882	9%
☐ Indivs under $200	$27,809	3%
☒ Other	$972,897	89%
Candidate	$931,291	86%
Party	$41,606	4%

Source of PAC Dollars by Sector

No PAC contributions reported

Source	Total	Pct
■ Business	$0	0%
▦ Labor	$0	0%
☐ Ideology/Single Issue	$0	0%

In-State vs. Out-of-State Contributions*

Source	Total	Pct
☐ In-State	$70,982	75%
■ Out-of-state	$23,900	25%
No state listed	$1,000	

* by large individual contributors ($200 & above)

Finance, Insurance & Real Estate	**$18,925**	
Commercial Banks	$1,200	
First Citizens Bank	$1,000	Indiv
Insurance	$2,500	
Consolidated National Life	$1,000	Indiv
National Security Life Insurance	$1,000	Indiv
Real Estate	$3,400	
Thompson Realty Corp	$1,000	Indiv
Accountants	$11,125	
McDaniel & Associates	$10,125	Indiv
Wilson, Price et al	$1,000	Indiv

Health	**$2,950**	
Health Professionals	$2,150	
None over $1,000		

Lawyers & Lobbyists	**$1,850**	
Lawyers & Lobbyists	$1,850	
None over $1,000		

Misc Business	**$6,900**	
Retail Sales	$5,400	
Amway Corp	$5,400	Indiv
Misc Manufacturing & Distributing	$1,000	
Smith & Butterfield Co	$1,000	Indiv

Transportation	**$12,950**	
Automotive	$11,050	
Prince Corp	$5,000	Indiv
ASC Inc	$1,000	Indiv
Crown Cadillac Olds Inc	$1,000	Indiv
Great Lakes Mazda Distributors	$1,000	Indiv
Smith Inc	$1,000	Indiv
Misc Transport	$1,000	
Kershaw Inc	$1,000	Indiv

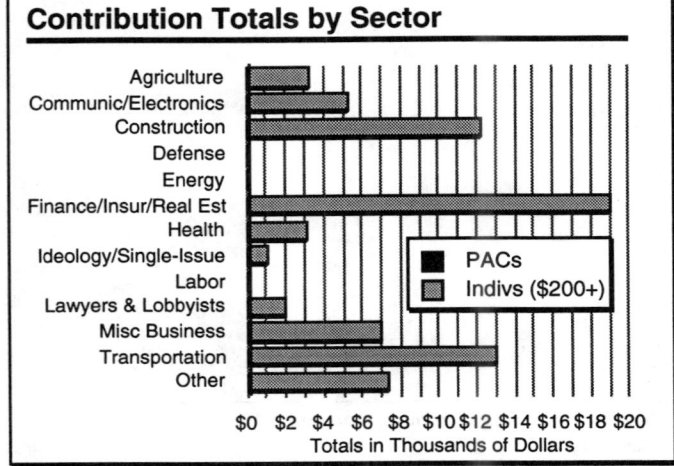

Contribution Totals by Sector

Agriculture
Communic/Electronics
Construction
Defense
Energy
Finance/Insur/Real Est
Health
Ideology/Single-Issue
Labor
Lawyers & Lobbyists
Misc Business
Transportation
Other

■ PACs
▦ Indivs ($200+)

$0 $2 $4 $6 $8 $10 $12 $14 $16 $18 $20
Totals in Thousands of Dollars

Ideological/Single-Issue

Ideological/Single-Issue	$1,011

Republican/Conservative....................................$1,011
   None over $1,000

Other & Unknown

Other	$7,250

Civil Servants/Public Officials $3,000
   US Government ....$2,000   Indiv
Retired..$4,250
   None over $1,000

Unknown	$23,007

   Homemakers/Non-income earners $1,700
   No Employer Listed or Found $3,920
   Employer Listed/Category Unknown $19,087
      Alfab Inc ....$1,000   Indiv
      Floyd H Mann Consultants ....$1,000   Indiv
      Hicks Inc...$1,000   Indiv
      Hold Enterprises ....$1,000   Indiv
      Lewis & Smith Supply ....$1,000   Indiv
      Network Marketing ....$1,000   Indiv
      Ozark Stripping Co.....................................$1,000   Indiv
      Profit Group Corp ....$1,000   Indiv
      Smith's Inc of Dothan ....$1,000   Indiv

Independent expenditures supporting Everett
   National Right to Life PAC $3,578

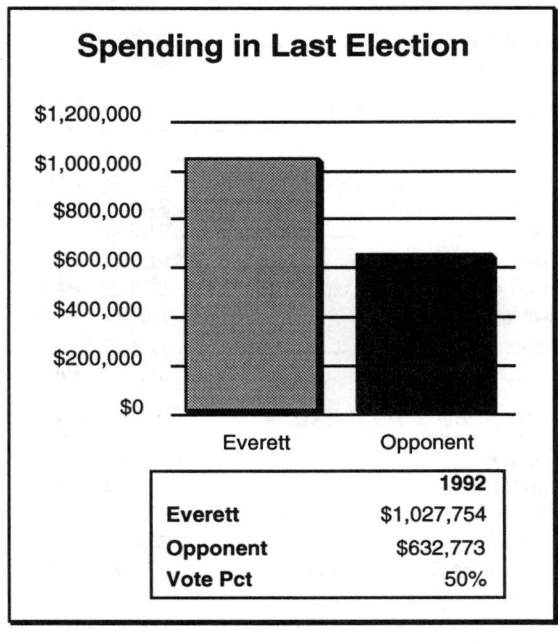

Spending in Last Election

	1992
Everett	$1,027,754
Opponent	$632,773
Vote Pct	50%

Thomas W. Ewing, R-Ill (15)

First elected: 1991

1991-92 Total Receipts: $700,864
1992 Year-end Cash: $123,473

1991-92 Committees & Subcommittees

Agriculture
Department Operations, Research and Foreign Agriculture

Public Works and Transportation
Aviation; Public Buildings and Grounds; Water Resources

Leading Contributors

Business

Agriculture $60,789

Crop Production & Basic Processing **$9,350**
   None over $1,500

Tobacco **$5,900**
   RJR Nabisco .... $2,500 PAC
   Eby-Brown Co .... $1,500 Indiv

Dairy **$4,000**
   Associated Milk Producers .... $3,500 PAC

Livestock **$3,700**
   National Cattlemen's Assn* .... $2,000 PAC

Agricultural Services/Products **$23,039**
   Illinois Agricultural Assn .... $4,839 PAC
   Archer-Daniels-Midland Corp .... $4,500 PAC
   FMC Corp .... $2,000 PAC
   Deere & Co .... $1,500 PAC
   Farm Credit Council .... $1,500 PAC
   Navistar International .... $1,500 PAC

Food Processing & Sales **$11,300**
   AE Staley Manufacturing Co .... $2,200 PAC
   Food Marketing Institute .... $1,500 PAC
   Quaker Oats .... $1,500 PAC

Forestry & Forest Products **$2,500**
   Westvaco Corp .... $2,000 PAC

Communications/Electronics $27,300

Printing & Publishing **$5,200**
   RR Donnelley & Sons .... $3,500 PAC/Ind

Media/Entertainment **$1,750**
   None over $1,500

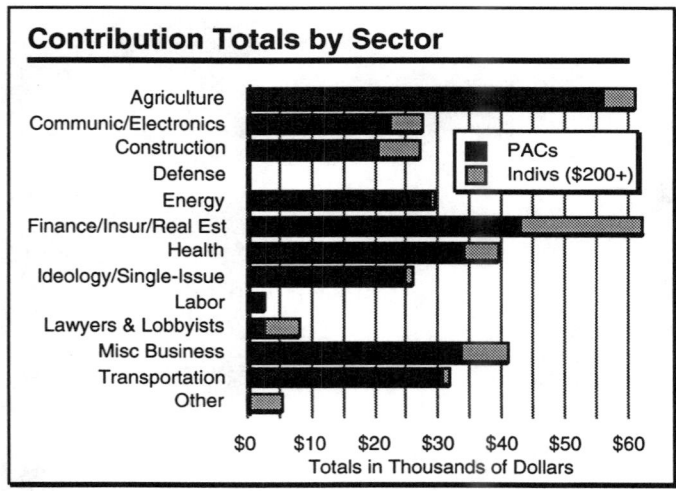

Contribution Totals by Sector

Agriculture
Communic/Electronics
Construction
Defense
Energy
Finance/Insur/Real Est
Health
Ideology/Single-Issue
Labor
Lawyers & Lobbyists
Misc Business
Transportation
Other

     PACs
     Indivs ($200+)

$0 $10 $20 $30 $40 $50 $60
Totals in Thousands of Dollars

Source of Funds in 1992 Election

Source	Total	Pct
PACs	$323,275	45%
Indivs $200+	$97,353	13%
Indivs under $200	$228,509	32%
Other	$76,323	11%
Candidate	$16,713	2%
Party	$31,507	4%

Source of PAC Dollars by Sector

Source	Total	Pct
Business	$268,289	91%
Labor	$2,500	1%
Ideology/Single Issue	$24,246	8%

In-State vs. Out-of-State Contributions*

Source	Total	Pct
In-State	$95,126	98%
Out-of-state	$2,227	2%
No state listed	$0	

* by large individual contributors ($200 & above)

Telephone Utilities **$19,850**
   Illinois Bell Telephone .... $6,500 PAC
   BellSouth Corp* .... $4,000 PAC
   GTE Corp .... $4,000 PAC
   AT&T .... $2,000 PAC

Construction $26,600

General Contractors **$8,000**
   Associated General Contractors .... $2,000 PAC
   Apcom Corp .... $1,500 Indiv

Home Builders **$7,300**
   National Assn of Home Builders .... $7,000 PAC

Special Trade Contractors **$2,350**
   National Roofing Contractors Assn .... $1,800 PAC

Building Materials & Equipment **$8,700**
   Caterpillar Tractor .... $5,000 PAC

Energy & Natural Resources $29,135

Oil & Gas **$12,150**
   Nicor Inc .... $2,100 PAC
   Petroleum Marketers Assn* .... $1,950 PAC
   Amoco Corp .... $1,500 PAC

Electric Utilities **$14,185**
   Illinois Power Co .... $7,350 PAC
   Central Illinois Public Service Co .... $3,000 PAC

Waste Management **$1,500**
   Waste Management Inc .... $1,500 PAC

Finance, Insurance & Real Estate $61,700

Commercial Banks **$16,350**
   American Bankers Assn .... $4,000 PAC
   Independent Bankers Assn .... $3,000 PAC

Securities & Investment **$6,000**
   Chicago Mercantile Exchange .... $2,000 PAC

Insurance **$14,500**
    National Assn of Life Underwriters .... $3,500   PAC
    Kemper Insurance .... $1,550   PAC

Real Estate **$23,000**
    National Assn of Realtors .... $15,250   PAC
    Hamilton Partners .... $1,500   Indiv
    Regency Associates .... $1,500   Indiv

Accountants **$1,650**
    None over $1,500

Health $39,000

Health Professionals **$34,500**
    American Medical Assn .... $20,000   PAC
    American Dental Assn .... $6,500   PAC
    American Academy of Ophthalmology .... $3,000   PAC

Hospitals/Nursing Homes **$2,400**
    American Health Care Assn .... $1,500   PAC

Pharmaceuticals/Health Products **$1,800**
    None over $1,500

Lawyers & Lobbyists $7,950

Lawyers & Lobbyists **$7,950**
    Hopkins & Sutter .... $1,500   PAC

Misc Business $40,558

Business Associations **$1,580**
    None over $1,500

Food & Beverage **$7,828**
    Pepsi-Cola General Bottlers .... $2,200   PAC
    McDonald's Corp .... $2,000   PAC
    National Restaurant Assn .... $2,000   PAC

Beer, Wine & Liquor **$2,500**
    Brown-Forman Distillers .... $1,500   PAC

Retail Sales **$9,050**
    Walgreen Co .... $1,500   PAC

Business Services **$4,950**
    Alarm Detection Systems .... $2,000   Indiv

Chemical & Related Manufacturing **$6,050**
    Stepan Co .... $3,300   PAC

Misc Manufacturing & Distributing **$5,950**
    Illinois Tool Works .... $1,750   PAC/Ind

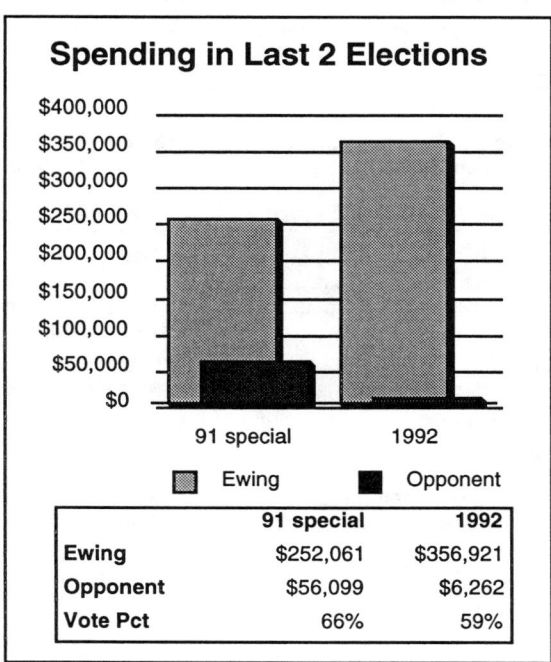

Spending in Last 2 Elections

	91 special	1992
Ewing	$252,061	$356,921
Opponent	$56,099	$6,262
Vote Pct	66%	59%

Transportation   **$33,004**

Air Transport **$9,260**
    United Parcel Service .... $5,000   PAC

Automotive **$11,950**
    National Auto Dealers Assn .... $10,500   PAC

Trucking **$5,544**
    Carters Moving & Storage .... $1,544   Indiv
    Pre Fab Transit Co .... $1,500   PAC

Railroads **$4,750**
    Union Pacific Corp .... $1,500   PAC

Sea Transport **$1,500**
    None over $1,500

Labor

Labor $2,500

Public Sector Unions **$2,500**
    National Assn Retired Federal Employees .... $2,000   PAC

Ideological/Single-Issue

Ideological/Single-Issue $25,546

Republican/Conservative **$2,100**
    None over $1,500

Leadership PACs **$13,075**
    Republican Leader's Fund (Bob Michel) .... $10,000   PAC

Pro-Life **$3,371**
    Illinois Right to Life .... $3,371   PAC

Gun Rights/Gun Control **$5,000**
    National Rifle Assn .... $5,000   PAC

Misc Issues **$1,500**
    Public Service Research Council .... $1,500   PAC

Other & Unknown

Other $5,150

Retired **$4,150**
    None over $1,500

Unknown $33,166

    No Employer Listed or Found $18,925
    Employer Listed/Category Unknown $13,981
        None over $1,500

* Contributions came from more than one affiliate or
subsidiary.

Harris W. Fawell, R-III (13)

First elected: 1984

1991-92 Total Receipts: $498,465
1992 Year-end Cash: $30,674

1991-92 Committees & Subcommittees

Education and Labor
Human Resources (Ranking Republican); Labor-Management Relations; Labor Standards

Science, Space and Technology
Energy; Science

Select Committee on Aging

Select Committee on Children, Youth and Families

Leading Contributors

Business

Agriculture		$14,098
Poultry & Eggs		**$1,500**
National Broiler Council	$1,500	PAC
Agricultural Services/Products		**$6,598**
George J Ball Inc	$1,500	Indiv
Navistar International	$1,500	PAC
Food Processing & Sales		**$5,500**
Food Marketing Institute	$3,000	PAC

Communications/Electronics		$14,849
Printing & Publishing		**$1,500**
None over $1,500		
Telephone Utilities		**$9,000**
BellSouth Corp*	$2,250	PAC
Illinois Bell Telephone	$2,250	PAC
AT&T	$2,000	PAC
Ameritech Corp	$1,500	PAC/Ind
Telecom Services & Equipment		**$2,399**
None over $1,500		

Construction		$44,124
General Contractors		**$15,950**
Associated General Contractors	$2,500	PAC
Pattermann Builders	$2,250	Indiv
Associated Builders & Contractors	$2,000	PAC
CBI Industries	$4,800	PAC
Home Builders		**$4,000**
National Assn of Home Builders	$4,000	PAC

Contribution Totals by Sector

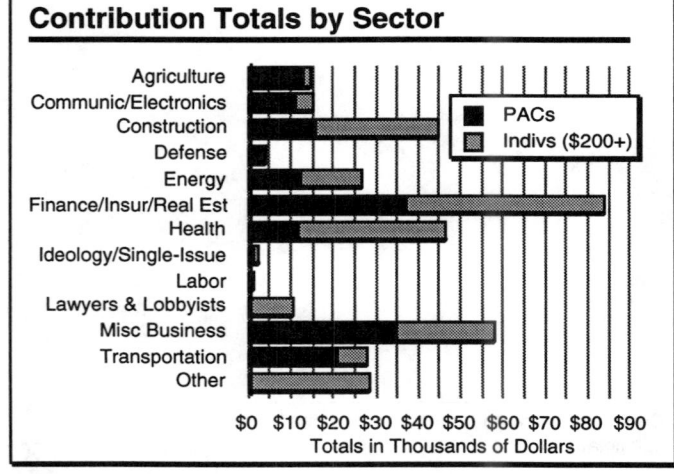

PACs
Indivs ($200+)

Agriculture
Communic/Electronics
Construction
Defense
Energy
Finance/Insur/Real Est
Health
Ideology/Single-Issue
Labor
Lawyers & Lobbyists
Misc Business
Transportation
Other

$0 $10 $20 $30 $40 $50 $60 $70 $80 $90
Totals in Thousands of Dollars

Source of Funds in 1992 Election

Source	Total	Pct
■ PACs	$179,934	36%
▨ Indivs $200+	$269,034	54%
□ Indivs under $200	$31,815	6%
⊠ Other	$17,682	4%
Candidate	$0	0%
Party	$2,019	0%

Source of PAC Dollars by Sector

Source	Total	Pct
■ Business	$156,957	99%
▨ Labor	$1,000	1%
□ Ideology/Single Issue	$750	0%

In-State vs. Out-of-State Contributions*

Source	Total	Pct
□ In-State	$264,334	99%
■ Out-of-state	$3,200	1%
No state listed	$1,500	

*** by large individual contributors ($200 & above)**

Special Trade Contractors		**$6,250**
McNulty Bros Co	$1,500	Indiv
Building Materials & Equipment		**$16,674**
Molex Inc	$9,650	Indiv
USG Corp	$3,000	Indiv
Caterpillar Tractor	$1,500	PAC

Defense		$3,800
Defense Aerospace		**$3,500**
None over $1,500		

Energy & Natural Resources		$26,200
Oil & Gas		**$5,250**
None over $1,500		
Electric Utilities		**$4,000**
Commonwealth Edison	$2,000	PAC
Waste Management		**$15,700**
Waste Management Inc	$14,600	PAC/Ind

Finance, Insurance & Real Estate		$83,620
Commercial Banks		**$11,100**
American Bankers Assn	$2,000	PAC
Harris Trust & Savings	$1,750	PAC/Ind
Citicorp	$1,500	PAC
Savings & Loans		**$5,320**
Mid America Federal Savings & Loan	$5,070	PAC/Ind
Securities & Investment		**$13,250**
Rasin Corp	$3,000	Indiv
Stein, Roe & Farnham	$3,000	Indiv
Huizenga Capital Management	$2,000	Indiv
Assn of Private Pension Plans	$1,500	PAC

Insurance $27,100
    Farmers Insurance Group ....$5,600 Indiv
    Blue Cross & Blue Shield Assn ....$4,500 PAC/Ind
    American Council of Life Insurance ....$2,500 PAC
    Kemper Insurance ....$2,250 PAC/Ind
    Allstate Insurance ....$1,500 PAC
    Health Insurance Assn of America......................$1,500 PAC
    National Assn of Independent Insurers...............$1,500 PAC
    National Assn of Life Underwriters......................$1,500 PAC
    Principal Mutual Life Insurance ....$1,500 PAC

Real Estate $15,100
    National Assn of Realtors ....$4,500 PAC
    Inland Group ....$3,000 Indiv
    John T Greene Realtor.................................$3,000 Indiv
    Oliver-Hoffmann Corp ....$2,000 Indiv

Accountants $2,500
    American Institute of CPA's ....$2,000 PAC

Misc Finance $9,250
    Healthcare Compare Corp ....$5,150 PAC/Ind

Health $45,875

Health Professionals $30,225
    American Medical Assn.................................$5,350 PAC
    Midwest Cardiovascular ....$3,250 Indiv
    Riveredge Hospital ....$2,850 Indiv
    American Podiatry Assn ....$2,000 PAC

Hospitals/Nursing Homes $7,150
    Good Samaritan Hospital ....$1,500 Indiv

Pharmaceuticals/Health Products $1,500
    None over $1,500

Misc Health $7,000
    Sub Women's Health Center ....$4,250 Indiv
    Midwest Heart Associates ....$1,500 Indiv

Lawyers & Lobbyists $10,250

Lawyers & Lobbyists $10,250
    None over $1,500

Spending in Last 3 Elections

	1988	1990	1992
Fawell	$289,190	$271,913	$574,347
Opponent	$45,760	$0	$4,327
Vote Pct	70%	66%	68%

Misc Business $57,186

Business Associations $2,000
    None over $1,500

Food & Beverage $8,450
    McDonald's Corp ....$3,400 PAC/Ind
    Pepsi-Cola General Bottlers ....$1,500 PAC

Retail Sales..$10,500
    National Assn of Chain Drug Stores ....$2,500 PAC
    Spiegel Inc ....$2,500 PAC

Misc Services $1,750
    Blake-Lamb Funeral Home ....$1,500 Indiv

Business Services $6,336
    Peterson & Co ....$5,136 Indiv

Lodging/Tourism $1,500
    None over $1,500

Chemical & Related Manufacturing $9,500
    Nalco Chemical Co ....$5,750 PAC/Ind
    FMC Corp ....$3,250 PAC/Ind

Steel Production $1,750
    Axia Inc ....$1,500 PAC

Misc Manufacturing & Distributing...................$14,400
    Award Emblem ....$2,900 Indiv
    International Sanitary Supply ....$2,000 PAC

Transportation $27,360

Air Transport...$10,160
    United Airlines ....$5,500 PAC/Ind
    United Parcel Service ....$2,650 PAC

Automotive $14,700
    National Auto Dealers Assn ....$6,500 PAC
    Village Pontiac GMC Inc ....$2,250 Indiv
    Auto Dealers & Drivers for Free Trade ....$1,500 PAC

Sea Transport..$1,500
    None over $1,500

Ideological/Single-Issue

Ideological/Single-Issue $1,750
    None over $1,500

Other & Unknown

Other $28,200

Civil Servants/Public Officials............................$3,000
    Argonne National Laboratory ....$1,750 Indiv

Education $3,000
    Palm Desert School District ....$2,000 Indiv

Retired $22,200
    None over $1,500

Unknown $69,929

    Homemakers/Non-income earners $12,560
    No Employer Listed or Found $23,680
    Generic Occupation/Category Unknown $3,900
    Employer Listed/Category Unknown $29,789
        TSC ....$2,864 Indiv
        Wright & Co ....$2,750 Indiv
        Meadowbrook Manor ....$2,000 Indiv
        Packer Engineering Inc ....$2,000 Indiv

* Contributions came from more than one affiliate or subsidiary.

Vic Fazio, D-Calif (3)

First elected: 1978

1991-92 Total Receipts: $1,993,452
1992 Year-end Cash: $281,802

1991-92 Committees & Subcommittees

Appropriations
Energy and Water Development; Legislative (Chairman); Military Construction

Select Committee on Hunger

Leading Contributors
Business

Agriculture		$160,739
Crop Production & Basic Processing	**$95,774**	
Sun-Diamond Growers*	$10,985	PAC
California Almond Growers Exchange	$10,000	PAC
Farmers' Rice Cooperative	$10,000	PAC
Sunkist Growers	$10,000	PAC
Tobacco	**$19,500**	
RJR Nabisco	$9,000	PAC
Dairy	**$16,000**	
None over $6,000		
Agricultural Services/Products	**$11,965**	
None over $6,000		
Food Processing & Sales	**$13,000**	
None over $6,000		

Communications/Electronics		$91,200
Media/Entertainment	**$52,050**	
National Cable Television Assn	$10,000	PAC
MCA Inc	$8,500	PAC/Ind
Telephone Utilities	**$22,750**	
Pacific Telesis Group	$10,000	PAC
Electronics Mfg & Services	**$7,000**	
None over $6,000		

Construction		$46,550
General Contractors	**$16,300**	
None over $6,000		
Home Builders	**$9,900**	
None over $6,000		
Construction Services	**$13,750**	
None over $6,000		

Source of Funds in 1992 Election

Source	Total	Pct
PACs	$1,147,938	57%
Indivs $200+	$583,346	29%
Indivs under $200	$203,082	10%
Other	$67,838	3%
Candidate	$0	0%
Party	$10,302	1%

Source of PAC Dollars by Sector

Source	Total	Pct
Business	$789,334	70%
Labor	$241,076	21%
Ideology/Single Issue	$101,500	9%

In-State vs. Out-of-State Contributions*

Source	Total	Pct
In-State	$383,196	67%
Out-of-state	$188,600	33%
No state listed	$3,500	

* by large individual contributors ($200 & above)

Defense		$95,025
Defense Aerospace	**$47,350**	
Northrop Corp	$10,000	PAC
Defense Electronics	**$21,000**	
AT&T	$11,000	PAC
Misc Defense	**$26,675**	
General Atomics	$10,000	PAC
Foundation Health Corp	$9,075	PAC

Energy & Natural Resources		$97,360
Oil & Gas	**$49,510**	
Coastal Corp	$9,000	PAC
Occidental Petroleum	$9,000	PAC
Misc Energy	**$12,600**	
None over $6,000		
Electric Utilities	**$25,500**	
Pacific Gas & Electric	$9,000	PAC
Southern California Edison	$7,000	PAC
Waste Management	**$7,500**	
None over $6,000		

Finance, Insurance & Real Estate		$272,781
Commercial Banks	**$51,050**	
American Bankers Assn	$10,000	PAC
BankAmerica Corp	$6,000	PAC/Ind
Savings & Loans	**$6,250**	
None over $6,000		
Finance/Credit Companies	**$8,000**	
None over $6,000		
Securities & Investment	**$39,100**	
Goldman, Sachs & Co	$6,000	PAC/Ind
Insurance	**$90,299**	
Independent Insurance Agents of America	$9,999	PAC
Management Compensation Group	$9,000	Indiv
National Assn of Life Underwriters	$9,000	PAC

Contribution Totals by Sector

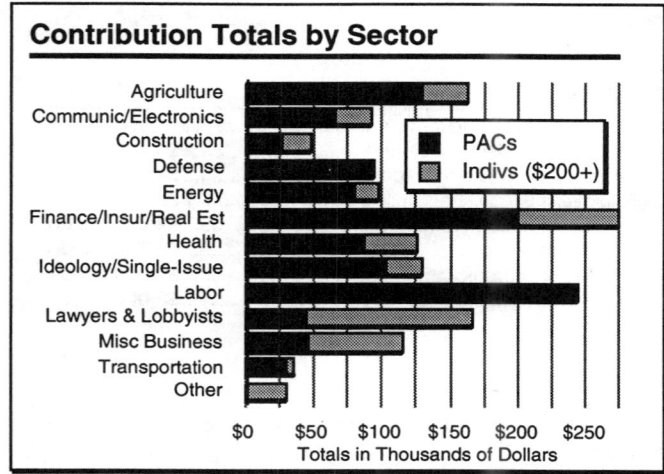

Agriculture
Communic/Electronics
Construction
Defense
Energy
Finance/Insur/Real Est
Health
Ideology/Single-Issue
Labor
Lawyers & Lobbyists
Misc Business
Transportation
Other

PACs
Indivs ($200+)

$0 $50 $100 $150 $200 $250
Totals in Thousands of Dollars

Real Estate **$51,932**
    National Assn of Realtors .... $10,000 PAC

Accountants **$15,300**
    American Institute of CPA's .... $6,000 PAC

Health $124,730

Health Professionals **$73,225**
    American Dental Assn .... $10,000 PAC
    Foundation Health Corp .... $7,200 Indiv
    Assn for the Advancement of Psychology .... $7,000 PAC

Hospitals/Nursing Homes **$22,455**
    None over $6,000

Health Services **$14,750**
    Foundation Health Corp .... $6,250 Indiv

Pharmaceuticals/Health Products **$9,750**
    None over $6,000

Lawyers & Lobbyists $165,504

Lawyers & Lobbyists **$165,504**
    Assn of Trial Lawyers of America .... $10,000 PAC
    Orrick, Herrington & Sutcliffe .... $8,000 PAC

Transportation $34,320

Air Transport **$10,220**
    United Parcel Service .... $7,720 PAC/Ind

Railroads **$8,000**
    None over $6,000

Misc Business $116,631

Beer, Wine & Liquor **$53,750**
    Gallo Winery .... $9,000 Indiv
    National Beer Wholesalers Assn .... $7,000 PAC

Retail Sales **$7,550**
    None over $6,000

Business Services **$29,631**
    None over $6,000

Labor

Labor $242,326

Building Trade Unions **$49,126**
    Carpenters & Joiners Union .... $10,000 PAC
    Sheet Metal Workers Union .... $10,000 PAC
    Laborers Union* .... $7,000 PAC
    Plumbers/Pipefitters Union .... $7,000 PAC
    Ironworkers Union .... $6,000 PAC

Industrial Unions **$43,000**
    Intl Brotherhood of Electrical Workers .... $10,000 PAC
    United Auto Workers .... $10,000 PAC

Transportation Unions **$48,950**
    Seafarers International Union* .... $10,500 PAC
    Air Line Pilots Assn .... $10,000 PAC
    Teamsters Union .... $10,000 PAC

Public Sector Unions **$74,650**
    American Federation of Teachers .... $10,000 PAC
    American Fedn of St/Cnty/Munic Employees .... $10,000 PAC
    National Education Assn .... $10,000 PAC
    National Assn of Letter Carriers .... $9,800 PAC
    National Assn Retired Federal Employees .... $8,000 PAC
    American Postal Workers Union .... $7,000 PAC
    International Assn of Firefighters .... $6,950 PAC

Misc Unions **$26,600**
    Service Employees International Union .... $10,000 PAC
    Food & Commercial Workers Union .... $9,850 PAC

Ideological/Single-Issue

Ideological/Single-Issue $128,450

Democratic/Liberal **$23,550**
    Harry S Truman Club .... $10,000 PAC

Leadership PACs **$11,500**
    Cmte for a Demo Consensus (Alan Cranston) .... $7,500 PAC

Pro-Israel **$36,550**
    None over $6,000

Pro-Choice **$13,350**
    National Abortion Rights Action League .... $9,500 PAC

Human Rights **$25,000**
    Human Rights Campaign Fund .... $10,000 PAC
    KidsPAC .... $10,000 PAC

Misc Issues **$18,500**
    National Council of Senior Citizens .... $10,000 PAC
    National Cmte to Preserve Social Security .... $8,500 PAC

Other & Unknown

Other $28,125

Retired **$11,275**
    None over $6,000

Unknown $111,965

    No Employer Listed or Found $38,265
    Employer Listed/Category Unknown $62,150
        None over $6,000

Independent expenditures supporting Fazio
    American Medical Assn $255,085
    Handgun Control Inc $20,778
    National Cmte to Preserve Social Security $13,735

Independent expenditures opposing Fazio
    National Rifle Assn $15,318
    National Freedom PAC $7,973

* Contributions came from more than one affiliate or
  subsidiary.

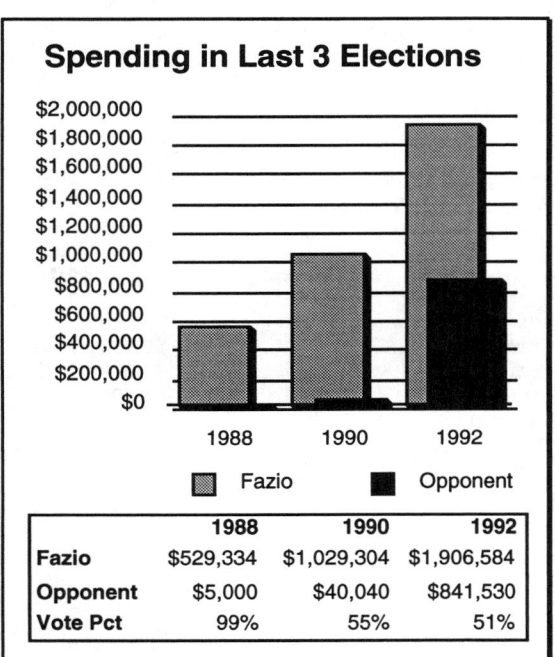

Spending in Last 3 Elections

	1988	1990	1992
Fazio	$529,334	$1,029,304	$1,906,584
Opponent	$5,000	$40,040	$841,530
Vote Pct	99%	55%	51%

Cleo Fields, D-La (4)

First elected: 1992

1991-92 Total Receipts:	$291,225
1992 Year-end Cash:	$1,044

1993-94 Committees & Subcommittees

Banking, Finance and Urban Affairs
Consumer Credit and Insurance; Housing and Community Development; International Development, Finance, Trade and Monetary Policy

Small Business
Minority Enterprise, Finance and Urban Development; SBA Legislation and the General Economy

Leading Contributors

Business

Agriculture	**$2,200**	
Food Processing & Sales **$1,000**		
Fleming Companies Inc $1,000		PAC

Communications/Electronics	**$6,500**	
Telephone Utilities................................... **$5,500**		
Southern Bell $3,000		PAC
US Long Distance of Louisiana.....................$1,500		Indiv
AT&T $1,000		PAC

Construction	**$6,850**	
General Contractors **$5,850**		
M Wormack General Contractor $2,000		Indiv
Construction Services **$1,000**		
Vernon F Meyer & Assoc $1,000		Indiv

Energy & Natural Resources	**$6,150**	
Oil & Gas **$4,450**		
Arkla Inc $1,000		PAC
Coastal Corp $1,000		PAC
Electric Utilities **$1,200**		
Southwestern Electric Power Co $1,000		PAC

Finance, Insurance & Real Estate	**$18,850**	
Commercial Banks **$2,700**		
First National Bank of Denham Springs..............$1,000		Indiv
Life Savings Bank $1,000		Indiv
Credit Unions **$1,000**		
Credit Union National Assn $1,000		PAC

Source of Funds in 1992 Election

Source	Total	Pct
■ PACs	$49,020	17%
▨ Indivs $200+	$197,700	68%
☐ Indivs under $200	$11,323	4%
▨ Other..........................	$33,182	11%
Candidate	$23,006	8%
Party	$0	0%

Source of PAC Dollars by Sector

Source	Total	Pct
■ Business	$29,170	57%
▨ Labor	$13,300	26%
☐ Ideology/Single Issue	$8,479	17%

In-State vs. Out-of-State Contributions*

Source	Total	Pct
☐ In-State	$176,150	90%
■ Out-of-state	$19,850	10%
No state listed......................	$1,700	

*** by large individual contributors ($200 & above)**

Securities & Investment **$3,000**		
Smith Barney $2,000		Indiv
First Commonwealth Securities $1,000		Indiv
Insurance **$4,300**		
National Assn of Life Underwriters......................$1,500		PAC
Real Estate **$5,600**		
Roy Carter Realtors $1,700		Indiv
National Assn of Realtors $1,000		PAC
Accountants **$1,500**		
American Institute of CPA's $1,500		PAC

Health $12,950

Health Professionals **$8,700**		
American Academy of Ophthalmology................$2,000		PAC
American Nurses Assn.................................$1,000		PAC
Hospitals/Nursing Homes **$1,750**		
None over $1,000		
Health Services **$1,500**		
Acadian Ambulance Service $1,000		Indiv
Pharmaceuticals/Health Products **$1,000**		
Luffey's Medical Supplies $1,000		Indiv

Lawyers & Lobbyists $50,420

Lawyers & Lobbyists **$50,420**		
Preis & Crawford $2,000		Indiv
Assn of Trial Lawyers of America $1,670		PAC
Simoneaux & Hudson $1,200		Indiv
Fayard & Fayard $1,000		Indiv
Jones & Tarver $1,000		Indiv
Matchett Attorneys at Law $1,000		Indiv

Contribution Totals by Sector

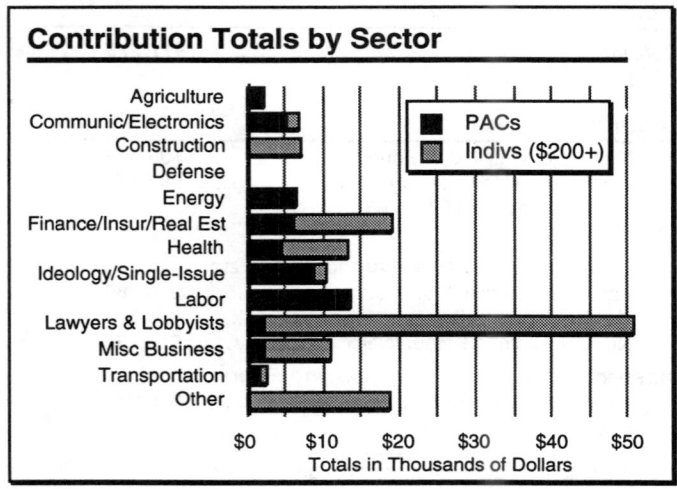

Totals in Thousands of Dollars

Misc Business $11,600

Beer, Wine & Liquor **$1,000**
   National Beer Wholesalers Assn .... $1,000   PAC
Retail Sales **$2,250**
   American Coin Video .... $2,000   Indiv
Business Services **$4,250**
   National Assessment Institute .... $2,000   Indiv
   AME Inc .... $1,000   Indiv
Casinos/Gambling **$3,000**
   Catfish Town Bingo .... $2,000   Indiv
   Valley Gaming .... $1,000   Indiv

Transportation $2,500

Automotive **$1,500**
   Rountree Cadillac .... $1,000   Indiv
Railroads **$1,000**
   Union Pacific Corp .... $1,000   PAC

Labor

Labor $13,300

Industrial Unions **$2,500**
   Machinists/Aerospace Workers Union ...... $2,500   PAC
Transportation Unions **$6,800**
   United Transportation Union .... $5,000   PAC
Public Sector Unions **$3,000**
   American Fedn of St/Cnty/Munic Employees ...... $3,000   PAC
Misc Unions **$1,000**
   AFL-CIO .... $1,000   PAC

Ideological/Single-Issue

Ideological/Single-Issue $10,179

Leadership PACs **$1,000**
   People Helping People (Maxine Waters) ..... $1,000   PAC
Pro-Israel **$5,700**
   Louisiana for American Security .... $5,000   PAC
Misc Issues **$3,479**
   Sierra Club .... $1,979   PAC
   National Toxics Campaign .... $1,000   Indiv

Other & Unknown

Other $18,450

Civil Servants/Public Officials **$8,200**
   Louisiana Senate .... $3,950   Indiv
   City of Baton Rouge .... $1,500   Indiv
   State of Louisiana .... $1,500   Indiv
   Louisiana House of Representatives ..... $1,000   Indiv
Education **$7,050**
   Camelot Career College .... $2,000   Indiv
   Southern University .... $1,550   Indiv
   Career Training Specialist .... $1,000   Indiv
   Drug Free School .... $1,000   Indiv
   Southern Law School .... $1,000   Indiv
Retired **$1,000**
   None over $1,000
Other **$2,200**
   US Army .... $1,000   Indiv

Unknown $89,200

   Homemakers/Non-income earners $1,000
   No Employer Listed or Found $30,600
   Generic Occupation/Category Unknown $37,700
   Employer Listed/Category Unknown $19,400
      Metro Plex Inc .... $2,000   Indiv
      Southern Media .... $2,000   Indiv
      Amioma Living Inc .... $1,000   Indiv
      Atlantic County Women Club .... $1,000   Indiv
      Bailey Investment .... $1,000   Indiv
      Carter & Associates .... $1,000   Indiv
      Harris & Associates .... $1,000   Indiv
      Le Senate .... $1,000   Indiv
      Mel Inc .... $1,000   Indiv
      R Harvey & Assoc .... $1,000   Indiv
      Rice Gregory & Assoc .... $1,000   Indiv
      Unglesby & Koch .... $1,000   Indiv

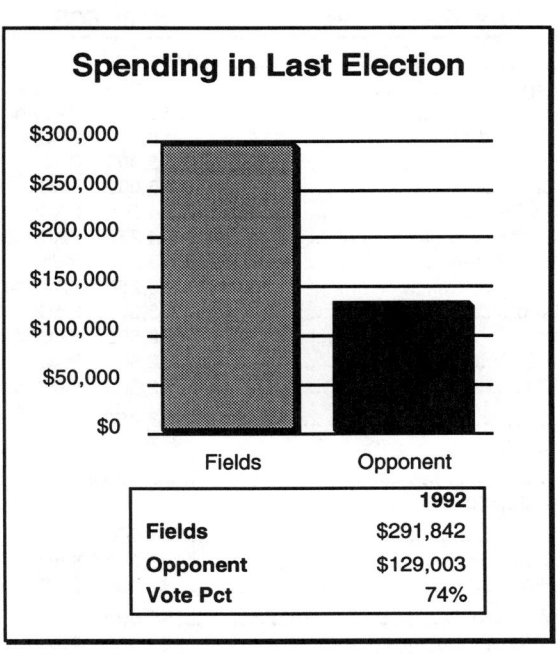

Spending in Last Election

	1992
Fields	$291,842
Opponent	$129,003
Vote Pct	74%

Jack Fields, R-Texas (8)

First elected: 1980

1991-92 Total Receipts: $757,980
1992 Year-end Cash: $46,066

1991-92 Committees & Subcommittees

Energy and Commerce
Health and the Environment; Telecommunications and Finance;
Transportation and Hazardous Materials

Merchant Marine and Fisheries
Coast Guard and Navigation (Ranking Republican); Merchant Marine

Leading Contributors

Business

Agriculture		$47,152	
Tobacco		**$12,500**	
RJR Nabisco	$4,000		PAC
US Tobacco Co	$4,000		PAC
Philip Morris	$2,500		PAC/Ind
Livestock		**$5,750**	
National Cattlemen's Assn*	$3,000		PAC
Agricultural Services/Products		**$4,750**	
Texas Farm Bureau	$2,500		PAC
Food Processing & Sales		**$17,750**	
Randall's Food Markets	$10,000		Indiv
Food Marketing Institute	$2,500		PAC
Forestry & Forest Products		**$4,902**	
None over $2,500			

Communications/Electronics		$71,521	
Media/Entertainment		**$27,721**	
National Assn of Broadcasters	$7,000		PAC
National Cable Television Assn	$5,500		PAC
Tele-Communications Inc	$5,000		PAC
Telephone Utilities		**$35,800**	
AT&T	$7,500		PAC
GTE Corp	$5,750		PAC
Southwestern Bell	$5,250		PAC/Ind
Ameritech Corp	$3,250		PAC
Telecom Services & Equipment		**$6,500**	
DSC Communications Corp	$2,500		PAC

Source of Funds in 1992 Election

Source	Total	Pct
■ PACs	$451,576	60%
▨ Indivs $200+	$246,350	32%
□ Indivs under $200	$47,129	6%
▨ Other	$12,925	2%
Candidate	$0	0%
Party	$0	0%

Source of PAC Dollars by Sector

Source	Total	Pct
■ Business	$411,316	94%
▨ Labor	$21,500	5%
□ Ideology/Single Issue	$6,450	1%

In-State vs. Out-of-State Contributions*

Source	Total	Pct
□ In-State	$219,050	90%
■ Out-of-state	$25,500	10%
No state listed	$750	

* by large individual contributors ($200 & above)

Construction		$21,500	
General Contractors		**$11,500**	
Fluor Corp	$3,000		PAC
Construction Services		**$6,500**	
None over $2,500			
Building Materials & Equipment		**$3,000**	
None over $2,500			

Defense		$4,250	
Misc Defense		**$4,250**	
Insilco Corp	$4,000		PAC

Energy & Natural Resources		$126,605	
Oil & Gas		**$101,505**	
Exxon Corp	$7,000		PAC/Ind
Shell Oil	$6,600		PAC/Ind
Atlantic Richfield	$6,050		PAC/Ind
Chevron Corp	$5,000		PAC
Coastal Corp	$5,000		PAC
Halliburton Co*	$4,500		PAC
Mitchell Energy & Development	$4,250		PAC/Ind
Quintana Petroleum	$3,250		Indiv
Texaco	$3,250		PAC/Ind
Amoco Corp	$3,000		PAC
Arkla Inc	$2,500		PAC/Ind
Marathon Oil	$2,500		PAC
Mobil Oil	$2,500		PAC/Ind
Mining		**$3,250**	
None over $2,500			
Misc Energy		**$5,050**	
None over $2,500			
Electric Utilities		**$11,600**	
Houston Industries	$3,000		PAC
Texas Utilities Co*	$3,000		PAC
Waste Management		**$4,000**	
Browning-Ferris Industries	$2,500		PAC

Contribution Totals by Sector

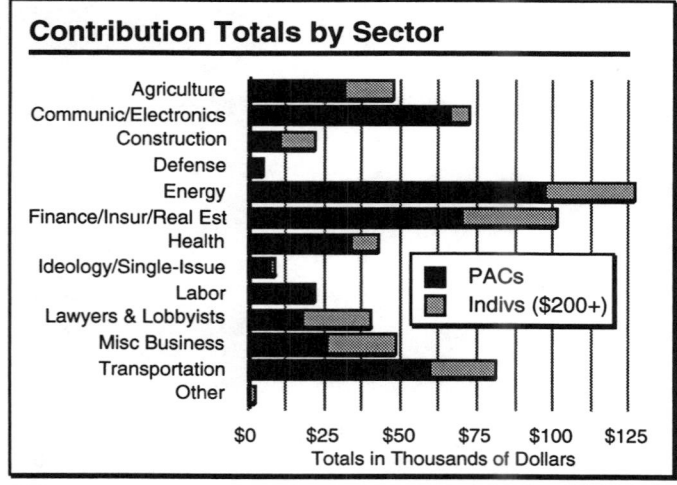

Agriculture
Communic/Electronics
Construction
Defense
Energy
Finance/Insur/Real Est
Health
Ideology/Single-Issue
Labor
Lawyers & Lobbyists
Misc Business
Transportation
Other

■ PACs
▨ Indivs ($200+)

$0 $25 $50 $75 $100 $125
Totals in Thousands of Dollars

Finance, Insurance & Real Estate $100,731

Commercial Banks **$25,650**
    JP Morgan & Co ....$5,000   PAC
    Citizens & Southern National Bank ....$4,500   PAC
    First City Bancorp of Texas ....$3,850   PAC/Ind

Securities & Investment **$10,750**
    None over $2,500

Insurance **$24,831**
    Richard E Tinsley Insurance Co ....$2,750   Indiv
    United Services Automobile Assn Group ....$2,750   PAC

Real Estate **$14,250**
    National Assn of Realtors ....$6,250   PAC

Accountants **$19,300**
    American Institute of CPA's ....$10,000   PAC

Misc Finance **$4,950**
    None over $2,500

Health $42,550

Health Professionals **$30,300**
    American Medical Assn......................................$10,000   PAC
    American Academy of Ophthalmology ....$2,500   PAC
    American Dental Assn ....$2,500   PAC

Pharmaceuticals/Health Products **$9,750**
    None over $2,500

Lawyers & Lobbyists $40,800

Lawyers & Lobbyists **$40,800**
    Baker & Botts ....$3,500   PAC/Ind
    Akin, Gump et al ....$2,750   PAC/Ind

Misc Business $47,607

Food & Beverage **$3,900**
    None over $2,500

Beer, Wine & Liquor **$6,000**
    None over $2,500

Misc Services **$5,500**
    Service Corp International ....$3,500   PAC/Ind

Business Services **$2,500**
    None over $2,500

Chemical & Related Manufacturing $21,050
    Dow Chemical ....$5,000   PAC
    Lyondell Petrochemical ....$2,950   Indiv
    Arco Chemical ....$2,500   Indiv

Misc Manufacturing & Distributing **$7,050**
    Hoechst Celanese Corp ....$2,500   PAC

Transportation $80,650

Air Transport **$12,250**
    Texas Air ....$7,000   PAC
    United Parcel Service ....$4,000   PAC

Automotive **$25,150**
    National Auto Dealers Assn ....$8,500   PAC
    Gulf States Toyota Inc..$8,000   Indiv

Railroads **$9,250**
    Union Pacific Corp ....$3,750   PAC/Ind
    Burlington Northern ....$2,500   PAC

Sea Transport **$33,000**
    CSX Corp* ....$4,550   PAC
    Hollywood Marine Inc ....$4,500   PAC

Labor

Labor $21,500

Transportation Unions **$21,500**
    Marine Engineers Union* ....$10,000   PAC
    Seafarers International Union ....$5,500   PAC
    Masters, Mates & Pilots Union ....$4,000   PAC

Ideological/Single-Issue

Ideological/Single-Issue $8,450

Gun Rights/Gun Control **$5,950**
    National Rifle Assn ....$4,950   PAC

Other & Unknown

Other $2,250
    None over $2,500

Unknown $69,250
    No Employer Listed or Found $35,450
    Generic Occupation/Category Unknown $8,000
    Employer Listed/Category Unknown $24,550
        None over $2,500

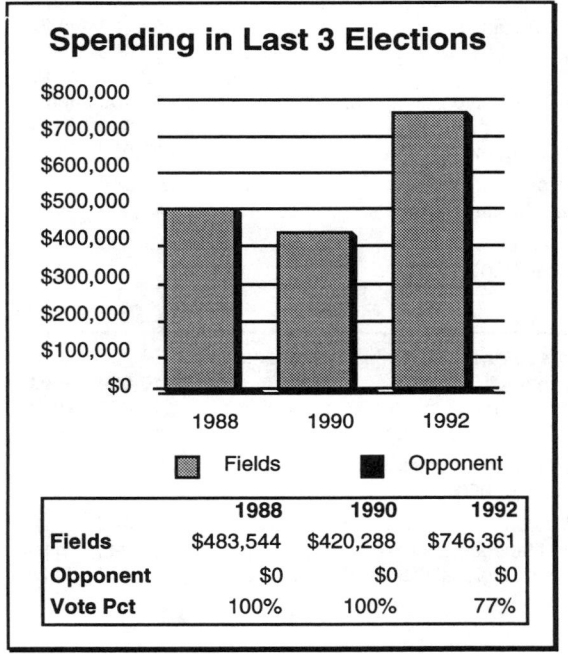

Spending in Last 3 Elections

	1988	1990	1992
Fields	$483,544	$420,288	$746,361
Opponent	$0	$0	$0
Vote Pct	100%	100%	77%

* Contributions came from more than one affiliate or subsidiary.

617

Bob Filner, D-Calif (50)

First elected: 1992

1991-92 Total Receipts: $842,594
1992 Year-end Cash: $822

1993-94 Committees & Subcommittees

Public Works and Transportation
Economic Development; Investigations and Oversight; Water Resources and the Environment

Veterans' Affairs
Hospitals and Health Care; Oversight and Investigations

Leading Contributors

Business

Agriculture	$4,750

None over $2,000

Communications/Electronics	$13,500

Media/Entertainment	$7,050	
Time Warner*	$2,000	PAC
Telephone Utilities	$3,300	
AT&T	$2,000	PAC

Construction	$19,000

General Contractors	$11,750	
BRH-Garver Inc	$2,500	Indiv
Pacific View Construction Co	$2,000	Indiv
Home Builders	$3,500	
National Assn of Home Builders	$2,500	PAC
Construction Services	$3,000	
Stein Partnership	$2,000	Indiv

Defense	$4,150

Defense Electronics	$4,150	
Cubic Corp	$3,500	PAC/Ind

Energy & Natural Resources	$5,500

Electric Utilities	$3,700	
Southern California Edison	$2,500	PAC

Source of Funds in 1992 Election

Source	Total	Pct
PACs	$267,797	32%
Indivs $200+	$320,370	38%
Indivs under $200	$89,485	11%
Other	$167,109	20%
Candidate	$150,055	18%
Party	$12,017	1%

Source of PAC Dollars by Sector

Source	Total	Pct
Business	$84,750	33%
Labor	$117,500	45%
Ideology/Single Issue	$57,157	22%

In-State vs. Out-of-State Contributions*

Source	Total	Pct
In-State	$287,220	90%
Out-of-state	$33,150	10%
No state listed	$0	

* by large individual contributors ($200 & above)

Finance, Insurance & Real Estate	$88,900

Commercial Banks	$6,000	
San Diego National Bank	$3,500	Indiv
Securities & Investment	$4,500	
None over $2,000		
Insurance	$7,300	
Golden Rule Insurance Co	$2,000	Indiv
Real Estate	$62,950	
Baldwin Building Co	$6,000	Indiv
PIA Sports Properties	$4,950	Indiv
De Anza Group Inc	$4,000	Indiv
So Cal Development Co	$3,400	Indiv
Oliver-McMillan	$3,000	Indiv
Telecu Industries	$3,000	Indiv
Hahn Co	$2,500	Indiv
Arnold Construction Co	$2,400	Indiv
National Assn of Realtors	$2,000	PAC
Resort Group Inc	$2,000	Indiv
Accountants	$3,300	
American Institute of CPA's	$2,000	PAC
Misc Finance	$3,850	
None over $2,000		

Health	$52,500

Health Professionals	$39,700	
American Medical Assn	$10,000	PAC
American Academy of Ophthalmology	$5,000	PAC
Anesthesia Service Medical Group	$3,000	PAC
Hospitals/Nursing Homes	$2,950	
None over $2,000		
Misc Health	$7,600	
Ob Gyn Management Co	$2,000	Indiv
San Diego Regional Cancer Center	$2,000	Indiv

Contribution Totals by Sector

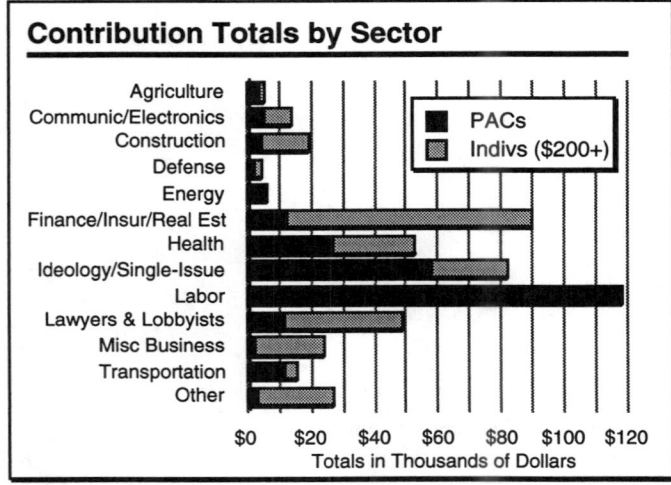

Agriculture, Communic/Electronics, Construction, Defense, Energy, Finance/Insur/Real Est, Health, Ideology/Single-Issue, Labor, Lawyers & Lobbyists, Misc Business, Transportation, Other

PACs
Indivs ($200+)

$0 $20 $40 $60 $80 $100 $120
Totals in Thousands of Dollars

Lawyers & Lobbyists $49,000

Lawyers & Lobbyists **$49,000**
Assn of Trial Lawyers of America	$10,000	PAC
Casey, Gerry et al	$4,000	Indiv
Milberg, Weiss et al	$2,750	Indiv
Appellate Defenders Inc	$2,500	Indiv
Peterson & Price	$2,250	Indiv
Federal Legislative Associates	$2,000	Indiv
Seltzer, Caplan et al	$2,000	Indiv

Misc Business $23,900

Food & Beverage **$5,000**
Premier Food Services Inc	$2,500	Indiv

Business Services **$8,250**
None over $2,000

Lodging/Tourism **$4,250**
Hotel del Coronado	$2,000	Indiv

Transportation $14,875

Automotive **$9,000**
National Auto Dealers Assn	$5,000	PAC
Americans for Free International Trade	$2,000	PAC

Sea Transport **$4,375**
None over $2,000

Labor

Labor $117,500

Building Trade Unions **$26,000**
Carpenters & Joiners Union	$10,000	PAC
Plumbers/Pipefitters Union	$5,000	PAC
Ironworkers Union	$4,000	PAC
Laborers' Political League	$3,000	PAC
Sheet Metal Workers Union	$2,500	PAC

Industrial Unions **$19,600**
Machinists/Aerospace Workers Union	$7,000	PAC
United Auto Workers	$6,500	PAC
Intl Brotherhood of Electrical Workers	$4,000	PAC

Transportation Unions **$18,000**
Teamsters Union	$6,000	PAC
Air Line Pilots Assn	$2,500	PAC
Amalgamated Transit Union	$2,000	PAC
Marine Engineers Union	$2,000	PAC

Public Sector Unions **$38,750**
American Fedn of St/Cnty/Munic Employees	$10,000	PAC
National Education Assn	$10,000	PAC
National Assn of Letter Carriers	$7,000	PAC
American Federation of Teachers	$5,000	PAC
International Assn of Firefighters	$2,500	PAC
National Assn Retired Federal Employees	$2,000	PAC

Misc Unions **$15,150**
Service Employees International Union	$7,500	PAC
Food & Commercial Workers Union	$5,000	PAC

Ideological/Single-Issue

Ideological/Single-Issue $81,357

Democratic/Liberal **$4,250**
Hollywood Women's Political Cmte	$3,000	PAC

Leadership PACs **$6,829**
None over $2,000

Foreign & Defense Policy **$2,378**
None over $2,000

Pro-Israel **$45,350**
City PAC	$5,000	PAC
National PAC	$5,000	PAC
Women's Alliance for Israel	$4,000	PAC
Joint Action Cmte for Political Affairs	$3,000	PAC
Women's Pro-Israel National PAC	$2,000	PAC

Pro-Choice **$2,000**
None over $2,000

Human Rights **$8,750**
Human Rights Campaign Fund	$7,500	PAC

Misc Issues **$9,800**
Sierra Club	$3,500	PAC
League of Conservation Voters	$2,000	PAC

Other & Unknown

Other $26,775

Civil Servants/Public Officials **$5,600**
US Department of Justice	$2,000	Indiv

Education **$7,525**
University of California	$2,100	Indiv
San Diego State University	$2,000	Indiv

Retired **$10,400**
None over $2,000

Other **$3,250**
None over $2,000

Unknown $79,070

Homemakers/Non-income earners	$5,150	
No Employer Listed or Found	$13,650	
Employer Listed/Category Unknown	$59,770	
Cushman Associates	$2,000	Indiv
David Engel Enterprises	$2,000	Indiv
MS Management	$2,000	Indiv
RS Consulting	$2,000	Indiv
Spreckels Building	$2,000	Indiv

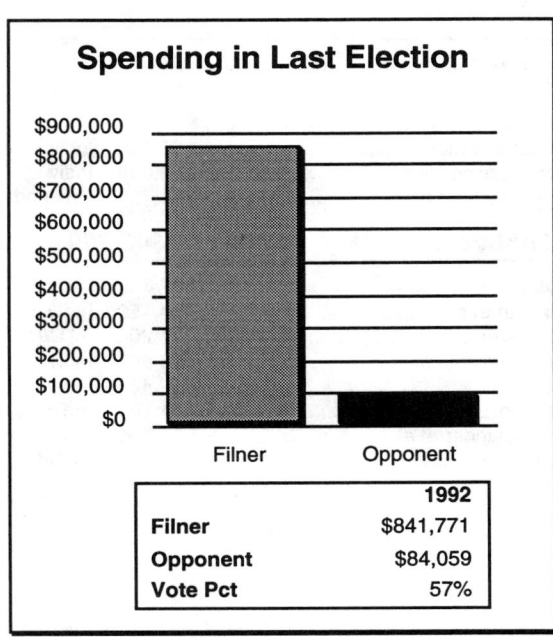

Spending in Last Election

	1992
Filner	$841,771
Opponent	$84,059
Vote Pct	57%

---

* Contributions came from more than one affiliate or subsidiary.

619

Eric D. Fingerhut, D-Ohio (19)

First elected: 1992

1991-92 Total Receipts: $617,946
1992 Year-end Cash: $6,465

1993-94 Committees & Subcommittees

Banking, Finance and Urban Affairs
Economic Growth and Credit Formation; International Development, Finance, Trade and Monetary Policy

Foreign Affairs
Asia and the Pacific; Economic Policy, Trade and Environment

Science, Space and Technology
Space

Leading Contributors

Business

Agriculture		$6,950
Food Processing & Sales $5,250		
Orlando Bakery $2,000	Indiv	

Communications/Electronics		$6,800
Printing & Publishing $2,300		
American Greetings Corp $2,000	Indiv	
Telephone Utilities $3,500		
AT&T $1,750	PAC	

Construction		$8,950
Special Trade Contractors $5,200		
Colejon Mechanical Corp $2,200	Indiv	
Centimark Corp $1,500	Indiv	

Energy & Natural Resources		$2,100
Waste Management $1,600		
None over $1,500		

Finance, Insurance & Real Estate		$62,550
Commercial Banks $3,050		
National City Corp $2,500	PAC	
Savings & Loans $1,750		
None over $1,500		
Finance/Credit Companies $2,500		
Gries Investment Co $2,000	Indiv	

Source of Funds in 1992 Election

Source	Total	Pct
PACs $210,017		33%
Indivs $200+ $275,992		44%
Indivs under $200 .... $120,654		19%
Other $22,929		4%
Candidate $1,000		0%
Party $16,646		3%

Source of PAC Dollars by Sector

Source	Total	Pct
Business $34,800		17%
Labor $112,449		56%
Ideology/Single Issue $53,000		26%

In-State vs. Out-of-State Contributions*

Source	Total	Pct
In-State $247,617		91%
Out-of-state $24,300		9%
No state listed $4,050		

* by large individual contributors ($200 & above)

Securities & Investment $4,000		
None over $1,500		
Insurance **$7,850**		
Associated Agencies Inc $2,000	Indiv	
National Assn of Life Underwriters $1,500	PAC	
Real Estate **$40,700**		
Forest City Enterprises Inc $25,350	Indiv	
National Assn of Realtors $5,000	PAC	
Chelm Management Co $2,000	Indiv	
Transcon Builders Inc $2,000	Indiv	
Misc Finance **$2,000**		
None over $1,500		

Health — $20,505

Health Professionals $6,755		
American Nurses Assn $2,000	PAC	
Hospitals/Nursing Homes **$12,200**		
Multi-Care Management $3,000	Indiv	
Shady Lawn Nursing Home $2,000	Indiv	
American Hospital Assn $1,750	PAC/Ind	

Lawyers & Lobbyists — $43,300

Lawyers & Lobbyists $43,300		
Kahn, Kleinman et al $4,750	Indiv	
Baker & Hostetler $4,200	PAC/Ind	
Hahn, Loeser & Parks $3,500	Indiv	
Weston Hurd $2,400	Indiv	
Arter & Hadden $1,700	Indiv	
Benesch, Friedlander et al $1,500	Indiv	
Hogan & Hartson $1,500	PAC/Ind	

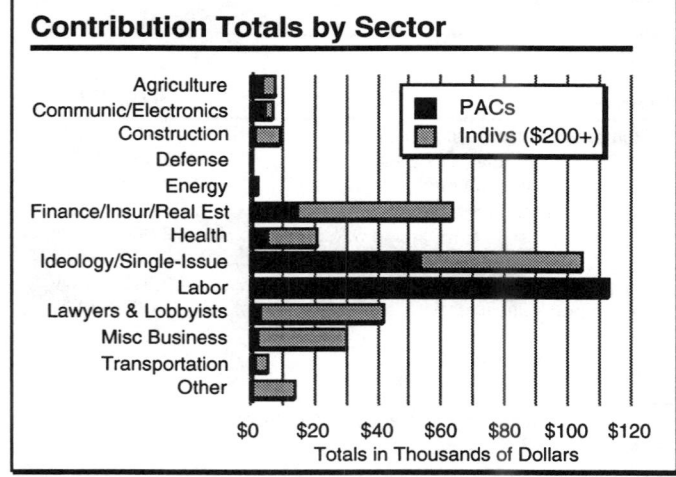

Contribution Totals by Sector

Legend: ■ PACs   ▨ Indivs ($200+)

Categories (top to bottom): Agriculture, Communic/Electronics, Construction, Defense, Energy, Finance/Insur/Real Est, Health, Ideology/Single-Issue, Labor, Lawyers & Lobbyists, Misc Business, Transportation, Other

$0 $20 $40 $60 $80 $100 $120
Totals in Thousands of Dollars

Misc Business	$29,475

Retail Sales **$7,700**
Antwerp Diamond Center Inc .... $2,000   Indiv
Cole National Corp .... $2,000   Indiv
Officemax Office Supplies .... $2,000   Indiv

Business Services **$6,375**
Management Recruiters International .... $2,000   Indiv

Chemical & Related Manufacturing **$1,950**
None over $1,500

Misc Manufacturing & Distributing **$9,550**
Premier Industrial Corp .... $2,000   Indiv
US Tool & Supply .... $2,000   Indiv
A Edelstein & Son .... $1,500   Indiv

Transportation	$4,750

Air Transport **$1,500**
None over $1,500

Automotive **$1,950**
None over $1,500

Labor

Labor	$112,449

Building Trade Unions **$16,500**
Carpenters & Joiners Union .... $5,000   PAC
Painters & Allied Trades Union .... $5,000   PAC
Sheet Metal Workers Union .... $2,500   PAC
Laborers' Political League .... $2,000   PAC

Industrial Unions **$34,300**
United Auto Workers .... $10,000   PAC
Communications Workers of America .... $5,000   PAC
Electronic Machine Furniture Workers .... $5,000   PAC
United Steelworkers .... $5,000   PAC
Rubber Cork Linoleum & Plastic Workers .... $3,000   PAC
Machinists/Aerospace Workers Union .... $2,500   PAC

Transportation Unions **$12,000**
Teamsters Union .... $5,000   PAC
Air Line Pilots Assn .... $2,000   PAC
International Longshoremen's Assn .... $1,500   PAC

Public Sector Unions **$30,150**
National Education Assn .... $10,000   PAC
National Assn of Letter Carriers .... $6,000   PAC
American Fedn of St/Cnty/Munic Employees ...... $5,000   PAC
American Federation of Teachers .... $2,600   PAC
International Assn of Firefighters .... $2,500   PAC
National Rural Letter Carriers Assn .... $2,500   PAC

Misc Unions **$19,499**
Bakery & Confectionery Workers local #19 .... $10,000   PAC
Food & Commercial Workers Union .... $4,999   PAC
AFL-CIO .... $3,500   PAC

Ideological/Single-Issue

Ideological/Single-Issue	$103,550

Democratic/Liberal **$5,850**
Fifth Horseman PAC .... $5,000   PAC

Leadership PACs **$3,500**
None over $1,500

Pro-Israel **$72,950**
City PAC .... $3,000   PAC
Heartland PAC .... $2,500   PAC
National PAC .... $2,000   PAC
Garden State PAC .... $1,500   PAC
MOPAC .... $1,500   PAC
Maryland Assn for Concerned Citizens .... $1,500   PAC

Pro-Choice **$3,250**
None over $1,500

Gun Rights/Gun Control **$2,000**
Handgun Control Inc .... $2,000   PAC

Human Rights **$5,500**
Human Rights Campaign Fund .... $4,500   PAC

Misc Issues **$10,500**
League of Conservation Voters .... $7,000   PAC
Sierra Club .... $3,500   PAC

Other & Unknown

Other	$13,400

Education **$7,000**
Cleveland Institute of Art .... $2,000   Indiv
Maple Heights Board of Education .... $2,000   Indiv
Ohio Diesel Technical Institute Inc .... $2,000   Indiv

Retired **$4,450**
None over $1,500

Unknown	$61,687

Homemakers/Non-income earners $2,050
No Employer Listed or Found $34,092
Employer Listed/Category Unknown $24,795
    Millbuilders .... $2,500   Indiv
    Metroplex Communications .... $2,000   Indiv

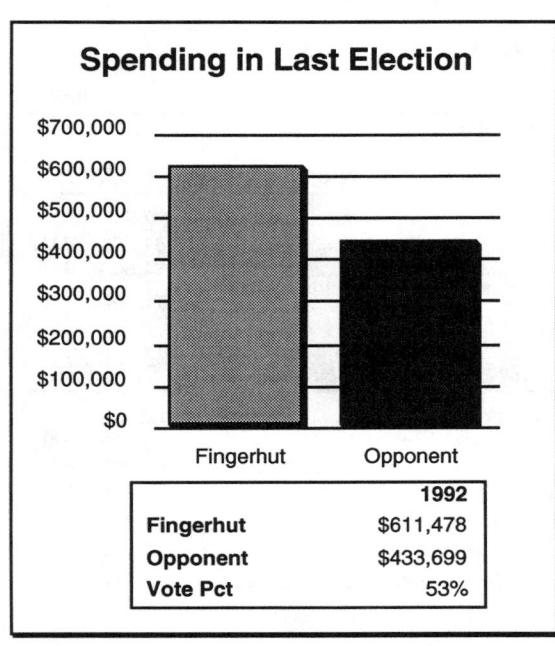

Spending in Last Election

	1992
Fingerhut	$611,478
Opponent	$433,699
Vote Pct	53%

Hamilton Fish Jr., R-NY (19)

First elected: 1968

1991-92 Total Receipts: $489,831
1992 Year-end Cash: $6,830

1991-92 Committees & Subcommittees

Judiciary (Ranking Republican)
Intellectual Property and Judicial Administration; Economic and Commercial Law (Ranking Republican)

Joint Economic Committee

Leading Contributors

Business

Agriculture	$19,750	
Dairy	**$2,500**	
Associated Milk Producers	$2,000	PAC
Agricultural Services/Products	**$2,500**	
Archer-Daniels-Midland Corp	$1,500	PAC
Food Processing & Sales	**$11,150**	
Food Marketing Institute	$5,000	PAC
Pepsico Inc	$5,000	PAC
Forestry & Forest Products	**$2,200**	
None over $1,500		

Communications/Electronics	$64,800	
Printing & Publishing	**$6,050**	
West Publishing	$2,500	PAC
Media/Entertainment	**$29,900**	
National Cable Television Assn	$10,000	PAC
National Assn of Broadcasters	$6,000	PAC
ASCAP	$3,250	PAC/Ind
CBS Inc	$3,000	Indiv
Bresnan Communications	$2,200	Indiv
MCA Inc	$1,500	PAC

Source of Funds in 1992 Election

Source	Total	Pct
PACs	$229,000	46%
Indivs $200+	$124,800	25%
Indivs under $200	$65,560	13%
Other	$80,471	16%
Candidate	$0	0%
Party	$10,476	2%

Source of PAC Dollars by Sector

Source	Total	Pct
Business	$251,350	90%
Labor	$26,250	9%
Ideology/Single Issue	$2,250	1%

In-State vs. Out-of-State Contributions*

Source	Total	Pct
In-State	$94,800	78%
Out-of-state	$26,900	22%
No state listed	$0	

* by large individual contributors ($200 & above)

Telephone Utilities	$26,350	
NYNEX Corp*	$5,000	PAC
AT&T	$4,000	PAC
BellSouth Corp*	$4,000	PAC
Pacific Telesis Group	$3,500	PAC
Bell Atlantic	$3,000	PAC/Ind
Ameritech Corp	$2,500	PAC
GTE Corp	$1,850	PAC
Southwestern Bell	$1,500	PAC
Electronics Mfg & Services	**$2,000**	
None over $1,500		

Construction	$6,200	
Construction Services	**$2,000**	
None over $1,500		

Defense	$1,500	
None over $1,500		

Energy & Natural Resources	$7,400	
Oil & Gas	**$5,000**	
Columbia Gas System*	$1,500	PAC
Texaco	$1,500	PAC
Electric Utilities	**$1,500**	
None over $1,500		

Finance, Insurance & Real Estate	$144,950	
Commercial Banks	**$19,000**	
American Bankers Assn	$6,000	PAC
Citicorp	$6,000	PAC
JP Morgan & Co	$5,000	PAC
Savings & Loans	**$4,200**	
US League of Savings Assns	$1,500	PAC
Finance/Credit Companies	**$2,750**	
None over $1,500		

Contribution Totals by Sector

Agriculture, Communic/Electronics, Construction, Defense, Energy, Finance/Insur/Real Est, Health, Ideology/Single-Issue, Labor, Lawyers & Lobbyists, Misc Business, Transportation, Other

PACs / Indivs ($200+)

$0 $25 $50 $75 $100 $125 $150
Totals in Thousands of Dollars

Securities & Investment $24,150
Goldman, Sachs & Co	$7,000	PAC/Ind
Morgan Stanley & Co	$7,000	PAC

Insurance $62,700
National Assn of Life Underwriters	$10,000	PAC
American Council of Life Insurance	$8,000	PAC
Travelers Corp	$8,000	PAC
ITT Corp*	$2,500	PAC
Independent Insurance Agents of America	$2,200	PAC
National Assn Mutual Insurance Companies	$2,000	PAC
National Assn of Independent Insurers	$2,000	PAC
National Assn of Prof Insurance Agents	$2,000	PAC
Aetna Life & Casualty	$1,500	PAC
Alliance of American Insurers	$1,500	PAC
American Insurance Assn	$1,500	PAC
Crum & Forster Insurance	$1,500	PAC
Health Insurance Assn of America	$1,500	PAC
National Assn of Life Companies	$1,500	PAC

Real Estate $13,650
National Assn of Realtors	$6,000	PAC
American Land Title Assn	$1,500	PAC

Accountants $11,700
American Institute of CPA's	$9,000	PAC
Coopers & Lybrand	$1,500	PAC

Misc Finance $5,800
None over $1,500

Health $17,900

Health Professionals $11,150
American Medical Assn*	$7,350	PAC

Pharmaceuticals/Health Products $6,500
Bristol-Myers Squibb	$1,500	PAC/Ind

Lawyers & Lobbyists $25,400

Lawyers & Lobbyists $25,400
Preston, Gates et al	$1,500	PAC/Ind
Skadden, Arps et al	$1,500	Indiv
Swidler & Berlin	$1,500	PAC/Ind

Misc Business $28,350

Food & Beverage $5,250
Pizza Hut Franchise Holders Assn	$2,500	PAC
Coca-Cola Co	$1,750	PAC

Retail Sales $1,950
None over $1,500

Misc Services $3,750
American Assn of Equipment Lessors	$3,500	PAC

Business Services $4,300
Alarm Industry Communications Cmte	$1,500	PAC

Lodging/Tourism $1,950
None over $1,500

Chemical & Related Manufacturing $2,700
WR Grace & Co	$1,500	PAC

Misc Manufacturing & Distributing $7,200
Corning Glass Works	$2,000	PAC

Transportation $13,100

Air Transport $4,900
United Parcel Service	$1,700	PAC
American Airlines	$1,500	PAC

Automotive $6,200
Auto Dealers & Drivers for Free Trade	$1,500	PAC
Ford Motor Co	$1,500	PAC

Railroads $1,500
None over $1,500

Labor

Labor $26,250

Building Trade Unions $10,800
Laborers' Political League	$4,000	PAC
Operating Engineers Union*	$3,800	PAC

Transportation Unions $4,200
Marine Engineers Dist 2 Maritime Officers	$2,500	PAC

Public Sector Unions $8,050
National Education Assn	$2,500	PAC
National Assn Retired Federal Employees	$2,000	PAC

Misc Unions $2,000
Food & Commercial Workers Union	$2,000	PAC

Ideological/Single-Issue

Ideological/Single-Issue $3,400
None over $1,500

Other & Unknown

Other $16,350

Retired $15,900
None over $1,500

Unknown $26,200
Homemakers/Non-income earners	$10,050	
No Employer Listed or Found	$3,650	
Generic Occupation/Category Unknown	$1,850	
Employer Listed/Category Unknown	$10,650	
Saul Partners	$2,000	Indiv

Spending in Last 3 Elections

	1988	1990	1992
Fish	$277,680	$411,614	$617,832
Opponent	$0	$729	$132,279
Vote Pct	75%	71%	60%

Legend: Fish, Opponent

* Contributions came from more than one affiliate or subsidiary.

Floyd H. Flake, D-NY (6)

First elected: 1986

1991-92 Total Receipts: $272,263
1992 Year-end Cash: $39,483

1991-92 Committees & Subcommittees

Banking, Finance and Urban Affairs
Financial Institutions Supervision, Regulation and Insurance; General Oversight; Housing and Community Development; International Development, Finance, Trade and Monetary Policy

Small Business
Regulation, Business Opportunity and Energy

Select Committee on Hunger

Leading Contributors

Business

Agriculture	$8,000	
Crop Production & Basic Processing	**$2,500**	
Florida Sugar Cane League	$1,000	PAC
Tobacco	**$3,000**	
Philip Morris	$1,000	PAC
RJR Nabisco	$1,000	PAC
Tobacco Institute	$1,000	PAC
Dairy	**$2,500**	
Associated Milk Producers	$2,500	PAC

Communications/Electronics	$4,250	
Media/Entertainment	**$1,000**	
ASCAP	$1,000	PAC
Telephone Utilities	**$3,250**	
New York Telephone	$2,000	PAC

Construction	$3,500	
General Contractors	**$2,000**	
Benjamin Development Corp	$2,000	Indiv
Home Builders	**$1,500**	
Fairmont Homes	$1,500	Indiv

Energy & Natural Resources	$2,550	
Oil & Gas	**$1,200**	
None over $1,000		

Source of Funds in 1992 Election

Source	Total	Pct
■ PACs	$142,490	52%
▨ Indivs $200+	$28,700	11%
□ Indivs under $200	$52,817	19%
▧ Other	$48,393	18%
Candidate	$0	0%
Party	$587	0%

Source of PAC Dollars by Sector

Source	Total	Pct
■ Business	$89,964	54%
▨ Labor	$75,766	46%
□ Ideology/Single Issue	$500	0%

In-State vs. Out-of-State Contributions*

Source	Total	Pct
□ In-State	$15,070	53%
■ Out-of-state	$13,350	47%
No state listed	$0	

* by large individual contributors ($200 & above)

Finance, Insurance & Real Estate $74,764

Commercial Banks	$32,450	
Chemical Bank	$5,500	PAC
American Bankers Assn	$5,000	PAC
Citicorp	$5,000	PAC
JP Morgan & Co	$3,000	PAC
Bankers Trust	$2,500	PAC
Chase Manhattan	$2,500	PAC
Barnett Banks Inc	$1,500	PAC
Citizens & Southern National Bank	$1,500	PAC
National Bankers Assn	$1,500	PAC
Savings & Loans	**$9,300**	
US League of Savings Assns*	$3,500	PAC
National Council of Savings Institutions*	$1,750	PAC
Anchor Savings Bank	$1,000	PAC
Roosevelt Savings Bank	$1,000	PAC
Credit Unions	**$5,000**	
Credit Union National Assn	$5,000	PAC
Finance/Credit Companies	**$2,000**	
Household International Inc	$1,500	PAC
Securities & Investment	**$11,750**	
Pryor, McClendon, Counts & Co	$4,500	Indiv
First Boston Corp	$2,000	PAC
American Express	$1,500	PAC
Commodity Exchange Inc	$1,000	PAC
Securities Industry Assn	$1,000	PAC
Insurance	**$1,264**	
None over $1,000		
Real Estate	**$11,000**	
National Assn of Realtors	$8,000	PAC
National Assn of Real Estate Brokers	$1,000	Indiv
Accountants	**$1,500**	
American Institute of CPA's	$1,500	PAC

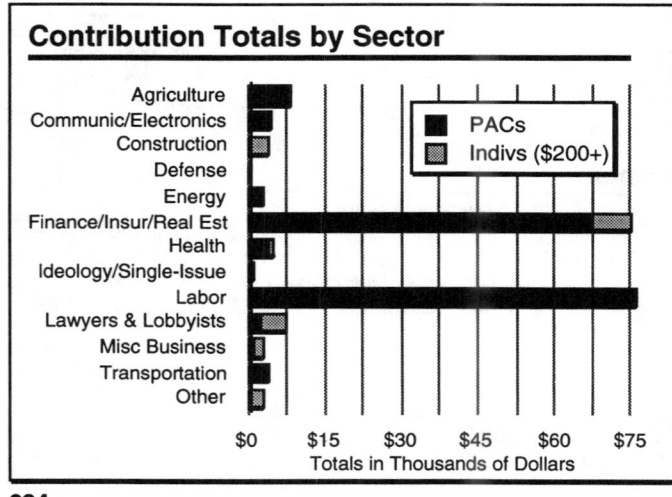

Contribution Totals by Sector

Legend: ■ PACs ▨ Indivs ($200+)

Categories: Agriculture, Communic/Electronics, Construction, Defense, Energy, Finance/Insur/Real Est, Health, Ideology/Single-Issue, Labor, Lawyers & Lobbyists, Misc Business, Transportation, Other

$0 $15 $30 $45 $60 $75

Totals in Thousands of Dollars

Health — $4,375

Health Professionals **$4,375**
    American Medical Assn* ....$3,500 PAC

Lawyers & Lobbyists — $7,000

Lawyers & Lobbyists **$7,000**
    Royer, Mehle & Babyak ....$2,000 Indiv
    Muldoon, Murphy & Faucette ....$1,500 Indiv
    Shaw, Pittman et al ....$1,500 PAC

Misc Business — $2,800

Misc Services **$1,550**
    Nu Clear Cleaners ....$1,550 Indiv

Transportation — $3,500

Air Transport **$3,000**
    United Parcel Service ....$2,500 PAC

Labor

Labor — $75,766

Building Trade Unions **$11,566**
    Laborers Union* ....$4,275 PAC
    Plumbers/Pipefitters Union ....$3,000 PAC
    AFL-CIO Bldg/Construction Trades Dept ....$2,291 PAC
    Ironworkers Union ....$1,000 PAC
    Operating Engineers Union ....$1,000 PAC

Industrial Unions **$16,700**
    United Auto Workers ....$5,000 PAC
    Communications Workers of America ....$2,500 PAC
    Machinists/Aerospace Workers Union ....$2,000 PAC
    United Steelworkers ....$2,000 PAC
    Rubber Cork Linoleum & Plastic Workers ....$1,500 PAC
    Ladies Garment Workers Union ....$1,200 PAC
    Intl Brotherhood of Electrical Workers ....$1,000 PAC

Transportation Unions **$17,600**
    Teamsters Union ....$7,500 PAC
    Marine Engineers Union* ....$3,000 PAC
    Transport Workers Union ....$3,000 PAC
    Seafarers International Union ....$2,500 PAC
    International Longshoremen's Assn ....$1,000 PAC

Public Sector Unions **$20,900**
    American Federation of Teachers ....$5,000 PAC
    American Fedn of St/Cnty/Munic Employees ......$5,000 PAC
    National Assn of Letter Carriers ....$3,150 PAC
    American Postal Workers Union ....$2,500 PAC
    National Education Assn ....$2,000 PAC
    National Assn Retired Federal Employees ....$1,000 PAC
    National Assn of Postmasters ....$1,000 PAC

Misc Unions **$9,000**
    Food & Commercial Workers Union ....$6,000 PAC
    Bakery, Confectionery & Tobacco Workers ....$1,000 PAC
    Service Employees International Union ....$1,000 PAC

Other & Unknown

Other — $2,700

Retired **$2,700**
    None over $1,000

Unknown — $4,945

    Employer Listed/Category Unknown $4,125
        Walker International Transportation ....$1,500 Indiv
        Daniel & Bell ....$1,000 Indiv

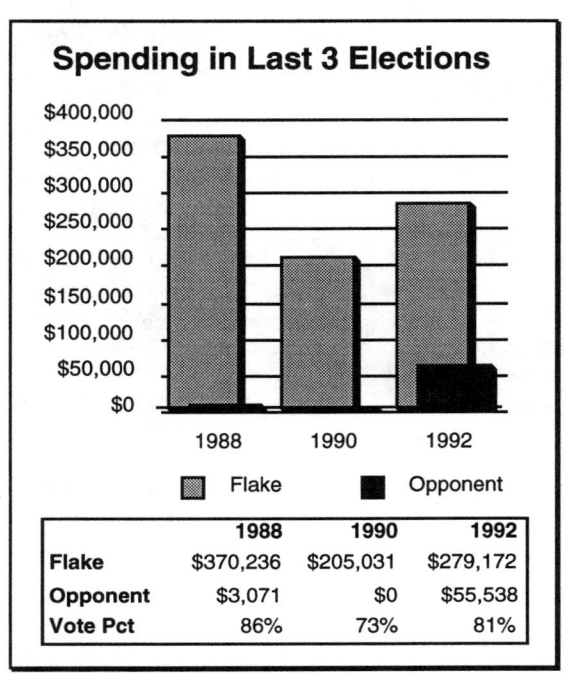

Spending in Last 3 Elections

	1988	1990	1992
Flake	$370,236	$205,031	$279,172
Opponent	$3,071	$0	$55,538
Vote Pct	86%	73%	81%

Legend: ▨ Flake ■ Opponent

---

* Contributions came from more than one affiliate or
subsidiary.

Thomas M. Foglietta, D-Pa (1)

First elected: 1980
1991-92 Total Receipts: $387,584
1992 Year-end Cash: $383,478

1991-92 Committees & Subcommittees

Armed Services
Military Installations and Facilities; Research and Development; Seapower and Strategic and Critical Materials

Foreign Affairs
Arms Control, International Security and Science; Asian and Pacific Affairs

Merchant Marine and Fisheries

Leading Contributors

Business

Agriculture $9,250

Crop Production & Basic Processing $4,500
   Ocean Spray Cranberries Inc .... $1,500   PAC
Food Processing & Sales $3,000
   Philadelphia Macaroni Co .... $2,750   Indiv

Communications/Electronics $14,750

Printing & Publishing $2,000
   None over $1,500
Media/Entertainment $6,000
   Spectacor .... $3,000   Indiv
Telephone Utilities $5,750
   AT&T .... $4,500   PAC

Construction $3,950

General Contractors $1,500
   None over $1,500
Construction Services $1,700
   None over $1,500

Defense $12,000

Defense Aerospace $3,500
   Grumman Corp .... $1,500   PAC
Defense Electronics $7,500
   SPD Technologies .... $3,000   PAC
   AEL Industries Inc .... $2,000   PAC
   Aydin Corp .... $1,500   Indiv

Source of Funds in 1992 Election

Source	Total	Pct
PACs	$168,450	43%
Indivs $200+	$134,736	34%
Indivs under $200	$8,040	2%
Other	$84,188	21%
Candidate	$0	0%
Party	$8,280	2%

Source of PAC Dollars by Sector

Source	Total	Pct
Business	$85,450	43%
Labor	$105,595	53%
Ideology/Single Issue	$9,000	4%

In-State vs. Out-of-State Contributions*

Source	Total	Pct
In-State	$102,736	78%
Out-of-state	$29,250	22%
No state listed	$2,750	

* by large individual contributors ($200 & above)

Energy & Natural Resources $7,200

Oil & Gas $4,000
   Atlantic Richfield .... $1,500   PAC

Finance, Insurance & Real Estate $28,650

Commercial Banks $4,600
   Continental Bank .... $1,500   PAC
Securities & Investment $1,750
   None over $1,500
Insurance $7,250
   Penn Mutual Life Insurance .... $3,500   PAC
   Cigna Corp .... $1,750   PAC
Real Estate $12,750
   National Assn of Realtors .... $6,000   PAC
   Canus Corp .... $2,000   Indiv
Accountants $1,500
   Pagnotti Enterprises .... $1,500   Indiv

Health $20,550

Health Professionals $12,550
   American Medical Assn* .... $6,350   PAC
   American Dental Assn .... $2,000   PAC
Hospitals/Nursing Homes $3,000
   American Hospital Assn .... $1,500   PAC
Health Services $1,750
   US Healthcare Inc .... $1,750   PAC
Misc Health $2,250
   Bob Brand Associates .... $2,000   Indiv

Contribution Totals by Sector

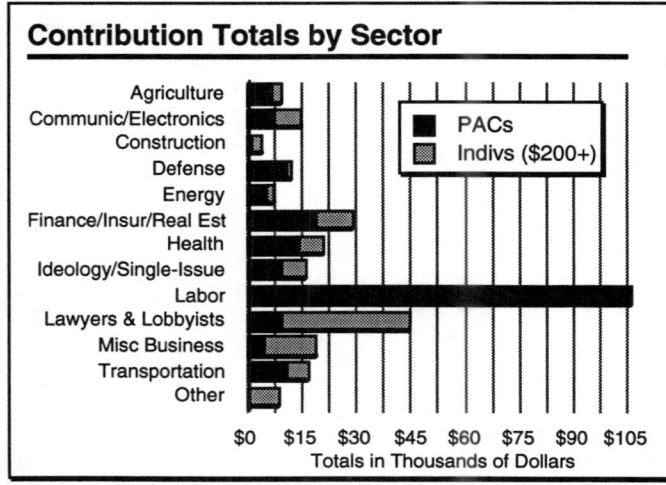

Legend: PACs, Indivs ($200+)

Sectors: Agriculture, Communic/Electronics, Construction, Defense, Energy, Finance/Insur/Real Est, Health, Ideology/Single-Issue, Labor, Lawyers & Lobbyists, Misc Business, Transportation, Other

Scale: $0 $15 $30 $45 $60 $75 $90 $105
Totals in Thousands of Dollars

Lawyers & Lobbyists $44,586

Lawyers & Lobbyists $44,586
Assn of Trial Lawyers of America	$6,000	PAC
SR Wojdak & Associates	$4,086	Indiv
Reid & Priest	$3,750	PAC/Ind
Cassidy & Associates	$3,000	Indiv
Peyser Associates Inc	$2,000	Indiv
Morgan, Lewis & Bockius	$1,750	Indiv
Obermayer, Rebman et al	$1,750	Indiv

Misc Business $18,350

Food & Beverage $2,500
None over $1,500

Business Services $3,450
Freedom Group	$1,500	Indiv

Chemical & Related Manufacturing $5,250
Pennsylvania Engineering Co	$2,000	Indiv

Misc Manufacturing & Distributing $3,500
Hosiery Corp of America	$1,500	Indiv

Transportation $16,350

Air Transport $5,550
Boeing Co	$2,000	PAC
United Parcel Service	$1,500	PAC

Sea Transport $8,550
Society for Relief of Distressed Pilots	$2,000	PAC
Holt Cargo Systems	$1,500	Indiv

Labor

Labor $105,595

Building Trade Unions $23,095
Carpenters & Joiners Union	$5,000	PAC
Roofers Union local #30	$4,500	PAC
Plumbers/Pipefitters #690	$3,645	PAC
Sheet Metal Workers Union	$3,000	PAC
Laborers Union*	$2,250	PAC
Operating Engineers Union*	$2,000	PAC
Ironworkers local #401	$1,500	PAC

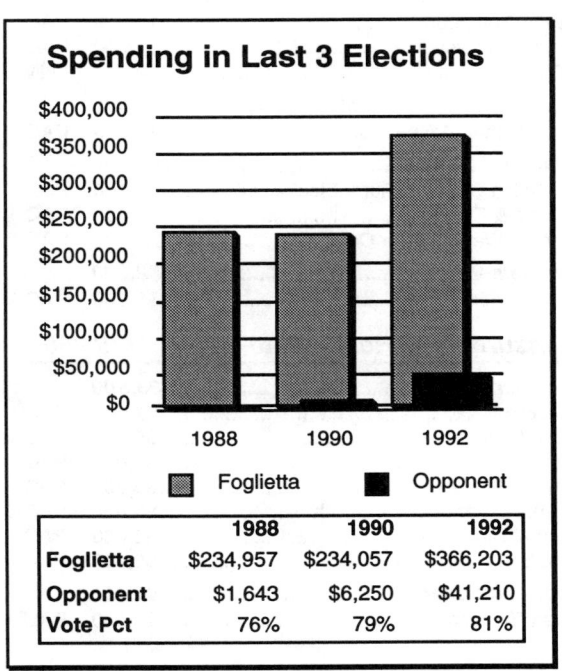

Spending in Last 3 Elections

	1988	1990	1992
Foglietta	$234,957	$234,057	$366,203
Opponent	$1,643	$6,250	$41,210
Vote Pct	76%	79%	81%

Industrial Unions $25,600
United Auto Workers	$8,000	PAC
Communications Workers Union #13000	$5,250	PAC
Intl Brotherhood of Electrical Workers*	$3,250	PAC
Electronic Machine Furniture Workers	$2,000	PAC
Machinists/Aerospace Workers Union	$1,500	PAC

Transportation Unions $31,000
Teamsters Union	$10,000	PAC
Marine Engineers Union*	$6,500	PAC
Maintenance of Way Employees	$4,000	PAC
International Longshoremen's Assn	$3,500	PAC
Seafarers International Union	$3,000	PAC
Transport Workers Union	$3,000	PAC

Public Sector Unions $20,750
American Fedn of St/Cnty/Munic Employees	$7,000	PAC
National Education Assn	$5,000	PAC
National Assn Retired Federal Employees	$4,000	PAC
American Postal Workers Union	$2,000	PAC

Misc Unions $5,150
Food & Commercial Workers Union	$2,000	PAC
Hotel/Restaurant Employees Union	$1,500	PAC

Ideological/Single-Issue

Ideological/Single-Issue $15,450

Democratic/Liberal $1,500
None over $1,500

Pro-Israel $9,950
National PAC	$5,000	PAC

Misc Issues $2,500
National Cmte to Preserve Social Security	$2,500	PAC

Other & Unknown

Other $8,300

Non-Profit Institutions $1,500
None over $1,500

Education $1,550
None over $1,500

Retired $5,000
None over $1,500

Unknown $29,800
No Employer Listed or Found	$10,300	
Generic Occupation/Category Unknown	$4,500	
Employer Listed/Category Unknown	$14,250	
Danella & Co	$2,000	Indiv
Fedullo & Hunter	$2,000	Indiv
Maggio Brothers	$1,500	Indiv

* Contributions came from more than one affiliate or subsidiary.

Thomas S. Foley, D-Wash (5)

First elected: 1964

1991-92 Total Receipts:	$561,826
1992 Year-end Cash:	$244,887

1991-92 Committees & Subcommittees

Speaker of the House
No committee assignments

Leading Contributors

Business

Agriculture $66,749

Crop Production & Basic Processing $17,250
    American Sugar Cane League ....$3,500   PAC
    American Crystal Sugar Corp ....$3,000   PAC
    National Assn of Wheat Growers ....$2,000   PAC

Tobacco $2,000
    None over $2,000

Dairy $4,000
    None over $2,000

Agricultural Services/Products $17,500
    American Veterinary Medical Assn ....$5,000   PAC
    Farm Credit Council ....$4,000   PAC
    National Council of Farmer Co-ops.....................$2,000   PAC

Food Processing & Sales $10,250
    Pepsico Inc ....$5,000   PAC

Forestry & Forest Products $14,749
    Weyerhaeuser Co* ....$2,500   Indiv
    Potlatch Corp ....$2,000   PAC

Communications/Electronics $29,300

Media/Entertainment $10,000
    National Cable Television Assn ....$5,000   PAC
    National Assn of Broadcasters...........................$2,000   PAC
    Viacom International ....$2,000   PAC

Telephone Utilities...$17,000
    AT&T ....$10,000   PAC

Source of Funds in 1992 Election

Source	Total	Pct
■ PACs	$404,990	71%
▨ Indivs $200+	$68,500	12%
☐ Indivs under $200	$15,739	3%
▩ Other................................	$85,180	15%
Candidate	$0	0%
Party	$12,583	2%

Source of PAC Dollars by Sector

Source	Total	Pct
■ Business	$303,208	71%
▨ Labor	$107,100	25%
☐ Ideology/Single Issue	$14,150	3%

In-State vs. Out-of-State Contributions*

Source	Total	Pct
☐ In-State	$44,050	64%
■ Out-of-state	$24,450	36%
No state listed	$0	

* by large individual contributors ($200 & above)

Construction $15,750

General Contractors $11,500
    Associated General Contractors ....$5,000   PAC
    Fluor Corp ....$5,000   PAC

Defense $6,000

Defense Aerospace $4,500
    Northrop Corp ....$2,500   PAC

Energy & Natural Resources $28,599

Oil & Gas...$14,099
    Occidental Petroleum* ....$2,500   PAC
    Columbia Gas System ....$2,000   PAC
    Mobil Oil ....$2,000   Indiv

Mining $5,000
    Kaiser Aluminum & Chemical ....$2,500   PAC

Electric Utilities $6,500
    ACRE (Action Cmte for Rural Electrification) ....$2,000   PAC
    Pacific Gas & Electric ....$2,000   PAC
    Washington Water Power Co ....$2,000   PAC

Waste Management $2,000
    Waste Management Inc ....$2,000   PAC

Finance, Insurance & Real Estate $79,950

Commercial Banks $33,500
    US Bancorp ....$7,000   PAC
    American Bankers Assn ....$5,000   PAC
    JP Morgan & Co ....$5,000   PAC
    Security Pacific Corp ....$3,500   PAC
    Central Bancshares of the South ....$3,000   PAC
    Continental Illinois Corp ....$2,000   PAC
    SeaFirst Bank ....$2,000   PAC

Securities & Investment $5,750
    American Express ....$2,000   PAC

Contribution Totals by Sector

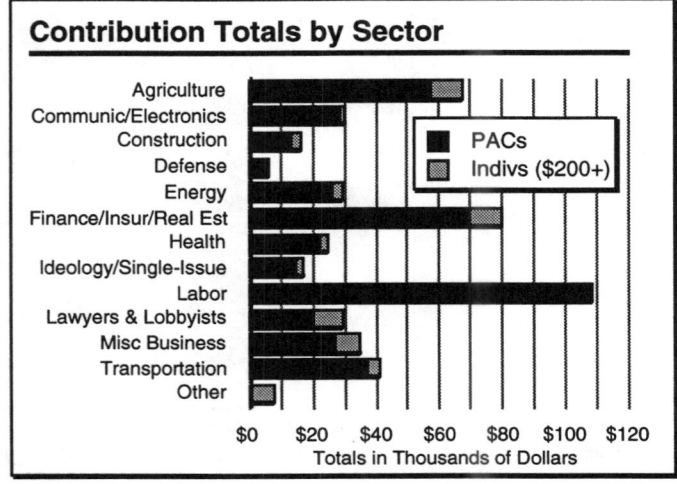

Agriculture
Communic/Electronics
Construction
Defense
Energy
Finance/Insur/Real Est
Health
Ideology/Single-Issue
Labor
Lawyers & Lobbyists
Misc Business
Transportation
Other

■ PACs
▨ Indivs ($200+)

$0 $20 $40 $60 $80 $100 $120
Totals in Thousands of Dollars

Insurance	$15,500	
American Council of Life Insurance	$3,000	PAC
Health Insurance Assn of America	$2,000	PAC
New England Mutual Life	$2,000	PAC
Northwestern Mutual Life	$2,000	PAC
Western United Life Insurance Co	$2,000	Indiv

Real Estate	$18,500	
National Assn of Realtors	$10,000	PAC
Century 21 Real Estate	$2,000	PAC
Federal National Mortgage Assn	$2,000	PAC/Ind

Accountants	$5,000	
American Institute of CPA's	$5,000	PAC

Health
$24,000

Health Professionals	$12,000	
American Medical Assn	$7,000	PAC
American Dental Assn	$5,000	PAC

Hospitals/Nursing Homes	$3,000	
American Health Care Assn	$2,000	PAC

Pharmaceuticals/Health Products	$8,000	
ICI Americas Inc	$2,000	PAC

Lawyers & Lobbyists
$28,810

Lawyers & Lobbyists	$28,810	
Assn of Trial Lawyers of America	$6,000	PAC
Williams & Jensen	$2,860	PAC
Akin, Gump et al	$2,000	PAC
Lukins & Annis	$2,000	Indiv
Shaw, Pittman et al	$2,000	PAC

Misc Business
$33,450

Beer, Wine & Liquor	$15,000	
National Beer Wholesalers Assn	$6,000	PAC
Stimson Lane Ltd	$5,000	PAC

Retail Sales	$10,000	
Huppin's Hi-Fi & Photo	$2,000	Indiv
International Council of Shopping Centers	$2,000	PAC
Montgomery Ward	$2,000	PAC
Spiegel Inc	$2,000	PAC

Chemical & Related Manufacturing	$4,000	
None over $2,000		

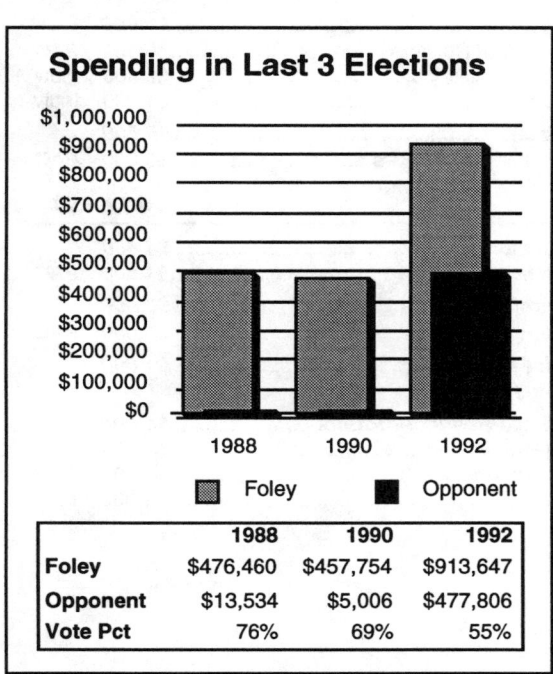

Spending in Last 3 Elections

	1988	1990	1992
Foley	$476,460	$457,754	$913,647
Opponent	$13,534	$5,006	$477,806
Vote Pct	76%	69%	55%

Transportation	$40,000	
Air Transport	**$21,000**	
Boeing Co	$7,000	PAC/Ind
United Parcel Service	$6,000	PAC
Federal Express Corp	$5,000	PAC
Automotive	**$11,500**	
Chrysler Corp	$6,000	PAC
Railroads	**$7,000**	
Union Pacific Corp	$5,000	PAC
Burlington Northern	$2,000	PAC

Labor

Labor	$107,100	
Building Trade Unions	**$19,100**	
Carpenters & Joiners Union	$10,000	PAC
Laborers' Political League	$7,000	PAC
Industrial Unions	**$13,000**	
Machinists/Aerospace Workers Union	$5,000	PAC
United Steelworkers	$2,500	PAC
Transportation Unions	**$26,000**	
Marine Engineers Union*	$6,500	PAC
Air Line Pilots Assn	$5,000	PAC
Seafarers International Union	$5,000	PAC
United Transportation Union	$5,000	PAC
Public Sector Unions	**$38,000**	
American Fedn of St/Cnty/Munic Employees	$10,000	PAC
National Assn of Letter Carriers	$10,000	PAC
National Education Assn	$10,000	PAC
National Assn Retired Federal Employees	$4,000	PAC
Misc Unions	**$11,000**	
Food & Commercial Workers Union	$10,000	PAC

Ideological/Single-Issue

Ideological/Single-Issue	$16,150	
Leadership PACs	**$2,500**	
House Leadership Fund (Tom Foley)	$2,500	PAC
Gun Rights/Gun Control	**$9,900**	
National Rifle Assn	$9,900	PAC

Other & Unknown

Other	$7,000	
Education	**$2,500**	
None over $2,000		
Retired	**$4,000**	
None over $2,000		

Unknown	$10,100	
No Employer Listed or Found	$2,850	
Employer Listed/Category Unknown	$6,750	
None over $2,000		

Independent expenditures supporting Foley
National Rifle Assn	$8,667

Independent expenditures opposing Foley
Ruff PAC	$5,355

---

* Contributions came from more than one affiliate or subsidiary.

629

Harold E. Ford, D-Tenn (9)

First elected: 1974

1991-92 Total Receipts:	$204,840
1992 Year-end Cash:	$4,640

1991-92 Committees & Subcommittees

Ways and Means
Human Resources (Chairman); Oversight

Select Committee on Aging

Leading Contributors

Business

Agriculture		$9,950	
Crop Production & Basic Processing		**$1,750**	
Federal Compress & Warehouse Co		$1,500	Indiv
Tobacco		**$2,700**	
Philip Morris		$1,500	PAC
RJR Nabisco		$1,000	PAC
Dairy		**$1,000**	
Dairymen Inc-Kentucky		$1,000	PAC
Poultry & Eggs		**$3,500**	
Tyson Foods		$3,500	PAC/Ind
Agricultural Services/Products		**$1,000**	
Drexel Chemical Co		$1,000	Indiv

Communications/Electronics		$2,750	
Telephone Utilities		**$2,000**	
BellSouth Corp*		$2,000	PAC

Construction		$3,200	
General Contractors		**$2,200**	
None over $1,000			
Construction Services		**$1,000**	
None over $1,000			

Energy & Natural Resources		$2,000	
Oil & Gas		**$1,000**	
Coastal Corp		$1,000	PAC
Mining		**$1,000**	
Phelps Dodge Corp		$1,000	PAC

Contribution Totals by Sector

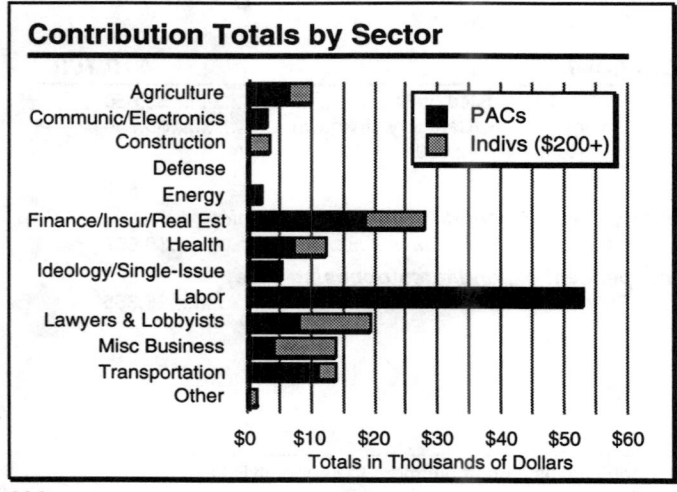

Agriculture
Communic/Electronics
Construction
Defense
Energy
Finance/Insur/Real Est
Health
Ideology/Single-Issue
Labor
Lawyers & Lobbyists
Misc Business
Transportation
Other

■ PACs
▨ Indivs ($200+)

$0 $10 $20 $30 $40 $50 $60
Totals in Thousands of Dollars

Source of Funds in 1992 Election

Source	Total	Pct
■ PACs	$118,450	56%
▨ Indivs $200+	$71,848	34%
☐ Indivs under $200	$7,508	4%
⊠ Other	$14,380	7%
Candidate	$0	0%
Party	$7,946	4%

Source of PAC Dollars by Sector

Source	Total	Pct
■ Business	$59,420	51%
▨ Labor	$52,500	45%
☐ Ideology/Single Issue	$5,000	4%

In-State vs. Out-of-State Contributions*

Source	Total	Pct
☐ In-State	$55,398	79%
■ Out-of-state	$14,450	21%
No state listed	$2,000	

* by large individual contributors ($200 & above)

Finance, Insurance & Real Estate		$27,500	
Commercial Banks		**$3,750**	
First Tennessee National Corp		$1,000	PAC
United American Bank		$1,000	Indiv
Savings & Loans		**$1,500**	
Leader Federal Savings & Loan		$1,500	PAC
Securities & Investment		**$2,750**	
Morgan, Keegan & Co		$1,500	Indiv
AG Edwards & Sons		$1,000	Indiv
Insurance		**$4,750**	
American Family Corp		$2,000	PAC
National Assn of Life Underwriters		$2,000	PAC
Real Estate		**$9,500**	
National Assn of Realtors		$6,000	PAC
Cooper Companies		$2,000	Indiv
Henry Turley Co		$1,000	Indiv
Accountants		**$5,000**	
American Institute of CPA's		$5,000	PAC

Health		$12,150	
Health Professionals		**$4,650**	
American Medical Assn		$1,500	PAC
Hospitals/Nursing Homes		**$2,000**	
American Hospital Assn		$1,000	PAC
Health Services		**$1,000**	
None over $1,000			
Pharmaceuticals/Health Products		**$4,000**	
Schering-Plough Corp		$1,500	PAC
Bristol-Myers Squibb		$1,000	PAC
Sterling Drug		$1,000	PAC

Lawyers & Lobbyists — $19,200

Lawyers & Lobbyists **$19,200**
US Strategies Corp .... $6,000 — Indiv
Assn of Trial Lawyers of America .... $5,000 — PAC
Farris, Hancock et al .... $2,000 — Indiv
Vinson & Elkins .... $2,000 — PAC
Cliff Madison Government Relations .... $1,000 — Indiv

Misc Business — $13,500

Food & Beverage **$2,500**
Coca-Cola Co .... $2,500 — PAC/Ind

Beer, Wine & Liquor **$2,000**
James B Beam Distilling Co .... $2,000 — PAC

Retail Sales **$3,000**
Cleo Inc .... $1,000 — Indiv
Fresh Ideas .... $1,000 — Indiv
JC Penney Co .... $1,000 — PAC

Business Services **$5,250**
Guardsmark Inc .... $2,000 — Indiv
Medshares Management Group .... $1,000 — Indiv
Naegele Outdoor Advertising .... $1,000 — Indiv

Transportation — $13,520

Air Transport **$7,000**
United Parcel Service .... $5,000 — PAC
General Electric .... $2,000 — PAC

Automotive **$5,500**
Bud Davis Cadillac .... $2,000 — Indiv
National Auto Dealers Assn .... $2,000 — PAC
Autozone Inc .... $1,000 — PAC

Trucking **$1,020**
American Trucking Assns .... $1,020 — PAC

Labor

Labor — $52,500

Building Trade Unions **$10,500**
Carpenters & Joiners Union .... $5,000 — PAC
Laborers' Political League .... $3,000 — PAC
Plumbers/Pipefitters Union .... $2,000 — PAC

Industrial Unions **$16,000**
United Auto Workers .... $6,500 — PAC
Intl Brotherhood of Electrical Workers .... $4,500 — PAC
Communications Workers of America .... $2,500 — PAC
Boilermakers Union .... $1,000 — PAC
Machinists/Aerospace Workers Union .... $1,000 — PAC

Transportation Unions **$6,500**
Teamsters Union .... $5,000 — PAC
United Transportation Union .... $1,000 — PAC

Public Sector Unions **$14,500**
National Education Assn .... $5,000 — PAC
American Fedn of St/Cnty/Munic Employees ...... $4,500 — PAC
National Assn of Letter Carriers .... $2,000 — PAC
American Postal Workers Union .... $1,000 — PAC
National Assn Retired Federal Employees .... $1,000 — PAC

Misc Unions **$5,000**
Food & Commercial Workers Union .... $3,500 — PAC
AFL-CIO .... $1,000 — PAC

Ideological/Single-Issue

Ideological/Single-Issue — *$5,000*

Leadership PACs **$1,000**
Democrats for the Future (Beryl Anthony) .... $1,000 — PAC

Pro-Israel **$1,000**
Tennesseans for Better Government .... $1,000 — PAC

Human Rights **$1,000**
Human Rights Campaign Fund .... $1,000 — PAC

Misc Issues **$2,000**
National Cmte to Preserve Social Security .... $2,000 — PAC

Other & Unknown

Other — $1,200
None over $1,000

Unknown — $27,298
Unknown $1,000
Citizens for Better Government .... $1,000 — PAC
No Employer Listed or Found $18,000
Employer Listed/Category Unknown $8,298
D Canale Companies .... $1,500 — Indiv
Hnedah Bobo Group .... $1,000 — Indiv
JM Services .... $1,000 — Indiv
Wharton, Wharton & Associates .... $1,000 — Indiv

---

Spending in Last 3 Elections

	1988	1990	1992
Ford	$364,330	$284,282	$198,070
Opponent	$0	$0	$0
Vote Pct	82%	58%	58%

Legend: Ford, Opponent

---

* Contributions came from more than one affiliate or subsidiary.

631

William D. Ford, D-Mich (13)

First elected: 1964

1991-92 Total Receipts: $681,981
1992 Year-end Cash: $6,768

1991-92 Committees & Subcommittees

Education and Labor (Chairman)
Postsecondary Education (Chairman)

Leading Contributors

Business

Agriculture	$20,350	
Crop Production & Basic Processing	**$7,350**	
United States Sugar Corp	$3,000	PAC
Tobacco	**$7,500**	
Philip Morris	$3,000	PAC
RJR Nabisco	$2,000	PAC
Tobacco Institute	$2,000	PAC
Dairy	**$2,500**	
None over $2,000		

Communications/Electronics	$26,450	
Media/Entertainment	**$2,000**	
None over $2,000		
Telephone Utilities	**$18,400**	
BellSouth Corp*	$7,000	PAC
Ameritech Corp*	$6,800	PAC
AT&T	$2,000	PAC
Computer Equipment & Services	**$4,300**	
Electronic Data Systems	$3,500	PAC

Energy & Natural Resources	$16,250	
Oil & Gas	**$5,100**	
Michigan Consolidated Gas	$3,100	PAC
Coastal Corp	$2,000	PAC
Nuclear Energy	**$2,850**	
KMS Fusion Inc	$2,850	PAC
Electric Utilities	**$6,600**	
Detroit Edison	$3,600	PAC
Consumers Power Co	$2,000	PAC

Contribution Totals by Sector

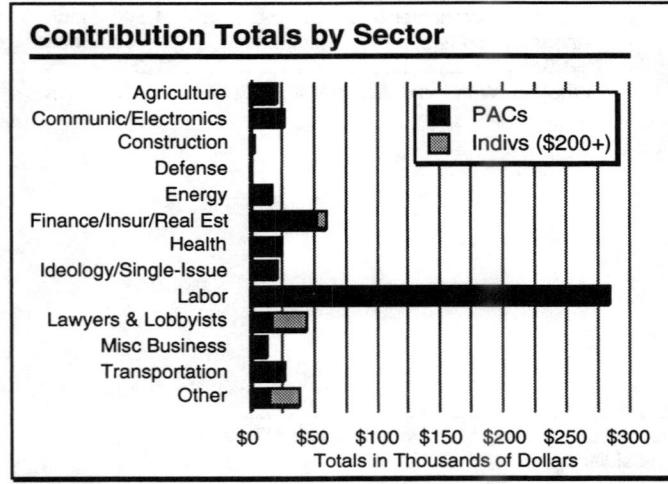

Agriculture
Communic/Electronics
Construction
Defense
Energy
Finance/Insur/Real Est
Health
Ideology/Single-Issue
Labor
Lawyers & Lobbyists
Misc Business
Transportation
Other

■ PACs
▨ Indivs ($200+)

$0 $50 $100 $150 $200 $250 $300
Totals in Thousands of Dollars

Source of Funds in 1992 Election

Source	Total	Pct
■ PACs	$520,850	74%
▨ Indivs $200+	$76,450	11%
☐ Indivs under $200	$49,254	7%
▨ Other	$59,616	8%
Candidate	$0	0%
Party	$29,639	4%

Source of PAC Dollars by Sector

Source	Total	Pct
■ Business	$193,175	39%
▨ Labor	$281,000	57%
☐ Ideology/Single Issue	$20,600	4%

In-State vs. Out-of-State Contributions*

Source	Total	Pct
☐ In-State	$19,250	26%
▨ Out-of-state	$55,700	74%
No state listed	$0	

* by large individual contributors ($200 & above)

Finance, Insurance & Real Estate	$59,425	
Commercial Banks	**$13,750**	
American Bankers Assn	$3,500	PAC
Securities & Investment	**$5,350**	
Investment Company Institute	$2,100	PAC
Insurance	**$19,000**	
CNA Financial Corp	$4,000	PAC
Blue Cross & Blue Shield Assn*	$3,250	PAC
Equitable Financial Services	$2,000	PAC
National Assn of Life Underwriters	$2,000	PAC
Real Estate	**$3,000**	
None over $2,000		
Accountants	**$10,000**	
American Institute of CPA's	$10,000	PAC
Misc Finance	**$6,200**	
None over $2,000		

Health	$24,200	
Health Professionals	**$18,700**	
American Dental Assn	$5,000	PAC
American Assn Oral & Maxillofacial Surgeons	$2,000	PAC
American Chiropractic Assn	$2,000	PAC
American Nurses Assn	$2,000	PAC
American Optometric Assn	$2,000	PAC
Pharmaceuticals/Health Products	**$5,000**	
Upjohn Co	$2,500	PAC

Lawyers & Lobbyists	$42,400	
Lawyers & Lobbyists	**$42,400**	
Assn of Trial Lawyers of America	$10,000	PAC
Patton, Boggs & Blow	$3,000	Indiv
Williams & Jensen	$3,000	Indiv
Squire, Sanders & Dempsey	$2,500	Indiv
Dykema, Gossett et al	$2,400	Indiv
Timmons & Co	$2,000	Indiv

Misc Business $11,800

Business Services **$2,400**
  None over $2,000

Misc Manufacturing & Distributing **$4,350**
  Corning Glass Works ....$2,000 PAC

Transportation $26,000

Air Transport **$17,000**
  United Parcel Service ....$10,500 PAC/Ind
  Northwest Airlines ....$4,500 PAC
  General Electric ....$2,000 PAC

Automotive **$6,000**
  Chrysler Corp ....$2,000 PAC
  Ford Motor Co ....$2,000 PAC

Trucking **$3,000**
  American Trucking Assns ....$3,000 PAC

Labor

Labor $282,200

Building Trade Unions **$48,750**
  Carpenters & Joiners Union ....$10,000 PAC
  Laborers' Political League ....$10,000 PAC
  Ironworkers Union ....$7,500 PAC
  Plumbers/Pipefitters Union ....$5,150 PAC
  Boilermakers Union local #169 ....$3,700 PAC
  Operating Engineers Union* ....$3,700 PAC
  Bricklayers Union ....$3,500 PAC
  AFL-CIO Bldg/Construction Trades Dept ....$2,000 PAC
  Sheet Metal Workers Union ....$2,000 PAC

Industrial Unions **$67,400**
  Intl Brotherhood of Electrical Workers ....$10,000 PAC
  United Auto Workers ....$10,000 PAC
  Communications Workers of America ....$8,500 PAC
  United Steelworkers ....$8,000 PAC
  Machinists/Aerospace Workers Union ....$7,300 PAC
  United Mine Workers ....$7,100 PAC
  Rubber Cork Linoleum & Plastic Workers ....$3,000 PAC
  Boilermakers Union ....$2,500 PAC
  Amalgamated Clothing & Textile Workers ....$2,000 PAC
  American Radio Assn (AFL-CIO) ....$2,000 PAC
  Electronic Machine Furniture Workers ....$2,000 PAC

Transportation Unions **$55,850**
  Air Line Pilots Assn ....$10,000 PAC
  Marine Engineers Union* ....$10,000 PAC
  Teamsters Union ....$10,000 PAC
  United Transportation Union ....$8,000 PAC
  Seafarers International Union ....$6,000 PAC
  Transport Workers Union ....$2,100 PAC
  Amalgamated Transit Union ....$2,000 PAC
  Assn of Flight Attendants ....$2,000 PAC

Public Sector Unions **$85,650**
  American Postal Workers Union ....$15,000 PAC
  American Federation of Teachers.......................$10,000 PAC
  American Fedn of St/Cnty/Munic Employees ....$10,000 PAC
  National Assn of Letter Carriers ....$10,000 PAC
  National Education Assn ....$10,000 PAC
  National Assn Retired Federal Employees ....$8,000 PAC
  International Assn of Firefighters ....$6,000 PAC
  National Assn of Postmasters ....$3,750 PAC
  National League of Postmasters ....$3,200 PAC
  National Rural Letter Carriers Assn ....$3,000 PAC
  Natl Star Route Mail Contractors Assn ....$2,500 PAC

Misc Unions **$24,550**
  Food & Commercial Workers Union ....$8,000 PAC
  Service Employees International Union ....$6,000 PAC
  AFL-CIO ....$5,500 PAC
  Hotel/Restaurant Employees Union ....$3,500 PAC

Ideological/Single-Issue

Ideological/Single-Issue $20,600

Democratic/Liberal **$2,500**
  National Cmte for an Effective Congress ....$2,500 PAC

Leadership PACs **$2,000**
  None over $2,000

Pro-Choice **$3,000**
  National Abortion Rights Action League ....$3,000 PAC

Human Rights **$11,000**
  KidsPAC ....$11,000 PAC

Other & Unknown

Other $36,400

Civil Servants/Public Officials **$3,500**
  Wayne County ....$2,500 Indiv

Education **$32,400**
  National Assn Trade & Technical Schools ....$9,000 PAC
  Assn of Independent Colleges & Schools ....$4,250 Indiv

Unknown $15,250

  Unknown $2,000
    Vocational PAC ....$2,000 PAC
  Homemakers/Non-income earners $2,700
  No Employer Listed or Found $6,000
  Employer Listed/Category Unknown $4,550
    None over $2,000

Independent expenditures supporting Ford
  Michigan 15th Cong Dist Democratic Org $2,364

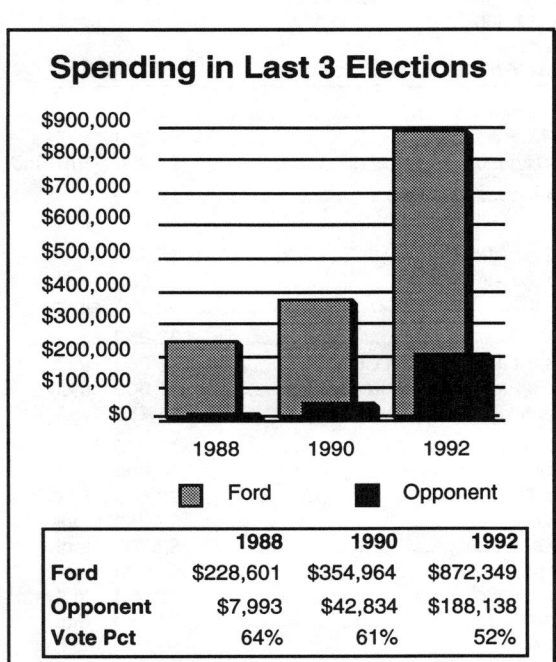

Spending in Last 3 Elections

	1988	1990	1992
Ford	$228,601	$354,964	$872,349
Opponent	$7,993	$42,834	$188,138
Vote Pct	64%	61%	52%

---

* Contributions came from more than one affiliate or
subsidiary.

Tillie Fowler, R-Fla (4)

1993-94 Committees & Subcommittees

Armed Services
Military Forces and Personnel; Military Installations and Facilities

Merchant Marine and Fisheries
Coast Guard and Navigation; Merchant Marine

Leading Contributors

Business

Agriculture $26,200

Crop Production & Basic Processing $1,750
    None over $1,500

Food Processing & Sales $21,150
    Winn-Dixie Stores .... $12,400 PAC/Ind
    Flowers Industries .... $2,000 PAC
    Hickory Meat Packing .... $2,000 Indiv
    Southeast Atlantic Corp .... $2,000 Indiv

Forestry & Forest Products $1,800
    Bryant Skinner Corp .... $1,500 Indiv

Communications/Electronics $10,250

Telephone Utilities $5,000
    AT&T .... $2,500 PAC/Ind

Electronics Mfg & Services $2,000
    Harris Corp .... $2,000 PAC

Computer Equipment & Services $2,250
    Computer Power Inc .... $2,250 Indiv

Construction $17,150

General Contractors $5,750
    Haskell Co .... $2,000 PAC

Home Builders $1,750
    None over $1,500

Building Materials & Equipment $9,000
    Florida Rock Industries .... $3,700 PAC/Ind
    Holmes Lumber Co .... $2,100 Indiv
    RW Fowler & Associates .... $2,000 Indiv

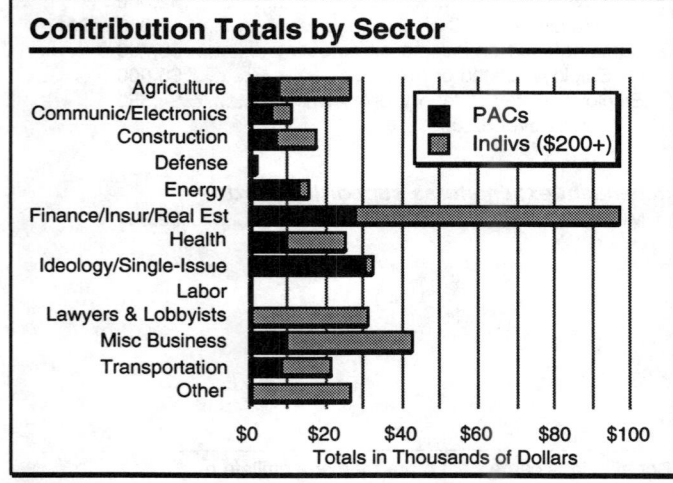

Contribution Totals by Sector

(Bar chart — Totals in Thousands of Dollars, scale $0 to $100)

PACs / Indivs ($200+)

Agriculture · Communic/Electronics · Construction · Defense · Energy · Finance/Insur/Real Est · Health · Ideology/Single-Issue · Labor · Lawyers & Lobbyists · Misc Business · Transportation · Other

---

Source of Funds in 1992 Election

Source	Total	Pct
PACs	$115,350	20%
Indivs $200+	$308,628	53%
Indivs under $200	$81,204	14%
Other	$72,202	13%
Candidate	$2,040	0%
Party	$60,185	10%

Source of PAC Dollars by Sector

Source	Total	Pct
Business	$88,000	75%
Labor	$0	0%
Ideology/Single Issue	$29,767	25%

In-State vs. Out-of-State Contributions*

Source	Total	Pct
In-State	$291,478	95%
Out-of-state	$16,400	5%
No state listed	$500	

* by large individual contributors ($200 & above)

Defense $1,750

Defense Aerospace $1,750
    None over $1,500

Energy & Natural Resources $15,250

Oil & Gas $6,700
    None over $1,500

Mining $1,800
    National Coal Assn .... $1,500 PAC

Misc Energy $3,000
    Cooper Industries .... $3,000 PAC

Electric Utilities $3,750
    None over $1,500

Finance, Insurance & Real Estate $96,868

Commercial Banks $8,700
    American National Bank .... $2,250 Indiv
    Barnett Banks Inc .... $2,200 PAC/Ind

Savings & Loans $2,500
    CalFed Inc .... $2,500 PAC

Securities & Investment $7,300
    CHT Corp .... $2,000 Indiv
    Merrill Lynch .... $2,000 Indiv

Insurance $22,650
    Independent Life Insurance Co .... $6,000 Indiv
    American Heritage Life Insurance ...... $2,000 Indiv
    Blue Cross & Blue Shield Assn* .... $1,750 Indiv

Real Estate $33,240
    National Assn of Realtors .... $10,000 PAC
    First Union Corp .... $3,500 PAC/Ind
    Regency Group .... $2,750 Indiv
    Hamilton Group Ltd .... $2,200 Indiv
    Odum Properties .... $2,000 Indiv
    Stokes-Collins Co .... $2,000 Indiv
    Phillips & Co .... $1,840 Indiv

First elected: 1992

1991-92 Total Receipts: $525,279
1992 Year-end Cash: $2,329

Accountants	$4,450	
Coopers & Lybrand	$2,500	PAC/Ind
Misc Finance	$17,028	
DDI Inc	$8,000	Indiv
Florida Stock & Land Co	$2,000	Indiv

Health — $24,600

Health Professionals	$18,450	
American Medical Assn*	$7,000	PAC
Hospitals/Nursing Homes	$2,950	
None over $1,500		
Pharmaceuticals/Health Products	$2,500	
None over $1,500		

Lawyers & Lobbyists — $30,207

Lawyers & Lobbyists	$30,207	
Ulmer, Murchison et al	$5,559	Indiv
Holland & Knight	$2,250	PAC/Ind
Gentry & Phillips	$2,000	Indiv
Gobelman & Love	$2,000	Indiv
Mahoney, Adams & Criser	$1,750	Indiv

Misc Business — $41,900

Food & Beverage	$5,450	
Eddy Corp	$2,000	Indiv
Retail Sales	$9,900	
Stein Mart Inc	$2,300	Indiv
Cain & Bultman Inc	$2,000	Indiv
Business Services	$11,750	
Shircliff Group Inc	$5,750	Indiv
Lodging/Tourism	$3,500	
Ocean Eleven Resorts	$2,000	Indiv
Chemical & Related Manufacturing	$3,300	
SCM Glidco Organics	$1,500	Indiv
Misc Manufacturing & Distributing	$2,700	
None over $1,500		
Textiles	$2,000	
Mussallem Oriental Rugs Inc	$2,000	Indiv

Transportation — $20,850

Air Transport	$1,500	
None over $1,500		
Automotive	$9,700	
Scott McCrae Automotive Group	$4,500	Indiv
Railroads	$5,400	
CSX Corp*	$5,400	Indiv
Sea Transport	$3,250	
None over $1,500		

Ideological/Single-Issue

Ideological/Single-Issue — $31,736

Republican/Conservative	$6,537	
Leader PAC	$5,000	PAC
Leadership PACs	$9,077	
Campaign America (Bob Dole)	$5,950	PAC
Republican Leader's Fund (Bob Michel)	$2,000	PAC
Womens Issues	$16,122	
Women's Campaign Fund	$10,000	PAC
Wish List	$5,672	PAC

Other & Unknown

Other — $25,820

Retired	$23,434	
None over $1,500		

Unknown — $83,564

Homemakers/Non-income earners	$36,978	
No Employer Listed or Found	$4,600	
Employer Listed/Category Unknown	$41,286	
Contract Services Co	$2,000	Indiv
Jacqueline Holmes & Associates	$2,000	Indiv

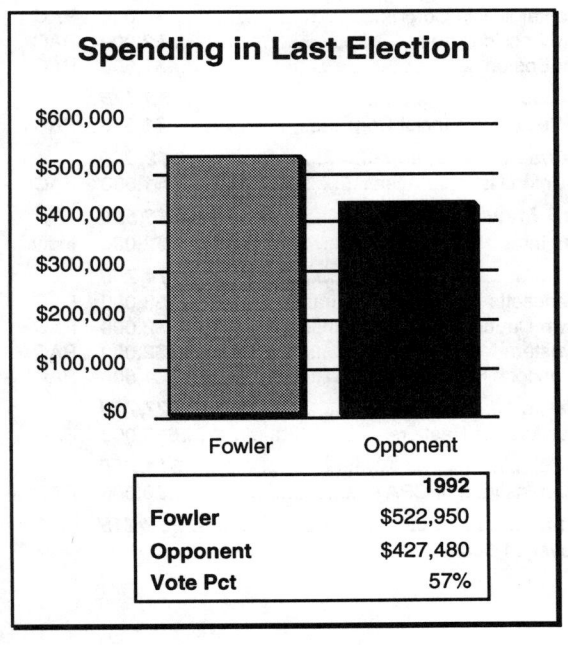

Spending in Last Election

	1992
Fowler	$522,950
Opponent	$427,480
Vote Pct	57%

* Contributions came from more than one affiliate or subsidiary.

Barney Frank, D-Mass (4)

First elected: 1980

1991-92 Total Receipts: $498,997
1992 Year-end Cash: $175,056

1991-92 Committees & Subcommittees

Banking, Finance and Urban Affairs
Financial Institutions Supervision, Regulation and Insurance; Housing and Community Development; International Development, Finance, Trade and Monetary Policy

Budget
Budget Process, Reconciliation and Enforcement; Defense, Foreign Policy and Space; Economic Policy, Projections and Revenues

Judiciary
Administrative Law and Governmental Relations (Chairman); Intellectual Property and Judicial Administration

Select Committee on Aging

Leading Contributors

Business

Agriculture	$4,250

Crop Production & Basic Processing $1,500
    Ocean Spray Cranberries Inc .... $1,500 PAC
Dairy $1,500
    Milk Industry Foundation .... $1,500 PAC

Communications/Electronics	$15,320

Printing & Publishing $3,050
    None over $1,500
Media/Entertainment $4,000
    None over $1,500
Telephone Utilities $6,270
    New England Telephone .... $3,220 PAC
    AT&T .... $2,000 PAC
Computer Equipment & Services $1,500
    None over $1,500

Construction	$8,950

General Contractors $2,050
    None over $1,500
Home Builders $6,000
    National Assn of Home Builders .... $3,000 PAC

Source of Funds in 1992 Election

Source	Total	Pct
■ PACs	$185,360	37%
▨ Indivs $200+	$117,318	24%
▦ Indivs under $200	$184,093	37%
▨ Other	$12,363	2%
Candidate	$0	0%
Party	$587	0%

Source of PAC Dollars by Sector

Source	Total	Pct
■ Business	$123,895	66%
▨ Labor	$48,450	26%
□ Ideology/Single Issue	$15,165	8%

In-State vs. Out-of-State Contributions*

Source	Total	Pct
□ In-State	$82,850	71%
■ Out-of-state	$33,318	29%
No state listed	$500	

* by large individual contributors ($200 & above)

Defense	$3,000

Defense Electronics $2,000
    None over $1,500

Energy & Natural Resources	$2,450

    None over $1,500

Finance, Insurance & Real Estate	$103,293

Commercial Banks $35,200
    JP Morgan & Co .... $7,500 PAC
    American Bankers Assn* .... $5,200 PAC
    Citizens & Southern National Bank .... $4,500 PAC
    Barnett Banks Inc .... $2,000 PAC
    Continental Illinois Corp .... $2,000 PAC
    Security Pacific Corp .... $2,000 PAC
    Bank of Boston .... $1,500 PAC
Savings & Loans $3,175
    Great Western Financial Corp .... $1,500 PAC
Credit Unions $2,000
    Credit Union National Assn .... $1,500 PAC
Securities & Investment $6,500
    Equidex Inc .... $2,000 Indiv
Insurance $14,700
    Massachusetts Mutual Life Insurance .... $3,000 PAC
    American Council of Life Insurance .... $2,000 PAC
    Northwestern Mutual Life .... $2,000 PAC
    John Hancock Financial Service .... $1,500 PAC
Real Estate $27,750
    National Assn of Realtors .... $10,000 PAC
Accountants $11,250
    American Institute of CPA's .... $8,000 PAC
Misc Finance $2,218
    None over $1,500

Contribution Totals by Sector

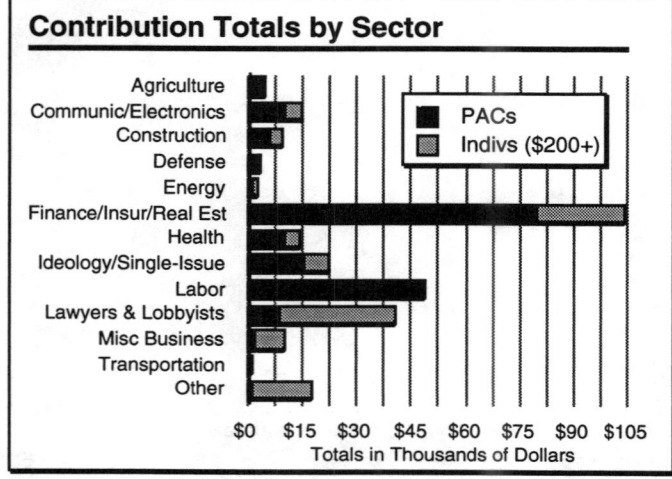

■ PACs
▨ Indivs ($200+)

Agriculture
Communic/Electronics
Construction
Defense
Energy
Finance/Insur/Real Est
Health
Ideology/Single-Issue
Labor
Lawyers & Lobbyists
Misc Business
Transportation
Other

$0 $15 $30 $45 $60 $75 $90 $105
Totals in Thousands of Dollars

Health $14,050

Health Professionals $8,350
   None over $1,500

Hospitals/Nursing Homes $2,700
   American Hospital Assn ....$2,000   PAC

Pharmaceuticals/Health Products $3,000
   None over $1,500

Lawyers & Lobbyists $40,175

Lawyers & Lobbyists $40,175
   Mintz, Levin et al ....$6,850   Indiv
   Powell, Goldstein et al ....$1,750   PAC/Ind
   Arnold & Porter* ....$1,500   PAC
   O'Neill & Athy ....$1,500   Indiv
   Patton, Boggs & Blow ....$1,500   Indiv

Misc Business $9,850

Food & Beverage $2,950
   Venus de Milo Restaurant ....$1,500   Indiv

Beer, Wine & Liquor $2,500
   National Beer Wholesalers Assn ....$1,500   PAC

Business Services $2,450
   None over $1,500

Labor

Labor $48,450

Building Trade Unions $8,250
   Plumbers/Pipefitters Union ....$2,000   PAC
   Laborers' Political League ....$1,750   PAC

Industrial Unions $10,000
   Intl Brotherhood of Electrical Workers ....$3,000   PAC
   United Auto Workers ....$3,000   PAC
   Ladies Garment Workers Union ....$1,500   PAC

Transportation Unions $4,250
   None over $1,500

Public Sector Unions $22,050
   American Fedn of St/Cnty/Munic Employees ......$5,000   PAC
   National Assn of Letter Carriers ....$5,000   PAC
   National Education Assn ....$3,050   PAC
   National Assn Retired Federal Employees ....$3,000   PAC
   American Postal Workers Union ....$1,500   PAC
   International Assn of Firefighters ....$1,500   PAC

Misc Unions $3,900
   Food & Commercial Workers Union ....$2,000   PAC

Ideological/Single-Issue

Ideological/Single-Issue $21,865

Pro-Israel $1,850
   None over $1,500

Human Rights $13,650
   Human Rights Campaign Fund ....$10,500   PAC/Ind

Misc Issues $3,250
   National Cmte to Preserve Social Security ....$2,750   PAC

Other & Unknown

Other $16,850

Education $3,200
   Crystal Springs School ....$1,500   Indiv

Retired $9,700
   None over $1,500

Other $2,750
   None over $1,500

Unknown $14,675

   Generic Occupation/Category Unknown $1,750
   Employer Listed/Category Unknown $11,475
     None over $1,500

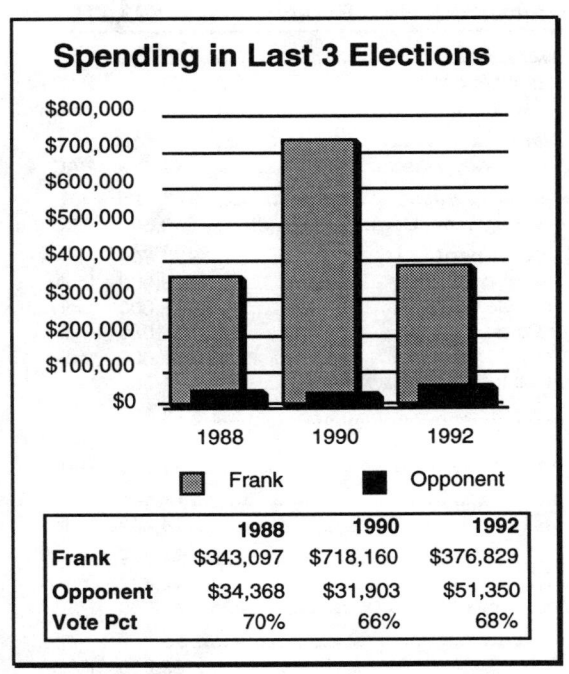

Spending in Last 3 Elections

	1988	1990	1992
Frank	$343,097	$718,160	$376,829
Opponent	$34,368	$31,903	$51,350
Vote Pct	70%	66%	68%

* Contributions came from more than one affiliate or
  subsidiary.

Bob Franks, R-NJ (7)

1993-94 Committees & Subcommittees

First elected: 1992
1991-92 Total Receipts: $460,998
1992 Year-end Cash: $7,007

Budget

Public Works and Transportation
Economic Development; Surface Transportation

Leading Contributors

Business

Agriculture		$3,950

Food Processing & Sales $3,700
  None over $1,500

Communications/Electronics		$9,600

Media/Entertainment $2,700
  None over $1,500

Telephone Utilities $5,500
  AT&T .... $2,500 PAC/Ind
  United Telecommunications .... $2,000 PAC

Construction		$23,850

General Contractors $8,650
  None over $1,500

Home Builders $7,000
  Carbro Construction Co .... $3,000 Indiv
  Berkson's Building Inc .... $2,000 Indiv

Construction Services $3,000
  None over $1,500

Building Materials & Equipment $5,000
  Pamic International .... $4,000 Indiv

Defense		$2,500

Defense Electronics $2,000
  Imo Industries Inc .... $2,000 PAC

Source of Funds in 1992 Election

Source	Total	Pct
PACs	$131,032	25%
Indivs $200+	$261,054	50%
Indivs under $200	$44,372	9%
Other	$82,329	16%
Candidate	$0	0%
Party	$68,473	13%

Source of PAC Dollars by Sector

Source	Total	Pct
Business	$102,547	82%
Labor	$12,500	10%
Ideology/Single Issue	$10,000	8%

In-State vs. Out-of-State Contributions*

Source	Total	Pct
In-State	$222,404	85%
Out-of-state	$37,800	15%
No state listed	$0	

* by large individual contributors ($200 & above)

Energy & Natural Resources		$21,970

Oil & Gas $6,250
  None over $1,500

Misc Energy $4,800
  Cooper Industries .... $3,000 PAC
  Foster Wheeler Corp .... $1,500 PAC/Ind

Electric Utilities $7,620
  Public Service Electric & Gas .... $2,000 PAC

Environmental Svcs/Equipment $1,800
  Hazchem Associates .... $1,800 Indiv

Finance, Insurance & Real Estate		$93,215

Commercial Banks $10,700
  American Bankers Assn* .... $3,150 PAC
  Citicorp .... $2,000 PAC/Ind

Savings & Loans $2,519
  US League of Savings Assns* .... $2,519 PAC

Finance/Credit Companies $11,000
  Beneficial Management Corp .... $10,500 PAC/Ind

Securities & Investment $30,600
  Hibbard, Brown & Co .... $13,000 Indiv
  LC Wegard & Co .... $3,000 Indiv
  SB Cantor Co .... $2,000 Indiv
  Smith Barney .... $2,000 Indiv
  Fuji Securities Inc .... $1,500 Indiv

Insurance $13,817
  Chubb Corp .... $1,750 PAC/Ind
  National Assn of Life Underwriters .... $1,500 PAC

Real Estate $13,500
  Atlantic Realty Co .... $4,000 Indiv

Accountants $4,879
  Wiss & Co .... $2,679 Indiv
  American Institute of CPA's .... $2,000 PAC

Misc Finance $5,700
  National Check Cashers Assn .... $2,000 PAC

Contribution Totals by Sector

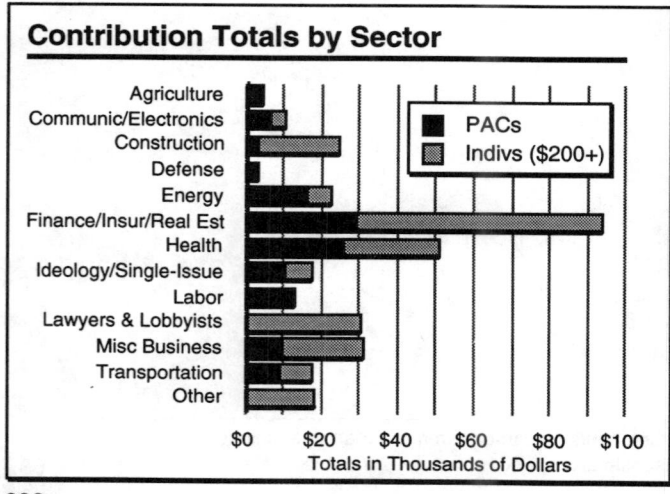

Totals in Thousands of Dollars

Health $50,350

Health Professionals **$27,600**
     American Medical Assn .... $5,000   PAC
     American Dental Assn .... $2,500   PAC
     American Academy of Ophthalmology .... $2,000   PAC
     American College of Emergency Physicians ...... $2,000   PAC
     Summit Medical Group .... $1,750   Indiv
     American Optometric Assn .... $1,500   PAC

Hospitals/Nursing Homes **$6,050**
     Overlook Hospital .... $1,800   Indiv
     St Barnabas Medical Center .... $1,750   Indiv

Pharmaceuticals/Health Products **$15,400**
     Schering-Plough Corp .... $5,000   PAC
     Bon-Art International .... $3,000   Indiv
     Johnson & Johnson .... $2,500   PAC/Ind

Lawyers & Lobbyists $30,100

Lawyers & Lobbyists **$30,100**
     Schwartz, Tobia & Stanziale .... $2,500   Indiv
     Gross & Novak .... $2,250   Indiv
     Bressler, Amery & Ross .... $2,000   Indiv
     Montgomery, McCracken et al .... $2,000   Indiv
     Podvey, Sachs et al .... $2,000   Indiv

Misc Business $30,341

Food & Beverage **$1,850**
     None over $1,500

Beer, Wine & Liquor **$1,500**
     None over $1,500

Misc Services **$3,250**
     Garden State Leasing Co .... $3,000   Indiv

Business Services **$10,100**
     Impact Inc .... $4,200   Indiv
     Kam Group Inc .... $2,000   Indiv

Lodging/Tourism **$2,500**
     None over $1,500

Misc Business **$2,750**
     National Assn of Wholesale-Distributors .... $1,500   PAC

Chemical & Related Manufacturing **$2,950**
     Therma-Systems Corp .... $2,000   Indiv

Misc Manufacturing & Distributing **$2,750**
     Flemington Fur Co .... $2,000   Indiv

Transportation $16,700

Air Transport **$3,000**
     United Parcel Service .... $2,000   PAC

Automotive **$9,250**
     National Auto Dealers Assn .... $2,850   PAC
     Autoland Inc .... $2,000   Indiv
     Toresco's Autoland .... $1,500   Indiv

Misc Transport **$2,250**
     Taggart/Fasola Group .... $2,250   Indiv

Labor

Labor $12,500

Building Trade Unions **$11,500**
     Laborers' Political League .... $5,000   PAC
     Operating Engineers Union* .... $5,000   PAC
     Carpenters & Joiners Union .... $1,500   PAC

Ideological/Single-Issue

Ideological/Single-Issue $16,750

Leadership PACs **$10,000**
     Cmte for an Affordable NJ (C. Whitman) .... $5,000   PAC
     Campaign America (Bob Dole) .... $2,000   PAC
     Republican Leader's Fund (Bob Michel) .... $2,000   PAC

Pro-Israel **$6,000**
     None over $1,500

Other & Unknown

Other $17,465

Civil Servants/Public Officials **$1,700**
     None over $1,500

Education **$1,750**
     None over $1,500

Retired **$12,765**
     None over $1,500

Unknown $55,960

     Homemakers/Non-income earners $6,150
     No Employer Listed or Found $6,000
     Employer Listed/Category Unknown $43,560
         None over $1,500

Spending in Last Election

	1992
Franks	$453,991
Opponent	$219,704
Vote Pct	53%

---

* Contributions came from more than one affiliate or subsidiary.

639

Gary Franks, R-Conn (5)

First elected: 1990

1991-92 Total Receipts: $650,466
1992 Year-end Cash: $18,140

1991-92 Committees & Subcommittees

Armed Services
Investigations; Military Personnel and Compensation; Readiness

Small Business
Exports, Tax Policy and Special Problems; SBA, the General Economy and Minority Enterprise Development

Select Committee on Aging

Leading Contributors

Business

Agriculture $36,450

Crop Production & Basic Processing	**$6,000**	
Sun-Diamond Growers*	$5,000	PAC
Tobacco	**$10,100**	
US Tobacco Co	$4,000	PAC/Ind
RJR Nabisco	$3,500	PAC
Dairy	**$3,900**	
Mid-America Dairymen	$2,900	PAC/Ind
Food Processing & Sales	**$10,300**	
Food Marketing Institute	$2,700	PAC
Pepsico Inc	$2,250	PAC/Ind
Ann's Deli	$2,000	Indiv
Forestry & Forest Products	**$4,700**	
Westvaco Corp	$2,000	PAC

Communications/Electronics $26,350

Printing & Publishing	**$2,600**	
None over $2,000		
Media/Entertainment	**$10,350**	
National Cable Television Assn	$4,000	PAC
Producer Group Inc	$2,000	Indiv
Telephone Utilities	**$2,750**	
None over $2,000		
Computer Equipment & Services	**$9,450**	
Photronics Corp	$4,950	Indiv

Construction $16,400

General Contractors	**$5,900**	
Associated General Contractors	$2,850	PAC

Source of Funds in 1992 Election

Source	Total	Pct
PACs	$293,259	42%
Indivs $200+	$229,222	33%
Indivs under $200	$78,109	11%
Other	$103,845	15%
Candidate	$2,685	0%
Party	$69,265	10%

Source of PAC Dollars by Sector

Source	Total	Pct
Business	$249,686	83%
Labor	$6,750	2%
Ideology/Single Issue	$44,629	15%

In-State vs. Out-of-State Contributions*

Source	Total	Pct
In-State	$141,772	67%
Out-of-state	$68,325	33%
No state listed	$7,125	

* by large individual contributors ($200 & above)

Home Builders	**$5,000**	
National Assn of Home Builders	$5,000	PAC
Special Trade Contractors	**$2,750**	
None over $2,000		

Defense $52,000

Defense Aerospace	**$29,000**	
United Technologies	$6,100	PAC
General Electric	$3,250	PAC
General Dynamics	$2,850	PAC
Textron Inc	$2,700	PAC/Ind
Northrop Corp	$2,400	PAC
Colt Industries	$2,000	PAC
Defense Electronics	**$17,500**	
Hughes Aircraft	$3,350	PAC/Ind
Eaton Corp	$3,000	PAC
Kaman Corp	$2,500	PAC
Misc Defense	**$5,500**	
FMC Corp	$2,250	PAC

Energy & Natural Resources $29,175

Oil & Gas	**$16,300**	
Exxon Corp	$2,000	PAC
F&S Oil Co	$2,000	Indiv
Petroleum Marketers Assn	$2,000	PAC
Misc Energy	**$5,600**	
Cooper Industries	$3,000	PAC
Energy Research Corp	$2,100	Indiv
Electric Utilities	**$4,925**	
United Illuminating Co	$2,625	PAC/Ind

Finance, Insurance & Real Estate $67,472

Commercial Banks	**$8,300**	
None over $2,000		
Savings & Loans	**$2,925**	
None over $2,000		

Contribution Totals by Sector

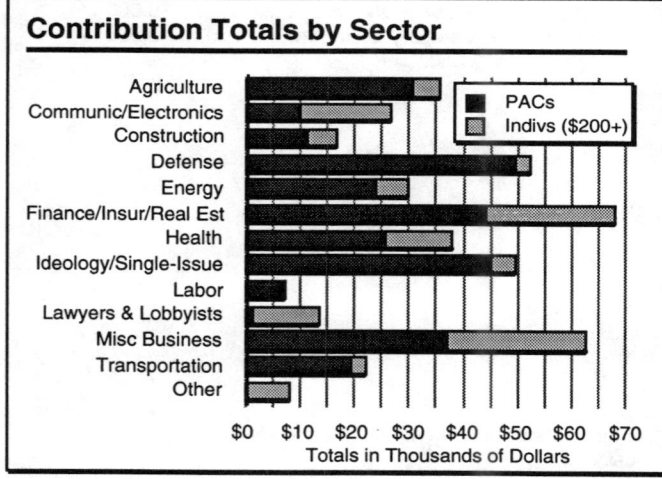

Agriculture
Communic/Electronics
Construction
Defense
Energy
Finance/Insur/Real Est
Health
Ideology/Single-Issue
Labor
Lawyers & Lobbyists
Misc Business
Transportation
Other

■ PACs
■ Indivs ($200+)

$0 $10 $20 $30 $40 $50 $60 $70
Totals in Thousands of Dollars

Securities & Investment	$5,450	
Smith Barney	$2,000	Indiv
Insurance	**$27,222**	
Travelers Corp	$5,000	PAC/Ind
Aetna Life & Casualty	$4,250	PAC/Ind
Independent Insurance Agents of America	$2,722	PAC
Golden Rule Insurance Co	$2,000	PAC
Surety Insurance Agency	$2,000	Indiv
Real Estate	**$15,625**	
National Assn of Realtors	$10,000	PAC
Accountants	**$5,700**	
None over $2,000		

Health $37,359

Health Professionals	$26,259	
American Medical Assn	$10,000	PAC
American Academy of Ophthalmology	$4,959	PAC
American Dental Assn	$3,000	PAC
American Chiropractic Assn	$2,500	PAC
Hospitals/Nursing Homes	**$6,000**	
New York City Hospital	$4,500	Indiv
Pharmaceuticals/Health Products	**$3,600**	
None over $2,000		

Lawyers & Lobbyists $13,125

Lawyers & Lobbyists	$13,125	
Carmody & Torrance	$2,250	Indiv

Misc Business $62,305

Food & Beverage	$11,050	
McDonald's Corp	$2,500	PAC
National Restaurant Assn	$2,000	PAC
Beer, Wine & Liquor	**$6,550**	
Brown-Forman Distillers	$3,250	PAC
Retail Sales	**$5,550**	
None over $2,000		
Misc Services	**$2,375**	
Sanders Mortuary	$2,375	Indiv
Business Services	**$8,600**	
None over $2,000		

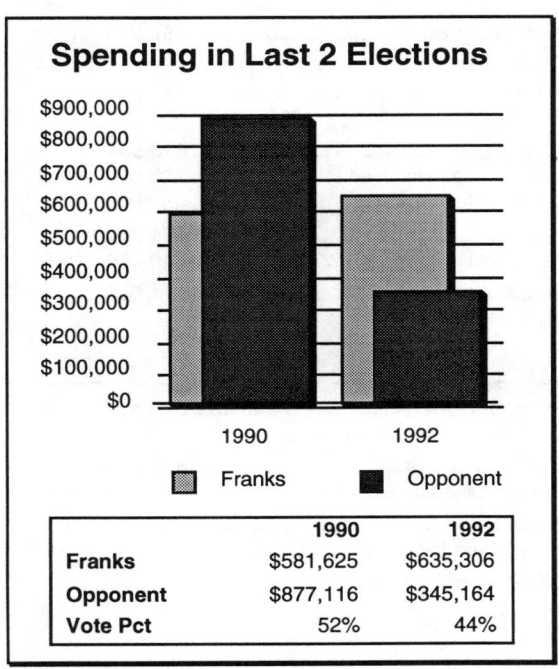

Spending in Last 2 Elections

	1990	1992
Franks	$581,625	$635,306
Opponent	$877,116	$345,164
Vote Pct	52%	44%

Chemical & Related Manufacturing	$7,800	
Union Carbide	$2,550	PAC
Technical Coatings Laboratory	$2,000	Indiv
Misc Manufacturing & Distributing	**$13,750**	
Stone Container Corp	$3,000	PAC
Farrel Corp	$2,250	Indiv

Transportation $21,950

Air Transport	$6,200	
United Parcel Service	$4,200	PAC/Ind
Automotive	**$13,250**	
National Auto Dealers Assn	$8,000	PAC
Americans for Free International Trade	$2,000	PAC
Auto Dealers & Drivers for Free Trade	$2,000	PAC
Railroads	**$2,000**	
Union Pacific Corp	$2,000	PAC/Ind

Labor

Labor $6,750

Transportation Unions	$3,500	
Marine Engineers Union*	$3,000	PAC

Ideological/Single-Issue

Ideological/Single-Issue $48,979

Republican/Conservative	$6,850	
GOP-5 Committee	$4,000	PAC
Leadership PACs	**$7,850**	
Cmte for an Affordable NJ (C. Whitman)	$5,000	PAC
Campaign America (Bob Dole)	$2,850	PAC
Foreign & Defense Policy	**$2,959**	
Veterans of Foreign Wars	$2,300	PAC
Pro-Israel	**$14,000**	
National PAC	$5,000	PAC
Citizens Organized PAC	$2,000	PAC
Hudson Valley PAC	$2,000	PAC
Pro-Choice	**$2,570**	
None over $2,000		
Gun Rights/Gun Control	**$9,900**	
National Rifle Assn	$9,900	PAC
Misc Issues	**$3,850**	
None over $2,000		

Other & Unknown

Other $7,775

Retired	$3,450	
None over $2,000		

Unknown $92,697

Homemakers/Non-income earners	$16,922	
No Employer Listed or Found	$37,075	
Generic Occupation/Category Unknown	$2,450	
Employer Listed/Category Unknown	$35,750	
FTC	$2,250	Indiv
Hansen & Co	$2,000	Indiv

Independent expenditures supporting Franks
American Medical Assn	$81,254

Independent expenditures opposing Franks
Clean Up Congress	$32,899

---

* Contributions came from more than one affiliate or subsidiary.

Martin Frost, D-Texas (24)

First elected: 1978

1991-92 Total Receipts: $1,241,725
1992 Year-end Cash: $8,276

1991-92 Committees & Subcommittees

Administration
Elections; Libraries and Memorials; Office Systems; Campaign Finance Reform Task Force

Rules
Legislative Process

Leading Contributors

Business

Agriculture	$42,050

Crop Production & Basic Processing $11,850
   None over $5,000
Dairy $14,500
   Associated Milk Producers .... $10,000   PAC
Food Processing & Sales $9,450
   None over $5,000

Communications/Electronics	$42,250

Media/Entertainment $9,750
   National Assn of Broadcasters .... $5,000   PAC
Telephone Utilities $12,000
   None over $5,000
Computer Equipment & Services $14,500
   Electronic Data Systems .... $8,000   PAC

Construction	$14,550

General Contractors $6,750
   None over $5,000

Defense	$43,000

Defense Aerospace $40,000
   General Dynamics .... $10,000   PAC
   LTV Aerospace & Defense Co .... $10,000   PAC
   Textron Inc .... $10,000   PAC

Source of Funds in 1992 Election

Source	Total	Pct
■ PACs	$666,804	54%
▨ Indivs $200+	$407,900	33%
□ Indivs under $200	$125,835	10%
⊠ Other	$42,823	3%
Candidate	$0	0%
Party	$2,297	0%

Source of PAC Dollars by Sector

Source	Total	Pct
■ Business	$433,054	64%
▨ Labor	$206,200	31%
□ Ideology/Single Issue	$33,250	5%

In-State vs. Out-of-State Contributions*

Source	Total	Pct
□ In-State	$353,500	87%
■ Out-of-state	$53,400	13%
No state listed	$0	

* by large individual contributors ($200 & above)

Energy & Natural Resources	$109,850

Oil & Gas $80,850
   Bass Brothers Enterprises .... $10,000   Indiv
   Enron Corp .... $6,250   PAC/Ind
   Enserch Corp .... $5,500   PAC
Electric Utilities $18,750
   Texas Utilities Co* .... $8,000   PAC
Waste Management $6,500
   None over $5,000

Finance, Insurance & Real Estate	$164,592

Commercial Banks $38,750
   NCNB Texas .... $5,000   PAC
Finance/Credit Companies $7,250
   None over $5,000
Securities & Investment $31,850
   None over $5,000
Insurance $30,550
   National Assn of Life Underwriters .... $8,500   PAC
   Northwestern Mutual Life .... $7,000   PAC
Real Estate $35,750
   National Assn of Realtors .... $10,000   PAC
Misc Finance $11,000
   None over $5,000

Health	$76,600

Health Professionals $50,550
   American Medical Assn .... $9,000   PAC
Hospitals/Nursing Homes $13,000
   American Hospital Assn .... $7,750   PAC
Health Services $7,250
   Girling Health Care Inc .... $6,000   Indiv
Pharmaceuticals/Health Products $5,550
   None over $5,000

Contribution Totals by Sector

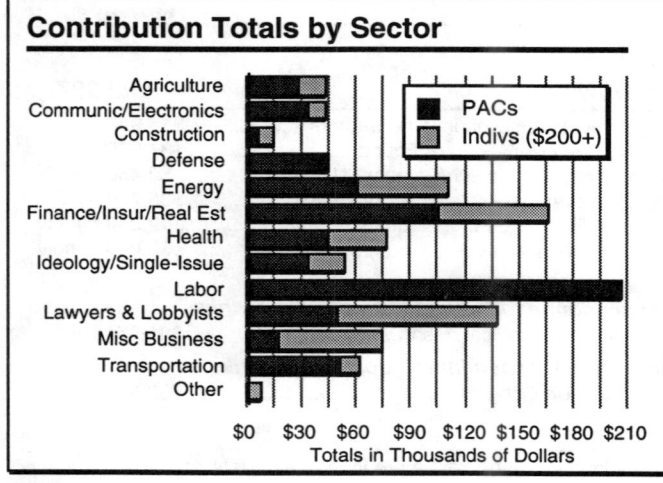

Agriculture, Communic/Electronics, Construction, Defense, Energy, Finance/Insur/Real Est, Health, Ideology/Single-Issue, Labor, Lawyers & Lobbyists, Misc Business, Transportation, Other

■ PACs
▨ Indivs ($200+)

$0 $30 $60 $90 $120 $150 $180 $210
Totals in Thousands of Dollars

Lawyers & Lobbyists $137,162

Lawyers & Lobbyists.....................................**$137,162**
    Assn of Trial Lawyers of America ....$15,000 PAC
    Akin, Gump et al...$8,487 PAC/Ind
    Baron & Budd ....$8,000 Indiv

Misc Business $89,000

Food & Beverage **$9,000**
    Dr Pepper Bottling Co ....$8,000 Indiv
Beer, Wine & Liquor **$26,750**
    None over $5,000
Retail Sales..**$11,950**
    None over $5,000
Business Services **$6,000**
    None over $5,000
Chemical & Related Manufacturing **$6,550**
    None over $5,000
Misc Manufacturing & Distributing...............**$23,150**
    Pillowtex Corp ....$9,000 Indiv
    MacAndrews & Forbes Group..........................$8,000 Indiv

Transportation $61,100

Air Transport **$27,100**
    American Airlines ....$10,000 PAC
    Federal Express Corp ....$5,000 PAC
Automotive **$16,000**
    National Auto Dealers Assn ....$8,000 PAC
Trucking..**$5,650**
    None over $5,000
Railroads...**$12,000**
    Burlington Northern ....$7,000 PAC/Ind

Labor

Labor $206,200

Building Trade Unions **$31,000**
    Carpenters & Joiners Union ....$9,500 PAC
    Laborers' Political League ....$6,000 PAC
    Plumbers/Pipefitters Union.............................$5,000 PAC
    Sheet Metal Workers Union ....$5,000 PAC
Industrial Unions **$53,300**
    Intl Brotherhood of Electrical Workers ....$10,000 PAC
    Machinists/Aerospace Workers Union ....$10,000 PAC
    United Auto Workers ....$10,000 PAC
    Communications Workers of America ....$8,300 PAC
    United Steelworkers ....$8,000 PAC
Transportation Unions **$49,000**
    Teamsters Union ....$10,000 PAC
    United Transportation Union ....$10,000 PAC
    Transport Workers Union ....$9,500 PAC
    Seafarers International Union ....$8,000 PAC
Public Sector Unions **$50,000**
    American Fedn of St/Cnty/Munic Employees ....$10,000 PAC
    National Assn of Letter Carriers ....$10,000 PAC
    National Education Assn ....$8,000 PAC
    American Federation of Teachers ....$7,500 PAC
    National Assn Retired Federal Employees ....$5,500 PAC
Misc Unions...**$22,900**
    Office & Professional Employees Union ....$12,500 PAC
    Food & Commercial Workers Union ....$7,500 PAC

Ideological/Single-Issue

Ideological/Single-Issue $53,300

Pro-Israel **$31,800**
    National PAC ....$5,000 PAC
Pro-Choice..**$7,000**
    None over $5,000
Misc Issues..**$5,000**
    National Cmte to Preserve Social Security ....$5,000 PAC

Other & Unknown

Other $7,500

    None over $5,000

Unknown $32,250

    Homemakers/Non-income earners $8,050
    Employer Listed/Category Unknown $23,200
        None over $5,000

Spending in Last 3 Elections

	1988	1990	1992
Frost	$438,949	$597,310	$1,549,556
Opponent	$0	$0	$105,061
Vote Pct	93%	100%	60%

---

* Contributions came from more than one affiliate or subsidiary.

Elizabeth Furse, D-Ore (1)

First elected: 1992

1991-92 Total Receipts: $785,545
1992 Year-end Cash: $7,255

1993-94 Committees & Subcommittees

Armed Services
Research and Technology

Banking, Finance and Urban Affairs
Consumer Credit and Insurance; Housing and Community Development

Merchant Marine and Fisheries
Environment and Natural Resources; Merchant Marine

Leading Contributors

Business

Agriculture		$5,242
Crop Production & Basic Processing		$1,650
None over $1,000		
Livestock		$1,000
None over $1,000		
Food Processing & Sales		$1,742
Ben & Jerry's Ice Cream	$1,500	Indiv

Communications/Electronics		$13,782
Printing & Publishing		$6,182
Ms Magazine	$1,000	Indiv
Media/Entertainment		$5,100
None over $1,000		
Telephone Utilities		$2,000
AT&T	$1,000	PAC
US West Inc	$1,000	PAC

Construction		$3,298
Construction Services		$2,480
None over $1,000		

Energy & Natural Resources		$5,900
Oil & Gas		$4,000
Jubitz Corp	$4,000	Indiv
Electric Utilities		$1,900
Pacificorp	$1,400	Indiv

Source of Funds in 1992 Election

Source	Total	Pct
■ PACs	$186,049	24%
▨ Indivs $200+	$235,786	30%
□ Indivs under $200	$355,196	45%
▨ Other	$14,818	2%
Candidate	$4,294	1%
Party	$10,524	1%

Source of PAC Dollars by Sector

Source	Total	Pct
■ Business	$26,500	14%
▨ Labor	$67,250	36%
□ Ideology/Single Issue	$90,597	49%

In-State vs. Out-of-State Contributions*

Source	Total	Pct
□ In-State	$157,792	76%
▨ Out-of-state	$50,089	24%
No state listed	$0	

*** by large individual contributors ($200 & above)**

Finance, Insurance & Real Estate — $18,724

Commercial Banks		$5,582
US Bancorp	$2,000	PAC
American Bankers Assn	$1,000	PAC
Securities & Investment		$2,750
Bear, Stearns & Co	$1,000	PAC
Real Estate		$4,153
Hasson Co	$1,703	Indiv
Coldwell Banker	$1,000	Indiv
Ralph Schlesinger Co	$1,000	Indiv
Misc Finance		$4,955
Public Finance Management	$1,000	Indiv

Health — $9,959

Health Professionals		$7,559
American Nurses Assn	$2,500	PAC
Hospitals/Nursing Homes		$1,500
ADS Management Inc	$1,000	Indiv

Lawyers & Lobbyists — $36,869

Lawyers & Lobbyists		$36,869
Assn of Trial Lawyers of America	$10,000	PAC
Stoel, Rives et al	$5,017	PAC/Ind
Williams & Troutwine	$2,000	Indiv
Law Offices of Jeffrey P Foote	$1,616	Indiv
Stoll, Stoll et al	$1,600	Indiv
Schwabe, Williamson & Wyatt	$1,500	Indiv
Gaylord & Eyerman	$1,300	Indiv
Burke, Wilson & McIlvaine	$1,000	Indiv
Foote, Wobbrock et al	$1,000	Indiv
Markowitz, Herbold et al	$1,000	Indiv
Roxanne Barton Conlin Law Firm	$1,000	Indiv

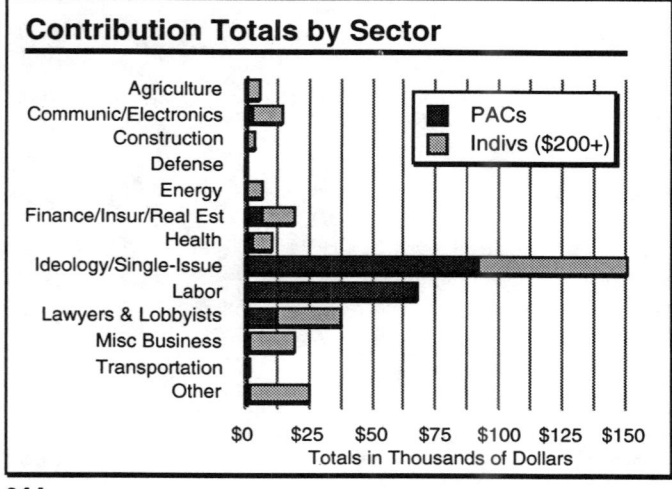

Contribution Totals by Sector

■ PACs
▨ Indivs ($200+)

Agriculture
Communic/Electronics
Construction
Defense
Energy
Finance/Insur/Real Est
Health
Ideology/Single-Issue
Labor
Lawyers & Lobbyists
Misc Business
Transportation
Other

$0 $25 $50 $75 $100 $125 $150
Totals in Thousands of Dollars

Misc Business	$18,570

Retail Sales...$2,455
   Powell's Books ....$1,000 Indiv

Misc Services $2,000
   None over $1,000

Business Services $6,335
   None over $1,000

Misc Manufacturing & Distributing $6,030
   Nike Inc ....$1,830 PAC/Ind
   Soloflex Inc ....$1,700 Indiv
   Norcrest China Co ....$1,500 Indiv

Transportation	$1,500

Air Transport $1,000
   Transwestern Helicopters Inc ....$1,000 Indiv

Labor

Labor	$67,250

Building Trade Unions $4,000
   Laborers' Political League ....$2,000 PAC
   Sheet Metal Workers Union ....$1,500 PAC

Industrial Unions $17,300
   Machinists/Aerospace Workers Union ....$7,500 PAC
   United Steelworkers ....$5,000 PAC
   United Auto Workers ....$3,000 PAC
   Intl Brotherhood of Electrical Workers ....$1,000 PAC

Transportation Unions $6,000
   Intl Longshoremen's/Warehousemen's Union .....$2,000 PAC
   Marine Engineers Union ....$2,000 PAC
   United Transportation Union ....$1,000 PAC

Public Sector Unions $24,200
   National Education Assn* ....$10,000 PAC
   American Fedn of St/Cnty/Munic Employees ......$5,000 PAC
   National Assn of Letter Carriers ....$4,500 PAC
   American Federation of Teachers ....$2,000 PAC
   International Assn of Firefighters ....$1,500 PAC
   American Postal Workers Union ....$1,000 PAC

Misc Unions $15,750
   Food & Commercial Workers Union ....$6,250 PAC
   AFL-CIO ....$5,000 PAC
   Service Employees International Union ......$4,500 PAC

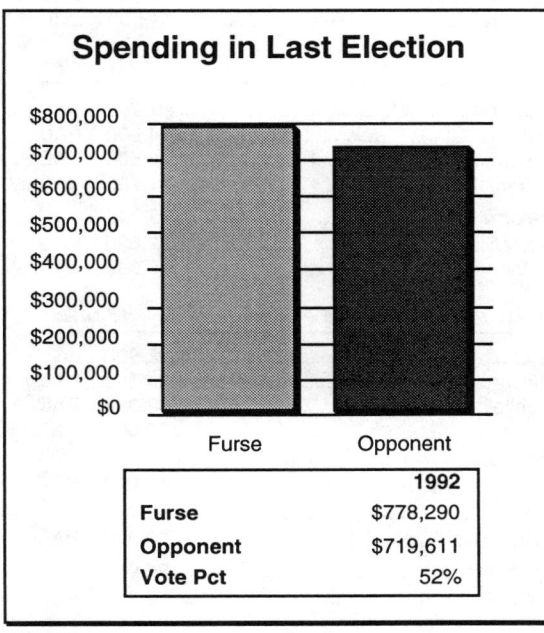

Spending in Last Election

	1992
Furse	$778,290
Opponent	$719,611
Vote Pct	52%

Ideological/Single-Issue

Ideological/Single-Issue	$150,439

Democratic/Liberal $30,504
   Hollywood Women's Political Cmte ....$7,500 PAC
   Operation Real Security ....$7,400 PAC
   Furse for Congress ....$3,006 Indiv
   National Cmte for an Effective Congress ......$2,500 PAC
   Independent Action ....$2,000 PAC

Leadership PACs $2,925
   Effective Government Cmte (Dick Gephardt) ......$1,000 PAC
   House Leadership Fund (Tom Foley) ....$1,000 PAC

Foreign & Defense Policy $16,148
   Council for a Livable World ....$5,748 PAC/Ind
   Ohio Freeze Voter ....$4,500 PAC
   Stop the Arms Race PAC ....$3,000 PAC
   Women's Action for Nuclear Disarmament ....$2,250 PAC/Ind

Pro-Israel $3,250
   None over $1,000

Pro-Choice $8,250
   National Abortion Rights Action League ....$5,000 PAC
   Voters for Choice ....$1,500 PAC/Ind

Gun Rights/Gun Control $3,000
   Handgun Control Inc ....$3,000 PAC

Womens Issues $60,305
   Emily's List ....$29,105 PAC/Ind
   Women's Campaign Fund ....$9,500 PAC
   National Organization for Women ....$5,000 PAC
   National Womens Political Caucus ....$4,000 PAC

Human Rights $8,950
   Human Rights Campaign Fund ....$7,500 PAC

Misc Issues $17,107
   Sierra Club ....$6,500 PAC
   League of Conservation Voters ....$4,556 PAC
   Oregon League of Conservation Voters ....$2,401 PAC/Ind

Other & Unknown

Other	$24,000

Non-Profit Institutions $2,200
   Foundation for Hearing Aid Research ....$1,000 Indiv
   Lincoln City Library ....$1,000 Indiv

Civil Servants/Public Officials $4,310
   City of Portland ....$2,710 Indiv

Education $6,992
   Cathlin Gabel School ....$1,624 Indiv
   Lewis & Clark College ....$1,000 Indiv
   San Luis Obispo School ....$1,000 Indiv

Other $8,248
   National Assn of Social Workers ....$1,500 PAC

Unknown	$62,895

   Homemakers/Non-income earners $22,064
   No Employer Listed or Found $15,799
   Generic Occupation/Category Unknown $1,710
   Employer Listed/Category Unknown $23,322
     Dennis Uniform ....$1,500 Indiv
     Nature's Fresh NW ....$1,500 Indiv
     Private Lines ....$1,450 Indiv
     Colum R Intertribe ....$1,245 Indiv
     Century Companies ....$1,000 Indiv
     M Sellin Ltd ....$1,000 Indiv

Independent expenditures supporting Furse
   Handgun Control Inc $13,616

* Contributions came from more than one affiliate or
  subsidiary.

Elton Gallegly, R-Calif (23)

First elected: 1986

1991-92 Total Receipts: $679,886
1992 Year-end Cash: $49,095

1991-92 Committees & Subcommittees

Foreign Affairs
Arms Control, International Security and Science; Europe and the Middle East

Interior and Insular Affairs
Insular and International Affairs; National Parks and Public Lands

Leading Contributors

Business

Agriculture $34,280

Crop Production & Basic Processing $8,284
Sunkist Growers .... $1,510 PAC
Tobacco $1,850
None over $1,500
Livestock $3,980
None over $1,500
Agricultural Services/Products $2,750
Ag-Land Services .... $1,500 Indiv
Food Processing & Sales $2,915
None over $1,500
Forestry & Forest Products $7,200
Stone Container Corp .... $5,000 PAC
Misc Agriculture $7,301
Boskovich Farms .... $4,501 Indiv

Communications/Electronics $16,680

Printing & Publishing $2,350
None over $1,500
Media/Entertainment $3,100
Salem Communications Corp .... $1,500 Indiv
Telephone Utilities $7,680
GTE Corp .... $2,450 PAC
Pacific Telesis Group .... $2,150 PAC
AT&T .... $1,880 PAC
Electronics Mfg & Services $2,700
Harris Corp .... $2,000 PAC

Source of Funds in 1992 Election

Source	Total	Pct
■ PACs	$195,705	27%
▨ Indivs $200+	$267,961	36%
☐ Indivs under $200	$155,496	21%
▨ Other	$118,027	16%
Candidate	$8,000	1%
Party	$72,066	10%

Source of PAC Dollars by Sector

Source	Total	Pct
■ Business	$160,370	84%
▨ Labor	$2,350	1%
☐ Ideology/Single Issue	$27,788	15%

In-State vs. Out-of-State Contributions*

Source	Total	Pct
☐ In-State	$256,661	96%
▨ Out-of-state	$11,300	4%
No state listed	$0	

* by large individual contributors ($200 & above)

Construction $43,575

General Contractors $17,726
Sergent Mechanical Sys .... $5,076 Indiv
Steve Bubalo Construction Co .... $4,000 Indiv
CA Rasmussen Co .... $3,000 Indiv
Associated General Contractors .... $1,500 PAC
Home Builders $6,850
National Assn of Home Builders .... $3,500 PAC
Special Trade Contractors $4,649
Sheet Metal/Air Conditioning Contractors .... $1,750 PAC
JH McDonough .... $1,549 Indiv
Building Materials & Equipment $13,750
PW Gillibrand Co .... $5,750 Indiv
Lee Bolin & Assoc .... $5,600 Indiv
Blue Star Ready Mix .... $1,900 Indiv

Defense $16,649

Defense Aerospace $9,900
Lockheed Corp .... $4,000 PAC
Textron Inc .... $2,500 PAC
Rockwell International .... $1,700 PAC/Ind
Defense Electronics $6,749
Hughes Aircraft .... $2,699 PAC
Whittaker Corp .... $2,300 PAC

Energy & Natural Resources $32,686

Oil & Gas $22,692
Litton Industries .... $4,250 PAC
Atlantic Richfield .... $2,934 PAC
Chevron Corp .... $2,000 PAC
Oxnard Refinery .... $1,800 Indiv
Phillips Petroleum .... $1,500 PAC
Electric Utilities $3,730
Southern California Edison .... $2,380 PAC
Waste Management $4,914
Hillside Rubbish Co .... $3,164 Indiv

Contribution Totals by Sector

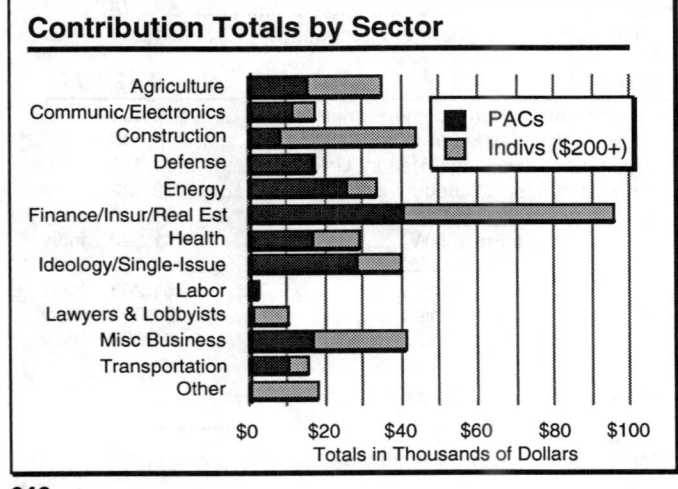

Agriculture
Communic/Electronics
Construction
Defense
Energy
Finance/Insur/Real Est
Health
Ideology/Single-Issue
Labor
Lawyers & Lobbyists
Misc Business
Transportation
Other

■ PACs
▨ Indivs ($200+)

$0 $20 $40 $60 $80 $100
Totals in Thousands of Dollars

Finance, Insurance & Real Estate — $95,270

Commercial Banks *$6,475*
- American Bankers Assn* .... $4,000 PAC
- BankAmerica Corp .... $1,950 PAC

Savings & Loans *$6,930*
- Great Western Financial Corp .... $2,430 PAC
- Home Savings of America .... $2,200 PAC

Securities & Investment *$1,800*
- None over $1,500

Insurance *$17,597*
- TransAmerica Corp* .... $8,700 PAC/Ind
- Farmers Group Inc .... $5,622 PAC

Real Estate *$54,038*
- National Assn of Realtors .... $8,000 PAC
- Century 21 Real Estate .... $6,550 PAC/Ind
- Assert Inc .... $4,336 Indiv
- Gelb Enterprises .... $3,150 Indiv
- Voit Companies .... $3,000 Indiv
- Dale Poe Development .... $2,500 Indiv
- Lowe Enterprises .... $2,400 Indiv
- Jerry B Epstein Management Co .... $2,300 Indiv
- Newhall Land & Farming Co .... $2,300 PAC
- Watt Industries .... $2,150 Indiv
- Bermant Development Co .... $1,500 Indiv

Accountants *$4,350*
- Vance, Thrift & Biller .... $2,750 Indiv

Misc Finance *$4,080*
- None over $1,500

Health — $28,715

Health Professionals *$16,460*
- American Medical Assn .... $6,000 PAC
- Cooperative of American Physicians .... $2,530 PAC
- American Academy of Ophthalmology .... $2,000 PAC

Hospitals/Nursing Homes *$2,350*
- None over $1,500

Pharmaceuticals/Health Products *$7,550*
- Amgen Inc .... $4,950 Indiv

Misc Health *$1,800*
- None over $1,500

Lawyers & Lobbyists — $10,095

Lawyers & Lobbyists *$10,095*
- Kindel & Anderson .... $2,190 Indiv
- Moriarity & Associates .... $1,650 Indiv

Misc Business — $40,948

Business Associations *$1,500*
- National Fedn of Independent Business ...... $1,500 PAC

Food & Beverage *$13,400*
- Cimm's Inc .... $7,400 Indiv
- National Restaurant Assn .... $2,000 PAC

Beer, Wine & Liquor *$6,150*
- National Beer Wholesalers Assn .... $5,000 PAC

Business Services *$7,148*
- Lyle Overby & Associates .... $2,998 Indiv
- Davis Group .... $2,100 Indiv

Misc Manufacturing & Distributing *$6,850*
- Bugle Boy Industries .... $6,000 Indiv

Transportation — $14,780

Air Transport *$4,030*
- United Parcel Service .... $3,530 PAC

Automotive *$9,050*
- National Auto Dealers Assn .... $2,850 PAC
- Galpin Motors .... $2,100 Indiv
- Auto Dealers & Drivers for Free Trade .... $1,500 PAC

Labor

Labor — $2,350

Public Sector Unions *$2,350*
- National Assn Retired Federal Employees ... $2,000 PAC

Ideological/Single-Issue

Ideological/Single-Issue — $39,488

Republican/Conservative *$11,250*
- None over $1,500

Pro-Israel *$5,500*
- National PAC .... $5,000 PAC

Gun Rights/Gun Control *$10,650*
- National Rifle Assn .... $9,900 PAC

Misc Issues *$10,088*
- Fair PAC .... $4,988 PAC
- Immigration PAC .... $2,500 PAC

Other & Unknown

Other — $17,620

Retired *$16,520*
- None over $1,500

Unknown — $65,333
- Homemakers/Non-income earners $13,498
- Generic Occupation/Category Unknown $3,280
- Employer Listed/Category Unknown $47,405
  - Lowe Associates .... $1,900 Indiv
  - Camacho Security Co .... $1,500 Indiv
  - Huber & Takasugi .... $1,500 Indiv

Independent expenditures opposing Gallegly
- Public Citizen $6,739

---

* Contributions came from more than one affiliate or subsidiary.

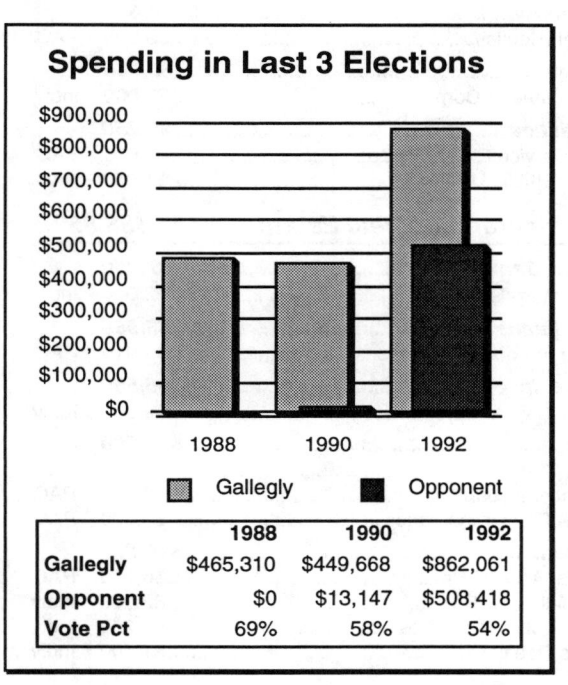

Spending in Last 3 Elections

	1988	1990	1992
Gallegly	$465,310	$449,668	$862,061
Opponent	$0	$13,147	$508,418
Vote Pct	69%	58%	54%

Legend: Gallegly, Opponent

Dean A. Gallo, R-NJ (11)

First elected: 1984
1991-92 Total Receipts: $567,280
1992 Year-end Cash: $20,723

1991-92 Committees & Subcommittees

Appropriations
District of Columbia (Ranking Republican); Energy and Water Development

Leading Contributors

Business

Agriculture		$14,350

Crop Production & Basic Processing **$1,500**
   Ocean Spray Cranberries Inc .... $1,500   PAC

Tobacco **$3,800**
   Philip Morris .... $1,500   PAC

Agricultural Services/Products **$1,750**
   None over $1,500

Food Processing & Sales **$6,800**
   Food Marketing Institute .... $2,200   PAC
   Nabisco Brands Inc .... $2,000   PAC
   Nature Food Centers .... $2,000   Indiv

Communications/Electronics $18,120

Telephone Utilities **$7,520**
   Bell Atlantic* .... $4,550   PAC
   AT&T .... $2,110   PAC

Electronics Mfg & Services **$4,450**
   Johanson Dielectrics Inc .... $2,200   Indiv

Computer Equipment & Services **$5,300**
   HF Henderson Industries .... $4,000   Indiv

Construction $33,950

General Contractors **$15,150**
   National Utility Contractors Assn .... $3,500   PAC
   Associated General Contractors .... $2,000   PAC

Home Builders **$13,700**
   National Assn of Home Builders .... $6,000   PAC
   Pineview Homes .... $3,700   Indiv
   Grove Associates .... $2,000   Indiv

Source of Funds in 1992 Election

Source	Total	Pct
PACs	$187,034	33%
Indivs $200+	$243,730	43%
Indivs under $200	$130,885	23%
Other	$6,105	1%
Candidate	$0	0%
Party	$539	0%

Source of PAC Dollars by Sector

Source	Total	Pct
Business	$144,234	78%
Labor	$27,950	15%
Ideology/Single Issue	$11,895	6%

In-State vs. Out-of-State Contributions*

Source	Total	Pct
In-State	$223,280	93%
Out-of-state	$17,450	7%
No state listed	$3,000	

* by large individual contributors ($200 & above)

Construction Services **$2,600**
   None over $1,500

Building Materials & Equipment **$2,500**
   Cerbo Lumber .... $2,000   Indiv

Defense $4,680

Defense Aerospace **$4,000**
   None over $1,500

Energy & Natural Resources $25,185

Oil & Gas **$7,335**
   Enserch Corp .... $1,535   PAC

Nuclear Energy **$4,300**
   General Atomics .... $3,500   PAC

Misc Energy **$3,050**
   Foster Wheeler Corp .... $2,000   Indiv

Electric Utilities **$9,250**
   Public Service Electric & Gas .... $4,600   PAC
   General Public Utilities .... $1,950   PAC

Finance, Insurance & Real Estate $58,869

Commercial Banks **$7,350**
   Oolie Enterprises .... $2,000   Indiv

Savings & Loans **$3,569**
   US League of Savings Assns* .... $3,019   PAC

Securities & Investment **$6,550**
   Wesray Capital Corp .... $2,000   Indiv

Insurance **$15,300**
   Chubb Corp .... $2,000   PAC
   Prudential Insurance .... $2,000   PAC
   Crum & Forster Insurance .... $1,500   PAC

Real Estate **$19,850**
   National Assn of Realtors .... $6,000   PAC
   Trammell Crow Co .... $2,000   Indiv
   Lane Webber Properties .... $1,750   Indiv
   Atlantic Realty Co .... $1,500   Indiv

Contribution Totals by Sector

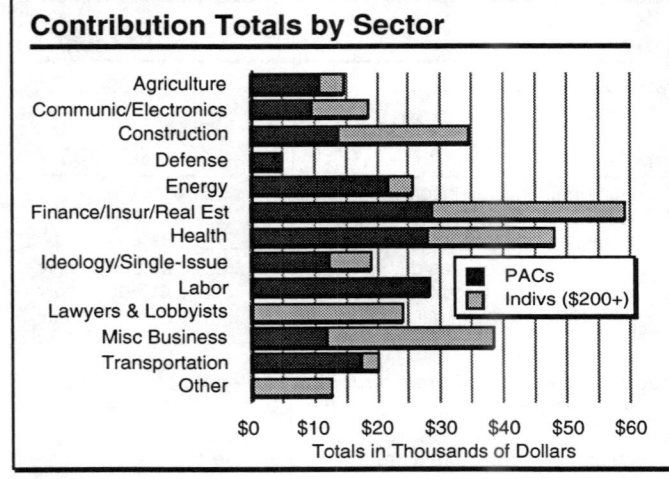

Agriculture
Communic/Electronics
Construction
Defense
Energy
Finance/Insur/Real Est
Health
Ideology/Single-Issue
Labor
Lawyers & Lobbyists
Misc Business
Transportation
Other

PACs
Indivs ($200+)

$0 $10 $20 $30 $40 $50 $60
Totals in Thousands of Dollars

Accountants **$3,250**
    None over $1,500

Misc Finance **$2,000**
    None over $1,500

Health $47,550

Health Professionals **$15,150**
    American Medical Assn* .... $7,850   PAC
    American Dental Assn .... $3,000   PAC

Hospitals/Nursing Homes **$6,100**
    St Clare's Hospital .... $3,850   Indiv

Pharmaceuticals/Health Products **$24,300**
    Warner-Lambert .... $4,750   PAC/Ind
    Schering-Plough Corp .... $3,750   PAC
    Bon-Art International .... $2,000   Indiv
    Merck & Co .... $2,000   PAC/Ind

Misc Health **$2,000**
    Medical Research .... $2,000   Indiv

Lawyers & Lobbyists $23,600

Lawyers & Lobbyists **$23,600**
    Cassidy & Associates .... $3,250   Indiv
    Cahill, Gordon et al .... $2,000   Indiv
    Montgomery, McCracken et al .... $1,650   Indiv

Misc Business $37,940

Food & Beverage **$4,950**
    None over $1,500

Beer, Wine & Liquor **$1,700**
    None over $1,500

Retail Sales **$3,800**
    Imperial Office Equipment .... $1,800   Indiv

Business Services **$9,000**
    Environmental Strategies .... $2,000   Indiv

Chemical & Related Manufacturing **$5,240**
    Stull Engraving .... $1,850   Indiv
    BASF Corp .... $1,750   Indiv

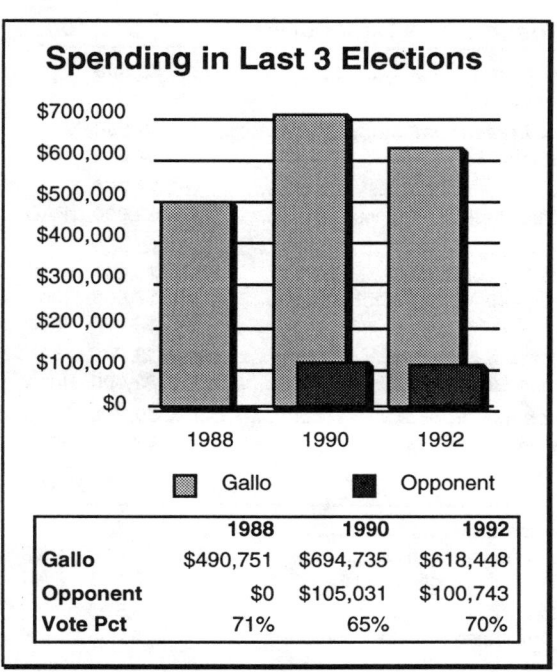

Spending in Last 3 Elections

	1988	1990	1992
Gallo	$490,751	$694,735	$618,448
Opponent	$0	$105,031	$100,743
Vote Pct	71%	65%	70%

Misc Manufacturing & Distributing **$7,800**
    Ohaus Scale Corp .... $3,000   Indiv
    Ohaus Management Group Inc .... $2,000   Indiv

Textiles **$2,000**
    Annin & Co .... $2,000   Indiv

Transportation $19,850

Air Transport **$5,450**
    United Parcel Service .... $4,450   PAC

Automotive **$6,500**
    National Auto Dealers Assn .... $2,500   PAC
    Auto Dealers & Drivers for Free Trade .... $2,000   PAC

Sea Transport **$7,500**
    Maersk Inc .... $2,500   PAC
    CSX Corp* .... $2,000   PAC

Labor

Labor $27,950

Building Trade Unions **$15,950**
    Laborers' Political League .... $5,000   PAC
    Operating Engineers #825 .... $4,200   PAC
    Carpenters & Joiners Union .... $3,250   PAC
    Ironworkers Union .... $2,500   PAC

Transportation Unions **$7,500**
    Marine Engineers Union* .... $5,000   PAC
    Air Line Pilots Assn .... $1,500   PAC

Public Sector Unions **$4,500**
    National Assn Retired Federal Employees .... $2,000   PAC
    National Assn of Letter Carriers .... $2,000   PAC

Ideological/Single-Issue

Ideological/Single-Issue $18,445

Leadership PACs **$2,000**
    Cmte for an Affordable NJ (C. Whitman) .... $2,000   PAC

Pro-Israel **$10,500**
    National PAC .... $5,000   PAC

Pro-Choice **$2,000**
    None over $1,500

Human Rights **$2,000**
    Human Rights Campaign Fund .... $2,000   PAC

Other & Unknown

Other $12,650

Civil Servants/Public Officials **$7,800**
    US Department of Justice .... $4,000   Indiv

Education **$2,850**
    CMMI at University of Medicine & Dentistry .... $2,000   Indiv

Retired **$2,000**
    None over $1,500

Unknown $84,670

    Homemakers/Non-income earners $8,400
    No Employer Listed or Found $44,503
    Generic Occupation/Category Unknown $2,100
    Employer Listed/Category Unknown $29,667
        A&S Holding Co .... $2,000   Indiv
        Bedford Management Co .... $2,000   Indiv
        Cypress Lakes at Boca Rio .... $2,000   Indiv
        Boonton Enterprises .... $1,500   Indiv

---

* Contributions came from more than one affiliate or
  subsidiary.

Sam Gejdenson, D-Conn (2)

First elected: 1980

1991-92 Total Receipts: $909,091
1992 Year-end Cash: $11,333

1991-92 Committees & Subcommittees

Administration
Accounts; Office Systems (Chairman); Campaign Finance Reform Task Force (Chairman)

Foreign Affairs
International Economic Policy and Trade (Chairman); Western Hemisphere Affairs

Interior and Insular Affairs
Energy and the Environment; Water, Power and Offshore Energy

Joint Committee on Printing

Leading Contributors

Business

Agriculture		$18,650	
Tobacco		**$3,250**	
H Willey Inc		$2,000	Indiv
Dairy		**$7,250**	
Mid-America Dairymen		$3,000	PAC
Associated Milk Producers		$2,500	PAC
Food Processing & Sales		**$2,700**	
None over $2,000			

Communications/Electronics		$26,000	
Media/Entertainment		**$5,000**	
None over $2,000			
Telephone Utilities		**$10,300**	
AT&T		$7,500	PAC/Ind
Telecom Services & Equipment		**$3,000**	
None over $2,000			
Electronics Mfg & Services		**$2,200**	
None over $2,000			
Computer Equipment & Services		**$4,000**	
None over $2,000			

Construction		$12,900	
General Contractors		**$3,650**	
None over $2,000			

Source of Funds in 1992 Election

Source	Total	Pct
■ PACs	$333,101	36%
▦ Indivs $200+	$258,611	28%
□ Indivs under $200	$215,412	23%
⊠ Other	$130,421	14%
Candidate	$85,000	9%
Party	$28,904	3%

Source of PAC Dollars by Sector

Source	Total	Pct
■ Business	$109,825	35%
▦ Labor	$106,381	34%
□ Ideology/Single Issue	$97,350	31%

In-State vs. Out-of-State Contributions*

Source	Total	Pct
□ In-State	$132,053	51%
■ Out-of-state	$124,558	49%
No state listed	$0	

* by large individual contributors ($200 & above)

Special Trade Contractors	**$5,500**	
North Haven Ceramic Tile & Floor	$4,000	Indiv
Building Materials & Equipment	**$2,000**	
None over $2,000		

Defense		$13,700	
Defense Aerospace		**$12,700**	
United Technologies		$5,200	PAC
General Dynamics		$5,000	PAC

Energy & Natural Resources		$12,125	
Oil & Gas		**$6,875**	
None over $2,000			

Finance, Insurance & Real Estate		$45,100	
Commercial Banks		**$3,500**	
None over $2,000			
Securities & Investment		**$8,550**	
Bear, Stearns & Co		$2,000	Indiv
Insurance		**$7,750**	
Connecticut Mutual Life Insurance		$2,000	PAC
Real Estate		**$15,300**	
National Assn of Realtors		$5,000	PAC
Aspen Square Management		$2,000	Indiv
Transcon Builders Inc		$2,000	Indiv
Accountants		**$2,800**	
Biederman Greenwald		$2,000	Indiv
Misc Finance		**$6,700**	
WR Family Associates		$2,000	Indiv

Health		$22,950	
Health Professionals		**$17,750**	
American Dental Assn		$5,000	PAC
American Chiropractic Assn		$2,000	PAC
Misc Health		**$3,500**	
Pain & Wellbeing Rehabilitation Clinic		$2,000	Indiv

Contribution Totals by Sector

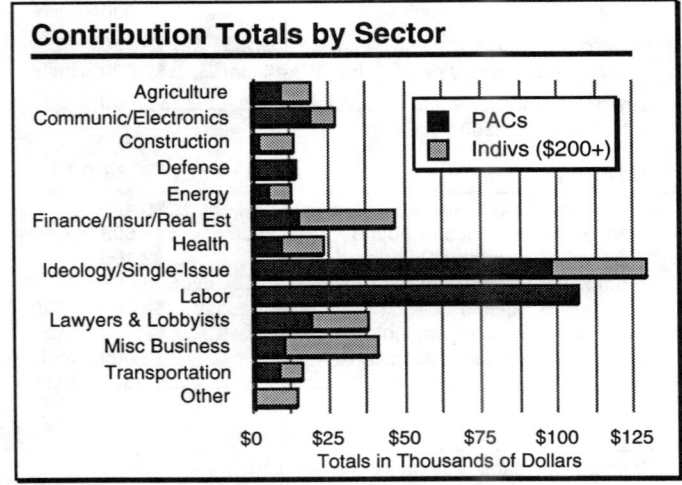

Agriculture
Communic/Electronics
Construction
Defense
Energy
Finance/Insur/Real Est
Health
Ideology/Single-Issue
Labor
Lawyers & Lobbyists
Misc Business
Transportation
Other

■ PACs
▦ Indivs ($200+)

$0 $25 $50 $75 $100 $125
Totals in Thousands of Dollars

Lawyers & Lobbyists $38,085

Lawyers & Lobbyists **$38,085**
   Assn of Trial Lawyers of America ....$10,000 PAC

Misc Business $45,052

Beer, Wine & Liquor **$4,627**
   Northeastern Distributing Co ....$2,000 Indiv

Retail Sales **$7,050**
   Radio Research Instrument Corp ....$2,000 Indiv
   Woodhaven Furniture Co ....$2,000 Indiv

Misc Services **$2,500**
   JC Ehrlich Co ....$2,500 Indiv

Business Services **$4,300**
   None over $2,000

Chemical & Related Manufacturing **$2,750**
   Philipp Brothers Chemical ....$2,750 Indiv

Misc Manufacturing & Distributing **$18,200**
   Institute of Scrap Recycling Industries ....$3,100 PAC
   Arrow Paper & Supply ....$2,500 Indiv
   MacAndrews & Forbes Group ....$2,500 Indiv
   Stratco Inc ....$2,000 Indiv

Textiles **$2,000**
   None over $2,000

Transportation $15,700

Air Transport **$6,750**
   Boeing Co ....$2,500 PAC
   United Parcel Service ....$2,000 PAC

Automotive **$7,700**
   None over $2,000

Labor

Labor $106,381

Building Trade Unions **$10,250**
   Carpenters & Joiners Union* ....$3,500 PAC
   Laborers' Political League ....$2,250 PAC
   Plumbers/Pipefitters Union ....$2,000 PAC

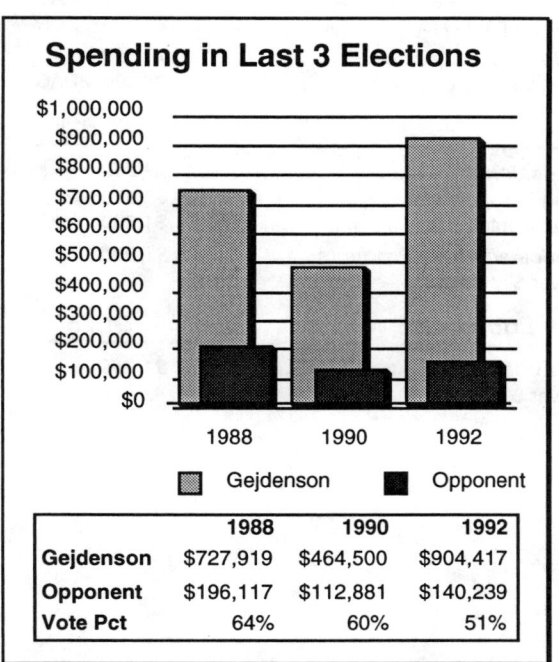

Spending in Last 3 Elections

	1988	1990	1992
Gejdenson	$727,919	$464,500	$904,417
Opponent	$196,117	$112,881	$140,239
Vote Pct	64%	60%	51%

Legend: ▨ Gejdenson   ■ Opponent

Industrial Unions $26,950

   Machinists/Aerospace Workers Union ....$9,500 PAC
   United Auto Workers ....$5,500 PAC
   Intl Brotherhood of Electrical Workers ....$5,450 PAC
   United Steelworkers ....$2,500 PAC

Transportation Unions **$20,250**
   Marine Engineers Union* ....$5,500 PAC
   Teamsters Union ....$5,000 PAC
   Maintenance of Way Employees ....$3,500 PAC
   Air Line Pilots Assn ....$3,000 PAC

Public Sector Unions **$43,331**
   American Fedn of St/Cnty/Munic Employees ....$12,000 PAC
   National Education Assn ....$9,000 PAC
   National Assn Retired Federal Employees ....$5,000 PAC
   American Federation of Teachers ....$4,000 PAC
   National Assn of Letter Carriers ....$4,000 PAC
   National Treasury Employees Union ....$2,961 PAC
   National Rural Letter Carriers Assn ....$2,000 PAC

Misc Unions **$5,600**
   AFL-CIO ....$2,500 PAC
   Food & Commercial Workers Union ....$2,000 PAC

Ideological/Single-Issue

Ideological/Single-Issue $129,360

Leadership PACs **$10,000**
   House Leadership Fund (Tom Foley) ....$5,000 PAC
   America's Leaders' Fund (Dan Rostenkowski) ....$2,000 PAC
   Effective Government Cmte (Dick Gephardt) ......$2,000 PAC

Foreign & Defense Policy **$5,000**
   Free Cuba PAC ....$5,000 PAC

Pro-Israel **$88,060**
   Desert Caucus ....$6,000 PAC
   National PAC ....$5,000 PAC
   North Jersey PAC ....$4,500 PAC
   Hudson Valley PAC ....$3,900 PAC
   Arizona Politically Interested Citizens ....$3,500 PAC
   Women's Alliance for Israel ....$3,500 PAC
   Joint Action Cmte for Political Affairs ....$3,000 PAC
   MOPAC ....$3,000 PAC
   St Louisians for Better Government ....$3,000 PAC
   Garden State PAC ....$2,750 PAC
   Citizens Organized PAC ....$2,500 PAC
   Multi-Issue PAC...$2,000 PAC

Human Rights **$11,600**
   KidsPAC ....$7,500 PAC

Misc Issues **$12,000**
   National Council of Senior Citizens.....................$5,000 PAC
   National Cmte to Preserve Social Security ....$4,000 PAC
   League of Conservation Voters ....$2,500 PAC

Other & Unknown

Other $14,151

Retired **$9,900**
   None over $2,000

Unknown $71,013

   Homemakers/Non-income earners $12,450
   No Employer Listed or Found $24,525
   Employer Listed/Category Unknown $32,538
     None over $2,000

* Contributions came from more than one affiliate or
  subsidiary.

George W. Gekas, R-Pa (17)

First elected: 1982

1991-92 Total Receipts: $112,141
1992 Year-end Cash: $62,800

1991-92 Committees & Subcommittees

Judiciary
Administrative Law and Governmental Relations (Ranking Republican); Crime and Criminal Justice

Select Committee on Intelligence

Leading Contributors

Business

Agriculture	**$4,800**	
Agricultural Services/Products	**$1,300**	
None over $1,000		
Food Processing & Sales	**$1,250**	
None over $1,000		

Communications/Electronics	**$7,600**	
Media/Entertainment	**$1,000**	
National Assn of Broadcasters	$1,000	PAC
Telephone Utilities	**$5,600**	
AT&T	$2,500	PAC

Construction	**$5,925**	
General Contractors	**$1,750**	
Associated General Contractors	$1,500	PAC
Home Builders	**$2,500**	
National Assn of Home Builders	$2,500	PAC
Special Trade Contractors	**$1,000**	
National Electrical Contractors Assn	$1,000	PAC

Energy & Natural Resources	**$3,575**	
Oil & Gas	**$1,500**	
Petroleum Marketers Assn	$1,000	PAC
Electric Utilities	**$1,400**	
None over $1,000		

Source of Funds in 1992 Election

Source	Total	Pct
■ PACs	$68,435	61%
▨ Indivs $200+	$10,830	10%
☐ Indivs under $200	$15,870	14%
▩ Other	$17,006	15%
Candidate	$0	0%
Party	$2,035	2%

Source of PAC Dollars by Sector

Source	Total	Pct
■ Business	$67,180	96%
▨ Labor	$1,500	2%
☐ Ideology/Single Issue	$1,300	2%

In-State vs. Out-of-State Contributions*

Source	Total	Pct
☐ In-State	$9,380	87%
▨ Out-of-state	$1,450	13%
No state listed	$0	

*** by large individual contributors ($200 & above)**

Finance, Insurance & Real Estate	**$26,755**	
Commercial Banks	**$1,850**	
American Bankers Assn	$1,000	PAC
Securities & Investment	**$1,000**	
Hillman Co	$1,000	Indiv
Insurance	**$5,555**	
American Council of Life Insurance	$2,000	PAC
Nationwide Corp	$1,150	PAC
National Assn of Life Underwriters	$1,000	PAC
Real Estate	**$10,175**	
National Assn of Realtors	$9,000	PAC
Eldorado Properties Corp	$1,000	Indiv
Accountants	**$7,500**	
American Institute of CPA's	$7,500	PAC

Health	**$5,025**	
Health Professionals	**$3,850**	
American Medical Assn	$2,850	PAC
American Dental Assn	$1,000	PAC
Pharmaceuticals/Health Products	**$1,000**	
None over $1,000		

Lawyers & Lobbyists	**$1,250**	
Lawyers & Lobbyists	**$1,250**	
None over $1,000		

Contribution Totals by Sector

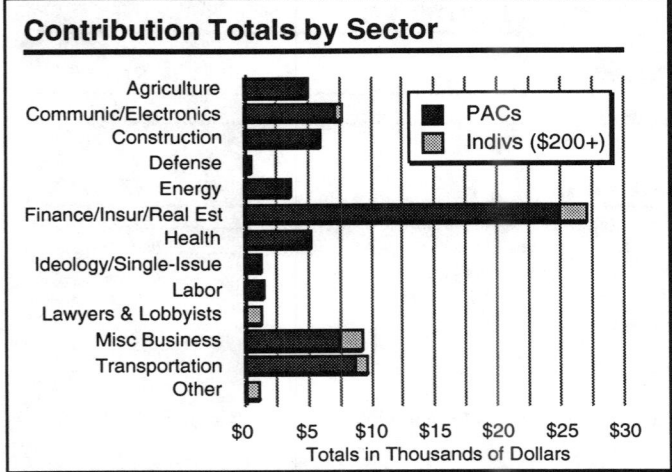

Agriculture
Communic/Electronics
Construction
Defense
Energy
Finance/Insur/Real Est
Health
Ideology/Single-Issue
Labor
Lawyers & Lobbyists
Misc Business
Transportation
Other

■ PACs
▨ Indivs ($200+)

$0 $5 $10 $15 $20 $25 $30
Totals in Thousands of Dollars

Misc Business   **$9,155**

Beer, Wine & Liquor **$1,500**
    National Beer Wholesalers Assn ....$1,000   PAC

Retail Sales **$1,530**
    None over $1,000

Steel Production **$1,600**
    Bethlehem Steel ....$1,600   PAC

Misc Manufacturing & Distributing **$2,000**
    Stone Container Corp ....$2,000   PAC

Transportation $9,500

Air Transport **$3,800**
    United Parcel Service ....$3,800   PAC/Ind

Automotive **$4,700**
    National Auto Dealers Assn ....$3,000   PAC
    Americans for Free International Trade ....$1,000   PAC

Labor

Labor   **$1,500**

Transportation Unions **$1,000**
    Marine Engineers Dist 2 Maritime Officers ....$1,000   PAC

Ideological/Single-Issue

Ideological/Single-Issue   **$1,300**
    None over $1,000

Other & Unknown

Other   **$1,100**
    None over $1,000

Unknown   **$2,950**
    Employer Listed/Category Unknown $2,000
        Famous Hot Weiner North ....$1,500   Indiv

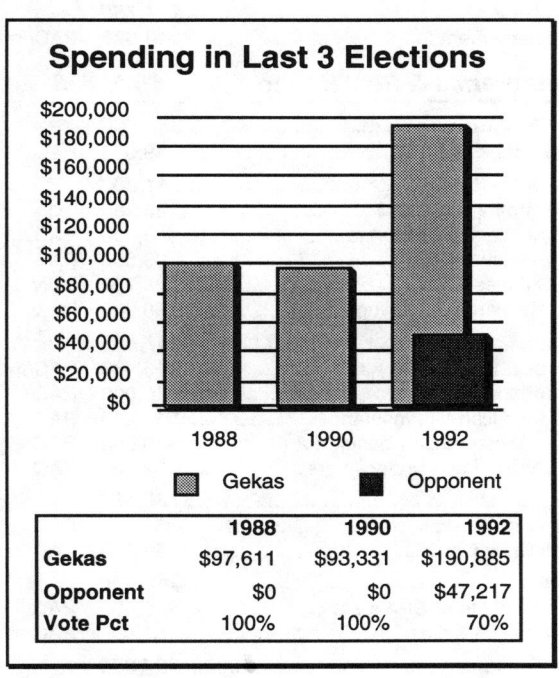

Spending in Last 3 Elections

	1988	1990	1992
Gekas	$97,611	$93,331	$190,885
Opponent	$0	$0	$47,217
Vote Pct	100%	100%	70%

Richard A. Gephardt, D-Mo (3)

First elected: 1976
1991-92 Total Receipts: $3,238,479
1992 Year-end Cash: $114,236

1991-92 Committees & Subcommittees

Budget

Leading Contributors

Business

Agriculture	$108,283	
Crop Production & Basic Processing	$21,700	
None over $7,500		
Tobacco	$22,848	
Philip Morris	$12,598	PAC/Ind
Dairy	$12,000	
Associated Milk Producers	$7,500	PAC
Agricultural Services/Products	$15,000	
None over $7,500		
Food Processing & Sales	$19,985	
None over $7,500		

Communications/Electronics	$191,855	
Printing & Publishing	$18,850	
None over $7,500		
Media/Entertainment	$96,255	
Walt Disney Co	$15,500	PAC/Ind
Time Warner*	$9,500	PAC/Ind
Telephone Utilities	$46,250	
Southwestern Bell	$10,750	PAC/Ind
GTE Corp	$8,000	PAC
AT&T	$7,500	PAC
Telecom Services & Equipment	$10,750	
None over $7,500		
Computer Equipment & Services	$17,500	
None over $7,500		

Construction	$81,297	
General Contractors	$34,985	
None over $7,500		
Home Builders	$12,050	
None over $7,500		
Construction Services	$21,262	
Sverdrup Corp	$9,000	PAC

Contribution Totals by Sector

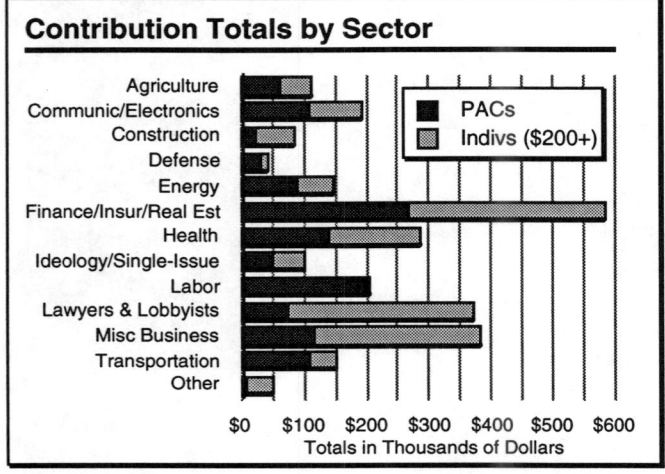

Agriculture
Communic/Electronics
Construction
Defense
Energy
Finance/Insur/Real Est
Health
Ideology/Single-Issue
Labor
Lawyers & Lobbyists
Misc Business
Transportation
Other

- PACs
- Indivs ($200+)

$0 $100 $200 $300 $400 $500 $600
Totals in Thousands of Dollars

Source of Funds in 1992 Election

Source	Total	Pct
PACs	$1,240,597	38%
Indivs $200+	$1,624,333	50%
Indivs under $200	$244,381	8%
Other	$129,305	4%
Candidate	$0	0%
Party	$3,337	0%

Source of PAC Dollars by Sector

Source	Total	Pct
Business	$988,527	80%
Labor	$199,933	16%
Ideology/Single Issue	$48,253	4%

In-State vs. Out-of-State Contributions*

Source	Total	Pct
In-State	$390,235	24%
Out-of-state	$1,230,248	76%
No state listed	$0	

* by large individual contributors ($200 & above)

Defense	$39,000	
Defense Aerospace	$38,750	
McDonnell Douglas	$18,250	PAC/Ind

Energy & Natural Resources	$144,800	
Oil & Gas	$80,500	
Coastal Corp	$11,000	PAC/Ind
Shell Oil	$8,250	PAC/Ind
Atlantic Richfield	$8,000	PAC/Ind
Electric Utilities	$19,300	
None over $7,500		
Waste Management	$31,750	
Waste Management Inc	$14,500	PAC/Ind

Finance, Insurance & Real Estate	$575,673	
Commercial Banks	$60,000	
Boatmens Bankshares	$9,000	PAC
Securities & Investment	$141,207	
Salomon Brothers	$22,185	Indiv
Chicago Mercantile Exchange	$10,000	PAC
Morgan Stanley & Co	$9,500	PAC
Edward D Jones & Co	$8,750	Indiv
Chicago Research & Trading Group	$8,000	Indiv
Insurance	$157,889	
Blue Cross & Blue Shield Assn*	$15,489	PAC/Ind
American Family Corp	$10,000	PAC
General American Life Insurance	$10,000	PAC
Independent Insurance Agents of America	$10,000	PAC
National Assn of Life Underwriters	$9,500	PAC
Real Estate	$125,677	
National Assn of Realtors	$9,999	PAC
Trammell Crow Co	$9,250	PAC/Ind
Accountants	$40,900	
American Institute of CPA's	$10,000	PAC
Arthur Andersen & Co	$9,000	PAC/Ind
Misc Finance	$37,000	
None over $7,500		

Health — $282,230

Health Professionals **$98,630**
American Chiropractic Assn .... $9,500 PAC

Hospitals/Nursing Homes **$67,500**
Hospice Care Inc .... $11,000 Indiv
American Health Care Assn .... $10,000 PAC

Health Services **$57,950**
Group Health Plan Inc .... $16,000 Indiv

Pharmaceuticals/Health Products **$41,500**
None over $7,500

Misc Health **$16,650**
None over $7,500

Lawyers & Lobbyists — $369,892

Lawyers & Lobbyists **$369,892**
Sills, Cummis et al .... $21,500 Indiv
Thompson & Mitchell .... $20,000 Indiv
Bryan, Cave et al .... $18,050 Indiv
Jones & Granger .... $15,000 Indiv
Assn of Trial Lawyers of America .... $10,000 PAC

Misc Business — $378,121

Food & Beverage **$9,500**
None over $7,500

Beer, Wine & Liquor **$151,100**
Anheuser-Busch .... $43,350 PAC/Ind
Gallo Winery .... $21,000 Indiv
Wine Institute .... $10,000 PAC

Retail Sales **$30,400**
None over $7,500

Business Services **$55,800**
None over $7,500

Casinos/Gambling **$25,771**
Circus Circus Enterprises .... $12,771 PAC/Ind

Lodging/Tourism **$9,250**
None over $7,500

Chemical & Related Manufacturing **$16,750**
None over $7,500

Steel Production **$9,000**
None over $7,500

Misc Manufacturing & Distributing **$46,750**
None over $7,500

Transportation — $146,996

Air Transport **$38,500**
Federal Express Corp .... $10,000 PAC
United Parcel Service .... $8,500 PAC

Automotive **$50,500**
Enterprise Leasing Co .... $10,000 PAC
Moog Automotive Inc .... $9,250 Indiv
National Auto Dealers Assn .... $8,000 PAC

Trucking **$26,246**
None over $7,500

Railroads **$15,000**
None over $7,500

Sea Transport **$13,750**
None over $7,500

Labor

Labor — $200,433

Building Trade Unions **$26,500**
None over $7,500

Industrial Unions **$36,784**
Communications Workers of America .... $7,500 PAC
Machinists/Aerospace Workers Union* .... $7,500 PAC

Transportation Unions **$55,850**
Seafarers International Union .... $10,000 PAC
Teamsters Union .... $10,000 PAC

Public Sector Unions **$58,800**
National Assn of Letter Carriers* .... $12,000 PAC
American Federation of Teachers .... $10,000 PAC
National Education Assn .... $10,000 PAC

Misc Unions **$22,499**
Food & Commercial Workers Union .... $9,499 PAC

Ideological/Single-Issue

Ideological/Single-Issue — $98,753

Democratic/Liberal **$8,000**
None over $7,500

Pro-Israel **$47,750**
Desert Caucus .... $7,500 PAC

Human Rights **$23,000**
None over $7,500

Other & Unknown

Other — $47,681

Civil Servants/Public Officials **$9,300**
None over $7,500

Education **$22,131**
None over $7,500

Retired **$13,950**
None over $7,500

Unknown — $205,782

Homemakers/Non-income earners $40,930
No Employer Listed or Found $16,827
Employer Listed/Category Unknown $146,725
None over $7,500

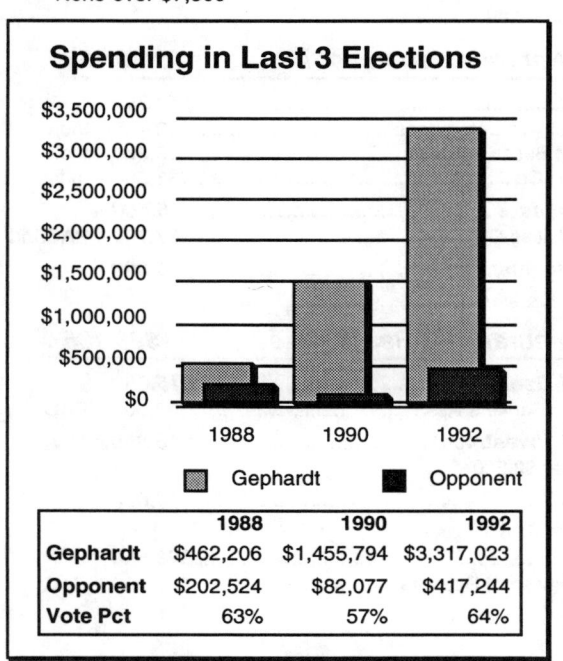

Spending in Last 3 Elections

	1988	1990	1992
Gephardt	$462,206	$1,455,794	$3,317,023
Opponent	$202,524	$82,077	$417,244
Vote Pct	63%	57%	64%

Legend: Gephardt / Opponent

---

* Contributions came from more than one affiliate or subsidiary.

Pete Geren, D-Texas (12)

First elected: 1989

1991-92 Total Receipts: $809,664
1992 Year-end Cash: $15,548

1991-92 Committees & Subcommittees

Public Works and Transportation
Aviation; Surface Transportation

Science, Space and Technology
Investigations and Oversight; Space

Veterans' Affairs
Education, Training and Employment

Leading Contributors

Business

Agriculture	$46,300	
Crop Production & Basic Processing $10,400		
None over $2,500		
Tobacco $5,000		
Philip Morris $2,500	PAC
Dairy $7,250		
Associated Milk Producers $5,000	PAC
Livestock $7,700		
National Cattlemen's Assn* $2,500	PAC
Agricultural Services/Products $7,750		
Texas Farm Bureau $2,500	PAC
Food Processing & Sales $6,000		
None over $2,500		

Communications/Electronics	$27,000	
Printing & Publishing $7,450		
Motherak Printing Co $4,500	Indiv
Telephone Utilities $8,500		
GTE Corp $3,000	PAC
Southwestern Bell $3,000	PAC/Ind
Electronics Mfg & Services $3,400		
None over $2,500		
Computer Equipment & Services $5,400		
None over $2,500		

Source of Funds in 1992 Election

Source	Total	Pct
■ PACs	$351,418	43%
▨ Indivs $200+	$372,412	46%
☐ Indivs under $200	$63,338	8%
⊠ Other	$29,564	4%
Candidate	$0	0%
Party	$7,068	1%

Source of PAC Dollars by Sector

Source	Total	Pct
■ Business	$320,588	90%
▨ Labor	$23,550	7%
☐ Ideology/Single Issue	$10,500	3%

In-State vs. Out-of-State Contributions*

Source	Total	Pct
☐ In-State	$355,162	96%
■ Out-of-state	$15,750	4%
No state listed	$200	

* by large individual contributors ($200 & above)

Construction	$36,929	
General Contractors $15,809		
Associated General Contractors $4,000	PAC
Home Builders $4,500		
National Assn of Home Builders $4,000	PAC
Construction Services $10,770		
Enserch Corp $2,500	PAC
Building Materials & Equipment $4,850		
None over $2,500		

Defense	$5,000	
Defense Electronics $3,350		
None over $2,500		

Energy & Natural Resources	$99,155	
Oil & Gas $79,355		
Bass Brothers Enterprises $13,485	Indiv
Robert M Bass Group Inc $8,970	Indiv
Young Oil Co $3,500	Indiv
Electric Utilities $15,500		
Texas Utilities Co* $7,700	PAC/Ind
Waste Management $4,000		
None over $2,500		

Finance, Insurance & Real Estate	$93,135	
Commercial Banks $15,650		
American Bankers Assn $3,000	PAC
Securities & Investment $10,850		
None over $2,500		
Insurance $9,650		
None over $2,500		
Real Estate $28,650		
National Assn of Realtors $10,000	PAC

Contribution Totals by Sector

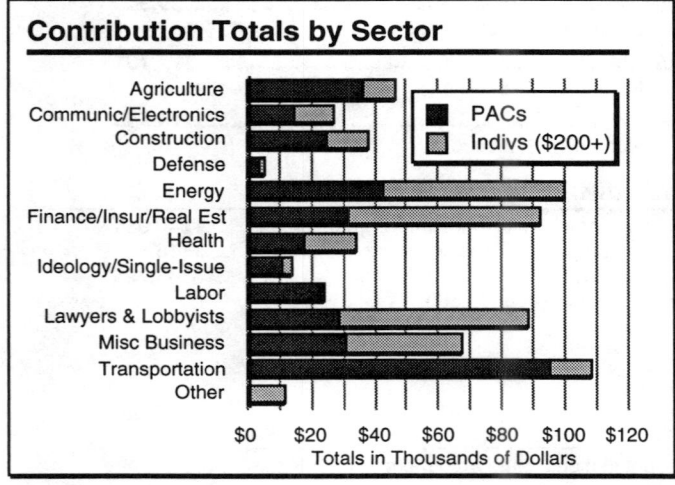

Agriculture
Communic/Electronics
Construction
Defense
Energy
Finance/Insur/Real Est
Health
Ideology/Single-Issue
Labor
Lawyers & Lobbyists
Misc Business
Transportation
Other

■ PACs
▨ Indivs ($200+)

$0 $20 $40 $60 $80 $100 $120
Totals in Thousands of Dollars

Accountants $2,600
    None over $2,500

Misc Finance $22,585
    None over $2,500

Health $33,100

Health Professionals $26,700
    American Medical Assn .... $9,700   PAC
Health Services $3,650
    Pacificare Health Systems .... $3,450   PAC/Ind

Lawyers & Lobbyists $87,469

Lawyers & Lobbyists $87,469
    Assn of Trial Lawyers of America .... $8,000   PAC
    Kelly, Hart & Hallman .... $6,000   Indiv
    Vinson & Elkins .... $5,500   PAC/Ind
    Winstead, Sechrest & Minick .... $4,000   PAC
    McDonald, Sanders & Ginsburg .... $3,620   Indiv
    Cantey, Hanger et al .... $3,000   Indiv
    Decker, McMackin & McClane .... $2,500   Indiv
    Thompson & Knight .... $2,500   Indiv

Misc Business $66,708

Food & Beverage $7,950
    National Restaurant Assn* .... $4,250   PAC
Beer, Wine & Liquor $16,050
    Miller Distributing-Fort Worth .... $4,400   Indiv
    National Beer Wholesalers Assn .... $3,000   PAC
Retail Sales $11,957
    JC Penney Co .... $2,500   PAC
Misc Services $6,201
    None over $2,500
Business Services $12,650
    None over $2,500
Chemical & Related Manufacturing $3,000
    None over $2,500
Misc Manufacturing & Distributing $4,750
    None over $2,500

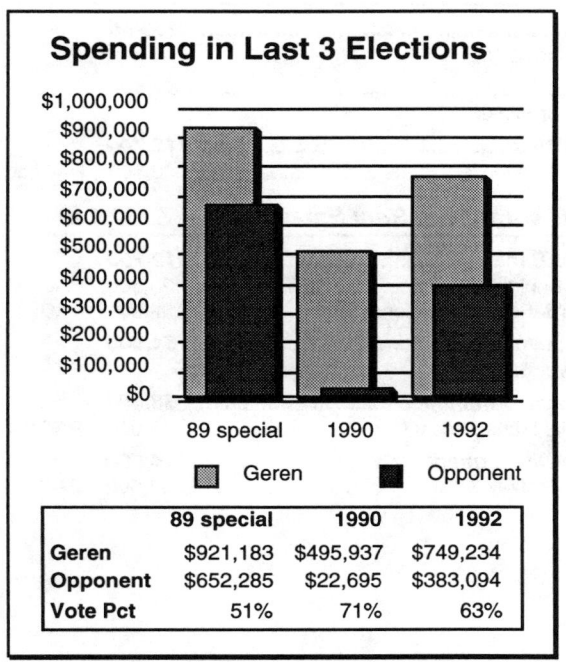

Spending in Last 3 Elections

	89 special	1990	1992
Geren	$921,183	$495,937	$749,234
Opponent	$652,285	$22,695	$383,094
Vote Pct	51%	71%	63%

(Legend: Geren, Opponent)

Transportation $107,709

Air Transport $63,800
    Federal Express Corp .... $11,000   PAC
    American Airlines .... $10,500   PAC/Ind
    General Dynamics .... $10,200   PAC
    Textron Inc .... $8,800   PAC
    United Parcel Service .... $4,500   PAC
    Aircraft Owners & Pilots Assn .... $4,000   PAC
    Southwest Airlines .... $3,500   Indiv
Automotive $19,450
    National Auto Dealers Assn .... $10,000   PAC
Trucking $4,400
    None over $2,500
Railroads $18,559
    Burlington Northern .... $9,500   PAC/Ind
    Union Pacific Corp .... $5,559   PAC

Labor

Labor $23,550

Industrial Unions $2,500
    None over $2,500
Transportation Unions $14,500
    Teamsters local #745 .... $5,000   PAC
    United Transportation Union .... $2,500   PAC
Public Sector Unions $5,050
    None over $2,500

Ideological/Single-Issue

Ideological/Single-Issue $13,500

Democratic/Liberal $2,750
    National Cmte for an Effective Congress .... $2,500   PAC
Gun Rights/Gun Control $5,000
    National Rifle Assn .... $5,000   PAC

Other & Unknown

Other $11,300

Retired $8,650
    None over $2,500

Unknown $74,645

    Homemakers/Non-income earners $22,650
    No Employer Listed or Found $21,000
    Employer Listed/Category Unknown $28,995
      None over $2,500

Independent expenditures supporting Geren
    National Rifle Assn $17,500

* Contributions came from more than one affiliate or
subsidiary.

Sam M. Gibbons, D-Fla (11)

First elected: 1962

1991-92 Total Receipts: $722,678
1992 Year-end Cash: $41,127

1991-92 Committees & Subcommittees

Ways and Means
Social Security; Trade (Chairman)

Joint Committee on Taxation

Leading Contributors

Business

Agriculture	$66,600	
Crop Production & Basic Processing	**$6,250**	
Florida Citrus Mutual	$3,000	PAC
Tobacco	**$25,250**	
Havatampa Inc	$4,250	Indiv
US Tobacco Co	$4,000	PAC
Culbro Corp	$3,500	Indiv
Cigar Assn of America	$3,000	PAC
Dairy	**$3,500**	
None over $2,500		
Poultry & Eggs	**$4,000**	
None over $2,500		
Agricultural Services/Products	**$11,750**	
Archer-Daniels-Midland Corp	$4,500	PAC/Ind
Food Processing & Sales	**$10,100**	
Food Marketing Institute	$3,000	PAC
Winn-Dixie Stores	$3,000	PAC/Ind
Forestry & Forest Products	**$4,000**	
None over $2,500		

Communications/Electronics	$31,500	
Media/Entertainment	**$7,500**	
None over $2,500		
Telephone Utilities	**$15,250**	
AT&T	$6,000	PAC
Southern Bell	$3,000	PAC
Computer Equipment & Services	**$5,000**	
None over $2,500		

Source of Funds in 1992 Election

Source	Total	Pct
■ PACs	$427,161	59%
▣ Indivs $200+	$177,474	24%
□ Indivs under $200	$72,926	10%
▨ Other	$51,790	7%
Candidate	$0	0%
Party	$7,173	1%

Source of PAC Dollars by Sector

Source	Total	Pct
■ Business	$419,625	95%
▣ Labor	$16,500	4%
□ Ideology/Single Issue	$4,000	1%

In-State vs. Out-of-State Contributions*

Source	Total	Pct
□ In-State	$115,324	65%
■ Out-of-state	$61,300	35%
No state listed	$0	

*** by large individual contributors ($200 & above)**

Construction	$28,100	
Home Builders	**$9,800**	
Walter Industries	$8,800	PAC/Ind
Building Materials & Equipment	**$14,300**	
Jim Walter Corp	$8,550	PAC/Ind

Defense	$10,000	
Defense Aerospace	**$7,000**	
None over $2,500		

Energy & Natural Resources	$39,119	
Oil & Gas	**$15,750**	
None over $2,500		
Mining	**$7,500**	
None over $2,500		
Electric Utilities	**$12,700**	
Teco Energy Inc	$3,500	PAC/Ind

Finance, Insurance & Real Estate	$127,149	
Commercial Banks	**$12,250**	
Barnett Banks Inc	$3,500	PAC
Citizens & Southern National Bank	$2,500	PAC
Savings & Loans	**$4,000**	
None over $2,500		
Finance/Credit Companies	**$3,000**	
Beneficial Management Corp	$3,000	PAC/Ind
Securities & Investment	**$14,500**	
Morgan Stanley & Co	$3,500	PAC

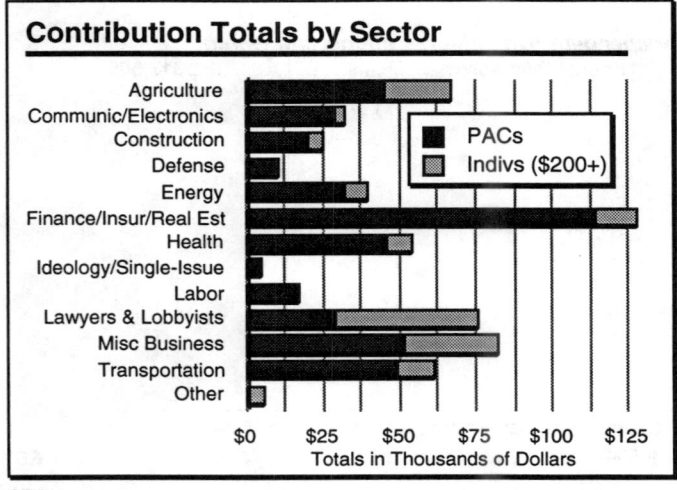

Contribution Totals by Sector

Agriculture
Communic/Electronics
Construction
Defense
Energy
Finance/Insur/Real Est
Health
Ideology/Single-Issue
Labor
Lawyers & Lobbyists
Misc Business
Transportation
Other

■ PACs
▨ Indivs ($200+)

$0 $25 $50 $75 $100 $125
Totals in Thousands of Dollars

Insurance **$60,949**
    National Assn of Life Underwriters .... $10,000   PAC
    American Family Corp .... $7,000   PAC
    Metropolitan Life Insurance .... $5,000   PAC
    Mutual Life Insurance of New York .... $4,000   PAC
    Northwestern Mutual Life .... $4,000   PAC
    Massachusetts Mutual Life Insurance .... $3,000   PAC
    Torchmark Corp .... $3,000   PAC
    American Council of Life Insurance .... $2,999   PAC

Real Estate **$14,750**
    National Assn of Realtors .... $8,000   PAC

Accountants **$16,950**
    American Institute of CPA's .... $10,000   PAC
    Coopers & Lybrand .... $2,500   PAC/Ind

Health $53,050

Health Professionals **$26,050**
    American Chiropractic Assn .... $4,500   PAC
    American Dental Assn .... $4,000   PAC
    T2 Medical Inc .... $3,000   PAC

Hospitals/Nursing Homes **$2,750**
    None over $2,500

Pharmaceuticals/Health Products **$23,250**
    SmithKline Beecham .... $3,000   PAC
    ICI Americas Inc .... $2,500   PAC

Lawyers & Lobbyists $75,100

Lawyers & Lobbyists **$75,100**
    McClure, Trotter & Mentz .... $5,000   Indiv
    Assn of Trial Lawyers of America .... $4,000   PAC
    MacFarland, Ferguson et al .... $3,750   Indiv
    Vinson & Elkins .... $3,000   PAC
    Holland & Knight .... $2,500   PAC/Ind

Misc Business $77,557

Food & Beverage **$3,300**
    None over $2,500

Beer, Wine & Liquor **$25,750**
    Florida Distillers Co .... $6,000   Indiv
    Bacardi Imports .... $5,000   Indiv

Retail Sales **$9,757**
    None over $2,500

Business Services **$5,250**
    None over $2,500

Chemical & Related Manufacturing **$11,300**
    None over $2,500

Misc Manufacturing & Distributing **$17,950**
    Corning Glass Works .... $7,000   PAC

Transportation $60,800

Air Transport **$11,500**
    United Parcel Service .... $5,500   PAC

Automotive **$22,750**
    Americans for Free International Trade .... $6,000   PAC
    National Auto Dealers Assn .... $6,000   PAC
    Auto Dealers & Drivers for Free Trade .... $2,500   PAC
    Ferman Motor Car Co .... $2,500   Indiv

Railroads **$4,250**
    Union Pacific Corp .... $3,000   PAC

Sea Transport **$21,300**
    Cruise PAC .... $4,000   PAC
    Miami Cruise PAC .... $4,000   PAC
    Sea-Land Corp .... $4,000   PAC
    Carnival Cruise Lines .... $3,000   Indiv
    Lykes Brothers Steamship Co .... $3,000   PAC/Ind

Labor

Labor   **$16,500**

Building Trade Unions **$2,500**
    Sheet Metal Workers Union .... $2,500   PAC

Transportation Unions **$4,500**
    United Transportation Union .... $3,000   PAC

Public Sector Unions **$8,500**
    National Education Assn .... $3,000   PAC

Ideological/Single-Issue

Ideological/Single-Issue   **$4,000**

Democratic/Liberal **$2,500**
    National Cmte for an Effective Congress .... $2,500   PAC

Other & Unknown

Other   **$5,350**
    None over $2,500

Unknown   **$22,424**
    Homemakers/Non-income earners $4,500
    Employer Listed/Category Unknown $16,400
        None over $2,500

Spending in Last 3 Elections

	1988	1990	1992
Gibbons	$382,889	$825,795	$960,511
Opponent	$0	$0	$49,644
Vote Pct	100%	68%	53%

Wayne T. Gilchrest, R-Md (1)

First elected: 1990

1991-92 Total Receipts: $394,794
1992 Year-end Cash: $2,582

1991-92 Committees & Subcommittees

Merchant Marine and Fisheries
Coast Guard and Navigation; Fisheries and Wildlife Conservation and the Environment

Science, Space and Technology
Science; Technology and Competitiveness

Select Committee on Aging

Select Committee on Hunger

Leading Contributors

Business

Agriculture $18,050

Crop Production & Basic Processing	**$4,800**	
Eversley Farm	$1,300	Indiv
Hybarc Farm	$1,000	Indiv
Tobacco	**$1,500**	
Tobacco Institute	$1,000	PAC
Poultry & Eggs	**$4,250**	
National Broiler Council	$2,000	PAC
Showell Poultry Co	$1,250	Indiv
Perdue Farms	$1,000	Indiv
Agricultural Services/Products	**$1,000**	
None over $1,000		
Food Processing & Sales	**$3,500**	
McCormick & Co	$1,500	PAC
Fleming Companies Inc	$1,000	PAC
Forestry & Forest Products	**$2,000**	
Westvaco Corp	$2,000	PAC

Communications/Electronics $5,750

Printing & Publishing	**$1,750**	
Uticom Systems Inc	$1,000	Indiv
Electronics Mfg & Services	**$2,700**	
North American Philips Corp	$1,700	PAC
Harris Corp	$1,000	PAC

Source of Funds in 1992 Election

Source	Total	Pct
■ PACs	$94,529	22%
▨ Indivs $200+	$95,767	22%
☐ Indivs under $200	$155,856	36%
⊠ Other	$88,528	20%
Candidate	$0	0%
Party	$52,841	12%

Source of PAC Dollars by Sector

Source	Total	Pct
■ Business	$80,101	83%
▨ Labor	$4,500	5%
☐ Ideology/Single Issue	$11,442	12%

In-State vs. Out-of-State Contributions*

Source	Total	Pct
☐ In-State	$88,267	93%
▨ Out-of-state	$6,750	7%
No state listed	$750	

* by large individual contributors ($200 & above)

Construction $11,500

General Contractors	**$10,250**	
Associated Builders & Contractors	$5,000	PAC
Associated General Contractors	$2,500	PAC
National Utility Contractors Assn	$1,500	PAC

Defense $4,650

Defense Aerospace	**$2,900**	
Thiokol	$1,550	PAC
Defense Electronics	**$1,000**	
Veda Inc	$1,000	PAC

Energy & Natural Resources $10,700

Oil & Gas	**$4,000**	
None over $1,000		
Misc Energy	**$3,000**	
Cooper Industries	$3,000	PAC
Electric Utilities	**$2,950**	
Baltimore Gas & Electric	$1,750	PAC
ACRE (Action Cmte for Rural Electrification)	$1,000	PAC

Finance, Insurance & Real Estate $20,950

Commercial Banks	**$6,900**	
MBNA Corp	$2,500	PAC/Ind
American Bankers Assn	$2,000	PAC
First Maryland Bancorp	$1,100	PAC
Citizens & Southern National Bank	$1,000	PAC
Securities & Investment	**$4,000**	
Legg Mason Inc	$1,450	Indiv
Tudor Investment Corp	$1,000	Indiv
Insurance	**$5,750**	
National Assn of Life Underwriters	$2,000	PAC
Liberty Mutual Insurance	$1,000	PAC
Real Estate	**$3,000**	
Continental Realty Corp	$1,000	Indiv

Contribution Totals by Sector

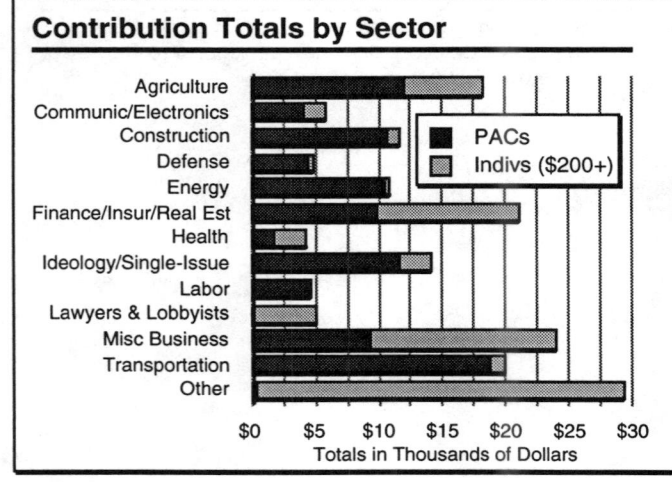

Agriculture
Communic/Electronics
Construction
Defense
Energy
Finance/Insur/Real Est
Health
Ideology/Single-Issue
Labor
Lawyers & Lobbyists
Misc Business
Transportation
Other

■ PACs
▨ Indivs ($200+)

$0 $5 $10 $15 $20 $25 $30
Totals in Thousands of Dollars

Health $4,100

Health Professionals $3,850
    None over $1,000

Lawyers & Lobbyists $4,943

Lawyers & Lobbyists...$4,943
    Mason, Ketterman & Morgan ....$1,000   Indiv
    Steptoe & Johnson ....$1,000   Indiv

Misc Business $23,801

Business Associations $2,000
    National Fedn of Independent Business ....$2,000   PAC
Food & Beverage $2,500
    Morrison Inc...$1,000   PAC
    National Restaurant Assn ....$1,000   PAC
Beer, Wine & Liquor $1,500
    National Beer Wholesalers Assn ....$1,000   PAC
Retail Sales...$2,500
    National Assn of Convenience Stores ....$1,000   PAC
Misc Manufacturing & Distributing $3,500
    Solo Cup..$1,500   Indiv
    Murray Corp ....$1,000   Indiv
Textiles $10,000
    Jasper Textiles ....$10,000   Indiv

Transportation $19,800

Air Transport $7,250
    United Parcel Service ....$4,500   PAC
    UNC Inc ....$1,000   PAC
Automotive $8,250
    Auto Dealers & Drivers for Free Trade ....$3,000   PAC
    Eaton Corp ....$3,000   PAC
    Americans for Free International Trade ....$2,000   PAC
Sea Transport..$3,800
    CSX Corp*...$3,000   PAC

Labor

Labor $4,500

Public Sector Unions $4,000
    National Assn Retired Federal Employees ....$4,000   PAC

Ideological/Single-Issue

Ideological/Single-Issue $13,942

Republican/Conservative.....................................$1,669
    None over $1,000
Leadership PACs...$4,000
    Campaign America (Bob Dole) ....$2,000   PAC
    Republican Leader's Fund (Bob Michel) ....$2,000   PAC
Pro-Choice...$1,750
    None over $1,000
Misc Issues..$6,023
    Sierra Club ....$4,773   PAC
    Public Service Research Council ....$1,000   PAC

Other & Unknown

Other $29,084

Civil Servants/Public Officials............................$1,950
    US Small Business Administration ....$1,000   Indiv
Retired $26,934
    None over $1,000

Unknown $20,040

    Homemakers/Non-income earners $4,550
    No Employer Listed or Found $5,700
    Generic Occupation/Category Unknown $2,840
    Employer Listed/Category Unknown $6,950
        Brookside Co ....$1,000   Indiv
        Celeste Industries ....$1,000   Indiv

Independent expenditures opposing Gilchrest
    National Rifle Assn $1,020

Spending in Last 2 Elections

	1990	1992
Gilchrest	$264,932	$395,104
Opponent	$771,809	$1,553,849
Vote Pct	57%	52%

* Contributions came from more than one affiliate or subsidiary.

Paul E. Gillmor, R-Ohio (5)

First elected: 1988

1991-92 Total Receipts: $244,817
1992 Year-end Cash: $72,967

1991-92 Committees & Subcommittees

Administration
Accounts (Ranking Republican); Elections

Banking, Finance and Urban Affairs
Financial Institutions Supervision, Regulation and Insurance; Housing and Community Development; International Development, Finance, Trade and Monetary Policy

Public Works and Transportation
Economic Development; Investigations and Oversight; Water Resources

Select Committee on Narcotics Abuse and Control

Leading Contributors

Business

Agriculture $17,787

Crop Production & Basic Processing	**$6,275**	
American Sugarbeet Growers Assn	$2,350	PAC
Tobacco	**$2,700**	
RJR Nabisco	$1,400	PAC
Dairy	**$2,900**	
Milk Marketing Inc	$1,400	PAC
Associated Milk Producers	$1,000	PAC
Poultry & Eggs	**$1,000**	
Cooper Hatchery Inc	$1,000	Indiv
Agricultural Services/Products	**$1,512**	
Ohio Farm Bureau Federation	$1,262	PAC
Food Processing & Sales	**$1,650**	
None over $1,000		
Forestry & Forest Products	**$1,250**	
None over $1,000		

Communications/Electronics $9,750

Telephone Utilities	**$7,700**	
AT&T	$2,250	PAC
BellSouth Corp*	$1,550	PAC
Ohio Bell Telephone	$1,500	PAC
Electronics Mfg & Services	**$1,400**	
North American Philips Corp	$1,400	PAC

Source of Funds in 1992 Election

Source	Total	Pct
■ PACs	$160,137	65%
▨ Indivs $200+	$46,145	19%
☐ Indivs under $200	$27,009	11%
⊠ Other	$11,526	5%
Candidate	$0	0%
Party	$259	0%

Source of PAC Dollars by Sector

Source	Total	Pct
■ Business	$156,487	98%
▨ Labor	$1,750	1%
☐ Ideology/Single Issue	$1,650	1%

In-State vs. Out-of-State Contributions*

Source	Total	Pct
☐ In-State	$44,153	96%
▨ Out-of-state	$1,742	4%
No state listed	$0	

* by large individual contributors ($200 & above)

Construction $10,350

General Contractors	**$1,900**	
None over $1,000		
Home Builders	**$3,150**	
National Assn of Home Builders	$2,000	PAC
Fleetwood Enterprises	$1,150	PAC
Special Trade Contractors	**$2,500**	
National Electrical Contractors Assn	$1,000	PAC
Building Materials & Equipment	**$2,800**	
Owens-Corning Fiberglas	$2,300	PAC

Defense $1,400

Defense Aerospace	**$1,400**	
None over $1,000		

Energy & Natural Resources $12,150

Oil & Gas	**$5,200**	
Petroleum Marketers Assn	$2,000	PAC
Mining	**$1,000**	
None over $1,000		
Electric Utilities	**$5,950**	
American Electric Power*	$2,900	PAC
Ohio Edison	$1,150	PAC

Finance, Insurance & Real Estate $62,192

Commercial Banks	**$22,650**	
American Bankers Assn*	$7,000	PAC
Chase Manhattan	$2,800	PAC
JP Morgan & Co	$2,500	PAC
Barnett Banks Inc	$1,500	PAC
Independent Bankers Assn	$1,300	PAC
National City Corp	$1,150	PAC/Ind
First Chicago Corp	$1,000	PAC
Society Corp	$1,000	PAC

Contribution Totals by Sector

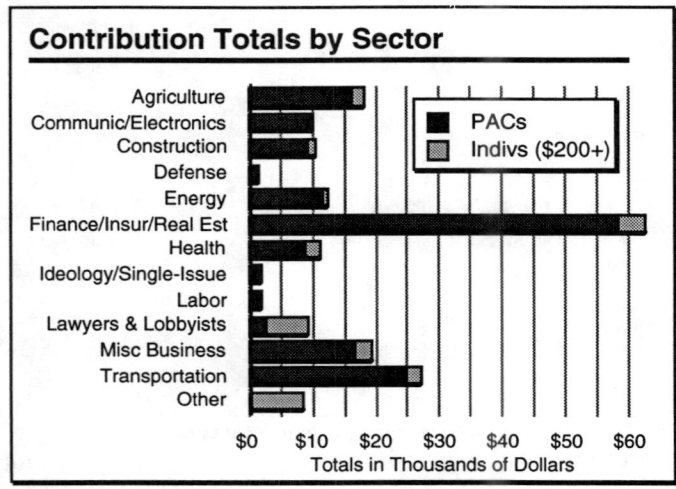

Agriculture
Communic/Electronics
Construction
Defense
Energy
Finance/Insur/Real Est
Health
Ideology/Single-Issue
Labor
Lawyers & Lobbyists
Misc Business
Transportation
Other

■ PACs
▨ Indivs ($200+)

$0 $10 $20 $30 $40 $50 $60
Totals in Thousands of Dollars

Finance/Credit Companies $1,050
  None over $1,000

Securities & Investment *$6,400*
  Goldman, Sachs & Co .... $1,000 PAC
  Morgan Stanley & Co .... $1,000 PAC

Insurance *$17,492*
  National Assn of Life Underwriters....................... $5,000 PAC
  Kemper Insurance .... $1,242 PAC/Ind
  National Assn of Independent Insurers .... $1,150 PAC
  Nationwide Corp .... $1,000 PAC
  Travelers Corp .... $1,000 PAC

Real Estate *$9,150*
  National Assn of Realtors .... $7,000 PAC

Accountants *$3,750*
  American Institute of CPA's .... $3,750 PAC

Health   **$10,850**

Health Professionals *$9,100*
  American Medical Assn....................................... $4,350 PAC
  American Academy of Ophthalmology .... $1,500 PAC

Pharmaceuticals/Health Products *$1,250*
  Syntex (USA) Inc .... $1,000 PAC

Lawyers & Lobbyists   **$9,100**

Lawyers & Lobbyists *$9,100*
  Cooper, Straub et al .... $1,000 Indiv

Misc Business   **$18,950**

Food & Beverage *$1,000*
  None over $1,000

Retail Sales *$1,000*
  None over $1,000

Chemical & Related Manufacturing *$1,300*
  None over $1,000

Misc Manufacturing & Distributing *$13,850*
  Brush Wellman .... $6,000 PAC
  Stone Container Corp .... $2,400 PAC
  Libbey-Owens-Ford.. $2,000 PAC
  Owens-Illinois .... $2,000 PAC

Transportation   **$26,900**

Air Transport *$12,800*
  United Parcel Service .... $5,400 PAC
  Federal Express Corp .... $5,000 PAC
  Aircraft Owners & Pilots Assn .... $1,000 PAC

Automotive *$8,050*
  National Auto Dealers Assn .... $3,900 PAC
  Ford Motor Co .... $2,400 PAC/Ind

Trucking *$3,900*
  None over $1,000

Railroads *$1,400*
  None over $1,000

Labor

Labor   **$1,750**

Public Sector Unions *$1,250*
  None over $1,000

Ideological/Single-Issue

Ideological/Single-Issue   **$1,650**
  None over $1,000

Other & Unknown

Other   **$8,403**

Education *$1,500*
  None over $1,000

Retired *$5,403*
  None over $1,000

Unknown   **$14,550**
  Homemakers/Non-income earners $1,750
  No Employer Listed or Found $1,000
  Generic Occupation/Category Unknown $1,250
  Employer Listed/Category Unknown $10,550
    Glasstech Inc .... $1,000 Indiv

Spending in Last 3 Elections

	1988	1990	1992
Gillmor	$769,548	$254,688	$254,988
Opponent	$850,819	$248	$0
Vote Pct	61%	69%	100%

* Contributions came from more than one affiliate or subsidiary.

663

Benjamin A. Gilman, R-NY (20)

First elected: 1972
1991-92 Total Receipts: $566,773
1992 Year-end Cash: $58,491

1991-92 Committees & Subcommittees

Foreign Affairs
Europe and the Middle East (Ranking Republican); International Operations

Post Office and Civil Service (Ranking Republican)
Investigations

Select Committee on Hunger

Select Committee on Narcotics Abuse and Control

Leading Contributors

Business

Agriculture $19,970

Crop Production & Basic Processing $6,995
None over $1,500

Dairy $7,750
Associated Milk Producers .... $7,000 PAC

Agricultural Services/Products $2,475
None over $1,500

Food Processing & Sales $1,875
None over $1,500

Communications/Electronics $9,675

Telephone Utilities $3,875
AT&T .... $2,000 PAC
New York Telephone .... $1,875 PAC/Ind

Computer Equipment & Services $2,500
HZI Research Center .... $2,000 Indiv

Construction $11,400

General Contractors $7,700
Ritangela Construction Corp .... $2,900 Indiv

Home Builders $2,000
None over $1,500

Defense $2,250

Defense Aerospace $1,750
None over $1,500

Source of Funds in 1992 Election

Source	Total	Pct
PACs	$212,397	37%
Indivs $200+	$193,516	34%
Indivs under $200	$148,816	26%
Other	$12,044	2%
Candidate	$0	0%
Party	$1,321	0%

Source of PAC Dollars by Sector

Source	Total	Pct
Business	$89,704	43%
Labor	$98,340	47%
Ideology/Single Issue	$20,425	10%

In-State vs. Out-of-State Contributions*

Source	Total	Pct
In-State	$152,781	81%
Out-of-state	$35,750	19%
No state listed	$3,750	

* by large individual contributors ($200 & above)

Energy & Natural Resources $6,880

Electric Utilities $6,380
Orange & Rockland Utilities .... $3,260 PAC

Finance, Insurance & Real Estate $30,819

Commercial Banks $7,544
Citicorp .... $2,499 PAC

Securities & Investment $3,150
None over $1,500

Insurance $5,625
Rhulen Agency .... $1,500 Indiv

Real Estate $12,650
National Assn of Realtors .... $5,500 PAC
Mesh Realty Corp .... $2,000 Indiv

Health $29,400

Health Professionals $18,700
American Medical Assn* .... $7,800 PAC
South Orange Obs Gyn .... $1,600 Indiv

Hospitals/Nursing Homes $1,775
Horton Hospital .... $1,525 Indiv

Pharmaceuticals/Health Products $8,675
Ciba-Geigy Corp .... $2,550 PAC/Ind
Hoffman-La Roche .... $2,250 PAC

Lawyers & Lobbyists $24,000

Lawyers & Lobbyists $24,000
Cassidy & Associates .... $3,875 Indiv
Swidler & Berlin .... $2,250 PAC/Ind
Rogers & Wells .... $1,750 Indiv
Granik, Silverman, Sandbar .... $1,500 Indiv

Contribution Totals by Sector

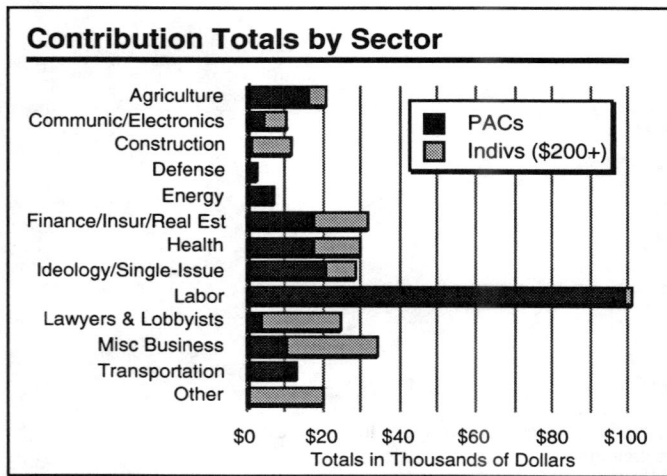

Agriculture, Communic/Electronics, Construction, Defense, Energy, Finance/Insur/Real Est, Health, Ideology/Single-Issue, Labor, Lawyers & Lobbyists, Misc Business, Transportation, Other

PACs / Indivs ($200+)

$0 $20 $40 $60 $80 $100
Totals in Thousands of Dollars

Misc Business $33,921

Food & Beverage **$3,200**
   None over $1,500

Retail Sales **$3,625**
   None over $1,500

Misc Services **$1,875**
   Duffy Leasing Corp ....$1,875   Indiv

Business Services **$5,500**
   Advo-System Inc ....$2,000   PAC
   GLM Security & Sound Inc ....$1,500   Indiv

Misc Business **$2,175**
   Regal Bag Co ....$1,500   Indiv

Misc Manufacturing & Distributing **$8,420**
   Monroe Wire & Cable Corp ....$2,150   Indiv

Textiles **$6,150**
   Bermaha Textile Co ....$2,300   Indiv

Transportation $12,655

Air Transport **$9,355**
   United Parcel Service.................................$4,980   PAC
   Chromalloy Gas Turbine Corp ....$2,000   PAC

Automotive **$2,500**
   Auto Dealers & Drivers for Free Trade ....$1,500   PAC

Labor

Labor $100,332

Building Trade Unions **$14,475**
   Carpenters & Joiners Union* ....$5,300   PAC
   Operating Engineers Union* ....$3,300   PAC
   Laborers' Political League ....$3,000   PAC

Industrial Unions **$10,732**
   United Auto Workers ....$3,655   PAC
   Intl Brotherhood of Electrical Workers* ....$3,192   Indiv

Transportation Unions $24,250
   Teamsters Union ....$7,075   PAC
   Air Line Pilots Assn ....$5,500   PAC
   International Longshoremen's Assn ....$4,500   PAC
   Marine Engineers Union* ....$3,000   PAC
   Transport Workers Union ....$2,800   PAC

Public Sector Unions **$49,500**
   National Assn of Letter Carriers ....$10,000   PAC
   American Postal Workers Union ....$7,500   PAC
   National Assn of Postmasters ....$5,525   PAC
   National Assn Retired Federal Employees ....$5,500   PAC
   American Federation of Teachers ....$4,600   PAC
   National Rural Letter Carriers Assn ....$3,000   PAC
   American Fedn of St/Cnty/Munic Employees ......$2,500   PAC
   National League of Postmasters ....$2,000   PAC
   National Assn of Postal Supervisors ....$1,500   PAC

Ideological/Single-Issue

Ideological/Single-Issue $28,125

Foreign & Defense Policy **$2,350**
   None over $1,500

Pro-Israel **$14,050**
   National PAC ....$5,000   PAC
   Maryland Assn for Concerned Citizens ......$1,500   PAC

Human Rights **$7,500**
   National Albanian American PAC ....$5,000   PAC
   Human Rights Campaign Fund ....$2,000   PAC

Misc Issues **$2,800**
   National Cmte to Preserve Social Security ....$1,500   PAC

Other & Unknown

Other $19,450

Civil Servants/Public Officials **$1,800**
   None over $1,500

Education **$3,300**
   None over $1,500

Retired **$9,000**
   None over $1,500

Other **$5,350**
   Syda Foundation ....$3,350   Indiv
   United Jewish Appeal ....$2,000   Indiv

Unknown $71,873
   Homemakers/Non-income earners $6,480
   No Employer Listed or Found $15,565
   Generic Occupation/Category Unknown $1,500
   Employer Listed/Category Unknown $48,328
      Finklestein, Kaplan et al ....$1,800   Indiv
      Gibraltar Co ....$1,600   Indiv
      Dutchess Center Co ....$1,500   Indiv
      HVAC Corp ....$1,500   Indiv
      Ira Green Inc ....$1,500   Indiv
      SMG Management Agency ....$1,500   Indiv

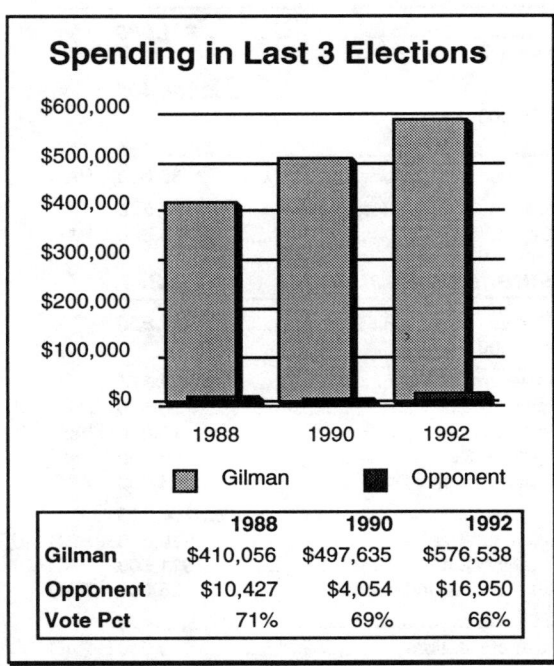

Spending in Last 3 Elections

	1988	1990	1992
Gilman	$410,056	$497,635	$576,538
Opponent	$10,427	$4,054	$16,950
Vote Pct	71%	69%	66%

* Contributions came from more than one affiliate or
subsidiary.

Newt Gingrich, R-Ga (6)

First elected: 1978

1991-92 Total Receipts: $2,507,668
1992 Year-end Cash: $25,365

1991-92 Committees & Subcommittees

Administration
Accounts; Procurement and Printing

Joint Committee on Printing

Leading Contributors

Business

Agriculture	$76,575

Crop Production & Basic Processing $11,225
  None over $5,000
Tobacco $9,500
  RJR Nabisco .... $5,000 PAC
Dairy $9,700
  Schwan's Sales Enterprises .... $5,700 Indiv
Poultry & Eggs $5,500
  None over $5,000
Food Processing & Sales $26,250
  Flowers Industries .... $12,500 PAC/Ind
Forestry & Forest Products $8,700
  None over $5,000

Communications/Electronics	$69,875

Printing & Publishing $5,200
  None over $5,000
Media/Entertainment $31,200
  National Cable Television Assn .... $10,000 PAC
Telephone Utilities $15,000
  None over $5,000
Electronics Mfg & Services $7,200
  None over $5,000
Computer Equipment & Services $6,550
  None over $5,000

Construction	$47,400

General Contractors $15,650
  None over $5,000

Contribution Totals by Sector

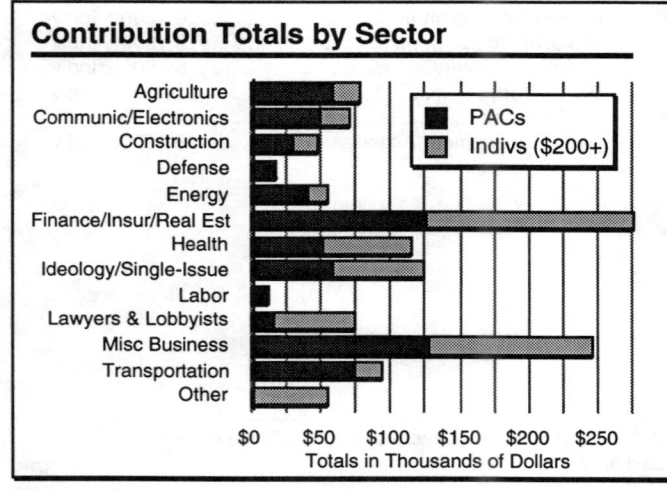

Agriculture
Communic/Electronics
Construction
Defense
Energy
Finance/Insur/Real Est
Health
Ideology/Single-Issue
Labor
Lawyers & Lobbyists
Misc Business
Transportation
Other

■ PACs
▨ Indivs ($200+)

$0 $50 $100 $150 $200 $250
Totals in Thousands of Dollars

Source of Funds in 1992 Election

Source	Total	Pct
■ PACs	$756,347	30%
▨ Indivs $200+	$778,188	30%
☐ Indivs under $200	$680,255	27%
▨ Other	$337,967	13%
Candidate	$0	0%
Party	$64,996	3%

Source of PAC Dollars by Sector

Source	Total	Pct
■ Business	$577,447	89%
▨ Labor	$11,000	2%
☐ Ideology/Single Issue	$57,456	9%

In-State vs. Out-of-State Contributions*

Source	Total	Pct
☐ In-State	$422,911	55%
▨ Out-of-state	$342,691	45%
No state listed	$6,500	

*** by large individual contributors ($200 & above)**

Home Builders $10,000
  National Assn of Home Builders .... $5,000 PAC
Special Trade Contractors $8,050
  None over $5,000
Building Materials & Equipment $10,950
  None over $5,000

Defense	$17,375

Defense Aerospace $13,125
  Lockheed Corp .... $5,500 PAC/Ind

Energy & Natural Resources	$54,130

Oil & Gas $31,980
  None over $5,000
Mining $6,400
  None over $5,000
Misc Energy $6,250
  Cooper Industries .... $5,000 PAC
Electric Utilities $7,500
  Southern Co* .... $5,500 PAC

Finance, Insurance & Real Estate	$274,247

Commercial Banks $20,850
  None over $5,000
Securities & Investment $63,375
  Morgan Stanley & Co .... $6,500 PAC/Ind
  Account Portfolios LP .... $5,800 Indiv
  Gilder, Gagnon & Co .... $5,000 Indiv
  National Venture Capital Assn .... $5,000 PAC
Insurance $84,513
  Golden Rule Insurance Co .... $20,565 PAC/Ind
  American Family Corp .... $11,500 PAC
  National Assn of Life Underwriters .... $5,000 PAC
Real Estate $56,459
  National Assn of Realtors .... $10,000 PAC

Accountants $14,850	
American Institute of CPA's $10,000	PAC
Misc Finance $25,450	
None over $5,000	

Health — $114,360

Health Professionals $75,510	
American Medical Assn $9,400	PAC
T2 Medical Inc $7,000	PAC
American Chiropractic Assn $5,000	PAC
American Dental Assn $5,000	PAC
Hospitals/Nursing Homes $11,650	
American Hospital Assn $5,000	PAC
Health Services $15,700	
Healthsouth Rehabilitation Corp $12,500	Indiv
Pharmaceuticals/Health Products $10,750	
None over $5,000	

Lawyers & Lobbyists — $73,759

Lawyers & Lobbyists $73,759	
Sutherland, Asbill & Brennan $5,600	Indiv
Kilpatrick & Cody $5,300	Indiv

Misc Business — $244,434

Business Associations $8,510	
National Fedn of Independent Business $5,010	PAC
Food & Beverage $72,049	
Cracker Barrel Old Country Store Inc $10,000	PAC
S&A Restaurant Corp $10,000	PAC
National Restaurant Assn $9,999	PAC
Coca-Cola Co $8,000	PAC/Ind
Outback Steakhouse Inc $7,500	PAC/Ind
Chili's Inc $6,000	PAC
Beer, Wine & Liquor $13,800	
National Beer Wholesalers Assn $9,500	PAC
Retail Sales $21,600	
None over $5,000	
Misc Services $6,000	
None over $5,000	
Business Services $23,625	
Crouse Communications $5,000	Indiv

Lodging/Tourism $7,150	
None over $5,000	
Chemical & Related Manufacturing $15,450	
None over $5,000	
Misc Manufacturing & Distributing $56,900	
Vollrath Co $10,000	PAC
Southwire Co $8,000	Indiv
Textiles $14,600	
None over $5,000	

Transportation — $93,365

Air Transport $46,615	
Aircraft Owners & Pilots Assn $10,000	PAC
United Parcel Service $10,000	PAC
Delta Airlines $9,800	PAC/Ind
General Electric $5,825	PAC/Ind
Automotive $29,200	
Americans for Free International Trade $7,500	PAC
National Auto Dealers Assn $5,000	PAC
Trucking $9,800	
None over $5,000	

Labor

Labor	**$11,000**
Transportation Unions $9,500	
Marine Engineers Union* $7,000	PAC

Ideological/Single-Issue

Ideological/Single-Issue	**$122,423**
Republican/Conservative $60,307	
Loose Group $10,000	PAC
Pro-Israel $36,700	
National PAC $5,000	PAC
Pro-Life $5,711	
None over $5,000	
Gun Rights/Gun Control $9,900	
National Rifle Assn $9,900	PAC
Misc Issues $5,555	
None over $5,000	

Other & Unknown

Other	**$54,370**
Civil Servants/Public Officials $8,770	
None over $5,000	
Retired $41,350	
None over $5,000	

Unknown	**$166,192**
Homemakers/Non-income earners $37,090	
No Employer Listed or Found $70,477	
Employer Listed/Category Unknown $55,825	
None over $5,000	

Independent expenditures supporting Gingrich
National Assn of Realtors $60,000

Independent expenditures opposing Gingrich
Public Citizen $82,522
Clean Up Congress $17,906

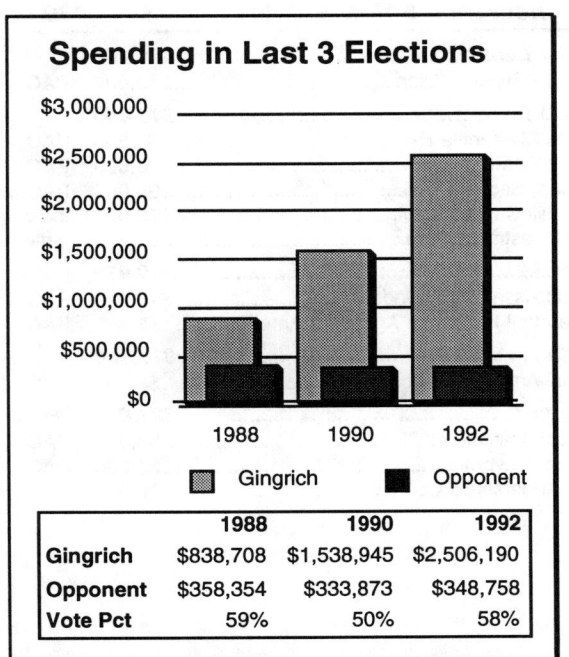

Spending in Last 3 Elections

	1988	1990	1992
Gingrich	$838,708	$1,538,945	$2,506,190
Opponent	$358,354	$333,873	$348,758
Vote Pct	59%	50%	58%

Legend: Gingrich, Opponent

---

* Contributions came from more than one affiliate or subsidiary.

Dan Glickman, D-Kan (4)

First elected: 1976

1991-92 Total Receipts: $873,194
1992 Year-end Cash: $18,743

1991-92 Committees & Subcommittees

Agriculture
Conservation, Credit and Rural Development; Department Operations, Research and Foreign Agriculture; Wheat, Soybeans and Feed Grains (Chairman)

Judiciary
Economic and Commercial Law; Intellectual Property and Judicial Administration

Science, Space and Technology
Technology and Competitiveness

Select Committee on Intelligence

Leading Contributors

Business

Agriculture $51,850

Crop Production & Basic Processing	**$17,350**	
Cargill Inc	$3,000	PAC/Ind
Poultry & Eggs	**$3,500**	
None over $2,500		
Agricultural Services/Products	**$10,150**	
None over $2,500		
Food Processing & Sales	**$17,000**	
Pepsico Inc	$2,550	PAC
ConAgra Inc	$2,500	PAC

Communications/Electronics $34,950

Printing & Publishing	**$4,950**	
None over $2,500		
Media/Entertainment	**$16,500**	
National Cable Television Assn	$5,000	PAC
Telephone Utilities	**$12,500**	
United Telecommunications	$5,000	PAC

Construction $7,250

Building Materials & Equipment	**$3,000**	
None over $2,500		

Source of Funds in 1992 Election

Source	Total	Pct
PACs	$421,726	48%
Indivs $200+	$312,126	35%
Indivs under $200	$94,730	11%
Other	$51,449	6%
Candidate	$0	0%
Party	$14,087	2%

Source of PAC Dollars by Sector

Source	Total	Pct
Business	$266,025	64%
Labor	$88,850	21%
Ideology/Single Issue	$63,700	15%

In-State vs. Out-of-State Contributions*

Source	Total	Pct
In-State	$142,187	46%
Out-of-state	$165,689	54%
No state listed	$4,250	

* by large individual contributors ($200 & above)

Defense $10,500

Defense Aerospace	**$8,000**	
Textron Inc	$2,500	PAC

Energy & Natural Resources $34,850

Oil & Gas	**$28,850**	
Sooner Pipe & Supply	$4,500	Indiv
Frances Oil & Gas Inc	$4,000	Indiv
Coastal Corp	$3,000	PAC
Koch Industries	$2,700	PAC/Ind
Waste Management	**$3,500**	
None over $2,500		

Finance, Insurance & Real Estate $148,439

Commercial Banks	**$20,100**	
American Bankers Assn	$9,000	PAC
Securities & Investment	**$45,450**	
Chicago Mercantile Exchange	$7,500	PAC
Chicago Board of Trade	$6,000	PAC
Goldman, Sachs & Co	$5,000	PAC/Ind
Forest Hill Capital Corp	$3,000	Indiv
Tudor Investment Corp	$2,500	Indiv
Insurance	**$39,939**	
National Assn of Life Underwriters	$10,000	PAC
Independent Insurance Agents of America	$5,499	PAC
Real Estate	**$17,800**	
National Assn of Realtors	$6,000	PAC
Accountants	**$21,050**	
American Institute of CPA's	$8,000	PAC
Coopers & Lybrand	$5,000	PAC
Arthur Andersen & Co	$2,500	PAC

Contribution Totals by Sector

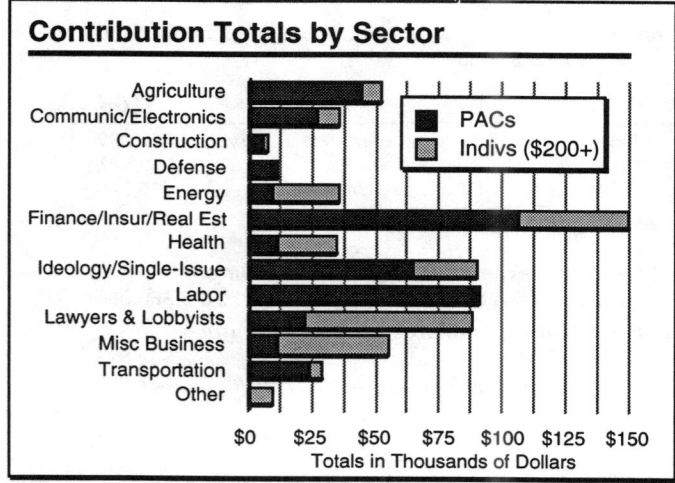

Agriculture
Communic/Electronics
Construction
Defense
Energy
Finance/Insur/Real Est
Health
Ideology/Single-Issue
Labor
Lawyers & Lobbyists
Misc Business
Transportation
Other

■ PACs
▨ Indivs ($200+)

$0 $25 $50 $75 $100 $125 $150
Totals in Thousands of Dollars

Health $34,130

Health Professionals $25,780
    Drs Kuhn & Kogan Chartered ....$4,000   Indiv
    American Medical Assn......................................$3,000   PAC

Hospitals/Nursing Homes $2,500
    None over $2,500

Pharmaceuticals/Health Products $5,250
    None over $2,500

Lawyers & Lobbyists $86,903

Lawyers & Lobbyists.................................$86,903
    Akin, Gump et al...$6,804   PAC/Ind
    Assn of Trial Lawyers of America ....$5,000   PAC
    Render, Kamas & Hammond ....$4,000   Indiv
    Johnston & Johnston...$2,850   Indiv

Misc Business $54,582

Food & Beverage $2,800
    None over $2,500

Beer, Wine & Liquor $6,900
    None over $2,500

Retail Sales...$7,657
    None over $2,500

Business Services $8,350
    Sutherland Capital Management ....$4,000   Indiv

Chemical & Related Manufacturing $4,250
    None over $2,500

Misc Manufacturing & Distributing $21,500
    Glickman Inc ....$4,000   Indiv

Transportation $27,850

Air Transport $23,250
    Aircraft Owners & Pilots Assn ....$7,000   PAC
    Boeing Co ....$3,750   PAC/Ind
    Beech Aircraft ....$2,500   PAC

Labor

Labor $89,550

Building Trade Unions $13,000
    Carpenters & Joiners Union ....$5,500   PAC
    Laborers' Political League ....$4,000   PAC
    Plumbers/Pipefitters Union................................$2,500   PAC

Industrial Unions $33,550
    Machinists/Aerospace Workers Union ....$10,000   PAC
    Intl Brotherhood of Electrical Workers ....$7,500   PAC
    United Auto Workers ....$6,000   PAC
    Rubber Cork Linoleum & Plastic Workers ....$5,000   PAC
    Communications Workers of America ....$2,500   PAC

Transportation Unions $11,500
    Teamsters Union ....$6,000   PAC

Public Sector Unions $24,500
    National Education Assn ....$10,000   PAC
    National Assn Retired Federal Employees ....$7,000   PAC
    American Fedn of St/Cnty/Munic Employees ......$2,500   PAC

Misc Unions...$7,000
    Food & Commercial Workers Union ....$6,000   PAC

Ideological/Single-Issue

Ideological/Single-Issue $88,589

Democratic/Liberal $6,450
    National Cmte for an Effective Congress ....$5,000   PAC

Leadership PACs $8,000
    House Leadership Fund (Tom Foley) ....$6,000   PAC

Pro-Israel $59,639
    Hudson Valley PAC...$5,000   PAC
    National PAC ....$5,000   PAC
    St Louisians for Better Government ....$2,500   PAC

Human Rights $8,500
    KidsPAC ....$8,000   PAC

Misc Issues..$5,500
    None over $2,500

Other & Unknown

Other $8,850

Civil Servants/Public Officials............$2,500
    None over $2,500

Retired $3,400
    None over $2,500

Unknown $51,708

    Homemakers/Non-income earners $11,601
    No Employer Listed or Found $8,850
    Employer Listed/Category Unknown $31,257
        None over $2,500

Independent expenditures opposing Glickman
    National Rifle Assn $52,080
    Eagle Forum $5,390

Spending in Last 3 Elections

	1988	1990	1992
Glickman	$545,755	$355,581	$1,046,769
Opponent	$149,035	$4,417	$392,137
Vote Pct	64%	71%	52%

Legend: Glickman, Opponent

Henry B. Gonzalez, D-Texas (20)

First elected: 1961

1991-92 Total Receipts:	$50,423
1992 Year-end Cash:	$18,039

1991-92 Committees & Subcommittees

Banking, Finance and Urban Affairs (Chairman)
Consumer Affairs and Coinage; Domestic Monetary Policy; General Oversight and Investigations; Housing and Community Development (Chairman); Policy Research and Insurance

Leading Contributors

Business

Construction	$1,000

Home Builders **$1,000**
    Ray Ellison Industries ....$1,000 PAC

Energy & Natural Resources	$1,250

Oil & Gas **$1,250**
    None over $1,000

Finance, Insurance & Real Estate	$3,500

Savings & Loans **$1,000**
    Texas Savings & Loan League ....$1,000 PAC

Securities & Investment **$1,000**
    Advantage Capital Corp ....$1,000 Indiv

Insurance **$1,500**
    National Assn of Life Underwriters ....$1,000 PAC
    Morton Companies ....$1,000 Indiv

Misc Finance **$1,000**
    McCombs Enterprises ....$1,000 Indiv

Lawyers & Lobbyists	$5,700

Lawyers & Lobbyists **$5,700**
    Assn of Trial Lawyers of America ....$5,000 PAC

Transportation	$3,000

Automotive **$3,000**
    National Auto Dealers Assn ....$2,000 PAC
    Tom Benson Chevrolet ....$1,000 Indiv

Source of Funds in 1992 Election

Source	Total	Pct
PACs	$11,525	23%
Indivs $200+	$17,900	35%
Indivs under $200	$13,615	27%
Other	$7,520	15%
Candidate	$0	0%
Party	$137	0%

Source of PAC Dollars by Sector

Source	Total	Pct
Business	$5,900	70%
Labor	$2,500	30%
Ideology/Single Issue	$0	0%

In-State vs. Out-of-State Contributions*

Source	Total	Pct
In-State	$16,400	92%
Out-of-state	$1,500	8%
No state listed	$0	

* by large individual contributors ($200 & above)

Contribution Totals by Sector

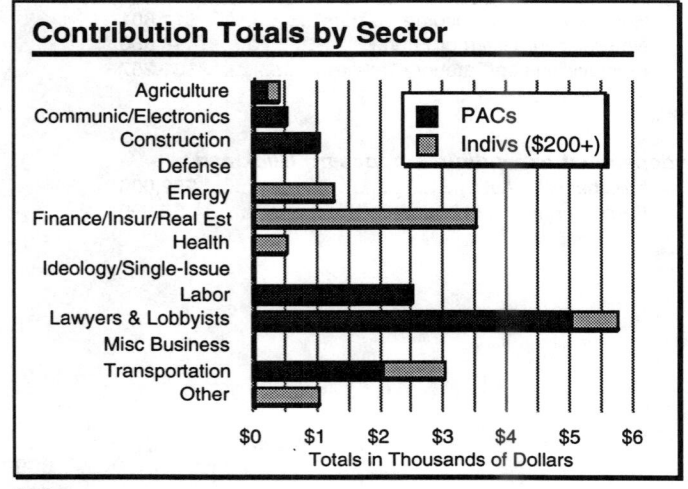

Legend: ■ PACs ▨ Indivs ($200+)

Sectors: Agriculture, Communic/Electronics, Construction, Defense, Energy, Finance/Insur/Real Est, Health, Ideology/Single-Issue, Labor, Lawyers & Lobbyists, Misc Business, Transportation, Other

Totals in Thousands of Dollars ($0 $1 $2 $3 $4 $5 $6)

Labor

Labor	$2,500

Public Sector Unions..$2,000
    National Education Assn ....$1,500 PAC

Other & Unknown

Other	$1,000

Retired..$1,000
    None over $1,000

Unknown	$9,750

No Employer Listed or Found $3,500
Generic Occupation/Category Unknown $1,000
Employer Listed/Category Unknown $5,250
    Jaffe Companies ....$3,250 Indiv
    Dement Companies ....$1,000 Indiv
    York International ....$1,000 Indiv

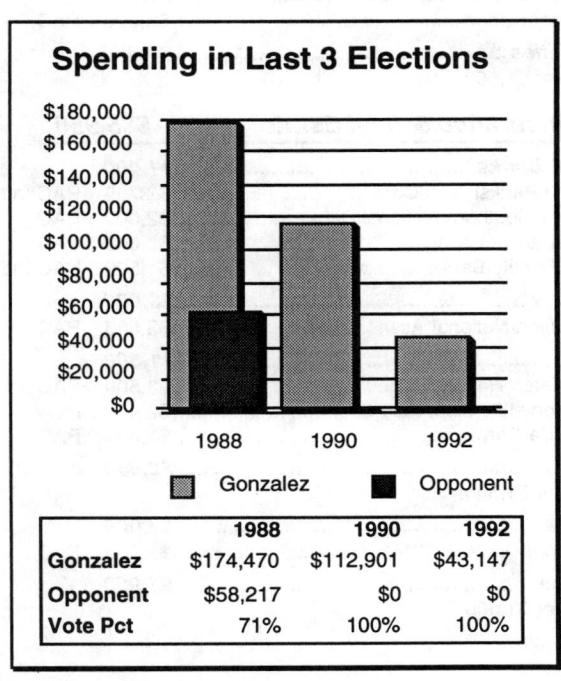

Spending in Last 3 Elections

	1988	1990	1992
Gonzalez	$174,470	$112,901	$43,147
Opponent	$58,217	$0	$0
Vote Pct	71%	100%	100%

Robert W. Goodlatte, R-Va (6)

First elected: 1992

1991-92 Total Receipts: $464,535
1992 Year-end Cash: $12,486

1993-94 Committees & Subcommittees

Agriculture
Livestock; Specialty Crops and Natural Resources

Judiciary
Administrative Law and Governmental Relations; Economic and
Commercial Law

Leading Contributors

Business

Agriculture $20,489

Tobacco	**$2,750**	
Philip Morris	$1,500	PAC
Dairy	**$1,500**	
None over $1,500		
Poultry & Eggs	**$1,500**	
National Broiler Council	$1,500	PAC
Food Processing & Sales	**$6,817**	
Pepsico Inc	$3,300	PAC/Ind
Flowers Industries	$2,000	PAC
Forestry & Forest Products	**$5,950**	
Westvaco Corp	$3,000	PAC

Communications/Electronics $7,696

Telephone Utilities	**$3,050**	
None over $1,500		
Computer Equipment & Services	**$2,156**	
None over $1,500		

Construction $13,150

General Contractors	**$7,700**	
Lanford Brothers Co	$2,000	Indiv
Associated General Contractors	$1,500	PAC
Building Materials & Equipment	**$3,700**	
Taylor-Ramsey Corp	$3,000	Indiv

Source of Funds in 1992 Election

Source	Total	Pct
■ PACs	$120,492	24%
▦ Indivs $200+	$149,194	30%
☐ Indivs under $200	$121,992	25%
▨ Other	$104,606	21%
Candidate	$57,951	12%
Party	$46,655	9%

Source of PAC Dollars by Sector

Source	Total	Pct
■ Business	$105,850	88%
☐ Labor	$2,000	2%
☐ Ideology/Single Issue	$12,024	10%

In-State vs. Out-of-State Contributions*

Source	Total	Pct
☐ In-State	$141,004	95%
■ Out-of-state	$7,400	5%
No state listed	$750	

* by large individual contributors ($200 & above)

Defense $4,250

Misc Defense	**$4,000**	
BDM International	$2,500	PAC/Ind
Tenneco Inc	$1,500	PAC

Energy & Natural Resources $18,050

Oil & Gas	**$8,950**	
Chevron Corp	$2,500	PAC
Mining	**$3,450**	
None over $1,500		
Misc Energy	**$4,000**	
Cooper Industries	$3,000	PAC
Electric Utilities	**$1,650**	
None over $1,500		

Finance, Insurance & Real Estate $35,950

Commercial Banks	**$11,400**	
Dominion Bankshares Corp	$2,750	PAC/Ind
Citizens & Southern National Bank	$2,000	PAC
Virginia Bankers Assn	$2,000	PAC
Central Fidelity Banks	$1,500	PAC/Ind
Credit Unions	**$3,000**	
Credit Union National Assn	$3,000	PAC
Insurance	**$11,300**	
Consolidated Healthcare Inc	$3,500	PAC
First Colony Life Insurance Co	$2,400	Indiv
Nationwide Corp	$1,800	PAC
Real Estate	**$2,650**	
None over $1,500		
Accountants	**$4,000**	
American Institute of CPA's	$2,500	PAC
Misc Finance	**$2,900**	
None over $1,500		

Contribution Totals by Sector

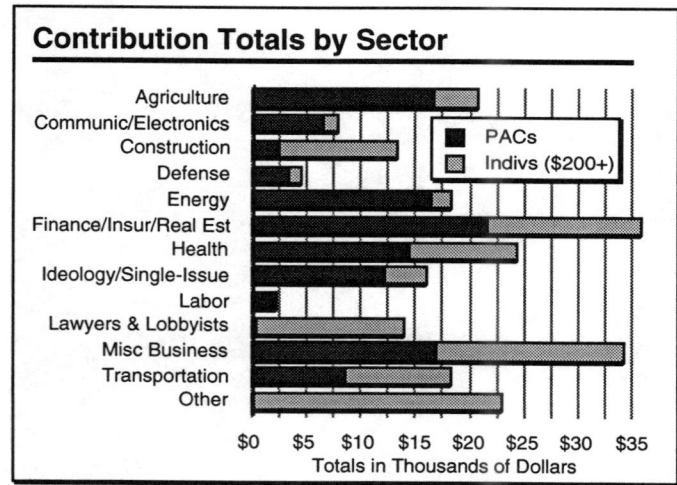

Agriculture, Communic/Electronics, Construction, Defense, Energy, Finance/Insur/Real Est, Health, Ideology/Single-Issue, Labor, Lawyers & Lobbyists, Misc Business, Transportation, Other

■ PACs
▦ Indivs ($200+)

$0 $5 $10 $15 $20 $25 $30 $35
Totals in Thousands of Dollars

Health — $24,200

Health Professionals $16,700
    American Medical Assn...........................$4,000 PAC
    American Academy of Ophthalmology ....$2,500 PAC
    Valley Nephrology ....$1,600 Indiv
Hospitals/Nursing Homes $5,000
    American Hospital Assn ....$1,500 PAC
Pharmaceuticals/Health Products $2,500
    None over $1,500

Lawyers & Lobbyists — $14,240

Lawyers & Lobbyists $14,240
    Glenn, Flippin et al ....$4,390 Indiv
    Woods, Rogers & Hazelgrove ....$2,300 Indiv
    Moss & Rocovich ....$2,000 Indiv

Misc Business — $34,114

Food & Beverage $3,500
    None over $1,500
Beer, Wine & Liquor $4,000
    National Beer Wholesalers Assn ....$2,000 PAC
    Bova Distributing Co ....$1,500 Indiv
Retail Sales $7,070
    Advance Stores ....$2,000 Indiv
    Entre Computers ....$1,820 Indiv
Misc Services $1,700
    None over $1,500
Business Services $2,750
    None over $1,500
Chemical & Related Manufacturing $4,400
    Harrington Corp ....$1,900 Indiv
Misc Manufacturing & Distributing $9,350
    McKendree & Co ....$2,000 Indiv
    Stone Container Corp ....$2,000 PAC
    Fabricated Metals Inc ....$1,500 Indiv

Transportation — $18,150

Air Transport $4,500
    Cambata Aviation ....$2,000 Indiv
Automotive $10,650
    National Auto Dealers Assn ....$5,000 PAC
    Avis Rent-a-Car ....$2,000 Indiv
Trucking $2,750
    None over $1,500

Labor

Labor — $2,000

Public Sector Unions $2,000
    National Assn Retired Federal Employees ....$1,500 PAC

Ideological/Single-Issue

Ideological/Single-Issue — $15,824

Republican/Conservative $9,324
    V-PAC ....$5,000 PAC
Leadership PACs $1,500
    None over $1,500
Misc Issues $3,000
    Right to Work PAC ....$2,000 PAC

Other & Unknown

Other — $22,725

Retired $19,575
    None over $1,500

Unknown — $38,190

    Homemakers/Non-income earners $7,350
    No Employer Listed or Found $6,100
    Employer Listed/Category Unknown $24,740
        None over $1,500

Independent expenditures supporting Goodlatte
    National Right to Life PAC $4,604

Spending in Last Election

	1992
Goodlatte	$452,048
Opponent	$592,070
Vote Pct	60%

Bill Goodling, R-Pa (19)

First elected: 1974

1991-92 Total Receipts: $200,014
1992 Year-end Cash: $4,312

1991-92 Committees & Subcommittees

Education and Labor (Ranking Republican)
Elementary, Secondary and Vocational Education (Ranking Republican); Postsecondary Education

Foreign Affairs
Europe and the Middle East

Leading Contributors

NOTE: Goodling reported taking no PAC funds during his 1992 campaign. The PACs listed below did report making contributions, however, and those contributions are recorded in the official FEC records.

Business

Agriculture		$4,000
Food Processing & Sales **$1,000**		
Snyders of Hanover $1,000	Indiv	
Forestry & Forest Products **$2,250**		
PH Glatfelter Co $1,250	Indiv	
Colony Papers Inc $1,000	Indiv	

Communications/Electronics		$4,400
Media/Entertainment **$3,300**		
Susquehanna Broadcasting $1,300	Indiv	
Cable TV of Carlisle $1,000	Indiv	
WSBA WARM 103 Radio $1,000	Indiv	

Construction		$6,550
General Contractors **$3,250**		
Adams Co Asphalt $1,750	Indiv	
Morton Building Inc $1,000	PAC	
Building Materials & Equipment **$3,300**		
Bradley Lifting Corp $1,300	Indiv	
Mann & Parker Lumber Co $1,000	Indiv	
Wolf Distributing Co $1,000	Indiv	

Energy & Natural Resources		$3,750
Mining **$3,650**		
Helm Coal Co $3,400	Indiv	

Source of Funds in 1992 Election

Source	Total	Pct
■ PACs	$0	0%
▨ Indivs $200+	$90,179	37%
☐ Indivs under $200	$88,789	36%
⊠ Other	$66,981	27%
Candidate	$0	0%
Party	$65,636	25%

Source of PAC Dollars by Sector

No PAC contributions reported

Source	Total	Pct
■ Business	$600	11%
▨ Labor	$0	0%
☐ Ideology/Single Issue	$4,800	89%

In-State vs. Out-of-State Contributions*

Source	Total	Pct
☐ In-State	$79,429	88%
■ Out-of-state	$10,750	12%
No state listed	$0	

* by large individual contributors ($200 & above)

Finance, Insurance & Real Estate		$4,075
Securities & Investment **$1,300**		
Hillman Co $1,300	Indiv	
Insurance **$1,825**		
Glatfelter Insurance Group $2,300	Indiv	

Health		$4,000
Health Professionals **$3,500**		
None over $1,000		

Lawyers & Lobbyists		$6,768
Lawyers & Lobbyists **$6,768**		
Johnson, Duffie et al $1,068	Indiv	

Misc Business		$9,450
Food & Beverage **$1,000**		
None over $1,000		
Retail Sales **$2,600**		
S Grumbacher & Son $1,600	Indiv	
Christmas Tree Hill $1,000	Indiv	
Misc Services **$3,450**		
Beauty Salon Operator $2,400	Indiv	
Misc Manufacturing & Distributing **$1,300**		
York Container Co $1,300	Indiv	

Transportation		$1,500
Automotive **$1,000**		
Saturn of Harrisburg $1,000	Indiv	

Contribution Totals by Sector

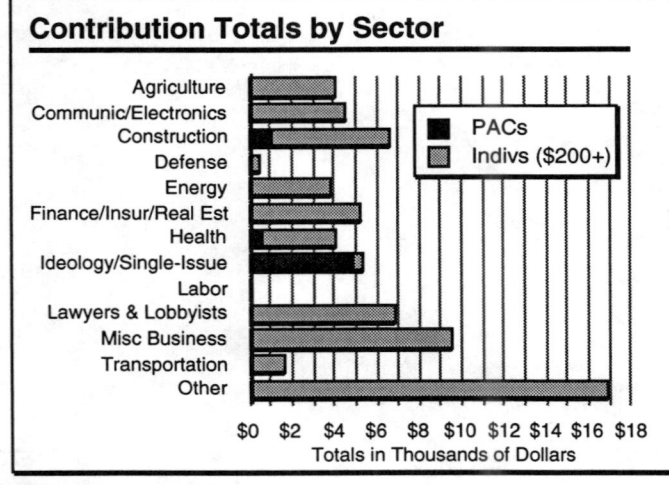

- Agriculture
- Communic/Electronics
- Construction
- Defense
- Energy
- Finance/Insur/Real Est
- Health
- Ideology/Single-Issue
- Labor
- Lawyers & Lobbyists
- Misc Business
- Transportation
- Other

■ PACs
▨ Indivs ($200+)

$0 $2 $4 $6 $8 $10 $12 $14 $16 $18
Totals in Thousands of Dollars

Ideological/Single-Issue

Ideological/Single-Issue	$5,300	
Republican/Conservative $5,300		
People for John Heinz Cmte $4,800		PAC

Other & Unknown

Other	$16,766	
Education...$7,500		
Triangle Tech Group $1,300		Indiv
Education Management Corp $1,000		Indiv
Rasmussen Business College $1,000		Indiv
Retired...$7,516		
None over $1,000		
Other $1,000		
None over $1,000		

Unknown	$28,620	
Homemakers/Non-income earners $1,750		
No Employer Listed or Found $10,950		
Employer Listed/Category Unknown $15,620		
J Giambalvo Motor Co $1,600		Indiv
Leonard Wherley Moving Systems Inc $1,470		Indiv
PII Affiliates $1,300		Indiv
Central Penn Sales $1,000		Indiv
KBA-Motter Corp $1,000		Indiv
Kruper, Danyo, Van Giesen $1,000		Indiv
Maple Press Co $1,000		Indiv

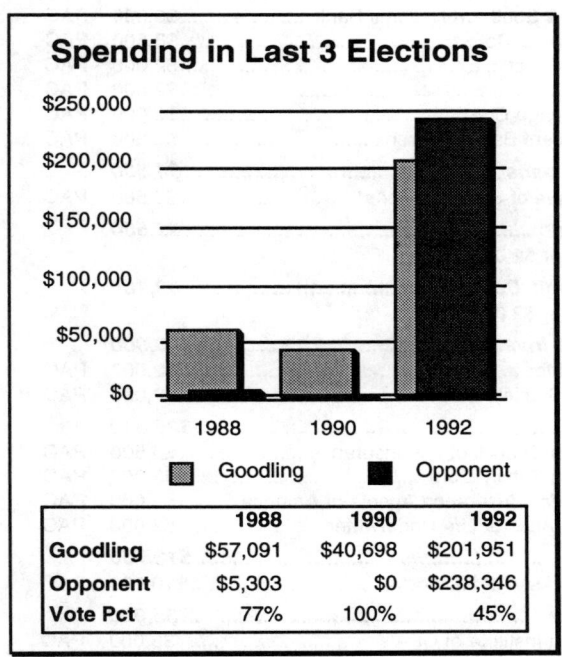

Spending in Last 3 Elections

	1988	1990	1992
Goodling	$57,091	$40,698	$201,951
Opponent	$5,303	$0	$238,346
Vote Pct	77%	100%	45%

Bart Gordon, D-Tenn (6)

First elected: 1984

1991-92 Total Receipts: $662,234
1992 Year-end Cash: $208,386

1991-92 Committees & Subcommittees

Rules
Legislative Process

Select Committee on Aging

Leading Contributors

Business

Agriculture	$29,500

Tobacco **$11,500**
    RJR Nabisco ....$3,500 PAC
    Philip Morris ....$3,000 PAC
    US Tobacco Co ....$2,500 PAC

Dairy **$7,000**
    Associated Milk Producers ....$3,000 PAC
    Dairymen Inc-Tennessee ....$3,000 PAC

Livestock **$4,500**
    Tennessee Walking Horse Breeders ....$2,500 PAC

Food Processing & Sales **$3,000**
    None over $2,000

Communications/Electronics	$20,200

Media/Entertainment **$5,400**
    ASCAP ....$2,000 PAC

Telephone Utilities **$12,500**
    BellSouth Corp* ....$6,000 PAC
    AT&T ....$4,000 PAC

Construction	$16,900

General Contractors **$11,750**
    Fluor Corp ....$10,000 PAC

Home Builders **$4,150**
    National Assn of Home Builders ....$2,750 PAC

Defense	$5,850

Defense Aerospace **$4,350**
    None over $2,000

Source of Funds in 1992 Election

Source	Total	Pct
PACs	$388,590	57%
Indivs $200+	$14,350	2%
Indivs under $200	$146,656	22%
Other	$130,518	19%
Candidate	$0	0%
Party	$18,730	3%

Source of PAC Dollars by Sector

Source	Total	Pct
Business	$272,110	70%
Labor	$105,550	27%
Ideology/Single Issue	$12,000	3%

In-State vs. Out-of-State Contributions*

Source	Total	Pct
In-State	$10,350	75%
Out-of-state	$3,500	25%
No state listed	$0	

* by large individual contributors ($200 & above)

Energy & Natural Resources	$17,500

Oil & Gas **$10,000**
    Columbia Gas System* ....$2,000 PAC

Electric Utilities **$2,500**
    None over $2,000

Waste Management **$2,500**
    Waste Management Inc ....$2,500 PAC

Finance, Insurance & Real Estate	$97,660

Commercial Banks **$28,700**
    American Bankers Assn ....$5,000 PAC
    Citizens & Southern National Bank ......$5,000 PAC
    JP Morgan & Co ....$3,500 PAC
    Bankers Trust ....$2,000 PAC
    Citicorp ....$2,000 PAC
    First Chicago Corp ....$2,000 PAC
    Independent Bankers Assn ....$2,000 PAC

Savings & Loans **$4,800**
    US League of Savings Assns* ....$3,500 PAC

Credit Unions **$2,500**
    None over $2,000

Finance/Credit Companies **$3,100**
    None over $2,000

Securities & Investment **$13,000**
    Dean Witter ....$2,000 PAC
    Morgan Stanley & Co ....$2,000 PAC

Insurance **$26,810**
    American Council of Life Insurance ......$3,500 PAC
    American Family Corp ....$3,000 PAC
    Independent Insurance Agents of America ....$3,000 PAC
    National Assn of Life Underwriters ......$3,000 PAC

Real Estate **$13,750**
    National Assn of Realtors ....$10,000 PAC

Accountants **$5,000**
    American Institute of CPA's ....$5,000 PAC

Contribution Totals by Sector

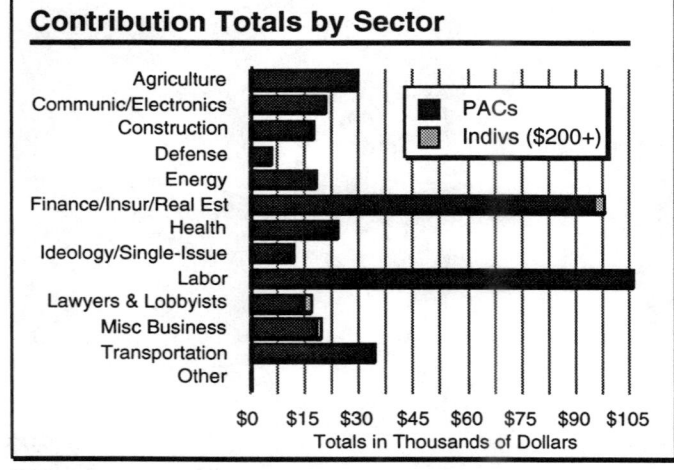

Legend: ■ PACs ▨ Indivs ($200+)

Categories: Agriculture, Communic/Electronics, Construction, Defense, Energy, Finance/Insur/Real Est, Health, Ideology/Single-Issue, Labor, Lawyers & Lobbyists, Misc Business, Transportation, Other

$0 $15 $30 $45 $60 $75 $90 $105
Totals in Thousands of Dollars

Health $23,750

Health Professionals **$15,750**
   American Medical Assn ....$4,850   PAC
   American Dental Assn ....$3,500   PAC
   National Assn of Pharmacists ....$2,500   PAC
Hospitals/Nursing Homes **$2,500**
   None over $2,000
Pharmaceuticals/Health Products **$5,500**
   Schering-Plough Corp ....$4,000   PAC

Lawyers & Lobbyists $16,750

Lawyers & Lobbyists **$16,750**
   Assn of Trial Lawyers of America ....$10,000   PAC

Misc Business $19,000

Beer, Wine & Liquor **$11,500**
   Wine Institute ....$2,500   PAC
Lodging/Tourism **$3,500**
   None over $2,000

Transportation $34,250

Air Transport **$18,500**
   Federal Express Corp ....$10,000   PAC
   United Parcel Service ....$3,500   PAC
Automotive **$9,250**
   National Auto Dealers Assn ....$3,000   PAC
Trucking **$2,500**
   None over $2,000
Railroads **$3,500**
   None over $2,000

Labor

Labor $105,550

Building Trade Unions **$16,000**
   Carpenters & Joiners Union ....$7,000   PAC
   Plumbers/Pipefitters Union ....$4,000   PAC
   Laborers' Political League ....$3,500   PAC
Industrial Unions **$39,500**
   United Steelworkers ....$15,000   PAC
   Rubber Cork Linoleum & Plastic Workers ....$8,000   PAC
   United Auto Workers ....$6,000   PAC
   Intl Brotherhood of Electrical Workers ....$3,000   PAC
   Communications Workers of America ....$2,500   PAC
Transportation Unions **$17,500**
   Transport Workers Union ....$3,500   PAC
   Air Line Pilots Assn ....$2,500   PAC
   Marine Engineers Dist 2 Maritime Officers ....$2,500   PAC
   Teamsters Union ....$2,500   PAC
Public Sector Unions **$28,550**
   National Assn Retired Federal Employees ....$7,000   PAC
   National Education Assn ....$6,500   PAC
   American Fedn of St/Cnty/Munic Employees ......$4,000   PAC
   National Assn of Letter Carriers ....$3,000   PAC
   American Postal Workers Union ....$2,000   PAC
Misc Unions **$4,000**
   Food & Commercial Workers Union ....$2,500   PAC

Ideological/Single-Issue

Ideological/Single-Issue $12,000

Democratic/Liberal **$2,500**
   National Cmte for an Effective Congress ....$2,500   PAC
Pro-Israel **$6,000**
   National PAC ....$5,000   PAC
Misc Issues **$3,500**
   National Cmte to Preserve Social Security ....$3,000   PAC

Other & Unknown

Unknown $4,100

   Employer Listed/Category Unknown $4,100
     None over $2,000

Spending in Last 3 Elections

	1988	1990	1992
Gordon	$454,346	$367,090	$988,920
Opponent	$12,635	$8,996	$181,515
Vote Pct	77%	67%	59%

---

* Contributions came from more than one affiliate or
subsidiary.

Porter J. Goss, R-Fla (14)

First elected: 1988

1991-92 Total Receipts: $419,508
1992 Year-end Cash: $106,397

1991-92 Committees & Subcommittees

Foreign Affairs
Arms Control, International Security and Science; Western Hemisphere Affairs

Merchant Marine and Fisheries
Coast Guard and Navigation; Fisheries and Wildlife Conservation and the Environment

Standards of Official Conduct

Leading Contributors

Business

Agriculture — $6,850

Crop Production & Basic Processing	$4,300	
Naples Tomato Growers	$3,000	Indiv
Livestock	$2,000	
Babcock Florida Co	$1,250	Indiv

Communications/Electronics — $9,252

Telephone Utilities	$3,500	
AT&T	$1,000	PAC
GTE Corp	$1,000	PAC
Southern Bell	$1,000	PAC
Telecom Services & Equipment	$1,000	
Palmer Communications	$1,000	PAC
Electronics Mfg & Services	$2,652	
Westinghouse Electric	$1,652	Indiv
Harris Corp	$1,000	PAC
Computer Equipment & Services	$1,300	
Fox Electronics	$1,300	Indiv

Construction — $7,150

General Contractors	$3,100	
Associated General Contractors	$1,000	PAC
Home Builders	$1,500	
Boran Craig Barber Contractor	$1,000	Indiv
Construction Services	$2,300	
Johnson Engineering Inc	$1,300	Indiv
Hole, Montez & Associates	$1,000	Indiv

Source of Funds in 1992 Election

Source	Total	Pct
PACs	$35,400	8%
Indivs $200+	$176,149	42%
Indivs under $200	$195,963	47%
Other	$11,996	3%
Candidate	$0	0%
Party	$4,100	1%

Source of PAC Dollars by Sector

Source	Total	Pct
Business	$33,400	93%
Labor	$0	0%
Ideology/Single Issue	$2,500	7%

In-State vs. Out-of-State Contributions*

Source	Total	Pct
In-State	$157,714	91%
Out-of-state	$15,335	9%
No state listed	$0	

* by large individual contributors ($200 & above)

Defense — $3,100

Defense Electronics	$3,100	
Loral Corp	$3,100	Indiv

Energy & Natural Resources — $2,650

Electric Utilities	$2,000	
ACRE (Action Cmte for Rural Electrification)	$1,000	PAC
Lee County Electric Coop Inc	$1,000	Indiv

Finance, Insurance & Real Estate — $38,235

Commercial Banks	$4,950	
Citizens & Southern National Bank	$2,000	PAC
C&S Bank	$1,000	Indiv
SunBanks	$1,000	PAC
Securities & Investment	$3,700	
Federated Investors Inc	$1,000	Indiv
Hixon Properties Inc	$1,000	Indiv
Insurance	$4,250	
Florida Agency Services Inc	$2,000	Indiv
Liberty Mutual Insurance	$1,000	PAC
Real Estate	$17,985	
Collier Enterprises	$2,000	Indiv
National Assn of Realtors	$2,000	PAC
Prudential Florida Realty	$1,900	Indiv
Cooper Companies	$1,835	Indiv
Lely Development Corp	$1,500	Indiv
Priscilla Murphy Real Estate	$1,500	Indiv
Bonita Bay Properties	$1,000	Indiv
First Union Corp	$1,000	PAC
Florida Real Estate Consultants	$1,000	Indiv
Lutgert Companies	$1,000	Indiv
Misc Finance	$6,500	
None over $1,000		

Contribution Totals by Sector

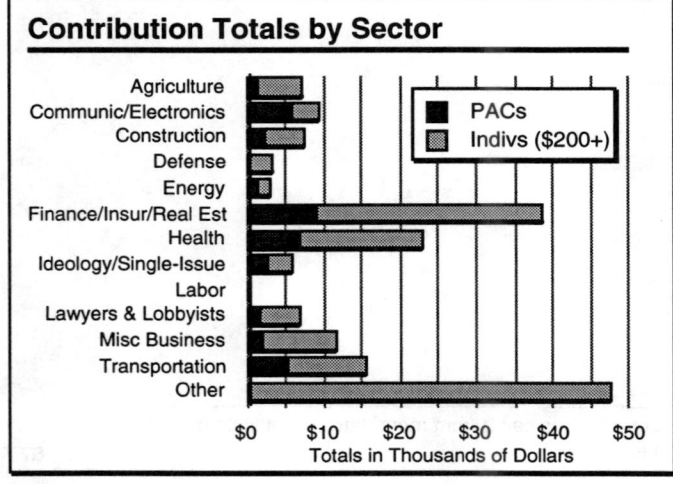

Agriculture
Communic/Electronics
Construction
Defense
Energy
Finance/Insur/Real Est
Health
Ideology/Single-Issue
Labor
Lawyers & Lobbyists
Misc Business
Transportation
Other

- PACs
- Indivs ($200+)

$0 $10 $20 $30 $40 $50
Totals in Thousands of Dollars

Health — $22,550

Health Professionals **$18,000**
    American Medical Assn* .... $3,000   PAC
    American Academy of Ophthalmology .... $1,000   PAC
    Cape Coral Medical Clinic .... $1,000   Indiv

Hospitals/Nursing Homes **$2,950**
    American Hospital Assn .... $1,500   PAC

Misc Health **$1,600**
    Health Management Assn .... $1,000   Indiv

Lawyers & Lobbyists — $6,461

Lawyers & Lobbyists **$6,461**
    Holland & Knight .... $1,500   PAC
    Cummings & Lockwood .... $1,000   Indiv

Misc Business — $11,250

Food & Beverage **$1,150**
    None over $1,000

Beer, Wine & Liquor **$1,200**
    None over $1,000

Misc Services **$1,000**
    None over $1,000

Business Services **$2,100**
    None over $1,000

Lodging/Tourism **$2,000**
    Hilton Grand Vacations .... $1,000   Indiv
    Royal Palm Travel .... $1,000   Indiv

Chemical & Related Manufacturing **$3,300**
    Goldberg, Goldstein et al .... $3,000   Indiv

Transportation — $15,250

Air Transport **$5,750**
    Barron Collier Co .... $3,500   Indiv
    Bar Harbor Airways .... $1,000   Indiv
    United Parcel Service .... $1,000   PAC

Automotive **$8,500**
    Palm Automotive .... $2,250   Indiv
    Americans for Free International Trade .... $1,000   PAC
    Auto Dealers & Drivers for Free Trade .... $1,000   PAC
    National Auto Dealers Assn .... $1,000   PAC
    Sam Galloway Ford .... $1,000   Indiv

Sea Transport **$1,000**
    Cruise PAC .... $1,000   PAC

Ideological/Single-Issue

Ideological/Single-Issue — $5,450

Republican/Conservative **$1,950**
    None over $1,000

Foreign & Defense Policy **$1,000**
    Free Cuba PAC .... $1,000   PAC

Pro-Israel **$2,500**
    National PAC .... $1,000   PAC

Other & Unknown

Other — $47,250

Retired **$47,000**
    None over $1,000

Unknown — $36,601

    Homemakers/Non-income earners $15,041
    No Employer Listed or Found $1,250
    Employer Listed/Category Unknown $22,810
        Wilson, Miller et al .... $2,000   Indiv
        Budd & Thompson .... $1,500   Indiv
        Gargiulo Inc .... $1,000   Indiv
        Lance Benefield .... $1,000   Indiv
        McHale, Ezzell & Co .... $1,000   Indiv
        Sanibel Marine & Investments .... $1,000   Indiv

Spending in Last 3 Elections

	1988	1990	1992
Goss	$836,224	$244,740	$414,185
Opponent	$200,296	$0	$16,880
Vote Pct	71%	100%	82%

Legend: Goss, Opponent

* Contributions came from more than one affiliate or subsidiary.

Bill Gradison, R-Ohio (2)

First elected: 1974

1991-92 Total Receipts: $111,258
1992 Year-end Cash: $458,452

1991-92 Committees & Subcommittees

Budget (Ranking Republican)

Ways and Means
Health (Ranking Republican)

Leading Contributors

NOTE: Gradison reported taking no PAC funds in his 1992 campaign. The PAC listed below did report making contributions, however, and those contributions are recorded in the official FEC records.

Business

Finance, Insurance & Real Esta	$12,793	
Securities & Investment	**$1,710**	
Morgenthaler Management Partners	$1,210	Indiv
Insurance	**$5,000**	
American Financial Corp	$1,250	Indiv
Golden Rule Insurance Co	$1,000	Indiv
Real Estate	**$1,000**	
Hart Realty	$1,000	Indiv
Accountants	**$4,000**	
Price Waterhouse	$4,000	PAC
Misc Finance	**$1,083**	
None over $1,000		

Health	$7,000	
Health Professionals	**$3,750**	
Cincinnati Eye Institute	$1,000	Indiv
Pharmaceuticals/Health Products	**$2,250**	
Pfizer Inc	$1,000	Indiv

Lawyers & Lobbyists	$9,000	
Lawyers & Lobbyists	**$9,000**	
McClure, Trotter & Mentz	$1,000	Indiv
Powers, Pyles & Sutter	$1,000	Indiv

Source of Funds in 1992 Election

Source	Total	Pct
PACs	$0	0%
Indivs $200+	$36,309	33%
Indivs under $200	$32,630	29%
Other	$42,319	38%
Candidate	$0	0%
Party	$0	0%

Source of PAC Dollars by Sector

No PAC contributions reported

Source	Total	Pct
Business	$4,200	100%
Labor	$0	0%
Ideology/Single Issue	$0	0%

In-State vs. Out-of-State Contributions*

Source	Total	Pct
In-State	$17,310	49%
Out-of-state	$17,999	51%
No state listed	$1,000	

* by large individual contributors ($200 & above)

Misc Business	$4,400	
Retail Sales	**$1,000**	
Cintas Corp	$1,000	Indiv
Misc Manufacturing & Distributing	**$1,900**	
Ashley F Ward Inc	$1,000	Indiv

Contribution Totals by Sector

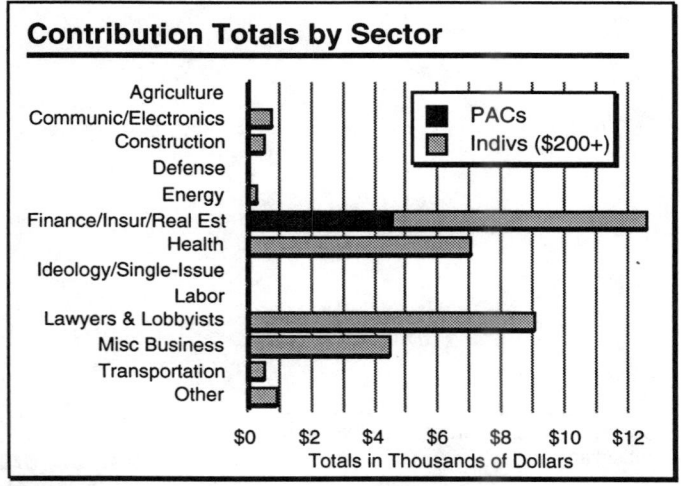

Legend: ■ PACs ▨ Indivs ($200+)

Categories: Agriculture, Communic/Electronics, Construction, Defense, Energy, Finance/Insur/Real Est, Health, Ideology/Single-Issue, Labor, Lawyers & Lobbyists, Misc Business, Transportation, Other

$0 $2 $4 $6 $8 $10 $12
Totals in Thousands of Dollars

Other & Unknown

Unknown $4,716

Homemakers/Non-income earners $1,550
Employer Listed/Category Unknown $2,666
    None over $1,000

Spending in Last 3 Elections

	1988	1990	1992
Gradison	$125,682	$124,331	$96,108
Opponent	$13,961	$5,350	$289
Vote Pct	72%	64%	70%

Rod Grams, R-Minn (6)

1993-94 Committees & Subcommittees

Banking, Finance and Urban Affairs
Consumer Credit and Insurance; Financial Institutions Supervision, Regulation and Deposit Insurance; Housing and Community Development

Science, Space and Technology
Energy; Technology, Environment and Aviation

Leading Contributors

Business

Agriculture		$28,700
Crop Production & Basic Processing	**$5,000**	
Cargill Inc	$4,250	PAC/Ind
Tobacco	**$4,750**	
RJR Nabisco	$3,000	PAC
Dairy	**$2,000**	
Schwan's Sales Enterprises	$2,000	Indiv
Agricultural Services/Products	**$2,100**	
None over $1,500		
Food Processing & Sales	**$9,350**	
General Mills	$5,050	Indiv
Forestry & Forest Products	**$5,500**	
None over $1,500		

Communications/Electronics		$8,150
Media/Entertainment	**$5,250**	
National Assn of Broadcasters	$3,000	PAC
Hubbard Broadcasting Co	$2,250	Indiv

Construction		$17,450
General Contractors	**$7,450**	
Associated General Contractors	$2,000	PAC
Home Builders	**$2,000**	
National Assn of Home Builders	$2,000	PAC
Special Trade Contractors	**$2,000**	
National Electrical Contractors Assn	$2,000	PAC
Building Materials & Equipment	**$5,500**	
Lyman Lumber Co	$1,500	Indiv

First elected: 1992

1991-92 Total Receipts:	$453,643
1992 Year-end Cash:	-$244

Source of Funds in 1992 Election

Source	Total	Pct
■ PACs	$138,784	27%
▨ Indivs $200+	$132,039	26%
☐ Indivs under $200	$167,455	33%
⊠ Other	$72,037	14%
Candidate	$0	0%
Party	$67,752	13%

Source of PAC Dollars by Sector

Source	Total	Pct
■ Business	$121,966	87%
▨ Labor	$1,000	1%
☐ Ideology/Single Issue	$17,838	13%

In-State vs. Out-of-State Contributions*

Source	Total	Pct
☐ In-State	$124,789	95%
■ Out-of-state	$7,250	5%
No state listed	$0	

*** by large individual contributors ($200 & above)**

Energy & Natural Resources		$25,800
Oil & Gas	**$20,200**	
Amoco Corp	$2,000	PAC
Dallas Energy PAC	$2,000	PAC
Koch Industries	$2,000	PAC
Atlantic Richfield	$1,500	PAC
Chevron Corp	$1,500	PAC
Exxon Corp	$1,500	PAC
Mining	**$1,500**	
None over $1,500		
Electric Utilities	**$3,600**	
None over $1,500		

Finance, Insurance & Real Estate		$26,500
Commercial Banks	**$2,200**	
None over $1,500		
Savings & Loans	**$1,800**	
None over $1,500		
Securities & Investment	**$3,850**	
Piper, Jaffray & Hopwood	$2,750	Indiv
Insurance	**$8,750**	
Golden Rule Insurance Co	$1,500	PAC/Ind
Real Estate	**$2,300**	
Burnet Realty	$1,500	Indiv
Misc Finance	**$7,350**	
IC Systems Inc	$4,000	Indiv

Contribution Totals by Sector

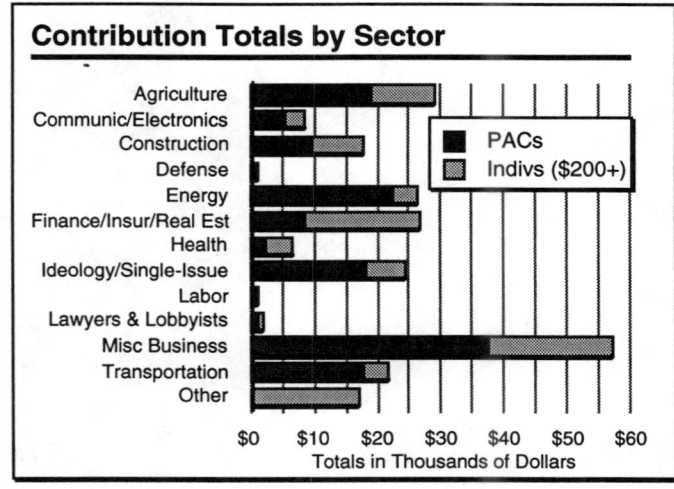

Agriculture
Communic/Electronics
Construction
Defense
Energy
Finance/Insur/Real Est
Health
Ideology/Single-Issue
Labor
Lawyers & Lobbyists
Misc Business
Transportation
Other

Legend: ■ PACs ▨ Indivs ($200+)

$0 $10 $20 $30 $40 $50 $60
Totals in Thousands of Dollars

Health $6,300

Health Professionals $2,550
    None over $1,500

Hospitals/Nursing Homes $1,500
    None over $1,500

Lawyers & Lobbyists $1,850

Lawyers & Lobbyists $1,850
    None over $1,500

Misc Business $56,640

Business Associations $2,540
    National Fedn of Independent Business .... $1,500   PAC

Food & Beverage $7,500
    National Restaurant Assn .... $2,000   PAC
    S&A Restaurant Corp .... $2,000   PAC

Beer, Wine & Liquor $7,250
    National Beer Wholesalers Assn .... $5,000   PAC
    Brown-Forman Distillers .... $1,500   PAC

Misc Services $4,150
    Great Clips Inc .... $1,900   Indiv

Business Services $4,250
    Ecolab Inc .... $2,250   PAC/Ind

Chemical & Related Manufacturing $12,600
    Dow Chemical .... $4,500   PAC
    FMC Corp .... $2,000   PAC
    UFE Inc .... $1,700   Indiv

Misc Manufacturing & Distributing $15,850
    Jostens Inc .... $4,000   Indiv
    Rock Island Co .... $2,000   Indiv
    Stone Container Corp .... $1,500   PAC

Transportation $21,276

Air Transport $2,300
    Honeywell Inc .... $2,300   PAC

Automotive $7,300
    National Auto Dealers Assn .... $3,000   PAC
    Minar Ford Inc .... $1,500   Indiv

Railroads $9,626
    Union Pacific Corp .... $5,000   PAC
    Burlington Northern .... $3,626   PAC/Ind

Ideological/Single-Issue

Ideological/Single-Issue $24,038

Republican/Conservative $6,774
    None over $1,500

Leadership PACs $3,702
    New Majority Leadership PAC (Vin Weber) .... $2,702   PAC

Pro-Life $6,425
    Minnesota Citizens Concerned for Life .... $4,975   PAC

Gun Rights/Gun Control $5,500
    National Rifle Assn .... $5,000   PAC

Other & Unknown

Other $16,800

Retired $16,800
    None over $1,500

Unknown $37,589

    Homemakers/Non-income earners $7,595
    No Employer Listed or Found $7,100
    Generic Occupation/Category Unknown $4,212
    Employer Listed/Category Unknown $18,682
        Fremont Industies .... $1,500   Indiv

Independent expenditures supporting Grams
    Minnesota Citizens Concerned for Life $32,974
    National Right to Life PAC $15,000

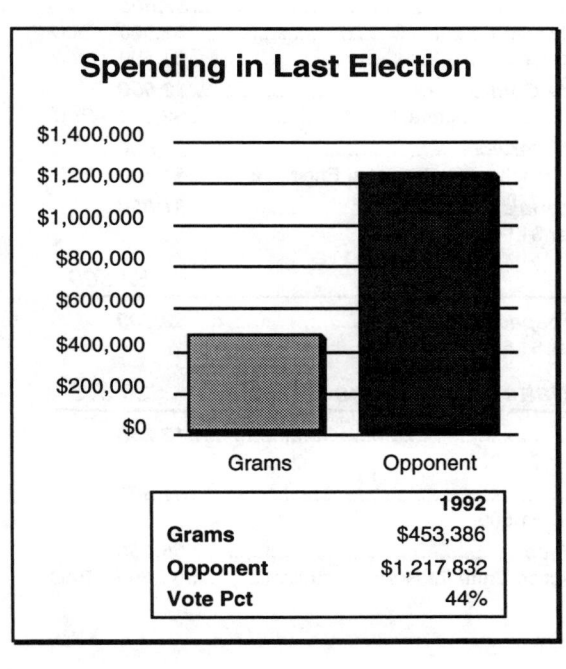

Spending in Last Election

	1992
Grams	$453,386
Opponent	$1,217,832
Vote Pct	44%

Fred Grandy, R-Iowa (5)

First elected: 1986

1991-92 Total Receipts: $382,626
1992 Year-end Cash: $174,722

1991-92 Committees & Subcommittees

Standards of Official Conduct

Ways and Means
Human Resources; Select Revenue Measures

Leading Contributors

Business

Agriculture $59,275

Crop Production & Basic Processing	**$7,775**	
American Crystal Sugar Corp	$1,500	PAC
Tobacco	**$6,000**	
RJR Nabisco	$2,000	PAC
US Tobacco Co	$2,000	PAC
Dairy	**$4,500**	
Associated Milk Producers	$2,500	PAC
Poultry & Eggs	**$1,500**	
National Broiler Council	$1,500	PAC
Livestock	**$4,000**	
National Cattlemen's Assn*	$2,500	PAC
National Pork Producers Council	$1,500	PAC
Agricultural Services/Products	**$19,750**	
Land O'Lakes Inc	$2,500	PAC
American Assn of Crop Insurers	$1,500	PAC
American Assn of Nurserymen	$1,500	PAC
Archer-Daniels-Midland Corp	$1,500	PAC
Deere & Co	$1,500	PAC
Farmland Industries	$1,500	PAC
Food Processing & Sales	**$15,750**	
ConAgra Inc	$2,500	PAC
Food Marketing Institute	$2,000	PAC
Metz Baking Co	$2,000	Indiv
AE Staley Manufacturing Co	$1,500	PAC
American Bakers Assn	$1,500	PAC

Source of Funds in 1992 Election

Source	Total	Pct
■ PACs	$296,149	77%
▨ Indivs $200+	$55,960	15%
☐ Indivs under $200	$17,496	5%
▧ Other	$13,021	3%
Candidate	$0	0%
Party	$328	0%

Source of PAC Dollars by Sector

Source	Total	Pct
■ Business	$282,523	96%
▨ Labor	$7,000	2%
☐ Ideology/Single Issue	$5,750	2%

In-State vs. Out-of-State Contributions*

Source	Total	Pct
☐ In-State	$38,510	69%
■ Out-of-state	$17,450	31%
No state listed	$0	

* by large individual contributors ($200 & above)

Communications/Electronics $29,150

Media/Entertainment	**$5,550**	
National Assn of Broadcasters	$2,650	PAC
Telephone Utilities	**$22,600**	
GTE Corp	$5,350	PAC
BellSouth Corp*	$3,750	PAC
US West Inc	$2,500	PAC
AT&T	$2,000	PAC
Bell Atlantic	$1,750	PAC

Construction $13,850

General Contractors	**$7,500**	
Irving F Jensen Co	$2,000	Indiv
WA Klinger Inc	$1,500	Indiv
Special Trade Contractors	**$2,000**	
National Electrical Contractors Assn	$2,000	PAC
Construction Services	**$1,500**	
National Society of Professional Engineers	$1,500	PAC
Building Materials & Equipment	**$1,850**	
None over $1,500		

Defense $2,500

Defense Aerospace	**$2,500**	
None over $1,500		

Energy & Natural Resources $20,505

Oil & Gas	**$12,255**	
None over $1,500		
Mining	**$1,500**	
None over $1,500		
Electric Utilities	**$5,750**	
ACRE (Action Cmte for Rural Electrification)*	$1,500	PAC

Contribution Totals by Sector

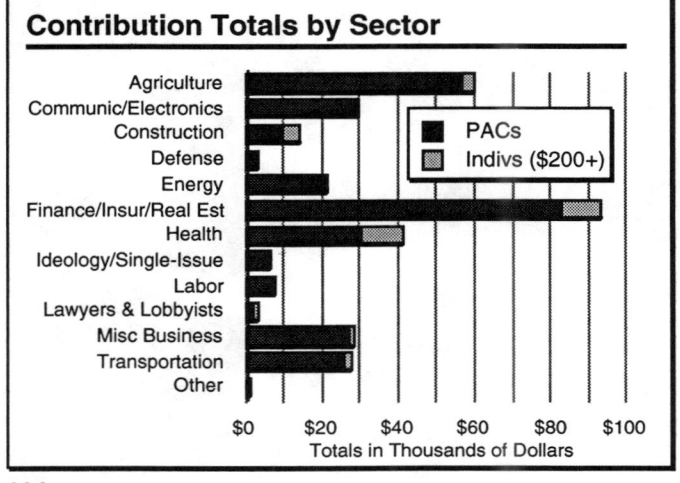

Agriculture
Communic/Electronics
Construction
Defense
Energy
Finance/Insur/Real Est
Health
Ideology/Single-Issue
Labor
Lawyers & Lobbyists
Misc Business
Transportation
Other

■ PACs
▨ Indivs ($200+)

$0 $20 $40 $60 $80 $100
Totals in Thousands of Dollars

Finance, Insurance & Real Estate — $93,049

Commercial Banks $10,800
    Independent Bankers Assn ....$2,500 — PAC
    Citicorp ....$2,000 — PAC

Securities & Investment $9,750
    Chicago Board of Trade ....$1,500 — PAC
    Merrill Lynch ....$1,500 — PAC

Insurance $57,499
    National Assn of Life Underwriters ....$7,500 — PAC
    Northwestern Mutual Life ....$3,400 — PAC/Ind
    American Family Corp ....$3,000 — PAC
    Mutual of Omaha ....$2,999 — PAC
    Massachusetts Mutual Life Insurance ....$2,500 — PAC
    Health Insurance Assn of America ....$2,000 — PAC
    Independent Insurance Agents of America ......$2,000 — PAC
    Metropolitan Life Insurance ....$2,000 — PAC
    Travelers Corp ....$2,000 — PAC
    Torchmark Corp ....$1,500 — PAC

Real Estate $6,500
    National Assn of Realtors ....$5,500 — PAC

Accountants $6,500
    American Institute of CPA's ....$5,000 — PAC

Health — $40,847

Health Professionals $28,397
    American Dental Assn ....$2,500 — PAC
    American Medical Assn ....$2,135 — PAC
    American Assn Oral & Maxillofacial Surgeons ....$2,000 — PAC
    American College of Emergency Physicians ....$1,500 — PAC

Hospitals/Nursing Homes $5,000
    American Hospital Assn ....$1,500 — PAC
    Manor Healthcare Corp ....$1,500 — PAC

Pharmaceuticals/Health Products $7,450
    None over $1,500

Lawyers & Lobbyists — $2,750

Lawyers & Lobbyists $2,750
    None over $1,500

Misc Business — $27,807

Business Associations $1,500
    None over $1,500

Food & Beverage $4,000
    National Restaurant Assn ....$2,000 — PAC

Beer, Wine & Liquor $4,000
    National Beer Wholesalers Assn ....$1,500 — PAC
    Wine & Spirits Wholesalers of America ....$1,500 — PAC

Retail Sales $6,257
    International Council of Shopping Centers ....$2,000 — PAC

Business Services $1,500
    None over $1,500

Chemical & Related Manufacturing $3,000
    FMC Corp ....$1,500 — PAC
    WR Grace & Co ....$1,500 — PAC

Misc Manufacturing & Distributing $5,200
    Stone Container Corp ....$2,500 — PAC

Transportation — $27,500

Air Transport $9,000
    United Parcel Service ....$4,000 — PAC
    General Electric ....$2,000 — PAC

Automotive $10,500
    National Auto Dealers Assn ....$6,500 — PAC
    Auto Dealers & Drivers for Free Trade ....$1,500 — PAC

Trucking $2,500
    None over $1,500

Railroads $4,000
    Chicago & North Western Transport ....$1,500 — PAC
    Union Pacific Corp ....$1,500 — PAC

Sea Transport $1,500
    CSX Corp* ....$1,500 — PAC

Labor

Labor — $7,000

Transportation Unions $1,500
    Marine Engineers Dist 2 Maritime Officers ....$1,500 — PAC

Public Sector Unions $5,500
    None over $1,500

Ideological/Single-Issue

Ideological/Single-Issue — $6,000

Misc Issues $3,000
    National Cmte to Preserve Social Security ....$3,000 — PAC

Other & Unknown

Unknown — $20,750

    No Employer Listed or Found $14,500
    Generic Occupation/Category Unknown $2,500
    Employer Listed/Category Unknown $3,250
        None over $1,500

Spending in Last 3 Elections

	1988	1990	1992
Grandy	$523,108	$322,563	$244,752
Opponent	$175,951	$45,203	$0
Vote Pct	64%	72%	99%

* Contributions came from more than one affiliate or subsidiary.

Gene Green, D-Texas (29)

First elected: 1992

1991-92 Total Receipts: $674,830
1992 Year-end Cash: $11,051

1993-94 Committees & Subcommittees

Education and Labor
Elementary, Secondary and Vocational Education; Labor-Management Relations; Postsecondary Education and Training

Government Operations
Commerce, Consumer and Monetary Affairs

Merchant Marine and Fisheries
Merchant Marine; Oceanography, Gulf of Mexico and the Outer Continental Shelf

Leading Contributors

Business

Agriculture — $15,550

Dairy	**$3,000**	
Associated Milk Producers	$3,000	PAC
Livestock	**$3,000**	
None over $1,500		
Food Processing & Sales	**$2,850**	
Randall's Food Markets	$2,500	Indiv
Forestry & Forest Products	**$4,350**	
Texas Paper Products	$3,000	Indiv

Communications/Electronics — $6,500

Telephone Utilities	**$6,500**	
GTE Corp	$2,500	PAC
AT&T	$1,500	PAC
United Telecommunications	$1,500	PAC

Construction — $11,300

General Contractors	**$7,100**	
Associated General Contractors	$2,500	PAC
Williams Brothers Construction	$2,000	Indiv
Universal Services	$1,500	PAC
Construction Services	**$3,450**	
None over $1,500		

Defense — $2,000

Misc Defense	**$1,500**	
Tenneco Inc	$1,500	PAC

Source of Funds in 1992 Election

Source	Total	Pct
PACs	$399,350	57%
Indivs $200+	$176,670	25%
Indivs under $200	$50,211	7%
Other	$75,994	11%
Candidate	$44,490	6%
Party	$27,845	4%

Source of PAC Dollars by Sector

Source	Total	Pct
Business	$171,597	44%
Labor	$195,100	50%
Ideology/Single Issue	$24,000	6%

In-State vs. Out-of-State Contributions*

Source	Total	Pct
In-State	$170,330	96%
Out-of-state	$6,290	4%
No state listed	$0	

by large individual contributors ($200 & above)

Energy & Natural Resources — $24,300

Oil & Gas	**$11,000**	
None over $1,500		
Electric Utilities	**$12,950**	
Texas Utilities Co	$7,500	PAC
ACRE (Action Cmte for Rural Electrification)	$3,350	PAC

Finance, Insurance & Real Estate — $62,250

Commercial Banks	**$5,000**	
Citizens & Southern National Bank	$1,500	PAC
Savings & Loans	**$2,000**	
US League of Savings Assns*	$2,000	PAC
Credit Unions	**$2,500**	
Credit Union National Assn	$2,000	PAC
Insurance	**$13,750**	
National Assn of Life Underwriters	$8,500	PAC
American General Insurance Co	$1,500	PAC
Real Estate	**$22,250**	
National Assn of Realtors	$20,000	PAC
Accountants	**$14,500**	
American Institute of CPA's	$12,500	PAC

Health — $41,997

Health Professionals	**$28,647**	
American Dental Assn	$6,097	PAC
American Medical Assn*	$5,450	PAC
American Chiropractic Assn	$4,000	PAC
American Academy of Ophthalmology	$2,000	PAC
American College of Emergency Physicians	$2,000	PAC
American Optometric Assn	$2,000	PAC
American Podiatry Assn	$1,500	PAC
Hospitals/Nursing Homes	**$11,500**	
Metro National Corp	$7,500	Indiv

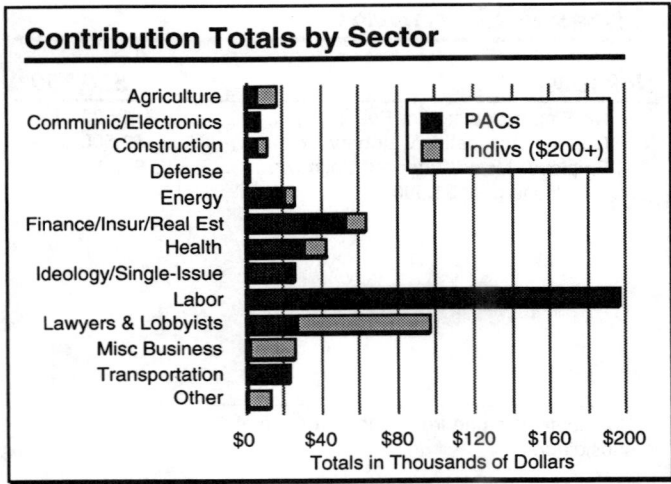

Contribution Totals by Sector

Agriculture, Communic/Electronics, Construction, Defense, Energy, Finance/Insur/Real Est, Health, Ideology/Single-Issue, Labor, Lawyers & Lobbyists, Misc Business, Transportation, Other

■ PACs ▩ Indivs ($200+)

$0 $40 $80 $120 $160 $200
Totals in Thousands of Dollars

Lawyers & Lobbyists — $96,376

Lawyers & Lobbyists *$96,376*
Assn of Trial Lawyers of America	$20,000	PAC
Helm, Pletcher et al	$7,000	Indiv
Glenn Vickery & Associates	$4,000	Indiv
Shelton Smith & Associates	$3,000	Indiv
Burrow & Williams	$2,500	Indiv
Vinson & Elkins	$1,850	PAC
Watson, Flynn & Bensik	$1,500	Indiv

Misc Business — $24,850

Beer, Wine & Liquor *$16,100*
Houston Distributing Co	$3,500	Indiv
Faust Distributing Co	$2,500	Indiv
Harris County Beer Wholesalers	$2,500	Indiv

Retail Sales *$2,000*
Academy Corp	$2,000	Indiv

Misc Manufacturing & Distributing *$2,600*
Enichem America	$1,850	Indiv

Transportation — $22,950

Air Transport *$5,050*
United Parcel Service	$4,200	PAC

Automotive *$11,850*
National Auto Dealers Assn	$11,350	PAC

Trucking *$2,350*
Central Freight Inc	$1,500	PAC

Railroads *$2,700*
Burlington Northern	$1,700	PAC

Labor

Labor — $195,100

Building Trade Unions *$21,750*
Laborers' Political League	$5,500	PAC
Plumbers/Pipefitters Union	$5,000	PAC
Carpenters & Joiners Union	$3,500	PAC
Ironworkers Union	$3,500	PAC
Sheet Metal Workers Union	$3,500	PAC

Industrial Unions — $78,000
United Steelworkers	$22,500	PAC
Communications Workers of America	$19,500	PAC
Machinists/Aerospace Workers Union	$10,000	PAC
United Auto Workers	$10,000	PAC
Intl Brotherhood of Electrical Workers	$9,000	PAC
Oil, Chemical & Atomic Workers Union	$2,500	PAC
Boilermakers Union	$2,000	PAC
United Paperworkers	$2,000	PAC

Transportation Unions *$44,850*
Seafarers International Union	$13,500	PAC
Teamsters Union	$13,500	PAC
United Transportation Union	$6,000	PAC
Transport Workers Union	$3,500	PAC
Air Line Pilots Assn	$2,500	PAC
Brotherhood of Locomotive Engineers	$2,000	PAC
International Longshoremen's Assn	$2,000	PAC

Public Sector Unions *$34,500*
American Federation of Teachers	$8,000	PAC
American Fedn of St/Cnty/Munic Employees	$5,000	PAC
National Assn of Letter Carriers	$5,000	PAC
National Assn of Postal Supervisors	$5,000	PAC
International Assn of Firefighters	$3,500	PAC
National Education Assn	$2,500	PAC
American Postal Workers Union	$2,000	PAC
National Assn Retired Federal Employees	$2,000	PAC

Misc Unions *$16,000*
AFL-CIO	$7,500	PAC
Food & Commercial Workers Union	$6,000	PAC
Office & Professional Employees Union	$2,500	PAC

Ideological/Single-Issue

Ideological/Single-Issue — $25,375

Leadership PACs *$1,500*
None over $1,500

Pro-Israel *$5,100*
None over $1,500

Gun Rights/Gun Control *$16,900*
National Rifle Assn	$16,900	PAC

Other & Unknown

Other — $12,269

Civil Servants/Public Officials *$6,219*
District Court Judge	$2,164	Indiv
State of Texas	$2,000	Indiv

Education *$2,850*
Houston Independent School District	$1,600	Indiv

Retired *$3,200*
None over $1,500

Unknown — $26,500
Homemakers/Non-income earners	$6,500	
Generic Occupation/Category Unknown	$9,600	
Employer Listed/Category Unknown	$9,150	
Texas Locators	$1,500	Indiv

Independent expenditures supporting Green
National Rifle Assn	$139,468	

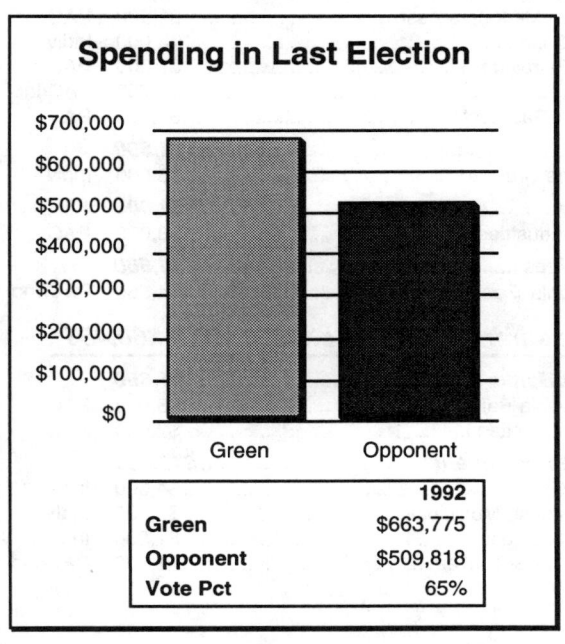

Spending in Last Election

	1992
Green	$663,775
Opponent	$509,818
Vote Pct	65%

---

* Contributions came from more than one affiliate or
subsidiary.

James C. Greenwood, R-Pa (8)

First elected: 1992

1991-92 Total Receipts: $732,618
1992 Year-end Cash: $5,914

1993-94 Committees & Subcommittees

Energy and Commerce
Commerce, Consumer Protection and Competitiveness; Health and the Environment

Leading Contributors

Business

Agriculture	$35,845	
Crop Production & Basic Processing	**$4,945**	
Farming & Music	$1,600	Indiv
Tobacco	**$3,000**	
US Tobacco Co	$2,500	PAC
Dairy	**$2,500**	
None over $1,500		
Agricultural Services/Products	**$8,150**	
Asplundh Tree Expert Co	$3,950	PAC
Nursery Supplies Inc	$3,000	Indiv
Food Processing & Sales	**$6,300**	
Flowers Industries	$2,000	PAC
Pepsico Inc	$2,000	PAC
Forestry & Forest Products	**$10,750**	
Willamette Industries	$3,000	PAC
Westvaco Corp	$2,000	PAC

Communications/Electronics	$8,712	
Printing & Publishing	**$3,712**	
Charles Kerr Ents Inc	$1,750	Indiv
Telephone Utilities	**$2,500**	
United Telecommunications	$1,500	PAC

Construction	$34,950	
General Contractors	**$13,550**	
Hankin Management Co	$2,000	Indiv
Home Builders	**$4,250**	
National Assn of Home Builders	$3,000	PAC

Contribution Totals by Sector

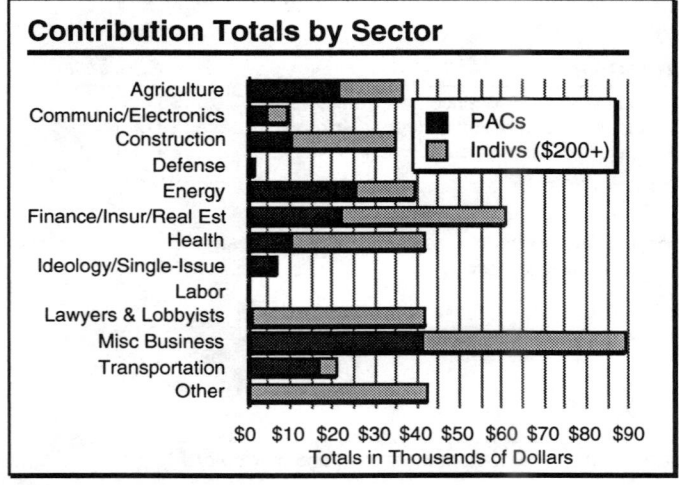

Agriculture
Communic/Electronics
Construction
Defense
Energy
Finance/Insur/Real Est
Health
Ideology/Single-Issue
Labor
Lawyers & Lobbyists
Misc Business
Transportation
Other

PACs
Indivs ($200+)

$0 $10 $20 $30 $40 $50 $60 $70 $80 $90
Totals in Thousands of Dollars

Source of Funds in 1992 Election

Source	Total	Pct
PACs	$180,377	23%
Indivs $200+	$379,944	49%
Indivs under $200	$150,899	19%
Other	$71,244	9%
Candidate	$0	0%
Party	$55,859	7%

Source of PAC Dollars by Sector

Source	Total	Pct
Business	$151,488	96%
Labor	$0	0%
Ideology/Single Issue	$6,524	4%

In-State vs. Out-of-State Contributions*

Source	Total	Pct
In-State	$346,814	93%
Out-of-state	$27,480	7%
No state listed	$4,400	

* by large individual contributors ($200 & above)

Special Trade Contractors	**$7,200**	
John Knoell & Sons Inc	$3,500	Indiv
Construction Services	**$2,500**	
National Society of Professional Engineers	$1,500	PAC
Building Materials & Equipment	**$7,450**	
Delaware Quarries Inc	$2,500	Indiv
Amquip Corp	$2,000	Indiv

Defense	$1,500	
None over $1,500		

Energy & Natural Resources	$39,100	
Oil & Gas	**$24,800**	
Sinkler Inc	$3,250	Indiv
Petroleum Marketers Assn	$2,500	PAC
Mauger & Co	$2,000	Indiv
Phillips Petroleum	$2,000	PAC
Sun Co	$1,750	PAC/Ind
Columbia Gas System*	$1,700	PAC
Mining	**$4,500**	
New Hope Crushed Stone	$3,000	Indiv
Misc Energy	**$3,000**	
Cooper Industries	$3,000	PAC
Electric Utilities	**$5,550**	
Philadelphia Electric	$4,550	PAC/Ind

Finance, Insurance & Real Estate	$60,455	
Commercial Banks	**$11,650**	
Pennsylvania Bankers Assn	$8,000	PAC
Chase Manhattan	$2,000	PAC
Securities & Investment	**$12,350**	
Hillman Co	$4,000	Indiv
First American Municipals	$2,000	Indiv
Butcher & Singer	$1,500	Indiv
Wheat First Securities	$1,500	PAC/Ind

Insurance	$15,480	
Noble, Lowndes, Johnson	$1,950	Indiv
PMA Reinsurance Co	$1,500	Indiv
Real Estate	**$11,550**	
None over $1,500		
Misc Finance	**$7,825**	
None over $1,500		

Health — $41,240

Health Professionals	$21,090	
American Medical Assn*	$3,000	PAC
Hospitals/Nursing Homes	**$10,250**	
Schirm Associates	$10,000	Indiv
Pharmaceuticals/Health Products	**$7,750**	
Merck & Co	$1,750	Indiv

Lawyers & Lobbyists — $41,475

Lawyers & Lobbyists	$41,475	
Begley, Carlin & Mandio	$4,500	Indiv
Dechert, Price & Rhoads	$2,300	Indiv
Curtin & Heefner	$2,100	Indiv
Fine, Kaplan & Black	$2,000	Indiv
McKissock & Hoffman	$1,850	Indiv
Baldi & Ceppanelo	$1,825	Indiv

Misc Business — $88,568

Business Associations	$6,437	
National Fedn of Independent Business	$5,000	PAC
Food & Beverage	**$12,250**	
National Restaurant Assn	$6,000	PAC
S&A Restaurant Corp	$2,000	PAC
Beer, Wine & Liquor	**$4,250**	
Pat Deon Beverages	$1,550	Indiv
Brown-Forman Distillers	$1,500	PAC
Retail Sales	**$6,000**	
Intrigue	$2,000	Indiv
Misc Services	**$2,751**	
None over $1,500		
Business Services	**$8,780**	
Lewis, Eckert, Robb & Co	$3,250	Indiv

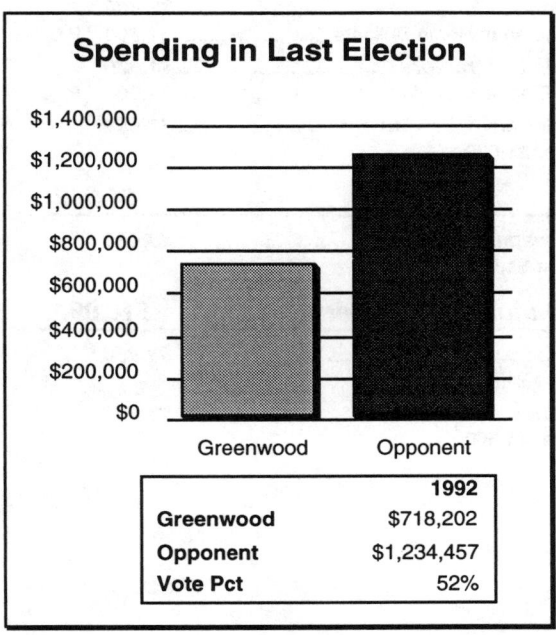

Spending in Last Election

	1992
Greenwood	$718,202
Opponent	$1,234,457
Vote Pct	52%

Lodging/Tourism	$2,100	
Black Bass Hotel	$1,500	Indiv
Misc Business	**$3,000**	
Philadelphia Suburban Water Co	$2,750	Indiv
Chemical & Related Manufacturing	**$22,500**	
Betz Laboratories	$14,050	PAC/Ind
Dow Chemical	$2,000	PAC
Penn Color	$2,000	Indiv
Misc Manufacturing & Distributing	**$19,400**	
Stone Container Corp	$5,000	PAC
Byers Choice Ltd	$4,000	Indiv
Pennfield Precision Inc	$2,000	Indiv
White Engineering Surface	$1,750	Indiv

Transportation — $20,250

Air Transport	$2,500	
Aircraft Owners & Pilots Assn	$2,000	PAC
Automotive	**$10,150**	
National Auto Dealers Assn	$5,000	PAC
Eaton Corp	$2,000	PAC
Railroads	**$6,000**	
Union Pacific Corp	$6,000	PAC

Ideological/Single-Issue

Ideological/Single-Issue — $6,724

Leadership PACs	$2,500	
Republican Leader's Fund (Bob Michel)	$2,000	PAC
Pro-Choice	**$2,500**	
National Abortion Rights Action League	$2,000	PAC

Other & Unknown

Other — $41,785

Civil Servants/Public Officials	$8,400	
Commonwealth of Pennsylvania	$5,700	Indiv
Bucks County	$2,000	Indiv
Education	**$4,700**	
Philadelphia Public School District	$2,000	Indiv
Retired	**$27,185**	
None over $1,500		
Other	**$1,500**	
None over $1,500		

Unknown — $116,102

Homemakers/Non-income earners	$26,520	
No Employer Listed or Found	$45,562	
Generic Occupation/Category Unknown	$4,700	
Employer Listed/Category Unknown	$39,320	
Carroll Engineering	$2,000	Indiv
Edgewood Village Marketing	$2,000	Indiv
Industrial Rehabilitation	$1,500	Indiv

* Contributions came from more than one affiliate or subsidiary.

Steve Gunderson, R-Wis (3)

First elected: 1980
1991-92 Total Receipts: $427,368
1992 Year-end Cash: $67,331

1991-92 Committees & Subcommittees

Agriculture
Conservation, Credit and Rural Development; Department Operations, Research and Foreign Agriculture; Livestock, Dairy and Poultry (Ranking Republican); Peanuts and Tobacco

Education and Labor
Elementary, Secondary and Vocational Education; Employment Opportunities (Ranking Republican); Postsecondary Education

Leading Contributors

Business

Agriculture	$89,216	
Crop Production & Basic Processing **$12,375**		
American Crystal Sugar Corp $1,600	PAC	
Tobacco **$5,400**		
US Tobacco Co $1,500	PAC	
Dairy **$16,400**		
Associated Milk Producers $6,000	PAC	
Mid-America Dairymen $4,000	PAC	
Milk Industry Foundation $1,800	PAC	
Poultry & Eggs **$3,900**		
National Turkey Federation $1,600	PAC	
National Broiler Council $1,500	PAC	
Livestock **$7,051**		
National Cattlemen's Assn* $2,900	PAC	
National Pork Producers Council $1,601	PAC	
Agricultural Services/Products **$19,950**		
Land O'Lakes Inc $3,100	PAC	
American Veterinary Medical Assn $3,000	PAC	
Deere & Co $2,500	PAC	
Food Processing & Sales **$17,740**		
Food Marketing Institute $3,440	PAC	
ConAgra Inc $2,800	PAC	
Jerome Foods Inc $2,250	Indiv	
American Meat Institute $1,800	PAC	
Trugman Nash Inc $1,600	Indiv	
Forestry & Forest Products **$5,400**		
National Presto Indust $4,750	Indiv	

Source of Funds in 1992 Election

Source	Total	Pct
■ PACs	$222,462	52%
■ Indivs $200+	$96,926	23%
□ Indivs under $200	$94,825	22%
⊠ Other....................	$13,155	3%
Candidate	$0	0%
Party	$6,319	1%

Source of PAC Dollars by Sector

Source	Total	Pct
■ Business	$207,616	99%
▨ Labor	$2,400	1%
□ Ideology/Single Issue	$600	0%

In-State vs. Out-of-State Contributions*

Source	Total	Pct
□ In-State	$85,601	88%
■ Out-of-state	$11,325	12%
No state listed	$0	

* by large individual contributors ($200 & above)

Communications/Electronics	$17,550	
Media/Entertainment **$2,350**		
None over $1,500		
Telephone Utilities........................... **$12,300**		
Ameritech Corp* $3,600	PAC	
AT&T $2,300	PAC	
GTE Corp $2,000	PAC	

Construction	$19,820	
General Contractors **$9,850**		
Hoffman Construction $4,000	Indiv	
Associated General Contractors $2,500	PAC	
Home Builders **$2,800**		
National Assn of Home Builders $2,800	PAC	
Special Trade Contractors **$4,320**		
National Electrical Contractors Assn ... $4,000	PAC	
Building Materials & Equipment **$1,850**		
None over $1,500		

Defense	$4,950	
Defense Aerospace **$3,450**		
None over $1,500		

Energy & Natural Resources	$10,090	
Oil & Gas... **$3,950**		
None over $1,500		
Electric Utilities **$3,420**		
None over $1,500		

Contribution Totals by Sector

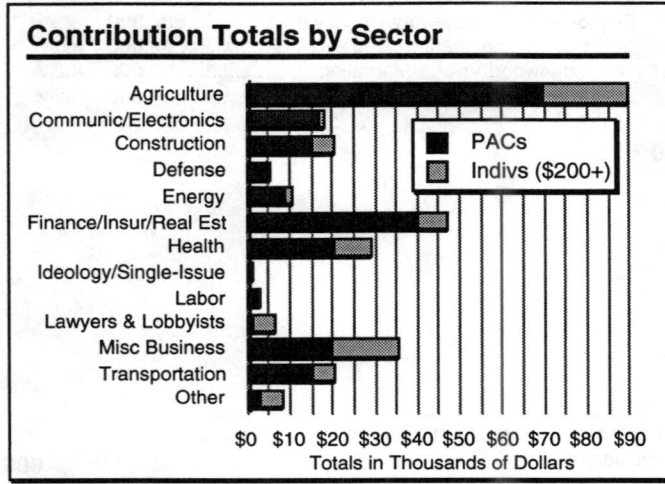

Agriculture
Communic/Electronics
Construction
Defense
Energy
Finance/Insur/Real Est
Health
Ideology/Single-Issue
Labor
Lawyers & Lobbyists
Misc Business
Transportation
Other

■ PACs
▨ Indivs ($200+)

$0 $10 $20 $30 $40 $50 $60 $70 $80 $90
Totals in Thousands of Dollars

Finance, Insurance & Real Estate — $46,320

Commercial Banks $18,960
    American Bankers Assn .... $10,000   PAC
    Independent Bankers Assn .... $1,900   PAC

Securities & Investment $3,500
    Chicago Mercantile Exchange .... $1,500   PAC

Insurance $13,700
    Northwestern Mutual Life .... $3,500   PAC/Ind
    American Council of Life Insurance .... $1,500   PAC

Real Estate $6,740
    National Assn of Realtors .... $6,740   PAC

Misc Finance $1,600
    None over $1,500

Health — $28,425

Health Professionals $21,250
    American Medical Assn .... $10,000   PAC
    Gundersen Clinic Ltd .... $4,750   Indiv
    American Dental Assn .... $2,500   PAC

Hospitals/Nursing Homes $2,800
    American Hospital Assn .... $1,900   PAC

Pharmaceuticals/Health Products $2,850
    None over $1,500

Misc Health $1,525
    None over $1,500

Lawyers & Lobbyists — $6,250

Lawyers & Lobbyists $6,250
    Williams & Jensen .... $2,550   PAC/Ind

Misc Business — $34,813

Business Associations $1,750
    None over $1,500

Food & Beverage $3,103
    National Restaurant Assn .... $2,000   PAC

Beer, Wine & Liquor $2,720
    National Beer Wholesalers Assn .... $1,900   PAC

Retail Sales $3,120
    None over $1,500

Misc Services $2,000
    None over $1,500

Business Services $3,000
    None over $1,500

Chemical & Related Manufacturing $2,250
    None over $1,500

Misc Manufacturing & Distributing $14,870
    SC Johnson & Son Inc .... $3,000   Indiv
    Ashley Furniture .... $2,000   Indiv
    Rice Lake Bearing Inc .... $2,000   Indiv
    Northern Engraving Corp .... $1,500   Indiv

Transportation — $19,858

Air Transport $4,340
    United Parcel Service .... $3,640   PAC

Automotive $12,268
    National Auto Dealers Assn .... $5,000   PAC
    Auto Dealers & Drivers for Free Trade ... $1,500   PAC

Misc Transport $1,750
    S&S Cycle Inc .... $1,500   Indiv

Labor

Labor — $2,400

Public Sector Unions $2,400
    National Assn Retired Federal Employees .... $2,000   PAC

Other & Unknown

Other — $7,890

Education $3,600
    Assn of Independent Colleges & Schools .... $1,600   PAC

Retired $3,790
    None over $1,500

Unknown — $22,060

    Homemakers/Non-income earners $5,600
    Employer Listed/Category Unknown $16,460
        Russ Cleary & Assoc .... $2,000   Indiv
        Cvikota Billing Service .... $1,500   Indiv

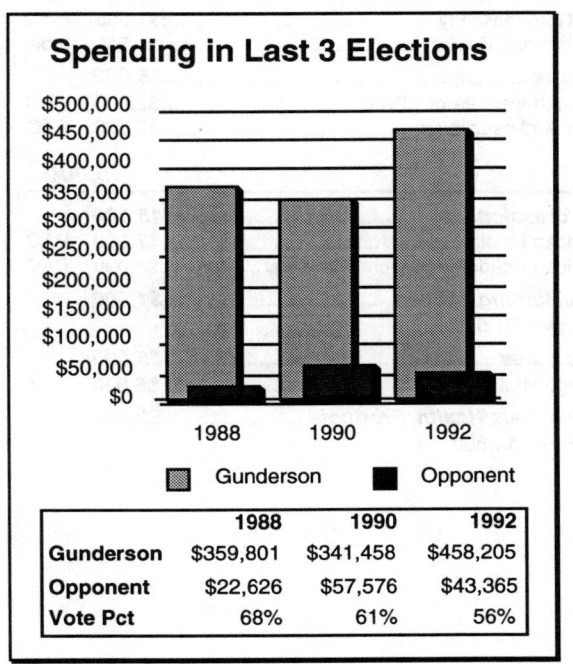

Spending in Last 3 Elections

	1988	1990	1992
Gunderson	$359,801	$341,458	$458,205
Opponent	$22,626	$57,576	$43,365
Vote Pct	68%	61%	56%

* Contributions came from more than one affiliate or subsidiary.

Luis V. Gutierrez, D-Ill (4)

First elected: 1992

1991-92 Total Receipts: $438,253
1992 Year-end Cash: $18,024

1993-94 Committees & Subcommittees

Banking, Finance and Urban Affairs
Consumer Credit and Insurance; Housing and Community Development

Veterans' Affairs
Hospitals and Health Care; Oversight and Investigations

Leading Contributors

Business

Agriculture	$10,250	
Food Processing & Sales **$7,250**		
Andy's Deli $2,000	Indiv	
Caminos Grocery $2,000	Indiv	

Communications/Electronics	$7,750	
Printing & Publishing **$1,800**		
None over $1,500		
Media/Entertainment **$3,000**		
Harriscope Broadcasting Corp $1,500	Indiv	
Telephone Utilities **$1,950**		
None over $1,500		

Construction	$23,269	
General Contractors **$7,000**		
Northwest Constructors $2,000	Indiv	
Home Builders **$6,000**		
National Assn of Home Builders $6,000	PAC	
Special Trade Contractors **$4,750**		
All Masonry Inc $3,000	Indiv	
Construction Services **$5,519**		
None over $1,500		

Energy & Natural Resources	$2,250	
Waste Management **$2,000**		
Waste Management Inc $2,000	PAC/Ind	

Source of Funds in 1992 Election

Source	Total	Pct
■ PACs	$187,945	43%
▥ Indivs $200+	$192,419	44%
□ Indivs under $200	$50,982	12%
⊠ Other	$6,907	2%
Candidate	$0	0%
Party	$0	0%

Source of PAC Dollars by Sector

Source	Total	Pct
■ Business	$76,800	40%
▨ Labor	$83,300	44%
□ Ideology/Single Issue	$30,506	16%

In-State vs. Out-of-State Contributions*

Source	Total	Pct
□ In-State	$173,299	91%
■ Out-of-state	$17,600	9%
No state listed	$1,000	

* by large individual contributors ($200 & above)

Finance, Insurance & Real Estate — $57,880

Commercial Banks **$2,450**		
None over $1,500		
Securities & Investment **$14,450**		
Reinoso & Co $5,000	Indiv	
Chicago Mercantile Exchange $3,500	PAC	
Insurance **$5,250**		
Near North Insurance Agency $3,000	Indiv	
Real Estate **$28,680**		
National Assn of Realtors $10,000	PAC	
Stein & Co $2,000	Indiv	
ERA Roman Realty $1,500	Indiv	
Renaissance Realty $1,500	Indiv	
Accountants **$5,000**		
American Institute of CPA's $2,000	PAC	
Arthur Andersen & Co $2,000	PAC	

Health — $25,000

Health Professionals **$15,500**		
American Medical Assn $7,000	PAC	
American Academy of Ophthalmology $6,000	PAC	
Hospitals/Nursing Homes **$1,500**		
None over $1,500		
Health Services **$5,000**		
Chicago HMO $5,000	Indiv	
Pharmaceuticals/Health Products **$2,250**		
None over $1,500		

Contribution Totals by Sector

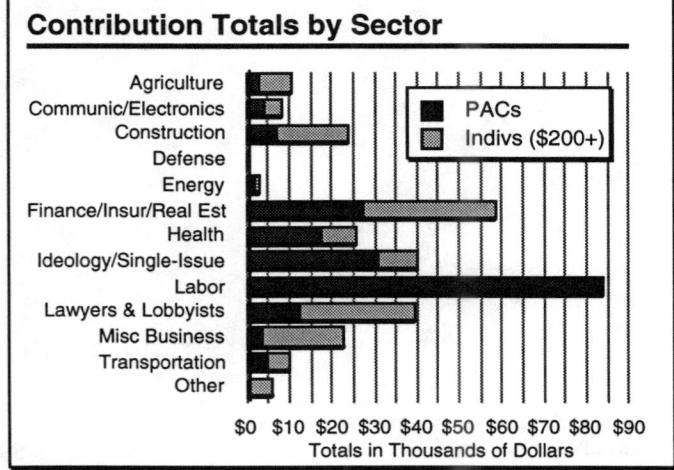

Totals in Thousands of Dollars

Lawyers & Lobbyists $38,750

Lawyers & Lobbyists **$38,750**
   Assn of Trial Lawyers of America ....$10,000   PAC
   Dickinson, Wright et al ....$1,500   Indiv

Misc Business $22,200

Food & Beverage **$4,900**
   Rezko Foods Inc ....$1,500   Indiv

Business Services **$10,000**
   Hugo's Cleaning Service Inc ....$4,250   Indiv
   Jasculca & Terman Associates ....$2,000   Indiv

Lodging/Tourism **$4,000**
   Custom Companies.............................$4,000   Indiv

Transportation $9,750

Air Transport **$2,250**
   None over $1,500

Automotive **$6,000**
   Milwaukee Avenue Auto Parts ....$1,500   Indiv

Trucking.. **$1,500**
   None over $1,500

Labor

Labor $83,300

Building Trade Unions **$12,600**
   Sheet Metal Workers Union ....$5,000   PAC
   Laborers' Political League ....$2,500   PAC
   Operating Engineers Union ....$2,500   PAC
   Plumbers/Pipefitters Union ....$2,000   PAC

Industrial Unions **$15,000**
   United Auto Workers ....$4,000   PAC
   Intl Brotherhood of Electrical Workers ....$3,500   PAC
   Machinists/Aerospace Workers Union ....$3,000   PAC
   United Steelworkers ....$2,000   PAC

Transportation Unions **$15,200**
   Teamsters Union ....$10,000   PAC
   United Transportation Union ....$2,000   PAC

Public Sector Unions **$19,000**
   National Education Assn ....$6,500   PAC
   American Fedn of St/Cnty/Munic Employees ......$6,000   PAC
   National Assn of Letter Carriers ....$2,500   PAC

Misc Unions.. **$21,500**
   AFL-CIO ....$9,000   PAC
   Food & Commercial Workers Union ....$6,000   PAC
   Hotel/Restaurant Employees Union ....$5,000   PAC

Ideological/Single-Issue

Ideological/Single-Issue $39,256

Leadership PACs **$6,000**
   America's Leaders' Fund (Dan Rostenkowski) ...$3,000   PAC
   Effective Government Cmte (Dick Gephardt) ......$1,500   PAC

Pro-Israel **$17,250**
   National PAC ....$5,000   PAC
   City PAC ....$3,000   PAC
   Joint Action Cmte for Political Affairs ....$2,000   PAC

Pro-Choice.. **$3,000**
   Voters for Choice ....$2,000   PAC

Human Rights **$9,998**
   Human Rights Campaign Fund............$4,998   PAC
   KidsPAC ....$2,500   PAC

Misc Issues.. **$2,000**
   National Cmte to Preserve Social Security ....$2,000   PAC

Other & Unknown

Other $5,600

Civil Servants/Public Officials **$3,300**
   City of Chicago ....$1,500   Indiv

Retired **$1,800**
   None over $1,500

Unknown $57,250

   Homemakers/Non-income earners $2,900
   No Employer Listed or Found $20,500
   Employer Listed/Category Unknown $33,850
      44 Video Inc ....$4,000   Indiv
      Rubinos & Mesia Engineering ....$2,500   Indiv
      Riley Group ....$2,000   Indiv
      Rezmar Corp ....$1,500   Indiv

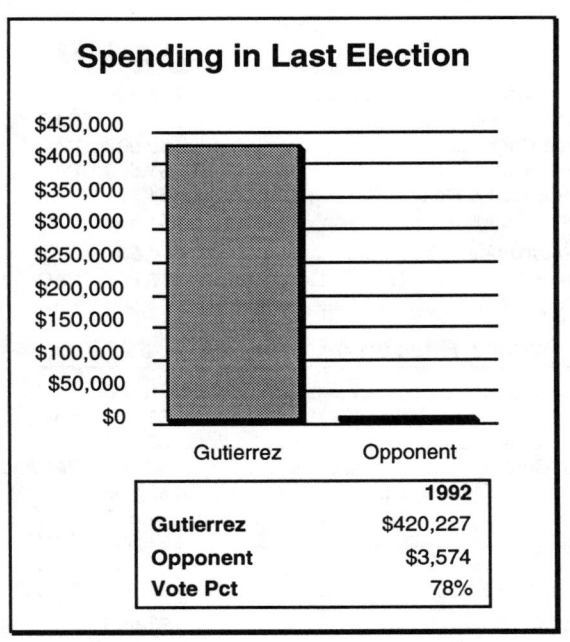

Spending in Last Election

	1992
Gutierrez	$420,227
Opponent	$3,574
Vote Pct	78%

Ralph M. Hall, D-Texas (4)

First elected: 1980

1991-92 Total Receipts: $520,216
1992 Year-end Cash: $38,176

1991-92 Committees & Subcommittees

Energy and Commerce
Health and the Environment; Telecommunications and Finance

Science, Space and Technology
Energy; Environment; Space (Chairman)

Leading Contributors

Business

Agriculture — $29,450

Crop Production & Basic Processing $1,500
   None over $1,500
Dairy $3,000
   Associated Milk Producers .... $2,000   PAC
Livestock $4,000
   National Cattlemen's Assn* .... $2,000   PAC
   Texas & Southwestern Cattle Raisers .... $2,000   PAC
Agricultural Services/Products $5,400
   Texas Farm Bureau .... $2,500   PAC
Food Processing & Sales $14,550
   Food Marketing Institute .... $2,000   PAC
   Nabisco Brands Inc .... $2,000   PAC
   Pepsico Inc .... $2,000   PAC
   Winn-Dixie Stores .... $2,000   PAC

Communications/Electronics — $38,650

Printing & Publishing $2,300
   AH Belo Corp .... $1,500   Indiv
Media/Entertainment $10,450
   National Assn of Broadcasters .... $2,500   PAC
   Prime Cable .... $2,000   Indiv
   Viacom International .... $2,000   PAC
Telephone Utilities $14,900
   AT&T .... $6,000   PAC
   GTE Corp .... $3,000   PAC
   Southwestern Bell .... $1,500   PAC
Telecom Services & Equipment $4,250
   Rockwell International .... $2,000   PAC

Source of Funds in 1992 Election

Source	Total	Pct
PACs	$349,590	66%
Indivs $200+	$97,974	18%
Indivs under $200	$42,882	8%
Other	$41,709	8%
Candidate	$0	0%
Party	$11,939	2%

Source of PAC Dollars by Sector

Source	Total	Pct
Business	$325,999	98%
Labor	$2,300	1%
Ideology/Single Issue	$5,450	2%

In-State vs. Out-of-State Contributions*

Source	Total	Pct
In-State	$89,374	91%
Out-of-state	$8,500	9%
No state listed	$0	

* by large individual contributors ($200 & above)

Electronics Mfg & Services $2,000
   None over $1,500
Computer Equipment & Services $4,750
   Texas Instruments .... $2,000   PAC

Construction — $11,250

General Contractors $7,250
   Associated General Contractors .... $2,500   PAC
   Petrofac Inc .... $1,750   Indiv
Home Builders $1,500
   None over $1,500
Building Materials & Equipment $1,500
   None over $1,500

Defense — $26,167

Defense Aerospace $11,500
   General Dynamics .... $2,000   PAC
   Lockheed Corp .... $2,000   PAC
   Gencorp Inc .... $1,500   PAC
   LTV Aerospace & Defense Co .... $1,500   PAC
   McDonnell Douglas .... $1,500   PAC
Defense Electronics $14,667
   E-Systems Inc .... $10,667   PAC/Ind
   Loral Corp .... $1,500   PAC

Energy & Natural Resources — $93,700

Oil & Gas $51,100
   Coastal Corp .... $5,000   PAC
   Atlantic Richfield .... $3,000   PAC
   Enserch Corp .... $2,800   PAC/Ind
   Columbia Gas System* .... $2,000   PAC
   Arkla Inc .... $1,500   PAC
   BP America .... $1,500   PAC
   Shell Oil .... $1,500   PAC
   USX Corp* .... $1,500   PAC
Mining $3,000
   None over $1,500

Contribution Totals by Sector

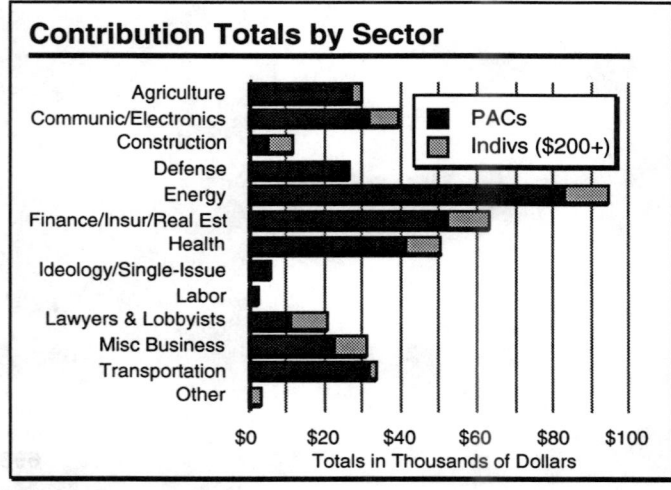

Legend: PACs, Indivs ($200+)

Agriculture
Communic/Electronics
Construction
Defense
Energy
Finance/Insur/Real Est
Health
Ideology/Single-Issue
Labor
Lawyers & Lobbyists
Misc Business
Transportation
Other

$0 $20 $40 $60 $80 $100

Totals in Thousands of Dollars

Nuclear Energy **$2,550**
    General Atomics ....$1,500   PAC

Electric Utilities **$37,050**
    Texas Utilities Co* ....$10,000   PAC
    Houston Industries ....$3,000   PAC
    Duke Power Co ....$1,500   PAC
    Southern California Edison ....$1,500   PAC

Finance, Insurance & Real Estate $62,463

Commercial Banks **$15,550**
    JP Morgan & Co ....$5,000   PAC
    Citizens & Southern National Bank ......$4,500   PAC
    American Bankers Assn ....$2,000   PAC

Finance/Credit Companies **$1,500**
    None over $1,500

Securities & Investment **$2,100**
    None over $1,500

Insurance **$17,813**
    Textron Inc ....$2,500   PAC
    Hibbs-Hallmark & Co ....$2,113   Indiv
    American Council of Life Insurance .....$2,000   PAC

Real Estate **$8,500**
    National Assn of Realtors ....$6,000   PAC

Accountants **$15,000**
    American Institute of CPA's ....$5,500   PAC
    Coopers & Lybrand ....$3,500   PAC
    Ernst & Young ....$2,500   PAC
    Arthur Andersen & Co ....$2,000   PAC
    Deloitte & Touche ....$1,500   PAC

Health $49,750

Health Professionals **$28,550**
    American Medical Assn ....$10,000   PAC
    American Dental Assn ....$3,000   PAC
    American Academy of Ophthalmology ....$2,000   PAC
    American Pharmaceutical Assn ....$1,500   PAC

Hospitals/Nursing Homes **$8,000**
    American Health Care Assn ....$5,000   PAC
    American Hospital Assn ....$1,500   PAC

Pharmaceuticals/Health Products **$13,200**
    Schering-Plough Corp ....$2,000   PAC
    Johnson & Johnson ....$1,500   PAC

Lawyers & Lobbyists $20,300

Lawyers & Lobbyists **$20,300**
    Assn of Trial Lawyers of America ....$5,000   PAC

Misc Business $30,707

Food & Beverage **$6,850**
    National Restaurant Assn* ....$3,500   PAC
    Old Spaghetti Warehouse ....$2,000   Indiv

Beer, Wine & Liquor **$4,500**
    National Beer Wholesalers Assn ....$1,500   PAC

Retail Sales **$3,007**
    None over $1,500

Business Services **$1,550**
    None over $1,500

Lodging/Tourism **$2,000**
    None over $1,500

Chemical & Related Manufacturing **$6,800**
    Dow Chemical ....$2,000   PAC

Misc Manufacturing & Distributing **$5,500**
    Hoechst Celanese Corp ....$1,500   PAC

Transportation $32,750

Air Transport **$8,500**
    United Parcel Service ....$3,500   PAC

Automotive **$17,000**
    National Auto Dealers Assn ....$10,000   PAC
    Auto Dealers & Drivers for Free Trade ....$1,500   PAC
    Libbey-Owens-Ford ....$1,500   PAC

Trucking **$2,250**
    None over $1,500

Railroads **$5,000**
    Burlington Northern ....$2,500   PAC
    Union Pacific Corp ....$2,000   PAC

Labor

Labor $2,300

Public Sector Unions **$2,300**
    National Assn Retired Federal Employees ....$2,000   PAC

Ideological/Single-Issue

Ideological/Single-Issue $5,450

Gun Rights/Gun Control **$4,950**
    National Rifle Assn ....$4,950   PAC

Other & Unknown

Other $2,530

Retired **$1,700**
    None over $1,500

Unknown $26,156

    No Employer Listed or Found $8,450
    Employer Listed/Category Unknown $15,056
        Madix Stone Fixtures ....$2,000   Indiv

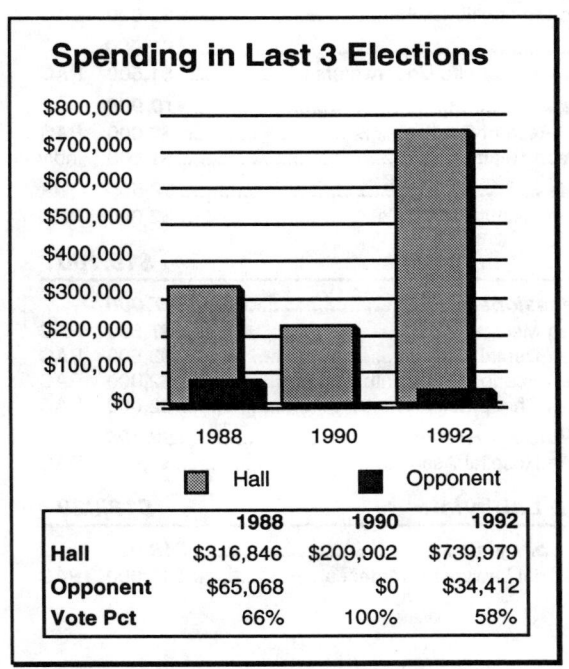

Spending in Last 3 Elections

	1988	1990	1992
Hall	$316,846	$209,902	$739,979
Opponent	$65,068	$0	$34,412
Vote Pct	66%	100%	58%

* Contributions came from more than one affiliate or subsidiary.

Tony P. Hall, D-Ohio (3)

First elected: 1978

1991-92 Total Receipts: $342,116
1992 Year-end Cash: $58,479

1991-92 Committees & Subcommittees

Rules
Rules of the House

Select Committee on Hunger (Chairman)

Leading Contributors

Business

Agriculture $11,100

Tobacco **$4,000**
   Philip Morris ....$2,000 PAC
Food Processing & Sales **$4,000**
   None over $1,500
Forestry & Forest Products **$1,500**
   Mead Corp ....$1,500 PAC

Communications/Electronics $24,830

Media/Entertainment **$5,530**
   National Cable Television Assn ....$3,400 PAC
   Continental Cablevision ....$1,630 Indiv
Telephone Utilities **$15,550**
   Ohio Bell Telephone ....$5,000 PAC
   BellSouth Corp* ....$4,500 PAC
   AT&T ....$3,000 PAC
   GTE Corp ....$1,550 PAC
Computer Equipment & Services **$3,500**
   None over $1,500

Construction $4,400

Building Materials & Equipment **$1,900**
   Price Brothers Co ....$1,500 PAC

Defense $5,000

Defense Aerospace **$2,000**
   None over $1,500
Misc Defense **$2,000**
   BDM International ....$2,000 PAC

Contribution Totals by Sector

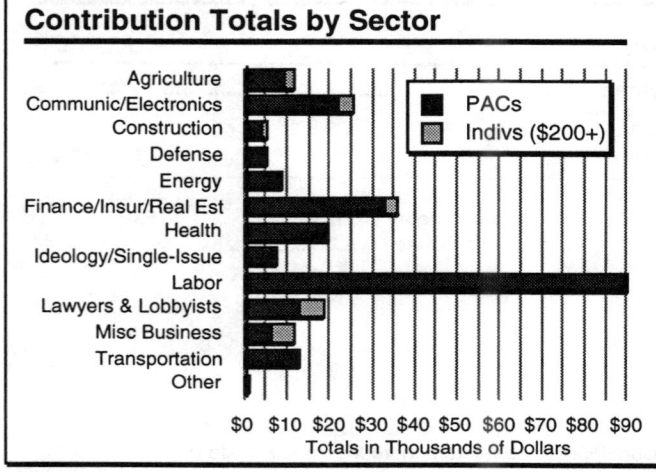

Totals in Thousands of Dollars

Source of Funds in 1992 Election

Source	Total	Pct
■ PACs	$235,200	66%
▨ Indivs $200+	$30,242	8%
□ Indivs under $200	$39,695	11%
⊠ Other...............................	$51,270	14%
Candidate	$0	0%
Party	$14,441	4%

Source of PAC Dollars by Sector

Source	Total	Pct
■ Business	$128,979	57%
▨ Labor	$89,850	40%
□ Ideology/Single Issue	$7,273	3%

In-State vs. Out-of-State Contributions*

Source	Total	Pct
□ In-State	$20,992	69%
■ Out-of-state	$9,250	31%
No state listed	$0	

* by large individual contributors ($200 & above)

Energy & Natural Resources $8,300

Oil & Gas **$1,500**
   None over $1,500
Electric Utilities **$6,300**
   Dayton Power & Light ....$3,000 PAC
   American Electric Power* ....$1,500 PAC

Finance, Insurance & Real Estate $35,700

Commercial Banks **$8,900**
   American Bankers Assn* ....$4,000 PAC
   Independent Bankers Assn ....$1,500 PAC
Securities & Investment **$4,000**
   Chicago Mercantile Exchange ....$2,000 PAC
Insurance **$7,000**
   National Assn of Life Underwriters ......$1,500 PAC
Real Estate **$10,900**
   National Assn of Realtors ....$8,000 PAC
   Mandelson Realty Co ....$1,600 Indiv
Accountants **$2,500**
   American Institute of CPA's ....$2,000 PAC

Health $19,100

Health Professionals **$17,000**
   American Medical Assn ....$7,500 PAC
   American Dental Assn ....$3,500 PAC
   American Academy of Ophthalmology ...$2,000 PAC
   American Chiropractic Assn* ....$2,000 PAC
Hospitals/Nursing Homes **$2,100**
   American Hospital Assn ....$1,900 PAC

Lawyers & Lobbyists $18,029

Lawyers & Lobbyists **$18,029**
   Assn of Trial Lawyers of America ....$10,000 PAC

Misc Business   **$11,150**

Business Services **$3,750**
    LM Berry & Co ....$2,500   PAC/Ind
Misc Manufacturing & Distributing **$4,000**
    Dayton Bag & Burlap ....$2,000   Indiv

Transportation   **$12,550**

Air Transport **$2,700**
    None over $1,500
Automotive **$4,150**
    Chrysler Corp ....$1,500   PAC
Trucking...**$2,000**
    Consolidated Freightways ....$1,500   PAC
Railroads...**$2,500**
    None over $1,500

Labor

Labor   **$89,850**

Building Trade Unions **$12,250**
    Laborers' Political League ....$4,000   PAC
    Carpenters & Joiners Union ....$3,000   PAC
    Plumbers/Pipefitters Union ....$2,000   PAC
    AFL-CIO Bldg/Construction Trades Dept ....$1,500   PAC
Industrial Unions **$33,400**
    United Auto Workers ....$9,000   PAC
    Electronic Machine Furniture Workers ....$7,450   PAC
    Rubber Cork Linoleum & Plastic Workers ....$4,700   PAC
    United Steelworkers ....$2,500   PAC
    Communications Workers of America ....$2,000   PAC
    Intl Brotherhood of Electrical Workers ....$2,000   PAC
    United Mine Workers ....$1,500   PAC
Transportation Unions **$9,700**
    Teamsters Union* ....$4,500   PAC
    United Transportation Union ....$2,000   PAC

Public Sector Unions **$30,700**
    National Education Assn ....$6,600   PAC
    National Assn Retired Federal Employees ....$6,000   PAC
    American Fedn of St/Cnty/Munic Employees ......$5,000   PAC
    National Assn of Letter Carriers ....$4,500   PAC
    National Rural Letter Carriers Assn ....$3,000   PAC
    American Postal Workers Union ....$1,600   PAC
    International Assn of Firefighters ....$1,500   PAC
    National Assn of Postal Supervisors ....$1,500   PAC
Misc Unions..**$3,800**
    Food & Commercial Workers Union ....$1,500   PAC

Ideological/Single-Issue

Ideological/Single-Issue   **$7,273**

Democratic/Liberal **$2,500**
    National Cmte for an Effective Congress ....$2,500   PAC
Misc Issues..**$3,000**
    National Cmte to Preserve Social Security ....$3,000   PAC

Other & Unknown

Unknown   **$8,312**

    No Employer Listed or Found $2,250
    Employer Listed/Category Unknown $6,062
        None over $1,500

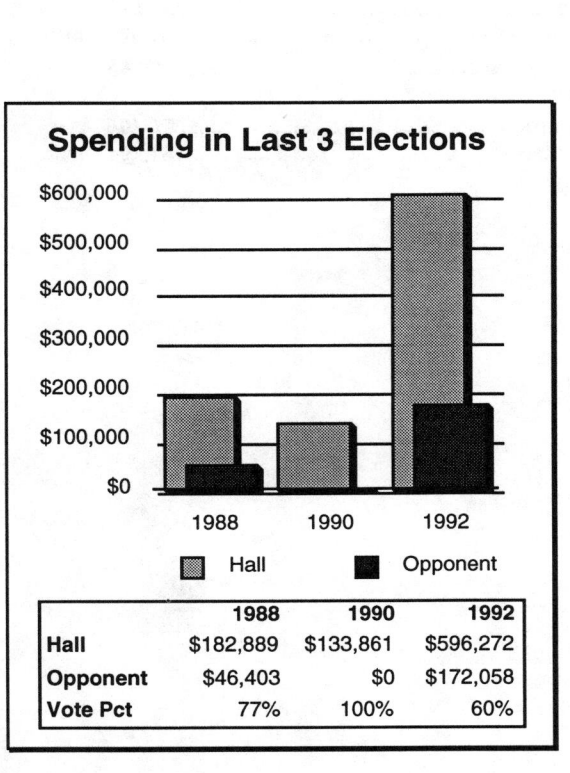

Spending in Last 3 Elections

	1988	1990	1992
Hall	$182,889	$133,861	$596,272
Opponent	$46,403	$0	$172,058
Vote Pct	77%	100%	60%

Legend: Hall, Opponent

---

* Contributions came from more than one affiliate or
subsidiary.

697

Dan Hamburg, D-Calif (1)

First elected: 1992

1991-92 Total Receipts: $642,592
1992 Year-end Cash: $5,057

1993-94 Committees & Subcommittees

Merchant Marine and Fisheries
Environment and Natural Resources; Fisheries Management

Public Works and Transportation
Economic Development; Surface Transportation; Water Resources
and the Environment

Leading Contributors

Business

Communications/Electronics	$3,540	
Printing & Publishing	$1,000	
Earthworks Press	$1,000	Indiv
Telephone Utilities	$2,000	
AT&T	$1,000	PAC
Pacific Telesis Group	$1,000	PAC

Construction	$2,415	
General Contractors	$1,175	
None over $1,000		

Energy & Natural Resources	$1,000	
Oil & Gas	$1,000	
None over $1,000		

Finance, Insurance & Real Estate	$2,200	
Securities & Investment	$1,250	
Hambrecht & Quist	$1,000	Indiv

Health	$8,625	
Health Professionals	$6,675	
American Nurses Assn	$2,000	PAC
American Academy of Ophthalmology	$1,000	PAC
Hospitals/Nursing Homes	$1,250	
American Health Care Assn	$1,000	PAC

Source of Funds in 1992 Election

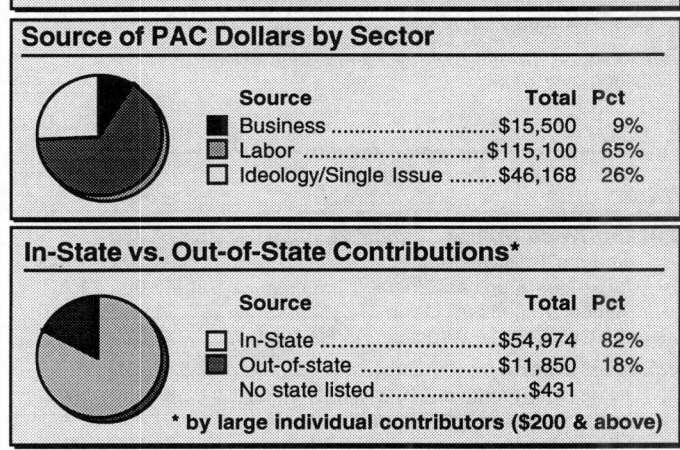

Source	Total	Pct
■ PACs	$185,507	28%
▨ Indivs $200+	$69,480	10%
□ Indivs under $200	$337,195	51%
⊠ Other	$73,801	11%
Candidate	$0	0%
Party	$29,841	4%

Source of PAC Dollars by Sector

Source	Total	Pct
■ Business	$15,500	9%
▨ Labor	$115,100	65%
□ Ideology/Single Issue	$46,168	26%

In-State vs. Out-of-State Contributions*

Source	Total	Pct
□ In-State	$54,974	82%
■ Out-of-state	$11,850	18%
No state listed	$431	

* by large individual contributors ($200 & above)

Lawyers & Lobbyists	$14,237	
Lawyers & Lobbyists	$14,237	
Assn of Trial Lawyers of America	$7,500	PAC
Summers, Compton et al	$1,500	Indiv

Misc Business | $7,645

Beer, Wine & Liquor	$2,541	
Mondavi Winery	$1,475	Indiv
Retail Sales	$1,025	
Real Goods Trading Co	$1,025	Indiv
Business Services	$1,685	
None over $1,000		
Lodging/Tourism	$1,194	
Rachel's Inn	$1,194	Indiv

Contribution Totals by Sector

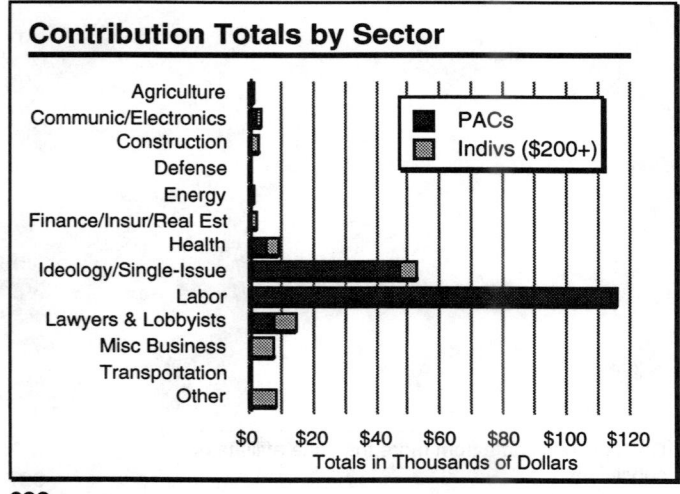

Labor

Labor	$115,350

Building Trade Unions **$16,250**
Carpenters & Joiners Union ....$5,000 PAC
Laborers' Political League ....$2,000 PAC
Operating Engineers Union* ....$2,000 PAC
Plumbers/Pipefitters Union ....$2,000 PAC
California State Pipe Trades Council ....$1,500 PAC
Ironworkers Union ....$1,500 PAC
Sheet Metal Workers Union* ....$1,250 Indiv
Painters & Allied Trades Union ....$1,000 PAC

Industrial Unions **$29,300**
United Auto Workers ....$10,000 PAC
Machinists/Aerospace Workers Union ....$7,500 PAC
Intl Brotherhood of Electrical Workers ....$5,000 PAC
Rubber Cork Linoleum & Plastic Workers ....$5,000 PAC
Communications Workers of America ....$1,000 PAC

Transportation Unions **$20,500**
Intl Longshoremen's/Warehousemen's Union .....$5,000 PAC
Teamsters Union ....$5,000 PAC
Air Line Pilots Assn ....$2,000 PAC
Marine Engineers Union ....$2,000 PAC
Seafarers International Union ....$2,000 PAC
United Transportation Union ....$1,500 PAC
Brotherhood of Locomotive Engineers ....$1,000 PAC

Public Sector Unions **$30,000**
American Fedn of St/Cnty/Munic Employees ....$10,000 PAC
National Education Assn ....$10,000 PAC
National Assn of Letter Carriers ....$4,500 PAC
American Federation of Teachers ....$2,500 PAC
International Assn of Firefighters ....$2,000 PAC
American Postal Workers Union ....$1,000 PAC

Misc Unions **$19,300**
Service Employees International Union ....$10,000 PAC
Food & Commercial Workers Union ....$5,000 PAC
AFL-CIO ....$2,500 PAC
Bakery, Confectionery & Tobacco Workers ....$1,500 PAC

Ideological/Single-Issue

Ideological/Single-Issue	$51,643

Democratic/Liberal **$10,825**
National Cmte for an Effective Congress ....$5,000 PAC
Hollywood Women's Political Cmte ....$2,500 PAC
Independent Action ....$1,000 PAC

Leadership PACs **$10,454**
24th Cong Dist of Calif PAC (Henry Waxman) ....$5,000 PAC
Victory USA (Vic Fazio) ....$2,000 PAC
Effective Government Cmte (Dick Gephardt) ......$1,954 PAC
House Leadership Fund (Tom Foley) ....$1,000 PAC

Foreign & Defense Policy **$3,820**
Council for a Livable World ....$3,290 PAC/Ind

Pro-Israel **$1,700**
National PAC ....$1,000 PAC

Pro-Choice **$3,750**
Voters for Choice ....$2,000 PAC/Ind
National Abortion Rights Action League ....$1,000 PAC

Human Rights **$6,000**
Human Rights Campaign Fund ....$5,000 PAC
KidsPAC ....$1,000 PAC

Misc Issues **$15,094**
League of Conservation Voters ....$5,000 PAC
Sierra Club ....$5,000 PAC
National Council of Senior Citizens....................$2,000 PAC
National Cmte to Preserve Social Security ....$1,500 PAC
California League of Conservation Voters ....$1,344 PAC

Other & Unknown

Other	$8,225

Non-Profit Institutions **$1,225**
Foundation for Hearing Aid Research ....$1,000 Indiv

Civil Servants/Public Officials **$3,200**
City of Los Gatos ....$1,000 Indiv
State of Minnesota ....$1,000 Indiv

Retired **$2,450**
None over $1,000

Unknown	$29,993

Homemakers/Non-income earners $1,500
No Employer Listed or Found $11,881
Generic Occupation/Category Unknown $7,987
Employer Listed/Category Unknown $8,625
   Woodstove & Sun ....$1,000 Indiv

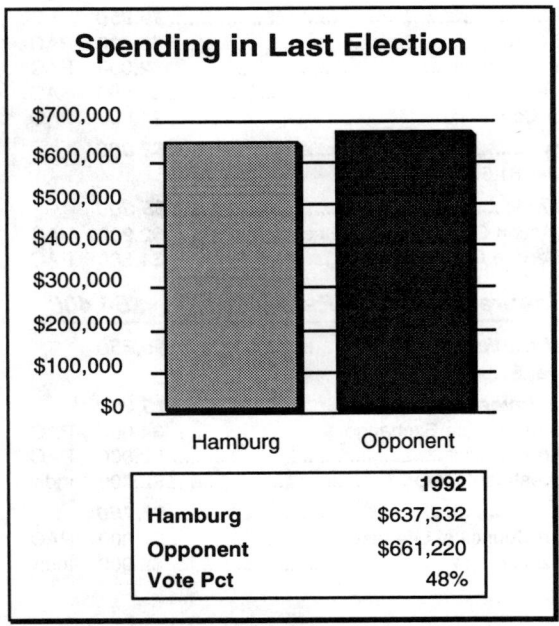

Spending in Last Election

	1992
Hamburg	$637,532
Opponent	$661,220
Vote Pct	48%

---

* Contributions came from more than one affiliate or subsidiary.

Lee H. Hamilton, D-Ind (9)

First elected: 1964

1991-92 Total Receipts: $485,788
1992 Year-end Cash: $66,788

1991-92 Committees & Subcommittees

Foreign Affairs
Arms Control, International Security and Science; Europe and the Middle East (Chairman); Human Rights and International Organizations

Joint Economic Committee (Vice Chairman)

Leading Contributors

Business

Agriculture $19,350

Crop Production & Basic Processing **$1,750**
  None over $1,500

Tobacco **$5,200**
  Philip Morris ....$1,500   PAC
  RJR Nabisco ....$1,500   PAC

Dairy **$4,000**
  Milk Marketing Inc ....$2,000   PAC
  Dairymen Inc ....$1,500   PAC

Agricultural Services/Products **$7,150**
  Indiana Farm Bureau ....$4,200   PAC

Communications/Electronics $15,500

Media/Entertainment **$2,500**
  None over $1,500

Telephone Utilities **$9,000**
  Indiana Bell Telephone ....$5,000   PAC
  AT&T ....$2,500   PAC

Telecom Services & Equipment **$1,500**
  None over $1,500

Electronics Mfg & Services **$1,500**
  None over $1,500

Construction $16,300

General Contractors **$6,300**
  KLM Construction Inc ....$3,000   Indiv

Home Builders **$6,000**
  National Assn of Home Builders ....$5,000   PAC

Source of Funds in 1992 Election

Source	Total	Pct
■ PACs	$199,150	41%
▨ Indivs $200+	$151,600	31%
☐ Indivs under $200	$120,983	25%
⊠ Other.......................	$14,418	3%
Candidate	$0	0%
Party	$513	0%

Source of PAC Dollars by Sector

Source	Total	Pct
■ Business	$129,000	64%
▨ Labor	$41,550	21%
☐ Ideology/Single Issue	$30,000	15%

In-State vs. Out-of-State Contributions*

Source	Total	Pct
☐ In-State	$18,800	12%
■ Out-of-state	$132,800	88%
No state listed	$0	

*** by large individual contributors ($200 & above)**

Construction Services **$2,000**
  None over $1,500

Building Materials & Equipment **$1,500**
  None over $1,500

Defense $11,300

Defense Aerospace **$7,800**
  General Dynamics ....$2,000   PAC
  McDonnell Douglas ....$2,000   PAC

Defense Electronics **$3,500**
  Aydin Corp ....$2,000   Indiv

Energy & Natural Resources $18,500

Oil & Gas **$9,950**
  Coastal Corp ....$3,500   PAC
  Dresser Industries ....$2,000   PAC
  USX Corp* ....$1,850   PAC
  Chevron Corp ....$1,500   PAC

Misc Energy **$2,000**
  None over $1,500

Electric Utilities **$5,300**
  ACRE (Action Cmte for Rural Electrification)* .....$2,200   PAC
  Public Service Co of Indiana ....$1,500   PAC

Finance, Insurance & Real Estate $54,400

Commercial Banks **$5,650**
  None over $1,500

Securities & Investment **$13,250**
  Chicago Mercantile Exchange ....$4,000   PAC
  American Express* ....$2,000   PAC
  Finial Investment Corp ....$2,000   Indiv

Insurance **$7,150**
  American Council of Life Insurance .....$2,000   PAC
  Omega Brokerage ....$2,000   Indiv

Contribution Totals by Sector

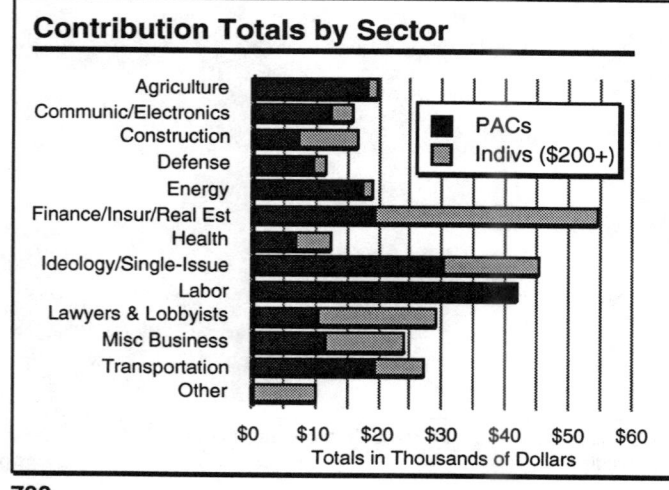

Legend: ■ PACs ▨ Indivs ($200+)

Sectors: Agriculture, Communic/Electronics, Construction, Defense, Energy, Finance/Insur/Real Est, Health, Ideology/Single-Issue, Labor, Lawyers & Lobbyists, Misc Business, Transportation, Other

Totals in Thousands of Dollars ($0 $10 $20 $30 $40 $50 $60)

Real Estate **$24,850**
    AKT Development Co ....$6,000   Indiv
    National Assn of Realtors ....$6,000   PAC
    Melvin Simon & Associates ....$3,000   Indiv
    MMM Invest Inc ....$2,000   Indiv

Accountants **$1,500**
    None over $1,500

Health $12,200

Health Professionals **$9,200**
    American Medical Assn* ....$2,100   PAC

Pharmaceuticals/Health Products **$2,500**
    None over $1,500

Lawyers & Lobbyists $28,750

Lawyers & Lobbyists **$28,750**
    Assn of Trial Lawyers of America ....$5,000   PAC
    Akin, Gump et al ....$2,500   PAC
    Neill & Co ....$2,500   Indiv
    Katz, Teller et al ....$1,500   Indiv

Misc Business $23,800

Food & Beverage **$3,000**
    None over $1,500

Beer, Wine & Liquor **$2,500**
    Joseph E Seagram & Sons ....$2,500   PAC

Retail Sales **$2,750**
    None over $1,500

Business Services **$6,800**
    Dun & Bradstreet ....$2,500   PAC

Misc Manufacturing & Distributing **$5,250**
    None over $1,500

Transportation $26,650

Air Transport **$11,900**
    Federal Express Corp ....$5,000   PAC
    United Parcel Service ....$2,900   PAC
    General Electric ....$2,000   PAC
    Boeing Co ....$1,500   PAC

Automotive **$6,750**
    Cummins Engine Co ....$2,750   Indiv
    National Auto Dealers Assn ....$2,000   PAC

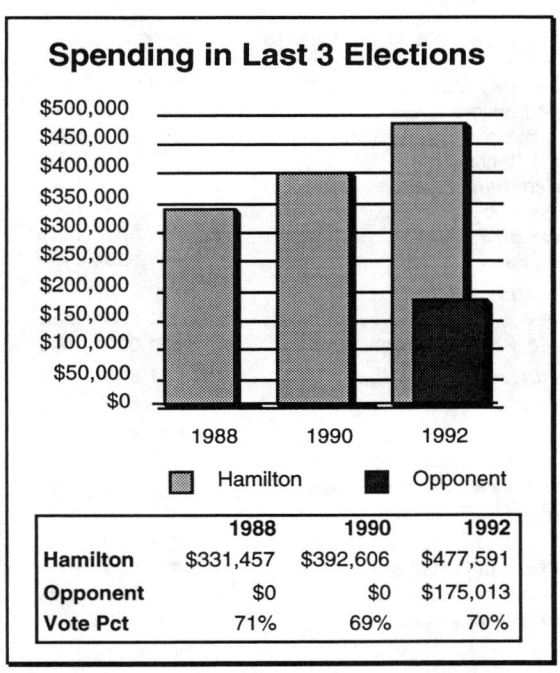

Spending in Last 3 Elections

	1988	1990	1992
Hamilton	$331,457	$392,606	$477,591
Opponent	$0	$0	$175,013
Vote Pct	71%	69%	70%

Legend: Hamilton / Opponent

Railroads **$1,500**
    None over $1,500

Sea Transport **$5,000**
    Star Trading & Marine Inc ....$2,000   Indiv

Misc Transport **$1,500**
    None over $1,500

Labor

Labor $41,550

Building Trade Unions **$6,250**
    Laborers' Political League ....$2,500   PAC
    AFL-CIO Bldg/Construction Trades Dept ....$1,500   PAC

Industrial Unions **$12,500**
    United Auto Workers ....$10,000   PAC

Transportation Unions **$7,600**
    Teamsters Union ....$5,000   PAC
    Marine Engineers Union ....$2,500   PAC

Public Sector Unions **$12,600**
    National Assn Retired Federal Employees ....$5,000   PAC
    American Fedn of St/Cnty/Munic Employees ......$2,600   PAC
    National Assn of Postmasters ....$1,500   PAC

Misc Unions **$2,600**
    Food & Commercial Workers Union ....$1,500   PAC

Ideological/Single-Issue

Ideological/Single-Issue $44,800

Democratic/Liberal **$5,500**
    National Cmte for an Effective Congress ....$2,500   PAC

Foreign & Defense Policy **$3,250**
    None over $1,500

Pro-Israel **$21,800**
    National PAC ....$5,000   PAC
    Citizens Organized PAC ....$2,500   PAC
    National Action Committee ....$2,500   PAC
    Florida Congressional Cmte ....$2,000   PAC
    Washington PAC ....$1,500   PAC

Gun Rights/Gun Control **$2,000**
    National Rifle Assn ....$2,000   PAC

Human Rights **$9,250**
    National Albanian American PAC ....$4,000   PAC
    Hellenic American Council ....$3,000   PAC

Misc Issues **$2,500**
    National Cmte to Preserve Social Security ....$2,000   PAC

Other & Unknown

Other $9,900

Education **$2,700**
    New York University ....$1,500   Indiv

Retired **$5,950**
    None over $1,500

Unknown $29,150

    Homemakers/Non-income earners $1,750
    No Employer Listed or Found $16,700
    Employer Listed/Category Unknown $10,450
        None over $1,500

---

* Contributions came from more than one affiliate or subsidiary.

Mel Hancock, R-Mo (7)

First elected: 1988

1991-92 Total Receipts: $393,638
1992 Year-end Cash: $96,147

1991-92 Committees & Subcommittees

Banking, Finance and Urban Affairs
Economic Stabilization; General Oversight and Investigations;
International Development, Finance, Trade and Monetary Policy

Public Works and Transportation
Aviation; Investigations and Oversight; Water Resources

Small Business
Procurement, Tourism and Rural Development (Ranking Republican);
Regulation, Business Opportunity and Energy

Leading Contributors

Business

Agriculture		$22,283	
Tobacco		**$2,500**	
RJR Nabisco		$2,500	PAC
Dairy		**$11,000**	
Mid-America Dairymen		$10,000	PAC
Associated Milk Producers		$1,000	PAC
Agricultural Services/Products		**$4,883**	
Missouri Farm Bureau/SW Dist		$2,600	PAC
Food Processing & Sales		**$1,900**	
Fleming Companies Inc		$1,000	PAC

Communications/Electronics		$8,600	
Media/Entertainment		**$2,000**	
KTXR		$1,000	Indiv
Telephone Utilities		**$6,300**	
AT&T		$3,500	PAC
Southwestern Bell		$1,000	PAC

Construction		$21,750	
General Contractors		**$11,000**	
Killian Construction Co		$6,000	Indiv
Associated Builders & Contractors		$1,500	PAC
Associated General Contractors		$1,000	PAC
National Utility Contractors Assn		$1,000	PAC
Special Trade Contractors		**$1,000**	
Sechler Electric Inc		$1,000	Indiv

Contribution Totals by Sector

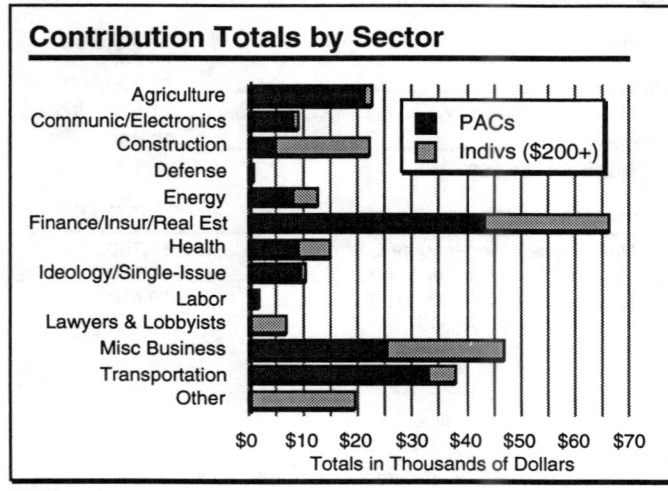

Totals in Thousands of Dollars

Source of Funds in 1992 Election

Source	Total	Pct
■ PACs	$164,430	42%
▨ Indivs $200+	$121,683	31%
□ Indivs under $200	$78,202	20%
▨ Other	$29,323	7%
Candidate	$0	0%
Party	$7,244	2%

Source of PAC Dollars by Sector

Source	Total	Pct
■ Business	$150,479	93%
▨ Labor	$1,500	1%
□ Ideology/Single Issue	$9,275	6%

In-State vs. Out-of-State Contributions*

Source	Total	Pct
□ In-State	$109,933	91%
■ Out-of-state	$11,350	9%
No state listed	$0	

*** by large individual contributors ($200 & above)**

Building Materials & Equipment	$9,250	
Tamko Asphalt Products Inc	$4,000	Indiv
Griesemer Stone Quarry	$2,000	Indiv
Tapjac Co Inc	$1,000	Indiv
Webco Engineering	$1,000	Indiv

Energy & Natural Resources	$12,200	
Oil & Gas	**$7,500**	
Empire Gas Corp	$2,000	Indiv
Morris Oil Co	$1,000	Indiv
Petroleum Marketers Assn	$1,000	PAC
Electric Utilities	**$4,200**	
Missouri ACRE	$3,200	PAC
Empire District Electric Co	$1,000	PAC

Finance, Insurance & Real Estate	$65,824	
Commercial Banks	**$19,549**	
Mercantile Bancorp	$3,600	PAC
American Bankers Assn*	$3,500	PAC
Commerce Bancshares	$1,724	PAC
Independent Bankers Assn	$1,500	PAC
Bank of Neosho	$1,000	Indiv
Commerce Bank	$1,000	Indiv
Marshfield Bank	$1,000	Indiv
Savings & Loans	**$2,675**	
Farm & Home Savings & Loan	$1,000	Indiv
US League of Savings Assns	$1,000	PAC
Securities & Investment	**$1,500**	
Morgan Stanley & Co	$1,000	PAC
Insurance	**$11,400**	
National Assn of Life Underwriters	$5,000	PAC
General American Life Insurance	$1,000	PAC
Shelter Mutual Insurance	$1,000	PAC
Real Estate	**$17,150**	
National Assn of Realtors	$10,000	PAC
H&T Apartments	$2,000	Indiv
Wilhoit Properties	$1,000	Indiv

Accountants **$7,800**
    American Institute of CPA's ....$5,000 PAC
    Elliott, Robinson & Co ....$2,000 Indiv

Misc Finance **$4,750**
    Progressive Finance Co ....$1,000 Indiv

Health $14,650

Health Professionals **$12,350**
    American Medical Assn* ....$6,350 PAC
    American Academy of Ophthalmology ....$1,500 PAC

Pharmaceuticals/Health Products **$1,450**
    None over $1,000

Lawyers & Lobbyists $6,675

Lawyers & Lobbyists **$6,675**
    Allen, Matkins et al ....$4,000 Indiv
    Vern Clark & Assoc ....$1,000 Indiv

Misc Business $46,576

Business Associations **$5,545**
    National Fedn of Independent Business ....$3,500 PAC
    Business Industry PAC ....$1,045 PAC
    Farm States Supply ....$1,000 Indiv

Food & Beverage **$5,879**
    National Restaurant Assn ....$2,000 PAC
    Ozarks Coca-Cola Bottling ....$1,000 Indiv
    Pepsi-Cola General Bottlers ....$1,000 PAC

Beer, Wine & Liquor **$4,200**
    National Beer Wholesalers Assn ....$2,500 PAC
    Duffy Distrution Inc ....$1,000 Indiv

Retail Sales **$9,002**
    Bass Pro Shops ....$4,000 Indiv

Business Services **$6,600**
    Federal Protection Inc ....$2,000 Indiv
    Missouri Neon Advertising Co ....$2,000 Indiv
    Alarm Industry Communications Cmte ....$1,000 PAC

Lodging/Tourism **$1,000**
    None over $1,000

Chemical & Related Manufacturing **$2,500**
    Dow Chemical ....$2,000 PAC

Misc Manufacturing & Distributing **$10,350**
    Leggett & Platt Inc ....$2,850 Indiv
    Stone Container Corp ....$2,500 PAC
    O&F Machine Products ....$2,000 Indiv
    Vi-Jon Laboratories ....$1,250 Indiv
    Hunter Engineering ....$1,000 PAC

Textiles **$1,000**
    Milliken & Co ....$1,000 Indiv

Transportation $37,650

Air Transport **$13,750**
    United Parcel Service ....$4,700 PAC
    Aircraft Owners & Pilots Assn ....$4,000 PAC
    United Airlines ....$1,500 PAC
    Trans World Airlines ....$1,000 PAC

Automotive **$13,850**
    National Auto Dealers Assn ....$8,000 PAC
    Aaron's Automotive ....$2,000 Indiv
    Auto Dealers & Drivers for Free Trade ....$2,000 PAC
    Americans for Free International Trade ....$1,000 PAC

Trucking **$2,850**
    Trailiner Corp ....$1,350 Indiv

Railroads **$6,200**
    Burlington Northern ....$4,700 PAC
    Union Pacific Corp ....$1,000 PAC

Sea Transport **$1,000**
    None over $1,000

Labor

Labor $1,500

Public Sector Unions **$1,000**
    National Assn Retired Federal Employees ....$1,000 PAC

Ideological/Single-Issue

Ideological/Single-Issue $10,275

Republican/Conservative **$1,325**
    None over $1,000

Gun Rights/Gun Control **$6,950**
    National Rifle Assn ....$6,950 PAC

Misc Issues **$1,500**
    Right to Work PAC ....$1,000 PAC

Other & Unknown

Other $19,000

Retired **$19,000**
    None over $1,000

Unknown $15,054

    Homemakers/Non-income earners $5,100
    Employer Listed/Category Unknown $9,475
        Consumers Markets Inc ....$1,000 Indiv
        Greene Country ....$1,000 Indiv
        Harry Cooper Supply ....$1,000 Indiv

Independent expenditures supporting Hancock
    National Right to Life PAC $2,330
    Missouri Citizens for Life $1,098

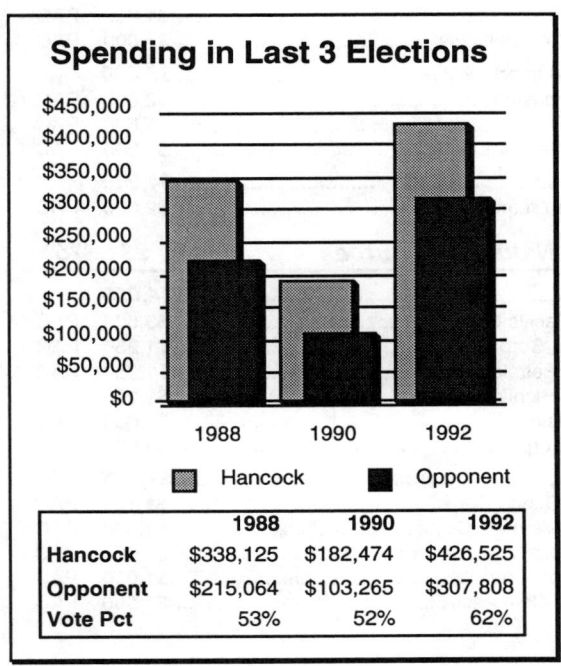

Spending in Last 3 Elections

	1988	1990	1992
Hancock	$338,125	$182,474	$426,525
Opponent	$215,064	$103,265	$307,808
Vote Pct	53%	52%	62%

---

* Contributions came from more than one affiliate or
subsidiary.

James V. Hansen, R-Utah (1)

First elected: 1980

1991-92 Total Receipts: $221,781
1992 Year-end Cash: $22,756

1991-92 Committees & Subcommittees

Armed Services
Military Installations and Facilities; Research and Development

Interior and Insular Affairs
National Parks and Public Lands; Water, Power and Offshore Energy (Ranking Republican)

Standards of Official Conduct (Ranking Republican)

Leading Contributors

Business

Agriculture	$4,250	
Livestock	**$1,750**	
National Cattlemen's Assn	$1,500	PAC
Forestry & Forest Products	**$1,000**	
None over $1,000		

Communications/Electronics	$4,500	
Media/Entertainment	**$1,000**	
National Cable Television Assn	$1,000	PAC
Telephone Utilities	**$2,500**	
US West Inc	$3,000	PAC
Electronics Mfg & Services	**$1,000**	
Ezra C Lundahl Inc	$1,000	Indiv

Construction	$8,000	
General Contractors	**$4,500**	
Associated General Contractors	$1,500	PAC
Jack B Parson Companies	$1,500	Indiv
Kier Corp	$1,000	Indiv
Home Builders	**$2,000**	
National Assn of Home Builders	$1,500	PAC
Construction Services	**$1,000**	
CH2M Hill	$1,000	PAC

Source of Funds in 1992 Election

Source	Total	Pct
■ PACs	$147,351	66%
▨ Indivs $200+	$46,285	21%
□ Indivs under $200	$22,226	10%
▧ Other	$5,919	3%
Candidate	$0	0%
Party	$3,154	1%

Source of PAC Dollars by Sector

Source	Total	Pct
■ Business	$127,100	91%
▨ Labor	$2,000	1%
□ Ideology/Single Issue	$10,950	8%

In-State vs. Out-of-State Contributions*

Source	Total	Pct
□ In-State	$34,785	75%
■ Out-of-state	$11,500	25%
No state listed	$0	

*** by large individual contributors ($200 & above)**

Defense	$33,750	
Defense Aerospace	**$20,900**	
Thiokol	$3,600	PAC
Lockheed Corp	$2,000	PAC
General Electric	$1,800	PAC
LTV Aerospace & Defense Co	$1,500	PAC
McDonnell Douglas*	$1,500	PAC
Northrop Corp	$1,500	PAC
Rockwell International	$1,500	PAC
Boeing Co	$1,000	PAC
Colt Industries	$1,000	PAC
General Dynamics	$1,000	PAC
Hercules Inc	$1,000	PAC
Martin Marietta Corp	$1,000	PAC
Textron Inc	$1,000	PAC
United Technologies	$1,000	PAC
Defense Electronics	**$8,600**	
Litton Industries	$2,000	PAC
AT&T	$1,500	PAC
Westinghouse Electric	$1,500	PAC
Misc Defense	**$4,250**	
General Atomics	$2,000	PAC

Energy & Natural Resources	$31,375	
Oil & Gas	**$14,050**	
Union Pacific Corp	$3,500	PAC
Chevron Corp	$1,250	PAC
Phillips Petroleum	$1,250	PAC
Atlantic Richfield	$1,000	PAC
BP America	$1,000	PAC
Exxon Corp	$1,000	PAC
Mining	**$7,975**	
Phelps Dodge Corp	$1,100	PAC
Cyprus Minerals Co	$1,000	PAC
Fluor Corp	$1,000	PAC
Kennecott Corp	$1,000	PAC
National Coal Assn	$1,000	PAC

Contribution Totals by Sector

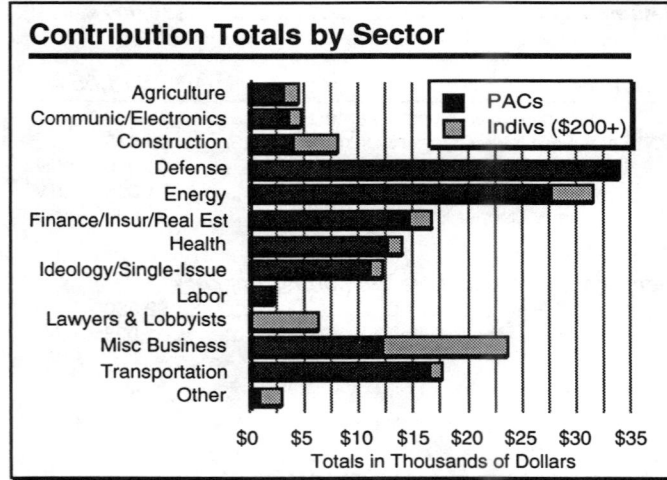

Totals in Thousands of Dollars

Categories: Agriculture, Communic/Electronics, Construction, Defense, Energy, Finance/Insur/Real Est, Health, Ideology/Single-Issue, Labor, Lawyers & Lobbyists, Misc Business, Transportation, Other

Legend: ■ PACs, ▨ Indivs ($200+)

Axis: $0, $5, $10, $15, $20, $25, $30, $35

Nuclear Energy **$1,750**
- Yankee Atomic Electric Co — $1,500 PAC

Misc Energy **$1,000**
- Bechtel Corp — $1,000 PAC

Electric Utilities **$3,100**
- ACRE (Action Cmte for Rural Electrification) — $1,000 PAC

Environmental Svcs/Equipment **$1,000**
- Montgomery Engineering — $1,000 PAC

Waste Management **$2,500**
- Envirocare of Utah — $2,000 Indiv

Finance, Insurance & Real Estate $16,450

Commercial Banks **$3,750**
- American Bankers Assn — $1,500 PAC
- First Security Bank — $1,000 Indiv

Insurance **$4,750**
- National Assn of Life Underwriters — $2,500 PAC
- American Family Corp — $1,000 PAC

Real Estate **$6,700**
- National Assn of Realtors — $6,500 PAC

Accountants **$1,000**
- American Institute of CPA's — $1,000 PAC

Health $13,700

Health Professionals **$12,200**
- American Medical Assn — $10,000 PAC
- American Academy of Ophthalmology — $2,000 PAC

Lawyers & Lobbyists $6,250

Lawyers & Lobbyists **$6,250**
- Green Callister Nebeker — $1,000 Indiv
- Timmons & Co — $1,000 Indiv

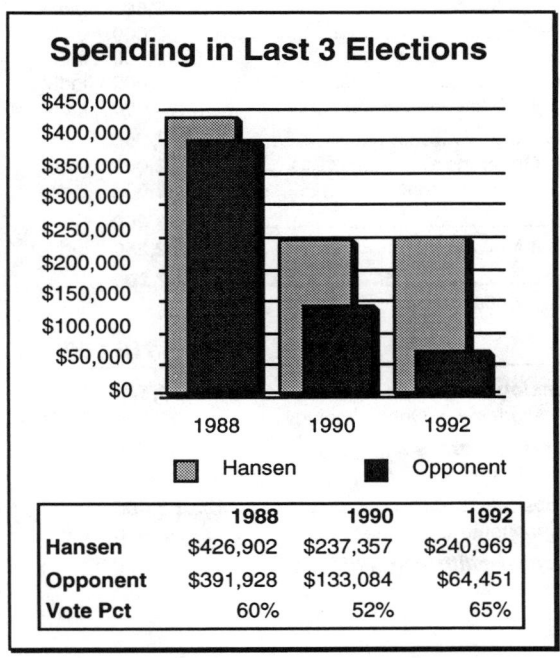

Spending in Last 3 Elections

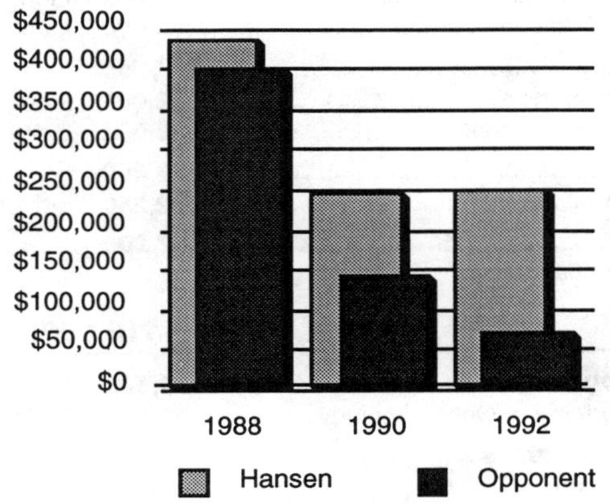

	1988	1990	1992
Hansen	$426,902	$237,357	$240,969
Opponent	$391,928	$133,084	$64,451
Vote Pct	60%	52%	65%

Misc Business $23,550

Beer, Wine & Liquor **$2,000**
- National Beer Wholesalers Assn — $2,000 PAC

Retail Sales **$3,800**
- Smith & Edwards — $1,800 Indiv
- International Council of Shopping Centers — $1,000 PAC

Business Services **$1,000**
- Cannon Industries — $1,000 Indiv

Recreation/Live Entertainment **$1,500**
- Lagoon Corp — $1,500 Indiv

Lodging/Tourism **$3,850**
- Holding's Little America — $1,500 Indiv
- Conference of National Park Concessioners — $1,000 PAC
- Marriott Corp — $1,000 PAC

Chemical & Related Manufacturing **$2,000**
- American Pacific Corp — $1,000 Indiv
- Huntsman Chemical Corp — $1,000 Indiv

Misc Manufacturing & Distributing **$9,000**
- Brush Wellman — $6,000 PAC
- Potomac Corp — $3,000 Indiv

Transportation $17,500

Air Transport **$6,750**
- Aircraft Owners & Pilots Assn — $3,000 PAC
- Delta Airlines — $1,500 PAC
- United Parcel Service — $1,250 PAC
- Williams International — $1,000 Indiv

Automotive **$9,250**
- National Auto Dealers Assn — $6,000 PAC
- Auto Dealers & Drivers for Free Trade — $2,000 PAC
- Americans for Free International Trade — $1,000 PAC

Labor

Labor $2,000

Public Sector Unions **$2,000**
- National Assn Retired Federal Employees — $1,500 PAC

Ideological/Single-Issue

Ideological/Single-Issue $11,950

Foreign & Defense Policy **$4,000**
- Veterans of Foreign Wars — $2,000 PAC
- National Assn of Arab-Americans — $1,000 PAC

Gun Rights/Gun Control **$7,450**
- National Rifle Assn — $6,450 PAC
- Safari Club International — $1,000 PAC

Other & Unknown

Other $2,700

Retired **$1,950**
- None over $1,000

Unknown $11,110

- Homemakers/Non-income earners — $1,000
- Generic Occupation/Category Unknown — $3,460
- Employer Listed/Category Unknown — $6,650
  - Redcon — $1,000 Indiv
  - Shipley Associates — $1,000 Indiv

* Contributions came from more than one affiliate or subsidiary.

Jane Harman, D-Calif (36)

First elected: 1992

1991-92 Total Receipts: $1,628,376
1992 Year-end Cash: $16,019

1993-94 Committees & Subcommittees

Armed Services
Military Forces and Personnel; Oversight and Investigations;
Research and Technology

Science, Space and Technology
Space; Technology, Environment and Aviation

Leading Contributors

Business

Communications/Electronics	$49,400	
Printing & Publishing **$11,000**		
Jostens Publishing Group	$2,500	Indiv
Art & Auction Magazine	$2,000	Indiv
Media/Entertainment **$28,400**		
Disney Channel*	$2,750	Indiv
MCA Inc	$2,700	PAC/Ind
Telephone Utilities **$3,250**		
None over $2,000		
Telecom Services & Equipment **$5,250**		
Loral Conic	$2,000	Indiv
Mobile Telecommunications Technologies	$2,000	Indiv

Construction	$5,900	
Home Builders **$2,000**		
Kaufman & Broad	$2,000	Indiv
Building Materials & Equipment **$2,700**		
None over $2,000		

Defense	$43,434	
Defense Aerospace **$23,184**		
Northrop Corp	$10,699	PAC/Ind
Rockwell International	$5,235	PAC/Ind
Lockheed Corp	$5,000	PAC
Defense Electronics **$20,250**		
Hughes Aircraft	$8,500	PAC/Ind
Loral Corp	$8,000	PAC/Ind
TRW Inc	$2,750	PAC/Ind

Source of Funds in 1992 Election

Source	Total	Pct
■ PACs	$198,208	12%
▨ Indivs $200+	$449,410	27%
☐ Indivs under $200	$148,766	9%
⊠ Other	$840,732	51%
Candidate	$823,000	50%
Party	$13,890	1%

Source of PAC Dollars by Sector

Source	Total	Pct
■ Business	$71,699	35%
▨ Labor	$65,040	32%
☐ Ideology/Single Issue	$66,446	33%

In-State vs. Out-of-State Contributions*

Source	Total	Pct
☐ In-State	$191,009	43%
■ Out-of-state	$252,001	57%
No state listed	$500	

* by large individual contributors ($200 & above)

Energy & Natural Resources	$4,200	
Mining **$3,000**		
American Premier Inc	$3,000	Indiv

Finance, Insurance & Real Estate	$71,950	
Securities & Investment **$45,300**		
Patricof & Co Ventures Inc	$3,500	Indiv
Brentwood Associates	$3,300	Indiv
Shearson Lehman Brothers	$3,000	Indiv
Goldman, Sachs & Co	$2,800	PAC/Ind
LT Funston & Co	$2,500	Indiv
Lazard Freres & Co	$2,500	Indiv
Argosy Group	$2,000	Indiv
Bessemer Venture Partners	$2,000	Indiv
Blackstone Group	$2,000	Indiv
Howard Alper Management	$2,000	Indiv
Real Estate **$18,250**		
Cloverleaf Group Inc	$3,000	Indiv
Maguire Thomas Partners	$2,000	Indiv
Accountants **$3,000**		
KPMG Peat Marwick	$2,250	Indiv
Misc Finance **$2,200**		
None over $2,000		

Health	$16,000	
Health Professionals **$8,500**		
American Academy of Ophthalmology	$2,000	PAC
Hospitals/Nursing Homes **$2,000**		
None over $2,000		
Health Services **$2,000**		
Kaiser Permanente	$2,000	Indiv
Pharmaceuticals/Health Products **$2,000**		
None over $2,000		

Contribution Totals by Sector

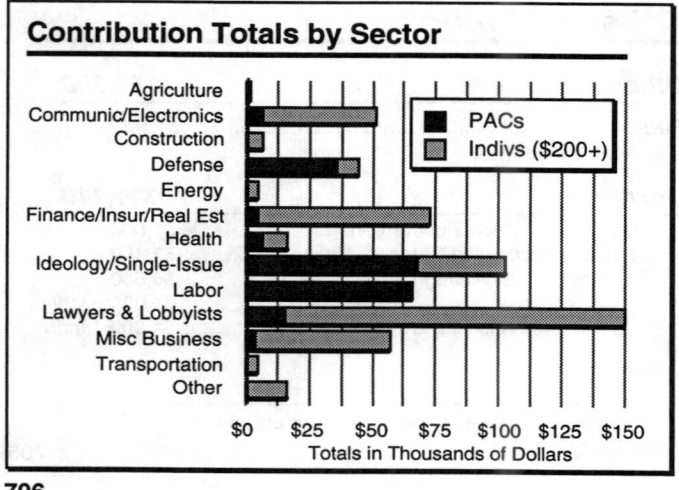

Agriculture
Communic/Electronics
Construction
Defense
Energy
Finance/Insur/Real Est
Health
Ideology/Single-Issue
Labor
Lawyers & Lobbyists
Misc Business
Transportation
Other

■ PACs
▨ Indivs ($200+)

$0 $25 $50 $75 $100 $125 $150
Totals in Thousands of Dollars

Lawyers & Lobbyists | $148,925

Lawyers & Lobbyists **$148,925**
Jones, Day et al	$39,900	PAC/Ind
Latham & Watkins	$10,014	Indiv
Manatt, Phelps et al	$5,250	PAC/Ind
Assn of Trial Lawyers of America	$5,000	PAC
Skadden, Arps et al	$3,750	Indiv
Weil, Gotshal & Manges	$3,500	Indiv
Wilmer, Cutler & Pickering	$3,000	Indiv
Hogan & Hartson	$2,250	Indiv
Akin, Gump et al	$2,100	PAC/Ind
Coblentz, Cohen et al	$2,000	Indiv
Cravath, Swaine & Moore	$2,000	Indiv
Kelly, McAuliffe et al	$2,000	Indiv
Tyre, Kamins et al	$2,000	Indiv

Misc Business | $55,350

Misc Services **$3,250**
None over $2,000		

Business Services **$17,500**
Grey Advertising Inc	$4,500	Indiv

Recreation/Live Entertainment **$4,200**
None over $2,000		

Steel Production **$2,000**
LTV Steel	$2,000	PAC

Misc Manufacturing & Distributing **$21,650**
Harman International Industries	$10,650	Indiv
JBL Consumer Products	$3,500	Indiv
21 International Holdings Inc	$2,500	Indiv

Transportation | $4,900

Air Transport **$2,000**
General Electric	$3,000	PAC/Ind

Spending in Last Election

	1992
Harman	$1,612,356
Opponent	$811,592
Vote Pct	48%

Labor

Labor | **$65,040**

Building Trade Unions **$12,500**
Bricklayers Union	$10,000	PAC
Laborers' Western Political League	$2,000	PAC

Industrial Unions **$20,500**
United Auto Workers	$10,000	PAC
Machinists/Aerospace Workers Union ...	$5,000	PAC
Communications Workers of America ...	$3,000	PAC
Intl Brotherhood of Electrical Workers ...	$2,500	PAC

Transportation Unions **$5,540**
Marine Engineers Union.....................	$2,500	PAC

Public Sector Unions **$18,000**
National Education Assn	$10,000	PAC
National Assn of Letter Carriers	$5,000	PAC
American Fedn of St/Cnty/Munic Employees ...	$3,000	PAC

Misc Unions **$8,500**
Food & Commercial Workers Union	$5,000	PAC
AFL-CIO	$3,500	PAC

Ideological/Single-Issue

Ideological/Single-Issue | **$101,546**

Democratic/Liberal **$22,500**
Hollywood Women's Political Cmte	$10,000	PAC
National Cmte for an Effective Congress ...	$5,000	PAC
Center for National Policy	$2,000	Indiv

Leadership PACs **$9,400**
Friends of Edelman	$2,400	PAC
House Leadership Fund (Tom Foley) ...	$2,000	PAC

Pro-Israel **$2,500**
None over $2,000		

Pro-Choice **$9,250**
National Abortion Rights Action League ...	$5,000	PAC

Womens Issues..**$40,932**
Emily's List	$11,087	PAC/Ind
Women's Campaign Fund	$9,000	PAC
Women's Political Committee	$5,000	PAC
National Organization for Women	$3,145	PAC
National Womens Political Caucus	$2,000	PAC

Human Rights **$9,250**
Human Rights Campaign Fund...........	$5,000	PAC

Misc Issues..**$7,714**
Sierra Club	$5,664	PAC/Ind

Other & Unknown

Other | **$16,250**

Education **$5,700**
University of Southern California	$2,450	Indiv

Retired **$7,050**
None over $2,000		

Unknown | **$67,900**
Homemakers/Non-income earners	$20,600	
No Employer Listed or Found	$7,900	
Generic Occupation/Category Unknown ...	$2,200	
Employer Listed/Category Unknown ...	$37,200	
DYG Group	$2,500	Indiv
Mary Boies & Associates	$2,000	Indiv
Sentura Creations	$2,000	Indiv

* Contributions came from more than one affiliate or
subsidiary.

Dennis Hastert, R-III (14)

First elected: 1986

1991-92 Total Receipts: $601,812
1992 Year-end Cash: $177,247

1991-92 Committees & Subcommittees

Energy and Commerce
Energy and Power; Health and the Environment

Government Operations
Commerce, Consumer and Monetary Affairs (Ranking Republican)

Select Committee on Hunger

Leading Contributors

Business

Agriculture	$43,792	
Crop Production & Basic Processing	$4,725	
None over $1,500		
Tobacco	$11,500	
RJR Nabisco	$4,000	PAC
US Tobacco Co	$2,500	PAC
Eby-Brown Co	$2,000	Indiv
Philip Morris	$1,500	PAC
Livestock	$3,240	
None over $1,500		
Agricultural Services/Products	$11,427	
Deere & Co	$2,000	PAC
American Veterinary Medical Assn	$1,500	PAC
Food Processing & Sales	$10,500	
Food Marketing Institute	$2,500	PAC
Nabisco Brands Inc	$2,000	PAC

Communications/Electronics	$47,900	
Printing & Publishing	$3,500	
La Salle Tribune	$3,000	Indiv
Media/Entertainment	$12,400	
National Cable Television Assn	$6,000	PAC
National Assn of Broadcasters	$3,000	PAC
Telephone Utilities	$30,200	
BellSouth Corp*	$8,500	PAC
Ameritech Corp*	$6,000	PAC
GTE Corp	$5,000	PAC
NYNEX Corp	$1,950	PAC
Pacific Telesis Group	$1,500	PAC
Southwestern Bell	$1,500	PAC

Source of Funds in 1992 Election

Source	Total	Pct
■ PACs	$317,156	53%
▨ Indivs $200+	$116,808	19%
☐ Indivs under $200	$135,020	22%
▧ Other	$32,828	5%
Candidate	$5	0%
Party	$544	0%

Source of PAC Dollars by Sector

Source	Total	Pct
■ Business	$304,163	97%
▨ Labor	$3,500	1%
☐ Ideology/Single Issue	$4,500	1%

In-State vs. Out-of-State Contributions*

Source	Total	Pct
☐ In-State	$113,158	98%
■ Out-of-state	$2,650	2%
No state listed	$1,000	

* by large individual contributors ($200 & above)

Construction	$29,000	
General Contractors	$9,200	
Associated General Contractors	$2,000	PAC
Furnas Electric Co	$2,000	Indiv
Sho-Deen Construction	$2,000	Indiv
Home Builders	$5,000	
National Assn of Home Builders	$5,000	PAC
Special Trade Contractors	$2,900	
None over $1,500		
Building Materials & Equipment	$10,500	
Caterpillar Tractor	$3,500	PAC
Elmer Larson Inc	$2,200	Indiv
Elmhurst-Chicago Stone Co	$2,000	Indiv

Defense	$1,500	
Defense Aerospace	$1,500	
None over $1,500		

Energy & Natural Resources	$32,150	
Oil & Gas	$11,600	
Petroleum Marketers Assn*	$1,850	PAC
Mining	$1,500	
None over $1,500		
Electric Utilities	$16,800	
Illinois Power Co	$2,200	PAC
Central Illinois Public Service Co	$1,800	PAC

Finance, Insurance & Real Estate	$72,646	
Commercial Banks	$19,690	
American Bankers Assn	$4,000	PAC
Merchants National Corp	$2,850	Indiv
Continental Illinois Corp	$2,000	PAC
First National Bank	$2,000	Indiv
First Chicago Corp	$1,500	PAC

Contribution Totals by Sector

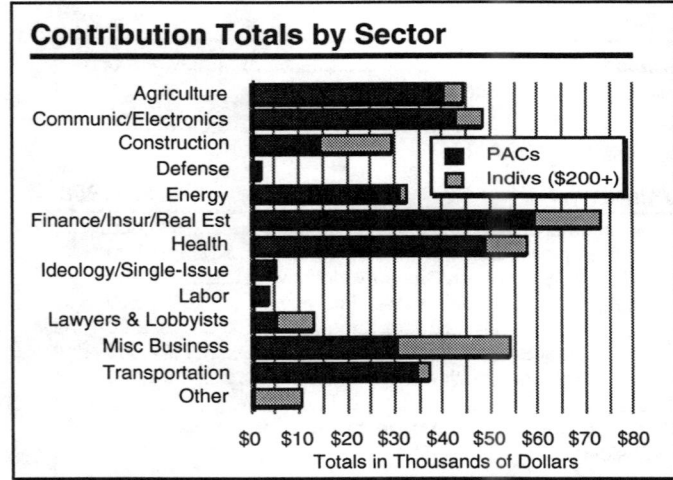

Agriculture
Communic/Electronics
Construction
Defense
Energy
Finance/Insur/Real Est
Health
Ideology/Single-Issue
Labor
Lawyers & Lobbyists
Misc Business
Transportation
Other

■ PACs
▨ Indivs ($200+)

$0 $10 $20 $30 $40 $50 $60 $70 $80
Totals in Thousands of Dollars

Securities & Investment $4,200
    Chicago Mercantile Exchange ....$1,500 PAC

Insurance $13,956
    American Family Corp ....$2,000 PAC
    Golden Rule Insurance Co ....$1,500 PAC
    National Assn of Independent Insurers.....$1,500 PAC

Real Estate $9,600
    National Assn of Realtors ....$7,000 PAC

Accountants $23,200
    American Institute of CPA's ....$10,000 PAC
    Arthur Andersen & Co ....$7,000 PAC
    Coopers & Lybrand ....$2,700 PAC/Ind

Health $57,000

Health Professionals $34,350
    American Medical Assn.......................$10,000 PAC
    American Dental Assn ....$6,500 PAC
    American College of Emergency Physicians.......$2,400 PAC
    American Academy of Ophthalmology ...$2,000 PAC
    American Soc Plastic & Reconstr Surgeons.....$1,500 PAC
    University of Chicago Medical Center....$1,500 Indiv

Hospitals/Nursing Homes $9,000
    American Hospital Assn ....$3,500 PAC
    American Health Care Assn ....$2,500 PAC
    Marianjoy Rehab Center ....$2,000 Indiv

Pharmaceuticals/Health Products $12,150
    Proprietary Association ....$1,600 PAC
    Pfizer Inc ....$1,500 PAC

Lawyers & Lobbyists $12,450

Lawyers & Lobbyists $12,450
    Rathje, Woodward et al ....$2,500 Indiv
    Crowell & Moring ....$1,500 PAC
    Jones, Day et al ....$1,500 PAC

Misc Business $53,725

Food & Beverage $12,050
    White Fence Farm Restaurant ....$3,000 Indiv
    McDonald's Corp ....$2,000 PAC/Ind
    Lincoln Inn Restaurant ....$1,700 Indiv
    Pepsi-Cola General Bottlers ....$1,600 PAC

Spending in Last 3 Elections

	1988	1990	1992
Hastert	$334,785	$312,555	$615,535
Opponent	$0	$0	$0
Vote Pct	74%	67%	67%

Retail Sales $3,000
    None over $1,500

Business Services $5,500
    Alarm Detection Systems ....$2,000 Indiv
    LM Berry & Co ....$1,500 PAC

Chemical & Related Manufacturing $13,000
    Safety-Kleen Corp ....$2,500 Indiv
    Dow Chemical ....$2,000 PAC
    Nalco Chemical Co ....$2,000 PAC
    FMC Corp ....$1,750 PAC
    Dial Corp ....$1,500 PAC

Misc Manufacturing & Distributing $17,900
    Commander Packaging Co ....$4,000 Indiv
    Aurora Cord & Cable ....$2,200 Indiv
    Ace Metal Refinishers ....$2,000 Indiv
    Owens-Illinois ....$2,000 PAC
    Stone Container Corp ....$2,000 PAC
    Libbey-Owens-Ford ....$1,500 PAC

Transportation $37,075

Air Transport $11,575
    United Parcel Service ....$4,400 PAC
    Federal Express Corp ....$3,000 PAC
    General Electric ....$1,500 PAC
    United Airlines ....$1,500 PAC

Automotive $12,750
    National Auto Dealers Assn ....$5,500 PAC
    Ford Motor Co ....$1,500 PAC
    General Motors....................................$1,500 PAC

Trucking $3,000
    None over $1,500

Railroads $8,250
    Union Pacific Corp ....$2,000 PAC

Sea Transport...$1,500
    None over $1,500

Labor

Labor $3,500

Public Sector Unions $2,500
    National Assn Retired Federal Employees.....$2,000 PAC

Ideological/Single-Issue

Ideological/Single-Issue $5,000

Misc Issues $4,000
    National Cmte to Preserve Social Security.....$4,000 PAC

Other & Unknown

Other $9,800

Retired $9,800
    None over $1,500

Unknown $23,683

    No Employer Listed or Found $1,700
    Generic Occupation/Category Unknown $3,200
    Employer Listed/Category Unknown $18,283
        Harding & Harding ....$1,500 Indiv

* Contributions came from more than one affiliate or
subsidiary.

Alcee L. Hastings, D-Fla (23)

First elected: 1992

1991-92 Total Receipts:	$310,070
1992 Year-end Cash:	$7,211

1993-94 Committees & Subcommittees

Foreign Affairs
Africa; Europe and the Middle East

Merchant Marine and Fisheries
Coast Guard and Navigation; Merchant Marine

Post Office and Civil Service
Oversight and Investigations

Leading Contributors

Business

Agriculture	$5,500	
Crop Production & Basic Processing	**$1,000**	
United States Sugar Corp	$1,000	PAC
Tobacco	**$1,500**	
Philip Morris	$1,500	PAC/Ind
Misc Agriculture	**$3,000**	
None over $1,000		

Communications/Electronics	$2,000	
Telephone Utilities	**$2,000**	
Southern Bell	$2,000	PAC

Construction	$7,400	
General Contractors	**$4,450**	
Adler Group Inc	$2,000	Indiv
Home Builders	**$2,200**	
Wade Development	$2,000	Indiv

Finance, Insurance & Real Estate	$15,450	
Commercial Banks	**$3,000**	
Intercontinental Bank	$1,000	Indiv
Seaway National Bank	$1,000	Indiv
Insurance	**$1,500**	
Fidelity Insurance Inc	$1,000	Indiv
Real Estate	**$7,250**	
American Marketing & Management	$3,000	Indiv
Accountants	**$2,500**	
None over $1,000		

Source of Funds in 1992 Election

Source	Total	Pct
■ PACs	$59,450	19%
▨ Indivs $200+	$145,101	48%
☐ Indivs under $200	$80,228	26%
▧ Other	$20,200	7%
Candidate	$20,200	7%
Party	$0	0%

Source of PAC Dollars by Sector

Source	Total	Pct
■ Business	$4,500	6%
▨ Labor	$52,000	75%
☐ Ideology/Single Issue	$13,007	19%

In-State vs. Out-of-State Contributions*

Source	Total	Pct
☐ In-State	$154,011	79%
■ Out-of-state	$41,300	21%
No state listed	$2,050	

*** by large individual contributors ($200 & above)**

Health	$16,950	
Health Professionals	**$15,550**	
None over $1,000		
Misc Health	**$1,400**	
Florida International Medical Assn	$1,000	Indiv

Lawyers & Lobbyists	$57,920	
Lawyers & Lobbyists	**$57,920**	
Tripp, Scott et al	$6,000	Indiv
Sylvester Lukis & Associates	$4,000	Indiv
Amlong & Amlong	$2,000	Indiv
Kurzban, Kurzban & Weinger	$2,000	Indiv
Mesirov, Gelman et al	$2,000	Indiv
Steel, Hector & Davis	$2,000	Indiv
Sonnett, Sale & Kuehne	$1,600	Indiv
Kluger, Peretz et al	$1,500	Indiv
Krupnick, Campbell et al	$1,500	Indiv

Misc Business	$6,901	
Beer, Wine & Liquor	**$4,200**	
Brown Distributing Co	$4,000	Indiv
Misc Services	**$1,801**	
Blockbuster Entertainment	$1,000	Indiv

Transportation	$5,500	
Automotive	**$5,500**	
Alamo Rent-a-Car	$4,000	Indiv
Lehman Buick	$1,500	Indiv

Contribution Totals by Sector

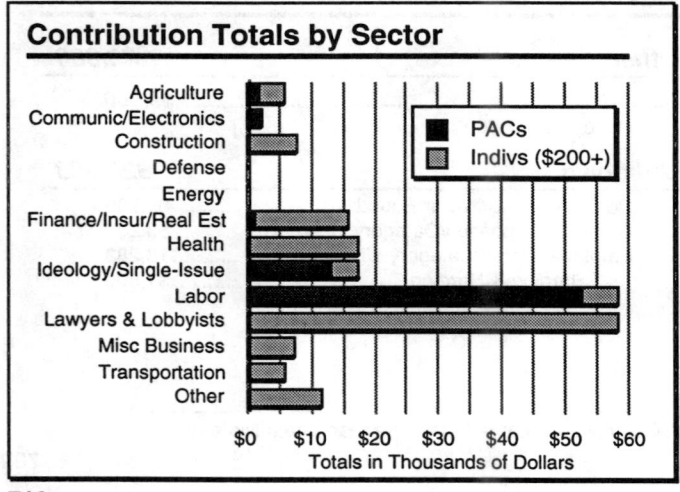

Agriculture
Communic/Electronics
Construction
Defense
Energy
Finance/Insur/Real Est
Health
Ideology/Single-Issue
Labor
Lawyers & Lobbyists
Misc Business
Transportation
Other

■ PACs
▨ Indivs ($200+)

$0 $10 $20 $30 $40 $50 $60
Totals in Thousands of Dollars

Labor

Labor		$58,000
Building Trade Unions	**$6,000**	
Asbestos Workers Union Local	$2,000	Indiv
Asbestos Workers local #60	$1,000	PAC
Laborers' Political League	$1,000	PAC
Plumbers/Pipefitters #519	$1,000	PAC
Sheet Metal Workers Union	$1,000	PAC
Industrial Unions	**$9,000**	
Machinists/Aerospace Workers Union	$3,000	PAC
United Auto Workers	$3,000	PAC
United Steelworkers	$2,000	PAC
Communications Workers of America	$1,000	PAC
Transportation Unions	**$25,500**	
Marine Engineers Union*	$15,000	PAC
Teamsters Union	$4,500	PAC
International Longshoremen's Assn*	$3,000	PAC
National Air Traffic Controllers Assn	$1,000	PAC
Transport Workers Union	$1,000	PAC
United Transportation Union	$1,000	PAC
Public Sector Unions	**$12,500**	
National Education Assn	$7,500	PAC
American Fedn of St/Cnty/Munic Employees	$5,000	PAC
Misc Unions	**$5,000**	
Food & Commercial Workers Union	$1,000	PAC

Ideological/Single-Issue

Ideological/Single-Issue		$17,007
Democratic/Liberal	**$1,000**	
None over $1,000		
Foreign & Defense Policy	**$2,000**	
Haitian-American Foundation	$2,000	Indiv
Pro-Israel	**$1,500**	
None over $1,000		
Pro-Choice	**$1,250**	
National Abortion Rights Action League	$1,000	PAC
Gun Rights/Gun Control	**$4,950**	
National Rifle Assn	$4,950	PAC
Human Rights	**$2,000**	
Human Rights Campaign Fund	$2,000	PAC
Misc Issues	**$3,000**	
National Council of Senior Citizens	$3,000	PAC

Other & Unknown

Other		$11,340
Civil Servants/Public Officials	**$3,250**	
Metro-Dade County	$2,000	Indiv
Education	**$5,000**	
None over $1,000		
Retired	**$1,150**	
None over $1,000		
Other	**$1,940**	
None over $1,000		

Unknown		$63,100
Homemakers/Non-income earners	$1,000	
No Employer Listed or Found	$41,400	
Generic Occupation/Category Unknown	$8,500	
Employer Listed/Category Unknown	$12,000	
Wade Industries	$6,000	Indiv
Curtoom Group Inc	$1,500	Indiv
IMDC Inc	$1,000	Indiv
Jaffe/Clayman PA	$1,000	Indiv

Spending in Last Election

Bar chart with y-axis from $0 to $350,000 in $50,000 increments.

	1992
Hastings	$314,285
Opponent	$15,622
Vote Pct	59%

* Contributions came from more than one affiliate or subsidiary.

Jimmy Hayes, D-La (7)

First elected: 1986

1991-92 Total Receipts: $507,046
1992 Year-end Cash: $42,064

1991-92 Committees & Subcommittees

Public Works and Transportation
Aviation; Investigations and Oversight; Water Resources (Vice-Chairman)

Science, Space and Technology
Science; Space

Leading Contributors

Business

Agriculture		$32,505

Crop Production & Basic Processing	**$6,000**	
American Sugar Cane League	$2,000	PAC
Tobacco	**$2,200**	
Philip Morris	$1,700	PAC
Dairy	**$1,600**	
None over $1,500		
Livestock	**$5,350**	
Texas & Southwestern Cattle Raisers	$2,500	PAC
National Cattlemen's Assn*	$2,350	PAC
Agricultural Services/Products	**$3,250**	
Freeport-McMoRan Inc	$2,000	PAC
Food Processing & Sales	**$5,200**	
Fleming Companies Inc	$2,000	PAC
Food Marketing Institute	$1,700	PAC
Forestry & Forest Products	**$8,905**	
Westvaco Corp	$2,000	PAC

Communications/Electronics		$9,400

Media/Entertainment	**$1,850**	
None over $1,500		
Telephone Utilities	**$6,300**	
BellSouth Corp*	$5,000	PAC

Construction		$40,580

General Contractors	**$15,730**	
Fluor Corp	$4,000	PAC
Associated General Contractors	$2,850	PAC
National Utility Contractors Assn	$2,330	PAC

Contribution Totals by Sector

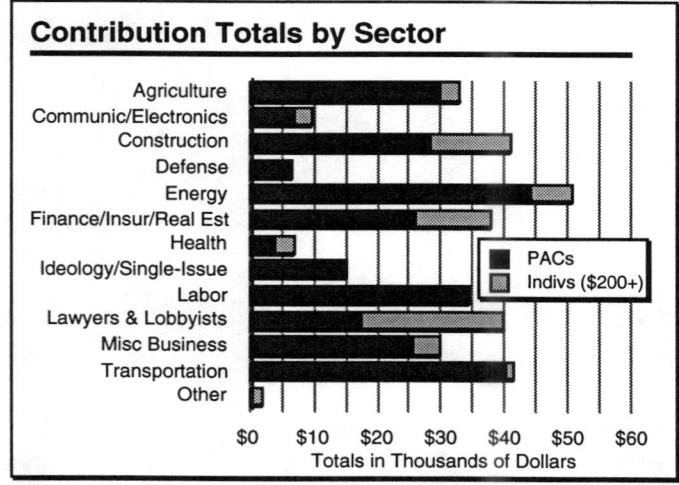

Agriculture
Communic/Electronics
Construction
Defense
Energy
Finance/Insur/Real Est
Health
Ideology/Single-Issue
Labor
Lawyers & Lobbyists
Misc Business
Transportation
Other

■ PACs
▨ Indivs ($200+)

$0 $10 $20 $30 $40 $50 $60
Totals in Thousands of Dollars

Source of Funds in 1992 Election

Source	Total	Pct
■ PACs	$240,552	47%
▨ Indivs $200+	$82,000	16%
☐ Indivs under $200	$36,388	7%
▨ Other	$148,243	29%
Candidate	$0	0%
Party	$15,687	3%

Source of PAC Dollars by Sector

Source	Total	Pct
■ Business	$226,017	82%
▨ Labor	$34,250	12%
☐ Ideology/Single Issue	$14,921	5%

In-State vs. Out-of-State Contributions*

Source	Total	Pct
☐ In-State	$52,900	65%
■ Out-of-state	$28,350	35%
No state listed	$200	

* by large individual contributors ($200 & above)

Home Builders	**$7,250**	
National Assn of Home Builders	$5,000	PAC
Construction Services	**$10,350**	
Vernon F Meyer & Assoc	$4,000	Indiv
John Chance & Assoc	$1,500	Indiv
Building Materials & Equipment	**$6,500**	
Dravo Corp	$1,500	PAC/Ind

Defense		$6,500

Defense Aerospace	**$4,650**	
Martin Marietta Corp	$1,600	PAC
Misc Defense	**$1,850**	
None over $1,500		

Energy & Natural Resources		$50,425

Oil & Gas	**$37,675**	
Graham Resources	$4,200	PAC/Ind
Columbia Gas System*	$2,600	PAC
Louisiana Land & Exploration	$2,000	PAC
Consolidated Natural Gas*	$1,575	PAC
Exxon Corp	$1,500	PAC
Mobil Oil	$1,500	PAC/Ind
Phillips Petroleum	$1,500	PAC
Mining	**$2,800**	
None over $1,500		
Electric Utilities	**$7,500**	
Entergy Corp*	$2,400	PAC

Finance, Insurance & Real Esta		$37,612

Insurance	**$15,262**	
Independent Insurance Agents of America	$6,050	PAC
National Assn of Life Underwriters	$5,000	PAC
Real Estate	**$17,850**	
National Assn of Realtors	$5,000	PAC
Misc Finance	**$4,200**	
None over $1,500		

Health $6,550

Health Professionals $4,800
    None over $1,500

Lawyers & Lobbyists $39,425

Lawyers & Lobbyists $39,425
    Assn of Trial Lawyers of America ....$10,000 PAC
    Jones, Walker et al ....$3,200 PAC/Ind
    Camp, Barsh & Tate ....$1,600 Indiv
    Long Law Firm ....$1,600 Indiv
    Mangham, Hardy et al ....$1,600 Indiv
    Holland & Hart ....$1,500 PAC

Misc Business $29,470

Food & Beverage $5,300
    Pepsi-Cola Bottlers Assn ....$2,000 PAC
Beer, Wine & Liquor $1,750
    National Beer Wholesalers Assn ....$1,500 PAC
Retail Sales $10,749
    International Council of Shopping Centers ....$9,999 PAC
Business Services $2,121
    None over $1,500
Lodging/Tourism $2,750
    Powell Group ....$2,000 Indiv
Chemical & Related Manufacturing $4,850
    Olin Corp ....$2,000 PAC
    WR Grace & Co ....$1,850 PAC

Transportation $41,000

Air Transport $26,300
    Federal Express Corp ....$10,000 PAC
    United Parcel Service ....$6,350 PAC
    American Airlines ....$2,850 PAC
    Boeing Co ....$2,200 PAC
Automotive $3,350
    Auto Dealers & Drivers for Free Trade ....$1,500 PAC
Railroads $5,750
    Union Pacific Corp ....$2,350 PAC
Sea Transport $4,850
    None over $1,500

Labor

Labor $34,250

Building Trade Unions $1,500
    Laborers' Political League ....$1,500 PAC
Industrial Unions $4,200
    Intl Brotherhood of Electrical Workers ....$2,000 PAC
Transportation Unions $18,800
    Air Line Pilots Assn ....$5,000 PAC
    Seafarers International Union ....$5,000 PAC
    Marine Engineers Union* ....$2,500 PAC
    Teamsters Union ....$2,500 PAC
    United Transportation Union ....$1,500 PAC
Public Sector Unions $7,250
    National Assn of Letter Carriers ....$2,500 PAC
    National League of Postmasters ....$1,500 PAC
Misc Unions $2,500
    Food & Commercial Workers Union ....$2,500 PAC

Ideological/Single-Issue

Ideological/Single-Issue $14,921

Leadership PACs $11,221
    Pelican PAC (Bennett Johnston) ....$5,000 PAC
    House Leadership Fund (Tom Foley) ....$2,500 PAC
Misc Issues $1,700
    National Cmte to Preserve Social Security ....$1,700 PAC

Other & Unknown

Other $1,700

    None over $1,500

Unknown $12,300

    Homemakers/Non-income earners $3,050
    Employer Listed/Category Unknown $8,800
        None over $1,500

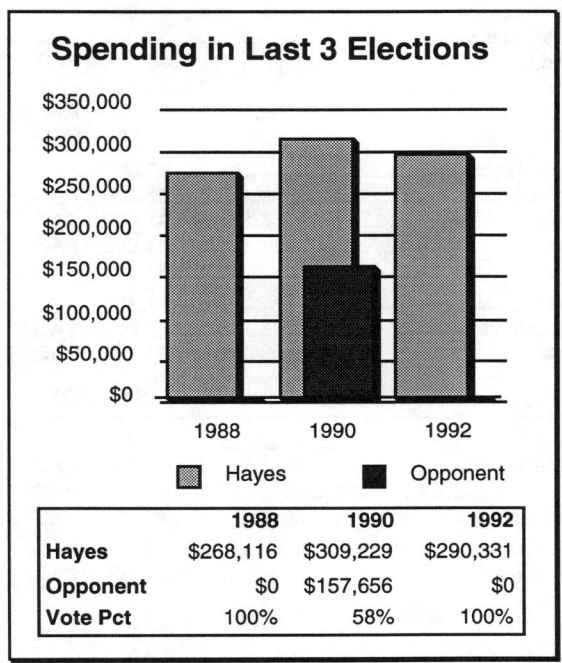

Spending in Last 3 Elections

	1988	1990	1992
Hayes	$268,116	$309,229	$290,331
Opponent	$0	$157,656	$0
Vote Pct	100%	58%	100%

Legend: Hayes, Opponent

* Contributions came from more than one affiliate or
subsidiary.

Joel Hefley, R-Colo (5)

First elected: 1986

1991-92 Total Receipts: $137,757
1992 Year-end Cash: $60,257

1991-92 Committees & Subcommittees

Armed Services
Investigations; Procurement and Military Nuclear Systems

Interior and Insular Affairs
Energy and the Environment; National Parks and Public Lands

Small Business
Antitrust, Impact of Deregulation and Ecology (Ranking Republican)

Leading Contributors

Business

Agriculture $10,975

Crop Production & Basic Processing **$4,775**
American Sugarbeet Growers Assn .... $1,500 PAC
American Crystal Sugar Corp .... $1,000 PAC

Tobacco **$2,000**
RJR Nabisco .... $1,000 PAC

Dairy **$1,500**
Royal Crest Dairy .... $1,000 Indiv

Livestock **$1,200**
National Cattlemen's Assn .... $1,000 PAC

Agricultural Services/Products **$1,000**
None over $1,000

Communications/Electronics $8,950

Media/Entertainment **$1,000**
Daniels & Associates .... $1,000 Indiv

Telephone Utilities **$4,500**
AT&T .... $2,000 PAC
US West Inc .... $2,000 PAC

Electronics Mfg & Services **$1,250**
North American Philips Corp .... $1,000 PAC

Computer Equipment & Services **$2,000**
Computer Sciences Corp .... $1,000 PAC

Source of Funds in 1992 Election

Source	Total	Pct
PACs	$99,515	72%
Indivs $200+	$14,200	10%
Indivs under $200	$13,996	10%
Other	$10,046	7%
Candidate	$0	0%
Party	$793	1%

Source of PAC Dollars by Sector

Source	Total	Pct
Business	$89,375	89%
Labor	$6,500	7%
Ideology/Single Issue	$4,000	4%

In-State vs. Out-of-State Contributions*

Source	Total	Pct
In-State	$11,000	83%
Out-of-state	$2,200	17%
No state listed	$0	

* by large individual contributors ($200 & above)

Construction $3,450

General Contractors **$1,950**
Associated General Contractors .... $1,000 PAC

Special Trade Contractors **$1,000**
National Electrical Contractors Assn .... $2,000 PAC

Defense $18,000

Defense Aerospace **$10,500**
Martin Marietta Corp .... $1,500 PAC
McDonnell Douglas .... $1,500 PAC
Northrop Corp .... $1,500 PAC
General Dynamics .... $1,000 PAC
LTV Aerospace & Defense Co .... $1,000 PAC
Lockheed Corp .... $1,000 PAC
Rockwell International .... $1,000 PAC
Textron Inc .... $1,000 PAC
United Technologies .... $1,000 PAC

Defense Electronics **$5,000**
Litton Industries .... $1,000 PAC
Loral Corp .... $1,000 PAC
Raytheon .... $1,000 PAC
TRW Inc .... $1,000 PAC

Misc Defense **$2,500**
Atlantic Research Corp .... $1,000 PAC
Insilco Corp .... $1,000 PAC

Energy & Natural Resources $11,150

Oil & Gas **$4,400**
Atlantic Richfield .... $1,000 PAC
Chevron Corp .... $1,000 PAC
Coastal Corp .... $1,000 PAC

Mining **$2,750**
Cyprus Minerals Co .... $1,000 PAC

Contribution Totals by Sector

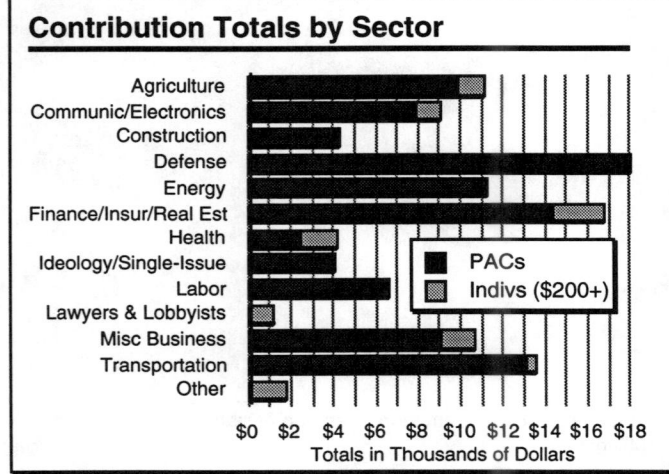

Agriculture
Communic/Electronics
Construction
Defense
Energy
Finance/Insur/Real Est
Health
Ideology/Single-Issue
Labor
Lawyers & Lobbyists
Misc Business
Transportation
Other

■ PACs
▨ Indivs ($200+)

$0 $2 $4 $6 $8 $10 $12 $14 $16 $18
Totals in Thousands of Dollars

Nuclear Energy $1,000
    General Atomics .... $1,000   PAC

Electric Utilities $2,500
    ACRE (Action Cmte for Rural Electrification) .... $1,000   PAC
    Public Service Co of Colorado .... $1,000   PAC

Finance, Insurance & Real Estate $16,650

Commercial Banks $1,950
    Norwest Corp .... $1,000   PAC

Insurance $3,500
    Security Life of Denver .... $1,000   PAC

Real Estate $5,950
    National Assn of Realtors .... $5,000   PAC

Accountants $4,000
    American Institute of CPA's .... $4,000   PAC

Health $4,050

Health Professionals $3,550
    American Academy of Ophthalmology .... $1,000   PAC

Lawyers & Lobbyists $1,040

Lawyers & Lobbyists $1,040
    None over $1,000

Misc Business $10,600

Beer, Wine & Liquor $1,700
    National Beer Wholesalers Assn .... $1,000   PAC

Retail Sales $3,000
    International Council of Shopping Centers .... $1,000   PAC

Chemical & Related Manufacturing $1,000
    Dow Chemical .... $1,000   PAC

Misc Manufacturing & Distributing $3,000
    Redmond Productions Inc .... $1,500   Indiv
    Ball Corp .... $1,000   PAC

Transportation $14,000

Air Transport $6,500
    United Parcel Service .... $3,000   PAC
    Boeing Co .... $1,000   PAC
    General Electric .... $1,000   PAC
    UNC Inc .... $1,000   PAC

Automotive $5,000
    National Auto Dealers Assn .... $3,500   PAC
    Phil Long Ford .... $1,000   Indiv

Railroads $1,500
    Union Pacific Corp .... $1,000   PAC

Misc Transport $1,000
    American Motorcyclist Assn .... $1,000   PAC

Labor

Labor $6,500

Transportation Unions $4,500
    Marine Engineers Dist 2 Maritime Officers .... $4,000   PAC

Public Sector Unions $2,000
    National Assn Retired Federal Employees .... $2,000   PAC

Ideological/Single-Issue

Ideological/Single-Issue $4,000

Gun Rights/Gun Control $3,500
    National Rifle Assn .... $3,500   PAC

Other & Unknown

Other $1,640

    None over $1,000

Unknown $2,070

    Employer Listed/Category Unknown $1,050
    None over $1,000

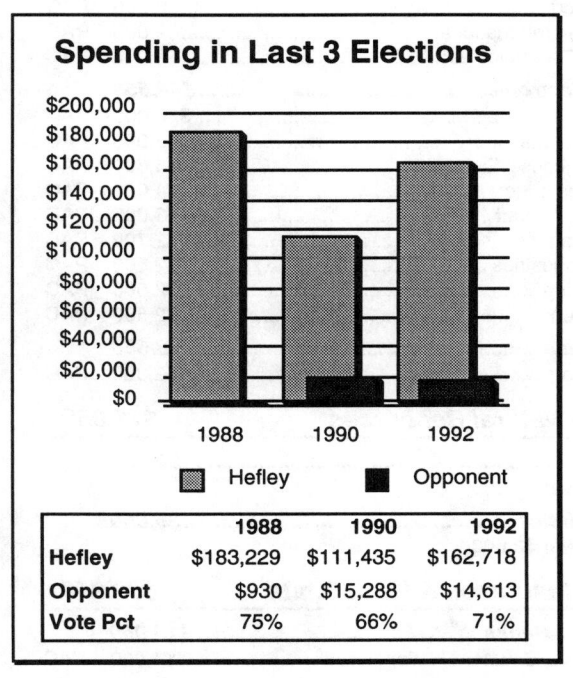

Spending in Last 3 Elections

	1988	1990	1992
Hefley	$183,229	$111,435	$162,718
Opponent	$930	$15,288	$14,613
Vote Pct	75%	66%	71%

W. G. "Bill" Hefner, D-NC (8)

First elected: 1974

1991-92 Total Receipts:	$566,690
1992 Year-end Cash:	$83,385

1991-92 Committees & Subcommittees

Appropriations
Defense; Military Construction (Chairman)

Leading Contributors

Business

Agriculture	$35,625

Crop Production & Basic Processing $5,025
  None over $2,000

Tobacco $13,500
  RJR Nabisco .... $6,000 PAC
  Philip Morris .... $4,500 PAC
  Tobacco Institute .... $2,000 PAC

Dairy $3,300
  Associated Milk Producers .... $2,000 PAC

Poultry & Eggs $3,500
  None over $2,000

Livestock $2,300
  None over $2,000

Agricultural Services/Products $2,000
  None over $2,000

Food Processing & Sales $6,000
  Food Lion Inc .... $3,000 PAC/Ind

Communications/Electronics | $18,000

Telephone Utilities $13,500
  Southern Bell .... $6,500 PAC
  AT&T* .... $4,850 Indiv

Computer Equipment & Services $3,000
  GEC-Marconi Electronic Systems Corp .... $2,500 PAC

Construction | $13,399

General Contractors $5,499
  None over $2,000

Home Builders $2,750
  None over $2,000

Contribution Totals by Sector

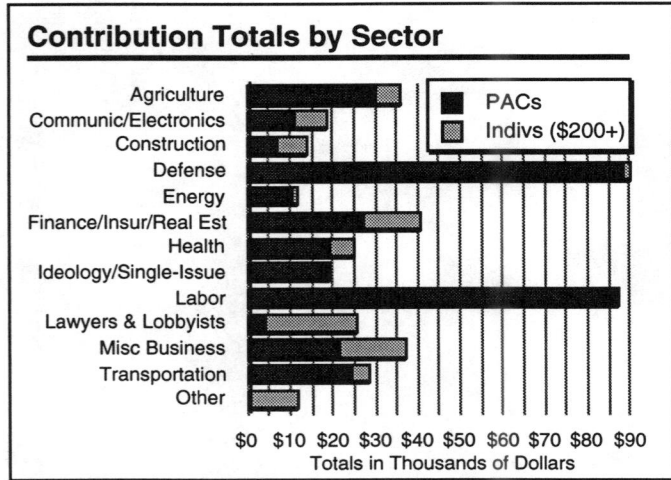

PACs
Indivs ($200+)

Agriculture
Communic/Electronics
Construction
Defense
Energy
Finance/Insur/Real Est
Health
Ideology/Single-Issue
Labor
Lawyers & Lobbyists
Misc Business
Transportation
Other

$0 $10 $20 $30 $40 $50 $60 $70 $80 $90
Totals in Thousands of Dollars

Source of Funds in 1992 Election

Source	Total	Pct
PACs	$355,739	62%
Indivs $200+	$112,444	20%
Indivs under $200	$60,024	10%
Other	$46,354	8%
Candidate	$0	0%
Party	$13,021	2%

Source of PAC Dollars by Sector

Source	Total	Pct
Business	$239,823	69%
Labor	$87,050	25%
Ideology/Single Issue	$18,450	5%

In-State vs. Out-of-State Contributions*

Source	Total	Pct
In-State	$65,250	58%
Out-of-state	$47,094	42%
No state listed	$0	

* by large individual contributors ($200 & above)

Building Materials & Equipment $3,650
  None over $2,000

Defense | $89,600

Defense Aerospace $38,500
  Martin Marietta Corp .... $7,000 PAC
  McDonnell Douglas* .... $4,500 PAC
  General Dynamics .... $3,000 PAC
  LTV Aerospace & Defense Co .... $3,000 PAC
  Gencorp Inc .... $2,500 PAC
  General Electric .... $2,500 PAC
  Grumman Corp .... $2,500 PAC
  Lockheed Corp .... $2,500 PAC
  Rockwell International .... $2,500 PAC
  United Technologies .... $2,000 PAC

Defense Electronics $44,550
  AT&T .... $10,000 PAC
  Imo Industries Inc .... $6,000 PAC
  Westinghouse Electric .... $5,000 PAC
  E-Systems Inc .... $4,000 PAC
  Hughes Aircraft .... $3,000 PAC
  AEL Industries Inc .... $2,700 PAC
  Litton Industries .... $2,500 PAC
  Loral Corp .... $2,500 PAC
  Raytheon .... $2,500 PAC

Misc Defense $6,550
  FMC Corp .... $2,300 PAC

Energy & Natural Resources | $11,050

Oil & Gas $2,000
  None over $2,000

Electric Utilities $6,050
  None over $2,000

Finance, Insurance & Real Estate | $39,840

Commercial Banks $10,950
  Citizens & Southern National Bank .... $4,000 PAC

Securities & Investment	$4,000	
None over $2,000		
Insurance	$6,950	
None over $2,000		
Real Estate	$13,190	
National Assn of Realtors	$9,940	PAC
Accountants	$2,500	
None over $2,000		

Health $24,400

Health Professionals	$15,800	
American Medical Assn	$5,350	PAC
American Dental Assn	$4,000	PAC
Pharmaceuticals/Health Products	$6,600	
Glaxo Inc	$3,000	PAC

Lawyers & Lobbyists $25,250

Lawyers & Lobbyists	$25,250	
Paul Magliocchetti Associates	$3,000	Indiv
Ginn, Edington et al	$2,500	Indiv
ETA Inc	$2,000	Indiv
Hyjek & Fix	$2,000	Indiv
Whitner Associates	$2,000	Indiv

Misc Business $36,558

Beer, Wine & Liquor	$4,000	
National Beer Wholesalers Assn	$2,000	PAC
Retail Sales	$3,000	
None over $2,000		
Business Services	$4,500	
None over $2,000		
Steel Production	$2,000	
None over $2,000		
Misc Manufacturing & Distributing	$5,500	
Hoechst Celanese Corp	$3,500	PAC
Textiles	$14,500	
Burlington Industries	$6,000	PAC
EJ Snyder & Sons	$3,000	Indiv
American Textile Manufacturers Institute	$2,500	PAC

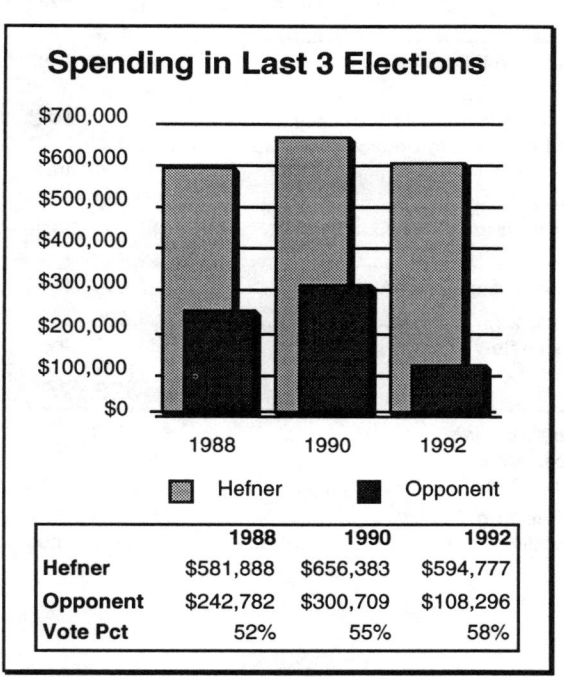

Spending in Last 3 Elections

	1988	1990	1992
Hefner	$581,888	$656,383	$594,777
Opponent	$242,782	$300,709	$108,296
Vote Pct	52%	55%	58%

Legend: ▨ Hefner ■ Opponent

Transportation $27,750

Air Transport	$12,500	
United Parcel Service	$3,500	PAC
Federal Express Corp	$3,000	PAC
Gulfstream Aerospace	$2,000	PAC
Automotive	$8,300	
National Auto Dealers Assn	$5,500	PAC
Trucking	$2,950	
None over $2,000		
Sea Transport	$2,500	
Southwest Marine	$2,500	PAC

Labor

Labor $87,050

Industrial Unions	$18,000	
Machinists/Aerospace Workers Union	$5,000	PAC
United Steelworkers	$5,000	PAC
Communications Workers of America	$2,500	PAC
United Auto Workers	$2,500	PAC
Transportation Unions	$25,500	
Teamsters Union	$7,500	PAC
United Transportation Union	$7,500	PAC
Air Line Pilots Assn	$6,000	PAC
Marine Engineers Dist 2 Maritime Officers	$3,000	PAC
Public Sector Unions	$35,550	
National Education Assn	$10,000	PAC
American Fedn of St/Cnty/Munic Employees	$5,500	PAC
National Assn Retired Federal Employees	$5,000	PAC
National Assn of Letter Carriers	$5,000	PAC
American Postal Workers Union	$2,000	PAC
International Assn of Firefighters	$2,000	PAC
Misc Unions	$8,000	
Food & Commercial Workers Union	$6,000	PAC

Ideological/Single-Issue

Ideological/Single-Issue $18,450

Democratic/Liberal	$2,500	
National Cmte for an Effective Congress	$2,500	PAC
Leadership PACs	$6,500	
House Leadership Fund (Tom Foley)	$3,000	PAC
America's Leaders' Fund (Dan Rostenkowski)	$2,000	PAC
Gun Rights/Gun Control	$5,950	
National Rifle Assn	$5,950	PAC
Misc Issues	$3,000	
National Cmte to Preserve Social Security	$2,000	PAC

Other & Unknown

Other $11,000

Education	$2,500	
None over $2,000		
Retired	$7,500	
None over $2,000		

Unknown $19,695

Homemakers/Non-income earners	$2,250	
Employer Listed/Category Unknown	$16,099	
G&G Leather Co	$2,000	Indiv

---

* Contributions came from more than one affiliate or subsidiary.

Paul B. Henry, R-Mich (3)

First elected: 1984

1991-92 Total Receipts: $349,444
1992 Year-end Cash: $342,492

1991-92 Committees & Subcommittees

Education and Labor
Elementary, Secondary and Vocational Education; Employment Opportunities; Health and Safety (Ranking Republican); Postsecondary Education

Science, Space and Technology
Space; Technology and Competitiveness

Select Committee on Aging

Leading Contributors

Business

Agriculture $12,850

Crop Production & Basic Processing	**$3,000**	
Mid-American Potato Co	$1,500	Indiv
Agricultural Services/Products	**$1,000**	
None over $1,000		
Food Processing & Sales	**$7,250**	
Holland American Wafer Co	$2,000	Indiv
Meijer Inc	$1,500	Indiv
D&W Food Centers Inc	$1,000	Indiv
Kent Provision	$1,000	Indiv
Spartan Stores Inc	$1,000	Indiv

Communications/Electronics $7,750

Telephone Utilities	**$7,025**	
Michigan Bell Telephone	$5,375	PAC
GTE Corp	$1,150	PAC

Construction $13,100

General Contractors	**$8,000**	
National Utility Contractors Assn	$3,500	PAC
Associated General Contractors	$1,500	PAC
Don Vos Construction Co	$1,000	Indiv
Owen Ames Kimball Co	$1,000	Indiv
Special Trade Contractors	**$1,800**	
National Assn of the Remodeling Industry	$1,000	PAC
Construction Services	**$1,800**	
National Society of Professional Engineers	$1,300	PAC
Building Materials & Equipment	**$1,500**	
TW Hager Lumber Co	$1,000	Indiv

Source of Funds in 1992 Election

Source	Total	Pct
■ PACs	$72,650	21%
▨ Indivs $200+	$115,600	33%
☐ Indivs under $200	$134,784	39%
▩ Other	$26,410	8%
Candidate	$0	0%
Party	$175	0%

Source of PAC Dollars by Sector

Source	Total	Pct
■ Business	$64,975	91%
▨ Labor	$5,450	8%
☐ Ideology/Single Issue	$1,273	2%

In-State vs. Out-of-State Contributions*

Source	Total	Pct
☐ In-State	$115,100	100%
▩ Out-of-state	$500	0%
No state listed	$0	

* by large individual contributors ($200 & above)

Energy & Natural Resources $4,950

Oil & Gas	**$3,550**	
Michigan Consolidated Gas	$1,100	PAC
Crystal Flash Petroleum	$1,000	Indiv
Electric Utilities	**$1,250**	
Consumers Power Co	$1,250	PAC

Finance, Insurance & Real Estate $19,800

Commercial Banks	**$2,450**	
None over $1,000		
Savings & Loans	**$1,150**	
Michigan League of Savings Institutions	$1,150	PAC
Credit Unions	**$3,375**	
Michigan Credit Union League	$3,375	PAC
Insurance	**$6,550**	
American Council of Life Insurance	$2,000	PAC
National Assn of Life Underwriters	$2,000	PAC
Paul Goebel Group	$1,500	Indiv
Real Estate	**$2,025**	
Hartger & Willard	$1,000	Indiv
Accountants	**$2,500**	
American Institute of CPA's	$2,500	PAC
Misc Finance	**$1,500**	
Merchants Service Bureau Inc	$1,000	Indiv

Health $29,675

Health Professionals	**$23,950**	
American Medical Assn	$5,000	PAC
American Dental Assn	$3,500	PAC
Hospitals/Nursing Homes	**$2,225**	
Metropolitan Hospital	$1,500	Indiv

Contribution Totals by Sector

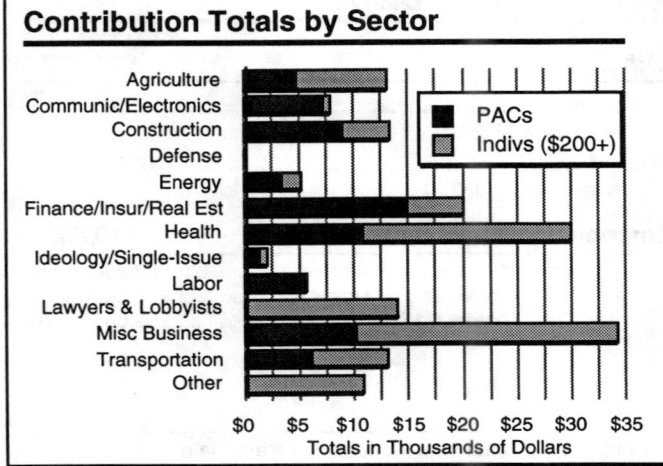

Legend: ■ PACs ▨ Indivs ($200+)

Categories: Agriculture, Communic/Electronics, Construction, Defense, Energy, Finance/Insur/Real Est, Health, Ideology/Single-Issue, Labor, Lawyers & Lobbyists, Misc Business, Transportation, Other

$0 $5 $10 $15 $20 $25 $30 $35
Totals in Thousands of Dollars

Pharmaceuticals/Health Products **$1,500**
    Upjohn Co ....$1,500   PAC

Misc Health **$1,750**
    Blodgett Memorial Medical Center ....$1,000   Indiv

Lawyers & Lobbyists $14,050

Lawyers & Lobbyists **$14,050**
    Varnum, Riddering et al ....$7,000   Indiv
    Warner, Norcross & Judd ....$2,500   Indiv
    Cholette, Perkins & Buchanan ....$1,000   Indiv
    Farr & Oosterhouse ....$1,000   Indiv

Misc Business $34,100

Food & Beverage **$4,500**
    National Restaurant Assn ....$2,000   PAC
    Russ Restaurant ....$1,500   Indiv

Retail Sales **$6,300**
    Amway Corp ....$4,050   PAC/Ind
    Model Coverall Service ....$1,000   Indiv

Chemical & Related Manufacturing **$6,400**
    Lacks Industries Inc ....$1,400   Indiv
    Cascade Engineering ....$1,000   Indiv
    Guardsman Chemical ....$1,000   Indiv
    Nicholas Plastics Inc ....$1,000   Indiv

Misc Manufacturing & Distributing **$15,950**
    Terryberry Co ....$3,500   Indiv
    Steelcase Inc ....$2,125   Indiv
    Custer Office Environments ....$1,000   Indiv
    Jostens Inc ....$1,000   PAC
    Knoll Group Office Furniture ....$1,000   Indiv
    Royce Rolls Ringer Co ....$1,000   Indiv
    Vans Industrial Equipment ....$1,000   Indiv
    Wolverine World Wide ....$1,000   Indiv

Transportation   **$12,950**

Air Transport **$3,200**
    United Parcel Service ....$3,200   PAC

Automotive **$9,250**
    Great Lakes Mazda Distributors ....$5,000   Indiv
    General Motors ....$1,250   PAC
    Auto Dealers & Drivers for Free Trade ....$1,000   PAC
    Jobbers Warehouse ....$1,000   Indiv

Labor

Labor $5,450

Public Sector Unions **$4,650**
    National Assn Retired Federal Employees ....$4,500   PAC

Ideological/Single-Issue

Ideological/Single-Issue $1,773

Human Rights **$1,000**
    KidsPAC ....$1,000   PAC

Other & Unknown

Other $10,750

Education **$1,225**
    Davenport College of Business ....$1,000   Indiv

Retired **$9,525**
    None over $1,000

Unknown $20,100

    Homemakers/Non-income earners $3,500
    No Employer Listed or Found $2,400
    Employer Listed/Category Unknown $14,200
        Locks Industries Inc ....$1,500   Indiv
        Bissell Inc ....$1,000   Indiv
        Lanco Corp & Alloy Exchange ....$1,000   Indiv
        Smiths Industries ....$1,000   Indiv
        TLC Service Inc ....$1,000   Indiv

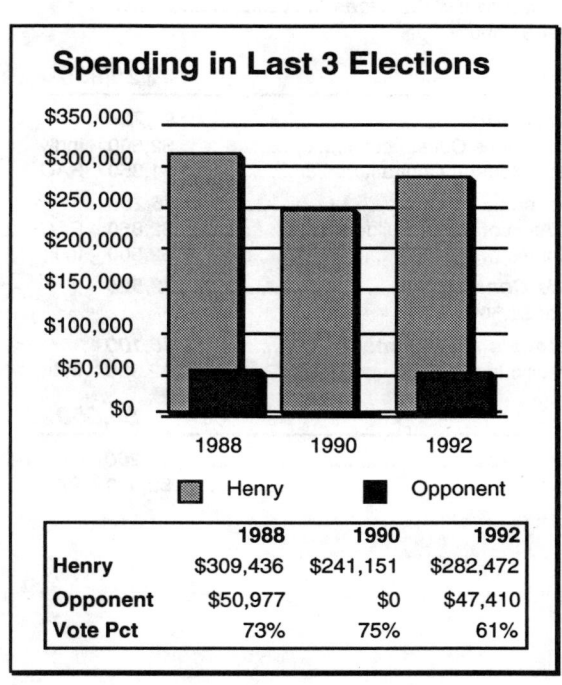

Spending in Last 3 Elections

	1988	1990	1992
Henry	$309,436	$241,151	$282,472
Opponent	$50,977	$0	$47,410
Vote Pct	73%	75%	61%

Wally Herger, R-Calif (2)

First elected: 1986

1991-92 Total Receipts:	$615,832
1992 Year-end Cash:	$225,763

1991-92 Committees & Subcommittees

Agriculture
Cotton, Rice and Sugar; Department Operations, Research and Foreign Agriculture; Domestic Marketing, Consumer Relations and Nutrition; Forests, Family Farms and Energy

Merchant Marine and Fisheries
Fisheries and Wildlife Conservation and the Environment; Oceanography, Great Lakes and Outer Continental Shelf

Select Committee on Narcotics Abuse and Control

Leading Contributors

Business

Agriculture	$155,748	
Crop Production & Basic Processing **$76,165**		
Farmers' Rice Cooperative	$6,600	PAC
Sunkist Growers	$6,000	PAC
Sun-Diamond Growers*	$5,800	PAC
California Almond Growers Exchange	$5,000	PAC
American Crystal Sugar Corp	$2,000	PAC
California Canning Peach Assn	$2,000	PAC
National Cotton Council	$1,850	PAC
Bransford Farms	$1,600	Indiv
Etchepare Ranches	$1,500	Indiv
Tobacco **$4,000**		
None over $1,500		
Dairy **$4,050**		
None over $1,500		
Poultry & Eggs **$3,200**		
None over $1,500		
Livestock **$16,975**		
None over $1,500		
Agricultural Services/Products **$15,204**		
California Farm Bureau Federation	$2,700	PAC
Farm Credit Council	$1,800	PAC
Food Processing & Sales **$18,054**		
Pacific Coast Producers	$5,000	PAC
Food Marketing Institute	$2,050	PAC
Pepsico Inc	$2,000	PAC

Source of Funds in 1992 Election

Source	Total	Pct
■ PACs	$221,689	36%
▨ Indivs $200+	$184,714	30%
□ Indivs under $200	$172,879	28%
⊠ Other.................................	$36,550	6%
Candidate	$0	0%
Party	$115	0%

Source of PAC Dollars by Sector

Source	Total	Pct
■ Business	$203,379	90%
▨ Labor	$15,700	7%
□ Ideology/Single Issue	$5,731	3%

In-State vs. Out-of-State Contributions*

Source	Total	Pct
□ In-State	$180,664	98%
■ Out-of-state	$4,000	2%
No state listed	$0	

* by large individual contributors ($200 & above)

Forestry & Forest Products	$12,000	
Simpson Investment Co	$2,750	PAC
Misc Agriculture..	$6,100	
None over $1,500		

Communications/Electronics	$9,350	
Media/Entertainment **$4,300**		
Bowling Proprietors Assn	$1,500	PAC
Telephone Utilities **$3,200**		
AT&T	$1,850	PAC
Computer Equipment & Services **$1,850**		
None over $1,500		

Construction	$25,850	
General Contractors **$9,725**		
Robinson & Sons Construction	$2,500	Indiv
Associated General Contractors	$1,850	PAC
Home Builders **$6,200**		
National Assn of Home Builders	$2,850	PAC
Drake Homes	$2,500	Indiv
Special Trade Contractors **$2,525**		
None over $1,500		
Building Materials & Equipment **$6,100**		
Sierra Pacific Industries	$2,350	Indiv

Defense	$6,550	
Defense Aerospace **$4,200**		
Northrop Corp	$2,000	PAC

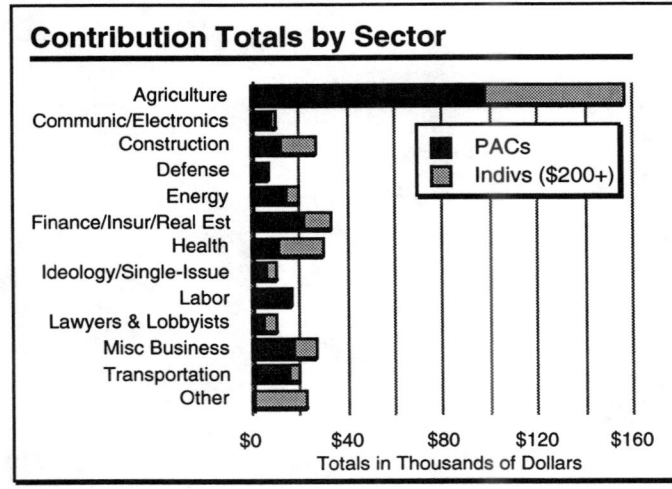

Contribution Totals by Sector

Agriculture
Communic/Electronics
Construction
Defense
Energy
Finance/Insur/Real Est
Health
Ideology/Single-Issue
Labor
Lawyers & Lobbyists
Misc Business
Transportation
Other

■ PACs
▨ Indivs ($200+)

$0 $40 $80 $120 $160
Totals in Thousands of Dollars

Energy & Natural Resources — $18,600

Oil & Gas **$11,850**
    Redding Auto-Truck Plaza .... $1,550   Indiv

Mining **$1,850**
    None over $1,500

Electric Utilities **$4,400**
    Pacific Gas & Electric .... $2,750   PAC

Finance, Insurance & Real Estate — $32,175

Commercial Banks **$6,900**
    Independent Bankers Assn .... $2,700   PAC

Credit Unions **$1,500**
    Credit Union National Assn .... $1,500   PAC

Securities & Investment **$2,500**
    Chicago Mercantile Exchange .... $2,000   PAC

Insurance **$5,250**
    Pacific Mutual Life .... $2,000   PAC

Real Estate **$12,625**
    National Assn of Realtors .... $6,500   PAC

Misc Finance **$1,800**
    None over $1,500

Health — $29,575

Health Professionals **$24,600**
    American Medical Assn .... $4,350   PAC
    Cooperative of American Physicians .... $1,850   PAC

Hospitals/Nursing Homes **$2,925**
    None over $1,500

Lawyers & Lobbyists — $9,250

Lawyers & Lobbyists **$9,250**
    Holland & Knight .... $1,600   PAC

Misc Business — $26,020

Food & Beverage **$2,150**
    None over $1,500

Beer, Wine & Liquor **$8,220**
    None over $1,500

Retail Sales — $4,400
    None over $1,500

Misc Services **$2,150**
    National Pest Control Assn .... $1,500   PAC

Chemical & Related Manufacturing **$2,000**
    None over $1,500

Misc Manufacturing & Distributing **$4,900**
    Stone Container Corp .... $2,350   PAC

Transportation — $18,650

Air Transport **$7,500**
    United Parcel Service .... $3,900   PAC
    Federal Express Corp .... $2,000   PAC

Automotive **$3,100**
    None over $1,500

Trucking **$2,050**
    None over $1,500

Sea Transport **$5,500**
    CSX Corp* .... $2,200   PAC

Labor

Labor — $15,700

Transportation Unions **$11,200**
    Marine Engineers Union* .... $9,500   PAC

Public Sector Unions **$4,500**
    National Assn Retired Federal Employees .... $4,500   PAC

Ideological/Single-Issue

Ideological/Single-Issue — $9,431

Republican/Conservative **$3,700**
    None over $1,500

Gun Rights/Gun Control **$3,350**
    National Rifle Assn .... $3,350   PAC

Misc Issues **$1,850**
    None over $1,500

Other & Unknown

Other — $21,475

Retired **$18,375**
    None over $1,500

Unknown — $31,100
    Homemakers/Non-income earners $6,700
    No Employer Listed or Found $2,800
    Generic Occupation/Category Unknown $2,950
    Employer Listed/Category Unknown $18,650
        None over $1,500

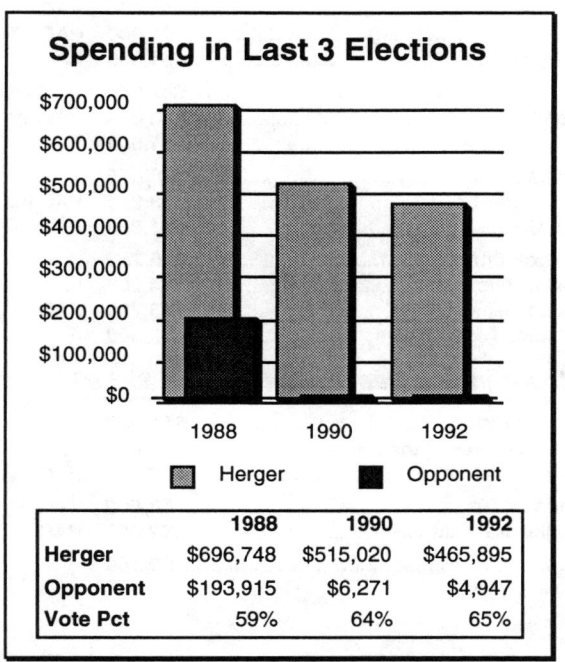

Spending in Last 3 Elections

	1988	1990	1992
Herger	$696,748	$515,020	$465,895
Opponent	$193,915	$6,271	$4,947
Vote Pct	59%	64%	65%

Legend: Herger, Opponent

---

* Contributions came from more than one affiliate or subsidiary.

Earl F. Hilliard, D-Ala (7)

First elected: 1992

1991-92 Total Receipts: $333,362
1992 Year-end Cash: $13,922

1993-94 Committees & Subcommittees

Agriculture
Environment, Credit and Rural Development; Livestock

Small Business
Minority Enterprise, Finance and Urban Development; Procurement,
Taxation and Tourism

Leading Contributors

Business

Agriculture $25,631

Crop Production & Basic Processing **$4,250**
    Alabama Peanut Producers Assn .... $3,000   PAC

Tobacco **$3,500**
    RJR Nabisco .... $2,000   PAC
    US Tobacco Co .... $1,000   PAC

Dairy **$1,000**
    Associated Milk Producers .... $1,000   PAC

Poultry & Eggs **$1,500**
    National Broiler Council .... $1,500   PAC

Agricultural Services/Products **$10,631**
    Alabama Farm Bureau Federation .... $10,631   PAC

Food Processing & Sales **$1,750**
    Supreme Beverage Co Inc .... $1,000   Indiv

Forestry & Forest Products **$2,500**
    None over $1,000

Communications/Electronics $11,800

Media/Entertainment **$3,800**
    Comcast Corp .... $3,500   PAC/Ind

Telephone Utilities **$7,500**
    Southern Bell .... $3,000   PAC
    AT&T .... $2,000   PAC
    Bremlee Mountain Telephone .... $1,000   Indiv
    United Telecommunications .... $1,000   PAC

Source of Funds in 1992 Election

Source	Total	Pct
PACs	$107,831	29%
Indivs $200+	$116,246	31%
Indivs under $200	$34,283	9%
Other	$112,601	30%
Candidate	$9,152	2%
Party	$37,899	10%

Source of PAC Dollars by Sector

Source	Total	Pct
Business	$106,231	67%
Labor	$32,000	20%
Ideology/Single Issue	$20,950	13%

In-State vs. Out-of-State Contributions*

Source	Total	Pct
In-State	$102,546	89%
Out-of-state	$12,200	11%
No state listed	$250	

* by large individual contributors ($200 & above)

Construction $5,800

General Contractors **$3,800**
    Associated Builders & Contractors .... $1,000   PAC
    HJ Russell & Co .... $1,000   Indiv
    Harbert Corp .... $1,000   Indiv

Home Builders **$2,000**
    National Assn of Home Builders .... $1,000   PAC
    Walter Industries .... $1,000   PAC

Energy & Natural Resources $43,750

Oil & Gas **$6,250**
    Alagasco Inc .... $2,000   PAC
    Chevron Corp .... $1,000   PAC
    Phillips Petroleum .... $1,000   PAC

Mining **$21,500**
    Drummond Co .... $20,000   PAC/Ind
    National Coal Assn .... $1,500   PAC

Electric Utilities **$5,250**
    Alabama Power Co .... $3,250   PAC/Ind
    Southern Co* .... $1,000   PAC

Waste Management **$10,750**
    Waste Away Group Inc .... $4,000   Indiv
    Waste Management Inc .... $3,750   PAC
    Wheelabrator Technologies .... $2,500   PAC

Finance, Insurance & Real Estate $26,900

Commercial Banks **$11,550**
    Central Bancshares of the South .... $8,000   PAC
    American Bankers Assn .... $2,000   PAC

Credit Unions **$2,000**
    Credit Union National Assn* .... $2,000   PAC

Insurance **$2,500**
    None over $1,000

Contribution Totals by Sector

Agriculture, Communic/Electronics, Construction, Defense, Energy, Finance/Insur/Real Est, Health, Ideology/Single-Issue, Labor, Lawyers & Lobbyists, Misc Business, Transportation, Other

PACs / Indivs ($200+)

$0 $5 $10 $15 $20 $25 $30 $35 $40 $45
Totals in Thousands of Dollars

Real Estate $7,850
    National Assn of Realtors ....$5,000   PAC
    Broadmoor Group ....$1,000   Indiv

Accountants $3,000
    American Institute of CPA's ....$2,500   PAC

Health — $10,000

Health Professionals $7,250
    American Chiropractic Assn ....$1,000   PAC
    American Optometric Assn ....$1,000   PAC
    Jefferson Clinic ....$1,000   Indiv

Health Services $1,000
    Home Healthcare ....$1,000   Indiv

Misc Health $1,000
    Midsouth Medical Distributors ....$1,000   Indiv

Lawyers & Lobbyists — $39,521

Lawyers & Lobbyists $39,521
    Hare, Wynn et al ....$6,496   Indiv
    Emond & Vines ....$6,000   Indiv
    Assn of Trial Lawyers of America ....$5,000   PAC
    Hollis, Pittman et al ....$5,000   Indiv
    Hogan, Smith et al ....$2,500   Indiv
    Fine, Geddie & Associates ....$2,000   Indiv
    Tanner & Guin ....$1,600   Indiv
    Baxley, Dillard & Dauphin ....$1,000   Indiv
    Haskell, Slaughter et al ....$1,000   Indiv
    Melton, Espy et al ....$1,000   Indiv

Misc Business — $10,850

Beer, Wine & Liquor $3,000
    National Beer Wholesalers Assn ....$2,500   PAC

Lodging/Tourism $1,000
    None over $1,000

Chemical & Related Manufacturing $1,250
    None over $1,000

Steel Production $2,000
    American Cast Iron & Pipe Co ....$2,000   Indiv

Misc Manufacturing & Distributing $2,500
    McWane Inc ....$1,000   Indiv
    Xerox Corp ....$1,000   PAC

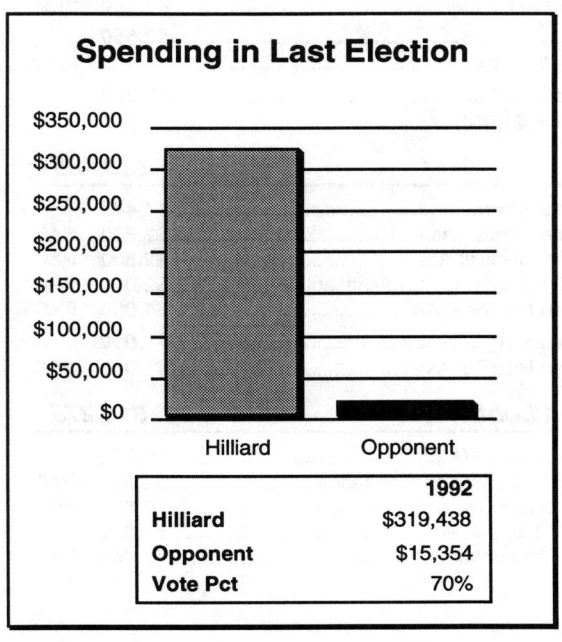

Spending in Last Election

	1992
Hilliard	$319,438
Opponent	$15,354
Vote Pct	70%

Transportation — $6,500

Air Transport $3,500
    United Parcel Service ....$3,000   PAC

Automotive $2,500
    National Auto Dealers Assn ....$2,000   PAC

Labor

Labor — $32,200

Building Trade Unions $1,000
    Laborers' Political League ....$1,000   PAC

Industrial Unions $14,000
    United Auto Workers ....$5,000   PAC
    Communications Workers of America .....$3,500   PAC
    United Steelworkers ....$3,000   PAC
    Rubber Cork Linoleum & Plastic Workers ...$2,500   PAC

Transportation Unions $4,000
    United Transportation Union ....$3,000   PAC
    Brotherhood of Locomotive Engineers ...$1,000   PAC

Public Sector Unions $10,500
    American Fedn of St/Cnty/Munic Employees ...$5,000   PAC
    National Education Assn ....$5,000   PAC

Misc Unions $2,700
    Food & Commercial Workers Union ......$2,500   PAC

Ideological/Single-Issue

Ideological/Single-Issue — $26,450

Leadership PACs $3,500
    Effective Government Cmte (Dick Gephardt) ...$1,500   PAC
    House Leadership Fund (Tom Foley) ......$1,000   PAC

Pro-Israel $12,000
    Americans for Good Government Inc .....$5,000   PAC
    Florida Congressional Cmte ....$1,000   PAC

Pro-Choice $1,000
    Voters for Choice ....$1,000   PAC

Gun Rights/Gun Control $9,950
    National Rifle Assn ....$9,950   PAC

Other & Unknown

Other — $1,750
    None over $1,000

Unknown — $32,775
    No Employer Listed or Found $20,625
    Employer Listed/Category Unknown $11,650
        MTG Partners.....................................$2,000   Indiv
        Cecil Jones & Assoc ....$1,000   Indiv
        Means, Thomas & Gillis ....$1,000   Indiv
        Stewart & Associates ....$1,000   Indiv
        Tricon Metal ....$1,000   Indiv
        United Shows of America....................$1,000   Indiv

* Contributions came from more than one affiliate or
subsidiary.

Maurice D. Hinchey, D-NY (26)

First elected: 1992

1991-92 Total Receipts: $374,264
1992 Year-end Cash: $5,484

1993-94 Committees & Subcommittees

Banking, Finance and Urban Affairs
Consumer Credit and Insurance; Financial Institutions Supervision, Regulation and Deposit Insurance; General Oversight, & Restoration of Failed Financial Institutions

Natural Resources
National Parks, Forests and Public Lands; Oversight and Investigations

Leading Contributors

Business

Agriculture — $2,650

Dairy	**$1,000**	
Associated Milk Producers	$1,000	PAC

Communications/Electronics — $4,000

Printing & Publishing	**$1,000**	
None over $1,000		
Telephone Utilities	**$3,000**	
United Telecommunications	$2,000	PAC
AT&T	$1,000	PAC

Construction — $21,200

Home Builders	**$5,250**	
Halmar Builders of New York	$5,000	Indiv
Construction Services	**$3,000**	
Ansaldo Industria	$3,000	Indiv
Building Materials & Equipment	**$12,000**	
Besicorp	$10,000	Indiv
Peckham Materials	$2,000	Indiv

Energy & Natural Resources — $4,150

Electric Utilities	**$3,200**	
Long Lake Energy Corp	$2,500	Indiv

Source of Funds in 1992 Election

Source	Total	Pct
PACs	$144,258	38%
Indivs $200+	$111,992	29%
Indivs under $200	$90,051	23%
Other	$38,402	10%
Candidate	$0	0%
Party	$15,439	4%

Source of PAC Dollars by Sector

Source	Total	Pct
Business	$28,575	22%
Labor	$63,480	50%
Ideology/Single Issue	$36,184	28%

In-State vs. Out-of-State Contributions*

Source	Total	Pct
In-State	$92,642	83%
Out-of-state	$18,650	17%
No state listed	$700	

* by large individual contributors ($200 & above)

Finance, Insurance & Real Estate — $21,050

Commercial Banks	**$3,000**	
Chase Manhattan	$2,000	PAC
Citicorp	$1,000	PAC
Savings & Loans	**$2,300**	
US League of Savings Assns	$2,000	PAC
Credit Unions	**$1,000**	
Credit Union National Assn	$1,000	PAC
Securities & Investment	**$10,000**	
Beale Lynch Partners Ltd	$2,500	Indiv
Glickenhaus & Co	$1,000	Indiv
Lazard Freres & Co	$1,000	Indiv
PaineWebber	$1,000	Indiv
Insurance	**$2,550**	
Fawcett Insurance	$1,000	Indiv
Real Estate	**$1,250**	
None over $1,000		

Health — $13,465

Health Professionals	**$11,440**	
American Dental Assn	$2,500	PAC
New York Medical Assn	$2,500	PAC
American Academy of Ophthalmology	$2,000	PAC
American Nurses Assn	$1,000	PAC
Hospitals/Nursing Homes	**$1,000**	
American Hospital Assn	$1,000	PAC

Lawyers & Lobbyists — $16,275

Lawyers & Lobbyists	**$16,275**	
Assn of Trial Lawyers of America	$2,500	PAC
Kelley, Drye & Warren	$2,500	Indiv
Leboeuf, Lamb et al	$1,000	PAC
Lowey, Dannenberg et al	$1,000	Indiv

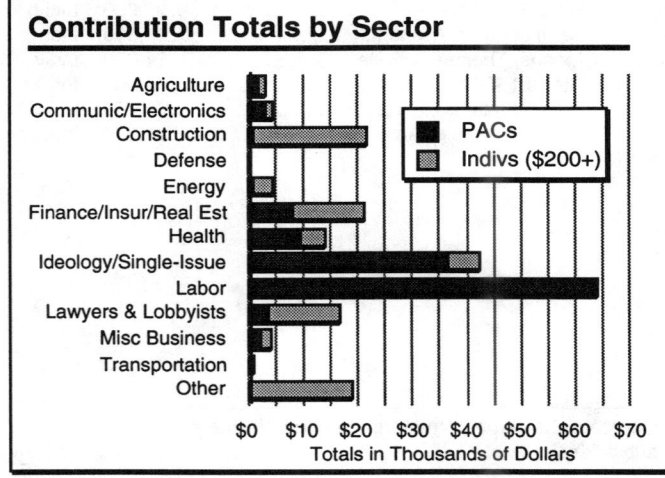

Contribution Totals by Sector

Legend: ■ PACs ▨ Indivs ($200+)

Categories: Agriculture, Communic/Electronics, Construction, Defense, Energy, Finance/Insur/Real Est, Health, Ideology/Single-Issue, Labor, Lawyers & Lobbyists, Misc Business, Transportation, Other

$0 $10 $20 $30 $40 $50 $60 $70
Totals in Thousands of Dollars

Misc Business   **$3,700**

Beer, Wine & Liquor ***$1,000***
     National Beer Wholesalers Assn ....$1,000   PAC

Steel Production ***$1,000***
     Stewart & Stevenson Services Inc ....$1,000   PAC

Labor

Labor	$63,480

Building Trade Unions ***$12,930***
     Operating Engineers Union* ....$6,350   PAC
     Carpenters & Joiners Union ....$5,000   PAC
     Ironworkers Union ....$1,080   PAC

Industrial Unions ***$10,500***
     Machinists/Aerospace Workers Union ....$5,000   PAC
     Intl Brotherhood of Electrical Workers ....$2,750   PAC
     Ladies Garment Workers Union ....$1,000   PAC
     United Paperworkers ....$1,000   PAC

Transportation Unions ***$5,000***
     Teamsters Union ....$3,500   PAC
     United Transportation Union ....$1,000   PAC

Public Sector Unions ***$28,550***
     American Fedn of St/Cnty/Munic Employees ....$10,000   PAC
     American Federation of Teachers ....$7,500   PAC
     National Education Assn ....$5,000   PAC
     National Assn of Letter Carriers ....$2,000   PAC
     International Assn of Firefighters ....$1,750   PAC
     National Assn Retired Federal Employees ....$1,000   PAC

Misc Unions ***$6,500***
     AFL-CIO ....$3,500   PAC
     Service Employees International Union ....$2,000   PAC
     Bakery, Confectionery & Tobacco Workers ....$1,000   PAC

Ideological/Single-Issue

Ideological/Single-Issue	$41,884

Democratic/Liberal ***$4,350***
     National Cmte for an Effective Congress ....$2,500   PAC
     Hollywood Women's Political Cmte ....$1,000   PAC

Leadership PACs ***$2,500***
     Effective Government Cmte (Dick Gephardt) ......$1,000   PAC
     House Leadership Fund (Tom Foley) ....$1,000   PAC

Pro-Choice ***$9,900***
     National Abortion Rights Action League ....$4,000   PAC
     Citizens for Family Planning ....$2,500   PAC

Gun Rights/Gun Control ***$4,950***
     National Rifle Assn ....$4,950   PAC

Human Rights ***$2,700***
     Human Rights Campaign Fund ....$2,500   PAC

Misc Issues ***$16,484***
     Sierra Club ....$8,784   PAC
     League of Conservation Voters ....$5,000   PAC
     Citizen Action of New York ....$1,000   PAC

Other & Unknown

Other	$18,650

Non-Profit Institutions ***$2,000***
     Foundation for Hearing Aid Research ....$2,000   Indiv

Civil Servants/Public Officials ***$1,000***
     None over $1,000

Education ***$7,200***
     New York City Board of Education ....$4,000   Indiv
     Highland Schools ....$1,500   Indiv

Retired ***$8,200***
     None over $1,000

Unknown	$28,977

     Homemakers/Non-income earners $5,450
     No Employer Listed or Found $4,650
     Employer Listed/Category Unknown $18,877
         Indeck Energy Services ....$3,000   Indiv
         Robbins, Green et al ....$1,500   Indiv
         Bio-Energy ....$1,000   Indiv
         Carroll Air Service ....$1,000   Indiv
         Indeck Power ....$1,000   Indiv
         Weidy Furniture ....$1,000   Indiv

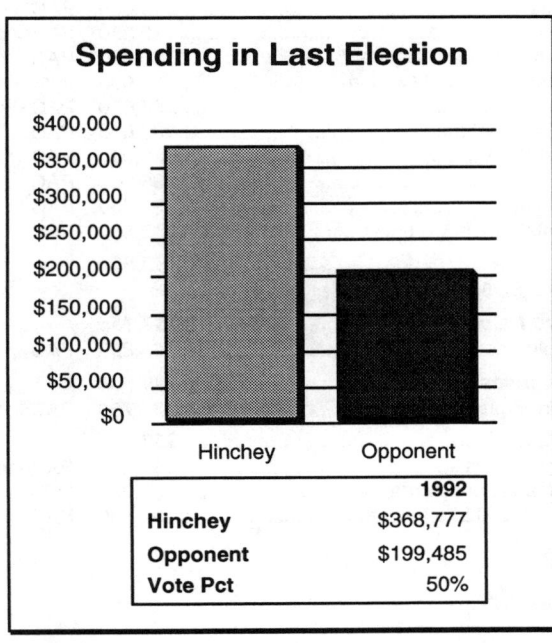

Spending in Last Election

	1992
Hinchey	$368,777
Opponent	$199,485
Vote Pct	50%

---

* Contributions came from more than one affiliate or subsidiary.

Peter Hoagland, D-Neb (2)

First elected: 1988

1991-92 Total Receipts: $711,298
1992 Year-end Cash: $13,744

1991-92 Committees & Subcommittees

Banking, Finance and Urban Affairs
Economic Stabilization; Financial Institutions Supervision, Regulation and Insurance

Interior and Insular Affairs
National Parks and Public Lands; Water, Power and Offshore Energy Resources

Judiciary
Crime and Criminal Justice

Leading Contributors

Business

Agriculture	$26,200	
Crop Production & Basic Processing	$4,500	
None over $2,500		
Dairy	$11,000	
Associated Milk Producers	$7,000	PAC
Mid-America Dairymen	$3,000	PAC
Agricultural Services/Products	$3,950	
Archer-Daniels-Midland Corp	$2,500	PAC
Food Processing & Sales	$4,050	
None over $2,500		

Communications/Electronics	$16,750	
Media/Entertainment	$2,500	
None over $2,500		
Telephone Utilities	$10,500	
AT&T	$4,500	PAC

Construction	$13,750	
Home Builders	$5,000	
National Assn of Home Builders	$5,000	PAC
Building Materials & Equipment	$4,750	
Phillips Manufacturing Co	$3,500	Indiv

Source of Funds in 1992 Election

Source	Total	Pct
PACs	$457,190	64%
Indivs $200+	$147,750	21%
Indivs under $200	$77,533	11%
Other	$37,001	5%
Candidate	$0	0%
Party	$10,412	1%

Source of PAC Dollars by Sector

Source	Total	Pct
Business	$267,079	58%
Labor	$163,338	36%
Ideology/Single Issue	$27,650	6%

In-State vs. Out-of-State Contributions*

Source	Total	Pct
In-State	$87,450	59%
Out-of-state	$60,300	41%
No state listed	$0	

* by large individual contributors ($200 & above)

Energy & Natural Resources	$5,500	
Oil & Gas	$2,500	
None over $2,500		
Electric Utilities	$3,000	
None over $2,500		

Finance, Insurance & Real Estate	$186,329	
Commercial Banks	$92,300	
American Bankers Assn	$10,000	PAC
JP Morgan & Co	$10,000	PAC
MNC Financial Inc	$6,500	PAC
Barnett Banks Inc	$5,500	PAC
Chase Manhattan	$5,500	PAC/Ind
Norwest Corp	$5,250	PAC/Ind
Citizens & Southern National Bank	$5,000	PAC
First National Bank of Omaha	$5,000	Indiv
Bankers Trust	$4,000	PAC
Firstier Financial Inc	$3,500	PAC
Chemical Bank	$3,000	PAC
Citicorp	$3,000	PAC
First Chicago Corp	$2,750	PAC
Continental Illinois Corp	$2,500	PAC
Savings & Loans	$3,500	
None over $2,500		
Finance/Credit Companies	$7,150	
Household International Inc	$3,800	PAC
Securities & Investment	$9,500	
American Express	$2,750	PAC/Ind
Insurance	$33,900	
Mutual of Omaha	$6,200	PAC/Ind
Physicians Mutual Insurance	$3,000	Indiv
Principal Mutual Life Insurance	$2,500	PAC

Contribution Totals by Sector

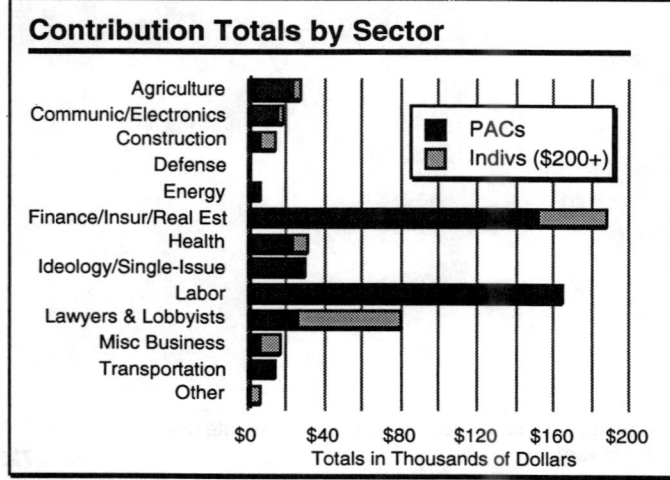

Agriculture
Communic/Electronics
Construction
Defense
Energy
Finance/Insur/Real Est
Health
Ideology/Single-Issue
Labor
Lawyers & Lobbyists
Misc Business
Transportation
Other

■ PACs
▨ Indivs ($200+)

$0 $40 $80 $120 $160 $200
Totals in Thousands of Dollars

Real Estate **$21,399**
    National Assn of Realtors ....$9,999 PAC

Accountants **$17,000**
    American Institute of CPA's ....$8,500 PAC
    Coopers & Lybrand ....$3,500 PAC
    Arthur Andersen & Co ....$2,500 PAC

Health   **$29,500**

Health Professionals **$21,400**
    American Academy of Ophthalmology ....$3,500 PAC
    American Chiropractic Assn* ....$2,950 PAC
    American Dental Assn ....$2,500 PAC

Hospitals/Nursing Homes **$2,500**
    None over $2,500

Pharmaceuticals/Health Products **$4,850**
    None over $2,500

Lawyers & Lobbyists   **$79,450**

Lawyers & Lobbyists **$79,450**
    Kutak, Rock & Campbell ....$10,650 PAC/Ind
    Assn of Trial Lawyers of America ....$10,000 PAC
    Akin, Gump et al ....$5,550 PAC/Ind
    Jenner & Block ....$3,000 Indiv
    Skadden, Arps et al ....$2,750 PAC/Ind
    Cleary, Gottlieb et al ....$2,550 Indiv

Misc Business   **$15,700**

Retail Sales **$3,750**
    None over $2,500

Business Services **$6,300**
    None over $2,500

Transportation   **$13,900**

Air Transport **$4,000**
    None over $2,500

Automotive **$2,700**
    None over $2,500

Railroads **$5,500**
    Union Pacific Corp ....$4,500 PAC/Ind

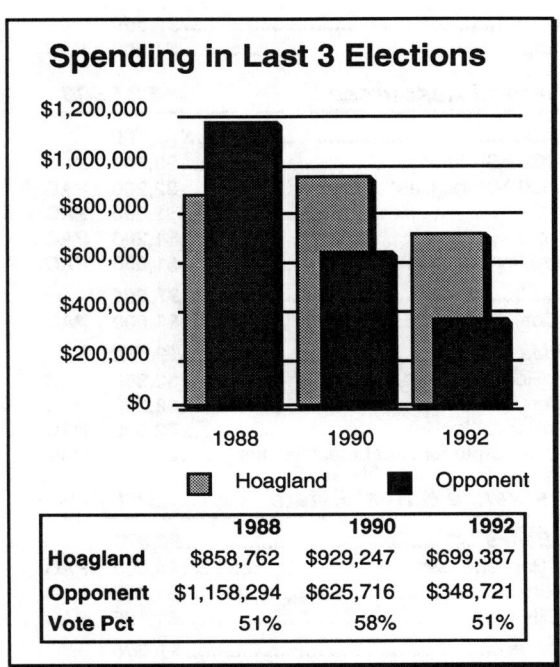

Spending in Last 3 Elections

	1988	1990	1992
Hoagland	$858,762	$929,247	$699,387
Opponent	$1,158,294	$625,716	$348,721
Vote Pct	51%	58%	51%

■ Hoagland   ■ Opponent

Labor

Labor   **$163,338**

Building Trade Unions **$16,000**
    Laborers' Political League ....$3,500 PAC
    Ironworkers Union ....$3,000 PAC
    Plumbers/Pipefitters Union....................$3,000 PAC

Industrial Unions **$55,889**
    Machinists/Aerospace Workers Union ...$10,000 PAC
    Rubber Cork Linoleum & Plastic Workers ....$10,000 PAC
    United Auto Workers ....$10,000 PAC
    Intl Brotherhood of Electrical Workers ....$8,000 PAC
    Communications Workers of America ......$7,389 PAC
    United Steelworkers ....$5,000 PAC

Transportation Unions **$33,500**
    Teamsters Union ....$10,000 PAC
    Air Line Pilots Assn ....$5,000 PAC
    Seafarers International Union ....$5,000 PAC
    Marine Engineers Union.......................$4,000 PAC
    Transport Workers Union ....$2,500 PAC

Public Sector Unions **$44,200**
    National Education Assn ....$10,000 PAC
    American Federation of Teachers...........$7,500 PAC
    National Assn of Letter Carriers ....$7,500 PAC
    National Assn Retired Federal Employees ....$7,000 PAC
    American Fedn of St/Cnty/Munic Employees ......$5,500 PAC
    American Postal Workers Union ....$2,500 PAC

Misc Unions **$13,749**
    AFL-CIO ....$4,000 PAC
    Food & Commercial Workers Union ......$3,499 PAC
    Service Employees International Union ...$3,000 PAC

Ideological/Single-Issue

Ideological/Single-Issue   **$28,350**

Democratic/Liberal **$2,700**
    National Cmte for an Effective Congress ...$2,500 PAC

Leadership PACs **$3,500**
    America's Leaders' Fund (Dan Rostenkowski) ....$2,500 PAC

Pro-Israel **$8,150**
    None over $2,500

Human Rights **$3,000**
    KidsPAC ....$3,000 PAC

Misc Issues **$8,000**
    Sierra Club ....$4,000 PAC
    National Cmte to Preserve Social Security ....$3,500 PAC

Other & Unknown

Other   **$6,050**

Retired **$3,100**
    None over $2,500

Unknown   **$20,000**

    Homemakers/Non-income earners $3,600
    Employer Listed/Category Unknown $14,650
        Sanford Management Co ....$4,000 Indiv

---

* Contributions came from more than one affiliate or subsidiary.

David L. Hobson, R-Ohio (7)

First elected: 1990
1991-92 Total Receipts: $360,267
1992 Year-end Cash: $81,974

1991-92 Committees & Subcommittees

Government Operations
Environment, Energy and Natural Resources; Human Resources and Intergovernmental Relations

Public Works and Transportation
Aviation; Investigations and Oversight; Surface Transportation

Standards of Official Conduct

Select Committee on Aging

Leading Contributors

Business

Agriculture	$11,650	
Tobacco	**$2,100**	
RJR Nabisco	$1,000	PAC
Dairy	**$2,750**	
Milk Marketing Inc	$1,250	PAC
Associated Milk Producers	$1,000	PAC
Agricultural Services/Products	**$3,000**	
Navistar International	$1,500	PAC
Freeport-McMoRan Inc	$1,000	PAC
Food Processing & Sales	**$2,500**	
Food Marketing Institute	$1,500	PAC
Nabisco Brands Inc	$1,000	PAC

Communications/Electronics	$13,750	
Media/Entertainment	**$3,000**	
National Cable Television Assn	$3,000	PAC
Telephone Utilities	**$8,900**	
Ohio Bell Telephone	$3,200	PAC
AT&T	$2,500	PAC
GTE Corp	$1,350	PAC
United Telecommunications	$1,000	PAC
Computer Equipment & Services	**$1,850**	
Electronic Data Systems	$1,500	PAC

Source of Funds in 1992 Election

Source	Total	Pct
PACs	$196,975	55%
Indivs $200+	$53,870	15%
Indivs under $200	$98,007	27%
Other	$11,415	3%
Candidate	$0	0%
Party	$170	0%

Source of PAC Dollars by Sector

Source	Total	Pct
Business	$183,677	93%
Labor	$9,783	5%
Ideology/Single Issue	$3,850	2%

In-State vs. Out-of-State Contributions*

Source	Total	Pct
In-State	$50,770	94%
Out-of-state	$3,100	6%
No state listed	$0	

* by large individual contributors ($200 & above)

Construction	$9,050	
General Contractors	**$5,600**	
Midwest Pipeliners	$2,000	Indiv
National Utility Contractors Assn	$1,500	PAC
Associated General Contractors	$1,000	PAC
Home Builders	**$2,600**	
National Assn of Home Builders	$1,700	PAC

Defense	$2,550	
Defense Aerospace	**$1,050**	
None over $1,000		
Misc Defense	**$1,500**	
Harsco Corp	$1,500	PAC

Energy & Natural Resources	$27,500	
Oil & Gas	**$16,700**	
Columbia Gas System*	$3,000	PAC
Consolidated Natural Gas*	$2,200	PAC
Marathon Oil	$1,600	PAC
Coastal Corp	$1,200	PAC
Texas Gas Transmission Corp	$1,050	PAC
Mining	**$1,000**	
National Coal Assn	$1,000	PAC
Electric Utilities	**$9,550**	
American Electric Power*	$2,350	PAC
Ohio Edison	$2,200	PAC
Dayton Power & Light	$2,000	PAC
ACRE (Action Cmte for Rural Electrification)	$1,100	PAC

Finance, Insurance & Real Estate	$41,225	
Commercial Banks	**$8,675**	
American Bankers Assn*	$4,000	PAC
Society Corp	$1,700	PAC
National City Corp	$1,175	PAC
Savings & Loans	**$1,000**	
Ohio Savings Assns League	$1,000	PAC

Contribution Totals by Sector

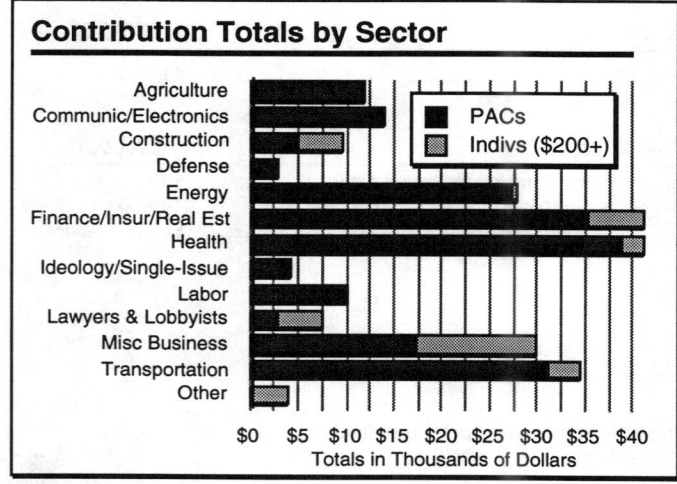

Agriculture, Communic/Electronics, Construction, Defense, Energy, Finance/Insur/Real Est, Health, Ideology/Single-Issue, Labor, Lawyers & Lobbyists, Misc Business, Transportation, Other

■ PACs
▨ Indivs ($200+)

$0 $5 $10 $15 $20 $25 $30 $35 $40
Totals in Thousands of Dollars

Insurance **$13,150**
    National Assn of Life Companies .... $2,500   PAC
    National Assn of Life Underwriters .... $2,000   PAC
    Independent Insurance Agents of America .... $1,500   PAC
    Metropolitan Life Insurance .... $1,500   PAC
    Blue Cross & Blue Shield Assn .... $1,350   PAC

Real Estate **$12,850**
    National Assn of Realtors .... $8,400   PAC
    Oberer Development Co .... $1,000   Indiv

Accountants **$3,500**
    American Institute of CPA's .... $3,500   PAC

Misc Finance **$1,100**
    None over $1,000

Health $41,052

Health Professionals **$30,152**
    American Medical Assn .... $9,700   PAC
    American Academy of Ophthalmology .... $3,000   PAC
    American College of Emergency Physicians .... $3,000   PAC
    American Podiatry Assn .... $2,850   PAC
    American Dental Assn* .... $2,400   PAC
    American Physical Therapy Assn .... $1,550   PAC
    American Optometric Assn .... $1,500   PAC
    American Chiropractic Assn* .... $1,300   PAC
    American Occupational Therapy Assn .... $1,002   PAC

Hospitals/Nursing Homes **$4,700**
    American Hospital Assn .... $2,750   PAC

Pharmaceuticals/Health Products **$6,200**
    Schering-Plough Corp .... $1,000   PAC

Lawyers & Lobbyists $7,250

Lawyers & Lobbyists **$7,250**
    Schwartz, Kelm et al .... $1,000   Indiv

Misc Business $30,600

Business Associations **$1,250**
    None over $1,000

Food & Beverage **$5,550**
    National Restaurant Assn .... $2,900   PAC
    Cooker Restaurants .... $2,000   Indiv

Retail Sales **$2,400**
    International Steel Wool Co .... $1,000   Indiv

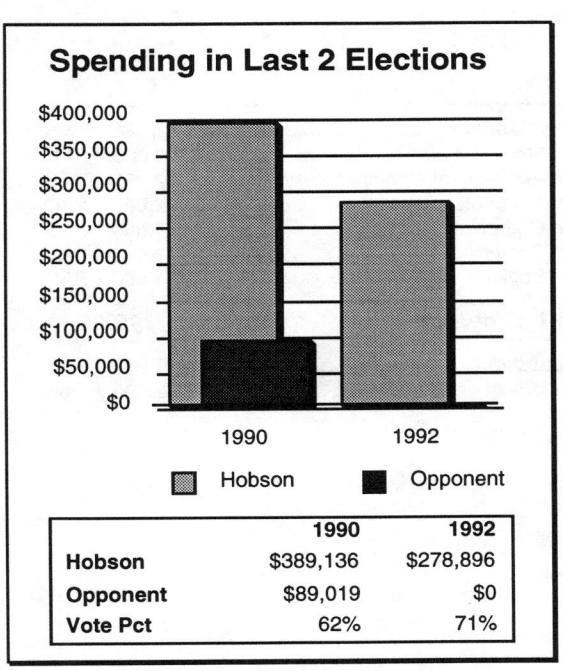

Spending in Last 2 Elections

	1990	1992
Hobson	$389,136	$278,896
Opponent	$89,019	$0
Vote Pct	62%	71%

Business Services **$5,400**
    NSC Consulting Corp .... $2,500   Indiv
    LM Berry & Co .... $1,700   PAC/Ind

Chemical & Related Manufacturing **$3,300**
    Dow Chemical .... $1,000   PAC

Misc Manufacturing & Distributing **$10,300**
    Hugo Bosca Co .... $2,200   Indiv
    Russell T Bundy Assoc .... $1,900   Indiv
    Hoechst Celanese Corp .... $1,350   PAC
    Corning Glass Works .... $1,000   PAC
    Graphic Paper Products .... $1,000   Indiv

Transportation $34,350

Air Transport **$16,600**
    United Parcel Service .... $4,750   PAC
    Airborne Freight Corp .... $3,000   PAC
    Federal Express Corp .... $3,000   PAC
    General Electric .... $1,500   PAC
    United Airlines .... $1,500   PAC
    American Airlines .... $1,150   PAC
    Aircraft Owners & Pilots Assn .... $1,000   PAC

Automotive **$11,400**
    National Auto Dealers Assn .... $2,700   PAC
    Americans for Free International Trade .... $2,000   PAC
    Auto Dealers & Drivers for Free Trade .... $2,000   PAC
    Honda of Marysville .... $1,950   Indiv
    Honda of America .... $1,600   Indiv

Trucking **$4,350**
    American Trucking Assns .... $1,100   PAC
    Roadway Services Inc .... $1,100   PAC

Railroads **$1,100**
    None over $1,000

Labor

Labor $9,783

Transportation Unions **$4,500**
    Air Line Pilots Assn .... $4,500   PAC

Public Sector Unions **$5,283**
    National Assn Retired Federal Employees .... $4,500   PAC

Ideological/Single-Issue

Ideological/Single-Issue $3,850

Republican/Conservative **$1,000**
    Southwest Ohio Concerned Citizens .... $1,000   PAC

Gun Rights/Gun Control **$1,100**
    National Rifle Assn .... $1,100   PAC

Misc Issues **$1,500**
    National Cmte to Preserve Social Security .... $1,500   PAC

Other & Unknown

Other $3,800

Retired **$3,050**
    None over $1,000

Unknown $14,820

    No Employer Listed or Found $2,350
    Employer Listed/Category Unknown $11,720
        Nutter Enterprises .... $1,000   Indiv
        UES Inc .... $1,000   Indiv

---

* Contributions came from more than one affiliate or subsidiary.

George J. Hochbrueckner, D-NY (1)

First elected: 1986

1991-92 Total Receipts: $530,966
1992 Year-end Cash: $1,850

1991-92 Committees & Subcommittees

Armed Services
Military Personnel and Compensation; Research and Development; Seapower and Strategic and Critical Materials

Merchant Marine and Fisheries
Coast Guard and Navigation; Fisheries and Wildlife Conservation and the Environment

Select Committee on Narcotics Abuse and Control

Leading Contributors

Business

Agriculture		$3,150
Dairy	$2,300	
Associated Milk Producers	$2,000	PAC

Communications/Electronics		$7,340
Electronics Mfg & Services	$1,500	
None over $1,500		
Computer Equipment & Services	$4,400	
EDO Corp	$2,600	Indiv

Construction		$6,225
General Contractors	$4,000	
Marancos Construction Corp	$2,000	Indiv
Construction Services	$1,725	
National Society of Professional Engineers	$1,500	PAC

Defense		$30,300
Defense Aerospace	$15,900	
Grumman Corp	$7,000	PAC
Defense Electronics	$9,750	
Loral Corp	$1,800	PAC
Misc Defense	$4,650	
General Atomics	$3,600	PAC

Energy & Natural Resources	$3,900
None over $1,500	

Source of Funds in 1992 Election

Source	Total	Pct
■ PACs	$296,600	54%
▨ Indivs $200+	$86,325	16%
☐ Indivs under $200	$114,825	21%
⊠ Other	$52,223	10%
Candidate	$0	0%
Party	$25,157	5%

Source of PAC Dollars by Sector

Source	Total	Pct
■ Business	$85,290	29%
▨ Labor	$177,799	60%
☐ Ideology/Single Issue	$31,550	11%

In-State vs. Out-of-State Contributions*

Source	Total	Pct
☐ In-State	$74,475	87%
■ Out-of-state	$10,850	13%
No state listed	$0	

* by large individual contributors ($200 & above)

Finance, Insurance & Real Estate		$32,150
Securities & Investment	$1,500	
None over $1,500		
Insurance	$7,975	
National Assn of Life Underwriters	$2,000	PAC
Metropolitan Life Insurance	$1,500	PAC
Real Estate	$18,400	
National Assn of Realtors	$10,000	PAC
Fisher Brothers Management Co	$2,500	Indiv
Sport Realty Co	$2,000	Indiv
Accountants	$1,675	
None over $1,500		
Misc Finance	$2,000	
None over $1,500		

Health		$24,175
Health Professionals	$22,325	
American Medical Assn*	$10,000	PAC
American Academy of Ophthalmology	$2,000	PAC
American Chiropractic Assn	$2,000	PAC
American Optometric Assn	$1,800	PAC
American Dental Assn	$1,500	PAC
American Podiatry Assn	$1,500	PAC

Lawyers & Lobbyists		$9,850
Lawyers & Lobbyists	$9,850	
Meltzer, Lippe et al	$2,800	Indiv

Contribution Totals by Sector

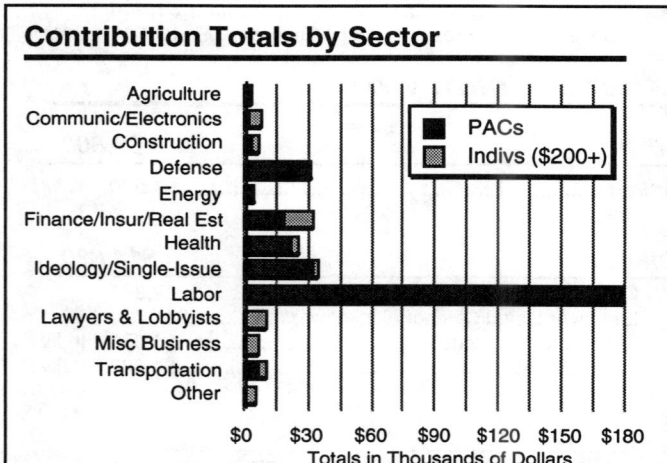

Legend: ■ PACs ▨ Indivs ($200+)

Categories (top to bottom): Agriculture, Communic/Electronics, Construction, Defense, Energy, Finance/Insur/Real Est, Health, Ideology/Single-Issue, Labor, Lawyers & Lobbyists, Misc Business, Transportation, Other

X-axis: $0 $30 $60 $90 $120 $150 $180
Totals in Thousands of Dollars

Misc Business   **$5,800**

Beer, Wine & Liquor **$2,000**
     Pindar Vineyards .... $2,000   Indiv

Business Services **$1,625**
     None over $1,500

Transportation   **$9,600**

Air Transport **$4,700**
     United Parcel Service .... $1,600   PAC
     Lawrence Aviation .... $2,000   Indiv

Automotive **$2,800**
     National Auto Dealers Assn .... $2,500   PAC

Sea Transport **$2,100**
     None over $1,500

Labor

Labor   **$178,249**

Building Trade Unions **$28,100**
     Sheet Metal Workers Union .... $7,500   PAC
     Laborers' Political League .... $6,000   PAC
     Carpenters & Joiners Union* .... $3,300   PAC
     Ironworkers Union .... $3,000   PAC
     Operating Engineers Union* .... $3,000   PAC
     Plumbers/Pipefitters Union .... $2,000   PAC
     AFL-CIO Bldg/Construction Trades Dept .... $1,500   PAC

Industrial Unions **$33,050**
     Machinists/Aerospace Workers Union ... $10,000   PAC
     United Auto Workers .... $6,300   PAC
     Communications Workers of America ... $5,000   PAC
     United Steelworkers .... $5,000   PAC
     Electronic Machine Furniture Workers ... $3,500   PAC

Transportation Unions **$46,200**
     Seafarers International Union .... $10,000   PAC
     Marine Engineers Union* .... $7,500   PAC
     Teamsters Union .... $5,000   PAC
     Boilermakers Union .... $4,250   PAC
     Brotherhood of Locomotive Engineers ... $4,200   PAC
     Air Line Pilots Assn .... $4,000   PAC
     International Longshoremen's Assn ...... $2,000   PAC
     Brotherhood of Railroad Signalmen ..... $1,600   PAC
     National Air Traffic Controllers Assn ... $1,500   PAC

Public Sector Unions **$56,400**
     American Federation of Teachers .... $10,000   PAC
     National Assn Retired Federal Employees ... $10,000   PAC
     National Assn of Letter Carriers .... $10,000   PAC
     National Education Assn .... $10,000   PAC
     American Fedn of St/Cnty/Munic Employees ... $6,000   PAC
     American Postal Workers Union .... $4,300   PAC
     International Assn of Firefighters .... $2,300   PAC

Misc Unions **$14,499**
     Food & Commercial Workers Union ..... $5,499   PAC
     AFL-CIO .... $3,000   PAC
     Service Employees International Union ... $3,000   PAC
     Bakery, Confectionery & Tobacco Workers ... $2,000   PAC

Ideological/Single-Issue

Ideological/Single-Issue   **$33,550**

Democratic/Liberal **$2,550**
     National Cmte for an Effective Congress ... $2,500   PAC

Leadership PACs **$5,500**
     House Leadership Fund (Tom Foley) ... $2,000   PAC
     Victory USA (Vic Fazio) .... $2,000   PAC

Pro-Israel **$5,500**
     Joint Action Cmte for Political Affairs ... $2,500   PAC

Human Rights **$7,500**
     Human Rights Campaign Fund .... $5,000   PAC
     KidsPAC .... $2,500   PAC

Misc Issues **$11,000**
     National Cmte to Preserve Social Security ... $5,000   PAC
     Sierra Club .... $3,000   PAC
     National Council of Senior Citizens ...... $2,000   PAC

Other & Unknown

Other   **$5,500**

Retired **$3,000**
     None over $1,500

Unknown   **$30,175**

     Homemakers/Non-income earners $5,925
     Generic Occupation/Category Unknown ... $2,225
     Employer Listed/Category Unknown $20,675
       Boyle, Shea et al .... $1,500   Indiv

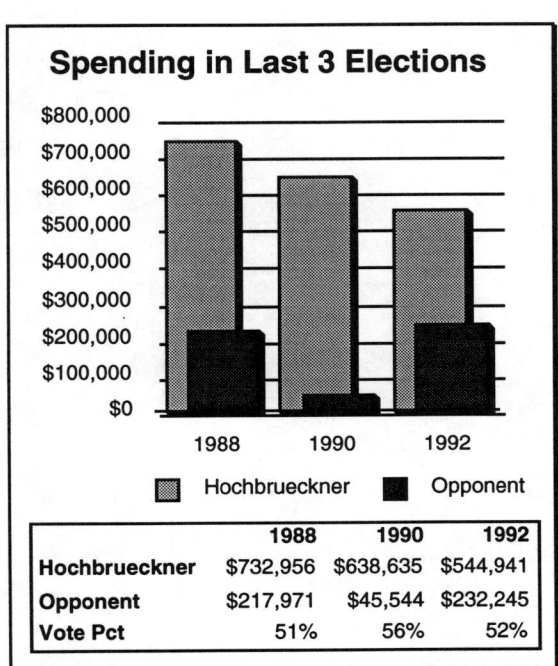

Spending in Last 3 Elections

	1988	1990	1992
Hochbrueckner	$732,956	$638,635	$544,941
Opponent	$217,971	$45,544	$232,245
Vote Pct	51%	56%	52%

Legend: ▨ Hochbrueckner   ■ Opponent

---

* Contributions came from more than one affiliate or
subsidiary.

Peter Hoekstra, R-Mich (2)

First elected: 1992

1991-92 Total Receipts: $101,362
1992 Year-end Cash: $4,582

1993-94 Committees & Subcommittees

Education and Labor
Labor-Management Relations; Labor Standards, Occupational Health and Safety; Postsecondary Education and Training

Public Works and Transportation
Economic Development; Water Resources and the Environment

Leading Contributors

NOTE: Hoekstra reported taking no PAC funds in his 1992 campaign. The PACs listed below did report making contributions, however, and those contributions are recorded in the official FEC records.

Business

Agriculture		$1,050
None over $1,000		

Communications/Electronics		$1,000
Telephone Utilities		$1,000
AT&T	$1,000	PAC

Construction		$2,000
General Contractors		$1,500
Thompson McCully Asphalt	$1,000	Indiv

Finance, Insurance & Real Estate		$2,700
Insurance		$1,700
Keuning Insurance Agency	$1,450	Indiv

Health		$1,950
Health Professionals		$1,950
None over $1,000		

Source of Funds in 1992 Election

Source	Total	Pct
■ PACs	$0	0%
Indivs $200+	$26,680	25%
Indivs under $200	$37,406	36%
▨ Other	$40,751	39%
Candidate	$26,801	26%
Party	$4,975	5%

Source of PAC Dollars by Sector

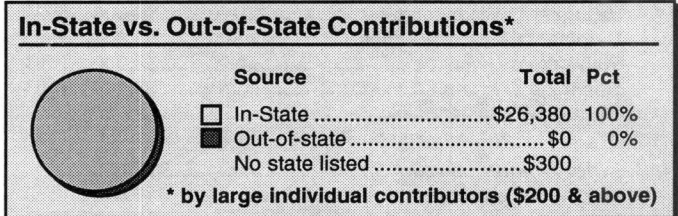

No PAC contributions reported

Source	Total	Pct
■ Business	$2,000	57%
Labor	$0	0%
□ Ideology/Single Issue	$1,500	43%

In-State vs. Out-of-State Contributions*

Source	Total	Pct
□ In-State	$26,380	100%
■ Out-of-state	$0	0%
No state listed	$300	

* by large individual contributors ($200 & above)

Misc Business		$3,700
Food & Beverage		$1,000
Brooks Beverage Management Inc	$1,000	Indiv
Retail Sales		$1,650
None over $1,000		

Transportation		$3,000
Automotive		$3,000
Prince Corp	$2,000	Indiv
Crown Cadillac Olds Inc	$1,000	Indiv

Contribution Totals by Sector

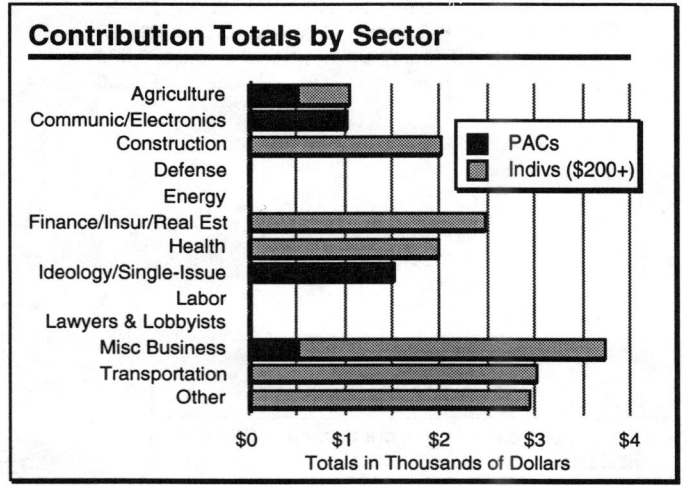

Agriculture
Communic/Electronics
Construction
Defense
Energy
Finance/Insur/Real Est
Health
Ideology/Single-Issue
Labor
Lawyers & Lobbyists
Misc Business
Transportation
Other

■ PACs
▨ Indivs ($200+)

$0 $1 $2 $3 $4
Totals in Thousands of Dollars

Ideological/Single-Issue

Ideological/Single-Issue	$1,500

Leadership PACs **$1,000**
    Republican Leader's Fund (Bob Michel) ....$1,000   PAC

Other & Unknown

Other	$2,900

Retired **$2,900**
    None over $1,000

Unknown	$10,380

    Homemakers/Non-income earners $1,750
    Employer Listed/Category Unknown $6,970
        Herman Miller Inc ....$1,470   Indiv

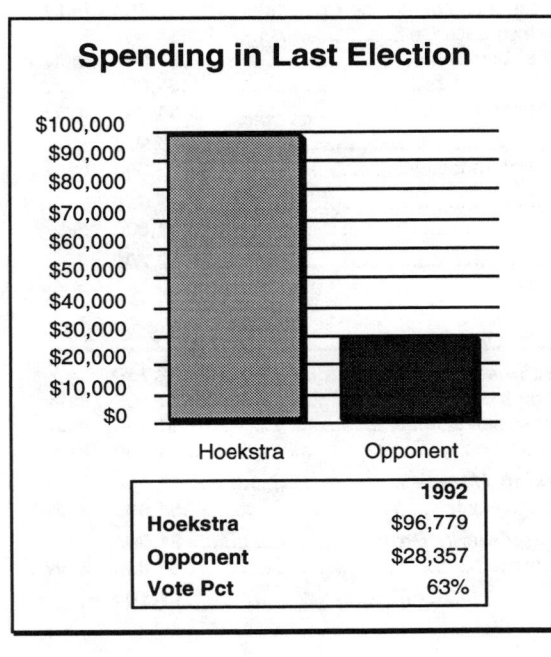

Spending in Last Election

	1992
Hoekstra	$96,779
Opponent	$28,357
Vote Pct	63%

Martin R. Hoke, R-Ohio (10)

First elected: 1992

1991-92 Total Receipts: $683,560
1992 Year-end Cash: $3,391

1993-94 Committees & Subcommittees

Budget

Science, Space and Technology
Space; Technology, Environment and Aviation

Leading Contributors

NOTE: Hoke reported taking no PAC funds in his 1992 campaign. The PAC listed below did report making a contribution, however, and that contribution is recorded in the official FEC records.

Business

Communications/Electronics	$11,900	
Printing & Publishing	*$3,200*	
American Greetings Corp	$3,000	Indiv
Media/Entertainment	*$3,000*	
WEOL/WNWV	$2,000	Indiv
North Coast Cable	$1,000	Indiv
Telecom Services & Equipment	*$2,650*	
Cellular Long Distance Co	$1,150	Indiv
Cellular One	$1,000	Indiv
Electronics Mfg & Services	*$2,800*	
Audiovox Corp	$1,500	Indiv

Construction	$13,800	
General Contractors	*$2,900*	
George R Hall Constracting	$1,000	Indiv
Home Builders	*$2,000*	
Bob Schmitt Homes	$2,000	Indiv
Special Trade Contractors	*$4,500*	
Clock Electric Inc	$1,900	Indiv
Lake Erie Electric	$1,200	Indiv
Crawford Industries	$1,000	Indiv
Building Materials & Equipment	*$4,400*	
Crawford Fitting Co	$2,000	Indiv

Energy & Natural Resources	$2,675	
Oil & Gas	*$2,675*	
BP America	$1,700	Indiv

Contribution Totals by Sector

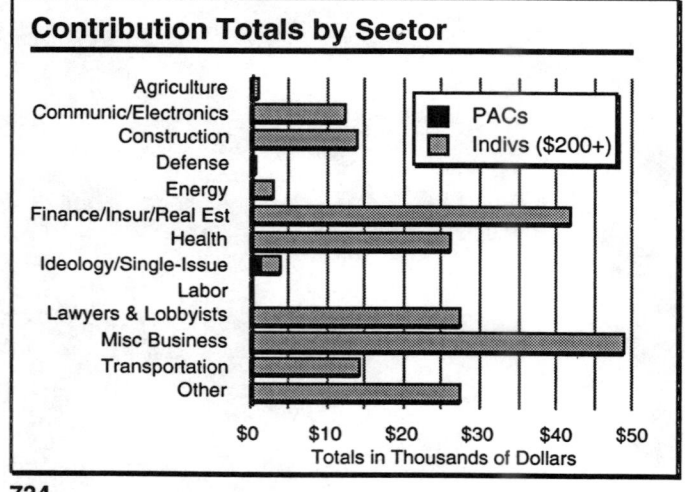

Agriculture
Communic/Electronics
Construction
Defense
Energy
Finance/Insur/Real Est
Health
Ideology/Single-Issue
Labor
Lawyers & Lobbyists
Misc Business
Transportation
Other

■ PACs
▨ Indivs ($200+)

$0 $10 $20 $30 $40 $50
Totals in Thousands of Dollars

Source of Funds in 1992 Election

Source	Total	Pct
■ PACs	$0	0%
▨ Indivs $200+	$291,096	40%
□ Indivs under $200	$114,162	16%
▨ Other	$330,266	45%
Candidate	$264,000	36%
Party	$66,266	9%

Source of PAC Dollars by Sector

No PAC contributions reported

Source	Total	Pct
■ Business	-$75	0%
▨ Labor	$0	0%
□ Ideology/Single Issue	$1,025	100%

In-State vs. Out-of-State Contributions*

Source	Total	Pct
□ In-State	$265,081	91%
■ Out-of-state	$25,515	9%
No state listed	$500	

* by large individual contributors ($200 & above)

Finance, Insurance & Real Estate	$40,415	
Commercial Banks	*$2,350*	
National City Corp	$1,100	Indiv
Securities & Investment	*$14,600*	
Morgenthaler Management Partners	$2,850	Indiv
Kemper Securities Group	$2,700	Indiv
Baker & Co	$2,000	Indiv
First Fiduciary Investment Counsel	$1,500	Indiv
Cumberland Associates	$1,000	Indiv
Kidder, Peabody	$1,000	Indiv
Ohio Co	$1,000	Indiv
Insurance	*$12,200*	
Central Reserve Life Insurance Co	$4,700	Indiv
Pie Mutual Insurance Co	$4,000	Indiv
Dickenson & Associates	$1,000	Indiv
JP Farley Corp	$1,000	Indiv
Pinkerton Insurance	$1,000	Indiv
Real Estate	*$5,915*	
Forest City Enterprises Inc	$3,000	Indiv
Accountants	*$2,650*	
Hebda & Co	$1,000	Indiv
Misc Finance	*$2,700*	
None over $1,000		

Health	$25,750	
Health Professionals	*$22,150*	
Drs Demarco & Irwin	$1,500	Indiv
Hummer Associates	$1,200	Indiv
FE Yuzon MD Inc	$1,000	Indiv
Hospitals/Nursing Homes	*$1,500*	
Eliza Jennings Home	$1,000	Indiv
Pharmaceuticals/Health Products	*$1,000*	
Invacare Corp	$1,000	Indiv
Misc Health	*$1,100*	
None over $1,000		

Lawyers & Lobbyists $27,032

Lawyers & Lobbyists $27,032
Baker & Hostetler	$6,100	Indiv
Seeley, Savidge & Aussem	$2,900	Indiv
Jones, Day et al	$2,700	Indiv
Thompson, Hine & Flory	$2,150	Indiv
Calfee, Halter & Griswold	$1,250	Indiv
Wickens, Herzer & Panza	$1,250	Indiv
Childs, Miller & Assoc	$1,000	Indiv
Kahn, Kleinman et al	$1,000	Indiv
Law Offices of Douglas Ehlke	$1,000	Indiv

Misc Business $48,779

Business Associations $1,500
Precision Metalforming Assn	$1,500	Indiv

Retail Sales $3,750
Sherwin-Williams Co	$2,000	Indiv

Business Services $9,579
Quicksilver Messenger Service	$1,329	Indiv
Tradesmen International	$1,250	Indiv
Accipiter Corp	$1,000	Indiv
Chimera Corp	$1,000	Indiv
GLM Security & Sound Inc	$1,000	Indiv
Jennie Jones Inc	$1,000	Indiv
McKinsey & Co	$1,000	Indiv
Success Group Inc	$1,000	Indiv

Recreation/Live Entertainment $1,000
Platinum Ent Inc	$1,000	Indiv

Chemical & Related Manufacturing $8,650
RPM Inc	$2,000	Indiv
Phillips Container Co	$1,900	Indiv
Mooney Chemicals	$1,500	Indiv
Day-Glo Color Corp	$1,000	Indiv

Steel Production $4,250
Sifco Industries Inc	$2,000	Indiv
Olympic Steel Inc	$1,000	Indiv

Misc Manufacturing & Distributing $19,300
Hy-Level Screw Products	$3,050	Indiv
Taft Business Machines	$2,250	Indiv
Nova Machine Products Corp	$1,500	Indiv
Dickey-Grabler Co	$1,300	Indiv
Avalon Precision Casting Co	$1,000	Indiv
Fusion Inc	$1,000	Indiv
Payne Investment Co	$1,000	Indiv
RW Beckett Corp	$1,000	Indiv
Ranpak Corp	$1,000	Indiv
Torq Corp	$1,000	Indiv
Varbros Corp	$1,000	Indiv
Windway Capital Corp	$1,000	Indiv

Transportation $13,700

Automotive $12,800
Anchor Tool & Die Co	$2,000	Indiv
S&S Auto	$2,000	Indiv
AJ Rose Manufacturing Co	$1,500	Indiv
Merrick Chevrolet	$1,300	Indiv
Eaton Corp	$1,250	Indiv
A&Z Auto	$1,000	Indiv
America's Body Co	$1,000	Indiv
Auto Accents	$1,000	Indiv

Trucking $1,000
None over $1,000

Ideological/Single-Issue

Ideological/Single-Issue $4,525

Republican/Conservative $2,025
Hoke for Congress Committee	$1,000	Indiv
Ohio Republican Party	$1,000	Indiv

Leadership PACs $1,000
Republican Leader's Fund (Bob Michel)	$1,000	PAC

Human Rights $1,000
None over $1,000

Other & Unknown

Other $27,000

Retired $26,500
None over $1,000

Unknown $74,870
Homemakers/Non-income earners	$21,000	
No Employer Listed or Found	$11,850	
Generic Occupation/Category Unknown	$5,450	
Employer Listed/Category Unknown	$36,570	
Amas Investments	$1,000	Indiv
Gen/Miller Corp	$1,000	Indiv
Maxus Investment Group	$1,000	Indiv
McGeen-Rohco Inc	$1,000	Indiv
Scott Fetzer Co	$1,000	Indiv
Strang Management Corp	$1,000	Indiv
Synerco Inc	$1,000	Indiv
Thrift & New	$1,000	Indiv

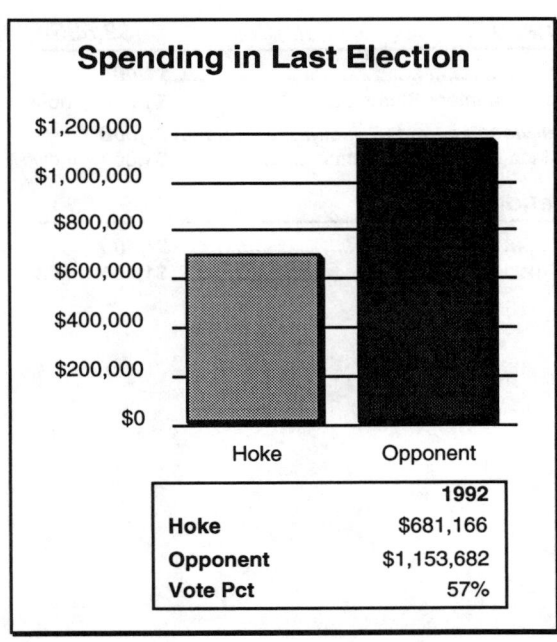

Spending in Last Election

	1992
Hoke	$681,166
Opponent	$1,153,682
Vote Pct	57%

Tim Holden, D-Pa (6)

1993-94 Committees & Subcommittees

Agriculture
Department Operations and Nutrition; Environment, Credit and Rural Development; Livestock

Armed Services
Military Acquisition; Oversight and Investigations

Leading Contributors

Business

Communications/Electronics	$4,750	
Telephone Utilities	**$4,000**	
AT&T	$4,000	PAC

Construction	$2,550	
General Contractors	**$1,000**	
None over $1,000		
Construction Services	**$1,000**	
Alfred Benesch & Co	$1,000	Indiv

Energy & Natural Resources	$2,900	
Electric Utilities	**$2,000**	
ACRE (Action Cmte for Rural Electrification)	$2,000	PAC

Finance, Insurance & Real Esta	$2,750	
Savings & Loans	**$1,000**	
US League of Savings Assns*	$1,000	PAC
Insurance	**$1,000**	
John B Hall Insurance	$1,000	Indiv
Real Estate	**$1,250**	
None over $1,000		

First elected: 1992

1991-92 Total Receipts:	$293,468
1992 Year-end Cash:	$9,118

Source of Funds in 1992 Election

Source	Total	Pct
PACs	$99,400	32%
Indivs $200+	$64,227	21%
Indivs under $200	$100,538	33%
Other	$43,490	14%
Candidate	$10,000	3%
Party	$32,387	11%

Source of PAC Dollars by Sector

Source	Total	Pct
Business	$9,300	8%
Labor	$91,350	80%
Ideology/Single Issue	$13,700	12%

In-State vs. Out-of-State Contributions*

Source	Total	Pct
In-State	$62,527	97%
Out-of-state	$1,700	3%
No state listed	$0	

*** by large individual contributors ($200 & above)**

Health	$3,700
Health Professionals	**$1,700**
None over $1,000	
Hospitals/Nursing Homes	**$2,000**
None over $1,000	

Lawyers & Lobbyists	$27,925	
Lawyers & Lobbyists	**$27,925**	
Riley & Fanelli	$6,350	Indiv
James J Curran Law Office	$2,000	Indiv
Williamson, Friedberg & Jones	$1,175	Indiv
SR Wojdak & Associates	$1,000	Indiv

Misc Business	$3,535	
Retail Sales	**$1,000**	
Boscov's Department Stores	$1,000	Indiv
Business Services	**$1,000**	
Mastiff Management Consutants	$1,000	Indiv

Transportation	$1,800	
Trucking	**$1,400**	
Fanelli Trucking	$1,400	Indiv

Contribution Totals by Sector

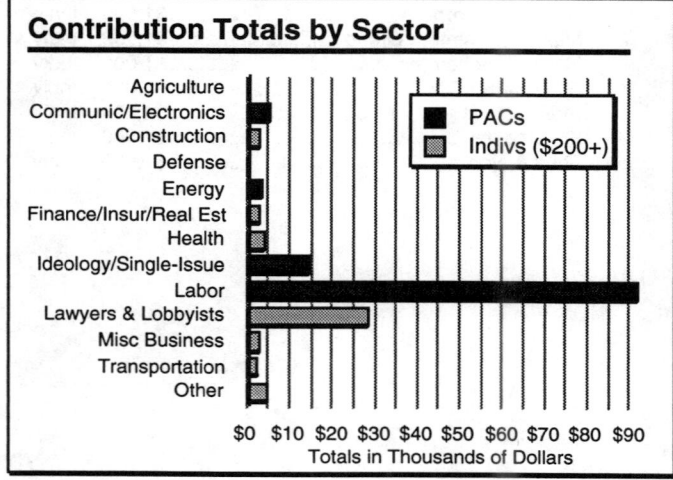

Agriculture
Communic/Electronics
Construction
Defense
Energy
Finance/Insur/Real Est
Health
Ideology/Single-Issue
Labor
Lawyers & Lobbyists
Misc Business
Transportation
Other

■ PACs
▨ Indivs ($200+)

$0 $10 $20 $30 $40 $50 $60 $70 $80 $90
Totals in Thousands of Dollars

Labor

Labor	$91,350	
Building Trade Unions	**$25,400**	
Ironworkers Union*	$7,250	PAC
Carpenters & Joiners Union	$7,000	PAC
Plumbers/Pipefitters Union*	$5,300	PAC
Laborers' Political League	$3,000	PAC
Sheet Metal Workers Union	$1,500	PAC
Industrial Unions	**$35,900**	
United Mine Workers	$5,100	PAC
Communications Workers of America* ...	$5,000	PAC
Machinists/Aerospace Workers Union ...	$5,000	PAC
United Auto Workers	$5,000	PAC
United Steelworkers	$5,000	PAC
Rubber Cork Linoleum & Plastic Workers ...	$4,000	PAC
Intl Brotherhood of Electrical Workers ...	$2,000	PAC
Amalgamated Clothing & Textile Workers ...	$1,500	PAC
Boilermakers Union	$1,000	PAC
Ladies Garment Workers Union	$1,000	PAC
Transportation Unions	**$10,250**	
Teamsters Union*	$5,000	PAC
Marine Engineers Union	$2,000	PAC
Air Line Pilots Assn	$1,000	PAC
United Transportation Union	$1,000	PAC
Public Sector Unions	**$13,500**	
American Fedn of St/Cnty/Munic Employees ...	$5,000	PAC
National Assn of Letter Carriers	$4,000	PAC
National Assn Retired Federal Employees ...	$2,000	PAC
American Postal Workers Union	$1,000	PAC
National Assn of Postmasters	$1,000	PAC
Misc Unions	**$6,300**	
Food & Commercial Workers Union	$5,000	PAC
AFL-CIO	$1,300	PAC

Ideological/Single-Issue

Ideological/Single-Issue	$14,200	
Democratic/Liberal	**$2,000**	
National Cmte for an Effective Congress ...	$2,500	PAC
Leadership PACs	**$2,000**	
Effective Government Cmte (Dick Gephardt) ...	$1,000	PAC
House Leadership Fund (Tom Foley) ...	$1,000	PAC
Gun Rights/Gun Control	**$4,950**	
National Rifle Assn	$4,950	PAC
Misc Issues	**$5,000**	
League of Conservation Voters	$5,000	PAC

Other & Unknown

Other	$5,000	
Education	**$1,000**	
Pottsville High School	$1,000	Indiv
Retired	**$3,400**	
None over $1,000		

Unknown	$17,117	
Homemakers/Non-income earners	$3,000	
No Employer Listed or Found	$3,400	
Generic Occupation/Category Unknown ...	$3,792	
Employer Listed/Category Unknown	$6,925	
McDevitt & Co	$1,000	Indiv
PLCB	$1,000	Indiv
Rose Corp	$1,000	Indiv

Independent expenditures supporting Holden
| National Rifle Assn .... | $4,000 | |

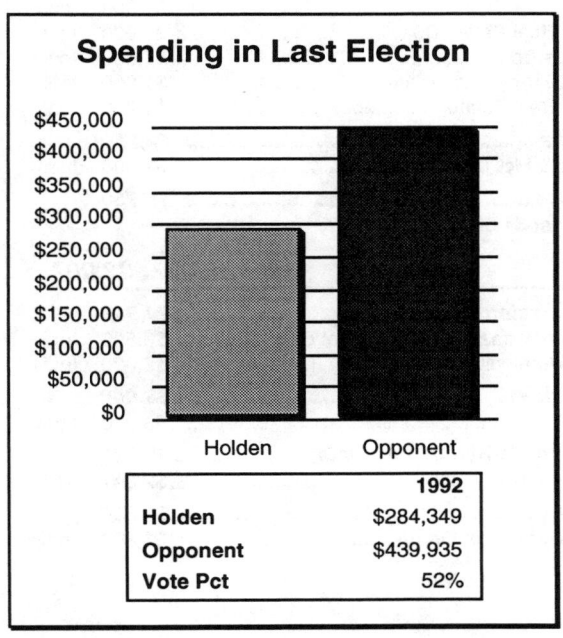

Spending in Last Election

	1992
Holden	$284,349
Opponent	$439,935
Vote Pct	52%

Steve Horn, R-Calif (38)

First elected: 1992

1991-92 Total Receipts: $436,093
1992 Year-end Cash: $493

1993-94 Committees & Subcommittees

Government Operations
Commerce, Consumer and Monetary Affairs; Information, Justice, Transportation and Agriculture

Public Works and Transportation
Aviation; Water Resources and the Environment

Leading Contributors

NOTE: Horn reported taking no PAC funds in his 1992 campaign. The PACs listed below did report making contributions, however, and those contributions are recorded in the official FEC records.

Business

Communications/Electronics $8,850

Printing & Publishing	**$1,400**	
None over $1,000		
Media/Entertainment	**$3,200**	
None over $1,000		
Telephone Utilities	**$2,500**	
Long Beach Press-Telegram Div	$2,000	Indiv
Computer Equipment & Services	**$1,750**	
Softie Inc	$1,000	Indiv

Construction $3,700

General Contractors	**$1,450**	
None over $1,000		
Construction Services	**$1,250**	
None over $1,000		

Defense $1,200

Defense Aerospace	**$1,000**	
Northrop Corp	$1,000	Indiv

Energy & Natural Resources $7,120

Oil & Gas	**$7,120**	
Atlantic Richfield	$3,620	Indiv
Western Petroleum Co	$1,000	Indiv

Source of Funds in 1992 Election

Source	Total	Pct
PACs	$0	0%
Indivs $200+	$274,867	56%
Indivs under $200	$88,180	18%
Other	$123,501	25%
Candidate	$58,217	12%
Party	$60,455	12%

Source of PAC Dollars by Sector

No PAC contributions reported

Source	Total	Pct
Business	$1,500	99%
Labor	$0	0%
Ideology/Single Issue	$18	1%

In-State vs. Out-of-State Contributions*

Source	Total	Pct
In-State	$250,432	92%
Out-of-state	$21,835	8%
No state listed	$1,000	

* by large individual contributors ($200 & above)

Finance, Insurance & Real Estate $37,450

Commercial Banks	**$4,250**	
Security Pacific Corp	$2,250	Indiv
F&M Bank of Long Beach	$1,000	Indiv
Securities & Investment	**$4,000**	
Brentwood Associates	$2,000	Indiv
Insurance	**$4,500**	
Hamman, Miller et al	$2,000	Indiv
Real Estate	**$16,200**	
Bixby Land Co	$3,000	Indiv
Bancap Investment Group	$2,000	Indiv
C Robert Langslet & Son Inc	$2,000	Indiv
Munco Inc	$1,500	Indiv
Houser Real Estate Co	$1,000	Indiv
Lansdale Co	$1,000	Indiv
Mike Silverman Associates	$1,000	Indiv
Sacher Real Estate	$1,000	Indiv
Accountants	**$2,250**	
Windes & McClaughry	$1,000	Indiv
Misc Finance	**$5,750**	
None over $1,000		

Health $32,007

Health Professionals	**$24,966**	
Alamitos Dermatological Medical Center	$3,500	Indiv
Brockside Medical Clinic	$2,000	Indiv
Health Services	**$3,000**	
FHP Inc	$3,000	Indiv
Pharmaceuticals/Health Products	**$2,341**	
MDT Corp	$2,341	Indiv
Misc Health	**$1,700**	
Memorial Medical Group	$1,500	Indiv

Contribution Totals by Sector

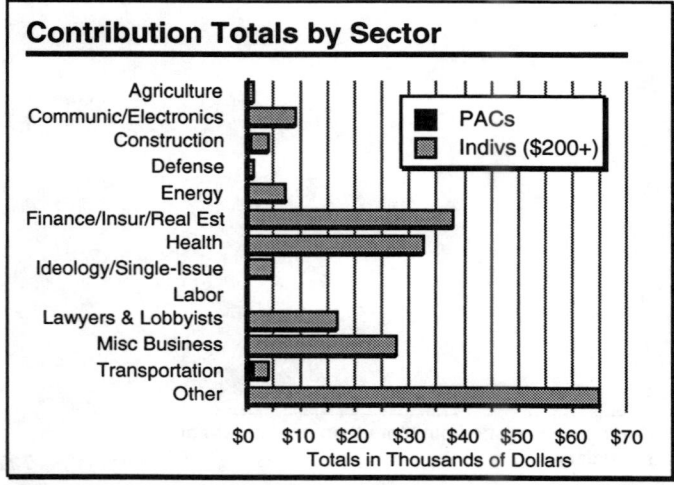

Agriculture
Communic/Electronics
Construction
Defense
Energy
Finance/Insur/Real Est
Health
Ideology/Single-Issue
Labor
Lawyers & Lobbyists
Misc Business
Transportation
Other

■ PACs
▨ Indivs ($200+)

$0 $10 $20 $30 $40 $50 $60 $70
Totals in Thousands of Dollars

Lawyers & Lobbyists $17,250

Lawyers & Lobbyists **$17,250**
    Sacks, Tierney & Kasen ....$3,000 Indiv
    O'Melveny & Myers ....$2,850 Indiv
    Thomas & Spaltro ....$1,900 Indiv
    Latham & Watkins ....$1,250 Indiv
    McDermott, Will & Emery ....$1,000 Indiv

Misc Business $26,968

Misc Services **$2,500**
    US Rentals Inc ....$2,000 Indiv
Business Services **$8,618**
    Athena Co ....$2,250 Indiv
Casinos/Gambling **$2,300**
    Resorts International ....$2,300 Indiv
Lodging/Tourism **$2,450**
    None over $1,000
Misc Business **$3,300**
    Coastal Wholesale Co ....$3,000 Indiv
Chemical & Related Manufacturing **$3,000**
    ICI Acrylics ....$2,000 Indiv
Misc Manufacturing & Distributing **$4,600**
    Downey Valve ....$2,000 Indiv

Transportation $3,702

Air Transport **$1,250**
    United Parcel Service ....$1,000 PAC
Automotive **$2,202**
    Boulevard Buick-GMC Truck ....$1,000 Indiv

Ideological/Single-Issue

Ideological/Single-Issue $4,465

Republican/Conservative **$4,465**
    None over $1,000

Other & Unknown

Other $64,537

Non-Profit Institutions **$2,250**
    None over $1,000
Education **$24,224**
    California State University ....$19,224 Indiv
    Long Beach Unified School District ....$3,250 Indiv
    Corona-Norco Unified School District ..$1,000 Indiv
Retired **$36,863**
    None over $1,000
Other **$1,000**
    Episcopal Church ....$1,000 Indiv

Unknown $66,686

    Homemakers/Non-income earners $34,131
    No Employer Listed or Found $1,650
    Employer Listed/Category Unknown ...$30,905
        Stansbury Co ....$4,000 Indiv
        Jaffe & Co ....$2,000 Indiv
        Newman-Brettin Co ....$2,000 Indiv
        Pacific Group ....$1,500 Indiv
        Gammaloy Ltd ....$1,250 Indiv
        William E Nicolai & Son ....$1,200 Indiv
        KTN Enterprises ....$1,000 Indiv
        Killingsworth Presentations ....$1,000 Indiv
        Murdoch Inc ....$1,000 Indiv
        RP Graham & Assoc ....$1,000 Indiv

Independent expenditures supporting Horn
    California Medical Assn $1,250

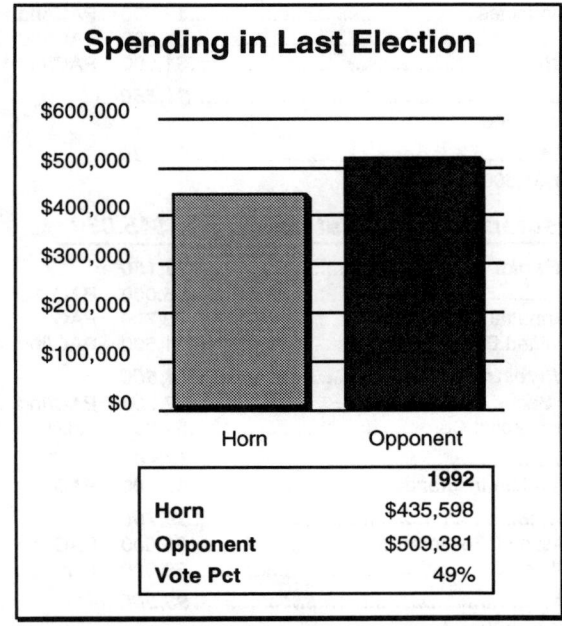

Spending in Last Election

	1992
Horn	$435,598
Opponent	$509,381
Vote Pct	49%

Amo Houghton, R-NY (31)

First elected: 1986

1991-92 Total Receipts: $363,139
1992 Year-end Cash: $213,487

1991-92 Committees & Subcommittees

Budget
Budget Process, Reconciliation and Enforcement; Economic Policy, Projections and Revenues (Ranking Republican)

Foreign Affairs
Africa; International Economic Policy and Trade

Select Committee on Aging

Leading Contributors

Business

Agriculture $16,400

Crop Production & Basic Processing	**$2,000**
National Grape Co-operative Assn	$1,500 PAC
Tobacco	**$3,200**
Philip Morris	$1,700 PAC/Ind
Dairy	**$2,750**
Associated Milk Producers	$1,500 PAC
Agricultural Services/Products	**$3,150**
None over $1,500	
Food Processing & Sales	**$3,800**
None over $1,500	
Forestry & Forest Products	**$1,500**
None over $1,500	

Communications/Electronics $43,150

Printing & Publishing	**$1,500**
None over $1,500	
Telephone Utilities	**$6,500**
AT&T	$3,000 PAC
Alltel Corp	$1,500 PAC
Telecom Services & Equipment	**$32,250**
Corning Inc	$30,050 Indiv
Electronics Mfg & Services	**$1,500**
None over $1,500	

Source of Funds in 1992 Election

Source	Total	Pct
■ PACs	$117,310	32%
▨ Indivs $200+	$181,298	50%
☐ Indivs under $200	$41,243	11%
⊠ Other	$23,288	6%
Candidate	$0	0%
Party	$2,089	1%

Source of PAC Dollars by Sector

Source	Total	Pct
■ Business	$91,880	86%
▨ Labor	$7,500	7%
☐ Ideology/Single Issue	$8,000	7%

In-State vs. Out-of-State Contributions*

Source	Total	Pct
☐ In-State	$103,548	57%
■ Out-of-state	$77,750	43%
No state listed	$0	

* by large individual contributors ($200 & above)

Construction $6,700

General Contractors	**$4,300**
Associated General Contractors	$2,500 PAC
Building Materials & Equipment	**$2,200**
Owens-Corning Fiberglas	$1,500 Indiv

Defense $3,500

Defense Aerospace	**$2,500**
None over $1,500	

Energy & Natural Resources $22,280

Oil & Gas	**$15,400**
Dresser Industries	$3,500 PAC/Ind
Texaco	$2,500 PAC/Ind
Exxon Corp	$1,500 PAC/Ind
Mining	**$1,550**
None over $1,500	
Electric Utilities	**$4,380**
None over $1,500	

Finance, Insurance & Real Estate $45,050

Commercial Banks	**$13,150**
Citicorp	$5,000 PAC
Chase Manhattan	$2,700 PAC
Marine Midland Banks	$1,500 PAC/Ind
Securities & Investment	**$14,600**
Goldman, Sachs & Co	$7,500 PAC/Ind
Meriwether Capital Corp	$2,000 Indiv
Insurance	**$3,900**
Metropolitan Life Insurance	$2,000 PAC
Real Estate	**$9,700**
National Assn of Realtors	$6,000 PAC
Solow Building Co	$2,000 Indiv
Misc Finance	**$3,500**
None over $1,500	

Contribution Totals by Sector

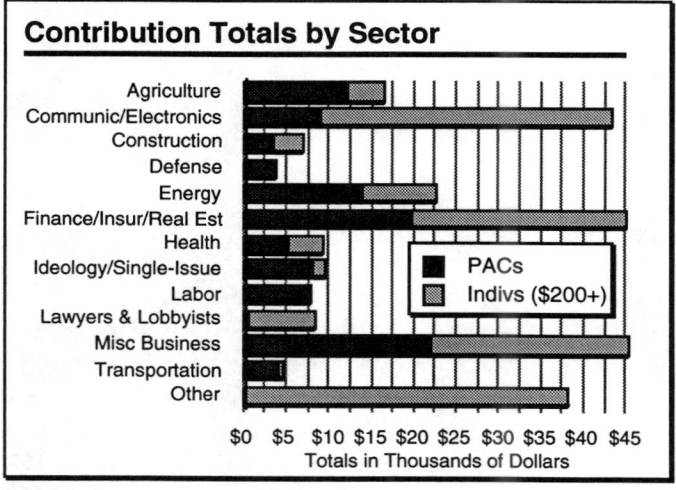

Agriculture
Communic/Electronics
Construction
Defense
Energy
Finance/Insur/Real Est
Health
Ideology/Single-Issue
Labor
Lawyers & Lobbyists
Misc Business
Transportation
Other

■ PACs
▨ Indivs ($200+)

$0 $5 $10 $15 $20 $25 $30 $35 $40 $45
Totals in Thousands of Dollars

Health | $9,000

Health Professionals *$5,400*
    American Dental Assn ...... $2,000   PAC

Pharmaceuticals/Health Products *$3,000*
    None over $1,500

Lawyers & Lobbyists | $8,300

Lawyers & Lobbyists *$8,300*
    None over $1,000

Misc Business | $45,098

Food & Beverage *$1,500*
    None over $1,500

Beer, Wine & Liquor *$1,900*
    None over $1,500

Retail Sales *$1,500*
    None over $1,500

Business Services *$2,400*
    None over $1,500

Chemical & Related Manufacturing *$7,250*
    Keene Corp ...... $3,000   Indiv
    Dow Corning Corp ...... $1,500   PAC/Ind

Misc Manufacturing & Distributing *$25,248*
    Corning Glass Works ...... $9,500   PAC
    Alcas Cutlery Corp ...... $3,048   PAC/Ind
    Stone Container Corp ...... $2,000   PAC
    PPG Industries ...... $1,500   Indiv

Transportation | $4,300

Air Transport *$1,600*
    None over $1,500

Automotive *$2,200*
    None over $1,500

Labor

Labor | $7,500

Building Trade Unions *$1,500*
    None over $1,500

Transportation Unions *$5,500*
    Air Line Pilots Assn ...... $2,500   PAC
    Marine Engineers Dist 2 Maritime Officers ...... $1,500   PAC

Ideological/Single-Issue

Ideological/Single-Issue | $9,250

Pro-Israel *$5,000*
    National PAC ...... $5,000   PAC

Gun Rights/Gun Control *$1,500*
    National Rifle Assn ...... $1,500   PAC

Other & Unknown

Other | $37,950

Retired *$33,850*
    None over $1,500

Other *$2,500*
    None over $1,500

Unknown | $30,200

    Homemakers/Non-income earners $14,200
    Employer Listed/Category Unknown $13,750
        None over $1,500

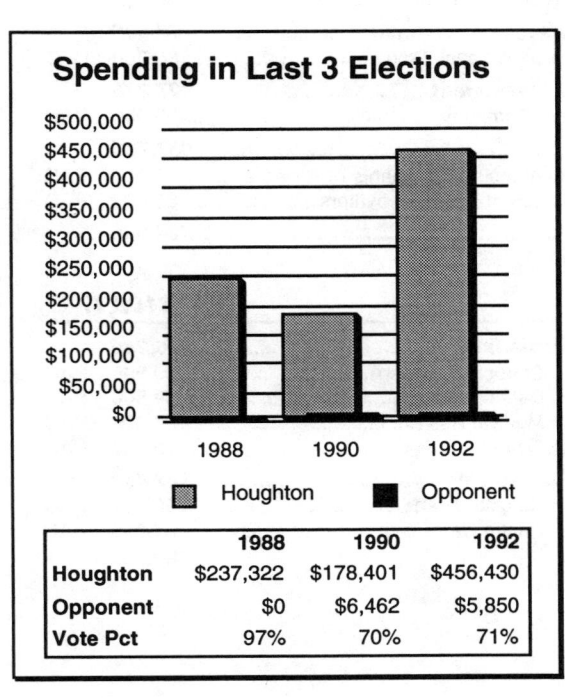

Spending in Last 3 Elections

	1988	1990	1992
Houghton	$237,322	$178,401	$456,430
Opponent	$0	$6,462	$5,850
Vote Pct	97%	70%	71%

Legend: ▨ Houghton   ■ Opponent

Steny H. Hoyer, D-Md (5)

First elected: 1981
1991-92 Total Receipts: $1,304,867
1992 Year-end Cash: $41,000

1991-92 Committees & Subcommittees

Administration
Elections; Libraries and Memorials; Procurement and Printing

Appropriations
Labor, Health and Human Services, Education and Related Agencies; Military Construction; Treasury, Postal Service and General Government

Leading Contributors

Business

Agriculture	**$39,960**

Crop Production & Basic Processing $7,950
  None over $5,000

Tobacco $12,200
  RJR Nabisco .... $5,000 PAC

Dairy $6,500
  None over $5,000

Food Processing & Sales $5,860
  None over $5,000

Communications/Electronics	**$47,933**

Media/Entertainment $16,950
  National Cable Television Assn .... $5,000 PAC

Telephone Utilities $17,000
  AT&T .... $5,250 PAC/Ind

Computer Equipment & Services $10,333
  None over $5,000

Construction	**$25,650**

General Contractors $14,350
  None over $5,000

Defense	**$15,740**

Defense Aerospace $8,000
  None over $5,000

Misc Defense $5,240
  None over $5,000

Contribution Totals by Sector

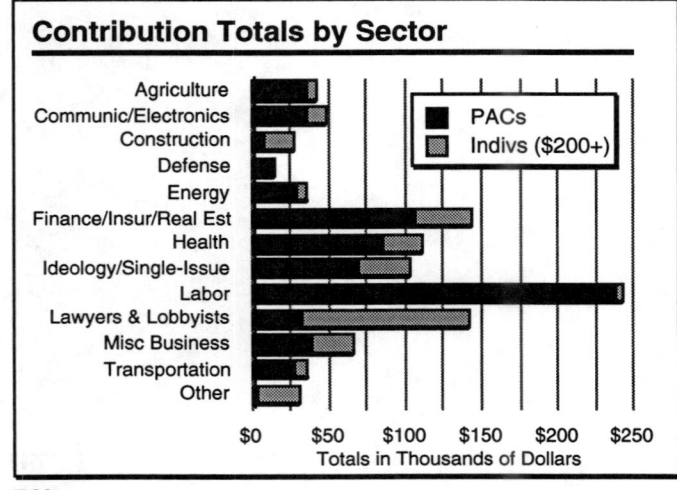

Totals in Thousands of Dollars

Source of Funds in 1992 Election

Source	Total	Pct
■ PACs	$705,642	53%
▨ Indivs $200+	$381,735	29%
▢ Indivs under $200	$156,325	12%
▨ Other	$90,781	7%
Candidate	$0	0%
Party	$30,066	2%

Source of PAC Dollars by Sector

Source	Total	Pct
■ Business	$402,061	57%
▨ Labor	$237,360	34%
▢ Ideology/Single Issue	$68,350	10%

In-State vs. Out-of-State Contributions*

Source	Total	Pct
▢ In-State	$237,413	62%
▨ Out-of-state	$143,802	38%
No state listed	$0	

* by large individual contributors ($200 & above)

Energy & Natural Resources	**$34,400**

Oil & Gas $23,950
  Coastal Corp .... $7,000 PAC

Electric Utilities $6,950
  None over $5,000

Finance, Insurance & Real Estate	**$142,320**

Commercial Banks $30,080
  American Bankers Assn* .... $7,620 PAC
  Citicorp .... $6,000 PAC
  Citizens & Southern National Bank .... $5,500 PAC

Credit Unions $9,500
  Credit Union National Assn .... $8,000 PAC

Securities & Investment $27,375
  Investment Company Institute .... $5,000 PAC

Insurance $37,750
  Independent Insurance Agents of America .... $6,000 PAC
  National Assn of Life Underwriters .... $6,000 PAC

Real Estate $24,965
  None over $5,000

Health	**$109,174**

Health Professionals $76,249
  American Chiropractic Assn .... $9,999 PAC
  American Dental Assn .... $9,500 PAC
  American Medical Assn .... $8,000 PAC
  American Optometric Assn .... $5,000 PAC

Hospitals/Nursing Homes $21,450
  American Hospital Assn .... $8,000 PAC
  American Health Care Assn .... $5,000 PAC

Lawyers & Lobbyists — $140,217

Lawyers & Lobbyists **$140,217**
- Assn of Trial Lawyers of America ....$10,000 PAC
- Akin, Gump et al ....$9,500 PAC/Ind
- Cassidy & Associates ....$8,971 Indiv
- Elliott & O'Brien ....$7,000 Indiv
- Meyers, Billingsley et al ....$5,200 Indiv

Misc Business — $65,232

Business Associations **$7,700**
- Greater Washington Board of Trade ....$7,000 PAC

Beer, Wine & Liquor **$16,950**
- None over $5,000

Retail Sales **$11,882**
- None over $5,000

Business Services **$14,725**
- None over $5,000

Transportation — $35,075

Air Transport **$13,750**
- United Parcel Service ....$7,500 PAC
- Federal Express Corp ....$5,000 PAC

Automotive **$9,350**
- Harbor Enterprises Inc ....$6,000 Indiv

Railroads **$5,625**
- None over $5,000

Labor

Labor — **$240,790**

Building Trade Unions **$37,150**
- Carpenters & Joiners Union ....$10,000 PAC
- Sheet Metal Workers Union ....$10,000 PAC
- Plumbers/Pipefitters Union* ....$5,900 PAC
- Laborers' Political League ....$5,500 PAC

Industrial Unions **$36,450**
- United Auto Workers ....$10,000 PAC
- United Mine Workers ....$5,500 PAC
- Communications Workers of America ....$5,400 PAC
- United Steelworkers ....$5,000 PAC

Transportation Unions **$56,010**
- Air Line Pilots Assn ....$10,000 PAC
- Seafarers International Union ....$10,000 PAC
- Teamsters Union ....$10,000 PAC
- Marine Engineers Union* ....$9,000 PAC
- United Transportation Union ....$7,000 PAC

Public Sector Unions **$90,000**
- National Assn of Letter Carriers ....$10,200 PAC
- American Federation of Teachers ....$10,000 PAC
- American Postal Workers Union ....$10,000 PAC
- National Education Assn ....$10,000 PAC
- National Treasury Employees Union ....$10,000 PAC
- National Assn Retired Federal Employees ....$9,000 PAC
- American Fedn of St/Cnty/Munic Employees ......$8,100 PAC
- International Assn of Firefighters ....$6,000 PAC

Misc Unions **$21,180**
- Food & Commercial Workers Union ....$7,500 PAC

Ideological/Single-Issue

Ideological/Single-Issue — **$101,890**

Democratic/Liberal **$8,065**
- None over $5,000

Pro-Israel **$45,575**
- National PAC ....$5,000 PAC

Pro-Choice **$6,000**
- National Abortion Rights Action League ....$5,500 PAC

Human Rights **$23,750**
- Human Rights Campaign Fund ....$10,500 PAC/Ind
- KidsPAC ....$10,000 PAC

Misc Issues **$16,600**
- National Cmte to Preserve Social Security ....$8,500 PAC
- Duc PAC ....$5,000 PAC

Other & Unknown

Other — **$29,180**

Civil Servants/Public Officials **$8,150**
- None over $5,000

Education **$10,120**
- None over $5,000

Retired **$9,000**
- None over $5,000

Unknown — **$63,925**

- Homemakers/Non-income earners $10,750
- Employer Listed/Category Unknown $50,375
  - None over $5,000

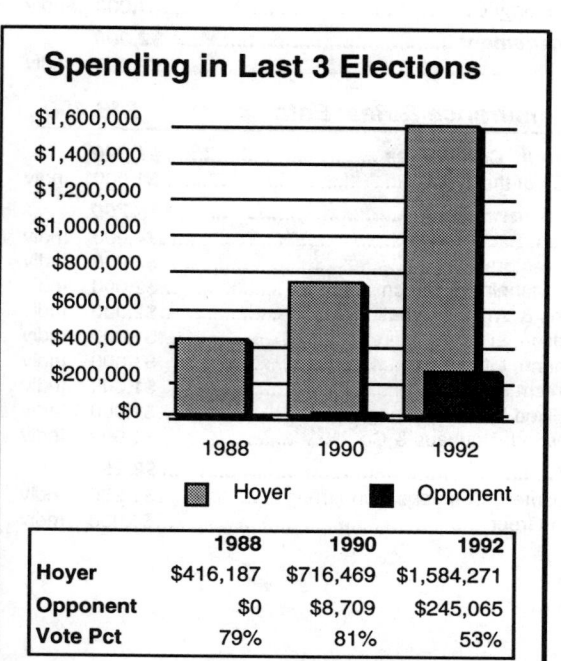

Spending in Last 3 Elections

	1988	1990	1992
Hoyer	$416,187	$716,469	$1,584,271
Opponent	$0	$8,709	$245,065
Vote Pct	79%	81%	53%

Legend: Hoyer, Opponent

* Contributions came from more than one affiliate or subsidiary.

Michael Huffington, R-Calif (22)

First elected: 1992

1991-92 Total Receipts: $5,443,247
1992 Year-end Cash: $8,071

1993-94 Committees & Subcommittees

Banking, Finance and Urban Affairs
Financial Institutions Supervision, Regulation and Deposit Insurance;
International Development, Finance, Trade and Monetary Policy

Small Business
Regulation, Business Opportunities and Technology; SBA Legislation
and the General Economy

Leading Contributors

Business

Agriculture	$4,900	
Crop Production & Basic Processing	**$4,000**	
Cypress Farms Inc	$2,000	Indiv
Dole Food Co	$1,000	Indiv
Sun World International	$1,000	Indiv

Communications/Electronics	$11,950	
Printing & Publishing	**$3,750**	
Johnson Publishing Co	$1,000	Indiv
Petersen Publishing Co	$1,000	Indiv
World of Communications Inc	$1,000	Indiv
Media/Entertainment	**$7,200**	
Crest Films Ltd	$2,000	Indiv
CBS Inc	$1,000	Indiv
IRS Media	$1,000	Indiv
MGM/UA	$1,000	Indiv
Telecom Services & Equipment	**$1,000**	
Metromedia Co	$1,000	Indiv

Construction	$5,200	
General Contractors	**$4,000**	
AG Spanos Development	$1,000	Indiv
Bechtel Corp	$1,000	Indiv
Building Materials & Equipment	**$1,000**	
Giant Group Ltd	$1,000	Indiv

Source of Funds in 1992 Election

Source	Total	Pct
■ PACs	$0	0%
▨ Indivs $200+	$174,660	3%
□ Indivs under $200	$79,447	1%
▧ Other	$5,192,728	95%
Candidate	$5,191,728	95%
Party	$1,000	0%

Source of PAC Dollars by Sector

No PAC contributions reported

Source	Total	Pct
■ Business	$0	0%
▨ Labor	$0	0%
□ Ideology/Single Issue	$0	0%

In-State vs. Out-of-State Contributions*

Source	Total	Pct
□ In-State	$112,060	65%
■ Out-of-state	$61,600	35%
No state listed	$0	

* by large individual contributors ($200 & above)

Energy & Natural Resources	$19,650	
Oil & Gas	**$17,650**	
Atlantic Richfield	$3,000	Indiv
Huffco Group Inc	$2,000	Indiv
Mesa Limited Partnership	$2,000	Indiv
Earle M Craig Jr Corp	$1,250	Indiv
Benson Mineral Group	$1,000	Indiv
Katch Go Petroleum	$1,000	Indiv
MT Halbouty Energy Co	$1,000	Indiv
Mosbasher Energy Co	$1,000	Indiv
Occidental Petroleum	$1,000	Indiv
Zilkha Energy Co	$1,000	Indiv
Waste Management	**$2,000**	
Sanifill Inc	$2,000	Indiv

Finance, Insurance & Real Esta	$46,450	
Finance/Credit Companies	**$1,000**	
Trust Co of the West	$1,000	Indiv
Securities & Investment	**$16,700**	
Goldman, Sachs & Co	$4,000	Indiv
AEA Investors	$2,000	Indiv
Green, Manning & Bunch	$2,000	Indiv
Hotchkis & Wiley International	$2,000	Indiv
Donaldson, Lufkin & Jenrette	$1,000	Indiv
Forstmann, Little & Co	$1,000	Indiv
Hambrecht & Quist	$1,000	Indiv
STW Fixed Income Management	$1,000	Indiv
Underwood, Neuhaus & Co	$1,000	Indiv
Insurance	**$2,250**	
Management Compensation Group	$1,250	Indiv
Holden Group	$1,000	Indiv

Contribution Totals by Sector

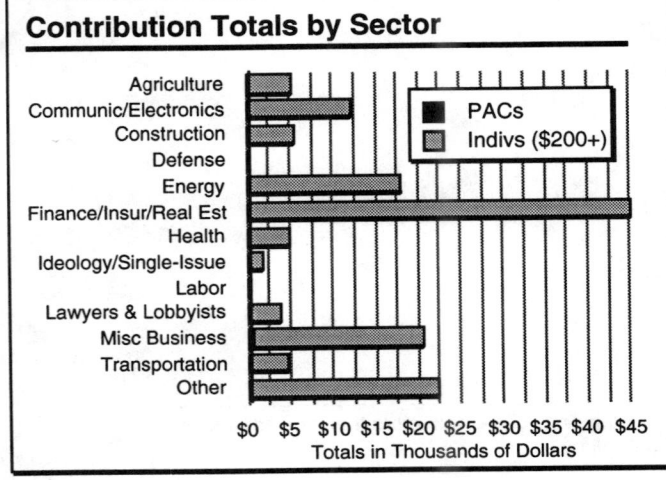

Totals in Thousands of Dollars

Real Estate $14,050

Gross Builders Inc	$2,000	Indiv
McNeil Real Estate Managment	$2,000	Indiv
Levy, Millender & Sinclair	$1,500	Indiv
Albert B Glickman & Assoc	$1,000	Indiv
Arnel Development Co	$1,000	Indiv
DRR Investments	$1,000	Indiv
Islay Investment	$1,000	Indiv
Melvin Simon & Associates	$1,000	Indiv

Misc Finance **$12,200**
None over $1,000

Health $4,700

Health Professionals **$4,700**
None over $1,000

Lawyers & Lobbyists $3,650

Lawyers & Lobbyists	**$3,650**	
Fulbright & Jaworski	$2,250	Indiv

Misc Business $20,300

Misc Services	**$2,500**	
Foothill Group	$1,000	Indiv
Business Services	**$6,000**	
Davis Group	$3,000	Indiv
Fell & Co Inc	$1,000	Indiv
Rockefeller Family & Assoc	$1,000	Indiv
Lodging/Tourism	**$2,000**	
First World Travel	$1,000	Indiv
Pleasant Travel Service	$1,000	Indiv
Chemical & Related Manufacturing	**$1,000**	
Contran Corp	$1,000	Indiv
Misc Manufacturing & Distributing	**$7,500**	
Crown Equipment Corp	$3,000	Indiv
Rainin Instrument Co	$2,000	Indiv
Northern Engraving Corp	$1,000	Indiv
Warnaco Inc	$1,000	Indiv

Transportation $4,500

Automotive	**$4,500**	
Cummins Engine Co	$2,000	Indiv
Tuttle Click Automotive Group	$1,500	Indiv
Galpin Motors	$1,000	Indiv

Ideological/Single-Issue

Ideological/Single-Issue $1,500

Republican/Conservative **$1,000**
None over $1,000

Other & Unknown

Other $22,210

Civil Servants/Public Officials	**$1,200**	
US Government	$1,000	Indiv

Retired **$19,560**
None over $1,000

Unknown $28,950

Homemakers/Non-income earners	$11,200	
No Employer Listed or Found	$2,200	
Generic Occupation/Category Unknown	$2,100	
Employer Listed/Category Unknown	$13,450	
Int Cable Casting Technologies	$1,900	Indiv
DJL	$1,200	Indiv
Pacific Air Industries	$1,200	Indiv
Starbuck, Tisdale & Assoc	$1,150	Indiv
Calpine Corp	$1,000	Indiv
HS Investments	$1,000	Indiv

Independent expenditures supporting Huffington

California Medical Assn	$2,500
Michael Towbes	$1,000

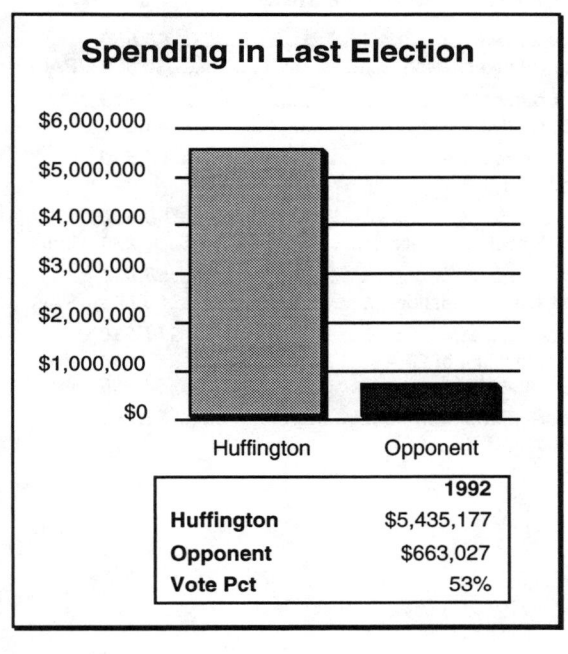

Spending in Last Election

	1992
Huffington	$5,435,177
Opponent	$663,027
Vote Pct	53%

William J. Hughes, D-NJ (2)

First elected: 1974

1991-92 Total Receipts: $513,720
1992 Year-end Cash: $116,489

1991-92 Committees & Subcommittees

Judiciary
Intellectual Property and Judicial Administration (Chairman); Crime and Criminal Justice

Merchant Marine and Fisheries
Coast Guard and Navigation; Fisheries and Wildlife Conservation and the Environment; Oceanography, Great Lakes and Outer Continental Shelf

Select Committee on Aging

Select Committee on Narcotics Abuse and Control

Leading Contributors

Business

Agriculture	$5,450	
Food Processing & Sales **$3,500**		
Food Marketing Institute $2,500	PAC	

Communications/Electronics	$52,400	
Printing & Publishing **$4,750**		
West Publishing $2,000	PAC	
Media/Entertainment **$34,850**		
Time Warner* $7,500	PAC	
MCA Inc $6,000	PAC/Ind	
ASCAP $3,000	PAC	
Viacom International $2,500	PAC	
Fox Inc $2,000	PAC/Ind	
Twentieth Century Fox $2,000	Indiv	
National Assn of Broadcasters............... $1,500	PAC	
Sony Corp/Columbia Pictures* $1,500	Indiv	
Walt Disney Co $1,500	PAC/Ind	
Telephone Utilities **$8,950**		
Bell Atlantic* $5,500	PAC	
Telecom Services & Equipment **$1,850**		
None over $1,500		
Computer Equipment & Services **$1,500**		
None over $1,500		

Source of Funds in 1992 Election

Source	Total	Pct
■ PACs	$220,075	42%
▨ Indivs $200+	$150,588	29%
□ Indivs under $200	$106,461	20%
▨ Other	$46,970	9%
Candidate	$0	0%
Party	$15,524	3%

Source of PAC Dollars by Sector

Source	Total	Pct
■ Business	$143,669	68%
▨ Labor	$62,500	29%
□ Ideology/Single Issue	$6,040	3%

In-State vs. Out-of-State Contributions*

Source	Total	Pct
□ In-State	$113,988	76%
■ Out-of-state	$36,050	24%
No state listed	$0	

* by large individual contributors ($200 & above)

Construction	$7,925	
General Contractors **$2,700**		
None over $1,500		
Construction Services **$3,225**		
Vaughn Organization $1,525	Indiv	

Energy & Natural Resources	$13,625	
Oil & Gas **$3,200**		
Columbia Gas System* $1,500	PAC	
Electric Utilities **$8,350**		
Public Service Electric & Gas $4,600	PAC	

Finance, Insurance & Real Estate	$48,419	
Commercial Banks **$8,850**		
American Bankers Assn $6,000	PAC	
Savings & Loans **$1,519**		
SAPEC, NJ (NJ Savings Assn) $1,519	PAC	
Securities & Investment **$5,550**		
None over $1,500		
Insurance **$6,800**		
Rollins, Burdick & Hunter $2,250	Indiv	
Real Estate **$8,950**		
National Assn of Realtors $5,000	PAC	
Accountants **$14,550**		
American Institute of CPA's $7,550	PAC	
Ford, Scott et al $1,900	Indiv	
Misc Finance **$1,700**		
None over $1,500		

Contribution Totals by Sector

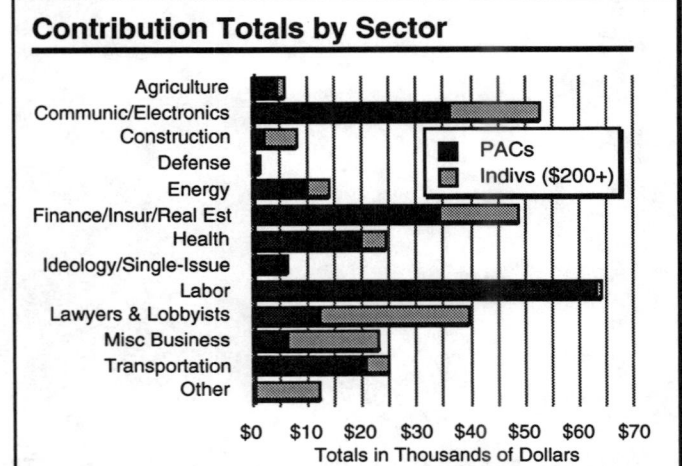

Agriculture
Communic/Electronics
Construction
Defense
Energy
Finance/Insur/Real Est
Health
Ideology/Single-Issue
Labor
Lawyers & Lobbyists
Misc Business
Transportation
Other

■ PACs
▨ Indivs ($200+)

$0 $10 $20 $30 $40 $50 $60 $70
Totals in Thousands of Dollars

Health $24,125

Health Professionals **$6,750**
    American Medical Assn ....$2,850   PAC

Pharmaceuticals/Health Products **$14,825**
    Merck & Co ....$2,450   PAC/Ind
    Johnson & Johnson ....$2,200   PAC
    Upjohn Co ....$2,000   PAC
    National Wholesale Druggists Assn ....$1,500   PAC

Lawyers & Lobbyists $40,200

Lawyers & Lobbyists **$40,200**
    Akin, Gump et al ....$3,000   PAC
    McGahn, Friss & Miller ....$3,000   Indiv
    Cooper, Perskie et al ....$2,350   Indiv
    Arnold & Porter ....$2,000   PAC
    Swidler & Berlin ....$1,500   PAC

Misc Business $22,910

Food & Beverage **$3,250**
    Cold Spring Fish & Supply Co ....$1,850   Indiv

Beer, Wine & Liquor **$2,000**
    None over $1,500

Business Services **$3,350**
    None over $1,500

Casinos/Gambling **$2,600**
    None over $1,500

Lodging/Tourism **$2,135**
    None over $1,500

Chemical & Related Manufacturing **$3,500**
    AK Pharma Inc ....$2,000   Indiv

Misc Manufacturing & Distributing **$2,550**
    Owens-Illinois ....$2,050   PAC

Transportation $24,650

Air Transport **$4,000**
    UNC Inc ....$2,000   PAC

Automotive **$4,350**
    National Auto Dealers Assn ....$1,500   PAC

Sea Transport **$15,300**
    Sea-Land Corp ....$3,900   PAC
    American Pilots Assn ....$2,500   PAC
    Society for Relief of Distressed Pilots ....$2,050   PAC

Labor

Labor $63,350

Building Trade Unions **$16,700**
    Operating Engineers Union* ....$5,700   PAC
    Carpenters & Joiners Union ....$5,000   PAC
    Laborers' Political League ....$3,000   PAC

Industrial Unions **$7,800**
    United Auto Workers ....$4,500   PAC
    Boilermakers Union ....$1,500   PAC

Transportation Unions **$20,350**
    Marine Engineers Union* ....$7,850   PAC
    Seafarers International Union ....$5,000   PAC
    Teamsters Union ....$5,000   PAC

Public Sector Unions **$16,500**
    National Education Assn ....$5,000   PAC
    National Assn Retired Federal Employees ....$4,000   PAC
    National Assn of Letter Carriers ....$3,000   PAC
    American Fedn of St/Cnty/Munic Employees ......$1,500   PAC

Misc Unions **$2,000**
    Food & Commercial Workers Union ....$1,500   PAC

Ideological/Single-Issue

Ideological/Single-Issue $6,040

Democratic/Liberal **$2,508**
    National Cmte for an Effective Congress ....$2,500   PAC

Misc Issues **$2,500**
    National Cmte to Preserve Social Security ....$1,500   PAC

Other & Unknown

Other $11,865

Civil Servants/Public Officials **$4,050**
    None over $1,500

Education **$2,715**
    None over $1,500

Retired **$5,100**
    None over $1,500

Unknown $40,053

    Homemakers/Non-income earners $5,933
    Employer Listed/Category Unknown $32,070
        Van Savage Agency ....$2,000   Indiv
        Galaxy Scientific Corp ....$1,900   Indiv
        Walker, Priviti & Holmes ....$1,550   Indiv
        Max Gurwicz Son Inc ....$1,500   Indiv

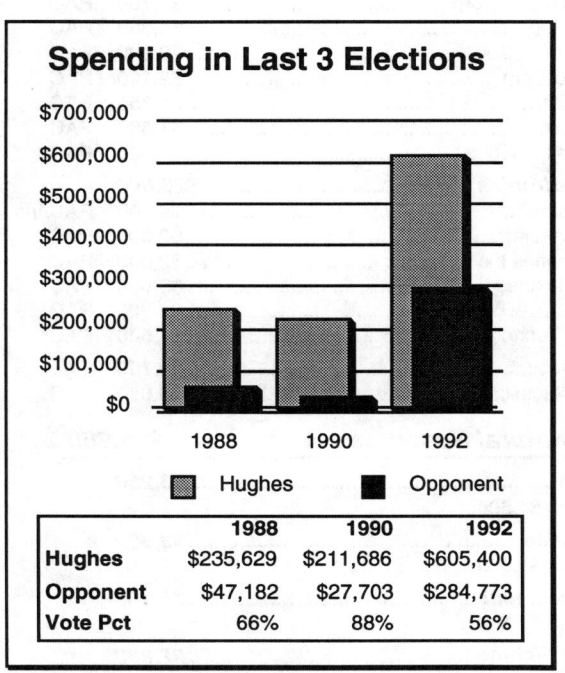

Spending in Last 3 Elections

	1988	1990	1992
Hughes	$235,629	$211,686	$605,400
Opponent	$47,182	$27,703	$284,773
Vote Pct	66%	88%	56%

---

* Contributions came from more than one affiliate or subsidiary.

Duncan Hunter, R-Calif (52)

First elected: 1980

1991-92 Total Receipts: $561,203
1992 Year-end Cash: $7,460

1991-92 Committees & Subcommittees

Armed Services
Research and Development; Seapower and Strategic and Critical Materials

Select Committee on Hunger

Leading Contributors

Business

Agriculture — $20,525

Crop Production & Basic Processing **$11,825**
American Sugarbeet Growers Assn	$2,000	PAC
Don Bee Farms	$2,000	Indiv

Livestock **$3,050**
National Cattlemen's Assn*	$1,800	PAC

Food Processing & Sales **$2,100**
None over $1,500

Communications/Electronics — $16,915

Media/Entertainment **$2,300**
None over $1,500

Telephone Utilities **$3,200**
Pacific Telesis Group	$1,700	PAC
BellSouth Corp*	$1,500	PAC

Electronics Mfg & Services **$3,040**
Titan Corp	$3,040	Indiv

Computer Equipment & Services **$7,625**
Questech Inc	$4,000	Indiv

Construction — $39,900

General Contractors **$29,200**
Fluor Corp	$4,000	PAC
RE Hazard Construction Co	$3,750	Indiv
Associated General Contractors	$3,500	PAC
Daley Corp	$3,250	Indiv
CE Wylie Construction Co	$2,500	Indiv
Luis E Garcia Inc	$2,200	Indiv

Home Builders **$3,000**
Brehm Communities	$2,000	Indiv

Source of Funds in 1992 Election

Source	Total	Pct
PACs	$237,167	39%
Indivs $200+	$204,958	34%
Indivs under $200	$93,267	15%
Other	$69,050	11%
Candidate	$0	0%
Party	$53,550	9%

Source of PAC Dollars by Sector

Source	Total	Pct
Business	$178,602	81%
Labor	$14,640	7%
Ideology/Single Issue	$26,450	12%

In-State vs. Out-of-State Contributions*

Source	Total	Pct
In-State	$155,558	76%
Out-of-state	$48,600	24%
No state listed	$0	

* by large individual contributors ($200 & above)

Construction Services **$4,050**
Apec Civil Engineering	$1,800	Indiv

Building Materials & Equipment **$2,350**
None over $1,500

Defense — $78,167

Defense Aerospace **$37,467**
Northrop Corp	$5,500	PAC
General Dynamics	$5,250	PAC/Ind
Rohr Industries	$3,206	PAC/Ind
Grumman Corp	$2,825	PAC
Martin Marietta Corp	$2,750	PAC
Gencorp Inc	$2,500	PAC
Textron Inc	$2,500	PAC
Lockheed Corp	$2,150	PAC
Interlake Inc	$1,750	PAC
Boeing Co	$1,500	PAC
McDonnell Douglas*	$1,500	PAC

Defense Electronics **$26,600**
Cubic Corp	$9,100	PAC/Ind
Hughes Aircraft	$3,000	PAC
Imo Industries Inc	$2,000	PAC
Litton Industries	$2,000	PAC
AT&T	$1,500	PAC
Chrysler Technologies Corp	$1,500	PAC

Misc Defense **$14,100**
General Atomics	$9,000	PAC

Energy & Natural Resources — $15,950

Oil & Gas **$6,250**
None over $1,500

Electric Utilities **$3,600**
None over $1,500

Waste Management **$2,100**
None over $1,500

Commercial Fishing **$2,000**
None over $1,500

Contribution Totals by Sector

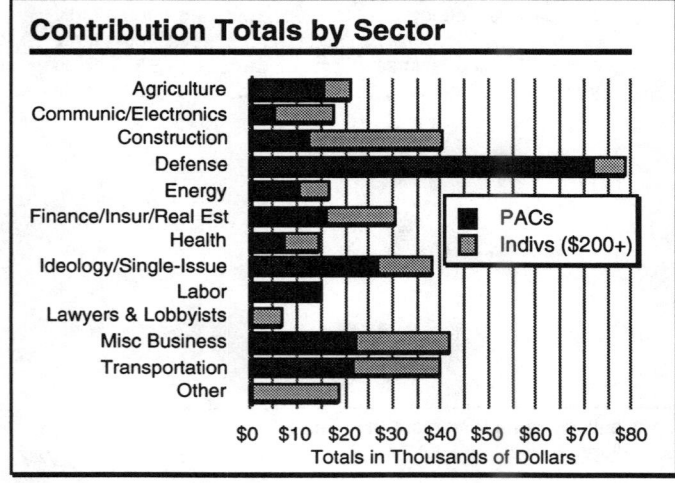

Totals in Thousands of Dollars

Legend: ■ PACs, ▨ Indivs ($200+)

Categories: Agriculture, Communic/Electronics, Construction, Defense, Energy, Finance/Insur/Real Est, Health, Ideology/Single-Issue, Labor, Lawyers & Lobbyists, Misc Business, Transportation, Other

Scale: $0, $10, $20, $30, $40, $50, $60, $70, $80

Finance, Insurance & Real Estate	$30,750	
Commercial Banks	**$5,450**	
American Bankers Assn	$3,500	PAC
Insurance	**$6,850**	
Independent Insurance Agents of America	$2,100	PAC
National Assn of Life Underwriters	$2,000	PAC
Real Estate	**$12,700**	
National Assn of Realtors	$4,000	PAC
Misc Finance	**$2,800**	
None over $1,500		

Health	$13,810	
Health Professionals	**$11,810**	
Assn for the Advancement of Psychology	$2,000	PAC
American Dental Assn	$1,500	PAC
American Optometric Assn	$1,500	PAC
Pharmaceuticals/Health Products	**$1,500**	
None over $1,500		

Lawyers & Lobbyists	$6,250	
Lawyers & Lobbyists	**$6,250**	
None over $1,500		

Misc Business	$41,175	
Food & Beverage	**$3,350**	
None over $1,500		
Beer, Wine & Liquor	**$9,400**	
National Beer Wholesalers Assn	$8,000	PAC
Lodging/Tourism	**$1,975**	
None over $1,500		
Misc Manufacturing & Distributing	**$5,900**	
Propulsion Controls Engineering	$2,100	Indiv
Textiles	**$15,500**	
Milliken & Co	$6,000	Indiv
Burlington Industries	$4,000	PAC
American Textile Manufacturers Institute	$2,000	PAC
Alice Manufacturing	$1,500	Indiv

Transportation	$40,225	
Air Transport	**$7,600**	
United Parcel Service	$3,500	PAC
North American Airlines	$3,000	Indiv
Automotive	**$4,750**	
National Auto Dealers Assn	$4,500	PAC
Sea Transport	**$21,750**	
National Steel & Shipbuilding	$7,400	PAC
Continental Maritime	$6,700	Indiv
Atlantic Marine/Atlantic Dry Dock	$3,000	PAC/Ind
Misc Transport	**$4,625**	
Alessio's Limousine	$4,000	Indiv

Labor

Labor	$14,640	
Transportation Unions	**$12,000**	
Marine Engineers Union*	$8,500	PAC
Seafarers International Union	$3,000	PAC
Public Sector Unions	**$2,140**	
National Assn Retired Federal Employees	$2,000	PAC

Ideological/Single-Issue

Ideological/Single-Issue	$37,750	
Republican/Conservative	**$14,450**	
Free Congress PAC	$5,000	PAC
Foreign & Defense Policy	**$3,000**	
Veterans of Foreign Wars	$3,000	PAC
Pro-Israel	**$10,050**	
National PAC	$5,000	PAC
Gun Rights/Gun Control	**$6,950**	
National Rifle Assn	$4,950	PAC
Safari Club International	$2,000	PAC
Misc Issues	**$2,300**	
None over $1,500		

Other & Unknown

Other	$17,985	
Retired	**$14,935**	
None over $1,500		
Other	**$1,500**	
None over $1,500		

Unknown	$49,808	
Homemakers/Non-income earners	$9,499	
Generic Occupation/Category Unknown	$5,78	
Employer Listed/Category Unknown	$33,925	
Science & Applied Technologies	$10,450	Indiv

Spending in Last 3 Elections

	1988	1990	1992
Hunter	$489,395	$376,408	$559,970
Opponent	$8,136	$0	$148,755
Vote Pct	74%	73%	53%

* Contributions came from more than one affiliate or subsidiary.

Tim Hutchinson, R-Ark (3)

First elected: 1992

1991-92 Total Receipts: $344,017
1992 Year-end Cash: $4,246

1993-94 Committees & Subcommittees

Public Works and Transportation
Economic Development; Surface Transportation; Water Resources and the Environment

Veterans' Affairs
Education, Training and Employment (Ranking Republican); Hospitals and Health Care

Leading Contributors

Business

Agriculture		$26,750

Crop Production & Basic Processing	**$7,000**	
Riceland Foods	$1,500	Indiv

Poultry & Eggs	**$6,000**	
Tyson Foods	$3,000	PAC/Ind
Simmons Industries	$1,000	Indiv

Agricultural Services/Products	**$1,750**	
None over $1,000		

Food Processing & Sales	**$9,000**	
Allan Canning Co	$2,000	Indiv
Harp's Food Stores Inc	$1,500	Indiv
Brown Packing Co	$1,000	Indiv
Fleming Companies Inc	$1,000	PAC
Pepsico Inc	$1,000	PAC
Winn-Dixie Stores	$1,000	PAC

Forestry & Forest Products	**$2,500**	
Willamette Industries	$1,000	PAC

Communications/Electronics		$2,500

Telephone Utilities	**$2,250**	
AT&T	$1,500	PAC

Construction		$8,450

General Contractors	**$2,950**	
None over $1,000		

Home Builders	**$1,300**	
ERC Properties	$1,300	Indiv

Special Trade Contractors	**$2,000**	
Fay Plumbing Heating Co	$2,000	Indiv

Building Materials & Equipment	**$2,200**	
Lewis Lumber & Manufacturing	$1,000	Indiv

Contribution Totals by Sector

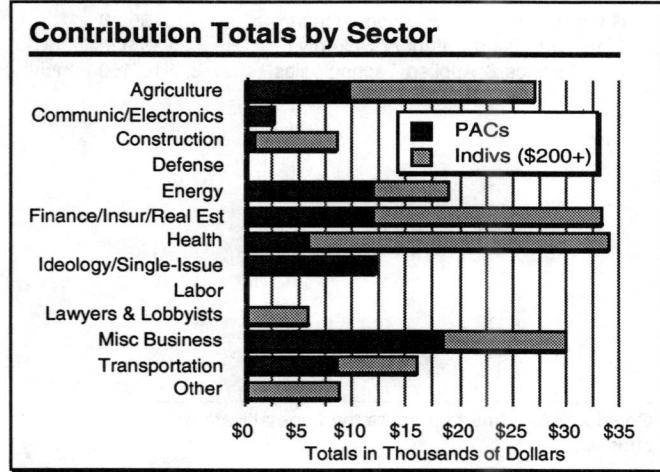

- Agriculture
- Communic/Electronics
- Construction
- Defense
- Energy
- Finance/Insur/Real Est
- Health
- Ideology/Single-Issue
- Labor
- Lawyers & Lobbyists
- Misc Business
- Transportation
- Other

PACs / Indivs ($200+)

$0 $5 $10 $15 $20 $25 $30 $35
Totals in Thousands of Dollars

Source of Funds in 1992 Election

Source	Total	Pct
PACs	$93,305	25%
Indivs $200+	$154,258	41%
Indivs under $200	$85,697	23%
Other	$40,718	11%
Candidate	$0	0%
Party	$35,961	10%

Source of PAC Dollars by Sector

Source	Total	Pct
Business	$68,433	85%
Labor	$0	0%
Ideology/Single Issue	$12,057	15%

In-State vs. Out-of-State Contributions*

Source	Total	Pct
In-State	$152,358	99%
Out-of-state	$1,400	1%
No state listed	$500	

* by large individual contributors ($200 & above)

Energy & Natural Resources		$18,750

Oil & Gas	**$12,250**	
Ashland Oil	$1,000	Indiv
Chevron Corp	$1,000	PAC
Continental Ozark Inc	$1,000	Indiv
Dallas Energy PAC	$1,000	PAC
Exxon Corp	$1,000	PAC
Mueller Oil & Gas	$1,000	Indiv
Phillips Petroleum	$1,000	PAC

Misc Energy	**$4,000**	
Cooper Industries	$3,000	PAC

Electric Utilities	**$2,500**	
Entergy Operations Inc	$1,000	PAC
Southwestern Electric Power Co	$1,000	PAC

Finance, Insurance & Real Estate		$33,100

Commercial Banks	**$5,850**	
Walton Enterprises Inc	$2,000	Indiv
Worthen Banking Corp	$1,000	PAC/Ind

Savings & Loans	**$1,000**	
US League of Savings Assns	$1,000	PAC

Credit Unions	**$1,000**	
Credit Union National Assn	$1,000	PAC

Securities & Investment	**$6,750**	
Stephens Inc	$5,500	Indiv

Insurance	**$4,250**	
National Assn of Life Underwriters	$3,000	PAC

Real Estate	**$12,500**	
National Assn of Realtors	$5,000	PAC
Cooper Communities Inc	$1,500	Indiv
Lindsey & Associates	$1,000	Indiv

Accountants	**$1,250**	
None over $1,000		

Health $33,800

Health Professionals $31,800
  Boozman-Hof Clinic ....$5,250   Indiv
  American Medical Assn.......................................$4,700   PAC
  American Chiropractic Assn................................$1,000   PAC
Misc Health $1,750
  Russellville Nursing Center ....$1,000   Indiv

Lawyers & Lobbyists $5,710

Lawyers & Lobbyists $5,710
  Jack, Lyon & Jones ....$1,000   Indiv

Misc Business $29,733

Business Associations $2,038
  Business Industry PAC ....$1,030   PAC
  National Fedn of Independent Business ....$1,000   PAC
Food & Beverage $1,250
  None over $1,000
Beer, Wine & Liquor $3,000
  National Beer Wholesalers Assn ....$2,500   PAC
Retail Sales $9,200
  Wal-Mart Stores ....$7,000   PAC/Ind
Lodging/Tourism $1,000
  None over $1,000
Chemical & Related Manufacturing $6,245
  Dow Chemical ....$5,000   PAC
Misc Manufacturing & Distributing $6,250
  Hendren Plastics ....$2,000   Indiv
  Stone Container Corp ....$1,000   PAC
  Whirlpool Corp ....$1,000   PAC

Transportation $15,750

Air Transport $3,000
  United Parcel Service ....$3,000   PAC
Automotive $6,500
  National Auto Dealers Assn ....$2,000   PAC
  Americans for Free International Trade ....$1,000   PAC
  Eaton Corp ....$1,000   PAC
  Hendren Ford ....$1,000   Indiv
  Superior Industries International ....$1,000   Indiv
Trucking...$5,250
  JB Hunt Transport ....$2,750   Indiv
  Arkansas Best Corp ....$1,000   Indiv
Railroads $1,000
  Union Pacific Corp ....$1,000   PAC

Ideological/Single-Issue

Ideological/Single-Issue $12,057

Republican/Conservative......................................$3,007
  Eagle Forum ....$2,000   PAC
  National Conservative Challengers PAC ....$1,000   PAC
Leadership PACs $2,750
  Republican Leader's Fund (Bob Michel) ....$2,000   PAC
Pro-Israel $2,800
  Congressional Action Cmte of Texas ....$1,800   PAC
  National PAC ....$1,000   PAC
Pro-Life $1,000
  National Right to Life PAC ....$1,000   PAC
Misc Issues $2,500
  English First..$1,000   PAC
  Right to Work PAC ....$1,000   PAC

Other & Unknown

Other $8,600

Civil Servants/Public Officials............................$1,500
  US Government...$1,000   Indiv
Retired $7,100
  None over $1,000

Unknown $39,558

  Homemakers/Non-income earners $20,500
  No Employer Listed or Found $3,400
  Generic Occupation/Category Unknown $3,250
  Employer Listed/Category Unknown $12,398
    Mount Aire Co ....$2,000   Indiv
    Fuller Enterprises ....$1,998   Indiv
    Mission Ministries Inc ....$1,500   Indiv
    Tompkins & Assoc ....$1,000   Indiv

Independent expenditures supporting Hutchinson
  National Right to Life PAC $10,080
  Arkansas Right to Life PAC.................................$2,336

Spending in Last Election

	1992
Hutchinson	$339,772
Opponent	$468,758
Vote Pct	50%

Earl Hutto, D-Fla (1)

First elected: 1978

1991-92 Total Receipts:	$298,700
1992 Year-end Cash:	$94,485

1991-92 Committees & Subcommittees

Armed Services
Military Installations and Facilities; Readiness (Chairman); Seapower and Strategic and Critical Materials

Merchant Marine and Fisheries
Coast Guard and Navigation; Fisheries and Wildlife Conservation and the Environment

Leading Contributors

Business

Agriculture	$11,500	
Crop Production & Basic Processing	**$2,500**	
Florida Citrus Mutual	$1,000	PAC
Food Processing & Sales	**$5,000**	
Winn-Dixie Stores	$2,000	PAC
Delchamps Inc	$1,000	Indiv
Fleming Companies Inc	$1,000	PAC
Food Marketing Institute	$1,000	PAC
Forestry & Forest Products	**$2,000**	
Champion International Corp	$1,500	PAC

Communications/Electronics	$7,950	
Media/Entertainment	**$1,750**	
Gulf World Inc	$1,000	Indiv
Telephone Utilities	**$3,950**	
Southern Bell	$3,950	PAC
Computer Equipment & Services	**$2,250**	
Visicom Labs	$2,250	Indiv

Construction	$9,000	
General Contractors	**$5,500**	
Associated General Contractors	$2,500	PAC
HG Harders & Sons	$1,000	Indiv
Phoenix Construction	$1,000	Indiv
Home Builders	**$2,000**	
National Assn of Home Builders	$2,000	PAC
Construction Services	**$1,500**	
Pacific Architects & Engineers	$1,000	Indiv

Contribution Totals by Sector

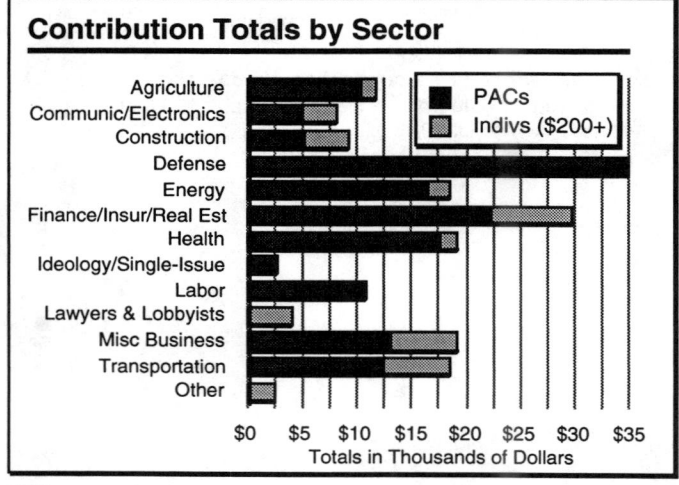

Totals in Thousands of Dollars

Source of Funds in 1992 Election

Source	Total	Pct
PACs	$144,704	48%
Indivs $200+	$45,380	15%
Indivs under $200	$80,853	27%
Other	$31,896	11%
Candidate	$0	0%
Party	$11,383	4%

Source of PAC Dollars by Sector

Source	Total	Pct
Business	$135,345	91%
Labor	$10,700	7%
Ideology/Single Issue	$2,500	2%

In-State vs. Out-of-State Contributions*

Source	Total	Pct
In-State	$40,130	88%
Out-of-state	$5,250	12%
No state listed	$0	

* by large individual contributors ($200 & above)

Defense	$34,850	
Defense Aerospace	**$23,650**	
Rockwell International	$2,550	PAC/Ind
Colt Industries	$2,000	PAC
Martin Marietta Corp	$2,000	PAC
McDonnell Douglas*	$2,000	PAC
Northrop Corp	$2,000	PAC
Beech Aircraft	$1,500	PAC
Grumman Corp	$1,500	PAC
Textron Inc	$1,500	PAC
United Technologies	$1,500	PAC
Sundstrand Corp	$1,100	PAC
Allied-Signal	$1,000	PAC
Boeing Co	$1,000	PAC
General Dynamics	$1,000	PAC
General Electric	$1,000	PAC
LTV Aerospace & Defense Co	$1,000	PAC
Lockheed Corp	$1,000	PAC
Defense Electronics	**$7,000**	
GTE Corp	$1,000	PAC
Harris Corp	$1,000	PAC
Loral Corp	$1,000	PAC
Westinghouse Electric	$1,000	PAC
Misc Defense	**$4,200**	
BDM International	$1,500	PAC
Mantech International	$1,000	PAC
Tenneco Inc	$1,000	PAC

Energy & Natural Resources	$18,300	
Oil & Gas	**$7,500**	
Chevron Corp	$1,500	PAC
Enserch Corp	$1,000	PAC
Mocar Oil	$1,000	Indiv
West Florida Natural Gas Co	$1,000	Indiv
Misc Energy	**$1,400**	
None over $1,000		

Electric Utilities **$8,900**
    Southern Co* ....$3,250 PAC
    ACRE (Action Cmte for Rural Electrification) ....$1,800 PAC
    Florida Power Corp ....$1,000 PAC

Finance, Insurance & Real Estate $29,620

Commercial Banks **$10,770**
    Barnett Banks Inc ....$4,000 PAC
    Amsouth Bancorp ....$2,000 PAC
    Sun Commercial Bank in Panama City ....$2,000 Indiv
    SunBanks ....$1,000 PAC

Savings & Loans **$1,000**
    Florida League of Financial Institutions ....$1,000 PAC

Insurance **$4,800**
    Blue Cross/Blue Shield of Florida ....$1,000 PAC
    Fisher Brown Inc ....$1,000 Indiv

Real Estate **$12,550**
    National Assn of Realtors ....$10,000 PAC
    Valparaiso Realty ....$1,000 Indiv

Health $18,950

Health Professionals **$17,550**
    American Medical Assn* ....$9,700 PAC
    American Dental Assn ....$2,500 PAC
    American Optometric Assn ....$2,500 PAC
    Florida Society of Anesthesiologists ....$1,500 PAC

Hospitals/Nursing Homes **$1,400**
    None over $1,000

Lawyers & Lobbyists $3,950

Lawyers & Lobbyists **$3,950**
    Jones & Welch ....$1,000 Indiv

Misc Business   **$18,905**

Business Associations **$3,545**
    National Fedn of Independent Business ....$2,500 PAC
    Business Industry PAC ....$1,045 PAC

Food & Beverage **$3,010**
    Coca-Cola Co ....$1,000 PAC

Beer, Wine & Liquor **$2,250**
    Lewis Bear Co ....$1,250 Indiv
    Gator Distributors Inc ....$1,000 Indiv

Retail Sales **$1,500**
    Abbott Military Tailors ....$1,000 Indiv

Business Services **$1,000**
    Michael Joy Corp ....$1,000 Indiv

Chemical & Related Manufacturing **$1,550**
    Air Products & Chemicals Inc ....$1,000 PAC

Misc Manufacturing & Distributing **$5,500**
    Stone Container Corp ....$5,000 PAC

Transportation $18,250

Air Transport **$2,500**
    United Parcel Service ....$2,500 PAC

Automotive **$7,550**
    National Auto Dealers Assn ....$4,000 PAC
    Cook-Whitehead Ford Inc ....$1,000 Indiv

Trucking **$1,450**
    A&A Transfer & Storage ....$1,450 Indiv

Sea Transport **$6,750**
    CSX Corp* ....$1,000 PAC
    Cruise PAC ....$1,000 PAC
    Lykes Brothers Steamship Co ....$1,000 PAC

Labor

Labor   **$10,700**

Transportation Unions **$7,500**
    Marine Engineers Union* ....$6,500 PAC
    Seafarers International Union ....$1,000 PAC

Public Sector Unions **$3,200**
    National Assn Retired Federal Employees ....$1,000 PAC
    National Assn of Letter Carriers ....$1,000 PAC

Ideological/Single-Issue

Ideological/Single-Issue   **$2,500**

Leadership PACs **$1,500**
    Effective Government Cmte (Dick Gephardt) ......$1,000 PAC

Other & Unknown

Other   **$2,300**

Retired **$1,550**
    None over $1,000

Unknown   **$7,150**

    Homemakers/Non-income earners $1,000
    Employer Listed/Category Unknown $6,150
        Rail Switching Services ....$1,000 Indiv

---

* Contributions came from more than one affiliate or
  subsidiary.

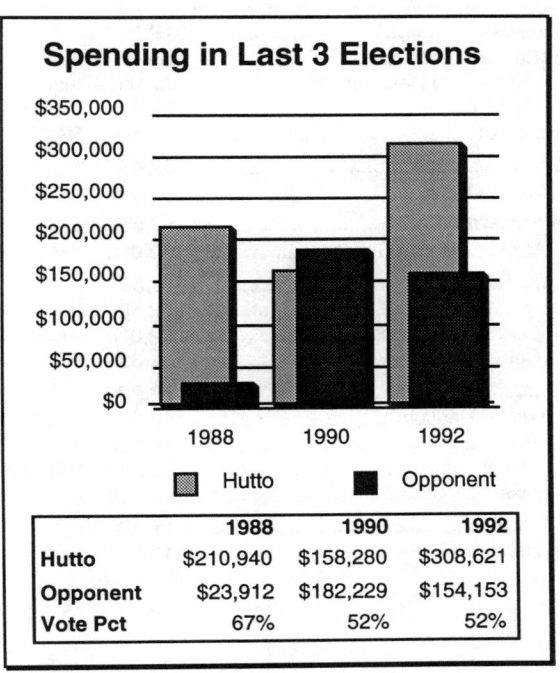

Spending in Last 3 Elections

	1988	1990	1992
Hutto	$210,940	$158,280	$308,621
Opponent	$23,912	$182,229	$154,153
Vote Pct	67%	52%	52%

Henry J. Hyde, R-Ill (6)

First elected: 1974

1991-92 Total Receipts:	$355,851
1992 Year-end Cash:	$134,632

1991-92 Committees & Subcommittees

Foreign Affairs
Arms Control, International Security and Science; Human Rights and International Organizations

Judiciary
Civil and Constitutional Rights (Ranking Republican); Economic and Commercial Law

Leading Contributors

Business

Agriculture	**$7,632**	
Tobacco	**$2,000**	
None over $1,500		
Food Processing & Sales	**$4,400**	
Food Marketing Institute	$1,700	PAC
Pepsico Inc	$1,500	PAC

Communications/Electronics	**$27,500**	
Printing & Publishing	**$4,300**	
RR Donnelley & Sons	$1,500	PAC/Ind
Media/Entertainment	**$7,500**	
National Cable Television Assn	$5,000	PAC
Telephone Utilities	**$13,000**	
Ameritech Corp*	$5,000	PAC
AT&T	$3,000	PAC

Construction	**$19,400**	
General Contractors	**$12,200**	
Norwood Builders	$2,500	Indiv
American Environmental Construction	$2,000	Indiv
Harbour Construction Co	$2,000	Indiv
Associated General Contractors	$1,500	PAC
Home Builders	**$2,500**	
National Assn of Home Builders	$2,000	PAC
Building Materials & Equipment	**$2,300**	
Elmhurst-Chicago Stone Co	$2,000	Indiv

Source of Funds in 1992 Election

Source	Total	Pct
■ PACs	$170,882	47%
■ Indivs $200+	$114,850	32%
☐ Indivs under $200	$48,574	13%
⊠ Other	$27,937	8%
Candidate	$0	0%
Party	$7,479	2%

Source of PAC Dollars by Sector

Source	Total	Pct
■ Business	$159,132	97%
■ Labor	$2,000	1%
☐ Ideology/Single Issue	$2,245	1%

In-State vs. Out-of-State Contributions*

Source	Total	Pct
☐ In-State	$104,350	91%
■ Out-of-state	$10,500	9%
No state listed	$0	

***by large individual contributors ($200 & above)**

Defense	**$3,000**	
Defense Aerospace	**$3,000**	
None over $1,500		

Energy & Natural Resources	**$9,900**	
Oil & Gas	**$6,600**	
Petroleum Marketers Assn*	$1,800	PAC/Ind
Electric Utilities	**$1,500**	
None over $1,500		

Finance, Insurance & Real Estate	**$79,150**	
Commercial Banks	**$19,500**	
American Bankers Assn	$5,000	PAC
First National Bank of Des Plaines	$2,000	Indiv
Northern Trust Co	$2,000	PAC
Barnett Banks Inc	$1,500	PAC
Savings & Loans	**$7,450**	
Fairfield Savings Bank	$2,000	Indiv
Securities & Investment	**$3,500**	
Hinsdale Assoc Financial Service	$2,000	Indiv
Insurance	**$18,500**	
Loews Corp*	$2,500	PAC
American Council of Life Insurance	$2,000	PAC
Travelers Corp	$1,500	PAC
Real Estate	**$18,900**	
National Assn of Realtors	$6,000	PAC
Inland Group	$4,000	Indiv
Century 21 Real Estate	$3,200	PAC/Ind
Greater Illinois Title Co	$2,000	Indiv
Accountants	**$11,100**	
American Institute of CPA's	$10,000	PAC

Contribution Totals by Sector

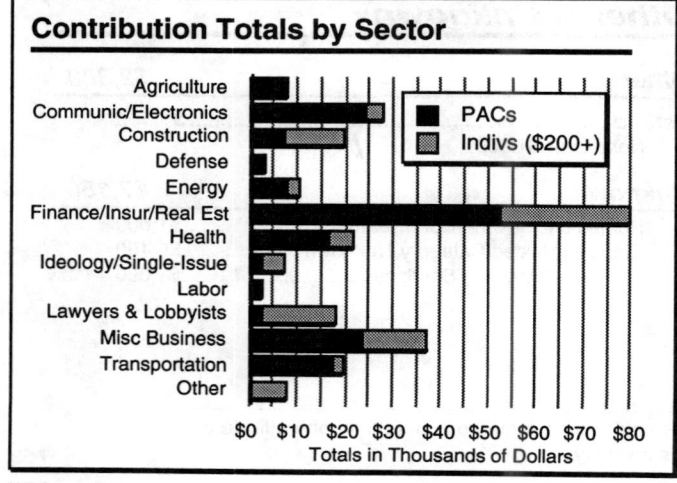

Horizontal bar chart comparing PACs (black) and Indivs ($200+) (gray) by sector:
Agriculture, Communic/Electronics, Construction, Defense, Energy, Finance/Insur/Real Est, Health, Ideology/Single-Issue, Labor, Lawyers & Lobbyists, Misc Business, Transportation, Other

$0 $10 $20 $30 $40 $50 $60 $70 $80
Totals in Thousands of Dollars

Health $21,200

Health Professionals *$15,400*
     American Medical Assn ....$10,000   PAC
     American Dental Assn ....$1,500   PAC

Hospitals/Nursing Homes *$2,100*
     None over $1,500

Pharmaceuticals/Health Products *$3,500*
     None over $1,500

Lawyers & Lobbyists $17,600

Lawyers & Lobbyists *$17,600*
     Schirott & Assoc ....$2,000   Indiv

Misc Business $36,900

Food & Beverage *$4,200*
     Pepsi-Cola General Bottlers ....$1,500   PAC

Beer, Wine & Liquor *$2,500*
     National Beer Wholesalers Assn ....$2,000   PAC

Retail Sales *$7,000*
     None over $1,500

Misc Services *$2,000*
     American Assn of Equipment Lessors ....$2,000   PAC

Business Services *$4,200*
     Peterson & Co ....$2,000   Indiv

Chemical & Related Manufacturing *$1,800*
     None over $1,500

Misc Manufacturing & Distributing *$11,250*
     Corning Glass Works ....$2,500   PAC
     Cabay & Co ....$2,000   Indiv
     Illinois Tool Works ....$2,000   PAC/Ind

Transportation $19,250

Air Transport *$3,600*
     United Parcel Service ....$3,000   PAC

Automotive *$10,400*
     National Auto Dealers Assn ....$5,000   PAC
     Americans for Free International Trade ....$2,000   PAC
     Auto Dealers & Drivers for Free Trade ....$1,500   PAC

Railroads *$3,250*
     Duchossois Industries ....$2,000   PAC

Labor

Labor $2,000
     None over $1,500

Ideological/Single-Issue

Ideological/Single-Issue $6,995

Republican/Conservative *$2,220*
     None over $1,500

Pro-Israel *$2,500*
     None over $1,500

Other & Unknown

Other $7,400

Retired *$6,900*
     None over $1,500

Unknown $20,300
     Homemakers/Non-income earners $1,700
     Generic Occupation/Category Unknown $2,200
     Employer Listed/Category Unknown $16,400
         Lawrence O'Brien ....$1,550   Indiv

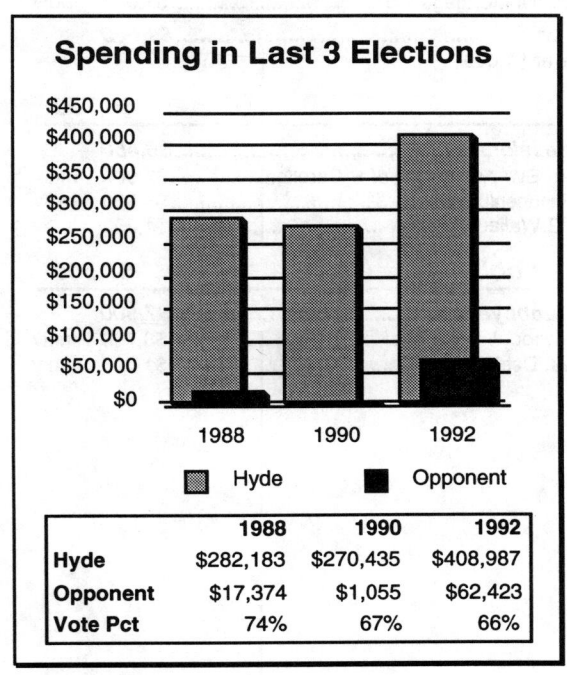

Spending in Last 3 Elections

	1988	1990	1992
Hyde	$282,183	$270,435	$408,987
Opponent	$17,374	$1,055	$62,423
Vote Pct	74%	67%	66%

* Contributions came from more than one affiliate or
subsidiary.

Robert D. Inglis, R-SC (4)

First elected: 1992

1991-92 Total Receipts: $226,577
1992 Year-end Cash: $11,214

1993-94 Committees & Subcommittees

Budget

Judiciary
Administrative Law and Governmental Relations; Economic and Commercial Law

Leading Contributors

NOTE: Inglis reported taking no PAC funds in his 1992 campaign. The PAC listed below did report making a contribution, however, and that contribution is recorded in the official FEC records.

Business

Agriculture		$5,250
Food Processing & Sales **$1,000**		
PYA/Monarch Inc $1,000	Indiv	
Forestry & Forest Products **$3,750**		
Union Camp Corp $3,250	Indiv	

Communications/Electronics		$2,000
Printing & Publishing **$1,000**		
A Press Inc $1,000	Indiv	
Media/Entertainment **$1,000**		
WFBC AM/FM Radio $1,000	Indiv	

Construction		$7,800
General Contractors **$1,700**		
Fluor Daniel Inc $1,700	Indiv	
Construction Services **$2,700**		
CRS Sirrine $1,250	Indiv	
Building Materials & Equipment **$3,400**		
Metromont Material Corp $2,000	Indiv	
General Equipment & Supply Co $1,400	Indiv	

Finance, Insurance & Real Estate		$14,787
Commercial Banks **$1,900**		
Carolina First Bank $1,000	Indiv	
Securities & Investment **$3,850**		
None over $1,000		
Insurance **$5,137**		
Equitable Life $1,457	Indiv	
Cooksey & Reynolds $1,250	Indiv	
Webb Insurance Agency $1,000	Indiv	
Real Estate **$1,900**		
Professional Mortgage Co $1,000	Indiv	
Misc Finance **$1,800**		
None over $1,000		

Health		$6,700
Health Professionals **$6,450**		
Southern Eye Associates of S Carolina $2,000	Indiv	
John M Huneniuk MD $1,500	Indiv	
James G Wallace MD PA $1,250	Indiv	

Lawyers & Lobbyists		$7,500
Lawyers & Lobbyists **$7,500**		
Leatherwood, Walker et al $3,700	Indiv	
Ogletree, Deakins et al $1,000	Indiv	

Source of Funds in 1992 Election

Source	Total	Pct
■ PACs	$1,200	0%
▨ Indivs $200+	$129,312	49%
□ Indivs under $200	$67,491	26%
▧ Other	$63,958	24%
Candidate	$10,000	4%
Party	$51,384	20%

Source of PAC Dollars by Sector

No PAC contributions reported

Source	Total	Pct
■ Business	$1,500	100%
▨ Labor	$0	0%
□ Ideology/Single Issue	$0	0%

In-State vs. Out-of-State Contributions*

Source	Total	Pct
□ In-State	$122,437	95%
■ Out-of-state	$6,875	5%
No state listed	$0	

* by large individual contributors ($200 & above)

Contribution Totals by Sector

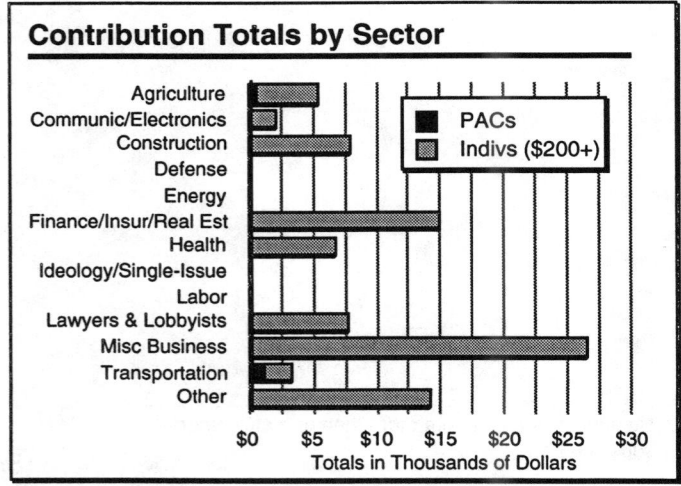

Agriculture
Communic/Electronics
Construction
Defense
Energy
Finance/Insur/Real Est
Health
Ideology/Single-Issue
Labor
Lawyers & Lobbyists
Misc Business
Transportation
Other

■ PACs
▨ Indivs ($200+)

$0 $5 $10 $15 $20 $25 $30
Totals in Thousands of Dollars

Misc Business $26,350

Misc Services **$2,000**
   American Rental Centers .... $2,000   Indiv

Chemical & Related Manufacturing **$6,000**
   Procter & Gamble .... $4,000   Indiv
   Nutex Inc .... $2,000   Indiv

Misc Manufacturing & Distributing **$5,500**
   Orderest Inc .... $4,000   Indiv
   Groome & Associates Inc .... $1,000   Indiv

Textiles **$11,250**
   Milliken & Co .... $5,250   Indiv
   Alice Manufacturing .... $2,500   Indiv
   Mayfair Mills Inc .... $1,300   Indiv
   Thomas Textile Machinery .... $1,000   Indiv

Transportation $3,250

Air Transport **$2,250**
   United Parcel Service .... $1,000   PAC

Automotive **$1,000**
   Michelin Tire Corp .... $1,000   Indiv

Other & Unknown

Other $13,950

Education **$1,950**
   Wofford College .... $1,500   Indiv

Retired **$11,600**
   None over $1,000

Unknown $43,225

   Homemakers/Non-income earners $13,775
   No Employer Listed or Found $4,400
   Employer Listed/Category Unknown $25,050
      Steller Communications .... $2,000   Indiv
      Alexander Machinery Inc .... $1,500   Indiv
      Hillcrest Offices .... $1,500   Indiv
      Edwards, Ballard et al .... $1,200   Indiv
      ABCO Industries Inc .... $1,000   Indiv
      General Equipment Co .... $1,000   Indiv
      Genesis Marketing Group .... $1,000   Indiv
      IT Fabrics Inc .... $1,000   Indiv
      Ivey Electric Co .... $1,000   Indiv
      Reeves International .... $1,000   Indiv

Independent expenditures supporting Inglis
   National Right to Life PAC $2,925

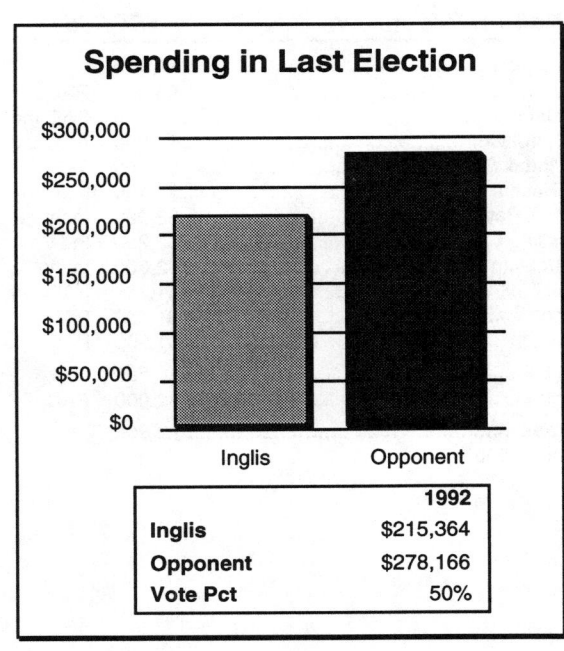

Spending in Last Election

	1992
Inglis	$215,364
Opponent	$278,166
Vote Pct	50%

James M. Inhofe, R-Okla (1)

First elected: 1986
1991-92 Total Receipts: $425,361
1992 Year-end Cash: $7,551

1991-92 Committees & Subcommittees

Merchant Marine and Fisheries
Coast Guard and Navigation; Merchant Marine

Public Works and Transportation
Aviation; Economic Development; Public Buildings and Grounds
(Ranking Republican)

Select Committee on Narcotics Abuse and Control

Leading Contributors

Business

Agriculture $19,225

Crop Production & Basic Processing $4,925
None over $1,500

Tobacco $3,600
Philip Morris .... $1,800 PAC
RJR Nabisco .... $1,500 PAC

Livestock $1,800
National Cattlemen's Assn* .... $1,800 PAC

Agricultural Services/Products $2,350
American Veterinary Medical Assn .... $1,500 PAC

Food Processing & Sales $5,400
None over $1,500

Communications/Electronics $16,050

Printing & Publishing $2,000
None over $1,500

Media/Entertainment $3,100
None over $1,500

Telephone Utilities $9,300
AT&T .... $3,500 PAC
Southwestern Bell .... $3,100 PAC
GTE Corp .... $2,700 PAC

Source of Funds in 1992 Election

	Source	Total	Pct
■	PACs	$227,931	49%
▨	Indivs $200+	$117,950	25%
□	Indivs under $200	$58,323	12%
⊠	Other	$65,669	14%
	Candidate	$0	0%
	Party	$59,072	13%

Source of PAC Dollars by Sector

	Source	Total	Pct
■	Business	$205,527	90%
▨	Labor	$10,250	4%
□	Ideology/Single Issue	$12,648	6%

In-State vs. Out-of-State Contributions*

	Source	Total	Pct
□	In-State	$100,600	85%
■	Out-of-state	$17,350	15%
	No state listed	$0	

* by large individual contributors ($200 & above)

Construction $12,700

General Contractors $3,350
None over $1,500

Special Trade Contractors $5,600
National Electrical Contractors Assn .... $3,000 PAC

Construction Services $1,900
None over $1,500

Defense $6,400

Defense Aerospace $6,150
None over $1,500

Energy & Natural Resources $64,805

Oil & Gas $57,505
Mapco Inc .... $5,850 PAC
Koch Industries .... $5,250 PAC/Ind
Phillips Petroleum .... $4,800 PAC/Ind
Sooner Pipe & Supply .... $4,000 Indiv
Samson Resources Co .... $3,150 Indiv
Helmerich & Payne .... $3,000 Indiv
Parker Drilling Co .... $2,200 Indiv
Citgo Petroleum Corp .... $2,000 Indiv
Sun Co .... $1,750 PAC/Ind
BP America .... $1,500 PAC
Chevron Corp .... $1,500 PAC

Misc Energy $2,500
McDermott Inc .... $2,000 PAC

Electric Utilities $2,800
None over $1,500

Contribution Totals by Sector

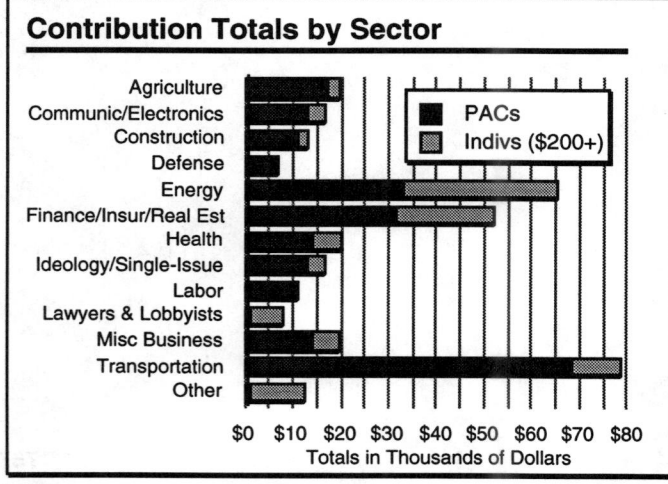

Agriculture
Communic/Electronics
Construction
Defense
Energy
Finance/Insur/Real Est
Health
Ideology/Single-Issue
Labor
Lawyers & Lobbyists
Misc Business
Transportation
Other

■ PACs
▨ Indivs ($200+)

$0 $10 $20 $30 $40 $50 $60 $70 $80
Totals in Thousands of Dollars

Finance, Insurance & Real Estate $51,421

Commercial Banks $2,750
   American Bankers Assn* ....$1,500 PAC

Credit Unions $2,000
   Credit Union National Assn ....$2,000 PAC

Securities & Investment $2,500
   Capital Advisors Inc ....$2,000 Indiv

Insurance $18,200
   Golden Rule Insurance Co ....$5,000 PAC/Ind
   Independent Insurance Agents of America ....$2,400 PAC
   Metropolitan Life Insurance ....$1,850 PAC
   Rich & Cartmill Inc ....$1,750 Indiv
   Casualty & Surety Agents Assn ....$1,650 PAC

Real Estate $9,221
   National Assn of Realtors ....$8,200 PAC

Accountants $2,500
   American Institute of CPA's ....$2,000 PAC

Misc Finance $13,450
   Ford Enterprises Co ....$2,000 Indiv

Health $19,850

Health Professionals $19,550
   American Medical Assn* ....$10,000 PAC
   American Dental Assn ....$1,700 PAC
   American Academy of Ophthalmology ....$1,500 PAC

Lawyers & Lobbyists $7,450

Lawyers & Lobbyists $7,450
   Doerner, Stuart et al ....$2,100 Indiv

Misc Business $19,301

Food & Beverage $2,850
   None over $1,500

Beer, Wine & Liquor $3,850
   National Beer Wholesalers Assn ....$2,850 PAC

Retail Sales $4,000
   None over $1,500

Business Services $2,650
   None over $1,500

Chemical & Related Manufacturing $2,800
   Dow Chemical ....$2,000 PAC

Misc Manufacturing & Distributing $1,600
   None over $1,500

Transportation $78,175

Air Transport $46,725
   American Airlines ....$8,600 PAC
   United Parcel Service ....$8,150 PAC
   Aircraft Owners & Pilots Assn ....$7,000 PAC
   Federal Express Corp ....$4,000 PAC
   Nordam Inc ....$2,500 Indiv
   Worldcorp Inc ....$2,350 PAC
   United Airlines ....$2,000 PAC
   General Electric ....$1,850 PAC

Automotive $16,550
   National Auto Dealers Assn ....$7,350 PAC
   Auto Dealers & Drivers for Free Trade ....$4,000 PAC
   Thrifty Rent A Car ....$2,750 Indiv

Trucking $3,150
   None over $1,500

Railroads $5,350
   Union Pacific Corp ....$1,500 PAC

Sea Transport $5,750
   CSX Corp* ....$3,050 PAC

Labor

Labor $10,250

Transportation Unions $8,250
   Marine Engineers Union* ....$3,350 PAC
   Transport Workers Union ....$3,350 PAC

Public Sector Unions $2,000
   None over $1,500

Ideological/Single-Issue

Ideological/Single-Issue $16,148

Republican/Conservative $4,350
   None over $1,500

Gun Rights/Gun Control $7,450
   National Rifle Assn ....$7,450 PAC

Misc Issues $2,089
   None over $1,500

Other & Unknown

Other $11,900

Retired $11,400
   None over $1,500

Unknown $13,700

   Homemakers/Non-income earners $5,250
   Employer Listed/Category Unknown $7,450
     None over $1,500

Independent expenditures supporting Inhofe
   National Right to Life PAC $6,313

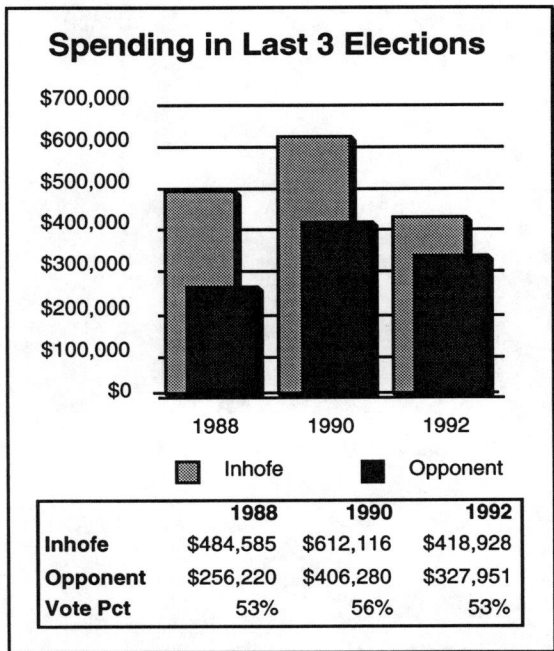

Spending in Last 3 Elections

	1988	1990	1992
Inhofe	$484,585	$612,116	$418,928
Opponent	$256,220	$406,280	$327,951
Vote Pct	53%	56%	53%

* Contributions came from more than one affiliate or subsidiary.

Jay Inslee, D-Wash (4)

1993-94 Committees & Subcommittees

Agriculture
Department Operations and Nutrition; Environment, Credit and Rural Development; Specialty Crops and Natural Resources

Science, Space and Technology
Energy; Technology, Environment and Aviation

Leading Contributors

Business

Agriculture	$3,750

Crop Production & Basic Processing	$3,000	
PJ Taggares Co	$3,000	Indiv

Finance, Insurance & Real Estate	$4,300

Commercial Banks	$3,500	
American Bankers Assn	$2,500	PAC
US Bancorp	$1,000	PAC

Health	$4,750

Health Professionals	$3,750	
American Dental Assn	$1,000	PAC
American Podiatry Assn	$1,000	PAC

Health Services	$1,000	
None over $1,000		

Lawyers & Lobbyists	$15,150

Lawyers & Lobbyists	$15,150	
Assn of Trial Lawyers of America	$5,000	PAC

Misc Business	$4,602

Retail Sales	$1,000	
Fred Meyer Inc	$1,000	PAC

Business Services	$1,500	
None over $1,000		

Recreation/Live Entertainment	$1,250	
None over $1,000		

First elected: 1992

1991-92 Total Receipts: $249,708
1992 Year-end Cash: $3,551

Source of Funds in 1992 Election

Source	Total	Pct
PACs	$98,886	39%
Indivs $200+	$53,719	21%
Indivs under $200	$50,025	20%
Other	$58,500	20%
Candidate	$43,500	17%
Party	$15,000	6%

Source of PAC Dollars by Sector

Source	Total	Pct
Business	$14,202	18%
Labor	$53,250	67%
Ideology/Single Issue	$12,272	15%

In-State vs. Out-of-State Contributions*

Source	Total	Pct
In-State	$44,634	88%
Out-of-state	$6,000	12%
No state listed	$232	

* by large individual contributors ($200 & above)

Contribution Totals by Sector

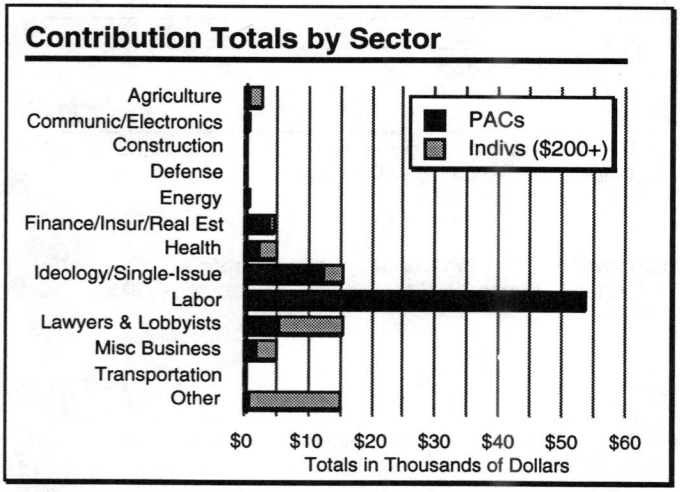

Totals in Thousands of Dollars

Labor

Labor	$53,250	
Building Trade Unions **$11,000**		
Sheet Metal Workers Union $3,500		PAC
Laborers' Political League $3,000		PAC
Operating Engineers #302 .... $2,500		PAC
Ironworkers Union $2,000		PAC
Industrial Unions **$10,750**		
Machinists/Aerospace Workers Union $5,000		PAC
Intl Brotherhood of Electrical Workers $2,500		PAC
United Steelworkers $1,500		PAC
Oil, Chemical & Atomic Workers Union $1,250		PAC
Transportation Unions **$10,000**		
Teamsters Union* $2,500		PAC
Intl Longshoremen's/Warehousemen's Union $2,000		PAC
Marine Engineers Union $2,000		PAC
Air Line Pilots Assn $1,000		PAC
Assn of Flight Attendants $1,000		PAC
United Transportation Union $1,000		PAC
Public Sector Unions **$13,500**		
National Education Assn $5,000		PAC
National Assn of Letter Carriers $3,000		PAC
American Federation of Teachers $2,000		PAC
International Assn of Firefighters $1,500		PAC
American Fedn of St/Cnty/Munic Employees $1,000		PAC
National Rural Letter Carriers Assn $1,000		PAC
Misc Unions **$8,000**		
AFL-CIO $5,000		PAC
Bakery, Confectionery & Tobacco Workers $1,000		PAC
Food & Commercial Workers Union $1,000		PAC
Service Employees International Union $1,000		PAC

Ideological/Single-Issue

Ideological/Single-Issue	$15,272	
Democratic/Liberal **$2,500**		
National Cmte for an Effective Congress $2,500		PAC
Leadership PACs **$2,000**		
Effective Government Cmte (Dick Gephardt) $1,000		PAC
House Leadership Fund (Tom Foley) $1,000		PAC
Pro-Choice **$4,250**		
National Abortion Rights Action League $4,000		PAC
Womens Issues **$1,522**		
None over $1,000		
Misc Issues **$5,000**		
League of Conservation Voters $3,000		PAC

Other & Unknown

Other	$14,757	
Civil Servants/Public Officials **$3,250**		
State of Washington $1,550		Indiv
Education **$3,700**		
Bellingham School District $1,000		Indiv
University of California $1,000		Indiv
Retired **$7,307**		
None over $1,000		

Unknown	$13,659	
Homemakers/Non-income earners $1,882		
No Employer Listed or Found $3,317		
Generic Occupation/Category Unknown $2,250		
Employer Listed/Category Unknown $6,210		
Central Washington Sales $1,000		Indiv
Heart of America Northwest $1,000		Indiv
Radar Electronics $1,000		Indiv

Independent expenditures supporting Inslee
Marilyn Knight $1,232

Spending in Last Election

	1992
Inslee	$246,159
Opponent	$351,909
Vote Pct	51%

* Contributions came from more than one affiliate or subsidiary.

Ernest Istook Jr., R-Okla (5)

First elected: 1992

1991-92 Total Receipts: $328,528
1992 Year-end Cash: $914

1993-94 Committees & Subcommittees

Appropriations
District of Columbia; Treasury, Postal Service and General Government

Leading Contributors

Business

Agriculture $8,350

Food Processing & Sales	$7,000	
Fleming Companies Inc	$5,500	PAC/Ind
Goodner Super Markets	$1,000	Indiv

Communications/Electronics $9,000

Printing & Publishing	$3,500	
Adams Investment Co	$3,000	Indiv
Media/Entertainment	$1,000	
KOCB-TV	$1,000	Indiv
Telephone Utilities	$4,500	
AT&T	$2,000	PAC
Southwestern Bell	$1,000	PAC
United Telecommunications	$1,000	PAC

Construction $1,500
None over $1,000

Energy & Natural Resources $36,000

Oil & Gas	$31,000	
Marlin Oil Corp	$4,100	Indiv
Mustang Fuel Corp	$4,000	Indiv
Phillips Petroleum	$2,500	PAC
Kuykendall Enterprises	$2,000	Indiv
Mustang Energy Corp	$2,000	PAC
Kerr-McGee	$1,500	PAC/Ind
Chevron Corp	$1,000	PAC
Halliburton Co	$1,000	PAC
Oneok Inc	$1,000	PAC
Ram Co	$1,000	Indiv
Red Stone Energies	$1,000	Indiv
Sun Co	$1,000	PAC

Source of Funds in 1992 Election

Source	Total	Pct
PACs	$72,277	20%
Indivs $200+	$88,455	24%
Indivs under $200	$73,973	20%
Other	$134,130	36%
Candidate	$83,442	23%
Party	$47,291	13%

Source of PAC Dollars by Sector

Source	Total	Pct
Business	$67,476	91%
Labor	$0	0%
Ideology/Single Issue	$7,000	9%

In-State vs. Out-of-State Contributions*

Source	Total	Pct
In-State	$83,730	96%
Out-of-state	$3,475	4%
No state listed	$1,250	

* by large individual contributors ($200 & above)

Misc Energy	$3,000	
Cooper Industries	$3,000	PAC
Electric Utilities	$1,500	
Public Service Co of Oklahoma	$1,000	PAC

Finance, Insurance & Real Estate $28,906

Commercial Banks	$5,600	
Community Bank	$1,700	Indiv
American Bankers Assn*	$1,500	PAC
First National Bank	$1,000	Indiv
United Community Bankers	$1,000	PAC
Credit Unions	$1,000	
Credit Union National Assn	$1,000	PAC
Insurance	$15,806	
Torchmark Corp	$2,500	PAC
Golden Rule Insurance Co	$2,326	PAC/Ind
National Assn of Life Underwriters	$2,000	PAC
Morris Insurance Agency	$1,330	Indiv
Farmers Insurance Group	$1,250	Indiv
Allbright Insurance	$1,000	Indiv
Globe Life Insurance	$1,000	Indiv
Independent Insurance Agents of America	$1,000	PAC
Mutual of Omaha	$1,000	PAC
Accountants	$4,000	
American Institute of CPA's	$2,000	PAC
Misc Finance	$1,500	
None over $1,000		

Contribution Totals by Sector

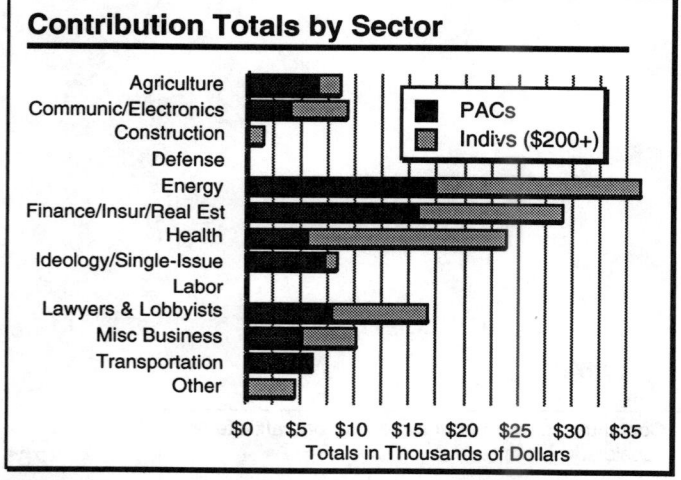

Totals in Thousands of Dollars

Health $23,700

Health Professionals **$20,200**
   American Medical Assn ....$5,000   PAC
   Radiology Associates ....$3,000   Indiv
Hospitals/Nursing Homes **$2,000**
   Amity Care Corp ....$2,000   Indiv
Misc Health **$1,000**
   None over $1,000

Lawyers & Lobbyists $16,450

Lawyers & Lobbyists **$16,450**
   Assn of Trial Lawyers of America ....$7,500   PAC

Misc Business $10,050

Beer, Wine & Liquor **$3,500**
   National Beer Wholesalers Assn ....$3,500   PAC
Business Services **$3,300**
   Ram Group Ltd ....$1,000   Indiv
Chemical & Related Manufacturing **$1,000**
   Dow Chemical ....$1,000   PAC
Misc Manufacturing & Distributing **$1,000**
   Pumpco Inc ....$1,000   Indiv

Transportation $6,000

Air Transport **$1,500**
   American Airlines ....$1,500   PAC
Automotive **$1,250**
   Eaton Corp ....$1,000   PAC
Railroads **$3,250**
   Union Pacific Corp ....$3,000   PAC

Ideological/Single-Issue

Ideological/Single-Issue $8,225

Republican/Conservative **$2,975**
   Eagle Forum ....$2,000   PAC
Leadership PACs **$2,000**
   Republican Leader's Fund (Bob Michel) ....$1,000   PAC
Foreign & Defense Policy **$1,000**
   Veterans of Foreign Wars ....$1,000   PAC
Misc Issues **$1,500**
   Right to Work PAC ....$1,250   PAC

Other & Unknown

Other $4,450

Retired **$3,250**
   None over $1,000

Unknown $10,300

   Homemakers/Non-income earners $4,000
   No Employer Listed or Found $3,050
   Employer Listed/Category Unknown $3,000
      American Guvasty ....$1,000   Indiv

Independent expenditures supporting Istook
   National Right to Life PAC $2,301

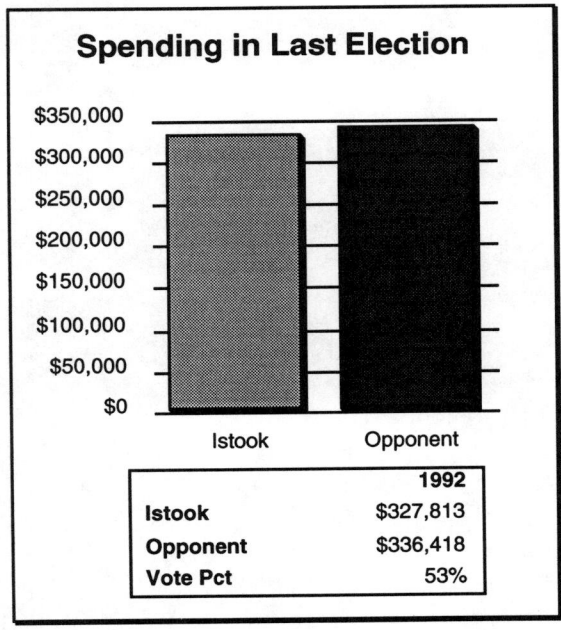

Spending in Last Election

	1992
Istook	$327,813
Opponent	$336,418
Vote Pct	53%

---

* Contributions came from more than one affiliate or subsidiary.

Andrew Jacobs Jr., D-Ind (10)

First elected: 1964

1991-92 Total Receipts: $15,690
1992 Year-end Cash: $33,505

1991-92 Committees & Subcommittees

Ways and Means
Oversight; Social Security (Chairman)

Leading Contributors

Finance, Insurance & Real Estate   **$1,200**

Insurance $1,200
    None over $1,000

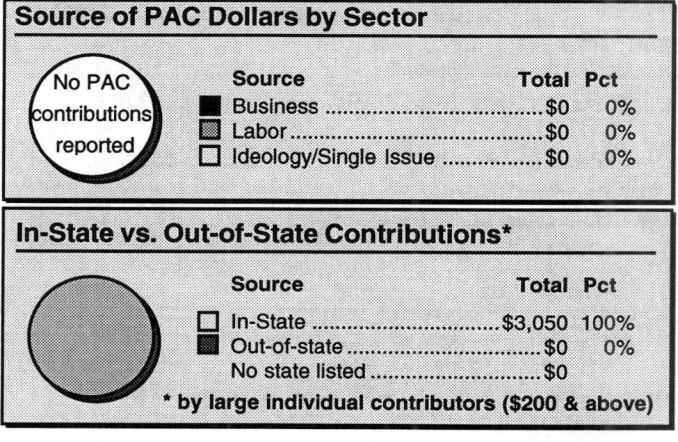

Source of Funds in 1992 Election

Source	Total	Pct
PACs	$0	0%
Indivs $200+	$3,050	19%
Indivs under $200	$9,726	61%
Other	$3,051	19%
Candidate	$0	0%
Party	$137	1%

Source of PAC Dollars by Sector

No PAC contributions reported

Source	Total	Pct
Business	$0	0%
Labor	$0	0%
Ideology/Single Issue	$0	0%

In-State vs. Out-of-State Contributions*

Source	Total	Pct
In-State	$3,050	100%
Out-of-state	$0	0%
No state listed	$0	

* by large individual contributors ($200 & above)

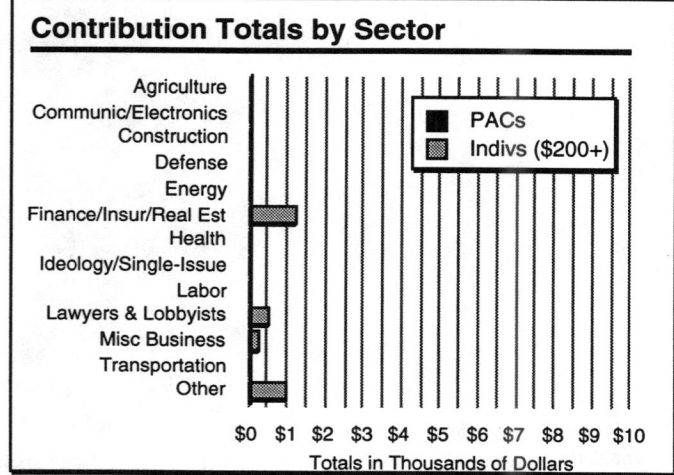

Contribution Totals by Sector

Agriculture
Communic/Electronics
Construction
Defense
Energy
Finance/Insur/Real Est
Health
Ideology/Single-Issue
Labor
Lawyers & Lobbyists
Misc Business
Transportation
Other

■ PACs
▨ Indivs ($200+)

$0 $1 $2 $3 $4 $5 $6 $7 $8 $9 $10
Totals in Thousands of Dollars

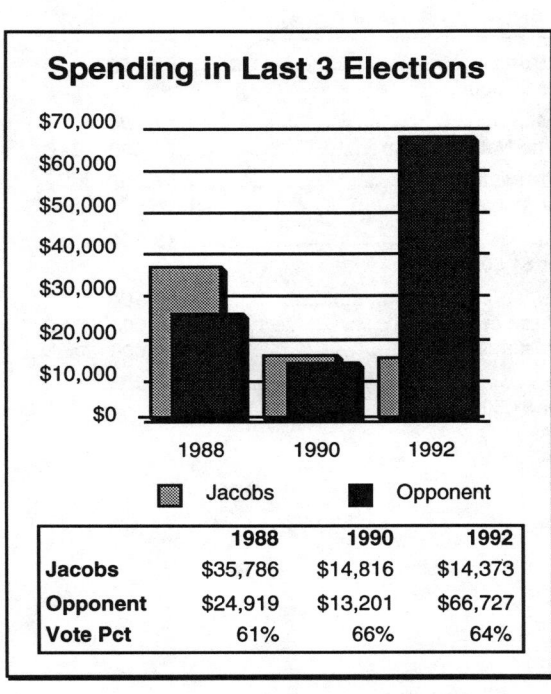

	1988	1990	1992
Jacobs	$35,786	$14,816	$14,373
Opponent	$24,919	$13,201	$66,727
Vote Pct	61%	66%	64%

William J. Jefferson, D-La (2)

First elected: 1990

1991-92 Total Receipts: $398,154
1992 Year-end Cash: $25,522

1991-92 Committees & Subcommittees

Education and Labor
Elementary, Secondary and Vocational Education; Postsecondary Education; Select Education

Merchant Marine and Fisheries
Fisheries and Wildlife Conservation and the Environment; Merchant Marine

Leading Contributors

Business

Agriculture	$13,050	
Crop Production & Basic Processing	**$3,650**	
None over $1,500		
Tobacco	**$5,800**	
RJR Nabisco	$3,000	PAC
Philip Morris	$1,500	PAC
Dairy	**$1,500**	
Associated Milk Producers	$1,500	PAC

Communications/Electronics	$8,600	
Telephone Utilities	**$8,100**	
BellSouth Corp*	$5,600	PAC
AT&T	$2,500	PAC

Construction	$8,600	
General Contractors	**$1,500**	
None over $1,500		
Construction Services	**$5,800**	
None over $1,500		

Defense	$4,600	
Defense Aerospace	**$3,100**	
Martin Marietta Corp	$1,800	PAC
Misc Defense	**$1,500**	
Avondale Industries	$1,500	PAC/Ind

Source of Funds in 1992 Election

Source	Total	Pct
■ PACs	$222,735	55%
▨ Indivs $200+	$129,725	32%
☐ Indivs under $200	$15,306	4%
▧ Other	$39,798	10%
Candidate	$0	0%
Party	$9,860	2%

Source of PAC Dollars by Sector

Source	Total	Pct
■ Business	$114,200	51%
▨ Labor	$97,599	43%
☐ Ideology/Single Issue	$14,000	6%

In-State vs. Out-of-State Contributions*

Source	Total	Pct
☐ In-State	$99,225	79%
■ Out-of-state	$25,950	21%
No state listed	-$500	

* by large individual contributors ($200 & above)

Energy & Natural Resources	$31,525	
Oil & Gas	**$15,675**	
Texaco	$2,000	PAC
Consolidated Natural Gas*	$1,800	PAC
Louisiana Land & Exploration	$1,625	PAC
Mining	**$6,600**	
Freeport-McMoRan Inc	$6,000	PAC/Ind
Misc Energy	**$4,000**	
McDermott Inc	$4,000	PAC
Electric Utilities	**$3,950**	
Entergy Corp*	$1,500	PAC

Finance, Insurance & Real Estate	$28,300	
Commercial Banks	**$2,550**	
None over $1,500		
Credit Unions	**$1,500**	
Credit Union National Assn	$1,500	PAC
Securities & Investment	**$1,500**	
None over $1,500		
Insurance	**$3,250**	
None over $1,500		
Real Estate	**$16,500**	
National Assn of Realtors	$10,000	PAC
Historic Restoration Inc	$2,000	Indiv
Misc Finance	**$2,000**	
None over $1,500		

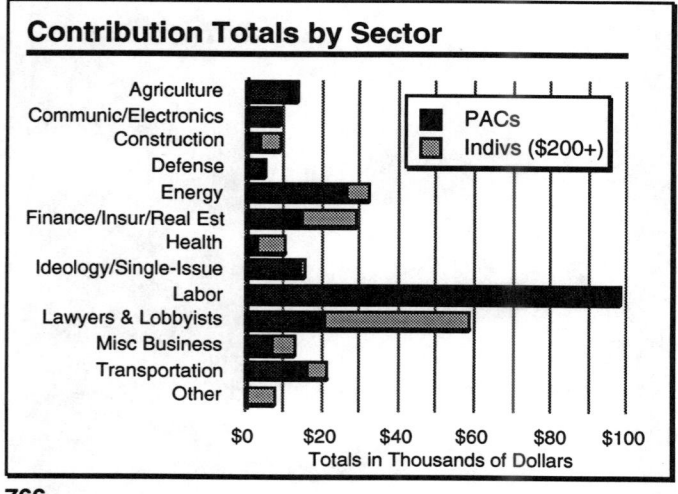

Contribution Totals by Sector

■ PACs
▨ Indivs ($200+)

Agriculture
Communic/Electronics
Construction
Defense
Energy
Finance/Insur/Real Est
Health
Ideology/Single-Issue
Labor
Lawyers & Lobbyists
Misc Business
Transportation
Other

$0 $20 $40 $60 $80 $100
Totals in Thousands of Dollars

Health $9,800

Health Professionals $7,800
  None over $1,500

Hospitals/Nursing Homes $1,500
  None over $1,500

Lawyers & Lobbyists $58,300

Lawyers & Lobbyists $58,300
  Assn of Trial Lawyers of America ....$11,000 PAC
  Thompson & Co ....$6,000 Indiv
  Jones, Walker et al ....$2,900 PAC/Ind
  Long Law Firm ....$2,500 Indiv
  St Martin, Lirette et al ....$2,000 Indiv
  Kutak, Rock & Campbell ....$1,800 PAC

Misc Business $12,500

Food & Beverage $3,000
  National Restaurant Assn ....$1,500 PAC

Beer, Wine & Liquor $1,500
  None over $1,500

Retail Sales $2,500
  None over $1,500

Business Services $4,250
  None over $1,500

Transportation $20,625

Air Transport $5,600
  United Parcel Service ....$5,300 PAC

Automotive $3,800
  Auto Dealers & Drivers for Free Trade ....$1,500 PAC

Railroads $2,300
  Union Pacific Corp ....$1,800 PAC

Sea Transport $8,425
  Lykes Brothers Steamship Co ....$2,125 PAC
  Sea-Land Corp ....$1,800 PAC

Labor

Labor $97,599

Building Trade Unions $13,800
  Laborers' Political League ....$3,500 PAC
  Sheet Metal Workers Union ....$2,500 PAC
  Plumbers/Pipefitters Union ....$2,000 PAC
  Ironworkers Union ....$1,500 PAC
  Operating Engineers Union ....$1,500 PAC

Industrial Unions $20,000
  United Steelworkers ....$6,000 PAC
  United Auto Workers ....$4,000 PAC
  Intl Brotherhood of Electrical Workers .....$3,000 PAC
  Communications Workers of America ....$2,500 PAC
  Boilermakers Union ....$1,500 PAC

Transportation Unions $23,600
  Seafarers International Union ....$9,000 PAC
  Teamsters Union ....$5,000 PAC
  International Longshoremen's Assn ....$2,500 PAC
  Marine Engineers Union ....$1,500 PAC
  United Transportation Union ....$1,500 PAC

Public Sector Unions $33,500
  American Federation of Teachers ....$15,000 PAC
  American Fedn of St/Cnty/Munic Employees ......$6,000 PAC
  American Postal Workers Union ....$4,500 PAC
  National Education Assn ....$3,000 PAC
  National Assn Retired Federal Employees ....$2,000 PAC

Misc Unions $6,699
  Food & Commercial Workers Union ....$3,499 PAC
  AFL-CIO ....$1,500 PAC

Ideological/Single-Issue

Ideological/Single-Issue $15,000

Leadership PACs $3,000
  Effective Government Cmte (Dick Gephardt) ......$3,000 PAC

Pro-Israel $9,000
  Louisiana for American Security ....$6,000 PAC

Human Rights $2,000
  Human Rights Campaign Fund ....$2,000 PAC

Other & Unknown

Other $7,050

Civil Servants/Public Officials $4,550
  None over $1,500

Education $2,000
  None over $1,500

Unknown $35,425

  No Employer Listed or Found $12,250
  Employer Listed/Category Unknown $23,175
    Systems Engineering & Mgmt Assoc ....$2,000 Indiv
    Luther Speight & Co ....$1,500 Indiv
    Murray, Braden et al ....$1,500 Indiv

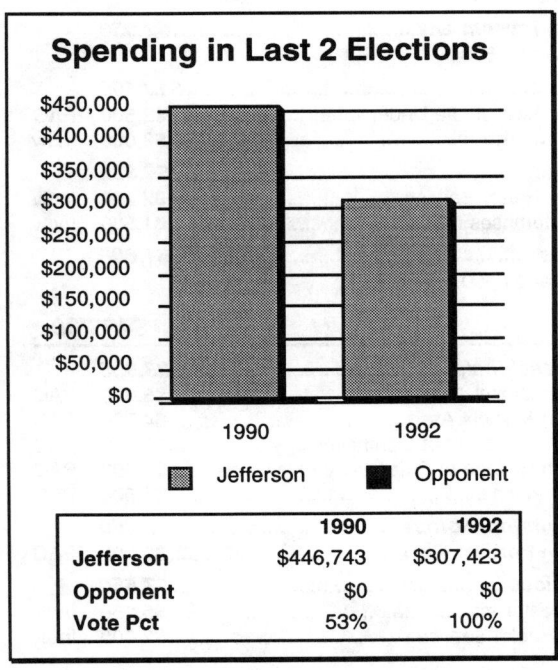

Spending in Last 2 Elections

	1990	1992
Jefferson	$446,743	$307,423
Opponent	$0	$0
Vote Pct	53%	100%

Legend: ▨ Jefferson ■ Opponent

---

* Contributions came from more than one affiliate or subsidiary.

767

Don Johnson, D-Ga (10)

1993-94 Committees & Subcommittees

First elected: 1992

1991-92 Total Receipts: $610,154
1992 Year-end Cash: $7,016

Armed Services
Military Installations and Facilities; Oversight and Investigations; Research and Technology

Science, Space and Technology
Investigations and Oversight; Science; Technology, Environment and Aviation

Leading Contributors

Business

Agriculture	$22,350	
Tobacco	**$1,500**	
None over $1,500		
Poultry & Eggs	**$4,500**	
Gold Kist	$3,500	PAC/Ind
Agricultural Services/Products	**$1,500**	
None over $1,500		
Food Processing & Sales	**$8,300**	
Dill's Food City	$2,500	Indiv
Golden Pantry Food Stores	$2,000	Indiv
General Mills	$1,500	PAC

Communications/Electronics	$7,700	
Printing & Publishing	**$2,000**	
None over $1,500		
Telephone Utilities	**$4,400**	
Southern Bell	$2,500	PAC

Construction	$7,100	
General Contractors	**$2,700**	
None over $1,500		
Building Materials & Equipment	**$2,400**	
Tri-State Distributors	$1,500	Indiv

Energy & Natural Resources	$17,850	
Oil & Gas	**$11,100**	
Ashland Oil	$4,000	PAC
Electric Utilities	**$5,750**	
Southern Co*	$3,250	PAC
ACRE (Action Cmte for Rural Electrification)	$2,500	PAC

Source of Funds in 1992 Election

Source	Total	Pct
■ PACs	$166,935	27%
▨ Indivs $200+	$184,502	30%
☐ Indivs under $200	$169,405	28%
▧ Other	$90,711	15%
Candidate	$73,246	12%
Party	$6,549	1%

Source of PAC Dollars by Sector

Source	Total	Pct
■ Business	$131,458	84%
▨ Labor	$19,800	13%
☐ Ideology/Single Issue	$4,800	3%

In-State vs. Out-of-State Contributions*

Source	Total	Pct
☐ In-State	$176,702	96%
■ Out-of-state	$7,700	4%
No state listed	$0	

* by large individual contributors ($200 & above)

Finance, Insurance & Real Estate — $61,260

Commercial Banks	$33,675	
American Bankers Assn*	$6,000	PAC
Citizens & Southern National Bank	$3,000	PAC
First Atlanta Corp	$2,100	PAC
Bankers Trust	$2,000	PAC
Chase Manhattan	$2,000	PAC
CB&T Bancshares	$1,750	PAC
First National Bank	$1,750	Indiv
Barnett Banks Inc	$1,500	PAC
Finance/Credit Companies	**$1,500**	
None over $1,500		
Securities & Investment	**$2,050**	
None over $1,500		
Insurance	**$12,799**	
National Assn of Life Underwriters	$2,500	PAC
TPA of America Inc	$2,000	Indiv
Real Estate	**$9,336**	
Connolly Realty Service	$2,250	Indiv
Selig Enterprises	$1,500	Indiv
Accountants	**$1,600**	
None over $1,500		

Health — $43,730

Health Professionals	$23,900	
American Dental Assn	$5,000	PAC
American Medical Assn	$4,700	PAC
American Academy of Ophthalmology	$3,000	PAC
American College of Emergency Physicians	$2,000	PAC
T2 Medical Inc	$1,500	PAC
Hospitals/Nursing Homes	**$5,950**	
American Hospital Assn	$3,000	PAC
Health Services	**$7,550**	
Healthmaster Inc	$5,250	Indiv
Central Health Services	$2,000	Indiv

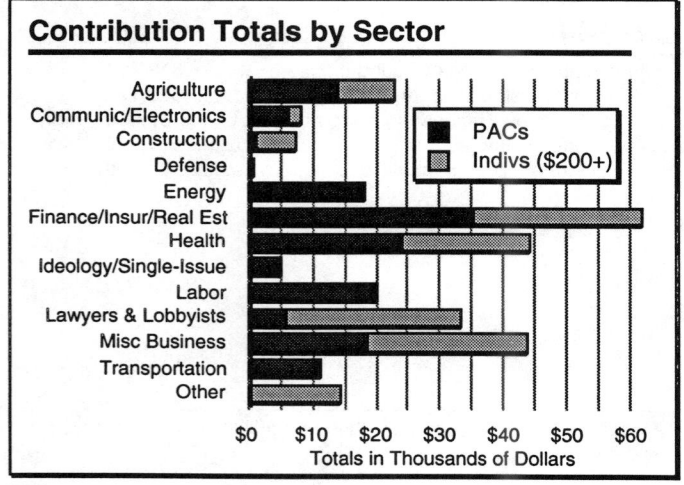

Contribution Totals by Sector

Agriculture, Communic/Electronics, Construction, Defense, Energy, Finance/Insur/Real Est, Health, Ideology/Single-Issue, Labor, Lawyers & Lobbyists, Misc Business, Transportation, Other

■ PACs ▨ Indivs ($200+)

$0 $10 $20 $30 $40 $50 $60
Totals in Thousands of Dollars

Pharmaceuticals/Health Products $2,700
    None over $1,500

Misc Health $3,630
    None over $1,500

Lawyers & Lobbyists $34,099

Lawyers & Lobbyists	$34,099	
Hurt, Richardson et al	$3,549	Indiv
King & Spalding	$3,050	PAC/Ind
Assn of Trial Lawyers of America	$2,500	PAC
Butler, Wooten et al	$2,000	Indiv
Powell, Goldstein et al	$1,950	PAC/Ind
Boller, Segars & Assoc	$1,700	Indiv

Misc Business $43,453

Business Associations	$2,008	
National Fedn of Independent Business	$2,000	PAC
Food & Beverage	**$5,000**	
Coca-Cola Co*	$3,200	PAC
Beer, Wine & Liquor	**$15,245**	
National Beer Wholesalers Assn	$6,250	PAC
Leon Farmer & Co	$4,000	Indiv
Retail Sales	**$4,850**	
None over $1,500		
Misc Services	**$2,750**	
Whitley, Garner Funeral	$1,500	Indiv
Misc Manufacturing & Distributing	**$11,450**	
Rock-Tenn Co	$4,000	Indiv
ASR Manufacturing Co	$2,000	Indiv
Adtec Sales Inc	$2,000	Indiv
Flowers Inc Balloons	$1,750	Indiv
Textiles	**$2,300**	
None over $1,500		

Transportation $10,950

Air Transport	$4,750	
United Parcel Service	$3,250	PAC
Automotive	**$4,200**	
National Auto Dealers Assn	$2,500	PAC

Labor   Labor

Labor $19,800

Building Trade Unions	$2,000	
None over $1,500		
Industrial Unions	**$2,000**	
None over $1,500		
Public Sector Unions	**$14,800**	
National Education Assn	$10,000	PAC
National Assn of Letter Carriers	$2,000	PAC

Ideological/Single-Issue

Ideological/Single-Issue $4,800

Leadership PACs	$3,500	
None over $1,500		

Other & Unknown

Other $13,879

Civil Servants/Public Officials	$5,609	
State of Georgia	$3,900	Indiv
Retired	**$7,270**	
None over $1,500		

Unknown $52,889

Homemakers/Non-income earners	$6,654	
No Employer Listed or Found	$7,619	
Employer Listed/Category Unknown	$37,166	
Mason Brothers	$2,250	Indiv
CE Smith Organization	$2,000	Indiv
Coggins Industries	$2,000	Indiv
Duplicating Systems	$1,693	Indiv
Ellis & Easterlin	$1,600	Indiv
Information Systems	$1,500	Indiv

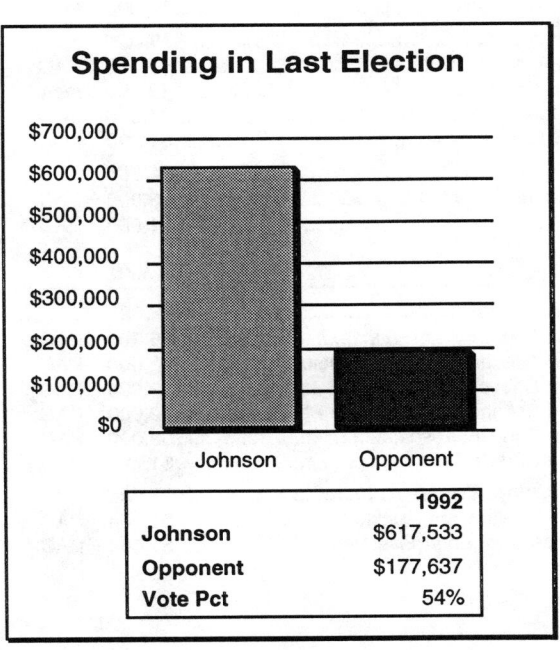

Spending in Last Election

	1992
Johnson	$617,533
Opponent	$177,637
Vote Pct	54%

* Contributions came from more than one affiliate or subsidiary.

Eddie Bernice Johnson, D-Texas (30)

First elected: 1992

1991-92 Total Receipts: $283,350
1992 Year-end Cash: $2,696

1993-94 Committees & Subcommittees

Public Works and Transportation
Investigations and Oversight; Public Buildings and Grounds; Surface Transportation

Science, Space and Technology
Science; Technology, Environment and Aviation

Leading Contributors

Business

Agriculture		$4,850
Crop Production & Basic Processing	**$1,000**	
Texas Sugar Beet Growers Assn	$1,000	PAC
Tobacco	**$1,850**	
RJR Nabisco	$1,350	PAC
Dairy	**$1,500**	
Associated Milk Producers	$1,000	PAC

Communications/Electronics		$9,600
Media/Entertainment	**$1,000**	
None over $1,000		
Telephone Utilities	**$4,500**	
GTE Corp	$2,000	PAC
AT&T	$1,500	PAC
Southwestern Bell	$1,000	PAC
Telecom Services & Equipment	**$2,250**	
DSC Communications Corp	$2,000	PAC
Computer Equipment & Services	**$1,850**	
Texas Instruments	$1,000	PAC

Defense		$2,100
Defense Aerospace	**$1,600**	
General Dynamics	$1,250	PAC

Energy & Natural Resources		$10,600
Oil & Gas	**$1,850**	
Enserch Corp	$1,000	PAC
Electric Utilities	**$8,250**	
Texas Utilities Co	$6,000	PAC
Central & South West Services	$1,000	PAC

Contribution Totals by Sector

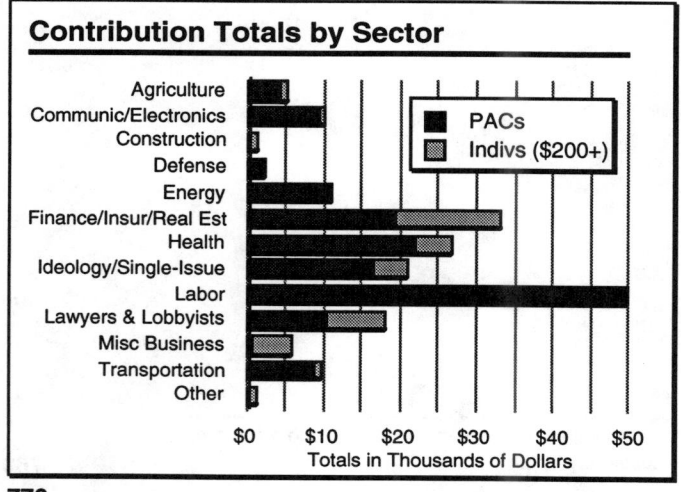

Totals in Thousands of Dollars

Source of Funds in 1992 Election

Source	Total	Pct
■ PACs	$112,176	40%
▨ Indivs $200+	$84,210	30%
☐ Indivs under $200	$67,951	24%
▨ Other	$19,313	7%
Candidate	$0	0%
Party	$600	0%

Source of PAC Dollars by Sector

Source	Total	Pct
■ Business	$85,230	56%
▨ Labor	$49,500	33%
☐ Ideology/Single Issue	$16,279	11%

In-State vs. Out-of-State Contributions*

Source	Total	Pct
☐ In-State	$61,200	86%
■ Out-of-state	$9,730	14%
No state listed	$13,280	

* by large individual contributors ($200 & above)

Finance, Insurance & Real Estate		$32,900
Commercial Banks	**$7,000**	
NCNB Texas	$2,500	PAC
Citizens & Southern National Bank	$1,500	PAC
American Bankers Assn	$1,000	PAC
Texas Commerce Bank/Dallas	$1,000	PAC
Securities & Investment	**$8,800**	
Goldman, Sachs & Co	$3,450	PAC/Ind
Morgan Stanley & Co	$2,000	Indiv
Kemper Securities Group	$1,650	Indiv
Southwest Securities Inc	$1,000	Indiv
Insurance	**$2,600**	
Unimark Insurance	$2,000	Indiv
Real Estate	**$10,000**	
National Assn of Realtors	$6,000	PAC
Trammell Crow Co	$2,000	Indiv
Lehndorf Management USA Ltd	$1,000	Indiv
Lomas & Nettleton Financial Corp	$1,000	Indiv
Accountants	**$4,500**	
American Institute of CPA's	$3,000	PAC
Ernst & Young	$1,000	PAC

Health		$26,477
Health Professionals	**$22,427**	
American Medical Assn	$6,700	PAC
American Academy of Ophthalmology	$3,000	PAC
American Chiropractic Assn	$2,000	PAC
American College of Emergency Physicians	$2,000	PAC
American Podiatry Assn	$2,000	PAC
American Nurses Assn	$1,727	PAC
Hospitals/Nursing Homes	**$2,950**	
American Health Care Assn	$1,000	PAC
National Medical Enterprises Inc	$1,000	PAC

Lawyers & Lobbyists $17,726

Lawyers & Lobbyists **$17,726**
  Assn of Trial Lawyers of America .... $5,000 PAC
  Johnson & Gibbs .... $2,500 PAC
  Heard, Goggan et al .... $1,500 Indiv
  Akin, Gump et al .... $1,126 PAC
  Weisbrod & Morgan .... $1,000 Indiv
  Winstead, Sechrest & Minick .... $1,000 PAC

Misc Business $5,600

Beer, Wine & Liquor **$2,850**
  None over $1,000
Business Services **$1,000**
  None over $1,000
Misc Manufacturing & Distributing **$1,500**
  None over $1,000

Transportation $9,527

Air Transport **$4,350**
  United Parcel Service .... $2,000 PAC
  American Airlines .... $1,850 PAC
Automotive **$4,677**
  National Auto Dealers Assn .... $3,250 PAC

Labor

Labor $49,500

Industrial Unions **$15,000**
  United Auto Workers .... $5,000 PAC
  United Steelworkers .... $5,000 PAC
  Communications Workers of America .... $2,500 PAC
  Machinists/Aerospace Workers Union .... $2,500 PAC
Transportation Unions **$14,750**
  Teamsters Union* .... $10,000 PAC
  Seafarers International Union .... $2,500 PAC
  Brotherhood of Locomotive Engineers .... $1,000 PAC
Public Sector Unions **$18,750**
  National Education Assn .... $7,500 PAC
  American Fedn of St/Cnty/Munic Employees ...... $5,000 PAC
  National Assn of Letter Carriers .... $3,500 PAC
  American Postal Workers Union .... $1,000 PAC
  International Assn of Firefighters .... $1,000 PAC
Misc Unions **$1,000**
  Food & Commercial Workers Union .... $1,000 PAC

Ideological/Single-Issue

Ideological/Single-Issue $20,709

Democratic/Liberal **$1,250**
  Hollywood Women's Political Cmte .... $1,000 PAC
Leadership PACs **$3,500**
  Effective Government Cmte (Dick Gephardt) ...... $1,000 PAC
  House Leadership Fund (Tom Foley) .... $1,000 PAC
  Victory USA (Vic Fazio) .... $1,000 PAC
Pro-Choice **$4,000**
  National Abortion Rights Action League .... $1,000 PAC
  Voters for Choice .... $1,000 PAC
Womens Issues **$7,959**
  Emily's List .... $3,029 PAC
  Women's Campaign Fund .... $2,000 PAC
  National Womens Political Caucus .... $1,000 PAC
Human Rights **$2,500**
  Human Rights Campaign Fund .... $2,500 PAC
Misc Issues **$1,000**
  None over $1,000

Other & Unknown

Other $1,200

Retired **$1,000**
  None over $1,000

Unknown $43,480

  No Employer Listed or Found $40,080
  Employer Listed/Category Unknown $3,400
    Aguirre Associates .... $1,000 Indiv

Spending in Last Election

	1992
Johnson	$282,734
Opponent	$1,754
Vote Pct	72%

* Contributions came from more than one affiliate or subsidiary.

Nancy L. Johnson, R-Conn (6)

First elected: 1982

1991-92 Total Receipts:	$596,412
1992 Year-end Cash:	$144,036

1991-92 Committees & Subcommittees

Standards of Official Conduct

Ways and Means
Health; Human Resources

Leading Contributors

Business

Agriculture		$18,250
Dairy		**$2,500**
None over $2,000		
Food Processing & Sales		**$6,000**
Pepsico Inc	$2,000	PAC
Forestry & Forest Products		**$8,500**
Westvaco Corp	$5,000	PAC

Communications/Electronics		$23,620
Media/Entertainment		**$2,000**
None over $2,000		
Telephone Utilities		**$15,770**
GTE Corp	$4,000	PAC
AT&T	$3,000	PAC
Telecom Services & Equipment		**$2,100**
None over $2,000		

Construction		$24,450
General Contractors		**$16,550**
Tilcon-Tomasso Construction	$7,500	Indiv
Associated General Contractors	$2,500	PAC
Home Builders		**$5,000**
National Assn of Home Builders	$5,000	PAC

Defense		$14,382
Defense Aerospace		**$6,200**
United Technologies	$3,000	PAC
Defense Electronics		**$8,182**
Kaman Corp	$3,182	PAC/Ind
Imo Industries Inc	$3,000	PAC

Source of Funds in 1992 Election

Source	Total	Pct
■ PACs	$337,312	57%
▨ Indivs $200+	$122,184	20%
□ Indivs under $200	$119,893	20%
⊠ Other	$17,023	3%
Candidate	$0	0%
Party	$1,266	0%

Source of PAC Dollars by Sector

Source	Total	Pct
■ Business	$314,322	91%
▨ Labor	$12,100	4%
□ Ideology/Single Issue	$18,100	5%

In-State vs. Out-of-State Contributions*

Source	Total	Pct
□ In-State	$98,034	80%
■ Out-of-state	$24,450	20%
No state listed	$0	

* by large individual contributors ($200 & above)

Energy & Natural Resources		$18,200
Oil & Gas		**$8,000**
None over $2,000		
Misc Energy		**$4,700**
Cooper Industries	$2,500	PAC
Electric Utilities		**$2,350**
None over $2,000		

Finance, Insurance & Real Estate		$130,985
Commercial Banks		**$6,430**
American Bankers Assn	$3,500	PAC/Ind
Securities & Investment		**$10,300**
John Head & Partners	$2,250	Indiv
Insurance		**$95,305**
Cigna Corp	$11,550	PAC/Ind
National Assn of Life Underwriters	$10,000	PAC
Travelers Corp	$8,950	PAC/Ind
Aetna Life & Casualty	$7,900	PAC/Ind
Hartford Insurance	$5,780	PAC/Ind
Phoenix Mutual Life Insurance	$3,675	PAC/Ind
Massachusetts Mutual Life Insurance	$3,200	PAC/Ind
American Council of Life Insurance	$3,000	PAC
Northwestern Mutual Life	$2,400	PAC/Ind
Connecticut Mutual Life Insurance	$2,350	PAC
American Family Corp	$2,000	PAC
Health Insurance Assn of America	$2,000	PAC
Metropolitan Life Insurance	$2,000	PAC
Real Estate		**$6,300**
National Assn of Realtors	$5,300	PAC
Accountants		**$7,250**
American Institute of CPA's	$2,500	PAC
Price Waterhouse	$2,500	Indiv
Misc Finance		**$3,200**
None over $2,000		

Contribution Totals by Sector

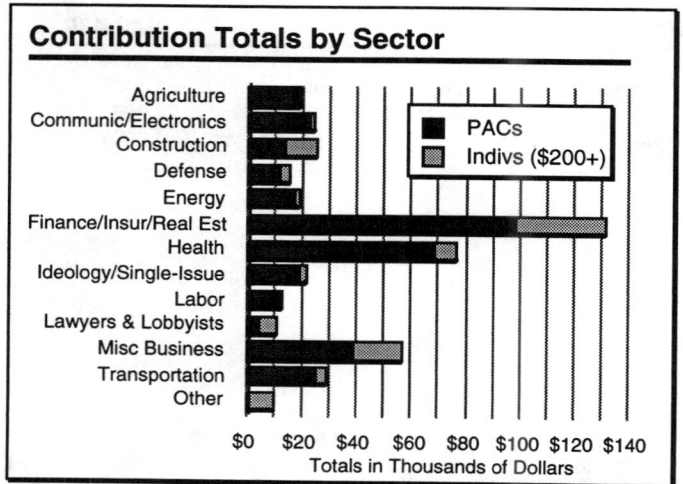

Agriculture
Communic/Electronics
Construction
Defense
Energy
Finance/Insur/Real Est
Health
Ideology/Single-Issue
Labor
Lawyers & Lobbyists
Misc Business
Transportation
Other

■ PACs
▨ Indivs ($200+)

$0 $20 $40 $60 $80 $100 $120 $140
Totals in Thousands of Dollars

Health — $76,200

Health Professionals $44,050
American Medical Assn .... $5,500 PAC
American College of Emergency Physicians .... $5,000 PAC
American Dental Assn .... $5,000 PAC
American Chiropractic Assn .... $3,500 PAC
American Assn Oral & Maxillofacial Surgeons .... $3,000 PAC
American Academy of Ophthalmology .... $2,500 PAC
American Podiatry Assn .... $2,000 PAC

Hospitals/Nursing Homes $11,850
American Hospital Assn .... $5,000 PAC
American Health Care Assn .... $2,500 PAC

Health Services $3,000
None over $2,000

Pharmaceuticals/Health Products $15,200
Kinetic Concepts Inc .... $2,500 PAC

Misc Health $2,100
None over $2,000

Lawyers & Lobbyists — $9,875

Lawyers & Lobbyists $9,875
McClure, Trotter & Mentz .... $2,000 Indiv

Misc Business — $56,132

Food & Beverage $2,500
National Restaurant Assn .... $2,000 PAC

Beer, Wine & Liquor $13,825
Brown-Forman Distillers .... $3,000 PAC
Smirnoff/Inglenook Distributors .... $3,000 PAC
Heublein Inc .... $2,325 PAC/Ind

Retail Sales $8,007
International Council of Shopping Centers .... $2,000 PAC

Business Services $6,850
Boardroom Consultants Inc .... $2,000 Indiv
Harry Gray Associates .... $2,000 Indiv

Lodging/Tourism $2,250
None over $2,000

Chemical & Related Manufacturing $8,300
Loctite Corp .... $2,000 Indiv

Misc Manufacturing & Distributing $12,200
Stanley Works .... $4,700 PAC/Ind
Barnes Group Inc .... $2,000 Indiv

Transportation — $28,328

Air Transport $10,900
Federal Express Corp .... $5,000 PAC
United Parcel Service .... $3,500 PAC

Automotive $10,428
Americans for Free International Trade .... $5,000 PAC

Trucking $3,000
None over $2,000

Railroads $2,000
None over $2,000

Sea Transport $2,000
None over $2,000

Labor

Labor — $12,100

Transportation Unions $3,500
None over $2,000

Public Sector Unions $8,100
National Assn Retired Federal Employees .... $5,000 PAC

Ideological/Single-Issue

Ideological/Single-Issue — $21,100

Womens Issues $14,250
Women's Campaign Fund .... $10,000 PAC
Wish List .... $2,000 PAC

Human Rights $2,350
Human Rights Campaign Fund .... $2,000 PAC

Other & Unknown

Other — $9,450

Retired $8,150
None over $2,000

Unknown — $24,434

No Employer Listed or Found $2,965
Employer Listed/Category Unknown $20,469
None over $2,000

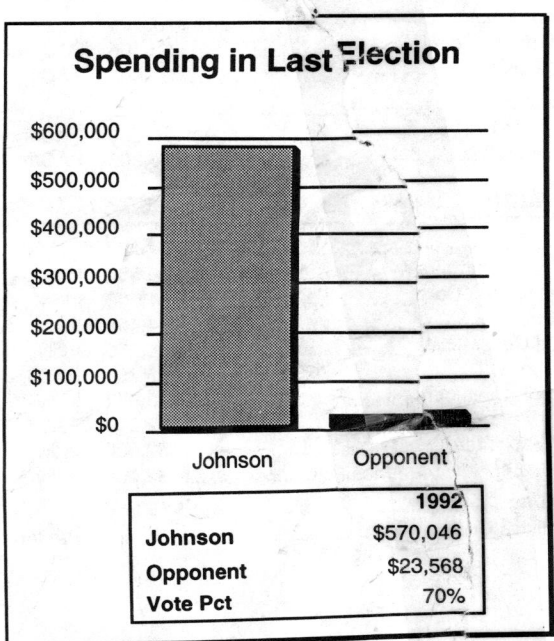

Spending in Last Election

	1992
Johnson	$570,046
Opponent	$23,568
Vote Pct	70%

Sam Johnson, R-Texas (3)

First elected: 1991

1991-92 Total Receipts: $776,652
1992 Year-end Cash: $13,717

1991-92 Committees & Subcommittees

Banking, Finance and Urban Affairs
General Oversight and Investigations; Housing and Community Development; International Development, Finance, Trade and Monetary Policy

Science, Space and Technology
Space

Small Business
Antitrust, Impact of Deregulation and Ecology

Leading Contributors

Business

Agriculture	$18,150	
Dairy	**$3,450**	
Associated Milk Producers	$2,000	PAC
Livestock	**$3,750**	
None over $2,000		
Agricultural Services/Products	**$2,250**	
None over $2,000		
Food Processing & Sales	**$6,450**	
Cullum Companies Inc	$2,000	Indiv

Communications/Electronics	$37,110	
Printing & Publishing	**$3,500**	
Today Newspapers Inc	$3,000	Indiv
Telephone Utilities	**$10,250**	
GTE Corp	$3,500	PAC
Southwestern Bell	$2,500	PAC
Contel	$2,000	PAC
Telecom Services & Equipment	**$5,250**	
DSC Communications Corp	$4,250	PAC/Ind
Computer Equipment & Services	**$16,360**	
EDS Corp	$4,750	Indiv
Electronic Data Systems	$3,760	PAC
Texas Instruments	$2,000	PAC

Contribution Totals by Sector

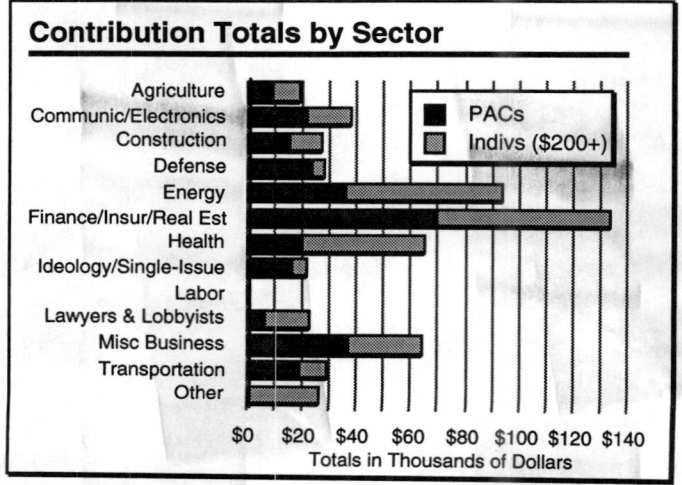

Totals in Thousands of Dollars

- Agriculture
- Communic/Electronics
- Construction
- Defense
- Energy
- Finance/Insur/Real Est
- Health
- Ideology/Single-Issue
- Labor
- Lawyers & Lobbyists
- Misc Business
- Transportation
- Other

Legend: PACs / Indivs ($200+)

$0 $20 $40 $60 $80 $100 $120 $140

Source of Funds in 1992 Election

Source	Total	Pct
■ PACs	$291,165	37%
▨ Indivs $200+	$341,523	44%
□ Indivs under $200	$111,897	14%
⊠ Other	$32,067	4%
Candidate	$0	0%
Party	$613	0%

Source of PAC Dollars by Sector

Source	Total	Pct
■ Business	$250,561	94%
▨ Labor	$100	0%
□ Ideology/Single Issue	$15,950	6%

In-State vs. Out-of-State Contributions*

Source	Total	Pct
□ In-State	$329,978	98%
■ Out-of-state	$7,500	2%
No state listed	$2,150	

* by large individual contributors ($200 & above)

Construction	$26,832	
General Contractors	**$6,982**	
Associated General Contractors	$2,500	PAC
Austin Industries	$2,000	Indiv
Home Builders	**$11,300**	
National Assn of Home Builders	$7,500	PAC
Fox & Jacobs	$2,250	Indiv
Building Materials & Equipment	**$7,250**	
Gifford, Hill & Co	$2,000	Indiv
Lennox Industries	$2,000	PAC

Defense	$27,555	
Defense Aerospace	**$13,505**	
Rockwell International	$2,505	PAC/Ind
Northrop Corp	$2,000	PAC
Defense Electronics	**$14,050**	
E-Systems Inc	$8,750	PAC/Ind
Imo Industries Inc	$4,300	PAC/Ind

Energy & Natural Resources	$93,175	
Oil & Gas	**$74,425**	
Mesa Limited Partnership	$6,550	Indiv
Texan Petroleum Corp	$4,500	Indiv
AG Hill Co	$4,400	Indiv
Guffey Oil Co	$4,250	Indiv
Hunt Oil Co	$3,250	PAC/Ind
Sunnybrook Development	$3,000	Indiv
American Petrofina	$2,000	PAC
Wesley West Interests	$2,000	Indiv
Western Co of North America	$2,000	Indiv
Electric Utilities	**$16,250**	
Texas Utilities Co*	$15,250	PAC/Ind

Finance, Insurance & Real Estate — $132,675

Commercial Banks **$34,240**
 NCNB Corp* ....$7,500 Indiv
 American Bankers Assn ....$4,065 PAC
 Citizens & Southern National Bank ....$4,000 PAC
 Chemical Bank* ....$2,500 PAC
 Texas American Bancshares ....$2,000 PAC

Savings & Loans **$3,250**
 US League of Savings Assns* ....$2,500 PAC

Credit Unions **$3,500**
 Credit Union National Assn ....$3,000 PAC

Finance/Credit Companies **$4,750**
 None over $2,000

Securities & Investment **$5,750**
 Southwest Securities Inc ....$2,000 Indiv

Insurance **$19,125**
 Unimark Insurance ....$2,500 Indiv
 Resource Deployment Inc ....$2,250 Indiv
 American National Insurance Co ....$2,000 PAC
 National Assn of Life Underwriters ....$2,000 PAC

Real Estate **$49,168**
 National Assn of Realtors ....$13,000 PAC
 Ebby Halliday Realtors ....$4,250 Indiv
 Industrial Properties Corp ....$3,750 Indiv
 Lawyers American Title Co ....$3,000 Indiv
 Vance C Miller Interests ....$3,000 Indiv
 Lehndorf Management USA Ltd ....$2,500 Indiv
 Worthing Companies ....$2,500 Indiv
 Paragon Group ....$2,250 Indiv
 Mortgage Bankers Assn of America ....$2,000 PAC

Misc Finance **$11,450**
 None over $2,000

Health — $64,459

Health Professionals **$58,959**
 American Medical Assn* ....$9,484 PAC
 Hunt Consolidated Inc ....$4,500 Indiv
 American Academy of Ophthalmology ....$3,500 PAC
 American Dental Assn ....$2,500 PAC
 Texas Back Institute ....$2,000 Indiv

Hospitals/Nursing Homes **$5,500**
 Heritage Manor ....$2,500 Indiv

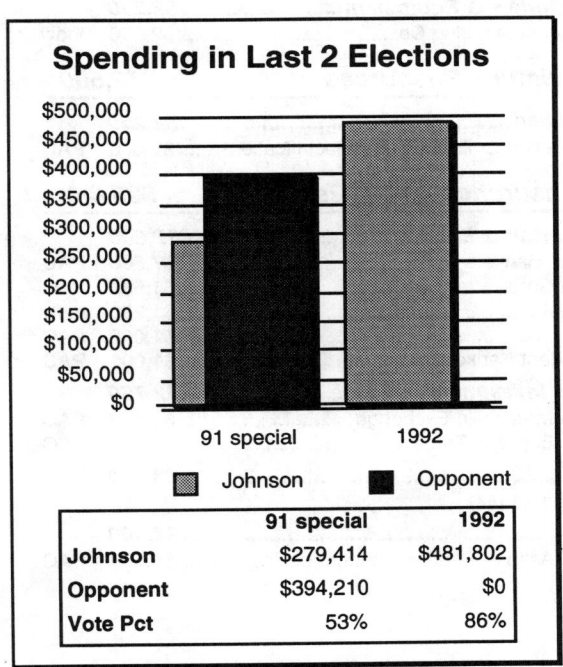

Spending in Last 2 Elections

	91 special	1992
Johnson	$279,414	$481,802
Opponent	$394,210	$0
Vote Pct	53%	86%

Legend: Johnson, Opponent

Lawyers & Lobbyists — $22,775

Lawyers & Lobbyists **$22,775**
 Johnson & Gibbs ....$2,750 PAC

Misc Business — $62,657

Food & Beverage **$14,800**
 National Restaurant Assn* ....$7,500 PAC
 McDonald's Corp ....$4,500 PAC/Ind

Beer, Wine & Liquor **$5,000**
 Ben E Keith Co ....$2,000 Indiv

Retail Sales **$5,007**
 JC Penney Co ....$2,000 PAC

Misc Services **$3,500**
 None over $2,000

Business Services **$6,350**
 Spaeth Communications Inc ....$2,000 Indiv
 Today's Temporary ....$2,000 Indiv

Chemical & Related Manufacturing **$12,500**
 Contran Corp ....$5,000 PAC
 Dow Chemical ....$4,000 PAC
 NL Industries ....$3,000 PAC

Misc Manufacturing & Distributing **$14,250**
 Hoechst Celanese Corp ....$5,000 PAC
 C-Koe Aluminum Inc ....$4,000 Indiv
 Stone Container Corp ....$2,000 PAC

Transportation — $27,878

Air Transport **$11,850**
 Addison Airport ....$5,000 Indiv
 Aircraft Owners & Pilots Assn ....$2,000 PAC
 United Parcel Service ....$2,000 PAC

Automotive **$15,528**
 National Auto Dealers Assn ....$8,500 PAC

Ideological/Single-Issue

Ideological/Single-Issue — $21,200

Republican/Conservative **$9,500**
 Conservative Victory Committee ....$5,000 PAC

Leadership PACs **$5,200**
 Republican Leader's Fund (Bob Michel) ....$5,000 PAC

Gun Rights/Gun Control **$3,500**
 National Rifle Assn ....$3,500 PAC

Other & Unknown

Other — $25,450

Education **$4,000**
 Southern Methodist University ....$2,000 Indiv

Retired **$19,200**
 None over $2,000

Unknown — $48,518

 Homemakers/Non-income earners $5,800
 No Employer Listed or Found $18,295
 Generic Occupation/Category Unknown $4,823
 Employer Listed/Category Unknown $19,600
  WE Cooper Investments ....$2,750 Indiv
  Brown Consolidated ....$2,000 Indiv
  Geo-Marine Inc ....$2,000 Indiv

---

* Contributions came from more than one affiliate or subsidiary.

Tim Johnson, D-SD (1)

First elected: 1986

1991-92 Total Receipts: $452,528
1992 Year-end Cash: $180,431

1991-92 Committees & Subcommittees

Agriculture
Conservation, Credit and Rural Development; Livestock, Dairy and Poultry; Wheat, Soybeans and Feed Grains

Interior and Insular Affairs
National Parks and Public Lands; Water, Power and Offshore Energy

Select Committee on Children, Youth and Families

Leading Contributors

Business

Agriculture	$51,275	
Crop Production & Basic Processing **$19,125**		
American Crystal Sugar Corp $2,000	PAC
National Assn of Wheat Growers $1,500	PAC
AG Processing Inc $1,000	PAC
American Sugarbeet Growers Assn $1,000	PAC
Florida Sugar Cane League $1,000	PAC
National Sunflower Assn $1,000	PAC
Dairy **$10,500**		
Associated Milk Producers $9,000	PAC
Mid-America Dairymen $1,000	PAC
Poultry & Eggs **$4,500**		
Tyson Foods $1,500	PAC
National Broiler Council $1,000	PAC
National Turkey Federation $1,000	PAC
United Egg Assn $1,000	PAC
Livestock **$3,900**		
National Cattlemen's Assn* $1,000	PAC
Agricultural Services/Products **$11,250**		
Land O'Lakes Inc $2,000	PAC
Archer-Daniels-Midland Corp $1,500	PAC
Farm Credit Council $1,500	PAC
American Assn of Crop Insurers $1,000	PAC
American Veterinary Medical Assn $1,000	PAC
National Council of Farmer Co-ops $1,000	PAC
Food Processing & Sales **$1,500**		
None over $1,000		

Source of Funds in 1992 Election

Source	Total	Pct
■ PACs	$221,153	48%
▨ Indivs $200+	$54,100	12%
□ Indivs under $200	$151,568	33%
▩ Other	$34,471	7%
Candidate	$0	0%
Party	$9,114	2%

Source of PAC Dollars by Sector

Source	Total	Pct
■ Business	$109,875	48%
▨ Labor	$105,650	47%
□ Ideology/Single Issue	$11,250	5%

In-State vs. Out-of-State Contributions*

Source	Total	Pct
□ In-State	$46,600	87%
■ Out-of-state	$7,250	13%
No state listed	$0	

*** by large individual contributors ($200 & above)**

Communications/Electronics	$8,750	
Printing & Publishing **$1,250**		
Miller, Freeman Inc $1,000	Indiv
Telephone Utilities **$6,750**		
US West Inc $2,500	PAC
AT&T $1,500	PAC/Ind
GTE Corp $1,000	PAC
US Telephone Assn $1,000	PAC

Construction	$5,400	
Home Builders **$2,000**		
National Assn of Home Builders $2,000	PAC
Building Materials & Equipment **$2,250**		
Larson Manufacturing Co $2,000	Indiv

Energy & Natural Resources	$2,500	
Electric Utilities **$2,250**		
ACRE (Action Cmte for Rural Electrification) $1,000	PAC

Finance, Insurance & Real Estate	$25,850	
Commercial Banks **$12,600**		
American Bankers Assn $7,500	PAC
Norwest Corp $1,500	PAC
Bank First $1,250	Indiv
Citicorp $1,000	PAC
Independent Bankers Assn $1,000	PAC
Securities & Investment **$2,750**		
Chicago Mercantile Exchange $1,500	PAC
Chicago Board of Trade $1,000	PAC
Insurance **$3,000**		
None over $1,000		
Real Estate **$7,500**		
National Assn of Realtors $6,500	PAC

Contribution Totals by Sector

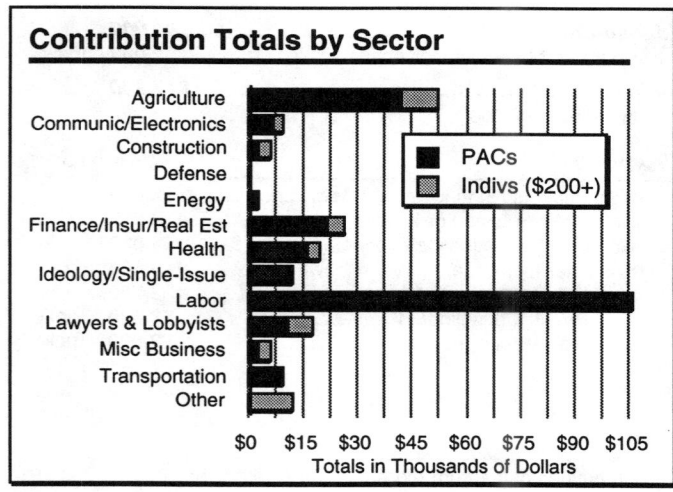

Agriculture, Communic/Electronics, Construction, Defense, Energy, Finance/Insur/Real Est, Health, Ideology/Single-Issue, Labor, Lawyers & Lobbyists, Misc Business, Transportation, Other

■ PACs
▨ Indivs ($200+)

$0 $15 $30 $45 $60 $75 $90 $105
Totals in Thousands of Dollars

Health $19,200

Health Professionals **$17,750**
    American Medical Assn ....$10,000 PAC
    American Academy of Ophthalmology ....$2,500 PAC
    Assn for the Advancement of Psychology ....$1,000 PAC

Hospitals/Nursing Homes **$1,250**
    American Hospital Assn ....$1,000 PAC

Lawyers & Lobbyists $17,100

Lawyers & Lobbyists **$17,100**
    Assn of Trial Lawyers of America ....$10,000 PAC
    Lynn, Jackson et al ....$1,500 Indiv
    Davenport, Evans et al ....$1,000 Indiv

Misc Business $5,600

Beer, Wine & Liquor **$1,000**
    None over $1,000

Retail Sales **$1,600**
    Feinsteins Clothing..$1,350 Indiv

Lodging/Tourism **$1,750**
    None over $1,000

Textiles...**$1,000**
    American Textile Manufacturers Institute ....$1,000 PAC

Transportation $8,750

Air Transport **$5,250**
    United Parcel Service...$3,750 PAC
    Aircraft Owners & Pilots Assn ....$1,000 PAC

Automotive **$3,000**
    National Auto Dealers Assn ....$3,000 PAC

Spending in Last 3 Elections

	1988	1990	1992
Johnson	$632,105	$463,625	$376,741
Opponent	$199,420	$211,617	$162,143
Vote Pct	72%	68%	69%

Labor

Labor $105,650

Building Trade Unions **$13,500**
    Laborers' Political League ....$3,500 PAC
    Carpenters & Joiners Union ....$3,000 PAC
    Sheet Metal Workers Union ....$2,500 PAC
    Plumbers/Pipefitters Union..................................$2,000 PAC
    AFL-CIO Bldg/Construction Trades Dept ....$1,500 PAC
    Operating Engineers Union ....$1,000 PAC

Industrial Unions **$42,900**
    United Auto Workers ....$10,000 PAC
    United Steelworkers ....$10,000 PAC
    Intl Brotherhood of Electrical Workers ....$9,500 PAC
    Machinists/Aerospace Workers Union ....$6,000 PAC
    Communications Workers of America ....$3,500 PAC
    Rubber Cork Linoleum & Plastic Workers ....$1,500 PAC
    AFL-CIO Allied Industrial Wrkrs ....$1,100 PAC

Transportation Unions **$20,250**
    Teamsters Union ....$7,500 PAC
    United Transportation Union ....$5,750 PAC
    Air Line Pilots Assn ....$3,000 PAC
    Marine Engineers Union......................................$2,000 PAC
    Seafarers International Union ....$1,000 PAC

Public Sector Unions **$24,000**
    American Postal Workers Union ....$5,000 PAC
    National Education Assn ....$5,000 PAC
    National Assn Retired Federal Employees ....$4,000 PAC
    American Fedn of St/Cnty/Munic Employees ......$3,500 PAC
    National Assn of Letter Carriers ....$3,000 PAC
    National League of Postmasters ....$1,000 PAC
    National Rural Letter Carriers Assn ....$1,000 PAC

Misc Unions..**$5,000**
    Food & Commercial Workers Union ....$4,000 PAC
    AFL-CIO ....$1,000 PAC

Ideological/Single-Issue

Ideological/Single-Issue $11,500

Democratic/Liberal **$2,500**
    National Cmte for an Effective Congress ....$2,500 PAC

Pro-Israel **$2,500**
    National PAC ....$1,000 PAC

Gun Rights/Gun Control **$3,000**
    National Rifle Assn ....$3,000 PAC

Misc Issues...**$3,500**
    National Cmte to Preserve Social Security ....$3,500 PAC

Other & Unknown

Other $11,450

Education **$4,750**
    University of Wyoming ....$3,000 Indiv

Retired **$6,000**
    None over $1,000

Unknown $7,350

    Homemakers/Non-income earners $1,000
    Employer Listed/Category Unknown $6,350
      Dougherty Consulting Services ....$2,000 Indiv

---

* Contributions came from more than one affiliate or
subsidiary.

Harry A. Johnston, D-Fla (19)

First elected: 1988

1991-92 Total Receipts: $348,039
1992 Year-end Cash: $155,908

1991-92 Committees & Subcommittees

Foreign Affairs
Europe and the Middle East; International Economic Policy and Trade; Western Hemisphere Affairs

Interior and Insular Affairs
National Parks and Public Lands; Water, Power and Offshore Energy

Leading Contributors

Business

Agriculture — $23,450

Crop Production & Basic Processing **$19,050**
Okeelanta Corp .... $6,000 Indiv
US Sugar Corp .... $2,000 Indiv
Florida Citrus Mutual .... $1,850 PAC
Savannah Foods & Industries .... $1,000 PAC
United States Sugar Corp .... $1,000 PAC

Dairy **$1,850**
Associated Milk Producers .... $1,500 PAC

Agricultural Services/Products **$2,100**
None over $1,000

Communications/Electronics — $7,900

Telephone Utilities **$5,350**
AT&T .... $2,050 PAC
GTE Corp .... $1,700 PAC
Southern Bell .... $1,600 PAC

Telecom Services & Equipment **$1,450**
None over $1,000

Construction — $7,400

General Contractors **$5,400**
Norman Construction .... $2,500 Indiv

Building Materials & Equipment **$1,750**
Rinker Materials Corp .... $1,750 Indiv

Defense — $4,950

Defense Aerospace **$4,650**
United Technologies .... $1,400 PAC

Contribution Totals by Sector

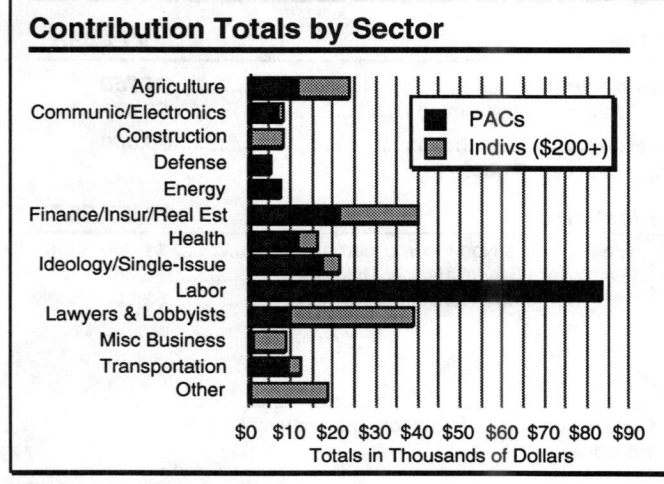

Agriculture, Communic/Electronics, Construction, Defense, Energy, Finance/Insur/Real Est, Health, Ideology/Single-Issue, Labor, Lawyers & Lobbyists, Misc Business, Transportation, Other

PACs / Indivs ($200+)

$0 $10 $20 $30 $40 $50 $60 $70 $80 $90
Totals in Thousands of Dollars

Source of Funds in 1992 Election

Source	Total	Pct
PACs	$179,300	49%
Indivs $200+	$121,846	33%
Indivs under $200	$31,996	9%
Other	$33,917	9%
Candidate	$0	0%
Party	$19,370	5%

Source of PAC Dollars by Sector

Source	Total	Pct
Business	$80,800	45%
Labor	$82,650	46%
Ideology/Single Issue	$17,246	10%

In-State vs. Out-of-State Contributions*

Source	Total	Pct
In-State	$113,346	93%
Out-of-state	$8,250	7%
No state listed	$250	

* by large individual contributors ($200 & above)

Energy & Natural Resources — $7,100

Oil & Gas **$1,450**
WR Grace & Co .... $1,450 PAC

Electric Utilities **$4,850**
ACRE (Action Cmte for Rural Electrification) .... $1,850 PAC
Florida Power & Light .... $1,000 PAC

Finance, Insurance & Real Estate — $39,000

Commercial Banks **$10,100**
Citizens & Southern National Bank .... $4,000 PAC
Barnett Banks Inc .... $1,700 PAC
SunBanks .... $1,000 PAC

Savings & Loans **$1,700**
Florida League of Financial Institutions .... $1,000 PAC

Securities & Investment **$1,800**
None over $1,000

Insurance **$2,850**
Blue Cross/Blue Shield of Florida .... $1,500 PAC
American Council of Life Insurance .... $1,150 PAC

Real Estate **$18,100**
National Assn of Realtors .... $6,500 PAC
Crocker & Co Develop .... $2,000 Indiv
Sidney Kohl Co .... $2,000 Indiv
Temple Development Co .... $1,000 Indiv

Misc Finance **$3,750**
None over $1,000

Health — $16,000

Health Professionals **$11,100**
American Medical Assn .... $5,000 PAC
American Academy of Ophthalmology .... $1,000 PAC
American Chiropractic Assn .... $1,000 PAC

Hospitals/Nursing Homes **$2,300**
American Hospital Assn .... $1,700 PAC

Health Services **$1,250**
    Atlantic Ambulance Service .... $1,000   Indiv

Pharmaceuticals/Health Products **$1,350**
    None over $1,000

Lawyers & Lobbyists $38,150

Lawyers & Lobbyists **$38,150**
    Assn of Trial Lawyers of America .... $5,000   PAC
    Searcy, Denney et al .... $5,000   Indiv
    Greenberg, Traurig et al .... $3,800   PAC/Ind
    Lytal & Reiter .... $2,300   Indiv
    Tripp, Scott et al .... $2,250   Indiv
    Jones, Foster et al .... $2,000   Indiv
    Holland & Knight .... $1,200   PAC
    Babbitt & Hazouri .... $1,000   Indiv
    Hogan & Hartson .... $1,000   PAC/Ind
    Sachs, Sax et al .... $1,000   Indiv

Misc Business $8,150

Beer, Wine & Liquor **$3,750**
    Brown Distributing Co .... $2,000   Indiv
    Todhunter International Inc .... $1,000   Indiv

Business Services **$1,000**
    None over $1,000

Misc Manufacturing & Distributing **$1,500**
    None over $1,000

Transportation $11,900

Air Transport **$4,200**
    United Parcel Service .... $3,000   PAC

Automotive **$6,500**
    National Auto Dealers Assn .... $4,000   PAC
    Alamo Rent-a-Car .... $2,000   Indiv

Labor

Labor $82,650

Building Trade Unions **$10,600**
    Sheet Metal Workers Union .... $3,500   PAC
    Laborers' Political League .... $3,000   PAC
    Carpenters & Joiners Union .... $2,000   PAC

Industrial Unions **$24,500**
    Communications Workers of America .... $5,700   PAC
    Machinists/Aerospace Workers Union .... $5,500   PAC
    United Steelworkers .... $5,000   PAC
    United Auto Workers .... $4,700   PAC
    IBEW local #728 .... $1,000   PAC

Transportation Unions **$24,650**
    Teamsters Union .... $10,000   PAC
    Marine Engineers Union* .... $6,500   PAC
    Air Line Pilots Assn .... $2,500   PAC
    Transport Workers Union .... $1,600   PAC
    United Transportation Union .... $1,350   PAC
    Amalgamated Transit Union .... $1,000   PAC
    Seafarers International Union .... $1,000   PAC

Public Sector Unions **$21,400**
    National Education Assn .... $7,500   PAC
    National Assn Retired Federal Employees .... $7,000   PAC
    American Fedn of St/Cnty/Munic Employees ...... $2,500   PAC
    National Assn of Letter Carriers .... $2,000   PAC
    American Postal Workers Union .... $1,050   PAC
    National Assn of Postmasters .... $1,000   PAC

Misc Unions **$1,500**
    Food & Commercial Workers Union .... $1,500   PAC

Ideological/Single-Issue

Ideological/Single-Issue $22,046

Democratic/Liberal **$2,500**
    National Cmte for an Effective Congress .... $2,500   PAC

Pro-Israel **$11,200**
    National PAC .... $5,000   PAC
    Florida Congressional Cmte .... $1,000   PAC
    National Action Committee .... $1,000   PAC

Pro-Choice **$1,000**
    National Abortion Rights Action League .... $1,000   PAC

Human Rights **$3,300**
    Human Rights Campaign Fund .... $2,500   PAC

Misc Issues **$2,750**
    National Cmte to Preserve Social Security .... $2,250   PAC

Other & Unknown

Other $17,900

Retired **$17,050**
    None over $1,000

Unknown $16,446

    Homemakers/Non-income earners $4,548
    No Employer Listed or Found $2,000
    Employer Listed/Category Unknown $9,398
        Industrial Plants Corp .... $1,000   Indiv

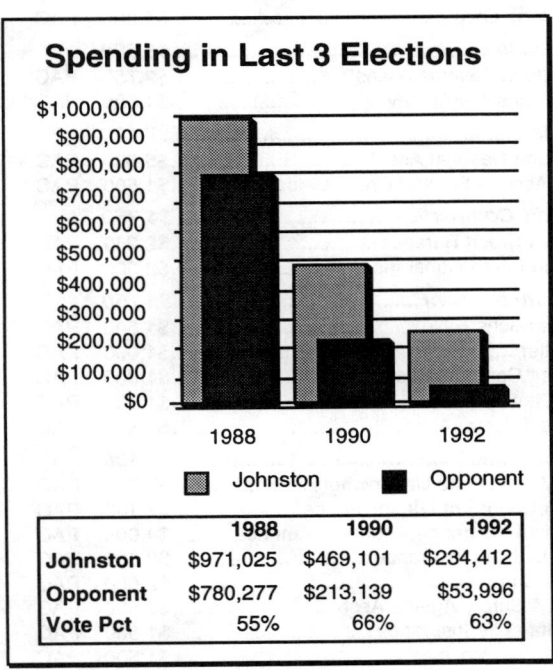

Spending in Last 3 Elections

	1988	1990	1992
Johnston	$971,025	$469,101	$234,412
Opponent	$780,277	$213,139	$53,996
Vote Pct	55%	66%	63%

Legend: Johnston, Opponent

---

* Contributions came from more than one affiliate or
  subsidiary.

Paul E. Kanjorski, D-Pa (11)

First elected: 1984

1991-92 Total Receipts: $311,016
1992 Year-end Cash: $63,183

1991-92 Committees & Subcommittees

Banking, Finance and Urban Affairs
Economic Stabilization; Financial Institutions Supervision, Regulation and Insurance; Housing and Community Development; Policy Research and Insurance

Post Office and Civil Service
Human Resources (Chairman)

Leading Contributors

Business

Agriculture		$5,100

Crop Production & Basic Processing $1,100
    None over $1,000

Dairy $3,500
    Mid-America Dairymen .... $2,000   PAC
    Associated Milk Producers .... $1,000   PAC

Communications/Electronics		$5,250

Telephone Utilities $4,000
    AT&T .... $3,000   PAC
    Bell Telephone of Pennsylvania .... $1,000   PAC

Construction		$4,500

General Contractors $1,750
    None over $1,000

Home Builders $2,750
    Fleetwood Enterprises .... $1,500   PAC

Defense		$1,000

    None over $1,000

Energy & Natural Resources		$4,350

Electric Utilities $3,600
    Pennsylvania Power & Light .... $2,350   PAC
    ACRE (Action Cmte for Rural Electrification) ...... $1,250   PAC

Source of Funds in 1992 Election

Source	Total	Pct
PACs	$235,360	75%
Indivs $200+	$27,552	9%
Indivs under $200	$36,450	12%
Other	$16,107	5%
Candidate	$0	0%
Party	$4,803	2%

Source of PAC Dollars by Sector

Source	Total	Pct
Business	$145,560	61%
Labor	$78,850	33%
Ideology/Single Issue	$12,450	5%

In-State vs. Out-of-State Contributions*

Source	Total	Pct
In-State	$21,252	77%
Out-of-state	$6,300	23%
No state listed	$0	

*** by large individual contributors ($200 & above)**

Finance, Insurance & Real Estate		$108,650

Commercial Banks $31,850
    American Bankers Assn .... $7,500   PAC
    Citicorp .... $2,500   PAC
    Citizens & Southern National Bank .... $2,500   PAC
    PNC Financial Corp* .... $2,500   PAC
    Barnett Banks Inc .... $2,000   PAC
    Chemical Bank .... $2,000   PAC
    Meridian Bancorp .... $1,800   PAC
    Mellon Bank .... $1,650   PAC
    Corestates Financial Corp .... $1,500   PAC
    Independent Bankers Assn .... $1,500   PAC
    First Chicago Corp .... $1,000   PAC

Savings & Loans $6,350
    US League of Savings Assns* .... $2,750   PAC
    Central Pennsylvania Savings .... $1,500   PAC/Ind

Credit Unions $7,100
    Credit Union National Assn* .... $5,600   PAC
    National Assn of Federal Credit Unions .... $1,500   PAC

Finance/Credit Companies $4,750
    Associated Credit Bureaus .... $2,250   PAC
    Household International Inc .... $2,000   PAC

Securities & Investment $6,750
    Goldman, Sachs & Co .... $1,500   PAC
    Dean Witter .... $1,000   PAC
    Investment Company Institute .... $1,000   PAC
    Morgan Stanley & Co .... $1,000   PAC
    Securities Industry Assn .... $1,000   PAC

Insurance $30,500
    National Assn of Life Underwriters .... $7,500   PAC
    American Council of Life Insurance .... $7,100   PAC
    Independent Insurance Agents of America ...... $4,000   PAC
    Penn Mutual Life Insurance .... $2,500   PAC
    Travelers Corp .... $2,000   PAC
    Casualty & Surety Agents Assn .... $1,500   PAC
    Metropolitan Life Insurance .... $1,500   PAC
    Prudential Insurance .... $1,500   PAC

Contribution Totals by Sector

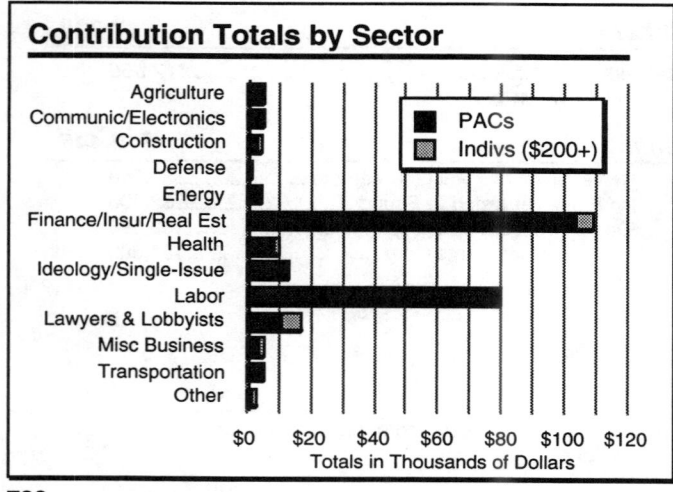

Legend: PACs, Indivs ($200+)

Sectors: Agriculture, Communic/Electronics, Construction, Defense, Energy, Finance/Insur/Real Est, Health, Ideology/Single-Issue, Labor, Lawyers & Lobbyists, Misc Business, Transportation, Other

Totals in Thousands of Dollars ($0, $20, $40, $60, $80, $100, $120)

Real Estate $8,600
    National Assn of Realtors ....$6,000   PAC
    Fricker Corp...$2,100   Indiv

Accountants $12,500
    American Institute of CPA's ....$10,000   PAC
    Coopers & Lybrand ....$1,000   PAC
    Pagnotti Enterprises ....$1,000   Indiv

Health $9,600

Health Professionals $8,100
    American Medical Assn.....................................$6,350   PAC

Pharmaceuticals/Health Products $1,500
    Merck & Co ....$1,000   PAC

Lawyers & Lobbyists $16,150

Lawyers & Lobbyists $16,150
    Assn of Trial Lawyers of America ....$10,000   PAC

Misc Business $4,900

Business Services $2,250
    Washington Financial Info Service.....................$1,250   Indiv

Misc Manufacturing & Distributing $1,000
    Owens-Illinois ....$1,000   PAC

Transportation $4,860

Air Transport $3,500
    United Parcel Service ....$3,500   PAC

Misc Transport $1,000
    None over $1,000

Labor

Labor $78,850

Building Trade Unions $16,200
    Plumbers/Pipefitters Union* ....$3,200   PAC
    Laborers' Political League ....$3,000   PAC
    Painters & Allied Trades Union ....$3,000   PAC
    Ironworkers Union ....$2,500   PAC
    Sheet Metal Workers Union ....$2,500   PAC
    Operating Engineers Union ....$1,000   PAC

Industrial Unions $17,600
    United Steelworkers ....$5,000   PAC
    United Auto Workers ....$4,000   PAC
    Machinists/Aerospace Workers Union ....$3,500   PAC
    United Mine Workers ....$2,000   PAC
    Boilermakers Union ....$1,000   PAC

Transportation Unions $13,250
    Marine Engineers Union* ....$6,500   PAC
    Teamsters Union ....$2,500   PAC
    National Air Traffic Controllers Assn ....$1,000   PAC

Public Sector Unions $30,300
    National Assn of Letter Carriers ....$7,000   PAC
    National Assn Retired Federal Employees ....$5,000   PAC
    National Education Assn ....$4,000   PAC
    American Postal Workers Union ....$3,000   PAC
    National League of Postmasters ....$2,500   PAC
    American Fedn of St/Cnty/Munic Employees ......$2,000   PAC
    Federal Managers' Assn ....$1,800   PAC
    National Assn of Postmasters ....$1,500   PAC
    American Federation of Govt Employees ....$1,000   PAC
    National Assn of Postal Supervisors ....$1,000   PAC

Misc Unions..$1,500
    Food & Commercial Workers Union ....$1,500   PAC

Ideological/Single-Issue

Ideological/Single-Issue $12,450

Democratic/Liberal $2,500
    National Cmte for an Effective Congress ....$2,500   PAC

Gun Rights/Gun Control $6,450
    National Rifle Assn ....$6,450   PAC

Misc Issues $3,500
    National Cmte to Preserve Social Security ....$3,500   PAC

Other & Unknown

Other $2,250

Retired $1,000
    None over $1,000

Unknown $7,752

    Generic Occupation/Category Unknown $1,500
    Employer Listed/Category Unknown....................$5,851
        Federal Jobs Digest ....$1,000   Indiv
        Frank Kelly Mgr Co ....$1,000   Indiv
        Robert Chacphin Assoc ....$1,000   Indiv

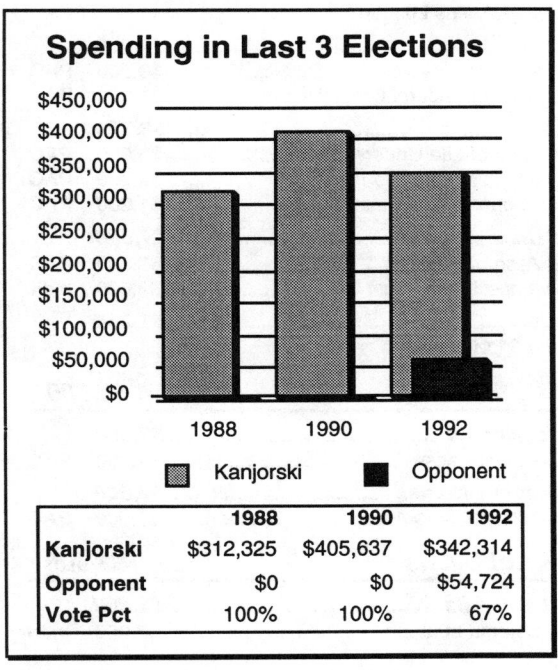

Spending in Last 3 Elections

	1988	1990	1992
Kanjorski	$312,325	$405,637	$342,314
Opponent	$0	$0	$54,724
Vote Pct	100%	100%	67%

Kanjorski   Opponent

---

* Contributions came from more than one affiliate or subsidiary.

Marcy Kaptur, D-Ohio (9)

First elected: 1982

1991-92 Total Receipts: $290,940
1992 Year-end Cash: $13,974

1991-92 Committees & Subcommittees

Appropriations
Agriculture, Rural Development, Food and Drug Administration and Related Agencies; Veterans Affairs, Housing and Urban Development, and Independent Agencies

Leading Contributors

Business

Agriculture	$20,550	
Crop Production & Basic Processing **$4,950**		
American Crystal Sugar Corp	$1,800	PAC
American Sugarbeet Growers Assn	$1,800	PAC
Dairy **$7,800**		
Associated Milk Producers	$4,000	PAC
Milk Marketing Inc	$2,800	PAC
Mid-America Dairymen	$1,000	PAC
Livestock **$1,550**		
National Pork Producers Council	$1,550	PAC
Agricultural Services/Products **$3,250**		
American Veterinary Medical Assn	$1,000	PAC
Farm Credit Council	$1,000	PAC
Food Processing & Sales **$1,000**		
None over $1,000		
Misc Agriculture **$1,000**		
State Aerial Farm	$1,000	Indiv

Communications/Electronics	$1,800	
Media/Entertainment **$1,800**		
ASCAP	$1,300	PAC

Construction	$5,550	
General Contractors **$1,000**		
National Utility Contractors Assn	$1,000	PAC
Construction Services **$1,000**		
Jacobs Engineering Group	$1,000	PAC
Building Materials & Equipment **$3,250**		
Owens-Corning Fiberglas	$3,000	PAC

Source of Funds in 1992 Election

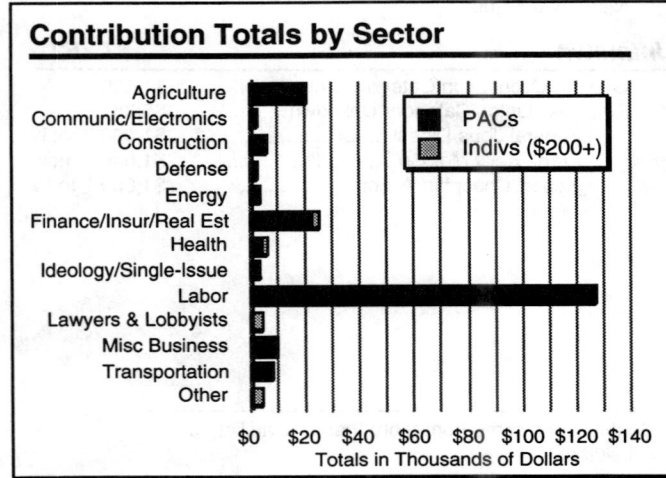

Source	Total	Pct
■ PACs	$208,305	65%
▨ Indivs $200+	$19,740	6%
☐ Indivs under $200	$55,010	17%
⊠ Other	$39,494	12%
Candidate	$0	0%
Party	$32,159	10%

Source of PAC Dollars by Sector

Source	Total	Pct
■ Business	$73,650	36%
▨ Labor	$126,435	62%
☐ Ideology/Single Issue	$2,500	1%

In-State vs. Out-of-State Contributions*

Source	Total	Pct
☐ In-State	$15,890	80%
■ Out-of-state	$3,850	20%
No state listed	$0	

* by large individual contributors ($200 & above)

Defense	$2,200	
Defense Aerospace **$2,500**		
None over $1,000		

Energy & Natural Resources	$3,300	
Electric Utilities **$1,600**		
ACRE (Action Cmte for Rural Electrification)	$1,600	PAC

Finance, Insurance & Real Estate	$24,500	
Commercial Banks **$2,250**		
Independent Bankers Assn	$1,800	PAC
Ohio Savings Assns League	$1,000	PAC
Credit Unions **$4,300**		
Credit Union National Assn	$3,000	PAC
National Assn of Federal Credit Unions	$1,300	PAC
Insurance **$8,700**		
National Assn of Life Underwriters	$5,000	PAC
Massachusetts Mutual Life Insurance	$2,000	PAC
American Council of Life Insurance	$1,200	PAC
Real Estate **$7,500**		
National Assn of Realtors	$5,500	PAC
Port Lawrence Title & Trust Co	$2,000	Indiv
Misc Finance **$1,250**		
None over $1,000		

Health	$5,500	
Health Professionals **$3,500**		
American Dental Assn	$1,000	PAC
Hospitals/Nursing Homes **$2,000**		
American Health Care Assn	$1,500	PAC

Lawyers & Lobbyists	$3,800	
Lawyers & Lobbyists **$3,800**		
Joseph, Gajarsa et al	$2,000	Indiv

Contribution Totals by Sector

Agriculture
Communic/Electronics
Construction
Defense
Energy
Finance/Insur/Real Est
Health
Ideology/Single-Issue
Labor
Lawyers & Lobbyists
Misc Business
Transportation
Other

■ PACs
▨ Indivs ($200+)

$0 $20 $40 $60 $80 $100 $120 $140
Totals in Thousands of Dollars

Misc Business $9,950

Food & Beverage **$1,000**
    Pepsi-Cola General Bottlers ....$1,000 PAC

Business Services **$1,150**
    None over $1,000

Misc Manufacturing & Distributing **$4,300**
    Owens-Illinois ....$2,250 PAC
    Libbey-Owens-Ford ....$1,000 PAC

Textiles **$2,500**
    Burlington Industries ....$2,000 PAC

Transportation $7,800

Air Transport **$2,650**
    United Parcel Service..............................$2,150 PAC/Ind

Automotive **$5,150**
    Chrysler Corp ....$2,300 PAC
    Ford Motor Co ....$1,600 PAC
    General Motors ....$1,000 PAC

Labor

Labor $126,635

Building Trade Unions **$27,450**
    Carpenters & Joiners Union ....$6,300 PAC
    Boilermakers Union local #85 ....$5,000 PAC
    Laborers' Political League ....$4,000 PAC
    Ironworkers Union ....$3,500 PAC
    Plumbers/Pipefitters Union* ....$3,150 PAC
    Operating Engineers Union ....$1,500 PAC
    AFL-CIO Bldg/Construction Trades Dept ....$1,000 PAC
    Heat/Frost/Asbestos Workers Union ....$1,000 PAC
    Sheet Metal Workers Union ....$1,000 PAC

Industrial Unions **$35,910**
    United Auto Workers ....$10,000 PAC
    Intl Brotherhood of Electrical Workers* ....$5,510 PAC
    Machinists/Aerospace Workers Union ....$5,500 PAC
    Boilermakers Union ....$5,000 PAC
    Communications Workers of America ....$2,500 PAC
    Electronic Machine Furniture Workers ....$2,500 PAC
    United Mine Workers ....$1,800 PAC
    Amalgamated Clothing & Textile Workers ....$1,000 PAC
    Ladies Garment Workers Union ....$1,000 PAC

Transportation Unions **$26,050**
    Teamsters Union* ....$10,000 PAC
    Air Line Pilots Assn ....$5,000 PAC
    International Longshoremen's Assn ....$3,000 PAC
    United Transportation Union ....$2,500 PAC
    Seafarers International Union ....$2,100 PAC
    Brotherhood of Railroad Signalmen ....$1,150 PAC

Public Sector Unions **$30,125**
    American Fedn of St/Cnty/Munic Employees ....$10,000 PAC
    National Assn Retired Federal Employees ....$4,000 PAC
    American Federation of Teachers ....$3,700 PAC
    National Education Assn ....$3,375 PAC
    National Assn of Letter Carriers ....$3,000 PAC
    American Postal Workers Union ....$1,500 PAC
    National Assn of Postmasters ....$1,500 PAC

Misc Unions **$7,100**
    Food & Commercial Workers Union ....$4,500 PAC
    AFL-CIO ....$1,300 PAC
    Hotel/Restaurant Employees Union ....$1,300 PAC

Ideological/Single-Issue

Ideological/Single-Issue $2,950

Democratic/Liberal **$2,950**
    National Cmte for an Effective Congress.............$2,500 PAC

Other & Unknown

Other $3,790

Retired **$3,790**
    None over $1,000

Unknown $4,000

    Employer Listed/Category Unknown $2,850
      Transworld Indust ....$1,000 Indiv

Spending in Last 3 Elections

	1988	1990	1992
Kaptur	$244,030	$211,524	$335,095
Opponent	$44,445	$200	$44,182
Vote Pct	81%	78%	74%

---

* Contributions came from more than one affiliate or
subsidiary.

John R. Kasich, R-Ohio (12)

First elected: 1982

1991-92 Total Receipts: $279,301
1992 Year-end Cash: $130,431

1991-92 Committees & Subcommittees

Armed Services
Procurement and Military Nuclear Systems; Readiness (Ranking Republican)

Budget
Defense, Foreign Policy and Space; Economic Policy, Projections and Revenues; Human Resources (Ranking Republican)

Leading Contributors

Business

Agriculture $10,950

Crop Production & Basic Processing $1,000
   None over $1,000

Dairy $5,200
   Associated Milk Producers .... $4,000   PAC

Food Processing & Sales $3,500
   Food Marketing Institute .... $1,550   PAC
   Michaels Finer Meats & Seafoods .... $1,000   Indiv

Communications/Electronics $5,300

Media/Entertainment $1,950
   None over $1,000

Telephone Utilities $3,000
   Ohio Bell Telephone .... $2,250   PAC

Construction $23,550

General Contractors $13,700
   Wallick Construction Co .... $3,500   Indiv
   TC Weiser Construction .... $2,500   Indiv
   Ruscilli Construction Co .... $2,000   Indiv
   Fishel Co .... $1,500   Indiv
   Associated General Contractors .... $1,350   PAC
   Johns Co .... $1,000   Indiv

Home Builders $2,750
   Virginia Homes .... $1,500   Indiv

Special Trade Contractors $4,750
   Shepherd Excavating Inc .... $2,000   Indiv
   Haslett Heating & Cooling Inc .... $1,000   Indiv

Building Materials & Equipment $2,350
   Davon Inc .... $1,000   Indiv

Source of Funds in 1992 Election

Source	Total	Pct
PACs	$113,970	41%
Indivs $200+	$147,375	53%
Indivs under $200	$13,821	5%
Other	$4,135	1%
Candidate	$0	0%
Party	$0	0%

Source of PAC Dollars by Sector

Source	Total	Pct
Business	$98,029	91%
Labor	$2,300	2%
Ideology/Single Issue	$7,550	7%

In-State vs. Out-of-State Contributions*

Source	Total	Pct
In-State	$146,675	100%
Out-of-state	$700	0%
No state listed	$0	

***by large individual contributors ($200 & above)**

Defense $15,850

Defense Aerospace $6,650
   General Electric .... $1,200   PAC

Defense Electronics $6,600
   AT&T .... $4,000   PAC
   GTE Corp .... $1,250   PAC

Misc Defense $2,600
   None over $1,000

Energy & Natural Resources $14,079

Oil & Gas $7,320
   Oxford Oil Co .... $1,500   Indiv
   Englefield Oil Corp .... $1,100   Indiv
   Ashland Oil .... $1,000   PAC

Electric Utilities $4,259
   American Electric Power* .... $3,909   PAC

Environmental Svcs/Equipment $1,500
   Batelle Memorial Institute .... $1,500   PAC

Waste Management $1,000
   Mid-American Waste Systems .... $1,000   PAC

Finance, Insurance & Real Estate $50,475

Commercial Banks $9,850
   Huntington Bancshares .... $3,250   PAC/Ind
   National City Corp .... $2,500   PAC
   American Bankers Assn* .... $2,000   PAC
   Banc One Corp .... $1,100   PAC/Ind
   Park National Bank .... $1,000   Indiv

Savings & Loans $1,500
   Ohio Savings Assns League .... $1,000   PAC

Securities & Investment $9,850
   Ohio Co .... $8,750   Indiv

Contribution Totals by Sector

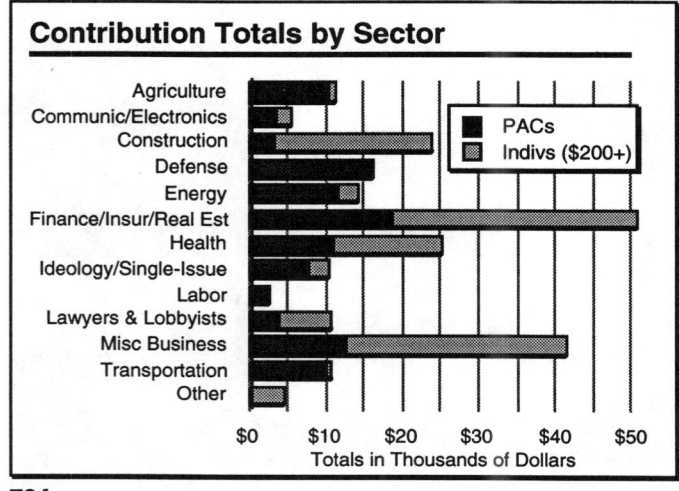

Legend: ■ PACs   ▨ Indivs ($200+)

Agriculture
Communic/Electronics
Construction
Defense
Energy
Finance/Insur/Real Est
Health
Ideology/Single-Issue
Labor
Lawyers & Lobbyists
Misc Business
Transportation
Other

$0 $10 $20 $30 $40 $50
Totals in Thousands of Dollars

Insurance	$13,000	
Nationwide Corp	$4,300	PAC
Garlikov & Associates	$2,000	Indiv
Harmon & Associates Life Insurance	$1,500	Indiv
National Assn of Life Underwriters	$1,500	PAC
Golden Rule Insurance Co	$1,000	PAC

Real Estate	$11,275	
Glimcher Co	$2,500	Indiv
National Assn of Realtors	$1,600	PAC
Don M Casto Organization	$1,000	Indiv
James A Rhodes & Associates	$1,000	Indiv
James Petropoulos Co Realtors	$1,000	Indiv
RJ Solove & Associates	$1,000	Indiv

Accountants	$2,000	
American Institute of CPA's	$1,000	PAC
Ernst & Young	$1,000	Indiv

Misc Finance	$3,000	
L Corp	$2,000	Indiv

Health $24,900

Health Professionals	$20,550	
American Physical Therapy Assn	$2,500	PAC
American Medical Assn	$2,350	PAC
American Dental Assn	$1,500	PAC
MA Bechtel MD Inc	$1,500	Indiv
American Academy of Ophthalmology	$1,000	PAC

Hospitals/Nursing Homes	$2,000	
None over $1,000		

Pharmaceuticals/Health Products	$1,600	
Abbott Laboratories	$1,600	PAC/Ind

Lawyers & Lobbyists $10,550

Lawyers & Lobbyists	$10,550	
Bricker & Eckler	$2,000	PAC
Chester, Hoffman et al	$1,600	Indiv
Baker & Hostetler	$1,500	PAC/Ind
Schottenstein, Zox & Dunn	$1,500	Indiv
Vorys, Sater et al	$1,250	PAC/Ind

Misc Business $41,100

Food & Beverage	$8,500	
Wendy's Corp	$3,000	Indiv
GD Ritzy's Inc	$1,750	Indiv
Chili's Inc	$1,000	PAC

Spending in Last 3 Elections

	1988	1990	1992
Kasich	$351,517	$278,977	$242,096
Opponent	$0	$47,815	$42,013
Vote Pct	79%	72%	71%

Retail Sales	$9,050	
The Limited Inc	$3,500	Indiv
Sun TV & Appliance Inc	$3,000	Indiv
Limited Inc	$1,000	PAC

Business Services	$2,500	
Leff Advertising & Public Relations	$1,250	Indiv
RD Zande & Assoc	$1,000	Indiv

Chemical & Related Manufacturing	$4,100	
Liqui-Box Corp	$1,000	Indiv
Yenkin Majestic Paint Co	$1,000	Indiv

Steel Production	$5,950	
Worthington Industries	$5,700	Indiv

Misc Manufacturing & Distributing	$8,700	
Stone Container Corp	$2,350	PAC
Kobacker Co	$2,000	Indiv
Russell T Bundy Assoc	$1,000	Indiv

Transportation $10,500

Air Transport	$1,500	
United Parcel Service	$1,250	PAC

Automotive	$8,500	
National Auto Dealers Assn	$6,500	PAC
Auto Dealers & Drivers for Free Trade	$1,500	PAC

Labor

Labor	$2,300	

Public Sector Unions	$2,300	
National Assn Retired Federal Employees	$2,000	PAC

Ideological/Single-Issue

Ideological/Single-Issue	$10,050	

Republican/Conservative	$1,000	
None over $1,000		

Foreign & Defense Policy	$1,000	
None over $1,000		

Pro-Israel	$5,500	
National PAC	$5,000	PAC

Gun Rights/Gun Control	$1,000	
National Rifle Assn	$1,000	PAC

Misc Issues	$1,550	
National Cmte to Preserve Social Security	$1,200	PAC

Other & Unknown

Other	$4,300	

Retired	$3,900	
None over $1,000		

Unknown	$31,350	
Homemakers/Non-income earners	$4,250	
No Employer Listed or Found	$10,250	
Employer Listed/Category Unknown	$16,850	
Ral Group Inc	$2,000	Indiv
Evans, Mechwart et al	$1,500	Indiv
Leveque Enterprises	$1,500	Indiv
Jomar Partnership	$1,000	Indiv
Waibel Electric Co	$1,000	Indiv

* Contributions came from more than one affiliate or subsidiary.

Joseph P. Kennedy II, D-Mass (8)

First elected: 1986
1991-92 Total Receipts: $769,635
1992 Year-end Cash: $228,528

1991-92 Committees & Subcommittees

Banking, Finance and Urban Affairs
Financial Institutions Supervision, Regulation and Insurance; Housing and Community Development; International Development, Finance, Trade and Monetary Policy

Veterans' Affairs
Hospitals and Health Care; Oversight and Investigations

Select Committee on Aging

Leading Contributors

Business

Agriculture	$3,900	
None over $2,000		

Communications/Electronics	$25,475	
Printing & Publishing	$2,300	
None over $2,000		
Media/Entertainment	$14,825	
EMI Records Group	$2,800	Indiv
Smith Broadcasting Group	$2,000	Indiv
Telephone Utilities	$3,950	
AT&T	$3,000	PAC
Computer Equipment & Services	$2,200	
Bolt, Beranek & Newman	$2,000	Indiv

Construction	$23,600	
General Contractors	$14,000	
JM Cashman Co	$5,000	Indiv
CRC Construction	$2,000	Indiv
Home Builders	$4,500	
None over $2,000		
Special Trade Contractors	$2,650	
None over $2,000		

Source of Funds in 1992 Election

Source	Total	Pct
PACs	$145,230	19%
Indivs $200+	$456,496	59%
Indivs under $200	$132,653	17%
Other	$35,393	5%
Candidate	$0	0%
Party	$287	0%

Source of PAC Dollars by Sector

Source	Total	Pct
Business	$55,125	39%
Labor	$81,075	57%
Ideology/Single Issue	$5,950	4%

In-State vs. Out-of-State Contributions*

Source	Total	Pct
In-State	$284,326	63%
Out-of-state	$169,320	37%
No state listed	$2,500	

* by large individual contributors ($200 & above)

Energy & Natural Resources	$22,525	
Oil & Gas	$3,275	
None over $2,000		
Misc Energy	$8,200	
Citizens Energy Corp	$6,650	Indiv
Environmental Svcs/Equipment	$7,300	
Thermo Electron Corp	$7,300	Indiv
Waste Management	$3,550	
None over $2,000		

Finance, Insurance & Real Estate	$133,036	
Commercial Banks	$12,475	
BankAmerica Corp	$2,000	Indiv
Securities & Investment	$32,150	
Bear, Stearns & Co	$5,450	Indiv
Chicago Mercantile Exchange	$5,325	PAC/Ind
Bostonian Group Inc	$2,250	Indiv
Insurance	$14,897	
None over $2,000		
Real Estate	$50,389	
National Assn of Realtors	$6,000	PAC
Melvin Simon & Associates	$4,000	Indiv
Beacon Companies	$3,750	Indiv
Corcoran, Jennison Co	$2,307	Indiv
Boston Financial Group	$2,250	Indiv
Telecu Industries	$2,000	Indiv
Accountants	$12,050	
Reznick, Fedder & Silverman	$3,000	Indiv
KPMG Peat Marwick	$2,250	Indiv
Morgan & Martindale CPAs	$2,000	Indiv
Misc Finance	$9,075	
First Winthrop Corp	$2,200	Indiv

Contribution Totals by Sector

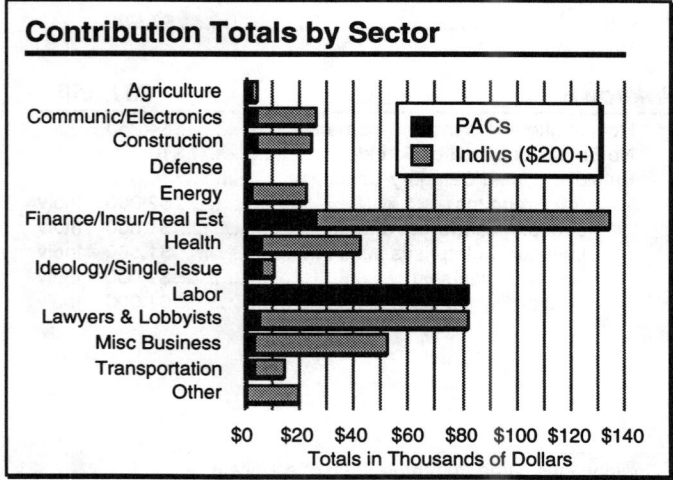

Agriculture, Communic/Electronics, Construction, Defense, Energy, Finance/Insur/Real Est, Health, Ideology/Single-Issue, Labor, Lawyers & Lobbyists, Misc Business, Transportation, Other

PACs
Indivs ($200+)

$0 $20 $40 $60 $80 $100 $120 $140
Totals in Thousands of Dollars

Health $41,525

Health Professionals **$12,475**
American Dental Assn ....$2,500   PAC

Hospitals/Nursing Homes **$12,250**
Continental Health Affiliates ....$3,000   Indiv

Health Services **$6,700**
Brester Ambulance Service ....$5,300   Indiv

Pharmaceuticals/Health Products **$4,500**
Amcare Medical Services ....$3,500   Indiv

Misc Health **$5,600**
None over $2,000

Lawyers & Lobbyists $82,521

Lawyers & Lobbyists **$82,521**
Cooley, Manion et al ....$10,650   Indiv
Morgan, Lewis & Bockius ....$5,000   Indiv
Crowe, Crowe & Vernaglia ....$3,000   Indiv
Connor & Hilliard ....$2,500   Indiv
Waite, Schneider et al ....$2,000   Indiv

Lobbyists/PR **$6,200**
None over $2,000

Misc Business $52,029

Food & Beverage **$7,400**
D'Angelo Sandwich Shop ....$2,325   Indiv
TS Enterprises ....$2,000   Indiv

Misc Services **$3,925**
Focus Leasing ....$2,325   Indiv

Business Services **$21,829**
McDermott, O'Neill & Associates ....$2,400   Indiv
Revmax Corp ....$2,200   Indiv
LTC Management ....$2,150   Indiv
Atlantic Advertising ....$2,000   Indiv

Lodging/Tourism **$4,050**
Beacon Hotel Corp ....$2,050   Indiv

Misc Manufacturing & Distributing **$2,675**
None over $2,000

Textiles **$4,200**
Korinos Village Embroidery ....$4,100   Indiv

Spending in Last 3 Elections

	1988	1990	1992
Kennedy	$1,186,852	$832,815	$768,393
Opponent	$17,288	$0	$0
Vote Pct	80%	72%	83%

Transportation $13,475

Air Transport **$3,275**
None over $2,000

Automotive **$9,050**
Rodman Ford Sales ....$3,750   Indiv
Tatone Buick ....$2,000   Indiv

Labor

Labor $81,075

Building Trade Unions **$20,750**
Ironworkers Union ....$8,750   PAC
Carpenters & Joiners Union ....$2,500   PAC
Operating Engineers Union ....$2,000   PAC
Plumbers/Pipefitters Union ....$2,000   PAC
Sheet Metal Workers Union ....$2,000   PAC

Industrial Unions **$18,700**
Intl Brotherhood of Electrical Workers ......$7,000   PAC
Machinists/Aerospace Workers Union ....$6,000   PAC
Communications Workers of America ....$3,500   PAC

Transportation Unions **$10,825**
Teamsters Union ....,.....................$2,500   PAC
International Longshoremen's Assn ....$2,300   PAC

Public Sector Unions **$18,100**
American Postal Workers Union ....$10,000   PAC
National Education Assn ....$3,200   PAC

Misc Unions **$12,700**
Food & Commercial Workers Union ....$7,500   PAC
Hotel/Restaurant Employees Union ....$5,000   PAC

Ideological/Single-Issue

Ideological/Single-Issue $10,675

Pro-Israel **$2,925**
None over $2,000

Human Rights **$4,750**
National Community Action Foundation ....$2,000   PAC

Other & Unknown

Other $19,107

Civil Servants/Public Officials **$6,625**
Registry of Motor Vehicle ....$2,000   Indiv

Education **$4,957**
None over $2,000

Retired **$3,475**
None over $2,000

Other **$2,250**
None over $2,000

Unknown $88,353

Homemakers/Non-income earners $4,180
No Employer Listed or Found $32,865
Employer Listed/Category Unknown $50,258
Casco Co ....$2,000   Indiv
DJL ....$2,000   Indiv

Barbara B. Kennelly, D-Conn (1)

First elected: 1982
1991-92 Total Receipts: $523,025
1992 Year-end Cash: $127,166

1991-92 Committees & Subcommittees

Ways and Means
Human Resources; Select Revenue Measures

Select Committee on Intelligence

Leading Contributors

Business

Agriculture	$14,650	
Tobacco	**$6,250**	
US Tobacco Co	$3,000	PAC
Philip Morris	$1,500	PAC
Food Processing & Sales	**$6,150**	
Food Marketing Institute	$2,000	PAC
Winn-Dixie Stores	$2,000	PAC
Forestry & Forest Products	**$2,000**	
Champion International Corp	$1,500	PAC

Communications/Electronics	$14,400	
Media/Entertainment	**$3,100**	
None over $1,500		
Telephone Utilities	**$9,200**	
AT&T	$3,600	PAC
GTE Corp	$2,150	PAC

Construction	$6,250	
General Contractors	**$1,750**	
None over $1,500		
Home Builders	**$4,200**	
National Assn of Home Builders	$3,500	PAC

Defense	$8,700	
Defense Aerospace	**$7,400**	
United Technologies	$4,100	PAC/Ind

Source of Funds in 1992 Election

	Source	Total	Pct
■	PACs	$335,981	63%
▨	Indivs $200+	$101,905	19%
□	Indivs under $200	$59,567	11%
▣	Other	$39,193	7%
	Candidate	$0	0%
	Party	$14,071	3%

Source of PAC Dollars by Sector

	Source	Total	Pct
■	Business	$272,058	82%
▨	Labor	$52,700	16%
□	Ideology/Single Issue	$8,841	3%

In-State vs. Out-of-State Contributions*

	Source	Total	Pct
□	In-State	$72,050	71%
■	Out-of-state	$29,555	29%
	No state listed	$0	

* by large individual contributors ($200 & above)

Energy & Natural Resources	$15,850	
Oil & Gas	**$6,550**	
Petroleum Marketers Assn	$2,100	PAC
Misc Energy	**$2,500**	
Combustion Engineering	$2,000	PAC
Electric Utilities	**$4,800**	
None over $1,500		

Finance, Insurance & Real Estate	$161,555	
Commercial Banks	**$9,100**	
Norstar Bancorp	$1,900	PAC
American Bankers Assn	$1,500	PAC
Credit Unions	**$4,000**	
Credit Union National Assn	$3,000	PAC
Finance/Credit Companies	**$2,000**	
None over $1,500		
Securities & Investment	**$13,050**	
Greenwich Capital Markets	$2,050	Indiv
National Venture Capital Assn	$2,000	PAC
Securities Industry Assn	$1,500	PAC
Insurance	**$111,305**	
Travelers Corp	$12,100	PAC/Ind
National Assn of Life Underwriters	$10,255	PAC/Ind
Aetna Life & Casualty	$8,650	PAC/Ind
American Council of Life Insurance	$8,000	PAC
ITT Corp*	$7,200	PAC
Cigna Corp	$6,500	PAC/Ind
Northwestern Mutual Life	$4,000	PAC
Health Insurance Assn of America	$3,000	PAC
Connecticut Mutual Life Insurance	$2,500	PAC
Management Compensation Group	$2,100	Indiv
American Family Corp	$2,000	PAC
American Insurance Assn	$2,000	PAC
Massachusetts Mutual Life Insurance ...	$2,000	PAC
Metropolitan Life Insurance	$2,000	PAC
Torchmark Corp	$2,000	PAC
Independent Insurance Agents of America	$1,800	PAC

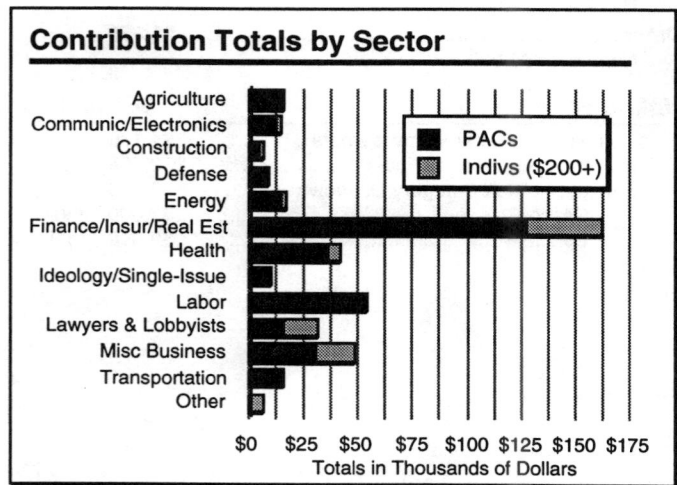

Contribution Totals by Sector

Legend: ■ PACs, ▨ Indivs ($200+)

Agriculture
Communic/Electronics
Construction
Defense
Energy
Finance/Insur/Real Est
Health
Ideology/Single-Issue
Labor
Lawyers & Lobbyists
Misc Business
Transportation
Other

$0 $25 $50 $75 $100 $125 $150 $175
Totals in Thousands of Dollars

Real Estate	....	$12,400	
National Assn of Realtors	....	$5,000	PAC
Accountants	....	**$8,400**	
American Institute of CPA's	....	$5,000	PAC
Coopers & Lybrand	....	$1,650	PAC

Health $40,400

Health Professionals	....	**$22,700**	
American Dental Assn	....	$10,000	PAC
American Medical Assn	....	$3,000	PAC
American Assn Oral & Maxillofacial Surgeons	....	$2,000	PAC
American College of Emergency Physicians	....	$2,000	PAC
Hospitals/Nursing Homes	....	**$8,100**	
American Hospital Assn	....	$2,000	PAC
Federation of American Health Systems	....	$1,500	PAC
Hughes Convalescent Hospital	....	$1,500	Indiv
Pharmaceuticals/Health Products	......	**$9,600**	
Pfizer Inc	....	$1,500	PAC

Lawyers & Lobbyists $30,375

Lawyers & Lobbyists	....	**$30,375**	
Assn of Trial Lawyers of America	....	$5,000	PAC
McClure, Trotter & Mentz	....	$4,000	Indiv
Verner, Liipfert et al	....	$2,375	PAC/Ind
Murtha, Cullina et al	....	$1,800	PAC/Ind

Misc Business $47,978

Beer, Wine & Liquor	....	**$13,600**	
Heublein Inc	....	$3,000	PAC
Smirnoff/Inglenook Distributors	....	$3,000	PAC
Wine & Spirits Wholesalers of America	....	$2,000	PAC
Hartford Distributors	....	$1,800	Indiv
Retail Sales	....	**$3,300**	
None over $1,500			
Misc Services	....	**$3,800**	
American Assn of Equipment Lessors	....	$2,500	PAC
Business Services	....	**$15,600**	
Pierce, Kennedy & Hearth	....	$7,300	Indiv
Advo-System Inc	....	$2,100	PAC

Misc Business	....	**$1,500**	
National Assn of Water Companies	....	$1,500	PAC
Chemical & Related Manufacturing	....	**$1,500**	
None over $1,500			
Misc Manufacturing & Distributing	....	**$6,100**	
Corning Glass Works	....	$2,500	PAC

Transportation $15,105

Air Transport	....	**$5,000**	
United Parcel Service	....	$4,000	PAC
Automotive	....	**$3,135**	
National Auto Dealers Assn	....	$2,100	PAC
Railroads	....	**$3,000**	
Union Pacific Corp	....	$1,500	PAC

Labor

Labor $52,700

Building Trade Unions	....	**$6,600**	
Laborers' Political League	....	$2,100	PAC
Carpenters Union/Connecticut	....	$1,500	PAC
Industrial Unions	....	**$10,700**	
Connecticut Union of Telephone Workers	....	$5,000	PAC
United Steelworkers	....	$2,500	PAC
Transportation Unions	....	**$11,850**	
Air Line Pilots Assn	....	$5,000	PAC
Teamsters Union	....	$2,500	PAC
Public Sector Unions	....	**$17,650**	
American Fedn of St/Cnty/Munic Employees	......	$5,000	PAC
National Education Assn	....	$4,150	PAC
National Assn of Letter Carriers	....	$2,500	PAC
National Assn Retired Federal Employees	....	$2,000	PAC
Misc Unions	....	**$5,900**	
Food & Commercial Workers Union	....	$2,000	PAC
Hotel/Restaurant Employees Union	....	$1,500	PAC

Ideological/Single-Issue

Ideological/Single-Issue $9,741

Democratic/Liberal	....	**$2,500**	
National Cmte for an Effective Congress	....	$2,500	PAC
Leadership PACs	....	**$1,510**	
None over $1,500			
Misc Issues	....	**$2,000**	
National Cmte to Preserve Social Security	....	$2,000	PAC

Other & Unknown

Other $6,100

| **Retired** | .... | **$4,500** | |
| None over $1,500 | | | |

Unknown $12,200

No Employer Listed or Found	....	$1,900	
Employer Listed/Category Unknown	....	$8,850	
None over $1,500			

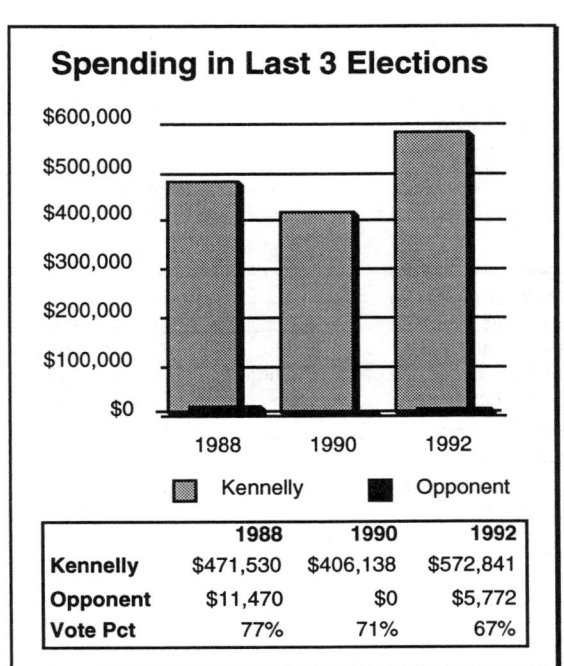

Spending in Last 3 Elections

	1988	1990	1992
Kennelly	$471,530	$406,138	$572,841
Opponent	$11,470	$0	$5,772
Vote Pct	77%	71%	67%

* Contributions came from more than one affiliate or
 subsidiary.

Dale E. Kildee, D-Mich (9)

First elected: 1976

1991-92 Total Receipts: $762,558
1992 Year-end Cash: $5,733

1991-92 Committees & Subcommittees

Administration
Elections; Office Systems

Budget
Economic Policy, Projections and Revenues (Chairman); Human Resources

Education and Labor
Elementary, Secondary and Vocational Education (Chairman); Human Resources; Labor-Management Relations; Postsecondary Education

Leading Contributors

Business

Agriculture	$28,810

Crop Production & Basic Processing	$10,810	
United States Sugar Corp	$3,500	PAC
Dairy	**$11,500**	
Associated Milk Producers	$8,000	PAC
Mid-America Dairymen	$3,000	PAC
Food Processing & Sales	**$2,500**	
None over $2,000		

Communications/Electronics	$24,060

Printing & Publishing	$3,050	
None over $2,000		
Media/Entertainment	**$6,000**	
National Assn of Broadcasters	$3,000	PAC
Telephone Utilities	**$12,010**	
Michigan Bell Telephone	$9,060	PAC
Computer Equipment & Services	**$2,000**	
Electronic Data Systems	$2,000	PAC

Construction	$3,770

General Contractors	$2,550
None over $2,000	

Source of Funds in 1992 Election

Source	Total	Pct
PACs	$463,805	59%
Indivs $200+	$100,773	13%
Indivs under $200	$138,238	18%
Other	$83,367	11%
Candidate	$40,000	5%
Party	$39,934	5%

Source of PAC Dollars by Sector

Source	Total	Pct
Business	$158,990	36%
Labor	$243,915	55%
Ideology/Single Issue	$43,832	10%

In-State vs. Out-of-State Contributions*

Source	Total	Pct
In-State	$77,932	77%
Out-of-state	$23,041	23%
No state listed	$0	

* by large individual contributors ($200 & above)

Energy & Natural Resources	$16,870

Oil & Gas	$7,500	
Michigan Consolidated Gas	$6,000	PAC
Electric Utilities	**$8,670**	
Detroit Edison	$4,610	PAC
Consumers Power Co	$3,050	PAC

Finance, Insurance & Real Estate	$34,380

Commercial Banks	$4,685	
None over $2,000		
Credit Unions	**$4,615**	
Michigan Credit Union League	$4,615	PAC
Insurance	**$18,500**	
Blue Cross & Blue Shield Assn*	$5,000	PAC
Prudential Insurance	$2,500	PAC
American Council of Life Insurance	$2,000	PAC
Accountants	**$2,000**	
American Institute of CPA's	$2,000	PAC

Health	$35,825

Health Professionals	$30,555	
American Medical Assn	$5,350	PAC
American Dental Assn	$2,500	PAC
American Assn Oral & Maxillofacial Surgeons	$2,000	PAC
American Podiatry Assn	$2,000	PAC
Hospitals/Nursing Homes	**$2,520**	
None over $2,000		
Pharmaceuticals/Health Products	**$2,000**	
None over $2,000		

Contribution Totals by Sector

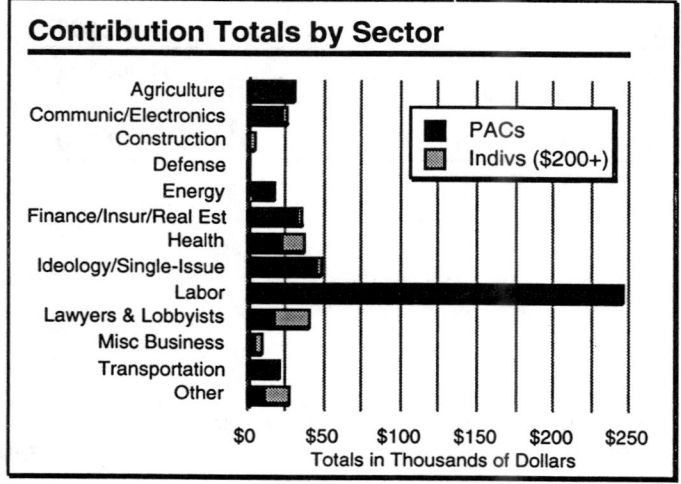

Agriculture
Communic/Electronics
Construction
Defense
Energy
Finance/Insur/Real Est
Health
Ideology/Single-Issue
Labor
Lawyers & Lobbyists
Misc Business
Transportation
Other

■ PACs
▨ Indivs ($200+)

$0 $50 $100 $150 $200 $250
Totals in Thousands of Dollars

Lawyers & Lobbyists $39,366

Lawyers & Lobbyists $39,366
Assn of Trial Lawyers of America	$10,000	PAC
Cassidy & Associates	$3,250	Indiv
Dow, Lohnes & Albertson	$2,250	PAC/Ind
Jarvis Co	$2,000	Indiv
Verner, Liipfert et al	$2,000	PAC/Ind

Misc Business $8,440

Food & Beverage $2,500
None over $2,000

Misc Manufacturing & Distributing $2,350
None over $2,000

Transportation $19,415

Automotive $17,790
Ford Motor Co	$6,940	PAC
Chrysler Corp	$6,610	PAC
General Motors	$3,770	PAC/Ind

Labor

Labor $244,135

Building Trade Unions $51,240
Carpenters & Joiners Union	$10,000	PAC
Laborers' Political League	$10,000	PAC
Plumbers/Pipefitters Union*	$8,300	PAC
Operating Engineers Union*	$5,500	PAC
Ironworkers Union	$5,000	PAC
Boilermakers Union local #169	$4,220	PAC
Sheet Metal Workers Union	$4,000	PAC
Bricklayers Union	$2,500	PAC

Industrial Unions $55,800
Intl Brotherhood of Electrical Workers	$10,000	PAC
United Auto Workers	$10,000	PAC
Rubber Cork Linoleum & Plastic Workers	$9,000	PAC
Communications Workers of America	$5,500	PAC
Machinists/Aerospace Workers Union	$5,000	PAC
United Mine Workers	$3,500	PAC
Amalgamated Clothing & Textile Workers	$2,500	PAC
Boilermakers Union	$2,000	PAC
Oil, Chemical & Atomic Workers Union	$2,000	PAC
United Steelworkers	$2,000	PAC

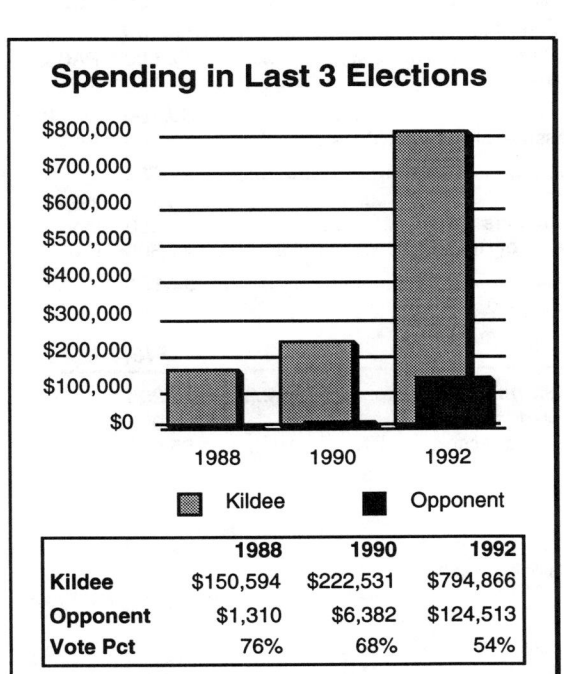

Spending in Last 3 Elections

	1988	1990	1992
Kildee	$150,594	$222,531	$794,866
Opponent	$1,310	$6,382	$124,513
Vote Pct	76%	68%	54%

Kildee   ▨   Opponent ■

Transportation Unions $40,170
Teamsters Union	$10,000	PAC
Air Line Pilots Assn	$8,500	PAC
Seafarers International Union	$6,000	PAC
United Transportation Union	$2,720	PAC
Trans Comm International Union	$2,700	PAC
Transport Workers Union	$2,500	PAC
Amalgamated Transit Union	$2,000	PAC
Marine Engineers Dist 2 Maritime Officers	$2,000	PAC

Public Sector Unions $71,075
American Federation of Teachers	$10,000	PAC
American Fedn of St/Cnty/Munic Employees	$10,000	PAC
American Postal Workers Union	$10,000	PAC
National Education Assn	$10,000	PAC
National Assn of Letter Carriers	$9,275	PAC
National Assn Retired Federal Employees	$8,000	PAC
National Assn of Postmasters	$5,500	PAC
International Assn of Firefighters	$2,550	PAC
National League of Postmasters	$2,000	PAC

Misc Unions $25,850
Food & Commercial Workers Union	$10,000	PAC
AFL-CIO	$5,250	PAC
Service Employees International Union	$5,000	PAC
Bakery, Confectionery & Tobacco Workers	$2,500	PAC

Ideological/Single-Issue

Ideological/Single-Issue $46,582

Democratic/Liberal $6,159
7th District Democratic Cmte	$5,159	PAC

Leadership PACs $4,500
None over $2,000

Pro-Israel $6,350
MOPAC	$2,500	PAC

Human Rights $12,600
KidsPAC	$8,100	PAC
National Community Action Foundation	$3,500	PAC

Misc Issues $15,450
National Cmte to Preserve Social Security	$7,500	PAC
Sierra Club	$4,850	PAC
National Council of Senior Citizens	$2,000	PAC

Other & Unknown

Other $28,010

Non-Profit Institutions $6,000
Mott Foundation	$4,000	Indiv

Education $17,750
National Assn Trade & Technical Schools	$7,500	PAC
Vocational PAC	$2,000	PAC

Retired $2,650
None over $2,000

Unknown $28,997
Homemakers/Non-income earners	$5,050	
No Employer Listed or Found	$8,550	
Generic Occupation/Category Unknown	$4,622	
Employer Listed/Category Unknown	$10,675	
MFO Co	$2,000	Indiv

---

* Contributions came from more than one affiliate or subsidiary.

Jay C. Kim, R-Calif (41)

1993-94 Committees & Subcommittees

Public Works and Transportation
Aviation; Economic Development; Surface Transportation

Small Business
Regulation, Business Opportunities and Technology

Leading Contributors

Business

Agriculture	$7,000

Food Processing & Sales **$4,000**
   None over $1,500

Communications/Electronics	$10,125

Telephone Utilities **$2,625**
   None over $1,500

Electronics Mfg & Services **$5,850**
   Ultimate Sound Int .... $3,200   Indiv

Construction	$21,650

General Contractors **$3,850**
   None over $1,500

Home Builders **$5,000**
   National Assn of Home Builders .... $5,000 PAC

Construction Services **$9,800**
   National Society of Professional Engineers .... $2,500 PAC

Building Materials & Equipment **$2,000**
   Pusan Steel Pipe Industries .... $2,000 Indiv

Defense	$2,750

Defense Aerospace **$1,750**
   None over $1,500

Energy & Natural Resources — $12,000

Oil & Gas **$5,000**
   None over $1,500

Electric Utilities **$3,000**
   Southern California Edison .... $3,000 PAC/Ind

Environmental Svcs/Equipment **$1,500**
   Montgomery Engineering .... $1,500 PAC

Waste Management **$2,000**
   Western Waste Industries .... $2,000 Indiv

Finance, Insurance & Real Estate — $45,700

Commercial Banks **$9,150**
   American Bankers Assn .... $2,500 PAC
   General Bank .... $1,800 Indiv

Insurance **$8,700**
   National Assn of Life Underwriters ...... $1,500 PAC

Real Estate **$21,750**
   Union Wide .... $5,750 Indiv
   Diamond Brothers .... $3,000 Indiv
   National Assn of Realtors .... $2,500 PAC

Accountants **$2,900**
   None over $1,500

Health — $48,195

Health Professionals **$45,295**
   American Medical Assn .... $10,000 PAC
   American Dental Assn .... $5,000 PAC

First elected: 1992

1991-92 Total Receipts: $735,483
1992 Year-end Cash: $28,312

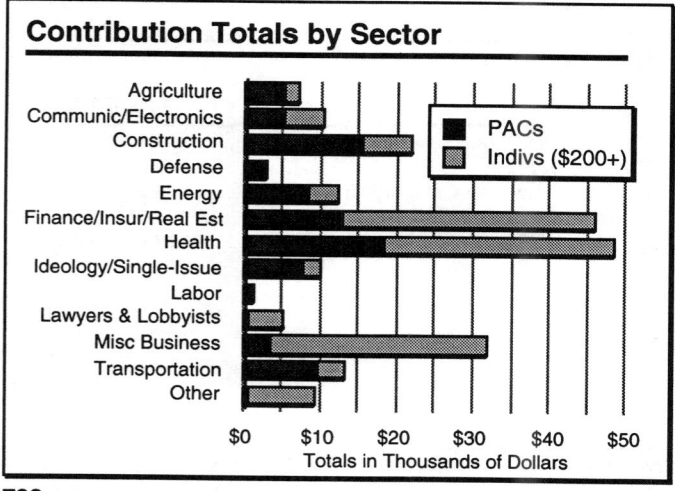

Contribution Totals by Sector

- Agriculture
- Communic/Electronics
- Construction
- Defense
- Energy
- Finance/Insur/Real Est
- Health
- Ideology/Single-Issue
- Labor
- Lawyers & Lobbyists
- Misc Business
- Transportation
- Other

■ PACs
▨ Indivs ($200+)

$0 $10 $20 $30 $40 $50
Totals in Thousands of Dollars

Lawyers & Lobbyists	$4,800

Lawyers & Lobbyists $4,800
  None over $1,000

Misc Business	$31,650

Food & Beverage $1,800
  None over $1,500

Beer, Wine & Liquor $5,050
  Foothill Beverage Co .... $2,000   Indiv

Retail Sales $7,350
  None over $1,500

Business Services $1,550
  None over $1,500

Lodging/Tourism $2,000
  None over $1,500

Misc Business $5,000
  None over $1,500

Misc Manufacturing & Distributing $5,350
  Overseas Packing Co .... $2,000   Indiv

Transportation	$12,900

Air Transport $2,000
  None over $1,500

Automotive $8,400
  National Auto Dealers Assn .... $5,000   PAC

Ideological/Single-Issue

Ideological/Single-Issue	$9,774

Republican/Conservative $3,074
  Lincoln Club of Orange County .... $2,500   PAC

Pro-Israel $1,500
  None over $1,500

Misc Issues $3,450
  Korean American Senior Citizen Assn .... $1,700   Indiv

Other & Unknown

Other	$9,205

Education $1,900
  None over $1,500

Retired $6,305
  None over $1,500

Unknown	$192,640

  Homemakers/Non-income earners $12,102
  No Employer Listed or Found $106,110
  Generic Occupation/Category Unknown $28,200
  Employer Listed/Category Unknown $46,228
    None over $1,500

Independent expenditures supporting Kim
  California Medical Assn $2,500

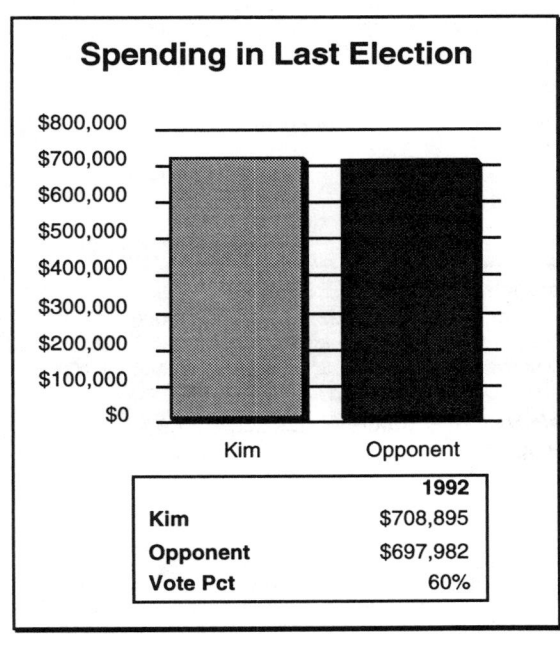

Spending in Last Election

	1992
Kim	$708,895
Opponent	$697,982
Vote Pct	60%

Peter T. King, R-NY (3)

1993-94 Committees & Subcommittees

First elected: 1992
1991-92 Total Receipts: $244,526
1992 Year-end Cash: $8,079

Banking, Finance and Urban Affairs
Consumer Credit and Insurance; Economic Growth and Credit Formation; International Development, Finance, Trade and Monetary Policy

Merchant Marine and Fisheries
Coast Guard and Navigation; Merchant Marine

Veteran's Affairs
Compensation, Pension and Insurance

Leading Contributors

Business

Agriculture		$4,900
Tobacco	**$2,500**	
RJR Nabisco	$2,000	PAC
Food Processing & Sales	**$1,900**	
Pepsico Inc	$1,000	PAC

Communications/Electronics		$4,692
Telephone Utilities	**$3,192**	
New York Telephone	$1,192	PAC
AT&T	$1,000	PAC
United Telecommunications	$1,000	PAC
Electronics Mfg & Services	**$1,000**	
Harris Corp	$1,000	PAC

Construction		$4,350
General Contractors	**$2,500**	
Benjamin Development Corp	$1,000	Indiv
Structure Tone Inc	$1,000	Indiv
Special Trade Contractors	**$1,550**	
Mathew's Industrial Piping Inc	$1,300	Indiv

Energy & Natural Resources		$6,550
Oil & Gas	**$5,650**	
Columbia Gas System*	$1,000	PAC

Source of Funds in 1992 Election

Source	Total	Pct
■ PACs	$117,550	39%
▨ Indivs $200+	$78,401	26%
☐ Indivs under $200	$43,901	15%
▨ Other	$58,981	20%
Candidate	$0	0%
Party	$58,981	20%

Source of PAC Dollars by Sector

Source	Total	Pct
■ Business	$64,587	66%
▨ Labor	$9,800	10%
☐ Ideology/Single Issue	$23,700	24%

In-State vs. Out-of-State Contributions*

Source	Total	Pct
☐ In-State	$62,101	88%
■ Out-of-state	$8,600	12%
No state listed	$7,700	

* by large individual contributors ($200 & above)

Finance, Insurance & Real Estate		$25,650
Commercial Banks	**$2,200**	
Chase Manhattan	$2,000	PAC
Credit Unions	**$2,000**	
Credit Union National Assn	$2,000	PAC
Securities & Investment	**$8,700**	
Morgan Stanley & Co	$3,000	PAC/Ind
Chicago Mercantile Exchange	$1,500	PAC
Cumberland Associates	$1,000	Indiv
Furman Selz Inc	$1,000	Indiv
Insurance	**$6,500**	
National Assn of Life Underwriters	$1,500	PAC
Casualty & Surety Agents Assn	$1,000	PAC
Health Insurance Assn of America	$1,000	PAC
Real Estate	**$2,500**	
Mack Companies	$2,000	Indiv
Accountants	**$2,750**	
American Institute of CPA's	$2,500	PAC
Misc Finance	**$1,000**	
None over $1,000		

Health		$15,050
Health Professionals	**$12,800**	
American Medical Assn	$5,000	PAC
American Academy of Ophthalmology ...	$4,000	PAC
American Optometric Assn	$2,500	PAC
Cmte for Quality Orthopedic Health Care ...	$1,000	PAC
Pharmaceuticals/Health Products ...	**$1,500**	
Schering-Plough Corp	$1,000	PAC

Contribution Totals by Sector

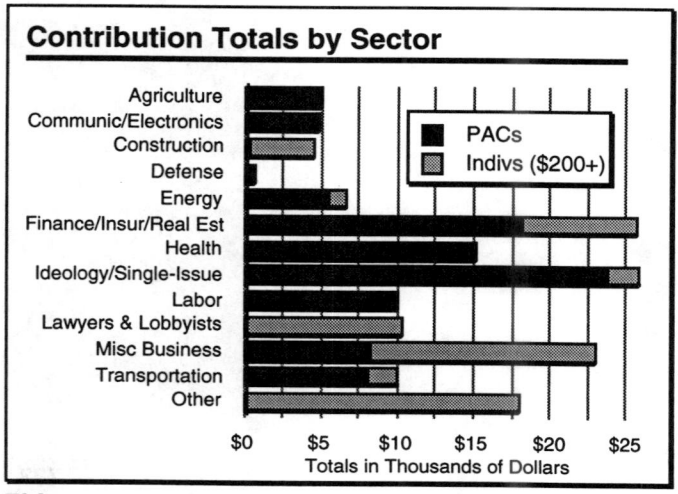

- Agriculture
- Communic/Electronics
- Construction
- Defense
- Energy
- Finance/Insur/Real Est
- Health
- Ideology/Single-Issue
- Labor
- Lawyers & Lobbyists
- Misc Business
- Transportation
- Other

■ PACs
▨ Indivs ($200+)

$0 $5 $10 $15 $20 $25
Totals in Thousands of Dollars

Lawyers & Lobbyists — $10,150

Lawyers & Lobbyists **$10,150**
    Colleran, O'Hara & Mills .... $4,000   Indiv
    Gardner, Carton & Douglas .... $1,000   Indiv
    O'Dwyer & Bernstein .... $1,000   Indiv

Misc Business — $23,710

Business Associations **$1,045**
    Business Industry PAC .... $1,045   PAC

Food & Beverage **$2,765**
    None over $1,000

Beer, Wine & Liquor **$3,000**
    National Beer Wholesalers Assn .... $3,000   PAC

Retail Sales **$7,300**
    Fortunoff's Inc .... $5,000   Indiv

Business Services **$3,750**
    Carpat Investments .... $2,000   Indiv

Misc Manufacturing & Distributing **$4,750**
    Estee Lauder Inc .... $3,000   Indiv
    Stone Container Corp .... $1,500   PAC

Transportation — $9,900

Air Transport **$2,800**
    United Parcel Service .... $1,800   PAC
    General Electric .... $1,000   PAC

Automotive **$2,300**
    Auto Dealers & Drivers for Free Trade .... $2,000   PAC

Railroads **$2,500**
    Union Pacific Corp .... $2,000   PAC

Sea Transport **$2,300**
    Apex Marine Corp .... $1,000   Indiv
    Liberty Maritime Corp .... $1,000   Indiv

Labor

Labor — $9,800

Transportation Unions **$4,800**
    Marine Engineers Union* .... $3,000   PAC
    Brotherhood of Locomotive Engineers .... $1,500   PAC

Public Sector Unions **$5,000**
    American Fedn of St/Cnty/Munic Employees ...... $5,000   PAC

Ideological/Single-Issue

Ideological/Single-Issue — $25,700

Republican/Conservative **$4,550**
    Mid-America Conservative PAC .... $4,250   PAC

Leadership PACs **$12,200**
    New Frontier Leadership PAC (Norman Lent) ... $10,000   PAC
    New Majority Leadership PAC (Vin Weber) .... $1,000   PAC
    Republican Leader's Fund (Bob Michel) .... $1,000   PAC

Pro-Israel **$3,000**
    National PAC .... $1,000   PAC

Pro-Life **$1,000**
    National Right to Life PAC .... $1,000   PAC

Gun Rights/Gun Control **$4,950**
    National Rifle Assn .... $4,950   PAC

Other & Unknown

Other — $17,826

Civil Servants/Public Officials **$10,750**
    Town of Oyster Bay .... $2,700   Indiv
    Town of Hempstead .... $2,550   Indiv
    Kings Cty District Attorney's Office .... $2,000   Indiv
    Nassau County Police Department .... $2,000   Indiv

Retired **$6,576**
    None over $1,000

Unknown — $17,710

    No Employer Listed or Found $10,110
    Employer Listed/Category Unknown $6,150
        Deforest & Dyer .... $1,000   Indiv
        Gem Elevator Co .... $1,000   Indiv

Independent expenditures supporting King
    National Right to Life PAC $6,229

Spending in Last Election

	1992
King	$263,345
Opponent	$1,127,239
Vote Pct	50%

---

* Contributions came from more than one affiliate or subsidiary.

Jack Kingston, R-Ga (1)

First elected: 1992

1991-92 Total Receipts: $439,846
1992 Year-end Cash: $20,963

1993-94 Committees & Subcommittees

Agriculture
Department Operations and Nutrition; Specialty Crops and Natural Resources

Merchant Marine and Fisheries
Fisheries Management; Merchant Marine

Leading Contributors

Business

Agriculture $28,450

Crop Production & Basic Processing **$7,450**
  Savannah Foods .... $2,700   Indiv
Poultry & Eggs **$3,500**
  None over $1,500
Food Processing & Sales **$10,300**
  Flowers Industries .... $7,000   PAC
  Claxton Bakery .... $1,500   Indiv
Forestry & Forest Products **$4,700**
  Union Camp Corp .... $1,750   PAC/Ind

Communications/Electronics $6,450

Telephone Utilities **$4,500**
  Southern Bell .... $1,500   PAC

Construction $8,100

General Contractors **$2,950**
  None over $1,500
Building Materials & Equipment **$3,250**
  Bradley Plywood Co .... $2,300   Indiv

Energy & Natural Resources $15,750

Oil & Gas **$8,350**
  Colonial Oil Industries Inc .... $2,250   Indiv
Misc Energy **$3,000**
  Cooper Industries .... $3,000   PAC
Electric Utilities **$3,450**
  Georgia Power Co .... $3,450   PAC/Ind

Source of Funds in 1992 Election

Source	Total	Pct
■ PACs	$113,985	25%
▨ Indivs $200+	$202,893	44%
☐ Indivs under $200	$101,787	22%
▧ Other	$46,181	10%
Candidate	$0	0%
Party	$31,000	7%

Source of PAC Dollars by Sector

Source	Total	Pct
■ Business	$105,551	86%
▨ Labor	$0	0%
☐ Ideology/Single Issue	$16,857	14%

In-State vs. Out-of-State Contributions*

Source	Total	Pct
☐ In-State	$196,893	98%
■ Out-of-state	$5,000	2%
No state listed	$500	

* by large individual contributors ($200 & above)

Finance, Insurance & Real Estate $65,240

Commercial Banks **$8,300**
  American Bankers Assn .... $2,000   PAC
Securities & Investment **$6,750**
  None over $1,500
Insurance **$36,320**
  Palmer & Cay Carswell Insurance .... $7,050   Indiv
  Casualty & Surety Agents Assn .... $5,000   PAC
  Independent Insurance Agents of America ... $3,500   PAC
  National Assn of Life Underwriters .... $2,000   PAC
Real Estate **$6,400**
  National Assn of Realtors .... $2,500   PAC
Accountants **$4,810**
  American Institute of CPA's .... $2,500   PAC
Misc Finance **$2,200**
  None over $1,500

Health $53,352

Health Professionals **$51,302**
  American Medical Assn .... $9,700   PAC
  Clark Eye Clinic .... $4,000   Indiv
  American Dental Assn .... $3,000   PAC
  Coastal Internal Medicine .... $2,500   Indiv
  Savannah Plastic Surgery .... $2,500   Indiv
  Neurological Institute of Savannah .... $1,800   Indiv

Lawyers & Lobbyists $9,375

Lawyers & Lobbyists **$9,375**
  Morris & Morris Attorneys .... $2,000   Indiv

Contribution Totals by Sector

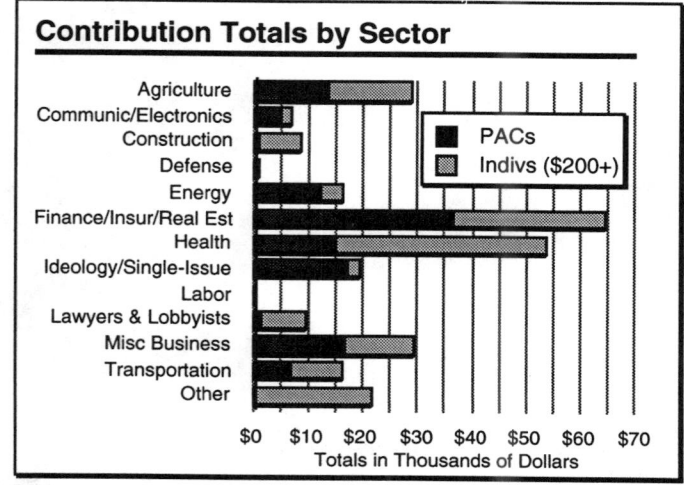

- Agriculture
- Communic/Electronics
- Construction
- Defense
- Energy
- Finance/Insur/Real Est
- Health
- Ideology/Single-Issue
- Labor
- Lawyers & Lobbyists
- Misc Business
- Transportation
- Other

■ PACs
▨ Indivs ($200+)

$0 $10 $20 $30 $40 $50 $60 $70
Totals in Thousands of Dollars

Misc Business $28,849

Business Associations **$1,500**
National Fedn of Independent Business .... $1,500 PAC

Food & Beverage **$4,200**
None over $1,500

Beer, Wine & Liquor **$3,900**
None over $1,500

Retail Sales **$5,050**
Gibson, McDonald Furniture .... $1,800 Indiv

Misc Manufacturing & Distributing **$9,548**
Stone Container Corp .... $5,000 PAC
Carson Products Co .... $2,750 Indiv

Transportation $15,911

Air Transport **$4,250**
United Parcel Service .... $4,000 PAC

Automotive **$8,261**
JC Lewis Motors .... $3,061 Indiv
National Auto Dealers Assn .... $2,000 PAC

Railroads **$1,500**
Sandersville Railroad Co .... $1,500 Indiv

Ideological/Single-Issue

Ideological/Single-Issue $19,107

Republican/Conservative **$8,687**
Eagle Forum .... $5,121 PAC
V-PAC .... $1,542 PAC

Pro-Life **$7,000**
Republican National Coalition for Life .... $4,000 PAC
Right to Life* .... $3,000 PAC

Misc Issues **$2,500**
None over $1,500

Other & Unknown

Other $21,450

Civil Servants/Public Officials **$2,500**
None over $1,500

Retired **$16,250**
None over $1,500

Other **$1,550**
None over $1,500

Unknown $53,267

Homemakers/Non-income earners $5,900
No Employer Listed or Found $3,750
Employer Listed/Category Unknown $42,617
Jepson Industries .... $2,000 Indiv
Luzon Group .... $2,000 Indiv
Archibalds .... $1,500 Indiv
Blount, Glass & Assoc .... $1,500 Indiv
Dale Critz Inc .... $1,500 Indiv
Newer Dimensions .... $1,500 Indiv

Independent expenditures supporting Kingston
National Right to Life PAC $5,267

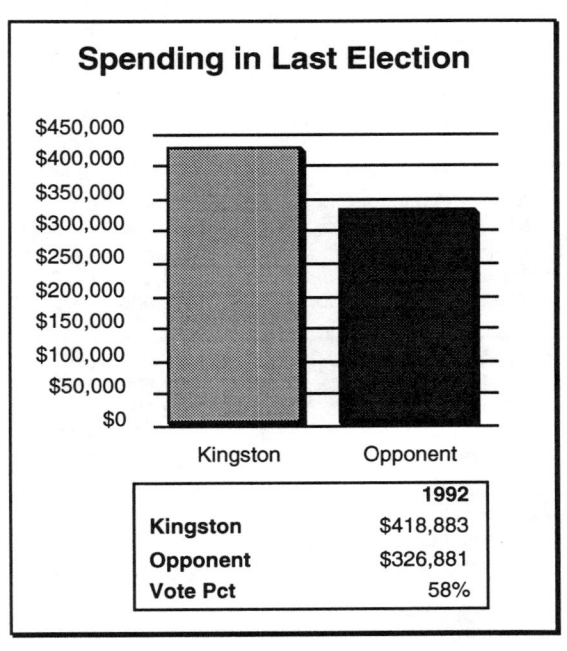

Spending in Last Election

	1992
Kingston	$418,883
Opponent	$326,881
Vote Pct	58%

* Contributions came from more than one affiliate or
  subsidiary.

Gerald D. Kleczka, D-Wis (4)

First elected: 1984
1991-92 Total Receipts: $334,070
1992 Year-end Cash: $76,093

1991-92 Committees & Subcommittees

Administration
Personnel and Police; Campaign Finance Reform Task Force

Banking, Finance and Urban Affairs
Financial Institutions Supervision, Regulation and Insurance; Housing and Community Development; International Development, Finance, Trade and Monetary Policy

Government Operations
Government Activities and Transportation; Legislation and National Security

Joint Committee on Printing

Leading Contributors

Business

Agriculture		$10,650
Crop Production & Basic Processing		$1,000
American Sugarbeet Growers Assn	$1,000	PAC
Tobacco		$3,000
Philip Morris	$1,000	PAC
RJR Nabisco	$1,000	PAC
Dairy		$5,000
Associated Milk Producers	$4,000	PAC
Mid-America Dairymen	$1,000	PAC

Communications/Electronics		$5,500
Telephone Utilities		$5,500
Ameritech Corp*	$2,750	PAC
AT&T	$1,000	PAC

Construction		$7,611
General Contractors		$2,361
None over $1,000		
Home Builders		$3,250
National Assn of Home Builders	$2,000	PAC
Manufactured Housing Institute	$1,000	PAC
Special Trade Contractors		$1,000
None over $1,000		
Construction Services		$1,000
Donohue & Associates	$1,000	PAC

Source of Funds in 1992 Election

Source	Total	Pct
PACs	$203,707	58%
Indivs $200+	$51,033	15%
Indivs under $200	$52,969	15%
Other	$41,699	12%
Candidate	$0	0%
Party	$15,888	5%

Source of PAC Dollars by Sector

Source	Total	Pct
Business	$128,707	61%
Labor	$75,800	36%
Ideology/Single Issue	$5,500	3%

In-State vs. Out-of-State Contributions*

Source	Total	Pct
In-State	$29,233	58%
Out-of-state	$21,600	42%
No state listed	$200	

* by large individual contributors ($200 & above)

Energy & Natural Resources — $6,600

Electric Utilities		$2,550
Wisconsin Electric Power Co	$1,250	PAC
ACRE (Action Cmte for Rural Electrification)	$1,000	PAC
Waste Management		$3,050
Waste Management Inc	$2,250	PAC/Ind

Finance, Insurance & Real Estate — $69,750

Commercial Banks		$13,350
American Bankers Assn	$4,000	PAC
Banc One Corp	$2,400	PAC
Independent Bankers Assn	$1,500	PAC
Norwest Corp	$1,500	PAC
First Wisconsin Corp	$1,450	PAC
Barnett Banks Inc	$1,000	PAC
Savings & Loans		$6,000
First Financial Savings	$1,700	PAC
National Council of Savings Institutions	$1,000	PAC
Security Savings & Loan	$1,000	Indiv
Securities & Investment		$11,200
Goldman, Sachs & Co	$3,500	PAC
First Boston Corp	$1,500	PAC
Morgan Stanley & Co	$1,000	PAC
PaineWebber	$1,000	PAC
Insurance		$14,550
Northwestern Mutual Life	$5,000	PAC
American Council of Life Insurance	$2,500	PAC
National Assn of Life Underwriters	$2,000	PAC
ITT Corp*	$1,500	PAC
Mortgage Insurance Companies of America	$1,500	PAC
Real Estate		$13,900
National Assn of Realtors	$10,000	PAC
Dhaliwal Enterprises Inc	$2,000	Indiv
Federal National Mortgage Assn	$1,000	PAC

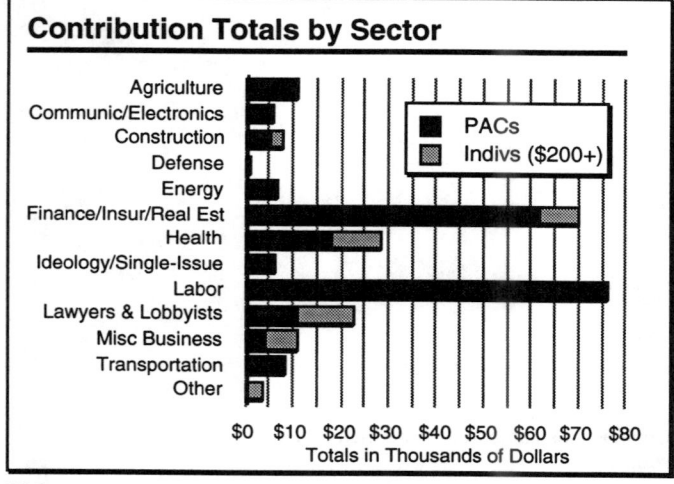

Contribution Totals by Sector

Legend: PACs; Indivs ($200+)

Categories: Agriculture, Communic/Electronics, Construction, Defense, Energy, Finance/Insur/Real Est, Health, Ideology/Single-Issue, Labor, Lawyers & Lobbyists, Misc Business, Transportation, Other

$0 $10 $20 $30 $40 $50 $60 $70 $80
Totals in Thousands of Dollars

Accountants	....	$9,000	
American Institute of CPA's	....	$7,000	PAC
Ernst & Young	....	$1,000	PAC

Misc Finance	....	$1,250	
MGIC Investment Corp	....	$1,250	Indiv

Health $27,750

Health Professionals	....	$22,250	
American Medical Assn	....	$3,350	PAC
American Optometric Assn	....	$2,500	PAC
American Assn of Nurse Anesthetists	......	$1,500	PAC
American Dental Assn	....	$1,500	PAC
American Academy of Ophthalmology	......	$1,000	PAC
American Chiropractic Assn	....	$1,000	PAC
American College of Emergency Physicians	......	$1,000	PAC

Hospitals/Nursing Homes	....	$3,700	
American Health Care Assn	....	$1,700	PAC
American Hospital Assn	....	$1,500	PAC

Pharmaceuticals/Health Products	......	$1,500	
ICN Pharmaceuticals	....	$1,000	Indiv

Lawyers & Lobbyists $22,461

Lawyers & Lobbyists	....	$22,461	
Assn of Trial Lawyers of America	......	$10,000	PAC
Broydrick & Associates	....	$2,000	Indiv
Fontheim & O'Rourke	....	$2,000	Indiv
Royer, Mehle & Babyak	....	$1,500	Indiv
Winburn & Associates	....	$1,500	Indiv
Campbell-Raupe Inc	....	$1,000	Indiv
Waterman & Associates	....	$1,000	Indiv

Misc Business $10,307

Food & Beverage	....	$1,000	
Pepsi-Cola General Bottlers	....	$1,000	PAC

Beer, Wine & Liquor	....	$1,000	
National Beer Wholesalers Assn	....	$1,000	PAC

Business Services	....	$2,250	
Zeppos, Remsick & Mueller	....	$1,000	Indiv

Misc Manufacturing & Distributing	......	$4,300	
SC Johnson & Son Inc	....	$3,000	Indiv

Transportation $8,150

Air Transport	....	$2,800	
United Parcel Service	....	$1,500	PAC

Automotive	....	$4,250	
National Auto Dealers Assn	....	$3,000	PAC
Auto Dealers & Drivers for Free Trade	......	$1,000	PAC

Labor

Labor $75,800

Building Trade Unions	....	$12,500	
Laborers Union*	....	$5,500	PAC
Carpenters & Joiners Union	....	$3,000	PAC
Sheet Metal Workers Union	....	$2,500	PAC
Operating Engineers Union	....	$1,000	PAC

Industrial Unions	....	$23,100	
United Auto Workers	....	$9,000	PAC
Machinists/Aerospace Workers Union	......	$6,000	PAC
United Steelworkers	....	$2,000	PAC
United Mine Workers	....	$1,500	PAC
AFL-CIO Allied Industrial Workers*	......	$1,050	PAC
Boilermakers Union	....	$1,000	PAC
Communications Workers of America	......	$1,000	PAC
Electronic Machine Furniture Workers	......	$1,000	PAC

Transportation Unions	....	$19,100	
Teamsters Union	....	$10,000	PAC
Air Line Pilots Assn	....	$5,000	PAC
United Transportation Union	....	$1,600	PAC
Amalgamated Transit Union	....	$1,000	PAC

Public Sector Unions	....	$17,700	
National Education Assn	....	$6,500	PAC
National Assn of Letter Carriers	....	$3,000	PAC
National Assn Retired Federal Employees	......	$2,000	PAC
American Fedn of St/Cnty/Munic Employees	......	$1,500	PAC
National Assn of Postmasters	....	$1,200	PAC
American Postal Workers Union	....	$1,000	PAC
National League of Postmasters	....	$1,000	PAC

Misc Unions	....	$3,400	
Food & Commercial Workers Union	......	$1,500	PAC

Ideological/Single-Issue

Ideological/Single-Issue $6,000

Democratic/Liberal	....	$3,000	
National Cmte for an Effective Congress	......	$2,500	PAC

Misc Issues	....	$3,000	
National Cmte to Preserve Social Security	......	$3,000	PAC

Other & Unknown

Other $3,500

Non-Profit Institutions	....	$1,000	
Foundation for Hearing Aid Research	......	$1,000	Indiv

Retired	....	$2,500	
None over $1,000			

Unknown $6,311

Homemakers/Non-income earners	....	$1,300	
Generic Occupation/Category Unknown	......	$2,150	
Employer Listed/Category Unknown	......	$2,361	
MRM Services Inc	....	$1,000	Indiv

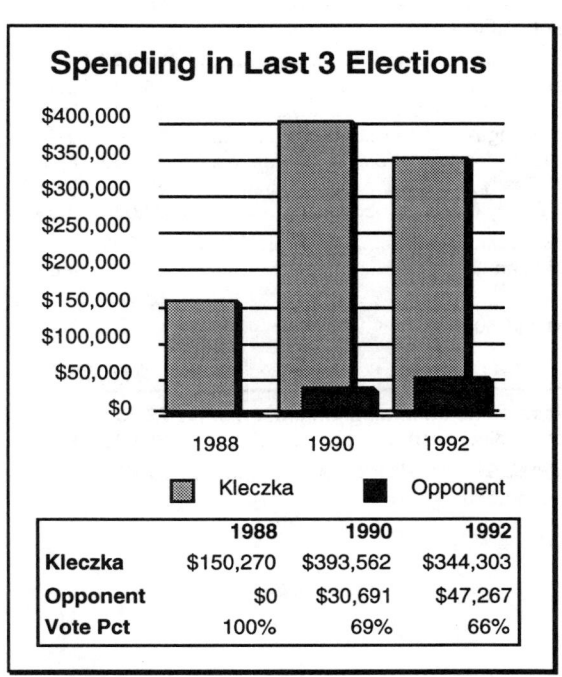

Spending in Last 3 Elections

	1988	1990	1992
Kleczka	$150,270	$393,562	$344,303
Opponent	$0	$30,691	$47,267
Vote Pct	100%	69%	66%

*Contributions came from more than one affiliate or subsidiary.

Herbert C. Klein, D-NJ (8)

First elected: 1992

1991-92 Total Receipts: $1,291,518
1992 Year-end Cash: $56,646

1993-94 Committees & Subcommittees

Banking, Finance and Urban Affairs
Economic Growth and Credit Formation; Financial Institutions Supervision, Regulation and Deposit Insurance; Housing and Community Development

Science, Space and Technology
Energy; Technology, Environment and Aviation

Leading Contributors

Business

Agriculture — $4,500

Food Processing & Sales $2,000
  None over $1,500

Forestry & Forest Products $1,500
  None over $1,500

Communications/Electronics — $10,600

Telephone Utilities $3,500
  AT&T .... $1,500 PAC
  New Jersey Bell Telephone .... $1,500 PAC

Telecom Services & Equipment $1,500
  Gemini Industries Inc .... $1,500 Indiv

Computer Equipment & Services $3,750
  None over $1,500

Construction — $10,600

General Contractors $1,500
  None over $1,500

Home Builders $1,500
  None over $1,500

Special Trade Contractors $1,800
  None over $1,500

Building Materials & Equipment $5,500
  Thermwell Products Co .... $2,500 Indiv
  New Thermal Corp .... $2,000 Indiv

Energy & Natural Resources — $2,300

Electric Utilities $2,300
  Public Service Electric & Gas .... $2,000 PAC

Source of Funds in 1992 Election

Source	Total	Pct
PACs	$173,920	13%
Indivs $200+	$236,117	18%
Indivs under $200	$187,017	14%
Other	$698,388	54%
Candidate	$639,000	49%
Party	$9,074	1%

Source of PAC Dollars by Sector

Source	Total	Pct
Business	$46,450	35%
Labor	$70,150	53%
Ideology/Single Issue	$16,547	12%

In-State vs. Out-of-State Contributions*

Source	Total	Pct
In-State	$212,867	90%
Out-of-state	$23,250	10%
No state listed	$0	

* by large individual contributors ($200 & above)

Finance, Insurance & Real Estate — $87,450

Commercial Banks $5,750
  American Bankers Assn* .... $3,000 PAC

Savings & Loans $2,000
  SAPEC, NJ (NJ Savings Assn) .... $2,000 PAC

Credit Unions $1,500
  None over $1,500

Securities & Investment $13,350
  JB Hanauer & Co .... $3,000 Indiv
  Smith Barney .... $3,000 Indiv
  Goldman, Sachs & Co .... $1,500 PAC/Ind

Insurance $7,000
  None over $1,500

Real Estate $45,300
  Hekemian & Co .... $18,000 Indiv
  National Assn of Realtors .... $5,000 PAC
  Edison Parking Associates .... $4,000 Indiv
  Square Industries .... $4,000 Indiv
  Monarch Realty .... $2,000 Indiv
  Point 88 Realty Co .... $2,000 Indiv

Accountants $7,800
  BDO Seidman .... $3,000 Indiv

Misc Finance $4,750
  None over $1,500

Health — $16,000

Health Professionals $12,750
  American Medical Assn .... $5,000 PAC

Pharmaceuticals/Health Products $1,950
  None over $1,500

Contribution Totals by Sector

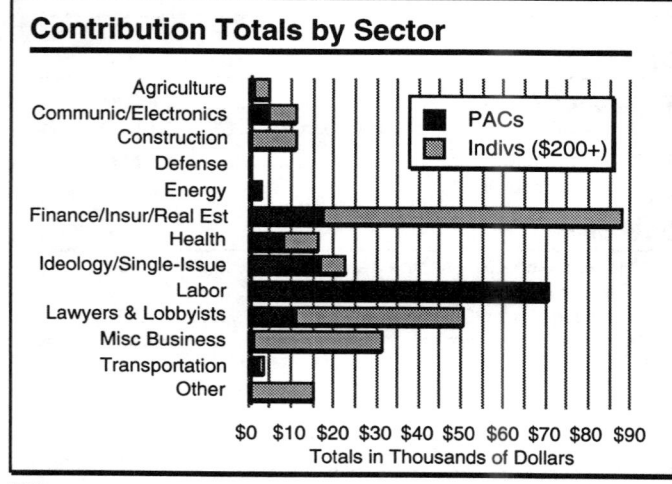

Legend: PACs, Indivs ($200+)

Categories: Agriculture, Communic/Electronics, Construction, Defense, Energy, Finance/Insur/Real Est, Health, Ideology/Single-Issue, Labor, Lawyers & Lobbyists, Misc Business, Transportation, Other

$0 $10 $20 $30 $40 $50 $60 $70 $80 $90
Totals in Thousands of Dollars

Lawyers & Lobbyists $49,792

Lawyers & Lobbyists **$49,792**
Assn of Trial Lawyers of America ....$10,000 PAC
Klein, Chapman et al ....$6,000 Indiv
Sills, Cummis et al ....$4,350 Indiv
Lynch, Martin Esqs ....$4,000 Indiv
Carella, Byrne et al ....$2,500 Indiv
Garrubbo, Dorian & Romankow ....$2,000 Indiv
Genova, Burns & Schott ....$2,000 Indiv
Taub & Taub ....$2,000 Indiv
Lowenstein, Sandler et al ....$1,500 Indiv

Misc Business $31,050

Food & Beverage **$2,000**
None over $1,500
Retail Sales **$5,550**
Shoes Plus ....$2,000 Indiv
Business Services **$2,500**
None over $1,500
Recreation/Live Entertainment **$4,000**
New Jersey Nets ....$4,000 Indiv
Lodging/Tourism **$2,000**
None over $1,500
Misc Business **$2,250**
C Goodman & Co ....$1,500 Indiv
Chemical & Related Manufacturing **$4,000**
Chemical Corp of America ....$3,000 Indiv
Misc Manufacturing & Distributing **$4,750**
None over $1,500
Textiles **$1,500**
Brawer Brothers Inc ....$1,500 Indiv

Transportation $3,350

None over $1,500

Spending in Last Election

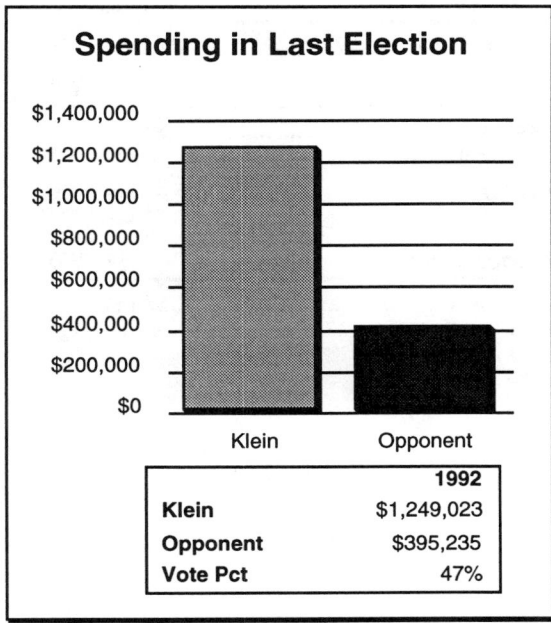

	1992
Klein	$1,249,023
Opponent	$395,235
Vote Pct	47%

Labor

Labor $70,150

Building Trade Unions **$20,200**
Operating Engineers Union* ....$5,600 PAC
Laborers' Political League ....$5,500 PAC
Carpenters & Joiners Union ....$5,000 PAC
Sheet Metal Workers Union ....$2,500 PAC
Industrial Unions **$23,650**
United Auto Workers ....$10,000 PAC
Electronic Machine Furniture Workers ....$3,900 PAC
Communications Workers of America ....$1,500 PAC
Electrical Radio & Machine Workers ....$1,500 PAC
Machinists/Aerospace Workers Union ....$1,500 PAC
Transportation Unions **$11,750**
Seafarers International Union ....$2,500 PAC
Marine Engineers Dist 2 Maritime Officers ....$1,500 PAC
Transport Workers Union ....$1,500 PAC
Public Sector Unions **$11,550**
American Fedn of St/Cnty/Munic Employees ...$5,000 PAC
National Assn of Letter Carriers ....$2,500 PAC
National Assn Retired Federal Employees ....$2,000 PAC
International Assn of Firefighters ....$1,500 PAC
Misc Unions **$3,000**
AFL-CIO ....$1,500 PAC

Ideological/Single-Issue

Ideological/Single-Issue $22,297

Democratic/Liberal **$3,500**
National Cmte for an Effective Congress ....$2,500 PAC
Leadership PACs **$2,500**
None over $1,500
Pro-Israel **$10,500**
None over $1,500
Gun Rights/Gun Control **$4,547**
Handgun Control Inc ....$4,547 PAC

Other & Unknown

Other $14,700

Civil Servants/Public Officials **$2,000**
Environmental Protection Agency ....$2,000 Indiv
Retired **$11,350**
None over $1,500

Unknown $46,575

Homemakers/Non-income earners $13,100
Generic Occupation/Category Unknown $3,750
Employer Listed/Category Unknown $28,850
Langan Engineering ....$1,500 Indiv
Rabinowitz & Co ....$1,500 Indiv

---

* Contributions came from more than one affiliate or
subsidiary.

Ron Klink, D-Pa (4)

1993-94 Committees & Subcommittees

Banking, Finance and Urban Affairs
Economic Growth and Credit Formation

Education and Labor
Labor-Management Relations; Postsecondary Education and Training

Small Business
Procurement, Taxation and Tourism; SBA Legislation and the General Economy

Leading Contributors

Business

Communications/Electronics	$6,700	
Telephone Utilities	**$5,300**	
AT&T	$5,000	PAC
Electronics Mfg & Services	**$1,000**	
Westinghouse Electric	$1,000	PAC

Construction	$3,000	
Home Builders	**$1,000**	
National Assn of Home Builders	$1,000	PAC
Special Trade Contractors	**$1,000**	
Bruce & Merriless	$1,000	Indiv
Building Materials & Equipment	**$1,000**	
Latrobe Construction Co	$1,000	Indiv

Defense	$4,000	
Defense Aerospace	**$2,500**	
Rockwell International	$1,000	PAC
Misc Defense	**$1,000**	
Foundation Health Corp	$1,000	PAC

Energy & Natural Resources	$6,350	
Oil & Gas	**$4,150**	
Sun Co	$1,000	PAC

First elected: 1992

1991-92 Total Receipts:	$422,391
1992 Year-end Cash:	$2,497

Source of Funds in 1992 Election

Source	Total	Pct
PACs	$131,047	31%
Indivs $200+	$36,228	9%
Indivs under $200	$113,115	27%
Other	$144,157	34%
Candidate	$112,458	26%
Party	$6,883	2%

Source of PAC Dollars by Sector

Source	Total	Pct
Business	$38,300	29%
Labor	$88,800	68%
Ideology/Single Issue	$3,000	2%

In-State vs. Out-of-State Contributions*

Source	Total	Pct
In-State	$29,153	89%
Out-of-state	$3,700	11%
No state listed	$2,375	

* by large individual contributors ($200 & above)

Finance, Insurance & Real Estate	$12,340	
Commercial Banks	**$1,750**	
American Bankers Assn	$1,000	PAC
Securities & Investment	**$2,000**	
Russell, Rea & Zappala	$1,500	PAC
Insurance	**$4,050**	
Golden Rule Insurance Co	$1,000	Indiv
National Assn of Life Underwriters	$1,000	PAC
Real Estate	**$3,700**	
National Assn of Realtors	$3,000	PAC

Misc Business	$4,200	
Food & Beverage	**$2,350**	
Dagwoods Restaurant	$1,000	Indiv

Health	$6,700	
Health Professionals	**$4,200**	
American Medical Assn	$2,000	PAC
Hospitals/Nursing Homes	**$1,750**	
American Hospital Assn	$1,000	PAC

Lawyers & Lobbyists	$8,050	
Lawyers & Lobbyists	**$8,050**	
Kirkpatrick & Lockhart	$3,000	PAC

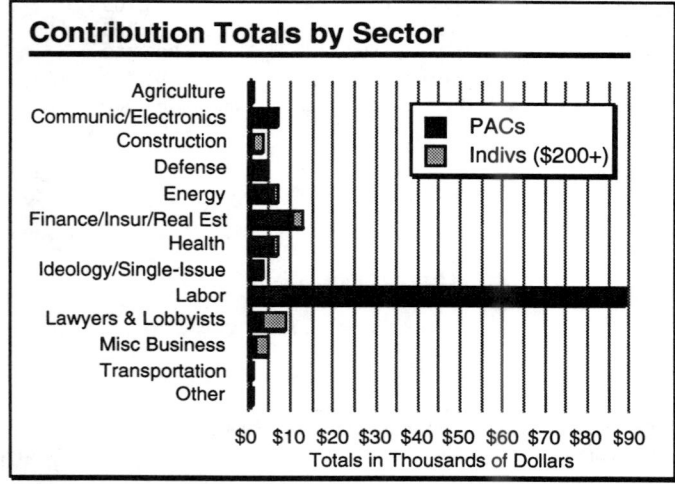

Contribution Totals by Sector

- Agriculture
- Communic/Electronics
- Construction
- Defense
- Energy
- Finance/Insur/Real Est
- Health
- Ideology/Single-Issue
- Labor
- Lawyers & Lobbyists
- Misc Business
- Transportation
- Other

■ PACs
▒ Indivs ($200+)

$0 $10 $20 $30 $40 $50 $60 $70 $80 $90
Totals in Thousands of Dollars

Labor

Labor	$88,800

Building Trade Unions $12,750
- Carpenters & Joiners Union ....$5,000   PAC
- Laborers' Political League ....$2,750   PAC
- Plumbers/Pipefitters Union* ....$2,500   PAC
- Operating Engineers Union ....$2,000   PAC

Industrial Unions $36,000
- Communications Workers of America* .....$7,000   PAC
- Electronic Machine Furniture Workers .....$5,000   PAC
- Intl Brotherhood of Electrical Workers .....$5,000   PAC
- Machinists/Aerospace Workers Union ....$5,000   PAC
- United Auto Workers ....$5,000   PAC
- United Steelworkers ....$5,000   PAC
- United Mine Workers ....$2,500   PAC
- Boilermakers Union ....$1,000   PAC

Transportation Unions $12,250
- Teamsters Union ....$5,000   PAC
- Air Line Pilots Assn ....$2,500   PAC
- Transport Workers Union ....$1,500   PAC
- Maintenance of Way Employees ....$1,000   PAC
- United Transportation Union ....$1,000   PAC

Public Sector Unions $21,500
- National Education Assn ....$10,000   PAC
- National Assn of Letter Carriers ....$4,000   PAC
- American Fedn of St/Cnty/Munic Employees ......$3,500   PAC
- International Assn of Firefighters ....$1,000   PAC
- National Assn Retired Federal Employees ....$1,000   PAC
- National Rural Letter Carriers Assn ......$1,000   PAC
- Postal Workers Union/Pittsburgh ....$1,000   PAC

Misc Unions $6,300
- Food & Commercial Workers Union ......$2,500   PAC
- Service Employees International Union ...$2,000   PAC
- Office & Professional Employees Union ..$1,000   PAC

Ideological/Single-Issue

Ideological/Single-Issue	$3,200

Leadership PACs $3,000
- Effective Government Cmte (Dick Gephardt) ......$1,000   PAC
- House Leadership Fund (Tom Foley) .....$1,000   PAC
- Victory USA (Vic Fazio) ....$1,000   PAC

Other & Unknown

Unknown	$19,788

- Homemakers/Non-income earners $1,950
- No Employer Listed or Found $11,600
- Employer Listed/Category Unknown $5,488
  - Rufus Inc ....$1,088   Indiv
  - Video House ....$1,000   Indiv

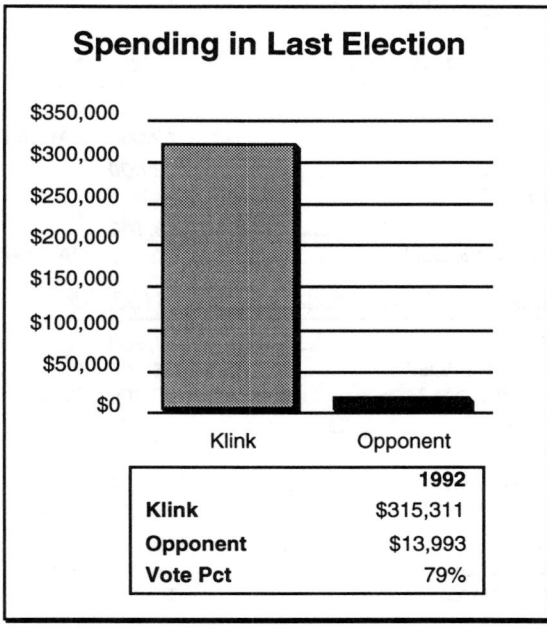

Spending in Last Election

	1992
Klink	$315,311
Opponent	$13,993
Vote Pct	79%

---

* Contributions came from more than one affiliate or subsidiary.

Scott L. Klug, R-Wis (2)

First elected: 1990

1991-92 Total Receipts: $879,091
1992 Year-end Cash: $57,373

1991-92 Committees & Subcommittees

Education and Labor
Elementary, Secondary and Vocational Education; Postsecondary Education; Select Education

Government Operations
Environment, Energy and Natural Resources; Government Activities and Transportation

Select Committee on Children, Youth and Families

Leading Contributors

Business

Agriculture	$41,064	
Crop Production & Basic Processing	**$5,528**	
Cargill Inc	$2,500	PAC
Tobacco	**$3,200**	
None over $2,000		
Dairy	**$11,025**	
Associated Milk Producers	$7,500	PAC
Mid-America Dairymen	$2,100	PAC
Agricultural Services/Products	**$3,250**	
Deere & Co	$2,000	PAC
Food Processing & Sales	**$10,211**	
Food Marketing Institute	$2,550	PAC
Fleming Companies Inc	$2,000	PAC
Forestry & Forest Products	**$6,200**	
None over $2,000		

Communications/Electronics	$31,300	
Printing & Publishing	**$5,550**	
None over $2,000		
Media/Entertainment	**$6,750**	
None over $2,000		
Telephone Utilities	**$14,900**	
Ameritech Corp*	$5,200	PAC
AT&T	$3,500	PAC
United Telecommunications	$3,000	PAC
Electronics Mfg & Services	**$4,100**	
None over $2,000		

Source of Funds in 1992 Election

Source	Total	Pct
PACs	$223,966	24%
Indivs $200+	$301,150	33%
Indivs under $200	$311,971	34%
Other	$82,596	9%
Candidate	$0	0%
Party	$62,120	7%

Source of PAC Dollars by Sector

Source	Total	Pct
Business	$221,154	97%
Labor	$1,500	1%
Ideology/Single Issue	$5,130	2%

In-State vs. Out-of-State Contributions*

Source	Total	Pct
In-State	$279,246	93%
Out-of-state	$21,100	7%
No state listed	$0	

* by large individual contributors ($200 & above)

Construction	$41,757	
General Contractors	**$17,491**	
Associated General Contractors	$3,000	PAC
Edward Kraemer & Sons Inc	$2,988	Indiv
Marshall Erdman & Associates	$2,700	Indiv
Home Builders	**$14,048**	
National Assn of Home Builders	$11,000	PAC
Special Trade Contractors	**$4,050**	
National Electrical Contractors Assn	$2,000	PAC
Construction Services	**$2,000**	
None over $2,000		
Building Materials & Equipment	**$4,168**	
None over $2,000		

Energy & Natural Resources	$22,361	
Oil & Gas	**$13,861**	
Koch Industries	$2,000	PAC/Ind
Mining	**$2,000**	
None over $2,000		
Electric Utilities	**$5,100**	
Wisconsin Power & Light	$2,550	PAC/Ind

Finance, Insurance & Real Estate	$103,484	
Commercial Banks	**$21,798**	
American Bankers Assn*	$8,300	PAC
Independent Bankers Assn	$2,400	PAC
Savings & Loans	**$2,150**	
None over $2,000		
Securities & Investment	**$13,920**	
Blunt, Ellis & Loewi	$5,277	Indiv
Insurance	**$28,176**	
National Assn of Life Underwriters	$6,000	PAC
Northwestern Mutual Life	$3,000	PAC

Contribution Totals by Sector

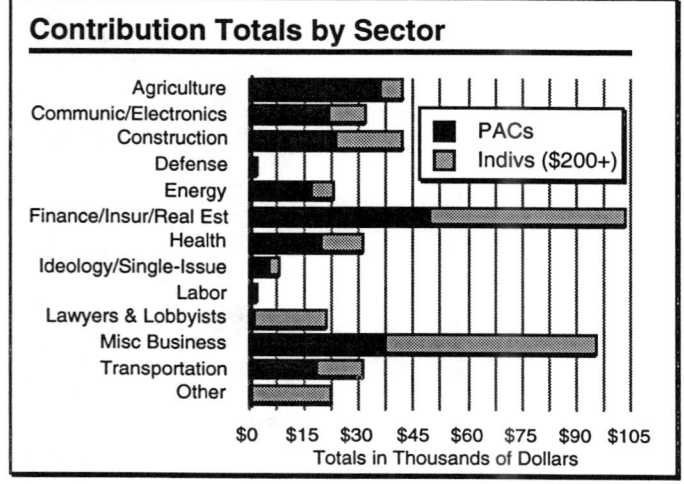

Agriculture, Communic/Electronics, Construction, Defense, Energy, Finance/Insur/Real Est, Health, Ideology/Single-Issue, Labor, Lawyers & Lobbyists, Misc Business, Transportation, Other

- PACs
- Indivs ($200+)

$0 $15 $30 $45 $60 $75 $90 $105
Totals in Thousands of Dollars

Real Estate $28,590
  National Assn of Realtors .... $9,440 PAC
  Century 21 Real Estate .... $2,000 PAC

Accountants $4,150
  American Institute of CPA's .... $2,000 PAC

Misc Finance $2,950
  None over $2,000

Health $30,760

Health Professionals $21,860
  American Medical Assn .... $10,000 PAC

Hospitals/Nursing Homes $2,200
  None over $2,000

Pharmaceuticals/Health Products $3,000
  None over $2,000

Misc Health $3,700
  None over $2,000

Lawyers & Lobbyists $20,295

Lawyers & Lobbyists $20,295
  Mohs, MacDonald & Widder .... $4,500 Indiv
  Foley & Lardner .... $2,500 Indiv

Misc Business $94,583

Business Associations $5,091
  National Fedn of Independent Business .... $2,500 PAC

Food & Beverage $17,460
  Pizza Hut Inc .... $7,518 Indiv
  National Restaurant Assn .... $5,000 PAC

Beer, Wine & Liquor $11,125
  National Beer Wholesalers Assn .... $6,900 PAC
  H&M Distributing Co .... $3,600 Indiv

Retail Sales $13,836
  Land's End Inc .... $3,886 Indiv

Misc Services $2,951
  None over $2,000

Business Services $6,400
  None over $2,000

Recreation/Live Entertainment $3,200
  None over $2,000

Misc Business $4,000
  Conney Safety Products Co .... $2,150 Indiv

Chemical & Related Manufacturing $9,135
  Dow Chemical .... $3,500 PAC
  WT Rogers Co .... $2,085 Indiv

Steel Production $2,000
  Milwaukee Valve Co .... $2,000 Indiv

Misc Manufacturing & Distributing $16,050
  SC Johnson & Son Inc .... $3,000 Indiv
  Penda Corp .... $2,250 Indiv
  Acme Equipment Corp .... $2,000 Indiv

Transportation $30,573

Automotive $22,031
  National Auto Dealers Assn .... $3,500 PAC
  Nelson Industries Inc .... $3,266 Indiv
  Ahrens Cadillac .... $2,000 Indiv
  Americans for Free International Trade .... $2,000 PAC
  Eaton Corp .... $2,000 PAC
  Zimbrick Inc .... $2,000 Indiv

Trucking $3,267
  None over $2,000

Railroads $2,700
  None over $2,000

Ideological/Single-Issue

Ideological/Single-Issue $7,780

Pro-Israel $3,500
  None over $2,000

Other & Unknown

Other $22,040

Civil Servants/Public Officials $7,373
  State of Wisconsin .... $6,538 Indiv

Education $3,617
  None over $2,000

Retired $10,050
  None over $2,000

Unknown $79,133

  Homemakers/Non-income earners $16,092
  Generic Occupation/Category Unknown $3,479
  Employer Listed/Category Unknown $58,966
    None over $2,000

Independent expenditures supporting Klug
  American Medical Assn $80,968

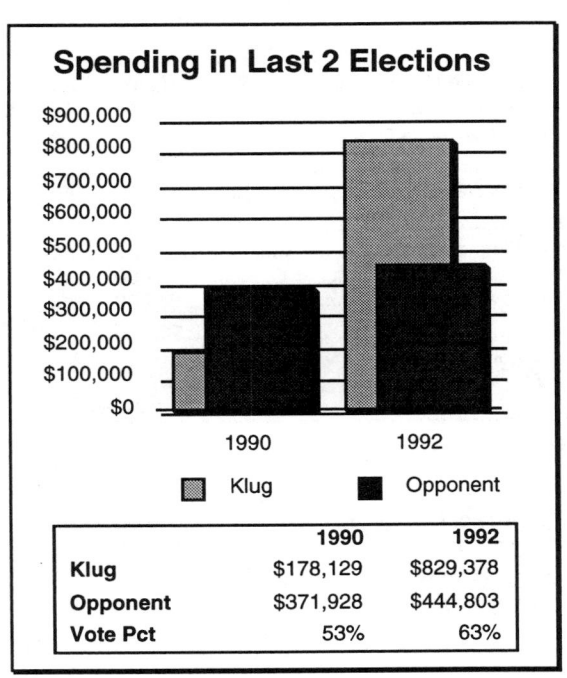

Spending in Last 2 Elections

	1990	1992
Klug	$178,129	$829,378
Opponent	$371,928	$444,803
Vote Pct	53%	63%

Klug   Opponent

---

* Contributions came from more than one affiliate or subsidiary.

Joseph K. Knollenberg, R-Mich (11)

First elected: 1992

1991-92 Total Receipts:	$476,906
1992 Year-end Cash:	$4,058

1993-94 Committees & Subcommittees

Banking, Finance and Urban Affairs
Consumer Credit and Insurance; Housing and Community Development

Small Business
Minority Enterprise, Finance and Urban Development; Procurement, Taxation and Tourism

Leading Contributors

Business

Agriculture		$4,750
Dairy		**$1,500**
None over $1,500		
Food Processing & Sales		**$2,000**
None over $1,500		

Communications/Electronics		$7,000
Telephone Utilities		**$3,000**
Michigan Bell Telephone	$2,000	PAC
Computer Equipment & Services		**$2,500**
DP Corporate Services Inc	$2,000	Indiv

Construction		$15,405
General Contractors		**$3,200**
None over $1,500		
Home Builders		**$4,900**
Robert R Jones Assoc Inc	$2,000	Indiv
National Assn of Home Builders	$1,500	PAC
Special Trade Contractors		**$2,250**
None over $1,500		
Building Materials & Equipment		**$4,500**
Intraco Corp	$3,500	Indiv

Defense		$1,500
Defense Aerospace		**$1,500**
None over $1,500		

Source of Funds in 1992 Election

Source	Total	Pct
■ PACs	$117,436	23%
▨ Indivs $200+	$184,146	36%
□ Indivs under $200	$139,695	27%
▧ Other	$66,841	13%
Candidate	$29,511	6%
Party	$34,245	7%

Source of PAC Dollars by Sector

Source	Total	Pct
■ Business	$104,540	90%
▨ Labor	$1,600	1%
□ Ideology/Single Issue	$9,724	8%

In-State vs. Out-of-State Contributions*

Source	Total	Pct
□ In-State	$174,396	95%
■ Out-of-state	$8,550	5%
No state listed	$700	

by large individual contributors ($200 & above)

Energy & Natural Resources		$12,650
Oil & Gas		**$6,950**
Michigan Consolidated Gas	$3,000	PAC
Electric Utilities		**$5,200**
Detroit Edison	$2,850	PAC/Ind

Finance, Insurance & Real Estate		$67,453
Commercial Banks		**$8,390**
Comerica Inc	$2,000	PAC
Fidelity Bank	$2,000	Indiv
Securities & Investment		**$1,750**
None over $1,500		
Insurance		**$35,138**
National Assn of Life Underwriters	$10,000	PAC
Allstate Insurance	$5,154	PAC/Ind
Flavay-Counihan Insurance	$3,884	Indiv
Real Estate		**$7,450**
National Assn of Realtors	$5,000	PAC
Accountants		**$9,825**
American Institute of CPA's	$5,000	PAC
Schellenberg & Associates	$2,000	Indiv
Follmer, Rudzewicz & Co	$1,500	Indiv
Misc Finance		**$2,900**
None over $1,500		

Health		$33,466
Health Professionals		**$29,400**
American Medical Assn	$5,000	PAC
American Academy of Ophthalmology	$4,000	PAC
American College of Emergency Physicians	$2,000	PAC
American Dental Assn	$2,000	PAC
Hospitals/Nursing Homes		**$2,566**
St Joseph Mercy Hospital	$2,066	Indiv

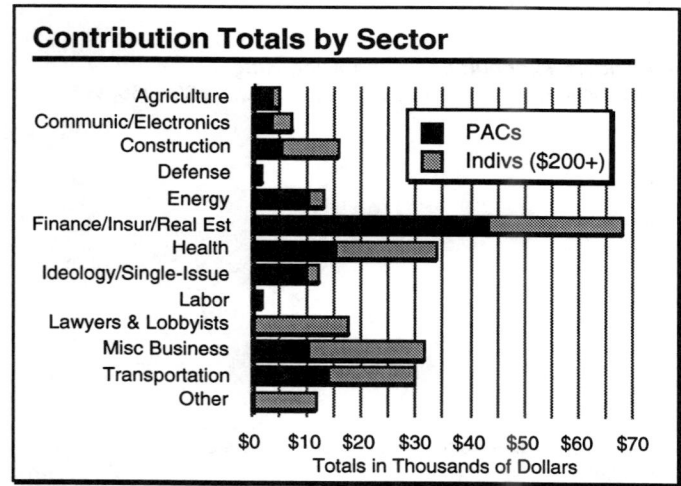

Contribution Totals by Sector

Legend: ■ PACs ▨ Indivs ($200+)

Categories: Agriculture, Communic/Electronics, Construction, Defense, Energy, Finance/Insur/Real Est, Health, Ideology/Single-Issue, Labor, Lawyers & Lobbyists, Misc Business, Transportation, Other

Totals in Thousands of Dollars ($0 $10 $20 $30 $40 $50 $60 $70)

Lawyers & Lobbyists $17,037

Lawyers & Lobbyists *$17,037*
    Basile & Hanlon ....$2,000   Indiv

Misc Business $31,100

Food & Beverage *$1,750*
    None over $1,500

Beer, Wine & Liquor *$3,750*
    Decanter Imports Inc ....$2,000   Indiv

Retail Sales *$3,050*
    None over $1,500

Misc Services *$2,250*
    Thayer-Rock Funeral Homes ....$2,000   Indiv

Business Services *$4,950*
    Helm Advertising ....$2,000   Indiv

Chemical & Related Manufacturing *$1,900*
    None over $1,500

Misc Manufacturing & Distributing *$13,000*
    Particle Measuring Systems Inc ....$5,250   Indiv
    Stone Container Corp ....$3,000   PAC
    Invetech Co ....$2,000   Indiv

Transportation $29,572

Automotive *$23,872*
    National Auto Dealers Assn ....$4,000   PAC
    Ford Motor Co ....$3,060   PAC/Ind
    General Motors ....$3,000   PAC
    Eaton Corp ....$2,200   PAC/Ind
    Budd Co ....$2,000   PAC
    Suburban Motors Co ....$2,000   Indiv
    Bill Cook Buick Inc ....$1,662   Indiv

Misc Transport *$4,000*
    Great Lakes Export Co ....$4,000   Indiv

Labor

Labor $1,600

Public Sector Unions *$1,500*
    None over $1,500

Ideological/Single-Issue

Ideological/Single-Issue $11,634

Foreign & Defense Policy *$3,660*
    Arab American-Caldean Council ....$1,660   Indiv

Pro-Life *$5,718*
    Right to Life* ....$5,718   PAC

Other & Unknown

Other $11,600

Education *$2,450*
    None over $1,500

Retired *$8,450*
    None over $1,500

Unknown $55,243

    Homemakers/Non-income earners $15,026
    No Employer Listed or Found $5,300
    Employer Listed/Category Unknown $34,117
        Tek ....$2,000   Indiv
        Wilkie & Co................................$2,000   Indiv
        Burns Aerospace ....$1,500   Indiv
        Yntema, Wood & Co ....$1,500   Indiv

Independent expenditures supporting Knollenberg
    Right to Life/Michigan $6,930
    National Right to Life PAC $2,960

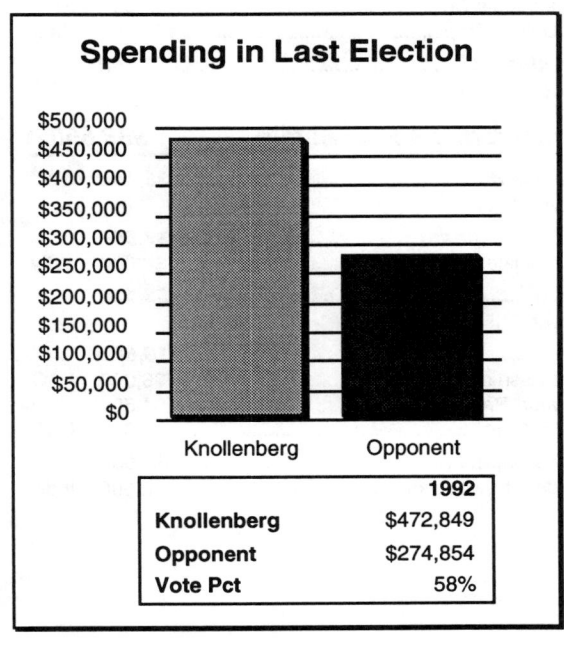

Spending in Last Election

	1992
Knollenberg	$472,849
Opponent	$274,854
Vote Pct	58%

---

* Contributions came from more than one affiliate or
subsidiary.

Jim Kolbe, R-Ariz (5)

First elected: 1984

1991-92 Total Receipts: $409,883
1992 Year-end Cash: $21,918

1991-92 Committees & Subcommittees

Appropriations
Commerce, Justice, State, the Judiciary and Related Agencies

Budget
Human Resources; Urgent Fiscal Issues

Leading Contributors

Business

Agriculture	$30,050	
Crop Production & Basic Processing	**$6,100**	
Sunkist Growers	$1,500	PAC
Livestock	**$14,150**	
National Cattlemen's Assn*	$1,500	PAC
Agricultural Services/Products	**$2,550**	
Salt River Valley Water Users	$1,800	PAC
Food Processing & Sales	**$3,100**	
None over $1,500		
Forestry & Forest Products	**$2,250**	
None over $1,500		

Communications/Electronics	$7,500	
Media/Entertainment	**$2,300**	
None over $1,500		
Telephone Utilities	**$5,200**	
US West Inc	$3,100	PAC

Construction	$14,850	
General Contractors	**$9,400**	
Sundt Corp	$3,400	Indiv
Associated General Contractors	$2,500	PAC
Special Trade Contractors	**$3,700**	
National Electrical Contractors Assn	$2,000	PAC

Source of Funds in 1992 Election

Source	Total	Pct
■ PACs	$143,400	35%
▨ Indivs $200+	$134,393	33%
□ Indivs under $200	$113,976	28%
▩ Other	$18,114	4%
Candidate	$0	0%
Party	$6,516	2%

Source of PAC Dollars by Sector

Source	Total	Pct
■ Business	$126,700	91%
▨ Labor	$2,750	2%
□ Ideology/Single Issue	$9,500	7%

In-State vs. Out-of-State Contributions*

Source	Total	Pct
□ In-State	$122,943	91%
■ Out-of-state	$11,450	9%
No state listed	$0	

* by large individual contributors ($200 & above)

Defense	$21,250	
Defense Aerospace	**$10,000**	
General Motors	$1,500	PAC
Defense Electronics	**$10,250**	
Hughes Aircraft	$3,000	PAC
AT&T	$2,500	PAC

Energy & Natural Resources	$14,050	
Oil & Gas	**$6,050**	
El Paso Co	$1,500	PAC
Southwest Gas Corp	$1,500	PAC
Mining	**$5,250**	
Cyprus Minerals Co	$2,000	PAC
Phelps Dodge Corp	$2,000	PAC
Electric Utilities	**$2,750**	
None over $1,500		

Finance, Insurance & Real Estate	$38,650	
Commercial Banks	**$6,150**	
None over $1,500		
Securities & Investment	**$7,500**	
DRD Associates Ltd	$4,000	Indiv
Insurance	**$3,150**	
None over $1,500		
Real Estate	**$13,600**	
National Assn of Realtors	$6,000	PAC
Cottonwood Properties	$1,500	Indiv
Del Webb Corp	$1,500	PAC
Misc Finance	**$6,000**	
Consolidated Investments	$2,500	Indiv

Contribution Totals by Sector

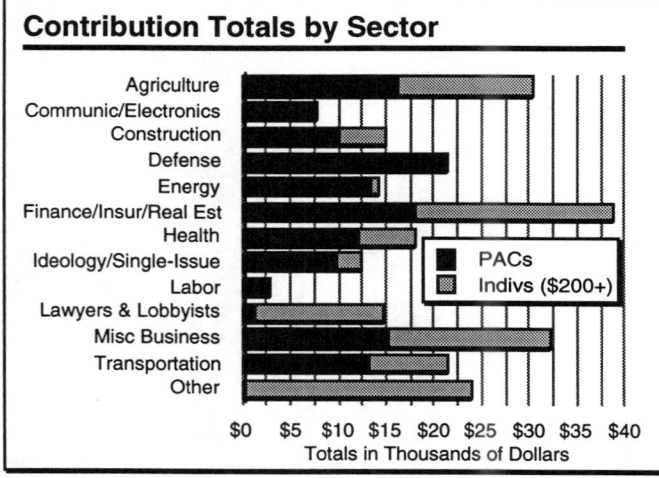

Agriculture
Communic/Electronics
Construction
Defense
Energy
Finance/Insur/Real Est
Health
Ideology/Single-Issue
Labor
Lawyers & Lobbyists
Misc Business
Transportation
Other

■ PACs
▨ Indivs ($200+)

$0 $5 $10 $15 $20 $25 $30 $35 $40
Totals in Thousands of Dollars

Health — $17,950

Health Professionals **$10,800**
    American Medical Assn .... $5,850   PAC
    American Dental Assn .... $1,500   PAC

Health Services **$2,200**
    None over $1,500

Pharmaceuticals/Health Products **$3,000**
    Abbott Laboratories .... $2,000   PAC

Lawyers & Lobbyists — $14,357

Lawyers & Lobbyists **$14,357**
    Crowell & Owens .... $2,000   Indiv

Misc Business — $32,060

Food & Beverage **$2,375**
    None over $1,500

Beer, Wine & Liquor **$5,000**
    Golden Eagle Distributors .... $2,000   Indiv
    National Beer Wholesalers Assn .... $1,500   PAC

Retail Sales **$5,350**
    National Automatic Merchandising Assn ..... $1,500   PAC

Business Services **$2,585**
    None over $1,500

Lodging/Tourism **$2,000**
    None over $1,500

Misc Business **$4,750**
    Capin Mercantile Corp .... $2,750   Indiv
    Finley Distributing Co .... $2,000   Indiv

Chemical & Related Manufacturing **$1,500**
    Dial Corp .... $1,500   PAC

Misc Manufacturing & Distributing **$6,000**
    National Tooling & Machining Assn .... $1,750   PAC
    Stone Container Corp .... $1,500   PAC

Transportation — $21,100

Air Transport **$3,750**
    United Parcel Service .... $3,000   PAC

Automotive **$15,650**
    National Auto Dealers Assn .... $4,500   PAC
    Jim Click Automotive Group .... $3,250   Indiv
    Americans for Free International Trade .... $2,000   PAC
    Auto Dealers & Drivers for Free Trade .... $1,500   PAC
    Bill Breck Dodge .... $1,500   Indiv

Railroads **$1,500**
    None over $1,500

Labor

Labor — $2,750

Public Sector Unions **$2,750**
    National Assn Retired Federal Employees .... $1,500   PAC

Ideological/Single-Issue

Ideological/Single-Issue — $12,200

Pro-Israel **$7,400**
    National PAC .... $5,000   PAC

Gun Rights/Gun Control **$4,000**
    National Rifle Assn .... $4,000   PAC

Other & Unknown

Other — $23,805

Education **$3,650**
    University of Arizona .... $2,900   Indiv

Retired **$18,405**
    None over $1,500

Unknown — $22,771

    Homemakers/Non-income earners $2,740
    Generic Occupation/Category Unknown $2,000
    Employer Listed/Category Unknown $18,031
        None over $1,500

Spending in Last 3 Elections

	1988	1990	1992
Kolbe	$434,665	$250,642	$469,053
Opponent	$0	$0	$66,089
Vote Pct	68%	65%	67%

Legend: ▨ Kolbe   ■ Opponent

---

* Contributions came from more than one affiliate or
  subsidiary.

Mike Kopetski, D-Ore (5)

First elected: 1990

1991-92 Total Receipts: $434,981
1992 Year-end Cash: $40,738

1991-92 Committees & Subcommittees

Agriculture
Department Operations, Research and Foreign Agriculture; Forests, Family Farms and Energy

Judiciary
Civil and Constitutional Rights; International Law, Immigration and Refugees

Science, Space and Technology
Science

Leading Contributors

Business

Agriculture $37,337

Crop Production & Basic Processing $4,750
   None over $1,500

Tobacco $7,500
   RJR Nabisco .... $5,500   PAC
   Philip Morris .... $1,500   PAC

Dairy $8,000
   Mid-America Dairymen .... $4,000   PAC
   Associated Milk Producers .... $2,000   PAC
   Darigold/Northwest Dairymens Assn ... $2,000   PAC

Agricultural Services/Products $6,350
   American Assn of Nurserymen .... $2,000   PAC
   American Veterinary Medical Assn ...... $1,500   PAC

Food Processing & Sales $2,835
   None over $1,500

Forestry & Forest Products $5,152
   Weyerhaeuser Co .... $2,652   PAC

Communications/Electronics $32,525

Media/Entertainment $7,000
   National Cable Television Assn .... $2,000   PAC

Telephone Utilities $23,025
   US West Inc .... $10,300   PAC/Ind
   BellSouth Corp* .... $2,500   PAC
   Ameritech Corp .... $1,500   PAC

Electronics Mfg & Services $1,750
   None over $1,500

Source of Funds in 1992 Election

Source	Total	Pct
■ PACs	$303,092	70%
▨ Indivs $200+	$37,050	9%
☐ Indivs under $200	$89,587	21%
⊠ Other	$5,689	1%
Candidate	$0	0%
Party	$887	0%

Source of PAC Dollars by Sector

Source	Total	Pct
■ Business	$184,769	58%
▨ Labor	$94,300	30%
☐ Ideology/Single Issue	$37,023	12%

In-State vs. Out-of-State Contributions*

Source	Total	Pct
☐ In-State	$23,700	68%
■ Out-of-state	$11,350	32%
No state listed	$400	

* by large individual contributors ($200 & above)

Construction $3,375

Home Builders $2,250
   National Assn of Home Builders .... $2,250   PAC

Defense $2,850

Defense Aerospace $1,500
   None over $1,500

Energy & Natural Resources $8,610

Oil & Gas $2,350
   None over $1,500

Mining $1,750
   Northwest Aluminum Co .... $1,500   Indiv

Electric Utilities $4,260
   ACRE (Action Cmte for Rural Electrification) .... $2,750   PAC

Finance, Insurance & Real Estate $35,075

Commercial Banks $14,125
   American Bankers Assn* .... $6,375   PAC
   US Bancorp .... $4,700   PAC/Ind

Savings & Loans $2,000
   US League of Savings Assns .... $2,000   PAC

Credit Unions $1,500
   Credit Union National Assn .... $1,500   PAC

Securities & Investment $3,250
   None over $1,500

Insurance $3,750
   Standard Insurance Co .... $1,750   PAC

Real Estate $7,400
   National Assn of Realtors .... $6,750   PAC

Accountants $2,050
   None over $1,500

Contribution Totals by Sector

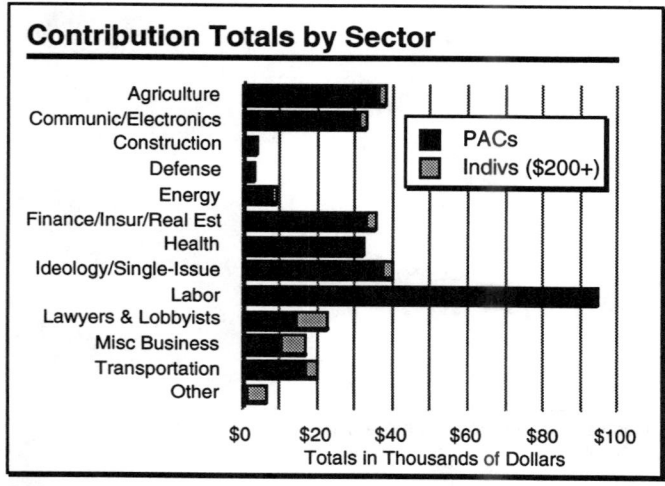

Agriculture
Communic/Electronics
Construction
Defense
Energy
Finance/Insur/Real Est
Health
Ideology/Single-Issue
Labor
Lawyers & Lobbyists
Misc Business
Transportation
Other

■ PACs
▨ Indivs ($200+)

$0 $20 $40 $60 $80 $100
Totals in Thousands of Dollars

Health — $31,850

Health Professionals $25,700
- American Medical Assn .... $8,450 — PAC
- American Academy of Ophthalmology .... $4,000 — PAC
- American Dental Assn .... $2,250 — PAC
- American Chiropractic Assn .... $2,000 — PAC
- American College of Emergency Physicians .... $2,000 — PAC
- American Nurses Assn .... $1,500 — PAC

Hospitals/Nursing Homes $4,000
- American Hospital Assn .... $2,500 — PAC

Pharmaceuticals/Health Products $1,900
- None over $1,500

Lawyers & Lobbyists — $22,100

Lawyers & Lobbyists $22,100
- Assn of Trial Lawyers of America .... $10,000 — PAC
- Ball, Janik & Novack .... $2,000 — Indiv
- Schwabe, Williamson & Wyatt .... $1,750 — Indiv

Misc Business — $16,407

Food & Beverage $2,000
- None over $1,500

Beer, Wine & Liquor $3,500
- National Beer Wholesalers Assn .... $2,500 — PAC

Retail Sales $4,757
- Fred Meyer Inc .... $2,500 — Indiv

Misc Manufacturing & Distributing $4,200
- Schnitzer Steel Industries .... $2,000 — Indiv

Transportation — $19,590

Air Transport $4,840
- Boeing Co .... $2,000 — PAC
- Aircraft Owners & Pilots Assn .... $1,500 — PAC

Automotive $10,500
- National Auto Dealers Assn .... $7,000 — PAC
- Americans for Free International Trade ...... $3,000 — PAC

Railroads $3,750
- James-Furman & Co .... $3,250 — Indiv

Labor

Labor — $94,300

Building Trade Unions $8,000
- Laborers' Political League .... $3,500 — PAC
- Plumbers/Pipefitters Union .... $2,000 — PAC

Industrial Unions $13,250
- United Auto Workers .... $3,750 — PAC
- Intl Brotherhood of Electrical Workers .... $2,500 — PAC
- Boilermakers Union .... $2,000 — PAC
- Rubber Cork Linoleum & Plastic Workers ..... $2,000 — PAC
- United Steelworkers .... $2,000 — PAC

Transportation Unions $29,050
- Teamsters Union .... $7,500 — PAC
- Marine Engineers Union* .... $6,000 — PAC
- Air Line Pilots Assn .... $5,000 — PAC
- Seafarers International Union .... $4,000 — PAC
- Intl Longshoremen's/Warehousemen's Union ..... $1,750 — PAC

Public Sector Unions $39,500
- American Fedn of St/Cnty/Munic Employees .... $10,000 — PAC
- National Education Assn* .... $10,000 — PAC
- National Assn Retired Federal Employees ..... $8,000 — PAC
- National Assn of Letter Carriers .... $4,000 — PAC
- National Rural Letter Carriers Assn .... $2,500 — PAC
- American Postal Workers Union .... $2,000 — PAC
- American Federation of Teachers .... $1,500 — PAC

Misc Unions $4,500
- Service Employees International Union .... $1,500 — PAC

Ideological/Single-Issue

Ideological/Single-Issue — $39,723

Democratic/Liberal $4,000
- National Cmte for an Effective Congress ..... $2,500 — PAC

Leadership PACs $5,561
- America's Leaders' Fund (Dan Rostenkowski) .... $2,500 — PAC
- House Leadership Fund (Tom Foley) .... $2,061 — PAC

Pro-Israel $4,450
- None over $1,500

Pro-Choice $2,000
- National Abortion Rights Action League ...... $1,500 — PAC

Gun Rights/Gun Control $14,850
- National Rifle Assn .... $14,850 — PAC

Human Rights $6,112
- Human Rights Campaign Fund .... $5,112 — PAC

Misc Issues $2,750
- National Cmte to Preserve Social Security ..... $2,000 — PAC

Other & Unknown

Other — $6,250

Non-Profit Institutions $2,000
- Foundation for Hearing Aid Research .... $2,000 — Indiv

Education $2,000
- City University .... $2,000 — Indiv

Unknown — $1,550
- None over $1,500

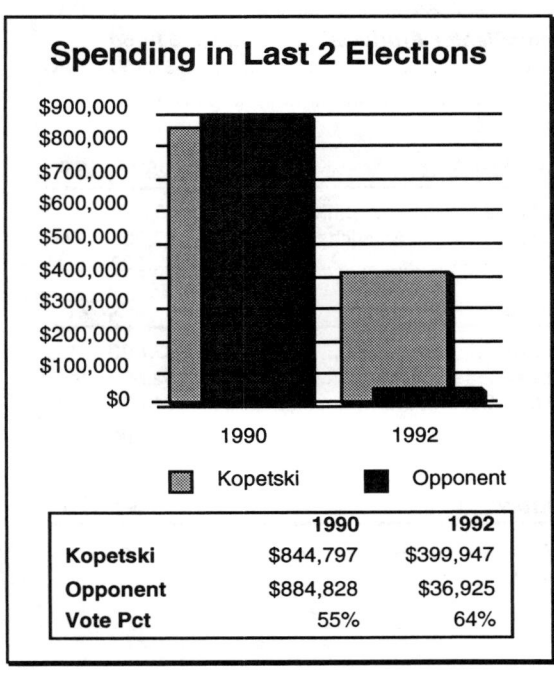

Spending in Last 2 Elections

	1990	1992
Kopetski	$844,797	$399,947
Opponent	$884,828	$36,925
Vote Pct	55%	64%

Legend: Kopetski (light), Opponent (dark)

* Contributions came from more than one affiliate or subsidiary.

811

Mike Kreidler, D-Wash (9)

First elected: 1992

1991-92 Total Receipts: $431,480
1992 Year-end Cash: $2

1993-94 Committees & Subcommittees

Energy and Commerce
Energy and Power; Health and the Environment

Veterans' Affairs
Hospitals and Health Care; Housing and Memorial Affairs; Oversight and Investigations

Leading Contributors

Business

Agriculture	$5,000	
Forestry & Forest Products	$5,000	
Weyerhaeuser Co*	$4,500	Indiv

Communications/Electronics	$2,500	
Telephone Utilities	$1,500	
US West Inc	$1,000	PAC

Construction	$1,000	
Building Materials & Equipment	$1,000	
Cedar Products	$1,000	Indiv

Energy & Natural Resources	$11,050	
Electric Utilities	$1,750	
Washington Water Power Co	$1,000	PAC
Commercial Fishing	$8,500	
Arctic Alaska Fisheries Corp	$4,500	PAC
Royal Seafood Inc	$2,000	Indiv

Finance, Insurance & Real Estate	$4,850	
Commercial Banks	$3,700	
American Bankers Assn	$2,500	PAC
US Bancorp	$1,000	PAC

Source of Funds in 1992 Election

Source	Total	Pct
PACs	$163,762	36%
Indivs $200+	$43,726	10%
Indivs under $200	$179,062	39%
Other	$69,004	15%
Candidate	$26,000	6%
Party	$34,524	8%

Source of PAC Dollars by Sector

Source	Total	Pct
Business	$62,002	34%
Labor	$93,775	51%
Ideology/Single Issue	$26,740	15%

In-State vs. Out-of-State Contributions*

Source	Total	Pct
In-State	$35,901	84%
Out-of-state	$6,825	16%
No state listed	$1,000	

*** by large individual contributors ($200 & above)**

Health — $44,068

Health Professionals	$38,575	
American Dental Assn	$10,000	PAC
American Optometric Assn	$9,000	PAC
American College of Emergency Physicians	$5,000	PAC
American Nurses Assn	$2,000	PAC
American Chiropractic Assn	$1,000	PAC
American Podiatry Assn	$1,000	PAC
Pacific Laser & Cataract Institute	$1,000	Indiv
Hospitals/Nursing Homes	$2,650	
American Health Care Assn	$1,000	PAC
American Hospital Assn	$1,000	PAC
Pharmaceuticals/Health Products	$1,650	
Immunex Corp	$1,150	PAC
Misc Health	$1,193	
None over $1,000		

Lawyers & Lobbyists — $15,065

Lawyers & Lobbyists	$15,065	
Assn of Trial Lawyers of America	$7,500	PAC
Preston, Gates et al	$2,500	Indiv

Misc Business — $6,577

Food & Beverage	$3,000	
Emerald Seafoods Inc	$2,000	Indiv
Golden Alaska Seafoods	$1,000	Indiv
Business Services	$2,000	
None over $1,000		

Transportation — $1,875

Sea Transport	$1,125	
None over $1,000		

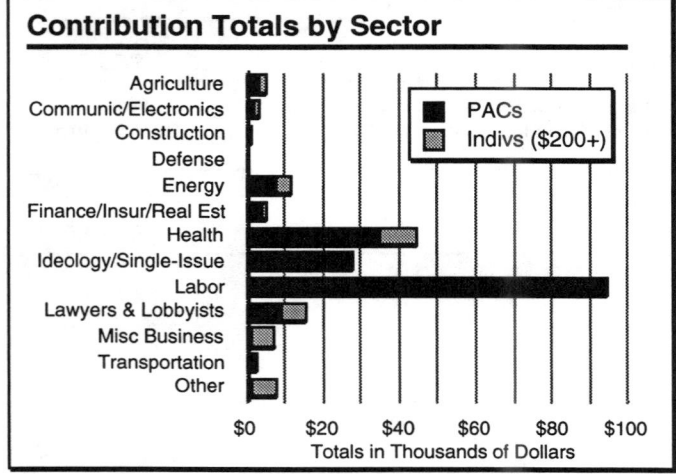

Contribution Totals by Sector

Agriculture
Communic/Electronics
Construction
Defense
Energy
Finance/Insur/Real Est
Health
Ideology/Single-Issue
Labor
Lawyers & Lobbyists
Misc Business
Transportation
Other

- PACs
- Indivs ($200+)

$0 $20 $40 $60 $80 $100
Totals in Thousands of Dollars

Labor

Labor	$93,775

Building Trade Unions **$13,000**
  Laborers Union* .... $4,000 PAC
  Carpenters & Joiners Union .... $3,000 PAC
  Operating Engineers Union* .... $2,500 PAC
  Sheet Metal Workers Union .... $2,500 PAC
  Plumbers/Pipefitters Union .... $1,000 PAC

Industrial Unions **$19,500**
  Machinists/Aerospace Workers Union .... $10,000 PAC
  Intl Brotherhood of Electrical Workers .... $5,000 PAC
  United Auto Workers .... $2,500 PAC
  Boilermakers Union .... $1,000 PAC
  United Steelworkers .... $1,000 PAC

Transportation Unions **$16,000**
  Intl Longshoremen's/Warehousemen's Union ..... $6,000 PAC
  Marine Engineers Union .... $3,000 PAC
  Teamsters Union .... $2,500 PAC
  Air Line Pilots Assn .... $1,000 PAC
  Assn of Flight Attendants .... $1,000 PAC

Public Sector Unions **$26,275**
  American Fedn of St/Cnty/Munic Employees .... $10,000 PAC
  National Education Assn .... $10,000 PAC
  American Federation of Teachers .... $2,000 PAC
  American Postal Workers Union .... $2,000 PAC
  National Assn Retired Federal Employees .... $2,000 PAC

Misc Unions **$19,000**
  Food & Commercial Workers Union .... $7,500 PAC
  AFL-CIO .... $6,500 PAC
  Service Employees International Union .... $3,000 PAC
  Bakery, Confectionery & Tobacco Workers .... $2,000 PAC

Ideological/Single-Issue

Ideological/Single-Issue	$27,240

Leadership PACs **$5,500**
  House Leadership Fund (Tom Foley) .... $2,000 PAC
  America's Leaders' Fund (Dan Rostenkowski) .... $1,000 PAC
  Effective Government Cmte (Dick Gephardt) ...... $1,000 PAC

Pro-Choice **$3,250**
  National Abortion Rights Action League .... $3,000 PAC

Human Rights **$5,500**
  Human Rights Campaign Fund .... $4,500 PAC
  KidsPAC .... $1,000 PAC

Misc Issues **$12,240**
  Sierra Club .... $7,000 PAC
  League of Conservation Voters .... $4,840 PAC

Other & Unknown

Other	$7,250

Civil Servants/Public Officials **$2,000**
  King County Prosecutors Office .... $1,500 Indiv

Education **$1,750**
  South Kitsap School District .... $1,000 Indiv

Retired **$2,500**
  None over $1,000

Other **$1,000**
  National Assn of Social Workers .... $1,000 PAC

Unknown	$5,993

  Homemakers/Non-income earners $3,000
  Employer Listed/Category Unknown $2,093
  None over $1,000

Independent expenditures supporting Kreidler
  Marilyn Knight $1,232

Spending in Last Election

	1992
Kreidler	$426,476
Opponent	$414,594
Vote Pct	52%

(Bar chart: Kreidler vs. Opponent, y-axis $0 to $450,000)

---

* Contributions came from more than one affiliate or subsidiary.

Jon Kyl, R-Ariz (4)

First elected: 1986

1991-92 Total Receipts: $616,154
1992 Year-end Cash: $493,753

1991-92 Committees & Subcommittees

Armed Services
Investigations; Research and Development

Government Operations
Employment and Housing; Legislation and National Security

Standards of Official Conduct

Leading Contributors

Business

Agriculture		**$28,126**

Crop Production & Basic Processing $5,067
   None over $2,000

Tobacco $2,850
   None over $2,000

Livestock $4,100
   Globe Corp ....$2,000   Indiv

Agricultural Services/Products $5,650
   Salt River Valley Water Users ....$3,100   PAC

Food Processing & Sales $9,900
   Shamrock Foods Co ....$2,200   Indiv

Communications/Electronics	**$14,150**

Telephone Utilities $5,850
   US West Inc ....$3,850   PAC/Ind

Telecom Services & Equipment $4,100
   Inter-Tel Corp ....$2,000   Indiv

Computer Equipment & Services $2,100
   None over $2,000

Construction	**$18,890**

General Contractors $14,090
   Associated General Contractors ....$2,500   PAC

Building Materials & Equipment $2,250
   None over $2,000

Source of Funds in 1992 Election

Source	Total	Pct
PACs	$162,818	26%
Indivs $200+	$327,202	53%
Indivs under $200	$76,349	12%
Other	$49,785	8%
Candidate	$355	0%
Party	$747	0%

Source of PAC Dollars by Sector

Source	Total	Pct
Business	$156,616	96%
Labor	$200	0%
Ideology/Single Issue	$6,100	4%

In-State vs. Out-of-State Contributions*

Source	Total	Pct
In-State	$311,915	96%
Out-of-state	$12,300	4%
No state listed	$0	

* by large individual contributors ($200 & above)

Defense	**$31,420**

Defense Aerospace $18,170
   Boeing Co ....$2,500   PAC
   Rockwell International ....$2,250   PAC

Defense Electronics $10,150
   None over $2,000

Misc Defense $3,100
   General Atomics ....$2,100   PAC

Energy & Natural Resources	**$31,150**

Oil & Gas $10,600
   None over $2,000

Mining $8,900
   Phelps Dodge Corp ....$5,200   PAC/Ind
   Cyprus Minerals Co ....$2,200   PAC

Misc Energy $3,500
   Bechtel Corp ....$3,000   PAC

Electric Utilities $6,250
   Salt River Project ....$2,000   Indiv

Finance, Insurance & Real Estate	**$88,450**

Commercial Banks $14,319
   Thunderbird Bank ....$2,600   Indiv
   BankAmerica Corp ....$2,000   PAC/Ind

Securities & Investment $8,580
   Kidder, Peabody ....$2,000   Indiv

Insurance $16,241
   National Assn of Life Underwriters ....$2,500   PAC
   Blue Cross & Blue Shield Assn* ....$2,350   Indiv

Real Estate $27,900
   National Assn of Realtors ....$5,100   PAC
   Marlin Group ....$4,000   Indiv
   Arizona One Pulve ....$2,000   Indiv
   DMB Associates ....$2,000   Indiv
   Pinnacle Peak Land Co ....$2,000   Indiv

Contribution Totals by Sector

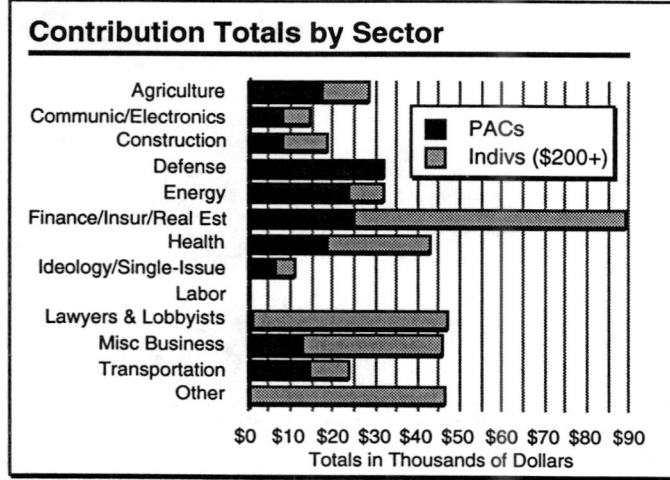

Legend: ■ PACs; ▨ Indivs ($200+)

Sectors: Agriculture, Communic/Electronics, Construction, Defense, Energy, Finance/Insur/Real Est, Health, Ideology/Single-Issue, Labor, Lawyers & Lobbyists, Misc Business, Transportation, Other

$0 $10 $20 $30 $40 $50 $60 $70 $80 $90
Totals in Thousands of Dollars

| Accountants | $7,200 | |
| Arthur Andersen & Co | $3,450 | PAC/Ind |

Misc Finance **$13,410**
Maricopa Partners	$4,000	Indiv
Consolidated Investments	$2,350	Indiv
Pinnacle West Capital Corp	$2,000	Indiv

Health — $42,190

Health Professionals **$35,740**
American Medical Assn	$8,000	PAC
American Academy of Ophthalmology	$3,500	PAC
American Dental Assn	$2,500	PAC

Pharmaceuticals/Health Products **$3,100**
None over $2,000

Misc Health **$2,350**
None over $2,000

Lawyers & Lobbyists — $46,550

Lawyers & Lobbyists **$46,550**
Jennings, Strouss & Salmon	$7,330	Indiv
Snell & Wilmer	$6,200	Indiv
Teilborg, Sanders & Parks	$3,700	Indiv
Ryley, Carlock & Applewhite	$3,000	Indiv
Lewis & Roca	$2,600	Indiv
Gallagher & Kennedy	$2,000	Indiv

Misc Business — $45,810

Food & Beverage **$3,000**
| Shannon M Inc | $2,000 | Indiv |

Beer, Wine & Liquor **$4,000**
| Hensley & Co | $2,000 | Indiv |

Retail Sales **$3,500**
| Leonards Luggage | $2,000 | Indiv |

Business Services **$8,660**
| Outdoor Systems Advertising | $2,000 | Indiv |

Lodging/Tourism **$3,750**
None over $2,000

Chemical & Related Manufacturing **$6,650**
| Dial Corp | $6,400 | PAC/Ind |

Misc Manufacturing & Distributing **$10,950**
Stone Container Corp	$2,500	PAC
Naumann, Hobbs Material Handling	$2,300	Indiv
Signature Industries	$2,000	Indiv

Transportation — $23,620

Air Transport **$3,870**
| United Parcel Service | $3,120 | PAC |

Automotive **$18,150**
National Auto Dealers Assn	$5,750	PAC
Western States Tire	$2,100	Indiv
Americans for Free International Trade	$2,000	PAC
Jim Click Automotive Group	$2,000	Indiv

Ideological/Single-Issue

Ideological/Single-Issue — $10,575

Republican/Conservative **$2,275**
None over $2,000

Pro-Israel **$2,950**
None over $2,000

Gun Rights/Gun Control **$4,200**
| National Rifle Assn | $4,200 | PAC |

Other & Unknown

Other — $46,210

Civil Servants/Public Officials **$4,900**
None over $2,000

Education **$6,100**
| Clinton Harley Corp | $2,000 | Indiv |

Retired **$33,910**
None over $2,000

Unknown — $59,535

Homemakers/Non-income earners	$11,500	
Generic Occupation/Category Unknown	$3,800	
Employer Listed/Category Unknown	$44,499	
Bid-Group Inc	$4,000	Indiv
Stuckey Investment Co	$3,000	Indiv
Castillo & Arnold	$2,000	Indiv
McCabe & Pietzsch	$2,000	Indiv
TCA Associates	$2,000	Indiv
Tom Hopkins International	$2,000	Indiv

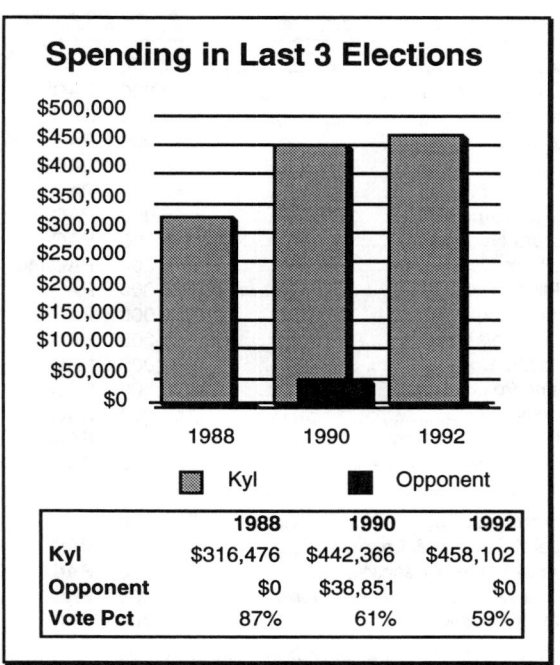

Spending in Last 3 Elections

	1988	1990	1992
Kyl	$316,476	$442,366	$458,102
Opponent	$0	$38,851	$0
Vote Pct	87%	61%	59%

* Contributions came from more than one affiliate or
   subsidiary.

John J. LaFalce, D-NY (29)

First elected: 1974

1991-92 Total Receipts: $588,616
1992 Year-end Cash: $765,913

1991-92 Committees & Subcommittees

Banking, Finance and Urban Affairs
Economic Stabilization; Financial Institutions Supervision, Regulation and Insurance; Housing and Community Development; International Development, Finance, Trade and Monetary Policy

Small Business (Chairman)
SBA, the General Economy and Minority Enterprise Development (Chairman)

Leading Contributors

Business

Agriculture	$12,000	
Dairy **$1,500**		
Associated Milk Producers $1,500	PAC	
Agricultural Services/Products **$2,000**		
None over $1,500		
Food Processing & Sales **$7,500**		
JCB Supermarkets $2,000	Indiv	
Rich Products Corp $2,000	Indiv	
Food Marketing Institute $1,500	PAC	

Communications/Electronics	$9,500	
Media/Entertainment **$2,000**		
None over $1,500		
Telephone Utilities **$4,000**		
AT&T $3,000	PAC	
Computer Equipment & Services **$2,000**		
None over $1,500		

Construction	$9,750	
General Contractors **$3,000**		
None over $1,500		
Home Builders **$2,000**		
National Assn of Home Builders $2,000	PAC	
Building Materials & Equipment **$3,000**		
Carborundum Co $2,000	Indiv	

Defense	$2,500	
Defense Aerospace **$2,000**		
Textron Inc $2,000	PAC	

Contribution Totals by Sector

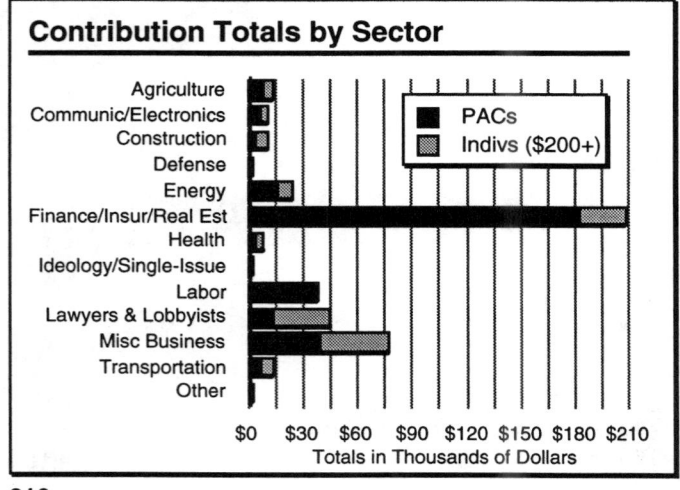

- Agriculture
- Communic/Electronics
- Construction
- Defense
- Energy
- Finance/Insur/Real Est
- Health
- Ideology/Single-Issue
- Labor
- Lawyers & Lobbyists
- Misc Business
- Transportation
- Other

■ PACs
▨ Indivs ($200+)

$0 $30 $60 $90 $120 $150 $180 $210
Totals in Thousands of Dollars

Source of Funds in 1992 Election

Source	Total	Pct
■ PACs	$312,270	52%
▨ Indivs $200+	$169,917	28%
☐ Indivs under $200	$27,983	5%
▨ Other	$91,900	15%
Candidate	$0	0%
Party	$13,904	2%

Source of PAC Dollars by Sector

Source	Total	Pct
■ Business	$274,841	88%
▨ Labor	$37,250	12%
☐ Ideology/Single Issue	$2,023	1%

In-State vs. Out-of-State Contributions*

Source	Total	Pct
☐ In-State	$123,267	73%
■ Out-of-state	$46,050	27%
No state listed	$0	

* by large individual contributors ($200 & above)

Energy & Natural Resources	$22,950	
Oil & Gas **$10,050**		
Occidental Petroleum $2,500	PAC	
BP America $2,000	PAC	
Petroleum Marketers Assn $2,000	PAC	
Electric Utilities **$2,600**		
New York State Electric & Gas Corp $1,600	PAC	
Waste Management **$9,300**		
Waste Management Inc $3,300	PAC	
Modern Landfill $3,000	Indiv	
Browning-Ferris Industries $2,000	PAC	

Finance, Insurance & Real Estate	$206,997	
Commercial Banks **$103,450**		
American Bankers Assn $10,000	PAC	
Chase Manhattan $10,000	PAC	
JP Morgan & Co $10,000	PAC	
Citicorp $8,500	PAC	
Bankers Trust $6,000	PAC	
First Chicago Corp $6,000	PAC	
Manufacturers Hanover $6,000	PAC	
Chemical Bank $5,200	PAC/Ind	
Marine Midland Banks $5,000	PAC	
BankAmerica Corp $4,000	PAC/Ind	
Continental Illinois Corp $4,000	PAC	
Security Pacific Corp $4,000	PAC	
Norstar Bancorp $3,000	PAC	
Barnett Banks Inc $2,000	PAC	
Citizens & Southern National Bank $2,000	PAC	
Assn of Bank Holding Companies $1,500	PAC	
M&T Bank $1,500	Indiv	
Savings & Loans **$19,350**		
Coast Federal Savings & Loan $5,000	PAC	
US League of Savings Assns* $3,200	PAC	
National Council of Savings Institutions* $3,000	PAC	
Anchor Savings Bank $1,700	PAC	
Finance/Credit Companies **$4,700**		
Household International Inc $2,000	PAC	

Securities & Investment	$15,950	
Prudential Securities	$2,750	PAC
Dean Witter	$2,500	PAC
National Venture Capital Assn	$2,500	PAC
American Express*	$2,000	PAC
Merrill Lynch	$1,500	PAC

Insurance	$11,950	
Northwestern Mutual Life	$2,000	PAC
Massachusetts Mutual Life Insurance	$1,500	PAC

Real Estate	$22,700	
National Assn of Realtors	$6,000	PAC
Snyder Corp	$2,000	Indiv

Accountants	$23,497	
American Institute of CPA's	$10,000	PAC
Ernst & Young	$3,000	PAC
Price Waterhouse	$2,997	PAC
Coopers & Lybrand	$2,500	PAC
Arthur Andersen & Co	$2,000	PAC
Deloitte & Touche	$2,000	PAC

Health $7,000

Health Professionals	$5,500	
None over $1,500		

Lawyers & Lobbyists $43,250

Lawyers & Lobbyists	$43,250	
Assn of Trial Lawyers of America	$5,000	PAC
Templeton & Co	$3,500	Indiv
Hodgson, Russ et al	$3,000	Indiv
Jaeckle, Fleischmann & Mugel	$2,250	Indiv
Kavinoky & Cook	$2,100	Indiv
Jones, Day et al	$2,000	PAC/Ind
Saperston & Day	$1,850	Indiv
Butera & Andrews	$1,500	Indiv

Misc Business $76,053

Business Associations	$14,000	
National Assn of Sm Bus Investment Cos	$10,000	PAC
International Franchise Assn	$1,500	PAC
Small Business Council of America	$1,500	PAC

Food & Beverage	$28,094	
Delaware North Companies	$17,250	Indiv
Pizza Hut Franchise Holders Assn	$5,000	PAC
Assn of KFC Franchisees Inc	$2,844	PAC

Spending in Last 3 Elections

	1988	1990	1992
LaFalce	$133,738	$145,079	$467,841
Opponent	$13,702	$0	$83,110
Vote Pct	73%	55%	55%

Beer, Wine & Liquor	$6,000	
National Beer Wholesalers Assn	$6,000	PAC

Retail Sales	$6,700	
Rainbow Factory Outlet Mall	$2,000	Indiv

Business Services	$4,950	
Gioia Management Inc	$2,000	Indiv

Chemical & Related Manufacturing	$3,000	
None over $1,500		

Misc Manufacturing & Distributing	$11,309	
Otis Elevator Co	$4,000	Indiv
Columbus, McKinnon	$2,000	Indiv

Transportation $13,250

Air Transport	$5,500	
National Air Cargo Inc	$2,000	Indiv
Enidine Inc	$1,500	Indiv
General Electric	$1,500	PAC

Automotive	$3,000	
None over $1,500		

Trucking	$3,500	
None over $1,500		

Labor

Labor	$37,250	

Building Trade Unions	$14,000	
Operating Engineers Union*	$5,500	PAC
Laborers' Political League	$3,000	PAC
Plumbers/Pipefitters Union	$2,500	PAC
Carpenters & Joiners Union	$2,000	PAC

Industrial Unions	$8,750	
United Steelworkers	$5,000	PAC
Electronic Machine Furniture Workers	$1,500	PAC

Transportation Unions	$4,000	
Teamsters Union	$3,500	PAC

Public Sector Unions	$8,500	
National Assn Retired Federal Employees	$3,000	PAC
National Education Assn	$3,000	PAC
American Postal Workers Union	$1,500	PAC

Misc Unions	$2,000	
Food & Commercial Workers Union	$2,000	PAC

Ideological/Single-Issue

Ideological/Single-Issue	$2,223	
None over $1,500		

Other & Unknown

Unknown	$39,458	
No Employer Listed or Found	$20,550	
Employer Listed/Category Unknown	$17,908	
Spartan Beverage Corp	$2,500	Indiv
Flickingers Food	$2,000	Indiv

Independent expenditures supporting LaFalce
National Right to Life PAC $3,646

---

* Contributions came from more than one affiliate or subsidiary.

Blanche Lambert, D-Ark (1)

First elected: 1992

1991-92 Total Receipts:	$439,343
1992 Year-end Cash:	$112,243

1993-94 Committees & Subcommittees

Agriculture
Department Operations and Nutrition

Energy and Commerce
Energy and Power; Transportation and Hazardous Materials

Merchant Marine and Fisheries
Coast Guard and Navigation; Environment and Natural Resources

Leading Contributors

Business

Agriculture	$41,475	
Crop Production & Basic Processing	**$19,925**	
Riceland Foods	$3,200	PAC/Ind
Tobacco	**$3,500**	
RJR Nabisco	$2,000	PAC
Poultry & Eggs	**$3,000**	
Tyson Foods	$3,000	PAC/Ind
Livestock	**$2,300**	
National Cattlemen's Assn*	$1,500	PAC
Agricultural Services/Products	**$4,250**	
None over $1,500		
Food Processing & Sales	**$6,500**	
Fleming Companies Inc	$2,500	PAC

Communications/Electronics	$13,600	
Media/Entertainment	**$3,000**	
None over $1,500		
Telephone Utilities	**$7,100**	
GTE Corp	$2,000	PAC/Ind

Construction	$8,300	
General Contractors	**$3,550**	
Associated General Contractors	$1,500	PAC
Special Trade Contractors	**$2,000**	
Cache Valley Electric Co	$2,000	Indiv
Building Materials & Equipment	**$2,000**	
Blytheville Winnelson Co	$2,000	Indiv

Source of Funds in 1992 Election

	Source	Total	Pct
■	PACs	$175,400	38%
▨	Indivs $200+	$127,384	28%
☐	Indivs under $200	$119,665	26%
⊠	Other	$34,899	8%
	Candidate	$4,000	1%
	Party	$23,255	5%

Source of PAC Dollars by Sector

	Source	Total	Pct
■	Business	$132,489	74%
▨	Labor	$24,000	13%
☐	Ideology/Single Issue	$22,550	13%

In-State vs. Out-of-State Contributions*

	Source	Total	Pct
☐	In-State	$93,212	73%
■	Out-of-state	$34,172	27%
	No state listed	$0	

* by large individual contributors ($200 & above)

Energy & Natural Resources	$23,500	
Oil & Gas	**$16,200**	
Ashland Oil	$1,500	PAC
Mining	**$1,500**	
None over $1,500		
Electric Utilities	**$4,800**	
Entergy Corp*	$1,500	PAC

Finance, Insurance & Real Estate	$52,649	
Commercial Banks	**$12,700**	
American Bankers Assn	$3,000	PAC
Worthen Banking Corp	$2,000	PAC/Ind
Securities & Investment	**$7,199**	
Stephens Inc	$4,450	Indiv
Insurance	**$15,300**	
National Assn of Life Underwriters	$3,000	PAC
Casualty & Surety Agents Assn	$1,500	PAC
Mutual of Omaha	$1,500	PAC
Real Estate	**$9,000**	
National Assn of Realtors	$5,000	PAC
Accountants	**$2,200**	
None over $1,500		
Misc Finance	**$5,750**	
Stephens Overseas Services	$5,250	PAC

Health	$19,300	
Health Professionals	**$13,800**	
American Dental Assn	$5,000	PAC
American Academy of Ophthalmology	$2,000	PAC
American College of Emergency Physicians	$2,000	PAC
Hospitals/Nursing Homes	**$2,000**	
American Hospital Assn	$1,500	PAC
Pharmaceuticals/Health Products	**$3,500**	
None over $1,500		

Contribution Totals by Sector

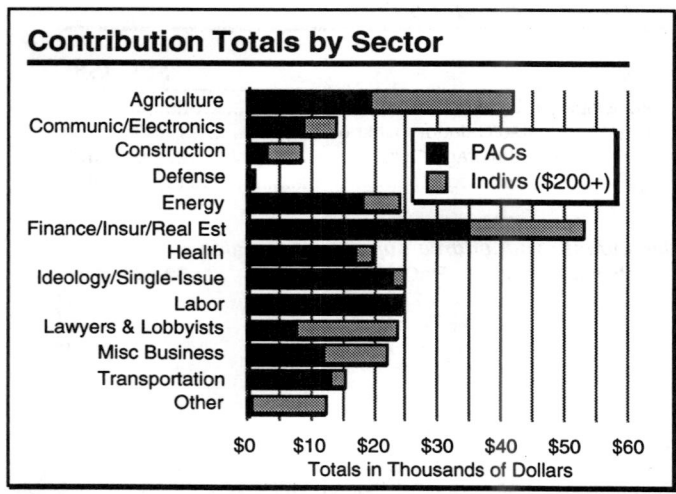

Agriculture, Communic/Electronics, Construction, Defense, Energy, Finance/Insur/Real Est, Health, Ideology/Single-Issue, Labor, Lawyers & Lobbyists, Misc Business, Transportation, Other

PACs / Indivs ($200+)

Totals in Thousands of Dollars

Lawyers & Lobbyists $23,432

Lawyers & Lobbyists **$23,432**
   Assn of Trial Lawyers of America ....$5,000 PAC
   Mitchell, Williams et al ....$1,600 Indiv

Misc Business $21,852

Food & Beverage **$4,250**
   Delaware North Companies ....$2,000 Indiv
Beer, Wine & Liquor **$1,750**
   None over $1,500
Retail Sales **$2,000**
   None over $1,500
Lodging/Tourism **$3,198**
   None over $1,500
Misc Business **$2,764**
   Blackhawk Warehouse & Leasing Co ....$2,264 Indiv
Chemical & Related Manufacturing **$5,050**
   Dow Chemical ....$2,500 PAC

Transportation $15,200

Air Transport **$4,000**
   Federal Express Corp ....$3,000 PAC
Automotive **$6,250**
   National Auto Dealers Assn ....$5,000 PAC
Trucking **$1,700**
   None over $1,500
Railroads **$2,250**
   None over $1,500

Labor

Labor $24,000

Industrial Unions **$5,500**
   United Auto Workers ....$5,000 PAC
Transportation Unions **$4,000**
   United Transportation Union ....$2,500 PAC
Public Sector Unions **$12,000**
   National Education Assn ....$4,000 PAC
   American Fedn of St/Cnty/Munic Employees ......$2,500 PAC
   National Assn of Letter Carriers ....$2,500 PAC
Misc Unions **$2,500**
   Food & Commercial Workers Union ....$2,500 PAC

Ideological/Single-Issue

Ideological/Single-Issue $24,500

Democratic/Liberal **$4,000**
   None over $1,500
Leadership PACs **$5,000**
   None over $1,500
Pro-Israel **$3,750**
   None over $1,500
Womens Issues **$10,500**
   Emily's List ....$5,000 PAC
   National Organization for Women ....$2,500 PAC
   Women's Campaign Fund ....$2,000 PAC

Other & Unknown

Other $12,175

Civil Servants/Public Officials **$2,400**
   None over $1,500
Retired **$9,025**
   None over $1,500

Unknown $25,440

   Homemakers/Non-income earners $2,450
   No Employer Listed or Found $11,840
   Generic Occupation/Category Unknown $2,150
   Employer Listed/Category Unknown $9,000
      None over $1,500

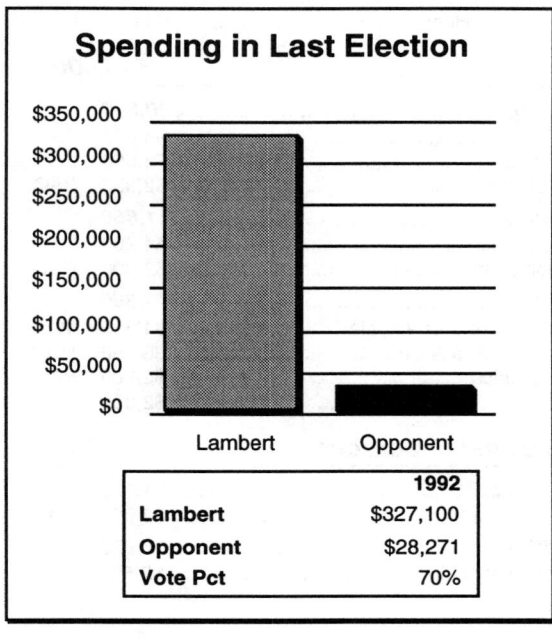

Spending in Last Election

	1992
Lambert	$327,100
Opponent	$28,271
Vote Pct	70%

---

* Contributions came from more than one affiliate or
subsidiary.

H. Martin Lancaster, D-NC (3)

First elected: 1986

1991-92 Total Receipts: $588,664
1992 Year-end Cash: $60,660

1991-92 Committees & Subcommittees

Armed Services
Military Personnel and Compensation; Readiness

Merchant Marine and Fisheries
Coast Guard and Navigation

Small Business
Exports, Tax Policy and Special Problems; Procurement, Tourism and Rural Development; Regulation, Business Opportunity and Energy

Leading Contributors

Business

Agriculture	**$83,359**	
Crop Production & Basic Processing	**$10,586**	
None over $2,000		
Tobacco	**$22,198**	
RJR Nabisco	$10,000	PAC
Philip Morris	$6,648	PAC
Dairy	**$5,700**	
Associated Milk Producers	$3,000	PAC
Poultry & Eggs	**$4,750**	
Tyson Foods	$2,900	PAC/Ind
Livestock	**$2,550**	
None over $2,000		
Agricultural Services/Products	**$5,125**	
None over $2,000		
Food Processing & Sales	**$28,550**	
Webco USA	$6,000	Indiv
Dixon Marketing Inc	$3,150	Indiv
Dunham & Smith Agencies Inc	$2,400	Indiv
Pepsico Inc	$2,100	PAC/Ind
Forestry & Forest Products	**$3,900**	
None over $2,000		

Source of Funds in 1992 Election

Source	Total	Pct
PACs	$300,165	50%
Indivs $200+	$175,609	29%
Indivs under $200	$96,273	16%
Other	$26,426	4%
Candidate	$0	0%
Party	$15,409	3%

Source of PAC Dollars by Sector

Source	Total	Pct
Business	$251,662	83%
Labor	$31,750	10%
Ideology/Single Issue	$19,800	7%

In-State vs. Out-of-State Contributions*

Source	Total	Pct
In-State	$92,103	53%
Out-of-state	$83,200	47%
No state listed	$0	

* by large individual contributors ($200 & above)

Communications/Electronics	**$16,925**	
Printing & Publishing	**$4,650**	
Downey Communications Inc	$2,400	Indiv
Exchange & Commissary News	$2,000	Indiv
Telephone Utilities	**$8,475**	
Southern Bell	$3,675	PAC
United Telecommunications	$3,600	PAC

Construction	**$12,500**	
General Contractors	**$6,600**	
Associated General Contractors	$3,350	PAC
TA Loving Co	$2,000	Indiv
Home Builders	**$3,250**	
National Assn of Home Builders	$3,000	PAC

Defense	**$46,000**	
Defense Aerospace	**$20,800**	
Textron Inc	$8,000	PAC
Boeing Co	$2,550	PAC
General Electric	$2,350	PAC
Defense Electronics	**$11,850**	
AT&T	$4,200	PAC
Imo Industries Inc	$2,000	PAC
Misc Defense	**$13,350**	
Military Distributors of Virginia	$4,300	Indiv
American Logistics Assn	$3,150	Indiv
General Atomics	$2,700	PAC
Tenneco Inc	$2,000	PAC

Energy & Natural Resources	**$14,575**	
Oil & Gas	**$4,600**	
Petroleum Marketers Assn	$2,000	PAC
Electric Utilities	**$7,875**	
Carolina Power & Light	$2,500	PAC

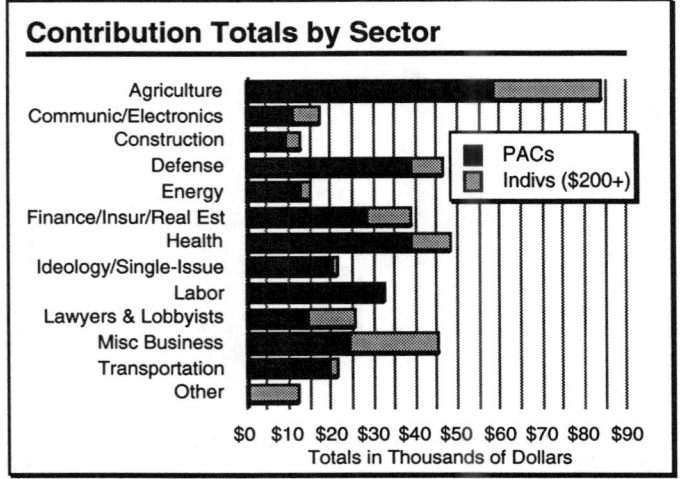

Contribution Totals by Sector

Agriculture, Communic/Electronics, Construction, Defense, Energy, Finance/Insur/Real Est, Health, Ideology/Single-Issue, Labor, Lawyers & Lobbyists, Misc Business, Transportation, Other

PACs / Indivs ($200+)

$0 $10 $20 $30 $40 $50 $60 $70 $80 $90
Totals in Thousands of Dollars

Finance, Insurance & Real Estate $38,650

Commercial Banks *$6,750*
   Citizens & Southern National Bank .... $2,000 PAC

Securities & Investment *$4,450*
   None over $2,000

Insurance *$11,900*
   Jefferson-Pilot Corp .... $5,000 PAC
   Independent Insurance Agents of America .... $3,350 PAC

Real Estate *$12,500*
   National Assn of Realtors .... $6,000 PAC
   S&K Sales Co .... $2,050 Indiv

Health $47,753

Health Professionals *$37,503*
   American Medical Assn .... $10,200 PAC
   Assn for the Advancement of Psychology .... $4,353 PAC
   American Academy of Ophthalmology .... $3,500 PAC
   American Dental Assn .... $2,000 PAC

Hospitals/Nursing Homes *$4,350*
   None over $2,000

Pharmaceuticals/Health Products *$5,650*
   Glaxo Inc .... $2,850 PAC

Lawyers & Lobbyists $25,200

Lawyers & Lobbyists *$25,200*
   Assn of Trial Lawyers of America .... $10,000 PAC

Misc Business $44,700

Food & Beverage *$7,050*
   None over $2,000

Beer, Wine & Liquor *$12,600*
   National Beer Wholesalers Assn .... $2,250 PAC

Retail Sales *$8,200*
   C Lloyd Johnson Co .... $3,400 Indiv

Misc Business *$2,050*
   None over $2,000

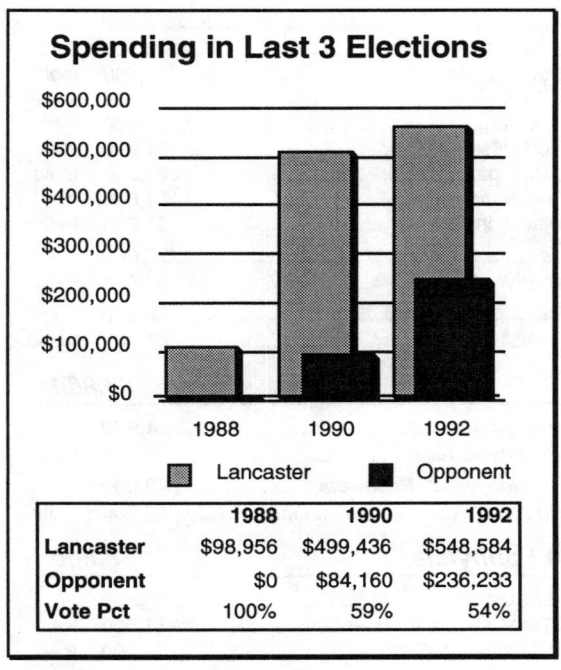

Spending in Last 3 Elections

	1988	1990	1992
Lancaster	$98,956	$499,436	$548,584
Opponent	$0	$84,160	$236,233
Vote Pct	100%	59%	54%

Misc Manufacturing & Distributing *$3,700*
   None over $2,000

Textiles *$6,300*
   American Textile Manufacturers Institute .... $2,550 PAC
   Burlington Industries .... $2,500 PAC

Transportation $21,100

Air Transport *$5,250*
   United Parcel Service .... $2,850 PAC

Automotive *$3,550*
   National Auto Dealers Assn .... $3,350 PAC

Railroads *$2,000*
   None over $2,000

Sea Transport *$8,600*
   None over $2,000

Labor

Labor $31,750

Transportation Unions *$16,000*
   Marine Engineers Union* .... $6,000 PAC
   Seafarers International Union .... $6,000 PAC
   Air Line Pilots Assn .... $2,500 PAC

Public Sector Unions *$12,850*
   National Assn Retired Federal Employees .... $6,000 PAC
   National Assn of Letter Carriers .... $5,000 PAC

Misc Unions *$2,050*
   None over $2,000

Ideological/Single-Issue

Ideological/Single-Issue $20,800

Democratic/Liberal *$2,750*
   National Cmte for an Effective Congress .... $2,500 PAC

Pro-Israel *$6,100*
   None over $2,000

Gun Rights/Gun Control *$5,000*
   National Rifle Assn .... $5,000 PAC

Misc Issues *$5,450*
   National Cmte to Preserve Social Security .... $3,250 PAC
   Sierra Club .... $2,000 PAC

Other & Unknown

Other $11,725

Education *$2,250*
   None over $2,000

Retired *$8,225*
   None over $2,000

Unknown $63,478

   Homemakers/Non-income earners $4,850
   No Employer Listed or Found $15,928
   Employer Listed/Category Unknown $42,700
      CWO Distribution .... $2,300 Indiv
      Ace Services Inc .... $2,000 Indiv

---

* Contributions came from more than one affiliate or
subsidiary.

Tom Lantos, D-Calif (12)

First elected: 1980

1991-92 Total Receipts: $499,867
1992 Year-end Cash: $510,190

1991-92 Committees & Subcommittees

Foreign Affairs
Asian and Pacific Affairs; Europe and the Middle East; International Operations

Government Operations
Employment and Housing (Chairman)

Select Committee on Aging

Leading Contributors

Business

Agriculture		$5,250
Food Processing & Sales	**...$4,250**	
Shelf Stable Foods Inc	$2,250	Indiv
Right Away Foods	$1,000	Indiv
Wornick Co	$1,000	Indiv

Communications/Electronics		$11,150
Printing & Publishing	**...$1,250**	
None over $1,000		
Media/Entertainment	**...$1,650**	
KTSF Channel 26	$1,000	Indiv
Telephone Utilities	**...$4,000**	
AT&T	$3,000	PAC
Computer Equipment & Services	**...$4,250**	
Atari Corp	$4,000	Indiv

Construction		$2,300
Home Builders	**...$1,000**	
Chudnow Construction Co	$1,000	Indiv
Building Materials & Equipment	**...$1,000**	
Echelon Corp	$1,000	Indiv

Defense		$4,000
Defense Aerospace	**...$2,000**	
Lockheed Corp	$1,000	PAC
Northrop Corp	$1,000	PAC
Defense Electronics	**...$2,000**	
Aydin Corp	$2,000	Indiv

Source of Funds in 1992 Election

Source	Total	Pct
■ PACs	$112,850	22%
▨ Indivs $200+	$106,080	21%
☐ Indivs under $200	$228,451	45%
▩ Other	$57,900	11%
Candidate	$0	0%
Party	$5,864	1%

Source of PAC Dollars by Sector

Source	Total	Pct
■ Business	$38,825	34%
▨ Labor	$67,758	60%
☐ Ideology/Single Issue	$7,185	6%

In-State vs. Out-of-State Contributions*

Source	Total	Pct
☐ In-State	$67,180	63%
■ Out-of-state	$38,900	37%
No state listed	$0	

* by large individual contributors ($200 & above)

Energy & Natural Resources		$3,100
Electric Utilities	**...$1,500**	
None over $1,000		

Finance, Insurance & Real Estate		$34,600
Commercial Banks	**...$1,000**	
None over $1,000		
Credit Unions	**...$1,300**	
None over $1,000		
Insurance	**...$1,000**	
None over $1,000		
Real Estate	**...$21,500**	
National Assn of Realtors	$6,500	PAC
Michael Enterprises	$1,500	Indiv
Irmas & Gold	$1,000	Indiv
Konheim Enterprises	$1,000	Indiv
Nathan Katz Realty	$1,000	Indiv
Praxis Development Group	$1,000	Indiv
Sade Development	$1,000	Indiv
Tom Lowenstein Co	$1,000	Indiv
Accountants	**...$7,000**	
American Institute of CPA's	$7,000	PAC
Misc Finance	**...$2,050**	
American Value Investment	$1,300	Indiv

Health		$7,850
Health Professionals	**...$4,850**	
American Medical Assn	$2,850	PAC
Pharmaceuticals/Health Products	**...$2,500**	
Alza Corp	$2,000	Indiv

Lawyers & Lobbyists		$6,500
Lawyers & Lobbyists	**...$6,500**	
Assn of Trial Lawyers of America	$1,000	PAC
Pillsbury, Madison & Sutro	$1,000	PAC

Contribution Totals by Sector

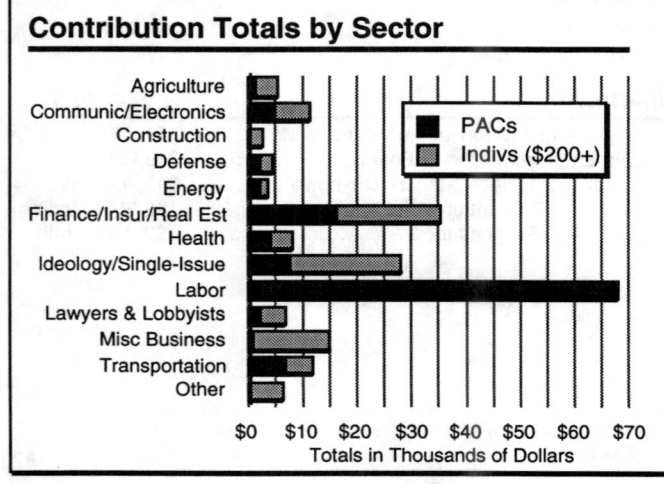

Agriculture, Communic/Electronics, Construction, Defense, Energy, Finance/Insur/Real Est, Health, Ideology/Single-Issue, Labor, Lawyers & Lobbyists, Misc Business, Transportation, Other

■ PACs
▨ Indivs ($200+)

$0 $10 $20 $30 $40 $50 $60 $70
Totals in Thousands of Dollars

Misc Business — $14,405

Food & Beverage **$5,030**
   American Licorice Co ....$4,530   Indiv

Beer, Wine & Liquor **$1,075**
   None over $1,000

Business Services **$1,000**
   None over $1,000

Lodging/Tourism **$1,000**
   None over $1,000

Chemical & Related Manufacturing **$2,500**
   Environmental Chemical Corp ....$2,500   Indiv

Misc Manufacturing & Distributing **$2,550**
   Judith Ann Inc ....$1,000   Indiv

Transportation — $11,250

Air Transport **$4,000**
   General Electric ....$1,500   PAC
   Boeing Co ....$1,000   PAC
   Federal Express Corp ....$1,000   PAC

Automotive **$7,250**
   Auto Dealers & Drivers for Free Trade ....$2,500   PAC
   Lloyd Wise Inc ....$2,250   Indiv
   General Motors ....$1,000   Indiv
   Saturn Car Dealership ....$1,000   Indiv

Labor

Labor — $67,758

Building Trade Unions **$11,000**
   Plumbers/Pipefitters Union* ....$6,000   PAC
   Laborers' Political League ....$2,000   PAC
   Operating Engineers Union* ....$1,500   PAC
   AFL-CIO Bldg/Construction Trades Dept ....$1,000   PAC

Industrial Unions — $10,500

   United Auto Workers ....$4,500   PAC
   Machinists/Aerospace Workers Union ....$1,500   PAC
   Amalgamated Clothing & Textile Workers ....$1,000   PAC
   Intl Brotherhood of Electrical Workers ....$1,000   PAC
   Ladies Garment Workers Union ....$1,000   PAC
   United Mine Workers ....$1,000   PAC

Transportation Unions **$28,050**
   Marine Engineers Union* ....$7,500   PAC
   Air Line Pilots Assn ....$6,000   PAC
   Teamsters Union ....$5,000   PAC
   Transport Workers Union ....$2,500   PAC
   Assn of Flight Attendants ....$1,500   PAC
   Seafarers International Union* ....$1,500   PAC
   United Transportation Union ....$1,500   PAC

Public Sector Unions **$12,250**
   National Assn Retired Federal Employees ....$3,500   PAC
   American Postal Workers Union ....$3,000   PAC
   National Education Assn ....$1,500   PAC
   American Fedn of St/Cnty/Munic Employees ......$1,000   PAC
   International Assn of Firefighters ....$1,000   PAC
   National Assn of Letter Carriers ....$1,000   PAC

Misc Unions **$5,958**
   Food & Commercial Workers Union ....$2,500   PAC
   Office & Professional Employees Union ....$2,000   PAC
   Hotel/Restaurant Employees Union ....$1,458   PAC

Ideological/Single-Issue

Ideological/Single-Issue — $27,735

Pro-Israel **$23,300**
   Westchester Allied PAC ....$2,000   PAC
   Washington PAC ....$1,500   PAC

Human Rights **$1,000**
   None over $1,000

Misc Issues **$2,685**
   National Cmte to Preserve Social Security ....$2,500   PAC

Other & Unknown

Other — $6,200

Retired **$5,950**
   None over $1,000

Unknown — $17,750

   Homemakers/Non-income earners $3,800
   No Employer Listed or Found $2,000
   Generic Occupation/Category Unknown $3,700
   Employer Listed/Category Unknown $8,250
      American Intertrade Group Inc ....$2,000   Indiv

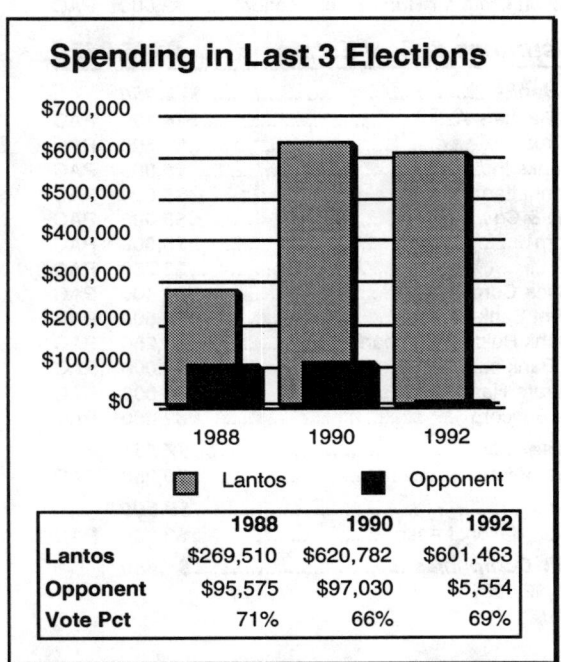

Spending in Last 3 Elections

	1988	1990	1992
Lantos	$269,510	$620,782	$601,463
Opponent	$95,575	$97,030	$5,554
Vote Pct	71%	66%	69%

---

* Contributions came from more than one affiliate or subsidiary.

Larry LaRocco, D-Idaho (1)

First elected: 1990

1991-92 Total Receipts: $598,847
1992 Year-end Cash: $2,042

1991-92 Committees & Subcommittees

Banking, Finance and Urban Affairs
Consumer Affairs and Coinage; Financial Institutions Supervision, Regulation and Insurance; International Development, Finance, Trade and Monetary Policy

Interior and Insular Affairs
National Parks and Public Lands; Water, Power and Offshore Energy

Leading Contributors

Business

Agriculture	$31,150	
Crop Production & Basic Processing	**$5,850**	
Amalgamated Sugar Co	$2,000	PAC
American Sugarbeet Growers Assn	$2,000	PAC
Tobacco	**$4,500**	
RJR Nabisco	$3,500	PAC
Dairy	**$9,000**	
Mid-America Dairymen	$4,500	PAC
Associated Milk Producers	$4,000	PAC
Livestock	**$2,500**	
National Cattlemen's Assn	$2,000	PAC
Food Processing & Sales	**$2,000**	
None over $2,000		
Forestry & Forest Products	**$6,050**	
Potlatch Corp	$2,500	PAC

Communications/Electronics	$22,750	
Media/Entertainment	**$11,000**	
Walt Disney Co	$10,000	PAC/Ind
Telephone Utilities	**$10,000**	
AT&T	$5,500	PAC
US West Inc	$3,000	PAC

Construction	$12,175	
General Contractors	**$2,700**	
Morrison-Knudsen	$2,200	PAC
Home Builders	**$8,250**	
National Assn of Home Builders	$6,500	PAC

Source of Funds in 1992 Election

Source	Total	Pct
■ PACs	$407,795	67%
▨ Indivs $200+	$70,540	12%
□ Indivs under $200	$108,561	18%
▨ Other	$25,206	4%
Candidate	$0	0%
Party	$18,360	3%

Source of PAC Dollars by Sector

Source	Total	Pct
■ Business	$261,542	64%
▨ Labor	$117,250	29%
□ Ideology/Single Issue	$27,200	7%

In-State vs. Out-of-State Contributions*

Source	Total	Pct
□ In-State	$27,842	41%
■ Out-of-state	$39,951	59%
No state listed	$200	

*** by large individual contributors ($200 & above)**

Defense	$2,000	
Defense Electronics	**$2,000**	
None over $2,000		

Energy & Natural Resources	$11,636	
Oil & Gas	**$2,750**	
Coastal Corp	$2,000	PAC
Mining	**$3,724**	
None over $2,000		
Electric Utilities	**$4,662**	
ACRE (Action Cmte for Rural Electrification)	$3,000	PAC

Finance, Insurance & Real Estate	$146,947	
Commercial Banks	**$72,350**	
American Bankers Assn*	$14,100	PAC
Bankers Trust	$6,500	PAC
Barnett Banks Inc	$5,000	PAC
Chase Manhattan	$5,000	PAC
JP Morgan & Co	$5,000	PAC
US Bancorp	$5,000	PAC
Citicorp	$3,750	PAC/Ind
BankAmerica Corp*	$3,400	PAC
Independent Bankers Assn	$2,500	PAC
Assn of Bank Holding Companies	$2,250	PAC
Chemical Bank	$2,000	PAC
Manufacturers Hanover	$2,000	PAC
West One Bancorp	$2,000	PAC
Savings & Loans	**$7,335**	
US League of Savings Assns*	$3,250	PAC
Credit Unions	**$9,500**	
Credit Union National Assn	$8,000	PAC
Finance/Credit Companies	**$5,450**	
None over $2,000		

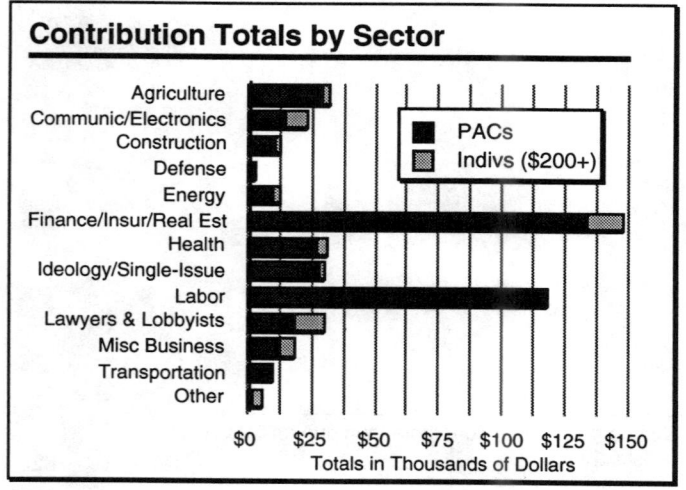

Contribution Totals by Sector

Agriculture, Communic/Electronics, Construction, Defense, Energy, Finance/Insur/Real Est, Health, Ideology/Single-Issue, Labor, Lawyers & Lobbyists, Misc Business, Transportation, Other

■ PACs
▨ Indivs ($200+)

$0 $25 $50 $75 $100 $125 $150
Totals in Thousands of Dollars

Securities & Investment $26,225
   Prudential Securities ....$4,000 PAC
   Dean Witter ....$3,350 PAC/Ind
   American Express* ....$3,000 PAC
   Merrill Lynch ....$2,000 PAC/Ind

Insurance $7,350
   None over $2,000

Real Estate $10,737
   National Assn of Realtors ....$2,000 PAC

Accountants $5,500
   American Institute of CPA's ....$5,000 PAC

Misc Finance $2,500
   Financial Services Council ....$2,000 Indiv

Health   **$30,186**

Health Professionals $25,742
   American Medical Assn* ....$14,450 PAC
   American Dental Assn ....$4,000 PAC

Hospitals/Nursing Homes $2,850
   None over $2,000

Lawyers & Lobbyists   **$29,095**

Lawyers & Lobbyists $29,095
   Assn of Trial Lawyers of America ....$10,000 PAC

Misc Business   **$17,900**

Beer, Wine & Liquor $6,000
   National Beer Wholesalers Assn ....$3,000 PAC

Retail Sales $2,750
   None over $2,000

Business Services $3,000
   None over $2,000

Transportation   **$9,050**

Air Transport $3,500
   General Electric ....$2,500 PAC

Railroads $4,050
   None over $2,000

Labor

Labor   **$117,250**

Building Trade Unions $24,000
   Carpenters & Joiners Union ....$8,000 PAC
   Laborers' Political League ....$7,000 PAC
   Ironworkers Union ....$6,500 PAC

Industrial Unions $28,500
   United Steelworkers ....$10,000 PAC
   Intl Brotherhood of Electrical Workers .....$7,000 PAC
   United Auto Workers ....$6,500 PAC

Transportation Unions $26,000
   Teamsters Union ....$9,000 PAC
   Air Line Pilots Assn ....$4,500 PAC
   Amalgamated Transit Union ....$2,500 PAC
   Maintenance of Way Employees ....$2,500 PAC
   Marine Engineers Union ....$2,000 PAC
   Trans Comm International Union ....$2,000 PAC

Public Sector Unions $29,250
   National Education Assn ....$10,000 PAC
   National Assn Retired Federal Employees ....$9,000 PAC
   American Postal Workers Union ....$4,000 PAC
   National Assn of Letter Carriers ....$4,000 PAC

Misc Unions $9,500
   Food & Commercial Workers Union ....$5,500 PAC
   AFL-CIO ....$2,000 PAC

Ideological/Single-Issue

Ideological/Single-Issue   **$29,450**

Democratic/Liberal $3,500
   National Cmte for an Effective Congress ....$2,500 PAC

Pro-Israel $2,750
   None over $2,000

Pro-Choice $5,000
   National Abortion Rights Action League ....$2,500 PAC
   Voters for Choice ....$2,500 PAC

Gun Rights/Gun Control $10,950
   National Rifle Assn ....$10,950 PAC

Human Rights $4,250
   Human Rights Campaign Fund ....$4,000 PAC

Misc Issues $2,500
   None over $2,000

Other & Unknown

Other   **$4,746**

   None over $2,000

Unknown   **$9,650**

   Employer Listed/Category Unknown $6,265
      None over $2,000

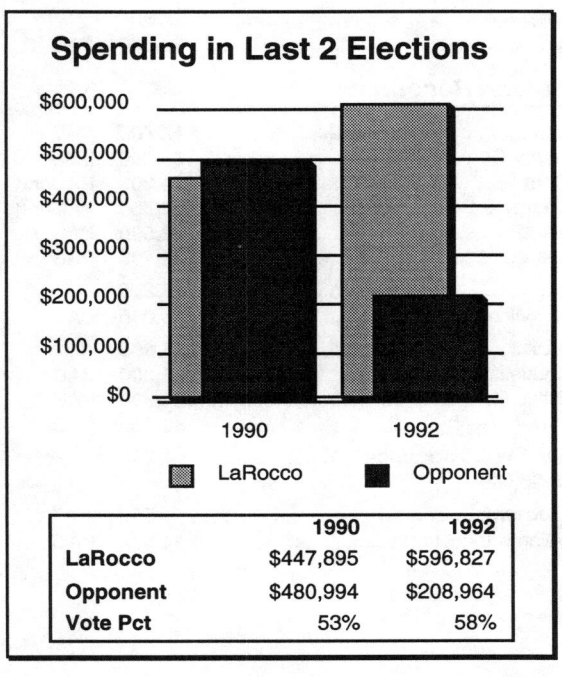

Spending in Last 2 Elections

	1990	1992
LaRocco	$447,895	$596,827
Opponent	$480,994	$208,964
Vote Pct	53%	58%

---

* Contributions came from more than one affiliate or
  subsidiary.

Greg Laughlin, D-Texas (14)

First elected: 1988

1991-92 Total Receipts: $608,011
1992 Year-end Cash: $79,691

1991-92 Committees & Subcommittees

Merchant Marine and Fisheries
Coast Guard and Navigation; Fisheries and Wildlife Conservation and the Environment

Public Works and Transportation
Aviation; Investigations and Oversight; Surface Transportation

Leading Contributors

Business

Agriculture	$42,300	
Crop Production & Basic Processing	**$7,400**	
None over $2,000		
Tobacco	**$5,850**	
RJR Nabisco	$3,000	PAC
Dairy	**$4,000**	
Associated Milk Producers	$2,000	PAC
Poultry & Eggs	**$3,250**	
Tyson Foods	$3,250	PAC/Ind
Livestock	**$11,700**	
National Cattlemen's Assn*	$2,500	PAC
Texas & Southwestern Cattle Raisers	$2,000	PAC
Agricultural Services/Products	**$6,100**	
Texas Farm Bureau	$3,000	PAC
Food Processing & Sales	**$3,000**	
None over $2,000		

Communications/Electronics	$14,100	
Telephone Utilities	**$10,350**	
GTE Corp	$3,500	PAC
AT&T	$2,500	PAC

Source of Funds in 1992 Election

Source	Total	Pct
PACs	$353,940	58%
Indivs $200+	$189,674	31%
Indivs under $200	$58,573	10%
Other	$12,651	2%
Candidate	$0	0%
Party	$7,127	1%

Source of PAC Dollars by Sector

Source	Total	Pct
Business	$272,196	76%
Labor	$73,000	20%
Ideology/Single Issue	$11,750	3%

In-State vs. Out-of-State Contributions*

Source	Total	Pct
In-State	$174,324	92%
Out-of-state	$14,600	8%
No state listed	$750	

* by large individual contributors ($200 & above)

Construction	$29,600	
General Contractors	**$22,750**	
Williams Brothers Construction	$6,000	Indiv
Associated General Contractors	$3,500	PAC
JD Abrams Co	$3,000	Indiv
Home Builders	**$2,750**	
National Assn of Home Builders	$2,750	PAC
Building Materials & Equipment	**$2,600**	
None over $2,000		

Defense	$8,800	
Defense Aerospace	**$7,500**	
Textron Inc	$4,000	PAC

Energy & Natural Resources	$79,653	
Oil & Gas	**$47,700**	
Valero Energy Corp	$8,250	Indiv
Coastal Corp	$4,200	PAC/Ind
Mitchell Energy & Development	$2,750	PAC/Ind
Enserch Corp	$2,500	PAC
BP America	$2,100	PAC
Misc Energy	**$7,200**	
Babcock & Wilcox*	$5,000	PAC
Electric Utilities	**$14,000**	
Houston Industries	$5,000	PAC
Texas Utilities Co*	$4,500	PAC
Central Power & Light	$2,250	PAC
Environmental Svcs/Equipment	**$4,250**	
None over $2,000		
Waste Management	**$5,503**	
Browning-Ferris Industries	$4,503	PAC

Contribution Totals by Sector

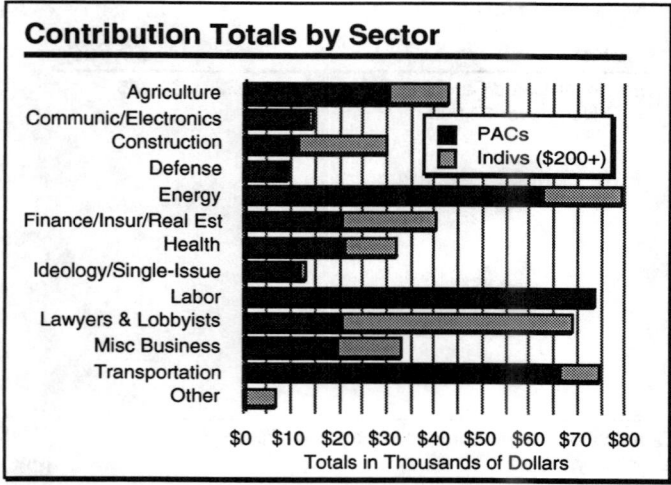

Agriculture
Communic/Electronics
Construction
Defense
Energy
Finance/Insur/Real Est
Health
Ideology/Single-Issue
Labor
Lawyers & Lobbyists
Misc Business
Transportation
Other

Legend: PACs / Indivs ($200+)

$0 $10 $20 $30 $40 $50 $60 $70 $80
Totals in Thousands of Dollars

Finance, Insurance & Real Estate — $39,622

Commercial Banks $15,000
  American Bankers Assn ....$5,000 PAC
  Victoria Bank & Trust ....$2,500 Indiv

Securities & Investment $3,750
  None over $2,000

Insurance $6,122
  Corroon & Black ....$2,000 Indiv

Real Estate $10,000
  National Assn of Realtors ....$6,000 PAC

Misc Finance $3,250
  None over $2,000

Health — $31,700

Health Professionals $27,350
  American Medical Assn................................$9,700 PAC
  American Academy of Ophthalmology ....$3,000 PAC
  American Dental Assn ....$2,250 PAC

Pharmaceuticals/Health Products $2,600
  None over $2,000

Lawyers & Lobbyists — $68,816

Lawyers & Lobbyists $68,816
  Assn of Trial Lawyers of America ....$9,700 PAC
  Hardy, Milutin et al ....$3,000 Indiv
  Vinson & Elkins ....$2,750 PAC
  Fisher, Gallagher et al ....$2,500 Indiv
  Helm, Pletcher et al ....$2,000 Indiv

Misc Business — $32,350

Beer, Wine & Liquor $4,250
  None over $2,000

Retail Sales $4,250
  Lack's Furniture ....$3,000 Indiv

Chemical & Related Manufacturing $14,350
  Dow Chemical ....$7,000 PAC
  FMC Corp ....$2,000 PAC

Misc Manufacturing & Distributing $2,750
  None over $2,000

Spending in Last 3 Elections

	1988	1990	1992
Laughlin	$600,114	$851,294	$530,139
Opponent	$645,988	$479,819	$13,425
Vote Pct	53%	54%	68%

Legend: Laughlin, Opponent

Transportation — $74,029

Air Transport $33,841
  Federal Express Corp ....$10,000 PAC
  Texas Air ....$6,500 PAC
  United Parcel Service ....$5,850 PAC
  American Airlines ....$4,000 PAC
  Aircraft Owners & Pilots Assn ....$3,000 PAC

Automotive $13,250
  National Auto Dealers Assn ....$8,250 PAC
  Auto Dealers & Drivers for Free Trade ....$2,000 PAC
  Avis Inc ....$2,000 PAC

Trucking..$4,100
  None over $2,000

Railroads $4,050
  None over $2,000

Sea Transport $17,838
  Hollywood Marine Inc ....$4,038 PAC
  CSX Corp* ....$2,000 PAC
  King Fisher Dredging ....$2,000 Indiv

Labor

Labor — $73,000

Building Trade Unions $13,250
  Carpenters & Joiners Union ....$5,500 PAC
  Laborers' Political League ....$3,000 PAC

Industrial Unions $14,250
  Communications Workers of America ....$5,000 PAC
  Intl Brotherhood of Electrical Workers ....$3,000 PAC
  United Auto Workers ....$3,000 PAC
  United Steelworkers ....$2,000 PAC

Transportation Unions $35,700
  Teamsters Union ....$7,500 PAC
  Air Line Pilots Assn ....$5,000 PAC
  United Transportation Union ....$4,500 PAC
  Marine Engineers Union* ....$4,000 PAC
  International Longshoremen's Assn ....$3,500 PAC
  Seafarers International Union ....$3,500 PAC

Public Sector Unions $9,500
  National Assn of Letter Carriers ....$5,000 PAC

Ideological/Single-Issue

Ideological/Single-Issue — $12,500

Pro-Israel $4,500
  Hudson Valley PAC.......................................$3,000 PAC

Gun Rights/Gun Control $4,500
  National Rifle Assn ....$4,500 PAC

Misc Issues $3,500
  National Cmte to Preserve Social Security ....$3,500 PAC

Other & Unknown

Other — $6,500

Retired $4,000
  None over $2,000

Unknown — $33,650

  Homemakers/Non-income earners $2,250
  No Employer Listed or Found $13,750
  Employer Listed/Category Unknown $15,700
    None over $2,000

---

* Contributions came from more than one affiliate or subsidiary.

Rick A. Lazio, R-NY (2)

1993-94 Committees & Subcommittees

First elected: 1992

1991-92 Total Receipts:	$283,788
1992 Year-end Cash:	$223

Banking, Finance and Urban Affairs
Consumer Credit and Insurance; Financial Institutions Supervision, Regulation and Deposit Insurance; Housing and Community Development

Budget

Leading Contributors

Business

Agriculture		$6,500
Crop Production & Basic Processing		**$1,000**
None over $1,000		
Food Processing & Sales		**$4,500**
Flowers Industries	$2,000	PAC
Phoenix Beverage Corp	$2,000	Indiv

Communications/Electronics		$5,250
Telephone Utilities		**$4,000**
AT&T	$2,000	PAC
NYNEX Corp*	$2,000	PAC
Computer Equipment & Services		**$1,250**
JW Systems Inc	$1,000	Indiv

Construction		$5,250
General Contractors		**$2,000**
JD Posillico Inc	$1,000	Indiv
National Utility Contractors Assn	$1,000	PAC
Special Trade Contractors		**$2,150**
National Electrical Contractors Assn	$1,000	PAC
Construction Services		**$1,100**
None over $1,000		

Source of Funds in 1992 Election

Source	Total	Pct
PACs	$43,663	13%
Indivs $200+	$91,452	27%
Indivs under $200	$106,421	31%
Other	$102,171	30%
Candidate	$18,000	5%
Party	$79,213	23%

Source of PAC Dollars by Sector

Source	Total	Pct
Business	$27,596	68%
Labor	$10,006	24%
Ideology/Single Issue	$3,274	8%

In-State vs. Out-of-State Contributions*

Source	Total	Pct
In-State	$83,737	93%
Out-of-state	$6,740	7%
No state listed	$0	

* by large individual contributors ($200 & above)

Energy & Natural Resources		$6,550
Oil & Gas		**$3,250**
Amoco Corp	$1,000	PAC
Electric Utilities		**$1,300**
None over $1,000		
Waste Management		**$2,000**
Remar Refuse Removal Corp	$2,000	Indiv

Finance, Insurance & Real Estate		$18,285
Savings & Loans		**$2,000**
Radcliffe Resources	$2,000	Indiv
Credit Unions		**$1,000**
Credit Union National Assn	$1,000	PAC
Finance/Credit Companies		**$1,000**
General Electric Credit Corp	$1,000	Indiv
Securities & Investment		**$1,900**
Dillon, Read & Co	$1,150	PAC/Ind
Insurance		**$3,000**
Brownyard WH Corp	$2,500	Indiv
Real Estate		**$8,485**
R-Three Investors	$2,585	Indiv
Batzar & Weinberg Realty Co	$1,000	Indiv
Federal Square Gardens	$1,000	Indiv
Parr Development Co	$1,000	Indiv

Contribution Totals by Sector

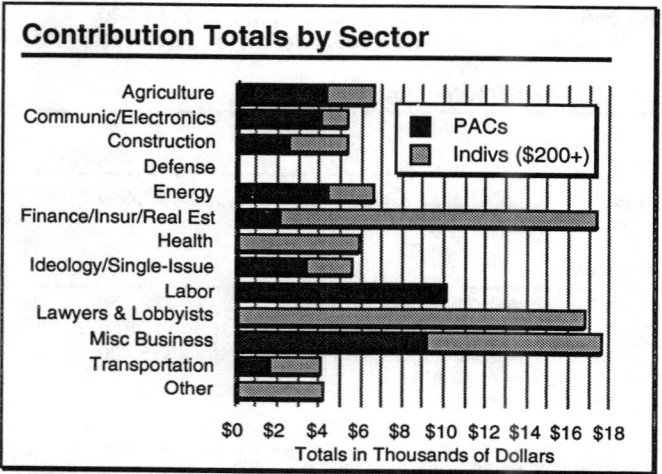

Agriculture
Communic/Electronics
Construction
Defense
Energy
Finance/Insur/Real Est
Health
Ideology/Single-Issue
Labor
Lawyers & Lobbyists
Misc Business
Transportation
Other

■ PACs
▨ Indivs ($200+)

$0 $2 $4 $6 $8 $10 $12 $14 $16 $18
Totals in Thousands of Dollars

Health | $5,850

Health Professionals **$5,850**
    Pilgrim Psychiatric Center .... $1,400   Indiv

Lawyers & Lobbyists | $16,490

Lawyers & Lobbyists **$16,490**
    Siben & Siben Law Offices .... $1,950   Indiv
    Glass, Lazio et al .... $1,250   Indiv
    Koeppel, Martone et al .... $1,000   Indiv
    Nixon, Hargrave et al .... $1,000   Indiv

Misc Business | $17,546

Business Associations **$1,045**
    Business Industry PAC .... $1,045   PAC

Food & Beverage **$3,250**
    Chili's Inc .... $1,000   PAC
    S&A Restaurant Corp .... $1,000   PAC

Beer, Wine & Liquor **$2,250**
    Clare Rose Inc .... $1,000   Indiv
    National Beer Wholesalers Assn .... $1,000   PAC

Retail Sales **$1,650**
    None over $1,000

Misc Services **$2,951**
    American Assn of Equipment Lessors .... $2,000   PAC

Business Services **$3,650**
    Curran & Connors Investment Co .... $1,000   Indiv

Textiles **$2,000**
    Burlington Industries .... $2,000   PAC

Transportation | $4,000

Air Transport **$1,500**
    United Parcel Service .... $1,000   PAC

Automotive **$1,500**
    Woodbury Automotive Warehouse .... $1,000   Indiv

Trucking **$1,000**
    Wallack Freight Lines Inc .... $1,000   Indiv

Labor

Labor | $10,006

Building Trade Unions **$1,406**
    None over $1,000

Transportation Unions **$7,500**
    Teamsters Union .... $5,000   PAC
    Air Line Pilots Assn .... $2,500   PAC

Public Sector Unions **$1,100**
    None over $1,000

Ideological/Single-Issue

Ideological/Single-Issue | $5,524

Republican/Conservative **$1,024**
    Lazio for a New Congress .... $1,000   Indiv

Leadership PACs **$3,250**
    New Frontier Leadership PAC (Norman Lent) ..... $1,000   PAC
    New Majority Leadership PAC (Vin Weber) .... $1,000   PAC
    Republican Leader's Fund (Bob Michel) .... $1,000   PAC

Pro-Israel **$1,250**
    None over $1,000

Other & Unknown

Other | $4,052

Civil Servants/Public Officials **$2,452**
    None over $1,000

Retired **$1,000**
    None over $1,000

Unknown | $26,050

    Homemakers/Non-income earners $4,200
    No Employer Listed or Found $5,650
    Employer Listed/Category Unknown $16,200
        American Maintenance Co .... $1,650   Indiv
        Gargano Inc .... $1,500   Indiv
        JDL Corp .... $1,300   Indiv
        Bauman & Kankis .... $1,000   Indiv
        Groton Equities Associates .... $1,000   Indiv
        Robins, Wells & Walser .... $1,000   Indiv

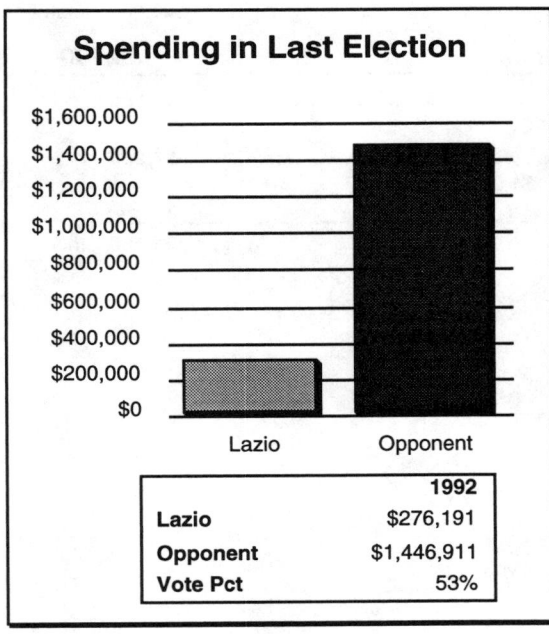

Spending in Last Election

	1992
Lazio	$276,191
Opponent	$1,446,911
Vote Pct	53%

* Contributions came from more than one affiliate or subsidiary.

Jim Leach, R-Iowa (1)

First elected: 1976

1991-92 Total Receipts: $213,649
1992 Year-end Cash: $759

1991-92 Committees & Subcommittees

Banking, Finance and Urban Affairs
Financial Institutions Supervision, Regulation and Insurance;
International Development, Finance, Trade and Monetary Policy
(Ranking Republican)

Foreign Affairs
Asian and Pacific Affairs (Ranking Republican); Europe and the
Middle East

Leading Contributors

Business

Agriculture	$2,250

Agricultural Services/Products	$1,500	
Diamond V Mills Inc	$1,000	Indiv

Communications/Electronics	$2,975

Printing & Publishing	$3,000	
Lee Enterprises Inc	$1,500	Indiv
McCleary, Cumming Co	$1,000	Indiv

Construction	$3,400

Building Materials & Equipment	$2,400
None over $1,000	

Energy & Natural Resources	$1,800

Oil & Gas	$1,050
None over $1,000	

Finance, Insurance & Real Estate	$7,300

Commercial Banks	$2,550
None over $1,000	

Insurance	$2,250
None over $1,000	

Misc Finance	$1,000
None over $1,000	

Source of Funds in 1992 Election

Source	Total	Pct
PACs	$0	0%
Indivs $200+	$59,703	28%
Indivs under $200	$136,786	64%
Other	$17,360	8%
Candidate	$10,000	5%
Party	$40	0%

Source of PAC Dollars by Sector

No PAC contributions reported

Source	Total	Pct
Business	$0	0%
Labor	$0	0%
Ideology/Single Issue	$0	0%

In-State vs. Out-of-State Contributions*

Source	Total	Pct
In-State	$55,033	100%
Out-of-state	$0	0%
No state listed	$3,550	

* by large individual contributors ($200 & above)

Health	$6,050

Health Professionals	$5,550
None over $1,000	

Lawyers & Lobbyists	$2,700

Lawyers & Lobbyists	$2,700
None over $1,000	

Misc Business	$4,750

Food & Beverage	$1,000	
Winifrieds Catering	$1,000	Indiv

Chemical & Related Manufacturing	$2,000	
Varied Investments Inc	$2,000	Indiv

Transportation	$3,700

Automotive	$1,000
None over $1,000	

Trucking	$1,200
None over $1,000	

Sea Transport	$1,500	
Alter Co	$1,500	Indiv

Contribution Totals by Sector

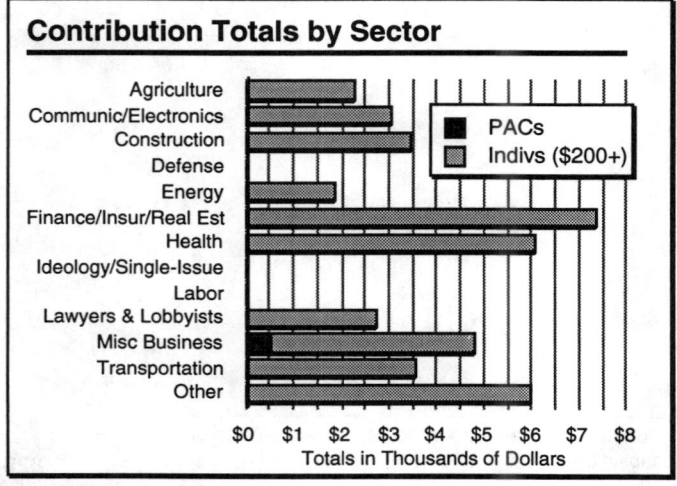

PACs
Indivs ($200+)

Agriculture
Communic/Electronics
Construction
Defense
Energy
Finance/Insur/Real Est
Health
Ideology/Single-Issue
Labor
Lawyers & Lobbyists
Misc Business
Transportation
Other

$0 $1 $2 $3 $4 $5 $6 $7 $8
Totals in Thousands of Dollars

Other & Unknown

Other $5,953

Retired..*$5,236*
　　None over $1,000

Unknown $18,180

　　Homemakers/Non-income earners $1,300
　　No Employer Listed or Found $9,850
　　Employer Listed/Category Unknown $7,030
　　　　Holden Foundation Seed ....$1,300　　Indiv

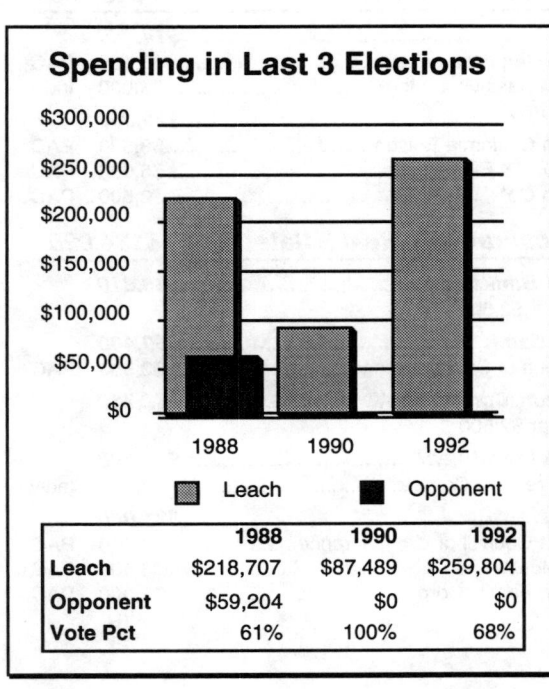

Spending in Last 3 Elections

	1988	1990	1992
Leach	$218,707	$87,489	$259,804
Opponent	$59,204	$0	$0
Vote Pct	61%	100%	68%

Richard H. Lehman, D-Calif (19)

First elected: 1982

1991-92 Total Receipts: $826,532
1992 Year-end Cash: $7,171

1991-92 Committees & Subcommittees

Energy and Commerce
Energy and Power; Telecommunications and Finance

Interior and Insular Affairs
Energy and the Environment; General Oversight and California Desert Lands (Chairman); Water, Power and Offshore Energy Resources

Leading Contributors

Business

Agriculture — $86,820

Crop Production & Basic Processing	**$52,470**	
California Almond Growers Exchange	$5,000	PAC
Sun-Diamond Growers*	$4,400	PAC
Sunkist Growers	$4,000	PAC
Tobacco	**$5,000**	
Philip Morris	$2,500	PAC
Dairy	**$6,500**	
None over $2,500		
Livestock	**$4,500**	
None over $2,500		
Agricultural Services/Products	**$9,600**	
California Westside Farmers Inc	$2,900	PAC
Food Processing & Sales	**$7,250**	
None over $2,500		

Communications/Electronics — $60,570

Misc Communications/Electronics	**$3,000**	
Pappas Telecasting Companies	$3,000	Indiv
Media/Entertainment	**$26,670**	
National Assn of Broadcasters	$9,500	PAC
Telephone Utilities	**$28,600**	
Pacific Telesis Group	$10,000	PAC
AT&T	$7,500	PAC

Source of Funds in 1992 Election

Source	Total	Pct
■ PACs	$526,345	62%
▨ Indivs $200+	$221,564	26%
□ Indivs under $200	$67,006	8%
▧ Other	$36,954	4%
Candidate	$0	0%
Party	$30,687	4%

Source of PAC Dollars by Sector

Source	Total	Pct
■ Business	$315,897	63%
▨ Labor	$152,760	31%
□ Ideology/Single Issue	$32,000	6%

In-State vs. Out-of-State Contributions*

Source	Total	Pct
□ In-State	$172,775	80%
■ Out-of-state	$43,643	20%
No state listed	$1,000	

*** by large individual contributors ($200 & above)**

Construction — $21,100

General Contractors	**$4,800**	
None over $2,500		
Home Builders	**$11,800**	
Beck Construction	$4,000	Indiv
National Assn of Home Builders	$3,000	PAC
Rural Builders of America PAC	$3,000	PAC
Building Materials & Equipment	**$3,500**	
None over $2,500		

Energy & Natural Resources — $45,250

Oil & Gas	**$14,750**	
Pacific Enterprises	$3,150	PAC
Robert M Bass Group Inc	$3,000	Indiv
Electric Utilities	**$29,000**	
Southern California Edison	$8,500	PAC
Pacific Gas & Electric	$5,000	PAC
Southern Co*	$2,500	PAC

Finance, Insurance & Real Estate — $134,020

Commercial Banks	**$8,310**	
None over $2,500		
Savings & Loans	**$9,400**	
US League of Savings Assns*	$3,500	PAC
Finance/Credit Companies	**$2,750**	
None over $2,500		
Securities & Investment	**$24,000**	
Lazard Freres & Co	$4,000	Indiv
Insurance	**$21,060**	
American Council of Life Insurance	$3,500	PAC
Pacific Mutual Life	$3,500	PAC
American Family Corp	$3,000	PAC

Contribution Totals by Sector

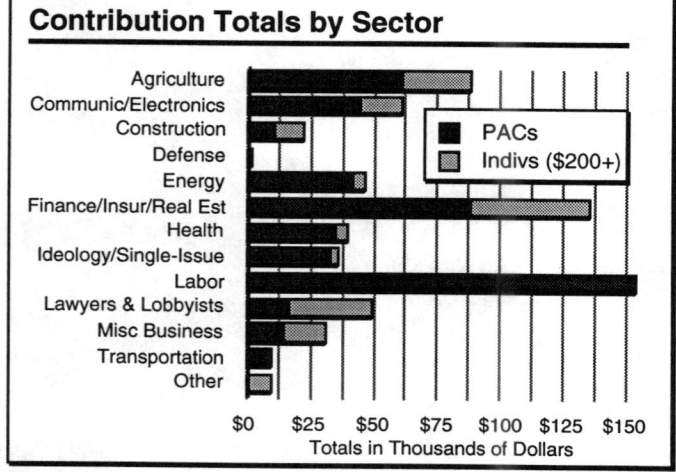

Agriculture
Communic/Electronics
Construction
Defense
Energy
Finance/Insur/Real Est
Health
Ideology/Single-Issue
Labor
Lawyers & Lobbyists
Misc Business
Transportation
Other

■ PACs
▨ Indivs ($200+)

$0 $25 $50 $75 $100 $125 $150
Totals in Thousands of Dollars

Real Estate **$50,100**
    National Assn of Realtors .... $10,000 PAC
    Gunner Andros Real Estate .... $8,000 Indiv
    Mortgage Bankers Assn of America .... $3,500 PAC
    AKT Development Co .... $3,000 Indiv

Accountants **$12,300**
    American Institute of CPA's .... $5,000 PAC
    Coopers & Lybrand .... $2,500 PAC

Misc Finance **$5,100**
    None over $2,500

Health $39,350

Health Professionals **$31,850**
    American Medical Assn .... $7,200 PAC
    American Dental Assn .... $5,500 PAC
    American Chiropractic Assn .... $5,000 PAC
    American Academy of Ophthalmology .... $4,000 PAC

Hospitals/Nursing Homes **$4,100**
    None over $2,500

Pharmaceuticals/Health Products **$2,500**
    None over $2,500

Lawyers & Lobbyists $48,493

Lawyers & Lobbyists **$48,493**
    Assn of Trial Lawyers of America .... $5,000 PAC

Misc Business $30,657

Beer, Wine & Liquor **$13,500**
    Gallo Winery .... $5,000 Indiv

Business Services **$6,050**
    None over $2,500

Casinos/Gambling **$4,000**
    None over $2,500

Transportation $8,850

Automotive **$2,700**
    None over $2,500

Railroads **$3,500**
    None over $2,500

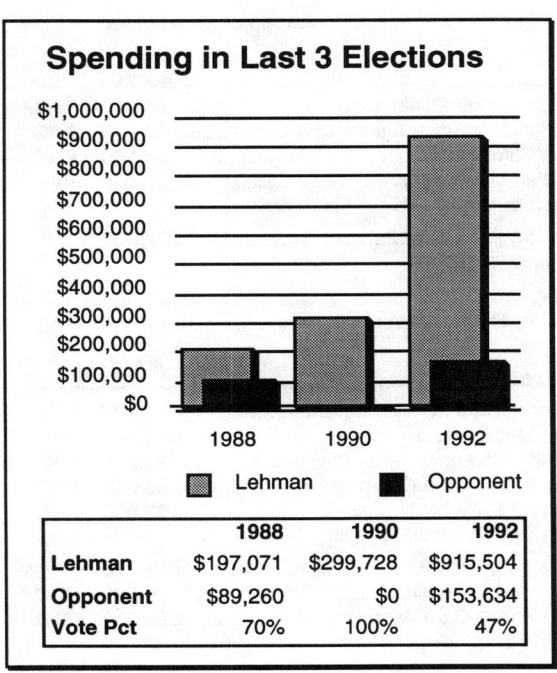

Spending in Last 3 Elections

	1988	1990	1992
Lehman	$197,071	$299,728	$915,504
Opponent	$89,260	$0	$153,634
Vote Pct	70%	100%	47%

Legend: ▨ Lehman   ■ Opponent

Labor

Labor $152,760

Building Trade Unions **$29,850**
    Carpenters & Joiners Union .... $8,500 PAC
    Laborers Union* .... $7,000 PAC
    Ironworkers Union .... $5,100 PAC
    Plumbers/Pipefitters Union .... $5,000 PAC
    Operating Engineers Union* .... $3,250 PAC

Industrial Unions **$34,750**
    Machinists/Aerospace Workers Union .... $10,000 PAC
    United Auto Workers .... $10,000 PAC
    Intl Brotherhood of Electrical Workers .... $8,000 PAC
    Rubber Cork Linoleum & Plastic Workers .... $4,000 PAC

Transportation Unions **$31,150**
    Teamsters Union .... $7,300 PAC
    United Transportation Union .... $7,000 PAC
    Marine Engineers Dist 2 Maritime Officers .... $5,500 PAC
    Air Line Pilots Assn .... $4,000 PAC

Public Sector Unions **$39,210**
    American Fedn of St/Cnty/Munic Employees .... $10,000 PAC
    National Education Assn .... $10,000 PAC
    National Assn of Letter Carriers .... $8,200 PAC
    National Assn Retired Federal Employees .... $7,000 PAC

Misc Unions **$17,800**
    Food & Commercial Workers Union .... $7,500 PAC
    Service Employees International Union .... $7,500 PAC

Ideological/Single-Issue

Ideological/Single-Issue $35,500

Democratic/Liberal **$2,500**
    None over $2,500

Leadership PACs **$12,000**
    24th Cong Dist of Calif PAC (Henry Waxman) .... $5,000 PAC
    Effective Government Cmte (Dick Gephardt) ...... $2,500 PAC

Pro-Choice **$7,500**
    National Abortion Rights Action League .... $5,500 PAC

Human Rights **$2,500**
    None over $2,500

Misc Issues **$9,000**
    National Cmte to Preserve Social Security .... $4,000 PAC
    Sierra Club .... $3,000 PAC

Other & Unknown

Other $9,500

Civil Servants/Public Officials **$3,900**
    None over $2,500

Retired **$3,800**
    None over $2,500

Unknown $43,705

    No Employer Listed or Found $2,950
    Generic Occupation/Category Unknown $6,640
    Employer Listed/Category Unknown $32,615
        Tolladay Corp .... $4,000 Indiv
        Lance Kashian & Co .... $3,900 Indiv

Independent expenditures supporting Lehman
    California Medical Assn $2,500

---

* Contributions came from more than one affiliate or subsidiary.

Sander Levin, D-Mich (12)

First elected: 1982

1991-92 Total Receipts: $1,028,481
1992 Year-end Cash: $98,288

1991-92 Committees & Subcommittees

District of Columbia
Government Operations and Metropolitan Affairs

Ways and Means
Health; Human Resources

Select Committee on Children, Youth and Families

Leading Contributors

Business

Agriculture	$17,825

Crop Production & Basic Processing $4,775
   None over $2,500

Dairy $4,200
   None over $2,500

Food Processing & Sales $3,350
   None over $2,500

Communications/Electronics	$28,950

Printing & Publishing $3,250
   None over $2,500

Media/Entertainment $5,750
   None over $2,500

Telephone Utilities $14,200
   Ameritech Corp* ....$6,000 PAC

Computer Equipment & Services $4,000
   Electronic Data Systems ....$3,000 PAC

Construction	$15,600

General Contractors $5,750
   Seligman & Associates ....$3,500 Indiv

Home Builders $4,000
   None over $2,500

Construction Services $2,800
   Smith, Hinchman & Grylls Assoc ....$2,800 Indiv

Building Materials & Equipment $2,550
   None over $2,500

Defense	$8,750

Defense Aerospace $7,000
   None over $2,500

Contribution Totals by Sector

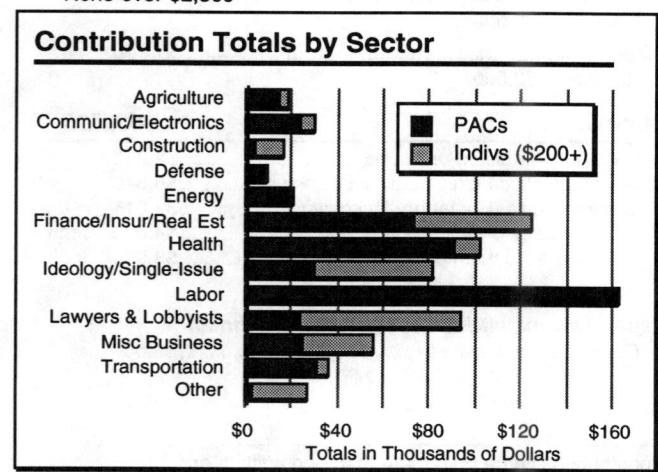

PACs
Indivs ($200+)

Agriculture
Communic/Electronics
Construction
Defense
Energy
Finance/Insur/Real Est
Health
Ideology/Single-Issue
Labor
Lawyers & Lobbyists
Misc Business
Transportation
Other

$0 $40 $80 $120 $160
Totals in Thousands of Dollars

Source of Funds in 1992 Election

Source	Total	Pct
PACs	$504,521	47%
Indivs $200+	$291,220	27%
Indivs under $200	$162,890	15%
Other	$113,104	11%
Candidate	$0	0%
Party	$55,604	5%

Source of PAC Dollars by Sector

Source	Total	Pct
Business	$308,596	62%
Labor	$161,340	32%
Ideology/Single Issue	$29,600	6%

In-State vs. Out-of-State Contributions*

Source	Total	Pct
In-State	$141,120	48%
Out-of-state	$150,100	52%
No state listed	$0	

* by large individual contributors ($200 & above)

Energy & Natural Resources	$20,050

Oil & Gas $10,200
   USX Corp ....$2,500 PAC

Electric Utilities $8,450
   Detroit Edison ....$3,900 PAC/Ind
   Consumers Power Co ....$2,800 PAC

Finance, Insurance & Real Estate	$123,549

Commercial Banks $10,600
   American Bankers Assn ....$2,500 PAC

Credit Unions $5,540
   Credit Union National Assn* ....$5,040 PAC

Securities & Investment $16,850
   None over $2,500

Insurance $42,999
   Blue Cross & Blue Shield Assn* ....$5,600 PAC/Ind
   Independent Insurance Agents of America ....$5,000 PAC
   American Family Corp ....$4,000 PAC
   Metropolitan Life Insurance ....$3,000 PAC
   Northwestern Mutual Life ....$2,500 PAC

Real Estate $32,200
   None over $2,500

Accountants $9,000
   American Institute of CPA's ....$5,000 PAC

Health	$100,597

Health Professionals $56,747
   American Medical Assn ....$10,000 PAC
   Assn for the Advancement of Psychology ....$9,997 PAC
   American Academy of Ophthalmology ....$3,500 PAC
   American Podiatry Assn ....$3,500 PAC
   American Soc Cataract/Refractive Surgery ....$2,500 PAC

Hospitals/Nursing Homes $15,850
   American Hospital Assn ....$6,000 PAC
   American Health Care Assn ....$5,000 PAC

Health Services $9,100
    None over $2,500

Pharmaceuticals/Health Products $16,900
    Kinetic Concepts Inc .... $4,000 PAC

Lawyers & Lobbyists $93,295

Lawyers & Lobbyists $93,295
    Assn of Trial Lawyers of America .... $5,000 PAC
    Akin, Gump et al .... $2,750 PAC
    Dickinson, Wright et al .... $2,750 Indiv
    Honigman, Miller et al .... $2,700 Indiv
    Arent, Fox et al .... $2,500 PAC/Ind

Misc Business $54,400

Beer, Wine & Liquor $5,550
    None over $2,500

Retail Sales $8,900
    New York Carpet World .... $3,000 Indiv

Misc Services $5,750
    None over $2,500

Business Services $10,250
    National Assn of Temporary Services .... $3,000 PAC

Chemical & Related Manufacturing $3,500
    None over $2,500

Steel Production $4,250
    None over $2,500

Misc Manufacturing & Distributing $13,100
    None over $2,500

Transportation $35,050

Air Transport $7,500
    None over $2,500

Automotive $23,600
    Chrysler Corp .... $8,000 PAC/Ind
    Ford Motor Co .... $4,000 PAC
    General Motors .... $3,200 PAC
    National Auto Dealers Assn .... $2,500 PAC

Railroads $3,450
    None over $2,500

Labor

Labor $161,640

Building Trade Unions $27,590
    Carpenters & Joiners Union* .... $6,800 PAC
    Laborers' Political League .... $4,500 PAC
    Sheet Metal Workers Union .... $4,500 PAC
    Plumbers/Pipefitters Union .... $3,400 PAC

Industrial Unions $38,600
    United Auto Workers .... $9,900 PAC
    Machinists/Aerospace Workers Union .... $5,500 PAC
    Intl Brotherhood of Electrical Workers .... $5,100 PAC
    Communications Workers of America .... $5,000 PAC
    United Steelworkers .... $5,000 PAC
    United Mine Workers .... $2,500 PAC

Transportation Unions $30,800
    Teamsters Union .... $10,000 PAC
    Seafarers International Union .... $6,000 PAC
    United Transportation Union .... $4,000 PAC
    Air Line Pilots Assn .... $3,000 PAC
    Amalgamated Transit Union .... $2,500 PAC

Public Sector Unions $49,450
    American Fedn of St/Cnty/Munic Employees .... $10,000 PAC
    National Education Assn .... $10,000 PAC
    National Assn of Letter Carriers .... $7,000 PAC
    American Federation of Teachers .... $6,500 PAC
    American Postal Workers Union .... $5,500 PAC
    National Assn Retired Federal Employees .... $3,500 PAC
    National Assn of Postmasters .... $3,100 PAC

Misc Unions $15,200
    Food & Commercial Workers Union .... $7,500 PAC
    Service Employees International Union .... $3,500 PAC

Ideological/Single-Issue

Ideological/Single-Issue $80,950

Democratic/Liberal $9,950
    None over $2,500

Pro-Israel $55,150
    National PAC .... $5,000 PAC
    MOPAC .... $2,500 PAC

Pro-Choice $3,150
    None over $2,500

Human Rights $3,950
    None over $2,500

Misc Issues $5,600
    National Cmte to Preserve Social Security .... $3,000 PAC

Other & Unknown

Other $26,250

Civil Servants/Public Officials $2,850
    None over $2,500

Education $4,850
    Oakland Community College .... $2,500 Indiv

Retired $15,150
    None over $2,500

Unknown $24,850

    Homemakers/Non-income earners $9,300
    No Employer Listed or Found $2,700
    Generic Occupation/Category Unknown $2,550
    Employer Listed/Category Unknown $10,300
        None over $2,500

* Contributions came from more than one affiliate or
subsidiary.

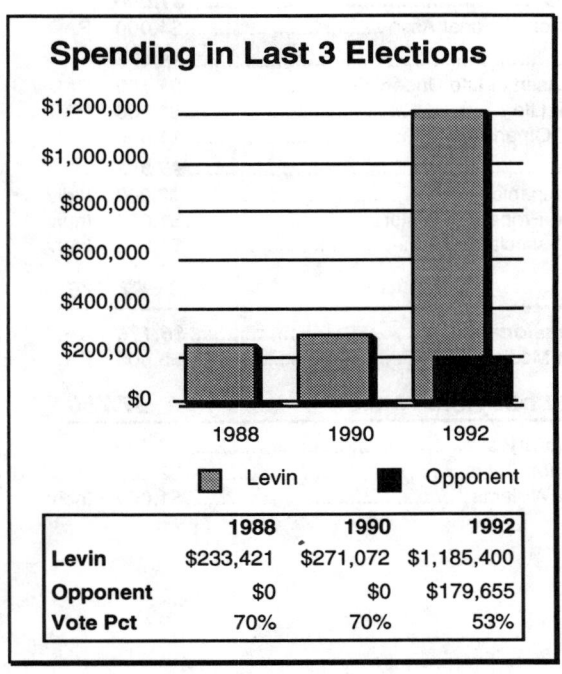

Spending in Last 3 Elections

	1988	1990	1992
Levin	$233,421	$271,072	$1,185,400
Opponent	$0	$0	$179,655
Vote Pct	70%	70%	53%

■ Levin   ■ Opponent

David A. Levy, R-NY (4)

First elected: 1992

1991-92 Total Receipts: $217,319
1992 Year-end Cash: $8,092

1993-94 Committees & Subcommittees

Foreign Affairs
Europe and the Middle East; International Operations

Public Works and Transportation
Aviation; Surface Transportation

Leading Contributors

Business

Agriculture	$4,925	
Tobacco	**$3,000**	
RJR Nabisco	$2,000	PAC
Philip Morris	$1,000	PAC
Food Processing & Sales	**$1,425**	
Pepsico Inc	$1,000	PAC

Communications/Electronics	$15,975	
Printing & Publishing	**$9,225**	
Inflight Newspapers Inc	$9,225	Indiv
Media/Entertainment	**$1,500**	
None over $1,000		
Telephone Utilities	**$3,750**	
NYNEX Corp*	$2,500	PAC
AT&T	$1,000	PAC
Electronics Mfg & Services	**$1,000**	
Harris Corp	$1,000	PAC

Construction	$3,625	
General Contractors	**$1,400**	
None over $1,000		
Construction Services	**$1,000**	
None over $1,000		

Source of Funds in 1992 Election

Source	Total	Pct
■ PACs	$60,880	23%
▨ Indivs $200+	$82,458	31%
☐ Indivs under $200	$56,178	21%
▧ Other	$69,317	26%
Candidate	$395	0%
Party	$57,914	22%

Source of PAC Dollars by Sector

Source	Total	Pct
■ Business	$50,170	89%
▨ Labor	$4,000	7%
☐ Ideology/Single Issue	$2,425	4%

In-State vs. Out-of-State Contributions*

Source	Total	Pct
☐ In-State	$76,425	95%
■ Out-of-state	$4,333	5%
No state listed	$1,450	

* by large individual contributors ($200 & above)

Energy & Natural Resources	$8,600	
Oil & Gas	**$4,100**	
Amoco Corp	$1,000	PAC
Electric Utilities	**$2,500**	
None over $1,000		
Waste Management	**$2,000**	
Browning-Ferris Industries	$2,000	PAC

Finance, Insurance & Real Estate	$16,708	
Commercial Banks	**$2,250**	
Chase Manhattan	$2,000	PAC
Credit Unions	**$1,000**	
Credit Union National Assn	$1,000	PAC
Insurance	**$6,475**	
National Assn of Life Underwriters	$1,500	PAC
New York Life	$1,500	PAC
Mutual of Omaha	$1,000	PAC
Real Estate	**$5,383**	
Mack Companies	$2,000	Indiv
Corporate Property Investors	$1,000	Indiv
Rodolitz Associates	$1,000	Indiv

Health	$7,575	
Health Professionals	**$6,175**	
American Medical Assn	$5,000	PAC

Lawyers & Lobbyists	$7,750	
Lawyers & Lobbyists	**$7,750**	
Meyer, Suozzi et al	$2,000	PAC/Ind
Hunton & Williams	$1,050	Indiv

Contribution Totals by Sector

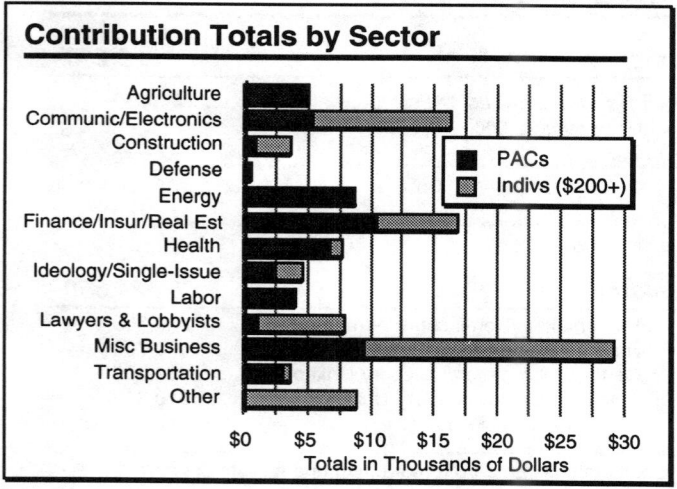

Agriculture, Communic/Electronics, Construction, Defense, Energy, Finance/Insur/Real Est, Health, Ideology/Single-Issue, Labor, Lawyers & Lobbyists, Misc Business, Transportation, Other

■ PACs
▨ Indivs ($200+)

$0 $5 $10 $15 $20 $25 $30
Totals in Thousands of Dollars

Misc Business $29,995

Business Associations **$1,045**
    Business Industry PAC ....$1,045   PAC
Food & Beverage **$1,200**
    Swan Club Restaurant ....$1,000   Indiv
Beer, Wine & Liquor **$5,000**
    National Beer Wholesalers Assn ....$5,000   PAC
Retail Sales **$13,450**
    Fortunoff's Inc ....$12,250   Indiv
Business Services **$6,600**
    Carpat Investments ....$5,000   Indiv
Chemical & Related Manufacturing **$1,000**
    None over $1,000
Misc Manufacturing & Distributing **$1,000**
    None over $1,000

Transportation $4,550

Air Transport **$1,500**
    Express Air Freight Unlimited ....$1,000   Indiv
    United Parcel Service ....$1,500   PAC
Automotive **$1,550**
    Eaton Corp ....$1,000   PAC

Labor

Labor $4,000

Building Trade Unions **$3,500**
    Laborers' Political League ....$3,000   PAC

Ideological/Single-Issue

Ideological/Single-Issue $4,425

Leadership PACs **$2,000**
    Republican Leader's Fund (Bob Michel) ....$1,000   PAC
Pro-Israel **$1,750**
    None over $1,000

Other & Unknown

Other $8,800

Civil Servants/Public Officials **$5,650**
    Town of Hempstead ....$2,750   Indiv
    Nassau County ....$1,300   Indiv
Retired **$2,250**
    None over $1,000

Unknown $21,350

    Homemakers/Non-income earners $2,000
    No Employer Listed or Found $9,350
    Employer Listed/Category Unknown $11,000
        Rubinstein Assoc ....$2,000   Indiv
        Assn for a Better Long Island ....$1,500   Indiv
        Morton Weber & Associates ....$1,500   Indiv

Spending in Last Election

	1992
Levy	$209,225
Opponent	$477,513
Vote Pct	50%

* Contributions came from more than one affiliate or subsidiary.

Jerry Lewis, R-Calif (40)

First elected: 1978

1991-92 Total Receipts: $471,956
1992 Year-end Cash: $264,213

1991-92 Committees & Subcommittees

Appropriations
Defense; Legislative (Ranking Republican)

Leading Contributors
Business

Agriculture	$40,900	
Crop Production & Basic Processing	**$15,350**	
Sunkist Growers	$5,000	PAC
Ocean Spray Cranberries Inc	$2,000	PAC
Tobacco	**$6,000**	
RJR Nabisco	$3,500	PAC
Dairy	**$6,350**	
None over $2,000		
Food Processing & Sales	**$10,600**	
Food Marketing Institute	$3,500	PAC
Connell Rice & Sugar Co	$2,000	Indiv

Communications/Electronics	$24,850	
Media/Entertainment	**$12,250**	
Walt Disney Co	$5,000	PAC/Ind
National Assn of Broadcasters	$3,500	PAC
National Cable Television Assn	$2,000	PAC
Telephone Utilities	**$8,500**	
Pacific Telesis Group	$4,000	PAC
Telecom Services & Equipment	**$2,000**	
New Bedford Panoramex Corp	$2,000	PAC
Computer Equipment & Services	**$2,000**	
Electronic Data Systems	$2,000	PAC

Construction	$16,250	
General Contractors	**$7,000**	
Associated General Contractors	$2,500	PAC

Contribution Totals by Sector

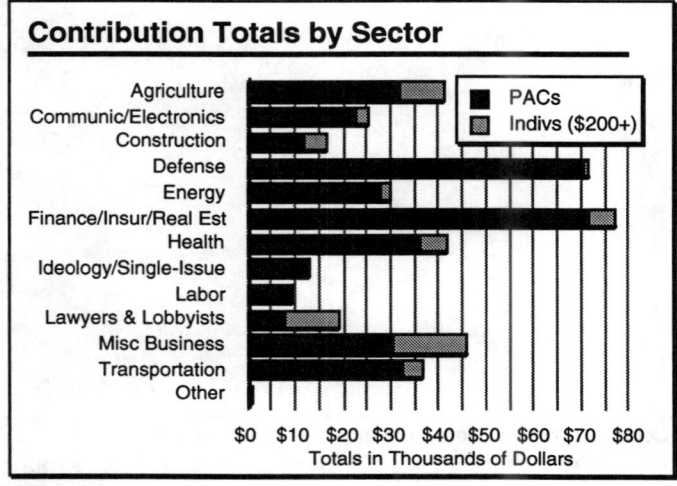

Agriculture
Communic/Electronics
Construction
Defense
Energy
Finance/Insur/Real Est
Health
Ideology/Single-Issue
Labor
Lawyers & Lobbyists
Misc Business
Transportation
Other

■ PACs
▨ Indivs ($200+)

$0 $10 $20 $30 $40 $50 $60 $70 $80
Totals in Thousands of Dollars

Source of Funds in 1992 Election

Source	Total	Pct
■ PACs	$358,045	76%
▨ Indivs $200+	$74,250	16%
☐ Indivs under $200	$14,349	3%
⊠ Other	$25,312	5%
Candidate	$0	0%
Party	$400	0%

Source of PAC Dollars by Sector

Source	Total	Pct
■ Business	$339,884	94%
▨ Labor	$9,000	2%
☐ Ideology/Single Issue	$12,086	3%

In-State vs. Out-of-State Contributions*

Source	Total	Pct
☐ In-State	$49,550	67%
■ Out-of-state	$24,050	33%
No state listed	$250	

* by large individual contributors ($200 & above)

Home Builders	$5,250	
National Assn of Home Builders	$5,000	PAC
Building Materials & Equipment	**$2,250**	
None over $2,000		

Defense	$72,195	
Defense Aerospace	**$39,945**	
General Dynamics	$5,750	PAC/Ind
Martin Marietta Corp	$4,500	PAC
Gencorp Inc	$4,000	PAC
Rockwell International	$4,000	PAC/Ind
Lockheed Corp	$3,000	PAC
Northrop Corp	$3,000	PAC
General Electric	$2,500	PAC/Ind
United Technologies	$2,500	PAC
Dyncorp	$2,000	PAC
McDonnell Douglas	$2,000	PAC
Defense Electronics	**$19,250**	
AT&T	$4,000	PAC
Hughes Aircraft	$3,000	PAC
Imo Industries Inc	$3,000	PAC
Misc Defense	**$13,000**	
General Atomics	$6,000	PAC
FMC Corp	$2,000	PAC

Energy & Natural Resources	$29,400	
Oil & Gas	**$15,600**	
Atlantic Richfield	$2,000	PAC
Coastal Corp	$2,000	PAC
Mining	**$2,250**	
None over $2,000		
Misc Energy	**$5,000**	
Bechtel Corp	$5,000	PAC
Electric Utilities	**$6,050**	
Southern California Edison	$3,000	PAC

Finance, Insurance & Real Estate — $77,000

Commercial Banks $11,000
   American Bankers Assn .... $5,000 PAC

Savings & Loans $2,250
   None over $2,000

Securities & Investment $6,500
   Chicago Mercantile Exchange .... $2,000 PAC
   Morgan Stanley & Co .... $2,000 PAC

Insurance $39,500
   National Assn of Life Underwriters .... $7,000 PAC
   American Council of Life Insurance .... $3,000 PAC
   Mutual of Omaha .... $3,000 PAC
   Pacific Mutual Life .... $3,000 PAC
   Delta Dental Plans Assn .... $2,000 PAC
   Independent Insurance Agents of America ...... $2,000 PAC
   Northwestern Mutual Life .... $2,000 PAC

Real Estate $15,750
   National Assn of Realtors .... $9,750 PAC

Misc Finance $2,000
   None over $2,000

Health — $41,289

Health Professionals $24,539
   American Medical Assn .... $7,500 PAC
   American Dental Assn .... $7,239 PAC
   National Assn of Pharmacists .... $2,000 PAC

Hospitals/Nursing Homes $6,250
   American Health Care Assn .... $2,500 PAC

Health Services $3,000
   None over $2,000

Pharmaceuticals/Health Products $5,500
   None over $2,000

Misc Health $2,000
   Victor Dalley Medical Group .... $2,000 Indiv

Lawyers & Lobbyists — $18,500

Lawyers & Lobbyists $18,500
   None over $1,500

Misc Business — $45,200

Food & Beverage $3,500
   McDonald's Corp .... $2,000 PAC

Beer, Wine & Liquor $10,000
   National Beer Wholesalers Assn .... $3,000 PAC
   Foothill Beverage Co .... $2,000 Indiv
   Wine & Spirits Wholesalers of America ...... $2,000 PAC

Retail Sales $7,500
   International Council of Shopping Centers ...... $2,000 PAC

Business Services $2,500
   None over $2,000

Casinos/Gambling $15,350
   Whiskey Pete's Casino .... $5,000 Indiv
   Circus Circus Enterprises .... $2,000 PAC

Misc Manufacturing & Distributing $3,000
   None over $2,000

Transportation — $36,050

Air Transport $14,500
   United Parcel Service .... $7,000 PAC
   Federal Express Corp .... $5,000 PAC

Automotive $12,500
   Americans for Free International Trade .... $5,000 PAC
   National Auto Dealers Assn .... $4,000 PAC

Trucking $2,500
   None over $2,000

Railroads $2,500
   None over $2,000

Sea Transport $2,050
   None over $2,000

Misc Transport $2,000
   None over $2,000

Labor

Labor — $9,000

Transportation Unions $6,500
   Marine Engineers Union* .... $6,500 PAC

Public Sector Unions $2,500
   None over $2,000

Ideological/Single-Issue

Ideological/Single-Issue — $12,586

Pro-Israel $5,000
   National PAC .... $5,000 PAC

Gun Rights/Gun Control $6,950
   National Rifle Assn .... $6,950 PAC

Other & Unknown

Unknown — $11,250

   No Employer Listed or Found $2,250
   Employer Listed/Category Unknown $8,000
     Lewis Jenkins & Associates .... $2,000 Indiv

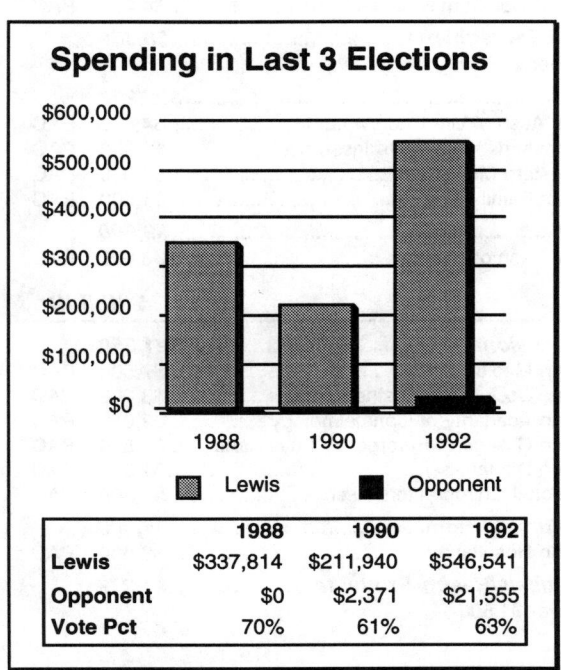

Spending in Last 3 Elections

	1988	1990	1992
Lewis	$337,814	$211,940	$546,541
Opponent	$0	$2,371	$21,555
Vote Pct	70%	61%	63%

* Contributions came from more than one affiliate or
subsidiary.

John Lewis, D-Ga (5)

First elected: 1986

1991-92 Total Receipts: $307,636
1992 Year-end Cash: $324,123

1991-92 Committees & Subcommittees

Interior and Insular Affairs
Insular and International Affairs; National Parks and Public Lands

Public Works and Transportation
Aviation; Public Buildings and Grounds; Surface Transportation

Select Committee on Aging

Leading Contributors

Business

Agriculture	$10,400

Crop Production & Basic Processing	$2,700
None over $1,500	

Poultry & Eggs	$2,500
None over $1,500	

Forestry & Forest Products	$1,600
None over $1,500	

Communications/Electronics	$14,600

Media/Entertainment	$4,000	
MCA Inc	$1,500	PAC/Ind

Telephone Utilities	$10,600	
Southern Bell	$7,500	PAC
AT&T	$1,850	PAC

Construction	$3,600

General Contractors	$2,400
None over $1,500	

Defense	$1,500

Defense Aerospace	$1,500
None over $1,500	

Source of Funds in 1992 Election

Source	Total	Pct
PACs	$229,245	71%
Indivs $200+	$52,650	16%
Indivs under $200	$22,587	7%
Other	$18,947	6%
Candidate	$0	0%
Party	$16,243	5%

Source of PAC Dollars by Sector

Source	Total	Pct
Business	$141,929	54%
Labor	$106,500	41%
Ideology/Single Issue	$13,621	5%

In-State vs. Out-of-State Contributions*

Source	Total	Pct
In-State	$36,000	69%
Out-of-state	$16,400	31%
No state listed	$250	

* by large individual contributors ($200 & above)

Energy & Natural Resources — $8,300

Oil & Gas	$1,500	
None over $1,500		

Electric Utilities	$3,550	
Southern Co*	$2,550	PAC

Waste Management	$3,000	
Waste Management Inc	$3,000	PAC

Finance, Insurance & Real Estate — $44,450

Commercial Banks	$6,950	
Citizens & Southern National Bank	$4,200	PAC

Securities & Investment	$3,500	
None over $1,500		

Insurance	$22,250	
National Assn of Life Underwriters	$4,000	PAC
Massachusetts Mutual Life Insurance	$2,000	PAC
Northwestern Mutual Life	$2,000	PAC
American Family Corp	$1,500	PAC

Real Estate	$9,900	
National Assn of Realtors	$3,600	PAC

Health — $30,629

Health Professionals	$21,350	
American Medical Assn	$7,500	PAC
American Society of Anesthesiologists	$3,000	PAC
American Academy of Ophthalmology	$2,000	PAC
American College of Emergency Physicians	$1,500	PAC
American Dental Assn	$1,500	PAC
International Chiropractors Assn	$1,500	PAC

Hospitals/Nursing Homes	$4,000	
American Hospital Assn	$2,500	PAC

Pharmaceuticals/Health Products	$4,279	
None over $1,500		

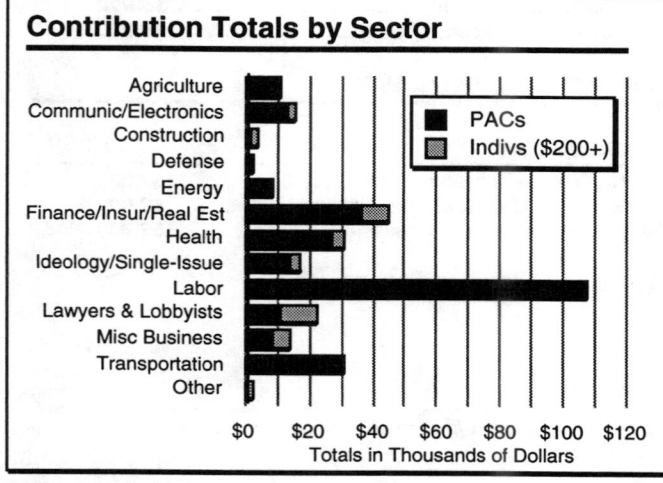

Contribution Totals by Sector

Agriculture
Communic/Electronics
Construction
Defense
Energy
Finance/Insur/Real Est
Health
Ideology/Single-Issue
Labor
Lawyers & Lobbyists
Misc Business
Transportation
Other

Legend: PACs / Indivs ($200+)

$0 $20 $40 $60 $80 $100 $120
Totals in Thousands of Dollars

Lawyers & Lobbyists	$21,500

Lawyers & Lobbyists	$21,500	
Assn of Trial Lawyers of America	$5,000	PAC
Alexander & Associates	$2,200	Indiv
King & Spalding	$2,000	PAC

Misc Business	$13,550

Food & Beverage	$3,500	
Coca-Cola Co	$2,500	PAC
Retail Sales	$1,500	
None over $1,500		
Business Services	$2,000	
None over $1,500		
Misc Manufacturing & Distributing	$2,150	
None over $1,500		

Transportation	$30,300

Air Transport	$21,550	
Federal Express Corp	$10,000	PAC
United Parcel Service	$7,200	PAC
Delta Airlines	$1,500	PAC
United Airlines	$1,500	PAC
Automotive	$3,500	
National Auto Dealers Assn	$1,500	PAC
Trucking	$2,550	
None over $1,500		
Railroads	$1,850	
None over $1,500		

Labor

Labor	$106,500

Building Trade Unions	$13,200	
Laborers' Political League	$4,000	PAC
Sheet Metal Workers Union	$2,500	PAC
Plumbers/Pipefitters Union	$2,000	PAC
Industrial Unions	$30,350	
United Auto Workers	$7,500	PAC
Intl Brotherhood of Electrical Workers	$5,200	PAC
United Steelworkers	$5,000	PAC
Communications Workers of America	$3,500	PAC
Machinists/Aerospace Workers Union	$3,000	PAC
Ladies Garment Workers Union	$2,350	PAC
Transportation Unions	$25,850	
Teamsters Union	$10,000	PAC
Air Line Pilots Assn	$5,000	PAC
Marine Engineers Union*	$3,000	PAC
Public Sector Unions	$27,400	
National Education Assn	$7,500	PAC
American Federation of Teachers	$5,000	PAC
American Fedn of St/Cnty/Munic Employees	$5,000	PAC
American Postal Workers Union	$2,050	PAC
National Assn Retired Federal Employees	$2,000	PAC
National Assn of Letter Carriers	$2,000	PAC
International Assn of Firefighters	$1,500	PAC
Misc Unions	$9,700	
Food & Commercial Workers Union	$3,350	PAC
AFL-CIO	$2,850	PAC
Hotel/Restaurant Employees Union	$1,500	PAC

Ideological/Single-Issue

Ideological/Single-Issue	$16,621

Pro-Israel	$7,600	
National PAC	$5,000	PAC
Human Rights	$3,121	
Human Rights Campaign Fund	$2,121	PAC
Misc Issues	$2,900	
National Cmte to Preserve Social Security	$2,400	PAC

Other & Unknown

Other	$1,500
None over $1,500	

Unknown	$11,250	
Homemakers/Non-income earners	$2,350	
No Employer Listed or Found	$2,700	
Employer Listed/Category Unknown	$5,200	
None over $1,500		

Spending in Last 3 Elections

	1988	1990	1992
Lewis	$101,540	$108,118	$248,867
Opponent	$6,047	$8,271	$57,850
Vote Pct	78%	76%	72%

---

* Contributions came from more than one affiliate or subsidiary.

Tom Lewis, R-Fla (16)

1991-92 Committees & Subcommittees

Agriculture
Cotton, Rice and Sugar; Domestic Marketing, Consumer Relations and Nutrition (Ranking Republican); Livestock, Dairy and Poultry

Science, Space and Technology
Space; Technology and Competitiveness (Ranking Republican)

Select Committee on Narcotics Abuse and Control

Leading Contributors

Business

Agriculture $86,543

Crop Production & Basic Processing	**$58,193**	
Okeelanta Corp	$9,000	Indiv
Florida Citrus Mutual	$5,000	PAC
United States Sugar Corp	$3,500	PAC
A Duda & Sons	$2,900	PAC
Florida Fruit & Vegetable Assn	$2,500	PAC/Ind
American Crystal Sugar Corp	$2,250	PAC
Indian River Citrus League	$2,250	Indiv
Fritz Stein Farms	$2,000	Indiv
Russakis Groves	$2,000	Indiv
Lewis Pope Farm	$1,800	Indiv
Alico Inc	$1,500	Indiv
American Sugarbeet Growers Assn	$1,500	PAC
Bernard Egan & Co	$1,500	Indiv
Sugar Cane Growers Co-op of Florida	$1,500	PAC
Riverfront Groves	$1,250	Indiv
Southern Minn Beet Sugar Co-op	$1,125	PAC
Ben Hill Griffin Inc	$1,000	Indiv
Naples Tomato Growers	$1,000	Indiv
Savannah Foods & Industries	$1,000	PAC
WE Schlechter & Sons	$1,000	Indiv
Dairy	**$5,400**	
Associated Milk Producers	$2,500	PAC
Dairymen Inc	$1,000	PAC
Schwan's Sales Enterprises	$1,000	Indiv
Poultry & Eggs	**$1,750**	
None over $1,000		
Livestock	**$3,900**	
Hilliard Brothers of Florida	$1,900	Indiv
National Cattlemen's Assn*	$1,250	PAC

First elected: 1982

1991-92 Total Receipts:	$296,405
1992 Year-end Cash:	$53,970

Source of Funds in 1992 Election

Source	Total	Pct
PACs	$127,015	43%
Indivs $200+	$79,692	27%
Indivs under $200	$67,217	23%
Other	$22,481	8%
Candidate	$0	0%
Party	$1,705	1%

Source of PAC Dollars by Sector

Source	Total	Pct
Business	$129,175	95%
Labor	$6,000	4%
Ideology/Single Issue	$250	0%

In-State vs. Out-of-State Contributions*

Source	Total	Pct
In-State	$77,392	97%
Out-of-state	$2,250	3%
No state listed	$0	

***by large individual contributors ($200 & above)**

Agricultural Services/Products	**$7,350**	
American Veterinary Medical Assn	$1,000	PAC
Farm Credit Council	$1,000	PAC
Freeport-McMoRan Inc	$1,000	PAC
Food Processing & Sales	**$8,700**	
Winn-Dixie Stores	$3,500	PAC
Food Marketing Institute	$1,500	PAC
Neill's Farm Fresh Produce	$1,250	Indiv
Rose Packing Co	$1,000	Indiv

Communications/Electronics $12,000

Telephone Utilities	**$9,750**	
Southern Bell	$5,000	PAC
AT&T	$2,000	PAC
GTE Corp	$1,250	PAC
United Telecommunications	$1,250	PAC
Electronics Mfg & Services	**$1,500**	
Harris Corp	$1,000	PAC

Construction $6,000

General Contractors	**$2,750**	
Associated General Contractors	$1,250	PAC
Ranger Construction	$1,000	Indiv
Home Builders	**$1,500**	
National Assn of Home Builders	$1,500	PAC
Special Trade Contractors	**$1,000**	
Dycom Industries Inc	$1,000	Indiv

Defense $6,750

Defense Aerospace	**$5,750**	
Textron Inc	$1,500	PAC
United Technologies	$1,000	PAC
Defense Electronics	**$1,000**	
None over $1,000		

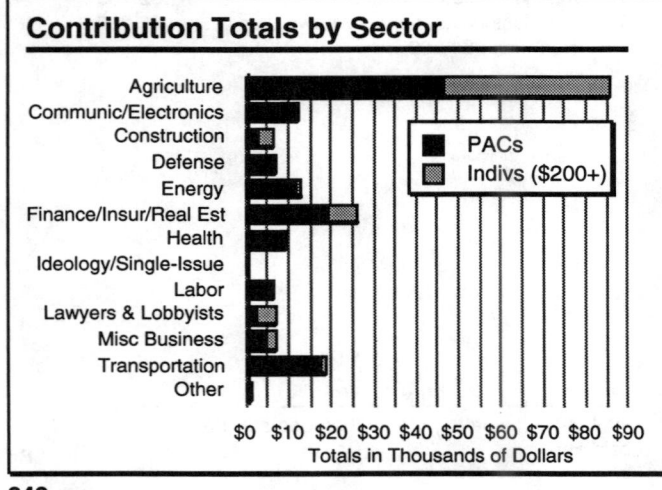

Contribution Totals by Sector

Agriculture
Communic/Electronics
Construction
Defense
Energy
Finance/Insur/Real Est
Health
Ideology/Single-Issue
Labor
Lawyers & Lobbyists
Misc Business
Transportation
Other

■ PACs
▨ Indivs ($200+)

$0 $10 $20 $30 $40 $50 $60 $70 $80 $90
Totals in Thousands of Dollars

Energy & Natural Resources — $12,600

Oil & Gas **$2,500**
    Kirchman Oil Corp ....$1,000   Indiv

Electric Utilities **$10,100**
    Florida Power & Light ....$2,500   PAC
    Southern Co* ....$2,000   PAC
    ACRE (Action Cmte for Rural Electrification) ......$1,500   PAC
    American Electric Power ....$1,000   PAC
    Florida Power Corp ....$1,000   PAC
    Teco Energy Inc ....$1,000   PAC

Finance, Insurance & Real Estate — $25,657

Commercial Banks **$8,250**
    Citizens & Southern National Bank ....$3,000   PAC
    Barnett Banks Inc ....$2,500   PAC
    SunBanks ....$2,000   PAC

Savings & Loans **$1,250**
    Florida League of Financial Institutions ....$1,000   PAC

Securities & Investment **$2,200**
    Andlinger & Co ....$1,000   Indiv

Insurance **$2,800**
    Blue Cross/Blue Shield of Florida ....$1,000   PAC

Real Estate **$9,907**
    National Assn of Realtors ....$6,000   PAC

Misc Finance **$1,250**
    None over $1,000

Health — $9,000

Health Professionals **$7,000**
    American Medical Assn ....$5,000   PAC
    American Academy of Ophthalmology ....$1,000   PAC

Health Services **$1,500**
    American Ambulance Assn ....$1,500   PAC

Lawyers & Lobbyists — $6,300

Lawyers & Lobbyists **$6,300**
    Holland & Knight ....$2,500   PAC/Ind
    Fleming, Haile & Shaw ....$1,250   Indiv

Misc Business — $6,500

Beer, Wine & Liquor **$3,000**
    Brown Distributing Co ....$2,000   Indiv

Casinos/Gambling **$1,000**
    Showboat Inc ....$1,000   PAC

Misc Manufacturing & Distributing **$1,000**
    Stone Container Corp ....$1,000   PAC

Transportation — $18,050

Air Transport **$11,000**
    Aircraft Owners & Pilots Assn ...$7,000   PAC
    United Parcel Service ....$2,500   PAC
    Boeing Co ....$1,000   PAC

Automotive **$5,800**
    National Auto Dealers Assn ....$4,000   PAC
    Americans for Free International Trade ....$1,000   PAC

Labor

Labor — $6,000

Transportation Unions **$3,500**
    Marine Engineers Dist 2 Maritime Officers ....$3,500   PAC

Misc Unions **$2,500**
    AFL-CIO ....$2,500   PAC

Other & Unknown

Other — $1,033

Retired **$1,033**
    None over $1,000

Unknown — $18,384

    Homemakers/Non-income earners $7,166
    No Employer Listed or Found $2,000
    Employer Listed/Category Unknown $8,968
        Berry ....$1,000   Indiv
        Gulf & Western Food ....$1,000   Indiv
        Tradcom International ....$1,000   Indiv

Spending in Last 3 Elections

	1988	1990	1992
Lewis	$256,081	$405,471	$363,795
Opponent	$0	$0	$96,522
Vote Pct	100%	100%	61%

*Contributions came from more than one affiliate or subsidiary.

Jim Ross Lightfoot, R-Iowa (3)

First elected: 1984

1991-92 Total Receipts: $623,098
1992 Year-end Cash: $8,356

1991-92 Committees & Subcommittees

Appropriations
Military Construction; Treasury, Postal Service and General Government

Leading Contributors

Business

Agriculture	$65,023	
Crop Production & Basic Processing	**$15,525**	
American Crystal Sugar Corp	$1,500	PAC
Tobacco	**$2,000**	
None over $1,500		
Dairy	**$11,000**	
Associated Milk Producers	$7,000	PAC
Mid-America Dairymen	$4,000	PAC
Livestock	**$4,200**	
Flying A Cattle Co	$1,500	Indiv
National Cattlemen's Assn*	$1,500	PAC
Agricultural Services/Products	**$21,298**	
Deere & Co	$5,000	PAC
Iowa Farm Bureau Federation	$4,948	PAC
Land O'Lakes Inc	$2,000	PAC
Food Processing & Sales	**$10,500**	
ConAgra Inc	$4,500	PAC
Food Marketing Institute	$2,500	PAC

Communications/Electronics	$20,100	
Printing & Publishing	**$3,750**	
McCleary, Cumming Co	$3,000	Indiv
Media/Entertainment	**$3,800**	
None over $1,500		
Telephone Utilities	**$10,750**	
GTE Corp	$3,000	PAC
AT&T	$2,500	PAC
NYNEX Corp	$1,500	PAC/Ind
US West Inc	$1,500	PAC
Electronics Mfg & Services	**$1,800**	
None over $1,500		

Source of Funds in 1992 Election

Source	Total	Pct
■ PACs	$259,952	38%
▨ Indivs $200+	$87,515	13%
□ Indivs under $200	$229,045	34%
⊠ Other	$106,810	16%
Candidate	$0	0%
Party	$80,221	12%

Source of PAC Dollars by Sector

Source	Total	Pct
■ Business	$225,660	89%
▨ Labor	$2,500	1%
□ Ideology/Single Issue	$24,400	10%

In-State vs. Out-of-State Contributions*

Source	Total	Pct
□ In-State	$74,623	85%
■ Out-of-state	$12,892	15%
No state listed	$0	

*** by large individual contributors ($200 & above)**

Construction	$16,800	
General Contractors	**$7,000**	
Associated General Contractors	$2,500	PAC
Home Builders	**$3,750**	
National Assn of Home Builders	$3,000	PAC
Special Trade Contractors	**$3,000**	
National Electrical Contractors Assn	$2,000	PAC
Building Materials & Equipment	**$3,050**	
Lennox Industries	$2,000	PAC

Defense	$6,000	
Defense Aerospace	**$6,000**	
Rockwell International	$2,500	PAC

Energy & Natural Resources	$23,642	
Oil & Gas	**$9,142**	
Petroleum Marketers Assn	$1,750	PAC
Mining	**$1,500**	
None over $1,500		
Misc Energy	**$3,000**	
Cooper Industries	$3,000	PAC
Electric Utilities	**$9,500**	
Iowa Resources Inc	$2,500	PAC
Midwest Energy Co	$2,500	PAC

Finance, Insurance & Real Estate	$36,650	
Commercial Banks	**$6,950**	
American Bankers Assn	$2,000	PAC
Hawkeye Bancorp	$2,000	PAC
Insurance	**$11,950**	
Mutual of Omaha	$2,000	PAC/Ind
Employers Mutual Casualty Co	$1,500	PAC/Ind

Contribution Totals by Sector

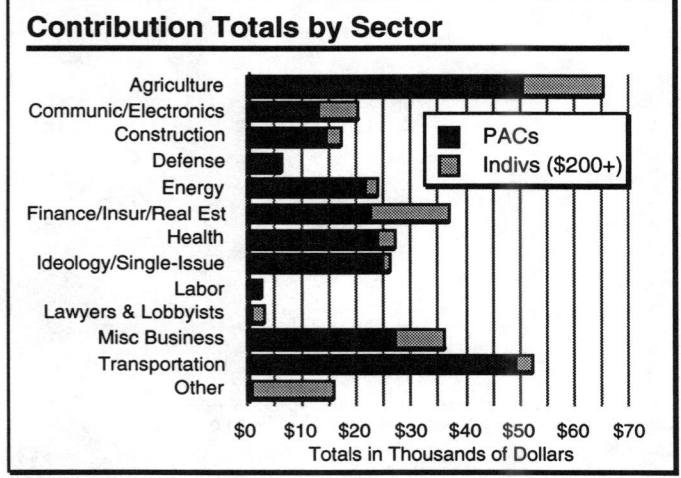

Agriculture
Communic/Electronics
Construction
Defense
Energy
Finance/Insur/Real Est
Health
Ideology/Single-Issue
Labor
Lawyers & Lobbyists
Misc Business
Transportation
Other

■ PACs
▨ Indivs ($200+)

$0 $10 $20 $30 $40 $50 $60 $70
Totals in Thousands of Dollars

Real Estate **$12,750**
    National Assn of Realtors .... $10,000 PAC
    Mid-America Group .... $2,000 Indiv

Misc Finance **$3,250**
    CIC Plan .... $2,750 Indiv

Health   **$26,846**

Health Professionals **$24,346**
    American Medical Assn .... $9,996 PAC
    American Chiropractic Assn .... $4,000 PAC
    American Dental Assn .... $3,000 PAC
    National Assn of Pharmacists .... $3,000 PAC

Pharmaceuticals/Health Products **$2,000**
    None over $1,500

Lawyers & Lobbyists   **$3,000**

Lawyers & Lobbyists **$3,000**
    None over $1,500

Misc Business   **$35,801**

Business Associations **$4,041**
    National Fedn of Independent Business .... $1,500 PAC

Food & Beverage **$3,000**
    None over $1,500

Beer, Wine & Liquor **$4,500**
    National Beer Wholesalers Assn .... $3,500 PAC

Retail Sales **$3,750**
    Wal-Mart Stores .... $1,750 PAC/Ind

Business Services **$1,800**
    None over $1,500

Chemical & Related Manufacturing **$3,750**
    Dow Chemical .... $1,500 PAC
    Dial Corp .... $1,500 PAC

Misc Manufacturing & Distributing **$13,960**
    Maytag Co .... $6,500 PAC
    Stone Container Corp .... $2,000 PAC
    Delong Sportswear .... $1,500 Indiv

Transportation   **$51,650**

Air Transport **$19,600**
    Aircraft Owners & Pilots Assn .... $10,000 PAC
    United Parcel Service .... $4,500 PAC

Automotive **$18,000**
    National Auto Dealers Assn .... $9,500 PAC
    Auto Dealers & Drivers for Free Trade .... $3,000 PAC
    Eaton Corp .... $3,000 PAC
    Americans for Free International Trade .... $2,000 PAC

Trucking **$4,550**
    PACEG Committee .... $2,000 PAC
    Ruan Companies .... $1,800 Indiv

Railroads **$7,500**
    Union Pacific Corp .... $5,000 PAC

Sea Transport **$2,000**
    None over $1,500

Labor

Labor   **$2,500**

Transportation Unions **$1,500**
    None over $1,500

Ideological/Single-Issue

Ideological/Single-Issue   **$25,900**

Republican/Conservative **$4,500**
    Eagle Forum .... $3,000 PAC

Pro-Israel **$5,500**
    None over $1,500

Pro-Life **$3,500**
    National Right to Life PAC .... $3,500 PAC

Gun Rights/Gun Control **$9,900**
    National Rifle Assn .... $9,900 PAC

Misc Issues **$2,000**
    None over $1,500

Other & Unknown

Other   **$15,350**

Retired **$13,950**
    None over $1,500

Unknown   **$11,213**

    No Employer Listed or Found $4,965
    Employer Listed/Category Unknown $5,248
        None over $1,500

Independent expenditures supporting Lightfoot
    National Right to Life PAC $2,904

Spending in Last 3 Elections

	1988	1990	1992
Lightfoot	$420,730	$418,134	$755,552
Opponent	$131,599	$63,591	$646,569
Vote Pct	64%	68%	49%

* Contributions came from more than one affiliate or subsidiary.

845

John Linder, R-Ga (4)

First elected: 1992

1991-92 Total Receipts: $516,357
1992 Year-end Cash: $1,219

1993-94 Committees & Subcommittees

Banking, Finance and Urban Affairs
Consumer Credit and Insurance; Financial Institutions Supervision, Regulation and Deposit Insurance

Science, Space and Technology
Technology, Environment and Aviation

Veterans' Affairs
Compensation and Health Care

Leading Contributors

Business

Agriculture $24,755

Tobacco	**$1,500**	
RJR Nabisco	$1,500	PAC
Poultry & Eggs	**$3,250**	
Gold Kist	$3,250	PAC/Ind
Livestock	**$2,000**	
National Cattlemen's Assn*	$1,500	PAC
Agricultural Services/Products	**$2,000**	
Deere & Co	$1,500	PAC
Food Processing & Sales	**$11,600**	
Flowers Industries	$5,000	PAC
American Bakers Assn	$1,500	PAC
Winn-Dixie Stores	$1,500	PAC
Forestry & Forest Products	**$3,905**	
Westvaco Corp	$2,000	PAC

Communications/Electronics $14,049

Telephone Utilities	**$5,510**	
Southern Bell	$2,750	PAC
AT&T	$1,500	PAC
Electronics Mfg & Services	**$3,339**	
Harris Corp	$2,000	PAC
Computer Equipment & Services	**$2,500**	
None over $1,500		

Source of Funds in 1992 Election

Source	Total	Pct
■ PACs	$187,978	35%
▨ Indivs $200+	$163,752	30%
☐ Indivs under $200	$117,410	22%
▧ Other	$72,217	13%
Candidate	$0	0%
Party	$31,100	6%

Source of PAC Dollars by Sector

Source	Total	Pct
■ Business	$164,613	82%
▨ Labor	$2,000	1%
☐ Ideology/Single Issue	$34,002	17%

In-State vs. Out-of-State Contributions*

Source	Total	Pct
☐ In-State	$149,992	92%
■ Out-of-state	$13,500	8%
No state listed	$0	

* by large individual contributors ($200 & above)

Construction $16,550

General Contractors	**$4,900**	
None over $1,500		
Home Builders	**$1,650**	
None over $1,500		
Special Trade Contractors	**$5,000**	
Sheet Metal/Air Conditioning Contractors	$4,500	PAC
Building Materials & Equipment	**$4,000**	
American Supply Assn	$1,500	PAC

Defense $2,750

Defense Aerospace	**$2,000**	
None over $1,500		

Energy & Natural Resources $21,500

Oil & Gas	**$16,000**	
Triton Inc	$4,500	Indiv
Gas Inc	$2,000	Indiv
Chevron Corp	$1,500	PAC
Misc Energy	**$3,000**	
Cooper Industries	$3,000	PAC
Electric Utilities	**$2,250**	
Georgia Power Co	$2,250	PAC

Finance, Insurance & Real Estate $85,017

Commercial Banks	**$16,917**	
American Bankers Assn	$5,000	PAC
Trust Co of Georgia	$2,000	PAC
Citizens & Southern National Bank	$1,917	PAC
Bank South Corp	$1,750	PAC
Finance/Credit Companies	**$2,000**	
Nationwide Credit	$2,000	Indiv
Securities & Investment	**$5,950**	
Account Portfolios LP	$4,000	Indiv

Contribution Totals by Sector

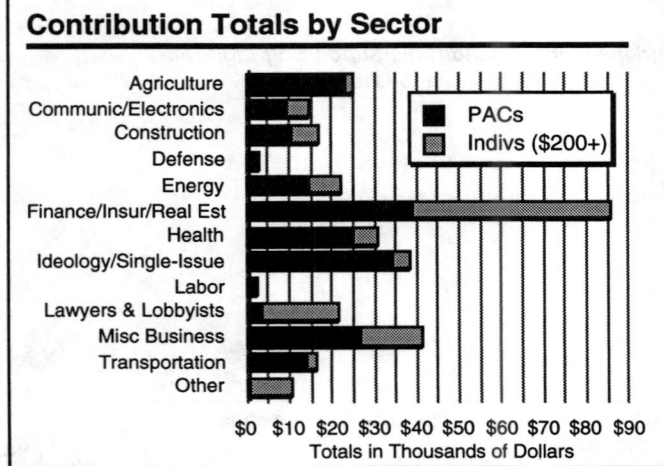

Agriculture
Communic/Electronics
Construction
Defense
Energy
Finance/Insur/Real Est
Health
Ideology/Single-Issue
Labor
Lawyers & Lobbyists
Misc Business
Transportation
Other

■ PACs
▨ Indivs ($200+)

$0 $10 $20 $30 $40 $50 $60 $70 $80 $90
Totals in Thousands of Dollars

Insurance **$23,250**
    Integrated Administration Services ....$6,000   Indiv
    American Family Corp ....$3,000   PAC
    Health Systems Management Co ....$3,000   Indiv
    Golden Rule Insurance Co ....$2,000   PAC/Ind
    Powell & Co ....$2,000   Indiv

Real Estate **$16,600**
    National Assn of Realtors ....$10,000   PAC

Accountants **$11,550**
    Ernst & Young ....$8,000   PAC/Ind
    Gunn & Mann ....$1,750   Indiv

Misc Finance **$7,750**
    Equifax Inc ....$2,750   PAC/Ind
    Noble Enterprises ....$2,000   Indiv

Health $30,550

Health Professionals **$28,050**
    American Medical Assn ....$10,800   PAC
    American Dental Assn......................................$10,000   PAC

Pharmaceuticals/Health Products **$1,500**
    None over $1,500

Lawyers & Lobbyists $20,750

Lawyers & Lobbyists **$20,750**
    Bauer, Deitch & Raines ....$4,500   Indiv
    Sutherland, Asbill & Brennan ....$4,000   Indiv
    King & Spalding..$3,250   PAC/Ind
    Fisher & Phillips ....$2,000   Indiv

Misc Business $40,544

Business Associations **$3,540**
    National Fedn of Independent Business ....$1,500   PAC

Food & Beverage **$7,250**
    Waffle House Inc ....$4,000   Indiv
    Coca-Cola Co ....$1,500   PAC

Beer, Wine & Liquor **$5,500**
    National Beer Wholesalers Assn ....$4,000   PAC

Business Services **$4,553**
    None over $1,500

Chemical & Related Manufacturing **$6,700**
    Dow Chemical ....$3,000   PAC

Misc Manufacturing & Distributing **$10,050**
    John H Harland Co ....$1,500   PAC
    Stone Container Corp ....$1,500   PAC

Transportation $15,650

Air Transport **$8,700**
    United Parcel Service......................................$8,000   PAC

Automotive **$4,700**
    Eaton Corp ....$3,000   PAC

Railroads **$1,500**
    Union Pacific Corp ....$1,500   PAC

Labor

Labor $2,000

Public Sector Unions **$2,000**
    National Assn Retired Federal Employees ....$2,000   PAC

Ideological/Single-Issue

Ideological/Single-Issue $39,452

Republican/Conservative **$20,391**
    Loose Group..$8,500   PAC
    Eagle Forum ....$5,500   PAC

Leadership PACs **$4,200**
    Fund for Southern Progress ....$1,500   PAC

Pro-Life **$4,000**
    National Right to Life PAC ....$4,000   PAC

Gun Rights/Gun Control **$4,950**
    National Rifle Assn ....$4,950   PAC

Misc Issues **$4,491**
    None over $1,500

Other & Unknown

Other $9,900

Retired **$7,200**
    None over $1,500

Unknown $42,650

    Homemakers/Non-income earners $14,650
    No Employer Listed or Found $2,250
    Generic Occupation/Category Unknown $3,000
    Employer Listed/Category Unknown $22,500
        HBR Capital ....$2,000   Indiv
        Mark Demoss & Associates ....$2,000   Indiv

Independent expenditures supporting Linder
    National Right to Life PAC $9,080

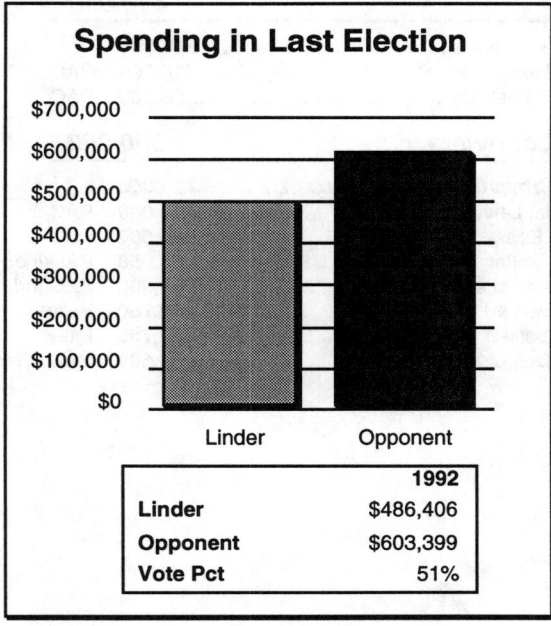

Spending in Last Election

	1992
Linder	$486,406
Opponent	$603,399
Vote Pct	51%

---

* Contributions came from more than one affiliate or subsidiary.

William O. Lipinski, D-Ill (3)

First elected: 1982

1991-92 Total Receipts: $556,335
1992 Year-end Cash: $23,597

1991-92 Committees & Subcommittees

Merchant Marine and Fisheries
Oceanography, Great Lakes and Outer Continental Shelf; Oversight and Investigations (Chairman)

Public Works and Transportation
Aviation; Public Buildings and Grounds; Surface Transportation

Leading Contributors

Business

Agriculture	$5,600	
Crop Production & Basic Processing	**$2,850**	
None over $1,500		

Communications/Electronics	$6,850	
Telephone Utilities	**$5,350**	
Ameritech Corp*	$4,350	PAC

Construction	$16,500	
General Contractors	**$6,500**	
Fluor Corp	$2,000	PAC
Associated General Contractors	$1,500	PAC
Home Builders	**$4,250**	
National Assn of Home Builders	$2,750	PAC
Morse Diesel International	$1,500	Indiv
Construction Services	**$4,500**	
Alfred Benesch & Co	$2,000	Indiv

Energy & Natural Resources	$6,250	
Oil & Gas	**$4,000**	
None over $1,500		

Finance, Insurance & Real Estate	$51,775	
Commercial Banks	**$4,600**	
Amalgamated Trust & Savings Bank	$1,500	Indiv
Securities & Investment	**$17,750**	
Chicago Board of Trade	$4,250	PAC/Ind
Chicago Mercantile Exchange	$3,500	PAC
First Boston Corp	$3,000	PAC/Ind
Goldman, Sachs & Co	$2,500	PAC/Ind

Source of Funds in 1992 Election

Source	Total	Pct
■ PACs	$317,850	57%
▨ Indivs $200+	$174,250	31%
☐ Indivs under $200	$53,596	10%
⊠ Other	$10,776	2%
Candidate	$0	0%
Party	$587	0%

Source of PAC Dollars by Sector

Source	Total	Pct
■ Business	$151,050	51%
▨ Labor	$124,000	42%
☐ Ideology/Single Issue	$20,442	7%

In-State vs. Out-of-State Contributions*

Source	Total	Pct
☐ In-State	$150,350	86%
■ Out-of-state	$23,900	14%
No state listed	$0	

* by large individual contributors ($200 & above)

Insurance	$5,250	
None over $1,500		
Real Estate	**$19,125**	
National Assn of Realtors	$5,750	PAC
Stein & Co	$3,000	Indiv
Ted Amdur & Associates	$3,000	Indiv
JMB Realty Corp	$1,625	Indiv
K&G Building Management	$1,500	Indiv
Accountants	**$2,900**	
Arthur Andersen & Co	$1,700	PAC/Ind
Misc Finance	**$2,150**	
None over $1,500		

Health	$18,950	
Health Professionals	**$16,800**	
American Medical Assn*	$10,000	PAC
American Dental Assn	$5,500	PAC

Lawyers & Lobbyists	$50,000	
Lawyers & Lobbyists	**$50,000**	
Assn of Trial Lawyers of America	$10,000	PAC
Kirkland & Ellis	$5,500	PAC
Hopkins & Sutter	$2,950	PAC/Ind
Linton, Mields et al	$2,900	PAC/Ind
Mayer, Brown & Platt	$2,750	Indiv
Sidley & Austin	$2,750	Indiv
Corboy & Demetrio	$2,500	Indiv

Contribution Totals by Sector

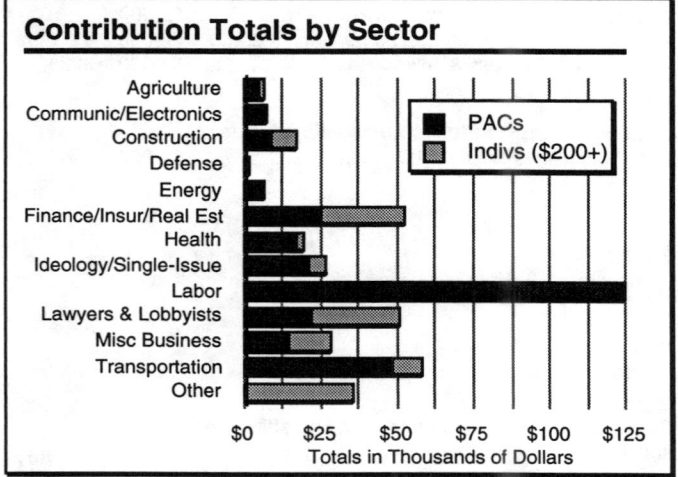

- Agriculture
- Communic/Electronics
- Construction
- Defense
- Energy
- Finance/Insur/Real Est
- Health
- Ideology/Single-Issue
- Labor
- Lawyers & Lobbyists
- Misc Business
- Transportation
- Other

Legend: ■ PACs, ▨ Indivs ($200+)

$0 $25 $50 $75 $100 $125

Totals in Thousands of Dollars

Misc Business — $27,950

Food & Beverage **$6,250**
    Pepsi-Cola General Bottlers .... $5,500   PAC

Business Services **$4,800**
    None over $1,500

Lodging/Tourism **$3,000**
    None over $1,500

Misc Manufacturing & Distributing **$7,300**
    John O'Connell Ltd .... $2,000   Indiv
    Owens-Illinois .... $1,500   PAC

Transportation — $57,000

Air Transport **$31,000**
    American Airlines .... $15,500   PAC/Ind
    Federal Express Corp .... $4,000   PAC
    United Airlines .... $3,500   PAC
    Aircraft Owners & Pilots Assn .... $2,500   PAC
    United Parcel Service .... $2,300   PAC

Automotive **$3,000**
    National Auto Dealers Assn .... $2,000   PAC

Trucking **$4,250**
    None over $1,500

Railroads **$10,750**
    Burlington Northern .... $2,500   PAC
    Santa Fe Southern Pacific .... $2,500   PAC

Sea Transport **$7,500**
    Matson Navigation .... $2,000   PAC
    Sea-Land Corp .... $2,000   PAC
    American President Lines .... $1,500   PAC

Labor

Labor — $124,000

Building Trade Unions **$25,500**
    Ironworkers Union .... $7,500   PAC
    Laborers' Political League .... $6,000   PAC
    Plumbers/Pipefitters Union .... $3,000   PAC
    Painters & Allied Trades Union .... $2,500   PAC
    Sheet Metal Workers Union .... $2,500   PAC
    AFL-CIO Bldg/Construction Trades Dept .... $1,500   PAC

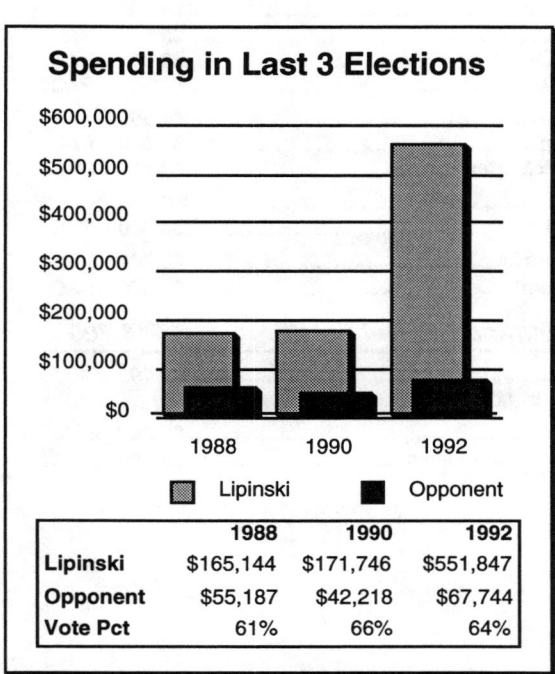

Spending in Last 3 Elections

	1988	1990	1992
Lipinski	$165,144	$171,746	$551,847
Opponent	$55,187	$42,218	$67,744
Vote Pct	61%	66%	64%

Legend: ▨ Lipinski   ■ Opponent

Industrial Unions — $25,000

    United Auto Workers .... $7,500   PAC
    Intl Brotherhood of Electrical Workers ...... $5,000   PAC
    Boilermakers Union .... $3,000   PAC
    United Steelworkers .... $2,500   PAC
    Central States Joint Board .... $2,000   PAC
    Machinists/Aerospace Workers Union ...... $2,000   PAC

Transportation Unions **$49,400**
    Teamsters Union .... $10,000   PAC
    Air Line Pilots Assn .... $6,000   PAC
    Marine Engineers Union* .... $5,500   PAC
    Transport Workers Union .... $5,500   PAC
    United Transportation Union .... $5,500   PAC
    Amalgamated Transit Union .... $4,500   PAC
    National Air Traffic Controllers Assn ...... $2,500   PAC
    Seafarers International Union .... $2,000   PAC
    Assn of Flight Attendants .... $1,500   PAC
    International Longshoremen's Assn .... $1,500   PAC

Public Sector Unions **$14,100**
    National Assn Retired Federal Employees .... $4,000   PAC
    American Federation of Teachers .... $2,500   PAC
    American Postal Workers Union .... $2,500   PAC
    American Fedn of St/Cnty/Munic Employees ...... $2,000   PAC
    National Assn of Letter Carriers .... $2,000   PAC

Misc Unions **$10,000**
    AFL-CIO .... $5,500   PAC
    Food & Commercial Workers Union .... $3,000   PAC

Ideological/Single-Issue

Ideological/Single-Issue — $25,617

Leadership PACs **$14,500**
    Citizens for Gary J Lapaille .... $8,000   PAC
    House Leadership Fund (Tom Foley) ...... $5,000   PAC

Pro-Israel **$5,125**
    None over $1,500

Misc Issues **$4,500**
    National Cmte to Preserve Social Security .... $4,000   PAC

Other & Unknown

Other — $35,050

Civil Servants/Public Officials **$30,375**
    City of Chicago .... $10,425   Indiv
    Chicago Park District .... $4,725   Indiv
    Cook County .... $4,550   Indiv
    State of Illinois .... $2,000   Indiv
    Chicago Transit Authority .... $1,725   Indiv

Retired **$4,425**
    None over $1,500

Unknown — $43,200

    Homemakers/Non-income earners $7,575
    No Employer Listed or Found $5,400
    Generic Occupation/Category Unknown $3,800
    Employer Listed/Category Unknown $26,425
        Burke, Smith & Williams .... $3,000   Indiv
        Lison, Pullman et al .... $3,000   Indiv
        Lake Development Enterprises .... $2,000   Indiv
        Schwatz, Cooper et al .... $2,000   Indiv
        Terry O'Brien & Co .... $2,000   Indiv

* Contributions came from more than one affiliate or subsidiary.

Robert L. Livingston, R-La (1)

First elected: 1977

1991-92 Total Receipts: $337,316
1992 Year-end Cash: $295,908

1991-92 Committees & Subcommittees

Administration
Elections (Ranking Republican); Personnel and Police

Appropriations
Defense; Foreign Operations, Export Financing and Related Programs

Leading Contributors

Business

Agriculture	$7,850

Crop Production & Basic Processing $2,000
　None over $1,500

Tobacco $2,500
　None over $1,500

Communications/Electronics	$5,250

Telephone Utilities $3,500
　BellSouth Corp* .... $3,500　PAC

Construction	$11,750

General Contractors $2,250
　None over $1,500

Construction Services $6,750
　Vernon F Meyer & Assoc .... $3,000　Indiv
　Walk, Haydel & Associates .... $2,000　Indiv

Defense	$57,200

Defense Aerospace $24,000
　Rockwell International .... $4,000　PAC
　General Electric .... $2,500　PAC
　Gencorp Inc .... $2,000　PAC
　Lockheed Corp .... $2,000　PAC
　Northrop Corp .... $2,000　PAC
　Textron Inc .... $2,000　PAC
　General Dynamics .... $1,500　PAC
　McDonnell Douglas .... $1,500　PAC

Source of Funds in 1992 Election

Source	Total	Pct
PACs	$133,247	40%
Indivs $200+	$101,000	30%
Indivs under $200	$69,924	21%
Other	$33,145	10%
Candidate	$0	0%
Party	$80	0%

Source of PAC Dollars by Sector

Source	Total	Pct
Business	$120,550	92%
Labor	$5,000	4%
Ideology/Single Issue	$5,200	4%

In-State vs. Out-of-State Contributions*

Source	Total	Pct
In-State	$81,000	81%
Out-of-state	$19,500	19%
No state listed	$0	

* by large individual contributors ($200 & above)

Defense Electronics $21,000
　Diagnostic Retrieval Systems .... $5,000　Indiv
　Hughes Aircraft .... $2,000　PAC
　Raytheon .... $2,000　PAC
　Westinghouse Electric .... $2,000　PAC
　TRW Inc .... $1,750　PAC

Misc Defense $12,200
　Avondale Industries .... $3,500　PAC/Ind
　Maersk Inc .... $2,700　PAC

Energy & Natural Resources	$31,800

Oil & Gas $19,600
　Texaco .... $2,500　PAC
　Columbia Gas System .... $2,300　PAC
　Graham Resources .... $1,500　PAC/Ind

Mining $5,500
　Dravo Corp .... $2,000　PAC
　Freeport-McMoRan Inc .... $3,500　PAC/Ind

Misc Energy $4,000
　McDermott Inc .... $4,000　PAC

Electric Utilities $2,700
　Entergy Corp* .... $1,950　PAC

Finance, Insurance & Real Estate	$11,700

Insurance $3,400
　None over $1,500

Real Estate $6,750
　National Assn of Realtors .... $5,000　PAC

Contribution Totals by Sector

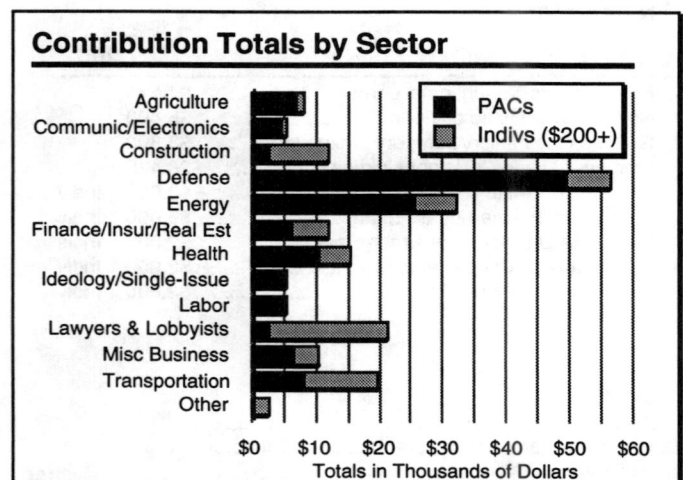

Agriculture
Communic/Electronics
Construction
Defense
Energy
Finance/Insur/Real Est
Health
Ideology/Single-Issue
Labor
Lawyers & Lobbyists
Misc Business
Transportation
Other

PACs
Indivs ($200+)

$0　$10　$20　$30　$40　$50　$60
Totals in Thousands of Dollars

Health $15,300

Health Professionals $12,800
    American Medical Assn...........................$5,000 PAC
    National Assn of Pharmacists ....$1,500 PAC

Hospitals/Nursing Homes $2,000
    None over $1,500

Lawyers & Lobbyists $21,100

Lawyers & Lobbyists $21,100
    Jones, Walker et al ....$3,000 PAC/Ind
    Porteous, Hainkel et al ....$2,000 Indiv

Misc Business $10,050

Retail Sales $2,250
    None over $1,500

Business Services $1,500
    None over $1,500

Chemical & Related Manufacturing $3,500
    None over $1,500

Transportation $18,800

Air Transport $2,000
    United Parcel Service ....$1,500 PAC

Automotive $2,000
    None over $1,500

Sea Transport...$12,500
    Pike Shipping Co/American Gulf Shipping ....$2,000 Indiv
    Trinity Marine Group ....$2,000 Indiv
    Edison Chouest Offshore ....$1,500 Indiv
    Lykes Brothers Steamship Co ....$1,500 PAC

Labor

Labor $5,000

Transportation Unions $5,000
    Marine Engineers Dist 2 Maritime Officers ....$3,000 PAC
    Seafarers International Union ....$1,500 PAC

Ideological/Single-Issue

Ideological/Single-Issue $5,200

Pro-Israel $3,000
    Louisiana for American Security ....$3,000 PAC

Other & Unknown

Other $2,500

Retired $2,000
    None over $1,500

Unknown $27,750

    Homemakers/Non-income earners $2,000
    No Employer Listed or Found $7,050
    Employer Listed/Category Unknown $18,200
        None over $1,500

Spending in Last 3 Elections

	1988	1990	1992
Livingston	$153,458	$108,207	$321,487
Opponent	$99,065	$0	$0
Vote Pct	79%	84%	100%

* Contributions came from more than one affiliate or subsidiary.

851

Marilyn Lloyd, D-Tenn (3)

First elected: 1974

1991-92 Total Receipts: $463,643
1992 Year-end Cash: $10,471

1991-92 Committees & Subcommittees

Armed Services
Military Personnel and Compensation; Procurement and Military Nuclear Systems

Science, Space and Technology
Energy (Chairwoman)

Select Committee on Aging

Leading Contributors

Business

Agriculture $12,250

Dairy **$2,000**
    Dairymen Inc-Tennessee .... $1,500 PAC

Food Processing & Sales **$4,300**
    None over $1,500

Forestry & Forest Products **$3,000**
    East Brainerd Lumber Co .... $2,000 Indiv

Communications/Electronics $3,600

Media/Entertainment **$2,000**
    None over $1,500

Telephone Utilities **$1,600**
    South Central Bell Telephone .... $1,600 PAC

Construction $8,150

General Contractors **$4,900**
    Fluor Corp .... $3,000 PAC

Construction Services **$3,000**
    None over $1,500

Defense $51,750

Defense Aerospace **$28,000**
    Martin Marietta Corp .... $6,500 PAC/Ind
    General Dynamics .... $4,500 PAC
    General Electric .... $2,500 PAC
    Boeing Co .... $2,000 PAC
    Grumman Corp .... $2,000 PAC
    Rockwell International .... $2,000 PAC
    LTV Aerospace & Defense Co .... $1,500 PAC

Source of Funds in 1992 Election

Source	Total	Pct
PACs	$272,250	57%
Indivs $200+	$86,222	18%
Indivs under $200	$67,455	14%
Other	$50,157	11%
Candidate	$0	0%
Party	$18,241	4%

Source of PAC Dollars by Sector

Source	Total	Pct
Business	$180,000	67%
Labor	$85,750	32%
Ideology/Single Issue	$2,000	1%

In-State vs. Out-of-State Contributions*

Source	Total	Pct
In-State	$78,422	91%
Out-of-state	$7,800	9%
No state listed	$0	

* by large individual contributors ($200 & above)

Defense Electronics **$12,750**
    AT&T .... $4,500 PAC
    Raytheon .... $3,500 PAC

Misc Defense **$11,000**
    General Atomics .... $8,000 PAC

Energy & Natural Resources $25,800

Oil & Gas **$7,000**
    Enserch Corp .... $1,500 PAC

Mining **$3,000**
    None over $1,500

Nuclear Energy **$3,850**
    Gilbert Associates .... $2,750 PAC

Misc Energy **$5,250**
    Bechtel Corp .... $3,000 PAC

Electric Utilities **$4,500**
    None over $1,500

Environmental Svcs/Equipment **$1,500**
    None over $1,500

Finance, Insurance & Real Estate $30,650

Commercial Banks **$4,750**
    None over $1,500

Insurance **$2,250**
    None over $1,500

Real Estate **$20,500**
    National Assn of Realtors .... $10,000 PAC
    CBL & Associates .... $5,250 Indiv
    Otho Brown Realty .... $2,000 Indiv

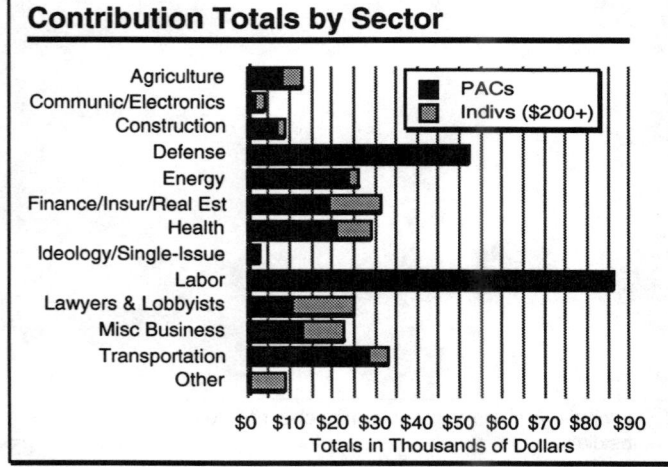

Contribution Totals by Sector

Legend: ■ PACs ▨ Indivs ($200+)

Categories (top to bottom): Agriculture, Communic/Electronics, Construction, Defense, Energy, Finance/Insur/Real Est, Health, Ideology/Single-Issue, Labor, Lawyers & Lobbyists, Misc Business, Transportation, Other

Axis: $0 $10 $20 $30 $40 $50 $60 $70 $80 $90
Totals in Thousands of Dollars

Health $28,722

Health Professionals **$18,200**
   American Medical Assn ....$7,350   PAC
   American Dental Assn ....$1,500   PAC
   American Optometric Assn ....$1,500   PAC

Hospitals/Nursing Homes **$4,772**
   National Health Corp ....$2,000   PAC

Pharmaceuticals/Health Products **$4,750**
   Schering-Plough Corp ....$3,500   PAC

Lawyers & Lobbyists $24,250

Lawyers & Lobbyists **$24,250**
   Assn of Trial Lawyers of America ....$10,000   PAC
   Witt, Gaither & Whitaker ....$1,500   Indiv

Misc Business $22,250

Food & Beverage **$2,500**
   None over $1,500

Retail Sales **$3,500**
   None over $1,500

Business Services **$2,250**
   Olan Mills Inc ....$2,000   Indiv

Chemical & Related Manufacturing **$1,500**
   None over $1,500

Misc Manufacturing & Distributing **$2,500**
   Hoechst Celanese Corp ....$1,500   PAC

Textiles **$8,500**
   Burlington Industries ....$3,500   PAC
   American Textile Manufacturers Institute ....$2,500   PAC

Transportation $32,450

Air Transport **$12,000**
   Federal Express Corp ....$10,000   PAC
   United Parcel Service ....$2,000   PAC

Automotive **$17,700**
   National Auto Dealers Assn ....$10,000   PAC
   Americans for Free International Trade ....$3,000   PAC
   Fox Toyota ....$1,700   Indiv
   Auto Dealers & Drivers for Free Trade ....$1,500   PAC

Railroads **$1,500**
   None over $1,500

Labor

Labor $86,000

Building Trade Unions **$16,500**
   Carpenters & Joiners Union ....$6,500   PAC
   Plumbers/Pipefitters Union ....$3,000   PAC
   Ironworkers Union ....$2,500   PAC
   Laborers' Political League ....$2,000   PAC
   AFL-CIO Bldg/Construction Trades Dept ....$1,500   PAC

Industrial Unions **$33,700**
   Machinists/Aerospace Workers Union ....$10,000   PAC
   Intl Brotherhood of Electrical Workers ....$7,500   PAC
   United Steelworkers ....$5,000   PAC
   United Auto Workers ....$3,500   PAC
   Communications Workers of America ....$2,500   PAC
   Rubber Cork Linoleum & Plastic Workers ....$2,000   PAC

Transportation Unions **$14,000**
   Teamsters Union ....$10,000   PAC
   Marine Engineers Dist 2 Maritime Officers ....$3,500   PAC

Public Sector Unions **$15,550**
   National Education Assn ....$10,000   PAC
   National Assn Retired Federal Employees ....$4,000   PAC

Misc Unions **$6,250**
   Food & Commercial Workers Union ....$3,000   PAC
   AFL-CIO ....$2,750   PAC/Ind

Ideological/Single-Issue

Ideological/Single-Issue $2,500
   None over $1,500

Other & Unknown

Other $8,250

Civil Servants/Public Officials **$3,750**
   City of Clinton ....$3,000   Indiv

Retired **$4,250**
   None over $1,500

Unknown $17,350
   Homemakers/Non-income earners $4,250
   Employer Listed/Category Unknown $11,850
      None over $1,500

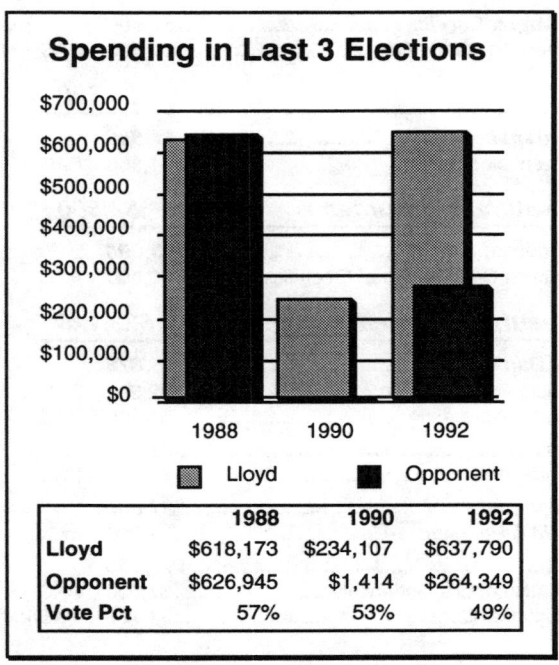

Spending in Last 3 Elections

	1988	1990	1992
Lloyd	$618,173	$234,107	$637,790
Opponent	$626,945	$1,414	$264,349
Vote Pct	57%	53%	49%

Jill L. Long, D-Ind (4)

1991-92 Committees & Subcommittees

Agriculture
Conservation, Credit and Rural Development; Livestock, Dairy and Poultry; Wheat, Soybeans and Feed Grains

Veterans' Affairs
Hospitals and Health Care; Oversight and Investigations

Select Committee on Hunger

Leading Contributors

Business

Agriculture $58,000

Crop Production & Basic Processing	**$12,200**	
American Crystal Sugar Corp	$1,500	PAC
American Sugarbeet Growers Assn	$1,500	PAC
Central Soya Co	$1,250	Indiv
National Cotton Council	$1,250	PAC
American Sugar Cane League	$1,000	PAC
Florida Sugar Cane League	$1,000	PAC
Dairy	**$23,500**	
Milk Marketing Inc	$10,000	PAC
Associated Milk Producers	$6,500	PAC
Mid-America Dairymen	$4,000	PAC
Dairymen Inc	$2,000	PAC
Dairymens Mountain Assn	$1,000	PAC
Poultry & Eggs	**$4,000**	
National Broiler Council	$2,000	PAC
National Turkey Federation	$1,000	PAC
United Egg Assn	$1,000	PAC
Livestock	**$3,050**	
National Pork Producers Council	$1,500	PAC
National Cattlemen's Assn	$1,000	PAC
Agricultural Services/Products	**$12,000**	
Indiana Farm Bureau	$5,000	PAC
Land O'Lakes Inc	$1,500	PAC
American Assn of Crop Insurers	$1,000	PAC
American Veterinary Medical Assn	$1,000	PAC
CF Industries	$1,000	PAC
National Council of Farmer Co-ops	$1,000	PAC

First elected: 1989

1991-92 Total Receipts: $375,147
1992 Year-end Cash: $15,090

Source of Funds in 1992 Election

Source	Total	Pct
■ PACs	$262,682	69%
▨ Indivs $200+	$29,556	8%
□ Indivs under $200	$63,544	17%
▧ Other	$25,587	7%
Candidate	$0	0%
Party	$7,072	2%

Source of PAC Dollars by Sector

Source	Total	Pct
■ Business	$125,605	48%
▨ Labor	$128,050	49%
□ Ideology/Single Issue	$8,152	3%

In-State vs. Out-of-State Contributions*

Source	Total	Pct
□ In-State	$26,356	89%
■ Out-of-state	$3,200	11%
No state listed	$0	

* by large individual contributors ($200 & above)

Food Processing & Sales	**$2,250**	
American Meat Institute	$1,250	PAC
Central Soya Co	$1,000	PAC
Forestry & Forest Products	**$1,000**	
None over $1,000		

Communications/Electronics $12,700

Telephone Utilities	**$10,500**	
Indiana Bell Telephone	$3,500	PAC
GTE Corp	$2,750	PAC
AT&T	$2,000	PAC
United Telecommunications	$1,000	PAC
Electronics Mfg & Services	**$1,500**	
North American Philips Corp	$1,500	PAC

Defense $1,500

Defense Aerospace	**$1,500**	
United Technologies	$1,500	PAC

Energy & Natural Resources $3,500

Electric Utilities	**$3,000**	
ACRE (Action Cmte for Rural Electrification)*	$3,000	PAC

Finance, Insurance & Real Estate $28,123

Commercial Banks	**$5,673**	
Independent Bankers Assn	$2,500	PAC
American Bankers Assn	$1,500	PAC
Credit Unions	**$1,000**	
Credit Union National Assn	$1,000	PAC
Securities & Investment	**$1,500**	
John Head & Partners	$1,000	Indiv
Insurance	**$11,150**	
National Assn of Life Underwriters	$7,500	PAC
Lincoln National Corp	$1,700	PAC/Ind

Contribution Totals by Sector

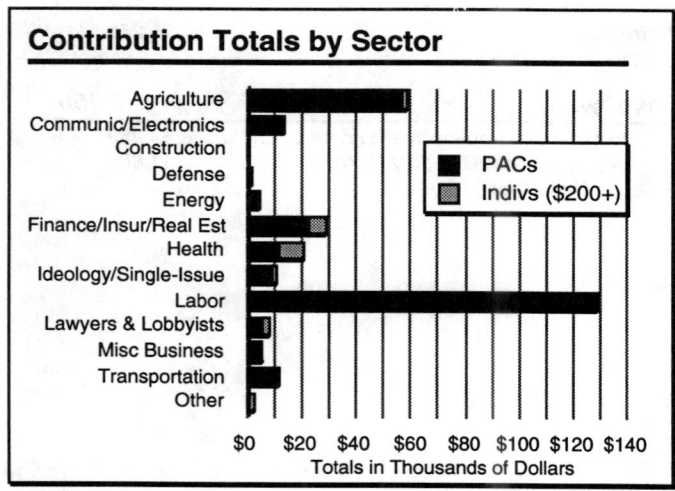

Legend: ■ PACs ▨ Indivs ($200+)

Categories: Agriculture, Communic/Electronics, Construction, Defense, Energy, Finance/Insur/Real Est, Health, Ideology/Single-Issue, Labor, Lawyers & Lobbyists, Misc Business, Transportation, Other

Totals in Thousands of Dollars
$0 $20 $40 $60 $80 $100 $120 $140

Real Estate **$9,000**
   National Assn of Realtors ....$6,000 PAC
   MMM Invest Inc ....$2,000 Indiv
   Schrader Real Estate Co ....$1,000 Indiv

Health   **$20,008**

Health Professionals **$16,508**
   American Medical Assn* ....$2,075 PAC
   American Academy of Ophthalmology ....$1,500 PAC
   American Podiatry Assn ....$1,000 PAC
   American Psychiatric Assn ....$1,000 PAC

Pharmaceuticals/Health Products **$3,000**
   ICI Americas Inc ....$1,000 PAC
   Merck & Co ....$1,000 PAC

Lawyers & Lobbyists   **$7,100**

Lawyers & Lobbyists **$7,100**
   Assn of Trial Lawyers of America ....$5,000 PAC

Misc Business   **$5,050**

Misc Manufacturing & Distributing **$2,700**
   Hoechst Celanese Corp ....$2,000 PAC

Textiles **$1,500**
   Burlington Industries ....$1,500 PAC

Transportation   **$10,830**

Air Transport **$1,080**
   General Electric ....$1,000 PAC

Automotive **$2,250**
   General Motors ....$1,250 PAC/Ind

Trucking **$7,500**
   North American Van Lines ....$7,500 PAC

Labor

Labor   **$128,250**

Building Trade Unions **$15,100**
   Sheet Metal Workers Union ....$5,000 PAC
   Laborers Union* ....$3,200 Indiv
   Plumbers/Pipefitters Union ....$2,000 PAC

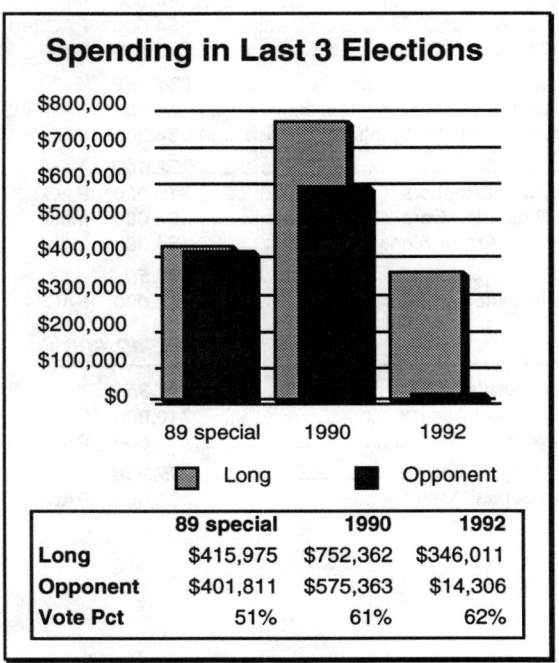

Spending in Last 3 Elections

	89 special	1990	1992
Long	$415,975	$752,362	$346,011
Opponent	$401,811	$575,363	$14,306
Vote Pct	51%	61%	62%

   Carpenters & Joiners Union ....$1,500 PAC
   Operating Engineers Union* ....$1,400 PAC
   AFL-CIO Bldg/Construction Trades Dept ....$1,000 PAC
   Bricklayers Union ....$1,000 PAC

Industrial Unions **$39,800**
   United Auto Workers ....$10,000 PAC
   Intl Brotherhood of Electrical Workers ....$7,500 PAC
   Rubber Cork Linoleum & Plastic Workers ....$7,000 PAC
   Machinists/Aerospace Workers Union ....$5,500 PAC
   Boilermakers Union ....$3,000 PAC
   United Mine Workers ....$2,500 PAC
   Electronic Machine Furniture Workers ....$2,000 PAC
   Ladies Garment Workers Union ....$1,000 PAC

Transportation Unions **$19,550**
   Teamsters Union ....$10,000 PAC
   United Transportation Union ....$2,000 PAC
   Amalgamated Transit Union ....$1,500 PAC
   Trans Comm International Union ....$1,500 PAC
   Transport Workers Union ....$1,500 PAC
   Air Line Pilots Assn ....$1,000 PAC
   Marine Engineers Dist 2 Maritime Officers ....$1,000 PAC

Public Sector Unions **$44,000**
   National Education Assn ....$13,500 PAC
   American Federation of Teachers ....$6,000 PAC
   American Fedn of St/Cnty/Munic Employees ......$5,000 PAC
   American Postal Workers Union ....$5,000 PAC
   National Assn Retired Federal Employees ....$5,000 PAC
   National Assn of Letter Carriers ....$3,000 PAC
   International Assn of Firefighters ....$2,000 PAC
   National Rural Letter Carriers Assn ....$2,000 PAC
   National Assn of Postmasters ....$1,500 PAC
   American Federation of Govt Employees ....$1,000 PAC

Misc Unions **$9,800**
   Food & Commercial Workers Union ....$6,500 PAC
   Service Employees International Union ....$2,000 PAC
   AFL-CIO ....$1,000 PAC

Ideological/Single-Issue

Ideological/Single-Issue   **$9,852**

Democratic/Liberal **$3,850**
   National Cmte for an Effective Congress ....$2,500 PAC
   Hollywood Women's Political Cmte ....$1,000 PAC

Pro-Choice **$2,500**
   Voters for Choice ....$2,500 PAC

Womens Issues **$2,502**
   National Organization for Women ....$1,000 PAC

Misc Issues **$1,000**
   Sierra Club ....$1,000 PAC

Other & Unknown

Other   **$1,750**
   None over $1,000

Unknown   **$4,450**
   Homemakers/Non-income earners $1,750
   Employer Listed/Category Unknown $2,450
      Swager Communications ....$1,000 Indiv

---

* Contributions came from more than one affiliate or subsidiary.

Nita M. Lowey, D-NY (18)

First elected: 1988

1991-92 Total Receipts: $1,153,196
1992 Year-end Cash: $215,816

1991-92 Committees & Subcommittees

Education and Labor
Elementary, Secondary and Vocational Education; Human Resources; Postsecondary Education

Merchant Marine and Fisheries
Coast Guard and Navigation; Fisheries and Wildlife Conservation and the Environment

Select Committee on Narcotics Abuse and Control

Leading Contributors

Business

Agriculture	$14,356	
Tobacco	**$2,750**	
Philip Morris	$2,500	PAC/Ind
Food Processing & Sales	**$4,356**	
None over $2,500		
Forestry & Forest Products	**$4,000**	
Richard Bauer & Co	$4,000	Indiv

Communications/Electronics	$16,500	
Printing & Publishing	**$5,500**	
None over $2,500		
Media/Entertainment	**$3,750**	
None over $2,500		
Telephone Utilities	**$3,500**	
None over $2,500		

Construction	$7,400	
General Contractors	**$2,900**	
None over $2,500		
Home Builders	**$3,500**	
None over $2,500		

Source of Funds in 1992 Election

Source	Total	Pct
PACs	$307,977	27%
Indivs $200+	$527,430	46%
Indivs under $200	$240,492	21%
Other	$77,504	7%
Candidate	$0	0%
Party	$657	0%

Source of PAC Dollars by Sector

Source	Total	Pct
Business	$101,858	33%
Labor	$146,750	48%
Ideology/Single Issue	$56,032	18%

In-State vs. Out-of-State Contributions*

Source	Total	Pct
In-State	$482,630	92%
Out-of-state	$44,050	8%
No state listed	$0	

* by large individual contributors ($200 & above)

Finance, Insurance & Real Estate — $191,792

Commercial Banks	**$4,000**	
Chemical Bank	$2,500	PAC/Ind
Securities & Investment	**$99,740**	
Goldman, Sachs & Co	$12,000	PAC/Ind
61 Associates	$9,000	Indiv
Bear, Stearns & Co	$8,044	Indiv
LC Wegard & Co	$6,000	Indiv
Shearson Lehman Brothers	$5,146	PAC/Ind
Cumberland Associates	$4,000	Indiv
James P Wolfensohn Inc	$4,000	Indiv
Loeb Partners Corp	$4,000	Indiv
Morgan Stanley & Co	$4,000	PAC/Ind
Lieber & Co	$3,000	Indiv
Insurance	**$24,952**	
National Assn of Life Underwriters	$5,000	PAC
Independent Insurance Agents of America	$4,202	PAC
Real Estate	**$52,000**	
National Assn of Realtors	$10,000	PAC
Benerofe Properties Corp	$4,000	Indiv
Swig, Weiler & Arnow Management Co	$4,000	Indiv
Accountants	**$7,500**	
American Institute of CPA's	$3,000	PAC

Health — $42,600

Health Professionals	**$37,350**	
American Medical Assn*	$10,000	PAC
American Nurses Assn	$3,500	PAC
Hospitals/Nursing Homes	**$5,250**	
American Hospital Assn	$4,000	PAC

Contribution Totals by Sector

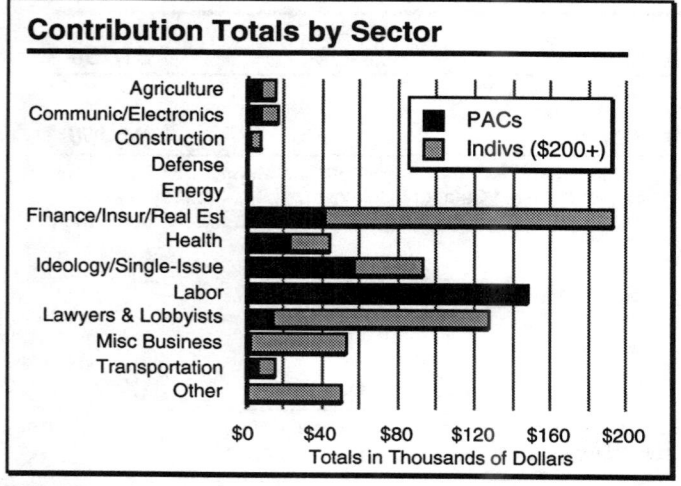

Agriculture, Communic/Electronics, Construction, Defense, Energy, Finance/Insur/Real Est, Health, Ideology/Single-Issue, Labor, Lawyers & Lobbyists, Misc Business, Transportation, Other

PACs / Indivs ($200+)

$0 $40 $80 $120 $160 $200
Totals in Thousands of Dollars

Lawyers & Lobbyists — $126,350

Lawyers & Lobbyists $126,350
Assn of Trial Lawyers of America	$10,000	PAC
Lowey, Dannenberg et al	$9,000	Indiv
Wachtell, Lipton et al	$9,000	Indiv
Kaplan & Kilsheimer	$7,500	Indiv
Cleary, Gottlieb et al	$7,000	Indiv
Skadden, Arps et al	$7,000	Indiv
Goodkind, Labaton & Rudoff	$6,000	Indiv
Kaye, Scholer et al	$5,800	Indiv
Simpson, Thacher & Bartlett	$5,200	Indiv
Milbank, Tweed et al	$3,000	Indiv
Milberg, Weiss et al	$3,000	Indiv
Migdal, Tenney et al	$2,500	Indiv

Misc Business — $52,050

Retail Sales $10,250
None over $2,500

Business Services $16,750
Kroll Associates	$4,000	Indiv
Kissinger Associates	$3,000	Indiv

Recreation/Live Entertainment $4,000
National Basketball Assn	$4,000	Indiv

Misc Manufacturing & Distributing $13,050
AFP Imaging Corp	$3,000	Indiv
Primary Industries Corp	$2,500	Indiv

Transportation — $14,050

Air Transport $3,500
None over $2,500

Sea Transport $10,050
Brewer Yacht Yard	$4,000	Indiv

Labor

Labor — $146,750

Building Trade Unions $21,750
Carpenters & Joiners Union	$5,000	PAC
Laborers' Political League	$5,000	PAC
Sheet Metal Workers Union	$2,500	PAC

Spending in Last 3 Elections

	1988	1990	1992
Lowey	$1,309,873	$911,766	$1,027,433
Opponent	$1,567,129	$15,356	$560,305
Vote Pct	50%	63%	56%

Industrial Unions $27,000
Communications Workers of America	$5,000	PAC
Machinists/Aerospace Workers Union	$5,000	PAC
Intl Brotherhood of Electrical Workers	$4,000	PAC
United Steelworkers	$3,000	PAC

Transportation Unions $37,500
Teamsters Union	$10,000	PAC
Marine Engineers Union*	$8,500	PAC
Air Line Pilots Assn	$7,500	PAC
Seafarers International Union	$3,500	PAC
United Transportation Union	$3,000	PAC

Public Sector Unions $51,000
American Federation of Teachers	$10,000	PAC
American Fedn of St/Cnty/Munic Employees	$10,000	PAC
National Assn of Letter Carriers	$10,000	PAC
National Education Assn	$7,500	PAC
National Assn Retired Federal Employees	$7,000	PAC

Misc Unions $9,500
Food & Commercial Workers Union	$6,000	PAC
Service Employees International Union	$2,500	PAC

Ideological/Single-Issue

Ideological/Single-Issue — $91,832

Democratic/Liberal $9,500
National Cmte for an Effective Congress	$2,500	PAC

Pro-Israel $22,650
Joint Action Cmte for Political Affairs	$3,500	PAC
Women's Pro-Israel National PAC	$2,500	PAC

Pro-Choice $8,800
National Abortion Rights Action League	$3,500	PAC

Womens Issues $20,644
None over $2,500

Human Rights $13,750
Human Rights Campaign Fund	$10,000	PAC
KidsPAC	$3,000	PAC

Misc Issues $14,500
Sierra Club	$10,000	PAC
National Cmte to Preserve Social Security	$4,500	PAC

Other & Unknown

Other — $49,750

Education $18,750
Monroe Business Institute	$4,500	Indiv
School of Visual Arts	$4,000	Indiv

Retired $25,200
None over $2,500

Other $4,500
None over $2,500

Unknown — $75,890
Homemakers/Non-income earners	$19,500	
Employer Listed/Category Unknown	$54,640	
Spitzer Engineering	$3,000	Indiv

* Contributions came from more than one affiliate or subsidiary.

Ronald K. Machtley, R-RI (1)

First elected: 1988
1991-92 Total Receipts: $608,563
1992 Year-end Cash: $54,332

1991-92 Committees & Subcommittees

Armed Services
Military Installations and Facilities; Readiness; Seapower and Strategic and Critical Materials

Government Operations
Employment and Housing (Ranking Republican)

Small Business
Procurement, Tourism and Rural Development

Select Committee on Children, Youth and Families

Leading Contributors

Business

Agriculture	$9,450	
Crop Production & Basic Processing	**$2,000**	
Warwick Land Co	$2,000	Indiv
Agricultural Services/Products	**$3,000**	
American Assn of Nurserymen	$1,500	PAC
Food Processing & Sales	**$2,700**	
None over $1,500		

Communications/Electronics	$12,400	
Media/Entertainment	**$5,950**	
GTech Corp	$3,000	Indiv
Telephone Utilities	**$3,750**	
NYNEX Corp*	$1,750	PAC
Computer Equipment & Services	**$1,500**	
None over $1,500		

Construction	$16,625	
General Contractors	**$5,700**	
Associated General Contractors	$2,500	PAC
Home Builders	**$4,000**	
National Assn of Home Builders	$4,000	PAC
Construction Services	**$5,225**	
None over $1,500		

Source of Funds in 1992 Election

Source	Total	Pct
PACs	$222,306	35%
Indivs $200+	$137,251	21%
Indivs under $200	$232,250	36%
Other	$46,756	7%
Candidate	$0	0%
Party	$35,552	6%

Source of PAC Dollars by Sector

Source	Total	Pct
Business	$162,165	74%
Labor	$41,125	19%
Ideology/Single Issue	$14,950	7%

In-State vs. Out-of-State Contributions*

Source	Total	Pct
In-State	$118,084	86%
Out-of-state	$18,867	14%
No state listed	$0	

* by large individual contributors ($200 & above)

Defense	$38,025	
Defense Aerospace	**$19,250**	
Textron Inc	$3,450	PAC/Ind
General Dynamics	$2,500	PAC/Ind
Grumman Corp	$2,000	PAC
McDonnell Douglas*	$2,000	PAC
Rockwell International	$2,000	PAC
United Technologies	$1,500	PAC
Defense Electronics	**$13,025**	
AT&T	$2,875	PAC
Raytheon	$2,250	PAC
Planning Research Corp	$2,000	PAC
GTE Corp	$1,500	PAC
Misc Defense	**$5,750**	
BDM International	$2,000	PAC
Atlantic Research Corp	$1,750	PAC

Energy & Natural Resources	$14,525	
Oil & Gas	**$6,575**	
None over $1,500		
Electric Utilities	**$3,400**	
New England Power Co	$1,900	PAC

Finance, Insurance & Real Estate	$43,032	
Commercial Banks	**$12,690**	
American Bankers Assn	$4,000	PAC
Bank of Boston*	$2,690	PAC
Norstar Bancorp	$1,900	PAC
Securities & Investment	**$2,950**	
None over $1,500		
Insurance	**$5,050**	
National Assn of Life Underwriters	$3,000	PAC
Real Estate	**$14,325**	
National Assn of Realtors	$10,000	PAC

Contribution Totals by Sector

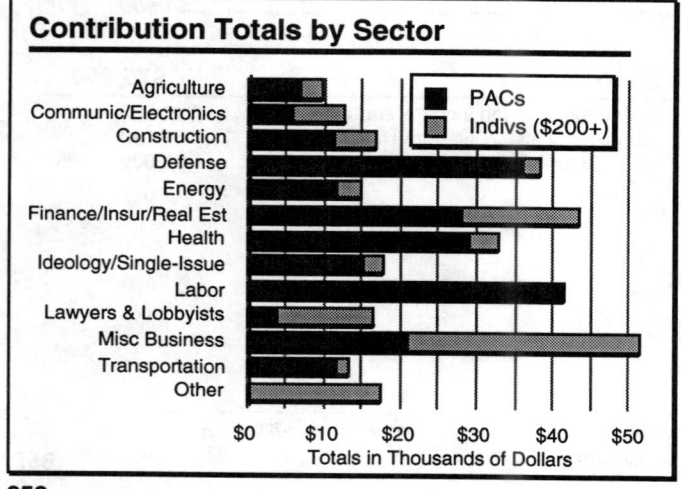

PACs
Indivs ($200+)

Agriculture
Communic/Electronics
Construction
Defense
Energy
Finance/Insur/Real Est
Health
Ideology/Single-Issue
Labor
Lawyers & Lobbyists
Misc Business
Transportation
Other

$0 $10 $20 $30 $40 $50
Totals in Thousands of Dollars

Accountants **$5,475**
    American Institute of CPA's .... $3,000   PAC

Misc Finance **$1,892**
    None over $1,500

Health $32,550

Health Professionals **$27,800**
    American Medical Assn ....$9,350   PAC
    American Dental Assn ....$4,500   PAC
    American Academy of Ophthalmology ....$3,100   PAC
    American Psychiatric Assn ....$2,450   PAC
    Cmte for Quality Orthopedic Health Care ....$1,500   PAC

Hospitals/Nursing Homes **$3,750**
    American Hospital Assn ....$1,500   PAC

Lawyers & Lobbyists $16,125

Lawyers & Lobbyists **$16,125**
    Hinckley, Allen et al ....$2,150   Indiv
    Reid & Priest ....$2,000   PAC

Misc Business $51,215

Business Associations **$3,030**
    None over $1,500

Food & Beverage **$5,750**
    National Restaurant Assn ....$3,500   PAC

Beer, Wine & Liquor **$10,335**
    National Beer Wholesalers Assn ....$5,500   PAC
    McLaughlin & Moran Inc ....$2,600   Indiv

Business Services **$5,050**
    None over $1,500

Lodging/Tourism **$2,550**
    None over $1,500

Chemical & Related Manufacturing **$2,500**
    None over $1,500

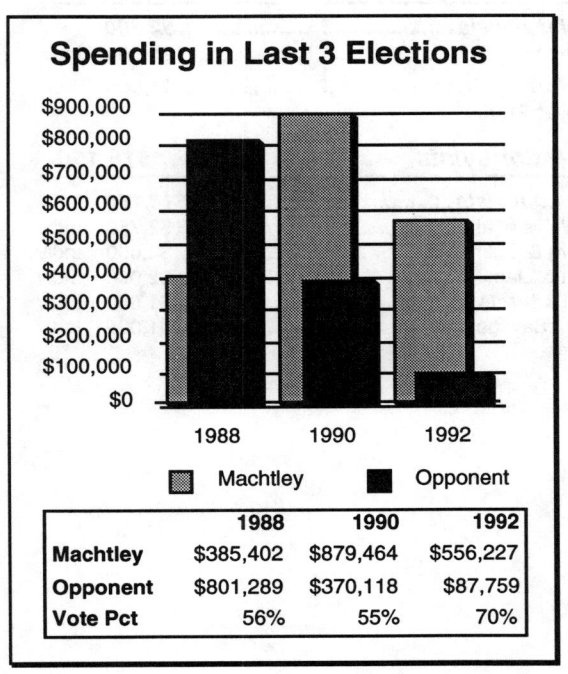

Spending in Last 3 Elections

	1988	1990	1992
Machtley	$385,402	$879,464	$556,227
Opponent	$801,289	$370,118	$87,759
Vote Pct	56%	55%	70%

Misc Manufacturing & Distributing **$13,750**
    M&F Case Co ....$2,525   Indiv
    Brown & Sharpe Manufacturing ....$2,000   Indiv
    Etco Inc ....$1,875   Indiv
    Hoechst Celanese Corp ....$1,500   PAC

Textiles **$7,000**
    American Textile Manufacturers Institute ....$2,000   PAC
    Hood Sails ....$2,000   Indiv
    Union Wadding Co ....$2,000   Indiv

Transportation $12,875

Air Transport **$4,300**
    United Parcel Service ....$4,300   PAC

Automotive **$6,500**
    Americans for Free International Trade ....$3,000   PAC
    Auto Dealers & Drivers for Free Trade ....$2,000   PAC
    National Auto Dealers Assn ....$1,500   PAC

Sea Transport **$1,575**
    None over $1,500

Labor

Labor $41,125

Transportation Unions **$17,500**
    Marine Engineers Union* ....$5,000   PAC
    Masters, Mates & Pilots Union ....$5,000   PAC
    Air Line Pilots Assn ....$3,500   PAC

Public Sector Unions **$23,125**
    National Assn Retired Federal Employees ....$7,000   PAC
    National Education Assn ....$5,625   PAC
    National Assn of Letter Carriers ....$2,000   PAC
    National Assn of Postmasters ....$2,000   PAC
    American Fedn of St/Cnty/Munic Employees ......$1,500   PAC
    American Postal Workers Union ....$1,500   PAC

Ideological/Single-Issue

Ideological/Single-Issue $17,350

Pro-Israel **$6,650**
    National PAC ....$5,000   PAC

Pro-Choice **$2,000**
    None over $1,500

Human Rights **$3,000**
    Human Rights Campaign Fund ....$2,000   PAC

Misc Issues **$5,500**
    National Cmte to Preserve Social Security ....$3,000   PAC
    Sierra Club ....$1,500   PAC

Other & Unknown

Other $17,297

Retired **$15,597**
    None over $1,500

Unknown $32,597

    Homemakers/Non-income earners $5,625
    No Employer Listed or Found $1,600
    Employer Listed/Category Unknown $24,122
        Goodwin, Loomis & Brittai ....$1,500   Indiv

Independent expenditures supporting Machtley
    National Assn of Realtors $45,100

---

* Contributions came from more than one affiliate or subsidiary.

Carolyn B. Maloney, D-NY (14)

First elected: 1992

1991-92 Total Receipts: $279,980
1992 Year-end Cash: $3,786

1993-94 Committees & Subcommittees

Banking, Finance and Urban Affairs
Consumer Credit and Insurance; Financial Institutions Supervision, Regulation and Deposit Insurance; Housing and Community Development

Government Operations
Environment, Energy and Natural Resources; Legislation and National Security

Leading Contributors

Business

Communications/Electronics		$8,793
Media/Entertainment		**$3,450**
ACTV Inc	$1,250	Indiv
Telephone Utilities		**$3,000**
AT&T	$2,000	PAC
New York Telephone	$1,000	PAC
Computer Equipment & Services		**$1,443**
None over $1,000		

Construction		$2,250
General Contractors		**$1,000**
None over $1,000		
Special Trade Contractors		**$1,000**
Grace Industries Inc	$1,000	Indiv

Finance, Insurance & Real Esta		$51,600
Finance/Credit Companies		**$3,000**
Primerica Corp	$3,000	Indiv
Securities & Investment		**$22,850**
Jennison Associates	$6,000	Indiv
Goldman, Sachs & Co	$3,750	Indiv
Blackstone Group	$1,500	Indiv
Hunt Alternative Fund	$1,200	Indiv
Cmte for Effective Government	$1,000	PAC
Morgan Stanley & Co	$1,000	Indiv
Wagner, Stott & Co	$1,000	Indiv
Wertheim, Schroder & Co	$1,000	Indiv

Insurance		$1,250
Equitable Life	$1,000	Indiv
Real Estate		**$21,750**
Trump Organization	$11,000	Indiv
Forest City Enterprises Inc	$5,000	Indiv
Bromley Companies	$1,000	Indiv
Fisher Brothers Management Co	$1,000	Indiv
Rudin Management Co	$1,000	Indiv
Misc Finance		**$2,750**
International Financial Group Inc	$1,000	Indiv

Health		$3,300
Health Professionals		**$2,300**
Infetech Inc	$1,000	Indiv
Hospitals/Nursing Homes		**$1,000**
None over $1,000		

Lawyers & Lobbyists		$18,150
Lawyers & Lobbyists		**$18,150**
Paul, Weiss et al	$2,750	Indiv
Goldberg & Gelman	$2,000	Indiv
Sullivan & Liapakis	$2,000	Indiv
Seward & Kissel	$1,650	Indiv
Gersten, Savage et al	$1,000	Indiv

Source of Funds in 1992 Election

Source	Total	Pct
■ PACs	$65,695	23%
▨ Indivs $200+	$148,468	53%
☐ Indivs under $200	$18,687	7%
⊠ Other..............................	$49,630	18%
Candidate	$37,045	13%
Party	$2,850	1%

Source of PAC Dollars by Sector

Source	Total	Pct
■ Business	$5,250	8%
▨ Labor	$55,000	83%
☐ Ideology/Single Issue	$6,250	9%

In-State vs. Out-of-State Contributions*

Source	Total	Pct
☐ In-State	$106,868	80%
■ Out-of-state	$26,650	20%
No state listed	$14,950	

* by large individual contributors ($200 & above)

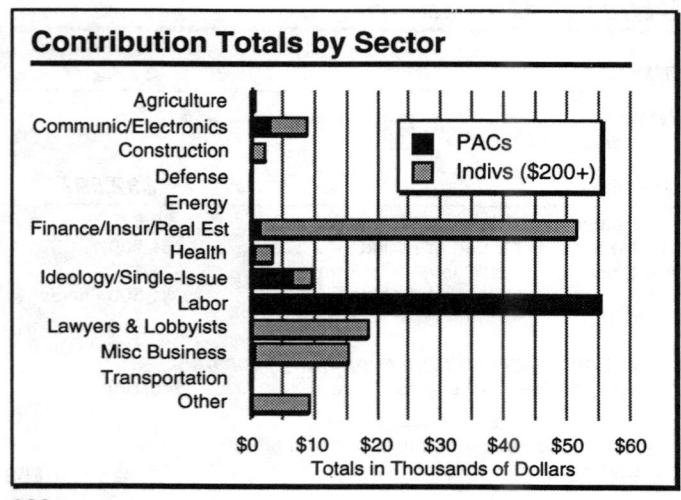

Contribution Totals by Sector

Categories (top to bottom): Agriculture, Communic/Electronics, Construction, Defense, Energy, Finance/Insur/Real Est, Health, Ideology/Single-Issue, Labor, Lawyers & Lobbyists, Misc Business, Transportation, Other

Legend: ■ PACs ▨ Indivs ($200+)

Totals in Thousands of Dollars ($0, $10, $20, $30, $40, $50, $60)

Misc Business $15,250

Food & Beverage **$1,500**
    Canard & Co ....$1,000   Indiv

Retail Sales **$3,800**
    Alexander's Department Store ....$1,000   Indiv
    Auto Sound Co ....$1,000   Indiv
    Barnes & Noble ....$1,000   Indiv

Misc Services **$1,000**
    Apex Studios Inc ....$1,000   Indiv

Business Services **$4,950**
    Creative Marketing Inc ....$2,000   Indiv
    Howard J Rubenstein Associates ....$1,250   Indiv

Misc Manufacturing & Distributing **$3,500**
    MacAndrews & Forbes Group ....$1,500   Indiv
    Black Clawson Co ....$1,000   Indiv

Labor

Labor $55,000

Building Trade Unions **$12,000**
    Carpenters & Joiners Union ....$7,500   PAC
    Operating Engineers Union* ....$3,500   PAC
    Laborers' Political League ....$1,000   PAC

Industrial Unions **$22,000**
    United Auto Workers ....$7,000   PAC
    Intl Brotherhood of Electrical Workers ....$6,000   PAC
    Communications Workers of America ....$2,500   PAC
    Ladies Garment Workers Union ....$2,500   PAC
    United Steelworkers ....$2,500   PAC
    Machinists/Aerospace Workers Union ....$1,000   PAC

Transportation Unions **$4,500**
    International Longshoremen's Assn ....$2,500   PAC
    Teamsters Union ....$1,000   PAC
    Transport Workers Union ....$1,000   PAC

Public Sector Unions **$10,500**
    American Federation of Teachers ....$7,500   PAC
    National Assn Retired Federal Employees ....$2,000   PAC
    National Assn of Letter Carriers ....$1,000   PAC

Misc Unions **$6,000**
    Service Employees International Union ....$3,500   PAC
    Retail, Wholesale & Dept Store Union ....$2,000   PAC

Ideological/Single-Issue

Ideological/Single-Issue $9,500

Leadership PACs **$1,000**
    House Leadership Fund (Tom Foley) ....$1,000   PAC

Foreign & Defense Policy **$2,000**
    SANE/Freeze Inc ....$1,000   PAC

Womens Issues **$3,000**
    National Organization for Women ....$1,250   PAC

Human Rights **$2,250**
    Human Rights Campaign Fund ....$2,000   PAC

Misc Issues **$1,000**
    National Council of Senior Citizens ....$1,000   PAC

Other & Unknown

Other $9,100

Education **$2,000**
    Stanley Kaplan Inc ....$1,500   Indiv

Retired **$4,200**
    None over $1,000

Other **$1,500**
    Hudson House Co ....$1,000   Indiv

Unknown $41,625

    Homemakers/Non-income earners $7,900
    No Employer Listed or Found $18,075
    Generic Occupation/Category Unknown $2,775
    Employer Listed/Category Unknown $12,775
        Brodsky Organization ....$1,000   Indiv
        Dow Jones ....$1,000   Indiv
        Durst Organization ....$1,000   Indiv
        Wagner & Stott ....$1,000   Indiv
        Wagner, FIschbein et al ....$1,000   Indiv

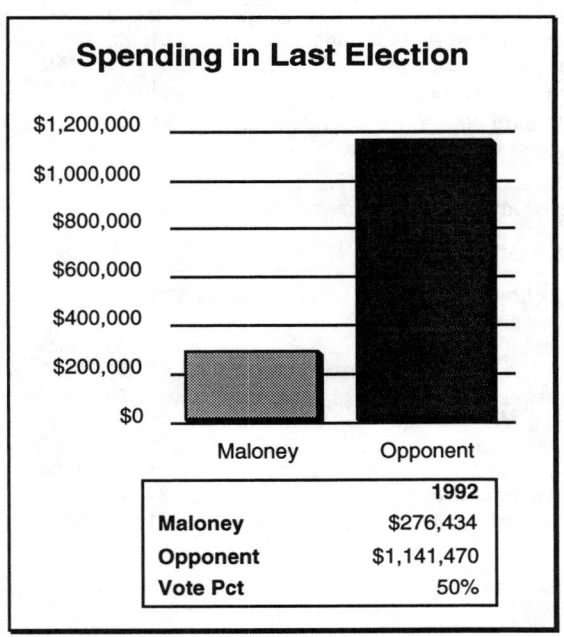

Spending in Last Election

	1992
Maloney	$276,434
Opponent	$1,141,470
Vote Pct	50%

---

* Contributions came from more than one affiliate or subsidiary.

David Mann, D-Ohio (1)

First elected: 1992

1991-92 Total Receipts:	$281,158
1992 Year-end Cash:	$2,863

1993-94 Committees & Subcommittees

Armed Services
Military Acquisition; Oversight and Investigations

Judiciary
Administrative Law and Governmental Relations; Crime and Criminal Justice; Economic and Commercial Law

Leading Contributors

Business

Agriculture	$2,550

Food Processing & Sales $1,300
  None over $1,000

Communications/Electronics	$5,750

Telephone Utilities $4,600
  Cincinnati Bell .... $2,750 PAC
  AT&T .... $1,250 PAC

Construction	$2,000

General Contractors $2,000
  None over $1,000

Finance, Insurance & Real Estate	$40,100

Commercial Banks $3,700
  Banc One Corp .... $1,000 PAC
  Central Bancorp .... $1,000 PAC

Securities & Investment $14,250
  Smith Barney .... $8,000 Indiv
  McDonald & Co Securities .... $3,000 PAC
  Merrill Lynch .... $2,000 Indiv

Insurance $10,000
  American Financial Corp .... $3,000 Indiv
  Chas H Bilz Insurance Agency .. $2,000 Indiv
  National Assn of Life Underwriters .. $1,500 PAC

Source of Funds in 1992 Election

Source	Total	Pct
■ PACs	$107,550	38%
▨ Indivs $200+	$102,668	36%
□ Indivs under $200	$62,580	22%
▨ Other	$8,763	3%
Candidate	$2,000	1%
Party	$403	0%

Source of PAC Dollars by Sector

Source	Total	Pct
■ Business	$47,700	45%
▨ Labor	$53,550	50%
□ Ideology/Single Issue	$5,000	5%

In-State vs. Out-of-State Contributions*

Source	Total	Pct
□ In-State	$74,518	73%
■ Out-of-state	$27,600	27%
No state listed	$500	

* by large individual contributors ($200 & above)

Real Estate $6,850
  Community Management .... $2,000 Indiv
  Hart Realty .... $1,000 Indiv
  Mid-America Development Co .... $1,000 Indiv
  Re/Max Premier .... $1,000 Indiv
  Stern-Hendy Properties Inc .... $1,000 Indiv

Accountants $3,500
  American Institute of CPA's .... $2,500 PAC

Misc Finance $1,050
  None over $1,000

Health	$19,650

Health Professionals $14,750
  American Medical Assn .... $2,000 PAC
  Middletown Radiologic Associates .... $1,250 Indiv
  American Chiropractic Assn .... $1,000 PAC
  American Podiatry Assn .... $1,000 PAC

Hospitals/Nursing Homes $1,250
  None over $1,000

Misc Health $3,450
  Wellington Ortho & Sports Medicine .... $2,250 Indiv

Lawyers & Lobbyists	$25,768

Lawyers & Lobbyists $25,768
  Keating, Muething & Klekamp .... $3,750 Indiv
  Calfee, Halter & Griswold .... $3,100 Indiv
  Assn of Trial Lawyers of America .... $2,500 PAC
  Katz, Teller et al .... $2,000 Indiv
  Taliaferro & Mann .... $1,250 Indiv
  Vorys, Sater et al .... $1,250 PAC
  Clohan & Dean .... $1,200 Indiv
  Waite, Schneider et al .... $1,200 Indiv
  Graydon, Head & Ritchey .... $1,000 Indiv

Contribution Totals by Sector

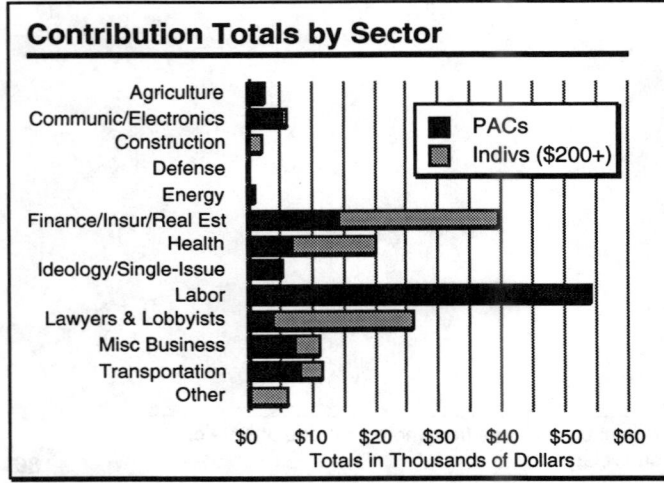

Legend: ■ PACs, □ Indivs ($200+)

Agriculture
Communic/Electronics
Construction
Defense
Energy
Finance/Insur/Real Est
Health
Ideology/Single-Issue
Labor
Lawyers & Lobbyists
Misc Business
Transportation
Other

$0 $10 $20 $30 $40 $50 $60
Totals in Thousands of Dollars

Misc Business — $10,950

Food & Beverage **$1,500**
   None over $1,000

Retail Sales **$2,500**
   National Assn of Chain Drug Stores .... $1,000   PAC

Business Services **$1,800**
   Stoner & Associates .... $1,300   Indiv

Chemical & Related Manufacturing **$3,800**
   Procter & Gamble .... $3,800   PAC/Ind

Misc Manufacturing & Distributing **$1,000**
   None over $1,000

Transportation — $11,500

Air Transport **$2,500**
   United Parcel Service .... $1,500   PAC
   General Electric .... $1,000   PAC

Automotive **$7,000**
   Auto Dealers & Drivers for Free Trade .... $2,500   PAC
   National Auto Dealers Assn .... $2,500   PAC
   Columbia Oldsmobile .... $1,500   Indiv

Railroads **$2,000**
   Chicago West Pullman .... $2,000   Indiv

Labor

Labor — $53,550

Building Trade Unions **$9,500**
   Carpenters & Joiners Union .... $3,000   PAC
   Plumbers/Pipefitters #59 .... $2,000   PAC
   Heat/Frost/Asbestos Workers Union .... $1,000   PAC
   Laborers' Political League .... $1,000   PAC
   Painters & Allied Trades Union .... $1,000   PAC
   Sheet Metal Workers Union .... $1,000   PAC

Industrial Unions **$22,650**
   Intl Brotherhood of Electrical Workers .... $5,000   PAC
   Machinists/Aerospace Workers Union .... $5,000   PAC
   United Auto Workers .... $5,000   PAC
   United Steelworkers .... $5,000   PAC
   Communications Workers of America .... $1,000   PAC

Transportation Unions **$1,400**
   None over $1,000

Public Sector Unions **$16,000**
   National Education Assn .... $5,000   PAC
   American Fedn of St/Cnty/Munic Employees ...... $3,000   PAC
   American Federation of Teachers .... $2,500   PAC
   National Assn of Letter Carriers .... $2,500   PAC
   International Assn of Firefighters .... $1,000   PAC

Misc Unions **$4,000**
   Food & Commercial Workers Union .... $2,500   PAC
   Service Employees International Union .... $1,000   PAC

Ideological/Single-Issue

Ideological/Single-Issue — $5,000

Leadership PACs **$3,000**
   Effective Government Cmte (Dick Gephardt) ...... $1,000   PAC
   House Leadership Fund (Tom Foley) .... $1,000   PAC
   Victory USA (Vic Fazio) .... $1,000   PAC

Pro-Israel **$1,000**
   National PAC .... $1,000   PAC

Other & Unknown

Other — $6,000

Civil Servants/Public Officials **$1,050**
   None over $1,000

Education **$2,200**
   Loyola University .... $2,000   Indiv

Retired **$2,750**
   None over $1,000

Unknown — $25,250

   Homemakers/Non-income earners $7,200
   No Employer Listed or Found $2,950
   Employer Listed/Category Unknown $15,100
      Beck Hospitality Inc .... $1,000   Indiv
      Broadcast Alchemy .... $1,000   Indiv
      Buslad, Funk & Zevely .... $1,000   Indiv
      Lawrence, Linder & McGrath Co .... $1,000   Indiv
      Radcliff Co .... $1,000   Indiv
      Ruvolo & Associates .... $1,000   Indiv

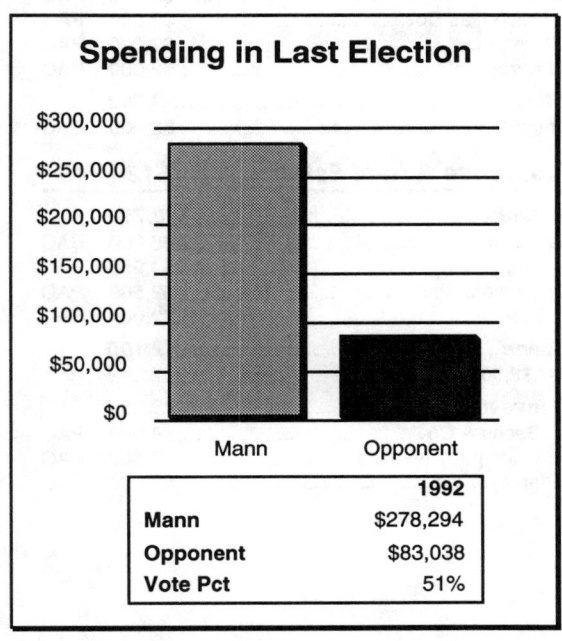

Spending in Last Election

	1992
Mann	$278,294
Opponent	$83,038
Vote Pct	51%

Thomas J. Manton, D-NY (7)

First elected: 1984

1991-92 Total Receipts: $643,780
1992 Year-end Cash: $108,919

1991-92 Committees & Subcommittees

Administration
Accounts; Personnel and Police

Energy and Commerce
Commerce, Consumer Protection and Competitiveness; Telecommunications and Finance; Transportation and Hazardous Materials

Merchant Marine and Fisheries
Fisheries and Wildlife Conservation and the Environment

Select Committee on Aging

Joint Committee on the Library

Leading Contributors

Business

Agriculture $33,899

Crop Production & Basic Processing	**$6,850**
Florida Sugar Cane League ....$2,000 PAC	
Tobacco	**$11,999**
Philip Morris ....$4,999 PAC	
RJR Nabisco ....$3,000 PAC	
Dairy	**$6,500**
Associated Milk Producers ....$5,500 PAC	
Agricultural Services/Products	**$2,250**
None over $2,000	
Food Processing & Sales	**$5,500**
Cumberland Packing Corp ....$4,000 Indiv	

Communications/Electronics $47,500

Media/Entertainment	**$27,500**
National Cable Television Assn ....$10,000 PAC	
Viacom International ....$5,000 PAC	
Time Warner* ....$3,000 PAC/Ind	
Kenmare Productions ....$2,000 Indiv	
Telephone Utilities	**$17,500**
AT&T ....$4,000 PAC	
Ameritech Corp ....$3,000 PAC	
BellSouth Corp* ....$2,500 PAC	
New York Telephone ....$2,500 PAC	
Telecom Services & Equipment	**$2,000**
None over $2,000	

Contribution Totals by Sector

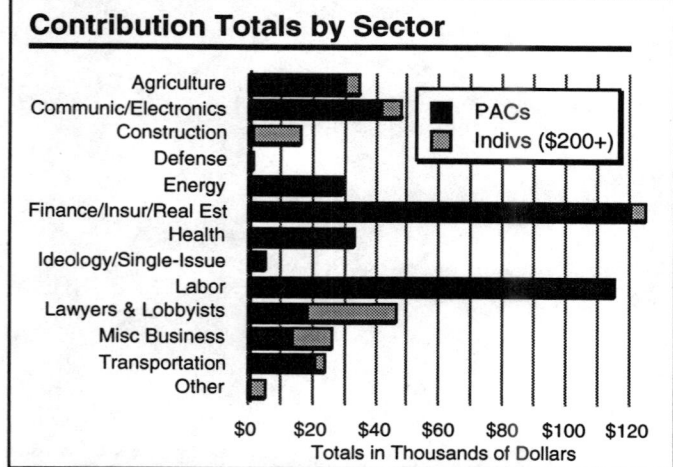

Agriculture
Communic/Electronics
Construction
Defense
Energy
Finance/Insur/Real Est
Health
Ideology/Single-Issue
Labor
Lawyers & Lobbyists
Misc Business
Transportation
Other

- PACs
- Indivs ($200+)

$0 $20 $40 $60 $80 $100 $120
Totals in Thousands of Dollars

Source of Funds in 1992 Election

Source	Total	Pct
PACs	$427,492	66%
Indivs $200+	$92,324	14%
Indivs under $200	$52,584	8%
Other	$71,517	11%
Candidate	$0	0%
Party	$287	0%

Source of PAC Dollars by Sector

Source	Total	Pct
Business	$305,231	72%
Labor	$114,300	27%
Ideology/Single Issue	$4,523	1%

In-State vs. Out-of-State Contributions*

Source	Total	Pct
In-State	$76,075	82%
Out-of-state	$16,249	18%
No state listed	$0	

* by large individual contributors ($200 & above)

Construction $15,900

General Contractors	**$3,250**
None over $2,000	
Special Trade Contractors	**$5,000**
Interphase Electric Co ....$2,000 Indiv	
Petri Mechanical ....$2,000 Indiv	
Building Materials & Equipment	**$5,850**
Nassau Door & Window ....$5,000 Indiv	

Energy & Natural Resources $28,833

Oil & Gas	**$19,033**
Columbia Gas System* ....$3,000 PAC	
Brooklyn Union Gas Co ....$2,000 PAC	
Coastal Corp ....$2,000 PAC	
Transco Energy Co* ....$2,000 PAC	
Electric Utilities	**$8,800**
Consolidated Edison of New York ....$2,000 PAC	

Finance, Insurance & Real Estate $124,749

Commercial Banks	**$20,750**
JP Morgan & Co ....$5,000 PAC	
Citicorp ....$4,950 PAC	
American Bankers Assn ....$2,500 PAC	
Bankers Trust ....$2,000 PAC	
Savings & Loans	**$2,100**
None over $2,000	
Securities & Investment	**$23,250**
Goldman, Sachs & Co ....$4,000 PAC	
Investment Company Institute ....$3,500 PAC	
Morgan Stanley & Co ....$2,500 PAC	

Insurance **$45,499**
 National Assn of Life Underwriters .... $10,000 PAC
 Independent Insurance Agents of America .... $6,499 PAC
 Equitable Financial Services .... $3,500 PAC
 Aetna Life & Casualty .... $2,000 PAC
 American Council of Life Insurance .... $2,000 PAC
 American Family Corp .... $2,000 PAC
 Cigna Corp .... $2,000 PAC
 Travelers Corp .... $2,000 PAC

Real Estate **$12,650**
 National Assn of Realtors .... $8,000 PAC

Accountants **$19,500**
 American Institute of CPA's .... $9,000 PAC
 Coopers & Lybrand .... $2,500 PAC
 Arthur Andersen & Co .... $2,000 PAC
 Ernst & Young .... $2,000 PAC
 Price Waterhouse .... $2,000 PAC
 Deloitte & Touche .... $2,000 PAC

Health $32,500

Health Professionals **$19,000**
 American Medical Assn* .... $10,000 PAC
 American Dental Assn .... $3,000 PAC
 American Academy of Ophthalmology .... $2,000 PAC

Hospitals/Nursing Homes **$3,000**
 American Hospital Assn .... $2,000 PAC

Pharmaceuticals/Health Products **$10,500**
 None over $2,000

Lawyers & Lobbyists $45,749

Lawyers & Lobbyists **$45,749**
 Assn of Trial Lawyers of America .... $10,000 PAC

Misc Business $25,600

Food & Beverage **$3,850**
 None over $2,000

Beer, Wine & Liquor **$5,200**
 Anheuser-Busch .... $2,500 PAC

Business Services **$8,250**
 Alarm Industry Communications Cmte .... $2,000 PAC

Misc Manufacturing & Distributing **$2,750**
 None over $2,000

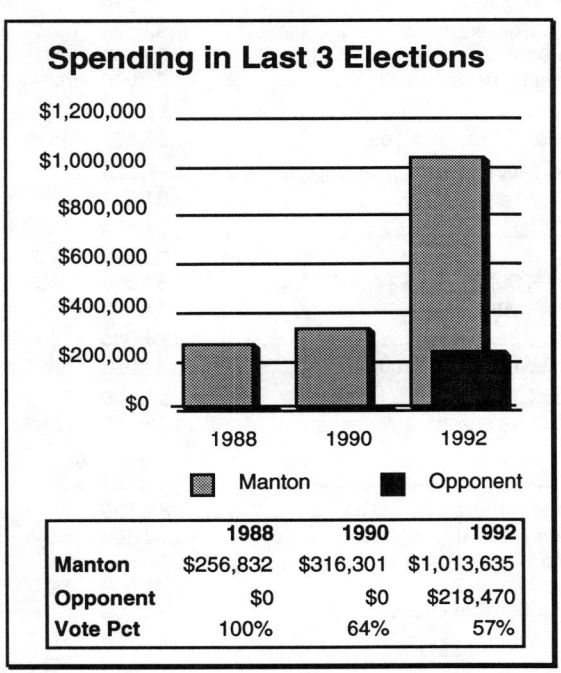

Spending in Last 3 Elections

	1988	1990	1992
Manton	$256,832	$316,301	$1,013,635
Opponent	$0	$0	$218,470
Vote Pct	100%	64%	57%

Transportation $23,500

Air Transport **$2,250**
 None over $2,000

Automotive **$8,500**
 Auto Dealers & Drivers for Free Trade .... $3,500 PAC

Railroads **$5,000**
 None over $2,000

Sea Transport **$4,500**
 None over $2,000

Misc Transport **$2,250**
 None over $2,000

Labor

Labor $114,300

Building Trade Unions **$26,200**
 Ironworkers Union .... $10,000 PAC
 Operating Engineers Union* .... $6,000 PAC
 Laborers Union* .... $5,700 PAC

Industrial Unions **$13,800**
 Machinists/Aerospace Workers Union .... $6,500 PAC
 Boilermakers Union .... $2,500 PAC
 United Auto Workers .... $2,000 PAC

Transportation Unions **$42,300**
 United Transportation Union .... $9,000 PAC
 Marine Engineers Union* .... $8,000 PAC
 Teamsters Union .... $6,000 PAC
 International Longshoremen's Assn .... $5,500 PAC
 Seafarers International Union .... $5,000 PAC
 Air Line Pilots Assn .... $2,500 PAC
 Brotherhood of Locomotive Engineers .... $2,000 PAC

Public Sector Unions **$26,500**
 American Fedn of St/Cnty/Munic Employees ...... $7,000 PAC
 American Postal Workers Union .... $5,000 PAC
 National Assn Retired Federal Employees .... $5,000 PAC
 National Assn of Letter Carriers .... $4,000 PAC
 National Education Assn .... $2,500 PAC

Misc Unions **$5,500**
 Food & Commercial Workers Union .... $2,000 PAC
 Service Employees International Union .... $2,000 PAC

Ideological/Single-Issue

Ideological/Single-Issue $4,773

Misc Issues **$2,500**
 National Cmte to Preserve Social Security .... $2,500 PAC

Other & Unknown

Other $5,150

Retired **$2,100**
 None over $2,000

Unknown $13,175

 Homemakers/Non-income earners $3,250
 Employer Listed/Category Unknown $8,975
  M Curley & Co Inc .... $2,000 Indiv

Independent expenditures supporting Manton
 National Right to Life PAC $4,807

---

* Contributions came from more than one affiliate or
subsidiary.

Donald Manzullo, R-Ill (16)

First elected: 1992

1991-92 Total Receipts:	$465,348
1992 Year-end Cash:	$5,908

1993-94 Committees & Subcommittees

Foreign Affairs
Economic Policy, Trade and Environment; International Operations

Small Business
Rural Enterprises, Exports and the Environment

Leading Contributors

Business

Agriculture	$10,750	
Crop Production & Basic Processing	**$2,000**	
None over $1,000		
Agricultural Services/Products	**$4,000**	
Deere & Co	$2,500	PAC
Archer-Daniels-Midland Corp	$1,000	PAC
Food Processing & Sales	**$4,750**	
Flowers Industries	$2,000	PAC
Fleming Companies Inc	$1,000	PAC

Communications/Electronics	$8,475	
Telephone Utilities	**$4,000**	
Illinois Bell Telephone	$1,500	PAC
AT&T	$1,000	PAC
United Telecommunications	$1,000	PAC
Telecom Services & Equipment	**$3,000**	
Cotter & Co	$3,000	Indiv

Construction	$13,900	
General Contractors	**$6,600**	
Sjostrom Construction	$3,400	Indiv
American Environmental Construction	$1,000	Indiv
Associated General Contractors	$1,000	PAC
Home Builders	**$2,000**	
National Assn of Home Builders	$2,000	PAC
Special Trade Contractors	**$4,800**	
Sunstrand	$2,200	Indiv
Sheet Metal/Air Conditioning Contractors	$1,100	PAC

Source of Funds in 1992 Election

Source	Total	Pct
■ PACs	$123,598	24%
▨ Indivs $200+	$157,666	30%
☐ Indivs under $200	$118,334	23%
⊠ Other	$117,922	23%
Candidate	$16,203	3%
Party	$58,172	11%

Source of PAC Dollars by Sector

Source	Total	Pct
■ Business	$86,367	71%
▨ Labor	$0	0%
☐ Ideology/Single Issue	$34,501	29%

In-State vs. Out-of-State Contributions*

Source	Total	Pct
☐ In-State	$153,166	97%
■ Out-of-state	$4,500	3%
No state listed	$0	

* by large individual contributors ($200 & above)

Energy & Natural Resources	$12,450	
Oil & Gas	**$8,250**	
Amoco Corp	$1,500	PAC
Exxon Corp	$1,000	PAC
Koch Industries	$1,000	PAC
Occidental Petroleum*	$1,000	PAC
Phillips Petroleum	$1,000	PAC
Sun Co	$1,000	PAC
Misc Energy	**$3,000**	
Cooper Industries	$3,000	PAC

Finance, Insurance & Real Estate	$23,550	
Commercial Banks	**$7,350**	
American Bankers Assn	$2,500	PAC
Amcore Bank	$1,000	Indiv
First National Bank	$1,000	Indiv
Savings & Loans	**$1,500**	
First Federal Savings & Loan	$1,500	Indiv
Securities & Investment	**$1,525**	
Hamilton Investments	$1,225	Indiv
Insurance	**$7,925**	
National Assn of Life Underwriters	$3,500	PAC
Casualty & Surety Agents Assn	$1,000	PAC
Kemper Insurance	$1,000	PAC
Real Estate	**$4,000**	
Rubloff Development Group	$3,000	Indiv
Accountants	**$1,250**	
Odling, Clark, Shelton & Assoc	$1,250	Indiv

Health	$24,400	
Health Professionals	**$21,700**	
Brookside Medical	$4,000	Indiv
American Dental Assn	$2,500	PAC
American Optometric Assn	$1,000	PAC
Lundholm Surgical Group	$1,000	Indiv

Contribution Totals by Sector

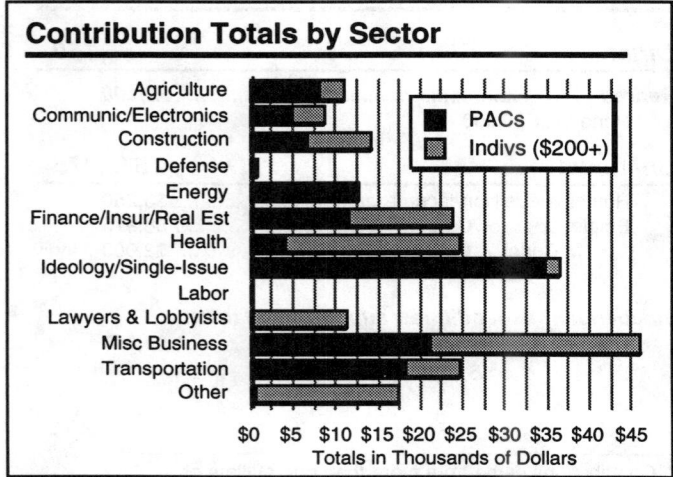

Legend: ■ PACs ▨ Indivs ($200+)

Sectors: Agriculture, Communic/Electronics, Construction, Defense, Energy, Finance/Insur/Real Est, Health, Ideology/Single-Issue, Labor, Lawyers & Lobbyists, Misc Business, Transportation, Other

$0 $5 $10 $15 $20 $25 $30 $35 $40 $45
Totals in Thousands of Dollars

Pharmaceuticals/Health Products	$2,000	
RITA Corp	$2,000	Indiv

Lawyers & Lobbyists — $11,044

Lawyers & Lobbyists	$11,044	
Schmalzle & Kroeger	$3,750	Indiv
Reese & Reese	$2,000	Indiv
Brassfield, Cowan et al	$1,000	Indiv

Misc Business — $47,104

Business Associations	$4,030	
National Fedn of Independent Business	$3,000	PAC
Business Industry PAC	$1,030	PAC
Food & Beverage	**$8,924**	
Manzullo's Restaurant	$3,924	Indiv
McDonald's Corp	$1,500	PAC
National Restaurant Assn	$1,000	PAC
Royal Crown Bottling Co	$1,000	Indiv
Retail Sales	**$1,275**	
None over $1,000		
Misc Services	**$2,300**	
American Assn of Equipment Lessors	$2,300	PAC
Business Services	**$1,580**	
None over $1,000		
Lodging/Tourism	**$1,500**	
John Evans Inn	$1,000	Indiv
Chemical & Related Manufacturing	**$3,745**	
Dow Chemical	$1,000	PAC
FMC Corp	$1,000	PAC
Misc Manufacturing & Distributing	**$23,250**	
Valley Countertops	$3,300	Indiv
Eclipse Inc	$3,150	Indiv
Stone Container Corp	$3,000	PAC
Ingersoll	$2,850	Indiv
Manzullo's Villa	$2,000	Indiv
Windway Capital Corp	$2,000	Indiv
Circle Boring	$1,750	Indiv
CDV Corp	$1,700	Indiv
Ingersoll Milling Machine Co	$1,250	Indiv
National Machine Tool Builders Assn	$1,000	PAC

Transportation — $24,432

Air Transport	$12,182	
Sundstrand Corp	$8,042	PAC/Ind
Woodward Governor Corp	$2,290	Indiv
Automotive	**$9,500**	
National Auto Dealers Assn	$5,000	PAC
Eaton Corp	$3,700	PAC/Ind
Railroads	**$2,250**	
Union Pacific Corp	$2,000	PAC

Ideological/Single-Issue

Ideological/Single-Issue	$36,201	
Republican/Conservative	**$8,047**	
Eagle Forum	$3,000	PAC
Conservative Leadership PAC	$1,723	PAC
United Republican Fund of Illinois	$1,000	PAC
Leadership PACs	**$3,250**	
Republican Leader's Fund (Bob Michel)	$2,000	PAC
New Majority Leadership PAC (Vin Weber)	$1,000	PAC
Pro-Life	**$4,563**	
Republican National Coalition for Life	$4,000	PAC
Gun Rights/Gun Control	**$9,900**	
National Rifle Assn	$9,900	PAC
Misc Issues	**$9,610**	
Right to Work PAC	$6,861	PAC
Ruff PAC	$1,249	PAC
Public Service Research Council	$1,000	PAC

Other & Unknown

Other	$17,125	
Civil Servants/Public Officials	**$1,000**	
None over $1,000		
Retired	**$14,875**	
None over $1,000		
Other	**$1,250**	
None over $1,000		

Unknown	$48,953	
Homemakers/Non-income earners	$5,950	
No Employer Listed or Found	$6,680	
Generic Occupation/Category Unknown	$1,675	
Employer Listed/Category Unknown	$34,548	
Elco Industries	$2,700	Indiv
Kostantocas, Traum et al	$1,250	Indiv
Connolly, Oliver et al	$1,050	Indiv
Aqua Arobic Systems	$1,000	Indiv
Guyner & Eichen	$1,000	Indiv
Kelco Industries Inc	$1,000	Indiv
Larson & Darby	$1,000	Indiv
Nisen & Elliott	$1,000	Indiv
Otto Engineering Inc	$1,000	Indiv
Prem Magnetics Inc	$1,000	Indiv
Ranger Ent Inc	$1,000	Indiv
Rogers Bros Investments	$1,000	Indiv
Suntec Industries	$1,000	Indiv
Zenith Cutter Co	$1,000	Indiv

Independent expenditures supporting Manzullo

National Right to Life PAC	$3,794	
National Rifle Assn	$2,208	

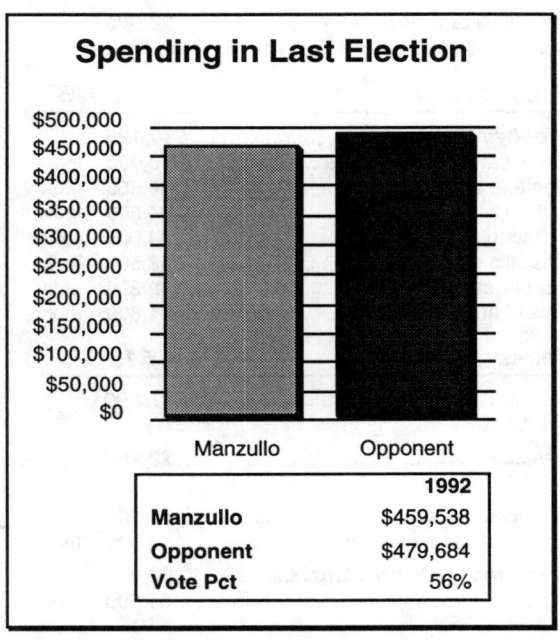

Spending in Last Election

	1992
Manzullo	$459,538
Opponent	$479,684
Vote Pct	56%

---

* Contributions came from more than one affiliate or subsidiary.

Marjorie Margolies-Mezvinsky, D-Pa (13)

First elected: 1992

1991-92 Total Receipts: $569,961
1992 Year-end Cash: $10,901

1993-94 Committees & Subcommittees

Energy and Commerce
Oversight and Investigations; Telecommunications and Finance

Government Operations
Commerce, Consumer and Monetary Affairs

Small Business
SBA Legislation and the General Economy

Leading Contributors

Business

Agriculture	$4,100

Forestry & Forest Products	$2,000	
Roosevelt Paper Co	$2,000	Indiv

Communications/Electronics	$15,250

Printing & Publishing	$6,250	
National Business Services	$3,000	Indiv
Media/Entertainment	$5,000	
None over $1,500		
Telephone Utilities	$4,000	
AT&T	$4,000	PAC

Construction	$1,500
None over $1,500	

Energy & Natural Resources	$5,250

Electric Utilities	$1,500	
None over $1,500		
Waste Management	$2,500	
Mid American Waste Systems	$2,000	Indiv

Finance, Insurance & Real Estate	$34,169

Commercial Banks	$3,250	
None over $1,500		
Securities & Investment	$10,969	
Prudential Securities	$3,519	Indiv
George Weiss Associates	$2,000	Indiv

Source of Funds in 1992 Election

Source	Total	Pct
PACs	$172,273	30%
Indivs $200+	$233,429	41%
Indivs under $200	$163,036	28%
Other	$7,707	1%
Candidate	$0	0%
Party	$7,707	1%

Source of PAC Dollars by Sector

Source	Total	Pct
Business	$54,300	35%
Labor	$51,050	33%
Ideology/Single Issue	$48,177	31%

In-State vs. Out-of-State Contributions*

Source	Total	Pct
In-State	$160,710	71%
Out-of-state	$66,369	29%
No state listed	$6,350	

* by large individual contributors ($200 & above)

Insurance	$6,150	
National Assn of Life Underwriters	$2,500	PAC
Real Estate	$8,750	
Toll Brothers Inc	$2,500	Indiv
Mortgage Bankers Assn of America	$2,000	PAC
Accountants	$3,250	
American Institute of CPA's	$2,000	PAC

Health	$30,760

Health Professionals	$21,860	
American Medical Assn	$5,000	PAC
American Nurses Assn	$3,500	PAC
Health Services	$5,500	
US Healthcare Inc	$5,500	PAC/Ind
Pharmaceuticals/Health Products	$2,000	
None over $1,500		

Lawyers & Lobbyists	$60,125

Lawyers & Lobbyists	$60,125	
Assn of Trial Lawyers of America	$10,000	PAC
Blank, Rome et al	$6,550	Indiv
Greenfield & Chimicles	$4,500	Indiv
Spector, Gadon et al	$4,000	Indiv
Fox, Rothschild et al	$2,500	Indiv
Ballard, Spahr et al	$2,250	Indiv
Wolf, Block et al	$1,800	Indiv

Misc Business	$15,025

Retail Sales	$1,800	
None over $1,500		
Misc Services	$2,250	
None over $1,500		
Business Services	$3,900	
American Protection Industries	$2,000	Indiv
Misc Manufacturing & Distributing	$3,075	
Tube City Inc	$1,600	Indiv

Contribution Totals by Sector

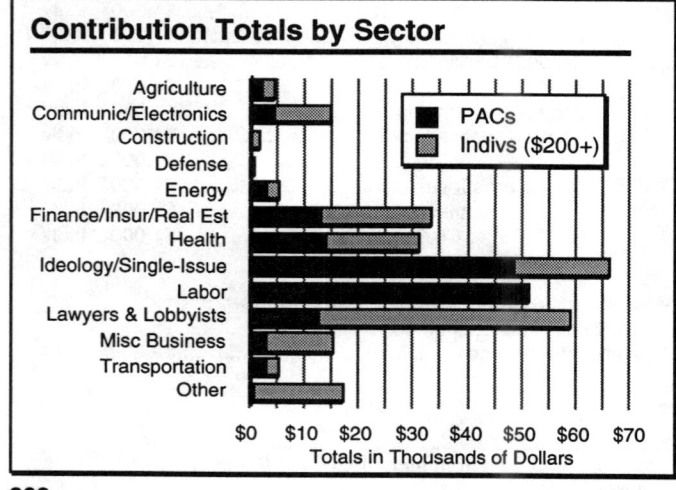

Legend: ■ PACs ▨ Indivs ($200+)

Categories: Agriculture, Communic/Electronics, Construction, Defense, Energy, Finance/Insur/Real Est, Health, Ideology/Single-Issue, Labor, Lawyers & Lobbyists, Misc Business, Transportation, Other

$0 $10 $20 $30 $40 $50 $60 $70
Totals in Thousands of Dollars

Transportation	$5,250	

Air Transport **$4,000**
   General Electric* ....$2,500   Indiv
   United Parcel Service ....$1,500   PAC

Labor

Labor	$51,050	

Building Trade Unions **$3,000**
   Operating Engineers #542 ....$1,500   PAC

Industrial Unions **$17,300**
   Communications Workers Union #13000 ....$5,000   PAC
   Rubber Cork Linoleum & Plastic Workers ....$5,000   PAC
   United Auto Workers ....$5,000   PAC

Transportation Unions **$5,500**
   Brotherhood of Locomotive Engineers ....$2,000   PAC

Public Sector Unions **$15,500**
   National Assn of Letter Carriers ....$7,000   PAC
   National Education Assn ....$5,000   PAC
   International Assn of Firefighters ....$2,000   PAC

Misc Unions **$9,750**
   Food & Commercial Workers Union ....$5,000   PAC
   Service Employees International Union ....$3,000   PAC
   AFL-CIO ....$1,750   PAC

Ideological/Single-Issue

Ideological/Single-Issue	$65,677	

Democratic/Liberal **$6,050**
   National Cmte for an Effective Congress ....$2,500   PAC

Leadership PACs **$3,542**
   None over $1,500

Pro-Israel **$9,100**
   Joint Action Cmte for Political Affairs ....$1,500   PAC

Pro-Choice **$2,500**
   National Abortion Rights Action League ....$2,000   PAC

Womens Issues **$31,187**
   Women's Campaign Fund ....$8,500   PAC
   Emily's List ....$6,237   PAC/Ind
   National Womens Political Caucus ....$5,000   PAC
   National Organization for Women ....$4,100   PAC

Human Rights **$7,069**
   Human Rights Campaign Fund ....$5,019   PAC

Misc Issues **$4,500**
   Sierra Club ....$3,500   PAC

Other & Unknown

Other	$16,600	

Civil Servants/Public Officials **$1,900**
   None over $1,500

Education **$6,100**
   University of Pennsylvania ....$3,100   Indiv

Retired **$7,900**
   None over $1,500

Unknown	$82,200	

   Homemakers/Non-income earners $32,500
   No Employer Listed or Found $23,800
   Generic Occupation/Category Unknown $4,500
   Employer Listed/Category Unknown $20,900
      Congressional Institue for the Future ....$2,000   Indiv
      Steiner, Segal et al ....$1,500   Indiv

Spending in Last Election

	1992
Margolies-Mezvinsky	$559,060
Opponent	$719,618
Vote Pct	50%

* Contributions came from more than one affiliate or
  subsidiary.

Edward J. Markey, D-Mass (7)

First elected: 1976

1991-92 Total Receipts: $444,628
1992 Year-end Cash: $131,110

1991-92 Committees & Subcommittees

Energy and Commerce
Energy and Power; Telecommunications and Finance (Chairman)

Interior and Insular Affairs
Energy and the Environment; National Parks and Public Lands;
Water, Power and Offshore Energy Resources

Leading Contributors

NOTE: Markey reported taking no PAC funds during his 1992 campaign.
The PAC listed below did report making a contribution , however, and
those contributions are recorded in the official FEC records.

Business

Agriculture $1,500

Food Processing & Sales	**$1,500**	
International Ice Cream Co	$1,500	Indiv

Communications/Electronics $75,900

Printing & Publishing	**$4,000**	
Newsweb Corp	$2,000	Indiv
Media/Entertainment	**$34,200**	
Viacom International	$5,300	Indiv
Hubbard Broadcasting Co	$2,750	Indiv
Time Warner*	$2,500	Indiv
National Assn of Broadcasters	$1,800	Indiv
NBC	$1,750	Indiv
Telephone Utilities	**$18,900**	
New England Telephone Co	$4,000	Indiv
AT&T	$3,750	Indiv
Pacific Telesis Group	$3,500	Indiv
Intellicall Inc	$2,000	Indiv
Telecom Services & Equipment	**$13,050**	
Pan American Satellite	$3,000	Indiv
Boston Technology	$2,500	Indiv
M/A-Com Inc	$2,000	Indiv
Computer Equipment & Services	**$5,000**	
Data General Corp	$2,250	Indiv
Bolt, Beranek & Newman	$1,500	Indiv

Source of Funds in 1992 Election

Source	Total	Pct
PACs	$0	0%
Indivs $200+	$335,675	75%
Indivs under $200	$58,569	13%
Other	$50,521	11%
Candidate	$0	0%
Party	$137	0%

Source of PAC Dollars by Sector

No PAC contributions reported

Source	Total	Pct
Business	-$1,850	0%
Labor	$0	0%
Ideology/Single Issue	-$250	0%

In-State vs. Out-of-State Contributions*

Source	Total	Pct
In-State	$164,200	50%
Out-of-state	$166,475	50%
No state listed	$3,500	

* by large individual contributors ($200 & above)

Construction $4,350

General Contractors	**$2,500**	
None over $1,500		

Defense $1,500

Misc Defense	**$1,500**	
Pacer Systems Inc	$1,500	Indiv

Energy & Natural Resources $16,275

Oil & Gas	**$5,225**	
None over $1,500		
Misc Energy	**$2,050**	
None over $1,500		
Electric Utilities	**$6,500**	
Intercontinental Energy Corp	$2,500	Indiv
Environmental Svcs/Equipment	**$1,500**	
None over $1,500		

Finance, Insurance & Real Estate $64,300

Commercial Banks	**$5,000**	
Fleet/Norstar	$1,500	Indiv
Securities & Investment	**$42,250**	
Federated Investors Inc	$9,000	Indiv
TransAmerica Corp*	$4,000	Indiv
Boston Stock Exchange	$2,500	Indiv
Salomon Brothers	$2,500	Indiv
Fidelity Investments Co	$2,000	Indiv
First Boston Corp	$2,000	Indiv
Goldman, Sachs & Co	$2,000	Indiv
T Rowe Price Associates	$2,000	Indiv
Merrill Lynch	$1,500	Indiv
Tucker, Anthony & Day	$1,500	Indiv

Contribution Totals by Sector

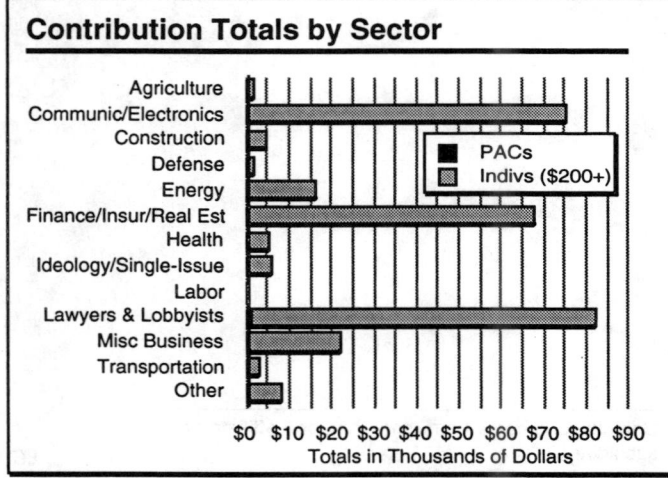

Agriculture
Communic/Electronics
Construction
Defense
Energy
Finance/Insur/Real Est
Health
Ideology/Single-Issue
Labor
Lawyers & Lobbyists
Misc Business
Transportation
Other

■ PACs
▨ Indivs ($200+)

$0 $10 $20 $30 $40 $50 $60 $70 $80 $90
Totals in Thousands of Dollars

Insurance	**$4,500**	
John Hancock Mutual Life Insurance	$2,000	Indiv
Real Estate	**$2,750**	
None over $1,500		
Accountants	**$6,800**	
Coopers & Lybrand	$3,250	Indiv
Feeley & Driscoll	$1,500	Indiv
Misc Finance	**$2,500**	
None over $1,500		

Health | | | **$5,000**

| **Health Professionals** .... | **$2,450** | |
| None over $1,500 | | |

Lawyers & Lobbyists | | | **$81,750**

Lawyers & Lobbyists	**$81,750**	
Cassidy & Associates	$7,300	Indiv
Mintz, Levin et al	$6,750	Indiv
Verner, Liipfert et al	$4,500	Indiv
Akin, Gump et al	$3,500	Indiv
Smith, McNulty & Kearney	$3,500	Indiv
Squire, Sanders & Dempsey	$3,000	Indiv
Thacher, Proffitt & Wood	$3,000	Indiv
Wunder, Diefenderfer et al	$3,000	Indiv
Kirkpatrick & Lockhart	$2,500	Indiv
O'Neill & Athy	$2,500	Indiv
Powell, Goldstein et al	$2,000	PAC/Ind
Murphy & Rennick	$1,500	Indiv
Swidler & Berlin	$1,500	Indiv
Wexler Group	$1,500	Indiv

Misc Business | | | **$21,750**

Food & Beverage	**$4,000**	
Michaels Place	$1,500	Indiv
Business Services	**$14,000**	
DMC Services Inc	$2,500	Indiv
Cullinane Group Inc	$1,500	Indiv
Misc Manufacturing & Distributing	**$1,500**	
None over $1,500		

Transportation | | | **$2,500**

| None over $1,500 | | |

Ideological/Single-Issue

Ideological/Single-Issue | | **$4,250**

| **Womens Issues** .... | **$1,500** | |
| None over $1,500 | | |

Other & Unknown

Other | | **$7,550**

Education	**$5,300**	
Harvard University	$1,500	Indiv
Retired	**$2,250**	
None over $1,500		

Unknown | | **$45,450**

No Employer Listed or Found	$14,550	
Generic Occupation/Category Unknown	$1,750	
Employer Listed/Category Unknown	$28,450	
Abry Communications	$2,000	Indiv
John Drew Co	$2,000	Indiv

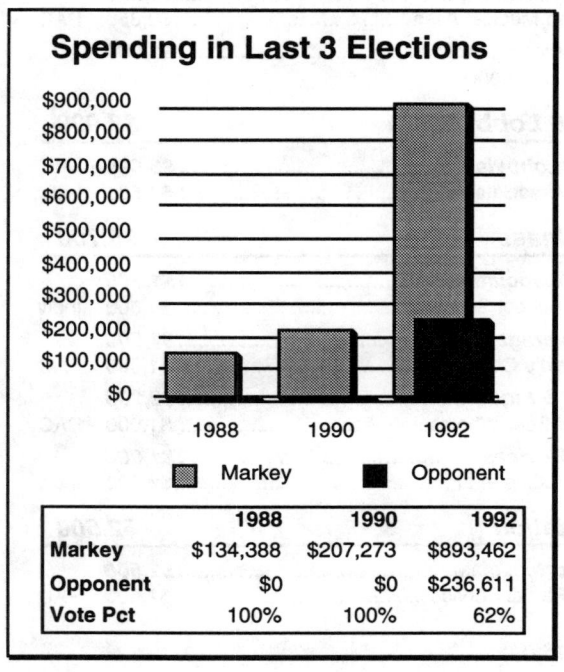

Spending in Last 3 Elections

	1988	1990	1992
Markey	$134,388	$207,273	$893,462
Opponent	$0	$0	$236,611
Vote Pct	100%	100%	62%

Markey   Opponent

---

* Contributions came from more than one affiliate or
subsidiary.

Matthew G. Martinez, D-Calif (31)

First elected: 1982

1991-92 Total Receipts: $119,807
1992 Year-end Cash: $13,570

1991-92 Committees & Subcommittees

Education and Labor
Elementary, Secondary and Vocational Education; Human Resources (Chairman); Labor-Management Relations

Government Operations
Commerce, Consumer and Monetary Affairs; Employment and Housing

Select Committee on Children, Youth and Families

Leading Contributors

Business

Agriculture	$1,569	
None over $1,000		

Communications/Electronics	$2,950	
Telephone Utilities	$2,700	
Pacific Telesis Group	$1,200	PAC
AT&T	$1,000	PAC

Construction	$3,723	
General Contractors	$1,000	
None over $1,000		
Construction Services	$1,500	
Pacifica Services Inc	$1,000	Indiv
Building Materials & Equipment	$1,223	
None over $1,000		

Defense	$2,000	
Defense Electronics	$1,250	
Raytheon	$1,000	PAC

Energy & Natural Resources	$2,050	
Waste Management	$1,200	
Browning-Ferris Industries	$1,000	PAC

Source of Funds in 1992 Election

Source	Total	Pct
■ PACs	$77,450	59%
▨ Indivs $200+	$35,573	27%
□ Indivs under $200	$5,991	5%
▧ Other	$11,339	9%
Candidate	$0	0%
Party	$10,996	8%

Source of PAC Dollars by Sector

Source	Total	Pct
■ Business	$31,718	42%
▨ Labor	$32,500	44%
□ Ideology/Single Issue	$10,500	14%

In-State vs. Out-of-State Contributions*

Source	Total	Pct
□ In-State	$26,273	76%
■ Out-of-state	$8,500	24%
No state listed	$800	

* by large individual contributors ($200 & above)

Finance, Insurance & Real Estate	$22,050	
Commercial Banks	$1,500	
American Bankers Assn	$1,000	PAC
Real Estate	$16,050	
National Assn of Realtors	$7,250	PAC
Telecu Industries	$6,000	Indiv
Accountants	$3,500	
American Institute of CPA's	$3,500	PAC

Health	$5,850	
Health Professionals	$4,850	
American Medical Assn	$3,850	PAC
Hospitals/Nursing Homes	$1,000	
None over $1,000		

Lawyers & Lobbyists	$3,999	
Lawyers & Lobbyists	$3,999	
MARC Associates	$1,500	Indiv

Misc Business	$6,700	
Business Associations	$1,500	
Kaplan School Supply	$1,500	Indiv
Food & Beverage	$1,500	
McDonald's Corp	$1,000	PAC
Beer, Wine & Liquor	$2,200	
National Beer Wholesalers Assn	$1,000	PAC
Business Services	$1,000	
Moss, McGee et al	$1,000	Indiv

Transportation	$2,500	
Air Transport	$2,500	
United Parcel Service	$2,500	PAC

Contribution Totals by Sector

Legend: ■ PACs, ▨ Indivs ($200+)

Sectors (top to bottom): Agriculture, Communic/Electronics, Construction, Defense, Energy, Finance/Insur/Real Est, Health, Ideology/Single-Issue, Labor, Lawyers & Lobbyists, Misc Business, Transportation, Other

$0 $5 $10 $15 $20 $25 $30 $35
Totals in Thousands of Dollars

Labor

Labor	$32,500

Building Trade Unions	**$5,500**	
Laborers' Political League	$4,000	PAC
Carpenters & Joiners Union	$1,000	PAC

Industrial Unions	**$8,500**	
United Auto Workers	$7,000	PAC
Intl Brotherhood of Electrical Workers	$1,000	PAC

Transportation Unions	**$4,500**	
Teamsters Union	$2,500	PAC
Marine Engineers Dist 2 Maritime Officers	$1,000	PAC
Trans Comm International Union	$1,000	PAC

Public Sector Unions	**$10,000**	
National Assn Retired Federal Employees	$4,000	PAC
National Assn of Letter Carriers	$2,000	PAC
National Education Assn	$1,500	PAC
International Assn of Firefighters	$1,000	PAC

Misc Unions	**$4,000**	
AFL-CIO	$2,500	PAC
Food & Commercial Workers Union	$1,500	PAC

Ideological/Single-Issue

Ideological/Single-Issue	$10,500

Human Rights	**$10,000**	
National Community Action Foundation	$10,000	PAC

Other & Unknown

Other	$5,400

Education	**$1,500**	
None over $1,000		

Retired	**$2,000**	
None over $1,000		

Other	**$1,500**	
National Community Action Foundation	$1,500	Indiv

Unknown	$8,500

No Employer Listed or Found	$1,000	
Generic Occupation/Category Unknown	$2,500	
Employer Listed/Category Unknown	$5,000	
Eagle Tool Co	$2,500	Indiv
Kaplan Industries	$1,000	Indiv

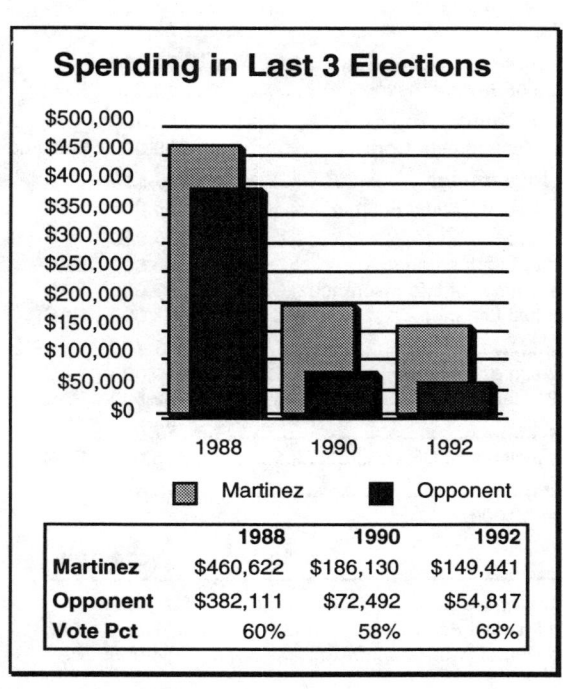

Spending in Last 3 Elections

	1988	1990	1992
Martinez	$460,622	$186,130	$149,441
Opponent	$382,111	$72,492	$54,817
Vote Pct	60%	58%	63%

Martinez   Opponent

Robert T. Matsui, D-Calif (5)

First elected: 1978

1991-92 Total Receipts: $656,875
1992 Year-end Cash: $384,523

1991-92 Committees & Subcommittees

Budget
Defense, Foreign Policy and Space; Economic Policy, Projections and Revenues; Human Resources

Ways and Means
Trade

Leading Contributors

Business

Agriculture	$28,875	
Crop Production & Basic Processing	**$13,325**	
California Almond Growers Exchange	$2,500	PAC
Tobacco	**$2,000**	
None over $2,000		
Food Processing & Sales	**$10,250**	
Yum Yum Donuts	$4,000	Indiv
Connell Rice & Sugar Co	$2,000	Indiv

Communications/Electronics	$31,200	
Media/Entertainment	**$7,300**	
National Assn of Broadcasters	$2,000	PAC
Telephone Utilities	**$17,150**	
Ameritech Corp	$6,000	PAC
AT&T	$3,300	PAC
GTE Corp	$2,500	PAC
Pacific Telesis Group	$2,300	PAC
Telecom Services & Equipment	**$2,000**	
Motorola Inc	$2,000	PAC
Computer Equipment & Services	**$3,450**	
Electronic Data Systems	$2,000	PAC

Construction	$7,475	
Home Builders	**$4,375**	
National Assn of Home Builders	$2,000	PAC

Defense	$4,500	
Defense Aerospace	**$3,500**	
None over $2,000		

Source of Funds in 1992 Election

Source	Total	Pct
■ PACs	$365,100	55%
▨ Indivs $200+	$88,300	13%
□ Indivs under $200	$89,735	14%
▨ Other	$119,154	18%
Candidate	$0	0%
Party	$5,864	1%

Source of PAC Dollars by Sector

Source	Total	Pct
■ Business	$322,325	85%
▨ Labor	$53,399	14%
□ Ideology/Single Issue	$4,615	1%

In-State vs. Out-of-State Contributions*

Source	Total	Pct
□ In-State	$58,950	42%
■ Out-of-state	$81,050	58%
No state listed	$500	

* by large individual contributors ($200 & above)

Energy & Natural Resources	$32,375	
Oil & Gas	**$17,825**	
Atlantic Richfield	$3,000	PAC/Ind
Pacific Enterprises	$3,000	PAC
Electric Utilities	**$11,050**	
Southern California Edison	$5,000	PAC
Pacific Gas & Electric	$2,800	PAC

Finance, Insurance & Real Estate	$112,150	
Commercial Banks	**$12,300**	
American Bankers Assn	$4,000	PAC
Barnett Banks Inc	$2,000	PAC
Savings & Loans	**$4,400**	
US League of Savings Assns*	$3,000	PAC
Finance/Credit Companies	**$11,000**	
Beneficial Management Corp	$9,000	PAC/Ind
Securities & Investment	**$16,550**	
National Venture Capital Assn	$6,000	PAC
Insurance	**$30,850**	
Metropolitan Life Insurance	$3,500	PAC
American Council of Life Insurance	$3,000	PAC
Pacific Mutual Life	$2,000	PAC
Real Estate	**$23,100**	
National Assn of Realtors	$10,000	PAC
Century 21 Real Estate	$2,500	PAC
Accountants	**$9,050**	
American Institute of CPA's	$5,000	PAC
Misc Finance	**$3,400**	
None over $2,000		

Health	$68,423	
Health Professionals	**$31,100**	
American Medical Assn	$8,850	PAC
American Dental Assn	$4,000	PAC

Contribution Totals by Sector

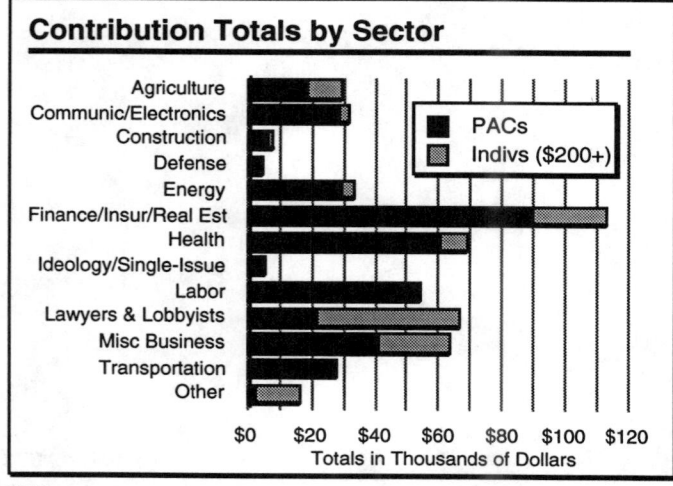

Agriculture
Communic/Electronics
Construction
Defense
Energy
Finance/Insur/Real Est
Health
Ideology/Single-Issue
Labor
Lawyers & Lobbyists
Misc Business
Transportation
Other

■ PACs
▨ Indivs ($200+)

$0 $20 $40 $60 $80 $100 $120
Totals in Thousands of Dollars

American Society of Anesthesiologists .... $3,000 PAC
American Academy of Ophthalmology .... $2,500 PAC
Anesthesia Service Medical Group .... $2,500 PAC

Hospitals/Nursing Homes **$19,423**
Federation of American Health Systems .... $5,500 PAC
American Hospital Assn .... $4,000 PAC
American Health Care Assn .... $2,500 PAC
California Assn of Hosp/Health Systems .... $2,123 PAC/Ind

Pharmaceuticals/Health Products **$14,900**
Pfizer Inc .... $2,000 PAC

Misc Health **$2,500**
None over $2,000

Lawyers & Lobbyists — $65,875

Lawyers & Lobbyists **$65,875**
Marks, Murase & White .... $8,000 Indiv
Assn of Trial Lawyers of America .... $5,000 PAC
Akin, Gump et al .... $4,500 PAC/Ind
McClure, Trotter & Mentz .... $4,000 Indiv

Misc Business — $62,352

Food & Beverage **$3,000**
National Restaurant Assn .... $2,000 PAC

Beer, Wine & Liquor **$18,800**
Gallo Winery .... $4,000 Indiv
Todhunter International Inc .... $4,000 Indiv
Florida Distillers Co .... $3,000 Indiv
Joseph E Seagram & Sons .... $2,000 PAC
Smirnoff/Inglenook Distributors .... $2,000 PAC

Retail Sales **$12,252**
International Council of Shopping Centers .... $2,000 PAC
National Assn of Convenience Stores .... $2,000 PAC

Misc Services **$6,300**
American Assn of Equipment Lessors .... $3,500 PAC

Business Services **$4,250**
None over $2,000

Misc Business **$3,000**
National Assn of Water Companies .... $3,000 PAC

Misc Manufacturing & Distributing **$9,250**
Xerox Corp .... $2,500 PAC/Ind
Corning Glass Works .... $2,000 PAC

Textiles **$2,500**
Jersey Sales Co Associates .... $2,500 Indiv

Spending in Last 3 Elections

	1988	1990	1992
Matsui	$638,688	$734,005	$1,421,123
Opponent	$7,695	$4,628	$24,150
Vote Pct	71%	60%	69%

Transportation — $27,600

Air Transport **$8,000**
United Parcel Service .... $3,500 PAC
General Electric .... $2,000 PAC
United Airlines .... $2,000 PAC

Automotive **$9,600**
Americans for Free International Trade .... $3,000 PAC
Chrysler Corp .... $2,500 PAC

Trucking **$4,500**
None over $2,000

Railroads **$4,000**
Union Pacific Corp .... $2,000 PAC

Labor

Labor — $53,399

Building Trade Unions **$4,600**
Plumbers/Pipefitters Union .... $2,000 PAC

Industrial Unions **$4,500**
United Auto Workers .... $4,500 PAC

Transportation Unions **$16,950**
Air Line Pilots Assn .... $5,000 PAC
United Transportation Union .... $5,000 PAC
Marine Engineers Union* .... $3,500 PAC

Public Sector Unions **$23,050**
American Federation of Teachers .... $5,000 PAC
National Assn Retired Federal Employees .... $3,000 PAC
National Assn of Letter Carriers .... $3,000 PAC
International Assn of Firefighters .... $2,800 PAC
American Fedn of St/Cnty/Munic Employees ...... $2,000 PAC
American Postal Workers Union .... $2,000 PAC

Misc Unions **$4,299**
Food & Commercial Workers Union .... $2,499 PAC

Ideological/Single-Issue

Ideological/Single-Issue — $4,915
None over $2,000

Other & Unknown

Other — $15,950

Education **$2,500**
None over $2,000

Retired **$11,200**
None over $2,000

Other **$2,250**
None over $2,000

Unknown — $6,250
Homemakers/Non-income earners $7,000
Employer Listed/Category Unknown $10,825
None over $2,000

Independent expenditures supporting Matsui
California Medical Assn $2,500

---

* Contributions came from more than one affiliate or
subsidiary.

Romano L. Mazzoli, D-Ky (3)

First elected: 1970

1991-92 Total Receipts: $223,091
1992 Year-end Cash: $6,743

1991-92 Committees & Subcommittees

Judiciary
Administrative Law and Governmental Relations; Economic and Commercial Law; International Law, Immigration and Refugees (Chairman)

Small Business
Antitrust, Impact of Deregulation and Ecology; SBA, the General Economy and Minority Enterprise Development

Select Committee on Narcotics Abuse and Control

Leading Contributors

Business

Finance, Insurance & Real Estate	$2,950
Commercial Banks	$1,400
None over $1,000	
Real Estate	$1,000
None over $1,000	

Health	$2,900
Health Professionals	$2,100
None over $1,000	

Lawyers & Lobbyists	$2,900
Lawyers & Lobbyists	$2,900
None over $1,000	

Source of Funds in 1992 Election

Source	Total	Pct
■ PACs	$0	0%
▨ Indivs $200+	$15,950	7%
☐ Indivs under $200	$202,157	91%
⊠ Other	$5,121	2%
Candidate	$0	0%
Party	$137	0%

Source of PAC Dollars by Sector

No PAC contributions reported

Source	Total	Pct
■ Business	$0	0%
▨ Labor..	$0	0%
☐ Ideology/Single Issue	$0	0%

In-State vs. Out-of-State Contributions*

Source	Total	Pct
☐ In-State	$14,900	100%
■ Out-of-state	$0	0%
No state listed	$0	

* by large individual contributors ($200 & above)

Contribution Totals by Sector

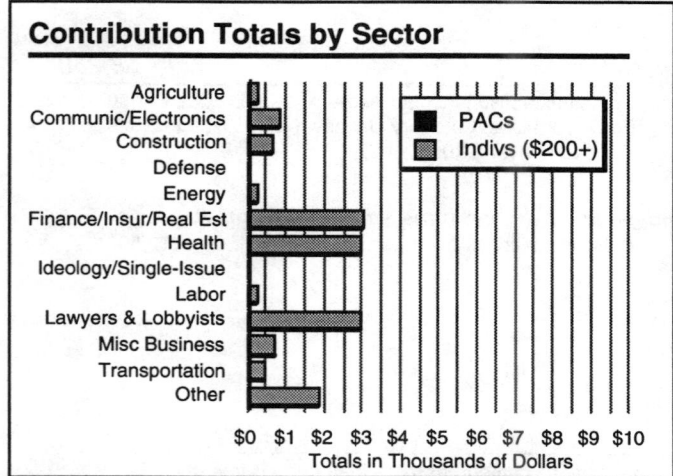

Agriculture
Communic/Electronics
Construction
Defense
Energy
Finance/Insur/Real Est
Health
Ideology/Single-Issue
Labor
Lawyers & Lobbyists
Misc Business
Transportation
Other

■ PACs
▨ Indivs ($200+)

$0 $1 $2 $3 $4 $5 $6 $7 $8 $9 $10
Totals in Thousands of Dollars

Other & Unknown

Other   **$1,800**

   None over $1,000

Unknown   **$1,300**

   None over $1,000

Independent expenditures supporting Mazzoli
   National Right to Life PAC $5,763

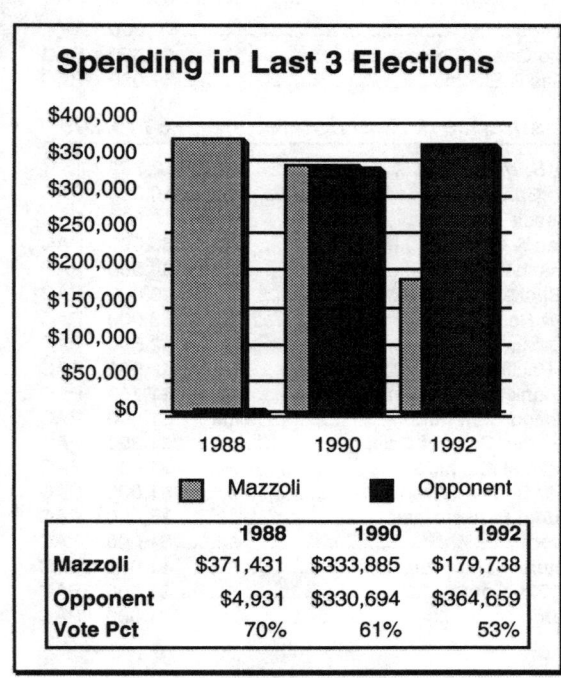

Spending in Last 3 Elections

	1988	1990	1992
Mazzoli	$371,431	$333,885	$179,738
Opponent	$4,931	$330,694	$364,659
Vote Pct	70%	61%	53%

Al McCandless, R-Calif (44)

First elected: 1982

1991-92 Total Receipts: $318,312
1992 Year-end Cash: $45,027

1991-92 Committees & Subcommittees

Banking, Finance and Urban Affairs
Consumer Affairs and Coinage (Ranking Republican); Financial Institutions Supervision, Regulation and Insurance; International Development, Finance, Trade and Monetary Policy

Government Operations
Government Information, Justice and Agriculture (Ranking Republican)

Leading Contributors

Business

Agriculture	$20,256	
Crop Production & Basic Processing	**$17,056**	
Richard Bagdasarian Inc	$3,500	Indiv
Sunkist Growers	$2,000	PAC
JG Boswell Co	$1,000	PAC
Agricultural Services/Products	**$1,250**	
American Veterinary Medical Assn	$1,000	PAC

Communications/Electronics	$9,600	
Printing & Publishing	**$2,800**	
West Publishing	$2,000	PAC
Telephone Utilities	**$5,800**	
AT&T	$1,500	PAC
GTE Corp	$1,200	PAC
Pacific Telesis Group	$1,000	PAC
United Telecommunications	$1,000	PAC

Construction	$17,392	
General Contractors	**$6,050**	
Fluor Corp	$2,000	PAC
Associated General Contractors	$1,000	PAC
Home Builders	**$4,550**	
National Assn of Home Builders	$2,000	PAC
Manufactured Housing Institute	$1,500	PAC
Special Trade Contractors	**$2,000**	
National Electrical Contractors Assn	$1,000	PAC
Construction Services	**$3,542**	
CH2M Hill	$1,000	PAC
Building Materials & Equipment	**$1,250**	
Johnson Machinery Co	$1,000	Indiv

Contribution Totals by Sector

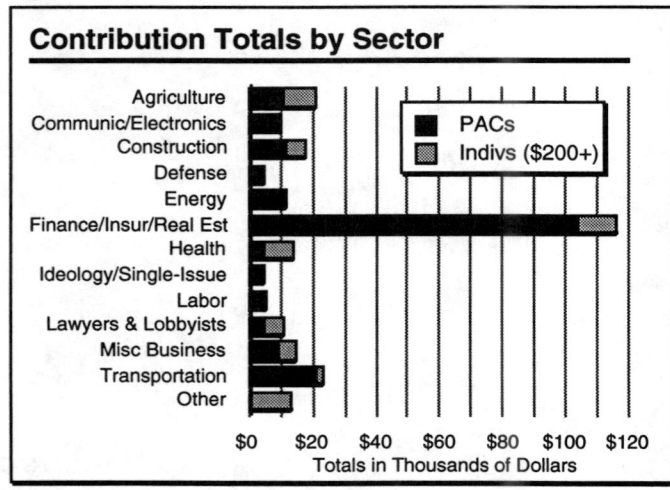

Agriculture
Communic/Electronics
Construction
Defense
Energy
Finance/Insur/Real Est
Health
Ideology/Single-Issue
Labor
Lawyers & Lobbyists
Misc Business
Transportation
Other

- PACs
- Indivs ($200+)

$0 $20 $40 $60 $80 $100 $120
Totals in Thousands of Dollars

Source of Funds in 1992 Election

Source	Total	Pct
PACs	$195,137	61%
Indivs $200+	$77,426	24%
Indivs under $200	$43,208	14%
Other	$2,541	1%
Candidate	$0	0%
Party	$270	0%

Source of PAC Dollars by Sector

Source	Total	Pct
Business	$184,624	95%
Labor	$5,000	3%
Ideology/Single Issue	$4,057	2%

In-State vs. Out-of-State Contributions*

Source	Total	Pct
In-State	$70,876	92%
Out-of-state	$6,550	8%
No state listed	$0	

* by large individual contributors ($200 & above)

Defense	$4,000	
Defense Aerospace	**$2,500**	
Northrop Corp	$2,000	PAC
Defense Electronics	**$1,500**	
TRW Inc	$1,500	PAC

Energy & Natural Resources	$11,000	
Oil & Gas	**$5,500**	
Atlantic Richfield	$1,000	PAC
Pacific Enterprises	$1,000	PAC
Union Oil	$1,000	PAC
Electric Utilities	**$4,300**	
San Diego Gas & Electric	$1,550	PAC
Pacific Gas & Electric	$1,000	PAC

Finance, Insurance & Real Estate	$115,249	
Commercial Banks	**$52,799**	
American Bankers Assn	$10,000	PAC
BankAmerica Corp	$6,000	PAC
JP Morgan & Co	$5,000	PAC
Chase Manhattan	$4,500	PAC
Barnett Banks Inc	$3,000	PAC
Citizens & Southern National Bank	$3,000	PAC
Citicorp	$2,500	PAC
Security Pacific Corp	$2,000	PAC
Assn of Bank Holding Companies	$1,750	PAC
First Chicago Corp	$1,500	PAC
First Interstate Bank of California	$1,399	PAC
Bankers Trust	$1,000	PAC
Consumer Bankers Assn	$1,000	PAC
Independent Bankers Assn	$1,000	PAC
MBNA Corp	$1,000	PAC
Manufacturers Hanover	$1,000	PAC
National City Corp	$1,000	PAC
Wells Fargo	$1,000	PAC

Savings & Loans $6,350
   US League of Savings Assns* .... $2,750 PAC
   Great Western Financial Corp .... $1,000 PAC
   Home Federal Savings & Loan .... $1,000 PAC
   National Council of Savings Institutions .... $1,000 PAC

Credit Unions $2,000
   Credit Union National Assn .... $2,000 PAC

Finance/Credit Companies $10,100
   Associated Credit Bureaus .... $4,500 PAC
   Household International Inc .... $2,100 PAC
   Beneficial Management Corp .... $2,000 PAC
   American Financial Services Assn .... $1,500 PAC

Securities & Investment $7,500
   Dean Witter .... $2,000 PAC
   American Express* .... $1,000 PAC
   Investment Company Institute .... $1,000 PAC

Insurance $5,500
   Fireman's Fund Insurance .... $1,000 PAC
   Mortgage Insurance Companies of America .... $1,000 PAC
   National Assn of Independent Insurers .... $1,000 PAC

Real Estate $17,250
   National Assn of Realtors .... $6,750 PAC
   Del Webb Corp .... $2,000 PAC
   Sunrise Co .... $2,000 Indiv
   Bedford Properties .... $1,000 PAC
   DRR Investments .... $1,000 Indiv

Accountants $9,850
   American Institute of CPA's .... $7,500 PAC
   Coopers & Lybrand .... $1,000 PAC

Misc Finance $3,900
   National Check Cashers Assn .... $1,500 PAC
   Equifax Inc .... $1,000 PAC

Health $13,600

Health Professionals $11,600
   American Medical Assn .... $3,850 PAC

Health Services $1,500
   Blythe Ambulance Service .... $1,500 Indiv

---

Lawyers & Lobbyists $10,250
Lawyers & Lobbyists $10,250
   Jones, Day et al .... $1,250 PAC
   Morrison & Foerster .... $1,000 Indiv

Misc Business $14,200
Beer, Wine & Liquor $2,000
   National Beer Wholesalers Assn .... $1,500 PAC
Retail Sales $2,750
   JC Penney Co .... $1,000 PAC
Business Services $2,750
   Dun & Bradstreet .... $1,000 PAC
Lodging/Tourism $1,200
   None over $1,000
Misc Business $1,000
   Heimark Distributing Co .... $1,000 Indiv
Chemical & Related Manufacturing $2,000
   SICPA Industries of America .... $1,000 Indiv
Misc Manufacturing & Distributing $2,000
   Stone Container Corp .... $2,000 PAC

Transportation $22,300

Air Transport $8,550
   United Parcel Service .... $5,500 PAC
   United Airlines .... $2,000 PAC

Automotive $13,000
   National Auto Dealers Assn .... $6,500 PAC
   Auto Dealers & Drivers for Free Trade .... $2,000 PAC
   Ford Motor Co .... $1,500 PAC
   Americans for Free International Trade .... $1,000 PAC
   Plaza Motors Inc .... $1,000 Indiv

Labor

Labor $5,000

Transportation Unions $3,000
   Marine Engineers Union* .... $3,000 PAC
Public Sector Unions $2,000
   National Assn Retired Federal Employees .... $2,000 PAC

Ideological/Single-Issue

Ideological/Single-Issue $4,057

Gun Rights/Gun Control $3,000
   National Rifle Assn .... $3,000 PAC
Misc Issues $1,057
   None over $1,000

Other & Unknown

Other $12,953

Retired $12,953
   None over $1,000

Unknown $11,250
   Homemakers/Non-income earners $3,900
   Employer Listed/Category Unknown $6,600
      Windtech Inc .... $1,250 Indiv

---

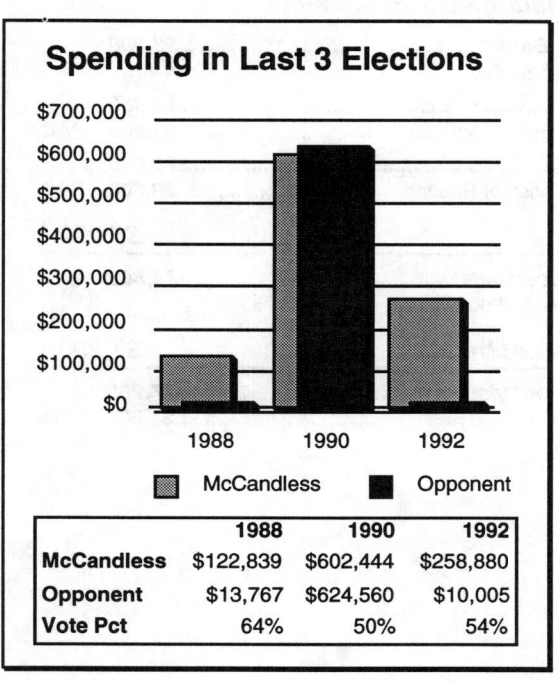

Spending in Last 3 Elections

	1988	1990	1992
McCandless	$122,839	$602,444	$258,880
Opponent	$13,767	$624,560	$10,005
Vote Pct	64%	50%	54%

McCandless   Opponent

---

* Contributions came from more than one affiliate or subsidiary.

Frank McCloskey, D-Ind (8)

First elected: 1982

1991-92 Total Receipts: $498,192
1992 Year-end Cash: $8,622

1991-92 Committees & Subcommittees

Armed Services
Investigations; Procurement and Military Nuclear Systems

Foreign Affairs
Arms Control, International Security and Science

Post Office and Civil Service
Investigations; Postal Operations and Services (Chairman)

Leading Contributors

Business

Agriculture	$8,750	
Crop Production & Basic Processing	**$4,300**	
American Crystal Sugar Corp	$2,000	PAC
Food Processing & Sales	**$1,500**	
None over $1,500		

Communications/Electronics	$7,000	
Printing & Publishing	**$1,750**	
None over $1,500		
Telephone Utilities	**$3,750**	
Indiana Bell Telephone	$3,000	PAC

Defense	$24,400	
Defense Aerospace	**$18,000**	
Textron Inc	$2,500	PAC
United Technologies	$2,000	PAC
General Dynamics	$1,500	PAC
General Motors	$1,500	PAC
Grumman Corp	$1,500	PAC
LTV Aerospace & Defense Co	$1,500	PAC
Lockheed Corp	$1,500	PAC
Defense Electronics	**$5,900**	
AT&T	$3,500	PAC

Source of Funds in 1992 Election

Source	Total	Pct
■ PACs	$329,069	62%
▨ Indivs $200+	$27,624	5%
□ Indivs under $200	$117,047	22%
▨ Other	$57,142	11%
Candidate	$0	0%
Party	$38,140	7%

Source of PAC Dollars by Sector

Source	Total	Pct
■ Business	$95,811	31%
▨ Labor	$188,250	60%
□ Ideology/Single Issue	$27,484	9%

In-State vs. Out-of-State Contributions*

Source	Total	Pct
□ In-State	$11,030	40%
■ Out-of-state	$16,594	60%
No state listed	$0	

* by large individual contributors ($200 & above)

Energy & Natural Resources	$12,250	
Mining	**$2,500**	
None over $1,500		
Misc Energy	**$3,500**	
Babcock & Wilcox	$3,000	PAC
Electric Utilities	**$4,250**	
ACRE (Action Cmte for Rural Electrification)*	$2,000	PAC
Waste Management	**$2,000**	
Waste Management Inc	$2,000	PAC

Finance, Insurance & Real Estate	$20,300	
Commercial Banks	**$3,800**	
None over $1,500		
Insurance	**$3,350**	
CNA Financial Corp	$1,600	PAC
Real Estate	**$10,500**	
National Assn of Realtors	$9,500	PAC

Health	$5,050	
Health Professionals	**$4,800**	
None over $1,500		

Lawyers & Lobbyists	$7,200	
Lawyers & Lobbyists	**$7,200**	
Hyjek & Fix	$1,500	Indiv

Contribution Totals by Sector

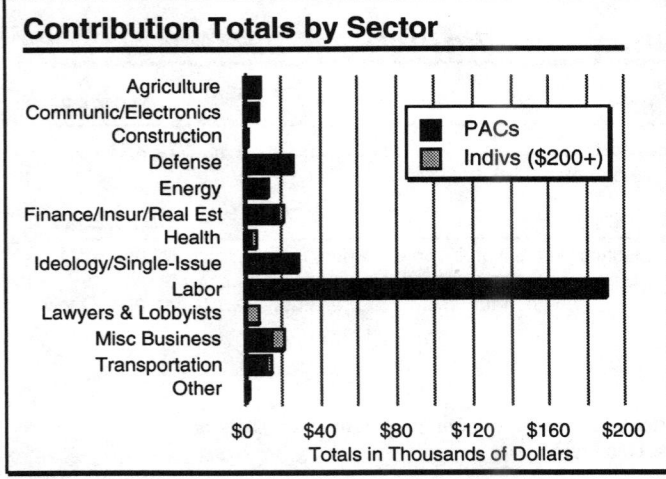

Agriculture, Communic/Electronics, Construction, Defense, Energy, Finance/Insur/Real Est, Health, Ideology/Single-Issue, Labor, Lawyers & Lobbyists, Misc Business, Transportation, Other

■ PACs
▨ Indivs ($200+)

$0 $40 $80 $120 $160 $200
Totals in Thousands of Dollars

Misc Business — $19,555

Retail Sales **$6,590**
- Direct Marketing Assn ....$2,240 PAC/Ind
- Third Class Mail Assn ....$2,000 PAC

Misc Services **$2,000**
- None over $1,500

Business Services **$8,625**
- Advo-System Inc ....$4,961 PAC
- Metcor Inc ....$3,414 Indiv

Transportation — $12,800

Air Transport **$10,800**
- United Parcel Service ....$8,200 PAC

Automotive **$1,500**
- None over $1,500

Labor

Labor — $189,750

Building Trade Unions **$25,700**
- Carpenters & Joiners Union ....$7,500 PAC
- Sheet Metal Workers Union ....$5,000 PAC
- Laborers' Political League ....$4,500 PAC
- Plumbers/Pipefitters Union ....$4,000 PAC
- Painters & Allied Trades Union ....$1,500 PAC

Industrial Unions **$59,000**
- United Mine Workers ....$10,500 PAC
- Machinists/Aerospace Workers Union ...$10,000 PAC
- United Auto Workers ....$10,000 PAC
- Intl Brotherhood of Electrical Workers ....$7,500 PAC
- Electronic Machine Furniture Workers ....$4,000 PAC
- Rubber Cork Linoleum & Plastic Workers ...$3,500 PAC
- Communications Workers of America .....$3,000 PAC
- United Steelworkers ....$2,500 PAC
- Boilermakers Union ....$2,000 PAC
- Amalgamated Clothing & Textile Workers ...$1,500 PAC
- Intl Ladies Garment Workers Union ....$1,500 Indiv

Transportation Unions — $19,850
- Air Line Pilots Assn ....$7,500 PAC
- Teamsters Union ....$7,500 PAC

Public Sector Unions — $71,200
- American Fedn of St/Cnty/Munic Employees ....$10,000 PAC
- American Postal Workers Union ....$10,000 PAC
- National Assn of Letter Carriers ....$10,000 PAC
- National Education Assn ....$10,000 PAC
- Natl Star Route Mail Contractors Assn ....$6,500 PAC
- National Assn Retired Federal Employees ....$4,000 PAC
- National Assn of Postmasters ....$3,700 PAC
- American Federation of Teachers ....$3,500 PAC
- National Assn of Postal Supervisors .....$3,050 PAC
- National Rural Letter Carriers Assn ....$2,850 PAC
- National League of Postmasters ....$2,500 PAC
- Federal Managers' Assn ....$1,500 PAC
- International Assn of Firefighters ....$1,500 PAC

Misc Unions — $14,000
- Food & Commercial Workers Union ......$6,000 PAC
- AFL-CIO ....$5,000 PAC
- Bakery, Confectionery & Tobacco Workers ....$1,500 PAC

Ideological/Single-Issue

Ideological/Single-Issue — $27,484

Democratic/Liberal **$5,000**
- National Cmte for an Effective Congress .....$5,000 PAC

Leadership PACs **$9,734**
- Effective Government Cmte (Dick Gephardt) ....$4,234 PAC
- America's Leaders' Fund (Dan Rostenkowski) ....$2,000 PAC
- House Leadership Fund (Tom Foley) ....$2,000 PAC

Foreign & Defense Policy **$3,000**
- Veterans of Foreign Wars ....$2,000 PAC

Misc Issues **$7,500**
- National Cmte to Preserve Social Security ....$3,500 PAC
- National Council of Senior Citizens ......$2,000 PAC
- Sierra Club ....$2,000 PAC

Other & Unknown

Unknown — $2,700
- Employer Listed/Category Unknown $2,700
  - None over $1,500

Independent expenditures opposing McCloskey
- Ruff PAC $2,201

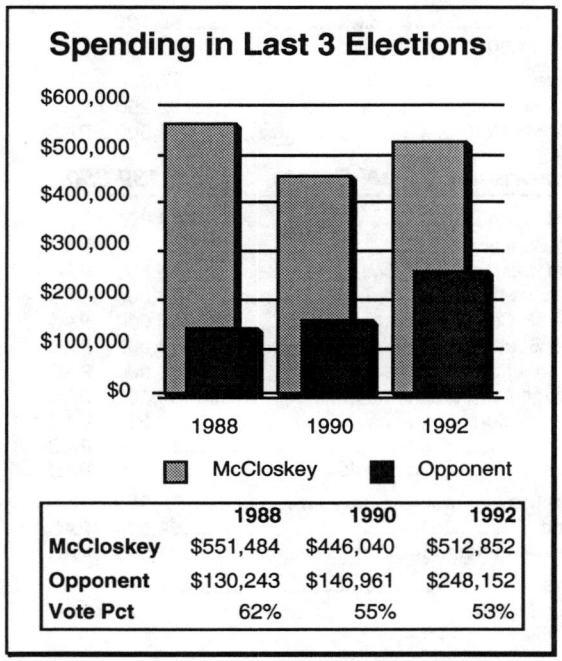

Spending in Last 3 Elections

	1988	1990	1992
McCloskey	$551,484	$446,040	$512,852
Opponent	$130,243	$146,961	$248,152
Vote Pct	62%	55%	53%

---

* Contributions came from more than one affiliate or subsidiary.

Bill McCollum, R-Fla (8)

First elected: 1980

1991-92 Total Receipts:	$642,785
1992 Year-end Cash:	$68,837

1991-92 Committees & Subcommittees

Banking, Finance and Urban Affairs
Financial Institutions Supervision, Regulation and Insurance; General Oversight and Investigations (Ranking Republican); International Development, Finance, Trade and Monetary Policy

Judiciary
Civil and Constitutional Rights; Crime and Criminal Justice; International Law, Immigration and Refugees (Ranking Republican)

Leading Contributors

Business

Agriculture — $35,850

Crop Production & Basic Processing $17,600
Florida Fruit & Vegetable Assn	$3,000	PAC/Ind
A Duda & Sons	$2,000	PAC
Eastgate Farms	$1,500	Indiv

Tobacco $4,500
RJR Nabisco	$3,000	PAC

Agricultural Services/Products $1,550
None over $1,500

Food Processing & Sales $10,500
Food Marketing Institute	$2,500	PAC
General Mills	$2,500	PAC/Ind
Winn-Dixie Stores	$2,000	PAC

Communications/Electronics — $35,200

Media/Entertainment $19,750
National Cable Television Assn	$8,500	PAC
National Assn of Broadcasters	$5,000	PAC
Walt Disney Co	$2,000	PAC

Telephone Utilities $12,150
AT&T	$3,500	PAC
Southern Bell	$3,500	PAC
GTE Corp	$2,500	PAC
United Telecommunications	$1,900	PAC

Computer Equipment & Services $1,500
None over $1,500

Construction — $12,750

General Contractors $4,500
None over $1,500

Source of Funds in 1992 Election

Source	Total	Pct
PACs	$300,830	47%
Indivs $200+	$213,275	33%
Indivs under $200	$84,766	13%
Other	$43,914	7%
Candidate	$0	0%
Party	$207	0%

Source of PAC Dollars by Sector

Source	Total	Pct
Business	$286,400	95%
Labor	$4,000	1%
Ideology/Single Issue	$12,000	4%

In-State vs. Out-of-State Contributions*

Source	Total	Pct
In-State	$187,925	89%
Out-of-state	$22,250	11%
No state listed	$2,000	

* by large individual contributors ($200 & above)

Home Builders $2,550
None over $1,500

Building Materials & Equipment $4,200
None over $1,500

Defense — $8,000

Defense Aerospace $7,000
Martin Marietta Corp	$6,500	PAC/Ind

Energy & Natural Resources — $15,300

Oil & Gas $6,000
Enron Corp	$2,000	PAC

Mining $1,500
None over $1,500

Electric Utilities $7,300
Southern Co*	$2,250	PAC
Florida Power Corp	$1,500	PAC

Finance, Insurance & Real Estate — $139,050

Commercial Banks $48,800
American Bankers Assn	$10,000	PAC
SunBanks	$5,500	PAC/Ind
Barnett Banks Inc	$5,000	PAC
JP Morgan & Co	$5,000	PAC
Citizens & Southern National Bank	$4,000	PAC
Chase Manhattan	$3,000	PAC
First Chicago Corp	$2,500	PAC
BankAmerica Corp	$2,000	PAC
Citicorp	$2,000	PAC
Assn of Bank Holding Companies	$1,500	PAC

Savings & Loans $6,000
CalFed Inc	$2,500	PAC
Great Western Financial Corp	$1,500	PAC

Credit Unions $1,500
None over $1,500

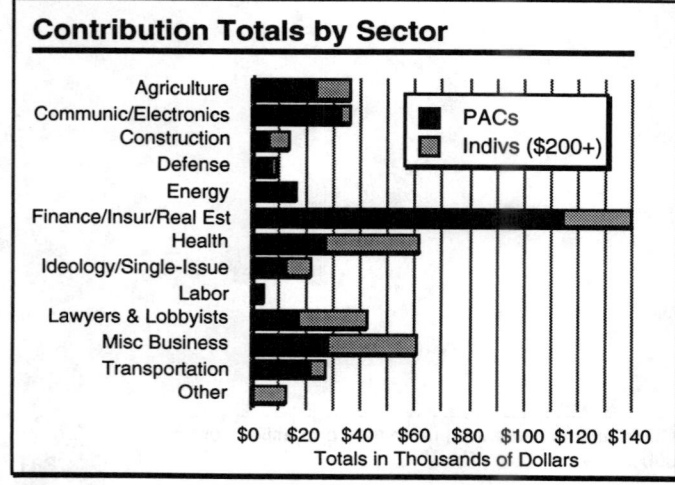

Contribution Totals by Sector

- PACs
- Indivs ($200+)

Agriculture
Communic/Electronics
Construction
Defense
Energy
Finance/Insur/Real Est
Health
Ideology/Single-Issue
Labor
Lawyers & Lobbyists
Misc Business
Transportation
Other

$0 $20 $40 $60 $80 $100 $120 $140

Totals in Thousands of Dollars

Finance/Credit Companies $1,500
  None over $1,500

Securities & Investment $6,750
  Prudential Securities .... $1,500 PAC

Insurance $34,450
  National Assn of Life Underwriters .... $5,000 PAC
  American Council of Life Insurance .... $3,000 PAC
  Independent Insurance Agents of America .... $2,500 PAC
  Travelers Corp .... $2,000 PAC
  Accredited Surety & Casualty Co .... $1,500 Indiv
  Kemper Insurance .... $1,500 PAC
  National Assn of Independent Insurers .... $1,500 PAC
  United Services Automobile Assn Group .... $1,500 PAC

Real Estate $24,100
  National Assn of Realtors .... $8,000 PAC
  First Union Corp .... $2,000 PAC
  Mortgage Bankers Assn of America .... $1,500 PAC

Accountants $12,700
  American Institute of CPA's .... $10,000 PAC
  Ernst & Young .... $1,500 PAC

Misc Finance $3,250
  None over $1,500

Health $60,400

Health Professionals $48,400
  American Medical Assn .... $10,000 PAC
  American Physical Therapy Assn .... $4,000 PAC
  American Dental Assn .... $3,000 PAC

Health Services $2,000
  LC Herring & Co .... $2,000 Indiv

Pharmaceuticals/Health Products $7,750
  None over $1,500

Lawyers & Lobbyists $41,600

Lawyers & Lobbyists $41,600
  Assn of Trial Lawyers of America .... $5,000 PAC
  Gray, Harris & Robinson .... $2,500 PAC/Ind
  Jones, Day et al .... $2,500 PAC/Ind
  Rumberger, Kirk et al .... $2,500 Indiv
  Holland & Knight .... $1,700 PAC
  Akin, Gump et al .... $1,500 PAC

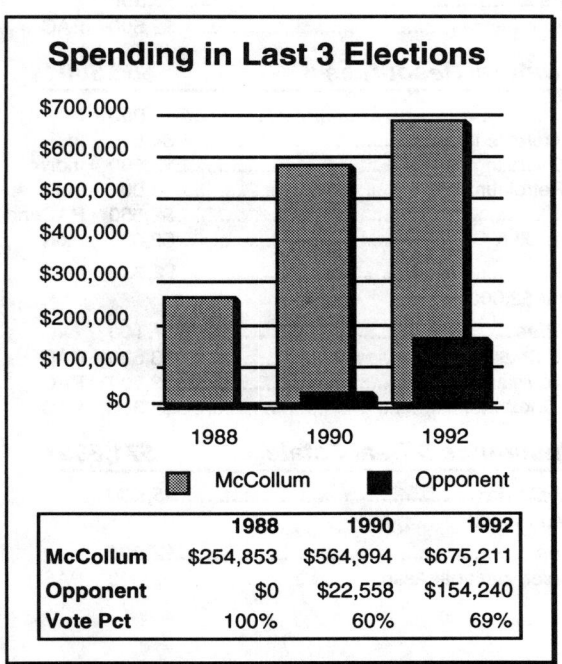

Spending in Last 3 Elections

	1988	1990	1992
McCollum	$254,853	$564,994	$675,211
Opponent	$0	$22,558	$154,240
Vote Pct	100%	60%	69%

▨ McCollum   ■ Opponent

Misc Business $59,700

Food & Beverage $20,450
  General Mills Restaurants .... $6,450 PAC/Ind
  Coca-Cola Bottling .... $3,500 Indiv
  National Restaurant Assn .... $2,000 PAC
  Olive Garden Restaurants .... $2,000 Indiv

Beer, Wine & Liquor $7,000
  National Beer Wholesalers Assn .... $4,000 PAC

Retail Sales $4,500
  None over $1,500

Business Services $3,850
  None over $1,500

Lodging/Tourism $7,950
  Walt Disney World .... $3,000 Indiv
  Marriott Corp .... $1,500 PAC

Chemical & Related Manufacturing $2,800
  None over $1,500

Misc Manufacturing & Distributing $9,400
  Daniels Manufacturing Corp .... $2,200 Indiv

Transportation $26,250

Air Transport $7,500
  United Parcel Service .... $3,000 PAC
  Delta Airlines .... $2,000 PAC
  General Electric .... $2,000 PAC

Automotive $15,250
  National Auto Dealers Assn .... $6,000 PAC
  Contemporary Cars Inc .... $3,000 Indiv
  Auto Dealers & Drivers for Free Trade .... $1,500 PAC

Labor

Labor $4,000

Transportation Unions $3,000
  Marine Engineers Union* .... $3,000 PAC

Ideological/Single-Issue

Ideological/Single-Issue $20,750

Pro-Israel $15,250
  Americans for Good Government Inc .... $2,000 PAC
  Florida Congressional Cmte .... $2,000 PAC

Misc Issues $2,500
  None over $1,500

Other & Unknown

Other $12,400

Education $3,500
  None over $1,500

Retired $7,200
  None over $1,500

Unknown $43,325

  Homemakers/Non-income earners $16,150
  No Employer Listed or Found $6,000
  Employer Listed/Category Unknown $20,925
    FLM Inc .... $2,000 Indiv

Independent expenditures supporting McCollum
  National Right to Life PAC $2,547

---

* Contributions came from more than one affiliate or
subsidiary.

Jim McCrery, R-La (5)

First elected: 1988

1991-92 Total Receipts: $768,933
1992 Year-end Cash: $63,367

1991-92 Committees & Subcommittees

Armed Services
Military Installations and Facilities; Military Personnel and Compensation; Research and Development

Budget
Defense, Foreign Policy and Space (Ranking Republican); Urgent Fiscal Issues

Leading Contributors

Business

Agriculture — $55,500

Crop Production & Basic Processing $12,400
None over $2,000

Tobacco $5,200
RJR Nabisco .... $3,300 PAC

Dairy $2,300
None over $2,000

Livestock $4,750
Jack Lawton Inc .... $4,500 Indiv

Agricultural Services/Products $4,100
None over $2,000

Food Processing & Sales $4,050
National Wholesale Grocers Assn ... $2,000 PAC

Forestry & Forest Products $21,200
International Paper Co .... $7,000 PAC
Georgia-Pacific Corp .... $2,800 PAC
Boise Cascade .... $2,000 PAC
Westvaco Corp .... $2,000 PAC

Communications/Electronics — $5,100

Telephone Utilities $4,100
BellSouth Corp* .... $4,100 PAC

Construction — $21,450

General Contractors $14,350
Delta Gulf Corp .... $4,000 Indiv
Madden Construction .... $2,000 Indiv

Contribution Totals by Sector

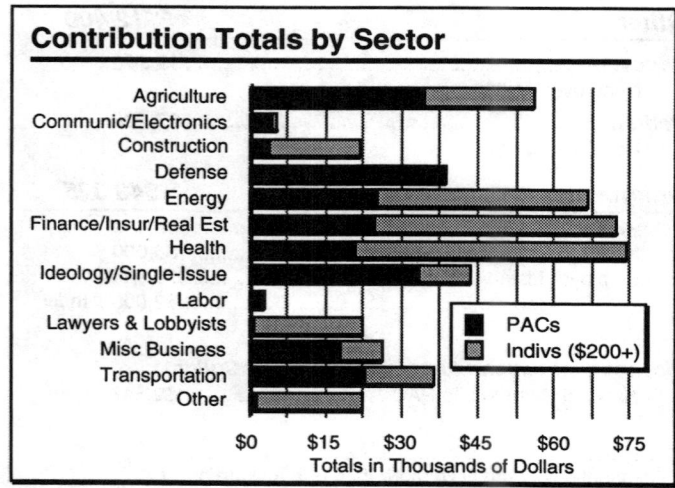

Agriculture
Communic/Electronics
Construction
Defense
Energy
Finance/Insur/Real Est
Health
Ideology/Single-Issue
Labor
Lawyers & Lobbyists
Misc Business
Transportation
Other

■ PACs
▨ Indivs ($200+)

$0 $15 $30 $45 $60 $75
Totals in Thousands of Dollars

Source of Funds in 1992 Election

Source	Total	Pct
■ PACs	$225,593	27%
▨ Indivs $200+	$337,404	41%
☐ Indivs under $200	$168,382	20%
⊠ Other	$92,680	11%
Candidate	$500	0%
Party	$74,917	9%

Source of PAC Dollars by Sector

Source	Total	Pct
■ Business	$189,950	84%
▨ Labor	$2,650	1%
☐ Ideology/Single Issue	$32,916	15%

In-State vs. Out-of-State Contributions*

Source	Total	Pct
☐ In-State	$314,554	94%
■ Out-of-state	$21,850	6%
No state listed	$1,000	

*** by large individual contributors ($200 & above)**

Home Builders $3,600
Calhoun Builders Inc .... $2,000 Indiv

Building Materials & Equipment $2,250
None over $2,000

Defense — $38,050

Defense Aerospace $23,600
Rockwell International .... $2,400 PAC
General Dynamics .... $2,300 PAC
Martin Marietta Corp .... $2,050 PAC

Defense Electronics $9,950
AT&T .... $6,000 PAC

Misc Defense $4,500
Avondale Industries .... $2,500 PAC

Energy & Natural Resources — $66,300

Oil & Gas $49,950
Kinsey Interests Inc .... $4,500 Indiv
Woods Operating Co .... $3,500 Indiv
Palmer Petroleum Inc .... $3,000 Indiv
Arkla Inc .... $2,550 PAC/Ind
Anderson Oil & Gas .... $2,000 Indiv

Mining $2,750
None over $2,000

Electric Utilities $11,100
Central & South West Services* ..... $3,500 PAC
Central Louisiana Electric .... $2,500 PAC
Entergy Corp* .... $2,350 PAC

Finance, Insurance & Real Estate — $71,850

Commercial Banks $5,600
None over $2,000

Credit Unions $2,000
Credit Union National Assn .... $2,000 PAC

Insurance **$26,000**
Independent Insurance Agents of America .... $5,200 PAC
National Assn of Life Underwriters .... $3,000 PAC
Prudential Insurance .... $3,000 PAC
Lincoln National Insurance .... $2,000 Indiv

Real Estate **$22,250**
Atco Investments .... $8,000 Indiv
Ross Investments .... $3,000 Indiv
Larkin Development Co .... $2,500 Indiv
Fairfield Development Co .... $2,000 Indiv

Accountants **$3,200**
KPMG Peat Marwick .... $2,200 Indiv

Misc Finance **$10,950**
None over $2,000

Health $74,100

Health Professionals **$62,100**
American Medical Assn .... $10,000 PAC
American Dental Assn .... $4,000 PAC
American Academy of Ophthalmology .... $3,000 PAC

Hospitals/Nursing Homes **$4,000**
None over $2,000

Pharmaceuticals/Health Products **$8,000**
Morris Dickson Co Ltd .... $6,000 Indiv

Lawyers & Lobbyists $22,050

Lawyers & Lobbyists **$22,050**
Hicks & Hubley .... $2,000 Indiv

Misc Business $25,600

Business Associations **$2,350**
None over $2,000

Food & Beverage **$3,550**
None over $2,000

Beer, Wine & Liquor **$8,000**
National Beer Wholesalers Assn .... $8,000 PAC

Chemical & Related Manufacturing **$4,550**
Dow Chemical .... $3,000 PAC

Misc Manufacturing & Distributing **$5,950**
Stone Container Corp .... $2,500 PAC
Grayson Co of Southwest Inc .... $2,000 Indiv

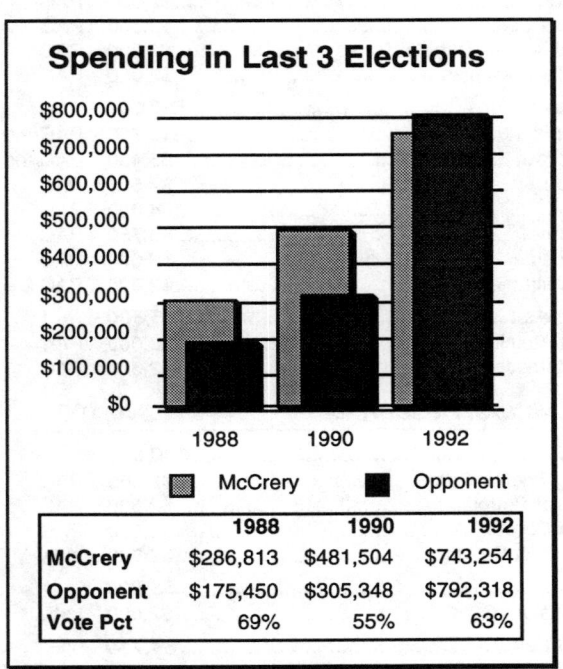

Spending in Last 3 Elections

	1988	1990	1992
McCrery	$286,813	$481,504	$743,254
Opponent	$175,450	$305,348	$792,318
Vote Pct	69%	55%	63%

Transportation **$35,732**

Air Transport **$5,800**
United Parcel Service .... $3,300 PAC
Federal Express Corp .... $2,500 PAC

Automotive **$18,382**
National Auto Dealers Assn .... $5,000 PAC
Rountree Cadillac .... $3,000 Indiv
Avis Rent-a-Car .... $2,382 Indiv
Americans for Free International Trade .... $2,000 PAC

Trucking **$2,750**
None over $2,000

Railroads **$3,700**
Union Pacific Corp .... $2,600 PAC

Sea Transport **$5,100**
None over $2,000

Labor

Labor **$2,650**

Public Sector Unions **$3,150**
None over $2,000

Ideological/Single-Issue

Ideological/Single-Issue **$42,916**

Republican/Conservative **$10,666**
Eagle Forum .... $2,416 PAC

Leadership PACs **$2,550**
Republican Leader's Fund (Bob Michel) .... $2,000 PAC

Pro-Israel **$23,250**
Florida Congressional Cmte .... $10,000 PAC
Louisiana for American Security .... $7,500 PAC

Misc Issues **$2,400**
None over $2,000

Other & Unknown

Other **$21,800**

Retired **$19,550**
None over $2,000

Unknown **$82,072**

Homemakers/Non-income earners $31,775
No Employer Listed or Found $6,800
Generic Occupation/Category Unknown $2,000
Employer Listed/Category Unknown $40,497
Otto Stores .... $3,000 Indiv
Woodard-Holland .... $2,800 Indiv
Hargrove, Guyton & Ramey .... $2,100 Indiv
Johnson Minerals Co .... $2,000 Indiv
Vowell Development .... $2,000 Indiv

* Contributions came from more than one affiliate or
subsidiary.

Dave McCurdy, D-Okla (4)

First elected: 1980

1991-92 Total Receipts: $556,174
1992 Year-end Cash: $53,387

1991-92 Committees & Subcommittees

Armed Services
Military Installations and Facilities; Research and Development

Science, Space and Technology

Select Committee on Intelligence (Chairman)

Leading Contributors

Business

Agriculture — $15,500

Livestock	**$4,000**	
National Cattlemen's Assn*	$2,250	PAC
Agricultural Services/Products	**$2,750**	
None over $2,000		
Food Processing & Sales	**$6,000**	
Food Marketing Institute	$2,500	PAC
Connell Rice & Sugar Co	$2,000	Indiv

Communications/Electronics — $14,700

Printing & Publishing	**$3,500**	
Lawton Constitution	$2,500	Indiv
Telephone Utilities	**$4,000**	
Southwestern Bell	$3,500	PAC
Computer Equipment & Services	**$5,750**	
Perot Group	$2,000	Indiv

Construction — $15,750

General Contractors	**$9,500**	
Yordi Construction Co	$2,000	Indiv
Construction Services	**$2,500**	
None over $2,000		
Building Materials & Equipment	**$2,250**	
None over $2,000		

Source of Funds in 1992 Election

Source	Total	Pct
■ PACs	$270,250	48%
▨ Indivs $200+	$209,650	37%
□ Indivs under $200	$59,850	11%
▨ Other	$28,798	5%
Candidate	$0	0%
Party	$12,824	2%

Source of PAC Dollars by Sector

Source	Total	Pct
■ Business	$231,450	84%
▨ Labor	$10,250	4%
□ Ideology/Single Issue	$33,500	12%

In-State vs. Out-of-State Contributions*

Source	Total	Pct
□ In-State	$93,700	45%
■ Out-of-state	$115,750	55%
No state listed	$0	

*** by large individual contributors ($200 & above)**

Defense — $129,450

Defense Aerospace	**$63,750**	
LTV Aerospace & Defense Co	$7,650	PAC/Ind
Textron Inc	$7,000	PAC
Rockwell International	$6,950	PAC/Ind
General Dynamics	$5,000	PAC
General Electric	$5,000	PAC
McDonnell Douglas*	$4,500	PAC
Martin Marietta Corp	$4,000	PAC
Lockheed Corp	$3,500	PAC
Gencorp Inc	$2,950	PAC
Boeing Co	$2,500	PAC
Grumman Corp	$2,500	PAC
Chromalloy Gas Turbine Corp	$2,200	PAC
United Technologies	$2,000	PAC
Defense Electronics	**$50,200**	
E-Systems Inc	$17,750	PAC/Ind
Loral Corp	$5,450	PAC/Ind
Raytheon	$4,500	PAC
AT&T	$4,000	PAC
GTE Corp	$3,750	PAC
Imo Industries Inc	$2,000	PAC
Texas Instruments	$2,000	PAC
Misc Defense	**$15,500**	
General Atomics	$6,000	PAC
BDM International	$2,500	PAC

Energy & Natural Resources — $40,100

Oil & Gas	**$30,600**	
Mustang Energy Corp	$2,500	PAC
Occidental Petroleum	$2,500	PAC
Enserch Corp	$2,000	PAC
Francis Oil & Gas Inc	$2,000	Indiv
Mining	**$3,000**	
Allied Custom Gypsum	$2,000	Indiv
Electric Utilities	**$4,750**	
Oklahoma Gas & Electric	$2,250	PAC/Ind

Contribution Totals by Sector

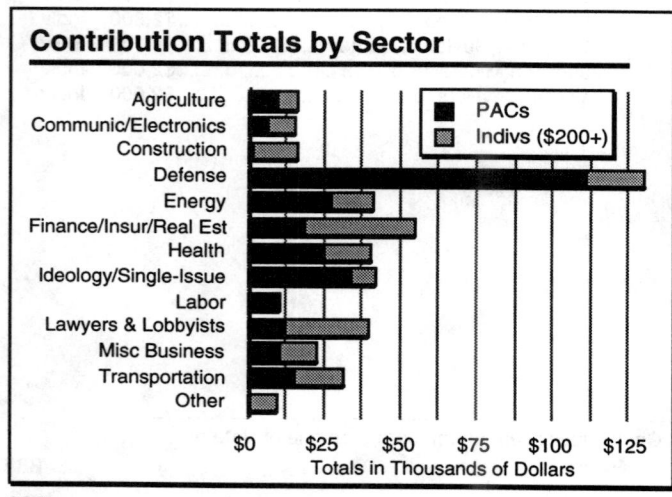

Agriculture
Communic/Electronics
Construction
Defense
Energy
Finance/Insur/Real Est
Health
Ideology/Single-Issue
Labor
Lawyers & Lobbyists
Misc Business
Transportation
Other

■ PACs
▨ Indivs ($200+)

$0 $25 $50 $75 $100 $125
Totals in Thousands of Dollars

Finance, Insurance & Real Estate — $54,350

Commercial Banks **$10,700**
   None over $2,000

Securities & Investment **$15,650**
   Goldman, Sachs & Co .... $5,250   PAC/Ind
   Chicago Mercantile Exchange .... $3,000   PAC

Insurance **$6,500**
   CL Frates & Co .... $2,000   Indiv

Real Estate **$14,350**
   National Assn of Realtors .... $4,100   PAC
   First Worthing Co .... $2,000   Indiv
   Worthing Companies .... $2,000   Indiv

Accountants **$2,700**
   None over $2,000

Misc Finance **$2,450**
   None over $2,000

Health — $39,800

Health Professionals **$23,050**
   American Medical Assn* .... $6,500   PAC
   American Dental Assn .... $2,750   PAC

Hospitals/Nursing Homes **$9,500**
   Continental Medical Systems Inc .... $5,000   Indiv

Pharmaceuticals/Health Products **$6,250**
   Glaxo Inc .... $2,000   PAC

Lawyers & Lobbyists — $39,050

Lawyers & Lobbyists **$39,050**
   Akin, Gump et al .... $3,500   PAC/Ind
   Hyjek & Fix .... $3,500   Indiv
   Burson-Marsteller .... $2,500   PAC
   Williams & Jensen .... $2,300   PAC/Ind

Misc Business — $22,100

Food & Beverage **$4,700**
   S&A Restaurant Corp .... $3,000   PAC

Retail Sales **$6,200**
   None over $2,000

Business Services **$5,000**
   None over $2,000

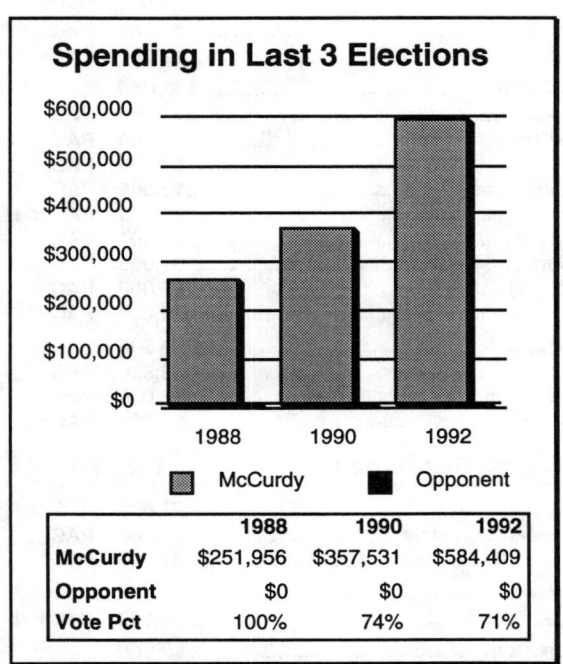

Spending in Last 3 Elections

	1988	1990	1992
McCurdy	$251,956	$357,531	$584,409
Opponent	$0	$0	$0
Vote Pct	100%	74%	71%

Transportation — $30,850

Air Transport **$16,150**
   Marquardt Manufacturing .... $3,000   Indiv
   American Airlines .... $2,750   PAC
   Canadair Challenger Inc .... $2,000   Indiv
   Earth Observation Satellite Co .... $2,000   Indiv
   United Parcel Service .... $2,000   PAC

Automotive **$9,950**
   National Auto Dealers Assn .... $2,750   PAC
   Short Brothers USA .... $2,000   Indiv

Trucking **$2,250**
   None over $2,000

Railroads **$2,250**
   None over $2,000

Labor

Labor — **$10,250**

Transportation Unions **$5,250**
   Marine Engineers Union .... $5,000   PAC

Public Sector Unions **$4,500**
   National Assn of Letter Carriers .... $2,500   PAC

Ideological/Single-Issue

Ideological/Single-Issue — **$41,250**

Foreign & Defense Policy **$7,500**
   Free Cuba PAC .... $6,000   PAC

Pro-Israel **$26,750**
   National PAC .... $5,000   PAC
   North Jersey PAC .... $5,000   PAC
   Hudson Valley PAC .... $3,000   PAC
   Pax PAC .... $2,500   PAC
   Westchester Allied PAC .... $2,000   PAC

Gun Rights/Gun Control **$2,500**
   National Rifle Assn .... $2,500   PAC

Misc Issues **$3,000**
   National Cmte to Preserve Social Security .... $3,000   PAC

Other & Unknown

Other — **$9,400**

Civil Servants/Public Officials **$3,200**
   None over $2,000

Retired **$2,450**
   None over $2,000

Other **$2,000**
   None over $2,000

Unknown — **$22,300**

   Homemakers/Non-income earners $2,000
   Employer Listed/Category Unknown $19,550
      Mintmire, Alagia & Day .... $2,500   Indiv

---

* Contributions came from more than one affiliate or subsidiary.

887

Joseph M. McDade, R-Pa (10)

First elected: 1962

1991-92 Total Receipts:	$375,429
1992 Year-end Cash:	$367,412

1991-92 Committees & Subcommittees

Appropriations (Ranking Republican)
Defense (Ranking Republican); Interior and Related Agencies

Small Business
SBA, the General Economy and Minority Enterprise Development

Leading Contributors

Business

Agriculture — $9,150

Tobacco	**$3,050**	
Tobacco Institute	$1,500	PAC
Dairy	**$2,500**	
None over $1,500		

Communications/Electronics — $11,550

Media/Entertainment	**$4,000**	
None over $1,500		
Telephone Utilities	**$6,250**	
Bell Atlantic*	$3,000	PAC
SLT Communications	$2,000	PAC/Ind

Construction — $9,667

Home Builders	**$4,500**	
National Assn of Home Builders	$4,500	PAC
Construction Services	**$1,667**	
None over $1,500		
Building Materials & Equipment	**$3,000**	
MIC Industries Inc	$2,000	Indiv

Source of Funds in 1992 Election

Source	Total	Pct
PACs	$242,172	65%
Indivs $200+	$91,600	24%
Indivs under $200	$7,560	2%
Other	$34,097	9%
Candidate	$0	0%
Party	$954	0%

Source of PAC Dollars by Sector

Source	Total	Pct
Business	$190,673	79%
Labor	$37,250	15%
Ideology/Single Issue	$14,100	6%

In-State vs. Out-of-State Contributions*

Source	Total	Pct
In-State	$28,450	31%
Out-of-state	$63,150	69%
No state listed	$0	

* by large individual contributors ($200 & above)

Defense — $93,350

Defense Aerospace — $49,000

General Dynamics	$6,000	PAC
McDonnell Douglas*	$5,000	PAC
Northrop Corp	$5,000	PAC
Rockwell International	$5,000	PAC
Martin Marietta Corp	$4,000	PAC
Gencorp Inc	$3,000	PAC
General Electric	$3,000	PAC
Grumman Corp	$3,000	PAC/Ind
Lockheed Corp	$3,000	PAC
Textron Inc	$3,000	PAC
Allied-Signal	$2,000	PAC
LTV Aerospace & Defense Co	$2,000	PAC

Defense Electronics — $33,850

AT&T	$4,500	PAC
Hughes Aircraft	$4,000	PAC
Raytheon	$4,000	PAC
SPD Technologies	$3,500	PAC
Loral Corp	$3,000	PAC/Ind
GTE Corp	$2,500	PAC
Kaman Corp	$2,000	PAC
Litton Industries	$2,000	PAC
TRW Inc	$2,000	PAC

Misc Defense — $10,500

AAI Corp	$2,500	PAC
Evergreen Information Technologies	$2,000	Indiv
Bath Iron Works	$1,500	PAC/Ind

Energy & Natural Resources — $15,300

Oil & Gas — $7,000

Petroleum Marketers Assn	$2,000	PAC
Tenneco Inc	$2,000	Indiv

Electric Utilities — $4,300

Philadelphia Electric	$1,500	PAC/Ind

Waste Management — $2,000

None over $1,500

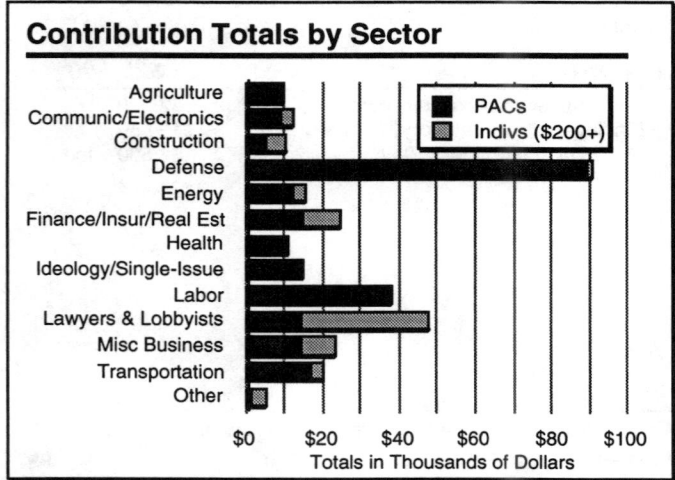

Contribution Totals by Sector

Agriculture, Communic/Electronics, Construction, Defense, Energy, Finance/Insur/Real Est, Health, Ideology/Single-Issue, Labor, Lawyers & Lobbyists, Misc Business, Transportation, Other

PACs / Indivs ($200+)

Totals in Thousands of Dollars

Finance, Insurance & Real Estate $24,074

Credit Unions **$2,000**
    Haddon Craftsmen Inc .... $2,000   Indiv

Insurance **$3,124**
    None over $1,500

Real Estate **$8,000**
    National Assn of Realtors .... $6,000   PAC
    Money Store Investment Corp .... $1,500   Indiv

Accountants **$8,500**
    Pagnotti Enterprises .... $5,000   Indiv
    American Institute of CPA's .... $2,500   PAC

Health $10,750

Health Professionals **$6,000**
    American Medical Assn .... $1,500   PAC

Hospitals/Nursing Homes **$1,500**
    None over $1,500

Pharmaceuticals/Health Products **$3,250**
    Connaught Laboratories .... $2,000   PAC

Lawyers & Lobbyists $46,849

Lawyers & Lobbyists **$46,849**
    Paul Magliocchetti Associates .... $10,000   Indiv
    Assn of Trial Lawyers of America .... $5,000   PAC
    Reid & Priest .... $5,000   PAC/Ind
    Vinson & Elkins .... $2,699   PAC/Ind
    Baker & Botts .... $2,000   PAC/Ind
    Morgan, Lewis & Bockius .... $2,000   Indiv
    Stanton & Associates .... $2,000   Indiv

Misc Business $23,700

Food & Beverage **$1,500**
    None over $1,500

Beer, Wine & Liquor **$4,500**
    Wine & Spirits Wholesalers of America .... $3,000   PAC

Retail Sales **$2,000**
    None over $1,500

Business Services **$2,000**
    Energy Partners Inc .... $2,000   Indiv

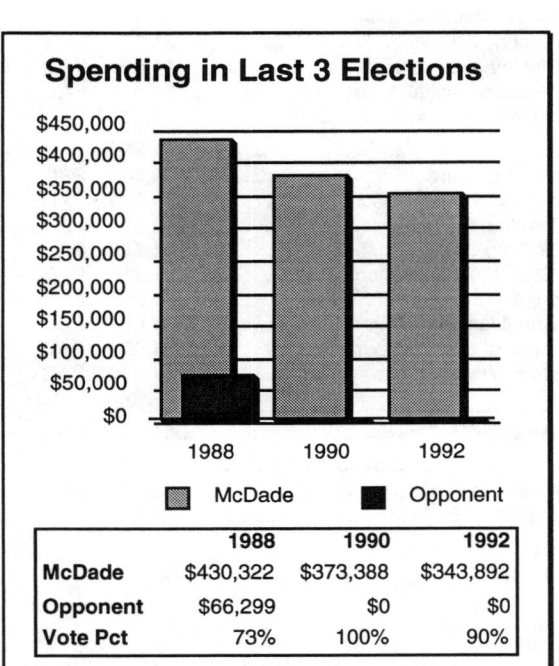

Chemical & Related Manufacturing $3,200
    Air Products & Chemicals Inc .... $2,000   PAC

Steel Production **$2,000**
    Bethlehem Steel .... $2,000   PAC

Misc Manufacturing & Distributing **$5,500**
    Hoechst Celanese Corp .... $2,000   PAC
    Pocal Industries .... $2,000   Indiv

Transportation $19,800

Air Transport **$4,000**
    Piasecki Aircraft Corp .... $2,000   Indiv

Trucking **$4,000**
    Roadway Services Inc .... $2,000   PAC

Railroads **$9,000**
    Duchossois Industries .... $7,000   PAC
    Delaware Otsego Corp .... $2,000   PAC

Sea Transport **$2,800**
    National Steel & Shipbuilding .... $2,000   PAC

Labor

Labor $37,250

Building Trade Unions **$14,000**
    Carpenters & Joiners Union .... $5,000   PAC
    Laborers' Political League .... $4,000   PAC
    AFL-CIO Bldg/Construction Trades Dept .... $2,000   PAC
    Plumbers/Pipefitters Union* .... $2,000   PAC

Industrial Unions **$3,500**
    None over $1,500

Transportation Unions **$11,750**
    Marine Engineers Dist 2 Maritime Officers .... $4,250   PAC
    Teamsters Union .... $3,500   PAC
    United Transportation Union .... $3,000   PAC

Public Sector Unions **$8,000**
    National Assn of Letter Carriers .... $3,000   PAC

Ideological/Single-Issue

Ideological/Single-Issue $14,100

Pro-Israel **$5,000**
    National PAC .... $5,000   PAC

Gun Rights/Gun Control **$4,950**
    National Rifle Assn .... $4,950   PAC

Human Rights **$2,000**
    National Community Action Foundation .... $2,000   PAC

Other & Unknown

Other $5,000

Retired **$4,000**
    None over $1,500

Unknown $14,083

    No Employer Listed or Found $3,500
    Employer Listed/Category Unknown $10,583
      MIC Industries Inc .... $2,000   Indiv

---

* Contributions came from more than one affiliate or
subsidiary.

Jim McDermott, D-Wash (7)

First elected: 1988

1991-92 Total Receipts: $266,146
1992 Year-end Cash: $68,692

1991-92 Committees & Subcommittees

District of Columbia
Fiscal Affairs and Health

Standards of Official Conduct

Ways and Means
Human Resources; Social Security

Leading Contributors

Business

Agriculture — $5,950

Poultry & Eggs	**$1,000**	
Tyson Foods	$1,000	PAC
Forestry & Forest Products	**$3,100**	
Klukwan Forest Products	$2,100	Indiv

Communications/Electronics — $7,060

Telephone Utilities	**$5,060**	
US West Inc	$1,460	PAC/Ind
BellSouth Corp*	$1,000	PAC
Electronics Mfg & Services	**$1,000**	
None over $1,000		

Construction — $1,850

General Contractors	**$1,350**	
None over $1,000		

Energy & Natural Resources — $10,607

Oil & Gas	**$1,750**	
None over $1,000		
Electric Utilities	**$2,900**	
None over $1,000		
Commercial Fishing	**$4,957**	
American Factory Trawler Assn	$2,257	PAC

Source of Funds in 1992 Election

Source	Total	Pct
■ PACs	$189,515	69%
▨ Indivs $200+	$26,250	10%
☐ Indivs under $200	$29,756	11%
☒ Other	$27,869	10%
Candidate	$0	0%
Party	$7,544	3%

Source of PAC Dollars by Sector

Source	Total	Pct
■ Business	$132,410	71%
▨ Labor	$46,900	25%
☐ Ideology/Single Issue	$7,675	4%

In-State vs. Out-of-State Contributions*

Source	Total	Pct
☐ In-State	$17,650	67%
■ Out-of-state	$8,600	33%
No state listed	$0	

*** by large individual contributors ($200 & above)**

Finance, Insurance & Real Estate — $56,200

Commercial Banks	**$12,500**	
American Bankers Assn	$3,500	PAC
JP Morgan & Co	$3,500	PAC
Barnett Banks Inc	$1,500	PAC
Seafirst National Bank	$1,000	Indiv
Security Pacific Corp	$1,000	PAC
US Bancorp	$1,000	PAC
Savings & Loans	**$3,000**	
US League of Savings Assns*	$2,000	PAC
Credit Unions	**$3,000**	
Credit Union National Assn	$2,500	PAC
Securities & Investment	**$5,400**	
Tucker, Anthony & Day	$1,050	Indiv
Morgan Stanley & Co	$1,000	PAC
National Venture Capital Assn	$1,000	PAC
Securities Industry Assn	$1,000	PAC
Insurance	**$16,350**	
American Family Corp	$3,000	PAC
American Council of Life Insurance	$2,000	PAC
Metropolitan Life Insurance	$2,000	PAC
Torchmark Corp	$1,500	PAC
National Structured Settlements Assn	$1,350	PAC
American Insurance Assn	$1,000	PAC
General American Life Insurance	$1,000	PAC
National Assn of Life Underwriters	$1,000	PAC
Northwestern Mutual Life	$1,000	PAC
Real Estate	**$6,100**	
National Assn of Realtors	$4,500	PAC
Accountants	**$9,000**	
American Institute of CPA's	$5,000	PAC
Peterson, Sullivan & Co	$4,000	Indiv

Contribution Totals by Sector

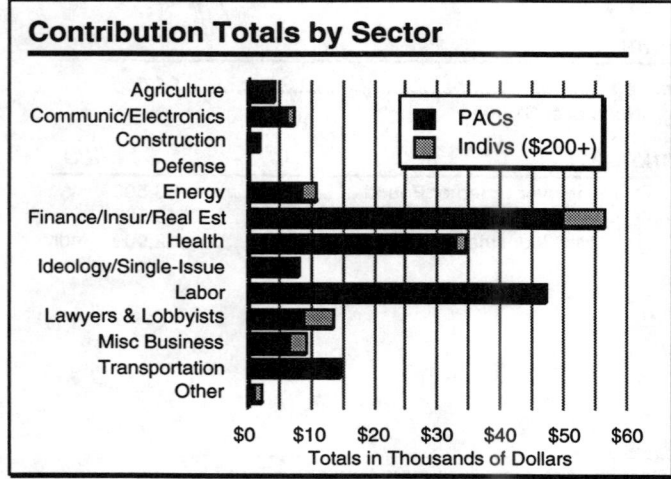

Agriculture, Communic/Electronics, Construction, Defense, Energy, Finance/Insur/Real Est, Health, Ideology/Single-Issue, Labor, Lawyers & Lobbyists, Misc Business, Transportation, Other

■ PACs
▨ Indivs ($200+)

$0 $10 $20 $30 $40 $50 $60
Totals in Thousands of Dollars

Health $33,900

Health Professionals $18,100
  American Academy of Ophthalmology ....$5,000 PAC
  American Psychiatric Assn ....$3,000 PAC
  American College of Emergency Physicians ....$1,850 PAC
  American Medical Assn.....................................$1,500 PAC
  American Podiatry Assn ....$1,500 PAC
  American Society of Anesthesiologists ....$1,500 PAC

Hospitals/Nursing Homes $3,700
  American Hospital Assn ....$1,850 PAC

Health Services $1,850
  None over $1,000

Pharmaceuticals/Health Products $9,750
  Schering-Plough Corp ....$4,000 PAC
  Ciba-Geigy Corp ....$1,000 PAC
  Invacare Corp ....$1,000 PAC

Lawyers & Lobbyists $13,200

Lawyers & Lobbyists $13,200
  Assn of Trial Lawyers of America ....$5,000 PAC
  Garvey, Schubert & Barer ....$1,350 PAC
  Preston, Gates et al ....$1,000 PAC/Ind

Misc Business $9,003

Food & Beverage $1,750
  None over $1,000

Beer, Wine & Liquor $4,303
  Wine & Spirits Wholesalers of America ....$2,803 PAC

Misc Manufacturing & Distributing $1,000
  None over $1,000

Transportation $14,250

Air Transport $3,400
  Boeing Co ....$2,000 PAC

Automotive $1,850
  Americans for Free International Trade ....$1,000 PAC

Trucking...$2,350
  American Trucking Assns ....$1,350 PAC

Railroads $2,200
  Burlington Northern ....$2,200 PAC

Sea Transport..$4,450
  Matson Navigation ....$1,500 PAC

Labor

Labor $46,900

Building Trade Unions $5,500
  Laborers' Political League ....$2,000 PAC
  Plumbers/Pipefitters Union ....$2,000 PAC
  AFL-CIO Bldg/Construction Trades Dept ....$1,000 PAC

Industrial Unions $8,500
  Intl Brotherhood of Electrical Workers ....$3,000 PAC
  United Auto Workers ....$2,500 PAC
  United Steelworkers ....$1,500 PAC
  United Mine Workers ....$1,000 PAC

Transportation Unions $14,750
  Air Line Pilots Assn ....$5,000 PAC
  Marine Engineers Union* ....$4,000 PAC
  Teamsters Union ....$2,500 PAC
  United Transportation Union ....$1,700 PAC

Public Sector Unions $12,900
  American Fedn of St/Cnty/Munic Employees ......$3,000 PAC
  National Assn Retired Federal Employees ....$3,000 PAC
  National Education Assn ....$1,350 PAC
  American Postal Workers Union ....$1,000 PAC
  International Assn of Firefighters ....$1,000 PAC
  National Assn of Letter Carriers ....$1,000 PAC

Misc Unions $5,250
  Food & Commercial Workers Union ....$2,000 PAC
  Hotel/Restaurant Employees Union ....$1,500 PAC
  Service Employees International Union ....$1,000 PAC

Ideological/Single-Issue

Ideological/Single-Issue $7,925

Leadership PACs $1,500
  America's Leaders' Fund (Dan Rostenkowski) ....$1,500 PAC

Human Rights $4,500
  Human Rights Campaign Fund............................$3,500 PAC
  KidsPAC ....$1,000 PAC

Misc Issues..$1,675
  National Cmte to Preserve Social Security ....$1,500 PAC

Other & Unknown

Other $2,000

Other $1,000
  None over $1,000

Unknown $4,890

  No Employer Listed or Found $1,400
  Employer Listed/Category Unknown $2,990
    Sullivan & Peterson ....$1,000 Indiv

Independent expenditures supporting McDermott
  Knight, Marilyn $1,232

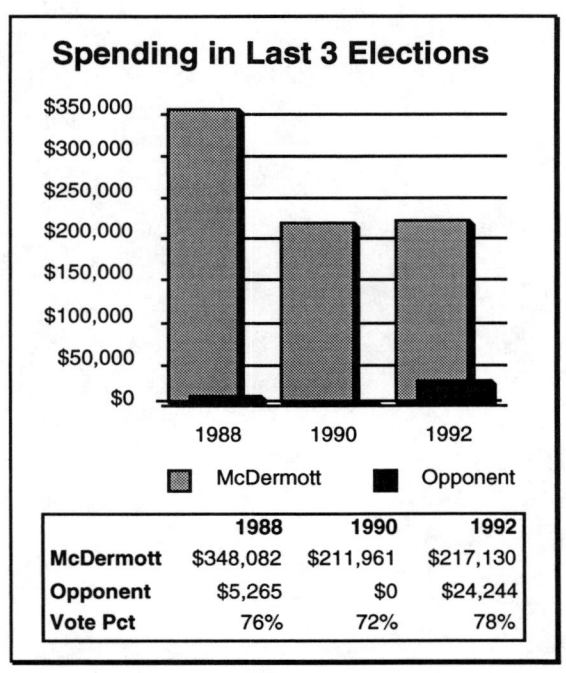

Spending in Last 3 Elections

	1988	1990	1992
McDermott	$348,082	$211,961	$217,130
Opponent	$5,265	$0	$24,244
Vote Pct	76%	72%	78%

McDermott   Opponent

---

* Contributions came from more than one affiliate or subsidiary.

Paul McHale, D-Pa (15)

First elected: 1992

1991-92 Total Receipts:	$222,578
1992 Year-end Cash:	$1,642

1993-94 Committees & Subcommittees

Armed Services
Military Acquisition; Readiness

Science, Space and Technology
Energy; Technology, Environment and Aviation

Leading Contributors

Business

Communications/Electronics	$4,000	
Printing & Publishing	**$2,000**	
FDR Publications	$1,000	Indiv
Rodale Press Inc	$1,000	Indiv
Telephone Utilities	**$2,000**	
AT&T	$2,000	PAC

Finance, Insurance & Real Estate	$1,250
None over $1,000	

Health	$3,750	
Health Professionals	**$3,500**	
American Podiatry Assn	$1,000	PAC

Lawyers & Lobbyists	$21,645	
Lawyers & Lobbyists	**$21,645**	
Assn of Trial Lawyers of America	$6,500	PAC
Leeson, Leeson & Leeson	$1,750	Indiv

Misc Business	$1,000
None over $1,000	

Source of Funds in 1992 Election

Source	Total	Pct
■ PACs	$109,450	43%
▨ Indivs $200+	$42,215	17%
☐ Indivs under $200	$45,059	18%
▩ Other	$55,651	22%
Candidate	$4,000	2%
Party	$34,947	14%

Source of PAC Dollars by Sector

Source	Total	Pct
■ Business	$11,500	10%
▨ Labor	$97,000	81%
☐ Ideology/Single Issue	$11,232	9%

In-State vs. Out-of-State Contributions*

Source	Total	Pct
☐ In-State	$41,315	98%
■ Out-of-state	$650	2%
No state listed	$0	

* by large individual contributors ($200 & above)

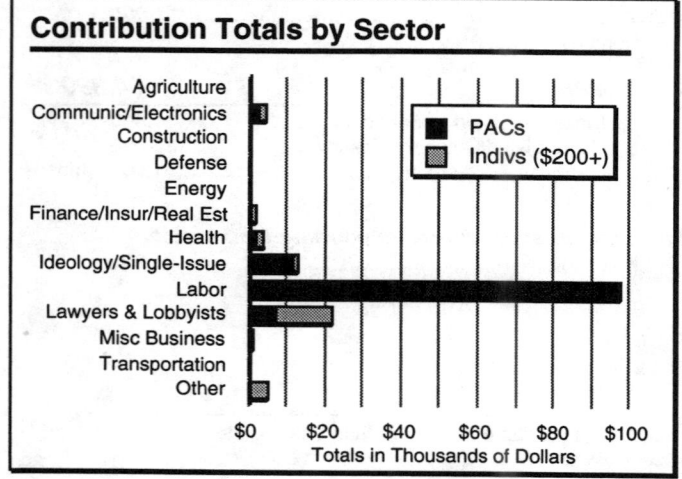

Contribution Totals by Sector

Agriculture
Communic/Electronics
Construction
Defense
Energy
Finance/Insur/Real Est
Health
Ideology/Single-Issue
Labor
Lawyers & Lobbyists
Misc Business
Transportation
Other

■ PACs
▨ Indivs ($200+)

$0 $20 $40 $60 $80 $100
Totals in Thousands of Dollars

Labor

Labor	$97,000	
Building Trade Unions **$2,000**		
Laborers' Political League $1,500		PAC
Industrial Unions **$38,500**		
United Auto Workers $10,000		PAC
United Steelworkers $10,000		PAC
Machinists/Aerospace Workers Union $5,000		PAC
Intl Brotherhood of Electrical Workers $4,000		PAC
Communications Workers of America* $3,000		PAC
Rubber Cork Linoleum & Plastic Workers $3,000		PAC
Electronic Machine Furniture Workers $1,000		PAC
United Mine Workers...$1,000		PAC
Transportation Unions **$13,500**		
United Transportation Union $5,000		PAC
Teamsters Union $2,500		PAC
Brotherhood of Locomotive Engineers $2,000		PAC
Maintenance of Way Employees $1,750		PAC
Air Line Pilots Assn $1,000		PAC
Public Sector Unions **$27,000**		
National Education Assn $10,000		PAC
American Fedn of St/Cnty/Munic Employees $6,000		PAC
National Assn of Letter Carriers $5,000		PAC
International Assn of Firefighters $3,000		PAC
National Assn Retired Federal Employees $1,500		PAC
National Rural Letter Carriers Assn $1,000		PAC
Misc Unions.. **$16,000**		
Food & Commercial Workers Union $8,000		PAC
Service Employees International Union $4,000		PAC
AFL-CIO $2,500		PAC
Bakery, Confectionery & Tobacco Workers $1,500		PAC

Ideological/Single-Issue

Ideological/Single-Issue	$12,532	
Democratic/Liberal **$2,800**		
National Cmte for an Effective Congress $2,500		PAC
Leadership PACs **$1,542**		
Effective Government Cmte (Dick Gephardt) $1,542		PAC
Pro-Israel **$2,000**		
South Carolinians for Representve Govt $1,000		PAC
Misc Issues.. **$5,690**		
League of Conservation Voters $4,440		PAC
National Council of Senior Citizens.....................$1,000		PAC

Other & Unknown

Other	$5,050	
Civil Servants/Public Officials............................. **$2,000**		
City of Easton $1,000		Indiv
Pennsylvania Liquor Control Board $1,000		Indiv
Retired **$2,800**		
None over $1,000		

Unknown	$12,920	
Homemakers/Non-income earners $3,200		
No Employer Listed or Found $3,550		
Employer Listed/Category Unknown $5,220		
None over $1,000		

Independent expenditures opposing McHale
US Federation of Small Businesses $1,853

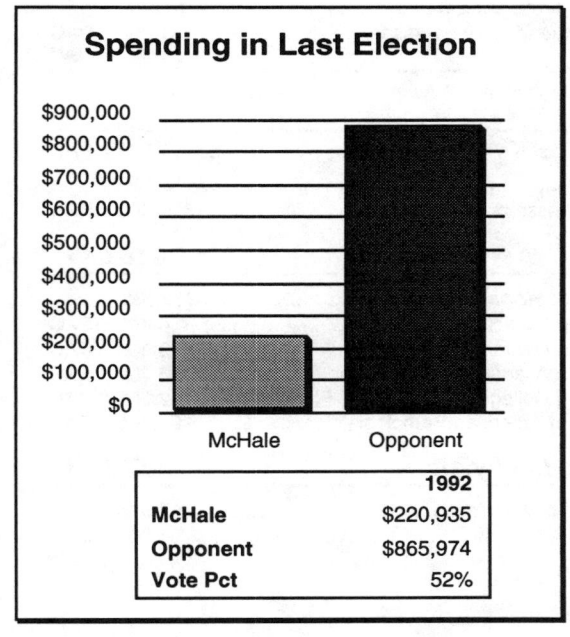

Spending in Last Election

	1992
McHale	$220,935
Opponent	$865,974
Vote Pct	52%

---

* Contributions came from more than one affiliate or subsidiary.

John M. McHugh, R-NY (24)

First elected: 1992

1991-92 Total Receipts:	$177,433
1992 Year-end Cash:	$6,282

1993-94 Committees & Subcommittees

Armed Services
Military Installations and Facilities; Oversight and Investigations

Government Operations
Employment, Housing and Aviation; Environment, Energy and Natural Resources

Leading Contributors

Business

Agriculture	$8,350	
Tobacco	**$2,000**	
Philip Morris	$1,000	PAC
RJR Nabisco	$1,000	PAC
Dairy	**$1,150**	
None over $1,000		
Agricultural Services/Products	**$1,500**	
Agway Inc	$1,000	PAC
Food Processing & Sales	**$1,500**	
Pepsico Inc	$1,000	PAC
Forestry & Forest Products	**$2,000**	
Champion International Corp	$1,000	PAC
International Paper Co	$1,000	PAC

Communications/Electronics	$4,700	
Printing & Publishing	**$1,200**	
None over $1,000		
Telephone Utilities	**$3,500**	
AT&T	$2,000	PAC
United Telecommunications	$1,000	PAC

Construction	$2,900	
General Contractors	**$2,900**	
Associated General Contractors	$1,000	PAC

Source of Funds in 1992 Election

Source	Total	Pct
■ PACs	$96,351	48%
▨ Indivs $200+	$29,373	15%
☐ Indivs under $200	$20,837	10%
⊠ Other	$55,388	27%
Candidate	$8,000	4%
Party	$25,516	13%

Source of PAC Dollars by Sector

Source	Total	Pct
■ Business	$66,076	68%
▨ Labor	$18,500	19%
☐ Ideology/Single Issue	$11,900	12%

In-State vs. Out-of-State Contributions*

Source	Total	Pct
☐ In-State	$28,073	96%
■ Out-of-state	$1,300	4%
No state listed	$0	

* by large individual contributors ($200 & above)

Energy & Natural Resources	$6,500	
Oil & Gas	**$3,650**	
Phillips Petroleum	$1,000	PAC
Mining	**$1,000**	
Alcoa	$1,000	PAC
Misc Energy	**$1,000**	
Sithe Energies Group	$1,000	Indiv

Finance, Insurance & Real Estate	$27,081	
Commercial Banks	**$6,981**	
American Bankers Assn	$2,500	PAC
JP Morgan & Co	$1,000	PAC
Savings & Loans	**$1,000**	
US League of Savings Assns	$1,000	PAC
Credit Unions	**$1,000**	
Credit Union National Assn	$1,000	PAC
Insurance	**$4,200**	
National Assn of Life Underwriters	$1,500	PAC
Real Estate	**$13,150**	
National Assn of Realtors	$10,000	PAC

Health	$16,645	
Health Professionals	**$15,395**	
American Medical Assn	$4,895	PAC
American Dental Assn	$3,500	PAC
American Academy of Ophthalmology	$3,000	PAC
American College of Emergency Physicians	$2,000	PAC
College of American Pathologists	$1,000	PAC

Lawyers & Lobbyists	$2,978	
Lawyers & Lobbyists	**$2,978**	
Hiscock & Barclay	$1,000	Indiv

Contribution Totals by Sector

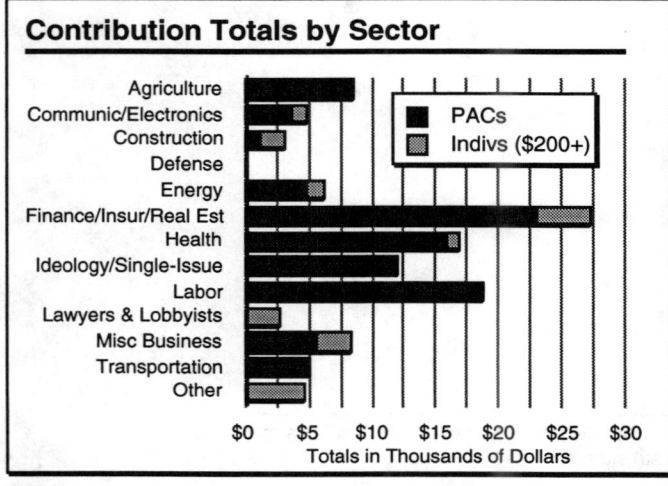

Legend: ■ PACs ▨ Indivs ($200+)

Categories: Agriculture, Communic/Electronics, Construction, Defense, Energy, Finance/Insur/Real Est, Health, Ideology/Single-Issue, Labor, Lawyers & Lobbyists, Misc Business, Transportation, Other

Totals in Thousands of Dollars ($0, $5, $10, $15, $20, $25, $30)

Misc Business $8,200

Food & Beverage **$1,950**
   National Restaurant Assn ....$1,000 PAC

Beer, Wine & Liquor **$2,400**
   National Beer Wholesalers Assn ....$2,000 PAC

Business Services **$1,000**
   None over $1,000

Lodging/Tourism **$1,100**
   None over $1,000

Misc Manufacturing & Distributing **$1,000**
   Corning Glass Works ....$1,000 PAC

Transportation $4,800

Air Transport **$2,300**
   United Parcel Service..$2,000 PAC

Automotive **$2,500**
   National Auto Dealers Assn ....$2,500 PAC

Labor

Labor $18,500

Building Trade Unions **$1,500**
   Carpenters & Joiners Union ....$1,000 PAC

Industrial Unions **$9,000**
   Machinists/Aerospace Workers Union ....$5,000 PAC
   Intl Brotherhood of Electrical Workers ....$2,500 PAC
   United Auto Workers ....$1,500 PAC

Transportation Unions **$2,000**
   Teamsters Union ....$2,000 PAC

Public Sector Unions **$6,000**
   American Federation of Teachers.......................$2,500 PAC
   American Fedn of St/Cnty/Munic Employees ......$2,500 PAC
   National Assn Retired Federal Employees ....$1,000 PAC

Ideological/Single-Issue

Ideological/Single-Issue $11,900

Leadership PACs **$2,000**
   Republican Leader's Fund (Bob Michel) ....$2,000 PAC

Gun Rights/Gun Control **$9,900**
   National Rifle Assn ....$9,900 PAC

Other & Unknown

Other $4,600

Civil Servants/Public Officials.................... **$2,700**
   New York State Legislature..................................$1,000 Indiv
   US Department of Agriculture ....$1,000 Indiv

Retired **$1,700**
   None over $1,000

Unknown $8,695

   No Employer Listed or Found $1,150
   Generic Occupation/Category Unknown $1,450
   Employer Listed/Category Unknown $6,095
     None over $1,000

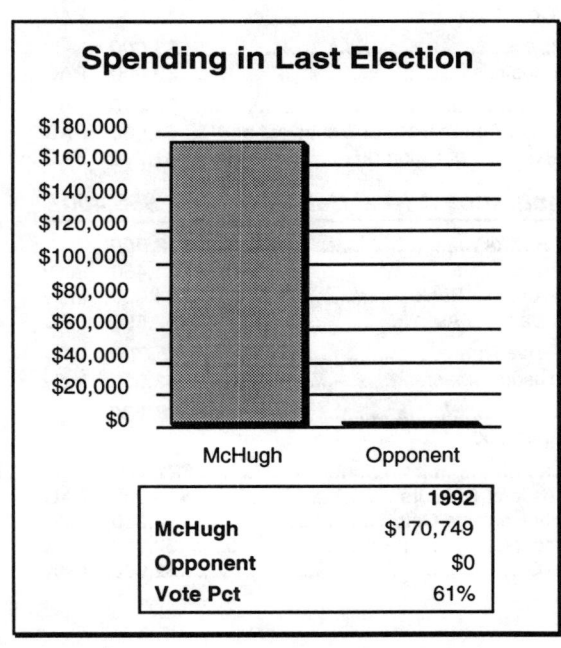

Spending in Last Election

	1992
McHugh	$170,749
Opponent	$0
Vote Pct	61%

Scott McInnis, R-Colo (3)

First elected: 1992

1991-92 Total Receipts:	$438,090
1992 Year-end Cash:	$3,638

1993-94 Committees & Subcommittees

Natural Resources
Energy and Mineral Resources

Small Business

Leading Contributors

Business

Agriculture — $13,600

Dairy	**$4,000**	
Robinson Dairy Inc	$2,000	Indiv
Livestock	**$3,700**	
Paragon Ranch Inc	$2,000	Indiv
Food Processing & Sales	**$3,250**	
Flowers Industries	$2,000	PAC

Communications/Electronics — $12,450

Printing & Publishing	**$3,000**	
Pueblo Chieftain	$2,000	Indiv
Media/Entertainment	**$4,200**	
None over $1,500		
Telephone Utilities	**$4,500**	
United Telecommunications	$2,000	PAC
AT&T	$1,500	PAC

Construction — $24,850

General Contractors	**$11,900**	
Phelps-Tointon Inc	$3,000	Indiv
Associated General Contractors	$2,500	PAC
GE Johnson Construction Co	$2,000	Indiv
Home Builders	**$4,750**	
National Assn of Home Builders	$2,000	PAC
Bellock Construction	$1,500	Indiv
Special Trade Contractors	**$3,000**	
Cobb Plumbing	$3,000	Indiv
Building Materials & Equipment	**$5,200**	
Burnett Construction	$4,000	Indiv

Contribution Totals by Sector

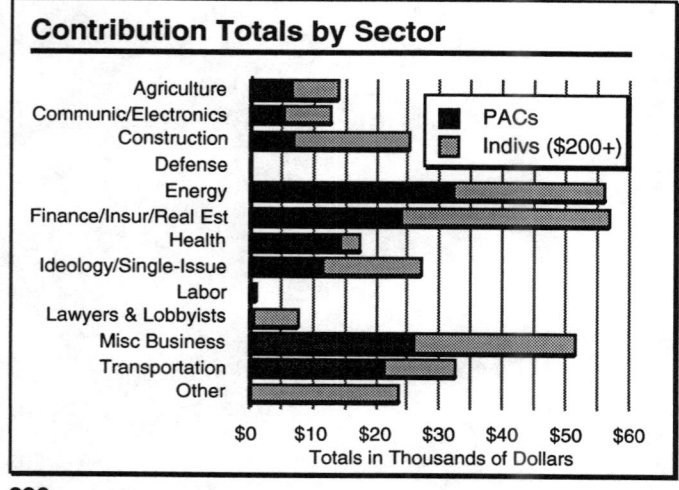

Totals in Thousands of Dollars

Source of Funds in 1992 Election

Source	Total	Pct
■ PACs	$144,614	29%
▨ Indivs $200+	$251,140	51%
☐ Indivs under $200	$19,415	4%
⊠ Other	$77,921	16%
Candidate	$0	0%
Party	$61,000	12%

Source of PAC Dollars by Sector

Source	Total	Pct
■ Business	$134,904	92%
▨ Labor	$1,000	1%
☐ Ideology/Single Issue	$11,174	8%

In-State vs. Out-of-State Contributions*

Source	Total	Pct
☐ In-State	$237,690	95%
■ Out-of-state	$13,200	5%
No state listed	$0	

* by large individual contributors ($200 & above)

Energy & Natural Resources — $55,478

Oil & Gas	**$46,228**	
Associated Natural Gas	$6,000	Indiv
Chevron Corp	$4,447	PAC
Ashland Oil	$4,000	PAC
Benson Mineral Group	$3,000	Indiv
Tom Vessels Oil & Gas	$3,000	Indiv
Dallas Energy PAC	$2,000	PAC
Fattor Petroleum	$2,000	Indiv
KN Energy Inc	$1,881	PAC/Ind
BWAB Inc	$1,750	Indiv
Amoco Corp	$1,500	PAC
Mining	**$2,000**	
National Coal Assn	$1,500	PAC
Misc Energy	**$3,000**	
Cooper Industries	$3,000	PAC
Electric Utilities	**$4,200**	
ACRE (Action Cmte for Rural Electrification)*	$2,000	PAC
Public Service Co of Colorado	$1,700	PAC/Ind

Finance, Insurance & Real Estate — $56,400

Commercial Banks	**$12,900**	
Alpine Bank	$4,450	Indiv
Colorado National Bank	$4,000	Indiv
American Bankers Assn	$2,500	PAC
Securities & Investment	**$5,700**	
Apollo Advisors	$3,000	Indiv
Insurance	**$8,200**	
None over $1,500		
Real Estate	**$21,200**	
National Assn of Realtors	$10,000	PAC
Community Holdings Corp	$2,250	Indiv
Broe Companies	$2,000	Indiv
Land Title Co	$2,000	Indiv

Accountants	$2,500	
American Institute of CPA's	$2,500	PAC
Misc Finance	**$5,400**	
High Valley Group Inc	$2,000	Indiv
Western Capital Investment	$1,750	Indiv

Health $17,200

Health Professionals	$15,500	
American Medical Assn	$10,000	PAC
American Dental Assn	$2,000	PAC

Lawyers & Lobbyists $7,400

Lawyers & Lobbyists	$7,400	
Brownstein, Hyatt et al	$1,500	Indiv

Misc Business $50,829

Business Associations	$4,500	
National Fedn of Independent Business	$4,500	PAC
Food & Beverage	**$7,000**	
Waffle House Inc	$2,500	Indiv
Pizza Hut Franchise Holders Assn	$1,500	PAC
Beer, Wine & Liquor	**$8,750**	
National Beer Wholesalers Assn	$4,000	PAC
Coors Industries	$2,500	PAC
Retail Sales	**$2,750**	
None over $1,500		
Misc Services	**$1,701**	
None over $1,500		
Business Services	**$5,383**	
Captiva Corp	$3,000	Indiv
Recreation/Live Entertainment	**$5,000**	
Vail Associates	$4,000	Indiv
Lodging/Tourism	**$5,150**	
Crested Butte Mountain Resort	$1,500	Indiv
Canon Inn	$2,000	Indiv

Chemical & Related Manufacturing	$6,495	
Dow Chemical	$2,000	PAC
NL Industries	$2,000	PAC/Ind
Steel Production	**$1,500**	
Hotsy Corp	$1,500	Indiv
Misc Manufacturing & Distributing	**$2,250**	
None over $1,500		

Transportation $32,030

Air Transport	$3,280	
United Parcel Service	$3,200	PAC/Ind
Automotive	**$15,750**	
National Auto Dealers Assn	$10,000	PAC
Eaton Corp	$2,000	PAC
Stevinson Auto	$2,000	Indiv
Trucking	**$3,500**	
Northwest Transport Service	$3,000	Indiv
Railroads	**$9,000**	
Southern Pacific Transport Co	$6,500	PAC/Ind

Ideological/Single-Issue

Ideological/Single-Issue $26,636

Republican/Conservative	$15,486	
Friends of Scott McInnis	$12,962	Indiv
Gun Rights/Gun Control	**$9,900**	
National Rifle Assn	$9,900	PAC

Other & Unknown

Other $23,129

Civil Servants/Public Officials	$1,929	
None over $1,500		
Retired	**$19,900**	
None over $1,500		

Unknown $76,966

Homemakers/Non-income earners	$8,300	
No Employer Listed or Found	$5,987	
Generic Occupation/Category Unknown	$43,050	
Employer Listed/Category Unknown	$19,629	
Anschutz Family Holding	$2,000	Indiv
Colorado Well Service	$1,800	Indiv

Independent expenditures supporting McInnis

American Medical Assn $184,910

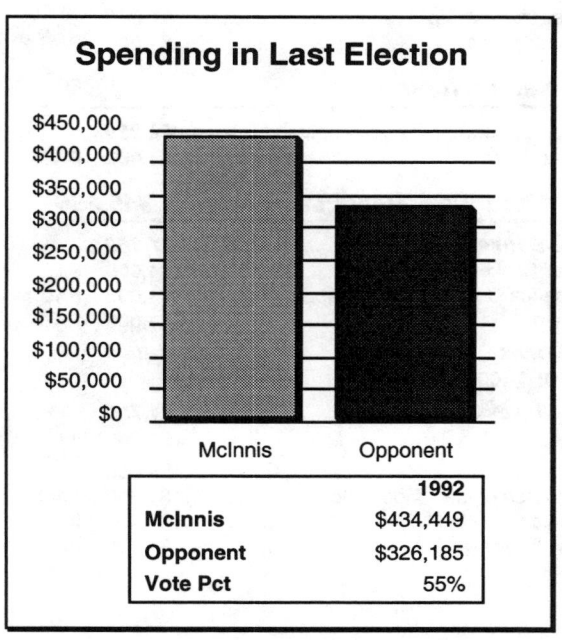

Spending in Last Election

	1992
McInnis	$434,449
Opponent	$326,185
Vote Pct	55%

* Contributions came from more than one affiliate or subsidiary.

Howard "Buck" McKeon, R-Calif (25)

First elected: 1992

1991-92 Total Receipts: $457,650
1992 Year-end Cash: $4,858

1993-94 Committees & Subcommittees

Education and Labor
Elementary, Secondary and Vocational Education; Labor-Management Relations; Postsecondary Education and Training

Public Works and Transportation
Aviation; Surface Transportation

Leading Contributors

Business

Agriculture $6,750

Crop Production & Basic Processing $1,000
  None over $1,000

Livestock $2,250
  Triple A Livestock Co .... $1,250   Indiv
  National Cattlemen's Assn* .... $1,000   PAC

Agricultural Services/Products $2,000
  Green Nursery .... $1,500   Indiv

Communications/Electronics $9,500

Printing & Publishing $4,500
  TV Fanfare Publications .... $2,500   Indiv
  Los Angeles Times .... $1,000   Indiv
  World of Communications Inc .... $1,000   Indiv

Media/Entertainment $1,500
  United Television Inc .... $1,500   Indiv

Telephone Utilities $3,000
  AT&T .... $1,000   PAC
  Pacific Telesis Group .... $1,000   PAC
  United Telecommunications .... $1,000   PAC

Construction $19,650

General Contractors $6,450
  Associated General Contractors .... $2,500   PAC
  CA Rasmussen Co .... $1,500   Indiv
  National Utility Contractors Assn .... $1,000   PAC

Home Builders $5,250

Source of Funds in 1992 Election

Source	Total	Pct
■ PACs	$96,525	21%
▨ Indivs $200+	$164,789	36%
□ Indivs under $200	$66,108	14%
▧ Other	$133,602	29%
Candidate	$126,000	27%
Party	$4,513	1%

Source of PAC Dollars by Sector

Source	Total	Pct
■ Business	$86,550	87%
▨ Labor	$0	0%
□ Ideology/Single Issue	$12,374	13%

In-State vs. Out-of-State Contributions*

Source	Total	Pct
□ In-State	$162,589	99%
■ Out-of-state	$2,000	1%
No state listed	$0	

* by large individual contributors ($200 & above)

National Assn of Home Builders .... $5,000   PAC

Special Trade Contractors $3,500
  Acedo Millwork .... $2,000   Indiv
  Ebensteiner Co .... $1,000   Indiv

Construction Services $3,250
  William Cloyd Inc Architect .... $2,950   Indiv

Building Materials & Equipment $1,200
  None over $1,000

Defense $3,750

Defense Aerospace $2,750
  Lockheed Corp .... $1,000   PAC

Defense Electronics $1,000
  Imo Industries Inc .... $1,000   PAC

Energy & Natural Resources $3,350

Oil & Gas $2,250
  Chevron Corp .... $1,000   PAC

Finance, Insurance & Real Estate $45,236

Commercial Banks $7,150
  American Bankers Assn .... $4,000   PAC
  BankAmerica Corp .... $1,600   PAC/Ind
  Wells Fargo .... $1,000   PAC

Savings & Loans $1,000
  None over $1,000

Securities & Investment $1,750
  Goldman, Sachs & Co .... $1,000   Indiv

Insurance $8,050
  National Assn of Life Underwriters .... $1,500   PAC
  New England Mutual Life .... $1,500   Indiv
  The New England .... $1,000   Indiv

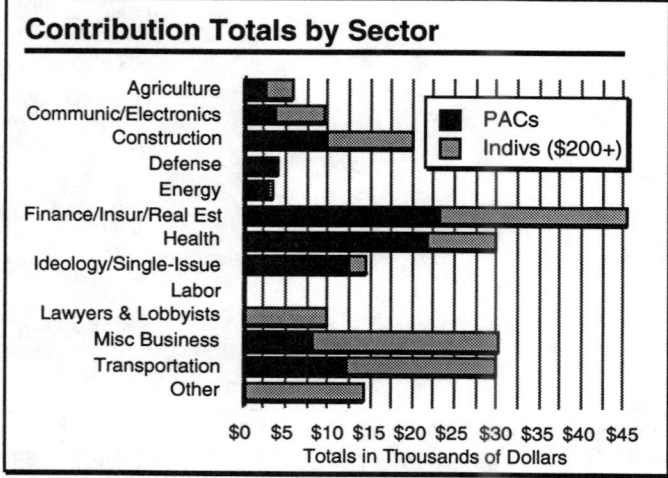

Contribution Totals by Sector

Agriculture, Communic/Electronics, Construction, Defense, Energy, Finance/Insur/Real Est, Health, Ideology/Single-Issue, Labor, Lawyers & Lobbyists, Misc Business, Transportation, Other

■ PACs
▨ Indivs ($200+)

$0 $5 $10 $15 $20 $25 $30 $35 $40 $45
Totals in Thousands of Dollars

Pacific Mutual Life	$1,000	PAC

Real Estate **$24,686**

National Assn of Realtors	$7,500	PAC
Newhall Land & Farming Co	$5,000	PAC/Ind
Guerdon Industries	$3,900	Indiv
RR Gable Inc	$1,250	Indiv

Misc Finance **$2,200**

First Financial Corp	$1,000	Indiv

Health $29,650

Health Professionals **$24,350**

American Medical Assn	$10,000	PAC
American Dental Assn	$5,000	PAC
American Academy of Ophthalmology	$3,000	PAC
American Optometric Assn	$1,000	PAC

Pharmaceuticals/Health Products **$4,000**

Baxter International Inc	$1,500	Indiv
Eli Lilly & Co	$1,000	PAC
McKesson Corp	$1,000	PAC

Lawyers & Lobbyists $10,149

Lawyers & Lobbyists **$10,149**

Kestler & Walsh	$2,850	Indiv
Nahin & Nahin	$1,700	Indiv
Latham & Watkins	$1,000	Indiv

Misc Business $29,899

Food & Beverage **$2,950**

Chili's Inc	$1,000	PAC
National Restaurant Assn	$1,000	PAC

Retail Sales **$17,350**

Howard & Phil's Western Wear	$13,100	Indiv
House of Fabrics Inc	$2,000	Indiv

Business Services **$3,849**
None over $1,000

Casinos/Gambling **$1,000**

Caesar's World	$1,000	PAC

Lodging/Tourism **$2,000**

Intl Assn Amusement Parks & Attractions	$1,500	PAC

Misc Manufacturing & Distributing **$1,500**

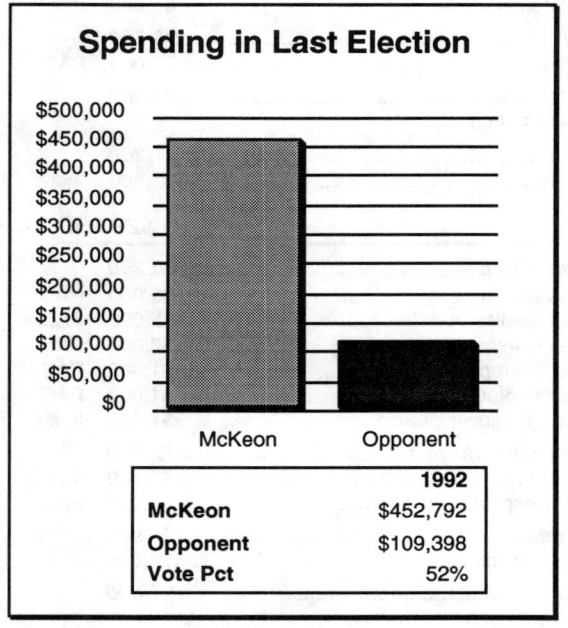

Spending in Last Election

	1992
McKeon	$452,792
Opponent	$109,398
Vote Pct	52%

Scully Sportswear Inc	$1,500	Indiv

Transportation $29,600

Air Transport **$4,000**

United Parcel Service	$4,000	PAC

Automotive **$24,600**

Magic Ford	$11,850	Indiv
National Auto Dealers Assn	$5,000	PAC
Antelope Vly Nissen Inc	$1,800	Indiv
Galpin Motors	$1,750	Indiv
Rexhall Industries	$1,700	Indiv
Auto Dealers & Drivers for Free Trade	$1,000	PAC
Eaton Corp	$1,000	PAC

Railroads **$1,000**

Union Pacific Corp	$1,000	PAC

Ideological/Single-Issue

Ideological/Single-Issue $14,374

Republican/Conservative **$1,024**
None over $1,000

Leadership PACs **$1,000**

Republican Leader's Fund (Bob Michel)	$1,000	PAC

Pro-Israel **$6,500**

National PAC	$5,000	PAC

Gun Rights/Gun Control **$4,950**

National Rifle Assn	$4,950	PAC

Misc Issues **$1,000**
None over $1,000

Other & Unknown

Other $14,000

Education **$1,250**
None over $1,000

Retired **$11,950**
None over $1,000

Unknown $47,605

Homemakers/Non-income earners	$10,250
Generic Occupation/Category Unknown	$1,400
Employer Listed/Category Unknown	$35,355

Magnum Enterprises	$3,500	Indiv
Western Pacific	$3,000	Indiv
Keysor Century	$2,500	Indiv
Hunt Companies	$2,000	Indiv
Magnum Enterprises	$3,500	Indiv
Santa Clarita Disposal	$1,500	Indiv
Weston Development	$1,200	Indiv
Commercial Casualty	$1,000	Indiv
Forest & Co	$1,000	Indiv
Gruber Systems	$1,000	Indiv
Lloyd R Andersen & Assoc	$1,000	Indiv
Luccese Boot	$1,000	Indiv
Norehart Land Co	$1,000	Indiv
Prime West Inc	$1,000	Indiv
Russell Associates	$1,000	Indiv

Independent expenditures supporting McKeon

California Medical Assn	$2,500

---

* Contributions came from more than one affiliate or subsidiary.

Cynthia McKinney, D-Ga (11)

1991-92 Total Receipts: $316,990
1992 Year-end Cash: $4,066

1993-94 Committees & Subcommittees

Agriculture
Department Operations and Nutrition; Environment, Credit and Rural Development; Foreign Agriculture and Hunger

Foreign Affairs
Economic Policy, Trade and Environment; Western Hemisphere Affairs

Leading Contributors

Business

Agriculture	$10,550	

Crop Production & Basic Processing **$2,000**
  Georgia Peanut Producers Assn .... $2,000 PAC

Tobacco **$3,250**
  Philip Morris .... $1,000 PAC
  US Tobacco Co .... $1,000 PAC

Dairy **$1,000**
  None over $1,000

Poultry & Eggs **$1,000**
  National Broiler Council .... $1,000 PAC

Food Processing & Sales **$1,500**
  Pepsico Inc .... $1,000 PAC

Forestry & Forest Products **$1,050**
  Georgia-Pacific Corp .... $1,050 PAC/Ind

Communications/Electronics	$7,650	

Media/Entertainment **$1,500**
  None over $1,000

Telephone Utilities **$5,500**
  AT&T .... $2,000 PAC
  Southern Bell .... $1,750 PAC
  United Telecommunications .... $1,000 PAC

Construction	$6,200	

General Contractors **$3,000**
  HJ Russell & Co .... $1,000 Indiv

Construction Services **$2,250**
  Law Companies Group .... $2,000 Indiv

Source of Funds in 1992 Election

Source	Total	Pct
PACs	$168,917	51%
Indivs $200+	$74,588	22%
Indivs under $200	$63,426	19%
Other	$26,015	8%
Candidate	$2,809	1%
Party	$16,956	5%

Source of PAC Dollars by Sector

Source	Total	Pct
Business	$68,000	39%
Labor	$59,650	34%
Ideology/Single Issue	$45,342	26%

In-State vs. Out-of-State Contributions*

Source	Total	Pct
In-State	$65,638	90%
Out-of-state	$7,700	10%
No state listed	$1,250	

* by large individual contributors ($200 & above)

Energy & Natural Resources	$6,600	

Oil & Gas **$2,400**
  American Food Investment .... $1,000 Indiv

Electric Utilities **$3,450**
  Southern Co* .... $2,750 PAC

Finance, Insurance & Real Estate	$15,770	

Commercial Banks **$2,050**
  First Atlanta Corp .... $1,000 PAC

Insurance **$7,020**
  Georgia US Corp .... $1,500 PAC
  National Assn of Life Underwriters .... $1,500 PAC
  Atlanta Life Insurance .... $1,000 Indiv

Real Estate **$3,750**
  First Union Corp .... $1,000 PAC

Accountants **$1,000**
  None over $1,000

Misc Finance **$1,200**
  Equifax Inc .... $1,200 Indiv

Health	$29,050	

Health Professionals **$24,250**
  American Dental Assn .... $5,000 PAC
  American Medical Assn .... $5,000 PAC
  American Nurses Assn .... $2,000 PAC
  American Chiropractic Assn .... $1,000 PAC
  American Podiatry Assn .... $1,000 PAC
  Kaufmann Diagnostic Clinic .... $1,000 Indiv

Hospitals/Nursing Homes **$2,800**
  Grady Hospital .... $1,000 Indiv
  Midtown Hospital .... $1,000 Indiv

Health Services **$1,000**
  Healthmaster Inc .... $1,000 Indiv

Misc Health **$1,000**
  None over $1,000

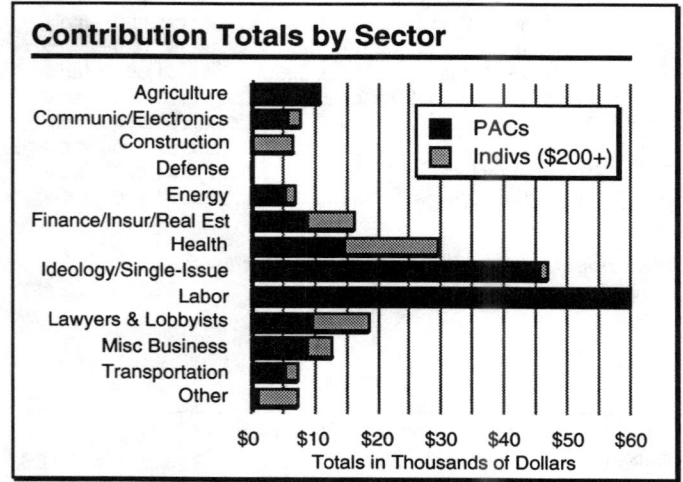

Contribution Totals by Sector

Agriculture
Communic/Electronics
Construction
Defense
Energy
Finance/Insur/Real Est
Health
Ideology/Single-Issue
Labor
Lawyers & Lobbyists
Misc Business
Transportation
Other

PACs
Indivs ($200+)

$0 $10 $20 $30 $40 $50 $60
Totals in Thousands of Dollars

Lawyers & Lobbyists $18,250

Lawyers & Lobbyists **$18,250**
    Assn of Trial Lawyers of America ....$7,500   PAC
    King & Spalding ....$1,250   PAC/Ind
    Arrington & Assoc ....$1,000   Indiv

Misc Business $12,650

Business Associations **$1,350**
    None over $1,000

Food & Beverage **$3,750**
    Coca-Cola Co ....$2,500   PAC/Ind
    Blimpie's ....$1,000   Indiv

Beer, Wine & Liquor **$2,800**
    National Beer Wholesalers Assn ....$2,000   PAC

Misc Services **$1,500**
    None over $1,000

Business Services **$1,250**
    None over $1,000

Lodging/Tourism **$2,000**
    Marriott Corp ....$2,000   PAC

Transportation $7,054

Air Transport **$4,500**
    United Parcel Service ....$4,000   PAC

Automotive **$1,154**
    None over $1,000

Labor

Labor $59,650

Building Trade Unions **$7,350**
    Carpenters & Joiners Union ....$2,500   PAC
    Laborers' Political League ....$2,500   PAC
    Sheet Metal Workers Union ....$2,000   PAC

Industrial Unions **$13,700**
    United Steelworkers ....$3,000   PAC
    United Auto Workers ....$2,500   PAC
    Intl Brotherhood of Electrical Workers ....$2,200   PAC
    Machinists/Aerospace Workers Union ....$2,000   PAC
    Communications Workers of America ....$1,500   PAC
    Electronic Machine Furniture Workers ....$1,500   PAC
    Amalgamated Clothing & Textile Workers ....$1,000   PAC

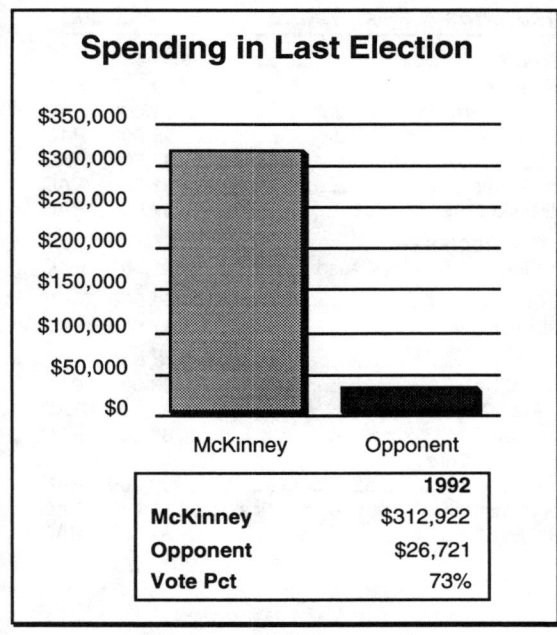

Spending in Last Election

	1992
McKinney	$312,922
Opponent	$26,721
Vote Pct	73%

Transportation Unions **$9,600**
    Teamsters Union ....$5,000   PAC
    Air Line Pilots Assn ....$1,000   PAC
    International Longshoremen's Assn ....$1,000   PAC
    United Transportation Union ....$1,000   PAC

Public Sector Unions **$21,000**
    National Education Assn ....$7,500   PAC
    American Fedn of St/Cnty/Munic Employees ......$5,000   PAC
    American Federation of Teachers ....$3,500   PAC
    National Assn of Letter Carriers ....$2,000   PAC
    National Assn Retired Federal Employees ....$1,000   PAC
    National Rural Letter Carriers Assn ....$1,000   PAC

Misc Unions **$8,000**
    Service Employees International Union ....$3,000   PAC
    AFL-CIO ....$2,500   PAC
    Food & Commercial Workers Union ....$2,500   PAC

Ideological/Single-Issue

Ideological/Single-Issue $46,342

Leadership PACs **$4,000**
    Effective Government Cmte (Dick Gephardt) ......$1,000   PAC
    House Leadership Fund (Tom Foley) ....$1,000   PAC
    People Helping People (Maxine Waters) ....$1,000   PAC

Foreign & Defense Policy **$1,634**
    Council for a Livable World ....$1,000   PAC

Pro-Choice **$2,000**
    Voters for Choice ....$1,000   PAC

Womens Issues **$27,500**
    Emily's List ....$15,000   PAC
    National Organization for Women ....$6,250   PAC
    Women's Campaign Fund ....$5,000   PAC
    National Womens Political Caucus ....$1,000   PAC

Human Rights **$4,500**
    Human Rights Campaign Fund ....$4,500   PAC

Misc Issues **$6,208**
    Sierra Club ....$4,458   PAC
    National Cmte to Preserve Social Security ....$1,000   PAC

Other & Unknown

Other $7,044

Civil Servants/Public Officials **$2,194**
    State of Georgia ....$1,744   Indiv

Retired **$3,250**
    None over $1,000

Unknown $22,020

Unknown **$1,000**
      Georgia Federal Elections Committee ....$1,000   PAC
Homemakers/Non-income earners **$1,250**
No Employer Listed or Found **$8,250**
Generic Occupation/Category Unknown **$2,500**
Employer Listed/Category Unknown **$9,020**
    Horizon Import ....$1,494   Indiv
    Lawmark International Corp ....$1,200   Indiv
    Payton Distributors ....$1,000   Indiv
    Ross Shoes ....$1,000   Indiv

---

* Contributions came from more than one affiliate or
subsidiary.

Alex McMillan, R-NC (9)

First elected: 1984

1991-92 Total Receipts: $345,961
1992 Year-end Cash: $212,977

1991-92 Committees & Subcommittees

Budget

Energy and Commerce
Commerce, Consumer Protection and Competitiveness (Ranking Republican); Health and the Environment

Leading Contributors

Business

Agriculture	$30,050	
Crop Production & Basic Processing	**$1,500**	
None over $1,500		
Tobacco	**$9,050**	
RJR Nabisco	$5,000	PAC
Philip Morris	$1,500	PAC
Agricultural Services/Products	**$2,500**	
American Veterinary Medical Assn	$1,500	PAC
Food Processing & Sales	**$10,700**	
Food Marketing Institute	$1,500	PAC
Pepsico Inc	$1,500	PAC
Forestry & Forest Products	**$3,100**	
Westvaco Corp	$1,500	PAC

Communications/Electronics	$19,250	
Media/Entertainment	**$5,000**	
National Assn of Broadcasters	$3,000	PAC
National Cable Television Assn	$2,000	PAC
Telephone Utilities	**$13,250**	
Southern Bell	$7,000	PAC
GTE Corp	$1,500	PAC

Construction	$6,750	
Home Builders	**$1,500**	
None over $1,500		
Building Materials & Equipment	**$3,250**	
Charlotte Pipe & Foundry	$2,000	Indiv

Contribution Totals by Sector

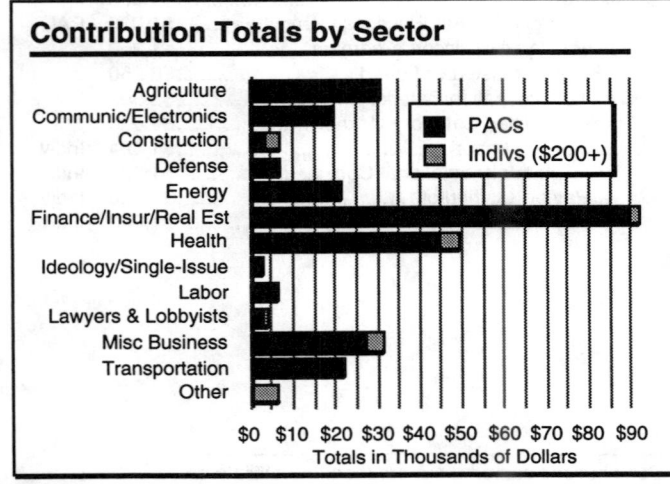

- PACs
- Indivs ($200+)

Agriculture
Communic/Electronics
Construction
Defense
Energy
Finance/Insur/Real Est
Health
Ideology/Single-Issue
Labor
Lawyers & Lobbyists
Misc Business
Transportation
Other

$0 $10 $20 $30 $40 $50 $60 $70 $80 $90
Totals in Thousands of Dollars

Source of Funds in 1992 Election

Source	Total	Pct
■ PACs	$268,000	77%
▨ Indivs $200+	$30,800	9%
☐ Indivs under $200	$28,644	8%
▧ Other	$18,517	5%
Candidate	$0	0%
Party	$0	0%

Source of PAC Dollars by Sector

Source	Total	Pct
■ Business	$261,750	97%
▨ Labor	$5,750	2%
☐ Ideology/Single Issue	$2,750	1%

In-State vs. Out-of-State Contributions*

Source	Total	Pct
☐ In-State	$27,050	88%
■ Out-of-state	$3,750	12%
No state listed	$0	

* by large individual contributors ($200 & above)

Defense	$6,500	
Defense Aerospace	**$3,000**	
None over $1,500		
Misc Defense	**$3,500**	
Insilco Corp	$3,000	PAC

Energy & Natural Resources	$20,850	
Oil & Gas	**$11,000**	
None over $1,500		
Mining	**$2,250**	
Reynolds Metals	$1,500	PAC
Electric Utilities	**$7,100**	
Duke Power Co	$1,500	PAC

Finance, Insurance & Real Estate	$92,200	
Commercial Banks	**$34,450**	
American Bankers Assn	$10,000	PAC
Citizens & Southern National Bank	$5,000	PAC
JP Morgan & Co	$5,000	PAC
Citicorp	$2,500	PAC
Barnett Banks Inc	$1,500	PAC
Security Pacific Corp	$1,500	PAC
Finance/Credit Companies	**$1,500**	
American Financial Services Assn	$1,500	PAC
Securities & Investment	**$4,900**	
Prudential Securities	$1,500	PAC
Insurance	**$28,650**	
Mutual of Omaha	$3,000	PAC
Jefferson-Pilot Corp	$2,500	PAC
American Council of Life Insurance	$2,000	PAC
American Family Corp	$2,000	PAC
Travelers Corp	$2,000	PAC
Independent Insurance Agents of America	$1,750	PAC
Capital Holding Corp	$1,500	PAC

Real Estate **$8,000**
    National Assn of Realtors ....$6,500 PAC

Accountants **$12,500**
    American Institute of CPA's ....$6,500 PAC
    Arthur Andersen & Co ....$2,000 PAC
    Coopers & Lybrand ....$2,000 PAC

Misc Finance **$2,200**
    Employee Stock Ownership Assn ....$1,500 PAC

Health   **$48,800**

Health Professionals **$25,750**
    American Medical Assn ....$10,000 PAC
    American Dental Assn ....$2,000 PAC
    American College of Emergency Physicians ....$1,500 PAC

Hospitals/Nursing Homes **$3,600**
    American Hospital Assn ....$2,000 PAC

Pharmaceuticals/Health Products **$19,450**
    Glaxo Inc ....$2,500 PAC
    Merck & Co ....$2,000 PAC
    Pfizer Inc ....$1,500 PAC
    Schering-Plough Corp ....$1,500 PAC

Lawyers & Lobbyists   **$3,750**

Lawyers & Lobbyists **$3,750**
    None over $1,500

Misc Business   **$31,050**

Food & Beverage **$1,500**
    None over $1,500

Retail Sales **$3,750**
    None over $1,500

Business Services **$1,750**
    None over $1,500

Chemical & Related Manufacturing **$6,250**
    Eastman Kodak/Chemicals Division ....$2,500 PAC

Misc Manufacturing & Distributing **$11,550**
    Hoechst Celanese Corp ....$3,500 PAC
    American Furniture Manufacturers Assn ....$2,000 PAC
    Stone Container Corp ....$2,000 PAC

Textiles **$3,250**
    None over $1,500

Transportation   **$21,500**

Air Transport **$4,050**
    United Parcel Service ....$2,000 PAC

Automotive **$11,250**
    National Auto Dealers Assn ....$4,500 PAC
    Americans for Free International Trade ....$2,000 PAC
    Auto Dealers & Drivers for Free Trade ....$1,500 PAC

Trucking **$2,200**
    None over $1,500

Railroads **$4,000**
    None over $1,500

Labor

Labor   **$5,750**

Transportation Unions **$4,250**
    Marine Engineers Union* ....$3,250 PAC

Public Sector Unions **$1,500**
    None over $1,500

Ideological/Single-Issue

Ideological/Single-Issue   **$2,750**
    None over $1,500

Other & Unknown

Other   **$6,050**

Retired **$5,800**
    None over $1,500

Unknown   **$5,800**

    Employer Listed/Category Unknown $4,500
        None over $1,500

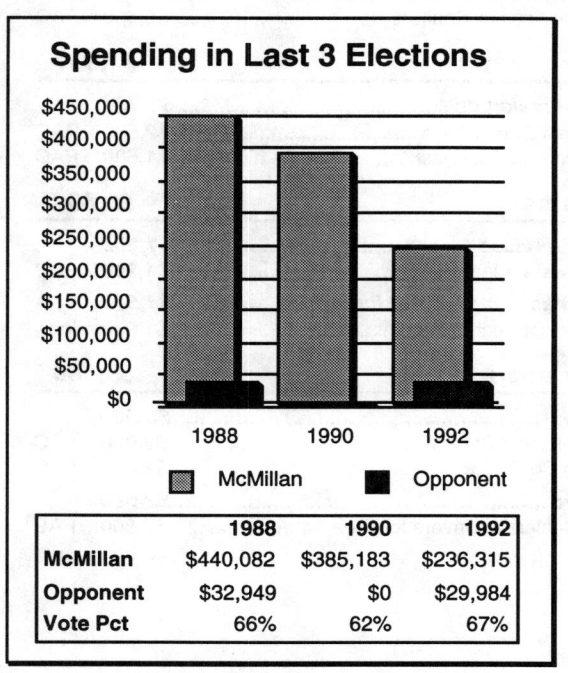

Spending in Last 3 Elections

	1988	1990	1992
McMillan	$440,082	$385,183	$236,315
Opponent	$32,949	$0	$29,984
Vote Pct	66%	62%	67%

Legend: McMillan, Opponent

---

* Contributions came from more than one affiliate or
subsidiary.

Michael R. McNulty, D-NY (21)

First elected: 1988

1991-92 Total Receipts: $220,997
1992 Year-end Cash: $68,572

1991-92 Committees & Subcommittees

Armed Services
Investigations; Procurement and Military Nuclear Systems

Post Office and Civil Service
Census and Population; Investigations; Postal Personnel and Modernization

Select Committee on Hunger

Leading Contributors

Business

Agriculture		$2,000
Dairy	*$1,000*	
Associated Milk Producers	$1,000	PAC
Food Processing & Sales	*$1,000*	
Connell Rice & Sugar Co	$1,000	Indiv

Communications/Electronics		$4,750
Telephone Utilities	*$4,750*	
AT&T	$2,500	PAC
BellSouth Corp*	$1,750	PAC

Construction		$1,000
None over $1,000		

Defense		$12,650
Defense Aerospace	*$10,200*	
General Electric	$1,700	PAC
General Dynamics	$1,500	PAC
LTV Aerospace & Defense Co	$1,500	PAC
Grumman Corp	$1,000	PAC
Martin Marietta Corp	$1,000	PAC
McDonnell Douglas*	$1,000	PAC
Rockwell International	$1,000	PAC
Textron Inc	$1,000	PAC
Defense Electronics	*$1,450*	
None over $1,000		
Misc Defense	*$1,000*	
Harsco Corp	$1,000	PAC

Contribution Totals by Sector

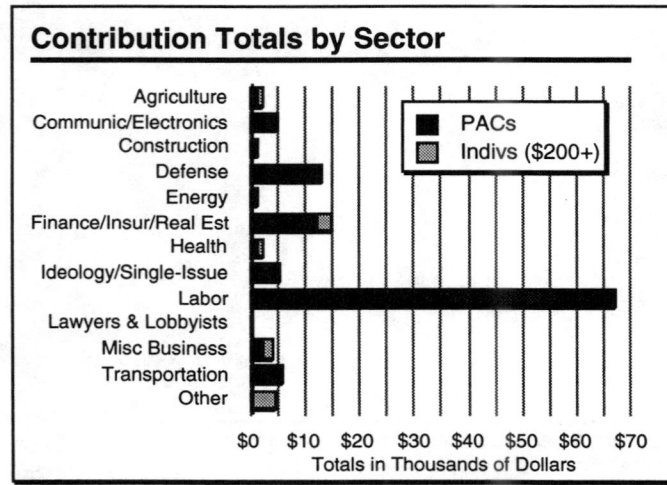

Legend: ■ PACs ▦ Indivs ($200+)

Agriculture
Communic/Electronics
Construction
Defense
Energy
Finance/Insur/Real Est
Health
Ideology/Single-Issue
Labor
Lawyers & Lobbyists
Misc Business
Transportation
Other

$0 $10 $20 $30 $40 $50 $60 $70
Totals in Thousands of Dollars

Source of Funds in 1992 Election

Source	Total	Pct
■ PACs	$126,286	56%
▤ Indivs $200+	$13,701	6%
□ Indivs under $200	$65,695	29%
▨ Other	$19,933	9%
Candidate	$0	0%
Party	$5,198	2%

Source of PAC Dollars by Sector

Source	Total	Pct
■ Business	$40,625	36%
▤ Labor	$66,800	59%
□ Ideology/Single Issue	$5,000	4%

In-State vs. Out-of-State Contributions*

Source	Total	Pct
□ In-State	$12,701	93%
■ Out-of-state	$1,000	7%
No state listed	$0	

* by large individual contributors ($200 & above)

Energy & Natural Resources		$1,000
None over $1,000		

Finance, Insurance & Real Estate		$14,425
Commercial Banks	*$1,100*	
Norstar Bancorp	$1,000	PAC
Finance/Credit Companies	*$1,000*	
Beneficial Management Corp	$1,000	PAC
Insurance	*$2,750*	
CNA Financial Corp	$1,000	PAC
Real Estate	*$7,750*	
National Assn of Realtors	$6,500	PAC

Health		$1,951
Health Professionals	*$1,751*	
American Dental Assn	$2,500	PAC
American Medical Assn*	$1,500	PAC

Misc Business		$3,800
Business Services	*$1,250*	
Advo-System Inc	$1,250	PAC
Misc Manufacturing & Distributing	*$1,500*	
Mechanical Technology Inc	$1,000	Indiv

Transportation		$5,500
Air Transport	*$3,000*	
United Parcel Service	$2,000	PAC
Boeing Co	$1,000	PAC
Automotive	*$2,500*	
Auto Dealers & Drivers for Free Trade	$2,500	PAC

Labor

Labor	$66,800

Building Trade Unions $11,100
Laborers' Political League $4,000	PAC
Operating Engineers Union* $2,600	PAC
Ironworkers Union $2,000	PAC
Plumbers/Pipefitters Union $2,000	PAC

Industrial Unions $9,000
Machinists/Aerospace Workers Union* $2,500	PAC
Intl Brotherhood of Electrical Workers $2,000	PAC
Boilermakers Union $1,500	PAC
United Auto Workers $1,200	PAC

Transportation Unions $17,900
Teamsters Union $7,500	PAC
Marine Engineers Dist 2 Maritime Officers $2,000	PAC
United Transportation Union $1,700	PAC
Air Line Pilots Assn $1,500	PAC
Seafarers International Union $1,500	PAC
Transport Workers Union $1,100	PAC
National Air Traffic Controllers Assn $1,000	PAC
Trans Comm International Union $1,000	PAC

Public Sector Unions $25,000
National Assn of Letter Carriers $7,000	PAC
National Assn Retired Federal Employees $4,000	PAC
American Postal Workers Union $3,500	PAC
American Fedn of St/Cnty/Munic Employees $3,000	PAC
National Assn of Postmasters $2,000	PAC
National League of Postmasters $2,000	PAC
National Assn of Postal Supervisors $1,500	PAC
Federal Managers' Assn $1,000	PAC
International Assn of Firefighters $1,000	PAC
National Rural Letter Carriers Assn $1,000	PAC

Misc Unions $3,800
Food & Commercial Workers Union $3,000	PAC

Ideological/Single-Issue

Ideological/Single-Issue	$5,000

Foreign & Defense Policy $1,000
Veterans of Foreign Wars $1,000	PAC

Pro-Israel $1,000
Washington PAC $1,000	PAC

Misc Issues $3,000
National Cmte to Preserve Social Security $3,000	PAC

Other & Unknown

Other	$4,250

Retired $3,050
None over $1,000

Unknown | $2,700 |
Employer Listed/Category Unknown $2,150
None over $1,000

Spending in Last 3 Elections

	1988	1990	1992
McNulty	$273,505	$149,204	$252,821
Opponent	$174,790	$23,299	$15,459
Vote Pct	62%	64%	63%

* Contributions came from more than one affiliate or subsidiary.

Martin T. Meehan, D-Mass (5)

First elected: 1992

1991-92 Total Receipts:	$812,181
1992 Year-end Cash:	$721

1993-94 Committees & Subcommittees

Armed Services
Military Forces and Personnel; Readiness; Research and Technology

Small Business
Regulation, Business Opportunities and Technology; SBA Legislation and the General Economy

Leading Contributors

NOTE: Meehan reported taking no PAC funds during his 1992 campaign. The PACs listed below did report making contributions, however, and those contributions are recorded in the official FEC records.

Business

Agriculture $6,000

Food Processing & Sales	$6,000	
Page International	$6,000	Indiv

Communications/Electronics $8,125

Printing & Publishing	$2,800	
Picken Printing	$2,200	Indiv
Telecom Services & Equipment	$1,000	
Artel Communications	$1,000	Indiv
Computer Equipment & Services	$3,000	
Wang Laboratories Inc	$2,000	Indiv

Construction $35,850

General Contractors	$11,800	
Suffolk Construction Co	$1,750	Indiv
Turco Plumbing	$1,100	Indiv
Methuen Construction Co	$1,000	Indiv
Middlesex Corp	$1,000	Indiv
Roads Corp	$1,000	Indiv
Special Trade Contractors	$12,750	
National Surface Cleaning	$3,100	Indiv
Franny Landscaping Co	$1,000	Indiv
US Seal Coating	$1,000	Indiv
Building Materials & Equipment	$11,300	
Bardon Trimount Inc	$2,000	Indiv
Boston Sand & Gravel	$2,000	Indiv
Newpro	$2,000	Indiv
Wakefield Concrete	$2,000	Indiv

Contribution Totals by Sector

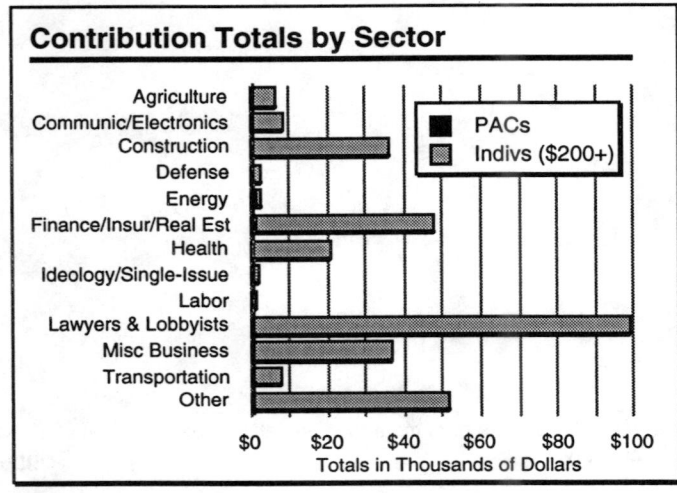

Totals in Thousands of Dollars

Source of Funds in 1992 Election

Source	Total	Pct
■ PACs	$0	0%
▨ Indivs $200+	$446,175	53%
☐ Indivs under $200	$182,529	22%
⊠ Other	$216,386	26%
Candidate	$166,168	20%
Party	$37,909	4%

Source of PAC Dollars by Sector

No PAC contributions reported

Source	Total	Pct
■ Business	$2,000	91%
▨ Labor	$200	9%
☐ Ideology/Single Issue	$0	0%

In-State vs. Out-of-State Contributions*

Source	Total	Pct
☐ In-State	$400,450	92%
■ Out-of-state	$36,650	8%
No state listed	$7,750	

* by large individual contributors ($200 & above)

Evered Bardon USA Inc	$1,000	Indiv
Guaranteed Aluminum Door & Window	$1,000	Indiv
Ideal Concrete Blozck	$1,000	Indiv

Defense $2,150

Defense Electronics	$1,650	
Raytheon Co	$1,650	Indiv

Energy & Natural Resources $1,950

Waste Management	$1,000	
Resource Controls Inc	$1,000	Indiv

Finance, Insurance & Real Estate $46,985

Commercial Banks	$1,150	
None over $1,000		
Savings & Loans	$1,800	
Massbank for Savings	$1,800	Indiv
Securities & Investment	$5,750	
Cohasset Capital Corp	$4,000	Indiv
Bear, Stearns & Co	$1,000	Indiv
Insurance	$8,050	
American Life Insurance Council	$2,000	Indiv
American Council of Life Insurance	$1,000	PAC
Corroon & Black	$1,000	Indiv
JH Albert Co	$1,000	Indiv
Real Estate	$26,785	
Corcoran, Jennison Co	$3,000	Indiv
Beacon Companies	$2,000	Indiv
John M Corcoran & Co	$2,000	Indiv
Keith Properties	$1,250	Indiv
Boston Capital Partners	$1,000	Indiv
Carpenter & Co	$1,000	Indiv
Congress Group Properties	$1,000	Indiv
Drummer Real Estate	$1,000	Indiv
Joseph R Mullins Co	$1,000	Indiv
Misc Finance	$3,200	
First Concord Financial	$1,500	Indiv

Health $20,310

Health Professionals $8,825
   None over $1,000

Hospitals/Nursing Homes $5,085
   ADS Management Inc .... $2,000   Indiv
   Middlesex County Hospital .... $1,450   Indiv

Health Services $4,000
   Shields Health Care .... $3,000   Indiv
   Frontline Ambulance .... $1,000   Indiv

Pharmaceuticals/Health Products $1,000
   Muro Pharmaceutical .... $1,000   Indiv

Misc Health $1,400
   Lowell Medical Instrument .... $1,000   Indiv

Lawyers & Lobbyists $99,249

Lawyers & Lobbyists $99,249
   Gilman, McLaughlin & Hanrahan .... $11,500   Indiv
   Gargiulo, Rudnick & Garguilo .... $3,000   Indiv
   Palmer & Dodge .... $2,525   Indiv
   Sarrouf, Tarricone & Fleming .... $2,500   Indiv
   Aucilla Law .... $2,200   Indiv
   Choate, Hall & Stewart .... $2,000   Indiv
   Mintz, Levin et al .... $1,950   Indiv
   Mahoney, Hawk & Goldings .... $1,700   Indiv
   Finnigan, Underwood et al .... $1,500   Indiv
   Legal Secretary .... $1,500   Indiv
   Buckley, Haight et al .... $1,000   Indiv
   Crowe, Crowe & Vernaglia .... $1,000   Indiv
   Donahue & Donahue .... $1,000   Indiv
   Driscoll & Marchand .... $1,000   Indiv
   Esdaile, Barrett et al .... $1,000   Indiv
   Foley, Hoag & Eliot .... $1,000   Indiv
   Goldman & Curtis .... $1,000   Indiv
   Goodwin, Proctor & Hoar .... $1,000   Indiv
   Halstrom Law Offices .... $1,000   Indiv
   Hogan & Roache .... $1,000   Indiv
   Joyce & Joyce .... $1,000   Indiv
   Sugarman & Sugarman .... $1,000   Indiv

Misc Business $36,106

Food & Beverage $7,425
   American Food Products .... $2,150   Indiv

Beer, Wine & Liquor $3,200
   DJ Reardon Co .... $2,000   Indiv

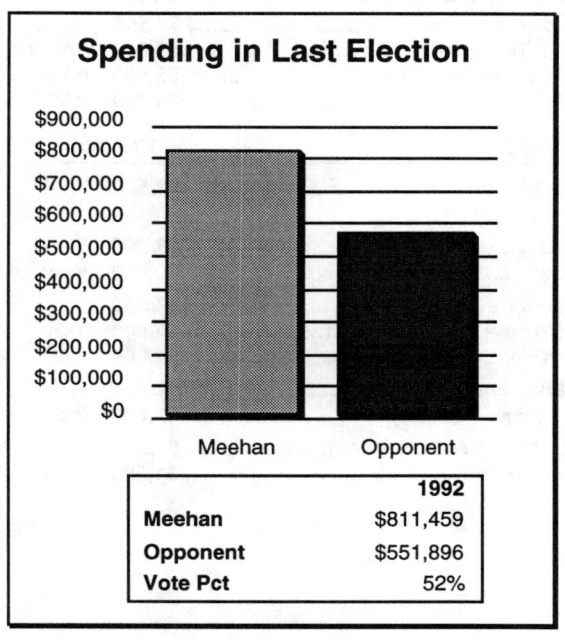

Spending in Last Election

	1992
Meehan	$811,459
Opponent	$551,896
Vote Pct	52%

Retail Sales $3,500
   Eastern Clothing Co .... $2,000   Indiv

Misc Services $1,000
   Boston Athletic Club .... $1,000   Indiv

Business Services $13,500
   Campaign Group .... $2,000   Indiv
   Pappas Management Corp .... $2,000   Indiv
   Issues Management Inc .... $1,000   Indiv
   McDermott, O'Neill & Associates .... $1,000   Indiv
   Minuteman Tech Serv .... $1,000   Indiv

Chemical & Related Manufacturing $1,000
   Eastern Minerals .... $1,000   Indiv

Misc Manufacturing & Distributing $4,931
   Anwelt Corp .... $1,000   Indiv
   Massachusetts Envelope Co .... $1,000   Indiv
   Nike Inc .... $1,000   Indiv
   Prelco Corp .... $1,000   Indiv

Transportation $7,150

Air Transport $1,700
   None over $1,000

Automotive $5,450
   Stanhope Garages .... $1,500   Indiv
   Gendron Auto Body .... $1,000   Indiv
   Iversen Ford .... $1,000   Indiv
   McCarthy's Portable Structures .... $1,000   Indiv

Ideological/Single-Issue

Ideological/Single-Issue $1,750

Democratic/Liberal $1,250
   None over $1,000

Other & Unknown

Other $51,199

Civil Servants/Public Officials $27,925
   City of Lowell .... $13,675   Indiv
   District Attorney's Office .... $2,250   Indiv
   Middlesex District Attorney's Office .... $2,000   Indiv
   Commonwealth of Massachusetts .... $1,775   Indiv
   Hanscom Air Force Base .... $1,200   Indiv
   Environmental Protection Agency .... $1,000   Indiv
   State of Massachusetts .... $1,000   Indiv

Education $4,950
   None over $1,000

Retired $17,924
   None over $1,000

Unknown $129,276

   Homemakers/Non-income earners $16,050
   No Employer Listed or Found $70,541
   Generic Occupation/Category Unknown $9,400
   Employer Listed/Category Unknown $33,285
      Flynn Enterprises .... $2,200   Indiv
      Atheneum Group .... $1,000   Indiv
      B&H Equipment Co .... $1,000   Indiv
      Choate Group .... $1,000   Indiv
      Dynamics Research Corp .... $1,000   Indiv
      HR McBride & Assoc .... $1,000   Indiv
      Middlesex Companies .... $1,000   Indiv

Carrie Meek, D-Fla (17)

1993-94 Committees & Subcommittees

Appropriations
Energy and Water Development; Military Construction

First elected: 1992

1991-92 Total Receipts: $574,719
1992 Year-end Cash: $113,605

Leading Contributors

Business

Agriculture	**$11,000**	
Crop Production & Basic Processing *$3,250*		
Okeelanta Corp $2,000	Indiv	
Tobacco *$3,500*		
RJR Nabisco $2,500	PAC	
Food Processing & Sales *$3,500*		
Winn-Dixie Stores $2,000	Indiv	

Communications/Electronics	**$6,250**	
Telephone Utilities *$5,250*		
Southern Bell $3,250	PAC	

Construction	**$5,450**	
General Contractors *$2,750*		
None over $1,500		
Construction Services *$1,700*		
None over $1,500		

Energy & Natural Resources	**$2,250**	
None over $1,500		

Finance, Insurance & Real Estate	**$17,550**	
Commercial Banks *$2,600*		
Citizens & Southern National Bank $1,500	PAC	
Insurance *$2,250*		
None over $1,500		
Real Estate *$9,000*		
National Assn of Realtors $5,000	PAC	
Accountants *$1,700*		
None over $1,500		

Source of Funds in 1992 Election

Source	Total	Pct
■ PACs $157,115		27%
▨ Indivs $200+ $188,984		32%
☐ Indivs under $200 ....$226,118		39%
⊠ Other $11,096		2%
Candidate $0		0%
Party $9,044		2%

Source of PAC Dollars by Sector

Source	Total	Pct
■ Business $57,200		37%
▨ Labor $68,350		44%
☐ Ideology/Single Issue $31,128		20%

In-State vs. Out-of-State Contributions*

Source	Total	Pct
☐ In-State $160,884		86%
▨ Out-of-state $25,550		14%
No state listed $0		

* by large individual contributors ($200 & above)

Health	**$66,900**	
Health Professionals *$15,400*		
American Medical Assn $2,500	PAC	
American College of Emergency Physicians $2,000	PAC	
American Dental Assn* $1,500	PAC	
Hospitals/Nursing Homes *$44,500*		
Hospice Care Inc $36,000	Indiv	
Humana Inc $2,000	PAC	
St Vincent's Hospital $2,000	Indiv	
Health Services *$5,250*		
Care Florida (HMO) $1,500	Indiv	
Home Intensive Care Inc $2,500	PAC	

Lawyers & Lobbyists	**$33,550**	
Lawyers & Lobbyists *$33,550*		
Greenberg, Traurig et al $5,800	PAC/Ind	
Assn of Trial Lawyers of America $5,000	PAC	
Holland & Knight $4,200	PAC/Ind	

Misc Business	**$19,850**	
Beer, Wine & Liquor *$2,500*		
None over $1,500		
Misc Services *$3,000*		
Roto Rooter $2,000	Indiv	
Business Services *$7,550*		
Owen Colliflower Court Reporting $2,000	Indiv	
Westbrook Family Enterprises Inc $2,000	Indiv	
Recreation/Live Entertainment *$2,450*		
Miami Dolphins $2,000	Indiv	
Misc Manufacturing & Distributing *$1,500*		
Miami River Recycling $1,500	Indiv	

Contribution Totals by Sector

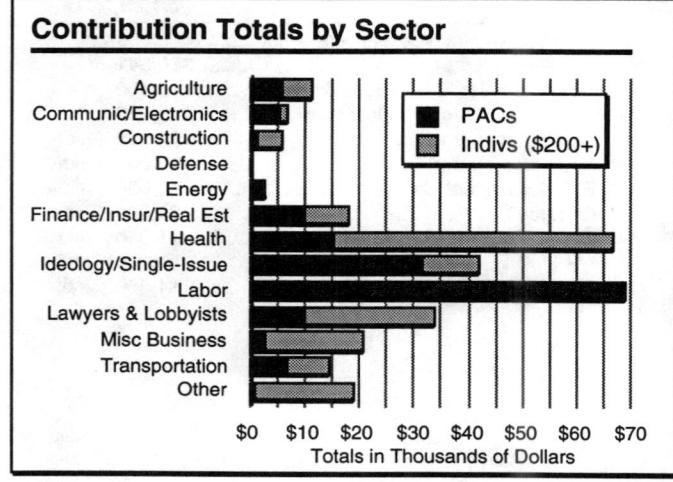

Agriculture
Communic/Electronics
Construction
Defense
Energy
Finance/Insur/Real Est
Health
Ideology/Single-Issue
Labor
Lawyers & Lobbyists
Misc Business
Transportation
Other

■ PACs
▨ Indivs ($200+)

$0 $10 $20 $30 $40 $50 $60 $70
Totals in Thousands of Dollars

Transportation $14,000

Automotive *$5,000*
    National Auto Dealers Assn .... $3,000   PAC

Sea Transport *$6,250*
    Harrmgton & Co .... $3,000   Indiv

Labor

Labor $68,350

Building Trade Unions *$7,600*
    Carpenters & Joiners Union .... $5,000   PAC

Industrial Unions *$17,000*
    Communications Workers of America .... $5,000   PAC
    Machinists/Aerospace Workers Union .... $5,000   PAC
    United Steelworkers .... $3,000   PAC
    United Auto Workers .... $2,500   PAC

Transportation Unions *$10,500*
    Teamsters Union .... $5,000   PAC
    United Transportation Union .... $2,000   PAC

Public Sector Unions *$26,250*
    National Education Assn .... $10,000   PAC
    American Federation of Teachers .... $5,000   PAC
    American Fedn of St/Cnty/Munic Employees ...... $5,000   PAC
    National Assn of Letter Carriers .... $3,000   PAC

Misc Unions *$7,000*
    Food & Commercial Workers Union .... $3,000   PAC
    AFL-CIO .... $2,000   PAC

Ideological/Single-Issue

Ideological/Single-Issue $41,428

Democratic/Liberal *$2,784*
    None over $1,500

Leadership PACs *$4,500*
    None over $1,500

Foreign & Defense Policy *$1,729*
    None over $1,500

Pro-Israel *$5,250*
    None over $1,500

Womens Issues *$17,415*
    Emily's List .... $5,151   PAC/Ind
    Women's Campaign Fund .... $5,000   PAC
    National Organization for Women .... $4,264   PAC
    National Womens Political Caucus .... $1,500   PAC

Human Rights *$3,000*
    Human Rights Campaign Fund .... $2,500   PAC

Misc Issues *$6,000*
    Greenvote .... $5,000   PAC

Other & Unknown

Other $18,450

Civil Servants/Public Officials *$7,150*
    City of Jacksonville .... $4,000   Indiv
    Miami Shores Police Department .... $2,000   Indiv

Education *$6,600*
    Hope Day Care.. $3,000   Indiv

Retired *$3,500*
    None over $1,500

Unknown $40,784

    Homemakers/Non-income earners $7,850
    No Employer Listed or Found $14,305
    Generic Occupation/Category Unknown $3,500
    Employer Listed/Category Unknown $15,129
        None over $1,500

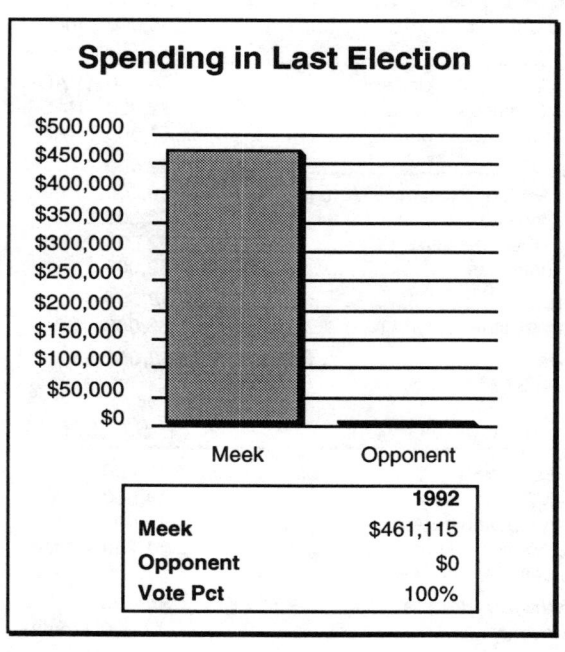

Spending in Last Election

	1992
Meek	$461,115
Opponent	$0
Vote Pct	100%

---

* Contributions came from more than one affiliate or
subsidiary.

Robert Menendez, D-NJ (13)

1993-94 Committees & Subcommittees

Foreign Affairs
International Operations; Western Hemisphere Affairs

Public Works and Transportation
Economic Development; Surface Transportation; Water Resources and the Environment

First elected: 1992

1991-92 Total Receipts: $668,659
1992 Year-end Cash: $23,018

Leading Contributors

Business

Agriculture	$14,000	
Tobacco	**$2,500**	
None over $1,500		
Dairy	**$4,000**	
Mendez Dairy Inc	$2,000	Indiv
Food Processing & Sales	**$6,250**	
None over $1,500		

Communications/Electronics	$14,800	
Printing & Publishing	**$3,500**	
None over $1,500		
Telephone Utilities	**$9,300**	
New Jersey Bell Telephone	$4,000	PAC/Ind
AT&T	$1,500	PAC
Bell Atlantic	$1,500	PAC/Ind

Construction	$25,050	
General Contractors	**$3,750**	
Cali Associates	$2,000	Indiv
Home Builders	**$10,000**	
National Assn of Home Builders	$10,000	PAC
Special Trade Contractors	**$3,300**	
None over $1,500		
Construction Services	**$7,000**	
Rivard Architects	$3,000	Indiv
Canger & Cassera	$2,000	Indiv

Source of Funds in 1992 Election

Source	Total	Pct
■ PACs	$226,497	33%
▨ Indivs $200+	$368,821	54%
☐ Indivs under $200	$71,787	11%
▧ Other	$10,633	2%
Candidate	$0	0%
Party	$9,079	1%

Source of PAC Dollars by Sector

Source	Total	Pct
■ Business	$108,794	47%
▨ Labor	$86,431	37%
☐ Ideology/Single Issue	$36,039	16%

In-State vs. Out-of-State Contributions*

Source	Total	Pct
☐ In-State	$314,121	89%
■ Out-of-state	$39,800	11%
No state listed	$14,600	

* by large individual contributors ($200 & above)

Energy & Natural Resources	$15,960	
Oil & Gas	**$5,500**	
International Matex	$2,000	Indiv
Electric Utilities	**$8,210**	
Public Service Electric & Gas	$2,810	PAC/Ind

Finance, Insurance & Real Estate	$74,284	
Commercial Banks	**$7,550**	
None over $1,500		
Savings & Loans	**$3,519**	
US League of Savings Assns*	$2,519	PAC
Securities & Investment	**$9,700**	
Enright & Co	$5,000	Indiv
Insurance	**$18,315**	
National Assn of Life Underwriters	$4,000	PAC
Prudential Insurance	$2,250	PAC/Ind
Chubb Corp	$1,500	PAC
Real Estate	**$22,600**	
National Assn of Realtors	$8,500	PAC
Applied Housing	$3,000	Indiv
Frederick Fish Investment Co	$2,000	Indiv
Square Industries	$2,000	Indiv
Accountants	**$8,600**	
American Institute of CPA's	$3,000	PAC
Misc Finance	**$3,000**	
None over $1,500		

Health	$37,950	
Health Professionals	**$26,700**	
American Dental Assn	$4,500	PAC
American Optometric Assn	$2,000	PAC
Pavonia Medical Associates	$1,750	Indiv
New Jersey Medical Assn	$1,500	PAC
Hospitals/Nursing Homes	**$4,000**	
Christ Hospital	$2,000	Indiv

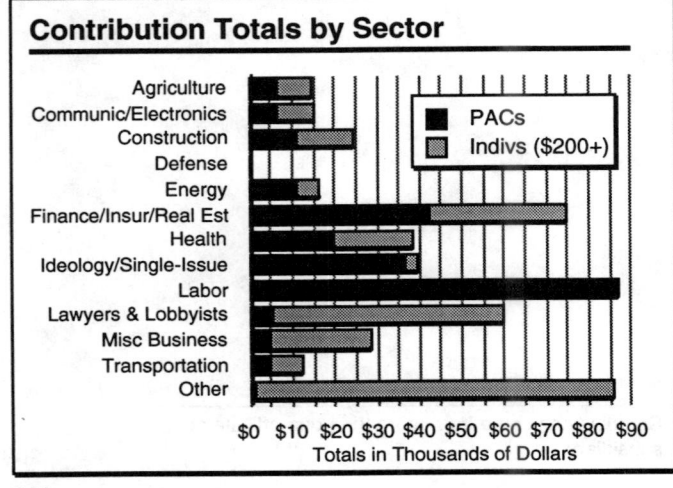

Contribution Totals by Sector

Agriculture, Communic/Electronics, Construction, Defense, Energy, Finance/Insur/Real Est, Health, Ideology/Single-Issue, Labor, Lawyers & Lobbyists, Misc Business, Transportation, Other

■ PACs
▨ Indivs ($200+)

$0 $10 $20 $30 $40 $50 $60 $70 $80 $90
Totals in Thousands of Dollars

Pharmaceuticals/Health Products **$6,050**
    None over $1,500

Lawyers & Lobbyists   **$60,200**

Lawyers & Lobbyists **$60,200**
Waters, McPherson et al	$11,500	Indiv
Assn of Trial Lawyers of America	$5,000	PAC
Scarinci & Hollenbeck	$2,500	Indiv
Leanza, Agrapidis & Kalebic	$2,000	Indiv
Nelson & Walrod	$2,000	Indiv
Patino-Treat & Rosen	$2,000	Indiv
Sills, Cummis et al	$2,000	Indiv

Misc Business   **$27,850**

Food & Beverage **$10,050**
El Unico Restaurant	$2,000	Indiv
Schuetzen Park	$2,000	Indiv

Retail Sales **$4,500**
    None over $1,500

Misc Services **$3,700**
Odorite	$2,000	Indiv

Business Services **$3,900**
    None over $1,500

Misc Manufacturing & Distributing **$3,300**
    None over $1,500

Transportation   **$11,900**

Air Transport **$2,550**
United Parcel Service	$2,250	PAC

Automotive **$5,600**
    None over $1,500

Trucking **$2,000**
    None over $1,500

Labor

Labor   **$86,431**

Building Trade Unions **$20,000**
Laborers' Political League	$6,000	PAC
Operating Engineers Union*	$6,000	PAC
Plumbers/Pipefitters #274	$5,000	PAC
Carpenters & Joiners Union	$3,000	PAC

Industrial Unions **$12,150**
United Auto Workers	$10,000	PAC

Transportation Unions **$25,781**
Seafarers International Union	$6,764	PAC
Marine Engineers Dist 2 Maritime Officers	$5,000	PAC
Teamsters Joint Council #73	$5,000	PAC
Trans Comm International Union	$4,267	PAC
Transport Workers Union	$1,500	PAC

Public Sector Unions **$19,500**
American Fedn of St/Cnty/Munic Employees	$7,500	PAC
National Education Assn	$5,000	PAC
National Assn of Letter Carriers	$3,500	PAC

Misc Unions **$9,000**
AFL-CIO	$5,000	PAC
Food & Commercial Workers Union	$2,500	PAC

Ideological/Single-Issue

Ideological/Single-Issue   **$38,789**

Democratic/Liberal **$6,050**
National Cmte for an Effective Congress	$5,050	PAC

Leadership PACs **$8,489**
Campaign for America (Frank Lautenberg)	$5,000	PAC

Foreign & Defense Policy **$10,000**
Free Cuba PAC	$10,000	PAC

Pro-Choice **$1,750**
    None over $1,500

Human Rights **$11,000**
Hispanic PAC USA	$6,500	PAC
Human Rights Campaign Fund	$2,000	PAC

Other & Unknown

Other   **$84,700**

Civil Servants/Public Officials **$38,900**
Union City Municipal Government	$28,350	Indiv
State of New Jersey	$6,000	Indiv

Education **$37,550**
Union City Board of Education	$30,150	Indiv
West New York Board of Education	$1,550	Indiv
Stevens Institute of Technology	$1,500	Indiv

Retired **$5,750**
    None over $1,500

Other **$2,500**
    None over $1,500

Unknown   **$107,421**

Homemakers/Non-income earners	$9,000	
No Employer Listed or Found	$28,650	
Generic Occupation/Category Unknown	$1,850	
Employer Listed/Category Unknown	$67,921	
PMK Engineers	$6,000	Indiv
Applied Companies	$4,000	Indiv
Albert E Sammartino	$3,000	Indiv
AAA Communications	$2,000	Indiv
Hindsight Inc	$2,000	Indiv
Union Kennedy Associates	$2,000	Indiv

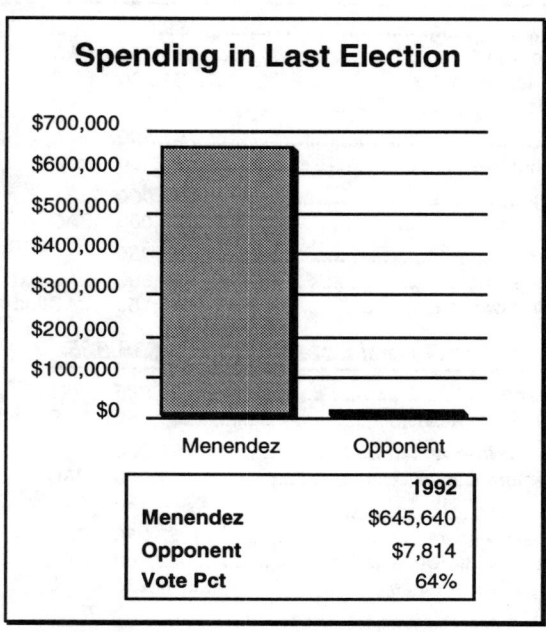

Spending in Last Election

	1992
Menendez	$645,640
Opponent	$7,814
Vote Pct	64%

---

* Contributions came from more than one affiliate or subsidiary.

Jan Meyers, R-Kan (3)

First elected: 1984

1991-92 Total Receipts: $440,290
1992 Year-end Cash: $403

1991-92 Committees & Subcommittees

Foreign Affairs
Europe and the Middle East; Western Hemisphere Affairs

Small Business
Regulation, Business Opportunity and Energy (Ranking Republican)

Select Committee on Aging

Leading Contributors

Business

Agriculture — $16,279

Agricultural Services/Products $5,604
Seabord Corp	$1,550	PAC
Archer-Daniels-Midland Corp	$1,250	PAC/Ind
Society of American Florists	$1,054	PAC
Deere & Co	$1,000	PAC

Food Processing & Sales $9,675
Pepsico Inc	$4,925	PAC
Food Marketing Institute	$1,900	PAC
Interstate Bakeries Corp	$1,250	Indiv

Communications/Electronics — $22,450

Printing & Publishing $6,825
Hallmark Cards	$5,750	PAC/Ind

Telephone Utilities $14,875
United Telecommunications	$7,500	PAC
AT&T	$3,000	PAC
Southwestern Bell	$2,025	PAC
BellSouth Corp*	$1,600	PAC

Construction — $20,450

General Contractors $7,750
Associated General Contractors	$2,900	PAC
Phillips Construction Co	$2,000	Indiv
Associated Builders & Contractors	$1,800	PAC
Builders Assn of Kansas City	$1,050	PAC

Home Builders $2,500
National Assn of Home Builders	$2,000	PAC

Source of Funds in 1992 Election

Source	Total	Pct
■ PACs	$211,395	48%
▨ Indivs $200+	$61,565	14%
☐ Indivs under $200	$145,995	33%
▨ Other	$24,835	6%
Candidate	$6,295	1%
Party	$13,500	3%

Source of PAC Dollars by Sector

Source	Total	Pct
■ Business	$169,924	83%
▨ Labor	$500	0%
☐ Ideology/Single Issue	$34,150	17%

In-State vs. Out-of-State Contributions*

Source	Total	Pct
☐ In-State	$54,640	90%
■ Out-of-state	$6,400	10%
No state listed	$0	

* by large individual contributors ($200 & above)

Special Trade Contractors $5,900
Sheet Metal/Air Conditioning Contractors	$2,400	PAC
National Electrical Contractors Assn	$2,000	PAC
American Subcontractors Assn	$1,000	PAC

Construction Services $2,000
None over $1,000

Building Materials & Equipment $2,300
Owens-Corning Fiberglas	$1,500	PAC

Defense — $3,400

Defense Aerospace $2,900
Allied-Signal	$1,900	PAC/Ind
Northrop Corp	$1,000	PAC

Energy & Natural Resources — $16,275

Oil & Gas $9,675
KPL Gas Service	$4,250	PAC
Petroleum Marketers Assn	$1,200	PAC
Ashland Oil	$1,000	PAC

Mining $1,500
Atkinson Industries	$1,500	Indiv

Nuclear Energy $1,000
General Atomics	$1,000	PAC

Electric Utilities $3,350
Utilicorp United Inc	$1,500	PAC/Ind
Kansas City Power & Light	$1,150	PAC/Ind

Finance, Insurance & Real Estate — $36,825

Commercial Banks $6,225
American Bankers Assn	$1,650	PAC

Securities & Investment $1,200
National Venture Capital Assn	$1,000	PAC

Insurance $13,450
Business Mens Assurance Co	$3,250	PAC
National Assn of Life Underwriters	$2,500	PAC
Kansas City Life Insurance	$1,250	PAC

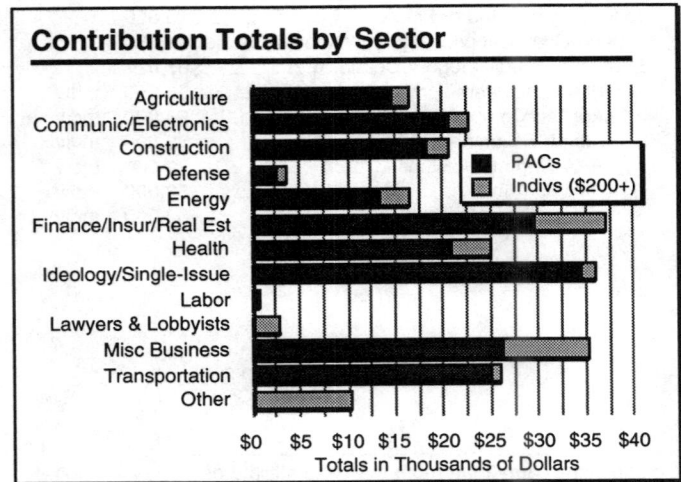

Contribution Totals by Sector

Agriculture, Communic/Electronics, Construction, Defense, Energy, Finance/Insur/Real Est, Health, Ideology/Single-Issue, Labor, Lawyers & Lobbyists, Misc Business, Transportation, Other

■ PACs
▨ Indivs ($200+)

$0 $5 $10 $15 $20 $25 $30 $35 $40
Totals in Thousands of Dollars

Real Estate	$8,350	
National Assn of Realtors	$3,000	PAC
JC Nichols Co	$2,100	PAC/Ind
Fishman Realty	$2,000	Indiv
Mortgage Bankers Assn of America	$1,000	PAC

Accountants	$3,500	
American Institute of CPA's	$3,000	PAC

Misc Finance	$2,850	
H&R Block	$2,400	PAC

Health $24,750

Health Professionals	$20,350	
American Medical Assn*	$10,000	PAC
American Academy of Ophthalmology	$1,000	PAC
American College of Emergency Physicians	$1,000	PAC
American Optometric Assn	$1,000	PAC
American Soc Plastic & Reconstr Surgeons	$1,000	PAC

Hospitals/Nursing Homes	$2,400	
American Hospital Assn	$1,900	PAC

Pharmaceuticals/Health Products	$1,750	
None over $1,000		

Lawyers & Lobbyists $2,700

Lawyers & Lobbyists	$2,700	
Logan & Logan	$1,050	Indiv

Misc Business $35,000

Business Associations	$3,000	
International Franchise Assn	$1,000	PAC

Food & Beverage	$12,050	
Pepsi-Cola General Bottlers	$5,000	PAC
McDonald's Corp	$2,000	PAC
National Restaurant Assn	$1,500	PAC
Pizza Hut Franchise Holders Assn	$1,000	PAC

Beer, Wine & Liquor	$2,500	
National Beer Wholesalers Assn	$1,750	PAC

Retail Sales	$3,450	
National Assn of Convenience Stores	$1,000	PAC

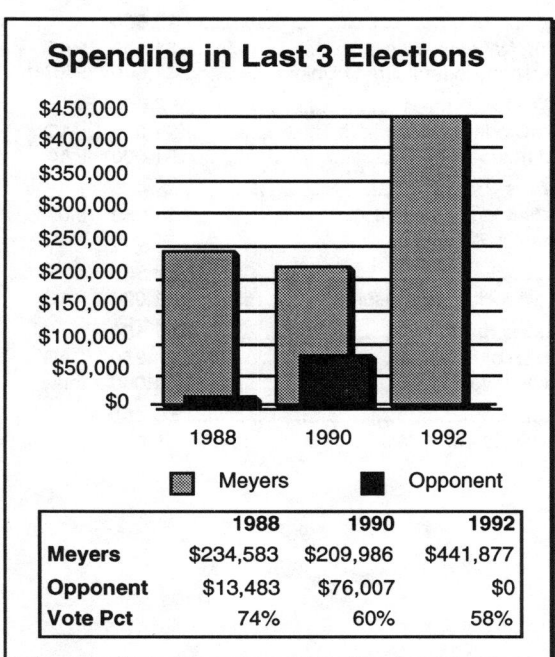

Spending in Last 3 Elections

	1988	1990	1992
Meyers	$234,583	$209,986	$441,877
Opponent	$13,483	$76,007	$0
Vote Pct	74%	60%	58%

Lodging/Tourism	$1,500	
None over $1,000		

Chemical & Related Manufacturing	$5,100	
Faultless Starch Co	$2,000	Indiv
Dow Chemical	$1,000	PAC

Misc Manufacturing & Distributing	$5,400	
IBT Inc	$2,000	Indiv
PPG Industries	$1,500	PAC

Transportation $25,820

Air Transport	$3,700	
United Parcel Service	$1,500	PAC

Automotive	$13,925	
National Auto Dealers Assn	$9,000	PAC
Auto Dealers & Drivers for Free Trade	$1,500	PAC
Ford Motor Co	$1,125	PAC
Americans for Free International Trade	$1,000	PAC

Trucking	$1,525	
Yellow Freight System	$1,400	PAC

Railroads	$6,670	
Kansas City Southern	$3,250	PAC/Ind
Burlington Northern	$2,020	PAC
Santa Fe Southern Pacific	$1,000	PAC

Ideological/Single-Issue

Ideological/Single-Issue $35,825

Republican/Conservative	$1,000	
Leader PAC	$1,000	PAC

Leadership PACs	$10,000	
Campaign America (Bob Dole)	$10,000	PAC

Foreign & Defense Policy	$1,000	
Veterans of Foreign Wars	$1,000	PAC

Pro-Israel	$7,725	
National PAC	$5,000	PAC

Pro-Choice	$1,700	
Republicans for Choice	$1,000	PAC

Gun Rights/Gun Control	$1,000	
Handgun Control Inc	$1,000	PAC

Womens Issues	$11,750	
Wish List	$7,500	PAC
Women's Campaign Fund	$3,000	PAC
National Womens Political Caucus	$1,000	PAC

Misc Issues	$1,400	
League of Conservation Voters	$1,000	PAC

Other & Unknown

Other $10,175

Education	$1,000	
Brown-Mackie Business College	$1,000	Indiv

Retired	$8,925	
None over $1,000		

Unknown $15,165

Homemakers/Non-income earners	$3,800	
Employer Listed/Category Unknown	$11,165	
Colonial Trading Co	$1,615	Indiv
HLI Group	$1,000	Indiv
John Head & Partners	$1,000	Indiv
Osborn Laboratories	$1,000	Indiv
Rig Industries	$1,000	Indiv

---

* Contributions came from more than one affiliate or subsidiary.

Kweisi Mfume, D-Md (7)

First elected: 1986

1991-92 Total Receipts: $255,269
1992 Year-end Cash: $123,136

1991-92 Committees & Subcommittees

Banking, Finance and Urban Affairs
Financial Institutions Supervision, Regulation and Insurance; Housing and Community Development

Small Business
SBA, the General Economy and Minority Enterprise Development

Select Committee on Narcotics Abuse and Control

Joint Economic Committee

Leading Contributors

Business

Agriculture		$5,050
Dairy		**$1,500**
Dairymen Inc	$1,000	PAC
Food Processing & Sales		**$2,700**
Connell Rice & Sugar Co	$1,000	Indiv

Communications/Electronics		$5,760
Printing & Publishing		**$1,070**
None over $1,000		
Telephone Utilities		**$1,400**
None over $1,000		
Computer Equipment & Services		**$1,850**
None over $1,000		

Construction		$5,290
General Contractors		**$2,450**
None over $1,000		
Home Builders		**$2,800**
National Assn of Home Builders	$1,300	PAC
Macks & Macks Inc	$1,000	Indiv

Energy & Natural Resources		$4,000
Oil & Gas		**$1,000**
Crown Central Petroleum	$1,000	PAC
Electric Utilities		**$2,500**
Baltimore Gas & Electric	$1,500	PAC

Source of Funds in 1992 Election

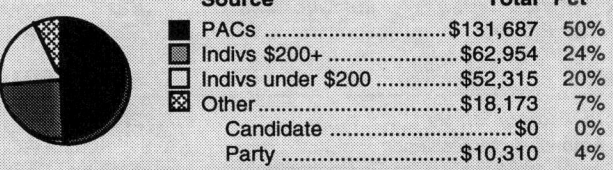

Source	Total	Pct
■ PACs	$131,687	50%
▨ Indivs $200+	$62,954	24%
☐ Indivs under $200	$52,315	20%
▨ Other	$18,173	7%
Candidate	$0	0%
Party	$10,310	4%

Source of PAC Dollars by Sector

Source	Total	Pct
■ Business	$63,080	51%
▨ Labor	$56,350	45%
☐ Ideology/Single Issue	$4,650	4%

In-State vs. Out-of-State Contributions*

Source	Total	Pct
☐ In-State	$53,054	83%
■ Out-of-state	$10,900	17%
No state listed	$0	

* by large individual contributors ($200 & above)

Finance, Insurance & Real Estate — $49,590

Commercial Banks		**$17,190**
American Bankers Assn	$3,000	PAC
National Bankers Assn	$3,000	PAC
MNC Financial Inc	$2,300	PAC
Barnett Banks Inc	$2,000	PAC
First Maryland Bancorp	$1,400	PAC
Mercantile Bankshares Corp	$1,400	PAC
Citicorp	$1,000	PAC
Citizens & Southern National Bank	$1,000	PAC
National City Corp	$1,000	PAC
Savings & Loans		**$2,000**
US League of Savings Assns	$2,000	PAC
Credit Unions		**$2,500**
Credit Union National Assn	$1,500	PAC
National Assn of Federal Credit Unions	$1,000	PAC
Finance/Credit Companies		**$2,000**
Associated Credit Bureaus	$1,000	PAC
Household International Inc	$1,000	PAC
Securities & Investment		**$5,400**
Pryor, McClendon, Counts & Co	$1,250	Indiv
Morgan Stanley & Co	$1,000	PAC
Insurance		**$2,850**
American Council of Life Insurance	$1,000	PAC
Real Estate		**$10,500**
National Assn of Realtors	$4,250	PAC
First Security Invest Co	$1,000	Indiv
Accountants		**$6,400**
American Institute of CPA's	$5,000	PAC

Contribution Totals by Sector

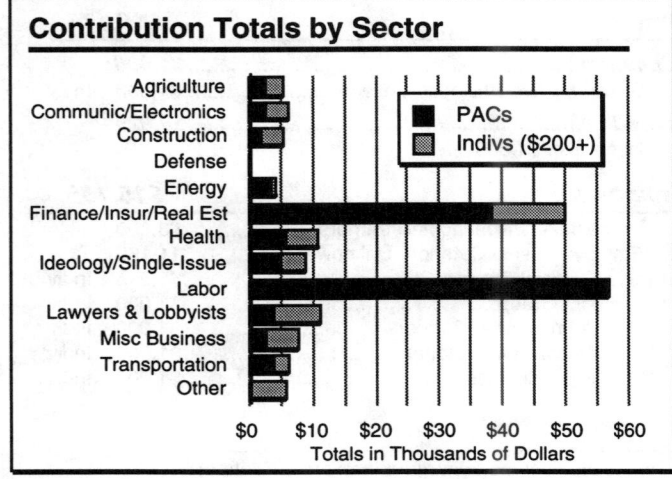

Legend: ■ PACs, ▨ Indivs ($200+)

Categories: Agriculture, Communic/Electronics, Construction, Defense, Energy, Finance/Insur/Real Est, Health, Ideology/Single-Issue, Labor, Lawyers & Lobbyists, Misc Business, Transportation, Other

Axis: $0, $10, $20, $30, $40, $50, $60
Totals in Thousands of Dollars

Health $10,570

Health Professionals **$6,820**
   American Medical Assn ....$2,250 PAC
   American Academy of Ophthalmology ....$2,000 PAC
   American Dental Assn ....$1,000 PAC

Hospitals/Nursing Homes **$2,600**
   Johns Hopkins Hospital ....$1,000 Indiv

Lawyers & Lobbyists $11,220

Lawyers & Lobbyists **$11,220**
   Assn of Trial Lawyers of America ....$2,500 PAC
   Gordon, Feinblatt et al ....$1,500 Indiv
   Snyder, Baron et al ....$1,250 Indiv
   Shaw, Pittman et al ....$1,000 PAC

Misc Business $7,600

Food & Beverage **$1,900**
   Hardee's Food Systems ....$1,000 PAC

Retail Sales **$1,450**
   JC Penney Co ....$1,000 PAC

Misc Services **$1,300**
   None over $1,000

Business Services **$1,000**
   None over $1,000

Transportation $5,790

Air Transport **$3,040**
   United Parcel Service ....$2,540 PAC

Sea Transport **$1,350**
   None over $1,000

Labor

Labor $56,350

Building Trade Unions **$6,900**
   Laborers' Political League ....$3,000 PAC
   AFL-CIO Bldg/Construction Trades Dept ....$1,500 PAC
   Operating Engineers Union ....$1,000 PAC
   Plumbers/Pipefitters Union ....$1,000 PAC

Industrial Unions **$18,650**
   United Steelworkers ....$5,000 PAC
   Machinists/Aerospace Workers Union ....$4,500 PAC
   United Auto Workers ....$3,000 PAC
   Intl Brotherhood of Electrical Workers ....$2,000 PAC
   Boilermakers Union ....$1,000 PAC

Transportation Unions **$13,000**
   Teamsters Union ....$5,500 PAC
   Marine Engineers Union* ....$3,000 PAC
   Masters, Mates & Pilots Union ....$1,500 PAC
   Amalgamated Transit Union ....$1,000 PAC

Public Sector Unions **$14,000**
   American Fedn of St/Cnty/Munic Employees ......$4,500 PAC
   National Education Assn ....$3,000 PAC
   American Postal Workers Union ....$2,000 PAC
   American Federation of Teachers ....$1,000 PAC
   National Assn Retired Federal Employees ....$1,000 PAC
   National Assn of Letter Carriers ....$1,000 PAC

Misc Unions **$3,800**
   Food & Commercial Workers Union ....$2,000 PAC

Ideological/Single-Issue

Ideological/Single-Issue $8,600

Pro-Israel **$3,850**
   None over $1,000

Human Rights **$1,000**
   Human Rights Campaign Fund ....$1,000 PAC

Misc Issues **$3,250**
   National Cmte to Preserve Social Security ....$3,250 PAC

Other & Unknown

Other $5,620

Retired **$2,520**
   None over $1,000

Other **$1,200**
   None over $1,000

Unknown $12,594

   Homemakers/Non-income earners $1,000
   No Employer Listed or Found $1,350
   Employer Listed/Category Unknown $10,244
     None over $1,000

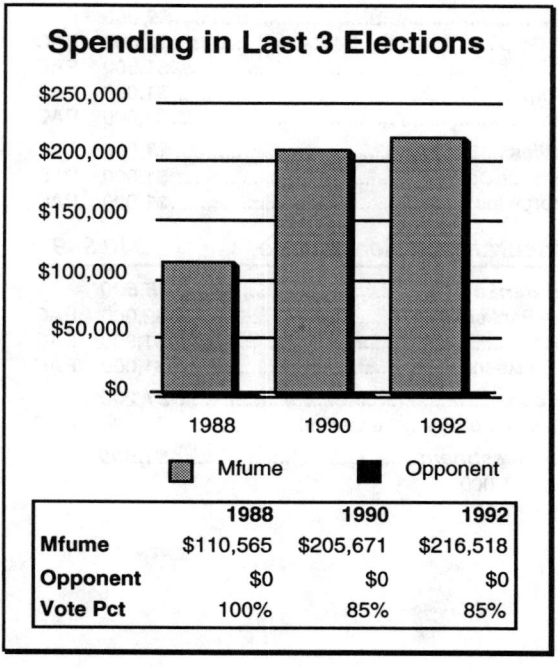

Spending in Last 3 Elections

	1988	1990	1992
Mfume	$110,565	$205,671	$216,518
Opponent	$0	$0	$0
Vote Pct	100%	85%	85%

* Contributions came from more than one affiliate or subsidiary.

John L. Mica, R-Fla (7)

First elected: 1992

| 1991-92 Total Receipts: | $598,764 |
| 1992 Year-end Cash: | $4,609 |

1993-94 Committees & Subcommittees

Government Operations
Environment, Energy and Natural Resources; Human Resources and Intergovernmental Relations

Public Works and Transportation
Aviation; Economic Development

Leading Contributors

Business

Agriculture	$19,300	
Crop Production & Basic Processing **$11,600**		
Okeelanta Corp $4,000		Indiv
Florida Fruit & Vegetable Assn $2,200		PAC/Ind
United States Sugar Corp $2,000		PAC
A Duda & Sons $1,400		PAC
Crittenden Fruit Co $1,000		Indiv
Florida Citrus Mutual $1,000		PAC
Tobacco **$2,000**		
RJR Nabisco $1,500		PAC
Agricultural Services/Products **$1,500**		
None over $1,000		
Food Processing & Sales **$3,500**		
Winn-Dixie Stores $2,000		PAC
Pepsico Inc $1,000		PAC

Communications/Electronics	$16,350	
Telephone Utilities **$5,000**		
Southern Bell $2,500		PAC
United Telecommunications $1,500		PAC
AT&T $1,000		PAC
Telecom Services & Equipment **$3,250**		
RF Communications $2,000		Indiv
More House Cellular $1,000		Indiv
Electronics Mfg & Services **$5,300**		
Harris Corp $4,550		PAC
Computer Equipment & Services **$1,500**		
Electronic Data Systems $1,000		PAC

Source of Funds in 1992 Election

Source	Total	Pct
■ PACs	$145,700	24%
▨ Indivs $200+	$96,229	16%
▢ Indivs under $200	$105,629	17%
▧ Other	$269,213	44%
Candidate	$185,000	30%
Party	$26,507	4%

Source of PAC Dollars by Sector

Source	Total	Pct
■ Business	$124,544	89%
▨ Labor	$1,000	1%
▢ Ideology/Single Issue	$13,700	10%

In-State vs. Out-of-State Contributions*

Source	Total	Pct
▢ In-State	$71,180	74%
▨ Out-of-state	$24,849	26%
No state listed	$200	

* by large individual contributors ($200 & above)

Construction	$4,650	
General Contractors **$2,450**		
Church & Tower of Florida $1,500		Indiv
Building Materials & Equipment **$1,000**		
None over $1,000		

Defense	$2,500	
Defense Aerospace **$2,500**		
Rockwell International $1,500		PAC

Energy & Natural Resources	$13,500	
Oil & Gas **$9,000**		
Chevron Corp $2,000		PAC
Sun Co $1,500		PAC
Enron Corp $1,000		PAC
Texaco $1,000		PAC
Electric Utilities **$3,000**		
Florida Power Corp $1,000		PAC
Teco Energy Inc $1,000		PAC

Finance, Insurance & Real Estate	$40,849	
Commercial Banks **$5,600**		
American Bankers Assn $2,000		PAC
SunBanks $1,200		PAC
Barnett Banks Inc $1,000		PAC
Savings & Loans **$1,200**		
Florida League of Financial Institutions $1,200		PAC
Securities & Investment **$1,000**		
None over $1,000		

Contribution Totals by Sector

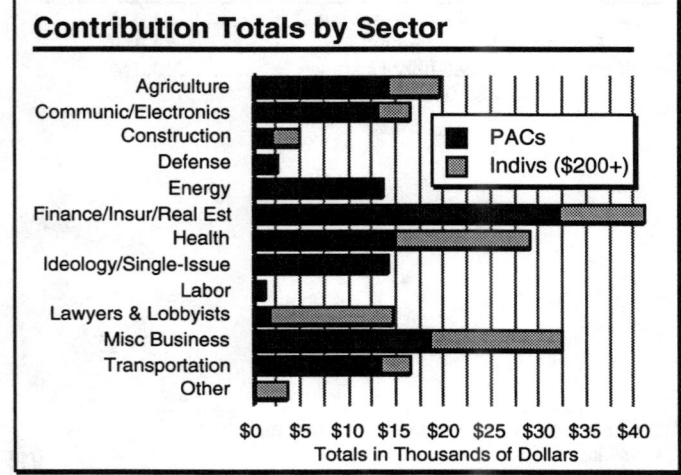

Agriculture
Communic/Electronics
Construction
Defense
Energy
Finance/Insur/Real Est
Health
Ideology/Single-Issue
Labor
Lawyers & Lobbyists
Misc Business
Transportation
Other

■ PACs
▨ Indivs ($200+)

$0 $5 $10 $15 $20 $25 $30 $35 $40
Totals in Thousands of Dollars

Insurance **$22,749**
 Northwestern Mutual Life .... $2,000   PAC
 Mutual of Omaha .... $1,500   PAC
 National Assn of Life Underwriters............ $1,500   PAC
 National Assn of Life Companies .... $1,250   PAC
 Blue Cross & Blue Shield Assn* .... $1,050   PAC
 Central Reserve Life Insurance Co .... $1,000   Indiv
 Insurance Associates .... $1,000   Indiv
 Mutual Life Insurance of New York .... $1,000   PAC

Real Estate **$9,350**
 National Assn of Realtors .... $5,000   PAC

Health $28,860

Health Professionals **$24,110**
 American Chiropractic Assn .... $5,000   PAC
 American Medical Assn............................. $5,000   PAC
 American Podiatry Assn .... $1,000   PAC

Hospitals/Nursing Homes **$1,650**
 American Hospital Assn .... $1,000   PAC

Pharmaceuticals/Health Products **$1,850**
 Eli Lilly & Co .... $1,000   PAC

Lawyers & Lobbyists $14,515

Lawyers & Lobbyists **$14,515**
 Bobo, Spicer et al .... $4,000   Indiv
 Pino & Dicks .... $2,499   Indiv
 Sylvester Lukis & Associates .... $1,000   Indiv

Misc Business $33,369

Business Associations **$2,545**
 National Fedn of Independent Business .... $1,500   PAC
 Business Industry PAC .... $1,045   PAC

Food & Beverage **$4,700**
 General Mills Restaurants .... $2,700   PAC
 Schenck Co .... $1,000   PAC/Ind

Beer, Wine & Liquor **$7,250**
 National Beer Wholesalers Assn .... $5,000   PAC
 ABC Liquors .... $1,000   Indiv

Retail Sales **$3,750**
 International Council of Shopping Centers .... $1,000   PAC
 Time & Sound Enterprises .... $1,000   Indiv

Misc Services **$1,000**
 Massey Services Inc .... $1,000   Indiv

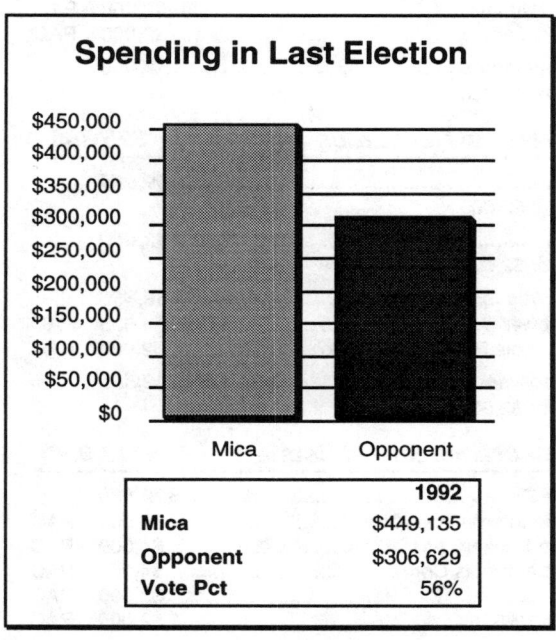

Spending in Last Election

	1992
Mica	$449,135
Opponent	$306,629
Vote Pct	56%

Business Services **$4,450**
 Mica Dudinsky & Associates .... $2,000   Indiv

Recreation/Live Entertainment **$1,474**
 Daytona Beach International Speedway .... $1,474   Indiv

Lodging/Tourism **$1,500**
 Tamar Inns Inc .... $1,000   Indiv

Chemical & Related Manufacturing **$3,250**
 Carbonic Industry .... $1,500   Indiv

Misc Manufacturing & Distributing **$3,750**
 Daniels Manufacturing Corp .... $2,000   Indiv

Transportation $16,300

Air Transport **$3,000**
 United Parcel Service .... $1,500   PAC

Automotive **$8,600**
 National Auto Dealers Assn .... $4,000   PAC
 Americans for Free International Trade .... $1,000   PAC
 Braman Enterprises .... $1,000   Indiv
 Eaton Corp .... $1,000   PAC

Railroads **$1,000**
 CSX Transportation Inc .... $1,000   PAC

Sea Transport **$3,000**
 Cruise PAC .... $1,500   PAC
 Hvide Shipping .... $1,000   Indiv

Labor

Labor   **$1,000**
 None over $1,000

Ideological/Single-Issue

Ideological/Single-Issue   **$13,950**

Leadership PACs **$2,000**
 Republican Leader's Fund (Bob Michel) .... $1,000   PAC

Foreign & Defense Policy **$3,500**
 Free Cuba PAC .... $3,500   PAC

Gun Rights/Gun Control **$4,950**
 National Rifle Assn .... $4,950   PAC

Misc Issues **$2,500**
 National Cmte to Preserve Social Security .... $1,000   PAC

Other & Unknown

Other   **$3,494**

Civil Servants/Public Officials **$1,950**
 Federal Maritime Commission .... $1,000   Indiv

Unknown   **$26,536**

 Homemakers/Non-income earners $5,375
 No Employer Listed or Found $7,680
 Employer Listed/Category Unknown $12,781
  Kellico .... $2,698   Indiv
  Bogan Aerotech .... $2,000   Indiv
  BSCF&B .... $1,000   Indiv
  Weiss & Stein .... $1,000   Indiv

Independent expenditures supporting Mica
 National Right to Life PAC $1,629

---

* Contributions came from more than one affiliate or subsidiary.

Robert H. Michel, R-Ill (18)

First elected: 1956

1991-92 Total Receipts:	$646,637
1992 Year-end Cash:	$252,205

1991-92 Committees & Subcommittees

Minority Leader

Leading Contributors

Business

Agriculture — $57,357

Crop Production & Basic Processing $3,000
None over $2,000

Tobacco $6,175
RJR Nabisco .... $3,000 PAC

Livestock $3,000
None over $2,000

Agricultural Services/Products $26,982
Archer-Daniels-Midland Corp .... $22,300 PAC/Ind
Deere & Co .... $2,000 PAC

Food Processing & Sales $15,700
AE Staley Manufacturing Co .... $5,000 PAC
Food Marketing Institute .... $3,000 PAC
Pepsico Inc .... $2,500 PAC
Ralphs Grocery Co .... $2,000 PAC

Communications/Electronics — $40,035

Printing & Publishing $2,500
None over $2,000

Media/Entertainment $14,000
National Assn of Broadcasters .... $5,000 PAC
Bowling Proprietors Assn .... $3,000 PAC

Telephone Utilities $18,785
Illinois Bell Telephone .... $4,285 PAC
GTE Corp .... $4,000 PAC
BellSouth Services .... $3,000 PAC
AT&T .... $2,000 PAC
Pacific Telesis Group .... $2,000 PAC

Computer Equipment & Services $2,250
None over $2,000

Source of Funds in 1992 Election

Source	Total	Pct
PACs	$403,027	62%
Indivs $200+	$115,085	18%
Indivs under $200	$100,327	16%
Other	$28,198	4%
Candidate	$0	0%
Party	$126	0%

Source of PAC Dollars by Sector

Source	Total	Pct
Business	$357,555	90%
Labor	$23,000	6%
Ideology/Single Issue	$15,000	4%

In-State vs. Out-of-State Contributions*

Source	Total	Pct
In-State	$77,435	68%
Out-of-state	$36,450	32%
No state listed	$1,200	

* by large individual contributors ($200 & above)

Construction — $24,545

General Contractors $9,165
Fluor Corp .... $3,000 PAC
Associated General Contractors .... $2,000 PAC

Home Builders $7,500
National Assn of Home Builders .... $7,500 PAC

Building Materials & Equipment $7,880
Caterpillar Tractor .... $6,630 PAC

Defense — $16,000

Defense Aerospace $11,500
Martin Marietta Corp .... $3,000 PAC
General Dynamics .... $2,000 PAC
Lockheed Corp .... $2,000 PAC

Defense Electronics $2,000
None over $2,000

Energy & Natural Resources — $25,385

Oil & Gas $9,000
None over $2,000

Mining $3,000
None over $2,000

Electric Utilities $9,885
Illinois Power Co .... $4,635 PAC
Central Illinois Public Service Co .... $2,000 PAC

Waste Management $2,500
None over $2,000

Finance, Insurance & Real Estate — $118,898

Commercial Banks $29,650
Exchange International Corp .... $5,000 PAC
American Bankers Assn .... $4,000 PAC
Continental Illinois Corp .... $4,000 PAC
Citicorp .... $3,000 PAC
Barnett Banks Inc .... $2,000 PAC

Contribution Totals by Sector

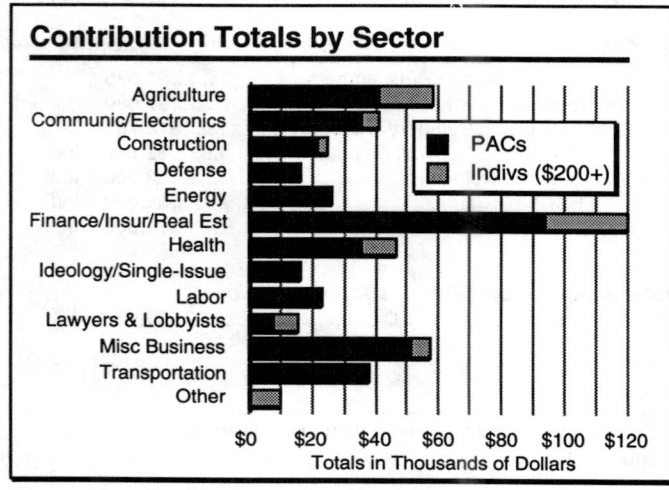

Categories (top to bottom): Agriculture, Communic/Electronics, Construction, Defense, Energy, Finance/Insur/Real Est, Health, Ideology/Single-Issue, Labor, Lawyers & Lobbyists, Misc Business, Transportation, Other

Legend: ■ PACs ☐ Indivs ($200+)

Totals in Thousands of Dollars: $0 $20 $40 $60 $80 $100 $120

Finance/Credit Companies **$4,000**
    Household International Inc ....$2,000 PAC

Securities & Investment **$16,750**
    Morgan Stanley & Co ....$5,000 PAC
    Chicago Mercantile Exchange ....$4,000 PAC
    Bear, Stearns & Co ....$2,000 PAC/Ind
    Chicago Board of Trade ....$2,000 PAC
    Sandler Capital Management ....$2,000 Indiv

Insurance **$40,448**
    National Assn of Life Underwriters......................$7,200 PAC
    Blue Cross & Blue Shield Assn ....$5,000 PAC/Ind
    Kemper Insurance ....$2,000 PAC
    Massachusetts Mutual Life Insurance ....$2,000 PAC
    Mutual of Omaha ....$2,000 PAC

Real Estate **$12,750**
    National Assn of Realtors ....$10,000 PAC

Accountants **$11,750**
    American Institute of CPA's ....$10,000 PAC

Health $46,025

Health Professionals **$30,100**
    American Medical Assn ....$10,000 PAC
    American Dental Assn ....$5,000 PAC
    National Assn of Pharmacists ....$3,000 PAC
    American Podiatry Assn ....$2,000 PAC

Hospitals/Nursing Homes **$10,175**
    Manor Healthcare Corp ....$2,500 PAC

Pharmaceuticals/Health Products **$5,500**
    None over $2,000

Lawyers & Lobbyists $15,250

Lawyers & Lobbyists **$15,250**
    None over $2,000

Misc Business $57,375

Food & Beverage **$3,500**
    National Restaurant Assn ....$2,000 PAC

Beer, Wine & Liquor **$14,000**
    National Beer Wholesalers Assn ....$4,000 PAC
    Smirnoff/Inglenook Distributors ....$2,000 PAC
    Wine & Spirits Wholesalers of America ....$2,000 PAC

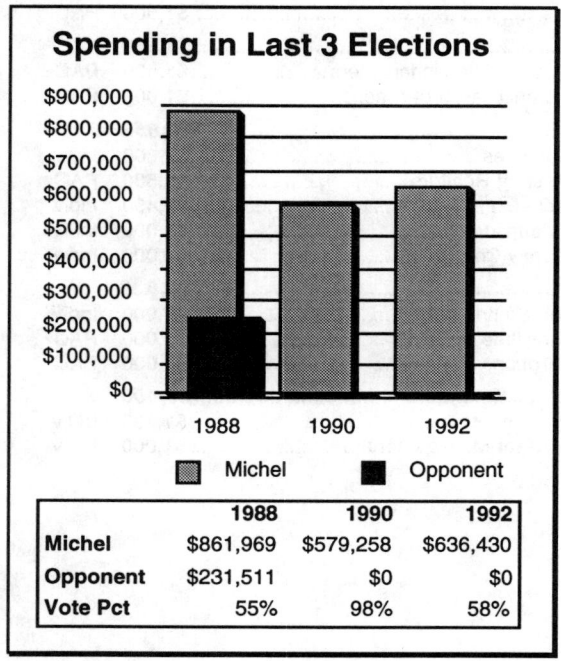

Spending in Last 3 Elections

	1988	1990	1992
Michel	$861,969	$579,258	$636,430
Opponent	$231,511	$0	$0
Vote Pct	55%	98%	58%

Legend: Michel, Opponent

Retail Sales **$10,450**
    International Council of Shopping Centers ....$2,000 PAC

Lodging/Tourism **$3,000**
    Marriott Corp ....$2,000 PAC

Misc Business **$3,000**
    None over $2,000

Chemical & Related Manufacturing **$5,250**
    None over $2,000

Misc Manufacturing & Distributing **$14,750**
    Corning Glass Works ....$3,000 PAC

Transportation $37,600

Air Transport **$16,325**
    United Parcel Service ....$6,510 PAC
    United Airlines ....$5,000 PAC

Automotive **$14,275**
    National Auto Dealers Assn ....$6,000 PAC
    Americans for Free International Trade ....$5,000 PAC

Railroads **$5,000**
    Union Pacific Corp ....$2,000 PAC

Labor

Labor   **$23,000**

Building Trade Unions **$2,000**
    Laborers' Political League ....$2,000 PAC

Transportation Unions **$9,000**
    Air Line Pilots Assn ....$5,000 PAC
    Marine Engineers Dist 2 Maritime Officers ....$4,000 PAC

Public Sector Unions **$10,000**
    National Rural Letter Carriers Assn ....$3,000 PAC
    National Assn of Letter Carriers ....$2,000 PAC

Ideological/Single-Issue

Ideological/Single-Issue   **$15,500**

Leadership PACs **$5,000**
    America 2000 Fund (Jim Thompson) ....$5,000 PAC

Pro-Israel **$5,500**
    National PAC ....$5,000 PAC

Gun Rights/Gun Control **$4,000**
    National Rifle Assn ....$4,000 PAC

Other & Unknown

Other   **$9,800**

Civil Servants/Public Officials **$2,250**
    None over $2,000

Retired **$6,550**
    None over $2,000

Unknown   **$23,870**

    Homemakers/Non-income earners $4,750
    No Employer Listed or Found $2,450
    Generic Occupation/Category Unknown $3,000
    Employer Listed/Category Unknown $13,670
        None over $2,000

Dan Miller, R-Fla (13)

1993-94 Committees & Subcommittees

Budget

Education and Labor
Elementary, Secondary and Vocational Education; Postsecondary Education and Training

Leading Contributors

Business

Agriculture	**$17,650**	
Crop Production & Basic Processing	**$5,300**	
Florida Citrus Mutual	$2,000	PAC
Manatee Fruit Co	$1,300	Indiv
Segrest Farms	$1,000	Indiv
Food Processing & Sales	**$10,250**	
Miller Enterprises	$5,250	Indiv
Winn-Dixie Stores	$1,500	PAC
Fleming Companies Inc	$1,000	PAC
Pepsico Inc	$1,000	PAC

Communications/Electronics	**$8,000**	
Media/Entertainment	**$1,000**	
WDUV Radio	$1,000	Indiv
Telephone Utilities	**$5,500**	
LDDS Communications	$2,000	Indiv
GTE Corp	$1,500	PAC
Southern Bell	$1,000	PAC
Electronics Mfg & Services	**$1,000**	
Harris Corp	$1,000	PAC

Construction	**$10,098**	
General Contractors	**$8,498**	
Neal, Adams & Burskirk	$3,398	Indiv
Gator Asphalt Highway Const	$1,500	Indiv
Associated General Contractors	$1,000	PAC
Special Trade Contractors	**$1,000**	
None over $1,000		

Source of Funds in 1992 Election

	Source	Total	Pct
■	PACs	$70,400	16%
▤	Indivs $200+	$160,559	35%
□	Indivs under $200	$97,988	22%
▨	Other	$124,246	27%
	Candidate	$122,500	27%
	Party	$500	0%

Source of PAC Dollars by Sector

	Source	Total	Pct
■	Business	$69,350	97%
▨	Labor	$0	0%
□	Ideology/Single Issue	$1,824	3%

In-State vs. Out-of-State Contributions*

	Source	Total	Pct
□	In-State	$150,909	96%
■	Out-of-state	$7,000	4%
	No state listed	$2,250	

* by large individual contributors ($200 & above)

Energy & Natural Resources	**$11,050**	
Oil & Gas	**$3,550**	
Ashland Oil	$2,000	PAC
Electric Utilities	**$2,250**	
Florida Power & Light	$1,000	PAC
Commercial Fishing	**$5,000**	
Segrest Fish Farms	$5,000	Indiv

Finance, Insurance & Real Estate	**$46,820**	
Commercial Banks	**$8,600**	
Barnett Banks Inc	$2,500	PAC/Ind
Citizens & Southern National Bank	$2,000	PAC
SunBanks	$1,500	PAC
Insurance	**$3,650**	
National Assn of Life Underwriters	$1,500	PAC
Health Insurance Assn of America	$1,000	PAC
Real Estate	**$20,850**	
Rickert Properties	$2,900	Indiv
National Assn of Realtors	$2,500	PAC
Neal & Neal	$2,450	Indiv
Pinellas Title Insurance	$1,000	Indiv
Trammell Crow Co	$1,000	Indiv
Accountants	**$6,820**	
Christopher, Smith et al	$2,000	Indiv
American Institute of CPA's	$1,000	PAC
Deloitte & Touche	$1,000	PAC
Misc Finance	**$6,400**	
Crouse Investment	$1,150	Indiv
Peninsula Asset Management	$1,000	Indiv

Contribution Totals by Sector

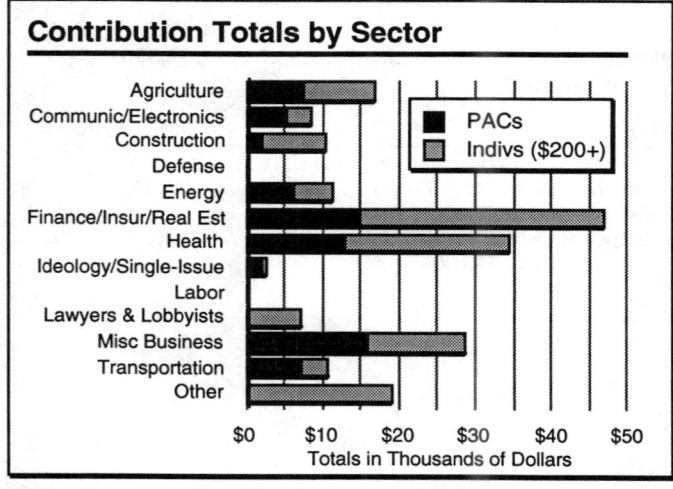

Legend: ■ PACs ▨ Indivs ($200+)

Categories: Agriculture, Communic/Electronics, Construction, Defense, Energy, Finance/Insur/Real Est, Health, Ideology/Single-Issue, Labor, Lawyers & Lobbyists, Misc Business, Transportation, Other

Totals in Thousands of Dollars ($0, $10, $20, $30, $40, $50)

Health $34,217

Health Professionals $27,350
American Medical Assn ....$5,000 PAC
American Optometric Assn ....$2,500 PAC
Eye Associates ....$1,500 Indiv
American Podiatry Assn ....$1,000 PAC

Hospitals/Nursing Homes $5,867
Brandon Hospital ....$2,000 Indiv
American Health Care Assn ....$1,500 PAC

Health Services $1,000
Novacare Inc ....$1,000 PAC

Lawyers & Lobbyists $6,749

Lawyers & Lobbyists $6,749
None over $1,000

Misc Business $28,450

Food & Beverage $8,500
National Restaurant Assn ....$6,500 PAC
Outback Steakhouse Inc ....$1,000 PAC

Beer, Wine & Liquor $4,000
National Beer Wholesalers Assn ....$4,000 PAC

Retail Sales $4,750
Beall's Department Store ....$1,500 Indiv

Business Services $2,000
Staff Leasing ....$2,000 Indiv

Recreation/Live Entertainment $1,000
Ringling Brothers Barnum & Bailey ....$1,000 Indiv

Chemical & Related Manufacturing $4,800
Continental Plastics ....$4,500 Indiv

Misc Manufacturing & Distributing $1,500
None over $1,000

Transportation $10,400

Air Transport $2,600
American Airlines ....$1,000 Indiv
United Parcel Service ....$1,000 PAC

Automotive $7,250
National Auto Dealers Assn ....$4,000 PAC
Eaton Corp ....$1,000 PAC

Ideological/Single-Issue

Ideological/Single-Issue $2,324

Leadership PACs $1,000
Republican Leader's Fund (Bob Michel) ....$1,000 PAC

Other & Unknown

Other $18,685

Civil Servants/Public Officials $2,250
Palm City Government ....$1,300 Indiv

Education $4,850
Manatee County School Board ....$1,000 Indiv

Retired $11,585
None over $1,000

Unknown $37,390

Homemakers/Non-income earners $16,738
No Employer Listed or Found $3,650
Generic Occupation/Category Unknown $3,500
Employer Listed/Category Unknown $13,002
Johnson Smith Co ....$2,000 Indiv
Harlee, Porges et al ....$1,800 Indiv
National Development Corp ....$1,200 Indiv
Dophin Aviation ....$1,000 Indiv
Michael Sanders & Co ....$1,000 Indiv
Southern Corp ....$1,000 Indiv
Townsend, Lassen ....$1,000 Indiv

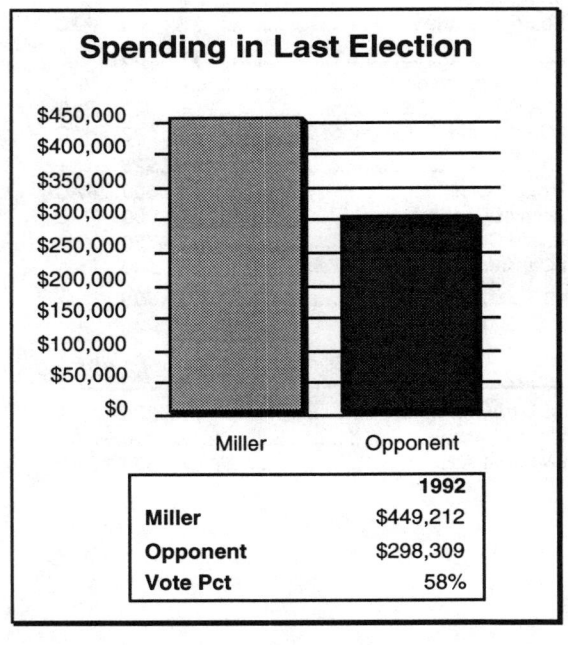

Spending in Last Election

	1992
Miller	$449,212
Opponent	$298,309
Vote Pct	58%

George Miller, D-Calif (7)

First elected: 1974

1991-92 Total Receipts: $542,532
1992 Year-end Cash: $328,659

1991-92 Committees & Subcommittees

Education and Labor
Elementary, Secondary and Vocational Education; Labor-Management Relations; Postsecondary Education

Interior and Insular Affairs (Chairman)
Insular and International Affairs; Water, Power and Offshore Energy (Chairman)

Select Committee on Children, Youth and Families

Leading Contributors

Business

Agriculture	$11,025

Crop Production & Basic Processing	$5,625
None over $1,500	

Livestock	$1,750
None over $1,500	

Communications/Electronics	$14,500

Media/Entertainment	$11,500	
MCA Inc	$2,000	PAC/Ind

Telephone Utilities	$2,500	
Pacific Telesis Group	$1,500	PAC

Construction	$11,050

General Contractors	$3,550	
None over $1,500		

Construction Services	$2,500	
None over $1,500		

Building Materials & Equipment	$4,000	
Morgan Equipment Co	$2,000	Indiv

Energy & Natural Resources	$55,341

Oil & Gas	$12,716	
Chevron Corp	$3,250	Indiv
Pacific Enterprises	$2,500	PAC
Atlantic Richfield	$2,000	PAC

Nuclear Energy	$2,750	
Westinghouse Electric	$1,750	PAC

Contribution Totals by Sector

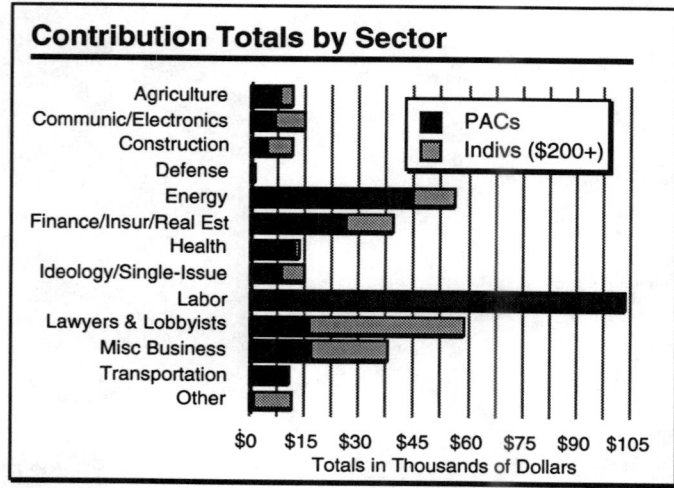

Totals in Thousands of Dollars

Source of Funds in 1992 Election

Source	Total	Pct
PACs	$261,290	48%
Indivs $200+	$137,299	25%
Indivs under $200	$81,326	15%
Other	$68,031	12%
Candidate	$0	0%
Party	$5,564	1%

Source of PAC Dollars by Sector

Source	Total	Pct
Business	$143,291	56%
Labor	$102,825	40%
Ideology/Single Issue	$8,590	3%

In-State vs. Out-of-State Contributions*

Source	Total	Pct
In-State	$68,749	51%
Out-of-state	$65,300	49%
No state listed	$0	

* by large individual contributors ($200 & above)

Misc Energy	$8,000	
Bechtel Corp	$7,000	PAC

Electric Utilities	$21,875	
Southern California Edison	$7,500	PAC
Pacific Gas & Electric	$4,500	PAC

Waste Management	$8,000	
Waste Management Inc	$4,500	PAC
Richmond Sanitary Service	$3,000	Indiv

Finance, Insurance & Real Estate	$38,600

Commercial Banks	$2,500	
BankAmerica Corp	$2,000	PAC

Securities & Investment	$5,750	
Chicago Board of Trade	$2,000	PAC

Insurance	$11,500	
Metropolitan Life Insurance	$3,000	PAC
Pacific Mutual Life	$2,000	PAC
American Council of Life Insurance	$1,500	PAC

Real Estate	$16,525	
Bedford Properties	$3,500	PAC
National Assn of Realtors	$3,000	PAC
Haas & Haynie Corp	$1,750	Indiv
American Capital Management	$1,500	Indiv

Accountants	$1,500	
None over $1,500		

Health	$13,225

Health Professionals	$11,225	
American Dental Assn	$4,000	PAC
American Medical Assn	$3,850	PAC

Lawyers & Lobbyists $58,424

Lawyers & Lobbyists **$58,424**
Assn of Trial Lawyers of America	$5,000	PAC
Winston & Strawn	$3,000	Indiv
Akin, Gump et al	$2,000	PAC
Nossaman, Gunther et al	$2,000	Indiv
Dickstein, Shapiro & Morin	$1,500	PAC
Kogovsek & Associates	$1,500	Indiv
Perkins Coie	$1,500	Indiv

Misc Business $37,500

Beer, Wine & Liquor **$5,500**
California Beer & Wine Wholesalers	$2,000	Indiv

Retail Sales **$1,500**
None over $1,500

Business Services **$5,100**
None over $1,500

Casinos/Gambling **$18,000**
Nevada Resort Assn	$5,000	PAC
Circus Circus Enterprises	$2,000	Indiv
Horseshoe Hotel & Casino	$2,000	Indiv

Lodging/Tourism **$2,000**
Conference of National Park Concessioners	$1,500	PAC

Misc Manufacturing & Distributing **$2,500**
Marwais Steel Co	$1,500	Indiv

Transportation $10,400

Air Transport **$6,800**
Federal Express Corp	$3,000	PAC
General Electric	$1,500	PAC

Railroads **$2,000**
None over $1,500

Labor

Labor $102,825

Building Trade Unions **$20,675**
Laborers Union*	$7,000	PAC
Plumbers/Pipefitters Union	$4,000	PAC
California State Pipe Trades Council	$2,000	PAC
Ironworkers Union	$1,875	PAC
Painters & Allied Trades Union	$1,500	PAC
Sheet Metal Workers Union	$1,500	PAC

Industrial Unions **$21,525**
Intl Brotherhood of Electrical Workers	$4,500	PAC
United Auto Workers	$4,000	PAC
Machinists/Aerospace Workers Union	$3,525	PAC
Communications Workers of America	$3,000	PAC
Oil, Chemical & Atomic Workers Union	$2,500	PAC
Boilermakers Union	$2,000	PAC
United Mine Workers	$2,000	PAC

Transportation Unions **$31,350**
Teamsters Union	$10,000	PAC
Intl Longshoremen's/Warehousemen's Union	$6,000	PAC
United Transportation Union	$4,500	PAC
Air Line Pilots Assn	$2,500	PAC
Amalgamated Transit Union	$2,000	PAC
Marine Engineers Union*	$2,000	PAC

Public Sector Unions **$19,525**
American Fedn of St/Cnty/Munic Employees	$5,000	PAC
National Assn of Letter Carriers*	$3,225	PAC
National Education Assn	$2,150	PAC
American Federation of Teachers	$2,000	PAC
National Assn Retired Federal Employees	$2,000	PAC
International Assn of Firefighters	$1,500	PAC
National Assn of Postmasters	$1,500	PAC

Misc Unions **$9,750**
Hotel/Restaurant Employees Union	$5,000	PAC
Food & Commercial Workers Union	$3,000	PAC

Ideological/Single-Issue

Ideological/Single-Issue $14,640

Democratic/Liberal **$4,500**
None over $1,500

Pro-Choice **$1,740**
None over $1,500

Human Rights **$4,000**
KidsPAC	$2,500	PAC

Misc Issues **$3,900**
Sierra Club	$2,750	PAC/Ind

Other & Unknown

Other $11,125

Non-Profit Institutions **$2,000**
Foundation for Hearing Aid Research	$2,000	Indiv

Education **$5,000**
Case Western Reserve University	$2,000	Indiv
Dalton School/NY Public School System	$2,000	Indiv

Retired **$2,900**
None over $1,500

Unknown $13,450

Employer Listed/Category Unknown	$11,225	
United Council Spanish Spkg	$1,500	Indiv

* Contributions came from more than one affiliate or subsidiary.

Spending in Last 3 Elections

	1988	1990	1992
Miller	$269,887	$448,026	$651,360
Opponent	$15,311	$47,912	$60,747
Vote Pct	68%	61%	70%

Norman Y. Mineta, D-Calif (15)

First elected: 1974

1991-92 Total Receipts: $967,049
1992 Year-end Cash: $197,336

1991-92 Committees & Subcommittees

Public Works and Transportation
Aviation; Investigations and Oversight; Surface Transportation (Chairman)

Science, Space and Technology
Space; Technology and Competitiveness

Leading Contributors

Business

Agriculture	$18,035

Food Processing & Sales $7,060
   None over $5,000

Communications/Electronics	$40,076

Media/Entertainment $6,500
   None over $5,000

Telephone Utilities $10,300
   None over $5,000

Electronics Mfg & Services $6,950
   None over $5,000

Computer Equipment & Services $12,576
   None over $5,000

Construction	$66,500

General Contractors $25,680
   Associated General Contractors .... $5,000   PAC

Construction Services $29,850
   American Consulting Engineers Council ...... $6,000   PAC

Building Materials & Equipment $8,000
   None over $5,000

Defense	$13,898

Defense Aerospace $8,798
   Lockheed Corp .... $8,548   PAC/Ind

Defense Electronics $5,100
   None over $5,000

Source of Funds in 1992 Election

Source	Total	Pct
■ PACs	$544,795	56%
▦ Indivs $200+	$263,401	27%
□ Indivs under $200	$110,299	11%
▨ Other	$51,903	5%
Candidate	$0	0%
Party	$3,499	0%

Source of PAC Dollars by Sector

Source	Total	Pct
■ Business	$403,137	73%
▦ Labor	$140,690	25%
□ Ideology/Single Issue	$11,552	2%

In-State vs. Out-of-State Contributions*

Source	Total	Pct
□ In-State	$146,454	56%
■ Out-of-state	$114,380	44%
No state listed	$205	

* by large individual contributors ($200 & above)

Energy & Natural Resources	$23,500

Oil & Gas $11,000
   None over $5,000

Electric Utilities $6,950
   None over $5,000

Finance, Insurance & Real Estate	$66,900

Commercial Banks $12,350
   None over $5,000

Securities & Investment $8,500
   None over $5,000

Insurance $18,200
   Independent Insurance Agents of America .... $5,000   PAC

Real Estate $24,000
   National Assn of Realtors .... $8,500   PAC

Health	$26,150

Health Professionals $16,275
   American Medical Assn .... $9,500   PAC

Pharmaceuticals/Health Products $8,025
   Syntex (USA) Inc .... $5,525   PAC

Lawyers & Lobbyists	$80,335

Lawyers & Lobbyists $80,335
   Assn of Trial Lawyers of America .... $10,000   PAC

Contribution Totals by Sector

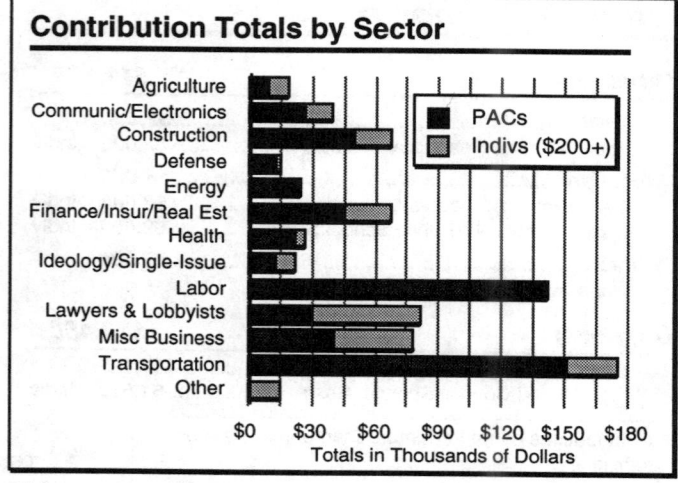

Agriculture
Communic/Electronics
Construction
Defense
Energy
Finance/Insur/Real Est
Health
Ideology/Single-Issue
Labor
Lawyers & Lobbyists
Misc Business
Transportation
Other

PACs
Indivs ($200+)

$0 $30 $60 $90 $120 $150 $180
Totals in Thousands of Dollars

Misc Business $77,834

Beer, Wine & Liquor *$6,500*
   None over $5,000

Business Services *$30,850*
   Outdoor Advertising Assn of America .... $5,500 PAC/Ind

Chemical & Related Manufacturing *$7,760*
   None over $5,000

Misc Manufacturing & Distributing *$10,874*
   None over $5,000

Transportation $174,359

Air Transport *$59,944*
   United Parcel Service .... $7,450 PAC
   Aircraft Owners & Pilots Assn .... $7,000 PAC
   Federal Express Corp .... $6,125 PAC

Automotive *$14,050*
   None over $5,000

Trucking *$45,665*
   Owner-Operator Independent Drivers Assn .... $5,000 PAC
   Roadway Services Inc* .... $5,000 PAC
   Yellow Freight System .... $5,000 PAC

Railroads *$29,000*
   ITEL Corp .... $5,000 PAC
   Union Pacific Corp .... $5,000 PAC

Sea Transport *$8,500*
   American President Lines .... $5,000 PAC

Misc Transport *$17,200*
   None over $5,000

Labor

Labor $140,690

Building Trade Unions *$20,220*
   Laborers Union* .... $6,000 PAC
   Carpenters & Joiners Union .... $5,500 PAC

Industrial Unions *$18,432*
   Machinists/Aerospace Workers Union .... $6,000 PAC
   United Auto Workers .... $6,000 PAC

Transportation Unions *$56,300*
   Air Line Pilots Assn .... $10,000 PAC
   Teamsters Union .... $10,000 PAC
   Transport Workers Union .... $7,000 PAC
   Amalgamated Transit Union .... $6,000 PAC
   Marine Engineers Union* .... $5,500 PAC

Public Sector Unions *$37,828*
   National Assn Retired Federal Employees .... $10,000 PAC
   National Assn of Letter Carriers* .... $6,988 PAC
   National Education Assn .... $6,500 PAC
   American Fedn of St/Cnty/Munic Employees ...... $5,500 PAC

Misc Unions *$7,910*
   None over $5,000

Ideological/Single-Issue

Ideological/Single-Issue $21,601

Democratic/Liberal *$7,949*
   None over $5,000

Other & Unknown

Other $15,696

Retired *$9,050*
   None over $5,000

Unknown $52,444

   Homemakers/Non-income earners $5,650
   No Employer Listed or Found $8,484
   Employer Listed/Category Unknown $37,560
      None over $5,000

Spending in Last 3 Elections

	1988	1990	1992
Mineta	$521,674	$644,962	$1,112,414
Opponent	$25,511	$624	$11,067
Vote Pct	67%	58%	64%

* Contributions came from more than one affiliate or
subsidiary.

David Minge, D-Minn (2)

First elected: 1992

1991-92 Total Receipts: $331,983
1992 Year-end Cash: $7,499

1993-94 Committees & Subcommittees

Agriculture
Environment, Credit and Rural Development; General Farm Commodities; Specialty Crops and Natural Resources

Science, Space and Technology
Science; Technology, Environment and Aviation

Leading Contributors

Business

Agriculture		$16,450

Crop Production & Basic Processing	$9,500	
Southern Minn Beet Sugar Co-op	$6,500	PAC
Dairy	$2,500	
Associated Milk Producers	$2,500	PAC
Agricultural Services/Products	$2,550	
None over $1,000		
Food Processing & Sales	$1,400	
General Mills	$1,000	PAC

Communications/Electronics		$4,250

Printing & Publishing	$2,900	
Deluxe Check Printing Inc	$2,900	Indiv
Telephone Utilities	$1,250	
US West Inc	$1,250	PAC

Energy & Natural Resources		$2,450

| Electric Utilities | $2,250 | |
| ACRE (Action Cmte for Rural Electrification) | $2,000 | PAC |

Finance, Insurance & Real Estate		$10,720

Commercial Banks	$2,700	
Independent Bankers Assn	$1,300	PAC
Credit Unions	$1,000	
Credit Union National Assn	$1,000	PAC
Insurance	$3,000	
National Assn of Life Underwriters	$1,500	PAC
Northwestern National Life	$1,000	PAC

Source of Funds in 1992 Election

	Source	Total	Pct
■	PACs	$164,228	48%
▨	Indivs $200+	$59,310	17%
☐	Indivs under $200	$87,631	25%
⊠	Other	$33,757	10%
	Candidate	$0	0%
	Party	$21,287	6%

Source of PAC Dollars by Sector

	Source	Total	Pct
■	Business	$34,210	22%
▨	Labor	$110,500	71%
☐	Ideology/Single Issue	$11,900	8%

In-State vs. Out-of-State Contributions*

	Source	Total	Pct
☐	In-State	$53,760	92%
■	Out-of-state	$4,850	8%
	No state listed	$500	

* by large individual contributors ($200 & above)

Real Estate	$1,020	
None over $1,000		
Misc Finance	$1,700	
None over $1,000		

Health		$5,024

Health Professionals	$3,324	
American Medical Assn	$1,000	PAC
Hospitals/Nursing Homes	$1,700	
American Health Care Assn	$1,000	PAC

Lawyers & Lobbyists		$11,686

Lawyers & Lobbyists	$11,686	
Faegre & Benson	$1,601	PAC/Ind
Popham, Haik et al	$1,300	PAC/Ind
Nelson, Oyen et al	$1,050	Indiv

Misc Business		$4,050

Retail Sales	$1,050	
Dayton Hudson Corp	$1,050	PAC/Ind
Business Services	$2,500	
Impact Plastics Advertising Inc	$2,500	Indiv

Transportation		$3,300

| Automotive | $1,300 | |
| National Auto Dealers Assn | $1,000 | PAC |

Contribution Totals by Sector

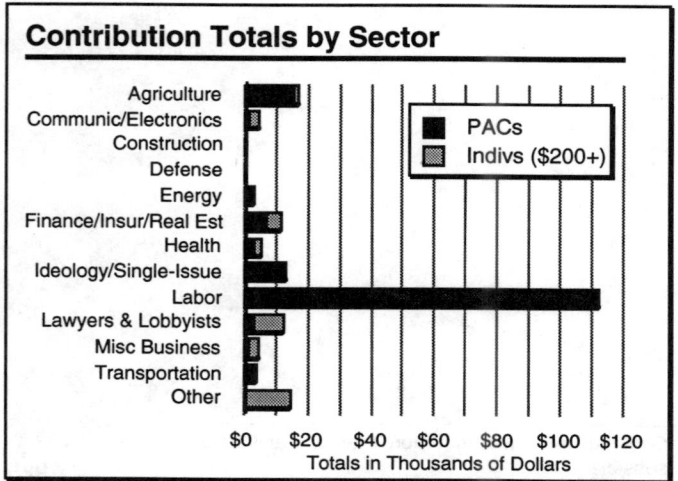

Agriculture
Communic/Electronics
Construction
Defense
Energy
Finance/Insur/Real Est
Health
Ideology/Single-Issue
Labor
Lawyers & Lobbyists
Misc Business
Transportation
Other

■ PACs
▨ Indivs ($200+)

$0 $20 $40 $60 $80 $100 $120
Totals in Thousands of Dollars

Labor

Labor $111,100

Building Trade Unions **$10,550**
Carpenters & Joiners Union	$4,500	PAC
Sheet Metal Workers Union	$2,500	PAC
Laborers' Political League	$1,500	PAC
Ironworkers Union	$1,000	PAC

Industrial Unions **$31,850**
United Auto Workers	$10,000	PAC
United Steelworkers	$10,000	PAC
Intl Brotherhood of Electrical Workers	$3,750	PAC
Machinists/Aerospace Workers Union	$3,500	PAC
Communications Workers of America	$2,500	PAC

Transportation Unions **$15,850**
Teamsters Union	$5,000	PAC
United Transportation Union	$4,000	PAC
National Air Traffic Controllers Assn	$2,000	PAC
Trans Comm International Union	$1,100	PAC
Air Line Pilots Assn	$1,000	PAC
Amalgamated Transit Union	$1,000	PAC
Brotherhood of Locomotive Engineers	$1,000	PAC

Public Sector Unions **$39,750**
American Federation of Teachers	$10,000	PAC
National Education Assn	$10,000	PAC
American Fedn of St/Cnty/Munic Employees	$7,500	PAC
National Assn Retired Federal Employees	$5,000	PAC
National Assn of Letter Carriers	$5,000	PAC

Misc Unions **$13,100**
Food & Commercial Workers Union	$6,500	PAC
AFL-CIO	$5,100	PAC
Service Employees International Union	$1,000	PAC

Ideological/Single-Issue

Ideological/Single-Issue $12,300

Democratic/Liberal **$2,640**
National Cmte for an Effective Congress	$2,500	PAC

Leadership PACs **$2,400**
Effective Government Cmte (Dick Gephardt)	$1,000	PAC
House Leadership Fund (Tom Foley)	$1,000	PAC

Pro-Choice **$1,250**
National Abortion Rights Action League	$1,000	PAC

Gun Rights/Gun Control **$1,000**
Handgun Control Inc	$1,000	PAC

Misc Issues **$4,560**
League of Conservation Voters	$2,790	PAC
National Cmte to Preserve Social Security	$1,000	PAC

Other & Unknown

Other $14,350

Civil Servants/Public Officials **$3,200**
State of Minnesota	$3,000	Indiv

Education **$4,200**
SW&WC ECSU	$1,900	Indiv
Montavideo Public School	$1,500	Indiv

Retired **$6,750**
None over $1,000

Unknown $20,040
No Employer Listed or Found	$8,490	
Generic Occupation/Category Unknown	$2,200	
Employer Listed/Category Unknown	$8,450	
Steiner-Copplum Contractor	$3,600	Indiv

Independent expenditures supporting Minge
Planned Parenthood of Minnesota	$4,933

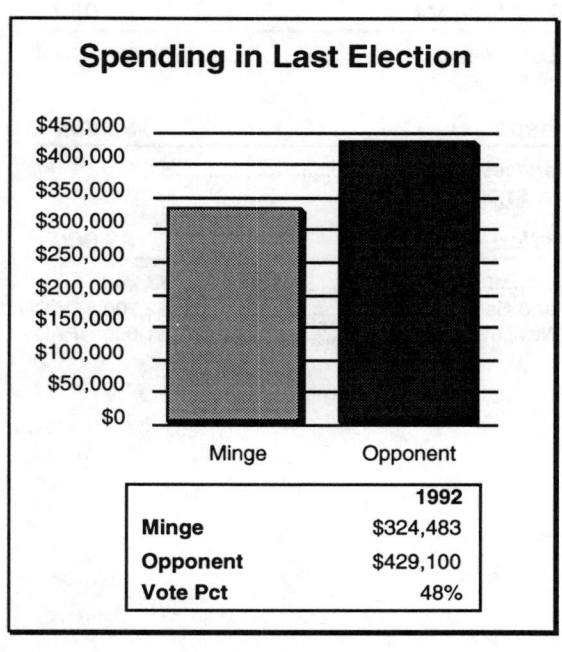

Spending in Last Election

	1992
Minge	$324,483
Opponent	$429,100
Vote Pct	48%

Patsy T. Mink, D-Hawaii (2)

First elected: 1990
(also served 1965-77)
1991-92 Total Receipts: $332,881
1992 Year-end Cash: $49,359

1991-92 Committees & Subcommittees

Education and Labor
Elementary, Secondary and Vocational Education; Labor-Management Relations; Postsecondary Education

Government Operations
Government Information, Justice and Agriculture; Human Resources and Intergovernmental Relations

Leading Contributors

Business

Agriculture	**$5,132**	
Crop Production & Basic Processing	$1,600	
None over $1,000		
Dairy	$1,500	
Associated Milk Producers	$1,500	PAC
Food Processing & Sales	$1,532	
None over $1,000		

Communications/Electronics	**$1,776**	
GTE Corp*	$1,626	PAC

Construction	**$5,850**	
General Contractors	$2,800	
WT Yoshimoto Corp	$1,750	Indiv
Construction Services	$2,850	
Gima, Yoshimori & Associates	$1,000	Indiv

Energy & Natural Resources	**$2,250**	
Oil & Gas	$1,500	
Pacific Resources	$1,500	PAC

Finance, Insurance & Real Estate	**$26,400**	
Commercial Banks	$6,350	
Bancorp Hawaii	$2,600	PAC
First Hawaiian Inc	$2,250	PAC
Central Pacific Bank	$1,000	PAC
Credit Unions	$1,500	
Credit Union National Assn	$1,500	PAC
Insurance	$1,500	
None over $1,000		
Real Estate	$11,650	
National Assn of Realtors	$10,000	PAC
Accountants	$5,000	
American Institute of CPA's	$5,000	PAC

Health	**$7,700**	
Health Professionals	$6,400	
American Nurses Assn	$1,500	PAC
Cytopath Inc	$1,000	Indiv
Hawaii Medical Assn	$1,000	PAC
Misc Health	$1,300	
Queen's Medical Center	$1,300	Indiv

Lawyers & Lobbyists	**$5,050**	
Lawyers & Lobbyists	$5,050	
None over $1,000		

Misc Business	**$2,800**	
Business Services	$1,150	
None over $1,000		

Transportation	**$3,900**	
Sea Transport	$3,700	
Alexander & Baldwin Inc	$2,700	PAC/Ind
Matson Navigation	$1,000	PAC

Source of Funds in 1992 Election

Source	Total	Pct
PACs	$113,425	34%
Indivs $200+	$56,482	17%
Indivs under $200	$151,655	45%
Other	$16,365	5%
Candidate	$0	0%
Party	$5,196	2%

Source of PAC Dollars by Sector

Source	Total	Pct
Business	$36,476	33%
Labor	$75,399	67%
Ideology/Single Issue	$1	0%

In-State vs. Out-of-State Contributions*

Source	Total	Pct
In-State	$53,082	94%
Out-of-state	$3,400	6%
No state listed	$0	

* by large individual contributors ($200 & above)

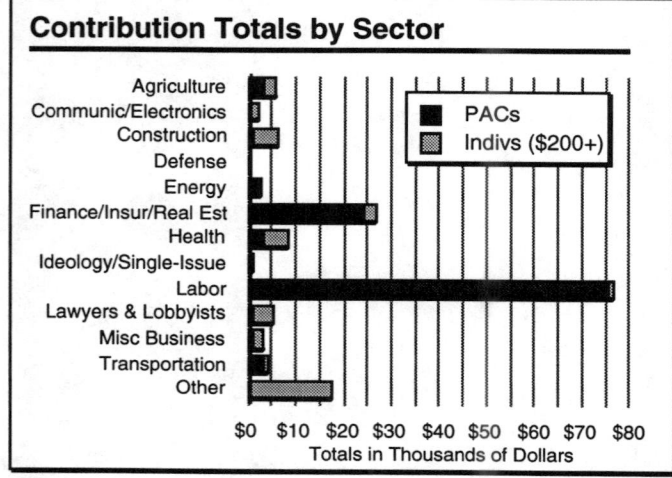

Contribution Totals by Sector

Legend: ■ PACs ▨ Indivs ($200+)

Sectors: Agriculture, Communic/Electronics, Construction, Defense, Energy, Finance/Insur/Real Est, Health, Ideology/Single-Issue, Labor, Lawyers & Lobbyists, Misc Business, Transportation, Other

$0 $10 $20 $30 $40 $50 $60 $70 $80
Totals in Thousands of Dollars

Labor

Labor		**$76,399**
Building Trade Unions	**$21,000**	
Carpenters & Joiners Union	$10,000	PAC
Laborers' Political League	$5,000	PAC
Operating Engineers Union*	$2,500	PAC
Plumbers/Pipefitters #675	$2,000	PAC
Industrial Unions	**$19,000**	
Machinists/Aerospace Workers Union	$10,000	PAC
Intl Brotherhood of Electrical Workers	$3,000	PAC
United Auto Workers	$3,000	PAC
Boilermakers Union	$1,000	PAC
Transportation Unions	**$13,700**	
Intl Longshoremen's/Warehousemen's Union	$6,200	PAC
Teamsters Union*	$3,500	PAC
Air Line Pilots Assn	$1,000	PAC
Marine Engineers Dist 2 Maritime Officers	$1,000	PAC
Seafarers International Union	$1,000	PAC
Public Sector Unions	**$18,699**	
National Assn Retired Federal Employees	$6,000	PAC
American Fedn of St/Cnty/Munic Employees	$4,999	PAC
National Education Assn	$3,300	PAC
National Assn of Letter Carriers	$3,000	PAC
Misc Unions	**$4,000**	
Food & Commercial Workers Union	$2,500	PAC
AFL-CIO	$1,500	PAC

Other & Unknown

Other		**$17,350**
Civil Servants/Public Officials	**$1,350**	
None over $1,000		
Education	**$1,350**	
None over $1,000		
Retired	**$11,850**	
None over $1,000		
Other	**$2,800**	
Hydrologist	$2,000	Indiv

Unknown		**$13,250**
No Employer Listed or Found	$2,200	
Employer Listed/Category Unknown	$9,650	
George A L Yuen Inc	$1,750	Indiv
C&C Hon	$1,050	Indiv

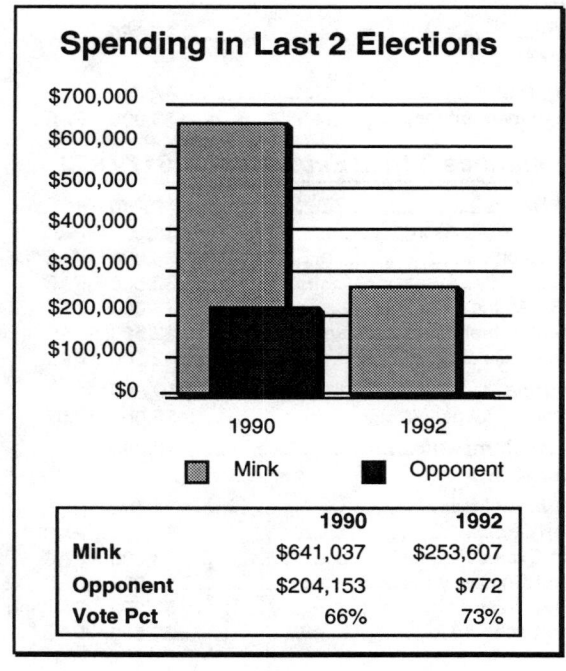

Spending in Last 2 Elections

	1990	1992
Mink	$641,037	$253,607
Opponent	$204,153	$772
Vote Pct	66%	73%

Legend: Mink / Opponent

---

* Contributions came from more than one affiliate or subsidiary.

Joe Moakley, D-Mass (9)

First elected: 1972

1991-92 Total Receipts: $869,410
1992 Year-end Cash: $287,002

1991-92 Committees & Subcommittees

Rules (Chairman)
Legislative Process; Rules of the House

Leading Contributors

Business

Agriculture $9,200

Dairy $2,700
None over $2,500

Food Processing & Sales $4,500
None over $2,500

Communications/Electronics $28,550

Media/Entertainment $6,800
National Cable Television Assn ....$2,500 PAC

Telephone Utilities $20,500
New England Telephone ....$5,500 PAC
AT&T ....$5,250 PAC/Ind
GTE Corp ....$4,500 PAC/Ind

Construction $50,600

General Contractors $31,600
Fluor Corp ....$7,000 PAC
Suffolk Construction Co ....$6,000 Indiv
JF White Contracting Co ....$3,500 Indiv
JM Cashman Co ....$3,500 Indiv

Home Builders $6,550
National Assn of Home Builders ....$4,000 PAC

Construction Services $6,950
Stone & Webster ....$4,500 PAC

Building Materials & Equipment $4,000
None over $2,500

Source of Funds in 1992 Election

Source	Total	Pct
■ PACs	$435,825	50%
■ Indivs $200+	$224,300	26%
□ Indivs under $200	$159,642	18%
⊠ Other	$49,780	6%
Candidate	$0	0%
Party	$587	0%

Source of PAC Dollars by Sector

Source	Total	Pct
■ Business	$315,550	74%
■ Labor	$110,200	26%
□ Ideology/Single Issue	$1,023	0%

In-State vs. Out-of-State Contributions*

Source	Total	Pct
□ In-State	$161,950	73%
■ Out-of-state	$60,850	27%
No state listed	$0	

* by large individual contributors ($200 & above)

Defense $9,550

Defense Aerospace $5,900
Textron Inc ....$3,000 PAC

Defense Electronics $2,500
Raytheon ....$2,500 PAC

Energy & Natural Resources $21,000

Oil & Gas $6,250
None over $2,500

Misc Energy $3,250
None over $2,500

Electric Utilities $5,650
None over $2,500

Waste Management $4,750
Waste Management Inc ....$3,000 PAC

Finance, Insurance & Real Estate $179,850

Commercial Banks $41,250
American Bankers Assn* ....$8,950 PAC
Bank of Boston ....$6,000 PAC/Ind
Citicorp ....$3,500 PAC
Barnett Banks Inc ....$3,000 PAC
Citizens & Southern National Bank ....$2,500 PAC
JP Morgan & Co ....$2,500 PAC

Savings & Loans $10,050
World Savings & Loan ....$3,000 Indiv

Finance/Credit Companies $2,700
None over $2,500

Securities & Investment $34,100
FMR Corp ....$8,000 PAC
American Express* ....$3,000 PAC
Investment Company Institute ....$3,000 PAC
Federated Investors Inc ....$2,500 PAC/Ind
Goldman, Sachs & Co ....$2,500 PAC

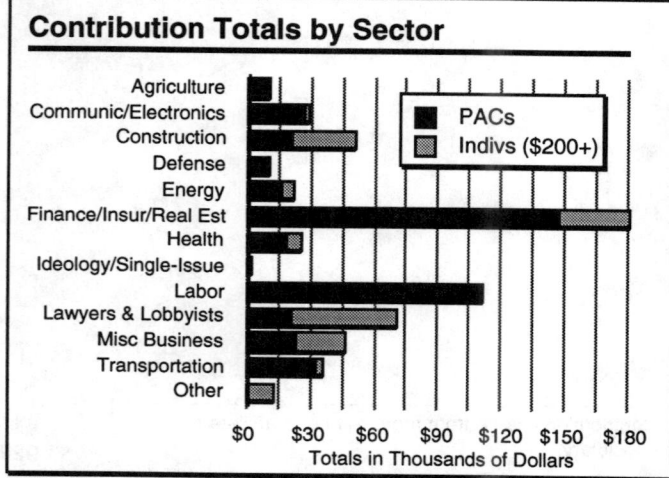

Contribution Totals by Sector

- Agriculture
- Communic/Electronics
- Construction
- Defense
- Energy
- Finance/Insur/Real Est
- Health
- Ideology/Single-Issue
- Labor
- Lawyers & Lobbyists
- Misc Business
- Transportation
- Other

■ PACs
▨ Indivs ($200+)

$0 $30 $60 $90 $120 $150 $180
Totals in Thousands of Dollars

Insurance	$48,150	
American Council of Life Insurance	$8,000	PAC
Massachusetts Mutual Life Insurance	$5,500	PAC
National Assn of Life Underwriters	$5,000	PAC
John Hancock Financial Service	$4,500	PAC
Independent Insurance Agents of America	$3,000	PAC

Real Estate	$29,400	
National Assn of Realtors	$10,000	PAC
Beacon Companies	$4,000	Indiv

| Accountants | $11,300 | |
| American Institute of CPA's | $10,000 | PAC |

Health — $24,700

Health Professionals	$12,800	
American Assn Oral & Maxillofacial Surgeons	$3,000	PAC
American Dental Assn	$2,500	PAC
American Medical Assn	$2,500	PAC

| Hospitals/Nursing Homes | $5,650 | |
| None over $2,500 | | |

| Pharmaceuticals/Health Products | $4,750 | |
| None over $2,500 | | |

Lawyers & Lobbyists — $72,175

Lawyers & Lobbyists	$72,175	
Assn of Trial Lawyers of America	$10,000	PAC
O'Neill & Athy	$3,750	Indiv
Coyne & Mahoney	$3,500	Indiv
Cassidy & Associates	$3,000	Indiv
Shaw, Pittman et al	$2,500	PAC/Ind

Misc Business — $45,575

| Food & Beverage | $5,000 | |
| None over $2,500 | | |

| Beer, Wine & Liquor | $10,175 | |
| None over $2,500 | | |

Business Services	$14,550	
Ackerley Communications	$2,500	Indiv
Alternate Concepts Inc	$2,500	Indiv

Spending in Last 3 Elections

	1988	1990	1992
Moakley	$273,488	$318,847	$1,072,222
Opponent	$0	$0	$12,616
Vote Pct	100%	70%	69%

Chemical & Related Manufacturing	$2,600	
None over $2,500		
Misc Manufacturing & Distributing	$3,550	
None over $2,500		

Transportation — $34,550

Air Transport	$18,600	
Aircraft Owners & Pilots Assn	$7,000	PAC
Federal Express Corp	$5,000	PAC
United Parcel Service	$3,000	PAC

| Automotive | $5,750 | |
| National Auto Dealers Assn | $2,500 | PAC |

| Trucking | $2,550 | |
| None over $2,500 | | |

| Railroads | $2,600 | |
| None over $2,500 | | |

| Sea Transport | $2,700 | |
| None over $2,500 | | |

Labor

Labor	$110,200	
Building Trade Unions	$17,200	
Laborers' Political League	$5,000	PAC
Sheet Metal Workers Union	$3,500	PAC
Ironworkers Union	$3,000	PAC

| Industrial Unions | $10,750 | |
| Intl Brotherhood of Electrical Workers | $2,500 | PAC |

Transportation Unions	$48,600	
Teamsters Union	$10,000	PAC
United Transportation Union	$10,000	PAC
Marine Engineers Union*	$8,500	PAC
Air Line Pilots Assn	$7,500	PAC
Seafarers International Union	$5,000	PAC

Public Sector Unions	$27,850	
National Assn of Letter Carriers	$10,000	PAC
American Fedn of St/Cnty/Munic Employees	$3,000	PAC
American Postal Workers Union	$3,000	PAC
National Assn Retired Federal Employees	$3,000	PAC

| Misc Unions | $5,800 | |
| Food & Commercial Workers Union | $3,000 | PAC |

Other & Unknown

Other	$12,150	
Retired	$6,450	
None over $2,500		
Other	$3,000	
None over $2,500		

Unknown	$50,450	
Homemakers/Non-income earners	$4,500	
Employer Listed/Category Unknown	$45,950	
None over $2,500		

* Contributions came from more than one affiliate or subsidiary.

Susan Molinari, R-NY (13)

First elected: 1990

1991-92 Total Receipts: $524,112
1992 Year-end Cash: $33,045

1991-92 Committees & Subcommittees

Education and Labor
Elementary, Secondary and Vocational Education; Employment Opportunities; Postsecondary Education

Public Works and Transportation
Aviation; Investigations and Oversight; Water Resources

Leading Contributors

Business

Agriculture $14,174

Crop Production & Basic Processing *$5,225*
  American Sugarbeet Growers Assn .... $1,500   PAC

Tobacco *$4,550*
  RJR Nabisco .... $2,350   PAC
  Philip Morris .... $1,500   PAC

Agricultural Services/Products *$2,799*
  None over $1,500

Food Processing & Sales *$1,600*
  None over $1,500

Communications/Electronics $18,050

Media/Entertainment *$6,500*
  National Assn of Broadcasters .... $2,500   PAC
  Bowling Proprietors Assn .... $1,500   PAC

Telephone Utilities *$6,550*
  AT&T .... $2,200   PAC/Ind
  New York Telephone .... $1,850   PAC
  BellSouth Corp* .... $1,500   PAC

Telecom Services & Equipment *$1,500*
  None over $1,500

Computer Equipment & Services *$2,000*
  Keystone Electronics .... $2,000   Indiv

Construction $28,300

General Contractors *$13,300*
  Associated General Contractors .... $2,600   PAC

Home Builders *$2,500*
  National Assn of Home Builders .... $1,500   PAC

Source of Funds in 1992 Election

Source	Total	Pct
PACs	$228,481	44%
Indivs $200+	$192,680	37%
Indivs under $200	$84,343	16%
Other	$18,608	4%
Candidate	$0	0%
Party	$1,134	0%

Source of PAC Dollars by Sector

Source	Total	Pct
Business	$174,233	78%
Labor	$16,300	7%
Ideology/Single Issue	$33,257	15%

In-State vs. Out-of-State Contributions*

Source	Total	Pct
In-State	$149,630	80%
Out-of-state	$36,750	20%
No state listed	$3,300	

* by large individual contributors ($200 & above)

Special Trade Contractors *$7,500*
  None over $1,500

Construction Services *$2,250*
  None over $1,500

Building Materials & Equipment *$2,750*
  None over $1,500

Defense $6,622

Defense Aerospace *$3,622*
  General Dynamics .... $1,500   PAC

Defense Electronics *$2,000*
  Diagnostic Retrieval Systems .... $2,000   Indiv

Energy & Natural Resources $11,900

Oil & Gas *$8,650*
  Brooklyn Union Gas Co .... $3,600   PAC/Ind

Electric Utilities *$2,250*
  None over $1,500

Finance, Insurance & Real Estate $79,430

Commercial Banks *$13,200*
  JP Morgan & Co .... $3,500   PAC
  Chase Manhattan .... $2,500   PAC
  Chemical Bank .... $2,000   PAC

Finance/Credit Companies *$5,500*
  Fort Hill Group .... $4,500   Indiv

Securities & Investment *$18,080*
  Dillon, Read & Co .... $7,080   PAC/Ind
  John Head & Partners .... $2,000   Indiv
  Monness, Crespi, Hardt & Co .... $2,000   Indiv
  New York Stock Exchange .... $1,500   PAC

Insurance *$16,150*
  American International Group Inc .... $4,500   PAC
  National Assn of Life Underwriters .... $2,000   PAC

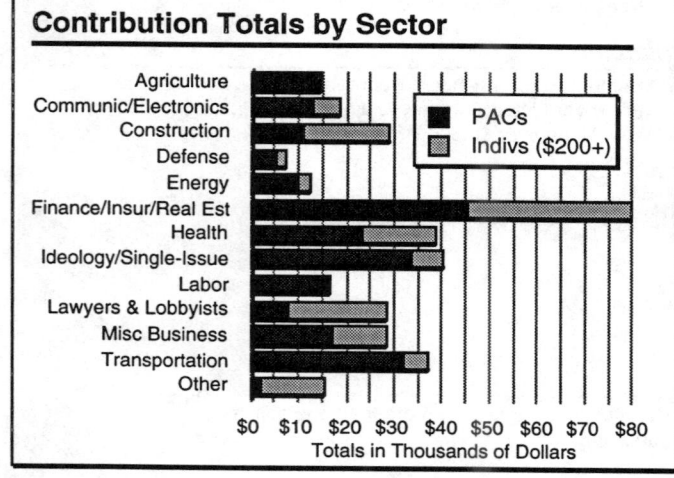

Contribution Totals by Sector

Agriculture
Communic/Electronics
Construction
Defense
Energy
Finance/Insur/Real Est
Health
Ideology/Single-Issue
Labor
Lawyers & Lobbyists
Misc Business
Transportation
Other

PACs
Indivs ($200+)

$0 $10 $20 $30 $40 $50 $60 $70 $80
Totals in Thousands of Dollars

Real Estate		$16,650	
National Assn of Realtors		$6,000	PAC
Mack Companies		$2,000	Indiv
Accountants		**$2,250**	
American Institute of CPA's		$2,000	PAC
Misc Finance		**$7,100**	
Bernard Baruch Organization		$3,000	Indiv

Health — $38,425

Health Professionals		$34,825	
American Medical Assn*		$10,000	PAC
American Academy of Ophthalmology		$4,675	PAC
American Dental Assn		$2,350	PAC
Hospitals/Nursing Homes		**$2,850**	
None over $1,500			

Lawyers & Lobbyists — $28,112

Lawyers & Lobbyists		$28,112	
Assn of Trial Lawyers of America		$5,000	PAC
Crowe, Crowe & Vernaglia		$2,000	Indiv
Fischbein, Badillo et al		$2,000	Indiv
Mudge, Rose et al		$2,000	Indiv

Misc Business — $28,150

Food & Beverage		$8,100	
National Restaurant Assn		$2,000	PAC
General Mills Restaurants		$1,500	PAC
Sirico's Catering		$1,500	Indiv
Beer, Wine & Liquor		**$2,500**	
National Beer Wholesalers Assn		$1,500	PAC
Retail Sales		**$6,050**	
None over $1,500			
Business Services		**$4,350**	
None over $1,500			
Steel Production		**$2,000**	
US Steel Corp		$2,000	Indiv
Misc Manufacturing & Distributing		**$2,100**	
None over $1,500			

Transportation — $36,800

Air Transport		$19,150	
Federal Express Corp		$7,000	PAC
United Parcel Service		$6,350	PAC
United Airlines		$1,500	PAC
Automotive		**$5,000**	
National Auto Dealers Assn		$2,000	PAC
Auto Dealers & Drivers for Free Trade		$1,500	PAC
Trucking		**$8,550**	
Victory Van Lines		$5,000	Indiv
Roadway Services Inc*		$1,500	PAC
Railroads		**$2,500**	
Union Pacific Corp		$2,250	PAC

Labor

Labor — $16,300

Building Trade Unions		$2,250	
Operating Engineers #15		$2,000	PAC
Transportation Unions		**$9,050**	
Marine Engineers Dist 2 Maritime Officers		$3,500	PAC
Air Line Pilots Assn		$2,500	PAC
Public Sector Unions		**$4,650**	
None over $1,500			

Ideological/Single-Issue

Ideological/Single-Issue — $39,907

Republican/Conservative		$5,500	
Fund to Keep America #1		$2,000	PAC
Pro-Israel		**$8,550**	
Stat PAC		$4,500	PAC
Pro-Choice		**$7,457**	
Republican Pro-Choice PAC		$5,000	PAC
Womens Issues		**$10,950**	
Women's Campaign Fund		$7,750	PAC
Wish List		$2,000	PAC
Human Rights		**$2,000**	
None over $1,500			
Misc Issues		**$3,950**	
National Cmte to Preserve Social Security		$3,700	PAC

Other & Unknown

Other — $15,350

Civil Servants/Public Officials		$4,200	
None over $1,500			
Education		**$1,900**	
None over $1,500			
Retired		**$6,250**	
None over $1,500			
Other		**$2,000**	
Council of Jewish Organizations		$1,500	Indiv

Unknown — $53,850

Homemakers/Non-income earners		$8,950	
No Employer Listed or Found		$17,750	
Generic Occupation/Category Unknown		$14,900	
Employer Listed/Category Unknown		$12,250	
Boathouse		$1,500	Indiv

* Contributions came from more than one affiliate or subsidiary.

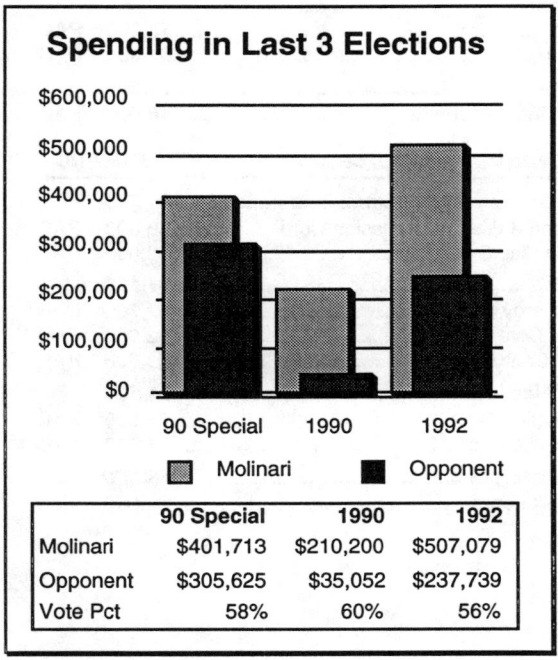

Spending in Last 3 Elections

	90 Special	1990	1992
Molinari	$401,713	$210,200	$507,079
Opponent	$305,625	$35,052	$237,739
Vote Pct	58%	60%	56%

Alan B. Mollohan, D-WVa (1)

First elected: 1982

1991-92 Total Receipts:	$484,159
1992 Year-end Cash:	$1,176

1991-92 Committees & Subcommittees

Appropriations
Commerce, Justice, State, the Judiciary and Related Agencies;
Veterans Affairs, Housing and Urban Development, and Independent
Agencies

Leading Contributors

Business

Agriculture	$24,425	
Crop Production & Basic Processing	**$5,125**	
American Sugarbeet Growers Assn	$1,500	PAC
Tobacco	**$7,500**	
RJR Nabisco	$3,500	PAC
Philip Morris	$2,500	PAC
Dairy	**$7,500**	
Associated Milk Producers	$5,000	PAC
Dairymen Inc	$1,500	PAC
Forestry & Forest Products	**$2,500**	
Westvaco Corp	$2,000	PAC

Communications/Electronics	$5,550	
Media/Entertainment	**$2,000**	
National Assn of Broadcasters	$2,000	PAC
Telephone Utilities	**$1,750**	
None over $1,500		
Computer Equipment & Services	**$1,600**	
Automation Research Systems Ltd	$1,600	Indiv

Construction	$11,550	
General Contractors	**$5,700**	
JF Allen Co	$2,000	Indiv
National Utility Contractors Assn	$2,000	PAC
Special Trade Contractors	**$3,300**	
Lang Brothers Inc	$2,000	Indiv

Source of Funds in 1992 Election

Source	Total	Pct
■ PACs	$238,369	49%
■ Indivs $200+	$151,350	31%
□ Indivs under $200	$50,581	10%
⊠ Other	$43,996	9%
Candidate	$25,000	5%
Party	$487	0%

Source of PAC Dollars by Sector

Source	Total	Pct
■ Business	$149,775	62%
■ Labor	$74,400	31%
□ Ideology/Single Issue	$18,650	8%

In-State vs. Out-of-State Contributions*

Source	Total	Pct
□ In-State	$102,250	68%
■ Out-of-state	$48,850	32%
No state listed	$0	

* by large individual contributors ($200 & above)

Defense	$53,950	
Defense Aerospace	**$32,800**	
Martin Marietta Corp	$6,500	PAC
United Technologies	$5,000	PAC
Grumman Corp	$4,600	PAC
Lockheed Corp	$4,000	PAC
Textron Inc	$3,000	PAC
Rockwell International	$2,500	PAC
General Dynamics	$1,500	PAC
McDonnell Douglas	$1,500	PAC
Defense Electronics	**$14,900**	
AT&T	$4,400	PAC
Imo Industries Inc	$2,000	PAC
TRW Inc	$2,000	PAC
GTE Corp	$1,500	PAC
Misc Defense	**$6,250**	
Mantech International	$6,000	PAC

Energy & Natural Resources	$38,400	
Oil & Gas	**$13,700**	
Consolidated Gas Transmission Corp	$3,500	PAC
Columbia Gas System*	$3,000	PAC
Mining	**$14,150**	
Five-J Energy Inc	$2,700	Indiv
Peabody Coal	$2,000	PAC
National Coal Assn	$1,500	PAC
Electric Utilities	**$4,550**	
ACRE (Action Cmte for Rural Electrification)	$2,000	PAC
Texas Utilities Co*	$1,500	PAC
Waste Management	**$6,000**	
Meadowfill Landfill	$6,000	Indiv

Contribution Totals by Sector

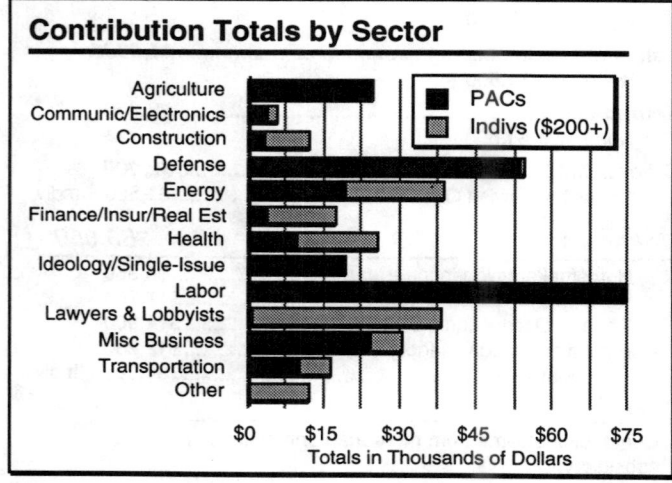

Agriculture
Communic/Electronics
Construction
Defense
Energy
Finance/Insur/Real Est
Health
Ideology/Single-Issue
Labor
Lawyers & Lobbyists
Misc Business
Transportation
Other

■ PACs
▨ Indivs ($200+)

$0 $15 $30 $45 $60 $75
Totals in Thousands of Dollars

Finance, Insurance & Real Estate — $16,870

Commercial Banks $5,350
    American Bankers Assn .... $2,000   PAC

Insurance $3,000
    None over $1,500

Real Estate $3,950
    None over $1,500

Health — $25,134

Health Professionals $16,384
    American Medical Assn .... $5,000   PAC

Hospitals/Nursing Homes $5,700
    Wheeling Hospital .... $2,250   Indiv
    American Hospital Assn .... $2,000   PAC

Pharmaceuticals/Health Products $1,850
    None over $1,500

Lawyers & Lobbyists — $37,900

Lawyers & Lobbyists $37,900
    Paul Magliocchetti Associates .... $11,000   Indiv
    Hyjek & Fix .... $6,500   Indiv
    Klett, Lieber et al .... $2,000   Indiv

Misc Business — $30,100

Misc Services $2,000
    None over $1,500

Business Services $1,750
    None over $1,500

Misc Business $4,000
    National Rural Water Assn .... $4,000   PAC

Chemical & Related Manufacturing $11,500
    Institute of Makers of Explosives .... $6,000   PAC
    Austin Powder Co .... $5,000   PAC/Ind

Steel Production $2,700
    Wheeling-Pittsburgh Steel .... $1,500   PAC

Misc Manufacturing & Distributing $5,900
    Corning Glass Works .... $5,000   PAC

Transportation — $16,200

Air Transport $3,800
    United Parcel Service .... $3,300   PAC

Automotive $7,400
    Short Brothers USA .... $3,700   Indiv
    National Auto Dealers Assn .... $2,500   PAC

Trucking $2,500
    American Trucking Assns .... $1,500   PAC

Railroads $1,500
    CSX Transportation Inc .... $1,500   PAC

Labor

Labor — $74,400

Building Trade Unions $14,000
    Carpenters & Joiners Union .... $4,500   PAC
    Laborers' Political League .... $4,000   PAC
    Ironworkers Union .... $3,500   PAC
    AFL-CIO Bldg/Construction Trades Dept .... $1,500   PAC

Industrial Unions $20,500
    United Auto Workers .... $6,500   PAC
    Machinists/Aerospace Workers Union .... $4,500   PAC
    United Mine Workers .... $3,000   PAC
    Boilermakers Union .... $2,000   PAC
    Intl Brotherhood of Electrical Workers .... $2,000   PAC

Transportation Unions $22,500
    Teamsters Union .... $7,500   PAC
    Air Line Pilots Assn .... $5,000   PAC
    Marine Engineers Dist 2 Maritime Officers .... $4,500   PAC
    United Transportation Union .... $3,500   PAC

Public Sector Unions $15,500
    National Assn Retired Federal Employees .... $4,000   PAC
    National Assn of Letter Carriers .... $3,500   PAC
    American Fedn of St/Cnty/Munic Employees ...... $2,500   PAC

Misc Unions $1,900
    Food & Commercial Workers Union .... $1,500   PAC

Ideological/Single-Issue

Ideological/Single-Issue — $18,850

Pro-Life $2,800
    Right to Life* .... $2,600   PAC

Gun Rights/Gun Control $9,900
    National Rifle Assn .... $9,900   PAC

Misc Issues $5,000
    National Cmte to Preserve Social Security .... $4,000   PAC

Other & Unknown

Other — $11,850

Civil Servants/Public Officials $2,000
    None over $1,500

Education $4,450
    Mountain State College .... $2,000   Indiv

Retired $5,400
    None over $1,500

Unknown — $28,746

    Homemakers/Non-income earners $2,100
    No Employer Listed or Found $7,200
    Generic Occupation/Category Unknown $1,666
    Employer Listed/Category Unknown $17,780
      None over $1,500

---

* Contributions came from more than one affiliate or subsidiary.

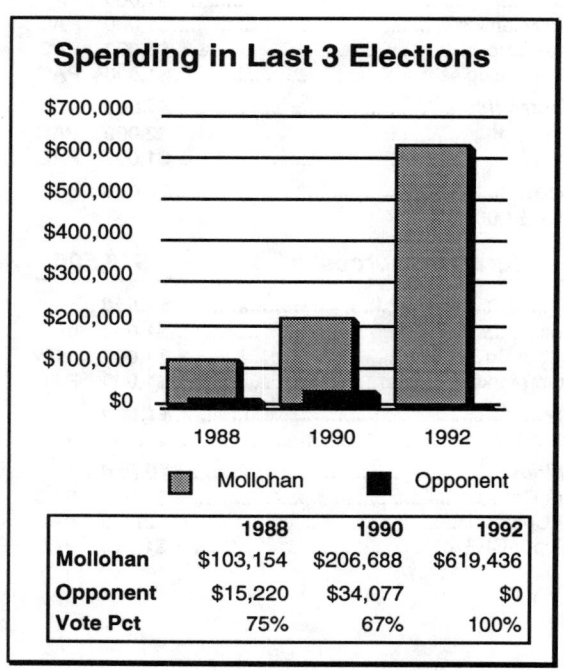

Spending in Last 3 Elections

	1988	1990	1992
Mollohan	$103,154	$206,688	$619,436
Opponent	$15,220	$34,077	$0
Vote Pct	75%	67%	100%

■ Mollohan   ■ Opponent

G. V. "Sonny" Montgomery, D-Miss (3)

First elected: 1966

1991-92 Total Receipts:	$172,603
1992 Year-end Cash:	$170,345

1991-92 Committees & Subcommittees

Armed Services
Military Installations and Facilities; Military Personnel and Compensation

Veterans' Affairs (Chairman)
Hospitals and Health Care (Chairman)

Leading Contributors

Business

Agriculture	$14,750	
Crop Production & Basic Processing	**$2,000**	
National Cotton Council	$1,000	Indiv
Tobacco	**$2,000**	
RJR Nabisco	$1,000	PAC
US Tobacco Co	$1,000	PAC
Poultry & Eggs	**$2,500**	
Cal-Maine Foods Inc	$1,000	Indiv
Sanderson Farms Inc	$1,000	Indiv
Agricultural Services/Products	**$1,250**	
None over $1,000		
Food Processing & Sales	**$3,500**	
Jitney-Jungle Inc	$1,000	PAC
Pepsico Inc	$1,000	PAC
Winn-Dixie Stores	$1,000	PAC
Forestry & Forest Products	**$1,700**	
International Paper Co	$1,000	PAC

Communications/Electronics	$11,000	
Media/Entertainment	**$5,500**	
National Assn of Broadcasters	$2,000	PAC
Imes Communications	$1,000	Indiv
Peavey Electronics	$1,000	Indiv
WCBI TV	$1,000	Indiv
Telephone Utilities	**$4,000**	
BellSouth Corp*	$4,000	PAC
Computer Equipment & Services	**$1,000**	
Electronic Data Systems	$1,000	PAC

Source of Funds in 1992 Election

Source	Total	Pct
■ PACs	$97,600	56%
▨ Indivs $200+	$43,743	25%
□ Indivs under $200	$17,020	10%
▧ Other	$14,377	8%
Candidate	$0	0%
Party	$137	0%

Source of PAC Dollars by Sector

Source	Total	Pct
■ Business	$90,400	94%
▨ Labor	$1,100	1%
□ Ideology/Single Issue	$5,000	5%

In-State vs. Out-of-State Contributions*

Source	Total	Pct
□ In-State	$41,643	95%
■ Out-of-state	$2,100	5%
No state listed	$0	

*** by large individual contributors ($200 & above)**

Construction	$7,148	
General Contractors	**$5,198**	
Associated General Contractors	$1,500	PAC
Fluor Corp	$1,000	PAC
Building Materials & Equipment	**$1,950**	
None over $1,000		

Defense	$15,750	
Defense Aerospace	**$9,750**	
Lockheed Corp	$2,000	PAC
Beech Aircraft	$1,500	PAC
Colt Industries	$1,000	PAC
Dyncorp	$1,000	PAC
General Dynamics	$1,000	PAC
Grumman Corp	$1,000	PAC
United Technologies	$1,000	PAC
Defense Electronics	**$5,000**	
Hughes Aircraft	$2,000	PAC
AT&T	$1,000	PAC
Misc Defense	**$1,000**	
None over $1,000		

Energy & Natural Resources	$18,500	
Oil & Gas	**$6,950**	
Ergon Inc	$1,000	Indiv
Maples Gas Co	$1,000	Indiv
Petroleum Marketers Assn	$1,000	PAC
Misc Energy	**$1,000**	
Babcock & Wilcox	$1,000	PAC
Electric Utilities	**$10,050**	
Southern Co*	$3,000	PAC
Entergy Corp*	$2,750	PAC
Mississippi ACRE	$1,000	PAC

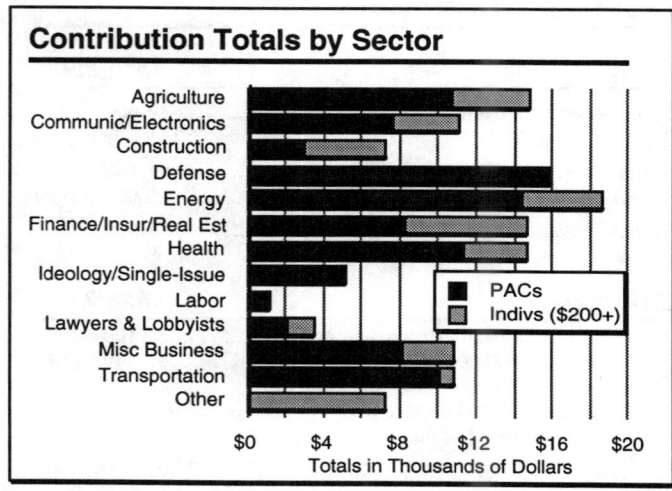

Contribution Totals by Sector

Agriculture
Communic/Electronics
Construction
Defense
Energy
Finance/Insur/Real Est
Health
Ideology/Single-Issue
Labor
Lawyers & Lobbyists
Misc Business
Transportation
Other

■ PACs
▨ Indivs ($200+)

$0 $4 $8 $12 $16 $20
Totals in Thousands of Dollars

Finance, Insurance & Real Estate — $14,600

Commercial Banks **$4,800**
    American Bankers Assn ....$1,000   PAC
    Carthage Bank ....$1,000   Indiv

Insurance **$2,200**
    None over $1,000

Real Estate **$4,250**
    National Assn of Realtors ....$3,000   PAC
    Paul Broadhead Interests Inc ....$1,000   Indiv

Accountants **$2,000**
    American Institute of CPA's ....$2,000   PAC

Health — $14,550

Health Professionals **$12,550**
    American Medical Assn ....$4,700   PAC
    American Dental Assn ....$3,000   PAC
    American Academy of Ophthalmology ....$1,000   PAC

Misc Health **$1,000**
    Boundary Health Care Corp ....$1,000   Indiv

Lawyers & Lobbyists — $3,450

Lawyers & Lobbyists **$3,450**
    Assn of Trial Lawyers of America ....$2,000   PAC

Misc Business — $10,700

Beer, Wine & Liquor **$2,950**
    National Beer Wholesalers Assn ....$1,500   PAC

Retail Sales **$2,600**
    National Assn of Convenience Stores ....$1,000   PAC

Misc Manufacturing & Distributing **$1,250**
    None over $1,000

Textiles **$2,000**
    Burlington Industries ....$2,000   PAC

Transportation — $10,695

Air Transport **$5,000**
    Federal Express Corp ....$2,000   PAC
    United Parcel Service ....$2,000   PAC
    Gulfstream Aerospace ....$1,000   PAC

Automotive **$5,200**
    National Auto Dealers Assn ....$3,500   PAC
    Auto Dealers & Drivers for Free Trade ....$1,500   PAC

Labor

Labor — $1,100

Public Sector Unions **$1,100**
    None over $1,000

Ideological/Single-Issue

Ideological/Single-Issue — $5,000

Foreign & Defense Policy **$2,000**
    Veterans of Foreign Wars ....$2,000   PAC

Gun Rights/Gun Control **$2,000**
    National Rifle Assn ....$2,000   PAC

Misc Issues **$1,000**
    National Assn for Uniformed Services ....$1,000   PAC

Other & Unknown

Other — $7,100

Retired **$6,200**
    None over $1,000

Unknown — $5,900

    Employer Listed/Category Unknown $5,700
        Howard Industries ....$1,000   Indiv

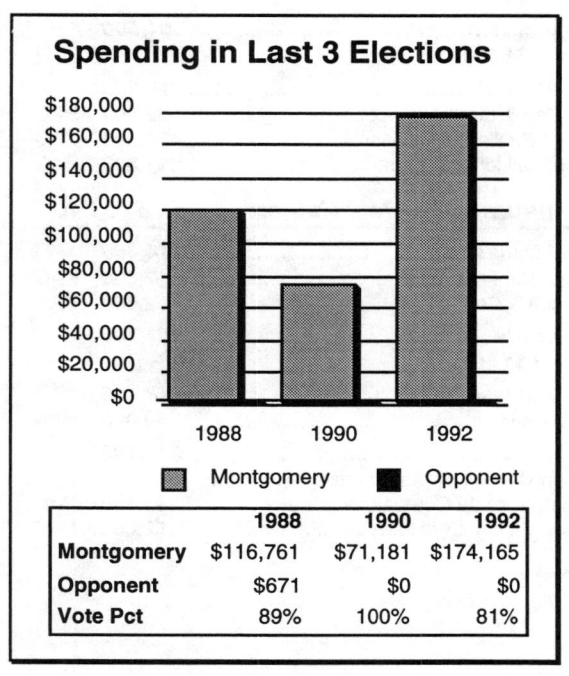

Spending in Last 3 Elections

	1988	1990	1992
Montgomery	$116,761	$71,181	$174,165
Opponent	$671	$0	$0
Vote Pct	89%	100%	81%

* Contributions came from more than one affiliate or subsidiary.

Carlos J. Moorhead, R-Calif (27)

First elected: 1972

1991-92 Total Receipts: $448,791
1992 Year-end Cash: $409,659

1991-92 Committees & Subcommittees

Energy and Commerce
Energy and Power (Ranking Republican); Telecommunications and Finance

Judiciary
Intellectual Property and Judicial Administration (Ranking Republican); Economic and Commercial Law

Leading Contributors

Business

Agriculture		$14,100
Crop Production & Basic Processing		**$2,500**
None over $1,500		
Tobacco		**$4,000**
US Tobacco Co	$2,000	PAC
Food Processing & Sales		**$7,100**
Nestle Enterprises Inc	$1,500	PAC

Communications/Electronics		$44,050
Printing & Publishing		**$1,500**
None over $1,500		
Media/Entertainment		**$27,300**
Walt Disney Co	$7,500	PAC
National Cable Television Assn	$5,000	PAC
Viacom International	$3,500	PAC
ASCAP	$3,000	PAC
National Assn of Broadcasters	$2,900	PAC
Telephone Utilities		**$12,250**
AT&T	$3,200	PAC
Pacific Telesis Group	$2,800	PAC
Telecom Services & Equipment		**$2,000**
None over $1,500		

Construction		$8,200
Construction Services		**$4,700**
Jacobs Engineering Group	$2,300	PAC
Parsons Corp	$1,500	PAC
Building Materials & Equipment		**$2,000**
None over $1,500		

Source of Funds in 1992 Election

Source	Total	Pct
■ PACs	$260,025	57%
▨ Indivs $200+	$37,050	8%
☐ Indivs under $200	$57,466	13%
▧ Other	$99,810	22%
Candidate	$0	0%
Party	$5,560	1%

Source of PAC Dollars by Sector

Source	Total	Pct
■ Business	$254,940	99%
▨ Labor	$1,000	0%
☐ Ideology/Single Issue	$1,750	1%

In-State vs. Out-of-State Contributions*

Source	Total	Pct
☐ In-State	$27,050	73%
■ Out-of-state	$10,000	27%
No state listed	$0	

* by large individual contributors ($200 & above)

Defense		$6,000
Defense Aerospace		**$4,500**
None over $1,500		

Energy & Natural Resources		$45,600
Oil & Gas		**$23,150**
Atlantic Richfield	$3,000	PAC
Columbia Gas System*	$2,000	PAC
Coastal Corp	$1,500	PAC
Mining		**$1,500**
None over $1,500		
Misc Energy		**$1,500**
None over $1,500		
Electric Utilities		**$17,150**
Pacific Gas & Electric	$2,000	PAC
American Public Power Assn	$1,500	PAC
Southern California Edison	$1,500	PAC

Finance, Insurance & Real Estate		$70,240
Commercial Banks		**$14,400**
American Bankers Assn	$7,500	PAC
JP Morgan & Co	$2,500	PAC
Savings & Loans		**$1,700**
None over $1,500		
Securities & Investment		**$8,100**
Capital Group	$2,000	Indiv
Insurance		**$19,100**
American Council of Life Insurance	$2,500	PAC
TransAmerica Life Companies	$2,100	PAC
American Family Corp	$2,000	PAC

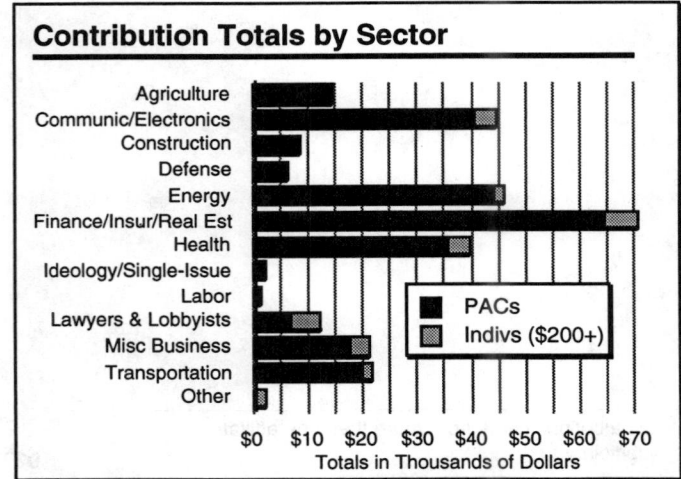

Contribution Totals by Sector

Agriculture
Communic/Electronics
Construction
Defense
Energy
Finance/Insur/Real Est
Health
Ideology/Single-Issue
Labor
Lawyers & Lobbyists
Misc Business
Transportation
Other

■ PACs
▧ Indivs ($200+)

$0 $10 $20 $30 $40 $50 $60 $70
Totals in Thousands of Dollars

Real Estate **$12,640**
    National Assn of Realtors ....$6,000 PAC
    American Land Title Assn ....$2,740 PAC

Accountants **$14,000**
    American Institute of CPA's ....$10,000 PAC
    Coopers & Lybrand ....$2,500 PAC

Health $39,150

Health Professionals **$21,350**
    American Medical Assn ....$10,000 PAC
    American Dental Assn ....$5,000 PAC
    American Optometric Assn ....$1,500 PAC

Pharmaceuticals/Health Products **$15,500**
    Merck & Co ....$2,000 PAC
    Syntex (USA) Inc ....$2,000 PAC

Lawyers & Lobbyists $12,050

Lawyers & Lobbyists **$12,050**
    Murphy & Demory Ltd ....$2,000 Indiv
    Jones, Day et al ....$1,500 PAC

Misc Business $20,900

Food & Beverage **$1,800**
    None over $1,500

Beer, Wine & Liquor **$2,000**
    National Beer Wholesalers Assn ....$1,500 PAC

Retail Sales **$2,650**
    None over $1,500

Business Services **$2,000**
    None over $1,500

Chemical & Related Manufacturing **$3,500**
    None over $1,500

Misc Manufacturing & Distributing **$7,550**
    Seastrom Manufacturing Co ....$2,000 Indiv
    Stone Container Corp ....$2,000 PAC

Transportation $21,200

Air Transport **$7,000**
    United Parcel Service ....$6,500 PAC

Automotive **$8,500**
    Americans for Free International Trade ....$2,000 PAC
    Auto Dealers & Drivers for Free Trade ....$2,000 PAC
    Ford Motor Co ....$1,500 PAC

Railroads **$4,000**
    None over $1,500

Ideological/Single-Issue

Ideological/Single-Issue   **$1,750**
    None over $1,500

Other & Unknown

Other   **$1,900**

Retired **$1,900**
    None over $1,500

Unknown   **$8,600**

    No Employer Listed or Found $1,500
    Employer Listed/Category Unknown $6,500
        None over $1,500

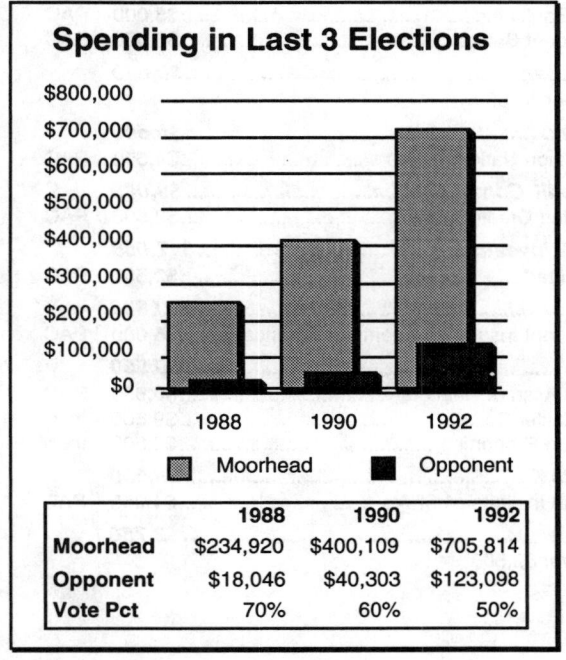

Spending in Last 3 Elections

	1988	1990	1992
Moorhead	$234,920	$400,109	$705,814
Opponent	$18,046	$40,303	$123,098
Vote Pct	70%	60%	50%

* Contributions came from more than one affiliate or subsidiary.

James P. Moran Jr., D-Va (8)

First elected: 1990

1991-92 Total Receipts: $924,029
1992 Year-end Cash: $1,455

1991-92 Committees & Subcommittees

Banking, Finance and Urban Affairs
Economic Stabilization; Financial Institutions Supervision, Regulation and Insurance; International Development, Finance, Trade and Monetary Policy

Post Office and Civil Service
Civil Service; Human Resources

Select Committee on Hunger

Leading Contributors

Business

Agriculture	$13,850

Crop Production & Basic Processing $6,850
　None over $2,500

Communications/Electronics	$29,475

Printing & Publishing $3,725
　None over $2,500
Media/Entertainment $4,050
　None over $2,500
Telephone Utilities $8,750
　None over $2,500
Computer Equipment & Services $12,950
　Planning Research Corp .... $4,500　PAC

Construction	$15,250

General Contractors $7,650
　None over $2,500
Home Builders $5,550
　National Assn of Home Builders .... $4,000　PAC

Defense	$23,042

Defense Aerospace $4,706
　None over $2,500
Defense Electronics $2,500
　None over $2,500
Misc Defense $15,836
　Mantech International .... $9,700　PAC
　BDM International .... $2,500　PAC

Contribution Totals by Sector

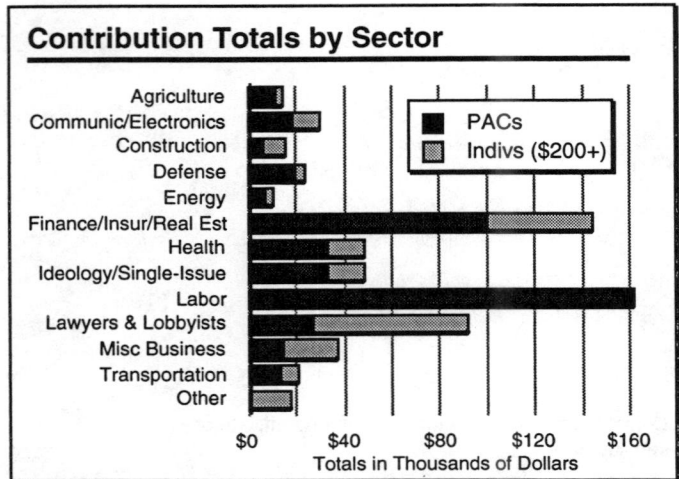

Totals in Thousands of Dollars

Source of Funds in 1992 Election

Source	Total	Pct
PACs	$434,521	47%
Indivs $200+	$291,463	31%
Indivs under $200	$173,013	19%
Other	$30,770	3%
Candidate	$0	0%
Party	$18,426	2%

Source of PAC Dollars by Sector

Source	Total	Pct
Business	$243,481	56%
Labor	$159,850	37%
Ideology/Single Issue	$32,163	7%

In-State vs. Out-of-State Contributions*

Source	Total	Pct
In-State	$190,335	68%
Out-of-state	$91,550	32%
No state listed	$0	

* by large individual contributors ($200 & above)

Energy & Natural Resources	$9,400

Oil & Gas $3,100
　None over $2,500
Electric Utilities $3,750
　None over $2,500

Finance, Insurance & Real Estate	$143,008

Commercial Banks $29,950
　MNC Financial Inc .... $6,600　PAC
　American Bankers Assn* .... $5,100　PAC
　Citizens & Southern National Bank .... $5,000　PAC
　Barnett Banks Inc .... $3,000　PAC
　Independent Bankers Assn .... $3,000　PAC
Savings & Loans $8,850
　None over $2,500
Credit Unions $5,500
　Credit Union National Assn .... $4,500　PAC
Finance/Credit Companies $9,000
　Associated Credit Bureaus .... $2,500　PAC
Securities & Investment $17,058
　Dean Witter* .... $2,500　PAC
Insurance $9,800
　Independent Insurance Agents of America .... $5,000　PAC
Real Estate $50,550
　National Assn of Realtors .... $9,650　PAC
　Mark Winkler Co .... $9,500　Indiv
　Abramson Properties .... $2,500　Indiv
Accountants $9,550
　American Institute of CPA's .... $4,250　PAC
Misc Finance $2,750
　None over $2,500

940

Health $48,037

Health Professionals **$39,837**
 American Medical Assn .... $5,350 PAC
 American Academy of Ophthalmology .... $4,137 PAC
 American Chiropractic Assn .... $3,000 PAC
 American Dental Assn .... $3,000 PAC
 American Nurses Assn .... $2,500 PAC
 American Psychiatric Assn .... $2,500 PAC

Pharmaceuticals/Health Products **$6,000**
 Merck & Co .... $3,000 PAC/Ind

Lawyers & Lobbyists $91,330

Lawyers & Lobbyists **$91,330**
 Assn of Trial Lawyers of America .... $12,500 PAC
 Cassidy & Associates .... $8,250 Indiv
 Hazel & Thomas .... $3,800 Indiv
 Akin, Gump et al .... $3,580 PAC/Ind
 Arnold & Porter .... $3,250 PAC/Ind
 Capitol Associates .... $3,250 Indiv
 US Strategies Corp .... $3,000 Indiv

Misc Business $36,390

Business Associations **$6,500**
 Greater Washington Board of Trade .... $5,000 PAC

Food & Beverage **$7,750**
 Hoffman Co .... $4,000 Indiv

Retail Sales **$8,750**
 None over $2,500

Business Services **$8,340**
 None over $2,500

Transportation $19,650

Air Transport **$4,250**
 United Parcel Service .... $4,000 PAC

Automotive **$11,400**
 Americans for Free International Trade .... $5,000 PAC

Spending in Last 2 Elections

	1990	1992
Moran	$883,216	$922,592
Opponent	$986,265	$413,395
Vote Pct	52%	56%

Labor

Labor $160,350

Building Trade Unions **$22,150**
 Laborers' Political League .... $6,000 PAC
 Sheet Metal Workers Union .... $4,500 PAC
 Plumbers/Pipefitters Union .... $4,000 PAC
 Carpenters & Joiners Union .... $3,000 PAC

Industrial Unions **$28,000**
 Intl Brotherhood of Electrical Workers .... $8,000 PAC
 Communications Workers of America .... $7,000 PAC
 United Auto Workers .... $6,000 PAC

Transportation Unions **$34,900**
 Teamsters Union .... $7,500 PAC
 Air Line Pilots Assn .... $6,500 PAC
 Seafarers International Union .... $6,500 PAC
 United Transportation Union .... $5,500 PAC

Public Sector Unions **$59,750**
 National Education Assn .... $11,000 PAC
 American Fedn of St/Cnty/Munic Employees .... $10,000 PAC
 American Postal Workers Union .... $6,000 PAC
 National Assn Retired Federal Employees .... $5,000 PAC
 International Assn of Firefighters .... $4,500 PAC
 National Assn of Letter Carriers .... $4,500 PAC
 American Federation of Teachers .... $4,000 PAC
 National Assn of Postmasters .... $3,000 PAC

Misc Unions **$15,550**
 Food & Commercial Workers Union .... $7,000 PAC
 AFL-CIO .... $3,500 PAC

Ideological/Single-Issue

Ideological/Single-Issue $48,030

Democratic/Liberal **$9,817**
 Moran for Congress .... $4,217 Indiv
 National Cmte for an Effective Congress .... $3,400 PAC

Foreign & Defense Policy **$4,850**
 National Assn of Arab-Americans .... $3,100 PAC/Ind

Pro-Choice **$10,750**
 National Abortion Rights Action League .... $7,000 PAC
 Voters for Choice .... $2,750 PAC

Human Rights **$5,950**
 None over $2,500

Misc Issues **$11,000**
 National Cmte to Preserve Social Security .... $7,000 PAC

Other & Unknown

Other $16,492

Civil Servants/Public Officials **$3,542**
 None over $2,500

Retired **$8,100**
 None over $2,500

Unknown $61,059

 Homemakers/Non-income earners $9,500
 No Employer Listed or Found $14,581
 Employer Listed/Category Unknown $35,778
  None over $2,500

---

* Contributions came from more than one affiliate or
subsidiary.

Constance A. Morella, R-Md (8)

First elected: 1986

1991-92 Total Receipts: $430,301
1992 Year-end Cash: $303,167

1991-92 Committees & Subcommittees

Post Office and Civil Service
Civil Service (Ranking Republican); Compensation and Employee Benefits

Science, Space and Technology
Environment; Technology and Competitiveness

Select Committee on Aging

Leading Contributors

Business

Agriculture	$4,850	
Food Processing & Sales $2,100		
None over $1,500		

Communications/Electronics	$21,250	
Printing & Publishing $3,400		
Downey Communications Inc $2,000		Indiv
Media/Entertainment $2,000		
None over $1,500		
Telephone Utilities $4,350		
Chesapeake & Potomac Telephone $2,000		PAC
AT&T $1,850		PAC
Telecom Services & Equipment $2,350		
Comsat $2,350		PAC
Computer Equipment & Services $6,800		
Richard S Carson & Assoc $3,200		Indiv

Construction	$17,700	
General Contractors $4,000		
Associated General Contractors $2,500		PAC
Special Trade Contractors $7,650		
Miller & Long Co $6,800		Indiv
Construction Services $3,500		
Loiederman Associates $2,000		Indiv
National Society of Professional Engineers $1,500		PAC
Building Materials & Equipment $1,850		
None over $1,500		

Source of Funds in 1992 Election

Source	Total	Pct
PACs	$184,373	43%
Indivs $200+	$101,251	24%
Indivs under $200	$126,356	29%
Other	$18,321	4%
Candidate	$0	0%
Party	$0	0%

Source of PAC Dollars by Sector

Source	Total	Pct
Business	$118,745	66%
Labor	$43,300	24%
Ideology/Single Issue	$18,350	10%

In-State vs. Out-of-State Contributions*

Source	Total	Pct
In-State	$91,060	90%
Out-of-state	$10,136	10%
No state listed	$0	

* by large individual contributors ($200 & above)

Defense	$9,400	
Defense Aerospace $3,750		
None over $1,500		
Defense Electronics $3,200		
None over $1,500		
Misc Defense $2,450		
Atlantic Research Corp $2,000		PAC

Energy & Natural Resources	$11,160	
Oil & Gas $2,000		
None over $1,500		
Misc Energy $3,100		
Bechtel Corp $3,000		PAC
Electric Utilities $6,060		
Baltimore Gas & Electric $4,100		PAC

Finance, Insurance & Real Estate	$37,150	
Commercial Banks $5,350		
Citizens & Southern National Bank $2,000		PAC
Securities & Investment $2,750		
None over $1,500		
Insurance $11,150		
Schoenke & Assoc $2,500		Indiv
GEICO Insurance $1,500		PAC
Real Estate $12,550		
National Assn of Realtors $6,500		PAC
Grady Management Inc $4,000		Indiv
Accountants $2,350		
Arthur Andersen & Co $1,500		Indiv
Misc Finance $3,000		
None over $1,500		

Contribution Totals by Sector

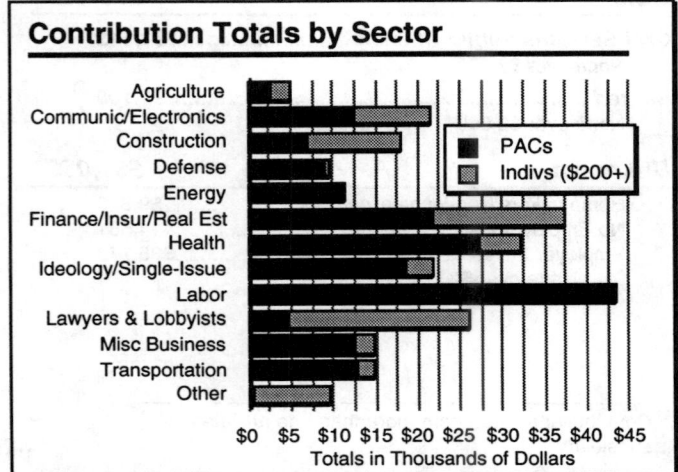

Agriculture
Communic/Electronics
Construction
Defense
Energy
Finance/Insur/Real Est
Health
Ideology/Single-Issue
Labor
Lawyers & Lobbyists
Misc Business
Transportation
Other

- PACs
- Indivs ($200+)

$0 $5 $10 $15 $20 $25 $30 $35 $40 $45
Totals in Thousands of Dollars

Health — $32,025

Health Professionals **$25,600**
   American Medical Assn .... $7,500 PAC
   American Academy of Ophthalmology .... $2,000 PAC
   American Podiatry Assn .... $2,000 PAC
Health Services **$1,500**
   None over $1,500
Pharmaceuticals/Health Products **$3,575**
   None over $1,500

Lawyers & Lobbyists — $25,970

Lawyers & Lobbyists **$25,970**
   Fulbright & Jaworski .... $3,100 Indiv
   Assn of Trial Lawyers of America .... $2,500 PAC
   Hewes, Morella, Gelban .... $2,000 Indiv
   Kendall & Associates .... $2,000 Indiv
   Cotten, Day & Selfon .... $1,500 Indiv

Misc Business — $14,515

Business Associations **$2,250**
   Greater Washington Board of Trade .... $2,000 PAC
Retail Sales **$2,600**
   None over $1,500
Business Services **$4,550**
   None over $1,500
Misc Manufacturing & Distributing **$2,550**
   Cosmetic, Toiletry & Fragrance Assn .... $1,550 PAC

Transportation — $14,500

Air Transport **$6,250**
   United Parcel Service .... $3,200 PAC
   General Electric .... $2,050 PAC
Automotive **$6,400**
   National Auto Dealers Assn .... $2,350 PAC
   Americans for Free International Trade .... $1,500 PAC

Labor

Labor — $43,300

Transportation Unions **$7,550**
   Air Line Pilots Assn .... $2,500 PAC
   Marine Engineers Dist 2 Maritime Officers .... $2,000 PAC
   National Air Traffic Controllers Assn .... $1,700 PAC
Public Sector Unions **$35,400**
   National Assn Retired Federal Employees .... $8,000 PAC
   National Assn of Letter Carriers .... $8,000 PAC
   American Postal Workers Union .... $3,000 PAC
   National Education Assn .... $2,850 PAC
   American Fedn of St/Cnty/Munic Employees ...... $2,500 PAC
   National League of Postmasters .... $2,000 PAC

Ideological/Single-Issue

Ideological/Single-Issue — $21,386

Pro-Israel **$2,636**
   None over $1,500
Womens Issues **$9,750**
   Women's Campaign Fund .... $6,000 PAC
   Wish List .... $2,000 PAC
Human Rights **$5,100**
   Human Rights Campaign Fund .... $5,000 PAC
Misc Issues **$2,200**
   National Cmte to Preserve Social Security .... $2,200 PAC

Other & Unknown

Other — $9,450

Education **$2,250**
   American University .... $2,000 Indiv
Retired **$4,950**
   None over $1,500
Other **$1,950**
   None over $1,500

Unknown — $19,435

   Homemakers/Non-income earners $3,460
   No Employer Listed or Found $2,195
   Employer Listed/Category Unknown $13,530
      Orkand Corp .... $7,875 Indiv
      Redmond Consulting .... $1,500 Indiv

---

Spending in Last 3 Elections

	1988	1990	1992
Morella	$821,574	$353,959	$328,516
Opponent	$460,847	$0	$73,047
Vote Pct	63%	74%	73%

Austin J. Murphy, D-Pa (20)

First elected: 1976

1991-92 Total Receipts:	$235,296
1992 Year-end Cash:	$37,124

1991-92 Committees & Subcommittees

Education and Labor
Health and Safety; Labor Standards (Chairman)

Foreign Affairs
International Economic Policy and Trade

Interior and Insular Affairs
Energy and the Environment; National Parks and Public Lands

Leading Contributors

Business

Agriculture		$8,050
Crop Production & Basic Processing	**$3,250**	
Florida Sugar Cane League	$1,000	PAC
Dairy	**$1,800**	
Associated Milk Producers	$1,500	PAC
Food Processing & Sales	**$1,800**	
Food Marketing Institute	$1,500	PAC

Communications/Electronics		$3,300
Telephone Utilities	**$2,550**	
Bell Telephone of Pennsylvania	$1,050	PAC

Construction		$500
Building Materials & Equipment	**$1,000**	
None over $1,000		

Energy & Natural Resources		$14,000
Oil & Gas	**$3,300**	
None over $1,000		
Mining	**$1,500**	
Cyprus Minerals Co	$1,000	PAC
Misc Energy	**$2,500**	
Babcock & Wilcox*	$2,500	PAC

Source of Funds in 1992 Election

Source	Total	Pct
■ PACs	$174,750	69%
▨ Indivs $200+	$11,100	4%
☐ Indivs under $200	$34,201	13%
⊠ Other	$34,540	14%
Candidate	$0	0%
Party	$19,745	8%

Source of PAC Dollars by Sector

Source	Total	Pct
■ Business	$69,300	38%
▨ Labor	$97,000	54%
☐ Ideology/Single Issue	$13,923	8%

In-State vs. Out-of-State Contributions*

Source	Total	Pct
☐ In-State	$8,350	75%
■ Out-of-state	$2,750	25%
No state listed	$0	

* by large individual contributors ($200 & above)

Electric Utilities		$5,200
Duquesne Light Co	$1,450	PAC
General Public Utilities	$1,250	PAC
ACRE (Action Cmte for Rural Electrification)	$1,000	PAC
Pennsylvania Power & Light	$1,000	PAC
Waste Management	**$1,000**	
None over $1,000		

Finance, Insurance & Real Estate		$12,600
Insurance	**$1,450**	
American Council of Life Insurance	$1,000	PAC
Real Estate	**$8,000**	
National Assn of Realtors	$8,000	PAC
Accountants	**$2,000**	
American Institute of CPA's	$2,000	PAC

Health		$14,800
Health Professionals	**$13,800**	
American Medical Assn	$10,000	PAC

Lawyers & Lobbyists		$3,300
Lawyers & Lobbyists	**$3,300**	
None over $1,000		

Misc Business		$16,200
Food & Beverage	**$10,000**	
S&A Restaurant Corp	$3,000	PAC
ARA Services Inc	$2,000	PAC
Chili's Inc	$2,000	PAC
National Restaurant Assn	$1,250	PAC
Misc Manufacturing & Distributing	**$3,800**	
Corning Glass Works	$2,500	PAC
Owens-Illinois	$1,000	PAC

Contribution Totals by Sector

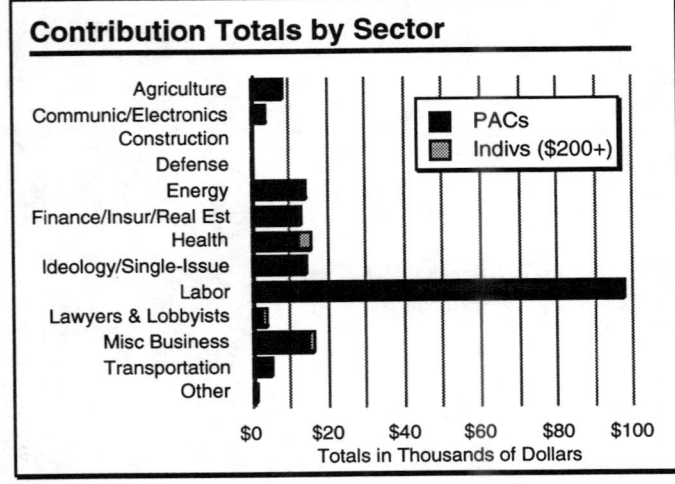

Legend: ■ PACs ▨ Indivs ($200+)

Sectors (top to bottom): Agriculture, Communic/Electronics, Construction, Defense, Energy, Finance/Insur/Real Est, Health, Ideology/Single-Issue, Labor, Lawyers & Lobbyists, Misc Business, Transportation, Other

Totals in Thousands of Dollars: $0 $20 $40 $60 $80 $100

Transportation $4,450

Automotive $1,500
    Auto Dealers & Drivers for Free Trade ....$1,500 PAC

Railroads $1,000
    Union Pacific Corp ....$1,000 PAC

Sea Transport $1,000
    None over $1,000

Labor

Labor $97,000

Building Trade Unions $22,550
    Laborers' Political League ....$6,500 PAC
    Plumbers/Pipefitters Union* ....$5,550 PAC
    Carpenters & Joiners Union ....$5,000 PAC
    Operating Engineers Union ....$2,750 PAC
    AFL-CIO Bldg/Construction Trades Dept ....$1,500 PAC
    Ironworkers Union ....$1,000 PAC

Industrial Unions $26,000
    United Auto Workers ....$10,000 PAC
    Intl Brotherhood of Electrical Workers ....$6,500 PAC
    Machinists/Aerospace Workers Union ....$5,500 PAC
    Boilermakers Union ....$1,750 PAC

Transportation Unions $21,150
    Marine Engineers Union* ....$7,000 PAC
    Teamsters Union ....$5,100 PAC
    Air Line Pilots Assn ....$5,000 PAC
    United Transportation Union ....$1,500 PAC
    Transport Workers Union ....$1,300 PAC

Public Sector Unions $24,550
    National Education Assn ....$9,000 PAC
    American Fedn of St/Cnty/Munic Employees ......$5,500 PAC
    National Assn Retired Federal Employees ....$3,000 PAC
    International Assn of Firefighters ....$2,500 PAC
    National Assn of Letter Carriers ....$2,500 PAC
    American Postal Workers Union ....$1,000 PAC

Misc Unions $2,750
    Hotel/Restaurant Employees Union ....$1,750 PAC
    Service Employees International Union ....$1,000 PAC

Ideological/Single-Issue

Ideological/Single-Issue $13,923

Gun Rights/Gun Control $10,400
    National Rifle Assn ....$9,900 PAC

Misc Issues $3,500
    National Cmte to Preserve Social Security ....$3,000 PAC

Other & Unknown

Unknown $1,950

    Employer Listed/Category Unknown $1,000
      None over $1,000

Independent expenditures supporting Murphy
    National Right to Life PAC $1,996

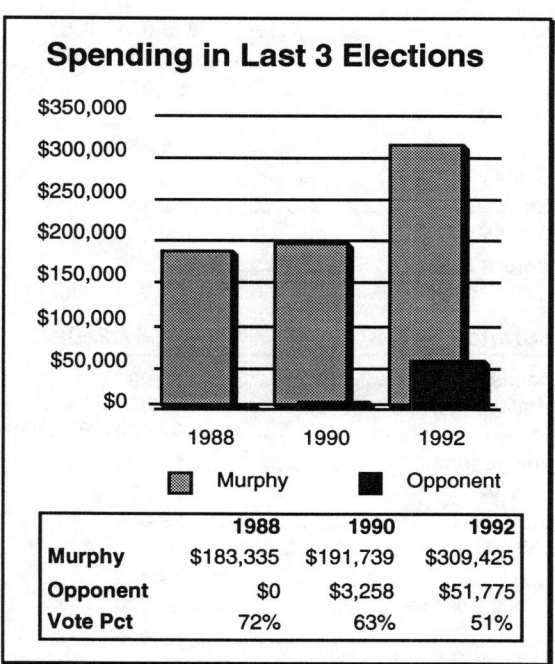

Spending in Last 3 Elections

	1988	1990	1992
Murphy	$183,335	$191,739	$309,425
Opponent	$0	$3,258	$51,775
Vote Pct	72%	63%	51%

---

* Contributions came from more than one affiliate or subsidiary.

John P. Murtha, D-Pa (12)

First elected: 1974
1991-92 Total Receipts: $935,459
1992 Year-end Cash: $174,483

1991-92 Committees & Subcommittees

Appropriations
Defense (Chairman); Interior and Related Agencies; Legislative

Leading Contributors

Business

Agriculture	**$17,600**
Tobacco	$5,500

None over $5,000

Communications/Electronics	**$23,533**
Computer Equipment & Services	$13,000

None over $5,000

Construction	**$31,200**
General Contractors	$14,200
George Zamias & Co	$5,000 Indiv
Special Trade Contractors	$6,000
Sargent Electric Co	$5,000 Indiv

Defense	**$231,200**
Defense Aerospace	$109,600
General Dynamics	$12,600 PAC/Ind
Textron Inc	$10,500 PAC/Ind
General Electric	$9,900 PAC
Rockwell International	$9,000 PAC/Ind
LTV Aerospace & Defense Co	$7,000 PAC
Martin Marietta Corp	$7,000 PAC
Lockheed Corp	$6,000 PAC
Grumman Corp	$5,500 PAC
Boeing Co	$5,000 PAC
Colt Industries	$5,000 PAC
United Technologies	$5,000 PAC

Source of Funds in 1992 Election

Source	Total	Pct
■ PACs	$540,060	57%
▨ Indivs $200+	$342,033	36%
☐ Indivs under $200	$42,576	5%
⊠ Other	$18,320	2%
Candidate	$0	0%
Party	$7,530	1%

Source of PAC Dollars by Sector

Source	Total	Pct
■ Business	$411,300	77%
▨ Labor	$107,850	20%
☐ Ideology/Single Issue	$15,600	3%

In-State vs. Out-of-State Contributions*

Source	Total	Pct
☐ In-State	$170,233	51%
■ Out-of-state	$166,600	49%
No state listed	$1,700	

* by large individual contributors ($200 & above)

Defense Electronics	**$83,400**
AT&T	$10,000 PAC
Raytheon	$9,500 PAC
Diagnostic Retrieval Systems	$6,000 Indiv
Westinghouse Electric	$5,900 PAC
Hughes Aircraft	$5,000 PAC
Texas Instruments	$5,000 PAC
Misc Defense	$38,200
Tenneco Inc	$6,000 PAC
General Atomics	$5,500 PAC

Energy & Natural Resources	**$93,000**
Oil & Gas	$49,250
USX Corp*	$13,000 PAC
Coastal Corp	$7,000 PAC
Mining	$8,950

None over $5,000

Misc Energy	**$5,250**

None over $5,000

Electric Utilities	**$19,800**

None over $5,000

Waste Management	**$7,500**
Chambers Development Co	$5,000 PAC/Ind

Finance, Insurance & Real Estate	**$61,250**
Commercial Banks	$22,000
Pittsburgh National Bank	$9,000 PAC
Mellon Bank	$7,000 PAC/Ind
Securities & Investment	$8,000

None over $5,000

Insurance	**$9,000**

None over $5,000

Real Estate	**$13,400**
National Assn of Realtors	$6,000 PAC
Accountants	$8,500

None over $5,000

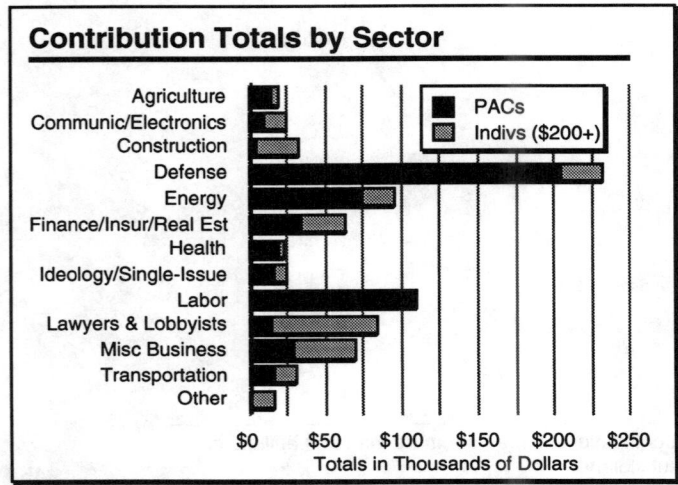

Contribution Totals by Sector

Agriculture, Communic/Electronics, Construction, Defense, Energy, Finance/Insur/Real Est, Health, Ideology/Single-Issue, Labor, Lawyers & Lobbyists, Misc Business, Transportation, Other

■ PACs ▨ Indivs ($200+)

$0 $50 $100 $150 $200 $250
Totals in Thousands of Dollars

Health $22,050

Health Professionals $7,750
    None over $5,000

Hospitals/Nursing Homes $8,800
    None over $5,000

Lawyers & Lobbyists $82,900

Lawyers & Lobbyists $82,900
    SR Wojdak & Associates .... $12,000 Indiv
    Cassidy & Associates .... $10,000 Indiv
    Hyjek & Fix .... $8,000 Indiv
    Assn of Trial Lawyers of America .... $5,000 PAC

Misc Business $67,600

Business Services $8,000
    None over $5,000

Chemical & Related Manufacturing $6,750
    None over $5,000

Steel Production $33,000
    Allegheny Ludlum Corp* .... $6,000 PAC

Misc Manufacturing & Distributing $11,200
    None over $5,000

Transportation $29,550

Air Transport $5,000
    None over $5,000

Railroads $10,800
    None over $5,000

Sea Transport $8,250
    None over $5,000

Labor

Labor $107,850

Building Trade Unions $33,500
    Ironworkers Union .... $9,000 PAC
    Laborers' Political League .... $7,000 PAC
    Carpenters & Joiners Union .... $5,000 PAC
    Plumbers/Pipefitters Union .... $5,000 PAC

Industrial Unions $28,500
    United Auto Workers .... $7,500 PAC
    United Mine Workers .... $5,000 PAC
    United Steelworkers .... $5,000 PAC

Transportation Unions $30,000
    Air Line Pilots Assn .... $10,000 PAC
    Teamsters Union .... $10,000 PAC
    Seafarers International Union .... $6,000 PAC

Public Sector Unions $9,800
    None over $5,000

Misc Unions $6,050
    None over $5,000

Ideological/Single-Issue

Ideological/Single-Issue $22,350

Pro-Israel $9,750
    None over $5,000

Gun Rights/Gun Control $7,450
    National Rifle Assn .... $7,450 PAC

Other & Unknown

Other $15,450

Education $6,650
    None over $5,000

Retired $7,300
    None over $5,000

Unknown $71,250

    Employer Listed/Category Unknown $66,600
        None over $5,000

Spending in Last 3 Elections

	1988	1990	1992
Murtha	$401,945	$1,097,107	$794,097
Opponent	$0	$5,951	$0
Vote Pct	100%	62%	100%

* Contributions came from more than one affiliate or subsidiary.

John T. Myers, R-Ind (7)

First elected: 1966

1991-92 Total Receipts: $340,979
1992 Year-end Cash: $62,387

1991-92 Committees & Subcommittees

Appropriations
Energy and Water Development (Ranking Republican); Agriculture, Rural Development, Food and Drug Administration and Related Agencies

Post Office and Civil Service
Compensation and Employee Benefits (Ranking Republican); Postal Personnel and Modernization

Leading Contributors

Business

Agriculture $28,000

Crop Production & Basic Processing *$6,500*
  None over $1,500
Tobacco *$2,000*
  None over $1,500
Dairy *$3,500*
  Associated Milk Producers .... $2,000 PAC
Poultry & Eggs *$1,500*
  None over $1,500
Livestock *$2,500*
  National Pork Producers Council .... $1,500 PAC
Agricultural Services/Products *$9,500*
  Indiana Farm Bureau .... $5,000 PAC
  American Veterinary Medical Assn .... $1,500 PAC
Food Processing & Sales *$2,500*
  None over $1,500

Communications/Electronics $14,700

Printing & Publishing *$2,500*
  Thomas J Lankford Inc .... $2,000 Indiv
Media/Entertainment *$3,000*
  Comcast Corp .... $3,000 PAC
Telephone Utilities *$7,700*
  Indiana Bell Telephone .... $3,750 PAC
  BellSouth Corp* .... $1,500 PAC

Source of Funds in 1992 Election

Source	Total	Pct
■ PACs	$199,534	59%
▦ Indivs $200+	$28,609	8%
□ Indivs under $200	$69,506	20%
⊠ Other	$43,330	13%
Candidate	$0	0%
Party	$6,000	2%

Source of PAC Dollars by Sector

Source	Total	Pct
■ Business	$162,099	87%
▨ Labor	$21,750	12%
□ Ideology/Single Issue	$3,250	2%

In-State vs. Out-of-State Contributions*

Source	Total	Pct
□ In-State	$10,059	35%
■ Out-of-state	$18,350	65%
No state listed	$0	

* by large individual contributors ($200 & above)

Construction $16,949

General Contractors *$4,150*
  None over $1,500
Home Builders *$3,000*
  National Assn of Home Builders .... $3,000 PAC
Construction Services *$7,099*
  Parsons Brinckerhoff Inc .... $1,500 Indiv
Building Materials & Equipment *$2,700*
  Caterpillar Tractor .... $1,500 PAC

Defense $4,700

Defense Aerospace *$4,200*
  Martin Marietta Corp .... $1,500 PAC

Energy & Natural Resources $37,599

Oil & Gas *$8,100*
  Petroleum Marketers Assn .... $2,000 PAC
Mining *$4,749*
  National Coal Assn .... $1,749 PAC
Nuclear Energy *$8,500*
  General Atomics .... $7,000 PAC
Misc Energy *$2,500*
  Bechtel Corp .... $1,500 PAC
Electric Utilities *$12,500*
  Public Service Co of Indiana .... $2,600 PAC
  Southern Indiana Gas & Electric .... $2,500 PAC
  ACRE (Action Cmte for Rural Electrification)* ... $1,850 PAC

Contribution Totals by Sector

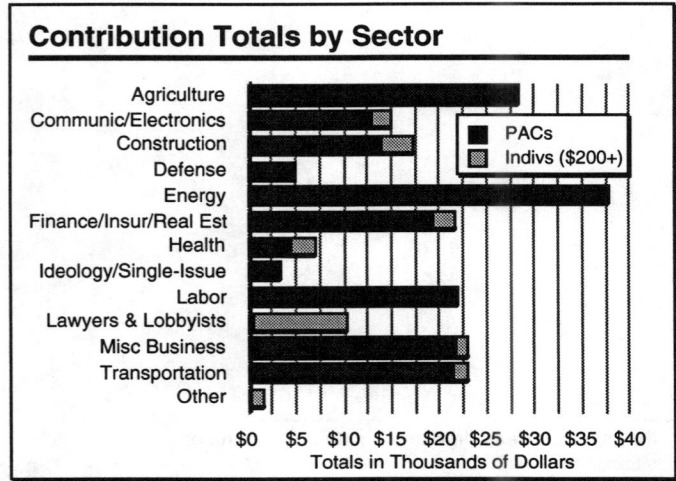

Agriculture
Communic/Electronics
Construction
Defense
Energy
Finance/Insur/Real Est
Health
Ideology/Single-Issue
Labor
Lawyers & Lobbyists
Misc Business
Transportation
Other

■ PACs
▨ Indivs ($200+)

$0 $5 $10 $15 $20 $25 $30 $35 $40
Totals in Thousands of Dollars

Finance, Insurance & Real Estate $21,501

Commercial Banks $6,175
  American Bankers Assn* ....$3,625 PAC

Insurance $5,386
  None over $1,500

Real Estate $8,190
  National Assn of Realtors ....$7,940 PAC

Health $6,650

Health Professionals $1,500
  None over $1,500

Hospitals/Nursing Homes $3,250
  None over $1,500

Pharmaceuticals/Health Products $1,900
  None over $1,500

Lawyers & Lobbyists $10,150

Lawyers & Lobbyists $10,150
  Cassidy & Associates ....$6,800 Indiv

Misc Business $22,800

Beer, Wine & Liquor $2,500
  National Beer Wholesalers Assn ....$2,500 PAC

Retail Sales $3,400
  None over $1,500

Misc Services $2,000
  None over $1,500

Business Services $2,300
  None over $1,500

Chemical & Related Manufacturing $3,850
  None over $1,500

Misc Manufacturing & Distributing $7,000
  Corning Glass Works ....$2,500 PAC
  Stone Container Corp ....$2,000 PAC

Transportation $22,600

Air Transport $6,500
  United Parcel Service ....$3,000 PAC
  UNC Inc ....$1,500 PAC

Automotive $10,300
  National Auto Dealers Assn ....$5,000 PAC
  Auto Dealers & Drivers for Free Trade ......$2,500 PAC
  Americans for Free International Trade ....$2,000 PAC

Trucking $1,500
  None over $1,500

Sea Transport $3,800
  American Waterways Operators ....$1,500 PAC

Labor

Labor $21,750

Transportation Unions $2,000
  None over $1,500

Public Sector Unions $19,750
  National Assn of Letter Carriers ....$6,500 PAC
  National Assn Retired Federal Employees ..$4,000 PAC
  American Postal Workers Union ....$2,000 PAC
  National League of Postmasters ....$2,000 PAC
  National Rural Letter Carriers Assn ....$2,000 PAC
  National Assn of Postmasters ....$1,500 PAC

Ideological/Single-Issue

Ideological/Single-Issue $3,250

Gun Rights/Gun Control $2,500
  National Rifle Assn ....$2,500 PAC

Other & Unknown

Unknown $3,609
  None over $1,500

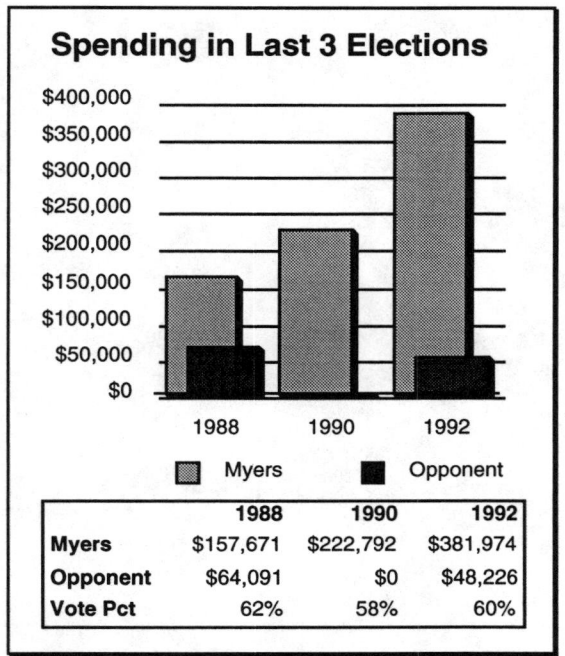

Spending in Last 3 Elections

	1988	1990	1992
Myers	$157,671	$222,792	$381,974
Opponent	$64,091	$0	$48,226
Vote Pct	62%	58%	60%

---

* Contributions came from more than one affiliate or subsidiary.

Jerrold Nadler, D-NY (8)

First elected: 1992
1991-92 Total Receipts: $49,685
1992 Year-end Cash: $9,178

1993-94 Committees & Subcommittees

Judiciary
Civil and Constitutional Rights; International Law, Immigration and Refugees

Public Works and Transportation
Economic Development; Surface Transportation; Water Resources and the Environment

Leading Contributors

Business

Communications/Electronics		$3,000
Media/Entertainment		*$1,000*
Motion Picture Assn of America	$1,000	Indiv
Telephone Utilities		*$2,000*
AT&T	$1,000	PAC
United Telecommunications	$1,000	PAC

Construction		$1,000
General Contractors		*$1,000*
Grow Tunneling Corp	$1,000	Indiv

Finance, Insurance & Real Estate		$8,250
Commercial Banks		*$3,500*
Chase Manhattan	$1,000	PAC
JP Morgan & Co	$1,000	PAC
Securities & Investment		*$2,750*
Goldman, Sachs & Co	$1,500	PAC/Ind
Insurance		*$2,000*
MLW Services Inc	$1,250	Indiv

Health		$7,500
Health Professionals		*$7,000*
American Medical Assn	$5,000	PAC
American College of Emergency Physicians	$1,000	PAC
American Nurses Assn	$1,000	PAC

Source of Funds in 1992 Election

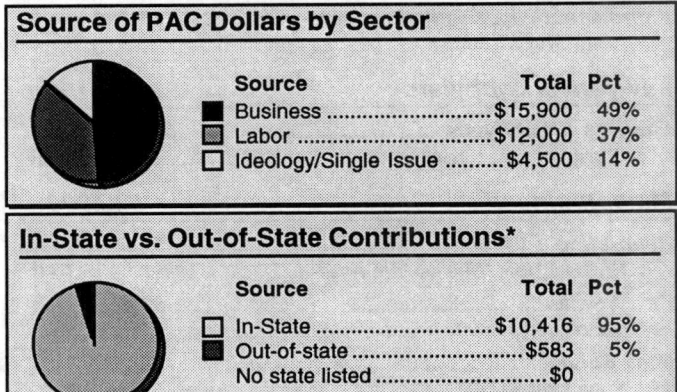

Source	Total	Pct
■ PACs	$37,750	67%
▨ Indivs $200+	$13,749	24%
☐ Indivs under $200	$786	1%
⊠ Other	$3,900	7%
Candidate	$1,000	2%
Party	$0	0%

Source of PAC Dollars by Sector

Source	Total	Pct
■ Business	$15,900	49%
▨ Labor	$12,000	37%
☐ Ideology/Single Issue	$4,500	14%

In-State vs. Out-of-State Contributions*

Source	Total	Pct
☐ In-State	$10,416	95%
■ Out-of-state	$583	5%
No state listed	$0	

* by large individual contributors ($200 & above)

Lawyers & Lobbyists		$1,499
Lawyers & Lobbyists		*$1,499*
None over $1,000		

Transportation		$1,000
Railroads		*$1,000*
None over $1,000		

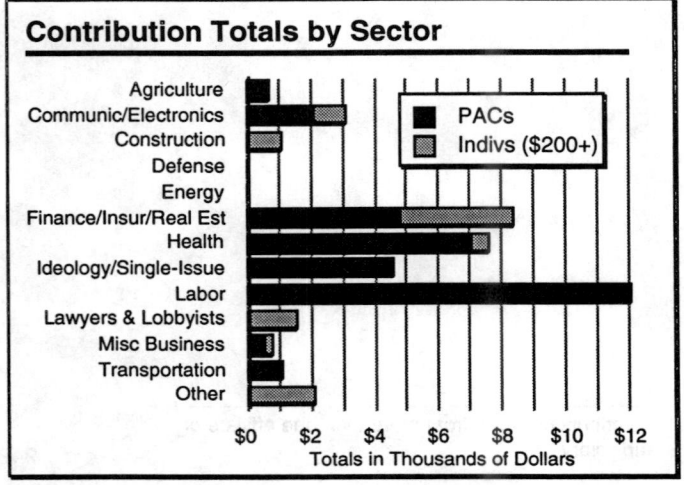

Contribution Totals by Sector

- Agriculture
- Communic/Electronics
- Construction
- Defense
- Energy
- Finance/Insur/Real Est
- Health
- Ideology/Single-Issue
- Labor
- Lawyers & Lobbyists
- Misc Business
- Transportation
- Other

■ PACs
▨ Indivs ($200+)

$0 $2 $4 $6 $8 $10 $12
Totals in Thousands of Dollars

Labor

Labor	$12,000

Industrial Unions **$2,500**
    United Auto Workers ....$2,500   PAC

Transportation Unions **$2,500**
    United Transportation Union ....$2,500   PAC

Public Sector Unions **$5,500**
    American Federation of Teachers ....$5,000   PAC

Misc Unions **$1,500**
    Food & Commercial Workers Union ....$1,000   PAC

Ideological/Single-Issue

Ideological/Single-Issue	$4,500

Leadership PACs **$1,500**
    Effective Government Cmte (Dick Gephardt) ......$1,000   PAC

Pro-Israel **$1,000**
    National PAC ....$1,000   PAC

Human Rights **$2,000**
    Human Rights Campaign Fund...........................$2,000   PAC

Other & Unknown

Other	$2,050

Retired **$1,750**
    None over $1,000

Unknown	$1,250

    Employer Listed/Category Unknown $1,250
        Barnert Associates ....$1,000   Indiv

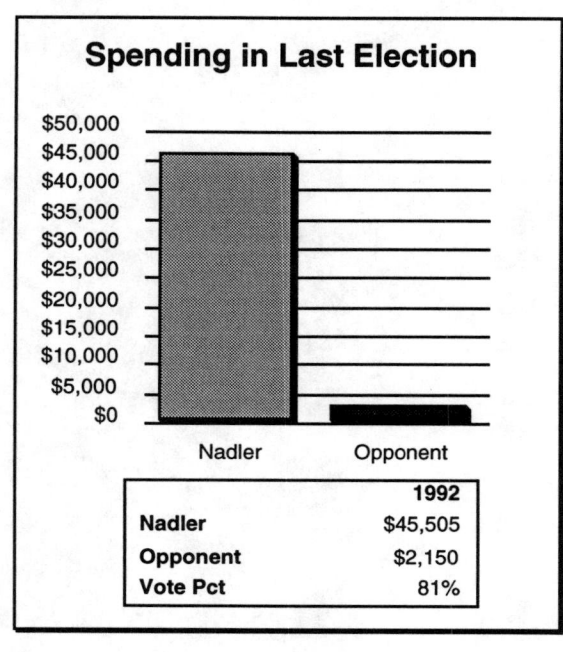

Spending in Last Election

	1992
Nadler	$45,505
Opponent	$2,150
Vote Pct	81%

* Contributions came from more than one affiliate or subsidiary.

951

William H. Natcher, D-Ky (2)

First elected: 1953

1991-92 Total Receipts: $6,623
1992 Year-end Cash: $0

1991-92 Committees & Subcommittees

Appropriations
Agriculture, Rural Development, Food and Drug Administration and Related Agencies; District of Columbia; Labor, Health and Human Services, and Education (Chairman)

Leading Contributors

Source of Funds in 1992 Election

Source	Total	Pct
PACs	$0	0%
Indivs $200+	$0	0%
Indivs under $200	$0	0%
Other	$24,393	100%
Candidate	$6,623	27%
Party	$17,770	73%

Source of PAC Dollars by Sector

No PAC contributions reported

Source	Total	Pct
Business	$0	0%
Labor	$0	0%
Ideology/Single Issue	$0	0%

In-State vs. Out-of-State Contributions*

No large contributions

Source	Total	Pct
In-State	$0	0%
Out-of-state	$0	0%
No state listed	$0	

* by large individual contributors ($200 & above)

Contribution Totals by Sector

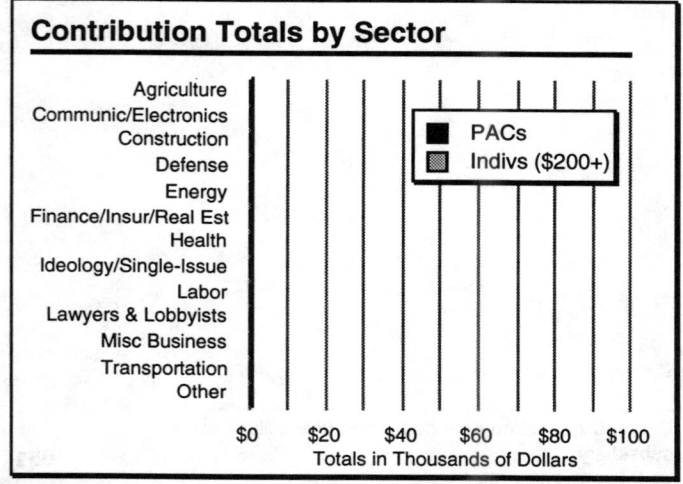

PACs
Indivs ($200+)

Agriculture
Communic/Electronics
Construction
Defense
Energy
Finance/Insur/Real Est
Health
Ideology/Single-Issue
Labor
Lawyers & Lobbyists
Misc Business
Transportation
Other

$0 $20 $40 $60 $80 $100
Totals in Thousands of Dollars

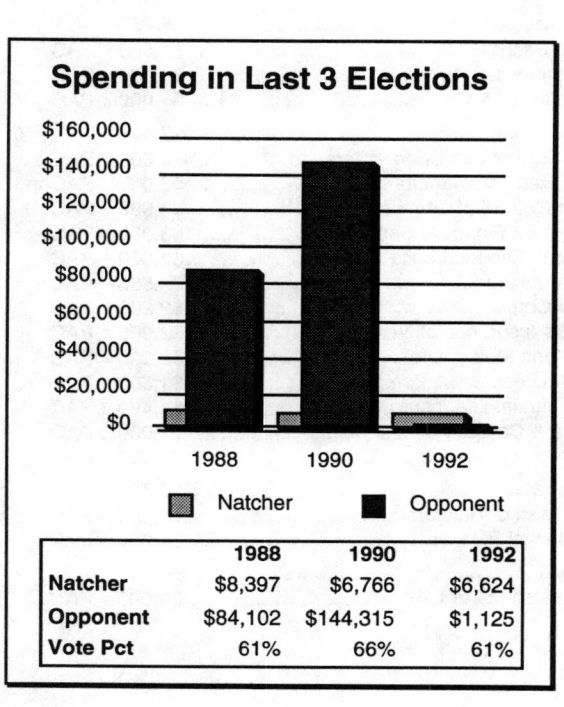

Spending in Last 3 Elections

	1988	1990	1992
Natcher	$8,397	$6,766	$6,624
Opponent	$84,102	$144,315	$1,125
Vote Pct	61%	66%	61%

Richard E. Neal, D-Mass (2)

First elected: 1988

1991-92 Total Receipts: $384,741
1992 Year-end Cash: $41,868

1991-92 Committees & Subcommittees

Banking, Finance and Urban Affairs
Domestic Monetary Policy; Financial Institutions Supervision, Regulation and Insurance; Housing and Community Development; International Development, Finance, Trade and Monetary Policy

Small Business
Regulation, Business Opportunity and Energy

Leading Contributors

Business

Agriculture — $9,700

Agricultural Services/Products	**$1,750**	
Farm Credit Council	$1,500	PAC
Food Processing & Sales	**$1,750**	
Food Marketing Institute	$1,000	PAC
Forestry & Forest Products	**$5,500**	
Westvaco Corp	$5,000	PAC

Communications/Electronics — $6,150

Printing & Publishing	**$2,000**	
Bassett Printing	$2,000	Indiv
Telephone Utilities	**$3,900**	
AT&T	$2,000	PAC
New England Telephone	$1,400	PAC

Construction — $4,100

General Contractors	**$1,000**	
None over $1,000		
Special Trade Contractors	**$2,000**	
Collins Electric Co	$1,750	Indiv

Defense — $3,300

Defense Aerospace	**$1,500**	
United Technologies	$1,000	PAC
Defense Electronics	**$1,800**	
Raytheon	$1,800	PAC

Energy & Natural Resources — $3,800

Oil & Gas	**$2,750**	
Bay State Gas Co	$1,750	PAC

Contribution Totals by Sector

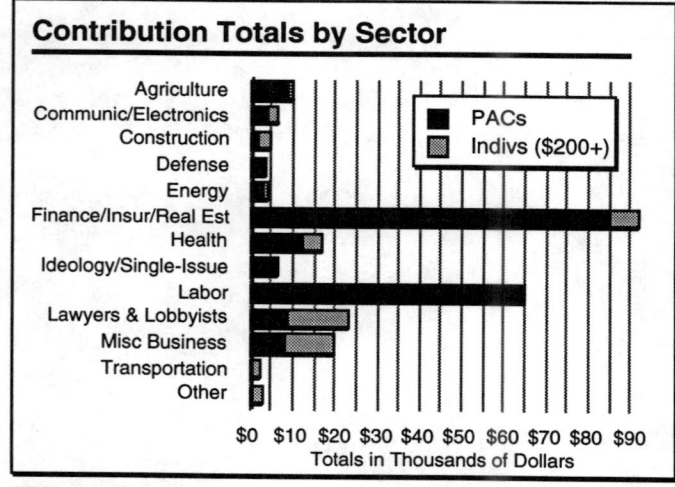

Agriculture
Communic/Electronics
Construction
Defense
Energy
Finance/Insur/Real Est
Health
Ideology/Single-Issue
Labor
Lawyers & Lobbyists
Misc Business
Transportation
Other

■ PACs
▨ Indivs ($200+)

$0 $10 $20 $30 $40 $50 $60 $70 $80 $90
Totals in Thousands of Dollars

Source of Funds in 1992 Election

Source	Total	Pct
■ PACs	$208,395	54%
▨ Indivs $200+	$76,769	20%
□ Indivs under $200	$94,232	24%
▨ Other	$5,682	1%
Candidate	$0	0%
Party	$1,137	0%

Source of PAC Dollars by Sector

Source	Total	Pct
■ Business	$132,199	65%
▨ Labor	$64,400	32%
□ Ideology/Single Issue	$5,723	3%

In-State vs. Out-of-State Contributions*

Source	Total	Pct
□ In-State	$65,519	87%
■ Out-of-state	$9,750	13%
No state listed	$1,500	

*** by large individual contributors ($200 & above)**

Finance, Insurance & Real Estate — $91,418

Commercial Banks	**$13,800**	
JP Morgan & Co	$4,000	PAC
Norstar Bancorp	$2,000	PAC
Bank of Boston	$1,750	PAC
Barnett Banks Inc	$1,000	PAC
Continental Illinois Corp	$1,000	PAC
First Chicago Corp	$1,000	PAC
Savings & Loans	**$2,050**	
None over $1,000		
Credit Unions	**$1,500**	
Credit Union National Assn	$1,000	PAC
Securities & Investment	**$5,450**	
Goldman, Sachs & Co	$1,500	PAC
Securities Industry Assn	$1,400	PAC
Morgan Stanley & Co	$1,000	PAC
Insurance	**$50,418**	
National Assn of Life Underwriters	$10,000	PAC
Massachusetts Mutual Life Insurance	$8,000	PAC/Ind
American Council of Life Insurance	$4,999	PAC
John Hancock Financial Service	$3,000	PAC
Metropolitan Life Insurance	$2,900	PAC
Prudential Insurance	$2,500	PAC
Travelers Corp	$2,200	PAC
Mutual Life Insurance of New York	$2,000	PAC
New England Mutual Life	$2,000	PAC
New York Life	$1,500	PAC
Principal Mutual Life Insurance	$1,400	PAC
Aetna Life & Casualty	$1,000	PAC
Chubb Corp	$1,000	PAC
Real Estate	**$12,700**	
National Assn of Realtors	$10,000	PAC
Boston Capital Partners	$1,000	Indiv
Accountants	**$4,500**	
American Institute of CPA's	$4,000	PAC

Health — $16,350

Health Professionals **$14,100**
   American Medical Assn ....$5,350 PAC
   American Dental Assn ....$4,000 PAC
   American Academy of Ophthalmology ....$2,000 PAC

Hospitals/Nursing Homes **$1,500**
   Bay State Medical Center ....$1,000 Indiv

Lawyers & Lobbyists — $23,050

Lawyers & Lobbyists **$23,050**
   Assn of Trial Lawyers of America ....$5,000 PAC
   Akin, Gump et al ....$1,800 PAC
   Keyes & Donnellan ....$1,400 Indiv
   Federal Legislative Associates ....$1,000 Indiv
   Jones, Day et al ....$1,000 PAC
   RG Flippo & Associates ....$1,000 Indiv

Misc Business — $19,200

Food & Beverage **$2,500**
   Abdow's Restaurant ....$1,250 Indiv

Beer, Wine & Liquor **$2,000**
   National Beer Wholesalers Assn ....$1,000 PAC

Recreation/Live Entertainment **$2,000**
   Riverside Park ....$2,000 Indiv

Lodging/Tourism **$2,500**
   Carroll Travel ....$1,500 Indiv
   Marriott Corp ....$1,000 PAC

Chemical & Related Manufacturing **$3,000**
   Astro Chemical ....$2,000 Indiv

Misc Manufacturing & Distributing **$5,400**
   Corning Glass Works ....$2,000 PAC
   HBA Cast Products ....$1,000 Indiv

Transportation — $2,200

Trucking **$1,950**
   None over $1,000

Labor

Labor — $64,400

Building Trade Unions **$19,000**
   Carpenters & Joiners Union ....$6,000 PAC
   Laborers' Political League ....$3,500 PAC
   Operating Engineers Union ....$3,100 PAC
   Ironworkers Union ....$2,500 PAC
   Sheet Metal Workers Union ....$1,500 PAC
   Plumbers/Pipefitters Union...........................$1,000 PAC

Industrial Unions **$18,900**
   Intl Brotherhood of Electrical Workers ....$5,700 PAC
   United Auto Workers ....$5,000 PAC
   Machinists/Aerospace Workers Union ....$3,900 PAC
   United Steelworkers ....$2,000 PAC
   Rubber Cork Linoleum & Plastic Workers ....$1,000 PAC

Transportation Unions **$9,600**
   Teamsters Union ....$7,500 PAC
   Transport Workers Union ....$1,000 PAC

Public Sector Unions **$14,900**
   National Assn Retired Federal Employees ....$4,000 PAC
   National Assn of Letter Carriers ....$4,000 PAC
   National Education Assn ....$4,000 PAC
   American Postal Workers Union ....$1,000 PAC
   International Assn of Firefighters ....$1,000 PAC

Misc Unions **$2,000**
   Food & Commercial Workers Union ....$2,000 PAC

Ideological/Single-Issue

Ideological/Single-Issue — $5,723

Leadership PACs **$3,000**
   Fund for a Democratic Majority (Ted Kennedy) ...$2,500 PAC

Misc Issues **$2,700**
   National Cmte to Preserve Social Security ....$2,800 PAC

Other & Unknown

Other — $2,250

Civil Servants/Public Officials **$1,000**
   None over $1,000

Unknown — $27,450

   No Employer Listed or Found $18,450
   Employer Listed/Category Unknown $8,500
      Steiger's ....$1,750 Indiv
      Resource Controls Inc ....$1,000 Indiv

Spending in Last 3 Elections

	1988	1990	1992
Neal	$268,094	$534,345	$336,327
Opponent	$0	$0	$102,179
Vote Pct	80%	100%	53%

Legend: Neal, Opponent

Stephen L. Neal, D-NC (5)

First elected: 1974

1991-92 Total Receipts: $493,627
1992 Year-end Cash: $3,697

1991-92 Committees & Subcommittees

Banking, Finance and Urban Affairs
Domestic Monetary Policy (Chairman); Financial Institutions Supervision, Regulation and Insurance; Housing and Community Development; International Development, Finance, Trade and Monetary Policy

Government Operations
Legislation and National Security

Leading Contributors

Business

Agriculture $33,125

Crop Production & Basic Processing **$7,625**
　None over $1,500

Tobacco **$16,250**
　RJR Nabisco* .... $12,250　Indiv
　Philip Morris .... $3,000　PAC

Dairy **$4,500**
　Associated Milk Producers .... $2,000　PAC
　Dairymen Inc-North Carolina .... $2,000　PAC

Poultry & Eggs **$2,500**
　Tyson Foods .... $1,500　PAC

Agricultural Services/Products **$2,000**
　None over $1,500

Communications/Electronics $12,650

Telephone Utilities **$9,750**
　Southern Bell .... $6,000　PAC
　AT&T .... $2,000　PAC

Computer Equipment & Services **$2,000**
　Electronic Data Systems .... $2,000　PAC

Construction $5,750

Home Builders **$3,500**
　Manufactured Housing Institute .... $1,500　PAC

Defense $2,500

Defense Aerospace **$2,000**
　Textron Inc .... $1,500　PAC

Contribution Totals by Sector

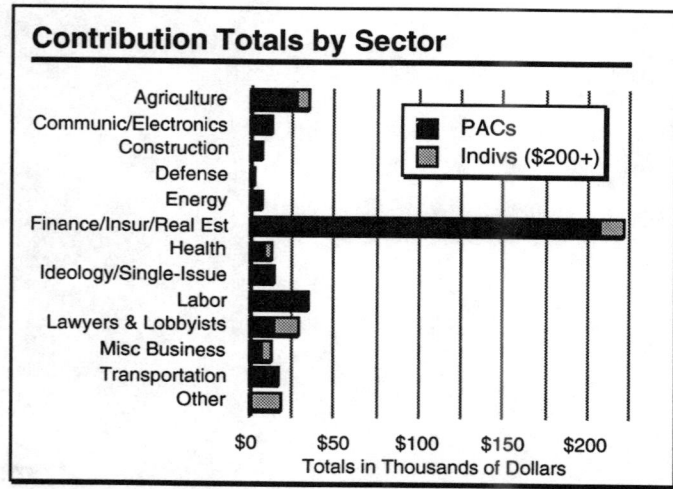

Agriculture
Communic/Electronics
Construction
Defense
Energy
Finance/Insur/Real Est
Health
Ideology/Single-Issue
Labor
Lawyers & Lobbyists
Misc Business
Transportation
Other

■ PACs
▨ Indivs ($200+)

$0　$50　$100　$150　$200
Totals in Thousands of Dollars

Source of Funds in 1992 Election

Source	Total	Pct
■ PACs	$338,570	67%
▨ Indivs $200+	$83,600	16%
☐ Indivs under $200	$56,214	11%
▧ Other	$28,556	6%
Candidate	$0	0%
Party	$18,313	4%

Source of PAC Dollars by Sector

Source	Total	Pct
■ Business	$296,420	86%
▨ Labor	$34,300	10%
☐ Ideology/Single Issue	$14,050	4%

In-State vs. Out-of-State Contributions*

Source	Total	Pct
☐ In-State	$73,600	88%
■ Out-of-state	$10,000	12%
No state listed	$0	

*** by large individual contributors ($200 & above)**

Energy & Natural Resources $6,050

Electric Utilities **$4,450**
　ACRE (Action Cmte for Rural Electrification) .... $2,000　PAC

Finance, Insurance & Real Estate $220,050

Commercial Banks **$112,900**
　American Bankers Assn .... $10,000　PAC
　Citicorp .... $10,000　PAC
　JP Morgan & Co .... $8,500　PAC
　Citizens & Southern National Bank .... $8,000　PAC
　Chase Manhattan .... $5,000　PAC
　Continental Illinois Corp .... $5,000　PAC
　Independent Bankers Assn .... $4,750　PAC
　BankAmerica Corp .... $4,500　PAC
　Banc One Corp .... $4,000　PAC
　First Chicago Corp .... $4,000　PAC
　Security Pacific Corp .... $4,000　PAC
　Assn of Bank Holding Companies .... $3,500　PAC
　Bankers Trust .... $3,000　PAC
　Barnett Banks Inc .... $3,000　PAC
　Chemical Bank .... $3,000　PAC
　Consumer Bankers Assn .... $2,500　PAC
　NCNB Corp .... $2,500　PAC/Ind
　Wachovia Bank & Trust .... $2,200　Indiv
　First Interstate Bank of California .... $2,000　PAC
　MBNA Corp .... $2,000　PAC
　MNC Financial Inc .... $2,000　PAC
　Manufacturers Hanover .... $2,000　PAC
　Mellon Bank .... $1,700　PAC

Savings & Loans **$4,500**
　First Federal Savings Bank .... $2,500　Indiv
　Great Western Financial Corp .... $2,000　PAC

Credit Unions **$11,750**
　Credit Union National Assn .... $10,000　PAC
　National Assn of Federal Credit Unions .... $1,750　PAC

Finance/Credit Companies $9,500
- Household International Inc ......$5,000 PAC
- American Financial Services Assn ......$1,500 PAC
- Beneficial Management Corp ......$1,500 PAC

Securities & Investment $21,950
- Chicago Board of Trade ......$4,000 PAC
- Dean Witter ......$3,000 PAC
- Chicago Mercantile Exchange ......$2,500 PAC
- First Boston Corp ......$2,000 PAC
- Public Securities Assn ......$1,900 PAC
- Merrill Lynch ......$1,500 PAC

Insurance $21,850
- Northwestern Mutual Life ......$4,000 PAC
- Massachusetts Mutual Life Insurance ......$3,000 PAC
- Acacia Mutual Life Insurance ......$1,500 PAC
- American International Group Inc ......$1,500 PAC
- Capital Holding Corp ......$1,500 PAC

Real Estate $21,100
- National Assn of Realtors ......$8,000 PAC
- First Union Corp ......$2,500 PAC
- Loan America Financial Corp ......$2,500 PAC
- Federal National Mortgage Assn ......$1,900 PAC

Accountants $15,000
- American Institute of CPA's ......$10,000 PAC
- Arthur Andersen & Co ......$2,000 PAC
- Coopers & Lybrand ......$2,000 PAC

Misc Finance $1,500
- None over $1,500

Health $11,850

Health Professionals $6,850
- American Medical Assn ......$2,850 PAC

Pharmaceuticals/Health Products $3,500
- Glaxo Inc ......$2,000 PAC

Lawyers & Lobbyists $28,400

Lawyers & Lobbyists $28,400
- Womble, Carlyle et al ......$5,650 Indiv
- Assn of Trial Lawyers of America ......$5,500 PAC
- Kirkpatrick & Lockhart ......$1,500 PAC
- Petree, Stockton & Robinson ......$1,500 Indiv
- SecuraPAC ......$1,500 PAC
- Shaw, Pittman et al ......$1,500 PAC

Spending in Last 3 Elections

	1988	1990	1992
Neal	$756,115	$647,331	$517,594
Opponent	$745,010	$174,574	$188,130
Vote Pct	53%	59%	53%

Neal / Opponent

Misc Business $12,445

Business Associations $1,500
- Kaplan School Supply ......$1,500 Indiv

Business Services $1,500
- None over $1,500

Textiles $6,250
- Burlington Industries ......$2,000 PAC
- American Textile Manufacturers Institute ......$1,500 PAC
- Unifi Inc ......$1,500 Indiv

Transportation $16,450

Air Transport $7,250
- United Parcel Service ......$3,000 PAC
- Boeing Co ......$2,000 PAC
- General Electric ......$1,500 PAC

Automotive $7,000
- National Auto Dealers Assn ......$3,500 PAC
- Ford Motor Co ......$2,500 PAC

Railroads $1,500
- None over $1,500

Labor

Labor $34,300

Transportation Unions $3,000
- Marine Engineers Dist 2 Maritime Officers ......$2,500 PAC

Public Sector Unions $28,550
- National Education Assn ......$12,000 PAC
- National Assn Retired Federal Employees ......$5,000 PAC
- American Fedn of St/Cnty/Munic Employees ......$4,000 PAC
- International Assn of Firefighters ......$2,000 PAC
- National Assn of Letter Carriers ......$2,000 PAC

Misc Unions $2,000
- Food & Commercial Workers Union ......$1,500 PAC

Ideological/Single-Issue

Ideological/Single-Issue $14,250

Democratic/Liberal $2,250
- National Cmte for an Effective Congress ......$2,050 PAC

Leadership PACs $1,500
- None over $1,500

Gun Rights/Gun Control $2,000
- National Rifle Assn ......$2,000 PAC

Misc Issues $7,500
- National Cmte to Preserve Social Security ......$4,000 PAC
- Sierra Club ......$2,000 PAC

Other & Unknown

Other $18,400

Civil Servants/Public Officials $1,500
- None over $1,500

Education $6,800
- Bowman Gray School of Medicine ......$4,250 Indiv

Retired $10,600
- None over $1,500

Unknown $12,150
- Homemakers/Non-income earners $1,900
- Employer Listed/Category Unknown $8,800
  - Kaplan Companies ......$1,500 Indiv

* Contributions came from more than one affiliate or subsidiary.

Jim Nussle, R-Iowa (2)

First elected: 1990

1991-92 Total Receipts: $867,359
1992 Year-end Cash: $5,194

1991-92 Committees & Subcommittees

Agriculture
Conservation, Credit and Rural Development; Cotton, Rice and Sugar; Wheat, Soybeans and Feed Grains

Banking, Finance and Urban Affairs
Economic Stabilization; General Oversight and Investigations; Policy Research and Insurance

Select Committee on Aging

Leading Contributors

Business

Agriculture	$91,932	
Crop Production & Basic Processing	**$18,975**	
Cargill Inc	$6,250	PAC/Ind
American Crystal Sugar Corp	$2,700	PAC
Tobacco	**$5,200**	
RJR Nabisco	$2,500	PAC
Dairy	**$7,350**	
Associated Milk Producers	$3,000	PAC
Poultry & Eggs	**$2,700**	
None over $2,500		
Livestock	**$5,150**	
National Cattlemen's Assn*	$3,850	PAC
Agricultural Services/Products	**$24,258**	
Iowa Farm Bureau Federation	$5,148	PAC
Archer-Daniels-Midland Corp	$3,000	PAC
Food Processing & Sales	**$22,449**	
ConAgra Inc	$6,000	PAC
American Meat Institute	$3,399	PAC
General Mills	$2,500	PAC
Iowa Packing Co	$2,500	Indiv
Forestry & Forest Products	**$3,600**	
None over $2,500		

Source of Funds in 1992 Election

Source	Total	Pct
■ PACs	$350,415	38%
▨ Indivs $200+	$217,003	23%
▦ Indivs under $200	$256,579	28%
⊠ Other	$103,335	11%
Candidate	$0	0%
Party	$80,139	9%

Source of PAC Dollars by Sector

Source	Total	Pct
■ Business	$314,824	94%
▨ Labor	$4,000	1%
☐ Ideology/Single Issue	$16,601	5%

In-State vs. Out-of-State Contributions*

Source	Total	Pct
☐ In-State	$188,888	88%
■ Out-of-state	$26,400	12%
No state listed	$0	

* by large individual contributors ($200 & above)

Communications/Electronics	$26,350	
Printing & Publishing	**$11,950**	
Babka Publishing Co	$4,850	Indiv
Woodward Communications	$2,750	Indiv
Telephone Utilities	**$11,900**	
United Telecommunications	$3,000	PAC
US West Inc	$2,550	PAC

Construction	$30,950	
General Contractors	**$7,200**	
Associated General Contractors	$2,500	PAC
Lockard Construction	$2,500	Indiv
Home Builders	**$5,300**	
National Assn of Home Builders	$4,500	PAC
Special Trade Contractors	**$8,400**	
Sheet Metal/Air Conditioning Contractors	$3,250	PAC
Building Materials & Equipment	**$10,050**	
None over $2,500		

Defense	$7,405	
Defense Aerospace	**$4,405**	
None over $2,500		

Energy & Natural Resources	$19,350	
Oil & Gas	**$7,650**	
None over $2,500		
Misc Energy	**$3,000**	
Cooper Industries	$3,000	PAC
Electric Utilities	**$8,700**	
Iowa Electric Light & Power	$2,750	PAC/Ind

Contribution Totals by Sector

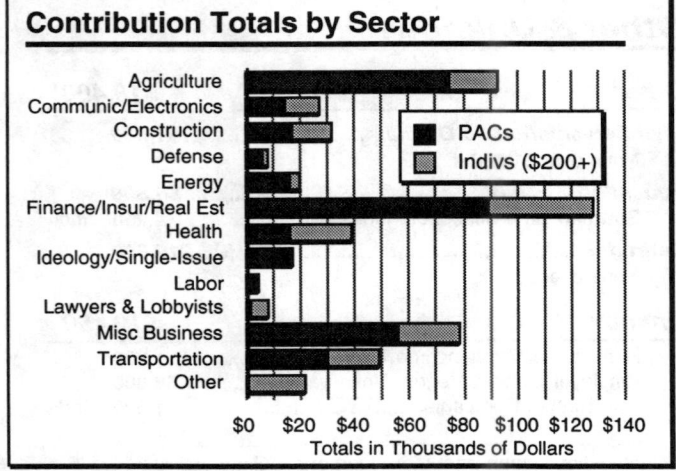

Agriculture
Communic/Electronics
Construction
Defense
Energy
Finance/Insur/Real Est
Health
Ideology/Single-Issue
Labor
Lawyers & Lobbyists
Misc Business
Transportation
Other

■ PACs
▨ Indivs ($200+)

$0 $20 $40 $60 $80 $100 $120 $140
Totals in Thousands of Dollars

Finance, Insurance & Real Estate $127,225

Commercial Banks *$43,150*
   Iowa Bankers Assn ....$10,000 PAC
   Hawkeye Bancorp ....$5,000 PAC
   Barnett Banks Inc ....$4,100 PAC
   First National Bank ....$2,500 Indiv

Securities & Investment *$16,850*
   Chicago Mercantile Exchange ....$3,000 PAC

Insurance *$33,800*
   National Assn of Life Underwriters.............$10,000 PAC
   Principal Mutual Life Insurance ....$2,650 PAC

Real Estate *$15,200*
   National Assn of Realtors ....$5,600 PAC

Accountants *$7,950*
   American Institute of CPA's ....$5,850 PAC

Misc Finance *$6,650*
   None over $2,500

Health $38,100

Health Professionals *$32,500*
   American Dental Assn ....$4,500 PAC
   American Medical Assn....................................$3,500 PAC

Pharmaceuticals/Health Products *$3,150*
   None over $2,500

Lawyers & Lobbyists $7,750

Lawyers & Lobbyists *$7,750*
   None over $2,000

Misc Business $77,677

Business Associations *$6,951*
   National Fedn of Independent Business ....$5,764 PAC

Food & Beverage *$14,850*
   National Restaurant Assn ....$6,000 PAC
   McDonald's Corp ....$3,250 PAC/Ind

Beer, Wine & Liquor *$6,850*
   National Beer Wholesalers Assn ....$5,500 PAC

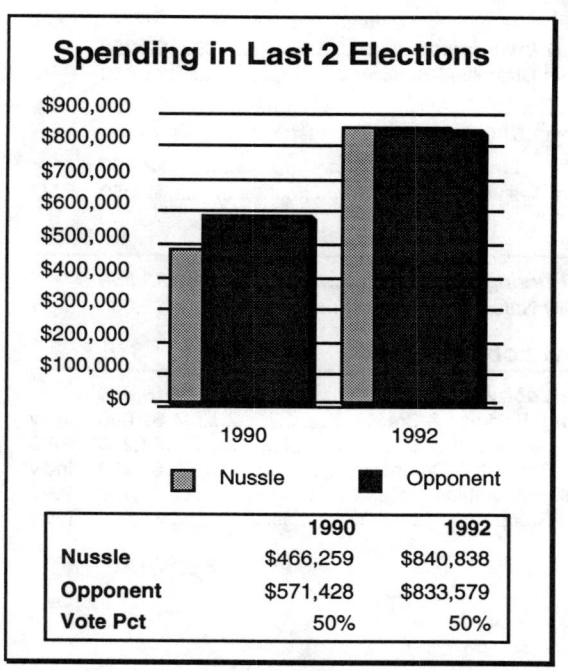

Spending in Last 2 Elections

	1990	1992
Nussle	$466,259	$840,838
Opponent	$571,428	$833,579
Vote Pct	50%	50%

Retail Sales *$6,000*
   None over $2,500

Business Services *$3,150*
   None over $2,500

Chemical & Related Manufacturing *$7,100*
   Dow Chemical ....$3,500 PAC

Misc Manufacturing & Distributing *$27,850*
   Maytag Co ....$5,500 PAC
   Stone Container Corp ....$5,000 PAC
   Flexsteel Industries ....$3,750 Indiv

Transportation $48,750

Air Transport *$4,600*
   United Parcel Service ....$3,200 PAC

Automotive *$26,750*
   National Auto Dealers Assn ....$5,000 PAC
   Auto Dealers & Drivers for Free Trade ....$3,000 PAC
   Eaton Corp ....$3,000 PAC
   PES Inc ....$3,000 Indiv
   Mike Finnin Motors ....$2,500 Indiv
   Truck Country of Iowa ....$2,500 Indiv

Trucking *$5,200*
   None over $2,500

Railroads *$8,050*
   Union Pacific Corp ....$5,500 PAC

Misc Transport *$3,450*
   Featherlite Mfg Inc ....$2,500 Indiv

Labor

Labor $4,000

Public Sector Unions *$4,000*
   National Assn Retired Federal Employees ....$4,000 PAC

Ideological/Single-Issue

Ideological/Single-Issue $16,801

Leadership PACs *$5,000*
   Campaign America (Bob Dole) ....$3,000 PAC

Pro-Life *$3,000*
   National Right to Life PAC ....$3,000 PAC

Misc Issues *$5,400*
   None over $2,500

Other & Unknown

Other $20,850

Retired *$18,600*
   None over $2,500

Unknown $34,488

   Homemakers/Non-income earners $11,800
   No Employer Listed or Found $3,650
   Employer Listed/Category Unknown $17,138
     None over $2,500

---

* Contributions came from more than one affiliate or
subsidiary.

959

James L. Oberstar, D-Minn (8)

First elected: 1974

1991-92 Total Receipts: $340,642
1992 Year-end Cash: $347,548

1991-92 Committees & Subcommittees

Budget
Human Resources (Chairman); Urgent Fiscal Issues

Public Works and Transportation
Aviation (Chairman); Economic Development (Vice Chairman); Investigations and Oversight; Public Buildings and Grounds; Water Resources

Leading Contributors

Business

Agriculture $13,650

Crop Production & Basic Processing	**$3,400**	
American Crystal Sugar Corp	$1,000	PAC
American Sugarbeet Growers Assn	$1,000	PAC
Southern Minn Beet Sugar Co-op	$1,000	PAC
Dairy	**$5,000**	
Associated Milk Producers	$4,000	PAC
Forestry & Forest Products	**$5,000**	
Potlatch Corp	$4,000	PAC

Communications/Electronics $7,500

Telephone Utilities	**$6,250**	
AT&T	$2,000	PAC/Ind
US West Inc	$2,000	PAC
GTE Corp	$1,000	PAC

Construction $10,200

General Contractors	**$5,750**	
National Utility Contractors Assn	$3,000	PAC
Construction Services	**$1,500**	
None over $1,000		
Building Materials & Equipment	**$1,450**	
None over $1,000		

Defense $3,500

Defense Aerospace	**$2,000**	
Lockheed Corp	$1,000	PAC
Martin Marietta Corp	$1,000	PAC
Misc Defense	**$1,500**	
BDM International	$1,000	PAC

Source of Funds in 1992 Election

Source	Total	Pct
■ PACs	$202,005	57%
▨ Indivs $200+	$45,600	13%
☐ Indivs under $200	$28,587	8%
▧ Other	$76,030	22%
Candidate	$0	0%
Party	$11,930	3%

Source of PAC Dollars by Sector

Source	Total	Pct
■ Business	$112,107	56%
▨ Labor	$80,500	40%
☐ Ideology/Single Issue	$9,023	4%

In-State vs. Out-of-State Contributions*

Source	Total	Pct
☐ In-State	$22,950	50%
■ Out-of-state	$22,650	50%
No state listed	$0	

* by large individual contributors ($200 & above)

Energy & Natural Resources $5,000

Oil & Gas	**$1,000**	
None over $1,000		
Mining	**$1,500**	
Cleveland-Cliffs Iron Co	$1,500	PAC
Electric Utilities	**$2,500**	
ACRE (Action Cmte for Rural Electrification)	$1,000	PAC
Northern States Power Co	$1,000	PAC

Finance, Insurance & Real Estate $7,850

Commercial Banks	**$2,000**	
Norwest Corp	$1,000	PAC
Securities & Investment	**$2,250**	
Investors Diversified Services	$1,000	PAC
Insurance	**$1,350**	
None over $1,000		
Real Estate	**$2,250**	
National Assn of Realtors	$2,250	PAC

Health $3,800

Hospitals/Nursing Homes	**$3,550**	
Pine City Nursing Home	$2,000	Indiv

Lawyers & Lobbyists $18,850

Lawyers & Lobbyists	**$18,850**	
Ginsburg, Feldman & Bress	$2,000	Indiv
Dorsey, Windhorst et al	$1,250	PAC
Squire, Sanders & Dempsey	$1,250	Indiv
Capital Partnerships Inc	$1,100	PAC
Hoving Group	$1,000	Indiv

Contribution Totals by Sector

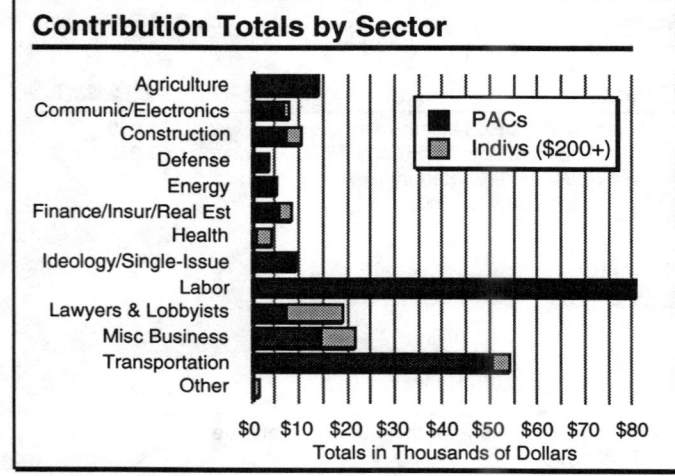

Agriculture, Communic/Electronics, Construction, Defense, Energy, Finance/Insur/Real Est, Health, Ideology/Single-Issue, Labor, Lawyers & Lobbyists, Misc Business, Transportation, Other

■ PACs
▨ Indivs ($200+)

$0 $10 $20 $30 $40 $50 $60 $70 $80
Totals in Thousands of Dollars

Misc Business $21,227

Beer, Wine & Liquor **$1,500**
   Joseph E Seagram & Sons ....$1,000 PAC

Misc Services **$2,500**
   American Assn of Equipment Lessors ....$2,500 PAC

Business Services **$9,077**
   Outdoor Advertising Assn of America ....$4,327 PAC/Ind
   Marketing Corp of America ....$1,000 Indiv

Lodging/Tourism **$3,400**
   American Hotel & Motel Assn ....$1,150 PAC
   American Society of Travel Agents ....$1,000 PAC

Chemical & Related Manufacturing **$1,000**
   Dial Corp ....$1,000 PAC

Steel Production **$2,250**
   None over $1,000

Transportation $53,530

Air Transport **$39,905**
   Aircraft Owners & Pilots Assn ....$10,000 PAC
   Federal Express Corp ....$5,000 PAC
   Northwest Airlines ....$5,000 PAC
   United Parcel Service ....$5,000 PAC
   American Assn of Airport Executives ....$3,655 PAC
   United Airlines ....$2,000 PAC
   Dallas-Fort Worth Air ....$1,000 Indiv
   Delta Airlines ....$1,000 PAC
   General Aviation Manufacturers Assn ....$1,000 PAC
   General Electric ....$1,000 PAC

Automotive **$4,000**
   National Auto Dealers Assn ....$3,000 PAC

Trucking **$3,750**
   American Trucking Assns ....$2,000 PAC
   Minnesota Truck Operators ....$1,000 PAC

Railroads **$2,625**
   Burlington Northern ....$1,000 PAC
   Union Pacific Corp ....$1,000 PAC

Sea Transport **$1,750**
   CSX Corp* ....$1,000 PAC

Misc Transport **$1,500**
   American Bus Assn ....$1,000 PAC

Spending in Last 3 Elections

	1988	1990	1992
Oberstar	$157,802	$229,262	$386,646
Opponent	$7,743	$16,681	$51,689
Vote Pct	75%	73%	59%

Labor

Labor $80,500

Building Trade Unions **$9,000**
   Laborers' Political League ....$4,000 PAC
   Carpenters & Joiners Union ....$2,500 PAC
   Operating Engineers Union ....$1,000 PAC
   Plumbers/Pipefitters Union ....$1,000 PAC

Industrial Unions **$14,400**
   United Steelworkers ....$5,000 PAC
   Machinists/Aerospace Workers Union ....$4,000 PAC
   United Auto Workers ....$1,500 PAC
   Amalgamated Clothing & Textile Workers ....$1,000 PAC
   Intl Brotherhood of Electrical Workers ....$1,000 PAC
   Ladies Garment Workers Union ....$1,000 PAC

Transportation Unions **$34,700**
   Air Line Pilots Assn ....$10,000 PAC
   United Transportation Union ....$5,000 PAC
   Assn of Flight Attendants ....$3,000 PAC
   Transport Workers Union ....$3,000 PAC
   Teamsters Union ....$2,500 PAC
   Amalgamated Transit Union ....$2,000 PAC
   National Air Traffic Controllers Assn ....$2,000 PAC
   Assn of Professional Flight Attendants ....$1,250 PAC
   Independent Fedn of Flight Attendants ....$1,250 PAC
   Trans Comm International Union ....$1,100 PAC
   International Longshoremen's Assn ....$1,000 PAC
   Marine Engineers Union ....$1,000 PAC

Public Sector Unions **$19,500**
   American Federation of Teachers ....$5,000 PAC
   National Assn Retired Federal Employees ....$3,000 PAC
   National Assn of Letter Carriers ....$2,500 PAC
   American Fedn of St/Cnty/Munic Employees ......$2,000 PAC
   Federal Managers' Assn ....$1,500 PAC
   International Assn of Firefighters ....$1,500 PAC
   American Postal Workers Union ....$1,000 PAC
   National Assn of Postal Supervisors ....$1,000 PAC

Misc Unions **$2,900**
   Food & Commercial Workers Union ....$2,000 PAC

Ideological/Single-Issue

Ideological/Single-Issue $9,023

Democratic/Liberal **$2,500**
   National Cmte for an Effective Congress ....$2,500 PAC

Gun Rights/Gun Control **$3,000**
   National Rifle Assn ....$3,000 PAC

Human Rights **$1,000**
   KidsPAC ....$1,000 PAC

Misc Issues **$2,000**
   National Cmte to Preserve Social Security ....$2,000 PAC

Other & Unknown

Other $1,450
   None over $1,000

Unknown $11,150
   Generic Occupation/Category Unknown $1,750
   Employer Listed/Category Unknown $9,150
    None over $1,000

---

* Contributions came from more than one affiliate or subsidiary.

David R. Obey, D-Wis (7)

First elected: 1969

1991-92 Total Receipts: $497,123
1992 Year-end Cash: $307,113

1991-92 Committees & Subcommittees

Appropriations
Foreign Operations, Export Financing and Related Programs (Chairman); Labor, Health and Human Services, Education and Related Agencies; Legislative

Joint Economic Committee

Leading Contributors

Business

Agriculture $32,625

Crop Production & Basic Processing	**$7,625**	
Ocean Spray Cranberries Inc	$2,000	PAC
American Sugarbeet Growers Assn	$1,500	PAC
Tobacco	**$2,000**	
None over $1,500		
Dairy	**$13,000**	
Associated Milk Producers	$9,000	PAC
Mid-America Dairymen	$3,000	PAC
Agricultural Services/Products	**$6,500**	
Land O'Lakes Inc	$2,500	PAC
Food Processing & Sales	**$1,750**	
None over $1,500		

Communications/Electronics $17,270

Media/Entertainment	**$4,250**	
National Cable Television Assn	$1,500	PAC
Telephone Utilities	**$6,800**	
AT&T	$3,000	PAC
Wisconsin Bell Telephone	$2,000	PAC
Electronics Mfg & Services	**$3,500**	
Westinghouse Electric	$2,500	PAC
Computer Equipment & Services	**$2,220**	
None over $1,500		

Construction $3,750
None over $1,500

Source of Funds in 1992 Election

Source	Total	Pct
■ PACs	$267,575	53%
▨ Indivs $200+	$82,355	16%
☐ Indivs under $200	$99,454	20%
⊠ Other	$54,597	11%
Candidate	$0	0%
Party	$7,008	1%

Source of PAC Dollars by Sector

Source	Total	Pct
■ Business	$134,225	51%
▨ Labor	$91,900	35%
☐ Ideology/Single Issue	$35,895	14%

In-State vs. Out-of-State Contributions*

Source	Total	Pct
☐ In-State	$5,100	6%
■ Out-of-state	$76,470	94%
No state listed	$785	

* by large individual contributors ($200 & above)

Defense $4,200

Defense Aerospace	**$3,500**	
General Dynamics	$2,000	PAC

Energy & Natural Resources $11,300

Oil & Gas	**$6,000**	
Michigan Consolidated Gas	$3,500	PAC
Electric Utilities	**$3,300**	
ACRE (Action Cmte for Rural Electrification)	$1,500	PAC
Waste Management	**$2,000**	
None over $1,500		

Finance, Insurance & Real Estate $30,550

Commercial Banks	**$4,250**	
American Bankers Assn	$3,000	PAC
Credit Unions	**$1,500**	
Credit Union National Assn	$1,500	PAC
Securities & Investment	**$2,000**	
Chicago Mercantile Exchange	$1,500	PAC
Insurance	**$13,500**	
Northwestern Mutual Life	$5,000	PAC
American Income Life Insurance	$2,000	Indiv
Blue Cross & Blue Shield Assn*	$2,000	PAC
Nationwide Corp*	$2,000	PAC
Rosen Associates Insurance	$2,000	Indiv
Real Estate	**$7,800**	
National Assn of Realtors	$3,750	PAC

Health $24,800

Health Professionals	**$17,750**	
American Medical Assn	$10,000	PAC
American Dental Assn	$4,500	PAC
American Podiatry Assn	$1,500	PAC

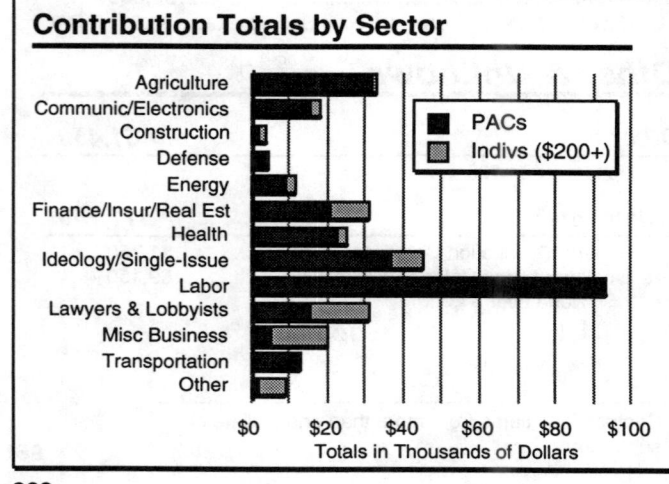

Contribution Totals by Sector

Agriculture
Communic/Electronics
Construction
Defense
Energy
Finance/Insur/Real Est
Health
Ideology/Single-Issue
Labor
Lawyers & Lobbyists
Misc Business
Transportation
Other

■ PACs
▨ Indivs ($200+)

$0 $20 $40 $60 $80 $100
Totals in Thousands of Dollars

Hospitals/Nursing Homes *$4,000*
    American Hospital Assn .... $3,000 PAC

Misc Health *$1,550*
    None over $1,500

Lawyers & Lobbyists $30,650

Lawyers & Lobbyists *$30,650*
    Assn of Trial Lawyers of America .... $10,000 PAC
    Cassidy & Associates .... $3,000 Indiv
    Neill & Co .... $2,000 Indiv
    Powell, Goldstein et al .... $1,500 PAC

Misc Business $19,200

Beer, Wine & Liquor *$2,250*
    Miller Brewing Co .... $1,500 PAC

Retail Sales *$2,000*
    Woodhaven Furniture Co .... $2,000 Indiv

Business Services *$1,500*
    None over $1,500

Steel Production *$1,500*
    None over $1,500

Misc Manufacturing & Distributing *$7,500*
    Orbit Manufacturing .... $2,000 Indiv

Transportation $12,500

Air Transport *$6,500*
    General Electric .... $2,000 PAC
    United Parcel Service .... $1,500 PAC

Trucking *$3,000*
    American Trucking Assns .... $1,500 PAC
    Yellow Freight System .... $1,500 PAC

Railroads *$2,000*
    None over $1,500

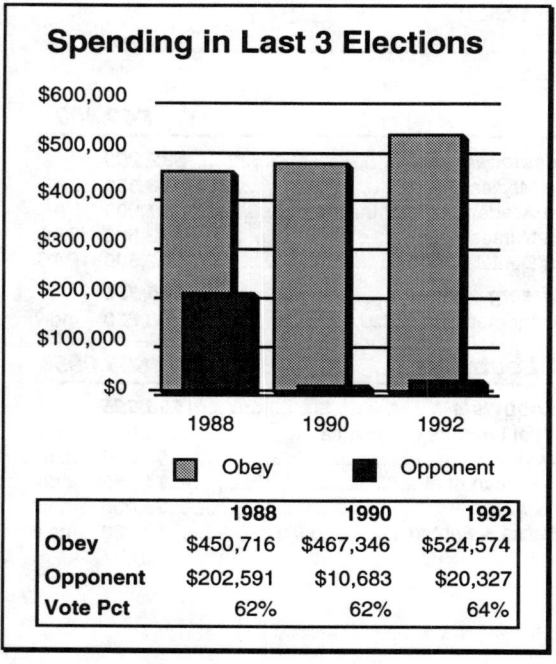

Spending in Last 3 Elections

	1988	1990	1992
Obey	$450,716	$467,346	$524,574
Opponent	$202,591	$10,683	$20,327
Vote Pct	62%	62%	64%

Labor

Labor $92,900

Building Trade Unions *$16,750*
    Laborers' Political League .... $6,000 PAC
    Plumbers/Pipefitters Union................................ $4,000 PAC
    Carpenters & Joiners Union .... $3,000 PAC
    Operating Engineers Union .... $2,250 PAC/Ind

Industrial Unions *$18,500*
    United Auto Workers .... $6,000 PAC
    Communications Workers of America .... $2,500 PAC
    Intl Brotherhood of Electrical Workers .... $2,000 PAC
    United Mine Workers .... $2,000 PAC
    United Paperworkers .... $1,500 PAC

Transportation Unions *$16,100*
    Air Line Pilots Assn .... $6,000 PAC
    Teamsters Union .... $5,000 PAC
    United Transportation Union .... $1,500 PAC

Public Sector Unions *$35,550*
    American Fedn of St/Cnty/Munic Employees ...... $9,000 PAC
    National Assn of Letter Carriers .... $6,000 PAC
    National Education Assn .... $6,000 PAC
    American Federation of Teachers .... $5,500 PAC
    National Assn Retired Federal Employees .... $3,000 PAC
    American Postal Workers Union .... $2,500 PAC

Misc Unions *$6,000*
    Food & Commercial Workers Union .... $2,000 PAC
    Office & Professional Employees Union .... $2,000 PAC

Ideological/Single-Issue

Ideological/Single-Issue $44,795

Foreign & Defense Policy *$4,500*
    American-Arab Anti-Discrimination Cmte .... $2,000 Indiv

Pro-Israel *$17,650*
    North Jersey PAC .... $4,000 PAC
    National PAC .... $2,000 PAC
    Hudson Valley PAC .... $1,500 PAC

Gun Rights/Gun Control *$3,000*
    National Rifle Assn .... $3,000 PAC

Human Rights *$17,525*
    National Community Action Foundation .... $8,000 PAC
    KidsPAC .... $5,000 PAC
    National Albanian American PAC .... $4,000 PAC

Misc Issues *$1,620*
    National Cmte to Preserve Social Security .... $1,500 PAC

Other & Unknown

Other $8,300

Education *$4,800*
    None over $1,500

Retired *$2,250*
    None over $1,500

Unknown $13,285

    Homemakers/Non-income earners $3,000
    No Employer Listed or Found $2,285
    Generic Occupation/Category Unknown $1,750
    Employer Listed/Category Unknown $6,250
        Loffredo & Volarich .... $2,000 Indiv

---

* Contributions came from more than one affiliate or
  subsidiary.

John W. Olver, D-Mass (1)

First elected: 1991

1991-92 Total Receipts: $1,416,201
1992 Year-end Cash: $3,502

1991-92 Committees & Subcommittees

Education and Labor
Elementary, Secondary and Vocational Education; Employment Opportunities; Labor-Management Relations

Science, Space and Technology
Environment; Technology and Competitiveness

Leading Contributors

Business

Agriculture	$7,500	
Dairy	$4,000	
None over $2,500		

Communications/Electronics	$18,650	
Printing & Publishing	$6,400	
Channing L Bete Co	$4,000	Indiv
Media/Entertainment	$7,300	
None over $2,500		
Telephone Utilities	$4,450	
None over $2,500		

Construction	$11,700	
General Contractors	$6,450	
None over $2,500		
Home Builders	$3,750	
National Assn of Home Builders	$2,500	PAC

Defense	$3,000	
Defense Electronics	$3,000	
Raytheon	$3,000	PAC

Energy & Natural Resources	$9,450	
Oil & Gas	$3,250	
None over $2,500		
Electric Utilities	$4,450	
None over $2,500		

Source of Funds in 1992 Election

Source	Total	Pct
PACs	$587,930	40%
Indivs $200+	$346,628	24%
Indivs under $200	$319,234	22%
Other	$212,917	15%
Candidate	$110,900	8%
Party	$79,733	5%

Source of PAC Dollars by Sector

Source	Total	Pct
Business	$80,000	15%
Labor	$343,099	65%
Ideology/Single Issue	$108,090	20%

In-State vs. Out-of-State Contributions*

Source	Total	Pct
In-State	$276,881	85%
Out-of-state	$50,697	15%
No state listed	$1,950	

* by large individual contributors ($200 & above)

Finance, Insurance & Real Estate — $48,591

Commercial Banks	$4,450	
None over $2,500		
Credit Unions	$3,000	
Credit Union National Assn	$3,000	PAC
Securities & Investment	$7,800	
Lazard Freres & Co	$3,000	Indiv
Insurance	$14,700	
Massachusetts Mutual Life Insurance	$5,000	PAC
AH Rist Insurance	$2,500	Indiv
Real Estate	$15,641	
None over $2,500		
Accountants	$2,750	
None over $2,500		

Health — $49,800

Health Professionals	$32,200	
American Medical Assn	$8,350	PAC
American Academy of Ophthalmology	$7,000	PAC
American Nurses Assn	$3,500	PAC
American Dental Assn	$2,500	PAC
Hospitals/Nursing Homes	$15,350	
ADS Management Inc	$3,650	Indiv

Lawyers & Lobbyists — $68,095

Lawyers & Lobbyists	$68,095	
Assn of Trial Lawyers of America	$10,000	PAC
Mintz, Levin et al	$5,300	Indiv
Lesser, Newman et al	$4,250	Indiv
Cassidy & Associates	$3,000	Indiv
Morse, Sacks & Fenton	$3,000	Indiv

Contribution Totals by Sector

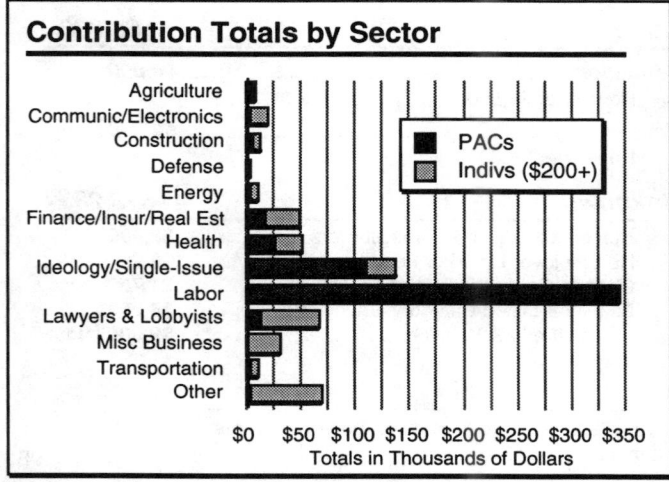

- Agriculture
- Communic/Electronics
- Construction
- Defense
- Energy
- Finance/Insur/Real Est
- Health
- Ideology/Single-Issue
- Labor
- Lawyers & Lobbyists
- Misc Business
- Transportation
- Other

Legend: ■ PACs, ▨ Indivs ($200+)

$0 $50 $100 $150 $200 $250 $300 $350
Totals in Thousands of Dollars

Misc Business	$30,287

Food & Beverage **$5,550**
None over $2,500

Retail Sales **$4,500**
Yankee Candle Co .... $3,000 Indiv

Business Services **$8,937**
None over $2,500

Misc Manufacturing & Distributing **$6,550**
Anwelt Corp .... $4,000 Indiv

Transportation	$8,725

Air Transport **$3,000**
None over $2,500

Misc Transport **$5,525**
Peter Pan Bus Lines .... $5,525 Indiv

Labor

Labor	$343,599

Building Trade Unions **$86,000**
Carpenters & Joiners Union* .... $20,000 PAC
Sheet Metal Workers Union .... $12,500 PAC
Laborers' Political League .... $12,000 PAC
Painters & Allied Trades Union .... $10,000 PAC
Operating Engineers Union .... $9,500 PAC
Bricklayers Union .... $8,000 PAC
Ironworkers Union .... $8,000 PAC
Plumbers/Pipefitters Union .... $4,000 PAC

Industrial Unions **$74,250**
United Auto Workers .... $18,000 PAC
Machinists/Aerospace Workers Union ..... $16,000 PAC
Intl Brotherhood of Electrical Workers ..... $15,500 PAC
United Steelworkers .... $7,000 PAC
Electronic Machine Furniture Workers ..... $4,500 PAC
Boilermakers Union .... $3,000 PAC
Ladies Garment Workers Union .... $3,000 PAC

Transportation Unions **$49,700**
Teamsters Union .... $20,000 PAC
Seafarers International Union .... $9,000 PAC
Marine Engineers Dist 2 Maritime Officers .... $5,500 PAC
Air Line Pilots Assn .... $5,000 PAC
Transport Workers Union .... $3,500 PAC
United Transportation Union .... $2,500 PAC

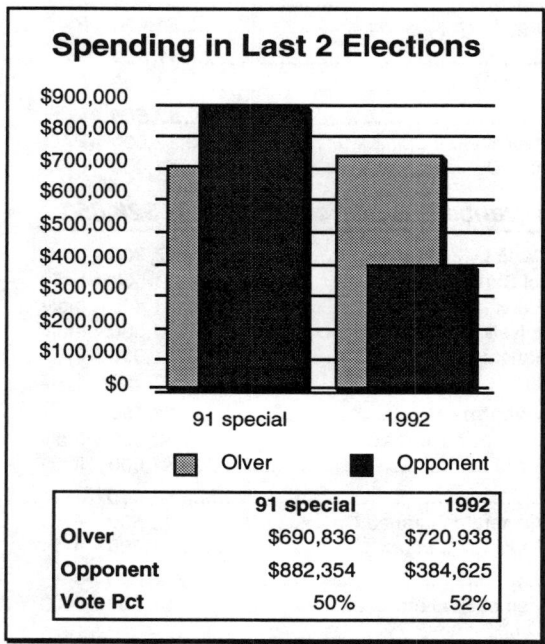

Spending in Last 2 Elections

	91 special	1992
Olver	$690,836	$720,938
Opponent	$882,354	$384,625
Vote Pct	50%	52%

Public Sector Unions **$96,350**
American Federation of Teachers .... $20,000 PAC
American Fedn of St/Cnty/Munic Employees .... $20,000 PAC
National Education Assn .... $20,000 PAC
National Assn Retired Federal Employees .... $10,000 PAC
American Postal Workers Union .... $8,500 PAC
National Assn of Letter Carriers .... $5,000 PAC
International Assn of Firefighters .... $3,500 PAC
National Rural Letter Carriers Assn .... $3,000 PAC

Misc Unions **$37,299**
Food & Commercial Workers Union .... $14,999 PAC
AFL-CIO .... $13,000 PAC
Service Employees International Union ..... $4,500 PAC

Ideological/Single-Issue

Ideological/Single-Issue	$136,683

Democratic/Liberal **$28,843**
National Cmte for an Effective Congress .... $5,150 PAC
Independent Action .... $3,500 PAC

Leadership PACs **$16,500**
Effective Government Cmte (Dick Gephardt) ...... $7,000 PAC
House Leadership Fund (Tom Foley) .... $5,000 PAC
Fund for a Democratic Majority (Ted Kennedy) ... $2,500 PAC

Pro-Israel **$11,750**
National PAC .... $6,000 PAC

Pro-Choice **$9,000**
National Abortion Rights Action League .... $5,000 PAC
Voters for Choice .... $4,000 PAC

Human Rights **$29,550**
Human Rights Campaign Fund .... $16,600 PAC
KidsPAC .... $9,000 PAC

Misc Issues **$35,837**
Sierra Club .... $13,500 PAC
League of Conservation Voters .... $8,892 PAC
National Cmte to Preserve Social Security .... $6,500 PAC
National Council of Senior Citizens .... $4,000 PAC

Other & Unknown

Other	$68,250

Non-Profit Institutions **$3,200**
MacArthur Foundation .... $2,500 Indiv

Civil Servants/Public Officials **$5,850**
None over $2,500

Education **$42,450**
Duke University .... $11,000 Indiv
University of Massachusetts .... $10,000 Indiv
Amherst College .... $6,700 Indiv
Harvard University .... $3,400 Indiv
Boston University .... $2,500 Indiv

Retired **$8,500**
None over $2,500

Other **$8,250**
National Assn of Social Workers .... $3,000 PAC

Unknown	$55,137

Homemakers/Non-income earners $7,800
No Employer Listed or Found $12,705
Employer Listed/Category Unknown $32,332
Contemporary Interiors .... $3,950 Indiv

Independent expenditures opposing Olver
East Coast Conservative PAC $2,987

---

* Contributions came from more than one affiliate or
subsidiary.

Solomon P. Ortiz, D-Texas (27)

First elected: 1982
1991-92 Total Receipts: $276,610
1992 Year-end Cash: $152,565

1991-92 Committees & Subcommittees

Armed Services
Military Installations and Facilities; Readiness; Seapower and Strategic and Critical Materials

Merchant Marine and Fisheries
Fisheries and Wildlife Conservation and the Environment; Merchant Marine

Select Committee on Narcotics Abuse and Control

Leading Contributors

Business

Agriculture $8,850

Crop Production & Basic Processing	**$2,600**	
Liska Farms	$1,000	Indiv
Food Processing & Sales	**$4,500**	
HE Butt Grocery Co	$1,500	Indiv
Sam Kane Beef Processors	$1,000	Indiv
Valley Beverage Inc	$1,000	Indiv

Communications/Electronics $9,400

Printing & Publishing	**$1,000**	
None over $1,000		
Telephone Utilities	**$4,500**	
Southwestern Bell	$3,500	PAC/Ind
AT&T	$1,000	PAC
Computer Equipment & Services	**$3,000**	
Texas Instruments	$3,000	PAC

Construction $19,518

General Contractors	**$5,800**	
Brown & Root	$1,000	PAC
Salazar Construction Co	$1,000	Indiv
Service Link	$1,000	Indiv
Special Trade Contractors	**$1,250**	
None over $1,000		
Building Materials & Equipment	**$12,468**	
CC Distributors	$9,000	Indiv
National Concrete Masonry Assn	$1,250	PAC
Valley Brick	$1,000	Indiv

Contribution Totals by Sector

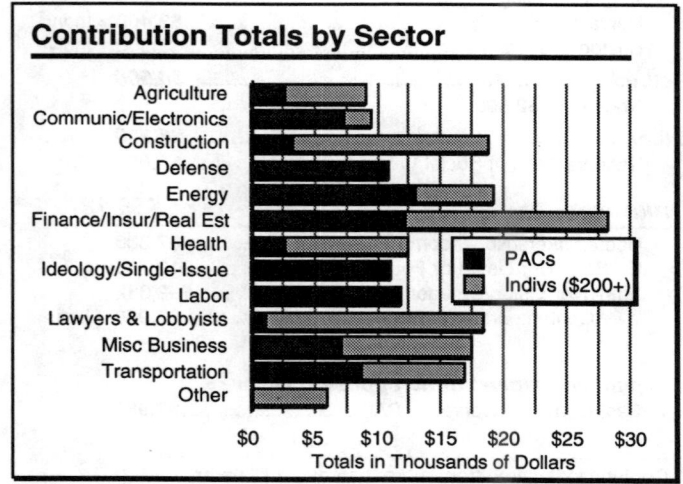

Agriculture
Communic/Electronics
Construction
Defense
Energy
Finance/Insur/Real Est
Health
Ideology/Single-Issue
Labor
Lawyers & Lobbyists
Misc Business
Transportation
Other

■ PACs
▨ Indivs ($200+)

$0 $5 $10 $15 $20 $25 $30
Totals in Thousands of Dollars

Source of Funds in 1992 Election

Source	Total	Pct
■ PACs	$99,518	36%
▨ Indivs $200+	$132,734	48%
☐ Indivs under $200	$20,446	7%
▨ Other	$24,049	9%
Candidate	$0	0%
Party	$287	0%

Source of PAC Dollars by Sector

Source	Total	Pct
■ Business	$67,668	75%
▨ Labor	$11,550	13%
☐ Ideology/Single Issue	$10,900	12%

In-State vs. Out-of-State Contributions*

Source	Total	Pct
☐ In-State	$114,184	87%
■ Out-of-state	$17,050	13%
No state listed	$1,500	

* by large individual contributors ($200 & above)

Defense $10,950

Defense Aerospace	**$5,750**	
Colt Industries	$1,000	PAC
Rockwell International	$1,000	PAC
Defense Electronics	**$3,000**	
GTE Corp	$3,000	PAC
Misc Defense	**$2,200**	
Stewart & Stevenson Services Inc	$1,200	PAC/Ind

Energy & Natural Resources $18,800

Oil & Gas	**$13,500**	
Tana Oil & Gas Corp	$2,000	Indiv
Coastal Corp	$1,000	PAC
Koch Industries	$1,000	PAC
Valero Energy Corp	$1,000	PAC
Misc Energy	**$1,000**	
Babcock & Wilcox*	$1,000	PAC
Electric Utilities	**$3,500**	
Central Power & Light	$2,000	PAC
Texas Utilities Co	$1,000	PAC

Finance, Insurance & Real Estate $28,050

Commercial Banks	**$7,200**	
International Bank of Laredo	$1,500	Indiv
American Bank	$1,400	Indiv
Brownsville National Bank	$1,000	Indiv
First City Bancorp of Texas	$1,000	PAC
NCNB Texas	$1,000	PAC
Securities & Investment	**$4,150**	
World Investment & Realty Corp	$2,000	Indiv
PaineWebber	$1,000	Indiv
Insurance	**$4,500**	
American General Insurance Co	$2,500	PAC
WC Dinn & Co	$1,000	Indiv
Real Estate	**$12,200**	
National Assn of Realtors	$7,000	PAC

Health | $12,150

Health Professionals *$10,450*
    American Medical Assn....................................$2,350   PAC
Pharmaceuticals/Health Products *$1,000*
    None over $1,000

Lawyers & Lobbyists | $18,150

Lawyers & Lobbyists *$18,150*
    Dan Alfaro Attorney at Law ....$1,000   Indiv
    Perry & Haas ....$1,000   Indiv

Misc Business | $17,200

Food & Beverage *$6,500*
    Albert Lee Co ....$1,000   Indiv
    Coca-Cola Co ....$1,000   PAC
Beer, Wine & Liquor *$3,000*
    L&F Distributors ....$2,000   Indiv
    National Beer Wholesalers Assn ....$1,000   PAC
Retail Sales *$1,200*
    None over $1,000
Business Services *$2,500*
    Contract Services Assn ....$1,300   PAC
Misc Manufacturing & Distributing *$3,500*
    Hoechst Celanese Corp ....$2,000   PAC
    Atlas & Iron Metal ....$1,500   Indiv

Transportation | $16,650

Air Transport *$2,750*
    Beech Aircraft ....$1,000   PAC
    United Parcel Service ....$1,000   PAC
Automotive *$7,000*
    National Auto Dealers Assn ....$3,000   PAC
    Shook Enterprises ....$2,000   Indiv
Railroads *$1,300*
    Union Pacific Corp ....$1,300   PAC
Sea Transport *$4,800*
    Marine Supply Sales ....$2,000   Indiv
    American Pilots Assn ....$1,000   PAC
    Port of Brownsville ....$1,000   Indiv

Labor

Labor | $11,550

Building Trade Unions *$2,000*
    Laborers' Political League ....$1,000   PAC
    Plumbers/Pipefitters Union...............................$1,000   PAC
Industrial Unions *$1,500*
    Intl Brotherhood of Electrical Workers ....$1,000   PAC
Transportation Unions *$7,000*
    Marine Engineers Dist 2 Maritime Officers ....$5,500   PAC
Public Sector Unions *$1,050*
    National Assn Retired Federal Employees ....$2,500   PAC
    American Postal Workers Union ....$1,000   PAC

Ideological/Single-Issue

Ideological/Single-Issue | $10,900

Gun Rights/Gun Control *$9,900*
    National Rifle Assn ....$9,900   PAC
Human Rights *$1,000*
    Latin American Manufacturers Assn ....$1,000   PAC

Other & Unknown

Other | $5,850

Education *$3,050*
    Ana G Mendez University ....$2,500   Indiv
Retired *$1,800*
    None over $1,000
Other *$1,000*
    Corpus Christi Army Depot ....$1,000   Indiv

Unknown | $34,834

    Homemakers/Non-income earners $8,500
    No Employer Listed or Found $2,750
    Generic Occupation/Category Unknown $2,700
    Employer Listed/Category Unknown $20,884
        Torres Enterprises ....$3,000   Indiv
        Gulf Marine Fabricators ....$1,384   Indiv
        Service Link..$1,000   Indiv
        Sky Management ....$1,000   Indiv
        TFPRA ....$1,000   Indiv
        Trane Export Inc ....$1,000   Indiv
        WL Dinn Co ....$1,000   Indiv

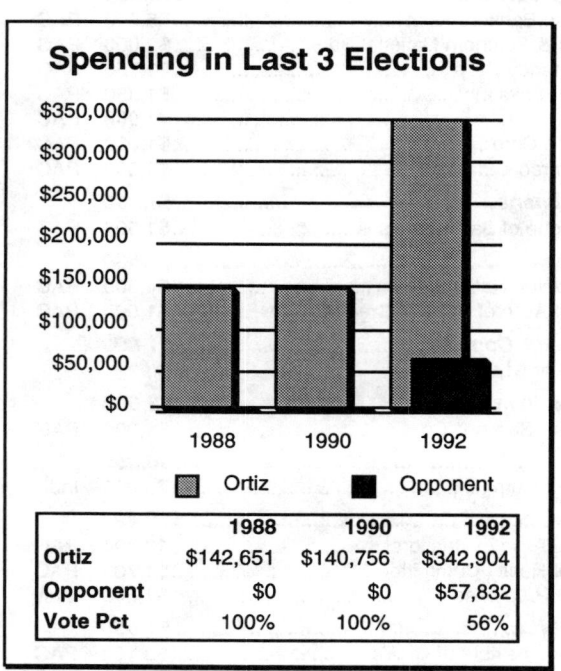

Spending in Last 3 Elections

	1988	1990	1992
Ortiz	$142,651	$140,756	$342,904
Opponent	$0	$0	$57,832
Vote Pct	100%	100%	56%

* Contributions came from more than one affiliate or
subsidiary.

Bill Orton, D-Utah (3)

First elected: 1990

1991-92 Total Receipts: $257,559
1992 Year-end Cash: $18,398

1991-92 Committees & Subcommittees

Banking, Finance and Urban Affairs
Financial Institutions Supervision, Regulation and Insurance; Housing and Community Development; International Development, Finance, Trade and Monetary Policy

Foreign Affairs
International Economic Policy and Trade

Small Business
Exports, Tax Policy and Special Problems

Leading Contributors

Business

Agriculture	$11,550	
Crop Production & Basic Processing	**$2,200**	
None over $1,000		
Dairy	**$4,800**	
Associated Milk Producers	$4,000	PAC
Livestock	**$1,800**	
National Cattlemen's Assn	$1,250	PAC
Food Processing & Sales	**$2,250**	
Murdock Healthcare	$2,000	Indiv

Communications/Electronics	$6,600	
Media/Entertainment	**$2,250**	
National Cable Television Assn	$1,000	PAC
Telephone Utilities	**$4,350**	
AT&T	$2,000	PAC
US West Inc	$1,600	PAC

Construction	$8,650	
General Contractors	**$1,350**	
Associated General Contractors	$1,350	PAC
Home Builders	**$6,900**	
National Assn of Home Builders	$5,500	PAC

Defense	$1,100	
None over $1,000		

Source of Funds in 1992 Election

	Source	Total	Pct
■	PACs	$190,995	72%
▨	Indivs $200+	$27,000	10%
□	Indivs under $200	$21,308	8%
▩	Other	$26,274	10%
	Candidate	$0	0%
	Party	$14,668	6%

Source of PAC Dollars by Sector

	Source	Total	Pct
■	Business	$139,864	61%
▨	Labor	$74,450	33%
□	Ideology/Single Issue	$14,250	6%

In-State vs. Out-of-State Contributions*

	Source	Total	Pct
□	In-State	$16,950	65%
■	Out-of-state	$9,050	35%
	No state listed	$1,000	

* by large individual contributors ($200 & above)

Energy & Natural Resources	$10,800	
Oil & Gas	**$6,450**	
Coastal Corp	$2,000	PAC
Chevron Corp	$1,350	PAC
Mining	**$1,500**	
Kennecott Corp	$1,500	PAC
Electric Utilities	**$1,850**	
ACRE (Action Cmte for Rural Electrification)	$1,350	PAC

Finance, Insurance & Real Estate	$60,394	
Commercial Banks	**$16,400**	
American Bankers Assn	$5,000	PAC
Citizens & Southern National Bank	$2,000	PAC
BankAmerica Corp	$1,750	PAC
Barnett Banks Inc	$1,350	PAC
Citicorp	$1,000	PAC
Utah Ban Corp	$1,000	PAC
Wells Fargo	$1,000	PAC
Savings & Loans	**$1,800**	
US League of Savings Assns	$1,500	PAC
Credit Unions	**$5,500**	
Credit Union National Assn	$4,500	PAC
National Assn of Federal Credit Unions	$1,000	PAC
Finance/Credit Companies	**$1,800**	
None over $1,000		
Securities & Investment	**$3,000**	
Goldman, Sachs & Co	$1,000	PAC
Insurance	**$6,350**	
Leucadia Corp	$3,000	Indiv
Real Estate	**$18,494**	
National Assn of Realtors	$13,494	PAC
National Realty Committee	$1,700	PAC
Bedford Properties	$1,500	Indiv
Accountants	**$7,050**	
American Institute of CPA's	$3,100	PAC
Arthur Andersen & Co	$2,850	PAC/Ind

Contribution Totals by Sector

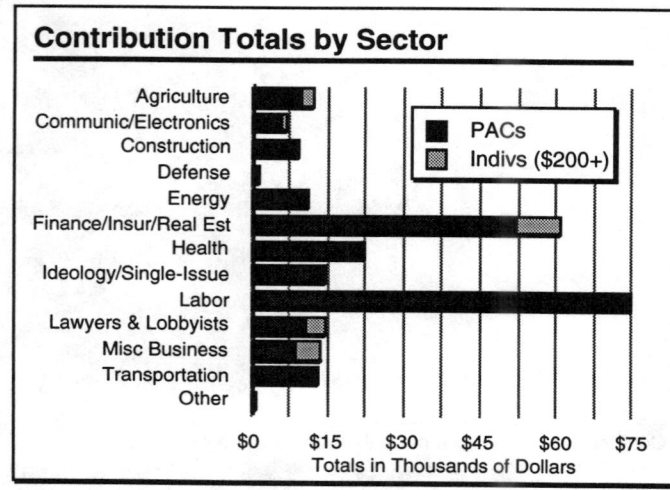

Agriculture
Communic/Electronics
Construction
Defense
Energy
Finance/Insur/Real Est
Health
Ideology/Single-Issue
Labor
Lawyers & Lobbyists
Misc Business
Transportation
Other

■ PACs
▨ Indivs ($200+)

$0 $15 $30 $45 $60 $75
Totals in Thousands of Dollars

Health $21,850

Health Professionals $14,300
   American Medical Assn.....................................$5,300 PAC
   American Dental Assn ....$3,000 PAC
   American Academy of Ophthalmology ....$2,000 PAC
   American College of Emergency Physicians ....$2,000 PAC
   American Chiropractic Assn ....$1,000 PAC

Hospitals/Nursing Homes $3,200
   American Hospital Assn ....$1,850 PAC
   Healthtrust Inc ....$1,000 PAC

Health Services $1,350
   Family Health Program Inc ....$1,000 PAC

Pharmaceuticals/Health Products $3,000
   Nu Skin International ....$2,000 PAC/Ind
   Abbott Laboratories ....$1,200 PAC

Lawyers & Lobbyists $14,150

Lawyers & Lobbyists $14,150
   Assn of Trial Lawyers of America ....$10,000 PAC
   Steptoe & Johnson ....$1,000 Indiv

Misc Business $13,150

Food & Beverage $4,000
   National Restaurant Assn ....$2,000 PAC
   McDonald's Corp ....$1,000 PAC

Retail Sales $2,150
   International Council of Shopping Centers ....$1,000 PAC

Business Services $1,500
   Peggy Fugal Advertising ....$1,000 Indiv

Chemical & Related Manufacturing $1,350
   Hercules Inc ....$1,100 PAC

Steel Production $2,500
   Geneva Steel Corp ....$2,500 Indiv

Transportation $12,720

Air Transport $3,450
   Delta Airlines ....$1,600 PAC
   Aircraft Owners & Pilots Assn ....$1,000 PAC

Automotive $7,150
   National Auto Dealers Assn ....$6,350 PAC

Railroads $1,600
   Union Pacific Corp ....$1,000 PAC

Labor

Labor $74,450

Building Trade Unions $20,650
   Carpenters & Joiners Union ....$6,000 PAC
   Laborers' Political League ....$6,000 PAC
   Sheet Metal Workers Union ....$4,000 PAC
   Plumbers/Pipefitters Union...............................$2,500 PAC
   Operating Engineers Union* ....$1,850 PAC

Industrial Unions $19,600
   United Steelworkers ....$10,000 PAC
   United Auto Workers ....$3,650 PAC
   United Mine Workers ....$1,650 PAC
   Intl Brotherhood of Electrical Workers ....$1,500 PAC
   Communications Workers of America ....$1,100 PAC
   Boilermakers Union ....$1,000 PAC

Transportation Unions $14,600
   Teamsters Union ....$10,000 PAC
   United Transportation Union ....$2,000 PAC
   Marine Engineers Union* ....$1,500 PAC

Public Sector Unions $16,800
   American Federation of Teachers ....$5,900 PAC
   National Assn of Letter Carriers ....$2,700 PAC
   National Assn Retired Federal Employees ....$2,500 PAC
   American Postal Workers Union ....$2,000 PAC
   International Assn of Firefighters ....$1,600 PAC
   National Rural Letter Carriers Assn ....$1,000 PAC

Misc Unions..$2,800
   AFL-CIO ....$1,300 PAC
   Hotel/Restaurant Employees Union ....$1,000 PAC

Ideological/Single-Issue

Ideological/Single-Issue $14,250

Democratic/Liberal $2,500
   National Cmte for an Effective Congress ....$2,500 PAC

Leadership PACs $1,000
   Victory USA (Vic Fazio) ....$1,000 PAC

Gun Rights/Gun Control $6,950
   National Rifle Assn ....$6,950 PAC

Misc Issues..$3,300
   National Cmte to Preserve Social Security ....$3,300 PAC

Other & Unknown

Unknown $5,300

   No Employer Listed or Found $2,200
   Employer Listed/Category Unknown....................$2,900
     None over $1,000

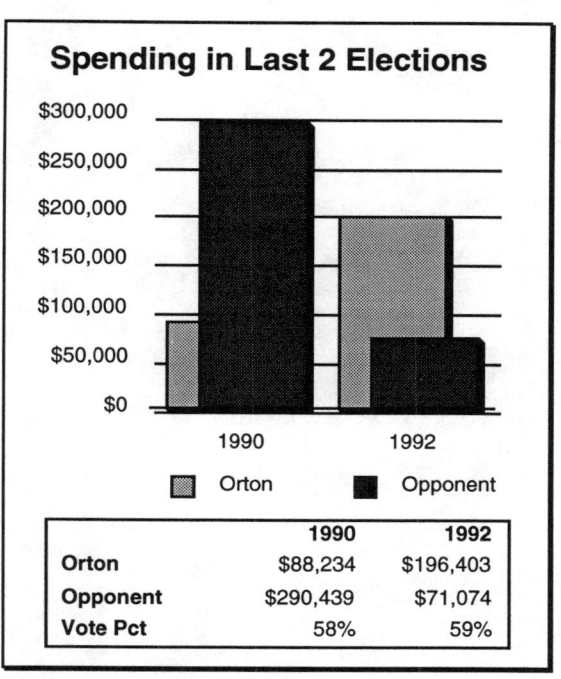

Spending in Last 2 Elections

	1990	1992
Orton	$88,234	$196,403
Opponent	$290,439	$71,074
Vote Pct	58%	59%

Orton   Opponent

* Contributions came from more than one affiliate or subsidiary.

969

Major R. Owens, D-NY (11)

First elected: 1982

1991-92 Total Receipts: $181,650
1992 Year-end Cash: $4,201

1991-92 Committees & Subcommittees

Education and Labor
Elementary, Secondary and Vocational Education; Labor-Management Relations; Labor Standards; Select Education (Chairman)

Government Operations
Government Activities and Transportation

Leading Contributors

Business

Agriculture	$1,000
None over $1,000	

Communications/Electronics	$3,100
Telephone Utilities	$2,750
AT&T	$2,750 PAC

Energy & Natural Resources	$1,125
None over $1,000	

Finance, Insurance & Real Estate	$7,125
Commercial Banks	$2,000
Chemical Bank	$1,000 PAC
Citicorp	$1,000 PAC
Securities & Investment	$2,875
Goldman, Sachs & Co	$1,250 PAC
Accountants	$1,000
American Institute of CPA's	$1,000 PAC

Health	$4,650
Health Professionals	$4,150
American Medical Assn*	$1,500 PAC
American Assn Oral & Maxillofacial Surgeons	$1,000 PAC

Lawyers & Lobbyists	$1,750
Lawyers & Lobbyists	$1,750
None over $1,000	

Source of Funds in 1992 Election

Source	Total	Pct
■ PACs	$89,972	49%
▨ Indivs $200+	$19,545	11%
☐ Indivs under $200	$53,890	30%
▥ Other	$18,380	10%
Candidate	$1,000	1%
Party	$587	0%

Source of PAC Dollars by Sector

Source	Total	Pct
■ Business	$18,600	21%
▨ Labor	$69,349	77%
☐ Ideology/Single Issue	$1,625	2%

In-State vs. Out-of-State Contributions*

Source	Total	Pct
☐ In-State	$13,100	68%
■ Out-of-state	$6,195	32%
No state listed	$250	

*by large individual contributors ($200 & above)

Misc Business	$2,950
Food & Beverage	$1,200
None over $1,000	
Misc Manufacturing & Distributing	$1,000
Jostens Inc	$1,000 PAC

Transportation	$1,100
Air Transport	$1,100
United Parcel Service	$1,100 PAC

Contribution Totals by Sector

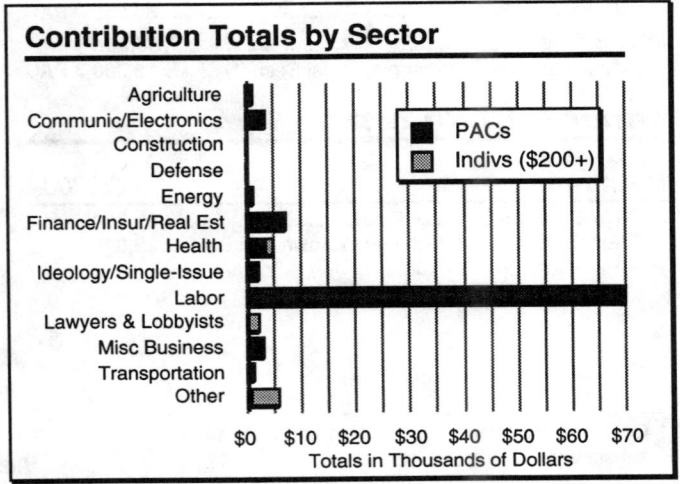

Totals in Thousands of Dollars

Labor

Labor	$69,349

Building Trade Unions **$6,750**
- Operating Engineers Union* ....$2,250   PAC
- Laborers' Political League ....$2,000   PAC
- Plumbers/Pipefitters Union ....$2,000   PAC

Industrial Unions **$13,125**
- United Auto Workers ....$5,000   PAC
- Communications Workers of America ....$1,750   PAC
- Ladies Garment Workers Union..........................$1,625   PAC
- Electronic Machine Furniture Workers ....$1,000   PAC
- Machinists/Aerospace Workers Union ....$1,000   PAC
- United Steelworkers ....$1,000   PAC

Transportation Unions **$21,750**
- Marine Engineers Union* ....$7,500   PAC
- Teamsters Union ....$5,000   PAC
- Air Line Pilots Assn ....$3,500   PAC
- Transport Workers Union ....$3,250   PAC
- Trans Comm International Union ....$1,000   PAC
- United Transportation Union ....$1,000   PAC

Public Sector Unions **$15,624**
- American Fedn of St/Cnty/Munic Employees ......$4,999   PAC
- American Federation of Teachers ....$4,225   PAC
- American Postal Workers Union ....$2,750   PAC
- National Education Assn ....$1,150   PAC
- National Assn Retired Federal Employees ....$1,000   PAC

Misc Unions **$12,100**
- Hospital/Health Care Union #1199 ....$5,000   PAC
- Food & Commercial Workers Union ....$4,850   PAC
- Service Employees International Union ....$1,250   PAC

Ideological/Single-Issue

Ideological/Single-Issue	$2,125

Human Rights **$1,000**
- Human Rights Campaign Fund ....$1,000   PAC

Misc Issues...**$1,000**
- None over $1,000

Other & Unknown

Other	$5,420

Non-Profit Institutions.............................**$1,045**
- None over $1,000

Education **$1,375**
- None over $1,000

Retired **$1,600**
- None over $1,000

Unknown	$10,050

- No Employer Listed or Found $8,575
- Generic Occupation/Category Unknown $1,000
  - None over $1,000

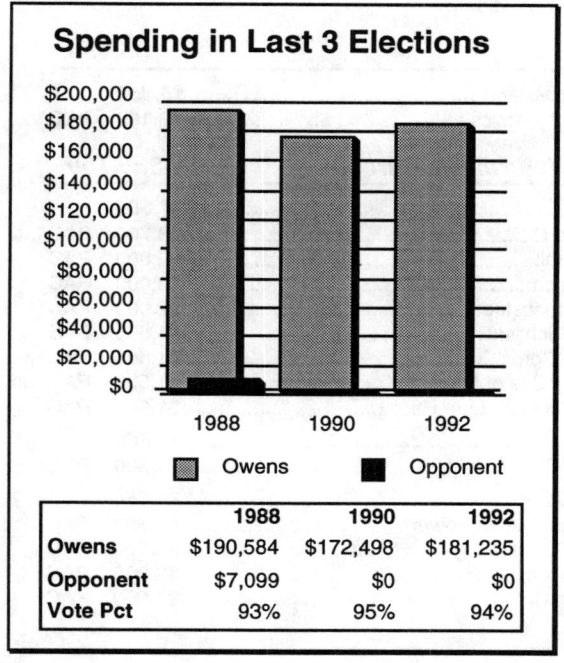

Spending in Last 3 Elections

	1988	1990	1992
Owens	$190,584	$172,498	$181,235
Opponent	$7,099	$0	$0
Vote Pct	93%	95%	94%

* Contributions came from more than one affiliate or subsidiary.

Michael G. Oxley, R-Ohio (4)

First elected: 1981

1991-92 Total Receipts: $491,631
1992 Year-end Cash: $32,084

1991-92 Committees & Subcommittees

Energy and Commerce
Commerce, Consumer Protection and Competitiveness; Energy and Power; Telecommunications and Finance

Select Committee on Narcotics Abuse and Control

Leading Contributors

Business

Agriculture	$27,600	
Crop Production & Basic Processing *$2,800*		
None over $1,500		
Tobacco *$3,000*		
None over $1,500		
Dairy *$5,000*		
Associated Milk Producers	$2,000	PAC
Milk Marketing Inc	$1,500	PAC
Agricultural Services/Products *$4,350*		
None over $1,500		
Food Processing & Sales *$10,250*		
Food Marketing Institute	$2,000	PAC
Forestry & Forest Products *$1,500*		
Mead Corp	$1,500	PAC

Communications/Electronics	$46,400	
Printing & Publishing *$1,500*		
None over $1,500		
Media/Entertainment *$12,400*		
National Assn of Broadcasters	$2,000	PAC
National Cable Television Assn	$2,000	PAC
Viacom International	$2,000	PAC
Telephone Utilities *$23,500*		
Ameritech Corp*	$5,000	PAC
BellSouth Corp*	$2,000	PAC
GTE Corp	$2,000	PAC
International Telecharge Inc	$2,000	PAC/Ind
Alltel Corp	$1,500	PAC
NYNEX Corp	$1,500	PAC
US Telephone Assn	$1,500	PAC
United Telecommunications	$1,500	PAC

Source of Funds in 1992 Election

	Source	Total	Pct
■	PACs	$279,025	57%
▨	Indivs $200+	$106,020	22%
□	Indivs under $200	$81,974	17%
▧	Other	$24,612	5%
	Candidate	$0	0%
	Party	$201	0%

Source of PAC Dollars by Sector

	Source	Total	Pct
■	Business	$272,225	100%
▨	Labor	$0	0%
□	Ideology/Single Issue	$500	0%

In-State vs. Out-of-State Contributions*

	Source	Total	Pct
□	In-State	$89,810	85%
■	Out-of-state	$15,460	15%
	No state listed	$250	

* by large individual contributors ($200 & above)

Telecom Services & Equipment *$5,000*		
None over $1,500		
Electronics Mfg & Services *$2,500*		
None over $1,500		
Computer Equipment & Services *$1,500*		
Electronic Data Systems	$1,500	PAC

Construction	$9,050	
General Contractors *$4,700*		
Kokosing Construction Co	$2,300	Indiv
Building Materials & Equipment *$1,850*		
None over $1,500		

Defense	$5,450	
Defense Aerospace *$5,450*		
General Dynamics	$3,100	PAC/Ind

Energy & Natural Resources	$65,750	
Oil & Gas *$31,600*		
Marathon Oil	$3,700	PAC/Ind
Ashland Oil	$2,000	PAC
BP America	$2,000	PAC
Dresser Industries	$2,000	PAC
Atlantic Richfield	$1,500	PAC
Chevron Corp	$1,500	PAC
Columbia Gas of Ohio	$1,500	PAC/Ind
Consolidated Natural Gas*	$1,500	PAC
Mining *$4,500*		
National Coal Assn	$1,500	PAC
Electric Utilities *$28,350*		
American Electric Power*	$5,500	PAC
Dayton Power & Light	$2,000	PAC
Ohio Edison	$2,000	PAC
Southern Co*	$2,000	PAC

Contribution Totals by Sector

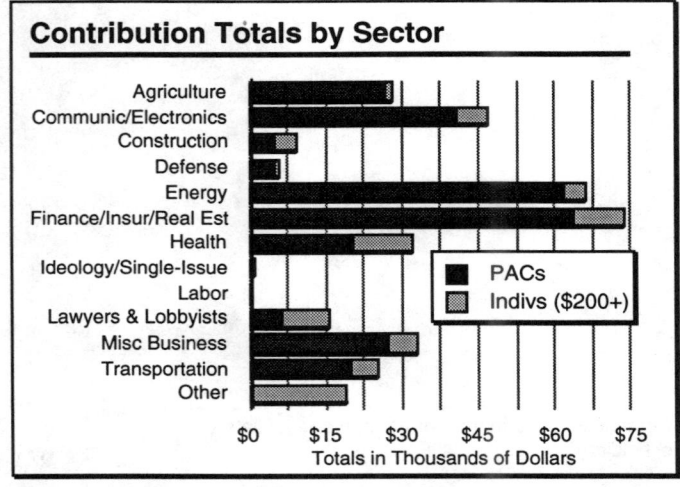

Agriculture
Communic/Electronics
Construction
Defense
Energy
Finance/Insur/Real Est
Health
Ideology/Single-Issue
Labor
Lawyers & Lobbyists
Misc Business
Transportation
Other

■ PACs
▨ Indivs ($200+)

$0 $15 $30 $45 $60 $75
Totals in Thousands of Dollars

Finance, Insurance & Real Estate — $73,200

Commercial Banks $11,400
    American Bankers Assn* .... $3,000   PAC
    Banc One Corp .... $1,750   PAC/Ind

Securities & Investment $15,350
    Shearson Lehman Brothers .... $1,500   PAC

Insurance $32,650
    Independent Insurance Agents of America .... $2,000   PAC
    Mutual of Omaha .... $2,000   PAC
    Travelers Corp .... $2,000   PAC
    Kemper Insurance .... $1,500   PAC
    National Assn of Life Underwriters .... $1,500   PAC
    Nationwide Corp .... $1,500   PAC

Real Estate $5,300
    National Assn of Realtors .... $1,500   PAC
    Society of Real Estate Appraisers .... $1,500   PAC

Accountants $7,500
    American Institute of CPA's .... $2,000   PAC
    Coopers & Lybrand .... $1,500   PAC
    Ernst & Young .... $1,500   PAC
    Deloitte & Touche .... $1,500   PAC

Health — $31,300

Health Professionals $17,050
    American Medical Assn .... $2,000   PAC
    American Dental Assn .... $1,500   PAC

Hospitals/Nursing Homes $2,250
    None over $1,500

Pharmaceuticals/Health Products $11,000
    Pfizer Inc .... $1,500   PAC

Lawyers & Lobbyists — $15,185

Lawyers & Lobbyists $15,185
    None over $1,500

Misc Business — $32,500

Food & Beverage $3,850
    None over $1,500

Beer, Wine & Liquor $2,000
    None over $1,500

Retail Sales $2,500
    None over $1,500

Misc Services $3,000
    American Assn of Equipment Lessors .... $3,000   PAC

Business Services $2,500
    None over $1,500

Chemical & Related Manufacturing $6,350
    None over $1,500

Steel Production $2,250
    Armco Inc .... $1,500   PAC

Misc Manufacturing & Distributing $8,800
    Corning Glass Works .... $2,000   PAC

Transportation — $25,175

Air Transport $5,050
    General Electric .... $2,000   PAC
    United Parcel Service .... $1,500   PAC

Automotive $11,375
    Ford Motor Co .... $2,500   PAC/Ind
    National Auto Dealers Assn .... $2,000   PAC

Trucking $2,850
    American Trucking Assns .... $1,500   PAC

Railroads $4,750
    Union Pacific Corp .... $2,000   PAC

Other & Unknown

Other — $18,385

Education $2,450
    None over $1,500

Retired $14,935
    None over $1,500

Unknown — $28,250

    Homemakers/Non-income earners $5,000
    No Employer Listed or Found $3,450
    Generic Occupation/Category Unknown $4,750
    Employer Listed/Category Unknown $15,050
        None over $1,500

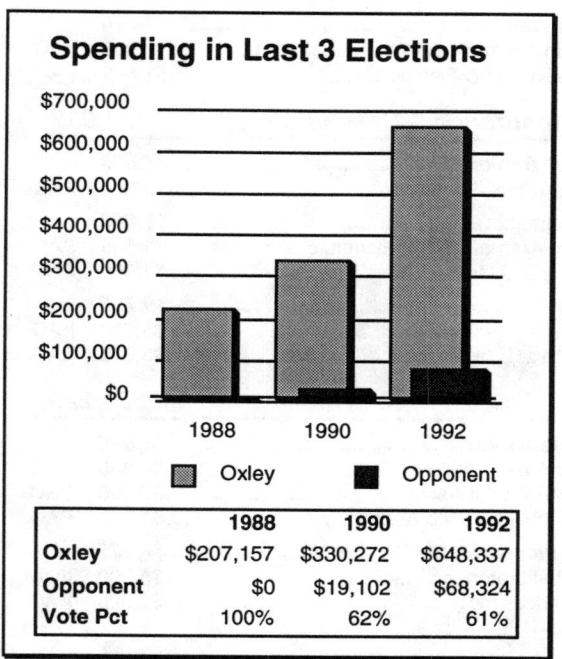

Spending in Last 3 Elections

	1988	1990	1992
Oxley	$207,157	$330,272	$648,337
Opponent	$0	$19,102	$68,324
Vote Pct	100%	62%	61%

* Contributions came from more than one affiliate or subsidiary.

Ron Packard, R-Calif (48)

First elected: 1982
1991-92 Total Receipts: $292,021
1992 Year-end Cash: $105,268

1991-92 Committees & Subcommittees

Public Works and Transportation
Investigations and Oversight (Ranking Republican); Surface Transportation; Water Resources

Science, Space and Technology
Science (Ranking Republican); Space

Leading Contributors

Business

Agriculture		$7,600
Crop Production & Basic Processing		**$2,250**
None over $1,500		
Food Processing & Sales		**$4,350**
Pepsico Inc	$1,500	PAC

Communications/Electronics		$14,425
Media/Entertainment		**$4,000**
Walt Disney Co	$3,000	PAC
Telephone Utilities		**$4,425**
None over $1,500		
Telecom Services & Equipment		**$1,500**
None over $1,500		
Computer Equipment & Services		**$3,500**
Orincon Corp of San Diego	$2,000	Indiv

Construction		$24,150
General Contractors		**$11,500**
Bechtel Corp	$3,500	PAC
Associated General Contractors	$2,500	PAC
National Utility Contractors Assn	$2,000	PAC
Home Builders		**$2,000**
National Assn of Home Builders	$2,000	PAC
Construction Services		**$6,750**
Ashland Oil	$1,500	PAC
Building Materials & Equipment		**$3,900**
Cubic Corp	$2,500	PAC

Contribution Totals by Sector

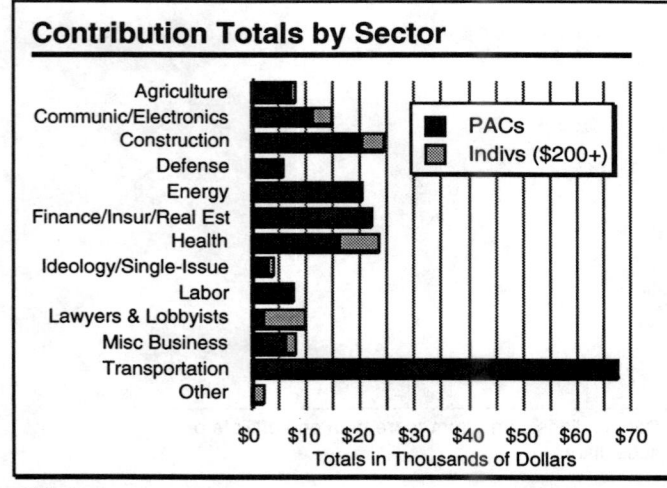

Agriculture
Communic/Electronics
Construction
Defense
Energy
Finance/Insur/Real Est
Health
Ideology/Single-Issue
Labor
Lawyers & Lobbyists
Misc Business
Transportation
Other

PACs
Indivs ($200+)

$0 $10 $20 $30 $40 $50 $60 $70
Totals in Thousands of Dollars

Source of Funds in 1992 Election

Source	Total	Pct
PACs	$191,832	66%
Indivs $200+	$33,950	12%
Indivs under $200	$38,641	13%
Other	$27,598	9%
Candidate	$0	0%
Party	$236	0%

Source of PAC Dollars by Sector

Source	Total	Pct
Business	$176,373	95%
Labor	$7,500	4%
Ideology/Single Issue	$2,750	1%

In-State vs. Out-of-State Contributions*

Source	Total	Pct
In-State	$14,950	44%
Out-of-state	$19,000	56%
No state listed	$0	

* by large individual contributors ($200 & above)

Defense		$5,646
Defense Aerospace		**$2,000**
Lockheed Corp	$2,000	PAC
Defense Electronics		**$3,646**
Hughes Aircraft	$3,146	PAC

Energy & Natural Resources		$20,000
Oil & Gas		**$5,500**
Pacific Enterprises	$1,500	PAC
Nuclear Energy		**$6,000**
General Atomics	$6,000	PAC
Electric Utilities		**$6,000**
Southern California Edison	$3,000	PAC
San Diego Gas & Electric	$1,500	PAC

Finance, Insurance & Real Estate		$21,900
Commercial Banks		**$4,500**
American Bankers Assn	$2,500	PAC
Insurance		**$6,000**
National Assn of Life Underwriters	$1,500	PAC
New England Mutual Life	$1,500	PAC
Real Estate		**$9,750**
National Assn of Realtors	$5,500	PAC
Irvine Co	$3,000	PAC

Health		$23,229
Health Professionals		**$13,600**
American Medical Assn	$5,350	PAC
American Dental Assn	$5,000	PAC
American Optometric Assn	$1,500	PAC
Pharmaceuticals/Health Products		**$7,729**
Mylan Laboratories	$5,000	Indiv
ICI Americas Inc	$1,529	PAC

Lawyers & Lobbyists $9,500

Lawyers & Lobbyists **$9,500**
   McConnell/Ferguson Group ....$3,000   Indiv
   Ferguson Co ....$1,500   Indiv

Misc Business $8,450

Beer, Wine & Liquor **$1,500**
   National Beer Wholesalers Assn ....$1,500   PAC
Retail Sales **$1,500**
   None over $1,500
Business Services **$1,650**
   None over $1,500
Lodging/Tourism **$2,000**
   None over $1,500

Transportation $67,373

Air Transport **$40,373**
   Federal Express Corp ....$7,000   PAC
   United Parcel Service ....$5,500   PAC
   General Dynamics ....$3,500   PAC
   Aircraft Owners & Pilots Assn ....$3,000   PAC
   Boeing Co ....$2,500   PAC
   Northrop Corp ....$2,500   PAC
   Martin Marietta Corp ....$2,000   PAC
   Grumman Corp ....$1,500   PAC
   United Airlines ....$1,500   PAC
Automotive **$12,500**
   National Auto Dealers Assn ....$6,000   PAC
   Auto Dealers & Drivers for Free Trade ......$1,500   PAC
   Rockwell International ....$1,500   PAC
Trucking **$6,500**
   Viking Freight ....$2,500   PAC
   American Trucking Assns ....$1,500   PAC
Railroads **$3,500**
   Union Pacific Corp ....$2,000   PAC
Sea Transport **$2,000**
   National Steel & Shipbuilding ....$2,000   PAC
Misc Transport **$2,500**
   None over $1,500

Labor

Labor $7,500

Transportation Unions **$6,500**
   Marine Engineers Dist 2 Maritime Officers ....$5,000   PAC
   Air Line Pilots Assn ....$1,500   PAC

Ideological/Single-Issue

Ideological/Single-Issue $3,750

Republican/Conservative **$2,750**
   Conservative Order of Good Guys ....$1,750   PAC

Other & Unknown

Other $2,050

Retired **$1,800**
   None over $1,500

Unknown $1,546

   No Employer Listed or Found $1,750
   Generic Occupation/Category Unknown $1,500
   Employer Listed/Category Unknown $1,750
     None over $1,500

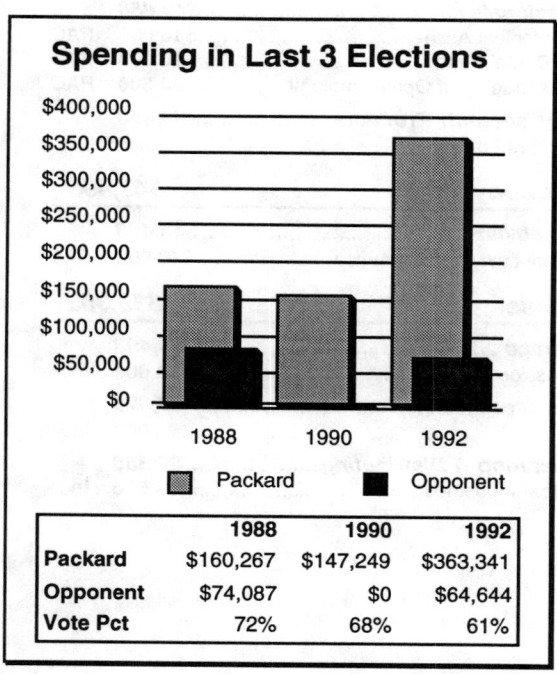

Spending in Last 3 Elections

	1988	1990	1992
Packard	$160,267	$147,249	$363,341
Opponent	$74,087	$0	$64,644
Vote Pct	72%	68%	61%

Frank Pallone Jr., D-NJ (6)

First elected: 1988

1991-92 Total Receipts: $924,079
1992 Year-end Cash: $3,297

1991-92 Committees & Subcommittees

Merchant Marine and Fisheries
Coast Guard and Navigation; Fisheries and Wildlife Conservation and the Environment; Oceanography, Great Lakes and Outer Continental Shelf

Public Works and Transportation
Surface Transportation; Water Resources

Select Committee on Aging

Leading Contributors

Business

Agriculture		$10,074
Tobacco		**$3,850**
RJR Nabisco	PAC	$3,850

Communications/Electronics		$13,550
Media/Entertainment		**$2,500**
None over $2,500		
Telephone Utilities		**$8,350**
AT&T	PAC	$3,600
Bell Atlantic*	PAC	$3,000

Construction		$41,000
General Contractors		**$19,250**
Paphian Enterprises	Indiv	$5,700
Sharp Construction Co	Indiv	$4,400
Home Builders		**$9,800**
National Assn of Home Builders	PAC	$7,000
Construction Services		**$5,325**
None over $2,500		
Building Materials & Equipment		**$4,850**
None over $2,500		

Energy & Natural Resources		$11,900
Electric Utilities		**$11,650**
Public Service Electric & Gas	PAC/Ind	$4,850

Source of Funds in 1992 Election

Source	Total	Pct
PACs	$530,379	57%
Indivs $200+	$224,680	24%
Indivs under $200	$151,135	16%
Other	$29,390	3%
Candidate	$0	0%
Party	$11,955	1%

Source of PAC Dollars by Sector

Source	Total	Pct
Business	$193,216	37%
Labor	$254,530	49%
Ideology/Single Issue	$68,385	13%

In-State vs. Out-of-State Contributions*

Source	Total	Pct
In-State	$185,935	83%
Out-of-state	$38,920	17%
No state listed	$0	

* by large individual contributors ($200 & above)

Finance, Insurance & Real Estate — $50,024

Insurance		$20,800
National Assn of Life Underwriters	PAC	$7,750
Independent Insurance Agents of America	PAC	$5,500
Real Estate		**$20,300**
National Assn of Realtors	PAC	$10,000
Accountants		**$3,724**
None over $2,500		

Health — $55,944

Health Professionals		$49,850
American Medical Assn*	PAC	$10,000
American Dental Assn	PAC	$5,000
American Academy of Ophthalmology	PAC	$4,500
Pharmaceuticals/Health Products		**$3,450**
None over $2,500		

Lawyers & Lobbyists — $43,493

Lawyers & Lobbyists		$43,493
Assn of Trial Lawyers of America	PAC	$10,000

Misc Business — $36,303

Food & Beverage		$8,493
HS Concessions Inc	Indiv	$4,600
Business Services		**$9,325**
Arinc Inc	Indiv	$4,000
Misc Manufacturing & Distributing		**$6,350**
Metallurgical Industries	Indiv	$4,550

Contribution Totals by Sector

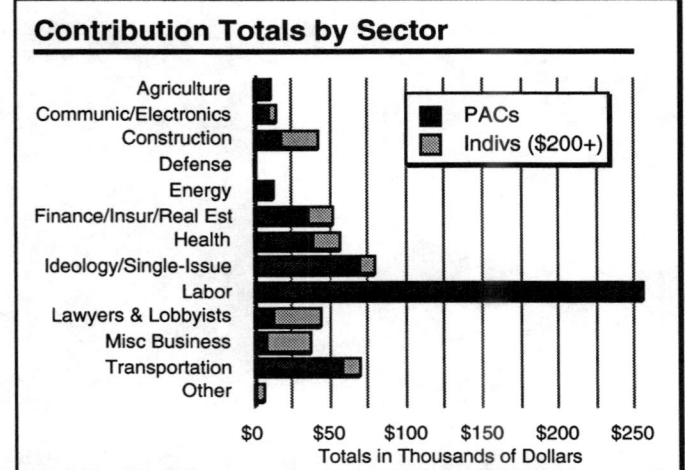

Legend: PACs, Indivs ($200+)

Agriculture
Communic/Electronics
Construction
Defense
Energy
Finance/Insur/Real Est
Health
Ideology/Single-Issue
Labor
Lawyers & Lobbyists
Misc Business
Transportation
Other

$0 $50 $100 $150 $200 $250
Totals in Thousands of Dollars

Transportation — $67,991

Air Transport **$14,200**
   Federal Express Corp .... $6,000   PAC

Automotive **$10,166**
   National Auto Dealers Assn .... $4,000   PAC
   Americans for Free International Trade .... $3,000   PAC

Trucking **$10,700**
   North American Van Lines .... $2,700   PAC

Railroads **$4,150**
   None over $2,500

Sea Transport **$23,200**
   Cruise PAC .... $6,500   PAC
   Bay Ship Management Inc .... $3,250   Indiv
   Sea-Land Corp .... $2,850   PAC

Misc Transport **$5,575**
   American Bus Assn .... $2,550   PAC

Labor

Labor — $255,030

Building Trade Unions **$58,350**
   Plumbers/Pipefitters Union* .... $9,900   PAC
   Ironworkers Union .... $8,250   PAC
   Operating Engineers Union* .... $8,075   PAC
   Carpenters & Joiners Union .... $8,025   PAC/Ind
   Sheet Metal Workers Union .... $7,500   PAC
   Laborers' Political League .... $7,400   PAC
   Heat/Frost/Asbestos Workers Union .... $3,000   PAC
   Bricklayers Union .... $2,500   PAC

Industrial Unions **$55,000**
   Rubber Cork Linoleum & Plastic Workers .... $11,000   PAC
   Machinists/Aerospace Workers Union .... $10,000   PAC
   United Auto Workers .... $10,000   PAC
   Intl Brotherhood of Electrical Workers .... $4,750   PAC
   Communications Workers of America .... $4,000   PAC
   United Steelworkers .... $4,000   PAC
   Electronic Machine Furniture Workers .... $3,000   PAC

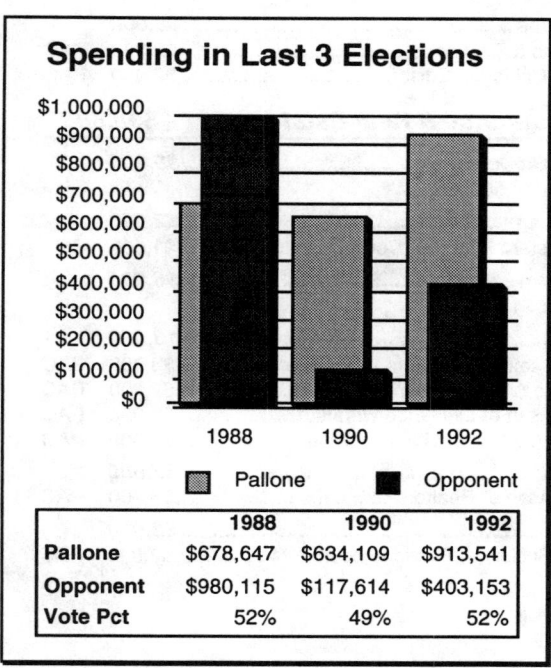

Spending in Last 3 Elections

	1988	1990	1992
Pallone	$678,647	$634,109	$913,541
Opponent	$980,115	$117,614	$403,153
Vote Pct	52%	49%	52%

Pallone   ■ Opponent

Transportation Unions **$67,630**
   Marine Engineers Union* .... $11,000   PAC
   Air Line Pilots Assn .... $10,000   PAC
   Seafarers International Union .... $10,000   PAC
   Teamsters Union .... $10,000   PAC
   Transport Workers Union .... $5,680   PAC
   International Longshoremen's Assn .... $3,500   PAC
   United Transportation Union .... $3,500   PAC
   Amalgamated Transit Union .... $3,000   PAC

Public Sector Unions **$55,300**
   National Assn of Letter Carriers .... $10,000   PAC
   National Education Assn .... $10,000   PAC
   American Postal Workers Union .... $7,000   PAC
   National Assn Retired Federal Employees .... $7,000   PAC
   International Assn of Firefighters .... $5,500   PAC
   American Federation of Teachers .... $5,350   PAC
   American Fedn of St/Cnty/Munic Employees ...... $5,000   PAC

Misc Unions **$18,750**
   AFL-CIO .... $7,350   PAC
   Food & Commercial Workers Union .... $6,500   PAC

Ideological/Single-Issue

Ideological/Single-Issue — $78,435

Democratic/Liberal **$8,500**
   National Cmte for an Effective Congress .... $5,000   PAC

Leadership PACs **$11,900**
   Effective Government Cmte (Dick Gephardt) ...... $3,000   PAC
   House Leadership Fund (Tom Foley) .... $3,000   PAC

Pro-Israel **$17,075**
   Pax PAC .... $3,000   PAC
   Joint Action Cmte for Political Affairs .... $2,500   PAC

Pro-Choice **$10,375**
   National Abortion Rights Action League .... $5,000   PAC
   Voters for Choice .... $2,500   PAC

Human Rights **$8,500**
   Human Rights Campaign Fund .... $5,500   PAC
   KidsPAC .... $3,000   PAC

Misc Issues **$21,735**
   Sierra Club .... $9,971   PAC
   League of Conservation Voters .... $4,270   PAC
   National Cmte to Preserve Social Security .... $3,500   PAC
   New Jersey Environmental Federation .... $2,994   PAC

Other & Unknown

Other — $5,000
   None over $2,500

Unknown — $71,242
   Homemakers/Non-income earners $8,100
   No Employer Listed or Found $25,050
   Employer Listed/Category Unknown $37,842
      None over $2,500

---

* Contributions came from more than one affiliate or subsidiary.

Leon E. Panetta, D-Calif (17)

First elected: 1976
1991-92 Total Receipts: $410,124
1992 Year-end Cash: $100,272

1991-92 Committees & Subcommittees

Administration
Elections; Personnel and Police; Campaign Finance Reform Task Force

Agriculture
Department Operations, Research and Foreign Agriculture; Domestic Marketing, Consumer Relations and Nutrition (Vice Chairman); Forests, Family Farms and Energy

Budget (Chairman)

Select Committee on Hunger

Leading Contributors

Business

Agriculture	$52,400	
Crop Production & Basic Processing **$22,650**		
Desert Grape Growers League/California $2,000	PAC	
Sunkist Growers $2,000	PAC	
California Almond Growers Exchange $1,500	PAC	
California Canning Peach Assn $1,500	PAC	
California Grape & Tree Fruit League $1,500	PAC	
Dairy **$5,500**		
Associated Milk Producers $2,000	PAC	
Milk Industry Foundation $1,500	PAC	
Poultry & Eggs **$2,500**		
None over $1,500		
Livestock **$2,500**		
National Cattlemen's Assn* $2,000	PAC	
Agricultural Services/Products **$8,500**		
American Assn of Crop Insurers $2,000	PAC	
Food Processing & Sales **$9,250**		
Food Marketing Institute $4,000	PAC	
Winn-Dixie Stores $2,000	PAC	

Communications/Electronics	$6,450	
Media/Entertainment **$1,500**		
None over $1,500		
Telephone Utilities **$3,950**		
AT&T $2,000	PAC	
Pacific Telesis Group $1,500	PAC	

Source of Funds in 1992 Election

	Source	Total	Pct
■	PACs	$239,250	56%
▨	Indivs $200+	$64,800	15%
□	Indivs under $200	$86,074	20%
▧	Other..................	$40,765	9%
	Candidate	$0	0%
	Party	$20,765	5%

Source of PAC Dollars by Sector

	Source	Total	Pct
■	Business	$167,900	71%
▨	Labor	$65,600	28%
□	Ideology/Single Issue	$2,000	1%

In-State vs. Out-of-State Contributions*

	Source	Total	Pct
□	In-State	$42,150	65%
■	Out-of-state	$22,650	35%
	No state listed	$0	

* by large individual contributors ($200 & above)

Construction	$3,200	
Home Builders **$2,000**		
Rural Builders of America PAC $2,000	PAC	

Defense	$1,500	
Defense Aerospace **$1,500**		
None over $1,500		

Energy & Natural Resources	$9,500	
Oil & Gas **$2,500**		
None over $1,500		
Electric Utilities **$6,000**		
Pacific Gas & Electric $2,000	PAC	
Southern California Edison $2,000	PAC	

Finance, Insurance & Real Estate	$38,800	
Commercial Banks **$6,300**		
None over $1,500		
Savings & Loans **$2,000**		
Great Western Financial Corp $1,500	PAC	
Securities & Investment **$6,000**		
None over $1,500		
Insurance **$13,000**		
Massachusetts Mutual Life Insurance $3,000	PAC	
Blue Cross & Blue Shield Assn* $2,500	PAC	
National Assn of Life Underwriters $2,000	PAC	
American Council of Life Insurance $1,500	PAC	
Real Estate **$7,500**		
National Assn of Realtors $6,000	PAC	
Accountants **$3,000**		
National Society of Public Accountants $2,000	PAC	

Contribution Totals by Sector

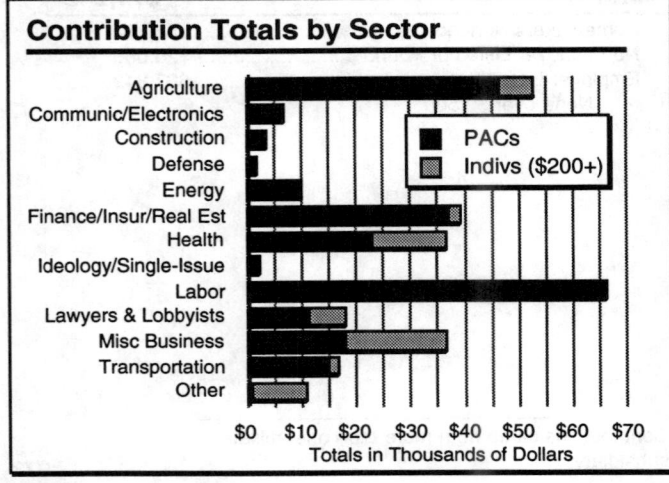

Agriculture
Communic/Electronics
Construction
Defense
Energy
Finance/Insur/Real Est
Health
Ideology/Single-Issue
Labor
Lawyers & Lobbyists
Misc Business
Transportation
Other

■ PACs
▨ Indivs ($200+)

$0 $10 $20 $30 $40 $50 $60 $70
Totals in Thousands of Dollars

Health $36,000

Health Professionals $13,750
    American Medical Assn.......................................$4,000 PAC
    American Dental Assn ....$3,000 PAC
    American Academy of Ophthalmology ....$2,000 PAC
Hospitals/Nursing Homes.............................$16,750
    Hospice Care Inc...$13,250 Indiv
    American Health Care Assn...............................$1,500 PAC
Pharmaceuticals/Health Products $5,000
    Glaxo Inc ....$2,000 PAC

Lawyers & Lobbyists $17,850

Lawyers & Lobbyists....................................$17,850
    Assn of Trial Lawyers of America ....$5,000 PAC

Misc Business $36,050

Beer, Wine & Liquor $25,750
    Gallo Winery..$15,000 Indiv
    Wine Institute ....$3,000 PAC
    Smirnoff/Inglenook Distributors ....$2,000 PAC
    National Beer Wholesalers Assn ....$1,500 PAC
Retail Sales...$3,700
    None over $1,500
Business Services $3,500
    Owen Colliflower Court Reporting ....$2,000 Indiv
    Advo-System Inc ....$1,500 PAC

Transportation $16,250

Air Transport $3,000
    None over $1,500
Automotive $6,000
    Americans for Free International Trade ....$3,000 PAC
Railroads..$5,500
    Union Pacific Corp ....$2,000 PAC

Labor

Labor $65,600

Building Trade Unions $11,000
    Carpenters & Joiners Union ....$5,000 PAC
    Laborers' Political League ....$4,000 PAC
Industrial Unions $6,500
    United Auto Workers ....$5,000 PAC
Transportation Unions $12,600
    Teamsters Union ....$10,000 PAC
    Air Line Pilots Assn ....$1,500 PAC
Public Sector Unions $31,000
    National Assn of Letter Carriers ....$7,000 PAC
    National Assn Retired Federal Employees ....$6,000 PAC
    American Fedn of St/Cnty/Munic Employees ......$5,000 PAC
    National Rural Letter Carriers Assn ....$3,000 PAC
    American Postal Workers Union ....$2,000 PAC
    National Assn of Postmasters ....$2,000 PAC
    National League of Postmasters ....$2,000 PAC
    National Education Assn ....$1,500 PAC
Misc Unions...$4,500
    Food & Commercial Workers Union ....$1,500 PAC
    Hotel/Restaurant Employees Union ....$1,500 PAC

Ideological/Single-Issue

Ideological/Single-Issue $2,000
    None over $1,500

Other & Unknown

Other $10,450

Retired $9,150
    None over $1,500

Unknown $4,750

    Employer Listed/Category Unknown....................$3,550
        Tom McLaughlin Opportunity Housing ....$2,000 Indiv

---

Spending in Last 3 Elections

	1988	1990	1992
Panetta	$252,336	$272,710	$513,958
Opponent	$69,563	$23,849	$72,384
Vote Pct	79%	74%	72%

Legend: Panetta, Opponent

---

* Contributions came from more than one affiliate or subsidiary.

Mike Parker, D-Miss (4)

First elected: 1988

1991-92 Total Receipts: $386,677
1992 Year-end Cash: $307,872

1991-92 Committees & Subcommittees

Budget
Budget Process, Reconciliation and Enforcement; Economic Policy, Projections and Revenues

Public Works and Transportation
Aviation; Surface Transportation; Water Resources

Leading Contributors

Business

Agriculture $38,900

Crop Production & Basic Processing $5,150
   None over $1,500

Tobacco $5,000
   RJR Nabisco .... $3,000   PAC
   Philip Morris .... $1,500   PAC

Dairy $5,000
   Associated Milk Producers .... $3,000   PAC
   Dairymen Inc-Mississippi .... $1,500   PAC

Poultry & Eggs $3,000
   National Broiler Council .... $1,500   PAC

Livestock $2,000
   National Cattlemen's Assn .... $1,500   PAC

Agricultural Services/Products $7,000
   First Mississippi Corp .... $2,000   PAC/Ind

Food Processing & Sales $6,750
   Food Marketing Institute .... $1,500   PAC
   Jitney-Jungle Inc .... $1,500   PAC
   Pepsico Inc .... $1,500   PAC

Forestry & Forest Products $5,000
   Georgia-Pacific Corp .... $1,500   PAC

Communications/Electronics $12,850

Telephone Utilities $12,050
   BellSouth Corp* .... $7,550   PAC/Ind
   AT&T .... $2,500   PAC
   Bay Springs Telephone Co .... $2,000   Indiv

Source of Funds in 1992 Election

Source	Total	Pct
■ PACs	$239,200	62%
▨ Indivs $200+	$103,286	27%
□ Indivs under $200	$28,236	7%
⊠ Other	$16,418	4%
Candidate	$0	0%
Party	$613	0%

Source of PAC Dollars by Sector

Source	Total	Pct
■ Business	$219,955	93%
▨ Labor	$5,500	2%
□ Ideology/Single Issue	$11,150	5%

In-State vs. Out-of-State Contributions*

Source	Total	Pct
□ In-State	$52,536	51%
▨ Out-of-state	$50,750	49%
No state listed	$0	

* by large individual contributors ($200 & above)

Construction $14,649

General Contractors $9,799
   Associated General Contractors .... $2,549   PAC
   Associated Builders & Contractors .... $1,500   PAC
   WE Blain & Sons Inc .... $1,500   Indiv

Home Builders $2,000
   National Assn of Home Builders .... $2,000   PAC

Special Trade Contractors $1,500
   None over $1,500

Energy & Natural Resources $41,850

Oil & Gas $22,400
   Ergon Inc .... $8,000   Indiv
   Lampton-Love Gas Co .... $2,000   Indiv
   Pace Oil Co .... $2,000   Indiv

Electric Utilities $18,600
   Southern Co* .... $5,250   PAC
   ACRE (Action Cmte for Rural Electrification) .... $4,000   PAC
   Entergy Corp* .... $2,750   PAC

Finance, Insurance & Real Estate $57,050

Commercial Banks $12,750
   American Bankers Assn .... $5,000   PAC
   Trustmark National Bank .... $2,500   Indiv
   Independent Bankers Assn .... $2,250   PAC

Savings & Loans $2,000
   None over $1,500

Securities & Investment $4,250
   None over $1,500

Insurance $24,850
   National Assn of Life Underwriters .... $10,000   PAC
   American Family Corp .... $5,000   PAC
   Independent Insurance Agents of America .... $2,850   PAC
   Dan Bottrell Agency .... $2,000   Indiv

Contribution Totals by Sector

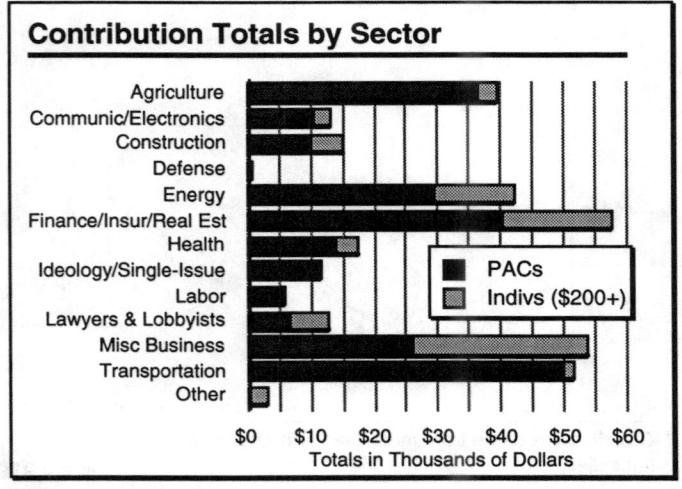

Agriculture, Communic/Electronics, Construction, Defense, Energy, Finance/Insur/Real Est, Health, Ideology/Single-Issue, Labor, Lawyers & Lobbyists, Misc Business, Transportation, Other

■ PACs   ▨ Indivs ($200+)

$0 $10 $20 $30 $40 $50 $60
Totals in Thousands of Dollars

Real Estate **$4,250**
National Assn of Realtors .... $3,000 PAC

Accountants **$2,000**
None over $1,500

Misc Finance **$5,450**
Gemini Investors Inc .... $5,000 Indiv

Health $17,247

Health Professionals **$15,847**
American Medical Assn .... $8,050 PAC
American Academy of Ophthalmology .... $2,000 PAC

Lawyers & Lobbyists $12,500

Lawyers & Lobbyists **$12,500**
Assn of Trial Lawyers of America .... $5,000 PAC

Misc Business $53,300

Business Associations **$1,700**
National Fedn of Independent Business .... $1,500 PAC

Food & Beverage **$6,700**
National Restaurant Assn .... $4,000 PAC
General Mills Restaurants .... $1,500 PAC

Beer, Wine & Liquor **$2,500**
National Beer Wholesalers Assn .... $2,500 PAC

Retail Sales **$2,750**
None over $1,500

Misc Services **$27,500**
Service Corp International .... $15,000 PAC/Ind
National Funeral Directors Assn .... $3,500 PAC

Casinos/Gambling **$2,000**
Lady Luck Casino & Hotel .... $2,000 Indiv

Lodging/Tourism **$1,500**
None over $1,500

Chemical & Related Manufacturing **$2,750**
Dow Chemical .... $2,000 PAC

Misc Manufacturing & Distributing **$2,750**
Stone Container Corp .... $1,500 PAC

Transportation $51,106

Air Transport **$35,056**
Federal Express Corp .... $10,000 PAC
Aircraft Owners & Pilots Assn .... $7,000 PAC
Texas Air .... $5,500 PAC
United Parcel Service .... $5,500 PAC
American Airlines .... $2,500 PAC
Delta Airlines .... $2,500 PAC

Automotive **$8,850**
National Auto Dealers Assn .... $6,000 PAC

Railroads **$2,500**
None over $1,500

Misc Transport **$2,100**
None over $1,500

Labor

Labor $5,500

Transportation Unions **$3,000**
None over $1,500

Public Sector Unions **$2,000**
None over $1,500

Ideological/Single-Issue

Ideological/Single-Issue $11,150

Foreign & Defense Policy **$2,000**
Veterans of Foreign Wars .... $2,000 PAC

Pro-Israel **$2,000**
None over $1,500

Gun Rights/Gun Control **$5,450**
National Rifle Assn .... $5,450 PAC

Misc Issues **$1,500**
National Cmte to Preserve Social Security .... $1,500 PAC

Other & Unknown

Other $2,800

Retired **$2,300**
None over $1,500

Unknown $20,489

Homemakers/Non-income earners $5,275
Employer Listed/Category Unknown $15,214
None over $1,500

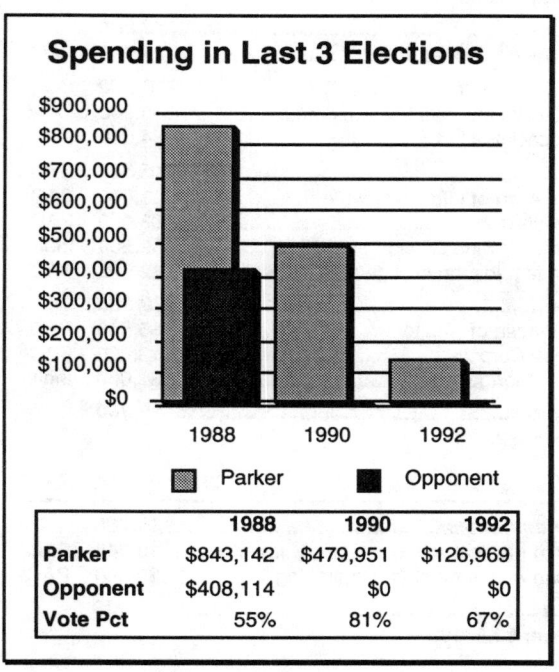

Spending in Last 3 Elections

	1988	1990	1992
Parker	$843,142	$479,951	$126,969
Opponent	$408,114	$0	$0
Vote Pct	55%	81%	67%

* Contributions came from more than one affiliate or subsidiary.

Ed Pastor, D-Ariz (2)

1991-92 Committees & Subcommittees

Education and Labor
Elementary, Secondary and Vocational Education; Labor-Management Relations; Select Education

Small Business
Procurement, Tourism and Rural Development; Regulation, Business Opportunities and Energy

Leading Contributors

Business

Agriculture		$30,536

Crop Production & Basic Processing	$8,100	
None over $2,500		
Tobacco	$9,250	
RJR Nabisco	$5,500	PAC
Dairy	$4,500	
Associated Milk Producers	$3,500	PAC
Food Processing & Sales	$3,200	
None over $2,500		

Communications/Electronics		$23,022

Media/Entertainment	$6,000	
National Cable Television Assn	$5,000	PAC
Telephone Utilities	$13,552	
US West Inc	$10,552	PAC/Ind

Construction		$22,500

General Contractors	$11,500	
Rodriguez Contracting	$6,000	Indiv
Home Builders	$3,500	
National Assn of Home Builders	$2,500	PAC
Construction Services	$2,700	
None over $2,500		
Building Materials & Equipment	$3,400	
None over $2,500		

Defense		$3,500

| Defense Aerospace | $3,000 | |
| None over $2,500 | | |

First elected: 1991

1991-92 Total Receipts: $928,664
1992 Year-end Cash: $33,368

Source of Funds in 1992 Election

Source	Total	Pct
PACs	$356,308	36%
Indivs $200+	$339,588	34%
Indivs under $200	$208,799	21%
Other	$81,016	8%
Candidate	$0	0%
Party	$68,897	7%

Source of PAC Dollars by Sector

Source	Total	Pct
Business	$142,338	40%
Labor	$183,443	52%
Ideology/Single Issue	$29,200	8%

In-State vs. Out-of-State Contributions*

Source	Total	Pct
In-State	$264,723	80%
Out-of-state	$65,315	20%
No state listed	$9,050	

*by large individual contributors ($200 & above)

Energy & Natural Resources		$16,950

Oil & Gas	$6,000	
Southwest Gas Corp	$2,500	PAC
Mining	$4,200	
Phelps Dodge Corp	$3,000	PAC
Electric Utilities	$3,000	
None over $2,500		

Finance, Insurance & Real Estate		$76,880

Commercial Banks	$4,100	
None over $2,500		
Credit Unions	$2,500	
Credit Union National Assn	$2,500	PAC
Securities & Investment	$16,700	
Alden Capital Markets Inc	$5,900	Indiv
DRD Associates Ltd	$4,650	Indiv
Insurance	$15,500	
National Assn of Life Underwriters	$3,000	PAC
Nationwide Corp	$3,000	PAC
Blue Cross & Blue Shield Assn*	$2,500	Indiv
Independent Insurance Agents of America	$2,500	PAC
Real Estate	$29,300	
National Assn of Realtors	$5,500	PAC
Del Webb Corp	$3,000	PAC
Kaufman Mortgage Co	$3,000	Indiv
Misc Finance	$6,330	
None over $2,500		

Health		$37,150

Health Professionals	$26,700	
American Medical Assn	$10,500	PAC
American Academy of Ophthalmology	$9,500	PAC
Misc Health	$5,800	
None over $2,500		

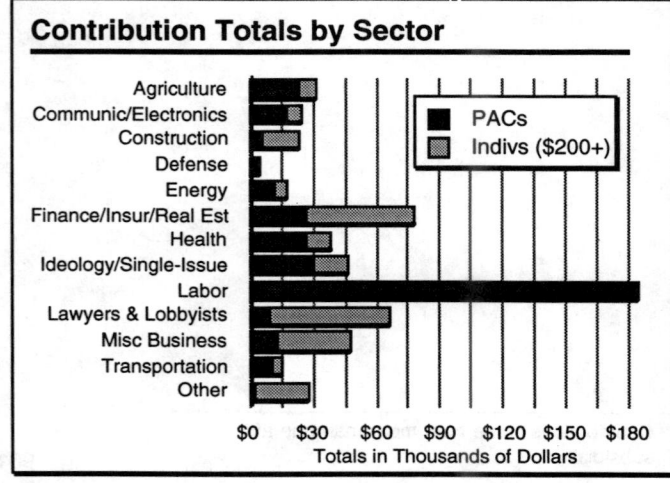

Contribution Totals by Sector

Categories: Agriculture, Communic/Electronics, Construction, Defense, Energy, Finance/Insur/Real Est, Health, Ideology/Single-Issue, Labor, Lawyers & Lobbyists, Misc Business, Transportation, Other

Legend: ■ PACs, ▨ Indivs ($200+)

Totals in Thousands of Dollars ($0, $30, $60, $90, $120, $150, $180)

Lawyers & Lobbyists — $65,309

Lawyers & Lobbyists $65,309
- Assn of Trial Lawyers of America .... $5,500 PAC
- Treon, Strick et al .... $4,000 Indiv
- Townsdin, Dybvig et al .... $3,100 Indiv
- Lewis & Roca .... $3,000 Indiv
- Linder, Chapa & Fields .... $2,500 Indiv

Misc Business — $46,530

Business Associations $3,282
- None over $2,500

Beer, Wine & Liquor $6,350
- None over $2,500

Retail Sales $6,598
- None over $2,500

Business Services $16,000
- Outdoor Systems Advertising .... $8,800 Indiv

Lodging/Tourism $2,500
- Canyon Ranch Health Spa .... $2,500 Indiv

Chemical & Related Manufacturing $3,750
- Dial Corp .... $2,750 PAC

Transportation — $14,050

Air Transport $4,750
- United Parcel Service .... $2,500 PAC

Automotive $3,050
- None over $2,500

Trucking $5,250
- None over $2,500

Labor

Labor — $183,443

Building Trade Unions $28,000
- Carpenters & Joiners Union .... $8,000 PAC
- Laborers Union* .... $8,000 PAC
- Plumbers/Pipefitters Union .... $6,000 PAC
- Sheet Metal Workers Union .... $5,000 PAC

Industrial Unions $47,499
- Machinists/Aerospace Workers Union .... $10,000 PAC
- United Auto Workers .... $10,000 PAC
- United Steelworkers .... $10,000 PAC
- Intl Brotherhood of Electrical Workers .... $9,500 PAC
- Communications Workers of America .... $5,499 PAC

Transportation Unions $39,800
- Teamsters Union .... $13,500 PAC
- Seafarers International Union .... $5,000 PAC
- United Transportation Union .... $4,500 PAC
- Marine Engineers Union* .... $3,500 PAC
- Trans Comm International Union .... $3,450 PAC
- Brotherhood of Locomotive Engineers .... $3,250 PAC
- Air Line Pilots Assn .... $2,500 PAC

Public Sector Unions $51,644
- American Fedn of St/Cnty/Munic Employees .... $16,000 PAC
- National Education Assn .... $8,000 PAC
- American Postal Workers Union .... $6,500 PAC
- Phoenix Firefighters #493 .... $5,344 PAC
- National Assn Retired Federal Employees .... $4,000 PAC
- National Assn of Letter Carriers .... $4,000 PAC
- American Federation of Teachers .... $2,500 PAC

Misc Unions $16,500
- Food & Commercial Workers Union .... $13,000 PAC

Ideological/Single-Issue

Ideological/Single-Issue — $45,050

Democratic/Liberal $7,750
- National Cmte for an Effective Congress .... $2,500 PAC

Leadership PACs $6,500
- Effective Government Cmte (Dick Gephardt) ...... $3,000 PAC
- House Leadership Fund (Tom Foley) .... $2,500 PAC

Pro-Israel $11,450
- None over $2,500

Pro-Choice $8,000
- National Abortion Rights Action League .... $5,000 PAC
- Voters for Choice .... $3,000 PAC

Human Rights $8,100
- Human Rights Campaign Fund .... $5,000 PAC

Misc Issues $3,000
- None over $2,500

Other & Unknown

Other — $27,120

Civil Servants/Public Officials $8,910
- US Government .... $4,000 Indiv

Education $7,950
- None over $2,500

Retired $7,420
- None over $2,500

Other $2,840
- None over $2,500

Unknown — $103,529
- Homemakers/Non-income earners $3,750
- No Employer Listed or Found $67,347
- Generic Occupation/Category Unknown $3,850
- Employer Listed/Category Unknown $28,582
  - None over $2,500

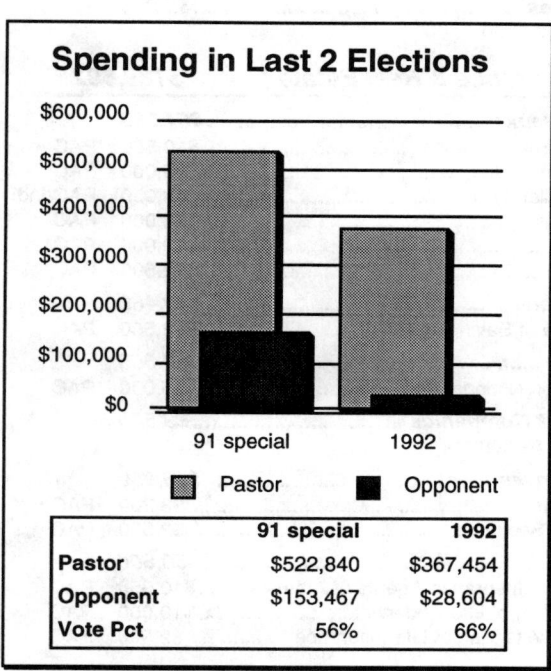

Spending in Last 2 Elections

	91 special	1992
Pastor	$522,840	$367,454
Opponent	$153,467	$28,604
Vote Pct	56%	66%

---

* Contributions came from more than one affiliate or subsidiary.

Bill Paxon, R-NY (27)

First elected: 1988

1991-92 Total Receipts: $845,163
1992 Year-end Cash: $5,784

1991-92 Committees & Subcommittees

Banking, Finance and Urban Affairs
Economic Stabilization; Financial Institutions Supervision, Regulation and Insurance; Housing and Community Development

Budget
Urgent Fiscal Issues

Veterans' Affairs
Housing and Memorial Affairs; Oversight and Investigations

Select Committee on Narcotics Abuse and Control

Leading Contributors

Business

Agriculture		$31,075

Crop Production & Basic Processing	$5,025	
None over $2,500		
Tobacco	$4,000	
None over $2,500		
Agricultural Services/Products	$3,750	
None over $2,500		
Food Processing & Sales	$16,550	
Rich Products Corp	$4,000	Indiv
Pepsico Inc	$2,500	PAC

Communications/Electronics		$28,450

Telephone Utilities	$20,950	
BellSouth Corp*	$8,000	PAC
NYNEX Corp*	$5,350	PAC

Construction		$63,185

General Contractors	$31,950	
ABC Paving Co	$5,000	Indiv
Dipizio Construction Co	$4,000	Indiv
Associated General Contractors	$2,500	PAC
Home Builders	$7,700	
National Assn of Home Builders	$7,500	PAC
Special Trade Contractors	$9,975	
None over $2,500		
Building Materials & Equipment	$11,110	
Gernatt Asphalt Products	$2,860	Indiv

Contribution Totals by Sector

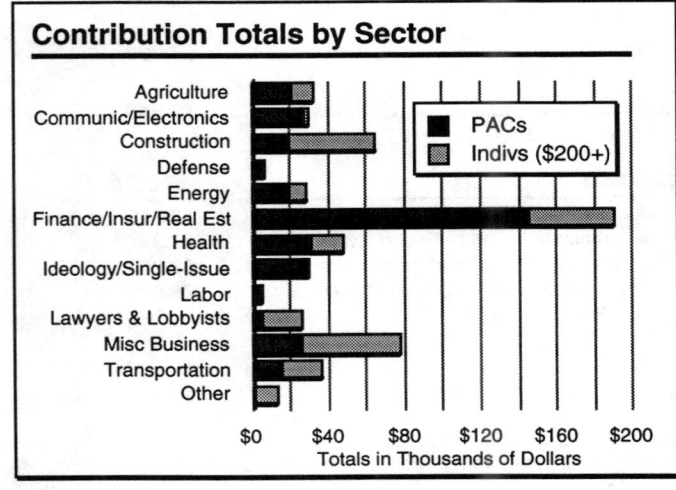

Agriculture
Communic/Electronics
Construction
Defense
Energy
Finance/Insur/Real Est
Health
Ideology/Single-Issue
Labor
Lawyers & Lobbyists
Misc Business
Transportation
Other

■ PACs
▨ Indivs ($200+)

$0 $40 $80 $120 $160 $200
Totals in Thousands of Dollars

Source of Funds in 1992 Election

	Source	Total	Pct
■	PACs	$329,412	39%
▨	Indivs $200+	$303,901	36%
☐	Indivs under $200	$171,034	20%
▨	Other	$40,816	5%
	Candidate	$0	0%
	Party	$6,026	1%

Source of PAC Dollars by Sector

	Source	Total	Pct
■	Business	$303,936	90%
▨	Labor	$4,850	1%
☐	Ideology/Single Issue	$28,500	8%

In-State vs. Out-of-State Contributions*

	Source	Total	Pct
☐	In-State	$285,201	96%
■	Out-of-state	$12,950	4%
	No state listed	$4,750	

*** by large individual contributors ($200 & above)**

Defense		$5,550

Defense Aerospace	$3,050	
None over $2,500		
Misc Defense	$2,500	
None over $2,500		

Energy & Natural Resources		$27,875

Oil & Gas	$17,650	
Noco Energy Corp	$4,000	Indiv
Mining	$2,500	
None over $2,500		
Electric Utilities	$5,225	
None over $2,500		

Finance, Insurance & Real Estate		$189,692

Commercial Banks	$54,550	
American Bankers Assn*	$10,500	PAC
Chase Manhattan	$5,000	PAC
Marine Midland Banks	$3,050	PAC/Ind
Barnett Banks Inc	$3,000	PAC
Citicorp	$3,000	PAC
JP Morgan & Co	$2,500	PAC
Savings & Loans	$10,480	
US League of Savings Assns*	$2,500	PAC
Credit Unions	$5,850	
Credit Union National Assn	$5,000	PAC
Finance/Credit Companies	$3,500	
None over $2,500		
Securities & Investment	$16,950	
Dean Witter	$3,200	PAC/Ind
Prudential Securities	$2,500	PAC
Insurance	$50,600	
Independent Insurance Agents of America	$10,050	PAC
National Assn of Life Underwriters	$10,000	PAC
Massachusetts Mutual Life Insurance	$2,500	PAC

Real Estate	$36,812	
National Assn of Realtors	$8,000	PAC
Ciminelli Companies	$4,000	Indiv
Mortgage Bankers Assn of America	$2,900	PAC
Farash Corp	$2,562	Indiv
Prime Real Estate Co	$2,500	Indiv
Accountants	**$8,350**	
American Institute of CPA's	$6,500	PAC
Misc Finance	**$2,600**	
None over $2,500		

Health $46,900

Health Professionals	$32,800	
American Medical Assn*	$9,850	PAC
American Academy of Ophthalmology	$3,700	PAC
American Chiropractic Assn	$2,500	PAC
Hospitals/Nursing Homes	**$8,150**	
None over $2,500		
Pharmaceuticals/Health Products	**$5,950**	
None over $2,500		

Lawyers & Lobbyists $25,350

Lawyers & Lobbyists	$25,350	
Nixon, Hargrave et al	$2,500	Indiv

Misc Business $76,301

Food & Beverage	$16,600	
Delaware North Companies	$7,000	Indiv
National Restaurant Assn	$3,350	PAC
Beer, Wine & Liquor	**$4,800**	
National Beer Wholesalers Assn	$4,000	PAC
Retail Sales	**$6,500**	
None over $2,500		
Misc Services	**$3,501**	
None over $2,500		
Business Services	**$5,300**	
None over $2,500		
Recreation/Live Entertainment	**$3,000**	
None over $2,500		

Lodging/Tourism	$4,500	
Hart Hotels Inc	$4,000	Indiv
Chemical & Related Manufacturing	**$3,000**	
None over $2,500		
Steel Production	**$4,850**	
None over $2,500		
Misc Manufacturing & Distributing	**$22,750**	
American Brass Co	$3,200	Indiv
American Precision Industries	$3,000	Indiv
Goulds Pumps Inc	$2,500	PAC

Transportation $34,730

Air Transport	$10,680	
United Parcel Service	$3,330	PAC
Enidine Inc	$3,000	Indiv
Moog Inc	$3,000	Indiv
Automotive	**$16,950**	
None over $2,500		
Trucking	**$4,100**	
None over $2,500		
Railroads	**$2,500**	
Union Pacific Corp	$2,500	PAC

Labor

Labor $4,850

Transportation Unions	$2,500	
Marine Engineers Dist 2 Maritime Officers	$2,500	PAC

Ideological/Single-Issue

Ideological/Single-Issue $29,150

Pro-Israel	$12,700	
National PAC	$5,000	PAC
Women's Alliance for Israel	$2,500	PAC
Gun Rights/Gun Control	**$9,900**	
National Rifle Assn	$9,900	PAC
Misc Issues	**$3,200**	
None over $2,500		

Other & Unknown

Other $12,554

Retired	$8,554	
None over $2,500		

Unknown $64,525

Homemakers/Non-income earners	$12,250
No Employer Listed or Found	$21,250
Employer Listed/Category Unknown	$29,025
None over $2,500	

Independent expenditures supporting Paxon
National Right to Life PAC $4,274

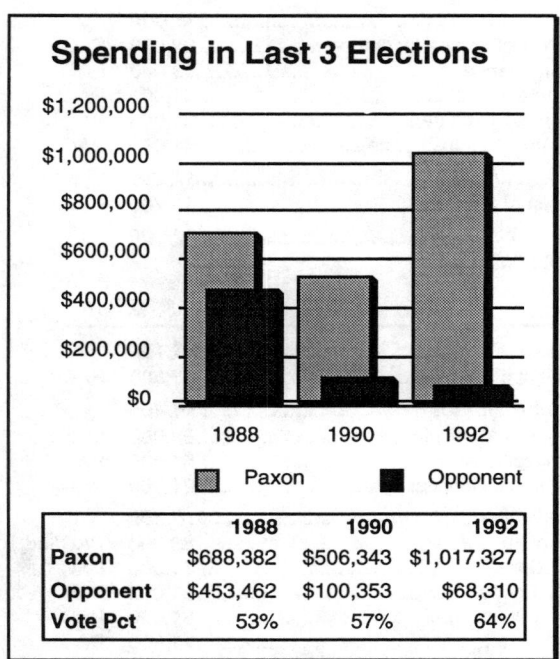

Spending in Last 3 Elections

Legend: ▨ Paxon ■ Opponent

	1988	1990	1992
Paxon	$688,382	$506,343	$1,017,327
Opponent	$453,462	$100,353	$68,310
Vote Pct	53%	57%	64%

---

* Contributions came from more than one affiliate or subsidiary.

Donald M. Payne, D-NJ (10)

First elected: 1988

1991-92 Total Receipts:	$358,688
1992 Year-end Cash:	$339,836

1991-92 Committees & Subcommittees

Education and Labor
Labor-Management Relations; Postsecondary Education; Select Education

Foreign Affairs
Africa

Government Operations
Human Resources and Intergovernmental Relations

Select Committee on Narcotics Abuse and Control

Leading Contributors

Business

Agriculture		**$8,000**	
Dairy		*$2,000*	
Associated Milk Producers		$1,000	PAC
Mid-America Dairymen		$1,000	PAC
Poultry & Eggs		*$1,000*	
Tyson Foods		$1,000	PAC
Agricultural Services/Products		*$1,500*	
Seabord Corp		$1,000	PAC
Food Processing & Sales		*$3,000*	
Connell Rice & Sugar Co		$2,000	Indiv

Communications/Electronics		**$8,680**	
Media/Entertainment		*$1,250*	
None over $1,000			
Telephone Utilities		*$6,630*	
Bell Atlantic*		$4,250	PAC
AT&T		$1,880	PAC/Ind

Construction		**$2,500**	
Home Builders		*$1,500*	
National Assn of Home Builders		$1,500	PAC

Energy & Natural Resources		**$5,900**	
Electric Utilities		*$5,400*	
Public Service Electric & Gas		$4,600	PAC

Contribution Totals by Sector

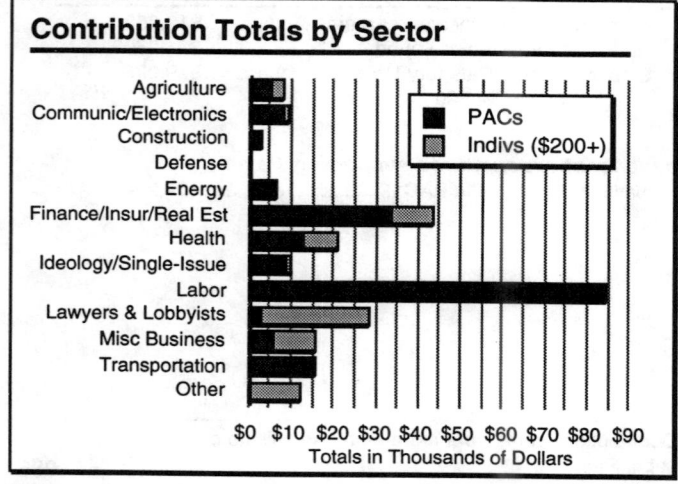

Totals in Thousands of Dollars

Source of Funds in 1992 Election

Source	Total	Pct
■ PACs	$183,606	50%
▨ Indivs $200+	$82,086	22%
□ Indivs under $200	$60,904	17%
▨ Other	$41,308	11%
Candidate	$0	0%
Party	$9,666	3%

Source of PAC Dollars by Sector

Source	Total	Pct
■ Business	$88,409	49%
▨ Labor	$83,360	46%
□ Ideology/Single Issue	$8,286	5%

In-State vs. Out-of-State Contributions*

Source	Total	Pct
□ In-State	$73,550	90%
▨ Out-of-state	$8,036	10%
No state listed	$500	

* by large individual contributors ($200 & above)

Finance, Insurance & Real Estate		**$42,919**	
Commercial Banks		*$4,100*	
American Bankers Assn		$1,000	PAC
Chemical Bank		$1,000	PAC
Savings & Loans		*$2,019*	
SAPEC, NJ (NJ Savings Assn)		$1,519	PAC
Finance/Credit Companies		*$7,500*	
Beneficial Management Corp		$7,500	PAC/Ind
Securities & Investment		*$5,100*	
Wesray Capital Corp		$2,000	Indiv
Prudential Securities		$1,000	PAC
Insurance		*$15,000*	
American Council of Life Insurance		$3,000	PAC
Prudential Insurance		$3,000	PAC
Mutual of Omaha		$1,000	PAC
Northwestern Mutual Life		$1,000	PAC
Principal Mutual Life Insurance		$1,000	PAC
Real Estate		*$7,200*	
National Assn of Realtors		$5,700	PAC
Accountants		*$2,000*	
None over $1,000			

Health		**$20,250**	
Health Professionals		*$5,100*	
American Dental Assn		$1,500	PAC
Hospitals/Nursing Homes		*$4,400*	
United Hospitals Medical Center		$2,000	Indiv
American Hospital Assn		$1,000	PAC
Orange Memorial Hospital		$1,000	Indiv
Pharmaceuticals/Health Products		*$10,250*	
Schering-Plough Corp		$3,500	PAC/Ind
Ciba-Geigy Corp		$1,000	PAC
Hoffman-La Roche		$1,000	PAC
Johnson & Johnson		$1,000	PAC
Merck & Co		$1,000	PAC

Lawyers & Lobbyists — $28,150

Lawyers & Lobbyists — $28,150

Lowenstein, Sandler et al	$7,550	Indiv
Assn of Trial Lawyers of America	$2,500	PAC
Brach, Eichler et al	$1,900	Indiv
Ashley & Charles	$1,250	Indiv
Frohling & Hanley	$1,250	Indiv
Carella, Byrne et al	$1,000	Indiv
Jordan, Schulte & Burchette	$1,000	Indiv

Misc Business — $14,980

Beer, Wine & Liquor — $2,230
Joseph E Seagram & Sons	$1,000	PAC

Retail Sales — $1,000
None over $1,000

Business Services — $4,000
The Writing Co	$2,000	Indiv

Lodging/Tourism — $2,500
Carlton Hotel	$1,000	Indiv
Robert Treat Hotel	$1,000	Indiv

Chemical & Related Manufacturing — $1,000
None over $1,000

Misc Manufacturing & Distributing — $3,750
Hoechst Celanese Corp	$2,500	PAC
Xerox Corp	$1,000	PAC

Transportation — $15,500

Air Transport — $13,500
United Parcel Service	$5,500	PAC
Federal Express Corp	$5,000	PAC
General Electric	$1,500	PAC
Texas Air	$1,000	PAC

Automotive — $1,500
Central Auto Body	$1,000	Indiv

Labor

Labor — $84,100

Building Trade Unions — $21,580
Operating Engineers Union*	$14,080	PAC
Laborers' Political League	$3,000	PAC
Plumbers/Pipefitters Union*	$2,000	PAC
Painters & Allied Trades Union	$1,000	PAC

Industrial Unions — $21,990
United Auto Workers	$10,000	PAC
Electrical Radio & Machine Workers	$3,000	PAC
Electronic Machine Furniture Workers	$2,500	PAC
Intl Brotherhood of Electrical Workers	$2,500	PAC
Ladies Garment Workers Union	$1,440	PAC
New Jersey Industrial Union Council	$1,300	PAC
Machinists/Aerospace Workers Union	$1,000	PAC

Transportation Unions — $19,700
Teamsters Union	$6,500	PAC
Air Line Pilots Assn	$3,500	PAC
Marine Engineers Dist 2 Maritime Officers	$2,000	PAC
United Transportation Union	$2,000	PAC
International Longshoremen's Assn	$1,750	PAC
Trans Comm International Union	$1,000	PAC

Public Sector Unions — $16,500
American Fedn of St/Cnty/Munic Employees	$7,500	PAC
National Education Assn	$3,500	PAC
American Postal Workers Union	$2,500	PAC
American Federation of Teachers	$1,000	PAC
National Assn Retired Federal Employees	$1,000	PAC

Misc Unions — $4,330
Food & Commercial Workers Union	$1,500	PAC
Service Employees International Union	$1,000	PAC

Ideological/Single-Issue

Ideological/Single-Issue — $9,572

Pro-Israel — $5,500
National PAC	$5,000	PAC

Human Rights — $1,000
Human Rights Campaign Fund	$1,000	PAC

Misc Issues — $1,500
National Cmte to Preserve Social Security	$1,500	PAC

Other & Unknown

Other — $11,620

Civil Servants/Public Officials — $3,590
County of Essex	$1,950	Indiv

Education — $3,840
Newark Board of Education	$1,090	Indiv

Retired — $3,500
None over $1,000

Unknown — $10,020

Homemakers/Non-income earners	$1,500	
No Employer Listed or Found	$1,700	
Employer Listed/Category Unknown	$6,820	
PMK Group	$1,500	Indiv
Berger Associates	$1,000	Indiv

Spending in Last 3 Elections

	1988	1990	1992
Payne	$413,338	$168,522	$285,455
Opponent	$0	$0	$24,777
Vote Pct	77%	82%	78%

---

* Contributions came from more than one affiliate or subsidiary.

987

Lewis F. Payne Jr., D-Va (5)

First elected: 1988

1991-92 Total Receipts: $419,768
1992 Year-end Cash: $13,540

1991-92 Committees & Subcommittees

Budget
Budget Process, Reconciliation and Enforcement; Community Development and Natural Resources

Public Works and Transportation
Aviation; Investigations and Oversight; Surface Transportation; Water Resources

Leading Contributors

Business

Agriculture — $28,300

Crop Production & Basic Processing	**$7,050**	
American Crystal Sugar Corp	$1,500	PAC
Tobacco	**$11,500**	
RJR Nabisco	$5,500	PAC
Philip Morris	$3,000	PAC
Dibrell Brothers Inc	$1,750	Indiv
Dairy	**$1,500**	
None over $1,500		
Livestock	**$1,500**	
National Cattlemen's Assn*	$1,500	PAC
Food Processing & Sales	**$1,500**	
None over $1,500		
Forestry & Forest Products	**$4,250**	
Westvaco Corp	$3,000	PAC

Communications/Electronics — $11,650

Printing & Publishing	**$1,700**	
None over $1,500		
Telephone Utilities	**$7,900**	
Bell Atlantic*	$2,500	PAC
AT&T	$2,250	PAC

Construction — $27,250

General Contractors	**$14,100**	
Associated General Contractors*	$3,750	Indiv
Construction Services	**$6,250**	
National Society of Professional Engineers	$4,500	PAC
Building Materials & Equipment	**$5,900**	
None over $1,500		

Source of Funds in 1992 Election

Source	Total	Pct
PACs	$218,944	52%
Indivs $200+	$141,070	33%
Indivs under $200	$58,430	14%
Other	$5,468	1%
Candidate	$0	0%
Party	$4,594	1%

Source of PAC Dollars by Sector

Source	Total	Pct
Business	$197,297	88%
Labor	$16,100	7%
Ideology/Single Issue	$10,850	5%

In-State vs. Out-of-State Contributions*

Source	Total	Pct
In-State	$131,410	94%
Out-of-state	$8,600	6%
No state listed	$0	

* by large individual contributors ($200 & above)

Defense — $4,250

Misc Defense	**$3,000**	
Tenneco Inc	$2,000	PAC

Energy & Natural Resources — $25,350

Oil & Gas	**$5,450**	
None over $1,500		
Mining	**$4,750**	
Reynolds Metals	$2,000	PAC/Ind
Misc Energy	**$7,500**	
Babcock & Wilcox	$6,000	PAC
Electric Utilities	**$7,150**	
ACRE (Action Cmte for Rural Electrification)	$3,500	PAC
Dominion Resources Inc	$1,900	PAC
American Electric Power*	$1,750	PAC

Finance, Insurance & Real Estate — $54,590

Commercial Banks	**$14,650**	
Citizens & Southern National Bank	$3,500	PAC
Virginia Bankers Assn	$3,500	PAC
Central Fidelity Banks	$2,000	PAC/Ind
Dominion Bankshares Corp	$1,500	PAC
Securities & Investment	**$4,700**	
None over $1,500		
Insurance	**$11,250**	
Blue Cross & Blue Shield Assn*	$2,500	PAC
Prudential Insurance	$1,500	PAC
Real Estate	**$17,590**	
National Assn of Realtors	$5,940	PAC
American Resort & Residential Devel Assn	$4,000	PAC
Accountants	**$2,500**	
American Institute of CPA's	$1,500	PAC

Contribution Totals by Sector

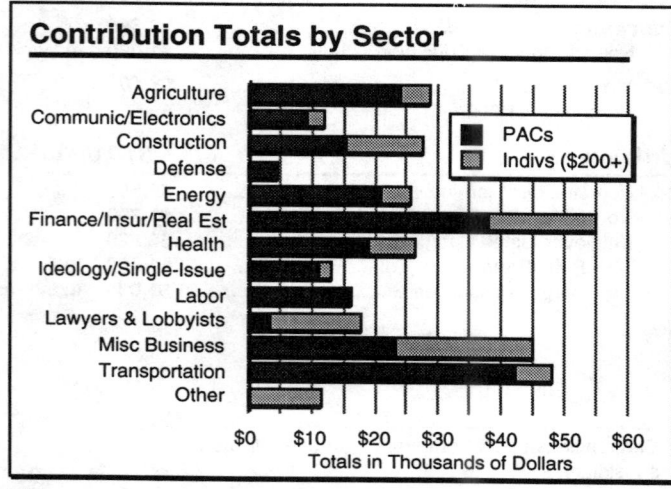

Totals in Thousands of Dollars

Agriculture, Communic/Electronics, Construction, Defense, Energy, Finance/Insur/Real Est, Health, Ideology/Single-Issue, Labor, Lawyers & Lobbyists, Misc Business, Transportation, Other

PACs / Indivs ($200+)

$0 $10 $20 $30 $40 $50 $60

Health — $25,950

Health Professionals **$18,200**
   American Medical Assn* ....$6,250 PAC
   American Academy of Ophthalmology ....$2,500 PAC
   American College of Emergency Physicians ....$2,000 PAC

Hospitals/Nursing Homes **$2,750**
   None over $1,500

Pharmaceuticals/Health Products **$3,500**
   None over $1,500

Misc Health **$1,500**
   None over $1,500

Lawyers & Lobbyists — $17,350

Lawyers & Lobbyists **$17,350**
   McGuire, Woods et al ....$4,950 PAC/Ind

Misc Business — $44,507

Food & Beverage **$4,750**
   General Mills Restaurants ....$2,000 PAC

Beer, Wine & Liquor **$4,250**
   National Beer Wholesalers Assn ....$1,750 PAC
   Associated Distributors ....$1,500 Indiv

Retail Sales **$4,507**
   None over $1,500

Misc Services **$1,700**
   None over $1,500

Business Services **$2,600**
   None over $1,500

Lodging/Tourism **$5,350**
   Wintergreen Resort ....$1,750 Indiv

Chemical & Related Manufacturing **$1,750**
   None over $1,500

Misc Manufacturing & Distributing **$11,000**
   American Furniture Manufacturers Assn ....$2,000 PAC
   Tultex Inc ....$2,000 Indiv
   Turbo Sales & Service ....$2,000 Indiv
   Hoechst Celanese Corp ....$1,500 PAC

Textiles **$7,500**
   Burlington Industries ....$5,000 PAC
   American Textile Manufacturers Institute ....$2,500 PAC

Transportation — $47,600

Air Transport **$22,650**
   Federal Express Corp ....$8,000 PAC
   United Parcel Service ....$6,500 PAC
   American Airlines ....$2,500 PAC
   Aircraft Owners & Pilots Assn ....$2,000 PAC

Automotive **$7,750**
   National Auto Dealers Assn ....$4,750 PAC

Trucking **$6,500**
   American Trucking Assns ....$2,250 PAC

Railroads **$8,300**
   Norfolk Southern Corp ....$2,050 PAC/Ind
   Union Pacific Corp ....$1,750 PAC
   Burlington Northern ....$1,500 PAC
   CSX Transportation Inc ....$1,500 PAC

Misc Transport **$1,500**
   None over $1,500

Labor

Labor — $16,100

Transportation Unions **$6,850**
   Air Line Pilots Assn ....$4,000 PAC
   United Transportation Union ....$1,500 PAC

Public Sector Unions **$8,250**
   National Assn of Letter Carriers ....$2,000 PAC
   National Education Assn ....$2,000 PAC
   American Federation of Teachers ....$1,500 PAC
   National Assn of Postal Supervisors ....$1,500 PAC

Ideological/Single-Issue

Ideological/Single-Issue — $12,870

Democratic/Liberal **$3,520**
   National Cmte for an Effective Congress ....$2,500 PAC

Gun Rights/Gun Control **$5,950**
   National Rifle Assn ....$5,950 PAC

Other & Unknown

Other — $11,250

Civil Servants/Public Officials **$3,400**
   Commonwealth of Virginia ....$1,500 Indiv

Retired **$6,150**
   None over $1,500

Unknown — $37,240

   Homemakers/Non-income earners $2,200
   No Employer Listed or Found $7,790
   Employer Listed/Category Unknown $27,000
      Donovan Data Systems ....$1,500 Indiv
      Robinson, Farmer, Cox Assoc ....$1,500 Indiv
      Tectonics II ....$1,500 Indiv

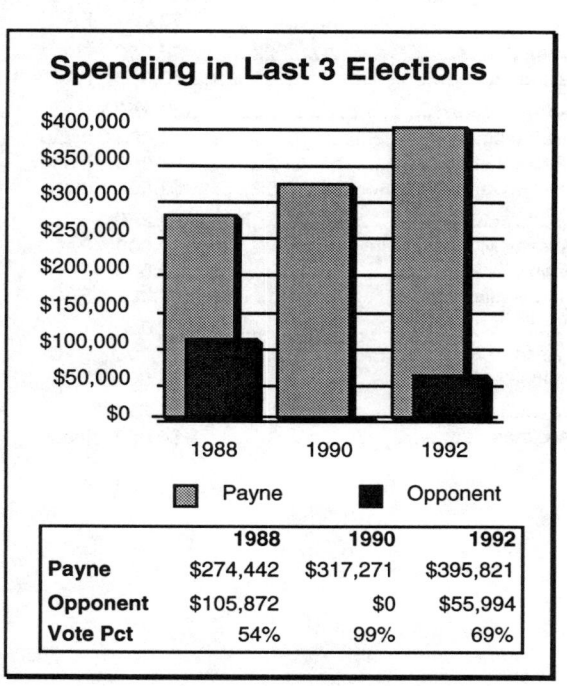

Spending in Last 3 Elections

	1988	1990	1992
Payne	$274,442	$317,271	$395,821
Opponent	$105,872	$0	$55,994
Vote Pct	54%	99%	69%

* Contributions came from more than one affiliate or subsidiary.

Nancy Pelosi, D-Calif (8)

First elected: 1987

1991-92 Total Receipts: $417,254
1992 Year-end Cash: $74,704

1991-92 Committees & Subcommittees

Appropriations
Commerce, Justice, State, the Judiciary and Related Agencies;
Treasury, Postal Service and General Government

Standards of Official Conduct

Leading Contributors

Business

Agriculture		$8,350

Crop Production & Basic Processing $3,850
  None over $1,500

Food Processing & Sales $1,500
  None over $1,500

Communications/Electronics	$10,500

Media/Entertainment $4,500
  None over $1,500

Telephone Utilities $3,000
  Pacific Telesis Group .... $2,500   PAC

Computer Equipment & Services $2,500
  None over $1,500

Construction	$7,000

General Contractors $3,000
  None over $1,500

Special Trade Contractors $2,000
  None over $1,500

Building Materials & Equipment $2,000
  None over $1,500

Defense	$4,500

Defense Aerospace $2,000
  None over $1,500

Defense Electronics $2,500
  AT&T .... $2,000   PAC

Source of Funds in 1992 Election

Source	Total	Pct
■ PACs	$204,689	48%
▦ Indivs $200+	$183,200	43%
□ Indivs under $200	$11,333	3%
▨ Other	$23,446	6%
Candidate	$0	0%
Party	$5,564	1%

Source of PAC Dollars by Sector

Source	Total	Pct
■ Business	$99,575	49%
▦ Labor	$95,750	47%
□ Ideology/Single Issue	$9,038	4%

In-State vs. Out-of-State Contributions*

Source	Total	Pct
□ In-State	$156,700	86%
■ Out-of-state	$26,500	14%
No state listed	$0	

* by large individual contributors ($200 & above)

Energy & Natural Resources — $11,250

Oil & Gas $2,500
  Robert M Bass Group Inc .... $1,500   Indiv

Misc Energy $3,000
  Bechtel Corp .... $3,000   PAC

Electric Utilities $5,250
  Pacific Gas & Electric .... $2,500   PAC
  Southern California Edison .... $1,500   PAC

Finance, Insurance & Real Estate — $86,700

Commercial Banks $8,500
  BankAmerica Corp .... $2,000   PAC
  Citicorp .... $2,000   PAC

Savings & Loans $5,200
  World Savings & Loan .... $3,000   PAC/Ind

Securities & Investment $20,250
  Hellman & Friedman .... $4,000   Indiv
  Kleiner, Perkins et al .... $3,000   Indiv
  Van Kasper & Co .... $1,500   Indiv

Insurance $12,250
  Massachusetts Mutual Life Insurance ... $2,000   PAC
  Metropolitan Life Insurance .... $2,000   PAC
  Pacific Mutual Life .... $2,000   PAC

Real Estate $25,000
  National Assn of Realtors .... $7,000   PAC
  AKT Development Co .... $5,000   Indiv

Misc Finance $14,750
  R&S Associates .... $4,000   Indiv

Contribution Totals by Sector

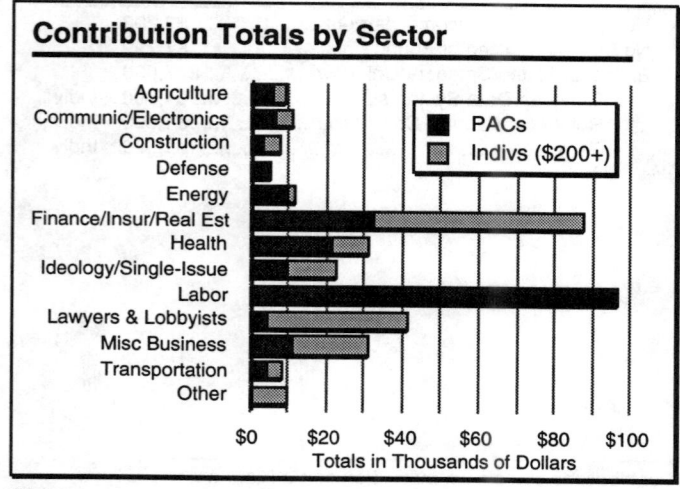

Agriculture
Communic/Electronics
Construction
Defense
Energy
Finance/Insur/Real Est
Health
Ideology/Single-Issue
Labor
Lawyers & Lobbyists
Misc Business
Transportation
Other

■ PACs
▦ Indivs ($200+)

$0 $20 $40 $60 $80 $100
Totals in Thousands of Dollars

Health $30,400

Health Professionals **$22,900**
  American Medical Assn.........................$7,350 PAC
  American Academy of Ophthalmology ....$3,500 PAC
  American Dental Assn ....$2,500 PAC

Hospitals/Nursing Homes **$2,500**
  None over $1,500

Pharmaceuticals/Health Products **$4,000**
  Syntex (USA) Inc ....$1,500 PAC

Lawyers & Lobbyists $40,525

Lawyers & Lobbyists **$40,525**
  Baker & McKenzie.............................$3,000 Indiv
  Heller, Ehrman et al ....$2,750 Indiv
  Howard, Rice et al ....$1,500 Indiv
  Ogilvy, Adams & Rinehart ....$1,500 Indiv

Misc Business $30,350

Food & Beverage **$2,500**
  None over $1,500

Beer, Wine & Liquor **$15,000**
  Gallo Winery....................................$5,000 Indiv
  Wine Institute ....$4,000 PAC

Retail Sales **$3,750**
  Gap Inc ....$1,500 PAC/Ind

Business Services **$3,500**
  None over $1,500

Recreation/Live Entertainment **$1,500**
  Robert Trent Jones International ....$1,500 Indiv

Lodging/Tourism **$3,100**
  None over $1,500

Transportation $8,000

Air Transport **$2,000**
  None over $1,500

Sea Transport **$3,000**
  None over $1,500

Misc Transport **$3,000**
  WJ Byrnes & Co ....$2,000 Indiv

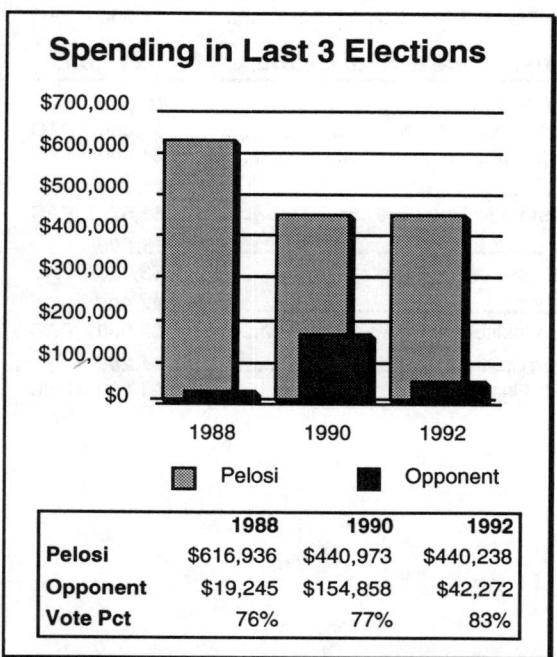

Spending in Last 3 Elections

	1988	1990	1992
Pelosi	$616,936	$440,973	$440,238
Opponent	$19,245	$154,858	$42,272
Vote Pct	76%	77%	83%

◻ Pelosi   ■ Opponent

Labor

Labor $95,750

Building Trade Unions **$12,000**
  Plumbers/Pipefitters Union....................$5,000 PAC
  Laborers' Political League ....$4,000 PAC
  AFL-CIO Bldg/Construction Trades Dept ....$1,500 PAC

Industrial Unions **$9,500**
  United Auto Workers ....$7,000 PAC

Transportation Unions **$37,300**
  Air Line Pilots Assn ....$7,500 PAC
  Teamsters Union ....$7,500 PAC
  Marine Engineers Union* ....$5,500 PAC
  Intl Longshoremen's/Warehousemen's Union .....$5,000 PAC
  Seafarers International Union* ....$4,500 PAC
  United Transportation Union ....$2,500 PAC
  Transport Workers Union ....$2,000 PAC
  Masters, Mates & Pilots Union ....$1,500 PAC

Public Sector Unions **$29,750**
  American Fedn of St/Cnty/Munic Employees ......$6,000 PAC
  National Assn of Letter Carriers ....$5,000 PAC
  National Assn Retired Federal Employees ....$3,000 PAC
  National Education Assn ....$3,000 PAC
  American Federation of Teachers ....$2,500 PAC
  American Postal Workers Union ....$2,500 PAC
  International Assn of Firefighters ....$1,500 PAC
  National Assn of Postmasters ....$1,500 PAC
  National Rural Letter Carriers Assn ....$1,500 PAC

Misc Unions **$7,200**
  Hotel/Restaurant Employees Union ....$3,000 PAC
  Food & Commercial Workers Union ....$2,500 PAC

Ideological/Single-Issue

Ideological/Single-Issue $22,288

Pro-Israel **$6,750**
  None over $1,500

Womens Issues **$6,788**
  National Organization for Women ....$2,090 PAC

Human Rights **$3,250**
  Human Rights Campaign Fund.....................$2,500 PAC

Misc Issues **$2,500**
  National Cmte to Preserve Social Security ....$1,500 PAC

Other & Unknown

Other $9,150

Education **$3,000**
  Dalton School/NY Public School System ....$2,000 Indiv

Retired **$5,250**
  None over $1,500

Unknown $23,050

  Homemakers/Non-income earners $4,250
  No Employer Listed or Found $1,500
  Generic Occupation/Category Unknown $3,500
  Employer Listed/Category Unknown $13,550
    None over $1,500

---

* Contributions came from more than one affiliate or subsidiary.

Timothy J. Penny, D-Minn (1)

First elected: 1982

1991-92 Total Receipts:	$244,518
1992 Year-end Cash:	$207,789

1991-92 Committees & Subcommittees

Agriculture
Conservation, Credit and Rural Development; Livestock, Dairy and Poultry; Wheat, Soybeans and Feed Grains (Vice Chairman)

Veterans' Affairs
Compensation, Pension and Insurance; Education, Training and Employment (Chairman)

Select Committee on Hunger

Leading Contributors

Business

Agriculture — $34,500

Crop Production & Basic Processing	**$7,100**	
American Crystal Sugar Corp	$2,000	PAC
Southern Minn Beet Sugar Co-op	$1,250	PAC
AG Processing Inc	$1,000	PAC
Cargill Inc	$1,000	PAC
Dairy	**$6,500**	
Associated Milk Producers	$3,500	PAC
Mid-America Dairymen	$1,500	PAC
Milk Industry Foundation	$1,500	PAC
Poultry & Eggs	**$3,000**	
National Broiler Council	$1,500	PAC
United Egg Assn	$1,000	PAC
Livestock	**$2,500**	
National Cattlemen's Assn*	$1,500	PAC
National Pork Producers Council	$1,000	PAC
Agricultural Services/Products	**$9,250**	
Land O'Lakes Inc	$3,000	PAC
American Veterinary Medical Assn	$1,000	PAC
Food Processing & Sales	**$5,150**	
Food Marketing Institute	$3,000	PAC
ConAgra Inc	$1,000	PAC
Forestry & Forest Products	**$1,000**	
Potlatch Corp	$1,000	PAC

Source of Funds in 1992 Election

Source	Total	Pct
■ PACs	$92,743	38%
▨ Indivs $200+	$11,450	5%
☐ Indivs under $200	$106,222	43%
⊠ Other	$34,480	14%
Candidate	$0	0%
Party	$677	0%

Source of PAC Dollars by Sector

Source	Total	Pct
■ Business	$87,243	93%
▨ Labor	$4,750	5%
☐ Ideology/Single Issue	$1,500	2%

In-State vs. Out-of-State Contributions*

Source	Total	Pct
☐ In-State	$4,450	39%
■ Out-of-state	$7,000	61%
No state listed	$0	

* by large individual contributors ($200 & above)

Communications/Electronics — $5,650

Media/Entertainment	**$1,000**	
None over $1,000		
Telephone Utilities	**$3,950**	
US West Inc	$2,500	PAC
GTE Corp	$1,000	PAC

Energy & Natural Resources — $3,200

Oil & Gas	**$1,000**	
Koch Industries	$1,000	PAC
Electric Utilities	**$1,700**	
Northern States Power Co	$1,000	PAC

Finance, Insurance & Real Estate — $14,650

Commercial Banks	**$5,500**	
American Bankers Assn	$3,000	PAC
Norwest Corp	$1,000	PAC
Insurance	**$1,750**	
Northwestern National Life	$1,550	PAC
Real Estate	**$3,000**	
National Assn of Realtors	$3,000	PAC
Accountants	**$2,000**	
American Institute of CPA's	$2,000	PAC
Misc Finance	**$1,200**	
Dearborn Financial Inc	$1,000	Indiv

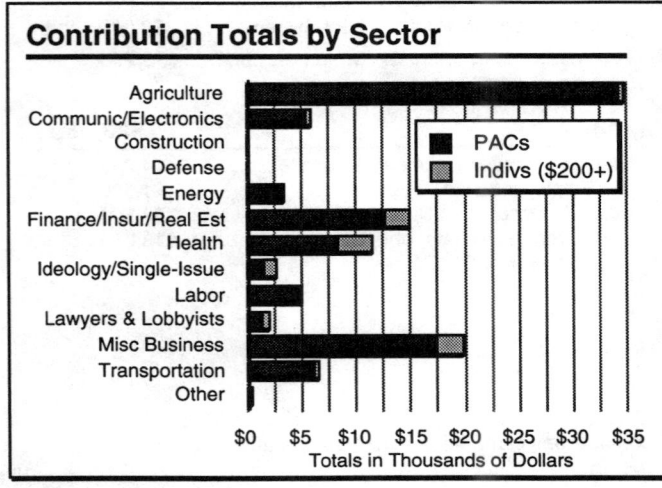

Contribution Totals by Sector

Agriculture, Communic/Electronics, Construction, Defense, Energy, Finance/Insur/Real Est, Health, Ideology/Single-Issue, Labor, Lawyers & Lobbyists, Misc Business, Transportation, Other

■ PACs
▨ Indivs ($200+)

$0 $5 $10 $15 $20 $25 $30 $35
Totals in Thousands of Dollars

Health $11,250

Health Professionals **$11,150**
    American Dental Assn .... $5,000 PAC
    American Medical Assn .... $2,500 PAC

Lawyers & Lobbyists $1,800

Lawyers & Lobbyists **$1,800**
    None over $1,000

Misc Business $19,643

Food & Beverage **$2,000**
    S&A Restaurant Corp .... $1,500 PAC

Beer, Wine & Liquor **$1,500**
    College City Beverage Inc .... $1,000 Indiv

Retail Sales **$10,893**
    Limited Inc .... $2,000 PAC
    Dayton Hudson Corp .... $1,500 PAC
    Spiegel Inc .... $1,500 PAC
    Gap Inc .... $1,000 Indiv
    May Department Stores .... $1,000 PAC
    National Assn of Chain Drug Stores ...... $1,000 PAC

Business Services **$2,500**
    Ecolab Inc .... $2,000 PAC

Misc Manufacturing & Distributing **$1,500**
    Minnesota Mining & Manufacturing (3M) .... $1,500 PAC

Transportation $6,400

Air Transport **$2,400**
    None over $1,000

Automotive **$2,500**
    National Auto Dealers Assn .... $2,500 PAC

Labor

Labor   **$4,750**

Transportation Unions **$1,100**
    Teamsters Union .... $1,000 PAC

Public Sector Unions **$2,900**
    National Education Assn .... $1,500 PAC

Ideological/Single-Issue

Ideological/Single-Issue   **$2,500**

Foreign & Defense Policy **$1,500**
    None over $1,000

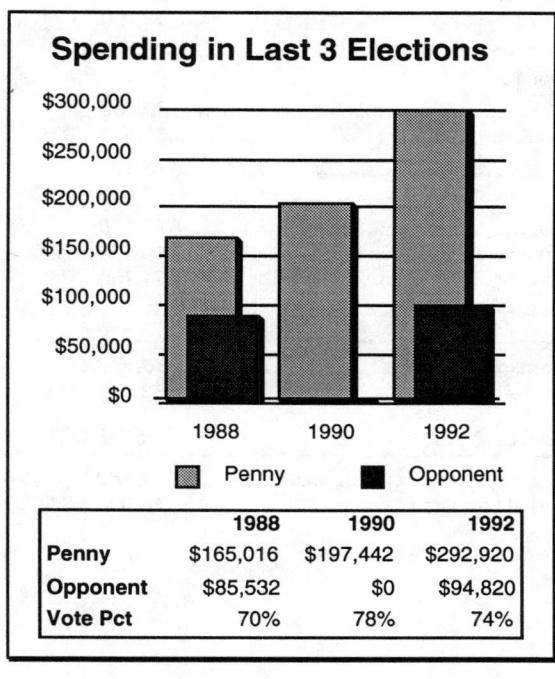

Spending in Last 3 Elections

	1988	1990	1992
Penny	$165,016	$197,442	$292,920
Opponent	$85,532	$0	$94,820
Vote Pct	70%	78%	74%

* Contributions came from more than one affiliate or subsidiary.

993

Collin C. Peterson, D-Minn (7)

First elected: 1990
1991-92 Total Receipts: $497,021
1992 Year-end Cash: $2,281

1991-92 Committees & Subcommittees

Agriculture
Cotton, Rice and Sugar; Livestock, Dairy and Poultry; Wheat, Soybeans and Feed Grains

Government Operations
Government Information, Justice and Agriculture; Legislation and National Security

Leading Contributors

Business

Agriculture — $64,667

Crop Production & Basic Processing	**$29,450**	
American Crystal Sugar Corp	$10,000	PAC
Southern Minn Beet Sugar Co-op	$2,750	PAC
American Sugarbeet Growers Assn	$2,100	PAC
AG Processing Inc	$1,500	PAC
National Cotton Council	$1,500	PAC
Tobacco	**$4,043**	
RJR Nabisco	$2,000	PAC
Philip Morris	$1,543	PAC
Dairy	**$14,250**	
Associated Milk Producers	$9,500	PAC
Mid-America Dairymen	$4,000	PAC
Poultry & Eggs	**$2,600**	
None over $1,500		
Agricultural Services/Products	**$8,300**	
American Veterinary Medical Assn	$1,500	PAC
Land O'Lakes Inc	$1,500	PAC
Food Processing & Sales	**$1,774**	
None over $1,500		
Forestry & Forest Products	**$3,000**	
Champion International Corp	$2,000	PAC

Communications/Electronics — $11,300

Printing & Publishing	**$2,500**	
West Publishing	$2,500	PAC
Telephone Utilities	**$8,800**	
US West Inc	$4,000	PAC
AT&T	$2,550	PAC

Source of Funds in 1992 Election

Source	Total	Pct
PACs	$321,007	64%
Indivs $200+	$22,050	4%
Indivs under $200	$99,063	20%
Other	$62,516	12%
Candidate	$0	0%
Party	$17,423	3%

Source of PAC Dollars by Sector

Source	Total	Pct
Business	$156,217	49%
Labor	$138,199	43%
Ideology/Single Issue	$26,321	8%

In-State vs. Out-of-State Contributions*

Source	Total	Pct
In-State	$17,150	78%
Out-of-state	$4,900	22%
No state listed	$0	

* by large individual contributors ($200 & above)

Energy & Natural Resources — $4,900

Electric Utilities	**$3,550**	
ACRE (Action Cmte for Rural Electrification)	$1,600	PAC

Finance, Insurance & Real Estate — $46,550

Commercial Banks	**$7,600**	
American Bankers Assn	$3,000	PAC
Independent Bankers Assn	$1,800	PAC
Savings & Loans	**$1,800**	
US League of Savings Assns*	$1,500	PAC
Credit Unions	**$2,000**	
Credit Union National Assn	$2,000	PAC
Securities & Investment	**$3,750**	
None over $1,500		
Insurance	**$3,950**	
American Family Corp	$2,000	PAC
Real Estate	**$15,200**	
National Assn of Realtors	$15,000	PAC
Accountants	**$12,250**	
American Institute of CPA's	$10,000	PAC
Ernst & Young	$1,750	PAC

Health — $8,300

Health Professionals	**$6,450**	
American Medical Assn	$3,350	PAC

Lawyers & Lobbyists — $14,150

Lawyers & Lobbyists	**$14,150**	
Assn of Trial Lawyers of America	$8,000	PAC

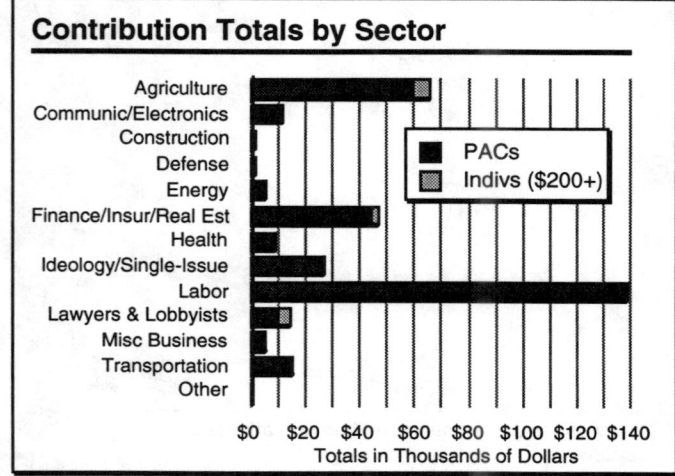

Contribution Totals by Sector

Agriculture
Communic/Electronics
Construction
Defense
Energy
Finance/Insur/Real Est
Health
Ideology/Single-Issue
Labor
Lawyers & Lobbyists
Misc Business
Transportation
Other

■ PACs
▨ Indivs ($200+)

$0 $20 $40 $60 $80 $100 $120 $140
Totals in Thousands of Dollars

Misc Business — $5,250

Beer, Wine & Liquor $1,700
   None over $1,500

Business Services $1,700
   None over $1,500

Transportation — $14,300

Air Transport $5,100
   Aircraft Owners & Pilots Assn .... $1,500 PAC

Automotive $6,700
   National Auto Dealers Assn .... $5,200 PAC
   Auto Dealers & Drivers for Free Trade .... $1,500 PAC

Trucking $1,500
   None over $1,500

Labor

Labor — $138,199

Building Trade Unions $19,500
   Carpenters & Joiners Union .... $6,000 PAC
   Sheet Metal Workers Union .... $5,500 PAC
   Ironworkers Union .... $3,000 PAC
   Laborers' Political League .... $2,500 PAC
   Plumbers/Pipefitters Union .... $1,500 PAC

Industrial Unions $40,950
   Machinists/Aerospace Workers Union .... $10,000 PAC
   United Steelworkers .... $10,000 PAC
   United Auto Workers .... $7,000 PAC
   Rubber Cork Linoleum & Plastic Workers .... $4,000 PAC
   Intl Brotherhood of Electrical Workers .... $3,500 PAC
   Communications Workers of America .... $2,100 PAC

Transportation Unions $28,350
   Teamsters Union* .... $10,000 PAC
   Seafarers International Union .... $5,000 PAC
   Air Line Pilots Assn .... $4,500 PAC
   Trans Comm International Union .... $1,700 PAC
   Transport Workers Union .... $1,500 PAC
   United Transportation Union .... $1,500 PAC

Public Sector Unions $43,499
   National Education Assn .... $10,000 PAC
   American Postal Workers Union* .... $7,500 PAC
   American Fedn of St/Cnty/Munic Employees ...... $7,499 PAC
   American Federation of Teachers .... $5,000 PAC
   National Assn of Letter Carriers .... $5,000 PAC
   National Assn Retired Federal Employees .... $3,000 PAC
   International Assn of Firefighters .... $2,000 PAC

Misc Unions $5,900
   Food & Commercial Workers Union .... $4,500 PAC

Ideological/Single-Issue

Ideological/Single-Issue — $26,321

Democratic/Liberal $8,348
   7th District DFL Campaign Cmte .... $5,848 PAC
   National Cmte for an Effective Congress .... $2,500 PAC

Pro-Israel $3,100
   MinnPAC .... $1,500 PAC

Gun Rights/Gun Control $10,400
   National Rifle Assn .... $9,900 PAC

Misc Issues $3,000
   National Cmte to Preserve Social Security .... $2,500 PAC

Other & Unknown

Unknown — $6,350

   No Employer Listed or Found $3,050
   Employer Listed/Category Unknown $2,600
     None over $1,500

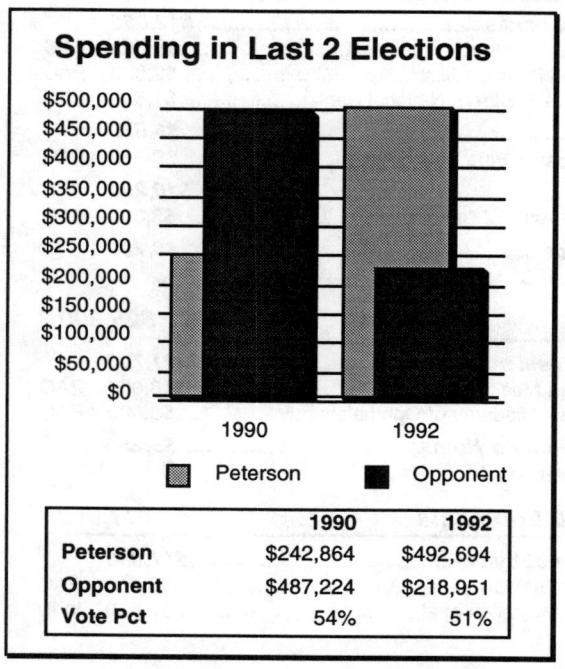

Spending in Last 2 Elections

	1990	1992
Peterson	$242,864	$492,694
Opponent	$487,224	$218,951
Vote Pct	54%	51%

Legend: Peterson, Opponent

* Contributions came from more than one affiliate or subsidiary.

Pete Peterson, D-Fla (2)

First elected: 1990

1991-92 Total Receipts: $400,867
1992 Year-end Cash: $25,352

1991-92 Committees & Subcommittees

Public Works and Transportation
Investigations and Oversight (Vice Chairman); Public Buildings and Grounds; Water Resources

Veterans' Affairs
Oversight and Investigations

Select Committee on Children, Youth and Families

Leading Contributors

Business

Agriculture		$25,050
Crop Production & Basic Processing **$8,500**		
None over $1,500		
Tobacco **$7,800**		
RJR Nabisco $5,200	PAC	
Dairy **$3,500**		
Associated Milk Producers $3,500	PAC	
Agricultural Services/Products **$2,350**		
None over $1,500		

Communications/Electronics		$14,050
Media/Entertainment **$1,600**		
None over $1,500		
Telephone Utilities **$10,000**		
Southern Bell $5,400	PAC	
GTE Corp $2,750	PAC	
AT&T $1,850	PAC	

Construction		$15,657
General Contractors **$8,057**		
AW & Associates $5,807	Indiv	
Home Builders **$2,750**		
National Assn of Home Builders $2,500	PAC	
Special Trade Contractors **$2,000**		
3-M Masonry $2,000	Indiv	
Building Materials & Equipment **$2,500**		
Jim Walter Corp $2,500	PAC	

Source of Funds in 1992 Election

Source	Total	Pct
■ PACs	$282,350	69%
▨ Indivs $200+	$63,731	16%
□ Indivs under $200	$52,677	13%
▧ Other	$10,840	3%
Candidate	$0	0%
Party	$8,881	2%

Source of PAC Dollars by Sector

Source	Total	Pct
■ Business	$145,000	53%
▨ Labor	$113,150	42%
□ Ideology/Single Issue	$14,250	5%

In-State vs. Out-of-State Contributions*

Source	Total	Pct
□ In-State	$57,380	91%
■ Out-of-state	$5,950	9%
No state listed	$0	

* by large individual contributors ($200 & above)

Defense		$3,200
Defense Aerospace **$2,950**		
General Dynamics $1,900	PAC	

Energy & Natural Resources		$11,800
Oil & Gas **$3,250**		
Occidental Petroleum $1,700	PAC	
Electric Utilities **$7,700**		
ACRE (Action Cmte for Rural Electrification) $1,850	PAC	

Finance, Insurance & Real Estate		$33,722
Commercial Banks **$12,050**		
Barnett Banks Inc $4,500	PAC	
American Bankers Assn $2,000	PAC	
Citizens & Southern National Bank $1,500	PAC	
Insurance **$5,572**		
Blue Cross & Blue Shield Assn* $2,350	PAC	
Real Estate **$10,250**		
National Assn of Realtors $8,000	PAC	
Misc Finance **$3,700**		
None over $1,500		

Health		$25,300
Health Professionals **$21,700**		
American Medical Assn* $10,000	PAC	
American Academy of Ophthalmology $3,000	PAC	
Hospitals/Nursing Homes **$3,250**		
None over $1,500		

Lawyers & Lobbyists		$17,000
Lawyers & Lobbyists **$17,000**		
Assn of Trial Lawyers of America $5,000	PAC	
Ausley, McMullen et al $2,650	Indiv	

Contribution Totals by Sector

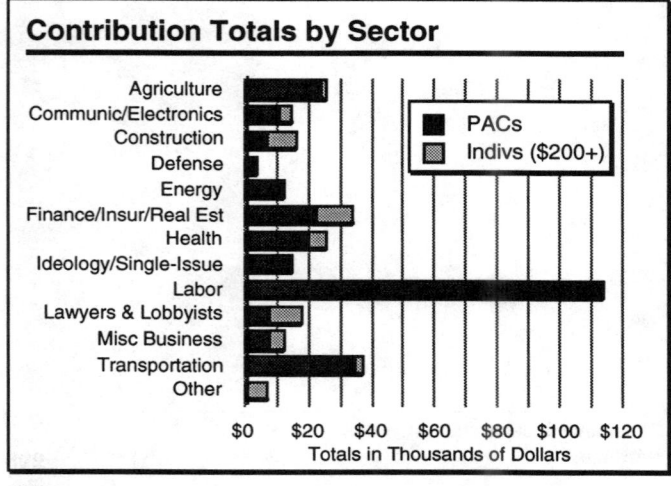

Agriculture
Communic/Electronics
Construction
Defense
Energy
Finance/Insur/Real Est
Health
Ideology/Single-Issue
Labor
Lawyers & Lobbyists
Misc Business
Transportation
Other

■ PACs
▨ Indivs ($200+)

$0 $20 $40 $60 $80 $100 $120
Totals in Thousands of Dollars

Misc Business $11,650

Retail Sales $2,500
   None over $1,500

Chemical & Related Manufacturing $2,700
   Olin Corp .... $1,700 PAC

Transportation $36,300

Air Transport $21,150
   Federal Express Corp .... $9,000 PAC
   United Parcel Service .... $6,400 PAC
   United Airlines .... $1,500 PAC

Automotive $8,250
   National Auto Dealers Assn .... $4,000 PAC
   Auto Dealers & Drivers for Free Trade ..... $1,500 PAC

Trucking $4,300
   None over $1,500

Railroads $2,250
   None over $1,500

Labor

Labor $113,150

Building Trade Unions $14,050
   Laborers' Political League .... $3,250 PAC
   Plumbers/Pipefitters Union .... $3,000 PAC
   Sheet Metal Workers Union .... $3,000 PAC
   Carpenters & Joiners Union .... $2,500 PAC

Industrial Unions $29,500
   United Auto Workers .... $10,000 PAC
   Communications Workers of America .... $4,000 PAC
   Machinists/Aerospace Workers Union ...... $3,550 PAC
   Intl Brotherhood of Electrical Workers ..... $3,000 PAC
   United Steelworkers .... $3,000 PAC

Transportation Unions $32,750
   Air Line Pilots Assn .... $7,500 PAC
   Seafarers International Union .... $7,500 PAC
   Marine Engineers Union* .... $3,500 PAC
   Teamsters Union .... $3,500 PAC
   Transport Workers Union .... $3,350 PAC
   United Transportation Union .... $2,200 PAC
   Amalgamated Transit Union .... $2,000 PAC

Public Sector Unions $30,100
   National Education Assn .... $10,000 PAC
   American Fedn of St/Cnty/Munic Employees ..... $7,500 PAC
   National Assn Retired Federal Employees ..... $3,000 PAC
   American Postal Workers Union .... $2,550 PAC
   National Assn of Letter Carriers .... $2,000 PAC

Misc Unions $6,750
   Food & Commercial Workers Union .... $2,500 PAC

Ideological/Single-Issue

Ideological/Single-Issue $14,250

Democratic/Liberal $2,500
   National Cmte for an Effective Congress ..... $2,500 PAC

Gun Rights/Gun Control $6,950
   National Rifle Assn .... $6,950 PAC

Misc Issues $3,450
   National Cmte to Preserve Social Security ..... $2,450 PAC

Other & Unknown

Other $6,150

Retired $4,400
   None over $1,500

Unknown $8,451

   Employer Listed/Category Unknown $6,636
      None over $1,500

Spending in Last 2 Elections

	1990	1992
Peterson	$306,104	$371,336
Opponent	$839,764	$22,639
Vote Pct	57%	73%

* Contributions came from more than one affiliate or subsidiary.

Tom Petri, R-Wis (6)

First elected: 1979

1991-92 Total Receipts: $433,702
1992 Year-end Cash: $55,773

1991-92 Committees & Subcommittees

Education and Labor
Elementary, Secondary and Vocational Education; Labor-Management Relations; Labor Standards (Ranking Republican); Postsecondary Education

Public Works and Transportation
Aviation; Surface Transportation; Water Resources (Ranking Republican)

Leading Contributors

Business

Agriculture — $33,250

Crop Production & Basic Processing $2,000		
Bog Farm Inc $1,000	Indiv
Ocean Spray Cranberries Inc $1,000	PAC
Dairy **$9,850**	
Associated Milk Producers $6,500	PAC
Mid-America Dairymen $2,100	PAC
Livestock **$1,150**	
None over $1,000	
Agricultural Services/Products **$4,550**	
Land O'Lakes Inc $1,400	PAC
Food Processing & Sales **$6,000**	
Food Marketing Institute $3,400	PAC
Forestry & Forest Products **$9,700**	
International Paper Co $2,000	PAC
Kimberly-Clark $2,000	PAC/Ind
Fort Howard Corp $1,800	PAC
Union Camp Corp $1,600	PAC
Scott Paper Co $1,000	PAC

Communications/Electronics — $9,810

Printing & Publishing $2,360	
Printing Industries of America $1,500	PAC
Telephone Utilities **$5,600**	
Wisconsin Bell Telephone $2,000	PAC
AT&T $1,500	PAC
GTE Corp $1,500	PAC

Source of Funds in 1992 Election

Source	Total	Pct
■ PACs	$204,000	46%
▨ Indivs $200+	$36,848	8%
□ Indivs under $200	$137,779	31%
⊠ Other	$60,075	14%
Candidate	$720	0%
Party	$14,201	3%

Source of PAC Dollars by Sector

Source	Total	Pct
■ Business	$187,870	95%
▨ Labor	$1,150	1%
□ Ideology/Single Issue	$8,750	4%

In-State vs. Out-of-State Contributions*

Source	Total	Pct
□ In-State	$24,675	67%
▨ Out-of-state	$12,173	33%
No state listed	$0	

* by large individual contributors ($200 & above)

Construction — $22,400

General Contractors $9,400	
Associated General Contractors $2,600	PAC
National Utility Contractors Assn $2,500	PAC
Associated Builders & Contractors $1,000	PAC
Home Builders **$1,200**	
National Assn of Home Builders* $2,200	PAC
Special Trade Contractors **$1,000**	
National Electrical Contractors Assn $1,000	PAC
Construction Services **$5,950**	
American Consulting Engineers Council $3,000	PAC
CH2M Hill $1,600	PAC
Building Materials & Equipment **$4,850**	
American Supply Assn $2,000	PAC
Caterpillar Tractor $1,000	PAC

Defense — $1,550

| Defense Aerospace .... $1,300 | |
| None over $1,000 | |

Energy & Natural Resources — $13,230

Oil & Gas $5,300	
Michigan Consolidated Gas $2,000	PAC
Amoco Corp $1,000	PAC
Electric Utilities **$5,680**	
Wisconsin Electric Power Co $2,400	PAC
Wisconsin Power & Light $1,380	PAC
Waste Management **$1,750**	
None over $1,000	

Contribution Totals by Sector

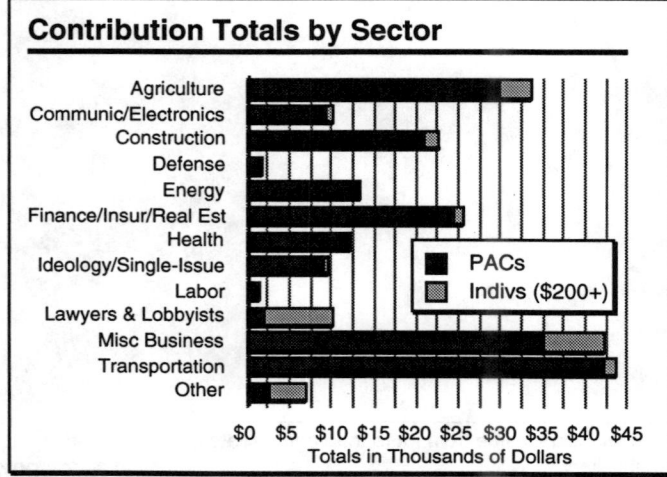

Agriculture
Communic/Electronics
Construction
Defense
Energy
Finance/Insur/Real Est
Health
Ideology/Single-Issue
Labor
Lawyers & Lobbyists
Misc Business
Transportation
Other

■ PACs
▨ Indivs ($200+)

$0 $5 $10 $15 $20 $25 $30 $35 $40 $45
Totals in Thousands of Dollars

Finance, Insurance & Real Estate — $25,250

Commercial Banks **$10,500**
First Wisconsin Corp ....$3,000 PAC
American Bankers Assn ....$1,500 PAC
JP Morgan & Co ....$1,300 PAC
Chemical Bank ....$1,100 PAC
Norwest Corp ....$1,000 PAC

Insurance **$10,050**
Northwestern Mutual Life ....$4,000 PAC
Cigna Corp ....$1,300 PAC
National Assn of Life Underwriters ....$1,000 PAC

Accountants **$2,000**
American Institute of CPA's ....$2,000 PAC

Misc Finance **$1,000**
None over $1,000

Health — $11,900

Health Professionals **$10,400**
American Medical Assn ....$10,000 PAC

Pharmaceuticals/Health Products **$1,500**
Eli Lilly & Co ....$1,000 PAC

Lawyers & Lobbyists — $9,823

Lawyers & Lobbyists **$9,823**
McMahon & Associates ....$1,000 Indiv
Waterman & Associates ....$1,000 Indiv

Misc Business — $41,900

Food & Beverage **$9,850**
National Restaurant Assn ....$5,000 PAC
McDonald's Corp ....$1,000 PAC
Pepsi-Cola General Bottlers ....$1,000 PAC

Beer, Wine & Liquor **$6,050**
National Beer Wholesalers Assn ....$5,800 PAC

Retail Sales **$6,900**
Spiegel Inc ....$1,300 PAC
May Department Stores ....$1,000 PAC

Business Services **$3,650**
National Assn of Temporary Services ....$1,000 PAC

Chemical & Related Manufacturing — $3,350
Dow Chemical ....$1,500 PAC

Misc Manufacturing & Distributing **$10,800**
SC Johnson & Son Inc ....$2,500 Indiv
Precision Metalforming Assn ....$2,000 PAC
Windway Capital Corp ....$2,000 Indiv
American Furniture Manufacturers Assn ....$1,200 PAC
Menasha Corp ....$1,000 PAC

Transportation — $43,340

Air Transport **$10,340**
United Parcel Service ....$5,490 PAC
United Airlines ....$1,300 PAC
Northwest Airlines ....$1,100 PAC
Aircraft Owners & Pilots Assn ....$1,000 PAC

Automotive **$12,800**
National Auto Dealers Assn ....$5,500 PAC
Americans for Free International Trade ......$4,000 PAC
Auto Dealers & Drivers for Free Trade ....$2,000 PAC

Trucking **$5,650**
American Trucking Assns ....$1,500 PAC
Consolidated Freightways ....$1,000 PAC

Railroads **$6,600**
Chicago & North Western Transport ....$1,100 PAC
Kansas City Southern ....$1,000 PAC
Union Pacific Corp ....$1,000 PAC

Sea Transport **$5,200**
Cruise PAC ....$2,000 PAC
American Commercial Barge Line Co ....$1,100 PAC

Misc Transport **$2,750**
National School Transport Assn ....$1,100 PAC

Labor

Labor — $1,150
None over $1,000

Ideological/Single-Issue

Ideological/Single-Issue — $9,250

Pro-Life **$1,000**
National Right to Life PAC ....$1,000 PAC

Gun Rights/Gun Control **$7,450**
National Rifle Assn ....$7,450 PAC

Other & Unknown

Other — $6,665

Education **$1,400**
None over $1,000

Retired **$4,265**
None over $1,000

Other **$1,000**
American Society of Assn Executives ....$1,000 PAC

Unknown — $7,800
No Employer Listed or Found $1,200
Employer Listed/Category Unknown $6,300
Rite Hite Corp ....$2,500 Indiv

Independent expenditures supporting Petri
Wisconsin Right to Life $3,780
National Right to Life PAC $3,285

---

* Contributions came from more than one affiliate or subsidiary.

Spending in Last 3 Elections

	1988	1990	1992
Petri	$187,714	$131,156	$775,594
Opponent	$19,815	$0	$319,363
Vote Pct	74%	100%	53%

Owen B. Pickett, D-Va (2)

First elected: 1986

1991-92 Total Receipts: $281,279
1992 Year-end Cash: $94,085

1991-92 Committees & Subcommittees

Armed Services
Military Personnel and Compensation; Readiness; Seapower and Strategic and Critical Materials

Merchant Marine and Fisheries
Coast Guard and Navigation; Merchant Marine

Veterans' Affairs
Housing and Memorial Affairs

Leading Contributors

Business

Agriculture	$7,650	
Crop Production & Basic Processing **$3,150**		
American Sugarbeet Growers Assn	$1,000	PAC
Florida Sugar Cane League	$1,000	PAC
Tobacco **$2,000**		
None over $1,000		
Food Processing & Sales **$2,000**		
Sandler Foods Inc	$1,000	Indiv

Communications/Electronics	$8,850	
Media/Entertainment **$1,000**		
Cox Cable Communications	$1,000	Indiv
Telephone Utilities **$3,600**		
AT&T	$1,500	PAC
Chesapeake & Potomac Telephone	$1,100	PAC
Telecom Services & Equipment **$4,000**		
Tabet Manufacturing Co	$4,000	Indiv

Construction	$4,000	
General Contractors **$2,000**		
National Utility Contractors Assn	$1,000	PAC
Home Builders **$1,000**		
National Assn of Home Builders	$1,000	PAC

Source of Funds in 1992 Election

Source	Total	Pct
■ PACs	$128,450	44%
▨ Indivs $200+	$94,535	32%
☐ Indivs under $200	$37,650	13%
⊠ Other	$32,754	11%
Candidate	$0	0%
Party	$14,160	5%

Source of PAC Dollars by Sector

Source	Total	Pct
■ Business	$103,550	79%
▨ Labor	$24,750	19%
☐ Ideology/Single Issue	$3,000	2%

In-State vs. Out-of-State Contributions*

Source	Total	Pct
☐ In-State	$92,885	98%
■ Out-of-state	$1,450	2%
No state listed	$200	

* by large individual contributors ($200 & above)

Defense	$21,650	
Defense Aerospace **$8,000**		
Colt Industries	$1,000	PAC
LTV Aerospace & Defense Co	$1,000	PAC
Lockheed Corp	$1,000	PAC
Martin Marietta Corp	$1,000	PAC
McDonnell Douglas	$1,000	PAC
Northrop Corp	$1,000	PAC
Rockwell International	$1,000	PAC
Defense Electronics **$1,100**		
Raytheon	$1,000	PAC
Misc Defense **$12,550**		
Tenneco Inc	$6,000	PAC
Mantech International	$2,000	PAC
Military Distributors of Virginia	$1,650	Indiv
Bath Iron Works	$1,000	PAC

Energy & Natural Resources	$10,100	
Oil & Gas **$3,500**		
None over $1,000		
Misc Energy **$1,000**		
Babcock & Wilcox	$1,000	PAC
Electric Utilities **$3,600**		
Dominion Resources Inc	$1,500	PAC
ACRE (Action Cmte for Rural Electrification)	$1,100	PAC
American Electric Power	$1,000	PAC
Waste Management **$1,000**		
Waste Management Inc	$1,000	PAC

Finance, Insurance & Real Estate	$49,450	
Commercial Banks **$9,850**		
Virginia Bankers Assn	$5,000	PAC
Citizens & Southern National Bank	$3,000	PAC
Securities & Investment **$1,000**		
Kidder, Peabody	$1,000	Indiv

Contribution Totals by Sector

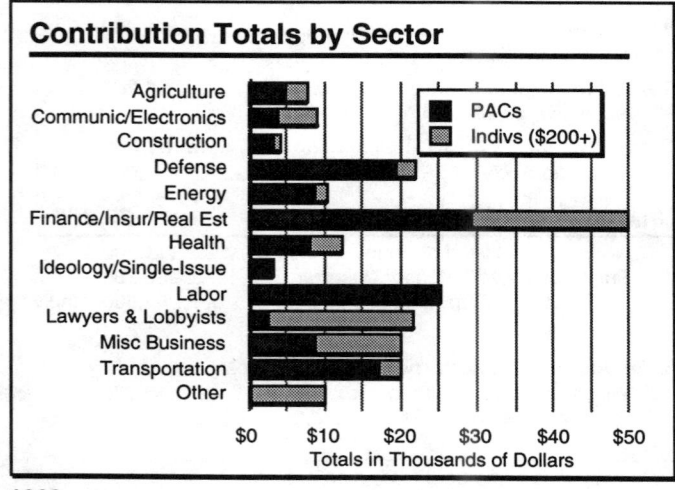

Legend: ■ PACs ▨ Indivs ($200+)

Sectors (top to bottom): Agriculture, Communic/Electronics, Construction, Defense, Energy, Finance/Insur/Real Est, Health, Ideology/Single-Issue, Labor, Lawyers & Lobbyists, Misc Business, Transportation, Other

Axis: $0 $10 $20 $30 $40 $50
Totals in Thousands of Dollars

Insurance $4,150
    Flagship Group ....$1,000   Indiv

Real Estate $8,750
    National Assn of Realtors ....$6,500   PAC

Accountants $12,000
    American Institute of CPA's ....$10,000   PAC
    Ernst & Young ....$1,000   PAC/Ind
    Goodman & Co ....$1,000   Indiv

Misc Finance $13,200
    None over $1,000

Health $12,050

Health Professionals $11,550
    American Academy of Ophthalmology ....$2,000   PAC
    First Hospital Corp ....$2,000   Indiv
    American Medical Assn....................................$1,850   PAC
    International Chiropractors Assn.........................$1,500   PAC
    American Dental Assn ....$1,000   PAC

Lawyers & Lobbyists $21,400

Lawyers & Lobbyists $21,400
    Breit, Drescher & Breit ....$4,000   Indiv
    Assn of Trial Lawyers of America ....$2,500   PAC
    Rutter & Montagna ....$1,500   Indiv
    Coates & Davenport ....$1,000   Indiv
    Kaufman & Canoles ....$1,000   Indiv
    Martin, Hopkins et al ....$1,000   Indiv
    Randolph G Flood & Assoc ....$1,000   Indiv
    Willcox & Savage ....$1,000   Indiv

Misc Business $19,700

Food & Beverage $2,250
    Bamboo Hut ....$1,000   Indiv

Beer, Wine & Liquor $12,500
    Associated Distributors ....$7,000   Indiv
    Wine & Spirits Wholesalers of America ....$3,500   PAC
    National Beer Wholesalers Assn ....$1,000   PAC

Retail Sales $1,900
    International Council of Shopping Centers ....$1,000   PAC

Chemical & Related Manufacturing $1,700
    Kay Chemical Co ....$1,200   Indiv

Spending in Last 3 Elections

	1988	1990	1992
Pickett	$414,011	$82,828	$373,047
Opponent	$189,391	$0	$190,447
Vote Pct	61%	75%	56%

Transportation $19,732

Air Transport $2,000
    United Parcel Service ....$2,000   PAC

Automotive $8,000
    National Auto Dealers Assn ....$5,000   PAC
    Americans for Free International Trade ....$1,000   PAC
    Ford Motor Co ....$1,000   PAC

Sea Transport $9,732
    Norfolk Shipbuilding & Drydock Corp ....$6,000   PAC
    American Pilots Assn ....$1,000   PAC

Labor

Labor $24,750

Transportation Unions $12,250
    Marine Engineers Union* ....$6,500   PAC
    Seafarers International Union ....$5,000   PAC

Public Sector Unions $12,500
    National Education Assn ....$3,500   PAC
    National Assn Retired Federal Employees ....$3,000   PAC
    American Postal Workers Union ....$2,000   PAC
    National Assn of Letter Carriers ....$2,000   PAC
    Natl Star Route Mail Contractors Assn ....$1,000   PAC

Ideological/Single-Issue

Ideological/Single-Issue $3,000

Foreign & Defense Policy $1,000
    Veterans of Foreign Wars ....$1,000   PAC

Misc Issues $1,500
    National Cmte to Preserve Social Security ....$1,500   PAC

Other & Unknown

Other $9,800

Civil Servants/Public Officials $1,450
    City of Virginia Beach ....$1,200   Indiv

Education $1,200
    ECPI Computer Institute ....$1,000   Indiv

Retired $7,150
    None over $1,000

Unknown $13,703

    Homemakers/Non-income earners $4,453
    Employer Listed/Category Unknown $8,500
        None over $1,000

---

* Contributions came from more than one affiliate or subsidiary.

J. J. Pickle, D-Texas (10)

First elected: 1963

1991-92 Total Receipts: $421,708
1992 Year-end Cash: $124,589

1991-92 Committees & Subcommittees

Ways and Means
Oversight (Chairman); Social Security

Joint Committee on Taxation

Leading Contributors

Business

Agriculture		$20,750

Crop Production & Basic Processing ... **$2,450**
  None over $1,500

Dairy ... **$1,500**
  None over $1,500

Poultry & Eggs ... **$3,000**
  Pilgrim's Pride Co ... $2,000   Indiv

Livestock ... **$4,400**
  National Cattlemen's Assn* ... $3,000   PAC

Agricultural Services/Products ... **$1,700**
  None over $1,500

Food Processing & Sales ... **$4,000**
  Winn-Dixie Stores ... $2,000   PAC

Forestry & Forest Products ... **$3,000**
  Temple-Inland ... $2,500   PAC

Communications/Electronics $22,200

Media/Entertainment ... **$3,350**
  None over $1,500

Telephone Utilities ... **$15,350**
  Ameritech Corp ... $3,500   PAC
  GTE Corp ... $3,000   PAC
  Southwestern Bell ... $2,000   PAC/Ind
  Pacific Telesis Group ... $1,500   PAC
  US Telephone Assn ... $1,500   PAC

Computer Equipment & Services ... **$2,500**
  None over $1,500

Source of Funds in 1992 Election

Source	Total	Pct
PACs	$263,432	61%
Indivs $200+	$102,017	24%
Indivs under $200	$43,886	10%
Other	$19,434	5%
Candidate	$0	0%
Party	$7,061	2%

Source of PAC Dollars by Sector

Source	Total	Pct
Business	$264,747	98%
Labor	$6,250	2%
Ideology/Single Issue	$0	0%

In-State vs. Out-of-State Contributions*

Source	Total	Pct
In-State	$77,165	76%
Out-of-state	$23,800	24%
No state listed	$1,052	

*** by large individual contributors ($200 & above)**

Construction $9,450

General Contractors ... **$6,200**
  Associated General Contractors ... $2,500   PAC

Building Materials & Equipment ... **$2,750**
  Lumberman's Investment ... $1,750   Indiv

Defense $4,500

Misc Defense ... **$2,500**
  Insilco Corp ... $2,500   PAC

Energy & Natural Resources $28,000

Oil & Gas ... **$20,300**
  Coastal Corp ... $2,000   PAC
  Columbia Gas System* ... $2,000   PAC
  Enron Corp ... $2,000   PAC

Mining ... **$2,500**
  None over $1,500

Electric Utilities ... **$4,000**
  Texas Utilities Co ... $3,000   PAC

Finance, Insurance & Real Estate $109,865

Commercial Banks ... **$12,706**
  American Bankers Assn ... $5,000   PAC
  Citizens & Southern National Bank ... $5,000   PAC

Savings & Loans ... **$1,700**
  None over $1,500

Securities & Investment ... **$22,200**
  Investment Company Institute ... $3,000   PAC
  Prudential Securities ... $2,500   PAC
  Dean Witter ... $2,000   PAC
  Merrill Lynch ... $2,000   PAC
  Morgan Stanley & Co ... $2,000   PAC
  National Venture Capital Assn ... $2,000   PAC
  American Express* ... $1,500   PAC

Contribution Totals by Sector

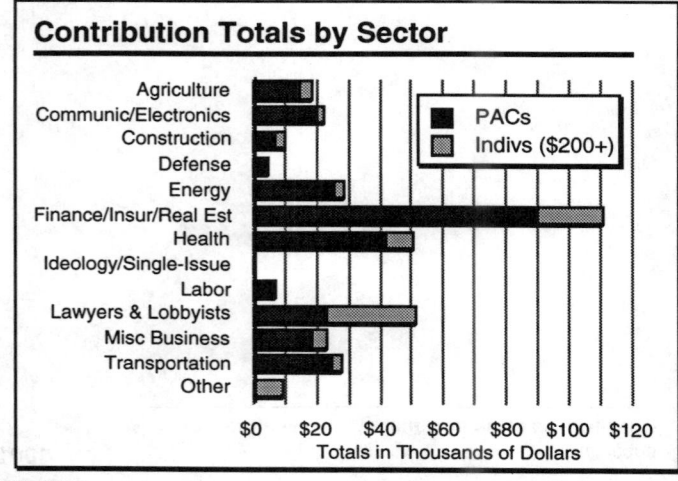

Totals in Thousands of Dollars

Insurance **$47,709**
    National Assn of Life Underwriters.....................$10,000   PAC
    Kentor, Waxman Insurance ....$3,459   Indiv
    American Council of Life Insurance ....$3,000   PAC
    TransAmerica Life Companies............................$2,000   PAC

Real Estate **$10,900**
    National Assn of Realtors ....$7,000   PAC
    Del Webb Corp ....$2,000   PAC

Accountants **$9,250**
    American Institute of CPA's ....$5,000   PAC

Misc Finance **$4,400**
    None over $1,500

Health $49,397

Health Professionals **$33,897**
    American Medical Assn* ....$10,097   PAC
    American Dental Assn ....$5,000   PAC
    American Academy of Ophthalmology ....$2,000   PAC
    American Assn Oral & Maxillofacial Surgeons ....$2,000   PAC
    American Chiropractic Assn...............................$2,000   PAC

Hospitals/Nursing Homes **$7,250**
    American Health Care Assn...............................$2,000   PAC

Health Services **$3,000**
    Girling Health Care Inc ....$2,000   Indiv

Pharmaceuticals/Health Products **$4,750**
    None over $1,500

Lawyers & Lobbyists $50,050

Lawyers & Lobbyists **$50,050**
    Assn of Trial Lawyers of America ....$5,000   PAC
    McClure, Trotter & Mentz ....$3,350   Indiv
    Jones, Day et al ....$3,000   PAC
    Johnson & Gibbs ....$2,500   PAC
    Clark, Thomas et al ....$2,400   Indiv
    Akin, Gump et al ....$2,000   PAC
    Bracewell & Patterson ....$2,000   PAC
    Long Law Firm ....$2,000   Indiv
    Vinson & Elkins ....$2,000   PAC

Spending in Last 3 Elections

	1988	1990	1992
Pickle	$172,921	$562,967	$363,561
Opponent	$0	$261,528	$117,934
Vote Pct	93%	65%	68%

Legend: Pickle, Opponent

Misc Business   **$20,150**

Food & Beverage **$2,450**
    None over $1,500

Beer, Wine & Liquor **$4,400**
    None over $1,500

Retail Sales.. **$6,300**
    International Council of Shopping Centers ....$2,000   PAC

Business Services **$1,700**
    None over $1,500

Misc Manufacturing & Distributing **$1,950**
    None over $1,500

Transportation $27,000

Air Transport **$8,500**
    United Parcel Service.......................................$4,000   PAC

Automotive **$12,500**
    Americans for Free International Trade ....$5,000   PAC
    National Auto Dealers Assn ....$5,000   PAC

Trucking **$2,500**
    None over $1,500

Railroads **$2,500**
    None over $1,500

Labor

Labor   **$6,250**

Public Sector Unions **$5,000**
    National Education Assn ....$2,500   PAC

Other & Unknown

Other   **$8,550**

Education **$1,650**
    None over $1,500

Retired **$5,300**
    None over $1,500

Unknown   **$16,852**

    No Employer Listed or Found $2,552
    Employer Listed/Category Unknown $13,900
        Partners Group..$2,400   Indiv

---

* Contributions came from more than one affiliate or subsidiary.

Richard W. Pombo, R-Calif (11)

First elected: 1992

1991-92 Total Receipts: $532,902
1992 Year-end Cash: $3,911

1993-94 Committees & Subcommittees

Agriculture
Environment, Credit and Rural Development; Livestock; Specialty Crops and Natural Resources

Merchant Marine and Fisheries
Coast Guard and Navigation

Natural Resources
Energy and Mineral Resources; Oversight and Investigations

Leading Contributors

Business

Agriculture $75,280

Crop Production & Basic Processing	**$43,030**	
Vaquero Farms	$9,500	Indiv
Calcot Ltd	$3,500	PAC
Sun-Diamond Growers*	$3,000	PAC
Alvarez Produce	$2,500	Indiv
Martin Farms	$2,230	Indiv
Vaquero Farms	$2,000	Indiv
Dave & Michael Petz Ranch	$1,750	Indiv
Tri-M Farms	$1,750	Indiv
Dairy	**$6,600**	
Western United Dairymens Assn	$2,200	PAC
Van Exel Dairy	$1,700	Indiv
Livestock	**$9,000**	
National Cattlemen's Assn*	$3,000	PAC
Agricultural Services/Products	**$4,500**	
California Farm Bureau Federation	$1,500	PAC
Food Processing & Sales	**$4,500**	
None over $1,500		
Forestry & Forest Products	**$2,400**	
None over $1,500		
Misc Agriculture	**$4,000**	
Degraaf Ranch	$2,000	Indiv

Source of Funds in 1992 Election

Source	Total	Pct
■ PACs	$152,486	26%
▨ Indivs $200+	$217,564	37%
☐ Indivs under $200	$144,295	25%
▨ Other	$73,794	13%
Candidate	$0	0%
Party	$73,296	12%

Source of PAC Dollars by Sector

Source	Total	Pct
■ Business	$109,686	75%
▨ Labor	$0	0%
☐ Ideology/Single Issue	$37,187	25%

In-State vs. Out-of-State Contributions*

Source	Total	Pct
☐ In-State	$189,514	88%
■ Out-of-state	$26,900	12%
No state listed	$0	

* by large individual contributors ($200 & above)

Communications/Electronics $9,300

Printing & Publishing	**$5,000**	
Commercial Press Inc	$2,000	Indiv
Crown Enterprises	$2,000	Indiv
Telephone Utilities	**$3,000**	
None over $1,500		

Construction $17,150

General Contractors	**$9,100**	
AG Spanos Development	$3,500	Indiv
Associated General Contractors	$2,500	PAC
AD Seeno Construction Co	$1,500	Indiv
Home Builders	**$3,050**	
National Assn of Home Builders	$2,000	PAC
Special Trade Contractors	**$2,500**	
None over $1,500		
Building Materials & Equipment	**$1,500**	
None over $1,500		

Defense $2,250

None over $1,500

Energy & Natural Resources $17,500

Oil & Gas	**$10,500**	
Atlantic Richfield	$2,000	PAC
Chevron Corp	$2,000	PAC
Mining	**$2,000**	
Lodestar Mining	$2,000	Indiv
Misc Energy	**$3,000**	
Cooper Industries	$3,000	PAC
Waste Management	**$2,000**	
Tracy Delta Disposal	$2,000	Indiv

Contribution Totals by Sector

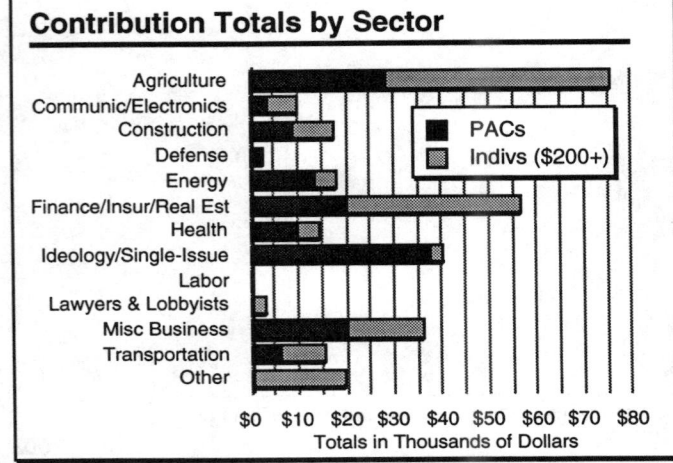

Agriculture
Communic/Electronics
Construction
Defense
Energy
Finance/Insur/Real Est
Health
Ideology/Single-Issue
Labor
Lawyers & Lobbyists
Misc Business
Transportation
Other

■ PACs
▨ Indivs ($200+)

$0 $10 $20 $30 $40 $50 $60 $70 $80
Totals in Thousands of Dollars

Finance, Insurance & Real Estate — $56,220

Commercial Banks $16,650
    Bank of Stockton .... $8,150 — PAC/Ind
    American Bankers Assn .... $3,500 — PAC
    Bank of Agriculture & Commerce ... $2,250 — Indiv
    Fieldstead & Co .... $2,000 — Indiv

Insurance $7,870
    Hastie Insurance .... $2,000 — Indiv
    National Assn of Life Underwriters ... $1,500 — PAC

Real Estate $24,750
    National Assn of Realtors .... $4,000 — PAC
    Pombo Real Estate .... $3,200 — Indiv
    Grupe Development Co .... $2,500 — Indiv
    Sassco Land Development .... $2,300 — Indiv
    Century 21 All Pro Real Estate ...... $1,500 — Indiv

Accountants $2,750
    American Institute of CPA's .... $2,500 — PAC

Misc Finance $1,750
    None over $1,500

Health — $14,275

Health Professionals $9,525
    American Medical Assn* .... $5,000 — PAC
    American Dental Assn .... $1,500 — PAC

Hospitals/Nursing Homes $1,750
    None over $1,500

Health Services $2,000
    None over $1,500

Lawyers & Lobbyists — $3,250

Lawyers & Lobbyists $3,250
    None over $1,500

Misc Business — $35,660

Business Associations $2,686
    National Fedn of Independent Business ... $1,500 — PAC

Beer, Wine & Liquor $1,500
    None over $1,500

Retail Sales $10,750
    Amway Corp .... $7,750 — PAC/Ind

Business Services $2,474
    None over $1,500

Chemical & Related Manufacturing ... $2,800
    Dow Chemical .... $1,500 — PAC

Misc Manufacturing & Distributing ... $12,250
    Libbey-Owens-Ford .... $2,000 — PAC
    Precision Metalforming Assn .... $2,000 — PAC
    Stone Container Corp .... $2,000 — PAC

Transportation — $15,000

Automotive $8,400
    Prince Corp .... $4,000 — Indiv
    Eaton Corp .... $2,000 — PAC

Trucking $4,650
    None over $1,500

Railroads $1,500
    Union Pacific Corp .... $1,500 — PAC

Ideological/Single-Issue

Ideological/Single-Issue — $39,837

Republican/Conservative $13,674
    Lincoln Club of Orange County ..... $5,000 — PAC
    Eagle Forum .... $3,000 — PAC

Pro-Life $9,000
    Right to Life* .... $5,000 — PAC
    Republican National Coalition for Life ... $4,000 — PAC

Gun Rights/Gun Control $9,450
    National Rifle Assn .... $4,950 — PAC
    Safari Club International .... $4,500 — PAC

Misc Issues $5,763
    Right to Work PAC .... $2,000 — PAC

Other & Unknown

Other — $19,075

Civil Servants/Public Officials $4,300
    US Government .... $2,950 — Indiv

Education $1,800
    None over $1,500

Retired $12,975
    None over $1,500

Unknown — $58,490

    Homemakers/Non-income earners ... $11,320
    No Employer Listed or Found $9,850
    Generic Occupation/Category Unknown ... $2,000
    Employer Listed/Category Unknown ... $35,320
        Bogetti Brothers .... $1,500 — Indiv

Independent expenditures supporting Pombo
    National Right to Life PAC $4,843

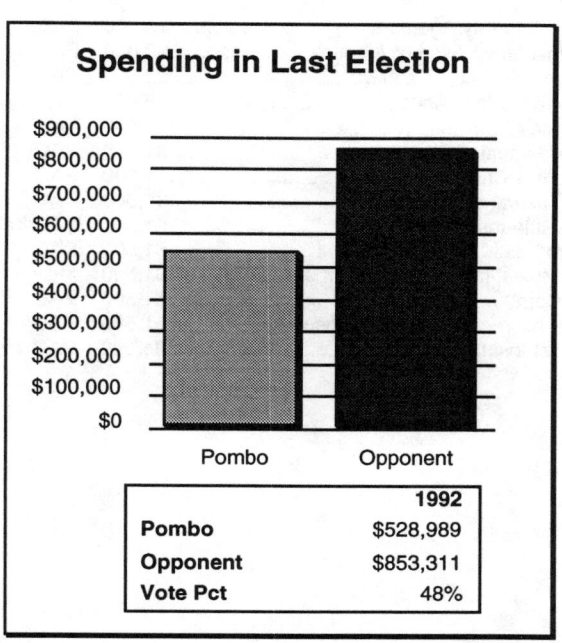

Spending in Last Election

	1992
Pombo	$528,989
Opponent	$853,311
Vote Pct	48%

---

* Contributions came from more than one affiliate or subsidiary.

Earl Pomeroy, D-ND (1)

First elected: 1992

1991-92 Total Receipts: $431,979
1992 Year-end Cash: $1,750

1993-94 Committees & Subcommittees

Agriculture
Department Operations Nutrition; Environment, Credit and Rural Development; General Farm Commodities; Specialty Crops and Natural Resources

Budget

Leading Contributors

Business

Agriculture $21,270

Crop Production & Basic Processing **$4,820**
    None over $1,500

Tobacco **$1,750**
    None over $1,500

Dairy **$3,000**
    Associated Milk Producers .... $2,000   PAC

Agricultural Services/Products **$9,450**
    American Assn of Crop Insurers .... $5,000   PAC

Communications/Electronics $3,000

Telephone Utilities **$1,500**
    None over $1,500

Construction $1,500

    None over $1,500

Energy & Natural Resources $17,395

Oil & Gas **$7,750**
    Ashland Oil .... $3,000   PAC

Mining **$1,500**
    None over $1,500

Electric Utilities **$8,145**
    ACRE (Action Cmte for Rural Electrification) ...... $2,000   PAC

Source of Funds in 1992 Election

Source	Total	Pct
PACs	$296,260	69%
Indivs $200+	$61,904	14%
Indivs under $200	$57,967	13%
Other	$15,848	4%
Candidate	$1,000	0%
Party	$10,000	2%

Source of PAC Dollars by Sector

Source	Total	Pct
Business	$183,473	63%
Labor	$97,650	33%
Ideology/Single Issue	$12,173	4%

In-State vs. Out-of-State Contributions*

Source	Total	Pct
In-State	$6,827	11%
Out-of-state	$55,077	89%
No state listed	$0	

by large individual contributors ($200 & above)

Finance, Insurance & Real Estate $106,628

Commercial Banks **$4,500**
    Norwest Corp .... $1,500   PAC

Insurance **$98,628**
    National Assn of Life Underwriters .... $10,000   PAC
    American Family Corp .... $6,000   Indiv
    Independent Insurance Agents of America .... $5,238   PAC
    American International Group Inc .... $4,270   PAC
    Northwestern Mutual Life .... $3,000   PAC
    Metropolitan Life Insurance .... $2,750   PAC/Ind
    Life USA Insurance Co .... $2,500   Indiv
    Mutual of Omaha .... $2,500   PAC
    American Council of Life Insurance .... $2,000   PAC
    Casualty & Surety Agents Assn .... $2,000   PAC
    Health Insurance Assn of America .... $2,000   PAC
    New York Life .... $2,000   PAC
    TransAmerica Insurance .... $2,000   PAC
    WR Berkley Corp .... $2,000   Indiv
    Principal Mutual Life Insurance .... $1,678   PAC
    Aetna Life & Casualty .... $1,500   PAC
    Allstate Insurance .... $1,500   PAC
    Golden Rule Insurance Co .... $1,500   PAC/Ind
    ITT Corp* .... $1,500   PAC
    Liberty Mutual Insurance .... $1,500   Indiv
    Loews Corp* .... $1,500   PAC
    National Assn of Independent Insurers .... $1,500   PAC
    Prudential Insurance .... $1,500   PAC

Contribution Totals by Sector

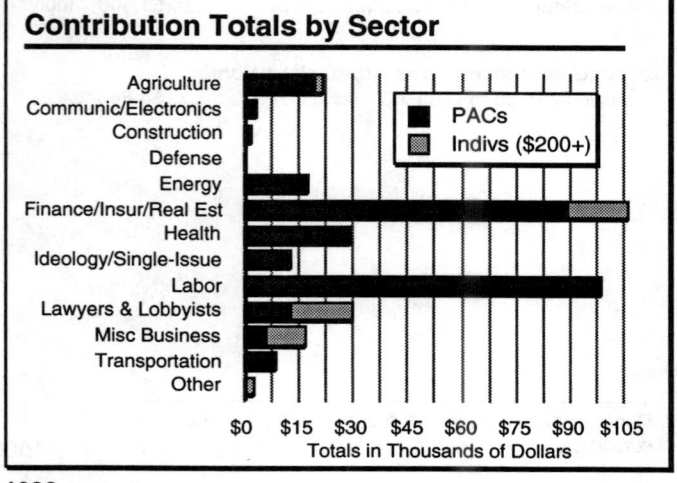

Legend: ■ PACs   ▨ Indivs ($200+)

Categories: Agriculture, Communic/Electronics, Construction, Defense, Energy, Finance/Insur/Real Est, Health, Ideology/Single-Issue, Labor, Lawyers & Lobbyists, Misc Business, Transportation, Other

$0 $15 $30 $45 $60 $75 $90 $105
Totals in Thousands of Dollars

Health $28,700

Health Professionals $20,750
    American Dental Assn ....$4,000 PAC
    American Podiatry Assn ....$3,000 PAC
    American Chiropractic Assn ....$2,500 PAC
    American Academy of Ophthalmology ....$2,000 PAC
    American College of Emergency Physicians ....$2,000 PAC
    American Optometric Assn ....$1,500 PAC

Hospitals/Nursing Homes $4,200
    American Hospital Assn ....$2,000 PAC
    American Health Care Assn ....$1,500 PAC

Pharmaceuticals/Health Products $3,250
    None over $1,500

Lawyers & Lobbyists $29,312

Lawyers & Lobbyists $29,312
    Assn of Trial Lawyers of America ....$10,000 PAC
    Rubinstein & Perry ....$6,750 Indiv

Misc Business $16,250

Beer, Wine & Liquor $3,500
    National Beer Wholesalers Assn ....$3,000 PAC

Business Services $4,250
    None over $1,500

Misc Manufacturing & Distributing $7,500
    Doranco Inc ....$7,500 Indiv

Transportation $8,250

Air Transport $5,000
    United Parcel Service ....$3,000 PAC
    American Airlines ....$1,500 PAC

Railroads $2,000
    Burlington Northern ....$2,000 PAC

Labor

Labor $97,900

Building Trade Unions $11,750
    Carpenters & Joiners Union ....$5,000 PAC
    Laborers' Political League ....$3,750 PAC
    Plumbers/Pipefitters Union......................$2,000 PAC

Industrial Unions $30,450
    United Auto Workers ....$10,000 PAC
    Machinists/Aerospace Workers Union ....$8,000 PAC
    United Steelworkers ....$5,000 PAC
    United Mine Workers ....$2,500 PAC
    Boilermakers Union ....$2,000 PAC

Transportation Unions $14,550
    Teamsters Union ....$5,000 PAC
    Air Line Pilots Assn ....$2,000 PAC
    United Transportation Union ....$2,000 PAC
    Brotherhood of Locomotive Engineers.................$1,500 PAC
    Marine Engineers Union.........................$1,500 PAC

Public Sector Unions $28,700
    National Education Assn ....$10,000 PAC
    National Assn of Letter Carriers ....$7,500 PAC
    American Postal Workers Union ....$3,000 PAC
    National Assn Retired Federal Employees ....$2,000 PAC
    International Assn of Firefighters ....$1,500 PAC
    National Treasury Employees Union ....$1,500 PAC

Misc Unions....................................$12,450
    Food & Commercial Workers Union ....$7,500 PAC
    AFL-CIO ....$3,500 PAC

Ideological/Single-Issue

Ideological/Single-Issue $12,423

Democratic/Liberal $2,508
    National Cmte for an Effective Congress ....$2,500 PAC

Leadership PACs................................$2,500
    None over $1,500

Human Rights $2,500
    KidsPAC ....$2,000 PAC

Misc Issues $3,000
    National Cmte to Preserve Social Security ....$2,000 PAC

Other & Unknown

Other $2,450
    None over $1,500

Unknown $10,122
    No Employer Listed or Found $3,572
    Employer Listed/Category Unknown $5,550
      None over $1,500

Spending in Last Election

	1992
Pomeroy	$430,228
Opponent	$140,639
Vote Pct	57%

---

* Contributions came from more than one affiliate or subsidiary.

John Porter, R-Ill (10)

First elected: 1980

1991-92 Total Receipts: $453,794
1992 Year-end Cash: $40,011

1991-92 Committees & Subcommittees

Appropriations
Foreign Operations, Export Financing and Related Programs; Labor,
Health and Human Services, and Education; Legislative

Select Committee on Aging

Leading Contributors

Business

Agriculture	$11,898	
Agricultural Services/Products	$4,450	
Navistar International	$2,500	PAC
Food Processing & Sales	$2,448	
None over $1,500		
Forestry & Forest Products	$2,500	
Westvaco Corp	$2,000	PAC

Communications/Electronics	$14,650	
Printing & Publishing	$2,900	
RR Donnelley & Sons	$1,700	PAC/Ind
Media/Entertainment	$2,250	
None over $1,500		
Telephone Utilities	$5,250	
Illinois Bell Telephone	$3,000	PAC
AT&T	$2,000	PAC
Telecom Services & Equipment	$2,750	
Motorola Inc	$2,750	PAC/Ind
Computer Equipment & Services	$1,500	
None over $1,500		

Construction	$13,600	
General Contractors	$3,750	
Blinderman Construction Co	$2,000	Indiv
Home Builders	$5,150	
National Assn of Home Builders	$4,500	PAC

Source of Funds in 1992 Election

	Source	Total	Pct
■	PACs	$160,299	35%
▨	Indivs $200+	$181,380	40%
□	Indivs under $200	$103,978	23%
▩	Other	$8,137	2%
	Candidate	$0	0%
	Party	$200	0%

Source of PAC Dollars by Sector

	Source	Total	Pct
■	Business	$140,898	89%
▨	Labor	$500	0%
□	Ideology/Single Issue	$16,307	10%

In-State vs. Out-of-State Contributions*

	Source	Total	Pct
□	In-State	$166,977	92%
■	Out-of-state	$14,203	8%
	No state listed	$0	

* by large individual contributors ($200 & above)

Construction Services	$1,500	
None over $1,500		
Building Materials & Equipment	$2,000	
None over $1,500		

Defense	$2,000	
Misc Defense	$1,500	
FMC Corp	$1,500	PAC

Energy & Natural Resources	$6,200	
Oil & Gas	$4,700	
Amoco Corp	$1,800	PAC/Ind

Finance, Insurance & Real Estate	$66,678	
Commercial Banks	$13,950	
American Bankers Assn	$3,000	PAC
Continental Illinois Corp	$3,000	PAC
First Chicago Corp	$2,050	PAC/Ind
Continental Bank	$1,500	Indiv
Securities & Investment	$13,350	
William Blair & Co	$2,500	Indiv
Chicago Mercantile Exchange	$2,000	PAC/Ind
Goldman, Sachs & Co	$1,750	Indiv
Harris Associates Ltd	$1,600	Indiv
Insurance	$9,028	
Kemper Insurance	$2,303	PAC/Ind
MMI Companies	$1,725	PAC
Real Estate	$14,850	
National Assn of Realtors	$8,500	PAC
Accountants	$9,000	
American Institute of CPA's	$6,000	PAC
Arthur Andersen & Co	$2,000	Indiv
Misc Finance	$5,000	
Lincoln Capital Management	$4,000	Indiv

Contribution Totals by Sector

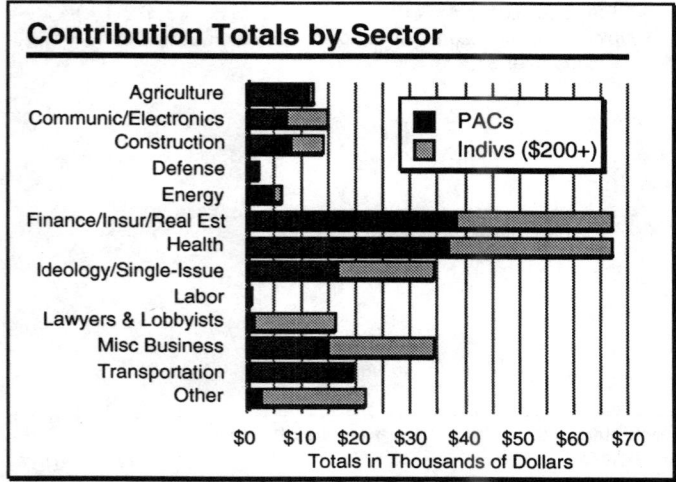

Agriculture
Communic/Electronics
Construction
Defense
Energy
Finance/Insur/Real Est
Health
Ideology/Single-Issue
Labor
Lawyers & Lobbyists
Misc Business
Transportation
Other

■ PACs
▨ Indivs ($200+)

$0 $10 $20 $30 $40 $50 $60 $70
Totals in Thousands of Dollars

Health — $66,511

Health Professionals $42,061
American Medical Assn	$10,400	PAC
American Dental Assn	$4,500	PAC
American Academy of Ophthalmology	$3,500	PAC
American Assn Oral & Maxillofacial Surgeons	$3,000	PAC
Day Surgicenters	$2,000	Indiv
American Physical Therapy Assn	$1,850	PAC

Hospitals/Nursing Homes $5,100
American Hospital Assn	$1,850	PAC

Health Services $2,000
Cancer Treatment Centers	$2,000	Indiv

Pharmaceuticals/Health Products $15,350
Baxter International Inc	$9,500	PAC/Ind
Abbott Laboratories	$2,000	PAC
GD Searle & Co	$1,500	PAC/Ind

Misc Health $2,000
None over $1,500

Lawyers & Lobbyists — $15,900

Lawyers & Lobbyists $14,400
Beacon Consulting Group	$3,500	Indiv

Misc Business — $33,350

Food & Beverage $3,350
None over $1,500

Retail Sales $5,150
None over $1,500

Business Services $2,900
Dun & Bradstreet	$2,000	PAC

Chemical & Related Manufacturing $6,300
CPI Inc	$2,000	Indiv

Steel Production $1,750
None over $1,500

Misc Manufacturing & Distributing $10,400
American National Can Co	$1,500	Indiv
Rey Marketing	$1,500	Indiv

Transportation — $19,050

Air Transport $3,500
United Parcel Service	$2,500	PAC

Automotive $13,000
National Auto Dealers Assn	$8,500	PAC
Americans for Free International Trade	$2,000	PAC
Auto Dealers & Drivers for Free Trade	$1,500	PAC

Railroads $2,050
None over $1,500

Ideological/Single-Issue

Ideological/Single-Issue — $34,457

Republican/Conservative $7,507
None over $1,500

Pro-Israel $15,300
National PAC	$5,000	PAC
City PAC	$2,000	PAC

Pro-Choice $4,450
Voters for Choice	$1,700	PAC

Human Rights $6,100
KidsPAC	$2,500	PAC
National Albanian American PAC	$2,000	PAC

Other & Unknown

Other — $21,410

Retired $18,910
None over $1,500

Other $1,500
American Society of Assn Executives	$1,500	PAC

Unknown — $36,681

Homemakers/Non-income earners	$7,631	
Employer Listed/Category Unknown	$28,800	
Kent Co	$2,000	Indiv
MacLean, Fogg Co	$2,000	Indiv
Golder/Thomas Investments	$1,850	Indiv
Pace Trans	$1,500	Indiv

Spending in Last 3 Elections

	1988	1990	1992
Porter	$212,630	$313,498	$485,778
Opponent	$62,560	$0	$34,948
Vote Pct	73%	68%	65%

Glenn Poshard, D-III (19)

First elected: 1988

1991-92 Total Receipts: $304,026
1992 Year-end Cash: $6,650

1991-92 Committees & Subcommittees

Public Works and Transportation
Aviation; Public Buildings and Grounds; Surface Transportation

Small Business
Environment and Employment; Procurement, Tourism and Rural Development

Leading Contributors

NOTE: Poshard reported taking no PAC funds during his 1992 campaign. The PACs listed below did report making contributions, however, and those contributions are recorded in the official FEC records.

Business

Communications/Electronics	$1,520
Media/Entertainment	$1,520
None over $1,000	

Construction	$1,350
General Contractors	$1,350
None over $1,000	

Energy & Natural Resources	$1,800
Oil & Gas	$1,300
Keller Oil Co	$1,000 Indiv

Finance, Insurance & Real Estate	$2,800
Insurance	$1,625
Golden Rule Insurance Co	$1,250 Indiv
Real Estate	$1,300
None over $1,000	

Health	$3,300
Health Professionals	$2,800
None over $1,000	

Source of Funds in 1992 Election

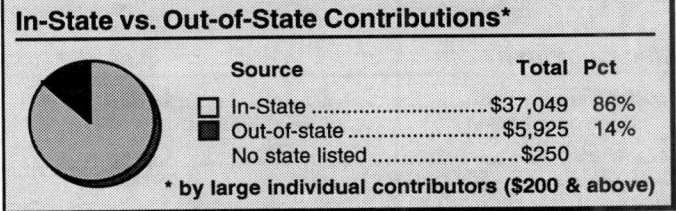

Source	Total	Pct
PACs	$0	0%
Indivs $200+	$43,224	14%
Indivs under $200	$247,442	78%
Other	$27,771	9%
Candidate	$4,483	1%
Party	$14,411	5%

Source of PAC Dollars by Sector

No PAC contributions reported

Source	Total	Pct
Business	$0	0%
Labor	$0	0%
Ideology/Single Issue	$0	0%

In-State vs. Out-of-State Contributions*

Source	Total	Pct
In-State	$37,049	86%
Out-of-state	$5,925	14%
No state listed	$250	

* by large individual contributors ($200 & above)

Lawyers & Lobbyists	$3,540
Lawyers & Lobbyists	$3,540
None over $1,000	

Misc Business	$2,350
Business Services	$1,000
None over $1,000	

Contribution Totals by Sector

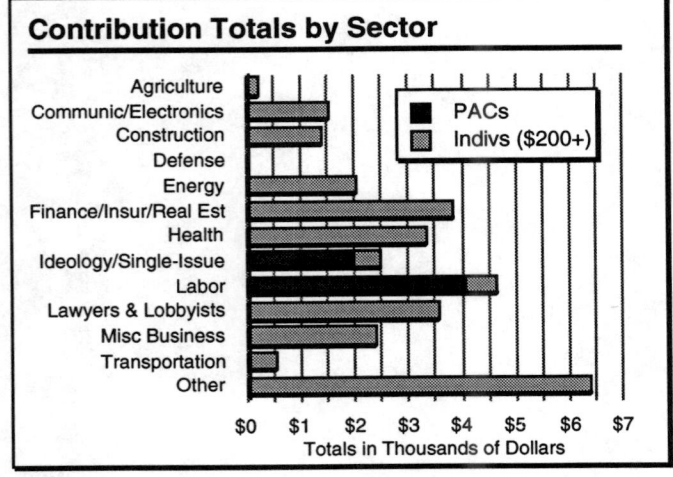

Agriculture
Communic/Electronics
Construction
Defense
Energy
Finance/Insur/Real Est
Health
Ideology/Single-Issue
Labor
Lawyers & Lobbyists
Misc Business
Transportation
Other

■ PACs
▨ Indivs ($200+)

$0 $1 $2 $3 $4 $5 $6 $7
Totals in Thousands of Dollars

Labor

Labor	$5,000

Building Trade Unions **$1,000**
    None over $1,000

Public Sector Unions.................................... **$4,000**
    American Federation of Teachers .... $3,000   PAC
    National Assn of Letter Carriers .... $1,000   PAC

Ideological/Single-Issue

Ideological/Single-Issue	$2,438

Pro-Life **$1,738**
    Illinois Right to Life .... $1,715   PAC

Other & Unknown

Other	$6,375

Civil Servants/Public Officials............................ **$2,750**
    None over $1,000

Education **$1,775**
    None over $1,000

Retired **$1,350**
    None over $1,000

Unknown	$16,789

    Homemakers/Non-income earners $1,400
    No Employer Listed or Found $10,350
    Employer Listed/Category Unknown $4,839
        Ligma Corp .... $1,600   Indiv

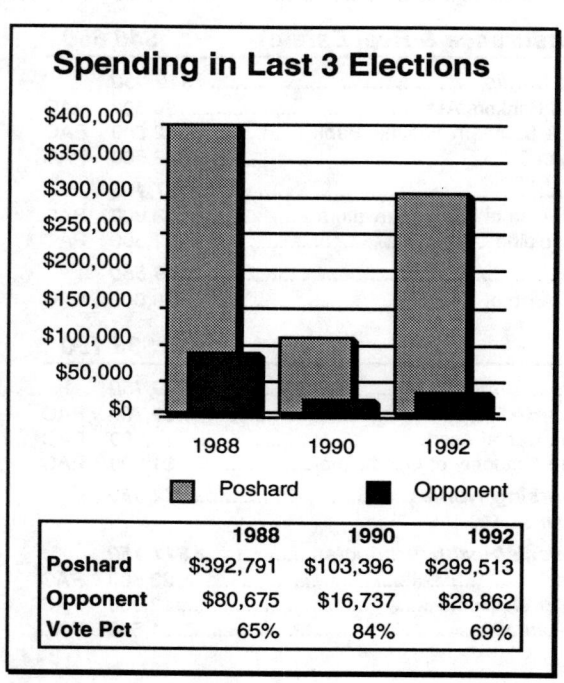

Spending in Last 3 Elections

	1988	1990	1992
Poshard	$392,791	$103,396	$299,513
Opponent	$80,675	$16,737	$28,862
Vote Pct	65%	84%	69%

David Price, D-NC (4)

First elected: 1986

1991-92 Total Receipts: $474,273
1992 Year-end Cash: $56,753

1991-92 Committees & Subcommittees

Appropriations
Agriculture, Rural Development, Food and Drug Administration and Related Agencies; Transportation and Related Agencies

Leading Contributors

Business

Agriculture	$37,161	
Crop Production & Basic Processing **$6,711**		
None over $1,500		
Tobacco **$11,050**		
RJR Nabisco	$6,000	PAC
Philip Morris	$2,850	PAC
Dairy **$3,500**		
Associated Milk Producers	$2,000	PAC
Poultry & Eggs **$2,500**		
Tyson Foods	$1,500	PAC
Livestock **$1,650**		
None over $1,500		
Agricultural Services/Products **$5,000**		
American Assn of Crop Insurers	$1,500	PAC
Food Processing & Sales **$6,750**		
Pepsico Inc	$2,500	PAC
Chatham Foods Inc	$1,500	Indiv

Communications/Electronics	$11,650	
Telephone Utilities **$8,300**		
Southern Bell	$4,200	PAC
AT&T	$2,000	PAC
Telecom Services & Equipment **$1,500**		
Northern Telecom	$1,500	PAC

Construction	$5,550	
General Contractors **$1,850**		
Associated General Contractors	$1,500	PAC
Home Builders **$3,700**		
Rural Builders of America PAC	$1,500	PAC

Contribution Totals by Sector

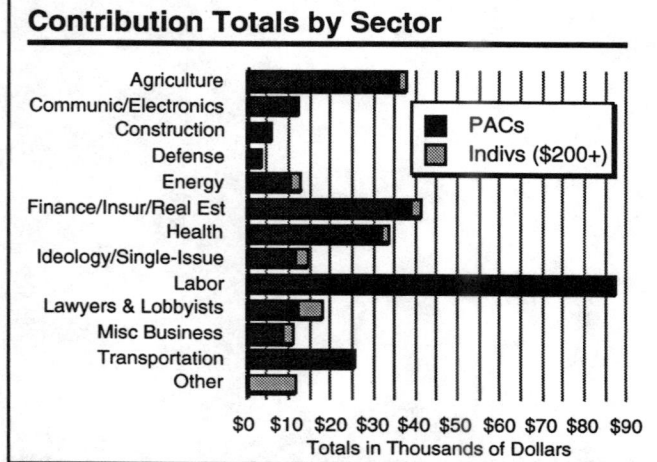

Agriculture
Communic/Electronics
Construction
Defense
Energy
Finance/Insur/Real Est
Health
Ideology/Single-Issue
Labor
Lawyers & Lobbyists
Misc Business
Transportation
Other

■ PACs
▨ Indivs ($200+)

$0 $10 $20 $30 $40 $50 $60 $70 $80 $90
Totals in Thousands of Dollars

Source of Funds in 1992 Election

Source	Total	Pct
■ PACs	$274,111	57%
▨ Indivs $200+	$45,385	9%
☐ Indivs under $200	$139,728	29%
▨ Other	$24,210	5%
Candidate	$0	0%
Party	$10,111	2%

Source of PAC Dollars by Sector

Source	Total	Pct
■ Business	$179,961	65%
▨ Labor	$86,900	31%
☐ Ideology/Single Issue	$11,209	4%

In-State vs. Out-of-State Contributions*

Source	Total	Pct
☐ In-State	$32,935	73%
■ Out-of-state	$12,450	27%
No state listed	$0	

* by large individual contributors ($200 & above)

Defense	$3,000	
Defense Aerospace **$2,500**		
None over $1,500		

Energy & Natural Resources	$12,350	
Oil & Gas **$2,700**		
None over $1,500		
Electric Utilities **$8,400**		
Carolina Power & Light	$3,100	PAC/Ind
ACRE (Action Cmte for Rural Electrification)	$1,750	PAC
Duke Power Co	$1,500	PAC

Finance, Insurance & Real Estate	$40,650	
Commercial Banks **$19,050**		
American Bankers Assn	$6,500	PAC
Citizens & Southern National Bank	$2,500	PAC
JP Morgan & Co	$2,500	PAC
Insurance **$7,100**		
National Assn of Life Underwriters	$3,000	PAC
Capital Holding Corp	$1,500	PAC
Real Estate **$9,550**		
National Assn of Realtors	$6,000	PAC

Health	$33,150	
Health Professionals **$19,150**		
American Medical Assn*	$9,700	PAC
American Dental Assn	$5,000	PAC
American Academy of Ophthalmology	$1,500	PAC
Hospitals/Nursing Homes **$2,850**		
None over $1,500		
Pharmaceuticals/Health Products **$11,150**		
Glaxo Inc	$3,500	PAC
Burroughs Wellcome	$2,000	PAC
Warner-Lambert	$1,500	PAC

Lawyers & Lobbyists $17,700

Lawyers & Lobbyists $17,700
    Assn of Trial Lawyers of America ....$10,000 PAC

Misc Business $10,835

Food & Beverage $2,685
    None over $1,500

Beer, Wine & Liquor $1,500
    National Beer Wholesalers Assn ....$1,500 PAC

Misc Manufacturing & Distributing $2,500
    Hoechst Celanese Corp ....$2,000 PAC

Textiles...$2,250
    Burlington Industries ....$1,500 PAC

Transportation $24,800

Air Transport $15,850
    Aircraft Owners & Pilots Assn ....$4,500 PAC
    United Parcel Service ....$3,350 PAC
    American Airlines ....$2,500 PAC
    Federal Express Corp ....$2,000 PAC
    Northwest Airlines ....$1,500 PAC

Automotive $2,500
    National Auto Dealers Assn ....$2,000 PAC

Trucking..$3,200
    American Trucking Assns ....$1,500 PAC
    Yellow Freight System ....$1,500 PAC

Railroads..$2,100
    None over $1,500

Labor

Labor $86,900

Building Trade Unions $2,500
    Laborers' Political League ....$1,500 PAC

Industrial Unions $10,500
    Intl Brotherhood of Electrical Workers ....$3,000 PAC
    United Auto Workers ....$3,000 PAC
    Communications Workers of America ....$2,500 PAC

Transportation Unions $45,050
    Teamsters Union ....$10,000 PAC
    Air Line Pilots Assn ....$9,000 PAC
    United Transportation Union ....$9,000 PAC
    Seafarers International Union ....$5,000 PAC
    Marine Engineers Union* ....$4,500 PAC
    Transport Workers Union ....$3,050 PAC
    Amalgamated Transit Union ....$2,500 PAC

Public Sector Unions $19,850
    American Federation of Teachers ....$5,000 PAC
    American Fedn of St/Cnty/Munic Employees ......$3,000 PAC
    National Education Assn ....$2,700 PAC
    National Assn of Letter Carriers ....$2,500 PAC
    American Postal Workers Union ....$1,500 PAC

Misc Unions $9,000
    Food & Commercial Workers Union ....$6,000 PAC

Ideological/Single-Issue

Ideological/Single-Issue $13,959

Democratic/Liberal $4,900
    National Cmte for an Effective Congress ....$2,500 PAC

Pro-Israel $6,100
    National PAC ....$5,000 PAC

Misc Issues $1,750
    None over $1,500

Other & Unknown

Other $11,200

Civil Servants/Public Officials $1,500
    None over $1,500

Education $3,300
    None over $1,500

Retired $5,550
    None over $1,500

Unknown $14,550

    No Employer Listed or Found $6,500
    Employer Listed/Category Unknown $7,050
      None over $1,500

Spending in Last 3 Elections

	1988	1990	1992
Price	$1,006,641	$793,291	$419,421
Opponent	$745,726	$890,838	$11,970
Vote Pct	58%	58%	65%

* Contributions came from more than one affiliate or
subsidiary.

Deborah Pryce, R-Ohio (15)

First elected: 1992

1991-92 Total Receipts: $558,617
1992 Year-end Cash: $1,874

1993-94 Committees & Subcommittees

Banking, Finance and Urban Affairs
Consumer Credit and Insurance; Financial Institutions Supervision, Regulation and Deposit Insurance; Housing and Community Development

Government Operations
Environment, Energy and Natural Resources

Leading Contributors

Business

Agriculture		$10,600
Tobacco		**$1,750**
None over $1,500		
Agricultural Services/Products		**$2,500**
None over $1,500		
Food Processing & Sales		**$4,100**
None over $1,500		

Communications/Electronics		$7,950
Printing & Publishing		**$1,750**
None over $1,500		
Telephone Utilities		**$5,700**
AT&T	$2,000	PAC

Construction		$25,450
General Contractors		**$12,400**
Borror Corp	$2,700	Indiv
Associated General Contractors	$2,000	PAC
Lincoln Construction Inc	$1,500	Indiv
Home Builders		**$6,250**
National Assn of Home Builders	$5,000	PAC
Special Trade Contractors		**$2,800**
None over $1,500		
Building Materials & Equipment		**$3,500**
Davon Inc	$2,000	Indiv

Source of Funds in 1992 Election

Source	Total	Pct
■ PACs	$211,227	35%
■ Indivs $200+	$201,221	34%
□ Indivs under $200	$117,857	20%
⊠ Other	$65,984	11%
Candidate	$0	0%
Party	$47,672	8%

Source of PAC Dollars by Sector

Source	Total	Pct
■ Business	$176,697	87%
■ Labor	$0	0%
□ Ideology/Single Issue	$27,157	13%

In-State vs. Out-of-State Contributions*

Source	Total	Pct
□ In-State	$194,410	97%
■ Out-of-state	$5,200	3%
No state listed	$0	

* by large individual contributors ($200 & above)

Energy & Natural Resources		$25,150
Oil & Gas		**$16,150**
Ashland Oil	$4,000	PAC
Columbia Gas System*	$3,100	PAC
Sun Co	$1,500	PAC
Mining		**$1,900**
None over $1,500		
Misc Energy		**$3,000**
Cooper Industries	$3,000	PAC
Electric Utilities		**$3,000**
American Electric Power*	$2,500	PAC

Finance, Insurance & Real Estate		$92,763
Commercial Banks		**$28,847**
Banc One Corp	$7,000	PAC/Ind
Huntington Bancshares	$5,750	PAC/Ind
American Bankers Assn*	$5,000	PAC
National City Corp	$3,750	PAC
Banc Ohio National Bank	$2,297	Indiv
NBD Bancorp	$1,500	PAC
Society Corp	$1,500	PAC
Securities & Investment		**$14,517**
Ohio Co	$6,751	Indiv
Banc One Capital Corp	$2,000	Indiv
Raymond James & Associates	$2,000	Indiv
Insurance		**$20,849**
National Assn of Life Underwriters	$5,000	PAC
Nationwide Corp	$5,000	PAC
Independent Insurance Agents of America	$2,000	PAC
Real Estate		**$24,550**
Don M Casto Organization	$4,000	Indiv
Galbreath Co	$3,000	Indiv
Mortgage Bankers Assn of America	$2,500	PAC
RJ Solove & Associates	$2,000	Indiv
Misc Finance		**$2,500**
None over $1,500		

Contribution Totals by Sector

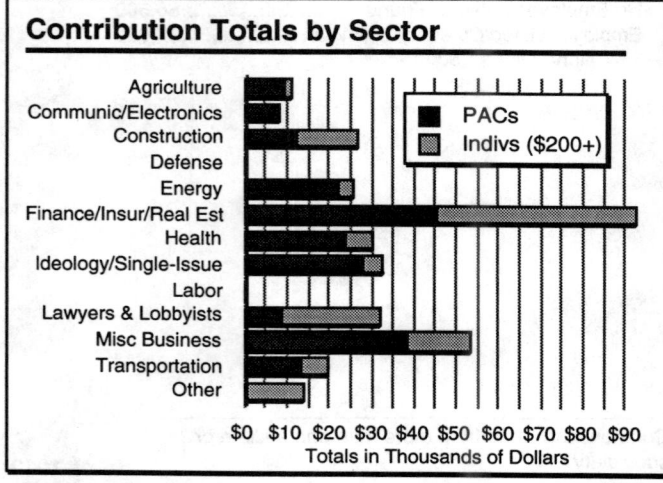

Agriculture, Communic/Electronics, Construction, Defense, Energy, Finance/Insur/Real Est, Health, Ideology/Single-Issue, Labor, Lawyers & Lobbyists, Misc Business, Transportation, Other

■ PACs
▨ Indivs ($200+)

$0 $10 $20 $30 $40 $50 $60 $70 $80 $90
Totals in Thousands of Dollars

Health $29,800

Health Professionals **$26,850**
   American Medical Assn ....$10,000 PAC
   American Dental Assn* ....$5,750 PAC
   American Academy of Ophthalmology ....$2,000 PAC
   American College of Emergency Physicians ....$2,000 PAC

Lawyers & Lobbyists $31,281

Lawyers & Lobbyists **$31,281**
   Assn of Trial Lawyers of America ....$5,000 PAC
   Harris, McClellan et al ....$3,150 Indiv
   Chester, Hoffman et al ....$2,180 Indiv
   Porter, Wright et al ....$1,500 Indiv

Misc Business $52,760

Business Associations **$2,780**
   None over $1,500

Food & Beverage **$16,000**
   National Restaurant Assn ....$8,000 PAC
   Pizza Hut Franchise Holders Assn ....$2,000 PAC
   White Castle System ....$2,000 PAC/Ind

Beer, Wine & Liquor **$5,500**
   National Beer Wholesalers Assn ....$5,000 PAC

Retail Sales **$3,000**
   Limited Inc ....$1,500 PAC

Misc Services **$1,501**
   None over $1,500

Business Services **$2,029**
   None over $1,500

Lodging/Tourism **$2,900**
   None over $1,500

Chemical & Related Manufacturing **$3,000**
   None over $1,500

Steel Production **$4,300**
   Worthington Industries ....$4,000 Indiv

Misc Manufacturing & Distributing **$11,500**
   Stone Container Corp ....$3,000 PAC
   Corning Glass Works ....$2,000 PAC

Transportation $19,699

Air Transport **$2,000**
   United Parcel Service ....$1,500 PAC

Automotive **$15,449**
   National Auto Dealers Assn ....$5,000 PAC
   Eaton Corp ....$2,000 PAC

Ideological/Single-Issue

Ideological/Single-Issue $31,941

Republican/Conservative **$5,847**
   Leader PAC ....$2,000 PAC
   Pryce for Congress ....$1,884 Indiv

Leadership PACs **$4,722**
   Campaign America (Bob Dole) ....$2,000 PAC
   Republican Leader's Fund (Bob Michel) ....$2,000 PAC

Foreign & Defense Policy **$1,500**
   None over $1,500

Gun Rights/Gun Control **$4,950**
   National Rifle Assn ....$4,950 PAC

Womens Issues **$11,972**
   Women's Campaign Fund ....$6,000 PAC
   Wish List ....$5,672 PAC

Other & Unknown

Other $13,600

Civil Servants/Public Officials **$6,550**
   City of Columbus ....$2,400 Indiv

Retired **$6,000**
   None over $1,500

Unknown $62,470

   Homemakers/Non-income earners $7,400
   No Employer Listed or Found $23,653
   Generic Occupation/Category Unknown $3,250
   Employer Listed/Category Unknown $28,167
      Johnson Family Diamond Cellar ....$3,500 Indiv
      Gerald Todaro & Associates ....$1,500 Indiv

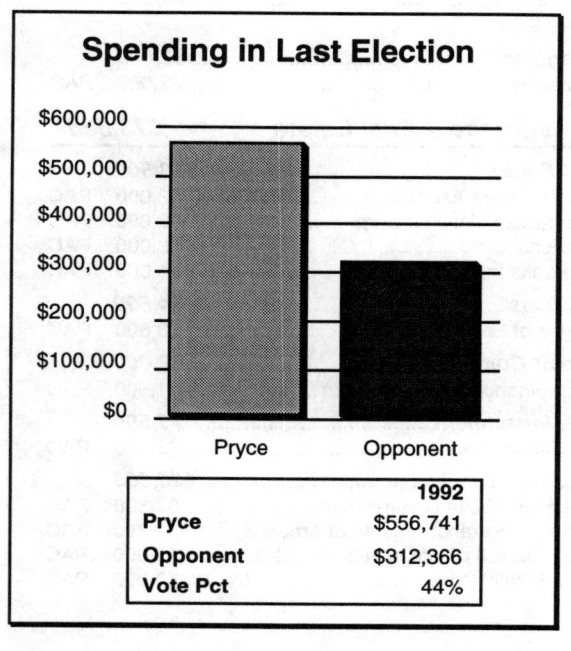

Spending in Last Election

	1992
Pryce	$556,741
Opponent	$312,366
Vote Pct	44%

* Contributions came from more than one affiliate or subsidiary.

James H. Quillen, R-Tenn (1)

1991-92 Committees & Subcommittees

Rules
Legislative Process (Ranking Republican)

Leading Contributors

Business

Agriculture $31,804

Crop Production & Basic Processing	**$8,250**	
American Crystal Sugar Corp	$1,500	PAC
Tobacco	**$5,500**	
Philip Morris	$2,000	PAC
Dairy	**$8,000**	
Associated Milk Producers	$5,000	PAC
Dairymen Inc-Tennessee	$2,000	PAC
Food Processing & Sales	**$4,000**	
Pepsico Inc	$2,000	PAC
Forestry & Forest Products	**$4,000**	
Blaylock Lumber Co	$2,000	Indiv

Communications/Electronics $18,250

Media/Entertainment	**$2,500**	
National Assn of Broadcasters	$2,000	PAC
Telephone Utilities	**$9,500**	
AT&T	$5,000	PAC
Computer Equipment & Services	**$4,000**	
Dynamic Decisions Inc	$4,000	Indiv

Construction $11,350

General Contractors	**$5,350**	
None over $1,500		
Home Builders	**$2,000**	
National Assn of Home Builders	$1,500	PAC
Construction Services	**$1,500**	
None over $1,500		
Building Materials & Equipment	**$1,500**	
None over $1,500		

Contribution Totals by Sector

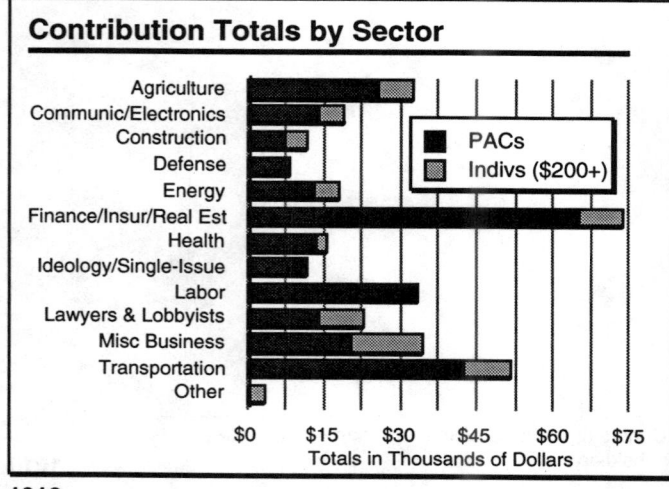

Totals in Thousands of Dollars

Source of Funds in 1992 Election

Source	Total	Pct
PACs	$267,050	59%
Indivs $200+	$72,805	16%
Indivs under $200	$7,950	2%
Other	$108,041	24%
Candidate	$0	0%
Party	$0	0%

Source of PAC Dollars by Sector

Source	Total	Pct
Business	$219,789	83%
Labor	$32,750	12%
Ideology/Single Issue	$11,400	4%

In-State vs. Out-of-State Contributions*

Source	Total	Pct
In-State	$46,300	64%
Out-of-state	$26,505	36%
No state listed	$0	

*** by large individual contributors ($200 & above)**

Defense $7,650

Defense Aerospace	**$2,500**	
None over $1,500		
Defense Electronics	**$4,000**	
Raytheon	$4,000	PAC

Energy & Natural Resources $17,300

Oil & Gas	**$8,000**	
Appalachian Oil Co	$1,500	Indiv
Nuclear Energy	**$2,800**	
Nuclear Fuel Services	$2,000	Indiv
Electric Utilities	**$3,500**	
None over $1,500		
Waste Management	**$2,000**	
Waste Management Inc	$2,000	PAC

Finance, Insurance & Real Estate $73,555

Commercial Banks	**$13,500**	
American Bankers Assn	$2,000	PAC
First Tennessee National Corp	$2,000	PAC
Third National Corp	$2,000	PAC
Barnett Banks Inc	$1,500	PAC
Savings & Loans	**$4,500**	
US League of Savings Assns*	$3,500	PAC
Finance/Credit Companies	**$2,000**	
American Financial Services Assn	$1,500	PAC
Securities & Investment	**$5,500**	
Morgan Stanley & Co	$2,000	PAC
Insurance	**$25,305**	
National Assn of Life Underwriters	$7,500	PAC
Independent Insurance Agents of America	$3,250	PAC
American Council of Life Insurance	$3,000	PAC
American Family Corp	$2,000	PAC

Real Estate **$14,250**
   National Assn of Realtors .... $10,000 PAC
   M&M Properties Inc .... $2,000 Indiv

Accountants **$7,500**
   American Institute of CPA's .... $7,500 PAC

Health $15,150

Health Professionals **$10,350**
   American Medical Assn .... $5,000 PAC
   American Podiatry Assn .... $2,000 PAC
   American Dental Assn .... $1,500 PAC

Pharmaceuticals/Health Products **$3,500**
   None over $1,500

Lawyers & Lobbyists $21,750

Lawyers & Lobbyists **$21,750**
   Assn of Trial Lawyers of America .... $10,000 PAC
   Webster, Chamberlain & Bean .... $2,000 Indiv
   Hill & Knowlton* .... $1,500 PAC/Ind

Misc Business $32,235

Food & Beverage **$3,535**
   Shoneys Inc .... $2,000 Indiv

Beer, Wine & Liquor **$6,750**
   None over $1,500

Retail Sales **$4,500**
   JC Penney Co .... $1,500 PAC

Chemical & Related Manufacturing **$4,000**
   Eastman Kodak/Chemicals Division .... $2,000 PAC

Misc Manufacturing & Distributing **$7,950**
   None over $1,500

Textiles **$3,750**
   North American Rayon .... $2,000 Indiv

Transportation   **$51,300**

Air Transport **$18,500**
   Federal Express Corp .... $10,000 PAC
   United Parcel Service .... $3,500 PAC
   Aircraft Owners & Pilots Assn .... $3,000 PAC

Automotive **$14,500**
   National Auto Dealers Assn .... $7,500 PAC
   Auto Dealers & Drivers for Free Trade .... $2,000 PAC
   Nickels Performance Systems .... $1,500 Indiv

Trucking **$3,750**
   None over $1,500

Railroads **$3,500**
   Norfolk Southern Corp .... $1,500 PAC

Sea Transport **$11,050**
   None over $1,500

Labor

Labor   **$32,750**

Industrial Unions **$1,500**
   None over $1,500

Transportation Unions **$13,750**
   Marine Engineers Union* .... $8,000 PAC
   Air Line Pilots Assn .... $3,500 PAC
   Seafarers International Union .... $2,000 PAC

Public Sector Unions **$17,500**
   National Assn of Letter Carriers .... $7,000 PAC
   National Assn Retired Federal Employees .... $6,000 PAC
   National Assn of Postmasters .... $2,000 PAC
   American Postal Workers Union .... $1,500 PAC

Ideological/Single-Issue

Ideological/Single-Issue   **$11,400**

Gun Rights/Gun Control **$9,900**
   National Rifle Assn .... $9,900 PAC

Other & Unknown

Other   **$3,000**

Retired **$2,000**
   None over $1,500

Unknown   **$7,250**
   Employer Listed/Category Unknown $6,750
     None over $1,500

Spending in Last 3 Elections

	1988	1990	1992
Quillen	$227,503	$263,291	$325,383
Opponent	$0	$0	$0
Vote Pct	80%	100%	68%

* Contributions came from more than one affiliate or subsidiary.

Jack Quinn, R-NY (30)

1993-94 Committees & Subcommittees

First elected: 1992
1991-92 Total Receipts: $206,843
1992 Year-end Cash: $7,583

Public Works and Transportation
Economic Development; Water Resources and the Environment

Veterans' Affairs
Education, Training and Employment; Oversight and Investigations

Leading Contributors

Business

Agriculture — $2,700

Dairy	**$1,200**	
Sorrento Cheese Co	$1,200	Indiv
Food Processing & Sales	**$1,500**	
Klass Ingredients Inc	$1,500	Indiv

Communications/Electronics — $2,800

Printing & Publishing	**$1,800**	
H&K Publications	$1,600	Indiv
Telephone Utilities	**$1,000**	
AT&T	$1,000	PAC

Construction — $10,100

General Contractors	**$5,250**	
Mader Construction Co	$3,000	Indiv
Special Trade Contractors	**$1,100**	
None over $1,000		
Building Materials & Equipment	**$3,750**	
Gernatt Asphalt Products	$1,200	Indiv
Clarence Materials Corp	$1,000	Indiv
Hamburg Overhead Door	$1,000	Indiv

Energy & Natural Resources — $2,700

Oil & Gas	**$2,500**	
Noco Energy Corp	$2,000	Indiv

Source of Funds in 1992 Election

Source	Total	Pct
■ PACs	$10,665	4%
▨ Indivs $200+	$125,650	48%
□ Indivs under $200	$57,826	22%
▤ Other	$67,900	26%
Candidate	$1,000	0%
Party	$60,198	23%

Source of PAC Dollars by Sector

Source	Total	Pct
■ Business	$10,625	95%
▨ Labor	$0	0%
□ Ideology/Single Issue	$616	5%

In-State vs. Out-of-State Contributions*

Source	Total	Pct
□ In-State	$120,800	97%
■ Out-of-state	$3,950	3%
No state listed	$900	

* by large individual contributors ($200 & above)

Finance, Insurance & Real Estate — $14,825

Commercial Banks	**$2,075**	
None over $1,000		
Securities & Investment	**$1,700**	
Fiscal Advisors & Marketing Inc	$1,500	Indiv
Real Estate	**$7,900**	
Ciminelli Companies	$2,200	Indiv
Benderson Development Co	$2,000	Indiv
Stuart Hunt Real Estate	$1,200	Indiv
EP Burke Realty	$1,000	Indiv
Accountants	**$2,950**	
American Institute of CPA's	$2,000	PAC

Health — $7,650

Health Professionals	**$3,700**	
New York Medical Assn	$1,500	PAC
Hospitals/Nursing Homes	**$2,200**	
Brylin Hospital	$2,000	Indiv
Pharmaceuticals/Health Products	**$1,500**	
Buffalo X-Ray Corp	$1,500	Indiv

Lawyers & Lobbyists — $8,595

Lawyers & Lobbyists	**$8,595**	
Hawkins, Delafield & Wood	$1,000	Indiv

Misc Business — $7,800

Food & Beverage	**$1,800**	
Resser Management	$1,000	Indiv
Business Services	**$1,000**	
None over $1,000		
Misc Manufacturing & Distributing	**$3,300**	
All-Flow Inc	$1,000	Indiv
Eden Tool Manufacturer	$1,000	Indiv

Contribution Totals by Sector

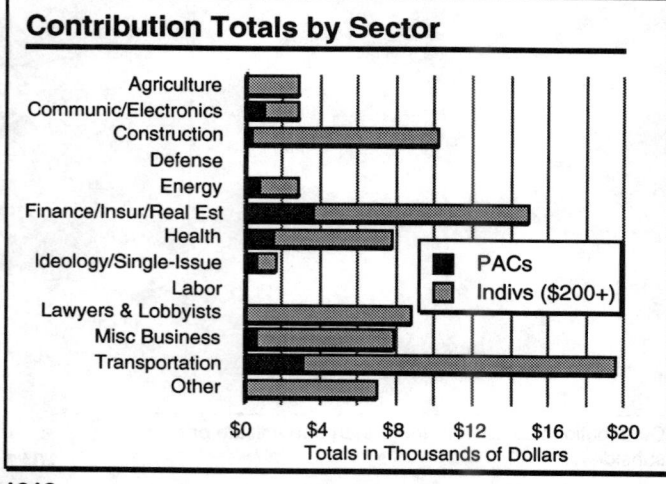

Agriculture
Communic/Electronics
Construction
Defense
Energy
Finance/Insur/Real Est
Health
Ideology/Single-Issue
Labor
Lawyers & Lobbyists
Misc Business
Transportation
Other

■ PACs
▨ Indivs ($200+)

$0 $4 $8 $12 $16 $20
Totals in Thousands of Dollars

Transportation $20,390

Air Transport $4,740
 Enidine Inc .... $4,740 Indiv

Automotive $10,200
 Ed Taylor Lincoln Mercury Inc .... $3,500 Indiv
 National Auto Dealers Assn .... $3,000 PAC
 West-Herr Ford Inc .... $2,000 Indiv
 Dunlop Tire Corp .... $1,000 Indiv

Trucking $5,450
 CID Group Inc .... $3,000 Indiv
 Sorrento Express .... $2,000 Indiv

Ideological/SIngle-Issue

Ideological/Single-Issue $1,566
 None over $1,000

Other & Unknown

Other $6,900

Civil Servants/Public Officials $2,800
 Town of Hamburg .... $1,700 Indiv

Retired $3,200
 None over $1,000

Unknown $50,865
 Homemakers/Non-income earners $6,900
 No Employer Listed or Found $11,150
 Employer Listed/Category Unknown $32,615
  Boehringert & Mannheim Inc .... $2,000 Indiv
  Marrano Marc Equity Corp .... $2,000 Indiv
  Summerset Exploration Inc .... $2,000 Indiv
  Superior Plan Magazine Fundrs .... $2,000 Indiv
  Environas Inc .... $1,400 Indiv
  Carpet Investments .... $1,000 Indiv
  Conax Buffalo .... $1,000 Indiv
  Envirocas Inc .... $1,000 Indiv
  JM Productions .... $1,000 Indiv
  Newbro Corp .... $1,000 Indiv
  Nolo Motor Fuels .... $1,000 Indiv
  Partners Press .... $1,000 Indiv
  Ralph J Vanner & Assoc .... $1,000 Indiv
  Snyder Tank Corp .... $1,000 Indiv

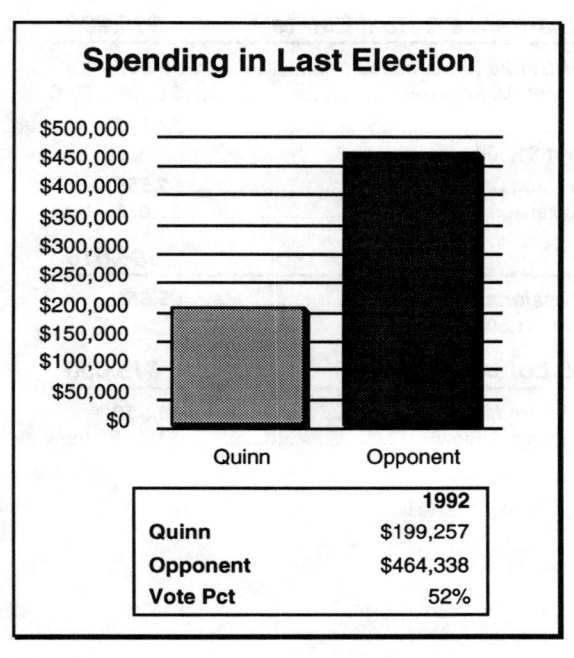

Spending in Last Election

	1992
Quinn	$199,257
Opponent	$464,338
Vote Pct	52%

Nick J. Rahall II, D-WVa (3)

First elected: 1976

1991-92 Total Receipts: $444,624
1992 Year-end Cash: $500,823

1991-92 Committees & Subcommittees

Interior and Insular Affairs
Mining and Natural Resources (Chairman); National Parks and Public Lands

Public Works and Transportation
Aviation; Surface Transportation; Water Resources

Leading Contributors

Business

Agriculture — $15,650

Crop Production & Basic Processing	$2,350	
None over $1,500		
Tobacco	$5,500	
RJR Nabisco	$3,000	PAC
Philip Morris	$1,500	PAC
Dairy	$5,800	
Associated Milk Producers	$3,000	PAC

Communications/Electronics — $5,550

Media/Entertainment	$2,000	
None over $1,500		
Telephone Utilities	$3,050	
Bell Atlantic*	$2,000	PAC

Construction — $12,340

General Contractors	$7,250	
Choice Construction Co	$2,000	Indiv
Construction Services	$3,340	
None over $1,500		

Defense — $2,300

Defense Aerospace	$2,300	
None over $1,500		

Source of Funds in 1992 Election

Source	Total	Pct
PACs	$246,158	52%
Indivs $200+	$83,650	18%
Indivs under $200	$42,728	9%
Other	$102,858	22%
Candidate	$0	0%
Party	$31,120	7%

Source of PAC Dollars by Sector

Source	Total	Pct
Business	$114,496	47%
Labor	$111,525	46%
Ideology/Single Issue	$17,798	7%

In-State vs. Out-of-State Contributions*

Source	Total	Pct
In-State	$12,150	15%
Out-of-state	$71,500	85%
No state listed	$0	

* by large individual contributors ($200 & above)

Energy & Natural Resources — $22,000

Oil & Gas	$14,350	
Ashland Oil	$2,000	PAC
Columbia Natural Resources	$2,000	PAC
Consolidated Gas Transmission Corp	$2,000	PAC
USX Corp*	$2,000	PAC
Occidental Petroleum	$1,500	PAC
Mining	$6,050	
Peabody Coal	$1,500	PAC
Pen Holdings	$1,500	Indiv
Electric Utilities	$1,600	
None over $1,500		

Finance, Insurance & Real Estate — $15,200

Commercial Banks	$6,500	
Independent Bankers Assn	$1,500	PAC
Insurance	$2,100	
None over $1,500		
Real Estate	$5,550	
Parking Management Inc	$2,050	Indiv

Health — $8,618

Health Professionals	$5,650	
None over $1,500		

Lawyers & Lobbyists — $15,050

Lawyers & Lobbyists	$15,050	
Patton, Boggs & Blow	$1,500	Indiv

Contribution Totals by Sector

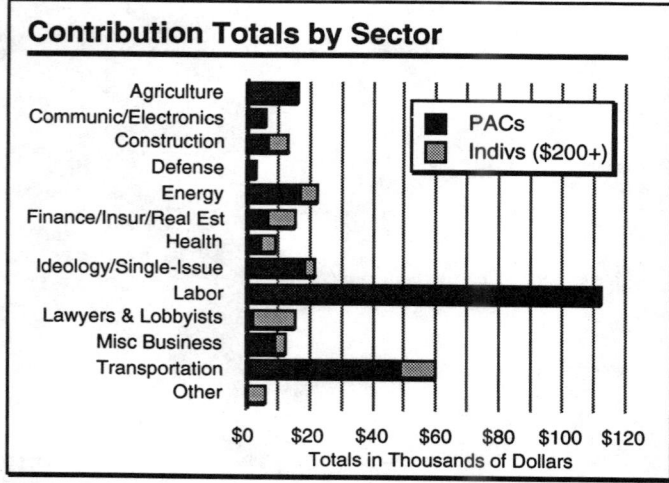

Agriculture
Communic/Electronics
Construction
Defense
Energy
Finance/Insur/Real Est
Health
Ideology/Single-Issue
Labor
Lawyers & Lobbyists
Misc Business
Transportation
Other

■ PACs
▨ Indivs ($200+)

$0 $20 $40 $60 $80 $100 $120
Totals in Thousands of Dollars

Misc Business $11,738

Beer, Wine & Liquor $2,350
    None over $1,500

Business Services $2,638
    None over $1,500

Lodging/Tourism $1,750
    None over $1,500

Chemical & Related Manufacturing $3,250
    Dial Corp .... $2,000 PAC

Transportation $58,800

Air Transport $15,250
    United Parcel Service .... $4,000 PAC
    Federal Express Corp .... $3,000 PAC
    Aircraft Owners & Pilots Assn .... $2,000 PAC

Automotive $5,500
    National Auto Dealers Assn .... $2,000 PAC
    Auto Dealers & Drivers for Free Trade ... $1,500 PAC

Trucking $24,300
    American Trucking Assns .... $2,500 PAC
    Consolidated Freightways .... $2,500 PAC
    Eastern Central Motor Carriers .... $2,250 PAC/Ind
    National Motor Freight Traffic Assn ...... $2,200 Indiv
    Yellow Freight System .... $2,000 PAC
    Interstate Carriers Conference .... $1,750 PAC
    Niagara Frontier Tarriff Bureau Inc ...... $1,650 Indiv
    National Tank Truck Carriers Inc .... $1,500 PAC
    Roadway Services Inc* .... $1,500 PAC

Railroads $4,750
    None over $1,500

Sea Transport $4,250
    None over $1,500

Misc Transport $4,750
    American Bus Assn .... $2,000 PAC

Labor

Labor $111,525

Building Trade Unions $15,500
    Laborers' Political League .... $6,000 PAC
    Carpenters & Joiners Union .... $2,500 PAC
    Ironworkers Union .... $2,500 PAC
    Plumbers/Pipefitters Union .... $2,000 PAC
    AFL-CIO Bldg/Construction Trades Dept ... $1,500 PAC

Industrial Unions $26,550
    Machinists/Aerospace Workers Union ...... $6,000 PAC
    United Auto Workers .... $5,500 PAC
    United Mine Workers .... $5,000 PAC
    United Steelworkers .... $5,000 PAC
    Intl Brotherhood of Electrical Workers ... $1,500 PAC

Transportation Unions $38,950
    Air Line Pilots Assn .... $10,000 PAC
    Teamsters Union .... $7,500 PAC
    Marine Engineers Dist 2 Maritime Officers ... $6,500 PAC
    United Transportation Union .... $6,500 PAC
    Amalgamated Transit Union .... $2,000 PAC
    Seafarers International Union .... $1,500 PAC

Public Sector Unions $26,625
    National Education Assn .... $7,500 PAC
    National Assn Retired Federal Employees ... $4,000 PAC
    International Assn of Firefighters .... $3,500 PAC
    American Fedn of St/Cnty/Munic Employees ... $3,000 PAC
    National Assn of Letter Carriers .... $2,000 PAC
    National Assn of Postmasters .... $1,575 PAC
    American Postal Workers Union .... $1,500 PAC

Misc Unions $3,900
    Food & Commercial Workers Union .... $2,000 PAC
    Hotel/Restaurant Employees Union .... $1,500 PAC

Ideological/Single-Issue

Ideological/Single-Issue $21,298

Democratic/Liberal $2,000
    None over $1,500

Foreign & Defense Policy $3,800
    American Task Force for Lebanon Policy ... $1,800 PAC

Gun Rights/Gun Control $10,150
    National Rifle Assn .... $10,150 PAC

Misc Issues $4,325
    National Cmte to Preserve Social Security ... $4,000 PAC

Other & Unknown

Other $5,800

Retired $3,750
    None over $1,500

Unknown $22,100

    Employer Listed/Category Unknown $20,300
      Donohue & Associates .... $2,000 Indiv
      Middle Atlantic Conference .... $1,600 Indiv

Spending in Last 3 Elections

	1988	1990	1992
Rahall	$152,271	$566,348	$309,313
Opponent	$32,039	$61,471	$150,822
Vote Pct	61%	52%	66%

---

* Contributions came from more than one affiliate or
subsidiary.

Jim Ramstad, R-Minn (3)

First elected: 1990
1991-92 Total Receipts: $1,010,791
1992 Year-end Cash: $317,719

1991-92 Committees & Subcommittees

Judiciary
Administrative Law and Governmental Relations; Crime and Criminal Justice

Small Business
Exports, Tax Policy and Special Problems; SBA, the General Economy and Minority Enterprise Development

Select Committee on Narcotics Abuse and Control

Leading Contributors

Business

Agriculture	$55,700	
Crop Production & Basic Processing	**$12,350**	
Cargill Inc	$4,000	PAC/Ind
American Crystal Sugar Corp	$3,700	PAC
Dairy	**$7,200**	
Mid-America Dairymen	$2,700	PAC
Associated Milk Producers	$2,500	PAC
Agricultural Services/Products	**$12,900**	
Ag-Chem Equipment Co	$4,000	Indiv
Food Processing & Sales	**$16,550**	
General Mills	$6,500	PAC/Ind
Pan O'Gold Baking	$4,000	Indiv
Forestry & Forest Products	**$4,350**	
None over $2,500		

Communications/Electronics	$35,450	
Printing & Publishing	**$11,250**	
West Publishing	$7,750	PAC/Ind
Media/Entertainment	**$7,500**	
Hubbard Broadcasting Co	$4,000	Indiv
Telephone Utilities	**$10,700**	
AT&T	$3,500	PAC
US West Inc	$2,500	PAC
Computer Equipment & Services	**$4,000**	
None over $2,500		

Source of Funds in 1992 Election

Source	Total	Pct
PACs	$258,016	25%
Indivs $200+	$469,267	46%
Indivs under $200	$270,972	27%
Other	$17,419	2%
Candidate	$0	0%
Party	$5,346	1%

Source of PAC Dollars by Sector

Source	Total	Pct
Business	$219,545	90%
Labor	$12,300	5%
Ideology/Single Issue	$11,620	5%

In-State vs. Out-of-State Contributions*

Source	Total	Pct
In-State	$428,167	91%
Out-of-state	$40,800	9%
No state listed	$0	

* by large individual contributors ($200 & above)

Construction	$26,222	
General Contractors	**$7,750**	
Ames Construction	$4,000	Indiv
Associated General Contractors	$2,500	PAC
Home Builders	**$7,000**	
National Assn of Home Builders	$7,000	PAC
Special Trade Contractors	**$4,672**	
None over $2,500		
Building Materials & Equipment	**$5,700**	
None over $2,500		

Defense	$3,300	
None over $2,500		

Energy & Natural Resources	$14,550	
Oil & Gas	**$8,300**	
None over $2,500		
Electric Utilities	**$2,500**	
None over $2,500		
Commercial Fishing	**$3,000**	
Fish 'N Dakota	$3,000	Indiv

Finance, Insurance & Real Estate	$159,375	
Commercial Banks	**$15,550**	
American Bankers Assn	$6,000	PAC
Norwest Corp	$2,500	PAC/Ind
Savings & Loans	**$4,750**	
Twin City Federal Savings & Loan	$2,500	Indiv
Securities & Investment	**$26,700**	
Piper, Jaffray & Hopwood	$4,800	PAC/Ind
SIT Investment Associates	$4,700	Indiv
Jundt Associates Inc	$4,000	Indiv
IDS Center	$3,000	Indiv

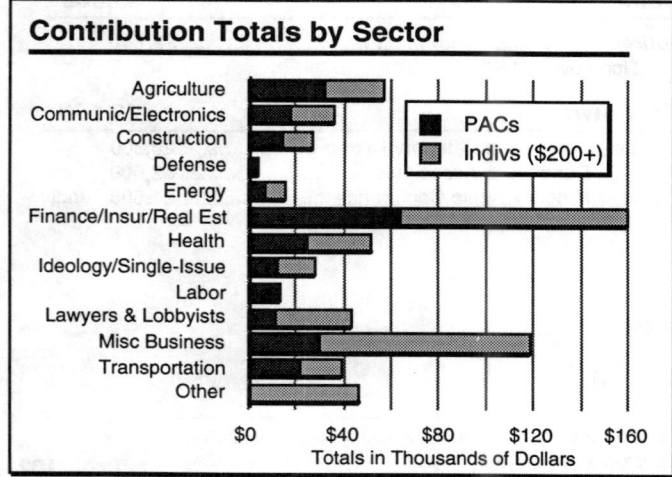

Contribution Totals by Sector

Categories (top to bottom): Agriculture, Communic/Electronics, Construction, Defense, Energy, Finance/Insur/Real Est, Health, Ideology/Single-Issue, Labor, Lawyers & Lobbyists, Misc Business, Transportation, Other

Legend: ■ PACs   ▨ Indivs ($200+)

X-axis: $0, $40, $80, $120, $160 — Totals in Thousands of Dollars

Insurance	$37,675	
National Assn of Life Underwriters	$8,000	PAC
Northwestern National Life	$3,600	PAC/Ind
St Paul Companies Inc	$2,750	PAC/Ind
Independent Insurance Agents of America	$2,725	PAC

Real Estate **$37,100**
National Assn of Realtors ....$7,700 PAC
Burnet Realty ....$7,100 Indiv
K Charles Development ....$4,000 Indiv

Accountants **$9,500**
American Institute of CPA's ....$5,700 PAC

Misc Finance **$25,600**
Whitney Management Co ....$2,700 Indiv
IC Systems Inc ....$2,500 Indiv

Health $50,445

Health Professionals **$26,445**
American Medical Assn.....................................$9,995 PAC
American Physical Therapy Assn ....$5,350 PAC
American Academy of Ophthalmology ....$3,500 PAC

Hospitals/Nursing Homes **$3,700**
None over $2,500

Pharmaceuticals/Health Products **$7,500**
Minntech ....$3,000 Indiv
Cherne Industries Inc ....$2,750 Indiv

Misc Health **$12,300**
Medical Industries ....$11,300 Indiv

Lawyers & Lobbyists $42,900

Lawyers & Lobbyists **$42,900**
Assn of Trial Lawyers of America ....$5,000 PAC
Popham, Haik et al ....$3,200 PAC/Ind
Shawn, Berger & Mann ....$3,000 Indiv
Opperman & Paquin ....$2,500 PAC

Misc Business $119,643

Food & Beverage **$8,800**
None over $2,500

Beer, Wine & Liquor **$4,000**
National Beer Wholesalers Assn ....$3,500 PAC

Retail Sales **$10,000**
Dayton Hudson Corp ....$3,300 PAC/Ind

Misc Services **$4,250**
None over $2,500

Business Services **$26,718**
Alarm Industry Communications Cmte ....$6,018 PAC
Wiken Promotions ....$4,000 Indiv
Proex Photo Studios ....$3,000 Indiv

Lodging/Tourism **$2,950**
None over $2,500

Chemical & Related Manufacturing **$10,850**
Hawkins Chemical Inc ....$2,900 Indiv

Misc Manufacturing & Distributing **$47,825**
Twin City Diecasting ....$8,975 Indiv
Katun Corp ....$4,500 Indiv
Jostens Inc ....$4,250 Indiv
High Country Fashions ....$2,750 Indiv
Stone Container Corp ....$2,500 PAC

Transportation $37,935

Air Transport **$7,650**
Northwest Airlines ....$3,500 PAC/Ind

Automotive **$23,300**
National Auto Dealers Assn ....$7,000 PAC

Misc Transport **$3,000**
None over $2,500

Labor

Labor $12,300

Transportation Unions **$4,850**
Air Line Pilots Assn ....$3,500 PAC

Public Sector Unions **$7,450**
National Assn Retired Federal Employees ....$3,000 PAC

Ideological/Single-Issue

Ideological/Single-Issue $26,945

Republican/Conservative..................................... **$3,000**
None over $2,500

Pro-Israel **$12,375**
None over $2,500

Gun Rights/Gun Control **$4,050**
National Rifle Assn ....$2,800 PAC

Misc Issues **$6,320**
National Cmte to Preserve Social Security ....$4,050 PAC

Other & Unknown

Other $45,575

Civil Servants/Public Officials **$2,800**
None over $2,500

Retired **$42,525**
None over $2,500

Unknown $82,092

Homemakers/Non-income earners $13,524
No Employer Listed or Found $18,050
Employer Listed/Category Unknown $49,268
    Clearwater Management Co ....$2,500 Indiv

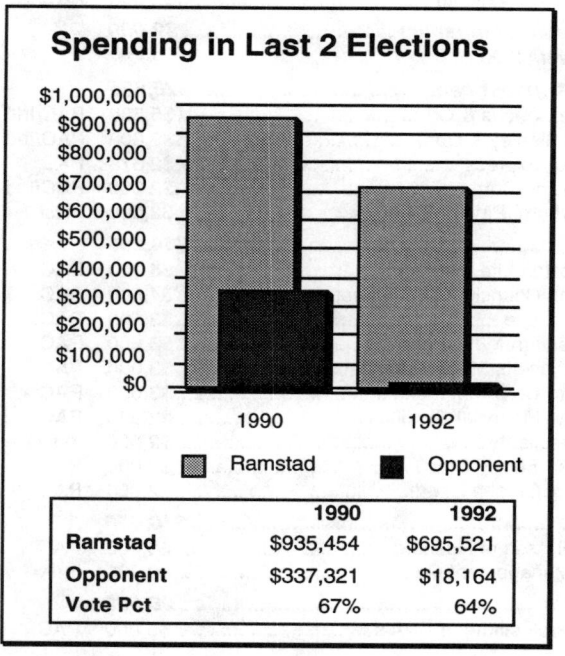

Spending in Last 2 Elections

	1990	1992
Ramstad	$935,454	$695,521
Opponent	$337,321	$18,164
Vote Pct	67%	64%

Legend: Ramstad, Opponent

Charles B. Rangel, D-NY (15)

First elected: 1970

1991-92 Total Receipts: $539,183
1992 Year-end Cash: $174,093

1991-92 Committees & Subcommittees

Ways and Means
Oversight; Select Revenue Measures (Chairman)

Select Committee on Narcotics Abuse and Control (Chairman)

Leading Contributors

Business

Agriculture	**$13,800**	
Tobacco	**$6,500**	
Philip Morris	$3,500	PAC
Food Processing & Sales	**$4,000**	
None over $2,000		

Communications/Electronics	**$27,675**	
Printing & Publishing	**$2,675**	
None over $2,000		
Media/Entertainment	**$7,750**	
Paramount Communications	$2,000	PAC
Telephone Utilities	**$14,250**	
AT&T	$3,000	PAC
Ameritech Corp	$3,000	PAC
GTE Corp	$2,000	PAC
Electronics Mfg & Services	**$2,000**	
None over $2,000		

Construction	**$5,650**	
General Contractors	**$3,650**	
Rexach Construction Co	$2,000	Indiv

Energy & Natural Resources	**$8,150**	
Electric Utilities	**$2,250**	
None over $2,000		

Contribution Totals by Sector

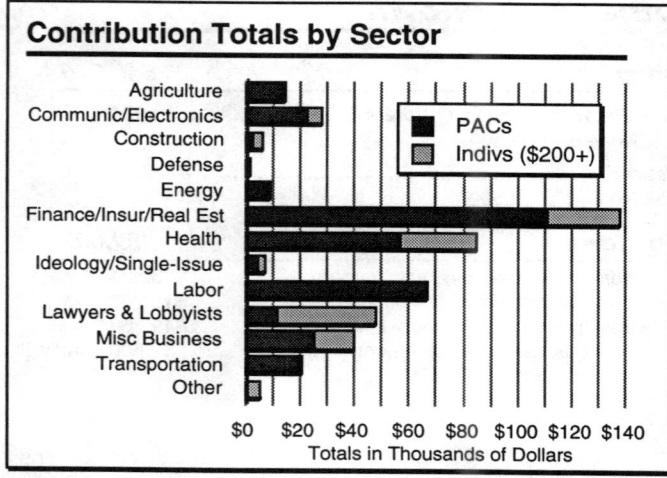

Totals in Thousands of Dollars

Source of Funds in 1992 Election

Source	Total	Pct
■ PACs	$325,850	60%
▨ Indivs $200+	$151,364	28%
□ Indivs under $200	$51,679	10%
⊠ Other	$10,427	2%
Candidate	$0	0%
Party	$137	0%

Source of PAC Dollars by Sector

Source	Total	Pct
■ Business	$268,488	79%
▨ Labor	$66,323	20%
□ Ideology/Single Issue	$3,750	1%

In-State vs. Out-of-State Contributions*

Source	Total	Pct
□ In-State	$61,450	41%
■ Out-of-state	$89,039	59%
No state listed	$875	

* by large individual contributors ($200 & above)

Finance, Insurance & Real Estate — $136,463

Commercial Banks	**$24,850**	
Republic National Bank of New York	$6,750	Indiv
American Bankers Assn	$5,000	PAC
Citicorp	$4,000	PAC
JP Morgan & Co	$2,500	PAC
Chase Manhattan	$2,050	PAC/Ind
Savings & Loans	**$7,043**	
National Council of Savings Institutions*	$2,918	PAC
US League of Savings Assns*	$2,000	PAC
Credit Unions	**$3,000**	
Credit Union National Assn	$2,000	PAC
Finance/Credit Companies	**$2,000**	
None over $2,000		
Securities & Investment	**$25,625**	
Goldman, Sachs & Co	$5,500	PAC/Ind
Morgan Stanley & Co	$2,800	PAC/Ind
American Express*	$2,375	PAC
First Boston Corp	$2,300	PAC/Ind
EM Warburg, Pincus & Co	$2,000	Indiv
Insurance	**$54,295**	
Metropolitan Life Insurance	$5,120	PAC
American Council of Life Insurance	$4,500	PAC
New York Life	$3,500	PAC
Northwestern Mutual Life	$3,500	PAC
Massachusetts Mutual Life Insurance	$3,000	PAC
Travelers Corp	$3,000	PAC
Equitable Financial Services	$2,625	PAC/Ind
AV Consultants	$2,000	Indiv
American Family Corp	$2,000	PAC
Mutual of Omaha	$2,000	PAC
Real Estate	**$10,050**	
National Assn of Realtors	$3,000	PAC
Rudin Management Co	$2,000	Indiv
Accountants	**$8,500**	
American Institute of CPA's	$5,000	PAC

Health $84,275

Health Professionals *$27,900*
    American Medical Assn* ....$5,500 PAC
    American Dental Assn ....$4,500 PAC
    American Assn Marriage/Family Therapy ....$3,000 PAC

Hospitals/Nursing Homes *$15,175*
    Hospital Hermanos Melendez ....$4,000 Indiv
    North General Hospital ....$2,875 Indiv
    Federation of American Health Systems ....$2,500 PAC

Pharmaceuticals/Health Products *$34,200*
    SmithKline Beecham ....$4,500 PAC
    Warner-Lambert ....$3,500 PAC
    Johnson & Johnson ....$3,250 PAC/Ind
    Pfizer Inc ....$2,300 PAC
    Bristol-Myers Squibb ....$2,100 PAC/Ind
    Merck & Co ....$2,000 PAC

Misc Health *$5,250*
    Managed Healthcare Systems Inc ....$4,000 Indiv

Lawyers & Lobbyists $47,414

Lawyers & Lobbyists *$47,414*
    Assn of Trial Lawyers of America ....$5,000 PAC
    Cassidy & Associates ....$4,489 Indiv
    Fox, Weinberg & Bennett ....$2,500 Indiv
    Black, Manafort et al ....$2,000 Indiv

Misc Business $39,075

Business Associations *$2,000*
    None over $2,000

Food & Beverage *$6,100*
    McDonald's Corp ....$2,000 PAC/Ind

Beer, Wine & Liquor *$7,000*
    None over $2,000

Retail Sales *$5,750*
    International Council of Shopping Centers ....$2,000 PAC

Misc Services *$3,050*
    None over $2,000

Business Services *$4,800*
    None over $2,000

Lodging/Tourism *$3,350*
    None over $2,000

Misc Manufacturing & Distributing *$4,550*
    None over $2,000

Transportation $19,900

Air Transport *$12,100*
    United Parcel Service ....$3,125 PAC
    United Airlines ....$3,000 PAC
    General Electric ....$2,850 PAC/Ind
    Federal Express Corp ....$2,000 PAC

Automotive *$3,800*
    Ford Motor Co ....$2,500 PAC

Labor

Labor $66,323

Building Trade Unions *$6,000*
    Laborers' Political League ....$3,000 PAC

Industrial Unions *$10,100*
    Intl Brotherhood of Electrical Workers ....$3,000 PAC
    United Auto Workers ....$3,000 PAC
    Machinists/Aerospace Workers Union ....$2,000 PAC

Transportation Unions *$22,100*
    Air Line Pilots Assn ....$10,000 PAC
    Teamsters Union ....$5,000 PAC
    International Longshoremen's Assn* ....$2,600 PAC
    United Transportation Union ....$2,500 PAC

Public Sector Unions *$26,000*
    American Fedn of St/Cnty/Munic Employees ......$7,000 PAC
    American Federation of Teachers ....$4,000 PAC
    National Assn Retired Federal Employees ....$4,000 PAC
    American Postal Workers Union ....$3,500 PAC
    National Assn of Letter Carriers ....$2,000 PAC
    National Rural Letter Carriers Assn ....$2,000 PAC

Misc Unions *$2,123*
    None over $2,000

Ideological/Single-Issue

Ideological/Single-Issue $6,750

Human Rights *$3,250*
    KidsPAC ....$2,500 PAC

Other & Unknown

Other $4,750

Retired *$2,150*
    None over $2,000

Unknown $30,200

    No Employer Listed or Found $11,025
    Employer Listed/Category Unknown $17,375
      None over $2,000

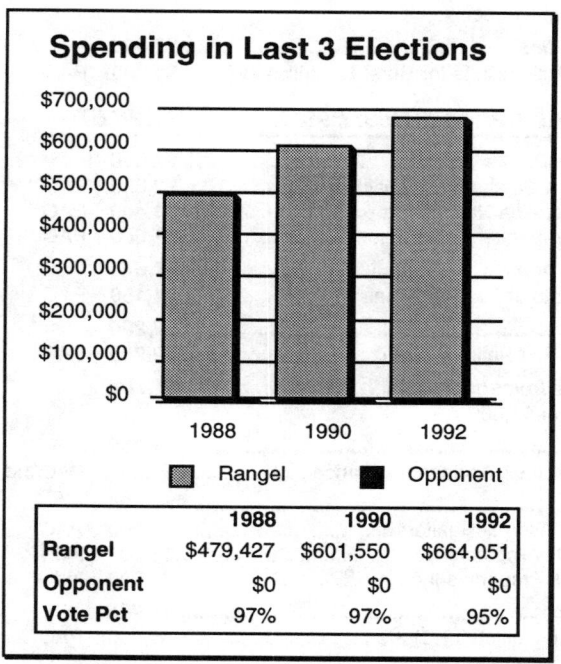

Spending in Last 3 Elections

	1988	1990	1992
Rangel	$479,427	$601,550	$664,051
Opponent	$0	$0	$0
Vote Pct	97%	97%	95%

---

* Contributions came from more than one affiliate or subsidiary.

Arthur Ravenel Jr., R-SC (1)

First elected: 1986
1991-92 Total Receipts: $282,816
1992 Year-end Cash: $0

1991-92 Committees & Subcommittees

Armed Services
Military Installations and Facilities; Military Personnel and Compensation

Merchant Marine and Fisheries
Fisheries and Wildlife Conservation and the Environment; Merchant Marine

Leading Contributors

Business

Agriculture	$11,500	
Crop Production & Basic Processing	**$2,050**	
None over $1,000		
Dairy	**$1,300**	
None over $1,000		
Food Processing & Sales	**$3,500**	
Winn-Dixie Stores	$3,000	PAC
Forestry & Forest Products	**$2,800**	
Westvaco Corp	$1,500	PAC

Communications/Electronics	$6,200	
Media/Entertainment	**$1,700**	
National Cable Television Assn	$1,000	PAC
Telephone Utilities	**$3,900**	
Southern Bell	$3,550	PAC

Construction	$8,650	
General Contractors	**$4,000**	
Associated General Contractors	$1,500	PAC
Sanders Brothers Construction Co	$1,000	Indiv
Home Builders	**$2,500**	
National Assn of Home Builders	$2,500	PAC
Building Materials & Equipment	**$1,100**	
None over $1,000		

Source of Funds in 1992 Election

Source	Total	Pct
■ PACs	$126,576	45%
▨ Indivs $200+	$57,900	20%
□ Indivs under $200	$56,436	20%
▧ Other	$41,904	15%
Candidate	$0	0%
Party	$0	0%

Source of PAC Dollars by Sector

Source	Total	Pct
■ Business	$103,071	85%
▨ Labor	$10,300	9%
□ Ideology/Single Issue	$7,525	6%

In-State vs. Out-of-State Contributions*

Source	Total	Pct
□ In-State	$52,550	91%
■ Out-of-state	$5,100	9%
No state listed	$250	

by large individual contributors ($200 & above)

Defense	$13,000	
Defense Aerospace	**$8,100**	
General Dynamics	$2,650	PAC/Ind
Lockheed Corp	$2,000	PAC
Defense Electronics	**$3,550**	
AT&T	$1,500	PAC
Misc Defense	**$1,350**	
Tenneco Inc	$1,000	PAC

Energy & Natural Resources	$4,700	
Oil & Gas	**$1,150**	
None over $1,000		
Electric Utilities	**$3,000**	
ACRE (Action Cmte for Rural Electrification)	$1,300	PAC

Finance, Insurance & Real Estate	$28,675	
Commercial Banks	**$6,650**	
Citizens & Southern National Bank	$2,350	PAC
South Carolina National Bank	$1,400	PAC
American Bankers Assn	$1,000	PAC
Savings & Loans	**$1,675**	
US League of Savings Assns*	$1,150	PAC
Credit Unions	**$2,200**	
Credit Union National Assn*	$2,200	PAC
Securities & Investment	**$1,700**	
None over $1,000		
Insurance	**$3,900**	
Colonial Life & Accident Insurance	$1,200	PAC/Ind
Real Estate	**$10,300**	
National Assn of Realtors	$6,000	PAC
Evans Development Co	$1,000	Indiv
Northfork Properties Inc	$1,000	Indiv
Accountants	**$1,900**	
American Institute of CPA's	$1,900	PAC

Contribution Totals by Sector

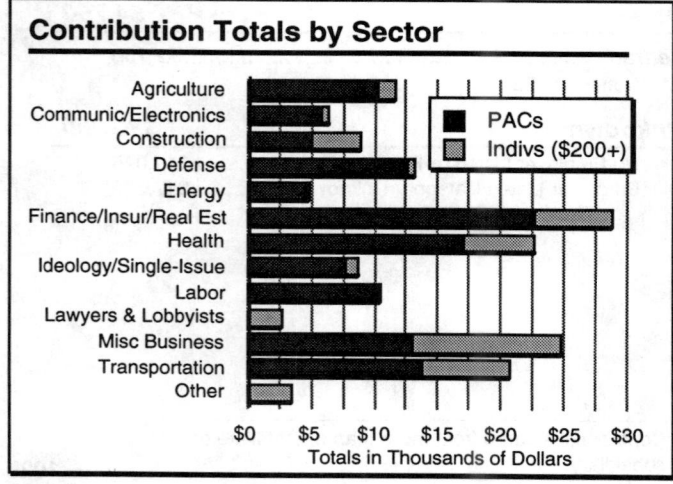

Agriculture
Communic/Electronics
Construction
Defense
Energy
Finance/Insur/Real Est
Health
Ideology/Single-Issue
Labor
Lawyers & Lobbyists
Misc Business
Transportation
Other

■ PACs
▨ Indivs ($200+)

$0 $5 $10 $15 $20 $25 $30
Totals in Thousands of Dollars

Health — $22,400

Health Professionals **$20,500**
    American Medical Assn .... $6,000   PAC
    American Chiropractic Assn .... $2,500   PAC
    American Dental Assn .... $2,500   PAC
    American Academy of Ophthalmology ..... $2,000   PAC
    American Podiatry Assn .... $1,000   PAC

Hospitals/Nursing Homes **$1,900**
    American Health Care Assn .... $1,200   PAC

Lawyers & Lobbyists — $2,550

Lawyers & Lobbyists **$2,550**
    Koenig, Ratner & Mott .... $1,000   Indiv

Misc Business — $24,496

Food & Beverage **$2,650**
    None over $1,000

Beer, Wine & Liquor **$3,300**
    National Beer Wholesalers Assn .... $2,550   PAC

Retail Sales **$1,500**
    Jack Eckerd Corp .... $1,000   PAC

Misc Services **$1,001**
    None over $1,000

Lodging/Tourism **$1,350**
    None over $1,000

Chemical & Related Manufacturing **$2,445**
    Dow Chemical .... $1,000   PAC

Steel Production **$6,000**
    MacAlloy Corp .... $6,000   Indiv

Textiles **$5,200**
    Milliken & Co .... $3,000   Indiv
    Chesterfield Yarn Mills .... $1,000   Indiv

Transportation — $21,550

Air Transport **$4,050**
    United Parcel Service .... $2,350   PAC
    Federal Express Corp .... $1,700   PAC

Automotive **$7,750**
    National Auto Dealers Assn .... $5,000   PAC
    Auto Dealers & Drivers for Free Trade .. $1,500   PAC

Sea Transport **$9,250**
    Metal Trades Inc .... $4,750   Indiv
    CSX Corp* .... $2,250   PAC
    Detyens Shipyards .... $1,000   Indiv

Labor

Labor — $10,300

Transportation Unions **$3,500**
    Marine Engineers Dist 2 Maritime Officers .... $2,500   PAC
    Seafarers International Union .... $1,000   PAC

Public Sector Unions **$6,800**
    National Assn Retired Federal Employees .... $3,000   PAC
    Federal Managers' Assn .... $1,400   PAC

Ideological/Single-Issue

Ideological/Single-Issue — $8,525

Pro-Israel **$6,000**
    National PAC .... $5,000   PAC

Gun Rights/Gun Control **$1,000**
    National Rifle Assn .... $1,000   PAC

Misc Issues **$1,525**
    League of Conservation Voters .... $1,000   PAC

Other & Unknown

Other — $3,350

Retired **$2,650**
    None over $1,000

Unknown — $18,900

    Homemakers/Non-income earners $2,200
    Employer Listed/Category Unknown $10,700
      Liollio Associates Inc .... $1,500   Indiv

Spending in Last 3 Elections

	1988	1990	1992
Ravenel	$118,702	$99,261	$561,793
Opponent	$82,035	$14,040	$53,380
Vote Pct	64%	66%	66%

* Contributions came from more than one affiliate or subsidiary.

John F. Reed, D-RI (2)

First elected: 1990

1991-92 Total Receipts: $748,808
1992 Year-end Cash: $6,837

1991-92 Committees & Subcommittees

Education and Labor
Elementary, Secondary and Vocational Education; Postsecondary Education

Judiciary
Administrative Law and Governmental Relations

Merchant Marine and Fisheries
Coast Guard and Navigation; Fisheries and Wildlife Conservation and the Environment

Leading Contributors

Business

Agriculture	$5,850	
Dairy	**$3,750**	
Associated Milk Producers	$2,000	PAC

Communications/Electronics	$18,400	
Printing & Publishing	**$2,000**	
None over $2,000		
Media/Entertainment	**$4,550**	
ASCAP	$2,000	PAC
Telephone Utilities	**$11,850**	
AT&T	$4,500	PAC
NYNEX Corp*	$2,350	PAC

Construction	$16,478	
General Contractors	**$2,000**	
Dimeo Construction Co	$2,000	Indiv
Home Builders	**$10,250**	
National Assn of Home Builders	$9,000	PAC
Special Trade Contractors	**$2,228**	
None over $2,000		

Defense	$23,050	
Defense Aerospace	**$20,850**	
Textron Inc	$17,350	PAC/Ind
General Dynamics	$3,500	PAC
Defense Electronics	**$2,200**	
Raytheon	$2,200	PAC

Contribution Totals by Sector

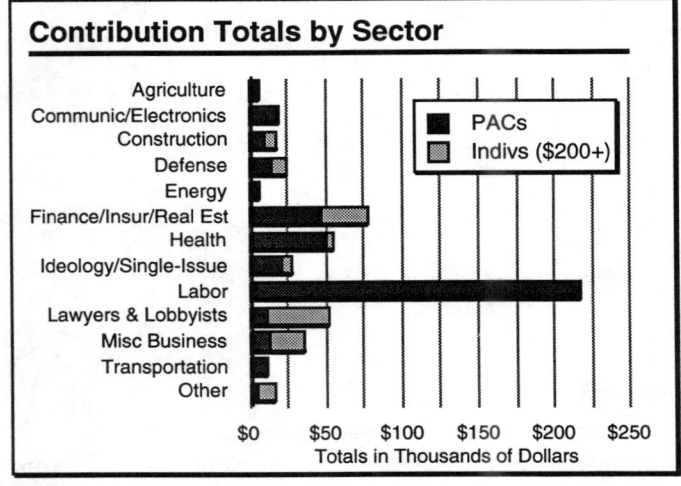

Totals in Thousands of Dollars

Source of Funds in 1992 Election

Source	Total	Pct
■ PACs	$415,690	55%
▨ Indivs $200+	$164,902	22%
☐ Indivs under $200	$158,730	21%
▨ Other	$20,485	3%
Candidate	$0	0%
Party	$13,915	2%

Source of PAC Dollars by Sector

Source	Total	Pct
■ Business	$178,534	43%
▨ Labor	$215,250	52%
☐ Ideology/Single Issue	$20,300	5%

In-State vs. Out-of-State Contributions*

Source	Total	Pct
☐ In-State	$118,977	72%
■ Out-of-state	$45,275	28%
No state listed	$0	

* by large individual contributors ($200 & above)

Energy & Natural Resources	$5,100	
None over $2,000		

Finance, Insurance & Real Estate	$76,014	
Commercial Banks	**$17,860**	
Fleet/Norstar	$5,250	Indiv
American Bankers Assn	$3,000	PAC
Norstar Bancorp	$2,900	PAC
Securities & Investment	**$10,600**	
Bear, Stearns & Co	$4,500	Indiv
Dean Witter	$4,000	PAC/Ind
Insurance	**$21,479**	
National Assn of Life Underwriters	$4,000	PAC
Independent Insurance Agents of America	$2,825	PAC
Prudential Insurance	$2,355	PAC
Connecticut Mutual Life Insurance	$2,000	PAC/Ind
Real Estate	**$16,475**	
National Assn of Realtors	$8,000	PAC
Accountants	**$8,350**	
American Institute of CPA's	$3,000	PAC
Ernst & Young	$2,200	PAC

Health	$53,145	
Health Professionals	**$45,945**	
American Medical Assn	$10,000	PAC
American Physical Therapy Assn	$5,650	PAC
American Optometric Assn	$4,550	PAC
American Dental Assn	$3,850	PAC
American College of Emergency Physicians	$3,000	PAC
American Podiatry Assn	$2,500	PAC
American Chiropractic Assn	$2,000	PAC
American Nurses Assn	$2,000	PAC
Cmte for Quality Orthopedic Health Care	$2,000	PAC
Hospitals/Nursing Homes	**$7,200**	
American Hospital Assn	$3,850	PAC

Lawyers & Lobbyists — $50,850

Lawyers & Lobbyists **$50,850**
Assn of Trial Lawyers of America	$10,000	PAC
Roberts, Carroll et al	$5,750	Indiv
Edwards & Angell	$3,450	Indiv
Williams & Jensen	$2,200	Indiv

Misc Business — $34,200

Food & Beverage **$3,500**
None over $2,000

Beer, Wine & Liquor **$11,700**
National Beer Wholesalers Assn	$4,400	PAC
McLaughlin & Moran Inc	$3,500	Indiv
Miller Brewing Co	$2,050	PAC

Business Services **$6,500**
Worrell, Passananti & Radoccia	$2,750	Indiv

Misc Manufacturing & Distributing **$7,100**
Hoechst Celanese Corp	$3,000	PAC

Transportation — $10,600

Automotive **$2,250**
National Auto Dealers Assn	$2,000	PAC

Sea Transport **$5,400**
None over $2,000

Labor

Labor — **$215,250**

Building Trade Unions **$38,300**
Carpenters & Joiners Union	$13,500	PAC
Laborers' Political League	$7,500	PAC
Sheet Metal Workers Union	$7,500	PAC
Plumbers/Pipefitters Union	$3,000	PAC
Ironworkers Union	$2,500	PAC
Bricklayers Union	$2,350	PAC

Industrial Unions **$55,800**
United Auto Workers	$12,500	PAC
Intl Brotherhood of Electrical Workers	$11,000	PAC
Machinists/Aerospace Workers Union	$10,000	PAC
United Steelworkers	$7,500	PAC
Boilermakers Union	$4,100	PAC
Communications Workers of America	$3,400	PAC
Electronic Machine Furniture Workers	$2,000	PAC

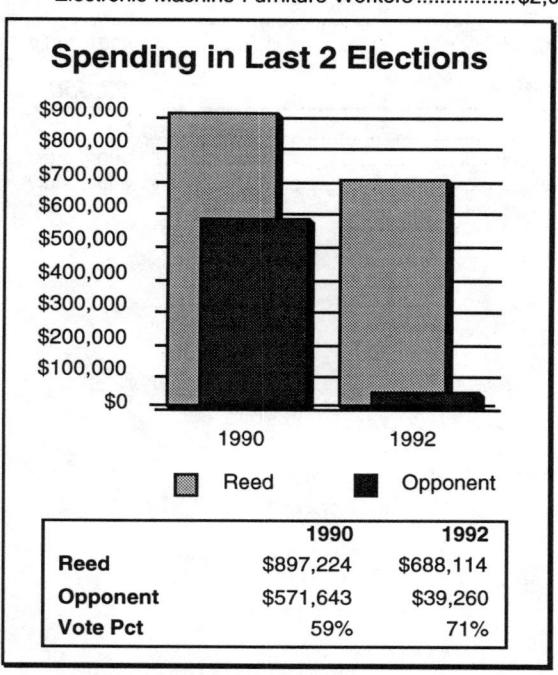

Spending in Last 2 Elections

	1990	1992
Reed	$897,224	$688,114
Opponent	$571,643	$39,260
Vote Pct	59%	71%

Reed / Opponent

Transportation Unions — $46,050

Seafarers International Union	$11,000	PAC
Teamsters Union	$10,000	PAC
Air Line Pilots Assn	$6,500	PAC
Marine Engineers Union*	$5,500	PAC
Amalgamated Transit Union	$4,500	PAC
Trans Comm International Union	$2,200	PAC
United Transportation Union	$2,000	PAC

Public Sector Unions **$60,050**
American Fedn of St/Cnty/Munic Employees	$14,700	PAC
American Federation of Teachers	$10,000	PAC
National Education Assn	$10,000	PAC
National Assn of Letter Carriers	$7,650	PAC
American Postal Workers Union	$6,000	PAC
National Assn Retired Federal Employees	$5,500	PAC
International Assn of Firefighters	$2,000	PAC
National Assn of Postmasters	$2,000	PAC

Misc Unions **$15,050**
Food & Commercial Workers Union	$9,000	PAC
Service Employees International Union	$3,000	PAC
AFL-CIO	$2,200	PAC

Ideological/Single-Issue

Ideological/Single-Issue — **$26,500**

Democratic/Liberal **$3,500**
National Cmte for an Effective Congress	$2,500	PAC

Pro-Israel **$8,650**
Hudson Valley PAC	$3,000	PAC

Human Rights **$4,850**
KidsPAC	$2,000	PAC

Misc Issues **$6,050**
National Cmte to Preserve Social Security	$3,700	PAC
Sierra Club	$2,000	PAC

Other & Unknown

Other — **$15,400**

Education **$9,100**
New York University	$3,500	Indiv

Other **$3,350**
National Assn of Social Workers	$2,050	PAC

Unknown — **$29,349**

Homemakers/Non-income earners	$6,400
Employer Listed/Category Unknown	$23,299
None over $2,000	

---

* Contributions came from more than one affiliate or subsidiary.

Ralph Regula, R-Ohio (16)

First elected: 1972

1991-92 Total Receipts: $168,665
1992 Year-end Cash: $12,012

1991-92 Committees & Subcommittees

Appropriations
Commerce, Justice, State, the Judiciary and Related Agencies;
District of Columbia; Interior and Related Agencies (Ranking
Republican)

Select Committee on Aging

Leading Contributors

Business

Agriculture — $4,706

Crop Production & Basic Processing	**$1,000**	
Okeelanta Corp	$1,000	Indiv
Agricultural Services/Products	**$1,000**	
Kurt O Laubiner Floral Supply	$1,000	Indiv
Food Processing & Sales	**$2,456**	
Superior Brand Meats	$1,000	Indiv

Communications/Electronics — $2,000

Printing & Publishing	**$2,000**	
Landoll Inc	$2,000	Indiv

Construction — $4,500

General Contractors	**$4,000**	
Dellagnese Companies	$2,000	Indiv
Highway Asphalt Co	$1,000	Indiv
Kokosing Construction Co	$1,000	Indiv

Energy & Natural Resources — $3,300

Oil & Gas	**$3,000**	
None over $1,000		

Finance, Insurance & Real Esta — $13,750

Real Estate	**$13,750**	
Forest City Enterprises Inc	$10,250	Indiv
Chapel Hill Properties	$2,000	Indiv
Westbrook Properties	$1,000	Indiv

Source of Funds in 1992 Election

Source	Total	Pct
PACs	$0	0%
Indivs $200+	$69,113	41%
Indivs under $200	$83,577	50%
Other	$15,975	9%
Candidate	$0	0%
Party	$3,182	2%

Source of PAC Dollars by Sector

No PAC contributions reported

Source	Total	Pct
Business	$0	0%
Labor	$0	0%
Ideology/Single Issue	$0	0%

In-State vs. Out-of-State Contributions*

Source	Total	Pct
In-State	$58,713	87%
Out-of-state	$8,400	13%
No state listed	$2,000	

* by large individual contributors ($200 & above)

Health — $4,400

Health Professionals	**$3,900**	
None over $1,000		

Lawyers & Lobbyists — $9,104

Lawyers & Lobbyists	**$9,104**	
Amer, Cunningham, Brennan & Co	$1,000	Indiv
Bergner, Boyette & Bockorny	$1,000	Indiv

Misc Business — $9,103

Food & Beverage	**$1,000**	
McDonald's Corp	$1,000	Indiv
Steel Production	**$6,300**	
Timken Co	$4,500	Indiv

Transportation — $3,550

Automotive	**$3,300**	
Brenlin Group	$2,000	Indiv
Goodyear	$1,000	Indiv

Contribution Totals by Sector

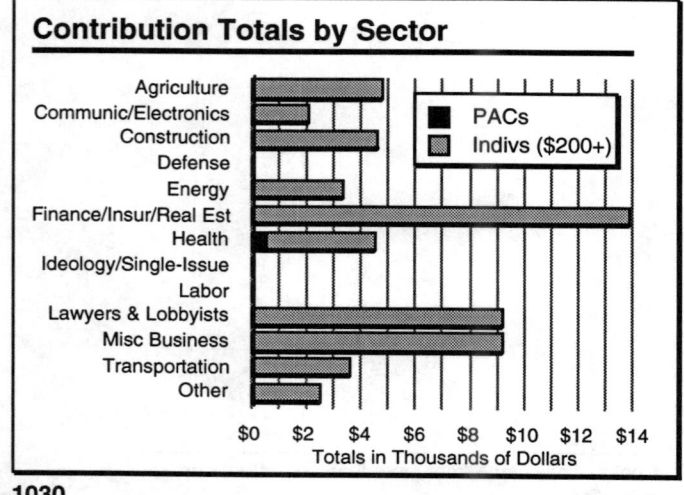

Totals in Thousands of Dollars

- PACs
- Indivs ($200+)

Categories: Agriculture, Communic/Electronics, Construction, Defense, Energy, Finance/Insur/Real Est, Health, Ideology/Single-Issue, Labor, Lawyers & Lobbyists, Misc Business, Transportation, Other

Other & Unknown

Other	$2,500

Retired...$2,000	
None over $1,000	

Unknown	$12,700

Homemakers/Non-income earners $2,150	
Employer Listed/Category Unknown $10,550	
Spagnuolo & Associates $2,000	Indiv
Carderon Automation $1,000	Indiv
Malcolm Maconachy $1,000	Indiv
McCoy Associates $1,000	Indiv
National Latex $1,000	Indiv
Roadway Services Inc $1,000	Indiv
Ross & Robertson $1,000	Indiv

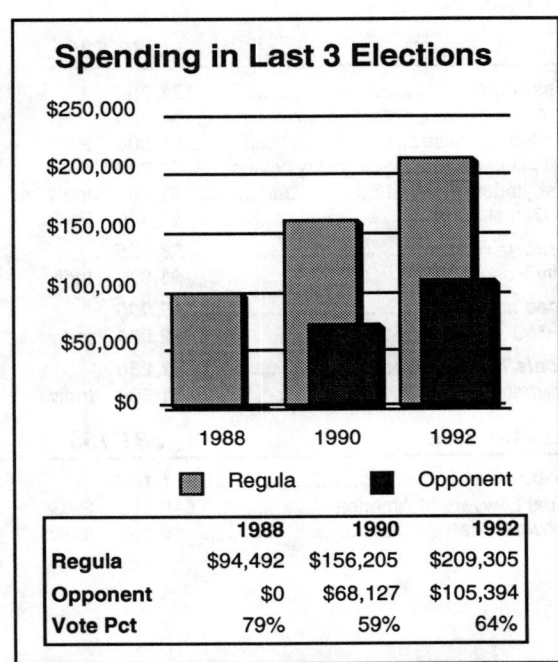

Spending in Last 3 Elections

	1988	1990	1992
Regula	$94,492	$156,205	$209,305
Opponent	$0	$68,127	$105,394
Vote Pct	79%	59%	64%

* Contributions came from more than one affiliate or subsidiary.

Mel Reynolds, D-Ill (2)

1993-94 Committees & Subcommittees

Ways and Means
Human Resources; Social Security

First elected: 1992
1991-92 Total Receipts: $532,031
1992 Year-end Cash: $1,032

Leading Contributors

Business

Agriculture		$7,450
Tobacco	**$3,500**	
Philip Morris.....................................	$2,000	PAC
RJR Nabisco	$1,500	PAC
Food Processing & Sales	**$2,950**	
General Mills	$1,500	PAC

Communications/Electronics		$5,950
Printing & Publishing	**$2,000**	
Commerce Clearing House	$2,000	Indiv
Telephone Utilities	**$3,750**	
AT&T	$1,500	PAC/Ind

Construction		$8,500
Home Builders	**$3,500**	
National Assn of Home Builders	$3,500	PAC
Construction Services	**$3,000**	
Globetrotter Engineering Corp	$2,000	Indiv
Building Materials & Equipment	**$2,000**	
Edward C Levy Co	$2,000	Indiv

Energy & Natural Resources		$2,000
None over $1,500		

Finance, Insurance & Real Estate		$51,250
Commercial Banks	**$11,600**	
Continental Illinois Corp	$3,000	PAC
Credit Unions	**$2,000**	
Credit Union National Assn	$2,000	PAC

Source of Funds in 1992 Election

Source	Total	Pct
■ PACs	$195,772	37%
▨ Indivs $200+	$178,260	34%
☐ Indivs under $200	$144,898	27%
▨ Other	$13,101	2%
Candidate	$10,000	2%
Party	$2,500	0%

Source of PAC Dollars by Sector

Source	Total	Pct
■ Business	$100,350	40%
▨ Labor	$72,100	29%
☐ Ideology/Single Issue	$77,420	31%

In-State vs. Out-of-State Contributions*

Source	Total	Pct
☐ In-State	$109,450	64%
■ Out-of-state	$62,810	36%
No state listed	$6,000	

* by large individual contributors ($200 & above)

Securities & Investment	....	$10,100	
Chicago Mercantile Exchange	....	$5,000	PAC/Ind
Ariel Capital Management	....	$1,900	Indiv
Insurance	....	**$6,250**	
National Assn of Life Underwriters	....	$3,000	PAC
New York Life	....	$1,500	PAC
Real Estate	....	**$17,650**	
National Assn of Realtors	....	$10,000	PAC
Accountants	....	**$2,000**	
American Institute of CPA's	....	$1,500	PAC
Misc Finance	....	**$1,650**	
None over $1,500			

Health — $30,525

Health Professionals	....	**$21,700**	
American Academy of Ophthalmology	....	$6,000	PAC
American Medical Assn	....	$5,000	PAC
American College of Emergency Physicians	....	$2,000	PAC
Rush Presbyterian Hospital	....	$1,750	Indiv
American Dental Assn	....	$1,500	PAC
Hospitals/Nursing Homes	....	**$2,025**	
Boston City Hospital	....	$1,825	Indiv
Health Services	....	**$3,000**	
Chicago HMO	....	$2,000	Indiv
Pharmaceuticals/Health Products	....	**$3,250**	
Baxter International Inc	....	$1,500	Indiv

Lawyers & Lobbyists — $31,150

Lawyers & Lobbyists	....	**$31,150**	
Assn of Trial Lawyers of America	....	$10,000	PAC
Mayer, Brown & Platt	....	$6,050	Indiv

Contribution Totals by Sector

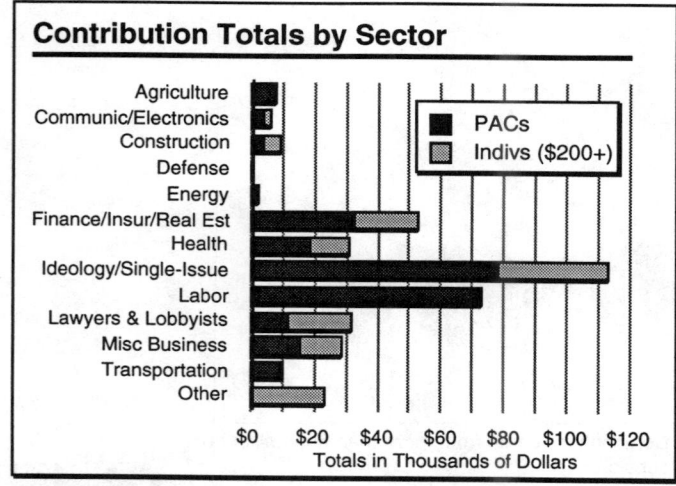

Legend: ■ PACs ▨ Indivs ($200+)

Agriculture
Communic/Electronics
Construction
Defense
Energy
Finance/Insur/Real Est
Health
Ideology/Single-Issue
Labor
Lawyers & Lobbyists
Misc Business
Transportation
Other

$0 $20 $40 $60 $80 $100 $120
Totals in Thousands of Dollars

Misc Business $28,100

Food & Beverage **$4,250**
    National Restaurant Assn .... $2,000   PAC

Retail Sales **$4,950**
    Montgomery Ward .... $1,500   PAC
    Walgreen Co .... $1,500   PAC

Misc Services **$2,200**
    American Assn of Equipment Lessors .... $2,000   PAC

Business Services **$2,750**
    None over $1,500

Recreation/Live Entertainment **$2,000**
    None over $1,500

Chemical & Related Manufacturing **$2,000**
    None over $1,500

Misc Manufacturing & Distributing **$6,650**
    Stone Container Corp .... $2,500   PAC
    Best Foam Fabricators .... $1,500   PAC/Ind

Transportation $9,500

Air Transport **$3,000**
    Federal Express Corp .... $2,500   PAC

Automotive **$6,000**
    Ford Motor Co .... $1,500   PAC
    National Auto Dealers Assn .... $1,500   PAC

Labor

Labor $72,100

Building Trade Unions **$9,500**
    Laborers' Political League .... $3,000   PAC
    Carpenters & Joiners Union .... $2,500   PAC
    Plumbers/Pipefitters Union .... $2,500   PAC

Industrial Unions **$10,000**
    Machinists/Aerospace Workers Union .... $5,000   PAC
    Communications Workers of America .... $2,000   PAC
    Intl Brotherhood of Electrical Workers .... $1,500   PAC

Transportation Unions **$14,500**
    Teamsters Union .... $5,000   PAC
    Air Line Pilots Assn .... $2,500   PAC
    International Longshoremen's Assn .... $2,500   PAC
    Amalgamated Transit Union .... $1,500   PAC
    United Transportation Union .... $1,500   PAC

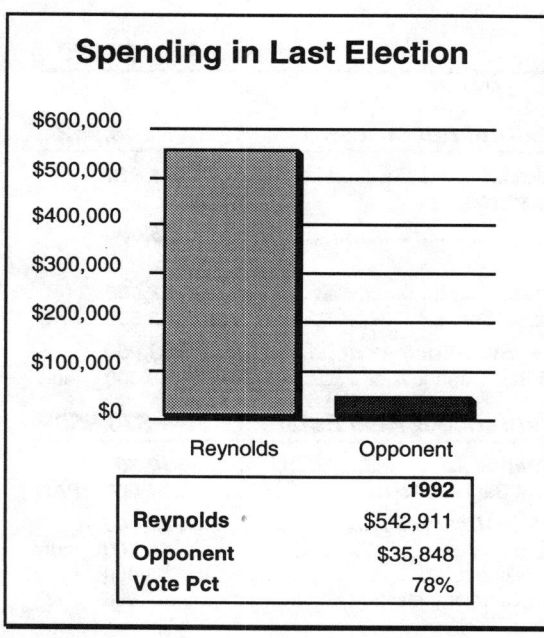

Spending in Last Election

	1992
Reynolds	$542,911
Opponent	$35,848
Vote Pct	78%

Public Sector Unions $30,600

    American Fedn of St/Cnty/Munic Employees ...... $8,500   PAC
    American Federation of Teachers .... $5,000   PAC
    National Assn of Letter Carriers .... $5,000   PAC
    National Education Assn .... $5,000   PAC
    American Postal Workers Union .... $2,000   PAC
    National Assn Retired Federal Employees .... $2,000   PAC

Misc Unions **$7,500**
    AFL-CIO .... $4,000   PAC
    Food & Commercial Workers Union .... $2,500   PAC

Ideological/Single-Issue

Ideological/Single-Issue $112,670

Democratic/Liberal **$3,000**
    None over $1,500

Leadership PACs **$12,500**
    America's Leaders' Fund (Dan Rostenkowski) .... $6,000   PAC
    House Leadership Fund (Tom Foley) .... $2,500   PAC

Pro-Israel **$80,671**
    Citizens Organized PAC .... $5,000   PAC
    City PAC .... $5,000   PAC
    National PAC .... $5,000   PAC
    Delaware Valley PAC .... $3,000   PAC
    Women's Pro-Israel National PAC .... $3,000   PAC
    Florida Congressional Cmte .... $2,500   PAC
    Heartland PAC .... $2,500   PAC
    Joint Action Cmte for Political Affairs .... $2,500   PAC
    San Franciscans for Good Government .... $2,500   PAC
    Americans for Good Government Inc .... $2,000   PAC
    Hudson Valley PAC .... $1,750   PAC
    ActionPAC .... $1,571   PAC
    Bi-County PAC .... $1,500   PAC
    National Action Committee .... $1,500   PAC

Pro-Choice **$1,500**
    None over $1,500

Human Rights **$8,999**
    Human Rights Campaign Fund .... $4,999   PAC
    KidsPAC .... $2,000   PAC

Misc Issues **$6,000**
    National Cmte to Preserve Social Security .... $6,000   PAC

Other & Unknown

Other $22,500

Civil Servants/Public Officials **$6,750**
    City of Chicago .... $3,600   Indiv

Education **$12,550**
    None over $1,500

Retired **$2,450**
    None over $1,500

Unknown $46,435

    Homemakers/Non-income earners $2,800
    No Employer Listed or Found $29,035
    Generic Occupation/Category Unknown $2,000
    Employer Listed/Category Unknown $12,600
        Ryan-Bernstein .... $2,000   Indiv

Independent expenditures supporting Reynolds
    National Cmte to Preserve Social Security $6,000

Bill Richardson, D-NM (3)

First elected: 1982

1991-92 Total Receipts: $680,154
1992 Year-end Cash: $409,373

1991-92 Committees & Subcommittees

Energy and Commerce
Health and the Environment; Telecommunications and Finance;
Transportation and Hazardous Materials

Interior and Insular Affairs
Energy and the Environment; National Parks and Public Lands

Select Committee on Aging

Select Committee on Intelligence

Leading Contributors

Business

Agriculture	$30,550

Crop Production & Basic Processing $3,800
   None over $2,500

Tobacco $7,500
   Philip Morris ....$2,500 PAC

Dairy $4,000
   Associated Milk Producers .... $2,500 PAC

Livestock $5,250
   None over $2,500

Agricultural Services/Products $4,250
   None over $2,500

Food Processing & Sales $4,500
   None over $2,500

Communications/Electronics	$75,500

Printing & Publishing $2,500
   None over $2,500

Media/Entertainment $36,250
   National Cable Television Assn .... $9,500 PAC
   Comcast Corp .... $5,000 PAC
   Viacom International .... $5,000 PAC
   Home Shopping Network Inc .... $2,500 PAC

Source of Funds in 1992 Election

Source	Total	Pct
■ PACs	$387,551	56%
▨ Indivs $200+	$142,278	20%
☐ Indivs under $200	$93,727	13%
▨ Other	$73,182	10%
Candidate	$0	0%
Party	$18,759	3%

Source of PAC Dollars by Sector

Source	Total	Pct
■ Business	$326,889	82%
▨ Labor	$50,199	13%
☐ Ideology/Single Issue	$20,450	5%

In-State vs. Out-of-State Contributions*

Source	Total	Pct
☐ In-State	$69,178	49%
■ Out-of-state	$72,650	51%
No state listed	$0	

* by large individual contributors ($200 & above)

Telephone Utilities $31,250
   AT&T .... $4,000 PAC
   US West Inc .... $4,000 PAC/Ind
   Ameritech Corp .... $3,500 PAC
   BellSouth Corp* .... $3,500 PAC
   GTE Corp .... $3,000 PAC
   Pacific Telesis Group .... $2,500 PAC

Telecom Services & Equipment $3,500
   None over $2,500

Construction	$9,250

General Contractors $4,500
   None over $2,500

Building Materials & Equipment $2,500
   None over $2,500

Defense	$2,850
   None over $2,500

Energy & Natural Resources	$48,562

Oil & Gas $31,812
   None over $2,500

Mining $5,000
   None over $2,500

Electric Utilities $7,000
   Texas Utilities Co* .... $2,500 PAC

Environmental Svcs/Equipment $3,000
   Advanced Sciences Inc .... $3,000 Indiv

Finance, Insurance & Real Estate	$78,950

Commercial Banks $10,300
   Independent Bankers Assn .... $4,000 PAC

Securities & Investment $22,500
   Weiss, Peck & Greer .... $3,500 Indiv
   Venture Advisers LP .... $3,000 Indiv
   Investment Company Institute .... $2,500 PAC

Contribution Totals by Sector

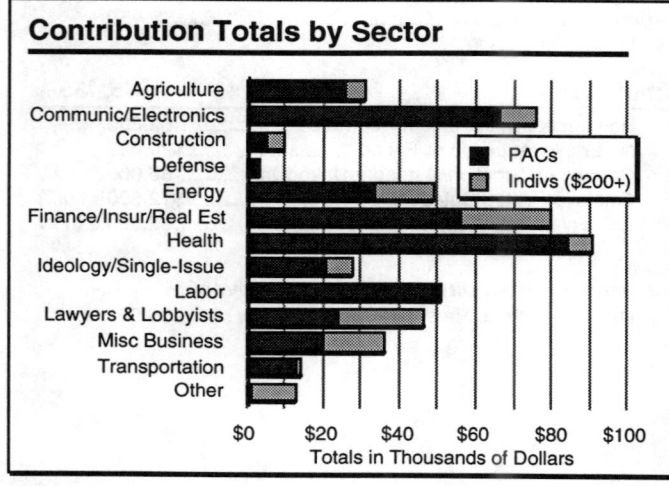

Categories (top to bottom): Agriculture, Communic/Electronics, Construction, Defense, Energy, Finance/Insur/Real Est, Health, Ideology/Single-Issue, Labor, Lawyers & Lobbyists, Misc Business, Transportation, Other

Legend: ■ PACs, ▨ Indivs ($200+)

Scale: $0, $20, $40, $60, $80, $100
Totals in Thousands of Dollars

Insurance $18,350
    National Assn of Life Underwriters .... $5,000 PAC
    American Family Corp .... $3,000 PAC

Real Estate $15,300
    National Assn of Realtors .... $6,000 PAC

Accountants $9,750
    American Institute of CPA's .... $7,500 PAC

Misc Finance $2,500
    None over $2,500

Health $90,260

Health Professionals $53,482
    American Physical Therapy Assn .... $9,000 PAC
    American Medical Assn* .... $8,982 PAC
    American Podiatry Assn .... $5,000 PAC
    American Dental Assn .... $4,000 PAC
    American College of Emergency Physicians .... $3,450 PAC
    American Chiropractic Assn .... $2,500 PAC

Hospitals/Nursing Homes $11,350
    American Health Care Assn .... $5,000 PAC
    American Hospital Assn .... $3,650 PAC

Health Services $6,500
    Family Health Program Inc .... $5,000 PAC

Pharmaceuticals/Health Products $16,050
    None over $2,500

Misc Health $2,878
    None over $2,500

Lawyers & Lobbyists $45,587

Lawyers & Lobbyists $45,587
    Assn of Trial Lawyers of America .... $7,500 PAC
    Akin, Gump et al .... $2,850 PAC/Ind

Misc Business $35,408

Food & Beverage $4,300
    None over $2,500

Beer, Wine & Liquor $3,500
    None over $2,500

Retail Sales $6,007
    None over $2,500

Business Services $8,900
    None over $2,500

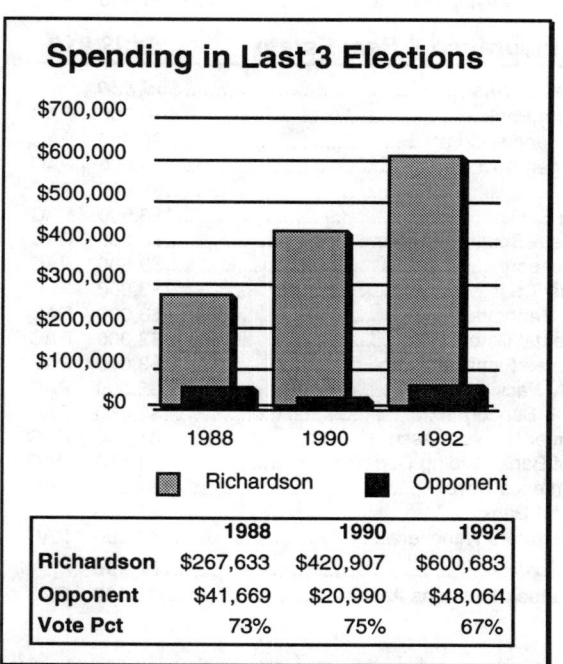

Spending in Last 3 Elections

	1988	1990	1992
Richardson	$267,633	$420,907	$600,683
Opponent	$41,669	$20,990	$48,064
Vote Pct	73%	75%	67%

Lodging/Tourism $4,800
    None over $2,500

Misc Manufacturing & Distributing $4,400
    None over $2,500

Transportation $14,000

Air Transport $4,500
    None over $2,500

Automotive $2,500
    None over $2,500

Railroads $6,000
    None over $2,500

Labor

Labor $50,199

Building Trade Unions $6,750
    Laborers' Political League .... $3,500 PAC

Industrial Unions $5,500
    None over $2,500

Transportation Unions $14,650
    Teamsters Union .... $5,000 PAC
    United Transportation Union .... $4,000 PAC

Public Sector Unions $18,800
    American Fedn of St/Cnty/Munic Employees ...... $5,000 PAC
    National Education Assn .... $5,000 PAC
    National Assn Retired Federal Employees .... $3,000 PAC

Misc Unions $4,499
    Food & Commercial Workers Union .... $3,499 PAC

Ideological/Single-Issue

Ideological/Single-Issue $27,200

Democratic/Liberal $4,000
    National Cmte for an Effective Congress .... $2,500 PAC

Pro-Israel $7,500
    None over $2,500

Gun Rights/Gun Control $3,000
    National Rifle Assn .... $2,500 PAC

Human Rights $3,500
    None over $2,500

Misc Issues $3,250
    None over $2,500

Other & Unknown

Other $12,650

Retired $9,200
    None over $2,500

Unknown $19,150

    Homemakers/Non-income earners $3,000
    Employer Listed/Category Unknown $15,200
        None over $2,500

* Contributions came from more than one affiliate or subsidiary.

1035

Tom Ridge, R-Pa (21)

First elected: 1982

1991-92 Total Receipts: $530,372
1992 Year-end Cash: $51,230

1991-92 Committees & Subcommittees

Banking, Finance and Urban Affairs
Economic Stabilization (Ranking Republican); Financial Institutions Supervision, Regulation and Insurance; Housing and Community Development

Post Office and Civil Service
Census and Population (Ranking Republican); Civil Service

Veterans' Affairs
Education, Training and Employment; Hospitals and Health Care

Leading Contributors

Business

Agriculture $19,550

Crop Production & Basic Processing	$4,350	
National Grape Co-operative Assn	$2,500	PAC
Tobacco	$2,000	
None over $1,500		
Dairy	$7,700	
Associated Milk Producers	$4,000	PAC
Milk Marketing Inc	$2,000	PAC
Agricultural Services/Products	$1,900	
Farm Credit Council	$1,500	PAC
Forestry & Forest Products	$2,500	
International Paper Co	$2,500	PAC/Ind

Communications/Electronics $13,700

Telephone Utilities	$9,000	
AT&T	$4,500	PAC
GTE Corp	$2,500	PAC
Electronics Mfg & Services	$3,000	
Westinghouse Electric	$3,000	PAC

Construction $20,050

General Contractors	$2,900	
Associated General Contractors	$1,500	PAC
Home Builders	$9,500	
National Assn of Home Builders	$7,500	PAC
Building Materials & Equipment	$7,400	
Wheatland Tube Co	$1,900	Indiv
Erie Sand & Gravel	$1,500	Indiv

Source of Funds in 1992 Election

Source	Total	Pct
■ PACs	$304,927	57%
▨ Indivs $200+	$115,425	22%
☐ Indivs under $200	$89,323	17%
▧ Other	$20,697	4%
Candidate	$0	0%
Party	$2,067	0%

Source of PAC Dollars by Sector

Source	Total	Pct
■ Business	$252,745	84%
▨ Labor	$43,200	14%
☐ Ideology/Single Issue	$5,000	2%

In-State vs. Out-of-State Contributions*

Source	Total	Pct
☐ In-State	$103,225	89%
■ Out-of-state	$12,200	11%
No state listed	$0	

* by large individual contributors ($200 & above)

Energy & Natural Resources $25,265

Oil & Gas	$14,965	
National Fuel Gas Corp	$2,800	PAC
Consolidated Natural Gas*	$2,165	PAC
USX Corp	$2,050	PAC
Columbia Gas System*	$2,000	PAC
Mining	$1,700	
None over $1,500		
Electric Utilities	$7,100	
General Public Utilities	$2,500	PAC
ACRE (Action Cmte for Rural Electrification)	$1,500	PAC
Waste Management	$1,500	
Chambers Development Co	$1,500	PAC

Finance, Insurance & Real Estate $133,910

Commercial Banks	$69,560	
American Bankers Assn	$10,000	PAC
PNC Financial Corp*	$6,860	PAC
JP Morgan & Co	$6,500	PAC
Citicorp	$5,000	PAC
Barnett Banks Inc	$3,500	PAC
Citizens & Southern National Bank	$3,500	PAC
PennBancorp	$3,500	PAC
Bankers Trust	$3,000	PAC
Chase Manhattan	$3,000	PAC
Continental Illinois Corp	$3,000	PAC
Corestates Financial Corp	$3,000	PAC
Security Pacific Corp	$2,500	PAC
Meridian Bancorp	$2,250	PAC
Consumer Bankers Assn	$1,750	PAC
Assn of Bank Holding Companies	$1,500	PAC
BankAmerica Corp	$1,500	PAC
Chemical Bank	$1,500	PAC
Manufacturers Hanover	$1,500	PAC
Savings & Loans	$4,750	
US League of Savings Assns*	$3,000	PAC

Contribution Totals by Sector

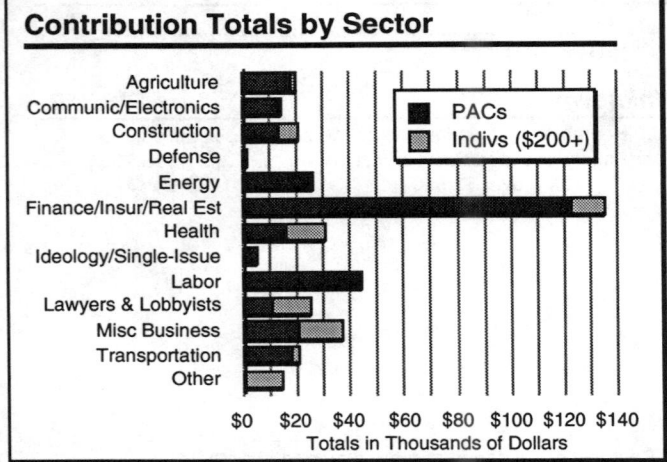

Agriculture
Communic/Electronics
Construction
Defense
Energy
Finance/Insur/Real Est
Health
Ideology/Single-Issue
Labor
Lawyers & Lobbyists
Misc Business
Transportation
Other

■ PACs
▨ Indivs ($200+)

$0 $20 $40 $60 $80 $100 $120 $140
Totals in Thousands of Dollars

Credit Unions **$3,400**
    Credit Union National Assn* ....$2,400   PAC

Finance/Credit Companies **$4,600**
    Household International Inc ....$2,000   PAC

Securities & Investment....................... **$16,500**
    Merrill Lynch ....$2,850   PAC/Ind
    American Express* ....$2,500   PAC
    Dean Witter ....$2,000   PAC
    Prudential Securities ....$2,000   PAC

Insurance **$13,000**
    Hubbard, Bert et al ....$1,750   Indiv
    Erie Insurance ....$1,500   Indiv
    Harleysville Insurance ....$1,500   PAC
    National Assn of Independent Insurers ....$1,500   PAC

Real Estate **$11,400**
    National Assn of Realtors ....$8,000   PAC
    American Land Title Assn ....$2,000   PAC

Accountants **$9,100**
    American Institute of CPA's ....$7,500   PAC

Misc Finance **$1,600**
    None over $1,500

Health $30,650

Health Professionals **$25,800**
    American Medical Assn* ....$9,850   PAC
    American Dental Assn ....$2,000   PAC

Hospitals/Nursing Homes **$2,000**
    None over $1,500

Pharmaceuticals/Health Products **$1,950**
    None over $1,500

Lawyers & Lobbyists $24,825

Lawyers & Lobbyists............................. **$24,825**
    Assn of Trial Lawyers of America ....$5,500   PAC
    Kirkpatrick & Lockhart ....$2,000   PAC/Ind

Misc Business $36,500

Food & Beverage **$2,700**
    None over $1,500

Retail Sales... **$11,650**
    International Council of Shopping Centers ....$7,000   PAC
    JC Penney Co ....$2,000   PAC

Spending in Last 3 Elections

	1988	1990	1992
Ridge	$370,619	$361,712	$705,861
Opponent	$0	$0	$15,800
Vote Pct	79%	100%	68%

Misc Services **$1,900**
    None over $1,500

Business Services **$4,400**
    Brabender Cox ....$2,000   Indiv

Lodging/Tourism **$1,600**
    None over $1,500

Chemical & Related Manufacturing **$3,450**
    None over $1,500

Steel Production **$4,750**
    Allegheny Ludlum Corp ....$1,500   PAC

Misc Manufacturing & Distributing **$4,300**
    None over $1,500

Transportation $19,970

Air Transport.. **$2,320**
    None over $1,500

Automotive **$13,550**
    National Auto Dealers Assn ....$10,000   PAC
    Ford Motor Co ....$1,500   PAC

Railroads **$3,000**
    None over $1,500

Labor

Labor $43,200

Building Trade Unions **$7,250**
    Ironworkers Union ....$2,000   PAC
    Laborers' Political League ....$2,000   PAC
    AFL-CIO Bldg/Construction Trades Dept ....$1,500   PAC
    Plumbers/Pipefitters Union* ....$1,500   PAC

Industrial Unions **$4,000**
    Intl Brotherhood of Electrical Workers ....$2,000   PAC

Transportation Unions **$17,250**
    Marine Engineers Dist 2 Maritime Officers ....$8,250   PAC
    Air Line Pilots Assn ....$6,000   PAC
    Transport Workers Union ....$1,500   PAC

Public Sector Unions **$14,700**
    National Assn of Letter Carriers ....$7,000   PAC
    American Postal Workers Union ....$2,000   PAC

Ideological/Single-Issue

Ideological/Single-Issue $6,250

Foreign & Defense Policy **$1,500**
    Veterans of Foreign Wars ....$1,500   PAC

Gun Rights/Gun Control **$3,000**
    National Rifle Assn ....$3,000   PAC

Other & Unknown

Other $12,250

Retired **$11,450**
    None over $1,500

Unknown $29,000

    No Employer Listed or Found $3,600
    Employer Listed/Category Unknown $25,150
        Dad's Products Co ....$1,850   Indiv

---

* Contributions came from more than one affiliate or
subsidiary.

Pat Roberts, R-Kan (1)

First elected: 1980

1991-92 Total Receipts: $313,020
1992 Year-end Cash: $110,891

1991-92 Committees & Subcommittees

Administration
Libraries and Memorials; Personnel and Police (Ranking Republican)

Agriculture
Department Operations, Research and Foreign Agriculture (Ranking Republican); Livestock, Dairy and Poultry; Wheat, Soybeans and Feed Grains

Joint Committee on the Library

Joint Committee on Printing

Leading Contributors

Business

Agriculture	$88,525	
Crop Production & Basic Processing	**$17,425**	
American Sugarbeet Growers Assn	$1,500	PAC
National Cotton Council	$1,500	PAC
National Assn of Wheat Growers	$1,300	PAC
Southern Minn Beet Sugar Co-op	$1,125	PAC
National Sunflower Assn	$1,050	PAC
AG Processing Inc	$1,000	PAC
American Cotton Shippers Assn	$1,000	PAC
American Crystal Sugar Corp	$1,000	PAC
American Sugar Cane League	$1,000	PAC
Cargill Inc	$1,000	PAC
Florida Sugar Cane League	$1,000	PAC
Sunkist Growers	$1,000	PAC
Tobacco	**$3,000**	
Philip Morris	$1,500	PAC
RJR Nabisco	$1,000	PAC
Dairy	**$4,000**	
Milk Industry Foundation	$2,000	PAC
Associated Milk Producers	$1,000	PAC
Schwan's Sales Enterprises	$1,000	Indiv
Poultry & Eggs	**$3,500**	
National Broiler Council	$1,500	PAC
National Turkey Federation	$1,000	PAC
United Egg Assn	$1,000	PAC

Source of Funds in 1992 Election

Source	Total	Pct
PACs	$185,085	59%
Indivs $200+	$38,337	12%
Indivs under $200	$43,718	14%
Other	$45,880	15%
Candidate	$0	0%
Party	$31	0%

Source of PAC Dollars by Sector

Source	Total	Pct
Business	$181,975	98%
Labor	$100	0%
Ideology/Single Issue	$3,500	2%

In-State vs. Out-of-State Contributions*

Source	Total	Pct
In-State	$24,000	63%
Out-of-state	$14,337	37%
No state listed	$0	

* by large individual contributors ($200 & above)

Livestock	$10,250	
National Cattlemen's Assn*	$4,000	PAC
Knight Feeders	$1,000	Indiv
National Pork Producers Council	$1,000	PAC
Pratt Feeders Inc	$1,000	Indiv
Ward Feed Yard	$1,000	Indiv
Western Star Ag Resources	$1,000	Indiv
Agricultural Services/Products	**$27,500**	
Farm Credit Council	$3,400	PAC
American Assn of Crop Insurers	$3,000	PAC
Archer-Daniels-Midland Corp	$2,000	PAC
Dow Chemical	$2,000	PAC
National Agricultural Chemicals Assn	$2,000	PAC/Ind
American Assn of Nurserymen	$1,500	PAC
American Veterinary Medical Assn	$1,500	PAC
Farmland Industries	$1,500	PAC
Monsanto Co	$1,500	PAC
National Council of Farmer Co-ops	$1,000	PAC
Food Processing & Sales	**$21,350**	
ConAgra Inc	$7,000	PAC
American Meat Institute	$1,500	PAC
Beef Products Inc	$1,500	Indiv
Pepsico Inc	$1,500	PAC
Food Marketing Institute	$1,000	PAC
IBP Inc	$1,000	PAC
Independent Bakers Assn	$1,000	PAC
Kellogg Co	$1,000	PAC
Nabisco Brands Inc	$1,000	PAC
National Food Processors Assn	$1,000	PAC
Misc Agriculture	**$1,000**	
None over $1,000		

Communications/Electronics	$7,600	
Telephone Utilities	**$6,100**	
AT&T	$2,500	PAC
Southwestern Bell	$1,100	PAC
Moundridge Telephone Co	$1,000	Indiv
United Telecommunications	$1,000	PAC

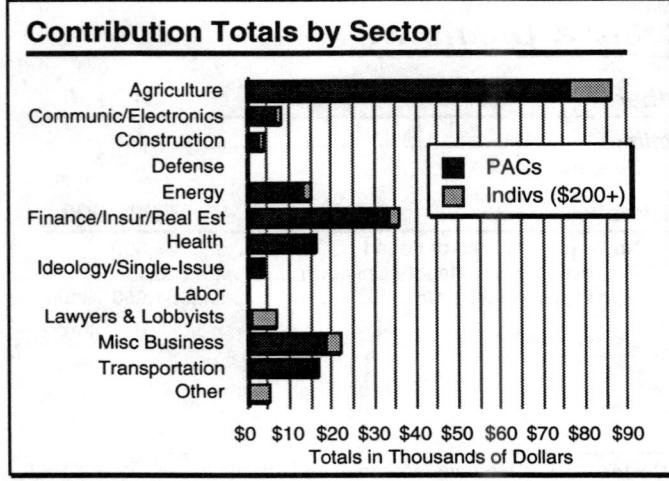

Contribution Totals by Sector

Agriculture
Communic/Electronics
Construction
Defense
Energy
Finance/Insur/Real Est
Health
Ideology/Single-Issue
Labor
Lawyers & Lobbyists
Misc Business
Transportation
Other

■ PACs
▦ Indivs ($200+)

$0 $10 $20 $30 $40 $50 $60 $70 $80 $90
Totals in Thousands of Dollars

Electronics Mfg & Services $1,500
    North American Philips Corp .... $1,500 PAC

Construction $3,500

General Contractors $3,000
    Associated General Contractors .... $1,000 PAC
    Morton Building Inc .... $1,000 PAC

Energy & Natural Resources $14,850

Oil & Gas $10,550
    KPL Gas Service .... $4,000 PAC
    Coastal Corp .... $1,000 PAC
    Kansas Natural Gas .... $1,000 Indiv
    Koch Industries .... $1,000 PAC
Mining $1,300
    Phelps Dodge Corp .... $1,300 PAC
Electric Utilities $2,500
    ACRE (Action Cmte for Rural Electrification) .... $1,000 PAC

Finance, Insurance & Real Estate $35,300

Commercial Banks $14,500
    American Bankers Assn .... $10,000 PAC
    Independent Bankers Assn .... $1,500 PAC
    First National Bank .... $1,250 Indiv
Savings & Loans $1,000
    US League of Savings Assns* .... $1,000 PAC
Securities & Investment $11,000
    Chicago Mercantile Exchange .... $6,000 PAC
    Chicago Board of Trade .... $5,000 PAC
Insurance $2,300
    National Assn of Independent Insurers .... $1,000 PAC
Real Estate $5,500
    National Assn of Realtors .... $5,500 PAC

Health $16,000

Health Professionals $10,500
    American Medical Assn* .... $10,000 PAC
Hospitals/Nursing Homes $1,250
    American Hospital Assn .... $1,000 PAC

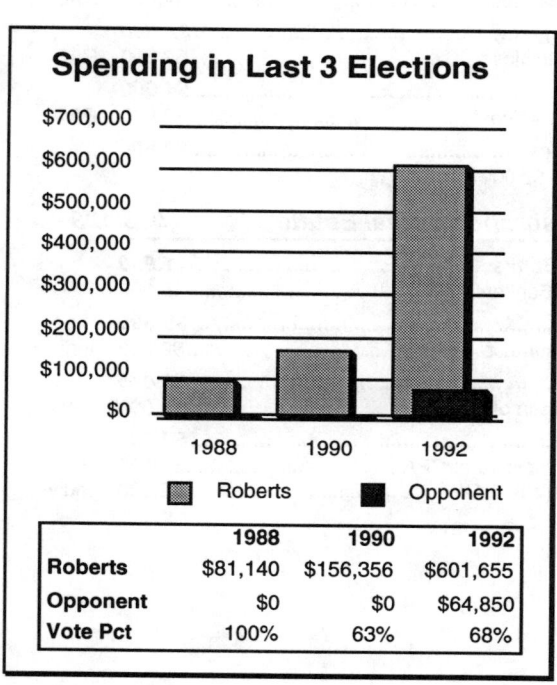

Spending in Last 3 Elections

	1988	1990	1992
Roberts	$81,140	$156,356	$601,655
Opponent	$0	$0	$64,850
Vote Pct	100%	63%	68%

Legend: Roberts, Opponent

Pharmaceuticals/Health Products $4,250
    Ciba-Geigy Corp .... $1,000 PAC
    Merck & Co .... $1,000 PAC

Lawyers & Lobbyists $6,787

Lawyers & Lobbyists $6,787
    Gordley & Associates .... $1,500 Indiv
    Lesher & Russell Inc .... $1,000 Indiv

Misc Business $21,500

Food & Beverage $1,250
    McDonald's Corp .... $1,000 PAC
Misc Services $2,500
    National Pest Control Assn .... $2,000 PAC
Business Services $2,000
    None over $1,000
Chemical & Related Manufacturing $9,850
    FMC Corp .... $5,000 PAC
    Dow Chemical .... $2,000 PAC/Ind
    Chemical Specialties Manufacturers Assn .... $1,500 PAC
Misc Manufacturing & Distributing $4,150
    International Sanitary Supply .... $1,000 PAC
    SC Johnson & Son Inc .... $1,000 Indiv
    Xerox Corp .... $1,000 PAC

Transportation $16,600

Air Transport $5,100
    United Parcel Service .... $3,600 PAC
    Boeing Co .... $1,000 PAC
Automotive $9,000
    National Auto Dealers Assn .... $6,500 PAC
    Auto Dealers & Drivers for Free Trade .... $1,500 PAC
    Americans for Free International Trade .... $1,000 PAC
Railroads $2,500
    Santa Fe Southern Pacific .... $1,000 PAC
    Union Pacific Corp .... $1,000 PAC

Ideological/Single-Issue

Ideological/Single-Issue $3,500

Gun Rights/Gun Control $3,000
    National Rifle Assn .... $3,000 PAC

Other & Unknown

Other $4,800

Education $1,000
    Brown-Mackie Business College .... $1,000 Indiv
Retired $3,800
    None over $1,000

Unknown $4,850

    Employer Listed/Category Unknown $4,350
        Morrison Enterprises .... $1,500 Indiv
        Great Bend Inc .... $1,000 Indiv

* Contributions came from more than one affiliate or subsidiary.

Tim Roemer, D-Ind (3)

First elected: 1990

1991-92 Total Receipts:	$467,094
1992 Year-end Cash:	$73,596

1991-92 Committees & Subcommittees

Education and Labor
Elementary, Secondary and Vocational Education; Postsecondary Education

Science, Space and Technology
Energy; Science; Technology and Competitiveness

Leading Contributors

Business

Agriculture $18,500

Crop Production & Basic Processing $4,300
　None over $2,000

Tobacco $2,500
　RJR Nabisco .... $2,000　PAC

Dairy $3,500
　Associated Milk Producers .... $3,000　PAC

Agricultural Services/Products $5,700
　Indiana Farm Bureau .... $5,000　PAC

Food Processing & Sales $2,000
　Connell Rice & Sugar Co .... $2,000　Indiv

Communications/Electronics $12,100

Telephone Utilities $8,600
　Indiana Bell Telephone .... $3,500　PAC
　AT&T .... $2,000　PAC

Construction $15,300

General Contractors $5,900
　None over $2,000

Home Builders $2,500
　None over $2,000

Construction Services $6,900
　John Chance & Assoc .... $4,000　Indiv

Source of Funds in 1992 Election

	Source	Total	Pct
■	PACs	$320,249	64%
▨	Indivs $200+	$105,027	21%
☐	Indivs under $200	$25,210	5%
▩	Other	$48,349	10%
	Candidate	$0	0%
	Party	$32,691	7%

Source of PAC Dollars by Sector

	Source	Total	Pct
■	Business	$146,998	48%
▨	Labor	$137,900	45%
☐	Ideology/Single Issue	$21,523	7%

In-State vs. Out-of-State Contributions*

	Source	Total	Pct
☐	In-State	$63,977	61%
■	Out-of-state	$40,300	39%
	No state listed	$750	

* by large individual contributors ($200 & above)

Defense $19,500

Defense Aerospace $14,000
　LTV Aerospace & Defense Co .... $3,000　PAC
　General Dynamics .... $2,500　PAC/Ind
　Textron Inc .... $2,500　PAC

Defense Electronics $4,000
　None over $2,000

Energy & Natural Resources $24,200

Oil & Gas $7,400
　BP America .... $2,000　PAC

Nuclear Energy $2,500
　General Atomics .... $2,000　PAC

Misc Energy $4,000
　Babcock & Wilcox* .... $3,000　PAC

Electric Utilities $7,800
　None over $2,000

Finance, Insurance & Real Estate $33,123

Commercial Banks $11,950
　American Bankers Assn .... $5,000　PAC

Insurance $9,698
　Gibson Insurance Agency .... $2,000　Indiv

Real Estate $6,475
　National Assn of Realtors .... $2,000　PAC

Accountants $4,500
　American Institute of CPA's .... $2,500　PAC
　Crowe, Chizek & Co .... $2,000　Indiv

Contribution Totals by Sector

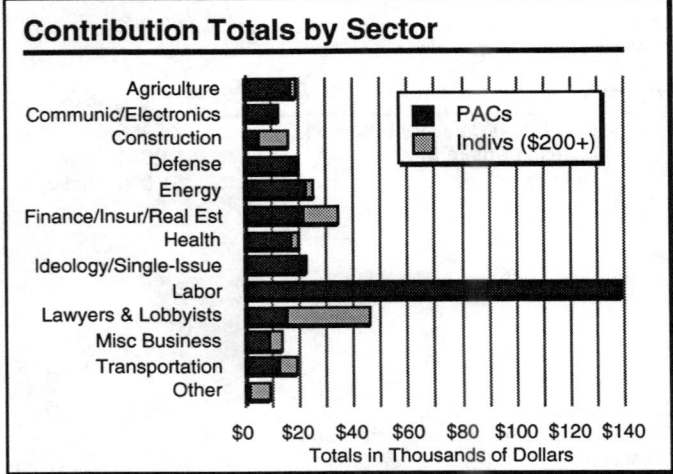

Agriculture
Communic/Electronics
Construction
Defense
Energy
Finance/Insur/Real Est
Health
Ideology/Single-Issue
Labor
Lawyers & Lobbyists
Misc Business
Transportation
Other

■ PACs
▨ Indivs ($200+)

$0　$20　$40　$60　$80　$100　$120　$140
Totals in Thousands of Dollars

Health $18,850

Health Professionals $14,800
   American Medical Assn ....$8,350   PAC
   American Dental Assn ....$3,000   PAC

Pharmaceuticals/Health Products $2,100
   None over $2,000

Lawyers & Lobbyists $45,270

Lawyers & Lobbyists $45,270
   Assn of Trial Lawyers of America ....$10,000   PAC
   Long Law Firm ....$2,500   Indiv
   Dutko & Associates ....$2,000   Indiv
   John C Walton Co ....$2,000   Indiv
   Williams & Jensen ....$2,000   PAC/Ind

Misc Business $12,750

Beer, Wine & Liquor $4,500
   National Beer Wholesalers Assn ....$2,500   PAC

Chemical & Related Manufacturing $2,000
   None over $2,000

Transportation $18,450

Air Transport $5,000
   United Parcel Service ....$2,000   PAC

Automotive $5,500
   National Auto Dealers Assn ....$3,000   PAC

Railroads $2,200
   None over $2,000

Sea Transport $3,850
   Edison Chouest Offshore ....$2,500   Indiv

Labor

Labor $137,900

Building Trade Unions $29,250
   Sheet Metal Workers Union ....$7,500   PAC
   Carpenters & Joiners Union ....$7,000   PAC
   Ironworkers Union ....$4,000   PAC
   Laborers' Political League ....$4,000   PAC
   Plumbers/Pipefitters Union ....$4,000   PAC

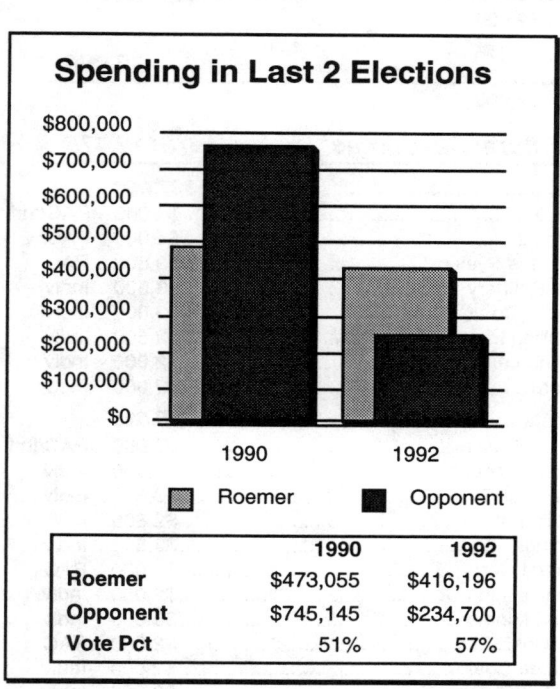

Spending in Last 2 Elections

	1990	1992
Roemer	$473,055	$416,196
Opponent	$745,145	$234,700
Vote Pct	51%	57%

Roemer   Opponent

Industrial Unions $55,600
   Machinists/Aerospace Workers Union ....$10,000   PAC
   Rubber Cork Linoleum & Plastic Workers ....$10,000   PAC
   United Auto Workers ....$10,000   PAC
   United Steelworkers ....$10,000   PAC
   Intl Brotherhood of Electrical Workers ....$6,000   PAC

Transportation Unions $17,300
   Teamsters Union ....$5,000   PAC
   Marine Engineers Union ....$3,500   PAC
   Air Line Pilots Assn ....$2,500   PAC
   United Transportation Union ....$2,500   PAC

Public Sector Unions $29,000
   National Education Assn ....$10,000   PAC
   National Assn Retired Federal Employees ....$5,000   PAC
   American Postal Workers Union ....$4,000   PAC
   National Assn of Letter Carriers ....$3,000   PAC

Misc Unions $6,750
   Food & Commercial Workers Union ....$4,000   PAC
   Service Employees International Union ....$2,000   PAC

Ideological/Single-Issue

Ideological/Single-Issue $22,523

Democratic/Liberal $2,500
   National Cmte for an Effective Congress ....$2,500   PAC

Leadership PACs $9,000
   Pelican PAC (Bennett Johnston) ....$9,000   PAC

Pro-Israel $2,000
   None over $2,000

Human Rights $2,500
   KidsPAC ....$2,000   PAC

Misc Issues $4,000
   National Cmte to Preserve Social Security ....$2,000   PAC
   Sierra Club ....$2,000   PAC

Other & Unknown

Other $8,645

Civil Servants/Public Officials $2,500
   None over $2,000

Education $4,500
   Notre Dame University ....$3,000   Indiv

Unknown $24,837
   No Employer Listed or Found $9,037
   Employer Listed/Category Unknown $15,100
     Trans-Tec Corp ....$3,500   Indiv

---

* Contributions came from more than one affiliate or subsidiary.

Harold Rogers, R-Ky (5)

First elected: 1980

1991-92 Total Receipts: $651,821
1992 Year-end Cash: $32,933

1991-92 Committees & Subcommittees

Appropriations
Commerce, Justice, State, the Judiciary and Related Agencies (Ranking Republican); Treasury, Postal Service and General Government

Budget
Budget Process, Reconciliation and Enforcement; Urgent Fiscal Issues (Ranking Republican)

Leading Contributors

Business

Agriculture — $57,750

Crop Production & Basic Processing $7,250
  None over $2,000

Tobacco $11,900
RJR Nabisco	$4,000	PAC
US Tobacco Co	$2,500	PAC

Dairy $6,000
Associated Milk Producers	$3,000	PAC
Dairymen Inc-Kentucky	$2,500	PAC

Livestock $4,000
Tennessee Walking Horse Breeders	$2,000	PAC

Agricultural Services/Products $5,800
Farmers Supply & Export Inc	$2,000	Indiv
Warner Fertilizer Co	$2,000	Indiv

Food Processing & Sales $15,800
Food Fair Inc	$2,700	Indiv
Fleming Companies Inc	$2,000	PAC
Food Marketing Institute	$2,000	PAC
Winn-Dixie Stores	$2,000	PAC

Forestry & Forest Products $6,500
Westvaco Corp	$5,000	PAC

Communications/Electronics — $25,850

Media/Entertainment $6,750
National Assn of Broadcasters	$6,000	PAC

Telephone Utilities $12,500
BellSouth Corp*	$6,000	PAC

Computer Equipment & Services $4,600
Electronic Data Systems	$2,000	PAC

Contribution Totals by Sector

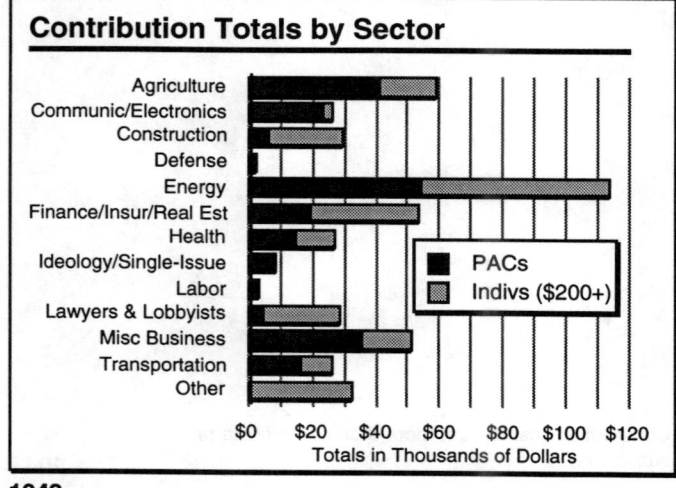

Agriculture
Communic/Electronics
Construction
Defense
Energy
Finance/Insur/Real Est
Health
Ideology/Single-Issue
Labor
Lawyers & Lobbyists
Misc Business
Transportation
Other

■ PACs
▨ Indivs ($200+)

$0 $20 $40 $60 $80 $100 $120
Totals in Thousands of Dollars

Source of Funds in 1992 Election

Source	Total	Pct
■ PACs	$233,590	34%
▨ Indivs $200+	$286,512	42%
☐ Indivs under $200	$89,959	13%
⊠ Other	$75,836	11%
Candidate	$0	0%
Party	$45,706	7%

Source of PAC Dollars by Sector

Source	Total	Pct
■ Business	$213,340	95%
▨ Labor	$2,500	1%
☐ Ideology/Single Issue	$7,950	4%

In-State vs. Out-of-State Contributions*

Source	Total	Pct
☐ In-State	$258,292	92%
■ Out-of-state	$23,000	8%
No state listed	$0	

* by large individual contributors ($200 & above)

Construction — $29,600

General Contractors $17,350
Hinkle Contracting Corp	$3,500	Indiv
Associated General Contractors	$2,500	PAC
Bizzack Construction	$2,000	Indiv
Ken Hiler Builder Inc	$2,000	Indiv

Home Builders $3,750
National Assn of Home Builders	$3,500	PAC

Construction Services $4,650
Vaughn & Melton Engineers	$3,400	Indiv

Building Materials & Equipment $3,250
  None over $2,000

Defense — $2,000

  None over $2,000

Energy & Natural Resources — $112,475

Oil & Gas $37,050
Ashland Oil	$7,000	PAC/Ind
Mapco Inc	$5,000	PAC
Columbia Gas System*	$3,500	PAC
Somerset Refinery Inc	$3,500	Indiv
Coleman Oil Co	$3,000	Indiv
Kinzer Drilling	$2,500	Indiv
Cumberland Lake Shell	$2,000	Indiv
Exxon Corp	$2,000	PAC

Mining $60,625
National Coal Assn	$7,000	PAC/Ind
Beech Fork Processing	$4,500	Indiv
Interstate Coal Co	$3,800	Indiv
Am Tar Mineral Co	$2,800	Indiv
Pen Holdings	$2,500	Indiv
Arch Mineral Corp	$2,000	PAC
Kiah Creek Mining Co	$2,000	Indiv
Manalapan Mining Co	$2,000	Indiv
Peabody Coal	$2,000	PAC
Sunny Ridge Coal	$2,000	Indiv
VM&M Rock Quarry	$2,000	Indiv

| Misc Energy | $4,000 | |
| Cooper Industries | $3,000 | PAC |

Electric Utilities	$10,300	
ACRE (Action Cmte for Rural Electrification)*	$3,000	PAC
Kentucky Utilities Co	$2,000	PAC

Finance, Insurance & Real Estate — $52,540

Commercial Banks	$19,050	
American Bankers Assn	$4,000	PAC
Inez Deposit Bank	$3,800	Indiv
Citizens National Bank	$3,650	Indiv
Citizens Bank	$2,000	Indiv

| Securities & Investment | $2,000 | |
| National Venture Capital Assn | $2,000 | PAC |

| Insurance | $6,700 | |
| Buchanan Insurance Agency | $2,000 | Indiv |

Real Estate	$19,490	
National Assn of Realtors	$8,940	PAC
Stearns Co	$4,000	Indiv

| Accountants | $4,300 | |
| None over $2,000 | | |

Health — $26,350

Health Professionals	$20,900	
American Medical Assn	$9,750	PAC
Asthma & Allergy Center	$2,000	Indiv

| Hospitals/Nursing Homes | $5,450 | |
| None over $2,000 | | |

Lawyers & Lobbyists — $29,050

Lawyers & Lobbyists	$29,050	
Baird, Baird et al	$3,000	Indiv
Cassidy & Associates	$2,250	Indiv
Reece, Lang & Breeding	$2,200	Indiv
Ham & Henry Attorneys	$2,000	Indiv

Misc Business — $50,700

Food & Beverage	$9,950	
Jerrico Inc	$2,000	PAC/Ind
National Restaurant Assn	$2,000	PAC

Beer, Wine & Liquor	$19,750	
Brown-Forman Distillers	$10,000	PAC
National Beer Wholesalers Assn	$4,000	PAC

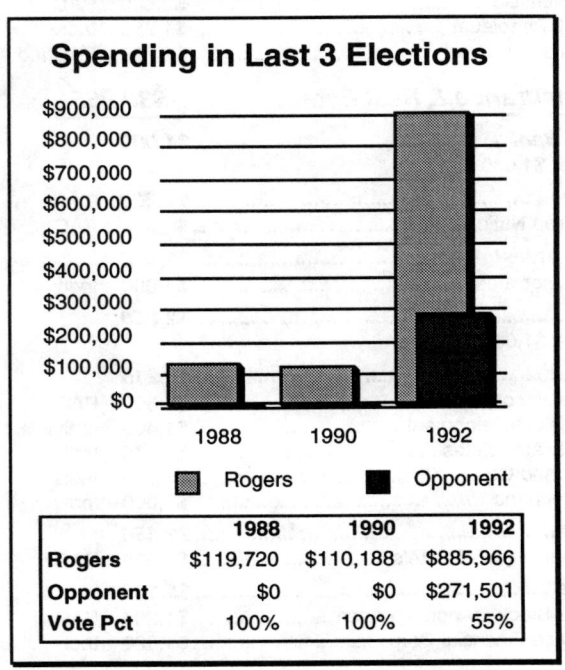

Spending in Last 3 Elections

	1988	1990	1992
Rogers	$119,720	$110,188	$885,966
Opponent	$0	$0	$271,501
Vote Pct	100%	100%	55%

| Retail Sales | $5,300 | |
| None over $2,000 | | |

| Business Services | $3,500 | |
| None over $2,000 | | |

| Misc Manufacturing & Distributing | $3,800 | |
| None over $2,000 | | |

| Textiles | $2,250 | |
| None over $2,000 | | |

Transportation — $25,800

| Air Transport | $4,500 | |
| United Parcel Service | $4,500 | PAC |

| Automotive | $5,500 | |
| National Auto Dealers Assn | $3,000 | PAC |

| Trucking | $3,500 | |
| None over $2,000 | | |

| Railroads | $5,000 | |
| Union Pacific Corp | $2,000 | PAC |

Sea Transport	$7,000	
Stardust Cruisers	$3,000	Indiv
CSX Corp*	$2,000	PAC
Lees Ford Dock	$2,000	Indiv

Labor

Labor	$2,500

| Transportation Unions | $2,000 | |
| Marine Engineers Dist 2 Retirees | $2,000 | PAC |

Ideological/Single-Issue

Ideological/Single-Issue	$7,950

| Gun Rights/Gun Control | $5,450 | |
| National Rifle Assn | $5,450 | PAC |

Other & Unknown

Other	$32,017

| Civil Servants/Public Officials | $9,387 | |
| None over $2,000 | | |

| Education | $3,580 | |
| None over $2,000 | | |

| Retired | $18,050 | |
| None over $2,000 | | |

Unknown	$50,500

Homemakers/Non-income earners	$17,050	
Employer Listed/Category Unknown	$30,950	
WE Elliott Enterprises	$2,000	Indiv

Independent expenditures supporting Rogers
| National Right to Life PAC | $5,195 |
| National Rifle Assn | $5,112 |

---

* Contributions came from more than one affiliate or subsidiary.

Dana Rohrabacher, R-Calif (45)

First elected: 1988
1991-92 Total Receipts: $311,608
1992 Year-end Cash: $52,281

1991-92 Committees & Subcommittees

District of Columbia
Fiscal Affairs and Health (Ranking Republican); Judiciary and Education

Science, Space and Technology
Space; Technology and Competitiveness

Leading Contributors

Business

Agriculture $2,550

Food Processing & Sales	**$1,500**	
Pepsico Inc	$1,000	PAC

Communications/Electronics $15,800

Printing & Publishing	**$3,350**	
Fisher Printing Inc	$1,000	Indiv
Media/Entertainment	**$4,050**	
New World Entertainment	$1,000	Indiv
Trans Atlantic Pictures	$1,000	Indiv
Telephone Utilities	**$3,250**	
GTE Corp	$1,300	PAC
Pacific Telesis Group	$1,300	PAC
Computer Equipment & Services	**$3,950**	
AST Research	$2,000	Indiv
Forbes Computer Group	$1,150	Indiv

Construction $12,450

General Contractors	**$8,350**	
Associated General Contractors	$1,800	PAC
Fluor Corp	$1,750	PAC
Mladen Buntich Construction Co	$1,750	Indiv
Steve Bubalo Construction Co	$1,000	Indiv
Special Trade Contractors	**$1,500**	
None over $1,000		
Building Materials & Equipment	**$2,050**	
Lumber & Truss Co	$1,000	Indiv

Source of Funds in 1992 Election

Source	Total	Pct
■ PACs	$108,926	35%
▨ Indivs $200+	$171,071	55%
☐ Indivs under $200	$28,746	9%
⊠ Other	$2,865	1%
Candidate	$0	0%
Party	$0	0%

Source of PAC Dollars by Sector

Source	Total	Pct
■ Business	$82,950	74%
▨ Labor	$0	0%
☐ Ideology/Single Issue	$29,202	26%

In-State vs. Out-of-State Contributions*

Source	Total	Pct
☐ In-State	$147,345	87%
■ Out-of-state	$22,376	13%
No state listed	$1,000	

*** by large individual contributors ($200 & above)**

Defense $13,290

Defense Aerospace	**$9,650**	
Northrop Corp	$3,250	PAC/Ind
McDonnell Douglas	$2,500	PAC/Ind
Rockwell International	$2,000	PAC/Ind
Defense Electronics	**$2,450**	
Hughes Aircraft	$1,750	PAC/Ind
Misc Defense	**$1,190**	
BDM International	$1,190	Indiv

Energy & Natural Resources $11,000

Oil & Gas	**$10,200**	
Atlantic Richfield	$2,500	PAC
Signal Hill Petroleum	$1,750	Indiv
Koch Industries	$1,500	PAC/Ind

Finance, Insurance & Real Estate $30,065

Commercial Banks	**$1,000**	
None over $1,000		
Credit Unions	**$1,200**	
Credit Union National Assn	$1,000	PAC
Securities & Investment	**$1,500**	
Krieble Associates	$1,000	Indiv
Insurance	**$2,350**	
None over $1,000		
Real Estate	**$16,215**	
National Assn of Realtors	$5,800	PAC
Bridgecreek Development	$1,400	Indiv
McCune & Associates	$1,375	Indiv
Cypress Land Co	$1,000	Indiv
Inland Group Inc	$1,000	Indiv
Accountants	**$2,450**	
American Institute of CPA's	$1,000	PAC
Misc Finance	**$5,100**	
Employee Stock Ownership Assn	$1,200	PAC
TDS Service Financial Corp	$1,000	Indiv

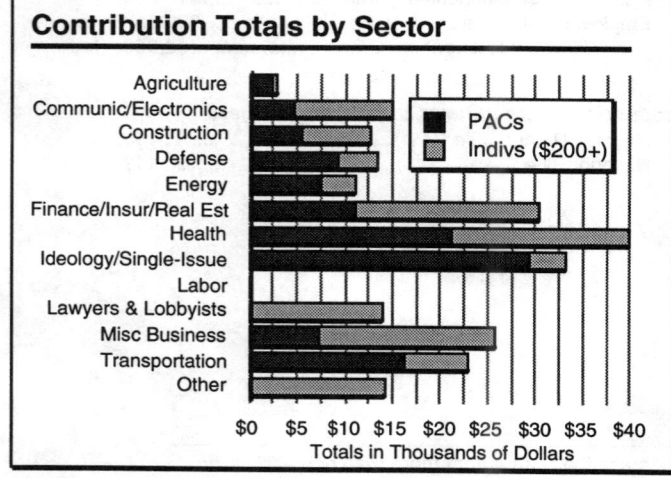

Contribution Totals by Sector

Agriculture
Communic/Electronics
Construction
Defense
Energy
Finance/Insur/Real Est
Health
Ideology/Single-Issue
Labor
Lawyers & Lobbyists
Misc Business
Transportation
Other

■ PACs
▨ Indivs ($200+)

$0 $5 $10 $15 $20 $25 $30 $35 $40
Totals in Thousands of Dollars

Health $39,710

Health Professionals $33,110
  American Chiropractic Assn .... $10,000 PAC
  American Medical Assn .... $7,850 PAC
  American Academy of Ophthalmology .... $1,000 PAC
Health Services $2,500
  Cancer Treatment Centers .... $1,500 Indiv
  Family Health Program Inc .... $1,000 PAC
Pharmaceuticals/Health Products $2,950
  St Ives Laboratories .... $2,500 Indiv

Lawyers & Lobbyists $13,750

Lawyers & Lobbyists $13,750
  Case, Schroeder et al .... $2,000 Indiv
  E Del Smith & Co .... $1,800 Indiv
  Riordan & McKinzie .... $1,750 Indiv
  Parker, Milliken et al .... $1,200 Indiv
  Shawn Steel & Associates .... $1,000 Indiv

Misc Business $25,580

Food & Beverage $3,530
  Vien/Dong Restaurant .... $1,200 Indiv
  Little Saigon Restaurant .... $1,000 Indiv
Beer, Wine & Liquor $1,500
  National Beer Wholesalers Assn .... $1,000 PAC
Retail Sales $3,900
  National Assn of Convenience Stores .... $1,000 PAC
Misc Services $1,500
  Tallon Termite & Pest Control .... $1,000 Indiv
Business Services $2,950
  None over $1,000
Lodging/Tourism $3,050
  Senven Seas Travel Agency .... $2,000 Indiv
Misc Business $2,650
  Price Transfer Inc .... $2,400 Indiv
Chemical & Related Manufacturing $4,000
  Sunshine Makers .... $2,000 Indiv
  Stauffer Chemical Trading .... $1,000 Indiv
Misc Manufacturing & Distributing $1,750
  YYK Enterprises .... $1,000 Indiv

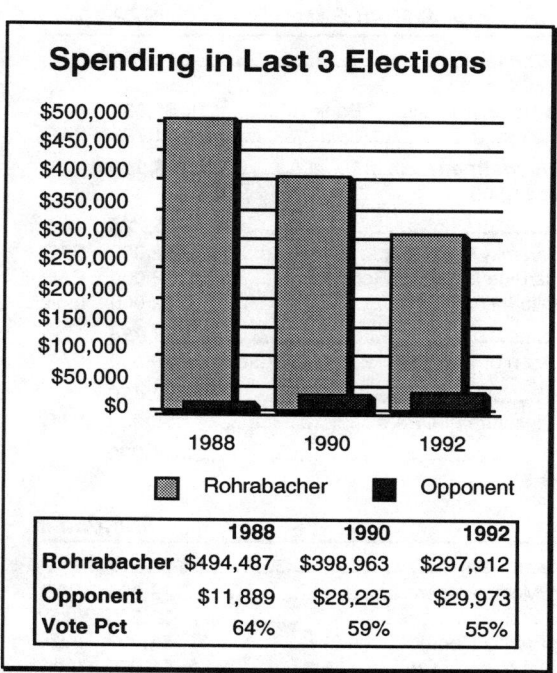

Spending in Last 3 Elections

	1988	1990	1992
Rohrabacher	$494,487	$398,963	$297,912
Opponent	$11,889	$28,225	$29,973
Vote Pct	64%	59%	55%

Transportation $22,700

Air Transport $5,500
  United Parcel Service .... $2,350 PAC
  Aircraft Owners & Pilots Assn .... $1,000 PAC
Automotive $12,150
  National Auto Dealers Assn .... $5,650 PAC
  California Diesel .... $2,000 Indiv
  Auto Dealers & Drivers for Free Trade .... $1,500 PAC
  Americans for Free International Trade .... $1,000 PAC
  Hitchcock Auto Resources .... $1,000 Indiv
Railroads $1,000
  Union Pacific Corp .... $1,000 PAC
Sea Transport $3,700
  Willow Industries .... $2,500 Indiv

Ideological/Single-Issue

Ideological/Single-Issue $32,952

Republican/Conservative $13,150
  American Citizens for Political Action .... $5,000 PAC
  America's PAC .... $4,000 PAC
Leadership PACs $2,502
  Campaign America (Bob Dole) .... $1,440 PAC
  Conservative Victory Fund (Steve Symms) .... $1,062 PAC
Foreign & Defense Policy $4,700
  Council for National Defense .... $4,600 PAC
Gun Rights/Gun Control $4,500
  National Rifle Assn .... $4,500 PAC
Human Rights $2,500
  Korean American National PAC .... $2,500 PAC
Misc Issues $5,600
  Howard Jarvis Taxpayers Assn .... $3,000 PAC
  Fair PAC .... $2,000 PAC

Other & Unknown

Other $13,950

Civil Servants/Public Officials $2,250
  None over $1,000
Retired $10,800
  None over $1,000

Unknown $50,226

  Homemakers/Non-income earners $6,300
  No Employer Listed or Found $9,390
  Generic Occupation/Category Unknown $4,150
  Employer Listed/Category Unknown $29,236
    National Rehabilitation Service .... $2,000 Indiv
    Van Halen Group .... $1,500 Indiv
    Cedillos Testing Co .... $1,000 Indiv
    Century Council .... $1,000 Indiv
    EL Management Inc .... $1,000 Indiv
    Failure Analysis Associates .... $1,000 Indiv
    Leetronics Inc .... $1,000 Indiv
    PE Fulton & Co .... $1,000 Indiv

Independent expenditures supporting Rohrabacher
  National Right to Life PAC $1,697

Ileana Ros-Lehtinen, R-Fla (18)

First elected: 1989

1991-92 Total Receipts: $662,069
1992 Year-end Cash: $7,076

1991-92 Committees & Subcommittees

Foreign Affairs
Human Rights and International Organizations; Western Hemisphere Affairs

Government Operations
Commerce, Consumer and Monetary Affairs; Government Information, Justice and Agriculture

Leading Contributors

Business

Agriculture		$25,853
Crop Production & Basic Processing	$10,465	
Okeelanta Corp	$3,500	Indiv
Tobacco	$1,790	
None over $1,500		
Agricultural Services/Products	$2,428	
None over $1,500		
Food Processing & Sales	$9,580	
Pepsico Inc	$2,000	PAC
Winn-Dixie Stores	$2,000	PAC

Communications/Electronics		$17,812
Printing & Publishing	$5,950	
Vista Magazine	$3,250	Indiv
Media/Entertainment	$1,550	
None over $1,500		
Telephone Utilities	$8,812	
Southern Bell	$4,142	PAC

Construction		$27,028
General Contractors	$9,850	
None over $1,500		
Home Builders	$3,750	
None over $1,500		
Special Trade Contractors	$3,150	
Century Plumbing Contr	$1,700	Indiv
Construction Services	$6,778	
Lannes & Garcia	$5,128	Indiv
Building Materials & Equipment	$3,500	
None over $1,500		

Contribution Totals by Sector

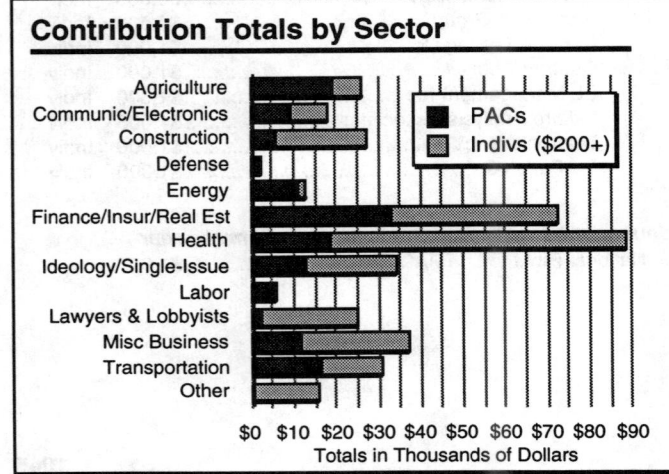

PACs
Indivs ($200+)

Agriculture
Communic/Electronics
Construction
Defense
Energy
Finance/Insur/Real Est
Health
Ideology/Single-Issue
Labor
Lawyers & Lobbyists
Misc Business
Transportation
Other

$0 $10 $20 $30 $40 $50 $60 $70 $80 $90
Totals in Thousands of Dollars

Source of Funds in 1992 Election

Source	Total	Pct
PACs	$147,844	22%
Indivs $200+	$339,211	51%
Indivs under $200	$149,223	23%
Other	$25,791	4%
Candidate	$0	0%
Party	$553	0%

Source of PAC Dollars by Sector

Source	Total	Pct
Business	$125,767	87%
Labor	$5,590	4%
Ideology/Single Issue	$12,530	9%

In-State vs. Out-of-State Contributions*

Source	Total	Pct
In-State	$295,461	90%
Out-of-state	$33,050	10%
No state listed	$10,661	

* by large individual contributors ($200 & above)

Defense		$2,130
Defense Aerospace	$2,130	
None over $1,500		

Energy & Natural Resources		$12,270
Oil & Gas	$3,640	
None over $1,500		
Electric Utilities	$6,730	
Southern Co*	$1,650	PAC
Florida Power & Light	$1,500	PAC

Finance, Insurance & Real Estate		$72,154
Commercial Banks	$14,120	
Barnett Banks Inc	$4,500	PAC
Citizens & Southern National Bank	$2,500	PAC
Citicorp	$1,780	PAC
Securities & Investment	$3,350	
None over $1,500		
Insurance	$15,728	
American Family Corp	$2,000	PAC
Blue Cross/Blue Shield of Florida	$2,000	PAC
Inter Atlantic Insurance	$2,000	Indiv
Real Estate	$23,856	
National Assn of Realtors	$6,000	PAC
Accountants	$9,450	
American Institute of CPA's	$5,000	PAC
Misc Finance	$4,200	
None over $1,500		

Health		$88,085
Health Professionals	$42,617	
American Medical Assn	$9,000	PAC
Emsa Inc	$2,500	Indiv
Interama Family Center	$2,000	Indiv
Mount Sinai Medical Center	$2,000	Indiv

JR Jannach MD & Assoc	$1,861	Indiv
American Dental Assn	$1,500	PAC
Miami Heart Institute	$1,500	Indiv

Hospitals/Nursing Homes **$16,189**
Hospice Care Inc	$4,000	Indiv
Clinica Fatima Inc	$2,078	Indiv
Victoria Hospital Ptrsh	$2,000	Indiv
Westchester General Hospital	$2,000	Indiv

Health Services **$13,261**
CAC Ramsay HMO	$3,495	Indiv
Central Medical Lab	$2,000	Indiv
Mederi Home Health	$2,000	Indiv
Pasteur Health Plan HMO	$1,988	Indiv
Care Florida (HMO)	$1,500	Indiv

Pharmaceuticals/Health Products **$7,740**
| Pharmed Group | $2,500 | Indiv |
| Doctors Medical Rental | $2,450 | Indiv |

Misc Health **$8,278**
| Miami Dade Health Plan | $2,000 | Indiv |

Lawyers & Lobbyists $25,558

Lawyers & Lobbyists **$25,558**
| Vierra Associates Inc | $1,500 | Indiv |

Misc Business $36,486

Food & Beverage **$3,000**
None over $1,500

Beer, Wine & Liquor **$6,550**
| Southern Wine & Spirits | $2,800 | PAC |
| Eagle Brands Inc | $2,000 | Indiv |

Retail Sales **$9,140**
| El Dorado Furniture | $2,500 | Indiv |
| Bal Harbour Shops | $1,500 | Indiv |

Misc Services **$1,500**
None over $1,500

Business Services **$9,370**
| Pan American & Assoc | $3,000 | Indiv |

Lodging/Tourism **$1,600**
None over $1,500

Chemical & Related Manufacturing **$2,300**
None over $1,500

Misc Manufacturing & Distributing **$2,026**
None over $1,500

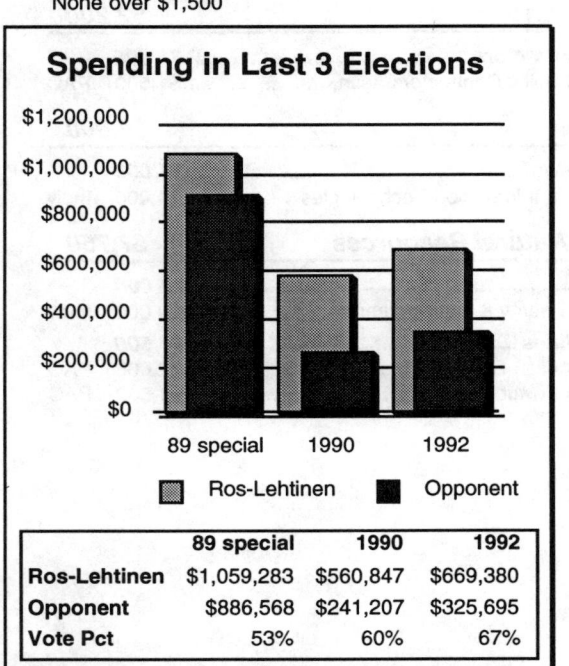

Spending in Last 3 Elections

	89 special	1990	1992
Ros-Lehtinen	$1,059,283	$560,847	$669,380
Opponent	$886,568	$241,207	$325,695
Vote Pct	53%	60%	67%

Legend: ▨ Ros-Lehtinen ■ Opponent

Transportation $30,361

Air Transport **$8,706**
Batch-Air Inc	$2,000	PAC
Southern Air Transport Inc	$2,000	Indiv
International Air Leases Inc	$1,756	Indiv
United Parcel Service	$1,500	PAC

Automotive **$12,140**
| National Auto Dealers Assn | $4,500 | PAC |
| Auto Dealers & Drivers for Free Trade | $2,000 | PAC |

Sea Transport **$9,015**
| Antilean Marine Shipping | $2,400 | Indiv |
| SEL Maduro | $2,000 | Indiv |

Labor

Labor $5,590

Transportation Unions **$3,500**
| Marine Engineers Union* | $3,000 | PAC |

Public Sector Unions **$2,090**
None over $1,500

Ideological/Single-Issue

Ideological/Single-Issue $33,570

Republican/Conservative **$1,640**
None over $1,500

Foreign & Defense Policy **$2,050**
None over $1,500

Pro-Israel **$23,680**
| National PAC | $5,000 | PAC |

Human Rights **$4,700**
| Miccosukee Tribe | $2,200 | Indiv |
| Pro Hispanic PAC | $1,500 | PAC |

Misc Issues **$1,500**
| National Cmte to Preserve Social Security | $1,500 | PAC |

Other & Unknown

Other $15,408

Education **$8,478**
| Lincoln-Marti Schools | $1,978 | Indiv |

Retired **$5,930**
None over $1,500

Unknown $90,754

Homemakers/Non-income earners	$14,601	
No Employer Listed or Found	$29,476	
Generic Occupation/Category Unknown	$2,328	
Employer Listed/Category Unknown	$44,349	
Pro-Eco Inc	$4,000	Indiv
Human Resources Int	$2,000	Indiv
International Maritime Corp	$1,500	Indiv
Project Advisory Board	$1,500	Indiv

Independent expenditures supporting Ros-Lehtinen
| National Right to Life PAC | $3,820 | |

---

* Contributions came from more than one affiliate or subsidiary.

Charlie Rose, D-NC (7)

First elected: 1972

1991-92 Total Receipts:	$395,280
1992 Year-end Cash:	$681,533

1991-92 Committees & Subcommittees

Administration (Chairman)

Agriculture
Cotton, Rice and Sugar; Department Operations, Research and Foreign Agriculture (Chairman); Livestock, Dairy and Poultry; Peanuts and Tobacco; Wheat, Soybeans and Feed Grains

Joint Committee on the Library (Vice Chairman)

Joint Committee on Printing (Chairman)

Leading Contributors

Business

Agriculture		$84,675
Crop Production & Basic Processing **$21,575**		
Alabama Peanut Producers Assn	$5,000	PAC
Virginia-Carolinas Peanut Membership Org	$2,000	PAC
Tobacco **$19,500**		
Philip Morris	$7,000	PAC
RJR Nabisco	$5,000	PAC
US Tobacco Co	$2,500	PAC
Tobacco Institute	$1,500	PAC/Ind
Dairy **$16,000**		
Associated Milk Producers	$10,000	PAC
Mid-America Dairymen	$3,500	PAC
Dairymen Inc-North Carolina	$1,500	PAC
Poultry & Eggs **$2,500**		
None over $1,500		
Agricultural Services/Products **$13,100**		
Dow Chemical	$2,000	PAC
Farm Credit Council	$1,500	PAC
Food Processing & Sales **$10,000**		
Connell Rice & Sugar Co	$2,000	Indiv
Food Lion Inc	$2,000	PAC
ConAgra Inc	$1,500	PAC
Forestry & Forest Products **$1,500**		
None over $1,500		

Source of Funds in 1992 Election

Source	Total	Pct
■ PACs	$251,535	60%
▨ Indivs $200+	$62,650	15%
☐ Indivs under $200	$19,783	5%
⊠ Other	$83,993	20%
Candidate	$0	0%
Party	$22,831	5%

Source of PAC Dollars by Sector

Source	Total	Pct
■ Business	$189,825	72%
▨ Labor	$62,000	24%
☐ Ideology/Single Issue	$10,500	4%

In-State vs. Out-of-State Contributions*

Source	Total	Pct
☐ In-State	$14,000	23%
■ Out-of-state	$46,700	77%
No state listed	$950	

* by large individual contributors ($200 & above)

Communications/Electronics		$29,700
Media/Entertainment **$5,200**		
National Cable Television Assn	$5,000	PAC
Telephone Utilities **$13,500**		
AT&T	$7,000	PAC
Southern Bell	$4,000	PAC
Telecom Services & Equipment **$2,500**		
Metromedia Co	$2,000	Indiv
Computer Equipment & Services **$8,000**		
Benchmark Systems Inc	$4,000	Indiv
Micro Research Industries	$3,000	Indiv

Construction		$2,200
General Contractors **$1,500**		
National Utility Contractors Assn	$1,500	PAC

Defense		$4,000
Misc Defense **$4,000**		
Evergreen Information Technologies	$4,000	Indiv

Energy & Natural Resources		$7,750
Oil & Gas **$3,000**		
Mitchell Energy & Development	$2,000	Indiv
Electric Utilities **$4,500**		
ACRE (Action Cmte for Rural Electrification)	$2,000	PAC
Carolina Power & Light	$1,500	PAC

Contribution Totals by Sector

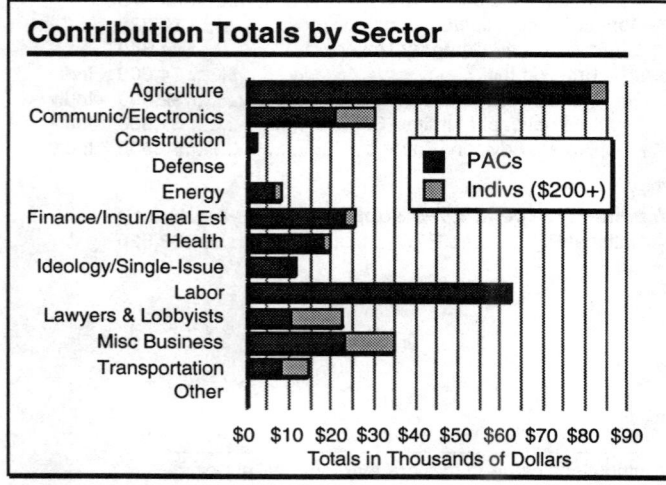

Agriculture
Communic/Electronics
Construction
Defense
Energy
Finance/Insur/Real Est
Health
Ideology/Single-Issue
Labor
Lawyers & Lobbyists
Misc Business
Transportation
Other

■ PACs
▨ Indivs ($200+)

$0 $10 $20 $30 $40 $50 $60 $70 $80 $90
Totals in Thousands of Dollars

Finance, Insurance & Real Estate $25,250

Commercial Banks **$8,500**
    American Bankers Assn ....$3,500 PAC
    Citizens & Southern National Bank ....$2,000 PAC

Securities & Investment **$3,100**
    Chicago Mercantile Exchange ....$2,500 PAC

Insurance **$3,350**
    None over $1,500

Real Estate **$8,300**
    National Assn of Realtors ....$6,000 PAC

Health $19,300

Health Professionals **$11,750**
    American Medical Assn.......................................$5,000 PAC
    American Dental Assn ....$3,500 PAC

Pharmaceuticals/Health Products **$6,550**
    ICI Americas Inc ....$1,500 PAC

Lawyers & Lobbyists $22,200

Lawyers & Lobbyists **$22,200**
    Assn of Trial Lawyers of America ....$10,000 PAC
    Cassidy & Associates ....$1,500 Indiv
    McNair Law Firm ....$1,500 Indiv

Misc Business $34,600

Food & Beverage **$10,400**
    National Restaurant Assn ....$3,000 PAC
    Shaw Food Services Co ....$2,900 Indiv
    Hardee's Food Systems....................................$2,500 PAC

Beer, Wine & Liquor **$3,700**
    Anheuser-Busch ....$2,000 PAC
    National Beer Wholesalers Assn ....$1,500 PAC

Retail Sales **$2,800**
    Intelligent Solutions Inc ....$2,800 Indiv

Misc Services **$2,200**
    National Pest Control Assn ....$2,000 PAC

Business Services **$5,000**
    None over $1,500

Chemical & Related Manufacturing $2,500
    None over $1,500

Misc Manufacturing & Distributing **$6,500**
    Corning Glass Works ....$2,000 PAC
    Xerox Corp ....$2,000 PAC/Ind

Textiles **$1,500**
    None over $1,500

Transportation $14,050

Air Transport **$2,500**
    United Parcel Service ....$1,500 PAC

Automotive **$9,200**
    Valley Motors...$4,500 Indiv
    National Auto Dealers Assn ....$2,500 PAC
    Auto Dealers & Drivers for Free Trade ....$1,500 PAC

Labor

Labor $62,000

Building Trade Unions **$7,500**
    Carpenters & Joiners Union ....$5,000 PAC

Industrial Unions **$11,500**
    Communications Workers of America ....$4,500 PAC
    Intl Brotherhood of Electrical Workers ....$4,500 PAC

Transportation Unions **$15,500**
    Teamsters Union ....$6,000 PAC
    Air Line Pilots Assn ....$2,500 PAC
    Marine Engineers Dist 2 Maritime Officers ....$2,500 PAC
    Trans Comm International Union ....$1,500 PAC

Public Sector Unions **$21,000**
    National Assn of Letter Carriers ....$10,000 PAC
    National Assn Retired Federal Employees ....$3,000 PAC
    National Education Assn ....$2,500 PAC
    National Rural Letter Carriers Assn ....$2,000 PAC
    American Postal Workers Union ....$1,500 PAC

Misc Unions **$6,500**
    Food & Commercial Workers Union ....$3,000 PAC
    Hotel/Restaurant Employees Union ....$2,500 PAC

Ideological/Single-Issue

Ideological/Single-Issue $11,000

Democratic/Liberal **$2,500**
    National Cmte for an Effective Congress ....$2,500 PAC

Leadership PACs **$2,000**
    America's Leaders' Fund (Dan Rostenkowski) ....$2,000 PAC

Pro-Israel **$5,500**
    National PAC ....$5,000 PAC

Other & Unknown

Unknown $6,850

    Employer Listed/Category Unknown $6,200
      None over $1,500

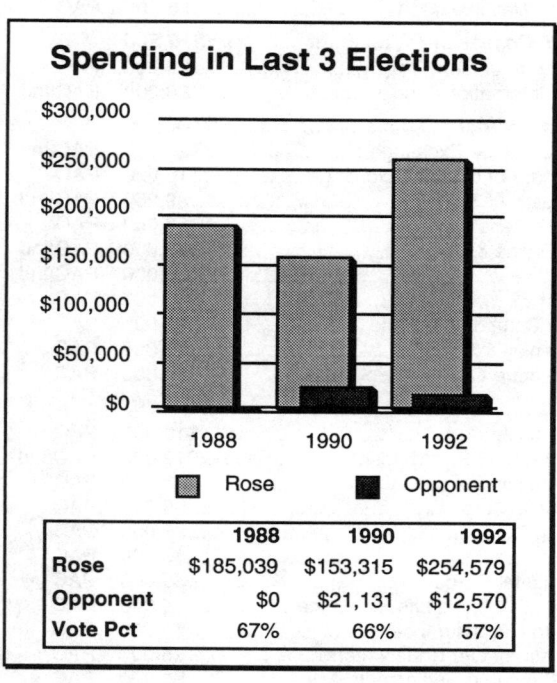

Spending in Last 3 Elections

	1988	1990	1992
Rose	$185,039	$153,315	$254,579
Opponent	$0	$21,131	$12,570
Vote Pct	67%	66%	57%

* Contributions came from more than one affiliate or subsidiary.

Dan Rostenkowski, D-Ill (5)

First elected: 1958

1991-92 Total Receipts: $1,587,234
1992 Year-end Cash: $1,245,721

1991-92 Committees & Subcommittees

Ways and Means (Chairman)
Trade

Joint Committee on Taxation (Vice Chairman)

Leading Contributors

Business

Agriculture		$61,500
Tobacco	*$22,000*	
US Tobacco Co	$10,000	PAC
RJR Nabisco	$6,000	PAC
Philip Morris	$5,000	PAC
Agricultural Services/Products	*$12,750*	
Archer-Daniels-Midland Corp	$5,000	PAC
Food Processing & Sales	*$11,250*	
Food Marketing Institute	$5,000	PAC

Communications/Electronics		$66,750
Media/Entertainment	*$17,250*	
National Assn of Broadcasters	$5,000	PAC
Telephone Utilities	*$35,000*	
Pacific Telesis Group	$7,000	PAC
Illinois Bell Telephone	$5,250	PAC/Ind
BellSouth Corp*	$5,000	PAC
GTE Corp	$5,000	PAC
US West Inc	$5,000	PAC

Construction		$36,250
General Contractors	*$17,250*	
Associated General Contractors ..	$5,000	PAC
Fluor Corp	$5,000	PAC
Home Builders	*$9,500*	
National Assn of Home Builders ..	$5,000	PAC

Defense		$22,750
Defense Aerospace	*$19,000*	
General Dynamics	$5,000	PAC
Northrop Corp	$5,000	PAC
Textron Inc	$5,000	PAC

Source of Funds in 1992 Election

Source	Total	Pct
■ PACs	$961,937	60%
▨ Indivs $200+	$359,131	22%
☐ Indivs under $200	$12,503	1%
⊠ Other	$265,536	17%
Candidate	$0	0%
Party	$12,023	1%

Source of PAC Dollars by Sector

Source	Total	Pct
■ Business	$836,105	89%
▨ Labor	$93,500	10%
☐ Ideology/Single Issue	$13,023	1%

In-State vs. Out-of-State Contributions*

Source	Total	Pct
☐ In-State	$208,300	58%
■ Out-of-state	$150,831	42%
No state listed	$0	

* by large individual contributors ($200 & above)

Energy & Natural Resources		$52,350
Oil & Gas	*$20,250*	
USX Corp*	$5,000	PAC
Waste Management	*$13,500*	
Waste Management Inc	$11,000	PAC/Ind

Finance, Insurance & Real Estate		$403,798
Commercial Banks	*$29,250*	
American Bankers Assn	$5,000	PAC
Barnett Banks Inc	$5,000	PAC
Credit Unions	*$5,250*	
Credit Union National Assn	$5,000	PAC
Finance/Credit Companies	*$19,500*	
Beneficial Management Corp	$9,500	PAC
Household International Inc	$6,000	PAC/Ind
Securities & Investment	*$124,600*	
Chicago Mercantile Exchange	$20,250	PAC/Ind
Chicago Board of Options Exchange ..	$10,000	PAC
Chicago Board of Trade	$9,250	PAC/Ind
American Express*	$6,000	PAC
Goldman, Sachs & Co	$6,000	PAC/Ind
Merrill Lynch	$6,000	PAC/Ind
Dean Witter	$5,000	PAC
Investment Company Institute	$5,000	PAC
Morgan Stanley & Co	$5,000	PAC
National Venture Capital Assn	$5,000	PAC
Insurance	*$144,198*	
American Family Corp	$10,000	PAC
Blue Cross & Blue Shield Assn* ..	$10,000	PAC/Ind
Prudential Insurance	$6,000	PAC
CNA Financial Corp	$5,000	PAC
Chubb Corp	$5,000	PAC
Cigna Corp	$5,000	PAC
Lincoln National Corp	$5,000	PAC
Massachusetts Mutual Life Insurance ..	$5,000	PAC
Metropolitan Life Insurance	$5,000	PAC
National Assn of Life Underwriters ..	$5,000	PAC
National Structured Settlements Assn ..	$5,000	PAC

Contribution Totals by Sector

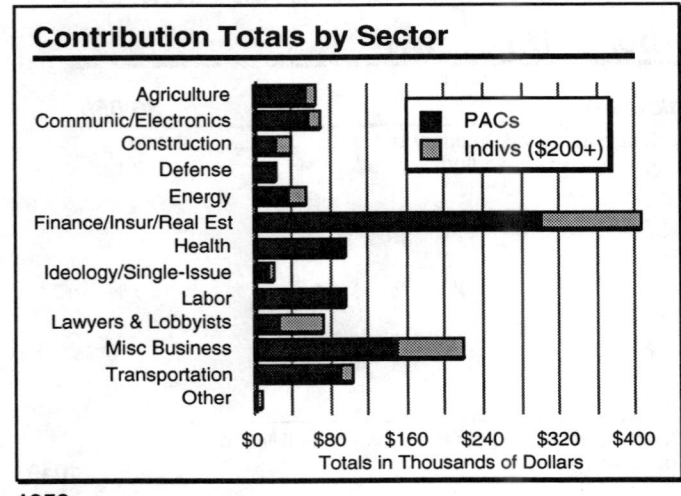

Agriculture, Communic/Electronics, Construction, Defense, Energy, Finance/Insur/Real Est, Health, Ideology/Single-Issue, Labor, Lawyers & Lobbyists, Misc Business, Transportation, Other

PACs / Indivs ($200+)

$0 $80 $160 $240 $320 $400
Totals in Thousands of Dollars

Northwestern Mutual Life ....$5,000 PAC
Torchmark Corp ....$5,000 PAC
TransAmerica Life Companies ....$5,000 PAC

Real Estate **$51,750**
National Assn of Realtors ....$10,000 PAC
National Realty Committee ....$6,000 PAC
National Apartment Assn ....$5,000 PAC

Accountants **$18,750**
American Institute of CPA's ....$10,000 PAC

Health $94,400

Health Professionals **$36,100**
American Dental Assn.....................................$10,000 PAC
American Medical Assn.....................................$10,000 PAC
American College of Emergency Physicians ....$5,000 PAC

Hospitals/Nursing Homes **$12,800**
American Hospital Assn ....$8,250 PAC
Federation of American Health Systems ....$5,000 PAC

Pharmaceuticals/Health Products **$45,500**
Baxter Healthcare Corp....................................$10,000 PAC
Abbott Laboratories ....$5,000 PAC
Glaxo Inc ....$5,000 PAC
Pfizer Inc ....$5,000 PAC

Lawyers & Lobbyists $70,081

Lawyers & Lobbyists **$70,081**
Skadden, Arps et al ....$5,500 PAC/Ind
Assn of Trial Lawyers of America ....$5,000 PAC
Lehrfeld, Canter, Henzke ....$5,000 Indiv

Misc Business $215,507

Food & Beverage **$28,000**
Pepsi-Cola General Bottlers ....$5,000 PAC

Beer, Wine & Liquor **$57,000**
Wine & Spirits Wholesalers of America ....$10,000 PAC
Wine Institute ....$10,000 PAC
Joseph E Seagram & Sons ....$6,250 PAC/Ind
Bacardi Imports ....$5,000 Indiv

Retail Sales.. **$49,507**
International Council of Shopping Centers ....$5,000 PAC
Limited Inc ....$5,000 PAC
May Department Stores ....$5,000 PAC
Spiegel Inc ....$5,000 PAC

Spending in Last 3 Elections

	1988	1990	1992
Rostenkowski	$428,607	$298,653	$1,455,455
Opponent	$0	$0	$83,293
Vote Pct	75%	79%	57%

Misc Services **$5,000**
American Assn of Equipment Lessors ....$5,000 PAC

Recreation/Live Entertainment **$5,000**
PGA Tour Inc..$5,000 PAC/Ind

Misc Business **$6,000**
National Assn of Wholesale-Distributors ....$5,000 PAC

Chemical & Related Manufacturing **$13,000**
El du Pont de Nemours & Co ....$5,000 PAC
Procter & Gamble ....$5,000 PAC

Misc Manufacturing & Distributing **$26,250**
American National Can Co ....$7,250 PAC/Ind

Transportation $100,750

Air Transport **$32,500**
United Airlines ....$7,000 PAC
Aircraft Owners & Pilots Assn ....$5,000 PAC
Gulfstream Aerospace ....$5,000 PAC
United Parcel Service ....$5,000 PAC

Automotive **$19,250**
Ford Motor Co ....$5,000 PAC
General Motors ....$5,000 PAC
National Auto Dealers Assn ....$5,000 PAC

Trucking **$16,750**
American Trucking Assns ....$5,000 PAC
Yellow Freight System ....$5,000 PAC

Railroads **$25,750**
Union Pacific Corp ....$10,000 PAC

Labor

Labor $93,500

Building Trade Unions **$20,500**
AFL-CIO Bldg/Construction Trades Dept ....$5,000 PAC
Carpenters & Joiners Union ....$5,000 PAC
Laborers' Political League ....$5,000 PAC
Plumbers/Pipefitters Union ....$5,000 PAC

Industrial Unions **$10,000**
United Auto Workers ....$5,000 PAC
United Mine Workers ....$5,000 PAC

Transportation Unions **$15,000**
Air Line Pilots Assn ....$5,000 PAC
Teamsters Union ....$5,000 PAC

Public Sector Unions **$35,500**
National Education Assn ....$10,000 PAC
National Rural Letter Carriers Assn ....$10,000 PAC
American Fedn of St/Cnty/Munic Employees ......$5,000 PAC
National Assn of Letter Carriers ....$5,000 PAC

Misc Unions... **$12,500**
Food & Commercial Workers Union ....$5,000 PAC
Hotel/Restaurant Employees Union ....$5,000 PAC

Ideological/Single-Issue

Ideological/Single-Issue $21,273

Pro-Israel **$7,250**
National PAC ....$5,000 PAC

Other & Unknown

Unknown $58,850

No Employer Listed or Found $16,800
Employer Listed/Category Unknown $39,050
None over $5,000

---

* Contributions came from more than one affiliate or subsidiary.

Toby Roth, R-Wis (8)

First elected: 1978

1991-92 Total Receipts: $589,778
1992 Year-end Cash: $239,081

1991-92 Committees & Subcommittees

Banking, Finance and Urban Affairs
Domestic Monetary Policy (Ranking Republican); Financial Institutions Supervision, Regulation and Insurance; Policy Research and Insurance

Foreign Affairs
Africa; Asian and Pacific Affairs; International Economic Policy and Trade (Ranking Republican)

Leading Contributors

Business

Agriculture		**$50,900**
Crop Production & Basic Processing		**$3,800**
None over $1,500		
Tobacco		**$5,050**
Philip Morris	$2,800	PAC
Dairy		**$11,000**
Associated Milk Producers	$5,300	PAC
Mid-America Dairymen	$3,000	PAC
Schreiber Foods	$1,700	Indiv
Agricultural Services/Products		**$5,000**
Land O'Lakes Inc	$2,000	PAC
Farm Credit Council	$1,500	PAC
Food Processing & Sales		**$4,350**
Pepsico Inc	$2,000	PAC
Forestry & Forest Products		**$18,450**
International Paper Co	$5,000	PAC
Fort Howard Corp	$2,400	PAC
Newark Paperboard Mill	$2,000	Indiv
Scott Paper Co	$2,000	PAC
Westvaco Corp	$2,000	PAC
Misc Agriculture		**$2,500**
Grey Fox Farm	$2,500	Indiv

Communications/Electronics		**$16,150**
Printing & Publishing		**$2,000**
Crystal Print	$1,500	Indiv
Telephone Utilities		**$9,600**
Ameritech Corp*	$6,300	PAC
AT&T	$2,300	PAC

Source of Funds in 1992 Election

	Source	Total	Pct
■	PACs	$292,200	50%
▨	Indivs $200+	$109,135	18%
☐	Indivs under $200	$158,188	27%
⊠	Other	$30,255	5%
	Candidate	$0	0%
	Party	$5,538	1%

Source of PAC Dollars by Sector

	Source	Total	Pct
■	Business	$270,435	93%
▨	Labor	$2,000	1%
☐	Ideology/Single Issue	$17,900	6%

In-State vs. Out-of-State Contributions*

	Source	Total	Pct
☐	In-State	$84,585	78%
■	Out-of-state	$24,550	22%
	No state listed	$0	

* by large individual contributors ($200 & above)

Electronics Mfg & Services		**$2,000**
North American Philips Corp	$1,500	PAC

Construction		**$22,200**
General Contractors		**$7,500**
J-Mark Construction	$2,000	Indiv
Home Builders		**$7,750**
National Assn of Home Builders	$5,000	PAC
Special Trade Contractors		**$3,800**
Suburban Electric	$2,250	Indiv
Building Materials & Equipment		**$2,000**
None over $1,500		

Defense		**$9,100**
Defense Aerospace		**$5,900**
None over $1,500		
Defense Electronics		**$2,700**
E-Systems Inc	$1,700	PAC

Energy & Natural Resources		**$18,300**
Oil & Gas		**$8,000**
Schmidt Oil Co	$2,700	Indiv
Mining		**$2,500**
Reynolds Metals	$2,500	PAC
Misc Energy		**$2,200**
Combustion Engineering	$2,200	PAC
Electric Utilities		**$5,600**
Wisconsin Electric Power Co	$1,800	PAC

Finance, Insurance & Real Estate		**$141,725**
Commercial Banks		**$69,025**
American Bankers Assn*	$10,000	PAC
JP Morgan & Co	$6,000	PAC
Chase Manhattan	$4,000	PAC
M&I Bank	$3,750	Indiv
Banc One Corp*	$3,350	PAC/Ind

Contribution Totals by Sector

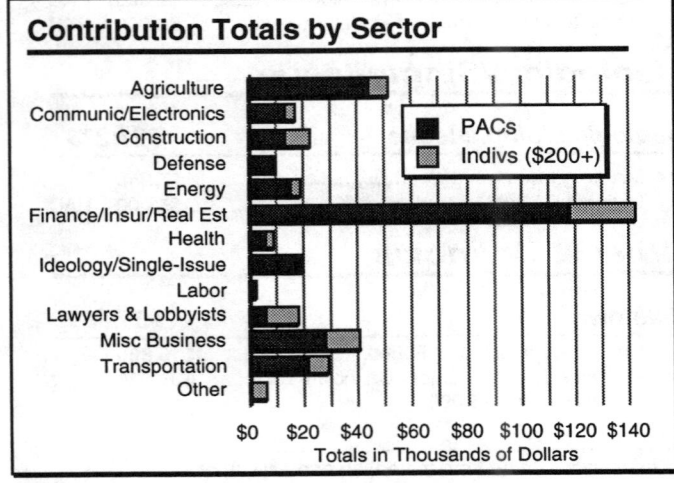

Agriculture, Communic/Electronics, Construction, Defense, Energy, Finance/Insur/Real Est, Health, Ideology/Single-Issue, Labor, Lawyers & Lobbyists, Misc Business, Transportation, Other

Legend: PACs, Indivs ($200+)

$0 $20 $40 $60 $80 $100 $120 $140
Totals in Thousands of Dollars

Independent Bankers Assn	$2,550	PAC
Citicorp	$2,500	PAC
First Wisconsin Corp	$2,500	PAC
Barnett Banks Inc	$2,000	PAC
Citizens & Southern National Bank	$2,000	PAC
Norwest Corp	$2,000	PAC
Northern Trust Co	$1,750	PAC
Assn of Bank Holding Companies	$1,500	PAC
First Interstate Bank of California	$1,500	PAC

Savings & Loans ... $7,000
US League of Savings Assns	$2,000	PAC
First Financial Savings	$1,650	PAC

Credit Unions ... $7,050
Credit Union National Assn	$4,500	PAC
Community First Credit	$1,550	Indiv

Finance/Credit Companies ... $2,000
Associated Credit Bureaus	$1,500	PAC

Securities & Investment ... $4,500
None over $1,500

Insurance ... $32,150
Northwestern Mutual Life	$4,000	PAC
Aid Assn for Lutherans	$3,450	PAC
American Council of Life Insurance	$2,000	PAC
National Assn of Life Underwriters	$2,000	PAC
American International Group Inc	$1,750	PAC
American Medical Security	$1,600	Indiv
Acacia Mutual Life Insurance	$1,500	PAC
Capital Holding Corp	$1,500	PAC
National Assn of Independent Insurers	$1,500	PAC

Real Estate ... $9,500
National Assn of Realtors	$6,000	PAC
Landmark Properties	$1,500	Indiv

Accountants ... $9,250
Arthur Andersen & Co	$4,000	PAC
American Institute of CPA's	$2,500	PAC
Ernst & Young	$1,500	PAC

Health — $8,800

Health Professionals ... $6,500
American Medical Assn	$3,350	PAC

Lawyers & Lobbyists — $17,610

Lawyers & Lobbyists ... $17,610
Baker & Botts	$2,000	PAC
Waterman & Associates	$2,000	Indiv
Hopkins & Sutter	$1,500	PAC

Misc Business — $39,610

Food & Beverage ... $6,400
National Restaurant Assn	$4,000	PAC

Business Services ... $3,350
Outdoor Advertising Assn of America	$1,500	PAC

Lodging/Tourism ... $6,350
American Hotel & Motel Assn	$2,000	PAC

Chemical & Related Manufacturing ... $5,000
None over $1,500

Misc Manufacturing & Distributing ... $13,350
Stone Container Corp	$3,000	PAC
SC Johnson & Son Inc	$2,500	Indiv

Transportation — $27,850

Air Transport ... $7,200
United Parcel Service	$3,400	PAC
United Airlines	$1,500	PAC

Automotive ... $10,500
Auto Dealers & Drivers for Free Trade	$4,000	PAC
National Auto Dealers Assn	$3,000	PAC

Trucking ... $4,750
None over $1,500

Sea Transport ... $3,650
Peterson Shipbuilding	$2,000	Indiv

Labor

Labor — $2,000

Public Sector Unions ... $2,000
National Assn Retired Federal Employees	$1,500	PAC

Ideological/Single-Issue

Ideological/Single-Issue — $19,300

Republican/Conservative ... $6,200
Conservative Victory Committee	$5,000	PAC

Gun Rights/Gun Control ... $11,100
National Rifle Assn	$9,900	PAC

Misc Issues ... $2,000
None over $1,500

Other & Unknown

Other — $5,500

Retired ... $4,750
None over $1,500

Unknown — $20,425
Homemakers/Non-income earners	$2,200	
No Employer Listed or Found	$4,825	
Employer Listed/Category Unknown	$13,200	
Utschig Enterprises	$2,100	Indiv

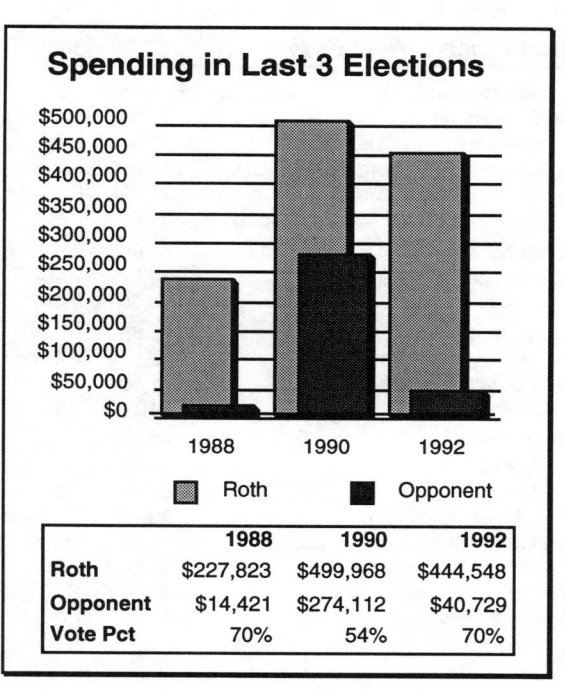

Spending in Last 3 Elections

	1988	1990	1992
Roth	$227,823	$499,968	$444,548
Opponent	$14,421	$274,112	$40,729
Vote Pct	70%	54%	70%

Roth / Opponent

---

* Contributions came from more than one affiliate or subsidiary.

1053

Marge Roukema, R-NJ (5)

First elected: 1980

1991-92 Total Receipts: $439,150
1992 Year-end Cash: $32,842

1991-92 Committees & Subcommittees

Banking, Finance and Urban Affairs
Financial Institutions Supervision, Regulation and Insurance; Housing and Community Development (Ranking Republican); International Development, Finance, Trade and Monetary Policy

Education and Labor
Elementary, Secondary and Vocational Education; Labor-Management Relations (Ranking Republican); Postsecondary Education

Select Committee on Hunger

Leading Contributors

Business

Agriculture	$11,900	
Crop Production & Basic Processing	**$1,850**	
None over $1,500		
Agricultural Services/Products	**$4,300**	
Chemical Producers & Distributors Assn	$2,500	PAC
Food Processing & Sales	**$2,500**	
Food Marketing Institute	$1,500	PAC
Forestry & Forest Products	**$3,250**	
None over $1,500		

Communications/Electronics	$13,775	
Telephone Utilities	**$10,475**	
AT&T	$2,975	PAC
New Jersey Bell Telephone	$2,000	PAC

Construction	$24,900	
General Contractors	**$10,500**	
Pike Construction Co	$3,000	Indiv
Associated General Contractors	$2,500	PAC
Home Builders	**$10,000**	
National Assn of Home Builders	$5,000	PAC
Liberty Homes Inc	$1,500	Indiv
Special Trade Contractors	**$1,500**	
None over $1,500		
Building Materials & Equipment	**$2,950**	
None over $1,500		

Contribution Totals by Sector

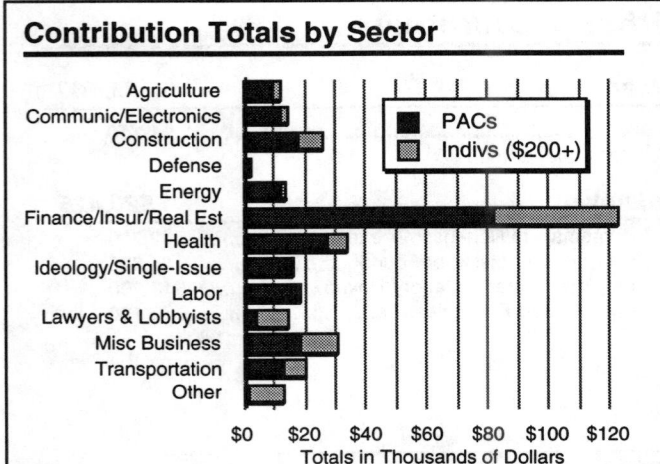

Agriculture
Communic/Electronics
Construction
Defense
Energy
Finance/Insur/Real Est
Health
Ideology/Single-Issue
Labor
Lawyers & Lobbyists
Misc Business
Transportation
Other

■ PACs
▨ Indivs ($200+)

$0 $20 $40 $60 $80 $100 $120
Totals in Thousands of Dollars

Source of Funds in 1992 Election

Source	Total	Pct
■ PACs	$224,598	51%
▨ Indivs $200+	$122,800	28%
☐ Indivs under $200	$76,799	17%
▧ Other	$14,953	3%
Candidate	$0	0%
Party	$80	0%

Source of PAC Dollars by Sector

Source	Total	Pct
■ Business	$193,074	86%
▨ Labor	$17,700	8%
☐ Ideology/Single Issue	$14,750	7%

In-State vs. Out-of-State Contributions*

Source	Total	Pct
☐ In-State	$111,740	91%
■ Out-of-state	$11,060	9%
No state listed	$0	

* by large individual contributors ($200 & above)

Defense	$2,250	
Defense Aerospace	**$2,250**	
None over $1,500		

Energy & Natural Resources	$12,850	
Oil & Gas	**$2,250**	
None over $1,500		
Mining	**$1,500**	
None over $1,500		
Electric Utilities	**$9,100**	
Public Service Electric & Gas	$4,600	PAC
Orange & Rockland Utilities	$2,500	PAC

Finance, Insurance & Real Estate	$123,485	
Commercial Banks	**$23,950**	
American Bankers Assn	$7,500	PAC
Chase Manhattan	$2,500	PAC
National Comm Bank of New Jersey	$2,000	Indiv
Chemical Bank	$1,500	PAC
Independent Bankers Assn	$1,500	PAC
Savings & Loans	**$9,069**	
US League of Savings Assns*	$4,519	PAC
Hudson City Savings Bank	$2,500	Indiv
Finance/Credit Companies	**$16,500**	
Beneficial Management Corp	$12,500	PAC/Ind
Associated Credit Bureaus	$1,500	PAC
Household International Inc	$1,500	PAC
Securities & Investment	**$30,062**	
Goldman, Sachs & Co	$4,500	PAC/Ind
Shearson Lehman Brothers	$3,500	PAC/Ind
Donaldson, Lufkin & Jenrette	$3,000	PAC/Ind
John Head & Partners	$2,000	Indiv
Morgan Stanley & Co	$1,500	PAC/Ind
PaineWebber	$1,500	PAC/Ind
Prudential Securities	$1,500	PAC

Insurance	$21,704	
Metropolitan Life Insurance	$2,604	PAC/Ind
American Council of Life Insurance	$1,500	PAC
Health Insurance Assn of America	$1,500	PAC
National Assn of Independent Insurers	$1,500	PAC
Prudential Insurance	$1,500	PAC/Ind

Real Estate	$17,150	
National Assn of Realtors	$2,500	PAC
Century 21 Real Estate	$2,000	PAC
Summit Associates Inc	$2,000	Indiv

Accountants	$2,500	
American Institute of CPA's	$2,500	PAC

Misc Finance	$2,050	
None over $1,500		

Health — $33,350

Health Professionals	$19,950	
American Medical Assn	$4,850	PAC/Ind
New Jersey Medical Assn	$3,500	PAC
American Assn Oral & Maxillofacial Surgeons	$3,000	PAC
American Podiatry Assn	$2,000	PAC

Pharmaceuticals/Health Products	$11,900	
Warner-Lambert	$2,000	PAC/Ind
Schering-Plough Corp	$1,700	PAC/Ind

Lawyers & Lobbyists — $13,700

Lawyers & Lobbyists	$13,700	
Fontheim & O'Rourke	$1,500	Indiv

Misc Business — $29,804

Food & Beverage	$3,000	
National Restaurant Assn	$2,000	PAC

Beer, Wine & Liquor	$3,004	
None over $1,500		

Retail Sales	$3,500	
None over $1,500		

Business Services	$5,500	
National Assn of Temporary Services	$2,000	PAC

Misc Business	$3,000	
Hudson Tank Terminals Corp	$2,000	Indiv

Chemical & Related Manufacturing	$2,700	
None over $1,500		

Misc Manufacturing & Distributing	$7,000	
Stone Container Corp	$2,500	PAC
Hoechst Celanese Corp	$2,000	PAC

Transportation — $19,500

Air Transport	$5,700	
United Parcel Service	$3,500	PAC

Automotive	$6,300	
General Automotive Specialty Co	$1,500	Indiv
National Auto Dealers Assn	$1,500	PAC

Trucking	$2,500	
None over $1,500		

Railroads	$3,500	
Gregg Co Ltd	$2,000	Indiv
Delaware Otsego Corp	$1,500	PAC

Sea Transport	$1,500	
None over $1,500		

Labor

Labor — $17,700

Transportation Unions	$5,700	
Air Line Pilots Assn	$3,000	PAC

Public Sector Unions	$12,000	
National Assn Retired Federal Employees	$4,000	PAC
National Education Assn	$2,500	PAC
American Fedn of St/Cnty/Munic Employees	$2,000	PAC

Ideological/Single-Issue

Ideological/Single-Issue — $15,850

Republican/Conservative	$1,850	
None over $1,500		

Leadership PACs	$2,750	
Cmte for an Affordable NJ (C. Whitman)	$2,250	PAC

Pro-Choice	$2,000	
Republicans for Choice	$2,000	PAC

Womens Issues	$4,000	
Wish List	$2,000	PAC
Women's Campaign Fund	$2,000	PAC

Misc Issues	$3,500	
National Cmte to Preserve Social Security	$3,000	PAC

Other & Unknown

Other — $12,600

Education	$2,300	
None over $1,500		

Retired	$9,800	
None over $1,500		

Unknown — $17,660

No Employer Listed or Found	$3,100	
Employer Listed/Category Unknown	$13,810	
Bolger & Co Inc	$2,000	Indiv
JF Fletcher & Son	$1,500	Indiv

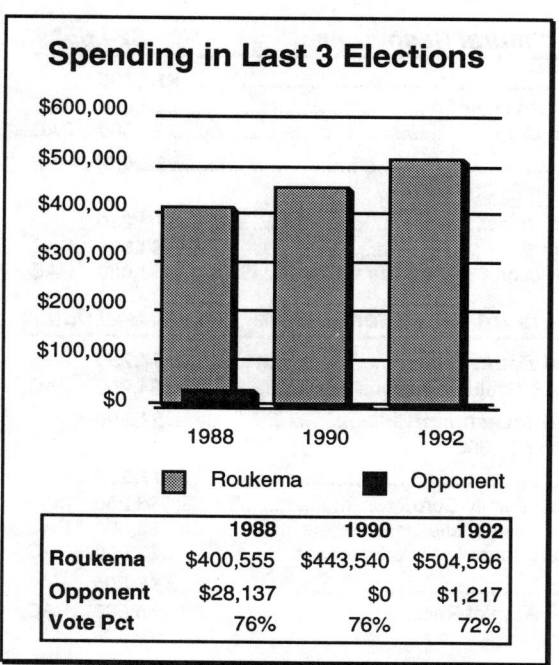

Spending in Last 3 Elections

	1988	1990	1992
Roukema	$400,555	$443,540	$504,596
Opponent	$28,137	$0	$1,217
Vote Pct	76%	76%	72%

* Contributions came from more than one affiliate or subsidiary.

J. Roy Rowland, D-Ga (8)

First elected: 1982

1991-92 Total Receipts: $454,319
1992 Year-end Cash: $120,061

1991-92 Committees & Subcommittees

Energy and Commerce
Commerce, Consumer Protection and Competitiveness; Health and the Environment; Oversight and Investigations

Veterans' Affairs
Compensation, Pension and Insurance; Hospitals and Health Care (Vice Chairman)

Select Committee on Children, Youth and Families

Leading Contributors

Business

Agriculture — $38,103

Crop Production & Basic Processing	**$5,350**	
None over $1,500		
Tobacco	**$11,503**	
RJR Nabisco	$6,000	PAC
Philip Morris	$1,753	PAC
US Tobacco Co	$1,500	PAC
Dairy	**$1,500**	
None over $1,500		
Poultry & Eggs	**$2,000**	
None over $1,500		
Livestock	**$2,000**	
National Cattlemen's Assn*	$1,500	PAC
Agricultural Services/Products	**$4,250**	
Freeport-McMoRan Inc	$1,500	PAC
Food Processing & Sales	**$6,750**	
Food Marketing Institute	$2,000	PAC
Pepsico Inc	$1,500	PAC
Forestry & Forest Products	**$3,750**	
None over $1,500		

Communications/Electronics — $24,000

Media/Entertainment	**$9,750**	
National Cable Television Assn	$4,000	PAC
National Assn of Broadcasters	$3,000	PAC
Telephone Utilities	**$13,250**	
Southern Bell	$7,500	PAC
AT&T	$2,500	PAC

Contribution Totals by Sector

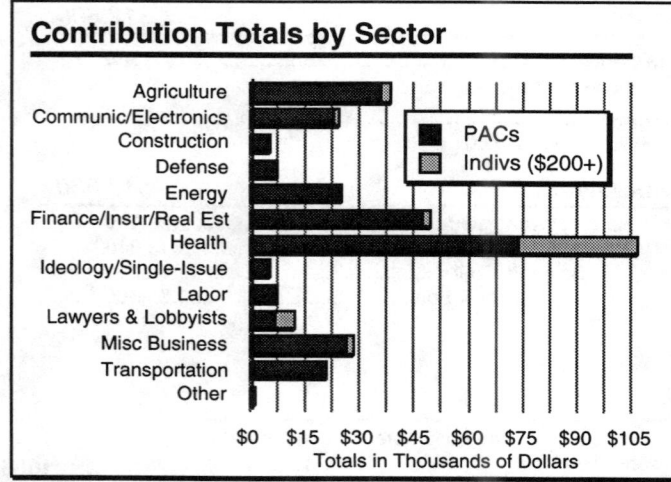

Totals in Thousands of Dollars

Source of Funds in 1992 Election

Source	Total	Pct
PACs	$286,099	62%
Indivs $200+	$54,033	12%
Indivs under $200	$60,231	13%
Other	$60,458	13%
Candidate	$0	0%
Party	$7,302	2%

Source of PAC Dollars by Sector

Source	Total	Pct
Business	$266,374	96%
Labor	$6,691	2%
Ideology/Single Issue	$4,500	2%

In-State vs. Out-of-State Contributions*

Source	Total	Pct
In-State	$46,785	87%
Out-of-state	$7,248	13%
No state listed	$0	

*** by large individual contributors ($200 & above)**

Construction — $5,000

Home Builders	**$2,500**	
National Assn of Home Builders	$2,500	PAC
Building Materials & Equipment	**$1,500**	
None over $1,500		

Defense — $7,000

Defense Aerospace	**$5,000**	
Lockheed Corp	$1,500	PAC
Defense Electronics	**$2,000**	
None over $1,500		

Energy & Natural Resources — $24,652

Oil & Gas	**$10,100**	
Atlanta Gas Light Co	$2,000	PAC
Chevron Corp	$2,000	PAC
Mining	**$2,802**	
None over $1,500		
Electric Utilities	**$10,250**	
Southern Co*	$4,500	PAC
ACRE (Action Cmte for Rural Electrification)	$3,000	PAC

Finance, Insurance & Real Estate — $49,000

Commercial Banks	**$7,750**	
Citizens & Southern National Bank	$4,250	PAC
Securities & Investment	**$1,500**	
None over $1,500		
Insurance	**$17,250**	
American Family Corp	$6,250	Indiv
National Assn of Life Underwriters	$2,500	PAC
American Council of Life Insurance	$2,000	PAC
Real Estate	**$5,500**	
National Assn of Realtors	$5,000	PAC

Accountants **$16,500**
    American Institute of CPA's ....$8,000 PAC
    Coopers & Lybrand ....$2,500 PAC
    Arthur Andersen & Co ....$2,000 PAC
    Deloitte & Touche ....$2,000 PAC
    Ernst & Young ....$1,500 PAC

Health $105,950

Health Professionals **$72,200**
    American Medical Assn* ....$9,450 PAC
    American Academy of Ophthalmology ....$6,000 PAC
    American College of Emergency Physicians ....$5,000 PAC
    American Dental Assn ....$4,500 PAC
    Clark Eye Clinic ....$4,000 Indiv
    American Assn Oral & Maxillofacial Surgeons ....$2,000 PAC
    American Soc Plastic & Reconstr Surgeons ....$2,000 PAC
    Assn for the Advancement of Psychology ....$2,000 PAC
    Kaufmann Diagnostic Clinic ....$2,000 Indiv
    American Podiatry Assn ....$1,500 PAC

Hospitals/Nursing Homes **$10,850**
    American Hospital Assn ....$4,000 PAC
    American Health Care Assn ....$2,500 PAC

Health Services **$2,250**
    None over $1,500

Pharmaceuticals/Health Products **$19,950**
    Schering-Plough Corp ....$4,500 PAC
    Merck & Co ....$2,500 PAC
    Eli Lilly & Co ....$1,500 PAC

Lawyers & Lobbyists $11,498

Lawyers & Lobbyists **$11,498**
    King & Spalding ....$2,000 PAC
    Ginn, Edington et al ....$1,548 Indiv

Misc Business   **$28,069**

Food & Beverage **$7,550**
    Coca-Cola Co* ....$4,500 PAC

Beer, Wine & Liquor **$3,250**
    National Beer Wholesalers Assn ....$2,000 PAC

Retail Sales **$2,000**
    None over $1,500

Business Services **$1,500**
    None over $1,500

Chemical & Related Manufacturing **$6,800**
    Dow Chemical ....$2,000 PAC
    Mallinckrodt Inc ....$2,000 PAC

Misc Manufacturing & Distributing **$3,769**
    Cosmetic, Toiletry & Fragrance Assn ....$2,069 PAC

Transportation $20,750

Air Transport **$7,000**
    United Parcel Service ....$3,000 PAC
    Delta Airlines ....$1,500 PAC

Automotive **$8,250**
    National Auto Dealers Assn ....$5,000 PAC

Trucking **$2,500**
    Watkins Associated Industries ....$1,500 PAC

Railroads **$3,000**
    None over $1,500

Labor

Labor   **$6,691**

Transportation Unions **$1,500**
    United Transportation Union ....$1,500 PAC

Public Sector Unions **$4,691**
    Southern States Police Benevolent Assn ....$2,491 PAC

Ideological/Single-Issue

Ideological/Single-Issue   **$5,000**

Gun Rights/Gun Control **$1,500**
    National Rifle Assn ....$1,500 PAC

Misc Issues **$1,500**
    None over $1,500

Other & Unknown

Unknown   **$5,335**

    Employer Listed/Category Unknown $3,885
      None over $1,500

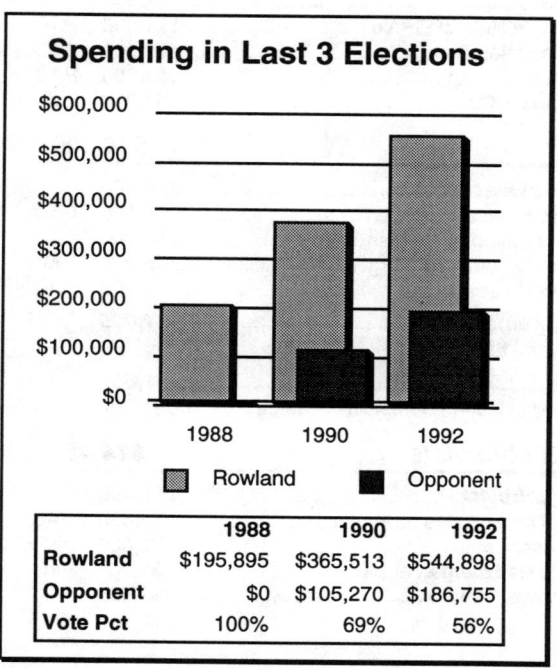

Spending in Last 3 Elections

	1988	1990	1992
Rowland	$195,895	$365,513	$544,898
Opponent	$0	$105,270	$186,755
Vote Pct	100%	69%	56%

* Contributions came from more than one affiliate or subsidiary.

Lucille Roybal-Allard, D-Calif (33)

First elected: 1992

1991-92 Total Receipts: $283,770
1992 Year-end Cash: $19,015

1993-94 Committees & Subcommittees

Banking, Finance and Urban Affairs
Consumer Credit and Insurance; Housing and Community Development

Small Business
Minority Enterprise, Finance and Urban Development; SBA Legislation and the General Economy

Leading Contributors

Business

Agriculture — $9,250

Crop Production & Basic Processing $1,500
  None over $1,000

Dairy $1,000
  Associated Milk Producers .... $1,000   PAC

Food Processing & Sales $6,250
  Americo .... $2,000   Indiv
  Jonsons Market Inc .... $1,250   Indiv
  El Rey Sausage Co .... $1,000   Indiv
  Pepsico Inc .... $1,000   PAC

Communications/Electronics — $5,750

Media/Entertainment $2,750
  Peg Yorkin Productions .... $1,000   Indiv

Telephone Utilities $3,000
  Pacific Telesis Group .... $1,000   PAC
  United Telecommunications .... $1,000   PAC

Construction — $3,102

Construction Services $1,500
  None over $1,000

Energy & Natural Resources — $1,500

Waste Management $1,000
  Waste Management Inc .... $1,000   PAC

Finance, Insurance & Real Estate — $26,750

Commercial Banks $1,750
  American Bankers Assn .... $1,000   PAC

Credit Unions $1,000
  Credit Union National Assn .... $1,000   PAC

Securities & Investment $1,500
  Yellin Co .... $1,000   Indiv

Insurance $1,250
  None over $1,000

Real Estate $16,500
  National Assn of Realtors .... $7,500   PAC
  Fisch Properties .... $2,000   Indiv
  Telecu Industries .... $2,000   Indiv
  Jaeger Development .... $1,000   Indiv
  Jonas & Assoc .... $1,000   Indiv

Accountants $4,500
  American Institute of CPA's .... $1,000   PAC
  Arthur Andersen & Co .... $1,000   PAC
  Coopers & Lybrand .... $1,000   PAC
  RJ Miranda & Co .... $1,000   Indiv

Health — $18,300

Health Professionals $14,500
  American Medical Assn .... $5,000   PAC
  American Chiropractic Assn .... $2,000   PAC
  American College of Emergency Physicians .... $2,000   PAC
  American Nurses Assn .... $1,000   PAC

Hospitals/Nursing Homes $1,000
  None over $1,000

Misc Health $1,800
  Community Health Foundation .... $1,300   Indiv

Lawyers & Lobbyists — $14,450

Lawyers & Lobbyists $14,450
  Assn of Trial Lawyers of America .... $5,000   PAC
  MARC Associates .... $2,000   Indiv
  Margolis, Hertzberg et al .... $1,000   Indiv
  O'Melveny & Myers .... $1,000   PAC

Source of Funds in 1992 Election

Source	Total	Pct
PACs	$133,587	47%
Indivs $200+	$74,122	26%
Indivs under $200	$69,980	24%
Other	$8,567	3%
Candidate	$0	0%
Party	$2,486	1%

Source of PAC Dollars by Sector

Source	Total	Pct
Business	$48,150	47%
Labor	$29,600	29%
Ideology/Single Issue	$24,119	24%

In-State vs. Out-of-State Contributions*

Source	Total	Pct
In-State	$59,956	89%
Out-of-state	$7,500	11%
No state listed	$0	

* by large individual contributors ($200 & above)

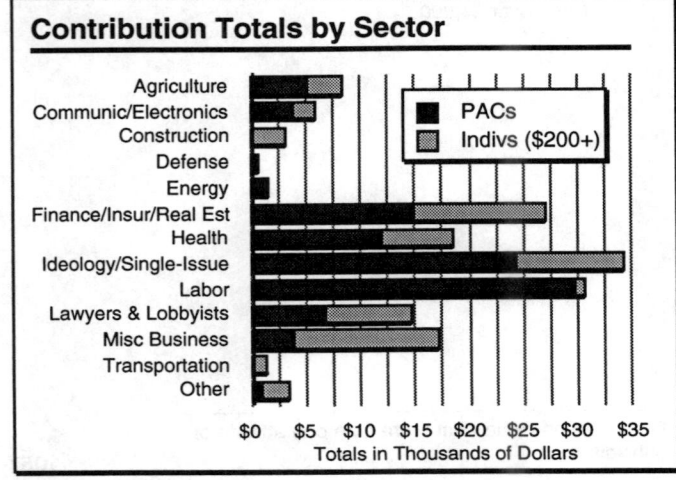

Contribution Totals by Sector

Categories: Agriculture, Communic/Electronics, Construction, Defense, Energy, Finance/Insur/Real Est, Health, Ideology/Single-Issue, Labor, Lawyers & Lobbyists, Misc Business, Transportation, Other

Legend: PACs, Indivs ($200+)

Totals in Thousands of Dollars ($0 $5 $10 $15 $20 $25 $30 $35)

Misc Business — $16,933

Food & Beverage **$1,900**
    McDonald's Corp ....$1,000   PAC

Beer, Wine & Liquor **$10,500**
    Gallo Winery ....$10,000   Indiv

Retail Sales **$1,000**
    None over $1,000

Business Services **$2,533**
    None over $1,000

Transportation — $1,250

Automotive **$1,250**
    Camino Real Chevrolet ....$1,000   Indiv

Labor

Labor — $30,350

Building Trade Unions **$1,250**
    Painters & Allied Trades Union/Calif ....$1,000   PAC

Industrial Unions **$9,350**
    United Auto Workers ....$5,000   PAC
    Machinists/Aerospace Workers Union ....$3,500   PAC

Transportation Unions **$6,500**
    Teamsters Union ....$5,000   PAC
    United Transportation Union ....$1,000   PAC

Public Sector Unions **$9,000**
    American Federation of Teachers ....$2,500   PAC
    American Fedn of St/Cnty/Munic Employees ......$2,500   PAC
    National Rural Letter Carriers Assn ....$1,500   PAC
    International Assn of Firefighters ....$1,000   PAC
    National Assn Retired Federal Employees ....$1,000   PAC

Misc Unions **$4,250**
    Service Employees International Union ....$2,500   PAC
    Food & Commercial Workers Union ....$1,000   PAC

Ideological/Single-Issue

Ideological/Single-Issue — $33,969

Leadership PACs **$2,500**
    Effective Government Cmte (Dick Gephardt) ......$1,000   PAC
    House Leadership Fund (Tom Foley) ....$1,000   PAC

Pro-Israel **$7,250**
    National PAC ....$5,000   PAC
    Women's Alliance for Israel ....$1,000   PAC

Womens Issues **$21,105**
    Emily's List ....$9,215   PAC/Ind
    National Organization for Women ....$3,090   PAC
    National Womens Political Caucus ....$2,500   PAC
    Women's Political Committee ....$2,500   PAC
    Women's Campaign Fund ....$1,000   PAC

Human Rights **$1,300**
    Hispanic PAC USA ....$1,000   PAC

Misc Issues **$1,064**
    None over $1,000

Other & Unknown

Other — $3,171

Education **$1,521**
    None over $1,000

Unknown — $9,800

    Generic Occupation/Category Unknown $1,000
    Employer Listed/Category Unknown $7,800
        Denver Inv Adv...$1,000   Indiv

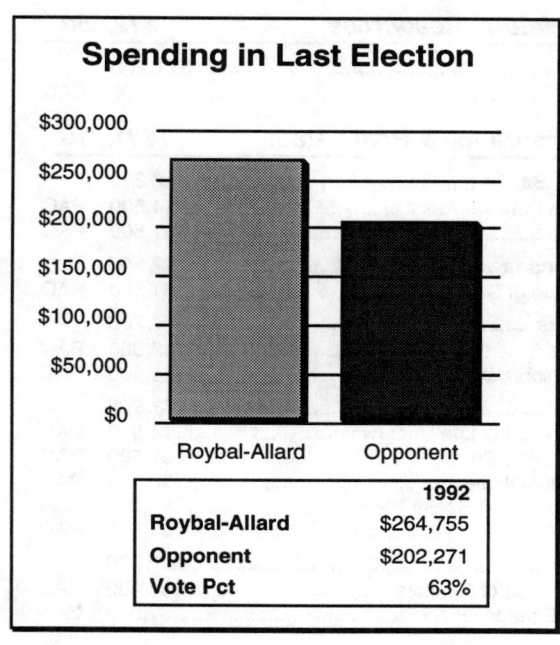

Spending in Last Election

	1992
Roybal-Allard	$264,755
Opponent	$202,271
Vote Pct	63%

Ed Royce, R-Calif (39)

First elected: 1992

1991-92 Total Receipts: $499,264
1992 Year-end Cash: $6,772

1993-94 Committees & Subcommittees

Foreign Affairs
Africa; Asia and the Pacific

Science, Space and Technology
Space; Technology, Environment and Aviation

Leading Contributors

Business

Agriculture — $19,800

Tobacco	**$5,500**	
RJR Nabisco	$2,000	PAC
US Tobacco Co	$2,000	PAC
Philip Morris	$1,500	PAC
Food Processing & Sales	**$6,750**	
ConAgra Inc	$2,000	PAC
Food Marketing Institute	$2,000	PAC
Forestry & Forest Products	**$2,000**	
None over $1,500		
Misc Agriculture	**$1,600**	
None over $1,500		

Communications/Electronics — $10,400

Printing & Publishing	**$2,200**	
None over $1,500		
Media/Entertainment	**$2,200**	
Walt Disney Co	$1,950	PAC
Telephone Utilities	**$3,250**	
None over $1,500		
Computer Equipment & Services	**$2,250**	
None over $1,500		

Construction — $20,400

General Contractors	**$7,650**	
Associated General Contractors	$2,500	PAC
Fluor Corp	$1,500	PAC
Home Builders	**$4,500**	
National Assn of Home Builders	$3,500	PAC

Source of Funds in 1992 Election

	Source	Total	Pct
■	PACs	$200,562	37%
▨	Indivs $200+	$195,886	36%
☐	Indivs under $200	$67,579	12%
⊠	Other	$81,328	15%
	Candidate	$10,000	2%
	Party	$47,091	9%

Source of PAC Dollars by Sector

	Source	Total	Pct
■	Business	$175,350	85%
▨	Labor	$2,000	1%
☐	Ideology/Single Issue	$29,045	14%

In-State vs. Out-of-State Contributions*

	Source	Total	Pct
☐	In-State	$187,361	96%
■	Out-of-state	$7,275	4%
	No state listed	$0	

* by large individual contributors ($200 & above)

Special Trade Contractors	**$2,700**	
None over $1,500		
Construction Services	**$2,100**	
None over $1,500		
Building Materials & Equipment	**$3,450**	
Orco Block Co	$1,750	Indiv

Defense — $6,250

Defense Aerospace	**$3,750**	
Rockwell International	$2,000	PAC
Defense Electronics	**$2,500**	
Hughes Aircraft	$2,000	PAC

Energy & Natural Resources — $12,650

Oil & Gas	**$11,400**	
Chevron Corp	$2,000	PAC

Finance, Insurance & Real Estate — $81,010

Commercial Banks	**$12,250**	
American Bankers Assn*	$4,500	PAC
Citicorp	$1,500	PAC
Savings & Loans	**$2,500**	
US League of Savings Assns*	$1,500	PAC
Credit Unions	**$4,700**	
California Credit Union League	$2,000	PAC
Credit Union National Assn	$1,500	PAC
Insurance	**$23,800**	
National Assn of Life Underwriters	$4,000	PAC
TransAmerica Corp*	$2,500	PAC
Pacific Mutual Life	$2,000	PAC
California Dental Health Plan	$1,950	Indiv
ITT Corp*	$1,500	PAC
Real Estate	**$21,780**	
National Assn of Realtors	$5,000	PAC
Tel Phil Enterprises Inc	$1,930	Indiv

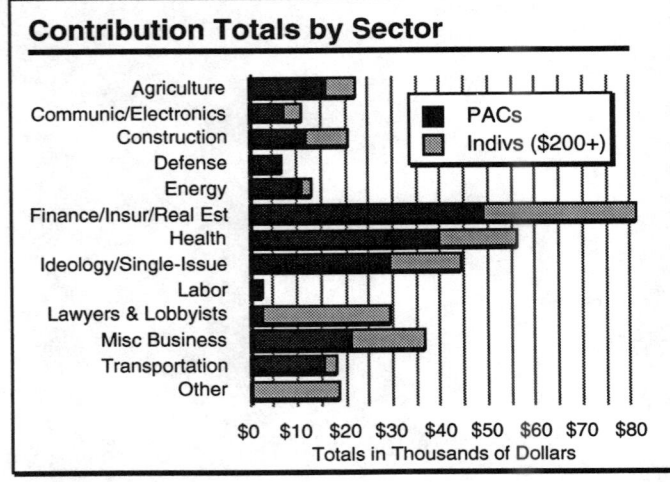

Contribution Totals by Sector

Sectors (top to bottom): Agriculture, Communic/Electronics, Construction, Defense, Energy, Finance/Insur/Real Est, Health, Ideology/Single-Issue, Labor, Lawyers & Lobbyists, Misc Business, Transportation, Other

Legend: ■ PACs ▨ Indivs ($200+)

$0 $10 $20 $30 $40 $50 $60 $70 $80
Totals in Thousands of Dollars

Accountants **$4,650**
    American Institute of CPA's .... $3,500   PAC

Misc Finance **$9,030**
    First Diversified Financial Service .... $4,000   Indiv

Health $55,792

Health Professionals **$39,667**
    American Medical Assn .... $7,500   PAC
    American Chiropractic Assn .... $5,000   PAC
    American Dental Assn .... $3,750   PAC
    American Academy of Ophthalmology .... $3,000   PAC
    American College of Emergency Physicians .... $2,000   PAC
    Cooperative of American Physicians .... $1,850   PAC
    American Optometric Assn .... $1,500   PAC

Hospitals/Nursing Homes **$5,900**
    American Health Care Assn .... $2,000   PAC

Health Services **$3,325**
    Family Health Program Inc .... $2,000   PAC

Pharmaceuticals/Health Products **$5,900**
    None over $1,500

Lawyers & Lobbyists $28,950

Lawyers & Lobbyists **$28,950**
    Federal Legislative Associates .... $2,000   Indiv
    Latham & Watkins .... $1,500   Indiv

Misc Business $38,250

Food & Beverage **$3,000**
    None over $1,500

Beer, Wine & Liquor **$5,900**
    National Beer Wholesalers Assn .... $3,000   PAC
    Triangle Distributing Co .... $1,900   Indiv

Retail Sales **$6,500**
    None over $1,500

Business Services **$3,150**
    National Assn of Temporary Services .... $1,500   PAC

Recreation/Live Entertainment **$2,050**
    Knott's Berry Farm .... $2,050   Indiv

Lodging/Tourism **$1,900**
    None over $1,500

Chemical & Related Manufacturing **$8,050**

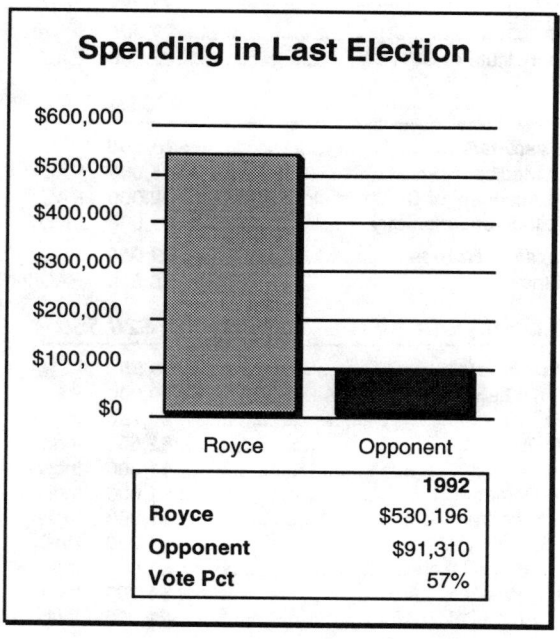

Spending in Last Election

	1992
Royce	$530,196
Opponent	$91,310
Vote Pct	57%

    Delst Chemical & Research Co .... $3,000   Indiv
    Procter & Gamble .... $1,500   PAC/Ind

Misc Manufacturing & Distributing **$6,700**
    Corning Glass Works .... $1,500   PAC
    Stone Container Corp .... $1,500   PAC

Transportation $17,800

Air Transport **$4,700**
    United Parcel Service .... $4,000   PAC

Automotive **$9,150**
    National Auto Dealers Assn .... $5,000   PAC
    Crevier BMW .... $1,500   Indiv

Railroads **$3,000**
    Union Pacific Corp .... $3,000   PAC

Labor

Labor   **$2,250**

Public Sector Unions **$2,000**
    National Assn Retired Federal Employees .... $1,500   PAC

Ideological/Single-Issue

Ideological/Single-Issue   **$43,768**

Republican/Conservative **$15,997**
    None over $1,500

Leadership PACs **$4,804**
    Republican Leader's Fund (Bob Michel) ...... $2,000   PAC

Pro-Israel **$6,750**
    National PAC .... $5,000   PAC

Gun Rights/Gun Control **$10,900**
    National Rifle Assn .... $9,900   PAC

Misc Issues **$4,567**
    Howard Jarvis Taxpayers Assn .... $2,000   PAC

Other & Unknown

Other   **$18,100**

Civil Servants/Public Officials **$5,600**
    Orange County .... $1,500   Indiv

Education **$2,750**
    United Education Institutes .... $1,750   Indiv

Retired **$9,250**
    None over $1,500

Unknown   **$45,811**

    Homemakers/Non-income earners $10,350
    Employer Listed/Category Unknown $33,861
        None over $1,500

---

* Contributions came from more than one affiliate or subsidiary.

Bobby L. Rush, D-Ill (1)

First elected: 1992
1991-92 Total Receipts: $257,455
1992 Year-end Cash: $112

1993-94 Committees & Subcommittees

Banking, Finance and Urban Affairs
Consumer Credit and Insurance; Housing and Community Development; International Development, Finance, Trade and Monetary Policy

Government Operations
Commerce, Consumer and Monetary Affairs; Employment, Housing and Aviation

Leading Contributors

Business

Agriculture		$5,500
Tobacco		**$2,500**
RJR Nabisco	$2,000	PAC
Dairy		**$1,000**
Associated Milk Producers	$1,000	PAC
Poultry & Eggs		**$1,000**
Tyson Foods	$1,000	PAC
Food Processing & Sales		**$1,000**
Brooks Sausage Co	$1,000	Indiv

Communications/Electronics		$3,500
Media/Entertainment		**$2,000**
Spring Creek Productions	$2,000	Indiv
Telephone Utilities		**$1,000**
AT&T	$1,000	PAC

Energy & Natural Resources		$9,000
Oil & Gas		**$6,000**
Coastal Corp	$5,000	PAC
Arkla Inc	$1,000	PAC
Electric Utilities		**$1,000**
Arkansas Power & Light	$1,000	Indiv
Waste Management		**$2,000**
Waste Management Inc	$2,000	PAC/Ind

Source of Funds in 1992 Election

Source	Total	Pct
PACs	$132,000	51%
Indivs $200+	$94,900	37%
Indivs under $200	$30,255	12%
Other	$5,150	2%
Candidate	$0	0%
Party	$5,150	2%

Source of PAC Dollars by Sector

Source	Total	Pct
Business	$61,300	51%
Labor	$38,550	32%
Ideology/Single Issue	$21,500	18%

In-State vs. Out-of-State Contributions*

Source	Total	Pct
In-State	$79,850	86%
Out-of-state	$3,250	4%
No state listed	$10,800	

* by large individual contributors ($200 & above)

Finance, Insurance & Real Estate		$28,850
Commercial Banks		**$2,750**
Worthen Banking Corp	$1,500	PAC
American Bankers Assn	$1,000	PAC
Securities & Investment		**$10,050**
C&D Commodities	$4,000	Indiv
Chicago Mercantile Exchange	$3,500	PAC
Insurance		**$5,250**
National Assn of Life Underwriters	$3,000	PAC
Near North Insurance Agency	$1,000	Indiv
Real Estate		**$7,500**
National Assn of Realtors	$5,000	PAC
Stein & Co	$1,000	Indiv
Accountants		**$3,300**
American Institute of CPA's	$2,500	PAC

Health		$19,550
Health Professionals		**$10,550**
American Medical Assn	$5,000	PAC
American Academy of Ophthalmology	$2,000	PAC
Illinois College of Optometry	$1,000	Indiv
Hospitals/Nursing Homes		**$9,000**
Humana Inc	$8,500	PAC/Ind

Lawyers & Lobbyists		$28,550
Lawyers & Lobbyists		**$28,550**
Assn of Trial Lawyers of America	$10,000	PAC
Mayer, Brown & Platt	$4,750	Indiv
Cherry & Flynn	$2,500	Indiv
American Bar Assn	$1,000	Indiv
Corboy & Demetrio	$1,000	Indiv
Hofeld & Schaffner	$1,000	Indiv
Kirkland & Ellis	$1,000	PAC
Power, Rogers & Lavin	$1,000	Indiv
Sachnoff & Weaver	$1,000	Indiv
Skadden, Arps et al	$1,000	Indiv

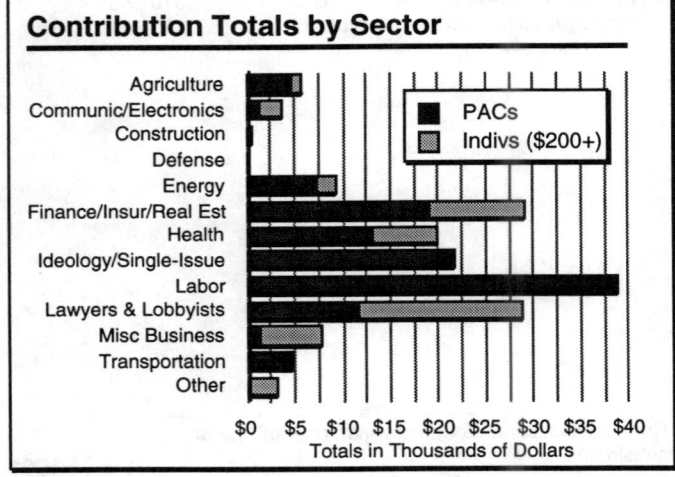

Contribution Totals by Sector

Legend: PACs, Indivs ($200+)

Categories: Agriculture, Communic/Electronics, Construction, Defense, Energy, Finance/Insur/Real Est, Health, Ideology/Single-Issue, Labor, Lawyers & Lobbyists, Misc Business, Transportation, Other

$0 $5 $10 $15 $20 $25 $30 $35 $40
Totals in Thousands of Dollars

Misc Business | $7,600

Business Services $5,600
    Jasculca & Terman Associates .... $3,500 Indiv
    Marmon Group .... $1,000 Indiv

Misc Manufacturing & Distributing $2,000
    Best Foam Fabricators .... $1,000 PAC

Transportation | $4,500

Air Transport $2,500
    United Parcel Service .... $2,500 PAC

Automotive $2,000
    National Auto Dealers Assn .... $1,000 PAC
    Warshawsky & Co/JC Whitney & Co .... $1,000 PAC

Labor

Labor | $38,550

Building Trade Unions $3,500
    Plumbers/Pipefitters Union .... $2,500 PAC
    Laborers' Political League .... $1,000 PAC

Industrial Unions $9,750
    Machinists/Aerospace Workers Union .... $5,000 PAC
    United Auto Workers .... $2,000 PAC
    Intl Brotherhood of Electrical Workers .... $1,000 PAC
    United Steelworkers .... $1,000 PAC

Transportation Unions $7,300
    Teamsters Union .... $5,000 PAC
    United Transportation Union .... $1,000 PAC

Public Sector Unions $9,500
    National Education Assn .... $5,000 PAC
    American Fedn of St/Cnty/Munic Employees ...... $1,000 PAC
    National Assn Retired Federal Employees .... $1,000 PAC
    National Assn of Letter Carriers .... $1,000 PAC

Misc Unions $8,500
    AFL-CIO .... $4,000 PAC
    Food & Commercial Workers Union .... $2,500 PAC
    Hotel/Restaurant Employees Union .... $1,000 PAC
    Service Employees International Union .... $1,000 PAC

Ideological/Single-Issue

Ideological/Single-Issue | $21,500

Democratic/Liberal $7,000
    Fifth Horseman PAC .... $5,000 PAC
    Hollywood Women's Political Cmte .... $2,000 PAC

Leadership PACs $7,000
    Citizens for Gary J Lapaille .... $3,000 PAC
    America's Leaders' Fund (Dan Rostenkowski) .... $1,000 PAC
    Effective Government Cmte (Dick Gephardt) ...... $1,000 PAC
    House Leadership Fund (Tom Foley) .... $1,000 PAC
    Victory USA (Vic Fazio) .... $1,000 PAC

Pro-Israel $2,000
    National PAC .... $2,000 PAC

Human Rights $3,750
    Human Rights Campaign Fund .... $2,500 PAC
    Pakistani Physicians PAC .... $1,000 PAC

Misc Issues $1,000
    National Cmte to Preserve Social Security .... $1,000 PAC

Other & Unknown

Other | $2,850

Retired $1,000
    None over $1,000

Unknown | $45,000

    No Employer Listed or Found $40,050
    Employer Listed/Category Unknown $3,950
        East Lake Management & Development ..... $1,000 Indiv
        Jaskula-Terman Chicago .... $1,000 Indiv

Spending in Last Election

	1992
Rush	$257,339
Opponent	$11,220
Vote Pct	83%

Martin Olav Sabo, D-Minn (5)

First elected: 1978
1991-92 Total Receipts: $408,981
1992 Year-end Cash: $39,370

1991-92 Committees & Subcommittees

Appropriations
Defense; District of Columbia; Transportation and Related Agencies

Budget
Budget Process, Reconciliation and Enforcement; Economic Policy, Projections and Revenues

Select Committee on Intelligence

Leading Contributors

Business

Agriculture		$17,900
Crop Production & Basic Processing		**$5,250**
Southern Minn Beet Sugar Co-op	$1,500	PAC
Tobacco		**$3,500**
Philip Morris	$1,500	PAC
Dairy		**$4,500**
Associated Milk Producers	$4,000	PAC
Agricultural Services/Products		**$2,800**
Land O'Lakes Inc	$2,500	PAC/Ind
Food Processing & Sales		**$1,850**
None over $1,500		

Communications/Electronics		$12,650
Printing & Publishing		**$3,000**
West Publishing	$3,000	PAC
Telephone Utilities		**$2,550**
US West Inc	$1,800	PAC
Computer Equipment & Services		**$6,700**
Control Data Corp	$4,250	Indiv

Construction		$4,650
Home Builders		**$3,450**
National Assn of Home Builders	$3,300	PAC

Source of Funds in 1992 Election

Source	Total	Pct
■ PACs	$247,703	61%
▨ Indivs $200+	$48,705	12%
□ Indivs under $200	$63,557	16%
⊠ Other	$49,153	12%
Candidate	$0	0%
Party	$3,449	1%

Source of PAC Dollars by Sector

Source	Total	Pct
■ Business	$141,036	58%
▨ Labor	$92,498	38%
□ Ideology/Single Issue	$8,070	3%

In-State vs. Out-of-State Contributions*

Source	Total	Pct
□ In-State	$19,217	39%
■ Out-of-state	$29,488	61%
No state listed	$0	

* by large individual contributors ($200 & above)

Defense		$43,500
Defense Aerospace		**$20,000**
McDonnell Douglas*	$3,000	PAC
Rockwell International	$2,500	PAC
General Dynamics	$2,000	PAC
Textron Inc	$2,000	PAC
General Electric	$1,500	PAC
Grumman Corp	$1,500	PAC
Martin Marietta Corp	$1,500	PAC
United Technologies	$1,500	PAC
Defense Electronics		**$17,750**
AT&T	$5,500	PAC
E-Systems Inc	$1,750	PAC
Hughes Aircraft	$1,500	PAC
Loral Corp	$1,500	PAC
Raytheon	$1,500	PAC
Misc Defense		**$5,750**
FMC Corp	$2,000	PAC
Alliant Techsystems Inc	$1,500	PAC

Energy & Natural Resources		$9,450
Oil & Gas		**$4,700**
Arkla Inc	$2,750	PAC/Ind
Misc Energy		**$2,500**
Energy Research Corp	$2,000	PAC
Electric Utilities		**$2,250**
None over $1,500		

Finance, Insurance & Real Estate		$15,810
Commercial Banks		**$4,450**
Norwest Corp	$3,000	PAC
Securities & Investment		**$3,410**
None over $1,500		

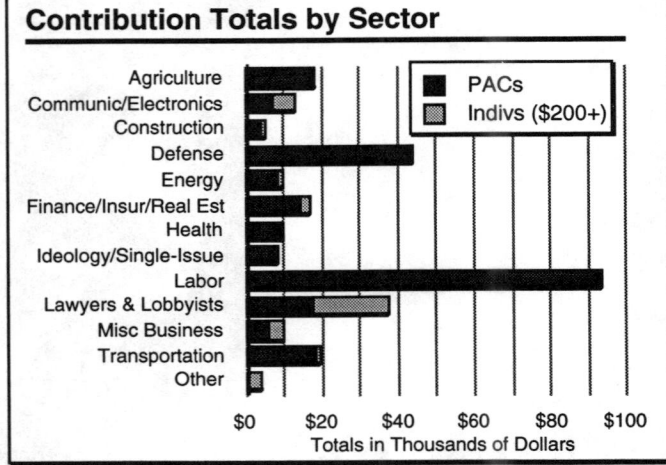

Contribution Totals by Sector

Agriculture, Communic/Electronics, Construction, Defense, Energy, Finance/Insur/Real Est, Health, Ideology/Single-Issue, Labor, Lawyers & Lobbyists, Misc Business, Transportation, Other

■ PACs
▨ Indivs ($200+)

$0 $20 $40 $60 $80 $100
Totals in Thousands of Dollars

Insurance **$3,350**
    Northwestern National Life ....$1,600 PAC

Real Estate **$2,750**
    National Assn of Realtors ....$2,750 PAC

Health   **$8,950**

Health Professionals **$6,450**
    American Medical Assn ....$3,350 PAC
    Cooperative of American Physicians ....$1,500 PAC

Hospitals/Nursing Homes **$1,500**
    None over $1,500

Lawyers & Lobbyists   **$36,981**

Lawyers & Lobbyists **$36,981**
    Cassidy & Associates ....$6,738 Indiv
    Assn of Trial Lawyers of America ....$5,500 PAC
    Opperman & Paquin ....$4,899 PAC
    Hill & Knowlton* ....$2,000 PAC/Ind
    Capital Partnerships Inc ....$1,500 PAC
    Hoving Group ....$1,500 Indiv
    Mullenholz & Brimsek ....$1,500 Indiv
    Paul Magliocchetti Associates ....$1,500 Indiv

Misc Business   **$9,350**

Beer, Wine & Liquor **$1,500**
    None over $1,500

Business Services **$1,500**
    None over $1,500

Misc Manufacturing & Distributing **$2,000**
    Recovery Engineering Inc ....$1,500 Indiv

Transportation   **$19,050**

Air Transport **$11,550**
    United Parcel Service ....$4,100 PAC
    Aircraft Owners & Pilots Assn ....$4,000 PAC
    Northwest Airlines ....$1,700 PAC

Trucking **$1,500**
    None over $1,500

Railroads **$1,750**
    None over $1,500

Misc Transport **$2,750**
    American Public Transit Assn ....$1,500 Indiv

Labor

Labor   **$92,498**

Building Trade Unions **$11,000**
    Laborers' Political League ....$5,000 PAC
    Carpenters & Joiners Union ....$2,500 PAC
    Plumbers/Pipefitters Union ....$2,000 PAC

Industrial Unions **$16,750**
    Machinists/Aerospace Workers Union ....$4,000 PAC
    United Auto Workers ....$3,500 PAC
    Intl Brotherhood of Electrical Workers* ....$3,000 PAC
    United Steelworkers ....$2,000 PAC

Transportation Unions **$28,750**
    Air Line Pilots Assn ....$10,000 PAC
    Teamsters Union ....$10,000 PAC
    Amalgamated Transit Union ....$4,250 PAC
    United Transportation Union ....$4,000 PAC

Public Sector Unions **$31,900**
    American Fedn of St/Cnty/Munic Employees ......$7,000 PAC
    National Assn of Letter Carriers* ....$5,300 PAC
    American Federation of Teachers ....$5,000 PAC
    National Education Assn ....$5,000 PAC
    American Postal Workers Union* ....$3,400 PAC
    National Assn Retired Federal Employees ....$3,000 PAC

Misc Unions **$4,098**
    Food & Commercial Workers Union ....$1,998 PAC

Ideological/Single-Issue

Ideological/Single-Issue   **$8,820**

Democratic/Liberal **$2,000**
    National Cmte for an Effective Congress ....$2,000 PAC

Human Rights **$2,750**
    None over $1,500

Misc Issues **$2,570**
    National Cmte to Preserve Social Security ....$2,000 PAC

Other & Unknown

Other   **$3,250**

Education **$1,950**
    University of North Dakota ....$1,500 Indiv

Unknown   **$7,450**

    Employer Listed/Category Unknown $7,200
      None over $1,500

Spending in Last 3 Elections

	1988	1990	1992
Sabo	$281,455	$321,644	$585,831
Opponent	$16,915	$0	$16,781
Vote Pct	72%	73%	63%

* Contributions came from more than one affiliate or subsidiary.

Bernard Sanders, I-Vt (1)

First elected: 1990

1991-92 Total Receipts: $586,682
1992 Year-end Cash: $19,231

1991-92 Committees & Subcommittees

Banking, Finance and Urban Affairs
Consumer Affairs and Coinage; Housing and Community Development; International Development, Finance, Trade and Monetary Policy

Government Operations
Government Information, Justice and Agriculture; Human Resources and Intergovernmental Relations

Leading Contributors

Business

Agriculture — $4,088

Crop Production & Basic Processing	$2,500	
None over $1,000		
Food Processing & Sales	$1,188	
Ben & Jerry's Ice Cream	$1,188	Indiv

Communications/Electronics — $1,700

Printing & Publishing	$1,450	
Hemmings Motor News	$1,000	Indiv

Construction — $2,000

Building Materials & Equipment	$2,000	
Natpro	$2,000	Indiv

Finance, Insurance & Real Esta — $2,950

Securities & Investment	$1,000	
Glickenhaus & Co	$1,000	Indiv
Real Estate	$1,450	
None over $1,000		

Source of Funds in 1992 Election

Source	Total	Pct
PACs	$147,057	25%
Indivs $200+	$63,403	11%
Indivs under $200	$364,535	62%
Other	$11,687	2%
Candidate	$0	0%
Party	$0	0%

Source of PAC Dollars by Sector

Source	Total	Pct
Business	$700	0%
Labor	$135,182	92%
Ideology/Single Issue	$10,600	7%

In-State vs. Out-of-State Contributions*

Source	Total	Pct
In-State	$13,357	21%
Out-of-state	$49,825	79%
No state listed	$221	

* by large individual contributors ($200 & above)

Health — $3,750

Health Professionals	$1,500	
Border Area Mental Health	$1,000	Indiv
Hospitals/Nursing Homes	$1,250	
None over $1,000		
Misc Health	$1,000	
Bob Brand Associates	$1,000	Indiv

Lawyers & Lobbyists — $1,750

Lawyers & Lobbyists	$1,750	
Burke, Wilson & McIlvaine	$1,000	Indiv

Misc Business — $3,200

Misc Services	$1,000	
None over $1,000		
Business Services	$1,250	
None over $1,000		

Contribution Totals by Sector

Legend: PACs, Indivs ($200+)

Categories: Agriculture, Communic/Electronics, Construction, Defense, Energy, Finance/Insur/Real Est, Health, Ideology/Single-Issue, Labor, Lawyers & Lobbyists, Misc Business, Transportation, Other

Totals in Thousands of Dollars: $0 $20 $40 $60 $80 $100 $120 $140

Labor

Labor $135,382

Building Trade Unions $21,500
Sheet Metal Workers Union	$6,000	PAC
Carpenters & Joiners Union	$5,500	PAC
Laborers' Political League	$3,000	PAC
Operating Engineers Union	$3,000	PAC
Plumbers/Pipefitters Union	$3,000	PAC
Ironworkers Union	$1,000	PAC

Industrial Unions $50,500
Machinists/Aerospace Workers Union	$15,000	PAC
United Auto Workers	$9,000	PAC
Intl Brotherhood of Electrical Workers	$7,500	PAC
Communications Workers of America	$5,500	PAC
Oil, Chemical & Atomic Workers Union	$3,000	PAC
Boilermakers Union	$2,000	PAC
United Steelworkers	$2,000	PAC
Amalgamated Clothing & Textile Workers	$1,500	PAC
Electronic Machine Furniture Workers	$1,500	PAC
United Mine Workers	$1,500	PAC
AFL-CIO Industrial Union Dept	$1,000	PAC

Transportation Unions $19,800
Teamsters Union	$15,000	PAC
Intl Longshoremen's/Warehousemen's Union	$1,500	PAC
Seafarers International Union	$1,500	PAC
Maintenance of Way Employees	$1,000	PAC

Public Sector Unions $29,700
National Education Assn	$14,000	PAC
National Assn of Letter Carriers	$7,000	PAC
American Fedn of St/Cnty/Munic Employees	$4,000	PAC
American Postal Workers Union	$1,500	PAC
International Assn of Firefighters	$1,500	PAC
National Assn Retired Federal Employees	$1,000	PAC

Misc Unions $13,882
Food & Commercial Workers Union	$10,000	PAC
Service Employees International Union	$2,382	PAC
AFL-CIO	$1,500	PAC

Ideological/Single-Issue

Ideological/Single-Issue $27,751

Democratic/Liberal $10,251
Sanders for Congress	$1,851	Indiv
Hollywood Women's Political Cmte	$1,000	PAC

Foreign & Defense Policy $2,000
Job with Peace Campaign	$1,900	Indiv

Pro-Choice $3,550
National Abortion Rights Action League	$1,000	PAC

Human Rights $4,000
KidsPAC	$2,000	PAC
Human Rights Campaign Fund	$1,000	PAC
National Community Action Foundation	$1,000	PAC

Misc Issues $7,750
League of Conservation Voters	$2,000	PAC
Sierra Club	$1,500	PAC
National Cmte to Preserve Social Security	$1,000	PAC

Other & Unknown

Other $13,140

Non-Profit Institutions $2,000
Foundation for Hearing Aid Research	$2,000	Indiv

Civil Servants/Public Officials $4,290
Equal Employment Opportunity Comm	$2,000	Indiv

Education $2,500
None over $1,000

Retired $3,250
None over $1,000

Other $1,100
None over $1,000

Unknown $14,174
Homemakers/Non-income earners	$1,400	
No Employer Listed or Found	$8,699	
Employer Listed/Category Unknown	$3,375	
Kayline Enterprises	$1,400	Indiv

Spending in Last 2 Elections

	1990	1992
Sanders	$569,772	$558,030
Opponent	$686,374	$82,585
Vote Pct	56%	58%

George E. Sangmeister, D-Ill (11)

First elected: 1988

1991-92 Total Receipts: $339,478
1992 Year-end Cash: $17,831

1991-92 Committees & Subcommittees

Judiciary
Crime and Criminal Justice; Intellectual Property and Judicial Administration

Public Works and Transportation
Aviation; Surface Transportation

Veterans' Affairs
Education, Training and Employment; Hospitals and Health Care

Leading Contributors

Business

Agriculture		$3,750
Crop Production & Basic Processing		$1,900
None over $1,000		
Dairy		$1,000
Associated Milk Producers	$1,000	PAC

Communications/Electronics		$20,850
Printing & Publishing		$1,600
West Publishing	$1,600	PAC
Media/Entertainment		$11,850
National Cable Television Assn	$5,000	PAC
National Assn of Broadcasters	$2,800	PAC
ASCAP	$1,500	PAC
Telephone Utilities		$7,400
AT&T	$5,500	PAC

Construction		$5,550
General Contractors		$3,000
K-Five Construction	$1,000	Indiv
PT Ferro Construction	$1,000	Indiv
TJ Lambrecht Construction	$1,000	Indiv
Home Builders		$1,000
Edon Construction Co	$1,000	Indiv
Building Materials & Equipment		$1,550
Elmhurst-Chicago Stone Co	$1,000	Indiv

Source of Funds in 1992 Election

Source	Total	Pct
PACs	$252,210	69%
Indivs $200+	$28,426	8%
Indivs under $200	$37,880	10%
Other	$48,121	13%
Candidate	$0	0%
Party	$32,159	9%

Source of PAC Dollars by Sector

Source	Total	Pct
Business	$97,960	39%
Labor	$137,200	55%
Ideology/Single Issue	$13,900	6%

In-State vs. Out-of-State Contributions*

Source	Total	Pct
In-State	$23,126	81%
Out-of-state	$5,300	19%
No state listed	$0	

* by large individual contributors ($200 & above)

Energy & Natural Resources		$5,950
Oil & Gas		$4,150
Amoco Corp	$1,500	PAC
Gas City Ltd	$1,000	Indiv
Midcon Corp	$1,000	PAC
Electric Utilities		$1,800
None over $1,000		

Finance, Insurance & Real Estate		$31,796
Commercial Banks		$9,670
American Bankers Assn	$2,000	PAC
New Lenox State Bank	$2,000	Indiv
First Chicago Corp	$1,500	PAC
Barnett Banks Inc	$1,000	PAC
South Holland Trust & Savings	$1,000	Indiv
Credit Unions		$1,000
Credit Union National Assn	$1,000	PAC
Securities & Investment		$2,250
Chicago Board of Trade	$1,000	PAC
Insurance		$5,276
Golden Rule Insurance Co	$3,200	PAC
Columbian Agency	$1,000	Indiv
Real Estate		$7,100
National Assn of Realtors	$6,000	PAC
Accountants		$6,500
American Institute of CPA's	$6,500	PAC

Health		$9,900
Health Professionals		$8,150
American Academy of Ophthalmology	$4,000	PAC
American Dental Assn	$1,300	PAC
American Podiatry Assn	$1,000	PAC
Pharmaceuticals/Health Products		$1,100
None over $1,000		

Contribution Totals by Sector

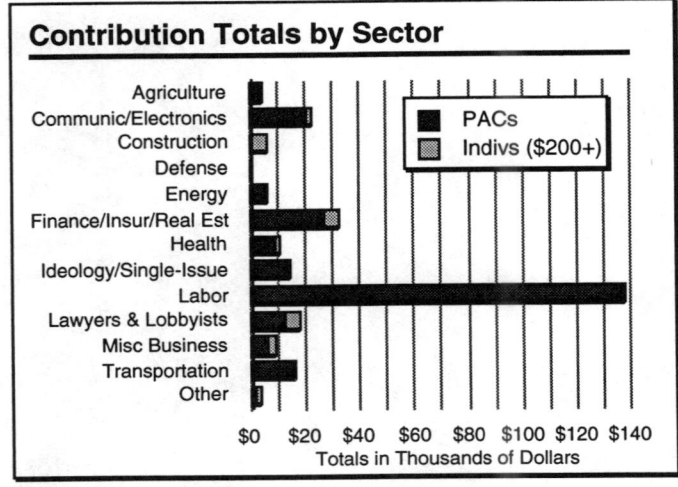

Agriculture
Communic/Electronics
Construction
Defense
Energy
Finance/Insur/Real Est
Health
Ideology/Single-Issue
Labor
Lawyers & Lobbyists
Misc Business
Transportation
Other

■ PACs
▨ Indivs ($200+)

$0 $20 $40 $60 $80 $100 $120 $140
Totals in Thousands of Dollars

Lawyers & Lobbyists — $17,500

Lawyers & Lobbyists **$17,500**
- Assn of Trial Lawyers of America .... $10,000 PAC
- Swidler & Berlin .... $1,000 PAC

Misc Business — $9,750

Retail Sales **$3,700**
- Montgomery Ward .... $1,500 PAC

Casinos/Gambling **$2,000**
- Empress River Casino .... $1,000 Indiv
- Fitzgerald's Casino & Hotel .... $1,000 Indiv

Steel Production **$1,100**
- None over $1,000

Transportation — $15,740

Air Transport **$4,040**
- United Airlines .... $1,300 PAC
- United Parcel Service .... $1,240 PAC
- Aircraft Owners & Pilots Assn .... $1,000 PAC

Automotive **$7,200**
- National Auto Dealers Assn .... $4,800 PAC
- Ford Motor Co .... $1,100 PAC
- Warshawsky & Co/JC Whitney & Co .... $1,000 PAC

Trucking **$2,100**
- None over $1,000

Railroads **$2,400**
- None over $1,000

Labor

Labor — **$137,200**

Building Trade Unions **$18,800**
- Carpenters & Joiners Union .... $5,000 PAC
- Laborers' Political League .... $3,000 PAC
- Plumbers/Pipefitters Union .... $3,000 PAC
- Sheet Metal Workers Union .... $2,500 PAC
- Ironworkers Union .... $2,000 PAC
- Operating Engineers Union* .... $2,000 PAC
- Bricklayers Union .... $1,000 PAC

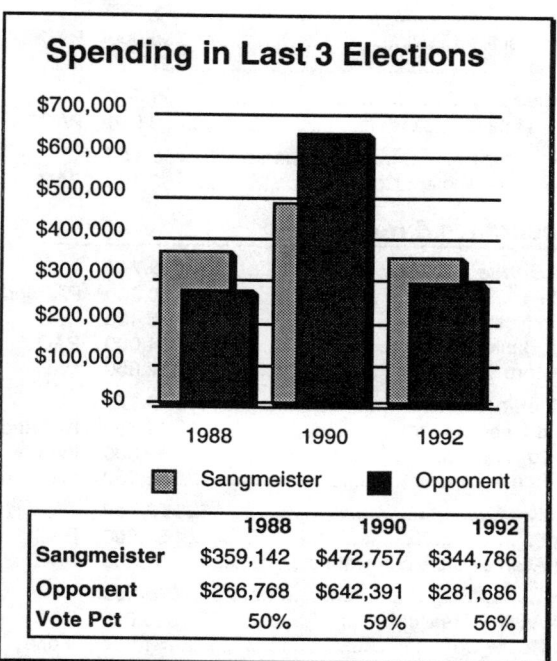

Spending in Last 3 Elections

	1988	1990	1992
Sangmeister	$359,142	$472,757	$344,786
Opponent	$266,768	$642,391	$281,686
Vote Pct	50%	59%	56%

Industrial Unions **$35,300**
- Machinists/Aerospace Workers Union .... $10,000 PAC
- United Auto Workers .... $10,000 PAC
- Boilermakers Union* .... $5,500 PAC
- Intl Brotherhood of Electrical Workers .... $5,500 PAC
- United Steelworkers .... $2,000 PAC
- Graphic Communications Union .... $1,000 PAC

Transportation Unions **$24,900**
- Teamsters Union .... $10,000 PAC
- Air Line Pilots Assn .... $3,500 PAC
- National Air Traffic Controllers Assn .... $3,000 PAC
- Marine Engineers Union* .... $2,500 PAC
- United Transportation Union .... $1,600 PAC
- Assn of Flight Attendants .... $1,000 PAC
- Trans Comm International Union .... $1,000 PAC

Public Sector Unions **$48,800**
- American Federation of Teachers .... $10,000 PAC
- American Fedn of St/Cnty/Munic Employees .... $10,000 PAC
- National Education Assn .... $7,800 PAC
- National Assn of Letter Carriers .... $7,500 PAC
- National Assn Retired Federal Employees .... $6,000 PAC
- American Postal Workers Union .... $3,000 PAC
- International Assn of Firefighters .... $2,000 PAC
- National Assn of Postmasters .... $1,500 PAC

Misc Unions **$9,400**
- Service Employees International Union .... $3,000 PAC
- AFL-CIO .... $2,800 PAC
- Food & Commercial Workers Union .... $2,300 PAC
- Bakery, Confectionery & Tobacco Workers ...... $1,000 PAC

Ideological/Single-Issue

Ideological/Single-Issue — **$13,900**

Democratic/Liberal **$2,500**
- National Cmte for an Effective Congress .... $2,500 PAC

Leadership PACs **$1,300**
- Effective Government Cmte (Dick Gephardt) ... $1,000 PAC

Human Rights **$2,000**
- KidsPAC .... $2,000 PAC

Misc Issues **$7,300**
- Sierra Club .... $3,000 PAC
- National Cmte to Preserve Social Security ...... $2,300 PAC
- National Council of Senior Citizens .... $2,000 PAC

Other & Unknown

Other — **$2,625**

Other **$1,000**
- None over $1,000

Unknown — **$3,775**

- Employer Listed/Category Unknown $3,075
  - None over $1,000

---

* Contributions came from more than one affiliate or subsidiary.

Rick Santorum, R-Pa (18)

First elected: 1990

1991-92 Total Receipts: $654,854
1992 Year-end Cash: $34,355

1991-92 Committees & Subcommittees

Budget
Community Development and Natural Resources; Economic Policy, Projections and Revenues

Veterans' Affairs
Education, Training and Employment

Select Committee on Children, Youth and Families

Leading Contributors

Business

Agriculture	**$7,095**	
Food Processing & Sales	$3,745	
None over $1,500		

Communications/Electronics	**$20,525**	
Media/Entertainment	$3,750	
None over $1,500		
Telephone Utilities	$4,200	
AT&T	$2,000	PAC
Bell Telephone of Pennsylvania	$1,700	PAC
Electronics Mfg & Services	$11,525	
Westinghouse Electric	$11,400	PAC/Ind

Construction	**$32,450**	
General Contractors	$12,850	
Dick Corp	$2,600	Indiv
Associated General Contractors	$2,500	PAC
Russell Industries	$1,900	Indiv
Home Builders	$10,200	
National Assn of Home Builders	$10,000	PAC
Special Trade Contractors	$6,700	
Sargent Electric Co	$3,350	Indiv
Sheet Metal/Air Conditioning Contractors	$1,500	PAC
Building Materials & Equipment	$2,500	
Beckwith Machinery Co	$1,500	Indiv

Defense	**$1,750**	
None over $1,500		

Source of Funds in 1992 Election

Source	Total	Pct
■ PACs	$265,454	38%
▨ Indivs $200+	$245,055	36%
▦ Indivs under $200	$113,971	17%
⊠ Other	$65,374	9%
Candidate	$0	0%
Party	$49,499	7%

Source of PAC Dollars by Sector

Source	Total	Pct
■ Business	$224,511	90%
▨ Labor	$4,800	2%
□ Ideology/Single Issue	$20,723	8%

In-State vs. Out-of-State Contributions*

Source	Total	Pct
□ In-State	$231,055	95%
■ Out-of-state	$12,850	5%
No state listed	$550	

* by large individual contributors ($200 & above)

Energy & Natural Resources — $57,277

Oil & Gas	**$29,627**	
USX Corp*	$11,327	PAC
Atlas Energy Group Inc	$3,200	Indiv
Consolidated Natural Gas*	$2,350	PAC
Columbia Gas System*	$1,600	PAC
Mobil Oil	$1,500	PAC/Ind
Sun Co	$1,500	PAC

Mining	**$8,850**	
Mine Safety Appliances Co	$3,650	PAC/Ind
Alcoa	$1,500	PAC
National Coal Assn	$1,500	PAC

Misc Energy	**$6,700**	
Cooper Industries	$5,000	PAC
Hansen Inc	$1,700	Indiv

Electric Utilities	**$6,500**	
Duquesne Light Co	$3,050	PAC/Ind

Waste Management	**$3,100**	
Chambers Development Co	$3,100	PAC

Finance, Insurance & Real Estate — $83,975

Commercial Banks	**$23,750**	
Mellon Bank	$10,200	PAC/Ind
Pittsburgh National Bank	$5,450	PAC
American Bankers Assn	$4,000	PAC
PennBancorp	$2,850	PAC

Securities & Investment	**$20,175**	
Federated Investors Inc	$9,750	PAC/Ind
Hillman Co	$3,800	Indiv
Russell, Rea & Zappala	$2,050	PAC/Ind

Insurance	**$9,750**	
ITT Corp*	$1,500	PAC
National Assn of Life Underwriters	$1,500	PAC

Real Estate	**$15,250**	
National Assn of Realtors	$10,000	PAC
Graham Realty Co	$1,850	Indiv
Barness Organization	$1,500	Indiv

Contribution Totals by Sector

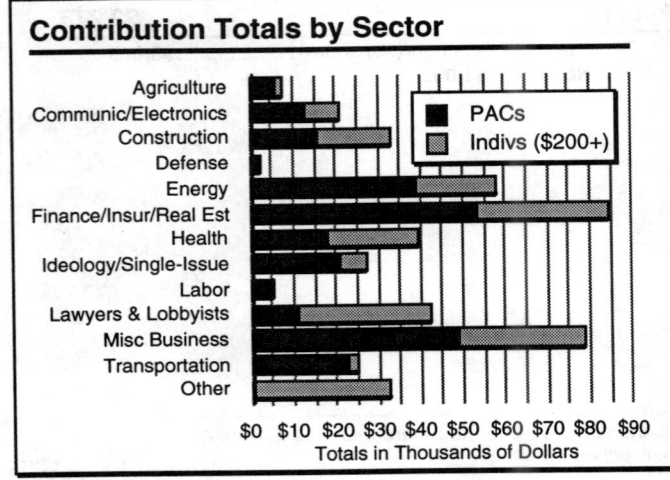

Agriculture, Communic/Electronics, Construction, Defense, Energy, Finance/Insur/Real Est, Health, Ideology/Single-Issue, Labor, Lawyers & Lobbyists, Misc Business, Transportation, Other

■ PACs
▦ Indivs ($200+)

$0 $10 $20 $30 $40 $50 $60 $70 $80 $90
Totals in Thousands of Dollars

Accountants	....	$14,500	
American Institute of CPA's	....	$6,500	PAC
Price Waterhouse	....	$2,900	Indiv
Urish Popeck & Co	....	$2,500	Indiv

Health — $38,710

Health Professionals	....	$28,035	
American Medical Assn*	....	$9,885	PAC
American Physical Therapy Assn	....	$3,000	PAC
Hospitals/Nursing Homes	....	$6,325	
North Hills Passavant Hospital	....	$1,500	Indiv
Pharmaceuticals/Health Products	....	$3,250	
None over $1,500			

Lawyers & Lobbyists — $41,905

Lawyers & Lobbyists	....	$41,905	
Kirkpatrick & Lockhart	....	$29,975	PAC/Ind
Houston, Houston & Donnelly	....	$3,000	Indiv
Reed, Smith et al	....	$3,000	PAC/Ind

Misc Business — $77,981

Business Associations	....	$5,780	
National Fedn of Independent Business	....	$4,750	PAC
Food & Beverage	....	$14,650	
National Restaurant Assn	....	$7,000	PAC
Eat 'n Park Resaurants Inc	....	$2,050	PAC/Ind
McDonald's Corp	....	$1,500	PAC/Ind
Beer, Wine & Liquor	....	$6,500	
National Beer Wholesalers Assn	....	$6,500	PAC
Misc Services	....	$1,501	
None over $1,500			
Business Services	....	$6,200	
Brabender Cox	....	$2,450	Indiv
Chemical & Related Manufacturing	....	$15,000	
Aristech Chemical Corp	....	$4,250	PAC/Ind
Sinclair & Rush Inc	....	$1,850	Indiv

Steel Production	....	$15,700	
Allegheny Ludlum Corp	....	$9,800	PAC/Ind
Misc Manufacturing & Distributing	....	$8,800	
PPG Industries	....	$2,750	PAC/Ind
Dynamet Inc	....	$1,900	Indiv

Transportation — $24,423

Air Transport	....	$2,850	
United Parcel Service	....	$2,350	PAC
Automotive	....	$15,100	
National Auto Dealers Assn	....	$8,600	PAC
Eaton Corp	....	$2,000	PAC
Auto Dealers & Drivers for Free Trade	....	$1,500	PAC
Railroads	....	$4,950	
Bessemer Railroad	....	$2,500	PAC
Union Switch & Signal	....	$1,700	Indiv

Labor

Labor		$4,800

Transportation Unions	....	$3,250	
Marine Engineers Union*	....	$3,000	PAC
Public Sector Unions	....	$1,550	
None over $1,500			

Ideological/Single-Issue

Ideological/Single-Issue		$26,923

Republican/Conservative	....	$4,100	
None over $1,500			
Leadership PACs	....	$3,000	
Republican Leader's Fund (Bob Michel)	....	$2,000	PAC
Pro-Israel	....	$4,500	
Hudson Valley PAC	....	$1,500	PAC
Pro-Life	....	$2,250	
None over $1,500			
Gun Rights/Gun Control	....	$10,900	
National Rifle Assn	....	$9,900	PAC

Other & Unknown

Other		$32,250

Civil Servants/Public Officials	....	$1,700	
None over $1,500			
Education	....	$7,650	
Education Management Corp	....	$1,500	Indiv
Sawyer School of Business	....	$1,500	Indiv
Retired	....	$21,900	
None over $1,500			

Unknown		$44,675

Homemakers/Non-income earners	....	$17,400
No Employer Listed or Found	....	$3,900
Employer Listed/Category Unknown	....	$23,375
None over $1,500		

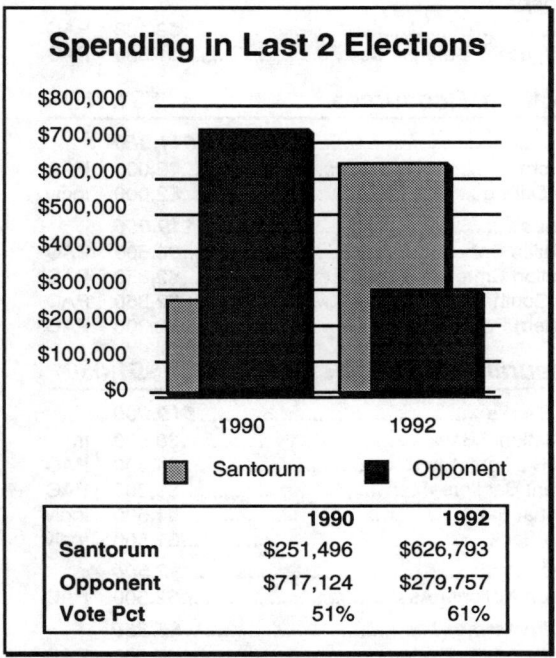

Spending in Last 2 Elections

	1990	1992
Santorum	$251,496	$626,793
Opponent	$717,124	$279,757
Vote Pct	51%	61%

Legend: Santorum, Opponent

* Contributions came from more than one affiliate or subsidiary.

1071

Bill Sarpalius, D-Texas (13)

First elected: 1988

1991-92 Total Receipts:	$521,447
1992 Year-end Cash:	$17,659

1991-92 Committees & Subcommittees

Agriculture
Conservation, Credit and Rural Development; Department Operations, Research and Foreign Agriculture; Livestock, Dairy and Poultry; Wheat, Soybeans and Feed Grains

Small Business
Antitrust, Impact of Deregulation and Ecology

Select Committee on Children, Youth and Families

Leading Contributors

Business

Agriculture — $107,381

Crop Production & Basic Processing $28,331

Southwest Peanut Membership Org	$2,850	PAC
National Cotton Council	$2,650	PAC
American Sugarbeet Growers Assn	$2,000	PAC
American Crystal Sugar Corp	$1,850	PAC

Tobacco $9,150

RJR Nabisco	$4,000	PAC
Philip Morris	$2,900	PAC

Dairy $6,150

Associated Milk Producers	$4,700	PAC

Poultry & Eggs $3,650

National Broiler Council	$2,300	PAC

Livestock $28,150

National Cattlemen's Assn*	$11,000	PAC
Livestock Marketing Assn	$6,550	PAC
Texas & Southwestern Cattle Raisers	$3,500	PAC
Cactus Feeders Inc	$2,500	Indiv
National Pork Producers Council	$1,600	PAC

Agricultural Services/Products $15,150

Texas Farm Bureau	$3,500	PAC
American Veterinary Medical Assn	$1,500	PAC

Food Processing & Sales $16,400

Food Marketing Institute	$2,550	PAC
Winn-Dixie Stores	$2,500	PAC
Beef Products Inc	$2,000	Indiv
Wright Brand Foods	$2,000	Indiv

Source of Funds in 1992 Election

Source	Total	Pct
■ PACs	$319,269	59%
▨ Indivs $200+	$123,517	23%
☐ Indivs under $200	$47,044	9%
▧ Other	$49,677	9%
Candidate	$0	0%
Party	$23,910	4%

Source of PAC Dollars by Sector

Source	Total	Pct
■ Business	$234,169	70%
▨ Labor	$73,150	22%
☐ Ideology/Single Issue	$25,700	8%

In-State vs. Out-of-State Contributions*

Source	Total	Pct
☐ In-State	$116,367	95%
■ Out-of-state	$6,650	5%
No state listed	$500	

* by large individual contributors ($200 & above)

Communications/Electronics — $8,200

Telephone Utilities $7,500

GTE Corp	$2,550	PAC
AT&T	$2,000	PAC
Southwestern Bell	$1,500	PAC

Construction — $6,800

General Contractors $5,400
None over $1,500

Defense — $6,150

Defense Aerospace $6,150

Dyncorp	$2,400	PAC
LTV Aerospace & Defense Co	$1,550	PAC

Energy & Natural Resources — $31,150

Oil & Gas $11,300

Coastal Corp	$2,000	PAC
Spradling Drilling	$2,000	Indiv

Electric Utilities $19,000

Texas Utilities Co*	$5,500	PAC
ACRE (Action Cmte for Rural Electrification)	$2,850	PAC
Central & South West Services*	$2,350	PAC
Southwestern Public Service Co	$2,300	PAC

Finance, Insurance & Real Estate — $51,050

Commercial Banks $19,900

Amarillo National Bank	$8,800	Indiv
American Bankers Assn	$4,000	PAC
Independent Bankers Assn	$3,300	PAC
First National Bank	$1,500	Indiv
Hale State Bank	$1,500	Indiv

Credit Unions $2,500

Credit Union National Assn	$2,500	PAC

Securities & Investment $5,850

Chicago Mercantile Exchange	$2,500	PAC

Contribution Totals by Sector

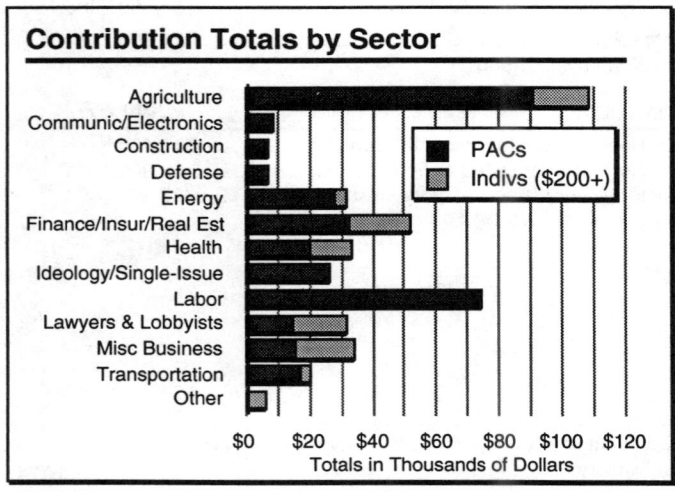

Agriculture
Communic/Electronics
Construction
Defense
Energy
Finance/Insur/Real Est
Health
Ideology/Single-Issue
Labor
Lawyers & Lobbyists
Misc Business
Transportation
Other

■ PACs
▨ Indivs ($200+)

$0 $20 $40 $60 $80 $100 $120
Totals in Thousands of Dollars

Insurance **$8,100**
National Assn of Life Underwriters ....$5,000   PAC
Ordway Saunders Insurance ....$1,500   Indiv

Real Estate **$11,400**
National Assn of Realtors ....$8,000   PAC

Accountants **$2,900**
Arthur Andersen & Co ....$2,000   PAC

Health   **$32,650**

Health Professionals **$29,350**
American Medical Assn ....$10,000   PAC
American Chiropractic Assn ....$2,000   PAC
American Dental Assn ....$2,000   PAC
American Academy of Ophthalmology ....$1,500   PAC

Pharmaceuticals/Health Products **$2,500**
None over $1,500

Lawyers & Lobbyists   **$31,250**

Lawyers & Lobbyists **$31,250**
Assn of Trial Lawyers of America ....$10,000   PAC
Anderson & Rodriguez ....$2,000   Indiv
Underwood, Wilson et al ....$2,000   Indiv
Akin, Gump et al ....$1,650   PAC/Ind

Misc Business   **$33,400**

Food & Beverage **$8,000**
Cantu Services ....$4,750   Indiv
National Restaurant Assn* ....$2,000   PAC

Beer, Wine & Liquor **$10,400**
North Country Distributing Co ....$3,400   Indiv
Coors Distributor ....$2,000   Indiv
Miller of Dallas ....$2,000   Indiv

Retail Sales **$4,250**
Chrysler Management Corp ....$2,900   Indiv

Business Services **$1,750**
None over $1,500

Chemical & Related Manufacturing **$4,050**
WR Grace & Co ....$1,550   PAC

Transportation   **$19,344**

Air Transport **$7,744**
Federal Express Corp ....$5,350   PAC
American Airlines ....$2,044   PAC

Automotive **$8,900**
National Auto Dealers Assn ....$5,700   PAC
Plains Chevrolet ....$2,000   Indiv

Railroads **$2,700**
Union Pacific Corp ....$2,000   PAC

Labor

Labor   **$73,150**

Building Trade Unions **$9,950**
Laborers' Political League ....$3,100   PAC
Plumbers/Pipefitters Union ....$2,500   PAC

Industrial Unions **$16,700**
Intl Brotherhood of Electrical Workers ....$6,500   PAC
United Auto Workers ....$5,500   PAC
United Steelworkers ....$2,000   PAC

Transportation Unions **$25,900**
Teamsters Union* ....$10,000   PAC
Seafarers International Union ....$5,000   PAC
United Transportation Union ....$4,400   PAC
Brotherhood of Locomotive Engineers.............$2,250   PAC
Air Line Pilots Assn ....$1,500   PAC

Public Sector Unions **$19,100**
National Assn Retired Federal Employees ....$4,000   PAC
National Assn of Letter Carriers ....$4,000   PAC
American Federation of Teachers ....$2,850   PAC
International Assn of Firefighters ....$2,850   PAC
American Postal Workers Union ....$2,000   PAC
National Assn of Postmasters ....$1,700   PAC

Misc Unions **$1,500**
None over $1,500

Ideological/Single-Issue

Ideological/Single-Issue   **$25,700**

Leadership PACs **$5,000**
House Leadership Fund (Tom Foley) ....$2,000   PAC

Pro-Israel **$4,350**
Hudson Valley PAC ....$3,500   PAC

Gun Rights/Gun Control **$12,900**
National Rifle Assn ....$12,900   PAC

Misc Issues **$2,450**
National Cmte to Preserve Social Security ....$2,450   PAC

Other & Unknown

Other   **$5,950**

Retired **$4,850**
None over $1,500

Unknown   **$24,361**
No Employer Listed or Found $7,161
Employer Listed/Category Unknown $15,700
Doucette Enterprises ....$2,000   Indiv
Maxor Corp ....$1,500   Indiv

Independent expenditures supporting Sarpalius
National Right to Life PAC $2,881

---

* Contributions came from more than one affiliate or subsidiary.

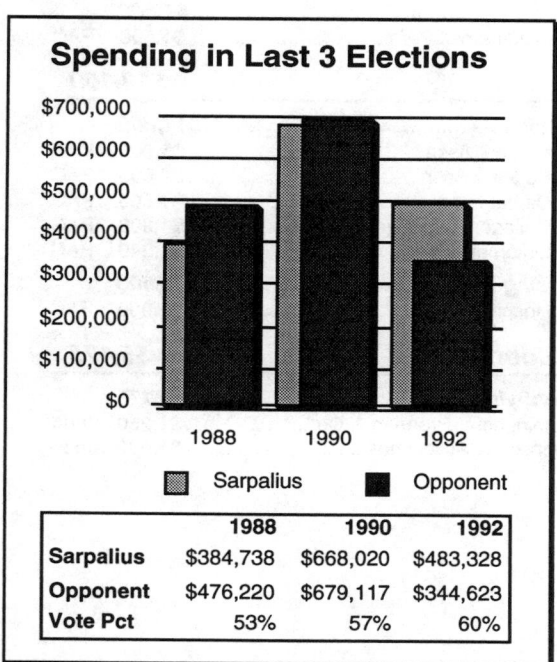

Spending in Last 3 Elections

	1988	1990	1992
Sarpalius	$384,738	$668,020	$483,328
Opponent	$476,220	$679,117	$344,623
Vote Pct	53%	57%	60%

Tom Sawyer, D-Ohio (14)

First elected: 1986

1991-92 Total Receipts: $195,200
1992 Year-end Cash: $34,362

1991-92 Committees & Subcommittees

Education and Labor
Elementary, Secondary and Vocational Education; Labor-Management Relations; Postsecondary Education

Foreign Affairs
Arms Control, International Security and Science

Post Office and Civil Service
Census and Population (Chairman)

Leading Contributors

Business

Agriculture	**$2,500**	
Dairy	**$2,500**	
Associated Milk Producers	$1,000	PAC
Milk Marketing Inc	$1,000	PAC

Communications/Electronics	**$8,000**	
Telephone Utilities	**$7,000**	
Ohio Bell Telephone	$3,500	PAC
AT&T	$2,500	PAC
Computer Equipment & Services	**$1,000**	
Electronic Data Systems	$1,000	PAC

Construction	**$1,250**	
None over $1,000		

Defense	**$3,500**	
Defense Aerospace	**$1,000**	
Gencorp Inc	$1,000	PAC
Defense Electronics	**$2,500**	
Loral Corp	$1,500	PAC
Imo Industries Inc	$1,000	PAC

Energy & Natural Resources	**$3,350**	
Electric Utilities	**$2,500**	
Centerior Energy Corp	$1,000	PAC
Ohio Edison	$1,000	PAC

Contribution Totals by Sector

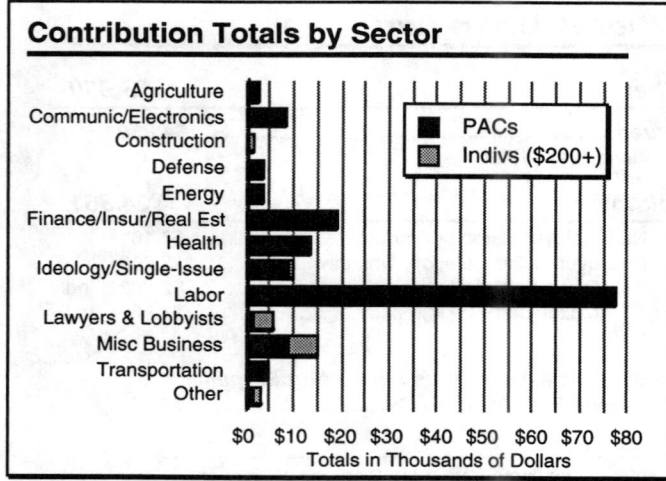

- Agriculture
- Communic/Electronics
- Construction
- Defense
- Energy
- Finance/Insur/Real Est
- Health
- Ideology/Single-Issue
- Labor
- Lawyers & Lobbyists
- Misc Business
- Transportation
- Other

■ PACs
▨ Indivs ($200+)

$0 $10 $20 $30 $40 $50 $60 $70 $80
Totals in Thousands of Dollars

Source of Funds in 1992 Election

Source	Total	Pct
■ PACs	$148,125	76%
▨ Indivs $200+	$20,650	11%
☐ Indivs under $200	$19,213	10%
⊠ Other	$7,486	4%
Candidate	$0	0%
Party	$1,324	1%

Source of PAC Dollars by Sector

Source	Total	Pct
■ Business	$62,425	42%
▨ Labor	$77,200	52%
☐ Ideology/Single Issue	$8,250	6%

In-State vs. Out-of-State Contributions*

Source	Total	Pct
☐ In-State	$18,782	91%
■ Out-of-state	$1,750	9%
No state listed	$0	

* by large individual contributors ($200 & above)

Finance, Insurance & Real Estate	**$18,500**	
Commercial Banks	**$3,500**	
National City Corp	$2,000	PAC
American Bankers Assn*	$1,500	PAC
Savings & Loans	**$1,000**	
Ohio Savings Assns League	$1,000	PAC
Insurance	**$5,750**	
American Council of Life Insurance	$1,000	PAC
Blue Cross & Blue Shield Assn	$1,000	PAC
Principal Mutual Life Insurance	$1,000	PAC
Real Estate	**$6,500**	
National Assn of Realtors	$6,200	PAC
Accountants	**$1,500**	
American Institute of CPA's	$1,500	PAC

Health	**$13,100**	
Health Professionals	**$11,600**	
American Medical Assn	$5,000	PAC
American Podiatry Assn	$2,000	PAC
American Dental Assn	$1,500	PAC
American College of Emergency Physicians	$1,000	PAC
American Optometric Assn	$1,000	PAC
Hospitals/Nursing Homes	**$1,500**	
American Hospital Assn	$1,000	PAC

Lawyers & Lobbyists	**$5,175**	
Lawyers & Lobbyists	**$5,175**	
Amer, Cunningham, Brennan & Co	$1,250	Indiv
Griffin, Johnson & Associates	$1,000	Indiv

Misc Business — $14,500

Retail Sales — $4,250
- Third Class Mail Assn ... $2,000 — PAC
- Revco DS Inc ... $1,000 — PAC

Chemical & Related Manufacturing — $6,000
- Go-Jo Industries ... $5,000 — Indiv
- Monsanto Co ... $1,000 — PAC

Misc Manufacturing & Distributing — $2,000
- BF Goodrich ... $2,000 — PAC

Transportation — $4,500

Air Transport — $2,000
- United Parcel Service ... $1,500 — PAC

Automotive — $1,500
- Goodyear ... $1,000 — PAC

Trucking — $1,000
- Roadway Services Inc ... $1,000 — PAC

Labor

Labor — $77,200

Building Trade Unions — $9,500
- Carpenters & Joiners Union ... $2,500 — PAC
- Laborers' Political League ... $2,500 — PAC
- Plumbers/Pipefitters Union ... $2,000 — PAC
- Operating Engineers Union ... $1,000 — PAC
- Painters & Allied Trades Union ... $1,000 — PAC

Industrial Unions — $17,200
- Rubber Cork Linoleum & Plastic Workers ... $6,500 — PAC
- United Auto Workers ... $5,000 — PAC
- Communications Workers of America ... $2,000 — PAC
- Boilermakers Union ... $1,000 — PAC

Transportation Unions — $18,500
- Teamsters Union ... $10,000 — PAC
- Marine Engineers Union* ... $3,500 — PAC
- Transport Workers Union ... $2,500 — PAC
- United Transportation Union ... $1,500 — PAC

Public Sector Unions — $29,500
- National Assn of Letter Carriers ... $8,000 — PAC
- National Assn Retired Federal Employees ... $4,500 — PAC
- American Fedn of St/Cnty/Munic Employees ... $3,000 — PAC
- American Postal Workers Union ... $3,000 — PAC
- National Education Assn ... $3,000 — PAC
- National Assn of Postmasters ... $1,500 — PAC
- National League of Postmasters ... $1,500 — PAC
- American Federation of Teachers ... $1,000 — PAC
- International Assn of Firefighters ... $1,000 — PAC
- National Assn of Postal Supervisors ... $1,000 — PAC
- National Rural Letter Carriers Assn ... $1,000 — PAC
- National Treasury Employees Union ... $1,000 — PAC

Misc Unions — $2,500
- Food & Commercial Workers Union ... $1,500 — PAC

Ideological/Single-Issue

Ideological/Single-Issue — $9,300

Pro-Israel — $6,250
- National PAC ... $5,000 — PAC

Pro-Choice — $1,550
- Voters for Choice ... $1,000 — PAC

Misc Issues — $1,000
- National Cmte to Preserve Social Security ... $1,000 — PAC

Other & Unknown

Other — $2,650

Education — $1,900
- National Assn Trade & Technical Schools ... $1,000 — PAC

Unknown — $5,882
- Homemakers/Non-income earners ... $1,000
- Employer Listed/Category Unknown ... $4,700
  None over $1,000

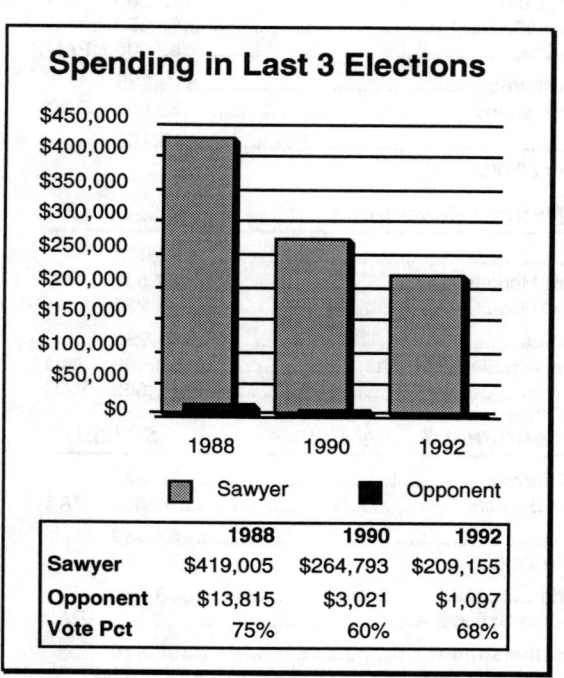

Spending in Last 3 Elections

	1988	1990	1992
Sawyer	$419,005	$264,793	$209,155
Opponent	$13,815	$3,021	$1,097
Vote Pct	75%	60%	68%

Legend: Sawyer / Opponent

---

* Contributions came from more than one affiliate or subsidiary.

H. James Saxton, R-NJ (3)

First elected: 1984
1991-92 Total Receipts: $647,329
1992 Year-end Cash: $279,382

1991-92 Committees & Subcommittees

Armed Services
Military Personnel and Compensation; Procurement and Military Nuclear Systems; Readiness

Merchant Marine and Fisheries
Fisheries and Wildlife Conservation and the Environment; Oceanography, Great Lakes and Outer Continental Shelf; Oversight and Investigations (Ranking Republican)

Select Committee on Aging

Leading Contributors

Business

Agriculture	$18,377	
Crop Production & Basic Processing	$3,742	
None over $2,000		
Tobacco	$3,500	
None over $2,000		
Agricultural Services/Products	$2,950	
None over $2,000		
Food Processing & Sales	$4,800	
None over $2,000		

Communications/Electronics	$12,110	
Media/Entertainment	$2,510	
Time Warner	$2,000	Indiv
Telephone Utilities	$5,600	
Bell Atlantic*	$5,100	PAC
Computer Equipment & Services	$2,500	
None over $2,000		

Construction	$28,950	
General Contractors	$11,750	
Fluor Corp	$3,000	PAC
Trataros Construction	$3,000	Indiv
Associated General Contractors	$2,000	PAC
Home Builders	$3,750	
National Assn of Home Builders	$3,500	PAC

Source of Funds in 1992 Election

Source	Total	Pct
■ PACs	$278,185	43%
▨ Indivs $200+	$158,933	25%
□ Indivs under $200	$185,320	29%
⊠ Other	$24,891	4%
Candidate	$0	0%
Party	$1,296	0%

Source of PAC Dollars by Sector

Source	Total	Pct
■ Business	$233,558	83%
▨ Labor	$22,000	8%
□ Ideology/Single Issue	$24,680	9%

In-State vs. Out-of-State Contributions*

Source	Total	Pct
□ In-State	$136,133	86%
■ Out-of-state	$22,550	14%
No state listed	$0	

* by large individual contributors ($200 & above)

Construction Services	$9,950	
Stone & Webster	$3,200	PAC/Ind
Remington & Vernick	$2,500	Indiv
Taylor, Wiseman & Taylor	$2,000	Indiv
Building Materials & Equipment	$2,500	
None over $2,000		

Defense	$39,225	
Defense Aerospace	$20,900	
General Electric	$3,000	PAC
Grumman Corp	$2,500	PAC
Lockheed Corp	$2,500	PAC
Martin Marietta Corp	$2,350	PAC
Northrop Corp	$2,000	PAC
Defense Electronics	$12,225	
Imo Industries Inc	$2,000	PAC
Misc Defense	$6,100	
None over $2,000		

Energy & Natural Resources	$25,347	
Oil & Gas	$12,680	
Petroleum Marketers Assn	$2,500	PAC
Majestic Oil Co	$2,250	Indiv
Electric Utilities	$10,999	
Public Service Electric & Gas	$4,599	PAC
General Public Utilities	$2,600	PAC

Finance, Insurance & Real Estate	$87,394	
Commercial Banks	$7,825	
American Bankers Assn	$2,000	PAC
Savings & Loans	$2,369	
None over $2,000		
Credit Unions	$3,250	
Credit Union National Assn	$2,500	PAC
Securities & Investment	$5,510	
None over $2,000		

Contribution Totals by Sector

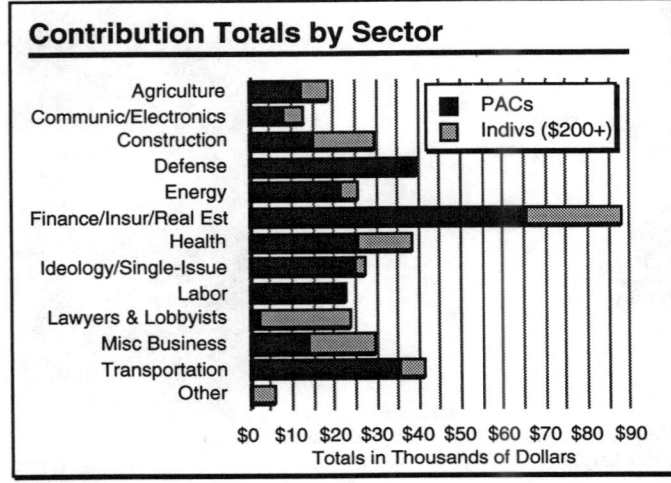

Legend: ■ PACs, ▨ Indivs ($200+)

Agriculture, Communic/Electronics, Construction, Defense, Energy, Finance/Insur/Real Est, Health, Ideology/Single-Issue, Labor, Lawyers & Lobbyists, Misc Business, Transportation, Other

$0 $10 $20 $30 $40 $50 $60 $70 $80 $90
Totals in Thousands of Dollars

Insurance **$41,840**
    Independent Insurance Agents of America .... $8,000   PAC
    National Assn of Life Underwriters .... $7,000   PAC
    McCay Corp .... $2,870   Indiv
    American Council of Life Insurance .... $2,500   PAC
    Casualty & Surety Agents Assn .... $2,000   PAC
    National Assn of Independent Insurers .... $2,000   PAC
    National Assn of Prof Insurance Agents .... $2,000   PAC
    Penn Mutual Life Insurance .... $2,000   PAC

Real Estate **$18,850**
    National Assn of Realtors .... $10,000   PAC
    Linpro Co .... $2,000   Indiv

Accountants **$5,500**
    American Institute of CPA's .... $5,000   PAC

Health $37,920

Health Professionals **$27,070**
    American Medical Assn* .... $5,450   PAC
    American Dental Assn .... $4,500   PAC
    American Physical Therapy Assn .... $2,000   PAC

Hospitals/Nursing Homes **$3,350**
    Seniors Management Inc .... $2,250   Indiv

Pharmaceuticals/Health Products **$6,000**
    None over $2,000

Lawyers & Lobbyists $23,619

Lawyers & Lobbyists **$23,619**
    Parker, McCay & Criscuolo .... $4,010   Indiv
    Montgomery, McCracken et al .... $2,500   Indiv
    McCarter & English .... $2,000   Indiv

Misc Business $28,975

Food & Beverage **$4,770**
    None over $2,000

Beer, Wine & Liquor **$2,750**
    National Beer Wholesalers Assn .... $2,000   PAC

Retail Sales **$5,200**
    Haddonfield Lumber Co .... $2,450   Indiv

Business Services **$3,500**
    None over $2,000

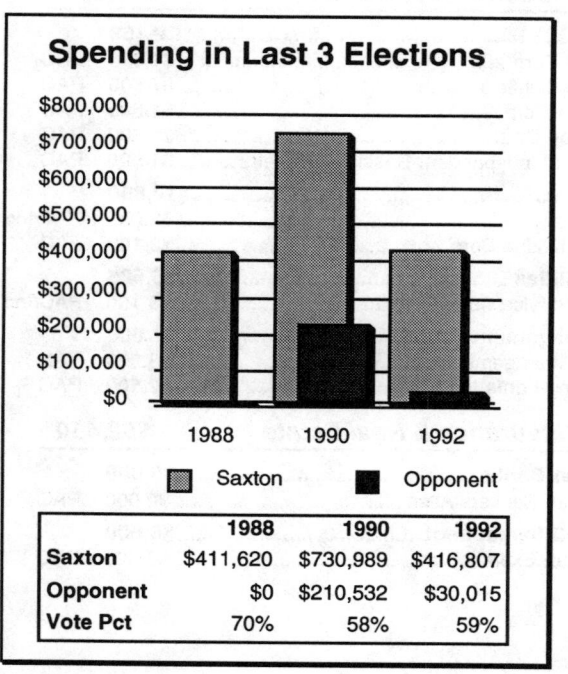

Spending in Last 3 Elections

	1988	1990	1992
Saxton	$411,620	$730,989	$416,807
Opponent	$0	$210,532	$30,015
Vote Pct	70%	58%	59%

Legend: Saxton / Opponent

Lodging/Tourism **$3,265**
    None over $2,000

Chemical & Related Manufacturing **$3,500**
    None over $2,000

Steel Production **$2,190**
    Sandmeyer Steel Co .... $2,190   Indiv

Transportation $40,950

Air Transport **$6,450**
    United Parcel Service .... $4,000   PAC

Automotive **$12,250**
    Auto Dealers & Drivers for Free Trade .... $5,000   PAC
    National Auto Dealers Assn .... $4,000   PAC

Railroads **$3,000**
    None over $2,000

Sea Transport **$16,800**
    CSX Corp* .... $3,000   PAC
    Society for Relief of Distressed Pilots .... $3,000   PAC
    American Pilots Assn .... $2,250   PAC
    Boat Owners Assn of the US .... $2,000   PAC
    Crowley Maritime .... $2,000   PAC

Labor

Labor $22,000

Transportation Unions **$13,000**
    Marine Engineers Dist 2 Maritime Officers .... $7,000   PAC
    Air Line Pilots Assn .... $2,500   PAC
    Teamsters Union .... $2,500   PAC

Public Sector Unions **$8,750**
    National Assn Retired Federal Employees .... $4,000   PAC
    National Assn of Letter Carriers .... $3,000   PAC

Ideological/Single-Issue

Ideological/Single-Issue $26,680

Leadership PACs **$2,000**
    Cmte for an Affordable NJ (C. Whitman) .... $2,000   PAC

Foreign & Defense Policy **$2,730**
    Veterans of Foreign Wars .... $2,000   PAC

Pro-Israel **$17,450**
    National PAC .... $5,000   PAC
    Pax PAC .... $2,500   PAC
    Women's Pro-Israel National PAC .... $2,500   PAC

Misc Issues **$3,500**
    National Cmte to Preserve Social Security .... $3,000   PAC

Other & Unknown

Other $5,550

Retired **$3,800**
    None over $2,000

Unknown $41,824

    Homemakers/Non-income earners $6,000
    Employer Listed/Category Unknown $33,824
        Demarco Enterprises .... $2,000   Indiv

* Contributions came from more than one affiliate or subsidiary.

Dan Schaefer, R-Colo (6)

First elected: 1983

1991-92 Total Receipts: $360,676
1992 Year-end Cash: $130,660

1991-92 Committees & Subcommittees

Energy and Commerce
Oversight and Investigations; Telecommunications and Finance; Transportation and Hazardous Materials

Leading Contributors

Business

Agriculture $29,600

Crop Production & Basic Processing	**$3,500**	
American Sugarbeet Growers Assn	$1,500	PAC
Tobacco	**$11,000**	
Philip Morris	$3,500	PAC
US Tobacco Co	$2,500	PAC
RJR Nabisco	$2,000	PAC
Tobacco Institute	$1,500	PAC
Dairy	**$4,000**	
Leprino Foods Co	$2,000	Indiv
Agricultural Services/Products	**$5,000**	
None over $1,500		
Food Processing & Sales	**$4,100**	
Food Marketing Institute	$3,000	PAC
Forestry & Forest Products	**$1,500**	
None over $1,500		

Communications/Electronics $40,290

Media/Entertainment	**$26,250**	
National Cable Television Assn	$10,000	PAC
National Assn of Broadcasters	$3,500	PAC
Viacom International	$3,000	PAC
Tele-Communications Inc	$2,500	PAC
Jones International	$2,000	PAC
Telephone Utilities	**$10,290**	
AT&T	$4,000	PAC
United Telecommunications	$1,500	PAC
Telecom Services & Equipment	**$2,500**	
None over $1,500		

Contribution Totals by Sector

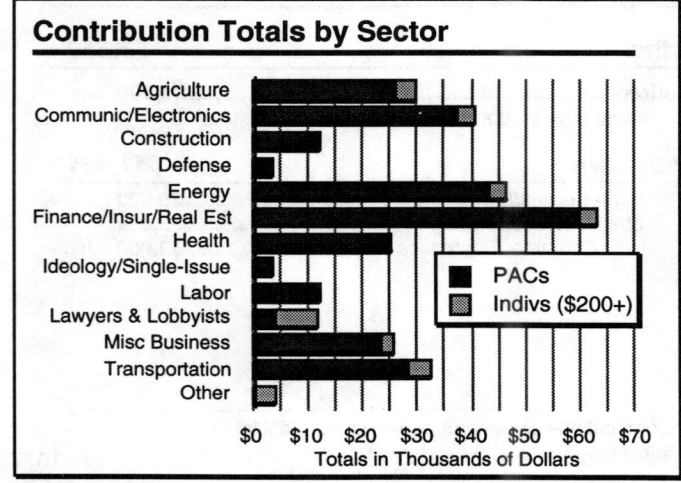

Totals in Thousands of Dollars

Source of Funds in 1992 Election

Source	Total	Pct
PACs	$272,484	76%
Indivs $200+	$37,155	10%
Indivs under $200	$31,933	9%
Other	$19,104	5%
Candidate	$0	0%
Party	$20	0%

Source of PAC Dollars by Sector

Source	Total	Pct
Business	$259,424	94%
Labor	$12,000	4%
Ideology/Single Issue	$3,200	1%

In-State vs. Out-of-State Contributions*

Source	Total	Pct
In-State	$29,905	80%
Out-of-state	$7,250	20%
No state listed	$0	

* by large individual contributors ($200 & above)

Construction $11,950

General Contractors	**$1,700**	
None over $1,500		
Construction Services	**$7,000**	
CH2M Hill	$3,500	PAC

Defense $3,500

Defense Aerospace	**$3,000**	
Martin Marietta Corp	$1,500	PAC

Energy & Natural Resources $46,034

Oil & Gas	**$19,159**	
Coastal Corp	$1,625	PAC
Atlantic Richfield	$1,500	PAC
Chevron Corp	$1,500	PAC
Marathon Oil	$1,500	PAC
Society of Independent Gasoline Marketrs	$1,500	PAC
Mining	**$10,850**	
Asarco Inc	$3,000	PAC/Ind
Phelps Dodge Corp	$2,100	PAC
Electric Utilities	**$8,525**	
Public Service Co of Colorado	$3,100	PAC/Ind
Waste Management	**$7,000**	
Waste Management Inc	$3,500	PAC
Browning-Ferris Industries	$2,500	PAC

Finance, Insurance & Real Estate $62,450

Commercial Banks	**$5,500**	
American Bankers Assn	$2,000	PAC
Securities & Investment	**$6,500**	
American Express*	$2,000	PAC

Insurance **$24,800**
 National Assn of Life Underwriters ....$5,000 PAC
 American Family Corp ....$4,000 PAC
 Security Life of Denver ....$3,000 PAC
 American Council of Life Insurance ....$2,000 PAC
 Mutual of Omaha ....$1,500 PAC

Real Estate **$8,150**
 National Assn of Realtors ....$6,000 PAC

Accountants **$17,000**
 American Institute of CPA's ....$8,500 PAC
 Arthur Andersen & Co ....$2,000 PAC
 Coopers & Lybrand ....$2,000 PAC
 Deloitte & Touche ....$2,000 PAC
 Ernst & Young ....$1,500 PAC

Health   *$24,750*

Health Professionals **$14,500**
 American Medical Assn ....$5,500 PAC
 American Dental Assn ....$3,500 PAC
 American Academy of Ophthalmology ....$2,000 PAC
 American Optometric Assn ....$1,500 PAC

Hospitals/Nursing Homes **$1,500**
 None over $1,500

Pharmaceuticals/Health Products **$8,250**
 Syntex (USA) Inc ....$3,000 PAC

Lawyers & Lobbyists   *$11,600*

Lawyers & Lobbyists **$11,600**
 Holland & Hart ....$2,000 PAC/Ind
 Montgomery, McCracken et al ....$1,500 Indiv

Misc Business   *$25,525*

Beer, Wine & Liquor **$2,500**
 None over $1,500

Retail Sales **$2,825**
 None over $1,500

Business Services **$4,500**
 Alarm Industry Communications Cmte ....$2,500 PAC
 Dun & Bradstreet ....$1,500 PAC

Lodging/Tourism **$1,850**
 None over $1,500

Chemical & Related Manufacturing **$5,100**
 Dow Chemical ....$1,500 PAC
 FMC Corp ....$1,500 PAC

Misc Manufacturing & Distributing **$7,250**
 Corning Glass Works ....$2,000 PAC
 Stone Container Corp ....$2,000 PAC
 Institute of Scrap Recycling Industries ....$1,700 PAC

Transportation   *$31,950*

Air Transport **$6,200**
 United Parcel Service ....$3,200 PAC
 General Electric ....$2,000 PAC

Automotive **$14,000**
 National Auto Dealers Assn ....$5,000 PAC
 Americans for Free International Trade ....$2,000 PAC
 Ford Motor Co ....$2,000 PAC
 Stevinson Auto ....$2,000 Indiv
 Auto Dealers & Drivers for Free Trade ....$1,500 PAC
 General Motors ....$1,500 PAC

Trucking **$1,750**
 None over $1,500

Railroads **$10,000**
 Burlington Northern ....$2,500 PAC
 Union Pacific Corp ....$2,000 PAC
 Norfolk Southern Corp ....$1,500 PAC
 Southern Pacific Transport Co ....$1,500 PAC/Ind

Labor

Labor   *$12,000*

Transportation Unions **$8,500**
 Marine Engineers Dist 2 Maritime Officers ....$6,500 PAC

Public Sector Unions **$3,500**
 National Assn Retired Federal Employees ....$2,000 PAC

Ideological/Single-Issue

Ideological/Single-Issue   *$3,200*

Gun Rights/Gun Control **$2,000**
 National Rifle Assn ....$1,500 PAC

Other & Unknown

Other   *$3,900*

Civil Servants/Public Officials **$2,150**
 None over $1,500

Unknown   *$5,030*

 Employer Listed/Category Unknown $4,030
  None over $1,500

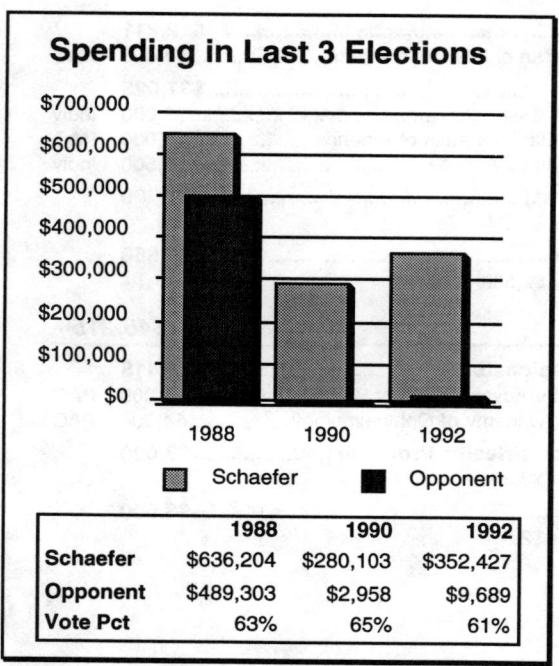

Spending in Last 3 Elections

	1988	1990	1992
Schaefer	$636,204	$280,103	$352,427
Opponent	$489,303	$2,958	$9,689
Vote Pct	63%	65%	61%

---

* Contributions came from more than one affiliate or subsidiary.

Lynn Schenk, D-Calif (49)

First elected: 1992

1991-92 Total Receipts: $1,150,104
1992 Year-end Cash: $23,509

1993-94 Committees & Subcommittees

Energy and Commerce
Telecommunications and Finance; Transportation and Hazardous Materials

Merchant Marine and Fisheries
Coast Guard and Navigation; Merchant Marine; Oceanography, Gulf of Mexico and the Outer Continental Shelf

Leading Contributors

Business

Agriculture		$12,500
Tobacco		**$4,000**
Brooke Group Ltd	$4,000	Indiv
Food Processing & Sales		**$8,250**
HJ Heinz Co	$5,000	Indiv

Communications/Electronics		$20,500
Printing & Publishing		**$4,750**
None over $2,500		
Media/Entertainment		**$6,750**
None over $2,500		
Telephone Utilities		**$2,750**
None over $2,500		
Computer Equipment & Services		**$4,000**
Dataquick	$4,000	Indiv

Construction		$5,450
Home Builders		**$3,500**
National Assn of Home Builders	$2,500	PAC

Energy & Natural Resources		$24,700
Oil & Gas		**$4,050**
None over $2,500		
Nuclear Energy		**$2,500**
General Atomics	$2,500	PAC/Ind
Electric Utilities		**$12,850**
Southern California Edison	$9,500	PAC/Ind
Commercial Fishing		**$5,300**
None over $2,500		

Source of Funds in 1992 Election

Source	Total	Pct
■ PACs	$300,129	26%
▨ Indivs $200+	$487,371	42%
☐ Indivs under $200	$169,826	15%
⊠ Other	$208,841	18%
Candidate	$180,000	15%
Party	$21,513	2%

Source of PAC Dollars by Sector

Source	Total	Pct
■ Business	$100,425	33%
▨ Labor	$124,100	41%
☐ Ideology/Single Issue	$77,401	26%

In-State vs. Out-of-State Contributions*

Source	Total	Pct
☐ In-State	$348,801	80%
■ Out-of-state	$86,650	20%
No state listed	$2,500	

* by large individual contributors ($200 & above)

Finance, Insurance & Real Estate — $103,386

Commercial Banks		**$18,600**
American Bankers Assn	$4,500	PAC
BankAmerica Corp	$3,500	PAC/Ind
San Diego National Bank	$2,750	Indiv
Savings & Loans		**$6,500**
None over $2,500		
Finance/Credit Companies		**$4,200**
Beneficial Management Corp	$4,000	PAC/Ind
Securities & Investment		**$10,000**
None over $2,500		
Insurance		**$12,211**
National Assn of Life Underwriters	$4,000	PAC
Real Estate		**$37,025**
Goldrich & Kest	$5,000	Indiv
Mortgage Bankers Assn of America	$3,000	PAC
Garden Homes Agency	$2,500	Indiv
Accountants		**$8,200**
None over $2,500		
Misc Finance		**$6,650**
None over $2,500		

Health — $46,215

Health Professionals		**$37,415**
Assn for the Advancement of Psychology	$7,000	PAC
American Academy of Ophthalmology	$4,000	PAC
Pharmaceuticals/Health Products		**$3,000**
None over $2,500		
Misc Health		**$3,500**
None over $2,500		

Contribution Totals by Sector

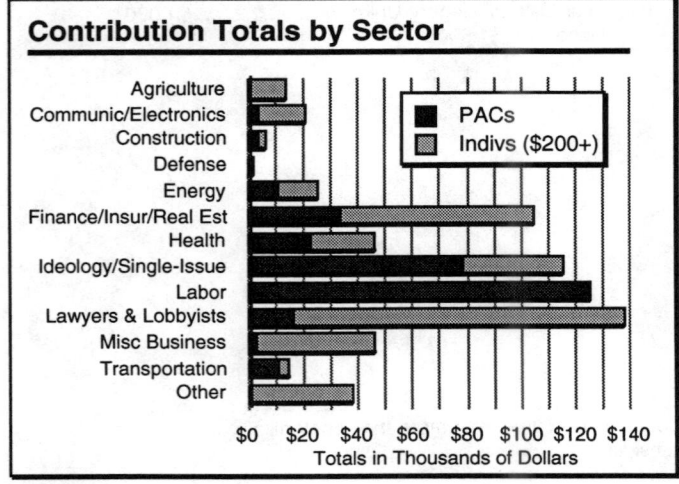

Totals in Thousands of Dollars

Lawyers & Lobbyists $139,642

Lawyers & Lobbyists $139,642
- Casey, Gerry et al .... $10,300 — Indiv
- Milberg, Weiss et al .... $10,250 — Indiv
- Assn of Trial Lawyers of America .... $10,000 — PAC
- Thorsnes, Bartolotta et al .... $3,500 — Indiv
- Peterson & Price .... $3,250 — Indiv
- Saxon, Dean et al .... $3,000 — Indiv
- Lorenz, Alhadeff et al .... $2,500 — Indiv

Misc Business $51,704

Food & Beverage $12,250
- Premier Catering .... $4,000 — Indiv
- Premier Food Services Inc .... $3,500 — Indiv

Retail Sales $6,250
- E-II Holdings .... $3,000 — Indiv

Misc Services $4,700
- None over $2,500

Business Services $14,954
- Assets Administration & Management .... $4,000 — Indiv

Lodging/Tourism $3,600
- None over $2,500

Misc Manufacturing & Distributing $5,750
- MacAndrews & Forbes Group .... $3,000 — Indiv

Transportation $13,550

Air Transport $5,000
- United Parcel Service .... $4,000 — PAC

Sea Transport $6,300
- None over $2,500

Labor

Labor $124,300

Building Trade Unions $21,700
- Carpenters & Joiners Union .... $8,000 — PAC
- Ironworkers Union .... $4,000 — PAC
- Laborers' Political League .... $3,000 — PAC
- Plumbers/Pipefitters Union .... $3,000 — PAC
- Sheet Metal Workers Union .... $2,500 — PAC

Industrial Unions $27,300
- Machinists/Aerospace Workers Union .... $7,000 — PAC
- United Auto Workers .... $6,500 — PAC
- Intl Brotherhood of Electrical Workers .... $6,000 — PAC
- United Steelworkers .... $5,000 — PAC

Transportation Unions $19,500
- Teamsters Union .... $5,000 — PAC
- Marine Engineers Union .... $4,500 — PAC
- Amalgamated Transit Union .... $2,500 — PAC
- Intl Longshoremen's/Warehousemen's Union .... $2,500 — PAC

Public Sector Unions $33,000
- National Education Assn .... $10,000 — PAC
- American Fedn of St/Cnty/Munic Employees .... $8,000 — PAC
- National Assn Retired Federal Employees .... $5,000 — PAC
- National Assn of Letter Carriers .... $3,500 — PAC
- International Assn of Firefighters .... $2,500 — PAC

Misc Unions $22,800
- Service Employees International Union .... $10,000 — PAC
- AFL-CIO .... $5,500 — PAC
- Food & Commercial Workers Union .... $5,500 — PAC

Ideological/Single-Issue

Ideological/Single-Issue $114,384

Democratic/Liberal $23,355
- Hollywood Women's Political Cmte .... $10,000 — PAC
- Independent Action .... $2,500 — PAC
- National Cmte for an Effective Congress .... $2,500 — PAC

Leadership PACs $6,429
- None over $2,500

Pro-Israel $19,200
- National PAC .... $5,000 — PAC

Pro-Choice $3,250
- None over $2,500

Womens Issues $42,163
- Emily's List .... $12,880 — PAC/Ind
- Women's Campaign Fund .... $10,000 — PAC
- Women's Political Committee .... $6,000 — PAC

Human Rights $7,000
- Human Rights Campaign Fund .... $4,500 — PAC

Misc Issues $11,987
- Sierra Club .... $5,000 — PAC
- League of Conservation Voters .... $4,487 — PAC

Other & Unknown

Other $36,861

Civil Servants/Public Officials $8,130
- US Department of Justice .... $4,000 — Indiv

Education $6,911
- None over $2,500

Retired $19,820
- None over $2,500

Unknown $92,835

- Homemakers/Non-income earners $21,650
- No Employer Listed or Found $20,965
- Employer Listed/Category Unknown $47,970
  - Gary Cypress & Co .... $4,000 — Indiv

Independent expenditures supporting Schenk
- Handgun Control Inc $20,962

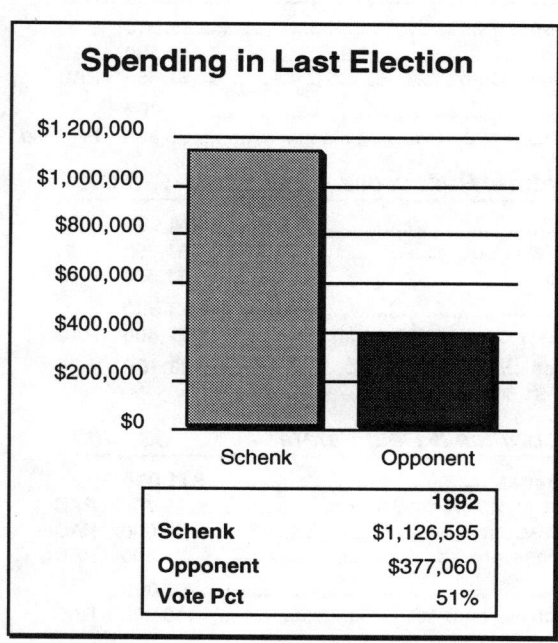

Spending in Last Election

	1992
Schenk	$1,126,595
Opponent	$377,060
Vote Pct	51%

Steven H. Schiff, R-NM (1)

First elected: 1988
1991-92 Total Receipts: $573,884
1992 Year-end Cash: $4,682

1991-92 Committees & Subcommittees

Government Operations
Government Information, Justice and Agriculture; Legislation and National Security

Judiciary
Administrative Law and Governmental Relations; Crime and Criminal Justice

Science, Space and Technology
Energy; Science

Leading Contributors

Business

Agriculture	$15,550	
Crop Production & Basic Processing	**$4,100**	
None over $1,500		
Tobacco	**$1,600**	
None over $1,500		
Livestock	**$5,750**	
National Cattlemen's Assn*	$2,100	PAC
Food Processing & Sales	**$3,000**	
None over $1,500		

Communications/Electronics	$23,255	
Media/Entertainment	**$4,905**	
National Cable Television Assn	$2,000	PAC
Telephone Utilities	**$11,700**	
GTE Corp	$2,400	PAC
US West Inc	$2,250	PAC/Ind
AT&T	$1,850	PAC/Ind
United Telecommunications	$1,800	PAC
Electronics Mfg & Services	**$3,200**	
North American Philips Corp	$2,000	PAC
Computer Equipment & Services	**$1,950**	
None over $1,500		

Source of Funds in 1992 Election

Source	Total	Pct
■ PACs	$183,610	32%
▦ Indivs $200+	$109,949	19%
☐ Indivs under $200	$270,897	47%
▨ Other	$9,428	2%
Candidate	$0	0%
Party	$1,108	0%

Source of PAC Dollars by Sector

Source	Total	Pct
■ Business	$154,951	83%
▦ Labor	$14,700	8%
☐ Ideology/Single Issue	$17,700	9%

In-State vs. Out-of-State Contributions*

Source	Total	Pct
☐ In-State	$105,894	96%
■ Out-of-state	$4,055	4%
No state listed	$0	

* by large individual contributors ($200 & above)

Construction	$14,300	
General Contractors	**$4,000**	
None over $1,500		
Home Builders	**$3,100**	
National Assn of Home Builders	$1,600	PAC
Joe W Roberts & Associates	$1,500	Indiv
Construction Services	**$3,700**	
None over $1,500		
Building Materials & Equipment	**$3,500**	
Western Building Supply	$2,300	Indiv

Defense	$13,849	
Defense Aerospace	**$9,050**	
Dyncorp	$2,500	PAC
Martin Marietta Corp	$1,650	PAC
Misc Defense	**$3,999**	
BDM International	$3,999	PAC/Ind

Energy & Natural Resources	$23,050	
Oil & Gas	**$14,950**	
Harvey E Yates Co	$1,750	Indiv
El Paso Co	$1,500	PAC
Mining	**$3,300**	
Phelps Dodge Corp	$2,400	PAC
Electric Utilities	**$3,100**	
None over $1,500		

Finance, Insurance & Real Estate	$37,400	
Commercial Banks	**$11,000**	
United New Mexico Financial Corp	$2,700	PAC
Barnett Banks Inc	$2,000	PAC
BankAmerica Corp	$1,500	PAC
Credit Unions	**$3,000**	
Credit Union National Assn	$3,000	PAC

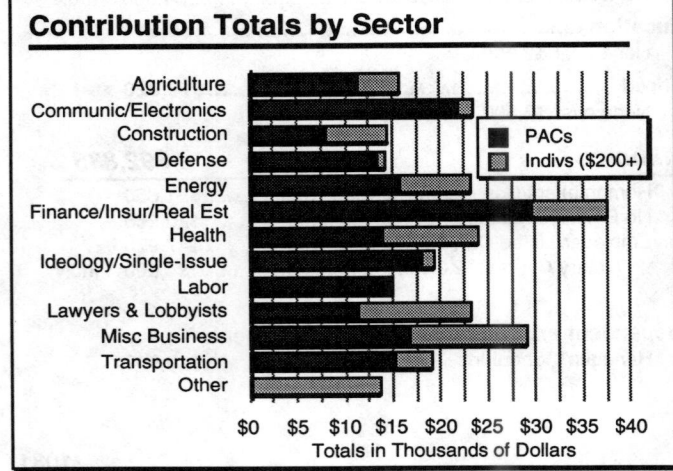

Contribution Totals by Sector

Agriculture, Communic/Electronics, Construction, Defense, Energy, Finance/Insur/Real Est, Health, Ideology/Single-Issue, Labor, Lawyers & Lobbyists, Misc Business, Transportation, Other

■ PACs
▦ Indivs ($200+)

$0 $5 $10 $15 $20 $25 $30 $35 $40
Totals in Thousands of Dollars

Insurance **$4,800**
    None over $1,500
Real Estate **$8,700**
    National Assn of Realtors ....$6,000 PAC
Accountants **$6,100**
    American Institute of CPA's ....$5,100 PAC
Misc Finance **$2,700**
    H&R Block ....$1,700 Indiv

Health $23,750

Health Professionals **$21,150**
    American Medical Assn ....$10,000 PAC
Pharmaceuticals/Health Products **$1,600**
    None over $1,500

Lawyers & Lobbyists $23,000

Lawyers & Lobbyists **$23,000**
    Assn of Trial Lawyers of America ....$10,000 PAC

Misc Business $28,801

Food & Beverage **$7,500**
    Coca-Cola Bottling ....$1,500 Indiv
Beer, Wine & Liquor **$5,350**
    National Beer Wholesalers Assn ....$4,350 PAC
Retail Sales **$3,050**
    None over $1,500
Misc Services **$1,501**
    None over $1,500
Business Services **$3,700**
    None over $1,500
Chemical & Related Manufacturing **$2,850**
    Dow Chemical ....$2,000 PAC
Misc Manufacturing & Distributing **$3,400**
    Stone Container Corp ....$2,000 PAC

Transportation $18,950

Air Transport **$5,650**
    United Parcel Service ....$3,800 PAC
Automotive **$9,200**
    National Auto Dealers Assn ....$2,300 PAC
    Auto Dealers & Drivers for Free Trade ....$1,500 PAC
Railroads **$2,600**
    Union Pacific Corp ....$1,500 PAC

Labor

Labor $14,700

Transportation Unions **$5,500**
    Marine Engineers Union* ....$5,500 PAC
Public Sector Unions **$9,200**
    National Education Assn ....$5,900 PAC
    National Assn Retired Federal Employees ....$3,000 PAC

Ideological/Single-Issue

Ideological/Single-Issue $19,150

Pro-Israel **$15,000**
    ChiliPAC ....$5,000 PAC
    Hudson Valley PAC ....$3,000 PAC
Gun Rights/Gun Control **$2,100**
    National Rifle Assn ....$1,900 PAC
Misc Issues **$1,800**
    National Cmte to Preserve Social Security ....$1,500 PAC

Other & Unknown

Other $13,500

Retired **$13,000**
    None over $1,500

Unknown $28,045

    Homemakers/Non-income earners $2,750
    No Employer Listed or Found $4,100
    Employer Listed/Category Unknown $20,145
        Styx Co ....$2,400 Indiv
        Kinney Agency Inc ....$1,500 Indiv

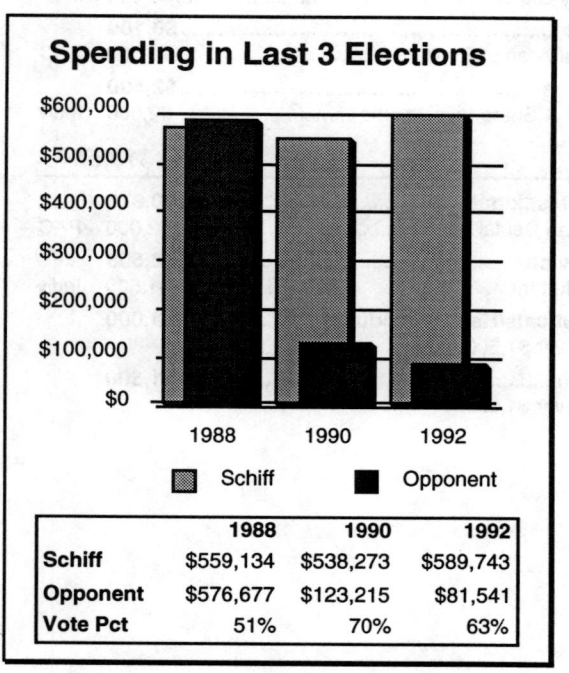

Spending in Last 3 Elections

	1988	1990	1992
Schiff	$559,134	$538,273	$589,743
Opponent	$576,677	$123,215	$81,541
Vote Pct	51%	70%	63%

Schiff   ■ *Opponent*

---

* Contributions came from more than one affiliate or
subsidiary.

Patricia Schroeder, D-Colo (1)

First elected: 1972

1991-92 Total Receipts: $361,845
1992 Year-end Cash: $612,243

1991-92 Committees & Subcommittees

Armed Services
Military Installations and Facilities (Chairwoman); Research and Development

Judiciary
Civil and Constitutional Rights; Intellectual Property and Judicial Administration

Post Office and Civil Service
Compensation and Employee Benefits

Select Committee on Children, Youth and Families (Chairwoman)

Leading Contributors

Business

Agriculture	$3,050
None over $1,500	

Communications/Electronics	$50,775

Printing & Publishing	$14,281	
West Publishing	$6,500	PAC
Continental Publications	$2,000	Indiv

Media/Entertainment	$30,250	
National Cable Television Assn	$8,000	PAC
MCA Inc	$4,000	PAC/Ind
ASCAP	$2,000	PAC
Mozark Productions	$2,000	Indiv
Time Warner*	$2,000	PAC
Fox Inc...	$1,500	PAC

Telephone Utilities	$4,740	
None over $1,500		

Construction	$2,250

Construction Services	$1,500	
None over $1,500		

Defense	$4,500

Defense Aerospace	$4,000	
None over $1,500		

Source of Funds in 1992 Election

Source	Total	Pct
PACs	$133,647	36%
Indivs $200+	$144,608	39%
Indivs under $200	$20,844	6%
Other................................	$72,035	19%
Candidate	$0	0%
Party	$11,189	3%

Source of PAC Dollars by Sector

Source	Total	Pct
Business	$79,904	60%
Labor	$46,100	35%
Ideology/Single Issue	$6,719	5%

In-State vs. Out-of-State Contributions*

Source	Total	Pct
In-State	$33,855	23%
Out-of-state	$110,503	77%
No state listed	$250	

* by large individual contributors ($200 & above)

Energy & Natural Resources	$7,200

Oil & Gas	$5,000	
None over $1,500		

Nuclear Energy	$1,500	
General Atomics	$1,500	PAC

Finance, Insurance & Real Estate	$18,462

Securities & Investment	$2,112	
None over $1,500		

Insurance	$5,750	
Security Life of Denver	$3,000	PAC

Real Estate	$6,100	
National Assn of Realtors	$1,500	PAC

Misc Finance	$2,500	
Wingler & Sharp Investments	$2,000	Indiv

Health	$18,584

Health Professionals	$10,975	
American Dental Assn	$2,000	PAC

Health Services	$2,500	
Qual-Med Inc	$1,500	Indiv

Pharmaceuticals/Health Products	$3,000	
None over $1,500		

Misc Health	$1,500	
None over $1,500		

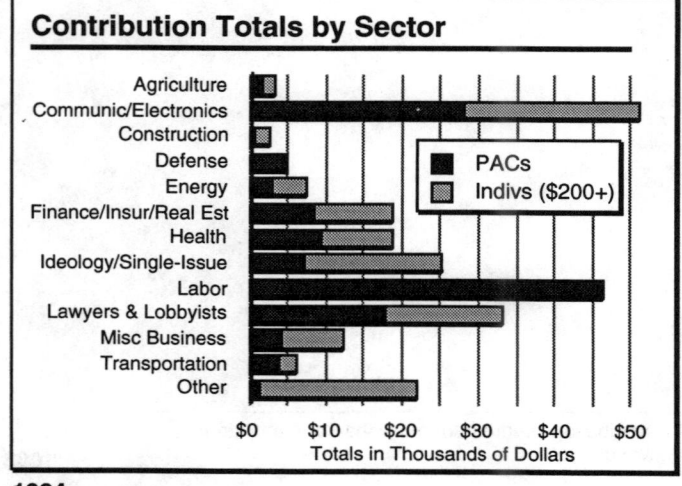

Contribution Totals by Sector

Categories (top to bottom): Agriculture, Communic/Electronics, Construction, Defense, Energy, Finance/Insur/Real Est, Health, Ideology/Single-Issue, Labor, Lawyers & Lobbyists, Misc Business, Transportation, Other

Legend: PACs, Indivs ($200+)

X-axis: $0, $10, $20, $30, $40, $50
Totals in Thousands of Dollars

Lawyers & Lobbyists — $32,906

Lawyers & Lobbyists $32,906
   Assn of Trial Lawyers of America ....$10,000 PAC
   Opperman & Paquin ....$4,500 PAC
   Kogovsek & Associates.......................................$2,000 Indiv
   Arnold & Porter...$1,750 PAC/Ind

Misc Business — $11,872

Food & Beverage $2,300
   None over $1,500

Retail Sales $2,700
   Direct Marketing Assn ....$1,500 PAC

Misc Services $1,500
   None over $1,500

Business Services $3,022
   None over $1,500

Misc Manufacturing & Distributing $1,500
   None over $1,500

Transportation — $6,100

Air Transport $4,500
   United Parcel Service ....$2,000 PAC

Labor

Labor — $46,100

Building Trade Unions $4,500
   Laborers' Political League ....$2,000 PAC

Industrial Unions $4,250
   Intl Brotherhood of Electrical Workers ....$3,500 PAC

Transportation Unions $16,000
   Teamsters Union ....$6,000 PAC
   Marine Engineers Dist 2 Maritime Officers ....$3,000 PAC
   Air Line Pilots Assn ....$2,500 PAC
   Assn of Flight Attendants ....$2,000 PAC

Public Sector Unions $19,250
   American Fedn of St/Cnty/Munic Employees ......$5,000 PAC
   National Assn Retired Federal Employees ....$3,000 PAC
   National Assn of Letter Carriers ....$3,000 PAC
   American Postal Workers Union ....$1,500 PAC

Misc Unions...$2,100
   Food & Commercial Workers Union ....$2,100 PAC

Ideological/Single-Issue

Ideological/Single-Issue — $24,760

Democratic/Liberal $13,212
   Hollywood Women's Political Cmte ....$2,500 PAC

Abortion Policy $4,400
   None over $1,500

Womens Issues...$3,579
   None over $1,500

Human Rights $2,569
   None over $1,500

Other & Unknown

Other — $21,544

Civil Servants/Public Officials $3,248
   None over $1,500

Education $6,076
   None over $1,500

Retired $10,370
   None over $1,500

Other $1,850
   None over $1,500

Unknown — $30,028

   Homemakers/Non-income earners $3,714
   No Employer Listed or Found $10,800
   Generic Occupation/Category Unknown $2,021
   Employer Listed/Category Unknown $13,493
     None over $1,500

Spending in Last 3 Elections

	1988	1990	1992
Schroeder	$217,503	$521,500	$398,749
Opponent	$26,040	$161,266	$0
Vote Pct	70%	64%	69%

* Contributions came from more than one affiliate or subsidiary.

Charles E. Schumer, D-NY (9)

First elected: 1980
1991-92 Total Receipts: $923,272
1992 Year-end Cash: $2,116,689

1991-92 Committees & Subcommittees

Banking, Finance and Urban Affairs
Financial Institutions Supervision, Regulation and Insurance; Housing and Community Development

Interior and Insular Affairs
Energy and the Environment

Judiciary
Crime and Criminal Justice (Chairman); Intellectual Property and Judicial Administration; International Law, Immigration and Refugees

Leading Contributors

Business

Agriculture		$4,000
Food Processing & Sales		$2,000
Royal Farms Inc	Indiv	$2,000

Communications/Electronics		$24,000
Media/Entertainment		$20,500
Paramount Communications	PAC	$15,000
ASCAP	PAC	$1,500
Telephone Utilities		$1,500
None over $1,500		

Construction		$1,500
None over $1,500		

Energy & Natural Resources		$1,500
None over $1,500		

Finance, Insurance & Real Estate		$407,246
Commercial Banks		$40,250
Republic National Bank of New York	Indiv	$13,000
JP Morgan & Co	PAC	$7,500
Chase Manhattan	PAC	$6,000
Commercial Bank of New York	Indiv	$6,000
Continental Illinois Corp	PAC	$3,000
Savings & Loans		$3,000
Emigrant Savings Bank	Indiv	$2,000
Finance/Credit Companies		$7,750
Rosenthal & Rosenthal	Indiv	$6,000

Source of Funds in 1992 Election

Source	Total	Pct
PACs	$187,114	20%
Indivs $200+	$490,350	53%
Indivs under $200	$50,346	5%
Other	$199,737	22%
Candidate	$0	0%
Party	$4,725	1%

Source of PAC Dollars by Sector

Source	Total	Pct
Business	$153,796	81%
Labor	$27,727	15%
Ideology/Single Issue	$8,400	4%

In-State vs. Out-of-State Contributions*

Source	Total	Pct
In-State	$425,550	88%
Out-of-state	$58,250	12%
No state listed	$3,750	

* by large individual contributors ($200 & above)

Securities & Investment		$221,996
Shearson Lehman Brothers	PAC/Ind	$13,500
Dean Witter	PAC/Ind	$11,750
Odyssey Partners	Indiv	$11,000
Donaldson, Lufkin & Jenrette	Indiv	$10,500
Morgan Stanley & Co	PAC/Ind	$10,446
Goldman, Sachs & Co	PAC/Ind	$10,300
Brown Brothers Harriman & Co	Indiv	$10,000
Merrill Lynch	PAC/Ind	$10,000
Wertheim, Schroder & Co	PAC/Ind	$9,000
Kohlberg, Kravis & Roberts	Indiv	$8,000
Neuberger & Berman	Indiv	$8,000
Bear, Stearns & Co	PAC/Ind	$6,500
PaineWebber	PAC/Ind	$6,500
James D Wolfensohn Inc	Indiv	$6,000
Clayton & Dubilier Inc	Indiv	$5,500
Chieftain Capital Management	Indiv	$5,000
DH Blair & Co	Indiv	$5,000
Gordon, Haskett Capital Corp	Indiv	$5,000
Investment Company Institute	PAC	$5,000
Triangle Industries	PAC	$5,000
First Boston Corp	PAC/Ind	$4,000
Glickenhaus & Co	Indiv	$4,000
James P Wolfensohn Inc	Indiv	$4,000
Mel Schnell & Co	Indiv	$4,000
Trian Group	Indiv	$4,000
Reich & Tang	Indiv	$3,000
Forstmann, Little & Co	Indiv	$2,000
Lasker, Stone & Stern	Indiv	$2,000
MJ Meehan & Co	Indiv	$2,000
Oppenheimer Holdings Inc	PAC	$2,000
Prudential Securities	PAC	$2,000
Rothschild Inc	Indiv	$2,000
Steinhardt Partners	Indiv	$2,000

Contribution Totals by Sector

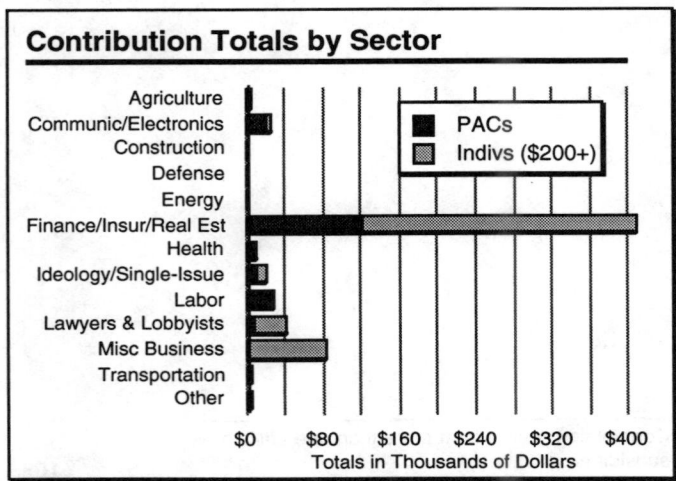

Agriculture
Communic/Electronics
Construction
Defense
Energy
Finance/Insur/Real Est
Health
Ideology/Single-Issue
Labor
Lawyers & Lobbyists
Misc Business
Transportation
Other

■ PACs
▨ Indivs ($200+)

$0 $80 $160 $240 $320 $400
Totals in Thousands of Dollars

Insurance	....	$35,500	
	Reliance Group Holdings	$10,000	PAC
	American International Group Inc	$5,000	PAC
	Metropolitan Life Insurance	$5,000	PAC
	American International Group	$4,500	Indiv
	American Council of Life Insurance	$4,000	PAC
	National Assn of Life Underwriters	$2,000	PAC

Insurance **$35,500**
  Reliance Group Holdings .... $10,000 PAC
  American International Group Inc .... $5,000 PAC
  Metropolitan Life Insurance .... $5,000 PAC
  American International Group .... $4,500 Indiv
  American Council of Life Insurance .... $4,000 PAC
  National Assn of Life Underwriters .... $2,000 PAC

Real Estate **$83,000**
  Sylvan Lawrence Co .... $18,000 Indiv
  Mack Companies .... $6,000 Indiv
  Milstein Properties .... $6,000 Indiv
  National Assn of Realtors .... $6,000 PAC
  Douglas Elliman-Gibbons & Ives .... $4,000 Indiv
  Philips International Holding Corp .... $4,000 Indiv
  Solow Building Co .... $4,000 Indiv
  World Wide Holdings Corp .... $4,000 Indiv
  Rentar Development Corp .... $3,500 Indiv
  Rudin Management Co .... $3,000 Indiv
  Edward S Gordon Co .... $2,000 Indiv
  Jack Resnick & Sons Inc .... $2,000 Indiv
  Nederlander Organization .... $2,000 Indiv
  Peter J Sharp & Co .... $2,000 Indiv
  Adco Group .... $1,500 Indiv

Accountants **$11,000**
  American Institute of CPA's .... $7,500 PAC

Misc Finance **$4,750**
  Ranieri, Wilson & Co .... $2,000 Indiv

Health — $9,350

Health Professionals **$3,350**
  American Medical Assn .... $2,850 PAC

Pharmaceuticals/Health Products **$4,500**
  Forest Laboratories Inc .... $4,000 Indiv

Lawyers & Lobbyists — $40,750

Lawyers & Lobbyists **$40,750**
  Schulte, Roth & Zabel .... $10,000 Indiv
  Assn of Trial Lawyers of America .... $5,000 PAC
  Skadden, Arps et al .... $4,250 Indiv
  Cadwalader, Wickersham & Taft .... $3,000 Indiv
  Debevoise & Plimpton .... $2,000 Indiv
  Singer, Netter & Dowd .... $2,000 Indiv
  Weil, Gotshal & Manges .... $2,000 Indiv
  Mintz, Levin et al .... $1,500 Indiv

Misc Business — **$81,250**

Retail Sales **$14,250**
  Rainbow Shops Inc .... $4,000 Indiv
  Burlington Coat Factory .... $2,000 Indiv
  Conway Stores .... $2,000 Indiv
  Gordon's Deep Discount .... $2,000 Indiv
  Rainbow Apparel Co .... $2,000 Indiv

Business Services **$6,000**
  Devon Group Inc .... $5,000 Indiv

Chemical & Related Manufacturing **$9,000**
  Transammonia Inc .... $6,000 Indiv
  GAF Corp .... $2,000 Indiv

Misc Manufacturing & Distributing **$46,750**
  Baby Togs Inc .... $10,000 Indiv
  Warnaco Inc .... $7,000 Indiv
  MacAndrews & Forbes Group .... $6,000 Indiv
  Pall Corp .... $6,000 Indiv
  Gitano Co .... $5,750 Indiv
  Skiva International Corp .... $4,000 Indiv
  Jordache Enterprises .... $3,000 Indiv
  Carolyne Roehm Inc .... $2,000 Indiv
  Estee Lauder Inc .... $2,000 Indiv

Transportation — $3,000

Air Transport **$2,500**
  Fairchild Corp .... $2,000 Indiv

Labor

Labor — **$27,727**

Building Trade Unions **$3,500**
  Laborers' Political League .... $3,000 PAC

Transportation Unions **$11,114**
  Seafarers International Union .... $5,114 PAC
  Teamsters Union .... $5,000 PAC

Public Sector Unions **$7,000**
  American Fedn of St/Cnty/Munic Employees ...... $5,000 PAC

Misc Unions **$5,113**
  Hotel/Restaurant Employees Union .... $2,614 PAC
  Food & Commercial Workers Union .... $1,999 PAC

Ideological/Single-Issue

Ideological/Single-Issue — **$18,650**

Pro-Israel **$12,750**
  National PAC .... $5,000 PAC

Gun Rights/Gun Control **$2,500**
  Handgun Control Inc .... $2,500 PAC

Womens Issues **$3,000**
  None over $1,500

Other & Unknown

Other — **$4,000**

Retired **$4,000**
  None over $1,500

Unknown — **$54,000**
  Homemakers/Non-income earners $28,500
  No Employer Listed or Found $13,250
  Employer Listed/Category Unknown $11,250
    Best Brands Home Products Inc .... $1,500 Indiv

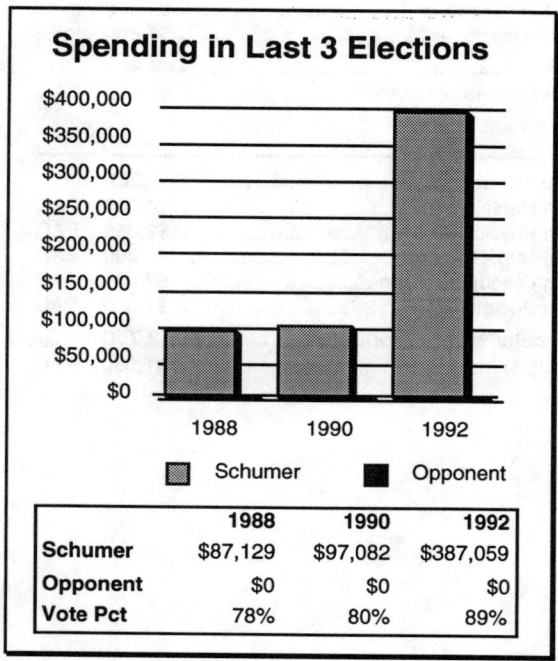

Spending in Last 3 Elections

	1988	1990	1992
Schumer	$87,129	$97,082	$387,059
Opponent	$0	$0	$0
Vote Pct	78%	80%	89%

Robert C. Scott, D-Va (3)

First elected: 1992

1991-92 Total Receipts: $510,776
1992 Year-end Cash: $18,915

1993-94 Committees & Subcommittees

Education and Labor
Human Resources; Postsecondary Education and Training; Select Education and Civil Rights

Judiciary
Economic and Commercial Law

Science, Space and Technology
Energy

Leading Contributors

Business

Agriculture	$7,750

Tobacco **$3,000**
   RJR Nabisco ....$3,000   PAC

Communications/Electronics	$2,400

   None over $1,500

Construction	$7,250

General Contractors **$3,750**
   None over $1,500

Home Builders **$2,500**
   National Assn of Home Builders ....$2,500   PAC

Defense	$6,000

Misc Defense **$6,000**
   Tenneco Inc ....$6,000   PAC

Energy & Natural Resources	$7,950

Oil & Gas **$4,100**
   Chevron Corp ....$1,500   PAC

Electric Utilities **$2,850**
   None over $1,500

Source of Funds in 1992 Election

Source	Total	Pct
■ PACs	$186,250	36%
▨ Indivs $200+	$128,803	25%
☐ Indivs under $200	$131,491	26%
⊠ Other	$66,676	13%
Candidate	$59,657	12%
Party	$3,594	1%

Source of PAC Dollars by Sector

Source	Total	Pct
■ Business	$103,435	51%
▨ Labor	$87,900	44%
☐ Ideology/Single Issue	$9,750	5%

In-State vs. Out-of-State Contributions*

Source	Total	Pct
☐ In-State	$117,353	92%
■ Out-of-state	$10,450	8%
No state listed	$1,000	

* by large individual contributors ($200 & above)

Finance, Insurance & Real Estate	$49,602

Commercial Banks **$12,600**
   American Bankers Assn* ....$6,500   PAC
   Citizens & Southern National Bank ....$2,000   PAC

Savings & Loans **$2,700**
   Virginia League of Savings Institutions ....$1,500   PAC

Securities & Investment **$3,100**
   None over $1,500

Insurance **$5,500**
   None over $1,500

Real Estate **$19,550**
   National Assn of Realtors ....$10,000   PAC
   General Services Corp ....$2,000   Indiv
   Kiln Creek Developer ....$1,850   Indiv

Accountants **$3,452**
   American Institute of CPA's ....$2,500   PAC

Health	$36,686

Health Professionals **$31,286**
   American Dental Assn ....$4,000   PAC
   American Physical Therapy Assn ....$2,085   PAC
   American Nurses Assn ....$2,000   PAC
   American Optometric Assn ....$2,000   PAC
   American Podiatry Assn ....$1,500   PAC

Pharmaceuticals/Health Products **$2,750**
   Syntex (USA) Inc ....$1,500   PAC

Contribution Totals by Sector

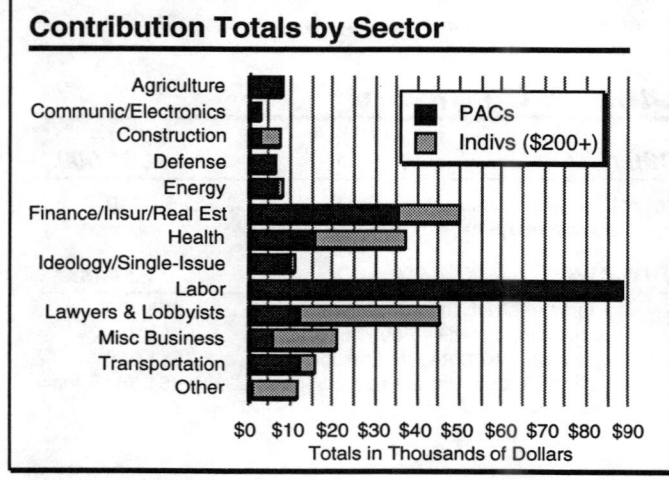

Agriculture
Communic/Electronics
Construction
Defense
Energy
Finance/Insur/Real Est
Health
Ideology/Single-Issue
Labor
Lawyers & Lobbyists
Misc Business
Transportation
Other

■ PACs
▨ Indivs ($200+)

$0 $10 $20 $30 $40 $50 $60 $70 $80 $90
Totals in Thousands of Dollars

Lawyers & Lobbyists $44,730

Lawyers & Lobbyists **$44,730**
Assn of Trial Lawyers of America	$10,000	PAC
Rutter & Montagna	$6,400	Indiv
Patten, Wornom & Watkins	$4,000	Indiv
Howell, Daugherty et al	$2,830	Indiv
Jones, Blechman et al	$2,500	Indiv
McGuire, Woods et al	$2,000	PAC/Ind
Willcox & Savage	$1,500	Indiv

Misc Business $20,400

Beer, Wine & Liquor **$6,000**
Associated Distributors	$2,000	Indiv
National Beer Wholesalers Assn	$2,000	PAC

Retail Sales **$4,550**
Virginia Specialty Store	$3,000	Indiv

Misc Services **$3,950**
Cooke Bros Funeral Chapel	$1,700	Indiv
Hampton Memorial Gardens	$1,500	Indiv

Business Services **$2,700**
C&W Associates	$2,700	Indiv

Misc Manufacturing & Distributing **$2,000**
None over $1,500

Transportation $15,450

Air Transport **$3,500**
United Parcel Service	$3,500	PAC

Automotive **$6,450**
National Auto Dealers Assn	$5,000	PAC

Railroads **$1,750**
None over $1,500

Sea Transport **$3,750**
Metro Machine Corp	$2,000	Indiv

Labor

Labor **$87,900**

Building Trade Unions **$10,200**
Carpenters & Joiners Union	$3,500	PAC
Laborers' Political League	$2,000	PAC
Bricklayers Union	$1,500	PAC

Industrial Unions **$23,500**
Machinists/Aerospace Workers Union	$5,500	PAC
Communications Workers of America	$5,000	PAC
United Steelworkers	$5,000	PAC
Intl Brotherhood of Electrical Workers	$4,000	PAC
United Mine Workers	$2,500	PAC

Transportation Unions **$22,500**
International Longshoremen's Assn	$6,000	PAC
Teamsters Union	$6,000	PAC
Seafarers International Union	$2,500	PAC
United Transportation Union	$2,500	PAC
Amalgamated Transit Union	$2,000	PAC
Marine Engineers Union	$1,500	PAC

Public Sector Unions **$20,600**
American Fedn of St/Cnty/Munic Employees	$6,000	PAC
National Education Assn	$6,000	PAC
National Assn of Letter Carriers	$3,000	PAC
American Postal Workers Union	$2,500	PAC
International Assn of Firefighters	$1,500	PAC

Misc Unions **$11,100**
Food & Commercial Workers Union	$6,000	PAC
AFL-CIO	$2,600	PAC
Bakery, Confectionery & Tobacco Workers	$1,500	PAC

Ideological/Single-Issue

Ideological/Single-Issue **$10,500**

Leadership PACs **$3,500**
None over $1,500

Human Rights **$2,500**
Human Rights Campaign Fund	$2,500	PAC

Misc Issues **$1,500**
None over $1,500

Other & Unknown

Other **$11,170**

Civil Servants/Public Officials **$3,320**
None over $1,500

Education **$4,300**
None over $1,500

Retired **$2,550**
None over $1,500

Unknown **$22,400**
Homemakers/Non-income earners	$3,050
No Employer Listed or Found	$5,600
Employer Listed/Category Unknown	$13,750

None over $1,500

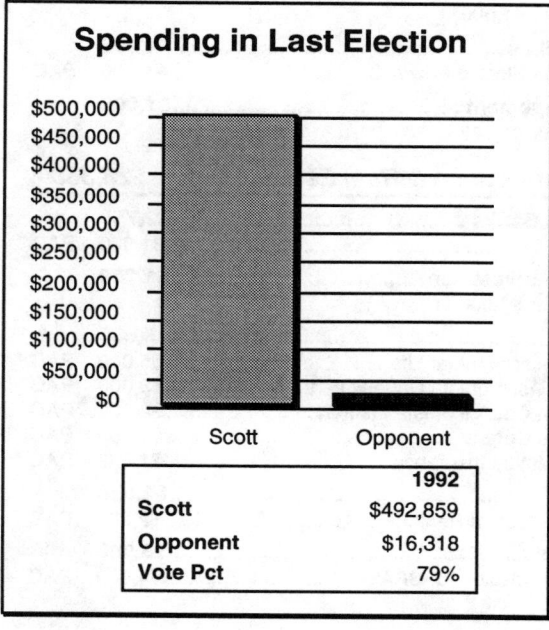

Spending in Last Election

	1992
Scott	$492,859
Opponent	$16,318
Vote Pct	79%

* Contributions came from more than one affiliate or subsidiary.

F. James Sensenbrenner Jr., R-Wis (9)

First elected: 1978

1991-92 Total Receipts: $283,602
1992 Year-end Cash: $138,787

1991-92 Committees & Subcommittees

Judiciary
Crime and Criminal Justice (Ranking Republican); Intellectual Property and Judicial Administration

Science, Space and Technology
Investigations and Oversight; Space (Ranking Republican)

Select Committee on Narcotics Abuse and Control

Leading Contributors

Business

Agriculture — $8,100

Dairy $3,500
    Associated Milk Producers .... $3,000   PAC

Agricultural Services/Products $1,250
    None over $1,000

Food Processing & Sales $1,750
    None over $1,000

Forestry & Forest Products $1,000
    None over $1,000

Communications/Electronics — $14,100

Printing & Publishing $1,000
    Quad Graphics .... $1,000   Indiv

Media/Entertainment $4,500
    National Cable Television Assn .... $3,000   PAC
    National Assn of Broadcasters .... $1,000   PAC

Telephone Utilities $7,100
    AT&T .... $3,800   PAC
    Ameritech Corp* .... $1,250   PAC
    GTE Corp .... $1,000   PAC

Electronics Mfg & Services $1,000
    Milwaukee Resistor Corp .... $1,000   Indiv

Construction — $5,850

General Contractors $1,850
    Associated General Contractors .... $1,350   PAC

Home Builders $2,000
    Harmony Homes Inc .... $1,000   Indiv
    National Assn of Home Builders .... $1,000   PAC

Source of Funds in 1992 Election

Source	Total	Pct
PACs	$75,709	27%
Indivs $200+	$56,025	20%
Indivs under $200	$110,871	39%
Other	$40,997	14%
Candidate	$0	0%
Party	$68	0%

Source of PAC Dollars by Sector

Source	Total	Pct
Business	$73,175	98%
Labor	$0	0%
Ideology/Single Issue	$1,850	2%

In-State vs. Out-of-State Contributions*

Source	Total	Pct
In-State	$54,245	97%
Out-of-state	$1,750	3%
No state listed	$0	

* by large individual contributors ($200 & above)

Special Trade Contractors $1,000
    National Electrical Contractors Assn ...... $1,000   PAC

Building Materials & Equipment $1,000
    Deltrol Controls .... $1,000   Indiv

Defense — $4,850

Defense Aerospace $4,350
    Rockwell International .... $1,500   PAC
    Martin Marietta Corp .... $1,000   PAC
    McDonnell Douglas .... $1,000   PAC

Energy & Natural Resources — $5,800

Oil & Gas $2,100
    None over $1,000

Electric Utilities $2,200
    Wisconsin Electric Power Co .... $1,200   PAC

Waste Management $1,000
    None over $1,000

Finance, Insurance & Real Estate — $28,350

Commercial Banks $2,750
    Norwest Corp .... $1,000   PAC

Securities & Investment $1,250
    None over $1,000

Insurance $15,600
    Northwestern Mutual Life .... $5,000   PAC
    National Assn of Life Underwriters .... $3,000   PAC
    American Council of Life Insurance .... $2,000   PAC
    Travelers Corp .... $2,000   PAC
    Liberty Mutual Insurance .... $1,000   PAC

Real Estate $2,550
    National Assn of Realtors .... $2,300   PAC

Accountants $5,000
    American Institute of CPA's .... $4,000   PAC

Contribution Totals by Sector

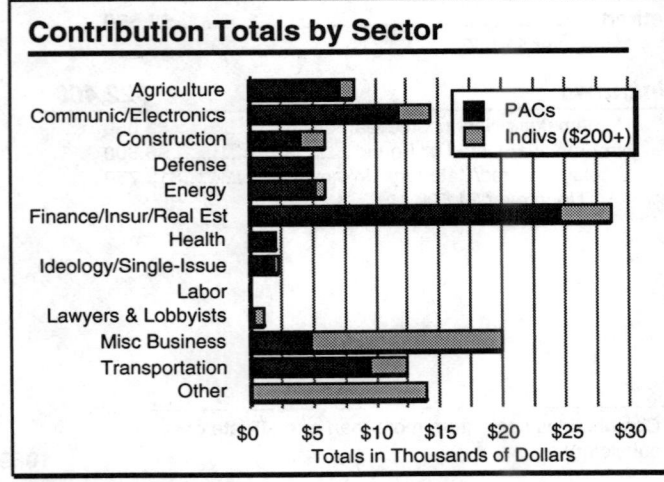

Legend: ■ PACs, ▨ Indivs ($200+)

Categories (top to bottom): Agriculture, Communic/Electronics, Construction, Defense, Energy, Finance/Insur/Real Est, Health, Ideology/Single-Issue, Labor, Lawyers & Lobbyists, Misc Business, Transportation, Other

Axis: $0, $5, $10, $15, $20, $25, $30 — Totals in Thousands of Dollars

Health $2,050

Health Professionals $1,550
    American Medical Assn.......................... $1,350 PAC

Lawyers & Lobbyists $1,100

Lawyers & Lobbyists $1,100
    None over $1,000

Misc Business $19,800

Beer, Wine & Liquor $2,250
    National Beer Wholesalers Assn .... $2,000 PAC
Misc Services $4,000
    PBC Producations Inc .... $4,000 Indiv
Misc Business $2,000
    Wiscold Inc .... $2,000 Indiv
Chemical & Related Manufacturing $1,500
    Essential Chemical Corp .... $1,000 Indiv
Misc Manufacturing & Distributing $8,800
    Western Metal Specialty .... $4,000 Indiv
    SC Johnson & Son Inc .... $2,000 Indiv

Transportation $12,225

Air Transport $2,475
    Boeing Co .... $2,000 PAC
Automotive $9,600
    National Auto Dealers Assn .... $4,000 PAC
    Briggs & Stratton Corp .... $2,550 Indiv
    Auto Dealers & Drivers for Free Trade .... $1,500 PAC
    Americans for Free International Trade .... $1,000 PAC

Ideological/Single-Issue

Ideological/Single-Issue $2,100

Gun Rights/Gun Control $1,000
    Handgun Control Inc .... $1,000 PAC

Other & Unknown

Other $13,775

Retired $13,525
    None over $1,000

Unknown $12,920

    Homemakers/Non-income earners $3,150
    Employer Listed/Category Unknown $8,800
        Taylor Electric Co .... $1,900 Indiv
        DFI Corp .... $1,000 Indiv
        Minahan & Peterson .... $1,000 Indiv

---

Spending in Last 3 Elections

	1988	1990	1992
Sensenbrenner	$288,505	$98,609	$457,292
Opponent	$14,686	$0	$24,260
Vote Pct	75%	100%	70%

Legend: ▨ Sensenbrenner   ■ Opponent

---

* Contributions came from more than one affiliate or subsidiary.

Jose E. Serrano, D-NY (16)

First elected: 1989

1991-92 Total Receipts: $116,483
1992 Year-end Cash: $41,830

1991-92 Committees & Subcommittees

Education and Labor
Labor-Management Relations; Postsecondary Education; Select Education

Small Business
Antitrust, Impact of Deregulation and Ecology; SBA, the General Economy and Minority Enterprise Development

Leading Contributors

Business

Agriculture — $2,500

Food Processing & Sales	**$1,000**	
Pepsico Inc	$1,000	PAC

Communications/Electronics — $5,700

Media/Entertainment	**$2,000**	
ASCAP	$1,500	PAC
Telephone Utilities	**$3,700**	
AT&T	$1,900	PAC

Defense — $1,500

Defense Electronics	**$1,500**	
Loral Corp	$1,500	PAC/Ind

Energy & Natural Resources — $1,200

None over $1,000

Finance, Insurance & Real Estate — $15,550

Commercial Banks	**$5,550**	
Citicorp	$3,000	PAC
Chemical Bank	$1,550	PAC
Real Estate	**$6,300**	
National Assn of Realtors	$6,000	PAC
Accountants	**$2,000**	
American Institute of CPA's	$2,000	PAC

Source of Funds in 1992 Election

Source	Total	Pct
PACs	$93,350	77%
Indivs $200+	$16,050	13%
Indivs under $200	$3,140	3%
Other	$8,314	7%
Candidate	$0	0%
Party	$4,821	4%

Source of PAC Dollars by Sector

Source	Total	Pct
Business	$40,050	43%
Labor	$48,000	52%
Ideology/Single Issue	$4,300	5%

In-State vs. Out-of-State Contributions*

Source	Total	Pct
In-State	$10,500	65%
Out-of-state	$5,550	35%
No state listed	$0	

* by large individual contributors ($200 & above)

Health — $10,000

Health Professionals	**$7,500**	
American Medical Assn*	$6,000	PAC
Hospitals/Nursing Homes	**$1,000**	
None over $1,000		
Pharmaceuticals/Health Products	**$1,500**	
None over $1,000		

Lawyers & Lobbyists — $4,300

Lawyers & Lobbyists	**$4,300**	
Cassidy & Associates	$1,800	Indiv

Misc Business — $1,750

Food & Beverage	**$1,400**	
McDonald's Corp	$1,000	PAC

Transportation — $3,000

Automotive	**$2,500**	
Auto Dealers & Drivers for Free Trade	$2,500	PAC

Contribution Totals by Sector

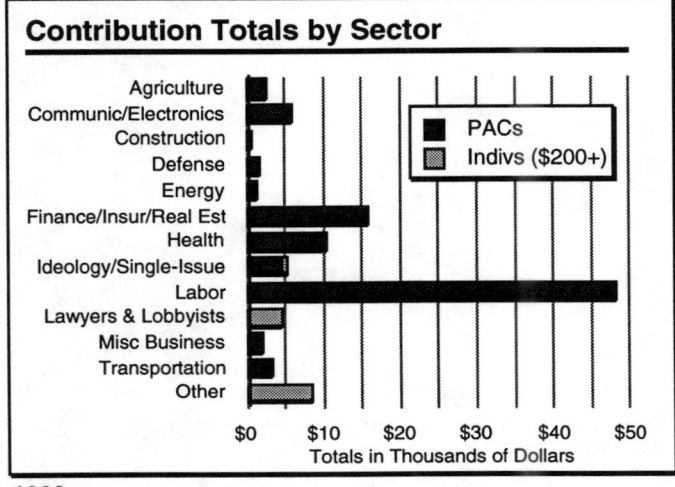

Legend: PACs; Indivs ($200+)

Agriculture
Communic/Electronics
Construction
Defense
Energy
Finance/Insur/Real Est
Health
Ideology/Single-Issue
Labor
Lawyers & Lobbyists
Misc Business
Transportation
Other

$0 $10 $20 $30 $40 $50
Totals in Thousands of Dollars

Labor

Labor	$48,000
Building Trade Unions	**$8,550**
Laborers Union*	$5,150 PAC
AFL-CIO Bldg/Construction Trades Dept	$1,400 PAC
Operating Engineers Union	$1,000 PAC
Plumbers/Pipefitters Union	$1,000 PAC
Industrial Unions	**$5,800**
Machinists/Aerospace Workers Union	$1,400 PAC
United Auto Workers	$1,400 PAC
Intl Brotherhood of Electrical Workers	$1,000 PAC
Transportation Unions	**$11,250**
Marine Engineers Union*	$2,500 PAC
Teamsters Union	$2,500 PAC
United Transportation Union	$1,900 PAC
Seafarers International Union	$1,000 PAC
Public Sector Unions	**$17,000**
National Education Assn	$7,300 PAC
American Fedn of St/Cnty/Munic Employees	$3,000 PAC
National Assn Retired Federal Employees	$2,500 PAC
American Postal Workers Union	$2,300 PAC
American Federation of Teachers	$1,000 PAC
Misc Unions	**$5,400**
Food & Commercial Workers Union	$2,000 PAC
AFL-CIO	$1,000 PAC
Retail, Wholesale & Dept Store Union	$1,000 PAC
Service Employees International Union	$1,000 PAC

Ideological/Single-Issue

Ideological/Single-Issue	$5,000
Human Rights	**$3,250**
Human Rights Campaign Fund	$1,000 PAC
KidsPAC	$1,000 PAC
Misc Issues	**$1,300**
National Cmte to Preserve Social Security	$1,300 PAC

Other & Unknown

Other	$8,000
Education	**$8,500**
Monroe Business Institute	$6,000 Indiv
Plaza Business Institute	$1,000 Indiv

Unknown	$2,000
Employer Listed/Category Unknown	$1,300
None over $1,000	

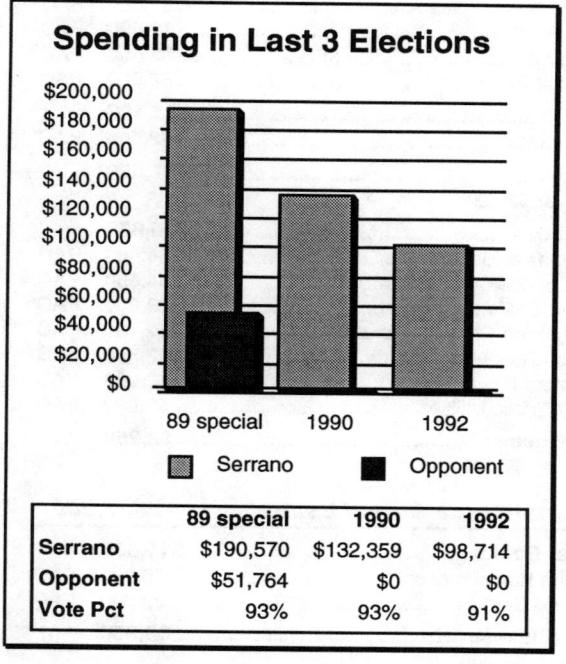

Spending in Last 3 Elections

Serrano / Opponent

	89 special	1990	1992
Serrano	$190,570	$132,359	$98,714
Opponent	$51,764	$0	$0
Vote Pct	93%	93%	91%

* Contributions came from more than one affiliate or subsidiary.

Philip R. Sharp, D-Ind (2)

First elected: 1974

1991-92 Total Receipts: $624,265
1992 Year-end Cash: $30,810

1991-92 Committees & Subcommittees

Energy and Commerce
Energy and Power (Chairman); Transportation and Hazardous Materials

Interior and Insular Affairs
Energy and the Environment; Water, Power and Offshore Energy

Leading Contributors

Business

Agriculture		$26,451

Tobacco **$2,250**
  None over $2,000

Agricultural Services/Products **$9,250**
  Navistar International .... $3,000 PAC

Food Processing & Sales **$9,801**
  Food Marketing Institute .... $3,601 PAC

Forestry & Forest Products **$2,000**
  None over $2,000

Communications/Electronics		$37,900

Media/Entertainment **$10,500**
  Comcast Corp .... $4,500 PAC
  Emmis Broadcasting Co .... $2,000 Indiv

Telephone Utilities **$26,400**
  Ameritech Corp* .... $5,000 PAC
  AT&T .... $4,000 PAC
  BellSouth Corp* .... $3,500 PAC
  US Telephone Assn .... $2,750 PAC
  GTE Corp .... $2,500 PAC
  Southwestern Bell .... $2,000 PAC

Construction		$21,600

General Contractors **$2,550**
  None over $2,000

Home Builders **$3,000**
  Centex Corp .... $3,000 PAC

Special Trade Contractors **$3,300**
  National Electrical Contractors Assn .... $3,000 PAC

Construction Services **$3,000**
  None over $2,000

Source of Funds in 1992 Election

Source	Total	Pct
PACs	$449,549	72%
Indivs $200+	$63,450	10%
Indivs under $200	$90,535	14%
Other	$21,460	3%
Candidate	$0	0%
Party	$5,879	1%

Source of PAC Dollars by Sector

Source	Total	Pct
Business	$354,020	79%
Labor	$88,850	20%
Ideology/Single Issue	$6,900	2%

In-State vs. Out-of-State Contributions*

Source	Total	Pct
In-State	$26,450	43%
Out-of-state	$35,300	57%
No state listed	$1,500	

* by large individual contributors ($200 & above)

Building Materials & Equipment **$9,750**
  Owens-Corning Fiberglas .... $2,500 PAC
  North American Insulation Mfrs Assn .... $2,000 PAC

Defense		$5,500

Defense Aerospace **$4,500**
  None over $2,000

Energy & Natural Resources		$116,791

Oil & Gas **$43,416**
  Columbia Gas System* .... $4,500 PAC
  USX Corp* .... $3,000 PAC
  Interstate Natural Gas Assn .... $2,066 PAC
  Atlantic Richfield .... $2,000 PAC
  Enron Corp .... $2,000 PAC
  Occidental Petroleum* .... $2,000 PAC

Mining **$11,400**
  Peabody Coal .... $2,500 PAC

Misc Energy **$7,550**
  None over $2,000

Electric Utilities **$50,675**
  Pacific Gas & Electric .... $4,500 PAC
  Public Service Co of Indiana .... $4,500 PAC
  Southern California Edison .... $3,000 PAC
  ACRE (Action Cmte for Rural Electrification)* .... $2,750 PAC
  Dominion Resources Inc .... $2,500 PAC
  Consumers Power Co .... $2,000 PAC
  General Public Utilities .... $2,000 PAC

Waste Management **$2,250**
  None over $2,000

Finance, Insurance & Real Estate		$57,300

Commercial Banks **$11,850**
  American Bankers Assn .... $5,000 PAC
  Banc One Corp .... $2,000 PAC

Securities & Investment **$5,850**
  None over $2,000

Contribution Totals by Sector

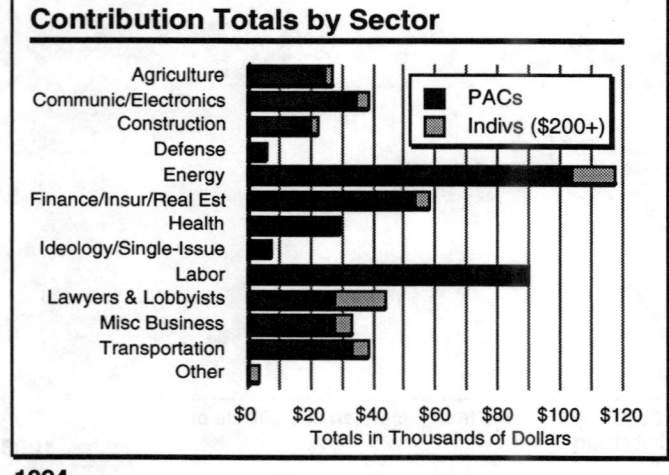

Categories: Agriculture, Communic/Electronics, Construction, Defense, Energy, Finance/Insur/Real Est, Health, Ideology/Single-Issue, Labor, Lawyers & Lobbyists, Misc Business, Transportation, Other

Legend: PACs (black), Indivs ($200+) (gray)

Totals in Thousands of Dollars — $0, $20, $40, $60, $80, $100, $120

Insurance **$13,100**
    American Family Corp .... $4,000 PAC
    American Council of Life Insurance .... $2,000 PAC
Real Estate **$6,700**
    National Assn of Realtors .... $6,500 PAC
Accountants **$18,200**
    American Institute of CPA's .... $10,000 PAC
    Coopers & Lybrand .... $2,500 PAC
    Arthur Andersen & Co .... $2,000 PAC
    Deloitte & Touche .... $2,000 PAC

Health

Health   **$28,750**

Health Professionals **$16,350**
    American Medical Assn* .... $5,650 PAC
    American Dental Assn .... $3,500 PAC
    American College of Emergency Physicians .... $3,000 PAC
    American Academy of Ophthalmology .... $2,500 PAC
Hospitals/Nursing Homes **$3,650**
    American Hospital Assn .... $3,150 PAC
Pharmaceuticals/Health Products **$8,250**
    Eli Lilly & Co .... $3,500 PAC

Lawyers & Lobbyists

Lawyers & Lobbyists   **$43,228**

Lawyers & Lobbyists **$43,228**
    Skadden, Arps et al .... $2,750 PAC/Ind
    Dickstein, Shapiro & Morin .... $2,500 PAC/Ind
    Hagemier, Allen & Smith .... $2,450 Indiv
    Crowell & Moring .... $2,300 PAC
    Akin, Gump et al .... $2,250 PAC/Ind
    Kirkland & Ellis .... $2,250 PAC/Ind
    Powell, Goldstein et al .... $2,150 PAC/Ind

Misc Business

Misc Business   **$32,800**

Food & Beverage **$3,950**
    None over $2,000
Beer, Wine & Liquor **$4,950**
    National Beer Wholesalers Assn .... $2,000 PAC
Retail Sales **$4,000**
    Woodhaven Furniture Co .... $2,000 Indiv
Business Services **$2,400**
    None over $2,000

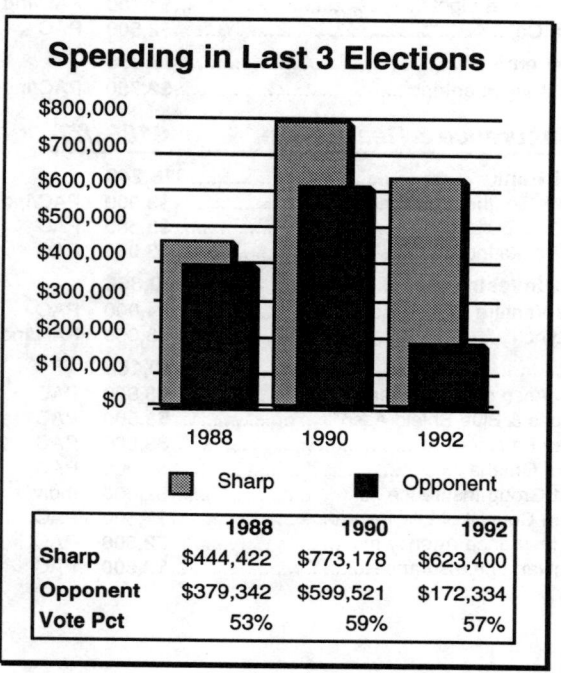

Spending in Last 3 Elections

	1988	1990	1992
Sharp	$444,422	$773,178	$623,400
Opponent	$379,342	$599,521	$172,334
Vote Pct	53%	59%	57%

Chemical & Related Manufacturing **$4,100**
    None over $2,000
Steel Production **$3,050**
    None over $2,000
Misc Manufacturing & Distributing **$9,500**
    Corning Glass Works .... $4,000 PAC
    Libbey-Owens-Ford .... $2,500 PAC

Transportation

Transportation   **$38,050**

Air Transport **$10,300**
    Federal Express Corp .... $5,000 PAC
    United Parcel Service .... $3,800 PAC
Automotive **$19,000**
    Cummins Engine Co .... $5,500 Indiv
    National Auto Dealers Assn .... $4,250 PAC
    Ford Motor Co .... $3,000 PAC
    General Motors .... $2,700 PAC
Railroads **$6,750**
    Union Pacific Corp .... $3,250 PAC

Labor

Labor   **$88,850**

Building Trade Unions **$16,400**
    Carpenters & Joiners Union .... $4,500 PAC
    Laborers' Political League .... $3,500 PAC
    Sheet Metal Workers Union .... $3,500 PAC
    Plumbers/Pipefitters Union .... $3,000 PAC
Industrial Unions **$23,400**
    United Auto Workers .... $10,000 PAC
    Intl Brotherhood of Electrical Workers .... $3,500 PAC
    United Mine Workers .... $3,150 PAC
    United Steelworkers .... $2,500 PAC
Transportation Unions **$14,550**
    Teamsters Union .... $10,000 PAC
    United Transportation Union .... $3,250 PAC
Public Sector Unions **$29,500**
    National Education Assn .... $10,000 PAC
    National Assn Retired Federal Employees .... $6,000 PAC
    National Assn of Letter Carriers .... $4,000 PAC
    National Rural Letter Carriers Assn .... $3,000 PAC
    American Postal Workers Union .... $2,000 PAC
Misc Unions **$5,000**
    AFL-CIO .... $2,000 PAC
    Food & Commercial Workers Union .... $2,000 PAC

Ideological/Single-Issue

Ideological/Single-Issue   **$7,350**

Democratic/Liberal **$2,650**
    National Cmte for an Effective Congress .... $2,500 PAC

Other & Unknown

Other   **$3,100**

Retired **$2,900**
    None over $2,000

Unknown   **$5,600**

    Employer Listed/Category Unknown $5,400
    None over $2,000

---

* Contributions came from more than one affiliate or subsidiary.

E. Clay Shaw Jr., R-Fla (22)

First elected: 1980

1991-92 Total Receipts: $948,514
1992 Year-end Cash: $116,312

1991-92 Committees & Subcommittees

Ways and Means
Human Resources (Ranking Republican); Oversight

Leading Contributors

Business

Agriculture	$37,750

Crop Production & Basic Processing $2,750
  None over $2,500
Tobacco $9,000
  US Tobacco Co .... $2,500 PAC
Agricultural Services/Products $5,350
  None over $2,500
Food Processing & Sales $18,650
  Fleming Companies Inc .... $6,000 PAC
  Winn-Dixie Stores .... $5,000 PAC
  Food Marketing Institute .... $4,000 PAC

Communications/Electronics	$48,949

Media/Entertainment $5,650
  None over $2,500
Telephone Utilities $17,850
  Southern Bell .... $5,000 PAC
  GTE Corp .... $2,500 PAC
Telecom Services & Equipment $3,049
  None over $2,500
Electronics Mfg & Services $21,800
  Harris Corp .... $11,250 PAC/Ind
  Sensormatic Electronics Corp .... $5,300 Indiv

Construction	$22,600

General Contractors $8,350
  Associated General Contractors .... $3,000 PAC
Home Builders $3,250
  None over $2,500

Source of Funds in 1992 Election

Source	Total	Pct
PACs	$440,351	45%
Indivs $200+	$335,535	34%
Indivs under $200	$117,443	12%
Other	$80,185	8%
Candidate	$0	0%
Party	$35,074	4%

Source of PAC Dollars by Sector

Source	Total	Pct
Business	$418,717	96%
Labor	$10,000	2%
Ideology/Single Issue	$9,250	2%

In-State vs. Out-of-State Contributions*

Source	Total	Pct
In-State	$293,585	88%
Out-of-state	$40,000	12%
No state listed	$0	

* by large individual contributors ($200 & above)

Special Trade Contractors $4,450
  None over $2,500
Building Materials & Equipment $4,200
  None over $2,500

Defense	$2,500
  None over $2,500

Energy & Natural Resources	$40,050

Oil & Gas $14,250
  None over $2,500
Electric Utilities $18,550
  Florida Power & Light .... $3,750 PAC/Ind
  Southern Co* .... $2,500 PAC
Waste Management $3,250
  Waste Management Inc .... $2,750 PAC/Ind

Finance, Insurance & Real Estate	$188,077

Commercial Banks $18,240
  Citizens & Southern National Bank .... $3,900 PAC/Ind
  Citicorp .... $3,500 PAC
  Barnett Banks Inc .... $3,000 PAC
Securities & Investment $20,350
  National Venture Capital Assn .... $4,000 PAC
  Merrill Lynch .... $3,000 PAC/Ind
Insurance $70,100
  National Assn of Life Underwriters .... $8,500 PAC
  Blue Cross & Blue Shield Assn* .... $3,500 PAC
  American Family Corp .... $3,000 PAC
  Mutual of Omaha .... $3,000 PAC
  Newport Group Insurance .... $2,600 Indiv
  American Council of Life Insurance .... $2,500 PAC
  Fidelity Insurance Agency Inc .... $2,500 PAC
  Metropolitan Life Insurance .... $2,500 PAC

Contribution Totals by Sector

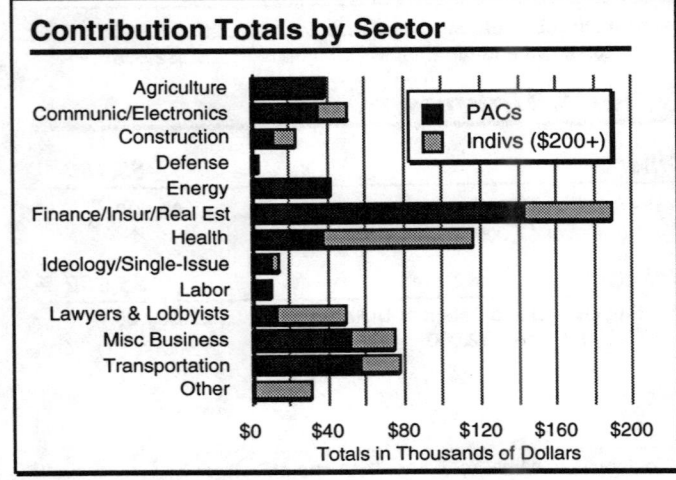

Agriculture
Communic/Electronics
Construction
Defense
Energy
Finance/Insur/Real Est
Health
Ideology/Single-Issue
Labor
Lawyers & Lobbyists
Misc Business
Transportation
Other

■ PACs
▨ Indivs ($200+)

$0 $40 $80 $120 $160 $200
Totals in Thousands of Dollars

Real Estate **$32,900**
    National Assn of Realtors .... $9,500   PAC
    Goodman Co .... $5,000   Indiv
    National Realty Committee .... $2,500   PAC

Accountants **$42,037**
    American Institute of CPA's .... $9,487   PAC
    Arthur Andersen & Co .... $8,250   PAC/Ind
    Price Waterhouse .... $7,000   PAC
    Coopers & Lybrand .... $5,000   PAC
    Deloitte & Touche .... $4,500   PAC
    Ernst & Young .... $3,850   PAC/Ind

Misc Finance **$3,650**
    None over $2,500

Health   **$115,445**

Health Professionals **$95,895**
    Anesthesia Professional Assn Inc .... $38,000   Indiv
    American Medical Assn .... $9,995   PAC
    American Dental Assn .... $4,500   PAC

Hospitals/Nursing Homes **$8,700**
    None over $2,500

Pharmaceuticals/Health Products **$10,600**
    None over $2,500

Lawyers & Lobbyists   **$48,163**

Lawyers & Lobbyists **$48,163**
    Tripp, Scott et al .... $4,000   Indiv
    Jordan, Schulte & Burchette .... $3,500   Indiv
    Gunster, Yoakley et al .... $3,273   Indiv

Misc Business   **$73,746**

Food & Beverage **$7,150**
    National Restaurant Assn .... $4,000   PAC

Beer, Wine & Liquor **$12,000**
    National Beer Wholesalers Assn .... $6,000   PAC

Retail Sales **$11,716**
    None over $2,500

Misc Services **$3,800**
    None over $2,500

Business Services **$16,950**
    Sensormatic Electronics Corp .... $6,250   PAC
    National Assn of Temporary Services .... $3,500   PAC

Spending in Last 3 Elections

	1988	1990	1992
Shaw	$455,578	$120,632	$1,138,425
Opponent	$36,084	$0	$936,960
Vote Pct	66%	98%	52%

Lodging/Tourism **$5,950**
    Gill Hotels .... $3,100   Indiv

Chemical & Related Manufacturing **$4,500**
    None over $2,500

Misc Manufacturing & Distributing **$6,750**
    None over $2,500

Transportation   **$76,700**

Air Transport **$10,350**
    United Parcel Service .... $3,500   PAC
    Federal Express Corp .... $3,000   PAC

Automotive **$29,650**
    Americans for Free International Trade .... $6,000   PAC
    National Auto Dealers Assn .... $6,000   PAC
    Alamo Rent-a-Car .... $4,750   Indiv

Trucking **$3,850**
    None over $2,500

Railroads **$7,500**
    Union Pacific Corp .... $5,000   PAC

Sea Transport **$20,150**
    National Marine Manufacturers Assn .... $8,000   PAC
    Cruise PAC .... $3,000   PAC

Misc Transport **$5,200**
    None over $2,500

Labor

Labor   **$10,000**

Transportation Unions **$6,000**
    Marine Engineers Dist 2 Maritime Officers .... $3,500   PAC
    Air Line Pilots Assn .... $2,500   PAC

Public Sector Unions **$3,000**
    None over $2,500

Ideological/Single-Issue

Ideological/Single-Issue   **$13,750**

Pro-Israel **$9,750**
    None over $2,500

Other & Unknown

Other   **$30,236**

Civil Servants/Public Officials **$3,100**
    None over $2,500

Retired **$23,636**
    None over $2,500

Unknown   **$65,336**

    Homemakers/Non-income earners $9,736
    No Employer Listed or Found $3,600
    Employer Listed/Category Unknown $51,050
        None over $2,500

Independent expenditures supporting Shaw
    National Assn of Realtors $125,209
    National Right to Life PAC $2,517

---

* Contributions came from more than one affiliate or subsidiary.

Christopher Shays, R-Conn (4)

First elected: 1987

1991-92 Total Receipts: $402,120
1992 Year-end Cash: $93,866

1991-92 Committees & Subcommittees

Budget
Budget Process, Reconciliation and Enforcement; Economic Policy, Projections and Revenues

Government Operations
Employment and Housing; Legislation and National Security

Select Committee on Narcotics Abuse and Control

Leading Contributors

Business

Agriculture		$11,200
Tobacco		**$3,900**
US Tobacco Co	$2,900	Indiv
American Brands	$1,000	Indiv
Food Processing & Sales		**$3,500**
Pepsico Inc	$2,500	PAC/Ind
Perrier Group of America	$1,000	Indiv
Forestry & Forest Products		**$3,300**
Westvaco Corp	$2,000	PAC
Champion International Corp	$1,300	PAC/Ind

Communications/Electronics		$14,049
Printing & Publishing		**$6,649**
Reader's Digest	$2,649	Indiv
McGraw-Hill Publications	$2,000	Indiv
Newsbank Inc	$1,000	Indiv
Media/Entertainment		**$1,750**
NBC	$1,000	Indiv
Telephone Utilities		**$4,650**
AT&T	$2,000	PAC
United Telecommunications	$1,000	PAC

Construction		$7,450
General Contractors		**$3,150**
Dorcal Associates	$1,000	Indiv
Tilcon-Tomasso Construction	$1,000	Indiv

Source of Funds in 1992 Election

Source	Total	Pct
PACs	$52,850	13%
Indivs $200+	$164,638	41%
Indivs under $200	$163,836	41%
Other	$20,796	5%
Candidate	$0	0%
Party	$800	0%

Source of PAC Dollars by Sector

Source	Total	Pct
Business	$38,500	77%
Labor	$7,900	16%
Ideology/Single Issue	$3,500	7%

In-State vs. Out-of-State Contributions*

Source	Total	Pct
In-State	$152,688	93%
Out-of-state	$11,800	7%
No state listed	$0	

by large individual contributors ($200 & above)

Home Builders		$3,000
National Assn of Home Builders	$2,000	PAC
Mercede & Sons	$1,000	Indiv
Building Materials & Equipment		**$1,000**
Manger Electric Co	$1,000	Indiv

Energy & Natural Resources		$2,300
Oil & Gas		**$1,500**
Tosco Corp	$1,000	Indiv

Finance, Insurance & Real Estate		$56,540
Commercial Banks		**$6,940**
People's Bank	$1,540	Indiv
Chase Manhattan	$1,000	PAC
JP Morgan & Co	$1,000	PAC
Norstar Bancorp	$1,000	PAC
Union Trust	$1,000	Indiv
Securities & Investment		**$20,750**
Philip K Meyer & Co	$2,000	Indiv
Merrill Lynch	$1,950	PAC/Ind
Donaldson, Lufkin & Jenrette	$1,500	Indiv
Kohlberg, Kravis & Roberts	$1,500	Indiv
Morgan Stanley & Co	$1,500	PAC/Ind
Wertheim, Schroder & Co	$1,500	Indiv
Goldman, Sachs & Co	$1,250	Indiv
Blackstone Group	$1,000	Indiv
Capital Partners	$1,000	Indiv
Lord, Abbett & Co	$1,000	Indiv
Prudential Securities	$1,000	PAC
SRG Associates	$1,000	Indiv
Insurance		**$5,000**
Connecticut Mutual Life Insurance	$2,000	PAC
Frank B Hall & Co	$1,000	Indiv

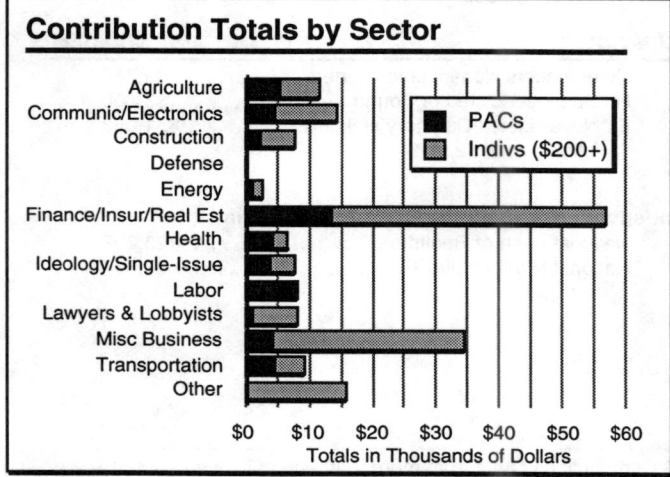

Contribution Totals by Sector

- Agriculture
- Communic/Electronics
- Construction
- Defense
- Energy
- Finance/Insur/Real Est
- Health
- Ideology/Single-Issue
- Labor
- Lawyers & Lobbyists
- Misc Business
- Transportation
- Other

Legend: PACs / Indivs ($200+)

$0 $10 $20 $30 $40 $50 $60
Totals in Thousands of Dollars

Real Estate $12,950
   Rockefeller Group .... $4,500 Indiv
   National Assn of Realtors .... $2,000 PAC
   CHC of Connecticut Inc .... $1,600 Indiv
   Albert B Ashforth Inc .... $1,300 Indiv
   Arredondo & Co .... $1,000 Indiv
   Cushman & Wakefield .... $1,000 Indiv

Accountants $5,750
   American Institute of CPA's .... $2,000 PAC
   Arthur Andersen & Co .... $1,000 Indiv
   Price Waterhouse .... $1,000 Indiv

Misc Finance $4,250
   First Equity Investment Bank .... $1,000 Indiv

Health   *$6,200*

Health Professionals $4,600
   American Academy of Ophthalmology .... $2,000 PAC

Pharmaceuticals/Health Products $1,600
   Ciba-Geigy Corp .... $1,350 PAC/Ind

Lawyers & Lobbyists   *$7,850*

Lawyers & Lobbyists $7,850
   Diserio, Martin et al .... $1,600 Indiv
   Wien, Malkin et al .... $1,000 Indiv

Misc Business   *$34,249*

Retail Sales $2,650
   None over $1,000

Misc Services $1,000
   None over $1,000

Business Services $14,800
   Personnel Corp of America .... $2,000 Indiv
   Wolsey & Co .... $2,000 Indiv
   Assets Administration & Management .... $1,500 Indiv
   Saatchi & Saatchi Advertising .... $1,500 Indiv
   AZ Marketing Services .... $1,000 Indiv

Steel Production $2,000
   Baldwin Technologies .... $2,000 Indiv

Misc Manufacturing & Distributing $11,349
   Emson Research .... $3,600 Indiv
   Farrel Corp .... $3,000 Indiv
   Xerox Corp .... $2,000 PAC
   Bridgeport Machines Inc .... $1,000 Indiv

Transportation   *$9,050*

Air Transport $2,050
   United Parcel Service .... $2,000 PAC

Automotive $5,000
   Auto Dealers & Drivers for Free Trade .... $2,000 PAC
   General Motors .... $1,000 Indiv
   Miller Automobile Corp .... $1,000 Indiv

Sea Transport $2,000
   Mormac Marine Group .... $1,000 Indiv

Labor

Labor   *$7,900*

Building Trade Unions $1,500
   Ironworkers Union .... $1,000 PAC
   Plumbers/Pipefitters Union .... $1,000 PAC

Industrial Unions $3,200
   Connecticut Union of Telephone Workers .... $2,000 PAC
   Intl Brotherhood of Electrical Workers .... $1,200 PAC

Transportation Unions $1,000
   Marine Engineers Dist 2 Maritime Officers .... $1,000 PAC

Public Sector Unions $2,000
   National Education Assn .... $2,000 PAC

Ideological/Single-Issue

Ideological/Single-Issue   *$7,400*

Pro-Israel $2,350
   None over $1,000

Human Rights $2,100
   Human Rights Campaign Fund .... $2,000 PAC

Misc Issues $2,400
   League of Conservation Voters .... $1,000 PAC

Other & Unknown

Other   *$15,600*

Retired $14,350
   None over $1,000

Unknown   *$34,600*

   Homemakers/Non-income earners $2,100
   No Employer Listed or Found $5,650
   Generic Occupation/Category Unknown $3,500
   Employer Listed/Category Unknown $23,350
       Roundtree Capital Corp .... $2,000 Indiv
       SAI Consulting Engineers .... $2,000 Indiv
       Stauffer Technology .... $2,000 Indiv
       Marvin Traub Consultants .... $1,500 Indiv
       Goni Housewares Corp .... $1,100 Indiv
       Barker Companies .... $1,000 Indiv
       Communication Supply Corp .... $1,000 Indiv
       Remington Profs Inc .... $1,000 Indiv
       Sun Hill Industries Inc .... $1,000 Indiv
       Winokur & Associates .... $1,000 Indiv
       Wright Juvente Services .... $1,000 Indiv

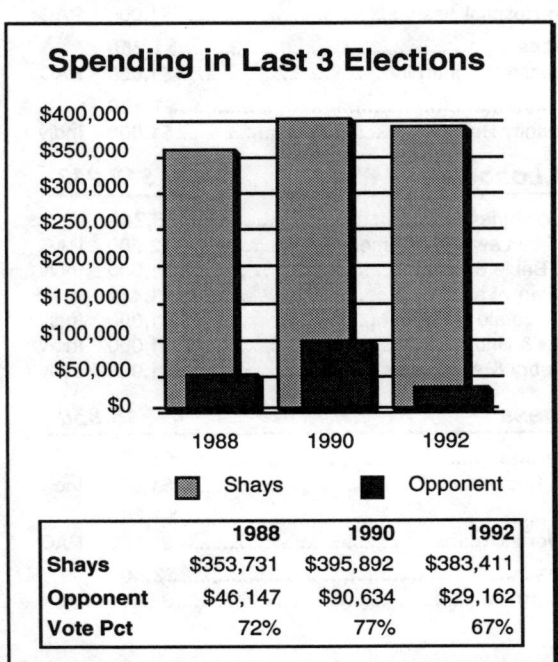

Spending in Last 3 Elections

	1988	1990	1992
Shays	$353,731	$395,892	$383,411
Opponent	$46,147	$90,634	$29,162
Vote Pct	72%	77%	67%

Karen Shepherd, D-Utah (2)

First elected: 1992

1991-92 Total Receipts: $646,636
1992 Year-end Cash: $23,437

1993-94 Committees & Subcommittees

Natural Resources
National Parks, Forests and Public Lands; Oversight and Investigations

Public Works and Transportation
Aviation; Economic Development; Water Resources and the Environment

Leading Contributors

Business

Communications/Electronics	$10,881	
Printing & Publishing	$2,731	
None over $1,000		
Media/Entertainment	$5,150	
Castle Rock Entertainment	$1,000	Indiv
Mirage Productions	$1,000	Indiv
Telephone Utilities	$2,000	
AT&T	$1,000	PAC
US West Inc	$1,000	PAC
Computer Equipment & Services	$1,000	
WordPerfect Corp	$1,000	Indiv

Construction	$1,250	
Building Materials & Equipment	$1,000	
American Standard Inc	$1,000	Indiv

Energy & Natural Resources	$2,000	
Oil & Gas	$1,500	
None over $1,000		

Finance, Insurance & Real Estate	$31,151	
Commercial Banks	$3,250	
Key Bank	$1,000	Indiv
Republic National Bank of New York	$1,000	Indiv
Savings & Loans	$2,900	
American Investment Bank	$2,900	Indiv
Securities & Investment	$9,550	
Jordan Co	$3,500	Indiv
Dougan & Associates	$2,000	Indiv

Source of Funds in 1992 Election

Source	Total	Pct
PACs	$201,601	30%
Indivs $200+	$173,464	26%
Indivs under $200	$257,278	38%
Other	$38,941	6%
Candidate	$914	0%
Party	$30,098	4%

Source of PAC Dollars by Sector

Source	Total	Pct
Business	$21,000	10%
Labor	$111,250	53%
Ideology/Single Issue	$78,436	37%

In-State vs. Out-of-State Contributions*

Source	Total	Pct
In-State	$82,601	58%
Out-of-state	$59,781	42%
No state listed	$0	

by large individual contributors ($200 & above)

Insurance	$12,551	
Leucadia Corp	$9,828	Indiv
Real Estate	$1,750	
None over $1,000		
Accountants	$1,150	
None over $1,000		

Health	$12,900	
Health Professionals	$7,900	
American Academy of Ophthalmology	$2,000	PAC
American Nurses Assn	$2,000	PAC
Hospitals/Nursing Homes	$2,350	
American Hospital Assn	$1,000	PAC
Health Services	$1,250	
Family Health Program Inc	$1,000	PAC
Misc Health	$1,400	
SI Community Health	$1,000	Indiv

Lawyers & Lobbyists	$18,243	
Lawyers & Lobbyists	$18,243	
Assn of Trial Lawyers of America	$2,500	PAC
Parsons, Behle & Latimer	$1,900	Indiv
Kimball, Parr et al	$1,412	Indiv
Butler, Fitzgerald & Potter	$1,000	Indiv
MacArthur & Uribe	$1,000	Indiv
Robert Debry & Associates	$1,000	Indiv

Misc Business	$15,850	
Food & Beverage	$2,100	
Santa Fe Restaurant	$1,000	Indiv
Retail Sales	$4,700	
Fred Meyer Inc	$1,500	PAC
Misc Services	$2,500	
Steiner Corp	$2,500	Indiv

Contribution Totals by Sector

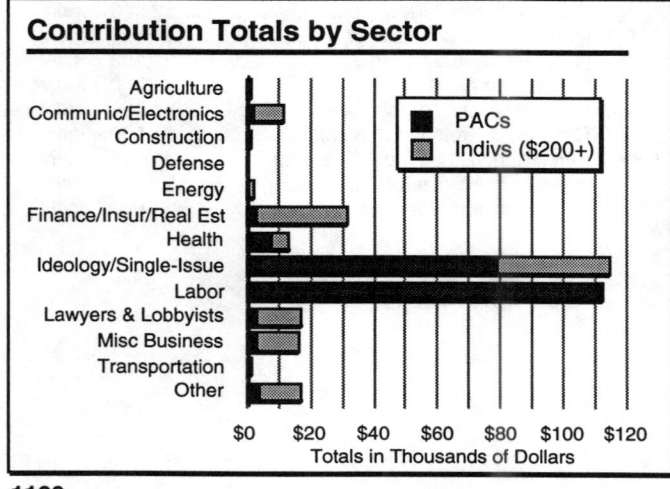

Agriculture
Communic/Electronics
Construction
Defense
Energy
Finance/Insur/Real Est
Health
Ideology/Single-Issue
Labor
Lawyers & Lobbyists
Misc Business
Transportation
Other

PACs
Indivs ($200+)

$0 $20 $40 $60 $80 $100 $120
Totals in Thousands of Dollars

Business Services $2,350
    None over $1,000

Lodging/Tourism $1,100
    None over $1,000

Misc Manufacturing & Distributing $1,900
    Crescent Cardboard Co .... $1,200   Indiv

Labor

Labor	$111,250	
Building Trade Unions **$11,000**		
Carpenters & Joiners Union $5,500	PAC	
Laborers' Political League $2,000	PAC	
Operating Engineers Union* $1,500	PAC	
Heat/Frost/Asbestos Workers Union $1,000	PAC	
Sheet Metal Workers Union $1,000	PAC	
Industrial Unions **$31,950**		
United Steelworkers $10,000	PAC	
Intl Brotherhood of Electrical Workers $8,000	PAC	
Machinists/Aerospace Workers Union $6,600	PAC	
United Auto Workers $3,000	PAC	
Boilermakers Union $1,550	PAC	
Communications Workers of America $1,500	PAC	
United Mine Workers $1,000	PAC	
Transportation Unions **$18,000**		
Teamsters Union $10,000	PAC	
Air Line Pilots Assn $2,000	PAC	
Marine Engineers Union $2,000	PAC	
United Transportation Union $2,000	PAC	
Assn of Flight Attendants $1,000	PAC	
Public Sector Unions **$35,300**		
American Fedn of St/Cnty/Munic Employees $10,000	PAC	
National Education Assn $10,000	PAC	
National Assn of Letter Carriers $4,000	PAC	
American Federation of Teachers $3,000	PAC	
International Assn of Firefighters $3,000	PAC	
National Assn Retired Federal Employees $3,000	PAC	
American Postal Workers Union $1,000	PAC	
National Rural Letter Carriers Assn $1,000	PAC	
Misc Unions **$15,000**		
AFL-CIO $7,500	PAC	
Food & Commercial Workers Union $5,000	PAC	
Bakery, Confectionery & Tobacco Workers $1,500	PAC	
Service Employees International Union $1,000	PAC	

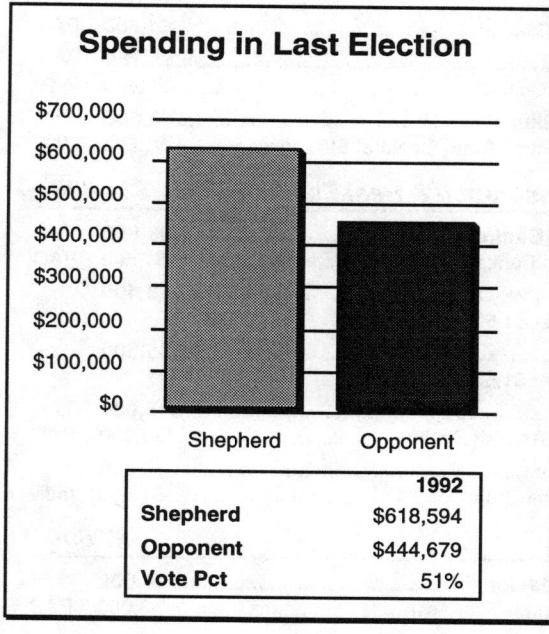

Spending in Last Election

	1992
Shepherd	$618,594
Opponent	$444,679
Vote Pct	51%

Ideological/Single-Issue

Ideological/Single-Issue	$113,886	
Democratic/Liberal **$14,750**		
Hollywood Women's Political Cmte $7,000	PAC	
National Cmte for an Effective Congress $3,000	PAC	
Fifth Horseman PAC $1,000	PAC	
Leadership PACs **$3,000**		
House Leadership Fund (Tom Foley) $2,000	PAC	
Effective Government Cmte (Dick Gephardt) ... $1,000	PAC	
Foreign & Defense Policy **$5,887**		
Council for a Livable World $4,537	PAC/Ind	
Women's Action for Nuclear Disarmament $1,250	PAC	
Pro-Israel **$6,750**		
Hudson Valley PAC $1,000	PAC	
Joint Action Cmte for Political Affairs $1,000	PAC	
Pro-Choice **$14,500**		
National Abortion Rights Action League $10,000	PAC	
Voters for Choice $3,750	PAC	
Womens Issues **$48,255**		
Emily's List $25,005	PAC/Ind	
Women's Campaign Fund $10,000	PAC	
National Womens Political Caucus $5,000	PAC	
National Organization for Women $2,750	PAC	
Human Rights **$9,000**		
Human Rights Campaign Fund $7,500	PAC	
KidsPAC $1,000	PAC	
Misc Issues **$11,744**		
Sierra Club $7,000	PAC	
League of Conservation Voters $2,994	PAC	

Other & Unknown

Other	$16,742	
Civil Servants/Public Officials **$1,200**		
Utah Department Of Employment Sec $1,000	Indiv	
Education **$2,842**		
University of Utah $4,774	Indiv	
Retired **$7,800**		
None over $1,000		
Other **$4,900**		
National Assn of Social Workers $3,500	PAC	

Unknown	$39,765
Homemakers/Non-income earners $11,623	
No Employer Listed or Found $4,921	
Generic Occupation/Category Unknown $1,350	
Employer Listed/Category Unknown $21,871	
Milcom Inc $3,300	Indiv
Summits Inc $2,000	Indiv
Pavelic & Levites $1,000	Indiv
Rosenblatt Investments $1,000	Indiv
STM Associates $1,000	Indiv
WLP Corp $1,000	Indiv

Independent expenditures supporting Shepherd
    Clean Up Congress $2,686

---

* Contributions came from more than one affiliate or subsidiary.

Bud Shuster, R-Pa (9)

First elected: 1972

1991-92 Total Receipts: $557,315
1992 Year-end Cash: $103,032

1991-92 Committees & Subcommittees

Public Works and Transportation
Aviation; Investigations and Oversight; Surface Transportation
(Ranking Republican)

Select Committee on Intelligence (Ranking Republican)

Leading Contributors

Business

Agriculture — $15,300

Crop Production & Basic Processing $4,800
    Ocean Spray Cranberries Inc .... $2,000   PAC
Livestock $1,500
    None over $1,500
Food Processing & Sales $6,500
    Martin's Famous Pastry Inc .... $1,750   Indiv

Communications/Electronics — $10,000

Printing & Publishing $1,500
    Don-Rey Media Group .... $1,500   Indiv
Telephone Utilities $5,500
    AT&T .... $3,000   PAC

Construction — $105,500

General Contractors $57,750
    George Zamias & Co .... $10,000   Indiv
    Associated General Contractors .... $8,000   PAC
    American Road & Transport Builders Assn .... $4,250   PAC
    Williams Brothers Construction .... $4,000   Indiv
    Fiore Construction Co .... $2,500   Indiv
    National Utility Contractors Assn .... $2,000   PAC
Home Builders $3,500
    National Assn of Home Builders .... $3,500   PAC
Special Trade Contractors $2,000
    None over $1,500

Source of Funds in 1992 Election

Source	Total	Pct
PACs	$187,250	34%
Indivs $200+	$335,229	60%
Indivs under $200	$18,174	3%
Other	$16,662	3%
Candidate	$0	0%
Party	$38	0%

Source of PAC Dollars by Sector

Source	Total	Pct
Business	$173,321	96%
Labor	$6,800	4%
Ideology/Single Issue	$500	0%

In-State vs. Out-of-State Contributions*

Source	Total	Pct
In-State	$144,000	43%
Out-of-state	$190,729	57%
No state listed	$0	

* by large individual contributors ($200 & above)

Construction Services $10,750
    National Society of Professional Engineers .... $2,000   PAC
    Parsons Corp* .... $1,500   PAC
Building Materials & Equipment $31,500
    New Enterprise Stone & Lime .... $10,500   Indiv
    National Crushed Stone Assn .... $5,000   PAC
    Bitrek Corp .... $3,000   Indiv
    Grove Worldwide .... $2,000   Indiv
    HB Mellot Estate Inc .... $2,000   Indiv
    Valley Quarries Inc .... $2,000   Indiv
    Vulcan Materials Co .... $2,000   PAC

Energy & Natural Resources — $17,050

Oil & Gas $5,800
    Ashland Oil .... $1,500   PAC
Mining $5,750
    Bradford Coal Co .... $2,000   Indiv
Electric Utilities $3,500
    ACRE (Action Cmte for Rural Electrification) .... $1,500   PAC

Finance, Insurance & Real Estate — $34,800

Commercial Banks $3,850
    American Bankers Assn* .... $1,500   PAC
Securities & Investment $3,400
    None over $1,500
Insurance $5,500
    None over $1,500
Real Estate $15,000
    National Assn of Realtors .... $6,000   PAC
Misc Finance $4,050
    Hawthorne Group Inc .... $1,500   Indiv

Health — $7,500

Health Professionals $6,000
    American Medical Assn .... $3,000   PAC

Contribution Totals by Sector

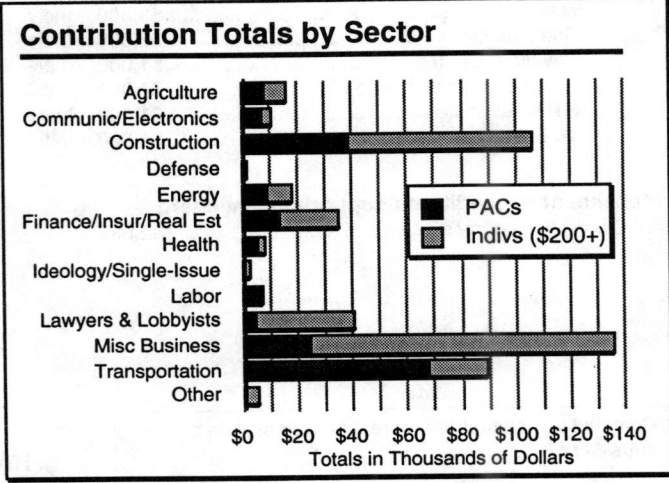

Agriculture
Communic/Electronics
Construction
Defense
Energy
Finance/Insur/Real Est
Health
Ideology/Single-Issue
Labor
Lawyers & Lobbyists
Misc Business
Transportation
Other

■ PACs
▨ Indivs ($200+)

$0 $20 $40 $60 $80 $100 $120 $140
Totals in Thousands of Dollars

Lawyers & Lobbyists $40,325

Lawyers & Lobbyists $40,325
Cassidy & Associates	$9,500	Indiv
Cameron Law Office	$3,000	Indiv
Cliff Madison Government Relations	$2,500	Indiv
Murphy & Rennick	$2,500	Indiv
Capital Partnerships Inc	$2,000	PAC/Ind
Gibson, Dunn & Crutcher	$1,500	Indiv
Orbovich, Fletcher & Lafond	$1,500	Indiv
Williams & Jensen	$1,500	PAC/Ind

Misc Business $135,050

Business Associations $2,000
Chamber of Commerce	$1,500	Indiv

Food & Beverage $6,000
Pistol Petes Pizza Parlor	$3,000	Indiv
No Name Restaurant	$2,500	Indiv

Retail Sales $7,500
Dream Machine Inc	$2,000	Indiv

Business Services $98,100
Ackerley Communications	$13,000	Indiv
Outdoor Advertising Assn of America	$10,500	PAC/Ind
Outdoor Systems Advertising	$10,000	Indiv
Reagan Outdoor Advertising	$6,500	Indiv
Gannett Outdoor	$6,000	Indiv
Matthew Outdoor Advertising Inc	$5,950	Indiv
Patrick Media Group	$4,800	Indiv
Whiteco Industries	$3,800	Indiv
ABC Advisors Inc	$3,500	Indiv
Gaess Outdoor Advertising Corp	$3,000	Indiv
Poa Acquisition Corp	$3,000	Indiv
Logan Communications	$2,500	Indiv
Allied Outdoor Advertising	$2,000	Indiv
Lamar Outdoor Advertising Corp	$2,000	Indiv
Adams Outdoor Advertising	$1,750	Indiv
Penn Advertising	$1,500	PAC

Lodging/Tourism $3,800
None over $1,500

Chemical & Related Manufacturing $5,000
Creative Pultrusions	$1,500	Indiv
Dial Corp	$1,500	PAC

Steel Production $2,950
None over $1,500

Misc Manufacturing & Distributing $7,500
Grove Manufacturing	$2,000	Indiv
Minnesota Mining & Manufacturing (3M)	$1,500	PAC

Transportation $88,425

Air Transport $26,500
Federal Express Corp	$10,000	PAC
United Parcel Service	$8,000	PAC
Aircraft Owners & Pilots Assn	$4,000	PAC

Automotive $6,221
National Auto Dealers Assn	$2,500	PAC

Trucking $18,750
American Trucking Assns	$3,000	PAC
North American Van Lines	$2,500	PAC
Roadway Services Inc	$2,500	PAC
Consolidated Freightways	$2,000	PAC

Railroads $25,954
ITEL Corp*	$3,204	Indiv
Duchossois Industries	$2,500	PAC
Norfolk Southern Corp	$2,000	PAC
Safetran Systems Corp	$2,000	Indiv
Union Pacific Corp	$2,000	PAC
Union Switch & Signal	$2,000	Indiv
Burlington Northern	$1,500	PAC
CSX Transportation Inc	$1,500	PAC
Consolidated Rail Corp	$1,500	PAC
Santa Fe Southern Pacific	$1,500	PAC

Sea Transport $2,000
None over $1,500

Misc Transport $9,000
International Taxicab Assn	$3,000	PAC
American Bus Assn	$2,000	PAC
Greyhound Lines	$1,500	PAC

Labor

Labor $6,800

Transportation Unions $6,000
United Transportation Union	$2,000	PAC

Ideological/Single Issue

Ideological/Single-Issue $2,000
None over $1,500

Other & Unknown

Other $5,000

Retired $5,000
None over $1,500

Unknown $46,100
Homemakers/Non-income earners	$6,000	
No Employer Listed or Found	$1,500	
Generic Occupation/Category Unknown	$1,500	
Employer Listed/Category Unknown	$37,100	
Lawruk Brant	$4,000	Indiv
Berman Co	$2,000	Indiv
Western Cullen Hayes	$2,000	Indiv
Martin Communications	$1,500	Indiv
PQ Industries	$1,500	Indiv

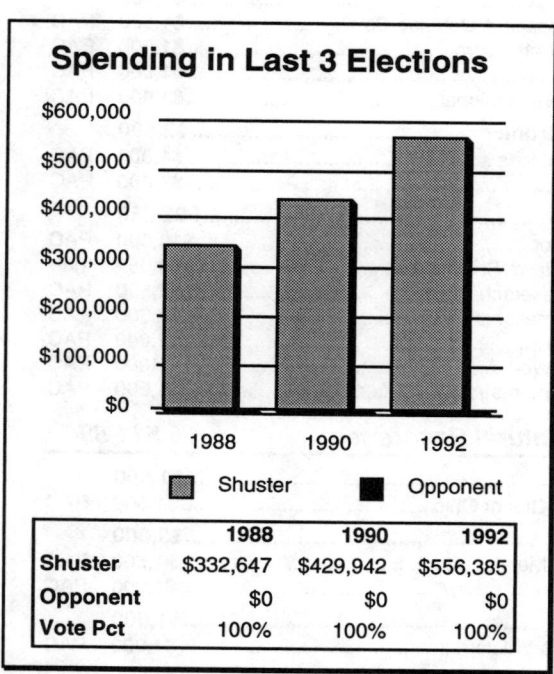

Spending in Last 3 Elections

	1988	1990	1992
Shuster	$332,647	$429,942	$556,385
Opponent	$0	$0	$0
Vote Pct	100%	100%	100%

Shuster / Opponent

* Contributions came from more than one affiliate or subsidiary.

Norman Sisisky, D-Va (4)

First elected: 1982

1991-92 Total Receipts: $257,047
1992 Year-end Cash: $72,679

1991-92 Committees & Subcommittees

Armed Services
Investigations; Military Installations and Facilities; Procurement and Military Nuclear Systems; Seapower and Strategic and Critical Materials

Small Business
Exports, Tax Policy and Special Problems (Chairman)

Select Committee on Aging

Leading Contributors

Business

Agriculture	$19,600	
Crop Production & Basic Processing	$1,100	
None over $1,000		
Tobacco	$6,500	
Philip Morris	$3,000	PAC
RJR Nabisco	$2,500	PAC
Dairy	$1,000	
None over $1,000		
Food Processing & Sales	$9,250	
Pepsico Inc	$6,000	PAC/Ind
Winn-Dixie Stores	$1,500	PAC
Nabisco Brands Inc	$1,000	PAC
Forestry & Forest Products	$1,000	
Union Camp Corp	$1,000	PAC

Communications/Electronics	$6,100	
Telephone Utilities	$2,750	
Chesapeake & Potomac Telephone	$1,000	PAC
Electronics Mfg & Services	$1,500	
Westinghouse Electric	$1,500	PAC
Computer Equipment & Services	$1,850	
Planning Research Corp	$1,500	PAC

Construction	$8,200	
General Contractors	$4,500	
Armada Hoffler Co	$1,500	Indiv
Associated General Contractors	$1,500	PAC
Specter Construction Co	$1,000	Indiv

Source of Funds in 1992 Election

Source	Total	Pct
■ PACs	$160,750	61%
▦ Indivs $200+	$44,984	17%
☐ Indivs under $200	$26,574	10%
⊠ Other	$29,566	11%
Candidate	$0	0%
Party	$7,227	3%

Source of PAC Dollars by Sector

Source	Total	Pct
■ Business	$121,600	78%
▨ Labor	$23,300	15%
☐ Ideology/Single Issue	$10,500	7%

In-State vs. Out-of-State Contributions*

Source	Total	Pct
☐ In-State	$41,234	92%
■ Out-of-state	$3,500	8%
No state listed	$0	

* by large individual contributors ($200 & above)

Special Trade Contractors	$1,000	
None over $1,000		
Building Materials & Equipment	$2,200	
Gray Lumber Co	$1,000	Indiv
Solite Corp	$1,000	Indiv

Defense	$39,550	
Defense Aerospace	$15,000	
Textron Inc	$3,500	PAC
McDonnell Douglas*	$2,500	PAC
Colt Industries	$1,500	PAC
Grumman Corp	$1,500	PAC
LTV Aerospace & Defense Co	$1,500	PAC
Martin Marietta Corp	$1,500	PAC
Lockheed Corp	$1,000	PAC
Rockwell International	$1,000	PAC
Defense Electronics	$2,500	
Litton Industries	$1,000	PAC
Raytheon	$1,000	PAC
Misc Defense	$22,050	
Tenneco Inc	$10,000	PAC
Newport News Shipbuilding	$3,050	Indiv
Atlantic Research Corp	$2,500	PAC
BDM International	$2,500	PAC
FMC Corp	$2,000	PAC
Bath Iron Works	$1,000	PAC
Mantech International	$1,000	PAC

Energy & Natural Resources	$11,884	
Oil & Gas	$1,500	
Columbia Gas of Ohio	$1,000	PAC
Mining	$3,000	
Reynolds Metals	$1,500	PAC
Pittston Co	$1,000	PAC
Misc Energy	$1,000	
Babcock & Wilcox	$1,000	PAC

Contribution Totals by Sector

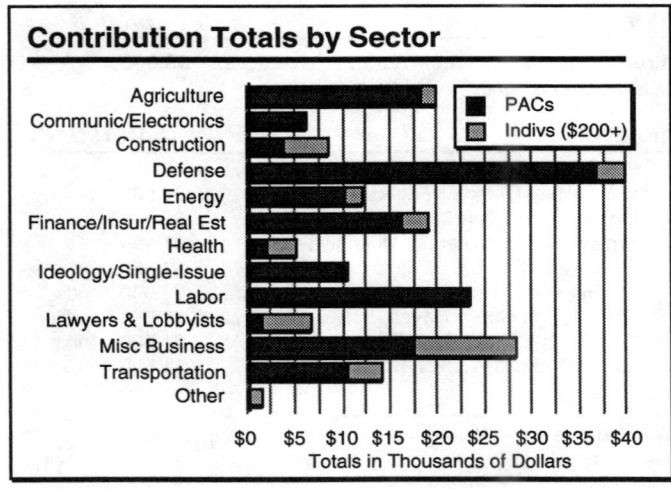

Legend: ■ PACs, ▦ Indivs ($200+)

Categories: Agriculture, Communic/Electronics, Construction, Defense, Energy, Finance/Insur/Real Est, Health, Ideology/Single-Issue, Labor, Lawyers & Lobbyists, Misc Business, Transportation, Other

Totals in Thousands of Dollars
$0 $5 $10 $15 $20 $25 $30 $35 $40

Electric Utilities **$4,884**
    ACRE (Action Cmte for Rural Electrification) .... $1,600   PAC
    Dominion Resources Inc .... $1,500   PAC
    American Electric Power .... $1,000   PAC

Waste Management **$1,500**
    Holly's Disposal .... $1,000   Indiv

Finance, Insurance & Real Estate   *$18,950*

Commercial Banks **$5,750**
    Virginia Bankers Assn .... $2,500   PAC
    Citizens & Southern National Bank .... $1,500   PAC

Insurance **$3,750**
    American Council of Life Insurance .... $1,000   PAC
    Equitable Financial Services .... $1,000   PAC

Real Estate **$7,750**
    National Assn of Realtors .... $5,500   PAC

Health   *$4,900*

Health Professionals **$4,900**
    American Medical Assn .... $1,500   PAC
    First Hospital Corp .... $1,500   Indiv

Lawyers & Lobbyists   *$6,450*

Lawyers & Lobbyists **$6,450**
    Coates & Davenport .... $1,000   Indiv

Misc Business   *$28,000*

Food & Beverage **$7,000**
    National Restaurant Assn .... $2,000   PAC
    Coca-Cola Co .... $1,500   PAC
    Pepsi-Cola Bottlers Assn .... $1,500   PAC
    Pepsi-Cola Bottling Co .... $1,000   Indiv

Beer, Wine & Liquor **$9,250**
    Anheuser-Busch .... $2,500   PAC
    National Beer Wholesalers Assn .... $2,250   PAC
    Associated Distributors .... $2,000   Indiv
    Brown Distributing Co .... $2,000   Indiv

Retail Sales **$2,750**
    Haynes Furniture Co .... $1,000   Indiv
    Standard Drug Stores .... $1,000   Indiv

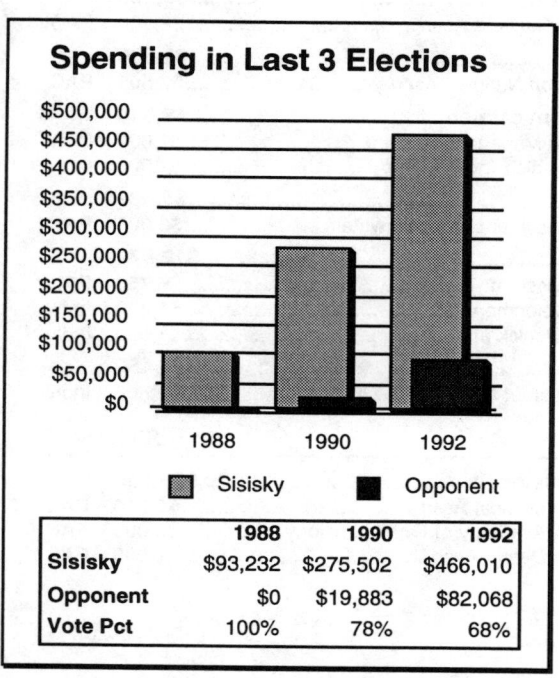

Spending in Last 3 Elections

Legend: Sisisky, Opponent

	1988	1990	1992
Sisisky	$93,232	$275,502	$466,010
Opponent	$0	$19,883	$82,068
Vote Pct	100%	78%	68%

Business Services **$1,750**
    National Council of Prof Services Firms .... $1,250   PAC

Chemical & Related Manufacturing **$1,000**
    None over $1,000

Misc Manufacturing & Distributing **$5,000**
    Stone Container Corp .... $2,000   PAC
    Hoechst Celanese Corp .... $1,000   PAC
    Jacobson Metal Co .... $1,000   Indiv

Transportation   *$14,000*

Air Transport **$2,500**
    General Electric .... $1,000   PAC

Automotive **$4,200**
    National Auto Dealers Assn .... $3,500   PAC

Trucking **$1,500**
    American Trucking Assns .... $1,000   PAC

Railroads **$2,000**
    CSX Corp* .... $1,000   PAC
    Norfolk Southern Corp .... $1,000   PAC/Ind

Sea Transport **$3,300**
    Moon Engineering Co .... $1,500   Indiv
    Elizabeth River Terminals Inc .... $1,000   Indiv

Labor

Labor   *$23,300*

Transportation Unions **$8,550**
    Teamsters Union .... $3,500   PAC
    Marine Engineers Dist 2 Maritime Officers .... $2,500   PAC
    United Transportation Union .... $2,000   PAC

Public Sector Unions **$12,500**
    National Assn Retired Federal Employees .... $4,000   PAC
    National Education Assn .... $3,500   PAC
    National Assn of Letter Carriers .... $2,000   PAC
    American Postal Workers Union .... $1,000   PAC

Ideological/Single-Issue

Ideological/Single-Issue   *$10,500*

Democratic/Liberal **$2,500**
    National Cmte for an Effective Congress .... $2,500   PAC

Pro-Israel **$2,500**
    National Action Committee .... $1,500   PAC
    Washington PAC .... $1,000   PAC

Gun Rights/Gun Control **$4,000**
    National Rifle Assn .... $4,000   PAC

Misc Issues **$1,500**
    National Cmte to Preserve Social Security .... $1,500   PAC

Other & Unknown

Other   *$1,300*

Retired **$1,000**
    None over $1,000

Unknown   *$7,650*

    Homemakers/Non-income earners $1,000
    Employer Listed/Category Unknown $6,650
      Earl Industries .... $1,000   Indiv

---

* Contributions came from more than one affiliate or subsidiary.

David E. Skaggs, D-Colo (2)

First elected: 1986

1991-92 Total Receipts: $659,719
1992 Year-end Cash: $17,460

1991-92 Committees & Subcommittees

Appropriations
Energy and Water Development; Treasury, Postal Service and General Government

Select Committee on Children, Youth and Families

Leading Contributors

Business

Agriculture	$10,175

Crop Production & Basic Processing $3,675
   None over $1,500

Dairy $3,250
   Associated Milk Producers .... $3,000   PAC

Communications/Electronics	$25,200

Printing & Publishing $1,500
   None over $1,500

Media/Entertainment $11,650
   Tele-Communications Inc .... $5,000   PAC/Ind
   National Cable Television Assn .... $2,000   PAC

Telephone Utilities $10,800
   US West Inc .... $6,500   PAC/Ind
   AT&T .... $2,000   PAC

Construction	$7,700

General Contractors $2,750
   None over $1,500

Home Builders $1,750
   National Assn of Home Builders .... $1,500   PAC

Construction Services $2,500
   Jacobs Engineering Group .... $2,000   PAC

Defense	$4,500

Defense Aerospace $3,000
   Martin Marietta Corp .... $3,000   PAC

Source of Funds in 1992 Election

Source	Total	Pct
■ PACs	$311,360	45%
▨ Indivs $200+	$150,636	22%
☐ Indivs under $200	$178,828	26%
⊠ Other	$53,287	8%
Candidate	$1,728	0%
Party	$39,542	6%

Source of PAC Dollars by Sector

Source	Total	Pct
■ Business	$120,515	40%
▨ Labor	$141,800	47%
☐ Ideology/Single Issue	$42,044	14%

In-State vs. Out-of-State Contributions*

Source	Total	Pct
☐ In-State	$127,017	85%
■ Out-of-state	$22,345	15%
No state listed	$0	

*** by large individual contributors ($200 & above)**

Energy & Natural Resources	$14,750

Oil & Gas $4,450
   Coastal Corp .... $2,000   PAC

Mining $1,750
   None over $1,500

Nuclear Energy $3,500
   General Atomics .... $3,000   PAC

Electric Utilities $3,600
   Public Service Co of Colorado .... $2,300   PAC/Ind

Finance, Insurance & Real Estate	$39,622

Commercial Banks $5,250
   American Bankers Assn .... $2,000   PAC

Credit Unions $2,500
   Credit Union National Assn .... $2,500   PAC

Securities & Investment $8,050
   Evergreen Management Corp .... $2,000   Indiv
   Kessler-Ehrlich Investments .... $2,000   Indiv

Insurance $5,000
   National Assn of Life Underwriters .... $3,000   PAC

Real Estate $12,872
   National Assn of Realtors .... $6,750   PAC
   Loup Development Co .... $1,500   Indiv
   Miller, Klutznick et al .... $1,500   Indiv

Misc Finance $5,450
   Hill, Carman et al .... $1,500   Indiv

Health	$30,150

Health Professionals $18,700
   American Medical Assn .... $9,700   PAC
   American Academy of Ophthalmology .... $3,000   PAC
   American Dental Assn .... $2,000   PAC

Contribution Totals by Sector

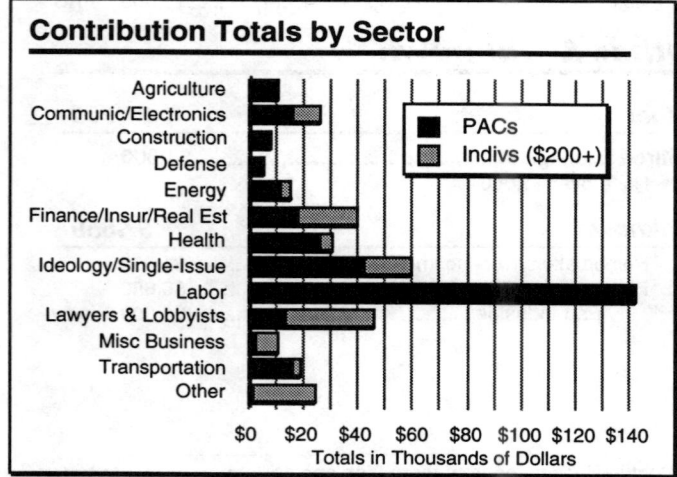

Agriculture
Communic/Electronics
Construction
Defense
Energy
Finance/Insur/Real Est
Health
Ideology/Single-Issue
Labor
Lawyers & Lobbyists
Misc Business
Transportation
Other

■ PACs
▨ Indivs ($200+)

$0 $20 $40 $60 $80 $100 $120 $140
Totals in Thousands of Dollars

Hospitals/Nursing Homes **$3,000**
National Jewish Hospital .... $2,500 Indiv
Pharmaceuticals/Health Products **$8,000**
Syntex (USA) Inc .... $6,000 PAC

Lawyers & Lobbyists $45,222

Lawyers & Lobbyists **$45,222**
Assn of Trial Lawyers of America .... $10,000 PAC
Haddon, Morgan & Foreman .... $4,000 Indiv
Buchanan, Gray et al .... $3,472 Indiv
Brownstein, Hyatt et al .... $2,000 Indiv
Kogovsek & Associates .... $2,000 Indiv
Holland & Hart .... $1,500 PAC
Rothberger, Appel et al .... $1,500 Indiv

Misc Business $10,450

Food & Beverage **$2,000**
Vicorp Restaurants .... $2,000 Indiv
Business Services **$3,250**
Neodata Services Inc .... $1,500 Indiv
Misc Manufacturing & Distributing **$2,000**
Corning Glass Works .... $2,000 PAC

Transportation $18,090

Air Transport **$11,740**
Aircraft Owners & Pilots Assn .... $3,000 PAC
United Parcel Service .... $3,000 PAC
Boeing Co .... $2,500 PAC
Trucking **$1,500**
None over $1,500
Misc Transport **$3,100**
Derby Cycle Corp .... $2,000 Indiv

Labor

Labor $141,800

Building Trade Unions **$18,500**
Carpenters & Joiners Union .... $5,500 PAC
Laborers' Political League .... $3,500 PAC
Sheet Metal Workers Union .... $3,500 PAC
Plumbers/Pipefitters Union .... $3,000 PAC

Industrial Unions **$35,550**
Intl Brotherhood of Electrical Workers .... $9,000 PAC
United Auto Workers .... $9,000 PAC
Machinists/Aerospace Workers Union .... $6,000 PAC
Rubber Cork Linoleum & Plastic Workers .... $5,000 PAC
Communications Workers of America .... $2,500 PAC
United Mine Workers .... $1,500 PAC
Transportation Unions **$35,150**
Marine Engineers Union* .... $11,500 PAC
Air Line Pilots Assn .... $7,500 PAC
Teamsters Union .... $6,000 PAC
United Transportation Union .... $3,500 PAC
Amalgamated Transit Union .... $2,000 PAC
Public Sector Unions **$39,500**
National Assn of Letter Carriers .... $9,000 PAC
National Assn Retired Federal Employees .... $8,000 PAC
American Fedn of St/Cnty/Munic Employees ...... $7,500 PAC
National Education Assn .... $5,000 PAC
National Rural Letter Carriers Assn .... $3,000 PAC
International Assn of Firefighters .... $1,500 PAC
National Treasury Employees Union .... $1,500 PAC
Misc Unions **$13,100**
Food & Commercial Workers Union .... $6,000 PAC
AFL-CIO .... $4,000 PAC
Bakery, Confectionery & Tobacco Workers .... $1,500 PAC

Ideological/Single-Issue

Ideological/Single-Issue $58,406

Democratic/Liberal **$14,672**
National Cmte for an Effective Congress .... $5,000 PAC
Leadership PACs **$1,500**
None over $1,500
Pro-Israel **$9,650**
National PAC .... $5,000 PAC
Joint Action Cmte for Political Affairs .... $1,500 PAC
Pro-Choice **$4,200**
National Abortion Rights Action League .... $3,000 PAC
Womens Issues **$2,750**
None over $1,500
Human Rights **$11,069**
Human Rights Campaign Fund .... $6,069 PAC
KidsPAC .... $4,500 PAC
Misc Issues **$13,075**
Sierra Club .... $5,550 PAC
National Cmte to Preserve Social Security .... $3,000 PAC
League of Conservation Voters .... $2,775 PAC

Other & Unknown

Other $23,580

Education **$2,480**
None over $1,500
Retired **$16,850**
None over $1,500
Other **$2,500**
None over $1,500

Unknown $24,576

Homemakers/Non-income earners $3,450
Employer Listed/Category Unknown $19,650
RKFV Ltd .... $2,500 Indiv
Lodestar Research Corp .... $2,000 Indiv

---

* Contributions came from more than one affiliate or subsidiary.

Joe Skeen, R-NM (2)

First elected: 1980

1991-92 Total Receipts: $387,893
1992 Year-end Cash: $91,360

1991-92 Committees & Subcommittees

Appropriations
Agriculture, Rural Development, Food and Drug Administration and Related Agencies (Ranking Republican); Interior and Related Agencies

Leading Contributors

Business

Agriculture	$70,631	
Crop Production & Basic Processing	**$24,131**	
National Cotton Council	$2,000	PAC
Southwest Peanut Membership Org	$1,250	PAC
Southern Minn Beet Sugar Co-op	$1,125	PAC
American Soybean Assn	$1,000	PAC
American Sugarbeet Growers Assn	$1,000	PAC
Florida Sugar Cane League	$1,000	PAC
National Assn of Wheat Growers	$1,000	PAC
Supima Assn of America	$1,000	PAC
Tobacco	**$2,000**	
Philip Morris	$1,000	PAC
RJR Nabisco	$1,000	PAC
Dairy	**$1,000**	
None over $1,000		
Poultry & Eggs	**$3,250**	
National Broiler Council	$1,500	PAC
National Turkey Federation	$1,250	PAC
Livestock	**$15,550**	
National Cattlemen's Assn*	$3,500	PAC
National Pork Producers Council	$1,000	PAC
National Wool Growers Assn	$1,000	PAC
Agricultural Services/Products	**$18,200**	
American Assn of Crop Insurers	$10,000	PAC
Farm Credit Council	$1,500	PAC
American Veterinary Medical Assn	$1,000	PAC
Farm Credit Bank of Texas	$1,000	PAC
IMC Fertilizer Inc	$1,000	PAC
Food Processing & Sales	**$6,500**	
American Meat Institute	$1,500	PAC
ConAgra Inc	$1,500	PAC
Food Marketing Institute	$1,500	PAC

Contribution Totals by Sector

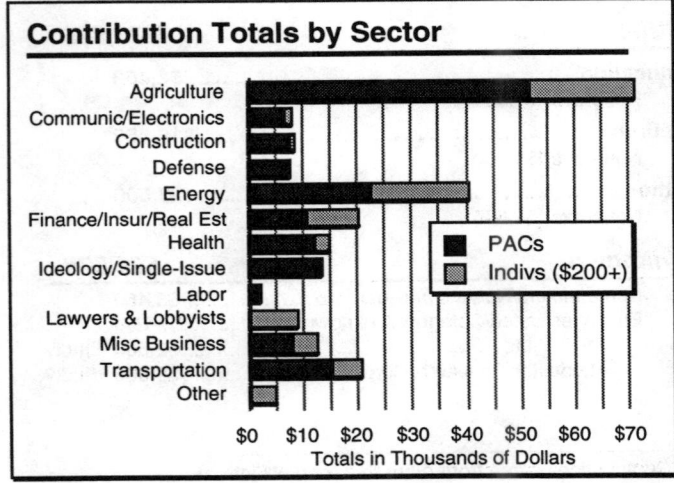

Agriculture
Communic/Electronics
Construction
Defense
Energy
Finance/Insur/Real Est
Health
Ideology/Single-Issue
Labor
Lawyers & Lobbyists
Misc Business
Transportation
Other

PACs
Indivs ($200+)

$0 $10 $20 $30 $40 $50 $60 $70
Totals in Thousands of Dollars

Source of Funds in 1992 Election

Source	Total	Pct
■ PACs	$160,125	41%
▨ Indivs $200+	$85,663	22%
□ Indivs under $200	$109,788	28%
⊠ Other	$32,317	8%
Candidate	$0	0%
Party	$5,606	1%

Source of PAC Dollars by Sector

Source	Total	Pct
■ Business	$141,050	91%
▨ Labor	$2,050	1%
□ Ideology/Single Issue	$12,600	8%

In-State vs. Out-of-State Contributions*

Source	Total	Pct
□ In-State	$63,863	76%
■ Out-of-state	$20,300	24%
No state listed	$500	

* by large individual contributors ($200 & above)

Communications/Electronics	$7,600	
Telephone Utilities	**$6,200**	
GTE Corp	$3,000	PAC
US West Inc	$2,200	PAC/Ind
National Telephone Co-op Assn	$1,000	PAC

Construction	$8,150	
General Contractors	**$4,200**	
Associated General Contractors	$2,500	PAC
National Utility Contractors Assn	$1,000	PAC
Special Trade Contractors	**$1,000**	
National Electrical Contractors Assn	$1,000	PAC
Construction Services	**$2,500**	
Jacobs Engineering Group	$1,000	PAC
National Society of Professional Engineers	$1,000	PAC

Defense	$7,500	
Defense Aerospace	**$6,000**	
Lockheed Corp	$1,500	PAC
Martin Marietta Corp	$1,000	PAC
Textron Inc	$1,000	PAC
Misc Defense	**$1,500**	
None over $1,000		

Energy & Natural Resources	$40,402	
Oil & Gas	**$24,002**	
El Paso Co	$2,000	PAC
Harvey E Yates Co	$1,500	Indiv
Hanson Oil Corp	$1,050	Indiv
Murphy Energy Corp	$1,006	Indiv
Atlantic Richfield	$1,000	PAC
Phillips Petroleum	$1,000	PAC
Shell Oil	$1,000	PAC
Yates Drilling Co	$1,000	Indiv

Mining **$6,350**
    Eddy County Potash .... $2,850   Indiv
    Phelps Dodge Corp .... $2,000   PAC

Misc Energy **$1,000**
    None over $1,000

Electric Utilities **$6,800**
    Southwestern Public Service Co .... $2,500   PAC
    ACRE (Action Cmte for Rural Electrification) .... $1,500   PAC
    Texas Utilities Co .... $1,000   PAC

Environmental Svcs/Equipment **$1,000**
    Cannon Consultants Inc .... $1,000   Indiv

Waste Management **$1,000**
    Waste Management Inc .... $1,000   PAC

Finance, Insurance & Real Estate   **$20,725**

Commercial Banks **$4,075**
    American Bankers Assn .... $1,000   PAC
    Independent Bankers Assn .... $1,000   PAC
    Western Commerce Bank .... $1,000   Indiv

Securities & Investment **$4,200**
    Craig Capital Corp .... $1,500   Indiv
    Chicago Board of Trade .... $1,000   PAC

Real Estate **$9,400**
    National Assn of Realtors .... $6,000   PAC
    KNB Investments .... $2,000   Indiv

Misc Finance **$2,550**
    None over $1,000

Health   **$14,332**

Health Professionals **$13,182**
    American Medical Assn .... $5,350   PAC
    American Dental Assn .... $3,000   PAC
    American Chiropractic Assn .... $2,000   PAC

Lawyers & Lobbyists   **$8,701**

Lawyers & Lobbyists **$8,701**
    Advocacy Group .... $3,000   Indiv
    Marchiondo, Vigil et al .... $1,000   Indiv
    McMahon & Associates .... $1,000   Indiv

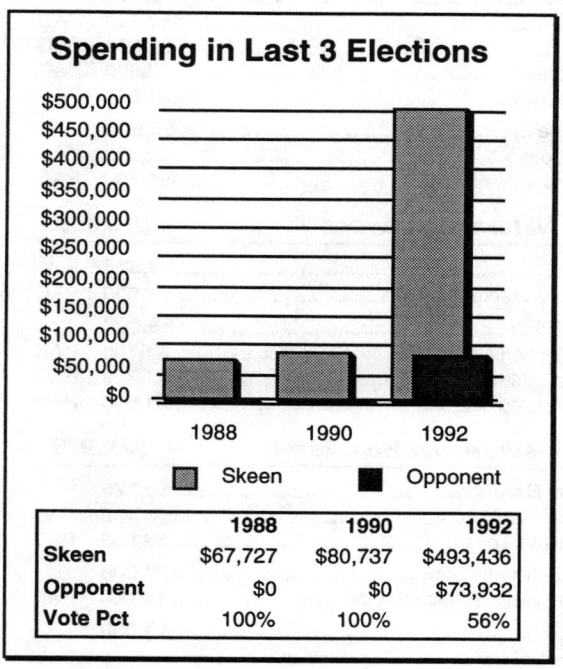

Spending in Last 3 Elections

	1988	1990	1992
Skeen	$67,727	$80,737	$493,436
Opponent	$0	$0	$73,932
Vote Pct	100%	100%	56%

Misc Business   **$12,300**

Food & Beverage **$2,500**
    Coca-Cola Bottling .... $2,000   Indiv

Beer, Wine & Liquor **$3,000**
    National Beer Wholesalers Assn .... $1,500   PAC

Retail Sales **$1,000**
    None over $1,000

Chemical & Related Manufacturing **$3,000**
    Dow Chemical .... $2,000   PAC
    Dial Corp .... $1,000   PAC

Misc Manufacturing & Distributing **$1,000**
    AFG Industries .... $1,000   Indiv

Transportation   **$20,600**

Air Transport **$6,000**
    United Parcel Service .... $3,000   PAC
    Aircraft Owners & Pilots Assn .... $2,000   PAC

Automotive **$12,100**
    National Auto Dealers Assn .... $4,500   PAC
    Forrest Tire Co .... $2,000   Indiv
    Auto Dealers & Drivers for Free Trade .... $1,500   PAC
    Patlex Corp .... $1,500   Indiv
    Americans for Free International Trade .... $1,000   PAC

Railroads **$2,500**
    Burlington Northern .... $1,000   PAC
    Union Pacific Corp .... $1,000   PAC

Labor   **$2,050**

Transportation Unions **$1,000**
    Marine Engineers Dist 2 Maritime Officers ..... $1,000   PAC

Public Sector Unions **$1,050**
    None over $1,000

Ideological/Single-Issue

Ideological/Single-Issue   **$13,100**

Foreign & Defense Policy **$1,000**
    Veterans of Foreign Wars .... $1,000   PAC

Pro-Israel **$5,500**
    ChiliPAC .... $1,000   PAC
    Florida Congressional Cmte .... $1,000   PAC

Gun Rights/Gun Control **$4,950**
    National Rifle Assn .... $4,950   PAC

Misc Issues **$1,650**
    National Cmte to Preserve Social Security ..... $1,000   PAC

Other & Unknown

Other   **$4,450**

Education **$1,000**
    American Indian Higher Ed Consortium .... $1,000   Indiv

Retired **$3,050**
    None over $1,000

Unknown   **$9,822**

    Employer Listed/Category Unknown $9,822
        TCOM LP .... $3,500   Indiv
        SIS Corp Inc .... $1,000   Indiv

* Contributions came from more than one affiliate or subsidiary.

Ike Skelton, D-Mo (4)

First elected: 1976

1991-92 Total Receipts: $310,017
1992 Year-end Cash: $194,795

1991-92 Committees & Subcommittees

Armed Services
Military Personnel and Compensation; Procurement and Military Nuclear Systems

Small Business
Procurement, Tourism and Rural Development (Chairman)

Select Committee on Aging

Leading Contributors

Business

Agriculture $26,625

Crop Production & Basic Processing $4,325
  None over $1,500

Tobacco $2,500
  None over $1,500

Dairy $9,000
  Associated Milk Producers ....$6,000 PAC
  Mid-America Dairymen ....$2,500 PAC

Livestock $2,500
  National Cattlemen's Assn* ....$1,500 PAC

Agricultural Services/Products $7,800
  Missouri Farm Bureau/W Central Dist ....$2,300 PAC
  Deere & Co ....$1,500 PAC
  Farm Credit Council ....$1,500 PAC

Communications/Electronics $11,250

Telephone Utilities $9,250
  Southwestern Bell ....$3,000 PAC
  United Telecommunications ....$3,000 PAC

Construction $4,875

General Contractors $2,625
  WJ Menefee Construction Co ....$1,625 Indiv

Construction Services $1,500
  None over $1,500

Defense $48,700

Defense Aerospace $30,500
  McDonnell Douglas* ....$4,500 PAC
  General Dynamics ....$3,500 PAC
  Northrop Corp ....$3,500 PAC
  Boeing Co ....$2,500 PAC
  General Electric ....$2,500 PAC
  Textron Inc ....$2,500 PAC
  Martin Marietta Corp ....$2,000 PAC
  Rockwell International ....$2,000 PAC
  LTV Aerospace & Defense Co ....$1,500 PAC

Defense Electronics $12,700
  AT&T ....$2,700 PAC
  GTE Corp ....$2,000 PAC
  Raytheon ....$2,000 PAC
  E-Systems Inc ....$1,500 PAC

Misc Defense $5,500
  Insilco Corp ....$2,500 PAC
  Olin Corp ....$1,500 PAC

Energy & Natural Resources $10,616

Oil & Gas $4,516
  Petroleum Marketers Assn ....$2,000 PAC

Electric Utilities $5,600
  ACRE (Action Cmte for Rural Electrification)* ......$1,700 PAC
  Utilicorp United Inc ....$1,700 PAC
  Union Electric ....$1,500 PAC

Finance, Insurance & Real Estate $29,975

Commercial Banks $10,725
  American Bankers Assn* ....$4,250 PAC
  Mercantile Bancorp ....$2,000 PAC

Securities & Investment $2,500
  National Venture Capital Assn ....$2,000 PAC

Insurance $8,950
  None over $1,500

Contribution Totals by Sector

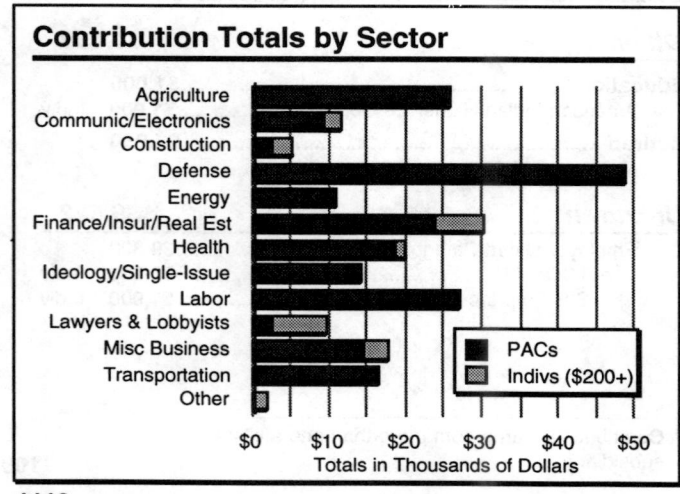

Agriculture
Communic/Electronics
Construction
Defense
Energy
Finance/Insur/Real Est
Health
Ideology/Single-Issue
Labor
Lawyers & Lobbyists
Misc Business
Transportation
Other

■ PACs
▨ Indivs ($200+)

$0 $10 $20 $30 $40 $50
Totals in Thousands of Dollars

Real Estate **$4,800**
    National Assn of Realtors .... $4,500   PAC
Accountants **$2,000**
    American Institute of CPA's .... $2,000   PAC

Health $19,600

Health Professionals **$18,000**
    American Medical Assn* .... $10,000   PAC
    American Dental Assn .... $5,000   PAC

Lawyers & Lobbyists $9,550

Lawyers & Lobbyists **$9,550**
    Assn of Trial Lawyers of America .... $2,500   PAC

Misc Business $17,489

Food & Beverage **$4,750**
    Pepsi-Cola General Bottlers .... $2,250   PAC
Beer, Wine & Liquor **$3,000**
    National Beer Wholesalers Assn .... $1,500   PAC
Lodging/Tourism **$3,650**
    None over $1,500
Misc Manufacturing & Distributing **$1,500**
    None over $1,500

Transportation $16,300

Air Transport **$3,500**
    United Parcel Service .... $3,000   PAC
Automotive **$8,200**
    National Auto Dealers Assn .... $8,000   PAC
Trucking **$1,600**
    None over $1,500
Railroads **$2,000**
    Kansas City Southern .... $1,500   PAC

Labor

Labor $26,900

Building Trade Unions **$6,200**
    Laborers' Political League .... $2,500   PAC
    Plumbers/Pipefitters Union .... $2,000   PAC
Industrial Unions **$4,500**
    Machinists/Aerospace Workers Union* .... $3,000   PAC
Transportation Unions **$6,500**
    Teamsters Union .... $3,500   PAC
Public Sector Unions **$5,200**
    None over $1,500
Misc Unions **$4,500**
    Food & Commercial Workers Union .... $2,000   PAC
    Hotel/Restaurant Employees Union .... $2,000   PAC

Ideological/Single-Issue

Ideological/Single-Issue $13,796

Pro-Israel **$2,000**
    None over $1,500
Gun Rights/Gun Control **$5,950**
    National Rifle Assn .... $5,950   PAC
Human Rights **$3,000**
    Health Care Concerns PAC .... $3,000   PAC
Misc Issues **$1,846**
    National Cmte to Preserve Social Security .... $1,500   PAC

Other & Unknown

Other $1,750

Retired **$1,750**
    None over $1,500

Unknown $5,450

    Employer Listed/Category Unknown $4,500
        None over $1,500

Independent expenditures supporting Skelton
    National Rifle Assn $7,411

Spending in Last 3 Elections

	1988	1990	1992
Skelton	$273,316	$306,485	$426,867
Opponent	$0	$7,137	$4,628
Vote Pct	72%	62%	70%

* Contributions came from more than one affiliate or subsidiary.

Jim Slattery, D-Kan (2)

First elected: 1982

1991-92 Total Receipts: $701,965
1992 Year-end Cash: $12,748

1991-92 Committees & Subcommittees

Banking, Finance and Urban Affairs

Energy and Commerce
Oversight and Investigations; Telecommunications and Finance; Transportation and Hazardous Materials

Veterans' Affairs
Education, Training and Employment (Vice Chairman); Hospitals and Health Care

Leading Contributors

Business

Agriculture	$20,200	
Dairy	**$2,500**	
Mid-America Dairymen	$2,000	PAC
Agricultural Services/Products	**$6,800**	
None over $2,000		
Food Processing & Sales	**$5,000**	
None over $2,000		

Communications/Electronics	$71,000	
Printing & Publishing	**$8,950**	
Hallmark Cards	$6,750	PAC/Ind
Montgomery Publications Inc	$2,000	Indiv
Media/Entertainment	**$10,750**	
National Assn of Broadcasters	$5,000	PAC
National Cable Television Assn	$3,000	PAC
ASCAP	$2,000	PAC
Telephone Utilities	**$46,050**	
Southwestern Bell	$7,550	PAC
Ameritech Corp	$7,500	PAC
BellSouth Corp*	$5,500	PAC
United Telecommunications	$4,500	PAC/Ind
Bell Atlantic	$4,000	PAC/Ind
Pacific Telesis Group	$3,500	PAC
US Telephone Assn	$3,500	PAC
NYNEX Corp	$2,500	PAC
GTE Corp	$2,000	PAC
US West Inc	$2,000	PAC
Telecom Services & Equipment	**$4,250**	
None over $2,000		

Contribution Totals by Sector

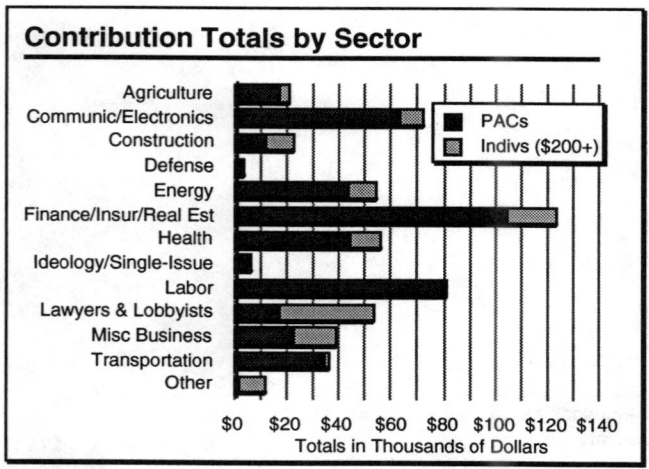

Agriculture
Communic/Electronics
Construction
Defense
Energy
Finance/Insur/Real Est
Health
Ideology/Single-Issue
Labor
Lawyers & Lobbyists
Misc Business
Transportation
Other

■ PACs
▦ Indivs ($200+)

$0 $20 $40 $60 $80 $100 $120 $140
Totals in Thousands of Dollars

Source of Funds in 1992 Election

Source	Total	Pct
■ PACs	$438,821	62%
▨ Indivs $200+	$171,445	24%
☐ Indivs under $200	$80,518	11%
▩ Other	$20,853	3%
Candidate	$0	0%
Party	$12,322	2%

Source of PAC Dollars by Sector

Source	Total	Pct
■ Business	$353,418	81%
▨ Labor	$80,500	18%
☐ Ideology/Single Issue	$4,750	1%

In-State vs. Out-of-State Contributions*

Source	Total	Pct
☐ In-State	$120,895	71%
■ Out-of-state	$50,550	29%
No state listed	$0	

* by large individual contributors ($200 & above)

Construction	$21,650	
General Contractors	**$5,200**	
Neosho Construction	$3,000	Indiv
Special Trade Contractors	**$3,500**	
National Electrical Contractors Assn ...	$3,000	PAC
Building Materials & Equipment	**$11,950**	
None over $2,000		

Defense	$3,000	
None over $2,000		

Energy & Natural Resources	$53,700	
Oil & Gas	**$24,400**	
KPL Gas Service	$5,900	PAC/Ind
Petroleum Marketers Assn	$5,000	PAC
Electric Utilities	**$21,800**	
Kansas City Power & Light	$3,000	PAC/Ind
Utilicorp United Inc	$2,600	PAC/Ind
Kansas Gas & Electric	$2,500	PAC/Ind
Waste Management	**$6,500**	
None over $2,000		

Finance, Insurance & Real Estate	$122,894	
Commercial Banks	**$20,895**	
American Bankers Assn	$7,500	PAC
Independent Bankers Assn	$2,000	PAC
JP Morgan & Co	$2,000	PAC
Savings & Loans	**$3,500**	
US League of Savings Assns*	$3,000	PAC
Securities & Investment	**$10,500**	
Investment Company Institute	$3,000	PAC
Insurance	**$46,699**	
National Assn of Life Underwriters	$10,000	PAC
American Family Corp	$3,000	PAC
American Council of Life Insurance	$2,999	PAC
American International Group Inc	$2,000	PAC

Mutual of Omaha ....$2,000 PAC
National Assn of Prof Insurance Agents ....$2,000 PAC
Northwestern Mutual Life ....$2,000 PAC

Real Estate **$16,500**
National Assn of Realtors...................................$10,000 PAC

Accountants **$18,250**
American Institute of CPA's ....$9,500 PAC
Arthur Andersen & Co ....$2,500 PAC
Ernst & Young ....$2,500 PAC

Misc Finance **$3,250**
None over $2,000

Health — $55,150

Health Professionals **$34,650**
American Medical Assn* ....$10,000 PAC
American Dental Assn ....$6,000 PAC

Hospitals/Nursing Homes **$8,250**
American Hospital Assn ....$3,250 PAC/Ind

Pharmaceuticals/Health Products **$9,750**
Glaxo Inc ....$2,000 PAC

Lawyers & Lobbyists — $53,300

Lawyers & Lobbyists **$53,300**
Verner, Liipfert et al ....$6,000 PAC/Ind
Williams & Jensen ....$3,000 PAC/Ind
Akin, Gump et al ....$2,000 PAC
Cameron Law Office ....$2,000 Indiv
Hubbell, Sawyer et al ....$2,000 Indiv
Wunder, Diefenderfer et al ....$2,000 Indiv

Misc Business — $38,505

Food & Beverage **$5,100**
Pepsi-Cola General Bottlers ....$3,000 PAC

Beer, Wine & Liquor **$5,500**
National Beer Wholesalers Assn ....$2,000 PAC

Retail Sales..**$7,200**
Payless Shoe Source ....$2,500 Indiv
Beachner Brothers ....$2,000 Indiv

Spending in Last 3 Elections

	1988	1990	1992
Slattery	$388,866	$504,861	$742,215
Opponent	$110,263	$84,568	$36,704
Vote Pct	73%	63%	56%

Business Services **$4,200**
None over $2,000

Chemical & Related Manufacturing **$8,405**
FMC Corp ....$4,000 PAC

Misc Manufacturing & Distributing **$3,500**
None over $2,000

Transportation — $35,499

Air Transport **$6,000**
Boeing Co ....$2,000 PAC
General Electric ....$2,000 PAC

Automotive **$10,000**
National Auto Dealers Assn ....$7,000 PAC

Railroads **$16,999**
Union Pacific Corp ....$3,499 PAC
Burlington Northern ....$2,750 PAC/Ind
Kansas City Southern ....$2,500 PAC/Ind
Southern Pacific Transport Co ....$2,000 PAC

Labor

Labor — $80,750

Building Trade Unions **$14,250**
Plumbers/Pipefitters Union* ....$5,500 PAC
Carpenters & Joiners Union ....$3,000 PAC
Laborers' Political League ....$2,500 PAC
Operating Engineers Union* ....$2,000 PAC

Industrial Unions **$28,250**
Rubber Cork Linoleum & Plastic Workers ....$8,000 PAC
United Auto Workers ....$6,500 PAC
Machinists/Aerospace Workers Union ....$5,500 PAC
Intl Brotherhood of Electrical Workers ....$2,500 PAC
United Steelworkers ....$2,000 PAC

Transportation Unions **$21,600**
United Transportation Union ....$9,000 PAC
Teamsters Union ....$6,000 PAC
Trans Comm International Union ....$2,100 PAC
Brotherhood of Locomotive Engineers................$2,000 PAC

Public Sector Unions **$13,650**
National Education Assn* ....$5,600 PAC
National Assn Retired Federal Employees ....$4,000 PAC

Misc Unions..**$3,000**
Food & Commercial Workers Union ....$2,500 PAC

Ideological/Single-Issue

Ideological/Single-Issue — $5,500

Democratic/Liberal **$2,750**
National Cmte for an Effective Congress ....$2,000 PAC

Other & Unknown

Other — $11,050

Retired **$6,950**
None over $2,000

Unknown — $38,915

Homemakers/Non-income earners $7,450
No Employer Listed or Found $12,165
Generic Occupation/Category Unknown $2,200
Employer Listed/Category Unknown $17,100
LDH Inc ....$2,000 Indiv

---

* Contributions came from more than one affiliate or subsidiary.

Louise M. Slaughter, D-NY (28)

First elected: 1986

1991-92 Total Receipts: $473,871
1992 Year-end Cash: $76,805

1991-92 Committees & Subcommittees

Budget
Defense, Foreign Policy and Space; Urgent Fiscal Issues

Rules
Rules of the House

Select Committee on Aging

Leading Contributors

Business

Agriculture	$14,400	
Crop Production & Basic Processing	**$4,400**	
American Crystal Sugar Corp	$1,500	PAC
Dairy	**$6,500**	
Associated Milk Producers	$3,000	PAC
Mid-America Dairymen	$1,500	PAC
Agricultural Services/Products	**$2,000**	
Farm Credit Council	$1,500	PAC

Communications/Electronics	$12,900	
Media/Entertainment	**$3,250**	
National Cable Television Assn	$2,000	PAC
Telephone Utilities	**$8,350**	
AT&T	$5,000	PAC
BellSouth Corp*	$1,750	PAC
Rochester Telephone Corp	$1,600	PAC/Ind

Construction	$3,500	
Home Builders	**$2,000**	
Wilmorite Inc	$1,500	Indiv
Construction Services	**$1,500**	
Joseph Lu Engineers	$1,500	Indiv

Defense	$1,500
None over $1,500	

Energy & Natural Resources	$3,100
None over $1,500	

Source of Funds in 1992 Election

Source	Total	Pct
PACs	$292,050	58%
Indivs $200+	$66,121	13%
Indivs under $200	$90,694	18%
Other	$52,022	10%
Candidate	$0	0%
Party	$27,466	5%

Source of PAC Dollars by Sector

Source	Total	Pct
Business	$117,924	41%
Labor	$157,248	54%
Ideology/Single Issue	$15,954	5%

In-State vs. Out-of-State Contributions*

Source	Total	Pct
In-State	$62,421	94%
Out-of-state	$3,700	6%
No state listed	$0	

* by large individual contributors ($200 & above)

Finance, Insurance & Real Estate	$48,874	
Commercial Banks	**$12,874**	
American Bankers Assn	$3,000	PAC
Citicorp	$2,574	PAC
JP Morgan & Co	$2,500	PAC
Savings & Loans	**$4,100**	
US League of Savings Assns	$1,500	PAC
Credit Unions	**$1,500**	
Credit Union National Assn	$1,500	PAC
Securities & Investment	**$11,000**	
Chicago Mercantile Exchange	$2,500	PAC
Morgan Stanley & Co	$2,000	PAC
PaineWebber	$1,500	PAC
Insurance	**$5,300**	
National Assn of Life Underwriters	$2,500	PAC
Real Estate	**$11,400**	
National Assn of Realtors	$6,000	PAC
Mortgage Bankers Assn of America	$2,000	PAC
Greenleaf Meadows	$1,500	Indiv
Accountants	**$2,000**	
American Institute of CPA's	$2,000	PAC

Health	$29,000	
Health Professionals	**$26,200**	
American Medical Assn	$15,000	PAC
American Nurses Assn	$3,500	PAC
American Podiatry Assn	$2,500	PAC
American Academy of Ophthalmology	$2,000	PAC
Hospitals/Nursing Homes	**$2,300**	
Vari-Care Inc	$1,700	Indiv

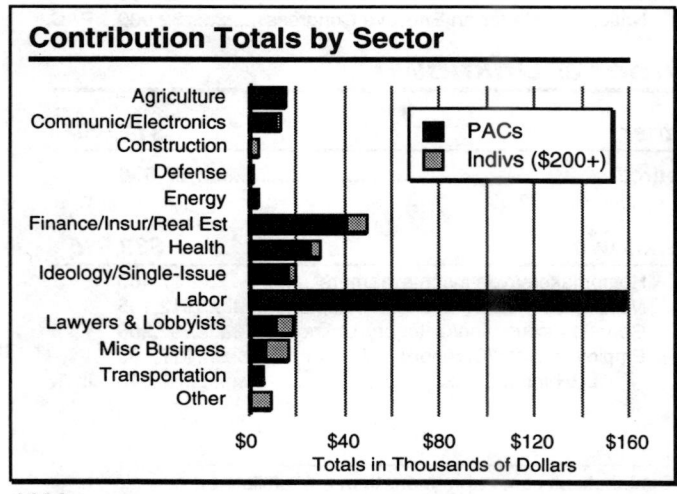

Contribution Totals by Sector

Legend: ■ PACs ▨ Indivs ($200+)

Agriculture
Communic/Electronics
Construction
Defense
Energy
Finance/Insur/Real Est
Health
Ideology/Single-Issue
Labor
Lawyers & Lobbyists
Misc Business
Transportation
Other

$0 $40 $80 $120 $160
Totals in Thousands of Dollars

Lawyers & Lobbyists $17,550

Lawyers & Lobbyists **$17,550**
 Assn of Trial Lawyers of America .... $10,000   PAC
 Harter, Secrest & Emery .... $1,700   Indiv

Misc Business $16,250

Food & Beverage **$2,500**
 National Restaurant Assn .... $2,000   PAC

Beer, Wine & Liquor **$1,750**
 None over $1,500

Misc Manufacturing & Distributing **$10,500**
 Hydroacoustics Inc .... $4,000   Indiv
 Xerox Corp .... $2,500   PAC
 Eastman Kodak .... $1,500   Indiv

Transportation $6,000

Air Transport **$1,500**
 None over $1,500

Trucking **$2,500**
 American Trucking Assns .... $1,500   PAC

Railroads **$2,000**
 None over $1,500

Labor

Labor $157,248

Building Trade Unions **$22,500**
 Operating Engineers Union* .... $5,500   PAC
 Carpenters & Joiners Union .... $5,000   PAC
 Laborers' Political League .... $5,000   PAC
 Plumbers/Pipefitters Union .... $2,000   PAC
 AFL-CIO Bldg/Construction Trades Dept .... $1,500   PAC
 Bricklayers Union .... $1,500   PAC

Spending in Last 3 Elections

	1988	1990	1992
Slaughter	$802,886	$322,216	$526,345
Opponent	$310,704	$24,712	$244,126
Vote Pct	57%	59%	55%

Industrial Unions **$35,200**
 Intl Brotherhood of Electrical Workers .... $10,000   PAC
 Machinists/Aerospace Workers Union .... $5,500   PAC
 United Auto Workers .... $5,500   PAC
 Amalgamated Clothing & Textile Workers* .... $2,700   PAC
 Electrical Radio & Machine Workers .... $2,500   PAC
 United Steelworkers .... $2,000   PAC
 Boilermakers Union .... $1,500   PAC
 Electronic Machine Furniture Workers .... $1,500   PAC
 Rubber Cork Linoleum & Plastic Workers .... $1,500   PAC
 United Mine Workers .... $1,500   PAC

Transportation Unions **$31,350**
 Air Line Pilots Assn .... $10,000   PAC
 United Transportation Union .... $7,500   PAC
 Amalgamated Transit Union .... $3,000   PAC
 Transport Workers Union .... $2,500   PAC
 Brotherhood of Railroad Signalmen .... $1,600   PAC
 Marine Engineers Dist 2 Maritime Officers .... $1,500   PAC
 Seafarers International Union .... $1,500   PAC

Public Sector Unions **$56,200**
 American Federation of Teachers .... $10,000   PAC
 American Fedn of St/Cnty/Munic Employees .... $10,000   PAC
 National Assn of Letter Carriers .... $10,000   PAC
 National Education Assn .... $10,000   PAC
 American Postal Workers Union .... $5,000   PAC
 National Assn Retired Federal Employees .... $4,000   PAC
 International Assn of Firefighters .... $1,500   PAC
 National Assn of Postmasters .... $1,500   PAC

Misc Unions **$11,998**
 Food & Commercial Workers Union .... $6,998   PAC
 Service Employees International Union .... $2,000   PAC

Ideological/Single-Issue

Ideological/Single-Issue $19,304

Democratic/Liberal **$4,150**
 National Cmte for an Effective Congress .... $2,500   PAC

Pro-Choice **$5,694**
 National Abortion Rights Action League .... $3,694   PAC
 Voters for Choice .... $2,000   PAC

Womens Issues **$3,100**
 None over $1,500

Human Rights **$2,000**
 None over $1,500

Misc Issues **$3,360**
 National Cmte to Preserve Social Security .... $2,250   PAC

Other & Unknown

Other $8,675

Non-Profit Institutions **$2,250**
 Foundation for Hearing Aid Research .... $2,000   Indiv

Education **$4,275**
 University of Rochester .... $1,725   Indiv

Retired **$1,750**
 None over $1,500

Unknown $18,946

 Homemakers/Non-income earners $4,246
 No Employer Listed or Found $5,100
 Employer Listed/Category Unknown $9,100
  None over $1,500

---

* Contributions came from more than one affiliate or
subsidiary.

Bob Smith, R-Ore (2)

First elected: 1982

1991-92 Total Receipts: $462,680
1992 Year-end Cash: $240,746

1991-92 Committees & Subcommittees

Agriculture
Conservation, Credit and Rural Development (Ranking Republican);
Forests, Family Farms and Energy; Livestock, Dairy and Poultry;
Wheat, Soybeans and Feed Grains

Interior and Insular Affairs
National Parks and Public Lands; Water, Power and Offshore Energy

Select Committee on Hunger

Leading Contributors

Business

Agriculture — $109,637

Crop Production & Basic Processing	**$14,425**	
American Crystal Sugar Corp	$1,350	PAC
American Sugarbeet Growers Assn	$1,350	PAC
National Assn of Wheat Growers	$1,200	PAC
Southern Minn Beet Sugar Co-op	$1,125	PAC
Amalgamated Sugar Co	$1,000	PAC
Smith Frozen Foods	$1,000	Indiv
Tobacco	**$4,350**	
Philip Morris	$1,350	PAC
RJR Nabisco	$1,000	PAC
US Tobacco Co	$1,000	PAC
Dairy	**$3,600**	
Dairymen Inc	$1,850	PAC
Poultry & Eggs	**$2,050**	
None over $1,000		
Livestock	**$18,900**	
Seneca Livestock Co	$4,000	Indiv
National Cattlemen's Assn	$1,200	PAC
Texas & Southwestern Cattle Raisers	$1,000	PAC
Agricultural Services/Products	**$14,400**	
American Assn of Crop Insurers	$5,000	PAC
Farm Credit Council	$1,700	PAC
FMC Corp	$1,500	PAC
American Assn of Nurserymen	$1,350	PAC
American Veterinary Medical Assn	$1,000	PAC
Land O'Lakes Inc	$1,000	PAC

Source of Funds in 1992 Election

Source	Total	Pct
PACs	$165,725	36%
Indivs $200+	$101,262	22%
Indivs under $200	$172,075	37%
Other	$23,618	5%
Candidate	$0	0%
Party	$1,545	0%

Source of PAC Dollars by Sector

Source	Total	Pct
Business	$146,825	95%
Labor	$1,000	1%
Ideology/Single Issue	$6,450	4%

In-State vs. Out-of-State Contributions*

Source	Total	Pct
In-State	$84,912	86%
Out-of-state	$14,350	14%
No state listed	$0	

* by large individual contributors ($200 & above)

Food Processing & Sales	**$7,650**	
American Meat Institute	$1,850	PAC
Food Marketing Institute	$1,850	PAC
ConAgra Inc	$1,500	PAC
Ampco Foods Inc	$1,000	PAC
Forestry & Forest Products	**$43,762**	
Louisiana-Pacific Corp	$5,350	PAC/Ind
Indian Hill Timber Co	$4,662	Indiv
Boise Cascade	$3,000	PAC
Willamette Industries*	$3,000	PAC
Snow Mountain Pine Ltd	$2,750	Indiv
Croman Corp	$2,700	Indiv
DR Johnson Lumber Co	$2,000	Indiv
Ellingson Lumber Co	$2,000	Indiv
Hanel Lumber Co	$2,000	Indiv
Ochoco Lumber Co	$1,750	Indiv
Hull Oakes Lumber Co	$1,500	Indiv
Kogap Lumber Manufacturing	$1,350	Indiv
Simpson Investment Co	$1,350	PAC
Eugene F Burrill Lumber Co	$1,000	Indiv
Stimson Lumber Co	$1,000	Indiv
Sun Studs Inc	$1,000	PAC

Communications/Electronics — $7,500

Media/Entertainment	**$1,000**	
KOBI-TV	$1,000	Indiv
Telephone Utilities	**$5,850**	
US West Inc	$2,000	PAC
Oregon Telephone Corp	$1,000	Indiv
United Telecommunications	$1,000	PAC

Construction — $12,800

General Contractors	**$5,700**	
Associated General Contractors	$2,500	PAC
Blount Inc	$1,000	PAC
Home Builders	**$1,000**	
National Assn of Home Builders	$1,000	PAC

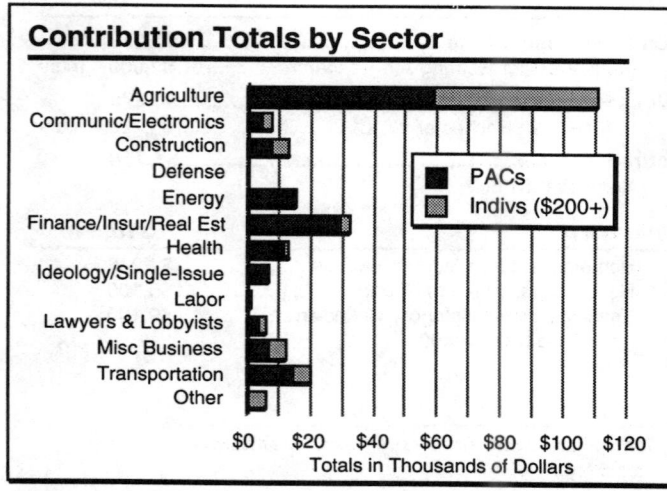

Contribution Totals by Sector

Agriculture
Communic/Electronics
Construction
Defense
Energy
Finance/Insur/Real Est
Health
Ideology/Single-Issue
Labor
Lawyers & Lobbyists
Misc Business
Transportation
Other

■ PACs
▨ Indivs ($200+)

$0 $20 $40 $60 $80 $100 $120
Totals in Thousands of Dollars

Special Trade Contractors	$1,000	
National Electrical Contractors Assn	$1,000	PAC
Building Materials & Equipment	**$5,100**	
Circle D Lumber	$2,000	Indiv
Contract Lumber Co	$1,000	Indiv

Energy & Natural Resources — $15,200

Oil & Gas	**$6,650**	
Litton Industries	$1,350	PAC
Coastal Corp	$1,000	PAC
Exxon Corp	$1,000	PAC
Mining	**$3,250**	
National Coal Assn	$1,000	PAC
Newmont Mining Corp	$1,000	PAC
Electric Utilities	**$4,350**	
ACRE (Action Cmte for Rural Electrification)	$1,350	PAC
Texas Utilities Co	$1,000	PAC

Finance, Insurance & Real Estate — $32,150

Commercial Banks	**$11,350**	
American Bankers Assn	$5,000	PAC
US Bancorp	$3,000	PAC
Independent Bankers Assn	$1,850	PAC
Credit Unions	**$1,000**	
Credit Union National Assn	$1,000	PAC
Securities & Investment	**$9,500**	
Chicago Board of Trade	$3,500	PAC
Chicago Mercantile Exchange	$3,500	PAC
New York Mercantile Exchange	$1,000	PAC
Insurance	**$2,500**	
National Assn of Life Underwriters	$1,000	PAC
Standard Insurance Co	$1,000	PAC
Real Estate	**$6,800**	
National Assn of Realtors	$4,350	PAC
Fairway Western Inc	$1,000	Indiv
Accountants	**$1,000**	
None over $1,000		

Spending in Last 3 Elections

	1988	1990	1992
Smith	$340,643	$284,700	$401,670
Opponent	$208,513	$0	$87,361
Vote Pct	63%	68%	67%

Health — $12,800

Health Professionals	**$9,350**	
American Medical Assn	$8,350	PAC
Pharmaceuticals/Health Products	**$2,850**	
Vitaline Corp	$1,000	Indiv

Lawyers & Lobbyists — $5,350

Lawyers & Lobbyists	**$5,350**	
Preston, Gates et al	$1,000	PAC

Misc Business — $11,850

Food & Beverage	**$2,350**	
National Restaurant Assn	$1,000	PAC
Beer, Wine & Liquor	**$1,400**	
None over $1,000		
Business Services	**$1,500**	
Resource Management International	$1,000	Indiv
Misc Manufacturing & Distributing	**$4,850**	
Stone Container Corp	$1,850	PAC
Pendleton Woolen Mills	$1,000	Indiv

Transportation — $19,200

Air Transport	**$6,700**	
United Parcel Service	$3,350	PAC
Aircraft Owners & Pilots Assn	$1,000	PAC
Transwestern Helicopters Inc	$1,000	Indiv
Automotive	**$7,350**	
National Auto Dealers Assn	$4,350	PAC
Auto Dealers & Drivers for Free Trade	$1,500	PAC
Americans for Free International Trade	$1,000	PAC
Railroads	**$2,350**	
James-Furman & Co	$1,000	Indiv
Union Pacific Corp	$1,000	PAC
Sea Transport	**$2,500**	
Brix Maritime Co	$2,000	Indiv

Labor

Labor	**$1,000**	
Transportation Unions	**$1,000**	
Marine Engineers Dist 2 Maritime Officers	$1,000	PAC

Ideological/Single-Issue

Ideological/Single-Issue	**$6,450**	
Gun Rights/Gun Control	**$5,600**	
National Rifle Assn	$5,500	PAC

Other & Unknown

Other	**$5,800**	
Retired	**$4,950**	
None over $1,000		
Unknown	**$13,800**	
Homemakers/Non-income earners	$2,650	
No Employer Listed or Found	$1,900	
Employer Listed/Category Unknown	$9,250	
Hart & Associates	$2,000	Indiv
Consep Membranes Inc	$1,000	Indiv

* Contributions came from more than one affiliate or subsidiary.

Christopher H. Smith, R-NJ (4)

First elected: 1980
1991-92 Total Receipts: $369,949
1992 Year-end Cash: $20,850

1991-92 Committees & Subcommittees

Foreign Affairs
Human Rights and International Organizations; International Operations

Veterans' Affairs
Education, Training and Employment (Ranking Republican); Hospitals and Health Care

Select Committee on Aging

Select Committee on Hunger

Leading Contributors

Business

Agriculture		$3,000
Food Processing & Sales		**$1,500**
Iowa Packing Co	$1,000	Indiv
Forestry & Forest Products		**$1,500**
Newark Group	$1,000	Indiv

Communications/Electronics		$8,525
Printing & Publishing		**$1,225**
Forbes Inc	$1,000	Indiv
Telephone Utilities		**$6,600**
Bell Atlantic*	$4,500	PAC
AT&T	$2,100	PAC/Ind

Construction		$5,350
General Contractors		**$1,250**
Associated General Contractors	$1,000	PAC
Home Builders		**$2,000**
Flatley Co	$1,000	Indiv
National Assn of Home Builders	$1,000	PAC
Construction Services		**$1,000**
Remington & Vernick	$1,000	Indiv

Defense		$1,000
Defense Electronics		**$1,000**
Imo Industries Inc	$1,000	PAC

Source of Funds in 1992 Election

Source	Total	Pct
PACs	$110,958	29%
Indivs $200+	$56,548	15%
Indivs under $200	$169,163	44%
Other	$51,946	13%
Candidate	$0	0%
Party	$25,066	6%

Source of PAC Dollars by Sector

Source	Total	Pct
Business	$41,934	45%
Labor	$30,390	33%
Ideology/Single Issue	$20,683	22%

In-State vs. Out-of-State Contributions*

Source	Total	Pct
In-State	$43,248	77%
Out-of-state	$12,600	23%
No state listed	$0	

* by large individual contributors ($200 & above)

Energy & Natural Resources		$5,550
Electric Utilities		**$5,050**
Public Service Electric & Gas	$5,050	PAC/Ind

Finance, Insurance & Real Estate		$19,634
Commercial Banks		**$1,975**
United Jersey Banks	$1,500	PAC
Savings & Loans		**$1,769**
SAPEC, NJ (NJ Savings Assn)	$1,519	PAC
Securities & Investment		**$1,900**
None over $1,000		
Insurance		**$3,490**
National Assn of Life Underwriters	$1,500	PAC
Rue Insurance Agency	$1,000	Indiv
Real Estate		**$9,500**
National Assn of Realtors	$8,000	PAC
Mid-State Abstract	$1,000	Indiv

Health		$8,410
Health Professionals		**$6,975**
American Medical Assn	$5,000	PAC

Lawyers & Lobbyists		$2,500
Lawyers & Lobbyists		**$2,500**
None over $1,000		

Misc Business		$3,325
None over $1,000		

Contribution Totals by Sector

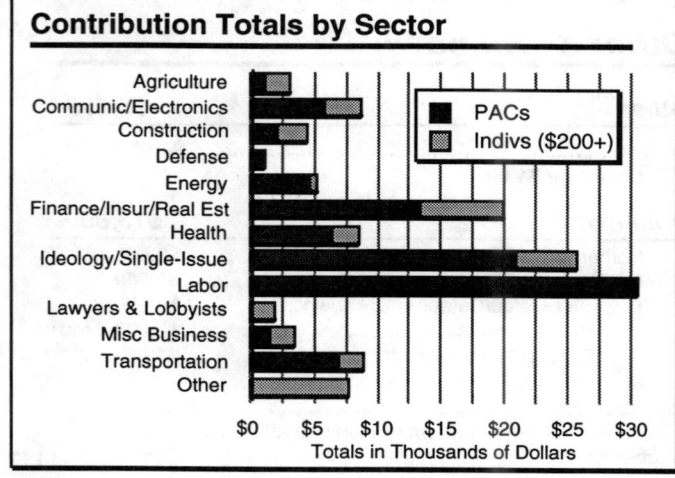

- Agriculture
- Communic/Electronics
- Construction
- Defense
- Energy
- Finance/Insur/Real Est
- Health
- Ideology/Single-Issue
- Labor
- Lawyers & Lobbyists
- Misc Business
- Transportation
- Other

PACs
Indivs ($200+)

$0 $5 $10 $15 $20 $25 $30
Totals in Thousands of Dollars

Transportation $8,650

Air Transport $2,900
    United Parcel Service ....$2,900   PAC
Automotive $5,250
    National Auto Dealers Assn ....$2,000   PAC
    Auto Dealers & Drivers for Free Trade ....$1,500   PAC

Labor

Labor $30,390

Building Trade Unions $9,475
    Operating Engineers Union* ....$3,500   PAC
    Carpenters & Joiners Union ....$2,500   PAC
    Laborers' Political League ....$2,000   PAC
    Plumbers/Pipefitters Union* ....$1,475   PAC
Industrial Unions $1,750
    Intl Brotherhood of Electrical Workers ....$1,000   PAC
Transportation Unions $11,500
    Air Line Pilots Assn ....$5,000   PAC
    International Longshoremen's Assn ....$2,500   PAC
    Marine Engineers Union* ....$2,000   PAC
    Masters, Mates & Pilots Union ....$1,000   PAC
    Seafarers International Union ....$1,000   PAC
Public Sector Unions $6,665
    International Assn of Firefighters ....$2,500   PAC
    National Assn Retired Federal Employees ....$2,500   PAC
    National Assn of Letter Carriers ....$1,525   PAC
Misc Unions $1,000
    Food & Commercial Workers Union ....$1,000   PAC

Ideological/Single-Issue

Ideological/Single-Issue $25,558

Republican/Conservative $1,683
    None over $1,000
Foreign & Defense Policy $3,000
    Veterans of Foreign Wars ....$3,000   PAC
Pro-Israel $5,000
    National PAC ....$5,000   PAC
Pro-Life $13,875
    Republican National Coalition for Life ....$4,000   PAC
    New Jersey Right to Life PAC ....$2,950   PAC
    Right to Life* ....$2,050   PAC
    Spring Lake Pro-Life ....$1,000   PAC
Misc Issues $2,000
    National Cmte to Preserve Social Security ....$2,000   PAC

Other & Unknown

Other $7,570

Education $1,360
    None over $1,000
Retired $5,225
    None over $1,000

Unknown $20,093

    No Employer Listed or Found $4,850
    Employer Listed/Category Unknown $15,243
        Ennis-Larosa Adv ....$1,500   Indiv
        Allen & Stults Co ....$1,000   Indiv
        Arch St Paul & Minneapolis ....$1,000   Indiv
        Danskin Agency ....$1,000   Indiv

Independent expenditures supporting Smith
    National Right to Life PAC $5,658

Spending in Last 3 Elections

	1988	1990	1992
Smith	$254,515	$292,826	$413,493
Opponent	$53,964	$55,772	$605,400
Vote Pct	66%	63%	62%

* Contributions came from more than one affiliate or subsidiary.

Lamar Smith, R-Texas (21)

First elected: 1986

1991-92 Total Receipts: $544,187
1992 Year-end Cash: $420,613

1991-92 Committees & Subcommittees

Judiciary
Economic and Commercial Law; International Law, Immigration and Refugees

Science, Space and Technology
Energy; Space

Select Committee on Children, Youth and Families

Leading Contributors

Business

Agriculture	$27,850	
Crop Production & Basic Processing	**$3,200**	
Rio Grande Valley Sugar Growers	$1,000	PAC
Livestock	**$14,800**	
National Cattlemen's Assn*	$2,300	PAC
Texas & Southwestern Cattle Raisers	$1,000	PAC
Agricultural Services/Products	**$2,500**	
Texas Farm Bureau	$2,500	PAC
Food Processing & Sales	**$6,350**	
HE Butt Grocery Co	$2,000	Indiv
Town & Country Food Stores	$2,000	Indiv
Food Marketing Institute	$1,300	PAC

Communications/Electronics	$26,000	
Printing & Publishing	**$5,000**	
Harte-Hanks Communications	$4,000	Indiv
Media/Entertainment	**$4,700**	
National Cable Television Assn	$2,500	PAC
National Assn of Broadcasters	$1,000	PAC
Telephone Utilities	**$9,200**	
AT&T	$3,500	PAC
GTE Corp	$3,000	PAC
Southwestern Bell	$1,300	PAC
Electronics Mfg & Services	**$1,500**	
Harris Corp	$1,000	PAC
Computer Equipment & Services	**$5,100**	
Sterling Software	$3,000	Indiv

Source of Funds in 1992 Election

Source	Total	Pct
■ PACs	$134,739	25%
▨ Indivs $200+	$197,810	36%
☐ Indivs under $200	$144,530	27%
⊠ Other	$67,108	12%
Candidate	$0	0%
Party	$2,844	1%

Source of PAC Dollars by Sector

Source	Total	Pct
■ Business	$129,008	98%
▨ Labor	$0	0%
☐ Ideology/Single Issue	$2,950	2%

In-State vs. Out-of-State Contributions*

Source	Total	Pct
☐ In-State	$191,477	97%
■ Out-of-state	$6,200	3%
No state listed	$0	

* by large individual contributors ($200 & above)

Construction	$17,750	
General Contractors	**$7,250**	
Browning Construction Co	$2,000	Indiv
HB Zachry Co	$2,000	Indiv
Associated General Contractors	$1,000	PAC
Embree Construction Group	$1,000	Indiv
Home Builders	**$5,300**	
National Assn of Home Builders	$2,300	PAC
Art Homes Inc	$2,000	Indiv
Ray Ellison Industries	$1,000	PAC
Building Materials & Equipment	**$4,050**	
Steves & Sons	$2,000	Indiv
Holt Companies	$1,000	Indiv

Defense	$6,950	
Defense Aerospace	**$3,200**	
None over $1,000		
Misc Defense	**$3,500**	
Insilco Corp	$3,000	PAC

Energy & Natural Resources	$49,350	
Oil & Gas	**$43,150**	
Earle M Craig Jr Corp	$4,000	Indiv
Bass Brothers Enterprises	$2,000	Indiv
Meredith Mallory Jr Invest	$2,000	Indiv
Newman Brothers Drilling	$2,000	Indiv
Osborn Heirs Co	$2,000	Indiv
Petro Engineer	$2,000	Indiv
Tesoro Petroleum Corp	$2,000	Indiv
Venus Oil Co	$2,000	Indiv
WB Osborn Oil & Gas	$2,000	Indiv
Loates Energy Oil & Gas	$1,950	Indiv
Valero Energy Corp	$1,500	Indiv
Del Ray Oil Co	$1,000	Indiv
Robert B Holt Co	$1,000	Indiv
Electric Utilities	**$6,200**	
Texas Utilities Co	$3,000	PAC

Contribution Totals by Sector

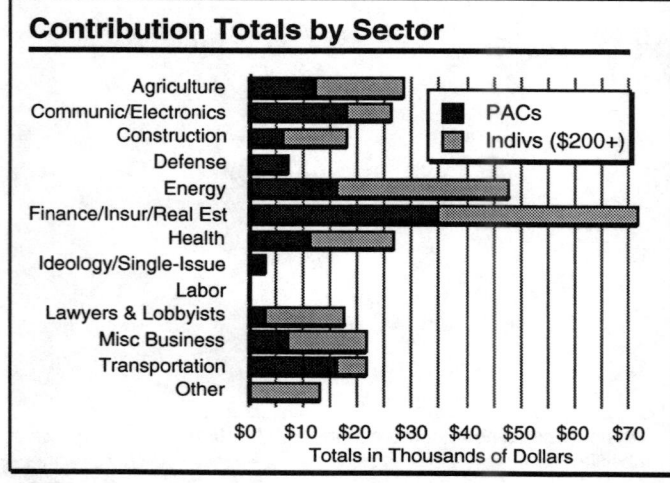

Totals in Thousands of Dollars

- PACs
- Indivs ($200+)

Categories: Agriculture, Communic/Electronics, Construction, Defense, Energy, Finance/Insur/Real Est, Health, Ideology/Single-Issue, Labor, Lawyers & Lobbyists, Misc Business, Transportation, Other

Scale: $0 $10 $20 $30 $40 $50 $60 $70

Houston Industries ....$2,000 PAC

Finance, Insurance & Real Estate $71,301

Commercial Banks $8,912
    Citizens & Southern National Bank ....$2,500 PAC
    American Bankers Assn ....$2,000 PAC
    Barnett Banks Inc ....$1,000 PAC

Securities & Investment $3,450
    Duncan Smith ....$1,000 Indiv
    Hixon Properties Inc ....$1,000 Indiv

Insurance $18,089
    American Council of Life Insurance ....$2,600 PAC
    United Services Automobile Assn Group ....$2,050 PAC
    National Assn of Life Underwriters.....................$2,000 PAC
    Catto & Catto ....$1,000 Indiv

Real Estate $13,950
    National Assn of Realtors ....$6,000 PAC
    Hovenden Co ....$2,000 Indiv
    Meek & Associates ....$1,000 Indiv

Accountants $6,000
    American Institute of CPA's ....$5,000 PAC

Misc Finance $20,600
    None over $1,000

Health $26,050

Health Professionals $23,050
    American Medical Assn* ....$7,300 PAC

Pharmaceuticals/Health Products $2,750
    None over $1,000

Lawyers & Lobbyists $17,349

Lawyers & Lobbyists $17,349
    Stubbeman, McRae & Sealy ....$5,000 Indiv
    Akin, Gump et al ....$1,600 PAC
    Matthews & Branscomb ....$1,499 Indiv
    Kaufman, Becker et al ....$1,000 Indiv

Misc Business $21,477

Food & Beverage $2,020
    None over $1,000

Beer, Wine & Liquor $2,500

Block Distributing ....$2,000 Indiv

Retail Sales $3,507
    National Assn of Convenience Stores ....$1,000 PAC

Misc Services $1,000
    None over $1,000

Business Services $4,500
    Atherton Capital Inc ....$1,000 Indiv
    Henry C Beck Co ....$1,000 Indiv

Chemical & Related Manufacturing $1,000
    Dow Chemical ....$1,000 PAC

Steel Production $2,000
    KLN Steel Products ....$2,000 Indiv

Misc Manufacturing & Distributing $2,900
    Crown Equipment Corp ....$1,000 Indiv

Transportation $21,300

Air Transport $4,200
    United Parcel Service ....$2,000 PAC
    Texas Air ....$1,100 PAC

Automotive $12,750
    National Auto Dealers Assn ....$6,800 PAC
    NAPA Auto Parts..$2,000 Indiv
    Auto Dealers & Drivers for Free Trade ....$1,500 PAC
    Americans for Free International Trade ....$1,000 PAC

Railroads $1,600
    None over $1,000

Sea Transport $2,500
    Lykes Brothers Steamship Co ....$2,000 Indiv

Ideological/Single-Issue

Ideological/Single-Issue $2,950

Misc Issues $2,600
    Fair PAC ....$1,000 PAC

Other & Unknown

Other $12,650

Retired $12,150
    None over $1,000

Unknown $28,658

    Homemakers/Non-income earners $11,750
    No Employer Listed or Found $1,700
    Generic Occupation/Category Unknown $3,000
    Employer Listed/Category Unknown $12,208
       Alamo Group ....$1,000 Indiv
       Patricia Z Johnson Interests ....$1,000 Indiv
       Promotion Network ....$1,000 Indiv
       Stringfellow Investments ....$1,000 Indiv

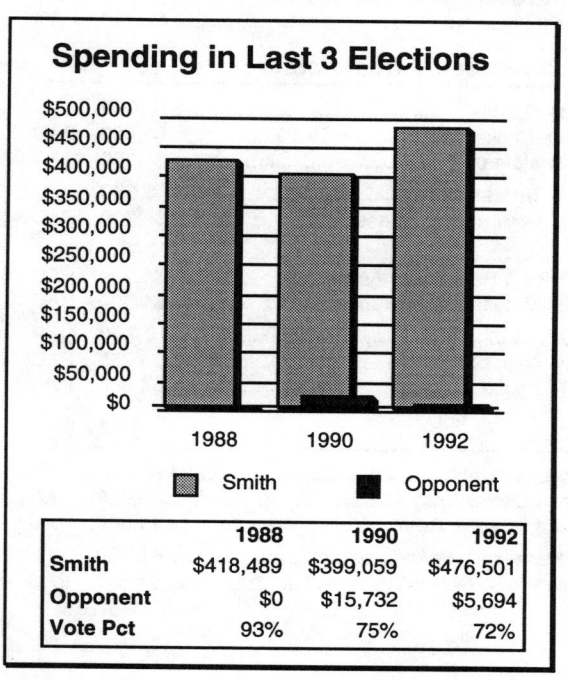

Spending in Last 3 Elections

	1988	1990	1992
Smith	$418,489	$399,059	$476,501
Opponent	$0	$15,732	$5,694
Vote Pct	93%	75%	72%

Legend: ▨ Smith   ■ Opponent

---

* Contributions came from more than one affiliate or subsidiary.

Neal Smith, D-Iowa (4)

First elected: 1958

1991-92 Total Receipts: $324,231
1992 Year-end Cash: $502,580

1991-92 Committees & Subcommittees

Appropriations
Agriculture, Rural Development, Food and Drug Administration and Related Agencies; Commerce, Justice, State, the Judiciary, and Related Agencies (Chairman); Labor, Health and Human Services, Education and Related Agencies

Small Business
SBA, the General Economy and Minority Enterprise Development

Leading Contributors

Business

Agriculture		$26,750
Crop Production & Basic Processing $7,000		
None over $1,500		
Dairy $4,000		
Associated Milk Producers $1,500	PAC	
Livestock $1,500		
National Pork Producers Council $1,500	PAC	
Agricultural Services/Products $6,750		
None over $1,500		
Food Processing & Sales $6,500		
Food Marketing Institute $2,000	PAC	
Kellogg Co $1,500	PAC	

Communications/Electronics		$17,650
Media/Entertainment $5,250		
National Cable Television Assn $3,000	PAC	
National Assn of Broadcasters $2,000	PAC	
Telephone Utilities $7,150		
US West Inc $3,000	PAC	
BellSouth Corp* $1,500	PAC	
Computer Equipment & Services $3,500		
Electronic Data Systems $1,500	PAC	

Construction		$6,350
General Contractors $2,000		
None over $1,500		
Home Builders $3,000		
National Assn of Home Builders $2,000	PAC	

Source of Funds in 1992 Election

	Source	Total	Pct
■	PACs	$209,300	61%
▨	Indivs $200+	$55,993	16%
☐	Indivs under $200	$5,287	2%
⊠	Other	$75,260	22%
	Candidate	$0	0%
	Party	$22,059	6%

Source of PAC Dollars by Sector

	Source	Total	Pct
■	Business	$141,200	68%
▨	Labor	$55,349	27%
☐	Ideology/Single Issue	$10,500	5%

In-State vs. Out-of-State Contributions*

	Source	Total	Pct
☐	In-State	$29,543	54%
■	Out-of-state	$24,950	46%
	No state listed	$0	

* by large individual contributors ($200 & above)

Defense		$16,000
Defense Aerospace $5,500		
General Electric $2,000	PAC	
Defense Electronics $10,000		
AT&T $2,500	PAC	
Computer Sciences Corp $2,500	PAC	
GTE Corp $2,000	PAC	

Energy & Natural Resources		$6,250
Electric Utilities $5,500		
ACRE (Action Cmte for Rural Electrification)* $2,500	PAC	
Iowa Resources Inc $2,000	PAC	

Finance, Insurance & Real Estate		$35,500
Commercial Banks $10,000		
American Bankers Assn* $1,500	PAC	
First Interstate of Iowa $1,500	PAC	
Securities & Investment $6,000		
National Venture Capital Assn $4,500	PAC	
Insurance $7,750		
Blue Cross & Blue Shield Assn $1,500	PAC	
Principal Mutual Life Insurance $1,500	PAC	
Real Estate $10,750		
National Assn of Realtors $5,750	PAC	
Iowa Realty Co $4,000	Indiv	

Health		$17,650
Health Professionals $15,600		
American Dental Assn $5,000	PAC	
American Podiatry Assn $1,500	PAC	
Hospitals/Nursing Homes $1,750		
American Hospital Assn $1,500	PAC	

Contribution Totals by Sector

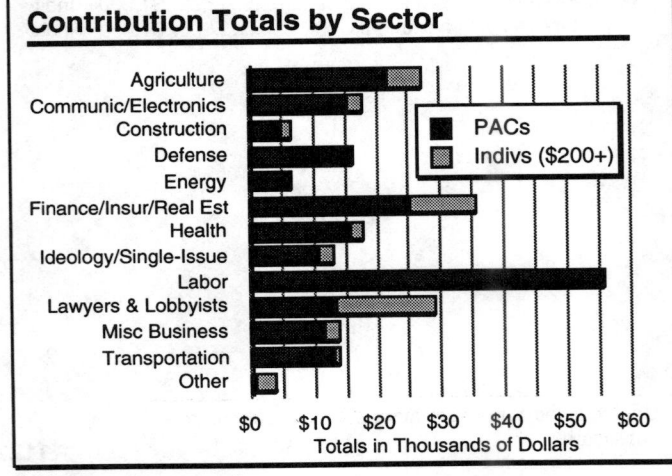

Agriculture
Communic/Electronics
Construction
Defense
Energy
Finance/Insur/Real Est
Health
Ideology/Single-Issue
Labor
Lawyers & Lobbyists
Misc Business
Transportation
Other

■ PACs
▨ Indivs ($200+)

$0 $10 $20 $30 $40 $50 $60
Totals in Thousands of Dollars

Lawyers & Lobbyists $28,743

Lawyers & Lobbyists $28,743
  Assn of Trial Lawyers of America .... $5,500 PAC
  Arent, Fox et al .... $2,000 PAC
  CR Associates .... $2,000 Indiv
  Neece, Cator & Associates .... $2,000 Indiv

Misc Business $13,800

Business Associations $1,500
  None over $1,500
Food & Beverage $1,750
  None over $1,500
Beer, Wine & Liquor $2,000
  None over $1,500
Business Services $3,750
  Ken Schlossberg Associates .... $1,500 Indiv
Lodging/Tourism $1,950
  None over $1,500
Misc Manufacturing & Distributing $1,500
  None over $1,500

Transportation $13,550

Air Transport $7,000
  United Parcel Service .... $3,500 PAC
  Aircraft Owners & Pilots Assn .... $3,000 PAC
Automotive $2,500
  National Auto Dealers Assn .... $1,500 PAC
Railroads $2,000
  None over $1,500

Labor

Labor $55,349

Building Trade Unions $12,500
  Carpenters & Joiners Union .... $5,000 PAC
  Laborers' Political League .... $5,000 PAC
  Plumbers/Pipefitters Union .... $2,000 PAC
Industrial Unions $3,100
  United Auto Workers .... $1,500 PAC
Transportation Unions $9,750
  Marine Engineers Union* .... $2,500 PAC
  Teamsters Union .... $2,500 PAC
  United Transportation Union .... $1,500 PAC
Public Sector Unions $21,000
  American Federation of Teachers .... $5,000 PAC
  American Fedn of St/Cnty/Munic Employees ...... $5,000 PAC
  National Education Assn .... $3,000 PAC
  National Assn Retired Federal Employees .... $2,000 PAC
  National Rural Letter Carriers Assn .... $1,500 PAC
Misc Unions $8,999
  Food & Commercial Workers Union .... $7,999 PAC

Ideological/Single-Issue

Ideological/Single-Issue $13,000

Foreign & Defense Policy $6,500
  Free Cuba PAC .... $5,500 PAC
Gun Rights/Gun Control $2,500
  National Rifle Assn .... $2,500 PAC
Misc Issues $2,500
  National Cmte to Preserve Social Security .... $2,500 PAC

Other & Unknown

Other $3,500

Education $1,500
  None over $1,500
Retired $1,500
  None over $1,500

Unknown $8,450

  Generic Occupation/Category Unknown $1,950
  Employer Listed/Category Unknown $4,500
    None over $1,500

Spending in Last 3 Elections

	1988	1990	1992
Smith	$83,474	$56,903	$197,159
Opponent	$0	$0	$11,178
Vote Pct	72%	98%	62%

* Contributions came from more than one affiliate or subsidiary.

Nick Smith, R-Mich (7)

1993-94 Committees & Subcommittees

First elected: 1992

1991-92 Total Receipts:	$228,408
1992 Year-end Cash:	$11,862

Agriculture
Environment, Credit and Rural Development; General Farm Commodities

Budget

Science, Space and Technology
Science; Technology, Environment and Aviation

Leading Contributors

Business

Agriculture	**$4,815**

Crop Production & Basic Processing	$2,200	
None over $1,000		
Agricultural Services/Products	$1,500	
Veterinarian	$1,000	Indiv

Construction	**$2,000**

Building Materials & Equipment	$1,200	
Addison Products	$1,000	Indiv

Energy & Natural Resources	**$1,200**

Oil & Gas	$1,200	
Patrick Petroleum	$1,000	Indiv

Finance, Insurance & Real Estate	**$9,900**

Insurance	$2,550	
None over $1,000		
Accountants	$4,500	
Ernst & Young	$1,000	Indiv
Misc Finance	$1,700	
None over $1,000		

Health	**$9,200**

Health Professionals	$8,700	
None over $1,000		

Source of Funds in 1992 Election

Source	Total	Pct
PACs	$0	0%
Indivs $200+	$78,192	34%
Indivs under $200	$49,634	22%
Other	$100,582	44%
Candidate	$97,500	43%
Party	$400	0%

Source of PAC Dollars by Sector

No PAC contributions reported

Source	Total	Pct
Business	$0	0%
Labor	$0	0%
Ideology/Single Issue	$0	0%

In-State vs. Out-of-State Contributions*

Source	Total	Pct
In-State	$74,692	96%
Out-of-state	$3,500	4%
No state listed	$0	

* by large individual contributors ($200 & above)

Lawyers & Lobbyists	**$1,050**

Lawyers & Lobbyists	$1,050	
None over $1,000		

Misc Business	**$3,300**

Food & Beverage	$1,500	
Fishbone's Cafe	$1,000	Indiv
Steel Production	$1,300	
Alro Steel	$1,000	Indiv

Transportation	**$6,400**

Automotive	$5,400	
Nippondenso America	$2,200	Indiv
Michigan Automotive	$2,000	Indiv
Trucking	$1,000	
Miller Trucking	$1,000	Indiv

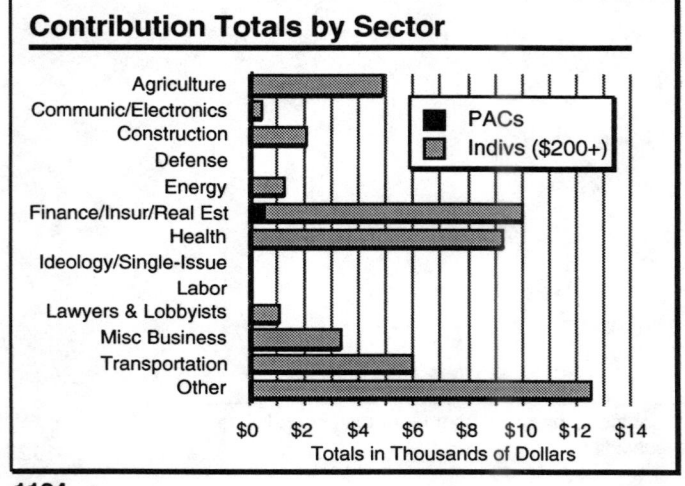

Contribution Totals by Sector

Agriculture, Communic/Electronics, Construction, Defense, Energy, Finance/Insur/Real Est, Health, Ideology/Single-Issue, Labor, Lawyers & Lobbyists, Misc Business, Transportation, Other

PACs
Indivs ($200+)

$0 $2 $4 $6 $8 $10 $12 $14
Totals in Thousands of Dollars

Other & Unknown

Other $12,427

Education..**$2,300**

    University of Michigan ....$2,000   Indiv

Retired...**$9,650**

    None over $1,000

Unknown $28,000

    Homemakers/Non-income earners $1,000

    No Employer Listed or Found $13,200

    Generic Occupation/Category Unknown $3,400

    Employer Listed/Category Unknown $10,400

        Greektown ....$2,000   Indiv

        Mackey Corp ....$1,150   Indiv

        Maci Corp ....$1,000   Indiv

Independent expenditures supporting Smith

    Right to Life/Michigan $2,494

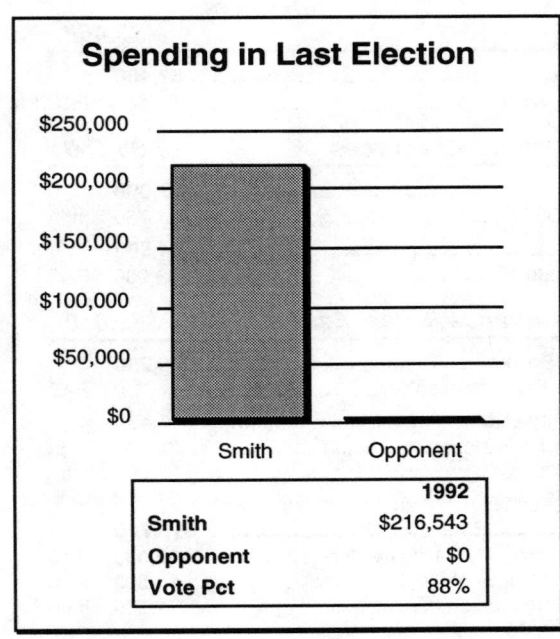

	1992
Smith	$216,543
Opponent	$0
Vote Pct	88%

Olympia J. Snowe, R-Maine (2)

First elected: 1978

1991-92 Total Receipts: $747,300
1992 Year-end Cash: $799

1991-92 Committees & Subcommittees

Foreign Affairs
Arms Control, International Security and Science; International Operations (Ranking Republican)

Select Committee on Aging

Joint Economic Committee

Leading Contributors

Business

Agriculture	$44,973	
Crop Production & Basic Processing	**$4,900**	
West Breeze Orchards	$2,150	Indiv
Tobacco	**$1,500**	
None over $1,500		
Dairy	**$4,500**	
West Lynn Creamery	$2,500	Indiv
Agricultural Services/Products	**$2,000**	
None over $1,500		
Food Processing & Sales	**$6,700**	
Mary Ann's Baking Co	$2,000	Indiv
Forestry & Forest Products	**$24,873**	
International Paper Co	$10,000	PAC
Boise Cascade	$3,000	PAC
Georgia-Pacific Corp	$2,273	PAC
Westvaco Corp	$2,000	PAC
Champion International Corp	$1,850	PAC

Communications/Electronics	$16,100	
Printing & Publishing	**$4,300**	
None over $1,500		
Telephone Utilities	**$6,050**	
AT&T	$2,000	PAC
NYNEX Corp*	$1,700	PAC
Telecom Services & Equipment	**$2,550**	
Comsat	$1,550	PAC

Contribution Totals by Sector

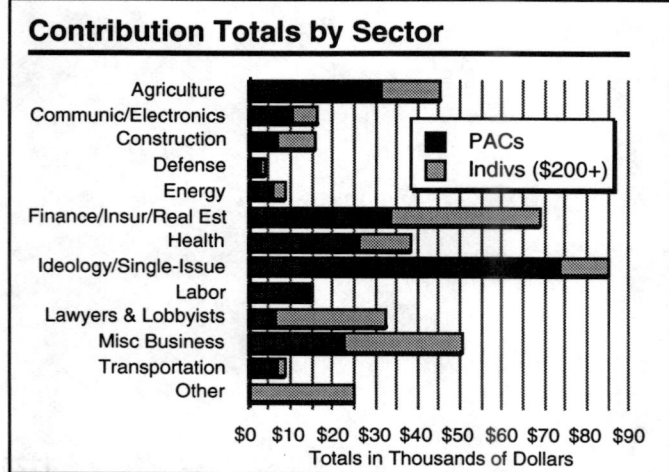

Legend: ■ PACs ▧ Indivs ($200+)

Agriculture
Communic/Electronics
Construction
Defense
Energy
Finance/Insur/Real Est
Health
Ideology/Single-Issue
Labor
Lawyers & Lobbyists
Misc Business
Transportation
Other

$0 $10 $20 $30 $40 $50 $60 $70 $80 $90
Totals in Thousands of Dollars

Source of Funds in 1992 Election

Source	Total	Pct
■ PACs	$239,559	30%
▧ Indivs $200+	$208,243	26%
□ Indivs under $200	$258,099	33%
▨ Other	$85,756	11%
Candidate	$0	0%
Party	$57,555	7%

Source of PAC Dollars by Sector

Source	Total	Pct
■ Business	$148,098	63%
▨ Labor	$14,750	6%
□ Ideology/Single Issue	$73,049	31%

In-State vs. Out-of-State Contributions*

Source	Total	Pct
□ In-State	$90,375	43%
■ Out-of-state	$117,468	57%
No state listed	$400	

* by large individual contributors ($200 & above)

Construction	$16,500	
General Contractors	**$8,200**	
Speedway Inc	$3,000	Indiv
Associated General Contractors	$2,750	PAC
Home Builders	**$2,750**	
None over $1,500		
Special Trade Contractors	**$2,250**	
None over $1,500		
Construction Services	**$1,500**	
None over $1,500		
Building Materials & Equipment	**$1,800**	
None over $1,500		

Defense	$3,468	
Misc Defense	**$2,468**	
Bath Iron Works	$2,468	PAC/Ind

Energy & Natural Resources	$8,450	
Oil & Gas	**$2,000**	
Webber Oil Co	$1,750	Indiv
Misc Energy	**$4,500**	
Cooper Industries	$3,000	PAC

Finance, Insurance & Real Estate	$69,650	
Commercial Banks	**$9,250**	
American Bankers Assn*	$4,750	PAC
Securities & Investment	**$14,450**	
John Head & Partners	$2,250	Indiv
William Blair & Co	$2,000	Indiv
Boston Co	$1,800	Indiv
Insurance	**$15,700**	
National Assn of Life Underwriters	$2,000	PAC
American Council of Life Insurance	$1,500	PAC
Dunlap Corp	$1,500	Indiv

Real Estate **$29,000**
    National Assn of Realtors .... $10,000   PAC
    AKT Development Co .... $8,250   Indiv
    Albert B Glickman & Assoc .... $2,000   Indiv
    SKK Development Co .... $2,000   Indiv

Health $37,700

Health Professionals **$28,200**
    American Medical Assn .... $10,000   PAC
    American Dental Assn .... $3,500   PAC
    American Nurses Assn .... $1,500   PAC
Hospitals/Nursing Homes **$2,700**
    None over $1,500
Pharmaceuticals/Health Products **$6,100**
    Kos Pharmaceuticals Inc .... $3,400   Indiv

Lawyers & Lobbyists $31,950

Lawyers & Lobbyists **$31,950**
    Assn of Trial Lawyers of America .... $5,000   PAC
    Verrill & Dana .... $1,750   Indiv
    Timmons & Co .... $1,500   Indiv

Misc Business $50,125

Business Associations **$3,530**
    National Fedn of Independent Business .... $1,500   PAC
Food & Beverage **$2,300**
    None over $1,500
Retail Sales **$9,700**
    Dexter Shoe Co .... $2,000   Indiv
    Ecology House .... $2,000   Indiv
    International Council of Shopping Centers .... $2,000   PAC
Business Services **$8,900**
    Institutional Shareholder Service .... $3,000   Indiv
Misc Manufacturing & Distributing ... **$10,700**
    Corning Glass Works .... $5,000   PAC
    Hoechst Celanese Corp .... $2,500   PAC
Textiles **$9,750**
    Milliken & Co .... $4,000   Indiv
    Robinson Manufacturing Co .... $3,000   Indiv

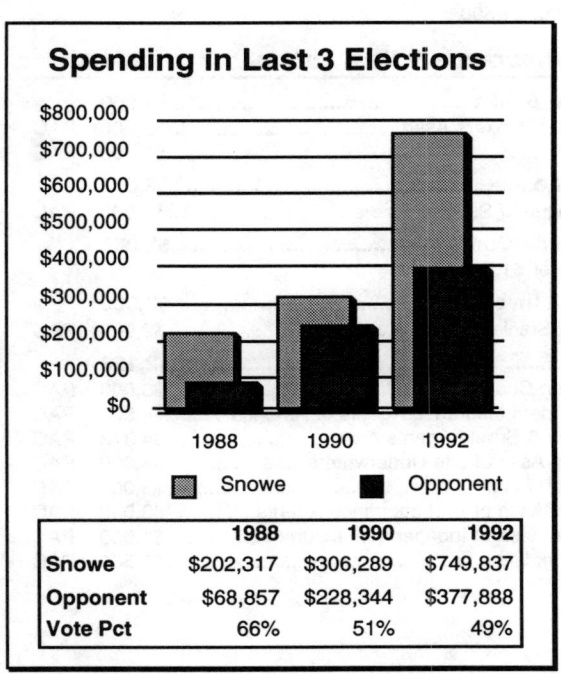

Spending in Last 3 Elections

	1988	1990	1992
Snowe	$202,317	$306,289	$749,837
Opponent	$68,857	$228,344	$377,888
Vote Pct	66%	51%	49%

Transportation $8,550

Air Transport **$2,850**
    General Electric .... $2,050   PAC
Automotive **$1,750**
    None over $1,500
Sea Transport **$2,250**
    None over $1,500

Labor

Labor $14,750

Industrial Unions **$1,750**
    None over $1,500
Transportation Unions **$10,500**
    Marine Engineers Union* .... $9,500   PAC
Public Sector Unions **$2,500**
    National Assn Retired Federal Employees .... $2,000   PAC

Ideological/Single-Issue

Ideological/Single-Issue $83,549

Republican/Conservative **$6,000**
    Leader PAC .... $5,000   PAC
Leadership PACs **$2,227**
    None over $1,500
Pro-Israel **$8,000**
    National PAC .... $5,000   PAC
Pro-Choice **$10,200**
    National Abortion Rights Action League .... $5,500   PAC
    Pro-Choice America .... $2,700   PAC
Gun Rights/Gun Control **$5,450**
    National Rifle Assn .... $5,450   PAC
Womens Issues **$27,172**
    Women's Campaign Fund .... $10,000   PAC
    National Womens Political Caucus .... $6,000   PAC
    Wish List .... $5,672   PAC
Human Rights **$13,500**
    Dynamis .... $10,000   PAC
Misc Issues **$9,250**
    National Cmte to Preserve Social Security .... $8,000   PAC

Other & Unknown

Other $24,400

Civil Servants/Public Officials **$1,900**
    None over $1,500
Education **$1,750**
    None over $1,500
Retired **$20,000**
    None over $1,500

Unknown $33,975

    Homemakers/Non-income earners $7,200
    No Employer Listed or Found $2,200
    Generic Occupation/Category Unknown $2,250
    Employer Listed/Category Unknown $22,325
        International Management Group .... $1,600   Indiv

Independent expenditures supporting Snowe
    National Cmte to Preserve Social Security $3,236

---

* Contributions came from more than one affiliate or subsidiary.

Gerald B. H. Solomon, R-NY (22)

First elected: 1978

1991-92 Total Receipts: $384,095
1992 Year-end Cash: $210,627

1991-92 Committees & Subcommittees

Rules (Ranking Republican)
Rules of the House

Leading Contributors

Business

Agriculture		$20,500
Tobacco	**$6,500**	
Philip Morris	$2,000	PAC
RJR Nabisco	$2,000	PAC
Dairy	**$3,650**	
Associated Milk Producers	$2,000	PAC
Agricultural Services/Products	**$2,250**	
Farm Credit Council	$1,500	PAC
Food Processing & Sales	**$2,500**	
Food Marketing Institute.............	$1,500	PAC
Forestry & Forest Products	**$4,600**	
International Paper Co	$2,000	PAC
Scott Paper Co	$1,600	PAC

Communications/Electronics		$16,500
Media/Entertainment	**$3,500**	
National Cable Television Assn	$2,500	PAC
Telephone Utilities	**$10,500**	
AT&T	$3,000	PAC
New York Telephone	$3,000	PAC
BellSouth Corp*	$2,250	PAC
Computer Equipment & Services	**$1,500**	
Electronic Data Systems	$1,500	PAC

Construction		$4,210
General Contractors	**$1,710**	
Associated General Contractors	$1,500	PAC

Source of Funds in 1992 Election

Source	Total	Pct
■ PACs	$282,680	74%
▦ Indivs $200+	$33,960	9%
☐ Indivs under $200	$54,851	14%
▨ Other	$12,604	3%
Candidate	$0	0%
Party	$0	0%

Source of PAC Dollars by Sector

Source	Total	Pct
■ Business	$209,323	74%
▦ Labor	$59,460	21%
☐ Ideology/Single Issue	$12,400	4%

In-State vs. Out-of-State Contributions*

Source	Total	Pct
☐ In-State	$16,660	50%
■ Out-of-state	$16,800	50%
No state listed	$500	

* by large individual contributors ($200 & above)

Defense		$11,500
Defense Aerospace	**$9,000**	
Northrop Corp	$2,000	PAC
General Dynamics	$1,500	PAC
McDonnell Douglas	$1,500	PAC
Defense Electronics	**$2,000**	
None over $1,500		

Energy & Natural Resources		$11,110
Oil & Gas	**$6,670**	
Petroleum Marketers Assn	$2,500	PAC
Electric Utilities	**$3,390**	
None over $1,500		

Finance, Insurance & Real Estate		$74,893
Commercial Banks	**$6,900**	
American Bankers Assn	$2,000	PAC
Citicorp	$2,000	PAC
Savings & Loans	**$2,660**	
US League of Savings Assns	$1,500	PAC
Finance/Credit Companies	**$2,000**	
None over $1,500		
Securities & Investment	**$3,000**	
Morgan Stanley & Co	$2,000	PAC
Insurance	**$42,123**	
American Council of Life Insurance	$8,000	PAC
Independent Insurance Agents of America	$4,500	PAC
Casualty & Surety Agents Assn	$4,373	PAC
National Assn of Life Underwriters	$4,000	PAC
American Family Corp	$3,000	PAC
National Assn of Prof Insurance Agents	$3,000	PAC
National Assn of Independent Insurers	$1,500	PAC
New York Life	$1,500	PAC

Contribution Totals by Sector

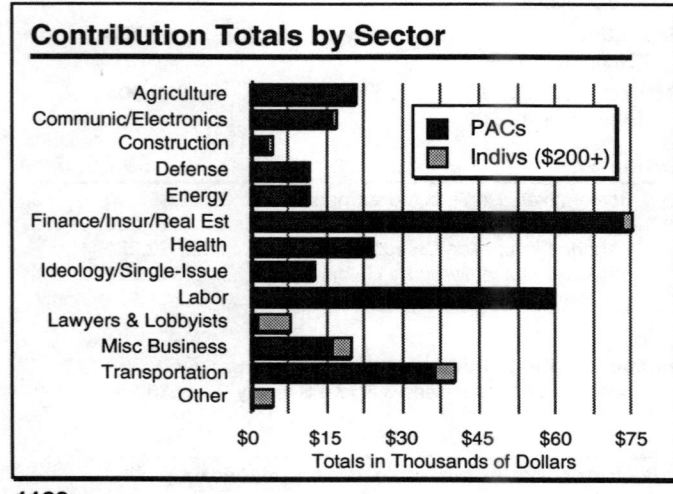

Agriculture
Communic/Electronics
Construction
Defense
Energy
Finance/Insur/Real Est
Health
Ideology/Single-Issue
Labor
Lawyers & Lobbyists
Misc Business
Transportation
Other

■ PACs
▦ Indivs ($200+)

$0 $15 $30 $45 $60 $75
Totals in Thousands of Dollars

Real Estate	....	**$11,000**	
National Assn of Realtors	....	$9,000	PAC
Accountants	....	**$5,000**	
American Institute of CPA's	....	$5,000	PAC

Health — *$23,910*

Health Professionals	....	**$17,410**	
American Medical Assn*	....	$10,000	PAC
American Dental Assn	....	$3,000	PAC
American Optometric Assn	....	$1,500	PAC
Pharmaceuticals/Health Products	....	**$6,000**	
Sterling Drug	....	$2,500	PAC
Ciba-Geigy Corp	....	$1,500	PAC

Lawyers & Lobbyists — *$7,210*

Lawyers & Lobbyists	....	**$7,210**	
Neill & Co	....	$1,750	Indiv
Evans Group	....	$1,500	Indiv

Misc Business — *$19,500*

Beer, Wine & Liquor	....	**$3,500**	
National Beer Wholesalers Assn	....	$1,500	PAC
Lodging/Tourism	....	**$3,050**	
Holiday Inns	....	$1,500	PAC
Chemical & Related Manufacturing	....	**$3,750**	
BASF Corp	....	$3,250	Indiv
Misc Manufacturing & Distributing	....	**$5,200**	
Corning Glass Works	....	$2,000	PAC
Textiles	....	**$2,000**	
American Textile Manufacturers Institute	....	$1,500	PAC

Transportation — *$39,460*

Air Transport	....	**$21,980**	
General Electric	....	$8,150	PAC/Ind
Federal Express Corp	....	$5,000	PAC
Aircraft Owners & Pilots Assn	....	$4,000	PAC
United Parcel Service	....	$2,280	PAC
Automotive	....	**$9,250**	
National Auto Dealers Assn	....	$3,000	PAC
Auto Dealers & Drivers for Free Trade	....	$1,500	PAC

Trucking	....	**$2,730**	
American Trucking Assns	....	$1,520	PAC
Railroads	....	**$3,000**	
Union Pacific Corp	....	$1,500	PAC
Sea Transport	....	**$2,500**	
None over $1,500			

Labor

Labor — *$59,460*

Building Trade Unions	....	**$6,000**	
Laborers' Political League	....	$3,000	PAC
Industrial Unions	....	**$5,000**	
Intl Brotherhood of Electrical Workers	....	$2,500	PAC
Transportation Unions	....	**$33,210**	
Air Line Pilots Assn	....	$10,000	PAC
Marine Engineers Dist 2 Maritime Officers	....	$10,000	PAC
Seafarers International Union	....	$5,500	PAC
Teamsters Union	....	$2,500	PAC
United Transportation Union	....	$2,140	PAC
Trans Comm International Union	....	$1,500	PAC
Public Sector Unions	....	**$15,250**	
National Assn of Letter Carriers	....	$11,400	PAC
National Assn Retired Federal Employees	....	$3,000	PAC

Ideological/Single-Issue

Ideological/Single-Issue — *$12,400*

Gun Rights/Gun Control	....	**$9,900**	
National Rifle Assn	....	$9,900	PAC
Misc Issues	....	**$2,500**	
National Cmte to Preserve Social Security	....	$2,000	PAC

Other & Unknown

Other — *$3,970*

Education	....	**$1,800**	
None over $1,500			
Retired	....	**$2,170**	
None over $1,500			

Unknown — *$10,520*

No Employer Listed or Found	....	$3,010	
Employer Listed/Category Unknown	....	$7,510	
None over $1,500			

Independent expenditures supporting Solomon
National Right to Life PAC $3,895

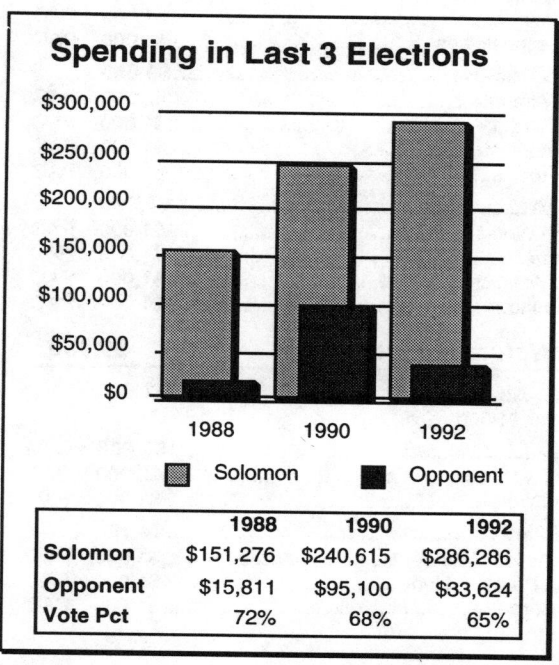

Spending in Last 3 Elections

	1988	1990	1992
Solomon	$151,276	$240,615	$286,286
Opponent	$15,811	$95,100	$33,624
Vote Pct	72%	68%	65%

---

* Contributions came from more than one affiliate or subsidiary.

Floyd D. Spence, R-SC (2)

First elected: 1970

1991-92 Total Receipts: $169,036
1992 Year-end Cash: $51,688

1991-92 Committees & Subcommittees

Armed Services
Military Installations and Facilities; Seapower and Strategic and Critical Materials (Ranking Republican)

Veterans' Affairs
Compensation, Pension and Insurance

Select Committee on Aging

Leading Contributors

Business

Agriculture		$11,000
Crop Production & Basic Processing $5,700		
American Crystal Sugar Corp $1,000	PAC	
American Sugarbeet Growers Assn $1,000	PAC	
Florida Sugar Cane League $1,000	PAC	
Tobacco $1,000		
None over $1,000		
Dairy $1,000		
Dairymen Inc $1,000	PAC	
Food Processing & Sales $1,000		
None over $1,000		
Forestry & Forest Products $1,000		
Union Camp Corp $1,000	PAC	

Communications/Electronics		$4,250
Telephone Utilities $3,500		
Southern Bell $3,500	PAC	

Construction		$5,450
General Contractors $2,700		
Fluor Corp $1,000	PAC	
RPR & Associates $1,000	Indiv	
Home Builders $1,000		
National Assn of Home Builders $1,000	PAC	
Construction Services $1,500		
Jacobs Engineering Group $1,000	PAC	

Source of Funds in 1992 Election

Source	Total	Pct
■ PACs	$108,900	64%
▨ Indivs $200+	$7,650	5%
☐ Indivs under $200	$44,269	26%
▩ Other	$8,217	5%
Candidate	$0	0%
Party	$0	0%

Source of PAC Dollars by Sector

Source	Total	Pct
■ Business	$107,450	95%
▨ Labor	$3,500	3%
☐ Ideology/Single Issue	$2,000	2%

In-State vs. Out-of-State Contributions*

Source	Total	Pct
☐ In-State	$5,250	69%
■ Out-of-state	$2,400	31%
No state listed	$0	

* by large individual contributors ($200 & above)

Defense		$32,850
Defense Aerospace $18,000		
General Dynamics $3,000	PAC	
Martin Marietta Corp $2,000	PAC	
McDonnell Douglas* $2,000	PAC	
Northrop Corp $1,500	PAC	
Colt Industries $1,000	PAC	
General Electric $1,000	PAC	
Grumman Corp $1,000	PAC	
LTV Aerospace & Defense Co $1,000	PAC	
Lockheed Corp $1,000	PAC	
Rockwell International $1,000	PAC	
Textron Inc $1,000	PAC	
United Technologies $1,000	PAC	
Defense Electronics $9,850		
Hughes Aircraft $2,500	PAC	
AT&T $1,600	PAC	
Litton Industries $1,000	PAC	
Loral Corp $1,000	PAC	
Misc Defense $5,000		
Bath Iron Works $1,000	PAC	
FMC Corp $1,000	PAC	
General Atomics $1,000	PAC	
Tenneco Inc $1,000	PAC	

Energy & Natural Resources		$9,850
Oil & Gas $1,000		
None over $1,000		
Misc Energy $3,000		
Babcock & Wilcox $2,000	PAC	
Bechtel Corp $1,000	PAC	
Electric Utilities $4,100		
ACRE (Action Cmte for Rural Electrification) $1,000	PAC	
Carolina Power & Light $1,000	PAC	
Scana Corp $1,000	PAC	

Contribution Totals by Sector

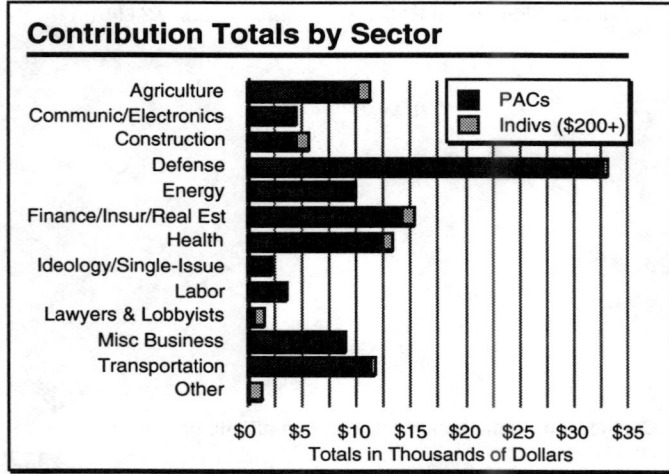

Legend: ■ PACs ▨ Indivs ($200+)

Agriculture
Communic/Electronics
Construction
Defense
Energy
Finance/Insur/Real Est
Health
Ideology/Single-Issue
Labor
Lawyers & Lobbyists
Misc Business
Transportation
Other

$0 $5 $10 $15 $20 $25 $30 $35
Totals in Thousands of Dollars

Finance, Insurance & Real Estate — $15,150

Commercial Banks **$3,100**
    Citizens & Southern National Bank .... $2,000 PAC
    South Carolina National Bank .... $1,000 PAC

Insurance **$6,250**
    Colonial Life & Accident Insurance .... $2,250 PAC/Ind
    Liberty Corp .... $1,000 PAC
    National Assn of Independent Insurers .... $1,000 PAC

Real Estate **$5,700**
    National Assn of Realtors .... $5,500 PAC

Health — $13,200

Health Professionals **$11,400**
    American Medical Assn .... $6,000 PAC
    American Chiropractic Assn .... $2,500 PAC
    American Dental Assn .... $2,000 PAC

Pharmaceuticals/Health Products **$1,300**
    None over $1,000

Lawyers & Lobbyists — $1,500

Lawyers & Lobbyists **$1,500**
    None over $1,000

Misc Business — $8,950

Beer, Wine & Liquor **$1,500**
    National Beer Wholesalers Assn .... $1,000 PAC

Retail Sales **$1,000**
    None over $1,000

Chemical & Related Manufacturing **$2,000**
    Eastman Kodak/Chemicals Division .... $1,000 PAC

Misc Manufacturing & Distributing **$1,700**
    Hoechst Celanese Corp .... $1,000 PAC

Textiles **$2,500**
    American Textile Manufacturers Institute .... $1,000 PAC

Transportation — $11,600

Air Transport **$4,000**
    United Parcel Service .... $3,500 PAC/Ind

Automotive **$6,500**
    National Auto Dealers Assn .... $5,000 PAC
    Auto Dealers & Drivers for Free Trade .... $1,500 PAC

Labor

Labor — $3,500

Transportation Unions **$3,500**
    Marine Engineers Dist 2 Maritime Officers .... $3,500 PAC

Ideological/Single-Issue

Ideological/Single-Issue — $2,000

Gun Rights/Gun Control **$2,000**
    National Rifle Assn .... $2,000 PAC

Other & Unknown

Other — $1,100
    None over $1,000

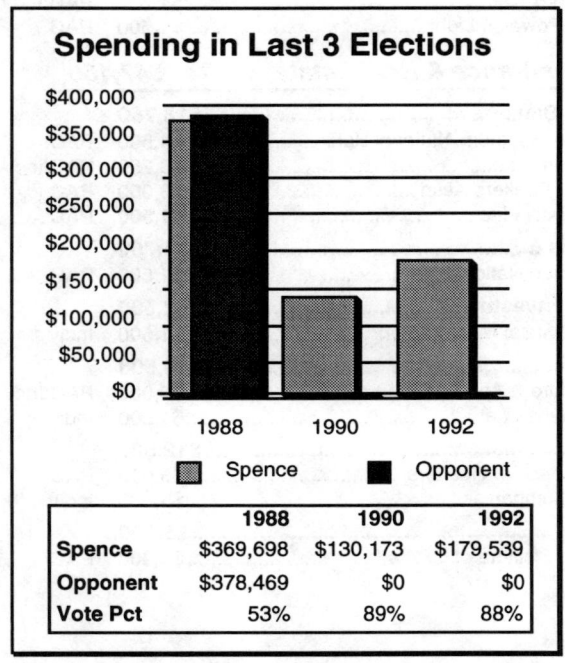

Spending in Last 3 Elections

	1988	1990	1992
Spence	$369,698	$130,173	$179,539
Opponent	$378,469	$0	$0
Vote Pct	53%	89%	88%

---

* Contributions came from more than one affiliate or subsidiary.

John M. Spratt Jr., D-SC (5)

First elected: 1982

1991-92 Total Receipts: $281,855
1992 Year-end Cash: $52,937

1991-92 Committees & Subcommittees

Armed Services
Investigations; Procurement and Military Nuclear Systems

Budget
Budget Process, Reconciliation and Enforcement; Defense, Foreign Policy and Space; Urgent Fiscal Issues

Leading Contributors

Business

Agriculture	$12,475

Crop Production & Basic Processing $1,725
  None over $1,500

Tobacco $2,500
  None over $1,500

Food Processing & Sales $2,500
  None over $1,500

Forestry & Forest Products $3,750
  None over $1,500

Communications/Electronics	$11,500

Telephone Utilities $7,750
  Southern Bell ....$4,000 PAC
  AT&T ....$3,000 PAC

Electronics Mfg & Services $1,500
  Westinghouse Electric ....$1,500 PAC

Construction	$8,600

General Contractors $6,750
  Fluor Corp ....$5,000 PAC

Defense	$23,900

Defense Aerospace $17,400
  Martin Marietta Corp ....$4,000 PAC
  Textron Inc ....$4,000 PAC
  General Dynamics ....$2,900 PAC/Ind
  Grumman Corp ....$1,500 PAC

Defense Electronics $5,500
  E-Systems Inc ....$1,500 PAC

Source of Funds in 1992 Election

Source	Total	Pct
■ PACs	$146,775	50%
▨ Indivs $200+	$87,050	30%
□ Indivs under $200	$28,736	10%
▧ Other	$30,173	10%
Candidate	$0	0%
Party	$11,329	4%

Source of PAC Dollars by Sector

Source	Total	Pct
■ Business	$137,800	91%
▨ Labor	$9,000	6%
□ Ideology/Single Issue	$4,750	3%

In-State vs. Out-of-State Contributions*

Source	Total	Pct
□ In-State	$38,800	45%
■ Out-of-state	$48,250	55%
No state listed	$0	

* by large individual contributors ($200 & above)

Energy & Natural Resources	$21,925

Oil & Gas $2,500
  None over $1,500

Nuclear Energy $9,000
  General Atomics ....$9,000 PAC

Misc Energy $2,000
  Bechtel Corp ....$1,500 PAC

Electric Utilities $7,925
  ACRE (Action Cmte for Rural Electrification) ....$2,925 PAC
  Duke Power Co ....$1,750 PAC/Ind
  Scana Corp ....$1,750 PAC/Ind
  Carolina Power & Light ....$1,500 PAC

Finance, Insurance & Real Estate	$47,150

Commercial Banks $13,750
  Citizens & Southern National Bank ....$4,500 PAC
  NCNB Corp ....$3,250 PAC/Ind
  American Bankers Assn ....$3,000 PAC
  Barnett Banks Inc ....$1,500 PAC

Credit Unions $1,750
  Credit Union National Assn ....$1,500 PAC

Securities & Investment $2,500
  Sterling Capital Management ....$1,500 Indiv

Insurance $10,500
  Colonial Life & Accident Insurance ....$5,000 PAC/Ind
  Barry, Evans et al ....$1,500 Indiv

Real Estate $12,500
  National Assn of Realtors ....$6,000 PAC
  Shelton Companies ....$3,000 Indiv

Accountants $5,500
  American Institute of CPA's ....$3,000 PAC

Contribution Totals by Sector

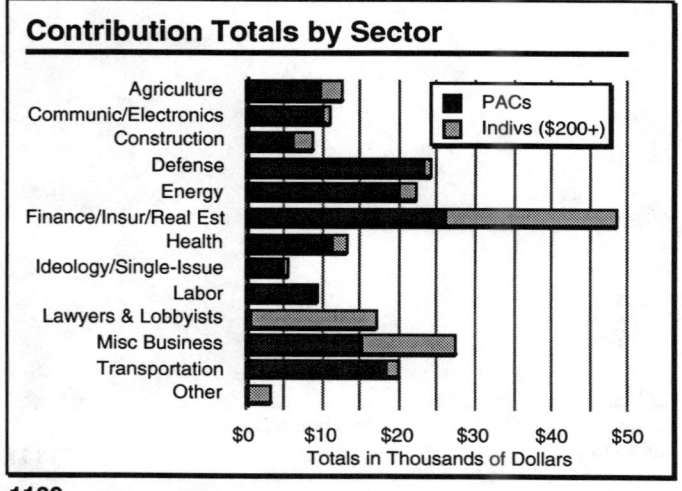

Legend: ■ PACs ▨ Indivs ($200+)

Categories: Agriculture, Communic/Electronics, Construction, Defense, Energy, Finance/Insur/Real Est, Health, Ideology/Single-Issue, Labor, Lawyers & Lobbyists, Misc Business, Transportation, Other

$0 $10 $20 $30 $40 $50
Totals in Thousands of Dollars

Health $12,950

Health Professionals $10,250
    American Medical Assn.............................$9,000   PAC
Hospitals/Nursing Homes $2,200
    None over $1,500

Lawyers & Lobbyists $16,950

Lawyers & Lobbyists $16,950
    Smith, Helms et al ....$2,250   Indiv
    Nelson, Mullins et al ....$1,750   Indiv
    Kennedy, Covington et al ....$1,500   Indiv

Misc Business $27,050

Retail Sales $2,000
    None over $1,500
Business Services $2,000
    None over $1,500
Chemical & Related Manufacturing $2,750
    FMC Corp ....$1,500   PAC
Misc Manufacturing & Distributing $6,900
    Hoechst Celanese Corp ....$4,000   PAC
Textiles $12,000
    Springs Mills ....$3,000   PAC
    Hamrick Mills ....$1,750   Indiv
    Springs Industries ....$1,750   Indiv
    Burlington Industries ....$1,500   PAC

Transportation $19,700

Air Transport $5,700
    United Parcel Service ....$2,500   PAC
Automotive $11,750
    National Auto Dealers Assn ....$5,000   PAC
    Torrington Co ....$5,000   PAC
Railroads $2,000
    None over $1,500

Labor

Labor $9,000

Building Trade Unions $1,500
    None over $1,500
Public Sector Unions $5,000
    None over $1,500
Misc Unions $1,500
    None over $1,500

Ideological/Single-Issue

Ideological/Single-Issue $5,500

Democratic/Liberal $2,500
    National Cmte for an Effective Congress ....$2,500   PAC
Human Rights $1,500
    None over $1,500

Other & Unknown

Other $2,950

Education $1,500
    University of North Carolina ....$1,500   Indiv

Unknown $18,950

    Homemakers/Non-income earners $2,950
    Employer Listed/Category Unknown $16,000
        Quest Capitol Corp ....$2,000   Indiv

---

Spending in Last 3 Elections

	1988	1990	1992
Spratt	$105,620	$173,157	$381,942
Opponent	$8,449	$0	$102,728
Vote Pct	70%	100%	61%

Pete Stark, D-Calif (13)

First elected: 1972

1991-92 Total Receipts: $634,494
1992 Year-end Cash: $400,792

1991-92 Committees & Subcommittees

District of Columbia
Fiscal Affairs and Health (Chairman); Government Operations and Metropolitan Affairs; Judiciary and Education

Ways and Means
Health; Select Revenue Measures

Select Committee on Narcotics Abuse and Control

Joint Economic Committee

Leading Contributors

Business

Agriculture		$5,550
Crop Production & Basic Processing	$1,750	
None over $1,500		
Food Processing & Sales	$3,500	
Food Marketing Institute	$2,000	PAC

Communications/Electronics		$8,500
Telephone Utilities	$3,750	
Pacific Telesis Group	$2,250	PAC
Computer Equipment & Services	$2,750	
Electronic Data Systems	$1,500	PAC

Construction		$3,250
Building Materials & Equipment	$2,000	
Jim Walter Corp	$2,000	PAC

Energy & Natural Resources		$4,500
Electric Utilities	$2,000	
Southern California Edison	$2,000	PAC/Ind

Source of Funds in 1992 Election

Source	Total	Pct
PACs	$348,944	55%
Indivs $200+	$110,800	17%
Indivs under $200	$69,656	11%
Other	$110,618	17%
Candidate	$0	0%
Party	$5,674	1%

Source of PAC Dollars by Sector

Source	Total	Pct
Business	$265,261	77%
Labor	$73,300	21%
Ideology/Single Issue	$7,211	2%

In-State vs. Out-of-State Contributions*

Source	Total	Pct
In-State	$18,250	17%
Out-of-state	$91,550	83%
No state listed	$0	

* by large individual contributors ($200 & above)

Finance, Insurance & Real Estate — $54,000

Commercial Banks		$1,750
None over $1,500		
Securities & Investment		$8,500
Liquidity Fund Investment	$2,500	Indiv
Investment Company Institute	$2,000	PAC
American Express*	$1,500	PAC
Insurance		$28,500
American Family Corp	$4,000	PAC
Blue Cross & Blue Shield Assn*	$2,500	PAC/Ind
Delta Dental Plans Assn	$2,000	PAC
Pacific Mutual Life	$2,000	PAC
Unum Life Insurance Co	$2,000	PAC
Real Estate		$7,250
National Assn of Realtors	$5,500	PAC
Accountants		$8,000
American Institute of CPA's	$5,000	PAC

Health — $193,401

Health Professionals		$113,401
American Podiatry Assn	$10,000	PAC
American Academy of Ophthalmology	$6,000	PAC
American Dental Assn	$6,000	PAC
American Medical Assn	$6,000	PAC
American Physical Therapy Assn	$6,000	PAC
American Assn Oral & Maxillofacial Surgeons	$5,000	PAC
American Chiropractic Assn	$5,000	PAC
American Optometric Assn	$5,000	PAC
American Assn of Nurse Anesthetists	$4,500	PAC
American College of Emergency Physicians	$3,250	PAC
American Occupational Therapy Assn	$3,001	PAC
American Society of Anesthesiologists	$3,000	PAC
National Assn of Pharmacists	$3,000	PAC
Cooperative of American Physicians	$2,500	PAC
American Assn of Bioanalysts	$2,000	PAC
American Soc Cataract/Refractive Surgery	$2,000	PAC
Assn for the Advancement of Psychology	$2,000	PAC
American Group Practice Assn	$1,500	PAC/Ind

Contribution Totals by Sector

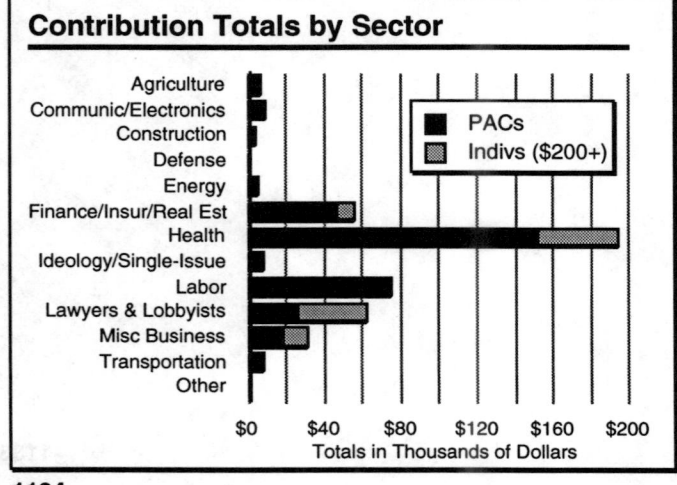

Agriculture, Communic/Electronics, Construction, Defense, Energy, Finance/Insur/Real Est, Health, Ideology/Single-Issue, Labor, Lawyers & Lobbyists, Misc Business, Transportation, Other

■ PACs
▨ Indivs ($200+)

$0 $40 $80 $120 $160 $200
Totals in Thousands of Dollars

Hospitals/Nursing Homes **$32,000**
    American Health Care Assn .... $10,000 PAC
    Manor Healthcare Corp .... $4,500 PAC
    American Hospital Assn .... $3,750 PAC
    Natl Assn of Private Psychiatric Hosp .... $3,000 PAC
    California Assn of Hosp/Health Systems .... $2,500 PAC

Health Services **$24,250**
    Family Health Program Inc .... $3,500 PAC
    Group Health Assn of America .... $2,500 PAC
    American Clinical Lab Assn .... $2,000 PAC
    Homedco Inc .... $2,000 PAC
    American Ambulance Assn .... $1,500 PAC
    National Renal Administrators Assn .... $1,500 PAC

Pharmaceuticals/Health Products **$19,500**
    American Orthotic & Prosthetic Assn .... $4,000 PAC
    Connaught Laboratories .... $2,000 PAC
    Invacare Corp .... $2,000 PAC
    Medical Equipment Suppliers .... $2,000 PAC
    Baxter Healthcare Corp .... $1,500 PAC

Misc Health **$4,250**
    None over $1,500

Lawyers & Lobbyists $61,210

Lawyers & Lobbyists **$61,210**
    Assn of Trial Lawyers of America .... $10,000 PAC
    Dyer, Ellis et al .... $4,500 Indiv
    Powell, Goldstein et al .... $2,500 PAC/Ind
    Arnold & Porter .... $2,000 PAC
    Copeland, Hatfield & Lowery .... $2,000 Indiv
    David Vienna & Associates .... $2,000 Indiv
    Davis & Harman .... $2,000 Indiv
    Hopkins & Sutter .... $2,000 PAC/Ind
    MARC Associates .... $2,000 Indiv
    White, Fine & Verville .... $2,000 Indiv
    Wunder, Diefenderfer et al .... $2,000 Indiv
    Williams & Jensen .... $1,560 PAC/Ind

Misc Business $29,700

Beer, Wine & Liquor **$8,000**
    Joseph E Seagram & Sons .... $2,000 PAC
    Wine & Spirits Wholesalers of America .... $2,000 PAC

Retail Sales **$6,000**
    National Assn of Chain Drug Stores .... $2,000 PAC

Misc Services **$2,000**
    National Funeral Directors Assn .... $2,000 PAC

Business Services **$8,750**
    Treacy Rhodes Consultants .... $2,000 Indiv
    Sierra Academy of Aeronautics .... $1,500 Indiv

Misc Manufacturing & Distributing **$2,750**
    Corning Glass Works .... $2,750 PAC

Transportation $7,500

Air Transport **$3,000**
    General Electric .... $2,000 PAC

Automotive **$2,500**
    None over $1,500

Labor

Labor $73,300

Building Trade Unions **$6,000**
    Laborers' Political League .... $2,000 PAC
    Plumbers/Pipefitters Union .... $2,000 PAC

Industrial Unions **$14,700**
    United Auto Workers .... $6,500 PAC
    Machinists/Aerospace Workers Union .... $4,000 PAC
    United Mine Workers .... $2,000 PAC

Transportation Unions **$20,500**
    Air Line Pilots Assn .... $10,000 PAC
    Teamsters Union .... $5,000 PAC
    United Transportation Union .... $2,000 PAC

Public Sector Unions **$25,600**
    National Assn of Letter Carriers .... $6,800 PAC
    American Fedn of St/Cnty/Munic Employees ...... $5,000 PAC
    National Assn Retired Federal Employees .... $5,000 PAC
    National Education Assn .... $1,500 PAC
    National Rural Letter Carriers Assn .... $1,500 PAC
    National Treasury Employees Union .... $1,500 PAC

Misc Unions **$6,500**
    Food & Commercial Workers Union .... $3,000 PAC
    Hotel/Restaurant Employees Union .... $2,500 PAC

Ideological/Single-Issue

Ideological/Single-Issue $7,211

Democratic/Liberal **$2,500**
    National Cmte for an Effective Congress .... $2,500 PAC

Misc Issues **$4,500**
    National Cmte to Preserve Social Security .... $4,500 PAC

Other & Unknown

Unknown $6,450

    Homemakers/Non-income earners $2,250
    Generic Occupation/Category Unknown $1,800
    Employer Listed/Category Unknown $1,950
    None over $1,500

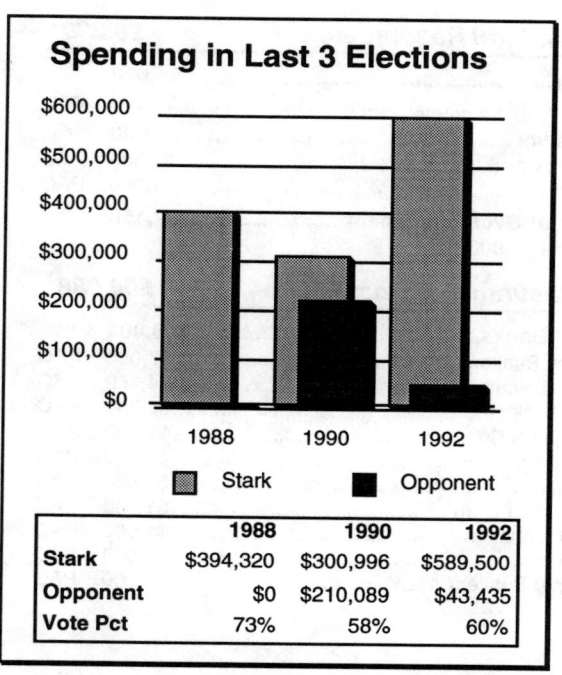

Spending in Last 3 Elections

	1988	1990	1992
Stark	$394,320	$300,996	$589,500
Opponent	$0	$210,089	$43,435
Vote Pct	73%	58%	60%

* Contributions came from more than one affiliate or subsidiary.

Cliff Stearns, R-Fla (6)

First elected: 1988

1991-92 Total Receipts: $374,016
1992 Year-end Cash: $112,117

1991-92 Committees & Subcommittees

Banking, Finance and Urban Affairs
Financial Institutions Supervision, Regulation and Insurance; Housing and Community Development; International Development, Finance, Trade and Monetary Policy

Veterans' Affairs
Housing and Memorial Affairs; Oversight and Investigations

Select Committee on Aging

Leading Contributors

Business

Agriculture $16,830

Crop Production & Basic Processing	**$7,000**	
Florida Fruit & Vegetable Assn	$1,750	PAC/Ind
Florida Citrus Mutual	$1,500	PAC
Florida Sugar Cane League	$1,000	PAC
Tobacco	**$1,500**	
RJR Nabisco	$1,000	PAC
Dairy	**$1,500**	
Associated Milk Producers	$1,000	PAC
Livestock	**$3,330**	
Alice Ann Farm	$1,830	Indiv
Hilliard Brothers of Florida	$1,000	Indiv
Agricultural Services/Products	**$1,000**	
None over $1,000		
Food Processing & Sales	**$2,500**	
Winn-Dixie Stores	$2,000	PAC

Communications/Electronics $8,500

Telephone Utilities	**$7,000**	
Southern Bell	$3,000	PAC
AT&T	$2,000	PAC
GTE Corp	$1,000	PAC
United Telecommunications	$1,000	PAC
Electronics Mfg & Services	**$1,000**	
Harris Corp	$1,000	PAC

Source of Funds in 1992 Election

Source	Total	Pct
■ PACs	$171,239	46%
▨ Indivs $200+	$91,864	25%
□ Indivs under $200	$67,710	18%
▨ Other	$42,830	11%
Candidate	$0	0%
Party	$-26	-0%

Source of PAC Dollars by Sector

Source	Total	Pct
■ Business	$161,480	94%
▨ Labor	$5,500	3%
□ Ideology/Single Issue	$4,135	2%

In-State vs. Out-of-State Contributions*

Source	Total	Pct
□ In-State	$88,295	97%
■ Out-of-state	$2,500	3%
No state listed	$0	

*** by large individual contributors ($200 & above)**

Construction $9,730

General Contractors	**$2,330**	
Associated General Contractors	$1,000	PAC
Home Builders	**$3,800**	
Manufactured Housing Institute	$2,000	PAC
Fleetwood Enterprises	$1,000	PAC
Building Materials & Equipment	**$3,350**	
Florida Crushed Stone Co	$2,350	Indiv

Defense $2,100

Defense Aerospace	**$1,500**	
Martin Marietta Corp	$1,000	PAC

Energy & Natural Resources $8,230

Misc Energy	**$1,000**	
Gates Energy	$1,000	Indiv
Electric Utilities	**$4,080**	
Florida Power & Light	$1,500	PAC
Southern Co*	$1,000	PAC
Environmental Svcs/Equipment	**$2,150**	
None over $1,000		

Finance, Insurance & Real Estate $94,088

Commercial Banks	**$28,804**	
American Bankers Assn	$7,000	PAC
Citizens & Southern National Bank	$4,150	PAC
Barnett Banks Inc	$3,750	PAC
JP Morgan & Co	$2,500	PAC
First Chicago Corp	$1,500	PAC
SunBanks	$1,500	PAC
BankAmerica Corp	$1,000	PAC
Chase Manhattan	$1,000	PAC
Citicorp	$1,000	PAC
Consumer Bankers Assn	$1,000	PAC

Contribution Totals by Sector

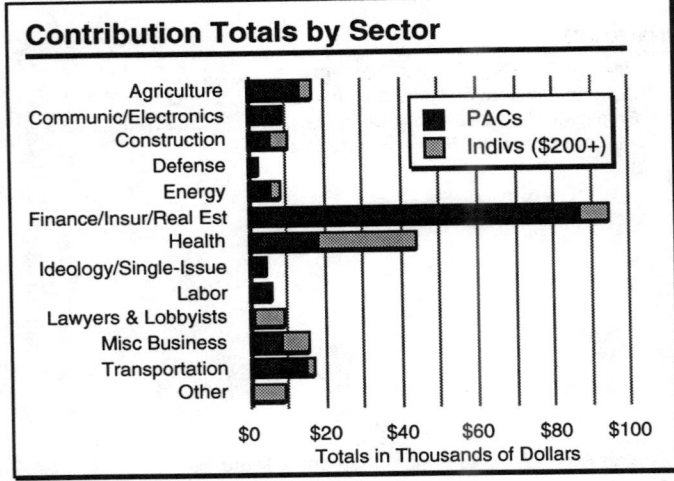

Agriculture
Communic/Electronics
Construction
Defense
Energy
Finance/Insur/Real Est
Health
Ideology/Single-Issue
Labor
Lawyers & Lobbyists
Misc Business
Transportation
Other

■ PACs
▨ Indivs ($200+)

$0 $20 $40 $60 $80 $100
Totals in Thousands of Dollars

Savings & Loans $2,000
    Great Western Financial Corp ....$1,000 PAC
    National Council of Savings Institutions ....$1,000 PAC

Credit Unions $4,350
    Credit Union National Assn ....$3,350 PAC
    National Assn of Federal Credit Unions ....$1,000 PAC

Finance/Credit Companies $5,000
    Associated Credit Bureaus ....$2,000 PAC
    Household International Inc ....$2,000 PAC

Securities & Investment $6,600
    Merrill Lynch ....$1,350 Indiv
    American Express ....$1,000 PAC
    Chicago Board of Trade ....$1,000 PAC
    Morgan Stanley & Co ....$1,000 PAC

Insurance $24,204
    National Assn of Life Underwriters ....$7,500 PAC
    Independent Insurance Agents of America ....$3,000 PAC
    Casualty & Surety Agents Assn ....$2,500 PAC
    National Assn of Prof Insurance Agents ....$2,000 PAC
    American Council of Life Insurance ....$1,000 PAC
    Blue Cross/Blue Shield of Florida ....$1,000 PAC
    Cigna Corp ....$1,000 PAC
    Metropolitan Life Insurance ....$1,000 PAC
    Prudential Insurance ....$1,000 PAC

Real Estate $15,380
    National Assn of Realtors ....$7,000 PAC
    American Land Title Assn ....$1,000 PAC
    First Union Corp ....$1,000 PAC
    Mortgage Bankers Assn of America ....$1,000 PAC

Accountants $7,750
    American Institute of CPA's ....$5,000 PAC
    National Society of Public Accountants ....$2,000 PAC

Health $43,003

Health Professionals $37,063
    American Medical Assn ....$9,700 PAC
    American Dental Assn ....$2,500 PAC
    American Academy of Ophthalmology ....$2,000 PAC
    Florida Society of Anesthesiologists ....$1,500 PAC
    Radiation Associates ....$1,500 Indiv

Hospitals/Nursing Homes $5,300
    Waterman Healthcare Systems Inc ....$3,000 Indiv
    American Hospital Assn ....$1,000 PAC

Spending in Last 3 Elections

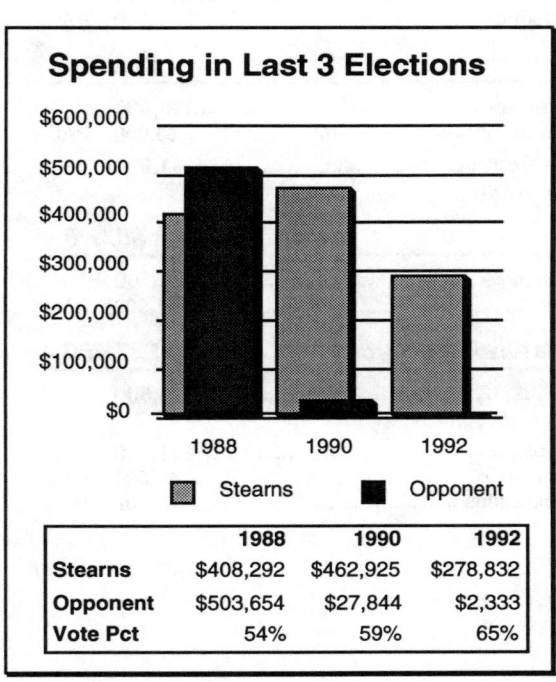

	1988	1990	1992
Stearns	$408,292	$462,925	$278,832
Opponent	$503,654	$27,844	$2,333
Vote Pct	54%	59%	65%

Lawyers & Lobbyists $8,436

Lawyers & Lobbyists $8,436
    Klein & Klein ....$2,000 Indiv
    Holland & Knight ....$1,000 PAC
    Williams & Jensen ....$1,000 Indiv

Misc Business $14,994

Food & Beverage $2,250
    None over $1,000

Beer, Wine & Liquor $1,250
    National Beer Wholesalers Assn ....$1,000 PAC

Business Services $1,500
    Koss/Olinger ....$1,000 Indiv

Lodging/Tourism $4,094
    Holiday Inns ....$1,750 PAC/Ind
    Plantation Inn ....$1,344 Indiv

Chemical & Related Manufacturing $2,600
    Trident Supply ....$1,800 Indiv

Misc Manufacturing & Distributing $1,000
    Stone Container Corp ....$1,000 PAC

Transportation $16,069

Air Transport $4,500
    United Parcel Service ....$3,000 PAC
    General Electric ....$1,000 PAC

Automotive $9,819
    National Auto Dealers Assn ....$6,000 PAC
    Auto Dealers & Drivers for Free Trade ....$1,500 PAC
    Americans for Free International Trade ....$1,000 PAC

Railroads $1,000
    CSX Transportation Inc ....$1,000 PAC

Labor

Labor $5,500

Transportation Unions $2,500
    Marine Engineers Union* ....$2,500 PAC

Public Sector Unions $3,000
    National Assn Retired Federal Employees ....$2,000 PAC

Ideological/Single-Issue

Ideological/Single-Issue $4,385

Foreign & Defense Policy $1,000
    Veterans of Foreign Wars ....$1,000 PAC

Gun Rights/Gun Control $1,500
    National Rifle Assn ....$1,500 PAC

Other & Unknown

Other $8,720

Education $2,750
    University of Florida ....$2,750 Indiv

Retired $4,420
    None over $1,000

Unknown $21,325

    Homemakers/Non-income earners $15,025
    Generic Occupation/Category Unknown $1,500
    Employer Listed/Category Unknown $4,550
        Waterman Center ....$1,000 Indiv

---

* Contributions came from more than one affiliate or
subsidiary.

Charles W. Stenholm, D-Texas (17)

First elected: 1978

1991-92 Total Receipts: $412,834
1992 Year-end Cash: $121,621

1991-92 Committees & Subcommittees

Agriculture
Conservation, Credit and Rural Development; Cotton, Rice and Sugar; Department Operations, Research and Foreign Agriculture; Livestock, Dairy and Poultry (Chairman); Peanuts and Tobacco

Budget
Budget Process, Reconciliation and Enforcement; Community Development and Natural Resources; Human Resources

Leading Contributors

Business

Agriculture	$144,303	
Crop Production & Basic Processing	**$31,075**	
National Cotton Council	$2,000	PAC
Southwest Peanut Membership Org	$1,800	PAC
American Crystal Sugar Corp	$1,500	PAC
Tobacco	**$6,500**	
US Tobacco Co	$2,000	PAC
RJR Nabisco	$1,500	PAC
Dairy	**$18,000**	
Associated Milk Producers	$4,000	PAC
Milk Industry Foundation	$2,500	PAC
Mid-America Dairymen	$1,500	PAC
Poultry & Eggs	**$11,000**	
National Broiler Council	$3,200	PAC
National Turkey Federation	$2,000	PAC
Tyson Foods	$2,000	PAC
United Egg Assn	$2,000	PAC
Livestock	**$19,450**	
National Cattlemen's Assn*	$4,000	PAC
Texas & Southwestern Cattle Raisers	$4,000	PAC
Livestock Marketing Assn	$1,500	PAC
National Pork Producers Council	$1,500	PAC
Agricultural Services/Products	**$29,000**	
American Veterinary Medical Assn	$5,000	PAC
Texas Farm Bureau	$4,000	PAC
American Assn of Crop Insurers	$1,500	PAC
American Feed Industry Assn	$1,500	PAC
Dow Chemical	$1,500	PAC
Farm Credit Council	$1,500	PAC
National Council of Farmer Co-ops	$1,500	PAC

Source of Funds in 1992 Election

Source	Total	Pct
PACs	$275,826	66%
Indivs $200+	$56,984	14%
Indivs under $200	$67,602	16%
Other	$18,422	4%
Candidate	$0	0%
Party	$6,150	1%

Source of PAC Dollars by Sector

Source	Total	Pct
Business	$276,182	99%
Labor	$900	0%
Ideology/Single Issue	$600	0%

In-State vs. Out-of-State Contributions*

Source	Total	Pct
In-State	$39,100	69%
Out-of-state	$17,584	31%
No state listed	$300	

*** by large individual contributors ($200 & above)**

Food Processing & Sales	$28,528	
ConAgra Inc	$4,000	PAC
American Meat Institute	$2,800	PAC
Food Marketing Institute	$2,500	PAC
Winn-Dixie Stores	$2,500	PAC
Beef Products Inc	$1,800	Indiv
Nabisco Brands Inc	$1,500	PAC

Communications/Electronics — $9,150

Media/Entertainment	$2,000	
National Assn of Broadcasters	$1,500	PAC
Telephone Utilities	**$5,850**	
GTE Corp	$3,000	PAC
Southwestern Bell	$1,500	PAC

Construction — $10,250

General Contractors	$8,300	
Associated Builders & Contractors	$3,000	PAC
Special Trade Contractors	**$1,600**	
None over $1,500		

Defense — $5,900

Defense Aerospace	$5,100	
Textron Inc	$1,500	PAC

Energy & Natural Resources — $27,400

Oil & Gas	$14,500	
None over $1,500		
Electric Utilities	**$11,400**	
Texas Utilities Co*	$4,000	PAC
Houston Industries	$2,000	PAC

Contribution Totals by Sector

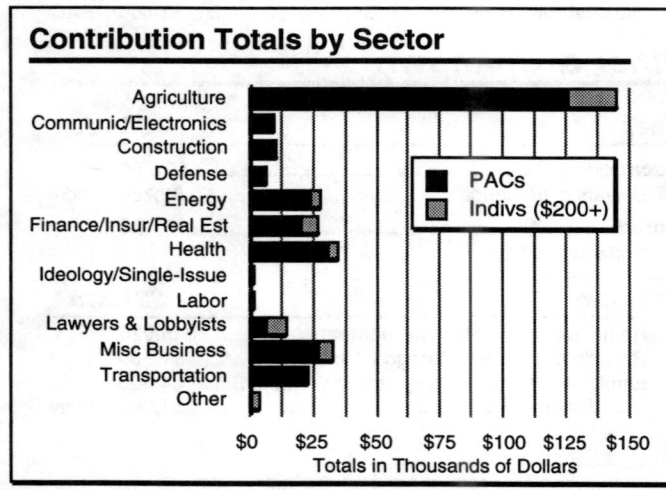

Agriculture
Communic/Electronics
Construction
Defense
Energy
Finance/Insur/Real Est
Health
Ideology/Single-Issue
Labor
Lawyers & Lobbyists
Misc Business
Transportation
Other

- PACs
- Indivs ($200+)

$0 $25 $50 $75 $100 $125 $150
Totals in Thousands of Dollars

Finance, Insurance & Real Estate — $25,950

Commercial Banks **$6,450**
   American Bankers Assn .... $2,500   PAC
Securities & Investment **$2,500**
   Chicago Board of Trade .... $1,500   PAC
Insurance **$6,750**
   National Assn of Life Underwriters .... $2,000   PAC
   American Council of Life Insurance .... $1,500   PAC
Real Estate **$6,900**
   National Assn of Realtors .... $6,300   PAC
Misc Finance **$3,050**
   None over $1,500

Health — $34,400

Health Professionals **$20,550**
   American Medical Assn .... $11,000   PAC/Ind
   American Academy of Ophthalmology .... $2,500   PAC
   American Society of Anesthesiologists .... $2,000   PAC
   American Dental Assn .... $1,500   PAC
Hospitals/Nursing Homes **$8,000**
   American Hospital Assn .... $5,500   PAC
Pharmaceuticals/Health Products **$5,350**
   None over $1,500

Lawyers & Lobbyists — $13,878

Lawyers & Lobbyists **$13,878**
   McLeod, Watkinson & Miller .... $1,550   Indiv
   Horty, Springer & Mattern .... $1,500   Indiv

Misc Business — $31,801

Business Associations **$1,500**
   National Fedn of Independent Business .... $1,500   PAC
Food & Beverage **$6,750**
   S&A Restaurant Corp .... $3,000   PAC
Beer, Wine & Liquor **$2,000**
   None over $1,500
Retail Sales **$4,600**
   None over $1,500
Misc Services **$2,001**
   National Pest Control Assn .... $1,500   PAC
Business Services **$2,550**
   Adcraft Agency .... $2,000   Indiv
Chemical & Related Manufacturing **$7,500**
   Dow Chemical .... $4,000   PAC
Misc Manufacturing & Distributing **$2,050**
   None over $1,500

Transportation — $22,150

Air Transport **$8,950**
   United Parcel Service .... $3,200   PAC
   UNC Inc .... $2,000   PAC
   American Airlines .... $1,500   PAC
   General Electric .... $1,500   PAC
Automotive **$10,500**
   National Auto Dealers Assn .... $8,500   PAC
Railroads **$2,350**
   None over $1,500

Other & Unknown

Other — $3,600

Retired **$2,500**
   None over $1,500

Unknown — $4,584

   Employer Listed/Category Unknown $2,934
     None over $1,500

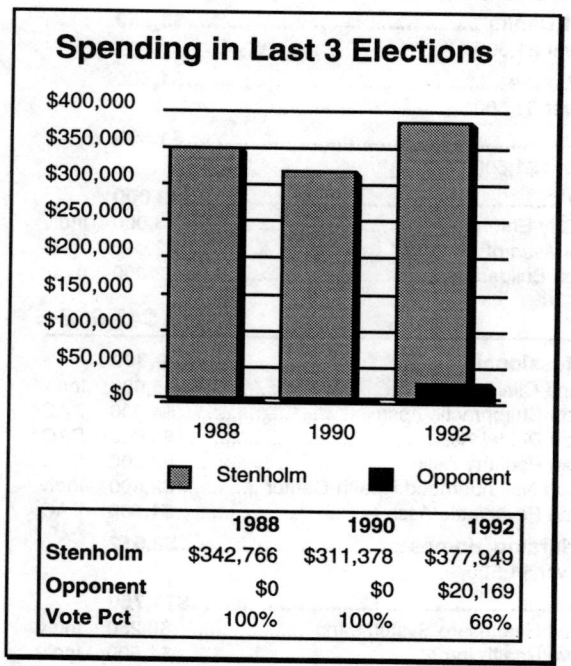

Spending in Last 3 Elections

	1988	1990	1992
Stenholm	$342,766	$311,378	$377,949
Opponent	$0	$0	$20,169
Vote Pct	100%	100%	66%

Legend: Stenholm, Opponent

---

* Contributions came from more than one affiliate or subsidiary.

Louis Stokes, D-Ohio (11)

First elected: 1968

1991-92 Total Receipts:	$391,172
1992 Year-end Cash:	$183,789

1991-92 Committees & Subcommittees

Appropriations
District of Columbia; Labor, Health and Human Services, Education, and Related Agencies; Veterans Affairs, Housing and Urban Development, and Independent Agencies

Standards of Official Conduct (Chairman)

Leading Contributors

Business

Agriculture	$10,375	
Crop Production & Basic Processing	$3,625	
None over $1,500		
Tobacco	$2,000	
None over $1,500		
Agricultural Services/Products	$1,750	
None over $1,500		
Food Processing & Sales	$2,000	
None over $1,500		

Communications/Electronics	$10,610	
Telephone Utilities	$5,060	
AT&T	$2,500	PAC
Ohio Bell Telephone	$2,310	PAC
Telecom Services & Equipment	$2,000	
Cleveland Telecommunications Corp	$2,000	Indiv
Electronics Mfg & Services	$2,500	
Atlantic Systems Inc	$2,500	Indiv

Construction	$14,750	
General Contractors	$6,250	
Ozanne Construction Co	$2,500	Indiv
Home Builders	$4,000	
Gross Builders Inc	$4,000	Indiv
Special Trade Contractors	$2,750	
Colejon Mechanical Corp	$2,000	Indiv

Contribution Totals by Sector

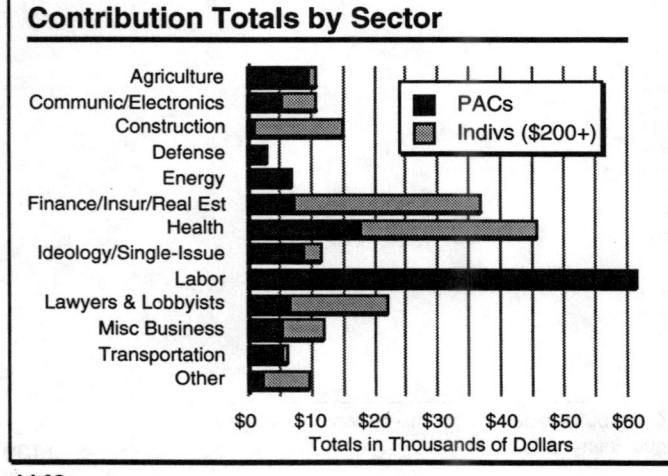

Totals in Thousands of Dollars

Agriculture
Communic/Electronics
Construction
Defense
Energy
Finance/Insur/Real Est
Health
Ideology/Single-Issue
Labor
Lawyers & Lobbyists
Misc Business
Transportation
Other

■ PACs
▨ Indivs ($200+)

$0 $10 $20 $30 $40 $50 $60

Source of Funds in 1992 Election

Source	Total	Pct
■ PACs	$149,293	37%
▨ Indivs $200+	$123,512	30%
☐ Indivs under $200	$18,933	5%
⊠ Other	$113,211	28%
Candidate	$0	0%
Party	$16,702	4%

Source of PAC Dollars by Sector

Source	Total	Pct
■ Business	$67,135	49%
▨ Labor	$61,150	45%
☐ Ideology/Single Issue	$8,610	6%

In-State vs. Out-of-State Contributions*

Source	Total	Pct
☐ In-State	$88,712	72%
■ Out-of-state	$33,800	28%
No state listed	$0	

* by large individual contributors ($200 & above)

Defense	$3,000	
Defense Aerospace	$1,500	
None over $1,500		
Defense Electronics	$1,500	
None over $1,500		

Energy & Natural Resources	$6,650	
Electric Utilities	$4,900	
Centerior Energy Corp	$4,400	PAC/Ind

Finance, Insurance & Real Estate	$36,250	
Commercial Banks	$3,250	
None over $1,500		
Savings & Loans	$1,500	
None over $1,500		
Insurance	$1,500	
None over $1,500		
Real Estate	$29,000	
Forest City Enterprises Inc	$23,000	Indiv
National Assn of Realtors	$2,000	PAC
Transcon Builders Inc	$2,000	Indiv

Health	$45,062	
Health Professionals	$30,300	
Cleveland Clinic	$5,000	Indiv
American Chiropractic Assn	$4,000	PAC
American Dental Assn	$4,000	PAC
American Podiatry Assn	$2,000	PAC
Cleveland Neighborhood Health Center	$2,000	Indiv
American Psychiatric Assn	$1,500	PAC
Hospitals/Nursing Homes	$2,512	
None over $1,500		
Misc Health	$11,750	
Managed Healthcare Systems Inc	$8,250	Indiv
Digestive Health Inc	$1,500	Indiv

Lawyers & Lobbyists — $21,550

Lawyers & Lobbyists $21,550
- Assn of Trial Lawyers of America .... $5,000 — PAC
- CR Associates .... $2,000 — Indiv
- MARC Associates .... $2,000 — Indiv
- Squire, Sanders & Dempsey .... $1,600 — Indiv
- Stanton & Associates .... $1,500 — Indiv

Misc Business — $11,850

Beer, Wine & Liquor $1,500
- None over $1,500

Retail Sales $1,500
- Antwerp Diamond Center Inc .... $1,500 — Indiv

Business Services $2,000
- None over $1,500

Steel Production $2,250
- LTV Corp* .... $1,750 — Indiv

Transportation — $6,000

Air Transport $5,000
- United Parcel Service .... $2,000 — PAC

Labor

Labor — $61,150

Building Trade Unions $5,000
- Laborers' Political League .... $1,500 — PAC

Industrial Unions $15,750
- United Auto Workers .... $10,000 — PAC
- Intl Brotherhood of Electrical Workers .... $1,500 — PAC

Transportation Unions $13,100
- Teamsters Union* .... $4,500 — PAC
- International Longshoremen's Assn .... $3,000 — PAC
- Marine Engineers Dist 2 Maritime Officers . $1,500 — PAC
- Transport Workers Union .... $1,500 — PAC

Public Sector Unions $22,100
- American Federation of Teachers .... $5,100 — PAC
- American Fedn of St/Cnty/Munic Employees . $5,000 — PAC
- National Assn of Letter Carriers .... $4,000 — PAC
- American Postal Workers Union .... $3,000 — PAC
- National Assn Retired Federal Employees .. $2,000 — PAC

Misc Unions $5,200
- Bakery & Confectionery Workers local #19 . $2,500 — PAC
- Food & Commercial Workers Union .... $2,000 — PAC

Ideological/Single-Issue

Ideological/Single-Issue — $11,460

Pro-Israel $7,850
- National PAC .... $5,000 — PAC

Misc Issues $2,110
- National Cmte to Preserve Social Security .. $2,000 — PAC

Other & Unknown

Other — $9,350

Civil Servants/Public Officials $2,100
- City of Brooklyn .... $1,500 — Indiv

Education $5,250
- None over $1,500

Unknown — $12,600

- No Employer Listed or Found $3,000
- Employer Listed/Category Unknown $9,600
  - None over $1,500

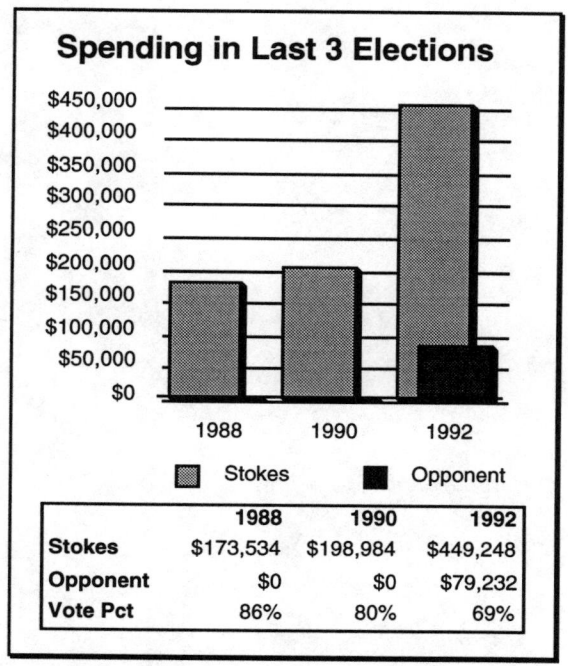

Spending in Last 3 Elections

	1988	1990	1992
Stokes	$173,534	$198,984	$449,248
Opponent	$0	$0	$79,232
Vote Pct	86%	80%	69%

Legend: ▨ Stokes   ■ Opponent

* Contributions came from more than one affiliate or subsidiary.

Ted Strickland, D-Ohio (6)

First elected: 1992

1991-92 Total Receipts: $238,391
1992 Year-end Cash: $3,308

1993-94 Committees & Subcommittees

Education and Labor
Elementary, Secondary and Vocational Education; Labor Standards
Occupational Health and Safety; Postsecondary Education and
Training

Small Business
Regulation, Business Opportunities and Technology; Rural Enterprises, Exports and the Environment

Leading Contributors

Business

Communications/Electronics — $1,000

Telephone Utilities	**$1,000**	
AT&T	$1,000	PAC

Finance, Insurance & Real Esta — $3,198

Insurance	**$3,198**	
Northwest Insurance	$1,700	Indiv

Health — $15,946

Health Professionals	**$13,446**	
Assn for the Advancement of Psychology	$9,957	PAC
Misc Health	**$2,000**	
Holzer Clinic Inc	$1,250	Indiv

Lawyers & Lobbyists — $6,750

Lawyers & Lobbyists	**$6,750**	
Assn of Trial Lawyers of America	$5,000	PAC

Source of Funds in 1992 Election

Source	Total	Pct
■ PACs	$112,457	41%
▨ Indivs $200+	$20,533	8%
☐ Indivs under $200	$72,531	27%
⊠ Other	$67,748	25%
Candidate	$12,755	5%
Party	$44,878	16%

Source of PAC Dollars by Sector

Source	Total	Pct
■ Business	$23,257	19%
▨ Labor	$89,199	73%
☐ Ideology/Single Issue	$10,500	9%

In-State vs. Out-of-State Contributions*

Source	Total	Pct
☐ In-State	$14,836	74%
■ Out-of-state	$5,189	26%
No state listed	$0	

*** by large individual contributors ($200 & above)**

Contribution Totals by Sector

Agriculture
Communic/Electronics
Construction
Defense
Energy
Finance/Insur/Real Est
Health
Ideology/Single-Issue
Labor
Lawyers & Lobbyists
Misc Business
Transportation
Other

■ PACs
▨ Indivs ($200+)

$0 $10 $20 $30 $40 $50 $60 $70 $80 $90
Totals in Thousands of Dollars

Labor

Labor $89,199

Building Trade Unions **$14,500**
  Plumbers/Pipefitters Union* .... $5,400   PAC
  Carpenters & Joiners Union .... $5,000   PAC
  Laborers' Political League .... $1,500   PAC
  Sheet Metal Workers Union .... $1,000   PAC

Industrial Unions **$32,200**
  Machinists/Aerospace Workers Union .... $5,000   PAC
  United Auto Workers .... $5,000   PAC
  United Steelworkers .... $5,000   PAC
  Intl Brotherhood of Electrical Workers .... $4,500   PAC
  Rubber Cork Linoleum & Plastic Workers .... $3,000   PAC
  United Mine Workers .... $3,000   PAC
  Communications Workers of America .... $2,500   PAC
  Amalgamated Clothing & Textile Workers .... $1,000   PAC
  Boilermakers Union .... $1,000   PAC
  Oil, Chemical & Atomic Workers Union .... $1,000   PAC

Transportation Unions **$11,000**
  Teamsters Union .... $5,000   PAC
  International Longshoremen's Assn .... $2,000   PAC
  Marine Engineers Union .... $2,000   PAC

Public Sector Unions **$26,000**
  National Education Assn .... $10,000 PAC
  American Fedn of St/Cnty/Munic Employees ...... $5,000   PAC
  National Assn Retired Federal Employees .... $4,000   PAC
  International Assn of Firefighters .... $3,000   PAC
  National Assn of Letter Carriers .... $2,000   PAC
  American Federation of Teachers .... $1,000   PAC
  American Postal Workers Union .... $1,000   PAC

Misc Unions **$5,499**
  Food & Commercial Workers Union .... $2,499   PAC
  Service Employees International Union .... $2,000   PAC

Ideological/Single-Issue

Ideological/Single-Issue $11,700

Democratic/Liberal **$2,700**
  National Cmte for an Effective Congress .... $2,500   PAC

Leadership PACs **$2,000**
  Effective Government Cmte (Dick Gephardt) ...... $1,000   PAC
  House Leadership Fund (Tom Foley) .... $1,000   PAC

Pro-Choice **$5,750**
  National Abortion Rights Action League .... $4,500   PAC

Misc Issues **$1,250**
  National Cmte to Preserve Social Security .... $1,000   PAC

Other & Unknown

Other $9,520

Civil Servants/Public Officials **$2,370**
  State of Ohio .... $1,300   Indiv

Education **$1,700**
  Ludlow Board of Education .... $1,000   Indiv

Other **$5,000**
  Appalachians for Community Action .... $4,500   PAC

Unknown $3,653

  Employer Listed/Category Unknown $2,903
    Revco .... $1,986   Indiv

Spending in Last Election

	1992
Strickland	$235,082
Opponent	$716,672
Vote Pct	51%

* Contributions came from more than one affiliate or
subsidiary.

Gerry E. Studds, D-Mass (10)

First elected: 1972

1991-92 Total Receipts: $1,438,264
1992 Year-end Cash: $19,799

1991-92 Committees & Subcommittees

Energy and Commerce
Energy and Power; Health and the Environment

Foreign Affairs

Merchant Marine and Fisheries (Chairman)
Coast Guard and Navigation; Fisheries and Wildlife Conservation and the Environment (Chairman); Merchant Marine

Select Committee on Aging

Leading Contributors
Business

Agriculture	$4,250

None over $2,500

Communications/Electronics	$38,750

Printing & Publishing $8,700
None over $2,500

Media/Entertainment $14,450
| Time Warner | $3,250 | PAC/Ind |
| National Cable Television Assn | $3,000 | PAC |

Telephone Utilities $14,600
| NYNEX Corp* | $6,000 | PAC |
| AT&T | $4,250 | PAC/Ind |

Defense	$3,750

Defense Electronics $3,500
| Raytheon | $3,500 | PAC |

Energy & Natural Resources	$32,400

Oil & Gas $5,250
None over $2,500

Commercial Fishing $22,200
American Factory Trawler Assn	$3,000	PAC
Arctic Alaska Fisheries Corp	$3,000	PAC
National Fisheries Institute	$2,500	PAC

Source of Funds in 1992 Election

Source	Total	Pct
■ PACs	$413,068	28%
▨ Indivs $200+	$343,845	23%
□ Indivs under $200	$666,711	45%
⊠ Other	$43,735	3%
Candidate	$0	0%
Party	$31,618	2%

Source of PAC Dollars by Sector

Source	Total	Pct
■ Business	$170,023	41%
▨ Labor	$168,800	41%
□ Ideology/Single Issue	$76,663	18%

In-State vs. Out-of-State Contributions*

Source	Total	Pct
□ In-State	$154,669	45%
■ Out-of-state	$186,926	55%
No state listed	$1,250	

* by large individual contributors ($200 & above)

Finance, Insurance & Real Estate	$28,700

Securities & Investment $8,500
None over $2,500

Insurance $3,850
None over $2,500

Real Estate $4,700
None over $2,500

Accountants $4,900
| American Institute of CPA's | $3,500 | PAC |

Misc Finance $4,000
None over $2,500

Health	$60,780

Health Professionals $42,430
American College of Emergency Physicians	$5,000	PAC
American Medical Assn	$4,500	PAC
American Podiatry Assn	$3,500	PAC
American Chiropractic Assn	$3,000	PAC
American Physical Therapy Assn	$2,500	PAC

Hospitals/Nursing Homes $9,750
| American Hospital Assn | $3,000 | PAC |
| American Health Care Assn | $2,500 | PAC |

Pharmaceuticals/Health Products $7,350
| Serono Laboratories | $2,500 | PAC |

Lawyers & Lobbyists	$61,150

Lawyers & Lobbyists $61,150
Assn of Trial Lawyers of America	$12,500	PAC
Preston, Gates et al	$3,500	PAC/Ind
Swidler & Berlin	$2,500	Indiv

Contribution Totals by Sector

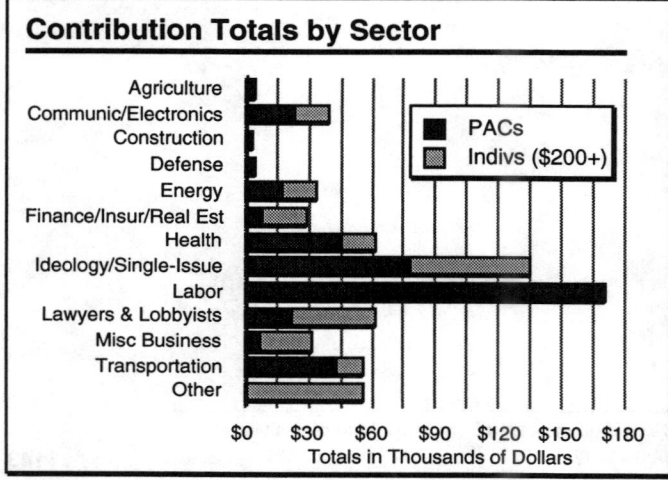

Totals in Thousands of Dollars

Misc Business — $30,918

Food & Beverage $9,450
    None over $2,500

Lodging/Tourism $2,950
    None over $2,500

Misc Manufacturing & Distributing $8,750
    Schnitzer Steel Industries .... $4,000   Indiv

Transportation — $55,200

Railroads $2,500
    None over $2,500

Sea Transport $51,900
    Sea-Land Corp .... $9,000   PAC
    American Pilots Assn .... $4,000   PAC
    Cruise PAC .... $4,000   PAC
    American President Lines .... $3,500   PAC
    Boat Owners Assn of the US .... $3,100   PAC
    Miami Cruise PAC .... $3,000   PAC
    World Explorer Cruises Inc .... $3,000   Indiv
    Carnival Cruise Lines .... $2,500   Indiv

Labor

Labor — $169,200

Building Trade Unions $15,750
    Laborers' Political League .... $5,250   PAC
    Sheet Metal Workers Union .... $4,000   PAC

Industrial Unions $37,050
    Machinists/Aerospace Workers Union .... $10,000   PAC
    United Auto Workers .... $10,000   PAC
    Intl Brotherhood of Electrical Workers .... $6,500   PAC
    Boilermakers Union .... $2,500   PAC

Transportation Unions $48,300
    Marine Engineers Union* .... $12,000   PAC
    Seafarers International Union* .... $10,200   PAC
    Teamsters Union* .... $5,000   PAC
    Masters, Mates & Pilots Union .... $3,000   PAC
    National Air Traffic Controllers Assn .... $3,000   PAC
    United Transportation Union .... $3,000   PAC

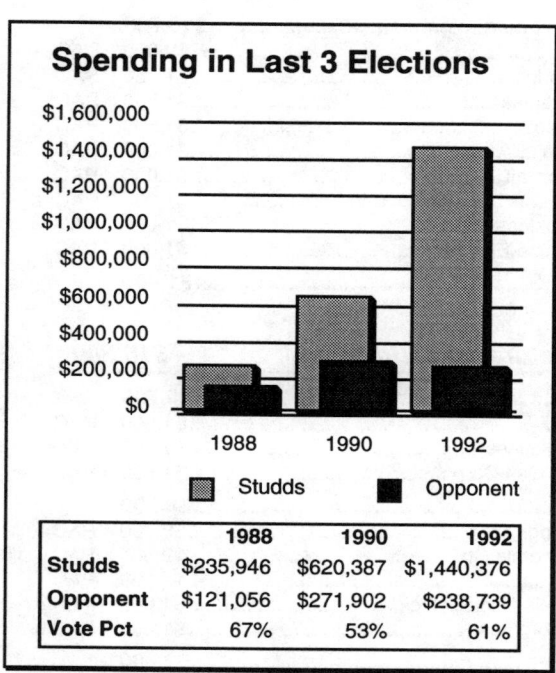

Spending in Last 3 Elections

	1988	1990	1992
Studds	$235,946	$620,387	$1,440,376
Opponent	$121,056	$271,902	$238,739
Vote Pct	67%	53%	61%

Legend: Studds / Opponent

Public Sector Unions $49,600
    National Education Assn .... $10,400   PAC/Ind
    National Assn Retired Federal Employees .... $10,000   PAC
    National Assn of Letter Carriers .... $10,000   PAC
    American Fedn of St/Cnty/Munic Employees ...... $8,500   PAC
    American Federation of Teachers .... $5,000   PAC
    International Assn of Firefighters .... $3,000   PAC
    American Postal Workers Union .... $2,500   PAC

Misc Unions $18,500
    Food & Commercial Workers Union .... $10,000   PAC
    AFL-CIO .... $3,500   PAC
    Service Employees International Union .... $3,000   PAC

Ideological/Single-Issue

Ideological/Single-Issue — $133,918

Democratic/Liberal $27,730
    Independent Action .... $5,000   PAC
    National Cmte for an Effective Congress .... $5,000   PAC

Leadership PACs $16,500
    24th Cong Dist of Calif PAC (Henry Waxman) .. $10,000   PAC
    Victory USA (Vic Fazio) .... $3,000   PAC
    Fund for a Democratic Majority (Ted Kennedy) ... $2,500   PAC

Foreign & Defense Policy $4,647
    None over $2,500

Pro-Choice $10,458
    National Abortion Rights Action League* .... $8,133   PAC

Human Rights $43,179
    Human Rights Campaign Fund .... $10,700   PAC/Ind
    KidsPAC .... $3,000   PAC

Misc Issues $28,154
    Sierra Club .... $10,000   PAC
    National Cmte to Preserve Social Security .... $5,000   PAC
    League of Conservation Voters .... $4,904   PAC

Other & Unknown

Other — $54,450

Non-Profit Institutions $3,250
    Foundation for Hearing Aid Research .... $3,000   Indiv

Civil Servants/Public Officials $3,750
    None over $2,500

Education $5,750
    None over $2,500

Retired $35,900
    None over $2,500

Other $5,800
    None over $2,500

Unknown — $82,615

    Homemakers/Non-income earners $5,375
    No Employer Listed or Found $39,515
    Generic Occupation/Category Unknown $3,200
    Employer Listed/Category Unknown $34,525
        None over $2,500

Independent expenditures supporting Studds
    National Cmte to Preserve Social Security $11,929

---

* Contributions came from more than one affiliate or
subsidiary.

Bob Stump, R-Ariz (3)

First elected: 1976

1991-92 Total Receipts: $233,476
1992 Year-end Cash: $43,638

1991-92 Committees & Subcommittees

Armed Services
Investigations; Research and Development

Veterans' Affairs (Ranking Republican)
Compensation, Pension and Insurance (Ranking Republican);
Hospitals and Health Care

Leading Contributors

Business

Agriculture — $29,150

Crop Production & Basic Processing	**$13,550**	
JM Accomazzo	$2,300	Indiv
Arizona Cotton Growers Assn	$1,500	PAC
Calcot Ltd	$1,500	PAC
National Cotton Council	$1,500	PAC
Florida Sugar Cane League	$1,000	PAC
Sunkist Growers	$1,000	PAC
Tobacco	**$3,500**	
RJR Nabisco	$2,000	PAC
Tobacco Institute	$1,000	PAC
Livestock	**$5,900**	
None over $1,000		
Agricultural Services/Products	**$3,000**	
Salt River Valley Water Users	$2,500	PAC
Food Processing & Sales	**$1,300**	
Fleming Companies Inc	$1,000	PAC

Communications/Electronics — $6,000

Telephone Utilities	**$3,200**	
US West Inc	$3,200	PAC
Telecom Services & Equipment	**$1,000**	
California Microwave Inc	$1,000	Indiv

Construction — $6,710

General Contractors	**$5,210**	
Associated General Contractors	$2,000	PAC
JWJ Contracting	$1,500	Indiv
Construction Services	**$1,000**	
None over $1,000		

Contribution Totals by Sector

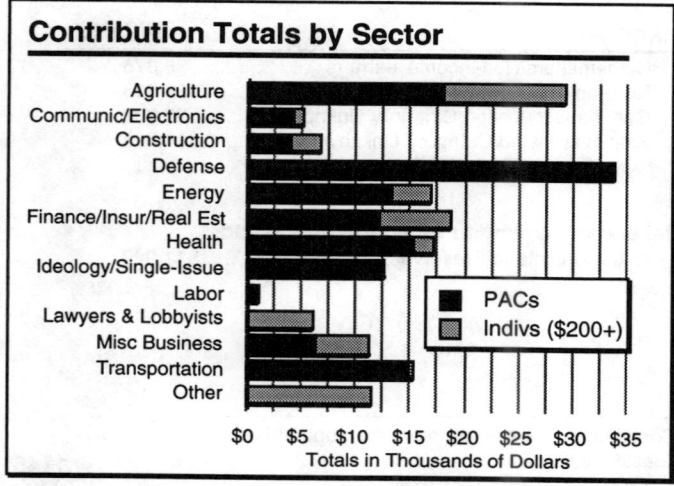

Agriculture
Communic/Electronics
Construction
Defense
Energy
Finance/Insur/Real Est
Health
Ideology/Single-Issue
Labor
Lawyers & Lobbyists
Misc Business
Transportation
Other

■ PACs
▨ Indivs ($200+)

$0 $5 $10 $15 $20 $25 $30 $35
Totals in Thousands of Dollars

Source of Funds in 1992 Election

Source	Total	Pct
■ PACs	$135,742	58%
▨ Indivs $200+	$58,510	25%
▢ Indivs under $200	$20,652	9%
▧ Other	$18,572	8%
Candidate	$0	0%
Party	$5,000	2%

Source of PAC Dollars by Sector

Source	Total	Pct
■ Business	$120,865	90%
▨ Labor	$1,000	1%
▢ Ideology/Single Issue	$12,150	9%

In-State vs. Out-of-State Contributions*

Source	Total	Pct
▢ In-State	$50,010	85%
▨ Out-of-state	$8,500	15%
No state listed	$0	

*by large individual contributors ($200 & above)

Defense — $33,565

Defense Aerospace	**$18,415**	
McDonnell Douglas*	$3,000	PAC
Martin Marietta Corp	$2,000	PAC
Lockheed Corp	$1,500	PAC
Northrop Corp	$1,500	PAC
Textron Inc	$1,500	PAC
Allied-Signal	$1,000	PAC
General Dynamics	$1,000	PAC
General Electric	$1,000	PAC
Grumman Corp	$1,000	PAC
LTV Aerospace & Defense Co	$1,000	PAC
Defense Electronics	**$13,750**	
AT&T	$2,000	PAC
E-Systems Inc	$1,750	PAC
Litton Industries	$1,500	PAC
Motorola Inc	$1,500	PAC
Harris Corp	$1,000	PAC
Hughes Aircraft	$1,000	PAC
Loral Corp	$1,000	PAC
Talley Industries	$1,000	PAC
Westinghouse Electric	$1,000	PAC
Misc Defense	**$1,400**	
None over $1,000		

Energy & Natural Resources — $16,800

Oil & Gas	**$5,500**	
El Paso Co	$1,500	PAC
Kaibab Industries	$1,500	Indiv
Southwest Gas Corp	$1,500	PAC
Mining	**$8,200**	
Phelps Dodge Corp	$2,700	PAC
Cyprus Minerals Co	$2,500	PAC
Asarco Inc	$1,000	PAC
Energy Fuels Nuclear Inc	$1,000	Indiv
National Coal Assn	$1,000	PAC
Electric Utilities	**$2,600**	
Arizona Public Service Co	$1,500	PAC

Finance, Insurance & Real Estate — $18,450

Commercial Banks $3,800
    American Bankers Assn .... $1,500   PAC
    Valley National Bank of Arizona .... $1,000   PAC

Securities & Investment $2,100
    Gage Communications Inc .... $1,500   Indiv

Insurance $2,550
    None over $1,000

Real Estate $9,250
    National Assn of Realtors .... $4,000   PAC
    Del Webb Corp .... $1,500   PAC

Health — $16,850

Health Professionals $13,350
    American Medical Assn .... $7,200   PAC
    American Academy of Ophthalmology .... $2,500   PAC
    American Dental Assn .... $1,500   PAC

Hospitals/Nursing Homes $1,500
    None over $1,000

Health Services $1,000
    Family Health Program Inc .... $1,000   PAC

Pharmaceuticals/Health Products $1,000
    None over $1,000

Lawyers & Lobbyists — $5,900

Lawyers & Lobbyists $5,900
    Ryley, Carlock & Applewhite .... $2,100   Indiv

Misc Business — $11,150

Beer, Wine & Liquor $2,800
    National Beer Wholesalers Assn .... $1,500   PAC
    Hensley & Co .... $1,000   Indiv

Retail Sales $1,000
    None over $1,000

Business Services $1,300
    None over $1,000

Casinos/Gambling $1,500
    Riverside Resort & Casino .... $1,500   Indiv

---

Chemical & Related Manufacturing $1,250
    Dial Corp .... $1,000   PAC

Misc Manufacturing & Distributing $3,000
    Stone Container Corp .... $2,500   PAC

Transportation — $15,200

Air Transport $4,600
    United Parcel Service .... $3,600   PAC
    Aircraft Owners & Pilots Assn .... $1,000   PAC

Automotive $8,300
    National Auto Dealers Assn .... $5,000   PAC
    Auto Dealers & Drivers for Free Trade .... $1,500   PAC
    Americans for Free International Trade ..... $1,000   PAC

Railroads $1,500
    Union Pacific Corp .... $1,000   PAC

Labor

Labor — $1,000

Public Sector Unions $1,000
    National Assn Retired Federal Employees ..... $1,000   PAC

Ideological/Single-Issue

Ideological/Single-Issue — $12,450

Gun Rights/Gun Control $9,900
    National Rifle Assn .... $9,900   PAC

Misc Issues $1,250
    None over $1,000

Other & Unknown

Other — $11,300

Retired $9,800
    None over $1,000

Unknown — $8,000

    Homemakers/Non-income earners $1,050
    Employer Listed/Category Unknown $6,200
      Arizona Rock Products Assn .... $1,000   Indiv
      JL Neal Family Limited Partnership .... $1,000   Indiv

Independent expenditures supporting Stump
    National Right to Life PAC $2,410

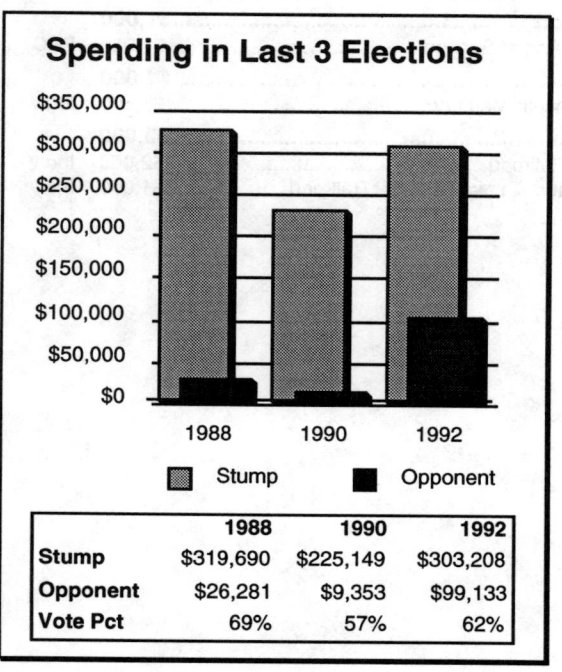

Spending in Last 3 Elections

	1988	1990	1992
Stump	$319,690	$225,149	$303,208
Opponent	$26,281	$9,353	$99,133
Vote Pct	69%	57%	62%

* Contributions came from more than one affiliate or subsidiary.

Bart Stupak, D-Mich (1)

First elected: 1992

1991-92 Total Receipts: $216,699
1992 Year-end Cash: $125

1993-94 Committees & Subcommittees

Armed Services
Military Acquisition; Military Forces and Personnel

Government Operations
Information, Justice, Transportation and Agriculture

Merchant Marine and Fisheries
Coast Guard and Navigation; Merchant Marine

Leading Contributors

Business

Agriculture	$2,500

Food Processing & Sales $2,000
   None over $1,000

Communications/Electronics	$2,200

Telephone Utilities $1,500
   AT&T ....$1,000 PAC

Construction	$3,450

Home Builders $1,000
   None over $1,000

Building Materials & Equipment $2,000
   Champion Inc ....$2,000 Indiv

Energy & Natural Resources	$6,250

Oil & Gas $2,500
   Krist Oil Co ....$2,000 Indiv

Waste Management $3,750
   City Management Corp ....$3,500 PAC/Ind

Finance, Insurance & Real Esta	$5,950

Securities & Investment $1,000
   Jennison Associates ....$1,000 Indiv

Insurance $1,600
   None over $1,000

Accountants $3,150
   American Institute of CPA's ....$2,000 PAC

Source of Funds in 1992 Election

Source	Total	Pct
PACs	$109,950	46%
Indivs $200+	$41,575	17%
Indivs under $200	$42,727	18%
Other	$45,214	19%
Candidate	$4,197	2%
Party	$36,517	15%

Source of PAC Dollars by Sector

Source	Total	Pct
Business	$14,550	14%
Labor	$70,250	68%
Ideology/Single Issue	$17,950	17%

In-State vs. Out-of-State Contributions*

Source	Total	Pct
In-State	$38,075	92%
Out-of-state	$3,500	8%
No state listed	$0	

* by large individual contributors ($200 & above)

Lawyers & Lobbyists	$16,000

Lawyers & Lobbyists $16,000
   Assn of Trial Lawyers of America ....$5,000 PAC

Misc Business	$3,925

Business Services $1,275
   None over $1,000

Lodging/Tourism $2,000
   None over $1,000

Transportation	$5,750

Air Transport $1,000
   United Parcel Service ....$1,000 PAC

Automotive $1,000
   Star Lincoln Mercury ....$1,000 Indiv

Railroads $3,000
   E&LS Railroad ....$2,000 Indiv
   Escanaba & Lake Superior Railroad ......$1,000 Indiv

Contribution Totals by Sector

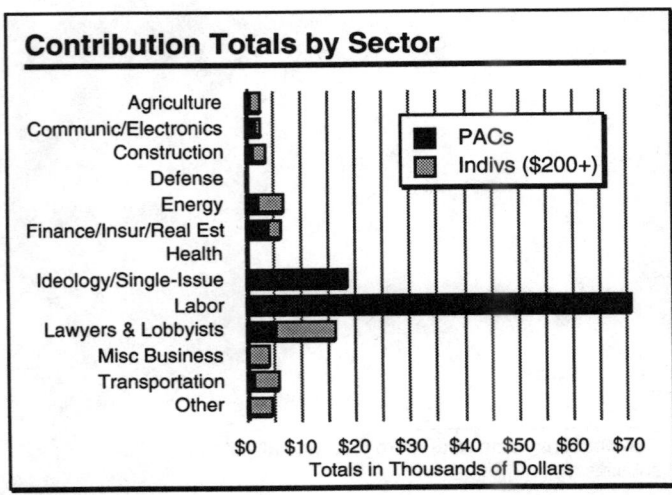

Agriculture
Communic/Electronics
Construction
Defense
Energy
Finance/Insur/Real Est
Health
Ideology/Single-Issue
Labor
Lawyers & Lobbyists
Misc Business
Transportation
Other

- PACs
- Indivs ($200+)

$0 $10 $20 $30 $40 $50 $60 $70
Totals in Thousands of Dollars

Labor

Labor	$70,250

Building Trade Unions **$18,450**
- Operating Engineers Union* .... $5,000   PAC
- Ironworkers Union .... $3,000   PAC
- Carpenters & Joiners Union .... $2,500   PAC
- Sheet Metal Workers Union .... $2,250   PAC
- Boilermakers Union local #169 .... $2,200   PAC
- Plumbers/Pipefitters Union* .... $2,000   PAC
- Laborers' Political League .... $1,000   PAC

Industrial Unions **$23,500**
- United Auto Workers .... $10,000   PAC
- Machinists/Aerospace Workers Union .... $2,500   PAC
- Communications Workers of America .... $2,000   PAC
- United Steelworkers .... $2,000   PAC
- AFL-CIO Allied Industrial Wrkrs .... $1,000   PAC
- Intl Brotherhood of Electrical Workers .... $1,000   PAC
- Oil, Chemical & Atomic Workers Union .... $1,000   PAC
- Rubber Cork Linoleum & Plastic Workers ..... $1,000   PAC
- United Paperworkers .... $1,000   PAC

Transportation Unions **$9,500**
- Teamsters Union .... $5,000   PAC
- Air Line Pilots Assn .... $2,000   PAC
- Seafarers International Union .... $1,000   PAC

Public Sector Unions **$9,300**
- American Fedn of St/Cnty/Munic Employees ..... $5,000   PAC
- International Assn of Firefighters .... $2,000   PAC
- National Assn Retired Federal Employees ..... $1,000   PAC
- National Assn of Letter Carriers .... $1,000   PAC

Misc Unions **$9,500**
- AFL-CIO .... $5,000   PAC
- Service Employees International Union .... $3,000   PAC
- Bakery, Confectionery & Tobacco Workers ..... $1,500   PAC

Ideological/Single-Issue

Ideological/Single-Issue	$17,950

Democratic/Liberal **$5,500**
- National Cmte for an Effective Congress .... $5,000   PAC

Leadership PACs **$2,500**
- Effective Government Cmte (Dick Gephardt) ...... $1,000   PAC
- House Leadership Fund (Tom Foley) .... $1,000   PAC

Pro-Israel **$1,000**
- MOPAC .... $1,000   PAC

Pro-Life **$2,000**
- National Right to Life PAC .... $2,000   PAC

Gun Rights/Gun Control **$4,950**
- National Rifle Assn .... $4,950   PAC

Misc Issues **$2,000**
- National Council of Senior Citizens .... $2,000   PAC

Other & Unknown

Other	$4,200

Retired **$3,800**
- None over $1,000

Unknown	$8,900

- Unknown $3,000
  - Democratic Leaders' Fund .... $3,000   PAC
- Homemakers/Non-income earners $5,400

Independent expenditures supporting Stupak
- National Rifle Assn $3,871

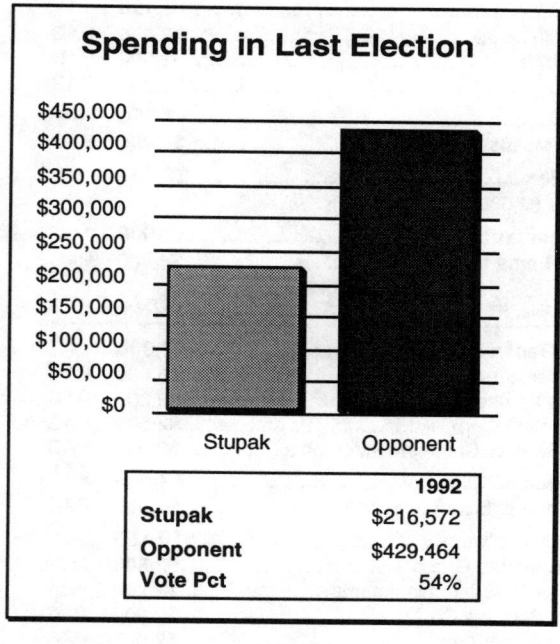

Spending in Last Election

	1992
Stupak	$216,572
Opponent	$429,464
Vote Pct	54%

---

* Contributions came from more than one affiliate or subsidiary.

Don Sundquist, R-Tenn (7)

First elected: 1982
1991-92 Total Receipts: $819,006
1992 Year-end Cash: $289,691

1991-92 Committees & Subcommittees

Ways and Means
Oversight; Select Revenue Measures

Leading Contributors

Business

Agriculture — $60,000

Crop Production & Basic Processing **$4,400**
None over $2,000

Tobacco **$16,100**
RJR Nabisco	$4,000	PAC
Conwood Co	$3,300	Indiv
Philip Morris	$3,000	PAC

Agricultural Services/Products **$6,000**
Deere & Co	$2,000	PAC
Drexel Chemical Co	$2,000	Indiv

Food Processing & Sales **$19,500**
Malone & Hyde Inc	$6,000	PAC/Ind
Fleming Companies Inc	$5,000	PAC
Food Marketing Institute	$3,000	PAC

Forestry & Forest Products **$11,000**
Westvaco Corp	$5,000	PAC
International Paper Co	$3,000	PAC

Communications/Electronics — $24,403

Printing & Publishing **$4,903**
Printing Industries of America	$2,503	PAC

Media/Entertainment **$3,500**
None over $2,000

Telephone Utilities **$11,800**
AT&T	$4,000	PAC
GTE Corp	$3,000	PAC

Source of Funds in 1992 Election

Source	Total	Pct
PACs	$355,884	43%
Indivs $200+	$238,380	29%
Indivs under $200	$150,978	18%
Other	$73,764	9%
Candidate	$0	0%
Party	$92	0%

Source of PAC Dollars by Sector

Source	Total	Pct
Business	$336,860	96%
Labor	$10,050	3%
Ideology/Single Issue	$5,037	1%

In-State vs. Out-of-State Contributions*

Source	Total	Pct
In-State	$214,880	90%
Out-of-state	$22,550	10%
No state listed	$0	

* by large individual contributors ($200 & above)

Construction — $21,250

General Contractors **$12,500**
Folk Construction Co	$4,000	Indiv

Building Materials & Equipment **$8,000**
Regal Corp	$2,000	Indiv
Schilling Enterprises	$2,000	Indiv

Defense — $4,500

Defense Aerospace **$3,000**
None over $2,000

Energy & Natural Resources — $32,700

Oil & Gas **$19,450**
Ashland Oil	$2,000	PAC
Coastal Fuels Inc	$2,000	Indiv
Mapco Inc	$2,000	PAC

Mining **$7,250**
Reynolds Metals	$3,000	PAC

Electric Utilities **$2,000**
None over $2,000

Waste Management **$3,000**
Browning-Ferris Industries	$2,000	PAC

Finance, Insurance & Real Estate — $144,927

Commercial Banks **$23,300**
First Tennessee National Corp	$6,000	PAC
Citizens & Southern National Bank	$3,000	PAC
Union Planters Corp	$2,500	PAC/Ind
National Bank of Commerce/Memphis	$2,000	PAC

Savings & Loans **$3,500**
Leader Federal Savings & Loan	$2,000	PAC

Securities & Investment **$19,150**
JMR Investments Group	$2,500	Indiv
Diaz-Verson Capital Investments	$2,000	Indiv
Goldman, Sachs & Co	$2,000	PAC
Public Securities Assn	$2,000	PAC

Contribution Totals by Sector

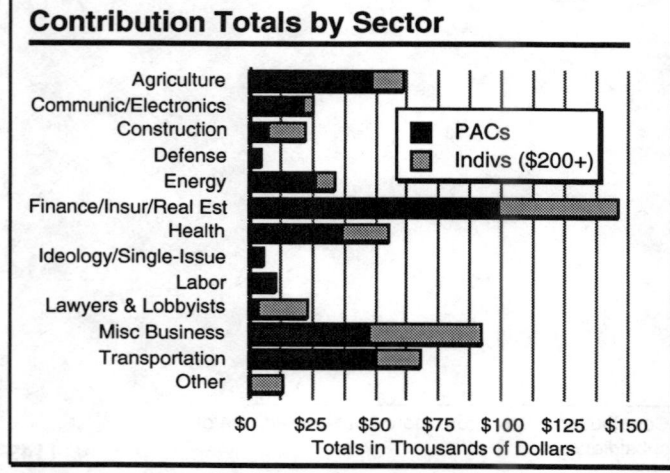

Agriculture, Communic/Electronics, Construction, Defense, Energy, Finance/Insur/Real Est, Health, Ideology/Single-Issue, Labor, Lawyers & Lobbyists, Misc Business, Transportation, Other

Legend: PACs, Indivs ($200+)

Totals in Thousands of Dollars ($0, $25, $50, $75, $100, $125, $150)

Insurance $52,161
    National Assn of Life Underwriters ....$7,500 PAC
    Massachusetts Mutual Life Insurance ....$4,500 PAC/Ind
    American Family Corp ....$4,000 PAC
    General American Life Insurance ....$3,000 PAC
    American Council of Life Insurance ....$2,500 PAC
    Independent Insurance Agents of America ....$2,100 PAC
    Mutual of Omaha ....$2,000 PAC
    New England Mutual Life ....$2,000 PAC
    Northwestern Mutual Life ....$2,000 PAC

Real Estate **$25,636**
    National Assn of Realtors ....$10,000 PAC
    Belz Enterprises ....$3,836 Indiv
    Trammell Crow Co ....$2,250 Indiv
    McGehee Realty & Mortgage ....$2,000 Indiv

Accountants **$10,780**
    American Institute of CPA's ....$5,000 PAC

Misc Finance **$8,900**
    Boyle Investment Co ....$4,000 Indiv

Health $53,850

Health Professionals **$29,900**
    American Medical Assn ....$5,500 PAC
    American Dental Assn ....$5,000 PAC

Hospitals/Nursing Homes **$4,500**
    None over $2,000

Pharmaceuticals/Health Products **$17,900**
    Schering-Plough Corp ....$7,000 PAC
    Danek Group ....$2,000 Indiv

Lawyers & Lobbyists $23,251

Lawyers & Lobbyists **$23,251**
    Heiskell, Donelson et al ....$4,750 Indiv
    Arent, Fox et al ....$2,000 Indiv
    McDonnell, Boyd et al ....$2,000 Indiv

Misc Business $91,296

Food & Beverage **$4,900**
    National Restaurant Assn ....$2,000 PAC

Beer, Wine & Liquor **$11,665**
    Wine & Spirits Wholesalers of America ....$2,500 PAC

Retail Sales **$12,100**
    Cleo Inc ....$3,400 Indiv
    International Council of Shopping Centers ....$2,000 PAC

Business Services **$26,650**
    Guardsmark Inc ....$21,750 Indiv
    Humphreys Cayman Ltd ....$2,000 Indiv

Casinos/Gambling **$3,500**
    Promus Companies ....$3,500 PAC

Lodging/Tourism **$4,000**
    None over $2,000

Misc Business **$2,500**
    Nordix Inc ....$2,000 Indiv

Chemical & Related Manufacturing **$8,981**
    Dow Chemical ....$2,000 PAC

Misc Manufacturing & Distributing **$12,900**
    Stone Container Corp ....$2,000 PAC

Transportation $66,850

Air Transport **$16,750**
    Federal Express Corp ....$10,000 PAC
    United Parcel Service ....$3,950 PAC

Automotive **$33,400**
    National Auto Dealers Assn ....$9,000 PAC
    Autozone Inc ....$8,000 PAC/Ind
    Americans for Free International Trade ....$5,000 PAC
    Dobbs Brothers Managment ....$3,000 Indiv
    Auto Dealers & Drivers for Free Trade ....$2,000 PAC

Trucking **$5,950**
    MS Carriers ....$2,000 Indiv

Railroads **$4,500**
    Norfolk Southern Corp ....$2,000 PAC

Sea Transport **$4,250**
    CSX Corp* ....$2,000 PAC

Misc Transport **$2,000**
    Continental Traffic Service ....$2,000 Indiv

Labor

Labor $10,050

Transportation Unions **$4,750**
    Marine Engineers Union* ....$4,750 PAC

Public Sector Unions **$4,800**
    National Assn Retired Federal Employees ....$2,500 PAC

Ideological/Single-Issue

Ideological/Single-Issue $5,037

Gun Rights/Gun Control **$3,500**
    National Rifle Assn ....$3,500 PAC

Other & Unknown

Other $12,450

Education **$2,500**
    None over $2,000

Retired **$9,450**
    None over $2,000

Unknown $40,063

    Homemakers/Non-income earners $15,407
    Employer Listed/Category Unknown $22,756
    None over $2,000

* Contributions came from more than one affiliate or subsidiary.

Spending in Last 3 Elections

	1988	1990	1992
Sundquist	$307,656	$451,944	$1,001,217
Opponent	$1,110	$0	$106,774
Vote Pct	80%	62%	62%

Dick Swett, D-NH (2)

First elected: 1990

1991-92 Total Receipts: $877,187
1992 Year-end Cash: $96,407

1991-92 Committees & Subcommittees

Public Works and Transportation
Aviation; Economic Development; Surface Transportation

Science, Space and Technology
Environment; Technology and Competitiveness

Select Committee on Aging

Leading Contributors

Business

Agriculture		$13,812
Poultry & Eggs	**$4,000**	
United Feather & Down Inc	$4,000	Indiv
Food Processing & Sales	**$5,712**	
Wornick Co	$2,712	Indiv
Trag's Market	$2,500	Indiv

Communications/Electronics		$29,000
Printing & Publishing	**$5,000**	
None over $2,500		
Media/Entertainment	**$5,000**	
None over $2,500		
Telephone Utilities	**$6,000**	
New England Telephone	$3,000	PAC
Computer Equipment & Services	**$12,500**	
Atari Corp	$6,000	Indiv
Phoenix Systems	$5,500	Indiv

Construction		$22,910
General Contractors	**$4,300**	
None over $2,500		
Home Builders	**$5,500**	
National Assn of Home Builders	$2,500	PAC
Construction Services	**$11,360**	
American Institute of Architects	$10,000	PAC

Source of Funds in 1992 Election

Source	Total	Pct
■ PACs	$408,900	46%
▨ Indivs $200+	$374,392	42%
□ Indivs under $200	$71,360	8%
⊠ Other	$44,076	5%
Candidate	$0	0%
Party	$26,991	3%

Source of PAC Dollars by Sector

Source	Total	Pct
■ Business	$140,950	36%
▨ Labor	$196,800	50%
□ Ideology/Single Issue	$55,753	14%

In-State vs. Out-of-State Contributions*

Source	Total	Pct
□ In-State	$54,924	15%
■ Out-of-state	$317,718	85%
No state listed	$500	

* by large individual contributors ($200 & above)

Defense		$15,700
Defense Aerospace	**$3,000**	
None over $2,500		
Defense Electronics	**$12,700**	
Aydin Corp	$7,000	PAC/Ind
Raytheon	$5,500	PAC

Energy & Natural Resources		$13,050
Oil & Gas	**$2,800**	
None over $2,500		
Waste Management	**$3,500**	
None over $2,500		
Commercial Fishing	**$4,000**	
Royal Seafood Inc	$4,000	Indiv

Finance, Insurance & Real Estate		$75,550
Commercial Banks	**$3,000**	
None over $2,500		
Securities & Investment	**$12,750**	
Cilluffo Associates	$3,500	Indiv
Insurance	**$12,500**	
Chubb Corp	$7,000	PAC/Ind
National Assn of Life Underwriters	$3,000	PAC
Real Estate	**$38,100**	
National Assn of Realtors	$6,900	PAC
Westwood Management Corp	$4,000	Indiv
Irmas & Gold	$3,000	Indiv
Mack Companies	$2,750	Indiv
Misc Finance	**$5,750**	
None over $2,500		

Health		$38,418
Health Professionals	**$26,168**	
American Medical Assn	$7,350	PAC
American Academy of Ophthalmology	$4,500	PAC

Contribution Totals by Sector

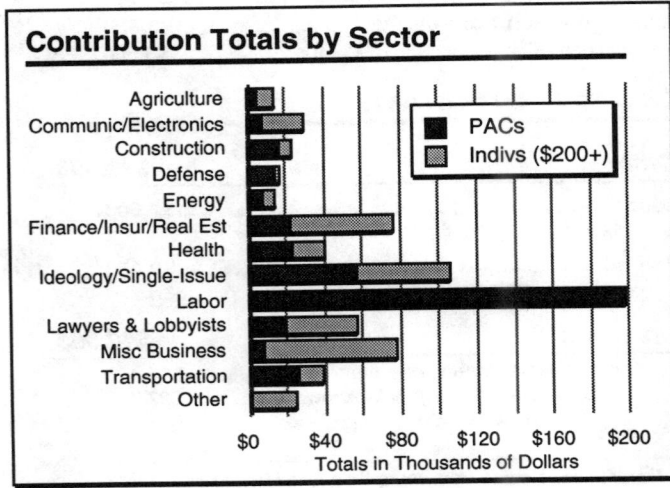

Agriculture
Communic/Electronics
Construction
Defense
Energy
Finance/Insur/Real Est
Health
Ideology/Single-Issue
Labor
Lawyers & Lobbyists
Misc Business
Transportation
Other

■ PACs
▨ Indivs ($200+)

$0 $40 $80 $120 $160 $200
Totals in Thousands of Dollars

Hospitals/Nursing Homes $2,500
   None over $2,500

Pharmaceuticals/Health Products $8,750
   Henley Group Inc .... $6,000   PAC/Ind

Lawyers & Lobbyists $55,177

Lawyers & Lobbyists $55,177
   Assn of Trial Lawyers of America .... $15,000   PAC
   Cotchett, Illston et al .... $4,000   Indiv
   Sulloway, Hollis et al .... $3,000   Indiv
   Powell, Goldstein et al .... $2,500   PAC

Misc Business $76,363

Food & Beverage $4,500
   None over $2,500

Retail Sales $5,750
   Jewelcor Inc .... $4,000   Indiv

Business Services $7,485
   AB Data .... $3,000   Indiv

Lodging/Tourism $2,850
   None over $2,500

Chemical & Related Manufacturing $3,000
   None over $2,500

Misc Manufacturing & Distributing $49,828
   Schnitzer Steel Industries .... $32,328   Indiv
   Chase Scientific Research .... $5,500   Indiv
   Guardian Industries Corp .... $2,500   Indiv

Transportation $37,750

Air Transport $18,600
   Federal Express Corp .... $8,000   PAC
   United Parcel Service .... $5,000   PAC

Automotive $6,400
   Shen Lincoln-Mercury .... $3,000   Indiv
   Auto Dealers & Drivers for Free Trade .... $2,500   PAC

Trucking $3,000
   None over $2,500

Sea Transport $8,000
   Apex Marine Corp .... $4,000   Indiv
   Liberty Maritime Corp .... $4,000   Indiv

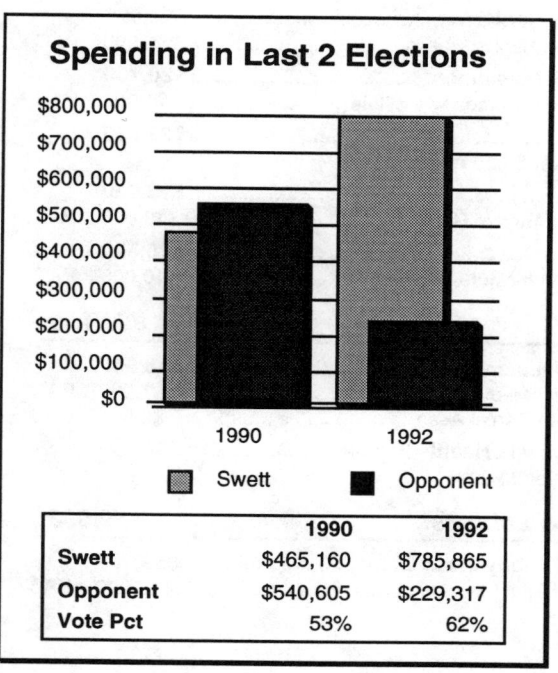

Spending in Last 2 Elections

	1990	1992
Swett	$465,160	$785,865
Opponent	$540,605	$229,317
Vote Pct	53%	62%

Swett   Opponent

Labor

Labor $196,800

Building Trade Unions $25,350
   Carpenters & Joiners Union .... $6,000   PAC
   Laborers' Political League .... $5,000   PAC
   Sheet Metal Workers Union .... $5,000   PAC
   Plumbers/Pipefitters Union .... $4,000   PAC

Industrial Unions $47,000
   Intl Brotherhood of Electrical Workers ...... $10,500   PAC
   United Auto Workers .... $10,000   PAC
   Machinists/Aerospace Workers Union .... $7,500   PAC
   Communications Workers of America .... $4,000   PAC
   Boilermakers Union .... $3,000   PAC
   Oil, Chemical & Atomic Workers Union ...... $2,500   PAC

Transportation Unions $37,000
   Teamsters Union .... $10,000   PAC
   Air Line Pilots Assn .... $7,500   PAC
   Marine Engineers Union* .... $7,500   PAC
   United Transportation Union .... $3,000   PAC

Public Sector Unions $59,050
   American Fedn of St/Cnty/Munic Employees .... $15,000   PAC
   National Assn of Letter Carriers .... $10,000   PAC
   National Education Assn .... $10,000   PAC
   American Federation of Teachers .... $7,500   PAC
   American Postal Workers Union .... $5,000   PAC
   National Assn Retired Federal Employees ...... $4,500   PAC

Misc Unions $28,400
   Food & Commercial Workers Union .... $10,000   PAC
   AFL-CIO .... $6,500   PAC
   Office & Professional Employees Union ...... $6,000   PAC
   Service Employees International Union .... $4,000   PAC

Ideological/Single-Issue

Ideological/Single-Issue $104,166

Democratic/Liberal $5,756
   National Cmte for an Effective Congress ...... $2,500   PAC

Leadership PACs $3,770
   None over $2,500

Foreign & Defense Policy $4,450
   Free Cuba PAC .... $3,450   PAC

Pro-Israel $60,157
   National PAC .... $5,000   PAC
   Hudson Valley PAC .... $4,000   PAC

Human Rights $14,000
   National Albanian American PAC .... $10,000   PAC
   KidsPAC .... $3,000   PAC

Misc Issues $16,033
   National Cmte to Preserve Social Security ...... $7,000   PAC
   Sierra Club .... $6,500   PAC

Other & Unknown

Other $24,050

Retired $18,000
   None over $2,500

Unknown $63,899

   Homemakers/Non-income earners $11,950
   No Employer Listed or Found $13,916
   Generic Occupation/Category Unknown $8,750
   Employer Listed/Category Unknown $29,283
     None over $2,500

* Contributions came from more than one affiliate or subsidiary.

Al Swift, D-Wash (2)

First elected: 1978

1991-92 Total Receipts: $914,905
1992 Year-end Cash: $22,730

1991-92 Committees & Subcommittees

Administration
Accounts; Elections (Chairman)

Energy and Commerce
Energy and Power; Transportation and Hazardous Materials (Chairman)

Leading Contributors

Business

Agriculture	$62,051

Tobacco	$8,500	
None over $5,000		
Food Processing & Sales	$16,876	
Food Marketing Institute	$6,250	PAC
Forestry & Forest Products	$24,250	
None over $5,000		

Communications/Electronics	$99,000

Media/Entertainment	$39,250	
National Assn of Broadcasters	$10,000	PAC
National Cable Television Assn	$10,000	PAC
Telephone Utilities	$43,850	
US West Inc	$10,000	PAC
BellSouth Corp*	$9,000	PAC
Ameritech Corp	$6,600	PAC
Pacific Telesis Group	$5,000	PAC
Telecom Services & Equipment	$9,000	
McCaw Cellular Communications	$5,000	PAC

Construction	$15,575

Construction Services	$6,325	
None over $5,000		
Building Materials & Equipment	$7,500	
None over $5,000		

Defense	$5,500

None over $5,000	

Source of Funds in 1992 Election

Source	Total	Pct
■ PACs	$649,844	70%
▨ Indivs $200+	$141,344	15%
☐ Indivs under $200	$80,553	9%
▩ Other	$53,916	6%
Candidate	$0	0%
Party	$10,752	1%

Source of PAC Dollars by Sector

Source	Total	Pct
■ Business	$506,885	79%
▨ Labor	$121,500	19%
☐ Ideology/Single Issue	$11,000	2%

In-State vs. Out-of-State Contributions*

Source	Total	Pct
☐ In-State	$56,008	40%
■ Out-of-state	$85,086	60%
No state listed	$250	

* by large individual contributors ($200 & above)

Energy & Natural Resources	$91,423

Oil & Gas	$35,250	
None over $5,000		
Mining	$8,923	
None over $5,000		
Electric Utilities	$11,950	
None over $5,000		
Waste Management	$29,050	
Browning-Ferris Industries	$7,000	PAC/Ind
Chambers Development Co	$5,000	PAC

Finance, Insurance & Real Estate	$112,000

Commercial Banks	$22,000	
American Bankers Assn	$5,000	PAC
Securities & Investment	$20,750	
Investment Company Institute	$7,000	PAC
Insurance	$29,750	
None over $5,000		
Real Estate	$13,050	
National Assn of Realtors	$10,000	PAC
Accountants	$20,500	
American Institute of CPA's	$10,000	PAC

Health	$29,150

Health Professionals	$18,900	
American Medical Assn*	$7,500	PAC
American Dental Assn	$5,500	PAC
Pharmaceuticals/Health Products	$6,500	
None over $5,000		

Lawyers & Lobbyists	$59,938

Lawyers & Lobbyists	$59,938	
Assn of Trial Lawyers of America	$10,000	PAC

Contribution Totals by Sector

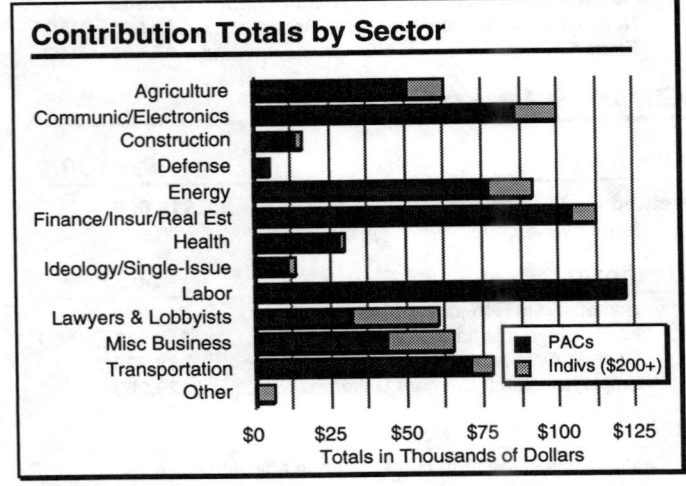

Agriculture
Communic/Electronics
Construction
Defense
Energy
Finance/Insur/Real Est
Health
Ideology/Single-Issue
Labor
Lawyers & Lobbyists
Misc Business
Transportation
Other

■ PACs
▨ Indivs ($200+)

$0 $25 $50 $75 $100 $125
Totals in Thousands of Dollars

Misc Business	$64,275

Food & Beverage $9,500
    None over $5,000

Beer, Wine & Liquor $9,000
    None over $5,000

Business Services $7,675
    None over $5,000

Chemical & Related Manufacturing $16,250
    None over $5,000

Misc Manufacturing & Distributing $16,050
    None over $5,000

Transportation

Transportation	$77,559

Air Transport $13,959
    Boeing Co ....$6,500 PAC/Ind

Automotive $15,350
    None over $5,000

Railroads $41,250
    Burlington Northern ....$14,250 PAC/Ind
    Union Pacific Corp ....$9,000 PAC

Labor

Labor	$121,500

Building Trade Unions $9,500
    None over $5,000

Industrial Unions $25,000
    United Auto Workers ....$6,500 PAC
    Intl Brotherhood of Electrical Workers .....$5,000 PAC

Transportation Unions $46,000
    Teamsters Union ....$10,000 PAC
    United Transportation Union ....$10,000 PAC
    Brotherhood of Locomotive Engineers ....$6,000 PAC
    Seafarers International Union ....$6,000 PAC

Public Sector Unions $33,000
    National Education Assn ....$10,000 PAC
    National Assn Retired Federal Employees ....$5,000 PAC
    National Assn of Letter Carriers ....$5,000 PAC

Misc Unions $8,000
    None over $5,000

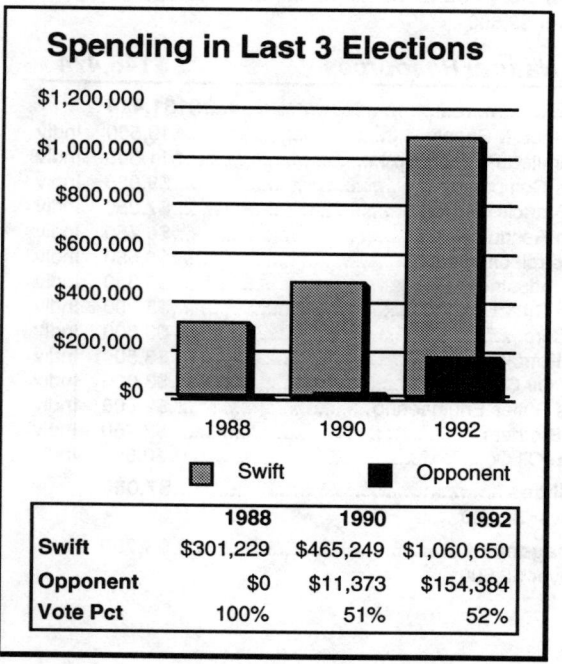

Spending in Last 3 Elections

	1988	1990	1992
Swift	$301,229	$465,249	$1,060,650
Opponent	$0	$11,373	$154,384
Vote Pct	100%	51%	52%

Ideological/Single-Issue

Ideological/Single-Issue	$13,000
    None over $5,000

Other & Unknown

Other	$6,100
    None over $5,000

Unknown	$24,158
    No Employer Listed or Found $7,350
    Employer Listed/Category Unknown $15,558
       None over $5,000

---

* Contributions came from more than one affiliate or
subsidiary.

Mike Synar, D-Okla (2)

First elected: 1978
1991-92 Total Receipts: $1,191,392
1992 Year-end Cash: $26,075

1991-92 Committees & Subcommittees

Energy and Commerce
Energy and Power; Health and the Environment; Telecommunications and Finance

Government Operations
Environment, Energy and Natural Resources (Chairman)

Judiciary
Economic and Commercial Law; Intellectual Property and Judicial Administration

Select Committee on Hunger

Leading Contributors

Business

Agriculture	$13,150	
Poultry & Eggs	$3,000	
None over $2,500		
Livestock	$3,950	
None over $2,500		
Food Processing & Sales	$5,800	
None over $2,500		

Communications/Electronics	$130,354	
Printing & Publishing	$12,950	
West Publishing	$5,000	Indiv
Donrey Media Group	$2,500	Indiv
Media/Entertainment	$71,754	
Walt Disney Co	$13,074	Indiv
Cox Cable Communications	$6,250	Indiv
MCA Inc	$6,000	Indiv
Tempo Enterprises	$6,000	Indiv
Paramount Pictures	$5,500	Indiv
Sony Corp/Columbia Pictures*	$5,000	Indiv
Turner Broadcasting System	$3,000	Indiv
United Video Inc	$2,550	Indiv
Time Warner*	$2,500	Indiv

Source of Funds in 1992 Election

Source	Total	Pct
PACs	$-350	-0%
Indivs $200+	$863,056	72%
Indivs under $200	$311,391	26%
Other	$18,850	2%
Candidate	$0	0%
Party	$1,555	0%

Source of PAC Dollars by Sector

No PAC contributions reported

Source	Total	Pct
Business	$0	0%
Labor	$0	0%
Ideology/Single Issue	$0	0%

In-State vs. Out-of-State Contributions*

Source	Total	Pct
In-State	$407,993	48%
Out-of-state	$443,734	52%
No state listed	$9,980	

* by large individual contributors ($200 & above)

Telephone Utilities	$33,950	
Chouteau Telephone Co	$12,000	Indiv
Totah Telephone Co	$4,900	Indiv
Cross Telephone Co	$2,500	Indiv
Telecom Services & Equipment	$7,750	
Fleetcall Inc	$4,700	Indiv

Construction	$19,350	
General Contractors	$13,400	
Roban Development Co	$3,000	Indiv
Yordi Construction Co	$3,000	Indiv
Construction Services	$2,850	
None over $2,500		

Energy & Natural Resources	$146,474	
Oil & Gas	$131,414	
Sooner Pipe & Supply	$13,550	Indiv
Mesa Limited Partnership	$11,500	Indiv
Williams Companies	$9,066	Indiv
Kaiser-Francis Oil Co	$7,250	Indiv
Samson Resources Co	$6,750	Indiv
Citgo Petroleum Corp	$6,550	Indiv
Anchor Industries	$5,350	Indiv
Frances Oil & Gas Inc	$5,000	Indiv
Enron Corp	$3,500	Indiv
Griffith Petroleum	$3,500	Indiv
Bankoff Oil Co	$3,000	Indiv
Willbros-Butler Engineering	$2,800	Indiv
Singer Brothers	$2,750	Indiv
Krumme Oil Co	$2,500	Indiv
Electric Utilities	$7,060	
None over $2,500		
Waste Management	$3,750	
None over $2,500		

Contribution Totals by Sector

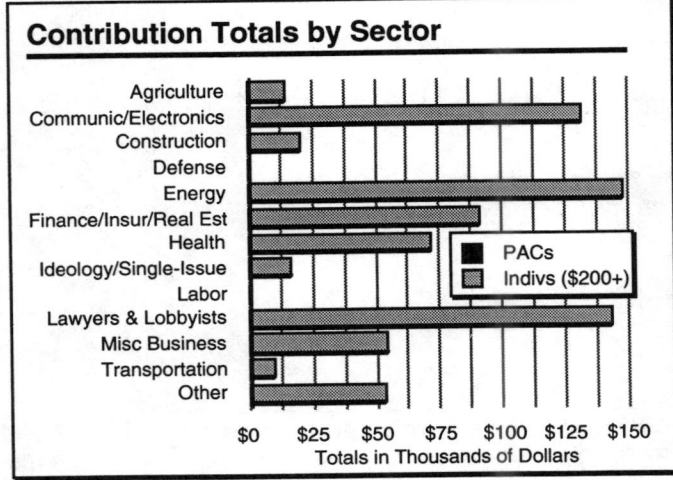

Agriculture
Communic/Electronics
Construction
Defense
Energy
Finance/Insur/Real Est
Health
Ideology/Single-Issue
Labor
Lawyers & Lobbyists
Misc Business
Transportation
Other

■ PACs
▨ Indivs ($200+)

$0 $25 $50 $75 $100 $125 $150
Totals in Thousands of Dollars

Finance, Insurance & Real Estate — $89,950

Commercial Banks **$11,300**
    Peoples National Bank .... $4,200   Indiv

Finance/Credit Companies **$8,750**
    Beneficial Management Corp .... $7,000   Indiv

Securities & Investment **$34,850**
    Salomon Brothers .... $9,000   Indiv
    Goldman, Sachs & Co .... $7,000   Indiv
    Shearson Lehman Brothers .... $5,500   Indiv
    Asset Management Co .... $3,000   Indiv

Insurance **$4,990**
    None over $2,500

Real Estate **$12,550**
    None over $2,500

Accountants **$8,560**
    None over $2,500

Misc Finance **$8,700**
    None over $2,500

Health — $70,361

Health Professionals **$20,471**
    St Michael Hospital .... $2,500   Indiv

Hospitals/Nursing Homes **$20,940**
    Guthrie Nursing Home .... $4,000   Indiv

Health Services **$9,500**
    Buford Properties .... $9,000   Indiv

Pharmaceuticals/Health Products **$16,200**
    Glaxo Inc .... $4,250   Indiv
    Genentech Inc .... $2,500   Indiv

Misc Health **$3,250**
    None over $2,500

Lawyers & Lobbyists — $143,121

Lawyers & Lobbyists **$143,121**
    David Vienna & Associates .... $9,000   Indiv
    Akin, Gump et al .... $8,750   Indiv
    Frasier & Frasier .... $6,999   Indiv
    Williams & Jensen .... $5,160   Indiv
    Wunder, Diefenderfer et al .... $3,750   Indiv
    Michael L Tiner & Assoc .... $3,000   Indiv

Spending in Last 3 Elections

	1988	1990	1992
Synar	$358,705	$631,839	$1,190,197
Opponent	$81,634	$62,793	$30,312
Vote Pct	65%	61%	56%

    Griffin, Johnson & Associates .... $2,750   Indiv
    Chapel, Riggs et al .... $2,500   Indiv
    Williams, Box et al .... $2,500   Indiv

Misc Business — $53,600

Food & Beverage **$4,850**
    None over $2,500

Beer, Wine & Liquor **$2,750**
    None over $2,500

Retail Sales **$5,500**
    None over $2,500

Business Services **$19,300**
    Fred Williamson & Associates .... $4,950   Indiv
    Dun & Bradstreet .... $2,500   Indiv

Misc Manufacturing & Distributing **$15,250**
    Madewell & Madewell .... $5,000   Indiv
    Yaffe Iron & Metal Co .... $2,750   Indiv

Transportation — $8,774

Automotive **$4,350**
    None over $2,500

Ideological/Single-Issue

Ideological/Single-Issue — $15,768

Democratic/Liberal **$9,050**
    None over $2,500

Pro-Israel **$3,500**
    None over $2,500

Other & Unknown

Other — $52,240

Civil Servants/Public Officials **$7,150**
    None over $2,500

Education **$15,250**
    None over $2,500

Retired **$25,540**
    None over $2,500

Other **$2,500**
    None over $2,500

Unknown — $118,833

    Homemakers/Non-income earners $20,850
    No Employer Listed or Found $26,500
    Employer Listed/Category Unknown $70,483
        Advanced Warnings .... $3,000   Indiv

Independent expenditures supporting Synar
    Small Business Coalition $10,364
    Petroleum Marketers Assn $10,200
    Teamsters local #523 .... $5,000

Independent expenditures opposing Synar
    National Rifle Assn $137,574

---

* Contributions came from more than one affiliate or subsidiary.

James M. Talent, R-Mo (2)

First elected: 1992

1991-92 Total Receipts: $924,820
1992 Year-end Cash: $10,004

1993-94 Committees & Subcommittees

Armed Services
Military Forces and Personnel; Research and Technology

Small Business
Minority Enterprise, Finance and Urban Development; SBA Legislation and the General Economy

Leading Contributors

Business

Agriculture — $29,190

Tobacco	**$8,400**	
US Tobacco Co	$5,000	PAC
RJR Nabisco	$3,400	PAC
Agricultural Services/Products	**$5,640**	
Missouri Farm Bureau/St Louis	$4,340	PAC
Food Processing & Sales	**$10,750**	
Fleming Companies Inc	$2,000	PAC
Flowers Industries	$2,000	PAC
Pepsico Inc	$2,000	PAC
Forestry & Forest Products	**$4,000**	
Westvaco Corp	$2,000	PAC

Communications/Electronics — $29,810

Printing & Publishing	**$3,860**	
Hallmark Cards	$2,500	PAC
Media/Entertainment	**$3,650**	
Cencom Cable Associates	$2,150	Indiv
Telephone Utilities	**$18,550**	
Southwestern Bell	$7,550	PAC/Ind
United Telecommunications	$5,500	PAC
GTE Corp	$4,000	PAC
Computer Equipment & Services	**$3,250**	
Tri Tek Information Systems Inc	$2,000	Indiv

Source of Funds in 1992 Election

Source	Total	Pct
PACs	$212,772	22%
Indivs $200+	$395,441	41%
Indivs under $200	$248,542	26%
Other	$107,829	11%
Candidate	$21,446	2%
Party	$47,600	5%

Source of PAC Dollars by Sector

Source	Total	Pct
Business	$184,597	91%
Labor	$0	0%
Ideology/Single Issue	$18,293	9%

In-State vs. Out-of-State Contributions*

Source	Total	Pct
In-State	$377,066	96%
Out-of-state	$14,300	4%
No state listed	$2,050	

* by large individual contributors ($200 & above)

Construction — $19,500

General Contractors	**$5,200**	
None over $2,000		
Home Builders	**$6,500**	
Rolwes Co	$4,000	Indiv
National Assn of Home Builders	$2,500	PAC
Special Trade Contractors	**$2,600**	
Engineered Fire Protection Inc	$2,100	Indiv
Building Materials & Equipment	**$4,200**	
Industrial Measurement Co	$2,000	Indiv

Defense — $2,750

Defense Aerospace	**$2,250**	
None over $2,000		

Energy & Natural Resources — $27,550

Oil & Gas	**$15,300**	
Schaeffer Manufacturing Co	$3,500	Indiv
Ashland Oil	$2,500	PAC
Chevron Corp	$2,000	PAC
Mining	**$4,000**	
Arch Mineral Corp	$2,250	PAC/Ind
Misc Energy	**$5,000**	
Cooper Industries	$5,000	PAC
Electric Utilities	**$3,250**	
Union Electric	$2,000	PAC

Finance, Insurance & Real Estate — $68,170

Commercial Banks	**$21,550**	
Mercantile Bancorp	$7,200	PAC
Boatmens Bankshares	$6,000	PAC
American Bankers Assn*	$4,500	PAC
Finance/Credit Companies	**$3,300**	
Household International Inc	$3,300	PAC

Contribution Totals by Sector

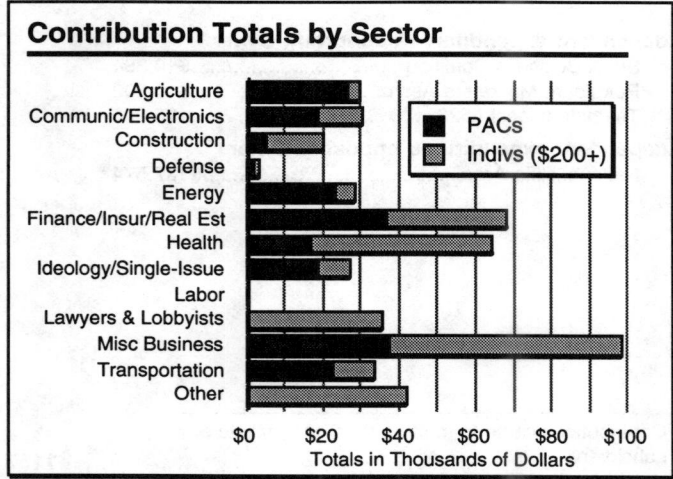

- Agriculture
- Communic/Electronics
- Construction
- Defense
- Energy
- Finance/Insur/Real Est
- Health
- Ideology/Single-Issue
- Labor
- Lawyers & Lobbyists
- Misc Business
- Transportation
- Other

Legend: PACs, Indivs ($200+)

$0 $20 $40 $60 $80 $100
Totals in Thousands of Dollars

Securities & Investment **$7,250**
    None over $2,000

Insurance **$14,700**
    General American Life Insurance .... $4,000   PAC
    Blue Cross & Blue Shield Assn* .... $3,450   PAC

Real Estate **$12,270**
    Health Facilities Management Corp .... $4,500   Indiv
    American Capital Corp .... $2,000   Indiv

Misc Finance **$6,300**
    Sunmark Capital Corp .... $2,000   Indiv

Health $63,600

Health Professionals **$38,100**
    American Medical Assn* .... $6,000   PAC
    American Dental Assn .... $3,500   PAC
    American Assn of Orthodontists .... $2,000   Indiv
    Metro Plastic & Reconstructive Surgeons .... $2,000   Indiv

Hospitals/Nursing Homes **$17,300**
    Community Care Centers .... $3,900   Indiv
    Mid America Long Term Care .... $3,500   Indiv
    Beverly Enterprises .... $3,000   PAC/Ind
    National Health Corp .... $3,000   PAC

Misc Health **$6,950**
    Tiffany Care Nursing Centers .... $2,250   Indiv

Lawyers & Lobbyists $35,719

Lawyers & Lobbyists **$35,719**
    Bryan, Cave et al .... $9,801   Indiv
    Lashall, Baer & Hamel .... $9,575   Indiv
    Armstrong, Teasdale et al .... $3,400   Indiv

Misc Business $99,818

Business Associations **$2,530**
    None over $2,000

Food & Beverage **$10,200**
    National Restaurant Assn .... $2,500   PAC
    Schollmeyers .... $2,000   Indiv

Beer, Wine & Liquor **$4,300**
    National Beer Wholesalers Assn .... $2,000   PAC

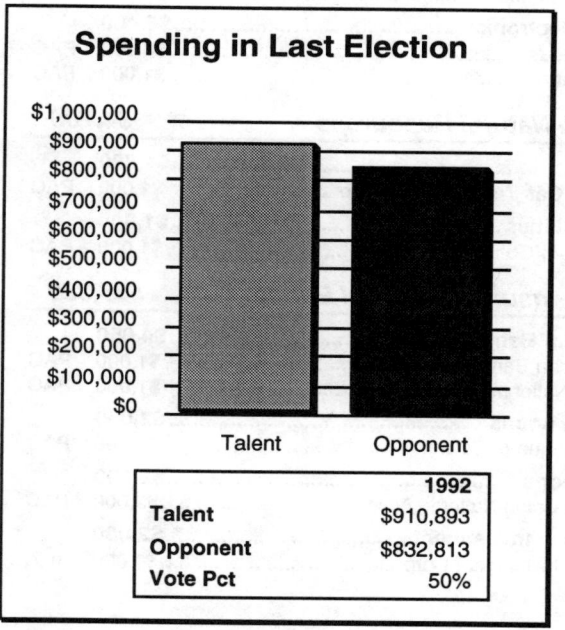

Spending in Last Election

	1992
Talent	$910,893
Opponent	$832,813
Vote Pct	50%

Retail Sales **$8,350**
    May Department Stores .... $2,500   PAC
    Coin Acceptors Inc .... $2,000   Indiv

Business Services **$7,200**
    Americare Properties Systems .... $2,500   Indiv

Chemical & Related Manufacturing **$12,450**
    Monsanto Co .... $4,900   PAC/Ind
    Tnemec Corp .... $2,000   Indiv

Steel Production **$8,500**
    Tubular Steel Inc .... $8,000   Indiv

Misc Manufacturing & Distributing **$41,987**
    Hunter Engineering .... $7,750   PAC
    Cambridge Engineering .... $4,500   Indiv
    Mark Andy Inc .... $4,000   Indiv
    Emerson Electric .... $3,500   PAC/Ind
    Stone Container Corp .... $3,000   PAC
    Crown Packaging .... $2,850   Indiv
    Vi-Jon Laboratories .... $2,050   Indiv
    Medart Inc .... $2,000   Indiv

Transportation $32,776

Automotive **$21,250**
    National Auto Dealers Assn .... $5,000   PAC
    Enterprise Rent-a-Car .... $4,750   Indiv
    Eaton Corp .... $3,000   PAC
    Felco Autoleasing .... $2,200   Indiv
    Enterprise Leasing Co .... $2,000   PAC

Trucking **$5,526**
    Unigroup Inc .... $3,276   PAC

Railroads **$3,000**
    Union Pacific Corp .... $3,000   PAC

Ideological/Single-Issue

Ideological/Single-Issue $25,843

Republican/Conservative **$8,368**
    Conservative Victory Committee .... $2,500   PAC
    Eagle Forum .... $2,500   PAC

Leadership PACs **$3,000**
    Republican Leader's Fund (Bob Michel) .... $2,000   PAC

Pro-Life **$12,225**
    Republican National Coalition for Life .... $4,000   PAC
    Pro-Life Citizens for a Better Society .... $2,025   PAC

Other & Unknown

Other $41,460

Retired **$36,510**
    None over $2,000

Unknown $121,120

    Homemakers/Non-income earners $21,587
    No Employer Listed or Found $46,904
    Employer Listed/Category Unknown $50,829
        Drury Displays .... $2,500   Indiv
        Behlmann Investments .... $2,250   Indiv
        Regency Group .... $2,000   Indiv

Independent expenditures supporting Talent
    National Rifle Assn $21,636
    National Right to Life PAC $4,816

---

* Contributions came from more than one affiliate or subsidiary.

John Tanner, D-Tenn (8)

First elected: 1988

1991-92 Total Receipts: $258,798
1992 Year-end Cash: $319,398

1991-92 Committees & Subcommittees

Armed Services
Investigations; Procurement and Military Nuclear Systems

Science, Space and Technology
Investigations and Oversight; Space; Technology and Competitiveness

Leading Contributors

Business

Agriculture	$27,400	
Crop Production & Basic Processing	**$10,150**	
National Cotton Council	$1,300	PAC
Florida Sugar Cane League	$1,000	PAC
Lee Wilson & Co	$1,000	Indiv
Southern Minn Beet Sugar Co-op	$1,000	PAC
US Beet Sugar Assn	$1,000	PAC
Tobacco	**$4,700**	
RJR Nabisco	$2,000	PAC
Philip Morris	$1,600	PAC
Dairy	**$4,300**	
Associated Milk Producers	$3,000	PAC
Livestock	**$1,350**	
Tennessee Walking Horse Breeders	$1,000	PAC
Agricultural Services/Products	**$2,100**	
None over $1,000		
Food Processing & Sales	**$2,300**	
None over $1,000		
Forestry & Forest Products	**$2,500**	
Westvaco Corp	$2,500	PAC

Communications/Electronics	$11,250	
Printing & Publishing	**$1,000**	
Union City Daily Messenger	$1,000	Indiv
Telephone Utilities	**$8,250**	
BellSouth Corp*	$6,500	PAC
United Telecommunications	$1,000	PAC
Telecom Services & Equipment	**$1,000**	
Northern Telecom	$1,000	PAC

Contribution Totals by Sector

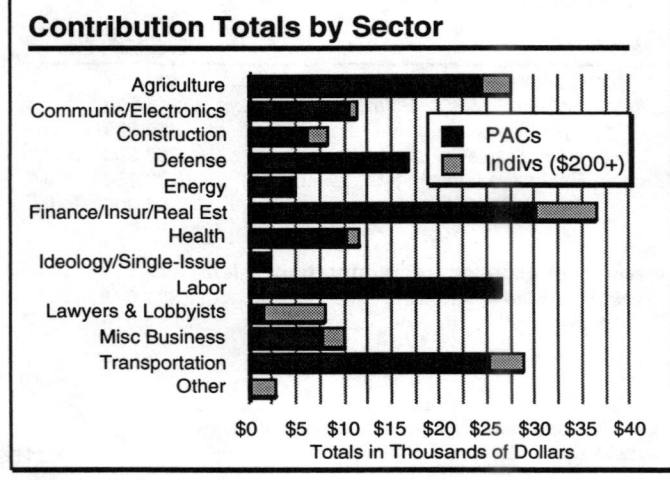

Agriculture
Communic/Electronics
Construction
Defense
Energy
Finance/Insur/Real Est
Health
Ideology/Single-Issue
Labor
Lawyers & Lobbyists
Misc Business
Transportation
Other

■ PACs
▨ Indivs ($200+)

$0 $5 $10 $15 $20 $25 $30 $35 $40
Totals in Thousands of Dollars

Source of Funds in 1992 Election

Source	Total	Pct
■ PACs	$164,239	62%
▨ Indivs $200+	$32,300	12%
☐ Indivs under $200	$29,107	11%
▨ Other	$40,875	15%
Candidate	$0	0%
Party	$10,223	4%

Source of PAC Dollars by Sector

Source	Total	Pct
■ Business	$134,989	83%
▨ Labor	$26,300	16%
☐ Ideology/Single Issue	$2,100	1%

In-State vs. Out-of-State Contributions*

Source	Total	Pct
☐ In-State	$25,550	79%
■ Out-of-state	$6,750	21%
No state listed	$0	

* by large individual contributors ($200 & above)

Construction	$8,050	
General Contractors	**$3,500**	
Tennessee Road Builders Assn	$1,250	PAC
Fluor Corp	$1,000	PAC
Home Builders	**$2,750**	
Haury & Smith	$1,250	Indiv
National Assn of Home Builders	$1,000	PAC

Defense	$16,450	
Defense Aerospace	**$9,550**	
Ford Motor Co	$1,000	PAC
General Dynamics	$1,000	PAC
Thiokol	$1,000	PAC
Defense Electronics	**$6,400**	
AT&T	$3,000	PAC
Raytheon	$1,000	PAC

Energy & Natural Resources	$4,700	
Oil & Gas	**$1,800**	
Texas Gas Transmission Corp	$1,000	PAC
Electric Utilities	**$1,300**	
Southern Co*	$1,000	PAC

Finance, Insurance & Real Estate	$36,389	
Commercial Banks	**$4,050**	
American Bankers Assn	$1,000	PAC
Third National Corp	$1,000	PAC
Savings & Loans	**$2,000**	
US League of Savings Assns*	$1,500	PAC
Credit Unions	**$2,000**	
Credit Union National Assn	$2,000	PAC
Securities & Investment	**$2,000**	
Tudor Investment Corp	$1,000	Indiv

Insurance **$18,289**
    Mutual of Omaha ....$3,000   PAC
    National Assn of Life Underwriters.....................$2,000   PAC
    Independent Insurance Agents of America.........$1,550   PAC
    Turner P Williams & Assoc ....$1,250   Indiv
    Casualty & Surety Agents Assn ....$1,100   PAC
    Union City Insurance ....$1,000   Indiv

Real Estate **$6,500**
    National Assn of Realtors ....$6,000   PAC

Accountants **$1,300**
    American Institute of CPA's ....$1,000   PAC

Health   *$11,500*

Health Professionals **$8,250**
    American Medical Assn.....................................$4,850   PAC
    American Dental Assn ....$2,500   PAC

Hospitals/Nursing Homes **$2,000**
    None over $1,000

Lawyers & Lobbyists   *$7,900*

Lawyers & Lobbyists **$7,900**
    None over $1,000

Misc Business   *$9,850*

Food & Beverage **$1,500**
    McDonald's Corp ....$1,250   PAC/Ind

Beer, Wine & Liquor **$1,750**
    National Beer Wholesalers Assn ....$1,000   PAC

Retail Sales **$1,000**
    International Council of Shopping Centers ....$1,000   PAC

Lodging/Tourism **$1,150**
    None over $1,000

Chemical & Related Manufacturing **$1,400**
    None over $1,000

Misc Manufacturing & Distributing **$2,000**
    Brother Industries ....$1,000   Indiv
    Maytag Co ....$1,000   PAC

Transportation   *$28,700*

Air Transport **$14,150**
    Federal Express Corp ....$10,000   PAC
    United Parcel Service ....$3,350   PAC

Automotive **$10,250**
    National Auto Dealers Assn ....$7,500   PAC
    Americans for Free International Trade ....$1,000   PAC
    Dobbs Brothers Managment ....$1,000   Indiv

Trucking **$2,800**
    All American Moving & Storage ....$2,000   Indiv

Railroads **$1,500**
    Norfolk Southern Corp ....$1,000   PAC

Labor

Labor   *$26,300*

Building Trade Unions **$1,000**
    None over $1,000

Industrial Unions **$10,300**
    Rubber Cork Linoleum & Plastic Workers ....$5,500   PAC
    Communications Workers of America ....$2,000   PAC
    Intl Brotherhood of Electrical Workers ....$2,000   PAC

Transportation Unions **$4,500**
    Teamsters Union ....$2,500   PAC
    Air Line Pilots Assn ....$1,000   PAC

Public Sector Unions **$9,500**
    National Education Assn ....$3,500   PAC
    National Assn Retired Federal Employees ....$2,000   PAC
    National Assn of Letter Carriers ....$2,000   PAC
    National Rural Letter Carriers Assn ....$1,000   PAC

Misc Unions **$1,000**
    None over $1,000

Ideological/Single-Issue

Ideological/Single-Issue   *$2,100*

Misc Issues **$1,600**
    National Cmte to Preserve Social Security ....$1,600   PAC

Other & Unknown

Other   *$2,550*

Civil Servants/Public Officials **$2,050**
    None over $1,000

Unknown   *$2,550*

    Employer Listed/Category Unknown $2,150
       None over $1,000

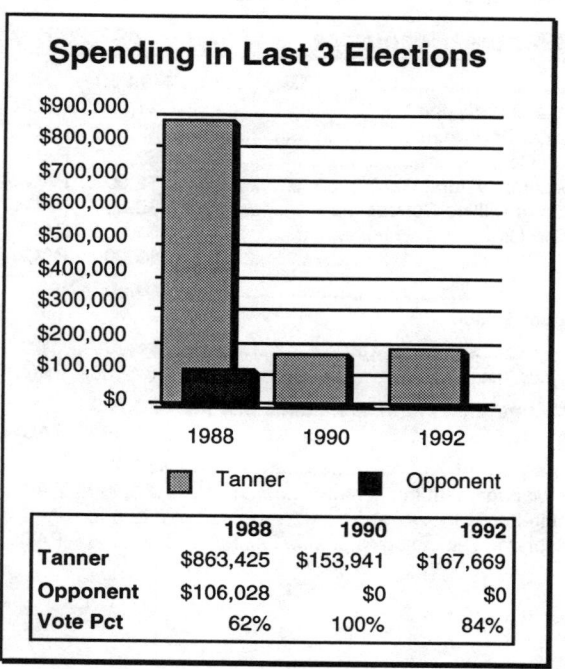

Spending in Last 3 Elections

	1988	1990	1992
Tanner	$863,425	$153,941	$167,669
Opponent	$106,028	$0	$0
Vote Pct	62%	100%	84%

* Contributions came from more than one affiliate or subsidiary.

W. J. "Billy" Tauzin, D-La (3)

First elected: 1980

1991-92 Total Receipts: $590,179
1992 Year-end Cash: $327,478

1991-92 Committees & Subcommittees

Energy and Commerce
Energy and Power; Telecommunications and Finance; Transportation and Hazardous Materials

Merchant Marine and Fisheries
Coast Guard and Navigation (Chairman); Fisheries and Wildlife Conservation and the Environment

Leading Contributors

Business

Agriculture		$38,919
Crop Production & Basic Processing	**$4,750**	
American Sugar Cane League	$2,000	PAC
Tobacco	**$10,169**	
RJR Nabisco	$3,500	PAC
Philip Morris	$2,669	PAC/Ind
US Tobacco Co	$2,500	PAC
Livestock	**$2,000**	
None over $2,000		
Agricultural Services/Products	**$3,250**	
None over $2,000		
Food Processing & Sales	**$12,250**	
Food Marketing Institute	$2,500	PAC
Winn-Dixie Stores	$2,000	PAC
Forestry & Forest Products	**$4,500**	
None over $2,000		

Communications/Electronics		$53,550
Media/Entertainment	**$13,000**	
National Assn of Broadcasters	$7,000	PAC
National Cable Television Assn	$2,000	PAC
Telephone Utilities	**$33,550**	
Ameritech Corp	$6,500	PAC
BellSouth Corp*	$4,500	PAC
Pacific Telesis Group	$3,000	PAC
Southwestern Bell	$2,250	PAC
LDDS Communications	$2,000	Indiv
Telecom Services & Equipment	**$5,000**	
Corning Glass Works	$2,000	PAC
Electronics Mfg & Services	**$2,000**	
General Instrument Corp	$2,000	PAC

Source of Funds in 1992 Election

Source	Total	Pct
■ PACs	$442,559	74%
▨ Indivs $200+	$107,650	18%
□ Indivs under $200	$22,905	4%
▨ Other	$28,121	5%
Candidate	$0	0%
Party	$11,206	2%

Source of PAC Dollars by Sector

Source	Total	Pct
■ Business	$422,860	95%
▨ Labor	$19,250	4%
□ Ideology/Single Issue	$2,500	1%

In-State vs. Out-of-State Contributions*

Source	Total	Pct
□ In-State	$68,250	64%
■ Out-of-state	$37,650	36%
No state listed	$1,000	

* by large individual contributors ($200 & above)

Construction		$14,350
General Contractors	**$4,750**	
Fluor Corp	$3,000	PAC
Construction Services	**$6,250**	
John Chance & Assoc	$3,750	Indiv

Defense		$5,000
Defense Aerospace	**$2,500**	
None over $2,000		
Defense Electronics	**$2,500**	
Diagnostic Retrieval Systems	$2,000	Indiv

Energy & Natural Resources		$97,200
Oil & Gas	**$49,850**	
Columbia Gas System*	$4,000	PAC
Occidental Petroleum*	$3,500	PAC
Chevron Corp	$2,500	PAC
Consolidated Natural Gas*	$2,000	PAC
Intl Assn of Drilling Contractors	$2,000	PAC
Marathon Oil	$2,000	PAC
Shell Oil	$2,000	PAC
Mining	**$9,500**	
None over $2,000		
Misc Energy	**$4,000**	
McDermott Inc	$2,500	PAC
Electric Utilities	**$20,750**	
Entergy Corp*	$2,100	PAC
Waste Management	**$10,000**	
Waste Management Inc	$3,000	PAC
Browning-Ferris Industries	$2,500	PAC
Wheelabrator Technologies	$2,000	PAC

Contribution Totals by Sector

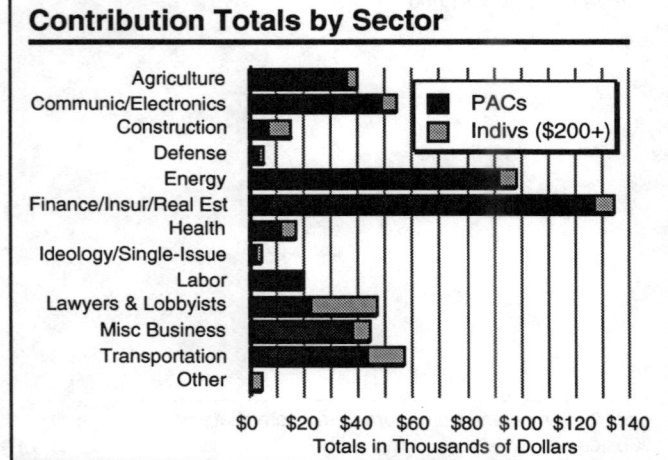

Totals in Thousands of Dollars

Finance, Insurance & Real Estate — $133,862

Commercial Banks $23,450
    American Bankers Assn .... $10,000   PAC
    JP Morgan & Co .... $3,000   PAC

Securities & Investment $19,500
    Prudential Securities .... $3,000   PAC
    First Boston Corp .... $2,000   PAC
    Morgan Stanley & Co .... $2,000   PAC

Insurance $30,212
    Independent Insurance Agents of America .... $3,062   PAC
    Mutual of Omaha .... $3,000   PAC
    National Assn of Life Underwriters .... $2,500   PAC
    American Family Corp .... $2,000   PAC

Real Estate $6,750
    National Assn of Realtors .... $5,000   PAC

Accountants $50,750
    American Institute of CPA's .... $10,000   PAC
    Arthur Andersen & Co .... $10,000   PAC
    Coopers & Lybrand .... $10,000   PAC
    Deloitte & Touche .... $10,000   PAC
    Ernst & Young .... $5,000   PAC
    Price Waterhouse .... $5,000   PAC

Misc Finance $2,700
    Hawthorne Group Inc .... $2,000   Indiv

Health — $16,279

Health Professionals $5,750
    American Dental Assn .... $2,500   PAC

Pharmaceuticals/Health Products $6,779
    None over $2,000

Lawyers & Lobbyists — $45,850

Lawyers & Lobbyists $45,850
    Assn of Trial Lawyers of America .... $10,000   PAC
    Akin, Gump et al .... $2,000   PAC
    Williams & Jensen .... $2,000   PAC/Ind

Misc Business — $43,100

Food & Beverage $8,800
    Coca-Cola Co* .... $4,000   PAC
    National Soft Drink Assn .... $2,000   PAC

Beer, Wine & Liquor $4,500
    National Beer Wholesalers Assn .... $2,500   PAC

Retail Sales $3,000
    None over $2,000

Business Services $3,450
    None over $2,000

Chemical & Related Manufacturing $20,350
    Dow Chemical .... $6,000   PAC

Misc Manufacturing & Distributing $2,000
    None over $2,000

Transportation — $56,150

Air Transport $3,000
    United Parcel Service .... $2,000   PAC

Automotive $9,750
    Auto Dealers & Drivers for Free Trade .... $5,000   PAC
    Americans for Free International Trade .... $2,500   PAC

Trucking $2,000
    None over $2,000

Railroads $6,300
    Union Pacific Corp .... $2,000   PAC

Sea Transport $34,700
    Edison Chouest Offshore .... $3,000   Indiv
    CSX Corp* .... $2,500   PAC
    Tenneco Inc .... $2,000   PAC

Labor

Labor — $19,250

Transportation Unions $13,500
    Seafarers International Union .... $5,000   PAC
    Marine Engineers Union* .... $4,500   PAC
    United Transportation Union .... $2,000   PAC

Public Sector Unions $5,250
    American Federation of Teachers .... $2,500   PAC
    National Assn Retired Federal Employees .... $2,000   PAC

Ideological/Single-Issue

Ideological/Single-Issue — $3,500
    None over $2,000

Other & Unknown

Other — $3,750

Retired $2,000
    None over $2,000

Unknown — $20,750
    No Employer Listed or Found $4,500
    Employer Listed/Category Unknown $16,000
    None over $2,000

Spending in Last 3 Elections

	1988	1990	1992
Tauzin	$707,085	$474,224	$311,112
Opponent	$0	$0	$0
Vote Pct	89%	88%	100%

---

* Contributions came from more than one affiliate or subsidiary.

Charles H. Taylor, R-NC (11)

First elected: 1990

1991-92 Total Receipts: $788,360
1992 Year-end Cash: $4,035

1991-92 Committees & Subcommittees

Interior and Insular Affairs
Energy and the Environment; National Parks and Public Lands; Water, Power and Offshore Energy Resources

Public Works and Transportation
Surface Transportation; Water Resources

Select Committee on Aging

Leading Contributors

Business

Agriculture — $61,000

Crop Production & Basic Processing	**$7,025**	
None over $2,000		
Tobacco	**$14,200**	
RJR Nabisco	$11,000	PAC
Dairy	**$3,250**	
Associated Milk Producers	$2,000	PAC
Livestock	**$2,000**	
None over $2,000		
Food Processing & Sales	**$4,450**	
None over $2,000		
Forestry & Forest Products	**$27,925**	
Champion International Corp	$3,500	PAC
Dendroi	$3,000	Indiv
Weyerhaeuser Co	$3,000	PAC
Willamette Industries	$2,500	PAC
National Forest Products Assn	$2,000	PAC
Westvaco Corp	$2,000	PAC

Communications/Electronics — $19,250

Telephone Utilities	**$15,250**	
Southern Bell	$8,000	PAC
Citizens Telephone Co	$4,000	Indiv
United Telecommunications	$2,500	PAC
Electronics Mfg & Services	**$2,300**	
None over $2,000		

Source of Funds in 1992 Election

Source	Total	Pct
■ PACs	$298,075	36%
▨ Indivs $200+	$165,661	20%
□ Indivs under $200	$231,855	28%
▧ Other	$141,341	17%
Candidate	$10,382	1%
Party	$64,121	8%

Source of PAC Dollars by Sector

Source	Total	Pct
■ Business	$246,892	85%
▨ Labor	$10,400	4%
□ Ideology/Single Issue	$33,496	12%

In-State vs. Out-of-State Contributions*

Source	Total	Pct
□ In-State	$147,961	89%
■ Out-of-state	$17,700	11%
No state listed	$0	

by large individual contributors ($200 & above)

Construction — $25,947

General Contractors	**$8,800**	
Associated General Contractors	$2,000	PAC
Home Builders	**$6,200**	
National Assn of Home Builders	$5,200	PAC
Building Materials & Equipment	**$8,847**	
LZC Corp	$2,000	Indiv
W Cramer Lumber Co	$2,000	Indiv

Defense — $2,600

Defense Aerospace	**$2,600**	
None over $2,000		

Energy & Natural Resources — $43,550

Oil & Gas	**$14,700**	
Exxon Corp	$2,100	PAC
Mining	**$2,350**	
None over $2,000		
Misc Energy	**$4,500**	
Cooper Industries	$4,500	PAC
Electric Utilities	**$21,000**	
Duke Power Co	$6,500	PAC
Carolina Power & Light	$4,500	PAC

Finance, Insurance & Real Estate — $48,400

Commercial Banks	**$10,500**	
Chase Manhattan	$2,350	PAC
Savings & Loans	**$2,100**	
Blue Ridge Savings Bank	$2,100	Indiv
Securities & Investment	**$2,675**	
None over $2,000		

Contribution Totals by Sector

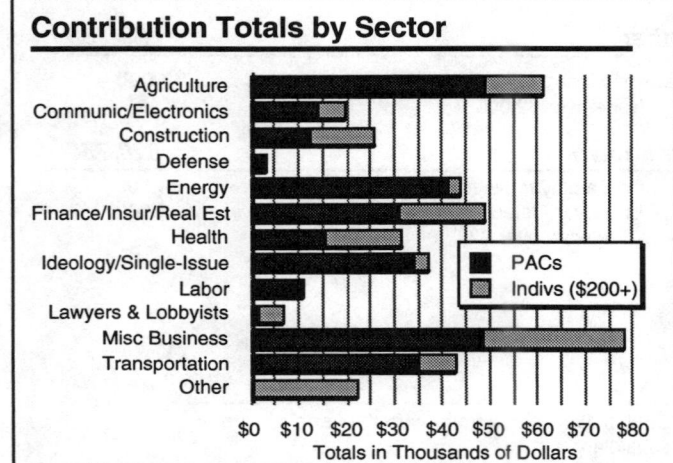

Agriculture
Communic/Electronics
Construction
Defense
Energy
Finance/Insur/Real Est
Health
Ideology/Single-Issue
Labor
Lawyers & Lobbyists
Misc Business
Transportation
Other

■ PACs
▨ Indivs ($200+)

$0 $10 $20 $30 $40 $50 $60 $70 $80
Totals in Thousands of Dollars

Insurance **$7,525**
   None over $2,000

Real Estate **$23,125**
   National Assn of Realtors ....$15,000 PAC
   Harrell Associates ....$2,000 Indiv

Health $31,100

Health Professionals **$23,750**
   American Medical Assn ....$9,400 PAC

Hospitals/Nursing Homes **$2,800**
   None over $2,000

Pharmaceuticals/Health Products **$4,550**
   Glaxo Inc ....$2,000 PAC

Lawyers & Lobbyists $6,800

Lawyers & Lobbyists **$6,800**
   None over $1,500

Misc Business $77,617

Business Associations **$7,117**
   National Fedn of Independent Business ....$5,930 PAC

Food & Beverage **$8,450**
   National Restaurant Assn ....$5,000 PAC

Beer, Wine & Liquor **$6,850**
   National Beer Wholesalers Assn ....$5,850 PAC

Retail Sales **$5,300**
   None over $2,000

Business Services **$6,000**
   Wackenhut Corp ....$3,000 PAC

Lodging/Tourism **$7,300**
   Westside Motels ....$3,500 Indiv
   Holiday Inns ....$2,000 Indiv

Chemical & Related Manufacturing **$6,500**
   Dow Chemical ....$3,000 PAC

Misc Manufacturing & Distributing **$18,300**
   Stone Container Corp ....$5,000 PAC
   Jackson Paper Co ....$3,000 Indiv
   American Furniture Manufacturers Assn ....$2,850 PAC

Textiles **$10,500**
   Stonecutter Mills Corp ....$4,250 Indiv
   Milliken & Co ....$2,000 Indiv

Transportation $42,425

Air Transport **$12,100**
   United Parcel Service ....$4,850 PAC
   Federal Express Corp ....$4,000 PAC

Automotive **$16,550**
   National Auto Dealers Assn ....$4,350 PAC
   Auto Dealers & Drivers for Free Trade ....$3,000 PAC
   Eaton Corp ....$3,000 PAC
   Americans for Free International Trade ....$2,000 PAC
   Cagle & Son Ford ....$2,000 Indiv

Trucking **$4,900**
   Youngblood Truck Lines ....$2,250 Indiv

Railroads **$5,850**
   None over $2,000

Sea Transport **$2,525**
   None over $2,000

Labor

Labor $10,400

Transportation Unions **$6,500**
   Marine Engineers Union* ....$5,000 PAC

Public Sector Unions **$3,900**
   National Assn Retired Federal Employees ....$3,000 PAC

Ideological/Single-Issue

Ideological/Single-Issue $36,496

Republican/Conservative **$6,397**
   None over $2,000

Pro-Israel **$2,300**
   None over $2,000

Pro-Life **$6,350**
   Right to Life* ....$4,350 PAC
   Republican National Coalition for Life ....$2,000 PAC

Gun Rights/Gun Control **$14,850**
   National Rifle Assn ....$14,850 PAC

Misc Issues **$5,150**
   None over $2,000

Other & Unknown

Other $21,789

Civil Servants/Public Officials **$2,700**
   None over $2,000

Retired **$19,389**
   None over $2,000

Unknown $29,325

   Homemakers/Non-income earners $2,250
   Employer Listed/Category Unknown $26,075
     Fails & Associates ....$2,000 Indiv

Independent expenditures supporting Taylor
   National Right to Life PAC $7,123

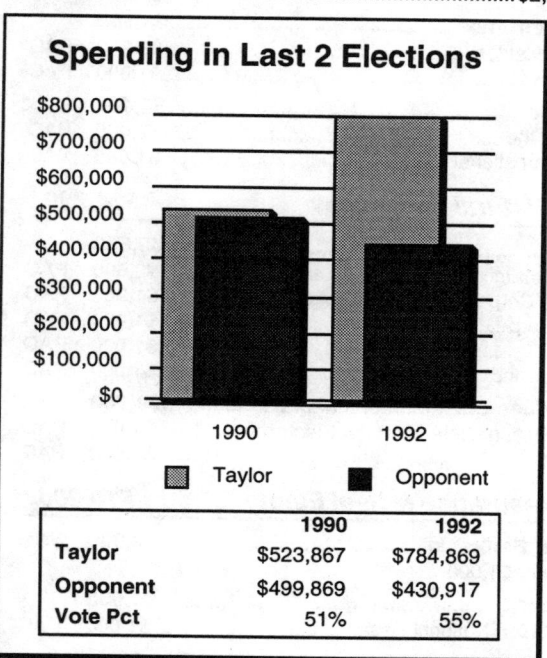

Spending in Last 2 Elections

	1990	1992
Taylor	$523,867	$784,869
Opponent	$499,869	$430,917
Vote Pct	51%	55%

---

* Contributions came from more than one affiliate or subsidiary.

Gene Taylor, D-Miss (5)

First elected: 1988
1991-92 Total Receipts: $330,357
1992 Year-end Cash: $2,918

1991-92 Committees & Subcommittees

Armed Services
Procurement and Military Nuclear Systems; Seapower and Strategic and Critical Materials

Merchant Marine and Fisheries
Coast Guard and Navigation; Merchant Marine; Oceanography, Great Lakes and Outer Continental Shelf

Leading Contributors

Business

Agriculture — $15,650

Crop Production & Basic Processing — $2,600
None over $1,000

Tobacco — $1,900
RJR Nabisco — $1,500 PAC

Dairy — $4,200
Dairymen Inc-Mississippi — $2,200 PAC
Associated Milk Producers — $2,000 PAC

Agricultural Services/Products — $1,650
None over $1,000

Food Processing & Sales — $3,400
Fleming Companies Inc — $1,000 PAC
Jitney-Jungle Inc — $1,000 PAC

Communications/Electronics — $12,500

Media/Entertainment — $2,900
Marine Life — $2,000 Indiv

Telephone Utilities — $7,900
BellSouth Corp* — $7,900 PAC

Computer Equipment & Services — $1,400
Advanced Technology Systems — $1,400 Indiv

Construction — $7,600

General Contractors — $4,250
Associated General Contractors — $1,400 PAC
Finlo Construction Co — $1,000 Indiv
Warren Paving Inc — $1,000 Indiv

Building Materials & Equipment — $2,700
Puckett Machinery — $1,500 Indiv

Source of Funds in 1992 Election

Source	Total	Pct
PACs	$158,535	47%
Indivs $200+	$99,902	30%
Indivs under $200	$66,539	20%
Other	$10,818	3%
Candidate	$0	0%
Party	$10,437	3%

Source of PAC Dollars by Sector

Source	Total	Pct
Business	$130,065	85%
Labor	$7,000	5%
Ideology/Single Issue	$15,150	10%

In-State vs. Out-of-State Contributions*

Source	Total	Pct
In-State	$78,152	79%
Out-of-state	$21,000	21%
No state listed	$350	

* by large individual contributors ($200 & above)

Defense — $29,270

Defense Aerospace — $16,210
Grumman Corp — $2,200 PAC
Gencorp Inc — $2,160 PAC
McDonnell Douglas* — $1,700 PAC
General Dynamics — $1,250 PAC
Colt Industries — $1,000 PAC
LTV Aerospace & Defense Co — $1,000 PAC
Lockheed Corp — $1,000 PAC
Northrop Corp — $1,000 PAC
Rockwell International — $1,000 PAC
Textron Inc — $1,000 PAC

Defense Electronics — $8,660
Litton Industries — $6,260 PAC
Raytheon — $1,000 PAC

Misc Defense — $4,400
Tenneco Inc — $2,000 PAC
BDM International — $1,500 PAC

Energy & Natural Resources — $14,700

Oil & Gas — $9,550
McDermott Inc — $2,600 PAC
Chevron Corp — $1,900 PAC
Exxon Corp — $1,000 PAC
Shell Oil — $1,000 PAC
Tidewater Inc — $1,000 PAC

Electric Utilities — $4,750
ACRE (Action Cmte for Rural Electrification)* — $2,000 PAC
Southern Co* — $2,000 PAC

Finance, Insurance & Real Estate — $10,200

Commercial Banks — $2,000
None over $1,000

Credit Unions — $1,000
Credit Union National Assn — $1,000 PAC

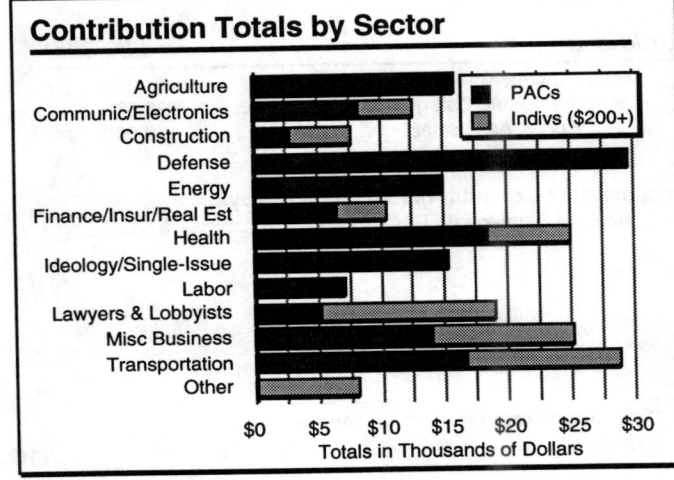

Contribution Totals by Sector

Legend: PACs, Indivs ($200+)

Agriculture
Communic/Electronics
Construction
Defense
Energy
Finance/Insur/Real Est
Health
Ideology/Single-Issue
Labor
Lawyers & Lobbyists
Misc Business
Transportation
Other

$0 $5 $10 $15 $20 $25 $30
Totals in Thousands of Dollars

Insurance $4,750
- American Family Corp .... $2,000 PAC
- National Assn of Life Underwriters .... $2,000 PAC

Real Estate $1,600
- None over $1,000

Health $24,720

Health Professionals $22,070
- American Medical Assn .... $9,695 PAC
- American Dental Assn .... $3,500 PAC
- American Academy of Ophthalmology .... $2,500 PAC
- Buddy Brice DDS .... $1,025 Indiv
- Cmte for Quality Orthopedic Health Care ...... $1,000 PAC
- Surgery Clinic of Hattiesburg .... $1,000 Indiv

Pharmaceuticals/Health Products $1,900
- Sterling Drug .... $1,900 PAC/Ind

Lawyers & Lobbyists $18,750

Lawyers & Lobbyists $18,750
- Assn of Trial Lawyers of America .... $4,500 PAC
- Minor, Benton & Guice .... $3,000 Indiv
- Jones & Wilson .... $1,000 Indiv
- Parsons & Taylor .... $1,000 Indiv

Misc Business $24,971

Food & Beverage $6,350
- RA Lesso Seafood Co .... $3,900 Indiv

Beer, Wine & Liquor $5,500
- National Beer Wholesalers Assn .... $3,500 PAC
- Rex Distributing Co .... $1,000 Indiv

Retail Sales $1,500
- None over $1,000

Misc Services $1,700
- Bradford O'Keefe Funeral Homes .... $1,700 Indiv

Business Services $1,000
- J Edward Connelly Associates .... $1,000 Indiv

Chemical & Related Manufacturing $3,000
- Dow Chemical .... $3,000 PAC

Misc Manufacturing & Distributing $3,871
- Stone Container Corp .... $2,000 PAC
- Karl Senner Inc .... $1,500 Indiv

Transportation $32,050

Air Transport $11,000
- Federal Express Corp .... $7,000 PAC
- United Parcel Service .... $4,000 PAC

Automotive $2,300
- Dearman Ford .... $1,000 Indiv

Sea Transport $18,750
- Gulf Coast Fabricators .... $4,000 Indiv
- Trinity Industries Inc .... $4,000 PAC/Ind
- Ryan Marine Shipbuilding & Repair .... $2,000 Indiv
- Donovan Marine Supply .... $1,500 Indiv
- LF Gaubert & Co .... $1,500 Indiv
- American Waterways Operators .... $1,000 PAC
- Edison Chouest Offshore .... $1,000 Indiv

Labor

Labor $7,000

Transportation Unions $4,000
- Marine Engineers Union* .... $4,500 PAC

Public Sector Unions $3,000
- National Assn Retired Federal Employees ...... $3,000 PAC

Ideological/Single-Issue

Ideological/Single-Issue $15,150

Leadership PACs $2,800
- America's Leaders' Fund (Dan Rostenkowski) .... $1,300 PAC
- Conservative Demo PAC (Charles Stenholm) ..... $1,000 PAC

Gun Rights/Gun Control $7,350
- National Rifle Assn .... $7,350 PAC

Human Rights $2,000
- KidsPAC .... $2,000 PAC

Misc Issues $3,000
- National Cmte to Preserve Social Security ...... $3,000 PAC

Other & Unknown

Other $8,031

Civil Servants/Public Officials $2,081
- US Department of Energy .... $1,081 Indiv
- Harrison County .... $1,000 Indiv

Retired $4,700
- None over $1,000

Unknown $31,125
- Homemakers/Non-income earners $5,218
- No Employer Listed or Found $7,700
- Employer Listed/Category Unknown $18,207
  - Fretz Culver Inc .... $2,500 Indiv
  - Engine Monitors .... $1,500 Indiv
  - Con-Tech Power Systems .... $1,000 Indiv
  - Dependable Abrasives .... $1,000 Indiv
  - GL Bannister Assoc .... $1,000 Indiv
  - Laitram Machinery Inc .... $1,000 Indiv
  - Leslie Hayes & Associates .... $1,000 Indiv
  - Ludie Toons Video .... $1,000 Indiv
  - Maples & Lomax .... $1,000 Indiv
  - McElroy Machine .... $1,000 Indiv

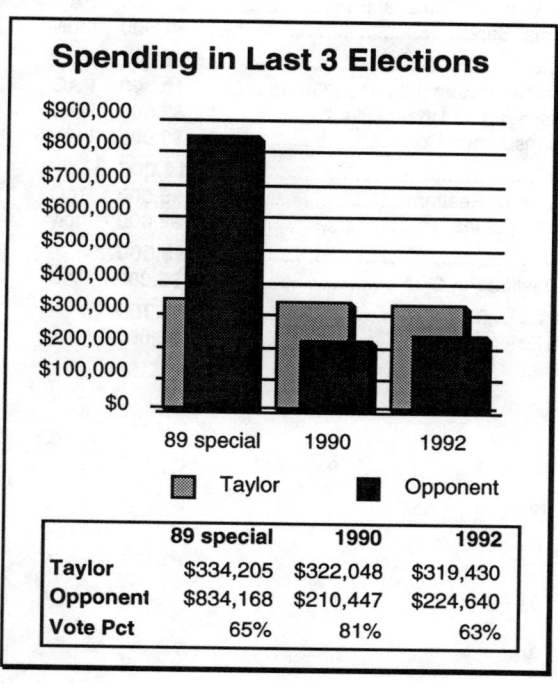

Spending in Last 3 Elections

Legend: ▨ Taylor ■ Opponent

	89 special	1990	1992
Taylor	$334,205	$322,048	$319,430
Opponent	$834,168	$210,447	$224,640
Vote Pct	65%	81%	63%

* Contributions came from more than one affiliate or subsidiary.

Frank M. Tejeda, D-Texas (28)

First elected: 1992

1991-92 Total Receipts: $302,873
1992 Year-end Cash: $1,384

1993-94 Committees & Subcommittees

Armed Services
Military Installations and Facilities; Oversight and Investigations; Research and Technology

Veterans' Affairs
Compensation, Pension and Insurance; Hospitals and Health Care

Leading Contributors

Business

Agriculture		$12,250
Tobacco	**$3,500**	
RJR Nabisco	$2,000	PAC
Livestock	**$3,500**	
None over $1,500		
Food Processing & Sales	**$3,500**	
L&H Packing Co	$2,000	Indiv
HE Butt Grocery Co	$1,500	Indiv

Communications/Electronics		$8,750
Printing & Publishing	**$3,000**	
Harte-Hanks Communications	$3,000	Indiv
Telephone Utilities	**$4,250**	
GTE Corp	$2,000	PAC
AT&T	$1,500	PAC

Construction		$20,350
General Contractors	**$8,000**	
HB Zachry Co	$3,000	PAC/Ind
Associated General Contractors ...	$1,500	PAC
Home Builders	**$9,850**	
National Assn of Home Builders	$6,100	PAC
Ray Ellison Industries	$3,000	PAC
Construction Services	**$2,500**	
Jones & Kell Architects	$2,500	Indiv

Source of Funds in 1992 Election

Source	Total	Pct
■ PACs	$131,725	43%
▨ Indivs $200+	$143,924	48%
☐ Indivs under $200	$13,648	5%
⊠ Other	$13,576	4%
Candidate	$13,267	4%
Party	$0	0%

Source of PAC Dollars by Sector

Source	Total	Pct
■ Business	$105,272	84%
▨ Labor	$11,700	9%
☐ Ideology/Single Issue	$7,950	6%

In-State vs. Out-of-State Contributions*

Source	Total	Pct
☐ In-State	$143,424	100%
■ Out-of-state	$0	0%
No state listed	$500	

* by large individual contributors ($200 & above)

Energy & Natural Resources		$19,050
Oil & Gas	**$13,000**	
Valero Energy Corp	$5,000	Indiv
Diamond Shamrock Inc	$2,500	PAC
Electric Utilities	**$6,050**	
Texas Utilities Co	$3,000	PAC
Central Power & Light	$2,050	PAC

Finance, Insurance & Real Estate		$57,497
Commercial Banks	**$13,500**	
Banker Industries	$3,500	Indiv
American Bankers Assn	$2,000	PAC
Citizens & Southern National Bank	$1,500	PAC
Frost National Bank	$1,500	Indiv
Insurance	**$19,797**	
United Services Automobile Assn Group	$10,000	PAC
National Assn of Life Underwriters	$3,500	PAC
Tower Life Insurance Co	$3,000	Indiv
Real Estate	**$14,000**	
National Assn of Realtors	$6,000	PAC
Schaeffer Properties	$2,000	Indiv
Accountants	**$5,500**	
American Institute of CPA's	$2,000	PAC
Misc Finance	**$3,700**	
McCombs Enterprises	$2,000	Indiv

Contribution Totals by Sector

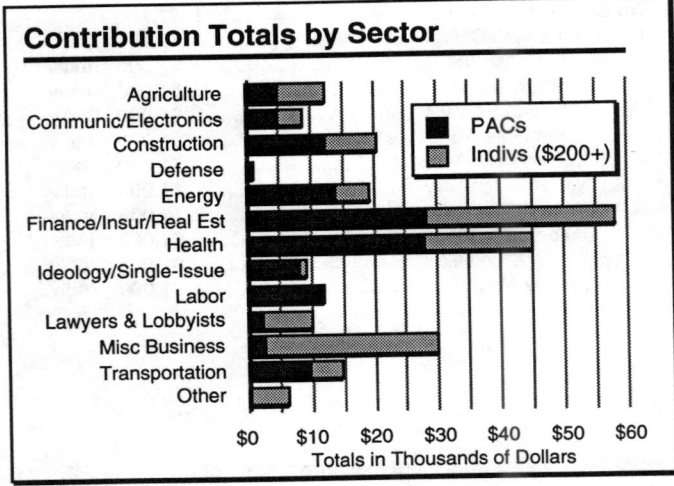

Categories: Agriculture, Communic/Electronics, Construction, Defense, Energy, Finance/Insur/Real Est, Health, Ideology/Single-Issue, Labor, Lawyers & Lobbyists, Misc Business, Transportation, Other

Legend: ■ PACs, ▨ Indivs ($200+)

Totals in Thousands of Dollars ($0 $10 $20 $30 $40 $50 $60)

Health $44,621

Health Professionals $36,771
    American Medical Assn.......................................$9,471 PAC
    American Academy of Ophthalmology ....$3,000 PAC
    American Dental Assn ....$3,000 PAC
    American Chiropractic Assn................................$2,000 PAC
    American College of Emergency Physicians ....$2,000 PAC
    Gonzaba Medical Group ....$2,000 Indiv
    Severance & Associates ....$1,750 Indiv

Pharmaceuticals/Health Products $7,750
    Kinetic Concepts Inc ....$7,750 PAC

Lawyers & Lobbyists $10,458

Lawyers & Lobbyists $10,458
    None over $1,000

Misc Business $29,530

Beer, Wine & Liquor $14,750
    Pabst Pearl Brewery Co ....$9,000 Indiv
    GLI Distributing ....$1,500 Indiv

Business Services $7,230
    Raba-Kistner Consultants ....$3,500 Indiv
    Atkins & Assoc ....$3,230 Indiv

Misc Business $2,000
    Halo Distributing Co ....$2,000 Indiv

Misc Manufacturing & Distributing $2,000
    None over $1,500

Transportation $14,300

Automotive $12,500
    National Auto Dealers Assn ....$8,000 PAC

Labor

Labor $11,700

Transportation Unions $2,000
    None over $1,500

Public Sector Unions $8,500
    American Fedn of St/Cnty/Munic Employees ......$6,000 PAC
    International Assn of Firefighters ....$2,000 PAC

Ideological/Single-Issue

Ideological/Single-Issue $8,950

Leadership PACs $2,000
    None over $1,500

Gun Rights/Gun Control $4,950
    National Rifle Assn ....$4,950 PAC

Other & Unknown

Other $5,750

Retired $5,250
    None over $1,500

Unknown $24,790

    Homemakers/Non-income earners $2,250
    Generic Occupation/Category Unknown $2,500
    Employer Listed/Category Unknown $18,590
        Mendelson & Mata ....$3,210 Indiv
        Torres Enterprises ....$3,000 Indiv
        Crain Co ....$2,880 Indiv

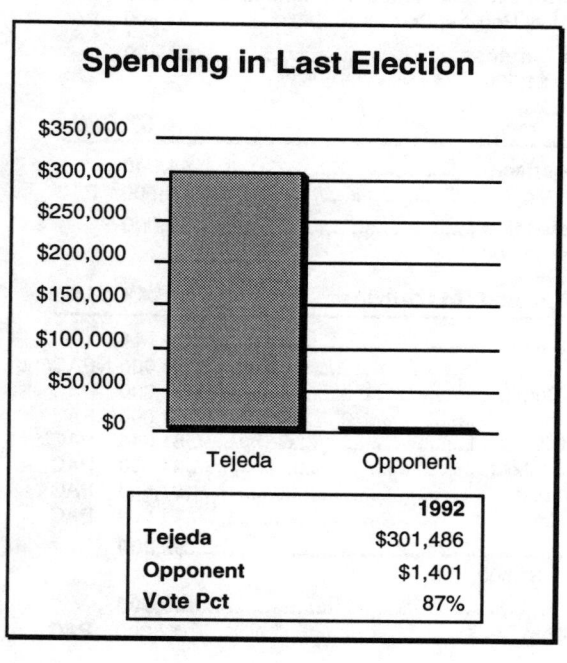

Spending in Last Election

	1992
Tejeda	$301,486
Opponent	$1,401
Vote Pct	87%

Bill Thomas, R-Calif (21)

First elected: 1978

1991-92 Total Receipts: $603,169
1992 Year-end Cash: $95,932

1991-92 Committees & Subcommittees

Administration (Ranking Republican)
Campaign Finance Reform Task Force (Ranking Republican)

Budget
Budget Process, Reconciliation and Enforcement (Ranking Republican); Urgent Fiscal Issues

Ways and Means
Trade

Leading Contributors

Business

Agriculture	$89,750	
Crop Production & Basic Processing	**$56,490**	
Desert Grape Growers League/California	$5,000	PAC
California Pistachio Assn	$4,500	PAC
Calcot Ltd	$3,037	PAC
JG Boswell Co	$3,000	PAC
National Cotton Council	$3,000	PAC
California Almond Growers Exchange	$2,000	PAC
Richard Bagdasarian Inc	$2,000	Indiv
Sun-Diamond Growers*	$2,000	PAC
Sunkist Growers	$1,750	PAC
Tobacco	**$3,250**	
None over $1,500		
Dairy	**$2,450**	
Dairymans Co-op Creamery Assn	$1,600	PAC
Livestock	**$5,850**	
National Cattlemen's Assn*	$2,750	PAC
Agricultural Services/Products	**$9,910**	
Zond Systems Inc	$2,400	Indiv
Friant Water PAC	$1,550	PAC
Food Processing & Sales	**$7,500**	
Food Marketing Institute	$2,000	PAC
Misc Agriculture	**$3,450**	
None over $1,500		

Source of Funds in 1992 Election

Source	Total	Pct
PACs	$281,436	47%
Indivs $200+	$195,289	32%
Indivs under $200	$58,172	10%
Other	$68,272	11%
Candidate	$0	0%
Party	$4,999	1%

Source of PAC Dollars by Sector

Source	Total	Pct
Business	$266,437	97%
Labor	$6,000	2%
Ideology/Single Issue	$1,000	0%

In-State vs. Out-of-State Contributions*

Source	Total	Pct
In-State	$171,989	88%
Out-of-state	$23,300	12%
No state listed	$0	

* by large individual contributors ($200 & above)

Communications/Electronics	$16,000	
Media/Entertainment	**$3,500**	
National Assn of Broadcasters	$1,500	PAC
Telephone Utilities	**$11,000**	
AT&T	$5,000	PAC
GTE Corp	$2,500	PAC
Pacific Telesis Group	$2,000	PAC

Construction	$13,150	
General Contractors	**$7,750**	
None over $1,500		
Home Builders	**$1,500**	
National Multi Housing Council	$1,500	PAC
Construction Services	**$2,250**	
None over $1,500		

Defense	$7,000	
Defense Aerospace	**$4,000**	
Northrop Corp	$1,500	PAC
Defense Electronics	**$2,000**	
None over $1,500		

Energy & Natural Resources	$43,444	
Oil & Gas	**$28,144**	
Mobil Oil	$3,000	PAC/Ind
Chevron Corp	$2,900	PAC
Shell Oil	$2,000	PAC
Union Oil	$1,944	PAC
Atlantic Richfield	$1,500	PAC
Enron Corp	$1,500	PAC
Texaco	$1,500	PAC
Mining	**$2,350**	
None over $1,500		
Misc Energy	**$3,500**	
Bechtel Corp	$2,000	PAC

Contribution Totals by Sector

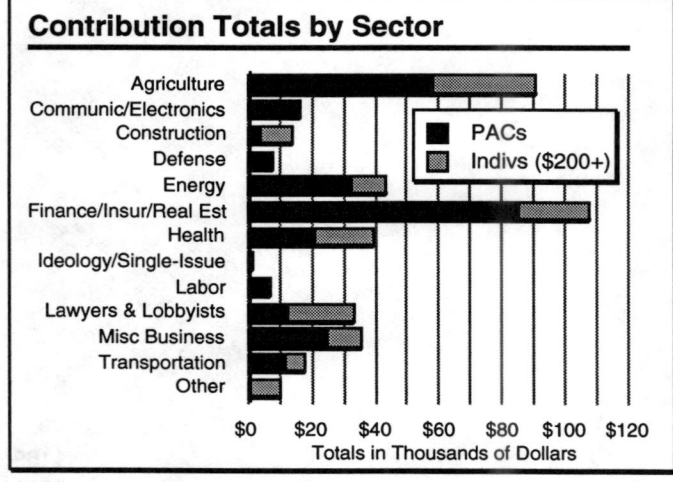

Legend: PACs, Indivs ($200+)

Sectors: Agriculture, Communic/Electronics, Construction, Defense, Energy, Finance/Insur/Real Est, Health, Ideology/Single-Issue, Labor, Lawyers & Lobbyists, Misc Business, Transportation, Other

Totals in Thousands of Dollars ($0, $20, $40, $60, $80, $100, $120)

Electric Utilities	$7,950	
Pacific Gas & Electric	$3,250	PAC
Southern California Edison	$1,500	PAC
Waste Management	**$1,500**	
None over $1,500		

Finance, Insurance & Real Estate $106,574

Commercial Banks	$12,400	
American Bankers Assn	$3,000	PAC
BankAmerica Corp	$3,000	PAC
Citicorp	$2,000	PAC
Security Pacific Corp	$1,500	PAC
Savings & Loans	**$3,000**	
Great Western Financial Corp	$1,500	PAC
US League of Savings Assns*	$1,500	PAC
Securities & Investment	**$9,625**	
Merrill Lynch	$2,000	PAC
American Express*	$1,500	PAC
Insurance	**$43,849**	
National Assn of Life Underwriters	$5,000	PAC
American Family Corp	$4,000	PAC
Pacific Mutual Life	$3,000	PAC
American Council of Life Insurance	$2,999	PAC
Travelers Corp	$2,000	PAC
Cigna Corp	$1,500	PAC
Fireman's Fund Insurance	$1,500	PAC
Independent Insurance Agents of America	$1,500	PAC
Torchmark Corp	$1,500	PAC
TransAmerica Life Companies	$1,500	PAC
Real Estate	**$24,875**	
National Assn of Realtors	$7,000	PAC
National Realty Committee	$3,000	PAC
Century 21 Real Estate	$2,500	PAC
National Assn Industrial & Office Parks	$1,500	PAC
Accountants	**$9,375**	
American Institute of CPA's	$5,000	PAC
Misc Finance	**$2,750**	
None over $1,500		

Health $39,050

Health Professionals	$27,050	
American Medical Assn	$7,000	PAC
Hospitals/Nursing Homes	**$3,000**	
National Medical Enterprises Inc	$1,500	PAC

Spending in Last 3 Elections

	1988	1990	1992
Thomas	$329,354	$496,845	$615,587
Opponent	$15,814	$690	$23,278
Vote Pct	71%	60%	65%

Pharmaceuticals/Health Products	$7,500	
Pfizer Inc	$2,000	PAC
Glaxo Inc	$1,500	PAC
Syntex (USA) Inc	$1,500	PAC

Lawyers & Lobbyists $32,275

Lawyers & Lobbyists	$32,275	
McClure, Trotter & Mentz	$6,000	Indiv
Assn of Trial Lawyers of America	$5,000	PAC
Borton, Petrini & Conron	$1,500	Indiv

Misc Business $35,257

Food & Beverage	$4,500	
National Restaurant Assn	$2,000	PAC
Beer, Wine & Liquor	**$8,950**	
Wine & Spirits Wholesalers of America	$2,500	PAC
Retail Sales	**$12,557**	
International Council of Shopping Centers	$9,000	PAC
Business Services	**$3,500**	
None over $1,500		
Textiles	**$2,000**	
American Textile Manufacturers Institute	$2,000	PAC

Transportation $17,150

Air Transport	$2,500	
None over $1,500		
Automotive	**$8,150**	
National Auto Dealers Assn	$2,000	PAC
Haddad Dodge	$1,500	Indiv
Jim Burke Ford	$1,500	Indiv
Trucking	**$3,250**	
None over $1,500		
Railroads	**$3,000**	
Union Pacific Corp	$2,000	PAC

Labor

Labor $6,250

Public Sector Unions	$6,000	
National Assn of Letter Carriers	$3,000	PAC
National Rural Letter Carriers Assn	$1,500	PAC

Ideological/Single-Issue $1,000
None over $1,500

Other & Unknown

Other $9,850

Civil Servants/Public Officials	$1,600	
None over $1,500		
Retired	**$6,750**	
None over $1,500		

Unknown $52,476

Homemakers/Non-income earners	$4,750
No Employer Listed or Found	$15,950
Generic Occupation/Category Unknown	$2,600
Employer Listed/Category Unknown	$29,176
None over $1,500	

---

* Contributions came from more than one affiliate or subsidiary.

Craig Thomas, R-Wyo (At Large)

First elected: 1989
1991-92 Total Receipts: $479,523
1992 Year-end Cash: $24,529

1991-92 Committees & Subcommittees

Banking, Finance and Urban Affairs
Consumer Affairs and Coinage; Economic Stabilization; Housing and Community Development

Government Operations
Human Resources and Intergovernmental Relations (Ranking Republican)

Interior and Insular Affairs
Energy and the Environment; Mining and Natural Resources; National Parks and Public Lands

Leading Contributors

Business

Agriculture		$32,075
Crop Production & Basic Processing	$6,175	
American Sugarbeet Growers Assn	$1,400	PAC
American Crystal Sugar Corp	$1,000	PAC
Tobacco	$3,600	
RJR Nabisco	$1,800	PAC
Livestock	$14,600	
National Cattlemen's Assn	$1,900	PAC
Texas & Southwestern Cattle Raisers	$1,000	PAC
Agricultural Services/Products	$3,400	
Freeport-McMoRan Inc	$1,000	PAC
Food Processing & Sales	$3,050	
None over $1,000		

Communications/Electronics		$9,900
Telephone Utilities	$9,150	
AT&T	$4,000	PAC
US West Inc	$4,000	PAC/Ind

Construction		$7,400
General Contractors	$2,500	
Associated General Contractors	$1,500	PAC
Home Builders	$2,400	
National Assn of Home Builders	$2,400	PAC

Source of Funds in 1992 Election

Source	Total	Pct
PACs	$222,053	46%
Indivs $200+	$96,425	20%
Indivs under $200	$143,016	30%
Other	$18,029	4%
Candidate	$0	0%
Party	$11,991	2%

Source of PAC Dollars by Sector

Source	Total	Pct
Business	$202,375	94%
Labor	$4,500	2%
Ideology/Single Issue	$7,750	4%

In-State vs. Out-of-State Contributions*

Source	Total	Pct
In-State	$86,925	90%
Out-of-state	$9,500	10%
No state listed	$0	

* by large individual contributors ($200 & above)

Special Trade Contractors		$1,250
National Electrical Contractors Assn	$1,000	PAC
Building Materials & Equipment		$1,000
Teton West Lumber	$1,000	Indiv

Defense		$2,900
Defense Aerospace	$1,900	
None over $1,000		
Misc Defense	$1,000	
Tenneco Inc	$1,000	PAC

Energy & Natural Resources		$67,350
Oil & Gas	$37,950	
Coastal Corp	$2,500	PAC
Columbia Gas System*	$2,000	PAC
Mountain Fuel Supply	$2,000	PAC
Enron Corp	$1,400	PAC
Exxon Corp	$1,400	PAC
Wold Oil & Gas Co	$1,250	Indiv
Amoco Corp	$1,000	PAC
Border Fuel Supply Corp	$1,000	Indiv
Rocky Mountain Energy Corp	$1,000	Indiv
Shell Oil	$1,000	PAC
Sun Co	$1,000	PAC
Texaco	$1,000	PAC
Williams Companies	$1,000	PAC
Mining	$13,450	
Cyprus Minerals Co	$2,500	PAC
National Coal Assn	$2,000	PAC
FMC Corp	$1,800	PAC
Peabody Coal	$1,400	PAC
Phelps Dodge Corp	$1,400	PAC
Misc Energy	$1,900	
None over $1,000		

Contribution Totals by Sector

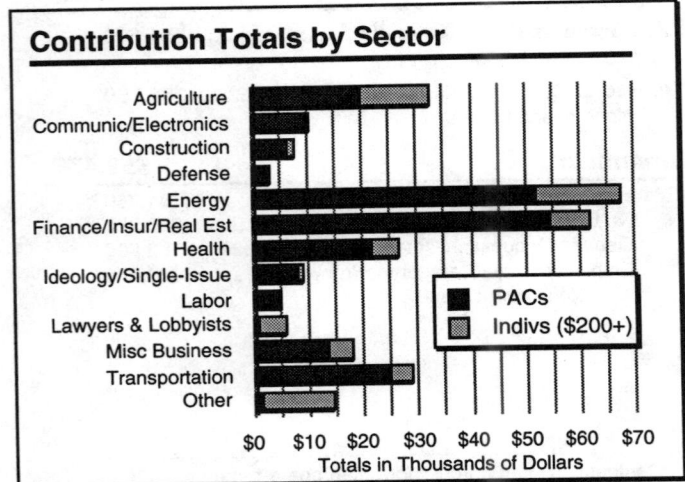

Agriculture
Communic/Electronics
Construction
Defense
Energy
Finance/Insur/Real Est
Health
Ideology/Single-Issue
Labor
Lawyers & Lobbyists
Misc Business
Transportation
Other

■ PACs
▨ Indivs ($200+)

$0 $10 $20 $30 $40 $50 $60 $70
Totals in Thousands of Dollars

Electric Utilities **$13,100**
    ACRE (Action Cmte for Rural Electrification)* ..... $2,900   PAC
    Basin Electric Power Co-op .... $2,000   PAC
    Public Service Co of Colorado .... $1,300   PAC
    Southern Co* .... $1,100   PAC

Finance, Insurance & Real Estate $61,275

Commercial Banks **$24,825**
    American Bankers Assn .... $7,500   PAC
    Norwest Corp .... $3,000   PAC
    Independent Bankers Assn .... $2,700   PAC
    Barnett Banks Inc .... $1,500   PAC
    Chase Manhattan .... $1,500   PAC
    First Chicago Corp .... $1,000   PAC
    JP Morgan & Co .... $1,000   PAC

Savings & Loans **$1,800**
    None over $1,000

Credit Unions **$3,000**
    Credit Union National Assn .... $3,000   PAC

Finance/Credit Companies **$1,900**
    Associated Credit Bureaus .... $1,500   PAC

Securities & Investment **$4,400**
    Friess Associates Inc .... $1,000   Indiv

Insurance **$5,150**
    National Assn of Life Underwriters .... $2,000   PAC
    National Assn of Independent Insurers .... $1,300   PAC

Real Estate **$10,600**
    National Assn of Realtors .... $8,500   PAC

Accountants **$7,400**
    American Institute of CPA's .... $7,000   PAC

Health $26,350

Health Professionals **$22,650**
    American Medical Assn .... $9,700   PAC
    American Academy of Ophthalmology .... $5,000   PAC
    American Dental Assn .... $1,400   PAC
    American Optometric Assn .... $1,000   PAC

Hospitals/Nursing Homes **$1,400**
    None over $1,000

Pharmaceuticals/Health Products **$2,300**
    Rhone-Poulenc Inc .... $1,000   PAC

Lawyers & Lobbyists $5,450

Lawyers & Lobbyists **$5,450**
    Burgess & Davis .... $1,000   Indiv
    Hooper, Hooper & Owen .... $1,000   Indiv

Misc Business $17,600

Food & Beverage **$2,250**
    National Restaurant Assn .... $1,000   PAC

Beer, Wine & Liquor **$3,000**
    National Beer Wholesalers Assn .... $3,000   PAC

Retail Sales **$3,250**
    JC Penney Co .... $1,250   PAC
    International Council of Shopping Centers .... $1,000   PAC

Lodging/Tourism **$4,200**
    American Hotel & Motel Assn .... $1,000   PAC

Misc Manufacturing & Distributing **$2,400**
    In-Situ Inc .... $1,000   Indiv

Transportation $28,500

Air Transport **$4,800**
    United Parcel Service .... $4,300   PAC

Automotive **$11,800**
    National Auto Dealers Assn .... $7,300   PAC
    Auto Dealers & Drivers for Free Trade .... $1,500   PAC
    Americans for Free International Trade .... $1,000   PAC
    Cody Chevrolet .... $1,000   Indiv

Trucking **$3,150**
    Northwest Transport Service .... $1,000   Indiv

Railroads **$7,850**
    Union Pacific Corp .... $5,500   PAC
    Burlington Northern .... $1,950   PAC

Labor

Labor $4,500

Public Sector Unions **$4,500**
    National Assn Retired Federal Employees .... $3,000   PAC
    National League of Postmasters .... $1,000   PAC

Ideological/Single-Issue

Ideological/Single-Issue $8,650

Gun Rights/Gun Control **$6,950**
    National Rifle Assn .... $6,450   PAC

Other & Unknown

Other $14,100

Retired **$12,100**
    None over $1,000

Other **$1,500**
    American Society of Assn Executives .... $1,000   PAC

Unknown $26,000

    Homemakers/Non-income earners $11,950
    Generic Occupation/Category Unknown $5,500
    Employer Listed/Category Unknown $8,550
        Neiman Sawmills Inc .... $1,000   Indiv
        Safecard Services Inc .... $1,000   Indiv
        Unicover Corp .... $1,000   Indiv

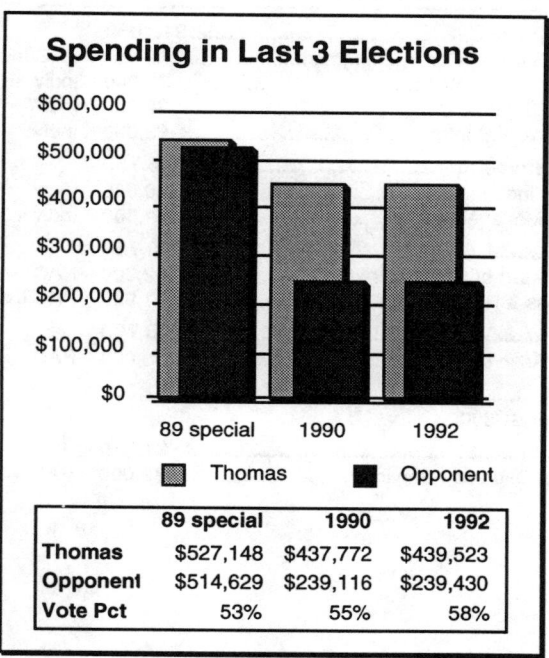

Spending in Last 3 Elections

	89 special	1990	1992
Thomas	$527,148	$437,772	$439,523
Opponent	$514,629	$239,116	$239,430
Vote Pct	53%	55%	58%

Legend: Thomas, Opponent

* Contributions came from more than one affiliate or subsidiary.

Ray Thornton, D-Ark (2)

First elected: 1990

1991-92 Total Receipts: $303,430
1992 Year-end Cash: $115,739

1991-92 Committees & Subcommittees

Government Operations
Government Activities and Transportation; Legislation and National Security

Science, Space and Technology
Investigations and Oversight; Science; Technology and Competitiveness

Leading Contributors

Business

Agriculture $27,150

Crop Production & Basic Processing $8,450
    Riceland Foods .... $2,500 PAC/Ind
Tobacco $3,000
    None over $1,500
Dairy $4,000
    Associated Milk Producers .... $4,000 PAC
Poultry & Eggs $4,500
    Tyson Foods .... $3,500 PAC/Ind
Livestock $2,300
    None over $1,500
Forestry & Forest Products $3,000
    None over $1,500

Communications/Electronics $11,800

Media/Entertainment $1,500
    None over $1,500
Telephone Utilities $9,300
    AT&T .... $2,500 PAC
    GTE Corp .... $1,500 PAC

Construction $6,500

General Contractors $2,750
    None over $1,500
Special Trade Contractors $1,500
    None over $1,500

Source of Funds in 1992 Election

Source	Total	Pct
PACs	$141,050	43%
Indivs $200+	$139,975	43%
Indivs under $200	$13,722	4%
Other	$33,991	10%
Candidate	$0	0%
Party	$25,708	8%

Source of PAC Dollars by Sector

Source	Total	Pct
Business	$82,650	59%
Labor	$51,900	37%
Ideology/Single Issue	$5,523	4%

In-State vs. Out-of-State Contributions*

Source	Total	Pct
In-State	$132,975	95%
Out-of-state	$7,000	5%
No state listed	$0	

* by large individual contributors ($200 & above)

Defense $2,000

Defense Electronics $1,500
    Raytheon .... $1,500 PAC

Energy & Natural Resources $11,425

Oil & Gas $5,450
    None over $1,500
Electric Utilities $3,250
    Entergy Corp* .... $1,750 PAC
Waste Management $1,725
    None over $1,500

Finance, Insurance & Real Estate $82,700

Commercial Banks $12,050
    Worthen Banking Corp .... $2,500 PAC/Ind
    First Jacksonville Bank .... $2,000 Indiv
    Twin City Bank .... $2,000 Indiv
    Union Bank of Benton .... $2,000 Indiv
Securities & Investment $44,750
    Stephens Inc .... $40,500 Indiv
    Meridian Management Co .... $1,500 Indiv
Insurance $10,750
    National Assn of Life Underwriters .... $2,000 PAC
    Blue Cross & Blue Shield Assn .... $1,900 PAC/Ind
Real Estate $8,700
    National Assn of Realtors .... $3,000 PAC
Accountants $1,700
    None over $1,500
Misc Finance $4,250
    Stephens Overseas Services .... $3,000 PAC

Contribution Totals by Sector

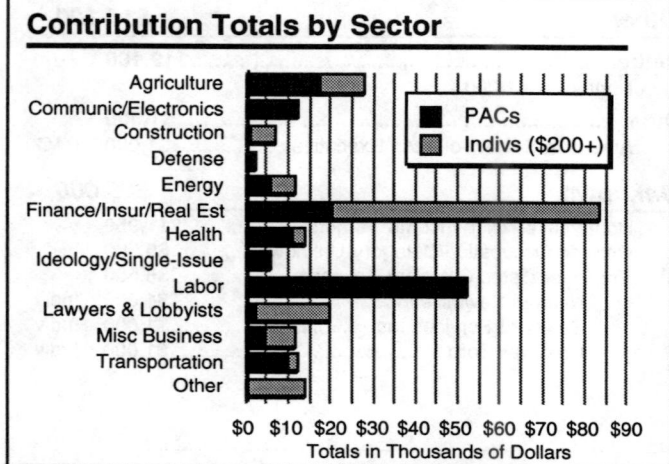

Agriculture, Communic/Electronics, Construction, Defense, Energy, Finance/Insur/Real Est, Health, Ideology/Single-Issue, Labor, Lawyers & Lobbyists, Misc Business, Transportation, Other

PACs / Indivs ($200+)

$0 $10 $20 $30 $40 $50 $60 $70 $80 $90
Totals in Thousands of Dollars

Health $13,350

Health Professionals $12,350
   American Medical Assn ....$5,000 PAC
   American Dental Assn ....$2,000 PAC

Lawyers & Lobbyists $19,050

Lawyers & Lobbyists $19,050
   Mitchell, Williams et al ....$4,150 Indiv
   Rose Law Firm ....$3,000 Indiv
   Friday, Eldredge & Clark ....$2,500 Indiv

Misc Business $11,300

Beer, Wine & Liquor $2,500
   None over $1,500

Misc Services $2,500
   Terminix ....$1,500 Indiv

Misc Manufacturing & Distributing $1,500
   None over $1,500

Transportation $11,700

Air Transport $3,200
   Central Flying Service ....$1,500 Indiv

Automotive $6,500
   National Auto Dealers Assn ....$5,500 PAC

Railroads $1,500
   Union Pacific Corp ....$1,500 PAC

Labor

Labor $51,900

Building Trade Unions $4,000
   Plumbers/Pipefitters Union ....$2,000 PAC
   Laborers' Political League ....$1,500 PAC

Industrial Unions $19,000
   United Auto Workers ....$5,500 PAC
   Intl Brotherhood of Electrical Workers ....$4,500 PAC
   United Steelworkers ....$3,000 PAC
   Machinists/Aerospace Workers Union ....$2,500 PAC
   Rubber Cork Linoleum & Plastic Workers ....$1,500 PAC

Transportation Unions $15,100
   Teamsters Union ....$6,000 PAC
   Marine Engineers Dist 2 Maritime Officers ....$2,000 PAC
   United Transportation Union ....$2,000 PAC
   Air Line Pilots Assn ....$1,500 PAC

Public Sector Unions $11,500
   National Assn Retired Federal Employees ....$4,000 PAC
   National Education Assn ....$2,500 PAC
   American Fedn of St/Cnty/Munic Employees ......$2,000 PAC
   American Postal Workers Union ....$2,000 PAC

Misc Unions $2,300
   Food & Commercial Workers Union ....$2,000 PAC

Ideological/Single-Issue

Ideological/Single-Issue $5,523

Gun Rights/Gun Control $4,500
   National Rifle Assn ....$4,500 PAC

Other & Unknown

Other $13,600

Civil Servants/Public Officials $3,750
   State of Arkansas ....$2,250 Indiv

Education $6,000
   Harding University ....$4,000 Indiv

Retired $3,350
   None over $1,500

Unknown $12,050

   Homemakers/Non-income earners $5,500
   Employer Listed/Category Unknown $5,150
     None over $1,500

Spending in Last 2 Elections

	1990	1992
Thornton	$678,429	$176,328
Opponent	$430,932	$6,212
Vote Pct	60%	74%

* Contributions came from more than one affiliate or subsidiary.

1175

Karen L. Thurman, D-Fla (5)

First elected: 1992

1991-92 Total Receipts:	$360,160
1992 Year-end Cash:	$7,553

1993-94 Committees & Subcommittees

Agriculture
Environment, Credit and Rural Development; Specialty Crops and Natural Resources

Government Operations
Employment, Housing and Aviation; Environment, Energy and Natural Resources; Information, Justice, Transportation and Agriculture

Leading Contributors

Business

Agriculture $28,375

Crop Production & Basic Processing **$14,925**
 Hancock Fidelity Citrus Groves .... $3,000 Indiv
 Florida Citrus Mutual .... $2,200 PAC
 United States Sugar Corp .... $2,000 PAC

Tobacco **$1,500**
 None over $1,500

Dairy **$3,100**
 Mid-America Dairymen .... $1,500 PAC

Livestock **$3,200**
 None over $1,500

Agricultural Services/Products **$1,650**
 None over $1,500

Food Processing & Sales **$4,000**
 Winn-Dixie Stores .... $2,500 PAC

Communications/Electronics $6,000

Telephone Utilities **$5,500**
 Southern Bell .... $2,500 PAC

Construction $3,200

General Contractors **$1,500**
 None over $1,500

Energy & Natural Resources $12,900

Oil & Gas **$5,450**
 Ashland Oil .... $2,250 PAC/Ind

Electric Utilities **$7,200**
 ACRE (Action Cmte for Rural Electrification) .... $4,000 PAC
 Florida Power & Light .... $2,000 PAC

Contribution Totals by Sector

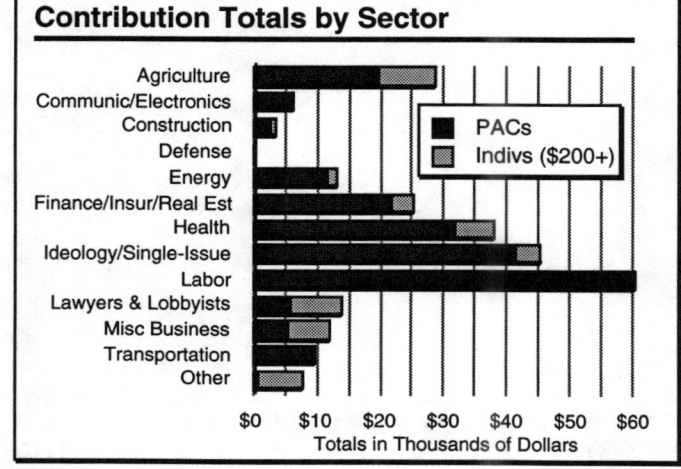

Agriculture
Communic/Electronics
Construction
Defense
Energy
Finance/Insur/Real Est
Health
Ideology/Single-Issue
Labor
Lawyers & Lobbyists
Misc Business
Transportation
Other

■ PACs
▨ Indivs ($200+)

$0 $10 $20 $30 $40 $50 $60
Totals in Thousands of Dollars

Source of Funds in 1992 Election

Source	Total	Pct
■ PACs	$202,744	56%
▨ Indivs $200+	$59,243	16%
☐ Indivs under $200	$69,452	19%
▧ Other	$29,526	8%
Candidate	$0	0%
Party	$5,955	2%

Source of PAC Dollars by Sector

Source	Total	Pct
■ Business	$112,157	53%
▨ Labor	$60,050	28%
☐ Ideology/Single Issue	$40,878	19%

In-State vs. Out-of-State Contributions*

Source	Total	Pct
☐ In-State	$44,301	85%
■ Out-of-state	$7,650	15%
No state listed	$362	

*** by large individual contributors ($200 & above)**

Finance, Insurance & Real Estate $24,911

Commercial Banks **$4,300**
 None over $1,500

Credit Unions **$1,500**
 Credit Union National Assn .... $1,500 PAC

Insurance **$6,750**
 Blue Cross & Blue Shield Assn* .... $1,750 PAC
 National Assn of Life Underwriters .... $1,500 PAC

Real Estate **$8,861**
 National Assn of Realtors .... $5,000 PAC

Accountants **$3,500**
 American Institute of CPA's .... $3,500 PAC

Health $37,354

Health Professionals **$30,654**
 American Dental Assn .... $5,000 PAC
 American Medical Assn .... $5,000 PAC
 American Academy of Ophthalmology .... $4,000 PAC
 American Nurses Assn .... $2,500 PAC
 American Chiropractic Assn .... $2,000 PAC
 American College of Emergency Physicians .... $2,000 PAC
 American Optometric Assn .... $2,000 PAC
 American Physical Therapy Assn .... $2,000 PAC
 Florida Society of Anesthesiologists .... $1,500 PAC

Hospitals/Nursing Homes **$6,450**
 Shands Corp .... $2,500 Indiv

Lawyers & Lobbyists $13,453

Lawyers & Lobbyists **$13,453**
 Assn of Trial Lawyers of America .... $5,000 PAC
 Taylor, Brian et al .... $2,000 Indiv

Misc Business — $13,657

Beer, Wine & Liquor **$2,000**
   National Beer Wholesalers Assn ....$2,000   PAC
Misc Services **$2,811**
   None over $1,500
Business Services **$5,339**
   George Lange Photography ....$2,000   Indiv

Transportation — $9,300

Air Transport **$1,500**
   None over $1,500
Automotive **$4,500**
   National Auto Dealers Assn ....$4,000   PAC
Sea Transport **$2,050**
   None over $1,500

Labor

Labor — $60,050

Industrial Unions **$24,200**
   Intl Brotherhood of Electrical Workers* ......$6,200   PAC
   United Auto Workers ....$6,000   PAC
   United Steelworkers ....$5,000   PAC
   Communications Workers of America ....$3,500   PAC
   Machinists/Aerospace Workers Union ....$2,500   PAC
Transportation Unions **$1,550**
   None over $1,500
Public Sector Unions **$28,500**
   National Education Assn ....$10,000   PAC
   American Fedn of St/Cnty/Munic Employees ......$5,000   PAC
   American Federation of Teachers ....$3,500   PAC
   National Assn of Letter Carriers ....$3,000   PAC
   National Rural Letter Carriers Assn ....$3,000   PAC
   National Assn Retired Federal Employees ......$2,000   PAC
   International Assn of Firefighters ....$1,500   PAC
Misc Unions **$5,300**
   Food & Commercial Workers Union ....$3,000   PAC

Ideological/Single-Issue

Ideological/Single-Issue — $44,712

Democratic/Liberal **$3,534**
   National Cmte for an Effective Congress ......$2,500   PAC
Leadership PACs **$3,900**
   None over $1,500
Pro-Choice **$2,500**
   National Abortion Rights Action League ......$1,500   PAC
Gun Rights/Gun Control **$9,900**
   National Rifle Assn ....$9,900   PAC
Womens Issues **$22,878**
   Emily's List ....$10,795   PAC/Ind
   National Organization for Women ....$5,083   PAC
   Women's Campaign Fund ....$5,000   PAC
   National Womens Political Caucus ....$1,500   PAC
Misc Issues **$2,000**
   National Cmte to Preserve Social Security ......$2,000   PAC

Other & Unknown

Other — $7,374

Civil Servants/Public Officials **$1,624**
   None over $1,500
Education **$3,500**
   Columbia University ....$3,000   Indiv
Retired **$1,750**
   None over $1,500

Unknown — $7,412

   Employer Listed/Category Unknown $5,062
     American Feed ....$2,250   Indiv

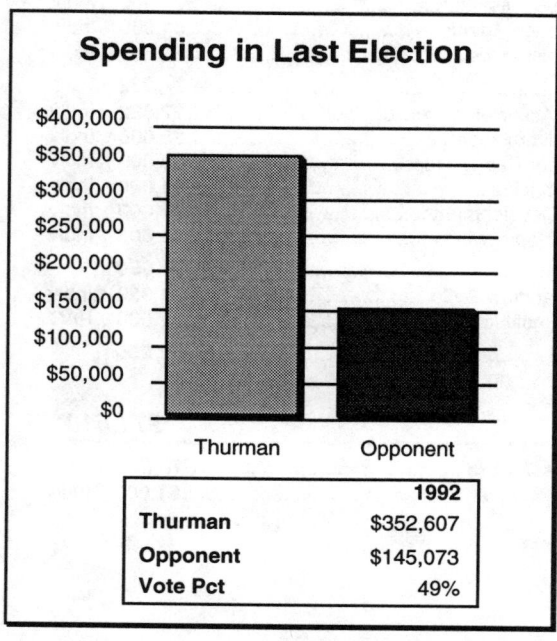

Spending in Last Election

	1992
Thurman	$352,607
Opponent	$145,073
Vote Pct	49%

* Contributions came from more than one affiliate or subsidiary.

Peter Torkildsen, R-Mass (6)

First elected: 1992

1991-92 Total Receipts: $453,507
1992 Year-end Cash: $2,072

1993-94 Committees & Subcommittees

Armed Services
Military Installations and Facilities; Research and Technology

Merchant Marine and Fisheries
Fisheries Management

Small Business
Regulation, Business Opportunities and Technology

Leading Contributors

NOTE: Torkildsen reported taking no PAC funds during his 1992 campaign. The PAC listed below did report making a contribution, however, and that contribution is recorded in the official FEC records.

Business

Agriculture		$1,500
Agricultural Services/Products	$1,000	
Blue Seal Feeds Inc	$1,000	Indiv

Communications/Electronics		$6,475
Printing & Publishing	$1,700	
None over $1,000		
Electronics Mfg & Services	$3,725	
Hewlett-Packard	$3,725	Indiv

Construction		$1,650
General Contractors	$1,400	
None over $1,000		

Defense		$1,100
Defense Electronics	$1,100	
Raytheon Co	$1,100	Indiv

Energy & Natural Resources		$1,250
Commercial Fishing	$1,000	
None over $1,000		

Source of Funds in 1992 Election

Source	Total	Pct
■ PACs	$0	0%
▨ Indivs $200+	$241,428	50%
☐ Indivs under $200	$180,351	37%
▧ Other	$60,162	12%
Candidate	$14,000	3%
Party	$34,556	7%

Source of PAC Dollars by Sector

No PAC contributions reported

Source	Total	Pct
■ Business	$1,000	100%
▨ Labor	$0	0%
☐ Ideology/Single Issue	$0	0%

In-State vs. Out-of-State Contributions*

Source	Total	Pct
☐ In-State	$229,603	95%
■ Out-of-state	$11,075	5%
No state listed	$750	

* by large individual contributors ($200 & above)

Finance, Insurance & Real Estate		$57,982
Commercial Banks	$2,100	
Bank of Boston	$1,500	Indiv
Finance/Credit Companies	$2,000	
Fort Hill Group	$2,000	Indiv
Securities & Investment	$18,700	
Fidelity Investments Co	$9,800	Indiv
PaineWebber	$1,700	Indiv
Baring America Asset Management	$1,500	Indiv
Cabot Partners	$1,000	Indiv
Kidder, Peabody	$1,000	Indiv
Insurance	$4,850	
Aetna Life & Casualty	$1,000	Indiv
Aim Insurance Agency	$1,000	Indiv
Schenck Insurance	$1,000	Indiv
Real Estate	$24,032	
Geraghty Associates Inc	$7,832	Indiv
Charles River Properties	$5,000	Indiv
Ambassador Realty Trust	$3,000	Indiv
Beal Companies	$1,000	Indiv
Howland Development	$1,000	Indiv
Winn Development Co	$1,000	Indiv
Accountants	$4,050	
Corner, Dandrow & Co	$1,350	Indiv
American Institute of CPA's	$1,000	PAC
Misc Finance	$2,250	
None over $1,000		

Health		$11,510
Health Professionals	$10,060	
Brigham & Women's Hospital	$1,000	Indiv

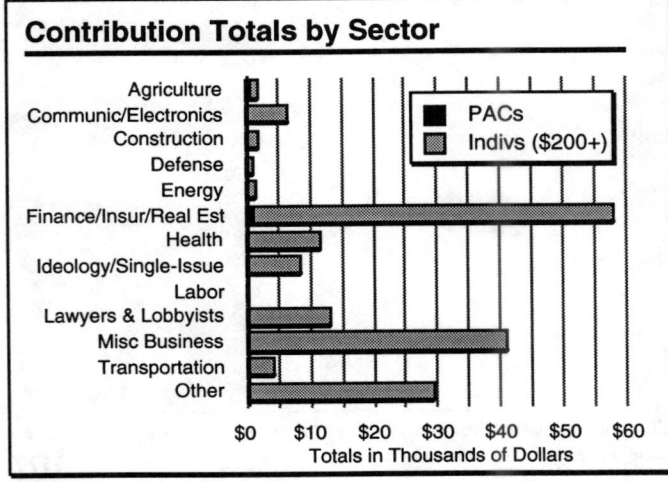

Contribution Totals by Sector

Legend: ■ PACs ▨ Indivs ($200+)

Categories: Agriculture, Communic/Electronics, Construction, Defense, Energy, Finance/Insur/Real Est, Health, Ideology/Single-Issue, Labor, Lawyers & Lobbyists, Misc Business, Transportation, Other

Totals in Thousands of Dollars ($0, $10, $20, $30, $40, $50, $60)

Lawyers & Lobbyists — $12,829

Lawyers & Lobbyists $12,829
Eckert, Seamans et al	$1,679	Indiv
Mintz, Levin et al	$1,500	Indiv
Kramer, Levin et al	$1,000	Indiv

Misc Business — $40,790

Food & Beverage $2,750
Fresh Water Fish Co	$1,000	Indiv
Roly's Restaurant	$1,000	Indiv

Beer, Wine & Liquor $1,750
Town & Country Liquors	$1,250	Indiv

Retail Sales $11,900
Christian Book Distributors Inc	$9,900	Indiv
Country Curtains	$1,500	Indiv

Business Services $15,040
PH Associates	$4,000	Indiv
Bain & Co	$2,000	Indiv
Arrow Advertising	$1,000	Indiv
Giardini & Russell Group	$1,000	Indiv

Chemical & Related Manufacturing $2,600
Cabot Corp	$2,000	Indiv

Misc Manufacturing & Distributing $6,750
Vacuum Barrier Corp	$3,000	Indiv
Joslin Displays Inc	$1,000	Indiv
New Balance Shoes	$1,000	Indiv
Peter Gray Corp	$1,000	Indiv

Transportation — $3,950

Automotive $2,500
Muzi Ford City	$2,500	Indiv

Ideological/Single-Issue

Ideological/Single-Issue — $8,355

Republican/Conservative $7,455
None over $1,000

Other & Unknown

Other — $29,089

Civil Servants/Public Officials $4,620
Commonwealth of Massachusetts	$2,950	Indiv
US Veterans Administration	$1,000	Indiv

Education $1,550
None over $1,000

Retired $22,349
None over $1,000

Unknown — $66,453
Homemakers/Non-income earners	$2,250	
No Employer Listed or Found	$19,108	
Generic Occupation/Category Unknown	$5,625	
Employer Listed/Category Unknown	$39,470	
Gem Line	$2,000	Indiv
Saltonstall & Co	$2,000	Indiv
Value Quest Ltd	$2,000	Indiv
Graham, Mays & Van Otterloo	$1,500	Indiv
AP Foundation	$1,400	Indiv
Sherbrooke Associates	$1,200	Indiv
American Fiber & Finishing	$1,000	Indiv
EM Parker Co	$1,000	Indiv
Greyrock Co	$1,000	Indiv
Implant Sciences Corp	$1,000	Indiv
New England Strategic Devel	$1,000	Indiv
Simons, Winslow et al	$1,000	Indiv
Struffolino & Struffolino	$1,000	Indiv
TA Communications Partners	$1,000	Indiv
Vanasse, Hansen & Brustlin	$1,000	Indiv

Spending in Last Election

	1992
Torkildsen	$451,434
Opponent	$671,110
Vote Pct	55%

Esteban E. Torres, D-Calif (34)

First elected: 1982

1991-92 Total Receipts: $169,451
1992 Year-end Cash: $63,139

1991-92 Committees & Subcommittees

Banking, Finance and Urban Affairs
Consumer Affairs and Coinage (Chairman); Housing and Community Development; International Development, Finance, Trade and Monetary Policy

Small Business
Environment and Employment; Procurement, Tourism and Rural Development

Leading Contributors

Business

Agriculture		$5,382

Crop Production & Basic Processing	$1,000	
None over $1,000		

Food Processing & Sales	$3,750	
Ace Wholesale	$2,000	Indiv
Mexican American Grocers Assn	$1,500	Indiv

Communications/Electronics		$12,905

Printing & Publishing	$4,200	
Hallmark Cards	$1,500	PAC/Ind
Hispanic Business Magazine	$1,000	Indiv
Maga Magazine	$1,000	Indiv

Telephone Utilities	$1,950	
Pacific Telesis Group	$1,350	PAC

Telecom Services & Equipment	$5,505	
New Bedford Panoramex Corp	$5,505	PAC/Ind

Computer Equipment & Services	$1,250	
Tamsco	$1,000	Indiv

Construction		$6,900

Home Builders	$3,350	
Manufactured Housing Institute	$1,000	PAC

Special Trade Contractors	$1,250	
National Electrical Contractors Assn	$1,000	PAC

Construction Services	$1,800	
Pacifica Services Inc	$1,000	Indiv

Source of Funds in 1992 Election

Source	Total	Pct
■ PACs	$49,300	27%
▨ Indivs $200+	$77,703	43%
□ Indivs under $200	$21,846	12%
⊠ Other	$31,490	17%
Candidate	$0	0%
Party	$11,038	6%

Source of PAC Dollars by Sector

Source	Total	Pct
■ Business	$36,089	65%
▨ Labor	$19,000	34%
□ Ideology/Single Issue	$314	1%

In-State vs. Out-of-State Contributions*

Source	Total	Pct
□ In-State	$58,053	75%
■ Out-of-state	$19,650	25%
No state listed	$0	

* by large individual contributors ($200 & above)

Defense		$2,500

Defense Aerospace	$1,500	
Northrop Corp	$1,500	PAC

Misc Defense	$1,000	
Luna Defense Systems Inc	$1,000	Indiv

Energy & Natural Resources		$2,500

Oil & Gas	$1,000	
None over $1,000		

Environmental Svcs/Equipment	$1,000	
Advanced Sciences Inc	$1,000	Indiv

Finance, Insurance & Real Esta		$24,250

Finance/Credit Companies	$1,000	
Tower Financial Corp	$1,000	Indiv

Securities & Investment	$1,000	
Saybrook Capital Corp	$1,000	Indiv

Insurance	$5,000	
Blue Cross of California	$2,500	PAC
American Council of Life Insurance	$1,000	PAC
Cumbre Inc	$1,000	Indiv

Real Estate	$13,250	
National Assn of Realtors	$5,000	PAC
Casden Co	$4,000	Indiv
Via Vista Corp	$2,000	Indiv
Funders Mortgage Co	$1,000	Indiv

Accountants	$2,500	
American Institute of CPA's	$1,000	PAC

Misc Finance	$1,500	
Towers Financial Corp	$1,000	Indiv

Contribution Totals by Sector

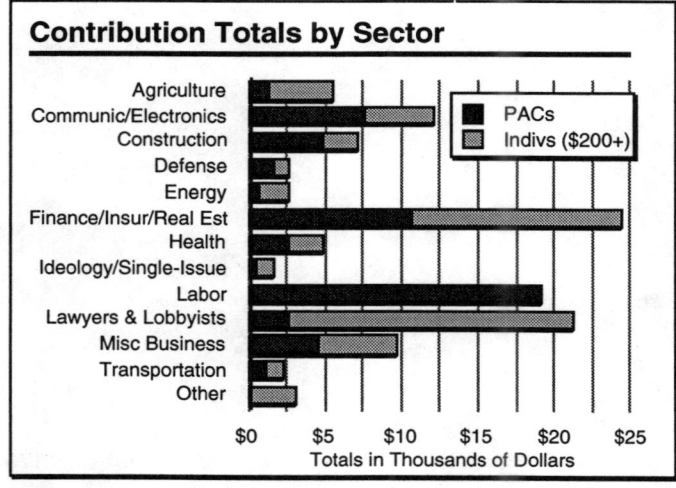

Agriculture, Communic/Electronics, Construction, Defense, Energy, Finance/Insur/Real Est, Health, Ideology/Single-Issue, Labor, Lawyers & Lobbyists, Misc Business, Transportation, Other

■ PACs ▨ Indivs ($200+)

$0 $5 $10 $15 $20 $25
Totals in Thousands of Dollars

Health $4,750

Health Professionals **$4,750**
  American Medical Assn ....$2,500 PAC

Lawyers & Lobbyists $21,100

Lawyers & Lobbyists **$21,100**
  Adorno & Zeder ....$3,500 Indiv
  Assn of Trial Lawyers of America ....$2,500 PAC
  Alcalde, Rousselot & Fay ....$1,000 Indiv
  Bloom, Dekom & Hergott ....$1,000 Indiv
  Margolis, Hertzberg et al ....$1,000 Indiv
  Rosato & Samuels ....$1,000 Indiv
  Ross & Scott ....$1,000 Indiv

Misc Business $9,584

Beer, Wine & Liquor **$1,824**
  National Beer Wholesalers Assn ....$1,000 PAC
Retail Sales **$1,000**
  None over $1,000
Misc Manufacturing & Distributing **$3,750**
  Philatron International ....$1,500 Indiv
  Marido Industrial Corp ....$1,000 Indiv

Transportation $2,178

Automotive **$1,678**
  None over $1,000

Labor

Labor $19,000

Building Trade Unions **$4,500**
  Laborers' Political League ....$4,000 PAC
Industrial Unions **$6,500**
  United Auto Workers ....$6,500 PAC
Public Sector Unions **$6,500**
  National Assn Retired Federal Employees ....$3,000 PAC
  National Assn of Letter Carriers ....$2,000 PAC
  National Education Assn ....$1,500 PAC
Misc Unions **$1,000**
  Food & Commercial Workers Union ....$1,000 PAC

Ideological/Single-Issue

Ideological/Single-Issue $1,564

Pro-Choice **$1,000**
  None over $1,000

Other & Unknown

Other $3,000

Civil Servants/Public Officials **$1,250**
  County of Los Angeles ....$1,000 Indiv
Retired **$1,750**
  None over $1,000

Unknown $17,493

  Employer Listed/Category Unknown $17,493
    Comprehensive Technologies International $3,000 Indiv
    Ace Group ....$1,500 Indiv
    Roselim Industries Inc ....$1,280 Indiv
    Hartland Funding ....$1,000 Indiv
    Perez & Associates ....$1,000 Indiv
    Perez Group ....$1,000 Indiv

Spending in Last 3 Elections

	1988	1990	1992
Torres	$227,098	$217,810	$254,092
Opponent	$149,886	$75,123	$131,271
Vote Pct	63%	61%	61%

Robert G. Torricelli, D-NJ (9)

First elected: 1982

1991-92 Total Receipts: $1,190,045
1992 Year-end Cash: $1,035,163

1991-92 Committees & Subcommittees

Foreign Affairs
Asian and Pacific Affairs; Western Hemisphere Affairs (Chairman)

Science, Space and Technology
Space; Technology and Competitiveness

Leading Contributors

Business

Agriculture — $28,350

Crop Production & Basic Processing $6,250
    None over $5,000
Dairy $7,000
    Associated Milk Producers .... $5,000   PAC
Food Processing & Sales $11,600
    None over $5,000

Communications/Electronics — $35,500

Media/Entertainment $15,750
    Pinelands Inc .... $5,000   Indiv
Telephone Utilities $9,650
    None over $5,000

Construction — $35,800

General Contractors $15,050
    None over $5,000
Special Trade Contractors $7,000
    None over $5,000
Building Materials & Equipment $5,750
    None over $5,000

Defense — $15,250

Defense Aerospace $12,750
    None over $5,000

Source of Funds in 1992 Election

Source	Total	Pct
PACs	$347,495	29%
Indivs $200+	$607,898	51%
Indivs under $200	$90,826	8%
Other	$155,952	13%
Candidate	$0	0%
Party	$12,576	1%

Source of PAC Dollars by Sector

Source	Total	Pct
Business	$186,268	56%
Labor	$106,950	32%
Ideology/Single Issue	$39,250	12%

In-State vs. Out-of-State Contributions*

Source	Total	Pct
In-State	$350,824	58%
Out-of-state	$256,675	42%
No state listed	$0	

* by large individual contributors ($200 & above)

Energy & Natural Resources — $23,899

Oil & Gas $7,550
    None over $5,000
Electric Utilities $14,299
    None over $5,000

Finance, Insurance & Real Estate — $104,669

Securities & Investment $31,900
    Wertheim, Schroder & Co .... $7,400   PAC/Ind
Insurance $21,450
    None over $5,000
Real Estate $26,750
    None over $5,000
Accountants $13,200
    Arthur Andersen & Co .... $6,500   Indiv

Health — $113,600

Health Professionals $75,500
    American Medical Assn* .... $10,000   PAC
Hospitals/Nursing Homes $18,250
    Hospice Care Inc .... $13,000   Indiv
Pharmaceuticals/Health Products $19,850
    Warner-Lambert .... $6,500   PAC/Ind

Lawyers & Lobbyists — $131,800

Lawyers & Lobbyists $131,800
    Assn of Trial Lawyers of America .... $5,000   PAC
    Sills, Cummis et al .... $5,000   Indiv

Contribution Totals by Sector

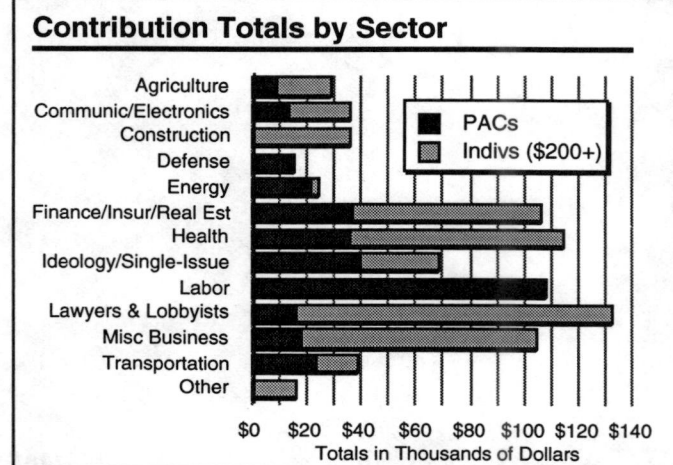

Legend: PACs; Indivs ($200+)

Categories: Agriculture, Communic/Electronics, Construction, Defense, Energy, Finance/Insur/Real Est, Health, Ideology/Single-Issue, Labor, Lawyers & Lobbyists, Misc Business, Transportation, Other

$0 $20 $40 $60 $80 $100 $120 $140
Totals in Thousands of Dollars

Misc Business $104,100

Beer, Wine & Liquor	**$13,250**
Gallo Winery	$10,000 Indiv
Retail Sales	**$9,500**
None over $5,000	
Business Services	**$15,800**
None over $5,000	
Casinos/Gambling	**$5,500**
None over $5,000	
Chemical & Related Manufacturing	**$10,000**
None over $5,000	
Misc Manufacturing & Distributing	**$34,800**
None over $5,000	
Textiles	**$7,000**
None over $5,000	

Transportation $38,200

Air Transport	**$14,750**
Texas Air	$5,500 PAC
Sea Transport	**$15,700**
None over $5,000	

Labor

Labor $106,950

Building Trade Unions	**$27,200**
Bricklayers Union	$6,000 PAC
Operating Engineers Union*	$6,000 PAC
Laborers' Political League	$5,000 PAC
Industrial Unions	**$13,000**
None over $5,000	
Transportation Unions	**$38,500**
Teamsters Union	$7,500 PAC
Marine Engineers Union*	$6,000 PAC
Masters, Mates & Pilots Union	$6,000 PAC
Public Sector Unions	**$23,750**
American Fedn of St/Cnty/Munic Employees	$5,000 PAC

Ideological/Single-Issue

Ideological/Single-Issue $68,000

Foreign & Defense Policy	**$21,150**
Free Cuba PAC	$10,000 PAC
Pro-Israel	**$33,150**
National PAC	$5,000 PAC
North Jersey PAC	$5,000 PAC

Other & Unknown

Other $15,250

Civil Servants/Public Officials	**$8,000**
None over $5,000	
Retired	**$5,050**
None over $5,000	

Unknown $119,099

Homemakers/Non-income earners	$45,050
No Employer Listed or Found	$16,524
Generic Occupation/Category Unknown	$5,100
Employer Listed/Category Unknown	$51,925
None over $5,000	

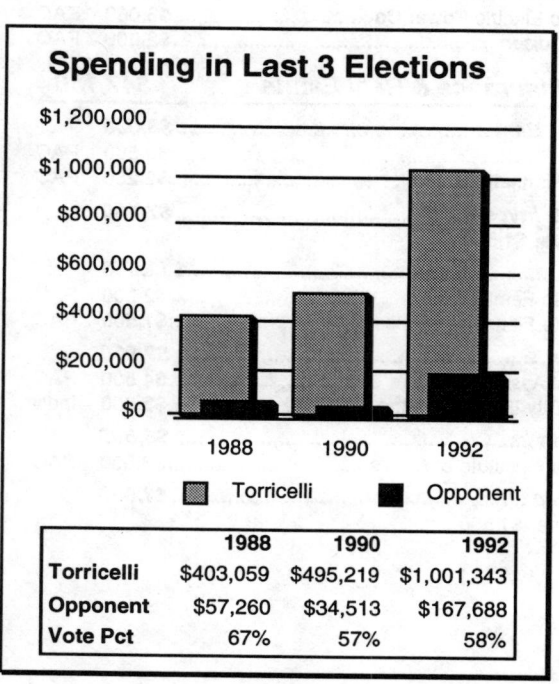

Spending in Last 3 Elections

	1988	1990	1992
Torricelli	$403,059	$495,219	$1,001,343
Opponent	$57,260	$34,513	$167,688
Vote Pct	67%	57%	58%

* Contributions came from more than one affiliate or subsidiary.

Edolphus Towns, D-NY (10)

First elected: 1982

1991-92 Total Receipts: $560,977
1992 Year-end Cash: $3,803

1991-92 Committees & Subcommittees

Energy and Commerce
Commerce, Consumer Protection and Competitiveness; Energy and Power; Health and the Environment

Government Operations
Environment, Energy and Natural Resources; Government Information, Justice and Agriculture

Select Committee on Narcotics Abuse and Control

Leading Contributors

Business

Agriculture	$37,045	
Crop Production & Basic Processing $3,000		
None over $1,500		
Tobacco $21,245		
RJR Nabisco $10,000	PAC	
Philip Morris $7,245	PAC	
US Tobacco Co $1,500	PAC	
Dairy $4,000		
Associated Milk Producers $3,000	PAC	
Agricultural Services/Products $1,800		
None over $1,500		
Food Processing & Sales $6,500		
Connell Rice & Sugar Co $3,000	Indiv	

Communications/Electronics	$54,000	
Printing & Publishing $3,350		
None over $1,500		
Media/Entertainment $40,400		
Time Warner* $13,100	Indiv	
National Cable Television Assn $10,000	PAC	
Viacom International $3,000	PAC	
Home Shopping Network Inc $2,500	PAC	
Black Entertainment Network $1,500	Indiv	
Telephone Utilities $7,250		
AT&T $3,000	PAC	
Electronics Mfg & Services $2,000		
Atlantic Systems Inc $2,000	Indiv	

Contribution Totals by Sector

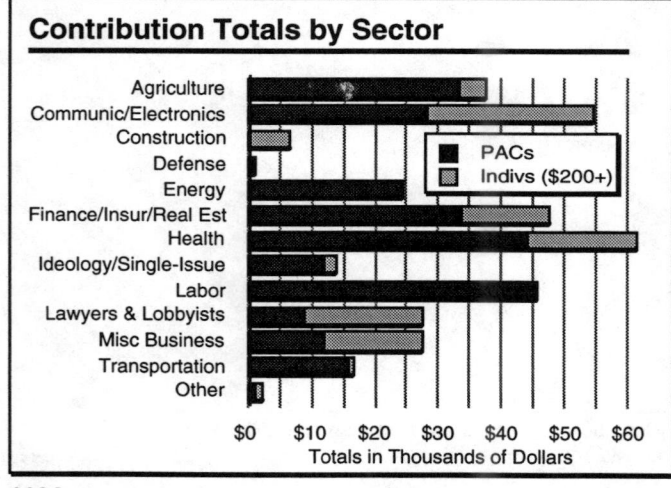

Agriculture
Communic/Electronics
Construction
Defense
Energy
Finance/Insur/Real Est
Health
Ideology/Single-Issue
Labor
Lawyers & Lobbyists
Misc Business
Transportation
Other

■ PACs
▨ Indivs ($200+)

$0 $10 $20 $30 $40 $50 $60
Totals in Thousands of Dollars

Source of Funds in 1992 Election

Source	Total	Pct
■ PACs	$242,365	43%
▨ Indivs $200+	$168,746	30%
☐ Indivs under $200	$96,165	17%
▧ Other	$57,976	10%
Candidate	$0	0%
Party	$4,275	1%

Source of PAC Dollars by Sector

Source	Total	Pct
■ Business	$198,608	78%
▨ Labor	$45,400	18%
☐ Ideology/Single Issue	$11,520	5%

In-State vs. Out-of-State Contributions*

Source	Total	Pct
☐ In-State	$102,171	65%
■ Out-of-state	$55,150	35%
No state listed	$11,425	

by large individual contributors ($200 & above)

Construction	$6,500	
General Contractors $2,400		
Black Contractors $1,800	Indiv	
Building Materials & Equipment $2,750		
Liberty Electric $2,500	Indiv	

Energy & Natural Resources	$24,213	
Oil & Gas $5,800		
None over $1,500		
Electric Utilities $17,513		
Potomac Electric Power Co $3,063	PAC	
Detroit Edison $2,000	PAC	

Finance, Insurance & Real Estate	$47,150	
Commercial Banks $8,000		
Citicorp $3,500	PAC	
Chase Manhattan $2,250	PAC	
Securities & Investment $7,150		
None over $1,500		
Insurance $12,550		
American Family Corp $2,000	PAC	
Equitable Financial Services $1,500	PAC	
Real Estate $9,950		
National Assn of Realtors $4,500	PAC	
Forest City Enterprises Inc $3,000	Indiv	
Accountants $5,500		
American Institute of CPA's $3,000	PAC	
Misc Finance $1,600		
None over $1,500		

Health $61,211

Health Professionals **$33,761**
    American Medical Assn* ....$10,000 PAC
    American Dental Assn ....$5,000 PAC
    American Podiatry Assn ....$3,500 PAC
    American Pharmaceutical Assn ....$1,500 PAC
    American Physical Therapy Assn ....$1,500 PAC

Hospitals/Nursing Homes **$3,350**
    None over $1,500

Pharmaceuticals/Health Products **$15,000**
    Merck & Co ....$1,500 PAC
    Upjohn Co ....$1,500 PAC

Misc Health **$9,100**
    Managed Healthcare Systems Inc ....$8,500 Indiv

Lawyers & Lobbyists $27,150

Lawyers & Lobbyists **$27,150**
    Assn of Trial Lawyers of America ....$5,000 PAC
    Fox, Weinberg & Bennett ....$3,500 Indiv
    Verner, Liipfert et al ....$1,500 PAC/Ind

Misc Business $27,025

Food & Beverage **$3,600**
    McDonald's Corp ....$2,100 PAC/Ind

Beer, Wine & Liquor **$2,000**
    None over $1,500

Business Services **$10,300**
    Echols & Co ....$2,500 Indiv
    Alarm Industry Communications Cmte ....$1,500 PAC

Misc Manufacturing & Distributing **$5,675**
    None over $1,500

Transportation $16,500

Air Transport **$6,500**
    United Parcel Service ....$6,500 PAC

Automotive **$7,500**
    Auto Dealers & Drivers for Free Trade ....$2,500 PAC

Trucking **$1,500**
    None over $1,500

Labor

Labor $45,400

Building Trade Unions **$6,000**
    Laborers' Political League ....$3,000 PAC

Industrial Unions **$5,000**
    None over $1,500

Transportation Unions **$19,300**
    Teamsters Union ....$5,000 PAC
    International Longshoremen's Assn* ....$4,100 PAC
    Air Line Pilots Assn ....$2,000 PAC
    Marine Engineers Dist 2 Maritime Officers ....$2,000 PAC
    United Transportation Union ....$2,000 PAC
    Transport Workers Union ....$1,700 PAC

Public Sector Unions **$12,000**
    American Fedn of St/Cnty/Munic Employees ......$5,000 PAC
    American Postal Workers Union ....$3,000 PAC
    National Education Assn ....$2,000 PAC

Misc Unions **$3,100**
    Food & Commercial Workers Union ....$2,000 PAC

Ideological/Single-Issue

Ideological/Single-Issue $13,520

Leadership PACs **$3,000**
    24th Cong Dist of Calif PAC (Henry Waxman) ....$2,000 PAC

Pro-Israel **$7,000**
    National PAC ....$5,000 PAC

Human Rights **$2,000**
    Human Rights Campaign Fund ....$2,000 PAC

Other & Unknown

Other $1,975

    None over $1,500

Unknown $61,585

    No Employer Listed or Found $46,435
    Generic Occupation/Category Unknown $3,800
    Employer Listed/Category Unknown $11,350
        None over $1,500

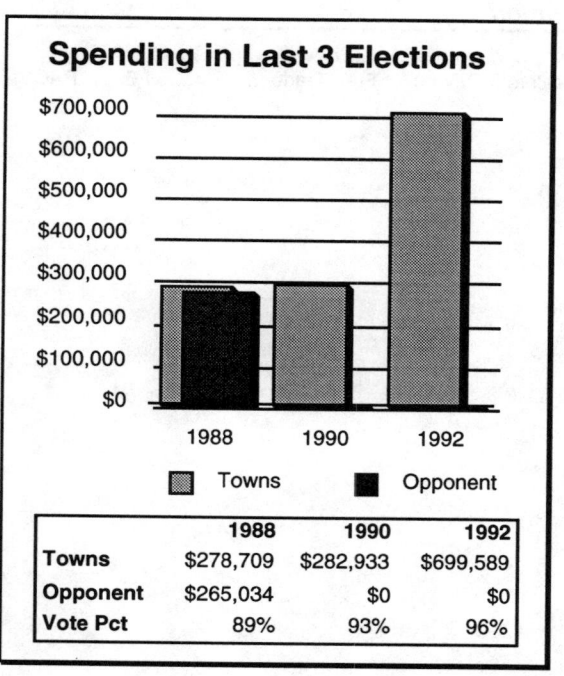

Spending in Last 3 Elections

	1988	1990	1992
Towns	$278,709	$282,933	$699,589
Opponent	$265,034	$0	$0
Vote Pct	89%	93%	96%

---

* Contributions came from more than one affiliate or subsidiary.

James A. Traficant Jr., D-Ohio (17)

First elected: 1984

1991-92 Total Receipts:	$155,474
1992 Year-end Cash:	$132,898

1991-92 Committees & Subcommittees

Public Works and Transportation
Aviation; Economic Development; Surface Transportation

Science, Space and Technology
Energy; Space

Select Committee on Narcotics Abuse and Control

Leading Contributors

Business

Agriculture		$2,200
Dairy		**$2,000**
Associated Milk Producers	$2,000	PAC

Communications/Electronics		$1,550
Telephone Utilities		**$1,300**
Ohio Bell Telephone	$1,300	PAC

Construction		$3,700
General Contractors		**$2,900**
PBS Construction	$1,400	Indiv
National Utility Contractors Assn	$1,000	PAC

Energy & Natural Resources		$1,200
Oil & Gas		**$1,000**
Lyden Oil Co	$1,000	Indiv

Finance, Insurance & Real Esta		$3,450
Real Estate		**$2,450**
Cafaro Co	$1,250	Indiv
Accountants		**$1,000**
None over $1,000		

Health		$4,550
Health Professionals		**$4,000**
American Medical Assn	$2,000	PAC

Source of Funds in 1992 Election

Source	Total	Pct
■ PACs	$85,120	51%
▨ Indivs $200+	$28,400	17%
☐ Indivs under $200	$39,132	23%
⊠ Other	$14,985	9%
Candidate	$0	0%
Party	$12,463	7%

Source of PAC Dollars by Sector

Source	Total	Pct
■ Business	$12,200	13%
▨ Labor	$79,270	86%
☐ Ideology/Single Issue	$1,000	1%

In-State vs. Out-of-State Contributions*

Source	Total	Pct
☐ In-State	$23,300	83%
■ Out-of-state	$4,900	17%
No state listed	$200	

*** by large individual contributors ($200 & above)**

Lawyers & Lobbyists		$1,850
Lawyers & Lobbyists		**$1,850**
None over $1,000		

Misc Business		$5,950
Steel Production		**$3,200**
Syro Steel Co	$1,300	Indiv
Standard Steel	$1,000	PAC
Textiles		**$1,000**
Burlington Industries	$1,000	PAC

Transportation		$2,650
Automotive		**$1,900**
Auto Dealers & Drivers for Free Trade	$1,500	PAC

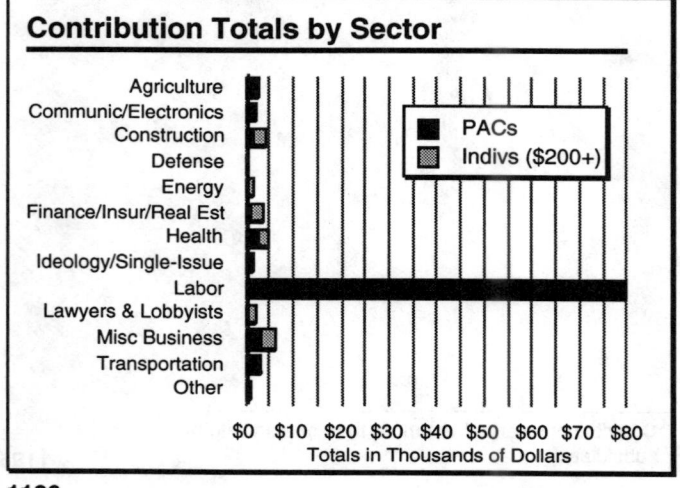

Contribution Totals by Sector

Agriculture
Communic/Electronics
Construction
Defense
Energy
Finance/Insur/Real Est
Health
Ideology/Single-Issue
Labor
Lawyers & Lobbyists
Misc Business
Transportation
Other

■ PACs
▨ Indivs ($200+)

$0 $10 $20 $30 $40 $50 $60 $70 $80
Totals in Thousands of Dollars

Labor

Labor	$79,520

Building Trade Unions **$8,500**
    Plumbers/Pipefitters Union ....$3,000   PAC
    Carpenters & Joiners Union ....$2,500   PAC
    Laborers' Political League ....$2,000   PAC
    Operating Engineers Union ....$1,000   PAC

Industrial Unions **$37,000**
    United Auto Workers ....$10,000   PAC
    United Steelworkers ....$5,300   PAC
    Boilermakers Union ....$5,000   PAC
    Intl Brotherhood of Electrical Workers ....$5,000   PAC
    Machinists/Aerospace Workers Union ....$5,000   PAC
    Electronic Machine Furniture Workers ....$4,200   PAC
    Rubber Cork Linoleum & Plastic Workers ....$1,500   PAC

Transportation Unions **$17,150**
    Air Line Pilots Assn ....$5,000   PAC
    Teamsters Union ....$5,000   PAC
    Marine Engineers Dist 2 Maritime Officers ....$2,000   PAC
    Trans Comm International Union ....$1,300   PAC
    Maintenance of Way Employees ....$1,250   PAC
    Assn of Flight Attendants ....$1,000   PAC

Public Sector Unions **$13,620**
    National Education Assn ....$7,000   PAC
    National Assn Retired Federal Employees ....$2,500   PAC
    American Postal Workers Union ....$1,500   PAC
    National League of Postmasters ....$1,000   PAC

Misc Unions **$3,250**
    AFL-CIO ....$1,500   PAC
    Food & Commercial Workers Union ....$1,500   PAC

Ideological/Single-Issue

Ideological/Single-Issue	$1,000

Foreign & Defense Policy **$1,000**
    None over $1,000

Other & Unknown

Unknown	$12,700

    Employer Listed/Category Unknown $12,150
        BJ Alan Co ....$1,600   Indiv
        Trumbell Corp ....$1,000   Indiv

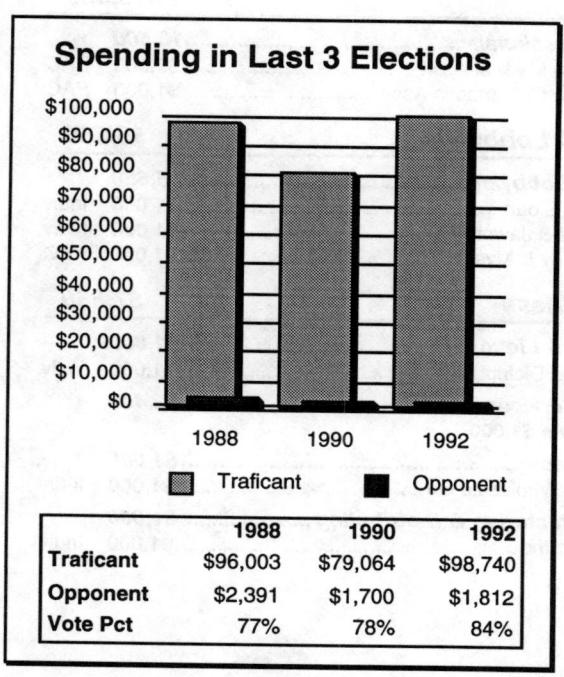

Spending in Last 3 Elections

	1988	1990	1992
Traficant	$96,003	$79,064	$98,740
Opponent	$2,391	$1,700	$1,812
Vote Pct	77%	78%	84%

Legend: Traficant / Opponent

Walter R. Tucker, D-Calif (37)

First elected: 1992

1991-92 Total Receipts: $283,230
1992 Year-end Cash: $5,644

1993-94 Committees & Subcommittees

Public Works and Transportation
Public Buildings and Grounds; Surface Transportation; Water Resources and the Environment

Small Business
Minority Enterprise, Finance and Urban Development; Regulation, Business Opportunities and Technology

Leading Contributors

Business

Agriculture	$7,500	

Crop Production & Basic Processing	$1,500	
None over $1,000		
Food Processing & Sales	$5,000	
Ralphs Grocery Co	$5,000	PAC

Communications/Electronics	$3,000	

Printing & Publishing	$1,000	
Printco Graphic Arts	$1,000	Indiv
Telephone Utilities	$1,500	
Pacific Telesis Group	$1,000	PAC

Construction	$2,000	

General Contractors	$1,500	
William Howell Construction	$1,000	Indiv

Energy & Natural Resources	$7,750	

Oil & Gas	$5,000	
Demenno & Kerdoon	$2,000	Indiv
World Oil Co	$2,000	Indiv
Electric Utilities	$2,500	
Southern California Edison	$2,500	PAC

Finance, Insurance & Real Estate	$16,125	

Commercial Banks	$3,000	
American Bankers Assn	$1,000	PAC
BankAmerica Corp	$1,000	PAC
Wells Fargo	$1,000	PAC
Securities & Investment	$1,150	
None over $1,000		

Insurance	$2,250	
Allstate Insurance	$1,750	Indiv
Real Estate	$6,750	
Telecu Industries	$2,000	Indiv
Morris Management Co	$1,000	Indiv
National Assn of Realtors	$1,000	PAC
Accountants	$1,000	
Thompson, Curtis, Brazilio & Assoc	$1,000	Indiv
Misc Finance	$1,975	
Hackman Equities	$1,250	Indiv

Health $13,500

Health Professionals	$13,500	
American Medical Assn	$5,000	PAC
American Chiropractic Assn	$1,000	PAC

Lawyers & Lobbyists $5,650

Lawyers & Lobbyists	$5,650	
Boren & Sloan	$1,000	Indiv
Fulbright & Jaworski	$1,000	Indiv
O'Melveny & Myers	$1,000	PAC

Misc Business $7,850

Beer, Wine & Liquor	$1,000	
Westside Distributors	$1,000	Indiv
Business Services	$2,400	
None over $1,000		
Misc Business	$1,000	
Coastal Wholesale Co	$1,000	Indiv
Misc Manufacturing & Distributing	$1,000	
Eurostar Inc	$1,000	Indiv

Source of Funds in 1992 Election

Source	Total	Pct
PACs	$65,100	19%
Indivs $200+	$131,590	39%
Indivs under $200	$52,256	15%
Other	$92,402	27%
Candidate	$34,950	10%
Party	$57,452	17%

Source of PAC Dollars by Sector

Source	Total	Pct
Business	$26,650	36%
Labor	$37,299	51%
Ideology/Single Issue	$9,250	13%

In-State vs. Out-of-State Contributions*

Source	Total	Pct
In-State	$125,840	97%
Out-of-state	$4,500	3%
No state listed	$1,000	

*** by large individual contributors ($200 & above)**

Contribution Totals by Sector

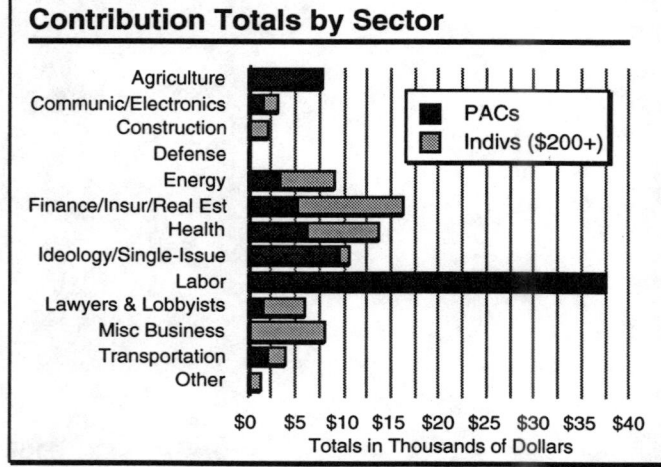

Agriculture
Communic/Electronics
Construction
Defense
Energy
Finance/Insur/Real Est
Health
Ideology/Single-Issue
Labor
Lawyers & Lobbyists
Misc Business
Transportation
Other

■ PACs
▨ Indivs ($200+)

$0 $5 $10 $15 $20 $25 $30 $35 $40
Totals in Thousands of Dollars

Transportation	$3,733

Air Transport **$2,000**
    United Parcel Service ....$2,000 PAC

Automotive **$1,000**
    Gateway Chevrolet..$1,000 Indiv

Labor

Labor	$37,299

Building Trade Unions **$6,500**
    Laborers' Political League ....$5,000 PAC
    Carpenters & Joiners Union ....$1,500 PAC

Industrial Unions **$12,250**
    Machinists/Aerospace Workers Union ....$5,000 PAC
    United Auto Workers ....$5,000 PAC
    Rubber Cork Linoleum & Plastic Workers ....$1,000 PAC

Transportation Unions **$8,050**
    Teamsters Union ....$5,000 PAC
    Marine Engineers Dist 2 Maritime Officers ....$2,000 PAC

Public Sector Unions.......................................**$6,000**
    American Fedn of St/Cnty/Munic Employees ......$3,000 PAC
    National Education Assn ....$2,500 PAC

Misc Unions **$4,499**
    Service Employees International Union ....$2,500 PAC
    AFL-CIO ....$1,000 PAC

Ideological/Single-Issue

Ideological/Single-Issue	$10,500

Leadership PACs **$3,000**
    Effective Government Cmte (Dick Gephardt) ......$1,000 PAC
    House Leadership Fund (Tom Foley) ....$1,000 PAC
    Victory USA (Vic Fazio)..$1,000 PAC

Pro-Israel **$7,250**
    National PAC ....$5,000 PAC
    Women's Alliance for Israel.................................$1,000 PAC

Other & Unknown

Other	$1,200

    None over $1,000

Unknown	$88,682

    No Employer Listed or Found $70,967
    Generic Occupation/Category Unknown $10,265
    Employer Listed/Category Unknown $7,450
        Dale Mason & Assoc....................................$1,000 Indiv
        Green, Goren & Marcus ....$1,000 Indiv
        Sinclair Corp..$1,000 Indiv

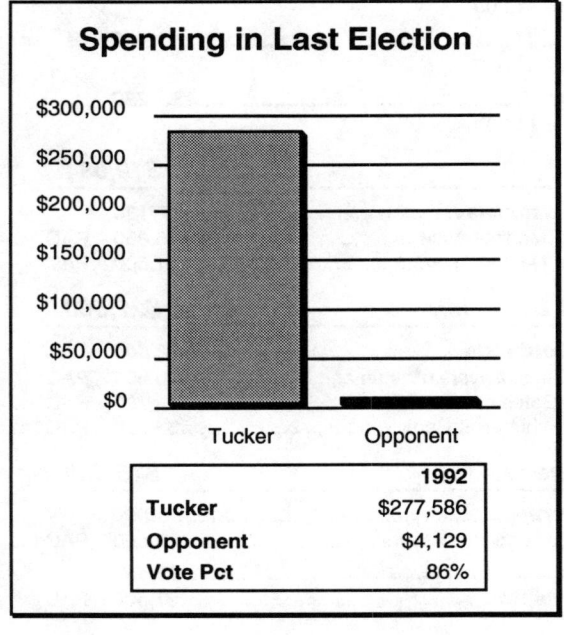

Spending in Last Election

	1992
Tucker	$277,586
Opponent	$4,129
Vote Pct	86%

Jolene Unsoeld, D-Wash (3)

First elected: 1988

1991-92 Total Receipts: $666,934
1992 Year-end Cash: $50,099

1991-92 Committees & Subcommittees

Education and Labor
Elementary, Secondary and Vocational Education; Labor-Management Relations; Postsecondary Education

Merchant Marine and Fisheries
Fisheries and Wildlife Conservation and the Environment; Merchant Marine

Select Committee on Aging

Leading Contributors

Business

Agriculture	$12,675	
Crop Production & Basic Processing $3,425		
None over $1,500		
Dairy $6,000		
Mid-America Dairymen $2,500	PAC	
Associated Milk Producers $2,000	PAC	
Darigold/Northwest Dairymens Assn $1,500	PAC	
Forestry & Forest Products $2,250		
None over $1,500		

Communications/Electronics	$17,450	
Printing & Publishing $3,200		
None over $1,500		
Media/Entertainment $10,250		
A&M Records $4,000	Indiv	
Peg Yorkin Productions $1,500	Indiv	
Telephone Utilities $1,500		
None over $1,500		
Computer Equipment & Services $2,000		
Business Computer Train $1,500	Indiv	

Construction	$2,450
None over $1,500	

Energy & Natural Resources	$29,431	
Oil & Gas $3,617		
Western Pioneer Inc $3,217	Indiv	

Electric Utilities	.... $2,200	
None over $1,500		
Commercial Fishing $22,864		
American Factory Trawler Assn $7,920	PAC/Ind	
Arctic Alaska Fisheries Corp $5,144	PAC/Ind	
Arctic Storm Inc $1,500	Indiv	

Finance, Insurance & Real Estate	$21,967	
Commercial Banks $12,800		
American Bankers Assn $7,500	PAC	
BankAmerica Corp* $2,000	PAC	
US Bancorp $2,000	PAC	
Savings & Loans $1,500		
None over $1,500		
Real Estate $1,500		
None over $1,500		
Misc Finance $3,269		
None over $1,500		

Health	$19,034	
Health Professionals $17,134		
American Medical Assn $5,350	PAC	
American Nurses Assn $1,500	PAC	

Lawyers & Lobbyists	$22,600	
Lawyers & Lobbyists $22,600		
Assn of Trial Lawyers of America $10,000	PAC	
Preston, Gates et al $2,700	PAC/Ind	
Garvey, Schubert & Barer $2,000	PAC/Ind	

Misc Business	$15,550	
Food & Beverage $8,000		
Pacific Seafood Processors $2,500	PAC/Ind	
Retail Sales $2,400		
Fred Meyer Inc $1,500	PAC	

Source of Funds in 1992 Election

Source	Total	Pct
■ PACs	$365,370	54%
▨ Indivs $200+	$118,409	18%
□ Indivs under $200	$170,011	25%
⊠ Other	$19,295	3%
Candidate	$0	0%
Party	$8,201	1%

Source of PAC Dollars by Sector

Source	Total	Pct
■ Business	$93,033	26%
▨ Labor	$197,050	55%
□ Ideology/Single Issue ..	$69,573	19%

In-State vs. Out-of-State Contributions*

Source	Total	Pct
□ In-State	$58,078	53%
■ Out-of-state	$51,700	47%
No state listed	$2,000	

*** by large individual contributors ($200 & above)**

Contribution Totals by Sector

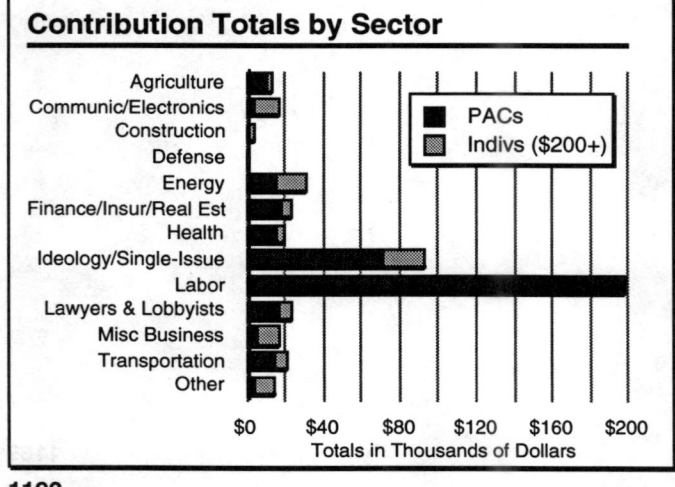

Agriculture
Communic/Electronics
Construction
Defense
Energy
Finance/Insur/Real Est
Health
Ideology/Single-Issue
Labor
Lawyers & Lobbyists
Misc Business
Transportation
Other

■ PACs
▨ Indivs ($200+)

$0 $40 $80 $120 $160 $200
Totals in Thousands of Dollars

Business Services	$2,400
None over $1,500	
Misc Manufacturing & Distributing	$1,750
None over $1,500	

Transportation $17,750

Railroads	$2,250	
Burlington Northern	$2,250	PAC
Sea Transport	**$14,000**	
Crowley Maritime	$3,250	PAC/Ind
Sea-Land Corp	$2,500	PAC
Tidewater Barge Lines	$2,000	Indiv
Totem Ocean Trailer Express	$2,000	PAC
Matson Navigation	$1,500	PAC

Labor

Labor $198,800

Building Trade Unions	$31,500	
Laborers Union*	$7,000	PAC
Carpenters & Joiners Union	$6,500	PAC
Sheet Metal Workers Union	$5,000	PAC
Ironworkers Union	$4,500	PAC
Operating Engineers Union*	$2,500	PAC
Plumbers/Pipefitters Union	$2,000	PAC
AFL-CIO Bldg/Construction Trades Dept	$1,500	PAC
Painters & Allied Trades Union	$1,500	PAC
Industrial Unions	**$50,300**	
Machinists/Aerospace Workers Union	$10,000	PAC
United Auto Workers	$10,000	PAC
United Steelworkers	$10,000	PAC
Intl Brotherhood of Electrical Workers	$9,000	PAC
Rubber Cork Linoleum & Plastic Workers	$4,000	PAC
Boilermakers Union	$3,000	PAC
Transportation Unions	**$55,200**	
Teamsters Union	$10,000	PAC
Seafarers International Union*	$9,500	PAC
Marine Engineers Union*	$8,250	PAC/Ind
Intl Longshoremen's/Warehousemen's Union	$7,000	PAC
Transport Workers Union	$4,000	PAC
Air Line Pilots Assn	$3,500	PAC
United Transportation Union	$3,000	PAC
Amalgamated Transit Union	$2,500	PAC
Trans Comm International Union	$2,300	PAC
Assn of Flight Attendants	$1,500	PAC

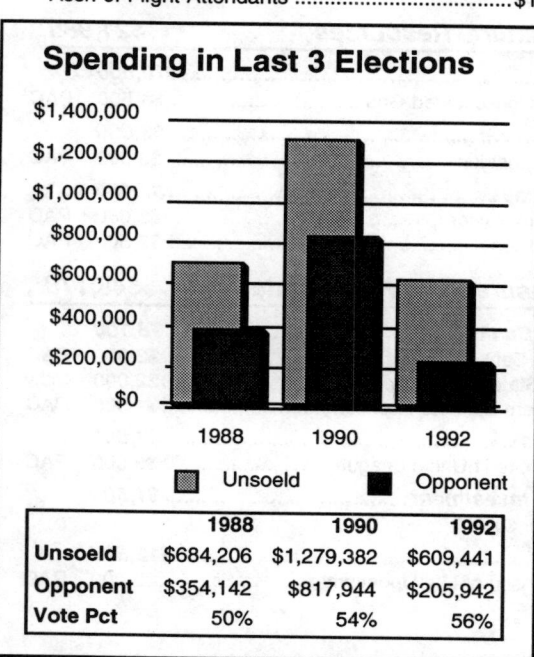

Spending in Last 3 Elections

	1988	1990	1992
Unsoeld	$684,206	$1,279,382	$609,441
Opponent	$354,142	$817,944	$205,942
Vote Pct	50%	54%	56%

Unsoeld   Opponent

Public Sector Unions	$47,000	
National Education Assn	$10,000	PAC
National Assn of Letter Carriers	$8,000	PAC
American Federation of Teachers	$7,500	PAC
National Assn Retired Federal Employees	$6,000	PAC
American Fedn of St/Cnty/Munic Employees	$5,000	PAC
American Postal Workers Union	$3,500	PAC
International Assn of Firefighters	$3,000	PAC
Misc Unions	**$14,800**	
Food & Commercial Workers Union	$5,000	PAC
AFL-CIO	$4,000	PAC
Service Employees International Union	$3,000	PAC

Ideological/Single-Issue

Ideological/Single-Issue $91,698

Democratic/Liberal	$9,200	
Hollywood Women's Political Cmte	$2,500	PAC
National Cmte for an Effective Congress	$2,200	PAC
Americans for Democratic Action	$1,500	PAC
Leadership PACs	**$5,000**	
America's Leaders' Fund (Dan Rostenkowski)	$2,500	PAC
Pro-Israel	**$7,500**	
Joint Action Cmte for Political Affairs	$1,500	PAC
Pro-Choice	**$8,575**	
Voters for Choice	$3,500	PAC/Ind
National Abortion Rights Action League	$2,000	PAC
Gun Rights/Gun Control	**$10,900**	
National Rifle Assn	$10,900	PAC
Womens Issues	**$22,985**	
National Organization for Women	$7,009	PAC
Emily's List	$5,126	PAC
Women's Campaign Fund	$3,000	PAC
Human Rights	**$10,000**	
Human Rights Campaign Fund	$10,000	PAC
Misc Issues	**$17,338**	
League of Conservation Voters	$6,088	PAC/Ind
Greenvote	$2,000	PAC
National Cmte to Preserve Social Security	$2,000	PAC
Sierra Club	$1,500	PAC

Other & Unknown

Other $13,400

Civil Servants/Public Officials	$1,800	
King County Prosecutors Office	$1,500	Indiv
Education	**$7,750**	
National Assn Trade & Technical Schools	$1,500	PAC
Retired	**$2,800**	
None over $1,500		

Unknown $13,629

No Employer Listed or Found	$4,679
Employer Listed/Category Unknown	$8,450
None over $1,500	

* Contributions came from more than one affiliate or subsidiary.

Fred Upton, R-Mich (6)

First elected: 1986

1991-92 Total Receipts: $432,851
1992 Year-end Cash: $107,399

1991-92 Committees & Subcommittees

Energy and Commerce
Commerce, Consumer Protection and Competitiveness; Oversight and Investigations

Select Committee on Hunger

Leading Contributors

Business

Agriculture — $21,000

Crop Production & Basic Processing **$3,000**
    National Grape Co-operative Assn .... $1,500   PAC

Tobacco **$1,500**
    RJR Nabisco .... $1,500   PAC

Dairy **$2,500**
    Associated Milk Producers .... $2,000   PAC

Livestock **$1,650**
    None over $1,500

Agricultural Services/Products **$3,000**
    None over $1,500

Food Processing & Sales **$6,350**
    Kellogg Co .... $2,750   PAC/Ind

Forestry & Forest Products **$2,000**
    None over $1,500

Communications/Electronics — $20,230

Printing & Publishing **$2,860**
    None over $1,500

Media/Entertainment **$6,300**
    National Assn of Broadcasters .... $2,000   PAC
    National Cable Television Assn .... $2,000   PAC

Telephone Utilities **$8,070**
    Michigan Bell Telephone .... $4,500   PAC
    AT&T .... $2,250   PAC

Telecom Services & Equipment **$1,500**
    None over $1,500

Computer Equipment & Services **$1,500**
    Electronic Data Systems .... $1,500   PAC

Source of Funds in 1992 Election

Source	Total	Pct
■ PACs	$149,585	35%
▨ Indivs $200+	$179,341	41%
□ Indivs under $200	$96,324	22%
▨ Other	$7,601	2%
Candidate	$0	0%
Party	$1,394	0%

Source of PAC Dollars by Sector

Source	Total	Pct
■ Business	$147,615	100%
▨ Labor	$50	0%
□ Ideology/Single Issue	$0	0%

In-State vs. Out-of-State Contributions*

Source	Total	Pct
□ In-State	$175,091	98%
■ Out-of-state	$4,250	2%
No state listed	$0	

* by large individual contributors ($200 & above)

Construction — $14,300

General Contractors **$9,200**
    Thompson McCully Asphalt .... $2,700   Indiv
    Associated General Contractors .... $2,000   PAC

Special Trade Contractors **$1,500**
    None over $1,500

Building Materials & Equipment **$3,600**
    None over $1,500

Defense — $3,250

Defense Aerospace **$3,250**
    None over $1,500

Energy & Natural Resources — $21,980

Oil & Gas **$10,000**
    Michigan Consolidated Gas .... $1,500   PAC

Misc Energy **$3,000**
    Cooper Industries .... $3,000   PAC

Electric Utilities **$7,480**
    Consumers Power Co .... $3,680   PAC
    Detroit Edison .... $2,500   PAC

Finance, Insurance & Real Estate — $45,170

Commercial Banks **$8,100**
    American Bankers Assn .... $2,000   PAC
    Peoples State Bank .... $2,000   Indiv
    Independent Bankers Assn .... $1,500   PAC

Credit Unions **$3,000**
    Michigan Credit Union League .... $3,000   PAC

Securities & Investment **$1,500**
    None over $1,500

Insurance **$12,320**
    National Assn of Life Underwriters .... $2,000   PAC

Contribution Totals by Sector

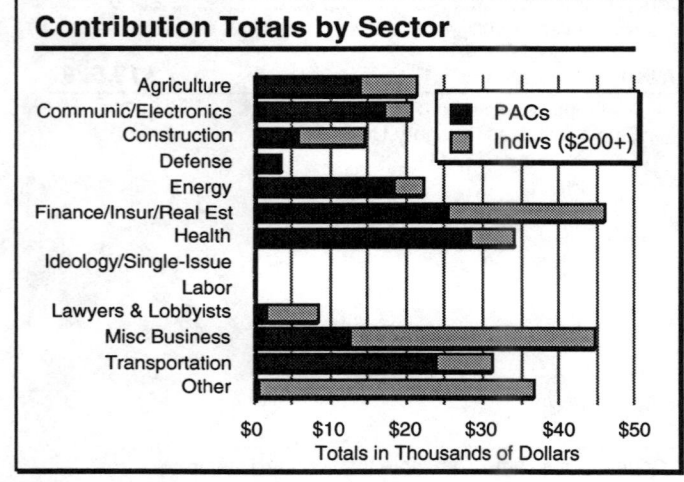

Agriculture
Communic/Electronics
Construction
Defense
Energy
Finance/Insur/Real Est
Health
Ideology/Single-Issue
Labor
Lawyers & Lobbyists
Misc Business
Transportation
Other

■ PACs
▨ Indivs ($200+)

$0 $10 $20 $30 $40 $50
Totals in Thousands of Dollars

Real Estate **$7,750**
   National Assn of Realtors ....$2,000   PAC

Accountants **$7,000**
   American Institute of CPA's ....$3,500   PAC

Misc Finance **$4,000**
   None over $1,500

Health $33,750

Health Professionals **$23,000**
   American Dental Assn ....$7,500   PAC
   American Medical Assn ....$6,500   PAC
   American Academy of Ophthalmology ....$3,500   PAC

Hospitals/Nursing Homes **$2,250**
   American Hospital Assn ....$1,500   PAC

Pharmaceuticals/Health Products **$8,500**
   Upjohn Co ....$3,000   PAC/Ind
   Glaxo Inc ....$1,500   PAC
   Warner-Lambert ....$1,500   PAC

Lawyers & Lobbyists $8,000

Lawyers & Lobbyists **$8,000**
   Jones, Day et al ....$1,500   PAC
   Kinney, Cook et al ....$1,500   Indiv

Misc Business $45,450

Food & Beverage **$3,250**
   None over $1,500

Retail Sales **$2,850**
   None over $1,500

Misc Services **$2,500**
   None over $1,500

Business Services **$2,200**
   None over $1,500

Lodging/Tourism **$2,250**
   None over $1,500

Chemical & Related Manufacturing **$2,000**
   None over $1,500

Misc Manufacturing & Distributing **$28,500**
   Whirlpool Corp ....$11,500   PAC/Ind
   Gast Manufacturing Corp ....$2,000   Indiv
   K&M Machine Fabricating Inc ....$2,000   Indiv
   Hanson International ....$1,500   Indiv
   Tobian Metals ....$1,500   Indiv

Transportation $30,995

Air Transport **$10,195**
   United Parcel Service ....$6,195   PAC
   General Electric ....$1,500   PAC

Automotive **$15,500**
   National Auto Dealers Assn ....$4,000   PAC
   General Motors ....$2,500   PAC
   Ford Motor Co ....$2,000   PAC
   Great Lakes Mazda Distributors ....$2,000   Indiv
   Holland Hitch Co ....$2,000   Indiv
   Chrysler Corp ....$1,500   PAC

Trucking **$3,400**
   None over $1,500

Other & Unknown

Other $36,370

Education **$2,500**
   None over $1,500

Retired **$32,370**
   None over $1,500

Unknown $46,961

   Homemakers/Non-income earners $19,100
   Employer Listed/Category Unknown $27,861
      Hess Industries Inc ....$1,500   Indiv

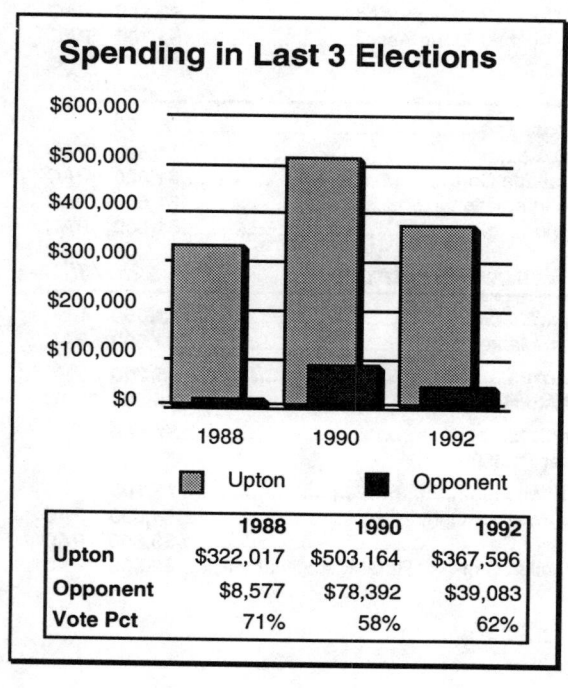

Spending in Last 3 Elections

	1988	1990	1992
Upton	$322,017	$503,164	$367,596
Opponent	$8,577	$78,392	$39,083
Vote Pct	71%	58%	62%

Tim Valentine, D-NC (2)

First elected: 1982

1991-92 Total Receipts: $443,499
1992 Year-end Cash: $5,853

1991-92 Committees & Subcommittees

Public Works and Transportation
Aviation; Surface Transportation; Water Resources

Science, Space and Technology
Science; Technology and Competitiveness (Chairman)

Leading Contributors

Business

Agriculture		$46,275	
Crop Production & Basic Processing		**$10,625**	
American Crystal Sugar Corp		$1,500	PAC
National Cotton Council		$1,500	PAC
Tobacco		**$19,850**	
RJR Nabisco*		$10,400	Indiv
Philip Morris		$5,500	PAC
US Tobacco Co		$2,000	PAC
Dairy		**$3,500**	
Associated Milk Producers		$2,000	PAC
Dairymen Inc-North Carolina		$1,500	PAC
Poultry & Eggs		**$2,500**	
National Broiler Council		$2,500	PAC
Livestock		**$1,750**	
None over $1,500			
Food Processing & Sales		**$4,250**	
MBM Corp		$2,000	Indiv
Pepsico Inc		$1,500	PAC
Forestry & Forest Products		**$2,500**	
Champion International Corp		$2,000	PAC

Communications/Electronics		$22,700	
Telephone Utilities		**$15,900**	
Southern Bell		$6,000	PAC
AT&T		$3,500	PAC
United Telecommunications		$3,000	PAC
GTE Corp		$1,600	PAC
Telecom Services & Equipment		**$2,000**	
Northern Telecom		$2,000	PAC

Source of Funds in 1992 Election

Source	Total	Pct
■ PACs	$237,040	52%
▨ Indivs $200+	$100,120	22%
☐ Indivs under $200	$71,477	16%
⊠ Other	$48,599	11%
Candidate	$25,000	5%
Party	$18,887	4%

Source of PAC Dollars by Sector

Source	Total	Pct
■ Business	$220,139	90%
▨ Labor	$14,800	6%
☐ Ideology/Single Issue	$10,213	4%

In-State vs. Out-of-State Contributions*

Source	Total	Pct
☐ In-State	$93,720	94%
■ Out-of-state	$6,400	6%
No state listed	$0	

*** by large individual contributors ($200 & above)**

Electronics Mfg & Services	$2,000
None over $1,500	
Computer Equipment & Services	**$2,200**
None over $1,500	

Construction		$18,900	
General Contractors		**$8,700**	
Associated General Contractors		$3,000	PAC
Home Builders		**$3,350**	
None over $1,500			
Building Materials & Equipment		**$6,100**	
National Concrete Masonry Assn		$2,300	PAC
National Crushed Stone Assn		$1,500	PAC

Defense		$8,500	
Defense Aerospace		**$8,500**	
Dyncorp		$1,500	PAC
Martin Marietta Corp		$1,500	PAC
Rockwell International		$1,500	PAC
Textron Inc		$1,500	PAC

Energy & Natural Resources		$25,700	
Oil & Gas		**$3,350**	
Petroleum Marketers Assn		$1,500	PAC
Nuclear Energy		**$5,250**	
General Atomics		$5,000	PAC
Misc Energy		**$1,500**	
None over $1,500			
Electric Utilities		**$15,100**	
Carolina Power & Light		$4,000	PAC
Duke Power Co		$3,600	PAC/Ind
ACRE (Action Cmte for Rural Electrification)		$2,500	PAC

Contribution Totals by Sector

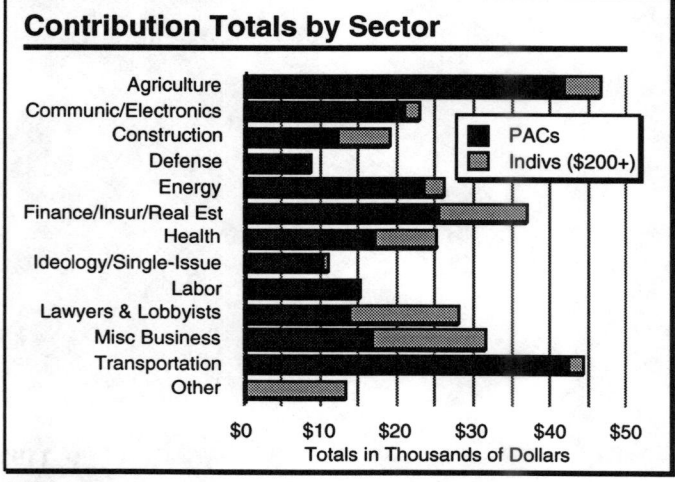

Agriculture
Communic/Electronics
Construction
Defense
Energy
Finance/Insur/Real Est
Health
Ideology/Single-Issue
Labor
Lawyers & Lobbyists
Misc Business
Transportation
Other

■ PACs
▨ Indivs ($200+)

$0 $10 $20 $30 $40 $50
Totals in Thousands of Dollars

Finance, Insurance & Real Estate   **$37,050**

Commercial Banks **$12,100**
    Citizens & Southern National Bank ....$3,000   PAC
    Centura Banks Inc ....$2,000   PAC
    Central Carolina Bank & Trust ....$1,850   PAC/Ind

Securities & Investment **$1,750**
    None over $1,500

Insurance **$9,200**
    National Assn of Life Underwriters ....$3,500   PAC
    Independent Insurance Agents of America ....$1,550   PAC

Real Estate **$13,400**
    National Assn of Realtors ....$8,000   PAC

Health   **$24,764**

Health Professionals **$7,500**
    None over $1,500

Hospitals/Nursing Homes **$3,014**
    American Hospital Assn ....$1,500   PAC

Pharmaceuticals/Health Products **$14,250**
    Glaxo Inc ....$6,000   PAC/Ind
    Burroughs Wellcome ....$3,000   PAC
    Merck & Co ....$1,500   PAC

Lawyers & Lobbyists   **$27,820**

Lawyers & Lobbyists **$27,820**
    Assn of Trial Lawyers of America ....$10,000   PAC

Misc Business   **$32,400**

Business Associations **$1,500**
    National Fedn of Independent Business ....$1,500   PAC

Food & Beverage **$2,800**
    Pearsall Operating Co ....$2,200   Indiv

Beer, Wine & Liquor **$1,500**
    None over $1,500

Retail Sales **$3,800**
    None over $1,500

Misc Services **$1,800**
    None over $1,500

Business Services **$3,350**
    None over $1,500

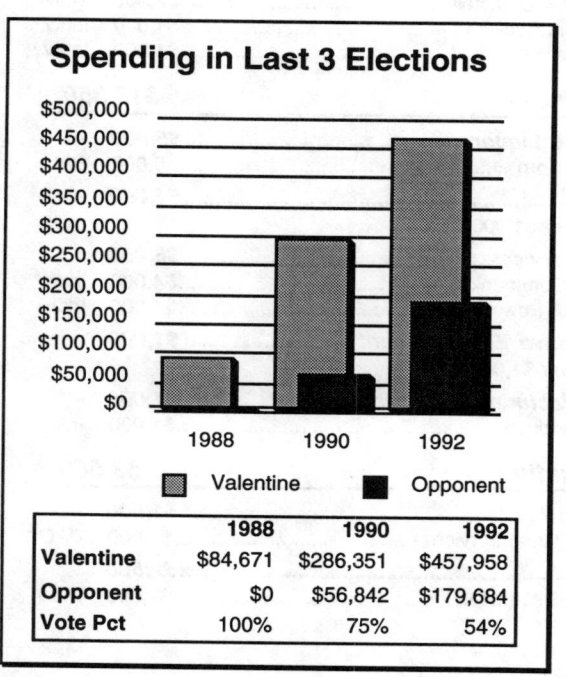

Spending in Last 3 Elections

	1988	1990	1992
Valentine	$84,671	$286,351	$457,958
Opponent	$0	$56,842	$179,684
Vote Pct	100%	75%	54%

Lodging/Tourism **$1,700**
    None over $1,500

Chemical & Related Manufacturing **$2,300**
    None over $1,500

Misc Manufacturing & Distributing **$6,450**
    American Furniture Manufacturers Assn ....$2,300   PAC
    Corning Glass Works ....$2,000   PAC

Textiles **$6,800**
    Harriet & Henderson Textiles ....$2,500   Indiv
    American Textile Manufacturers Institute ....$1,500   PAC

Transportation   **$44,050**

Air Transport **$27,850**
    Aircraft Owners & Pilots Assn ....$9,000   PAC
    American Airlines ....$5,500   PAC
    Federal Express Corp ....$5,000   PAC
    United Parcel Service ....$4,500   PAC

Automotive **$6,400**
    National Auto Dealers Assn ....$3,500   PAC
    Eaton Corp ....$1,900   PAC/Ind

Trucking **$4,700**
    Yellow Freight System ....$2,000   PAC
    American Trucking Assns ....$1,500   PAC

Railroads **$2,600**
    None over $1,500

Misc Transport **$2,500**
    Tourmobile Co ....$1,500   Indiv

Labor

Labor   **$14,800**

Transportation Unions **$4,750**
    Marine Engineers Dist 2 Maritime Officers ....$2,000   PAC
    National Air Traffic Controllers Assn ....$1,500   PAC

Public Sector Unions **$8,050**
    National Assn Retired Federal Employees ....$5,000   PAC
    National Assn of Letter Carriers ....$2,000   PAC

Ideological/Single-Issue

Ideological/Single-Issue   **$10,713**

Democratic/Liberal **$2,500**
    National Cmte for an Effective Congress ....$2,500   PAC

Leadership PACs **$2,500**
    None over $1,500

Misc Issues **$4,700**
    National Cmte to Preserve Social Security ....$2,700   PAC
    Sierra Club ....$2,000   PAC

Other & Unknown

Other   **$13,000**

Education **$2,200**
    Duke University ....$1,750   Indiv

Retired **$9,700**
    None over $1,500

Unknown   **$18,850**

    Generic Occupation/Category Unknown $1,900
    Employer Listed/Category Unknown $15,800
      Wimbley-Gregory & Co ....$2,000   Indiv

---

* Contributions came from more than one affiliate or subsidiary.

Nydia M. Velazquez, D-NY (12)

First elected: 1992

1991-92 Total Receipts: $477,373
1992 Year-end Cash: $14,698

1993-94 Committees & Subcommittees

Banking, Finance and Urban Affairs
Consumer Credit and Insurance; Economic Growth and Credit Formation; General Oversight, Investigations & Resolution for Failed Institutions; Housing and Community Development

Small Business
Minority Enterprise, Finance and Urban Development

Leading Contributors

Business

Agriculture	$1,000	
None over $1,000		

Communications/Electronics	$4,250	
Telephone Utilities	$2,500	
AT&T	$1,000	PAC
New York Telephone	$1,000	PAC

Construction	$2,600	
General Contractors	$2,400	
Research Construction	$1,000	Indiv

Energy & Natural Resources	$1,500	
Oil & Gas	$1,500	
Coastal Corp	$1,000	PAC

Finance, Insurance & Real Estate	$16,550	
Commercial Banks	$8,750	
American Bankers Assn	$3,500	PAC
Chase Manhattan	$1,000	PAC
Citicorp	$1,000	PAC
JP Morgan & Co	$1,000	PAC
Savings & Loans	$1,000	
None over $1,000		
Securities & Investment	$4,100	
Shearson Lehman Brothers	$1,300	PAC/Ind
Laidlaw Holdings	$1,000	Indiv
Insurance	$2,000	
Sedgwick James Inc	$2,000	Indiv

Source of Funds in 1992 Election

Source	Total	Pct
PACs	$159,900	33%
Indivs $200+	$109,745	23%
Indivs under $200	$99,208	21%
Other	$112,658	23%
Candidate	$8,500	2%
Party	$4,138	1%

Source of PAC Dollars by Sector

Source	Total	Pct
Business	$35,550	26%
Labor	$75,150	54%
Ideology/Single Issue	$27,691	20%

In-State vs. Out-of-State Contributions*

Source	Total	Pct
In-State	$71,845	68%
Out-of-state	$33,400	32%
No state listed	$3,750	

*** by large individual contributors ($200 & above)**

Health — $15,300

Health Professionals	$8,800	
American Medical Assn	$5,000	PAC
American Nurses Assn	$2,000	PAC
Pharmaceuticals/Health Products	$6,000	
Merck & Co	$1,000	PAC
Pfizer Inc	$1,000	PAC/Ind
Schering-Plough Corp	$1,000	PAC
Syntex (USA) Inc	$1,000	PAC

Lawyers & Lobbyists — $11,515

Lawyers & Lobbyists	$11,515	
O'Dwyer & Bernstein	$2,500	Indiv
Fischbein, Badillo et al	$1,000	Indiv
McAuliffe, Kelly et al	$1,000	Indiv

Misc Business — $15,350

Beer, Wine & Liquor	$5,000	
Bacardi Corp	$5,000	PAC
Retail Sales	$1,000	
None over $1,000		
Business Services	$6,900	
Robles Communications	$4,000	Indiv
Fingerhut Powers	$1,000	Indiv
Recreation/Live Entertainment	$1,000	
None over $1,000		
Misc Manufacturing & Distributing	$1,000	
Avon Products	$1,000	PAC

Transportation — $3,500

Air Transport	$1,000	
United Parcel Service	$1,000	PAC
Trucking	$2,500	
Azteca Enterprises Inc	$2,500	Indiv

Contribution Totals by Sector

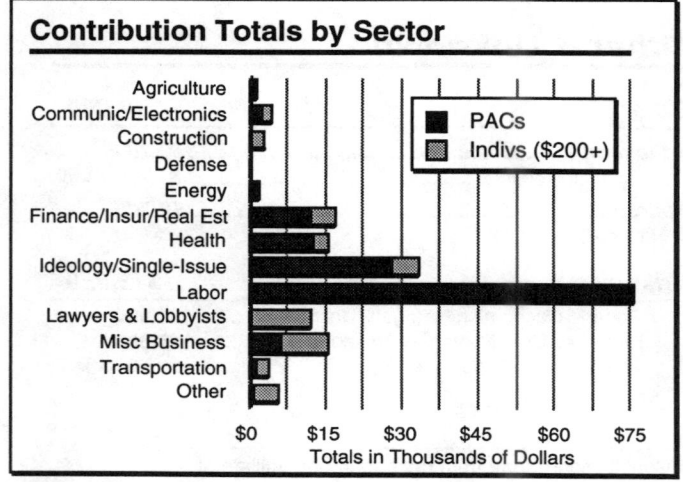

Categories (top to bottom): Agriculture, Communic/Electronics, Construction, Defense, Energy, Finance/Insur/Real Est, Health, Ideology/Single-Issue, Labor, Lawyers & Lobbyists, Misc Business, Transportation, Other

Legend: ■ PACs ▨ Indivs ($200+)

Scale: $0, $15, $30, $45, $60, $75
Totals in Thousands of Dollars

Labor

Labor	$75,150

Building Trade Unions **$5,000**
    Carpenters & Joiners Union .... $5,000   PAC

Industrial Unions **$26,300**
    Communications Workers of America .... $6,000   PAC
    United Auto Workers .... $5,000   PAC
    United Mine Workers .... $5,000   PAC
    Electrical Radio & Machine Workers .... $4,000   PAC
    Ladies Garment Workers Union .... $4,000   PAC
    Utilty Workers Union of America .... $2,000   PAC

Transportation Unions **$20,350**
    Teamsters Union .... $10,000   PAC
    TransAmerica Corp* .... $7,000   PAC
    International Longshoremen's Assn* .... $2,850   PAC

Public Sector Unions **$15,500**
    American Federation of Teachers .... $10,000   PAC
    American Fedn of St/Cnty/Munic Employees ...... $5,000   PAC

Misc Unions **$8,000**
    Food & Commercial Workers Union .... $5,000   PAC
    Retail, Wholesale & Dept Store Union .... $2,000   PAC
    Service Employees International Union .... $1,000   PAC

Ideological/Single-Issue

Ideological/Single-Issue	$32,941

Leadership PACs **$2,500**
    Effective Government Cmte (Dick Gephardt) ...... $1,000   PAC
    House Leadership Fund (Tom Foley) .... $1,000   PAC
Pro-Israel **$2,000**
    None over $1,000
Pro-Choice **$2,250**
    National Abortion Rights Action League .... $2,000   PAC
Womens Issues **$17,641**
    Emily's List .... $10,000   PAC
    Women's Campaign Fund .... $5,000   PAC
    National Womens Political Caucus .... $1,000   PAC
Human Rights **$8,300**
    Hispanic PAC USA .... $3,000   PAC
    Human Rights Campaign Fund .... $3,000   PAC

Other & Unknown

Other	$5,630

Civil Servants/Public Officials **$2,550**
    New York State Division for Women .... $1,400   Indiv
Education **$1,600**
    None over $1,000

Unknown	$62,300

    Homemakers/Non-income earners $4,000
    No Employer Listed or Found $34,150
    Generic Occupation/Category Unknown $7,400
    Employer Listed/Category Unknown $16,550
        Olayan Development Corp .... $1,300   Indiv
        Grana .... $1,000   Indiv
        Hanes Pubbeatin .... $1,000   Indiv
        Labor Research Assn .... $1,000   Indiv
        Monte Moving Co .... $1,000   Indiv
        Ramirez & Ramirez .... $1,000   Indiv

Spending in Last Election

	1992
Velazquez	$441,446
Opponent	$4,590
Vote Pct	77%

---

* Contributions came from more than one affiliate or
subsidiary.

Bruce F. Vento, D-Minn (4)

First elected: 1976

1991-92 Total Receipts: $280,123
1992 Year-end Cash: $86,382

1991-92 Committees & Subcommittees

Banking, Finance and Urban Affairs
Economic Stabilization; Financial Institutions Supervision, Regulation and Insurance; Housing and Community Development

Interior and Insular Affairs
National Parks and Public Lands (Chairman); Water, Power and Offshore Energy

Select Committee on Aging

Leading Contributors

Business

Agriculture	$10,950

Crop Production & Basic Processing **$4,250**
American Crystal Sugar Corp .... $1,500 PAC
Southern Minn Beet Sugar Co-op .... $1,250 PAC
American Sugarbeet Growers Assn .... $1,000 PAC
Dairy **$5,500**
Associated Milk Producers .... $5,000 PAC
Agricultural Services/Products **$1,200**
None over $1,000

Communications/Electronics	$7,425

Printing & Publishing **$2,000**
West Publishing .... $2,000 PAC
Telephone Utilities **$3,875**
US West Inc .... $1,500 PAC
AT&T .... $1,125 PAC
GTE Corp .... $1,000 PAC
Computer Equipment & Services **$1,550**
National Computer Systems .... $1,050 PAC

Construction	$6,500

Home Builders **$6,125**
National Assn of Home Builders .... $4,500 PAC
Manufactured Housing Institute .... $1,000 PAC

Energy & Natural Resources	$2,226

Electric Utilities **$1,726**
ACRE (Action Cmte for Rural Electrification) .... $1,351 PAC

Contribution Totals by Sector

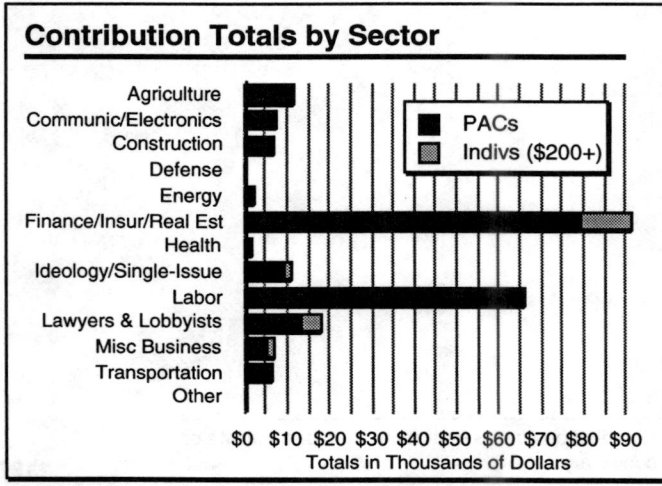

Agriculture
Communic/Electronics
Construction
Defense
Energy
Finance/Insur/Real Est
Health
Ideology/Single-Issue
Labor
Lawyers & Lobbyists
Misc Business
Transportation
Other

■ PACs
▨ Indivs ($200+)

$0 $10 $20 $30 $40 $50 $60 $70 $80 $90
Totals in Thousands of Dollars

Source of Funds in 1992 Election

Source	Total	Pct
■ PACs	$206,495	71%
▨ Indivs $200+	$20,820	7%
☐ Indivs under $200	$31,693	11%
▨ Other	$32,510	11%
Candidate	$0	0%
Party	$11,895	4%

Source of PAC Dollars by Sector

Source	Total	Pct
■ Business	$130,764	64%
▨ Labor	$65,524	32%
☐ Ideology/Single Issue	$9,070	4%

In-State vs. Out-of-State Contributions*

Source	Total	Pct
☐ In-State	$4,070	20%
■ Out-of-state	$16,750	80%
No state listed	$0	

***by large individual contributors ($200 & above)**

Finance, Insurance & Real Estate	$91,250

Commercial Banks **$19,575**
American Bankers Assn .... $7,500 PAC
Norwest Corp .... $4,000 PAC
Citizens & Southern National Bank .... $1,500 PAC
Independent Bankers Assn .... $1,300 PAC
Barnett Banks Inc .... $1,000 PAC
Security Pacific Corp .... $1,000 PAC
Savings & Loans **$6,150**
US League of Savings Assns* .... $3,650 PAC
American Savings Bank .... $1,000 PAC
National Council of Savings Institutions .... $1,000 PAC
Credit Unions **$4,100**
Credit Union National Assn .... $3,100 PAC
National Assn of Federal Credit Unions .... $1,000 PAC
Finance/Credit Companies **$1,650**
Associated Credit Bureaus .... $1,000 PAC
Securities & Investment **$29,950**
Federated Investors Inc .... $9,000 PAC/Ind
Goldman, Sachs & Co .... $7,000 PAC/Ind
Investment Company Institute .... $3,500 PAC
First Boston Corp .... $1,500 PAC
Morgan Stanley & Co .... $1,500 PAC
Public Securities Assn .... $1,250 PAC
American Express* .... $1,050 PAC
Kidder, Peabody .... $1,000 PAC
Miller & Schroeder Financial Group .... $1,000 Indiv
PaineWebber .... $1,000 PAC
Insurance **$8,025**
American Council of Life Insurance .... $3,000 PAC
American International Group Inc .... $1,500 PAC
Northwestern National Life .... $1,100 PAC
National Assn of Life Underwriters .... $1,000 PAC

Real Estate **$14,250**

    National Assn of Realtors .... $8,000   PAC
    Century 21 Real Estate .... $2,500   PAC
    American Land Title Assn .... $1,500   PAC
    Federal National Mortgage Assn .... $1,000   PAC

Accountants **$6,500**

    American Institute of CPA's .... $6,000   PAC

Misc Finance **$1,050**

    None over $1,000

Health $1,150

Health Professionals **$1,150**

    None over $1,000

Lawyers & Lobbyists $17,388

Lawyers & Lobbyists **$17,388**

    Opperman & Paquin .... $5,063   PAC
    Assn of Trial Lawyers of America .... $5,000   PAC
    Fontheim & O'Rourke .... $1,500   Indiv

Misc Business $6,600

Business Services **$2,000**

    Beverly Group Inc .... $2,000   Indiv

Lodging/Tourism **$1,100**

    Conference of National Park Concessioners .... $1,000   PAC

Chemical & Related Manufacturing **$2,000**

    Dial Corp .... $2,000   PAC

Misc Manufacturing & Distributing **$1,000**

    None over $1,000

Transportation $6,025

Air Transport **$3,025**

    United Parcel Service .... $1,250   PAC
    General Electric .... $1,000   PAC

Automotive **$1,000**

    National Auto Dealers Assn .... $1,000   PAC

Railroads **$1,500**

    Burlington Northern .... $1,500   PAC

Labor

Labor $65,524

Building Trade Unions **$8,500**

    Plumbers/Pipefitters Union .... $2,500   PAC
    Laborers' Political League .... $2,000   PAC
    AFL-CIO Bldg/Construction Trades Dept .... $1,000   PAC
    Operating Engineers Union .... $1,000   PAC
    Sheet Metal Workers Union .... $1,000   PAC

Industrial Unions **$14,600**

    Machinists/Aerospace Workers Union .... $5,000   PAC
    United Auto Workers .... $4,000   PAC
    United Steelworkers .... $2,000   PAC
    Amalgamated Clothing & Textile Workers .... $1,000   PAC
    Electronic Machine Furniture Workers .... $1,000   PAC
    Ladies Garment Workers Union .... $1,000   PAC

Transportation Unions **$15,150**

    Teamsters Union* .... $10,000   PAC
    Air Line Pilots Assn .... $2,500   PAC
    Trans Comm International Union .... $1,050   PAC

Public Sector Unions **$22,825**

    American Federation of Teachers .... $5,100   PAC
    American Postal Workers Union* .... $3,850   PAC
    National Assn of Letter Carriers* .... $3,575   PAC
    American Fedn of St/Cnty/Munic Employees ...... $3,100   PAC
    National Assn Retired Federal Employees .... $3,000   PAC
    National Education Assn .... $2,300   PAC
    National League of Postmasters .... $1,000   PAC

Misc Unions **$4,449**

    AFL-CIO .... $2,050   PAC
    Food & Commercial Workers Union .... $1,999   PAC

Ideological/Single-Issue

Ideological/Single-Issue $10,570

Democratic/Liberal **$2,500**

    National Cmte for an Effective Congress .... $2,500   PAC

Human Rights **$4,000**

    KidsPAC .... $2,000   PAC
    Human Rights Campaign Fund .... $1,000   PAC
    National Community Action Foundation .... $1,000   PAC

Misc Issues **$4,070**

    National Cmte to Preserve Social Security .... $1,500   PAC
    Sierra Club .... $1,070   PAC
    Natural Resources Defense Council .... $1,000   Indiv

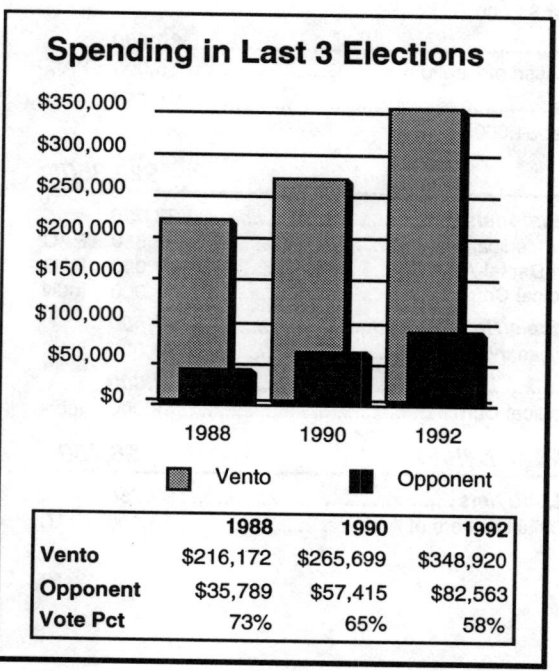

Spending in Last 3 Elections

	1988	1990	1992
Vento	$216,172	$265,699	$348,920
Opponent	$35,789	$57,415	$82,563
Vote Pct	73%	65%	58%

---

* Contributions came from more than one affiliate or subsidiary.

Peter J. Visclosky, D-Ind (1)

First elected: 1984
1991-92 Total Receipts: $276,028
1992 Year-end Cash: $50,939

1991-92 Committees & Subcommittees

Appropriations
Foreign Operations, Export Financing and Related Programs;
Treasury, Postal Service and General Government

Leading Contributors

Business

Agriculture	$6,400	
Dairy **$1,500**		
Associated Milk Producers $1,500	PAC	
Agricultural Services/Products **$1,200**		
None over $1,000		
Food Processing & Sales **$3,200**		
Wiseway Super Food Centers $2,000	Indiv	

Communications/Electronics	$7,250	
Telephone Utilities **$7,250**		
Indiana Bell Telephone $3,000	PAC	
AT&T $2,500	PAC	
United Telecommunications $1,000	PAC	

Construction	$4,900	
General Contractors **$1,400**		
None over $1,000		
Home Builders **$2,000**		
National Assn of Home Builders $2,000	PAC	
Building Materials & Equipment **$1,500**		
Crawford Supply Co $1,000	Indiv	

Energy & Natural Resources	$10,750	
Oil & Gas **$6,250**		
USX Corp* $3,300	PAC	
Welsh Oil $1,000	Indiv	

Source of Funds in 1992 Election

Source	Total	Pct
■ PACs	$189,415	69%
▨ Indivs $200+	$52,325	19%
□ Indivs under $200	$30,845	11%
⊠ Other	$3,880	1%
Candidate	$0	0%
Party	$887	0%

Source of PAC Dollars by Sector

Source	Total	Pct
■ Business	$71,885	34%
▨ Labor	$120,050	57%
□ Ideology/Single Issue	$17,716	8%

In-State vs. Out-of-State Contributions*

Source	Total	Pct
□ In-State	$42,365	81%
■ Out-of-state	$9,960	19%
No state listed	$0	

* by large individual contributors ($200 & above)

Electric Utilities	$3,500	
Public Service Co of Indiana	$2,000	PAC
Northern Indiana Public Service Co	$1,000	PAC
Waste Management	**$1,000**	
Waste Management Inc	$1,000	PAC

Finance, Insurance & Real Estate | $12,400

Commercial Banks	$3,700	
American Bankers Assn	$1,500	PAC
Peoples Bank	$1,000	Indiv
Insurance	**$1,250**	
None over $1,000		
Real Estate	**$5,200**	
National Assn of Realtors	$5,000	PAC
Accountants	**$1,750**	
None over $1,000		

Health | $26,350

Health Professionals	$22,850	
American Medical Assn*	$4,550	PAC
American Dental Assn	$1,000	PAC
Goel Medical Corp	$1,000	Indiv
Pharmaceuticals/Health Products	**$1,500**	
ICI Americas Inc	$1,000	PAC
Misc Health	**$2,000**	
Suniti Medical Corp	$2,000	Indiv

Lawyers & Lobbyists | $8,750

Lawyers & Lobbyists	$8,750	
Assn of Trial Lawyers of America	$3,000	PAC

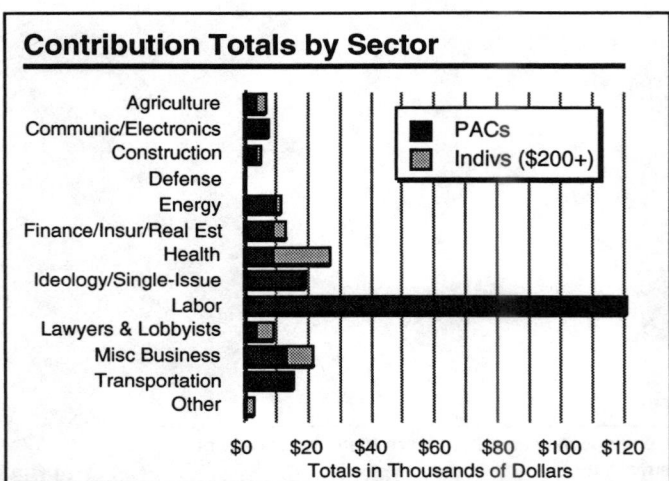

Contribution Totals by Sector

- Agriculture
- Communic/Electronics
- Construction
- Defense
- Energy
- Finance/Insur/Real Est
- Health
- Ideology/Single-Issue
- Labor
- Lawyers & Lobbyists
- Misc Business
- Transportation
- Other

■ PACs
▨ Indivs ($200+)

$0 $20 $40 $60 $80 $100 $120
Totals in Thousands of Dollars

Misc Business $20,955

Food & Beverage $2,470
   National Restaurant Assn .... $1,500   PAC

Beer, Wine & Liquor $3,000
   National Beer Wholesalers Assn .... $1,000   PAC
   Valpo Beverages Inc .... $1,000   Indiv
   Wine & Spirits Wholesalers of America .... $1,000   PAC

Misc Services $2,000
   Progress Pump Inc .... $2,000   Indiv

Business Services $4,660
   Whiteco Industries .... $2,000   Indiv

Steel Production $7,425
   LTV Steel .... $1,800   PAC
   Inland Steel .... $1,775   PAC/Ind
   Bethlehem Steel .... $1,600   PAC
   National Steel Corp .... $1,000   PAC

Transportation $14,940

Air Transport $10,440
   Federal Express Corp .... $6,000   PAC
   United Parcel Service .... $1,940   PAC
   Aircraft Owners & Pilots Assn .... $1,000   PAC
   United Airlines .... $1,000   PAC

Trucking $2,500
   American Trucking Assns .... $1,000   PAC

Railroads $2,000
   CSX Transportation Inc .... $1,000   PAC

Labor

Labor $120,050

Building Trade Unions $25,300
   Ironworkers Union .... $5,000   PAC
   Plumbers/Pipefitters Union .... $5,000   PAC
   Sheet Metal Workers Union .... $5,000   PAC
   Carpenters & Joiners Union .... $4,000   PAC
   Laborers' Political League .... $3,500   PAC
   AFL-CIO Bldg/Construction Trades Dept ...... $1,000   PAC
   Operating Engineers Union .... $1,000   PAC

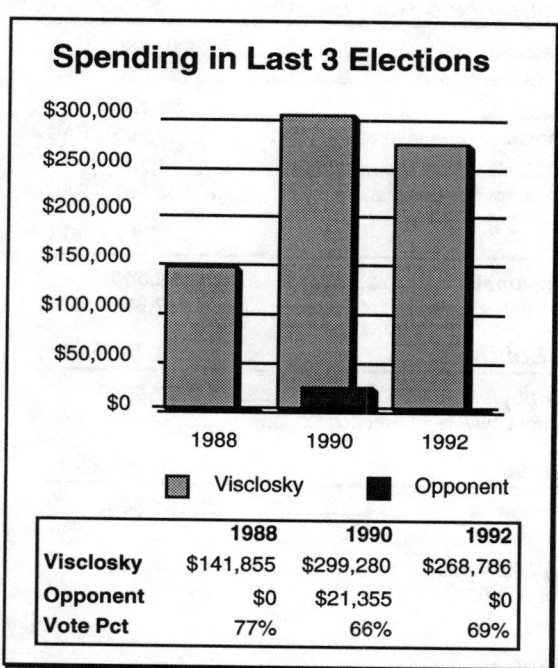

Spending in Last 3 Elections

	1988	1990	1992
Visclosky	$141,855	$299,280	$268,786
Opponent	$0	$21,355	$0
Vote Pct	77%	66%	69%

Industrial Unions $40,500
   United Auto Workers .... $10,000   PAC
   United Steelworkers .... $10,000   PAC
   Machinists/Aerospace Workers Union .... $5,500   PAC
   Rubber Cork Linoleum & Plastic Workers .... $5,000   PAC
   Intl Brotherhood of Electrical Workers .... $3,500   PAC
   Boilermakers Union .... $2,500   PAC
   Amalgamated Clothing & Textile Workers .... $1,000   PAC
   Electronic Machine Furniture Workers .... $1,000   PAC
   United Mine Workers .... $1,000   PAC

Transportation Unions $24,950
   Teamsters Union .... $10,000   PAC
   Air Line Pilots Assn .... $6,000   PAC
   United Transportation Union .... $2,100   PAC
   Transport Workers Union .... $2,000   PAC
   International Longshoremen's Assn .... $1,500   PAC
   Assn of Flight Attendants .... $1,000   PAC

Public Sector Unions $25,800
   National Education Assn .... $10,000   PAC
   American Fedn of St/Cnty/Munic Employees ...... $4,000   PAC
   National Assn Retired Federal Employees .... $3,000   PAC
   American Federation of Teachers .... $2,000   PAC
   National Assn of Letter Carriers .... $2,000   PAC
   American Postal Workers Union .... $1,500   PAC
   National Rural Letter Carriers Assn .... $1,500   PAC
   International Assn of Firefighters .... $1,000   PAC

Misc Unions $3,500
   Food & Commercial Workers Union .... $2,000   PAC
   AFL-CIO .... $1,000   PAC

Ideological/Single-Issue

Ideological/Single-Issue $18,466

Democratic/Liberal $2,500
   National Cmte for an Effective Congress .... $2,500   PAC

Leadership PACs $1,216
   House Leadership Fund (Tom Foley) .... $1,216   PAC

Pro-Israel $6,750
   National PAC .... $5,000   PAC

Human Rights $7,000
   Human Rights Campaign Fund .... $5,000   PAC
   KidsPAC .... $2,000   PAC

Other & Unknown

Other $2,540

Civil Servants/Public Officials $1,440
   Lake County .... $1,220   Indiv

Unknown $8,725

   Homemakers/Non-income earners $4,000
   No Employer Listed or Found $1,775
   Generic Occupation/Category Unknown $1,250
   Employer Listed/Category Unknown $1,700
     None over $1,000

* Contributions came from more than one affiliate or subsidiary.

Harold L. Volkmer, D-Mo (9)

First elected: 1976

1991-92 Total Receipts:	$354,612
1992 Year-end Cash:	$2,883

1991-92 Committees & Subcommittees

Agriculture
Department Operations, Research and Foreign Agriculture; Forests, Family Farms and Energy (Chairman); Livestock, Dairy and Poultry; Wheat, Soybeans and Feed Grains

Science, Space and Technology
Space

Select Committee on Aging

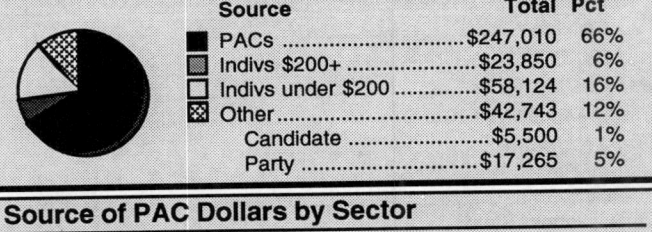

Source of Funds in 1992 Election

Source	Total	Pct
■ PACs	$247,010	66%
▨ Indivs $200+	$23,850	6%
□ Indivs under $200	$58,124	16%
⊠ Other	$42,743	12%
Candidate	$5,500	1%
Party	$17,265	5%

Source of PAC Dollars by Sector

Source	Total	Pct
■ Business	$137,408	57%
▨ Labor	$89,150	37%
□ Ideology/Single Issue	$15,400	6%

In-State vs. Out-of-State Contributions*

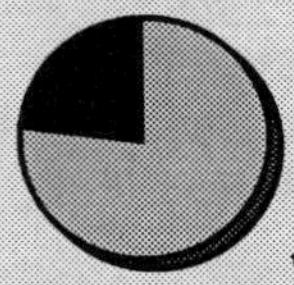

Source	Total	Pct
□ In-State	$18,300	77%
■ Out-of-state	$5,550	23%
No state listed	$0	

* by large individual contributors ($200 & above)

Leading Contributors

Business

Agriculture — $63,508

Crop Production & Basic Processing ***$10,325***
None over $1,500

Tobacco ***$5,250***
Philip Morris .... $3,250 PAC
RJR Nabisco .... $1,500 PAC

Dairy ***$20,500***
Associated Milk Producers .... $10,000 PAC
Mid-America Dairymen .... $9,000 PAC

Livestock ***$2,650***
None over $1,500

Agricultural Services/Products ***$12,683***
Missouri Farm Bureau/NE Dist .... $3,300 PAC
American Cyanimid .... $1,500 PAC

Food Processing & Sales ***$4,850***
Anheuser-Busch .... $1,500 PAC

Forestry & Forest Products ***$6,250***
None over $1,500

Communications/Electronics — $7,600

Telephone Utilities ***$6,100***
AT&T .... $2,800 PAC
Southwestern Bell .... $1,500 PAC

Construction — $5,200

Construction Services ***$2,750***
Jacobs Engineering Group .... $2,250 PAC

Contribution Totals by Sector

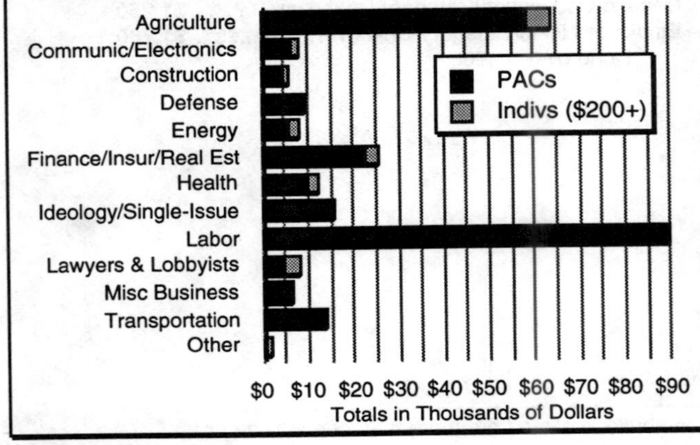

Agriculture
Communic/Electronics
Construction
Defense
Energy
Finance/Insur/Real Est
Health
Ideology/Single-Issue
Labor
Lawyers & Lobbyists
Misc Business
Transportation
Other
PACs
Indivs ($200+)
$0 $10 $20 $30 $40 $50 $60 $70 $80 $90
Totals in Thousands of Dollars

Defense — $9,000

Defense Aerospace ***$6,500***
Rockwell International .... $2,000 PAC

Defense Electronics ***$2,500***
None over $1,500

Energy & Natural Resources — $8,000

Oil & Gas ***$2,500***
Ayers Oil Co .... $1,500 Indiv

Electric Utilities ***$4,500***
ACRE (Action Cmte for Rural Electrification)* .... $3,500 PAC

Finance, Insurance & Real Estate — $25,200

Commercial Banks ***$10,550***
American Bankers Assn .... $7,000 PAC

Insurance ***$6,450***
General American Life Insurance .... $2,000 PAC

Real Estate ***$6,700***
National Assn of Realtors .... $5,950 PAC

Health — $11,900

Health Professionals ***$9,500***
American Medical Assn* .... $7,500 PAC

Lawyers & Lobbyists — $7,550

Lawyers & Lobbyists ***$7,550***
Assn of Trial Lawyers of America .... $2,500 PAC

Misc Business — $6,250

Food & Beverage ***$1,500***
None over $1,500

Beer, Wine & Liquor ***$1,500***
None over $1,500

Transportation	$13,400

Air Transport $2,600
    None over $1,500

Automotive $9,000
    National Auto Dealers Assn .... $8,000 PAC

Labor

Labor	$89,150

Building Trade Unions $20,900
    Carpenters & Joiners Union .... $10,000 PAC
    Sheet Metal Workers Union .... $4,800 PAC
    Laborers' Political League .... $2,000 PAC
    Plumbers/Pipefitters Union .... $2,000 PAC

Industrial Unions $29,150
    Intl Brotherhood of Electrical Workers .... $9,000 PAC
    Machinists/Aerospace Workers Union* .... $7,000 PAC
    United Auto Workers .... $6,000 PAC
    Gas Workers local #5-6 (OCAW) .... $2,500 PAC
    Communications Workers of America .... $2,300 PAC

Transportation Unions $9,550
    Teamsters Union .... $6,000 PAC
    United Transportation Union .... $2,000 PAC

Public Sector Unions $25,050
    National Education Assn .... $10,000 PAC
    National Assn Retired Federal Employees .... $7,000 PAC
    National Assn of Letter Carriers* .... $2,250 PAC
    National Assn of Postmasters .... $2,000 PAC
    American Postal Workers Union .... $1,500 PAC

Misc Unions $4,500
    Food & Commercial Workers Union .... $2,000 PAC
    AFL-CIO .... $1,500 PAC

Ideological/Single-Issue

Ideological/Single-Issue	$15,400

Leadership PACs $2,500
    None over $1,500

Gun Rights/Gun Control $10,400
    National Rifle Assn .... $9,900 PAC

Misc Issues $1,500
    National Cmte to Preserve Social Security .... $1,500 PAC

Other & Unknown

Unknown	$2,350

    Employer Listed/Category Unknown $1,650
      None over $1,500

Independent expenditures supporting Volkmer
    National Right to Life PAC $1,901

Spending in Last 3 Elections

	1988	1990	1992
Volkmer	$210,841	$238,679	$511,550
Opponent	$9,565	$36,045	$139,860
Vote Pct	68%	58%	48%

* Contributions came from more than one affiliate or
subsidiary.

Barbara F. Vucanovich, R-Nev (2)

First elected: 1982

1991-92 Total Receipts: $684,022
1992 Year-end Cash: $3,849

1991-92 Committees & Subcommittees

Appropriations
Agriculture , Rural Development, Food and Drug Administration and Related Agencies; Legislative

Interior and Insular Affairs
Mining and Natural Resources (Ranking Republican); National Parks and Public Lands

Leading Contributors

Business

Agriculture $34,750

Crop Production & Basic Processing **$9,300**
Lee Wilson & Co .... $2,000 Indiv

Tobacco **$3,500**
None over $2,000

Livestock **$9,850**
National Cattlemen's Assn .... $4,000 PAC
Peccole Ranch .... $2,000 Indiv

Agricultural Services/Products **$3,850**
None over $2,000

Food Processing & Sales **$7,250**
ConAgra Inc .... $4,000 PAC

Communications/Electronics $11,450

Telephone Utilities **$10,700**
Pacific Telesis Group .... $3,200 PAC
AT&T .... $2,000 PAC
United Telecommunications .... $2,000 PAC

Construction $23,220

General Contractors **$10,530**
Associated General Contractors .... $2,500 PAC

Home Builders **$2,900**
National Assn of Home Builders .... $2,500 PAC

Special Trade Contractors **$4,000**
None over $2,000

Building Materials & Equipment **$4,690**
Cashman Equipment Co .... $2,000 Indiv

Source of Funds in 1992 Election

Source	Total	Pct
■ PACs	$256,119	35%
▦ Indivs $200+	$211,703	29%
☐ Indivs under $200	$145,488	20%
▨ Other	$126,650	17%
Candidate	$48,000	6%
Party	$62,329	8%

Source of PAC Dollars by Sector

Source	Total	Pct
■ Business	$221,569	86%
▦ Labor	$10,500	4%
☐ Ideology/Single Issue	$26,591	10%

In-State vs. Out-of-State Contributions*

Source	Total	Pct
☐ In-State	$180,420	85%
■ Out-of-state	$30,908	15%
No state listed	$0	

* by large individual contributors ($200 & above)

Defense $6,409

Defense Aerospace **$4,034**
Gencorp Inc .... $2,034 PAC

Energy & Natural Resources $55,700

Oil & Gas **$19,600**
Alamo Truck Stop Horseshoe Club .... $2,000 Indiv
Exxon Corp .... $2,000 PAC
Southwest Gas Corp .... $2,000 PAC

Mining **$25,100**
Independence Mining Co .... $3,150 Indiv
National Coal Assn .... $3,000 PAC
Phelps Dodge Corp .... $2,400 PAC

Electric Utilities **$10,500**
Sierra Pacific Resources .... $4,000 PAC
ACRE (Action Cmte for Rural Electrification) .... $2,000 PAC

Finance, Insurance & Real Estate $52,840

Commercial Banks **$10,500**
BankAmerica Corp .... $3,000 PAC
American Bankers Assn .... $2,500 PAC
US Bancorp .... $2,000 PAC

Securities & Investment **$2,600**
None over $2,000

Insurance **$5,250**
National Assn of Life Underwriters .... $2,000 PAC

Real Estate **$27,740**
National Assn of Realtors .... $9,940 PAC
Summa Corp .... $5,000 PAC
Diversified Realty .... $3,000 Indiv
Del Webb Corp .... $2,500 PAC

Accountants **$4,500**
American Institute of CPA's .... $3,500 PAC

Misc Finance **$2,250**
None over $2,000

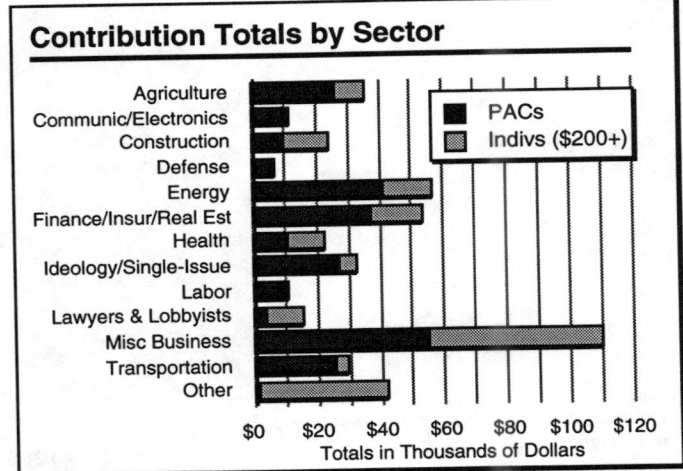

Contribution Totals by Sector

- Agriculture
- Communic/Electronics
- Construction
- Defense
- Energy
- Finance/Insur/Real Est
- Health
- Ideology/Single-Issue
- Labor
- Lawyers & Lobbyists
- Misc Business
- Transportation
- Other

■ PACs
▦ Indivs ($200+)

$0 $20 $40 $60 $80 $100 $120
Totals in Thousands of Dollars

Health $21,510

Health Professionals $18,010
   American Medical Assn.................................$4,500 PAC
   Century Clinic..$3,210 Indiv

Pharmaceuticals/Health Products $2,000
   None over $2,000

Lawyers & Lobbyists $15,908

Lawyers & Lobbyists....................................$15,908
   None over $1,500

Misc Business $108,745

Business Associations $3,045
   National Fedn of Independent Business ....$2,000 PAC

Food & Beverage $8,200
   National Restaurant Assn ....$5,500 PAC

Beer, Wine & Liquor $7,100
   National Beer Wholesalers Assn ....$6,000 PAC

Retail Sales..$8,000
   IGT Inc..$2,000 Indiv

Misc Services $2,000
   American Housekeeping ....$2,000 Indiv

Business Services $4,000
   None over $2,000

Casinos/Gambling $52,000
   Circus Circus Enterprises ....$8,500 PAC/Ind
   Whiskey Pete's Casino ....$7,000 Indiv
   Caesar's World ....$6,500 PAC
   California Hotel & Casino PAC ....$5,000 PAC
   Palace Station Hotel & Casino ....$5,000 PAC/Ind
   Barbary Coast Hotel ....$2,000 Indiv
   Harrah's..$2,500 PAC
   Lady Luck Casino & Hotel ....$2,000 Indiv
   Mirage Hotel & Casino ....$2,000 Indiv
   Sierra Development Co ....$2,000 PAC

Lodging/Tourism $9,650
   Hilton Hotel Corp ....$2,000 Indiv

Chemical & Related Manufacturing $9,750
   FMC Corp ....$6,000 PAC

Misc Manufacturing & Distributing $2,000
   Stone Container Corp ....$2,000 PAC

Transportation $29,100

Air Transport $6,500
   United Parcel Service ....$4,000 PAC
   Aircraft Owners & Pilots Assn ....$2,000 PAC

Automotive $14,100
   National Auto Dealers Assn ....$6,500 PAC
   Americans for Free International Trade ....$2,000 PAC

Railroads $5,500
   Union Pacific Corp ....$2,000 PAC

Labor

Labor $10,500

Public Sector Unions $9,500
   National Assn Retired Federal Employees ....$8,000 PAC

Ideological/Single-Issue

Ideological/Single-Issue $32,091

Republican/Conservative $13,500
   Leader PAC..$5,000 PAC
   Eagle Forum ....$3,000 PAC

Pro-Life $7,500
   Republican National Coalition for Life ....$4,000 PAC
   National Right to Life PAC ....$3,500 PAC

Gun Rights/Gun Control $10,400
   National Rifle Assn ....$9,900 PAC

Other & Unknown

Other $40,890

Retired $39,640
   None over $2,000

Unknown $28,000

   Employer Listed/Category Unknown $25,750
     None over $2,000

Spending in Last 3 Elections

	1988	1990	1992
Vucanovich	$614,828	$441,075	$686,379
Opponent	$430,155	$41,287	$198,888
Vote Pct	57%	59%	48%

Robert S. Walker, R-Pa (16)

First elected: 1976

1991-92 Total Receipts:	$134,434
1992 Year-end Cash:	$11,278

1991-92 Committees & Subcommittees

Science, Space and Technology (Ranking Republican)

Leading Contributors

Business

Agriculture	$9,550	
Crop Production & Basic Processing	**$1,000**	
None over $1,000		
Tobacco	**$2,000**	
Philip Morris	$1,000	PAC
RJR Nabisco	$1,000	PAC
Dairy	**$1,000**	
Milk Industry Foundation	$1,000	PAC
Agricultural Services/Products	**$2,700**	
Pennfield Corp	$1,000	Indiv
Forestry & Forest Products	**$1,000**	
Walter H Weaber & Sons	$1,000	Indiv

Communications/Electronics	$12,250	
Printing & Publishing	**$2,000**	
RR Donnelley & Sons	$1,000	PAC
Media/Entertainment	**$3,900**	
QVC Network	$3,250	Indiv
Telephone Utilities	**$3,850**	
AT&T	$1,000	PAC
GTE Corp	$1,000	PAC
Computer Equipment & Services	**$1,500**	
None over $1,000		

Construction	$7,800	
General Contractors	**$2,200**	
Paul Risk Associates	$1,000	Indiv
Building Materials & Equipment	**$5,100**	
Armstrong World Industries Inc	$1,000	Indiv
Binkley & Ober Inc	$1,000	Indiv

Contribution Totals by Sector

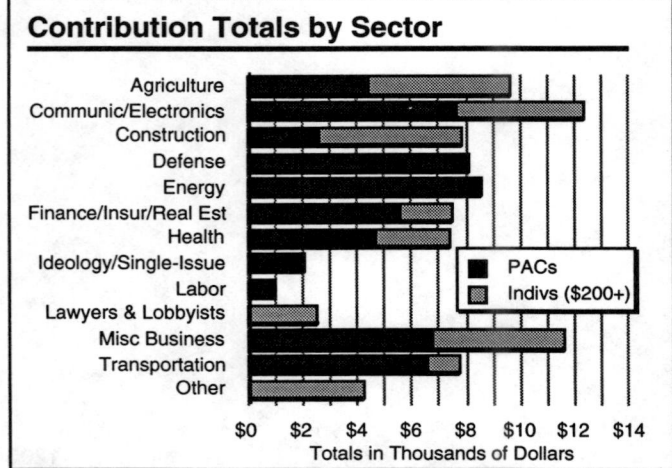

Agriculture
Communic/Electronics
Construction
Defense
Energy
Finance/Insur/Real Est
Health
Ideology/Single-Issue
Labor
Lawyers & Lobbyists
Misc Business
Transportation
Other

PACs
Indivs ($200+)

$0 $2 $4 $6 $8 $10 $12 $14
Totals in Thousands of Dollars

Source of Funds in 1992 Election

Source	Total	Pct
■ PACs	$58,350	43%
▨ Indivs $200+	$46,266	34%
□ Indivs under $200	$24,901	19%
⊠ Other	$4,917	4%
Candidate	$345	0%
Party	$172	0%

Source of PAC Dollars by Sector

Source	Total	Pct
■ Business	$54,250	95%
▨ Labor	$900	2%
□ Ideology/Single Issue	$2,000	4%

In-State vs. Out-of-State Contributions*

Source	Total	Pct
□ In-State	$44,066	95%
■ Out-of-state	$2,200	5%
No state listed	$0	

* by large individual contributors ($200 & above)

Defense	$8,000	
Defense Aerospace	**$6,500**	
General Dynamics	$1,000	PAC
Martin Marietta Corp	$1,000	PAC
Rockwell International	$1,000	PAC
Thiokol	$1,000	PAC
Defense Electronics	**$1,500**	
None over $1,000		

Energy & Natural Resources	$8,500	
Oil & Gas	**$2,000**	
None over $1,000		
Mining	**$2,000**	
Alcoa	$1,000	PAC
Nuclear Energy	**$1,000**	
Gilbert Associates	$1,000	PAC
Electric Utilities	**$2,500**	
Pennsylvania Power & Light	$1,500	PAC
Waste Management	**$1,000**	
Waste Management Inc	$1,000	PAC

Finance, Insurance & Real Estate	$7,450	
Commercial Banks	**$1,200**	
American Bankers Assn	$1,000	PAC
Insurance	**$1,000**	
National Assn of Life Underwriters	$1,000	PAC
Real Estate	**$2,000**	
National Assn of Realtors	$1,000	PAC
Accountants	**$1,950**	
American Institute of CPA's	$1,000	PAC
Misc Finance	**$1,000**	
Employee Stock Ownership Assn	$1,000	PAC

Health $7,316

Health Professionals **$3,216**
    American Medical Assn ....$1,000 PAC
Pharmaceuticals/Health Products **$4,000**
    Warner-Lambert ....$1,000 PAC

Lawyers & Lobbyists $2,500

Lawyers & Lobbyists **$2,500**
    None over $1,000

Misc Business $11,550

Food & Beverage **$2,050**
    None over $1,000
Retail Sales **$1,500**
    None over $1,000
Chemical & Related Manufacturing **$1,000**
    Air Products & Chemicals Inc ....$1,000 PAC
Misc Manufacturing & Distributing **$3,950**
    Fuller Co ....$1,000 PAC/Ind
    J Walter Miller Co ....$1,000 Indiv

Transportation $7,700

Air Transport **$2,000**
    General Electric ....$1,500 PAC
Automotive **$4,000**
    Auto Dealers & Drivers for Free Trade ....$1,000 PAC
    National Auto Dealers Assn ....$1,000 PAC
Misc Transport **$1,000**
    Krapf Coaches Inc ....$1,000 Indiv

Ideological/Single-Issue

Ideological/Single-Issue $2,000

Gun Rights/Gun Control **$1,000**
    National Rifle Assn ....$1,000 PAC

Other & Unknown

Other $4,150

Retired **$3,200**
    None over $1,000

Unknown $13,750

    Homemakers/Non-income earners $2,000
    No Employer Listed or Found $1,600
    Employer Listed/Category Unknown $9,900
        APL Industries ....$1,000 Indiv
        Horst Group Inc ....$1,000 Indiv
        Showcase of Fashions ....$1,000 Indiv

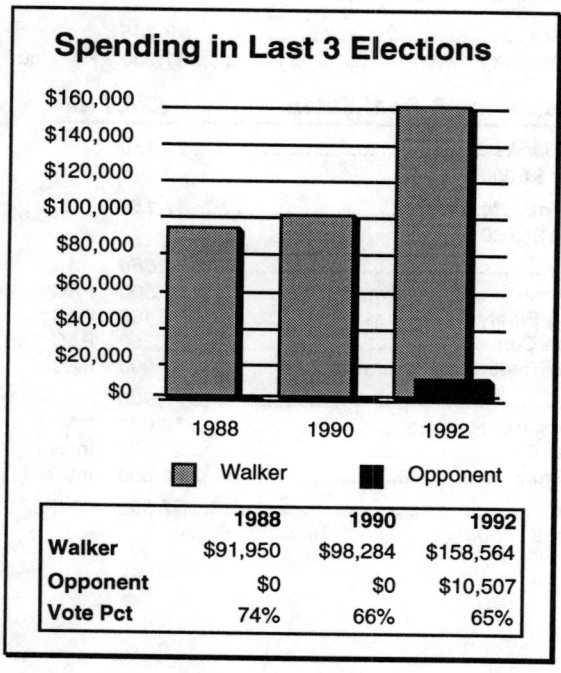

Spending in Last 3 Elections

	1988	1990	1992
Walker	$91,950	$98,284	$158,564
Opponent	$0	$0	$10,507
Vote Pct	74%	66%	65%

Walker   Opponent

James T. Walsh, R-NY (25)

First elected: 1988
1991-92 Total Receipts: $284,162
1992 Year-end Cash: $30,264

1991-92 Committees & Subcommittees

Administration
Elections; Office Systems (Ranking Republican); Campaign Finance Reform Task Force

Agriculture
Department Operations, Research and Foreign Agriculture; Livestock, Dairy and Poultry

Select Committee on Children, Youth and Families

Leading Contributors

Business

Agriculture		$15,600
Crop Production & Basic Processing		**$3,850**
American Sugarbeet Growers Assn	$1,000	PAC
Dairy		**$3,050**
Agri-Mark Inc	$1,000	PAC
Poultry & Eggs		**$1,000**
None over $1,000		
Livestock		**$1,000**
None over $1,000		
Agricultural Services/Products		**$4,700**
Farm Credit Council	$1,200	PAC
Agway Inc	$1,000	PAC
National Council of Farmer Co-ops	$1,000	PAC
Food Processing & Sales		**$2,000**
ConAgra Inc	$1,500	PAC

Communications/Electronics		$8,150
Telephone Utilities		**$4,750**
BellSouth Corp*	$2,250	PAC
AT&T	$2,000	PAC
Telecom Services & Equipment		**$2,000**
United Radio Service	$2,000	Indiv
Electronics Mfg & Services		**$1,000**
North American Philips Corp	$1,000	PAC

Source of Funds in 1992 Election

Source	Total	Pct
■ PACs	$82,495	27%
▨ Indivs $200+	$56,050	18%
☐ Indivs under $200	$134,836	44%
▧ Other	$35,781	12%
Candidate	$0	0%
Party	$30,193	10%

Source of PAC Dollars by Sector

Source	Total	Pct
■ Business	$76,286	95%
▨ Labor	$3,500	4%
☐ Ideology/Single Issue	$717	1%

In-State vs. Out-of-State Contributions*

Source	Total	Pct
☐ In-State	$53,850	99%
■ Out-of-state	$700	1%
No state listed	$0	

* by large individual contributors ($200 & above)

Construction		$3,400
General Contractors		**$2,000**
Associated General Contractors	$1,000	PAC
Building Materials & Equipment		**$1,100**
None over $1,000		

Defense		$1,700
Defense Aerospace		**$1,700**
United Technologies	$1,700	PAC

Energy & Natural Resources		$2,345
Electric Utilities		**$2,345**
Niagara Mohawk Power Corp	$1,300	PAC/Ind

Finance, Insurance & Real Estate		$28,116
Commercial Banks		**$1,150**
None over $1,000		
Securities & Investment		**$1,150**
None over $1,000		
Insurance		**$11,666**
National Assn of Life Underwriters	$2,500	PAC
Casualty & Surety Agents Assn	$1,466	PAC
Nationwide Corp	$1,250	PAC
Farmers & Traders Life Insurance	$1,000	PAC
Real Estate		**$11,900**
National Assn of Realtors	$8,000	PAC
Edgewater Co	$1,500	Indiv
Pioneer Group	$1,300	Indiv
Misc Finance		**$1,300**
None over $1,000		

Contribution Totals by Sector

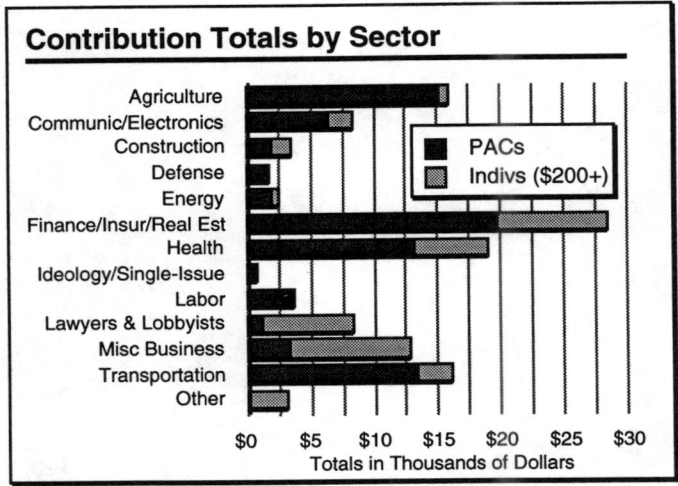

Agriculture, Communic/Electronics, Construction, Defense, Energy, Finance/Insur/Real Est, Health, Ideology/Single-Issue, Labor, Lawyers & Lobbyists, Misc Business, Transportation, Other

PACs
Indivs ($200+)

$0 $5 $10 $15 $20 $25 $30
Totals in Thousands of Dollars

Health $18,800

Health Professionals **$15,900**
    American Medical Assn* .... $8,450 PAC
    American Optometric Assn .... $1,500 PAC
    American Dental Assn .... $1,000 PAC
Hospitals/Nursing Homes **$1,400**
    None over $1,000
Pharmaceuticals/Health Products **$1,500**
    Bristol-Myers Squibb .... $1,000 PAC

Lawyers & Lobbyists $8,100

Lawyers & Lobbyists **$8,100**
    Costello, Cooney & Fearon .... $1,800 Indiv
    Cherundolo, Bottar & Del Duchetto .... $1,750 Indiv
    Hancock & Estabrook .... $1,000 Indiv
    Swidler & Berlin .... $1,000 PAC

Misc Business $12,600

Beer, Wine & Liquor **$1,900**
    Best Brands Beverages .... $1,900 Indiv
Retail Sales **$1,750**
    None over $1,000
Misc Services **$2,050**
    Coyne Textile Services .... $1,300 Indiv
Business Services **$4,000**
    Carpat Investments .... $4,000 Indiv
Misc Manufacturing & Distributing **$2,400**
    Goulds Pumps Inc .... $1,900 PAC

Transportation $15,825

Air Transport **$7,925**
    General Electric .... $4,000 PAC
    United Parcel Service .... $3,925 PAC
Automotive **$4,500**
    National Auto Dealers Assn .... $3,500 PAC
    Chrysler Corp .... $1,000 PAC
Trucking **$3,200**
    North American Van Lines .... $2,000 PAC/Ind
    TH Kinsella Inc .... $1,200 Indiv

Labor

Labor $3,500

Transportation Unions **$2,500**
    Marine Engineers Dist 2 Maritime Officers .... $2,500 PAC
Public Sector Unions **$1,500**
    National Assn Retired Federal Employees .... $1,000 PAC

Other & Unknown

Other $2,950

Retired **$2,950**
    None over $1,000

Unknown $14,750

    No Employer Listed or Found $1,400
    Employer Listed/Category Unknown $12,550
        Burns Brothers Inc .... $1,800 Indiv

Independent expenditures supporting Walsh
    National Right to Life PAC $4,037

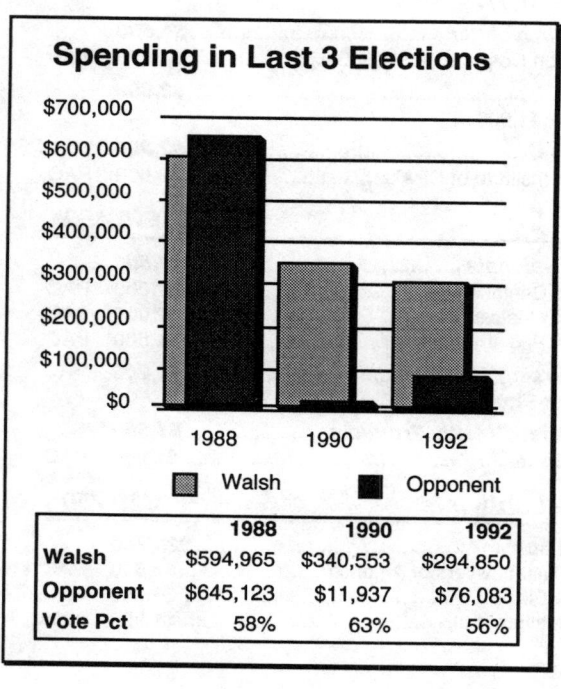

Spending in Last 3 Elections

	1988	1990	1992
Walsh	$594,965	$340,553	$294,850
Opponent	$645,123	$11,937	$76,083
Vote Pct	58%	63%	56%

Walsh   Opponent

Craig Washington, D-Texas (18)

First elected: 1989

1991-92 Total Receipts: $185,635
1992 Year-end Cash: $6,996

1991-92 Committees & Subcommittees

Education and Labor
Elementary, Secondary and Vocational Education; Labor-Management Relations; Postsecondary Education

Judiciary
Civil and Constitutional Rights; Crime and Criminal Justice

Select Committee on Narcotics Abuse and Control

Leading Contributors

Business

Agriculture		**$9,400**
Crop Production & Basic Processing	**$1,950**	
Imperial Holly Corp	$1,700	Indiv
Tobacco	**$2,750**	
RJR Nabisco	$2,250	PAC
Dairy	**$2,000**	
Associated Milk Producers	$2,000	PAC
Food Processing & Sales	**$2,000**	
Randall's Food Markets	$1,000	Indiv

Communications/Electronics		**$10,250**
Media/Entertainment	**$1,500**	
National Cable Television Assn	$1,000	PAC
Telephone Utilities	**$7,500**	
AT&T	$3,000	PAC
GTE Corp	$2,500	PAC
Southwestern Bell	$1,500	PAC

Construction		**$2,450**
General Contractors	**$2,000**	
Williams Brothers Construction	$2,000	Indiv

Energy & Natural Resources		**$10,900**
Oil & Gas	**$4,650**	
Texas Eastern Gas Transmission	$1,500	PAC
Coastal Corp	$1,000	PAC

Source of Funds in 1992 Election

Source	Total	Pct
■ PACs	$118,750	62%
▨ Indivs $200+	$42,300	22%
☐ Indivs under $200	$9,449	5%
⊠ Other	$21,436	11%
Candidate	$0	0%
Party	$6,501	3%

Source of PAC Dollars by Sector

Source	Total	Pct
■ Business	$59,350	46%
▨ Labor	$64,600	50%
☐ Ideology/Single Issue	$5,000	4%

In-State vs. Out-of-State Contributions*

Source	Total	Pct
☐ In-State	$40,050	95%
■ Out-of-state	$2,250	5%
No state listed	$0	

* by large individual contributors ($200 & above)

Electric Utilities		**$4,500**
Houston Industries	$3,000	PAC
Texas Utilities Co	$1,000	PAC
Waste Management	**$1,750**	
Browning-Ferris Industries	$1,750	PAC

Finance, Insurance & Real Estate		**$11,000**
Commercial Banks	**$3,000**	
NCNB Texas	$2,000	PAC
Citizens & Southern National Bank	$1,000	PAC
Credit Unions	**$1,250**	
None over $1,000		
Securities & Investment	**$1,500**	
First Boston Corp	$1,000	Indiv
Insurance	**$2,000**	
None over $1,000		
Accountants	**$2,000**	
American Institute of CPA's	$2,000	PAC

Health		**$10,450**
Health Professionals	**$7,500**	
American Dental Assn	$2,000	PAC
American Medical Assn	$2,000	PAC
American Podiatry Assn	$1,500	PAC
Hospitals/Nursing Homes	**$1,200**	
None over $1,000		
Pharmaceuticals/Health Products	**$1,500**	
Upjohn Co	$1,000	PAC

Lawyers & Lobbyists		**$29,750**
Lawyers & Lobbyists	**$29,750**	
Assn of Trial Lawyers of America	$7,500	PAC
Vinson & Elkins	$1,500	PAC
Helm, Pletcher et al	$1,250	Indiv

Contribution Totals by Sector

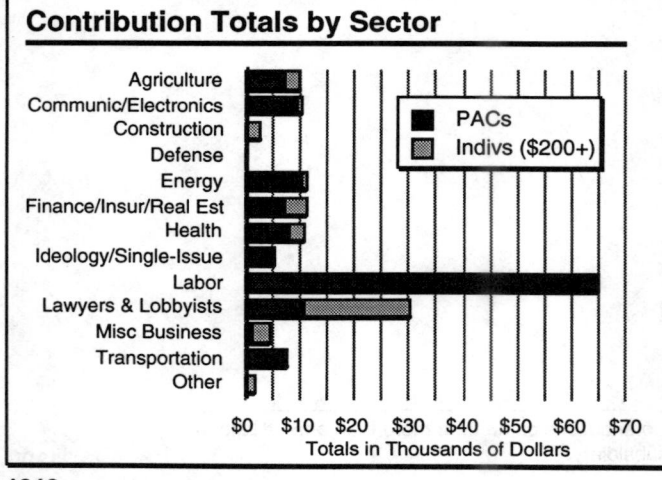

Agriculture
Communic/Electronics
Construction
Defense
Energy
Finance/Insur/Real Est
Health
Ideology/Single-Issue
Labor
Lawyers & Lobbyists
Misc Business
Transportation
Other

■ PACs
▨ Indivs ($200+)

$0 $10 $20 $30 $40 $50 $60 $70
Totals in Thousands of Dollars

Misc Business		$4,150

Food & Beverage **$1,000**
    Cody's Restaurant ....$1,000   Indiv
Beer, Wine & Liquor **$2,250**
    National Beer Wholesalers Assn ....$1,000   PAC

Transportation		$7,250

Air Transport **$2,250**
    United Parcel Service ....$1,500   PAC
Automotive **$5,000**
    National Auto Dealers Assn ....$5,000   PAC

Labor

Labor		$64,600

Building Trade Unions **$10,500**
    Laborers' Political League ....$3,500   PAC
    Plumbers/Pipefitters Union ....$3,000   PAC
    Carpenters & Joiners Union ....$2,500   PAC
    Sheet Metal Workers Union ....$1,000   PAC
Industrial Unions **$13,500**
    Intl Brotherhood of Electrical Workers ...$4,500   PAC
    United Steelworkers ....$4,000   PAC
    United Auto Workers ....$1,500   PAC
    Ladies Garment Workers Union ....$1,000   PAC
    Machinists/Aerospace Workers Union ...$1,000   PAC
Transportation Unions **$18,800**
    Teamsters Union ....$10,000   PAC
    Air Line Pilots Assn ....$6,500   PAC
    Trans Comm International Union ....$1,300   PAC
Public Sector Unions **$19,300**
    American Fedn of St/Cnty/Munic Employees ...$5,000   PAC
    American Postal Workers Union ....$3,000   PAC
    National Assn of Letter Carriers ....$2,800   PAC
    American Federation of Teachers ....$2,500   PAC
    National Education Assn ....$2,500   PAC
    National Assn Retired Federal Employees ...$2,000   PAC
Misc Unions **$2,500**
    Food & Commercial Workers Union ....$2,000   PAC

Ideological/Single-Issue

Ideological/Single-Issue		$5,000

Pro-Israel **$1,000**
    National Action Committee ....$1,000   PAC
Human Rights **$3,000**
    Human Rights Campaign Fund ....$2,000   PAC
    KidsPAC ....$1,000   PAC
Misc Issues **$1,000**
    National Cmte to Preserve Social Security ...$1,000   PAC

Other & Unknown

Other		$1,500

Civil Servants/Public Officials **$1,000**
    None over $1,000

Unknown		$4,550

    Employer Listed/Category Unknown $4,050
      None over $1,000

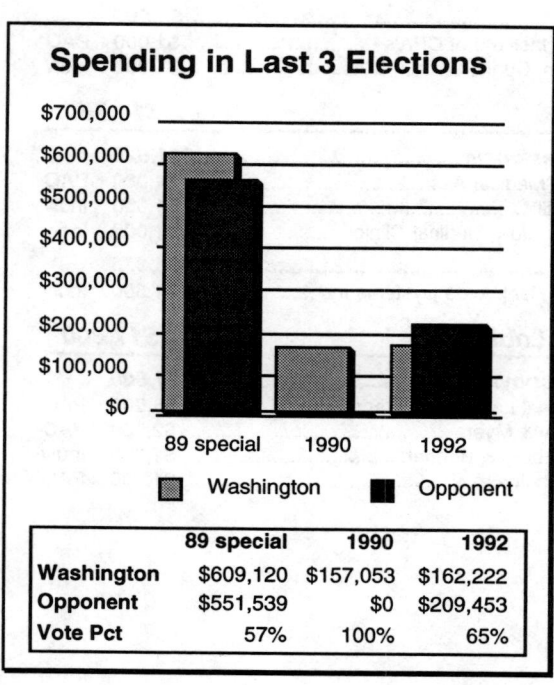

Spending in Last 3 Elections

	89 special	1990	1992
Washington	$609,120	$157,053	$162,222
Opponent	$551,539	$0	$209,453
Vote Pct	57%	100%	65%

    ■ Washington   ■ Opponent

Maxine Waters, D-Calif (35)

First elected: 1990

1991-92 Total Receipts: $191,510
1992 Year-end Cash: $11,274

1991-92 Committees & Subcommittees

Banking, Finance and Urban Affairs
Consumer Affairs and Coinage; General Oversight and Investigations; Housing and Community Development; International Development, Finance, Trade and Monetary Policy

Veterans' Affairs
Oversight and Investigations

Leading Contributors

Business

Agriculture — $6,000

Tobacco	**$3,000**	
RJR Nabisco	$2,000	PAC
Dairy	**$1,500**	
Associated Milk Producers	$1,500	PAC
Food Processing & Sales	**$1,000**	
Nabisco Brands Inc	$1,000	PAC

Communications/Electronics — $13,650

Printing & Publishing	**$5,000**	
Essence Communications	$1,500	Indiv
Media/Entertainment	**$6,250**	
Gordy Co	$1,000	Indiv
Motown Record Co	$1,000	Indiv

Construction — $3,400

General Contractors	**$1,400**	
None over $1,000		
Construction Services	**$2,000**	
KDG Architecture & Planning	$1,000	Indiv

Energy & Natural Resources — $2,000

Waste Management	**$1,000**	
None over $1,000		

Source of Funds in 1992 Election

Source	Total	Pct
PACs	$91,890	46%
Indivs $200+	$78,606	39%
Indivs under $200	$15,183	8%
Other	$15,053	8%
Candidate	$0	0%
Party	$9,672	5%

Source of PAC Dollars by Sector

Source	Total	Pct
Business	$35,294	38%
Labor	$50,650	54%
Ideology/Single Issue	$7,102	8%

In-State vs. Out-of-State Contributions*

Source	Total	Pct
In-State	$55,875	71%
Out-of-state	$22,481	29%
No state listed	$250	

* by large individual contributors ($200 & above)

Finance, Insurance & Real Estate — $20,475

Securities & Investment	**$8,150**	
Goldman, Sachs & Co	$1,500	PAC
First Boston Corp	$1,000	Indiv
Merrill Lynch	$1,000	Indiv
Muriel Siebert & Co	$1,000	Indiv
Real Estate	**$8,775**	
Telecu Industries	$3,000	Indiv
National Assn of Realtors	$2,500	PAC
Jonas & Assoc	$1,000	Indiv
Peter W Dauterive & Associates	$1,000	Indiv
Accountants	**$2,500**	
American Institute of CPA's	$1,000	PAC
Thompson, Curtis, Brazilio & Assoc	$1,000	Indiv

Health — $14,750

Health Professionals	**$11,625**	
American Medical Assn	$4,000	PAC
Dr Gus Gill	$1,000	Indiv
Vernon-Century Medical Clinic	$1,000	Indiv
Misc Health	**$2,275**	
Managed Healthcare Systems Inc	$1,500	Indiv

Lawyers & Lobbyists — $11,800

Lawyers & Lobbyists	**$11,800**	
Assn of Trial Lawyers of America	$5,000	PAC
O'Melveny & Myers	$2,000	PAC
Fox, Weinberg & Bennett	$1,000	Indiv
Manatt, Phelps et al	$1,000	PAC

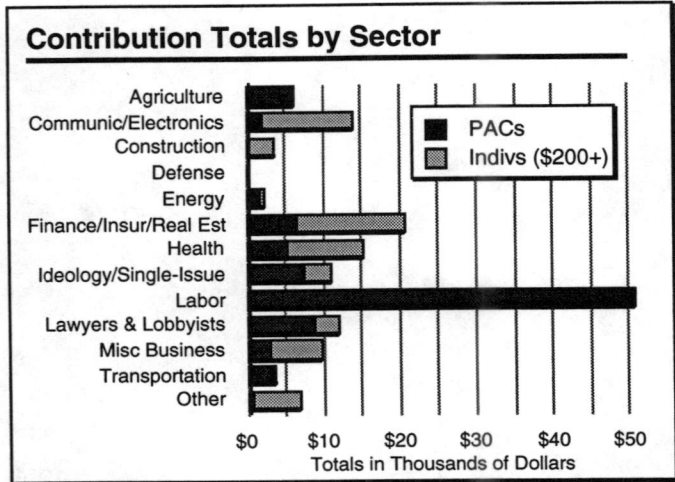

Contribution Totals by Sector

Agriculture, Communic/Electronics, Construction, Defense, Energy, Finance/Insur/Real Est, Health, Ideology/Single-Issue, Labor, Lawyers & Lobbyists, Misc Business, Transportation, Other

PACs / Indivs ($200+)

$0 $10 $20 $30 $40 $50
Totals in Thousands of Dollars

Misc Business $9,594

Retail Sales $1,000
    None over $1,000

Misc Services $2,000
    El Centro De La Raza ....$2,000   Indiv

Business Services $2,250
    None over $1,000

Misc Manufacturing & Distributing $2,500
    Avon Products ....$1,000   PAC
    Kobacker Co ....$1,000   Indiv

Transportation $3,250

Air Transport $2,500
    United Parcel Service ....$2,500   PAC

Labor

Labor $50,650

Building Trade Unions $8,000
    Laborers Union* ....$5,000   PAC
    Operating Engineers Union* ....$2,500   PAC

Industrial Unions $11,550
    United Auto Workers ....$7,500   PAC
    Boilermakers Union ....$1,000   PAC
    Electronic Machine Furniture Workers ......$1,000   PAC

Transportation Unions $9,000
    Teamsters Union ....$5,000   PAC
    Transport Workers Union ....$2,000   PAC

Public Sector Unions $18,800
    American Fedn of St/Cnty/Munic Employees ......$4,500   PAC
    National Assn of Letter Carriers ....$4,000   PAC
    American Federation of Teachers* ....$3,800   PAC
    National Assn Retired Federal Employees ......$2,000   PAC
    National Education Assn ....$1,500   PAC
    American Postal Workers Union ....$1,000   PAC
    National Assn of Postmasters ....$1,000   PAC

Misc Unions $3,300
    Food & Commercial Workers Union ....$1,500   PAC
    Service Employees International Union .....$1,000   PAC

Ideological/Single-Issue

Ideological/Single-Issue $10,852

Democratic/Liberal $1,250
    None over $1,000

Pro-Choice $2,500
    Voters for Choice ....$1,500   PAC

Womens Issues $5,038
    National Organization for Women ....$3,090   PAC

Human Rights $1,000
    Human Rights Campaign Fund ....$1,000   PAC

Misc Issues $1,064
    National Cmte to Preserve Social Security ....$1,000   PAC

Other & Unknown

Other $6,475

Civil Servants/Public Officials $1,000
    Deputy City Attorney ....$1,000   Indiv

Education $2,625
    Drew Univ School of Medicine & Science ....$1,000   Indiv

Retired $1,050
    None over $1,000

Other $1,800
    None over $1,000

Unknown $18,756

    Homemakers/Non-income earners $1,000
    No Employer Listed or Found $5,456
    Generic Occupation/Category Unknown $2,000
    Employer Listed/Category Unknown $10,300
        Community Thrift & Loan ....$2,000   Indiv
        Pacific Institute ....$1,000   Indiv
        Promothon Development Association ....$1,000   Indiv

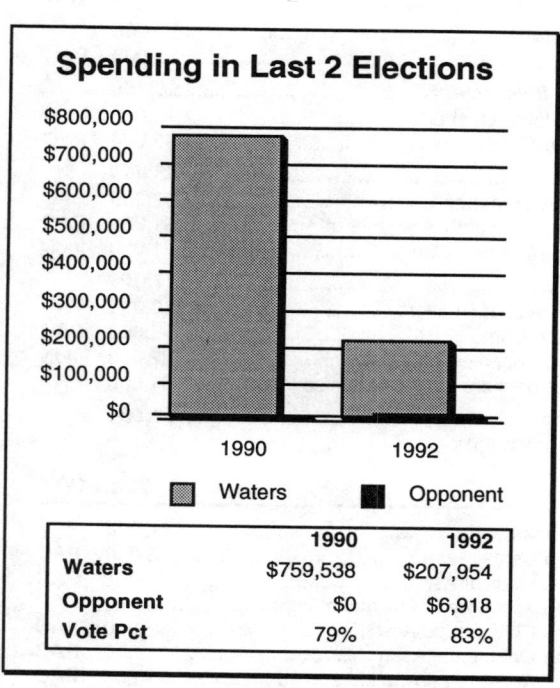

Spending in Last 2 Elections

	1990	1992
Waters	$759,538	$207,954
Opponent	$0	$6,918
Vote Pct	79%	83%

Legend: Waters, Opponent

* Contributions came from more than one affiliate or subsidiary.

1213

Melvin Watt, D-NC (12)

First elected: 1992

1991-92 Total Receipts: $483,601
1992 Year-end Cash: $2,887

1993-94 Committees & Subcommittees

Banking, Finance and Urban Affairs
Consumer Credit and Insurance; Housing and Community Development; International Development, Finance, Trade and Monetary Policy

Judiciary
Administrative Law and Governmental Relations; Economic and Commercial Law

Post Office and Civil Service
Postal Operations and Services

Leading Contributors

Business

Agriculture	$12,850	
Crop Production & Basic Processing	**$1,500**	
None over $1,000		
Tobacco	**$5,500**	
RJR Nabisco	$3,500	PAC
Philip Morris	$1,500	PAC
Dairy	**$2,500**	
Associated Milk Producers	$2,000	PAC
Food Processing & Sales	**$2,150**	
Pepsico Inc	$2,000	PAC

Communications/Electronics	$11,150	
Media/Entertainment	**$4,150**	
Kaplan Broadcasting Inc	$3,400	Indiv
Telephone Utilities	**$6,500**	
Southern Bell	$4,500	PAC
AT&T	$1,500	PAC

Construction	$3,700	
Home Builders	**$2,500**	
National Assn of Home Builders	$2,500	PAC

Energy & Natural Resources	$6,950	
Oil & Gas	**$1,250**	
None over $1,000		

Contribution Totals by Sector

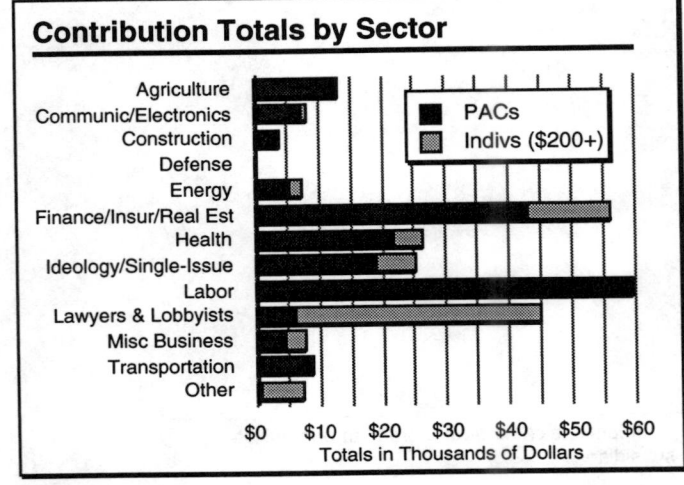

Agriculture
Communic/Electronics
Construction
Defense
Energy
Finance/Insur/Real Est
Health
Ideology/Single-Issue
Labor
Lawyers & Lobbyists
Misc Business
Transportation
Other

■ PACs
▨ Indivs ($200+)

$0 $10 $20 $30 $40 $50 $60
Totals in Thousands of Dollars

Source of Funds in 1992 Election

Source	Total	Pct
■ PACs	$203,732	41%
▨ Indivs $200+	$135,590	28%
□ Indivs under $200	$92,199	19%
⊠ Other	$61,104	12%
Candidate	$43,500	9%
Party	$17,575	4%

Source of PAC Dollars by Sector

Source	Total	Pct
■ Business	$111,200	59%
▨ Labor	$58,750	31%
□ Ideology/Single Issue	$18,605	10%

In-State vs. Out-of-State Contributions*

Source	Total	Pct
□ In-State	$98,640	73%
■ Out-of-state	$35,750	27%
No state listed	$200	

*** by large individual contributors ($200 & above)**

Electric Utilities	$5,700	
Duke Power Co	$3,200	PAC/Ind
Carolina Power & Light	$1,500	PAC
ACRE (Action Cmte for Rural Electrification)	$1,000	PAC

Finance, Insurance & Real Estate	$54,200	
Commercial Banks	**$16,150**	
American Bankers Assn	$4,000	PAC
Citizens & Southern National Bank	$3,500	PAC
JP Morgan & Co	$1,000	PAC
NC Alliance of Community Financial Insts	$1,000	PAC
NCNB Corp	$1,000	Indiv
Savings & Loans	**$2,000**	
US League of Savings Assns	$2,000	PAC
Securities & Investment	**$6,750**	
Bowles, Hollowell et al	$2,000	Indiv
Prudential Securities	$2,000	PAC
Insurance	**$5,350**	
National Assn of Life Underwriters	$2,000	PAC
Independent Insurance Agents of America	$1,350	PAC
Cameron M Harris & Co	$1,000	Indiv
Real Estate	**$21,000**	
National Assn of Realtors	$10,000	PAC
First Union Corp	$6,000	PAC
Shelton Companies	$2,000	Indiv
Mortgage Bankers Assn of America	$1,000	PAC
Misc Finance	**$1,950**	
None over $1,000		

Health	$26,000	
Health Professionals	**$22,000**	
American Dental Assn	$5,000	PAC
American Medical Assn	$5,000	PAC
American Academy of Ophthalmology	$3,000	PAC
American Chiropractic Assn	$2,000	PAC
American Optometric Assn	$1,500	PAC
American Nurses Assn	$1,000	PAC

Hospitals/Nursing Homes **$1,000**
  None over $1,000

Pharmaceuticals/Health Products **$3,000**
  Glaxo Inc .... $1,500   PAC
  Hynes Sales Co .... $1,000   Indiv

Lawyers & Lobbyists $44,550

Lawyers & Lobbyists **$44,550**
  Ferguson, Stein et al .... $9,400   Indiv
  Assn of Trial Lawyers of America .... $5,000   PAC
  Smith, Helms et al .... $2,750   Indiv
  Williams & Jensen .... $2,100   PAC/Ind
  Keker & Brockett .... $2,000   Indiv
  Lewis, White & Clay .... $1,000   Indiv
  Sutherland, Asbill & Brennan .... $1,000   Indiv
  Taft, Taft & Haigler .... $1,000   Indiv

Misc Business $7,500

Food & Beverage **$1,750**
  Hardee's Food Systems .... $1,000   PAC

Retail Sales **$2,000**
  Belk Stores Services .... $1,000   Indiv

Business Services **$1,000**
  None over $1,000

Lodging/Tourism **$1,000**
  Marriott Corp .... $1,000   PAC

Transportation $8,500

Air Transport **$4,300**
  United Parcel Service .... $2,300   PAC
  American Airlines .... $2,000   PAC

Automotive **$4,000**
  National Auto Dealers Assn .... $3,500   PAC

Labor

Labor   **$58,950**

Industrial Unions **$14,250**
  United Auto Workers .... $5,000   PAC
  Intl Brotherhood of Electrical Workers .... $3,000   PAC
  Communications Workers of America .... $2,500   PAC
  Amalgamated Clothing & Textile Workers .... $1,750   PAC
  Machinists/Aerospace Workers Union .... $1,500   PAC

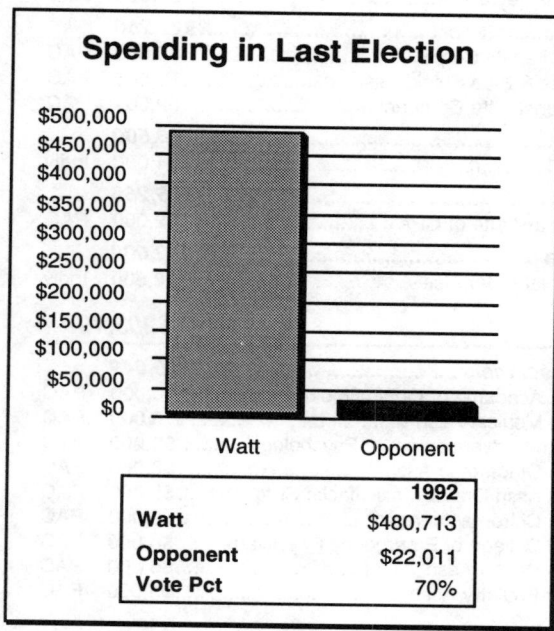

Spending in Last Election

	1992
Watt	$480,713
Opponent	$22,011
Vote Pct	70%

Transportation Unions **$15,000**
  Teamsters Union .... $10,000   PAC
  United Transportation Union .... $2,000   PAC
  Seafarers International Union .... $1,500   PAC

Public Sector Unions **$23,500**
  American Fedn of St/Cnty/Munic Employees ...... $7,500   PAC
  National Assn of Letter Carriers .... $5,000   PAC
  National Education Assn .... $5,000   PAC
  National Assn Retired Federal Employees .... $2,000   PAC
  American Federation of Teachers .... $1,500   PAC
  National Rural Letter Carriers Assn .... $1,000   PAC

Misc Unions **$6,200**
  Bakery, Confectionery & Tobacco Workers .... $2,500   PAC
  Food & Commercial Workers Union .... $2,500   PAC
  Service Employees International Union .... $1,200   PAC/Ind

Ideological/Single-Issue

Ideological/Single-Issue   **$22,755**

Democratic/Liberal **$5,450**
  Independent Action .... $2,500   PAC

Leadership PACs **$3,000**
  Effective Government Cmte (Dick Gephardt) ...... $1,000   PAC
  House Leadership Fund (Tom Foley) .... $1,000   PAC
  Victory USA (Vic Fazio) .... $1,000   PAC

Pro-Israel **$2,000**
  Joint Action Cmte for Political Affairs .... $1,000   PAC

Gun Rights/Gun Control **$1,000**
  Handgun Control Inc .... $1,000   PAC

Womens Issues **$1,500**
  None over $1,000

Human Rights **$5,700**
  Human Rights Campaign Fund .... $5,000   PAC

Misc Issues **$3,000**
  National Cmte to Preserve Social Security .... $2,000   PAC

Other & Unknown

Other   **$6,900**

Non-Profit Institutions **$2,250**
  Foundation for Hearing Aid Research .... $2,000   Indiv

Civil Servants/Public Officials **$1,050**
  None over $1,000

Education **$1,000**
  None over $1,000

Retired **$1,450**
  None over $1,000

Other **$1,150**
  None over $1,000

Unknown   **$59,640**

  No Employer Listed or Found $41,690
  Employer Listed/Category Unknown $16,300
    Hubberman & Gantt .... $1,500   Indiv
    Crossland Group .... $1,000   Indiv
    Harper Companies International .... $1,000   Indiv
    Harris Land Co .... $1,000   Indiv
    Interstate Townson Lane .... $1,000   Indiv
    Lewisville Trading Co .... $1,000   Indiv
    Metrolina Dodge Inc .... $1,000   Indiv
    Wakefield & Associates .... $1,000   Indiv

Henry A. Waxman, D-Calif (29)

First elected: 1974

1991-92 Total Receipts: $682,214
1992 Year-end Cash: $432,414

1991-92 Committees & Subcommittees

Energy and Commerce
Commerce, Consumer Protection and Competitiveness; Health and the Environment (Chairman)

Government Operations
Commerce, Consumer and Monetary Affairs; Human Resources and Intergovernmental Relations

Select Committee on Aging

Leading Contributors

Business

Agriculture		$10,700

Agricultural Services/Products	$6,000	
American Veterinary Medical Assn	$5,000	PAC

Food Processing & Sales	$3,500	
None over $2,000		

Communications/Electronics		$58,250

Media/Entertainment	$44,750	
MCA Inc	$7,000	PAC/Ind
National Assn of Broadcasters	$5,000	PAC
National Cable Television Assn	$5,000	PAC
Recording Industry Assn of America	$3,000	PAC/Ind
Paramount Communications	$2,500	PAC
Capitol-EMI Music	$2,000	Indiv
Falcon Cable TV	$2,000	Indiv
Viacom International	$2,000	PAC
Walt Disney Co	$2,000	Indiv
Warner Brothers	$2,000	Indiv

Telephone Utilities	$11,500	
AT&T	$4,000	PAC
Pacific Telesis Group	$4,000	PAC

Telecom Services & Equipment	$2,000	
None over $2,000		

Construction		$3,000
None over $2,000		

Source of Funds in 1992 Election

Source	Total	Pct
■ PACs	$402,915	58%
▨ Indivs $200+	$191,691	28%
☐ Indivs under $200	$36,537	5%
⊠ Other	$62,019	9%
Candidate	$0	0%
Party	$11,248	2%

Source of PAC Dollars by Sector

Source	Total	Pct
■ Business	$308,500	78%
▨ Labor	$63,750	16%
☐ Ideology/Single Issue	$21,564	5%

In-State vs. Out-of-State Contributions*

Source	Total	Pct
☐ In-State	$125,341	66%
■ Out-of-state	$63,850	34%
No state listed	$1,500	

* by large individual contributors ($200 & above)

Energy & Natural Resources		$26,000

Oil & Gas	$13,500	
Pacific Enterprises	$6,000	PAC

Electric Utilities	$10,500	
Southern California Edison	$7,000	PAC/Ind

Finance, Insurance & Real Estate		$51,500

Commercial Banks	$3,500	
None over $2,000		

Finance/Credit Companies	$2,500	
East-West Capital Associates	$2,500	Indiv

Securities & Investment	$10,000	
Investment Company Institute	$3,000	PAC
Morgan Stanley & Co	$2,000	PAC

Insurance	$21,250	
American Family Corp	$5,000	PAC
Blue Cross & Blue Shield Assn*	$3,500	PAC
TransAmerica Life Companies	$2,000	PAC

Real Estate	$6,500	
Casden Co	$4,000	Indiv

Accountants	$5,250	
American Institute of CPA's	$2,000	PAC

Misc Finance	$2,000	
EJ Financial Enterprise	$2,000	Indiv

Health		$203,199

Health Professionals	$126,049	
American Academy of Ophthalmology	$10,000	PAC
American Medical Assn*	$10,000	PAC
Assn for the Advancement of Psychology	$9,000	PAC
American Optometric Assn	$8,000	PAC
American Assn Oral & Maxillofacial Surgeons	$5,000	PAC
American Chiropractic Assn	$5,000	PAC
American College of Emergency Physicians	$5,000	PAC
American Dental Assn	$5,000	PAC
American Podiatry Assn	$5,000	PAC

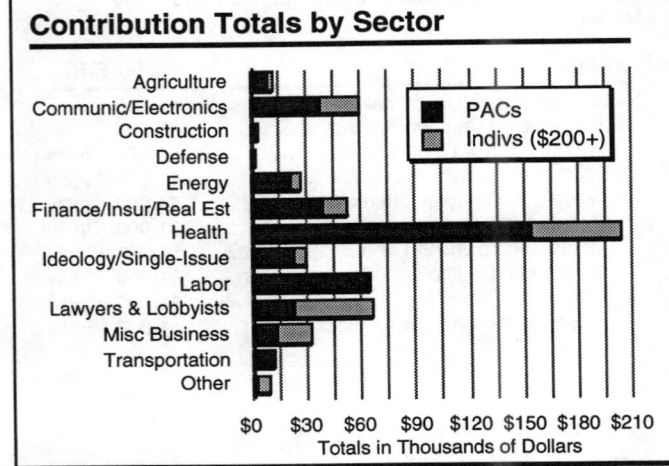

Contribution Totals by Sector

Legend: ■ PACs ▨ Indivs ($200+)

Agriculture
Communic/Electronics
Construction
Defense
Energy
Finance/Insur/Real Est
Health
Ideology/Single-Issue
Labor
Lawyers & Lobbyists
Misc Business
Transportation
Other

$0 $30 $60 $90 $120 $150 $180 $210
Totals in Thousands of Dollars

American Psychiatric Assn	$5,000	PAC
Anesthesia Service Medical Group	$5,000	PAC
Cooperative of American Physicians	$5,000	PAC
Cmte for Quality Orthopedic Health Care	$2,700	PAC
National Assn of Pharmacists	$2,500	PAC
American Pharmaceutical Assn	$2,000	PAC
American Soc Plastic & Reconstr Surgeons	$2,000	PAC
American Society of Internal Medicine	$2,000	Indiv
International Chiropractors Assn	$2,000	PAC

Hospitals/Nursing Homes ... $31,250

American Hospital Assn	$10,000	PAC
National Medical Enterprises Inc	$5,000	PAC
Federation of American Health Systems	$3,000	PAC
Manor Healthcare Corp	$3,000	PAC
Humana Inc	$2,500	PAC
Natl Assn of Private Psychiatric Hosp	$2,000	PAC

Health Services ... $15,500

| Family Health Program Inc | $3,000 | PAC |
| Group Health Assn of America | $2,000 | PAC |

Pharmaceuticals/Health Products ... $25,600

| Pharmavite Corp | $4,000 | Indiv |
| Proprietary Association | $2,500 | PAC |

Misc Health ... $4,800

None over $2,000

Lawyers & Lobbyists | $65,350

Lawyers & Lobbyists ... $65,350

Assn of Trial Lawyers of America	$5,000	PAC
MARC Associates	$5,000	Indiv
Akin, Gump et al	$3,000	PAC/Ind
Lyon & Lyon	$3,000	Indiv
O'Melveny & Myers	$3,000	Indiv
Arnold & Porter	$2,000	PAC
Griffin, Johnson & Associates	$2,000	Indiv
R Duffy Wall & Associates	$2,000	PAC/Ind
Wexler Group	$2,000	PAC/Ind
White, Fine & Verville	$2,000	Indiv

Misc Business | $31,750

Beer, Wine & Liquor ... $16,000

Gallo Winery	$8,000	Indiv
Iron Horse Vineyards	$2,000	Indiv
Wine Institute	$2,000	PAC

Spending in Last 3 Elections

	1988	1990	1992
Waxman	$191,334	$287,505	$718,695
Opponent	$15,449	$1,830	$143,526
Vote Pct	72%	69%	61%

Retail Sales	$5,000	
None over $2,000		
Business Services	$3,000	
None over $2,000		

Transportation | $11,500

Air Transport ... $3,000

| United Parcel Service | $2,000 | PAC |

Automotive ... $8,500

| Americans for Free International Trade | $5,000 | PAC |
| Auto Dealers & Drivers for Free Trade | $2,000 | PAC |

Labor

Labor | $63,750

Building Trade Unions ... $6,500

Laborers' Political League	$2,000	PAC
Painters & Allied Trades Union	$2,000	PAC
Plumbers/Pipefitters Union	$2,000	PAC

Industrial Unions ... $7,250

| United Auto Workers | $5,000 | PAC |

Transportation Unions ... $15,000

| Teamsters Union | $7,500 | PAC |
| United Transportation Union | $7,000 | PAC |

Public Sector Unions ... $24,500

American Fedn of St/Cnty/Munic Employees	$10,000	PAC
National Assn Retired Federal Employees	$5,000	PAC
National Assn of Letter Carriers	$5,000	PAC
American Federation of Teachers	$4,000	PAC

Misc Unions ... $10,500

Food & Commercial Workers Union	$6,000	PAC
Service Employees International Union	$2,500	PAC
Hotel/Restaurant Employees Union	$2,000	PAC

Ideological/Single-Issue

Ideological/Single-Issue | $29,064

Leadership PACs ... $10,000

| 24th Cong Dist of Calif PAC (Henry Waxman) | $10,000 | PAC |

Pro-Israel ... $4,500

None over $2,000

Human Rights ... $9,000

| KidsPAC | $5,000 | PAC |

Misc Issues ... $4,564

| National Cmte to Preserve Social Security | $2,500 | PAC |

Other & Unknown

Other | $8,150

Education ... $3,250

| Stanford University | $2,000 | Indiv |

Other ... $2,000

| National Assn of Social Workers | $2,000 | PAC |

Unknown | $20,792

No Employer Listed or Found	$6,300	
Employer Listed/Category Unknown	$14,042	
None over $2,000		

Independent expenditures supporting Waxman

| California Medical Assn | $2,500 |

---

* Contributions came from more than one affiliate or subsidiary.

Curt Weldon, R-Pa (7)

First elected: 1986

1991-92 Total Receipts: $465,223
1992 Year-end Cash: $34,613

1991-92 Committees & Subcommittees

Armed Services
Procurement and Military Nuclear Systems; Seapower and Strategic and Critical Materials

Merchant Marine and Fisheries
Fisheries and Wildlife Conservation and the Environment; Oceanography, Great Lakes and Outer Continental Shelf

Select Committee on Children, Youth and Families

Leading Contributors

Business

Agriculture		$6,500
Crop Production & Basic Processing		$1,500
None over $1,500		
Tobacco		$1,600
None over $1,500		
Forestry & Forest Products		$2,000
Scott Paper Co	$2,000	PAC

Communications/Electronics		$10,200
Media/Entertainment		$5,000
QVC Network	$4,000	Indiv
Telephone Utilities		$2,000
Bell Telephone of Pennsylvania	$1,500	PAC
Computer Equipment & Services		$2,000
None over $1,500		

Construction		$6,800
General Contractors		$2,850
None over $1,500		
Building Materials & Equipment		$2,450
None over $1,500		

Defense		$34,900
Defense Aerospace		$19,650
Boeing Co	$4,650	PAC
Textron Inc	$4,000	PAC
Colt Industries	$2,000	PAC

Defense Electronics		$9,950
Aydin Corp	$3,000	Indiv
Misc Defense		$5,300
FMC Corp	$1,700	PAC

Energy & Natural Resources		$21,600
Oil & Gas		$10,950
Atlantic Richfield	$2,850	PAC/Ind
Sun Co	$1,500	PAC
Electric Utilities		$5,000
Philadelphia Electric	$3,600	PAC
Waste Management		$3,650
Waste Management Inc	$2,850	PAC

Finance, Insurance & Real Estate		$33,500
Commercial Banks		$1,550
None over $1,500		
Securities & Investment		$1,750
Hillman Co	$1,500	Indiv
Insurance		$15,550
Glatfelter Insurance Group	$2,600	Indiv
National Assn of Life Underwriters	$2,000	PAC
Cigna Corp	$1,900	PAC
Independent Insurance Agents of America	$1,800	PAC
Real Estate		$13,100
National Assn of Realtors	$8,000	PAC
Berwind Property Group	$2,000	Indiv
Henderson Group	$1,550	Indiv

Source of Funds in 1992 Election

Source	Total	Pct
■ PACs	$185,187	40%
▨ Indivs $200+	$100,701	22%
☐ Indivs under $200	$159,217	34%
⊠ Other	$20,118	4%
Candidate	$0	0%
Party	$3,447	1%

Source of PAC Dollars by Sector

Source	Total	Pct
■ Business	$129,250	70%
▨ Labor	$50,925	28%
☐ Ideology/Single Issue	$3,423	2%

In-State vs. Out-of-State Contributions*

Source	Total	Pct
☐ In-State	$84,526	86%
■ Out-of-state	$13,425	14%
No state listed	$0	

* by large individual contributors ($200 & above)

Contribution Totals by Sector

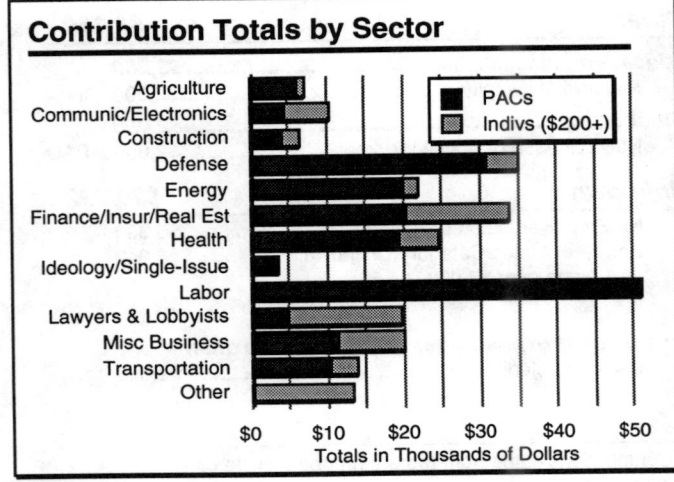

Agriculture
Communic/Electronics
Construction
Defense
Energy
Finance/Insur/Real Est
Health
Ideology/Single-Issue
Labor
Lawyers & Lobbyists
Misc Business
Transportation
Other

■ PACs
▨ Indivs ($200+)

$0 $10 $20 $30 $40 $50
Totals in Thousands of Dollars

Health $24,500

Health Professionals $15,850
    American Medical Assn* .... $10,000 PAC
    American Academy of Ophthalmology .... $2,000 PAC
Hospitals/Nursing Homes $2,300
    None over $1,500
Pharmaceuticals/Health Products $5,450
    SmithKline Beecham .... $2,600 PAC

Lawyers & Lobbyists $19,400

Lawyers & Lobbyists $19,400
    Reid & Priest .... $2,400 PAC/Ind
    Paul Magliocchetti Associates .... $1,500 Indiv

Misc Business $19,600

Retail Sales $2,550
    None over $1,500
Misc Services $1,550
    None over $1,500
Business Services $2,300
    None over $1,500
Chemical & Related Manufacturing $6,050
    Pennwalt Corp .... $1,800 PAC
Misc Manufacturing & Distributing $3,750
    None over $1,500

Transportation $13,450

Air Transport $5,850
    United Parcel Service .... $3,900 PAC
    Piasecki Aircraft Corp .... $1,950 Indiv
Railroads $2,300
    Union Pacific Corp .... $2,000 PAC
Sea Transport $3,000
    None over $1,500

Labor

Labor $50,925

Building Trade Unions $20,675
    Painters & Allied Trades Union .... $5,000 PAC
    Sheet Metal Workers Union .... $5,000 PAC
    Plumbers/Pipefitters Union* .... $3,575 PAC
    Laborers' Political League .... $3,000 PAC
    Roofers Union local #30 .... $2,300 PAC
Industrial Unions $8,350
    Machinists/Aerospace Workers Union .... $3,000 PAC
    United Auto Workers .... $2,500 PAC
    Intl Brotherhood of Electrical Workers .... $2,100 PAC
Transportation Unions $15,300
    Air Line Pilots Assn .... $5,000 PAC
    Teamsters Union .... $5,000 PAC
    Marine Engineers Union* .... $3,000 PAC
Public Sector Unions $6,600
    International Assn of Firefighters .... $2,000 PAC

Ideological/Single-Issue

Ideological/Single-Issue $3,423

Misc Issues $2,000
    National Cmte to Preserve Social Security .... $2,000 PAC

Other & Unknown

Other $12,821

Non-Profit Institutions $2,750
    Demoss Foundation .... $2,000 Indiv
Civil Servants/Public Officials $2,550
    None over $1,500
Retired $6,100
    None over $1,500

Unknown $24,680

    Homemakers/Non-income earners $3,200
    No Employer Listed or Found $5,980
    Employer Listed/Category Unknown $15,000
        Industrial Rehabilitation .... $3,000 Indiv

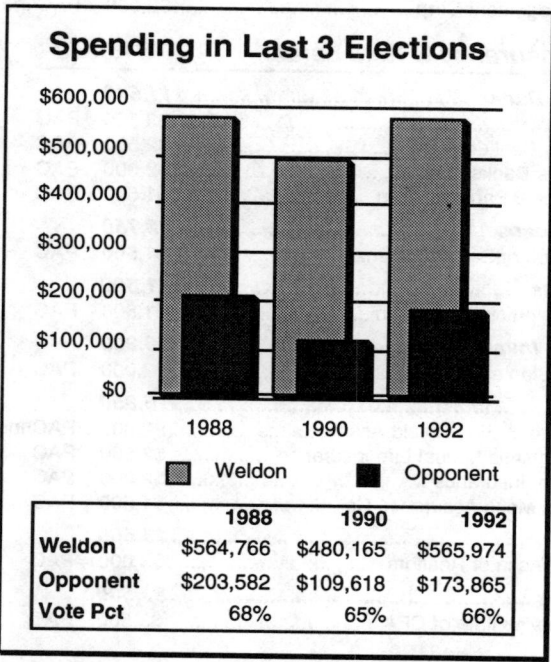

Spending in Last 3 Elections

	1988	1990	1992
Weldon	$564,766	$480,165	$565,974
Opponent	$203,582	$109,618	$173,865
Vote Pct	68%	65%	66%

Weldon   Opponent

* Contributions came from more than one affiliate or subsidiary.

Alan Wheat, D-Mo (5)

First elected: 1982

1991-92 Total Receipts:	$488,439
1992 Year-end Cash:	$76,049

1991-92 Committees & Subcommittees

District of Columbia
Government Operations and Metropolitan Affairs (Chairman);
Judiciary and Education

Rules
Legislative Process

Select Committee on Children, Youth and Families

Select Committee on Hunger

Leading Contributors

Business

Agriculture — $22,033

Crop Production & Basic Processing **$3,250**
  None over $1,500

Tobacco **$2,000**
  RJR Nabisco .... $2,000 PAC

Dairy **$12,500**
  Mid-America Dairymen .... $6,500 PAC
  Associated Milk Producers .... $6,000 PAC

Food Processing & Sales **$2,000**
  None over $1,500

Communications/Electronics — $38,200

Printing & Publishing **$11,150**
  Hallmark Cards .... $8,750 PAC/Ind

Media/Entertainment **$8,300**
  National Cable Television Assn .... $4,000 PAC
  National Assn of Broadcasters .... $2,000 PAC
  ASCAP .... $1,500 PAC

Telephone Utilities **$17,750**
  Southwestern Bell .... $6,000 PAC
  United Telecommunications .... $4,250 PAC/Ind
  AT&T .... $2,500 PAC
  GTE Corp .... $2,000 PAC

Construction — $6,000

General Contractors **$2,500**
  Heavy Constructors Assn .... $1,500 PAC

Building Materials & Equipment **$2,500**
  Payless Cashways Lumber .... $2,000 Indiv

Source of Funds in 1992 Election

Source	Total	Pct
■ PACs	$344,588	70%
▨ Indivs $200+	$71,818	15%
□ Indivs under $200	$44,546	9%
▧ Other	$28,124	6%
Candidate	$0	0%
Party	$1,087	0%

Source of PAC Dollars by Sector

Source	Total	Pct
■ Business	$169,918	50%
▨ Labor	$153,135	45%
□ Ideology/Single Issue	$19,750	6%

In-State vs. Out-of-State Contributions*

Source	Total	Pct
□ In-State	$40,348	56%
■ Out-of-state	$31,470	44%
No state listed	$0	

* by large individual contributors ($200 & above)

Defense — $3,500

Defense Aerospace **$3,500**
  Allied-Signal .... $3,000 PAC/Ind

Energy & Natural Resources — $13,900

Oil & Gas **$3,000**
  None over $1,500

Electric Utilities **$7,000**
  Utilicorp United Inc .... $3,500 PAC/Ind
  ACRE (Action Cmte for Rural Electrification)* ..... $1,500 PAC

Waste Management **$3,900**
  City Management Corp .... $2,000 PAC/Ind

Finance, Insurance & Real Estate — $45,840

Commercial Banks **$11,540**
  Citicorp .... $3,500 PAC
  American Bankers Assn .... $2,500 PAC
  Boatmens Bankshares .... $2,000 PAC
  Independent Bankers Assn .... $1,500 PAC

Savings & Loans **$2,750**
  US League of Savings Assns .... $1,500 PAC

Credit Unions **$1,500**
  Credit Union National Assn .... $1,500 PAC

Securities & Investment **$6,200**
  Morgan Stanley & Co .... $2,000 PAC

Insurance **$15,850**
  Blue Cross & Blue Shield Assn* .... $2,800 PAC/Ind
  Massachusetts Mutual Life Insurance .... $2,500 PAC
  Prudential Insurance .... $2,000 PAC
  Business Mens Assurance Co .... $1,500 PAC

Real Estate **$3,500**
  National Assn of Realtors .... $3,000 PAC

Accountants **$3,500**
  American Institute of CPA's .... $3,500 PAC

Contribution Totals by Sector

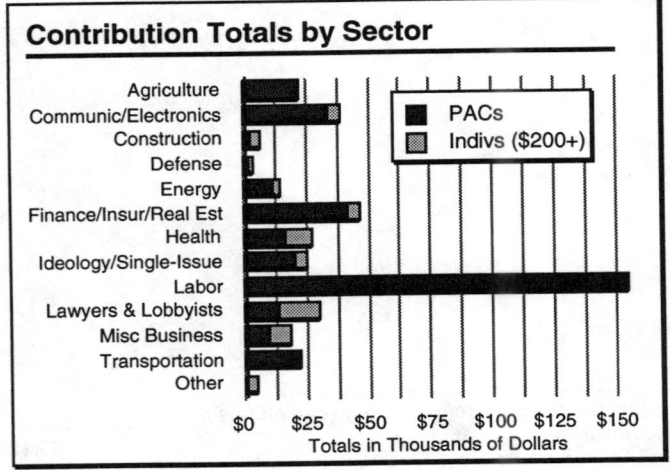

Agriculture
Communic/Electronics
Construction
Defense
Energy
Finance/Insur/Real Est
Health
Ideology/Single-Issue
Labor
Lawyers & Lobbyists
Misc Business
Transportation
Other

■ PACs
▨ Indivs ($200+)

$0 $25 $50 $75 $100 $125 $150
Totals in Thousands of Dollars

Health — $26,550

Health Professionals **$14,000**
  American Medical Assn* ....$6,650   PAC
  American Dental Assn ....$2,000   PAC
  Cleveland Chiropractic College.....................$2,000   Indiv

Hospitals/Nursing Homes **$4,050**
  Government Employees Hospital Assn ....$1,800   Indiv
  Humana Inc ....$1,750   PAC/Ind

Pharmaceuticals/Health Products **$8,000**
  Certified Safety ....$2,500   Indiv
  Bristol-Myers Squibb ....$1,500   PAC

Lawyers & Lobbyists — $29,110

Lawyers & Lobbyists **$29,110**
  Assn of Trial Lawyers of America ....$10,000   PAC
  Craft, Fridkin et al ....$3,200   Indiv
  Benson & Mckay ....$2,000   Indiv
  Hubbell, Sawyer et al ....$1,660   Indiv

Misc Business — $17,445

Food & Beverage **$4,250**
  Pepsi-Cola General Bottlers ....$2,000   PAC

Beer, Wine & Liquor **$3,500**
  Joseph E Seagram & Sons ....$1,500   PAC/Ind

Retail Sales **$2,000**
  None over $1,500

Business Services **$4,945**
  None over $1,500

Transportation — $22,000

Air Transport **$6,500**
  Federal Express Corp ....$3,000   PAC
  United Parcel Service ....$2,500   PAC

Automotive **$2,000**
  None over $1,500

Trucking **$6,000**
  Yellow Freight System ....$5,500   PAC

Railroads **$7,000**
  Kansas City Southern ....$4,000   PAC
  Union Pacific Corp ....$1,500   PAC

Labor

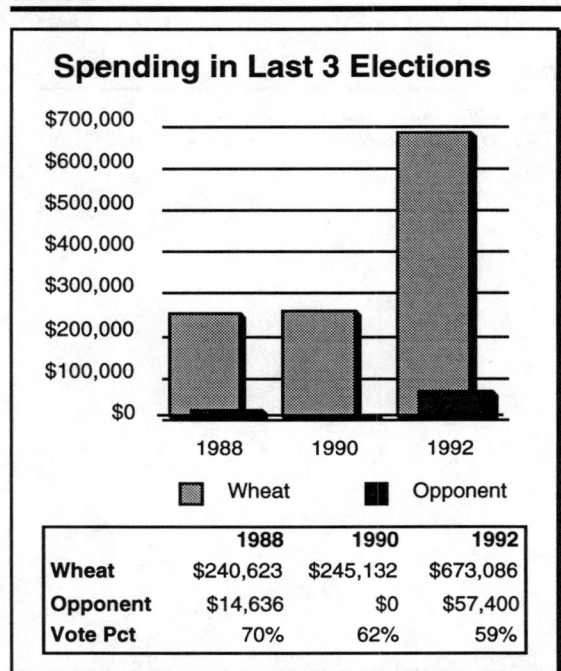

Spending in Last 3 Elections

	1988	1990	1992
Wheat	$240,623	$245,132	$673,086
Opponent	$14,636	$0	$57,400
Vote Pct	70%	62%	59%

Legend: ▨ Wheat   ■ Opponent

Labor — $153,385

Building Trade Unions **$21,900**
  Laborers' Political League ....$5,400   PAC
  Plumbers/Pipefitters Union* ....$4,000   PAC
  Painters & Allied Trades Union ....$3,000   PAC
  Carpenters & Joiners Union ....$2,500   PAC
  Sheet Metal Workers Union ....$2,500   PAC

Industrial Unions **$44,400**
  Intl Brotherhood of Electrical Workers ....$10,000   PAC
  Machinists/Aerospace Workers Union ....$10,000   PAC
  United Auto Workers ....$10,000   PAC
  United Steelworkers ....$5,000   PAC
  Boilermakers Union ....$4,000   PAC
  Communications Workers of America ....$1,900   PAC

Transportation Unions **$29,200**
  Teamsters Union ....$6,000   PAC
  Air Line Pilots Assn ....$5,000   PAC
  United Transportation Union ....$5,000   PAC
  Seafarers International Union ....$4,000   PAC
  Marine Engineers Union* ....$2,500   PAC
  Brotherhood of Locomotive Engineers.............$2,000   PAC
  Amalgamated Transit Union ....$1,500   PAC

Public Sector Unions **$46,600**
  American Federation of Teachers....................$10,000   PAC
  National Education Assn ....$10,000   PAC
  American Fedn of St/Cnty/Munic Employees ......$8,500   PAC
  American Postal Workers Union ....$5,500   PAC
  National Assn Retired Federal Employees ....$5,000   PAC
  National Assn of Letter Carriers ....$4,000   PAC

Misc Unions **$11,285**
  Food & Commercial Workers Union ....$6,000   PAC
  AFL-CIO ....$2,000   PAC
  Service Employees International Union ....$2,000   PAC

Ideological/Single-Issue

Ideological/Single-Issue — $24,338

Democratic/Liberal **$5,038**
  National Cmte for an Effective Congress ....$2,500   PAC
  Wheat for Congress ....$2,038   Indiv

Leadership PACs **$2,500**
  None over $1,500

Pro-Israel **$10,050**
  National PAC ....$5,000   PAC
  St Louisians for Better Government ....$3,000   PAC

Human Rights **$5,750**
  Health Care Concerns PAC ....$2,000   PAC
  KidsPAC ....$2,000   PAC

Other & Unknown

Other — **$4,020**

Retired **$2,020**
  None over $1,500

Unknown — **$8,300**

  No Employer Listed or Found $3,150
  Employer Listed/Category Unknown $4,900
    None over $1,500

---

* Contributions came from more than one affiliate or subsidiary.

Jamie L. Whitten, D-Miss (1)

First elected: 1941

1991-92 Total Receipts: $82,667
1992 Year-end Cash: $251,170

1991-92 Committees & Subcommittees

Appropriations (Chairman)
Agriculture, Rural Development, Food and Drug Administration and Related Agencies (Chairman)

Leading Contributors

Business

Agriculture $10,600

Dairy	**$3,000**	
Associated Milk Producers	$2,000	PAC
Dairymen Inc-Mississippi	$1,000	PAC
Agricultural Services/Products	**$4,300**	
American Veterinary Medical Assn	$2,500	PAC
Farm Credit Council	$1,000	PAC
Food Processing & Sales	**$1,000**	
Nabisco Brands Inc	$1,000	PAC
Forestry & Forest Products	**$2,000**	
Westvaco Corp	$1,000	PAC

Communications/Electronics $2,000

Telephone Utilities	**$2,000**	
Southern Bell	$2,000	PAC

Construction $1,000

General Contractors	**$1,000**	
Fluor Corp	$1,000	PAC

Energy & Natural Resources $2,900

Oil & Gas	**$1,000**	
Petroleum Marketers Assn	$1,000	PAC
Electric Utilities	**$1,900**	
Mississippi ACRE	$1,000	PAC

Source of Funds in 1992 Election

Source	Total	Pct
■ PACs	$30,700	37%
▨ Indivs $200+	$550	1%
☐ Indivs under $200	$5,387	7%
⊠ Other	$46,167	56%
Candidate	$0	0%
Party	$137	0%

Source of PAC Dollars by Sector

Source	Total	Pct
■ Business	$26,200	91%
▨ Labor	$1,050	4%
☐ Ideology/Single Issue	$1,500	5%

In-State vs. Out-of-State Contributions*

Source	Total	Pct
☐ In-State	$550	100%
■ Out-of-state	$0	0%
No state listed	$0	

* by large individual contributors ($200 & above)

Finance, Insurance & Real Estate $2,200

Commercial Banks	**$1,200**	
American Bankers Assn	$1,000	PAC
Real Estate	**$1,000**	
National Assn of Realtors	$1,000	PAC

Health $1,300

Health Professionals	**$1,300**	
American Medical Assn	$1,000	PAC

Lawyers & Lobbyists $5,000

Lawyers & Lobbyists	**$5,000**	
Assn of Trial Lawyers of America	$5,000	PAC

Misc Business $1,500

Beer, Wine & Liquor	**$1,000**	
National Beer Wholesalers Assn	$1,000	PAC

Contribution Totals by Sector

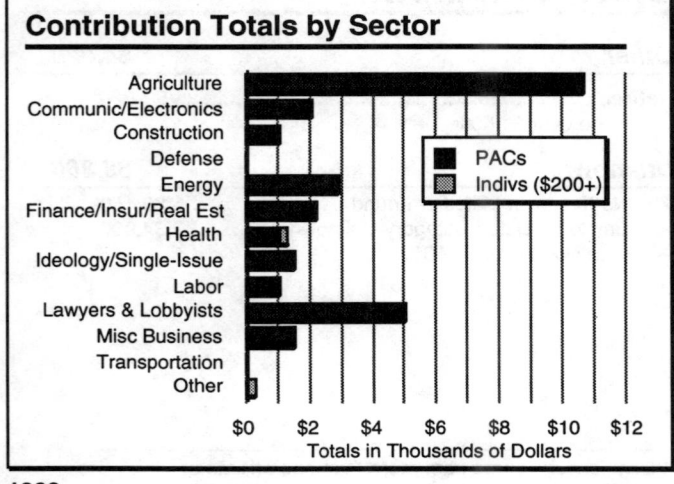

■ PACs
▨ Indivs ($200+)

Totals in Thousands of Dollars

Labor

Labor	$1,050

Public Sector Unions...$1,050
    National Assn of Letter Carriers ....$2,000   PAC

Ideological/Single-Issue

Ideological/Single-Issue	$1,500

Gun Rights/Gun Control $1,000
    National Rifle Assn ....$1,000   PAC

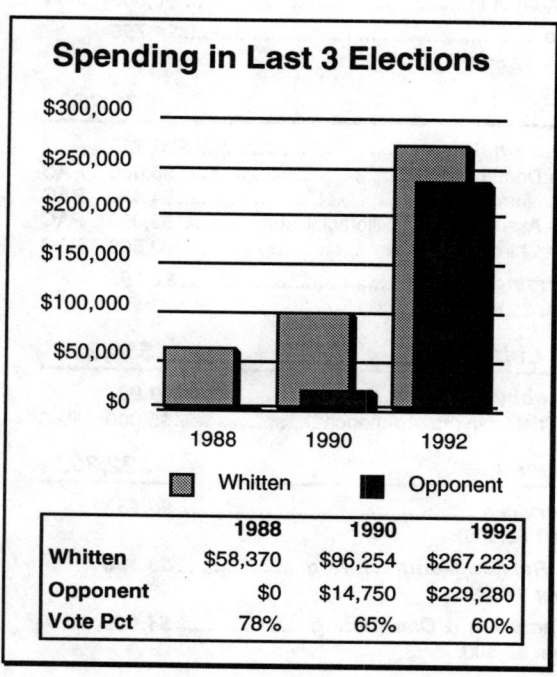

Spending in Last 3 Elections

	1988	1990	1992
Whitten	$58,370	$96,254	$267,223
Opponent	$0	$14,750	$229,280
Vote Pct	78%	65%	60%

Pat Williams, D-Mont (1)

First elected: 1978

1991-92 Total Receipts: $1,208,424
1992 Year-end Cash:　　$68,395

1991-92 Committees & Subcommittees

Education and Labor
Elementary, Secondary and Vocational Education; Labor-Management Relations (Chairman); Postsecondary Education; Select Education

Interior and Insular Affairs
National Parks and Public Lands

Leading Contributors

Business

Agriculture	**$38,700**	
Crop Production & Basic Processing	**$5,600**	
None over $2,500		
Tobacco	**$4,000**	
RJR Nabisco	$2,500	PAC
Dairy	**$4,300**	
Associated Milk Producers	$3,000	PAC
Poultry & Eggs	**$4,000**	
Tyson Foods	$3,000	PAC
Livestock	**$15,650**	
None over $2,500		

Communications/Electronics	**$19,178**	
Printing & Publishing	**$2,750**	
None over $2,500		
Media/Entertainment	**$7,528**	
Spring Creek Productions	$3,000	Indiv
Telephone Utilities	**$6,750**	
AT&T	$4,000	PAC

Energy & Natural Resources	**$15,550**	
Oil & Gas	**$3,850**	
None over $2,500		
Mining	**$4,000**	
None over $2,500		
Electric Utilities	**$5,250**	
ACRE (Action Cmte for Rural Electrification)*	$2,500	PAC

Source of Funds in 1992 Election

	Source	Total	Pct
■	PACs	$501,005	39%
■	Indivs $200+	$246,090	19%
□	Indivs under $200	$386,739	30%
▨	Other	$164,460	13%
	Candidate	$0	0%
	Party	$99,296	8%

Source of PAC Dollars by Sector

	Source	Total	Pct
■	Business	$108,388	23%
■	Labor	$282,509	59%
□	Ideology/Single Issue	$90,097	19%

In-State vs. Out-of-State Contributions*

	Source	Total	Pct
□	In-State	$117,170	49%
■	Out-of-state	$123,670	51%
	No state listed	$0	

* by large individual contributors ($200 & above)

Finance, Insurance & Real Estate	**$41,710**	
Commercial Banks	**$4,300**	
None over $2,500		
Securities & Investment	**$5,910**	
None over $2,500		
Insurance	**$13,750**	
New York Life	$3,000	PAC
Real Estate	**$3,800**	
None over $2,500		
Accountants	**$7,950**	
Nanas, Stern et al	$6,000	Indiv
Misc Finance	**$4,750**	
None over $2,500		

Health	**$31,350**	
Health Professionals	**$26,850**	
American Dental Assn	$5,000	PAC
American Nurses Assn	$4,450	PAC
American Assn Oral & Maxillofacial Surgeons	$3,000	PAC
American Chiropractic Assn	$2,500	PAC
Hospitals/Nursing Homes	**$2,750**	
None over $2,500		

Lawyers & Lobbyists	**$50,927**	
Lawyers & Lobbyists	**$50,927**	
Assn of Trial Lawyers of America	$5,000	PAC

Misc Business	**$22,303**	
Business Services	**$6,437**	
None over $2,500		
Chemical & Related Manufacturing	**$3,300**	
None over $2,500		
Misc Manufacturing & Distributing	**$4,000**	
None over $2,500		

Contribution Totals by Sector

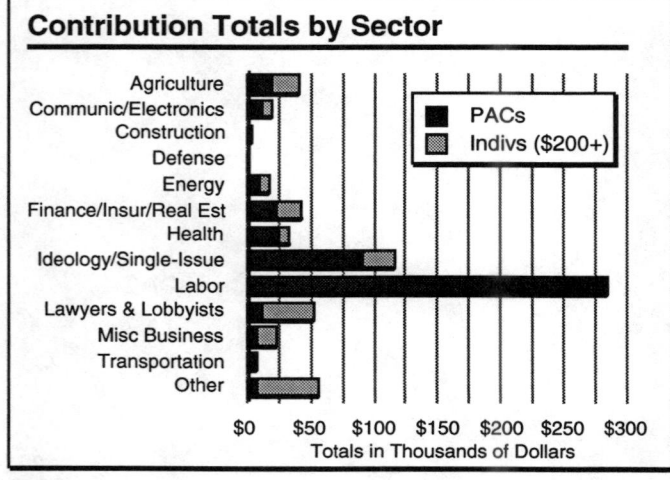

Agriculture
Communic/Electronics
Construction
Defense
Energy
Finance/Insur/Real Est
Health
Ideology/Single-Issue
Labor
Lawyers & Lobbyists
Misc Business
Transportation
Other

■ PACs
▨ Indivs ($200+)

$0　$50　$100　$150　$200　$250　$300
Totals in Thousands of Dollars

Transportation	$7,000

Railroads..$4,000
　None over $2,500

Labor

Labor	$282,709

Building Trade Unions **$60,750**
　Carpenters & Joiners Union ....$10,000　PAC
　Ironworkers Union ....$10,000　PAC
　Laborers' Political League ....$10,000　PAC
　Operating Engineers Union* ....$10,000　PAC
　Plumbers/Pipefitters Union ....$10,000　PAC
　Sheet Metal Workers Union ....$5,000　PAC

Industrial Unions **$73,190**
　United Mine Workers ....$10,500　PAC
　Communications Workers of America................$10,000　PAC
　Machinists/Aerospace Workers Union ....$10,000　PAC
　United Auto Workers ....$10,000　PAC
　United Steelworkers ....$10,000　PAC
　Intl Brotherhood of Electrical Workers ....$7,700　PAC/Ind
　Boilermakers Union ....$5,500　PAC
　Oil, Chemical & Atomic Workers Union ....$2,690　PAC

Transportation Unions **$53,800**
　Air Line Pilots Assn ....$10,000　PAC
　Teamsters Union ....$10,000　PAC
　United Transportation Union ....$10,000　PAC
　Amalgamated Transit Union ....$5,000　PAC
　Marine Engineers Union ....$5,000　PAC
　Trans Comm International Union ....$4,000　PAC

Public Sector Unions **$61,469**
　National Assn of Letter Carriers ....$10,000　PAC
　National Education Assn ....$10,000　PAC
　American Fedn of St/Cnty/Munic Employees ......$9,999　PAC
　American Federation of Teachers ....$9,750　PAC
　American Postal Workers Union ....$9,000　PAC
　National Assn Retired Federal Employees ....$4,000　PAC

Misc Unions **$33,500**
　Food & Commercial Workers Union ....$10,000　PAC
　Service Employees International Union ....$10,000　PAC
　AFL-CIO ....$6,500　PAC
　Bakery, Confectionery & Tobacco Workers ....$3,500　PAC

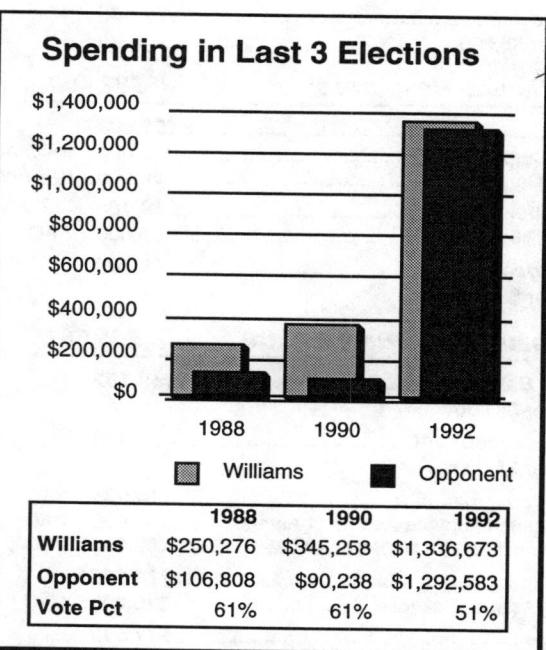

Spending in Last 3 Elections

	1988	1990	1992
Williams	$250,276	$345,258	$1,336,673
Opponent	$106,808	$90,238	$1,292,583
Vote Pct	61%	61%	51%

Ideological/Single-Issue

Ideological/Single-Issue	$113,747

Democratic/Liberal **$19,134**
　Hollywood Women's Political Cmte ....$5,000　PAC
　National Cmte for an Effective Congress ....$5,000　PAC
　Independent Action ....$4,000　PAC

Leadership PACs **$16,500**
　America's Leaders' Fund (Dan Rostenkowski) ....$6,500　PAC
　House Leadership Fund (Tom Foley) ....$4,500　PAC
　Effective Government Cmte (Dick Gephardt) ......$3,000　PAC

Pro-Israel **$5,750**
　None over $2,500

Pro-Choice **$11,300**
　Voters for Choice ....$5,300　PAC/Ind
　National Abortion Rights Action League ....$5,000　PAC

Womens Issues **$4,050**
　None over $2,500

Human Rights **$20,500**
　Human Rights Campaign Fund..........................$7,500　PAC
　KidsPAC ....$7,500　PAC
　National Community Action Foundation ....$5,500　PAC

Misc Issues **$35,676**
　Sierra Club ....$9,776　PAC
　League of Conservation Voters ....$8,750　PAC/Ind
　National Cmte to Preserve Social Security ....$7,500　PAC

Other & Unknown

Other	$56,057

Non-Profit Institutions **$4,450**
　None over $2,500

Civil Servants/Public Officials **$3,600**
　None over $2,500

Education **$12,417**
　University of Montana ....$3,017　Indiv

Retired **$26,940**
　None over $2,500

Other **$8,650**
　None over $2,500

Unknown	$48,703

　Homemakers/Non-income earners $5,300
　No Employer Listed or Found $6,525
　Generic Occupation/Category Unknown $9,275
　Employer Listed/Category Unknown $27,603
　　None over $2,500

Independent expenditures supporting Williams
　National Abortion Rights Action League $77,885
　Montana Hunters-Anglers PAC $11,396
　National Cmte to Preserve Social Security $8,617
Independent expenditures opposing Williams
　Eagle Forum $5,559

---

* Contributions came from more than one affiliate or
subsidiary.

Charles Wilson, D-Texas (2)

First elected: 1972
1991-92 Total Receipts: $1,188,912
1992 Year-end Cash: $25,171

1991-92 Committees & Subcommittees

Appropriations
Defense; Foreign Operations, Export Financing and Related Programs

Select Committee on Intelligence

Leading Contributors

Business

Agriculture		$51,091
Crop Production & Basic Processing	.... $5,800	
None over $5,000		
Dairy	.... $14,000	
Associated Milk Producers	.... $11,000	PAC
Food Processing & Sales	.... $8,500	
None over $5,000		
Forestry & Forest Products	.... $18,000	
Temple-Inland	.... $16,000	PAC/Ind

Communications/Electronics		$14,178
Computer Equipment & Services	.... $5,350	
None over $5,000		

Construction		$27,750
General Contractors	.... $10,500	
None over $5,000		
Home Builders	.... $5,000	
National Assn of Home Builders	.... $5,000	PAC
Construction Services	.... $8,750	
None over $5,000		

Defense		$210,650
Defense Aerospace	.... $125,700	
Textron Inc	.... $14,500	PAC/Ind
LTV Aerospace & Defense Co	.... $13,750	PAC/Ind
Fairchild Aircraft Corp	.... $10,500	Indiv
Martin Marietta Corp	.... $10,500	PAC
Northrop Corp	.... $10,000	PAC
McDonnell Douglas*	.... $8,000	PAC

Source of Funds in 1992 Election

Source	Total	Pct
■ PACs	.... $638,825	53%
▨ Indivs $200+	.... $464,533	38%
☐ Indivs under $200	.... $49,824	4%
⊠ Other	.... $60,978	5%
Candidate	.... $15,000	1%
Party	.... $30,398	2%

Source of PAC Dollars by Sector

Source	Total	Pct
■ Business	.... $400,773	64%
▨ Labor	.... $182,050	29%
☐ Ideology/Single Issue	.... $42,600	7%

In-State vs. Out-of-State Contributions*

Source	Total	Pct
☐ In-State	.... $234,033	51%
■ Out-of-state	.... $228,600	49%
No state listed	.... $1,900	

* by large individual contributors ($200 & above)

Henley Group Inc	.... $7,000	PAC
Grumman Corp	.... $6,000	PAC
General Electric	.... $5,800	PAC
Gencorp Inc	.... $5,000	PAC
General Dynamics	.... $5,000	PAC
Defense Electronics	.... $69,450	
Loral Corp	.... $10,200	PAC/Ind
Texas Instruments	.... $10,000	PAC
Imo Industries Inc	.... $9,500	PAC/Ind
Raytheon	.... $5,500	PAC
Diagnostic Retrieval Systems	.... $5,000	Indiv
TRW Inc	.... $5,000	PAC/Ind
Misc Defense	.... $15,500	
None over $5,000		

Energy & Natural Resources		$82,400
Oil & Gas	.... $63,800	
Coastal Corp	.... $15,000	PAC/Ind
Enserch Corp	.... $6,200	PAC/Ind
Electric Utilities	.... $8,100	
Texas Utilities Co	.... $5,000	PAC
Waste Management	.... $9,000	
None over $5,000		

Finance, Insurance & Real Estate		$65,681
Commercial Banks	.... $9,182	
None over $5,000		
Securities & Investment	.... $6,450	
None over $5,000		
Insurance	.... $16,936	
Independent Insurance Agents of America	.... $7,000	PAC
National Assn of Life Underwriters	.... $7,000	PAC
Real Estate	.... $14,100	
National Assn of Realtors	.... $10,000	PAC
Misc Finance	.... $11,513	
None over $5,000		

Contribution Totals by Sector

Legend: ■ PACs, ▨ Indivs ($200+)

Categories (top to bottom): Agriculture, Communic/Electronics, Construction, Defense, Energy, Finance/Insur/Real Est, Health, Ideology/Single-Issue, Labor, Lawyers & Lobbyists, Misc Business, Transportation, Other

X-axis: $0, $50, $100, $150, $200, $250
Totals in Thousands of Dollars

Health $48,550

Health Professionals **$34,250**
    American Medical Assn ....$7,500   PAC
    American Chiropractic Assn ....$5,000   PAC
    American Dental Assn ....$5,000   PAC

Pharmaceuticals/Health Products **$9,000**
    Henley Group Inc ....$9,000   Indiv

Lawyers & Lobbyists $118,090

Lawyers & Lobbyists **$118,090**
    Assn of Trial Lawyers of America ....$10,000   PAC
    Paul Magliocchetti Associates ....$10,000   Indiv
    Umphrey, Swearingen et al ....$10,000   Indiv
    Akin, Gump et al ....$7,700   PAC/Ind
    Vinson & Elkins ....$7,162   PAC/Ind
    Jamail & Kolius ....$6,000   Indiv

Misc Business $67,500

Beer, Wine & Liquor **$8,400**
    National Beer Wholesalers Assn ....$7,500   PAC

Misc Services **$17,500**
    Service Corp International ....$10,500   PAC/Ind

Business Services **$13,950**
    None over $5,000

Misc Manufacturing & Distributing **$20,700**
    Mag Instruments Inc ....$13,000   Indiv

Transportation $60,816

Air Transport **$17,600**
    American Airlines ....$5,000   PAC

Automotive **$11,500**
    National Auto Dealers Assn ....$10,000   PAC

Trucking **$8,000**
    Rollind Truck Leasing Corp ....$5,000   Indiv

Sea Transport **$20,716**
    Orange Shipbuilding ....$10,666   Indiv

Spending in Last 3 Elections

	1988	1990	1992
Wilson	$309,355	$740,342	$1,164,599
Opponent	$0	$124,884	$351,132
Vote Pct	88%	56%	56%

Legend: ▨ Wilson ■ Opponent

Labor

Labor $183,050

Building Trade Unions **$29,500**
    Laborers' Political League ....$7,750   PAC
    Carpenters & Joiners Union ....$5,500   PAC
    Plumbers/Pipefitters Union ....$5,000   PAC

Industrial Unions **$44,250**
    United Auto Workers ....$10,000   PAC
    Communications Workers of America ......$8,500   PAC
    United Steelworkers ....$8,000   PAC
    Intl Brotherhood of Electrical Workers ....$5,000   PAC

Transportation Unions **$56,000**
    Marine Engineers Union* ....$10,000   PAC
    Seafarers International Union ....$10,000   PAC
    Teamsters Union ....$10,000   PAC
    United Transportation Union ....$8,000   PAC
    Air Line Pilots Assn ....$6,000   PAC
    Transport Workers Union ....$5,000   PAC

Public Sector Unions **$37,800**
    National Education Assn ....$10,000   PAC
    National Assn Retired Federal Employees ....$7,000   PAC
    National Assn of Letter Carriers ....$6,000   PAC

Misc Unions **$15,500**
    None over $5,000

Ideological/Single-Issue

Ideological/Single-Issue $47,600

Leadership PACs **$7,000**
    House Leadership Fund (Tom Foley) ....$5,000   PAC

Pro-Israel **$11,700**
    None over $5,000

Pro-Choice **$9,000**
    National Abortion Rights Action League ....$6,000   PAC

Gun Rights/Gun Control **$9,900**
    National Rifle Assn ....$9,900   PAC

Misc Issues **$9,500**
    National Cmte to Preserve Social Security ....$5,500   PAC

Other & Unknown

Other $23,100

Education **$5,200**
    None over $5,000

Retired **$16,500**
    None over $5,000

Unknown $89,500

    Homemakers/Non-income earners $19,300
    No Employer Listed or Found $24,000
    Employer Listed/Category Unknown $45,000
      None over $5,000

Independent expenditures supporting Wilson
    National Cmte to Preserve Social Security $5,085

---

* Contributions came from more than one affiliate or subsidiary.

Bob Wise, D-WVa (2)

First elected: 1982
1991-92 Total Receipts: $295,894
1992 Year-end Cash: $145,069

1991-92 Committees & Subcommittees

Budget
Community Development and Natural Resources; Economic Policy, Projections and Revenues; Human Resources

Government Operations
Employment and Housing; Government Information, Justice and Agriculture (Chairman)

Select Committee on Aging

Leading Contributors

Business

Agriculture — $15,225

Crop Production & Basic Processing	**$3,775**	
American Sugarbeet Growers Assn	$1,000	PAC
Tobacco	**$7,700**	
RJR Nabisco	$5,000	PAC
Philip Morris	$1,700	PAC
Tobacco Institute	$1,000	PAC
Dairy	**$2,000**	
Associated Milk Producers	$1,000	PAC
Dairymen Inc	$1,000	PAC

Communications/Electronics — $14,800

Printing & Publishing	**$7,000**	
West Publishing	$5,000	PAC
Cambridge Information Group	$2,000	Indiv
Media/Entertainment	**$1,000**	
None over $1,000		
Telephone Utilities	**$5,800**	
AT&T	$2,500	PAC
Bell Atlantic*	$1,050	PAC

Construction — $5,175

General Contractors	**$4,000**	
National Utility Contractors Assn	$2,000	PAC
American Road & Transport Builders Assn	$1,000	PAC
Associated General Contractors	$1,000	PAC

Contribution Totals by Sector

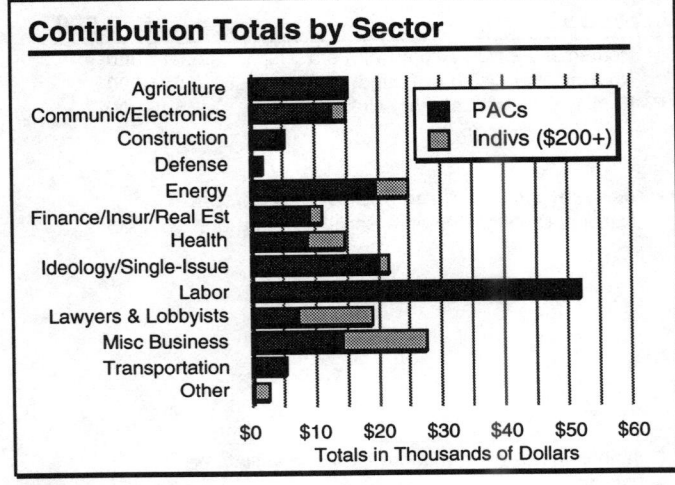

Totals in Thousands of Dollars

Source of Funds in 1992 Election

Source	Total	Pct
PACs	$169,200	56%
Indivs $200+	$51,225	17%
Indivs under $200	$54,418	18%
Other	$24,670	8%
Candidate	$0	0%
Party	$5,019	2%

Source of PAC Dollars by Sector

Source	Total	Pct
Business	$97,500	58%
Labor	$51,400	30%
Ideology/Single Issue	$19,700	12%

In-State vs. Out-of-State Contributions*

Source	Total	Pct
In-State	$32,650	65%
Out-of-state	$17,950	35%
No state listed	$0	

*by large individual contributors ($200 & above)

Defense — $1,500

Defense Aerospace	**$1,500**	
None over $1,000		

Energy & Natural Resources — $24,325

Oil & Gas	**$20,225**	
Columbia Natural Resources	$6,575	PAC
Eastern American Energy Corp	$2,000	Indiv
Consolidated Gas Transmission Corp	$1,500	PAC
Washington Gas Light Co	$1,500	PAC
Ashland Oil	$1,250	PAC
Natural Gas Transportation Co	$1,250	Indiv
Consolidated Natural Gas*	$1,150	PAC
Atlantic Richfield	$1,000	PAC
Occidental Petroleum	$1,000	PAC
Mining	**$3,100**	
National Coal Assn	$1,000	PAC
National Council of Coal Lessors	$1,000	PAC
Electric Utilities	**$1,000**	
None over $1,000		

Finance, Insurance & Real Estate — $10,250

Commercial Banks	**$3,500**	
American Bankers Assn	$2,000	PAC
Insurance	**$1,000**	
None over $1,000		
Accountants	**$5,000**	
American Institute of CPA's	$4,000	PAC

Health — $14,550

Health Professionals	**$8,475**	
American Medical Assn	$2,000	PAC
General Anesthesia Services Inc	$1,625	Indiv
Greenbrier Anesthesia Services	$1,000	Indiv

Hospitals/Nursing Homes *$3,375*
    American Hospital Assn .... $2,000 PAC

Pharmaceuticals/Health Products *$2,000*
    Rhone-Poulenc Inc .... $1,000 PAC

Lawyers & Lobbyists $18,600

Lawyers & Lobbyists *$18,600*
    Opperman & Paquin .... $5,000 PAC
    King, Betts & Allen .... $1,500 Indiv
    Hostler & Segal .... $1,000 Indiv
    Hoving Group .... $1,000 Indiv
    Vaughan & Withrow .... $1,000 Indiv

Misc Business $27,275

Food & Beverage *$1,500*
    Pepsi-Cola Bottlers Assn .... $1,500 PAC

Beer, Wine & Liquor *$1,000*
    None over $1,000

Retail Sales *$5,750*
    Bright of America .... $4,000 Indiv
    Fruth Pharmacies .... $1,000 Indiv

Business Services *$3,500*
    Charles Ryan & Associates .... $1,000 Indiv
    White Consulting Group .... $1,000 Indiv

Chemical & Related Manufacturing *$7,900*
    Union Carbide .... $2,100 PAC
    FMC Corp .... $1,500 PAC
    Monsanto Co .... $1,500 PAC

Steel Production *$1,000*
    LTV Corp* .... $1,000 PAC

Misc Manufacturing & Distributing *$6,375*
    McJunkin Corp .... $3,875 Indiv
    BF Goodrich .... $1,500 PAC
    Hoechst Celanese Corp .... $1,000 PAC

Transportation $5,250

Automotive *$1,000*
    National Auto Dealers Assn .... $1,000 PAC

Trucking *$1,500*
    American Trucking Assns .... $1,000 PAC

Railroads *$1,500*
    CSX Transportation Inc .... $1,000 PAC

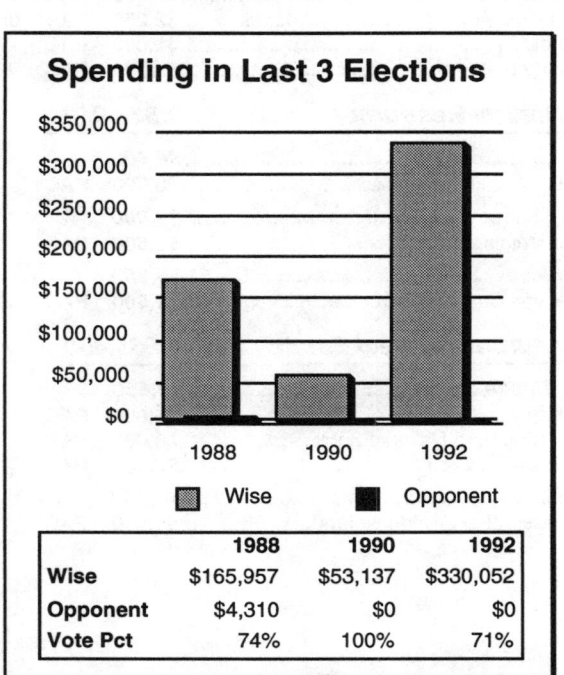

Spending in Last 3 Elections

	1988	1990	1992
Wise	$165,957	$53,137	$330,052
Opponent	$4,310	$0	$0
Vote Pct	74%	100%	71%

Labor

Labor $51,400

Building Trade Unions *$6,500*
    Carpenters & Joiners Union .... $2,500 PAC
    Laborers' Political League .... $2,500 PAC
    Plumbers/Pipefitters Union .... $1,000 PAC

Industrial Unions *$11,000*
    United Auto Workers .... $5,000 PAC
    Machinists/Aerospace Workers Union .... $2,000 PAC
    United Mine Workers .... $1,500 PAC

Transportation Unions *$12,500*
    Teamsters Union .... $5,000 PAC
    Masters, Mates & Pilots Union .... $2,000 PAC
    United Transportation Union .... $1,500 PAC
    Air Line Pilots Assn .... $1,000 PAC
    Marine Engineers Union .... $1,000 PAC
    Trans Comm International Union .... $1,000 PAC

Public Sector Unions *$19,500*
    American Fedn of St/Cnty/Munic Employees .... $5,000 PAC
    National Assn of Letter Carriers .... $3,500 PAC
    National Assn Retired Federal Employees .... $3,000 PAC
    American Postal Workers Union .... $2,500 PAC
    National Education Assn .... $2,500 PAC
    International Assn of Firefighters .... $1,000 PAC
    National Assn of Postmasters .... $1,000 PAC

Misc Unions *$1,900*
    Food & Commercial Workers Union .... $1,500 PAC

Ideological/Single-Issue

Ideological/Single-Issue $21,700

Democratic/Liberal *$3,500*
    National Cmte for an Effective Congress .... $2,500 PAC

Leadership PACs *$1,000*
    Cmte for America's Future (Robert Byrd) .... $1,000 PAC

Pro-Israel *$3,750*
    Hudson Valley PAC .... $3,000 PAC

Pro-Choice *$3,000*
    National Abortion Rights Action League .... $1,500 PAC
    Voters for Choice .... $1,500 PAC

Gun Rights/Gun Control *$7,450*
    National Rifle Assn .... $7,450 PAC

Human Rights *$1,000*
    None over $1,000

Misc Issues *$2,000*
    National Cmte to Preserve Social Security .... $2,000 PAC

Other & Unknown

Other $2,450

Non-Profit Institutions *$1,000*
    Ford Foundation .... $1,000 Indiv

Unknown $6,950

    Homemakers/Non-income earners $1,500
    Employer Listed/Category Unknown $4,950
        Di Trapano & Jackson .... $1,000 Indiv
        RMS Management .... $1,000 Indiv

* Contributions came from more than one affiliate or
subsidiary.

Frank R. Wolf, R-Va (10)

First elected: 1980

1991-92 Total Receipts: $452,307
1992 Year-end Cash: $79,889

1991-92 Committees & Subcommittees

Appropriations
Transportation and Related Agencies; Treasury, Postal Service and General Government (Ranking Republican)

Select Committee on Children, Youth and Families (Ranking Republican)

Select Committee on Hunger

Leading Contributors

Business

Agriculture	$4,500	
Food Processing & Sales	**$1,950**	
None over $1,500		

Communications/Electronics	$23,700	
Media/Entertainment	**$2,300**	
None over $1,500		
Telephone Utilities	**$5,050**	
United Telecommunications	$3,000	PAC
Computer Equipment & Services	**$15,150**	
Universal Systems Inc	$7,000	Indiv
Viar & Co	$2,000	Indiv
Electronic Data Systems	$1,700	PAC

Construction	$17,756	
General Contractors	**$7,806**	
Rocks Engineering Co	$2,250	Indiv
Associated General Contractors	$1,500	PAC
Home Builders	**$3,250**	
NV Homes	$2,000	Indiv
Special Trade Contractors	**$3,500**	
National Electrical Contractors Assn	$2,000	PAC
Construction Services	**$2,200**	
None over $1,500		

Source of Funds in 1992 Election

Source	Total	Pct
PACs	$180,302	40%
Indivs $200+	$133,872	30%
Indivs under $200	$123,339	27%
Other	$14,794	3%
Candidate	$0	0%
Party	$280	0%

Source of PAC Dollars by Sector

Source	Total	Pct
Business	$154,026	86%
Labor	$17,360	10%
Ideology/Single Issue	$6,900	4%

In-State vs. Out-of-State Contributions*

Source	Total	Pct
In-State	$120,172	90%
Out-of-state	$13,700	10%
No state listed	$0	

* by large individual contributors ($200 & above)

Defense — $48,400

Defense Aerospace	$9,650	
Dyncorp	$2,000	PAC
Grumman Corp	$1,600	PAC
Defense Electronics	**$23,450**	
E-Systems Inc	$5,700	PAC
Planning Research Corp	$3,750	PAC
AT&T	$3,250	PAC
TRW Inc	$2,500	PAC
Hughes Aircraft	$1,500	PAC
Misc Defense	**$15,300**	
BDM International	$8,500	PAC/Ind
Atlantic Research Corp	$2,250	PAC/Ind
Tenneco Inc	$2,000	PAC
Mantech International	$1,500	PAC

Energy & Natural Resources — $16,912

Oil & Gas	$8,462	
Mobil Oil	$3,000	PAC
Mining	**$3,000**	
Reynolds Metals	$2,500	PAC
Electric Utilities	**$4,250**	
ACRE (Action Cmte for Rural Electrification)	$1,500	PAC

Finance, Insurance & Real Estate — $65,450

Commercial Banks	$13,650	
Virginia Bankers Assn	$5,000	PAC
Citizens & Southern National Bank	$3,000	PAC
Crestar Financial Corp	$2,500	PAC
Insurance	**$4,300**	
National Assn of Life Underwriters	$1,500	PAC

Contribution Totals by Sector

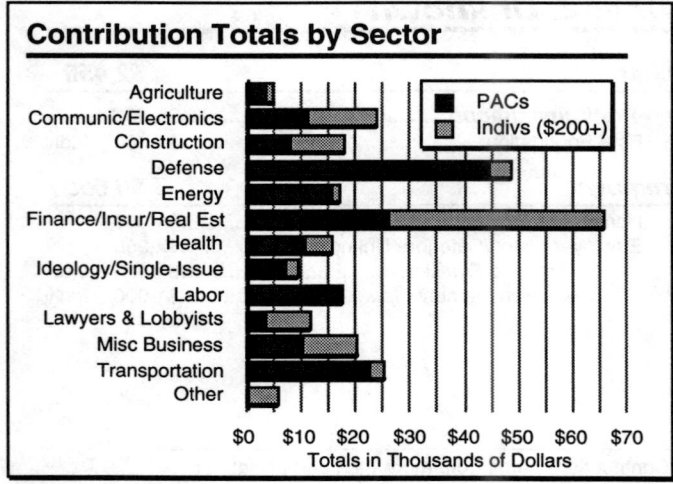

Agriculture, Communic/Electronics, Construction, Defense, Energy, Finance/Insur/Real Est, Health, Ideology/Single-Issue, Labor, Lawyers & Lobbyists, Misc Business, Transportation, Other

Legend: PACs, Indivs ($200+)

$0 $10 $20 $30 $40 $50 $60 $70
Totals in Thousands of Dollars

Real Estate **$40,750**
- Hazel-Peterson Companies .... $8,500 Indiv
- National Assn of Realtors .... $6,250 PAC
- West Group Corp .... $5,250 Indiv
- Clemente Development Co .... $2,000 Indiv
- Doggett Enterprises .... $2,000 Indiv
- Fairlakes Realty .... $2,000 Indiv
- J&R Enterprises .... $2,000 Indiv
- Broyhill Enterprises .... $1,500 Indiv

Accountants **$4,250**
- National Society of Public Accountants .... $1,500 PAC

Misc Finance **$2,000**
- None over $1,500

Health $15,300

Health Professionals **$12,150**
- American Medical Assn .... $5,000 PAC
- American Dental Assn .... $2,500 PAC

Pharmaceuticals/Health Products **$2,900**
- None over $1,500

Lawyers & Lobbyists $11,633

Lawyers & Lobbyists **$11,633**
- Hazel & Thomas .... $2,208 Indiv

Misc Business $19,997

Business Associations **$4,500**
- Greater Washington Board of Trade .... $4,000 PAC

Food & Beverage **$2,050**
- None over $1,500

Business Services **$6,212**
- NRP Inc .... $2,000 Indiv

Chemical & Related Manufacturing **$2,162**
- Ethyl Corp .... $1,500 PAC/Ind

Misc Manufacturing & Distributing **$2,000**
- Xerox Corp .... $1,500 PAC

Transportation $24,800

Air Transport **$10,250**
- Aircraft Owners & Pilots Assn .... $4,500 PAC
- United Parcel Service .... $3,500 PAC

Automotive **$8,300**
- National Auto Dealers Assn .... $5,500 PAC

Trucking **$3,250**
- American Trucking Assns .... $2,000 PAC

Misc Transport **$1,500**
- None over $1,500

Labor

Labor $17,360

Transportation Unions **$8,700**
- Air Line Pilots Assn .... $7,500 PAC

Public Sector Unions **$8,660**
- National Assn Retired Federal Employees .... $5,000 PAC

Ideological/Single-Issue

Ideological/Single-Issue $9,150

Pro-Israel **$7,000**
- National PAC .... $5,000 PAC

Other & Unknown

Other $5,500

Civil Servants/Public Officials **$2,750**
- None over $1,500

Retired **$1,750**
- None over $1,500

Unknown $31,700
- Homemakers/Non-income earners $13,550
- Generic Occupation/Category Unknown $1,750
- Employer Listed/Category Unknown $16,150
  - Vectre Corp .... $2,000 Indiv

Spending in Last 3 Elections

	1988	1990	1992
Wolf	$758,365	$511,853	$431,829
Opponent	$241,445	$93,659	$191,260
Vote Pct	68%	62%	64%

Lynn Woolsey, D-Calif (6)

First elected: 1992

1991-92 Total Receipts: $523,181
1992 Year-end Cash: $3,112

1993-94 Committees & Subcommittees

Budget

Education and Labor
Elementary, Secondary and Vocational Education; Human Resources; Labor-Management Relations

Government Operations
Information, Justice, Transportation and Agriculture

Leading Contributors

Business

Agriculture	$2,375	
Dairy	$1,250	
None over $1,000		

Communications/Electronics	$5,849	
Telephone Utilities	$2,000	
AT&T	$1,000	PAC
Pacific Telesis Group	$1,000	PAC
Computer Equipment & Services	$2,499	
Broderbund Software	$1,499	Indiv

Energy & Natural Resources	$1,750	
Waste Management	$1,000	
Waste Management Inc	$1,000	PAC

Finance, Insurance & Real Estate	$23,700	
Commercial Banks	$9,000	
BankAmerica Corp	$3,500	PAC
American Bankers Assn*	$2,000	PAC
Citizens & Southern National Bank	$1,000	PAC
Exchange Bank	$1,000	Indiv
Wells Fargo	$1,000	PAC
Securities & Investment	$6,450	
Hambrecht & Quist	$1,300	Indiv
Bear, Stearns & Co	$1,250	Indiv
Montgomery Securities Inc	$1,250	Indiv

Source of Funds in 1992 Election

Source	Total	Pct
■ PACs	$187,592	36%
▨ Indivs $200+	$83,202	16%
☐ Indivs under $200	$217,879	41%
▨ Other	$39,482	7%
Candidate	$28,300	5%
Party	$10,124	2%

Source of PAC Dollars by Sector

Source	Total	Pct
■ Business	$36,550	19%
▨ Labor	$98,850	53%
☐ Ideology/Single Issue	$52,341	28%

In-State vs. Out-of-State Contributions*

Source	Total	Pct
☐ In-State	$74,852	91%
■ Out-of-state	$7,650	9%
No state listed	$700	

* by large individual contributors ($200 & above)

Real Estate	$4,600	
National Assn of Realtors	$1,000	PAC
Misc Finance	$2,500	
None over $1,000		

Health	$10,255	
Health Professionals	$5,750	
American Chiropractic Assn	$2,000	PAC
American Nurses Assn	$2,000	PAC
American Optometric Assn	$1,000	PAC
Pharmaceuticals/Health Products	$3,005	
Syntex (USA) Inc	$2,500	PAC

Lawyers & Lobbyists	$22,750	
Lawyers & Lobbyists	$22,750	
Assn of Trial Lawyers of America	$10,000	PAC
Belli & Belli	$1,000	Indiv
Howard, Rice et al	$1,000	Indiv
Mediator & Attorney	$1,000	Indiv

Misc Business	$9,000	
Food & Beverage	$2,000	
None over $1,000		
Beer, Wine & Liquor	$2,150	
Wine Institute	$1,250	PAC
Business Services	$3,100	
None over $1,000		

Contribution Totals by Sector

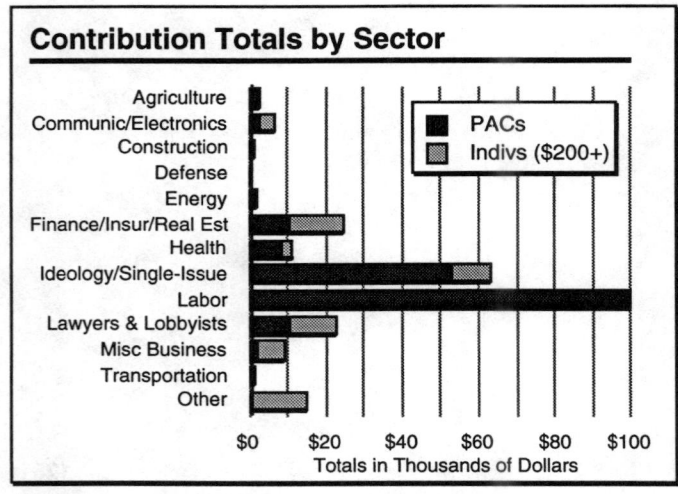

Legend: ■ PACs ▨ Indivs ($200+)

Categories: Agriculture, Communic/Electronics, Construction, Defense, Energy, Finance/Insur/Real Est, Health, Ideology/Single-Issue, Labor, Lawyers & Lobbyists, Misc Business, Transportation, Other

Totals in Thousands of Dollars ($0 $20 $40 $60 $80 $100)

Labor

Labor $98,850

Building Trade Unions **$19,000**
Carpenters & Joiners Union .... $10,000   PAC
Laborers Union* .... $4,000   PAC
Operating Engineers Union* .... $2,000   PAC
Ironworkers Union .... $1,000   PAC
Plumbers/Pipefitters Union .... $1,000   PAC
Sheet Metal Workers Union .... $1,000   PAC

Industrial Unions **$16,100**
Machinists/Aerospace Workers Union .... $5,100   PAC
United Auto Workers .... $5,000   PAC
Intl Brotherhood of Electrical Workers .... $4,000   PAC
Communications Workers of America .... $1,000   PAC
Rubber Cork Linoleum & Plastic Workers .... $1,000   PAC

Transportation Unions **$19,000**
Teamsters Union .... $7,500   PAC
Intl Longshoremen's/Warehousemen's Union ..... $5,000   PAC
Air Line Pilots Assn .... $2,000   PAC
Marine Engineers Union .... $2,000   PAC
Transport Workers Union .... $1,000   PAC

Public Sector Unions **$27,500**
National Education Assn .... $10,000   PAC
American Fedn of St/Cnty/Munic Employees ...... $5,000   PAC
National Assn Retired Federal Employees .... $5,000   PAC
National Assn of Letter Carriers .... $4,500   PAC
American Federation of Teachers .... $1,000   PAC
International Assn of Firefighters .... $1,000   PAC

Misc Unions **$17,250**
Service Employees International Union .... $10,000   PAC
Food & Commercial Workers Union .... $5,000   PAC
AFL-CIO .... $1,000   PAC
Bakery, Confectionery & Tobacco Workers .... $1,000   PAC

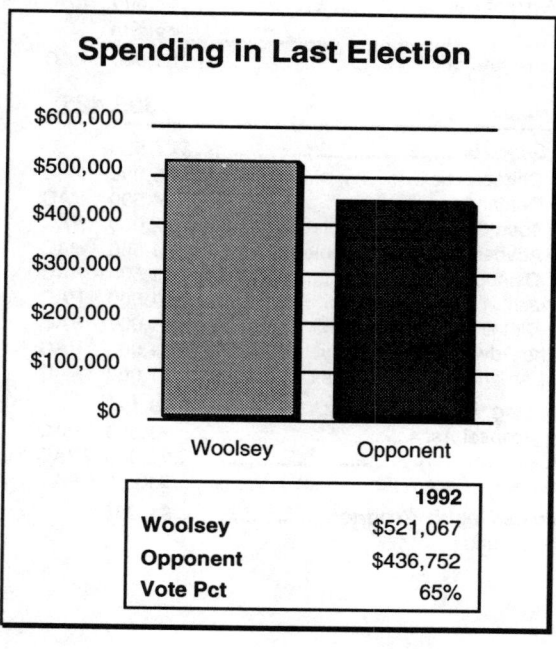

Spending in Last Election

	1992
Woolsey	$521,067
Opponent	$436,752
Vote Pct	65%

Ideological/Single-Issue

Ideological/Single-Issue $62,819

Democratic/Liberal **$4,850**
National Cmte for an Effective Congress .... $2,500   PAC
Hollywood Women's Political Cmte .... $1,000   PAC

Leadership PACs **$6,234**
Effective Government Cmte (Dick Gephardt) ...... $1,954   PAC
AmeriPAC (Steny Hoyer) .... $1,000   PAC
House Leadership Fund (Tom Foley) .... $1,000   PAC
Victory USA (Vic Fazio) .... $1,000   PAC

Pro-Israel **$1,350**
None over $1,000

Pro-Choice **$3,750**
Voters for Choice .... $1,250   PAC/Ind
California Abortion Rights Action League .... $1,000   PAC
National Abortion Rights Action League .... $1,000   PAC

Womens Issues **$36,583**
Emily's List .... $10,493   PAC
Women's Campaign Fund .... $8,500   PAC
National Organization for Women .... $5,562   PAC
National Womens Political Caucus .... $2,500   PAC
Women's Political Committee .... $2,000   PAC
Marin Women's PAC .... $1,250   PAC

Human Rights **$5,773**
Human Rights Campaign Fund .... $4,523   PAC
Bay Area Non-Partisan Alliance .... $1,000   PAC

Misc Issues **$2,950**
National Cmte to Preserve Social Security .... $1,000   PAC

Other & Unknown

Other $14,130

Education **$1,240**
None over $1,000

Retired **$8,900**
None over $1,000

Other **$3,250**
Network Ministries Tenderloin Distr .... $2,000   Indiv

Unknown $18,140

Homemakers/Non-income earners $2,500
No Employer Listed or Found $6,010
Generic Occupation/Category Unknown $1,400
Employer Listed/Category Unknown $8,230
    Codding Enterprises .... $1,150   Indiv
    Compass Associates .... $1,000   Indiv
    Electric Shadow Productions .... $1,000   Indiv

---

* Contributions came from more than one affiliate or subsidiary.

Ron Wyden, D-Ore (3)

First elected: 1980

1991-92 Total Receipts:	$233,749
1992 Year-end Cash:	$328,099

1991-92 Committees & Subcommittees

Energy and Commerce
Health and the Environment; Oversight and Investigations; Telecommunications and Finance

Small Business
Regulation, Business Opportunity and Energy (Chairman)

Select Committee on Aging

Leading Contributors

Business

Agriculture — $7,150

Crop Production & Basic Processing $1,300
    None over $1,000

Agricultural Services/Products $2,500
    American Veterinary Medical Assn .... $2,000   PAC

Food Processing & Sales $1,600
    Safeway Stores .... $1,100   PAC

Forestry & Forest Products $1,750
    None over $1,000

Communications/Electronics — $9,350

Media/Entertainment $3,000
    National Assn of Broadcasters .... $1,000   PAC
    National Cable Television Assn .... $1,000   PAC

Telephone Utilities $3,750
    US West Inc .... $1,000   PAC

Telecom Services & Equipment $1,150
    None over $1,000

Energy & Natural Resources — $7,000

Oil & Gas $1,700
    None over $1,000

Mining $2,600
    Northwest Aluminum Co .... $2,000   Indiv

Electric Utilities $1,700
    Detroit Edison .... $1,000   PAC

Source of Funds in 1992 Election

Source	Total	Pct
■ PACs	$123,675	50%
▨ Indivs $200+	$19,150	8%
□ Indivs under $200	$49,060	20%
⊠ Other	$54,009	22%
Candidate	$0	0%
Party	$12,495	5%

Source of PAC Dollars by Sector

Source	Total	Pct
■ Business	$98,825	80%
▨ Labor	$16,850	14%
□ Ideology/Single Issue	$7,250	6%

In-State vs. Out-of-State Contributions*

Source	Total	Pct
□ In-State	$11,750	66%
■ Out-of-state	$6,150	34%
No state listed	$0	

* by large individual contributors ($200 & above)

Finance, Insurance & Real Estate — $20,850

Commercial Banks $5,800
    US Bancorp .... $3,050   PAC
    Citizens & Southern National Bank .... $1,000   PAC

Securities & Investment $6,500
    Investment Company Institute .... $1,000   PAC
    Morgan Stanley & Co .... $1,000   PAC
    National Venture Capital Assn .... $1,000   PAC
    Prudential Securities .... $1,000   PAC

Insurance $2,450
    None over $1,000

Real Estate $3,600
    National Assn of Realtors .... $3,600   PAC

Accountants $2,500
    American Institute of CPA's .... $1,000   PAC

Health — $35,425

Health Professionals $24,525
    American Chiropractic Assn .... $5,000   PAC
    American Dental Assn .... $4,500   PAC
    American Assn Oral & Maxillofacial Surgeons .... $2,000   PAC
    American Academy of Ophthalmology .... $1,500   PAC
    American Osteopathic Assn .... $1,500   PAC
    National Assn of Pharmacists .... $1,500   PAC
    American Dietetic Assn .... $1,000   PAC
    Assn for the Advancement of Psychology .... $1,000   PAC
    College of American Pathologists .... $1,000   PAC

Hospitals/Nursing Homes $8,100
    American Hospital Assn .... $3,500   PAC
    Manor Healthcare Corp .... $2,000   PAC
    American Health Care Assn .... $1,250   PAC

Pharmaceuticals/Health Products $1,500
    None over $1,000

Contribution Totals by Sector

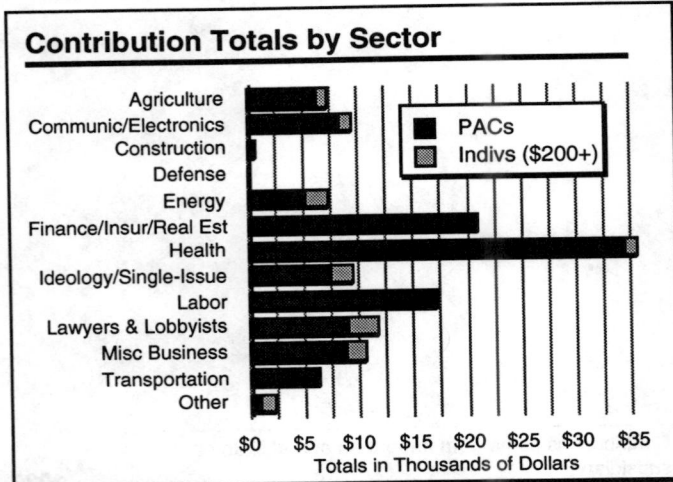

Agriculture, Communic/Electronics, Construction, Defense, Energy, Finance/Insur/Real Est, Health, Ideology/Single-Issue, Labor, Lawyers & Lobbyists, Misc Business, Transportation, Other

■ PACs   ▨ Indivs ($200+)

$0 $5 $10 $15 $20 $25 $30 $35
Totals in Thousands of Dollars

Lawyers & Lobbyists $11,650

Lawyers & Lobbyists *$11,650*
    Assn of Trial Lawyers of America .... $5,500   PAC
    Schwabe, Williamson & Wyatt .... $2,000   Indiv

Misc Business $10,450

Beer, Wine & Liquor *$4,000*
    National Beer Wholesalers Assn .... $1,500   PAC
    Coast Distributing Co .... $1,000   Indiv
    Joseph E Seagram & Sons .... $1,000   PAC

Retail Sales *$2,250*
    None over $1,000

Misc Manufacturing & Distributing *$3,050*
    Corning Glass Works .... $1,000   PAC

Transportation $6,200

Air Transport *$2,200*
    United Parcel Service .... $1,000   PAC

Automotive *$1,500*
    Americans for Free International Trade .... $1,000   PAC

Railroads *$1,000*
    None over $1,000

Sea Transport *$1,500*
    Southwest Marine .... $1,000   PAC

Labor

Labor $16,850

Building Trade Unions *$1,000*
    None over $1,000

Industrial Unions *$2,750*
    United Auto Workers .... $1,500   PAC
    United Steelworkers .... $1,000   PAC

Transportation Unions *$5,000*
    Teamsters Union .... $2,500   PAC
    Marine Engineers Dist 2 Maritime Officers .... $1,000   PAC
    United Transportation Union .... $1,000   PAC

Public Sector Unions *$6,000*
    National Assn of Letter Carriers .... $2,000   PAC
    National Education Assn* .... $1,500   PAC
    American Fedn of St/Cnty/Munic Employees ...... $1,000   PAC

Misc Unions *$2,100*
    Food & Commercial Workers Union .... $1,500   PAC

Ideological/Single-Issue

Ideological/Single-Issue $9,250

Pro-Israel *$3,500*
    None over $1,000

Pro-Choice *$1,500*
    National Abortion Rights Action League .... $1,500   PAC

Human Rights *$2,750*
    Human Rights Campaign Fund .... $1,000   PAC
    KidsPAC .... $1,000   PAC

Misc Issues *$1,500*
    National Cmte to Preserve Social Security .... $1,500   PAC

Other & Unknown

Other $3,000

Non-Profit Institutions *$2,000*
    Foundation for Hearing Aid Research .... $2,000   Indiv

Unknown $3,400
    Homemakers/Non-income earners $1,000
    Generic Occupation/Category Unknown $1,000
    Employer Listed/Category Unknown $1,900
    Natures Food .... $1,000   Indiv

Spending in Last 3 Elections

	1988	1990	1992
Wyden	$287,996	$693,855	$357,402
Opponent	$0	$4,436	$6,656
Vote Pct	99%	81%	77%

* Contributions came from more than one affiliate or subsidiary.

Albert R. Wynn, D-Md (4)

First elected: 1992

1991-92 Total Receipts: $565,665
1992 Year-end Cash: $185,179

1993-94 Committees & Subcommittees

Banking, Finance and Urban Affairs
Consumer Credit and Insurance; Housing and Community Development

Foreign Affairs
Economic Policy, Trade and Environment; Western Hemisphere Affairs

Post Office and Civil Service
Census, Statistics and Postal Personnel

Leading Contributors

Business

Agriculture $7,500

Tobacco	*$5,000*	
RJR Nabisco	$3,000	PAC
Food Processing & Sales	*$1,500*	
None over $1,500		

Communications/Electronics $6,200

Telephone Utilities	*$3,000*	
None over $1,500		
Computer Equipment & Services	*$2,000*	
MCSI Technologies	$2,000	Indiv

Construction $4,650

General Contractors	*$4,200*	
Potomac Development Corp	$2,000	Indiv

Energy & Natural Resources $5,575

Oil & Gas	*$2,925*	
Washington Gas Light Co	$1,500	PAC
Electric Utilities	*$2,000*	
None over $1,500		

Finance, Insurance & Real Estate $36,050

Commercial Banks	*$13,250*	
American Bankers Assn	$6,000	PAC
MNC Financial Inc	$2,000	PAC
Mercantile Bankshares Corp	$2,000	PAC

Source of Funds in 1992 Election

Source	Total	Pct
■ PACs	$233,377	41%
▨ Indivs $200+	$122,736	21%
☐ Indivs under $200	$57,527	10%
▧ Other	$159,132	28%
Candidate	$140,000	24%
Party	$12,557	2%

Source of PAC Dollars by Sector

Source	Total	Pct
■ Business	$91,125	36%
▨ Labor	$133,650	53%
☐ Ideology/Single Issue	$25,308	10%

In-State vs. Out-of-State Contributions*

Source	Total	Pct
☐ In-State	$101,886	83%
■ Out-of-state	$20,400	17%
No state listed	$450	

* by large individual contributors ($200 & above)

Insurance	*$3,050*	
National Assn of Life Underwriters	$1,500	PAC
Real Estate	*$17,750*	
National Assn of Realtors	$10,000	PAC
Mortgage Bankers Assn of America	$1,500	PAC

Health $36,000

Health Professionals	*$26,600*	
American Medical Assn*	$8,500	PAC
American Academy of Ophthalmology	$4,000	PAC
American Chiropractic Assn	$2,000	PAC
American College of Emergency Physicians	$2,000	PAC
American Dental Assn	$2,000	PAC
Hospitals/Nursing Homes	*$6,000*	
Manor Healthcare Corp	$3,500	Indiv
American Hospital Assn	$2,000	PAC
Health Services	*$1,900*	
None over $1,500		

Lawyers & Lobbyists $35,750

Lawyers & Lobbyists	*$35,750*	
Assn of Trial Lawyers of America	$10,000	PAC
Gallagher, Evelius & Jones	$2,500	Indiv
Denny Miller Associates	$2,000	Indiv

Misc Business $9,400

Business Associations	*$3,000*	
Greater Washington Board of Trade	$3,000	PAC
Retail Sales	*$2,500*	
None over $1,500		

Transportation $4,700

Automotive	*$4,450*	
National Auto Dealers Assn	$4,000	PAC

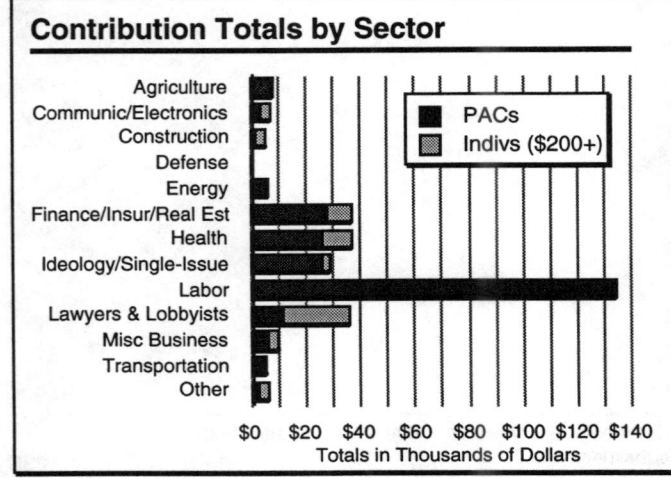

Contribution Totals by Sector

Agriculture
Communic/Electronics
Construction
Defense
Energy
Finance/Insur/Real Est
Health
Ideology/Single-Issue
Labor
Lawyers & Lobbyists
Misc Business
Transportation
Other

■ PACs
▨ Indivs ($200+)

$0 $20 $40 $60 $80 $100 $120 $140
Totals in Thousands of Dollars

Labor

Labor	$133,650	
Building Trade Unions **$26,250**		
Carpenters & Joiners Union $7,500	PAC	
Sheet Metal Workers Union $4,500	PAC	
Plumbers/Pipefitters Union $4,000	PAC	
Baltimore Bldg & Constr Trades Council $3,500	PAC	
Bricklayers Union $2,000	PAC	
Laborers' Political League $2,000	PAC	
Operating Engineers Union* $1,750	PAC	
Industrial Unions **$34,500**		
Machinists/Aerospace Workers Union $10,000	PAC	
United Auto Workers $7,500	PAC	
Communications Workers of America $6,500	PAC	
United Steelworkers $5,000	PAC	
Intl Brotherhood of Electrical Workers $3,500	PAC	
Transportation Unions **$22,400**		
Teamsters Union $10,000	PAC	
Air Line Pilots Assn $5,000	PAC	
Amalgamated Transit Union $4,550	PAC	
Public Sector Unions **$39,500**		
American Fedn of St/Cnty/Munic Employees $10,000	PAC	
National Education Assn $10,000	PAC	
National Assn of Letter Carriers $5,500	PAC	
American Federation of Teachers $5,000	PAC	
American Postal Workers Union $3,500	PAC	
National Assn Retired Federal Employees $2,000	PAC	
International Assn of Firefighters $1,500	PAC	
Misc Unions **$11,000**		
Food & Commercial Workers Union $6,600	PAC	
Bakery, Confectionery & Tobacco Workers $2,000	PAC	

Ideological/Single-Issue

Ideological/Single-Issue	$28,408	
Democratic/Liberal **$2,558**		
National Cmte for an Effective Congress $2,500	PAC	
Leadership PACs **$5,000**		
House Leadership Fund (Tom Foley) $2,000	PAC	
Pro-Israel **$9,300**		
National PAC $5,000	PAC	
Pro-Choice **$3,800**		
Voters for Choice $2,500	PAC	
Human Rights **$4,250**		
Human Rights Campaign Fund $2,500	PAC	
Filipino PAC $1,750	PAC	
Misc Issues **$2,500**		
Sierra Club $2,000	PAC	

Other & Unknown

Other	$5,600
Civil Servants/Public Officials **$3,350**	
None over $1,500	

Unknown	$60,336	
No Employer Listed or Found $43,186		
Generic Occupation/Category Unknown $1,500		
Employer Listed/Category Unknown $15,650		
Classics $2,250	Indiv	
Night Life Enterprises $2,000	Indiv	

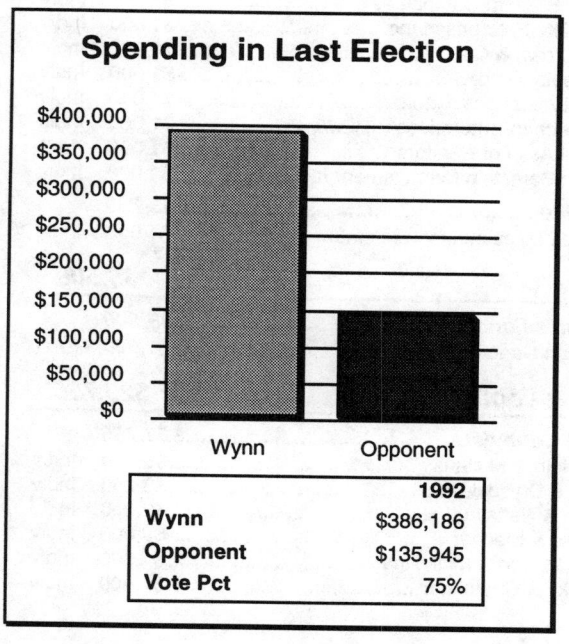

Spending in Last Election

	1992
Wynn	$386,186
Opponent	$135,945
Vote Pct	75%

* Contributions came from more than one affiliate or subsidiary.

1237

Sidney R. Yates, D-Ill (9)

First elected: 1948
1991-92 Total Receipts: $227,671
1992 Year-end Cash: $52,684

1991-92 Committees & Subcommittees

Appropriations
Foreign Operations, Export Financing and Related Programs; Interior and Related Agencies (Chairman)

Leading Contributors

Business

Agriculture $1,000

Agricultural Services/Products $1,000
   None over $1,000

Communications/Electronics $11,250

Printing & Publishing $5,250
   Cornhusker Printing .... $2,000   Indiv
   Adler & Adler Publishing .... $1,500   Indiv
   Chas Levy Co .... $1,000   Indiv
Media/Entertainment $5,000
   American Symphony Orchestra League .... $1,000   Indiv

Construction $2,750

Home Builders $1,000
   Holladay Corp .... $1,000   Indiv
Construction Services $1,000
   None over $1,000

Defense $1,000

Defense Aerospace $1,000
   None over $1,000

Energy & Natural Resources $3,100

Misc Energy $1,750
   Energy Research Corp .... $1,000   PAC
Waste Management $1,000
   Waste Management Inc .... $1,000   PAC

Source of Funds in 1992 Election

Source	Total	Pct
PACs	$34,350	15%
Indivs $200+	$157,150	69%
Indivs under $200	$33,448	15%
Other	$2,860	1%
Candidate	$0	0%
Party	$287	0%

Source of PAC Dollars by Sector

Source	Total	Pct
Business	$10,100	32%
Labor	$14,250	45%
Ideology/Single Issue	$7,500	24%

In-State vs. Out-of-State Contributions*

Source	Total	Pct
In-State	$25,700	16%
Out-of-state	$131,350	84%
No state listed	$0	

* by large individual contributors ($200 & above)

Finance, Insurance & Real Estate $42,200

Commercial Banks $1,000
   None over $1,000
Securities & Investment $6,150
   James D Wolfensohn Inc .... $1,500   Indiv
   Chicago Board of Trade .... $1,000   Indiv
Insurance $1,000
   None over $1,000
Real Estate $29,800
   Tower Companies .... $12,000   Indiv
   Lerner Companies .... $5,000   Indiv
   Westbrook Development Co .... $1,500   Indiv
   Charles E Smith Companies .... $1,000   Indiv
   Forest City Enterprises Inc .... $1,000   Indiv
   Henry Crown & Co .... $1,000   Indiv
   JMB Realty Corp .... $1,000   Indiv
   Lerner Enterprises .... $1,000   Indiv
   Miles Lerman Enterprises .... $1,000   Indiv
   National Assn of Realtors .... $1,000   PAC
   Norman Bernstein Management Inc .... $1,000   Indiv
Misc Finance $3,750
   Klutznick Investments .... $1,000   Indiv

Health $5,500

Health Professionals $5,500
   American Dental Assn .... $2,000   PAC

Lawyers & Lobbyists $23,750

Lawyers & Lobbyists $23,750
   Silverstein & Mullens .... $5,000   Indiv
   Caplin & Drysdale .... $3,000   Indiv
   Koteen & Naftalin .... $2,000   Indiv
   Linowes & Blocher .... $2,000   Indiv
   Burke, Wilson & McIlvaine .... $1,000   Indiv
   Sonosky & Chernikoff .... $1,000   Indiv

Contribution Totals by Sector

Legend: PACs; Indivs ($200+)

Agriculture
Communic/Electronics
Construction
Defense
Energy
Finance/Insur/Real Est
Health
Ideology/Single-Issue
Labor
Lawyers & Lobbyists
Misc Business
Transportation
Other

$0 $5 $10 $15 $20 $25 $30 $35 $40 $45
Totals in Thousands of Dollars

Misc Business — $9,550

Retail Sales $1,050
    None over $1,000
Business Services $5,500
    Wyse Advertising Inc .... $2,000   Indiv
Misc Manufacturing & Distributing $1,500
    Miltec Corp .... $1,000   Indiv

Transportation — $0

Automotive $1,500
    Warshawsky & Co/JC Whitney & Co ..... $1,000   PAC
Railroads $1,000
    Midland Manufacturing Corp .... $1,000   Indiv

Labor

Labor — $14,250

Building Trade Unions $1,500
    Laborers' Political League .... $2,000   PAC
Public Sector Unions $11,500
    National Education Assn .... $6,500   PAC
    National Assn of Letter Carriers .... $2,000   PAC
    American Fedn of St/Cnty/Munic Employees ..... $1,000   PAC
    American Postal Workers Union .... $1,000   PAC
    National Assn Retired Federal Employees ..... $1,000   PAC

Ideological/Single-Issue

Ideological/Single-Issue — $30,250

Pro-Israel $18,750
    San Franciscans for Good Government ..... $2,500   PAC
Womens Issues $2,800
    None over $1,000
Human Rights $6,250
    KidsPAC .... $2,000   PAC
    Human Rights Campaign Fund .... $1,000   PAC
    Mille Lacs Band of Ojibwe .... $1,000   Indiv
Misc Issues $2,250
    National Cmte to Preserve Social Security ..... $1,000   PAC

Other & Unknown

Other — $22,300

Non-Profit Institutions $11,550
    Smithsonian Institution .... $2,250   Indiv
    Blum-Kovler Foundation .... $1,000   Indiv
    Phillips Collection .... $1,000   Indiv
Civil Servants/Public Officials $1,500
    Cook County Circuit Court .... $1,000   Indiv
Education $1,450
    None over $1,000
Retired $5,800
    None over $1,000
Other $2,000
    None over $1,000

Unknown — $22,264

    Homemakers/Non-income earners $1,250
    Employer Listed/Category Unknown $20,300
        Hieronimus & Co .... $2,500   Indiv
        MICI .... $2,000   Indiv
        Natl Inst for Conserv of Cultural Propty ..... $2,000   Indiv
        Bauman Foundation .... $1,500   Indiv
        Cheyenne Corp .... $1,000   Indiv
        Woodrow Wilson Center .... $1,000   Indiv

Spending in Last 3 Elections

	1988	1990	1992
Yates	$122,900	$839,106	$228,812
Opponent	$36,837	$15,164	$12,599
Vote Pct	66%	71%	68%

C. W. Bill Young, R-Fla (10)

First elected: 1970

1991-92 Total Receipts: $274,122
1992 Year-end Cash: $156,032

1991-92 Committees & Subcommittees

Appropriations
Defense; Labor, Health and Human Services, Education and Related Agencies

Select Committee on Intelligence

Leading Contributors

Business

Agriculture	$6,300	
Crop Production & Basic Processing	**$1,000**	
Florida Citrus Mutual	$1,000	PAC
Agricultural Services/Products	**$1,300**	
American Veterinary Medical Assn	$1,000	PAC
Food Processing & Sales	**$3,500**	
Winn-Dixie Stores	$2,000	PAC
Food Marketing Institute	$1,000	PAC

Communications/Electronics	$2,250	
Computer Equipment & Services	**$1,750**	
EDO Corp	$1,250	Indiv

Construction	$8,000	
General Contractors	**$3,500**	
National Utility Contractors Assn	$1,500	PAC
Associated General Contractors	$1,000	PAC
Home Builders	**$3,000**	
National Assn of Home Builders	$1,500	PAC
Walter Industries	$1,000	PAC
Building Materials & Equipment	**$1,500**	
Jim Walter Corp	$1,500	PAC

Source of Funds in 1992 Election

Source	Total	Pct
■ PACs	$165,250	60%
▨ Indivs $200+	$30,650	11%
☐ Indivs under $200	$32,799	12%
▨ Other	$45,423	17%
Candidate	$0	0%
Party	$5,000	2%

Source of PAC Dollars by Sector

Source	Total	Pct
■ Business	$170,900	97%
▨ Labor	$2,350	1%
☐ Ideology/Single Issue	$2,250	1%

In-State vs. Out-of-State Contributions*

Source	Total	Pct
☐ In-State	$20,800	69%
■ Out-of-state	$9,350	31%
No state listed	$0	

* by large individual contributors ($200 & above)

Defense — $91,250

Defense Aerospace	$47,750	
Textron Inc	$7,000	PAC
Martin Marietta Corp	$5,250	PAC
General Electric	$5,000	PAC
Gencorp Inc	$4,500	PAC
Northrop Corp	$4,000	PAC
Lockheed Corp	$3,500	PAC
McDonnell Douglas*	$3,500	PAC
Boeing Co	$3,000	PAC
Grumman Corp	$3,000	PAC
Rockwell International	$3,000	PAC
LTV Aerospace & Defense Co	$1,500	PAC
United Technologies	$1,500	PAC
General Dynamics	$1,000	PAC
Hercules Inc	$1,000	PAC
Defense Electronics	**$35,000**	
E-Systems Inc	$10,000	PAC
TRW Inc	$4,000	PAC
Hughes Aircraft	$3,500	PAC
AT&T	$3,000	PAC
GTE Corp	$2,000	PAC
Harris Corp	$2,000	PAC
Loral Corp	$1,500	PAC
Raytheon	$1,500	PAC
Cubic Corp	$1,000	PAC
Honeywell*	$1,000	PAC
Texas Instruments	$1,000	PAC
Westinghouse Electric	$1,000	PAC
Misc Defense	***$8,500***	
General Atomics	$3,000	PAC
Alliant Techsystems Inc	$1,000	PAC
BDM International	$1,000	PAC
Olin Corp	$1,000	PAC
Tenneco Inc	$1,000	PAC

Contribution Totals by Sector

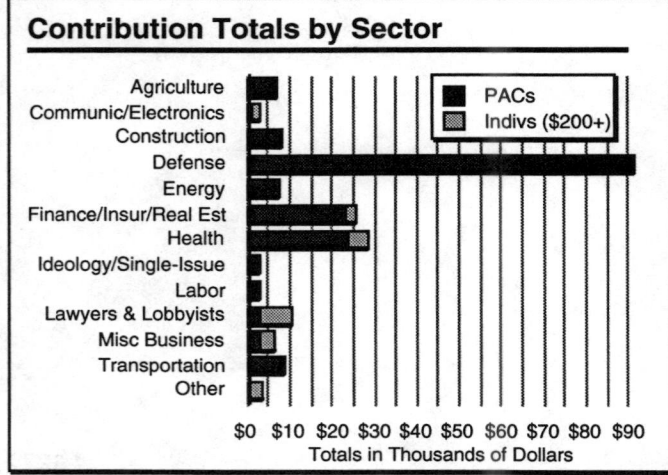

Agriculture
Communic/Electronics
Construction
Defense
Energy
Finance/Insur/Real Est
Health
Ideology/Single-Issue
Labor
Lawyers & Lobbyists
Misc Business
Transportation
Other

■ PACs
▨ Indivs ($200+)

$0 $10 $20 $30 $40 $50 $60 $70 $80 $90
Totals in Thousands of Dollars

Energy & Natural Resources — $7,050

Oil & Gas **$1,500**
    Louisiana Land & Exploration ....$1,000 PAC
Electric Utilities **$4,550**
    Florida Power Corp ....$2,000 PAC
    Florida Power & Light ....$1,500 PAC

Finance, Insurance & Real Estate — $26,500

Commercial Banks **$4,000**
    Citizens & Southern National Bank ....$3,500 PAC
Securities & Investment **$1,500**
    None over $1,000
Insurance **$4,750**
    Blue Cross & Blue Shield Assn* ....$2,500 PAC
    Frank B Hall & Co ....$1,000 Indiv
Real Estate **$16,000**
    National Assn of Realtors ....$15,000 PAC
    First Union Corp ....$1,000 PAC

Health — $28,100

Health Professionals **$22,350**
    American Medical Assn ....$10,000 PAC
    American Dental Assn ....$5,000 PAC
    American Academy of Ophthalmology ....$2,500 PAC
    American Chiropractic Assn ....$2,000 PAC
    American Optometric Assn ....$1,000 PAC
Hospitals/Nursing Homes **$3,250**
    Southern Management Services ....$2,000 Indiv
    American Health Care Assn ....$1,000 PAC
Health Services **$1,000**
    Qual-Med Inc ....$1,000 Indiv
Misc Health **$1,500**
    Tri-City Medical Products ....$1,500 Indiv

Lawyers & Lobbyists — $9,950

Lawyers & Lobbyists **$9,950**
    Florida Business Associates ....$1,000 Indiv
    Hand, Arendall et al ....$1,000 Indiv
    Holland & Knight ....$1,000 PAC
    Yerrid, Knopik & Valenzuela ....$1,000 Indiv

Misc Business — $5,850

Beer, Wine & Liquor **$1,500**
    National Beer Wholesalers Assn ....$1,500 PAC
Misc Manufacturing & Distributing **$1,500**
    Danka Industries ....$1,000 Indiv

Transportation — $8,500

Automotive **$6,500**
    National Auto Dealers Assn ....$4,500 PAC
    Americans for Free International Trade ....$2,000 PAC
Sea Transport **$1,000**
    None over $1,000

Labor

Labor — $2,350

Public Sector Unions **$2,350**
    National Assn Retired Federal Employees ....$2,000 PAC

Ideological/Single-Issue

Ideological/Single-Issue — $2,250

Human Rights **$1,000**
    KidsPAC ....$1,000 PAC
Misc Issues **$1,000**
    National Cmte to Preserve Social Security ....$1,000 PAC

Other & Unknown

Other — $3,200

Education **$1,000**
    None over $1,000
Retired **$2,200**
    None over $1,000

Unknown — $5,600

    Homemakers/Non-income earners $1,000
    Employer Listed/Category Unknown $4,100
      None over $1,000

Independent expenditures supporting Young
    National Right to Life PAC $3,747

Spending in Last 3 Elections

	1988	1990	1992
Young	$208,320	$201,188	$459,861
Opponent	$23,655	$0	$201,333
Vote Pct	73%	100%	57%

---

* Contributions came from more than one affiliate or subsidiary.

Don Young, R-Alaska (1)

First elected: 1973
1991-92 Total Receipts: $867,848
1992 Year-end Cash: -$94

1991-92 Committees & Subcommittees

Interior and Insular Affairs (Ranking Republican)
Water, Power and Offshore Energy

Merchant Marine and Fisheries
Coast Guard and Navigation; Fisheries and Wildlife Conservation and the Environment (Ranking Republican)

Post Office and Civil Service
Postal Operations and Services; Postal Personnel and Modernization (Ranking Republican)

Leading Contributors

Business

Agriculture		$44,531
Crop Production & Basic Processing **$6,475**		
None over $2,500		
Tobacco **$3,500**		
None over $2,500		
Livestock **$2,600**		
None over $2,500		
Agricultural Services/Products **$2,700**		
None over $2,500		
Food Processing & Sales **$7,250**		
Winn-Dixie Stores $3,500	PAC	
Forestry & Forest Products **$20,506**		
Klukwan Forest Products $2,956	Indiv	

Communications/Electronics		$25,100
Media/Entertainment **$3,450**		
None over $2,500		
Telephone Utilities **$14,000**		
GCI $8,000	Indiv	
Alascom Inc $2,500	Indiv	
Telecom Services & Equipment **$5,250**		
Pacific Telecom Inc $5,250	Indiv	

Source of Funds in 1992 Election

Source	Total	Pct
■ PACs	$376,835	40%
▨ Indivs $200+	$319,142	34%
□ Indivs under $200	$134,452	14%
▨ Other	$102,062	11%
Candidate	$0	0%
Party	$80,443	9%

Source of PAC Dollars by Sector

Source	Total	Pct
■ Business	$265,895	74%
▨ Labor	$61,242	17%
□ Ideology/Single Issue	$34,350	10%

In-State vs. Out-of-State Contributions*

Source	Total	Pct
□ In-State	$209,492	66%
■ Out-of-state	$109,150	34%
No state listed	-$250	

* by large individual contributors ($200 & above)

Construction		$38,550
General Contractors **$28,250**		
Alaska Interstate Construction $8,000	Indiv	
Fluor Corp $4,350	PAC	
Associated General Contractors $2,500	PAC	
Special Trade Contractors **$3,950**		
None over $2,500		
Construction Services **$4,950**		
None over $2,500		

Defense		$8,000
Defense Aerospace **$6,500**		
None over $2,500		

Energy & Natural Resources		$181,497
Oil & Gas **$118,495**		
Veco International Inc $27,790	Indiv	
Atlantic Richfield $14,950	PAC/Ind	
Exxon Corp $10,500	PAC/Ind	
BP America $6,450	PAC/Ind	
Chevron Corp $5,500	PAC	
Western Pioneer Inc $4,500	Indiv	
Mapco Inc $3,750	PAC	
Halliburton Co $3,000	PAC	
Petro Star Inc $2,500	Indiv	
Shell Oil $2,500	PAC	
Mining **$14,400**		
National Coal Assn $4,500	PAC	
Misc Energy **$2,500**		
Babcock & Wilcox* $2,500	PAC	
Electric Utilities **$18,350**		
None over $2,500		
Commercial Fishing **$23,602**		
Trident Seafoods Corp $4,500	Indiv	
Commercial Fishing $3,550	Indiv	
National Fisheries Institute $3,000	PAC	

Contribution Totals by Sector

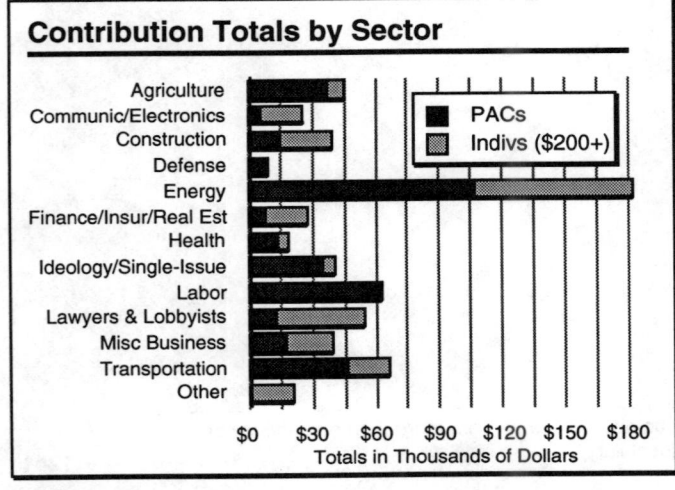

Agriculture
Communic/Electronics
Construction
Defense
Energy
Finance/Insur/Real Est
Health
Ideology/Single-Issue
Labor
Lawyers & Lobbyists
Misc Business
Transportation
Other

■ PACs
▨ Indivs ($200+)

$0 $30 $60 $90 $120 $150 $180
Totals in Thousands of Dollars

Finance, Insurance & Real Estate — $28,200

Commercial Banks $2,950
  None over $2,500

Insurance $4,450
  None over $2,500

Real Estate $15,350
  Cook Inlet Region Inc .... $5,950   Indiv
  Koniag Inc .... $3,900   Indiv

Accountants $2,950
  None over $2,500

Health — $17,400

Health Professionals $15,900
  American Medical Assn* .... $8,200   PAC

Lawyers & Lobbyists — $53,055

Lawyers & Lobbyists $53,055
  Robertson, Monagle & Eastaugh .... $4,900   Indiv
  Dyer, Ellis et al .... $4,075   Indiv
  Hopkins & Sutter .... $3,000   PAC/Ind
  Van Ness, Feldman et al .... $3,000   PAC/Ind

Misc Business — $38,215

Food & Beverage $5,865
  None over $2,500

Retail Sales $5,450
  None over $2,500

Business Services $8,200
  Porcaro Blankenship Advertising .... $2,750   Indiv

Lodging/Tourism $4,900
  None over $2,500

Misc Manufacturing & Distributing $7,500
  None over $2,500

Transportation — $65,250

Air Transport $13,800
  Federal Express Corp .... $3,000   PAC
  Alaska Airlines .... $2,500   PAC

Automotive $7,250
  National Auto Dealers Assn .... $3,000   PAC

Trucking $5,450
  Lynden Transport Inc .... $3,500   Indiv

Railroads $4,000
  Union Pacific Corp .... $3,000   PAC

Sea Transport $33,750
  CSX Corp* .... $7,500   PAC
  Crowley Maritime .... $3,000   PAC
  Totem Ocean Trailer Express .... $3,000   PAC
  American Pilots Assn .... $2,500   PAC

Labor

Labor — $61,692

Building Trade Unions $6,100
  Carpenters & Joiners Union .... $2,750   PAC

Transportation Unions $32,050
  Seafarers International Union* .... $10,600   PAC
  Marine Engineers Union* .... $8,000   PAC
  Teamsters Union* .... $6,450   PAC
  Air Line Pilots Assn .... $6,000   PAC

Public Sector Unions $21,500
  National Assn of Letter Carriers .... $7,000   PAC
  National Assn Retired Federal Employees ...... $4,000   PAC
  American Postal Workers Union .... $3,000   PAC
  National Assn of Postmasters .... $2,500   PAC

Ideological/Single-Issue

Ideological/Single-Issue — $39,350

Leadership PACs $5,950
  Campaign America (Bob Dole) .... $5,000   PAC

Pro-Israel $5,450
  None over $2,500

Gun Rights/Gun Control $17,850
  National Rifle Assn .... $14,850   PAC
  Safari Club International .... $3,000   PAC

Misc Issues $4,500
  National Cmte to Preserve Social Security ...... $3,500   PAC

Other & Unknown

Other — $19,950

Civil Servants/Public Officials $6,050
  None over $2,500

Retired $7,700
  None over $2,500

Other $4,500
  Arctic Slope Regional Corp .... $4,500   Indiv

Unknown — $59,089

  Homemakers/Non-income earners $3,750
  No Employer Listed or Found $5,300
  Employer Listed/Category Unknown $49,039
    None over $2,500

Independent expenditures supporting Young
  National Right to Life PAC $8,057

Independent expenditures opposing Young
  Public Citizen $6,900

Spending in Last 3 Elections

	1988	1990	1992
Young	$626,377	$564,759	$873,486
Opponent	$402,477	$164,732	$438,110
Vote Pct	63%	52%	47%

* Contributions came from more than one affiliate or subsidiary.

Bill Zeliff, R-NH (1)

First elected: 1990

1991-92 Total Receipts: $762,283
1992 Year-end Cash: $2,691

1991-92 Committees & Subcommittees

Government Operations
Commerce, Consumer and Monetary Affairs; Human Resources and Intergovernmental Relations

Public Works and Transportation
Surface Transportation; Water Resources

Small Business
Environment and Employment; Procurement, Tourism and Rural Development

Leading Contributors

Business

Agriculture		$31,850	
Tobacco		**$5,500**	
RJR Nabisco	$2,500		PAC
Philip Morris	$2,000		PAC
Agricultural Services/Products		**$5,500**	
Veterinarian	$3,000		Indiv
Food Processing & Sales		**$11,450**	
Food Marketing Institute	$2,500		PAC
Granite State Packing Co	$2,500		Indiv
Pepsico Inc	$2,000		PAC
Forestry & Forest Products		**$8,400**	
JD Cahill Co	$5,500		Indiv

Communications/Electronics		$44,640	
Printing & Publishing		**$2,500**	
Penmor Lithographers	$2,000		Indiv
Telephone Utilities		**$10,450**	
NYNEX Corp*	$5,000		PAC
Computer Equipment & Services		**$28,940**	
Cabletron Systems Inc	$28,940		Indiv

Construction		$35,730	
General Contractors		**$15,200**	
Speedway Inc	$5,000		Indiv
Associated General Contractors	$2,500		PAC
HJ Stabile & Son	$2,500		Indiv
Home Builders		**$5,930**	
National Assn of Home Builders	$4,500		PAC

Source of Funds in 1992 Election

Source	Total	Pct
■ PACs	$324,915	41%
▨ Indivs $200+	$311,417	39%
□ Indivs under $200	$104,335	13%
▨ Other	$60,136	8%
Candidate	$0	0%
Party	$53,421	7%

Source of PAC Dollars by Sector

Source	Total	Pct
■ Business	$284,267	91%
▨ Labor	$3,000	1%
□ Ideology/Single Issue	$24,450	8%

In-State vs. Out-of-State Contributions*

Source	Total	Pct
□ In-State	$222,238	72%
■ Out-of-state	$87,399	28%
No state listed	$200	

* by large individual contributors ($200 & above)

Special Trade Contractors		$8,400	
Sheet Metal/Air Conditioning Contractors	$4,000		PAC
National Electrical Contractors Assn	$2,000		PAC
Construction Services		**$2,500**	
None over $2,000			
Building Materials & Equipment		**$3,700**	
None over $2,000			

Defense		$15,000	
Defense Aerospace		**$7,500**	
Lockheed Corp	$4,000		PAC
Textron Inc	$2,000		PAC
Defense Electronics		**$6,500**	
Raytheon	$6,000		PAC

Energy & Natural Resources		$28,115	
Oil & Gas		**$6,150**	
None over $2,000			
Electric Utilities		**$12,915**	
None over $2,000			
Waste Management		**$6,100**	
Waste Management Inc*	$6,100		PAC

Finance, Insurance & Real Estate		$101,772	
Commercial Banks		**$8,580**	
First New Hampshire Banks	$3,630		Indiv
Securities & Investment		**$4,750**	
None over $2,000			
Insurance		**$43,142**	
Chubb Corp	$7,000		PAC
Liberty Mutual Insurance	$5,200		Indiv
National Assn of Life Underwriters	$5,000		PAC
American International Group Inc	$4,352		PAC
New England Mutual Life	$2,500		PAC
Independent Insurance Agents of America	$2,200		PAC
ITT Corp*	$2,000		PAC

Contribution Totals by Sector

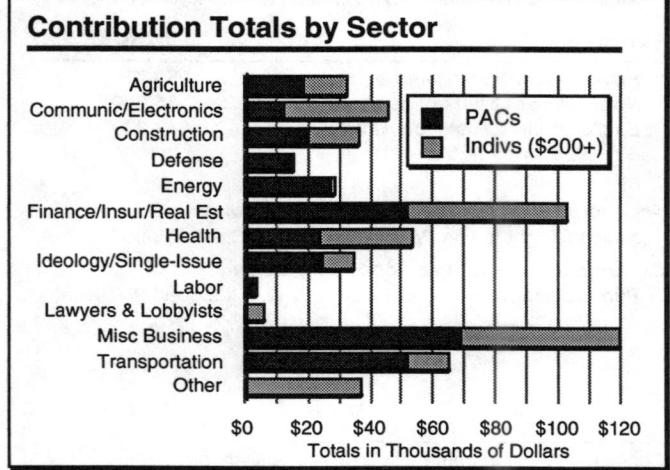

Agriculture
Communic/Electronics
Construction
Defense
Energy
Finance/Insur/Real Est
Health
Ideology/Single-Issue
Labor
Lawyers & Lobbyists
Misc Business
Transportation
Other

■ PACs
▨ Indivs ($200+)

$0 $20 $40 $60 $80 $100 $120
Totals in Thousands of Dollars

Real Estate	$42,050	
National Assn of Realtors	$10,000	PAC
Tare & Foss Realtors	$4,000	Indiv
Leland Properties	$3,500	Indiv
Tinkham Realty	$2,500	Indiv
Tamposi Co	$2,440	Indiv
Savory Square Realty	$2,100	Indiv

Health — $53,010

Health Professionals	$25,860	
American Medical Assn	$10,000	PAC
American Dental Assn	$6,500	PAC
American Academy of Ophthalmology	$2,500	PAC
Hospitals/Nursing Homes	$12,050	
McKerley Management Services	$5,550	Indiv
American Hospital Assn	$2,000	PAC
Supt Residential Care Facility	$2,000	Indiv
Pharmaceuticals/Health Products	$13,000	
Henley Group Inc	$12,500	Indiv

Lawyers & Lobbyists — $5,600

Lawyers & Lobbyists	$5,600	
Rath, Young et al	$2,800	Indiv

Misc Business — $119,254

Business Associations	$7,850	
National Fedn of Independent Business	$7,000	PAC
Food & Beverage	$28,170	
National Restaurant Assn	$10,000	PAC
ARA Services Inc	$2,500	PAC
Varsity Beverage	$2,050	Indiv
Beer, Wine & Liquor	$10,300	
National Beer Wholesalers Assn	$7,500	PAC
Retail Sales	$14,034	
GL Enterprises	$6,000	Indiv
International Council of Shopping Centers	$2,000	PAC
National Assn of Convenience Stores	$2,000	PAC
Misc Services	$3,700	
None over $2,000		
Business Services	$10,400	
O'Neil, Griffin & Associates	$2,800	Indiv
Harman Management Corp	$2,000	Indiv

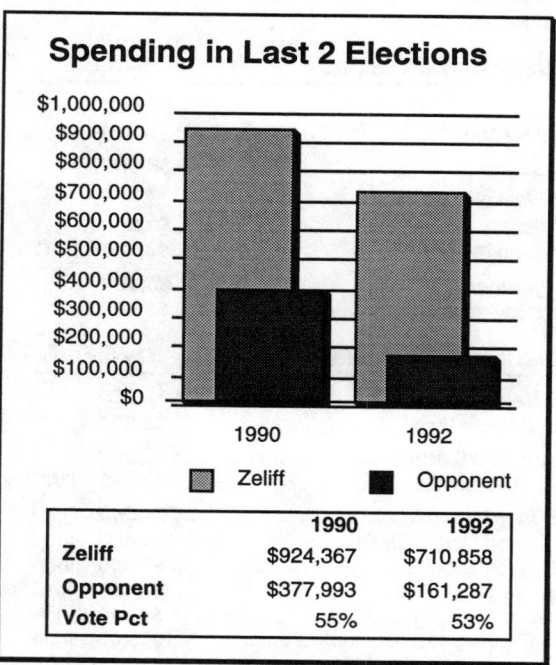

Spending in Last 2 Elections

Zeliff / Opponent (bar chart, 1990 and 1992)

	1990	1992
Zeliff	$924,367	$710,858
Opponent	$377,993	$161,287
Vote Pct	55%	53%

Recreation/Live Entertainment	$2,500	
Morrell Corp	$2,500	Indiv
Lodging/Tourism	$14,450	
American Hotel & Motel Assn	$4,000	PAC
Marriott Corp	$2,500	PAC/Ind
Christmas Inn	$2,000	Indiv
Chemical & Related Manufacturing	$8,850	
Dow Chemical	$3,500	PAC
WR Grace & Co	$2,350	PAC
Misc Manufacturing & Distributing	$15,050	
Tyco Laboratories	$3,000	Indiv
Foss Manufacturing Co	$2,500	Indiv
Stone Container Corp	$2,500	PAC

Transportation — $64,200

Air Transport	$28,850	
Henley Group Inc	$15,000	PAC
United Parcel Service	$6,500	PAC
General Electric	$2,600	PAC/Ind
United Airlines	$2,000	PAC
Automotive	$26,100	
National Auto Dealers Assn	$11,300	PAC
Auto Dealers & Drivers for Free Trade	$4,500	PAC
Trucking	$3,750	
None over $2,000		
Misc Transport	$3,000	
None over $2,000		

Labor

Labor	$3,000	
Public Sector Unions	$2,000	
None over $2,000		

Ideological/Single-Issue

Ideological/Single-Issue	$34,499	
Republican/Conservative	$3,099	
None over $2,000		
Pro-Israel	$9,700	
None over $2,000		
Gun Rights/Gun Control	$9,900	
National Rifle Assn	$9,900	PAC
Human Rights	$8,300	
National Albanian American PAC	$5,000	PAC

Other & Unknown

Other	$36,884	
Civil Servants/Public Officials	$4,880	
New Hampshire Housing Authority	$2,380	Indiv
Village at Loon Mtn	$2,000	Indiv
Retired	$28,504	
None over $2,000		
Other	$2,000	
Christmas Farm Inn	$2,000	Indiv

Unknown	$48,000	
Homemakers/Non-income earners	$12,200	
No Employer Listed or Found	$6,600	
Employer Listed/Category Unknown	$28,050	
None over $2,000		

* Contributions came from more than one affiliate or subsidiary.

Dick Zimmer, R-NJ (12)

First elected: 1990

1991-92 Total Receipts: $929,560
1992 Year-end Cash: $35,038

1991-92 Committees & Subcommittees

Government Operations
Commerce, Consumer and Monetary Affairs; Government Activities and Transportation

Science, Space and Technology
Environment; Space

Select Committee on Aging

Leading Contributors

Business

Agriculture — $31,250

Crop Production & Basic Processing	**$7,450**	
None over $2,500		
Tobacco	**$4,950**	
RJR Nabisco	$4,600	PAC/Ind
Dairy	**$8,950**	
Johanna Farms	$5,050	Indiv
Associated Milk Producers	$3,500	PAC
Agricultural Services/Products	**$2,500**	
None over $2,500		
Food Processing & Sales	**$6,000**	
None over $2,500		

Communications/Electronics — $33,300

Printing & Publishing	**$10,950**	
Forbes Inc	$10,250	Indiv
Media/Entertainment	**$3,900**	
None over $2,500		
Telephone Utilities	**$10,750**	
AT&T*	$6,000	Indiv
New Jersey Bell Telephone	$2,500	PAC
Electronics Mfg & Services	**$4,950**	
None over $2,500		
Computer Equipment & Services	**$2,750**	
None over $2,500		

Source of Funds in 1992 Election

Source	Total	Pct
■ PACs	$213,664	23%
▨ Indivs $200+	$535,242	57%
☐ Indivs under $200	$90,355	10%
▨ Other	$105,299	11%
Candidate	$0	0%
Party	$16,448	2%

Source of PAC Dollars by Sector

Source	Total	Pct
■ Business	$189,211	87%
▨ Labor	$14,200	6%
☐ Ideology/Single Issue	$15,025	7%

In-State vs. Out-of-State Contributions*

Source	Total	Pct
☐ In-State	$462,992	88%
■ Out-of-state	$61,800	12%
No state listed	$9,250	

*** by large individual contributors ($200 & above)**

Construction — $25,478

General Contractors	**$9,000**	
Associated General Contractors	$3,000	PAC
Home Builders	**$3,800**	
None over $2,500		
Construction Services	**$4,578**	
None over $2,500		
Building Materials & Equipment	**$6,850**	
None over $2,500		

Defense — $7,150

Defense Aerospace	**$5,800**	
None over $2,500		

Energy & Natural Resources — $25,800

Oil & Gas	**$7,050**	
None over $2,500		
Misc Energy	**$3,500**	
Cooper Industries	$3,000	PAC
Electric Utilities	**$8,250**	
Public Service Electric & Gas	$4,100	PAC
Waste Management	**$6,500**	
Advanced Environmental Tech Corp	$5,500	Indiv

Finance, Insurance & Real Estate — $176,766

Commercial Banks	**$11,250**	
American Bankers Assn	$3,000	PAC
Finance/Credit Companies	**$23,300**	
Beneficial Management Corp	$22,850	PAC/Ind
Securities & Investment	**$64,500**	
Wesray Capital Corp	$11,400	Indiv
Gilder, Gagnon & Co	$7,000	Indiv
Goldman, Sachs & Co	$4,750	PAC/Ind
Commodities Corp	$4,000	Indiv
Financial Planning Analysts Inc	$3,200	Indiv

Contribution Totals by Sector

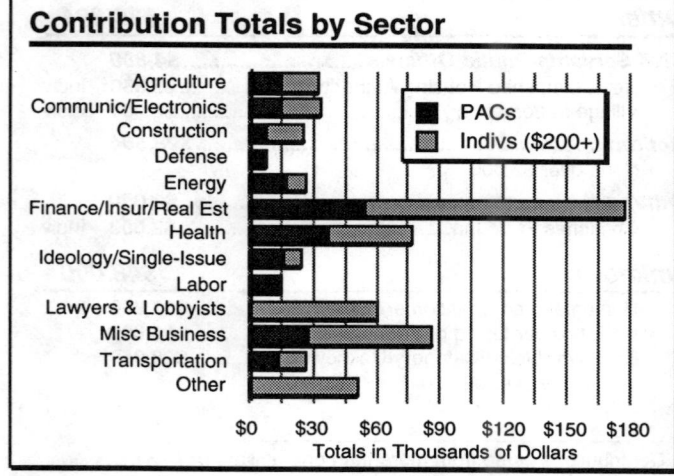

Agriculture
Communic/Electronics
Construction
Defense
Energy
Finance/Insur/Real Est
Health
Ideology/Single-Issue
Labor
Lawyers & Lobbyists
Misc Business
Transportation
Other

■ PACs
▨ Indivs ($200+)

$0 $30 $60 $90 $120 $150 $180
Totals in Thousands of Dollars

Insurance	$25,447	
Chubb Corp	$4,000	PAC

Real Estate	$25,800	
National Assn of Realtors	$5,000	PAC

Accountants	$8,150	
American Institute of CPA's	$5,200	PAC

Misc Finance	$15,450	
Gund Investment Corp	$5,000	Indiv

Health — $76,375

Health Professionals	$22,875	
American Medical Assn	$5,295	PAC

Pharmaceuticals/Health Products	$49,250	
Johnson & Johnson	$17,550	PAC/Ind
Schering-Plough Corp	$6,750	PAC/Ind
Rhone-Poulenc Inc	$6,000	PAC
Merck & Co	$3,900	PAC/Ind
Warner-Lambert	$3,150	PAC/Ind

Misc Health	$2,750	
None over $2,500		

Lawyers & Lobbyists — $59,375

Lawyers & Lobbyists	$59,375	
Norris, McLaughlin & Marcus	$5,125	Indiv
Mintz, Girgan et al	$3,400	Indiv
Cahill, Gordon et al	$3,000	Indiv
Cravath, Swaine & Moore	$2,900	Indiv
Amoroso, Mattia & Wyman	$2,650	Indiv

Misc Business — $84,650

Food & Beverage	$5,300	
National Restaurant Assn	$4,000	PAC

Beer, Wine & Liquor	$6,050	
National Beer Wholesalers Assn	$3,850	PAC

Retail Sales	$13,750	
Petrie Stores Corp	$5,000	Indiv
Flemington Department Store	$2,500	Indiv

Business Services	$23,850	
Matthew Outdoor Advertising Inc	$4,000	Indiv
Dun & Bradstreet	$3,450	PAC/Ind
Princeton Public Affairs	$2,500	Indiv

Misc Business	$3,100	
None over $2,500		

Chemical & Related Manufacturing	$8,250	
None over $2,500		

Misc Manufacturing & Distributing	$18,650	
Flemington Fur Co	$5,200	Indiv
Hoechst Celanese Corp	$4,700	PAC/Ind
Ohaus Scale Corp	$2,900	Indiv

Transportation — $26,400

Air Transport	$5,500	
United Parcel Service	$2,750	PAC

Automotive	$19,650	
Ditschman/Flemington Ford	$5,750	Indiv
National Auto Dealers Assn	$4,350	PAC

Labor

Labor	$14,200

Transportation Unions	$5,500	
Marine Engineers Union*	$5,000	PAC

Public Sector Unions	$6,400	
National Assn Retired Federal Employees	$5,000	PAC

Ideological/Single-Issue

Ideological/Single-Issue	$23,825

Leadership PACs	$4,000	
Cmte for an Affordable NJ (C. Whitman)	$4,000	PAC

Pro-Israel	$16,700	
Hudson Valley PAC	$4,000	PAC

Other & Unknown

Other	$50,600

Civil Servants/Public Officials	$4,200	
None over $2,500		

Retired	$44,200	
None over $2,500		

Unknown	$117,309

Homemakers/Non-income earners	$30,450
No Employer Listed or Found	$33,350
Employer Listed/Category Unknown	$53,000
None over $2,500	

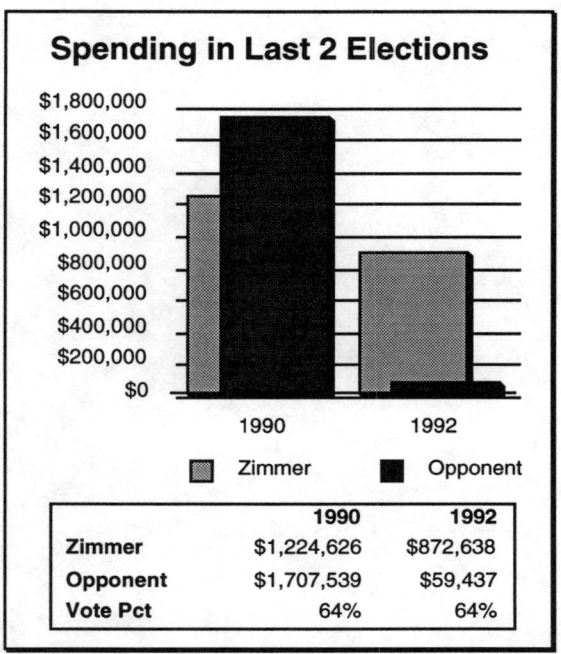

Spending in Last 2 Elections

	1990	1992
Zimmer	$1,224,626	$872,638
Opponent	$1,707,539	$59,437
Vote Pct	64%	64%

* Contributions came from more than one affiliate or subsidiary.

5.

PAC Profiles

pen Secrets

Introduction to the PAC Profiles

The final section of Open Secrets provides a directory of every political action committee that gave $20,000 or more in the 1991-92 election cycle. In all, these PACs contributed $178.2 million to congressional candidates — 94 percent of the total given by all PACs in the 1992 elections.

The PACs are listed alphabetically by the name of the PAC sponsor, or the name of the PAC itself where there is no other sponsor.

What's included in the PAC profiles:

Short name of the PAC or PAC sponsor. This is the name used elsewhere in the book to identify the PAC. The term "sponsor" is used simply to identify the group whose members contribute to the PAC, and does not imply a formal relationship between the PAC and the organization. Many PACs are officially connected with their sponsoring organization; others operate independently, even though the PAC's contributors all work for the same company or belong to the same trade association, labor union or other organization.

Official name of the PAC. The only abbreviation is the use of "PAC" for "Political Action Committee"

Total contributions in the 1991-92 election cycle.

Alabama Power Co		$114,275	179 Candidates	Dems:	54.4%
Alabama Power Co Employees Federal PAC (APC Employees Federal PAC)			Avg House: $619	House:	78.0%
Birmingham, AL	Southern Co	Electric Utilities	Avg Sen: $720	Incumb:	77.9%

Location of the PAC's headquarters.

Category or thumbnail description. See Appendix A for the complete list of categories used to classify the PACs and other contributors in this book.

Affiliated organization. When an organization is listed here, it means the PAC is one of several affiliated with the parent group. In the case of leadership PACs operated by members of Congress or other political figures, the name of the PAC's sponsor is listed here.

Percentage of total dollars that went to Democratic or Republican candidates. Whichever party got more than 50 percent is listed.

Number of federal candidates receiving contributions from the PAC in 1991-92.

Alabama Farm Bureau Federation		$86,511	72 Candidates	Dems:	61.2%
ELECT - the PAC of Alabama Farm Bureau Federation			Avg House: $1,239	House:	63.0%
Montgomery, AL		Farm Orgs	Avg Sen: $1,143	Incumb:	84.3%

Average contribution to House candidates in 1991-92.

Average contribution to Senate candidates in 1991-92.

Percentage of dollars that went to incumbents.

Percentage of dollars that went to House or Senate candidates. The group that got the biggest share is listed.

PAC Sponsor or Related Group/PAC Name	Affiliate	1991-92 Total	Where the money went...		
24th Congressional Dist of Calif PAC 24th Congressional District of California PAC Beverly Hills, CA	Rep Henry Waxman (D-Calif) Dem Leaders	$79,000	15 Candidates Avg House: $6,364 Avg Sen: $2,250	Dems: 100.0% House: 88.6% Incumb: 69.6%	
AAI Corp AAI Corporation PAC Hunt Valley, MD	United Industrial Corp Defense R&D†	$40,447	30 Candidates Avg House: $1,296 Avg Sen: $1,521	Repubs: 59.1% House: 73.7% Incumb: 95.3%	
Abbott Laboratories Abbott Laboratories Better Government Fund Abbott Park, IL	Pharmaceuticals†	$157,193	168 Candidates Avg House: $682 Avg Sen: $1,935	Repubs: 57.6% House: 58.1% Incumb: 79.1%	
ACRE (Action Committee for Rural Electrification) Action Committee for Rural Electrification (ACRE) Washington, DC	Rural Electric	$572,555	386 Candidates Avg House: $1,095 Avg Sen: $5,039	Dems: 76.7% House: 66.5% Incumb: 79.2%	
Advo-System Inc Advo-System, Inc PAC (AdvoPAC) Windsor, CT	Mail Advertising	$56,961	44 Candidates Avg House: $1,224 Avg Sen: $1,371	Dems: 86.5% Senate: 50.6% Incumb: 89.4%	
AEL Industries Inc AEL Industries Inc PAC (AEL PAC) Montgomeryville, PA	Defense Electronics	$32,350	19 Candidates Avg House: $1,607 Avg Sen: $2,063	Dems: 82.4% House: 74.5% Incumb: 96.9%	
Aetna Life & Casualty Aetna Life and Casualty Company PAC Hartford, CT	Insurance	$196,500	147 Candidates Avg House: $906 Avg Sen: $2,618	Repubs: 53.1% House: 50.7% Incumb: 86.1%	
AFL-CIO AFL-CIO Committee on Political Education/Political Contributions Committee Washington, DC	Labor Unions	$835,120	296 Candidates Avg House: $2,309 Avg Sen: $6,691	Dems: 98.8% House: 72.2% Incumb: 50.0%	
AFL-CIO Bldg/Construction Trades Dept Political Educational Fund of the Building and Construction Trades Department Washington, DC	AFL-CIO Building Trade Unions	$228,704	218 Candidates Avg House: $953 Avg Sen: $1,582	Dems: 95.3% House: 79.1% Incumb: 88.4%	
AFL-CIO Industrial Union Dept Industrial Union Department AFL-CIO Voluntary Fund Washington, DC	AFL-CIO Manufacturing Unions	$28,700	75 Candidates Avg House: $318 Avg Sen: $800	Dems: 95.6% House: 72.1% Incumb: 77.3%	
AG Processing Inc AG Processing Inc PAC, AGPAC Omaha, NE	Grain	$44,050	59 Candidates Avg House: $718 Avg Sen: $846	Repubs: 56.9% House: 75.0% Incumb: 88.1%	
Agri-Mark Inc Agri-Mark Inc PAC AGRI-PAC Methuen, MA	Dairy	$29,450	42 Candidates Avg House: $601 Avg Sen: $1,286	Repubs: 61.1% House: 69.4% Incumb: 94.1%	
Air Line Pilots Assn Air Line Pilots Association PAC Washington, DC	Air Transport Unions	$1,260,593	312 Candidates Avg House: $3,636 Avg Sen: $7,231	Dems: 87.0% House: 79.3% Incumb: 80.6%	
Air Products & Chemicals Inc Air Products Political Alliance Trexlertown, PA	Chemicals	$73,450	79 Candidates Avg House: $687 Avg Sen: $1,888	Repubs: 79.3% House: 58.9% Incumb: 78.9%	
Airborne Freight Corp Airborne Freight Corporation PAC (ABXPAC) Wilmington, OH	Air Freight	$20,550	14 Candidates Avg House: $1,572 Avg Sen: $1,280	Repubs: 76.2% House: 68.9% Incumb: 82.2%	
Aircraft Owners & Pilots Assn Aircraft Owners and Pilots Association PAC Frederick, MD	General Aviation	$482,695	168 Candidates Avg House: $2,399 Avg Sen: $4,968	Dems: 55.6% House: 68.1% Incumb: 91.1%	
Akin, Gump et al Akin, Gump, Strauss, Hauer & Feld Civic Action Committee Washington, DC	Lawyers	$304,656	220 Candidates Avg House: $1,197 Avg Sen: $1,991	Dems: 81.8% House: 66.0% Incumb: 93.5%	
Alabama Farm Bureau Federation Elect - The PAC of Alabama Farm Bureau Federation Montegomery, AL	Farm Orgs	$131,231	75 Candidates Avg House: $1,885 Avg Sen: $1,500	Dems: 75.3% House: 71.8% Incumb: 66.1%	
Alabama Peanut Producers Assn Peanut PAC of Alabama, PAC of Alabama Peanut Producers Association Dothan, AL	Misc Crops	$73,450	51 Candidates Avg House: $1,332 Avg Sen: $1,792	Dems: 97.3% House: 70.7% Incumb: 71.4%	

† PAC sponsor has other major interests in addition to this primary category

Alabama Power Co
Alabama Power Co Employees Federal PAC (APC Employees Federal PAC)
Birmingham, AL — Southern Co — Electric Utilities — **$92,050** — 165 Candidates; Avg House: $519; Avg Sen: $727 — Dems: 58.3%; House: 75.5%; Incumb: 80.2%

Alarm Industry Communications Committee
Alarm Industry Communications Committee PAC
Bethesda, MD — Security Services — **$66,368** — 44 Candidates; Avg House: $1,308; Avg Sen: $1,917 — Dems: 60.8%; House: 55.2%; Incumb: 97.0%

Alcoa
Alcoa Employees Political Fund
Pittsburgh, PA — Metal Mining/Process† — **$45,450** — 54 Candidates; Avg House: $749; Avg Sen: $1,083 — Repubs: 50.8%; House: 64.2%; Incumb: 94.0%

Allegheny Ludlum Steel Corp
Allegheny Ludlum Corporation PAC (AL-PAC)
Pittsburgh, PA — Allegheny Ludlum — Steel — **$31,600** — 8 Candidates; Avg House: $2,933; Avg Sen: $7,000 — Repubs: 68.3%; House: 55.7%; Incumb: 71.5%

Allied-Signal
Allied-Signal PAC
Morristown, NJ — Defense Aerospace† — **$196,000** — 162 Candidates; Avg House: $748; Avg Sen: $3,420 — Dems: 50.3%; House: 51.1%; Incumb: 88.7%

Allstate Insurance
Allstate Insurance Company PAC
Northbrook, IL — Sears — Insurance — **$76,200** — 67 Candidates; Avg House: $835; Avg Sen: $1,800 — Repubs: 65.4%; House: 50.4%; Incumb: 82.8%

Alltel Corp
Alltel Corporation PAC (APAC)
Hudson, OH — Phone Utilites — **$94,818** — 106 Candidates; Avg House: $784; Avg Sen: $1,253 — Dems: 56.0%; House: 67.0%; Incumb: 94.4%

Amalgamated Clothing & Textile Workers
Amalgamated Clothing and Textile Workers Union - PAC (ACTWU-PAC)
New York, NY — Clothing/Textile Wrkrs — Manufacturing Unions — **$269,892** — 213 Candidates; Avg House: $845; Avg Sen: $2,993 — Dems: 97.1%; House: 54.1%; Incumb: 61.6%

Amalgamated Sugar Co
Amalgamated Sugar Company PAC; The
Ogden, UT — Valhi Inc — Sugar — **$24,500** — 24 Candidates; Avg House: $944; Avg Sen: $1,250 — Repubs: 55.1%; House: 69.4%; Incumb: 61.2%

Amalgamated Transit Union
Amalgamated Transit Union-COPE
Washington, DC — Misc Transport Union — **$428,490** — 246 Candidates; Avg House: $1,371; Avg Sen: $3,506 — Dems: 97.8%; House: 65.3%; Incumb: 64.8%

Amax Inc
Amax Inc Concerned Citizens Fund
Washington, DC — Mining — **$33,900** — 47 Candidates; Avg House: $575; Avg Sen: $1,033 — Repubs: 71.5%; House: 54.3%; Incumb: 73.5%

America's Leaders' Fund
America's Leaders' Fund (aka Chicago Campaign Committee)
Chicago, IL — Rep Dan Rostenkowski (D-Ill) — Dem Leaders — **$120,703** — 64 Candidates; Avg House: $1,633; Avg Sen: $4,333 — Dems: 100.0%; House: 78.5%; Incumb: 64.4%

America's PAC
America's PAC
Herndon, VA — Repub/Conservative† — **$28,000** — 9 Candidates; Avg House: $3,250; Avg Sen: $1,750 — Repubs: 82.1%; House: 69.6%; Incumb: 23.2%

American Academy of Ophthalmology
American Academy of Ophthalmology Inc Political Committee ("OPHTHOPAC")
San Francisco, CA — Eye Doctors — **$870,027** — 334 Candidates; Avg House: $2,391; Avg Sen: $4,134 — Dems: 63.3%; House: 80.5%; Incumb: 60.5%

American Airlines
American Airlines PAC
Washington, DC — Airlines — **$257,570** — 130 Candidates; Avg House: $1,772; Avg Sen: $2,735 — Dems: 73.0%; House: 69.5%; Incumb: 89.8%

American Ambulance Assn
American Ambulance Association Federal PAC (aka AMBU-PAC)
Washington, DC — Health Care Svcs — **$55,425** — 62 Candidates; Avg House: $782; Avg Sen: $1,167 — Dems: 51.9%; House: 62.1%; Incumb: 88.3%

American Assn for Marriage & Family Therapy
American Association for Marriage & Family Therapy
Washington, DC — Health Practitioners — **$37,800** — 43 Candidates; Avg House: $793; Avg Sen: $1,083 — Dems: 77.5%; House: 63.0%; Incumb: 88.1%

American Assn of Airport Executives
American Association of Airport Executives Good Government Committee
Alexandria, VA — Aviation Services — **$43,112** — 33 Candidates; Avg House: $1,015; Avg Sen: $2,217 — Dems: 71.5%; House: 58.9%; Incumb: 99.4%

American Assn of Crop Insurers
American Association of Crop Insurers PAC (AACI PAC)
Washington, DC — Ag Services† — **$152,726** — 77 Candidates; Avg House: $1,592; Avg Sen: $3,134 — Dems: 62.6%; House: 57.3%; Incumb: 91.7%

PAC Sponsor or Related Group/PAC Name	Affiliate	1991-92 Total	Where the money went...		
American Assn of Equipment Lessors AAEL Lease-PAC Arlington, VA	Rentals†	$139,600	80 Candidates Avg House: $1,605 Avg Sen: $2,114	Repubs: 51.1% House: 66.7% Incumb: 57.3%	
American Assn of Nurse Anesthetists American Association of Nurse Anesthetists Separate Segregated Fund (CRNA-PAC) Park Ridge, IL	Nurses	$45,300	52 Candidates Avg House: $830 Avg Sen: $938	Dems: 72.7% House: 58.6% Incumb: 81.0%	
American Assn of Nurserymen Nursery Industry PAC Washington, DC	Florists	$34,950	39 Candidates Avg House: $990 Avg Sen: $583	Repubs: 80.0% House: 85.0% Incumb: 92.8%	
American Assn of Oral & Maxillofacial Surgeons Oral and Maxillofacial Surgery PAC (OMSPAC) Rosemont, IL	Dentists	$163,000	71 Candidates Avg House: $2,068 Avg Sen: $2,667	Dems: 62.9% House: 55.8% Incumb: 87.4%	
American Bakers Assn American Bakers Association Bread PAC Washington, DC	Food Processors	$61,975	52 Candidates Avg House: $649 Avg Sen: $2,309	Repubs: 93.5% Senate: 63.3% Incumb: 56.0%	
American Bankers Assn American Bankers Association BANKPAC Washington, DC	Commercial Banks	$1,498,388	443 Candidates Avg House: $3,055 Avg Sen: $5,790	Dems: 51.6% House: 79.5% Incumb: 80.0%	
American Bus Assn BusPAC-PAC of the American Bus Association Washington, DC	Bus Services	$78,450	79 Candidates Avg House: $897 Avg Sen: $1,319	Dems: 78.5% House: 69.7% Incumb: 91.1%	
American Cement Alliance American Cement Alliance Inc Washington, DC	Stone/Concrete	$27,100	28 Candidates Avg House: $747 Avg Sen: $1,365	Repubs: 53.3% Senate: 50.4% Incumb: 99.1%	
American Chiropractic Assn American Chiropractic Association PAC Arlington, VA	Chiropractors	$641,746	206 Candidates Avg House: $2,428 Avg Sen: $6,161	Dems: 73.7% House: 63.2% Incumb: 65.5%	
American Citizens for Political Action American Citizens for Political Action Washington, DC	Repub/Conservative	$26,490	28 Candidates Avg House: $956 Avg Sen: $875	Repubs: 96.2% House: 83.0% Incumb: 49.2%	
American Collectors Assn American Collectors Association Inc ACPAC Minneapolis, MN	Credit Reporting	$27,900	59 Candidates Avg House: $432 Avg Sen: $833	Repubs: 90.3% House: 82.1% Incumb: 87.8%	
American College of Emergency Physicians National Emergency Medicine PAC of the American College of Emergency Physicians Irving, TX	Doctors	$330,725	177 Candidates Avg House: $1,833 Avg Sen: $2,031	Dems: 73.8% House: 80.3% Incumb: 64.4%	
American Commercial Barge Line Co American Commercial Barge Line Co/Jeffboat Inc - PAC (ACBL/JFFBT) Jeffersonville, IN	CSX Corp	Sea Transport	$52,250	59 Candidates Avg House: $852 Avg Sen: $1,250	Repubs: 71.6% House: 88.0% Incumb: 97.1%
American Consulting Engineers Council American Consulting Engineers PAC (ACE/PAC) Washington, DC	Engineers	$95,500	113 Candidates Avg House: $675 Avg Sen: $1,363	Repubs: 52.9% House: 60.0% Incumb: 79.8%	
American Cotton Shippers Assn Cmte Organized for the Trading of Cotton - PAC of the Amer Cotton Shippers Assn Washington, DC	Cotton	$35,000	33 Candidates Avg House: $1,043 Avg Sen: $1,100	Dems: 54.0% House: 68.6% Incumb: 97.1%	
American Council of Life Insurance American Council of Life Insurance, Life Insurance PAC Washington, DC	Life Insurance	$577,430	308 Candidates Avg House: $1,525 Avg Sen: $3,528	Dems: 59.4% House: 67.4% Incumb: 89.0%	
American Crystal Sugar Corp American Crystal Sugar PAC Moorheard, MN	Sugar	$297,015	243 Candidates Avg House: $1,049 Avg Sen: $2,076	Dems: 70.9% House: 71.3% Incumb: 89.3%	
American Cyanimid American Cyanamid Company Good Government Fund Washington, DC	Pharmaceuticals†	$32,400	31 Candidates Avg House: $638 Avg Sen: $1,900	Dems: 62.0% Senate: 58.6% Incumb: 87.7%	
American Dental Assn American Dental PAC Washington, DC	Dentists	$1,419,958	433 Candidates Avg House: $2,918 Avg Sen: $6,133	Dems: 60.8% House: 78.7% Incumb: 71.5%	

† PAC sponsor has other major interests in addition to this primary category

PAC Sponsor or Related Group/PAC Name	Affiliate	1991-92 Total	Where the money went...		
American Dietetic Assn American Dietetic Association PAC, The Washington, DC	Health Practitioners	$45,750	60 Candidates Avg House: $599 Avg Sen: $1,176	Dems: 83.6% House: 56.3% Incumb: 61.8%	
American Electric Power American Electric Power Committee for Responsible Government; The Columbus, OH	Electric Utilities	$99,000	121 Candidates Avg House: $715 Avg Sen: $1,202	Repubs: 52.8% House: 67.9% Incumb: 92.2%	
American Express American Express Company Committee for Responsible Governmennt Washington, DC	Securities†	$141,425	141 Candidates Avg House: $807 Avg Sen: $1,795	Dems: 70.0% House: 64.5% Incumb: 91.3%	
American Factory Trawler Assn American Factory Trawler Association PAC Washington, DC	Comml Fishing	$23,299	13 Candidates Avg House: $1,839 Avg Sen: $1,688	Dems: 91.9% House: 71.0% Incumb: 69.1%	
American Family Corp American Family PAC (AF-PAC) Washington, DC	Health Insurance	$503,000	152 Candidates Avg House: $3,071 Avg Sen: $4,000	Dems: 59.3% House: 69.0% Incumb: 81.1%	
American Federation of Government Employees American Federation of Government Employees' PAC Washington, DC	Fedl Worker Unions	$173,243	164 Candidates Avg House: $823 Avg Sen: $1,873	Dems: 98.4% House: 59.9% Incumb: 71.8%	
American Federation of Musicians American Federation of Musicians - Tempo Political Contributions Committee New York, NY	Entrtainment Unions	$31,750	74 Candidates Avg House: $371 Avg Sen: $497	Dems: 96.8% Senate: 51.6% Incumb: 89.0%	
American Federation of Teachers American Federation of Teachers Committee on Political Education Washington, DC	Amer Fedn of Teachers	Teachers	$1,111,250	261 Candidates Avg House: $3,676 Avg Sen: $7,603	Dems: 97.0% House: 73.1% Incumb: 67.5%
American Fedn of State, County & Munic Employees American Federation of State County & Municipal Employees - PEOPLE, Qualified Washington, DC	Local Govt Unions	$1,950,365	387 Candidates Avg House: $4,806 Avg Sen: $6,767	Dems: 97.3% House: 83.5% Incumb: 60.1%	
American Feed Industry Assn Feed Industry PAC (FIPAC/AFIA) Arlington, VA	Animal Feed/Health	$29,112	50 Candidates Avg House: $548 Avg Sen: $629	Repubs: 81.5% House: 54.6% Incumb: 72.8%	
American Financial Services Assn American Financial Services Assn PAC Washington, DC	Credit/Loans	$105,124	80 Candidates Avg House: $935 Avg Sen: $2,957	Repubs: 53.7% House: 57.8% Incumb: 82.1%	
American Furniture Manufacturers Assn American Furniture Manufacturers Association PAC High Point, NC	Furniture	$86,750	76 Candidates Avg House: $986 Avg Sen: $1,523	Repubs: 77.3% House: 61.4% Incumb: 84.5%	
American Gas Assn Gas Employees PAC Arlington, VA	Natural Gas	$49,700	90 Candidates Avg House: $476 Avg Sen: $755	Dems: 61.9% House: 67.1% Incumb: 84.3%	
American General Insurance Co American General PAC Houston, TX	American General Corp	Insurance†	$54,460	44 Candidates Avg House: $1,078 Avg Sen: $1,447	Repubs: 57.7% Senate: 50.5% Incumb: 75.4%
American Health Care Assn American Health Care Association PAC (AHCA-PAC) Washington, DC	Nursing Homes	$381,019	333 Candidates Avg House: $936 Avg Sen: $2,019	Dems: 66.4% House: 66.1% Incumb: 77.0%	
American Home Products Corp American Home Products Corporation-AHP Good Government Fund New York, NY	Pharmaceuticals†	$56,400	66 Candidates Avg House: $613 Avg Sen: $1,410	Repubs: 59.8% House: 50.0% Incumb: 95.2%	
American Horse Council American Horse Council, Inc Committee on Legislation and Taxation (COLT) Washington, DC	Livestock	$20,700	33 Candidates Avg House: $530 Avg Sen: $850	Dems: 82.1% House: 58.9% Incumb: 86.2%	
American Hospital Assn PAC of the American Hospital Association Chicago, IL	Hospitals	$576,488	335 Candidates Avg House: $1,486 Avg Sen: $3,140	Dems: 69.9% House: 74.0% Incumb: 81.9%	
American Hotel & Motel Assn American Hotel Motel PAC Washington, DC	Hotels/Motels	$131,475	177 Candidates Avg House: $651 Avg Sen: $1,150	Dems: 54.3% House: 70.3% Incumb: 87.5%	

PAC Sponsor or Related Group / PAC Name / Location	Affiliate	1991-92 Total	Candidates	Averages	Percentages
American Institute of Architects American Institute of Architect's Quality Government Fund Washington, DC	Architects	$33,625	46 Candidates	Avg House: $737 Avg Sen: $700	Dems: 68.8% House: 85.4% Incumb: 82.8%
American Institute of CPA's American Institute of Certified Public Accountants Effective Legis Cmte (AICPA) New York, NY	Accountants	$1,542,851	405 Candidates	Avg House: $3,612 Avg Sen: $5,247	Dems: 55.6% House: 83.3% Incumb: 82.8%
American Insurance Assn American Insurance Association PAC Washington, DC	Insurance	$100,529	128 Candidates	Avg House: $674 Avg Sen: $1,246	Dems: 66.9% House: 69.0% Incumb: 91.2%
American International Group American International Group Employee PAC New York, NY	Insurance	$189,190	124 Candidates	Avg House: $1,216 Avg Sen: $2,181	Dems: 64.1% House: 54.0% Incumb: 79.8%
American Land Title Assn Title Industry PAC Washington, DC	Title Insurance	$100,889	106 Candidates	Avg House: $715 Avg Sen: $1,804	Dems: 64.8% House: 58.9% Incumb: 94.0%
American Meat Institute American Meat Institute PAC Arlington, VA	Meat Processors	$105,629	109 Candidates	Avg House: $823 Avg Sen: $1,336	Repubs: 62.4% House: 60.8% Incumb: 88.5%
American Medical Assn American Medical Association PAC Washington, DC	Doctors	$2,936,558	537 Candidates	Avg House: $5,452 Avg Sen: $5,663	Repubs: 51.4% House: 91.7% Incumb: 69.7%
American Motorcyclist Assn American Motorcyclist PAC Westerville, OH	Motorcycles	$50,525	81 Candidates	Avg House: $537 Avg Sen: $908	Repubs: 73.6% House: 65.9% Incumb: 80.2%
American Nuclear Energy Council American Nuclear Energy Council Federal PAC Washington, DC	Nuclear Energy	$25,053	50 Candidates	Avg House: $390 Avg Sen: $854	Dems: 70.0% House: 59.1% Incumb: 98.0%
American Nurses Assn American Nurses' Association PAC (ANA-PAC) Washington, DC	Nurses	$311,019	198 Candidates	Avg House: $1,415 Avg Sen: $2,337	Dems: 90.6% House: 73.7% Incumb: 45.4%
American Occupational Therapy Assn American Occupational Therapy PAC Rockville, MD	Health Practitioners	$81,363	87 Candidates	Avg House: $712 Avg Sen: $1,444	Dems: 73.7% House: 54.3% Incumb: 72.7%
American Optometric Assn American Optometric Association PAC Alexandria, VA	Eye Doctors	$398,366	252 Candidates	Avg House: $1,333 Avg Sen: $2,894	Dems: 69.0% House: 70.9% Incumb: 71.0%
American Orthotic & Prosthetic Assn American Orthotic & Prosthetic Association PAC (AOPAPAC) Alexandria, VA	Medical Supplies	$32,100	22 Candidates	Avg House: $1,182 Avg Sen: $1,610	Dems: 90.7% Senate: 50.2% Incumb: 86.0%
American Osteopathic Assn PAC of the American Osteopathic Association (AOHA-PAC) Alexandria, VA	Misc MD Specialists	$22,350	29 Candidates	Avg House: $636 Avg Sen: $1,143	Dems: 64.0% House: 59.7% Incumb: 94.6%
American PAC/Bellevue American PAC Bellevue, WA	Repub/Conservative†	$20,900	50 Candidates	Avg House: $407 Avg Sen: $500	Repubs: 92.3% House: 85.7% Incumb: 10.5%
American Pharmaceutical Assn American Pharmaceutical Association PAC Washington, DC	Pharmacists	$132,072	117 Candidates	Avg House: $817 Avg Sen: $1,830	Dems: 64.3% House: 50.1% Incumb: 81.8%
American Physical Therapy Assn American Physical Therapy Congressional Action Committee Alexandria, VA	Health Practitioners	$198,441	135 Candidates	Avg House: $1,331 Avg Sen: $1,749	Dems: 73.3% House: 63.7% Incumb: 75.3%
American Pilots Assn American Pilots' Association PAC Washington, DC	Sea Transport	$36,350	35 Candidates	Avg House: $1,028 Avg Sen: $1,100	Dems: 69.5% House: 84.9% Incumb: 96.6%
American Podiatry Assn Podiatry PAC Bethesda, MD	Misc MD Specialists	$401,000	231 Candidates	Avg House: $1,409 Avg Sen: $3,140	Dems: 69.7% House: 65.7% Incumb: 75.9%

† PAC sponsor has other major interests in addition to this primary category

American Postal Workers Union Political Fund Committee of the American Postal Workers Union, AFL-CIO Washington, DC	Amer Postal Workers Union Postal Unions	$892,290	331 Candidates Avg House: $2,411 Avg Sen: $4,341	Dems: 96.3% House: 76.7% Incumb: 80.7%
American President Lines American President Lines Ltd PAC (APT/PAC) Oakland, CA	American Presidents Co Sea Transport†	$109,462	110 Candidates Avg House: $757 Avg Sen: $1,764	Dems: 59.2% House: 58.1% Incumb: 83.6%
American Psychiatric Assn Corporation for the Advancement of Psychiatry PAC (CAPPAC) Washington, DC	Psychiatrist/Psychol	$164,980	150 Candidates Avg House: $1,014 Avg Sen: $1,417	Dems: 87.2% House: 71.9% Incumb: 67.8%
American Public Power Assn Public Ownership of Electric Resources PAC (POWERPAC) Washington, DC	Electric Utilities	$30,900	58 Candidates Avg House: $518 Avg Sen: $588	Dems: 83.2% House: 77.2% Incumb: 91.4%
American Rental Assn American Rental Association PAC (ARAPAC) Moline, IL	Rentals	$28,148	49 Candidates Avg House: $503 Avg Sen: $1,001	Repubs: 94.7% House: 75.1% Incumb: 41.3%
American Resort & Residential Development Assn American Resort & Residential Development Ass'n PAC Washington, DC	Real Estate Devel†	$24,300	29 Candidates Avg House: $919 Avg Sen: $625	Dems: 82.5% House: 79.4% Incumb: 91.8%
American Road & Transport Builders Assn American Road & Transportation Builders Association (ARTBA) - 525 PAC Washington, DC	Heavy Construction	$34,450	46 Candidates Avg House: $760 Avg Sen: $583	Dems: 67.3% House: 94.9% Incumb: 96.8%
American Society of Anesthesiologists American Society of Anesthesiologists Political Action Cmte (ASAPAC) Park Ridge, IL	Misc MD Specialists	$112,450	99 Candidates Avg House: $992 Avg Sen: $1,538	Dems: 63.0% House: 64.4% Incumb: 59.7%
American Society of Association Executives American Society of Association Executives A-PAC Washington, DC	Other	$61,500	97 Candidates Avg House: $486 Avg Sen: $1,083	Repubs: 61.4% House: 57.7% Incumb: 71.5%
American Society of Cataract & Refractive Surgery American Society of Cataract & Refractive Surgery PAC (aka EYEPAC) Fairfax, VA	Eye Doctors	$72,050	47 Candidates Avg House: $1,381 Avg Sen: $1,588	Dems: 85.4% House: 55.6% Incumb: 63.2%
American Society of Consultant Pharmacists American Society of Consultant Pharmacists PAC (ASCP PAC) Arlington, VA	Pharmacists	$21,400	28 Candidates Avg House: $732 Avg Sen: $833	Dems: 72.9% House: 65.0% Incumb: 90.7%
American Society of Plastic & Reconstructive Surgeons PAC of the Amer Soc of Plastic & Reconstr Surgeons Inc (ASPRS) PLASTYPAC Arlington Heights, IL	Misc MD Specialists	$85,700	90 Candidates Avg House: $876 Avg Sen: $1,202	Dems: 50.0% House: 70.5% Incumb: 73.2%
American Society of Travel Agents American Society of Travel Agents PAC Alexandria, VA	Travel Agents	$51,575	187 Candidates Avg House: $238 Avg Sen: $446	Dems: 60.1% House: 70.6% Incumb: 93.4%
American Soybean Assn American Soybean Association PAC (SOYPAC) St Louis, MO	Grain	$35,207	71 Candidates Avg House: $428 Avg Sen: $750	Repubs: 53.8% House: 68.0% Incumb: 98.0%
American Speech-Language-Hearing Assn American Speech-Language-Hearing Association PAC Rockville, MD	Health Practitioners	$57,681	68 Candidates Avg House: $635 Avg Sen: $1,192	Dems: 84.4% Senate: 53.7% Incumb: 61.1%
American Stores Co American Stores Company Federal PAC Salt Lake City, UT	Food Stores†	$26,750	12 Candidates Avg House: $417 Avg Sen: $2,833	Repubs: 56.1% Senate: 95.3% Incumb: 68.2%
American Sugar Cane League American Sugar Cane League PAC Thibodaux, LA	Sugar	$197,925	262 Candidates Avg House: $595 Avg Sen: $1,794	Dems: 75.6% House: 68.3% Incumb: 90.0%
American Sugarbeet Growers Assn American Sugarbeet Growers Association PAC Washington, DC	Sugar	$311,707	286 Candidates Avg House: $933 Avg Sen: $2,127	Dems: 68.5% House: 74.5% Incumb: 88.0%
American Supply Assn American Supply Association PAC Chicago, IL	Pipe Products†	$55,525	72 Candidates Avg House: $642 Avg Sen: $1,132	Repubs: 82.0% House: 61.3% Incumb: 68.4%

PAC Sponsor or Related Group/PAC Name	Affiliate	1991-92 Total	Where the money went...		
American Systems Corp American Systems Corporation PAC (ASC-PAC) Chantilly, VA	Defense Electronics†	$20,200	34 Candidates Avg House: $526 Avg Sen: $783	Repubs: 60.6% House: 65.1% Incumb: 95.0%	
American Textile Manufacturers Institute American Textile Manufacturers Institute, Inc Committee for Good Government Washington, DC	Textiles	$131,375	103 Candidates Avg House: $1,029 Avg Sen: $2,720	Dems: 65.5% House: 68.9% Incumb: 96.7%	
American Trucking Assns Trucking PAC of the American Trucking Associations' Inc Washington, DC	Trucking Companies	$354,619	275 Candidates Avg House: $1,012 Avg Sen: $2,604	Dems: 62.8% House: 64.8% Incumb: 90.9%	
American Veterinary Medical Assn American Veterinary Medical Association PAC (Avmapac) Washington, DC	Veterinary	$301,000	307 Candidates Avg House: $868 Avg Sen: $1,776	Dems: 59.3% House: 77.6% Incumb: 88.5%	
American Waterways Operators American Waterways Operators-PAC Arlington, VA	Sea Transport	$66,094	91 Candidates Avg House: $637 Avg Sen: $1,452	Dems: 52.7% House: 78.0% Incumb: 94.2%	
Americans for Democratic Action Americans for Democratic Action Inc PAC Washington, DC	Dem/Liberal	$53,650	54 Candidates Avg House: $649 Avg Sen: $2,081	Dems: 99.1% Senate: 50.4% Incumb: 33.7%	
Americans for Free International Trade Americans for Free International Trade Political Action Committee Inc Washington, DC	Japanese Auto Dlrs	$475,150	192 Candidates Avg House: $1,702 Avg Sen: $7,000	Repubs: 79.9% House: 58.8% Incumb: 72.2%	
Americans for Good Government Inc Americans for Good Government Inc Jasper, AL	Pro-Israel	$166,750	98 Candidates Avg House: $1,070 Avg Sen: $2,743	Dems: 57.4% Senate: 60.9% Incumb: 71.8%	
AmeriPAC: The Fund for a Greater America AmeriPAC: The Fund for a Greater America Washington, DC	Rep Steny Hoyer (D-Md) Dem Leaders	$31,500	47 Candidates Avg House: $674 Avg Sen: $500	Dems: 100.0% House: 98.4% Incumb: 34.9%	
Ameritech Corp American Information Technologies Corporation PAC (Ameritech PAC) Chicago, IL	Ameritech Phone Utilites	$255,132	112 Candidates Avg House: $2,097 Avg Sen: $2,818	Dems: 57.5% House: 68.2% Incumb: 91.7%	
Amoco Corp Amoco PAC Chicago, IL	Oil & Gas†	$264,750	230 Candidates Avg House: $764 Avg Sen: $4,065	Repubs: 73.3% House: 58.5% Incumb: 61.3%	
Amsouth Bancorp Amsouth PAC Birmingham, AL	Commercial Banks	$65,750	20 Candidates Avg House: $3,268 Avg Sen: $3,400	Dems: 59.6% House: 84.5% Incumb: 45.2%	
Anesthesia Service Medical Group Anesthesia Service Medical Group Inc Good Government Fund San Diego, CA	Misc MD Specialists	$40,930	26 Candidates Avg House: $1,497 Avg Sen: $1,833	Dems: 58.0% House: 73.1% Incumb: 32.8%	
Anheuser-Busch Anheuser-Busch Companies Inc PAC (AB-PAC) St. Louis, MO	Beer†	$126,080	119 Candidates Avg House: $830 Avg Sen: $1,969	Dems: 67.9% House: 62.5% Incumb: 81.8%	
ARA Services Inc ARA Services PAC (ARA PAC) Philadelphia, PA	Restaurants†	$33,197	23 Candidates Avg House: $1,059 Avg Sen: $2,321	Dems: 50.6% House: 51.1% Incumb: 77.3%	
Archer-Daniels-Midland Corp Archer Daniels Midland Company-ADM PAC Decatur, IL	Grain Traders†	$282,750	132 Candidates Avg House: $1,541 Avg Sen: $3,010	Dems: 50.4% Senate: 54.3% Incumb: 73.4%	
Arctic Alaska Fisheries Corp Arctic Alaska Fisheries Corp PAC Seattle, WA	Comml Fishing	$31,344	13 Candidates Avg House: $2,137 Avg Sen: $2,850	Dems: 93.9% House: 54.5% Incumb: 50.1%	
Arent, Fox et al Arent, Fox Civic Participation Fund Washington, DC	Lawyers	$55,450	70 Candidates Avg House: $630 Avg Sen: $1,136	Dems: 85.3% House: 53.4% Incumb: 80.6%	
Arizona Politically Interested Citizens Arizona Politically Interested Citizens Phoenix, AZ	Pro-Israel	$53,900	47 Candidates Avg House: $590 Avg Sen: $1,852	Dems: 68.0% Senate: 72.2% Incumb: 85.2%	

† PAC sponsor has other major interests in addition to this primary category

Arizona Public Service Co		$24,150	45 Candidates	Repubs: 68.5%
Arizona Public Service Company PAC (APSPAC)			Avg House: $490	House: 73.1%
Phoenix, AZ	Electric Utilities		Avg Sen: $722	Incumb: 92.8%

Arkansas Power & Light		$23,500	40 Candidates	Dems: 85.7%
Arkansas Power & Light Company Employees' Energy PAC			Avg House: $453	House: 56.0%
Little Rock, AR	Entergy Corp	Electric Utilities	Avg Sen: $941	Incumb: 79.2%

Arkla Inc		$33,400	32 Candidates	Dems: 87.1%
Arkla, Inc PAC or ArklaPAC			Avg House: $929	House: 66.8%
Shreveport, LA	Natural Gas		Avg Sen: $1,388	Incumb: 97.9%

Arkla Inc		$26,250	18 Candidates	Dems: 86.7%
Entex (Arkla, Inc) Better Government Committee			Avg House: $1,393	House: 74.3%
Houston, TX	Natural Gas		Avg Sen: $1,688	Incumb: 77.1%

Armco Inc		$46,100	35 Candidates	Repubs: 53.4%
Armco Employees' PAC (APAC)			Avg House: $1,117	House: 63.0%
Washington, DC	Steel		Avg Sen: $1,894	Incumb: 90.1%

Arnold & Porter		$79,174	81 Candidates	Dems: 88.0%
Arnold & Porter Partners PAC			Avg House: $912	House: 59.9%
Washington, DC	Lawyers		Avg Sen: $1,086	Incumb: 88.1%

Arthur Andersen & Co		$209,873	99 Candidates	Dems: 70.0%
Arthur Andersen & Co PAC			Avg House: $1,972	House: 63.9%
Washington, DC	Accountants		Avg Sen: $2,444	Incumb: 84.5%

Asarco Inc		$24,769	35 Candidates	Repubs: 63.7%
Asarco Employees PAC (ASARCOPAC)			Avg House: $600	House: 58.1%
New York, NY	Metal Mining/Process†		Avg Sen: $943	Incumb: 85.5%

ASCAP		$174,710	136 Candidates	Dems: 86.5%
ASCAP Legislative Fund for The Arts			Avg House: $1,081	House: 63.1%
New York, NY	Music Production		Avg Sen: $1,923	Incumb: 92.2%

Ashland Oil		$186,311	119 Candidates	Repubs: 58.3%
Ashland Oil PAC for Employees (PACE)			Avg House: $1,345	House: 75.1%
Russell, KY	Oil Refining/Mkting†		Avg Sen: $3,097	Incumb: 61.8%

Assn for the Advancement of Psychology		$273,743	130 Candidates	Dems: 90.1%
Psychologists for Legislative Action Now (Plan)			Avg House: $1,659	House: 53.3%
Colorado Springs, CO	Psychiatrist/Psychol		Avg Sen: $3,066	Incumb: 70.9%

Assn of American Publishers		$21,650	32 Candidates	Dems: 72.3%
Association of American Publishers PAC			Avg House: $579	House: 56.1%
Washington, DC	Publishing		Avg Sen: $864	Incumb: 100.0%

Assn of Bank Holding Companies		$59,200	46 Candidates	Dems: 59.2%
Association of Bank Holding Companies PAC (ABHC PAC)			Avg House: $1,064	House: 68.3%
Washington, DC	Commercial Banks		Avg Sen: $2,344	Incumb: 94.1%

Assn of Flight Attendants		$221,100	152 Candidates	Dems: 98.7%
Association of Flight Attendants PAC ("Flight PAC")			Avg House: $776	Senate: 55.4%
Washington, DC	Air Transport Unions		Avg Sen: $4,900	Incumb: 52.4%

Assn of Independent Colleges & Schools		$24,050	28 Candidates	Dems: 59.8%
Association of Independent Colleges and Schools PAC			Avg House: $877	House: 87.5%
Washington, DC	Vocational/Tech Educ		Avg Sen: $750	Incumb: 100.0%

Assn of Private Pension Plans		$27,956	37 Candidates	Dems: 51.3%
Association of Private Pension & Welfare Plans			Avg House: $682	House: 68.3%
Washington, DC	Securities		Avg Sen: $1,075	Incumb: 91.4%

Assn of Professional Flight Attendants		$32,275	95 Candidates	Dems: 90.8%
Association of Professional Flight Attendants PAC (APFA PAC)			Avg House: $301	House: 67.2%
Eugless, TX	Air Transport Unions		Avg Sen: $469	Incumb: 81.5%

Assn of Trial Lawyers of America		$2,361,135	386 Candidates	Dems: 92.3%
Association of Trial Lawyers of America PAC			Avg House: $5,965	House: 85.4%
Washington, DC	Assn of Trial Lawyers	Lawyers	Avg Sen: $7,188	Incumb: 64.5%

Associated Builders & Contractors		$184,150	146 Candidates	Repubs: 92.4%
Associated Builders and Contractors PAC (ABC/PAC)			Avg House: $885	House: 60.6%
Washington, DC	Builders Assns†		Avg Sen: $3,630	Incumb: 65.7%

PAC Sponsor or Related Group / PAC Name / City	Affiliate	Category	1991-92 Total	Candidates	Avg House / Avg Sen	Party	House/Senate	Incumb
Associated Credit Bureaus Associated Credit Bureaus PAC Houston, TX		Credit/Loans	$75,600	58 Candidates	Avg House: $1,132 Avg Sen: $2,375	Dems: 57.0%	House: 74.9%	Incumb: 98.7%
Associated General Contractors Associated General Contractors PAC Washington, DC	Assoc Genl Contractors	Heavy Construction	$669,249	315 Candidates	Avg House: $1,691 Avg Sen: $5,486	Repubs: 76.5%	House: 70.5%	Incumb: 72.8%
Associated Milk Producers Cmte for Thorough Agricultural Pol Education of Associated Milk Producers San Antonio, TX		Dairy	$877,550	356 Candidates	Avg House: $2,294 Avg Sen: $4,207	Dems: 78.8%	House: 85.0%	Incumb: 84.5%
AT&T American Telephone & Telegraph Company Inc PAC (AT&T PAC) New York, NY		Long Distance†	$1,303,035	593 Candidates	Avg House: $2,091 Avg Sen: $2,896	Dems: 62.4%	House: 82.7%	Incumb: 81.1%
Atlanta Gas Light Co Atlanta Gas Light Company for Good Government Committee, Inc. Atlanta, GA		Natural Gas	$20,250	16 Candidates	Avg House: $946 Avg Sen: $3,500	Dems: 80.2%	House: 65.4%	Incumb: 58.5%
Atlantic Marine/Atlantic Dry Dock Atlantic Marine, Inc & Atlantic Dry Dock Corp Separate Segregated Fund Jacksonville, FL		Shipbuilding/Repair	$24,250	21 Candidates	Avg House: $1,074 Avg Sen: $1,500	Repubs: 56.7%	House: 75.3%	Incumb: 73.2%
Atlantic Research Corp Atlantic Research Corporation PAC Alexandria, VA	Sequa Corp	Weapons Systems†	$66,750	60 Candidates	Avg House: $981 Avg Sen: $1,375	Dems: 58.0%	House: 58.8%	Incumb: 99.2%
Atlantic Richfield Arco PAC, Atlantic Richfield Company Los Angeles, CA		Oil & Gas†	$323,534	193 Candidates	Avg House: $1,218 Avg Sen: $4,269	Repubs: 72.5%	House: 61.7%	Incumb: 76.2%
Auto Dealers & Drivers for Free Trade Auto Dealers and Driver for Free Trade PAC Jamaica, NY		Japanese Auto Dlrs	$538,550	237 Candidates	Avg House: $1,844 Avg Sen: $3,691	Repubs: 61.8%	House: 62.3%	Incumb: 86.9%
Autozone Inc Autozone Inc Committee for Responsible Government Memphis, TN		Truck/Auto Parts	$27,000	17 Candidates	Avg House: $1,731 Avg Sen: $1,125	Repubs: 61.1%	House: 83.3%	Incumb: 68.5%
Avondale Industries Avondale Industries Political Action Fund New Orleans, LA		Naval Ships†	$21,600	19 Candidates	Avg House: $1,079 Avg Sen: $1,300	Dems: 58.6%	House: 69.9%	Incumb: 91.7%
Babcock & Wilcox Babcock & Wilcox Company Good Government Fund; The New Orleans, LA	McDermott Inc	Power Plant Constr†	$87,900	66 Candidates	Avg House: $1,212 Avg Sen: $1,542	Dems: 72.0%	House: 57.9%	Incumb: 92.0%
Baker & Botts Bluebonnet Fund (Baker & Botts), The Houston, TX		Lawyers	$74,391	52 Candidates	Avg House: $1,148 Avg Sen: $1,964	Repubs: 52.6%	House: 52.5%	Incumb: 88.6%
Baker & Hostetler Baker & Hostetler PAC Cleveland, OH		Lawyers	$35,084	45 Candidates	Avg House: $602 Avg Sen: $1,270	Dems: 68.4%	House: 56.6%	Incumb: 78.3%
Bakery & Confectionery Workers local #19 Bakery & Confectionary Workers International Union Local No. 19 Political Organization Cleveland, OH		Food Svc Unions	$28,175	7 Candidates	Avg House: $4,025 Avg Sen: $0	Dems: 100.0%	House: 100.0%	Incumb: 39.7%
Bakery Confectionery & Tobacco Workers Bakery, Confectionery and Tobacco Workers International Union PAC Kensington, MD		Food Svc Unions	$193,900	130 Candidates	Avg House: $1,302 Avg Sen: $2,024	Dems: 99.7%	House: 67.2%	Incumb: 45.5%
Ball Corp Ball Corporation PAC (BAC PAC) Muncie, IN		Glass Products†	$47,020	52 Candidates	Avg House: $644 Avg Sen: $1,396	Repubs: 77.1%	Senate: 53.4%	Incumb: 86.1%
Baltimore Gas & Electric Baltimore Gas and Electric Company PAC (BG&E PAC) Baltimore, MD		Gas & Electric Util†	$83,575	71 Candidates	Avg House: $1,225 Avg Sen: $962	Repubs: 59.8%	House: 85.0%	Incumb: 80.0%
Banc One Corp Banc One PAC Columbus, OH		Commercial Banks	$122,025	95 Candidates	Avg House: $1,135 Avg Sen: $1,884	Dems: 55.5%	House: 70.7%	Incumb: 82.5%

† PAC sponsor has other major interests in addition to this primary category

Bank of Boston Bank of Boston Federal PAC Boston, MA	Commercial Banks	$33,650	38 Candidates Avg House: $819 Avg Sen: $1,179	Dems: 78.5% House: 75.5% Incumb: 91.8%
Bank of New York Bank of New York Company PAC-BNY PAC New York, NY	Commercial Banks	$22,395	13 Candidates Avg House: $1,377 Avg Sen: $2,500	Repubs: 58.7% House: 55.4% Incumb: 20.7%
Bank of Stockton Bank of Stockton PAC Stockton, CA	Commercial Banks	$27,855	7 Candidates Avg House: $3,214 Avg Sen: $5,000	Repubs: 100.0% Senate: 53.9% Incumb: 37.7%
Bank South Corp Cmte on Public Affairs of Bank South Corporation and its Subsidiaries (BSCPA) Atlanta, GA	Commercial Banks	$21,900	27 Candidates Avg House: $669 Avg Sen: $3,175	Repubs: 51.8% House: 73.3% Incumb: 31.1%
BankAmerica BankAmerica Federal Election Fund San Francisco, CA	Commercial Banks	$279,377	158 Candidates Avg House: $1,484 Avg Sen: $2,529	Repubs: 52.6% House: 61.1% Incumb: 69.0%
Bankers Trust Bankers Trust PAC New York, NY	Commercial Banks	$105,200	62 Candidates Avg House: $1,513 Avg Sen: $2,938	Dems: 70.1% House: 77.7% Incumb: 92.9%
Barnett Banks of Florida Barnett People for Better Govt Inc - Fed a PAC of Barnett Banks of Florida Jacksonville, FL	Commercial Banks	$428,133	234 Candidates Avg House: $1,518 Avg Sen: $3,103	Repubs: 53.2% House: 66.7% Incumb: 87.7%
Baroid Corp Baroid Corporation- PAC Houston, TX	Oilfield Services	$44,200	33 Candidates Avg House: $721 Avg Sen: $2,179	Repubs: 85.1% Senate: 69.0% Incumb: 26.2%
Barrack, Rodos & Bacine Barrack, Rodos & Bacine PAC Philadelphia, PA	Lawyers	$29,950	21 Candidates Avg House: $944 Avg Sen: $1,927	Dems: 88.3% Senate: 70.8% Incumb: 65.1%
Bass Brothers Enterprises Bass Brothers Enterprises Inc PAC Fort Worth, TX	Oilfield Services	$44,500	16 Candidates Avg House: $3,167 Avg Sen: $2,286	Dems: 84.3% House: 64.0% Incumb: 91.0%
Bath Iron Works Bath Iron Works Corp PAC Arlington, VA	Naval Ships†	$35,700	36 Candidates Avg House: $965 Avg Sen: $1,125	Dems: 74.0% House: 81.1% Incumb: 95.1%
Baxter Healthcare Corp Baxter Healthcare Corporation PAC Deerfield, IL	Medical Supplies†	$83,140	71 Candidates Avg House: $1,037 Avg Sen: $1,389	Dems: 50.9% House: 54.9% Incumb: 86.7%
BDM International BDM International, Inc. PAC (BDM-PAC) Mclean, VA	Defense R&D†	$122,050	68 Candidates Avg House: $1,527 Avg Sen: $2,395	Repubs: 59.4% House: 58.8% Incumb: 85.2%
Bear, Stearns & Co Bear, Stearns and Co Political Campaign Committee New York, NY	Investmtent Banking†	$88,950	68 Candidates Avg House: $934 Avg Sen: $2,091	Dems: 86.0% Senate: 51.7% Incumb: 49.7%
Bechtel Corp Bechtel Group, Inc PAC San Francisco, CA	Power Plant Constr†	$142,847	92 Candidates Avg House: $1,373 Avg Sen: $2,200	Dems: 58.5% House: 69.2% Incumb: 90.2%
Bedford Properties Bedford Properties, Inc PAC Lafayette, CA	Real Estate Devel†	$26,250	15 Candidates Avg House: $1,750 Avg Sen: $1,750	Repubs: 63.8% House: 60.0% Incumb: 43.8%
Beech Aircraft Beech Aircraft PAC (BEECHPAC) Wichita, KS Raytheon	Aircraft Mfr†	$30,800	29 Candidates Avg House: $965 Avg Sen: $1,278	Dems: 64.9% House: 62.7% Incumb: 99.0%
Bell Atlantic Bell Atlantic Corporation PAC Philadelphia, PA	Phone Utilites†	$125,751	110 Candidates Avg House: $898 Avg Sen: $2,395	Dems: 60.8% House: 65.7% Incumb: 94.4%
Bell Telephone of Pennsylvania Bell Telephone Company of Pennsylvania PAC (Pa Bell PAC) Harrisburg, PA Bell Atlantic	Phone Utilites	$28,400	26 Candidates Avg House: $985 Avg Sen: $2,375	Repubs: 60.7% House: 83.3% Incumb: 89.4%

BellSouth Corp
Bellsouth Federal PAC (Bellsouth Fed PAC)
Atlanta, GA — BellSouth — Phone Utilites
$155,694
133 Candidates — Dems: 61.2%
Avg House: $1,059 — House: 73.5%
Avg Sen: $1,619 — Incumb: 89.7%

BellSouth Services
Bellsouth Services Federal PAC
Birmingham, AL — BellSouth — Phone Utilites
$88,750
102 Candidates — Repubs: 58.1%
Avg House: $750 — House: 71.8%
Avg Sen: $1,471 — Incumb: 98.9%

Beneficial Management Corp
Beneficial Management Corporation and Affiliated Corporations PAC
Peapack, NJ — Credit/Loans†
$158,300
118 Candidates — Dems: 58.0%
Avg House: $1,268 — House: 79.3%
Avg Sen: $1,724 — Incumb: 77.8%

LM Berry & Co
L. M. Berry and Company PAC
Dayton, OH — BellSouth — Mail Advertising†
$57,782
65 Candidates — Repubs: 98.3%
Avg House: $700 — House: 65.4%
Avg Sen: $1,818 — Incumb: 28.3%

Bethlehem Steel
Bethlehem Steel Good Government Committee
Bethlehem, PA — Steel
$56,170
42 Candidates — Repubs: 54.3%
Avg House: $1,237 — House: 70.5%
Avg Sen: $1,660 — Incumb: 92.9%

Betz Laboratories
Betz Laboratories, Inc PAC (Betz PAC)
Trevose, PA — Chemicals
$21,250
11 Candidates — Repubs: 97.7%
Avg House: $1,625 — House: 76.5%
Avg Sen: $5,000 — Incumb: 25.9%

Blue Cross & Blue Shield Assn
CAREPAC, The Blue Cross and Blue Shield Association PAC
Washington, DC — Blue Cross — Health Insurance
$195,801
208 Candidates — Dems: 61.4%
Avg House: $811 — House: 69.6%
Avg Sen: $1,487 — Incumb: 90.1%

Blue Cross of California
Blue Cross of California PAC
Woodland Hills, CA — Blue Cross — Health Insurance
$20,150
22 Candidates — Dems: 70.2%
Avg House: $893 — House: 66.5%
Avg Sen: $964 — Incumb: 74.0%

Blue Cross/Blue Shield of Florida
Florida Health PAC
Jacksonville, FL — Blue Cross — Health Insurance
$38,550
38 Candidates — Dems: 59.3%
Avg House: $981 — House: 89.1%
Avg Sen: $2,100 — Incumb: 61.6%

Boat Owners Assn of the US
Boat Owners Association of the United States (BOAT/US) PAC
Alexandria, VA — Recreational Boats†
$36,600
38 Candidates — Dems: 59.1%
Avg House: $952 — House: 85.8%
Avg Sen: $1,040 — Incumb: 93.2%

Boatmens Bankshares
BoBancPAC, a PAC of Boatmen's Bancshares, Inc
St Louis, MO — Commercial Banks
$38,315
18 Candidates — Repubs: 51.1%
Avg House: $2,171 — House: 79.3%
Avg Sen: $1,979 — Incumb: 66.8%

Boeing Co
Boeing Company PAC (BPAC)
Seattle, WA — Aircraft Mfr†
$336,100
171 Candidates — Dems: 55.3%
Avg House: $1,494 — House: 62.7%
Avg Sen: $4,180 — Incumb: 94.0%

Boilermakers Union
International Brotherhood of Boilermakers, In Sp Bldrs, Bkmths, Frgrs & Hlprs-Le
Kansas City, KS — Manufacturing Unions†
$398,100
218 Candidates — Dems: 95.6%
Avg House: $1,573 — House: 70.7%
Avg Sen: $2,961 — Incumb: 70.4%

Boise Cascade
Boise Cascade Political Fund
Boise, ID — Paper/Pulp†
$69,000
32 Candidates — Repubs: 92.0%
Avg House: $1,729 — House: 60.1%
Avg Sen: $3,438 — Incumb: 45.6%

JG Boswell Co
J.G. Boswell Company Employees' PAC
Los Angeles, CA — Cotton
$47,250
34 Candidates — Repubs: 67.7%
Avg House: $891 — Senate: 56.6%
Avg Sen: $2,432 — Incumb: 82.0%

Bowling Proprietors Assn
Bowling Proprietors Assn of America PAC
Arlington, TX — Amusement Centers
$67,100
81 Candidates — Repubs: 88.4%
Avg House: $793 — House: 78.0%
Avg Sen: $983 — Incumb: 87.9%

BP America
BPA-PAC (The BP America PAC)
Cleveland, OH — Oil & Gas†
$105,650
107 Candidates — Repubs: 60.1%
Avg House: $760 — House: 62.6%
Avg Sen: $1,975 — Incumb: 92.4%

Bracewell & Patterson
Bracewell & Patterson PAC
Washington, DC — Lawyers
$38,000
44 Candidates — Dems: 83.4%
Avg House: $847 — House: 80.3%
Avg Sen: $938 — Incumb: 93.4%

Bricklayers Union
International Union of Bricklayers and Allied Craftsmen PAC
Washington, DC — Building Trade Unions
$238,700
140 Candidates — Dems: 96.5%
Avg House: $1,269 — House: 55.8%
Avg Sen: $2,827 — Incumb: 70.4%

† PAC sponsor has other major interests in addition to this primary category

Bristol-Myers Squibb
Bristol-Myers Company PAC
New York, NY   Pharmaceuticals†

$127,725

141 Candidates	Repubs: 55.8%
Avg House: $621	House: 52.0%
Avg Sen: $1,801	Incumb: 87.1%

Brotherhood of Locomotive Engineers
Brotherhood of Locomotive Engineers Legislative League
Cleveland, OH   Locomotive Engrs Union   Railroad Unions

$262,113

213 Candidates	Dems: 95.8%
Avg House: $1,080	House: 72.9%
Avg Sen: $1,998	Incumb: 53.0%

Brotherhood of Railroad Signalmen
Brotherhood of Railroad Signalmen PAC
Mt. Prospect, IL   Railroad Unions

$110,410

130 Candidates	Dems: 98.2%
Avg House: $701	House: 66.6%
Avg Sen: $1,452	Incumb: 82.1%

Brown & Root
Brownbuilders PAC of Brown & Root, Inc Employees
Houston, TX   Halliburton Co   Heavy Construction†

$80,657

86 Candidates	Repubs: 74.3%
Avg House: $882	House: 77.7%
Avg Sen: $1,200	Incumb: 76.6%

Brown & Williamson Tobacco
Brown & Williamson Tobacco Corporation Employee PAC aka EMPAC
Louisville, KY   Batus Inc   Tobacco

$57,700

70 Candidates	Dems: 60.4%
Avg House: $508	Senate: 55.0%
Avg Sen: $1,984	Incumb: 93.5%

Brown-Forman Distillers
Brown-Forman Non-Partisan Committee for Responsible Government
Louisville, KY   Wine & Liquor†

$154,600

128 Candidates	Repubs: 78.8%
Avg House: $981	House: 62.2%
Avg Sen: $1,950	Incumb: 68.0%

Browning-Ferris Industries
Browning-Ferris Industries PAC (BFI PAC)
Houston, TX   Waste Mgmt

$148,606

151 Candidates	Dems: 53.4%
Avg House: $788	House: 63.7%
Avg Sen: $1,742	Incumb: 81.2%

Brush Wellman
Brush Wellman Good Government Fund
Cleveland, OH   Industl/Comml Equip

$41,500

12 Candidates	Repubs: 95.2%
Avg House: $4,100	Senate: 50.6%
Avg Sen: $3,000	Incumb: 56.6%

Buchanan Ingersoll
Buchanan Ingersoll Professional Corp Cmte for Effective Govt "BIPC PAC"
Pittsburgh, PA   Lawyers

$22,450

16 Candidates	Dems: 59.7%
Avg House: $383	Senate: 84.6%
Avg Sen: $2,714	Incumb: 54.8%

Burlington Industries
Burlington Industries Good Government Committee
Greensboro, NC   Textiles†

$148,675

99 Candidates	Dems: 74.9%
Avg House: $1,394	House: 77.8%
Avg Sen: $2,063	Incumb: 80.0%

Burlington Northern Inc
Burlington Northern Employees Voluntary Good Government Fund
Seattle, WA   Burlington Northern   Railroads

$76,850

97 Candidates	Dems: 60.8%
Avg House: $670	House: 64.5%
Avg Sen: $1,187	Incumb: 81.6%

Burlington Northern Railroad
Burlington Northern Railroad RailPAC (BN RailPAC)
Fort Worth, TX   Burlington Northern   Railroads

$218,256

188 Candidates	Dems: 62.6%
Avg House: $1,057	House: 74.5%
Avg Sen: $1,634	Incumb: 88.3%

Burroughs Wellcome
Burroughs Wellcome Co Good Government Fund
Res Triangle Park, NC   Pharmaceuticals

$24,100

30 Candidates	Repubs: 55.0%
Avg House: $754	House: 75.1%
Avg Sen: $1,000	Incumb: 85.5%

Burson-Marsteller
Burson-Marsteller PAC
Washington, DC   Lobbyists/PR

$68,575

78 Candidates	Dems: 65.4%
Avg House: $678	House: 52.4%
Avg Sen: $1,305	Incumb: 84.8%

Business Industry PAC
Business Industry PAC
Washington, DC   Pro-Business Assns

$133,431

109 Candidates	Repubs: 93.1%
Avg House: $1,007	House: 67.2%
Avg Sen: $2,189	Incumb: 29.5%

Cablevision Systems Corp
Cablevision Systems Corporation PAC
Woodbury, NY   Cable TV

$24,550

22 Candidates	Dems: 50.7%
Avg House: $629	Senate: 64.2%
Avg Sen: $1,969	Incumb: 95.9%

Caesars World
Caesars World PAC
Mill Valley, CA   Casinos/Gambling†

$22,000

10 Candidates	Dems: 61.4%
Avg House: $1,833	House: 50.0%
Avg Sen: $2,750	Incumb: 90.9%

Calcot Ltd
Calcot Ltd Federal PAC
Bakersfield, CA   Cotton

$65,832

40 Candidates	Repubs: 50.8%
Avg House: $1,655	House: 65.4%
Avg Sen: $1,629	Incumb: 80.0%

CalFed Inc
CalFed Inc Public Affairs Committee
Los Angeles, CA   Savings & Loans†

$23,750

12 Candidates	Repubs: 100.0%
Avg House: $1,705	House: 79.0%
Avg Sen: $5,000	Incumb: 23.2%

California Almond Growers Exchange
Blue Diamond Growers PAC
Sacramento, CA — Fruit/Veg
$61,991

18 Candidates	Repubs: 52.4%
Avg House: $3,320	House: 80.3%
Avg Sen: $4,064	Incumb: 90.3%

California Assn of Hosp/Health Systems
California Hospitals PAC-FED
Sacramento, CA — Hospitals
$57,253

40 Candidates	Dems: 79.6%
Avg House: $1,134	House: 61.4%
Avg Sen: $2,456	Incumb: 47.0%

California Avocado Advocate
California Avocado Advocate - Federal
Escondido, CA — Fruit/Veg
$22,350

35 Candidates	Dems: 50.3%
Avg House: $640	House: 88.8%
Avg Sen: $625	Incumb: 94.4%

California Bankers Assn
California Bankers Association Federal PAC (aka CalBankPAC)
San Francisco, CA — American Bankers Assn — Commercial Banks
$29,000

15 Candidates	Repubs: 69.0%
Avg House: $2,000	House: 89.7%
Avg Sen: $1,500	Incumb: 17.2%

California Canning Peach Assn
California Canning Peach Association PAC (aka Peach-PAC)
Lafayette, CA — Fruit/Veg
$26,660

31 Candidates	Repubs: 61.9%
Avg House: $744	House: 69.8%
Avg Sen: $1,342	Incumb: 90.6%

California Farm Bureau Federation
California Farm Bureau Federation PAC (Farm PAC)
Sacramento, CA — Farm Orgs
$35,549

23 Candidates	Repubs: 81.9%
Avg House: $1,015	House: 57.1%
Avg Sen: $5,083	Incumb: 67.7%

California League of Savings Institutions
California League of Savings Institutions FEDPAC
Los Angeles, CA — US League of Savings Assns — Savings & Loans
$29,250

31 Candidates	Repubs: 76.9%
Avg House: $644	House: 57.3%
Avg Sen: $2,500	Incumb: 65.8%

Campaign America
Campaign America
Washington, DC — Sen Bob Dole (R-Kans) — Repub Leaders
$388,236

85 Candidates	Repubs: 100.0%
Avg House: $2,303	Senate: 70.3%
Avg Sen: $7,803	Incumb: 40.9%

Campaign for America
Campaign for America
Livingston, NJ — Sen Frank Lautenberg (D-NJ) — Dem Leaders
$26,000

5 Candidates	Dems: 100.0%
Avg House: $5,000	Senate: 80.8%
Avg Sen: $5,250	Incumb: 42.3%

Capital Holding Corp
Capital Holding PAC - CAP-PAC
Louisville, KY — Insurance
$98,800

84 Candidates	Dems: 61.4%
Avg House: $863	House: 50.7%
Avg Sen: $1,930	Incumb: 86.5%

Cargill Inc
Cargill, Incorporated PAC
Minneapolis, MN — Crop Production†
$112,000

74 Candidates	Repubs: 80.4%
Avg House: $1,330	House: 66.5%
Avg Sen: $2,083	Incumb: 60.3%

Carolina Power & Light
Employees Federal PAC - Carolina Power & Light Co
Raleigh, NC — Electric Utilities
$93,550

93 Candidates	Dems: 62.8%
Avg House: $894	House: 71.7%
Avg Sen: $1,472	Incumb: 85.4%

Carpenters & Joiners Union
Carpenters Committee on Political Action
Los Angeles, CA — Carpenters Union — Building Trade Unions
$58,250

14 Candidates	Dems: 78.5%
Avg House: $3,325	House: 57.1%
Avg Sen: $6,250	Incumb: 12.9%

Carpenters & Joiners Union
Carpenters' Legislative Improvement Committee
Washington, DC — Carpenters Union — Building Trade Unions
$1,369,682

313 Candidates	Dems: 95.2%
Avg House: $4,080	House: 79.8%
Avg Sen: $6,193	Incumb: 58.3%

Carpenters Union/Connecticut
Connecticut Carpenters Legislative Improvement Committee
Norwalk, CT — Carpenters Union — Building Trade Unions
$28,000

6 Candidates	Dems: 67.9%
Avg House: $4,667	House: 100.0%
Avg Sen: $0	Incumb: 64.3%

Casualty & Surety Agents Assn
National Association of Casualty & Surety Agents PAC (NACSAPAC)
Bethesda, MD — Insurance
$163,321

143 Candidates	Repubs: 55.7%
Avg House: $1,034	House: 72.2%
Avg Sen: $1,568	Incumb: 67.8%

Caterpillar Tractor
Caterpillar Tractor Co Committee for Effective Govt
Peoria, IL — Constr Equipment†
$92,480

80 Candidates	Repubs: 87.7%
Avg House: $879	House: 56.1%
Avg Sen: $1,933	Incumb: 69.6%

CB&T Bancshares
CB&T Bancshares, Inc Federal Political Action Comittee
Columbus, GA — Commercial Banks
$54,700

15 Candidates	Dems: 85.8%
Avg House: $3,838	House: 56.1%
Avg Sen: $3,429	Incumb: 52.0%

CBI Industries
CBI Industries PAC (CBIPAC)
Oak Brook, IL — Heavy Construction†
$22,000

29 Candidates	Repubs: 88.6%
Avg House: $600	Senate: 72.7%
Avg Sen: $842	Incumb: 54.5%

† PAC sponsor has other major interests in addition to this primary category

Centerior Energy Corp
Centerior Fund a PAC of the Centerior Energy Corp
Independence, OH — Electric Utilities — **$45,473**

53 Candidates	Dems: 82.0%
Avg House: $710	House: 64.0%
Avg Sen: $1,365	Incumb: 90.9%

Central Bancshares of the South
Central Bancshares of the South, Inc PAC ("Central BancPAC")
Birmingham, AL — Commercial Banks — **$62,350**

18 Candidates	Dems: 76.7%
Avg House: $3,686	House: 82.8%
Avg Sen: $2,688	Incumb: 49.5%

Century 21 Real Estate
Century 21 PAC (CEN-PAC)
Washington, DC — Metropolitan Life — Real Estate Agents — **$101,500**

67 Candidates	Dems: 50.2%
Avg House: $1,354	House: 54.7%
Avg Sen: $1,769	Incumb: 80.3%

CF Industries
CF Industries Employees' Good Government Fund
Long Grove, IL — Ag Chemicals† — **$64,110**

89 Candidates	Dems: 60.1%
Avg House: $575	House: 67.3%
Avg Sen: $1,497	Incumb: 87.0%

CH2M Hill
CH2M Hill PAC Inc
Corvallis, OR — Engineers† — **$122,103**

136 Candidates	Repubs: 53.0%
Avg House: $748	House: 68.6%
Avg Sen: $1,598	Incumb: 88.7%

Chambers Development Co
Chambers Development Company Inc PAC
Penn Hills, PA — Waste Mgmt — **$67,250**

42 Candidates	Repubs: 50.6%
Avg House: $1,129	House: 48.7%
Avg Sen: $2,682	Incumb: 76.7%

Champion International Corp
Champion International Corporation PAC
Stamford, CT — Paper/Pulp† — **$107,227**

98 Candidates	Dems: 52.3%
Avg House: $889	House: 64.7%
Avg Sen: $1,895	Incumb: 85.3%

Charter Medical Corp
Charter Medical Corporation Employee Committee for Good Government
Macon, GA — Hospitals — **$22,800**

19 Candidates	Dems: 74.3%
Avg House: $858	Senate: 54.8%
Avg Sen: $1,786	Incumb: 74.3%

Chase Manhattan
Chase Manhattan Corporation PAC - (ChasePAC)
New York, NY — Commercial Banks† — **$282,013**

155 Candidates	Repubs: 61.6%
Avg House: $1,739	House: 75.9%
Avg Sen: $2,127	Incumb: 72.6%

Chemical Bank
Chemical Bank Fund for Good Government
New York, NY — Commercial Banks — **$140,000**

127 Candidates	Dems: 64.6%
Avg House: $1,005	House: 71.1%
Avg Sen: $1,446	Incumb: 86.6%

Chemical Manufacturers Assn
Chemical Manufacturers Association PAC
Washington, DC — Chemicals — **$26,279**

52 Candidates	Repubs: 59.1%
Avg House: $463	House: 82.9%
Avg Sen: $900	Incumb: 85.7%

Chemical Producers & Distributors Assn
Chemical Producers and Distributors Association PAC (CPDA-PAC)
Washington, DC — Ag Chemicals — **$21,800**

21 Candidates	Dems: 64.2%
Avg House: $933	House: 77.1%
Avg Sen: $1,667	Incumb: 86.2%

Chesapeake & Potomac Telephone
Chesapeake & Potomac Telephone Company Federal PAC, C&P of Md Va WVa
Washington, DC — Bell Atlantic — Phone Utilites — **$33,000**

31 Candidates	Dems: 69.5%
Avg House: $1,000	House: 90.9%
Avg Sen: $3,000	Incumb: 79.1%

Chevron Corp
Chevron Employees PAC
San Francisco, CA — Oil & Gas — **$386,581**

223 Candidates	Repubs: 72.2%
Avg House: $1,289	House: 63.7%
Avg Sen: $4,384	Incumb: 59.2%

Chicago & North Western Transport
North Western Officers Trust Account - Chicago & North Western Transportation Co
Chicago, IL — Railroads — **$61,050**

64 Candidates	Repubs: 52.0%
Avg House: $719	House: 55.4%
Avg Sen: $1,603	Incumb: 87.7%

Chicago Board of Options Exchange
Chicago Board of Options Exchange Inc PAC
Chicago, IL — Commodity Investment — **$74,500**

42 Candidates	Dems: 68.5%
Avg House: $1,724	House: 67.1%
Avg Sen: $1,885	Incumb: 98.7%

Chicago Board of Trade
Auction Markets PAC of the Chicago Board of Trade aka AMPAC/CBT
Chicago, IL — Commodity Investment — **$311,100**

165 Candidates	Dems: 68.7%
Avg House: $1,313	House: 51.1%
Avg Sen: $3,387	Incumb: 84.6%

Chicago Mercantile Exchange
Commodity Futures Political Fund of the Chicago Mercantile Exchange
Chicago, IL — Commodity Investment — **$492,750**

201 Candidates	Dems: 72.8%
Avg House: $1,748	House: 55.4%
Avg Sen: $5,000	Incumb: 82.2%

Chili's Inc
Chili's Inc PAC
Dallas, TX — Restaurants — **$64,500**

44 Candidates	Repubs: 80.6%
Avg House: $1,355	House: 65.1%
Avg Sen: $1,731	Incumb: 45.0%

PAC Sponsor or Related Group/PAC Name	Affiliate	1991-92 Total	Where the money went...		
Chrysler Corp Chrysler Corporation Political Support Committee Highland Park, MI	Auto Manufacturers†	$204,886	159 Candidates Avg House: $1,093 Avg Sen: $1,933	Dems: 73.6% House: 65.1% Incumb: 92.7%	
Chubb Corp Chubb Corporation PAC "ChubbPAC" Warren, NJ	Insurance	$107,305	88 Candidates Avg House: $1,107 Avg Sen: $1,577	Dems: 53.8% House: 69.1% Incumb: 78.6%	
Ciba-Geigy Corp Ciba-Geigy Employee Good Government Fund Ardsley, NY	Pharmaceuticals†	$140,200	146 Candidates Avg House: $828 Avg Sen: $1,493	Repubs: 57.8% House: 69.1% Incumb: 91.2%	
Cigna Corp Cigna Corporation PAC Philadelphia, PA	Insurance	$236,250	192 Candidates Avg House: $952 Avg Sen: $2,677	Repubs: 56.2% House: 64.9% Incumb: 80.2%	
Cincinnati Bell Cincinnati Bell Inc Federal PAC Cincinnati, OH	Phone Utilites	$32,364	18 Candidates Avg House: $1,675 Avg Sen: $2,044	Dems: 52.9% House: 62.1% Incumb: 80.2%	
Circus Circus Enterprises Circus Circus Enterprises Inc PAC (aka CC-PAC) San Francisco, CA	Casinos/Gambling†	$69,714	35 Candidates Avg House: $2,058 Avg Sen: $1,936	Dems: 75.5% Senate: 52.8% Incumb: 87.0%	
Citicorp Citicorp Voluntary Political Fund Federal Washington, DC	Commercial Banks†	$346,852	200 Candidates Avg House: $1,723 Avg Sen: $1,957	Dems: 54.7% House: 83.9% Incumb: 91.6%	
Citizens & Southern National Bank Citizens and Southern Corporation Better Government Committee Atlanta, GA C&S/Sovran Corp	Commercial Banks	$430,767	219 Candidates Avg House: $1,956 Avg Sen: $2,033	Dems: 61.8% House: 85.8% Incumb: 82.9%	
Citizens Concerned for the National Interest Citizens Concerned for the National Interest Chicago, IL	Pro-Israel	$75,500	11 Candidates Avg House: $0 Avg Sen: $7,050	Repubs: 60.3% Senate: 93.4% Incumb: 86.8%	
Citizens Organized PAC Citizens Organized PAC Los Angeles, CA	Pro-Israel	$192,750	34 Candidates Avg House: $2,205 Avg Sen: $7,326	Dems: 64.5% Senate: 87.4% Incumb: 85.3%	
Citizens Savings Financial Corp Citizens Savings Financial Corporation Excellence in Government Fund (CitPAC) Ft Lauderdale, FL	Savings & Loans	$21,000	10 Candidates Avg House: $750 Avg Sen: $4,125	Dems: 100.0% Senate: 78.6% Incumb: 85.7%	
City PAC City PAC (City PAC) Deerfield, IL	Pro-Israel	$84,000	40 Candidates Avg House: $1,565 Avg Sen: $2,824	Dems: 71.4% Senate: 57.1% Incumb: 61.3%	
Cleveland-Cliffs Iron Co Cleveland-Cliffs Iron Company PAC (CliffsPAC) Cleveland, OH	Metal Mining/Process	$38,400	46 Candidates Avg House: $785 Avg Sen: $928	Repubs: 70.7% House: 61.3% Incumb: 68.9%	
Clorox Co Clorox Employees' PAC Oakland, CA	Household Chemicals	$20,000	29 Candidates Avg House: $556 Avg Sen: $909	Repubs: 80.0% House: 50.0% Incumb: 62.5%	
CNA Financial Corp CNA Financial Corporation Citizens for Good Government Chicago, IL Loews Corp	Insurance	$43,825	43 Candidates Avg House: $1,180 Avg Sen: $604	Dems: 67.0% House: 83.5% Incumb: 88.4%	
Coast Federal Savings & Loan Coast FEDPAC - A PAC of Coast Savings and Loan Granada Hills, CA	Savings & Loans	$38,200	18 Candidates Avg House: $1,477 Avg Sen: $3,800	Repubs: 98.7% House: 50.3% Incumb: 66.0%	
Coastal Corp Coastal Corp. Employee Action Fund Houston, TX	Natural Gas†	$332,875	157 Candidates Avg House: $1,819 Avg Sen: $3,094	Dems: 75.3% House: 66.7% Incumb: 82.2%	
Coca-Cola Co Coca-Cola Company Nonpartisan Committee for Good Government Atlanta, GA Coca-Cola	Soft Drinks†	$198,990	199 Candidates Avg House: $826 Avg Sen: $1,645	Dems: 60.3% House: 64.8% Incumb: 78.3%	
Coffield, Ungaretti et al Coffield Ungaretti Harris & Slavin PAC Chicago, IL	Lawyers	$34,450	31 Candidates Avg House: $893 Avg Sen: $1,216	Dems: 86.4% Senate: 56.5% Incumb: 48.6%	

† PAC sponsor has other major interests in addition to this primary category

College of American Pathologists College of American Pathologists PAC Washington, DC Misc MD Specialists	**$52,500**	61 Candidates Repubs: 53.3% Avg House: $837 House: 82.9% Avg Sen: $1,000 Incumb: 81.0%
Colonial Life & Accident Insurance COLPAC - The PAC of Colonial Life & Accident Insurance Company Columbia, SC Insurance	**$37,850**	28 Candidates Dems: 65.7% Avg House: $1,152 House: 67.0% Avg Sen: $2,083 Incumb: 86.5%
Colt Industries Colt Industries Inc Voluntary Political Committee New York, NY Defense Aerospace†	**$111,200**	101 Candidates Repubs: 56.5% Avg House: $1,054 House: 65.4% Avg Sen: $1,203 Incumb: 85.6%
Columbia Gas of Ohio Columbia Gas Distribution Employees Political Action Fund Columbus, OH Columbia Gas System Natural Gas	**$23,827**	35 Candidates Dems: 51.8% Avg House: $643 House: 70.2% Avg Sen: $888 Incumb: 76.6%
Columbia Natural Resources Columbia Employees Political Action Fund Charleston, WV Columbia Gas System Oil & Gas	**$91,175**	92 Candidates Dems: 51.4% Avg House: $1,006 House: 75.0% Avg Sen: $949 Incumb: 83.4%
Combustion Engineering Combustion Engineering Inc PAC (ComPAC) Stamford, CT Power Plant Constr†	**$67,819**	81 Candidates Dems: 63.9% Avg House: $709 House: 59.6% Avg Sen: $1,142 Incumb: 92.5%
Comcast Corp Comcast Corporation PAC Philadelphia, PA Cable TV	**$146,290**	59 Candidates Dems: 62.4% Avg House: $1,925 House: 56.6% Avg Sen: $3,969 Incumb: 90.1%
Committee for a Democratic Consensus Committee for a Democratic Consensus; The Washington, DC Sen Alan Cranston (D-Calif) Dem Leaders	**$89,446**	44 Candidates Dems: 100.0% Avg House: $1,404 Senate: 59.2% Avg Sen: $2,941 Incumb: 59.8%
Committee for America's Future Committee for America's Future Washington, DC Sen Robert Byrd (D-WVa) Dem Leaders	**$47,000**	14 Candidates Dems: 100.0% Avg House: $1,000 Senate: 93.6% Avg Sen: $4,000 Incumb: 100.0%
Committee for an Affordable New Jersey Committee for an Affordable New Jersey-Federal Piscataway, NJ Christine Todd Whitman Non-federal Leaders	**$61,500**	16 Candidates Repubs: 100.0% Avg House: $3,844 House: 100.0% Avg Sen: $0 Incumb: 29.7%
Committee for Effective Government Committee for Effective Government New York, NY Investmtent Banking	**$41,500**	31 Candidates Dems: 90.4% Avg House: $938 Senate: 63.9% Avg Sen: $1,767 Incumb: 48.2%
Committee for Quality Orthopedic Health Care Committee for Quality Orthopaedic Health Care Inc Washington, DC Misc MD Specialists	**$150,802**	166 Candidates Dems: 56.9% Avg House: $762 House: 68.7% Avg Sen: $1,573 Incumb: 74.6%
Communications Workers of America CWA-COPE Political Contributions Committee Washington, DC Communications Workers Commun Unions	**$935,768**	296 Candidates Dems: 98.3% Avg House: $2,657 House: 71.8% Avg Sen: $6,181 Incumb: 50.0%
Commodity Exchange Inc Commodity Exchange Inc PAC (ComPAC) Washington, DC Commodity Investment	**$41,950**	40 Candidates Dems: 72.6% Avg House: $873 House: 58.3% Avg Sen: $1,458 Incumb: 95.2%
Commonwealth Edison Commonwealth Edison PAC Chicago, IL Electric Utilities	**$36,085**	57 Candidates Dems: 62.9% Avg House: $552 House: 68.8% Avg Sen: $938 Incumb: 85.5%
Communications Workers Union #13000 Local 13000 CWA AFL-CIO Philadelphia, PA Communications Workers Commun Unions	**$75,750**	14 Candidates Dems: 100.0% Avg House: $5,063 House: 80.2% Avg Sen: $7,500 Incumb: 49.8%
Computer Sciences Corp Computer Sciences Corporation PAC (CSC PAC) El Segundo, CA Computer Services†	**$93,150**	86 Candidates Dems: 60.6% Avg House: $891 House: 60.3% Avg Sen: $1,609 Incumb: 92.2%
Comsat ComsatPAC Washington, DC Satellite Communic	**$77,550**	65 Candidates Dems: 54.0% Avg House: $936 House: 55.5% Avg Sen: $1,816 Incumb: 93.2%
ConAgra Inc ConAgra Good Government Association Omaha, NE Food Processors†	**$300,038**	127 Candidates Repubs: 68.8% Avg House: $1,781 House: 54.0% Avg Sen: $3,800 Incumb: 82.4%

PAC Sponsor / PAC Name / Location	Affiliate	1991-92 Total	Where the money went...		
Conference of National Park Concessioners Conference of National Park Concessioners PAC (CONPAC) Waynesville, NC	Lodging/Tourism	$20,150	28 Candidates Avg House: $735 Avg Sen: $681	Dems: 54.1% House: 73.0% Incumb: 86.3%	
Congressional Action Committee of Texas Congressional Action Committee of Texas Houston, TX	Pro-Israel	$27,400	37 Candidates Avg House: $771 Avg Sen: $583	Dems: 58.4% House: 87.2% Incumb: 44.7%	
Connaught Laboratories Connaught Laboratories, Inc Political Action Swiftwater, PA	Pharmaceuticals	$32,700	35 Candidates Avg House: $683 Avg Sen: $1,455	Repubs: 52.6% Senate: 48.9% Incumb: 86.7%	
Connecticut Mutual Life Insurance Connecticut Mutual Life Insurance Co-PAC (CM-PAC;/CM PAC;/CML PAC) Hartford, CT	Life Insurance	$63,100	58 Candidates Avg House: $1,009 Avg Sen: $1,250	Dems: 57.0% House: 62.4% Incumb: 83.4%	
Connecticut Union of Telephone Workers PAC for Education - CUTW Hamden, CT	Communication Unions	$33,500	7 Candidates Avg House: $4,750 Avg Sen: $5,000	Dems: 79.1% House: 85.1% Incumb: 55.2%	
Conservative Victory Committee Conservative Victory Committee Alexandria, VA	Repub/Conservative	$96,022	51 Candidates Avg House: $1,859 Avg Sen: $2,111	Repubs: 99.2% House: 79.4% Incumb: 13.8%	
Consolidated Freightways Consolidated Freightways Inc PAC Menlo Park, CA	Trucking Companies†	$93,400	86 Candidates Avg House: $820 Avg Sen: $1,667	Repubs: 51.7% House: 51.8% Incumb: 76.3%	
Consolidated Gas Transmission Corp CNG Transmission Corporation "CONCEPT" Clarksburg, WV	Natural Gas	$20,300	24 Candidates Avg House: $867 Avg Sen: $811	Dems: 78.8% House: 64.0% Incumb: 86.5%	
Consolidated Natural Gas Consolidated Natural Gas Service Co Inc Executives' Political Fund (CONPAC) Pittsburgh, PA	Natural Gas	$44,262	49 Candidates Avg House: $800 Avg Sen: $1,066	Dems: 66.6% House: 54.2% Incumb: 87.3%	
Consolidated Rail Corp Consolidated Rail Corp Good Govt Fund (Conrail Good Govt Fund) Philadelphia, PA	Railroads	$64,850	89 Candidates Avg House: $682 Avg Sen: $1,062	Dems: 69.9% House: 82.0% Incumb: 92.9%	
Consumer Bankers Assn Consumer Bankers Association PAC, The Arlington, VA	Banks	$33,250	35 Candidates Avg House: $788 Avg Sen: $1,600	Dems: 60.8% House: 66.3% Incumb: 97.6%	
Consumers Power Co Consumers Power Company Employees for Better Government - Federal Jackson, MI	CMS Energy Corp Gas & Electric Util†	$116,580	88 Candidates Avg House: $1,386 Avg Sen: $1,103	Dems: 62.6% House: 82.0% Incumb: 83.6%	
Continental Illinois Corp Political Participation Fund of Continental Illinois Corp Chicago, IL	Commercial Banks	$90,750	73 Candidates Avg House: $1,284 Avg Sen: $1,071	Dems: 64.5% House: 83.5% Incumb: 80.7%	
Contran Corp Contran Corporation PAC (ConPAC) Dallas, TX	NL Industries Chemicals†	$31,500	20 Candidates Avg House: $1,900 Avg Sen: $1,467	Repubs: 96.8% Senate: 69.8% Incumb: 50.8%	
Cooper Industries Cooper Industries PAC (CIPAC) Houston, TX	Power Plant Constr†	$345,500	109 Candidates Avg House: $2,821 Avg Sen: $4,340	Repubs: 98.1% House: 68.6% Incumb: 34.9%	
Cooperative of American Physicians Cooperative of American Physicians Federal Action Committee (CAP/FAC) Los Angeles, CA	Doctors	$121,530	73 Candidates Avg House: $1,386 Avg Sen: $2,443	Dems: 69.2% House: 58.2% Incumb: 61.9%	
Coopers & Lybrand Coopers & Lybrand PAC Washington, DC	Accountants	$239,403	142 Candidates Avg House: $1,439 Avg Sen: $2,748	Dems: 65.5% House: 66.7% Incumb: 89.2%	
Coors Industries Political Action Coors Employees (PACE) Golden, CO	Beer	$29,210	41 Candidates Avg House: $717 Avg Sen: $701	Repubs: 91.4% House: 73.6% Incumb: 41.8%	
Corestates Financial Corp Corestates Financial Corp PAC (CorePAC) Philadelphia, PA	Commercial Banks	$30,750	31 Candidates Avg House: $728 Avg Sen: $1,750	Dems: 52.2% House: 54.5% Incumb: 56.9%	

† PAC sponsor has other major interests in addition to this primary category

Corning Glass Works
Corning Glass Works Employees PAC
Corning, NY
Glass Products†
$242,750

119 Candidates		Repubs: 60.6%
Avg House: $1,818		House: 71.2%
Avg Sen: $2,917		Incumb: 80.6%

Cosmetic, Toiletry & Fragrance Assn
Cosmetic, Toiletry & Fragrance Association PAC
Washington, DC
Cosmetics
$35,669

40 Candidates		Dems: 51.8%
Avg House: $829		House: 86.0%
Avg Sen: $1,667		Incumb: 97.8%

Council for a Livable World
Council for a Livable World
Boston, MA
Council for a Livable World
Pro-Peace
$77,104

31 Candidates		Dems: 100.0%
Avg House: $47		Senate: 99.8%
Avg Sen: $2,750		Incumb: 26.7%

Council for a Livable World
Peace PAC
Boston, MA
Council for a Livable World
Pro-Peace
$51,702

49 Candidates		Dems: 97.7%
Avg House: $1,055		House: 100.0%
Avg Sen: $0		Incumb: 30.1%

Council for National Defense
Council for National Defense Inc, The
Springfield, VA
Pro-Defense
$55,995

71 Candidates		Repubs: 100.0%
Avg House: $761		House: 74.7%
Avg Sen: $885		Incumb: 28.7%

Cracker Barrel Old Country Store Inc
Cracker Barrel Old Country Store Inc PAC
Lebanon, TN
Restaurants
$31,250

16 Candidates		Repubs: 92.8%
Avg House: $2,344		House: 60.0%
Avg Sen: $1,643		Incumb: 42.4%

Credit Union National Assn
Credit Union Legislative Action Council of Credit Union National Association
Washington, DC
Credit Union Natl Assn
Credit Unions
$522,970

261 Candidates		Dems: 67.7%
Avg House: $1,648		House: 70.6%
Avg Sen: $4,155		Incumb: 74.5%

Crestar Financial Corp
Crestar Financial Corporation Responsible Government Fund
Richmond, VA
Commercial Banks
$31,825

51 Candidates		Repubs: 64.2%
Avg House: $665		House: 87.8%
Avg Sen: $433		Incumb: 70.9%

Crowell & Moring
Crowell & Moring PAC
Washington, DC
Lawyers
$41,900

61 Candidates		Dems: 61.9%
Avg House: $670		House: 72.0%
Avg Sen: $734		Incumb: 95.2%

Crowley Maritime
Crowley Maritime Federal PAC
Oakland, CA
Sea Transport
$41,696

43 Candidates		Repubs: 50.1%
Avg House: $809		House: 58.2%
Avg Sen: $1,340		Incumb: 70.0%

Cruise PAC
Cruise PAC
Washington, DC
Sea Transport
$66,500

48 Candidates		Dems: 57.9%
Avg House: $1,257		House: 69.9%
Avg Sen: $1,818		Incumb: 76.7%

Crum & Forster Insurance
Crum & Forster Voluntary PAC
Basking Ridge, NJ
Insurance
$55,830

74 Candidates		Repubs: 67.7%
Avg House: $641		House: 59.7%
Avg Sen: $1,023		Incumb: 77.6%

CSX Transportation Inc
CSX Transportation Inc PAC
Washington, DC
CSX Corp
Railroads†
$184,525

179 Candidates		Dems: 62.7%
Avg House: $862		House: 70.1%
Avg Sen: $1,905		Incumb: 90.2%

Cubic Corp
Cubic Employees' PAC (CuePAC)
San Diego, CA
Defense Electronics†
$32,347

19 Candidates		Repubs: 86.1%
Avg House: $1,756		House: 81.5%
Avg Sen: $1,500		Incumb: 83.8%

Cyprus Minerals Co
Cyprus Minerals Company PAC/Cyprus PAC
Englewood, CO
Metal Mining/Process†
$86,123

49 Candidates		Repubs: 69.0%
Avg House: $1,140		Senate: 60.3%
Avg Sen: $2,733		Incumb: 84.8%

Dairymen Inc
Dairymen Inc-Special Pol Agricultural Community Education (DI-SPACE)
Louisville, KY
Dairy
$85,519

88 Candidates		Dems: 64.7%
Avg House: $849		House: 66.5%
Avg Sen: $1,365		Incumb: 91.1%

Dairymen Inc-Georgia
Dairymen Inc-Georgia Committee for Political Action (DI-GCFPA)
Culloden, GA
Dairymen Inc
Dairy
$21,800

17 Candidates		Dems: 93.1%
Avg House: $863		House: 63.3%
Avg Sen: $8,000		Incumb: 80.7%

Dairymens Mountain Assn
Political Action Trust PAC (PAT-PAC)
Thornton, CO
Dairy
$28,350

15 Candidates		Dems: 70.5%
Avg House: $1,706		House: 54.1%
Avg Sen: $2,167		Incumb: 38.3%

Dallas Energy PAC
Dallas Energy PAC (DalEnPAC)
Dallas, TX
Oil & Gas
$56,500

27 Candidates		Repubs: 100.0%
Avg House: $1,389		Senate: 77.9%
Avg Sen: $2,444		Incumb: 31.0%

Darigold/Northwest Dairymens Assn
Darigold PAC
Waterloo, IA   Dairy

$23,500

19 Candidates	Dems:	50.0%
Avg House: $1,458	House:	74.5%
Avg Sen: $857	Incumb:	50.0%

Dayton Hudson Corp
Dayton Hudson Corporation Committee for Effective Federal Government
Minneapolis, MN   Department Stores

$63,350

103 Candidates	Repubs:	62.4%
Avg House: $560	House:	77.7%
Avg Sen: $936	Incumb:	75.5%

Dean Witter Reynolds
Dean Witter Reynolds PAC
New York, NY   Sears   Securities

$136,150

117 Candidates	Dems:	63.1%
Avg House: $990	House:	69.8%
Avg Sen: $1,957	Incumb:	82.7%

Deere & Co
Deere & Company Civic Action Fund
Moline, IL   Farm Equipment†

$103,900

76 Candidates	Repubs:	89.5%
Avg House: $1,123	House:	60.5%
Avg Sen: $2,050	Incumb:	63.9%

Deere & Co/Illinois
Deere & Company PAC - Illinois (Deere PAC - Illinois)
Moline, IL   Deere & Co   Farm Equipment†

$25,950

33 Candidates	Repubs:	94.2%
Avg House: $708	House:	65.5%
Avg Sen: $994	Incumb:	31.6%

Del Webb Corp
Del Webb Corporation Employees PAC
Phoenix, AZ   Real Estate Devel

$37,040

21 Candidates	Repubs:	56.8%
Avg House: $1,328	House:	68.1%
Avg Sen: $5,900	Incumb:	85.8%

Delaware Valley PAC
Delaware Valley PAC
Bensalem, PA   Pro-Israel

$95,000

71 Candidates	Dems:	62.2%
Avg House: $683	Senate:	71.3%
Avg Sen: $2,184	Incumb:	80.6%

Deloitte & Touche
Touche Ross Partners Federal PAC (TRPAC)
Washington, DC   Accountants

$124,504

72 Candidates	Dems:	67.9%
Avg House: $1,527	House:	67.5%
Avg Sen: $2,382	Incumb:	87.5%

Delta Airlines
Delta Airlines Inc PAC
Atlanta, GA   Airlines

$122,250

92 Candidates	Dems:	65.4%
Avg House: $1,060	House:	61.5%
Avg Sen: $2,238	Incumb:	92.3%

Delta Dental Plans Assn
Delta Dental Plans Association PAC (DELTAPAC)
Chicago, IL   Health Insurance

$34,800

20 Candidates	Dems:	67.0%
Avg House: $1,130	Senate:	67.5%
Avg Sen: $2,350	Incumb:	97.1%

Desert Caucus
Desert Caucus
Tucson, AZ   Pro-Israel

$178,550

48 Candidates	Dems:	75.2%
Avg House: $1,077	Senate:	81.9%
Avg Sen: $8,125	Incumb:	81.6%

Desert Grape Growers League/California
Desert Grape Growers League of California PAC
Palm Desert, CA   Fruit/Veg

$26,350

14 Candidates	Repubs:	65.8%
Avg House: $1,363	House:	62.0%
Avg Sen: $5,000	Incumb:	96.2%

Detroit Edison
Detroit Edison PAC-EDPAC-Federal
Detroit, MI   Electric Utilities

$100,520

89 Candidates	Dems:	65.2%
Avg House: $1,150	House:	80.0%
Avg Sen: $1,055	Incumb:	92.0%

Dial Corp
Greyhound Good Government Project
Phoenix, AZ   Household Chemicals†

$98,650

105 Candidates	Repubs:	60.6%
Avg House: $801	House:	66.5%
Avg Sen: $1,455	Incumb:	92.0%

Diamond Shamrock R&M Inc
Diamond Shamrock R&M Inc Employee PAC
San Antonio, TX   Oil Refining/Mkting

$20,625

18 Candidates	Repubs:	75.8%
Avg House: $1,167	House:	84.8%
Avg Sen: $1,042	Incumb:	39.4%

Diamond Walnut Growers
Diamond Walnut Growers Inc PAC
Pleasanton, CA   Sun-Diamond Growers   Fruit/Veg

$34,800

15 Candidates	Repubs:	64.1%
Avg House: $1,618	House:	51.1%
Avg Sen: $4,250	Incumb:	79.9%

Dickstein, Shapiro & Morin
Dickstein, Shapiro & Morin PAC
Washington, DC   Lawyers

$108,700

129 Candidates	Dems:	66.2%
Avg House: $743	House:	58.8%
Avg Sen: $1,042	Incumb:	94.9%

Dillon, Read & Co
Dillon Read PAC
New York, NY   Travelers Corp   Investmtent Banking

$21,950

12 Candidates	Dems:	54.4%
Avg House: $1,779	House:	56.7%
Avg Sen: $1,900	Incumb:	40.8%

Direct Selling Assn
Direct Selling Association PAC
Washington, DC   Direct Sales

$22,400

30 Candidates	Dems:	60.9%
Avg House: $646	House:	72.1%
Avg Sen: $1,250	Incumb:	85.5%

† PAC sponsor has other major interests in addition to this primary category

PAC Sponsor or Related Group / PAC Name / Location	Affiliate	1991-92 Total	Candidates	Avg House	Avg Sen	Party/%	House/Senate %	Incumb %
Walt Disney Co Walt Disney Company Employees' PAC Burbank, CA	Movies/Resorts†	$97,450	69 Candidates	$1,132	$2,011	Repubs: 56.4%	House: 54.6%	Incumb: 83.1%
Distilled Spirits Council Distilled Spirits Council PAC Washington, DC	Wine & Liquor	$67,901	85 Candidates	$697	$1,364	Dems: 80.6%	House: 73.9%	Incumb: 95.2%
Dominion Resources Inc Committee for Responsible Govt-Dominion Resources Inc Richmond, VA	Electric Utilities	$53,875	64 Candidates	$896	$678	Dems: 62.0%	House: 79.9%	Incumb: 78.9%
Donaldson, Lufkin & Jenrette Donaldson, Lufkin & Jenrette Better Government Fund New York, NY — Equitable Life	Securities	$29,325	19 Candidates	$750	$2,333	Dems: 57.4%	Senate: 79.5%	Incumb: 56.5%
RR Donnelley & Sons R R Donnelley & Sons Company PAC Chicago, IL	Publishing†	$52,400	46 Candidates	$795	$1,675	Repubs: 88.1%	Senate: 57.5%	Incumb: 59.2%
Dorsey, Windhorst et al Dorsey Political Fund Minneapolis, MN	Lawyers	$21,539	32 Candidates	$685	$651	Dems: 81.9%	House: 66.7%	Incumb: 75.3%
Dow Chemical Dow Chemical Company Employees' PAC Freeport, TX	Chemicals†	$109,500	43 Candidates	$2,079	$6,100	Repubs: 74.9%	House: 72.2%	Incumb: 61.2%
Dow Chemical/Agricultural Executives Dow Chemical Company Agricultural Executive PAC Indianapolis, IN — Dow Chemical	Ag Chemicals†	$36,050	36 Candidates	$952	$1,250	Repubs: 53.1%	House: 79.2%	Incumb: 86.8%
Dow Chemical/Eastern Employees Dow Eastern Employees PAC of the Dow Chemical Company (DEEPAC) Strongsville, OH — Dow Chemical	Chemicals†	$25,450	33 Candidates	$682	$1,667	Repubs: 91.5%	House: 80.3%	Incumb: 64.6%
Dow Chemical/HQ Unit Dow Chemical Company-Headquarters Unit Employees PAC; The Midland, MI — Dow Chemical	Chemicals†	$94,000	86 Candidates	$957	$1,833	Repubs: 80.3%	House: 71.3%	Incumb: 56.9%
Dow Chemical/Midwest Midwest Area PAC - Employees of the Dow Chemical Company (MAPAC) Midland, MI — Dow Chemical	Chemicals†	$27,700	22 Candidates	$1,210	$1,750	Repubs: 83.8%	House: 87.4%	Incumb: 54.9%
Dow Chemical/SE Region Empac (Employees' PAC, S. E. Region, The Dow Chemical Company) Plaquemine, LA — Dow Chemical	Chemicals†	$72,450	57 Candidates	$1,201	$2,000	Repubs: 64.1%	House: 86.2%	Incumb: 59.8%
Dow Chemical/Western Employees Western Employees PAC of the Dow Chemical Co (WESPAC) Pittsburg, CA — Dow Chemical	Chemicals†	$39,300	44 Candidates	$633	$2,063	Repubs: 91.6%	House: 58.0%	Incumb: 41.5%
Dravo Corp Dravo Employees for Better Government Fund Pittsburgh, PA	Misc Mining†	$44,000	37 Candidates	$1,010	$1,614	Repubs: 55.1%	House: 59.7%	Incumb: 95.5%
Dresser Industries Dresser Industries PAC (DIPAC) Dallas, TX	Oilfield Services	$86,415	70 Candidates	$965	$1,908	Repubs: 78.7%	House: 55.9%	Incumb: 85.2%
Drummond Co Drummond Company Inc PAC (DPAC) Birmingham, AL	Coal	$47,350	24 Candidates	$2,623	$1,333	Dems: 84.7%	House: 72.0%	Incumb: 34.0%
DSC Communications Corp DSC Communications Corporation PAC DSCPAC Washington, DC	Communication Equip	$62,200	56 Candidates	$1,107	$1,125	Dems: 60.3%	House: 78.3%	Incumb: 89.5%
El du Pont de Nemours & Co E I du Pont de Nemours & Company Good Government Fund Wilmington, DE — du Pont	Chemicals†	$49,881	63 Candidates	$652	$1,455	Dems: 52.1%	House: 67.9%	Incumb: 84.0%
du Pont Merck du Pont Merck Program for Active Citizenship Inc Washington, DC	Pharmaceuticals	$41,917	43 Candidates	$761	$1,469	Repubs: 78.5%	House: 54.4%	Incumb: 74.2%

PAC Sponsor or Related Group/PAC Name	Affiliate	1991-92 Total	Where the money went...		

Duchossois Industries
Duchossois Industries Inc PAC
Elmhurst, IL — Railroad Equipment — **$23,000**

13 Candidates	Repubs: 65.2%
Avg House: $1,600	House: 69.6%
Avg Sen: $2,333	Incumb: 85.9%

Duke Power Co
Employees Federal PAC - Duke Power Company
Charlotte, NC — Electric Utilities — **$50,650**

46 Candidates	Repubs: 61.1%
Avg House: $1,132	House: 87.2%
Avg Sen: $929	Incumb: 77.7%

Dun & Bradstreet
PAC of the Dun & Bradstreet Corporation
Washington, DC — Market Research† — **$128,350**

102 Candidates	Repubs: 52.5%
Avg House: $899	Senate: 50.2%
Avg Sen: $2,081	Incumb: 91.4%

Duquesne Light Co
Duquesne Light Company Federal PAC (FEDUPAC)
Pittsburgh, PA — Electric Utilities — **$52,750**

49 Candidates	Repubs: 50.5%
Avg House: $792	House: 58.6%
Avg Sen: $2,185	Incumb: 83.9%

Dynamis
Dynamis
Palo Alto, CA — Ethnic Groups — **$25,000**

5 Candidates	Repubs: 60.0%
Avg House: $5,000	House: 100.0%
Avg Sen: $0	Incumb: 70.0%

Dyncorp
Dyncorp Federal PAC
Reston, VA — Defense Aerospace† — **$48,075**

49 Candidates	Dems: 58.6%
Avg House: $978	House: 85.4%
Avg Sen: $1,000	Incumb: 91.4%

E-Systems/Corporate Division
E-Systems Corporate Division PAC
Dallas, TX — E-Systems — Defense Electronics — **$115,509**

113 Candidates	Dems: 54.4%
Avg House: $999	House: 78.7%
Avg Sen: $1,119	Incumb: 84.9%

E-Systems/Greenville Division
E-Systems (Greenville Division) PAC
Greenville, TX — E-Systems — Defense Electronics — **$22,445**

33 Candidates	Dems: 51.9%
Avg House: $711	House: 88.7%
Avg Sen: $1,070	Incumb: 93.0%

Eagle Forum
Eagle Forum PAC
Alton, IL — Repub/Conservative — **$148,361**

101 Candidates	Repubs: 96.0%
Avg House: $1,445	House: 85.7%
Avg Sen: $1,629	Incumb: 32.6%

Eastern Airlines
Eastern Airlines PAC
Miami, FL — Continental Airlines — Airlines — **$26,250**

11 Candidates	Dems: 103.8%
Avg House: $4,000	Senate: 84.8%
Avg Sen: $2,225	Incumb: 100.0%

Eastman Kodak/Chemicals Division
EASTPAC-PAC of Eastman Chemicals Division Eastman Kodak Company
Kingsport, TN — Eastman Kodak — Chemicals — **$26,450**

30 Candidates	Repubs: 55.0%
Avg House: $890	House: 84.1%
Avg Sen: $840	Incumb: 86.6%

Eaton Corp
Eaton Corporation Public Policy Association
Cleveland, OH — Truck/Auto Parts† — **$218,600**

118 Candidates	Repubs: 93.5%
Avg House: $1,561	House: 71.4%
Avg Sen: $3,472	Incumb: 23.3%

Jack Eckerd Corp
Eckerd Committee for Responsible Government EckPAC
Clearwater, FL — Drug Stores — **$33,750**

51 Candidates	Repubs: 63.0%
Avg House: $540	House: 70.4%
Avg Sen: $1,429	Incumb: 77.0%

Ecolab Inc
Ecolab Inc PAC
St Paul, MN — Business Services† — **$25,650**

34 Candidates	Repubs: 54.2%
Avg House: $728	House: 76.6%
Avg Sen: $857	Incumb: 72.7%

Edison Electric Institute
Power PAC of the Edison Electric Institute
Washington, DC — Electric Utilities — **$84,614**

164 Candidates	Repubs: 57.4%
Avg House: $501	House: 81.1%
Avg Sen: $591	Incumb: 87.0%

Effective Government Committee
Effective Government Committee
Washington, DC — Rep Richard Gephardt (D-Mo) — Dem Leaders — **$204,425**

147 Candidates	Dems: 100.0%
Avg House: $1,294	House: 89.2%
Avg Sen: $3,667	Incumb: 43.8%

El Paso Co
El Paso Company PAC (PASPAC)
El Paso, TX — Burlington Resources — Natural Gas† — **$49,050**

44 Candidates	Dems: 50.4%
Avg House: $1,055	House: 79.6%
Avg Sen: $1,429	Incumb: 92.5%

Electrical Radio & Machine Workers
Int'l Union of Electronic Electrical Salaried Machine/Furniture Workers AFL-CIO
East Rutherford, NJ — Manufacturing Unions — **$25,900**

14 Candidates	Dems: 100.0%
Avg House: $1,608	House: 80.7%
Avg Sen: $5,000	Incumb: 44.8%

Electronic Data Systems
Electronic Data Systems Employees' PAC
Washington, DC — General Motors — Computer Services — **$226,616**

188 Candidates	Dems: 60.7%
Avg House: $1,070	House: 74.1%
Avg Sen: $1,890	Incumb: 84.6%

† PAC sponsor has other major interests in addition to this primary category

Electronic Machine Furniture Workers		$307,102	155 Candidates		Dems:	99.5%
IUE COPE Int'l Union/Electronic Electrical Tech Salaried Mach Workers AFL-CIO			Avg House: $1,478		House:	60.6%
Washington, DC	Communication Unions†		Avg Sen: $4,137		Incumb:	57.7%
Eli Lilly & Co		$195,530	125 Candidates		Repubs:	72.8%
Eli Lilly and Company PAC			Avg House: $806		Senate:	61.2%
Indianapolis, IN	Pharmaceuticals†		Avg Sen: $3,863		Incumb:	64.0%
Emerson Electric		$22,500	12 Candidates		Repubs:	70.0%
Emerson PAC (EMPAC)			Avg House: $1,321		Senate:	58.9%
St Louis, MO	Industl/Comml Equip†		Avg Sen: $2,650		Incumb:	84.4%
Emily's List		$365,318	65 Candidates		Dems:	97.6%
Emily's List			Avg House: $5,390		House:	84.1%
Washington, DC	Womens Issues		Avg Sen: $7,258		Incumb:	4.5%
Employee Stock Ownership Assn		$58,707	61 Candidates		Repubs:	70.3%
Employee Stock Ownership Association Inc PAC			Avg House: $872		House:	81.7%
Washington, DC	Misc Financial Svcs		Avg Sen: $1,788		Incumb:	97.0%
English First		$25,250	28 Candidates		Repubs:	94.1%
English First Political Victory Fund			Avg House: $817		House:	84.2%
Springfield, VA	Misc Issues		Avg Sen: $2,000		Incumb:	7.9%
English Language PAC		$35,851	49 Candidates		Repubs:	75.3%
English Language PAC			Avg House: $443		Senate:	64.2%
Washington, DC	Immigration PAC	Misc Issues	Avg Sen: $1,150		Incumb:	63.6%
Enron Corp		$130,550	134 Candidates		Repubs:	52.7%
Enron PAC			Avg House: $776		House:	60.6%
Houston, TX	Natural Gas†		Avg Sen: $1,642		Incumb:	90.5%
Enserch Corp		$147,785	127 Candidates		Dems:	64.1%
Enserch Corporation Employees Political Support Association			Avg House: $1,075		House:	68.4%
Dallas, TX	Natural Gas†		Avg Sen: $1,417		Incumb:	93.9%
Entergy Operations Inc		$30,000	60 Candidates		Dems:	66.2%
Empac Employees of Entergy Operations Inc PAC			Avg House: $446		House:	69.8%
Jackson, MS	Entergy Corp	Electric Utilities	Avg Sen: $696		Incumb:	90.7%
Entergy Services Inc		$50,125	85 Candidates		Dems:	61.5%
MSU System Services Inc			Avg House: $556		House:	73.3%
New Orleans, LA	Entergy Corp	Gas & Electric Util†	Avg Sen: $705		Incumb:	91.5%
Enterprise Leasing Co		$23,500	8 Candidates		Repubs:	53.2%
Enterprise Leasing Company PAC			Avg House: $2,750		House:	70.2%
St Louis, MO	Car/Truck Rental		Avg Sen: $3,500		Incumb:	76.6%
Equitable Financial Services		$110,350	91 Candidates		Dems:	71.8%
Equitable Financial Services PAC (EQUI-PAC)			Avg House: $955		House:	51.1%
New York, NY	Equitable Life	Insurance†	Avg Sen: $1,688		Incumb:	90.1%
Ernst & Young		$236,296	178 Candidates		Dems:	63.6%
Ernst & Whinney PAC			Avg House: $1,045		House:	54.8%
Washington, DC	Accountants		Avg Sen: $2,069		Incumb:	78.3%
Exchange International Corp		$21,900	18 Candidates		Dems:	61.4%
Exchange International Corporation Community Action			Avg House: $1,069		House:	63.5%
Chicago, IL	Commercial Banks		Avg Sen: $1,600		Incumb:	66.0%
Exxon Corp		$327,850	255 Candidates		Repubs:	82.5%
Exxon Corporation PAC (EXPAC)			Avg House: $833		House:	56.4%
Houston, TX	Oil & Gas†		Avg Sen: $4,438		Incumb:	60.1%
Fair PAC		$23,988	16 Candidates		Repubs:	72.9%
FAIR PAC			Avg House: $1,544		House:	70.8%
Washington, DC	Misc Issues		Avg Sen: $1,000		Incumb:	58.3%
Family Health Program Inc		$94,713	67 Candidates		Dems:	63.7%
FHP, Inc - Health Services PAC (FHP-HESPAC)			Avg House: $1,193		House:	59.2%
Fountain Valley, CA	HMOs		Avg Sen: $1,982		Incumb:	59.9%
Farm Credit Council		$170,023	208 Candidates		Dems:	56.7%
Farm Credit Council PAC/Farm Credit PAC			Avg House: $665		House:	63.8%
Washington, DC	Ag Services		Avg Sen: $1,369		Incumb:	87.7%

Farmers Group Inc
Farmers Group Inc PAC
Los Angeles, CA

$29,542

Insurance

65 Candidates		Repubs: 92.2%
Avg House:	$379	House: 69.4%
Avg Sen:	$823	Incumb: 60.2%

Farmers' Rice Cooperative
Farmers' Rice Cooperative Fund
Sacramento, CA

$52,200

Misc Crops

20 Candidates		Dems: 58.9%
Avg House:	$2,509	House: 52.9%
Avg Sen:	$2,733	Incumb: 91.0%

Farmland Industries
Farmland Industries PAC (Farmland/PAC)
Kansas City, MO

$49,050

Ag Services†

49 Candidates		Repubs: 56.2%
Avg House:	$851	House: 64.2%
Avg Sen:	$1,463	Incumb: 92.9%

Federal Express Corp
Federal Express Corporation PAC "FEPAC"
Memphis, TN

$740,975

Express Delivery

221 Candidates		Dems: 68.2%
Avg House:	$3,291	House: 68.8%
Avg Sen:	$3,528	Incumb: 90.3%

Federal Managers' Assn
Federal Managers' Association PAC
Washington, DC

$63,725

Fedl Worker Unions

64 Candidates		Dems: 78.9%
Avg House:	$833	House: 62.7%
Avg Sen:	$1,484	Incumb: 92.5%

Federal National Mortgage Assn
Federal National Mortgage Association PAC ("Fannie PAC")
Washington, DC

$62,725

Mortgage Banking

76 Candidates		Dems: 70.5%
Avg House:	$717	House: 72.0%
Avg Sen:	$1,352	Incumb: 96.0%

Federated Investors Inc
Financial Services Political Committee
Pittsburgh, PA

$39,550

Securities

31 Candidates		Dems: 57.5%
Avg House:	$1,159	Senate: 53.1%
Avg Sen:	$1,400	Incumb: 92.4%

Federation of American Health Systems
Federation of American Health Systems PAC
Washington, DC

$179,850

Hospitals

150 Candidates		Dems: 59.4%
Avg House:	$951	House: 61.4%
Avg Sen:	$2,044	Incumb: 81.2%

Fertilizer Institute
Fert PAC
Washington, DC

$22,550

Ag Chemicals

43 Candidates		Dems: 51.2%
Avg House:	$405	House: 55.6%
Avg Sen:	$833	Incumb: 95.6%

Fifth Horseman PAC
Fifth Horseman PAC
Elgin, IL

$109,000

Dem/Liberal

24 Candidates		Dems: 95.4%
Avg House:	$3,727	Senate: 57.8%
Avg Sen:	$5,250	Incumb: 15.1%

Fireman's Fund Insurance
Fireman's Fund Employees' Committee for Responsible Government
Novato, CA

$86,570

Insurance

112 Candidates		Repubs: 53.1%
Avg House:	$723	House: 67.6%
Avg Sen:	$905	Incumb: 77.8%

First Alabama Bancshares
First Alabama Bancshares Inc PAC
Birmingham, AL

$26,400

Commercial Banks

13 Candidates		Dems: 52.6%
Avg House:	$1,855	House: 77.3%
Avg Sen:	$3,000	Incumb: 39.4%

First Atlanta Corp
First Atlanta Corporation Fund for Better Government
Atlanta, GA

$32,465

Commercial Banks

34 Candidates		Dems: 65.9%
Avg House:	$799	House: 61.5%
Avg Sen:	$1,389	Incumb: 45.3%

First Boston Corp
First Boston-PAC (FB-PAC); The
New York, NY

$96,500

Investmtent Banking

66 Candidates		Dems: 75.7%
Avg House:	$1,287	House: 62.7%
Avg Sen:	$1,895	Incumb: 92.8%

First Chicago Corp
First Chicago Corp Government Affairs c/o The First National Bank of Chicago
Chicago, IL

$129,153

Commercial Banks

109 Candidates		Dems: 60.2%
Avg House:	$1,143	House: 74.3%
Avg Sen:	$1,340	Incumb: 84.9%

First Interstate Bank of California
First Interstate Bank of California PAC
Los Angeles, CA   *First Interstate*

$27,284

Commercial Banks

24 Candidates		Repubs: 71.2%
Avg House:	$1,071	House: 51.0%
Avg Sen:	$1,215	Incumb: 70.7%

First Nationwide Bank
First Nationwide Bank PAC
San Francisco, CA   *Ford Motor Co*

$21,854

Savings & Loans

16 Candidates		Dems: 79.4%
Avg House:	$719	Senate: 73.7%
Avg Sen:	$2,013	Incumb: 37.8%

First Tennessee National Corp
First Tennessee National Corp Federal PAC (First Tennessee Banks Federal PAC)
Memphis, TN

$25,800

Commercial Banks

14 Candidates		Dems: 62.0%
Avg House:	$1,660	House: 64.3%
Avg Sen:	$2,300	Incumb: 96.9%

First Union Corp
First Union Corporation Employees Good Government "F" Fund
Charlotte, NC

$58,550

Mortgage Banking

63 Candidates		Dems: 50.5%
Avg House:	$893	House: 77.8%
Avg Sen:	$1,300	Incumb: 34.8%

† PAC sponsor has other major interests in addition to this primary category

PAC Sponsor or Related Group/PAC Name	Affiliate	1991-92 Total	Where the money went...	
First Wisconsin Corp First Wisconsin Civic Affairs Committee Milwaukee, WI	Commercial Banks	$23,600	20 Candidates Avg House: $1,025 Avg Sen: $1,800	Repubs: 68.4% House: 69.5% Incumb: 87.3%
Fleetwood Enterprises Fleetwood Enterprises, Inc PAC Riverside, CA	Mobile Homes†	$32,930	50 Candidates Avg House: $567 Avg Sen: $1,025	Repubs: 54.5% House: 68.9% Incumb: 75.7%
Fleishman-Hillard Inc Fleishman-Hillard PAC Washington, DC	Lobbyists/PR	$29,750	50 Candidates Avg House: $559 Avg Sen: $723	Repubs: 57.1% House: 73.3% Incumb: 87.6%
Fleming Companies Inc Fleming Companies Inc Committee for Responsible Government Oklahoma City, OK	Food Wholesalers	$171,500	101 Candidates Avg House: $1,388 Avg Sen: $2,881	Repubs: 79.0% House: 64.7% Incumb: 55.7%
Florida Citrus Mutual Florida Citrus Mutual PAC Inc Lakeland, FL	Fruit/Veg	$47,850	47 Candidates Avg House: $967 Avg Sen: $1,367	Dems: 51.8% House: 82.9% Incumb: 74.1%
Florida Congressional Committee Florida Congressional Committee Miami, FL	Pro-Israel	$158,250	59 Candidates Avg House: $1,383 Avg Sen: $4,222	Dems: 50.1% Senate: 72.0% Incumb: 86.7%
Florida Fruit & Vegetable Assn Florida Fruit & Vegetable Ass'n PAC FFVA-PAC Orlando, FL	Fruit/Veg	$34,552	42 Candidates Avg House: $842 Avg Sen: $750	Dems: 55.6% House: 80.5% Incumb: 79.2%
Florida Medical Assn Florida Medical PAC Jacksonville, FL	American Medical Assn — Doctors	$37,100	15 Candidates Avg House: $2,543 Avg Sen: $1,500	Dems: 60.9% House: 96.0% Incumb: 39.1%
Florida Power & Light Good Government Management Ass'n Florida Power & Light Company Employee's PAC Juno Beach, FL	FPL Group — Electric Utilities	$72,700	86 Candidates Avg House: $756 Avg Sen: $1,346	Repubs: 52.3% House: 75.9% Incumb: 71.0%
Florida Power Corp PAC of Florida Power Corporation Employees (Power PAC) St Petersburg, FL	Electric Utilities	$42,590	64 Candidates Avg House: $659 Avg Sen: $700	Dems: 53.4% House: 83.6% Incumb: 75.5%
Florida Society of Anesthesiologists Florida Society of Anesthesiology PAC FSA-PAC St Petersburg, FL	Misc MD Specialists	$24,650	32 Candidates Avg House: $731 Avg Sen: $2,000	Dems: 52.7% House: 91.9% Incumb: 51.7%
Florida Sugar Cane League Florida Sugar Cane League PAC Clewiston, FL	Sugar	$167,075	191 Candidates Avg House: $774 Avg Sen: $1,397	Dems: 75.2% House: 74.1% Incumb: 94.3%
Flowers Industries Flowers PAC Thomasville, GA	Food Processors	$171,000	58 Candidates Avg House: $2,553 Avg Sen: $4,600	Repubs: 97.7% House: 70.2% Incumb: 14.0%
Fluor Corp Fluor Corporation Public Affairs Committee (Fluor PAC) Irvine, CA	Heavy Construction†	$333,058	157 Candidates Avg House: $1,659 Avg Sen: $3,569	Repubs: 56.8% House: 59.3% Incumb: 83.1%
FMC Corp FMC Corporation Good Government Program Chicago, IL	Chemicals†	$261,760	197 Candidates Avg House: $1,053 Avg Sen: $2,561	Repubs: 63.8% House: 64.8% Incumb: 78.9%
FMR Corp FMR Corp PAC Boston, MA	Securities	$33,922	23 Candidates Avg House: $1,561 Avg Sen: $1,341	Dems: 61.2% House: 64.4% Incumb: 64.1%
Food & Commercial Workers Union Active Ballot Club, A Dept of United Food & Commercial Workers Int'l Union Washington, DC	Food/Commercial Wrkrs Union — Retail Unions†	$1,488,961	388 Candidates Avg House: $3,495 Avg Sen: $6,143	Dems: 97.2% House: 79.1% Incumb: 57.6%
Food Marketing Institute Food Marketing Institute PAC (Food PAC) Washington, DC	Food Stores	$531,778	327 Candidates Avg House: $1,328 Avg Sen: $3,763	Repubs: 64.5% House: 71.7% Incumb: 81.8%
Ford Motor Co Ford Motor Company Civic Action Fund Detroit, MI	Auto Manufacturers†	$287,984	237 Candidates Avg House: $1,058 Avg Sen: $2,388	Dems: 52.9% House: 76.8% Incumb: 87.2%

Fort Howard Corp		$46,950	33 Candidates	Repubs: 96.8%
Fort Howard Corporation PAC			Avg House: $672	Senate: 67.1%
Green Bay, WI	Paper/Pulp		Avg Sen: $3,150	Incumb: 52.6%

Foundation Health Corp		$22,569	10 Candidates	Dems: 71.2%
Foundation Health Corporation PAC			Avg House: $2,096	House: 55.7%
Rancho Cordova, CA	Defense Services†		Avg Sen: $2,499	Incumb: 91.1%

Fox Inc		$53,700	46 Candidates	Dems: 85.1%
FOXPAC (Fox Inc and Subsidiaries)			Avg House: $1,098	House: 57.3%
Beverly Hills, CA	Movies/TV		Avg Sen: $1,291	Incumb: 85.2%

Free Cuba PAC		$159,000	59 Candidates	Dems: 64.5%
Free Cuba PAC Inc			Avg House: $2,328	House: 52.7%
Miami, FL	Foreign Policy		Avg Sen: $3,270	Incumb: 77.4%

Freeport-McMoRan Inc		$132,550	109 Candidates	Dems: 53.0%
Freeport-McMoRan Inc Citizenship Committee			Avg House: $861	Senate: 54.5%
Washington, DC	Ag Chemicals†		Avg Sen: $1,853	Incumb: 88.7%

Friant Water PAC		$27,900	14 Candidates	Repubs: 66.0%
Friant Water PAC			Avg House: $2,031	House: 58.2%
Delano, CA	Ag Services		Avg Sen: $1,942	Incumb: 69.5%

Fulbright & Jaworski		$71,343	76 Candidates	Dems: 70.8%
Freedom Fund; The			Avg House: $837	House: 56.3%
Houston, TX	Lawyers		Avg Sen: $1,113	Incumb: 83.4%

Fund for a Democratic Majority			$185,530	43 Candidates	Dems: 100.0%
Fund for a Democratic Majority				Avg House: $1,588	Senate: 85.5%
Washington, DC	Sen Edward Kennedy (D-Mass)	Dem Leaders		Avg Sen: $6,097	Incumb: 46.4%

Fund for California's Future		$20,999	13 Candidates	Repubs: 100.0%
Fund for California's Future			Avg House: $1,583	House: 90.5%
Rancho Cucamonga, CA	Non-federal Leaders		Avg Sen: $2,000	Incumb: 4.8%

Fund for Southern Progress			$42,500	41 Candidates	Repubs: 98.8%
Fund for Southern Progress				Avg House: $676	House: 58.8%
Columbia, SC	Carroll Campbell (R-SC)	Non-federal Leaders		Avg Sen: $4,375	Incumb: 15.9%

Future Leaders PAC			$22,205	26 Candidates	Repubs: 100.0%
Future Leaders PAC				Avg House: $854	House: 100.0%
Washington, DC	Rep Jerry Lewis (R-Calif)	Repub Leaders		Avg Sen: $0	Incumb: 11.6%

Garden State PAC		$59,950	52 Candidates	Dems: 56.6%
Garden State PAC			Avg House: $730	Senate: 65.9%
Roseland, NJ	Pro-Israel		Avg Sen: $1,646	Incumb: 72.6%

Garvey, Schubert & Barer		$42,600	45 Candidates	Dems: 81.9%
Garvey, Schubert & Barer PAC			Avg House: $852	House: 66.0%
Washington, DC	Lawyers		Avg Sen: $1,208	Incumb: 73.1%

Gencorp Inc		$116,029	80 Candidates	Dems: 60.2%
GenCorp Inc PAC (GENPAC)			Avg House: $1,346	House: 71.9%
Fairlawn, OH	Defense Aerospace†		Avg Sen: $1,811	Incumb: 98.2%

Genentech Inc		$79,200	72 Candidates	Dems: 64.3%
Genentech Inc PAC			Avg House: $748	Senate: 57.5%
So San Francisco, CA	Pharmaceuticals		Avg Sen: $1,687	Incumb: 79.5%

General American Life Insurance		$90,500	61 Candidates	Dems: 51.4%
General American Life Associates' Federal PAC			Avg House: $1,297	House: 53.0%
St Louis, MO	Insurance		Avg Sen: $1,771	Incumb: 79.6%

General Atomics		$305,550	96 Candidates	Dems: 64.0%
General Atomics PAC			Avg House: $3,183	House: 61.5%
San Diego, CA	Nuclear Plant Constr†		Avg Sen: $3,215	Incumb: 88.6%

General Aviation Manufacturers Assn		$38,050	53 Candidates	Dems: 51.9%
GAMAPAC (General Aviation Manufacturers Association PAC)			Avg House: $595	House: 64.1%
Washington, DC	Aircraft Mfr		Avg Sen: $1,138	Incumb: 90.3%

General Dynamics		$436,482	219 Candidates	Dems: 61.2%
General Dynamics Corporation Voluntary Political Contribution Plan			Avg House: $1,733	House: 71.5%
St Louis, MO	Defense Aerospace†		Avg Sen: $3,196	Incumb: 93.5%

† PAC sponsor has other major interests in addition to this primary category

General Electric
Non-Partisan Political Support Committee for General Electric Company Employees
Fairfield, CT   Aerospace Equip†

$683,350

417 Candidates	Dems:	58.7%
Avg House: $1,254	House:	59.3%
Avg Sen: $3,058	Incumb:	85.2%

General Instrument Corp
General Instrument Corporation PAC (GIPAC)
Washington, DC   Electronics Mfg

$37,250

29 Candidates	Repubs:	80.5%
Avg House: $729	Senate:	76.5%
Avg Sen: $1,676	Incumb:	77.2%

General Mills
General Mills Inc PAC (GM PAC)
Minneapolis, MN   Food Processors†

$100,850

89 Candidates	Repubs:	57.0%
Avg House: $768	Senate:	53.5%
Avg Sen: $1,929	Incumb:	80.7%

General Mills Restaurants
General Mills Restaurants Inc Empl Good Govt Fund (Red Lobster Emp Gd Govt Fd)
Orlando, FL   General Mills   Restaurants

$84,083

84 Candidates	Repubs:	69.4%
Avg House: $838	House:	59.8%
Avg Sen: $1,408	Incumb:	79.8%

General Motors
Civic Involvement Program/General Motors Corp.
Detroit, MI   Auto Manufacturers†

$232,480

158 Candidates	Repubs:	56.7%
Avg House: $1,013	House:	53.2%
Avg Sen: $3,025	Incumb:	84.2%

General Public Utilities
General Public Utilities Political Participation Association
Washington, DC   Electric Utilities

$84,576

84 Candidates	Repubs:	52.1%
Avg House: $873	House:	70.2%
Avg Sen: $1,576	Incumb:	86.1%

Georgia Peanut Producers Assn
Georgia Peanut Producers Association PAC
Blakely, GA   Misc Crops

$34,000

17 Candidates	Dems:	84.6%
Avg House: $1,712	House:	65.4%
Avg Sen: $2,938	Incumb:	76.5%

Georgia Power Co
Georgia Power Company Federal PAC Inc
Atlanta, GA   Southern Co   Electric Utilities

$72,550

110 Candidates	Dems:	58.1%
Avg House: $647	House:	77.5%
Avg Sen: $730	Incumb:	65.6%

Georgia US Corp
Georgia U S Federal PAC
Atlanta, GA   Insurance

$22,150

18 Candidates	Dems:	65.2%
Avg House: $1,008	House:	59.1%
Avg Sen: $1,810	Incumb:	46.7%

Georgia-Pacific Corp
G-P Employees Fund of Georgia-Pacific Corporation
Washington, DC   Georgia-Pacific   Forest Products†

$124,092

81 Candidates	Repubs:	58.9%
Avg House: $995	Senate:	55.1%
Avg Sen: $2,736	Incumb:	77.1%

Glass Molders Pottery Plastics Workers
Glass, Molders, Pottery, Plastics & Allied Workers Int'l Union - Pol Ed League
Media, PA   Glass, Molders Union   Manufacturing Unions

$40,000

28 Candidates	Dems:	100.0%
Avg House: $725	Senate:	63.8%
Avg Sen: $3,188	Incumb:	46.2%

Glaxo Inc
Glaxo Inc Democracy Fund
Research Triangle, NC   Pharmaceuticals

$175,522

115 Candidates	Dems:	54.4%
Avg House: $1,173	House:	59.5%
Avg Sen: $2,735	Incumb:	89.8%

Gold Kist
Gold Kist Political Action for Farmers Inc
Atlanta, GA   Poultry/Egg†

$44,300

30 Candidates	Dems:	81.9%
Avg House: $1,200	House:	65.0%
Avg Sen: $3,250	Incumb:	69.5%

Golden Rule Financial Corp
Golden Rule Financial Corporation - PAC
Indianapolis, IN   Insurance

$127,576

107 Candidates	Repubs:	50.2%
Avg House: $1,052	House:	69.3%
Avg Sen: $1,704	Incumb:	72.9%

Goldman, Sachs & Co
GSMMI Holdings Inc PAC aka Goldman Sachs PAC
Washington, DC   Investmtent Banking

$186,558

120 Candidates	Dems:	77.0%
Avg House: $1,453	House:	74.0%
Avg Sen: $1,940	Incumb:	86.7%

Columbia Gas System
Columbia Gas Employees Political Action Fund
Wilmington, DE   Columbia Gas System   Natural Gas

$122,750

112 Candidates	Repubs:	53.7%
Avg House: $925	House:	65.5%
Avg Sen: $1,692	Incumb:	87.7%

BF Goodrich
BF Goodrich PAC
Akron, OH   Industl/Comml Equip†

$49,700

51 Candidates	Repubs:	56.2%
Avg House: $771	House:	52.7%
Avg Sen: $1,382	Incumb:	75.5%

WR Grace & Co
GracePAC
New York, NY   Chemicals†

$133,795

104 Candidates	Repubs:	58.5%
Avg House: $992	House:	59.3%
Avg Sen: $2,269	Incumb:	85.4%

Graham Resources
Graham Resources Inc PAC / Graham PAC
Covington, LA   Oil & Gas

$22,750

29 Candidates	Dems:	67.7%
Avg House: $815	House:	85.9%
Avg Sen: $640	Incumb:	92.1%

PAC Sponsor or Related Group/PAC Name	Affiliate	1991-92 Total	Where the money went...		
Graphic Communications Union Graphic Communications International Union Political Contributions Committee Washington, DC	Communication Unions	$69,400	69 Candidates Avg House: $759 Avg Sen: $1,600	Dems: 98.9% House: 59.1% Incumb: 46.8%	
Great Lakes Sugar Beet Growers Great Lakes Sugar Beet Growers PAC (GLSBGPAC) Saginaw, MI	Sugar	$69,965	123 Candidates Avg House: $568 Avg Sen: $580	Repubs: 51.3% House: 91.7% Incumb: 94.6%	
Great Western Financial Corp Great Western Financial Corporation Good Government Committee Beverly Hills, CA	Savings & Loans	$73,580	80 Candidates Avg House: $859 Avg Sen: $1,231	Repubs: 51.5% House: 78.2% Incumb: 86.1%	
Greater Washington Board of Trade Federal Commerce & Industry PAC of the Greater Washington Board of Trade Washington, DC	Chambers of Commerce	$62,750	39 Candidates Avg House: $1,734 Avg Sen: $1,125	Dems: 71.5% House: 85.7% Incumb: 85.3%	
Greenvote Greenvote Boston, MA	Environment Policy	$98,850	66 Candidates Avg House: $975 Avg Sen: $2,700	Dems: 94.9% Senate: 54.6% Incumb: 30.2%	
Grocery Manufacturers of America Grocery Manufacturers of America Inc PAC ('GMA PAC') Washington, DC	Food Processors	$35,200	57 Candidates Avg House: $524 Avg Sen: $819	Repubs: 57.4% House: 58.1% Incumb: 86.4%	
Group Health Assn of America Group Health Association of America Prepaid Group Practice (PAC) Washington, DC	HMOs	$23,850	23 Candidates Avg House: $1,050 Avg Sen: $1,000	Dems: 83.2% House: 74.8% Incumb: 85.3%	
Grumman Corp Grumman PAC Bethpage, NY	Defense Aerospace†	$250,350	171 Candidates Avg House: $1,244 Avg Sen: $2,422	Dems: 66.3% House: 69.0% Incumb: 94.2%	
GTE Corp GTE Corporation Good Government Club Washington, DC	Phone Utilites†	$615,977	384 Candidates Avg House: $1,378 Avg Sen: $2,958	Dems: 52.0% House: 73.6% Incumb: 85.3%	
Gulf Power Co Gulf Power Employees' Committee for Responsible Government, Inc Pensacola, FL	Southern Co / Electric Utilities	$21,650	50 Candidates Avg House: $458 Avg Sen: $364	Dems: 52.7% House: 80.4% Incumb: 54.0%	
Gulfstream Aerospace Gulfstream Aerospace PAC Savannah, GA	Chrysler Corp / Aircraft Mfr	$31,620	19 Candidates Avg House: $1,681 Avg Sen: $1,628	Dems: 76.6% House: 69.1% Incumb: 84.2%	
H&R Block H & R Block PAC (BlockPAC) Kansas City, MO	Tax Services	$20,100	20 Candidates Avg House: $850 Avg Sen: $1,313	Dems: 57.5% Senate: 52.2% Incumb: 88.8%	
Halliburton Co Halliburton PAC Duncan, OK	Oilfield Services†	$90,512	57 Candidates Avg House: $1,056 Avg Sen: $2,500	Repubs: 81.8% Senate: 58.0% Incumb: 56.1%	
Hallmark Cards Hallmark PAC-Federal HALLPAC-Federal Kansas City, MO	Greeting Cards	$144,000	69 Candidates Avg House: $1,245 Avg Sen: $3,772	Repubs: 79.0% Senate: 60.2% Incumb: 68.1%	
Handgun Control Inc Handgun Control Inc PAC (HCI PAC) Washington, DC	Anti-Guns	$156,112	102 Candidates Avg House: $1,256 Avg Sen: $3,123	Dems: 87.0% House: 70.0% Incumb: 42.1%	
Hardee's Food Systems Hardee's Food Systems Inc Good Government Fund Rocky Mount, NC	Restaurants	$31,750	41 Candidates Avg House: $743 Avg Sen: $750	Repubs: 64.6% House: 79.5% Incumb: 70.9%	
Harris Corp Harris Corporation-Federal PAC Melbourne, FL	Electronics Mfg†	$206,490	117 Candidates Avg House: $1,093 Avg Sen: $4,238	Repubs: 96.8% Senate: 51.3% Incumb: 53.0%	
Harsco Corp Harsco Corporation PAC Camp Hill, PA	Weapons Systems†	$50,975	65 Candidates Avg House: $645 Avg Sen: $1,650	Repubs: 57.2% House: 70.9% Incumb: 91.2%	
Hartford Insurance Hartford Insurance Group - PAC Hartford, CT	ITT Corp / Insurance	$100,480	103 Candidates Avg House: $855 Avg Sen: $1,418	Dems: 59.9% House: 69.0% Incumb: 88.5%	

† PAC sponsor has other major interests in addition to this primary category

PAC Sponsor / Name / Location	Affiliate	1991-92 Total	Candidates / Averages	Party / Chamber / Incumb.
Hawaiian Sugar Planters Assn Hawaiian Sugar Planters' Association-PAC (Hawaiian Sugar-PAC) Aiea, HI	Sugar	$61,975	130 Candidates Avg House: $380 Avg Sen: $863	Dems: 73.4% House: 63.8% Incumb: 92.4%
Health Insurance Assn of America Health Insurance PAC of the Health Insurance Association of America Washington, DC	Health Insurance	$232,177	241 Candidates Avg House: $789 Avg Sen: $1,722	Repubs: 61.7% House: 66.6% Incumb: 77.1%
Healthtrust Inc Healthtrust Inc-the Hospital Company PAC Nashville, TN	Hospitals	$21,550	38 Candidates Avg House: $511 Avg Sen: $725	Dems: 62.6% House: 66.4% Incumb: 58.0%
Heartland PAC Heartland PAC Washington, DC	Pro-Israel	$85,250	55 Candidates Avg House: $750 Avg Sen: $2,217	Dems: 69.8% Senate: 78.0% Incumb: 73.3%
Heat/Frost/Asbestos Workers Union International Association of Heat & Frost Insulators and Asbestos Workers P A C Washington, DC	Building Trade Unions	$40,800	35 Candidates Avg House: $912 Avg Sen: $1,778	Dems: 84.6% House: 55.9% Incumb: 48.4%
Henley Group Inc Henley Group Inc Employees Cmte for Sensible Gov't (Henley COSIGN) Hampton, NH	Medical Supplies†	$77,200	28 Candidates Avg House: $3,135 Avg Sen: $2,246	Repubs: 52.1% House: 52.8% Incumb: 67.6%
Hercules Inc Hercules Inc Voluntary Nonpartisan Political Contributions Cmte (Hercules PCC) Wilmington, DE	Chemicals†	$32,125	38 Candidates Avg House: $816 Avg Sen: $1,000	Dems: 66.2% House: 81.3% Incumb: 89.1%
Heublein Heublein Employees' Political Participation Committee Farmington, CT Grand Metropolitan	Wine & Liquor	$65,129	66 Candidates Avg House: $865 Avg Sen: $1,400	Dems: 77.7% House: 67.8% Incumb: 91.6%
Hewlett-Packard Hewlett-Packard Company PAC (HP PAC) Palo Alto, CA	Electronics Mfg†	$58,800	47 Candidates Avg House: $633 Avg Sen: $3,273	Repubs: 75.7% Senate: 61.2% Incumb: 46.0%
Hiram Walker & Sons Hiram Walker & Sons Inc PAC (Hiram Walker PAC) Detroit, MI	Wine & Liquor	$31,300	33 Candidates Avg House: $752 Avg Sen: $1,400	Dems: 77.5% House: 55.3% Incumb: 90.7%
Hispanic PAC USA Hispanic PAC USA Inc Washington, DC	Ethnic Groups	$36,000	16 Candidates Avg House: $2,250 Avg Sen: $0	Dems: 99.3% House: 100.0% Incumb: 12.5%
Hoechst Celanese Corp Hoechst Celanese Corporation PAC Somerville, NJ	Synthetic Fibers†	$186,700	132 Candidates Avg House: $1,254 Avg Sen: $1,983	Repubs: 52.8% House: 69.2% Incumb: 88.0%
Hoffman-La Roche Hoffmann-La Roche Inc Good Government Committee Nutley, NJ	Pharmaceuticals†	$66,600	69 Candidates Avg House: $818 Avg Sen: $1,453	Repubs: 59.2% House: 65.1% Incumb: 89.2%
Hogan & Hartson Hogan & Hartson PAC Washington, DC	Lawyers	$51,700	85 Candidates Avg House: $472 Avg Sen: $936	Dems: 72.3% House: 54.7% Incumb: 91.0%
Holiday Inns INN/PAC Int'l Assn of Holiday Inns Inc PAC Memphis, TN Bass PLC	Hotels/Motels	$27,500	41 Candidates Avg House: $649 Avg Sen: $875	Repubs: 62.7% House: 87.3% Incumb: 82.7%
Holland & Hart Holland & Hart Federal PAC Washington, DC	Lawyers	$54,143	38 Candidates Avg House: $1,077 Avg Sen: $2,179	Dems: 64.0% House: 51.7% Incumb: 91.7%
Holland & Knight Holland & Knight Committee for Effective Government Washington, DC	Lawyers	$85,872	79 Candidates Avg House: $930 Avg Sen: $1,619	Dems: 62.0% House: 66.0% Incumb: 84.1%
Hollywood Marine Inc Hollywood Marine Inc PAC Houston, TX	Sea Transport	$29,488	19 Candidates Avg House: $1,299 Avg Sen: $2,500	Dems: 53.7% House: 66.1% Incumb: 92.7%
Hollywood Women's Political Committee Hollywood Women's Political Committee Culver City, CA	Dem/Liberal†	$278,500	82 Candidates Avg House: $2,967 Avg Sen: $4,568	Dems: 99.3% House: 63.9% Incumb: 31.6%

PAC Sponsor / Affiliate / Category	1991-92 Total	Candidates / Avg	Where the money went
Home Savings of America Home Savings of America PAC Mill Valley, CA — HF Ahmanson & Co — Savings & Loans	$34,950	26 Candidates Avg House: $1,379 Avg Sen: $1,278	Repubs: 52.8% House: 67.1% Incumb: 78.5%
Home Shopping Network Inc Home Shopping Network Inc PAC (HSN PAC) Clearwater, FL — Cable TV	$27,500	24 Candidates Avg House: $1,147 Avg Sen: $1,143	Dems: 69.1% House: 70.9% Incumb: 100.0%
Homedco Inc Homedco Inc PAC Fountain Valley, CA — Home Health Svcs†	$22,250	18 Candidates Avg House: $1,167 Avg Sen: $1,375	Dems: 73.0% House: 62.9% Incumb: 82.0%
Honeywell Inc Honeywell Employees Citizenship Fund Minneapolis, MN — Honeywell — Aerospace Equipt†	$34,400	46 Candidates Avg House: $618 Avg Sen: $1,017	Repubs: 66.4% House: 55.7% Incumb: 66.1%
Hopkins & Sudder HS Political Fund Chicago, IL — Lawyers	$65,715	104 Candidates Avg House: $551 Avg Sen: $1,018	Dems: 59.2% House: 72.1% Incumb: 90.0%
Hotel/Restaurant Employees Union Hotel Employees & Restaurant Employees Int'l Union TIP - "To Insure Progress" Washington, DC — Food Svc Unions	$333,524	259 Candidates Avg House: $1,018 Avg Sen: $2,504	Dems: 91.5% House: 64.4% Incumb: 81.1%
HOUPAC Houpac Houston, TX — Oil & Gas	$77,750	94 Candidates Avg House: $492 Avg Sen: $1,578	Repubs: 90.3% Senate: 58.8% Incumb: 38.3%
House Leadership Fund House Leadership Fund; The Washington, DC — Rep Thomas Foley (D-Wash) — Dem Leaders	$244,056	136 Candidates Avg House: $1,732 Avg Sen: $6,000	Dems: 100.0% House: 95.1% Incumb: 54.1%
Household International Inc Household International Inc & Subsidiary Companies PAC (Housepac) Prospect Heights, IL — Credit/Loans	$188,932	134 Candidates Avg House: $1,181 Avg Sen: $1,948	Dems: 51.0% House: 58.8% Incumb: 71.2%
Houston Industries Houston Industries PAC Houston, TX — Electric Utilities†	$63,000	35 Candidates Avg House: $1,828 Avg Sen: $1,667	Dems: 62.7% House: 84.1% Incumb: 84.9%
Howard Jarvis Taxpayers Assn Howard Jarvis Taxpayers Assn PAC Los Angeles, CA — Tax Policy	$48,497	22 Candidates Avg House: $1,816 Avg Sen: $4,667	Repubs: 100.0% House: 71.1% Incumb: 25.8%
Hudson Valley PAC Hudson Valley PAC Spring Valley, NY — Pro-Israel	$266,965	134 Candidates Avg House: $1,193 Avg Sen: $3,872	Dems: 65.4% Senate: 58.0% Incumb: 87.7%
Huffy Corp Huffy Corporation PAC ("HuffyPAC") Miamisburg, OH — Bicycles†	$21,184	15 Candidates Avg House: $1,068 Avg Sen: $2,100	Repubs: 67.9% House: 50.4% Incumb: 74.0%
Hughes Aircraft Hughes Aircraft Company Active Citizenship Fund Los Angeles, CA — General Motors — Defense Electronics†	$220,270	149 Candidates Avg House: $1,301 Avg Sen: $2,278	Dems: 52.3% House: 72.1% Incumb: 86.5%
Human Rights Campaign Fund Human Rights Campaign Fund PAC Washington, DC — Gay/Lesbian	$713,040	190 Candidates Avg House: $3,557 Avg Sen: $5,046	Dems: 92.8% House: 82.3% Incumb: 48.3%
Humana Inc HUMPAC - A PAC Sponsored by Humana Inc Louisville, KY — Hospitals†	$61,425	45 Candidates Avg House: $1,286 Avg Sen: $1,496	Dems: 75.7% House: 58.6% Incumb: 55.1%
Hunter Engineering Hunter Engineering Company PAC Bridgeton, MO — Industl/Comml Equip	$23,721	8 Candidates Avg House: $1,960 Avg Sen: $10,000	Repubs: 100.0% House: 57.8% Incumb: 54.8%
ICI Americas Inc ICI Americas PAC Wilmington, DE — Pharmaceuticals†	$84,487	102 Candidates Avg House: $665 Avg Sen: $1,281	Dems: 62.7% House: 59.0% Incumb: 94.0%
Illinois Bell Telephone Illinois Bell Citizenship Responsibility Committee Chicago, IL — Ameritech — Phone Utilites	$56,235	23 Candidates Avg House: $2,399 Avg Sen: $2,925	Dems: 55.9% House: 89.6% Incumb: 86.1%

† PAC sponsor has other major interests in addition to this primary category

PAC Sponsor or Related Group / PAC Name	Affiliate	1991-92 Total	Where the money went...		
Illinois Power Co Illinois Power Employees' Federal PAC Decatur, IL	Gas & Electric Util†	$42,111	26 Candidates Avg House: $1,665 Avg Sen: $1,497	Repubs: 58.8% House: 75.1% Incumb: 79.0%	
Illinois Tool Works Illinois Tool Works Inc PAC Glenview, IL	Industl/Comml Equip	$25,900	38 Candidates Avg House: $604 Avg Sen: $831	Repubs: 92.3% House: 58.3% Incumb: 65.1%	
IMC Fertilizer Inc IMC Fertilizer Inc PAC Northbrook, IL	Imcera Group Ag Chemicals	$21,000	37 Candidates Avg House: $485 Avg Sen: $1,250	Repubs: 61.4% House: 76.2% Incumb: 81.9%	
Immunex Corp Immunex Corp PAC Seattle, WA	Pharmaceuticals	$20,245	25 Candidates Avg House: $780 Avg Sen: $855	Repubs: 54.8% House: 57.8% Incumb: 43.2%	
Imo Industries Inc Imo Industries Inc PAC Lawrenceville, NJ	Defense Electronics†	$110,923	59 Candidates Avg House: $1,678 Avg Sen: $3,000	Repubs: 59.9% House: 75.7% Incumb: 78.0%	
Independent Action Independent Action Inc Washington, DC	Sen Tom Harkin/Rep Mo Udall Dem/Liberal	$116,318	40 Candidates Avg House: $2,049 Avg Sen: $3,702	Dems: 99.1% Senate: 60.5% Incumb: 30.1%	
Independent Bakers Assn BakePAC - The PAC of the Independent Bakers Association Washington, DC	Food Processors	$33,620	92 Candidates Avg House: $265 Avg Sen: $650	Repubs: 89.7% House: 53.6% Incumb: 66.8%	
Independent Bankers Assn Independent Bankers - PAC Washington, DC	Commercial Banks	$401,060	312 Candidates Avg House: $1,085 Avg Sen: $2,321	Dems: 62.3% House: 70.3% Incumb: 85.3%	
Independent Federation of Flight Attendants Independent Federation of Flight Attendants Jet PAC New York, NY	Air Transport Unions	$26,925	71 Candidates Avg House: $333 Avg Sen: $531	Dems: 90.6% House: 65.5% Incumb: 89.6%	
Independent Insurance Agents of America Independent Insurance Agents of America Inc PAC (InsurPAC) Washington, DC	Insurance	$589,798	278 Candidates Avg House: $1,746 Avg Sen: $3,612	Dems: 59.8% House: 65.7% Incumb: 83.7%	
Independent Petroleum Assn of America Independent Assn of America Wildcatters Fund (IPAA Wildcatters Fund) Washington, DC	Oil & Gas	$39,950	59 Candidates Avg House: $613 Avg Sen: $835	Repubs: 52.7% House: 64.5% Incumb: 74.3%	
Indiana Bell Telephone Indiana Bell Telephone Company, Incorporated PAC (InBellPAC) Indianapolis, IN	Ameritech Phone Utilites	$45,250	14 Candidates Avg House: $3,209 Avg Sen: $4,975	Dems: 54.2% House: 78.0% Incumb: 99.3%	
Indiana Farm Bureau Indiana Farm Bureau Inc Elect PAC Inc Indianapolis, IN	Farm Orgs	$45,250	10 Candidates Avg House: $4,406 Avg Sen: $5,000	Repubs: 66.3% House: 77.9% Incumb: 77.9%	
Insilco Corp Insilco Corporation PAC "InsilcoPAC" Midland, TX	Weapons Systems†	$77,000	33 Candidates Avg House: $2,056 Avg Sen: $2,667	Repubs: 71.4% Senate: 52.0% Incumb: 96.1%	
Institute of Scrap Recycling Industries ISRI PAC Washington, DC	Recycling	$54,315	71 Candidates Avg House: $761 Avg Sen: $785	Dems: 66.3% House: 81.2% Incumb: 95.2%	
Intel Corp Intel PAC Santa Clara, CA	Computer Equipment	$26,600	33 Candidates Avg House: $723 Avg Sen: $1,114	Repubs: 68.2% House: 70.7% Incumb: 60.1%	
Intergraph Corp Intergraph Corporation PAC Huntsville, AL	Computer Equipment	$29,600	19 Candidates Avg House: $1,513 Avg Sen: $1,725	Dems: 87.3% House: 76.7% Incumb: 96.6%	
International Assn of Drilling Contractors International Association of Drilling Contractors PAC Houston, TX	Oilfield Services	$27,310	20 Candidates Avg House: $1,003 Avg Sen: $1,728	Repubs: 61.5% Senate: 63.3% Incumb: 84.4%	
International Assn of Firefighters Int'l Assn of Firefighters Interested in Registration and Education PAC Washington, DC	Intl Assn of Firefighters Public Safety	$562,153	324 Candidates Avg House: $1,517 Avg Sen: $2,996	Dems: 93.9% House: 75.3% Incumb: 61.4%	

PAC Sponsor or Related Group/PAC Name	Affiliate	1991-92 Total	Where the money went...		
International Brotherhood of Electrical Workers (IBEW) International Brotherhood of Electrical Workers Committee on Political Education Washington, DC — IBEW — Electrical Workers		$1,517,592	387 Candidates Avg House: $3,657 Avg Sen: $5,438	Dems: 96.1% House: 79.3% Incumb: 57.7%	
International Chemical Workers Union International Chemical Workers Union Labor's Investment In Voter Education Akron, OH — Manufacturing Unions		$31,700	74 Candidates Avg House: $320 Avg Sen: $720	Dems: 100.0% House: 54.6% Incumb: 41.6%	
International Chiropractors Assn International Chiropractors PAC Arlington, VA — Chiropractors		$35,550	40 Candidates Avg House: $787 Avg Sen: $1,750	Dems: 86.9% House: 77.5% Incumb: 79.9%	
International Council of Shopping Centers International Council of Shopping Centers Inc PAC (ICSC PAC) Alexandria, VA — Retail Trade		$280,399	186 Candidates Avg House: $1,219 Avg Sen: $2,952	Repubs: 58.7% House: 67.4% Incumb: 84.1%	
International Longshoremen's/Warehousemen's Union International Longshoremen's & Warehousemen's Union - Political Action Fund San Francisco, CA — Sea Transport Unions		$181,751	59 Candidates Avg House: $2,449 Avg Sen: $5,836	Dems: 98.6% House: 64.7% Incumb: 43.9%	
International Longshoremens Assn Int'l Longshoremen's Association AFL-CIO Cmte on Pol Education ILA-COPE New York, NY — Intl Longshoremen Assn — Sea Transport Unions		$187,050	89 Candidates Avg House: $2,120 Avg Sen: $2,024	Dems: 92.3% House: 81.6% Incumb: 65.0%	
International Paper Co Voluntary Contributors for Better Govt: Employees of Int'l Paper Company Washington, DC — Paper/Pulp†		$218,860	93 Candidates Avg House: $1,380 Avg Sen: $4,732	Repubs: 89.8% Senate: 58.4% Incumb: 70.5%	
International Taxicab Assn International Taxicab Association PAC Kensington, MD — Taxis		$22,500	14 Candidates Avg House: $1,667 Avg Sen: $1,500	Repubs: 51.1% House: 66.7% Incumb: 84.4%	
Interstate Natural Gas Assn Interstate Natural Gas Association of America PAC Washington, DC — Natural Gas		$87,443	90 Candidates Avg House: $696 Avg Sen: $1,862	Dems: 67.0% House: 54.1% Incumb: 93.4%	
Invacare Corp Invacare Corp PAC aka INVA PAC Elyria, OH — Medical Supplies		$50,150	30 Candidates Avg House: $1,368 Avg Sen: $2,195	Dems: 72.8% House: 51.8% Incumb: 87.0%	
Investment Company Institute Investment Mgmt PAC of the Investment Company Institute (IMPAC) Washington, DC — Securities		$192,150	97 Candidates Avg House: $1,682 Avg Sen: $3,000	Dems: 80.2% House: 65.7% Incumb: 93.8%	
Investors Diversified Services IDS PAC Minneapolis, MN — American Express — Securities†		$29,650	49 Candidates Avg House: $537 Avg Sen: $841	Dems: 63.4% House: 68.8% Incumb: 92.8%	
Ironworkers Union Ironworkers Political Action League Washington, DC — Building Trade Unions		$530,280	200 Candidates Avg House: $2,345 Avg Sen: $4,576	Dems: 92.7% House: 75.2% Incumb: 66.7%	
Irvine Co Irvine Company Employees' PAC, The Newport Beach, CA — Real Estate Devel		$44,100	30 Candidates Avg House: $1,298 Avg Sen: $1,815	Dems: 57.1% House: 58.8% Incumb: 66.5%	
ITEL Corp ITEL Corporation PAC Chicago, IL — Communication Equip†		$57,150	39 Candidates Avg House: $1,050 Avg Sen: $2,063	Dems: 80.3% Senate: 57.7% Incumb: 86.9%	
ITT Corp Corporate Citizenship Committee (ITT) New York, NY — Insurance†		$101,300	154 Candidates Avg House: $545 Avg Sen: $1,212	Repubs: 76.3% House: 68.9% Incumb: 73.8%	
Jacobs Engineering Group JEG Good Government Committee Pasadena, CA — Engineers		$63,657	60 Candidates Avg House: $951 Avg Sen: $1,422	Dems: 70.8% House: 68.7% Incumb: 96.0%	
Jefferson-Pilot Corp Jefferson-Pilot Corp Federal Good Govt Cmte Jefferson-Pilot FEDPAC Greensboro, NC — Insurance†		$27,500	8 Candidates Avg House: $2,750 Avg Sen: $5,500	Repubs: 70.9% House: 60.0% Incumb: 60.0%	
Jim Walter Corp Jim Walter Corporation PAC (JWCPAC) Tampa, FL — Walter Industries — Bldg Materials		$64,650	56 Candidates Avg House: $1,027 Avg Sen: $1,577	Dems: 80.7% House: 66.7% Incumb: 83.8%	

† PAC sponsor has other major interests in addition to this primary category

PAC Sponsor or Related Group/PAC Name	Affiliate	1991-92 Total	Where the money went...		

John Hancock Financial Service
John Hancock Financial Services PAC
Boston, MA — Insurance†
$60,875

60 Candidates	Dems: 64.6%
Avg House: $941	House: 58.7%
Avg Sen: $1,142	Incumb: 84.2%

Johnson & Gibbs
Fund for Quality In Government
Dallas, TX — Lawyers
$28,850

27 Candidates	Dems: 69.7%
Avg House: $1,255	House: 82.7%
Avg Sen: $714	Incumb: 85.8%

Johnson & Johnson
Johnson & Johnson Employees' Good Government Fund
New Brunswick, NJ — Personal Health Prod†
$89,400

89 Candidates	Dems: 54.9%
Avg House: $868	House: 70.9%
Avg Sen: $1,625	Incumb: 90.2%

Joint Action Committee for Political Affairs
Joint Action Committee for Political Affair
Highland Park, IL — Pro-Israel
$205,000

111 Candidates	Dems: 97.1%
Avg House: $1,307	House: 55.5%
Avg Sen: $3,802	Incumb: 62.1%

Jones International
Jones International Ltd PAC
Englewood, CO — Cable TV
$42,950

27 Candidates	Repubs: 55.2%
Avg House: $1,017	Senate: 71.6%
Avg Sen: $2,050	Incumb: 69.7%

Jones, Day et al
Jones, Day, Reavis & Pogue Good Government Fund
Cleveland, OH — Lawyers
$176,082

150 Candidates	Dems: 50.1%
Avg House: $898	House: 59.1%
Avg Sen: $2,116	Incumb: 72.6%

K Mart Corp
K Mart Corporation PAC
Troy, MI — Department Stores
$54,100

136 Candidates	Repubs: 65.6%
Avg House: $311	House: 63.2%
Avg Sen: $765	Incumb: 71.5%

Kaiser Aluminum & Chemical
Kaiser Aluminum & Chemical Corporation PAC
Oakland, CA — Metal Mining/Process†
$24,500

31 Candidates	Dems: 58.4%
Avg House: $673	House: 71.4%
Avg Sen: $1,400	Incumb: 83.7%

Kaiser Engineers Inc
Kaiser Engineers, Inc PAC
Oakland, CA — Engineers
$49,646

52 Candidates	Dems: 78.5%
Avg House: $1,054	House: 70.1%
Avg Sen: $815	Incumb: 71.4%

Kaman Corp
Kaman Corporation Good Government Fund
Bloomfield, CT — Defense Electronics†
$35,582

22 Candidates	Dems: 71.2%
Avg House: $1,505	House: 71.9%
Avg Sen: $2,000	Incumb: 100.0%

Kansas City Southern
Kansas City Southern Employees PAC
Kansas City, MO — Railroads†
$99,725

94 Candidates	Dems: 64.2%
Avg House: $939	House: 62.1%
Avg Sen: $1,348	Incumb: 90.7%

Kellogg Co
Kellogg Better Government Committee
Battle Creek, MI — Food Processors
$70,700

82 Candidates	Dems: 58.4%
Avg House: $765	House: 68.2%
Avg Sen: $1,184	Incumb: 89.8%

Kemper Corp
Kemper Corporation Political Action Fund
Long Grove, IL — Insurance†
$24,800

37 Candidates	Repubs: 66.5%
Avg House: $592	House: 59.7%
Avg Sen: $833	Incumb: 88.7%

Kemper Insurance
Kemper Campaign Fund
Long Grove, IL — Insurance
$42,100

63 Candidates	Repubs: 66.0%
Avg House: $608	House: 78.0%
Avg Sen: $1,028	Incumb: 91.3%

Kerr-McGee
Kerr-McGee Corporation PAC
Oklahoma City, OK — Oil Refining/Mkting†
$48,250

57 Candidates	Repubs: 56.0%
Avg House: $592	Senate: 53.4%
Avg Sen: $1,355	Incumb: 91.7%

Kidder, Peabody
Nonpartisan Political Support Committee for Kidder, Peabody Employees
New York, NY — General Electric — Securities
$28,366

26 Candidates	Dems: 78.8%
Avg House: $800	Senate: 57.7%
Avg Sen: $1,488	Incumb: 43.2%

KidsPAC
KidsPAC
Cambridge, MA — Childrens Rights
$440,600

137 Candidates	Dems: 95.5%
Avg House: $2,510	House: 62.1%
Avg Sen: $5,964	Incumb: 73.7%

Kimberly-Clark
Kimberly-Clark Good Government Committee
Neenah, WI — Paper/Pulp†
$28,155

37 Candidates	Repubs: 76.9%
Avg House: $569	Senate: 51.5%
Avg Sen: $1,115	Incumb: 75.5%

Kinetic Concepts Inc
Kinetic Concepts Inc PAC (KCIPAC)
San Antonio, TX — Medical Supplies
$51,100

34 Candidates	Dems: 72.9%
Avg House: $1,648	House: 67.7%
Avg Sen: $1,269	Incumb: 68.2%

PAC Sponsor / PAC Name / Location	Affiliate	Category	1991-92 Total	Candidates	Avg House	Avg Sen	Dems/Repubs	House/Senate	Incumb
King & Spalding — King & Spalding Nonpartisan Committee for Good Government — Atlanta, GA		Lawyers	$55,400	53 Candidates	$1,114	$888	Dems: 74.8%	House: 74.4%	Incumb: 85.0%
Kirkland & Ellis — Kirkland & Ellis PAC — Chicago, IL		Lawyers	$79,219	51 Candidates	$1,207	$1,983	Dems: 90.5%	Senate: 57.6%	Incumb: 69.5%
Kirkpatrick & Lockhart — Kirkpatrick & Lockhart PAC — Pittsburgh, PA		Lawyers	$67,969	47 Candidates	$1,123	$2,389	Repubs: 55.1%	House: 57.8%	Incumb: 75.6%
Koch Industries — Koch Industries Inc PAC (KochPAC) — Wichita, KS		Oil & Gas†	$64,500	46 Candidates	$1,176	$2,042	Repubs: 83.0%	House: 62.0%	Incumb: 65.1%
Korean American National PAC — Korean American National PAC — Oakland, CA		Ethnic Groups	$21,000	7 Candidates	$2,500	$3,083	Repubs: 100.0%	Senate: 88.1%	Incumb: 76.2%
Kraft Inc — Kraft, Inc PAC — Glenview, IL	Philip Morris	Food Processors	$33,352	48 Candidates	$599	$1,111	Repubs: 68.1%	House: 70.0%	Incumb: 81.0%
Kroger Co — Kroger Better Government Committee/ KROPAC — Cincinnati, OH		Food Stores	$22,200	29 Candidates	$643	$1,214	Repubs: 64.2%	House: 60.8%	Incumb: 67.6%
Kutak, Rock & Campbell — Kutak Rock & Campbell PAC — Washington, DC		Lawyers	$54,900	64 Candidates	$648	$1,319	Dems: 87.2%	House: 53.1%	Incumb: 74.0%
Laborers' Political League — Laborers' Political League — Washington, DC	Laborers Union	Building Trade Unions	$1,387,406	409 Candidates	$3,079	$5,425	Dems: 94.1%	House: 78.6%	Incumb: 68.7%
Laborers' Western Political League — Laborers' Western Political League — Sacramento, CA	Laborers Union	Building Trade Unions	$49,300	24 Candidates	$1,544	$3,583	Dems: 100.0%	House: 56.4%	Incumb: 64.5%
Ladies Garment Workers Union — International Ladies Garment Workers Union Campaign Commmittee — New York, NY		Manufacturing Unions	$296,301	271 Candidates	$852	$2,567	Dems: 96.0%	House: 66.8%	Incumb: 70.4%
Land O'Lakes Inc — Land O'Lakes Inc PAC — Minneapolis, MN		Ag Chemicals†	$79,525	58 Candidates	$1,196	$1,794	Dems: 56.5%	House: 61.6%	Incumb: 77.4%
Leader PAC — Leader PAC — Fairfax, VA		Repub/Conservative	$61,500	35 Candidates	$1,515	$10,000	Repubs: 100.0%	House: 83.7%	Incumb: 27.6%
League of Conservation Voters — League of Conservation Voters Inc PAC — Washington, DC		Environment Policy	$413,139	120 Candidates	$3,200	$4,524	Dems: 92.4%	House: 75.9%	Incumb: 31.7%
Leboeuf, Lamb et al — Leboeuf, Lamb, Leiby & MacRae PAC — New York, NY		Lawyers	$33,253	39 Candidates	$711	$1,310	Dems: 52.9%	House: 59.8%	Incumb: 78.8%
Lennox Industries — Lennox PAC (Len PAC) — Dallas, TX		Constr Products†	$22,000	19 Candidates	$1,200	$1,111	Repubs: 90.9%	House: 54.5%	Incumb: 77.3%
Libbey-Owens-Ford — Libbey-Owens-Ford Co PAC — Toledo, OH		Glass Products†	$29,750	24 Candidates	$1,269	$1,205	Repubs: 83.2%	House: 55.5%	Incumb: 54.6%
Liberty Mutual Insurance — Liberty Mutual Insurance Company PAC — Boston, MA		Proprty Insurance	$70,300	59 Candidates	$862	$2,250	Repubs: 89.8%	House: 55.2%	Incumb: 60.2%
Limited Inc — Limited, Inc PAC — Columbus, OH		Clothing Stores	$65,300	49 Candidates	$851	$2,346	Repubs: 64.4%	Senate: 46.7%	Incumb: 66.3%

† PAC sponsor has other major interests in addition to this primary category

Lincoln Club of Northern California
Lincoln Club of Northern California
Menlo Park, CA — Repub/Conservative — $36,000

9 Candidates   Repubs: 100.0%
Avg House: $4,167   House: 69.4%
Avg Sen: $3,667   Incumb: 20.8%

Lincoln Club of Orange County
Lincoln Club Of Orange County
Costa Mesa, CA — Repub/Conservative — $66,250

17 Candidates   Repubs: 100.0%
Avg House: $3,354   House: 60.8%
Avg Sen: $6,250   Incumb: 20.4%

Lincoln National Corp
Lincoln National Corporation PAC
Fort Wayne, IN — Lincoln National — Insurance — $30,700

32 Candidates   Dems: 58.1%
Avg House: $907   House: 65.0%
Avg Sen: $1,194   Incumb: 96.7%

Litton Industries
Litton Industries Inc Employees Political Assistance Committee (LEPAC)
Beverly Hills, CA — Defense Electronics† — $140,229

109 Candidates   Repubs: 54.9%
Avg House: $1,015   House: 59.4%
Avg Sen: $2,187   Incumb: 87.7%

Lockheed Corp
Lockheed Employees PAC
Calabasas, CA — Defense Aerospace† — $338,537

211 Candidates   Dems: 54.8%
Avg House: $1,418   House: 72.9%
Avg Sen: $2,480   Incumb: 90.8%

Loews Corp
Loews Corporation/Lorillard Public Affairs Committee (LOPAC)
New York, NY — Insurance† — $41,460

74 Candidates   Dems: 53.6%
Avg House: $468   House: 70.0%
Avg Sen: $1,038   Incumb: 79.5%

Lone Star Fund
Lone Star Fund
Dallas, TX — Martin Frost (D-Texas) — Dem Leaders — $38,500

72 Candidates   Dems: 100.0%
Avg House: $535   House: 98.7%
Avg Sen: $500   Incumb: 67.5%

Longs Drugs Stores Inc
Longs Drugs Good Government Council
Walnut Creek, CA — Drug Stores — $22,350

33 Candidates   Repubs: 56.8%
Avg House: $634   House: 70.9%
Avg Sen: $813   Incumb: 65.5%

Loose Group
Loose Group; The
Union City, GA — Repub/Conservative — $53,500

10 Candidates   Repubs: 100.0%
Avg House: $5,250   House: 58.9%
Avg Sen: $5,500   Incumb: 18.7%

Loral Corp
Civic Action Fund - Loral Systems Group
Akron, OH — Defense Electronics† — $146,865

119 Candidates   Dems: 71.0%
Avg House: $1,028   House: 61.6%
Avg Sen: $1,920   Incumb: 93.2%

Louisiana for American Security
Louisiana for American Security PAC
Baton Rouge, LA — Pro-Israel — $36,500

13 Candidates   Dems: 56.2%
Avg House: $3,182   House: 95.9%
Avg Sen: $750   Incumb: 75.3%

Louisiana Land & Exploration
Louisiana Land and Exploration Company PAC (LL&E-PAC); The
New Orleans, LA — Oilfield Services† — $39,375

44 Candidates   Dems: 65.7%
Avg House: $639   Senate: 57.8%
Avg Sen: $1,264   Incumb: 82.9%

Louisiana-Pacific Corp
Louisiana-Pacific Corp Federal PAC
Portland, OR — Forest Products† — $32,350

26 Candidates   Repubs: 93.2%
Avg House: $1,383   House: 77.0%
Avg Sen: $931   Incumb: 76.8%

LTV Aerospace & Defense Co
LTV Aerospace and Defense Company Active Citizenship Campaign
Dallas, TX — LTV Corp — Defense Aerospace† — $157,851

113 Candidates   Dems: 71.8%
Avg House: $1,440   House: 77.6%
Avg Sen: $1,265   Incumb: 97.5%

LTV Steel
LTV Steel Active Citizenship Campaign
Cleveland, OH — LTV Corp — Steel — $45,500

56 Candidates   Dems: 81.8%
Avg House: $745   House: 76.9%
Avg Sen: $1,167   Incumb: 83.8%

Lykes Brothers Steamship Co
Lykes Bros Steamship Co Inc Active Citizenship Campaign
New Orleans, LA — Sea Transport — $43,775

43 Candidates   Dems: 70.2%
Avg House: $801   House: 64.0%
Avg Sen: $1,969   Incumb: 97.0%

Machinists/Aerospace Workers #837
Aerospace District Lodge 837-IAMAW-PAC
Hazelwood, MO — Machinists/Aerospace Wrkrs — Mfg Unions — $35,000

11 Candidates   Dems: 100.0%
Avg House: $3,000   House: 85.7%
Avg Sen: $5,000   Incumb: 72.9%

Machinists/Aerospace Workers Union
Machinists Non-Partisan Political League
Washington, DC — Machinists/Aerospace Wrkrs — Mfg Unions — $1,606,296

347 Candidates   Dems: 97.3%
Avg House: $4,389   House: 83.3%
Avg Sen: $6,407   Incumb: 55.4%

Maersk Inc
Maersk Good Government Fund Maersk Inc PAC
Madison, NJ — Sea Transport† — $39,750

26 Candidates   Repubs: 54.8%
Avg House: $1,544   House: 69.9%
Avg Sen: $1,494   Incumb: 87.8%

		1991-92 Total	Where the money went...			
Maintenance of Way Employees Maintenance of Way Political League Detroit, MI	Railroad Unions	$147,725	143 Candidates Avg House: $868 Avg Sen: $1,500	Dems: 96.5% House: 63.5% Incumb: 79.5%		
Mallinckrodt Inc Mallinckrodt, Inc PAC St Louis, MO	Chemicals	$30,600	31 Candidates Avg House: $714 Avg Sen: $2,125	Repubs: 53.1% House: 58.3% Incumb: 84.5%		
Manatt, Phelps et al Golden State PAC Los Angeles, CA	Lawyers	$71,260	81 Candidates Avg House: $755 Avg Sen: $1,194	Dems: 76.8% House: 61.5% Incumb: 92.6%		
Manor Healthcare Corp Manor Healthcare Federal PAC Silver Spring, MD	Nursing Homes	$73,700	49 Candidates Avg House: $1,317 Avg Sen: $1,775	Dems: 62.7% House: 51.8% Incumb: 82.1%		
Mantech International Mantech International Corp PAC Alexandria, VA	Defense Services†	$37,515	28 Candidates Avg House: $1,496 Avg Sen: $871	Dems: 78.7% House: 83.7% Incumb: 85.7%		
Manufactured Housing Institute Manufactured Housing Institute PAC (MHI PAC) Arlington, VA	Mobile Homes	$81,840	83 Candidates Avg House: $704 Avg Sen: $1,820	Repubs: 50.8% House: 53.3% Incumb: 87.1%		
Manufacturers Hanover Manufacturers Hanover Association for Responsible Government Fund New York, NY	Commercial Banks†	$67,550	68 Candidates Avg House: $834 Avg Sen: $1,471	Dems: 60.0% House: 63.0% Incumb: 95.6%		
Manville Corp Manville Corporation PAC Washington, DC	Forest Products†	$72,900	79 Candidates Avg House: $595 Avg Sen: $2,118	Repubs: 58.5% House: 50.6% Incumb: 96.9%		
Mapco Inc Mapco Inc PAC Tulsa, OK	Oil Refining/Mkting†	$134,450	136 Candidates Avg House: $645 Avg Sen: $2,442	Repubs: 86.4% House: 52.8% Incumb: 61.7%		
Marathon Oil Marathon Oil Company Employees Political Action Commttee (MEPAC) Findlay, OH	USX Corp Oil & Gas	$79,950	68 Candidates Avg House: $935 Avg Sen: $2,300	Dems: 50.5% House: 65.5% Incumb: 87.4%		
Marine Engineers District 2 Maritime Officers District 2 Marine Engineers Beneficial Assn-Associated Maritime Officers Brooklyn, NY	Marine Engineers Union Sea Transport Unions	$827,650	321 Candidates Avg House: $2,493 Avg Sen: $3,379	Dems: 62.9% House: 87.3% Incumb: 92.2%		
Marine Engineers District 2 Retirees District 2 Marine Engineers Beneficial Assn-Assoc Maritime Officers, Retirees Brooklyn, NY	Marine Engineers Union Sea Transport Unions	$63,274	56 Candidates Avg House: $986 Avg Sen: $3,000	Repubs: 73.1% House: 81.0% Incumb: 97.6%		
Marine Engineers Union Marine Engineers' Beneficial Assn Pol Action Fund (MEBA Pol Action Fund) Washington, DC	Sea Transport Unions	$705,550	237 Candidates Avg House: $2,547 Avg Sen: $4,526	Dems: 90.0% House: 67.2% Incumb: 62.3%		
Marine Fireman's Union Marine Fireman's Union Political Action Fund San Francisco, CA	Seafarers Intl Union Sea Transport Unions	$26,890	15 Candidates Avg House: $789 Avg Sen: $3,800	Dems: 100.0% Senate: 70.7% Incumb: 34.4%		
Marine Midland Banks Marine Midland Banks Inc Buffalo, NY	Commercial Banks	$34,335	57 Candidates Avg House: $586 Avg Sen: $700	Repubs: 51.2% House: 83.7% Incumb: 87.4%		
Marion Laboratories Marion Laboratories Inc PAC (MLPAC) Kansas City, MO	Dow Chemical Pharmaceuticals	$24,650	29 Candidates Avg House: $564 Avg Sen: $1,318	Repubs: 70.8% Senate: 58.8% Incumb: 95.5%		
Marriott Corp Marriott PAC Bethesda, MD	Hotels/Motels†	$118,950	104 Candidates Avg House: $853 Avg Sen: $1,797	Repubs: 64.9% House: 51.7% Incumb: 63.0%		
Martin Marietta Corp Martin Marietta Corporation PAC Bethesda, MD	Defense Aerospace†	$510,820	303 Candidates Avg House: $1,368 Avg Sen: $3,059	Dems: 51.5% House: 65.9% Incumb: 87.1%		
Maryland Assn for Concerned Citizens Maryland Association for Concerned Citizens PAC Pikesville, MD	Pro-Israel	$70,000	49 Candidates Avg House: $986 Avg Sen: $2,536	Dems: 70.0% Senate: 50.7% Incumb: 79.3%		

† PAC sponsor has other major interests in addition to this primary category

Massachusetts Mutual Life Insurance Massachusetts Mutual Life Insurance Company PAC Springfield, MA Life Insurance	**$282,338**	141 Candidates Avg House: $1,817 Avg Sen: $2,610	Dems: 68.0% House: 68.2% Incumb: 75.9%
Masters, Mates & Pilots Union Masters, Mates and Pilots Political Contribution Fund Linthicum Heights, MD Masters, Mates & Pilots Sea Transport Unions	**$143,865**	93 Candidates Avg House: $1,227 Avg Sen: $2,625	Dems: 82.5% House: 61.4% Incumb: 83.8%
Matson Navigation Matson Federal Election Committee San Francisco, CA Alexander & Baldwin Inc Sea Transport	**$52,500**	42 Candidates Avg House: $960 Avg Sen: $1,896	Dems: 69.8% House: 53.0% Incumb: 85.7%
May Department Stores May Department Stores Company PAC (MayPAC) St Louis, MO Department Stores	**$124,550**	176 Candidates Avg House: $575 Avg Sen: $1,636	Repubs: 77.5% House: 71.1% Incumb: 73.1%
Maytag Co Maytag Good Government Committee Newton, IA Appliances	**$54,500**	79 Candidates Avg House: $633 Avg Sen: $868	Repubs: 92.2% House: 69.7% Incumb: 63.3%
MBNA Corp MBNA Corp Federal Political Committee Newark, DE Commercial Banks	**$60,000**	35 Candidates Avg House: $1,621 Avg Sen: $2,167	Dems: 56.7% House: 78.3% Incumb: 71.7%
MCA Inc MCA PAC Universal City, CA Movies/TV†	**$182,650**	94 Candidates Avg House: $1,543 Avg Sen: $2,533	Dems: 83.0% Senate: 52.7% Incumb: 74.5%
McCaw Cellular Communications McCaw Cellular Communications Inc PAC Kirkland, WA Cellular Phones	**$63,320**	68 Candidates Avg House: $677 Avg Sen: $1,334	Dems: 79.4% House: 48.1% Incumb: 75.4%
McDermott Inc Better Government Fund of McDermott Incorporated New Orleans, LA Power Plant Constr†	**$34,700**	27 Candidates Avg House: $1,224 Avg Sen: $1,500	Dems: 68.0% House: 74.1% Incumb: 97.1%
McDonald's Corp McDonald's Corporation PAC Oak Brook, IL Restaurants	**$232,900**	189 Candidates Avg House: $759 Avg Sen: $4,074	Repubs: 73.4% House: 52.8% Incumb: 66.5%
McDonnell Douglas McDonnell Douglas Good Government Fund St Louis, MO Defense Aerospace†	**$251,050**	168 Candidates Avg House: $1,298 Avg Sen: $2,567	Dems: 56.9% House: 73.4% Incumb: 97.6%
McDonnell Douglas Helicopter McDonnell Douglas Helicopter Company PAC Mesa, AZ McDonnell Douglas Defense Aerospace	**$50,225**	59 Candidates Avg House: $770 Avg Sen: $1,250	Dems: 62.5% House: 75.1% Incumb: 97.5%
MCI Telecommunications MCI Telecommunications PAC (MCI PAC) Washington, DC Long Distance	**$73,300**	119 Candidates Avg House: $516 Avg Sen: $1,175	Dems: 71.4% House: 71.2% Incumb: 93.9%
McKesson Corp McKesson Corp Employees Political Fund San Francisco, CA Pharm Sales†	**$42,500**	31 Candidates Avg House: $1,045 Avg Sen: $2,167	Repubs: 69.4% House: 54.1% Incumb: 49.4%
Mead Corp Mead Corporation Effective Citizenship Fund Dayton, OH Paper/Pulp†	**$67,450**	60 Candidates Avg House: $974 Avg Sen: $1,425	Repubs: 79.6% House: 57.8% Incumb: 72.6%
Medco Containment Services Medco Containment Services Inc PAC Corp (Medco Rx PAC) Elmwood Park, NJ Pharmaceuticals	**$41,200**	17 Candidates Avg House: $1,920 Avg Sen: $3,143	Dems: 93.3% Senate: 53.4% Incumb: 67.3%
Medical Equipment Suppliers National Association of Medical Equipment Suppliers Inc PAC (NAMESPAC) Alexandria, VA Medical Supplies	**$47,500**	59 Candidates Avg House: $755 Avg Sen: $1,042	Dems: 70.5% House: 73.2% Incumb: 93.2%
Mellon Bank Bipartisan PAC Mellon Bank Corporation (BIPAC/MBC) Pittsburgh, PA Mellon Bank Corp Commercial Banks	**$51,304**	61 Candidates Avg House: $670 Avg Sen: $1,641	Repubs: 53.0% House: 64.0% Incumb: 83.1%
Menasha Corp Menasha Corporation PAC (aka Menasha Pac) Neenah, WI Packaging†	**$23,500**	33 Candidates Avg House: $565 Avg Sen: $1,050	Repubs: 91.5% House: 55.3% Incumb: 66.0%

PAC Sponsor or Related Group/PAC Name	Affiliate	1991-92 Total	Where the money went...		
Mercantile Bancorp Mercantile Bancorporation Inc (Federal) PAC St Louis, MO	Commercial Banks	$46,475	20 Candidates Avg House: $2,058 Avg Sen: $3,900	Repubs: 77.1% House: 66.4% Incumb: 71.1%	
Merck & Co Merck & Co, Inc PAC (Merck PAC) Rahway, NJ	Pharmaceuticals†	$138,050	147 Candidates Avg House: $723 Avg Sen: $1,857	Dems: 54.0% House: 62.3% Incumb: 81.9%	
Meridian Bancorp/Reading, Pa Meridian Bancorp Inc PAC Reading, PA	Commercial Banks	$26,850	36 Candidates Avg House: $707 Avg Sen: $907	Repubs: 70.0% House: 76.3% Incumb: 66.8%	
Merrill Lynch Merrill Lynch PAC Washington, DC	Securities†	$191,264	137 Candidates Avg House: $927 Avg Sen: $2,533	Repubs: 53.4% Senate: 53.0% Incumb: 83.6%	
Metropolitan Life Insurance Metropolitan Employees' Political Participation Fund A New York, NY	Metropolitan Life Life Insurance†	$266,342	175 Candidates Avg House: $1,277 Avg Sen: $2,252	Dems: 67.1% House: 61.4% Incumb: 83.9%	
Miami Cruise PAC Miami Cruise PAC Miami, FL	Sea Transport	$36,750	29 Candidates Avg House: $1,304 Avg Sen: $1,107	Dems: 77.5% House: 49.7% Incumb: 79.6%	
Michigan Bell Telephone Michigan Bell Telephone Company PAC (MICHBELLPAC) Detroit, MI	Ameritech Phone Utilites	$86,687	29 Candidates Avg House: $3,007 Avg Sen: $2,500	Dems: 62.0% House: 97.1% Incumb: 87.8%	
Michigan Consolidated Gas Michigan Consolidated Gas Company Federal PAC aka Michcon Fer PAC Detroit, MI	Natural Gas	$86,700	44 Candidates Avg House: $1,879 Avg Sen: $1,970	Dems: 66.0% House: 71.5% Incumb: 86.5%	
Michigan Credit Union League Michigan Credit Union League Legislative Action Fund Detroit, MI	Credit Union Natl Assn Credit Unions	$33,460	20 Candidates Avg House: $1,673 Avg Sen: $0	Dems: 59.5% House: 100.0% Incumb: 88.3%	
Michigan Farm Bureau Michigan Farm Bureau PAC Lansing, MI	Farm Orgs	$22,319	8 Candidates Avg House: $2,790 Avg Sen: $0	Repubs: 97.8% House: 100.0% Incumb: 28.3%	
Mid Manhattan PAC Mid Manhattan PAC (Mid PAC) New York, NY	Pro-Israel	$41,250	36 Candidates Avg House: $487 Avg Sen: $1,882	Dems: 70.3% Senate: 77.6% Incumb: 52.1%	
Mid-America Dairymen Mid-America Dairymen Inc Agricultural & Dairy Educational Political Trust Adept Springfield, MO	Dairy	$343,371	209 Candidates Avg House: $1,496 Avg Sen: $2,638	Dems: 73.9% House: 78.9% Incumb: 84.3%	
Midcon Corp Midcon Corp-PAC Lombard, IL	Occidental Petroleum Natural Gas	$27,900	32 Candidates Avg House: $670 Avg Sen: $1,692	Dems: 60.2% House: 60.0% Incumb: 92.1%	
Milk Industry Foundation Ice Cream & Milk PAC, PAC of the Int'l Ice Cream Assn & Milk Industry Foundation Washington, DC	Dairy	$132,600	105 Candidates Avg House: $876 Avg Sen: $2,381	Repubs: 71.3% House: 51.5% Incumb: 94.1%	
Milk Marketing Inc Milk Marketing Inc PAC Strongsville, OH	Dairy	$84,700	59 Candidates Avg House: $1,368 Avg Sen: $1,811	Dems: 64.0% House: 80.8% Incumb: 90.5%	
Miller & Chevalier Miller & Chevalier Chartered PAC Washington, DC	Lawyers	$20,600	32 Candidates Avg House: $629 Avg Sen: $708	Dems: 74.0% House: 79.4% Incumb: 89.1%	
Minn-Dak Farmers Co-op Minn-Dak Farmers Cooperative PAC (MDFPAC) Wahpeton, ND	Sugar	$51,275	112 Candidates Avg House: $426 Avg Sen: $595	Dems: 57.6% House: 75.6% Incumb: 90.7%	
Minnesota Mining & Manufacturing (3M) Minnesota Mining & Manufacturing Company PAC (3M PAC) St. Paul, MN	Industl/Comml Equipt†	$76,750	100 Candidates Avg House: $595 Avg Sen: $1,556	Repubs: 75.2% House: 63.5% Incumb: 66.8%	
MinnPAC MinnPAC Minneapolis, MN	Pro-Israel	$33,250	46 Candidates Avg House: $592 Avg Sen: $969	Dems: 69.9% House: 53.4% Incumb: 71.4%	

† PAC sponsor has other major interests in addition to this primary category

Mississippi Power Co
Mississippi Power Company Employees Committee for Responsible Federal Government
Gulfport, MS   Southern Co   Electric Utilities

$26,450

51 Candidates	Repubs: 51.4%
Avg House: $461	House: 57.5%
Avg Sen: $625	Incumb: 86.0%

MMI Companies
MMI Companies PAC
Bannockburn, IL   Insurance

$23,475

31 Candidates	Dems: 70.3%
Avg House: $649	House: 55.3%
Avg Sen: $955	Incumb: 85.1%

MNC Financial Inc
MNC Financial PAC-Federal Fund
Washington, DC   MNC Financial   Commercial Banks

$39,800

19 Candidates	Dems: 84.2%
Avg House: $2,053	House: 77.4%
Avg Sen: $2,250	Incumb: 91.2%

Mobil Oil
Mobil Oil Corporation PAC (aka Mobil PAC)
Fairfax, VA   Oil & Gas†

$195,750

183 Candidates	Repubs: 92.8%
Avg House: $640	House: 50.7%
Avg Sen: $3,446	Incumb: 58.8%

Monsanto Co
Monsanto Citizenship Fund
St. Louis, MO   Monsanto   Chemicals†

$113,955

98 Candidates	Repubs: 79.3%
Avg House: $717	Senate: 50.9%
Avg Sen: $2,900	Incumb: 69.8%

Montgomery Engineering
James M Montgomery Consulting Engineers Inc/Employee PAC
Pasadena, CA   Environmental Svcs

$20,250

29 Candidates	Dems: 67.9%
Avg House: $631	House: 65.4%
Avg Sen: $875	Incumb: 65.4%

Montgomery Ward
Montgomery Ward & Co Incorporated PAC aka WardPAC
Chicago, IL   Department Stores†

$51,250

49 Candidates	Dems: 54.6%
Avg House: $904	Senate: 52.4%
Avg Sen: $1,220	Incumb: 86.3%

MOPAC
MOPAC
Troy, MI   Pro-Israel

$68,300

64 Candidates	Dems: 100.0%
Avg House: $915	House: 63.0%
Avg Sen: $1,488	Incumb: 66.3%

JP Morgan & Co
Morgan Companies PAC (MorganPAC)
New York, NY   Commercial Banks†

$423,050

145 Candidates	Dems: 53.8%
Avg House: $2,951	House: 77.4%
Avg Sen: $2,818	Incumb: 86.3%

Morgan Stanley & Co
Morgan Stanley Better Government Fund
New York, NY   Morgan Stanley   Investmtent Banking†

$220,196

115 Candidates	Dems: 65.3%
Avg House: $1,709	House: 71.4%
Avg Sen: $2,739	Incumb: 92.8%

Morrison Inc
Morrison's PAC
Mobile, AL   Food Services†

$46,250

73 Candidates	Repubs: 90.3%
Avg House: $555	House: 70.8%
Avg Sen: $964	Incumb: 60.0%

Morrison-Knudsen
Morrison-Knudsen PAC
Boise, ID   Heavy Construction†

$107,675

122 Candidates	Dems: 64.7%
Avg House: $731	House: 61.8%
Avg Sen: $1,327	Incumb: 92.6%

Mortgage Bankers Assn of America
Mortgage Bankers Association of America PAC
Washington, DC   Mortgage Banking

$220,900

208 Candidates	Repubs: 53.2%
Avg House: $924	House: 76.1%
Avg Sen: $2,029	Incumb: 67.3%

Mortgage Insurance Companies of America
Mortgage Insurance PAC
Washington, DC   Insurance†

$37,050

45 Candidates	Dems: 52.1%
Avg House: $605	Senate: 52.6%
Avg Sen: $1,219	Incumb: 91.1%

Morton Building Inc
Morton Building Inc PAC
Morton, IL   Heavy Construction

$27,500

41 Candidates	Repubs: 89.1%
Avg House: $625	House: 81.8%
Avg Sen: $1,000	Incumb: 63.6%

Motorola Inc
Motorola Employees Good Government Committee
Washington, DC   Communication Equip†

$98,445

113 Candidates	Repubs: 57.7%
Avg House: $632	House: 55.2%
Avg Sen: $1,633	Incumb: 86.9%

Multi-Issue PAC
Multi-Issue PAC (MI-PAC)
Highland Park, IL   Pro-Israel

$88,750

74 Candidates	Dems: 100.0%
Avg House: $475	Senate: 72.1%
Avg Sen: $2,783	Incumb: 38.0%

Mutual Life Insurance of New York
Mutual Life Insurance Company of New York Mony PAC
New York, NY   Insurance

$51,750

44 Candidates	Dems: 70.0%
Avg House: $1,098	House: 59.4%
Avg Sen: $1,267	Incumb: 79.7%

Mutual of Omaha
General Agents Association PAC (COMPAC)
Winston Salem, NC   Mutual of Omaha   Insurance

$49,950

57 Candidates	Repubs: 88.0%
Avg House: $694	House: 57.0%
Avg Sen: $1,344	Incumb: 61.9%

PAC Sponsor or Related Group/PAC Name	Affiliate	1991-92 Total	Candidates	Avg House	Avg Sen	Party %	Chamber %	Incumb %
Mutual of Omaha Mutual of Omaha Companies PAC (IMPAC) Omaha, NE	Mutual of Omaha Insurance	$125,646	98 Candidates	Avg House: $1,184	Avg Sen: $1,583	Repubs: 54.3%	House: 69.8%	Incumb: 83.4%
Nabisco Brands Inc Nabisco Brands, Inc Program for Active Citizenship (NABPAC) East Hanover, NJ	RJR Nabisco Food Processors	$108,400	129 Candidates	Avg House: $775	Avg Sen: $1,125	Dems: 53.9%	House: 75.1%	Incumb: 85.7%
Nalco Chemical Co Nalco Chemical Company PAC Naperville, IL	Chemicals	$31,550	27 Candidates	Avg House: $809	Avg Sen: $1,780	Repubs: 88.9%	Senate: 56.4%	Incumb: 45.2%
National Abortion Rights Action League National Abortion Rights Action League - PAC NARAL-PAC Washington, DC	Natl Abortion Rts Action Lge Pro-Choice	$503,046	165 Candidates	Avg House: $2,792	Avg Sen: $4,527	Dems: 91.5%	House: 78.2%	Incumb: 44.2%
National Action Committee National Action Committee - NACPAC Miami, FL	Pro-Israel	$143,949	74 Candidates	Avg House: $967	Avg Sen: $3,552	Dems: 65.8%	Senate: 69.1%	Incumb: 83.3%
National Aggregates Assn National Aggregates Association PAC (SandPAC) Sivler Spring, MD	Stone/Concrete	$25,900	58 Candidates	Avg House: $405	Avg Sen: $567	Repubs: 76.6%	House: 67.2%	Incumb: 69.1%
National Air Traffic Controllers Assn National Air Traffic Controllers Association PAC (aka NATCA PAC) Washington, DC	Air Transport Unions	$87,400	72 Candidates	Avg House: $1,154	Avg Sen: $1,513	Dems: 90.0%	House: 79.2%	Incumb: 85.2%
National Albanian American PAC National Albanian American PAC Palm Beach Gardens, FL	Ethnic Groups	$90,000	14 Candidates	Avg House: $5,750	Avg Sen: $7,333	Repubs: 73.3%	House: 51.1%	Incumb: 77.8%
National Apartment Assn Apartment Political Committee of the National Apartment Association Washington, DC	Building Mgmt	$21,450	20 Candidates	Avg House: $850	Avg Sen: $2,333	Dems: 51.3%	House: 67.4%	Incumb: 72.0%
National Assn for Home Care National Association for Home Care Congressional Action Committee Washington, DC	Home Health Svcs	$32,982	39 Candidates	Avg House: $858	Avg Sen: $849	Dems: 93.3%	House: 65.0%	Incumb: 79.6%
National Assn for Uniformed Services National Association for Uniformed Services PAC Springfield, VA	Misc Issues	$21,485	23 Candidates	Avg House: $855	Avg Sen: $1,309	Repubs: 59.5%	House: 75.6%	Incumb: 82.5%
National Assn of Arab-Americans NAAA PAC Washington, DC	Foreign Policy	$31,613	26 Candidates	Avg House: $1,105	Avg Sen: $1,680	Dems: 63.6%	House: 73.4%	Incumb: 39.4%
National Assn of Broadcasters National Association of Broadcasters Television and Radio PAC Washington, DC	TV/Radio	$493,951	203 Candidates	Avg House: $1,978	Avg Sen: $4,129	Dems: 53.9%	House: 64.0%	Incumb: 90.1%
National Assn of Chain Drug Stores National Association of Chain Drug Stores Inc PAC Alexandria, VA	Drug Stores†	$91,050	70 Candidates	Avg House: $1,045	Avg Sen: $1,792	Dems: 57.4%	House: 52.8%	Incumb: 80.7%
National Assn of Convenience Stores National Association of Convenience Stores Alexandria, VA	Department Stores	$105,695	125 Candidates	Avg House: $680	Avg Sen: $1,542	Repubs: 80.6%	House: 65.0%	Incumb: 66.4%
National Assn of Federal Credit Unions National Association of Federal Credit Unions PAC (NAFCUPAC) Arlington, VA	Credit Unions	$69,750	87 Candidates	Avg House: $744	Avg Sen: $1,250	Dems: 69.2%	House: 82.1%	Incumb: 92.6%
National Assn of Home Builders BUILD PAC of the National Association of Home Builders Washington, DC	Natl Assn of Home Bldrs Resid Construction†	$1,072,926	422 Candidates	Avg House: $2,256	Avg Sen: $4,826	Repubs: 55.7%	House: 78.9%	Incumb: 74.5%
National Assn of Independent Insurers National Association of Independent Insurers PAC Des Plaines, IL	Insurance	$241,725	176 Candidates	Avg House: $813	Avg Sen: $3,411	Repubs: 82.7%	Senate: 53.6%	Incumb: 79.6%
National Assn of Insurance Brokers National Association of Insurance Brokers PAC (NAIBPAC) Washington, DC	Insurance	$49,350	72 Candidates	Avg House: $598	Avg Sen: $913	Dems: 53.2%	House: 63.0%	Incumb: 89.3%

† PAC sponsor has other major interests in addition to this primary category

National Assn of Letter Carriers Committee on Letter Carriers Pol Education (Letter Carriers Pol Action Fund) Washington, DC	Letter Carriers Union	**$1,634,277** Postal Unions	378 Candidates Avg House: $3,913 Avg Sen: $7,250	Dems: 89.8% House: 78.5% Incumb: 68.4%
National Assn of Life Companies National Association of Life Cos PAC (NALC/PAC) Washington, DC	Life Insurance†	**$80,900**	88 Candidates Avg House: $716 Avg Sen: $1,404	Repubs: 52.2% House: 54.9% Incumb: 78.9%
National Assn of Life Underwriters National Association of Life Underwriters PAC Washington, DC	Life Insurance	**$1,371,600**	440 Candidates Avg House: $2,759 Avg Sen: $5,340	Dems: 53.8% House: 76.2% Incumb: 73.2%
National Assn of Pharmacists National Association of Pharmacists PAC Alexandria, VA	Pharmacists†	**$154,900**	106 Candidates Avg House: $1,223 Avg Sen: $2,125	Dems: 80.6% House: 61.6% Incumb: 88.3%
National Assn of Postal Supervisors National Association of Postal Supervisors PAC Washington, DC	Postal Unions	**$137,050**	172 Candidates Avg House: $727 Avg Sen: $1,250	Dems: 83.4% House: 79.0% Incumb: 79.6%
National Assn of Postmasters NAPUS PAC for Postmasters Alexandria, VA	Postal Unions	**$334,195**	281 Candidates Avg House: $1,020 Avg Sen: $1,841	Dems: 86.3% House: 69.3% Incumb: 85.1%
National Assn of Private Psychiatric Hospitals National Association of Private Psychiatric Hospitals/PAC Washington, DC	Hospitals	**$92,950**	69 Candidates Avg House: $999 Avg Sen: $2,091	Dems: 68.6% House: 50.5% Incumb: 86.0%
National Assn of Professional Insurance Agents Professional Insurance Agents PAC Alexandria, VA	Insurance	**$146,224**	145 Candidates Avg House: $860 Avg Sen: $1,533	Repubs: 53.0% House: 66.5% Incumb: 88.3%
National Assn of Realtors Realtors PAC Chicago, IL Natl Assn of Realtors	Real Estate Agents	**$2,950,138**	540 Candidates Avg House: $5,592 Avg Sen: $4,412	Dems: 55.0% House: 91.2% Incumb: 78.9%
National Assn of Retired Federal Employees National Association of Retired Federal Employees PAC (NARFE-PAC) Washington, DC	Fedl Worker Unions	**$1,437,250**	455 Candidates Avg House: $2,985 Avg Sen: $4,826	Dems: 80.5% House: 85.6% Incumb: 79.4%
National Assn of Small Business Investment Companies National Association of Small Business Investment Companies PAC Washington, DC	Small Business Assns†	**$30,750**	14 Candidates Avg House: $1,477 Avg Sen: $4,833	Dems: 55.3% House: 52.9% Incumb: 100.0%
National Assn of Social Workers National Association of Social Workers Political Action for Candidate Election Silver Spring, MD Natl Assn of Social Workers	Social Workers	**$180,746**	179 Candidates Avg House: $818 Avg Sen: $1,761	Dems: 98.2% House: 63.8% Incumb: 47.3%
National Assn of Temporary Services National Association of Temporary Services PAC Alexandria, VA	Employment Agencies	**$74,500**	62 Candidates Avg House: $1,049 Avg Sen: $1,909	Repubs: 75.2% House: 71.8% Incumb: 40.9%
National Assn of Trade & Technical Schools National Association of Trade and Technical Schools PAC Washington, DC	Vocational/Tech Educ	**$80,800**	55 Candidates Avg House: $1,333 Avg Sen: $2,250	Dems: 68.4% House: 75.9% Incumb: 91.9%
National Assn of Truck Stop Operators National Association of Truck Stop Operators Alexandria, VA	Trucking Companies	**$57,903**	89 Candidates Avg House: $591 Avg Sen: $1,000	Repubs: 64.1% House: 77.5% Incumb: 78.4%
National Assn of Water Companies National Association of Water Companies PAC (NAWC - PAC) Washington, DC	Water Utilities	**$86,200**	102 Candidates Avg House: $670 Avg Sen: $1,286	Dems: 55.9% House: 56.7% Incumb: 85.0%
National Assn of Wheat Growers National Association of Wheat Growers PAC (WHEATPAC) Washington, DC	Grain	**$37,525**	46 Candidates Avg House: $759 Avg Sen: $960	Dems: 68.3% House: 66.8% Incumb: 93.7%
National Assn of Wholesale-Distributors Wholesaler-Distributor PAC of the National Association of Wholesale-Distributors Washington, DC	Wholesale Trade	**$102,459**	132 Candidates Avg House: $551 Avg Sen: $1,842	Repubs: 87.3% House: 58.6% Incumb: 61.3%
National Auto Dealers Assn Dealers Election Action Cmte of the Nat'l Automobile Dealers Assn (NADA) Mclean, VA	Auto Dealers	**$1,784,375**	449 Candidates Avg House: $3,840 Avg Sen: $5,153	Repubs: 60.7% House: 86.7% Incumb: 69.4%

PAC Sponsor or Related Group/PAC Name	Affiliate	1991-92 Total	Where the money went...		
National Automatic Merchandising Assn National Automatic Merchandising Association PAC (NAMAPAC) Chicago, IL	Retail Trade	$20,025	36 Candidates Avg House: $545 Avg Sen: $750	Dems: 58.4% House: 92.5% Incumb: 97.5%	
National Beer Wholesalers Assn National Beer Wholesalers' Association PAC (NBWA PAC) Falls Church, VA	Liquor Wholesalers	$977,081	453 Candidates Avg House: $1,902 Avg Sen: $4,082	Repubs: 62.5% House: 77.9% Incumb: 74.9%	
National Broiler Council National Broiler Council PAC Washington, DC	Poultry/Egg	$183,750	147 Candidates Avg House: $1,013 Avg Sen: $2,037	Dems: 53.0% House: 62.3% Incumb: 86.7%	
National Cable Television Assn National Cable Television Association's PAC (Cable PAC) Washington, DC	Cable TV	$636,199	167 Candidates Avg House: $3,207 Avg Sen: $5,986	Dems: 53.4% House: 65.0% Incumb: 92.3%	
National Cattlemen's Assn National Cattlemen's Association PAC Englewood, CO	Natl Cattlemens Assn Livestock	$297,670	258 Candidates Avg House: $946 Avg Sen: $2,087	Repubs: 55.0% House: 67.0% Incumb: 77.5%	
National City Corp National City Corporation PAC (aka National City PAC or NC PAC) Cleveland, OH	Commercial Banks	$65,980	57 Candidates Avg House: $1,153 Avg Sen: $1,173	Repubs: 57.1% House: 76.9% Incumb: 68.1%	
National Coal Assn COALPAC - The PAC of the National Coal Association Washington, DC	Coal	$239,848	163 Candidates Avg House: $997 Avg Sen: $4,361	Repubs: 75.3% House: 58.2% Incumb: 66.2%	
National Committee for an Effective Congress National Committee for an Effective Congress Washington, DC	Dem/Liberal	$650,750	222 Candidates Avg House: $2,702 Avg Sen: $4,242	Dems: 100.0% House: 78.5% Incumb: 55.0%	
National Committee to Preserve Social Secur National Committee to Preserve Social Security PAC Washington, DC	Elderly/Soc Security	$941,650	347 Candidates Avg House: $2,348 Avg Sen: $5,134	Dems: 88.1% House: 75.0% Incumb: 82.3%	
National Community Action Foundation Community Action Program-PAC (SSF of National Community Action Foundation Inc) Washington, DC	Health/Welfare	$120,350	40 Candidates Avg House: $2,493 Avg Sen: $3,706	Dems: 87.5% Senate: 52.4% Incumb: 81.1%	
National Concrete Masonry Assn National Concrete Masonry Association PAC Herndon, VA	Stone/Concrete	$43,759	67 Candidates Avg House: $611 Avg Sen: $788	Repubs: 55.8% House: 71.2% Incumb: 97.4%	
National Congressional Club National Congressional Club Raleigh, NC	Sen Jesse Helms (R-NC) Repub Leaders	$34,476	16 Candidates Avg House: $1,841 Avg Sen: $2,844	Repubs: 100.0% House: 58.8% Incumb: 34.2%	
National Cooperative Business Assn Cooperative League of the USA PAC (Nat'l Coop Business PAC) Washington, DC	Business Assns	$25,479	41 Candidates Avg House: $579 Avg Sen: $738	Dems: 53.6% House: 68.1% Incumb: 82.5%	
National Cotton Council National Cotton Council Committee for the Advancement of Cotton Memphis, TN	Cotton	$183,739	143 Candidates Avg House: $1,066 Avg Sen: $2,077	Dems: 62.3% House: 65.0% Incumb: 98.5%	
National Council of Farmer Co-ops National Council of Farmer Cooperatives Political Action Commitee (Co-op PAC) Washington, DC	Farm Orgs	$128,000	148 Candidates Avg House: $697 Avg Sen: $1,406	Dems: 69.1% House: 61.6% Incumb: 91.6%	
National Council of Savings Institutions National Council of Savings Institutions (THRIFTPAC) Washington, DC	Natl Council of Savings Insts Savings & Loans	$64,542	92 Candidates Avg House: $658 Avg Sen: $1,106	Dems: 68.3% House: 84.6% Incumb: 92.0%	
National Council of Senior Citizens National Council of Senior Citizens PAC Washington, DC	Elderly/Soc Security	$221,750	74 Candidates Avg House: $2,232 Avg Sen: $5,211	Dems: 100.0% House: 55.4% Incumb: 42.5%	
National Crushed Stone Assn National Stone Association STONEPAC Washington, DC	Stone/Concrete	$50,875	56 Candidates Avg House: $836 Avg Sen: $1,212	Repubs: 63.8% House: 69.0% Incumb: 82.6%	
National Education Assn National Education Association PAC Washington, DC	Natl Education Assn Teachers	$2,329,622	409 Candidates Avg House: $5,626 Avg Sen: $6,249	Dems: 95.7% House: 87.7% Incumb: 54.6%	

† PAC sponsor has other major interests in addition to this primary category

National Electrical Contractors Assn
Electrical Construction PAC-Nat'l Electrical Contractors Assn Inc (ECPAC)
Bethesda, MD — Electr Contractors
$163,500
97 Candidates — Repubs: 84.7%
Avg House: $1,380 — House: 63.3%
Avg Sen: $2,727 — Incumb: 69.4%

National Farmers Organization
National Farmers Organization (Grass Roots in Politics)
Washington, DC — Farm Orgs
$34,125
63 Candidates — Dems: 80.5%
Avg House: $473 — House: 63.8%
Avg Sen: $709 — Incumb: 80.4%

National Farmers Union PAC
National Farmers Union PAC (NATFARMPAC)
Denver, CO — Farm Orgs
$49,875
112 Candidates — Dems: 97.1%
Avg House: $349 — House: 64.5%
Avg Sen: $670 — Incumb: 63.6%

National Federation of Business & Professional Womens Clubs
National Federation of Business & Professional Women's Clubs Inc PAC; The
Washington, DC — Business Assns
$35,500
70 Candidates — Dems: 90.8%
Avg House: $500 — House: 83.1%
Avg Sen: $545 — Incumb: 25.4%

National Federation of Federal Employees
National Federation of Federal Employees Public Affairs Council
Washington, DC — Fedl Worker Unions
$25,200
70 Candidates — Dems: 93.8%
Avg House: $378 — House: 67.5%
Avg Sen: $328 — Incumb: 74.4%

National Federation of Independent Business
National Federation of Independent Business Free Enterprise PAC
San Mateo, CA — Small Business Assns
$293,587
171 Candidates — Repubs: 86.9%
Avg House: $1,441 — House: 73.6%
Avg Sen: $3,690 — Incumb: 44.9%

National Fisheries Institute
National Fisheries Institute Fisheries PAC (FishPAC)
Arlington, VA — Comml Fishing
$47,268
36 Candidates — Dems: 56.5%
Avg House: $876 — House: 51.9%
Avg Sen: $2,844 — Incumb: 91.4%

National Forest Products Assn
Forest Industries PAC
Washington, DC — Forest Products†
$51,547
56 Candidates — Repubs: 61.2%
Avg House: $773 — House: 62.9%
Avg Sen: $1,364 — Incumb: 81.2%

National Fuel Gas Corp
National Fuel Gas Federal PAC (NFG FEDPAC)
Buffalo, NY — Natural Gas
$30,600
39 Candidates — Repubs: 55.1%
Avg House: $705 — House: 64.5%
Avg Sen: $986 — Incumb: 88.6%

National Funeral Directors Assn
National Funeral Directors Assn of the U S Inc PAC (NFDA-PAC)
Milwaukee, WI — Funeral Services
$28,000
20 Candidates — Dems: 83.9%
Avg House: $1,615 — House: 75.0%
Avg Sen: $1,000 — Incumb: 85.7%

National League of Postmasters
National League of Postmasters PAC
Alexandria, VA — Postal Unions
$216,400
243 Candidates — Dems: 76.1%
Avg House: $756 — House: 69.8%
Avg Sen: $1,519 — Incumb: 92.3%

National Machine Tool Builders Assn
Machine Toolpac
Mclean, VA — Industl/Comml Equip
$57,100
80 Candidates — Repubs: 64.5%
Avg House: $503 — House: 52.8%
Avg Sen: $1,348 — Incumb: 84.9%

National Marine Manufacturers Assn
National Marine Manufacturers Association PAC
Washington, DC — Shipbuilding/Repair
$73,000
43 Candidates — Repubs: 57.1%
Avg House: $1,435 — House: 66.8%
Avg Sen: $2,689 — Incumb: 93.8%

National Medical Enterprises Inc
National Medical Enterprises Inc PAC
Santa Monica, CA — Hospitals†
$84,575
88 Candidates — Dems: 52.8%
Avg House: $701 — House: 56.4%
Avg Sen: $1,845 — Incumb: 57.6%

National Multi Housing Council
National Multi Housing Council PAC
Washington, DC — Resid Construction
$39,770
52 Candidates — Dems: 61.4%
Avg House: $682 — House: 65.1%
Avg Sen: $991 — Incumb: 86.3%

National Organization for Women
NOW/PAC (National Organization for Women PAC)
Washington, DC — Womens Issues
$322,385
102 Candidates — Dems: 89.2%
Avg House: $2,942 — House: 81.2%
Avg Sen: $4,660 — Incumb: 11.5%

National PAC
National PAC
Washington, DC — Pro-Israel
$684,000
175 Candidates — Dems: 64.6%
Avg House: $3,442 — House: 69.4%
Avg Sen: $5,667 — Incumb: 81.4%

National Pest Control Assn
National Pest Control Association PAC
Dunn Loring, VA — Pest Control
$56,200
47 Candidates — Dems: 50.4%
Avg House: $1,153 — House: 71.8%
Avg Sen: $1,321 — Incumb: 96.0%

National Pork Producers Council
National Pork Producers Council Pork PAC
Des Moines, IA — Livestock
$155,031
162 Candidates — Dems: 51.5%
Avg House: $755 — House: 57.0%
Avg Sen: $1,482 — Incumb: 87.7%

National Propane Gas Assn
National Propane Gas Association PAC (PropanePAC)
Lisle, IL
LPG
$21,600

43 Candidates	Repubs: 57.6%
Avg House: $391	House: 59.7%
Avg Sen: $870	Incumb: 89.1%

National Realty Committee
National Realty PAC (RealPAC)
Washington, DC
Real Estate Devel
$64,141

58 Candidates	Dems: 71.5%
Avg House: $1,043	House: 71.6%
Avg Sen: $1,303	Incumb: 91.0%

National Restaurant Assn
National Restaurant Association PAC
Washington, DC
Natl Restaurant Assn
Restaurants
$560,447

235 Candidates	Repubs: 77.4%
Avg House: $2,013	House: 72.6%
Avg Sen: $4,659	Incumb: 61.2%

National Rifle Assn
NRA Political Victory Fund
Washington, DC
Pro-Guns
$1,735,946

346 Candidates	Repubs: 63.3%
Avg House: $4,902	House: 85.0%
Avg Sen: $5,790	Incumb: 60.2%

National Right to Life PAC
National Right To Life PAC
Washington, DC
Right to Life
Pro-Life
$231,614

147 Candidates	Repubs: 88.4%
Avg House: $1,473	House: 78.9%
Avg Sen: $2,191	Incumb: 33.7%

National Roofing Contractors Assn
Natl Roofing Contractors Assoc RoofPAC
Washington, DC
Subcontractors
$40,300

54 Candidates	Repubs: 91.3%
Avg House: $587	House: 55.3%
Avg Sen: $1,125	Incumb: 55.3%

National Rural Letter Carriers Assn
National Rural Letter Carriers' Association PAC
Alexandria, VA
Postal Unions
$526,528

359 Candidates	Dems: 86.0%
Avg House: $1,010	House: 60.4%
Avg Sen: $4,826	Incumb: 75.2%

National Rural Water Assn
WaterPAC - National Rural Water Association Political Committee
Duncan, OK
Water Utilities
$30,200

24 Candidates	Dems: 84.9%
Avg House: $1,216	House: 64.4%
Avg Sen: $1,464	Incumb: 98.3%

National Screw Machines Products Assn
National Screw Machines Products Association-PAC (NSMPA-PAC)
Brecksville, OH
Industl/Comml Equip
$43,500

40 Candidates	Repubs: 100.0%
Avg House: $521	Senate: 71.3%
Avg Sen: $1,938	Incumb: 35.6%

National Society of Professional Engineers
National Society of Professional Engineers - PAC (NSPE-PAC)
Alexandria, VA
Engineers
$82,050

70 Candidates	Repubs: 61.1%
Avg House: $1,118	House: 81.7%
Avg Sen: $1,500	Incumb: 77.9%

National Society of Public Accountants
National Society of Public Accountants PAC
Alexandria, VA
Accountants
$24,950

28 Candidates	Repubs: 63.7%
Avg House: $935	House: 75.0%
Avg Sen: $781	Incumb: 88.0%

National Soft Drink Assn
Soft Drink PAC
Washington, DC
Soft Drinks
$52,814

72 Candidates	Dems: 52.8%
Avg House: $648	House: 68.8%
Avg Sen: $1,031	Incumb: 91.7%

National Solid Wastes Management Assn
National Solid Wastes Management Association Waste PAC
Washington, DC
Waste Mgmt
$27,750

24 Candidates	Dems: 75.7%
Avg House: $1,286	House: 64.9%
Avg Sen: $975	Incumb: 96.4%

National Star Route Mail Contractors Assn
National Star Route Mail Contractors PAC (StarPAC)
Washington, DC
Postal Unions
$31,975

23 Candidates	Dems: 77.7%
Avg House: $1,404	House: 92.2%
Avg Sen: $1,250	Incumb: 95.3%

National Steel & Shipbuilding
National Steel and Shipbuilding Company PAC (aka Nassco PAC)
San Diego, CA
Shipbuilding/Repair
$54,384

25 Candidates	Repubs: 75.4%
Avg House: $2,007	House: 66.4%
Avg Sen: $2,607	Incumb: 86.4%

National Structured Settlements Assn
National Structured Settlements PAC
Washington, DC
Life Insurance
$35,100

35 Candidates	Dems: 81.5%
Avg House: $1,042	House: 77.2%
Avg Sen: $889	Incumb: 85.8%

National Telephone Co-op Assn
National Telephone Cooperative Assn Telephone Education Cmte Organization
Washington, DC
Phone Utilites
$84,492

161 Candidates	Dems: 70.1%
Avg House: $462	House: 73.3%
Avg Sen: $836	Incumb: 91.1%

National Tooling & Machining Assn
Tooling & Machining PAC of the National Tooling and Machining Association
Ft Washington, MD
Industl/Comml Equip
$57,560

64 Candidates	Repubs: 84.2%
Avg House: $758	House: 68.5%
Avg Sen: $1,513	Incumb: 85.2%

National Treasury Employees Union
National Treasury Employees Union PAC (TEPAC)
Washington, DC
Fedl Worker Unions
$181,160

136 Candidates	Dems: 95.8%
Avg House: $991	House: 52.0%
Avg Sen: $2,050	Incumb: 78.5%

† PAC sponsor has other major interests in addition to this primary category

National Turkey Federation National Turkey Federation Political Action Commitee/TURPAC Reston, VA		**$54,650** Poultry/Egg	51 Candidates — Repubs: 52.6% Avg House: $975 — House: 64.2% Avg Sen: $1,303 — Incumb: 96.7%
National Utility Contractors Assn National Utility Contractors Assn Legislative Information & Action Committee Arlington, VA		**$203,580** Heavy Construction	179 Candidates — Repubs: 61.6% Avg House: $1,058 — House: 84.2% Avg Sen: $1,897 — Incumb: 82.1%
National Venture Capital Assn National Venture Capital Association PAC (NVCA PAC) Washington, DC		**$220,492** Venture Capital	98 Candidates — Dems: 53.5% Avg House: $1,475 — Senate: 55.9% Avg Sen: $3,848 — Incumb: 85.0%
National Wholesale Grocers Assn National American Wholesale Grocers' Association PAC: NAWGAPAC Falls Church, VA		**$83,839** Food Wholesalers	138 Candidates — Repubs: 93.3% Avg House: $584 — House: 79.4% Avg Sen: $721 — Incumb: 73.8%
National Womens Political Caucus National Women's Political Caucus Campaign Support Committee Washington, DC	Natl Womens Pol Caucus Womens Issues	**$69,800**	36 Candidates — Dems: 94.3% Avg House: $1,531 — House: 70.2% Avg Sen: $5,200 — Incumb: 5.0%
National Womens Political Caucus National Women's Political Caucus Victory Fund (NWPC) Washington, DC	Natl Womens Pol Caucus Womens Issues	**$136,220**	55 Candidates — Dems: 87.9% Avg House: $2,135 — House: 75.2% Avg Sen: $4,817 — Incumb: 13.9%
National Wool Growers Assn National Wool Growers Assn-PAC (RAMS-Responsible Acti) Englewood, CO		**$25,850** Sheep/Wool	37 Candidates — Repubs: 60.1% Avg House: $654 — House: 58.2% Avg Sen: $771 — Incumb: 91.1%
Nationwide Corp Nationwide Political Participation Committee Columbus, OH	Nationwide Mutual Insurance Insurance	**$69,634**	60 Candidates — Repubs: 66.5% Avg House: $1,022 — House: 76.3% Avg Sen: $2,063 — Incumb: 63.8%
Navistar International Navistar International Transportation Corp Good Gov't Cmte Chicago, IL		**$40,500** Farm Equipment	27 Candidates — Repubs: 72.2% Avg House: $1,203 — Senate: 52.5% Avg Sen: $1,932 — Incumb: 81.5%
NBD Bancorp NBD Bancorp Inc PAC (NBDPAC) Detroit, MI	Natl Bank of Detroit Commercial Banks	**$21,508**	37 Candidates — Dems: 58.0% Avg House: $518 — House: 74.7% Avg Sen: $908 — Incumb: 90.2%
NCNB Corp NCNB Corporation PAC (NCNB PAC) Charlotte, NC		**$33,750** Commercial Banks	57 Candidates — Dems: 70.4% Avg House: $593 — House: 89.6% Avg Sen: $583 — Incumb: 97.0%
NCNB Texas NCNB Texas PAC Dallas, TX	NCNB Corp Commercial Banks	**$49,050**	38 Candidates — Dems: 62.6% Avg House: $1,395 — House: 79.6% Avg Sen: $1,000 — Incumb: 87.8%
NCR Corp NCR Corporation PAC Dayton, OH		**$23,350** Computers†	43 Candidates — Dems: 52.5% Avg House: $406 — House: 54.0% Avg Sen: $896 — Incumb: 96.8%
Nestle Enterprises Inc Nestle Enterprises Inc PAC Solon, OH		**$83,867** Food & Beverage	113 Candidates — Dems: 68.4% Avg House: $536 — House: 56.9% Avg Sen: $1,505 — Incumb: 61.0%
Nevada Resort Assn Nevada Resort Association PAC Las Vegas, NV		**$47,000** Casinos/Gambling†	26 Candidates — Dems: 78.7% Avg House: $1,538 — Senate: 57.5% Avg Sen: $2,077 — Incumb: 89.4%
New England Mutual Life New England Mutual Life Insurance Company PAC/New England Life PAC (NELPAC) Boston, MA		**$80,850** Life Insurance	67 Candidates — Dems: 62.4% Avg House: $1,141 — House: 73.4% Avg Sen: $1,433 — Incumb: 86.5%
New England Power Co New England Electric PAC Establ by New England Power Service Co (NEEPAC) Westborough, MA		**$34,100** Electric Utilities	50 Candidates — Dems: 63.6% Avg House: $640 — House: 75.1% Avg Sen: $850 — Incumb: 90.9%
New England Telephone & Telegraph New England Telephone and Telegraph Company Federal PAC (NET-FED-PAC) Boston, MA	NYNEX Phone Utilites	**$42,020**	24 Candidates — Dems: 74.9% Avg House: $1,975 — House: 89.3% Avg Sen: $900 — Incumb: 85.0%
New Frontier Leadership PAC New Frontier Leadership PAC (NFL PAC) Arlington, VA	Rep Norman Lent (R-NY) Repub Leaders	**$21,550**	16 Candidates — Repubs: 90.7% Avg House: $1,347 — House: 100.0% Avg Sen: $0 — Incumb: 35.0%

New Jersey Bell Telephone
New Jersey Bell Telephone Company Federal PAC (NJB PAC)
Newark, NJ — Bell Atlantic — Phone Utilites

$47,900	20 Candidates	Dems: 59.0%
	Avg House: $2,311	House: 91.7%
	Avg Sen: $4,000	Incumb: 89.6%

New Jersey Environmental Federation
Clean Water/Vote Environment
Washington, DC — NJ Environmental Fedn — Environment Policy

$21,172	10 Candidates	Dems: 100.0%
	Avg House: $2,805	House: 92.8%
	Avg Sen: $512	Incumb: 55.8%

New Jersey Medical Assn
New Jersey Medical PAC
Lawrenceville, NJ — American Medical Assn — Doctors

$38,700	14 Candidates	Repubs: 80.4%
	Avg House: $2,764	House: 100.0%
	Avg Sen: $0	Incumb: 30.4%

New Majority Leadership PAC
New Majority Leadership PAC
New Ulm, MN — Rep Vin Weber (R-Minn) — Repub Leaders

$38,054	51 Candidates	Repubs: 100.0%
	Avg House: $746	House: 100.0%
	Avg Sen: $0	Incumb: 10.5%

New York Life
New York Life PAC - Federal Fund (New York Life PAC - Federal)
New York, NY — Life Insurance

$134,150	102 Candidates	Dems: 61.8%
	Avg House: $1,049	House: 60.2%
	Avg Sen: $2,136	Incumb: 79.9%

New York Medical Assn
New York Medical PAC
Lake Success, NY — American Medical Assn — Doctors

$94,653	28 Candidates	Dems: 64.3%
	Avg House: $3,492	House: 92.2%
	Avg Sen: $2,451	Incumb: 86.7%

New York Mercantile Exchange
New York Mercantile Exchange PAC Inc
New York, NY — Securities

$43,100	37 Candidates	Dems: 65.5%
	Avg House: $944	House: 54.8%
	Avg Sen: $1,625	Incumb: 83.8%

New York State Electric & Gas Corp
New York State Electric & Gas Corporation PAC (NYSEGPAC)
Binghamton, NY — Gas & Electric Util†

$26,620	33 Candidates	Repubs: 61.3%
	Avg House: $819	House: 83.1%
	Avg Sen: $750	Incumb: 95.6%

New York Stock Exchange
New York Stock Exchange Inc PAC (NYSE PAC)
Washington, DC — Stock Exchanges

$58,650	56 Candidates	Dems: 65.6%
	Avg House: $770	Senate: 50.1%
	Avg Sen: $1,633	Incumb: 97.4%

New York Telephone
New York Telephone Federal PAC
New York, NY — NYNEX — Phone Utilites

$51,710	39 Candidates	Repubs: 53.7%
	Avg House: $1,339	House: 90.6%
	Avg Sen: $1,215	Incumb: 82.5%

Newhall Land & Farming Co
Newhall Land and Farming Company PAC (NEWPAC)
Valencia, CA — Real Estate Devel

$28,650	22 Candidates	Repubs: 86.0%
	Avg House: $919	House: 57.8%
	Avg Sen: $3,025	Incumb: 41.5%

Nike Inc
Nike Inc PAC
Beaverton, OR — Shoes†

$46,369	51 Candidates	Repubs: 64.4%
	Avg House: $656	Senate: 54.7%
	Avg Sen: $1,335	Incumb: 76.8%

NL Industries
NL Industries Inc PAC
Houston, TX — Chemicals

$43,246	57 Candidates	Repubs: 97.7%
	Avg House: $530	Senate: 60.8%
	Avg Sen: $1,052	Incumb: 26.1%

Norfolk Southern Corp
Norfolk Southern Corporation Good Government Fund
Norfolk, VA — Norfolk Southern — Railroads†

$175,820	186 Candidates	Dems: 61.8%
	Avg House: $847	House: 74.2%
	Avg Sen: $1,419	Incumb: 93.7%

Norstar Bancorp
Norstar Bancorp Inc PAC
Providence, RI — Fleet/Norstar Financial Group — Commer Banks

$65,000	65 Candidates	Dems: 65.7%
	Avg House: $880	House: 62.3%
	Avg Sen: $1,289	Incumb: 82.3%

North American Philips Corp
North American Philips Corporation PAC
Washington, DC — Philips Group — Electronics Mfg†

$69,450	63 Candidates	Repubs: 81.4%
	Avg House: $940	House: 66.3%
	Avg Sen: $1,671	Incumb: 83.4%

North American Van Lines
North American Van Lines, Inc PAC (NAPAC)
Fort Wayne, IN — Norfolk Southern — Trucking Companies

$53,350	52 Candidates	Dems: 65.5%
	Avg House: $864	House: 79.4%
	Avg Sen: $3,667	Incumb: 98.5%

North Jersey PAC
North Jersey PAC
New York, NY — Pro-Israel

$136,750	86 Candidates	Dems: 73.9%
	Avg House: $909	Senate: 57.0%
	Avg Sen: $3,000	Incumb: 83.2%

Northern States Power Co
Northern States Power Employee Political Interest Committee
Minneapolis, MN — Gas & Electric Util†

$30,395	45 Candidates	Dems: 73.3%
	Avg House: $563	House: 55.6%
	Avg Sen: $900	Incumb: 88.0%

† PAC sponsor has other major interests in addition to this primary category

PAC Sponsor or Related Group/PAC Name	Affiliate	1991-92 Total	Candidates	Avg House / Avg Sen	Party/Chamber/Incumb
Northern Telecom Northern Telecom Inc PAC Nashville, TN	Communication Equip	$42,554	57 Candidates	Avg House: $668 Avg Sen: $1,042	Dems: 50.2% House: 70.6% Incumb: 80.0%
Northern Trust Co Northern Trust Company Good Government Committee Chicago, IL	Commercial Banks	$20,400	30 Candidates	Avg House: $663 Avg Sen: $750	Repubs: 52.9% House: 77.9% Incumb: 77.0%
Northrop Corp Northrop Employees PAC (aka NEPAC) San Francisco, CA	Defense Aerospace†	$360,015	212 Candidates	Avg House: $1,327 Avg Sen: $3,202	Repubs: 55.2% House: 62.6% Incumb: 85.9%
Northwest Airlines Northwest Airlines PAC St Paul, MN	Airlines	$156,224	103 Candidates	Avg House: $1,270 Avg Sen: $2,150	Dems: 66.5% House: 58.5% Incumb: 90.6%
Northwestern Mutual Life Northwestern Mutual Life Insurance Company Federal PAC (NML FEDPAC) Milwaukee, WI	Life Insurance	$240,580	110 Candidates	Avg House: $2,026 Avg Sen: $2,563	Dems: 61.4% House: 64.8% Incumb: 88.0%
Northwestern National Life NWNL Federal PAC Minneapolis, MN	Life Insurance	$23,940	26 Candidates	Avg House: $886 Avg Sen: $1,014	Dems: 52.2% House: 70.3% Incumb: 76.0%
Norwest Corp Norwest Corporation PAC (Norwest PAC) Minneapolis, MN	Commercial Banks	$80,700	75 Candidates	Avg House: $1,042 Avg Sen: $1,191	Dems: 63.1% House: 74.9% Incumb: 91.0%
NYNEX Corp NYNEX Federal PAC New York, NY	NYNEX Phone Utilites†	$111,790	98 Candidates	Avg House: $909 Avg Sen: $1,984	Repubs: 60.1% House: 61.0% Incumb: 73.9%
O'Melveny & Myers O'Melveny & Myers PAC Washington, DC	Lawyers	$75,204	60 Candidates	Avg House: $1,053 Avg Sen: $1,577	Dems: 64.8% Senate: 50.3% Incumb: 47.5%
Occidental Oil & Gas Occidental Oil & Gas Corp PAC (OOGPAC) (aka Cities Service Oil & Gas Corp PAC) Tulsa, OK	Occidental Petroleum Oil & Gas	$46,850	75 Candidates	Avg House: $514 Avg Sen: $1,067	Repubs: 91.9% House: 65.8% Incumb: 56.8%
Occidental Petroleum Occidental Petroleum Corporation PAC Los Angeles, CA	Oil & Gas†	$179,900	98 Candidates	Avg House: $1,269 Avg Sen: $3,500	Dems: 59.8% House: 50.8% Incumb: 76.9%
Ocean Spray Cranberries Inc Ocean Spray PAC Lakeville-Middlebo, MA	Fruit/Veg	$137,950	123 Candidates	Avg House: $1,011 Avg Sen: $1,412	Dems: 70.1% House: 63.8% Incumb: 96.0%
Office & Professional Employees Union Office and Professional Employees International Union-Voice of the Electorate Washington, DC	Office/Prof Employees Misc Labor Unions	$158,950	84 Candidates	Avg House: $1,370 Avg Sen: $3,283	Dems: 100.0% House: 50.9% Incumb: 58.7%
Ogden Corp Ogden Corporation Political Action Fund New York, NY	Waste Mgmt††	$29,950	35 Candidates	Avg House: $723 Avg Sen: $1,186	Dems: 64.8% House: 53.1% Incumb: 85.0%
Ohio Bankers Assn Ohio Bankers Political Campaign Committee Columbus, OH	American Bankers Assn Commercial Banks	$24,200	12 Candidates	Avg House: $1,745 Avg Sen: $5,000	Repubs: 69.0% House: 79.3% Incumb: 62.0%
Ohio Bell Telephone Ohio Bell Telephone Company Federal PAC; The (OBT PAC) Cleveland, OH	Ameritech Phone Utilites	$47,380	22 Candidates	Avg House: $2,209 Avg Sen: $1,000	Dems: 54.7% House: 97.9% Incumb: 92.5%
Ohio Freeze Voter Freeze Voter Washington, DC	Pro-Peace	$22,000	5 Candidates	Avg House: $2,000 Avg Sen: $5,333	Dems: 100.0% Senate: 72.7% Incumb: 0.0%
Oil, Chemical & Atomic Workers Union Oil, Chemical & Atomic Workers Int'l Union Cmte on Pol Educ Fund (OCAW-COPE) Denver, CO	Oil Chemical & Atomic Wkrs Energy Unions	$102,790	81 Candidates	Avg House: $1,048 Avg Sen: $1,764	Dems: 96.1% House: 57.1% Incumb: 51.7%
Olin Corp Olin Corporation Good Government Fund Washington, DC	Chemicals†	$47,332	47 Candidates	Avg House: $850 Avg Sen: $1,419	Dems: 50.4% House: 61.0% Incumb: 91.0%

Operating Engineers Union
Engineers Pol Education Cmte (EPEC)/Int'l Union of Operating Engineers
Washington, DC   Bldg Trade Unions   **$410,850**

315 Candidates	Dems:	93.7%
Avg House: $972	House:	64.8%
Avg Sen: $3,491	Incumb:	71.9%

Operating Engineers Union Local #12
Operating Engineers Local 12 Voluntary Legislative Fund
Pasadena, CA   Operating Engineers Union   Bldg Trade Unions   **$33,594**

12 Candidates	Dems:	100.0%
Avg House: $2,513	House:	52.4%
Avg Sen: $3,200	Incumb:	43.2%

Operating Engineers Union Local #15
International Union of Operating Engineers Local 15 PAC
New York, NY   Operating Engineers Union   Bldg Trade Unions   **$29,650**

13 Candidates	Dems:	66.3%
Avg House: $2,065	House:	69.7%
Avg Sen: $3,000	Incumb:	44.7%

Operating Engineers Union Local #3
SELEC: Supporters of Engineers Local 3 Endorsed Candiates
San Francisco, CA   Operating Engineers Union   Bldg Trade Unions   **$32,790**

33 Candidates	Dems:	100.0%
Avg House: $773	House:	56.6%
Avg Sen: $1,582	Incumb:	44.3%

Operating Engineers Union Local #68
International Union of Operating Engineers Local 68 PAC
West Caldwell, NJ   Operating Engineers Union   Bldg Trade Unions   **$35,125**

17 Candidates	Dems:	88.6%
Avg House: $2,066	House:	100.0%
Avg Sen: $0	Incumb:	65.0%

Operating Engineers Union Local #825
Int'l Union of Operating Engineers Lo 825 Pol Action and Education Cmte
Little Falls, NJ   Operating Engineers Union   Bldg Trade Unions   **$54,225**

20 Candidates	Dems:	62.6%
Avg House: $2,957	House:	98.2%
Avg Sen: $500	Incumb:	59.5%

Operation Real Security
Operation Real Security PAC
Jerome, AZ   Dem/Liberal   **$29,837**

11 Candidates	Dems:	100.0%
Avg House: $7,400	Senate:	84.4%
Avg Sen: $2,799	Incumb:	-2.4%

Opperman & Paquin
Opperman & Paquin Political Fund
Minneapolis, MN   Lawyers   **$82,229**

31 Candidates	Dems:	93.3%
Avg House: $3,021	House:	58.8%
Avg Sen: $2,314	Incumb:	87.7%

Orange & Rockland Utilities
Orange and Rockland Utilities, Inc Employees' PAC (OREPAC)
Pearl River, NY   Gas & Electric Util†   **$34,735**

31 Candidates	Dems:	58.5%
Avg House: $933	House:	56.4%
Avg Sen: $1,683	Incumb:	96.5%

Orrick, Herrington & Sutcliffe
Orrick, Herrington & Sutcliffe PAC
San Francisco, CA   Lawyers   **$38,400**

20 Candidates	Dems:	97.4%
Avg House: $2,144	House:	50.3%
Avg Sen: $1,736	Incumb:	34.6%

Oryx Energy Co
Oryx Energy Company PAC (Oryx Energy Pac)
Dallas, TX   Oil & Gas   **$34,000**

37 Candidates	Repubs:	73.5%
Avg House: $458	Senate:	67.7%
Avg Sen: $1,769	Incumb:	42.6%

Osteopathic PAC
Osteopathic PAC
Washington, DC   Misc MD Specialists   **$49,950**

69 Candidates	Dems:	69.6%
Avg House: $655	House:	74.8%
Avg Sen: $1,050	Incumb:	78.6%

Outback Steakhouse Inc
Outback Steakhouse Inc PAC
Tampa, FL   Restaurants   **$26,000**

40 Candidates	Repubs:	94.2%
Avg House: $655	House:	73.1%
Avg Sen: $636	Incumb:	34.6%

Outboard Marine Corp
Outboard Marine Corporation PAC (OMCPAC)
Waukegan, IL   Shipbuilding/Repair   **$31,150**

45 Candidates	Repubs:	77.5%
Avg House: $585	House:	63.9%
Avg Sen: $1,023	Incumb:	70.8%

Outdoor Advertising Assn of America
Outdoor Advertising PAC (OAPAC)
Washington, DC   Outdoor Advertising   **$211,500**

104 Candidates	Dems:	63.1%
Avg House: $1,079	Senate:	63.3%
Avg Sen: $4,182	Incumb:	86.2%

Owens-Corning Fiberglas
Owens-Corning Fiberglas Corporation Employees' Better Government Fund
Toledo, OH   Bldg Materials†   **$63,634**

52 Candidates	Repubs:	64.6%
Avg House: $787	Senate:	58.0%
Avg Sen: $2,049	Incumb:	82.7%

Owens-Illinois
Owens-Illinois Inc Employees Good Citizenship Fund
Toledo, OH   Kohlberg, Kravis & Roberts   Glass Products†   **$53,550**

41 Candidates	Repubs:	62.6%
Avg House: $1,278	House:	71.6%
Avg Sen: $1,382	Incumb:	85.4%

Paccar Inc
Paccar Employees Political Action Fund
Bellevue, WA   Truck Mfrs†   **$34,250**

23 Candidates	Repubs:	79.6%
Avg House: $1,304	House:	53.3%
Avg Sen: $1,778	Incumb:	62.8%

Pacific Enterprises
Pacific Enterprises Political Assistance Committee
Los Angeles, CA   Natural Gas†   **$99,230**

75 Candidates	Dems:	63.3%
Avg House: $955	Senate:	50.9%
Avg Sen: $2,104	Incumb:	72.5%

† PAC sponsor has other major interests in addition to this primary category

Pacific Gas & Electric
Pacific Gas and Electric Company Employees' Federal Good Government Fund
San Francisco, CA — Gas & Electric Util†

$140,235 — 87 Candidates — Avg House: $1,561 — Avg Sen: $1,754 — Dems: 60.9% — House: 71.2% — Incumb: 88.0%

Pacific Mutual Life
Pacific Mutual Life Insurance Company PAC (PMPAC)
Newport Beach, CA — Life Insurance

$103,250 — 65 Candidates — Avg House: $1,358 — Avg Sen: $2,071 — Dems: 62.0% — House: 57.9% — Incumb: 72.4%

Pacific Resources
Pacific Resources PAC
Honolulu, HI — Oil Refining/Mkting

$21,800 — 30 Candidates — Avg House: $509 — Avg Sen: $1,443 — Dems: 65.8% — House: 53.7% — Incumb: 90.8%

Pacific Telesis Group
Pacific Telesis Group Federal PAC (Pacific Telesis Federal PAC)
San Francisco, CA — Phone Utilites†

$310,762 — 194 Candidates — Avg House: $1,471 — Avg Sen: $2,160 — Dems: 61.8% — House: 74.3% — Incumb: 85.1%

Pacificare Health Systems
Carepac-the PAC Of Pacificare Health Systems Inc
Cypress, CA — HMOs

$23,000 — 28 Candidates — Avg House: $788 — Avg Sen: $906 — Repubs: 59.8% — House: 68.5% — Incumb: 71.7%

PaineWebber
PaineWebber Fund for Better Government
New York, NY — Securities

$85,475 — 61 Candidates — Avg House: $921 — Avg Sen: $2,048 — Dems: 68.7% — Senate: 62.3% — Incumb: 85.7%

Painters & Allied Trades Union
Int'l Brotherhood of Painters & Allied Trades Political Action Together Pol Cmte
Washington, DC — Painters & Allied Trades — Building Trade Unions

$279,002 — 172 Candidates — Avg House: $1,379 — Avg Sen: $2,549 — Dems: 93.7% — House: 67.7% — Incumb: 50.9%

Paramount Communications
Gulf + Western Industries Inc PAC
New York, NY — Movies/TV†

$92,250 — 41 Candidates — Avg House: $2,307 — Avg Sen: $2,250 — Dems: 79.4% — House: 55.0% — Incumb: 85.1%

Parsons Corp
Parsons Corporation PAC
Pasadena, CA — Ralph M Parsons Co — Engineers†

$24,800 — 25 Candidates — Avg House: $1,128 — Avg Sen: $643 — Dems: 71.8% — House: 81.8% — Incumb: 79.8%

Paul, Hastings et al
Paul, Hastings, Janofsky & Walker PAC
Washington, DC — Lawyers

$32,300 — 25 Candidates — Avg House: $592 — Avg Sen: $1,938 — Dems: 62.9% — Senate: 78.0% — Incumb: 81.4%

Pax PAC
Pax PAC
New York, NY — Pro-Israel

$40,750 — 46 Candidates — Avg House: $758 — Avg Sen: $1,179 — Dems: 81.0% — House: 59.5% — Incumb: 65.6%

Peabody Coal
Peabody PAC
St Louis, MO — Coal

$78,213 — 66 Candidates — Avg House: $839 — Avg Sen: $1,981 — Repubs: 51.6% — Senate: 50.6% — Incumb: 93.2%

Pelican PAC
Pelican PAC
Seattle, WA — Sen J Bennett Johnston (D-La) — Dem Leaders

$93,284 — 25 Candidates — Avg House: $3,500 — Avg Sen: $3,804 — Dems: 100.0% — Senate: 77.5% — Incumb: 84.2%

Penn Mutual Life Insurance
Penn Mutual PAC
Philadelphia, PA — Life Insurance

$43,650 — 31 Candidates — Avg House: $1,275 — Avg Sen: $2,100 — Dems: 74.2% — House: 76.0% — Incumb: 93.7%

JC Penney Co
J C Penney Company PAC (Penney PAC)
Dallas, TX — Department Stores†

$195,615 — 222 Candidates — Avg House: $767 — Avg Sen: $1,387 — Dems: 57.6% — House: 70.9% — Incumb: 89.9%

Pennsylvania Power & Light
Pennsylvania Power & Light Co People for Good Government
Allentown, PA — Electric Utilities

$23,600 — 22 Candidates — Avg House: $944 — Avg Sen: $1,417 — Repubs: 56.1% — House: 64.0% — Incumb: 88.8%

Pennzoil Co
Pennzoil PAC
Houston, TX — Oil Refining/Mkting†

$32,600 — 52 Candidates — Avg House: $618 — Avg Sen: $654 — Dems: 63.0% — House: 73.9% — Incumb: 94.6%

Pepsi-Cola Bottlers Assn
Pepsi-Cola Bottlers Association-PAC
Irving, TX — Beverage Bottling

$49,300 — 52 Candidates — Avg House: $944 — Avg Sen: $962 — Dems: 62.5% — House: 74.7% — Incumb: 79.5%

Pepsi-Cola General Bottlers
Pepsi-Cola General Bottlers PAC
Rolling Meadows, IL — Beverage Bottling

$79,695 — 57 Candidates — Avg House: $1,294 — Avg Sen: $1,813 — Dems: 55.1% — House: 71.5% — Incumb: 88.4%

Pepsico Inc
Pepsico Concerned Citizens Fund
Purchase, NY

Soft Drinks/Food†

$297,074

194 Candidates	Repubs: 65.4%
Avg House: $1,286	House: 73.6%
Avg Sen: $3,270	Incumb: 69.6%

Petroleum Marketers Assn
Petroleum Marketers Association of America Small Businessmen's Committee
Washington, DC

Gas Stations†

$262,325

236 Candidates	Repubs: 63.3%
Avg House: $875	House: 68.4%
Avg Sen: $2,677	Incumb: 77.6%

Pfizer Inc
Pfizer PAC
New York, NY

Pharmaceuticals†

$188,100

162 Candidates	Repubs: 52.1%
Avg House: $787	House: 51.9%
Avg Sen: $2,382	Incumb: 83.7%

Pharmaceutical Manufacturers Assn
Pharmaceutical Manufacturers Association Better Government Committee
Washington, DC

Pharmaceuticals

$36,981

52 Candidates	Repubs: 53.2%
Avg House: $524	House: 53.8%
Avg Sen: $1,220	Incumb: 79.0%

Phelps Dodge Corp
Phelps Dodge Employees Fund for Good Government
Phoenix, AZ

Metal Mining/Process

$84,800

52 Candidates	Repubs: 73.2%
Avg House: $1,397	House: 57.7%
Avg Sen: $2,112	Incumb: 86.3%

Philadelphia Electric
Philadelphia Electric Company Federal PAC (PECOPAC)
Philadelphia, PA

Gas & Electric Util

$86,050

84 Candidates	Repubs: 54.0%
Avg House: $820	House: 61.9%
Avg Sen: $1,806	Incumb: 64.7%

Philip Morris
Philip Morris PAC (aka PHIL-PAC)
New York, NY

Tobacco/Food†

$624,049

366 Candidates	Dems: 62.2%
Avg House: $1,489	House: 74.0%
Avg Sen: $2,862	Incumb: 84.5%

Phillips Petroleum
Phillips Petroleum Company PAC
Bartlesville, OK

Oil & Gas†

$171,689

155 Candidates	Repubs: 72.3%
Avg House: $971	House: 74.1%
Avg Sen: $1,854	Incumb: 49.6%

Phoenix Firefighters #493
Phoenix Firefighters local 493 FIRE PAC Committee
Phoenix, AZ

Public Safety

$20,869

10 Candidates	Dems: 99.0%
Avg House: $2,006	House: 67.3%
Avg Sen: $2,610	Incumb: 49.2%

Phoenix Mutual Life Insurance
Phoenix Mutual Life Insurance Company PAC (PML-PAC)
Hartford, CT

Life Insurance

$33,575

43 Candidates	Dems: 58.7%
Avg House: $638	House: 53.2%
Avg Sen: $1,047	Incumb: 82.1%

Physicians Interindemnity
Physicians Interindemnity/FED-PAC
Glendale, CA

Doctors

$26,430

18 Candidates	Dems: 88.8%
Avg House: $1,370	House: 51.8%
Avg Sen: $1,676	Incumb: 32.9%

Pillsbury Co
Pillsbury Company PAC
Minneapolis, MN   Grand Metropolitan

Food Processors†

$24,610

33 Candidates	Repubs: 68.5%
Avg House: $630	House: 58.9%
Avg Sen: $1,078	Incumb: 93.5%

Pillsbury, Madison & Sutro
Pillsbury, Madison & Sutro PAC
San Francisco, CA

Lawyers

$47,749

35 Candidates	Repubs: 52.4%
Avg House: $750	Senate: 69.6%
Avg Sen: $2,078	Incumb: 50.8%

Pinkerton Tobacco
Pinkerton Tobacco Company PAC
Richmond, VA

Tobacco

$66,475

64 Candidates	Dems: 50.2%
Avg House: $766	House: 51.9%
Avg Sen: $1,684	Incumb: 90.2%

Pittsburgh National Bank
Pittsburgh National Bank Bipartisan Voluntary PAC (PNBVOLPAC)
Pittsburgh, PA   PNC Financial Corp   Commercial Banks

$48,600

46 Candidates	Dems: 60.6%
Avg House: $997	House: 71.8%
Avg Sen: $1,245	Incumb: 85.1%

Pittston Co
Pittston Company PAC
Greenwich, CT

Coal†

$52,950

65 Candidates	Repubs: 51.3%
Avg House: $671	House: 53.3%
Avg Sen: $1,076	Incumb: 83.0%

Pizza Hut Franchise Holders Assn
IPHFHA Inc PAC Inc
Wichita, KS   Pizza Hut   Restaurants

$48,000

23 Candidates	Repubs: 63.5%
Avg House: $1,615	Senate: 56.2%
Avg Sen: $2,700	Incumb: 58.3%

Planning Research Corp
Emhart PAC
Mclean, VA   Black & Decker   Computers†

$50,600

45 Candidates	Dems: 52.7%
Avg House: $1,068	House: 80.2%
Avg Sen: $1,429	Incumb: 90.3%

Plumbers/Pipefitters Union
United Assn of Journeymen and Apprentices of the Plumb and Pipeftrs Indus
Washington, DC

Building Trade Unions

$835,456

309 Candidates	Dems: 96.2%
Avg House: $2,289	House: 73.7%
Avg Sen: $5,518	Incumb: 69.0%

† PAC sponsor has other major interests in addition to this primary category

Potato Chip & Snack Food Assn SnackPAC-Potato Chip/Snack Food Ass'n PAC Alexandria, VA *Food Processors*	**$40,530**	54 Candidates Avg House: $629 Avg Sen: $1,227	Repubs: 57.9% House: 66.7% Incumb: 91.1%
Potlatch Corp Potlatch Employees' Political Fund San Francisco, CA *Forest Products†*	**$49,350**	29 Candidates Avg House: $1,402 Avg Sen: $2,643	Repubs: 59.8% House: 62.5% Incumb: 60.5%
Potomac Electric Power Co Pepco PAC Washington, DC *Electric Utilities*	**$39,313**	40 Candidates Avg House: $960 Avg Sen: $1,050	Dems: 79.4% House: 73.3% Incumb: 94.9%
Powell, Goldstein et al Powell, Goldstein, Frazer & Murphy PAC Atlanta, GA *Lawyers*	**$123,285**	139 Candidates Avg House: $677 Avg Sen: $1,307	Dems: 88.5% House: 50.0% Incumb: 85.7%
PPG Industries PPG Employees Voluntary Political Campaign Fund Pittsburgh, PA *Glass Products†*	**$41,000**	38 Candidates Avg House: $680 Avg Sen: $1,846	Repubs: 87.8% Senate: 58.5% Incumb: 58.5%
Precision Metalforming Assn Precision Metalforming Association PAC Richmond Hts., OH *Metal Products*	**$36,750**	39 Candidates Avg House: $680 Avg Sen: $2,143	Repubs: 99.3% House: 59.2% Incumb: 33.3%
Premark International Premark International, Inc PAC Deerfield, IL *Plastic/Rubber†*	**$20,700**	29 Candidates Avg House: $400 Avg Sen: $879	Repubs: 87.9% Senate: 80.7% Incumb: 44.7%
Preston, Gates et al Preston, Thorgrimson, Ellis & Holman PAC Washington, DC *Lawyers*	**$114,839**	161 Candidates Avg House: $681 Avg Sen: $881	Dems: 70.6% House: 79.5% Incumb: 89.4%
Price Waterhouse Price Waterhouse Partners' PAC Washington, DC *Accountants*	**$92,047**	52 Candidates Avg House: $1,447 Avg Sen: $2,567	Dems: 62.5% House: 58.2% Incumb: 98.9%
Principal Mutual Life Insurance Principal Mutual Life Insurance Company - Federal PAC Des Moines, IA *Insurance*	**$103,777**	97 Candidates Avg House: $865 Avg Sen: $1,746	Dems: 57.4% House: 60.8% Incumb: 87.1%
Printing Industries of America Printing Industries of America PAC (Print PAC) Arlington, VA *Printing*	**$105,502**	87 Candidates Avg House: $634 Avg Sen: $2,569	Repubs: 93.4% Senate: 63.3% Incumb: 56.4%
Procter & Gamble Procter & Gamble Co Good Government Committee; The (aka P&G PAC) Cincinnati, OH *Household Chemicals†*	**$77,200**	90 Candidates Avg House: $684 Avg Sen: $1,429	Repubs: 51.7% House: 61.1% Incumb: 90.3%
Professionals in Advertising PAC Professionals in Advertising PAC New York, NY *Advertising/PR*	**$22,900**	27 Candidates Avg House: $608 Avg Sen: $1,536	Dems: 72.0% House: 53.1% Incumb: 97.8%
Proprietary Association Proprietary Association's PAC; The Washington, DC *Pharmaceuticals*	**$35,725**	40 Candidates Avg House: $795 Avg Sen: $1,357	Repubs: 62.2% House: 73.4% Incumb: 111.2%
Prudential Insurance Prudential Insurance Company of America Federal PAC ("Prudential PAC") Newark, NJ *Insurance†*	**$262,360**	157 Candidates Avg House: $1,098 Avg Sen: $3,466	Dems: 66.4% Senate: 50.2% Incumb: 79.7%
Prudential Securities Prudential-Bache Securities Inc PAC New York, NY *Prudential Insurance* *Securities*	**$138,475**	122 Candidates Avg House: $910 Avg Sen: $1,717	Repubs: 52.2% House: 57.8% Incumb: 68.7%
Public Securities Assn Public Securities Association Washington, DC *Securities*	**$135,239**	140 Candidates Avg House: $832 Avg Sen: $1,555	Dems: 69.5% House: 70.1% Incumb: 89.5%
Public Service Co of Indiana Public Service Company of Indiana Inc PAC (PSI-PAC) Plainfield, IN *Electric Utilities*	**$31,500**	25 Candidates Avg House: $950 Avg Sen: $2,500	Repubs: 57.1% House: 60.3% Incumb: 95.2%
Public Service Electric & Gas Public Service Electric and Gas Company PAC (PEGPAC) Newark, NJ *Gas & Electric Util†*	**$121,537**	120 Candidates Avg House: $1,068 Avg Sen: $835	Dems: 51.3% House: 83.5% Incumb: 88.1%

PAC Sponsor or Related Group/PAC Name	Affiliate	1991-92 Total	Where the money went...		
Public Service Research Council Public Service PAC Reston, VA	Anti-Union	$140,553	172 Candidates Avg House: $608 Avg Sen: $2,174	Repubs: 98.3% House: 64.4% Incumb: 50.8%	
Puget Sound Power & Light Puget Power Good Government Committee - Federal Bellevue, WA	Electric Utilities	$26,727	20 Candidates Avg House: $899 Avg Sen: $3,088	Repubs: 86.2% House: 53.8% Incumb: 27.7%	
Quaker Oats Public Interest Committee of the Quaker Oats Company; The Chicago, IL	Food Processors	$26,128	42 Candidates Avg House: $520 Avg Sen: $827	Repubs: 61.2% House: 55.7% Incumb: 71.3%	
Ralphs Grocery Co Ralphs Grocery Company PAC Compton, CA	Food Stores	$21,034	14 Candidates Avg House: $1,178 Avg Sen: $2,313	Repubs: 51.2% House: 56.0% Incumb: 28.9%	
Raytheon Raytheon Company PAC Lexington, MA	Defense Electronics†	$255,525	167 Candidates Avg House: $1,459 Avg Sen: $1,772	Dems: 63.2% House: 73.6% Incumb: 93.0%	
Recording Industry Assn of America Recording Industry Assn of America Inc PAC Washington, DC	Music Production	$61,110	75 Candidates Avg House: $743 Avg Sen: $1,000	Dems: 93.5% House: 65.6% Incumb: 83.6%	
Reed Smith Reed Smith PAC Washington, DC	Lawyers	$34,350	18 Candidates Avg House: $842 Avg Sen: $4,042	Repubs: 51.7% Senate: 70.6% Incumb: 72.3%	
Reid & Priest Reid & Priest PAC Washington, DC	Lawyers	$46,700	46 Candidates Avg House: $1,059 Avg Sen: $904	Dems: 66.6% House: 74.8% Incumb: 95.2%	
Reliance Group Holdings Reliance Group Holdings Inc PAC (ReliancePAC) New York, NY	Insurance	$31,544	10 Candidates Avg House: $2,000 Avg Sen: $5,848	Repubs: 58.8% Senate: 55.6% Incumb: 62.0%	
Republican Leader's Fund Republican Leader's Fund Washington, DC	Rep Bob Michel (R-Ill) Repub Leaders	$169,000	96 Candidates Avg House: $1,760 Avg Sen: $0	Repubs: 100.0% House: 100.0% Incumb: 16.6%	
Republican National Coalition for Life Republican National Coalition for Life PAC (RNC/LIFE PAC) Alton, IL	Pro-Life	$85,750	38 Candidates Avg House: $2,356 Avg Sen: $1,600	Repubs: 100.0% House: 90.7% Incumb: 36.7%	
Republicans for Choice Republicans for Choice Alexandria, VA	Pro-Choice†	$34,788	39 Candidates Avg House: $740 Avg Sen: $1,728	Repubs: 100.0% House: 70.2% Incumb: 40.1%	
Retail, Wholesale & Department Store Union Retail, Wholesale & Department Store Union COPE (RWDSU COPE) New York, NY	Retail Unions	$28,335	21 Candidates Avg House: $894 Avg Sen: $4,083	Dems: 100.0% House: 56.8% Incumb: 15.5%	
Reynolds Metals Reynolds Metals Company Political Participation Program Fund (RAPPP) Richmond, VA	Metal Mining/Process	$81,675	55 Candidates Avg House: $1,410 Avg Sen: $1,639	Repubs: 79.1% House: 63.9% Incumb: 74.3%	
Rhone-Poulenc Inc Rhone-poulenc Inc PAC (RPAC) Princeton, NJ	Pharmaceuticals†	$63,750	60 Candidates Avg House: $1,025 Avg Sen: $1,278	Repubs: 78.0% House: 82.0% Incumb: 91.0%	
Riceland Foods Riceland Foods Inc PAC (Riceland PAC) Stuttgart, AR	Misc Crops†	$32,000	19 Candidates Avg House: $1,542 Avg Sen: $1,929	Dems: 90.6% House: 57.8% Incumb: 96.9%	
Right to Work PAC Right to Work PAC Springfield, VA	Anti-Union	$205,151	120 Candidates Avg House: $1,362 Avg Sen: $3,450	Repubs: 98.3% House: 66.4% Incumb: 22.5%	
RJR Nabisco RJR PAC RJR Nabisco Inc Winston-Salem, NC	Tobacco/Food†	$845,363	398 Candidates Avg House: $1,944 Avg Sen: $3,500	Dems: 57.0% House: 81.0% Incumb: 81.4%	
Roadway Services Inc Roadway Services Inc REXPAC Akron, OH	Trucking Companies	$61,225	71 Candidates Avg House: $770 Avg Sen: $1,364	Dems: 53.9% House: 75.5% Incumb: 98.4%	

† PAC sponsor has other major interests in addition to this primary category

Rockwell International
Rockwell International Corporation Good Government Committee
Pittsburgh, PA
Defense Aerospace†
$340,164

223 Candidates	Repubs: 53.7%
Avg House: $1,210	House: 66.5%
Avg Sen: $3,331	Incumb: 87.4%

Rohm & Haas Co
Rohm and Haas Employees Association for Better Government
Philadelphia, PA
Chemicals†
$33,780

41 Candidates	Repubs: 66.0%
Avg House: $669	House: 71.3%
Avg Sen: $1,940	Incumb: 70.1%

Roofers Union local #30
Composition Roofers Local Union #30 Political Action & Education Fund
Philadelphia, PA
Building Trade Unions
$30,050

10 Candidates	Dems: 69.0%
Avg House: $2,756	House: 73.4%
Avg Sen: $4,000	Incumb: 76.7%

Rorer Group Inc
Rorer Group Inc - RorPAC
Fort Washington, PA
Pharmaceuticals
$28,500

53 Candidates	Repubs: 90.2%
Avg House: $512	House: 73.7%
Avg Sen: $625	Incumb: 74.7%

Roundtable PAC
Roundtable PAC
New York, NY
Pro-Israel
$30,000

31 Candidates	Dems: 80.0%
Avg House: $656	Senate: 65.0%
Avg Sen: $1,300	Incumb: 75.0%

Rubber Cork Linoleum & Plastic Workers Union
COPE Cmte of the United Rubber Cork Linoleum and Plastic Wrkrs of Amer AFL-CIO
Akron, OH
Manufacturing Unions
$505,730

202 Candidates	Dems: 99.8%
Avg House: $2,218	House: 75.4%
Avg Sen: $4,135	Incumb: 52.4%

Ruff PAC
Ruff PAC
Washington, DC
Tax Policy
$47,357

57 Candidates	Repubs: 100.0%
Avg House: $795	House: 85.6%
Avg Sen: $1,136	Incumb: 24.6%

Rural Builders of America PAC
Rural Builders of America PAC - (RBAPAC)
Washington, DC
Resid Construction†
$40,750

36 Candidates	Dems: 83.4%
Avg House: $1,112	House: 79.1%
Avg Sen: $1,214	Incumb: 92.6%

Russell, Rea & Zappala
Citizens for Effective Representative Government
Pittsburgh, PA
Securities
$21,550

17 Candidates	Dems: 61.5%
Avg House: $1,027	House: 52.4%
Avg Sen: $2,050	Incumb: 36.2%

Ryder System Inc
Ryder System, Inc Committee for Effective Government
Miami, FL
Car/Truck Rental
$50,361

70 Candidates	Dems: 63.0%
Avg House: $652	House: 73.8%
Avg Sen: $1,015	Incumb: 83.9%

S&A Restaurant Corp
S & A Restaurant Corp Employees PAC
Dallas, TX
Restaurants
$143,500

59 Candidates	Repubs: 85.4%
Avg House: $1,651	Senate: 50.5%
Avg Sen: $4,531	Incumb: 45.0%

Safari Club International
Safari Club International PAC
Edina, MN   *Safari Club Intl*   *Pro-Guns†*
$73,850

39 Candidates	Repubs: 88.5%
Avg House: $1,804	House: 83.1%
Avg Sen: $2,500	Incumb: 43.1%

Safeco Corp
Safeco-PAC
Seattle, WA
Insurance†
$44,750

24 Candidates	Repubs: 96.7%
Avg House: $1,733	House: 58.1%
Avg Sen: $2,083	Incumb: 6.2%

Safeway Stores
Safeway Stores, Incorporated PAC Safepac
Oakland, CA   *Kohlberg, Kravis, Roberts*   *Food Stores*
$37,285

35 Candidates	Repubs: 83.4%
Avg House: $636	Senate: 55.6%
Avg Sen: $2,306	Incumb: 43.7%

Sailor's Union of the Pacific
Sailor's Union of the Pacific Political Fund
San Francisco, CA   *Seafarers Intl Union*   *Sea Transport Unions*
$23,140

15 Candidates	Dems: 100.0%
Avg House: $470	Senate: 85.1%
Avg Sen: $2,814	Incumb: 19.9%

St Louisians for Better Government
St Louisians for Better Government
St Louis, MO
Pro-Israel
$138,250

50 Candidates	Dems: 80.1%
Avg House: $1,224	Senate: 74.3%
Avg Sen: $4,893	Incumb: 80.1%

Salomon Brothers
Salomon Brothers Inc PAC
New York, NY
Securities†
$55,850

56 Candidates	Dems: 51.9%
Avg House: $645	Senate: 57.3%
Avg Sen: $1,684	Incumb: 98.2%

Salt River Valley Water Users
Salt River Valley Water Users' Assn PolInvolvement Cmte
Phoenix, AZ
Ag Services†
$34,476

25 Candidates	Repubs: 62.3%
Avg House: $1,374	House: 71.7%
Avg Sen: $1,393	Incumb: 78.3%

San Diego Community PAC
San Diego Community PAC Inc aka SANCPAC
San Diego, CA
Pro-Israel
$26,500

20 Candidates	Repubs: 60.4%
Avg House: $917	Senate: 79.2%
Avg Sen: $1,500	Incumb: 92.5%

PAC Sponsor or Related Group/PAC Name	Affiliate	1991-92 Total	Where the money went...			
San Diego Gas & Electric San Diego Gas & Electric Co. Citizens for Good Government Committee San Diego, CA		$28,775	43 Candidates Avg House: $678 Avg Sen: $631		Dems: 51.8% House: 82.5% Incumb: 88.4%	
		Gas & Electric Util†				
San Franciscans for Good Government San Franciscans for Good Government San Francisco, CA		$72,500	25 Candidates Avg House: $2,125 Avg Sen: $3,265		Dems: 71.7% Senate: 76.5% Incumb: 96.5%	
		Pro-Israel				
Sandoz Pharmaceuticals Sandoz Pharmaceuticals Corp PAC East Hanover, NJ	Sandoz	$27,650	73 Candidates Avg House: $344 Avg Sen: $497		Repubs: 70.9% House: 68.3% Incumb: 90.2%	
		Pharmaceuticals†				
SANE/Freeze Inc SANE/Freeze PAC Washington, DC	SANE/Freeze	$20,394	12 Candidates Avg House: $806 Avg Sen: $2,593		Dems: 100.0% Senate: 76.3% Incumb: 17.5%	
		Pro-Peace				
Santa Fe International Corp Santa Fe International Corporation PAC Alhambra, CA		$39,784	30 Candidates Avg House: $544 Avg Sen: $2,391		Repubs: 89.7% Senate: 78.1% Incumb: 67.7%	
		Oilfield Services†				
Santa Fe Southern Pacific Santa Fe Southern Pacific Corporation PAC Chicago, IL		$61,500	84 Candidates Avg House: $600 Avg Sen: $1,155		Repubs: 63.4% House: 62.4% Incumb: 86.4%	
		Railroads†				
SAPEC, NJ (NJ Savings Assn) SAPEC, N J Cranford, NJ	US League of Savings Assns	$23,328	16 Candidates Avg House: $1,458 Avg Sen: $0		Dems: 51.0% House: 100.0% Incumb: 75.8%	
		Savings & Loans				
Savannah Foods & Industries Savannah Foods & Industries Inc Nonpartisan Cmte for Better Federal Govt Savannah, GA		$24,000	30 Candidates Avg House: $688 Avg Sen: $1,250		Dems: 75.0% House: 68.8% Incumb: 93.8%	
		Sugar†				
Scana Corp Scana Corporation Federal PAC Columbia, SC		$26,700	14 Candidates Avg House: $1,070 Avg Sen: $3,667		Dems: 73.8% Senate: 41.2% Incumb: 90.6%	
		Gas & Electric Util†				
Schering-Plough Corp Schering - Plough Corporation Better Government Fund Madison, NJ		$186,050	90 Candidates Avg House: $1,721 Avg Sen: $2,650		Dems: 51.3% House: 54.6% Incumb: 74.7%	
		Pharmaceuticals†				
Scott Paper Co Scott Paper Company PAC (ScottPAC) Washington, DC		$81,298	96 Candidates Avg House: $680 Avg Sen: $1,409		Repubs: 71.2% House: 61.9% Incumb: 74.2%	
		Paper/Pulp†				
Sea-Land Corp Sea-Land Good Government Fund Sea-Land Industries Inc Washington, DC	CSX Corp	$174,025	110 Candidates Avg House: $1,319 Avg Sen: $2,928		Dems: 53.8% House: 69.7% Incumb: 95.2%	
		Sea Transport†				
Seafarers International Union Seafarers Political Activity Donation (SPAD) Camp Springs, MD	Seafarers Intl Union	$916,796	300 Candidates Avg House: $2,679 Avg Sen: $5,091		Dems: 91.3% House: 73.9% Incumb: 75.4%	
		Sea Transport Unions				
SeaFirst Bank Seafirst Associates-National Olympia, WA	BankAmerica	$21,150	15 Candidates Avg House: $1,440 Avg Sen: $1,350		Repubs: 55.6% House: 68.1% Incumb: 36.2%	
		Commercial Banks				
Joseph E Seagram & Sons Joseph E Seagram & Sons, Inc PAC New York, NY		$208,000	119 Candidates Avg House: $1,140 Avg Sen: $3,923		Dems: 82.5% House: 51.0% Incumb: 79.3%	
		Wine & Liquor†				
GD Searle & Co G D Searle & Co PAC (Searle PAC) Skokie, IL	Monsanto	$26,000	29 Candidates Avg House: $750 Avg Sen: $1,222		Dems: 57.7% House: 57.7% Incumb: 76.9%	
		Pharmaceuticals				
Sears Sears PAC Chicago, IL		$55,800	94 Candidates Avg House: $510 Avg Sen: $1,115		Repubs: 84.1% House: 74.0% Incumb: 59.0%	
		Retail Trade†				
SecuraPAC SecuraPAC Washington, DC	Arnold & Porter	$28,700	41 Candidates Avg House: $682 Avg Sen: $786		Dems: 61.0% House: 80.8% Incumb: 87.6%	
		Lobbyists/PR				
Securities Industry Assn Securities Industry PAC Washington, DC		$120,448	138 Candidates Avg House: $781 Avg Sen: $1,447		Dems: 67.0% House: 77.2% Incumb: 95.4%	
		Securities				

† PAC sponsor has other major interests in addition to this primary category

PAC Sponsor or Related Group/PAC Name	Affiliate	1991-92 Total	Where the money went...		
Security Life of Denver Security Life of Denver Insurance Company PAC (Security Life PAC) Denver, CO	Life Insurance	$31,500	26 Candidates Avg House: $1,103 Avg Sen: $1,417	Repubs: 55.6% House: 59.5% Incumb: 57.9%	
Security Pacific Corp Security Pacific Corporation Active Citizenship Today Committee (SPACT) Los Angeles, CA	Commercial Banks	$105,500	80 Candidates Avg House: $1,216 Avg Sen: $1,591	Dems: 58.2% House: 66.8% Incumb: 87.7%	
Senate Victory Fund Senate Victory Fund PAC Jackson, MS	Sen Thad Cochran (R-Miss) — Repub Leaders	$107,000	29 Candidates Avg House: $500 Avg Sen: $3,804	Repubs: 100.0% Senate: 99.5% Incumb: 57.9%	
Service Corp International Service Corporation International PAC (SRV/PAC) Houston, TX	Funeral Services	$35,000	20 Candidates Avg House: $1,633 Avg Sen: $2,100	Repubs: 51.4% House: 70.0% Incumb: 83.6%	
Service Employees International Union Service Employees Int'l Union COPE Political Campaign Cmte Washington, DC	Misc Unions	$743,781	248 Candidates Avg House: $2,378 Avg Sen: $6,006	Dems: 98.1% House: 65.5% Incumb: 45.8%	
Services Group of America Services Group of America PAC Seattle, WA	Food Wholesalers†	$27,850	10 Candidates Avg House: $2,583 Avg Sen: $3,783	Repubs: 97.8% House: 55.7% Incumb: 9.9%	
Shaw, Pittman et al Shaw, Pittman, Potts and Trowbridge PAC Washington, DC	Lawyers	$102,850	113 Candidates Avg House: $830 Avg Sen: $1,154	Dems: 70.2% House: 68.6% Incumb: 92.9%	
Shearson Lehman Brothers Action Fund of Shearson Lehman Hutton Inc New York, NY	American Express — Securities	$164,200	129 Candidates Avg House: $879 Avg Sen: $2,150	Dems: 65.7% Senate: 52.4% Incumb: 69.2%	
Sheet Metal Workers Union Sheet Metal Workers International Association Political Action League (PAL) Washington, DC	Sheet Metal Workers — Building Trade Unions	$742,354	230 Candidates Avg House: $2,913 Avg Sen: $4,724	Dems: 95.5% House: 74.5% Incumb: 57.9%	
Sheet Metal/Air Conditioning Contractors Sheet Metal and Air Conditioning Contractors' PAC Vienna, VA	Plumbing/Air Cond	$161,401	98 Candidates Avg House: $966 Avg Sen: $4,000	Repubs: 94.7% Senate: 54.5% Incumb: 55.7%	
Shell Oil Shell Oil Company Employees' Political Awareness Committee Houston, TX	Oil & Gas†	$130,500	120 Candidates Avg House: $852 Avg Sen: $2,265	Repubs: 59.4% House: 65.3% Incumb: 89.6%	
Sierra Club Sierra Club Committee on Political Education San Francisco, CA	Environment Policy	$608,680	214 Candidates Avg House: $2,619 Avg Sen: $4,081	Dems: 96.6% House: 77.9% Incumb: 45.7%	
Silver State PAC Silver State PAC Las Vegas, NV	Pro-Israel	$29,557	48 Candidates Avg House: $337 Avg Sen: $974	Dems: 86.8% Senate: 69.2% Incumb: 65.3%	
Simpson Investment Co Simpson Investment Company PAC (aka Simpson Pol Act Cmte/SIMPAC) Seattle, WA	Forest Products†	$86,150	49 Candidates Avg House: $1,279 Avg Sen: $2,957	Repubs: 86.4% House: 51.9% Incumb: 53.0%	
Skadden, Arps et al Skadden Arps PAC Washington, DC	Lawyers	$95,717	73 Candidates Avg House: $988 Avg Sen: $1,831	Dems: 66.3% Senate: 53.6% Incumb: 96.3%	
Smirnoff/Inglenook Distributors Smirnoff/Inglenook Distributors PAC Hartford, CT	Wine & Liquor	$84,000	64 Candidates Avg House: $1,191 Avg Sen: $1,647	Dems: 78.0% House: 66.7% Incumb: 94.0%	
SmithKline Beecham Smithkline Beckman PAC (SKB-PAC) Philadelphia, PA	Pharmaceuticals†	$74,300	70 Candidates Avg House: $929 Avg Sen: $1,529	Dems: 50.5% House: 65.0% Incumb: 83.8%	
Smokeless Tobacco Council Smokeless Tobacco Council Inc PAC (STCPAC) Washington, DC	Tobacco	$40,550	48 Candidates Avg House: $633 Avg Sen: $1,650	Dems: 61.2% House: 59.3% Incumb: 96.9%	
Society Corp Society Corporation PAC Cleveland, OH	Commercial Banks	$30,692	25 Candidates Avg House: $1,004 Avg Sen: $2,400	Dems: 53.6% House: 68.7% Incumb: 56.3%	

Society of American Florists
Society of American Florists PAC (SAF-PAC)
Alexandria, VA — Florists — **$55,878**

98 Candidates	Repubs: 85.1%
Avg House: $471	House: 70.7%
Avg Sen: $1,168	Incumb: 82.5%

Society of Independent Gasoline Marketers
Society of Independent Gasoline Marketers of America
Reston, VA — Gas Stations — **$48,150**

61 Candidates	Dems: 64.1%
Avg House: $791	House: 85.5%
Avg Sen: $778	Incumb: 96.7%

Society of Real Estate Appraisers
Society of Real Estate Appraisers PAC (APPAC)
Washington, DC — Real Estate Svcs — **$34,450**

58 Candidates	Dems: 70.7%
Avg House: $504	House: 74.6%
Avg Sen: $1,250	Incumb: 72.9%

South Central Bell Telephone
South Central Bell Telephone Company Federal PAC (SCB FPAC)
Birmingham, AL — BellSouth — Phone Utilites — **$64,510**

36 Candidates	Dems: 76.9%
Avg House: $1,518	House: 68.2%
Avg Sen: $2,929	Incumb: 98.5%

Southdown Inc
Southdown Inc PAC
Houston, TX — Stone/Concrete — **$23,000**

18 Candidates	Dems: 65.2%
Avg House: $1,167	Senate: 54.4%
Avg Sen: $1,389	Incumb: 73.9%

Southeastern Peanut Assn
Southeastern Peanut PAC (Georgia)
Albany, GA — Misc Crops — **$25,600**

12 Candidates	Dems: 100.0%
Avg House: $1,943	House: 53.1%
Avg Sen: $2,875	Incumb: 95.9%

Southern Bell
Southern Bell Telephone and Telegraph Company Federal PAC (SOBELL PAC)
Birmingham, AL — BellSouth — Phone Utilites — **$519,207**

241 Candidates	Dems: 64.3%
Avg House: $2,175	House: 89.7%
Avg Sen: $2,140	Incumb: 79.1%

Southern California Edison
Federal Citizenship Responsibility Group/the Southern California Edison Company
Rosemead, CA — Electric Utilities — **$264,485**

135 Candidates	Dems: 75.5%
Avg House: $1,563	House: 55.5%
Avg Sen: $2,890	Incumb: 65.2%

Southern Co
Southern Company Services PAC
Atlanta, GA — Southern Co — Electric Utilities — **$75,450**

165 Candidates	Dems: 51.7%
Avg House: $400	House: 69.5%
Avg Sen: $678	Incumb: 82.6%

Southern Minnesota Beet Sugar Co-op
Southern Minnesota Sugar Cooperative PAC
Renville, MN — Sugar — **$120,400**

164 Candidates	Dems: 62.7%
Avg House: $704	House: 81.2%
Avg Sen: $904	Incumb: 82.5%

Southern Natural Resources
Sonat Inc PAC
Birmingham, AL — Natural Gas† — **$61,100**

44 Candidates	Dems: 81.2%
Avg House: $810	Senate: 59.4%
Avg Sen: $2,792	Incumb: 91.5%

Southern Nuclear Operating Co
Southern Nuclear Operating Co Inc Employees PAC (Southern Nuclear PAC)
Birmingham, AL — Southern Co — Nuclear Energy† — **$30,100**

66 Candidates	Dems: 53.3%
Avg House: $428	House: 72.6%
Avg Sen: $550	Incumb: 67.9%

Southern Pacific Transport Co
Southern Pacific Transportation Company PAC
San Francisco, CA — Railroads — **$62,600**

72 Candidates	Dems: 59.7%
Avg House: $637	Senate: 58.3%
Avg Sen: $1,177	Incumb: 86.9%

Southern Wine & Spirits
Southern Wine & Spirits PAC
Miami, FL — Wine & Liquor — **$30,000**

19 Candidates	Dems: 89.0%
Avg House: $1,000	Senate: 50.0%
Avg Sen: $2,500	Incumb: 62.7%

Southland Corp
Southland Corporation Employee's PAC; The
Dallas, TX — Department Stores — **$33,058**

44 Candidates	Dems: 61.8%
Avg House: $644	House: 60.4%
Avg Sen: $1,007	Incumb: 89.3%

Southtrust Corp
Southtrust Corporation Committee for Good Government
Birmingham, AL — Commercial Banks — **$42,700**

27 Candidates	Dems: 55.0%
Avg House: $1,369	House: 67.3%
Avg Sen: $2,390	Incumb: 43.3%

Southwest Gas Corp
Southwest Gas Corporation PAC
Phoenix, AZ — Natural Gas — **$20,700**

14 Candidates	Repubs: 54.1%
Avg House: $1,409	House: 74.9%
Avg Sen: $1,733	Incumb: 85.5%

Southwest Marine
Southwest Marine Inc PAC
San Diego, CA — Shipbuilding/Repair — **$50,400**

30 Candidates	Dems: 53.8%
Avg House: $1,441	House: 65.8%
Avg Sen: $2,464	Incumb: 68.5%

Southwest Peanut Membership Organization
Southwest Peanut PAC
Washington, DC — Misc Crops — **$101,100**

116 Candidates	Dems: 73.0%
Avg House: $778	House: 67.7%
Avg Sen: $1,166	Incumb: 86.8%

† PAC sponsor has other major interests in addition to this primary category

Southwestern Bell Southwestern Bell Corporation Employee Federal PAC (SWB EMPAC or EMPAC) St Louis, MO		**$250,630** Phone Utilites†	141 Candidates Avg House: $1,680 Avg Sen: $2,335	Dems: 60.1% House: 80.4% Incumb: 85.1%	
SPD Technologies SPD Technologies Inc PAC Philadelphia, PA		**$28,250** Defense Electronics	14 Candidates Avg House: $2,136 Avg Sen: $1,583	Dems: 63.2% House: 83.2% Incumb: 92.4%	
Spiegel Inc Spiegel Inc Executive PAC (SEPAC) Oak Brook, IL		**$68,650** Mail Order	58 Candidates Avg House: $967 Avg Sen: $1,813	Dems: 50.6% House: 57.8% Incumb: 89.1%	
Springs Mills Springs Mills Inc PAC (SpringsPAC) Fort Mill, SC		**$22,200** Textiles	25 Candidates Avg House: $980 Avg Sen: $750	Dems: 56.3% House: 66.2% Incumb: 84.2%	
AE Staley Manufacturing Co Staley PAC of A E Staley Manufacturing Company Decatur, IL	Tate & Lyle PLC	**$28,893** Food Processors†	18 Candidates Avg House: $2,045 Avg Sen: $913	Repubs: 52.6% House: 77.9% Incumb: 91.3%	
Stephens Overseas Services Stephens Overseas Services PAC Little Rock, AR		**$52,950** Misc Financial Svcs	19 Candidates Avg House: $2,661 Avg Sen: $3,556	Dems: 70.7% Senate: 60.4% Incumb: 79.7%	
Sterling Drug Sterling Drug Inc PAC SterlPAC New York, NY	Eastman Kodak	**$40,925** Pharmaceuticals	49 Candidates Avg House: $706 Avg Sen: $1,192	Repubs: 74.7% House: 62.1% Incumb: 81.7%	
Stone & Webster Stone & Webster PAC New York, NY		**$43,800** Engineers†	39 Candidates Avg House: $1,152 Avg Sen: $1,071	Dems: 68.4% House: 65.8% Incumb: 90.2%	
Stone Container Corp Stone Container Corporation PAC Chicago, IL		**$352,450** Paper Packaging†	161 Candidates Avg House: $2,090 Avg Sen: $2,814	Repubs: 91.1% House: 82.4% Incumb: 59.0%	
Storage Technology Corp Storage Technology Corporation PAC Inc Louisville, CO		**$29,208** Computer Equipment	36 Candidates Avg House: $580 Avg Sen: $1,100	Repubs: 65.9% Senate: 60.3% Incumb: 69.7%	
Sullivan & Worcester Sullivan & Worcester PAC Washington, DC		**$43,600** Lawyers	42 Candidates Avg House: $889 Avg Sen: $1,786	Dems: 87.4% House: 71.3% Incumb: 80.5%	
Sun Co Sun Company Inc PAC Radnor, PA		**$113,050** Oil Refining/Mkting†	101 Candidates Avg House: $844 Avg Sen: $2,389	Repubs: 88.0% House: 62.0% Incumb: 34.5%	
Sun-Maid Growers of California Sun-Maid Growers of California PAC Pleasanton, CA	Sun-Diamond Growers	**$29,900** Fruit/Veg	19 Candidates Avg House: $1,325 Avg Sen: $2,000	Repubs: 65.2% House: 53.2% Incumb: 71.6%	
SunBanks Sun Banks Inc PAC (Sun BANKPAC) Tallahassee, FL	SunTrust Banks	**$59,782** Commercial Banks	66 Candidates Avg House: $823 Avg Sen: $1,242	Dems: 51.7% House: 73.0% Incumb: 72.2%	
Sundstrand Corp Sundstrand Good Government Pledge Program Rockford, IL		**$29,479** Aerospace Equipt†	50 Candidates Avg House: $682 Avg Sen: $491	Repubs: 84.3% House: 71.7% Incumb: 73.0%	
Sunkist Growers Sunkist Growers, Inc PAC Sherman Oaks, CA		**$133,360** Fruit/Veg	74 Candidates Avg House: $1,693 Avg Sen: $2,168	Repubs: 50.4% House: 72.4% Incumb: 91.8%	
Sunsweet Growers Sunsweet Growers Inc PAC Pleasanton, CA	Sun-Diamond Growers	**$41,985** Fruit/Veg	18 Candidates Avg House: $1,874 Avg Sen: $3,250	Repubs: 60.7% House: 53.5% Incumb: 78.6%	
Sverdrup Corp SVGGS Fund Maryland Heights, MO		**$26,000** Engineers†	8 Candidates Avg House: $3,125 Avg Sen: $3,375	Dems: 61.5% Senate: 51.9% Incumb: 100.0%	
Swidler & Berlin Swidler & Berlin PAC Washington, DC		**$60,525** Lawyers	59 Candidates Avg House: $888 Avg Sen: $1,316	Dems: 79.8% House: 58.7% Incumb: 92.9%	

PAC Sponsor or Related Group/PAC Name	Affiliate	1991-92 Total	Where the money went...		

Syntex (USA) Inc
Syntex (U S A) Inc Employee PAC
Palo Alto, CA — Pharmaceuticals†
$121,644
81 Candidates	Dems: 71.0%
Avg House: $1,230	House: 57.6%
Avg Sen: $2,147	Incumb: 60.6%

T2 Medical Inc
T2 Medical Inc PAC (T2-PAC)
Alpharetta, GA — Doctors
$29,500
16 Candidates	Repubs: 54.2%
Avg House: $1,833	House: 74.6%
Avg Sen: $1,875	Incumb: 64.4%

Teamsters Union
Democratic Republican Independent Voter Education Committee
Washington, DC — Teamsters
$2,442,552
428 Candidates	Dems: 95.2%
Avg House: $5,695	House: 86.7%
Avg Sen: $5,818	Incumb: 61.1%

Teamsters Union Local #745
Local 745 Drive
Dallas, TX — Teamsters Union — Teamsters
$29,000
7 Candidates	Dems: 51.7%
Avg House: $4,167	House: 86.2%
Avg Sen: $4,000	Incumb: 44.8%

Teco Energy Inc
Teco Energy Inc PAC (TEPAC)
Tampa, FL — Electric Utilities†
$22,453
20 Candidates	Repubs: 57.9%
Avg House: $953	House: 67.9%
Avg Sen: $1,801	Incumb: 83.3%

Tele-Communications Inc
Tele-Communications, Inc PAC (TCI PAC)
Denver, CO — Cable TV
$112,500
51 Candidates	Repubs: 60.3%
Avg House: $1,466	Senate: 62.2%
Avg Sen: $3,182	Incumb: 85.8%

Tenneco Inc
Tenneco Inc. Employees Good Govt Fund (aka Tenneco Employees Good Govt Fund)
Houston, TX — Naval Ships/Natural Gas†
$170,750
104 Candidates	Dems: 56.8%
Avg House: $1,562	House: 70.4%
Avg Sen: $1,870	Incumb: 90.0%

Tennessee Walking Horse Breeders
Tennessee Walking Horse Breeders & Exhibitors Assoc
Nashville, TN — Livestock
$25,500
14 Candidates	Dems: 70.6%
Avg House: $1,643	Senate: 54.9%
Avg Sen: $2,000	Incumb: 94.1%

Texaco
Texaco Political Involvement Committee
White Plains, NY — Oil & Gas
$176,489
187 Candidates	Repubs: 70.2%
Avg House: $714	House: 63.9%
Avg Sen: $2,195	Incumb: 80.6%

Texas & Southwestern Cattle Raisers
Texas & Southwestern Cattle Raisers PAC
Fort Worth, TX — Livestock
$49,100
46 Candidates	Dems: 50.2%
Avg House: $1,063	House: 88.8%
Avg Sen: $1,100	Incumb: 89.8%

Texas Air
Texas Air Corporation PAC (TAC PAC)
Houston, TX — Airlines
$110,550
73 Candidates	Repubs: 53.4%
Avg House: $1,258	House: 58.0%
Avg Sen: $2,109	Incumb: 93.3%

Texas Cattle Feeders Assn
Beef-PAC (Beef PAC of Texas Cattle Feeders Association)
Amarillo, TX — Natl Cattlemens Assn — Feedlots
$121,700
124 Candidates	Repubs: 55.3%
Avg House: $903	House: 74.9%
Avg Sen: $1,386	Incumb: 82.7%

Texas Eastern Gas Transmission
Texas Eastern PAC
Houston, TX — Panhandle Eastern Corp — Natural Gas†
$77,900
103 Candidates	Dems: 61.4%
Avg House: $583	House: 66.6%
Avg Sen: $1,857	Incumb: 91.7%

Texas Farm Bureau
Texas Farm Bureau Friends of Agriculture Fund (AGFUND), Inc
Waco, TX — Farm Orgs
$44,279
15 Candidates	Dems: 54.2%
Avg House: $3,163	House: 100.0%
Avg Sen: $0	Incumb: 79.0%

Texas Gas Transmission Corp
Texas Gas Transmission Corporation PAC
Owensboro, KY — Transco Energy Co — Natural Gas
$25,000
37 Candidates	Dems: 66.4%
Avg House: $585	House: 63.2%
Avg Sen: $920	Incumb: 96.8%

Texas Instruments
Constructive Citizenship Program of Texas Instruments
Dallas, TX — Computer Equipment††
$107,800
79 Candidates	Dems: 69.1%
Avg House: $1,128	House: 68.0%
Avg Sen: $2,464	Incumb: 87.9%

Texas Utilities Co
Texas Utilities Company PAC
Dallas, TX — Texas Utilities Co — Electric Utilities
$86,800
95 Candidates	Dems: 57.1%
Avg House: $783	House: 69.5%
Avg Sen: $1,472	Incumb: 85.2%

Texas Utilities Co
Texas Utilities Company Power PAC
Dallas, TX — Texas Utilities Co — Electric Utilities
$41,500
42 Candidates	Dems: 69.3%
Avg House: $1,050	House: 88.5%
Avg Sen: $679	Incumb: 83.1%

Texas Utilities Co
Operations Employees' PAC of Texas Utilities Electric Co
Dallas, TX — Texas Utilities Co — Electric Utilities
$47,900
25 Candidates	Dems: 75.2%
Avg House: $2,039	House: 97.9%
Avg Sen: $500	Incumb: 79.3%

† PAC sponsor has other major interests in addition to this primary category

Texas Utilities Electric Co/TP&L Div Texas Utilities Electric Company TP&L Division Employee PAC-EM-PAC Dallas, TX	Texas Utilities Co	**$26,550** Electric Utilities	26 Candidates Avg House: $1,297 Avg Sen: $500	Dems: 55.9% House: 83.0% Incumb: 100.0%
Textron Inc Textron Inc PAC Providence, RI	Defense Aerospace†	**$398,850**	185 Candidates Avg House: $1,911 Avg Sen: $3,423	Dems: 66.6% House: 74.2% Incumb: 96.0%
TGI Friday's Inc TGI Friday's Incorporated Employees PAC Addison, TX	Restaurants	**$32,000**	37 Candidates Avg House: $760 Avg Sen: $1,083	Repubs: 92.2% House: 59.4% Incumb: 45.3%
Thiokol Morton Thiokol PAC Ogden, UT	Defense Aerospace†	**$71,025**	75 Candidates Avg House: $719 Avg Sen: $1,724	Dems: 52.9% House: 58.8% Incumb: 91.6%
Time Warner Warner Communications Inc PAC New York, NY	Broadcast/Movies†	**$138,000**	57 Candidates Avg House: $1,818 Avg Sen: $3,250	Dems: 72.5% Senate: 56.5% Incumb: 81.5%
Tobacco Institute Tobacco Institute PAC Washington, DC	Tobacco	**$183,950**	222 Candidates Avg House: $761 Avg Sen: $1,500	Dems: 50.4% House: 83.2% Incumb: 94.8%
Torchmark Corp Torchmark Corporation Political Action Committe (TORCH-PAC) Birmingham, AL	Insurance	**$204,184**	107 Candidates Avg House: $1,324 Avg Sen: $2,927	Repubs: 59.7% Senate: 55.9% Incumb: 72.1%
Torrington Co Torrington Company PAC Torrington, CT	Ingersoll-Rand	**$20,828** Truck/Auto Parts†	19 Candidates Avg House: $1,207 Avg Sen: $1,007	Dems: 67.9% House: 63.8% Incumb: 85.6%
Totem Ocean Trailer Express Totem Ocean Trailer Express Inc/Foss Maritime Company PAC (Tote/Foss PAC) Seattle, WA	Sea Transport	**$34,250**	26 Candidates Avg House: $1,095 Avg Sen: $1,673	Dems: 56.0% House: 51.2% Incumb: 76.6%
Trailer Train Co Trailer Train Co Employees' PAC Chicago, IL	Railroad Services†	**$23,850**	30 Candidates Avg House: $711 Avg Sen: $1,071	Dems: 63.7% House: 68.5% Incumb: 93.7%
Trans Comm International Union Responsible Citizens Pol League - A Project of the Trans Comm Intl Union (TCU) Rockville, MD	Misc Transport Union	**$421,230**	319 Candidates Avg House: $973 Avg Sen: $3,478	Dems: 96.1% House: 63.8% Incumb: 68.7%
TransAmerica Corp TransAmerica Corporation PAC (TransPAC) San Francisco, CA	TransAmerica	**$32,425** Insurance	14 Candidates Avg House: $1,116 Avg Sen: $3,917	Dems: 55.3% Senate: 72.5% Incumb: 37.9%
TransAmerica Insurance TransAmerica Insurance Company PAC Woodland Hills, CA	TransAmerica	**$35,750** Insurance	17 Candidates Avg House: $2,027 Avg Sen: $2,350	Repubs: 93.3% House: 73.7% Incumb: 49.6%
TransAmerica Life Companies TransAmerica Life Companies PAC "TALCPAC" Los Angeles, CA	TransAmerica	**$45,400** Life Insurance	53 Candidates Avg House: $656 Avg Sen: $1,542	Dems: 62.3% House: 59.2% Incumb: 78.5%
Transco Energy Co Transco Energy Company PAC Houston, TX	Natural Gas	**$25,900**	38 Candidates Avg House: $483 Avg Sen: $1,021	Dems: 73.9% Senate: 55.2% Incumb: 91.5%
Transport Workers Union Transport Workers Union Political Contributions Committee New York, NY	Misc Transport Union	**$414,830**	238 Candidates Avg House: $1,505 Avg Sen: $3,064	Dems: 97.3% House: 72.9% Incumb: 74.3%
Travelers Corp Travelers Corporation PAC (T-PAC); The Hartford, CT	Insurance†	**$230,219**	107 Candidates Avg House: $1,699 Avg Sen: $3,083	Repubs: 62.9% House: 53.1% Incumb: 84.4%
Trust Co of Georgia Trust Company of Georgia Good Government Group Atlanta, GA	SunTrust Banks	**$32,775** Commercial Banks	40 Candidates Avg House: $702 Avg Sen: $1,483	Repubs: 50.2% House: 72.8% Incumb: 29.7%
TRW Inc TRW Good Government Fund Lyndhurst, OH	Defense Electronics†	**$153,175**	143 Candidates Avg House: $970 Avg Sen: $1,571	Dems: 50.6% House: 75.4% Incumb: 89.2%

Turner Broadcasting System
Turner Broadcasting System PAC Inc
Atlanta, GA — Cable TV — **$74,770**

49 Candidates	Dems:	55.4%
Avg House: $1,069	Senate:	54.2%
Avg Sen: $2,385	Incumb:	100.0%

Tyson Foods
Tyson Foods Inc PAC (TYPAC)
Springdale, AR — Poultry/Egg† — **$171,850**

106 Candidates	Dems:	81.7%
Avg House: $1,279	House:	58.8%
Avg Sen: $2,622	Incumb:	82.5%

UNC Inc
UNC Incorporated Public Responsibility Fund
Annapolis, MD — Aerospace Equip† — **$49,186**

25 Candidates	Dems:	64.0%
Avg House: $1,733	House:	63.4%
Avg Sen: $2,570	Incumb:	82.6%

Union Camp Corp
Union Camp Corporation PAC
Wayne, NJ — Paper/Pulp† — **$77,810**

57 Candidates	Repubs:	73.8%
Avg House: $899	Senate:	52.6%
Avg Sen: $2,560	Incumb:	49.0%

Union Carbide
Union Carbide Corporation PAC
New York, NY — Chemicals — **$27,150**

32 Candidates	Dems:	53.2%
Avg House: $786	House:	72.4%
Avg Sen: $1,071	Incumb:	85.3%

Union Electric
Union Electric Company Federal PAC (UEFEDPAC)
St Louis, MO — Electric Utilities — **$22,250**

26 Candidates	Repubs:	59.3%
Avg House: $693	House:	62.2%
Avg Sen: $1,400	Incumb:	88.5%

Union Oil
Union Oil (Unocal) Political Awareness Fund
Los Angeles, CA — Oil & Gas† — **$129,424**

126 Candidates	Repubs:	70.8%
Avg House: $672	Senate:	50.1%
Avg Sen: $2,162	Incumb:	62.2%

Union Pacific Corp
Union Pacific Fund for Effective Government
Washington, DC — Railroads† — **$684,680**

305 Candidates	Repubs:	66.8%
Avg House: $1,677	House:	62.7%
Avg Sen: $5,214	Incumb:	70.8%

United Airlines
United Airlines PAC
Chicago, IL — Airlines — **$198,428**

159 Candidates	Dems:	57.4%
Avg House: $1,124	House:	69.7%
Avg Sen: $1,724	Incumb:	92.7%

United Auto Workers
UAW - V - CAP (UAW Voluntary Community Action Program)
Detroit, MI — Manufacturing Unions — **$2,231,917**

410 Candidates	Dems:	98.2%
Avg House: $5,339	House:	87.1%
Avg Sen: $6,301	Incumb:	57.2%

United Co
United Co PAC, The
Bristol, VA — Coal — **$40,450**

55 Candidates	Repubs:	61.7%
Avg House: $696	House:	65.4%
Avg Sen: $824	Incumb:	68.4%

United Egg Assn
United Egg Association PAC (EggPAC)
Decatur, GA — Poultry/Egg — **$67,250**

68 Candidates	Dems:	52.7%
Avg House: $801	House:	56.0%
Avg Sen: $1,410	Incumb:	93.2%

United Illuminating Co
Electric Employees Committee of the United Illuminating Company
New Haven, CT — Electric Utilities — **$39,025**

38 Candidates	Dems:	67.9%
Avg House: $720	Senate:	52.0%
Avg Sen: $1,692	Incumb:	86.4%

United Mine Workers
United Mine Workers of America - Coal Miners PAC
Washington, DC — Mine Workers — **$459,600**

244 Candidates	Dems:	97.5%
Avg House: $1,585	House:	69.3%
Avg Sen: $3,256	Incumb:	68.0%

United Paperworkers
United Paperworkers International Union Political Education Program
Washington, DC — Manufacturing Unions — **$86,000**

68 Candidates	Dems:	97.7%
Avg House: $1,087	House:	65.7%
Avg Sen: $1,900	Incumb:	49.4%

United Parcel Service
UPSPAC
Greenwich, CT — Express Delivery — **$1,454,487**

524 Candidates	Dems:	54.2%
Avg House: $2,646	House:	81.7%
Avg Sen: $3,554	Incumb:	84.2%

United Services Automobile Assn Group
United Services Automobile Association Group PAC (USAA Group PAC)
San Antonio, TX — Proprty Insurance — **$78,200**

73 Candidates	Repubs:	64.2%
Avg House: $1,078	House:	74.4%
Avg Sen: $1,053	Incumb:	67.0%

United States Sugar Corp
United States Sugar Corp-employee Stock Ownership Plan PAC
Clewiston, FL — Sugar — **$58,850**

42 Candidates	Dems:	78.8%
Avg House: $1,324	House:	78.8%
Avg Sen: $1,786	Incumb:	60.9%

United Steelworkers
United Steelworkers of America Political Action Fund
Pittsburgh, PA — Manufacturing Unions — **$1,253,949**

253 Candidates	Dems:	99.0%
Avg House: $4,634	House:	81.3%
Avg Sen: $7,226	Incumb:	51.5%

† PAC sponsor has other major interests in addition to this primary category

PAC Sponsor or Related Group/PAC Name	Affiliate	1991-92 Total	Where the money went...		
United Technologies United Technologies Corporation, PAC Washington, DC *Defense Aerospace†*		$285,540	215 Candidates Avg House: $1,045 Avg Sen: $2,566	Dems: 54.6% House: 64.0% Incumb: 91.2%	
United Telecommunications United Telecommunications, Inc PAC (UNIPAC) Westwood, KS	United Telecom *Phone Utilites†*	$424,060	259 Candidates Avg House: $1,305 Avg Sen: $3,838	Repubs: 66.8% House: 69.2% Incumb: 63.7%	
United Transportation Union Transportation Political Education League Cleveland, OH *Railroad Unions*		$1,097,550	380 Candidates Avg House: $2,390 Avg Sen: $6,453	Dems: 97.1% House: 72.5% Incumb: 67.4%	
Unum Life Insurance Co Unum PAC Portland, ME *Insurance*		$46,550	39 Candidates Avg House: $822 Avg Sen: $1,857	Dems: 58.5% Senate: 55.9% Incumb: 77.9%	
Upjohn Co Upjohn Employees PAC Kalamazoo, MI *Pharmaceuticals*		$124,950	128 Candidates Avg House: $905 Avg Sen: $1,208	Dems: 62.0% House: 71.0% Incumb: 91.2%	
US Bancorp US Bancorp PAC Portland, OR	US Bancorp *Commercial Banks*	$60,000	25 Candidates Avg House: $2,422 Avg Sen: $2,343	Dems: 52.5% House: 72.7% Incumb: 52.7%	
US Bancorp US Bancorp PAC-A Portland, OR	US Bancorp *Commercial Banks*	$28,041	10 Candidates Avg House: $3,094 Avg Sen: $2,128	Repubs: 57.0% House: 77.2% Incumb: 65.7%	
US Beet Sugar Assn United States Beet Sugar Association PAC Washington, DC *Sugar*		$52,432	75 Candidates Avg House: $647 Avg Sen: $876	Dems: 78.1% House: 71.6% Incumb: 80.4%	
US Federation of Small Businesses US Federation of Small Businesses PAC (Small Biz PAC) Washington, DC *Small Business Assns*		$22,500	18 Candidates Avg House: $786 Avg Sen: $1,545	Repubs: 75.6% Senate: 75.6% Incumb: 17.8%	
US Healthcare Inc US Healthcare Inc PAC (USHC-PAC) Blue Bell, PA *HMOs*		$28,918	32 Candidates Avg House: $811 Avg Sen: $1,174	Dems: 54.6% House: 61.7% Incumb: 63.5%	
US League of Savings Assns US League-Savings Association Political Elections Committee Washington, DC *Savings & Loans*		$198,215	164 Candidates Avg House: $1,198 Avg Sen: $1,257	Dems: 63.0% House: 81.0% Incumb: 81.3%	
US Telephone Assn United States Telephone Assn PAC Washington, DC *Phone Utilites*		$170,619	148 Candidates Avg House: $894 Avg Sen: $1,875	Dems: 57.8% House: 56.6% Incumb: 90.1%	
US Tobacco Co US Tobacco Executives, Administrators and Managers PAC (USTEAM PAC) Greenwich, CT	US Tobacco *Tobacco*	$427,250	177 Candidates Avg House: $1,811 Avg Sen: $5,152	Repubs: 57.0% House: 61.5% Incumb: 72.0%	
US West Inc US West Inc PAC (US West PAC) Denver, CO	US West *Phone Utilites*	$266,822	144 Candidates Avg House: $1,670 Avg Sen: $2,682	Dems: 54.4% House: 72.6% Incumb: 77.3%	
USAir Corp US-Air PAC (aka Allegheny PAC) Arlington, VA *Airlines*		$31,720	52 Candidates Avg House: $497 Avg Sen: $948	Dems: 56.4% House: 61.2% Incumb: 99.2%	
USX Corp USXPAC Washington, DC *Oil & Gas†*		$106,827	93 Candidates Avg House: $979 Avg Sen: $2,107	Dems: 65.8% House: 72.4% Incumb: 89.9%	
Utilicorp United Inc Utilicorp United Inc Employee PAC aka Utilicorp United Employee PAC Kansas City, MO *Gas & Electric Util†*		$42,825	30 Candidates Avg House: $854 Avg Sen: $2,575	Repubs: 65.0% Senate: 60.1% Incumb: 94.8%	
Utility Workers Union of America Utility Workers Union of America Political Contributions Committee Washington, DC *Energy Unions*		$26,550	37 Candidates Avg House: $591 Avg Sen: $1,111	Dems: 96.2% House: 62.3% Incumb: 64.4%	
V-PAC V-PAC Sterling, VA *Repub/Conservative*		$43,846	39 Candidates Avg House: $1,036 Avg Sen: $2,750	Repubs: 100.0% House: 87.5% Incumb: 3.4%	

PAC Sponsor or Related Group/PAC Name	Affiliate	1991-92 Total	Where the money went...		

Valero Energy Corp
Valero Energy Corporation PAC (VALPAC)
San Antonio, TX — Oil Refining/Mkting†
$39,500
22 Candidates	Dems: 76.0%
Avg House: $1,895	House: 91.1%
Avg Sen: $1,167	Incumb: 74.7%

Van Ness, Feldman et al
Van Ness, Feldman, Sutcliffe & Curtis PAC
Washington, DC — Lawyers
$40,099
62 Candidates	Dems: 69.1%
Avg House: $558	House: 58.5%
Avg Sen: $833	Incumb: 90.3%

Verner, Liipfert et al
Verner, Liipfert, Bernhard, McPherson & Hand PAC
Washington, DC — Lawyers
$175,192
119 Candidates	Dems: 90.0%
Avg House: $946	Senate: 56.8%
Avg Sen: $2,552	Incumb: 94.3%

Veterans of Foreign Wars
Veterans of Foreign Wars PAC Inc
Washington, DC — Pro-Defense
$102,675
96 Candidates	Repubs: 58.5%
Avg House: $953	House: 75.2%
Avg Sen: $1,700	Incumb: 92.7%

Viacom International
Viacom International Inc PAC Corporation
New York, NY — Cable TV
$123,250
62 Candidates	Dems: 66.9%
Avg House: $2,097	House: 61.3%
Avg Sen: $1,837	Incumb: 95.7%

Victory USA
Victory USA
Sacramento, CA — Rep Vic Fazio (D-Calif) — Dem Leaders
$91,100
86 Candidates	Dems: 98.9%
Avg House: $989	House: 90.1%
Avg Sen: $3,000	Incumb: 36.8%

Viking Freight
Viking Freight, Inc PAC (VIKPAC)
San Jose, CA — Roadway Services — Trucking Companies
$39,200
35 Candidates	Repubs: 67.5%
Avg House: $1,008	House: 61.7%
Avg Sen: $1,364	Incumb: 69.3%

Vinson & Elkins
National Good Government Fund; The
Houston, TX — Lawyers
$119,660
79 Candidates	Dems: 70.3%
Avg House: $1,604	House: 63.0%
Avg Sen: $1,355	Incumb: 84.8%

Virginia Bankers Assn
Virginia Bankpac
Richmond, VA — American Bankers Assn — Commercial Banks
$37,000
12 Candidates	Dems: 50.0%
Avg House: $3,083	House: 100.0%
Avg Sen: $0	Incumb: 64.9%

Virginia-Carolinas Peanut Membership Organization
Virginia - Carolina's Peanut PAC
Washington, DC — Misc Crops
$26,750
41 Candidates	Dems: 80.4%
Avg House: $608	House: 68.2%
Avg Sen: $773	Incumb: 91.0%

Vorys, Sater et al
VSS&P FEDPAC
Columbus, OH — Lawyers
$23,850
27 Candidates	Repubs: 53.9%
Avg House: $714	House: 74.8%
Avg Sen: $1,000	Incumb: 79.0%

Voters for Choice
Voters for Choice/Friends of Family Planning
Washington, DC — Pro-Choice
$265,450
183 Candidates	Dems: 88.6%
Avg House: $1,142	House: 70.2%
Avg Sen: $3,963	Incumb: 42.4%

Vulcan Materials Co
Vulcan Materials Company-PAC
Birmingham, AL — Bldg Materials†
$43,950
61 Candidates	Dems: 61.5%
Avg House: $547	House: 59.7%
Avg Sen: $1,362	Incumb: 77.9%

Wal-Mart Stores
Wal-Mart Stores Inc PAC for Responsible Government
Bentonville, AR — Department Stores
$51,700
57 Candidates	Repubs: 90.8%
Avg House: $658	Senate: 54.2%
Avg Sen: $1,333	Incumb: 66.4%

Walgreen Co
Walgreen PAC
Deerfield, IL — Drug Stores
$24,850
32 Candidates	Repubs: 50.7%
Avg House: $707	House: 59.8%
Avg Sen: $909	Incumb: 67.8%

Warner-Lambert
Warner-Lambert PAC ("WALPAC")
Morris Plains, NJ — Health Care Products†
$96,355
94 Candidates	Dems: 64.7%
Avg House: $925	House: 67.2%
Avg Sen: $1,316	Incumb: 84.1%

Warshawsky & Co/JC Whitney & Co
Warshawsky & Co/JC Whitney & Co PAC
Chicago, IL — Truck/Auto Parts
$25,500
28 Candidates	Dems: 70.6%
Avg House: $896	House: 84.3%
Avg Sen: $1,000	Incumb: 72.5%

Washington PAC
Washington PAC
Washington, DC — Pro-Israel
$202,020
157 Candidates	Dems: 72.6%
Avg House: $798	Senate: 53.8%
Avg Sen: $2,717	Incumb: 84.4%

Waste Management Inc
Waste Management Inc Employees' Better Government Fund ("WMI PAC")
Oak Brook, IL — Waste Mgmt — Waste Mgmt
$452,689
372 Candidates	Dems: 67.7%
Avg House: $1,039	House: 68.9%
Avg Sen: $1,955	Incumb: 82.9%

† PAC sponsor has other major interests in addition to this primary category

Watkins Associated Industries Watkins Associated Industries Inc Employees for Good Government Committee (Watkins-PAC) Atlanta, GA	Trucking Companies†	$20,950	19 Candidates Avg House: $1,335 Avg Sen: $600	Dems: 64.4% House: 82.8% Incumb: 72.5%
Watkins-Johnson Co Watkins-Johnson PAC Palo Alto, CA	Defense Electronics	$24,000	5 Candidates Avg House: $3,000 Avg Sen: $7,500	Repubs: 93.8% Senate: 62.5% Incumb: 27.1%
Wells Fargo Wells Fargo & Company Impact Fund San Francisco, CA	Commercial Banks	$71,715	55 Candidates Avg House: $1,137 Avg Sen: $1,793	Dems: 55.4% House: 65.0% Incumb: 62.2%
Wertheim Schroder & Co Wertheim Schroder & Co Incorporated PAC New York, NY	Securities	$23,250	7 Candidates Avg House: $3,667 Avg Sen: $3,063	Dems: 100.0% Senate: 52.7% Incumb: 47.3%
West Publishing West Publishing Company PAC (West Publishing PAC) Minneapolis, MN	Publishing	$108,900	53 Candidates Avg House: $1,978 Avg Sen: $2,292	Dems: 82.0% House: 72.6% Incumb: 91.2%
Western United Dairymens Assn Western United Dairymen's Association Federal PAC Modesto, CA	Dairy	$21,942	15 Candidates Avg House: $1,484 Avg Sen: $1,420	Dems: 61.0% House: 67.6% Incumb: 67.9%
Westinghouse Electric Westinghouse Electric Corporation Employees Political Participation Program Pittsburgh, PA	Electronics Mfg†	$214,800	189 Candidates Avg House: $978 Avg Sen: $1,836	Dems: 62.8% House: 70.1% Incumb: 94.1%
Westvaco Corp Westvaco Corporation Political Participation Program New York, NY	Paper/Pulp†	$245,200	85 Candidates Avg House: $2,495 Avg Sen: $4,071	Repubs: 78.7% House: 65.1% Incumb: 63.9%
Wexler Group Wexler Group PAC; The Washington, DC Hill & Knowlton	Lobbyists/PR	$72,684	100 Candidates Avg House: $649 Avg Sen: $927	Dems: 82.6% House: 64.3% Incumb: 94.5%
Weyerhaeuser Co Weyerhaeuser Company Special Shareholders PAC St. Paul, MN Weyerhaeuser	Paper/Pulp†	$81,750	73 Candidates Avg House: $844 Avg Sen: $1,850	Repubs: 71.9% House: 54.7% Incumb: 58.1%
Weyerhaeuser Co Weyerhaeuser Company PAC Federal Way, WA Weyerhaeuser	Paper/Pulp†	$53,047	18 Candidates Avg House: $2,909 Avg Sen: $3,045	Repubs: 81.8% House: 71.3% Incumb: 22.9%
Wheelabrator Technologies Wheelabrator Technologies Inc Sensible Government Fund Hampton, NH Waste Management Inc	Waste Mgmt	$77,800	64 Candidates Avg House: $1,093 Avg Sen: $1,486	Dems: 68.6% House: 61.8% Incumb: 74.6%
Whirlpool Corp Whirlpool PAC Benton Harbor, MI	Appliances	$28,850	49 Candidates Avg House: $436 Avg Sen: $876	Repubs: 100.0% Senate: 51.6% Incumb: 54.9%
Willamette Industries Willamette Industries PAC (WILPAC) Portland, OR	Forest Products†	$53,056	43 Candidates Avg House: $987 Avg Sen: $2,167	Repubs: 88.1% House: 63.2% Incumb: 37.9%
Williams & Jensen Williams & Jensen PC PAC (W & J PAC) Washington, DC	Lawyers	$90,469	135 Candidates Avg House: $587 Avg Sen: $963	Dems: 62.1% House: 68.1% Incumb: 92.3%
Williams Companies Williams Companies PAC ("Willco PAC"); The Tulsa, OK	Natural Gas	$36,275	48 Candidates Avg House: $569 Avg Sen: $1,167	Dems: 52.2% House: 51.8% Incumb: 83.7%
Wine & Spirits Wholesalers of America Wine and Spirits Wholesalers of America PAC Washington, DC	Liquor Wholesalers	$177,478	122 Candidates Avg House: $1,383 Avg Sen: $1,675	Dems: 66.6% House: 71.7% Incumb: 89.5%
Wine Institute Wine Institute PAC San Francisco, CA	Wine & Liquor	$105,026	49 Candidates Avg House: $1,690 Avg Sen: $2,997	Dems: 84.6% House: 51.5% Incumb: 93.6%
Winn-Dixie Stores Sunbelt Good Government Committee of Winn-Dixie Stores, Inc. Jacksonville, FL	Food Stores	$228,250	106 Candidates Avg House: $1,687 Avg Sen: $3,519	Repubs: 63.6% House: 58.4% Incumb: 73.7%

PAC Sponsor or Related Group/PAC Name	Affiliate	1991-92 Total	Where the money went...		
Winstead, Sechrest & Minick Winstead, McGuire, Sechrest & Minick PC PAC Dallas, TX	Lawyers	$20,250	15 Candidates Avg House: $1,442 Avg Sen: $750	Dems: 65.4% House: 92.6% Incumb: 95.1%	
Wisconsin Bell Telephone Wisconsin Bell Employees Federal PAC Milwaukee, WI	Ameritech Phone Utilites	$26,100	14 Candidates Avg House: $1,723 Avg Sen: $2,383	Repubs: 51.1% House: 72.6% Incumb: 73.2%	
Wish List Wish List New York, NY	Womens Issues†	$73,109	19 Candidates Avg House: $3,848 Avg Sen: $0	Repubs: 100.0% House: 100.0% Incumb: 29.0%	
Wolf, Block et al Tercentenary Fund Philadelphia, PA	Lawyers	$32,200	28 Candidates Avg House: $913 Avg Sen: $1,318	Dems: 60.6% Senate: 45.0% Incumb: 51.2%	
Women for: Women for: Beverly Hills, CA	Human Rights†	$20,877	17 Candidates Avg House: $675 Avg Sen: $2,555	Dems: 99.0% Senate: 61.2% Incumb: 1.2%	
Women's Alliance for Israel Women's Alliance for Israel Beverly Hills, CA	Pro-Israel	$209,000	67 Candidates Avg House: $1,342 Avg Sen: $5,448	Dems: 59.8% Senate: 75.6% Incumb: 77.8%	
Women's Campaign Fund Women's Campaign Fund Inc Washington, DC	Womens Issues	$513,067	96 Candidates Avg House: $5,167 Avg Sen: $6,583	Dems: 76.1% House: 84.6% Incumb: 14.6%	
Women's Political Committee Women's Political Committee Los Angeles, CA	Womens Issues	$57,100	14 Candidates Avg House: $3,513 Avg Sen: $4,833	Dems: 100.0% Senate: 50.8% Incumb: 0.0%	
Women's Pro-Israel National PAC Women's Pro-Israel National PAC ("WIN PAC") Washington, DC	Pro-Israel	$155,550	88 Candidates Avg House: $846 Avg Sen: $3,461	Repubs: 52.1% Senate: 69.0% Incumb: 78.1%	
World Savings & Loan World Savings and Loan Association PAC (WorldPAC) Oakland, CA	Savings & Loans	$22,750	10 Candidates Avg House: $688 Avg Sen: $3,000	Dems: 97.8% Senate: 65.9% Incumb: 41.8%	
Xerox Corp Team Xerox PAC ("TXP") Stamford, CT	Office Machines†	$49,500	43 Candidates Avg House: $1,016 Avg Sen: $1,545	Dems: 55.6% House: 65.7% Incumb: 87.9%	
Yankee Atomic Electric Co Yankee Atomic Electric Company-PAC (Yankee PAC) Bolton, MA	Nuclear Energy†	$20,150	35 Candidates Avg House: $577 Avg Sen: $571	Repubs: 68.5% House: 80.2% Incumb: 85.6%	
Yellow Freight System Yellow Freight System Inc PAC Shawnee Mission, KS	Trucking Companies	$170,409	139 Candidates Avg House: $877 Avg Sen: $2,733	Dems: 68.8% House: 57.1% Incumb: 93.2%	

† PAC sponsor has other major interests in addition to this primary category

Appendix A: Industry & Interest Group Categories

This is a listing of the detailed categories used in classifying all the contributors that gave money to federal candidates in the 1992 elections. Included are the category name, the total in 1991-92 contributions, and a breakdown of the totals by PACs and political parties.

Classification of contributors is not always a straightforward matter, particularly when the contributor has multiple interests or multiple sources of revenue. Many corporate PACs have been assigned multiple categories — a primary code based on their single largest source of income, and as many as six alternate codes encompassing smaller, but significant revenue sources. Throughout this book, and in the listings below, the category assigned to a particular contribution depends both on the interests of the contributor *and the congressional committee assignments of the recipient.* This is particularly relevant in the defense sector, as many defense contractors earn the majority of their revenues from non-defense activities. In such cases, the contributions are classified as defense-related *only when they are made to a member who sits on a defense-related committee.* (For that reason, totals in the defense sector can be considered very conservative.) A similar procedure was used for all other diversified companies.

In most cases, individual contributors are classified according to the economic interests of their employer. Contributions from non-income earning spouses and children are classified according to the economic interest of the income earner within the family. Thus a bank president, his wife and children would all be classified under "commercial banking" unless the wife had a job as well, in which case she would be classified separately.

Individual contributors are classified under the ideological/single-issue categories only if they contributed to an ideological or single-issue PAC. Even then, the contribution is considered ideological only if the candidate who received the contribution also drew money from an ideological PAC with similar interests. The following example illustrates the procedure used: If a real estate developer contributes both to a pro-Israel PAC and to a candidate who received direct contributions from pro-Israel PACs, the contribution would be classified under "pro-Israel." If the donor gave to someone who got no money from pro-Israel PACs, it would be classified under "real estate." In the case of ideological contributors, non-income earning spouses and children are *not* classified as ideological givers unless they themselves have contributed to an ideological PAC.

Detailed profiles of the spending patterns of each major industry group can be found in the "Industry Profile" section of this book, on pages 41-93.

Agriculture

	Total	PAC Pct	Dem Pct	Repub Pct
Crop Production & Basic Processing				
Cotton	$453,751	78%	53%	47%
Sugar cane & sugar beets	$1,801,818	83%	69%	31%
Vegetables, fruits and tree nuts	$1,188,860	60%	42%	58%
Wheat, corn, soybeans and cash grain	$189,413	69%	43%	57%
Other commodities (including rice, peanuts, honey)	$472,177	81%	77%	22%
Farmers, crop unspecified	$1,762,630	7%	46%	54%
TOTAL	**$5,868,649**	**54%**	**55%**	**45%**
Tobacco				
Tobacco & Tobacco products	$2,818,861	81%	53%	47%
Dairy				
Milk & dairy producers	$2,107,911	83%	63%	37%
Livestock & Poultry				
Livestock	$1,476,005	40%	39%	61%
Feedlots & related livestock services	$153,900	79%	40%	60%
Poultry & eggs	$891,174	59%	62%	38%
Sheep and wool producers	$30,600	84%	40%	60%
TOTAL	**$2,551,679**	**50%**	**47%**	**53%**
Agricultural Services & Products				
Agricultural services, diversified	$625,743	79%	52%	48%
Agricultural chemicals (fertilizers & pesticides)	$552,635	90%	48%	51%
Animal feed & health products	$128,262	43%	19%	80%
Veterinarians	$413,615	73%	55%	45%
Farm machinery & equipment	$320,297	58%	20%	80%
Grain traders & terminals	$462,575	64%	51%	49%
Farm organizations & cooperatives	$604,564	99%	58%	42%
Florists & nursery services	$362,329	28%	35%	65%
TOTAL	**$3,470,020**	**73%**	**47%**	**53%**

Food Processing & Sales

	Total	PAC Pct	Dem Pct	Repub Pct
Food & beverage products and services, diversified	$582,289	66%	40%	60%
Food and kindred products manufacturing	$1,818,855	65%	34%	66%
Meat processing & products	$334,720	38%	38%	62%
Food stores	$1,792,143	50%	39%	60%
Food wholesalers	$580,057	53%	39%	60%
TOTAL	**$5,108,064**	**57%**	**37%**	**62%**

Forestry & Forest Products

	Total	PAC Pct	Dem Pct	Repub Pct
Forestry & Forest Products	$1,253,349	43%	24%	76%
Paper & pulp mills and paper manufacturing	$1,455,994	76%	26%	74%
TOTAL	**$2,709,343**	**61%**	**25%**	**75%**

Other & Unclassified

	Total	PAC Pct	Dem Pct	Repub Pct
Misc Agriculture	$257,597	0%	33%	67%
TOTAL	**$257,597**	**0%**	**33%**	**67%**

Communications & Electronics

	Total	PAC Pct	Dem Pct	Repub Pct
Printing & Publishing				
Book, newspaper & periodical publishing	$1,674,934	13%	56%	43%
Commercial printing & typesetting	$647,556	17%	41%	58%
Greeting card publishing	$221,761	65%	28%	72%
Misc printing & publishing	$515,330	0%	80%	19%
TOTAL	**$3,059,581**	**15%**	**55%**	**44%**
Broadcasting, Motion Pictures & Entertainment				
Broadcasting & motion pictures, diversified	$478,265	29%	81%	19%
Motion picture production & distribution	$2,596,760	13%	87%	13%
Television production	$570,666	16%	87%	13%
Commercial TV & radio stations	$1,075,656	46%	57%	43%
Cable & satellite TV operators	$2,226,214	54%	55%	44%
Recorded Music & music production	$591,482	40%	88%	12%
Bands, orchestras & other live music production	$126,200	0%	78%	20%
Amusement/recreation centers & movie theaters	$353,539	26%	41%	59%
TOTAL	**$8,018,782**	**32%**	**72%**	**28%**
Telephone Utilities				
Local & regional telephone utilities	$4,518,436	88%	55%	44%
Long-distance telephone utilities	$1,385,963	86%	60%	40%
TOTAL	**$5,904,399**	**88%**	**56%**	**43%**
Telecommunications Services & Equipment				
Telephone & communications equipment	$482,048	57%	48%	52%
Cellular systems and equipment	$187,195	39%	58%	42%
Satellite communications	$115,450	74%	60%	40%
Other communications sServices	$14,200	58%	30%	70%
Telecommunications, unclassified	$110,447	7%	55%	44%
TOTAL	**$909,340**	**49%**	**52%**	**48%**
Electronics Manufacturing & Services				
Electronics manufacturing & services	$1,088,233	42%	37%	63%
Computer Equipment & Services				
Computer manufacturing & services, diversified	$498,735	14%	61%	38%
Computers, components & accessories	$746,873	26%	46%	54%
Data processing & computer services	$697,028	42%	51%	47%
Computer software	$270,318	8%	35%	63%
TOTAL	**$2,212,954**	**26%**	**50%**	**49%**
Other & Unclassified				
Misc communications & electronics	$39,175	1%	63%	37%

Construction

	Total	PAC Pct	Dem Pct	Repub Pct
General Contractors				
Builders associations	$192,778	96%	7%	93%
Public works, industrial & commercial construction	$3,623,909	42%	38%	61%

	Total	PAC Pct	Dem Pct	Repub Pct
Construction, unclassified or diversified	$2,683,507	0%	49%	51%
TOTAL	**$6,500,194**	**26%**	**42%**	**58%**

Home Builders

Residential construction	$2,017,905	59%	46%	54%
Mobile home construction	$198,270	59%	33%	67%
TOTAL	**$2,216,175**	**59%**	**45%**	**55%**

Special Trade Contractors

Special trade contractors, diversified	$580,886	12%	41%	58%
Electrical contractors	$436,146	37%	38%	62%
Plumbing, heating & air conditioning	$513,447	33%	33%	67%
Landscaping & excavation services	$155,949	0%	47%	53%
TOTAL	**$1,686,428**	**24%**	**38%**	**61%**

Construction Services

Engineering, architecture & construction mgmt, diversified	$1,327,535	45%	59%	41%
Architectural services	$574,357	6%	72%	28%
Surveying	$72,128	40%	35%	65%
TOTAL	**$1,974,020**	**33%**	**62%**	**38%**

Building Materials & Equipment

Building materials, diversified	$461,334	39%	50%	50%
Stone, clay, glass & concrete products	$963,985	28%	36%	64%
Lumber & wood products	$548,351	5%	33%	66%
Plumbing & pipe products	$315,230	18%	32%	68%
Electrical supply	$160,922	0%	33%	66%
Construction equipment	$318,400	30%	22%	78%
Other construction-related products	$101,450	32%	23%	71%
TOTAL	**$2,869,672**	**23%**	**35%**	**64%**

Defense

	Total	PAC Pct	Dem Pct	Repub Pct

Defense Aerospace

Defense areospace contractors	$4,748,928	92%	55%	44%
TOTAL	**$4,748,928**	**92%**	**55%**	**44%**

Defense Electronics

Defense electronic contractors	$2,433,503	86%	56%	44%
TOTAL	**$2,433,503**	**86%**	**56%**	**44%**

Misc Defense

Defense research & development	$333,099	87%	45%	54%
Defense shipbuilders	$250,013	88%	55%	45%
Defense nuclear contractors	$11,200	0%	79%	21%
Ground-based & other weapons systems	$351,947	94%	50%	50%
Defense-related services	$162,949	68%	67%	33%
Defense, unclassified	$37,121	0%	53%	47%
TOTAL	**$1,146,329**	**83%**	**53%**	**47%**

Energy & Natural Resources

	Total	PAC Pct	Dem Pct	Repub Pct

Oil & Gas

Major (multinational) oil & gas producers	$2,699,335	84%	26%	74%
Independent oil & gas producers	$2,048,958	26%	39%	61%
Natural gas transmission & distribution	$2,393,866	76%	59%	41%
Oilfield service, equipment & exploration	$1,039,863	43%	33%	67%
Petroleum refining & marketing	$1,136,686	54%	36%	63%
Gasoline service stations	$522,515	66%	44%	56%
Fuel oil dealers	$78,047	5%	44%	56%
LPG/liquid propane dealers & producers	$63,550	34%	41%	59%
Oil & gas, diversified or unclassified	$1,645,123	22%	41%	59%
TOTAL	**$11,627,943**	**55%**	**40%**	**60%**

Mining

Mining, diversified	$119,210	34%	41%	59%
Coal mining	$918,336	60%	39%	61%
Metal mining & processing	$685,217	70%	38%	62%
Non-metallic mining	$89,334	55%	41%	59%

	Mining services & equipment	$32,663	8%	30%	70%
	TOTAL	**$1,844,760**	**61%**	**38%**	**62%**

Misc Energy

Energy, Natural Resources and Environment	$18,850	0%	17%	83%
Power plant construction & equipment	$713,803	97%	33%	67%
Nuclear plant construction, equipment & svcs	$231,075	94%	66%	34%
Alternate energy production & services	$32,250	49%	71%	29%
Misc energy production & distribution	$285,694	0%	61%	39%
TOTAL	**$1,281,672**	**79%**	**46%**	**54%**

Electric Utilities

Electric power utilities	$2,748,642	84%	58%	42%
Gas & electric utilities	$1,145,674	90%	50%	50%
Rural electric cooperatives	$661,154	96%	73%	27%
TOTAL	**$4,555,470**	**87%**	**58%**	**42%**

Environmental Services & Equipment

Environmental services, equipment & consulting	$187,347	31%	74%	25%

Waste Management

Waste management	$1,529,834	55%	56%	44%

Commercial Fishing

Commercial fishing	$313,509	35%	72%	27%

Finance, Insurance & Real Estate

	Total	PAC Pct	Dem Pct	Repub Pct
Commercial Banks				
Commercial banks & bank holding companies	$10,349,223	71%	52%	48%
Savings & Loans				
Savings banks and savings & loans	$1,318,827	70%	53%	47%
Misc Banks				
Banks & lending institutions, unclassified	$847,098	7%	48%	52%
Credit Unions				
Credit unions	$697,305	95%	65%	35%
Finance/Credit Companies				
Credit agencies & finance companies	$1,042,551	55%	51%	49%
Securities & Investment				
Securities, commodities & investment, diversified	$285,350	0%	49%	51%
Security brokers & investment companies	$10,383,262	17%	59%	41%
Investment banking	$3,149,515	21%	61%	38%
Commodity brokers & dealers	$1,325,102	72%	71%	29%
Stock exchanges	$136,150	61%	68%	32%
Venture capital	$656,843	34%	49%	51%
TOTAL	**$15,936,222**	**23%**	**60%**	**40%**
Insurance				
Insurance companies, brokers & agents, diversified	$9,155,955	54%	47%	53%
Accident & health insurance	$1,273,400	87%	55%	45%
Life insurance	$4,283,249	82%	57%	43%
Property & casualty insurance	$232,174	73%	35%	65%
TOTAL	**$14,944,778**	**65%**	**50%**	**50%**
Real Estate				
Real estate, diversified	$1,937,926	0%	56%	44%
Real Estate developers & subdividers	$3,797,455	8%	57%	43%
Real estate agents & managers	$7,626,300	40%	53%	46%
Title insurance & title abstract offices	$286,712	37%	49%	51%
Mobile home dealers & parks	$52,488	0%	42%	57%
Building operators & managers	$1,903,331	1%	58%	41%
Mortgage bankers & brokers	$801,285	44%	55%	45%
Other real estate services	$67,058	57%	59%	40%
TOTAL	**$16,472,555**	**24%**	**55%**	**45%**
Accountants				
Accountants	$4,877,052	51%	55%	45%

Misc Finance

	Total	PAC Pct	Dem Pct	Repub Pct
Misc financial services & consulting	$157,046	5%	53%	47%
Credit reporting services & collection agencies	$142,915	43%	36%	64%
Tax return services	$42,475	47%	56%	44%
Other financial services	$342,440	42%	46%	54%
Other finance, diversified or unclassified	$3,921,389	0%	45%	54%
TOTAL	**$4,606,265**	**5%**	**45%**	**54%**

Health

	Total	PAC Pct	Dem Pct	Repub Pct
Health Professionals				
Physicians	$11,939,475	32%	50%	49%
Psychiatrists & psychologists	$920,126	50%	84%	15%
Optometrists & ophthalmologists	$1,719,077	78%	60%	40%
Other physician specialists	$2,182,598	44%	50%	49%
Dentists	$2,281,306	70%	57%	43%
Chiropractors	$920,007	76%	70%	29%
Nurses	$481,420	74%	81%	19%
Pharmacists	$364,763	85%	70%	30%
Other non-physician health practitioners	$572,073	81%	74%	25%
Health professionals, unclassified	$40,946	1%	92%	6%
TOTAL	**$21,421,791**	**46%**	**56%**	**44%**
Hospitals & Nursing Homes				
Hospitals	$2,369,306	49%	64%	36%
Nursing homes	$1,239,146	40%	65%	34%
Drug & alcohol treatment hospitals	$5,000	0%	100%	0%
Health care institutions, diversified	$25,308	3%	58%	42%
TOTAL	**$3,638,760**	**46%**	**65%**	**35%**
Health Services				
Health care services	$243,446	29%	71%	28%
Home care services	$138,560	43%	73%	27%
HMOs	$448,789	41%	59%	40%
Outpatient health services (incl drug & alcohol)	$194,015	11%	66%	34%
Optical services (glasses & contact lenses)	$19,850	22%	39%	61%
Medical laboratories	$68,412	7%	61%	39%
AIDS treatment & testing	$9,200	0%	89%	11%
TOTAL	**$1,122,272**	**30%**	**65%**	**35%**
Pharmaceuticals/Health Products				
Health care products	$191,060	51%	56%	44%
Medical supplies manufacturing & sales	$787,026	41%	49%	51%
Personal health care products	$157,100	78%	47%	53%
Pharmaceutical manufacturing	$3,147,717	76%	47%	53%
Pharmaceutical wholesale/retail	$156,468	33%	37%	63%
TOTAL	**$4,439,371**	**67%**	**47%**	**53%**
Other & Unclassified				
Health, education & human resources, unclassified	$1,088,045	0%	61%	39%

Lawyers & Lobbyists

	Total	PAC Pct	Dem Pct	Repub Pct
Lawyers & Law Firms				
Attorneys & law firms	$38,233,716	16%	73%	27%
Misc legal services	$3,775	0%	65%	35%
TOTAL	**$38,237,491**	**16%**	**73%**	**27%**
Lobbyists & Public Relations				
Lobbyists & public relations	$4,353,571	6%	73%	27%
Registered foreign agents	$1,467,682	0%	68%	32%
TOTAL	**$5,821,253**	**5%**	**72%**	**28%**

Miscellaneous Business

	Total	PAC Pct	Dem Pct	Repub Pct
Business Associations				
General business associations	$92,254	94%	75%	24%
Chambers of commerce	$114,290	57%	62%	37%
Small business organizations	$369,231	99%	21%	79%
Pro-business organizations	$143,181	96%	9%	91%
General commerce, unclassified or diversified	$215,710	0%	38%	58%
TOTAL	**$934,666**	**70%**	**33%**	**66%**
Food & Beverage				
NOTE: Food manufacturers are listed under Agriculture				
Artificial sweeteners and food additives	$14,700	24%	54%	46%
Restaurants & drinking establishments	$2,994,793	45%	35%	64%
Food catering & food services	$130,840	35%	40%	58%
Confectionary processors & manufacturers	$111,490	20%	34%	66%
Fish Processing	$168,410	13%	46%	54%
Non-alcoholic beverages	$388,539	70%	51%	49%
Beverage bottling & distribution	$255,265	53%	48%	52%
TOTAL	**$4,064,037**	**46%**	**38%**	**61%**
Beer, Wine & Liquor				
Beer	$347,864	46%	51%	49%
Wine & distilled spirits manufacturing	$1,356,172	59%	67%	33%
Beer & liquor wholesalers	$2,273,554	52%	50%	50%
Liquor stores	$95,627	1%	58%	42%
Alcohol, unclassified	$6,400	0%	62%	38%
TOTAL	**$4,079,617**	**52%**	**56%**	**44%**
Retail Sales				
Retail trade, diversified	$580,229	64%	45%	55%
Apparel & accessory stores	$564,284	16%	54%	46%
Consumer electronics & computer stores	$122,350	0%	51%	48%
Department, variety & convenience stores	$998,206	69%	42%	58%
Furniture & appliance stores	$284,881	0%	46%	54%
Hardware & building materials stores	$98,547	0%	40%	59%
Miscellaneous retail stores	$908,808	1%	65%	34%
Catalog & mail order houses	$225,963	42%	48%	51%
Direct sales	$209,979	24%	16%	84%
Vending machine sales & services	$79,170	0%	37%	62%
Drug stores	$457,696	43%	52%	48%
TOTAL	**$4,530,113**	**33%**	**49%**	**51%**
Misc Services				
Equipment rental & leasing	$324,813	50%	43%	57%
Funeral services	$306,098	21%	62%	38%
Laundries & dry cleaners	$119,264	3%	43%	57%
Miscellaneous repair services	$31,765	0%	44%	54%
Pest control	$156,520	44%	50%	50%
Physical fitness centers	$84,190	0%	50%	49%
Video tape rental	$42,550	0%	55%	45%
Other services	$423,750	1%	57%	42%
TOTAL	**$1,488,950**	**20%**	**52%**	**47%**
Business Services				
Beauty & barber shops	$75,363	0%	62%	37%
Advertising & public relations services	$1,256,983	2%	59%	40%
Direct mail advertising services	$198,916	58%	38%	62%
Outdoor advertising services	$644,017	37%	59%	41%
Commercial photography, art & graphic design	$217,155	0%	57%	41%
Employment agencies	$382,844	22%	47%	53%
Management consultants & services	$1,697,109	0%	53%	47%
Marketing research services	$211,325	55%	53%	47%
Security services	$374,126	34%	44%	55%
Other business services	$2,520,185	3%	59%	39%
TOTAL	**$7,578,023**	**10%**	**56%**	**44%**
Recreation & Live Entertainment				
Professional sports, arenas & related equip & svcs	$265,427	4%	61%	39%
Amusement parks	$28,650	0%	21%	79%

Misc recreation/entertainment	$177,415	5%	72%	27%
TOTAL	**$471,492**	**4%**	**62%**	**37%**

Casinos & Gambling

Casinos, racetracks & gambling	$740,605	31%	69%	31%

Lodging/Tourism

Lodging & tourism, diversified	$76,350	26%	49%	51%
Hotels & motels	$1,014,488	29%	48%	52%
Resorts	$127,933	14%	49%	51%
Travel agents	$376,368	18%	58%	41%
TOTAL	**$1,595,139**	**25%**	**50%**	**49%**

Other Miscellaneous Non-Manufacturing Business

Water Utilities	$157,050	74%	54%	46%
Wholesale trade	$344,191	33%	38%	62%
Warehousing	$109,090	0%	40%	60%
TOTAL	**$610,331**	**38%**	**42%**	**58%**

Chemical & Related Manufacturing

Chemicals	$2,184,662	57%	31%	68%
Explosives	$23,300	54%	74%	26%
Household cleansers & chemicals	$266,042	66%	44%	56%
Plastics & rubber processing & products	$528,022	12%	24%	76%
Paints, solvents & coatings	$74,393	20%	29%	71%
Adhesives & sealants	$12,200	20%	34%	66%
TOTAL	**$3,088,619**	**49%**	**31%**	**68%**

Steel Production

Steel production	$870,603	32%	38%	62%

Misc Manufacturing & Distributing

Manufacturing	$233,421	0%	32%	67%
Manmade fibers	$194,800	96%	47%	53%
Heavy industrial manufacturing	$135,877	0%	62%	38%
Smelting and non-petroleum refining	$76,440	0%	44%	56%
Industrial/commercial equipment & materials	$1,651,109	29%	26%	74%
Recycling of scrap metal, paper, plastics, etc.	$220,346	26%	65%	35%
Personal products manufacturing, diversified	$80,504	0%	41%	59%
Clothing & accessories	$802,122	1%	61%	39%
Shoes & leather products	$227,913	24%	52%	48%
Toiletries & cosmetics	$344,012	16%	47%	53%
Jewelry	$291,270	2%	79%	21%
Toys	$63,659	0%	37%	63%
Sporting goods sales & manufacturing	$73,015	4%	47%	52%
Household & office products	$215,248	15%	42%	58%
Furniture & wood products	$378,034	23%	32%	68%
Office machines	$130,763	42%	42%	58%
Household appliances	$158,950	54%	32%	68%
Fabricated metal products	$540,047	8%	28%	71%
Hardware & tools	$80,665	8%	23%	77%
Electroplating, polishing & related services	$58,225	7%	26%	74%
Small arms & ammunition	$43,381	0%	31%	69%
Electrical lighting products	$13,100	0%	41%	59%
Paper, glass & packaging materials	$222,678	19%	39%	61%
Paper packaging materials	$502,071	71%	18%	81%
Glass products	$461,372	82%	34%	66%
Metal cans & containers	$41,750	44%	34%	66%
Precision instruments	$76,675	0%	34%	65%
Optical instruments & lenses	$33,200	0%	12%	87%
Photographic equipment & supplies	$22,450	0%	49%	47%
Clocks & watches	$8,500	53%	74%	26%
TOTAL	**$7,381,597**	**27%**	**39%**	**61%**

Textiles

Textiles & fabrics	$1,044,215	34%	56%	43%

Transportation

	Total	PAC Pct	Dem Pct	Repub Pct
Air Transport				
Airlines	$1,242,710	77%	61%	38%
Air freight	$51,000	45%	21%	78%
Express delivery services	$2,224,752	99%	59%	41%
Aircraft manufacturers	$423,090	81%	56%	44%
Aircraft parts & equipment	$913,962	68%	47%	53%
General aviation (private pilots)	$491,356	98%	55%	45%
Aviation services & airports	$155,237	33%	53%	47%
Space vehicles & components	$35,150	67%	64%	36%
Air transport, diversified	$117,954	8%	42%	58%
TOTAL	**$5,655,211**	**83%**	**56%**	**44%**
Automotive				
Auto manufacturers	$786,478	77%	55%	45%
Truck/automotive parts & accessories	$840,264	44%	25%	75%
Auto dealers, new & used	$3,211,769	56%	36%	64%
Auto dealers, Japanese imports	$1,231,814	82%	28%	72%
Auto repair	$76,294	4%	56%	43%
Car & truck rental agencies	$298,468	29%	46%	53%
Misc automotive	$49,417	0%	38%	62%
TOTAL	**$6,494,504**	**59%**	**36%**	**64%**
Trucking				
Trucking companies & services	$1,702,073	57%	49%	51%
Truck & trailer manufacturers	$86,750	47%	23%	77%
Misc trucking	$32,733	11%	35%	65%
TOTAL	**$1,821,556**	**56%**	**48%**	**52%**
Railroads				
Railroads	$1,929,846	88%	49%	51%
Railroad industry services	$71,254	61%	75%	25%
Manufacturers of railroad equipment	$146,915	27%	31%	69%
Misc railroad transportation	$31,981	0%	37%	62%
TOTAL	**$2,179,996**	**82%**	**48%**	**52%**
Sea Transport				
Ship building & repair	$526,466	50%	47%	53%
Sea freight & passenger services	$1,347,755	63%	56%	44%
Sea transport, diversified	$188,130	1%	64%	36%
TOTAL	**$2,062,351**	**54%**	**54%**	**46%**
Misc Transport				
Buses & Taxis	$57,725	23%	62%	38%
Bus services	$207,305	51%	65%	35%
Taxicabs	$108,436	21%	56%	44%
Local freight & delivery services	$83,700	3%	44%	56%
Motorcycles, snowmobiles & other motorized vehicles	$73,275	88%	27%	73%
Bicycles & other non-motorized recreational transport	$22,434	99%	36%	64%
Motor homes & camper trailers	$24,851	0%	16%	84%
Pleasure boats	$61,200	77%	52%	47%
Recreational transport, diversified	$9,500	0%	26%	74%
Other transportation	$127,646	0%	29%	66%
TOTAL	**$776,072**	**36%**	**48%**	**51%**

Labor

	Total	PAC Pct	Dem Pct	Repub Pct
Building Trade Unions				
Building trade unions	$6,904,679	99%	94%	6%
Industrial Unions				
Communications & hi-tech unions	$1,426,390	100%	98%	1%
Intl Brotherhood of Electrical Workers (IBEW)	$1,575,999	99%	96%	3%
Mining unions	$459,600	100%	98%	2%
Energy-related unions (non-mining)	$137,840	100%	96%	1%
Manufacturing unions	$6,906,117	100%	98%	1%
TOTAL	**$10,505,946**	**100%**	**98%**	**2%**

Transportation Unions

	Total	PAC Pct	Dem Pct	Repub Pct
Transportation unions	$1,750	0%	100%	0%
Air transport unions	$1,657,643	100%	89%	11%
Teamsters Union	$2,532,956	100%	94%	5%
Railroad unions	$1,622,854	100%	97%	3%
Mechant marine & longshoremen unions	$3,125,766	100%	82%	18%
Other transportation unions	$1,279,765	100%	97%	3%
TOTAL	**$10,220,734**	**100%**	**91%**	**9%**

Public Sector Unions

	Total	PAC Pct	Dem Pct	Repub Pct
Federal employees unions	$1,882,828	100%	84%	16%
State & local govt employee unions	$1,955,613	100%	97%	2%
Teachers unions	$3,477,117	100%	96%	3%
US Postal Service unions & associations	$3,822,198	100%	89%	10%
Police & firefighters unions & associations	$610,625	99%	93%	6%
TOTAL	**$11,748,381**	**100%**	**92%**	**8%**

Misc Unions

	Total	PAC Pct	Dem Pct	Repub Pct
Labor unions, diversified	$869,240	96%	99%	1%
Agricultural labor unions	$1,940	48%	100%	0%
General commercial unions	$1,250	0%	80%	20%
Food service & related unions	$570,217	97%	95%	5%
Retail trade unions	$1,518,786	100%	97%	2%
Commercial service unions	$1,950	100%	100%	0%
Entertainment unions	$31,750	100%	97%	3%
Health worker unions	$15,980	100%	81%	0%
Other commercial unions	$744,681	100%	98%	1%
Other unions	$164,063	100%	100%	0%
TOTAL	**$3,919,857**	**99%**	**97%**	**2%**

Ideological/Single-Issue

	Total	PAC Pct	Dem Pct	Repub Pct
Republican/Conservative				
Republican/Conservative	$2,479,934	32%	2%	97%
Democratic/Liberal				
Democratic/Liberal	$2,658,027	52%	98%	1%
Leadership PACs				
Democratic leadership PAC	$1,342,037	100%	100%	0%
Republican leadership PAC	$851,893	99%	1%	99%
Democratic officials, candidates & former members	$26,384	100%	100%	0%
Republican officials, candidates & former members	$10,050	100%	0%	100%
State & local candidate committees	$210,571	100%	27%	73%
TOTAL	**$2,440,935**	**99%**	**59%**	**41%**
Foreign & Defense Policy				
Foreign policy	$355,259	67%	61%	38%
Defense policy, Pro-Defense	$191,985	92%	25%	75%
Defense policy, Pro-Peace	$370,918	53%	92%	0%
TOTAL	**$918,162**	**67%**	**66%**	**30%**
Pro-Israel				
Pro-Israel	$7,401,113	54%	71%	29%
Abortion Policy				
Abortion policy, Pro-Life	$486,407	85%	11%	89%
Abortion policy, Pro-Choice	$1,317,768	65%	84%	15%
TOTAL	**$1,804,175**	**71%**	**64%**	**35%**
Gun Rights/Gun Control				
Pro-Guns	$1,854,555	98%	35%	65%
Anti-Guns	$169,512	95%	84%	16%
TOTAL	**$2,024,067**	**98%**	**39%**	**61%**
Womens Issues				
Womens issues	$3,725,735	42%	84%	9%
Human Rights				
Human Rights	$74,507	28%	99%	1%
Gay & lesbian rights & issues	$928,654	82%	90%	8%

Minority/ethnic groups	$365,619	65%	55%	45%
Childrens' rights	$453,800	100%	96%	4%
Health & welfare policy	$512,855	29%	89%	11%
TOTAL	**$2,335,435**	**70%**	**86%**	**13%**

Misc Issues

Third-party committees	$15,769	15%	46%	0%
Consumer groups	$7,535	61%	100%	0%
Fiscal & tax policy	$111,404	86%	4%	96%
Elderly issues/social security	$1,167,425	100%	90%	10%
Animal rights	$24,850	21%	100%	0%
Labor, anti-union	$374,006	92%	1%	98%
Environmental policy	$1,633,398	73%	94%	5%
Other single-issue/ideological groups	$209,944	64%	30%	69%
TOTAL	**$3,544,331**	**83%**	**76%**	**23%**

Other & Unknown

	Total	PAC Pct	Dem Pct	Repub Pct
Non-Profit Institutions				
Non-Profits	$130,204	0%	89%	10%
Non-profit foundations	$222,569	0%	61%	39%
Museums, art galleries, libraries, etc.	$165,447	0%	71%	28%
TOTAL	**$518,220**	**0%**	**71%**	**28%**
Civil Servants/Public Officials				
Civil servant/public employee	$2,995,085	0%	62%	37%
Public official (elected or appointed)	$152,295	0%	60%	40%
Courts & justice system	$345,231	0%	71%	28%
TOTAL	**$3,492,611**	**0%**	**63%**	**36%**
Education				
Schools & colleges	$2,355,025	0%	72%	26%
Medical schools	$207,488	0%	78%	22%
Law schools	$145,745	0%	85%	14%
Technical, business and vocational schools & services	$373,522	34%	59%	41%
Public school teachers, administrators & officials	$674,494	0%	78%	21%
Education, unclassified	$585,559	0%	66%	29%
TOTAL	**$4,341,833**	**3%**	**72%**	**27%**
Retired				
Retired	$15,930,210	0%	45%	54%
Other				
Welfare & Social Work	$392,566	48%	89%	10%
Military	$125,803	0%	46%	50%
Other	$662,357	9%	70%	35%
TOTAL	**$1,180,726**	**21%**	**74%**	**29%**
Homemakers & Other Non-Income Earners				
Homemakers, students & other non-income earners	$13,650,755	0%	48%	51%
Unknown				
Unknown PACs	$85,426	100%	75%	22%
No employer listed or found	$33,504,033	0%	49%	51%
Generic occupation - impossible to assign category	$3,021,287	0%	46%	52%
Employer listed but category unknown	**$34,413,382**	**0%**	**51%**	**48%**

Appendix B: Members' Totals by Sector

The charts below show the industry-by-industry breakdown of contributions received by each member of Congress elected (or already in office) in 1992. The figures include both PACs and individual contributions of $200 or more. They are shown in thousands of dollars, rounded off to the nearest $1,000. A brief rundown of the industries and interest groups included in each sector can be found on pages 42-43. Detailed explanations and analyses of their spending patterns are provided on pages 44-93.

One important caveat: Senate totals cover the period 1987-92, *but do not include individual contributions made before 1989.* The totals for senators elected in 1988 will therefore be low, since most of their individual contributions were received in 1987-88. (PAC contributions for the entire 1987-1992 period are included). The totals for House members cover the 1991-92 election cycle.

To help identify the leading recipients of funds from a particular sector, members who rank in the top 10 percent of each sector are marked with an asterisk (*). The top-ranking recipient from each sector is marked with a dagger (†).

Senate

Name	Agriculture	Comm/Elec	Construction	Defense	Energy	Finance	Health	Law/Lobby	Transport	Misc Bus	Labor	Ideol
Akaka, Daniel K. (D-Hawaii).	$67	$53	$126	$25	$43	$174	$63	$87	$65	$85	$412*	$241
Baucus, Max (D-Mont).	$159	$132	$46	$4	$163	$532	$188	$264	$110	$227	$268	$232
Bennett, Robert F. (R-Utah).	$34	$33	$14	$22	$80	$102	$36	$23	$62	$63	$0	$28
Bentsen, Lloyd (D-Texas).	$154	$140	$97	$92	$348*	$745	$192	$205	$156	$236	$185	$94
Biden, Joseph R. Jr. (D-Del).	$9	$132	$35	$4	$21	$224	$42	$234	$25	$107	$286	$178
Bingaman, Jeff (D-NM).	$60	$23	$25	$127	$130	$140	$93	$121	$41	$52	$273	$241
Bond, Christopher S. (R-Mo).	$360*	$160	$183*	$106	$235	$848*	$261	$249	$198*	$510*	$30	$146
Boren, David L. (D-Okla).	$67	$36	$24	$4	$201	$212	$49	$172	$23	$70	$0	$21
Boxer, Barbara (D-Calif).	$42	$485*	$63	$4	$33	$363	$287	$687*	$28	$258	$327	$848*
Bradley, Bill (D-NJ).	$76	$528†	$200*	$38	$197	$1930†	$313*	$1060†	$133	$496*	$228	$282
Breaux, John B. (D-La).	$206	$187	$80	$54	$348*	$414	$167	$283	$264*	$273	$151	$64
Brown, Hank (R-Colo).	$205	$173	$140*	$52	$245	$567	$115	$167	$126	$301	$22	$186
Bryan, Richard H. (D-Nev).	$25	$33	$46	$1	$31	$170	$81	$66	$52	$162	$312	$173
Bumpers, Dale (D-Ark).	$271	$66	$67	$29	$178	$278	$94	$214	$77	$130	$66	$38
Burns, Conrad (R-Mont).	$95	$90	$29	$12	$71	$68	$10	$22	$82	$52	$0	$118
Byrd, Robert C. (D-WVa).	$79	$42	$41	$106	$127	$157	$41	$40	$61	$70	$234	$59
Campbell, Ben N. (D-Colo).	$101	$53	$8	$3	$99	$126	$83	$130	$40	$77	$270	$144
Chafee, John H. (R-RI).	$53	$79	$72	$78	$66	$373	$146	$38	$80	$136	$25	$77
Coats, Daniel R. (R-Ind).	$344*	$235*	$367†	$359†	$390*	$821*	$517*	$188	$246*	$611*	$7	$268
Cochran, Thad (R-Miss).	$309*	$29	$46	$81	$92	$136	$76	$72	$50	$79	$25	$29
Cohen, William S. (R-Maine).	$72	$59	$60	$98	$25	$233	$77	$64	$25	$107	$36	$152
Conrad, Kent (D-ND).	$285*	$47	$19	$10	$279	$246	$98	$170	$74	$101	$331	$168
Coverdell, Paul (R-Ga).	$231	$59	$116	$4	$111	$472	$146	$226	$77	$370	$0	$156
Craig, Larry E. (R-Idaho).	$232	$40	$62	$13	$232	$163	$51	$27	$87	$103	$6	$65
D'Amato, Alfonse M. (R-NY).	$175	$209	$326*	$146	$121	$1540*	$234	$505	$152	$528*	$129	$204
Danforth, John C. (R-Mo).	$77	$125	$59	$80	$93	$271	$90	$33	$160	$148	$11	$78
Daschle, Tom (D-SD).	$244	$153	$36	$11	$81	$548	$322*	$291	$111	$288	$325	$237
DeConcini, Dennis (D-Ariz).	$101	$117	$40	$137	$80	$328	$98	$121	$48	$105	$180	$114
Dodd, Christopher J. (D-Conn).	$96	$219*	$95	$54	$55	$1120*	$211	$339	$92	$186	$307	$257
Dole, Bob (R-Kan).	$430*	$230*	$100	$66	$319*	$795*	$186	$268	$246*	$359	$10	$91
Domenici, Pete V. (R-NM).	$91	$42	$50	$101	$368*	$307	$90	$107	$69	$129	$34	$71
Dorgan, Byron L. (D-ND).	$99	$28	$4	$2	$49	$161	$57	$54	$41	$72	$219	$62
Durenberger, Dave (R-Minn).	$207	$93	$91	$52	$93	$382	$308*	$81	$118	$220	$70	$236
Exon, Jim (D-Neb).	$150	$154	$33	$161*	$67	$298	$75	$138	$267*	$121	$292	$181
Faircloth, Lauch (R-NC).	$195	$45	$89	$15	$62	$166	$71	$44	$87	$194	$0	$97
Feingold, Russell (D-Wis).	$20	$40	$11	$0	$2	$86	$105	$204	$5	$57	$235	$124

* Ranks in top 10% of House in receipts from this sector
† Leading House recipient of funds from this sector

1324

Breakdown of Contributions by Industry & Interest Group Sectors
Totals in Thousands of Dollars

Senate

Name	Agriculture	Comm/Elec	Construction	Defense	Energy	Finance	Health	Law/Lobby	Transport	Misc Bus	Labor	Ideol
Feinstein, Dianne (D-Calif).	$134	$375*	$137	$17	$72	$780*	$329*	$707*	$93	$405*	$299	$543*
Ford, Wendell H. (D-Ky).	$183	$97	$57	$15	$266	$291	$81	$188	$197*	$178	$240	$39
Glenn, John (D-Ohio).	$38	$79	$70	$169*	$114	$384	$173	$251	$85	$203	$396*	$294
Gore, Al (D-Tenn).	$92	$212	$72	$121	$91	$385	$128	$307	$123	$131	$397*	$191
Gorton, Slade (R-Wash).	$173	$121	$85	$82	$137	$204	$56	$59	$158	$155	$13	$98
Graham, Bob (D-Fla).	$148	$157	$132	$33	$150	$546	$226	$464	$125	$265	$193	$145
Gramm, Phil (R-Texas).	$635†	$212	$364*	$217*	$1061†	$1572*	$624†	$785*	$307*	$914†	$26	$267
Grassley, Charles E. (R-Iowa).	$209	$120	$72	$11	$63	$323	$193	$88	$125	$149	$8	$140
Gregg, Judd (R-NH).	$39	$45	$27	$20	$36	$160	$86	$35	$37	$103	$0	$21
Harkin, Tom (D-Iowa).	$257	$111	$42	$72	$70	$491	$353*	$311	$94	$177	$682†	$744*
Hatch, Orrin G. (R-Utah).	$143	$107	$113	$69	$116	$252	$227	$74	$91	$225	$13	$72
Hatfield, Mark O. (R-Ore).	$242	$109	$79	$73	$173	$275	$100	$126	$124	$135	$118	$102
Heflin, Howell (D-Ala).	$421*	$168	$77	$64	$283	$403	$112	$496	$112	$167	$200	$221
Helms, Jesse (R-NC).	$318*	$79	$109	$31	$110	$271	$135	$83	$94	$321	$1	$363
Hollings, Ernest F. (D-SC).	$179	$437*	$73	$148	$122	$387	$143	$559*	$331†	$368	$154	$114
Inouye, Daniel K. (D-Hawaii).	$58	$148	$64	$114	$27	$426	$142	$171	$145	$179	$173	$235
Jeffords, James M. (R-Vt).	$102	$33	$59	$13	$28	$111	$60	$7	$34	$79	$96	$58
Johnston, J. Bennett (D-La).	$171	$102	$91	$189*	$664*	$307	$105	$305	$123	$143	$138	$211
Kassebaum, Nancy (R-Kan).	$28	$22	$16	$3	$27	$81	$24	$11	$12	$40	$3	$18
Kempthorne, Dirk (R-Idaho).	$223	$54	$60	$17	$113	$110	$28	$21	$63	$103	$0	$44
Kennedy, Edward M. (D-Mass).	$12	$48	$23	$21	$21	$208	$122	$178	$20	$116	$131	$72
Kerrey, Bob (D-Neb).	$139	$68	$17	$9	$42	$182	$84	$78	$84	$46	$469*	$259
Kerry, John (D-Mass).	$40	$353*	$145*	$10	$68	$853*	$143	$670*	$42	$380*	$8	$299
Kohl, Herb (D-Wis).	$1	$0	$0	$0	$0	$0	$0	$0	$2	$0	$2	$0
Lautenberg, Frank R. (D-NJ).	$45	$141	$138*	$66	$76	$558	$222	$321	$196*	$211	$377*	$443*
Leahy, Patrick J. (D-Vt).	$87	$115	$11	$15	$10	$106	$17	$115	$12	$71	$82	$74
Levin, Carl (D-Mich).	$93	$145	$95	$113	$88	$615	$168	$508*	$131	$328	$405*	$868*
Lieberman, Joseph I. (D-Conn).	$26	$38	$54	$9	$33	$349	$65	$151	$44	$157	$87	$166
Lott, Trent (R-Miss).	$190	$106	$81	$94	$154	$198	$49	$38	$106	$199	$23	$135
Lugar, Richard G. (R-Ind).	$302*	$93	$102	$57	$107	$296	$119	$76	$114	$193	$3	$40
Mack, Connie (R-Fla).	$188	$120	$133	$77	$173	$432	$179	$117	$163	$258	$26	$190
McCain, John (R-Ariz).	$152	$131	$83	$143	$161	$337	$257	$103	$167	$246	$53	$204
McConnell, Mitch (R-Ky).	$375*	$76	$144*	$30	$391*	$392	$215	$189	$103	$296	$3	$322
Metzenbaum, Howard (D-Ohio).	$11	$41	$14	$7	$17	$35	$46	$38	$25	$34	$347*	$405*
Mikulski, Barbara A. (D-Md).	$47	$93	$45	$159*	$47	$221	$179	$180	$53	$151	$329	$248
Mitchell, George J. (D-Maine).	$40	$28	$20	$21	$27	$172	$107	$20	$24	$51	$144	$93
Moseley-Braun, Carol (D-Ill).	$36	$69	$24	$1	$21	$229	$127	$357	$26	$108	$282	$451*
Moynihan, Daniel P. (D-NY).	$17	$82	$84	$14	$70	$469	$119	$140	$59	$123	$195	$117
Murkowski, Frank H. (R-Alaska).	$65	$76	$89	$55	$239	$210	$70	$103	$149	$150	$20	$85
Murray, Patty (D-Wash).	$11	$21	$1	$0	$25	$24	$40	$41	$14	$23	$258	$200
Nickles, Don (R-Okla).	$230	$99	$106	$142	$637*	$432	$184	$179	$137	$209	$4	$117
Nunn, Sam (D-Ga).	$133	$85	$82	$114	$75	$410	$82	$179	$52	$182	$41	$36
Packwood, Bob (R-Ore).	$192	$332*	$47	$9	$101	$572	$303*	$289	$267*	$371*	$95	$306
Pell, Claiborne (D-RI).	$21	$74	$33	$29	$39	$305	$74	$129	$49	$86	$285	$394*
Pressler, Larry (R-SD).	$117	$132	$59	$9	$68	$462	$90	$93	$167	$165	$18	$251
Pryor, David (D-Ark).	$227	$36	$21	$5	$61	$289	$82	$119	$46	$76	$62	$18
Reid, Harry (D-Nev).	$58	$79	$119	$53	$166	$233	$235	$271	$110	$499*	$266	$185
Riegle, Donald W. Jr. (D-Mich).	$58	$56	$28	$20	$67	$480	$80	$75	$113	$86	$256	$135
Robb, Charles S. (D-Va).	$78	$64	$36	$64	$107	$184	$60	$36	$52	$83	$135	$76
Rockefeller, John IV (D-WVa).	$107	$174	$80	$11	$231	$641	$482*	$287	$132	$301	$242	$227
Roth, William V. Jr. (R-Del).	$40	$43	$38	$35	$71	$243	$76	$26	$65	$91	$22	$62
Sarbanes, Paul S. (D-Md).	$11	$11	$23	$4	$7	$109	$14	$18	$27	$38	$286	$81
Sasser, Jim (D-Tenn).	$107	$43	$69	$119	$52	$374	$90	$58	$74	$102	$301	$144
Shelby, Richard C. (D-Ala).	$193	$165	$100	$172*	$272	$646	$226	$423	$108	$152	$156	$184
Simon, Paul (D-Ill).	$133	$195	$60	$10	$80	$553	$236	$644*	$99	$309	$599*	$892†

* Ranks in top 10% of House of Representatives in receipts from this sector
† Leading House recipient of funds from this sector

Breakdown of Contributions by Industry & Interest Group Sectors
Totals in Thousands of Dollars

Senate

Name	Agriculture	Comm/Elec	Construction	Defense	Energy	Finance	Health	Law/Lobby	Transport	Misc Bus	Labor	Ideol
Simpson, Alan K. (R-Wyo).	$86	$88	$54	$23	$194	$243	$64	$61	$84	$117	$6	$27
Smith, Robert C. (R-NH).	$70	$35	$95	$95	$78	$202	$76	$24	$62	$144	$3	$113
Specter, Arlen (R-Pa).	$241	$315*	$297*	$205*	$343*	$1195*	$531*	$911*	$175	$802*	$255	$385
Stevens, Ted (R-Alaska).	$36	$148	$34	$199*	$139	$151	$51	$104	$103	$67	$113	$54
Thurmond, Strom (R-SC).	$96	$42	$68	$120	$59	$217	$87	$112	$44	$139	$2	$103
Wallop, Malcolm (R-Wyo).	$82	$47	$33	$84	$238	$189	$53	$42	$69	$102	$6	$83
Warner, John W. (R-Va).	$98	$46	$111	$207*	$120	$258	$61	$120	$113	$134	$34	$74
Wellstone, Paul (D-Minn).	$21	$22	$3	$0	$6	$18	$19	$42	$4	$16	$274	$115
Wofford, Harris (D-Pa).	$37	$104	$65	$10	$122	$345	$156	$724*	$34	$163	$464*	$391*

House of Representatives

Name	Agriculture	Comm/Elec	Construction	Defense	Energy	Finance	Health	Law/Lobby	Transport	Misc Bus	Labor	Ideol
Abercrombie, Neil (D-Hawaii).	$9	$4	$14	$2	$5	$26	$3	$14	$14	$7	$116	$11
Ackerman, Gary L. (D-NY).	$6	$19	$15	$2	$4	$115	$64*	$24	$19	$37	$186*	$26
Allard, Wayne (R-Colo).	$87*	$19	$16	$2	$40	$38	$27	$5	$30	$37	$23	$12
Andrews, Michael A. (D-Texas).	$28	$40	$20	$18	$116*	$203*	$81*	$112*	$35	$61*	$41	$12
Andrews, Robert E. (D-NJ).	$14	$15	$31*	$1	$15	$45	$45	$47	$12	$22	$166*	$24
Andrews, Thomas H. (D-Maine).	$7	$17	$6	$13	$4	$58	$42	$55	$8	$17	$213*	$94*
Applegate, Douglas (D-Ohio).	$8	$4	$2	$0	$8	$7	$2	$1	$10	$2	$39	$2
Archer, Bill (R-Texas).	$3	$0	$0	$0	$4	$19	$4	$3	$0	$6	$0	$0
Armey, Dick (R-Texas).	$23	$18	$22	$17	$31	$66	$11	$4	$30	$34	$0	$10
Aspin, Les (D-Wis).	$32	$30	$24	$221*	$39	$131*	$37	$116*	$32	$89*	$100	$98*
Bacchus, Jim (D-Fla).	$30	$25	$23	$22	$14	$136*	$99*	$72*	$21	$26	$178*	$54*
Bachus, Spencer (R-Ala).	$17	$18	$48*	$1	$29	$98	$33	$37	$9	$47	$0	$13
Baesler, Scotty (D-Ky).	$14	$2	$20	$0	$9	$25	$19	$13	$19	$8	$2	$0
Baker, Bill (R-Calif).	$29	$15	$36*	$3	$19	$112	$36	$13	$22	$61*	$1	$24
Baker, Richard H. (R-La).	$22	$13	$24	$4	$32	$203*	$49	$61*	$38	$37	$2	$7
Ballenger, Cass (R-NC).	$34	$14	$13	$5	$14	$26	$15	$5	$25	$57	$1	$9
Barcia, James A. (D-Mich).	$9	$7	$7	$1	$14	$17	$20	$6	$14	$19	$38	$16
Barlow, Tom (D-Ky).	$9	$2	$1	$0	$3	$8	$6	$6	$6	$1	$58	$6
Barrett, Bill (R-Neb).	$63*	$11	$12	$0	$12	$78	$25	$2	$20	$30	$1	$7
Barrett, Thomas (D-Wis).	$6	$8	$4	$0	$3	$35	$25	$28	$10	$9	$65	$7
Bartlett, Roscoe G. (R-Md).	$8	$5	$13	$1	$23	$10	$7	$1	$9	$21	$0	$13
Barton, Joe L. (R-Texas).	$40	$69*	$38*	$42*	$137*	$93	$51	$41	$54*	$60	$1	$17
Bateman, Herbert H. (R-Va).	$34	$12	$34*	$104*	$42	$76	$30	$18	$38	$45	$16	$10
Becerra, Xavier (D-Calif).	$5	$7	$5	$2	$1	$20	$20	$23	$2	$7	$54	$14
Beilenson, Anthony C. (D-Calif).	$1	$57*	$7	$0	$2	$81	$25	$77*	$2	$30	$0	$48
Bentley, Helen Delich (R-Md).	$27	$17	$37*	$17	$41	$76	$24	$51	$84*	$69*	$51	$12
Bereuter, Doug (R-Neb).	$35	$8	$10	$6	$7	$104	$13	$6	$14	$11	$2	$1
Berman, Howard L. (D-Calif).	$5	$102*	$6	$4	$6	$70	$32	$82*	$12	$34	$78	$27
Bevill, Tom (D-Ala).	$12	$9	$18	$6	$40	$18	$7	$22	$12	$1	$11	$5
Bilbray, James (D-Nev).	$8	$9	$7	$22	$20	$50	$50	$37	$11	$62*	$91	$25
Bilirakis, Michael (R-Fla).	$45	$58*	$23	$3	$40	$73	$109*	$16	$16	$46	$12	$19
Bishop, Sanford (D-Ga).	$14	$3	$5	$0	$6	$60	$25	$18	$10	$18	$36	$15
Blackwell, Lucien E. (D-Pa).	$3	$3	$10	$5	$5	$22	$13	$47	$10	$10	$102	$6
Bliley, Thomas J. Jr. (R-Va).	$89*	$52*	$8	$6	$64*	$101	$87*	$24	$33	$55	$3	$3
Blute, Peter (R-Mass).	$2	$7	$7	$1	$7	$30	$32	$14	$4	$31	$0	$14

* Ranks in top 10% of House/Senate in PAC receipts from this sector in 1991-92
† Ranks as leading House/Senate recipient in PAC receipts from this sector in 1991-92

Breakdown of Contributions by Industry & Interest Group Sectors
Totals in Thousands of Dollars

Name	Agriculture	Comm/Elec	Construction	Defense	Energy	Finance	Health	Law/Lobby	Transport	Misc Bus	Labor	Ideol
Boehlert, Sherwood (R-NY).	$18	$16	$13	$6	$13	$37	$20	$7	$27	$28	$55	$10
Boehner, John A. (R-Ohio).	$64*	$24	$32*	$4	$17	$45	$29	$2	$22	$52	$1	$11
Bonilla, Henry (R-Texas).	$36	$17	$17	$2	$62*	$67	$34	$13	$11	$37	$0	$9
Bonior, David E. (D-Mich).	$82*	$88*	$19	$18	$42	$160*	$83*	$56	$89*	$59	$287*	$85*
Borski, Robert A. (D-Pa).	$2	$13	$23	$11	$11	$37	$18	$41	$38	$36	$150*	$13
Boucher, Rick (D-Va).	$35	$59*	$9	$9	$59*	$102	$47	$30	$26	$26	$51	$7
Brewster, Bill (D-Okla).	$37	$16	$20	$4	$72*	$26	$53	$24	$33	$34	$15	$15
Brooks, Jack (D-Texas).	$21	$84*	$16	$12	$34	$85	$26	$71*	$35	$36	$92	$17
Browder, Glen (D-Ala).	$16	$6	$4	$22	$8	$19	$12	$14	$6	$10	$24	$4
Brown, Corrine (D-Fla).	$5	$10	$9	$0	$5	$11	$10	$15	$7	$3	$57	$48
Brown, George E. Jr. (D-Calif).	$49	$49*	$26	$66*	$49*	$43	$16	$43	$22	$14	$173*	$69*
Brown, Sherrod (R-Ohio).	$3	$7	$3	$1	$5	$49	$28	$40	$9	$19	$148*	$49
Bryant, John (D-Texas).	$29	$54*	$5	$1	$31	$54	$64*	$85*	$33	$27	$100	$13
Bunning, Jim (R-Ky).	$64*	$42*	$24	$5	$56*	$178*	$68*	$28	$53*	$90*	$8	$6
Burton, Dan (R-Ind).	$30	$26	$19	$3	$15	$88	$37	$11	$32	$50	$10	$45
Buyer, Steve (R-Ind).	$64*	$7	$24	$1	$15	$24	$21	$2	$10	$38	$0	$5
Byrne, Leslie L. (D-Va).	$8	$9	$2	$4	$7	$25	$38	$34	$9	$9	$150*	$90*
Callahan, Sonny (R-Ala).	$52	$21	$21	$2	$36	$53	$45	$10	$34	$31	$21	$3
Calvert, Ken (R-Calif).	$24	$11	$35*	$4	$12	$66	$21	$17	$27	$28	$1	$21
Camp, Dave (R-Mich).	$64*	$16	$18	$0	$22	$29	$23	$13	$15	$85*	$5	$7
Canady, Charles T. (R-Fla).	$20	$2	$6	$1	$7	$12	$5	$5	$5	$10	$0	$10
Cantwell, Maria (D-Wash).	$7	$9	$0	$0	$20	$27	$30	$35	$6	$15	$143*	$67*
Cardin, Benjamin L. (D-Md).	$14	$10	$8	$3	$10	$131*	$94*	$36	$24	$40	$32	$23
Carr, Bob (D-Mich).	$37	$40	$52*	$53*	$46*	$78	$29	$119*	$129*	$61*	$134	$56*
Castle, Michael N. (R-Del).	$15	$13	$16	$2	$15	$205*	$32	$47	$30	$55	$12	$4
Chapman, Jim (D-Texas).	$35	$8	$8	$39*	$34	$18	$22	$20	$21	$13	$32	$10
Clay, William L. (D-Mo).	$8	$10	$1	$0	$2	$22	$20	$18	$9	$15	$157*	$13
Clayton, Eva (D-NC).	$15	$7	$1	$1	$3	$26	$32	$21	$2	$5	$136	$75*
Clement, Bob (D-Tenn).	$33	$27	$21	$4	$25	$56	$23	$27	$77*	$44	$73	$10
Clinger, William F. (R-Pa).	$9	$10	$12	$1	$19	$21	$7	$7	$45*	$19	$11	$1
Clyburn, Jim (D-SC).	$10	$9	$4	$0	$14	$30	$18	$29	$10	$14	$29	$18
Coble, J. Howard (R-NC).	$32	$36	$11	$4	$15	$52	$26	$11	$19	$55	$4	$13
Coleman, Ronald D. (D-Texas).	$33	$9	$22	$29*	$30	$43	$19	$58	$45*	$31	$182*	$63*
Collins, Barbara-Rose (D-Mich).	$7	$14	$3	$3	$9	$7	$5	$6	$17	$8	$87	$16
Collins, Cardiss (D-Ill).	$3	$24	$1	$1	$4	$93	$12	$34	$9	$11	$57	$3
Collins, Mac (R-Ga).	$8	$5	$3	$1	$10	$20	$10	$6	$10	$15	$3	$14
Combest, Larry (R-Texas).	$55	$7	$5	$5	$19	$29	$16	$2	$15	$8	$0	$1
Condit, Gary (D-Calif).	$87*	$8	$5	$2	$6	$23	$15	$10	$3	$12	$43	$4
Conyers, John Jr. (D-Mich).	$4	$49*	$9	$7	$6	$20	$3	$40	$11	$9	$94	$4
Cooper, Jim (D-Tenn).	$2	$0	$4	$0	$3	$7	$13	$7	$1	$3	$0	$3
Coppersmith, Sam (D-Ariz).	$3	$5	$2	$0	$0	$10	$5	$47	$2	$7	$35	$23
Costello, Jerry F. (D-Ill).	$6	$8	$42*	$3	$7	$38	$24	$85*	$21	$31	$73	$5
Cox, C. Christopher (R-Calif).	$10	$13	$46*	$6	$13	$97	$35	$60	$38	$38	$2	$32
Coyne, William J. (D-Pa).	$2	$6	$1	$0	$13	$63	$31	$19	$3	$9	$71	$0
Cramer, Bud (D-Ala).	$22	$26	$15	$10	$24	$30	$29	$16	$35	$18	$53	$14
Crane, Philip M. (R-Ill).	$5	$4	$4	$0	$1	$13	$16	$5	$2	$7	$0	$5
Crapo, Michael D. (R-Idaho).	$91*	$17	$16	$2	$39	$51	$40	$9	$23	$30	$0	$20
Cunningham, Randy (R-Calif).	$17	$18	$21	$68*	$24	$39	$18	$15	$68*	$49	$21	$49
Danner, Pat (D-Mo).	$15	$6	$4	$0	$6	$24	$43	$22	$16	$15	$80	$29
Darden, Buddy (D-Ga).	$27	$10	$9	$44*	$20	$47	$26	$22	$18	$30	$33	$6
de la Garza, Kika (D-Texas).	$145*	$5	$3	$0	$4	$31	$5	$11	$9	$5	$0	$2
Deal, Nathan (D-Ga).	$27	$7	$3	$1	$14	$49	$47	$8	$15	$19	$17	$8
DeFazio, Peter A. (D-Ore).	$11	$3	$2	$0	$3	$16	$9	$13	$23	$5	$95	$9
DeLauro, Rosa (D-Conn).	$10	$23	$24	$11	$7	$78	$61*	$76*	$34	$22	$218*	$150*
DeLay, Tom (R-Texas).	$22	$17	$24	$17	$42	$40	$21	$21	$44*	$32	$4	$8

* Ranks in top 10% of Senate in receipts from this sector
† Leading Senate recipient of funds from this sector

Breakdown of Contributions by Industry & Interest Group Sectors
Totals in Thousands of Dollars

Name	Agriculture	Comm/Elec	Construction	Defense	Energy	Finance	Health	Law/Lobby	Transport	Misc Bus	Labor	Ideol
Dellums, Ronald V. (D-Calif).	$3	$13	$3	$1	$1	$8	$11	$18	$6	$9	$58	$11
Derrick, Butler (D-SC).	$55	$32	$21	$5	$43	$169*	$50	$51	$33	$46	$42	$13
Deutsch, Peter (D-Fla).	$15	$9	$10	$0	$7	$90	$39	$57	$15	$27	$71	$21
Diaz-Balart, Lincoln (R-Fla).	$21	$15	$11	$0	$5	$29	$27	$21	$10	$12	$31	$20
Dickey, Jay (R-Ark).	$20	$3	$5	$0	$9	$20	$15	$12	$4	$14	$0	$1
Dicks, Norm (D-Wash).	$32	$15	$16	$99*	$36	$24	$16	$47	$33	$21	$87	$3
Dingell, John D. (D-Mich).	$46	$126*	$19	$8	$95*	$167*	$76*	$98*	$120*	$74*	$117	$22
Dixon, Julian C. (D-Calif).	$3	$7	$5	$7	$2	$11	$5	$3	$4	$5	$18	$7
Dooley, Calvin (D-Calif).	$146*	$13	$4	$2	$10	$31	$24	$22	$8	$7	$60	$10
Doolittle, John T. (R-Calif).	$56	$16	$29*	$4	$36	$55	$19	$12	$32	$31	$7	$31
Dornan, Robert K. (R-Calif).	$14	$6	$10	$20	$8	$12	$8	$3	$15	$17	$3	$105*
Dreier, David (R-Calif).	$25	$15	$16	$2	$11	$108	$22	$18	$19	$39	$1	$6
Duncan, Jimmy Jr. (R-Tenn).	$15	$6	$14	$2	$14	$54	$19	$11	$32	$14	$11	$6
Dunn, Jennifer (R-Wash).	$40	$16	$9	$2	$21	$71	$20	$11	$23	$46	$1	$36
Durbin, Richard J. (D-Ill).	$60*	$14	$8	$2	$9	$70	$42	$34	$37	$23	$147*	$30
Edwards, Chet (D-Texas).	$39	$10	$12	$58*	$30	$55	$36	$17	$25	$20	$98	$13
Edwards, Don (D-Calif).	$4	$30	$5	$1	$6	$21	$12	$30	$3	$10	$83	$11
Emerson, Bill (R-Mo).	$144*	$11	$11	$6	$21	$46	$23	$14	$41	$39	$11	$14
Engel, Eliot L. (D-NY).	$19	$9	$1	$5	$2	$63	$30	$20	$5	$7	$133	$53*
English, Glenn (D-Okla).	$63*	$24	$3	$3	$26	$61	$12	$22	$14	$12	$17	$11
English, Karan (D-Ariz).	$5	$4	$1	$0	$3	$9	$19	$11	$4	$3	$40	$68*
Eshoo, Anna G. (D-Calif).	$5	$12	$11	$2	$4	$56	$43	$40	$3	$19	$136	$169*
Espy, Mike (D-Miss).	$66*	$18	$6	$1	$14	$27	$14	$12	$15	$9	$68	$22
Evans, Lane (D-Ill).	$8	$4	$0	$3	$1	$14	$9	$21	$3	$5	$127	$18
Everett, Terry (R-Ala).	$3	$4	$13	$0	$0	$18	$3	$2	$13	$7	$0	$1
Ewing, Thomas W. (R-Ill).	$61*	$27	$27	$0	$29	$62	$39	$8	$31	$41	$3	$26
Fawell, Harris W. (R-Ill).	$14	$15	$44*	$4	$26	$84	$46	$10	$27	$57	$1	$2
Fazio, Vic (D-Calif).	$161†	$91*	$47*	$92*	$97*	$273*	$125*	$166*	$34	$117*	$242*	$128*
Fields, Cleo (D-La).	$2	$7	$7	$0	$6	$19	$13	$50	$3	$11	$13	$10
Fields, Jack (R-Texas).	$47	$72*	$22	$4	$127*	$101	$43	$41	$81*	$48	$22	$8
Filner, Bob (D-Calif).	$5	$14	$19	$4	$6	$89	$53	$49	$15	$24	$118	$81*
Fingerhut, Eric D. (D-Ohio).	$7	$7	$9	$0	$2	$63	$21	$43	$5	$29	$112	$104*
Fish, Hamilton Jr. (R-NY).	$20	$65*	$6	$2	$7	$145*	$18	$25	$13	$28	$26	$3
Flake, Floyd H. (D-NY).	$8	$4	$4	$0	$3	$75	$4	$7	$4	$3	$76	$1
Foglietta, Thomas M. (D-Pa).	$9	$15	$4	$12	$7	$29	$21	$45	$16	$18	$106	$15
Foley, Thomas S. (D-Wash).	$67*	$29	$16	$6	$29	$80	$24	$29	$40	$33	$107	$16
Ford, Harold E. (D-Tenn).	$10	$3	$3	$0	$2	$28	$12	$19	$14	$14	$53	$5
Ford, William D. (D-Mich).	$20	$26	$3	$1	$16	$59	$24	$42	$26	$12	$282*	$21
Fowler, Tillie (R-Fla).	$26	$10	$17	$2	$15	$97	$25	$30	$21	$42	$0	$32
Frank, Barney (D-Mass).	$4	$15	$9	$3	$2	$103	$14	$40	$1	$10	$48	$22
Franks, Bob (R-NJ).	$4	$10	$24	$3	$22	$93	$50	$30	$17	$30	$13	$17
Franks, Gary (R-Conn).	$36	$26	$16	$52*	$29	$67	$37	$13	$22	$62*	$7	$49
Frost, Martin (D-Texas).	$42	$50*	$15	$43*	$110*	$165*	$77*	$137*	$61*	$81*	$206*	$53*
Furse, Elizabeth (D-Ore).	$5	$14	$3	$0	$6	$19	$10	$37	$2	$19	$67	$150*
Gallegly, Elton (R-Calif).	$34	$17	$44*	$17	$33	$95	$29	$10	$15	$41	$2	$39
Gallo, Dean A. (R-NJ).	$14	$18	$34*	$5	$25	$59	$48	$24	$20	$38	$28	$18
Gejdenson, Sam (D-Conn).	$19	$29	$13	$14	$12	$45	$23	$38	$16	$43	$106	$129*
Gekas, George W. (R-Pa).	$5	$8	$6	$0	$4	$27	$5	$1	$10	$9	$2	$1
Gephardt, Richard A. (D-Mo).	$108*	$192†	$81*	$39*	$145*	$576†	$282†	$370†	$147*	$378†	$200*	$99*
Geren, Pete (D-Texas).	$46	$27	$37*	$5	$99*	$93	$33	$87*	$108*	$67*	$24	$14
Gibbons, Sam M. (D-Fla).	$67*	$32	$24	$10	$39	$127*	$53	$75*	$61*	$81*	$17	$4
Gilchrest, Wayne T. (R-Md).	$18	$6	$12	$5	$11	$21	$4	$5	$20	$24	$5	$14
Gillmor, Paul E. (R-Ohio).	$18	$10	$10	$1	$12	$62	$11	$9	$27	$19	$2	$2
Gilman, Benjamin A. (R-NY).	$20	$10	$11	$2	$7	$31	$29	$24	$13	$34	$100	$28
Gingrich, Newt (R-Ga).	$77*	$70*	$47*	$17	$54*	$274*	$114*	$74*	$93*	$244*	$11	$122*

* Ranks in top 10% of House in receipts from this sector
† Leading House recipient of funds from this sector

Breakdown of Contributions by Industry & Interest Group Sectors
Totals in Thousands of Dollars

Name	Agriculture	Comm/Elec	Construction	Defense	Energy	Finance	Health	Law/Lobby	Transport	Misc Bus	Labor	Ideol
Glickman, Dan (D-Kan).	$52	$35	$7	$11	$35	$148*	$34	$87*	$28	$55	$90	$89*
Gonzalez, Henry B. (D-Texas).	$0	$1	$1	$0	$1	$1	$1	$6	$3	$0	$3	$0
Goodlatte, Robert W. (R-Va).	$20	$8	$13	$4	$18	$36	$24	$14	$18	$34	$2	$16
Goodling, Bill (R-Pa).	$4	$4	$7	$0	$4	$4	$4	$7	$2	$9	$0	$5
Gordon, Bart (D-Tenn).	$30	$20	$17	$6	$18	$98	$24	$17	$34	$19	$106	$12
Goss, Porter J. (R-Fla).	$7	$9	$7	$3	$3	$38	$23	$6	$13	$10	$0	$5
Gradison, Bill (R-Ohio).	$0	$1	$1	$0	$0	$13	$7	$9	$1	$4	$0	$0
Grams, Rod (R-Minn).	$29	$8	$17	$1	$26	$27	$6	$2	$21	$57	$1	$24
Grandy, Fred (R-Iowa).	$59	$29	$14	$3	$21	$93	$41	$3	$28	$28	$7	$6
Green, Gene (D-Texas).	$16	$7	$11	$2	$24	$62	$42	$96*	$23	$25	$195*	$25
Greenwood, James C. (R-Pa).	$36	$9	$35*	$2	$39	$60	$41	$41	$20	$89*	$0	$7
Gunderson, Steve (R-Wis).	$89*	$18	$20	$5	$10	$46	$28	$6	$20	$35	$2	$1
Gutierrez, Luis V. (D-Ill).	$10	$8	$23	$0	$2	$58	$25	$39	$10	$22	$83	$39
Hall, Ralph M. (D-Texas).	$29	$39	$11	$26	$94*	$62	$50	$20	$33	$31	$2	$5
Hall, Tony P. (D-Ohio).	$11	$25	$4	$5	$8	$36	$19	$18	$13	$11	$90	$7
Hamburg, Dan (D-Calif).	$1	$4	$2	$0	$1	$2	$9	$14	$0	$8	$115	$52*
Hamilton, Lee H. (D-Ind).	$19	$16	$16	$11	$19	$54	$12	$29	$27	$24	$42	$45
Hancock, Mel (R-Mo).	$22	$9	$22	$1	$12	$66	$15	$7	$38	$47	$2	$10
Hansen, James V. (R-Utah).	$4	$5	$8	$34*	$31	$16	$14	$6	$18	$24	$2	$12
Harman, Jane (D-Calif).	$1	$49*	$6	$43*	$4	$72	$16	$149*	$5	$55	$65	$102*
Hastert, Dennis (R-Ill).	$44	$48*	$29*	$2	$32	$73	$57*	$12	$37	$54	$4	$5
Hastings, Alcee L. (D-Fla).	$6	$2	$7	$0	$0	$15	$17	$58	$6	$7	$58	$17
Hayes, Jimmy (D-La).	$33	$9	$41*	$7	$50*	$38	$7	$39	$41	$29	$34	$15
Hefley, Joel (R-Colo).	$11	$9	$3	$18	$11	$17	$4	$1	$14	$11	$7	$4
Hefner, W. G. "Bill" (D-NC).	$36	$18	$13	$90*	$11	$40	$24	$25	$28	$37	$87	$18
Henry, Paul B. (R-Mich).	$13	$8	$13	$0	$5	$20	$30	$14	$13	$34	$5	$2
Herger, Wally (R-Calif).	$156*	$9	$26	$7	$19	$32	$30	$9	$19	$26	$16	$9
Hilliard, Earl F. (D-Ala).	$26	$12	$6	$0	$44	$27	$10	$40	$7	$11	$32	$26
Hinchey, Maurice D. (D-NY).	$3	$4	$21	$0	$4	$21	$13	$16	$1	$4	$63	$42
Hoagland, Peter (D-Neb).	$26	$17	$14	$1	$6	$186*	$30	$79*	$14	$16	$163*	$28
Hobson, David L. (R-Ohio).	$12	$14	$9	$3	$28	$41	$41	$7	$34	$30	$10	$4
Hochbrueckner, George (D-NY).	$3	$7	$6	$30*	$4	$32	$24	$10	$10	$6	$178*	$34
Hoekstra, Peter (R-Mich).	$1	$1	$2	$0	$0	$3	$2	$0	$3	$4	$0	$2
Hoke, Martin R. (R-Ohio).	$1	$12	$14	$1	$3	$40	$26	$27	$14	$49	$0	$5
Holden, Tim (D-Pa).	$1	$5	$3	$1	$3	$3	$4	$28	$2	$3	$91	$14
Horn, Steve (R-Calif).	$1	$9	$4	$1	$7	$37	$32	$17	$4	$27	$0	$4
Houghton, Amo (R-NY).	$16	$43*	$7	$4	$22	$45	$9	$8	$4	$45	$8	$9
Hoyer, Steny H. (D-Md).	$40	$48*	$26	$14	$34	$142*	$109*	$140*	$35	$65*	$241*	$102*
Huffington, Michael (R-Calif).	$5	$12	$5	$0	$20	$46	$5	$4	$5	$20	$0	$2
Hughes, William J. (D-NJ).	$5	$52*	$8	$1	$14	$48	$24	$40	$25	$23	$63	$6
Hunter, Duncan (R-Calif).	$21	$17	$40*	$78*	$16	$31	$14	$6	$40	$41	$15	$38
Hutchinson, Tim (R-Ark).	$27	$3	$8	$0	$19	$33	$34	$6	$16	$30	$0	$12
Hutto, Earl (D-Fla).	$12	$8	$9	$35*	$18	$30	$19	$4	$18	$19	$11	$3
Hyde, Henry J. (R-Ill).	$8	$28	$19	$3	$10	$79	$21	$18	$19	$37	$2	$7
Inglis, Robert D. (R-SC).	$5	$2	$8	$0	$0	$15	$7	$8	$3	$26	$0	$0
Inhofe, James M. (R-Okla).	$19	$16	$13	$6	$65*	$51	$20	$7	$78*	$19	$10	$16
Inslee, Jay (D-Wash).	$3	$1	$0	$0	$1	$4	$5	$15	$0	$5	$53	$15
Istook, Ernest Jr. (R-Okla).	$8	$9	$2	$0	$36	$29	$24	$16	$6	$10	$0	$8
Jacobs, Andrew Jr. (D-Ind).	$0	$0	$0	$0	$0	$1	$0	$0	$0	$0	$0	$0
Jefferson, William J. (D-La).	$16	$9	$9	$5	$29	$28	$10	$58	$21	$13	$98	$15
Johnson, Don (D-Ga).	$22	$8	$7	$1	$18	$61	$44	$34	$11	$43	$20	$5
Johnson, Eddie B. (D-Texas).	$5	$10	$1	$2	$11	$33	$26	$18	$10	$6	$50	$21
Johnson, Nancy L. (R-Conn).	$18	$24	$24	$14	$18	$131*	$76*	$10	$28	$56	$12	$21
Johnson, Sam (R-Texas).	$18	$37	$27	$28	$93*	$133*	$64*	$23	$28	$63*	$0	$21
Johnson, Tim (D-SD).	$51	$9	$5	$0	$3	$26	$19	$17	$9	$6	$106	$12

* Ranks in top 10% of House of Representatives in receipts from this sector
† Leading House recipient of funds from this sector

Breakdown of Contributions by Industry & Interest Group Sectors
Totals in Thousands of Dollars

Name	Agriculture	Comm/Elec	Construction	Defense	Energy	Finance	Health	Law/Lobby	Transport	Misc Bus	Labor	Ideol
Johnston, Harry A. (D-Fla).	$23	$8	$7	$5	$7	$39	$16	$38	$12	$8	$83	$22
Kanjorski, Paul E. (D-Pa).	$5	$5	$5	$1	$4	$109	$10	$16	$5	$5	$79	$12
Kaptur, Marcy (D-Ohio).	$21	$2	$6	$2	$3	$25	$6	$4	$8	$10	$127	$3
Kasich, John R. (R-Ohio).	$11	$5	$24	$16	$14	$50	$25	$11	$11	$41	$2	$10
Kennedy, Joseph P. II (D-Mass).	$4	$25	$24	$1	$23	$133*	$42	$83*	$13	$52	$81	$11
Kennelly, Barbara B. (D-Conn).	$15	$14	$6	$9	$16	$162*	$40	$30	$15	$48	$53	$10
Kildee, Dale E. (D-Mich).	$29	$24	$4	$0	$17	$34	$36	$39	$19	$8	$244*	$47
Kim, Jay C. (R-Calif).	$7	$10	$22	$3	$12	$46	$48	$5	$13	$32	$1	$10
King, Peter T. (R-NY).	$5	$5	$4	$1	$7	$26	$15	$10	$10	$24	$10	$26
Kingston, Jack (R-Ga).	$28	$6	$8	$1	$16	$65	$53	$9	$16	$29	$0	$19
Kleczka, Gerald D. (D-Wis).	$11	$6	$8	$1	$7	$70	$28	$22	$8	$10	$76	$6
Klein, Herbert C. (D-NJ).	$5	$11	$11	$0	$2	$87	$16	$50	$3	$31	$70	$22
Klink, Ron (D-Pa).	$1	$7	$3	$4	$6	$12	$7	$8	$1	$4	$89	$3
Klug, Scott L. (R-Wis).	$41	$31	$42*	$2	$22	$103	$31	$20	$31	$95*	$2	$8
Knollenberg, Joseph (R-Mich).	$5	$7	$15	$2	$13	$67	$33	$17	$30	$31	$2	$12
Kolbe, Jim (R-Ariz).	$30	$8	$15	$21	$14	$39	$18	$14	$21	$32	$3	$12
Kopetski, Mike (D-Ore).	$37	$33	$3	$3	$9	$35	$32	$22	$20	$16	$94	$40
Kreidler, Mike (D-Wash).	$5	$3	$1	$0	$11	$5	$44	$15	$2	$7	$94	$27
Kyl, Jon (R-Ariz).	$28	$14	$18	$31*	$31	$88	$42	$47	$24	$46	$0	$11
LaFalce, John J. (D-NY).	$12	$10	$10	$3	$23	$207*	$7	$43	$13	$76*	$37	$2
Lambert, Blanche (D-Ark).	$41	$14	$8	$1	$24	$53	$19	$23	$15	$22	$24	$25
Lancaster, H. Martin (D-NC).	$83*	$17	$13	$46*	$15	$39	$48	$25	$21	$45	$32	$21
Lantos, Tom (D-Calif).	$5	$11	$2	$4	$3	$35	$8	$7	$11	$14	$68	$28
LaRocco, Larry (D-Idaho).	$31	$23	$12	$2	$12	$147*	$30	$29	$9	$18	$117	$29
Laughlin, Greg (D-Texas).	$42	$14	$30*	$9	$80*	$40	$32	$69*	$74*	$32	$73	$13
Lazio, Rick A. (R-NY).	$7	$5	$5	$0	$7	$18	$6	$16	$4	$18	$10	$6
Leach, Jim (R-Iowa).	$2	$3	$3	$0	$2	$7	$6	$3	$4	$5	$0	$0
Lehman, Richard H. (D-Calif).	$87*	$61*	$21	$2	$45*	$134*	$39	$48	$9	$31	$153*	$36
Levin, Sander (D-Mich).	$18	$29	$16	$9	$20	$124	$101*	$93*	$35	$54	$162*	$81*
Levy, David A. (R-NY).	$5	$16	$4	$1	$9	$17	$8	$8	$4	$30	$4	$4
Lewis, Jerry (R-Calif).	$41	$25	$16	$71*	$29	$77	$41	$19	$36	$45	$9	$13
Lewis, John (D-Ga).	$10	$15	$4	$2	$8	$44	$31	$22	$30	$14	$107	$17
Lewis, Tom (R-Fla).	$85*	$12	$6	$7	$13	$26	$9	$6	$18	$7	$6	$0
Lightfoot, Jim Ross (R-Iowa).	$65*	$20	$17	$6	$24	$37	$27	$3	$52*	$36	$3	$26
Linder, John (R-Ga).	$25	$14	$17	$3	$22	$85	$31	$21	$16	$41	$2	$38
Lipinski, William O. (D-Ill).	$6	$7	$17	$1	$6	$52	$19	$50	$57*	$28	$124	$26
Livingston, Robert L. (R-La).	$10	$5	$12	$57*	$30	$12	$15	$21	$19	$10	$5	$5
Lloyd, Marilyn (D-Tenn).	$12	$4	$8	$52*	$26	$31	$29	$24	$32	$22	$86	$3
Long, Jill L. (D-Ind).	$58	$13	$0	$2	$4	$28	$20	$7	$11	$5	$128	$10
Lowey, Nita M. (D-NY).	$14	$17	$7	$1	$2	$192*	$43	$126*	$14	$52	$147*	$92*
Machtley, Ronald K. (R-RI).	$9	$12	$17	$38*	$15	$43	$33	$16	$13	$51	$41	$17
Maloney, Carolyn B. (I-NY).	$1	$10	$2	$0	$0	$52	$3	$18	$0	$14	$55	$10
Mann, David (D-Ohio).	$3	$6	$2	$0	$1	$40	$20	$26	$12	$11	$54	$5
Manton, Thomas J. (D-NY).	$34	$48*	$16	$1	$29	$125	$33	$46	$24	$26	$114	$5
Manzullo, Donald (R-Ill).	$11	$8	$14	$1	$12	$24	$24	$11	$24	$46	$0	$36
Margolies-Mezvinsky, M. (D-Pa).	$4	$15	$2	$1	$5	$33	$31	$60	$5	$15	$51	$66*
Markey, Edward J. (D-Mass).	$2	$76*	$4	$2	$16	$64	$5	$82*	$3	$22	$0	$4
Martinez, Matthew G. (D-Calif).	$2	$3	$4	$2	$2	$22	$6	$4	$3	$7	$33	$11
Matsui, Robert T. (D-Calif).	$29	$31	$7	$5	$32	$112	$68*	$66*	$28	$62*	$53	$5
Mazzoli, Romano L. (D-Ky).	$0	$1	$1	$0	$0	$3	$3	$3	$0	$1	$0	$0
McCandless, Al (R-Calif).	$20	$10	$17	$4	$11	$115	$14	$10	$22	$14	$5	$4
McCloskey, Frank (D-Ind).	$9	$7	$1	$24	$12	$20	$5	$7	$13	$20	$190*	$27
McCollum, Bill (R-Fla).	$36	$35	$13	$8	$15	$139*	$60*	$42	$26	$60*	$4	$21
McCrery, Jim (R-La).	$56	$5	$21	$38*	$66*	$72	$74*	$22	$36	$26	$3	$43
McCurdy, Dave (D-Okla).	$16	$15	$16	$129*	$40	$54	$40	$39	$31	$22	$10	$41

* Ranks in top 10% of House in receipts from this sector
† Leading House recipient of funds from this sector

Breakdown of Contributions by Industry & Interest Group Sectors
Totals in Thousands of Dollars

Name	Agriculture	Comm/Elec	Construction	Defense	Energy	Finance	Health	Law/Lobby	Transport	Misc Bus	Labor	Ideol
McDade, Joseph M. (R-Pa).	$9	$12	$10	$91*	$15	$24	$11	$47	$20	$23	$37	$14
McDermott, Jim (D-Wash).	$6	$7	$2	$0	$11	$56	$34	$13	$14	$9	$47	$8
McHale, Paul (D-Pa).	$1	$4	$1	$1	$1	$1	$4	$22	$1	$1	$97	$13
McHugh, John M. (R-NY).	$8	$5	$3	$0	$7	$27	$17	$3	$5	$8	$19	$12
McInnis, Scott (R-Colo).	$14	$12	$25	$0	$55*	$56	$17	$7	$32	$51	$1	$27
McKeon, Howard (R-Calif).	$6	$10	$20	$4	$3	$45	$30	$10	$30	$30	$0	$14
McKinney, Cynthia (D-Ga).	$11	$8	$6	$0	$7	$16	$29	$18	$7	$13	$60	$46
McMillan, Alex (R-NC).	$30	$19	$7	$7	$21	$92	$49	$4	$22	$31	$6	$3
McNulty, Michael R. (D-NY).	$2	$5	$1	$13	$1	$14	$2	$0	$6	$4	$67	$5
Meehan, Martin T. (D-Mass).	$6	$8	$36*	$2	$2	$47	$20	$99*	$7	$36	$1	$2
Meek, Carrie (D-Fla).	$11	$6	$5	$0	$2	$18	$67*	$34	$14	$20	$68	$41
Menendez, Robert (D-NJ).	$14	$15	$25	$1	$16	$74	$38	$60	$12	$28	$86	$39
Meyers, Jan (R-Kan).	$16	$22	$20	$3	$16	$37	$25	$3	$26	$35	$1	$36
Mfume, Kweisi (D-Md).	$5	$6	$5	$0	$4	$50	$11	$11	$6	$8	$56	$9
Mica, John L. (R-Fla).	$19	$16	$5	$3	$14	$41	$29	$15	$16	$32	$1	$14
Michel, Robert H. (R-Ill).	$57	$40*	$25	$16	$25	$119	$46	$15	$38	$57	$23	$16
Miller, Dan (R-Fla).	$16	$8	$10	$0	$11	$47	$34	$7	$10	$28	$0	$2
Miller, George (D-Calif).	$11	$15	$11	$1	$55*	$39	$13	$58	$10	$38	$103	$15
Mineta, Norman Y. (D-Calif).	$18	$40*	$67*	$14	$24	$67	$26	$80*	$174†	$78*	$141*	$22
Minge, David (D-Minn).	$16	$4	$0	$0	$2	$11	$5	$12	$3	$4	$111	$12
Mink, Patsy T. (D-Hawaii).	$5	$2	$6	$0	$2	$26	$8	$5	$4	$3	$76	$1
Moakley, Joe (D-Mass).	$9	$29	$51*	$10	$21	$180*	$25	$72*	$35	$46	$110	$1
Molinari, Susan (R-NY).	$14	$18	$28*	$7	$12	$79	$38	$28	$37	$28	$16	$40
Mollohan, Alan B. (D-WVa).	$24	$6	$12	$54*	$38	$17	$25	$38	$16	$30	$74	$19
Montgomery, "Sonny" (D-Miss).	$15	$11	$7	$16	$19	$15	$15	$3	$11	$11	$1	$5
Moorhead, Carlos J. (R-Calif).	$14	$44*	$8	$6	$46*	$70	$39	$12	$21	$21	$1	$2
Moran, James P. Jr. (D-Va).	$14	$29	$15	$23	$9	$143*	$48	$91*	$20	$36	$160*	$48
Morella, Constance A. (R-Md).	$5	$21	$18	$9	$11	$37	$32	$26	$15	$15	$43	$21
Murphy, Austin J. (D-Pa).	$8	$3	$1	$1	$14	$13	$15	$3	$4	$16	$97	$14
Murtha, John P. (D-Pa).	$18	$24	$31*	$230†	$93*	$61	$22	$83*	$30	$68*	$108	$22
Myers, John T. (R-Ind).	$28	$15	$17	$5	$38	$22	$7	$10	$23	$23	$22	$3
Nadler, Jerrold (D-NY).	$1	$3	$1	$0	$0	$8	$8	$1	$1	$1	$12	$5
Natcher, William H. (D-Ky).	$0	$0	$0	$0	$0	$0	$0	$0	$0	$0	$0	$0
Neal, Richard E. (D-Mass).	$10	$6	$4	$3	$4	$91	$16	$23	$2	$19	$64	$6
Neal, Stephen L. (D-NC).	$33	$13	$6	$3	$6	$220*	$12	$28	$16	$12	$34	$14
Nussle, Jim (R-Iowa).	$92*	$26	$31*	$7	$19	$127*	$38	$8	$48*	$78*	$4	$17
Oberstar, James L. (D-Minn).	$14	$8	$10	$4	$5	$8	$4	$19	$54*	$21	$81	$9
Obey, David R. (D-Wis).	$33	$17	$4	$4	$11	$31	$25	$31	$13	$19	$93	$45
Olver, John W. (D-Mass).	$8	$19	$12	$3	$9	$49	$50	$68*	$9	$30	$344†	$137*
Ortiz, Solomon P. (D-Texas).	$9	$9	$19	$11	$19	$28	$12	$18	$17	$17	$12	$11
Orton, Bill (D-Utah).	$12	$7	$9	$1	$11	$60	$22	$14	$13	$13	$74	$14
Owens, Major R. (D-NY).	$1	$3	$0	$0	$1	$7	$5	$2	$1	$3	$69	$2
Oxley, Michael G. (R-Ohio).	$28	$46*	$9	$5	$66*	$73	$31	$15	$25	$33	$0	$1
Packard, Ron (R-Calif).	$8	$14	$24	$6	$20	$22	$23	$10	$67*	$8	$8	$4
Pallone, Frank Jr. (D-NJ).	$10	$14	$41*	$1	$12	$50	$56*	$43	$68*	$36	$255*	$78*
Panetta, Leon E. (D-Calif).	$52	$6	$3	$2	$10	$39	$36	$18	$16	$36	$66	$2
Parker, Mike (D-Miss).	$39	$13	$15	$1	$42	$57	$17	$13	$51*	$53	$6	$11
Pastor, Ed (D-Ariz).	$31	$23	$23	$4	$17	$77	$37	$65*	$14	$47	$183*	$45
Paxon, Bill (R-NY).	$31	$28	$63*	$6	$28	$190*	$47	$25	$35	$76*	$5	$29
Payne, Donald M. (D-NJ).	$8	$9	$3	$0	$6	$43	$20	$28	$16	$15	$84	$10
Payne, Lewis F. Jr. (D-Va).	$28	$12	$27*	$4	$25	$55	$26	$17	$48*	$45	$16	$13
Pelosi, Nancy (D-Calif).	$8	$11	$7	$5	$11	$87	$30	$41	$8	$30	$96	$22
Penny, Timothy J. (D-Minn).	$35	$6	$0	$0	$3	$15	$11	$2	$6	$20	$5	$3
Peterson, Collin C. (D-Minn).	$65*	$11	$1	$1	$5	$47	$8	$14	$14	$5	$138*	$26
Peterson, Pete (D-Fla).	$25	$14	$16	$3	$12	$34	$25	$17	$36	$12	$113	$14

* Ranks in top 10% of House of Representatives in receipts from this sector
† Leading House recipient of funds from this sector

Breakdown of Contributions by Industry & Interest Group Sectors
Totals in Thousands of Dollars

Name	Agriculture	Comm/Elec	Construction	Defense	Energy	Finance	Health	Law/Lobby	Transport	Misc Bus	Labor	Ideol
Petri, Tom (R-Wis).	$33	$10	$22	$2	$13	$25	$12	$10	$43*	$42	$1	$9
Pickett, Owen B. (D-Va).	$8	$9	$4	$22	$10	$49	$12	$21	$20	$20	$25	$3
Pickle, J. J. (D-Texas).	$21	$22	$9	$5	$28	$110	$49	$50	$27	$20	$6	$1
Pombo, Richard W. (R-Calif).	$75*	$9	$17	$2	$18	$56	$14	$3	$15	$36	$0	$40
Pomeroy, Earl (D-ND).	$21	$3	$2	$0	$17	$107	$29	$29	$8	$16	$98	$12
Porter, John (R-Ill).	$12	$15	$14	$2	$6	$67	$67*	$14	$19	$33	$1	$34
Poshard, Glenn (D-Ill).	$0	$2	$1	$0	$2	$3	$3	$4	$1	$2	$5	$2
Price, David (D-NC).	$37	$12	$6	$3	$12	$41	$33	$18	$25	$11	$87	$14
Pryce, Deborah (R-Ohio).	$11	$8	$25	$1	$25	$93	$30	$31	$20	$53	$0	$32
Quillen, James H. (R-Tenn).	$32	$18	$11	$8	$17	$74	$15	$22	$51*	$32	$33	$11
Quinn, Jack (R-NY).	$3	$3	$10	$0	$3	$15	$8	$9	$20	$8	$0	$2
Rahall, Nick J. II (D-WVa).	$16	$6	$12	$2	$22	$15	$9	$15	$59*	$12	$112	$21
Ramstad, Jim (R-Minn).	$56	$35	$26	$3	$15	$159*	$50	$43	$38	$120*	$12	$27
Rangel, Charles B. (D-NY).	$14	$28	$6	$1	$8	$136*	$84*	$47	$20	$39	$66	$7
Ravenel, Arthur Jr. (R-SC).	$12	$6	$9	$13	$5	$29	$22	$3	$21	$24	$10	$9
Reed, John F. (D-RI).	$6	$18	$16	$23	$5	$76	$53	$51	$11	$34	$215*	$27
Regula, Ralph (R-Ohio).	$5	$2	$5	$0	$3	$14	$4	$9	$4	$9	$0	$0
Reynolds, Mel (D-Ill).	$7	$6	$9	$0	$2	$51	$31	$31	$10	$28	$72	$113*
Richardson, Bill (D-NM).	$31	$76*	$9	$3	$49*	$79	$90*	$46	$14	$35	$50	$27
Ridge, Tom (R-Pa).	$20	$14	$20	$1	$25	$134*	$31	$25	$20	$37	$43	$6
Roberts, Pat (R-Kan).	$86*	$8	$4	$0	$15	$35	$16	$7	$17	$22	$0	$4
Roemer, Tim (D-Ind).	$19	$12	$15	$20	$24	$33	$19	$45	$18	$13	$138*	$23
Rogers, Harold (R-Ky).	$58	$26	$30*	$2	$112*	$53	$26	$29	$26	$51	$3	$8
Rohrabacher, Dana (R-Calif).	$3	$15	$12	$13	$11	$30	$40	$14	$23	$26	$0	$33
Ros-Lehtinen, Ileana (R-Fla).	$26	$18	$27	$2	$12	$72	$88*	$26	$30	$36	$6	$34
Rose, Charlie (D-NC).	$85*	$30	$2	$0	$8	$25	$19	$22	$14	$35	$62	$11
Rostenkowski, Dan (D-Ill).	$62*	$67*	$36*	$23	$52*	$404*	$94*	$70*	$101*	$216*	$94	$21
Roth, Toby (R-Wis).	$51	$16	$22	$9	$18	$142*	$9	$18	$28	$40	$2	$19
Roukema, Marge (R-NJ).	$12	$14	$25	$2	$13	$123	$33	$14	$20	$30	$18	$16
Rowland, J. Roy (D-Ga).	$38	$24	$5	$7	$25	$49	$106*	$11	$21	$28	$7	$5
Roybal-Allard, Lucille (D-Calif).	$8	$6	$3	$1	$2	$27	$18	$14	$1	$17	$30	$34
Royce, Ed (R-Calif).	$22	$10	$20	$6	$13	$81	$56*	$29	$18	$36	$2	$44
Rush, Bobby L. (D-Ill).	$6	$4	$0	$0	$9	$29	$20	$29	$5	$8	$39	$22
Sabo, Martin Olav (D-Minn).	$18	$13	$5	$44*	$9	$16	$9	$37	$19	$9	$92	$9
Sanders, Bernard (I-Vt).	$4	$2	$2	$0	$0	$3	$4	$2	$0	$3	$135	$28
Sangmeister, George E. (D-Ill).	$4	$22	$6	$0	$6	$32	$10	$18	$16	$9	$137	$14
Santorum, Rick (R-Pa).	$7	$21	$32*	$2	$57*	$84	$39	$42	$19	$33	$73	$26
Sarpalius, Bill (D-Texas).	$107*	$8	$7	$6	$31	$51	$33	$31	$5	$15	$77	$9
Sawyer, Tom (D-Ohio).	$3	$8	$1	$4	$3	$19	$13	$5	$41	$29	$22	$27
Saxton, H. James (R-NJ).	$18	$12	$29*	$39*	$25	$87	$38	$24	$41	$29	$12	$27
Schaefer, Dan (R-Colo).	$30	$40*	$12	$4	$46*	$62	$25	$12	$32	$26	$12	$3
Schenk, Lynn (D-Calif).	$13	$24	$5	$2	$25	$103	$46	$140*	$14	$49	$124	$114*
Schiff, Steven H. (R-NM).	$16	$23	$14	$14	$23	$37	$24	$23	$19	$29	$15	$19
Schroeder, Patricia (D-Colo).	$3	$51*	$2	$5	$7	$18	$19	$33	$6	$12	$46	$25
Schumer, Charles E. (D-NY).	$4	$30	$2	$1	$2	$407*	$9	$41	$3	$75*	$28	$19
Scott, Robert C. (D-Va).	$8	$2	$7	$6	$8	$50	$37	$45	$15	$20	$88	$11
Sensenbrenner, Jim (R-Wis).	$8	$14	$6	$5	$6	$28	$2	$1	$12	$20	$0	$2
Serrano, Jose E. (D-NY).	$3	$6	$0	$2	$1	$16	$10	$4	$3	$2	$48	$5
Sharp, Philip R. (D-Ind).	$26	$38	$22	$6	$117*	$57	$29	$43	$38	$33	$89	$7
Shaw, E. Clay Jr. (R-Fla).	$38	$49*	$23	$3	$40	$188*	$115*	$48	$77*	$74*	$10	$14
Shays, Christopher (R-Conn).	$11	$14	$7	$0	$2	$57	$6	$8	$9	$34	$8	$7
Shepherd, Karen (D-Utah).	$1	$11	$1	$0	$2	$31	$13	$17	$1	$16	$111	$114*
Shuster, Bud (R-Pa).	$15	$10	$106†	$1	$17	$35	$8	$40	$88*	$135*	$7	$2
Sisisky, Norman (D-Va).	$20	$6	$8	$40*	$12	$19	$5	$6	$14	$28	$23	$11
Skaggs, David E. (D-Colo).	$10	$25	$8	$5	$15	$40	$30	$45	$18	$10	$142*	$58*

* Ranks in top 10% of House in receipts from this sector
† Leading House recipient of funds from this sector

1332

Breakdown of Contributions by Industry & Interest Group Sectors
Totals in Thousands of Dollars

Name	Agriculture	Comm/Elec	Construction	Defense	Energy	Finance	Health	Law/Lobby	Transport	Misc Bus	Labor	Ideol
Skeen, Joe (R-NM).	$71*	$8	$8	$8	$40	$21	$14	$9	$21	$12	$2	$13
Skelton, Ike (D-Mo).	$26	$11	$5	$49*	$11	$30	$20	$10	$16	$17	$27	$14
Slattery, Jim (D-Kan).	$20	$71*	$22	$3	$54*	$123	$55*	$53	$35	$39	$81	$6
Slaughter, Louise M. (D-NY).	$14	$13	$4	$2	$3	$49	$29	$18	$6	$16	$157*	$19
Smith, Bob (R-Ore).	$110*	$8	$13	$0	$15	$32	$13	$5	$19	$12	$1	$6
Smith, Christopher H. (R-NJ).	$3	$9	$5	$1	$6	$20	$8	$3	$9	$3	$30	$26
Smith, Lamar (R-Texas).	$28	$26	$18	$7	$47*	$71	$26	$17	$21	$21	$0	$3
Smith, Neal (D-Iowa).	$27	$18	$6	$16	$6	$36	$18	$29	$14	$14	$55	$13
Smith, Nick (R-Mich).	$5	$0	$2	$0	$1	$10	$9	$1	$6	$3	$0	$0
Snowe, Olympia J. (R-Maine).	$45	$16	$17	$3	$8	$70	$38	$32	$9	$50	$15	$84*
Solomon, Gerald B. H. (R-NY).	$21	$17	$4	$12	$11	$75	$24	$7	$39	$20	$59	$12
Spence, Floyd D. (R-SC).	$11	$4	$5	$33*	$10	$15	$13	$2	$12	$9	$4	$2
Spratt, John M. Jr. (D-SC).	$12	$12	$9	$24	$22	$47	$13	$17	$20	$27	$9	$6
Stark, Pete (D-Calif).	$6	$9	$3	$0	$5	$54	$193*	$61*	$8	$30	$73	$7
Stearns, Cliff (R-Fla).	$17	$9	$10	$2	$8	$94	$43	$8	$16	$15	$6	$4
Stenholm, Charles (D-Texas).	$144*	$9	$10	$6	$27	$26	$34	$14	$22	$32	$1	$1
Stokes, Louis (D-Ohio).	$10	$11	$15	$3	$7	$36	$45	$22	$6	$12	$61	$11
Strickland, Ted (D-Ohio).	$1	$1	$0	$0	$1	$3	$16	$7	$0	$1	$89	$12
Studds, Gerry E. (D-Mass).	$4	$39	$2	$4	$32	$29	$61*	$61	$55*	$31	$169*	$134*
Stump, Bob (R-Ariz).	$29	$6	$7	$34*	$17	$18	$17	$6	$15	$11	$1	$12
Stupak, Bart (D-Mich).	$3	$2	$3	$0	$6	$6	$0	$16	$6	$4	$70	$18
Sundquist, Don (R-Tenn).	$60*	$24	$21	$5	$33	$145*	$54*	$23	$67*	$91*	$10	$5
Swett, Dick (D-NH).	$14	$29	$23	$16	$13	$76	$38	$55	$38	$76*	$197*	$104*
Swift, Al (D-Wash).	$62*	$99*	$16	$6	$91*	$112	$29	$60	$78*	$64*	$122	$13
Synar, Mike (D-Okla).	$13	$130*	$19	$0	$146*	$90	$70*	$143*	$9	$54	$1	$16
Talent, James M. (R-Mo).	$29	$30	$20	$3	$28	$68	$64*	$36	$33	$100*	$0	$26
Tanner, John (D-Tenn).	$27	$11	$8	$16	$5	$36	$12	$8	$29	$10	$26	$2
Tauzin, W.J. "Billy" (D-La).	$39	$54*	$14	$5	$97*	$134*	$16	$46	$56*	$43	$19	$4
Taylor, Charles H. (R-NC).	$61*	$19	$26	$3	$44	$48	$31	$7	$42*	$78*	$10	$36
Taylor, Gene (D-Miss).	$16	$13	$8	$29*	$15	$10	$25	$19	$31	$25	$7	$15
Tejeda, Frank M. (D-Texas).	$12	$9	$20	$1	$19	$57	$45	$10	$14	$30	$12	$9
Thomas, Bill (R-Calif).	$90*	$16	$13	$7	$43	$107	$39	$32	$17	$35	$6	$1
Thomas, Craig (R-Wyo).	$32	$10	$7	$3	$67*	$61	$26	$5	$29	$18	$5	$9
Thornton, Ray (D-Ark).	$27	$12	$7	$2	$11	$83	$13	$19	$12	$11	$52	$6
Thurman, Karen L. (D-Fla).	$28	$6	$3	$0	$13	$25	$37	$13	$9	$14	$60	$45
Torkildsen, Peter (R-Mass).	$2	$6	$2	$1	$1	$58	$12	$13	$4	$41	$0	$8
Torres, Esteban E. (D-Calif).	$5	$12	$7	$3	$3	$24	$5	$21	$2	$10	$19	$2
Torricelli, Robert G. (D-NJ).	$28	$36	$36*	$15	$24	$105	$114*	$132*	$38	$104*	$107	$68*
Towns, Edolphus (D-NY).	$37	$54*	$7	$1	$24	$47	$61*	$27	$17	$27	$45	$14
Traficant, James A. Jr. (D-Ohio).	$2	$2	$4	$0	$1	$3	$5	$2	$3	$6	$80	$1
Tucker, Walter R. (D-Calif).	$8	$3	$2	$0	$8	$16	$14	$6	$4	$8	$37	$11
Unsoeld, Jolene (D-Wash).	$13	$16	$2	$1	$29	$22	$19	$23	$19	$16	$199*	$92*
Upton, Fred (R-Mich).	$21	$20	$14	$3	$22	$45	$34	$8	$31	$45	$0	$0
Valentine, Tim (D-NC).	$46	$23	$19	$9	$26	$37	$25	$28	$44*	$32	$15	$11
Velazquez, Nydia M. (D-NY).	$1	$4	$3	$0	$2	$17	$15	$12	$4	$15	$75	$33
Vento, Bruce F. (D-Minn).	$11	$7	$7	$0	$2	$91	$1	$17	$6	$7	$66	$11
Visclosky, Peter J. (D-Ind).	$6	$7	$5	$0	$11	$12	$26	$9	$15	$21	$120	$18
Volkmer, Harold L. (D-Mo).	$64*	$8	$5	$9	$8	$25	$12	$8	$13	$6	$89	$15
Vucanovich, Barbara (R-Nev).	$35	$11	$23	$6	$56*	$53	$22	$16	$29	$109*	$11	$32
Walker, Robert S. (R-Pa).	$10	$12	$8	$8	$9	$7	$7	$3	$8	$12	$1	$2
Walsh, James T. (R-NY).	$16	$8	$3	$2	$2	$28	$19	$8	$16	$13	$4	$1
Washington, Craig (D-Texas).	$9	$10	$2	$0	$11	$11	$10	$30	$7	$4	$65	$5
Waters, Maxine (D-Calif).	$6	$14	$3	$0	$2	$20	$15	$12	$3	$10	$51	$11
Watt, Melvin (D-NC).	$13	$11	$4	$0	$7	$54	$26	$45	$9	$8	$59	$23
Waxman, Henry A. (D-Calif).	$11	$58*	$3	$2	$26	$52	$203*	$65*	$12	$32	$64	$29

* Ranks in top 10% of House of Representatives in receipts from this sector
† Leading House recipient of funds from this sector

Breakdown of Contributions by Industry & Interest Group Sectors
Totals in Thousands of Dollars

Name	Agriculture	Comm/Elec	Construction	Defense	Energy	Finance	Health	Law/Lobby	Transport	Misc Bus	Labor	Ideol
Weldon, Curt (R-Pa).	$7	$10	$7	$35*	$22	$34	$25	$19	$13	$20	$51	$3
Wheat, Alan (D-Mo).	$22	$38	$6	$4	$14	$46	$27	$29	$22	$17	$153*	$24
Whitten, Jamie L. (D-Miss).	$11	$2	$1	$0	$3	$2	$1	$5	$0	$2	$1	$2
Williams, Pat (D-Mont).	$39	$19	$2	$1	$16	$42	$31	$51	$7	$22	$283*	$114*
Wilson, Charles (D-Texas).	$51	$14	$28*	$211*	$82*	$66	$49	$118*	$61*	$68*	$183*	$48
Wise, Bob (D-WVa).	$15	$15	$5	$2	$24	$10	$15	$19	$5	$27	$51	$22
Wolf, Frank R. (R-Va).	$5	$24	$18	$48*	$17	$65	$15	$12	$25	$20	$17	$9
Woolsey, Lynn (D-Calif).	$2	$6	$1	$0	$2	$24	$10	$23	$1	$9	$99	$63*
Wyden, Ron (D-Ore).	$7	$9	$1	$0	$7	$21	$35	$12	$6	$10	$17	$9
Wynn, Albert R. (D-Md).	$8	$6	$5	$0	$6	$36	$36	$36	$5	$9	$134	$28
Yates, Sidney R. (D-Ill).	$1	$11	$3	$1	$3	$42	$6	$24	$0	$10	$14	$30
Young, C. W. Bill (R-Fla).	$6	$2	$8	$91*	$7	$27	$28	$10	$9	$6	$2	$2
Young, Don (R-Alaska).	$45	$25	$39*	$8	$181†	$28	$17	$53	$65*	$38	$62	$39
Zeliff, Bill (R-NH).	$32	$45*	$36*	$15	$28	$102	$53	$6	$64*	$119*	$3	$34
Zimmer, Dick (R-NJ).	$31	$33	$25	$7	$26	$177*	$76*	$59	$26	$85*	$14	$24

* Ranks in top 10% of House in receipts from this sector
† Leading House recipient of funds from this sector

Appendix C: State Delegation Index

The supplementary index below lists all members of each state's congressional delegation — district by district — as of November 1992 . A number of changes have taken place since that time, but this was the membership of the U.S. Congress immediately after the 1992 general elections.

Members are listed by state and district. The page number indicates the location of that member's two-page campaign finance profile. Readers wishing to find all other references to the members listed here should consult the regular index.

43	Ken Calvert (D)	484
44	Al McCandless (R)	878
45	Dana Rohrabacher (R)	1044
46	Robert K. Dornan (R)	578
47	C. Christopher Cox (R)	532
48	Ron Packard (R)	974
49	Lynn Schenk (D)	1080
50	Bob Filner (D)	618
51	Randy "Duke" Cunningham (R)	542
52	Duncan Hunter (R)	748

Colorado

Senate

	Hank Brown (R)	198
	Ben Nighthorse Campbell (D)	208

House of Representatives

1	Patricia Schroeder (D)	1084
2	David E. Skaggs (D)	1106
3	Scott McInnis (R)	896
4	Wayne Allard (R)	382
5	Joel Hefley (R)	714
6	Dan Schaefer (R)	1078

Connecticut

Senate

	Christopher J. Dodd (D)	232
	Joseph I. Lieberman (D)	302

House of Representatives

1	Barbara B. Kennelly (D)	788
2	Sam Gejdenson (D)	650
3	Rosa DeLauro (D)	554
4	Christopher Shays (R)	1098
5	Gary Franks (R)	640
6	Nancy L. Johnson (R)	772

Delaware

Senate

	William V. Roth Jr. (R)	348
	Joseph R. Biden Jr. (D)	184

House of Representatives

| At Large | Michael N. Castle (R) | 496 |

Florida

Senate

	Bob Graham (D)	258
	Connie Mack (R)	308

House of Representatives

1	Earl Hutto (D)	752
2	Pete Peterson (D)	996
3	Corrine Brown (D)	466
4	Tillie Fowler (R)	634
5	Karen L. Thurman (D)	1176
6	Cliff Stearns (R)	1136
7	John L. Mica (R)	916

8	Bill McCollum (R)	882
9	Michael Bilirakis (R)	438
10	C. W. Bill Young (R)	1240
11	Sam M. Gibbons (D)	658
12	Charles T. Canady (R)	488
13	Dan Miller (R)	920
14	Porter J. Goss (R)	678
15	Jim Bacchus (D)	398
16	Tom Lewis (R)	842
17	Carrie Meek (D)	908
18	Ileana Ros-Lehtinen (R)	1046
19	Harry A. Johnston (D)	778
20	Peter Deutsch (D)	562
21	Lincoln Diaz-Balart (R)	564
22	E. Clay Shaw Jr. (R)	1096
23	Alcee L. Hastings (D)	710

Georgia

Senate

	Sam Nunn (D)	330
	Paul Coverdell (R)	220

House of Representatives

1	Jack Kingston (R)	796
2	Sanford Bishop (D)	440
3	Mac Collins (R)	518
4	John Linder (R)	846
5	John Lewis (D)	840
6	Newt Gingrich (R)	666
7	George "Buddy" Darden (D)	546
8	J. Roy Rowland (D)	1056
9	Nathan Deal (D)	550
10	Don Johnson (D)	768
11	Cynthia McKinney (D)	900

Hawaii

Senate

	Daniel K. Inouye (D)	278
	Daniel K. Akaka (D)	176

House of Representatives

| 1 | Neil Abercrombie (D) | 378 |
| 2 | Patsy T. Mink (D) | 928 |

Idaho

Senate

	Larry E. Craig (R)	222
	Dirk Kempthorne (R)	286

House of Representatives

| 1 | Larry LaRocco (D) | 824 |
| 2 | Michael D. Crapo (R) | 540 |

Illinois

Senate

	Paul Simon (D)	356
	Carol Moseley-Braun (D)	320

House of Representatives

1	Bobby L. Rush (D)	1062
2	Mel Reynolds (D)	1032
3	William O. Lipinski (D)	848
4	Luis V. Gutierrez (D)	692
5	Dan Rostenkowski (D)	1050
6	Henry J. Hyde (R)	754
7	Cardiss Collins (D)	516
8	Philip M. Crane (R)	538
9	Sidney R. Yates (D)	1238
10	John Porter (R)	1008
11	George E. Sangmeister (D)	1068
12	Jerry F. Costello (D)	530
13	Harris W. Fawell (R)	610
14	Dennis Hastert (R)	708
15	Thomas W. Ewing (R)	608
16	Donald Manzullo (R)	866
17	Lane Evans (D)	604
18	Robert H. Michel (R)	918
19	Glenn Poshard (D)	1010
20	Richard J. Durbin (D)	586

Indiana

Senate

Richard G. Lugar (R)	306
Daniel R. Coats (R)	212

House of Representatives

1	Peter J. Visclosky (D)	1200
2	Philip R. Sharp (D)	1094
3	Tim Roemer (D)	1040
4	Jill L. Long (D)	854
5	Steve Buyer (R)	478
6	Dan Burton (R)	476
7	John T. Myers (R)	948
8	Frank McCloskey (D)	880
9	Lee H. Hamilton (D)	700
10	Andrew Jacobs Jr. (D)	764

Iowa

Senate

Charles E. Grassley (R)	262
Tom Harkin (D)	266

House of Representatives

1	Jim Leach (R)	830
2	Jim Nussle (R)	958
3	Jim Ross Lightfoot (R)	844
4	Neal Smith (D)	1122
5	Fred Grandy (R)	684

Kansas

Senate

Bob Dole (R)	234
Nancy Landon Kassebaum (R)	284

House of Representatives

1	Pat Roberts (R)	1038
2	Jim Slattery (D)	1112
3	Jan Meyers (R)	912
4	Dan Glickman (D)	668

Kentucky

Senate

Wendell H. Ford (D)	250
Mitch McConnell (R)	312

House of Representatives

1	Tom Barlow (D)	412
2	William H. Natcher (D)	952
3	Romano L. Mazzoli (D)	876
4	Jim Bunning (R)	474
5	Harold Rogers (R)	1042
6	Scotty Baesler (D)	402

Louisiana

Senate

J. Bennett Johnston (D)	282
John B. Breaux (D)	196

House of Representatives

1	Robert L. Livingston (R)	850
2	William J. Jefferson (D)	766
3	W.J. "Billy" Tauzin (D)	1162
4	Cleo Fields (D)	614
5	Jim McCrery (R)	884
6	Richard H. Baker (R)	406
7	Jimmy Hayes (D)	712

Maine

Senate

William S. Cohen (R)	216
George J. Mitchell (D)	318

House of Representatives

1	Thomas H. Andrews (D)	388
2	Olympia J. Snowe (R)	1126

Maryland

Senate

Paul S. Sarbanes (D)	350
Barbara A. Mikulski (D)	316

House of Representatives

1	Wayne T. Gilchrest (R)	660
2	Helen Delich Bentley (R)	428
3	Benjamin L. Cardin (D)	492
4	Albert R. Wynn (D)	1236
5	Steny H. Hoyer (D)	742
6	Roscoe G. Bartlett (R)	418
7	Kweisi Mfume (D)	914
8	Constance A. Morella (R)	942

Massachusetts

Senate

Edward M. Kennedy (D)	288
John Kerry (D)	292

House of Representatives

1	John W. Olver (D)	964
2	Richard E. Neal (D)	954
3	Peter Blute (R)	446
4	Barney Frank (D)	636
5	Martin T. Meehan (D)	906
6	Peter Torkildsen (R)	1178
7	Edward J. Markey (D)	870
8	Joseph P. Kennedy II (D)	786
9	Joe Moakley (D)	930
10	Gerry E. Studds (D)	1144

Michigan

Senate

	Donald W. Riegle Jr. (D)	342
	Carl Levin (D)	300

House of Representatives

1	Bart Stupak (D)	1148
2	Peter Hoekstra (R)	732
3	Paul B. Henry (R)	718
4	Dave Camp (R)	486
5	James A. Barcia (D)	410
6	Fred Upton (R)	1192
7	Nick Smith (R)	1124
8	Bob Carr (D)	494
9	Dale E. Kildee (D)	790
10	David E. Bonior (D)	454
11	Joseph K. Knollenberg (R)	806
12	Sander Levin (D)	834
13	William D. Ford (D)	632
14	John Conyers Jr. (D)	524
15	Barbara-Rose Collins (D)	514
16	John D. Dingell (D)	570

Minnesota

Senate

	Dave Durenberger (R)	240
	Paul Wellstone (D)	372

House of Representatives

1	Timothy J. Penny (D)	992
2	David Minge (D)	926
3	Jim Ramstad (R)	1022
4	Bruce F. Vento (D)	1198
5	Martin Olav Sabo (D)	1064
6	Rod Grams (R)	682
7	Collin C. Peterson (D)	994
8	James L. Oberstar (D)	960

Mississippi

Senate

	Thad Cochran (R)	214
	Trent Lott (R)	304

House of Representatives

1	Jamie L. Whitten (D)	1222
2	Mike Espy (D)	602
3	G. V. "Sonny" Montgomery (D)	936
4	Mike Parker (D)	980
5	Gene Taylor (D)	1166

Missouri

Senate

	John C. Danforth (R)	226
	Christopher S. Bond (R)	188

House of Representatives

1	William L. Clay (D)	500
2	James M. Talent (R)	1158
3	Richard A. Gephardt (D)	654
4	Ike Skelton (D)	1110
5	Alan Wheat (D)	1220
6	Pat Danner (D)	544
7	Mel Hancock (R)	702
8	Bill Emerson (R)	592
9	Harold L. Volkmer (D)	1202

Montana

Senate

	Max Baucus (D)	178
	Conrad Burns (R)	204

House of Representatives

At Large	Pat Williams (D)	1224

Nebraska

Senate

	Jim Exon (D)	242
	Bob Kerrey (D)	290

House of Representatives

1	Doug Bereuter (R)	430
2	Peter Hoagland (D)	726
3	Bill Barrett (R)	414

Nevada

Senate

	Harry Reid (D)	340
	Richard H. Bryan (D)	200

House of Representatives

1	James Bilbray (D)	436
2	Barbara F. Vucanovich (R)	1204

New Hampshire

Senate

	Robert C. Smith (R)	360
	Judd Gregg (R)	264

House of Representatives

1	Bill Zeliff (R)	1244
2	Dick Swett (D)	1152

New Jersey

Senate

	Bill Bradley (D)	194
	Frank R. Lautenberg (D)	296

House of Representatives

1	Robert E. Andrews (D)	386
2	William J. Hughes (D)	746
3	H. James Saxton (R)	1076
4	Christopher H. Smith (R)	1118
5	Marge Roukema (R)	1054
6	Frank Pallone Jr. (D)	976
7	Bob Franks (R)	638
8	Herbert C. Klein (D)	800
9	Robert G. Torricelli (D)	1182
10	Donald M. Payne (D)	986
11	Dean A. Gallo (R)	648
12	Dick Zimmer (R)	1246
13	Robert Menendez (D)	910

New Mexico

Senate

	Pete V. Domenici (R)	236
	Jeff Bingaman (D)	186

House of Representatives

1	Steven H. Schiff (R)	1082
2	Joe Skeen (R)	1108
3	Bill Richardson (D)	1034

New York

Senate

	Daniel Patrick Moynihan (D)	322
	Alfonse M. D'Amato (R)	224

House of Representatives

1	George J. Hochbrueckner (D)	730
2	Rick A. Lazio (R)	828
3	Peter T. King (R)	794
4	David A. Levy (R)	836
5	Gary L. Ackerman (D)	380
6	Floyd H. Flake (D)	624
7	Thomas J. Manton (D)	864
8	Jerrold Nadler (D)	950
9	Charles E. Schumer (D)	1086
10	Edolphus Towns (D)	1184
11	Major R. Owens (D)	970
12	Nydia M. Velazquez (D)	1196
13	Susan Molinari (R)	932
14	Carolyn B. Maloney (D)	860
15	Charles B. Rangel (D)	1024
16	Jose E. Serrano (D)	1092
17	Eliot L. Engel (D)	594
18	Nita M. Lowey (D)	856
19	Hamilton Fish Jr. (R)	622
20	Benjamin A. Gilman (R)	664
21	Michael R. McNulty (D)	904
22	Gerald B. H. Solomon (R)	1128
23	Sherwood Boehlert (R)	448
24	John M. McHugh (R)	894
25	James T. Walsh (R)	1208
26	Maurice D. Hinchey (D)	724
27	Bill Paxon (R)	984
28	Louise M. Slaughter (D)	1114
29	John J. LaFalce (D)	816
30	Jack Quinn (R)	1018
31	Amo Houghton (R)	740

North Carolina

Senate

	Jesse Helms (R)	274
	Lauch Faircloth (R)	244

House of Representatives

1	Eva Clayton (D)	502
2	Tim Valentine (D)	1194
3	H. Martin Lancaster (D)	820
4	David Price (D)	1012
5	Stephen L. Neal (D)	956
6	J. Howard Coble (R)	510
7	Charlie Rose (D)	1048
8	W. G. "Bill" Hefner (D)	716
9	Alex McMillan (R)	902
10	Cass Ballenger (R)	408
11	Charles H. Taylor (R)	1164
12	Melvin Watt (D)	1214

North Dakota

Senate

	Kent Conrad (D)	218
	Byron L. Dorgan (D)	238

House of Representatives

At Large	Earl Pomeroy (D)	1006

Ohio

Senate

	John Glenn (D)	252
	Howard M. Metzenbaum (D)	314

House of Representatives

1	David Mann (D)	862
2	Bill Gradison (R)	680
3	Tony P. Hall (D)	696
4	Michael G. Oxley (R)	972
5	Paul E. Gillmor (R)	662
6	Ted Strickland (D)	1142
7	David L. Hobson (R)	728
8	John A. Boehner (R)	450
9	Marcy Kaptur (D)	782
10	Martin R. Hoke (R)	734
11	Louis Stokes (D)	1140
12	John R. Kasich (R)	784
13	Sherrod Brown (D)	470
14	Tom Sawyer (D)	1074
15	Deborah Pryce (R)	1014
16	Ralph Regula (R)	1030
17	James A. Traficant Jr. (D)	1186
18	Douglas Applegate (D)	390
19	Eric D. Fingerhut (D)	620

Oklahoma

Senate
David L. Boren (D) 190
Don Nickles (R) 328

House of Representatives
1 James M. Inhofe (R) 758
2 Mike Synar (D) 1156
3 Bill Brewster (D) 460
4 Dave McCurdy (D) 886
5 Ernest Istook Jr. (R) 762
6 Glenn English (D) 596

Oregon

Senate
Mark O. Hatfield (R) 270
Bob Packwood (R) 332

House of Representatives
1 Elizabeth Furse (D) 644
2 Bob Smith (R) 1116
3 Ron Wyden (D) 1234
4 Peter A. DeFazio (D) 552
5 Mike Kopetski (D) 810

Pennsylvania

Senate
Arlen Specter (R) 362
Harris Wofford (D) 374

House of Representatives
1 Thomas M. Foglietta (D) 626
2 Lucien E. Blackwell (D) 442
3 Robert A. Borski (D) 456
4 Ron Klink (D) 802
5 William F. Clinger (R) 506
6 Tim Holden (D) 736
7 Curt Weldon (R) 1218
8 James C. Greenwood (R) 688
9 Bud Shuster (R) 1102
10 Joseph M. McDade (R) 888
11 Paul E. Kanjorski (D) 780
12 John P. Murtha (D) 946
13 Marjorie Margolies-Mezvinsky (D) ... 868
14 William J. Coyne (D) 534
15 Paul McHale (D) 892
16 Robert S. Walker (R) 1206
17 George W. Gekas (R) 652
18 Rick Santorum (R) 1070
19 Bill Goodling (R) 674
20 Austin J. Murphy (D) 944
21 Tom Ridge (R) 1036

Rhode Island

Senate
Claiborne Pell (D) 334
John H. Chafee (R) 210

House of Representatives
1 Ronald K. Machtley (R) 858
2 John F. Reed (D) 1028

South Carolina

Senate
Strom Thurmond (R) 366
Ernest F. Hollings (D) 276

House of Representatives
1 Arthur Ravenel Jr. (R) 1026
2 Floyd D. Spence (R) 1130
3 Butler Derrick (D) 560
4 Robert D. Inglis (R) 756
5 John M. Spratt Jr. (D) 1132
6 Jim Clyburn (D) 508

South Dakota

Senate
Larry Pressler (R) 336
Tom Daschle (D) 228

House of Representatives
At Large Tim Johnson (D) 776

Tennessee

Senate
Al Gore (D) 254
Jim Sasser (D) 352

House of Representatives
1 James H. Quillen (R) 1016
2 John J. "Jimmy" Duncan Jr. (R) 582
3 Marilyn Lloyd (D) 852
4 Jim Cooper (D) 526
5 Bob Clement (D) 504
6 Bart Gordon (D) 676
7 Don Sundquist (R) 1150
8 John Tanner (D) 1160
9 Harold E. Ford (D) 630

Texas

Senate
Lloyd Bentsen (D) 182
Phil Gramm (R) 260

House of Representatives
1 Jim Chapman (D) 498
2 Charles Wilson (D) 1226
3 Sam Johnson (R) 774
4 Ralph M. Hall (D) 694
5 John Bryant (D) 472
6 Joe L. Barton (R) 420
7 Bill Archer (R) 392
8 Jack Fields (R) 616
9 Jack Brooks (D) 462
10 J. J. Pickle (D) 1002
11 Chet Edwards (D) 588

12	Pete Geren (D)	656
13	Bill Sarpalius (D)	1072
14	Greg Laughlin (D)	826
15	E. "Kika" de la Garza (D)	548
16	Ronald D. Coleman (D)	512
17	Charles W. Stenholm (D)	1138
18	Craig Washington (D)	1210
19	Larry Combest (R)	520
20	Henry B. Gonzalez (D)	670
21	Lamar Smith (R)	1120
22	Tom DeLay (R)	556
23	Henry Bonilla (R)	452
24	Martin Frost (D)	642
25	Michael A. Andrews (D)	384
26	Dick Armey (R)	394
27	Solomon P. Ortiz (D)	966
28	Frank M. Tejeda (D)	1168
29	Gene Green (D)	686
30	Eddie Bernice Johnson (D)	770

Utah

Senate

	Orrin G. Hatch (R)	268
	Robert F. Bennett (R)	180

House of Representatives

1	James V. Hansen (R)	704
2	Karen Shepherd (D)	1100
3	Bill Orton (D)	968

Vermont

Senate

	Patrick J. Leahy (D)	298
	James M. Jeffords (R)	280

House of Representatives

1	Bernard Sanders (I)	1066

Virginia

Senate

	John W. Warner (R)	370
	Charles S. Robb (D)	344

House of Representatives

1	Herbert H. Bateman (R)	422
2	Owen B. Pickett (D)	1000
3	Robert C. Scott (D)	1088
4	Norman Sisisky (D)	1104
5	Lewis F. Payne Jr. (D)	988
6	Robert W. Goodlatte (R)	672
7	Thomas J. Bliley Jr. (R)	444
8	James P. Moran Jr. (D)	940
9	Rick Boucher (D)	458
10	Frank R. Wolf (R)	1230
11	Leslie L. Byrne (D)	480

Washington

Senate

	Slade Gorton (R)	256
	Patty Murray (D)	326

House of Representatives

1	Maria Cantwell (D)	490
2	Al Swift (D)	1154
3	Jolene Unsoeld (D)	1190
4	Jay Inslee (D)	760
5	Thomas S. Foley (D)	628
6	Norm Dicks (D)	568
7	Jim McDermott (D)	890
8	Jennifer Dunn (R)	584
9	Mike Kreidler (D)	812

West Virginia

Senate

	Robert C. Byrd (D)	206
	John D. Rockefeller IV (D)	346

House of Representatives

1	Alan B. Mollohan (D)	934
2	Bob Wise (D)	1228
3	Nick J. Rahall II (D)	1020

Wisconsin

Senate

	Herb Kohl (D)	294
	Russell Feingold (D)	246

House of Representatives

1	Les Aspin (D)	396
2	Scott L. Klug (R)	804
3	Steve Gunderson (R)	690
4	Gerald D. Kleczka (D)	798
5	Thomas Barrett (D)	416
6	Tom Petri (R)	998
7	David R. Obey (D)	962
8	Toby Roth (R)	1052
9	F. James Sensenbrenner Jr. (R)	1090

Wyoming

Senate

	Malcolm Wallop (R)	368
	Alan K. Simpson (R)	358

House of Representatives

At Large	Craig Thomas (R)	1172

Index

Note: **Boldface page numbers** indicate main entries

Symbols

Ryder System Inc 82, 1302

S

S&A Restaurant Corp 78, 1302
Sabo, Martin Olav (D-Minn) 132, 138, **1064–1065**
Safari Club International 1302
Safeco Corp 1302
Safeway Stores 1302
Sailor's Union of the Pacific 1302
Saint Louisians for Better Government 1302
Salomon Brothers 27, 28, 29, 66, 112, 122, 1302
Salt River Valley Water Users 1302
San Diego Community PAC 1302
San Diego Gas & Electric 1303
San Franciscans for Good Government 1303
San Franciscans Getting Things Done 91
Sanders, Bernard (I-Vt) 34, 136, 148, **1066–1067**
Sandoz Pharmaceuticals 1303
SANE/Freeze Inc 1303
Sanford, Terry 48, 66, 87, 102, 104, 114
Sangmeister, George E. (D-Ill) 152, 158, 166, **1068–1069**
Santa Fe International Corp 1303
Santa Fe Southern Pacific 1303
Santorum, Rick (R-Pa) 29, 138, 166, **1070–1071**
SAPEC, NJ (NJ Savings Assn) 1303
Sarbanes, Paul S. (D-Md) 102, 114, **350–351**
Sarpalius, Bill (D-Texas) 130, 164, **1072–1073**
Sasser, Jim (D-Tenn) 72, 98, 102, 104, 116, **352–353**
Savage, Gus 158, 164
Savannah Foods & Industries 1303
Sawyer, Tom (D-Ohio) 142, 146, 156, **1074–1075**
Saxton, H. James (R-NJ) 134, 154, **1076–1077**
Scana Corp 1303
Schaefer, Dan (R-Colo) 144, **1078–1079**
Schenk, Lynn (D-Calif) 75, **1080–1081**
Schering-Plough Corp 68, 71, 1303
Scheuer, James H. 144, 162
Science, Space and Technology Committee, House 162-163
Schiff, Steven H. (R-NM) 148, 152, 162, **1082–1083**
Schnitzer Steel Industries 29, 79
Schroeder, Patricia (D-Colo) 34, 52, 134, 152, 156, **1084–1085**
Schulze, Dick 150, 168
Schumer, Charles E. (D-NY) 65, 66, 67, 136, 150, 152, **1086–1087**
Scott Paper Co 49, 1303
Scott, Robert C. (D-Va) **1088–1089**
Sea transport industry contributions 80-81, **83**
Sea-Land Corp 1303
Seafarers International Union 24, 28, 84, 87, 110, 120, 155, 159, 160, 1303
SeaFirst Bank 1303
Seagram & Sons, Joseph E 17, 76, 78, 1303
Searle & Co, GD 1303
Sears 78, 118, 1303
SecuraPAC 1303
Securities Industry Assn 1303

Securities industry contributions 26, 30, 64-65, **66**
Security Life of Denver 1304
Security Pacific Corp 1304
Senate: Cost of elections in recent years 2; Committee profiles 96-127; Contributions from 27; Member profiles 176-375; Reelection rates 5
Senate Majority Fund 91
Senate Victory Fund 91, 1304
Sendelsky, Leonard R. 56
Sensenbrenner, F. James Jr. (R-Wis) 152, 162, **1090–1091**
Serrano, Jose E. (D-NY) 142, 164, **1092–1093**
Service Corp International 1304
Service Employees International Union 24, 1304
Services Group of America 1304
Seymour, John F. 47, 48, 49, 51, 55, 56, 57, 61, 62, 65, 67, 70, 71, 77, 78, 81, 82, 83, 96, 108, 116, 124
Sharp, Philip R. (D-Ind) 61, 62, 63, 144, 150, **1094–1095**
Shaw, E. Clay Jr. (R-Fla) 15, 29, 69, 70, 73, 82, 168, **1096–1097**
Shaw, Pittman et al 1304
Shays, Christopher (R-Conn) 138, 148, **1098–1099**
Shearson Lehman Brothers 26, 1304
Sheet Metal Workers Union 17, 24, 86, 1304
Sheet Metal/Air Conditioning Contractors 54, 1304
Shelby, Richard C. (D-Ala) 19, 53, 59, 61, 63, 66, 72, 75, 100, 102, 108, **354–355**
Shell Oil 151, 155, 1304
Shepherd, Karen (D-Utah) 29, 90, **1100–1101**
Shuster, Bud (R-Pa) 55, 56, 57, 77, 81, 83, 158, **1102–1103**
Sierra Club 25, 88, 93, 151, 155, 1304
Sierra Pacific Resources 110
Sikorski, Gerry 52, 69, 75, 85, 87, 144, 156
Sills, Cummis et al 29
Silver State PAC 1304
Simon, Paul (D-Ill) 72, 104, 114, 118, 120, **356–357**
Simpson, Alan K. (R-Wyo) 110, 118, 126, **358–359**
Simpson Investment Co 49, 1304
Sisisky, Norman (D-Va) 134, 164, **1104–1105**
Skadden, Arps et al 27, 74, 1304
Skaggs, David E. (D-Colo) 132, **1106–1107**
Skeen, Joe (R-NM) 132, **1108–1109**
Skelton, Ike (D-Mo) 134, 164, **1110–1111**
Slattery, Jim (D-Kan) 53, 73, 136, 144, 166, **1112–1113**
Slaughter, D. French Jr. 152, 162, 164
Slaughter, Louise M. (D-NY) 138, 160, **1114–1115**
Small Business Committee, House 164-165
Small Business Committee, Senate 124-125
Smirnoff/Inglenook Distributors 78, 1304
Smith Barney 27, 28, 102
Smith, Bob (R-Ore) 49, 130, 150, **1116–1117**
Smith, Christopher H. (R-NJ) 146, 166, **1118–1119**
Smith, Lamar (R-Texas) 152, 162, **1120–1121**
Smith, Lawrence J. 132
Smith, Neal (D-Iowa) 91, 132, 164, **1122–1123**
Smith, Nick (R-Mich) 19, **1124–1125**
Smith, Robert C. (R-NH) 100, 110, **360–361**
SmithKline Beecham 1304

Thornburgh, Dick 15, 55, 56, 57, 63, 77, 78, 79
Thornton, Ray (D-Ark) 29, 148, 162, **1174–1175**
Thurman, Karen L. (D-Fla) **1176–1177**
Thurmond, Strom (R-SC) 100, 118, 120, 126, **366–367**
Timber industry contributions 46-47, **49**
Time Warner 17, 25, 27, 28, 50, 52, 98, 104, 106, 112, 114, 120, 122, 152, 1308
Tobacco industry 46-47, **48**
Tobacco Institute 17, 46, 48, 1308
Toll Brothers Inc 56
Torchmark Corp 1308
Torkildsen, Peter (R-Mass) 19, **1178–1179**
Torres, Esteban E. (D-Calif) 136, 164, **1180–1181**
Torricelli, Robert G. (D-NJ) 69, 73, 75, 77, 146, 162, **1182–1183**
Torrington Co 1308
Totem Ocean Trailer Express 1308
Towns, Edolphus (D-NY) 35, 144, 148, **1184–1185**
Traficant, James A. Jr. (D-Ohio) 158, 162, **1186–1187**
Trailer Train Co 1308
Trans Comm International Union 87, 1308
TransAmerica Corp 1308
TransAmerica Insurance 1308
TransAmerica Life Companies 1308
Transco Energy Co 1308
Transport Workers Union 87, 159, 1308
Transportation industry contributions 43, 44-45, **80-83**; Average contributions to House committees 39
Travelers Corp 1308
Traxler, Bob 132
Trucking industry contributions 80-81, **83**
Trust Co of Georgia 1308
TRW Inc 58, 1308
Tucker, Walter R. (D-Calif) 35, **1188–1189**
Turner Broadcasting System 53, 1309
Tyson Foods 28, 46, 96, 1309

U

UNC Inc 1309
Unidentified contributors, members with highest proportion 35
Union Camp Corp 49, 1309
Union Carbide 1309
Union City (NJ) Municipal Government 29
Union City Board of Education 29
Union Electric 1309
Union Oil 1309
Union Pacific Corp 25, 80, 83, 106, 108, 112, 118, 145, 159, 1309
Unions see Labor
United Airlines 80, 82, 159, 1309
United Auto Workers 17, 24, 84, 87, 114, 120, 128, 133, 138, 140, 142, 147, 148, 152, 156, 160, 163, 164, 166, 1309
United Co 63, 1309
United Egg Assn 1309
United Illuminating Co 1309
United Mine Workers 25, 86, 151, 1309

United Paperworkers 1309
United Parcel Service 24, 44, 80, 82, 98, 104, 106, 112, 116, 122, 128, 133, 138, 142, 148, 156, 159, 163, 164, 166, 168, 1309
United Services Automobile Assn Group 1309
United States Sugar Corp 1309
United States Surgical Corp 17
United Steelworkers 17, 24, 29, 84, 86, 160, 1309
United Technologies 58, 100, 120, 135, 1310
United Telecommunications 50, 53, 1310
United Transportation Union 24, 84, 87, 98, 110, 120, 126, 133, 145, 159, 160, 1310
University of California 27, 28
Unsoeld, Jolene (D-Wash) 142, 154, **1190–1191**
Unum Life Insurance Co 1310
Upjohn Co 71, 1310
Upton, Fred (R-Mich) 144, **1192–1193**
US Bancorp 1310
US Beet Sugar Assn 1310
US Federation of Small Businesses 1310
US Healthcare Inc 71, 1310
US League of Savings Assns 137, 1310
US Telephone Assn 1310
US Tobacco Co 17, 25, 27, 28, 46, 48, 96, 98, 104, 114, 120, 122, 124, 168, 1310
US West 50, 53, 1310
USAir Corp 1310
USX Corp 60, 62, 1310
Utilicorp United Inc 1310
Utility Workers Union of America 1310

V

V-PAC 1310
Valentine, Tim (D-NC) 158, 162, **1194–1195**
Valero Energy Corp 1311
Van Ness, Feldman et al 1311
Vander Jagt, Guy 168
Veco International Inc 29, 151, 155
Velazquez, Nydia M. (D-NY) 35, **1196–1197**
Vento, Bruce F. (D-Minn) 34, 136, 150, **1198–1199**
Verner, Liipfert et al 74, 1311
Veterans of Foreign Wars 93, 1311
Veterans' Affairs Committee, House 166-167
Veterans' Affairs Committee, Senate 126-127
Viacom International 53, 145, 1311
Victory USA 91, 1311
Viking Freight 1311
Vinson & Elkins 74, 1311
Virginia Bankers Assn 1311
Virginia-Carolinas Peanut Membership Organization 1311
Visclosky, Peter J. (D-Ind) 132, **1200–1201**
Volkmer, Harold L. (D-Mo) 48, 130, 162, **1202–1203**
von Reichbauer, Pete 49
Vorys, Sater et al 1311
Voters for Choice 88, 92, 1311
Vucanovich, Barbara F. (R-Nev) 63, 77, 132, 150, **1204–1205**
Vulcan Materials Co 54, 57, 1311

W

Wachtell, Lipton et al 27
Wal-Mart Stores 78, 1311
Walgreen Co 1311
Walker, Robert S. (R-Pa) 162, **1206–1207**
Wall Street *see Securities industry contributions*
Wallop, Malcolm (R-Wyo) 100, 108, 124, **368–369**
Walsh, James T. (R-NY) 128, 130, **1208–1209**
Walt Disney Co 27, 50, 52, 116, 118, 152, 1270
Walter Industries 54, 57
Warner, John W. (R-Va) 100, 110, 122, **370–371**
Warner-Lambert 28, 71, 1311
Warshawsky & Co/JC Whitney & Co 1311
Washington, Craig (D-Texas) 142, 152, **1210–1211**
Washington PAC 90, 1311
Waste Management Inc 17, 25, 27, 28, 60, 108, 110, 112, 116, 122, 124, 1311
Waters, Maxine (D-Calif) 91, 136, 166, **1212–1213**
Watkins Associated Industries 1312
Watkins-Johnson Co 1312
Watson, Thomas J. 17
Watt, Melvin (D-NC) 35, **1214–1215**
Waxman, Henry A. (D-Calif) 69, 70, 71, 73, 91, 144, 148, **1216–1217**
Ways and Means Committee, House 168-169
Weber, Vin 91, 132
Weidner, Don 70
Weiss, Ted 136, 146, 148
Weldon, Curt (R-Pa) 134, 154, **1218–1219**
Wells Fargo 1312
Wellstone, Paul (D-Minn) 108, 120, 124, **372–373**
Wertheim Schroder & Co 1312
West Publishing 52, 1312
Western United Dairymens Assn 1312
Westinghouse Electric 50, 1312
Westvaco Corp 46, 49, 1312
Weyerhaeuser Co 49, 1312
Wheat, Alan (D-Mo) 140, 160, **1220–1221**
Wheelabrator Technologies 1312
Whirlpool Corp 1312
Whitman, Christine Todd 91
Whitten, Jamie L. (D-Miss) 132, **1222–1223**
Willamette Industries 1312
Williams & Jensen 27, 74, 1312
Williams Companies 62, 1312
Williams, Pat (D-Mont) 15, 85, 86, 142, 150, **1224–1225**
Williamson, Richard 79
Willkie, Farr & Gallagher 27
Wilson, Charles (D-Texas) 19, 59, 62, 132, **1226–1227**
Wine & Spirits Wholesalers of America 76, 78, 1312
Wine Institute 78, 1312
Winn-Dixie Stores 46, 49, 1312
Winstead, Sechrest & Minick 1313
Wirth, Tim 100, 102, 104, 108
Wisconsin Bell Telephone 1313
Wise, Bob (D-WVa) 138, 148, **1228–1229**
Wish List 90, 1313

Wofford, Harris (D-Pa) 15, 28, 72, 75, 85, 86, 89, 110, 114, 124, **374–375**
Wolf, Block et al 1313
Wolf, Frank R. (R-Va) 132, **1230–1231**
Wolpe, Howard 146, 162
Women for: 1313
Women's Alliance for Israel 90, 1313
Women's Campaign Fund 25, 88, 90, 1313
Women's issue PACs and contributions 88-89, **90**
Women's Political Committee 1313
Women's Pro-Israel National PAC 90, 1313
Woolsey, Lynn (D-Calif) **1232–1233**
World Savings & Loan 1313
WR Grace & Co 76, 79, 110, 1276
Wright, Jim 91
Wunder, Diefenderfer et al 27
Wyden, Ron (D-Ore) 144, 164, **1234–1235**
Wylie, Chalmers P. 136, 166
Wynn, Albert R. (D-Md) 35, **1236–1237**

X

Xerox Corp 1313

Y

Yankee Atomic Electric Co 1313
Yates, Sidney R. (D-Ill) 34, 132, **1238–1239**
Yatron, Gus 146, 156
Yeakel, Lynn 89, 90
Yellow Freight System 80, 83, 110, 1313
Young, C. W. Bill (R-Fla) 59, 132, **1240–1241**
Young, Don (R-Alaska) 29, 61, 62, 83, 150, 154, 156, **1242–1243**

Z

Zeliff, Bill (R-NH) 29, 73, 77, 78, 148, 158, 164, **1244–1245**
Zimmer, Dick (R-NJ) 29, 71, 73, 148, 162, **1246–1247**